Where We Were

In Vietnam

A Comprehensive Guide to the
Firebases, Military Installations and
Naval Vessels of the Vietnam War

Michael P. Kelley

Hellgate Press
Central Point, Oregon

Where We Were in Vietnam

Published by Hellgate Press

Hellgate Press
An Imprint of PSI Research
P.O. Box 3727
Central Point, OR 97502

info@psi-research.com

Interior design: Michael P. Kelley and Harley B. Patrick
Cover design: Erin Kelley/Zinc Designs and Mark Hannah
Editing: Harley B. Patrick

Library of Congress Cataloging-in-Publication Data

Kelley, Michael, 1946-
Where We Were : a comprehensive guide to the firebases and military installations of the Vietnam War / Michael Kelley
p.cm.
ISBN 1-55571-625-3 (paper)
1. Vietnamese Conflict, 1961-1975—Dictionaries. 2. Military bases, American—Vietnam—Dictionaries. 3. Military bases, American—Vietnam—Maps. 4. Vietnam—Gazetteers. I. Title.

DS557.7 .K45 2002
959.704'3'03—dc21 2001051682

Printed and bound in the United States of America
First Edition 10 9 8 7 6 5 4 3 2

Disclaimer

While a very substantial effort has been made to ensure the accuracy of the data presented in this manuscript, its complete accuracy simply cannot be guaranteed. Transposition and transcription errors were, and will forever remain, common among official military reports and as long as there are historians available to compound the problem with their own inadvertent contributions.

Readers will likely encounter numerous errors and omissions throughout the text and no one should rely on any of the material presented here as completely factual without independent verification. Nonetheless, the author does believe that the greater part of the information presented here remains both substantially correct and reliable.

Unfortunately, transposition errors introduced during the translation of grid coordinate data into relative location narrative seem to have occurred with inordinate regularity. To resolve the issue where a stated, relative location appears to conflict with a known or presumed location, the reader should give the greatest weight to the grid coordinate and plot it on an appropriate map.

Reporting Errors and Omissions

The author encourages and welcomes readers to report errors or omissions. He also welcomes additional grid coordinate, factual or anecdotal information of any sort related to any facility of the Vietnam War. It is his ultimate goal to make *WHERE WE WERE* the most comprehensive and most accurate reference of its kind. Readers may contact the author via an e-mail address provided at **www.wherewewere.com**.

More Praise for Michael Kelley's *Where We Were in Vietnam …*

"More than a prodigious feat of research, Mike Kelley's labor of love will be an invaluable resource—for scholars, for historians, and for the rest of us who want to know more about *Where We Were*."

~ Bernard Edelman
Editor of *Dear America: Letters Home from Vietnam* and *Centenarians: The Story of the 20th Century by the Americans Who Lived It*

"In the metaphorical sense, Americans may still be unsure 'where we were' in Vietnam. In the geographical sense, though, Mike Kelley's remarkable work will help veterans and any others who want to know exactly where U.S. forces were situated in that beautiful and troubled land. Kelley's astonishing and prodigious research literally puts America's Vietnam experience on the map."

~ Arnold R. Isaacs
Author of *Vietnam Shadows: The War, Its Ghosts, and Its Legacy*

"I am in awe of what Michael Kelley has produced in this amazing book. His massive and inclusive compilation of firebases and other military installations will instantly become a classic reference work of the Vietnam War."

~ Marc Leepson, Arts Editor, *The VVA Veteran*
Author of *Saving Monticello*

"The attention to detail in this volume is astonishing. If you were going to invest in just one reference book on the Vietnam War, this would be the one."

~ Eric James Schroeder
Lecturer in American Studies at UC Davis
Author of *Vietnam, We've All Been There: Interviews with American Writers*

About the Author

Michael "M-60" Kelley served as a rifleman and machine gunner with D Company, 1st/502d Infantry, 101st Airborne Division from Nov69 until badly wounded Sep70. Drafted immediately upon graduation from Sacramento State College (BA, Art), he has since established himself as one of the better-known artists whose focus has been the Vietnam experience. His works hang in numerous museums and private collections in the U.S. and around the world. Over the past decade, drawing has taken a back seat to writing, and his articles have appeared in *the Washington Post, Boston Globe, Chicago Sun Times,* and *Vietnam Magazine*, among others. His military awards include the Combat Infantryman Badge, Bronze Star, Purple Heart, Air Medal, and ARCOM.

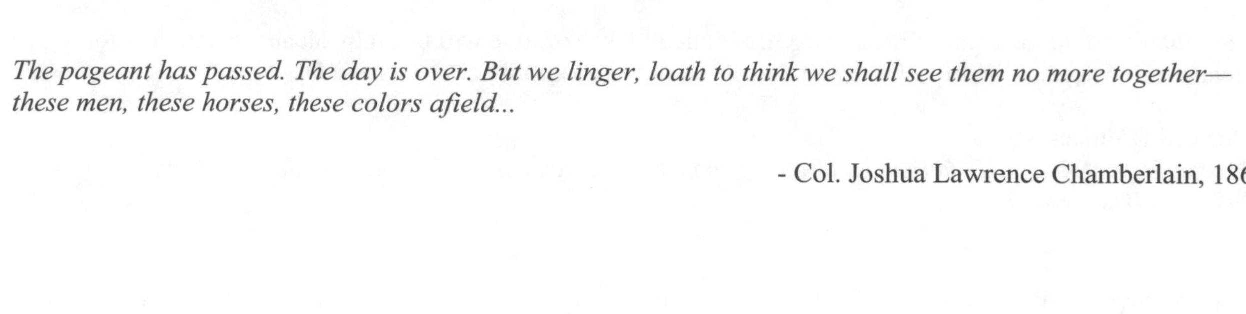

The pageant has passed. The day is over. But we linger, loath to think we shall see them no more together—these men, these horses, these colors afield...

- Col. Joshua Lawrence Chamberlain, 1865

And there were now the French forts, some downright ridiculous in their exact imitation of the North African "Beau Geste" type (you would almost expect Gary Cooper and Marlene Dietrich to stand atop one of the crenelated towers in tender embrace...), others of the squattish, ugly looking, deeply-dug-in modern bunker type. As I was to learn later, the fortifications of Indochina had had their "architectural periods" just like any other works of man., based upon the local terrain, the availability of materials, the enemy's combat potential, and the state of the art of military engineering.

- Bernard Fall, 1953, *Street Without Joy*

There were installations as big as cities with 30,000 citizens, once we dropped in to feed supply to one man. God knows what kind of Lord Jim phoenix numbers he was doing there, all he said to me was, "You didn't see a thing, right Chief? You weren't even here." There were posh fat air-conditioned camps like comfortable middle-class scenes with the violence tacit, "far away"; camps named for commanders' wives, LZ Thelma, LZ Betty Lou; number-named hilltops in trouble where I didn't want to stay; trail, paddy, swamp, deep hairy bush, scrub, swale, village, even city, where the ground couldn't drink up what the action spilled, it made you careful where you walked.

- Michael Herr, 1968, *Dispatches*

Dedication

This book is dedicated *to* the memory of my dear friend, Larry Keister, killed in action while with B Company, 3d/506th Infantry, near Phan Thiet, 26 Jan 69, and to that of Stephen T. "Doc Smitty" Smith, who while serving as the 3d platoon medic for D Company, 1st/502d Infantry (D/1st/502d Inf), triggered a land mine that first took his legs, 16 Sep 70, and then his last breath, 21 Sep. 70.

It is also dedicated to:

Donald "Donnie" Smith, D/1st/502d Inf and B/3d/506th Inf, KIA, 10 May 70.

Trinh Trong, our beloved Kit Carson Scout, who died of wounds received near Firebase Birmingham, 13 June 70. At his death, Trong had faithfully served D/1st/502d Inf for more than three years.

Michael Gross, who died in a grenade blast near Firebase Birmingham, 13 June 70.

The 250 killed and 1,280 wounded of the 1st Battalion, 502d Inf, suffered between December 1967 and February 1972.

The many comrades with whom I served in D/1st/502d Inf, 101st Abn Div and especially: Bob "Sonny" Smialowski, Ron Johnson, Gary Moutray, Howard "Chico" Mikkali, "Ranger" Bart Sacher, Phil "Phool" Moralez, Jose "M-79" Rentas, John Eastman, Bill Armer, Fred Wilkerson, Norman McCormick, Rick Schmierer, Lou "Teach" Zefran, Jim "Tweety Bird" Nelson, Ray "Soap Eater" Corey, Dale Bowman, Keith Hoskins, Manny Gallegos, Bill Bourne, Howard "Howie" Depoy, Wayne Earnest, Glen Hilsinger, Terry "Rotten" Lawton, Mert Johnson, Ed "Ole Daddy" Schoettelkotte, Bob Wakefield, Bill Weaver, Vail "Shep" Sheppard, Mike Slemmons, Tiny, Glenn Wasko, Jerry Shemwell, Carl Luukkonnen, KCS "Toi," "Top" Henry Hudson, Ken South, Dick Nolte, Peter Smith, Ralph Heinz, Garry Thornely, Pete Grasser and Stephen Rader.

Blake "*Oh Lord, Stuck in Lodi Again*" Mutschler and Jeffrey Grass, B-2-1 BCT, Ft. Ord, CA.

Jim Zwit, D/2d/501st Delta Raider, and Dr. Charley Carroll, 85th Evac Hospital surgeon.

My parents, who served their countries honorably during WWII (Father a U.S. Army AAA Lt., and Mother an RCAF Cpl.), only to endure the agony of seeing two sons then escape death in Vietnam by the slimmest of margins.

My brother, Bill Kelley, who served as a U.S. Navy Corpsman attached to the 1st Marine Air Wing flying medevacs out of Ky Ha/Chu Lai (HMM-262, MABS 36/MAG 36 and MABS 12/MAG 12, Dec. '66-Dec. '67). He was a good soldier and, when not tormenting me, a wonderful brother as well.

Beverly Currey, my mother-in-law, who, shortly before losing her battle with cancer in 1998, waved me to her bedside and surprised us all by whispering that she'd thought of a title for this manuscript (then in its infancy). "You should call it *Where We Really Were When You Only Thought You Knew Where We Were*," she said. In my heart, Bev, that will always be its true title.

My uncle, Robert E. Kelley, a rifleman/platoon leader with the 36th Texas Inf. He earned a battlefield commission and three Purple Hearts during his service in North African and Italian campaigns of WWII.

Joe Currey, my father-in-law, who was aboard the USS *West Virginia* when she was sunk at Pearl Harbor and later served aboard the USS *San Francisco,* whose 17 battle stars are the second highest total of the war (one of those stars was earned in the *Third Savo*, 12-13 Nov 42, one of the bloodiest, most intense sea battles of WWII).

My dear friends John Middlesworth (A Bty/1st/ 11th Arty, 1st Mar Div, '69), Lee Pittman (6/31st Inf, 9th Inf Div and 25th Inf Div, '70-'71), Doug Durham (A Co/3d Recon Bn, 3d Marine Div, '65-'66), and David Graham (6th/29th Arty, 4th Inf Div, '67-'68), for their service to country, steadfast loyalty and support over the years, and, above all, for their comradeship and good cheer. I owe them all at least a million good laughs!

Mary Roche, who suffered my monumental immaturity and failings as a husband and as the father of her child, only to have me further evade those responsibilities via military service and the Vietnam War.

Christopher, with the hope it serves to remind him that anything is possible if one is willing to commit and to sacrifice, and with the hope his future holds the fulfillment his childhood was denied.

Erin, my immensely talented and beautiful daughter, whom I left first for the Army and then Vietnam when she was but one and one- half years of age. Regretfully, I would again fail her several times during my sometimes chaotic life, but I am indeed blessed by, and extraordinarily proud of, what she has become and made of her life.

And finally, to Cathryn, my very dear wife of more than twenty-two years, who stood by me (weathering the storm, actually) through thick and thin, enduring my intemperance and selfishness over the first twelve years of our marriage only to effectively lose me again to the pages of this book for five or six more. Why she saw fit to hang on I'll never comprehend, but I'm extremely pleased and honored that she did.

Contents

Preface

Late in the afternoon of September 16, 1970, my platoon mounted the crest of a small hill and began setting up our night defensive position.

Exhausted from the climb and tattered uniform drenched with sweat, I first caught my breath and then voraciously wolfed-down a can of C-ration pineapple bits, relishing every drop of its sweet, thick, thirst-quenching juice. Soon afterwards, I rose unsteadily to my feet, then located and set about teaching a new squad-member named Hopson how best to deploy and integrate his claymore mine and trip flare into our perimeter's defenses. It was while teaching him that crucial skill that I heard Doc Smitty call my name from somewhere over my left shoulder.

Stephen T. Smith was the last platoon medic who served the platoon during my tour in Vietnam. Most everyone called him "Doc," as was the case with practically every Army medic assigned to a line unit in my war. Others of us routinely thought of him as Doc Smitty.

Doc Smitty was the only adopted son of an elderly Indianapolis couple and a conscientious objector. I have no memory of him ever carrying a weapon except, perhaps, a .45 pistol. He stood roughly six feet tall, was quite slender and rarely anything but cheerful. Sunglasses were a permanent fixture on his face and he combed his dark brown hair straight back from his face. He brushed his teeth after every meal and is brushing his teeth in the only picture I ever took of him. A vague memory of a slight lisp also sticks with me as well.

At the time of his death, he was sporting a thin mustache.

Despite a moderately severe case of dysentery that had been dogging me for several days before the climb, I was in a good mood for several reasons. All three platoons were moving to rendezvous on the hill for extraction the next morning following a tough and harrowing three-week mission combing the rugged hill mass of a mountain upon which sat a newly reopened firebase someone told me had once been a Marine firebase named "Blitz."[1] We were headed for the rear, a few days rest, and that was good news indeed. Our platoon leader, 1Lt. Kenneth South, suggested I report to the 326th Medical Battalion for treatment of the disabling condition once we got in, so the prospect of some "ghost" time was buoying my spirits as well. But, most importantly, I was so "short" I had to reach up to tie my shoes!

"Forty-three days and a wake-up," I'd fired back in glee earlier that morning when a buddy had teasingly asked me how many days I had left in-country. Then for emphasis I'd added, "Short!"

Turning toward the sound of Smitty's voice, I was puzzled to discover that he wasn't where his voice suggested he should be. The small clearing was empty, and that confused me greatly. Coincident with my turning came another odd sensation, as though a handful of something had been lightly tossed in my face. A practical joke perhaps?

"What sort of idiot would pull a fool stunt like that?" I asked myself, perplexed at the absurd prospect someone might engage in such inappropriate tom-foolery after the exhausting earlier climb. But other than Smitty calling my name, I heard no other sound and the balance of my senses weren't adding enough data to the equation to help me make much sense of that unfolding, timeless moment either.

Nothing made much sense, that is, until my nose caught the first ominous whiff of the distinctive odor that always attends the detonation of a high explosive. That first whiff triggered a realization that several potential solutions to the puzzle existed and none of the alternatives bade well for the future.

My gaze was then drawn to the foreground by some movement there. A series of surreal, copper-colored liquids were cascading from manifold perforations in my chest, head, arm and stomach in what seemed perfectly parallel streams arching to the ground at my feet. The severity of my predicament crashed home; something had gone terribly wrong and I was in deep, deep trouble.

"Oh God," the thought flashed through my mind, "a claymore cooked-off."

My first reflexive presumption was that one of the very lethal claymore mines we were deploying at the time had detonated accidentally. But whatever had happened, it was abundantly clear that the balance of my

---

[1] FSB Blitz was at YC 766-962, on Hill 861 (Dong Mang Chan), roughly twenty-five kilometers due S of Hue, twenty-three kilometers SW of Phu Bai and nine kilometers WSW of FSB Brick.

life was going to be measured in seconds, not years. Confused about all else, I was certain of one thing: I was about to die.

I recall people frozen in shock around me, and remember going to my knees and then rolling onto my back thinking that was what should be done. I gazed into the jungle canopy directly above my clearing and marveled at the beauty of the golden light dancing among the leaves. I don't remember feeling pain of any sort; instead, a profound calm and peacefulness enveloped my senses. The lights would soon go out, I knew, and that would be the end of it all.

My thoughts shifted to how the news of my death would affect the family, particularly my wife and daughter. As those thoughts arose, a cold wind of profound sorrow and remorse swept over me; my dismal performance as a husband and father would shortly end with the ultimate betrayal and abandonment, scarring them all forever.

Oddly, there was no fear, just a deep, profound sense of melancholy.

I was certain the lights would fade out at any moment, but they did not fade. Instead, faces started popping into and out of the limited, vertical cone of vision that remained available to me. Freeze-framed images and remote sound bites of encouragement stick in my memory of the moment. I recall Ranger Bart Sacher, Ron Johnson and Manny Gallegos telling me to hang on while they frantically applied bandages. A medic from another platoon, ashen with shock, was unable to start an IV because of his trembling hands, though he tried repeatedly. I remember feeling concern that the memory of his failure might one day haunt him.

And still the lights would not go out. How could that be?

It would be a few days before I knew the cause, but everyone else on Hill 222 at that moment knew someone's last footstep had found the detonator of a very powerful land mine. [2]

Years later I would learn that the resulting blast had thrown Doc Smitty vertically some thirty feet into the air, slamming him against the base of a massive branch hanging from an ancient teak that had been guarding our clearing for perhaps hundreds of years before our rude intrusion. His shattered body then apparently skidded back down the teak's trunk, coming to rest among its fluted roots, sitting upright and facing out in an almost natural pose.

So great was the force of the explosion that his belt and belt loops were the only clothing still adorning his body.

Blackened with dirt and the scorching heat of the blast, no one was really certain of the victim's identity. Ron Johnson recalls Lt. South cradling the broken body gently in his arms, tears streaming down his cheeks as he yelled for Doc Smitty's help.

By coincidence, I was later told, a dustoff medevac helicopter just happened to have been nearby on a routine, non-urgent mission at the moment our own radios came to life with the first frantic calls for help. To this day, I continue to draw breath as a result of that most fortuitous circumstance and the medevac's diversion to our small hilltop.

The helicopter soon landed in a whirlwind of dirt and debris, and within seconds I was hastily and unceremoniously tossed onto its cold, metal floor and left completely alone for what seemed an eternity. The inattention helped cement a growing conviction that I'd been given-up as a hopeless case. A sudden flurry of activity soon resulted in something being locked in-place on the bulkhead directly above me. Moments later we were airborne in a desperate, red-lined run for help.

During the flight, breathing was rapidly becoming a labor, so I yanked at the pant leg of one of the medics otherwise focused on the "something" above me. A green-helmeted figure bent to my beckoning. "What's up?" he asked as though we were on a Sunday drive.

"I can't breathe," I gasped and, in response, he spun around to sort through an assortment of gear littering the floor between the cockpit and the cabin, soon returning with a small, green oxygen bottle and its attached facemask. "Here," he said matter-of-factly as he pressed the mask to my face, "hold this tight. The guy upstairs is in bad shape and we need to work on him." Then, as quickly as he'd come, the green-helmeted figure was gone. He was gone in a flash that's for certain, but the import of the few words he'd uttered lingered for me to

---

[2] Apart from Smith, four others of us were wounded in the explosion: Keith Hoskins (Madison IN), Terry Lawton (Genoa, IL), Herbert Hopson and me.

ponder and gel into the first sign I might actually survive the day. To that point, I'd presumed being ignored was an indication that little could be done for me, and today it is with some guilt that I recall the relief those words brought with them, and that Smitty's suffering served to bring me hope.

Perhaps ten minutes later we flared into the landing pad adjacent the emergency entrance of the 85th Evacuation Hospital at Phu Bai. Still expecting the lights to go out at any second, I remained completely conscious throughout all the uncomfortable preliminary proceedings until actually anesthetized on the operating room table. Just before the lights did go out, a surgeon with a mustache and the nametag "Carroll" quite painfully introduced me to the first of many chest tubes.

It was many—and I mean many—hours after I'd awoken from my initial surgery when Smitty was finally wheeled into the ICU and propped-up in a bed immediately to my right. It was only then that I realized just what the "something" above me in the medevac had been.

Doc Smitty was in terrible shape.

Below the waist, he was little more than human wreckage; pure hamburger. Above the waist, excepting his hands, not a single wound was visible. Both legs had been removed above the knees, and huge, green, baby diaper-like pads were wrapped around each stump.

Nurses hung unit after unit of blood for Smitty, but as quickly as his veins could absorb the transfusions, the precious liquid inexorably ran out the other end, filling the green pads in minutes. The replacement cycle of pads and blood bags evolved into a seemingly endless blur, the image and implications of which became very disturbing. I soon found myself resisting any temptation to look his way as much to preclude attracting his attention as to avoid the horror of his condition.

Through it all Smitty kept up a steady stream of encouragement. "Don't worry Kelley, we'll be okay," he would whisper softly, over and over. Unfortunately, the myriad of tubes snaked down my nostrils and mouth prohibited reciprocity of any sort apart from an occasional nod, and that circumstance greatly frustrated my desire to properly acknowledge his thoughtful gestures and offer some reassurance of my own. I would have been lying of course, because it was a certainty things would never be okay again for Smitty.

On the morning of September 21, 1970, a nurse informed me that my friend's kidneys had failed and that he would be flown to the 3rd Field Hospital in Saigon and to what I remember her saying was the only dialysis unit available in South Vietnam. They soon bundled him up and gurneyed him out to a waiting aircraft on the nearby runway.

I have no memory of our saying good-bye to one another and would guess he was unconscious at the time.

Some hours later the same nurse again stopped at my bedside and gently broke the news to me that Doc Smitty had lost his final battle during the flight south. There were tears in her eyes.

As my own eyes began to well with tears of loss and loneliness, I told her that I was relieved Doc's suffering had come to an end, and that his death was likely for the best given the nature of his horrific wounds. She thought about what I'd said for a moment and then, unable to speak, reached out for my hand and squeezed it in understanding.

Several months later, while a patient at Letterman Army Hospital in San Francisco (and suffering greatly from the complications of my severe wounds and numerous surgeries), a Special Forces sergeant, whom I'd first met at Camp Zama's 249th General Hospital[3] during the second leg of my homeward journey, was by coincidence assigned to my 6th floor room. This second intersection of our paths allowed a much more detailed accounting of the events preceding each of our wounding. He asked the name of the firebase we'd been working from when Smitty hit the mine. I responded by saying it had been "Blitz" and that its site was roughly twenty-five kilometers south of Hue.

"I think you're mistaken," he responded authoritatively, "my teams worked that AO a lot and we never heard of a Firebase Blitz. Firebase Brick is in that area, though, and I'll bet that's where you were."

Well, I knew there was indeed a Firebase Brick in my battalion's AO, and was also vaguely aware that it was in the general vicinity of the base I thought to be Blitz. Though puzzled by his declaration and by how I'd

---

[3] Camp Zama was a U.S. Army base in Japan, and its huge wards were used throughout the war as a waypoint on the journey home for Vietnam War casualties thought too ill to endure the rigors of a single-hop, direct flight home from Vietnam.

otherwise been informed, I chalked-up the confusion to the fog of war and adopted Brick as the proper name. After all, the man had worked the area extensively in a capacity much more likely to arm him with an accurate grasp of the firebase inventory than me so it seemed reasonable to presume his analysis accurate.

From that point on, when relating the circumstance of my wounding, I told everyone I'd been hit a few kilometers east-southeast of FSB Brick.

In the late 1980's, a veteran to whom I'd described the physical layout of FSB Brick offered that he'd spent many months within Brick's perimeter himself and that my descriptions did not at all resemble the place. That surprising revelation rekindled my concern about the base's actual name and resulted in a series of inquiries to the Department of Defense. DOD's responses proved fruitless apart from the fact they did lead to the very important discovery that nearly all U.S. Army records from the Vietnam era had been transferred to the National Archives about the time my search had begun.

A subsequent inquiry to the National Archives and Records Administration (NARA) alerted me to the availability of two very important collections stored in its Archives II Textual Reference Branch: Battalion *Annual Historical Supplements* and Battalion *Daily Staff Journal or Duty Officer's Log*. A request for the September 16, 1970, 1st/502d Infantry Battalion *Daily Staff Journal* promptly followed and, only a month or so later, the copies were in hand bringing with them a definitive answer; my initial recollection had been accurate.[4] FSB Blitz not only existed, but its grid coordinate put it only two kilometers west-northwest of Smitty's hill; precisely where my initial memories had said it should be.

For whatever reason, the Army built two, mutually supportive firebases within ten kilometers of one another and christened them with names far too similar in sound and spelling for an environment where even the slightest of errors could cost men's lives. My battalion had indeed reopened FSB Blitz in September 1970, and it sat atop a huge hill mass only nine kilometers west-southwest of then existing FSB Brick.

That series of events coupled with my own combat experience, curiosity and a few other seminal events along the way, led to the birth of this manuscript.

One positive result of the Brick/Blitz confusion was an ever-expanding file folder in which I religiously compiled firebase/LZ names and grid coordinate information. While an associate member of the California Vietnam Veterans Memorial Commission between 1984 and 1991, that database expanded rapidly as firebase information slowly emerged from commission research, correspondence and from a significant acceleration in the publication of first-person accounts of the war. As the years slipped by, my skills at helping veterans locate historical data, unit associations and their long-lost comrades also increased exponentially.

By our memorial's dedication in December 1988, my reputation as a resource had been well established and, as a result, frequent inquiries found their way to me through the veteran community and news media. One such inquiry brought with it the acquaintance of a gentleman whose writings would later play a major role in the decision to embark on this perilous journey. A few days before the dedication, Ray Bows flew in to Sacramento and looked me up at the commission's headquarters.

Ray was the owner of Bows and Sons Publishing Company and had just released his own book, *Vietnam Military Lore—1959-1973*. He was in Sacramento both to attend the dedication and to market his product. At our first meeting, Ray handed me a copy and I in turn promised him that I'd do what I could to promote it, but cautioned that I was overwhelmed with the upcoming dedication and that it might be quite a while before I could spend any time with my nose among its pages.

That evening, I somehow found a spare moment to thumb through Ray's tome and, to my great surprise and delight, even that cursory review made it readily apparent Bows' book was both an unusual and important resource. Much enthused by the unexpected discovery, I grabbed my word processor and quickly drafted a one-page press release that was in the mailbox of every major California daily newspaper and TV station at the Capitol Press Center the very next morning. The release may not have helped Ray sell many books, but we've been friends ever since.

---

[4] I must emphasize here the exceedingly high quality of service provided by NARA's staff. I found them not only to be consummate professionals, but also thoughtful, considerate and exceedingly eager to help in any way possible. In fact, virtually all my dealings with agencies of the federal government (among them DOD, NARA, U.S. Navy, USMC, U.S. Army, NIMA, NPRC, USGS, Library of Congress, Army Center for Military History and the Army Military History Institute) have belied the widely-held notion that government employees are generally incompetent or otherwise unconcerned about the quality or quantity of service they provide. It was indeed rare that I was offered anything but competent and high-quality service.

Ray is a coin expert and the primary focus of the book was, oddly enough, slot machine tokens coined by U.S. military installations during the "American War" in Vietnam. Military Payment Certificates (MPC) used as cash in lieu of American greenbacks were also featured, as were the military awards of the various combatants.

Slot machines were ubiquitous among the many enlisted men's and officers' clubs that blossomed wherever units built their homes in Vietnam; however, following a big embezzlement scandal in 1968, the machines were generally banished from U.S. military facilities. From the early 1960s until the machines were removed in 1968, each facility produced its own unique token design and the designs were then cut and stamped by companies based in Japan and the U.S. Ray's exposure to the history of each facility was a natural by-product of his research into the history of each token, and the more he learned about the coins, the more he learned about the installations using them.

Most all had been named to honor the memory of a soldier lost in battle. Typically, those honored had either distinguished themselves, or the circumstance of their death was of historical significance to the unit or to the war. Ray apparently soon found himself as taken by the stories of these men and women as with slot machine tokens and, as a result, his book evolved into as much a history of military installations as it was a reference for tokens, currency and awards.

In early 1999, Bows released an epic follow-up to his initial effort. This time, rather than slot machine tokens and MPC, he instead focused exclusively on the history of named military installations and the stories of the men and women in whose honor they had been named. Meticulously and laboriously researched, *Vietnam Military Lore–Legends, Shadows And Heroes* is indeed a remarkable achievement.

At 1,179 pages and tipping the scales at over five pounds, it is a monster of a book! And, while his first work is now out of print and difficult to find, *Vietnam Military Lore– Legends, Shadows And Heroes* is still in print and available for purchase as this book goes to print (see Appendix H for more information in that regard).

Bows' *Vietnam Military Lore—1959-1973* became a mainstay of my reference collection and, when the decision to commit to *Where We Were* was made in 1996, his labor of love was in part the stimulus for that decision. Not only did his efforts provide inspiration, but also a significant portion of the data used in this manuscript was compiled from information found in both of Ray's efforts, as well as from other data he graciously provided as I struggled to construct this encyclopedia.

Les Hines, an Americal Division helicopter crew chief in 1968-69 who flew southern I Corps with the 123d Aviation Company's *Pelicans*, also provided significant inspiration. Les is a very important contributor to the Americal Association's remarkable website at *www.americal.org*. Hines and his cohorts have spent countless hours transcribing literally thousands of pages of after-action, operational and historical reports (as well as *The Army Reporter* of the era in almost its entirety) and, as a byproduct, compiled a listing of several hundred I Corps firebases now posted on the Americal Association's site. It was Les who enthusiastically urged me to "go for it" when I asked him if he thought a firebase book made any sense. Both before and after my decision, he graciously provided access to his data, asking nothing in return except that I do a good job. His contributions to the scholarship of the war both within and apart from this text are immense by any measure, as is his generosity and thoughtfulness.

There were many others who helped me navigate through the maze of this mammoth project as well, and I've done my best to recognize them all in the acknowledgment section of this manuscript. Sadly, it wasn't until after I'd committed to the undertaking that I started keeping track of all contributors' names, so some who deserve to be listed have gone without mention and I report that oversight with great remorse.

In the fall of 1971, and shortly after my release from Letterman Hospital, Doc Smitty's parents drove out to Sacramento, the only purpose of their trip to meet me and hear the details of their son's last days on earth firsthand. Over what seemed an eternity (but which could not have been more than a few minutes), I nervously related every detail still clear in my shattered memory. The anxiety of the telling grew steadily as my story progressed until it simply overwhelmed me. In desperation, I fabricated a thin excuse and fled the room in panic.

I never heard from Doc's parents again and my abandonment of them remains one of the great regrets of my life.

Many years later, Howard "Chico" Mikkali, our platoon leader's RTO that fateful day, told me a story that is the source of much guilt for him. While the rest of us were placing our mines and trip flares, Chico and Doc decided a game of cards would be an appropriate recreation. Neither possessed the requisite card deck and, exhausted from the climb up our little hill, they flipped a coin to decide which of the two would be responsible for bumming a deck from one of the riflemen setting up the perimeter. Doc Smitty lost the toss, wandered into my squad's position to ask me for a deck and called to me at the precise moment his footstep found the mine.

The memory of winning that toss has burdened Chico ever since, I think, though he did nothing wrong, and was a good soldier and a good friend throughout the war.

Steven "Doc Smitty" Smith died selflessly, his only apparent concern for my well-being and that of the patients around him. He died without complaint and fighting valiantly to the very end. I also know that Doc Smitty would have given his life to save any one of us, his friends in the Third Platoon, had it come to that in battle.

He may have died for his country or for no good reason at all, but whatever the reasons he was taken, I hope that in at least some small measure his death has taught the living a lesson, and that my own ending might be marked by such courage and selflessness.

As for my own wounds, how I survived them is beyond me because by any measure, I should have died that beautiful, sun-splashed autumn day in September 1970.

Certainly I also owe my life in great part to my comrades of Delta Company, the crew of that miraculous medevac, a wonderful surgeon named Charley Carroll and other staff at the 85th Evac Hospital, but there was some other force at work that day; something just beyond the reach of my comprehension.

I'd sensed the presence of that force months before Smitty triggered the mine and, oddly enough, was calmed by its presence immediately after the blast.

Though not a spiritually or religiously inclined person by most measures, it was nonetheless evident to me something greater than the reality of smoke and fury drifting across that clearing was at work and, for lack of a better description, "Divine Intervention" will have to suffice. Now no guardian angel or anything of that nature appeared before me, but the whole experience felt preordained; as though I was outside and above my body watching the events unfold more as an observer than a participant. I recall a distinct feeling that the stage had been set and the script written long before our arrival on that small hilltop.

Why the good Lord—or the accidental intersection of time and fate—conspired to deliver me alive and kicking at the far end of that tunnel I'll never comprehend, but at times I must admit to having been struck by the compelling feeling this book might have been the reason I was spared. Perhaps the force had other plans for me?

My work here has been a labor of love and is dedicated to many people, but in great part to Steve Smith's memory and also to the memory of the best friend of my high school years, Larry Keister.

Larry took a semester break during his third year as a pre-veterinary student at the University of California, Davis, and was quickly drafted into the Army as a result of that unfortunate lapse. By September 1968, he was in Vietnam, assigned to B Company, 3d/506th Infantry, 101st Airborne Division. On January 26, 1969, while carrying his squad's M-60 machine gun, Larry was killed (along with his platoon's Vietnamese Kit Carson Scout) by a command-detonated mine near Phan Thiet.[5] With him died much of the spirit of his family. And with him, died part of me.

Most of what I've done as an artist and writer has its roots in the memory of these two men, as well as in many fond and often laughter-filled memories of the many comrades with whom it was my privilege to serve as an American soldier in the war of our generation.

Michael Kelley
Sacramento, California
September 16, 2001

[5] AN 744-266 is the grid coordinate of that action, a spot situated in a ravine along the eastern slope of Hill 906, some two kilometers northeast of its peak, and twelve and one-half kilometers west to west-northwest of Thien Giao.

Introduction

While most of us who served in Vietnam, Laos, Cambodia, Thailand, their adjacent waters and even North Vietnam, recall vividly the names of the places we served, we were at the same time often uncertain of the precise location of those memory-filled sites, even when we were standing upon them. Thirty years later, that uncertainty has been greatly exacerbated by the ravages of time and our steadily fading memories.

We knew them as Camp Sally or as LZ Loon or as Firebase Blue or as OP-57 or Wunder Beach or Vung Tau or Xuan Loc or My Tho, but ask most veterans to pinpoint those places on a map today and it's likely they would have a very difficult time putting a finger on the spot.

Adding to the confusion for those who returned to Vietnam after the war is the fact the Vietnamese have virtually erased every trace of what they call the "American War." And whatever the Vietnamese might have overlooked, the jungle, monsoons and soil erosion have erased for them. Many veterans return convinced they can easily locate the images locked in their minds only to discover the terrain no longer resembles the crystal-clear photos stored in their memory banks.

The erasure of the former American presence is generally the result of two very powerful forces, one political and the other pragmatic.

The Vietnamese are an extremely resourceful people and while perhaps economically poor from a western point of view, they are quite rich in the skills and resolve it takes to exploit a practical use for every scrap material available to them. As recyclers, Americans are pure amateurs by comparison. During the war, the NVA and the VC demonstrated those skills by turning our trash into weapons later used against us, while the South Vietnamese converted much of it to shelter, souvenirs and furniture. The same was likely true of the French experience as well.

When the Americans left in 1973, those bases not taken by the ARVN often disappeared practically overnight; dismantled by nearby villagers intent on improving their homes or in marketing the material as industry. When the NVA/NLF overwhelmed the ARVN in the Final Offensive of 1973, most military facilities were abandoned and soon evaporated as the people dismantled and put to use every scrap of material left behind.

Perhaps as an expression of their nationalism, the victors also embarked on a conscious effort to eradicate even the most faint evidence of an American—and French—presence. What the scavengers might have missed or were unable to recycle, the government plowed under and reclaimed for farms, home sites or parks. More than a few of our old bases were reclaimed as military facilities that remain in use today, while some American-built seaports and airfields have been recycled into civilian facilities that will most likely remain in use for decades to come.

Returning U.S. veterans now often find themselves both astonished and befuddled by the almost total absence of our former presence. Places they thought would be simple to locate are instead almost impossible to position under the heavy footprints of intentional erasure, population growth, cultivation and the inexorable processes of Mother Nature as an artist and sculptor. "There" is simply no longer there, in many instances.

And while our memories fade and forces march ahead to reshape the landscape in anticipation of our return, there are other factors at work now hindering our efforts to find where we were during the war. One important factor is the language barrier; another is our predisposition to spell formal place names phonetically.

Take for example the main basecamp of the U.S. 1st Infantry Division. It was built near the village of Di An and took that name as its own official name.

In Vietnamese, Di An is pronounced *zee-anh* with a soft *a* and, as a result, many who once called the base their home spell the name simply as they heard it spoken. Today a veteran might spell Di An as *Zeon*, or perhaps *Xeon*. In other words, one must consider human nature when researching names provided by the men who served in Vietnam.

Another good example of the problem is a small Army Engineer base camp and quarry site that was situated near National Highway 14 and the town of Phu Nhon. To honor the memories of two fallen combat engineers, the site was named, or possibly renamed, Weigt-Davis.

During my research, I first became aware of the facility rather late in the process and was told its spelling was *Weight-Davis.* In fact, most anyone who'd been there confirmed that spelling and official reports often spelled it that way as well. A small number spelled it *Waite-Davis*, and still others, *Wake-Davis*. Subsequent efforts to unveil the name's origin were completely frustrated by the fact nobody by the last name Weight, (or Wait, Waite or Wake) was listed as a casualty of the war despite the fact everyone familiar with its history insisted those honored had indeed both been killed in the war.

Though rare, facilities were sometimes named to honor living soldiers—one who'd been badly wounded perhaps, or one for whom there was widespread adulation and respect. Alert to that potential, my instincts suggested that might be the case for Weigt-Davis and, if correct, establishing the men's identities would be a virtual impossibility because for privacy reasons, the names of our wounded have never been made part of the public record.

I hammered at the puzzle for months but it was only by some propitious quirk of fate that a correspondent who'd been forwarded one of my many inquiries provided the answer. Weigt-Davis, he noted, had been named to honor Army Sp4 Stephen L. Weigt, and Sp4 Robert S. Davis, both of whom were killed March 21, 1969. End of mystery.

In general, the proper spelling of Vietnamese place-names is problematic at best as there seems to be little spelling consistency for them even among the Vietnamese themselves. For example, Da Nang is variously spelled *Da Nang, Da-Nang, DaNang* and *Danang*, with similar variants common to virtually any multi-syllabic Vietnamese place-name.

By the same token, two-syllable place-names that one might instinctively presume consist of two separate words are often instead simply one. Most central highland, two-syllable village names that include the prefix *Plei* are broken into two words; however, by far the most common spelling of Plei Ku, for example, is *Pleiku.*

Apart from obvious problems associated with contrasts between Vietnamese and English pronunciations of the same letters or letter groupings, phonetic variations in which pronunciation is even the same can produce a wide range of spelling variants. Phu Bai becomes *Fou Bai, Fu Bai, Fu Bi, Fu B, Phou Bai*, and so on.

As a general rule of thumb where Vietnamese place names are concerned, if it's possible for a spelling variant to exist, then it will. In that regard, when a first attempt at locating a place name in the alphabetized section of this text is thwarted, I'd suggest the reader approach the name from as many points on the phonetic spelling compass as they can possibly imagine!

Transcription and Transposition Errors

While a substantial effort was made to ensure the accuracy of the data presented in this manuscript, apart from those introduced by the author, transposition and transcription errors were, and will forever remain, common among official military reports. Consider the fact most official reports were compiled or transcribed by nineteen-year olds woefully lacking in military experience or any real interest in the task at hand. But even where interest and experience might have been abundant, errors were commonplace. Consider too, that as long as there are historians around to compound the problem with our own inadvertent contributions, such errors will remain forever problematic.

Readers will likely encounter numerous errors and omissions throughout the text and no one should rely on any of the material presented here as completely factual without independent verification. Nonetheless, I do believe that the greater part of the information presented here remains both substantially correct and reliable.

Unfortunately, transposition errors introduced during the translation of grid coordinate data into relative location narrative seem to have occurred with inordinate regularity. The most typical of these errors is a 180-degree transposition. For example, a facility may be posted as having been fifteen kilometers north-northwest (NNW) of a village, when it was in fact fifteen kilometers south-southeast (SSE) of that village. Where the relative location appears to conflict with a known or presumed location, the reader should give the greatest weight to the grid coordinate itself and simply plot the grid on an appropriate map.

Terminology

Readers unfamiliar with the terminology of the war will encounter a host of words and phrases that may be puzzling in both their nature and frequent convolutions. Words such as Firebase, Fire Support Base, Forward

Fire Support Base, Patrol Base, Fire Support Patrol Base, LZ, Landing Zone, Camp and Basecamp are ubiquitous. At the same time, their application and origins are often unclear. There's a good reason for that: their origins and definitions have always been unclear!

There were conventions, to be sure, but those conventions often varied from unit to unit, or from division to division, or from military region to military region, or from year to year. There are no hard and fast definitions for these terms, though I'll try to define them in a way that might help the reader make some sense of them all:

Firebase and Fire Support Base (*often abbreviated as FB, FSB, FSSB, FSPB, FFSP, among other variants*): Firebases were ground installations designed to house artillery and/or mortar units firing in support of maneuvering infantry elements and of other bases within the range of their weapons. Firebases typically housed infantry security forces and communication elements, units that varied in size according to the dictates of the terrain, the number of artillery pieces in place, the estimated size of nearby enemy forces and degree of threat.

Most were generally circular in design (or built in any shape necessary to conform to the terrain) and contained any number of artillery pieces and/or mortars defended by various combinations of exterior concertina wire, trenches, sandbagged bunkers/foxholes and dirt berms. Although landing pads for helicopters were normally built within or adjacent to most firebases, aircraft were not usually housed or maintained upon them.

Some firebases existed for only a few days or hours, while others evolved into permanent positions that remained open for many years. In some areas, firebases were opened seasonally; that is, closed and reopened in concert with the monsoon rains on a cyclical basis. Some firebases were built in one location and subsequently relocated several times yet retained the same name in every move, while others remained entirely in one location yet were renamed several times during their life span. Others still were reclassified periodically from LZs to FSBs to Camps and to Basecamps in concert with their changing size, available facilities or at the whims of new tenants or commanders.

Landing Zones and LZs: The terms "Landing Zone" (LZ) and "Firebase" (FSB) were often used interchangeably and many were known both as LZs and FSBs at the same time or at different stages of their use. For example, by tradition, the U.S. Army's 1st Cavalry Division called nearly all its firebases LZs, while the 101st Airborne Division called them firebases. And they did that despite the fact many of these facilities were otherwise identical.

The term "Landing Zone" also often simply referred to anyplace a helicopter might land; that is, any undefended clearing in the jungle. In some cases, small LZs later grew into firebases as contact with the enemy was made and the battlefield expanded. Artillery was then added to support the surrounding infantry operations and still later that firebase might expand into a full-fledged, permanent Landing Zone or Basecamp over time and as tactical dictates evolved.

The general distinction between a permanent Landing Zone and a Fire Support Base (if there was any at all) was that a permanent LZ was often much larger than a FSB and, although they may have also provided artillery fire support as one of their functions, they typically also contained facilities designed to house helicopters and their supporting units, ground transportation, POL facilities, engineering elements, ammo supply dumps, medical and even recreational facilities, most of which were absent in a typical FSB. LZ Betty at Phan Thiet and LZ Sally near Hue are good examples of large, permanent LZs.

Camps and Basecamps: The term "Camp" was typically attached to facilities much larger than permanent LZs or firebases. Camps often grew to house multi-battalion, multi-brigade, or even division-sized elements. On the other hand, the term was also frequently assigned to small cantonments and compounds often sited within larger bases and home to very small, specialized units. Where Camp Eagle near Hue may have held 15,000 troops, Camp Hurt on the Cau Mau Peninsula might have held 100 or fewer.

French Forts and Airfields: The French built a staggering number of forts, fortresses and pillbox-style fortifications during their war and, when the Americans began arriving in significant numbers, it was not uncommon for them to first establish residence within or adjacent to old French positions. That is particularly true where airfields were concerned. Many French airfields and forts were also later occupied by the Japanese during WWII, and in some cases, expanded and improved by them as well. It's also true that many former French military facilities were put to use by the armies of both North and South Vietnam during the American War.

In fact, on March 15, 1962, and during Operation Shufly, the first U.S. helicopter force to serve in the war was flown to and housed in a former French air facility. That day, carrier-borne helicopters of USMC Helicopter Squadron HMM 362 launched from the deck of the USS *Princeton* at a point some twenty-five kilometers from the coast of South Vietnam and bound for the old, dilapidated, French and WWII Japanese airfield at Soc Trang, located in the Mekong Delta near Khanh Hung. Soc Trang was approximately 140 kilometers south-southwest of Saigon and twenty-five kilometers east of the mouth of the Hau Giang River, a place considered practically in the middle of nowhere at that point in the conflict. Replaced by an Army aviation unit two years later, the Marine elements at Soc Trang were among the very few U.S. Marine Corps units to have operated in any Combat Tactical Zone other than I Corps.

Final Observations

If one gains nothing else from thumbing through these many pages, it is my hope that he/she will at least be instilled with awe and appreciation for the immense physical labors, infrastructure and resources invested in the American War. I certainly was. Moral questions aside, the engineering and construction effort undertaken by the U.S. during its involvement is simply astonishing by any measure one might care to employ.[6]

For those of us who served in Vietnam, extrapolating our imagination out to the reality we know existed beyond the thousands of entries listed here, brings with it a sobering appreciation of our significance in the bigger picture that was the war. Individually, we were but mere pixels of color on a gargantuan canvas of drama that stretched to the horizon and beyond. While one might casually invoke the cliché that we were simply "cogs in a wheel," it would be far more accurate to say that we were actually little more than a few molecules on the tooth of a cog of one very big wheel! As my knowledge grew in concert with the labor invested in my research here, I found that realization both humbling and fascinating.

Thousands upon thousands of firebases and basecamps were built, dismantled and sometimes rebuilt again. Hundreds, even thousands of men and untold quantities of materials and supplies were needed to construct any one of them. Once built, hundreds and sometimes thousands of men were needed to house, operate and defend each of them. The breadth and depth of the undertaking simply staggers the mind.

Many, if not most, of the facilities listed in this text represent an investment of perhaps millions, or even many millions of dollars and, simultaneously, oceans of sweat, blood and tears invested by the men who built them. Each facility represents unfathomable effort and sacrifice, and perhaps more importantly, for every entry found here, at least a thousand stories yet to be told.

Built with the fire of youth and forged in the heat of battle, they were our homes, often our salvation, and frequently our refuge from a battlefront that always extended a full 360 degrees around us no matter where we stood and held the ground.

But why this book? Actually I had little choice in the matter. My significant veteran community experience made it abundantly clear there existed a great need for access to this sort of information but no place one might go to find it all in one convenient package. The need was within my abilities to fill, I thought, but what started as the inkling of an idea to build such a place quickly germinated into a few preliminary architectural sketches and then into a roaring fire beyond my ability to control. Once the first nails had been hammered into the framing, the project simply billowed into an obsession that often overwhelmed my desire to do much of anything else. My wife and family can no doubt attest to that unfortunate fact.

To be perfectly honest about it, when the manuscript was approaching 150 pages (some three years before these thoughts were transcribed), it was my distinct impression the journey was nearing its end. Little did I know that what I had in my grasp was the tail, not the body, of one very large and very hungry tiger!

---

[6] The same can be said for the French War as well. See "French Fort" and "de Lattre Line" entries in the Glossary.

The first leg of the journey is now over and it is my fervent hope these pages and their words become a very accurate and important resource for Vietnam veterans, their families, students of the American War and future generations that might pause to look back.

My sincere hope is that this manuscript will also help us all to determine just exactly where we were during our Vietnam experience and, in some cases, facilitate visits and even revisits to those many memory-intensive and far-off points once filled with thunder, light and hope. For some of us, a small few perhaps, discovering where we were in that long-ago dreamscape might help in our understanding of just where it is we are now, what it is that we have become and where the journey might next lead us.

Those of us who served in the combat zone left that far-away place, one way or the other, more than thirty years before these words were typed. But for many of us, the Vietnam experience still hovers at the edge of our consciousness, as though it all happened yesterday.

The smell of wet grass after a summer storm, the echo of a distant helicopter thumping its way through a morning sky, the image of a tree line silhouetted against a bank of rain clouds on a humid afternoon—any of these might carry us back in an instant. That said, it would be wrong for non-veterans to presume that such flashbacks are inherently unpleasant, wrenching experiences. Frankly, I'm of the opinion they take veterans back to the good far more often than to the bad. In fact, stereotypes of the Vietnam veteran notwithstanding, I'm also convinced that the war emotionally strengthened many more of us than it might have damaged or destroyed.

Though an infantryman and grievously wounded myself, I can only tell you that my war was indeed filled with far more laughter and wonder than it was with tears and horror.

Nothing in my lifetime has ever approached the intensity of emotion or heights of experience of that which painted the eleven months I spent in the mountains south and west of Hue. Nothing. It's also true that I would not part with those memories for the world, and experience tells me that I'm hardly alone in that regard.

For those of us who served in the American War in Vietnam, it is the people, the sounds and smells, the places we lived, worked and nurtured with our sweat and our blood that will remain inextricably woven into the fibers of our memory and character, forever part of us and who we may yet become. Where we were is in great part, after all, who we are.

Reference Guides

Guide to Standard Reference Notes

The reader will likely encounter a large number of unfamiliar acronyms and phrases throughout this text. To obviate any misunderstanding, a large glossary of abbreviations and acronyms can be found among the last pages of this manuscript. Additionally, many of the same abbreviations and acronyms are also listed within the body of the alphabetical listings to facilitate their interpretation. The frequency of a certain number of key phrases and acronyms is very high, and it would be appropriate for the reader to review a number of the most significant conventions before tackling the main body of the text.

Common terms, phrases and acronyms the reader will encounter while navigating *Where We Were* include:

Americal List

A comprehensive listing of Americal, USMC, 101st Abn and 1st Cav firebases/LZs in I Corps, and also 1st Cav LZs in III Corps, compiled by Mr. Les Hines and available on the website of the Americal Association at *www.americal.org/firebase.htm.*

AMS

Army Map Service. See DMA.

DMA

Defense Mapping Agency. The DMA produced most of the topographic maps used during the American War. That agency was preceded in that responsibility by the AMS (Army Map Service) and later superseded by the National Imagery and Mapping Agency (NIMA) as the maker of U.S. military's maps.

Grid Coordinates

Unless otherwise stated, 6-digit grid coordinates reference DMA L-7014, L-7015 or L-7016 series, 1:50,000 scale maps, while 2 and 4-digit coordinates reference AMS or DMA L-509 or L-1501 series JOG 1:250,000 scale maps and/or DMA ONCs and TPCs (see below).

Height/Altitude

Unless otherwise stated, all height and altitude references are in meters. Airfield altitude/elevation are normally listed as "El." or "EL." To convert meters to feet, multiply by 3.2808. To convert feet to meters, multiply by .3048.

JOG

Joint Operational Graphics. A series of 1:250,000 scale topographical maps of the Army Map Service and the Defense Mapping Agency of the L-509 and L-1501 series. See "L-509 Series."

L-509 Series

The L-509 series JOG (Joint Operations Graphics) maps (sometimes listed L509) were produced by the DMA for tactical and strategic planning. At 1:250,000 scale, they are of a larger scale than the L-7014 series but still highly-detailed, color, topographical maps. These maps were normally used at Battalion and higher levels and likely rarely used in the field. The L-509 series was superseded by the L-1501 JOG series of the same maps. For more detail and ordering information about these products, refer to the Table of Contents.

L-1501 Series

See "L-509 Series."

L-7014 Series

L-7014 series maps (sometimes listed as L7014) were produced by the DMA for tactical use. They are large-scale, highly-detailed, 1:50,000 scale, color, topographical maps used at the platoon and company level in Vietnam. In other words, these are the maps with which most Infantrymen were intimately familiar. For more detail and ordering information about these products, refer to the Table of Contents.

NIMA Gazetteer

Refers to the National Imagery and Mapping Agency's gazetteer of Vietnamese place and terrain feature names available on CD-ROM from the USGS. This extensive gazetteer (covers the entire planet excluding the U.S.) is also available in a two-volume, hard copy version as well. In this text, the term is often shortened to simply "NIMA," or "NIMA Gaz." For more detail and ordering information about these products, refer to the Table of Contents.

NOAA

National Oceanic and Atmospheric Administration. An agency that among other things markets small scale aeronautical charts (see TPC and ONC) produced by the DMA that were relied upon heavily in the research of this text.

NPIA Gazetteer

MACV/Vietnamese National Police Gazetteer of Hamlet Evaluation System (HES) villages, 1971-73. A large, detailed village listing that includes six-digit grid coordinates and corresponding VC names for each site. The file is held in the NARA Center for Electronic Records at College Park, MD. In this text, the term is often abbreviated as NPIA or NPIA Gaz.

ONC
Operational Navigation Charts produced by DMA and marketed through NOAA. These maps are 1:1,000,000 scale, color, topographical, aeronautical charts in which the color scheme denotes altitude rather than terrain composition.

TAD
Tactical Aerodrome Directory of South Vietnam. A comprehensive guide to all airfields and heliports in operation as of its publication date. Published periodically by the DMA with a requirement that all previous issues be destroyed.

TPC
Tactical Pilotage Charts produced by DMA and marketed through NOAA. These maps are 1:500,000 scale, color, topographical, aeronautical charts in which the color scheme denotes altitude rather than terrain composition.

UTM
Universal Transverse Mercator projection grid zone system. A global, grid overlay used for most map reading in Vietnam and as the reference for all grid coordinates noted in this publication. The two- character alpha designator preceding the numeric portion of a grid coordinate designates the UTM grid zone to which the numeric portion of the grid relates. To view the general UTM Zones overlying SVN, refer to the UTM Grid Zone map in mapping section at the front of this publication. For an explanation of the system, refer to the map reading section of this text.

VHPA Battle Index
Very large, chronological index of operations, aircraft losses and battles available on the Vietnam Helicopter Pilot Association's website: www. vhpa.org/info/panel/battle/.

XXIV Corps Grid or Index
Large index of III MAF, 101st Abn, and 5th Inf Div (Mech) FSB/LZ locations compiled by XXIX Corps HQ in April 1970. Discovered at National Archives by Don Armstrong, who then generously gave this project a copy. Includes a listing of proposed FSB names from each unit (XXIX Corps had taken away the responsibility for naming new FSBs from individual commands by April 1970, and required each to submit a list of its preferences).

Guide to Military Regions and Corps Tactical Zones

For tactical purposes, South Vietnam was divided into various military regions that carried different names at different points in the war. The most prominent designations were the four Corps Tactical Zones (CTZs) called I Corps CTZ, II Corps CTZ, III Corps CTZ, IV Corps CTZ and the Special Capitol CTZ centered on Saigon. These regions ran from north to south, with I Corps being the northernmost CTZ. On 1 Jul 70, the Corps CTZs were re-designated as Military Regions (MRs) 1 through 4, numbers that corresponded with the prior Corps numbering.

Each CTZ or region contained a number of SVN provinces and none of the provinces were less than 100% within a given region, except perhaps the area of the Special Capitol Zone including Saigon. **Important Note:** Province boundaries and names were apparently absorbed into one another or otherwise changed rather frequently during the war (particularly in IV Corps), and caution must be exercised when dealing with a location based on a province name (that is, a given location may have been located in several different provinces as a function of time).

The provinces located within each Corps CTZ or subsequent Military Region for most of the war were as follows (provinces that existed for only a portion of the war are in parenthesis):

I Corps

A.k.a. I CTZ or Military Region 1 and commonly pronounced *one corps;* northernmost of the five CTZs in SVN, consisting of the following five Provinces and the Island of Cu Lau Re:

Quang Nam Province	Quang Tri Province
Quang Ngai Province	Thua Thien Province
Quang Tin Province	(Quang Da Province)

II Corps
A.k.a. II CTZ (Combat Tactical Zone), commonly pronounced *two corps*; 2d northernmost of the five CTZs in SVN and consisting of the following 12 Provinces:

Binh Dinh Province	Ninh Thuan Province
Binh Thuan Province	Phu Bon Province
Darlac Province	Phu Yen Province
Khan Hoa Province	Pleiku Province
Kontum Province	Quang Duc Province
Lam Dong Province	Tuyen Duc Province
(Gia Lai Province)	(Thanh Hoa Province)
(Dak Lak Province)	

III Corps
A.k.a. III CTZ (Combat Tactical Zone), commonly pronounced *three corps*; 2d southernmost of the five CTZs in SVN, consisting of the following 11 Provinces and a Special CTZ within its boundaries:

Binh Duong Province	Long An Province
Bien Hoa Province	Long Khanh Province
Binh Long Province	Phuoc Long Province
Binh Tuy Province	Phuoc Tuy Province
Gia Dinh Province	Tay Ninh Province
Hau Nghia Province	Special Capital Zone (Saigon)
	(Phuoc Thanh Province)

IV Corps
A.k.a. IV CTZ (Combat Tactical Zone), commonly pronounced *four corps*; the southernmost of the five CTZs in SVN, consisting of the following 16 Provinces and the islands of Con Son and Dao Phu Quoc:

An Giang Province	Phong Dinh Province
An Xuyen Province	Sa Dec Province
Ba Xuyen Province	Vinh Binh Province
Bac Lieu Province	Vinh Long Province
Chau Doc Province	(Ben Tre Province)
Chuong Thien Province	(Ca Mau Province)
Dinh Tuong Province	(Can Tho Province)
Go Cong Province	(My Tho Province)
Kien Giang Province	(Rach Gia Province)
Kien Hoa Province	(Soc Trang Province)
Kien Phong Province	(Tra Vinh Province)
Kien Tuong Province	

Military Regions in Laos

During SF Operations Hotfoot/White Star, 1959-62, the U.S. military designated five military regions in Laos, naming them:

MR1 (containing Luang Prabang)
MR2 (containing Xiangkhoang)
MR3 (containing Khammouane)
MR4 (containing Pakse, its largest city, Saravane, Vapikham Thuong and dominated by the Bolovens Plateau)
MR5 (containing the capital, Vientiane)

These five Military Regions divided Laos into four, horizontal zones, with MR1 at the northern end and MR4 at the southern end. MR 2 was split in half vertically by MR5, with MR5 in the SW and MR2 in the NW.

NVA/VC Military Regions

MACV normally assigned a three-digit number to each enemy "base area." Base Areas were geographic regions that intelligence had determined were used by the NVA or VC for staging, training, re-supplying, recuperation or tactical operations. These areas could migrate to other areas, or disappear or reappear from year-to-year in concert with the enemy's strategic or tactical goals.

The first digit of each three-digit group represents the country in which the zone was located (1 and 4 indicate SVN; 3 and 7 indicate Cambodia; 6 indicates Laos), while the last two digits of each three-digit grouping simply indicate the sequential order in which the zones were discovered and are not code for a geographical zone. Base Areas are often also referred to as "Operational Areas" using the same numbering system. The manner in which enemy Operational Areas were given alphabetical assignments was not discovered during this research. See main alphabetical entry for detail regarding any particular region in the small sampling that follows:

Base Area 100	Quang Tin Prov, I Corps
Base Area 101	Quang Tri Prov, I Corps
Base Area 112	Quang Nam Prov, I Corps
Base Area 114	Thua Thien Prov, I Corps
Base Area 116	Quang Nam Prov, I Corps
Base Area 117	Americal AO. I Corps
Base Area 121	Quang Ngai Prov (?) I Corps
Base Area 202	BR 130-307. Pleiku Prov, II Corps
Base Area 226	BR 72-63. Binh Dinh Prov, II Corps
Base Area 237	II Corps
Base Area 238	Kontum/Darlac Prov, II Corps
Base Area 302	YS. Long Khanh Prov, III Corps
Base Area 303	Southern III Corps
Base Area 350	Area in Cambodia along the border and just N of the Fishhook & Loc Ninh
Base Area 351	An area of appx 100 sq. km in the Fishhook, Cambodia
Base Area 352	An area in the Fishhook of Cambodia
Base Area 353	N of Tay Ninh along the Cambodian border
Base Area 354	XT. Along the Cambodian border N of the Parrot's Beak and NE of Tay Ninh
Base Area 367	Area in Cambodia forming the S half of the Parrot's Beak
Base Area 483	The NE portion of Base Area 483 was in Chuong Thien Prov, S of Can Tho
Base Area 609	YB. Cambodia in Tri-border area
Base Area 604	XD. NVA staging area along the HCMT and centered around Tchepone, Laos
Base Area 610	XD/YD(?) See Base Areas 604, Laos
Base Area 611	XD. In Laos to the W of the A Shau Valley. See Base Areas 604, Laos
Base Area 618	XD/YD. Quang Tri Prov, I Corps
Base Area 701	YV. Adjacent Darlac Prov, II Corps
Base Area 702	YA 90-75. Chu Pa Mtn area 20 km NW of Plei Mrong. Kontum/Pleiku Provs, II Corps
Base Area 704	VS/WT/VS/WS, Cambodia, straddled the Mekong River at the border of SVN
Base Area 707	Cambodia
Base Area 740	YU. Located in Cambodia and along the SVN border SW of Ban Me Thuot
Base Area Do Xa	BS 410-079. Just south of the I Corps-II Corps border. Quang Nam Prov, I Corps
Binh Dai Secret Zone	XS 86-26. Eastern Kien Hoa Prov, IV Corps
Cam Son Secret Zone	XS 2-4. Located W and WNW of Dong Tam. Dinh Tuong Prov, IV Corps
Cong Cam Son Secret Zone	See Op Coronado, late '67. III Corps (?)
Hon Heo Secret Zone	CP 05-33. Along coast appx 18 km S of Nha Trang. Khanh Hoa Prov, II Corps
Interzone NAMBO	S 1/4 of SVN
Interzone V	N 3/4s of SVN
Khe Sanh Front HQ	XD 38-63 to 50-70. Located in Laos generally 16 km W of Khe Sanh Combat Base
Long Noggin Secret Zone	XT. Binh Duong and Binh Long Prov border, III Corps
Man Lyr Base Area	Cambodia opposite Quang Duc Prov in II Corps
Mao Tao Secret Zone	YS. Near Gia Ray and Nui Chua Chan Mtn. Phuoc Tuy Prov, III Corps
May Tao Secret Zone	Phuoc Tuy Prov. III Corps
Minh Dam Secret Zone	YS. Phuoc Tuy Prov, III Corps

Operational Area "101"	YD 4-4 (?) Hai Lang Forest. Thau Thien/Quang Tri Provs border area (?) I Corps
Operational Area "A"	YD 01-66. Quang Tri Prov, I Corps
Operational Area "B"	YD 54-17. Thua Thien Prov, I Corps
Operational Area "C"	AT 97-52. Quang Nam Prov, I Corps
Operational Area "D"	BT 18-18. Quang Tin Prov, I Corps
Operational Area "E"	BS 39-73. Quang Ngai Prov, I Corps

Guide to Lesser-Known Provinces of South Vietnam

It is not widely understood that the names of numerous provinces and province boundaries changed at various times during the American War in Vietnam (a phenomena that has continued in post-war Vietnam). As a result, the reader will encounter references to provinces and province locations that may seem contradictory or inconsistent with other, factual accounts and other research material. In many cases, the apparent contradiction or error may actually not be what it seems.

For example, it is possible for the same village or terrain feature to have been in Phouc Thanh Province early in the war, but in Phuoc Long Province later in the war. Other province name or boundary changes produce numerous, similar situations that can make positive identification problematic.

Because U.S. casualty data was compiled by province at time of casualty, the same confusion affects our ability to accurately interpret casualty data found in such resources as the DOD's Combat Area Casualty File. For example, it is not uncommon to find a 1964 casualty listed in a province that does not appear on a 1967 provincial map of South Vietnam.

Tracking these changes is exceedingly difficult and the author was unable to find any authoritative guide to the sequence of such changes. However, the following synopsis of former provinces may assist the reader in sorting out problems that arise from the predisposition of the Vietnamese to change political boundaries at an extraordinary pace.

Ben Tre Province (XS/XR)

In what later became known as IV Corps and absorbed into what became primarily Kien Hoa Prov(?) Thought to have ceased existence at some point shortly before or during early U.S. presence in SVN(?) Actual dates of existence unknown. IV Corps.

Ca Mau Province (VR/WR/VQ/WQ)

In what later became known as IV Corps and absorbed into what became primarily An Xuyen Prov. Thought to have ceased existence at some point shortly before or during early U.S. presence in SVN(?) Actual dates of existence unknown. IV Corps.

Can Tho Province (WR)

In what later became known as IV Corps and absorbed into what later became primarily Chuong Thien Prov. Thought to have ceased existence at some point shortly before or during early U.S. presence in SVN(?) Actual dates of existence unknown. IV Corps.

Dak Lak Province (YV/ZV/ZU/AQ/AP/BQ/BP)

In what later became known as II Corps and absorbed into what became primarily Darlac Prov. Thought to have ceased existence at some point shortly before or during early U.S. presence in SVN(?) Actual dates of existence unknown. II Corps.

Gia Lai Province (YA/ZA/AR)

In what later became known as II Corps. Appears to have been roughly the same size as, and absorbed within, Pleiku Prov. Thought to have ceased existence at some point shortly before or during early U.S. presence in SVN(?) Actual dates of existence unknown. II Corps.

My Tho Province (WS/XS)

In what later became known as IV Corps and absorbed into what became primarily Go Cong and Dinh Tuong Prov(?) Thought to have ceased existence at some point shortly before or during early U.S. presence in SVN(?) Actual dates of existence unknown. IV Corps.

Phuoc Thanh Province (XT/YT)

In what later became known as III Corps and later absorbed into what became the southern half of Phuoc Long Prov. Thought to have ceased existence at some point shortly before or during early U.S. presence in SVN(?) Actual dates of existence unknown. III Corps.

Quang Da Province (YC/ZC/AT/BT)

In what later became known as I Corps and apparently absorbed into what became primarily Quang Nam Prov. Thought to have ceased existence at some point shortly before or during early U.S. presence in SVN(?) Actual dates of existence unknown. I Corps.

Rach Gia Province (VR/WR/WS)

In what later became known as IV Corps and absorbed into what became primarily Kien Giang Prov. Thought to have ceased existence at some point shortly before or during early U.S. presence in SVN(?) Actual dates of existence unknown. IV Corps.

Soc Trang Province (WR/XR)

In what later became known as IV Corps and absorbed into what became primarily Bac Lieu Prov. Thought to have ceased existence at some point shortly before or during early U.S. presence in SVN(?) Actual dates of existence unknown. IV Corps.

Thanh Hoa Province (BP/CP)

In what later became known as II Corps and appears to have been renamed or absorbed into what became primarily Khanh Hoa Prov. Thought to have ceased existence at some point shortly before or during early U.S. presence in SVN(?) Actual dates of existence unknown. II Corps.

Tra Vinh Province (WR/XR)

In what later became known as IV Corps and absorbed into what became primarily Vinh Binh Prov. Thought to have ceased existence shortly before or during early U.S. presence in SVN(?) Actual dates of existence unknown.

Guide to Principal Roadway Systems of South Vietnam

During the American War in Vietnam, the road system of SVN was broken-down into five major groupings by cartographers. In order of quality and importance, starting with the most significant, those groups were:

QL National and International routes - Shield symbol

LTL Inter-provincial routes - Circular symbol

TL Provincial routes - Triangular symbol

Route Supplementary roads - Rectangular symbol (often abbreviated as "Rte.")

HL Communal routes - Diamond-shaped symbol

National, Inter-provincial, Provincial, and Communal roadways all appear to have been numbered using a two-digit numbering system (e.g., QL-1, LTL-23, TL-49 and HL-13), while Supplementary routes all appear to have been numbered using a three-digit system (e.g., Highway or Route 547). As a general rule throughout this publication, National routes (QLs) are referred to as "QL," Inter-provincial routes (LTLs) are referred to as "Highways," as are Provincial routes (TLs) and Communal routes (HLs). Supplementary routes are normally referred to as "Route," though sometimes also as "Highway."

Despite the hierarchy of the naming system, very little of the country's road network was paved. With the exceptions of the internal portions of the bigger cities and most of QL-1, roads in SVN were almost entirely dirt roads of dubious quality and generally poorly maintained. The weather and enemy activity made securing and maintaining them a very difficult task.

Primary Roadway Designation (Alpha Order)

Highway

"Highway" and "Route" are terms used interchangeably and informally in this text to identify Provincial routes (TLs), and Supplementary routes in particular, but often also for any road that is identified.

HL

Designator for Communal routes of the SVN road system. Normally identified by two digits in a diamond-shaped map symbol. Typically joined small towns with one another and ordinarily did not cross provincial borders and were almost all dirt roads. Lowest-quality roads.

Inter-provincial Route (See LTL)

LTL

Designator for Inter-provincial routes of the SVN road system. Normally identified by two digits enclosed in a circular map symbol. LTL routes were secondary to QL routes (major National and International routes), and the second-highest level system in SVN.

QL

Designator for major National and International routes of the SVN road system. Typically identified by one or two digits enclosed in a shield map symbol. The highest quality routes in SVN.

Route

Designator for Supplementary roads of the SVN road system. Typically identified by three digits enclosed in a rectangular map symbol. One step above Communal routes (HLs) in quality.

Route Coloniale

A general term for roads of the French Colonial period built before or during the 1st Indochina War, and then secured by the French Army during its war with the Vietminh. Normally designated by the initials "R. C." and followed by a route number, as in "R. C. 4."

Supplementary Route (See Route)

TL

Designator for Provincial routes of the SVN road system. Typically identified by two-digits in a triangular-shaped map symbol. Third in the hierarchy of road identifiers behind major National and International roads (QLs) and Inter-provincial roads (LTLs). A step in quality above. Supplementary roads (see routes).

Map Reading 101

How to Locate Grid Coordinates on Military Maps

The guidelines for locating a point on a map represented by a specific grid coordinate are not as difficult to learn as one might think. With an understanding of a few fundamental rules and the right map in hand, not only is the process actually quite simple, but the same procedures apply to virtually every military map, and most civilian maps, regardless of their origin.

In order to pinpoint grid coordinate locations, one must of course acquire the proper map or maps related to the grid coordinates they seek to plot. Instructions that should facilitate access to a wide variety of high-quality Vietnam era military maps are to be found among the appendices of this text, and it would also be wise to spend some time familiarizing one's self with the UTM grid overlay illustrations printed among the map section.

First, let's explore some background information that should help provide a fundamental understanding of military map coordinates:

The following was transcribed/paraphrased from http://mapping.usgs.gov/mac/isb/pubs/factsheets/fs15799.html:

Universal Transverse Mercator (UTM) Grid

USGS Fact Sheet Number 157-99 (February 1999)

Map projections: The most convenient way to identify points on the curved surface of the Earth is with a system of reference lines called parallels of latitude and meridians of longitude. On some maps, the meridians and parallels appear as straight lines. On most modern maps, however, the meridians and parallels appear as curved lines. These differences are due to the mathematical treatment required to portray a curved surface on a flat surface so that important properties of the map (such as distance and aerial accuracy) are shown with minimum distortion. Systems that portray the round Earth on a flat surface are called map projections.

Grids: To simplify the use of maps and to avoid the inconvenience of pinpointing locations on curved reference lines, cartographers superimpose on the map a rectangular grid consisting of two sets of straight, parallel lines, uniformly spaced, each set perpendicular to the other. This grid is designed so that any point on the map can be designated by its latitude and longitude or by its grid coordinates, and a reference in one system can be converted into a reference in another system. Such grids are usually identified by the name of the particular projection for which they are designed.

The Universal Transverse Mercator grid: The National Imagery and Mapping Agency (NIMA) (formerly the Defense Mapping Agency) adopted a special grid for military use throughout the world called the Universal Transverse Mercator (UTM) grid. In this grid, the world is divided into 60 north-south zones, each covering a strip 6° wide in longitude. These zones are numbered consecutively beginning with Zone 1, between 180° and 174° west longitude, and progressing eastward to Zone 60, between 174° and 180° east longitude… In each zone, coordinates are measured north and east in meters. (One meter equals 39.37 inches, or slightly more than 1 yard.) The northing values are measured continuously from zero at the Equator, in a northerly direction. Southerly values are similarly measured from the Equator, south. A central meridian through the middle of each 6° zone is assigned an easting value of 500,000 meters. Grid values to the west of this central meridian are less than 500,000; to the east, more than 500,000.

UTM gridlines: The UTM grid is shown on USGS and NIMA maps of most all scales. On large scale maps such as 1;25,000 or 1:50,000 (DMA L-7014 series for example), the UTM grid lines are indicated at intervals of 1,000 meters by either blue ticks in the margins of the map and/or solid gridlines. Smaller scale maps of say the 1:100,000 and 1:250,000 scale typically show solid, blue gridlines at 10 kilometer (10,000 meters) intervals but normally lack any 1 kilometer ticking. Larger scale maps of the 1:500,000 to 1:000,000 range and up (NIMA TPC's and ONC's for example), normally show solid, blue gridlines at 100 kilometer intervals with blue ticks at 10 kilometer intervals along the 100 kilometer gridlines and along the edge of the maps.

Detailed UTM grid information is available in several NIMA-produced technical publications available for sale to the public. See http://mapping.usgs.gov/mac/nimamaps/index.html.

"A" and "Z" Beginning Grid Coordinates in Vietnam: A Note of Caution

In both south and North Vietnam, the 108 degree East Longitudinal line forms the boundary between the "A" and "Z" UTM Grid Zones. Although the "A" and "Z" UTM zones range from only 20 to 30 kilometers in width (width varies with latitude), the visible portions of each are still based on a partially "invisible" 100 by 100 km square grid-square. The "Z" and "A" UTM zones differ in the following, important respects:

> The left hand (west) side of the "Z" zone is the 00 (zero-zero) line, and the "Z" zone is cut off by the A Zone just beyond the "Z" Zone's 20 (two-zero) vertical grid line. That is, the "Z" Zone starts at zero on the west and runs easterly a bit more than 20 kilometers before being cut off by the "A" Zone.
>
> By contrast, in the "A" zone, the <u>right</u> (east) vertical side is the 00 (zero-zero) line for the "B" UTM grid-zone, and everything to the immediate <u>left</u> of that line's (west) edge lies roughly between the "A" Zone's 70 (seven-zero and the 99 (nine-nine) vertical grid line of the "A" UTM grid-zone.

In other words, in mind's eye, one should imagine both the "Z" and "A" zones as being squares with 100 kilometer sides that have been folded against one another (or cut off) on a vertical axis such that most of the right hand side of "Z" zone and most of the left hand side of the "A" zone is no longer visible. The need to compensate for the curvature of the earth in the UTM projection is the reason for this odd circumstance.

One will also notice that the farther north one goes in these two particular UTM zones, the narrower they become. Near Da Nang in I Corps, the two zones are both only approximately 22 kilometers in width, while near Phan Thiet in southern II Corps where the two zones meet the ocean, they are each about 27 kilometers wide.

Because of the unique physical characteristics of these two grid-zones, the reader should be alert to the following axioms when reading or creating grid coordinates in the "A" and "Z" Zones in South Vietnam (in fact, any grid coordinate specific to Vietnam that does not follow these rules is in error.):

a) No "Z" beginning grid coordinate can possibly begin with a numeral greater than "2"
b) No "A" beginning grid coordinate can possibly begin with a numeral lower than "7"

Declination

Declination is a map-reading term indicating the degree of variation between true-north and magnetic-north for a given location. Not only does magnetic-north rarely coincide with true-north, but the location of magnetic-north is in a constant state of flux and may shift significantly over time.

Declination allows us to orient a map to "true-north" for actual land navigation, but it has nothing at all to do with finding a point on a map while sitting thousands of miles from the terrain it represents.

While it is true the term is of little importance where locating points on a map might be concerned, it is an extremely important concept to master if one intends to take map and compass in hand, and then actually set out on foot to visit some particular spot on the earth. If the reader intends to use maps in the field, it is imperative they study this aspect of map reading in great detail, and that's particularly true if one intends to use map and compass while exploring the US, where declination is much greater problem than it was in Vietnam.

During the second Indochina War and for most of South Vietnam, declination between true and magnetic-north was very small. In fact, declination typically did not exceed 1 degree of arc and, as a result, map reading, map orientation and plotting positions were relatively simple tasks. That circumstance was one of the few elements of good luck that fell our way during the war because it no doubt saved lives and reduced stress due to the ease it offered in reporting accurate locations for artillery fire missions, airstrikes and one's own location.

For most daily needs at the infantry platoon-level during the war, map declinations were so small that they were generally ignored as insignificant. Typically, our compass readings were relayed and recorded as true azimuths for all practical purposes (i.e. magnetic and true-north were considered synonymous). [7]

The legend or map identification portions along the edge of a military topographical map always contain declination measured <u>at the time the map was drawn or revised</u>. Because magnetic-north shifts over time, the

---

[7] By contrast, Map Declination in California is typically 17½ degrees. Reliance on magnetic north can result in huge errors were the declination is that high!

declinations are date-sensitive and should not be trusted if a map is old. When using a compass to find locations in the real world, always confirm the current declination registered for the area you plan to navigate.

Map Scales

The terms "large scale" and "small scale" are easily misunderstood because the terms are expressed in ratios of scale in which detail increases as the numeric ratio decreases; just the opposite of what our numeric-instincts suggest should be the case. In other words, a "large scale" map shows much greater detail and typically covers a much smaller area than a "small scale map." For example, a 1:50,000 scale map is a "large scale" map that shows much greater detail, but at the same time much less overall coverage, than a 1:1,000,000 "small scale" map of the same geographical area.

Where finding a precise location using military grid coordinate is concerned, the larger the map scale, the better.

Most tactical military maps used in Vietnam by US Troops ranged anywhere in scale from 1:15,000 to 1:1,000,000 or smaller, depending on the level of command and necessities of the mission. Large scale maps were typically the maps of choice used at the company and platoon levels in the field, while smaller scale maps were common at the brigade, division, corps and MACV headquarters levels.

1:15,000 and 1:25,000 scale maps provided the greatest detail, but covered such small areas of land that their use was very limited and actually quite rare. Though less detail is shown at 1:50,000 scale (1 centimeter equals 0.5 kilometer, or about 1.25 km per inch), that scale proved to be the best all-around scale needed for tactical operations at the platoon and company level. As a result, the 1:50,000 scale map became the map of choice for most of the war where US forces were concerned.

Maps at the progressively smaller scales of 1:100,000 (1 centimeter equals 1 kilometer), 1:250,000 (1" equals appx 4 miles), 1:500,000 (1" equals appx 8 miles), and 1:1,000,000 (1" equals appx 16 miles) cover progressively larger land surface areas and were typically used in strategic and regional planning at higher levels of command.

Contour Intervals

A contour interval is the distance in vertical altitude between contour lines drawn on a topographic map. As a logical result, the closer the interval lines are to one another, the steeper the slope of the terrain. The contour interval used in a map is clearly marked in the legend of the map along the bottom or side margins. Standard contour intervals are shown by solid contour lines, but where the slope is very gradual, supplementary interval (sometimes also called "intermediate" and/or "auxiliary") lines are sometimes employed and expressed by broken lines. Where military tactical, aeronautical and nautical maps are concerned, the interval distance may be expressed in meters, feet or fathoms, and close attention should be paid to those distinctions.

As the scale of a map varies, so does the distance between contour intervals. Contour intervals for the maps typical to Vietnam are:

Series	Scale	Contour Interval	Supplementary Interval	Type
DMA L-7014	1:50,000	20 meters	10 meters	Tactical
DMA L-701	1:100,000	?	?	Tactical/Strategic
DMA L-1501	1:250,000	100 meters	50 meters	Strategic
DMA L-1501A	1:250,000	100 meters	50 meters	Aeronautical
DMA L-509	1:250,000	100 meters	50 meters	Strategic
DMA L-509A	1:250,000	100 meters	50 meters	Aeronautical
DMA TPC	1:500,000	500 feet	250 and 100 feet	Aeronautical
DMA ONC	1:1,000,000	1,000 feet	500 feet	Aeronautical

Grid Coordinates

All grids listed in this text are applicable to any Defense Mapping Agency (DMA) or National Imagery and Mapping Agency (NIMA) map series. Among these are the L-509 series, the L-701 series, the L-1501 series, the L-7014 series, Joint Operation Graphics (JOG's), Tactical Pilotage Charts (TPCs), and Operational Navigation Charts, all of which are discussed in detail elsewhere.

Most grids references in this text were originally plotted on Defense Mapping Agency (DMA) L-7014 series 1:50,000 scale maps, L-1501 series 1:250,000 JOGs and various 1:500,000 Tactical Pilotage Charts (TPC's).

In all cases, listed grids reference the same UTM grid-zone system common to all these maps, and practically any given grid coordinate can be plotted on any DMA map with relative ease and reasonable accuracy.

Where the L-7014 series[8] is concerned, gridlines (N/S and E/W lines perpendicular to one another) are marked on each map that create a pattern of squares 1,000 meters (1 kilometer) on a side (for future reference, try also to visualize each one-kilometer square as also being subdivided into ten 100 meter increments by "imaginary" grid lines). These 1-kilometer grid-squares are then grouped into larger UTM grid-zones (typically about 100 by 100 kilometers) that are assigned a two-letter alpha identifier. Any grid coordinate plotted within a given grid-zone is preceded by the same 2-letter alpha (for example: XT, YD, AS and so on) that are 100 kilometers on a side. Intersections of these various vertical and horizontal grid lines form the basis of establishing grid coordinates. In fact, a grid coordinate can be thought of as a point on a map created by the intersection of two specified lines.

Where L-509, L-1501, TPC's are concerned, gridlines are marked in solid blue lines that are spaced 10 kilometers apart (for future reference, also try also to visualize each 10 x 10 kilometer square as also being subdivided into ten 1 kilometer increments by "imaginary" secondary grid lines).

All Proper Grid Coordinates are Numerically Symmetrical:

Every properly transcribed grid coordinate must be numerically symmetrical. That is, the number of numerals in a grid must be divisible by two. For example, XT 01, YA 7829, BN 235021 and CP 45560032 are all numerically legitimate grid coordinates because the number of digits in each is divisible by two, while grids XT 0, YA 782, BN 23502 and CP 4556003 are inherently erroneous because they are not divisible by two.

Grid coordinates normally include two, four, six or eight (and sometimes even ten) numeric characters.

Although while in most military documents grids are not ordinarily split to recognize the symmetry, the numbers are theoretically split at the center such that YD30 would read as YD 3-0, YD3906 as YD 39-06, YD395068 as YD 395-068, and YD39520684 as YD 3952-0684.

Where printed grids are not physically separated into equal left and right groupings, reading a solid string of four six or eight numbers often results in transcription and interpretive errors; hence, splitting printed grid coordinates with the use of a hyphen tends to minimize such errors. Accordingly, virtually all grids cited in this text are listed in a split format in order to facilitate their comprehension and ease of use.

The Left Half of a Grid Coordinate is an Easterly Measurement, the Right Half a Northerly Measurement:

1. Perhaps the easiest way to understand military grid coordinates is simply to think of them as points on a map represented by the distance in kilometers, measured first due east from the southwest-corner of a specific UTM grid-zone, and then measured due north from that easterly point.

Take for example the coordinate **YD 395-068**.

Each three-digit numeric grouping identifies a point on a map. The left-half numerals (in this case, "395") identify a point due east of the southwest-corner (YD 000-000) of the **"YD" or "Yankee-Delta" Grid-Zone** (a point where three other grid-zones also meet), while the right-half numerals ("068"), represent a point due north of the easterly point defined by the left-half numerals.

In our example, the easterly point we seek is 39.5 kilometers due east of the intersection of the YD 000 vertical and YD 000 horizontal gridlines (that is, the southwest-corner of the "YD" Grid-Zone). The right-hand numeric ("068") specifies a point 6.8 kilometers due north of the easterly point. That northerly point is the point on the map represented by the entire coordinate and it is the place we seek. It really is just that simple.

2. Another way to think of grid coordinates is to imagine that the left-hand half of the coordinate identifies the eastern position of an imaginary gridline running due north/south, and that the right-hand half of the coordinate identifies the northern position an imaginary gridline running due east/west. The intersection of these two lines is the point on the map the grid coordinate identifies.

Accordingly, in our example the left-hand grouping ("395") identifies an imaginary easterly, **vertical** gridline that is located 39.5 kilometers east of the extreme southwest-corner of the "YD" grid zone (i.e., "YD 000-000"). The right-hand grouping of three digits ("068") specifies an imaginary northerly, **horizontal** gridline located 6.8 kilometers north of the extreme southwest corner of the "YD" grid zone. The point where these two lines intersect is the location the grid coordinate identifies.

---

[8] The L-7014 map series Index Map can be seen at: //www.rjsmith.com/images/kelley/Index-L7014s.jpg

Hints for Dealing with Grid Coordinates:

a) The more numeric characters a grid contains, the more refined and exact the location it pinpoints.

b) When reading a map, always remember the axiom: **grid coordinates are read first from left to the right, then up**. "To the right and up," was a phrase the Army incessantly drilled into the minds of its trainees. Commit that phrase to memory and pinpointing grid coordinates on US military maps will become a relatively simple task. In other words, all grids are read "Easterly, then Northerly."

c) All military grid coordinates define a point by its distance first due east, and then due north of the southwest-corner of the UTM grid-zone specified by the two alpha characters preceding the numeric portion of the grid. For example, XT 835-293 defines a point that is first 83.5 kilometers due east and then 29.3 kilometers due north of the extreme southwest corner (XT 000-000) of the "XT" UTM grid-zone.

d) As a general rule, most firebases were built on the highest point available, so it is reasonable to presume that the highest terrain feature in a given grid-square may be the likely location of a firebase or LZ. On the other hand, many were actually built on valley floors, so there is no hard and fast rule on which we can rely. The same may or may not be true for battle sites and other "event" or terrain feature locations. In some instances, US bases were so large they occupied several square kilometers or even several square miles (Long Binh or Tan Son Nhut Airbase for example), and a grid might only represent the approximate geographical center of the facility or perhaps just some random point selected somewhere within it.

f) Never bet your life on a grid coordinate calculated by anyone other than yourself.

Two-Digit Grid Coordinates:

For the purposes of this text and in most other applications, a two-digit grid coordinate simply tells us that the location it identifies is somewhere within a 10 kilometer-by-10 kilometer square located immediately to the northeast of the point on the map identified by the coordinate.

For example, the two-digit grid, **"YD 3-1"** tells us that the specified feature should be located somewhere in the 10 kilometer x 10 kilometer square (100 square-kilometers) immediately northeast of a point 30 kilometers east, and then 10 kilometers north of the southwest corner of the specified YD grid-zone,

While only two-digits appear in the grid, develop the habit of mentally adding a "zero" after each digit such that YD 3-1 becomes YD 30-10. That should help simplify the interpretation two-digit grid coordinates.

Two-digit coordinates are common to large gazetteers of geographic place and feature names. For example, the NIMA (National Imagery and Mapping Agency, formerly DMA) Gazetteer of Vietnam lists over 59,000 Vietnam place names in this format.

While not of the greatest accuracy, even a two-digit coordinate does significantly simplify the process of finding a location by focusing our attention to a reasonably manageable target zone that is only 10 x 10 kilometers in size.

Four-Digit Grid Coordinates:

A four-digit grid coordinate may represent a specific location, or it might also represent a general location that is simply within a one or two kilometer radius of the point it identifies. Of much greater accuracy than a two-digit coordinate, a four-digit coordinate focuses our attention on a target search zone that falls within an area of roughly only about 3.2 square kilometers.

For our purposes, four-digit grid coordinates (such as YD 39-06) will normally reference "general" locations within a two-kilometer radius of the point identified by the coordinates.

Six-Digit Grid Coordinates:

As we learned in the preceding example, a four-digit grid coordinate only refines our search area to within about 2-kilometer radius of the exact point it seeks to identify (again, that's an area of about 3.2 square-kilometers, or 988 acres, or 1 1/2 square miles!). While that is a much more precise search area than the 100 square-kilometer search zone offered by a two-digit grid, if we are calling for artillery fire or air strikes on an attacking enemy, a four digit grid is far too inaccurate a measurement to ensure that the explosives we've ordered won't land in our own position! But if we refine a grid coordinate to six digit accuracy, then it becomes a very accurate tool for pinpointing our location, or that of the enemy.

Presume our target grid is **YD 395-068**. This coordinate is roughly accurate to the area within a 100-meter radius of the point it identifies (an area roughly equivalent to 8 acres). That's because it further breaks down a 1 x 1 kilometer grid-square into one hundred squares that are 100 x 100 meter in size. In other words:

a) The digit "5" in "395' means that the target point relative to the "39" vertical gridline is 5 tenths of a kilometer (500 meters) to its east (i.e., halfway between the gridlines "39" and "40").

b) The digit “8” in the second-half of the grid coordinate (“068”) means that the target point relative to the “06” horizontal gridline is 8 tenths of a kilometer (800 meters) to its north.

Eight-Digit Grid Coordinates:

An eight-digit grid coordinate is an extremely precise indicator, theoretically accurate to within 10 meters.

Eight-digit grids were almost never employed for everyday map reading during the war (except at the artillery FDC level) because it was virtually impossible to pinpoint a location that precisely on a 1:50,000 scale map. While rare, eight-digit coordinates do appear in this text, and most of those relate to Special Forces camps.

An eight-digit grid pinpoints a site to roughly within a 30-foot radius of its actual location. That’s an area roughly equivalent to the area of a three-car residential garage and is definitely close enough for government work. When Steve Sherman, a noted Special Forces historian who assisted in this project, was asked what the eight-digit coordinates for SF camps he’d supplied us were meant to identify, Steve chuckled and said, “Perhaps it was the flagpole?”

An exercise in plotting grid coordinates follows on the next page.

Plotting a Grid Coordinate on a Military Map: An Exercise

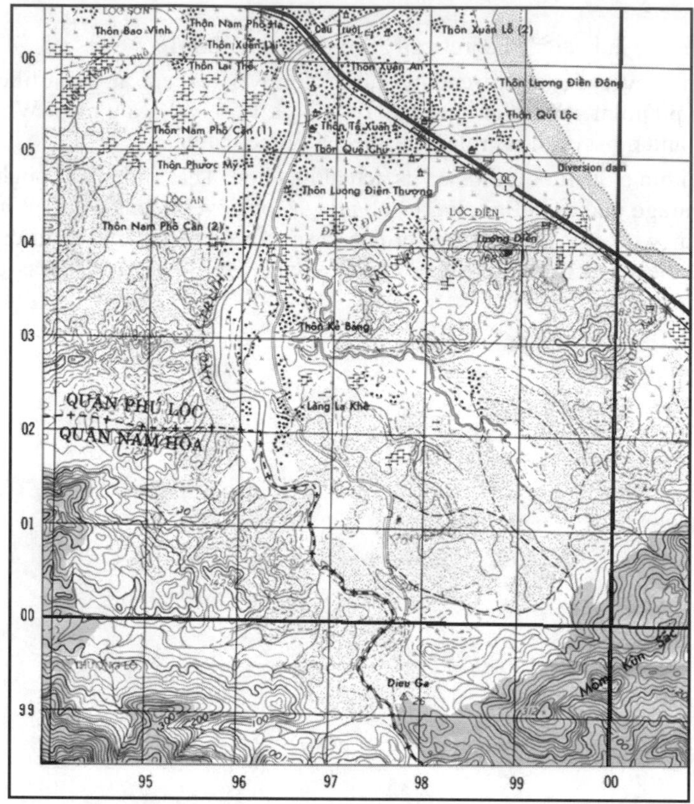

Figure 1. SW corner of map sheet "Q Phu Loc," Stock # L-7014-6541-1, slightly edited for ease of viewing. Note bold "00" N/S and E/W gridlines marking the boundaries of 4 UTM grid zones: YD, ZD, YC and ZC. Note that gridlines are spaced at one- kilometer intervals.

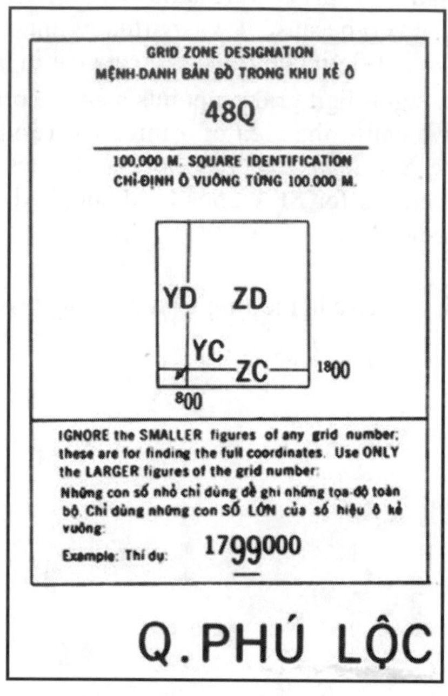

Figure 2. The grid zone legend from the same map sheet. Note how the "00" lines correspond with those on Figure 1.

Plotting the Grid "YD 967-062":

Keeping in mind the axiom, "to the right (east) and up (north)," and using **Figure 1** as our map, we can now attempt to pinpoint the location of a hypothetical grid coordinate. The grid for this exercise will be **YD 967-062**. Find the "96" vertical gridline in the **"YD"** grid-zone along the bottom of the map and to the left of the bold "00" vertical gridline. Put your finger on the bottom gridline at a point approximately 600 meters to the east (right) of the "96" vertical gridline (i.e., a point 6/10ths of the distance between the "96" and "97" gridlines).

Now run your finger due north along our imaginary "967" gridline until it meets a point roughly 200 meters above the "06" horizontal gridline. Your finger should be resting on a QL-1 highway bridge. If it is, you've just found the point on this map represented by the grid "YD 967-062."

Now try the plotting the location of **ZC 993-991**. Correctly plotted, this grid identifies a mountain peak near the southeast corner of Figure 1.

End of Exercise

Military Maps of Vietnam

Provinces, Military Regions, Principal Cities, Terrain Features and UTM* Grid Zone Overlays

***Universal Transverse Mercator Grid Zone Designator**: Origin of the two-letter alphabetical designation preceding a military grid coordinate.

Index to Maps by Number Sort

Index to Maps by Alpha Sort

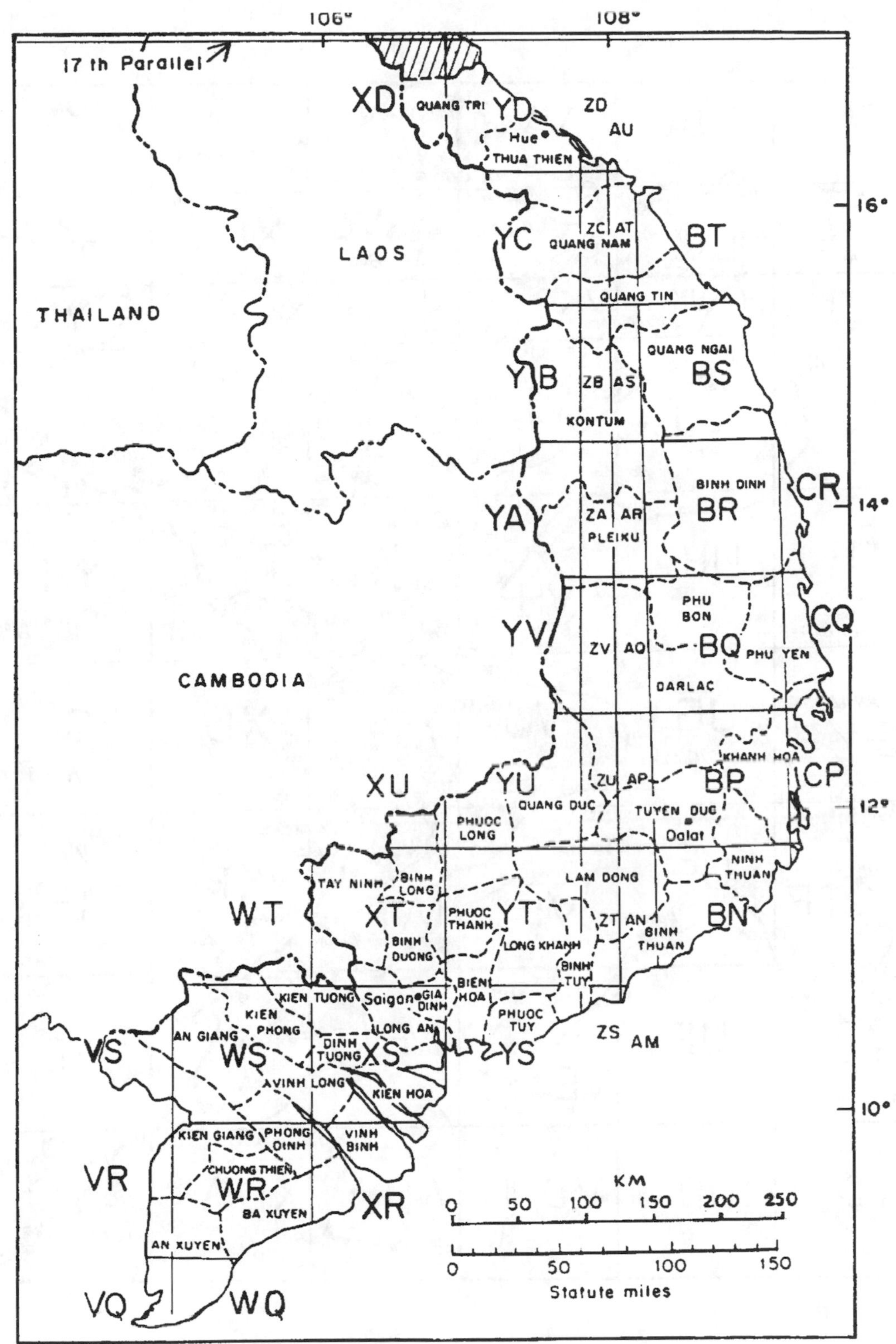

SVN UTM Grid Zone Overlay - circa 1963

Province names/boundaries in III and IV Corps here differ significantly from those in existence for the majority of American presence in RVN, 1965-73. For example, present here is Phouc Thanh; absent here are Go Cong, Sa Dec, Chau Doc, and Bac Lieu. Image courtesy of the USMC and *Khe Sanh Veteran* Magazine.

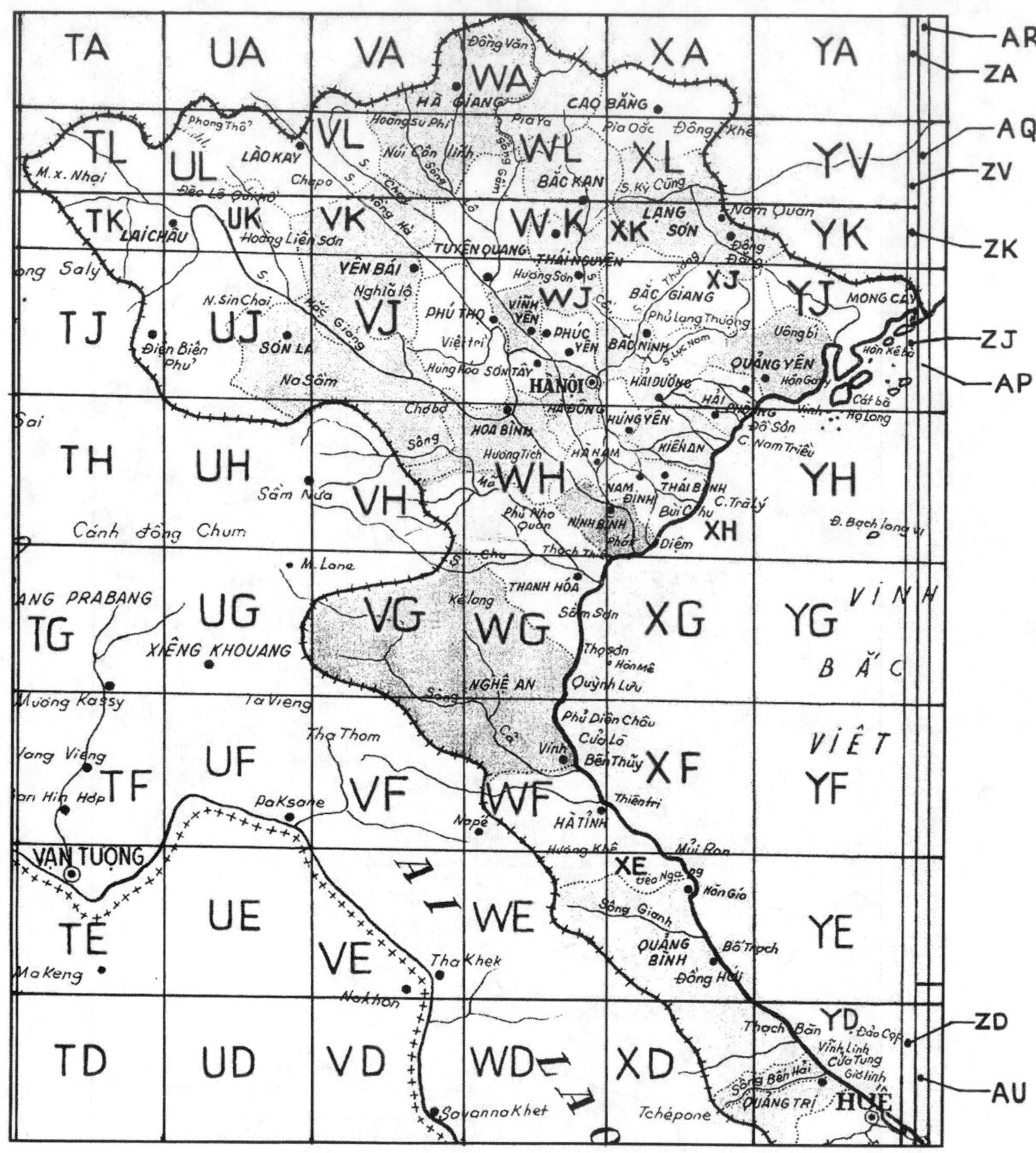

North Vietnam UTM Grid Zone Overlay and Province Borders - circa 1967
Overlay and boundaries are approximate only. Underlying image from Vietnamese map of unknown origin provided courtesy of Bob Peragallo. Overlay per author.

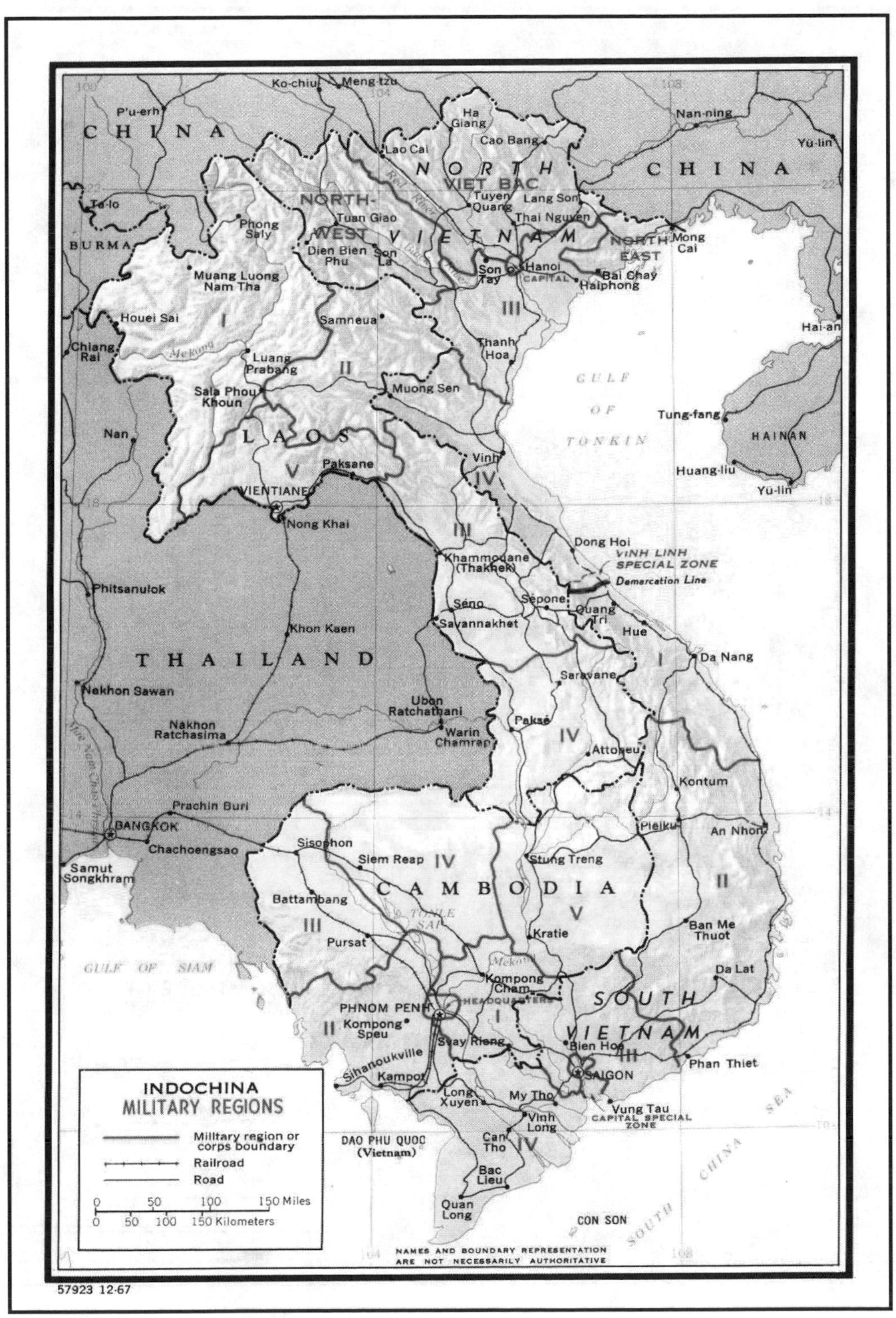

Military Region of Cambodia/Laos/NVN/SVN as of December 1967 - CIA Map

South Vietnam Provinces and Military Regions as of June, 1967 - CIA Map
(Compare III & IV Corps' province names/boundaries here with those of the Map 1)

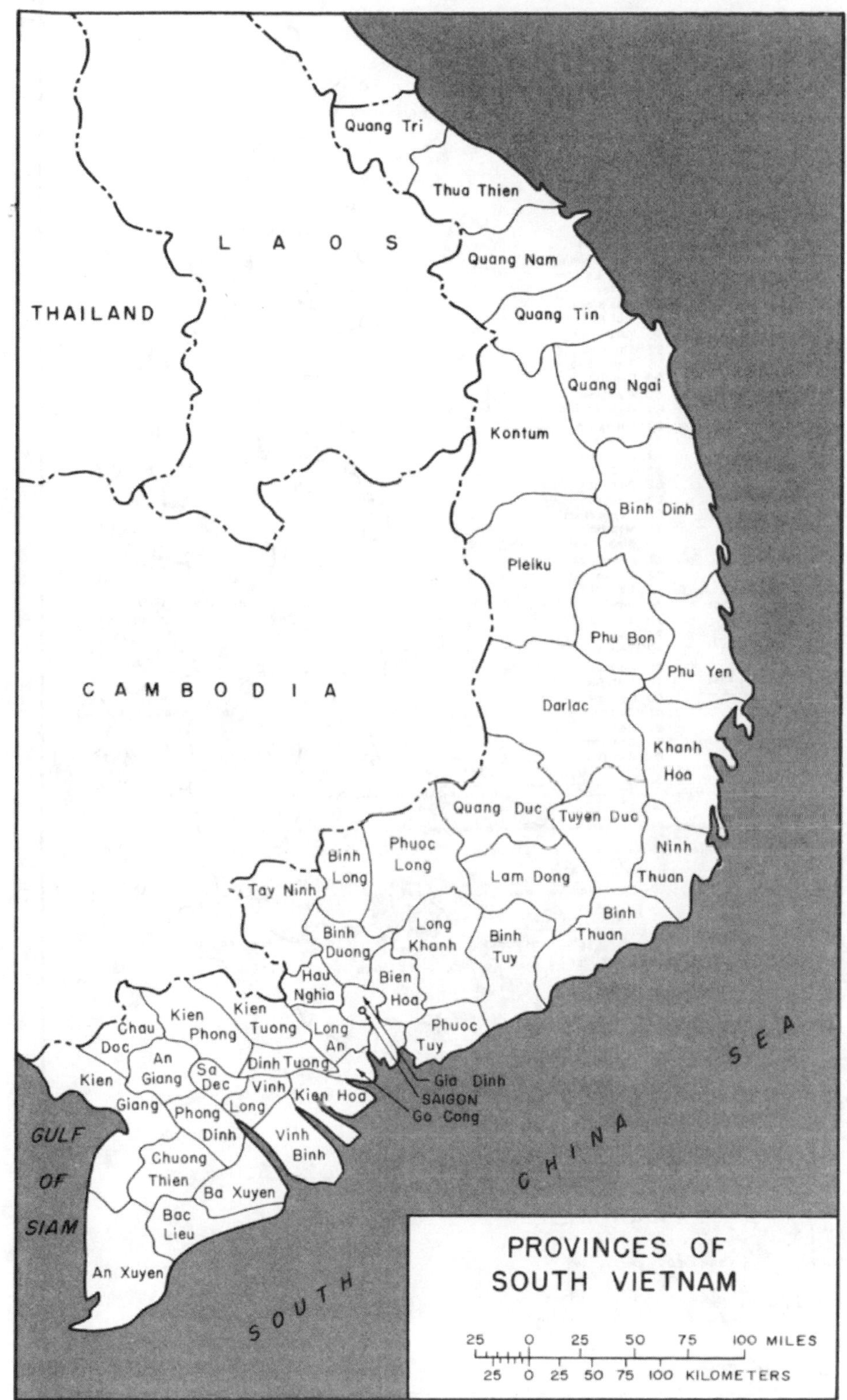

South Vietnam Provinces - Circa 1970

Courtesy Dept. of the Army, *Vietnam Studies, Base Development in South Vietnam 1965-1970*

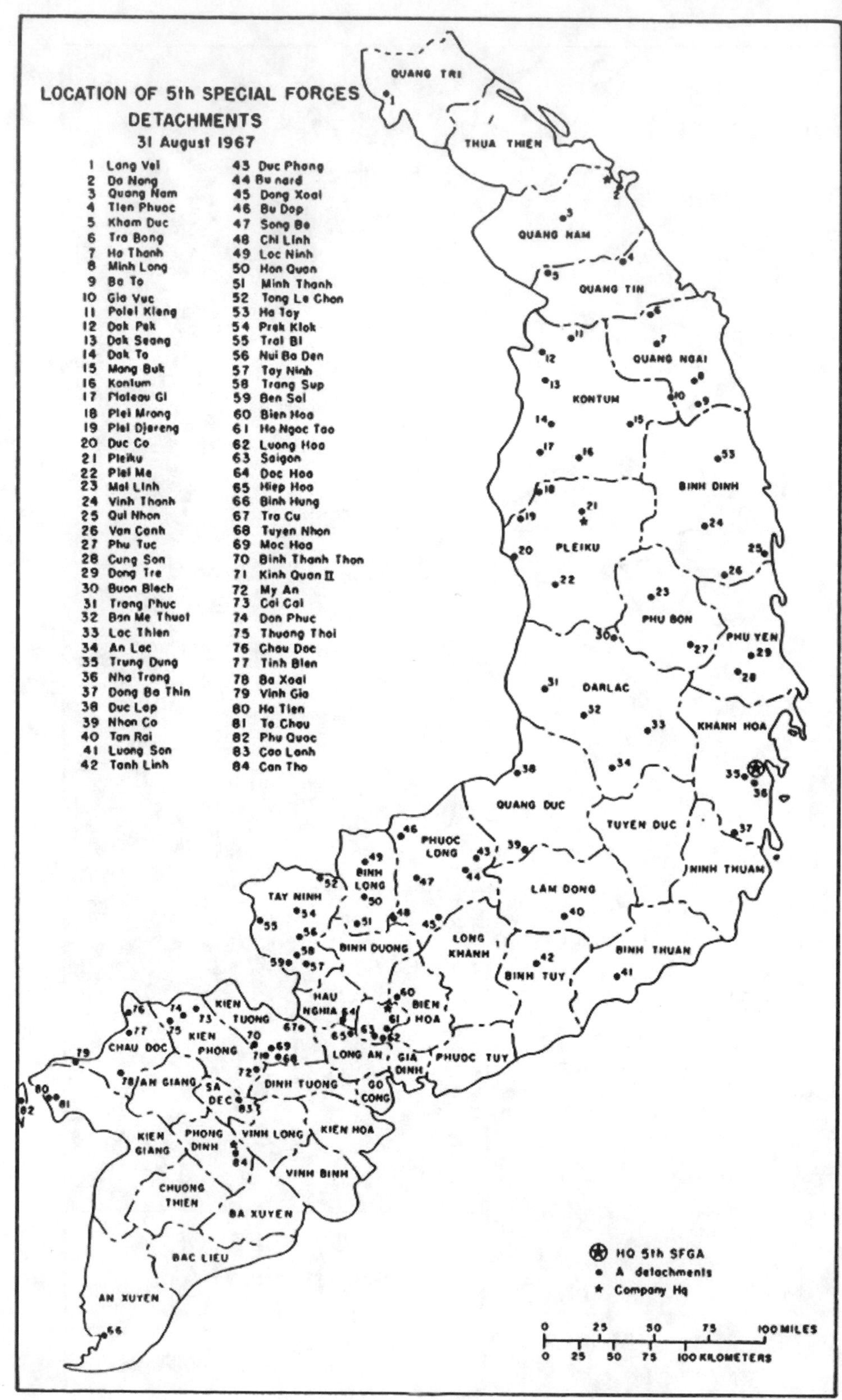

Special Forces Camp Locations – August 1967
Dept. of the Army Vietnam Studies, *US Army Special Forces 1961-1971*

South Vietnam's Tactical & Jet-Capable Airfields – 1968
Courtesy Dept. of the Army, *Vietnam Studies, Base Development In South Vietnam 1965-1970*

I MR MAJOR ROAD NET & AIRFIELDS

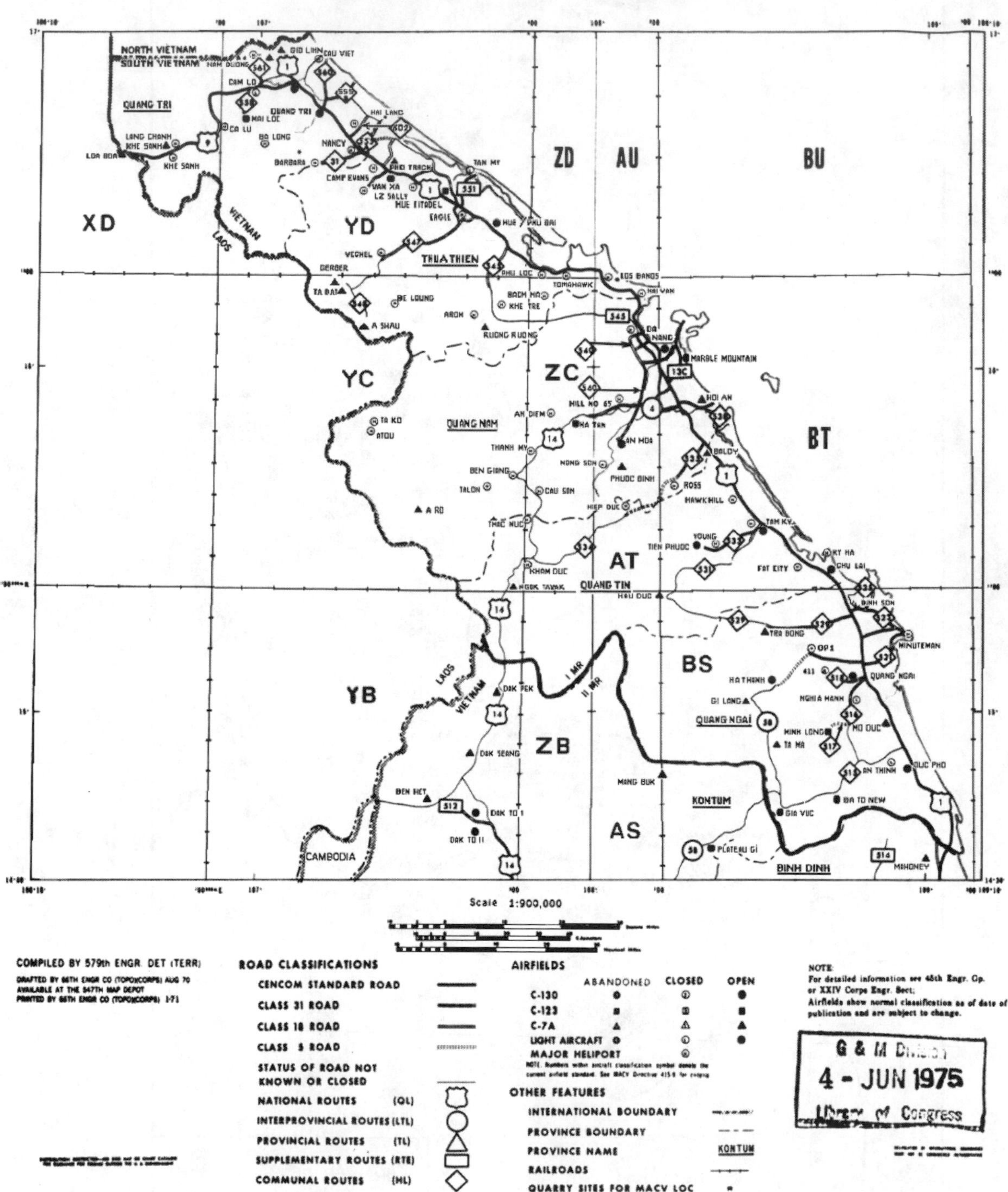

I Corps/Military Region 1 - Sheet 1 of 4. Compiled by 579th Engr. Det (Terrain), August 1970

Geography and Maps Div., Library of Congress Call No. 86-694430 G8021 .P2 svar .U51

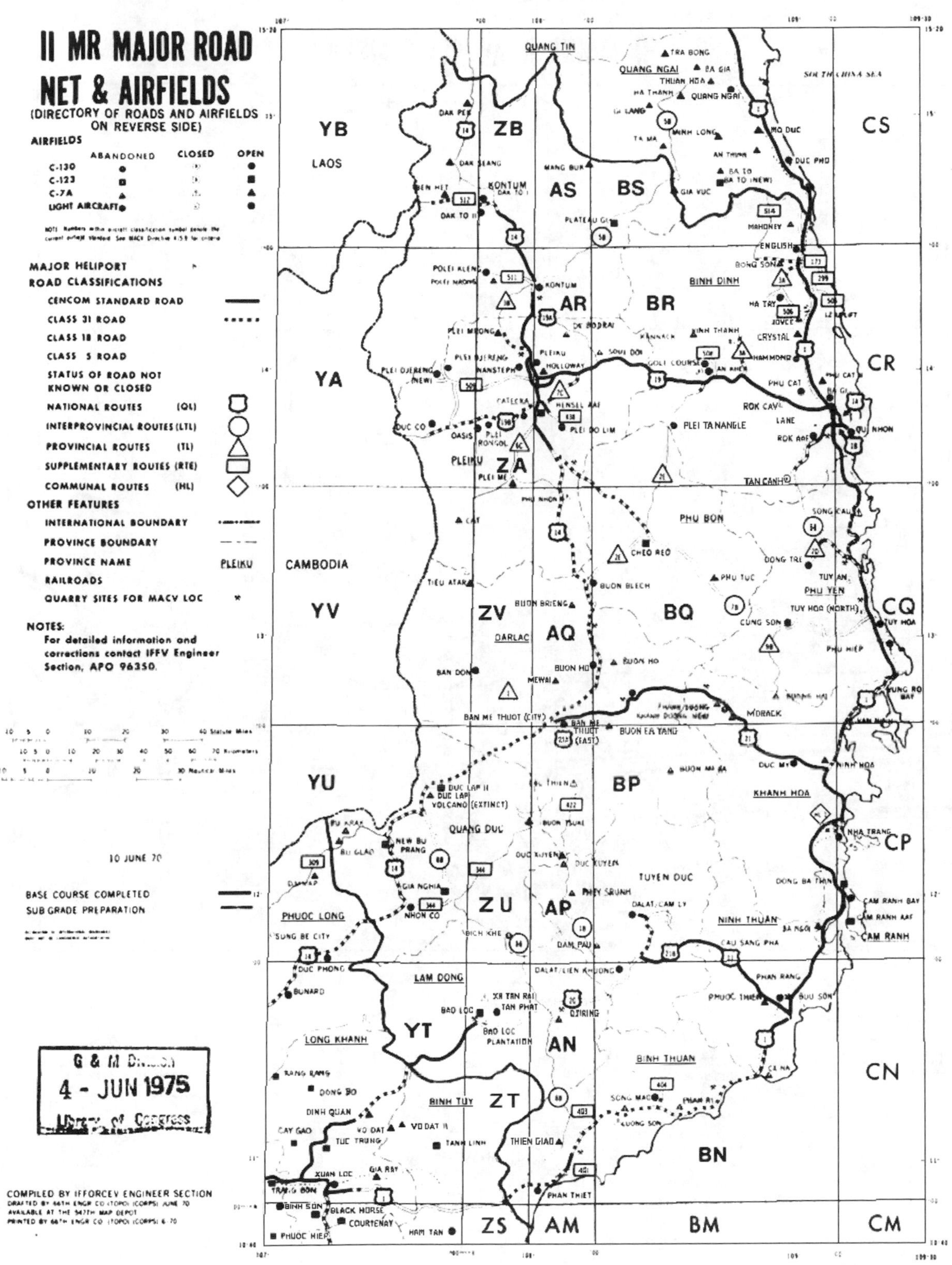

I Corps/Military Region 2 - Sheet 2 of 4. Compiled by IFFV Engr. Sect. June 1970

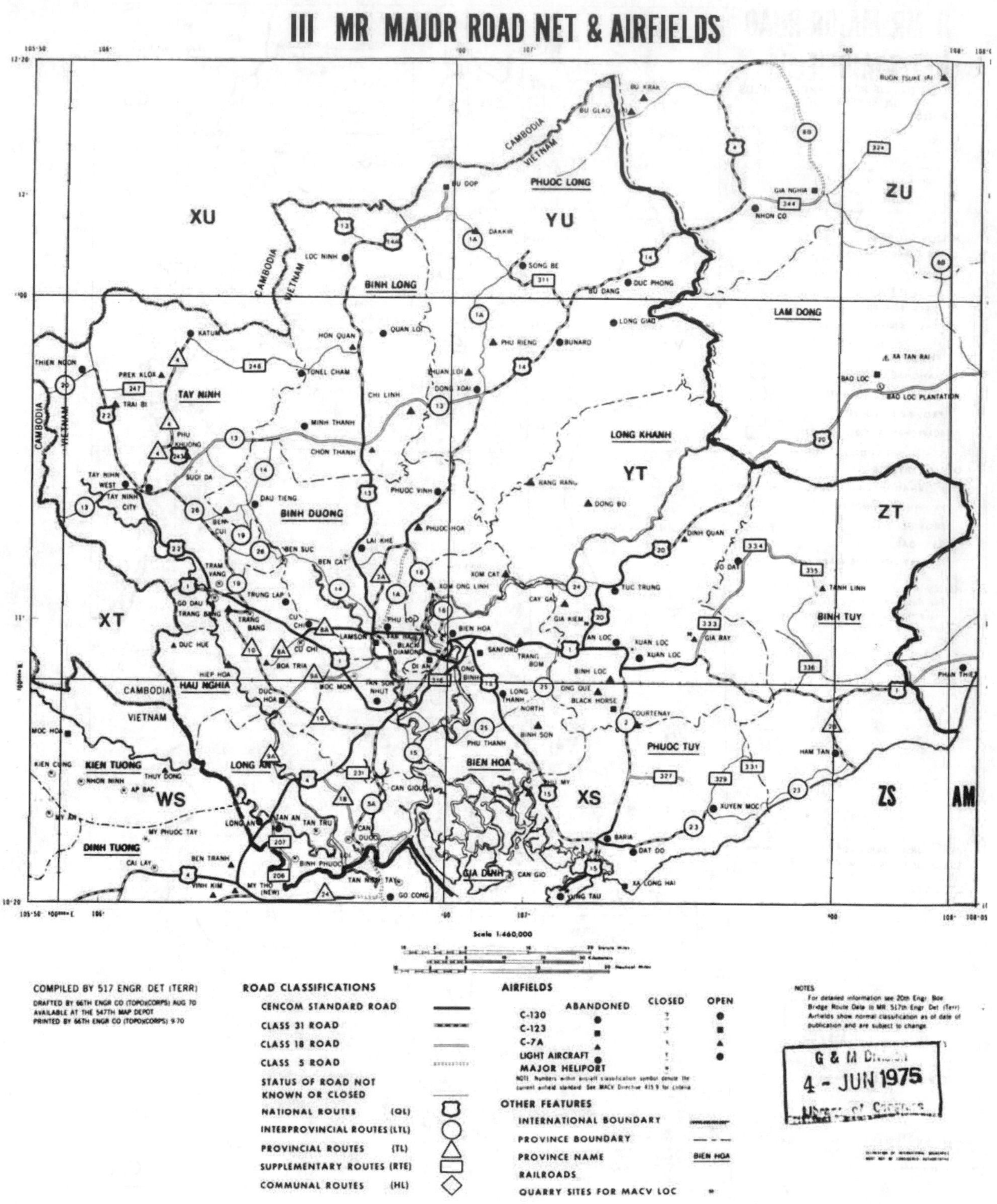

III Corps/Military Region 3 - Sheet 3 of 4. Compiled by 517th Engr. Det., September 1970
Available at the Geography and Maps Div., Library of Congress Call No. 86-694430 G8021 .P2 svar .U51

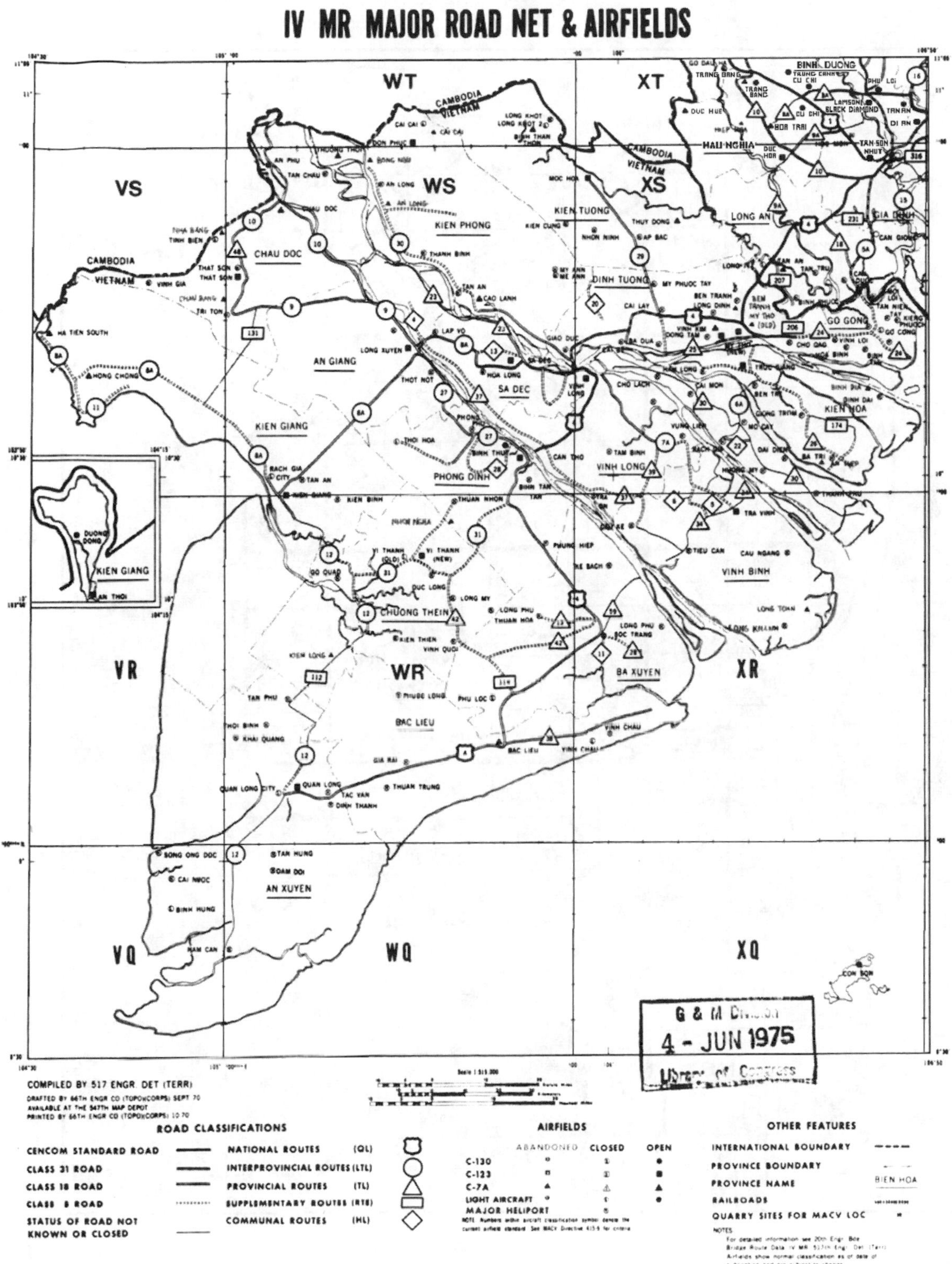

III Corps/Military Region 4 - Sheet 4 of 4. Compiled by 517th Engr. Det., August 1970
Geography and Maps Div., Library of Congress Call No. 86-694430 G8021 .P2 svar .U51

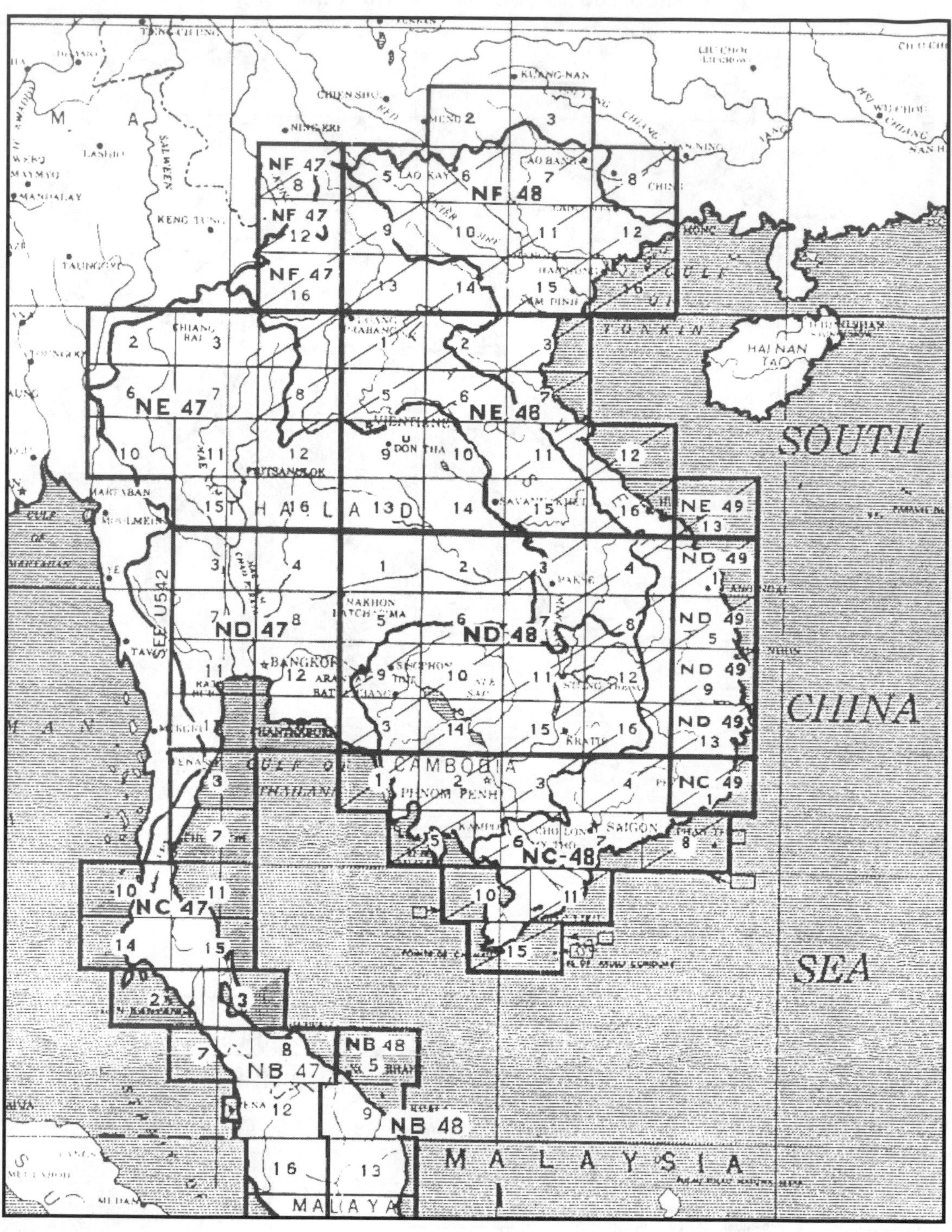

NIMA L-509/L-1501 Series, Joint Operations Graphics (JOG) 1:250,000 scale Map Index
(NIMA JOG Maps are available through the US Geological Survey, Denver)

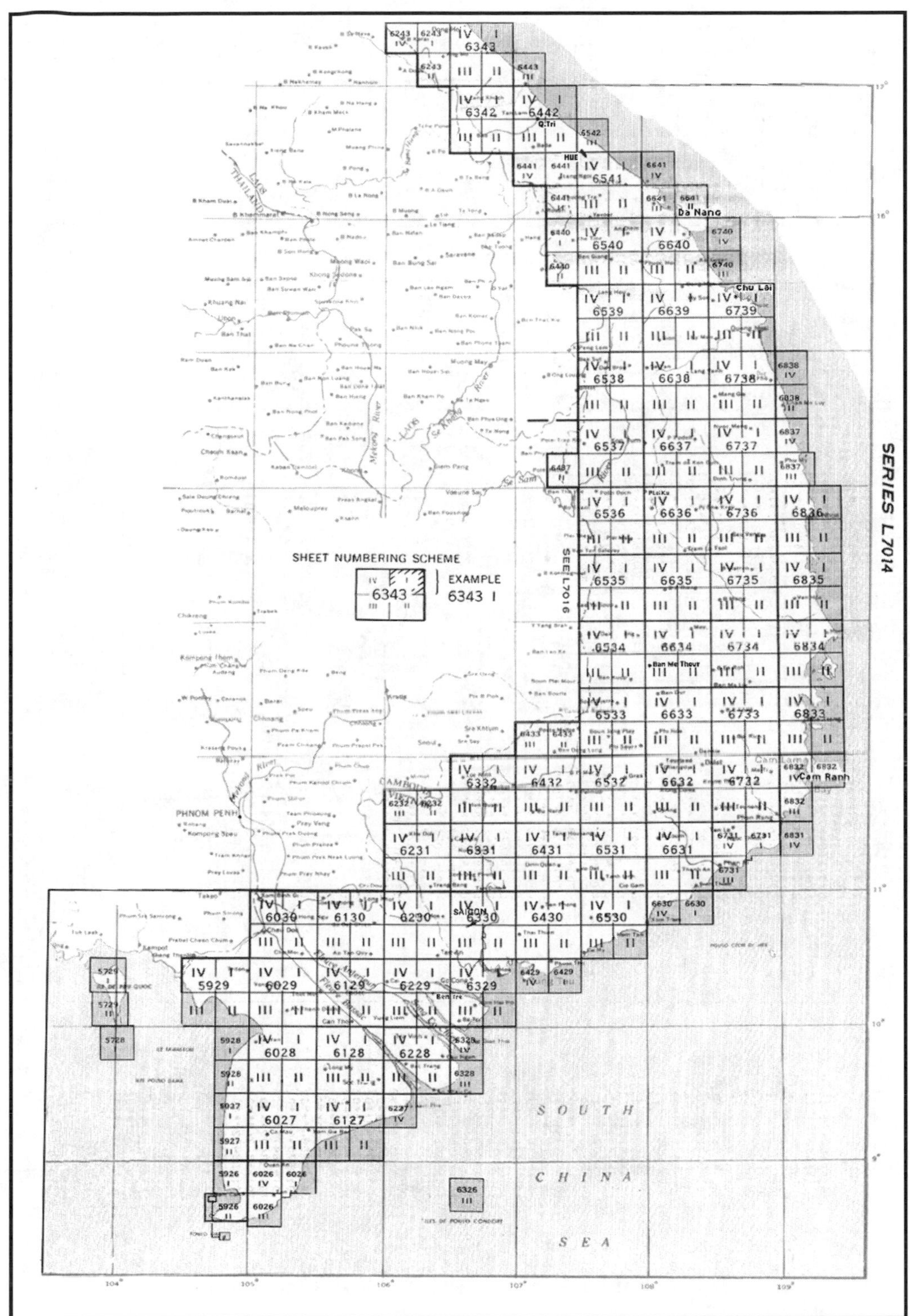

South Vietnam DMA 1:50,000 scale L-7014 Series Index Map (edited)
(These maps are available through the US Geological Survey, Denver)

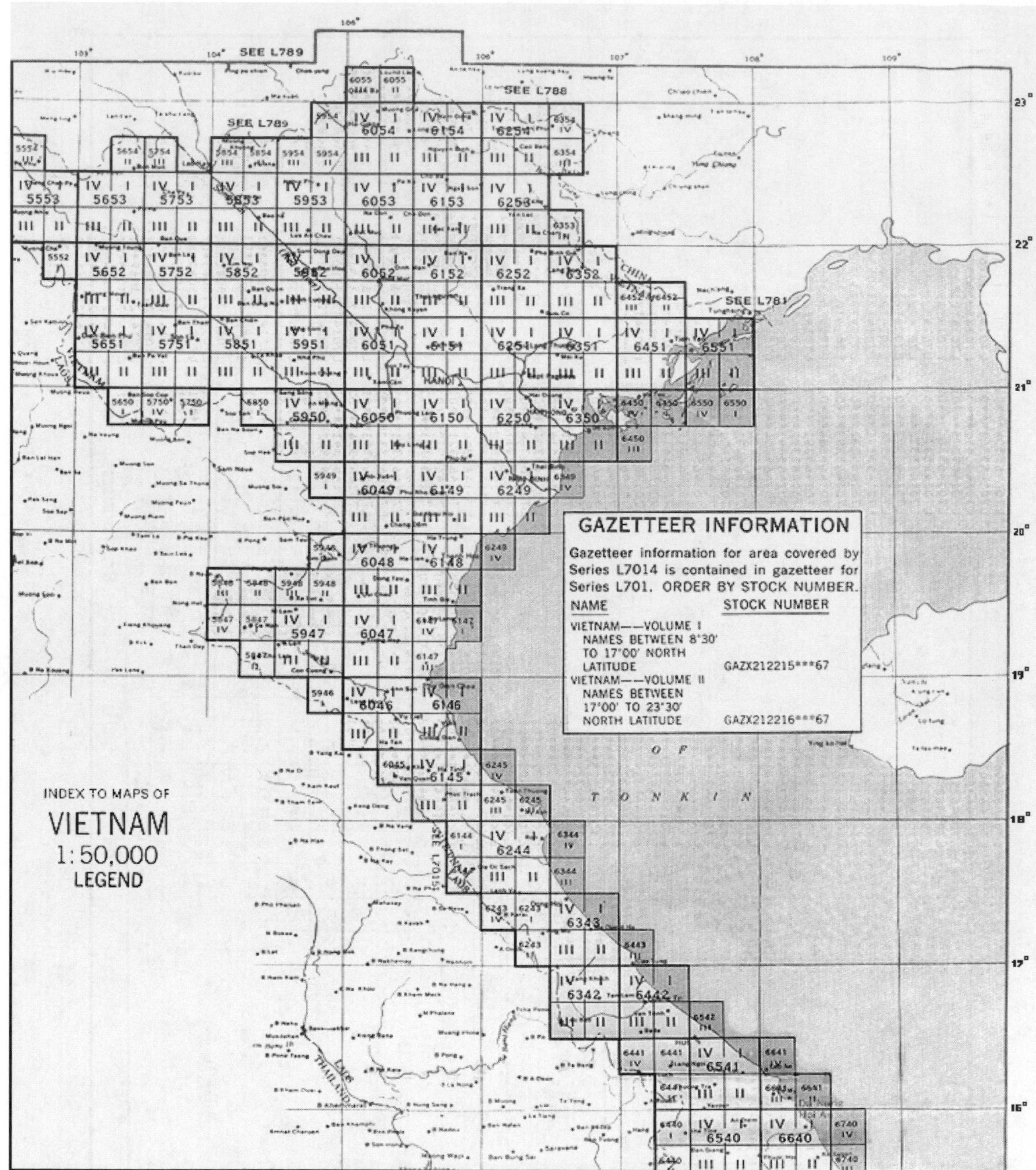

North Vietnam DMA 1:50,000 scale L-7014 Series Index Map (edited)

Coverage is primarily of North Vietnam, although a portion of northern South Vietnam is also shown. (These maps are available through the US Geological Survey, Denver)

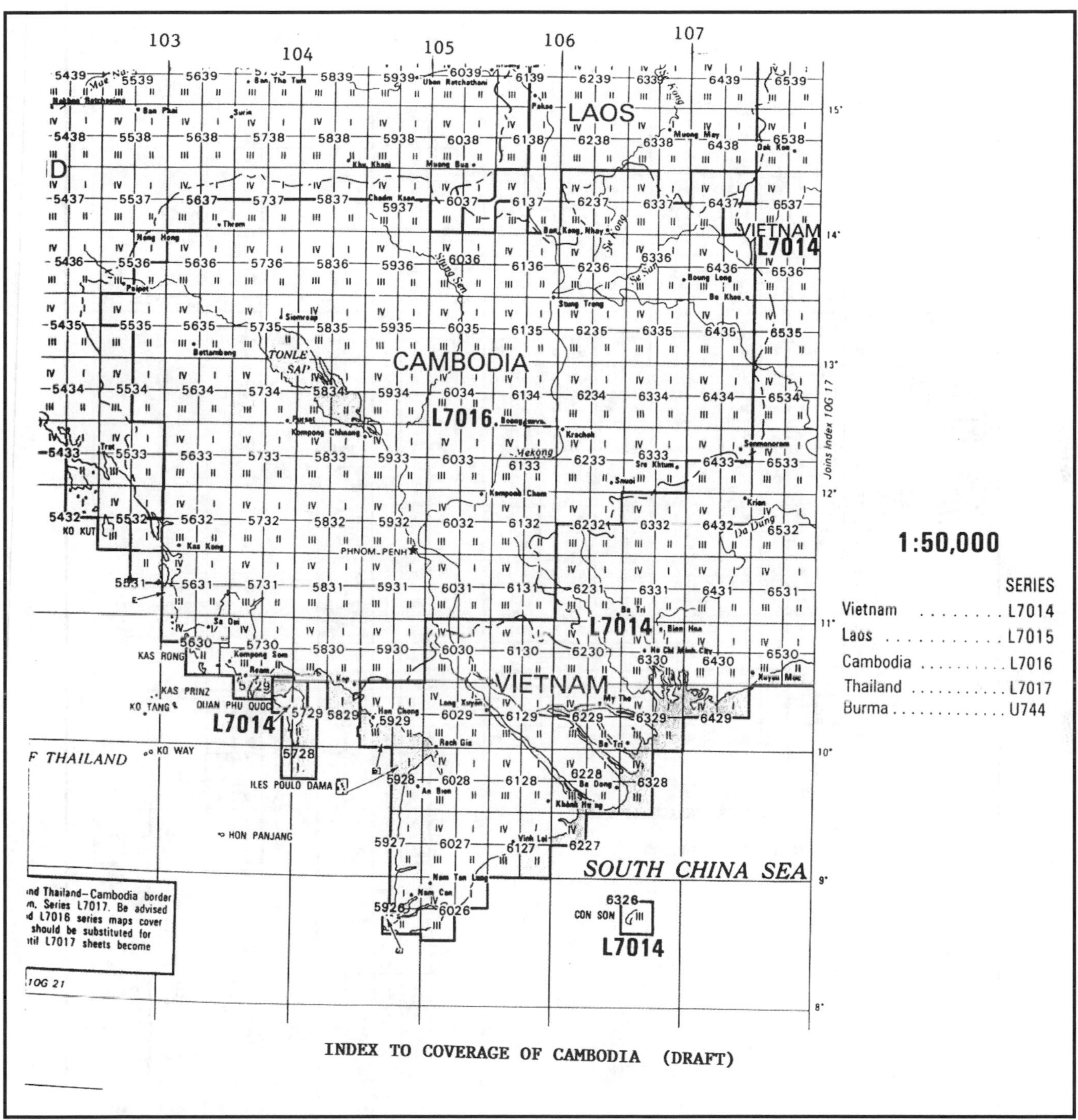

Cambodia DMA/NIMA 1:50,000 scale L-7016 Map Index

Courtesy of US Geological Survey & John McCammon

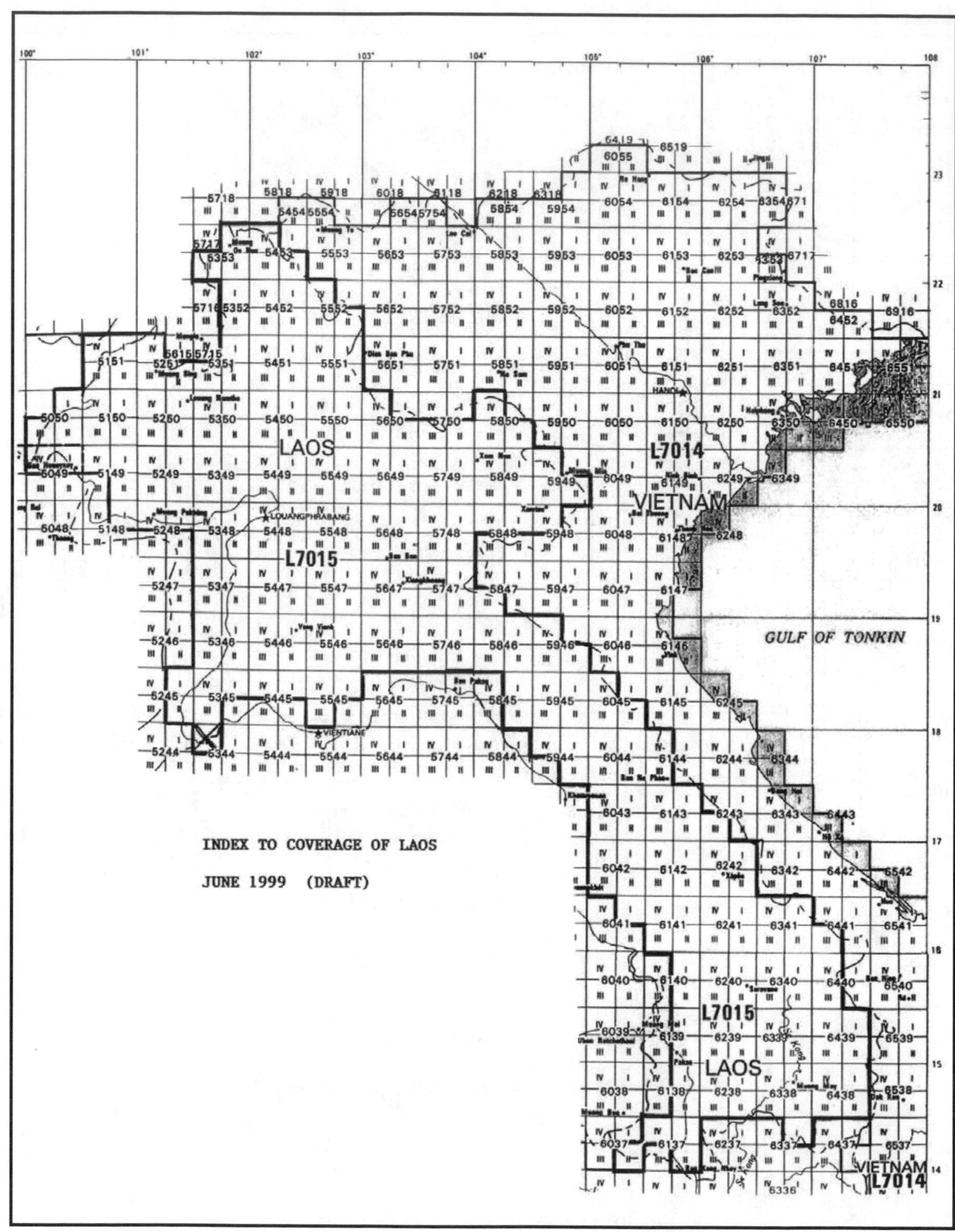

Laos DMA/NIMA 1:50,000 scale L-7015 Map Index
Courtesy of US Geological Survey & John McCammon

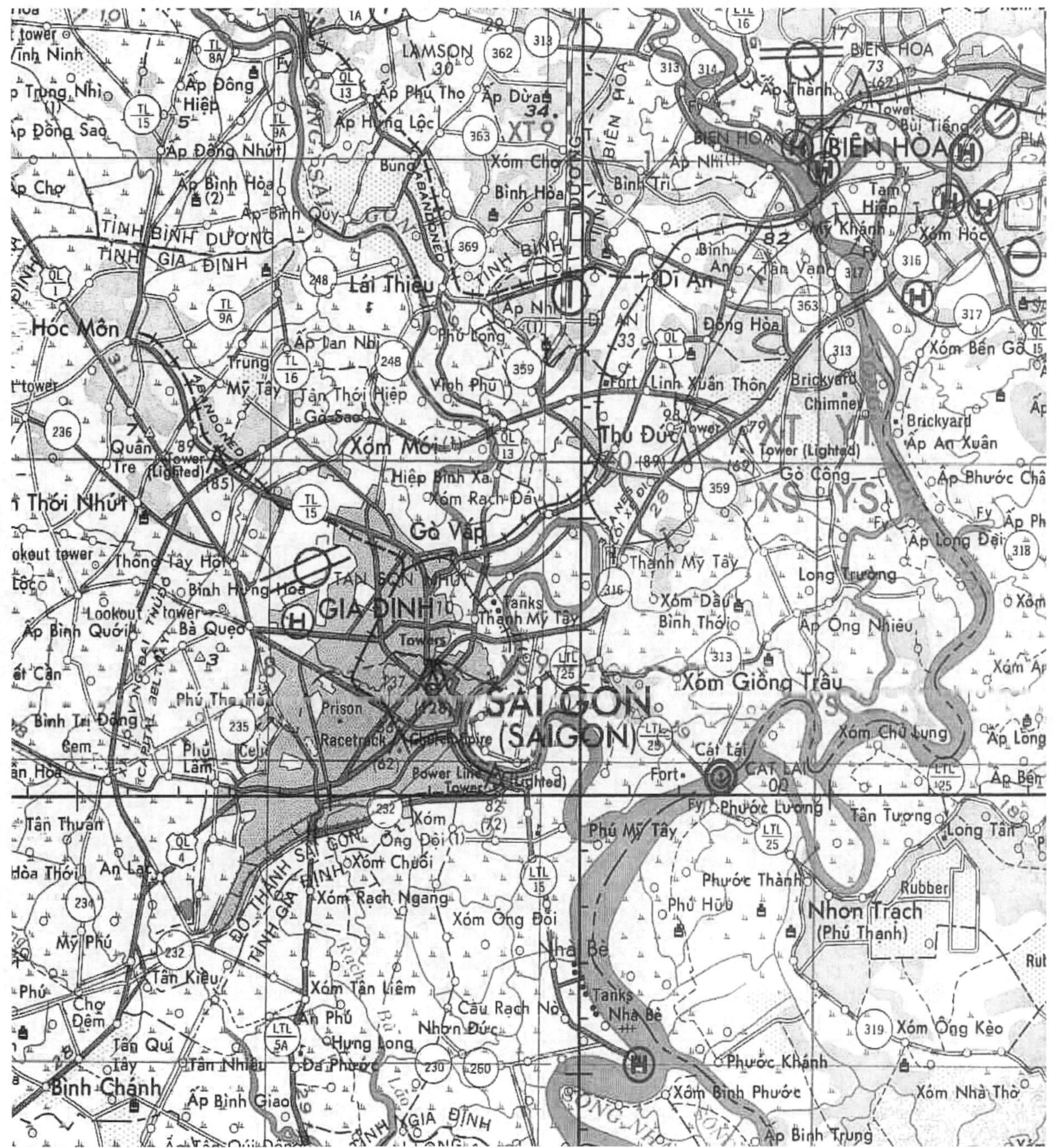

Saigon Area, per DMA Joint Operations Graphic (JOG), 1:250,000 scale, NC48-07 Map

Tan Son Nhut Airbase is at NW edge of city. Bien Hoa Airbase is at upper right, with Long Binh Post to its WSW.Grid Zone is ‘‘XS.” Note UTM zone intersection of “XS,” “XT,” “YT” and “YS” at upper right-center of map. Image courtesy of Jim Henthorn.

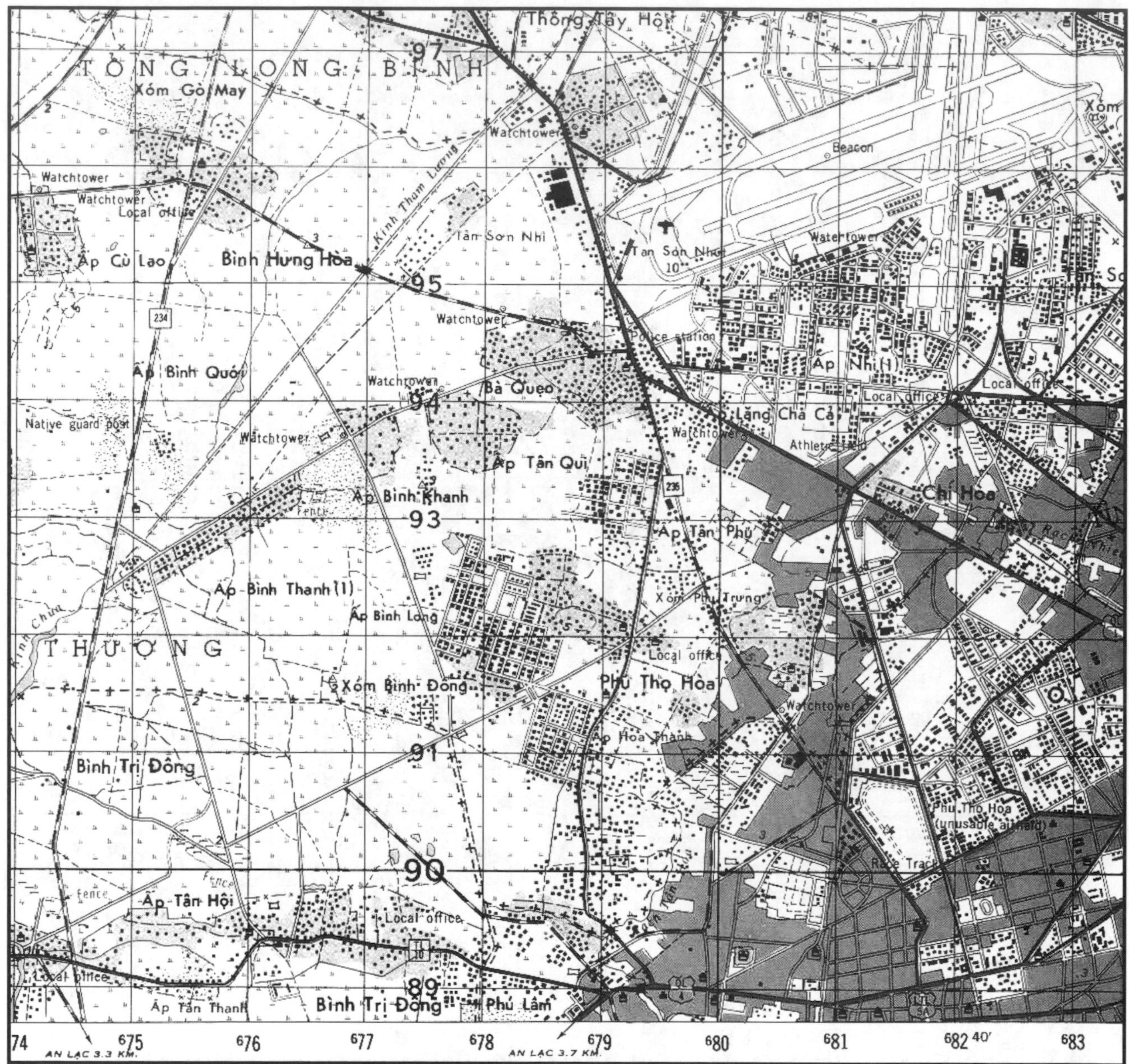

Tan Son Nhut Airbase and NW corner of Saigon, per DMA 1:50,000 scale, L-7014-6330-4 Map

UTM grid zone is XS. MACV HQ and ARVN Joint General Staff HQ were located in the area immediately SE of the intersection of the two main runways, at roughly XS 825-953. QL-1 is the dark SE/NW road skirting the southwest edge of the airbase. The Phu Tho (Saigon) Race Track is clearly visible at XS 815-905.

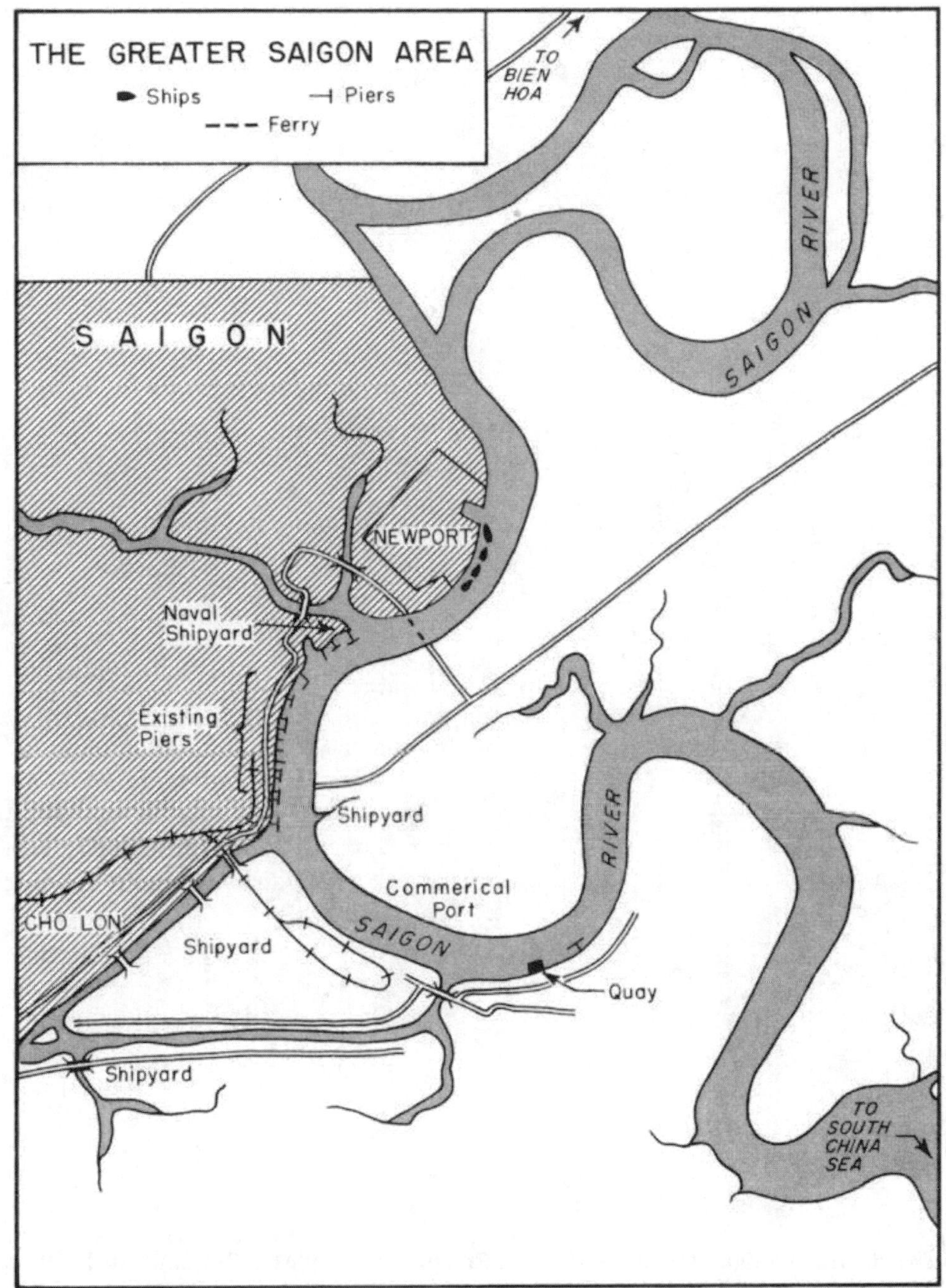

Saigon Shipyards, Commercial/Naval Port Facilities and Newport
All features are in grid square XS 8-9. Image courtesy Dept. of The Army, *Vietnam Studies,Base Development in South Vietnam 1965-1970*, p 144.

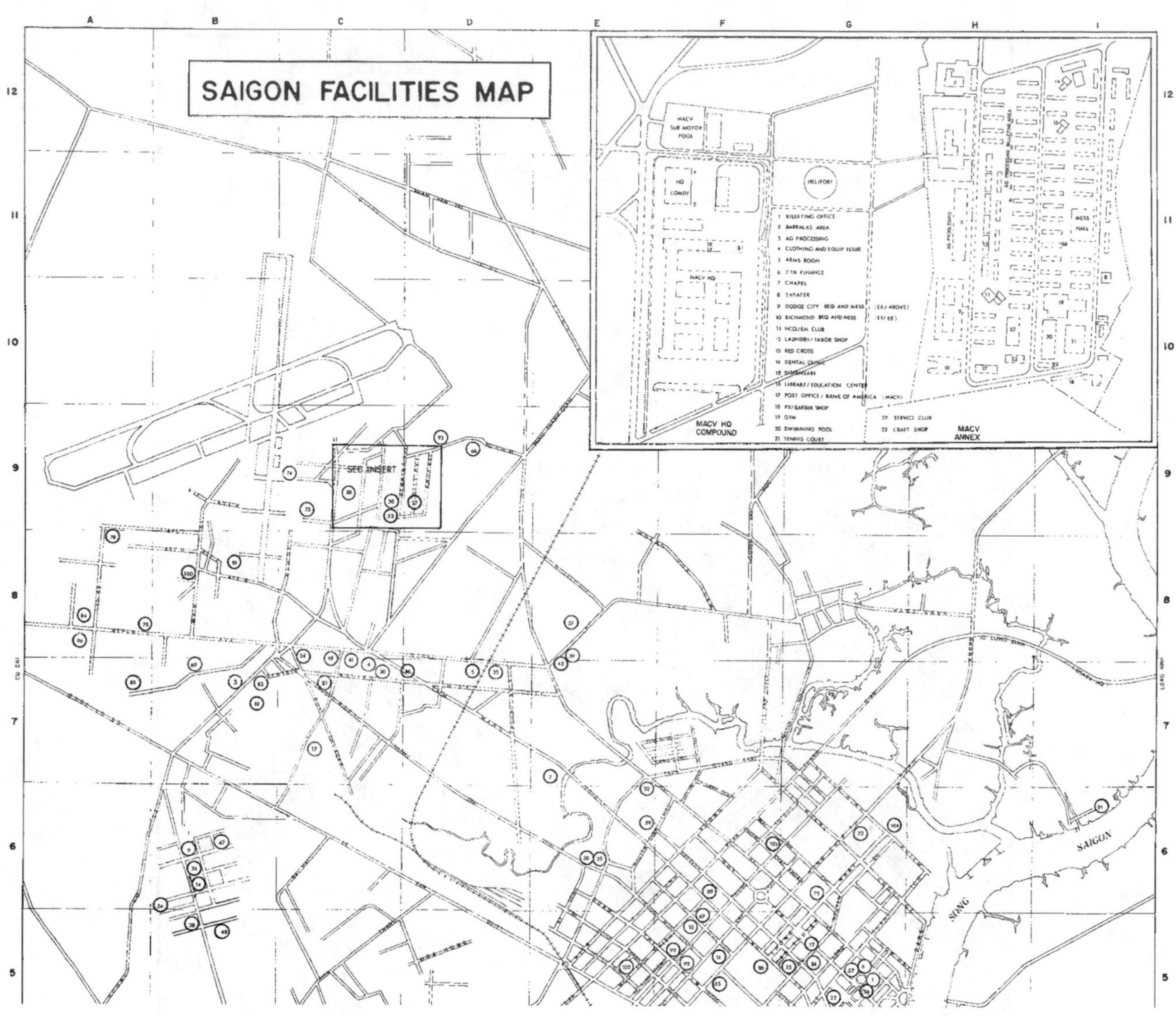

North 1/2 of Saigon Facilities Map, 3d Ed., prepared by MACV J2, June 1969, printed by 66th Engr Co (Topo) Nov69

Grid squares are 1 km square and match those of Saigon's L-7014-6330-4, 1:50k scale map. Grid zone is 'XS.' Vertical gridlines from E to W run sequentially from XS 80 to 89, while horizontal gridlines from S to N run from 93 to 99; hence, grid for intersection of Tan Son Nhut runways is apx XS 820-960.

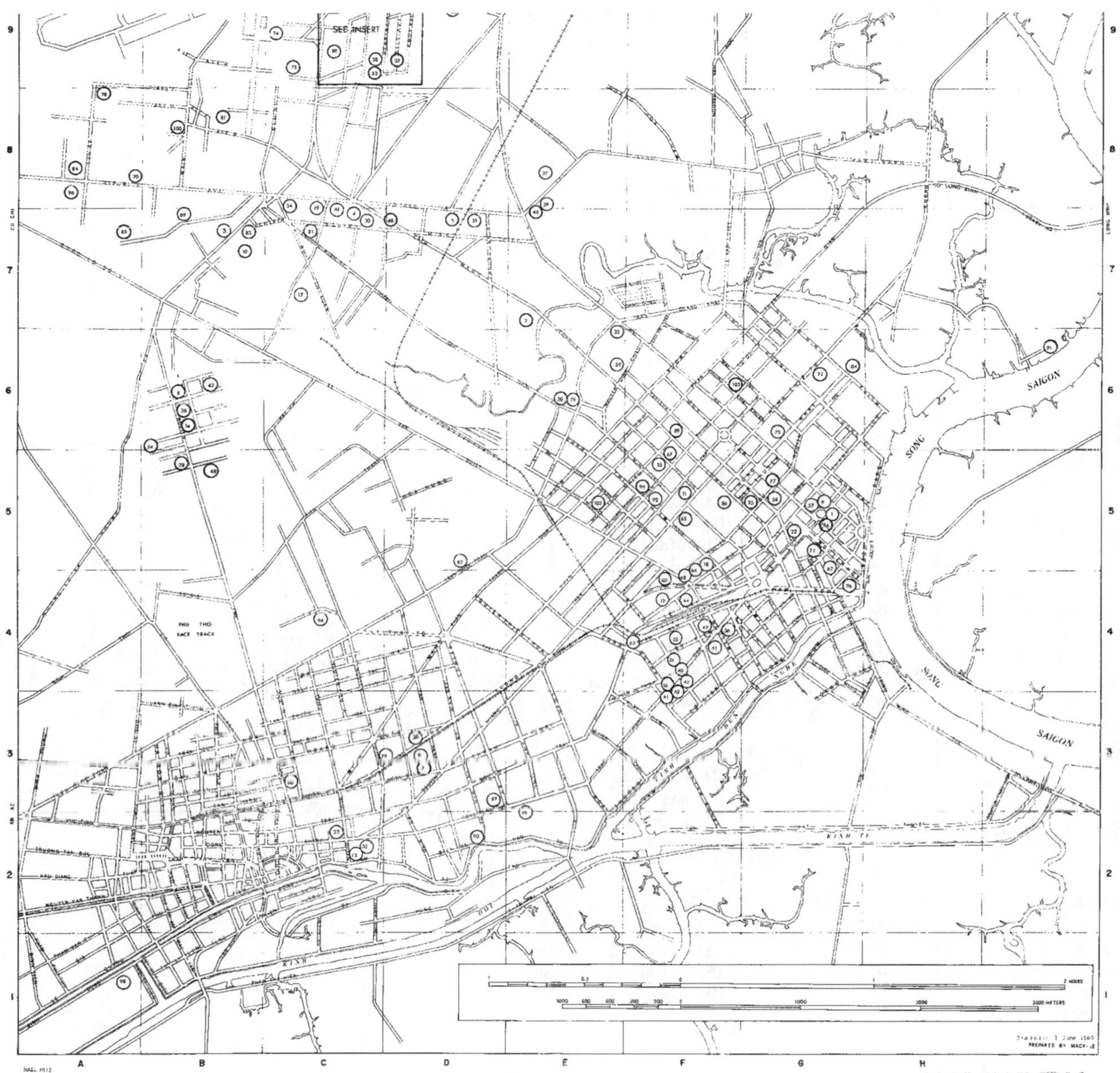

South 1/2 of Saigon Facilities Map, 3d Ed., prepared by MACV J2, June 1969, printed by 66th Engr Co (Topo) November 1969

Grid zone is "XS." Vertical gridlines from E to W run sequentially from XS 80 to 89, while horizontal gridlines for this portion of the map run S to N from 87 to 93; hence, grid for Phu Tho Race Track is apx XS 815-905.

Saigon Facilities Map Locator

Per 1 Jun 69, 3d Edition, MACV J2 Saigon Facilities Map, printed by 66th Engr Co (Topo) 11-69

BOQs

Ambassador	1	G5
Arkansas	2	E7
BOQ #1	3	B7
BOQ #2	4	C7
BOQ #3	5	D7
Brinks	6	G5
Buis	7	D3
Five Oceans	8	D3
Florida Bar	9	B6
Geneva #2	10	B7
Geneva	10	B7
Hergert	11	F5
Hialeah	9	B6
Hoa Lu	12	F4
Hong Kong	13	C2
Idaho	14	B6
Le Qui Don	15	F5
Lucky	13	C2
Massachusetts	4	C7
Metropole	16	F4
Meyerkord (PX)	18	F5
Missouri	17	C7
Newport	19	C8
Nhan Vi	20	D3
North Pole	7	D3
Pax	21	C7
Rex	22	G5
Savoy Palace	23	C2
Splendid	24	G5
Stone	13	C2
White/Blair House	25	G5

BEQs

Annapolis	26	B6
Barracks	27	Inset
Battle Creek **	28	B5
BEQ #1	29	E6
Billings	30	C7
Bui Ven	31	F4
Butte	32	E7
Capitol (MP's)	33	C2
Columbia	34	C8
Connecticut	35	D7
Dai Nam (Wabash)	36	F4
Den Bigh *	37	E8
Dodge City	38	C9
Helena **	39	E8
Hung Doa	40	F4
International	41	F3
Iowa	21	C7
Kalamazoo *	42	B6
Ky Son Annex	43	F4
Ky Son	43	F4
Le Lai	44	F4
Louisiana	45	E7-8
Medford	46	D7
Metropole Annex	16	F4
Montana	48	B5
Muskegon	9	B6
Pennsylvania	49	F4
Phoenix City	50	E6
Plaza	51	F4
Ponderosa Cmpd	52	F8
Richmond	53	C9
Royal Oaks	54	B6
Smith	36	F4
St. George	33	C2
Utah	37	E8
Wabash Inn	36	F4
Walling	55	F4
White	13	C2

*Closing Jul69
**Closing Sep69

Hotels:

Caravelle	56	G5
Continental	57	G5
Khai Minh	59	E6
Majestic	60	G5

Hospitals/Clinics:

3rd Field	61	C8
218th Med Dispensary	62	F3-4
Dental Clinic	63	F4

Recreational Facilities:

Bowling Alley	64	F4-5
Circle Sportif-Tennis	65	F5
Crafts Shop		Inset
Golf Course	66	D9
Library, Lincoln	67	F5
Library, Spec Serv	68	F4
Swimming pool	69	B7
TSN Theater #1	96	A8
TSN Theater #2	70	A8
USO, Saigon	71	G5
USO, TSN	4	C7

Miscellaneous Facilities:

7th AF HQ	100	B8
7th Finance (Capitol)	33	C2
8th Aerial Port	81	B8
AFRTS	72	G6
Air America Term.	73	C9
Air Terminal Civil	74	C9
ATCO, Tri-Services	74	C9
Camp Alpha	78	A8
Cathedral	77	G5
COFAT	79	D3
Comm Entertain.	80	C3
Eighth Aerial Port	81	B8
FWMAO	82	D5
Heliport	84	A8
Hold Baggage Stg	85	A7
HQ Area Cmd	83	B7
Independence Palace	86	F5
International House	87	G5
JUSPAO #1	22	G5
MACV #1	89	F6
MACV HQ	88	C9
MACV Sub-Motor Pool		Inset
MACV Trng Aids	90	D2
Naval Forces, VN	92	F5
Naval Supt Activity	99	F5
Navy Oceanographic	91	I6
NSA, Saigon	99	F5
Oceanographic Off	91	I6
PA&E	93	D9
Phu Tho Motor Pool	94	C4
Post Eng's Cmpd	95	E3-3
Provost Marshall	97	D3
PX/TSN Theater #1	96	A-8
PX, Cholon	79	D3
Red Cross	89	F6
Rice Mill Area	98	A1
TSN Theater #2	70	A8F4
US Army Procurmnt	27	B6
US Embassy Annex	76	G4
US Embassy	75	G6
USAID #1	101	E5
USAID #2	102	F4
USAID #3	43	F4
Viet-American Assoc	103	F6
Zoo/Park/Museum	104	G6

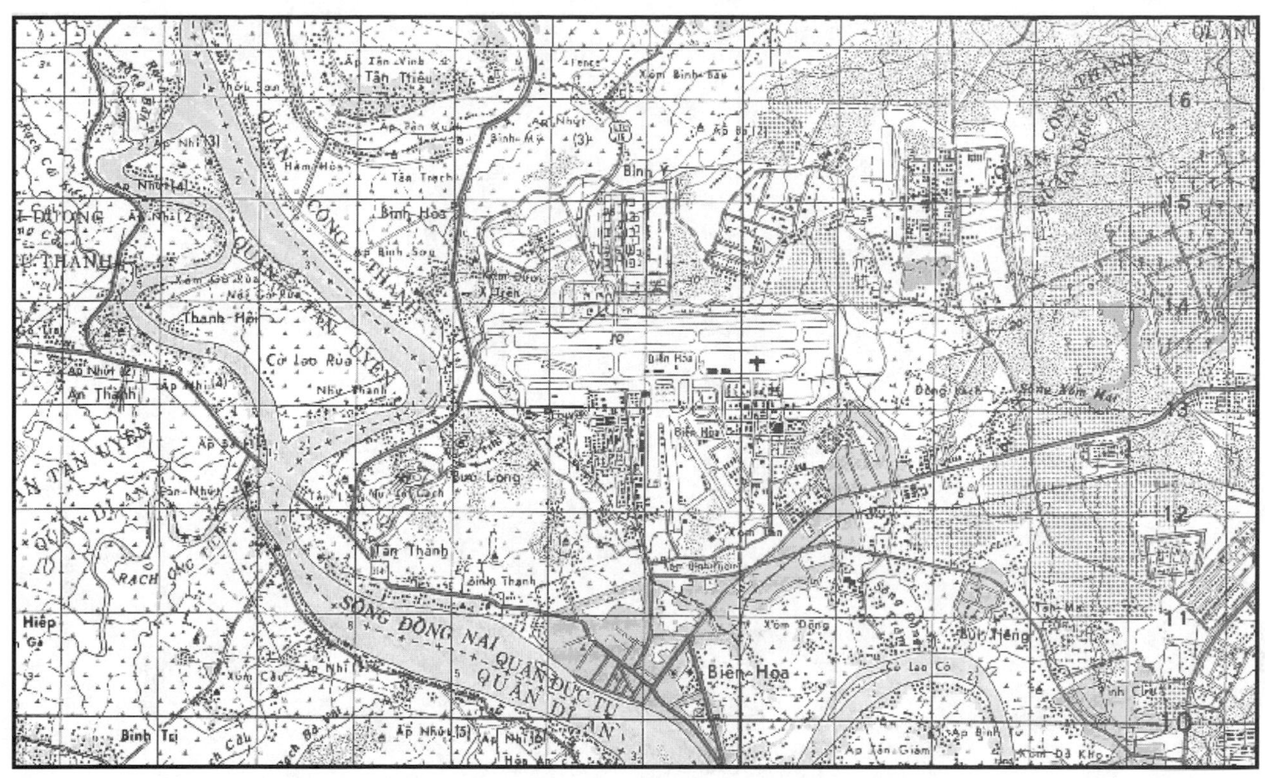

Bien Hoa Airbase, per L7014-6330-1 and 6331-2 DMA Maps

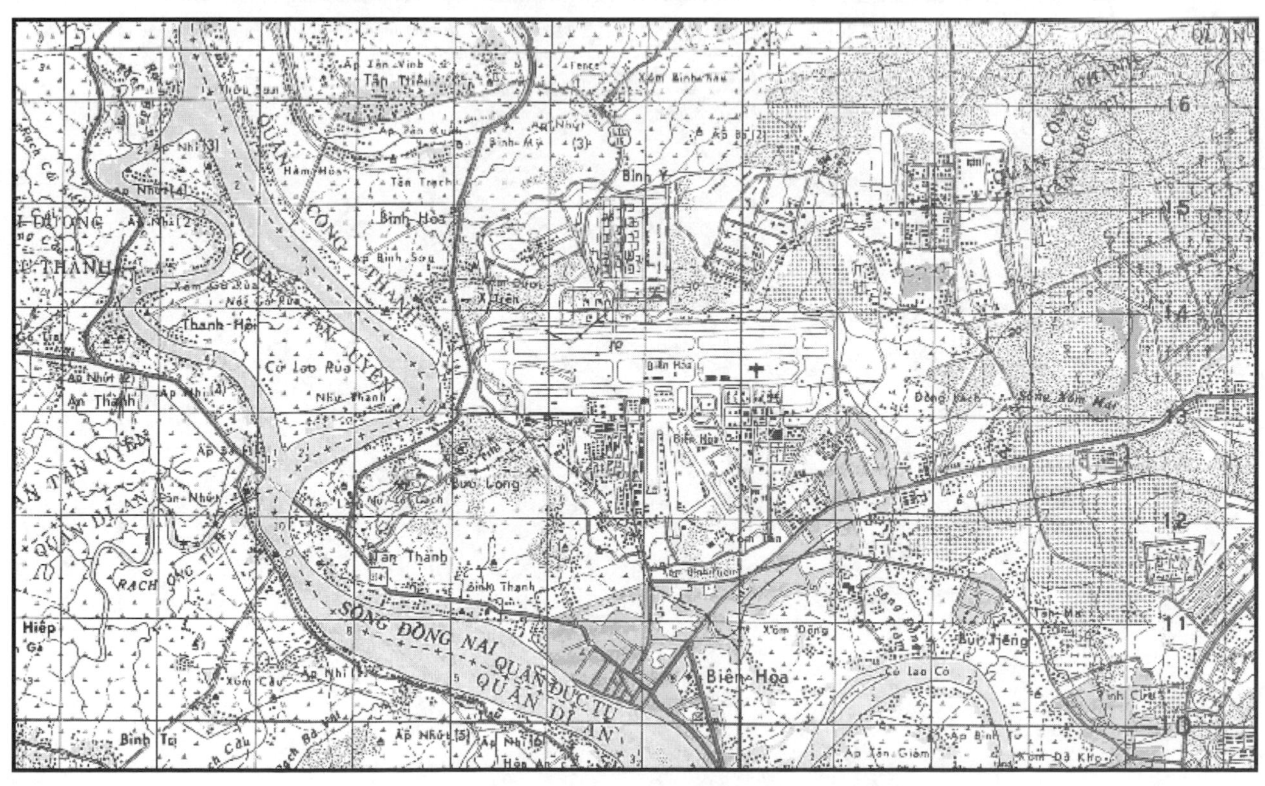

Long Binh Post, per L7014-6330-1 DMA Map
Images courtesy of WUG

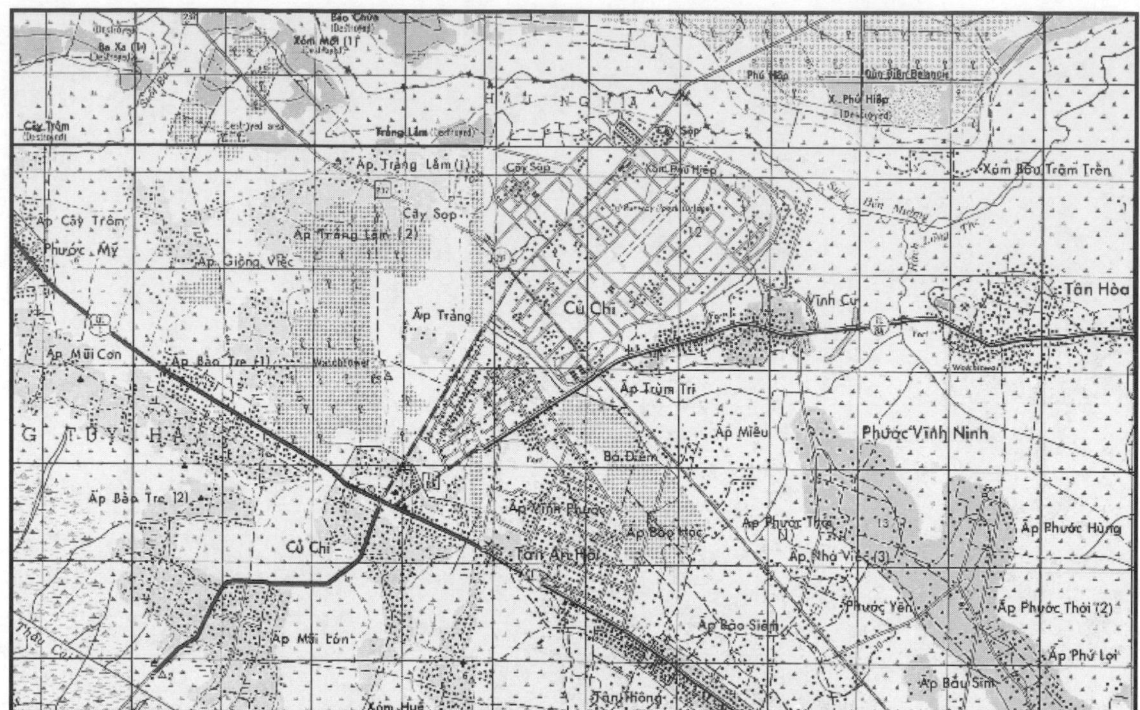

Cu Chi area per DMA 1:50,000 scale L-7014-6630-4 Map
Image courtesy of Steve Sherman.

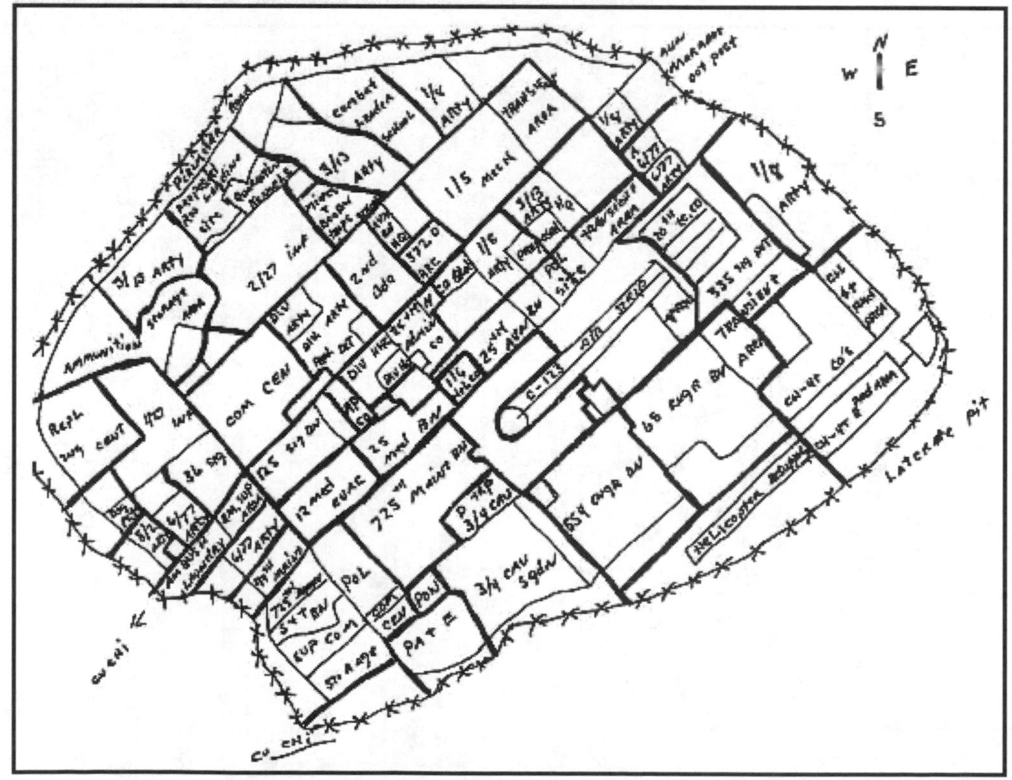

Map of Cu Chi Combat Base circa 1967, with Unit Locations Annotated. National Archives Image
(Courtesy of the 25th Infantry Division Association Archives, and gift of Vernon C. Smith)

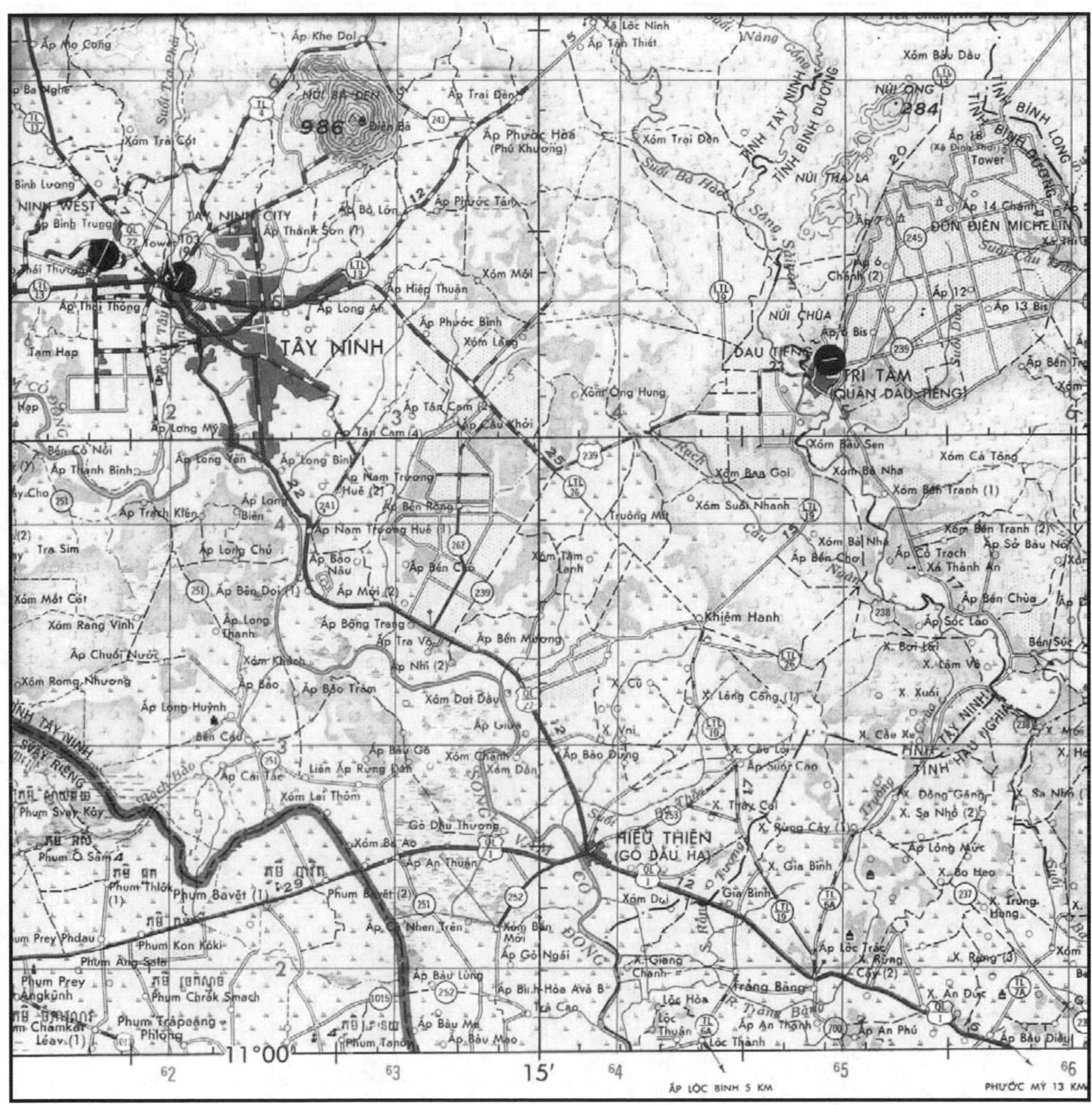

Tay Ninh, Dau Tieng, Nui Ba Den and Area Northwest of Saigon in UTM Grid Zone "XT"
Per L-1501 series, NC 48-03, 1;250,000 scale, JOG Map
Operational Area of the 25th Infantry, 1st Infantry and 1st Cavalry Divisions, et al.

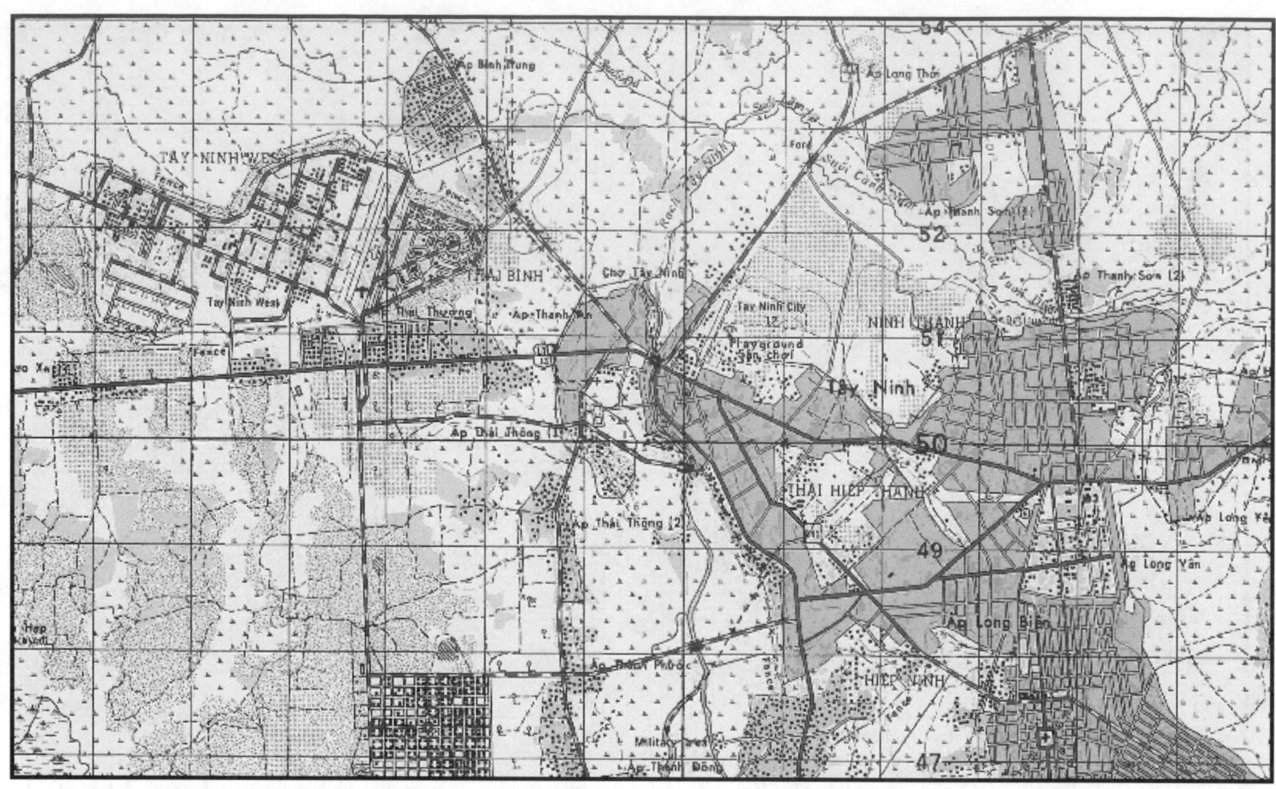

Tan Ninh West Airfield and Tay Ninh City per DMA Map L-7014-6231-4, 1:50,000 scale
Images courtesy of WUG

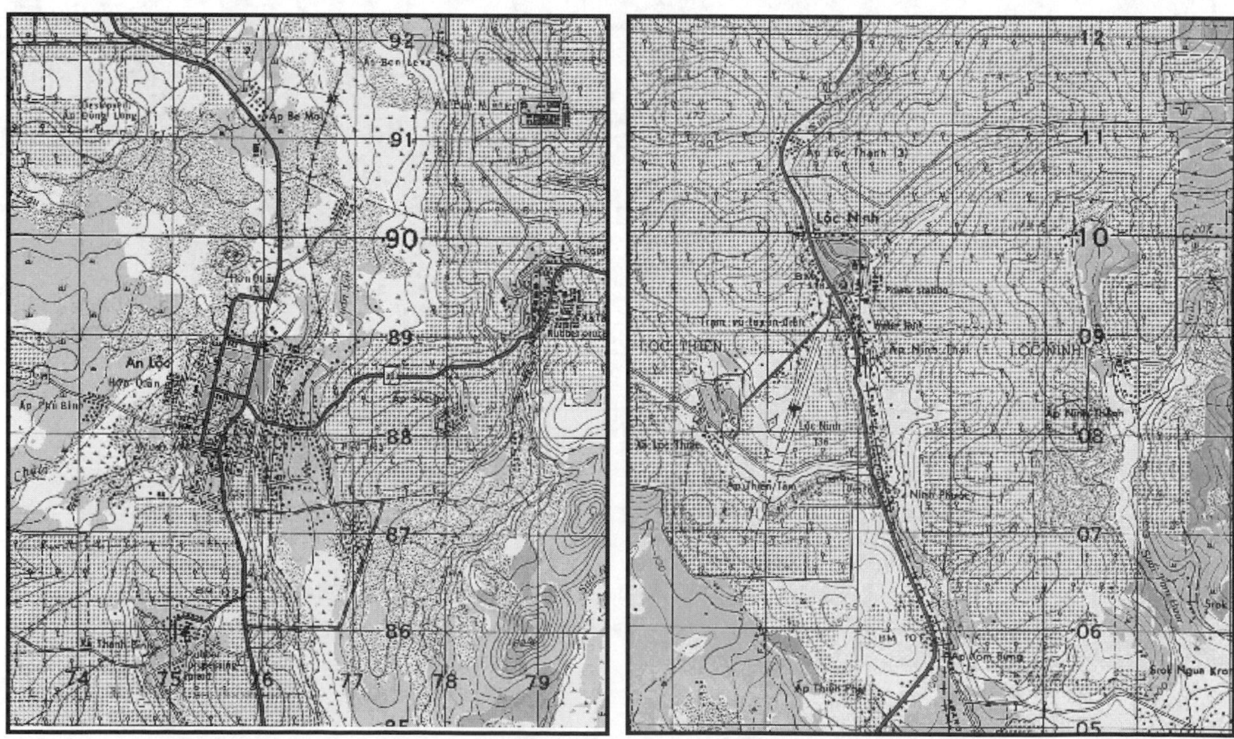

An Loc per DMA Map L-7014-6332-3, 1:50k

Loc Ninh DMA Map L-7014-6332-4, 1:50k

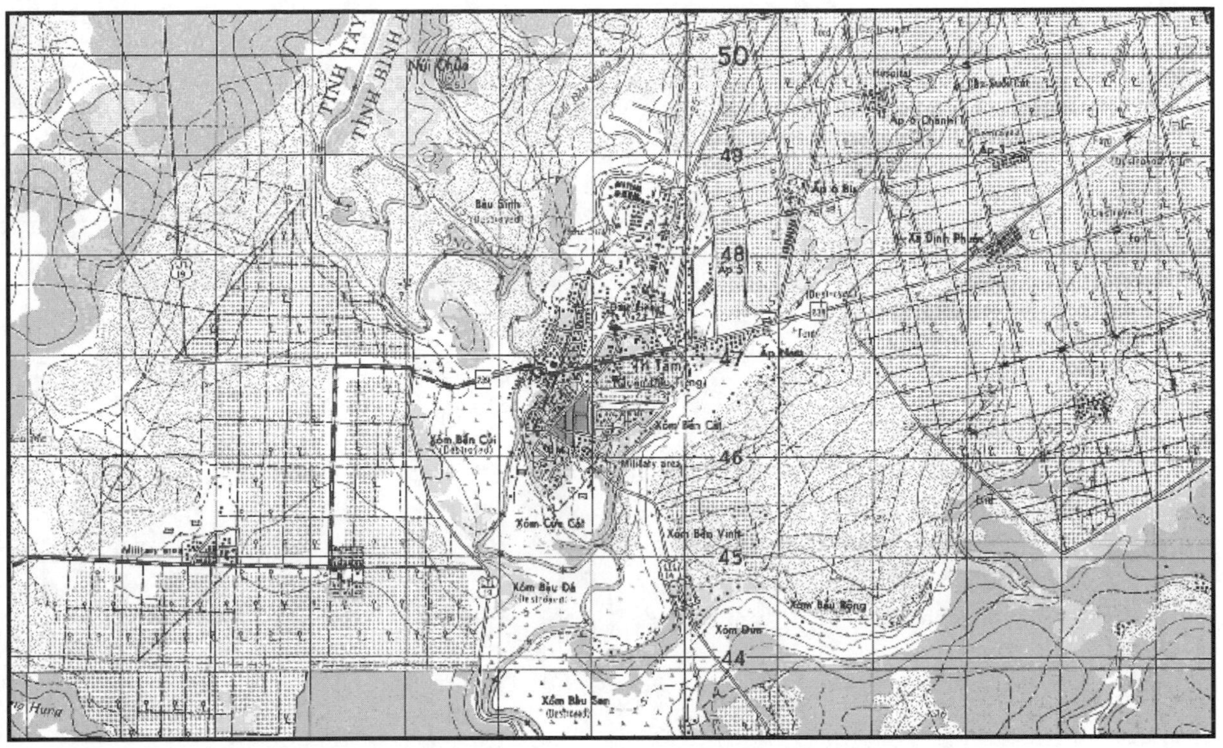

Dau Tieng Basecamp and Airfield per L-7014-6231-2 and 6231-1 DMA Maps

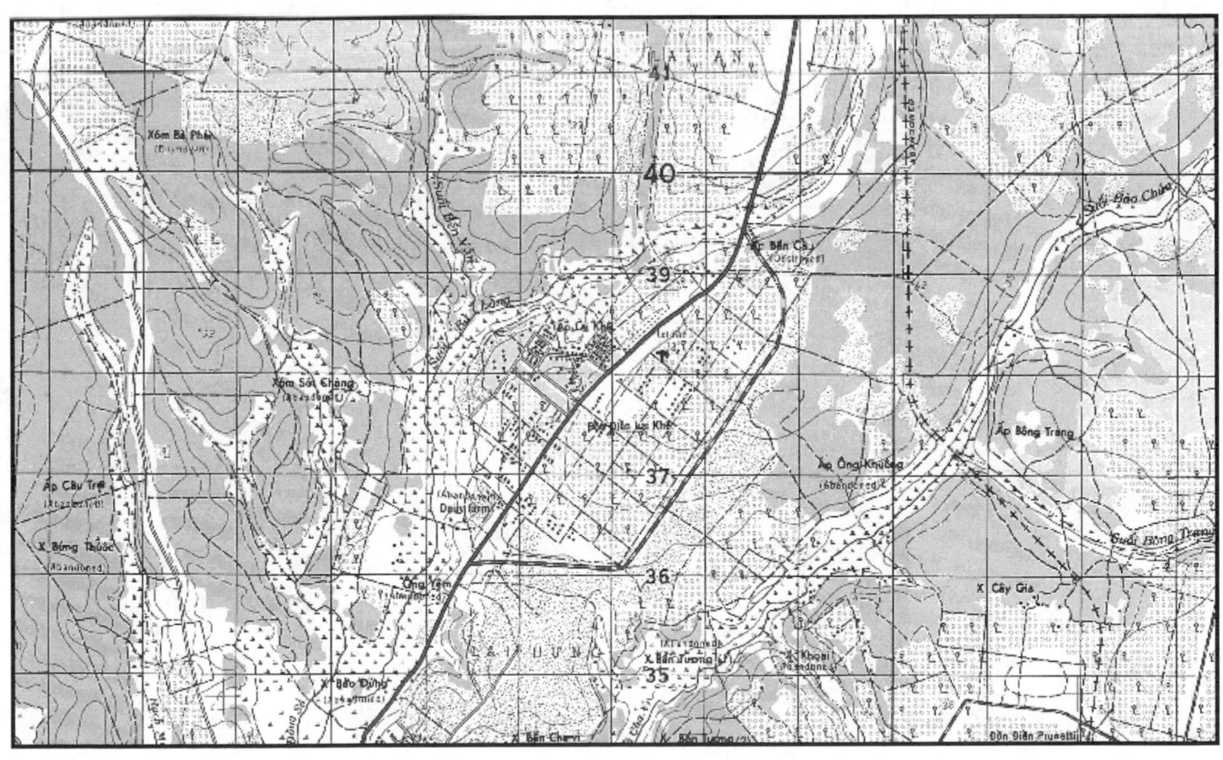

Lai Khe Airfield per L-7014-6331-4 and 6331-3 DMA Maps
Images courtesy of WUG

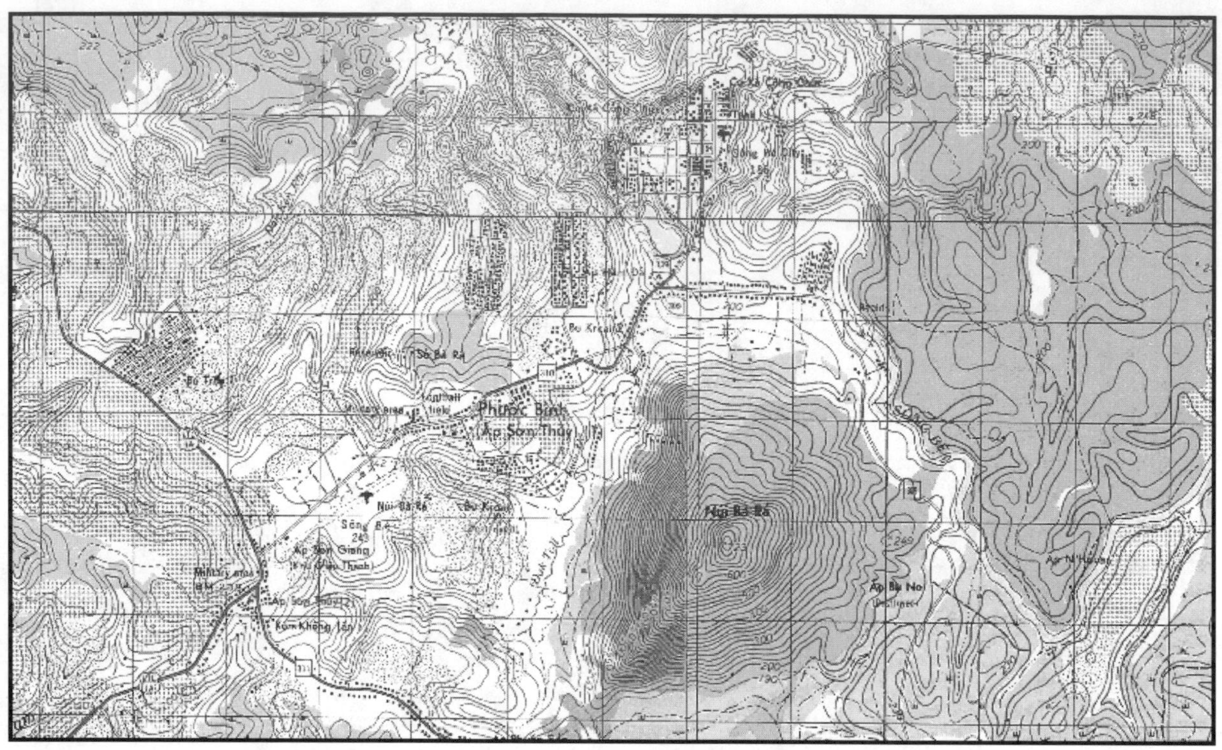

Phuoc Vinh Airfield per L-7014-6331-1 and 6331-2 DMA Map

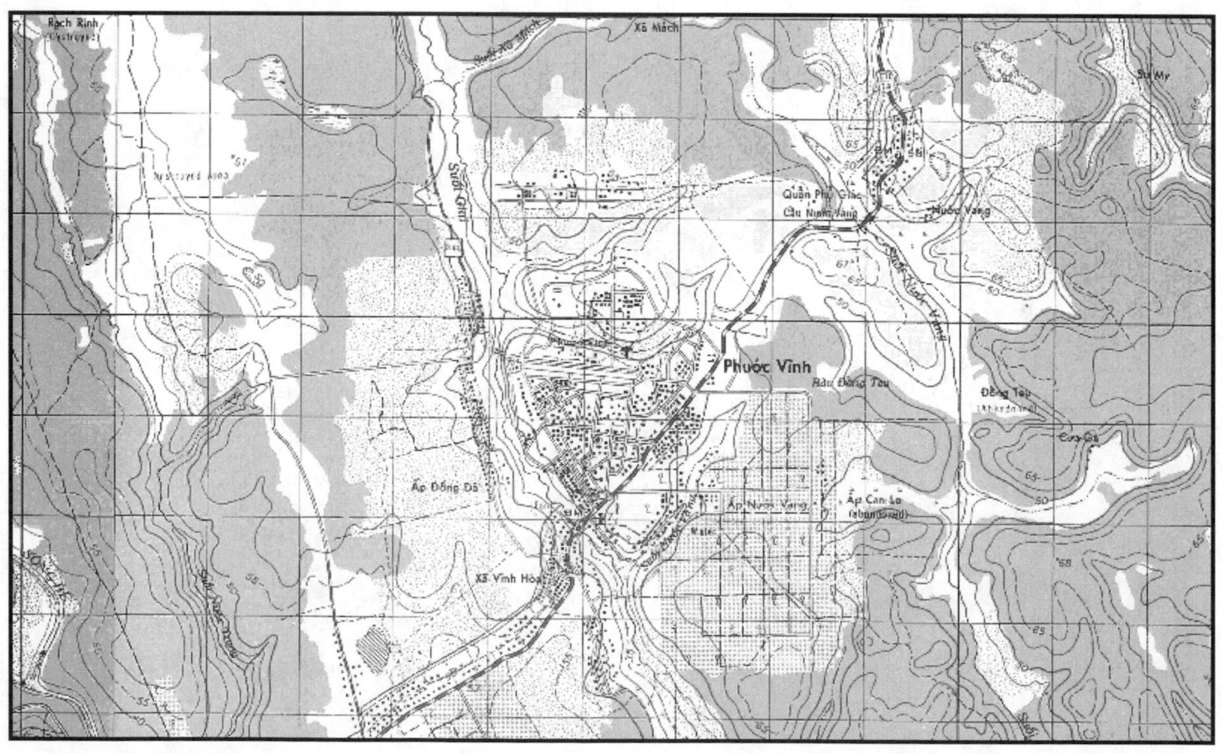

Song Be Airfield, Phuoc Binh, and Song Be City Airfield per L-7014-6332-1 and 6432-4 DMA Map
Images courtesy of WUG

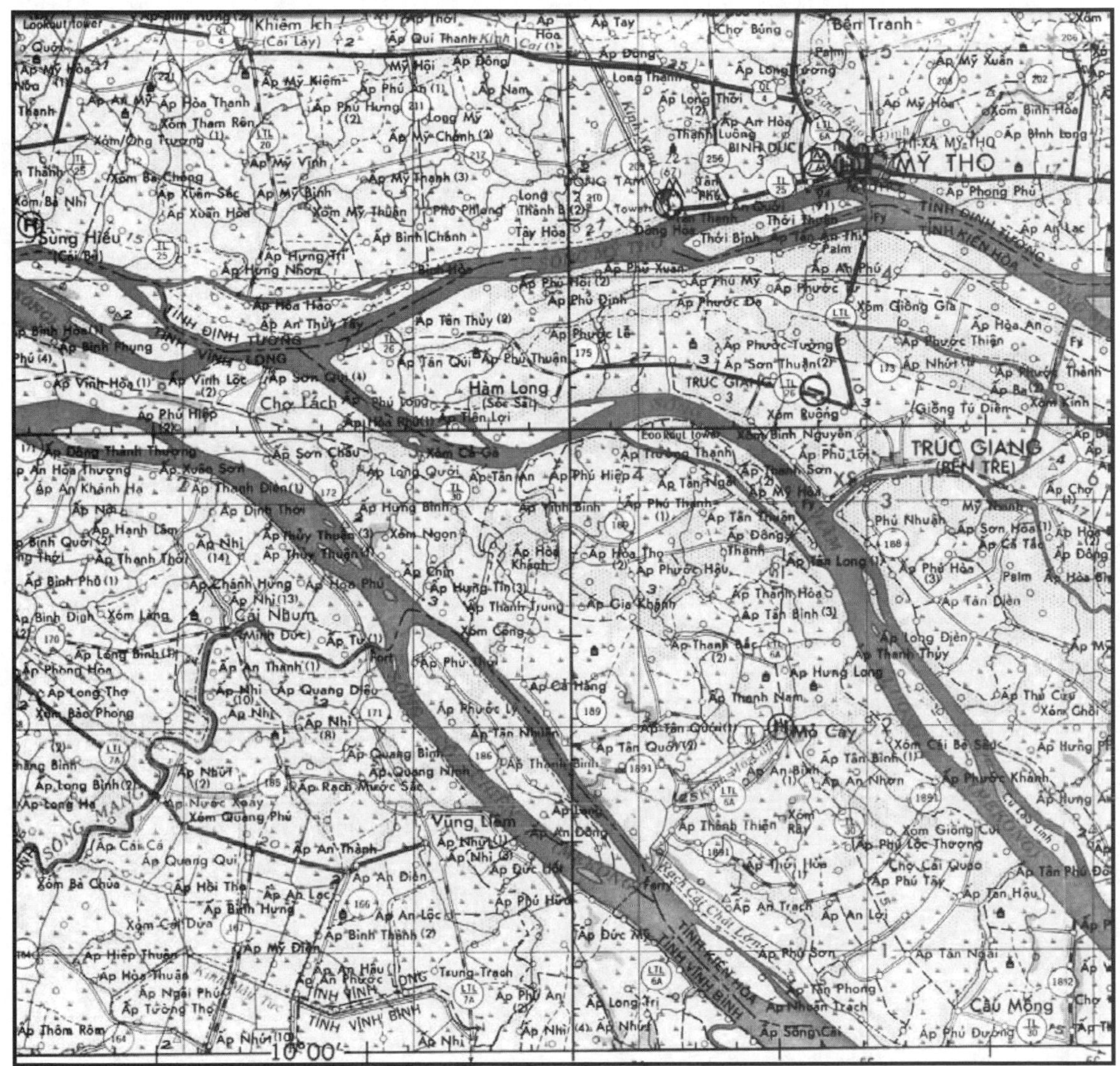

Dong Tam, My Tho, Ben Tre (Truc Giang) and the Mekong River Area Southwest of Saigon
Per DMA NC48-07 JOG, 1:250,000 scale Map

Using land dredged from the river, Dong Tam was built as the basecamp of the US Army's 9th Infantry Division and other elements of the Mobile Riverine Force (MRF). Image courtesy of Jim Henthorn.

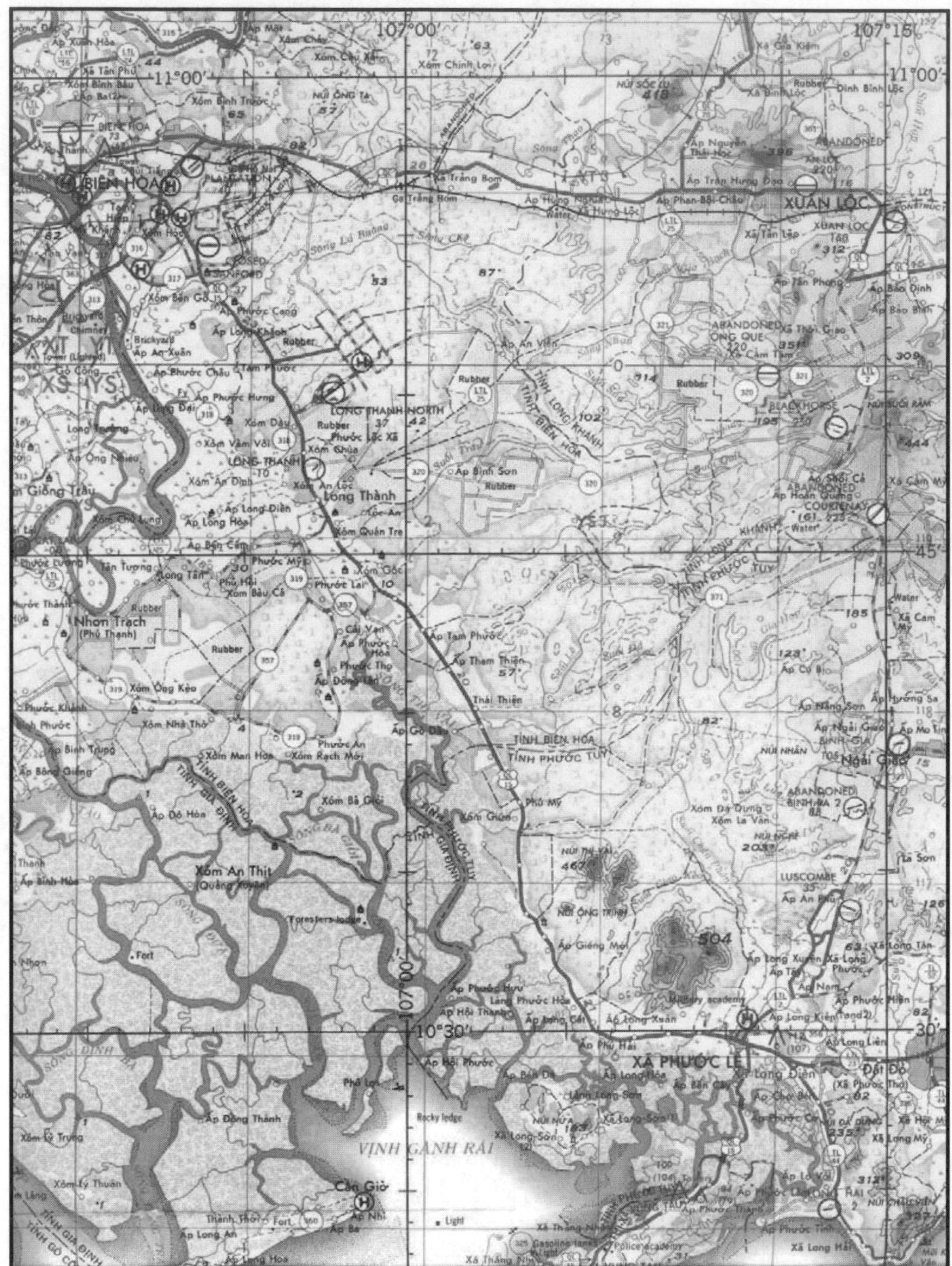

Portion of DMA Joint Operations Graphic (JOG) NC 48-07, 1:250,000 scale Map

Bien Hoa Airbase, Long Binh Post (Plantation Airfield) and Long Thanh (Bearcat) are in upper-left quad; Xuan Loc and Blackhorse (11th ACR) in upper-right quad; Nui Dat/Luscombe Airfield (1st ATF) and a portion of the Vung Tau Peninsula in lower right quad; Rung Sat Special Zone in lower-left. Image courtesy of Jim Henthorne and is on-line at: www.nexus.net/~911gfx/vietnam/maps/nc48-07/nc48_07d.jpg.

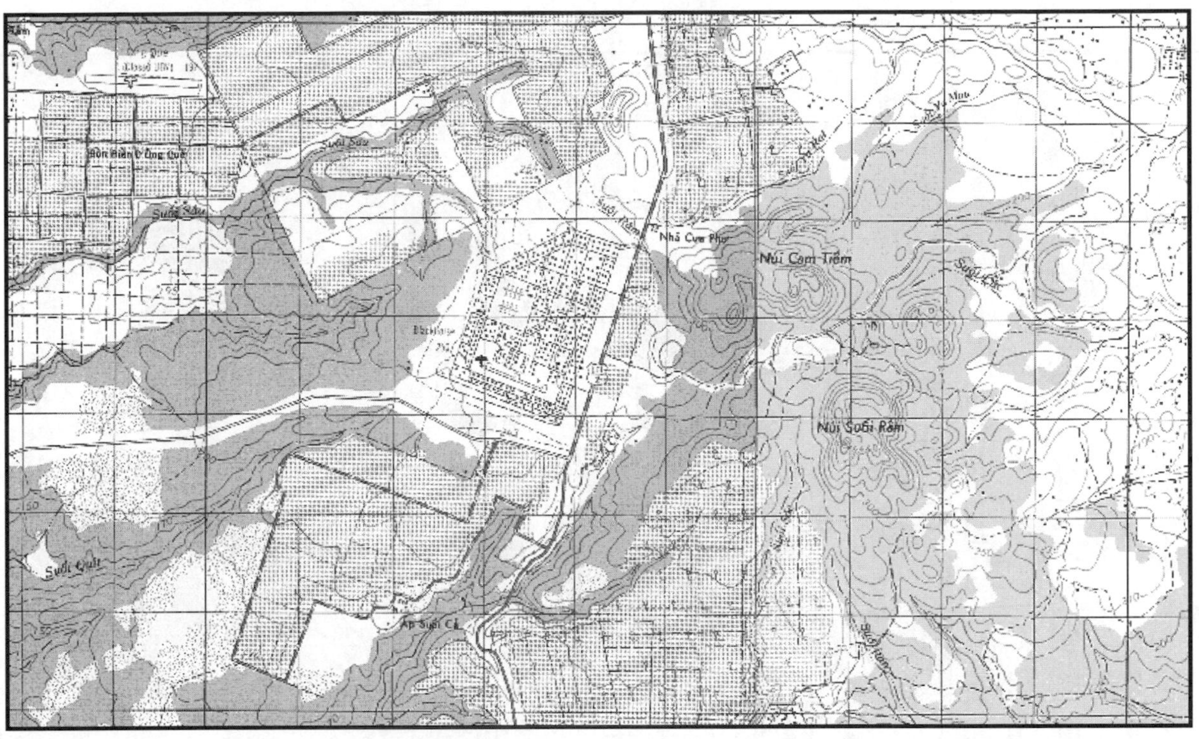

Xuan Loc City/QL-1 per L-7014-6430-4 and 6430-1, DMA Maps

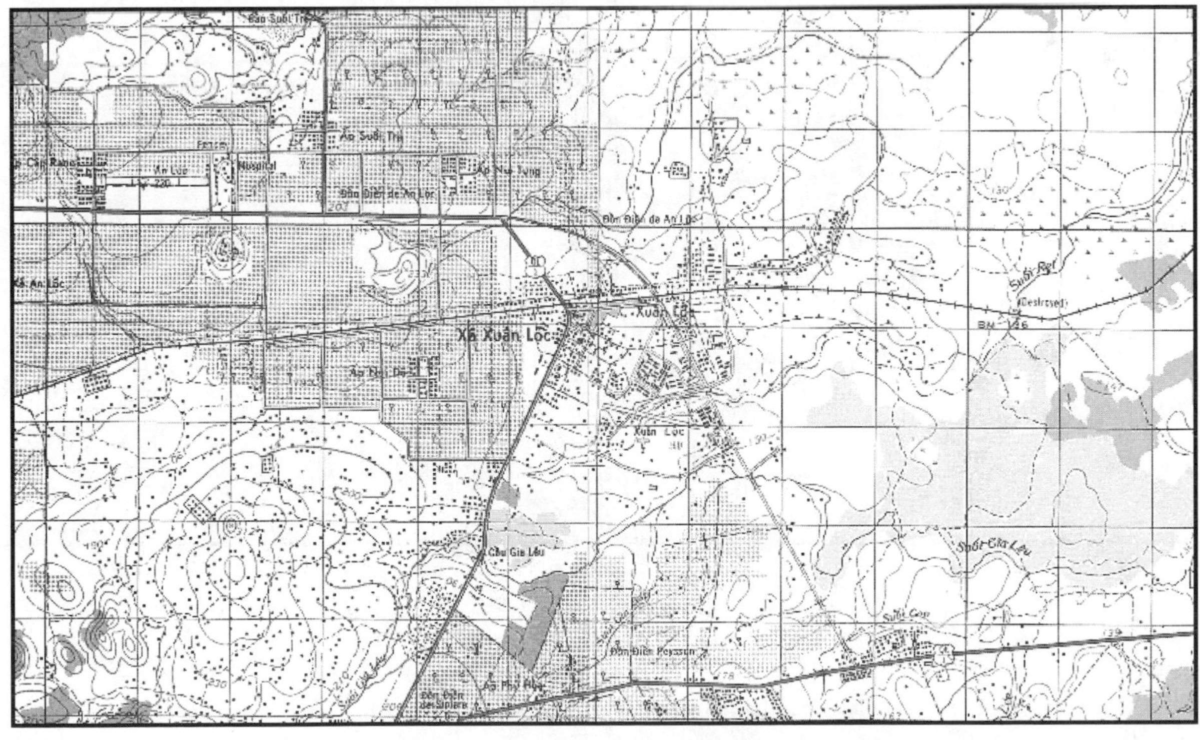

Blackhorse Airfield and Basecamp per L-7014-6430-4 and 6430-1 DMA Maps
Images courtesy of WUG

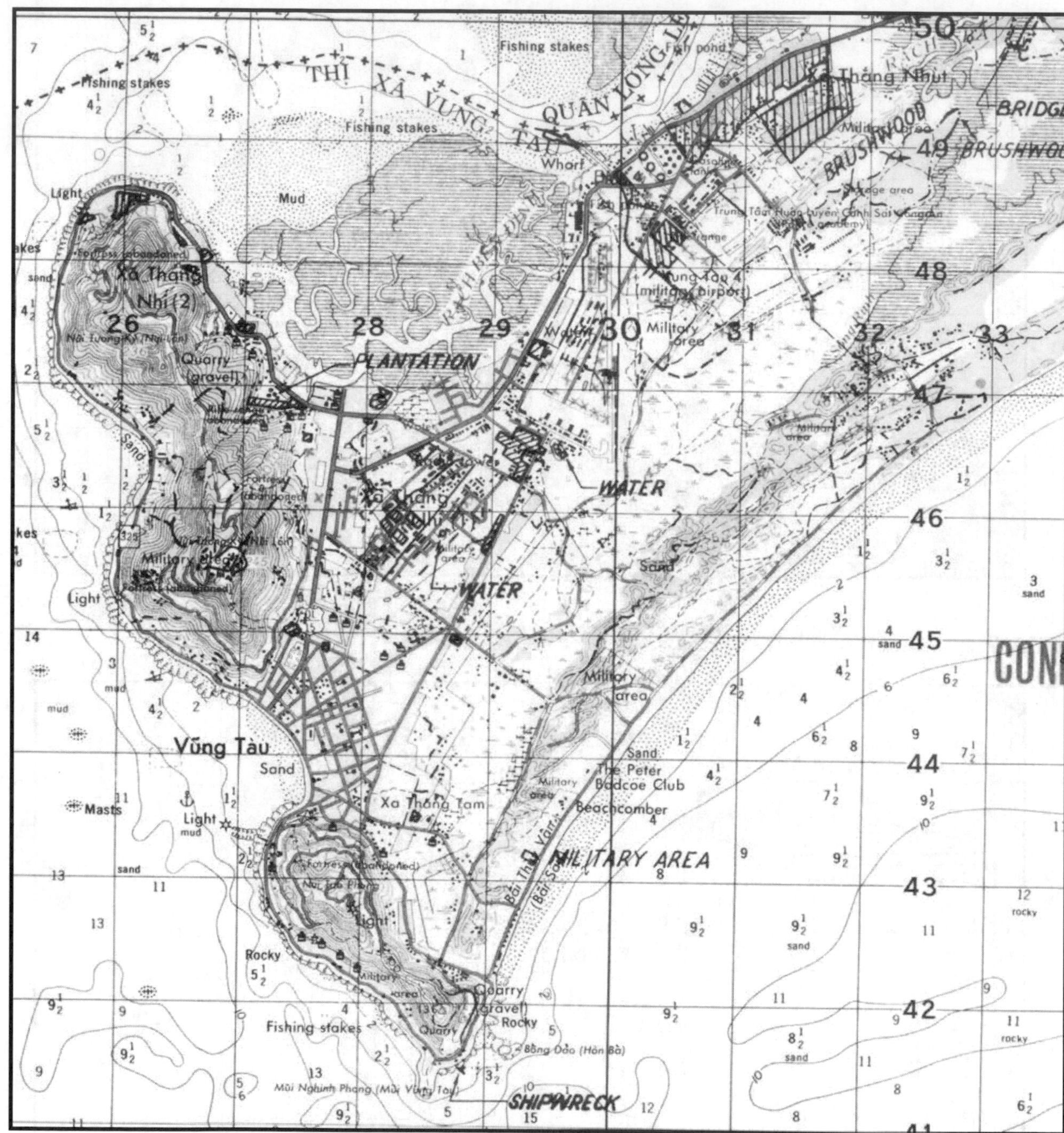

Vung Tau Peninsula per DMA L-7014-6429 4, 1:50,000 scale Map
UTM Grid Zone is "YS"

Image courtesy of Garry Adams, 6RAR, 1st ATF, 1969-70.

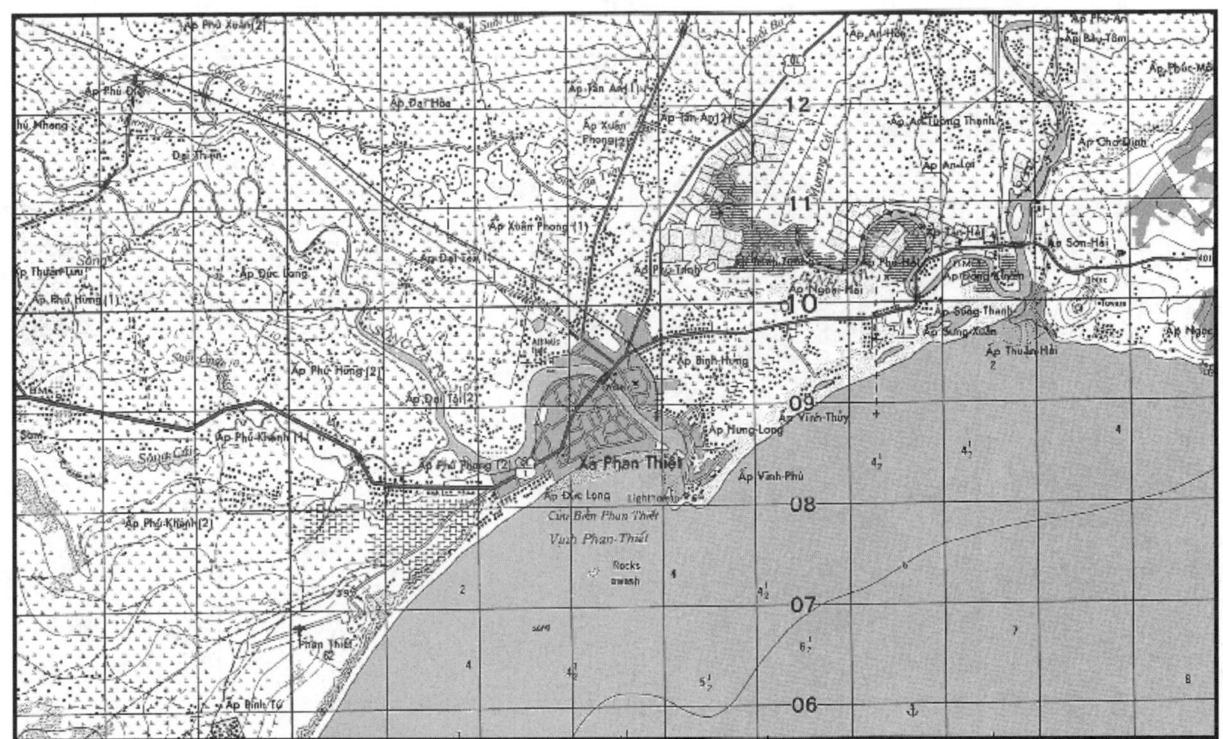

Phan Thiet Airfield/LZ Betty and Phan Thiet City, per L-7014-6630-4 DMA Map

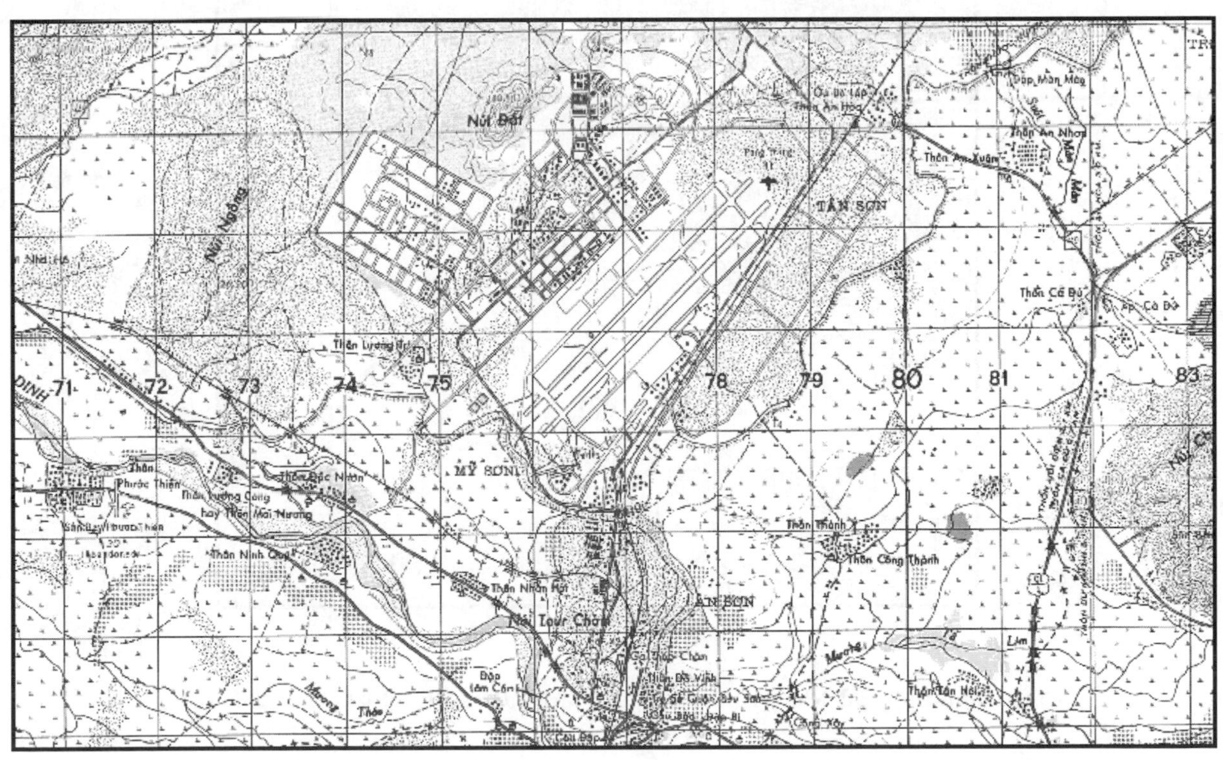

Phan Rang Airbase per L-7014-6732-2 DMA Map

Images courtesy of WUG

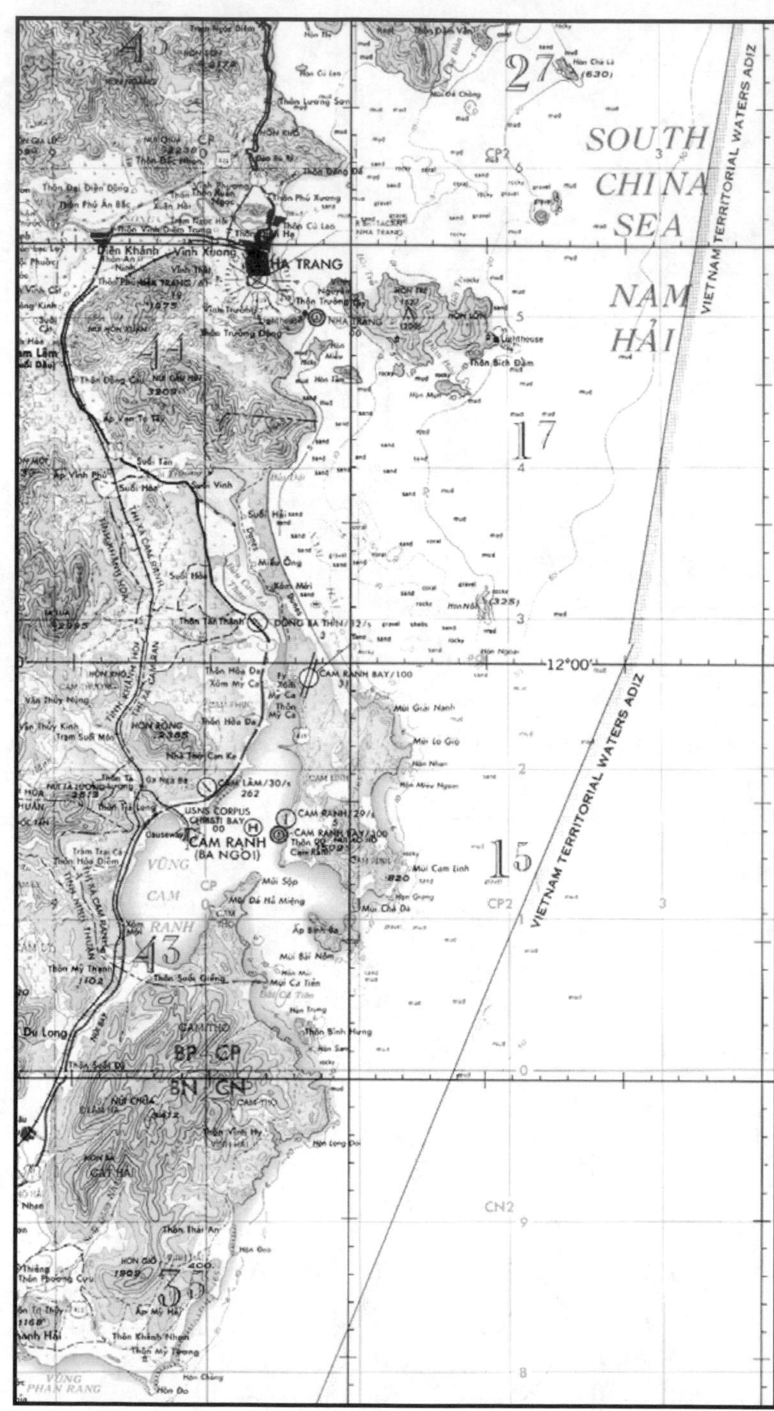

Cam Ranh Bay and Nha Trang Area, per DMA JOG NC 49-01, 1:250,000 scale Map

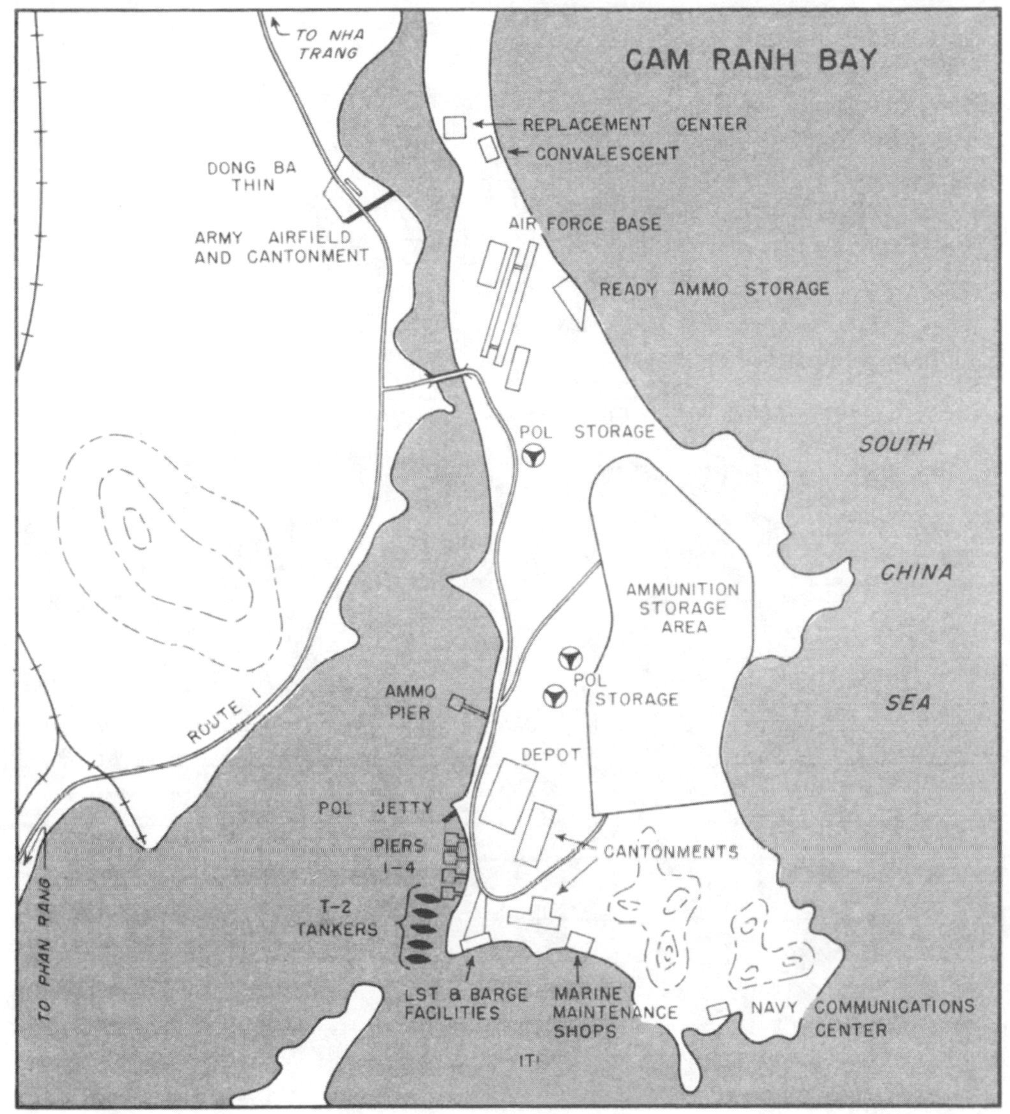

Cam Ranh Bay Facilities Map
Courtesy Dept. of The Army. *Vietnam Studies, Base Development in South Vietnam 1965-1970*, p 56

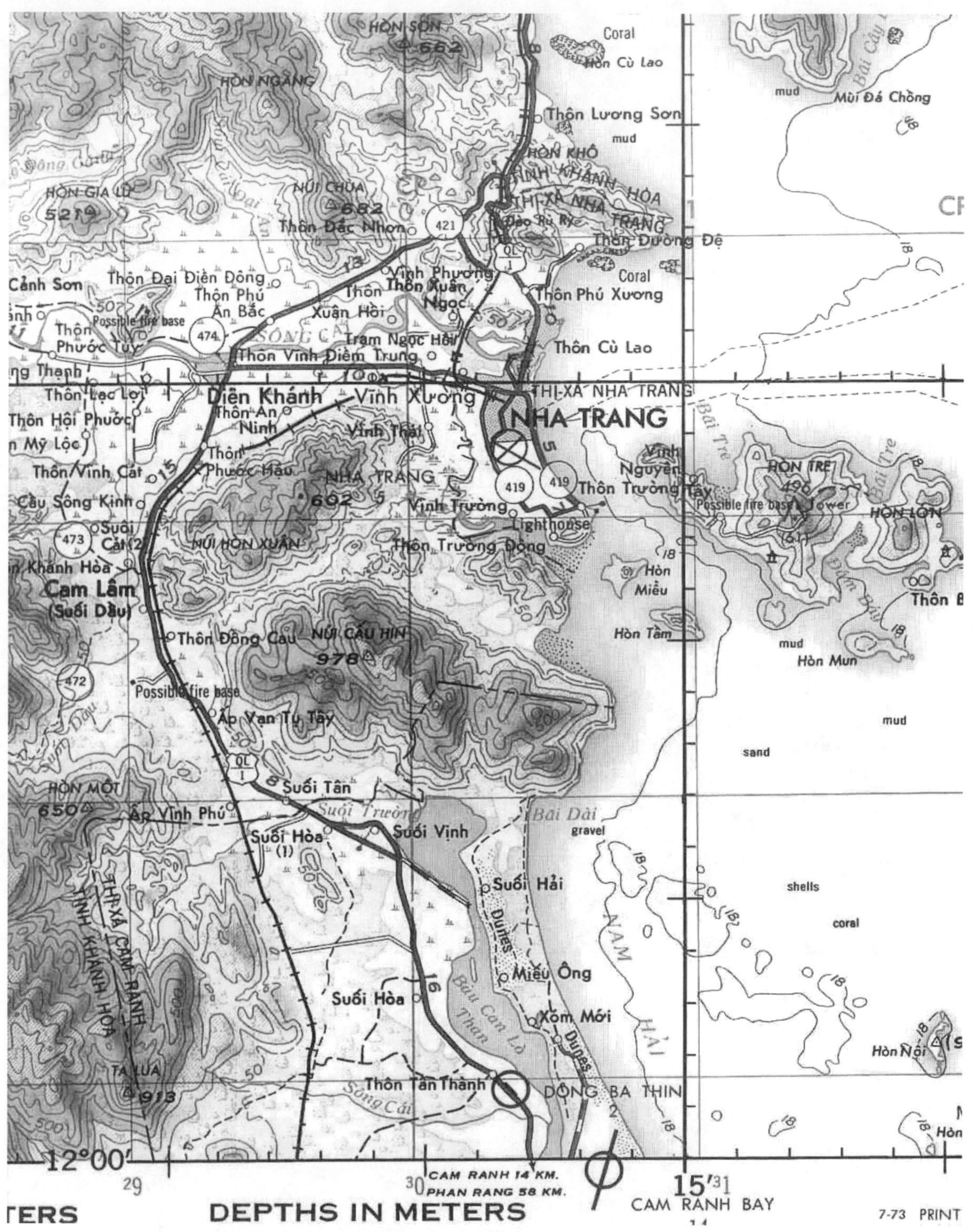

Nha Trang Area, per DMA JOG ND49-13, 1:250,000 scale Map
Image courtesy of Jim Henthorn

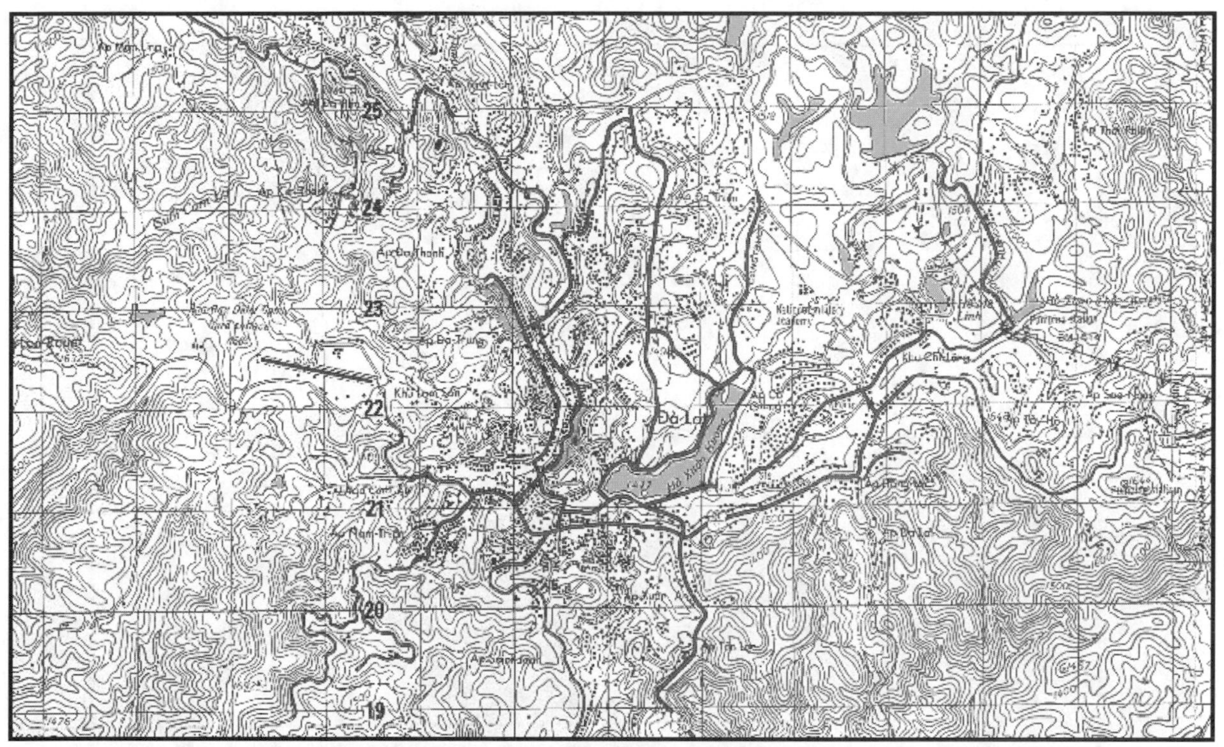

Dalat/Cam Ly Airfield and Dalat City per L-7014-6633-2 and 6632-1 DMA Maps

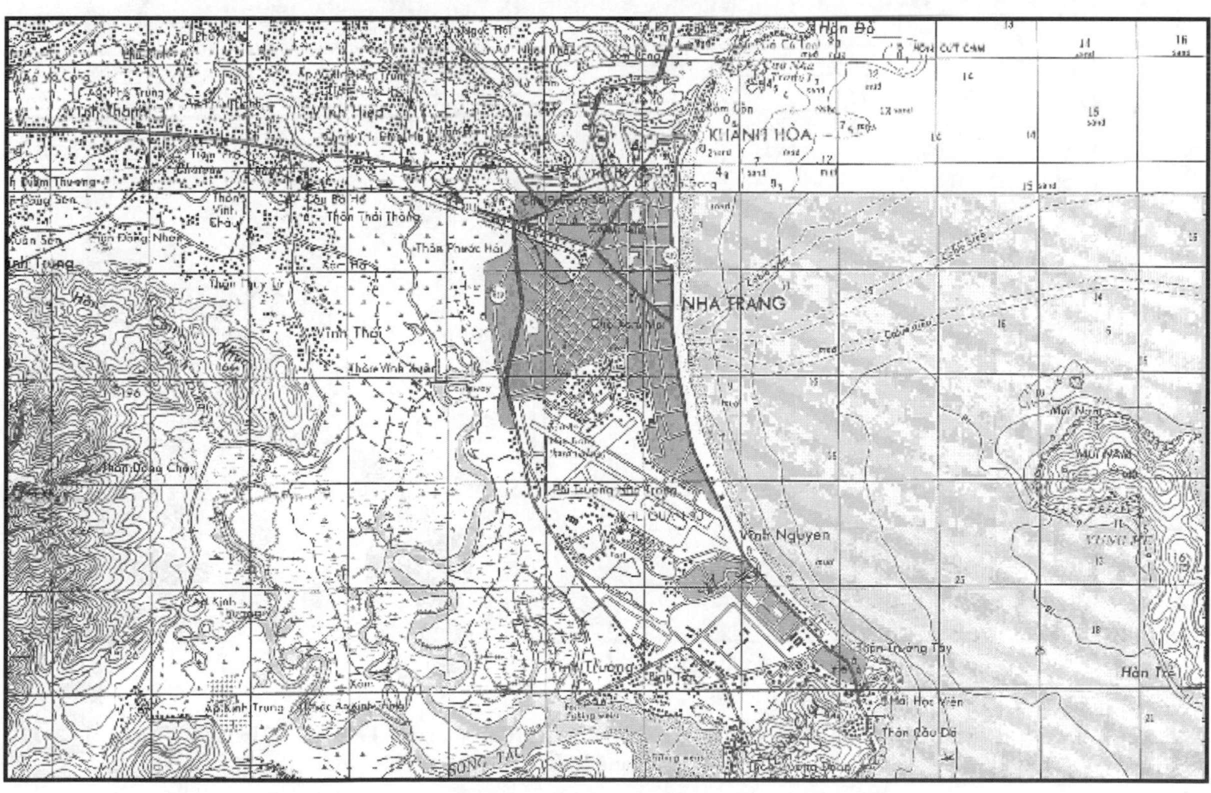

Nha Trang City and Airfield, per L-7014-6833-4 and 6833-3 DMA Maps
Images courtesy of WUG

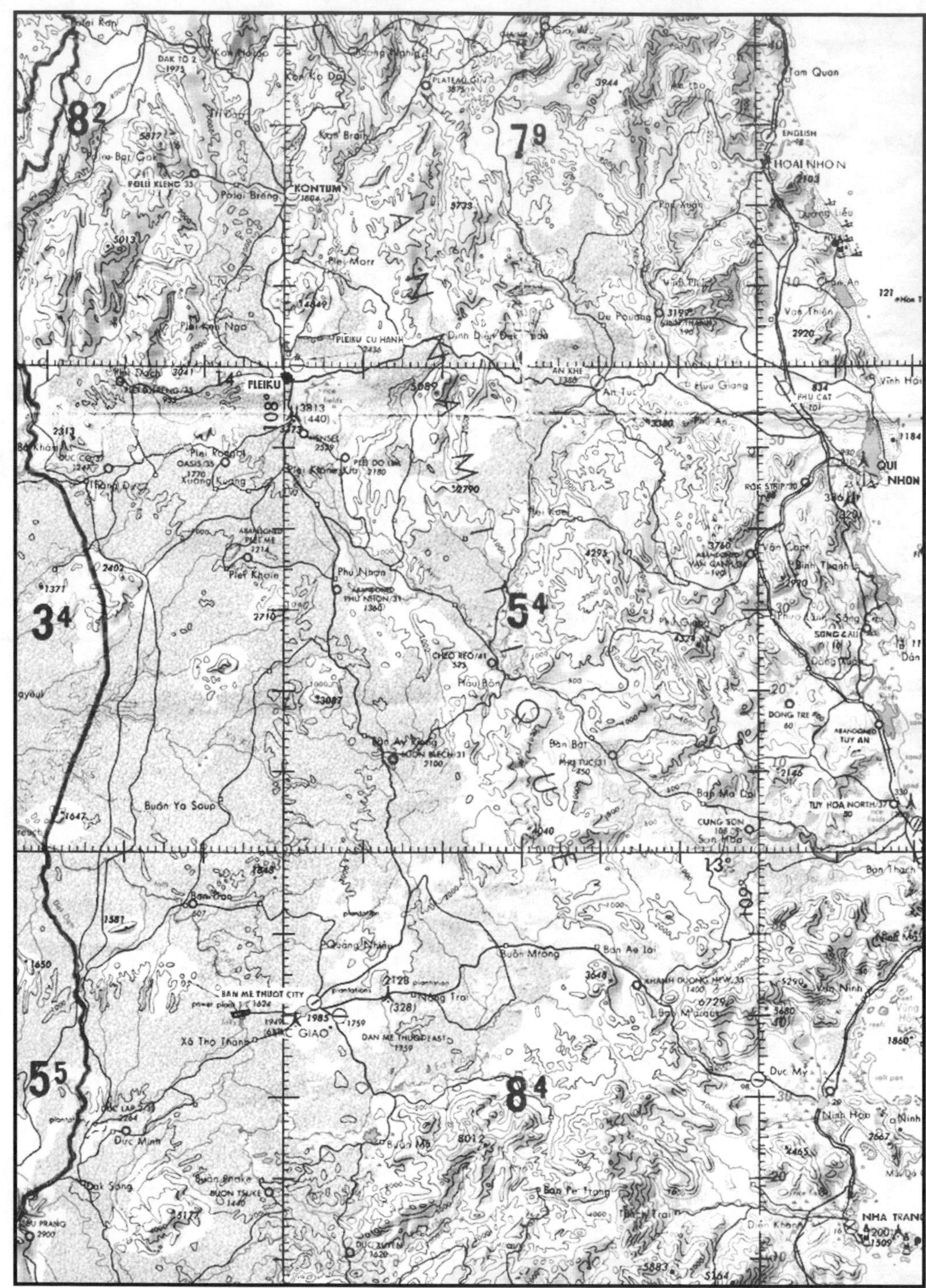

Portion of ONC K-10 with QL-19/14 Corridor Across Top 1/3 of Image

Ql-19 ran W from Qui Nhon to An Khe, through Mang Yang Pass, to Pleiku, then N along QL-14 to Kontum and Dak To.

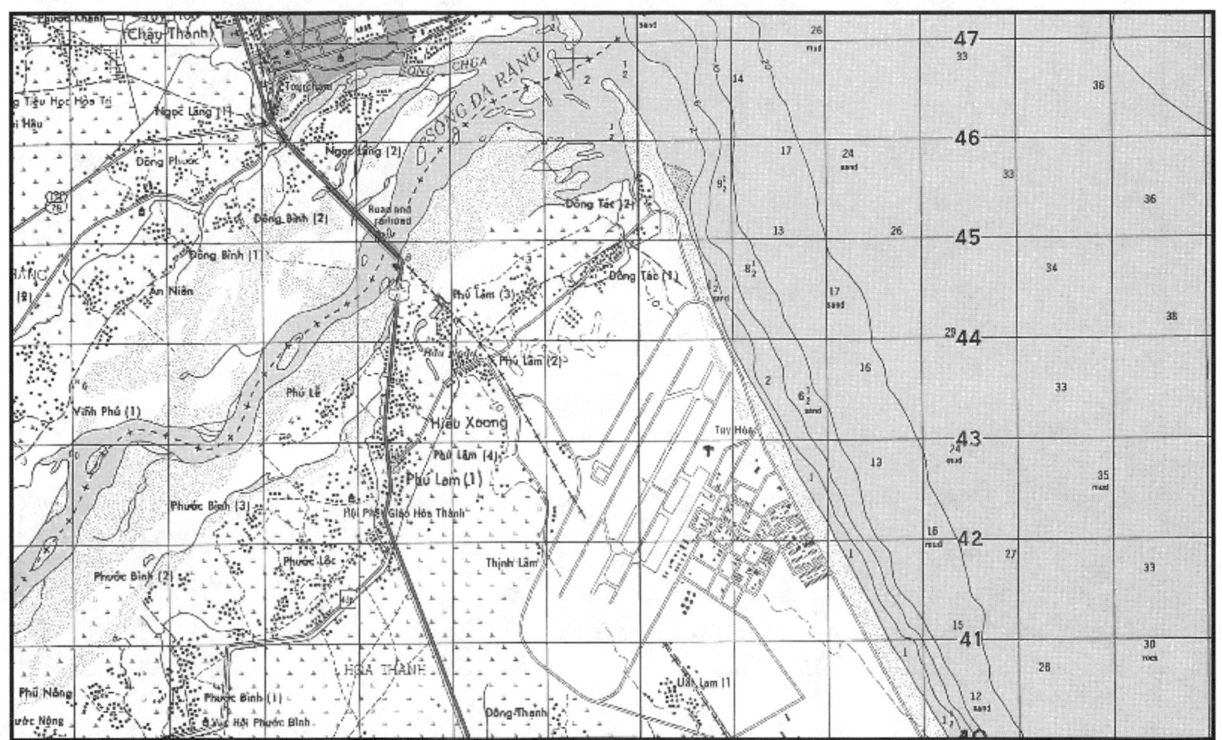

Tuy Hoa Airfield per L-7014-6835-2 and 6834-1, DMA Maps

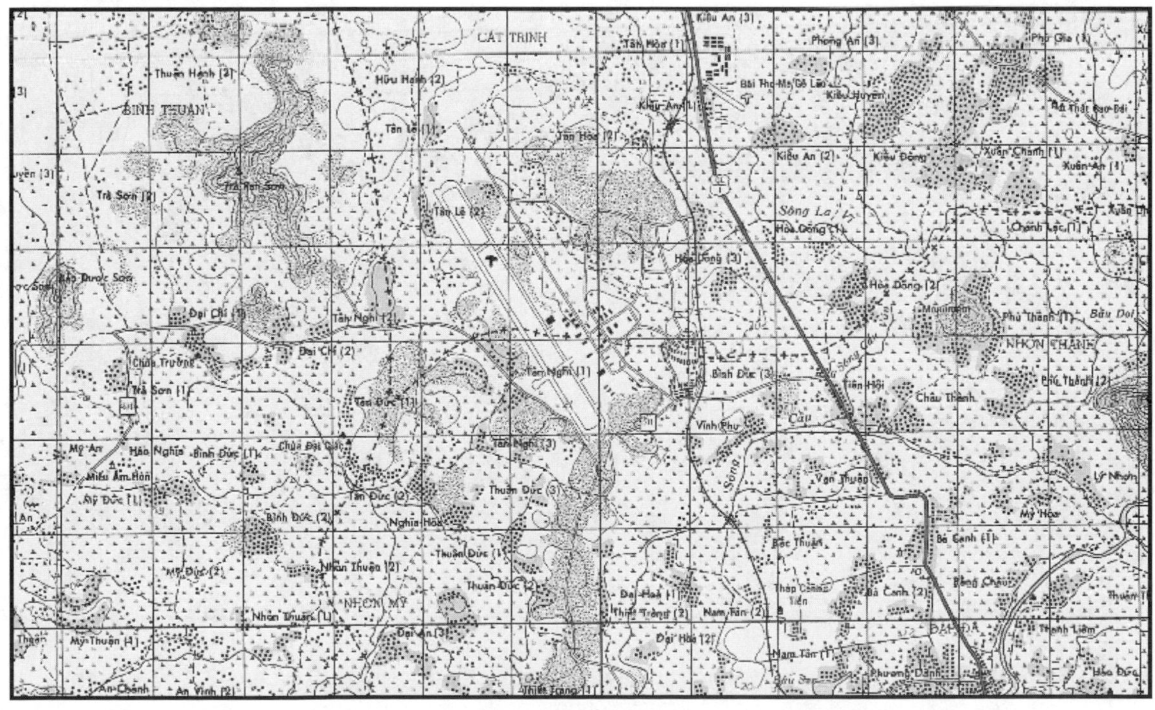

Phu Cat Airbase per L-7014-6837-3 and 6836-4 DMA Maps
Images courtesy of WUG

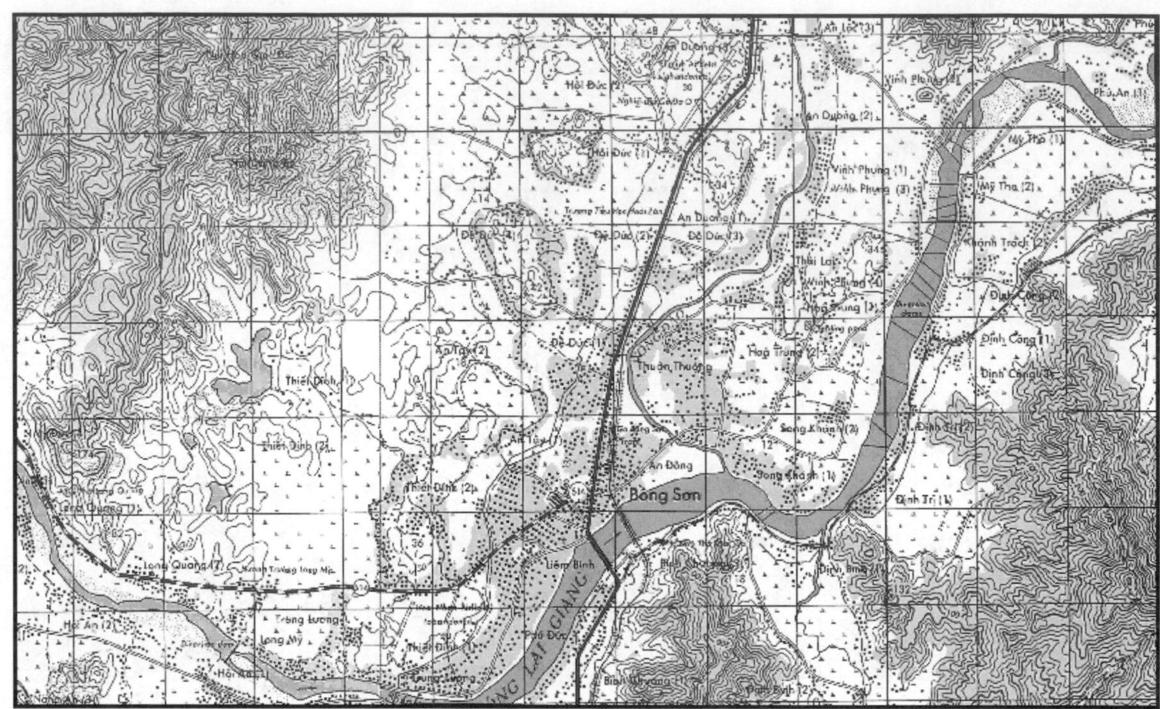

Bong Son Airfield, Bong Son and LZ English per L-7014-6737-1 and 6837-4, DMA Maps

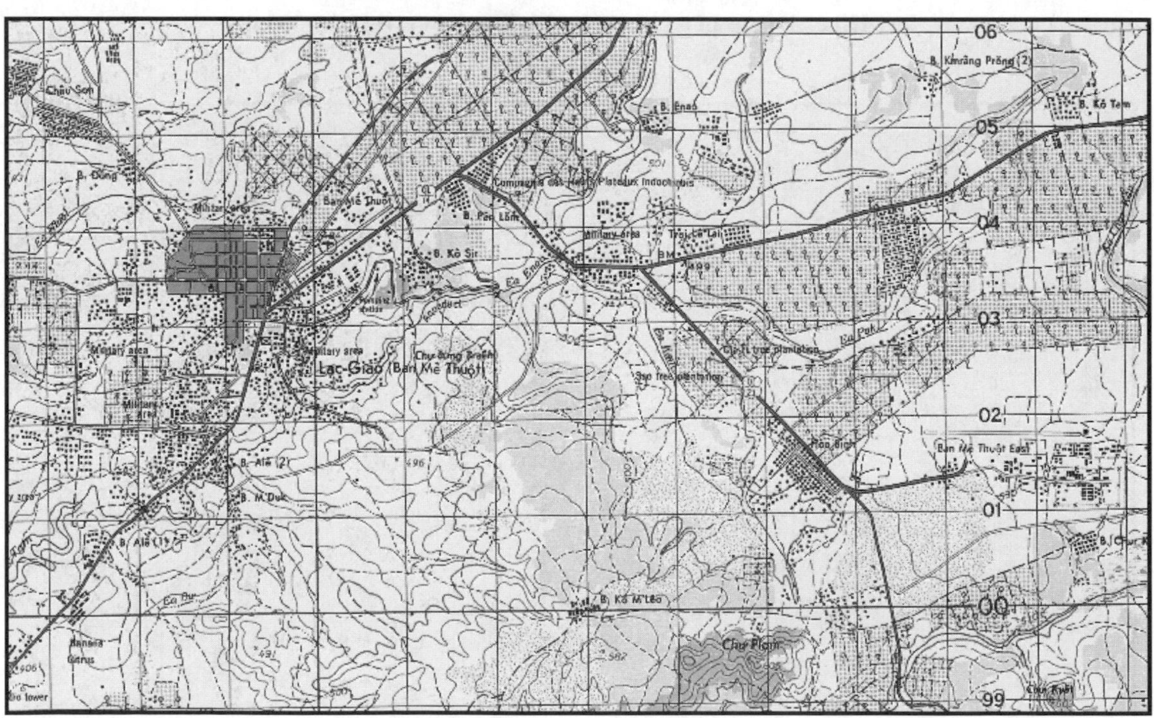

Ban Me Thuot Airfield and Ban Me Thuot East Airfield, per L-7014-6634-3 DMA Map
Images courtesy of WUG

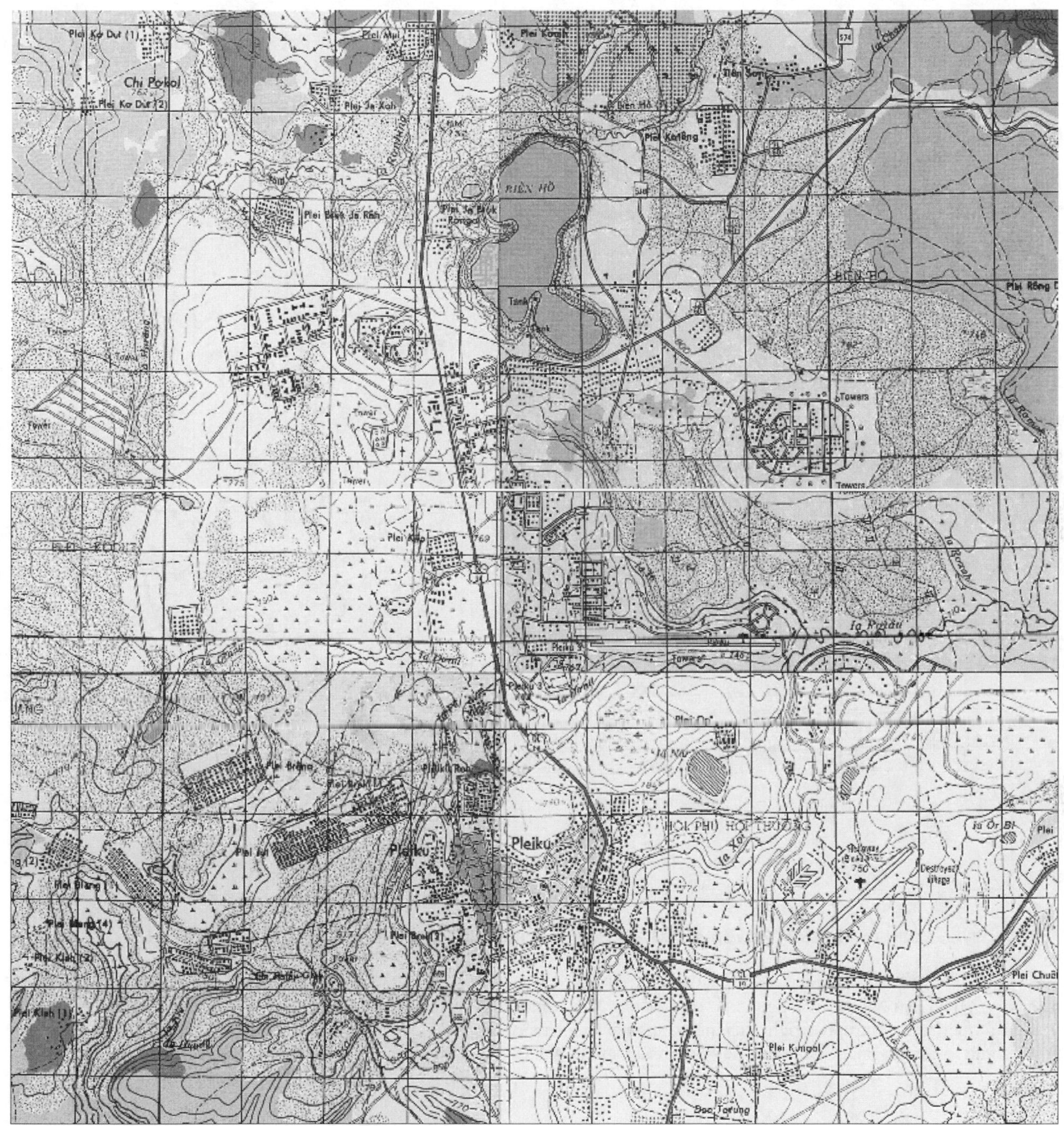

Pleiku, Camp Holloway (with Pleiku Area Airfield) and Pleiku/Cu Hanh Airfield
per DMA L-7014 Series 1:50,000 scale Maps

Camp Holloway and its Pleiku Area Airfield are at lower right. Pleiku/Cu Hanh AF is the due east/west runway at the right-center of this map. Image courtesy of Steve Sherman

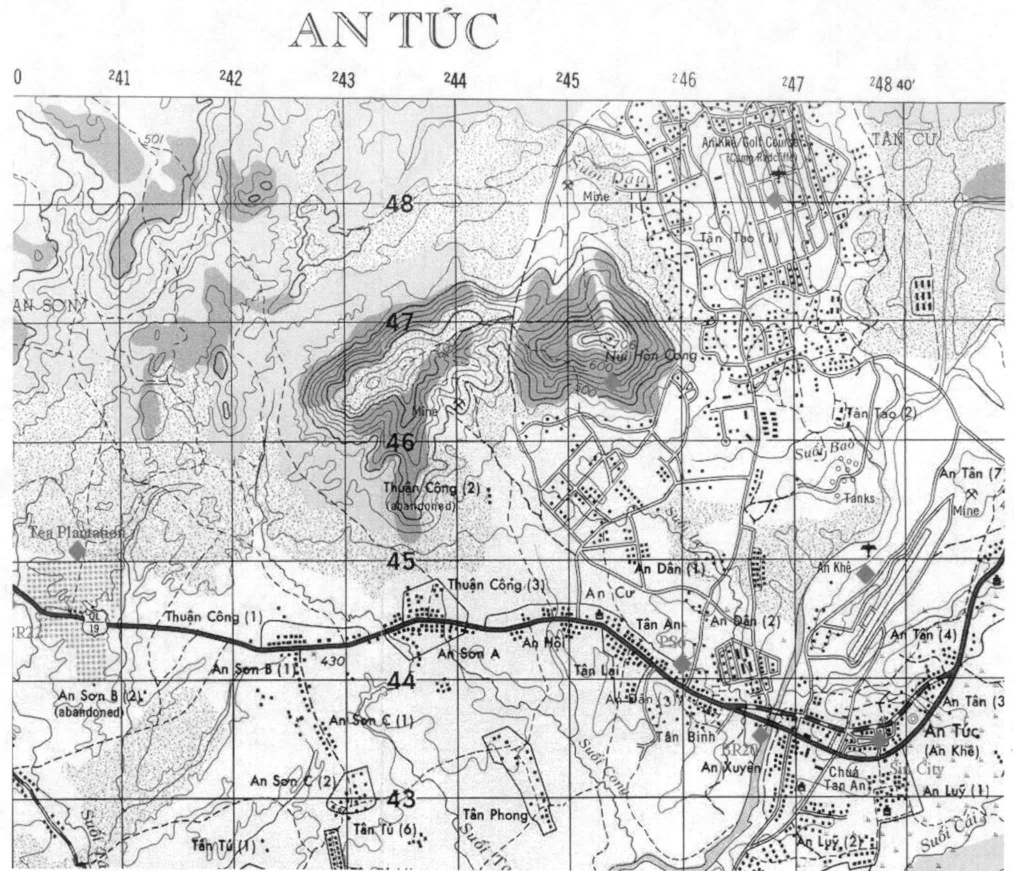

Portion of L-7014-6736-4 DMA 1:50,000 scale map of An Khe/Camp Radcliff/QL-19

Grid zone is "BR." The original home of the 1st Cav Division and later, the 173d Abn Bde and 4th Inf Divisions. Note Golf Course Airfield and Nui Hon Cong (a.k.a. Hong Kong Mtn, which had signal site at its peak and was incorporated within Camp Radcliff's perimeter) in upper right quadrant. Original French airfield, Sin City, Bridge Site 20 and Pump Station 6 are in the lower-right quadrant. Image Courtesy Ray Smith & 1st/69th Armor Association at: www.rjsmith.com/topo_map.html

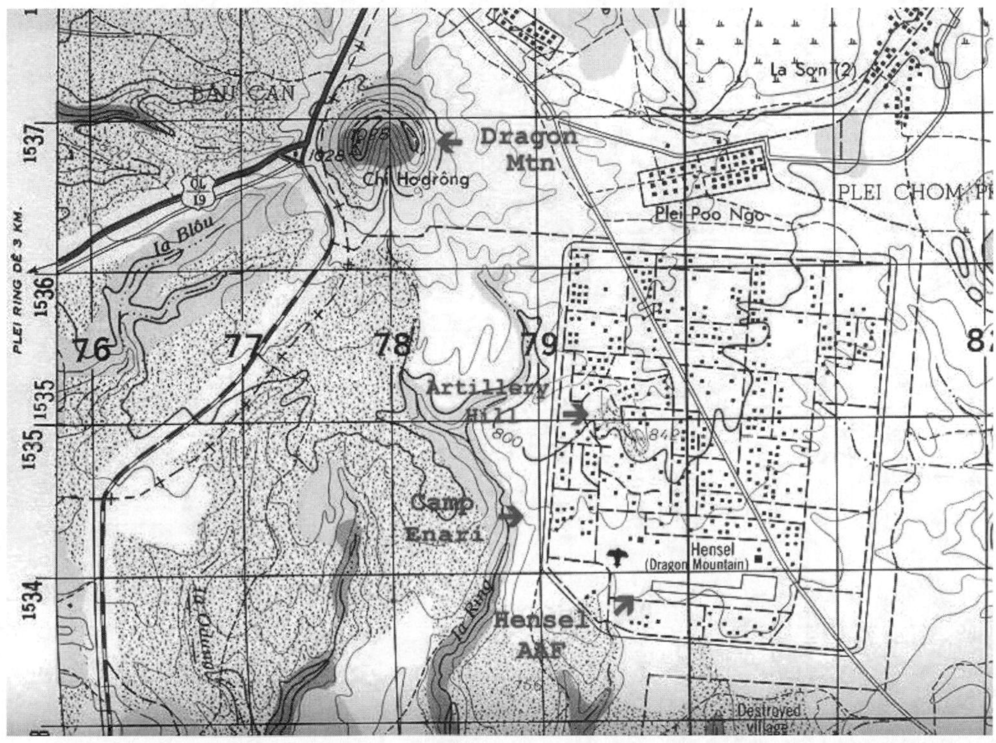

Camp Enari - Home of the 4th Infantry Division 1966-68, Pleiku Province, II Corps

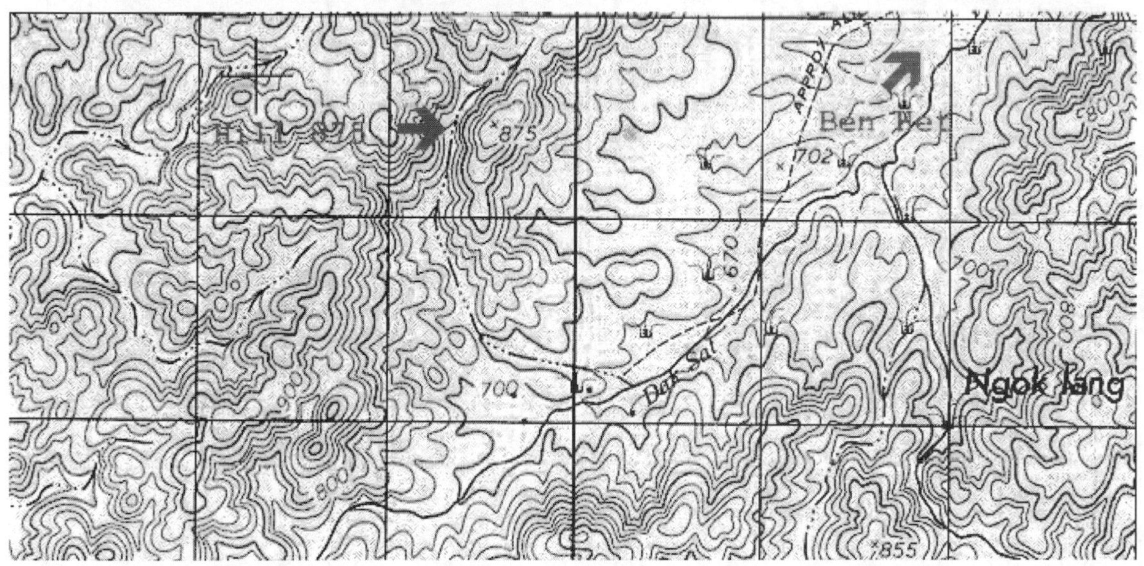

Hill 875 - Elements of the 173rd Abn Bde and 4th Infantry Division heavily engaged here or nearby during Battle of Dak To, November 1966. Pleiku Province, II Corps

Images courtesy of Ray Smith and 1st/69th Armor Assn, at http://www.rjsmith.com/topo_map.html

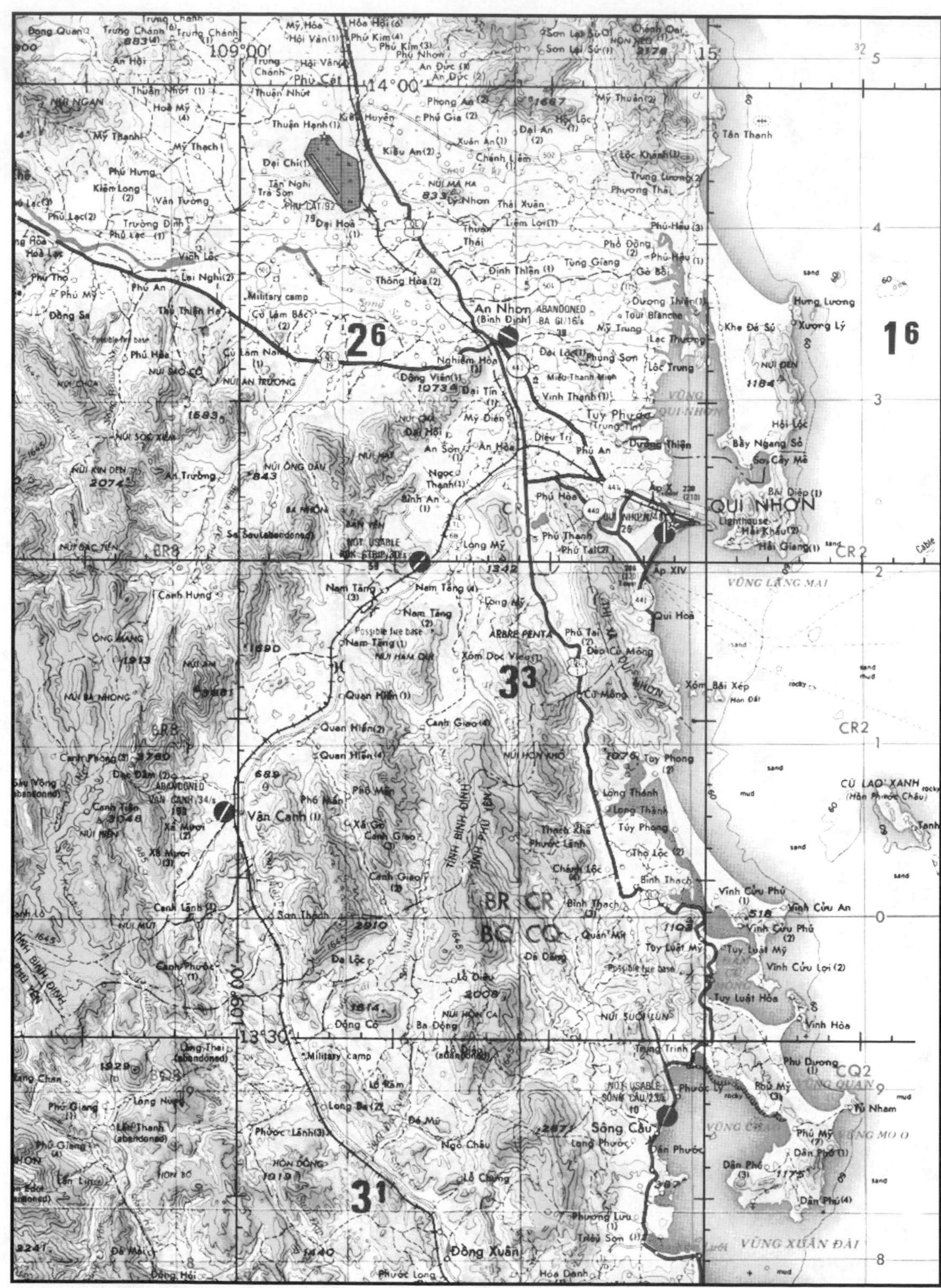

Qui Nhon Area Per DMA ND49-09 1:250,000 scale Joint Operations Graphics
Intersection of grid zones BR, CR, BQ & CQ at lower center of image. Phu Cat AB at upper center.

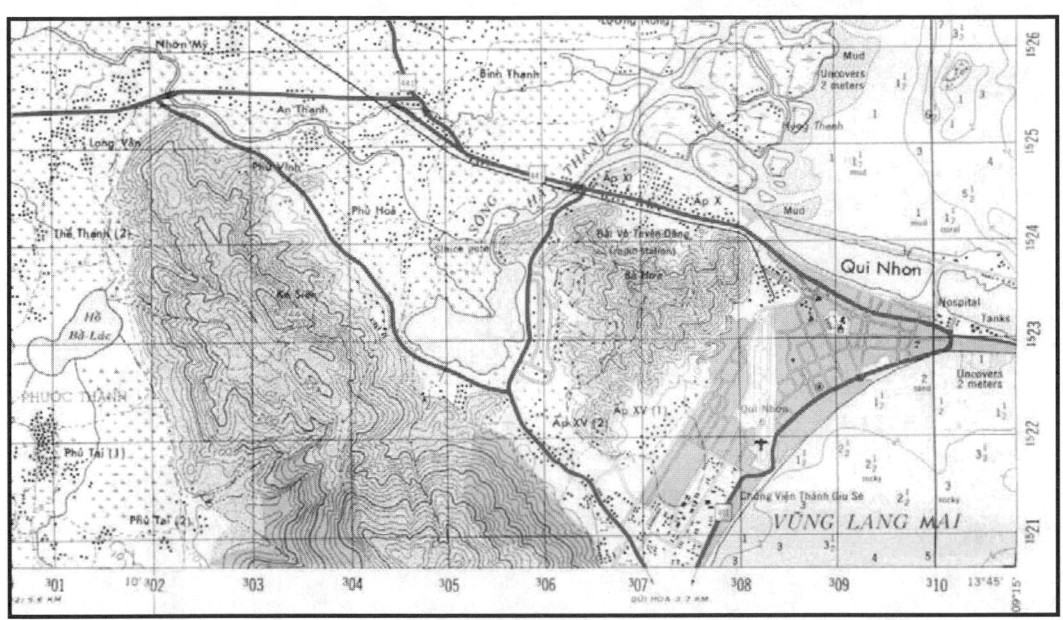

Qui Nhon City per portion of L-7014-6836-4 DMA 1:50,000 scale map

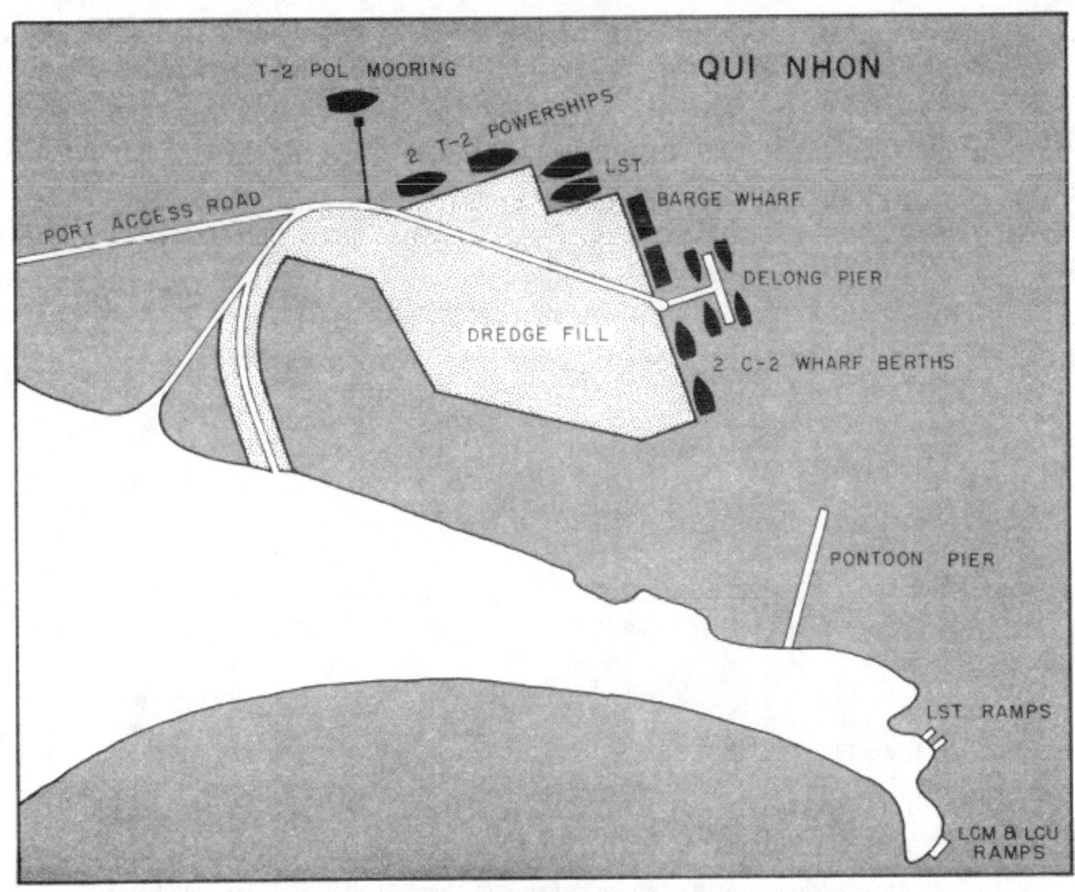

Qui Nhon Port
Courtesy Dept. of the Army. *Base Development In South Vietnam 1965-1970*, p 58.

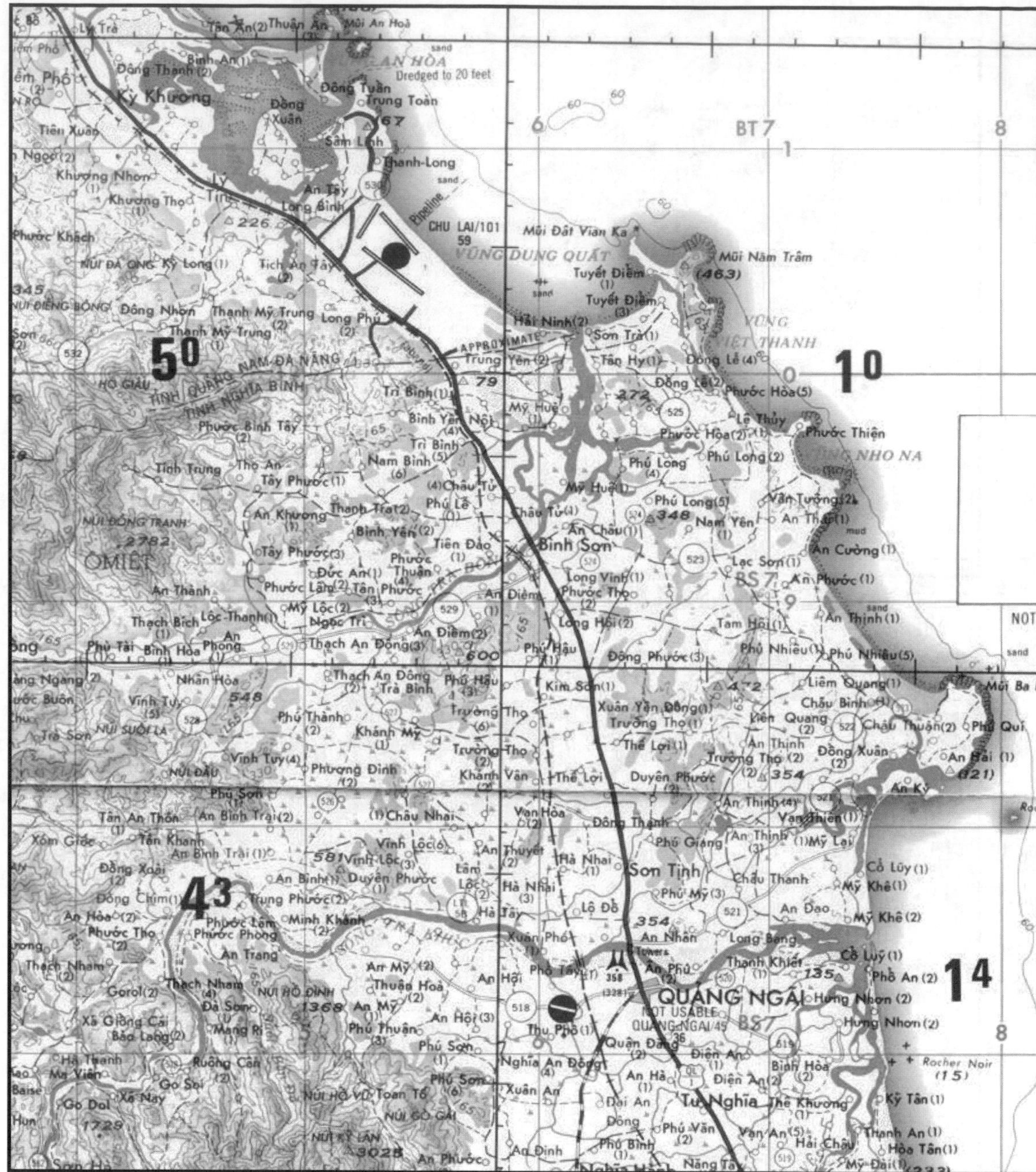

Chu Lai, Quang Ngai and Batangan Peninsula, per DMA 1:250,000 scale map ND 49-01

The Chu Lai Airfield/Combat base complex is located in the rectangular road network immediately to the left of the inscription for "Vung Dung Quat." Chu Lai was first a USMC HQ and Airbase for the 1st Marine Division. The Army's Americal Division later added its HQ here as well. The infamous My Lai (4) massacre site was at the south end of the Batangan Peninsula (near BS 73-77), about 10 kilometers northeast of Quang Ngai. The Batangan was much dreaded by US troops as perhaps the most heavily mined and booby-trapped area in Vietnam. US forces lost many men to the mines here, and the resulting frustration contributed to the tragedy that exploded at My Lai (4). Images courtesy of Jim Henthorn.

(UTM Grid Zones are "BT" above "Vung Viet Thanh" and "BS" below that bay.)

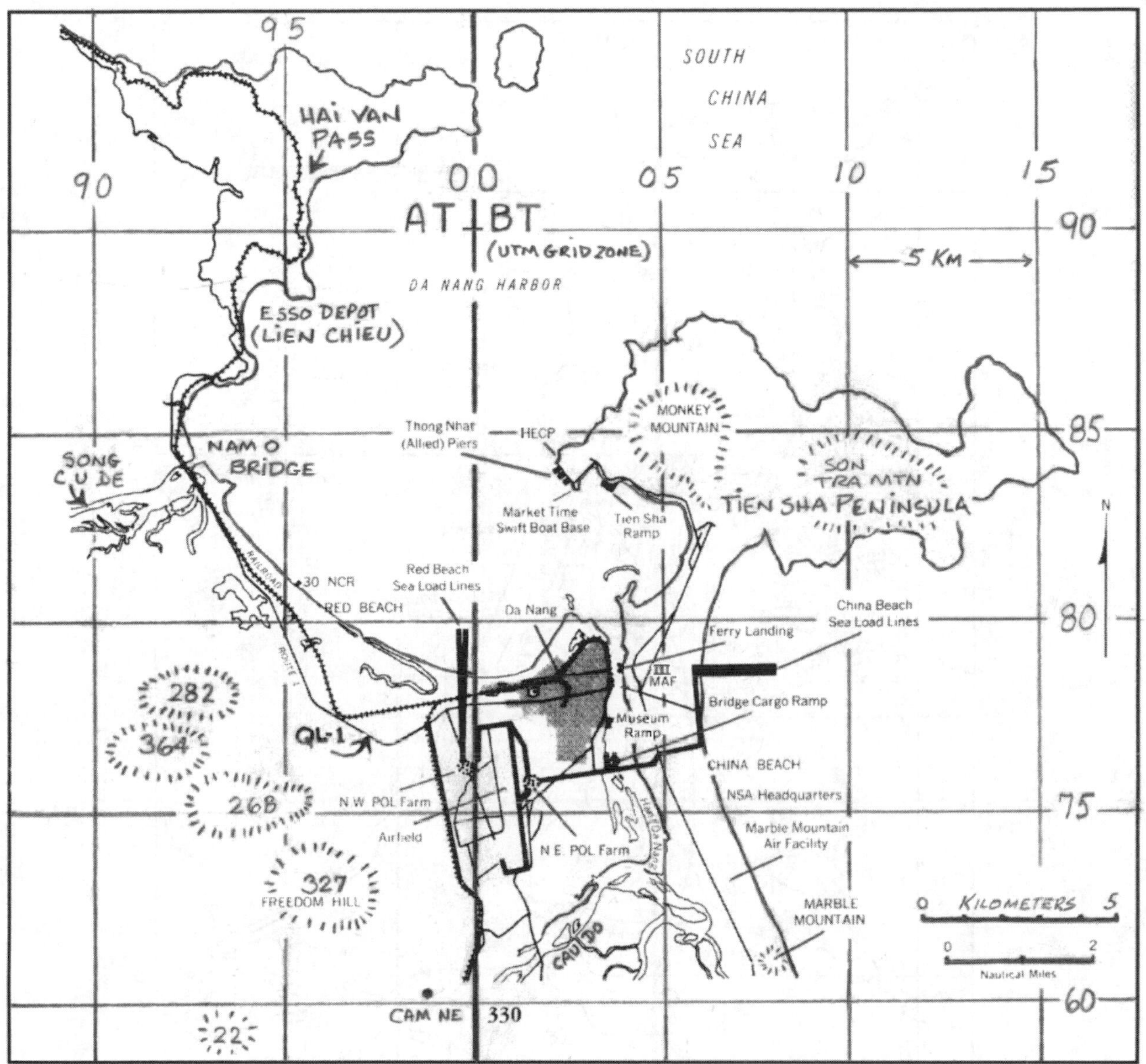

Da Nang Area Map

Image adapted from USMC History & Museums Division's *US Marines in Vietnam-1954-1973, An Anthology and Annotated Bibliography,* p 330, and apparently originally printed in the *US Naval Proceedings, Naval Review, 1971*, in article entitles *Maritime Support of the Campaign in I Corps*, by Cmdr Frank C. Collins, Jr., USN.

UTM Grid Zones include "AT" and "BT." Gridlines and handwritten annotations per author.

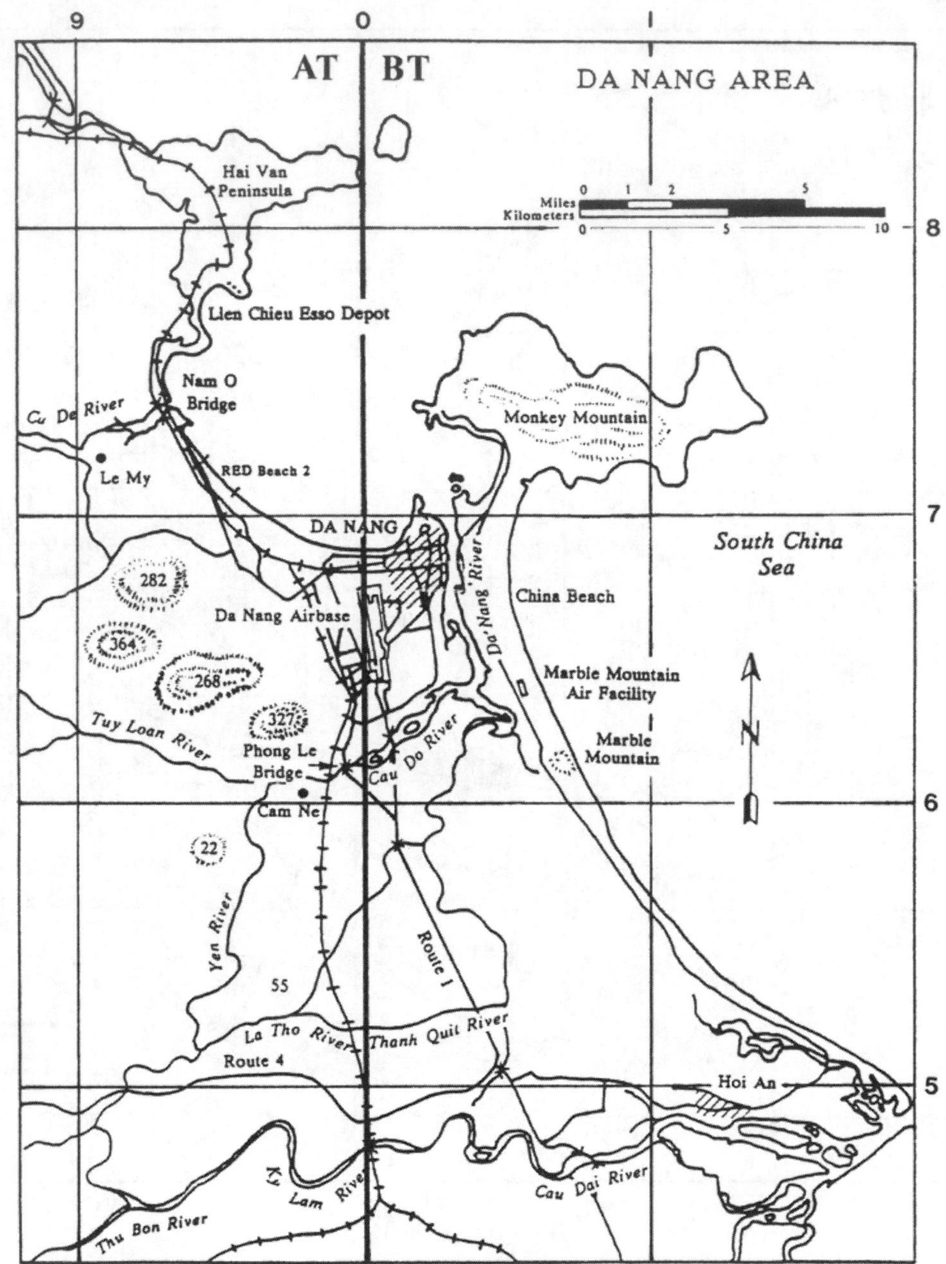

Da Nang Area Map

Da Nang Area - Per image adapted from USMC History & Museums Division's *US Marines in Vietnam-1965,* page 60. Gridlines per author.

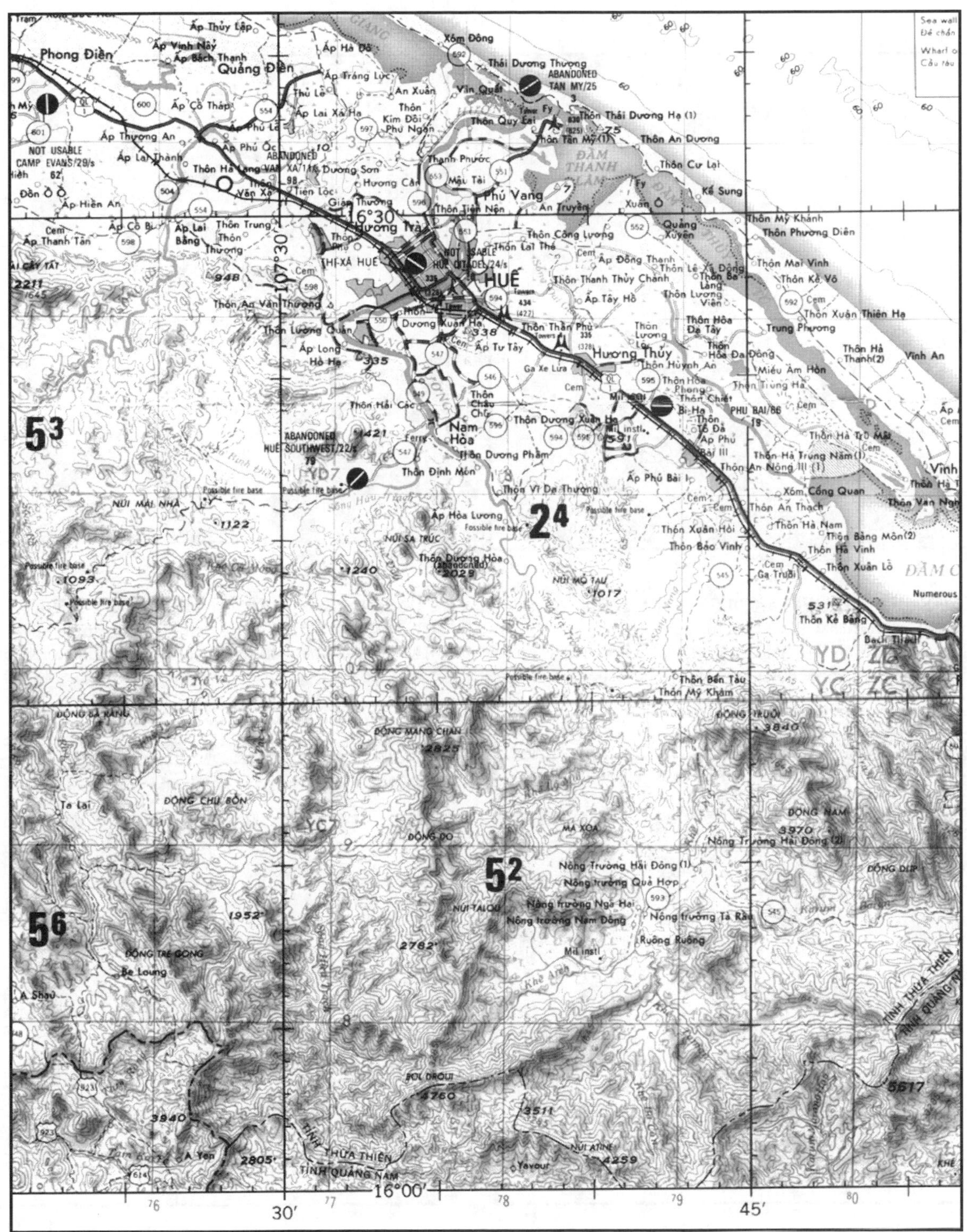

Hue area per DMA NE48-16, 1:250,000 scale JOG map

Included are Camp Evans, LZ Sally (Van Xa airfield symbol), Camp Eagle, Eagle Beach (Tan My), Vinh Loc Island, Phu Bai AF, FSB Birmingham (Hue SW airfield symbol), Ruong Ruong Valley & Dam Cau Hai Bay.

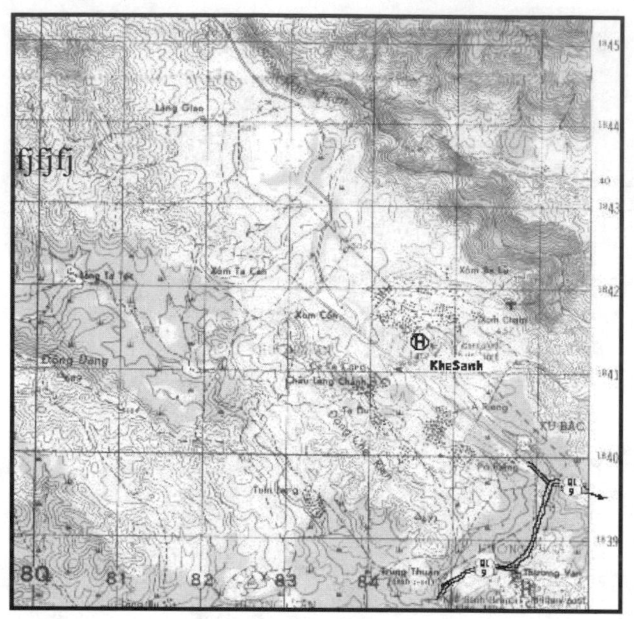

Khe Sanh, per L-7014-6342-3 DMA 1:50k Map
QL-9 is at SE corner with Rte 608 heading NW just to W of Sanh Heliport and Airfield. Hills 950 (Hickory Hill) and 1015 are at Map's upper edge to N and NNE respectively.

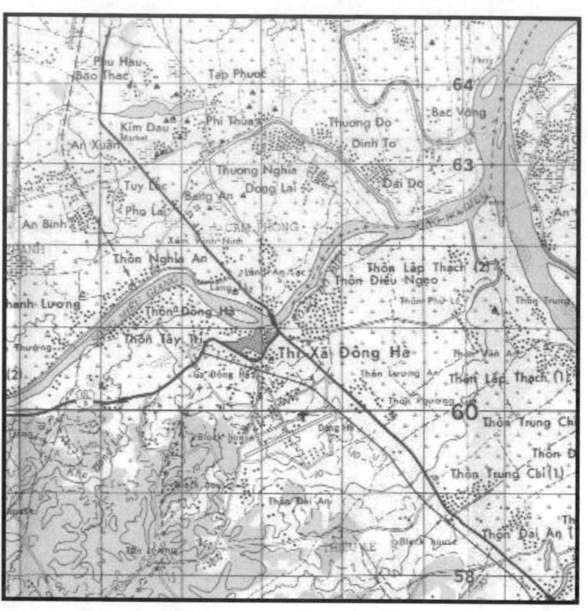

Dong Ha, per L-7014-6442-4 DMA 1:50k Map
QL 1 is the NW to SE road, with QL-9 branching W Khe from at Dong Ha City. The river flowing to NE meets. Cua Viet at the ocean, apx 13 km to NE of city

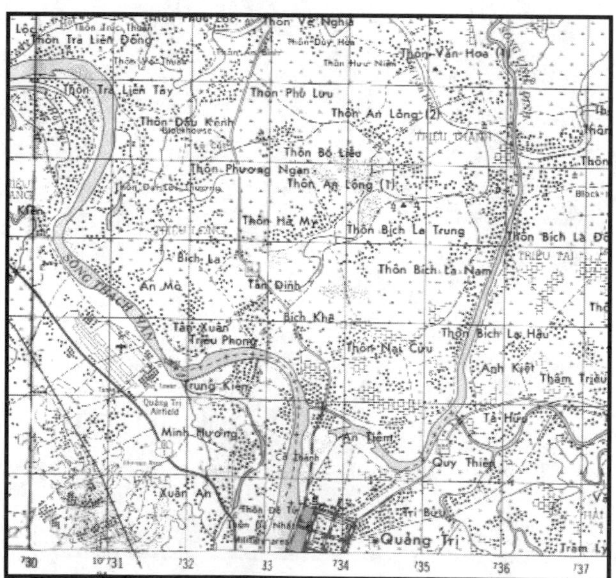

Quang Tri, per L-7014-6442-4 DMA 1:50k Map
Quang Tri Airfield is along QL-1 in SW quadrant of map. Not shown La Vang Airfield, apx 1 km due S of the city.

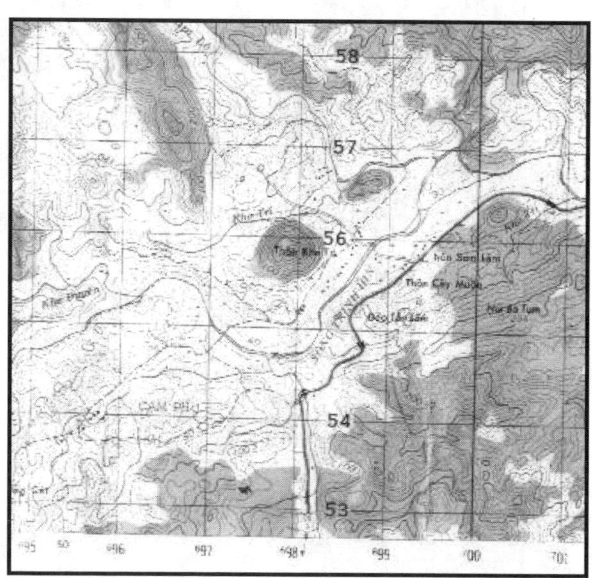

The Rockpile, per L-7014-66342-1 DMA 1:50k Map
Rockpile is at center of image, and small hill1 km to its NE is the "Little Rockpile." Portion of Razorback Ridge is in the NW quadrant, and QL-9 is in the SE quadrant

(All images courtesy of George Neville)

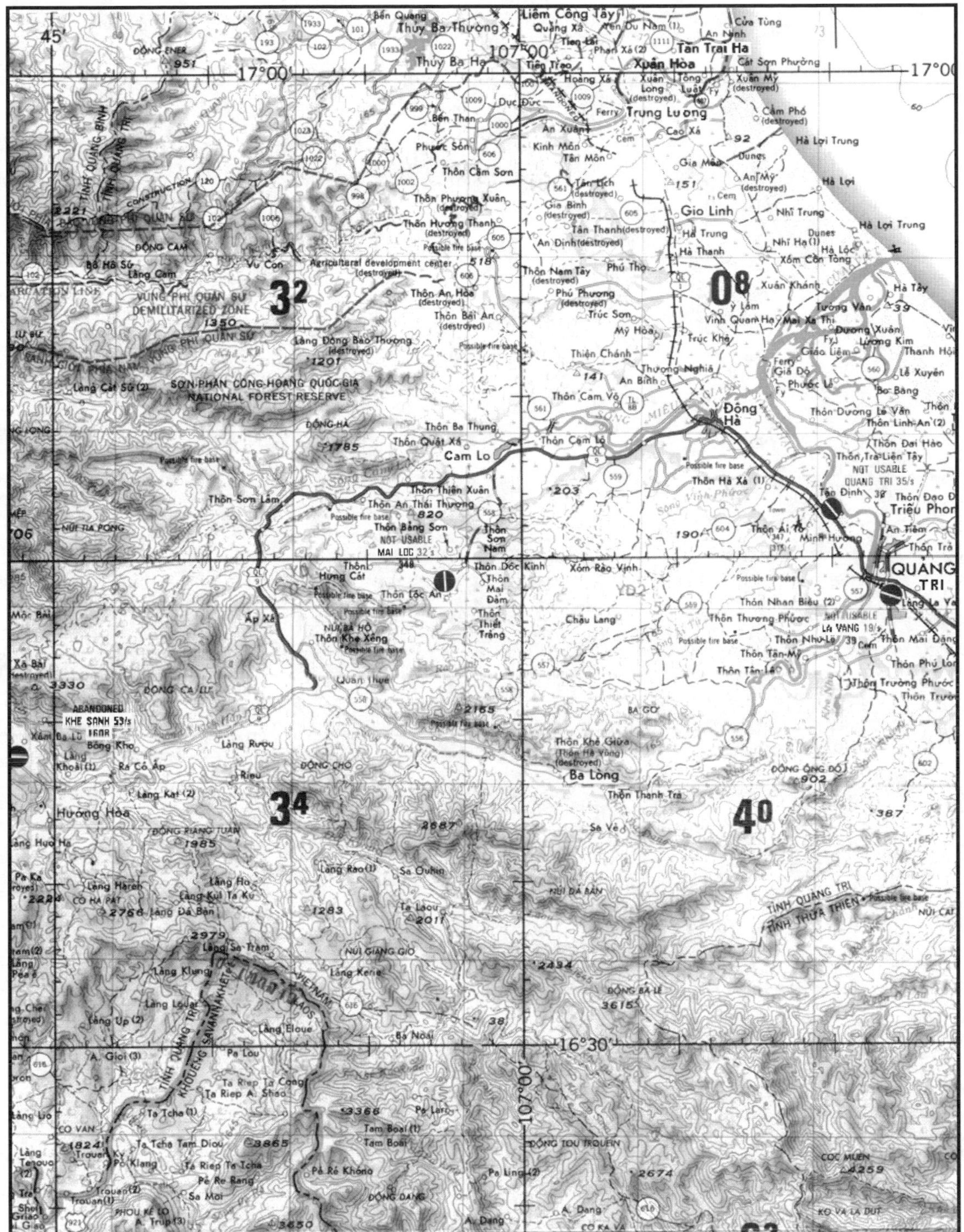

Quang Tri, Khe Sanh, the DMZ and West, per DMA NE48-16 JOG 1:250,000 Scale Map

Shown are Khe Sanh (extreme left-center), portions of the Vietnam and Laotian Salients, Mai Loc, QL-9, Cam Lo, Gio Linh, Dong Ha, DMZ, Ben Hai River (17th Parallel), Cau Viet, QL-1, the *Street Without Joy* and Quang Tri City with its 2 airfields. Left 1/3 of map is in the "XD" grid zone while right 2/3d's in the "YD" grid zone.

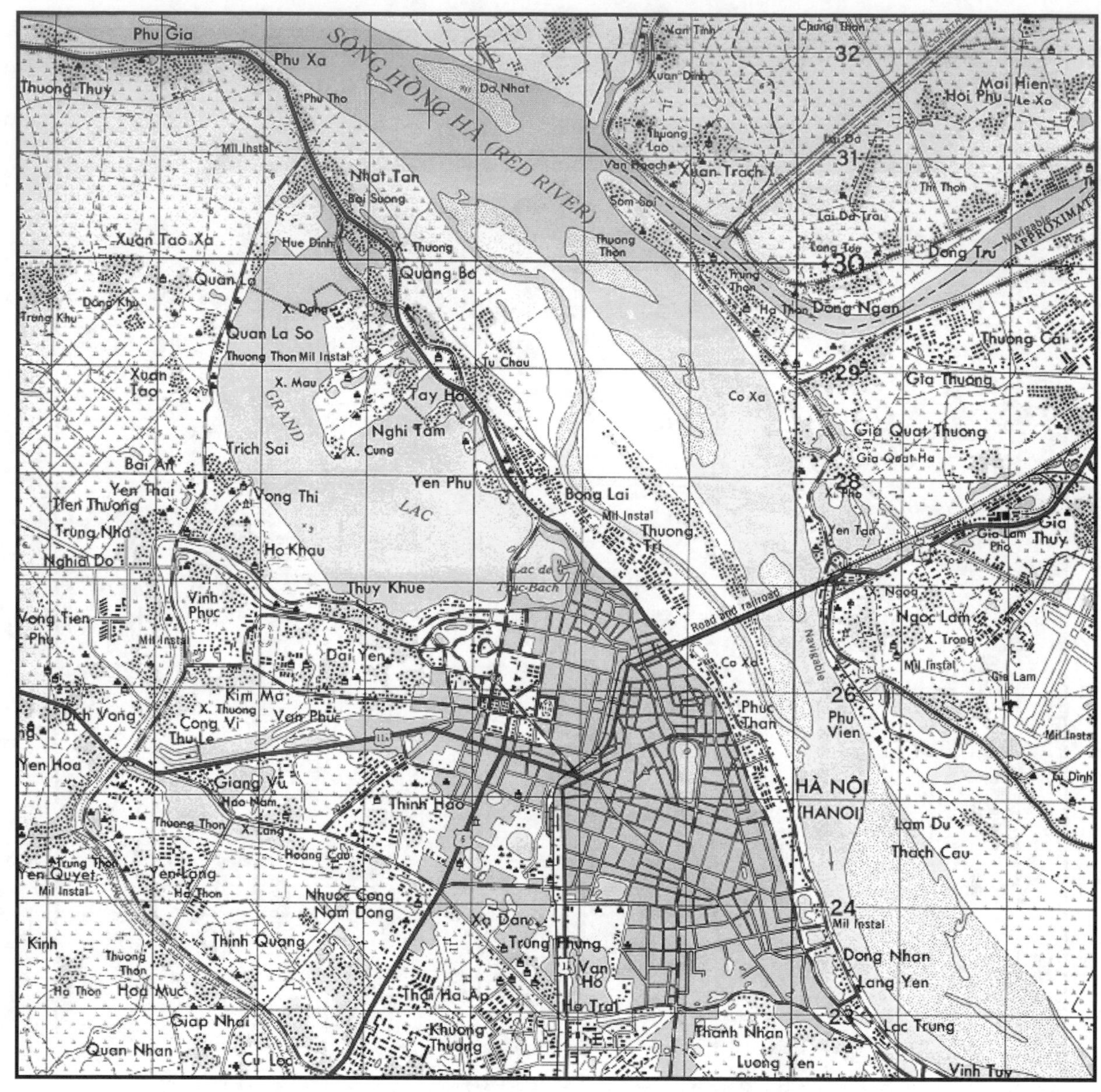

1:50,000 scale image of Hanoi per DMA L-7014-6151-2 Map

Image courtesy of the University of California, Berkeley, and is available on the internet at www.lib.berkeley.edu/EART/digital/viet-1.gif

Numerical Listings

Facility/Feature Name, Grid Coordinate, a.k.a. Name/History/Province/CTZ

Unless otherwise stated, 6-digit grid coordinates reference DMA L-7014, L-7015 or L-7016 series, 1:50,000 scale maps, while 2- and 4-digit coordinates reference AMS/DMA/NIMA 1:250,000, 1:500,000 and 1:1,000,000 scale maps. Unless otherwise stated, all heights are in meters. To convert meters to feet, multiply by 3.2808; feet to meters, multiply by .3048.

1 ATF (XT 98-13 and YS 43-67)
See Australian Task Force HQ, AAAGV, AAFV HQ AATTV and AFV in Major HQs Section. Bien Hoa/Phuoc Tuy Pr, III Corps.

1 RATF (XT 98-13 & YS 43-67)
See Australian Task Force HQ, AAAGV, AAFV HQ AATTV, and AFV in Major HQs Section. Bien Hoa/Phuoc Tuy Pr, III Corps.

1, Firebase (XT 73-85?)
See Firebase 1. Binh Long Pr, III Corps.

1, Firebase (YB 805-215)
See Firebase 1. Kontum Pr, II Corps.

1, Firebase (ZB 005-215?)
See Firebase 1. Kontum Pr, II Corps.

1, FOB (various)
See FOB 1. Quang Tri/Thua Thien Pr, I Corps.

1, LZ (AQ 827-618)
Apx 1 km ESE Plei Tung Se, 17 km WSW Buon Blech AF and 2 km WNW Hill 628. 10Mar66. Pleiku Pr, II Corps.

1, LZ (BN 828-628)
See One, LZ. Ninh Thuan Pr, II Corps.

1, LZ (BP 907-760)
Near the Suoi Nha Chay River, apx 7 km SW Ninh Hoa. 16Apr67. Khanh Hoa Pr, II Corps.

1, LZ (BR 600-469)
Apx 12 km ENE An Khe and 9 km WNW Binh Khe. 14Dec65. Binh Dinh Pr, II Corps.

1, LZ (BR 726-772)
Apx 1 km S Phu Huu (3) and 10 km SSW Hoai An. 30Oct66. Binh Dinh Pr, II Corps.

1, LZ (BR 745-544)
Apx 16 km WNW Vinh Thanh AF and 2 km N An Ninh (2). 28Dec65. Binh Dinh Pr, II Corps.

1, LZ (BS 523-823)
Apx 1 km E Phuong Dinh (4)/Rte 526, apx 16 km NW Quang Ngai. 21Apr66. Quang Ngai Pr, I Corps.

1, LZ (BT 132-203)
A.k.a. Nui Vu, Hill 488 and LZ 2. 11Sep67. See also Nui Vu. Quang Tin Pr, I Corps.

1, LZ (XS 458-760)
Apx 8 km Thu Thua and 15 km ESE Tuyen Nhon. 18Apr66. Long An Pr, III Corps.

1, LZ (XT 244-965)
Along Rte 246, 11 km NW Katum and 2 km S Cambodia. 22Feb67. Tay Ninh Pr, III Corps.

1, LZ (XT 924-285)
Apx 16 km NNW Bien Hoa and 2 km SSE Xa Binh Co. 22May67. Bien Hoa Pr?, III Corps.

1, LZ (YA 872-356)
Immed S the Ia Grouille River, apx 10 km S Plei Djereng New AF and 1 km S Rte 566. 4Jan66. Pleiku Pr, II Corps.

1, LZ (YA 935-589)
Apx 16 km NNE Plei Djereng New AF and 1.5 km NE Hill 1019. 18Jun66. Pleiku Pr, II Corps.

1, LZ (YB 891-405)
Apx 2 km WSW Lang Dak Sang and 16 km NNE Ben Het. 18Apr66. Kontum Pr, II Corps.

1 Camp (SF Camp) (n/a)
SF camp when Lao neutrality declared, 23Jul62. FTT 46 here then, per *Special Forces at War*. MR3, Laos.

1-Oh-Worst Pad (BT 173-078)
Apx 32 km NW Chu Lai and 9 km NNE old Hau Duc. Per Tommy Poppell, the S-4 helo pad at FSB Professional was nicknamed the One-Oh-Worst Pad apparently to honor 101st Abn's stalwart performance in adj sector of perimeter during mid '69 attack. At time, 1st Bde/101st Abn was opcon to Americal Div and operating with the 1st/46th Inf during Op Lamar Plain. Quang Tin Pr, I Corps.

1st (generally)
See also First entries.

1st, FSB (YC 864-833)
See FSB Fist. Thua Thien Pr, I Corps.

1st Australian Field Hospital (YS 28-43)
At Vung Tau. Phuoc Tuy Pr, III Corps.

1st Australian Logistics Supt Grp (YS 28-43)
At Vung Tau. Phuoc Tuy Pr, III Corps.

1st Australian Supt Compound (YS 28-43)
Site of Peter Badcoe Club, Vung Tau, apx 60 km ESE Saigon. Grid apx. Phuoc Tuy Pr, III Corps.

1st Australian Task Force (XT 98-13 & YS 43-67)
See Australian Task Force HQ, AAAGV, AAFV HQ AATTV, and AFV in Major HQs Section. Bien Hoa/Phuoc Tuy Pr, III Corps.

1st CAG (n/a)
1st Combined Action Grp, USMC. Its TAOR included all Quang Tin and Quang Ngai Prvs, including Tam Ky and Quang Ngai cities. I Corps.

1st Cavalry Division (n/a)
See Division Level Command Section for detailed history. Note: On 28Jun68, USARPAC issued Gen Order 325 redesignated 1st Cav to be the "1st Air Cavalry Division" (thereby making official its already popular nickname) eff 1Jul68. However, term "Air Cavalry Division" was revoked by DOA directive issued 26Aug68, and thereafter, official name of Div became: 1st Cavalry Division (Airmobile). Same orders affected 101st Abn Div.[1]

1st CTZ MSF Camp (BT 065-733)
A.k.a. Camp Shay? Apx 2 km W Marble Mtn AF and 5 km SE Da Nang AB. 5th SF. Info/grid per *SF Order of Battle.* Shifted to Border Rangers Cmd. Quang Nam Pr, I Corps.

1st FFV HQ/CORDS Club (CP 04-55)
At Nha Trang. 1FFV (1st Field Force) was corps-level cmd. Grid apx. See IFFV in Major HQs Section for detail. Khanh Hoa Pr, II Corps.

1st Indochina War (n/a)
See Glossary.

1st Infantry Division (n/a)
See Division Level Command Section.

1st Marine Amtrac Bn Compound (YD 34-68)
At Cua Viet naval base, apx 16 km N Quang Tri, near point where Dong Ha R and Cua Viet Rivers enter Gulf of Tonkin. Described in *Combat Medic*, pp 88-89, as follows: "Overlooking the Dong Ha River, the cmpd was a dug-in installation set up in defensive posture with watchtowers, concertina wire, trenches and bunkers. These bunkers weren't [your typical] sandbagged-holes, but the best bunkers in country-buried, derelict Amtracs capable of withstanding direct hits from just about anything the gooks had to throw at them." Quang Tri Pr, I Corps.

1st Marine Division (n/a)
See Division Level Command Section.

1st Marine Medical Bn (AT/BT)
Likely at Chu Lai or Da Nang. Hosp for 1st Mar Div. Quang Nam or Quang Tin, I Corps.

1st Philippine Civic Action Group (XT 175-517)
See PHILCAG. Tay Ninh Pr, III Corps.

1st Royal Australian TF HQ (XT 98-13 & YS 43-67)
Between 25May65-2May66 was known as HQ AAFV, with its HQ'd in Saigon suptg 1 Bn RAR at Bien Hoa AB (and attached to US 173d Abn Bde). From 3May66-15Mar72 was given own Phuoc Tuy Pr TAOR and HQ moved to Nui Dat/Luscombe AF. See Australian Task Force HQ in Major HQs Section. III Corps.

1st SF Grp (n/a)
See Major HQs Section.

2, FSB (XT 270-780)
See Firebase 2. Tay Ninh Pr, III Corps.

2, FSB (YS 46-83)
See Firebase 2. Phuoc Tuy Pr, III Corps.

2, FSB (YB or ZB?)
See Firebase 2. Kontum Pr, II Corps.

2, FOB (ZA & AR)
See FOB 2. Kontum Pr, II Corps.

2, LZ (AQ 775-640)
Apx 23 km WNW Buon Blech AF, 6 km N Plei Tung Thang, 2 km S Chu De Mtn and 3 km E Chu Amung (Hill 589). 10Feb66. Darlac Pr, II Corps.

2, LZ (BN 819-623)
A.k.a. LZ Two. Apx 18 km due S Phan Rang, 2 km due W Thon Son Hai, 2 km W the ocean and 12 km E QL-1. 9Mar67. Ninh Thuan Pr, II Corps.

2, LZ (BP 850-729)
Apx 13 km SW Ninh Hoa and 3 km NW Hon Ba Mtn. 16Apr67. Khanh Hoa Pr, II Corps.

2, LZ (BR 388-532)
Apx 1 km SE Kon Barr and 13 km NW An Khe. 9Apr67. Binh Dinh Pr, II Corps.

2, LZ (BR 588-477)
A.k.a. Hill 814 and Hon Ong Binh Mtn. Apx 12 km ENE An Khe. 14Dec65. Binh Dinh Pr, II Corps.

2, LZ (BR 736-778)
Apx 1 km SW Kim Son (2) and 20 km NW Phu My/QL-1. 30Oct66. Binh Dinh Pr, II Corps.

2, LZ (BS 8-2?)
Apx 3 km NNE LZ Dog, 8 km NNE Bong Son and just W QL-1. Used during Op Masher/White Wing, 28Jan-6Mar66. Details of Ops and site in *A Contagion of War* vol., *Vietnam Experience* series, pp 32-48, map on p 38. 2d/7th Cav, 1st Cav LZ. Binh Dinh Pr, II Corps.

2, LZ (BT 132-203)
A.k.a. Nui Vu, Hill 488 and LZ 1. 11Sep67. See Nui Vu. Quang Tin Pr, I Corps.

2, LZ (XS 464-764)
Apx 7 km Thu Thua and 16 km ESE Tuyen Nhon. 18Apr66. Long An Pr, III Corps.

2, LZ (XT 949-253)
Along LTL-16, apx 3 km NNW Tan Uyen and 13 km NE Phu Loi. 22May67. Bien Hoa Pr, III Corps.

2, LZ (YA 888 395)
7 km SSE Plei Djereng New AF and 1 km WSW Plei Ya Po (1)/Rte 568. 18Apr66. Pleiku Pr, II Corps.

2, LZ (YA 938-578)
Immed N Hill 745 and apx 15 km NNE Plei Djereng New AF. 18Jun66. Pleiku Pr, II Corps.

2 Alfa, LZ (BN 826-613)
See Two Alfa. Ninh Thuan Pr, II Corps.

2 Camp (SF Camp) (n/a)
SF camp in Laos when it declared neutrality (23Jul62). FTT 5 here then, per *Special Forces at War*. MR3, Laos.

2 Camp, (Kontum) (ZA 236 863)
See FOB 2. Kontum Pr, II Corps.

2 Step Snake (n/a)
See Two-Step Snake in Glossary.

2d CAG (n/a)
2d Combined Action Grp, USMC. HQ was ENE Hoi An and apx 1 km SW CAP 2-4-3. Geographic TAOR included all Quang Nam Pr, inc Da Nang and Hoi An. CAP 2-4-3 and 2d CAG HQ AOs on map at CAP website www.capmarine.com. Quang Nam Pr, I Corps.

2d CTZ MSF Camp (AR 765-474)
At Pleiku. 5th SF. Closed and assets moved to Kontum MSF. Info/grid per *SF Order of Battle.* Pleiku Pr, II Corps.

2d FFV Headquarters (YT 055-115)
A.k.a. HQ, IIFFV (2d Field Force, VN). Just N of Long Binh Post. Also listed at YT 048-106. See Plantation Cmpd in alpha listings, and IIFFV in Corps Level Cmd Section. Bien Hoa Pr, III Corps.

2d Indochina War (n/a)
See Glossary.

2d Marine Division (n/a)
See Division Level Command Section.

2d Surgical Hospital (n/a)
Mobile Army MASH Unit at Qui Nhon '66-67 (CR 09-23), then moved to Chu Lai '67 (BT 54-06) as part of Task Force Oregon, then to Lai Khe, '68 (XT 77-37) with 1st Inf Div. Grids apx. I, II/III Corps.

2d Thai Position (TJ 94-66)
Defensive position apx 1.5 km NE Dien Bien Phu main CP and immed N Strongpoint E2. In Muong Thanh Valley, apx 290 km W Hanoi. French strongpoint during Op Castor, 20Nov53-7May54. Grid apx. NVN.

3, Camp (SF Camp) (n/a)
SF camp in Laos when it declared neutrality (23Jul62). FTT 25 here then. Per *Special Forces at War*. MR4, Laos.

3, FOB (various)
See FOB 3. Quang Tri Pr, I Corps.

3, FSB (YB or ZB?)
See Firebase 3. Kontum Pr, II Corps.

3, LZ (BN 698-798)
12 km W Phan Rang. 17Mar67. Ninh Thuan Pr, II Corps.

3, LZ (BN 825-585)
A.k.a. LZ Three. Apx 21 km due S Phan Rang, 28 km S Phan Rang AF, 5 km SSW Thon Son Hai/LZ One, and 2 km from coast. Mar67. Ninh Thuan Pr, II Corps.

3, LZ (BP 874-768)
Near the Suoi Nha Chay River, apx 9 km WSW Ninh Hoa. 16Apr67. Khanh Hoa Pr, II Corps.

3, LZ (BR 744-514)
Apx 1 km SW Dong Quan and 16 km SW Vinh Thanh AF. 30Dec65. Binh Dinh Pr, II Corps.

3, LZ (BR 755-813)
Along TL-3A, apx 7 km SSW Hoai An. 30Oct66. Binh Dinh Pr, II Corps.

3, LZ (XS 478-768)
Apx 7 km Thu Thua and 4 km NNW Ap Hoa Lac. 18Apr68. Long An Pr, III Corps.

3, LZ (XT 205-976)
Apx 15 km NW Katum and 2 km S Cambodia. 22Mar67. Tay Ninh Pr, III Corps.

3, LZ (YA 832-342)
Apx 9 km N Duc Co AF. 4Jan66. Pleiku Pr, II Corps.

3, LZ (YB 889-375)
Immed NE Dak Ro Bong (1) and 21 km NW Dak To 2 AF. 18Apr66. Kontum Pr, II Corps.

3 Bees, The (n/a)
See Three Bees in Glossary.

3 Church, FSB (YA 850-455?)
See 3 Tango. Pleiku Pr, II Corps.

3 Golf, LZ (YA 859-457)
A.k.a. Three Golf and LZ 3g. Apparently at site of what became Plei Djereng New AF. Described as having been E of LZ 504-C, in vic of Plei Toun and Plei Chorr. As early as Oct-Nov66 was Bn Fwd Supt base, and described as large, sprawling almost circular FSB that was fwd HQ and resupply point for 3d Bde/25th Inf Div. See *Rites of Passage*, pp 33, 34, 44. Pleiku Pr, II Corps.

3 RAAF Hospital (n/a)
At Butterworth, Malaysia, not in Vietnam. ANZAC troops whose wounds exceeded Vung Tau's 1st Australian Field Hospital's capabilities were sent here, per Eddie Tricker.

3 Sisters (YD 810-184)
See Three Sisters. Thua Thien Pr, I Corps.

3 Sisters, FSB (YD 808-186)
See Three Sisters. Thua Thien Pr, I Corps.

3 Sisters, OP (YD 808-186)
See Three Sisters. Thua Thien Pr, I Corps.

3t, LZ (YA 850-455)
A.k.a. LZ Three Tango and Three Church(?). If grid is correct, was appx 3 km SW Plei Djereng New AF, 2 km S of Rte 567 and 38 km W of Pleiku. 1st/22d Inf, 4th Div in '66-67. Picture and discussion at http://grunt.space.swri.edu/LouTplei.htm. Possibly named for call-sign of A/1st/22d Inf. Apparently also an SF camp nearby. Listed grid is for an LZ 3t, Mar-Apr67. Pleiku Pr, II Corps.

3 Tango, FSB (YA 850-455?)
See 3T, LZ. Pleiku Pr, II Corps.

3d ARVN Ranger Grp HQ (XS 865-968)
Adj to Newport Bridge, NE Saigon. Gia Dinh Pr, III Corps.

3d Bde/82d Abn Div Trains (XS 808-027)
Inside Tan Son Nhut AB, along W to NW edge and 1 km due N the SW end of main rwy. Home of 3d/82 Supt Bn, 3d Bde/82d Abn, Oct68-Mar69. Gia Dinh Pr, III Corps.

3d CAG (n/a)
3d Combined Action Grp, USMC. TAOR covered all Thua Thien Pr, including Hue/Phu Bai. I Corps.

3d Field Hospital (XS 826-938)
A.k.a. Saigon Adventist Hosp. At 10 Tan Son Hoa St., Saigon, apx 1.5 km SSE Tan Son Nhut AB and across from main gate, 1 km S MACV HQ Cmpd. Opened Apr65. Informally a.k.a. 3d Surgical Hosp until arrival of actual 3d Surgical Hosp, Aug65, after which name became "3d Field." In '73, transferred to Seventh Day Adventist religious org and became known as Saigon Adventist Hosp. Tan Son Nhut Heliport (XS 810-946) was adj to site, with its H-4 pad used for Hosp and H-5 pad for mortuary. Gia Dinh Pr, III Corps.

3d Marine Division (n/a)
See Division Level Command Section.

3d Med Bn Field Hospital (YD 885-149?)
USMC Hosp at Phu Bai CB, apx 12 km SE Hue. Later either renamed or replaced by Army's 85th Evac Hosp? Thua Thien Pr, I Corps.

3d Surgical Hospital (XT/XS/WS)
Mobile Army MASH Unit first at Bien Hoa (XT 988-129) '65-67, then moved to Dong Tam (XS 41-45) to serve the 9th Inf Div AO, then to Binh Thuy (WS 80-13?), Sep69, and attached to 29th Evac Hosp. Grids are apx. III Corps.

3d Vietnam (n/a)
See Glossary.

3g, LZ (YA 859-457)
See 3 Golf. Pleiku Pr, II Corps.

4, FOB (BT 07-71)
See FOB 4. Quang Nam Pr, I Corps.

4, FSB (YB 9-1?)
Hill 664. See Firebase 4. Kontum Pr, II Corps.

4, LZ (AQ 765-330)
Adj Buon Ya Wam, apx 10 km ENE Ban Don AF. 4Mar67. Darlac Pr, II Corps.

4, LZ (BN 676-797)
14 km W Phan Rang. 17Mar67. Ninh Thuan Pr, II Corps.

4, LZ (BP 808-765)
17 km WSW Ninh Hoa. 16Apr67. Khanh Hoa Pr, II Corps.

4, LZ (BR 580-500)
Apx 3 km E An Dien Nam, 500 meters E Hill 606 and 12 km NE An Khe. 15Dec65. Binh Dinh Pr, II Corps.

4, LZ (BS 875-070)
Just W QL-1 and surrounded on 3 sides by hamlets & rice paddies of Phung Du (BS 875-063) directly S, Phung Du 2 just to NW, and Tan Thanh 2 (BS 880-075). Apx 3 km N LZ 2 and 11 km NNE Bong Son. Site of heavy fighting for elements of 2d/7th and 2d/12th Cav, 1st Cav during Op Masher/White Wing, 28Jan-6Mar66. Discussion of Masher/White Wing and this LZ in *A Contagion of War* vol., *Vietnam Experience* series, pp 32-48, with map on p 38. Grids per NIMA. Binh Dinh Pr, II Corps.
4, LZ (XS 487-765)
Apx 6 km Thu Thua and 3 km N Ap Hoa Lac. 18Apr66. Long An Pr, III Corps.
4, LZ (YB 896-368)
Apx 3 km S Lang Dak Kla and 12 km NNE Ben Het. 18Apr66. Kontum Pr, II Corps.
4 Noes (n/a)
See Glossary.
4-11 Road (BS 64-72 to BS 53-72)
A.k.a. Hill 4-11 Road and Rte 518. Ran from Quang Ngai to FSB/LZ 4-11. Opened beginning 11Sep69 by 26th Engr Bn with 11th LIB as security. Quang Ngai Pr, I Corps.
4-11, FSB/LZ (BS 539-732)
A.k.a. Hill 4-11 and LZ 411. Apx 5 km WNW Quang Ngai AF, 3 km S Song Tra Khuc River and adj Thuon Hoa. 11th LIB and ARVN here. 4-11, FSB or Hill 4-11. Carl Caputo, A/3rd/1st Inf Oct68-Oct69, helped build 4-11 and says that immed prior to its const SSgt Joseph H. Kelley and Sgt Bobby L. McCoy (A Co) were both KIA 1Jul69, and recalls men of Co recommended FSB be named FSB Kelley/McCoy; instead Bn named it FSB 4-11 (and mostly called Hill 4-11), per at www.hill4-11.org/ photos/ caputophotos/caputophotos-1.html (courtesy Richard White). Also listed at BS 539-731, Americal List. Quang Ngai Pr, I Corps.
4-12, LZ (BT 016-630)
See 412. Quang Nam Pr, I Corps.
4-H Division (n/a)
See Glossary.
4e, LZ (YA)
N of LZ 18m, W of Pleiku and E of Plei Djereng? A/1st/14th Inf/25th Div here, Oct66. See *Rites of Passage*, p 22. Pleiku Pr, II Corps.
4th Replacement Depot (AR 802-350)
A.k.a. 4th Repo-Depot and 4th Repel-Depot. At Camp Enari apx 13 km SSE Pleiku. 4th Div replacement in-country processing and trng here. 11-C mortarmen course was 2-3 wks, per John Linn. Pleiku Pr, II Corps.
4th Transportation Cmd HQ (XS 8-9)
US Army's 4th Trans Cmd HQ, responsible for running Saigon Port and later Newport. In Saigon port complex area formerly known as M&M Piers (constructed by *Messageries Mairitimes*, a French Co). After Newport constructed, the 4th TC's HQ remained at its original loc. Gia Dinh Pr, III Corps.
5 Cents (YC 865-838)
See Five Cents. Thua Thien Pr, I Corps.
5 Fingers, FSB (n/a)
See Five Fingers. Pleiku/Binh Dinh Pr?, II Corps.
5 Hills, The (n/a)
See Five Hills. The. NVN.
5 Mountains (BT 065-730)
Five, marble, out-croppings known as Marble Mtns. Apx 5 km SE Da Nang, immed S Marble Mtn AF and along coast. See Marble Mtn. Quang Nam Pr, I Corps.
5, FOB (AQ & YA)
See FOB 5. Pleiku/Darlac Pr, II Corps.
5, FSB (YB 990-153)
See Firebase 5. Kontum Pr, II Corps.
5, LZ (BP 552-865)
See Five, LZ. Khanh Hoa Pr, II Corps.
5, LZ (BP 845-772)
Immed NE Hon Ong Mtn, apx 12 km WSW Ninh Hoa. 16Apr67. Khanh Hoa Pr, II Corps.
5, LZ (XT 275-965)
Apx 8 km NW Katum and 3 km S Cambodia. 22Feb67. Tay Ninh Pr, III Corps.
5, LZ (YA 900-333)
Apx 10 km NE Duc Co and 1.5 km E Chu Bak (Hill 577). 4Jan66. Pleiku Pr, II Corps.
5, LZ (YB 888-430)
Immed SW Dak Nay Puey and 3 km NNW Lang Dak Sang. 18Apr66. Kontum Pr, II Corps.
5-E, Camp (XS 8-9)
On outskirts of Saigon. Japanese POW camp that among others, held 209 known US POWs at end of WWII. 120 of those POW's were from 36th Div's 2d Bn, 131st Field Arty (a.k.a. "The Lost Bn," Texas Natl Guard), which had been captured as unit when it mistakenly landed in Java. 86 others were from Cruiser *USS Houston*, which had been sunk 28Feb42. Camp 5-E was one objective of *Project Embankment*. Data per *Vietnam Military Lore, Legends, Shadows, and Heroes*, p 11. See also Project Embankment and Camp Poet. Gia Dinh Pr, III Corps.
5th Infantry Div (Mech) (n/a)
See Division Level Command Section.
5th Marine Division (n/a)
See Division Level Command Section.
5th Med Field Hospital (PR 7-3)
Bangkok, Thailand, May66-Nov70.
5th Precinct (XS 8-9)
See Precinct Five. Gia Dinh Pr, III Corps.
5th SF Group (n/a)
See Major HQs Section.
5th Special Forces HQ Grp (CP 04-53)
At Nha Trang. Khanh Hoa Pr, II Corps.
5th Trans Terminal Cmd Cmpd (BT 03-77?)
See Camp Baxter. Quang Nam Pr, I Corps.
6, Checkpoint (YD 476-376)
See Checkpoint 6. Thau Thien Pr?, I Corps.
6, FOB (XT 958-001)
See FOB 6. Gia Dinh Pr, III Corps.
6, FSB (YB 935-188)
Hill 1001. See Firebase 6. Kontum Pr, II Corps.
6a, LZ (YA 883-502)
Apx 6 km NNE Plei Djereng. 18Jun66. Pleiku Pr, II Corps.
6-Month Extensions (n/a)
See DEROS in Glossary.
6th Convalescent Center (CP 053-322)
At Cam Ranh Bay. 1,300 bed facility under 44th Med Bde/43d Med Grp and later 68th Med Grp. In '68, 44th Med was largest Hosp in Vietnam. Khanh Hoa Pr, II Corps.

7, FSB (ZA 025-933?)
See Firebase 7. Kontum Pr, II Corps.

7, FSB (ZB 060-267?)
See Firebase 7. Kontum Pr, II Corps.

7, LZ (BR 807-530)
Adj Tung Chanh (6), apx 10 km WNW Phu Cat/QL-1. 27Dec65. Binh Dinh Pr, II Corps.

7 Step Snake (n/a)
See Seven-Step Snake in Glossary.

7th Air Force (n/a)
See Major HQs Section.

7th Air Force HQ (XS 812-947)
At intersection of Avenue B and Main St. on Tan Son Nhut AB, apx 1.2 km WSW MACV HQ and 2.3 km ESE the SW end of the main rwy. Gia Dinh Pr, III Corps.

7th Day Adventist Hospital (XS 841-940)
Apx 2 km SE Tan Son Nhut AB and 3 km NNW Independence Palace, Saigon. Not same as Saigon Adventist Hosp. See 3d Field Hosp. Gia Dinh Pr, III Corps.

7th Day Adventist Church (XS 841-940)
Apx 2 km SE Tan Son Nhut AB and 3 km NNW Independence Palace. Gia Dinh Pr, III Corps.

7th Finance (MACV Annex) (XS 831-954)
In MACV Annex, Tan Son Nhut AB, Saigon and just E MACV HQ Cmpd. Gia Dinh Pr, III Corps.

7th Surgical Hospital (n/a)
Mobile Army MASH Unit, first at Cu Chi (XT 65-16), '66-67, then at Long Giao/Blackhorse (YS 437-963) in 67, where it served 11th ACR until leaving VN in May69. Hau Nghia and Long Khanh III Corps.

8, Checkpoint (YD 519-348)
See Checkpoint 8. Thua Thien Pr, I Corps.

8, LZ (YT 108-995)
Apx 17 km WNW Bunard AF and 2 km S Bu Mun Xau. 11Mar66. Phuoc Long Pr, III Corps.

8a, LZ (YA 815-575)
Apx 13 km NNW Plei Djereng New AF and 3 km NW the Se San River. 17Jun66. Kontum Pr, II Corps.

8 Inch Hill (BR 88-03?)
Apparently an 8" howitzer Bty or Bn position described as having been 500 meters N LZ Uplift. 173d Abn, '70. Binh Dinh Pr, II Corps.

8 Klickville (YD 7-2? or YD 7-3?)
Greg Mills describes site as hamlet in white coastal sands apparently just N or NW Hue. Was landmark in AO of 1st/502d Inf, 101st Abn, Spring/Summer '68. Likely named in reference to its distance from a patrol base (possibly An Lo Bridge or Quang Dien?). Thua Thien Pr, I Corps.

8th Aerial Port (XS 819-962)
Tan Son Nhut AB. Gia Dinh Pr, III Corps.

8th Field Hospital (CP/BR/CQ)
First Army Hosp in VN, Apr62. Originally at Nha Trang, (CP 039-520), then An Khe, '70 (BR 48-43?), then Tuy Hoa, '71 (CQ 17-47?). 500 beds. II Corps.

8th Field Hospital (CP 040-523)
In the Long Van Cmpd, apx 1.2 km ESE the NW end of Nha Trang AF main rwy and 500 meters from ocean. Was the first Army Field Hosp in VN. Grid is for Long Van AF (Nha Trang AB). Khanh Hoa Pr, II Corps.

8th RRFS (YD 874-145?)
A.k.a. 8th Radio Research Field Station (ASA). If grid correct, was apx 2 km WNW Hill 180 and 12 km SE Hue. Possibly at N end of Camp Hochmuth and on W side of QL-1 directly across QL-1 from 85th Evac Hosp and N end of Phu Bai AF's main rwy. Thua Thien Pr, I Corps.

9, Resolution (n/a)
See COSVN Resolution Nine in Glossary.

9 Camp, NMCB (BT 03-76)
A.k.a. Da Nang East. Later renamed Camp Adenir to honor SD3 Restituto Adenir, USN, KIA 28Oct65, dedicated 21Nov65. See Camp Adenir. Quang Nam Pr, I Corps.

9 RAR Handshake (n/a)
See Glossary.

9a, LZ (YA 828-562)
On N bank Se San River, apx 12 km NNW Plei Djereng New AF. 17Jun66. Pleiku Pr, II Corps.

9th Field Hospital (CP 04-55?)
Nha Trang, Jul65-Sep68. Khanh Hoa Pr, II Corps.

9th Infantry Division (n/a)
See Division Level Command Section.

9th MEB (AT/BT)
See Divisional Command Section.

9th MEF (AT/BT)
See Divisional Command Section.

10-Alfa, LZ (YA)
See 10 Alpha. Pleiku Pr, II Corps.

10-Alpha, LZ (YA 7-2?)
A.k.a. LZ Ten-Alpha. *Battles in the Monsoon* (pp 267-268) puts site at abnd former US airstrip, 10 km W Duc Co near Cambodian border. Major battle here 28-29May66. On morning of 28May66 during Op Paul Revere, B/2d/35th Inf inserted here during rainstorm and into midst of NVA Rgt HQ. NVA were thought to have been at LZ 11-Alpha, and insertions under TF Tyson were to take place at LZs 10-Alpha and 12-Alpha in order to cut off NVA retreating from simultaneous insertion at 11-Alpha. Not expecting Americans to move in a storm, enemy had taken shelter, leaving five-12.7mm AA MGs unmanned. Enemy initially scattered, but that night organized Bn-sized counter-attack that lasted 2 days. By afternoon of 28May66, B/2d/35th was down to 65 men when reinforced by A/1st/35th Inf. At apx 1:30 a.m. 29May66, NVA attacked and overran unit, forcing cmdr to call arty in on own position. The next morning, plt sweeping perimeter was ambushed and pinned-down while NVA again attacked LZ. Arty pieces were flown in under fire and immed began firing point-blank into NVA. Recon/1st/35th and C/2d/35th also arrived to reinforce A/B Cos. A-1As and F-105s strafed, napalmed and bombed in supt. 7 helos lost and all but 150 men of A & B/1st/35th Inf, 4th Div were KIA/WIA, filling Qui Nhon's hospital to capacity. CACF suggests 32 KIA for those dates in Pleiku Pr, so reasonable to expect apx 100-120 WIA as well. Site used for 27 more days, then abnd. Pleiku Pr, II Corps. [2 3]

10, OP (BT 0-6?)
See OP 10. Quang Nam Pr, I Corps.

11, LZ (XT 357-792)
Apx 12 km S Katum and 7 km SSW Bo Tuc. 6Mar67. Tay Ninh Pr, III Corps.

11, LZ, Heliport (BT 01-76?)
See Goodsell Heliport. Quang Nam Pr, I Corps.
11a, LZ (BR 821-578)
Near An Diem (3) and 16 km NNW Phu Cat/QL-1. 29Dec65. Binh Dinh Pr, II Corps.
11-Alfa, LZ (YA)
See 10 Alpha. Pleiku Pr, II Corps.
11-Alpha, LZ (YA)
See 10 Alpha. Pleiku Pr, II Corps.
11-Bravo, FSB (YU 323-498)
See Eleven-Bravo. Phuoc Long Pr, III Corps.
11th Armored Cavalry Rgt (n/a)
See Division Level Command Section.
11th Light Infantry Bde (n/a)
See Division Level Command Section.
12, LZ (YA 753-234)
Apx 9 km WSW Duc Co AF and 1 km N QL-19. 8Jan66. Pleiku Pr, II Corps.
12, LZ (YB 882-351)
Immed N Dak Iao, apx 13 km NW Dak To 2 AF and 2.5 km W QL-14. 18Apr66. Kontum Pr, II Corps.
12, LZ (YT 082-425)
Along Rte 350/Song Be River immed S Bao Phung, apx 14 km SE Phouc Vinh AF. 9Mar66. Binh Duong Pr, III Corps.
12-Alfa, LZ (YA)
See 10 Alpha. Pleiku Pr, II Corps.
12-Alpha, LZ (YA)
See LZ 10 Alpha. Pleiku Pr, II Corps.
12th Evac Hospital (XT 65-14?)
Semi-Mobile Army Hosp at Cu Chi Basecamp, Dec66-Dec70. 317 beds. Hau Nghia Pr, III Corps.
12, FSB (YB 874-256)
See Firebase 12. Kontum Pr, II Corps.
13, FSB (YB 916-259)
See Firebase 13. Kontum Pr, II Corps.
13, LZ (BR 794-582)
Apx 3 km W An Diem (3) and 17 km NW Phu Cat/QL-1. 28Dec65. Binh Dinh Pr, II Corps.
14, FSB (YA 939-912?)
See Firebase 14. Kontum Pr, II Corps.
14, LZ (YB 804-466)
Apx 1 km E of Laos, 13 km WSW Dak Sut and 3 km NE Ngok Lang Lo (Hill 903). 18Apr66. Kontum Pr, II Corps.
14th Aerial Port (CP 053-166)
A.k.a. Cam Ranh Bay AF. W side Cam Ranh Peninsula apx 7 km S the major AF there. Khanh Hoa Pr, II Corps.
15, FSB (YB 855-185)
See Firebase 15. Kontum Pr, II Corps.
15, LZ (YB 775-527)
Immed NW Dak Hon, apx 15 km W Dak Sut and 2 km W Hill 1051. 18Apr66. Kontum Pr, II Corps.
16, FSB (YB 815-151)
See Firebase 16. Kontum Pr, II Corps.
16, LZ (XT 875-483)
Apx 3 km due W Phu Cat/QL-1, and 2 km SE Hoi Vanh (4). 9Jun67. Binh Duong Pr, III Corps.
17, LZ (YB 842-482)
Apx 9 km ESE Dak Sut, 1.5 km NW Dak Hun and 2 km due W Nui Pon (Hill 976). 18Apr67. Kontum Pr, II Corps.
17a, LZ (YA 905-482)
Apx 5 km NE Plei Djereng New AF and 3 km W Chu Kan Yan Mtn (Hill 864). 18Jun66. Pleiku Pr, II Corps.
17th Field Hospital (XS/BR/CR)
Saigon-Cholon, 66-68, then An Khe (BR 48-43?), '68, then Qui Nhon (CR 080-230?), '69, then An Khe, Oct69. Left VN Aug70. 30 beds. II/III Corps.
17th Parallel (XD/YD)
Ran through DMZ, from XD 53-80 to YD 27-81 and met ocean apx 2 km S mouth of Song Ben Hai River. Was 17º North Latitude and apx dividing line between NVN & SVN. Crossed VN/Lao border apx 17 km NW Ban Kapay. See DMZ and McNamara's Wall. NVN/SVN/Laos.
18m, LZ (YA or YB)
Atop large hill W of Pleiku. 1st/14th Inf/25th Div here, 16Oct66. See *Rites of Passage*, p 20. Pleiku Pr, II Corps.
18th Surgical Hospital (n/a)
Mobile Army MASH Unit first at Pleiku (AR 780-480?) with 4th Div, Jun66-Dec67, then Lai Khe (XT 77-38), Dec67, then Quang Tri (YD 541-318?), Feb68-Mar69, then Camp Evans (Gia Le, YD 309-556?) then back to Quang Tri when elements of 3d Mar Div sent home, Dec69. 70 beds. Grids apx. I, II/III Corps.
19th Eng Logistical Depot (CR 0-1)
See Valley A, Valley F and Long My Valley. Binh Dinh Pr, II Corps.
19th Hole, LZ (YA 83-21?)
A.k.a. LZ Nineteenth Hole. Apx 3 km N Plei Girao Kla, 7 km SSW Duc Co SF Camp, 18 km NNW Chu Pong Mtn, 8 km E Cambodia, 8 km N LZ Golf and 35 km NW Plei Me. Spelled "Nineteen Hole" by Shelby Stanton; however, "Nineteenth Hole" or "19th Hole" are likely correct. 1st Cav. See *Ia Drang Valley* map in *The Rise and Fall of the American Army*, pp 368-369, and *Incursion*, p 252. Grid apx. Pleiku Pr, II Corps.
20, FSB (XT 78-48)
See Firebase 20. Binh Duong Pr, III Corps.
20-A (n/a)
A.k.a. Twenty Alternate. Gen. Van Pao's Meo Guerrilla and CIA HQ. Northern Laos.
20th Eng Bde HQ (YT 016-153)
See Castle Cmpd. Bien Hoa Pr, III Corps.
20, Site (TG 79-24 or RD 09-68)
See Lima Site-20 SF Camp. Laos.
20, FSB (YB 823-082)
See Firebase 20. Kontum Pr, II Corps.
20, FSB (XT 78-48)
See Firebase 20. Binh Duong Pr, III Corps.
21, FSB (n/a)
See Firebase 21. II Corps?
21, LZ (AQ 915-380)
Apx 16 km NW Buon Ho and 2 km S Ban Boi. 5Mar66. Darlac Pr, II Corps.
21, LZ (XT 380-856)
At Bo Tuc/Rte 246, apx 7 km SE Katum. 6Mar67. Tay Ninh Pr, III Corps.
21, LZ (ZV 156-726)
Apx 16 km NE Tieu Atar AF and 6 km SE Tieu Atar Mtn. 10Mar66. Pleiku Pr, II Corps.

21a, LZ (YA 939-474)
Apx 7 km ENE Plei Djereng New AF and 1 km SE Chu Kan Yan Mtn (Hill 864). 18Jun66. Pleiku Pr, II Corps.
22, FSB (XS 83-86)
A.k.a. FSB Twenty-Two. Apx 5 km S Saigon, along E edge of main N/S hwy, apx 8 km N Ap Phuoc Khanh and 8 km NNW Nha Be. 5th/12th Inf, 3d/7th Inf, 199th LIB. Gia Dinh Pr, III Corps.
22, LZ (ZV 142-712)
Apx 15 km NE Tieu Atar AF and 1 km N the Ya Drang River. 10Mar66. Pleiku Pr, II Corps.
22 Step Snake (n/a)
See Twenty-Two Step Snake in Glossary.
22d Replacement Depot (CP 07-27)
At Cam Ranh Bay. One of 2 major US Army personnel replacement depots in SVN and sister of 90th Replacement Depot at Long Binh. Khanh Hoa Pr, II Corps.
22d Surgical Hospital (YT/YD)
MUST Unit (Self-Contained, Portable), at Long Binh (YT 04-07?), Dec67-Jan68, then Phu Bai, Jan68-Oct69 (YD 885-149), with 101st Abn. Bien Hoa and Thua Thien Pr, III and I Corps.
23, FSB (n/a)
See Firebase 23. II Corps?
23, LZ (ZV 180-674)
Apx 15 km ENE Tieu Atar AF, 6 km NW Chu Amung and 40 km WNW Buon Blech. 10Mar66. Pleiku Pr, II Corps.
23a, LZ (YA 861-463)
At Plei Doch, apx 1 km N Plei Djereng New AF. 18Jun66. Pleiku Pr, II Corps.
23d Infantry Division (n/a)
See Division Level Command Section.
24, FSB (YB 90-12?)
See Firebase 24. Kontum Pr, II Corps.
24, LZ (ZV 190-733)
Apx 7 km ESE Tieu Atar Mtn and 33 km WNW Buon Blech AF. 10Mar66. Pleiku Pr, II Corps.
24th Evac Hospital (Semi-Mobile) (YT 046-070)
At Long Binh, Jul66-Nov72. Also operated US Army POW Hosp after Aug69. Bien Hoa Pr, III Corps.
24th Evac Hospital Heliport (YT 046-076)
See Long Binh (24th Evac) Hosp Heliport. Bien Hoa Pr, III Corps.
25, FSB (YB 9-3?)
See Firebase 25. Kontum Pr, II Corps.
25th Infantry Division (n/a)
See Division Level Command Section.
25th Infantry Div Minutiae (n/a)
See Shotgun, Operation.
25th Medical Bn Hospital (XT 65-14)
At Cu Chi. Suptd 25th Inf Div. Hau Nghia Pr, III Corps.
26, FSB (n/a)
See Firebase 26. II Corps?
26th Engineers Base Camp (BT 439-075)
Apx 10 km W Chu Lai, 3 km W Khuong Quang and2 km W of QL-1. Americal. Quang Tin Pr, I Corps.
27, FSB (n/a)
See Firebase 27. II Corps?
27r, LZ (YA 851-168)
Apx 8 km due S Duc Co AF and 2 km SE Plei Girao Kla. 3Sep66. Pleiku Pr, II Corps.
27t, LZ (YA 838-186)
At Plei Girao Kla/Rte 569, apx 6 km S Duc Co AF. 3Sep66. Pleiku Pr, II Corps.
27th Evac Hospital (BT 54-06)
At Chu Lai CB. See 27th Surgical Hosp. Americal List. Grid apx. Quang Tin Pr, I Corps.
27th Surgical Hospital (BT 54-06)
Mobile Army MASH Unit, Chu Lai, Mar68-Jun71, Americal Div/23d Inf Div. Quang Tin Pr, I Corps.
27th Trans Bn Cmpd (BR 95-42 or CR 03-16?)
A.k.a. Camp Vasquez. At Phu Tai, near Qui Nhon. In '72, consisted of 134 buildings, capable of suptg 900 troops. 2d ARVN Trans Bn replaced US units here 24Mar72. Binh Dinh Pr, II Corps.
28, FSB (YB 86-14?)
See Firebase 28. Kontum Pr, II Corps.
28, LZ (XT 828-477)
Apx 12 km NNE Lai Khe and 13 km WSW Phuoc Vinh AF. Binh Duong Pr, III Corps.
28f, LZ (YA 932-149)
Apx 14 km SE Duc Co AF. 2Sep66. Pleiku Pr, II Corps.
28h, LZ (YA 958-118)
Apx 6 km WSW Plei Tenau and 2 km ESE Plei Gong Ly Brand. 2Sep66. Pleiku Pr, II Corps.
29, FSB (YB 839-223)
See Firebase 29. Kontum Pr, II Corps.
29a, LZ (ZA 053-145)
Apx 14 km NW Plei Me and 1 km SW Plei Bon Ga. 10May66. Pleiku Pr, II Corps.
28a, LZ (ZV? 992-138)
Grid does not exist. Possibly AQ 992-138? NARA data. 19May66. Darlac Pr, II Corps.
28b LZ (ZV? 944-175)
Grid does not exist. Possibly AQ 944-175? NARA data. 14May66. Darlac Pr, II Corps.
28c, LZ (ZV? 921-154)
Grid does not exist. Possibly AQ 921-154? NARA data. 14May66. Darlac Pr, II Corps.
29c, LZ (ZA 081-131)
Immed N Plei Kung Xorr and 11 km NW Plei Me. 10May66. Pleiku Pr, II Corps.
29f, LZ (ZA 023-161)
Apx 15 km SW Oasis AF and 17 km NW Plei Me. 10May66. Pleiku Pr, II Corps.
29th Evac Hospital (WS?)
Semi-Mobile Army Hosp at Can Tho/Binh Thuy (WS 840-108?), May68-Oct69, 237 beds. Binh Tuy Pr, III Corps.
30-Day Extensions (n/a)
See DEROS in Glossary.
30, FSB (YB 971-267)
See Firebase 30. Kontum Pr, II Corps.
30, LZ/FSB (XD 58-46)
Apx 7 km E LZ 31, 8 km NE Aloui, 18 km ENE Tchepone and 28 km WNW Khe Sanh. ARVN LZ during Lam Son 719, opened 22Feb71. Good Lam Son 719 map at www.americal.org/174/ map4.htm. Laos.
30b, LZ (ZA 110-140)
Apx 10 km NNE Plei Me and immed NE Plei Kuenh Xom. 8Sep66. Pleiku Pr, II Corps.

30c, LZ (ZA 142-200)
Apx 8 km SSE Oasis AF and 2 km SW Plei La Meur/Rte 563. 8Sep66. Pleiku Pr, II Corps.
30x, LZ (ZA 163-104)
At Plei Le Tott, apx 6 km N Plei Me and 1 km W Rte TL-6C. 15Sep66. Pleiku Pr, II Corps.
30 Minute Island (BN 63-42)
A.k.a. Cu Lao Hon. 1 x 2 km-sized island apx 8 km due E Tuy Phong and 42 km SSW Phan Rang. Known Caribou pilots as "30 Minute Island" because as one passed it, they were apx 30 minutes from touchdown at Cam Ranh. Apparently there was much speculation among Caribou pilots as to whether it would be possible to land here, but "Before I boarded my freedom bird, there were Caribou tire tracks on island; some damn fool actually did land on it!" Quote per and good photo at www.petester.com/html/VNPICS003.html. II Corps.
31, FSB (YB 895-443)
Apx 3 km due N Dak Seang AF, 10 km E Laos, 27 km NNW Dak To and 65 km NW Kontum. Grid per Phil Landis and 4th Div Daily Journal of May '68. 4th Div. Kontum Pr, II Corps.
31, LZ (AQ 955-645)
Along QL-14, apx 7 km NW Buon Blech AF. 7Mar66. Darlac Pr, II Corps.
31, LZ/FSB (XD 51-46)
A.k.a. Hill #31. Apx 7 km N Aloui, 34 km WNW Khe Sanh and 11 km NW FSB Alpha. ARVN LZ during Lam Son 719. Suffered classic NVA tank attack by T-34 tanks and suptg NVA Inf. 2 assault waves were repulsed by ARVN, but 3d overran hill and ARVN fled into jungle. LZ 31 was only friendly FSB completely overrun during Lam Son 719. 1st major tank-to-tank battle of war also fought nearby, when ARVN 1st/11th Armored Cav performed "brilliantly" by destroying 16 PT-76 and 6 T-54s with no friendly losses. Lam Son 719 map at www.americal.org/174/map4htm. See also Lam Son 719. Laos. [4]
31st Med Field Hospital (SB 8-5)
At Khorat AFB, Jun62-May70. Thailand.
32, FSB (YA?)
See Firebase 32. II Corps?
32, LZ (AQ 873-523)
Apx 3 km S Ban Dung and 15 km SW Buon Blech AF. 7-8Mar66. Also listed at AQ 870-530. Darlac Pr, II Corps.
33, FSB (YA?)
See Firebase 33. II Corps?
33, LZ (AQ 830-546)
Apx 2 km E Chu Ktey Mtn and 17 km WSW Buon Blech AF. 7Mar66. Darlac Pr, II Corps.
34, FSB (YA?)
See Firebase 34. II Corps?
34 Alpha (n/a)
A.k.a. 34-A Operations. Clandestine ops in NVN.
34-A Operations (n/a)
A.k.a. 34-A. Code for clandestine NVN ops.
34th Engineer Bn Camp (XU 683-228)
On W side QL-13, apx 6 km NE Ap Thanh Vinh, 2 km S Cambodian border and 15 km NNW Loc Ninh. Engr Camp/Quarry of unknown name here, May-Jun70. 34th Engrs/20th Engr Bde here suptg Cambodian Incursion. Data per Frank Penk, Jr. Binh Long Pr, III Corps.
35b, LZ (YA 841-090)
Along the Ia Keng River, apx 3 km E Plei The. 21May66. Pleiku Pr, II Corps.
36b, LZ (YA 904-060)
Apx 6 km NNE Chu Pong Mtn and 26 km W Plei Me AF. 21May66. Pleiku Pr, II Corps.
36g, LZ (YA 962-022)
Apx 7 km due E Chu Pong Mtn and 20 km WSW Plei Me AF. 3Sep66. Pleiku Pr, II Corps.
36j, LZ (YA 976-055)
Apx 2 km SE the Ia Drang River and 10 km ENE Chu Pong Mtn. 2Sep66. Pleiku Pr, II Corps.
36th Evac Hospital (YS 300-473)
Semi-mobile Army Hosp. At Vung Tau. Provided care and prep for evac of patients to US, Mar66-Nov69, 400 beds. Facility and adj Army AF transferred to 3d Corps ARVN's control on 19Nov70, and renamed Camp Nguyen Van Nhut. A post-turnover inspection was held by MACV/JGS IG, 14Jun72, per Ray Bows. Phuoc Tuy Pr, III Corps.
38y, LZ (ZA 108-108)
Apx 7 km NW Plei Me and 1 km SE Plei Xorr. 15Sep66. Pleiku Pr, II Corps.
39th Bn Compound (XS 82-96)
At Tan Son Nhut AB, Saigon, and also at Vung Tau. Home of 39th Signal Bn. Later renamed Camp Gaylor after 39th moved to Vung Tau. See also Camp Gaylor. Gia Dinh and Phuoc Tuy Prvs, III Corps.
40, LZ (ZV 073-845)
Along the Ya Lop River, 3 km NNE peak of Tieu Teo Mtn and 5 km WNW Hill 711. 14Mar66. Pleiku Pr, II Corps.
41, LZ (XT 368-828)
Apx 8 km SSE Katum and 3 km SSW Bo Tuc. 6Mar67. Tay Ninh Pr, III Corps.
41, LZ (ZV 130-847)
Apx 3 km NNE Hill 711 and 22 km SSW Plei Me. 14Mar66. Pleiku Pr, II Corps.
42, LZ (ZV 150-888)
N of the Ya Lop River apx 9 km WSW Chu Don Mtn and 16 km S Plei Me. 14Mar66. Pleiku Pr, II Corps.
42d ARVN Rgt HQ (ZA 226-535)
Just S Pleiku/Nansteph AF, apx 1 km W QL-14 and 6 km NNW Pleiku. Elements of 1st/92d Arty here mid '68. Grid in 4th Div Op Rpt per Craig Miller. Pleiku Pr, II Corps.
44b, LZ (YV 995-988)
Apx 12 km ESE Chu Pong Mtn and 17 km WSW Plei Me. 3Sep66. Pleiku Pr, II Corps.
44th STZ (Special Tactical Zone) (WS)
See MACV Team 50. Kien Phong Pr, IV Corps.
45a, LZ (ZA 090-002)
Along the Ia Takouk River, apx 8 km SW Plei Me. 14May66. Pleiku Pr, II Corps.
45b, LZ (ZA 066-001)
Apx 17 km ESE Chu Pong Mtn and 11 km WSW Plei Me. 14May66. Pleiku Pr, II Corps.
45e, LZ (ZV 018-958)
Apx 17 km SW Plei Me and 15 km ESE Chu Pong Mtn. 14May66. Pleiku Pr, II Corps.
45h, LZ (ZV 053-908)
Apx 18 km SSW Plei Me and 21 km SE Chu Pong Mtn. 14May66. Pleiku Pr, II Corps.

45th Surgical Hospital (XT 202-508)
A.k.a. Wratten Memorial Hosp. MUST Unit (Self-Contained, Portable) Hosp at Tay Ninh, Oct66-Oct70. Grid is est. See also Wratten. Tay Ninh Pr, III Corps.

46b, LZ (ZA 185-907)
Apx 6 km WNW Kontum and immed N Plei Konang/Rte 511. 10May66. Kontum Pr, II Corps.

46e, LZ (ZV 163-967)
Apx 9 km due S Plei Me and 6 km WNW Chu Don Mtn. 10May66. Pleiku Pr, II Corps.

46f, LZ (ZA 104-963)
On W bank Krong Poko River, 8 km ENE Polei Kleng and 16 km NW Kontum. 10May66. Kontum Pr, II Corps.

46i, LZ (ZA 118-994)
Apx 15 km NW Kontum and 8 km ENE Polei Kleng. 10May66. Kontum Pr, II Corps.

46th SF Company Ops Det A-41 (n/a)
At Royal Thai Army Spec Warfare Ctr, Thailand. Per *Rangers A War* at p 275, was only formally designated SF Ranger unit in War, and also ranger Adv team to RTA. 10-week Thai Ranger course included 3 phases: 5 wk course near Lopburi; a 3 wk mtn trng course in Kanchanaburi Mtns; and 2 wk course in coastal swamps around Sattahip and Chantaburi. Thailand.

50 State EM Club (XS 040-331)
At Shannon-Wright Cmpd, Vinh Long AAF. See Shannon-Wright. Vinh Long Pr, IV Corps.

51st Field Hospital (XS 82-96)
At Tan Son Nhut AB, Oct65-Jun71. Gia Dinh Pr, III Corps.

54, LZ (XT 680-713)
Apx 6 km NE Minh Thanh AF and 4 km E Xa An Hoa/Rte 245. 30Jun66. Binh Long Pr, III Corps.

54th Trans Bn Compound (CR 03-16?)
See Camp Addison. Binh Dinh Pr, II Corps.

55, OP (YD 549-086)
See OP 55. Thua Thien Pr, I Corps.

56, OP (YD 855-133)
See OP 56. Thua Thien Pr, I Corps.

61, LZ (ZV 125-485)
Apx 17 km SW Tieu Atar AF and 3 km SE Buon Ya Soup. 25-28Mar66. II Corps.

62, LZ (ZV 075-540)
Apx 1 km E the Ya Soup River and 10 km SSE Tieu Atar AF. 25Mar66. Darlac Pr, II Corps.

66, LZ (BR 850-500)
Adj Hoi Vanh (2), apx 6 km NW Phu Cat/QL-1. 30Dec65. Binh Dinh Pr, II Corps.

67th Evac Hospital (CR/AR)
Semi-Mobile Army Evac Hosp at Qui Nhon (CR 080-230), Mar66-Feb72; Pleiku (AR 804-470), Feb72-Mar73. 400 beds in '69. Pleiku Pr, II Corps.

70, Camp (WH?)
Apx 80 km from Camp E-5 at Ngoc Lac. Vietminh POW Camp for in early '50's. In '54, and over a 30-day period, 120 of 250 inmates here died from drinking contaminated water. Discussed in *Prisoners of Hope*, p 7. NVN.

71stEvac Hospital (AR 804-470)
Semi-Mobile Army Hosp at Pleiku, Nov66-Dec70. 400 beds in '69. Served 4th Div. Grid apx. Pleiku Pr, II Corps.

74th Field Hospital (YT 046-076)
At Long Binh Post, Sep68-Aug69 Operated by New York Army Reserve Unit. Until Aug69, also operated the US Army Prisoner of War Hosp. Bien Hoa Pr, III Corps.

77 Heliport, Camp (XS 771-988)
Apx 5 km NW Tan Son Nhut AB. "Heliport #539, El. 13'. At 10°50'30"N-106°37'15"E," per Feb73 TAD. Gia Dinh Pr, III Corps.

81, LZ (AQ 855-835)
Along QL-14, apx 16 km S Phu Nhon and 3 km ENE Chu Krah Mtn. 25Mar66. Pleiku Pr, II Corps.

82, LZ (AQ 922-677)
Apx 12 km NNW Buon Blech AF and 2 km W QL-14. 25Mar66. Pleiku Pr, II Corps.

82d Abn Bde (n/a)
See Division Level Command Section.

82d Abn Bde R&R Center (XT 862-158)
At Phu Loi. See Phu Loi CB. Binh Duong Pr, III Corps.

82d Abn Bde Repl Center (XT 86-15?)
82d Abn Replacement Ctr was at or near Phu Loi. See Phu Loi CB. Binh Duong Pr, III Corps.

83, LZ (AQ 925-686)
Along QL-14, apx 13 km NNW Buon Blech AF and 2 km due E peak of Chu Dre Mtn. 25Mar66. Pleiku Pr, II Corps.

84, LZ (AQ 840-790)
N of the Ea Hok River, apx 21 km SSW Phu Nhon. 25Mar66. Pleiku Pr, II Corps.

85, LZ (AQ 906-795)
Along QL-14, apx 21 km ESE Phu Nhon. 25Mar66. Pleiku Pr, II Corps.

85, Site (UH 68-60)
See Lima Site 85. Laos.

85th Evac Hospital (YD 879-146)
Along NW edge of Phu Bai Airport rwy, adj and E QL-1, across road from Camp Hochmuth. Here '69-Dec71, Thua Thien Pr, I Corps.

85th Evac Hospital (CR/YD)
Semi-Mobile Army Hosp at Qui Nhon (CR 080-230), Aug65-69, then Phu Bai (YD 879-146), '69-Dec71, serving 101st Abn. 133 beds in '69. Binh Dinh and Thua Thien Prvs, I/II Corps.

86, LZ (AQ 798-783)
Along the Ea Ok River, apx 22 km SSW Phu Nhon and 4 km SW Chu Krah Mtn. 28Mar66. Pleiku Pr, II Corps.

90th Replacement Depot (YT 04-07)
Transient troop billet within Tan Son Nhut AB built beginning 5May65. 1st named "Tent City," then "Tent City Alpha" when other tent cities built at Pershing Field and Camp Davies. At some point was renamed Camp Alpha. Later became site of 90th Replacement Depot, the major personnel replacement center in SVN, consisting of 90th Replacement Bn (18th, the 178th, the 259th and 381st Replacement Cos). In '66, 90th was moved to Long Binh, and Camp Alpha became personnel out-processing facility. Sister to 22d Replacement Depot at Cam Ranh Bay. Listed grid is for Long Binh Post. Bien Hoa Pr, III Corps.

91, LZ (ZV 203-803)
Apx 25 km NE Tieu Atar AF, 1 km NNW Hill 263 and km 36 NW Buon Blech AF. 28Mar66. Pleiku Pr, II Corps.

92, LZ (ZV 198-777)
Apx 23 km NE Tieu Atar AF and 35 km NW Buon Blech AF. 28Mar66. Pleiku Pr, II Corps.

91st Evac Hospital (CQ/BT)
Semi-Mobile Army Hosp. At Tuy Hoa (CQ 17-47), Dec66-Jul69, then Chu Lai (BT 555-035), Jul69-Nov71. 325 Beds. I/II Corps.

92d Engineer Bn Camp (XT 322-090)
See Duc Hue Engr Camp. Hau Nghia Pr, III Corps.

93, LZ (AQ 750-813)
Near the Ea Kmok River, apx 22 km SE Phu Nhon. 28Mar66. Pleiku Pr, II Corps.

93d Evac Hospital (YT 04-07?)
Semi-Mobile Army Hosp. At Long Binh Post, Nov65-Apr71. 250 beds. Bien Hoa Pr, III Corps.

95th Evac Hospital (BT 01-76?)
Semi-Mobile Army Hosp. At Da Nang, Mar68-Mar73. 320 Beds. Quang Nam Pr, I Corps.

100 P Alley (XS 82-96)
A.k.a. One Hundred P, One Hundred Piaster and 100 Piaster Alley. Labyrinth of muddy alleys across from main gate at Tan Son Nhut AB. Described as somewhat dangerous area populated by military misfits, AWOLs and deserters. reportedly named for nominal fee AWOL troops had to pay villagers to house them until curfew was over and they could sneak back onto base. Grid is for Tan Son Nhut AB. Data per *Vietnam Military Lore, 1959-1973*, p 171. Gia Dinh Pr, III Corps.

100 Piaster Alley (XS 82-96)
See 100 P Alley. Gia Dinh Pr, III Corps.

101, FSB (YB 858-139)
See Firebase 101. Kontum Pr, II Corps.

101, LZ/FSB (YD)
Per Jim Corbett, was cut by 326th Engrs in 2d quarter '70, SW of Hue and on hill described as an upside-down bowl. Apparently built as a showcase firebase, it was opened with an elaborate ceremony. Thua Thien Pr, I Corps.

101st Airborne Division (n/a)
See Division Level Command Section for detailed history. Note: On 28Jun68, US Army, Pacific issued Gen Order 325 which reorganized the 101st Abn into Army's 2d Airmobile (AMBL) Div (1st Cav being the first). Same order redesignated Div as "101st Air Cavalry Division" eff 1Jul68. However, term "Air Cavalry Division" was revoked by Dept of Army directive issued 26Aug68, and thereafter, official name became: 101st Airborne Division (Airmobile). Same order affected 1st Cav Div. [5]

101st Pad (BT 173-078)
See 1-Oh-Worst Pad. Quang Tin Pr, I Corps.

105 Degrees and Rising (n/a)
See American Radio Service.

106, LZ (XT 970-363)
Apx 2 km Xom Suoi Dai, 8 km ESE Phu Giao and 13 km NNE Tan Uyen. 9Feb66. Binh Duong Pr, III Corps.

140, LZ (BR 665-815)
Apx 3 km ESE Nhon Son and 14 km WSW Hoai An. 23Feb66. Binh Dinh Pr, II Corps.

151, LZ (BR 708-832)
Apx 5 km NW Kim Son and 10 km ESE Hoai An. 23Feb66. Binh Dinh Pr, II Corps.

151st Infantry, Co D (n/a)
See Indiana Rangers and Atterbury East. III Corps.

152, LZ (BR 720-881)
Near Dinh Ban, apx 9 km WNW Hoai An. 23Feb66. Binh Dinh Pr, II Corps.

157, LZ (BR 841-754)
Apx 9 km NW Phu My/QL-1 and 4 km WSW Lac Son. 25Feb66. Binh Dinh Pr, II Corps.

158, LZ (BR 837-772)
Overlooking 506 Valley, apx 13 km NNW Phu My and 10 km SSE Hoai An. 25Feb66. Binh Dinh Pr, II Corps.

160, LZ (BR 879-775)
Apx 11 km NNE Phu My and 6 km W QL-1. 26Feb66. Binh Dinh Pr, II Corps.

161, LZ (BR 875-779)
Apx 12 km NNE Phu My and 6 km W QL-1. 26Feb66. Binh Dinh Pr, II Corps.

173, Firebase (n/a)
Newsletter of 173d Abn. Printed by Pacific Stars & Stripes in Tokyo, Japan. Its mailing address was "Firebase 173, 173d Abn Bde, APO 96250."

173rd Airborne Bde (n/a)
See Division Level Command Section.

173d Abn Drop Zone (XT 329-030)
Drop Zone for only Bde-sized combat jump by US forces during VN War, when 173d Abn jumped from C-130s during Op Junction City. Jump zone ran from XT 329-030 to XT 343-030 and was apx 300 meters wide running about 150 meters to either side of a line between XT 329 to XT 343. DZ was generally 3 km N Katum. Info/grid per Butch Sincock. Tay Ninh Pr, III Corps.

184, LZ (BR 864-826)
Apx 8 km SE Hoai An and 15 km NNE Phu My. 22Feb66. Binh Dinh Pr, II Corps.

185, LZ (BR 862-843)
Apx 6 km ESE Hoai An and 4 km WNW Van Dinh Thuong. 22Feb66. Binh Dinh Pr, II Corps.

196th Lt Inf Bde Fwd CP (XT 120-630)
Apx 12 km NNW Tay Ninh West AF, W QL-22 and 17 km WNW Nui Ba Den. Here during Op Gadsden (Junction City), 1-21Feb67, per Les Hines. Tay Ninh Pr, III Corps.

196th Light Infantry Bde (n/a)
See Division Level Command Section.

198th Light Infantry Bde (n/a)
See Division Level Command Section.

199th Light Infantry Bde (n/a)
See Division Level Command Section.

202, FSB (YB 821-078)
See Firebase 202. Kontum Pr, II Corps.

218th Dispensary (XS 854-900)
Apx 1.5 km SSW Independence Palace, Saigon. Gia Dinh Pr, III Corps.

249th General Hospital (n/a)
At Camp Zama Japan. Major US Army Hosp for patients transferred from VN's Evac hospitals. Apparently differed from the US Army Hosp, Camp Zama?

271, LZ (YA 819-178)
Immed W Plei Girao Ket/Rte 569, apx 8 km SSE Duc Co AF. 17Sep66. Pleiku Pr, II Corps.

311th Field Hospital (BR 95-42?)
Ohio Army Reserve Hosp. Originally at Qui Nhon, Oct68-early '69, then Phu Thanh (YS 032-870?) until leaving, Aug69. 240 beds. II/III Corps.

312th Evac Hospital (n/a)
Semi-Mobile Army Hosp. A North Carolina Army Reserve Hosp, Chu Lai (BT 54-06?), Sep68-Aug69. 325 beds. Quang Tin Pr, I Corps.

362d Compound (BP 23-24)
Krause Barracks, Dalat. Home of 362d Signal Co. Was Japanese Army Hosp in WWII. Tuyen Duc Pr, II Corps.

394th Trans Bn Terminal (CR 090-230)
At Qui Nhon Port, apx 240 mi. NE Saigon. See Qui Nhon Port. Binh Dinh Pr, II Corps.

398, Camp (YS?)
See FSB RedCatcher. Long Khanh Pr?, III Corps.

411 Road (BS)
See 4-11, Road. Quang Ngai Pr, I Corps.

411, FSB (BS 539-732)
See FSB 4-11. Quang Ngai Pr, I Corps.

412, LZ (BT 016-630)
A.k.a. Whiskey Tower, Camp Middlesworth and possibly FSBs Phong Luc I or II (BT 015-625). Apx 4.5 km E to ENE Hill 55 and 13 km due S Da Nang AB. 1st/1st Mar, 67,68,69. A Bty, 1st/11th Mar also. Map at http://1stbn1st marines.org/hs/images/ MarkedDaiLocMap.jpg. See also Whiskey Tower. Quang Nam Pr, I Corps.

413, LZ (BT 075-655)
A.k.a. FSB Cau Ha/Cau Ha CB. Just SE Nang Cau/Rte 543, apx 11 km SE Da Nang AB and 12 km NW Hoi An. 14May68. XXIV Corps Index per grid Don Armstrong. Also listed at BT 070-656. Quang Nam Pr, I Corps.

432, LZ (AT 916-583)
A.k.a. Dai Loc and Hill 37. Apx 18 km SSW Da Nang AB, 20 km ENE Ha Tan. Apr70 XXIV Corps grid per Don Armstrong. Quang Nam Pr, I Corps.

497, FSB (BT 189-047)
See Firebase 497. Quang Ngai Pr, I Corps.

501st Army Field Depot (SB 8-5)
At Khorat AFB, Jun62-May70. Thailand.

502d Light Infantry Bde (YU 344-375)
Col Hank Emerson's amusing name for makeshift unit assembled to reopen of Bu Gia Map AF, May66. Consisted of 1 plt 326th Engrs, 17-men of Bu Prang RF Co, 30 Montagnard porters, squad of VN Natl Police who were interpreters, 3d Co, 4th/9th ARVN Rgt, its Recondo Plt, 30 Montagnard trackers (Apache Plt) and its US and US SF Advisors. Reopening discussed in *Battles in the Monsoon*, pp 228-229. Phuoc Long Pr, III Corps.

504C, LZ (YA?)
A.k.a. LZ Punch Bowl? Said to have been in Punch Bowl Valley, W of Pleiku near Plei Djereng and Hill 745. Built apx 25Oct66 by 1st/14th Inf/25th Div, and by 29Oct66 was true FSB complete with arty/mortars. 10' high x 25' wide sign (of painted sandbags) in shape of the 25th Div patch was built on side of steep hill to N of LZ, and, in ceremony 2Nov66, the Bn CO (a Col Proctor) dedicated sign and renamed surrounding area Dragon Valley (previously Punch Bowl Valley). Closed soon after, but site reused, 7Dec67. Bn-sized FSB with 2 Cos manning perimeter and one on "the hill behind them." See *Rites of Passage*, pp 32, 39, 152l. Pleiku Pr, II Corps.

506 Valley (BR 80-84 to 86-77)
Valley of Hwy 506, between Ha Tay and pass near Lac Son, apx 18 km due S Bong Son and 9 km W Ql-1. Grid is on valley floor 3 km WSW LZ Uplift, 8 km N Phu My and 3.5 km W QL-1. Scene of 1st Cav Ops in Sep66 and major VC/NVA staging area throughout war. 173d Abn AO, '68-70. On SE corner of mapsheet L-7014-6737-1, per Ken Burrington. Binh Dinh Pr, II Corps.

506th Field Depot (YT 04-07?)
Originally at Camp Davies, and then at Long Binh in '67, where it became billed as largest Field depot in world! Grid is for Long Binh Post. Bien Hoa Pr, III Corps.

509 Bravo (ZB)
Possibly 584th Engrs nickname for bridge on Rte 509, N Dak To, between 509's intersection with QL-14 at ZB 04-28 and Toumorong at ZB 09-48. Kontum Pr?, II Corps.

509 Bridge, The (ZB)
See 509 Bravo. Kontum Pr?, II Corps.

515 Valley (BS 68-42)
A.k.a. Song Tra Cau Valley. E by NE orientation, apx 15 km NNW Duc Pho AF, 15 km NE Ba To New AF, 14 km SSW Mo Duc, and 15 km W of coast. Valley through which Hwy 515 traversed and also valley of Song Tra Cau River. Americal List. Quang Ngai Pr, I Corps.

523d Field Hospital (CP 04-53)
At Nha Trang. Attached to 8th Field Hosp, Sep65-Sep68. Khanh Hoa Pr, II Corps.

554th Eng Bn Camp (XT 742-328)
See Ben Cat Engr. Binh Duong Pr, III Corps.

588th Eng Bn Camp (XT 089-470)
See 588th Engr Bn Camp. Tay Ninh Pr, III Corps.

707, LZ (n/a)
Americal list. No data. I Corps.

1032 Ford (XD)
Significant bombing target near intersection where Rte 9 (coming out of Quang Tri Pr) crossed the primary N/S section of the HCMT. Laos.

4181 May Bay My (n/a)
See Glossary.

Alphabetical Listings

ALPHA

Facility/Feature Name, Grid Coordinate, a.k.a. Name/History/Province/CTZ

Unless otherwise stated, 6-digit grid coordinates reference DMA L-7014, L-7015 or L-7016 series, 1:50,000 scale maps, while 2 and 4-digit coordinates reference AMS/DMA/NIMA 1:250,000, 1:500,000 and 1:1,000,000 scale maps. Unless otherwise stated, all heights are in meters. To convert meters to feet, multiply by 3.2808; feet to meters, multiply by .3048.

A (n/a)
One of many Viet place-name prefixes meaning "village."
A, FSB (YB 8-1?)
See Firebase A. Kontum Pr, II Corps.
a, LZ (BR 487-573)
Immed SW De Hohca/Rte 508, apx 13 km WSW Vinh Thanh AF. 6De65. Binh Dinh Pr, II Corps.
a, LZ (XT 470-680)
Apx 16 km WNW Minh Thanh AF and 6 km E Ap Cha Do. 23Mar67. Tay Ninh Pr, III Corps.
a, LZ (YC 845-024)
Apx 3 km NE Dak Klan and 12 km WNW Ngok Tavak AF. Quang Tin Pr, I Corps.
A, Valley (CR 0-1?)
See Valley A. Binh Dinh Pr, II Corps.
A 1, FSB (YD 270-736)
A.k.a. Alpha 1. Apx 23 km NNW Quang Tri, 8 km SSE mouth of Ben Hai River/NVN border and in coastal sands 4 km from coast. Also listed at YD 269-732 and 270-732. On maps at: http://wmcbride.space. swri.edu/visit/maps/cuamap.jpg, and p 90, *US Marines in Vietnam, Fighting the North Vietnamese*, *1967*. Quang Tri Pr, I Corps.
A 1, Strongpoint (TJ 9-6)
A.k.a. Anne-Marie 1. Immed W A2 and apx 3.8 mi NW Main CP at DBP. In Muong Thanh Valley apx 290 km W Hanoi. French strongpoint during Op Castor, 20Nov53-7May54. See Dien Bien Phu. NVN.
A 2, FSB (YD 214-738)
A.k.a. Gio Linh, Alpha 2, Camp Hill, The Alamo and possibly LZ Cheyenne (YD 211-739). Just W QL-1 about 25 km NW Quang Tri, 3 km SE Kinh Mon and 10 km SSW mouth of Ben Hai River/ also Gio Linh. On map at p 90, *US Marines in Vietnam, Fighting the North Vietnamese*, *1967*. NVN border. ARVN, USMC and 5th Inf. See Quang Tri Pr, I Corps.
A 2, Strongpoint (TJ)
A.k.a. Anne-Marie 2. Immed E A1 and 4 mi NNW main CP at DBP. In Muong Thanh Valley apx 290 km W Hanoi. French strongpoint during Op Castor, 20Nov53-7May54. In Muong Thanh Valley. See Dien Bien Phu. NVN.
A 3, FSB (YD 174-721)
FSB, a.k.a. Alpha 3. Apx 24 km NW Quang Tri, 5 km W QL-1, and 6 km ENE Con Thien (A-4). ARVN and USMC. Location on map at p 90, *US Marines in Vietnam, Fighting the North Vietnamese*, *1967*. Quang Tri Pr, I Corps.
A 3, Strongpoint (TJ 9-6)
A.k.a. Anne-Marie 3. Apx 3.5 mi NW main CP at DBP, immed due S A1 and SW A2. In Muong Thanh Valley apx 290 km W Hanoi. French strongpoint during Op Castor, 20Nov53-7May54. See Dien Bien Phu. NVN.
A 4, FSB (YD 113-703)
A.k.a. FSB Alpha 4, Con Thien, and Hill of Angels. Apx 10 km W Gio Linh CB, 7 km WSW FSB A-3 and 28 km NW Quang Tri. On map at p 90, *US Marines in Vietnam, Fighting the North Vietnamese*, *1967*. See also Con Thien. Quang Tri Pr, I Corps.
A 4, Strongpoint (TJ 9-6)
A.k.a. Anne-Marie 4. Apx 3.3 mi NNW main CP at DBP and situated in Muong Thanh Valley apx 290 km W Hanoi. French strongpoint during Op Castor, 20Nov53-7May54. See Dien Bien Phu. NVN.
A 5, FSB (YD 09-64?)
Apx 7 km NNW Cam Lo, 6 km SW FSB A 4, 5.5 km N to NNW FSB 6, and 19 km WNW Dong Ha. Location description based on map at p 90, *US Marines in Vietnam, Fighting the North Vietnamese*, *1967*. Grid is est. Quang Tri Pr, I Corps.
A 6, FSB (YD 11-59?)
Just N Cam Lo River, apx 2 km NW Cam Lo, 18 km W to WSW Dong Ha, 6 km WSW FSB 3 and 5.5 km S to SSE FSB A 5. Location description based on map at p 90, *US Marines in Vietnam, Fighting the North Vietnamese, 1967*. Grid is est. Quang Tri Pr, I Corps.
A-22, A-23, A-24 (n/a)
See Glossary.
A-102, Camp? (BQ 7-8?)
Per Ben Youmans, described in a website guestbook as having been apx 50 km NW Tuy Hoa. Description suggests it was 20 km NW Dong Tre, and near Dong Hoi? Listed grid square is estimate. A-102 designation may not refer to 5th SF Det A-102, which according to official Army SF History, was only in A Shau Valley (63-66) and Tien Phuoc (65-70)? Phu Yen Pr, II Corps.
A-102, Camp (BT 105-102)
A.k.a. Tien Phuoc SF Camp. SF/CIDG camp in Song Chang/Song Tien River Valley along Rte 585, apx 20 km WSW Tam Ky AF and 43 km W to WNW Chu Lai. See Tien Phuoc SF Camp. Quang Tin Pr, I Corps.
A-102, Camp (YC 499-837)
A.k.a. A Shau SF Camp and apparently as 5th SF Grp Det A-102 Camp. At A Shau AF, apx 3 km NW A Shau ville,

slightly N A Sap, 14 km SE Ta Bat and 43 km SW Hue. 5th SF Grp Det A-102, and A-233, here Oct66. See A Shau SF Camp. Thua Thien Pr, I Corps.

A-102, CIDG Camp (BS 565-318)
A.k.a. CIDG Camp A-102 and apparently as Ba To New? CIDG Camp on upper reaches of Tra Bong River, apx 27 km SSW Quang Ngai, 26 km WSW Duc Pho, 95 km NNW Phu Cat and same grid as Ba To New AF. A-102 designation may not refer to 5th SF Det A-102, which according to official Army SF History, was only in A Shau Valley (63-66) and Tien Phuoc (65-70)? Americal list. Quang Ngai Pr, I Corps.

A-106, Camp (BS 558-327)
A.k.a. Ba To. Apx 18 km ENE Gia Vuc AF, 26 km WSW Duc Pho AF and 43 km NW LZ English. Mar 65, ARVN Rangers here Sep 70. At other site prior to Mar 65. Americal List. Quang Ngai Pr, I Corps.

A Battalion Training Area (XT 050-687?)
ARVN training area apx 16 km NW Saigon. See Quang Trung Trng Camp. Gia Dinh Pr?, II Corps.

A Bung (XD/YD)
On road leading S from QL-9 to A Shau Valley. A Dong, A Ngo, A Le, A Bung, A Shau and A Sap are along that road and through valley. Thua Thien Pr?, I Corps.

A Cham SF Camp (BN 711-845)
Possibly a.k.a. Phuoc Thien SF Camp. Apx 6 km SW Phan Rang AB, 11 km WNW Phan Rang, and at or near Phuoc Thien AF. 5th SF. Info/grid per *SF Order of Battle.* See Phuoc Thien. Ninh Thuan Pr, II Corps.

A Dong (XD/YD)
Ville S Da Krong Bridge between QL-9 and A Luoi. A Dong, A Ngo, A Le, A Bung, A Shau and A Sap are spread out along road through valley. Thua Thien Pr, I Corps.

A Le (YD 2-0?)
Ville S Da Krong Bridge on road leading south from QL-9 to A Shau Valley. A Dong, A Ngo, A Le, A Bung, A Shau and A Sap are spread out along that road and through valley. NIMA Gaz lists A Le Thien at YD 2-0. Thua Thien Pr, I Corps.

A Loui (XD 52-39)
Actually Aloui. In Laos, apx 33 km W Khe Sanh, 12 km SW LZ Ranger South and 17 km due E LZ Liz. Focus of Lam Son 719. ARVN Abn unit here. Good Lam Son 719 FSB map at www.americal.org/174/map4.htm. Do not confuse with A Luoi SF Camp. Laos.

A Luoi (n/a)
Mapsheet name of L-7014-6441-4. SVN/Cambodia.

A Luoi (YC 388-992)
In the A Shau Valley, apx 40 km WSW Hue. SF CIDG camps and AFs along Hwy 548 at A Luoi, Ta Bat and A Shau hamlets in A Shau Valley were closed Mar66 due to NVA pressure. For 2 years area then exclusively NVA controlled but, in May68, 1st Cav reentered Valley for several weeks. In Aug68, the 101st Abn spent 17 days patrolling valley and again in Mar69 reentered for 3 separate ops over a 167-day period known overall as Op Kentucky Jumper. Thua Thien Pr, I Corps.

A Luoi 1 Airfield (YD 386-003)
At N end of A Shau Valley, apx 10 km ENE Dong Ap Bia (Hamburger Hill) and 40 km WSW Hue. Abnd airstrip/SF camp at ville of A Luoi 1. Seized and reopened as "LZ Stallion" by 1st Bde/1st Cav, 24Apr68, during Op Delaware.[6] Between 29Apr-3May69, 8th Engr Bn, 1st Cav rebuilt AF to handle C-123s/C-130s. Do not confuse with Aloui in Laos. Thua Thien Pr, I Corps.

A Luoi Airfield (YC 386-998)
Apx 10 km ENE Dong Ap Bia (Hamburger Hill) and 40 km WSW Hue. "Insecure, abnd 1Jun68, AF # VA1-59," in Aug69 TAD per Frank Penk, Jr; not in Feb73 TAD. Thua Thien Pr, I Corps.

A Luoi Mountain (YD 407-036)
A.k.a. Dong Re Lao, Signal Mtn and Eagle's Nest. *LRRP Company Command* incorrectly refers to site as A Luoi Mtn. See Signal Hill/Mtn and Eagle's Nest. Thua Thien Pr, I Corps.

A Luoi SF Camp (YC 388-992)
A.k.a. FOB A Shau. In A Shau Valley apx 10 km ENE Dong Ap Bia (Hamburger Hill) and 40 km WSW Hue. 5th SF. Grid per *SF Order of Battle.* Thua Thien Pr, I Corps.

A Ngo (XD/YD)
Ville S of the Da Krong Bridge on road leading S from QL-9 to A Shau Valley. A Dong, A Ngo, A Le, A Bung, A Shau and A Sap are spread out along that road and through valley. Thua Thien Pr, I Corps.

A Rho, Camp (YC)
Likely variant of A Ro SF Camp (YC 668-258) or Aroh (YC 8-8). See A Ro, or Aroh for detail. Spelled "A Rho" in DA Chief, Mil Hist records summary which also puts Det A-414 here '64. Thua Thien or Quang Nam Pr, I Corps.

A Ro (n/a)
Mapsheet name of L-7014-6440-2. SVN/Cambodia.

A Ro Airfield (YC 669-251)
A.k.a. Aroh AF. Apx 12 km E Laotian border, 110 km W Tam Ky per TPC K-10A. Listed as, "Abnd. rwy mortared, AF # VA1-268," in Aug69 TAD per Frank Penk, Jr. Not in Feb73 TAD. El. 2,034'. Also listed at YC 668-258 per *SF Order of Battle.* Thua Thien Pr, I Corps.

A Ro SF Camp (YC 668-258)
A.k.a. Aroh SF Camp. Apx 12 km E of Laos, 110 km W Tam Ky. 5th SF Grp, Det. A-414, Dec64. Relocated to Ha Thanh. Grid per *SF Order of Battle.* Quang Nam Pr, I Corps.

A Sap (n/a)
Mapsheet name of L-7014-6441-2. SVN/Cambodia.

A Sap (YC 497-830)
Ville in A Shau Valley apx 14 km SSE Ta Bat and 45 km SW Hue. Thua Thien Pr, I Corps.

A Sap Airfield (YC 497-834)
See A Shau AF. Thua Thien Pr, I Corps.

A Sap River (YC 456-915)
A.k.a. Rao Lao. Ran SE to NW through center of A Shau Valley. Thua Thien Pr, I Corps.

A Shau (YC 524-812)
Along Hwy 548, at S end of A Shau Valley, apx 3 km SE A Shau AF. Thau Thien Pr, I Corps.

A Shau (SF FOB) (YC 499-837)
A.k.a. FOB Ta Bat (old). At A Sap and S end of A Shau Valley, 9 km WNW Be Loung. 5th SF. Grid per *SF Order of Battle.* Thua Thien Pr, I Corps.

A Shau, Camp (YC 388-992)
See A Luoi. Thua Thien Pr, I Corps.

A Shau Airfield (YC 498-835)
Apx 3 km NW A Shau, slightly N A Sap, 14 km SE Ta Bat and 43 km SW Hue. Maj. Bernard Fisher awarded MOH for lndg his A-1 Skyraider here after NVA had overrun camp, 10Mar65, to rescue downed Skyraider pilot (Maj. Dafford Meyer). Per ONC J-11. "Abnd. rwy mortared, ARVN, probably mined, AF # VA1-60," in Aug69 TAD per Frank Penk, Jr. Also listed at YC 497-834. Thua Thien Pr, I Corps.

A Shau SF Camp (YC 499-837)
A.k.a. 5th SF Grp Det A-102 Camp. At A Shau AF, apx 3 km NW A Shau, slightly N A Sap, 14 km SE Ta Bat and 43 km SW Hue. At 0300 hrs on 9Mar66, 95th Rgt, 365th NVA Div attacked 380 CIDG and SF Troops here. 1st/1st Marines were to reinforce but fog prevented their insertion. At 1630 hrs 10Mar66, Col House, CO HMM-163 was told to take his sixteen H-34 helos plus Huey gunships of VMO-2 and rescue survivors. As they arrived, the surrounded CIDG troops panicked and rushed helos. A wild melee ensued during which helicopter crews were forced to physically evict (in some cases even shoot) friendlies to achieve lift off. Col House and several other helos were shot down on LZ. 69 CIDG and 4 US SF troops were taken out that day. Those left at camp (including Col House) evaded into jungle and on 11Mar65 were found by H-34s some distance from A Shau. The RF troops again panicked as they were boarding, and A Shau scenario was repeated with more RF troops being shot to lighten loads. 12Mar65, HMM-163 found more survivors and for 3d time RF panicked and even began shooting one another to gain a spot on H-34s. 34 RFs, 2 Marines and several SF Adv were rescued that day and one HMM-163 helo received 126 bullet holes during evac. During entire Op, 21 of HMM-163's 24 H-34 helos suffered major damage. [7] Was closed after being overrun, and its assets then shifted to Tien Phuoc (Quang Tin Pr). Grid per *SF Order of Battle.* Thua Thien Pr, I Corps.

A Shau Valley (YD 36-03 to YC 53-88)
NW to SE running 30-mile-long x 2-mile-wide valley parallel to Lao border, apx 45 km SW Hue. In it were Hwy 548, and villes of A Shau, A Sap, A Luoi, Kon Tom, Ta Bat, Lan Nam, Lang Ka Kou, La Dut, as well as 2 AFs (A Luoi and A Shau AF). A Shau SF Camp/AF here also with 5th SF, Det A-102, Oct65, 5th SF Grp, Det. A-113, Dec64. Though numerous ops were mounted in valley over the years, complete control was never relinquished by NVA. Allied ops were suspended each Fall in anticipation of monsoons and great difficulty of resupply/supt of troops. Also known as Base Area 611, staging area of 6th and 9th NVA Rgt in '68-69. SF CIDG Camps/AFs at A Luoi, Ta Bat and A Shau were closed Mar66 due to enemy pressure. For 2 years area then became exclusively NVA controlled, but in May68, 1st Cav reentered Valley for a few weeks, leaving after only one sustained engagement in which it knocked-out a Soviet-made PT-76 tank. In Aug68, 101st Abn spent 17 days patrolling valley and again in Mar69 (2d Bde/101st Abn) they reentered for 3 separate ops over a 167 day period that were known overall as Kentucky Jumper. Unlike many prior ops, NVA stood its ground during Kentucky Jumper op, in battles such as "Bloody Ridge"(Dong A Tay). Infamous Hamburger Hill battle took place along W side of valley during Aug69, with 101st pulling out 11Aug69. On 20Jun69 after 27th Engrs, 18th Engr Bde completed W end of Hwy 547 (Camp Eagle to A Shau), 80 APCs of 3d/5th Cav, 101st Abn and 1st ARVN 3d Sqdn, 7th CAV entered valley as 1st allied armor to roam A Shau. Later, heavy armor of 3d/5thCav and 2d/34th Armor also entered and even climbed to top of Dong Ap Bia (Hamburger Hill) as part of Op Montgomery Rendezvous. During Lam Son 719, Mar71, elements of 101st and ARVN again entered valley to screen Hue and as diversion for Laotian Incursion. For maps see: L7014-6441-4 (A Luoi), which inc the N end of A Shau and Hamburger Hill, and L7014-6441-2 (A Sap) which inc bulk of the A Shau Valley and its southern regions. Thua Thien Pr, I Corps. [8 9]

A Team (n/a)
See Glossary.

A Valley (CR 0-1?)
See Valley A. Binh Dinh Pr, II Corps.

AA, LZ (BR)
See LZ Alpha-Alpha. Binh Dinh Pr, II Corps.

Aachen I, FSB (XT 644-330)
A.k.a. Aachen II. Along LTL-14, apx 13 km WSW Lai Khe, 2 km NW Xa Bung Cong, 8 km due W Ben Cat and 37 km NNW Tan Son Nhut AB. Named after 1st Inf Div WWII battle site. Opened 1Apr69?, and apparently reopened as Aachen II, May69? 1st/7th Arty; 1st Inf Div AO. On *Low Level Hell* and *Charlie Company* (p 6) maps. Binh Duong Pr, III Corps. [10]

Aachen II, FSB (XT 644-330)
A.k.a. Aachen I. See Aachen I for location. Binh Duong Pr, III Corps. [11]

Aaron, FSB (YD 797-108)
See FSB Arrow. Thua Thien Pr, I Corps.

Aaron, LZ (BR 817-677)
Apx 2 km NE Hoi San, 9 km W Phu My and 26 km NNW Phu Cat AB. Opened 30Nov66? Binh Dinh Pr, II Corps.

AB&T Cave Bar (CP 0-1)
Alaska Barge and Transport, a civilian contractor, built a this bar inside a natural cave within their cmpd at South Beach at Cam Ranh Bay. [12] Khanh Hoa Pr, II Corps.

AB&T Compound (CP 05-16?)
On what was known as South Beach of the Cam Ranh Bay Peninsula. HQ of civilian contractor, Alaska Barge and Transport. Co. built bar in natural cave there known as the AB&T Cave Bar. Grid apx. Khanh Hoa Pr, II Corps.

Abbey, LZ (BR 747-818)
See Abby, LZ. Binh Dinh Pr, II Corps.

Abby, LZ (BR 747-818)
Also spelled Abbey. Grid is in valley of Crow's Foot, at or adj to Phu Xuan, 6 km SE Ha Tay, 40 km NNW Phu Cat AB. In existence 30Nov66. 4th Div AO, '70. Per John Linn, was fwd FSB and B/2d/35th Inf, Jul70. 173d Abn apparently here Feb70. Name/grid per Jim Claeys. Binh Dinh Pr, II Corps.

Able, LZ (BR 807-953)
Along S bank of Song An Lo, apx 5 km due W Bong Son AF and 10 km SW LZ English. In existence 30Nov66. Binh Dinh Pr, II Corps.

Above the First (n/a)
Motto of 1st Avn Bn, 1st Inf Div.

Abraham, LZ (YD 115-699)
Apx 26 km WNW Quang Tri, 6 km N to NNW Cam Lo and QL-9, 5 km NW Phu Phuong and near FSB A-1. Apr70 XXIV Corps grid per Don Armstrong. Quang Tri Pr, I Corps.

Accelerated Pacification Campaign (n/a)
See Glossary.

Accessory Pack, C-Ration (n/a)
See Glossary.

Ace, LZ (BR 713-931)
Apx 15 km WSW Bong Son AF and 20 km SW LZ English. In existence 30Nov66. Binh Dinh Pr, II Corps.

Ace, LZ (BT 140-446)
At or near site of LZ Baldy, and possibly its predecessor? Apx 14 km S Hoi An, 27 km NNW Tam Ky and just W QL-1. 2d/1st Inf, 196th LIB, Americal here Jan68. Americal list. Quang Nam/Quang Tin Pr border, I Corps.

Ace, LZ (YD 123-687)
Apx 16 km NW Dong Ha and 7 km due N Cam Lo. Apr70 XXIV Corps grid per Don Armstrong. Quang Tri Pr, I Corps.

Ace, LZ (ZA 064-760)
Along Ya Krong Bolah River, at or near Polei Tum, apx 23 km SW Kontum. 7Feb66. Kontum Pr, II Corps.

Acme, USS (n/a)
MSO-508. Minesweeper, Ocean, per Ralph Fries.

Action, LZ/FSB (BR 264-471)
Along QL-19E between Pleiku/Qui Nhon, near Mang Yang Pass apx 23 km W An Khe, 24 km ESE Suoi Doi and 48 km due E Pleiku. Described as "just some concertina wire surrounding a few sandbagged bunkers, home to one [2d/17th Arty 105mm] Bty." 1st/69th Armor and M-42 Dusters of 4th/60th Arty provided security here and at various strongpoints along QL-19E. Base was a…wet" (alcohol permitted) FSB in '68-69, with troops allowed 2 cans of 3.2% beer a day. 100 lb. blocks of ice trucked-in from Pleiku regularly provided refrigeration and cold beer was always available at 50¢ a can! Burned-out hulk of an ambush-destroyed M-42 sat on S side of road at base's entrance."[13] 2d/17th Arty here 5Dec69, C Bty, 7th/15th Arty here later? Map is L-7014-6636-1. Binh Dinh/Kontum Pr border, II Corps.

Ada, LZ (BR 015-239)
Apx 33 km SE Pleiku, 13 km ESE Plei Do Lim AF and 18 km ENE My Thach. C Bty, 6th/29th Arty here Dec69. 4th Div 31Jan70 grid per Jim Henderson. Pleiku Pr, II Corps.

Adams, Camp (Phu Tai) (CR 026-160?)
If grid correct, was along E side of QL-1, apx 8 km SW Qui Nhon AF, and 4 km NNW Cu Mong. Engr Cantonment, Phu Tai (different Camp Adams at Quang Tri). Named to honor Col Carroll E. Adams, CO 937th Engr Grp, KIA 12May70, 16 km SE Pleiku when his helo was shot down (Maj Gen John A. Dillard, Cmdr US Army Engr Cmd VN, KIA same flight). Adams Hwy, road connecting Pleiku and Phu Tai, also named after Col Adams (promoted to BGen posthumously). Data per *Vietnam Military lore 1959-1973*. Also listed at BR 999-245. Binh Dinh Pr, II Corps.

Adams, Camp (Quang Tri) (YD 309-556?)
At Quang Tri. Named to honor SWF2 Cody E Adams, USN, Seabee, CMU-301 rwy repair, Khe Sanh CB. KIA, 16Apr68, by NVA Arty at very end of siege of Khe Sanh while repairing equip damaged in previous bombardments. Grid is for Quang Tri AF. Data per Ray Bows. Quang Tri Pr, I Corps.

Adam, FSB (CR 001-740)
On Nui Mieu hill mass overlooking coast apx 8 km distant, 22 km ESE Ha Tay AF, 26 km SW Bong Son and 13 km NW Phu My. 30Nov66. Binh Dinh Pr, II Corps.

Adams, FSB (AN 825-548)
Along LTL-8B, at or near Ap Gia Bac, apx 45 km due N Phan Thiet. 4Jul68. Also listed at AN 835-548, per Jerry Berry, which is 1 km E listed grid. Lam Dong Pr, II Corps.

Adams, LZ (XT 868-273)
Apx 14 km SE Lai Khe, 7 km SE Xom Trum Thap, 13 km WSW Khu Tru Mat, 20 km NNW Bien Hoa AB and 12 km N to NNE Phu Loi. Per Peter Cole, is mentioned in 1st Cav VN *Yearbook* Aug65-Dec69, p 88. Grid per Eric Weil, 7th Cav, 1st Cav. Binh Duong Pr, III Corps.

Adams Highway (BR)
Road connecting Pleiku and Phu Tai. Named to honor Col Carroll E. Adams, CO 937th Engr Grp, KIA 12May70, 16 km. SE Pleiku, when his helo was shot down (Maj Gen John A. Dillard, Cmdr US Army Engr Cmd VN KIA same flight). Camp Adams at Phu Tai also named for Col Adams (became BGen posthumously). Binh Dinh/Pleiku Prvs, II Corps.

ADAMS Huts (n/a)
See Glossary.

Adams Road (YU/XT)
NVA/VC infiltration route from Cambodian border near YU 10-35 through mtns E Song Be and Phuoc Binh, sweeping in curve along W edge of N/S mtn range, 1st to SE then back to SW toward Saigon, skirting Dong Xoai to its E and then SW through Phuoc Vinh area at XT 96-50. On map in *Rangers at War* at p 325. Origin of name unknown. Phuoc Long Pr, III Corps.

Addison, Camp (BR 95-42 or CR 03-16?)
Said to have been at Phu Tai, near Qui Nhon. DOD rpt lists it NE Qui Nhon but that would be in ocean? Phu Tai is apx 8 km SW Qui Nhon? Originally known as 54th Trans Bn Cmpd. Transferred to RVNAF near 14Jul71, and then dismantled by 22d ARVN Div, 14Aug71. Combined MACV-JGS IG Post-turnover inspection of dismantled base done 30May72. Binh Dinh Pr, II Corps.

Adenir, Camp (BT 06-73)
A.k.a. Da Nang East. Immed W Marble Mtn AF, apx 5 km ESE Da Nang AB. Originally Naval Mobile CB Camp 9. Named to honor SD3 Restituto Adenir, USN, KIA 28Oct65, dedicated 21Nov65. MCB-11 Seabees here 3Feb66-13Oct66. Per David Schill, "BUL2 Donald Haskins and SD3 Restituto P. Adenir were assigned to NMCB-9, one of 1st Seabee Bns deployed to supt the Marines in VN. Main camp was across from Marble Mt. AF, and one of NMCB-9's projects was the const of the Da Nang Naval Hosp adj to their camp. On night of Oct. 28, 1965, the enemy attacked the air facility, the hosp job site, and the Seabee camp. Haskins and Adenir were among those killed by a rain of mortar rounds. Adenir died that night, while Haskins died of his wounds on 31Oct. As a result, Camp Adenir was the name given to the camp attacked, and Haskins' name was given to Camp Haskins North and

South, near Red Beach. As an additional note to the ground attack story, NMCB-9 Seabees wounded in the attack were presented 93 Purple Hearts by the III MAF CG, LtG Lew Walt, which is likely the record for most Seabees wounded in one incident (VN)." Grid is est. Quang Nam Pr, I Corps. [14]

Adrian Messenger, The List of (XS 8-9)
See Glossary.

ADSID Sensors (n/a)
See Glossary.

Advance, USS (n/a)
MSO-510. Minesweeper, Ocean, per Ralph Fries.

Advance Base Rach Soi (WS 149-004)
Built along canal near Kien Giang AF, apx 8 km SE Rach Gia. Brown Water Navy, Seabees and Seals here '70. Data per PBR Forces Assn at www.pbr-fva.org/. Kien Giang Pr, IV Corps.

Advance Base Tinh Bien (WS)
See Tinh Bien Advance Base. Chau Doc Pr, IV Corps.

Advanced Tactical Bases (n/a)
See Glossary.

Adventist Hospital, Saigon (XS 82-97)
See 3d Field Hosp. Gia Dinh Pr, III Corps.

Advisory Team 50 Compound (WS 695-561?)
Renamed Crum Cmpd in '68. Near Coa Lanh, apx 4 km E Mekong River, 22 km ENE Long Xuyen, 22 km NNW Sa Dec and 48 km NNW Can Tho. Kien Phong Pr, IV Corps.

Advisory Team One (XD 84-54)
Apx 38 km WNW Mai Loc, 22 km NNW Khe Sanh CB and 65 km W NW Quang Tri. Code for secret Recon/Radio monitoring site built on Hill 1739 (a.k.a. Tiger Tooth Mtn or Dong Voi Mep), Jun64. ASA radio intel units under cover name "Advsy Team One" had 2 LZs built on Hill 1739 to provide recon/radio monitoring capabilities. One LZ was on crest and other downslope; named simply, LZs "Crest" and "Hill." ARVN and USMC troops also employed to build/secure site. High winds/downdrafts made lndg difficult. By 22Jun64, 100 ARVN and 73 Marines manned site. Quang Tri Pr, I Corps. [15]

Aeroport de Pochentong (VT 8-7)
A.k.a. Phnom Penh Intl Airport and Yean Than Antaracheat Airport. At 11°33'00"N-104°51'00"E. NIMA data. Cambodia.

Aeroportes (n/a)
See Glossary.

AFRTS Saigon (XS 866-926)
Apx 700 meters NE of US Embassy. Armed Forces Radio & TV Station. See AFVN and American Radio Service in Glossary. Gia Dinh Pr, III Corps.

AFVN & AFVN TV (n/a)
See Glossary.

AFVN TV Saigon (XS 866-926)
See AFRTS Saigon. Gia Dinh Pr, III Corps.

Agence France Presse (n/a)
See Glossary.

Agerholm, USS (n/a)
DD-826. Destroyer, per Ralph Fries.

Agnew BOQ (XS 8-9)
158 Pasteur St., Saigon. US officers billet Mar65, 38 rms. Named to honor civilian real estate officer Donald W Agnew, killed by VC bomb blast 24Dec64, while at Brink BOQ. Data per *Vietnam Military Lore, 1959-1973*. Gia Dinh Pr, III Corps.

Agricultural Development Center (YD 04-53)
Apx 8 km due W Mai Loc, 4 km S of QL-9 and 15 km SW Cam Lo. Quang Tri Pr, I Corps.

Agricultural Development Center (YD 090-695)
Apx 30 km NW Quang Tri. Perhaps the Dinh Dien Ag Dev Ctr? Quang Tri Pr, I Corps.

Agrovilles (n/a)
See Glossary.

Ai Tu Airfield (YD 343-509)
See Ai Tu CB and Quang Tri AF. Quang Tri Pr, I Corps.

Ai Tu Combat Base (YD 340-505)
ARVN armor base on SW bank Thach Han River, apx 3 km NW Quang Tri and on W side of QL-1. Straddled QL-1 and enclosed small AF at its NE edge (and on E side of QL-1). Base diagram in *The Marines in Vietnam 1954-1973*, p 154. Quang Tri Pr, I Corps.

Aigle Azur (n/a)
See Glossary.

Air America (n/a)
See Glossary.

Air America Terminal, Saigon (XS 822-952)
At Tan Son Nhut AB, apx 300 meters WSW MACV HQ. Gia Dinh Pr, III Corps.

Air Cofat (XS 830-895?)
A.k.a. the COFAT Cmpd? Nickname of NSA Saigon's air transport service that was HQ'd in bldg once owned by French Cofat Cigarette Co. Unit flew C-47, C-117, TC-45J, HU-16, and H-46 acft from Tan Son Nhut AB. By mid-68, Air Cofat delivering apx 300,000 to 400,000 lb. of supplies and 3,500 passengers per month. Gia Dinh Pr, III Corps. [16]

Air Force BEQ (XS 8-9)
At 150-156 Tran Hung Dao St., Saigon. Data per *Vietnam Military Lore, 1959-1973*. Gia Dinh Pr, III Corps.

Air Force BEQ (XS 8-9)
At 6 Hoan Hoa Tham St., Saigon. Data per *Vietnam Military Lore, 1959-1973*. Gia Dinh Pr, III Corps.

Air Force BEQ (XS 8-9)
At 72 Tran Tan Phat St., Saigon. Data per *Vietnam Military Lore, 1959-1973*. Gia Dinh Pr, III Corps.

Air Force BEQ (XS 8-9)
At 88 Phan Thanh Gian St. (originally AF #2), Jan65-68, 57 rms, Saigon. Data per *Vietnam Military Lore, 1959-1973*. Gia Dinh Pr, III Corps.

Air Force BOQ (XS 8-9)
At 138A Nguyen Hue St., Saigon. Data per *Vietnam Military Lore, 1959-1973*. Gia Dinh Pr, III Corps.

Air Force BOQ (XS 8-9)
At 149 Nguyen Hue St., Saigon. Data per *Vietnam Military Lore, 1959-1973*. Gia Dinh Pr, III Corps.

Air Force BOQ (XS 8-9)
At 590 Vo Di Nguy St., Saigon. Data per *Vietnam Military Lore, 1959-1973*. Gia Dinh Pr, III Corps.

Air Force No. 1 BEQ (XS 8-9)
At 39 Hong Thap Tu St. (field grade officers), Saigon. Jun65, 16 rms. Data per *Vietnam Military Lore, 1959-1973*. Gia Dinh Pr, III Corps.

Air Force No. 2 BEQ (XS 8-9)
Later renamed Air Force BEQ, Saigon. At 88 Phan Thanh Gian St. (originally AF #2), Jan65-68, 57 rms, XS 8-

Saigon. Data per *Vietnam Military Lore, 1959-1973*. Gia Dinh Pr, III Corps.

Air Ground Air Service (n/a)
See Glossary.

Air Laos (n/a)
See Glossary.

Air Viet & Air Viat (n/a)
See Glossary.

Air Viet-Nam (n/a)
See Glossary.

Airborne, FSB (YD 354-071)
On ridge running parallel to A Shau Valley, apx 42 km WSW Hue Citadel AF, 5 km SE FSB Goodman and 3 km NW FSB Pepper. 101st Abn. 12-13May69 night Sapper attack here detailed in *Secrets of the Viet Cong*, pp283-285. Elements of 6th NVA Rgt and 46 men of K-12 Sapper Bn hit 3 Arty Btys protected by 1 rifle Co (A/2/501st Inf, C/2/11th Arty and elements of B&C/2/319th Arty) with 22 US KIA and 61 WIA. Also discussed in *Hamburger Hill*. Also listed at 355-070. Thua Thien Pr, I Corps.

Airborne Resupply Company (n/a)
See Glossary.

Air-Ground Air Service (n/a)
See Glossary.

Ajax, USS (n/a)
AR-6. Repair ship.

AK Valley (BT)
In E Que Son Valley. Americal List. Quang Nam or Quang Tin Pr, I Corps.

Akuna III (n/a)
See Rescue, Operation.

Akuna Jack (n/a)
See Glossary.

AL, LZ (BR 622-550)
In Vinh Thanh Valley, apx 16 km NE An Khe and 6 km due S Vinh Thanh AF. 5Nov65. Binh Dinh Pr, II Corps.

AL, LZ (ZT 211-501)
Apx 30 km SSE Bao Loc and 45 km NNW Phan Thiet. 5Feb67. Lam Dong Pr, II Corps.

Alabama BOQ (XS 8-9)
At 143 Cong Guynh St., Saigon. Data per *Vietnam Military Lore, 1959-1973*. Gia Dinh Pr, III Corps.

Alabama, FSB/LZ (WS 943-504 or XS 944-503?)
Listed as FSB Alabama 30Jan68, and LZ Alabama 1Feb68. Presumed to have been only one Alabama, but proper grid zone unknown. If in WS, was apx 16 km NE Sa Dec. If in XS, was near ocean, apx 10 km ENE Go Cong AF. Dinh Tuong or Go Cong Pr, IV Corps.

Alamo, LZ (XD 915-351)
Apx 9 km SE Khe Sanh CB, 4 km due S Lang Kat. Apr70 XXIV Corps grid per Don Armstrong. Quang Tri Pr, I Corps.

Alamo, LZ (YA 950-880)
A.k.a. Hill 1124 and possibly LZ Cat (YA 947-896)? Apx 8 km SW Polei Kleng, 28 km due W Kontum and 33 km SSW Dak To 2 AF. A & D/1st/12th Inf, 4th Div, '68. Ground attack 13May68. 2d Bde/4th Inf apparently operating out of this position in Apr69. Cited in *Time Heals No Wounds*, p 183's 1st/12th Inf Radio Log excerpt. 4th Div FSB. Grid per Harry Dilkes. Map: L-7014-6537-4? See also LZs Brillo-Pad, Bunker-Hill, Bingo OP Hill, XYZ Pad and Hill 1124. Kontum Pr, II Corps.

Alamo, The (BT 030-643)
Along W side of QL-1, adj to Viem Tay (2), just W Song Ving Dien River, and apx 12 km S to SSE Da Nang AB. Apparently 1st/1st Mar position. On map at http://1stbn1stmarines.org/hs/images/ MarkedDaiLocMap.jpg. Data per John Middlesworth. Quang Nam Pr, I Corps.

Alamo, The (XD 858-384)
In '62, SF A Det occupied abnd French military post (concrete structures built in apx '52) just off Rte 9 near Khe Sanh ville. Site became known as "The Old French Fort" and also nicknamed "The Alamo" by SF advisors there. See also BV-33 and Khe Sanh SF Camp (old). Quang Tri Pr, I Corps. [17]

Alamo, The (XD 218-732)
A.k.a. Camp Hill. Nickname of Gio Linh CB. *1968 Yearbook* of *Encyclopedia Britannica* has a photo of sign here which read, "*Camp Hill, Gio Linh, The Alamo of Vietnam*." See also Gio Linh. Quang Tri Pr, I Corps.

Alamo, USS (n/a)
LSD-33. Lndg. Ship, Dock, per Ralph Fries.

Alamo BEQ (XS 8-9)
At 119 Tran Hung Dao St., Apr 65, 19 rms, Saigon. Named to honor MSgt Gabriel R. Alamo, KIA 6Jul64 at Nam Dong CIDG Camp in battle where Capt. R. C. Donlan became 1st MOH recipient in VN, SF Det A-726. Data per *Vietnam Military Lore, 1959-1973*. Gia Dinh Pr, III Corps.

Alamo Lounge (WS 840-108)
Apx 26 km due S Sa Dec, 3 km NW Can Tho and 120 km SW Saigon, at Can Tho Army AF. Named to honor MSgt Gabriel R. Alamo, KIA 6Jul64 at Nam Dong CIDG Camp in battle where Capt. R. C. Donlan became 1st recipient of MOH in VN. SF Det A-726. Phong Dinh Pr, IV Corps.

Alanbrooke, FSB (YS 460-786)
A.k.a. Allen Brook. Apx 1 km W Rte-2, 11 km N Nui Dat, 5 km WNW Ngai Giao. 161 Bty, RNZA (Martin's Bty 13May67-14Apr68) FSB set here 5-19Sep67. On 1ATF NCO trng map per John Hollett. Also listed at YS 450-780. 1ATF AO. Named to honor Gen Alanbrooke of WWII fame? Phuoc Tuy Pr, III Corps.

Alaska Barge and Transport (n/a)
See Glossary.

Alaska, LZ (XD 980-623)
Apx 16 km NW Mai Loc, 37 km WNW Quang Tri. Apr70 XXIV Corps grid per Don Armstrong. Quang Tri Pr, I Corps.

Albany, LZ (YA 943-043)
Apx 7 km NW peak of Chu Pong Mtn, 3 km NNE LZ X-Ray, 52 km SW Pleiku and 17 km W Plei Me. Site of major ambush and near annihilation of LTC Robert McDade's 2d/7th Cav, 17-18 Nov65, suffering 83% casualties, 155 KIA and 261 WIA, part of Ia Drang Valley battle NE Chu Pong Mtn. Grid per LtGen Hal Moore. LZ Detroit built very near this site (YA 935-050). Pleiku Pr, II Corps.

Albatross, Operation (n/a)
Code name for French Forces' planned break-out from Siege of Dien Bien Phu in 1954. NVN.

Albatross, USS (n/a)
MSC-289. Minesweeper, Coastal, per Ralph Fries.

Albemarle, USS (n/a)
A.k.a. AV 5. MSTS fleet. Operated as helicopter repair ship for Army under name *USS Corpus Christi Bay*. See also *Corpus Christi Bay, USS.*
Alcatraz POW Camp (XJ)
Inmate's nickname for POW camp near Hanoi. On map at www.soft-vision.com/hanoi/frame.html. NVN.
Alderson, FSB (YS 306-647)
Apx 13.5 km WSW Nui Dat, 2 km E FSB Tess, 3.5 km ESE FSB South Dakota. On 1ATF NCO trng map per John Hollett. Phuoc Tuy Pr, III Corps.
Alexandre de Rhodes (n/a)
See Rhodes, Alexandre de, in Glossary.
Alfa (various)
See also A and Alpha entries.
Alfa, LZ (BS 545-830)
Along Hwy 527, apx 14 km NW Quang Ngai and 12 km SSW Binh Son. Quang Ngai Pr, I Corps.
Alfa, LZ (BS 557-825)
See Chau Ngai (4). Quang Ngai Pr, I Corps.
Alfa, LZ (XS 281-569)
Apx 17 km WNW Ben Tranh AF, and 9 km NE Cai Lay. Dinh Tuong Pr, IV Corps.
Alfa-Alfa, LZ (BR)
See LZ Alpha-Alpha.
Alice, FSB (XU 827-113)
Apx 10 km ENE Loc Ninh and 5 km N Srok Proai. 1st/7th Inf, '69, AO Commanche Warrior. Grid per Frank Penk, Jr. Tay Ninh Pr, III Corps.
Alice, LZ (XS 135-602)
Grid Puts site apx 14 km NW Cai Lay and 20 km SE Thuy Dong AF. 6Jul69. Dinh Tuong Pr, IV Corps.
Alice, LZ (XT 231-435)
Grid Puts site adj to Long My and apx 4 km S Tay Ninh. 10Jul67. Tay Ninh Pr, III Corps.
Alisoun, FSB (YS 659-682)
Along N side of Rte-329, 24 km due E Nui Dat, 5 km ENE FSB Beth, and 7 km WNW FSB Feathers. Named after Bty CO's wife. 5Oct70, 161 Bty's deployment here met with near disaster when it ran into tail end of a VC ambush compromised by captured intel. During skirmish, enemy rounds whistled by Bty's Bn Sgt Major, "who expressed his astonishment at temerity of a soldier so lacking in discipline as to shoot at a senior Warrant officer, war or no war!" [18] 161 Bty, RNZA (Master's Bty 6Sep70-8May71) FSB set here 6-13Oct70. Also spelled Allisoon in one text. On 1ATF NCO trng map per John Hollett. Also listed at YS 65-68. Phuoc Tuy Pr, III Corps.
All American, FSB (XT 743-002)
Apx 5 km S FSB Harrison, 7 km NW Tan Son Nhut AB, 9 km WNW Camp Red Ball and 7 km N FSB Hardcore. Built by 1st/505th Inf during Op Toan Thang, Sep or Oct68 and home to that 3d Bde/82d Abn Bn from Oct68-Mar69. Name was motto of 82d Abn, and also reflects Div's red, white and blue patch sporting the letters "AA" under its Abn tab. Data per Butch Sincock. Gia Dinh Pr, III Corps.
All American II, FSB (XT 755-304)
Grid puts site apx 3 km SSE Ben Cat, and 34 km N Tan Son Nhut AB. Gia Dinh Pr, III Corps.
Allen Brook, Operation (n/a)
4May-24Aug68. USMC op W Hoi An. Also a.k.a. Allenbrook. 1,017 NVA/VC KIA, per *VN Order of Battle*, pp 9-14. Quang Nam Pr, I Corps.
Allen M. Sumner, USS (n/a)
DD-692. 7th Flt Destroyer, per Ralph Fries.
Allenbrook, Operation (n/a)
See Allen Brook, Op.
Allanbrooke, FSB (YS 450-780)
W of LTL-2, apx 3 km WNW Binh Gia and 11 km NNE Nui Dat/Luscombe AF. Likely a 1ATF base. Phuoc Tuy Pr, III Corps.
Alligator Lake (AT or BT)
SW Go Noi Island in Phu Loc Basin, E Spider Lake. 1st Mar Div. Quang Nam Pr, I Corps.
Allison, LZ (XT 308-460)
See Allyson. Tay Ninh Pr, III Corps.
Allons, FSB (XT 760-963)
Apx 6 km due N An Loc and 13 km SSE Loc Ninh AF. 1Jun69. Binh Long Pr, III Corps.
Allons I, FSB (XT 721-985)
A.k.a. FSB Allons and LZ Bravo. Along QL-13, apx 9 km SSW Loc Ninh and 11 km NNW An Loc. FSBs Allons I, II and Liz ran in string along QL-13, all within 10 km of S Loc Ninh and all within 2 km of one another. 11th ACR here. Grid per Frank Penk, Jr. Binh Long Pr, III Corps.
Allons II, FSB (XU 724-008)
Along QL-13, apx 7 km SSW Loc Ninh and 13 km NNW An Loc. FSBs Allons I, II and Liz ran in string along QL-13, all within 10 km of S Loc Ninh and all within 2 km of one another. 11th ACR here. Americal list. Grid per Frank Penk, Jr. Binh Long Pr, III Corps.
Allyson, LZ (XT 308-460)
A.k.a. Allison. Apx 7 km SE Tay Ninh, 19 km SW Dau Tieng. Tay Ninh Pr, III Corps.
Alma, LZ (n/a)
1st Cav FSB/LZ. No data. Name per Jim Claeys.
Almond, LZ (YD 129-589)
Apx 2 km ESE Cam Lo, and 21 km WNW Quang Tri. Apr70 XXIV Corps grid per Don Armstrong. Quang Tri Pr, I Corps.
Almost Hill 766 (BR 66-65?)
Within 6 km NE Vinh Thanh and on E side Vinh Thanh Valley. Apparently visible from Vinh Phuc 4 & 5, and from old French fort at Vinh Thanh. Given nickname because inaccurate maps led US troops to believe they were on Hill 766 during battle here, but were instead on adj, unmapped hill. Site of major, May66 fight involving 1st/12th Cav, 1st Cav, during Op Crazy Horse, featured in *Battles in the Monsoon*, pp 73-93. Grid is est. Site may be nearer BR 67-63? See also LZ Hereford. Binh Dinh Pr, II Corps.
Aloha State, SS (n/a)
Commercial transport under govt contract, per Ralph Fries.
Along, Baie d' (YJ 1-1)
A.k.a. Vinh Ha Long. Bay at 20°55'N-107°05'E. On NF48-16 JOG. NVN.
Aloui (XD 52-39)
Sometimes spelled A Loui (2 words). Apx 33 km W Khe Sanh, 12 km SW LZ Ranger South and 17 km due E LZ Liz. A focus of Lam Son 719, ARVN Abn here. Good map

of Lam Son 719 FSBs at www.americal.org/174/map4.htm. Laos. Do not confuse with A Luoi SF Camp. Laos.

Alpha, Camp (XS 819-962)
Transient troop billet within perimeter of Tan Son Nhut AB. 1st named "Tent City," then "Tent City Alpha" when other tent cities built at Pershing Field and Camp Davies. Initially const 5May65. Became site of 90th Replacement Depot, the major replacement center in VN, consisting of 90th Replacement Bn, which included 18th, 178th, 259th and 381st Replacement Cos. In '66, 90th Replacement Depot was moved to Long Binh and Alpha became a personnel out-processing facility. Per Ray Bows' *Vietnam Military Lore, 1959-1973*, on 29Jan73, an honor guard of apx 50 US personnel gave final salute as US flag was lowered and then base officially turned-over to SVN Govt. Moments after ceremony ended, "Vietnamese looters, both military and civilian, ransacked the camp and carried off everything in Camp Alpha that wasn't securely affixed." Later, looters dismantled most of the bldgs/fixtures as well, and left facility in ruins, a fate likely common to most US facilities at some point after war ended. Was very last US facility to close at end of US involvement in SVN and, interestingly enough, 28Jan73, the day before its flag was actually lowered, marks cut-off date for award of the Vietnam Service Medal. Listed grid is for Tan Son Nhut AB. Gia Dinh Pr, III Corps. [19]

Alpha, Camp (XT 760-893?)
A.k.a. Thunder Five and An Loc Basecamp. At An Loc along QL-13 (Thunder Road), apx 90 km N Saigon, 18 km S Loc Ninh and 33 km NW Dong Xoai. Per *Father Soldier Son*, p 9 and 167, in Aug68, was on N edge of An Loc as Bde or Bn HQ of 1st Inf Div and/or 1st/28th Inf, and also used as R&R center for 1st Div troops. Described in detail throughout that book, but author Nathaniel Tripp noted that upon his unit's arrival to take over base from its prior occupants, Alpha was on red clay knoll that was a "revolting mess when we arrived. Strewn with garbage and infested with rats...The fighting holes had collapsed and were filled with putrid water." Binh Long Pr, III Corps.

Alpha, FSB (XT 924-285)
Apx 16 km NNE Bien Hoa AB. 17May67. Also listed at XT 950-220. Bien Hoa Pr, III Corps.

Alpha, FSB (YS 390-740)
Apx 7 km NW Nui Dat. 7Dec67. Phuoc Tuy Pr, III Corps.

Alpha, LZ (BS 545-830)
See Alfa. Quang Ngai Pr, I Corps.

Alpha, LZ (BS 557-825)
See Chau Ngai (4). Quang Ngai Pr, I Corps.

Alpha, LZ/FSB (XD 59-38)
Apx 8 km E Aloui and 26 km WSW Khe Sanh, along QL-9. An ARVN FSB in Laos during Lam Son 719, 8Feb-6Apr71. Good Lam Son 719 FSB map at www.americal.org/174/map4.htm. Laos.

Alpha, LZ (XS 166-109)
Apx 39 km SW Truc Giang/Ben Tre, and 16 km E Khu Tru Mat. 26Mar67. Also listed at XS 188-111, which is apx 2 km E listed grid. Vinh Long Pr, IV Corps.

Alpha, LZ (XS 281-569)
See Alfa. Dinh Tuong Pr, IV Corps.

Alpha, LZ/FSB (XT 270-010)
A.k.a. LZ Alpha (New). In Cambodia, apx 10 km SSW Duc Hue AF, 8 km NNW tip Parrot's Beak and apx 2 km from SVN border. Opened 10May70 per *11th ACR Cambodia Invasion AAR, 1st Cav Div, May-Jun70*, courtesy Lou Rochat. [20] Cambodia.

Alpha, LZ (XT 789-460)
See Thunder I. Binh Duong Pr, III Corps.

Alpha, LZ (YS 610-703)
Apx 18 km E to ENE Nui Dat/Luscombe, and 5 km WNW Xuyen Moc. '65. Phuoc Tuy Pr, III Corps.

Alpha (New), LZ (XT 270-010)
Apx 10 km SSW Duc Hue AF, 9 km ESE Chantrea and 10 km NNE tip of Parrot's Beak. 1st Cav. Cambodia.

Alpha, Outpost (XD 85-41?)
S and outside main perimeter of Khe Sanh CB (1st/26th Mar Sector). Was along S side of Hill 558 road, S of the Bn position at the "Rock Quarry" and also S of Bravo Outpost. Outpost of 1st/9th Mar. Mislabeled map of site at p 388 of *Valley of Decision*. Grid est. Quang Tri Pr, I Corps.

Alpha 1, FSB (YD 270-236)
See A-1, FSB. Quang Tri Pr, I Corps.

Alpha 2, FSB (YD 214-738)
See A-2, Quang Tri Pr, I Corps.

Alpha 3, FSB (YD 174-721)
See A-3, Quang Tri Pr, I Corps.

Alpha 4, FSB (YD 113-703)
See A-4 or Con Thien. Quang Tri Pr, I Corps.

Alpha 6, Mountain (BT 058-710)
Apx 8 km SE Da Nang AB. Quang Nam Pr, Corps.

Alpha-Alpha, LZ (BR)
A.k.a. LZ AA and LZ Double Alpha. Apparently in very general vic of Phu Cat AB? Described as having been adj to the Oregon Trail, surrounded on 3-sides by higher ground, and having extremely limited fields of fire. 1st/14th Inf/25th Div here, Jan67. See *Rites of Passage*, p 236, 240, 247. Binh Dinh Pr, II Corps.

Alpha Ammo Storage Area (CP 095-230)
On Cam Ranh Bay Peninsula, apx 3 km SW the S end of main AF rwy. 1 of 3 ammo stg areas here renamed 12Jul69 for 3 KIA EOD personnel. Grid is apx. See also Black, McKinley or Moore Ammo Stg. Khanh Hoa Pr, II Corps.

Alpha CAC (YD?)
See CAC Listings. I Corps.

Alpha CAP (YD?)
See CAP Alpha. Thua Thien Pr, I Corps.

Alpha Med (YD 887-148)
USMC Field Hosp at Phu Bai in '66. Grid is that of Phu Bai AF. See also Charlie Med. Thua Thien Pr, I Corps.

Alpha New, LZ (XT 270-010)
See LZ/FSB Alpha at grid. Cambodia.

Alpine, FSB (XD 761-531)
A.k.a. Hill 665. Apx 1.7 km SW Nguon Rao, 16 km SSE FSB Argonne, 25 km WNW Ca Lu, 14 km NW Khe Sanh CB and 57 km due W Quang Tri. In '67, 3d Recon Bn, 3d Mar Div teams Breaker and Hawk suffered 100% casualties and several MIA in contacts on this hill. In '68, one 3d Div Marine was killed by a Tiger near Alpine and later a member of a 3d Recon Bn team observing near Alpine was attacked and badly mauled by perhaps same Tiger. In second incident, Tiger was shot and killed, but not

before inflicting wounds that led to medical retirement of Sgt Richard P. Goolden. 3d Mar Div and 101st Abn. Also listed at XD 755-530, but that is thought to be in error. See Hill 665 for more detail. Quang Tri Pr, I Corps. [21]

ALSG (YS 26-86)
A.k.a. Australian Logistical Supt Grp Cmpd at Vung Tau and Camp Khuu-Ngoc-Tuoc (after transfer to ARVN). See those entries for addnl detail. Phuoc Tuy Pr, III Corps.

Aludra, USS (n/a)
AF-55. Aux Refrig.

Aluoi (YC 388-992)
Actually A Loui. Hamlet/SF camp in northern A Shau Valley. See A Luoi for detail. Thua Thien Pr, I Corps.

Alvarado, FSB (YU 175-105)
Apx 3 km N Phouc Binh, 42 km due E Loc Ninh, 2 to 3 km W Song Be City AF, 6 km NE Song Be AF and 47 km ENE An Loc. 2d/12th Cav, 1st Cav, Aug-69. Grid per Frank Penk, Jr. Phuoc Long Pr, III Corps.

Amarillo (n/a)
6Apr70, XXIV Corps future-use 5th Div FSB name.

Amaranth, Operation (WJ)
22-24Feb52. Fighting withdrawal of all French forces from Hoa Binh Salient (apx 40 km WSW Hanoi) following Battle for Hoa Binh, Nov51-Feb52. Ordered by Gen. Salan after series of costly battles which isolated French trying to hold the Salient. Beginning 22Feb52, retreat was effected by over 200 trucks and 600 porters in several stages back up Road No. 6 toward Hanoi, under constant arty (30,000 rnds) and air cover. Others escaped by boat via Black River, fighting desperately to break through Vietminh encirclement, moving both N and E. Last elements reached Xuan Mai on 24Feb52. See Hoa Binh, Battle of. Data per *Street Without Joy*, pp 59-60. NVN.

Amazon, LZ (YS 397-627)
Apx 3 km N Phuoc Le and 6 km SW Nui Dat. 17Oct66. Phuoc Tuy Pr, III Corps.

Ambassador BEQ (n/a)
US enlisted billet at 7/9 Cong Truong St., Lam Son or Saigon? Jul62-68, 35 rms. Data per *Vietnam Military Lore, 1959-1973*. Gia Dinh Pr, Gia Dinh Pr, III Corps.

Amber, LZ (XD 987-589)
Apx 35 km WNW Quang Tri, 2 km W peak of Dong Ha Mtn and 5 km NNE the Rockpile. Apr70 XXIV Corps grid per Don Armstrong. Quang Tri Pr, I Corps.

Ambush Alley (XS 3-4)
Apparently a portion of Rte 210 near Dong Tam that ran from XS 39-43, NW to XS 36-44. In *Doc: Platoon Medic* (p 16, 102), describes it as, "…running straight and narrow through rice paddies and green undergrowth between Vinh Kim and Dong Tam." Also says it was along QL-4, but that may not be correct? Plt Patrol Base Cougar was built along "Widow-Maker Alley," a road branching off this road. Dinh Tuong Pr, IV Corps.

Ambush at PK 3 (AR 809-460?)
See PK 3. Pleiku Pr, II Corps.

Amelia (various)
See Emelia, LZ/FSB.

Amelia, FSB (BR ?)
Possible sp variant of LZ Emelia (BR 477-595). Mentioned on 129th AHC's webpage at www. vhfcn.org/129th/ 129thhist.htm. Per John Linn, 4th Div here May70, so likely was near Bong Son and probably N or NE An Khe. If properly Emelia, was apx 15 km N An Khe. See also Emelia. Binh Dinh Pr?, II Corps.

Amelia, LZ (BR 477-595)
See Emelia. Binh Dinh Pr, II Corps.

America, USS (n/a)
A.k.a. CVA-66 with CVW-6, 10Apr68-16Dec68; with CVW-8, 5Jun72-24Mar73; with CVW-9, 10Apr70-21Dec70. [22]

Americal 1st Bde FSSE (BT 290-230)
At Tam Ky AF. Forward Service and Supt Element for Americal. Americal list. Quang Tin Pr, I Corps.

Americal Division (n/a)
See 23d Inf Division in Division Level Cmd Section for history. Only "named" US Div to serve in Vietnam. Motto was *Under the Southern Cross*.

American, LZ (XD 977-615)
Apx 37 km WNW Quang Tri. Apr70 XXIV Corps grid per Don Armstrong. Quang Tri Pr, I Corps.

American Challenger, SS (n/a)
Commercial transport under govt contract, per Ralph Fries.

American Hawk, SS (n/a)
Commercial transport under govt contract, per Ralph Fries.

American Legion Post 34 (XS 8-9)
In Saigon, but precise location unknown. Mentioned *Vietnam Military Lore* website at www.namlore.com/ legend1.htm. See also VFW. Gia Dinh Pr, III Corps.

American Mail, SS (n/a)
Commercial transport under govt contract, per Ralph Fries.

American Racer, SS (n/a)
Commercial transport under govt contract, per Ralph Fries. See Evacuation of Da Nang.

American Radio Service (n/a)
See Glossary.

American Robin, SS (n/a)
Merchant ship under govt contract, per Ralph Fries.

Amleang Airfield (n/a)
Apx 65 km WNW Phnom Penh, per DMA TPC K-10D. El. 250'. Cambodia.

Ammo Supply Point-1 (BT 01-74)
See ASP-1. Quang Nam Pr, I Corps.

Amphibious Ready Group Alpha (n/a)
See Glossary.

Amy, LZ (BS 475-542)
Apx 6 km Minh Long AF, 7 km E FSB Warrior, 24 km SW Quang Ngai and 17 km SSE Ha Thanh AF. Also listed at BS 473-526. Americal list. Quang Ngai Pr, I Corps.

Amy, LZ (YA 608-518)
Apx 4 km from Cambodia and 24 km due W Plei Djereng. 12Jan66. Kontum Pr, I Corps.

An Cu, Dam (AT 8-9)
Lagoon at 16°13'N-108°03'E. On ND49-01 JOG. Quang Nam Pr, I Corps.

An Diem CAP (ZC)
CAP 1-3-2, 1st CAG, Binh Son District, per Tim Duffie. Quang Ngai Pr, I Corps.

An Diem Heliport (ZC 085-572)
Along LTL-4 in Song Vu Gia River valley, apx 39 km SW Da Nang AB and 8 km ENE Ha Tay. Heliport #500, El. 66', at15°53'N 107°53'E, per Feb73 TAD. See also FSB Shangri-La and LZ Vulture. Quang Nam Pr, I Corps.

An Diem SF Camp (ZC 090-574)
In narrow river valley, apx 39 km WSW Da Nang AB and 8 km WNW Ha Tay. 5th SF. Moved to Nam Dong. Info/grid per *SF Order of Battle*. Quang Nam Pr, I Corps.

An Dinh (n/a)
Mapsheet name of L-7014-6343-1. NVN only.

An Dinh 2 (BR 389-448)
Ville on QL-19, apx 3 km ESE LZ Schueller and 2 km SE Bridge 23. Binh Dinh Pr, II Corps.

An Do, FSB (YD 659-203)
See FSB T-Bone. Thua Thien Pr, I Corps.

An Duong Vuong, FSB (YD 336-107)
A.k.a. Co Pung Mtn, Hill 1615 and apparently FSB Co Pung? At N end of A Shau Valley, apx 12 km due N FSB Destiny (Dong Ap Bia/Hamburger Hill), 11 km NNW A Luoi AF and 40 km due W Hue. Opened 9May71, by 3d/54th ARVN Rgt during Lam Son 720, and closed11Jun71. 54th Rgt CP here. Data courtesy Cliff Snyder.[23] See Co Pung. Thua Thien Pr, I Corps.

An Giang Airfield (WS 521-416)
See Long Xuyen AF. IV Corps.

An Giang Province (VS/WS/WT)
One of 16 southern provs forming IV Corps.

An Hai Bridge (AN 879-105)
Rte 401 bridge, apx 4 km ENE Phan Thiet. Binh Thuan Pr, II Corps.

An Hiep (various)
Common Viet place-name. Sites inc: BR 830-905 and BR 821-901 in Binh Dinh Pr, and CR 040-367 in Phu Yen Pr; a "New Life" Hamlet due E Ben Het in YB, and at XS 711-096 in Kien Hoa Pr, IV Corps.

An Hiep (YB?)
New Life Hamlet said to have been due E Ben Het. Kontum Pr?, II Corps.

An Hiep Airfield (XS 711-096)
Apx 42 km SE My Tho, 3 km from Mekong River and 28 km ENE Tra Vinh AF/Phu Vinh. Listed as, "Field unserviceable, AF # VA4-180," in Aug69 TAD per Frank Penk, Jr. Not in Feb73 TAD. Kien Hoa Pr, IV Corps.

An Hoa, Baie de (BT 5-1)
A.k.a. Vung An Hoa. Bay at 15°29'N-108°41'E. On ND49-01 JOG. Quang Tin Pr, I Corps.

An Hoa, Cape (BT 5-1)
See Cape An Hoa. Quang Tin Pr, I Corps.

An Hoa, Mui (BT 5-1)
Coastal point at 15°31'N-108°41'E. On ND49-01 JOG. Quang Tin Pr, I Corps.

An Hoa, Pointe (BT 5-1)
See Pointe An Hoa. Quang Tin Pr, I Corps.

An Hoa, Vung (BT 5-1)
Bay at 15°29'N-108°41'E. On ND49-01 JOG. Quang Tin Pr, I Corps.

An Hoa Airfield (AT 874-475)
Apx 30 km SSW Da Nang, 28 km WSW Hoi An, 27 km W Baldy AF and 8 km N Phuoc Binh AF, per TPC K-10A. El. 66'. C-130, C-123, C-7, capable, AF # VA1-257. On map L-7014-6640. Quang Nam Pr, I Corps.

An Hoa ARVN HQ (AT 87-48?)
A.k.a. Duc Duc. Apx 30 km SSW Da Nang, 28 km WSW Hoi An, 27 km W Baldy AF and 8 km N Phuoc Binh AF. See Duc Duc. Quang Nam Pr, I Corps.

An Hoa Basin (AT 85-53)
See Arizona Territory. Quang Nam Pr, I Corps.

An Hoa Railroad Bridge (YD 737-228)
Apparent misspelling. Grid is for An Lo RR Bridge. Thau Thien Pr, I Corps.

An Hoa CAP (AT 87-48?)
CAP November 3, 2d CAG. Per Tim Duffie. Quang Nam Pr, I Corps.

An Hoa Combat Base (AT 874-475)
3d Mar Div HQ in '66. Apx 35 km SW Da Nang and 27 km WNW LZ Baldy. Described in *Bonnie Sue*, as a "sprawling complex of bunkers and barbed wire set on a low hill overlooking the Vu Gia River." Also Americal AO. 2d/5th Marines cantonment and Marine AF here. L-7014-6640-4 map. Quang Nam Pr, I Corps.

An Hoa Heliport (AT 873-467)
Apx 2-3 km S to SSE An Hoa AF and 33 km SSW Da Nang AB. Heliport #501 El. 49', Fuel-Refueling point at Da Nang. Emerg fuel available for F/W acft, at 15°47'N 108°05'E, per Feb73 TAD. Quang Nam Pr, I Corps.

An Hoa Industrial Complex (AT 92-53)
Roughly 18-30 km SW Da Nang. At confluence of 2 rivers, area included Nong Son Coal Mine, a hydro-electric power unit, water purification and fertilizer plant complex a.k.a. "Suicide Dam." Discussed in *Not Going Home Alone*, pp 178-180, which states coal mine was apparently only such mine SVN and that area was VC R-20 (Doc Lap) Bn AO. 3d/9th and 2d/5th Marine AO, 66. ARVN HQ at Duc Duc was here. L-7014-6640-4 map. Quang Nam Pr, I Corps.

An Hoa Outpost (BS 475-864)
A.k.a. Hill 141. Apx 15 km WSW Binh Son, 23 km NW Quang Ngai, 2 km S Rte 529 and overlooking Vinh Tuy Valley. Remote outpost of 936th RF Co, overrun night of 18-19Mar66, with 31 KIA, 85 MIA and 30 survivors. Assaulted by relief force of 3d/7th Mar and 5th ARVN Abn Bn on 19Mar66, during Op Texas, per *USMC in Vietnam, 1966*, p 120-21, 271. Also listed at 470-860. Quang Ngai Pr, I Corps.

An Hoi (YD 38-64)
Apx 52 km NW Hue. Ville that was northern limit of Op Carmargue, Jul53. Near listed grid. See Carmargue, Operation. Quang Tri Pr, I Corps.

An Hou, Cape (BT 5-1)
See Cape An Hou. Quang Tin Pr, I Corps.

An Khe (BR 48-43)
A.k.a. An Tuc. Along QL-19, about 60 km NW Qui Nhon, 60 km ESE Pleiku. El. 1,380'. Site of Camp Radcliff. See Camp Radcliff for detailed history of 1st Cav HQ here, and Hon Cong Mtn, Sin City and LZ Logan. On L-7014-6736-4 map per Ken Burrington. Binh Dinh Pr, II Corps.[24]

An Khe, Dam (BS 92-28)
Lagoon at 14°43'N-109°04'E. On ND49-05 JOG. Binh Dinh Pr, II Corps.

An Khe (An Tuc) (n/a)
Mapsheet L-7014-6736-4. Actual name: An Tuc (An Khe).

An Khe AAF (BR 478-447)
See An Khe AF. Binh Dinh Pr, II Corps.

An Khe Airfield (BR 478-447)
A.k.a. An Khe Army AF (AAF). Apx 3 km SE An Khe Golf Course AF, 40 km due W Phu Cat 1 AF and 64 km WNW Qui Nhon. Major AF of the 2 An Khe area AFs.

(smaller strip was at NW corner of Camp Radcliff). On TPC K-10A. El. 1,380', 4,300' conc rwy. *Infantry in Vietnam* has good map of site at p 265. At 13°57'42"N-108°39'57"E. Binh Dinh Pr, II Corps.

An Khe Gold Airfield (BR 468-483?)
Likely variant of helo pad known as the Golf Course. Described in one text as tactical AF at An Khe/Camp Radcliff, which better describes An Khe AF at BR 478-447? Binh Dinh Pr, II Corps.

An Khe Hairpin Curve (BR 582-438)
See Hairpin Curve, The. Binh Dinh Pr, II Corps.

An Khe Pass (BR 582-438)
Adj Nui Cav Rui on QL-19, apx 11 km E An Khe/Camp Radcliff and 10 km WNW Binh Khe. Described as very steep pass, that by '68-69 was heavily defoliated to minimize ambush potential (as was Mang Yang Pass). 1st/69th Armor provided security for road. Convoys of 54th Trans Bn made numerous trips between Pleiku and Qui Nhon carrying 105mm, 155mm rnds to Arty positions along road as well as 500 lb bombs destined for New Pleiku AB. See L-7014-6736-1 map at 1st/69th Armor website. Binh Dinh Pr, II Corps.

An Khe POL Depot (BR)
See An Khe Storage Depot. Binh Dinh Pr, II Corps.

An Khe SF Camp (BR 481-433)
Apx 3 km due S An Khe AF, 4 km SE An Tuc. 5th SF. Moved to Qui Nhon. Grid per *SF Order of Battle.* Binh Dinh Pr, II Corps.

An Khe Storage Depot (BR)
55,000 barrel capacity POL stg facility that received POL products via Qui Nhon/An Khe Pipeline and pumped them on to Pleiku along QL-19. See Pump Station 1 and An Khe-Pleiku Pipeline. Binh Dinh Pr, II Corps.

An Khe Golf Course Airfield (BR 462-478)
A.k.a. Golf Course AAF, Camp Radcliff AF and The Golf Course. Within perimeter of Camp Radcliff, apx 2 km NE peak of Hon Cong Mtn, 4 km NNW An Khe AF, and 5 km NNW An Tuc. Huge helicopter LZ/pad for vast helo assets of 1st Cav. Named "The Golf Course" after 1st Cav's CG Wright selected site in Aug65, and told advance team (inc 1st Bde, 101st Abn) to, "Cut brush until we have a golf course." Per *Chickenhawk,* p 107, it was apx 3,000' by 4,000' in size when 1st built. In *Baptism*, 77, author described it in '65 as, "a huge helicopter pad; just an open grass-covered, stump-riddled field. At any one time, on it sat hundreds of helicopters." Aug69 TAD courtesy Frank Penk, Jr. states, "alternate LZ for An Khe, hvy helo trfc ARVN 15Oct68, AF # VA2-261." Binh Dinh Pr, II Corps.

An Khe-Pleiku Pipeline (BR/AR/ZA)
105-km-long, above-ground, 6" petroleum pipeline that ran along QL-19 between POL Tank Farm at An Khe Stg Terminal to Pleiku Stg Terminal. Operated/secured by 647th QM Co, which manned 5 pump station sites along line. Water testing of new line began 17May68 and completed on 14Sep68, when Diesel fuel replaced water. Between 14Sep68 and 31Dec68, 119,869 barrels of Diesel, 95,778 barrels of JP-4 and 83,401 barrels of Mogas were pumped from An Khe to Pleiku; equivalent of 2,555, five-thousand gallon tanker-truck trips. During '68, 64th repaired 1,586 major breaks caused by enemy action, accidents and theft. See Pump Station 1. Binh Dinh/Pleiku Pr, II Corps. [25]

An Khe-Qui Nhon Pipeline (BR)
See Pump Station 1 and An Khe-Pleiku Pipeline. Binh Dinh Pr, II Corps.

An Lac (old) SF Camp (AP 916-497)
Adj Buin Rocat, apx 4 km ENE Duc Xuyen AF and 55 km SSE Ban Me Thuot. 5th SF. Det A-234 (was 124), Oct65. Info/grid per *SF Order of Battle.* See Krong Kno. Darlac Pr, II Corps.

An Lac Airfield (AP 882-478)
See Duc Xuyen AF. Darlac Pr, II Corps.

An Lac Hamlet, Battle of (BR 995-825)
On edge of large lagoon, 3 km W of ocean, 20 km SE Bong Son, 6 km E Ql-1 and 5 km NE Xuan Thanh. Took place 2-4Jan68. L-7014-6737-4 map, per Ken Burrington. Binh Dinh Pr, II Corps.

An Lac SF Camp (AP 8647-4847)
Apx 5 km SSW Duc Xuyen AF, 32 km SSW Lac Thien and 10 km SW An Lac (Old). 5th SF. Later became RF/PF camp. Info/grid per *SF Order of Battle.* Darlac Pr, II Corps.

An Lao (n/a)
Mapsheet name of L-7014-6738-2. SVN.

An Lao River (BS/BR)
Mouth is at BS 95-02, apx 7 km due E LZ English and 13 km NE Bong Son. On NE 1/4 of L-7014-6737-1 map, per Ken Burrington. Binh Dinh Pr, II Corps.

An Lao Valley (BR/BS)
Runs N to S from BS 73-23 to BR 80-90, then turns NE near Bong Son to meet ocean apx 13 km NE that city. [26] Narrow, 35-km-long Valley of Song An Lo River, edged by steep mtns. Focus of Op Masher/White Wing 28Jan-3Feb66, which was conducted to clear VC from this valley. Involved were Col Hal (LZ X-Ray) Moore's 3d Bde/1st Cav, as well as 2d/9th Marines, Korean Capitol and ARVN 22d Divs. On NE 1/4 L-7014-6737-1 map, per Ken Burrington. Binh Dinh Pr, II Corps. [27]

An Lau Heliport (BT 221-073)
At head of Song Chang River Valley, apx 13 km SE Tien Phuoc AF and 14 km SW Tam Ky AF. Heliport #502, El. 115', at 15°22'15"N-108°25'00"E, per Feb73 TAD. Quang Tin Pr, I Corps.

An Lo Airfield (YD 639-275)
See Van Xa AF. Thua Thien Pr, I Corps.

An Lo Bridge (YD 623-303)
QL-1 bridge across Song Bo, apx 15 km NW Hue and 3 km NNW LZ Sally. 2d Bde/101st Abn pulled security here in '68. 3d Mar Div/101st Abn here at various times. Thua Thien Pr, I Corps.

An Lo Bridge, FSB (YD 624-302)
Apx 15 km NW Hue and 3 km NNW LZ Sally. Small 101st Abn base in '68. Grid per Don Armstrong. See An Lo Bridge for location. Thua Thien Pr, I Corps.

An Lo Railroad Bridge (YD 737-228)
Listed as An Hoa RR Bridge? Thau Thien Pr, I Corps.

An Lo Valley (BS)
See An Lao Valley. Binh Dinh Pr, II Corps.

An Loc (various)
Common Viet place-name and pinpointing proper site can be problematic. US experience was focused at XT 76-88 in Binh Long Pr (90 km N Saigon), at YT 42-11 (55 km ENE

Saigon) and at BT 0-4 (25 km S Da Nang). Towns with same name were near YS 1-9 (25 km E Saigon), YD 7-3 (N Hue), BR 9-3 (20 km SW Qui Nhon), XT 9-9 (15 km ENE An Loc at XT 76-88) and BS 8-0 (near LZ English in Binh Dinh Pr). SVN.

An Loc (XT 76-88)
Apx 4 km SW Quan Loi, 22 km due S Loc Ninh, 26 km, N Minh Thanh AF, 17 km due E tip of Fishhook and 65 km NE Tay Ninh. In 1930's, plantation workers at nearby Quan Loi were frequently on-strike protesting poor working conditions. French plantation mgr responded to an extended strike by inviting strike leaders to his Quan Loi mansion to negotiate. There they were seized and taken to city's beautiful cobble-stone town square, disemboweled and beheaded in front of townspeople, no doubt ending strike, [28] *Father Soldier Son*, p 9, tells us a Camp Alpha (a.k.a. Thunder Five) here as Bde or Bn HQ of 1st Div and/or 1st/28th Inf. SF Det 34, 2d/3d Inf/199th LIB, 1st Cav 2d Bde Supt area here. Binh Long Pr, III Corps.

An Loc (YT 43-12)
Ville along QL-1, apx 5 km WNW Xuan Loc and 43 km E Bien Hoa AB. Site of An Loc Non-Directional Beacon facility. Long Khanh Pr, III Corps.

An Loc, FSB (XT 780-990)
Apx 8 km E QL-13, 11 km SE Loc Ninh AF and 2 km NE Srok Baveng. Jan68. Tay Ninh Pr, III Corps.

An Loc (Hon Quan) (n/a)
Mapsheet name of L-7014-6332-3. SVN.

An Loc Airfield (AP 882-478)
See Duc Xuyen AF. Tuyen Duc Pr, II Corps.

An Loc Airfield (YT 411-101)
Just N QL-1 apx 43 km E Bien Hoa AB, 4 km NE Xuan Loc AF and 63 km ENE Tan Son Nhut AB. "Check security, Pvt AF # VA3-47," in Aug69 TAD per Frank Penk, Jr. Not in Feb73 TAD. Long Khanh Pr, III Corps.

An Loc Basecamp (XT 760-893?)
A.k.a. Camp Alpha and FSB Thunder V. Along QL-13 (Thunder Road) immed N An Loc, apx 90 km N Saigon, 18 km S Loc Ninh and 33 km NW Dong Xoai. Per *Father Soldier Son*, p 9, a Camp Alpha was here as Bde or Bn HQ of 1st Inf Div and/or 1st/28th Inf. SF Det 34, 2d/3d Inf, 199th LIB, 1st Cav 2d Bde Supt area here. Grid is est. Binh Long Pr, III Corps.

An Loc NDB (YT 43-12)
Non-Directional Air Nav Beacon site. At An Loc, on N side of QL-1, apx 5 km WNW Xuan Loc, 43 km E Bien Hoa AB and 62 km ENE Tan Son Nhut AB. Long Khanh Pr, III Corps.

An Loc Radio Facility (YT 42-11)
Apx 5 km NE Xuan Loc. Air nav radio site here per TPC K-10D. Long Khanh Pr, III Corps.

An Loc, Battle of (XT 76-88)
Known to NVA as Binh Long City. On 13Apr72, NVA launched fierce attack with apx 40 tanks and suptg Inf. NVA T-54's penetrated to within yards of US Adv's cmd bunker but were stopped by last-chance gunship attack. 2 Cobras of Bty F, 79th Arty, 1st Cav (a.k.a. Blue Max, crewed by CWO Barry McIntyre, Maj. Larry McKay, 1Lt Steve Shields, and Capt. Bill Causey) armed with newly-developed 2.75" HEAT rockets (previously untested in combat), came to rescue. Armor had never been attacked by helos in combat before three T-54's were destroyed as they were about to overrun US CP. McIntyre and McKay's first rockets destroyed lead tank, thus becoming 1st helo pilots ever to destroy enemy tank. Over next month, repeated assaults were made upon surrounded besieged city. Finally, at midnight 10May72, apx 5,000 NVA arty rnds began raining in as prelude to final battle. At 4am on 11May72, NVA Inf and tanks advanced from N, NE and NW, but in desperate fighting were finally halted. Defending An Loc were 7th and 8th Inf Rgt, 5th RVN Div, 1st Abn Bde and elite 81st Abn Ranger Grp. Factor contributing to NVA defeat was inexperience of NVA armor which often moved without Inf supt and were vulnerable to M72 LAW. More than 100 NVA armored vehicles were destroyed by ARVN troops and US helos. NVA suffered est 30,000 casualties and ARVN over 600 dead. See Easter Offensive. Binh Long Pr, III Corps. [29]

An Loc, Plantation de (YT 42-11)
Plantation de An Loc, a.k.a. Don Dien An Loc. Apx 5 km NE Xuan Loc. Long Khanh Pr, III Corps.

An Long (n/a)
Mapsheet name of L-7014-6030-2. SVN.

An Long, Camp (WS 5616-0750)
See Cai Cai. IV Corps.

An Long, Camp (XS 030-912)
See Moc Hoa. IV Corps.

An Long Airfield (WS 427-821)
On E bank of Mekong River, apx 14 km S Cambodian border, 16 km SW Don Phuoc AF, 8 km NNW Ap An Minh and 45 km NW Cao Lanh. "Security questionable, SVN Directorate of Civ Avn, 4Nov68, for security contact G3 Air, IV Corps TOC, Clsd to C-123, (C-7), For combat essential or higher priority, AF # VA4-33," in Aug69 TAD per Frank Penk, Jr. Not in Feb73 TAD. Also listed at WS 40-85. Kien Tuong Pr, IV Corps.

An Long Heliport (WS 400-885)
On E bank of Mekong River, apx 14 km S Cambodian border, 16 km SW Don Phuoc AF and 45 km NW Cao Lanh. "Heliport #503, El. 7', sod, at 10°45'N 105°22'E," per Feb73 TAD. Kien Tuong Pr, IV Corps.

An Long SF Camp (WS 409-854)
On E bank of Mekong River, apx 14 km S Cambodia, 16 km SW Don Phuoc AF, 8 km NNW Ap An Minh and 45 km NW Cao Lanh. 5th SF Grp, Det. A-213, Dec64, Det. A-425 (was 324), Oct65. Moved to Thuong Tho. Grid per *SF Order of Battle.* Kien Tuong Pr, IV Corps.

An Long Veng Airfield (n/a)
3,500' rwy, apx 95 km NNE Siemreap, 12 km S Thai border, 65 km E Samrong AF. El. 191'. Cambodia.

An Luong, Mui (BT 1-5)
A.k.a. Pointe An Luong. Coastal point at 15°53'N-108°22'E. On ND49-01 JOG. Quang Nam Pr, I Corps.

An My (XT 85-08)
Apx 20 km due N Saigon. On 1Feb68, US Armored Cav and Inf Units met VC here in two-day battle at start of Tet '68. Binh Duong Pr, III Corps.

An My Outpost (XT 835-173)
Apx 20 km due N Saigon. '67. Binh Duong Pr, III Corps.

An My 3 CAP (BT 220-295?)
CAP 2-2-3, 2d CAG and CAP Charlie 3, 2d CAG. Dai Loc District, Quang Nam Pr, I Corps.

An Nhon (BR 96-36)
Along QL-1, apx 18 km NW Qui Nhon, 4 km NW Ba Gi AF and 12 km SE Phu Cat AF. Noted as being birthplace of communist insurgency movement in SE Asia. Possibly 1st Cav elements here early '66. Binh Dinh Pr, II Corps.
An Nhut Tan, FSB (XS 655-667)
Apparent FSB location. If grid correct, was along Song Vam Co Dong River apx 11 km SSE Ben Luc and 12 km ENE Tan An. Long An Pr, III Corps.
An Ninh Corridor (XT 35-15)
Generally 25 to 30 km W Cu Chi and 25 km SSE Tay Ninh. Enemy infiltration route from Angel's Wing E toward Cu Chi and Saigon. Traversed Nui Ba Den, Tri Tam as well as the Straight-Edge and Renegade Woods. FSB Jackson and Patrol Bases Harris and Kotrc (among others) were positioned in corridor. Hau Nghia Pr, III Corps.
An On 1/4 CUPP (BT 02-74)
Per Ed Saragoza, this CUPP team was along QL-1 near Finger Lake, apx 3 km S Da Nang, late '70/early '71. Quang Nam Pr, I Corps.
An Phong (various)
Common Viet place-name. Sites inc: BR 4-3, BR 6-4, BS 4-8, BS 7-5, BS 7-6, WR 1-9 and WS 4-7. All SVN.
An Phong (I) CAP (n/a)
See CAP 1-3-9. 1st CAG. Quang Tin or Quang Ngai Pr, I Corps.
An Phong CAP (n/a)
CAP 1-3-9, 1st CAG. See CAP 1-3-9 and OP George. Info per CAP Website. I Corps.
An Phu Heliport (WS 106-945)
On W bank of Mekong River, apx 4 km from Cambodia, 15 km NNW Chau Duc AF, 12 km due N Chau Phu. "Heliport #504, El. 10', wooden. End of F/W strip, by cmpd." at 10°48'30"N-105°05'30"E, per Feb73 TAD. Chau Doc Pr, IV Corps.
An Phu SF Camp (WS 105-945)
On W bank of Mekong River, apx 4 km from Cambodia, 15 km NNW Chau Duc AF, and 12 km due N Chau Phu. 5th SF Grp, Det. A-424 (was 6), Oct65, Det. A-6, Dec64. Moved to Phu Quoc. Grid per *SF Order of Battle*. Chau Doc Pr, IV Corps.
An Phu, Camp (WT 143-052)
See Phu Hiep. IV Corps.
An Quang, Battle of (BR 98-84)
A.k.a. Battle of Dam Tra O. Along E edge of Dam Tra O lagoon, apx 17 km SW Bong Son. Took place Jun67. L-7014-6837-4 map, per Ken Burrington. Binh Dinh Pr, II Corps.
An Son Airfield (BR 950-270)
A.k.a. Lane Army AF. Apx 14 km WNW Qui Nhon AF, 5 km due N ROK Strip AF10 km SSW Ba Gi AF and 18 km SSE Phu Cat AB. 7th Sqdn, 17th Cav here 71-72. See Lane AAF. Binh Dinh Pr, II Corps.
An Son SF Camp (XD 840-385)
Apx 5 km S Khe Sanh CB, and on S side of QL-9. 5th SF. See Khe Sanh SF Camp. Grid per *SF Order of Battle.* Quang Tri Pr, I Corps.
An Tan (BT 513-048)
Along QL-1 apx 3 km due W Chu Lai AF and 24 km SE Tam Ky AF. Americal List. Quang Tin Pr, I Corps.
An Tan, Camp (AT 937-706)
Along Hwy 540, apx 9 km SW Da Nang AB. Quang Nam Pr, I Corps.
An Tan Bridge (BT 497-065)
Along QL-1 apx 4 km due W Chu Lai AF and 22 km SE Tam Ky AF. Apparently destroyed or attacked Apr70. Americal List. Quang Tin Pr, I Corps.
An Thai, Thon (YD 36-54?)
See Thon An Thai. Quang Tri Pr, I Corps.
An Thanh (n/a)
Mapsheet name of L-7014-6231-3. SVN/Cambodia.
An Thinh Airfield (BS 718-425)
Near Song Tra Cau River, apx 7 km W QL-1, 11 km WNW Duc Pho and 12 km SSW Mo Duc AF. "No info, AF # VA1-115," Aug69 TAD per Frank Penk, Jr. Not in Feb73 TAD. Quang Ngai Pr, I Corps.
An Thoampoi Island (US 95-05?)
A.k.a. An Thoi Island, Ile d' An Thomapoi and Quan Do An Thoampoi. At S end of Phu Quoc island, just S of An Thoi AF. NIMA data. Gulf of Thailand, IV Corps.
An Thoi (US 940-070)
At S end of Phu Quoc Island in Gulf of Thailand, apx 25 km SSE Duong Dong, and 65 km SW Ha Tien. Among other things, AF here used to shuttle NVA/VC POWs from mainland SVN. Home of MP advisor camp, HQ for large POW camp, and Mobile Advsy Team IV-44 (trained 1 RF Co and 1 PF Plt). Per Ben Youmans, SVN Govt POW camp here held as many as 35,000 NVA/VC POWs.[30] Youmans also says An Thoi was also known for producing most superior Nouc Mam in SVN; its fish fermentation plant was in ville near MAT Team camp. He adds that An Thoi had a beautiful natural harbor whose water was clearest he has ever seen; from air, bottom was visible even many hundreds of yards off-shore. Beach composed of fine white powder, less coarse than sand. Photos of An Thoi and POW Camp at www.petester.com/toc.html. IV Corps.
An Thoi Airfield (US 940-070)
At S tip of Dao Phu Quoc Island, 65 km SW Ha Tien, 25 km S Duong Dong AF and 62 km from mainland SVN, per TPC K-10D. El. 16', 3,600' steel-mat rwy. USN operated, at 10°00'51"N-104°01'51"E. Gulf of Thailand, IV Corps.
An Thoi Island (US 95-05?)
See An Thoampoi Island. Gulf of Thailand, IV Corps.
An Thoi NSA (US 93-07)
Apparently at S tip of Dao Phu Quoc Island, 65 km SW Ha Tien, 25 km S Duong Dong AF and 62 km from SVN mainland. USN Supt Activity, '65-71, per MRF Assn Website. Gulf of Thailand, IV Corps.
An Thoi POW Camp (US 940-070)
See An Thoi. Gulf of Thailand, IV Corps.
An Thoi, Ile d' (US 95-05?)
See An Thoampoi Is. Kien Giang Pr?, IV Corps.
An Thomapoi, Ile d' (US 9-0)
See An Thomapoi Is. Kien Giang Pr, IV Corps.
An Thrach CAP (BT 010-233?)
Delta 2, 2d CAG. Quang Nam Pr, I Corps.
An Trach Relocation Ville (YD 345-625)
Apx 7 km due N Quang Tri. 69. Quang Tri Pr, I Corps.
An Tri (WS 97-40)
See Giao Duc. Dinh Tuong Pr, IV Corps.

An Tuc (An Khe) (n/a)
Mapsheet name of L-7014-6736-4. SVN.
An Tuc (BR 47-44)
See An Khe. Binh Dinh Pr, II Corps.
An Tuc Airfield (BR 478-447)
See An Khe AF. Binh Dinh Pr, II Corps.
An Tuc SF Camp (BR 481-433)
Along QL-19 near An Khe, 41 km due W Phu Cat AB. 5th SF camp. Det A-107, Oct65. Grid per *SF Order of Battle*. See An Khe. Binh Dinh Pr, II Corps.
An Vieng, Plantation de (YS 2-9)
A.k.a. Don Dien An Vieng. Apx 38 km W Saigon. Bien Hoa and/or Gia Dinh Pr, III Corps.
An Xuan Cu Airfield (WR 169-139)
See Quan Long City AF. An Xuyen Pr, IV Corps.
An Xuyen Province (VR/VQ/WR/WQ)
One of 16 southern provs forming IV Corps.
An Yen, Mui (US 9-1)
Coastal point at 10°04'N-104°02'E. On NC48-05 JOG. Kien Giang Pr, IV Corps.
An Yen, Pointe (US 9-1)
See Pointe An Yen. Kien Giang Pr, IV Corps.
An Yo, Pointe (BR 9-9)
See Pointe An Yo. Binh Dinh Pr, II Corps.
Anari, Camp (AR 802-350)
See Enari, Camp. Pleiku Pr, II Corps.
Anchor, LZ (BR 943-854)
Apx 3 km E Van An and 15 km SE Bong Son. 30Oct66. Binh Dinh Pr, II Corps.
Anchor, LZ (XD 815-473)
Apx 2 km Ap La Vien, 53 km W Quang Tri. Apr70 XXIV Corps grid per Don Armstrong. Quang Tri Pr, I Corps.
Anchor Airfield (VQ 988-674)
See Nam Can AF (a.k.a. Solid Anchor AF). An Xuyen Pr, IV Corps.
Anchorage, USS (n/a)
LSD 36. See Frequent Wind.
Andaung Pech Airfield (n/a)
A.k.a. Bo Kheo AF. Apx 345 km NE Phnom Penh and 85 km WSW Pleiku SVN. Natl Geo map. El. 984'. Cambodia.
Andell, FSB/LZ (AN 8-2 or 8-3?)
Per *Currahee History, 1Feb69-31Dec69*, p 26, was built N of Thien Giao by TF 3-506 during Op Double Eagle III, Phase II, around 17Dec68. 3d/506th Inf/101st Abn and 105mms here per Jerry Berry. Binh Thuan Pr?, II Corps.
Andersen, FSB (YT 215-125)
A.k.a. FSB Anderson. Apx 22 km due E Bien Hoa, 25 km WNW Xuan Loc, 2 km N QL-1 and 7 km SE FSB Harrison. Deliberately built on low, bull-dozed hill astride main VC infiltration rte and attacked 3 times during Tet '68 as result. On 18Feb68, following 150 rnd mortar barrage, 2 waves of VC struck, resulting in 8 Aussie KIA and 22 WIA. Was also hit 20Feb68 and 28Feb68. 161 Bty, RNZA (Martin's Bty 13May67-14Apr68) FSB set here 13Feb-1Mar68, and 13Feb-1Mar68 under Hitching's. 3 RAR TF tactical HQ, A Trp of A Sqdn, 3d US Cav, Engr Trp and med howitzers of Bty B/2d/35th US Arty here during those battles. On 1ATF NCO trng map per John Hollett. Also listed at YT 200-120 and YT 209-127. 199th LIB and 1ATF. Bien Hao Pr, III Corps.
Anderson, FSB (YT 215-125)
See Andersen. Bien Hoa Pr, III Corps.
Anderson, Richard B., USS (n/a)
A.k.a. DD 786. On 5Apr72, during Easter Offensive, Destroyers *Joseph Strauss* and *Richard B. Anderson* fired on Ben Hai Bridge in N half of DMZ. See *Stickell, USS.* [31]
Anderson Trail (AT/BT?)
Per Col Harvey Barnum, Jr.(MOH), trail was in area S of Da Nang patrolled by H/2d/9th Mar, in '65. Specific loc and name origin unknown. Quang Nam Pr?, I Corps. [32]
Andersonville SF Camp (YT 740-331)
Possibly a.k.a. Tuc Trung SF Camp. Along Rte 334 at S edge of Vo Dat, within 2 km E Vo Dat AF, and 36 km NW Xuan Loc. 5th SF. Grid per *SF Order of Battle*. See Tuc Trung. Long Khanh Pr, III Corps.
Andr, FSB (YT?)
See Andre. Long Khanh Pr?, III Corps.
Andre, FSB (YT 262-461)
Remote site apx 30 km E Phuoc Vinh AF, 10 km SSE Rang Mang, and 41 km NE Bien Hoa AB. Cited in *2d/7th Cav, 1st Cav Div Unit History* for'70 and '71, at p 6, per Peter Cole. Long Khanh Pr, III Corps.
Andrea, FSB (BP 193-279)
Apx 5 km NNW Dalat and 6 km SSE Ap Dang Gia Dit. 2d/17th Arty here, 17Oct70. Data per Jack Picciolo. Tuyen Duc Pr II Corps.
Andrea, FSB (YS 268-572)
On Long Son Island, apx 20 km SW Nui Dat, 13 km N Vung Tau, 3 km from ocean and 5 km SW QL-15. Built on solid-rock summit of Hill 84, and 1st opened when single, 161 Bty RNZA L-5 cannon and 8t gunners deployed here 4Ap70. Named to honor GPO's (Gun Position Officer) Flavel's daughter. Site was manned by gun and 17 PF Viet soldiers suptg HQ ATF's D and E Plts while they searched island for rocket sites threatening Vung Tau. A PF threw cigarette into unused powder-charge pit one night, causing intense blaze exposing all to sniper fire. 161 Bty, RNZA (Andrew's Bty 18Sep-6Sep70) set here 4-17Apr70. See Long Son Island. On 1ATF NCO trng map per John Hollett. Phuoc Tuy Pr, III Corps.
Andrews, FSB (YU 489-031)
Apx 7 km ESE Duc Phong AF/SF Camp, 52 km NE Dong Xoai and 122 km NE Saigon. Cited in 30th Arty ORLL. *1st Cav. Op Rpt, May-Jul70*, p 18, per Peter Cole. Phuoc Long Pr, III Corps.
Andrews, Julie (n/a)
See Shotgun, Operation.
Androscoggin, USCGC (n/a)
WHEC-68. 4Dec67-4Aug68. Sqdn 3 CGC, during Coast Guard's 2d deployment. Engaged NVA Trawler in duel on 29-30Feb68, involving exchange of 5", MG and recoilless rifle fire. Other cutters and VNN craft soon joined battle, eventually beaching trawler apx 18 km S Nha Trang vic Hon Heo Secret Zone. Discussed in *Brown Water, Black Berets*, p 126-31. Market Time TF-115. SVN.
Andy, LZ (BR 797-895)
Apparently a.k.a. or very near site of LZ Betsy (BR 808-884), apx 8 km SW Bong Son, 7 km N Ha Tay AF. 30Oct66. Binh Dinh Pr, II Corps.

Andy, LZ (BS 921-221)
Along QL-1, apx 8 km N Gia An, 21 km NNE LZ English, 20 km SE Duc Pho and 3 km WSW FSB Charlie Brown. 22May67. Listed as being in II Corps, but grid appears to be in I Corps? Quang Ngai Pr, I Corps.

Andy, LZ (XT 820-910)
A.k.a. Quan Loi Basecamp and Rocket City? At or near Quan Loi, apx 12 km NNE An Loc, 12 km SE Loc Ninh AF, 10 km W FSB Vivian and 9 km E QL-13. Also listed at XT 810-910 and 825-909. Binh Long, Pr, III Corps.

Andy, Patrol Base (XT 557-226)
Apx 10 km NW Cu Chi. Mar69. Hau Nghia Pr, III Corps.

Angel of Dien Bien Phu, The (n/a)
See Glossary.

Angel, FSB (YD 186-487)
Apx 10 km E Mai Loc, 15 km WSW Quang Tri and N Ba Long Valley. USMC. Also listed at YD 186-488 and either relocated or grid in error. Quang Tri Pr, I Corps.

Angel, FSB (YD 206-488)
Apx 11 km E Mai Loc, 14 km WSW Quang Tri. XXIV Corps grid. Likely same FSB Angel as that at YD 186-487. Was either relocated or grid in error. Quang Tri Pr, I Corps.

Angel's Wing (XT 25-20)
Cambodian wing-shaped border feature just N Parrot's Beak and apx 60 km WNW Saigon. ARVN's III Corps HQ launched Op Toan Thang 41 into this region of Cambodia at 0800, 14Apr71. 3-day op was suptd by US 25th Inf Div from within SVN, since no US forces or Adv were allowed in Cambodia at time. Cambodia/SVN.

Anh Nua Thuong CAP (n/a)
CAP 3-4-1, 3rd CAG. Thua Thien Pr, I Corps.

Animal, LZ (XD 888-587)
Apx 45 km WNW Quang Tri and 18 km N Khe Sanh. Apr70 XXIV Corps grid per Don Armstrong. Quang Tri Pr, I Corps.

Anlong Veng Airfield (n/a)
3,500' rwy, apx 95 km NNE Siemreap, 12 km S Thai border, 65 km E Samrong AF. El. 191'. Cambodia.

Ann, FSB/LZ (XT 084-816)
A.k.a. FSBs Anne and Phi Ma? Near Thien Ngon AF, apx 8 km S Cambodian border and 35 km NNW Tay Ninh. Also listed at XT 084-898 by Frank Penk, which is at point where QL-22 meets Cambodian border, 7 km NNW Thien Ngon? Listed grid per 30th Arty ORLL. See Phi Ma. Tay Ninh Pr, III Corps.

Ann, FSB/LZ (XT 364-488)
Apx 12 km WNW Dau Tieng AF and 12 km due E Tay Ninh. Grid per Frank Penk, Jr. Tay Ninh Pr, III Corps.

Ann, FSB/LZ (XT 987-815)
Apx 8 km NW Dong Xoai AF. 1st Cav. Name/grid per Dan Gillotti, 15th Arty. Tay Ninh Pr, III Corps.

Ann, FSB/LZ (XU 720-098)
Apx 1 km W QL-13, and 7 km SSW Loc Ninh. 1st/5th Cav, '69. Grid per Frank Penk, Jr. Binh Long Pr, III Corps.

Ann, FSB/LZ (YD 559-039)
A.k.a. LZ/FSB Anne. Apx 1 km ENE FSB Veghel site, 16 km WSW FSB Birmingham, 34 km WSW Phu Bai and 23 km SW Hue. Thua Thien Pr, I Corps.

Ann, LZ (BR 384-223)
Apx 68 km due W Qui Nhon, 26 km SSW An Khe and 8 km NNW Plei Niang. 2d/17th Arty here supt 1st Cav, 13Dec68. Data per Jack Picciolo. Binh Dinh Pr, II Corps.

Ann, LZ (BS 655-960)
A.k.a. FSB Annie. On Batangan Peninsula, apx 17 km SE Chu Lai AB, 8 km due S Tuyet Diem, 6 km E QL-1 and 11 km NNE LZ Dottie. Americal list. Quang Ngai Pr, I Corps.

Ann, LZ (YD 559-039)
See FSB Ann. Thua Thien Pr, I Corps.

Ann Arbor BEQ (XS 8-9)
Lot 80, Phu Tho Hoa St., Saigon. Data per *Vietnam Military Lore, 1959-1973*. Gia Dinh Pr, III Corps.

Ann Margaret (XT)
Nickname given an area of Iron Triangle along Song Saigon. See Iron Triangle.

Ann Margaret, Outpost (XT 664-171)
A.k.a. OP Ann Margaret. A twin-bunker position along road NE Cu Chi AF. Description and photos of position in *On Point* (photo section between pp 140-141) put it just outside the wire of the 1st/8th and 6th/77th Arty's position and within view of the Cu Chi CB perimeter bunkers along the NNE edge of the base. The 2 bunker post was likely named to honor its resemblance to the physical features of film starlet Ann Margaret who toured VN with the USO & Bob Hope shows. Per *Rangers At War-LRRPs*, p. 138, it guarded the wooden bridge that lead to Fihol Rubber Plantation. 6Apr66. Hau Nghia Pr, III Corps.

Ann's House (BP)
Notorious bar, restaurant and bordello in Dalat. Apparently run by lady named "Big Ann." Discussed in *Charlie Ranger*, p 174-176. Tuyen Duc Pr, II Corps.

Anna, FSB (XU 686-520)
In Cambodia, apx 27 km from SVN border, 23 km NNE Snuol, 12 km ENE Phum Anhchanh and 44 km N to NNW Loc Ninh (SVN). Cited in *1st Cav Div Op Rpt of May-Jul70*, at pp 37, 38, per Peter Cole. Grid per *11th ACR Cambodia Invasion AAR, 1st Cav Div, May-Jun70*, courtesy Lou Rochat. [33] III Corps.

Annam (n/a)
See Glossary.

Annamite Cordillera (n/a)
Chain of sometimes precipitous mtns up to 5,000' in height that form spine of most of VN. Covered with a triple-canopy growth of Teak, Mahogany and other tropical hardwoods, the lush jungle is cut by rushing rivers and deep gorges but very few lakes. What few openings exist in canopy allow elephant grasses to grow to heights of 10'-12'.

Annapolis, USS (n/a)
AGMR-1. Aux Ship, per Ralph Fries.

Annapolis BEQ/BOQ (XS 813-923)
A.k.a. Annapolis Hotel BEQ/BOQ. At Lot 158-168, Phu Tho Hoa St., Saigon. Data per *Vietnam Military Lore, 1959-1973*. Pictures/other data re site at www.mrfa.organnapolis1.htm. Gia Dinh Pr, III Corps.

Anne, FSB (XT 084-816)
See Ann, FSB, at grid. Tay Ninh Pr, III Corps.

Anne, FSB/LZ (YD 290-402)
A.k.a. Dong On Do and LZ/FSB Ann. Apx 13 km SSW Quang Tri, 24 km ESE Mai Loc26 km WNW Camp Evans. Elements of 4th/60th, E/71st and I/29th (Dusters, Quads, Searchlights) here late 67-Jan68. 1st/44th Arty here, per

Paul Kopsick. XXIV Corps grid per Don Armstrong. Also listed at YD 289-402. Quang Tri Pr, I Corps.

Anne, FSB (YD 559-039)
See Ann, FSB at grid. Thua Thien Pr, I Corps.

Anne, FSB (YS 551-775)
Apx 15 km NE Nui Dat, 9.5 km E Le Loi, 2 km SE FSB Friendship. On 1ATF NCO trng map per John Hollett. Phuoc Tuy Pr, III Corps.

Anne-Marie Strongpoints (TJ 9-6)
In Muong Thanh Valley (Dien Bien Phu) apx 290 km W Hanoi. A series of French defensive strongpoints at DBP a.k.a. A1, A2, A3, and A-4 and referred to as the "Ann-Maries." "Much farther to NE [of main complex], over 3 miles away, 3 little hills stood out at foot of a high mtn; this position had the name of Anne-Marie and was held by Thai of 3d Thai Bn."[34] Op Castor, 20Nov53-7May54. See A-1, A-2, and Dien Bien Phu. NVN.

Annette, LZ (YD 070-634)
Apx 7 km NW Cam Lo and 27 km WNW Quang Tri. Apr70 XXIV Corps grid per Don Armstrong. Quang Tri Pr, I Corps.

Annex #4, USARV Mess (YT 04-07)
USARV Mess Association a.k.a. Nelson Inn. At Long Binh. See Nelson Inn. Bien Hoa Pr, III Corps.

Annie, LZ (BS 655-960)
A.k.a. FSB Ann. On Batangan Peninsula, apx 17 km SE Chu Lai AB, 8 km due S Tuyet Diem, 6 km E QL-1 and 11 km NNE LZ Dottie. Americal list. Quang Ngai Pr, I Corps.

Annie, FSB (XT 198-878)
Apx 35 km due N Tay Ninh, 4 km W FSB Patti and 14 km WSW Katum AF. Tay Ninh Pr, III Corps.

Anta Village (YA 940-010)
Deserted ville at eastern base of Chu Pong Mtn, apx 55 km SW Pleiku and immed SW LZ X-Ray (Ia Drang battle site). Staging area for NVA 32d Rgt in '65. See LZ X-Ray, Chu Pong, Albany and Ia Drang River. Pleiku Pr, II Corps.

Antelope, USS (n/a)
PG 86. Patrol Gunboat.

Antenna Valley (AT 90-36)
A.k.a. the Hiep Duc Valley. Generally 10 km SSE An Hoa, WNW LZ Ross, SW FSB Ryder and 25 km SW LZ Baldy. Per *Not Going Home Alone*, p 189, given name because of large number of USMC RTOs killed there in mid to late '66 (RTOs were prime target and antennas on radios they carried made them easy to pinpoint). Another source indicates the ubiquitous antennas of USMC Bn HQs that dotted valley during 1st major op there was source of name? During Op Mississippi, was evacuated of all civilians in Fall '66, who were relocated to My Loc (2). Also listed at AT 91-37 and AT 84-34. 1st Mar Div, Americal List. Quang Nam Pr, I Corps.

Anthoi Islands (US 95-05?)
See An Thoampoi Island. Kien Giang Pr?, IV Corps.

Anti-Corruption Movement (n/a)
See Glossary.

Anvil, LZ (XD 835-645)
Apx 6 km S Ben Hai River, 23 km N Khe Sanh CB, 53 km WNW Quang Tri and 31 km WNW Cam Lo. Apr70 XXIV Corps grid per Don Armstrong. Quang Tri Pr, I Corps.

Anyen Point (US 9-1)
See Point An Yen. Kien Giang Pr, IV Corps.

Anzac, HMAS (n/a)
Australian Escort ship serving under US 7th Flt.

ANZAC Compound (YS 43-68)
See Nui Dat (Australian-New Zealand Army Corps).

ANZAC Forces (n/a)
See 1ATF in Major HQs Section.

Anzio, FSB (YD 929-072)
A.k.a. FSB La Son. Near Thon Xuan Hoa, apx 9 km SSE Phu Bai, 10 km E FSB Arsenal and just W QL-1. HQ 2d/505th Inf, 82d Abn Sep68 and in 2d Bde/101st Abn AO in '69-71. Also listed at YD 934-072 per XXIV Corps Index courtesy of Armstrong. Thua Thien Pr, I Corps.

Ao Ho, Lac (CP 05-14)
Freshwater lake apx 3 km W Qui Nhon. On NC49-01 JOG. Khanh Hoa Pr, II Corps.

Ao Xom Luoampoi (CQ 0-8)
Bay at 13°23'N-109°14'E. Phu Yen Pr, II Corps.

Ap An Tri (WS 97-40)
See Giao Duc. Dinh Tuong Pr, IV Corps.

Ap Bac (various) (XS/WS)
Name Ap Bac was ubiquitous in III/IV Corps, and because several significant actions occurred near places with this name, care must be used in determining site. Some examples are in grid squares: XS 1-7, 15-72, 29-55, 9-4, 8-6 and WS 4-7. III/IV Corps.

Ap Bac Heliport (XS 153-727)
Apx 14 km WSW Thuy Dog AF and 68 km WSW Tan Son Nhut AB/Saigon. "Heliport #505, El. 7', sod, confined by barbed wire and antennas, at 10°36'30"N-106°03'10"E," per Feb73 TAD. Kien Tuong Pr, IV Corps.

Ap Bac II, Battle of (n/a)
Battle of Ap Bac II occurred 27May67, when 514th VC Bn and 2d Bde/US 25th Inf Div fought here. US elements were A & C/5th/60th Inf (Mech), A/3d/47th Inf, 9th Div. IV Corps?

Ap Bac SF Camp (XS 153-727)
Apx 15 km WSW Thuy Dong AF, 45 km NW My Tho and 65 km WSW Saigon. Home of 5th SF Det. A-416 (was 221), Oct65. Moved to Kinh Quan I. Grid per *SF Order of Battle*. Kien Tuong Pr, IV Corps.

Ap Bac, Battle of ('63) (XS 29-55)
In Mekong Delta apx 65 km SW Saigon, 22 km NW My Tho, 5 km N Kinh Cai Canal and 1 km SSW Ap Tan Thoi. Site of infamous 2Jan63 Battle of Ap Bac, during which ARVN 7th Inf Div outnumbered VC by 10-1, but were defeated. The ARVN traded 5 helos, 80+ dead and over 100 WIA for 18 VC dead and 39 WIA.[35] Generally regarded as 1st major battle of ARVN and a clear harbinger of how difficult future would be. An entire chapter is devoted to Ap Bac in *A Bright Shining Lie*, p 203-263. See Tan Thoi. Kien Tuong Pr, IV Corps.

Ap Bac, Battle of ('67) (XS 84-66)
Battle took place Jun67, and not to be confused with infamous '63 Battle of Ap Bac. On N bank of Rach Nui Creek apx 1 km E Ap Bac, 7 km S to SSE Can Giuoc and 23 km due S Saigon. Involved 2d/46th ARVNs, 3d/47th and 4th/47th Inf (Riverine), 9th Inf MRF and VC 5th Nha Be Bn, during Op Concordia I. 46 US KIA, 150 WIA, and 255 VC KIA. Gia Dinh Pr?, III Corps.

Ap Bau Bang, FSB (XT 78-48)
A.k.a. Firebase 20. See Firebase 20 for detail. Binh Duong Pr, III Corps.

Ap Bau Bang (XT 79-46)
On QL-13, between War Zones C and D, apx 40 km S An Loc, 10 km N Lai Khe, 28 km due E Tri Tamand, and 26 km NNE Ben Cat. Site of Battle of Ap Bau Bang I, 15Nov65, 1st major engagement of 1st Inf Div in War. In action, 2d/2d Inf, 1st Inf Div was attacked by 272d & 273d Rgts/9th NVA Div. 2d battle of Ap Bau Bang took place during Op Junction City, Mar-Apr67 (see FSB 20). 161 Bty, RNZA (Kenning's Bty 13Jun65-13Jun66) FSB set here 23-27Sep65. Binh Duong Pr, III Corps.

Ap Bau Bang II (XT 78-48)
On QL-13 apx 1,500 meters N Ap Bau Bang. Battle of Ap Bau Bang II took place 19-20Mar67, during Op Junction City. A/3d/5th Cav and B/7th/9th Arty (both 9th Inf Div units opcon to 1st Inf Div) were attacked at FSPB 14 (apx 48 km N Saigon. B & C Trps reinforced base after initial VC mortar and ground attack. 2 more assaults were then repulsed by armor, 29 airstrikes and 2,148 arty rounds. 227 NVA KIA. See Firebase 20 for other detail. Cited in *Doc: Platoon Medic*, p 15. Binh Duong Pr, III Corps.

Ap Baw Bang (XT 79-46)
See Ap Bau Bang. Binh Duong Pr, III Corps.

Ap Ben Do (XS 820-600?)
See Doi Ma Creek, Battle of. NPIA Gaz lists villes of this name at XS 820-600, XS 736-640, XS 736-640, and YT 016-015. Long An Pr, III Corps.

Ap Binh Thuy (XS 632-998)
Apx 5 km NE Duc Hoa AF and 17 km WNW Tan Son Nhut AB. Also listed at XT 632-998, which is apx 15 km SW Loc Ninh in Binh Long Pr and thought to be in error. A & C Cos 2d/14th Inf, 25th ID, here during Op Toan Thang II, '68. Hau Nghia Pr, III Corps.

Ap Binh Trung SF Camp? (XT 165-554)
Apx 4 km N Tay Ninh W AF on main NW border road, perhaps 6 km NW Tay Ninh. Unknown if US or ARVN camp? Listed on webpage of 187th AHC's Bn Supp extracts at: www.kbi.org/187thahc/ incident_67.htm. Tay Ninh Pr, III Corps.

Ap Bu Gia Map Airfield (YU 340-368)
See Djamap AF. Phuoc Long Pr, III Corps.

Ap Cao Xa 3, FSB (XT 110-490)
A.k.a. FSB Elsenberg. At Ap Cao Xa, apx 6 km SW Tay Ninh West AF, and 3 km ENE Ben Soi. 15Feb69. Tay Ninh Pr, III Corps.

Ap Cau Cay (n/a)
Mapsheet name of L-7014-6431-4. SVN.

Ap Cha Do, Battle of (XT 413-683)
Area apx 3 km SSE of what later became FSB Gold (XT 386-705), some 16 km NE Nui Ba Den. During Op Attleboro, Dec 66, 1st/28th Inf, 1st Inf Div defeated elements of 272d VC and 101st NVA Rgts in this battle. See FSB Gold. Tay Ninh Pr, III Corps.

Ap Da Chong (WJ 3-2)
See Notre Dame Rock. NVN.

Ap Dinh Ba (n/a)
Mapsheet name of L-7014-6530-1. SVN.

Ap Do Moi (n/a)
See Glossary.

Ap Do Trong (YD 671-311)
A.k.a. Ap Duc Trong. Apx 10 km NW Hue, 6 km NE LZ Sally and 4 km E QL-1. B & C/1st/502d Inf hvy contact here 3Mar68. Bn CO, his RTO, Bn S-2 and Cmd Pilot all wounded in C&C bird. Bn S-2 DOA at Camp Evans. 9-11Mar68, 1st/502d Inf again had heavy contact here; 8 KIA, 17 WIA, 2 MIA/KIA. Thua Thien Pr, I Corps.

Ap Doan Van (n/a)
Mapsheet name of L-7014-6433-2. SVN/Cambodia.

Ap Don, Outpost (XT 801-061)
Apx 7 km due N Tan Son Nhut AB and 11 km due W Di An. Gia Dinh Pr?, III Corps.

Ap Dong (XS 320-985)
Possibly Ap Dong (2)? Ville at N edge of Tan Son Nhut AB. Site of heavy fighting during day-long Battle of Ap Dong, 2Feb68, involving a Trp of 1st Sqdn, 4th Cav, elements of 2d/27th Inf, 25th Inf Div and 3d Sqdn, 4th Cav. Gia Dinh Pr, III Corps.

Ap Dong An, FSB (BS 760-835?)
A.k.a. FSB Dong An. If Dong An at listed grid is correct site, was along Rte 521, apx 16 km NE Quang Ngai and near mouth of Song Chau Me Dong. Rte 521 runs from coast above My Lai to QL-1, apx 3 km N of Quang Ngia. No other data. Quang Ngia Pr?, I Corps.

Ap Dong Lang (YD-680-318)
Apx 10 km NW Hue and 7 km NE LZ Sally. Apr68 A/1st/502d Inf, 101st Abn hvy contact here, 6 KIA, 23 WIA. Thua Thien Pr, I Corps.

Ap Duc Trong (YD 67-31)
A.k.a. Ap Do Trong. Apx 10 km NW Hue and 7 km NE LZ Sally. B/C Cos/1st/502d Inf hvy contact here 3Mar68. Bn CO, his RTO, Bn S-2 and cmd pilot all wounded when C&C bird hit by ground fire. Bn S-2 DOA at Camp Evans. 9-11Mar68, 1s/502d Inf again had heavy contact here; 8 KIA, 17 WIA, 2 MIA/KIA. Thua Thien Pr, I Corps.

Ap Gia-Bac (n/a)
Mapsheet name of L-7014-6631-4. SVN.

Ap Gu, Battle of (XT 43-85?)
29Mar-1Apr67 during Op Junction City. See LZ George for location. Discussed in detail in *Cedar Falls-Junction City*. Tay Ninh Pr, III Corps.

Ap Kim Ngoc (YD 772-119)
On S bank of Song Ta Trach River, apx 1.5 km SE Nam Hoa District HQ and 9 km due South Hue. D/1st/502d Inf trained RF Plts here in early '70. Ferry site here was still in use in 1990. Thua Thien Pr, I Corps.

Ap Lai Bang (n/a)
Mapsheet name of L-7014-6441-1. SVN.

Ap Lai Bang (YD 608-255)
Ville on E Bank of Song Bo River along Rte 598 apx 16 km W Hue. Apparently battle site in '68 involving 2d Bde/101st Abn. Thua Thien Pr, I Corps.

Ap Lai Xa (YD 638-310)
Apx 13 km NW Citadel AF and 10 km ESE Camp Evans. A/1st/502d Inf, 101st Abn had hvy contact here 29Feb68, then returned 2Mar68 for another op. Near Thua Thien/Quang Tri Pr border, I Corps.

Ap Long Linh (Hai Long) (n/a)
Mapsheet L-7014-6630-1. True name is: Hai Long (Ap Long Linh). SVN.

Ap Long Thoi (XT 250-470)
Apx 4 km SSE Tay Ninh and 11 km S Nui Ba Den. Tay Ninh Pr, III Corps.
Ap Long Thonh Airfield (WS 521-416)
See Long Xuyen AF. Chau Doc Pr, IV Corps.
Ap Luong Tay (n/a)
Mapsheet name of L-7014-6631-2. SVN.
Ap Nam CAP (AT 93-84?)
Possibly along QL-1, apx 1 km S Nam O Bridge and directly W Red Beach. Hotel 1, 3rd CAG per Tim Duffie. Thua Thien Pr, I Corps.
Ap Nam O (AT 94-83)
Ville on QL-1 about 1 km S Nam O Bridge and directly W Red Beach. Quang Tri Pr, I Corps.
Ap Nong Thoampoi (YS 5-6)
A.k.a. Long Thoi. Vicinity of Dat Do, NE Vung Tau. Phuoc Tuy Pr, III Corps.
Ap Quan Nam (2) (AT 8-8)
A.k.a. Le My. Quang Nam Pr, I Corps.
Ap Ray (XS)
See Doi Ma Creek, Battle. Long An Pr, III Corps.
Ap Son Thuy (Phuoc Binh) (n/a)
Mapsheet name of L-7014-6332-1. SVN.
Ap Suoi Nghe, FSB (YS 43-71)
Apx 2 km W Rte-2 and 5 km N Nui Dat on S edge of Binh Ba Rubber Plantation. 161 Bty, RNZA (Martin's Bty 28Apr67-6Apr68) FSB set here 6-9Aug67 See Slope 30. Phuoc Tuy Pr, III Corps.
Ap Tan Hoa, FSB (XT 440-056)
Apx 12 km ESE Duc Hue AF, 10 km WNW Khiem Cuong and 40 km WNW Saigon. Dec68. Hau Nghia Pr, III Corps.
Ap Tan Hoa Airfield (XT 437-071)
See Hiep Hoa AF. Hau Nghia Pr, III Corps.
Ap Tan Thanh (XS 671-614)
A.k.a. Camp Scott and Tan Tru. See FSB Tan Tru. Long An Pr, III Corps.
Ap Tan Thoi (XS 29-56)
Ville 1,500 meters N Ap Bac and apx 62 km SW Saigon. Report of VC Co here Dec63 led to 1st Battle of Ap Bac. See Tan Thoi and Ap Bac. Dinh Tuong Pr, IV Corps.
Ap Tau O Bridge (XT 76-75)
On QL-13, 16 km S An Loc. A Trp 1st Sqdn, 4th Cav, attached 1st Inf Div, ambushed here by 272d VC Rgt 8Jun66, during Op El Paso II. III Corps.
Ap Tau O (XT 76-75)
See Minh Thanh Road. III Corps.
Ap Tay, FSB? (YS 390-620)
Apparently a.k.a. or adj to town of Hoa Long, at intersection of QL-2, QL-15 and LTL-23, apx 3 km SSW Nui Dat and 4 km NE Ba Ria. French Fort here used as FSB by 161 Bty, RNZA. See French Fort (Ap Tay). Elements of ANZAC 1ATF here at various times. Phuoc Tuy Pr, III Corps.
Ap Thai Thong 2 (XT 187-494)
At NW corner of Tay Ninh, apx 2 km E Tay Ninh West AF. Attacked/occupied by NVA, 10-11Sep68, and retaken by SVN Marine counterattack on 12Sep68, but attack met heavy resistance and was unable to secure ville until 0930 hrs, 13Sep68. [36] Tay Ninh Pr, III Corps.
Ap Thai Thong (XT 191-502)
At NW corner of Tay Ninh, apx 2 km E Tay Ninh West AF. Attacked and occupied by NVA forces 10-11Sep68 and retaken by SVN Marine counterattack on 12Sep68. [37] Tay Ninh Pr, III Corps.
Ap Thonh Nguyen Airfield (YS 135-935)
See Long Thanh AF. Bien Hoa Pr, III Corps.
Ap Trai (XT 635-243)
Apx 7 km due N Cu Chi CB. 2d/14th Inf, 25th Inf Div and 2d/49th ARVN Rgt, joint ops here Summer '69. Data per www.en.com/users/kramsey/ dragons.html. Dinh Tuong Pr?, III Corps.
Apache, FSB? (XS 883-989)
Possible FSB? N of QL-1 at Hiep Binh Xa, apx 7 km ENE Tan Son Nhut AB and 3 km SW Thu Duc. 15Dec68. Gia Dinh Pr, III Corps.
Apache, Fort (various)
See Fort Apache.
Apache, FSB (YD 629-222)
Apx 9 km due W Hue, 7 km SSE An Lo Bridge and 15 km NNW FSB Birmingham. Recon, 1st/502d Inf, here 26Oct68, per 1st/502d Inf '68 Bn Hist Supp. Thua Thien Pr, I Corps.
Apache, FSB (YT 730-245)
Apx 8 km SSE Vo Dat and 75 km E to ENE Bien Hoa AB. 7Dec70-28Feb71. Binh Tuy Pr, III Corps.
Apache, LZ (n/a)
1st/35th Inf, 4th Div here. No data. II Corps.
Apache, OP (YD 629-223)
See OP Apache. Thua Thien Pr, I Corps.
Apache Platoon (n/a)
See Glossary.
Apache Snow, Operation (n/a)
10May-7Jun69. Joint op of USMC's 9th Marines and elements of 2d Bde/101st Abn. 977 rptd enemy KIA, per *VN Order of Battle*, pp 9-14. Thua Thien Pr, I Corps.
Ape, LZ (BN 284-582)
Apx 14 km due N Song Mao AF, 66 km NE Phan Thiet and 4 km E Rte 404. 2Mar67. Binh Thuan Pr, II Corps.
APL-5 (n/a)
Auxiliary Personnel, Light. USN Non-Self-Propelled barracks ship/barge. SVN.
APL-26, USS (n/a)
USN Auxiliary Personnel Lighter used as barracks barge housing elements of MRF. Had 2 boilers for steam/hot water, and evaporators that produced over 24,000 gal of drinking water daily, 2 generators for elect and AC. Also had minor surgery ward and sick bay. Joined TF-117, Apr67 as "hotel" for USN boat crews and USA 9th Inf Div (Riverine Inf). Supt a River Assault Div (RAD) and its staff, two 9th Div rifle Cos and their HHC, as well as USN EOD team and 2 Tugs (YTB-784 and YTB-785). Plied Mekong Delta and Rung Sat Special Zone, III, IV Corps.
APL-27 (n/a)
Barracks Barge (non-self-propelled), per Ralph Fries.
APL-30 (n/a)
Auxiliary Personnel, Light. USN Non-Self-Propelled barracks ship/barge. SVN
Apollo, FSB (BP 147-007)
A.k.a. LZ Apollo. At or near Dalat/Lien Khuong AF, along southern outskirts of Duc Trong, apx 22 km SSW Dalat, 10

km ESE Thanh Binh, and 65 km WNW Phan Rang. 2 sections of B Bty/2d/17th FA here 1May-15Jul70 and Oct-Nov70, supt 5th/22nd Arty. Data per Nolan Putman and Jack Picciolo. Also listed at BP 149-007. Tuyen Duc Pr, III Corps.

Apollo, FSB (XT 637-507)
Apx 19 km NW Lai Khe and 16 km SW Chon Thanh AF. FSPB. Binh Duong Pr, III Corps.

Apollo, FSB (YD 7-0)
On bald hill (Hill 378 or possibly Nui Sa Truc, Hill 416) apx 4.5 km due S FSB Birmingham and 15 km due S Hue. 101st Abn and/or 82d Abn? Thua Thien Pr, I Corps.

Apollo, LZ (various)
See FSB Apollo. I Corps and III Corps.

Apowan, Baie d' (YH 1-9)
Bay at 20°43'N-107°02'E. On NF48-16 JOG. NVN.

Apple, FSB (YT 280-100)
Along QL-1, apx 28 km E Bien Hoa. A Trp/3d Sqdn/5th Cav here. 30Apr68. Bien Hoa Pr, III Corps.

Apple, LZ (BQ 97-66)
Apx 26 NNW Tuy Hoa, immed N Trung Thanh, SW Trung Luong, SW LZ Eagle and S LZ Axe. Involved in Battle of Dong Tre, Op Nathan Hale, Jun66. Major fight here of 2d/7th Cav, 1st Cav, 24Jun66. Discussed at length in *The Fields of Bamboo*, pp 149-156 et al. Phu Yen Pr, II Corps.

Apple, LZ (YD 305-554)
Near QL-1 and immed W of Quang Tri AF, about 5 km NW Quang Tri. Apr70 XXIV Corps grid per Don Armstrong. Quang Tri Pr, I Corps.

Apple Island (BT 040-561)
Apple-shaped island in Song Thu Bon River, apx 10 km WSW Hoi An, 20 km SSE Da Nang AB and 3 km W QL-1. Quang Nam Pr, I Corps.

April, LZ (XT 161-421)
Apx 2 km due S Long My and 6 km SW Tay Ninh. 8Jan66. Tay Ninh Pr, III Corps.

April, FSB/LZ (ZA 058-409)
Apx 23 km WSW Pleiku and 16 km WNW Catecka AF. Dec69-31Oct70. 4th Div AO, '70. Bty B/6th/29th Arty here Dec69. Also listed at ZA 088-409 (per 31Jan704th Div ORLL, courtesy Jim Henderson) which, if accurate, was 18 km WSW Pleiku, 15 km WNW Catecka, 14 km NNW Oasis. Name per Jim Claeys. 4th Div 31Jan70 ORLL grid per Jim Henderson. Pleiku Pr, II Corps.

Aquarius, FSB (AQ 889-016)
A.k.a. FSB Ban Me Thuot East (?) or LZ Doris K.(AQ 887-011)? Apx 1 km E FSB Doris K, 1 km SE Ban Me Thuot East AF and 10 km ESE Ban Me Thuot. Bty C/2d/17th Arty here, Nov70-Apr71. Grid/arty info per Nolan Putman. Darlac Pr, II Corps.

Aquarius, LZ (BR 457-600)
Along road between An Khe and Kannack AF, apx 7 km SE Kannack, 15 km N An Khe and 4 km NW De Ponang. 4th Div AO, '70; Bty B/4th/42d Arty here May70. Name/grid per Jim Claeys. Also listed at BR 455-602. Binh Dinh Pr, II Corps.

Arab, FSB (YD 142-617)
On N side of QL-9, apx 20 km WNW Quang Tri, 4 km NE Cam Lo. XXIV Corps grid. Quang Tri Pr, I Corps.

Aranyaprathet Airfield (TA 2-1)
Apx 8 km from Cambodia, 210 km due E Bangkok per Feb67 Natl Geo map. El. 150'. Thailand.

Araphaho (n/a)
6Apr70, XXIV Corps future-use 5th Div FSB name.

Arc En Ciel (n/a)
Famous Saigon restaurant. Referenced in *Street Without Joy*, p 139. Gia Dinh Pr, I Corps.

ARC LAPES (n/a)
See Glossary.

ARC LIGHT (n/a)
See Glossary.

Archer (n/a)
6Apr70, XXIV Corps future 101st Abn FSB name.

Archer, FSB (YS 203-847)
On E side of QL-15, apx 38 km SE Bien Hoa, 12 km NW FSB Nelson and 38 km NW Nui Dat. 161 Bty, RNZA (Hitching's Bty 14Apr68-18Mar69) FSB set here 18-21Jul68. On 1ATF NCO trng map per John Hollett. Also listed YS 20-84. Bien Hoa Pr, III Corps.

Archimedes Patti, Major (WJ 88-25)
See Glossary.

Archipel Fai Tsi Long (YH 5-9)
Vicinity of Long Chau. NIMA data. NVN.

Area, FSB (YT 515-665)
See Ares. Long Khanh Pr, III Corps.

Area Dog, FSB (BS 88-01?)
See LZ English. Binh Dinh Pr, II Corps.

Area Crossroads, FSB (BQ 071-715)
A.k.a. FSB Crossroads? Apx 5 km NNE Ban Bok, 13 km NNE Buon Blech AF and 20 km SW Cheo Reo/Hou Bon. Bty B/2d/17th Arty supt 1st/8th Cav, 1st Cav, 21Jun66. Data per Jack Picciolo. Phu Bon Pr, II Corps.

Arequier, Pointe de l' (ZJ 0-6)
See Pointe Arequier. NVN.

Ares, FSB (YT 515-665)
Apx 11 km NW Lot Tan, 46 km ESE Dong Xoai, 42 km NNW Vo Dat and 74 km NE Bien Hoa AB. Opened 23Oct70 at this grid. Also listed at YT 492-665 on 28Feb71 rpt. 1st/12th Cav Data per *1st Cav Div Op Rpt, ending 31Oct70*, courtesy Peter Cole. Sometimes spelled Aries. Long Khanh Pr, III Corps.

Ares, LZ (XD 901-550)
See Aries. Quang Tri Pr, I Corps.

Argonne, FSB (XD 676-573)
A.k.a. Hill 1308. Apx 2 km E Laotian border, 13 km S southern edge of DMZ, 3 km SW Dong Sa Mui (Hill 1550) and 15 km due W FSB Neville. Used for observation into Laos and portions of Ho Chi Minh Trail. On 29Mar69, while trying to reopen base, helo carrying a 3d Recon Bn, 3d Mar Div advance team was shot down on LZ with 6 KIA, 11 WIA from crash and rescue attempts. On 2d day, 8 more KIA and 23 WIA were suffered by elements taking hill. On 21Mar69, LTC George Sargent, Jr. CO 1st/4th Marines was KIA here by mortar fire. PFC Robert Jenkins awarded MOH during attack here 5Mar69. Also listed at XD 675-573 in XXIV Corps Index and XD 756-532 in *The Final Formation*, p 130. Map at p 58, *US Marines in Vietnam-1969*. Quang Tri Pr, I Corps.

Aries, FSB (YT 515-665)
See Ares. Long Khanh Pr, III Corps.

Aries, LZ (XD 901-550)
Apx 15 km NNE Khe Sanh CB, and 44 km due W Quang Tri. Apr70 XXIV Corps grid per Don Armstrong. Quang Tri Pr, I Corps.
Arizona (n/a)
See Project Arizona in Glossary.
Arizona Territory, The (AT 85-53)
A.k.a. An Hoa Basin. Large, broad plain generally NE An Hoa, SW Hill 55, W Go Noi Island, immed N Football Island and dominated by confluence of Song Vu Gia and Song Thu Bon. Area between those rivers in Dai Loc and Duc Duc Districts was given name to reflect its wild-west characteristics and danger. Noted for its dense foliage, booby traps, mines and ubiquitous enemy forces. Most units dreaded operating in this area. USMC and Americal. Quang Nam Pr, I Corps.
Arizona, LZ (XD 966-616)
Apx 22 km NE Khe Sanh, 38 km WNW Quang Tri. Apr70 XXIV Corps grid per Don Armstrong. Quang Tri Pr, I Corps.
Arkansas, FSB (915-403)
On N bank of Mekong, apx 9 km ENE Sa Dec. 30Jan68 and 30Apr68. Dinh Tuong Pr?, IV Corps.
Arlington (n/a)
6Apr70, XXIV Corps future-use 5th Div FSB name.
Arlington, USS (n/a)
AGMR-2. Aux Ship, per Ralph Fries.
Arm'ee Clandestine (n/a)
See Glossary.
Armageddon, FSB (BR 420-645)
A.k.a. LZ Armageddon. At or adj (W?) Kannack AF, 18 km WNW Vinh Thanh AF, 22 km NNW An Khe and 80 km NW Qui Nhon. 8Oct69-31Oct70. 4th Div AO, '70. Per John Linn, B/2d/35th Inf here Jan 70, and was small FSB whose name put fear in his comrade's minds. Mentioned on 129th AHC's webpage at www.vhfcn. rg/129th/129thhist. htm. Also spelled Armagedden and Armegeddon. Name/grid per Jim Claeys Binh Dinh Pr, II Corps.
Armed Forces Council (n/a)
See Glossary.
Armed Forces Institute (n/a)
See Cu Chi University.
Armed Forces Radio and TV (n/a)
See Glossary.
Armegedon, FSB (BR 420-645)
See Armageddon, FSB. Binh Dinh Pr, II Corps.
Armor School, ARVN (XT 92-00?)
See ARVN Armor School. Binh Duong Pr, III Corps.
Army Boats in Vietnam (n/a)
See Glossary.
Army Education Center (n/a)
See Glossary.
Army Reporter, The (n/a)
See Glossary.
Army Vessel Lt Col John U.D. Page (n/a)
See *Lt Col John U.D. Page*.
Arnn, Camp (WS 13-84?)
On S bank of Song Hau Giang River at Chau Phu, apx 2 km E Cambodia, 3 km NW Chau Doc AF and 75 km NE Ha Tien. HQ of SF Det B-42. Camp named to honor its CO, Maj. John O. Arnn, US Army SF, KIA 26Dec65, shot by VC snipers while leading unit run (units Ops Sgt also KIA on that run). Data per V*ietnam Military lore 1959-1973*. Chau Doc Pr, IV Corps. [38]
Arnold J. Isbell, USS (n/a)
DD-869, per Ralph Fries.
Arnold Trail, LZ (BR 726-607)
Apx 12 km due E Vinh Thanh AF, 17 km W NW Phu Cat AB and 10 km SW Hoi San. 30Apr70-31Oct70. 4th Div AO. Name/grid per Jim Claeys. See also Arnold's Trail. Binh Dinh Pr, II Corps.
Aro, Camp (YC 6-2)
See A Ro or Aroh. Quang Nam Pr, I Corps.
Aroh (YC 67-25)
See A Ro. Thua Thien Pr, I Corps.
Aroh Airfield (YC 669-251)
See A Ro AF. Thua Thien Pr, I Corps.
Aroh Heliport (YC 815-848)
A.k.a. A Ro Heliport. Apx 35 km due S Hue, 60 km WNW Da Nang. Heliport #507, El. 427', at 16°08'N 107°39'E, per Feb73 TAD. Thua Thien Pr, I Corps.
Aroh, Camp (YC 81-85)
In Ruong Ruong Valley, apx 60 km WNW Da Nang. Possible SF camp here with SF Det 414. There was an SF camp at A Ro (YC 6-2), but there is also an Aroh ville at listed grid. Thua Thien Pr, I Corps.
Arron, FSB (YD 797-108)
Apparent error or variant of FSB Arrow, as grid is identical. See Arrow, FSB. Thua Thien Pr, I Corps.
Arrow, FSB (YD 798-107)
A.k.a. Nui Dong Hoai and FSB Panther II. Apx 3.5 km NNW FSB Arsenal, 9 km WSW Phu Bai and 4 km SE Nam Hoa. Possibly 82d Abn? Likely built in '68 and closed by Fall '69. Author in area, Nov69-Sep70, but unaware of FSB here then. Also listed at YD 800-100, 20Nov69. Thua Thien Pr, I Corps.
Arrow, FSB (YS 481-565)
Apx 12 km SSE Nui Dat, 5.5 km SSW FSB Horseshoe, 2.5 km NW FSB Thrust. Per 1ATF NCO trng map. Phuoc Tuy Pr, III Corps.
Arsenal, FSB (YD 812-080)
A.k.a. FSB Panther III, FSB Victory(?), Nui Khe Tre, and Hill 140. Apx 8 km SW Phu Bai, 10 km ESE FSB Birmingham, 9 km SE Pohl Bridge, 7 km SE Nam Hoa Dist. HQ and 600 meters E Song Ta Trach River. 1st/502d Inf here, '69-71. Per 101st Abn ORLL of 9Dec69, p 40, beginning 4Jul69, Engrs built 7 km road from Camp Eagle to what had once been FSB Panther III (82d Abn rpts put it on Hill 46, YD 810-060, and say it was attacked by 50 sappers, 29Aug68?), and site was reopened/renamed as Arsenal. Possibly only FSB to have enemy who attacked it buried within its perimeter. During attack night of 6Apr70, against C/1st/502d Inf and 2d/11th Arty, NVA soldier who penetrated wire was killed while directing RPG fire from 4-hole outhouse at S end of FSB. Men of C Co then built grave on spot and marked it with sign reading, "*Here Lies an NVA Soldier Who Knows Death By Another Name. C Company, 1st/502d Infantry*." Author also recalls sign in front of mess tent reading: "*Kill 3 Rats and take them to the medical tent for a 2 Day In-Country R&R*" (Bubonic Plague was problematic; hence effort to eradicate rats). Author also recalls a Bn Cmdr here beseeching troops to,

"Kill me a gook and I'll give you a 2 Day R&R;" hence, 3 rats apparently equaled 1 human in Vietnam War math. 321st Arty, several Btys 105mm and 81mm plt here as well. See Bob Kalsu in Glossary, Ripcord and Panther III. Thua Thien Pr, I Corps.

Arsenal Road (YD 827-137 to 812-080)
101st Abn ORLL of 9Dec69, states that beginning 4Jul69, Engrs built 7 km road from Camp Eagle to FSB Arsenal. Thua Thien Pr, I Corps.

Arthur, LZ (XD 920-591)
Apx 6 km W QL-9, about 12 km NE Khe Sanh CB, 42 km due W Quang Tri and 22 km WSW Cam Lo. Apr70 XXIV Corps grid per Don Armstrong. Quang Tri Pr, I Corps.

Article 15 (n/a)
See Glossary.

Artillery Base 4 (YS 410-870)
Apx 18 km NNW Nui Dat/Luscombe AF, and 11 km SSW Blackhorse AF. 2Apr68. Long Khanh/Phuoc Tuy Pr border, III Corps.

Artillery Base I (XT 280-690)
Along TL-4, apx 12 km N Nui Ba Den, 20 km NNE Tay Ninh. 22Feb67. Also listed at XT 270-690, 15Mar67. Tay Ninh Pr, III Corps.

Artillery Base I (XT 709-815)
If grid correct, was 8 km SW An Loc and 16 km NE Minh Thanh AF. 7Jul66. Binh Long Pr, III Corps.

Artillery Base I (XT 75-34?)
A.k.a. The French Fort. Along QL-4 apx 2 km from Ben Cat at NE corner of Iron Triangle. 3d Bde/1st Inf Div and 155-mm Bty here during Op Cedar Falls. Data per *Cedar Falls-Junction City*, which describes it as being near Arty bases II and III. Binh Duong Pr, III Corps.

Artillery Base II (XT 280-790)
A.k.a. Firebase II or 2, Patrol Base II and FSB Cayalya. Along Rte 4 at Prek Klok, apx 32 km NE Tay Ninh, 12 km SSW Katum, 5 km SE Artillery Base I and 18 km S Cambodia. SF Camp/airstrip here built '67. Battle of Prek Klok II here 10Mar67, during Op Junction City, when 2d/2d Inf (Mech), 2d/33d Arty and elements of 168th Engr Bn were attacked by 272d VC Rgt. At 2208 hrs, VC initiated heavy mortar/grnd attack answered by US counter-bty and recon by fire. By midnight battle was over. 3 US KIA, 38 WIA, 197 NVA KIA. Tay Ninh Pr, III Corps.

Artillery Base II (XT 770-780)
If grid correct, was apx 2 km E An Loc and 21 km SSE Loc Ninh. 8Jul66. Binh Long Pr, III Corps.

Artillery Base III (XT 290-815)
Along E side of TL-4, apx 9 km SSW Katum AF, and 32 km N to NNE Tay Ninh. 22Feb67. Tay Ninh Pr, III Corps.

Artillery Base IV (XT 330-920)
N Katum AF, apx 43 km NNE Tay Ninh, and 6 km from Cambodia. 15Mar67. Tay Ninh Pr, III Corps.

Artillery Base V (XT 350-920)
Apx 2 km E Arty Base IV, 3 km NE Katum AF. 15Mar67. Tay Ninh Pr, III Corps.

Artillery Base VI (XT 270-970)
Apx 1 km S Cambodia, 9 km NW Arty Base IV, and 10 km NNW Katum AF and 46 km N Tay Ninh. 15Mar67. Tay Ninh Pr, III Corps.

Artillery Base VII (XT 240-960)
Apx 3 km SW Arty Base VI, 10 km NW Katum AF and 45 km due N Tay Ninh. 15Mar67. Tay Ninh Pr, III Corps.

Artillery Firsts (n/a)
See Glossary.

Artillery Hill (AR 228-532)
No such grid exists. See Artillery Hill at ZA 228-532. Pleiku Pr, II Corps.

Artillery Hill (AR 797-348)
A.k.a. Hill 842 and possibly Signal Mtn? Per 1st/69th Armor website map, was within perimeter of Camp Enari, along its W central edge. Some data suggests hill was called Signal Mtn? Pleiku Pr, II Corps.

Artillery Hill (BT 434-039)
A.k.a. Arty Hill and LZ Artillery Hill. In river valley apx 10 km W Chu Lai, 23 km SE Tam Ky and about 5k W QL-1 at its closest point. Possibly same Artillery Hill as that at BT 515-040? Americal List. Quang Tin Pr, I Corps.

Artillery Hill (YB 999-130)
A.k.a. FSB Yankee and Hill 1314. Apx 1 km due W Dak To 2 AF and 6 km W Tanh Can. Possibly within perimeter of AF. Grid per Nolan Putman. Kontum Pr, II Corps.

Artillery Hill (ZA 228-533)
A.k.a. FSBs Kelly and Dragon? Along W edge of QL-14, apx 5 km NNW Pleiku, 1 km SW Bien Ho Lake, 6 km WNW Pleiku/Cu Hanh AF and 5 km SSW Plei Mui. 30Apr70-31Jul70. 92d Arty here Jun68. 52d Arty Grp Cantonment here, inc. Bty A/7th/15th F Arty (hvy) and 1st/92d Arty. Per Tom Rethard, "Artillery Hill was really just that, a big hill right across the road from PA&E area in Pleiku." 4th Div base, and likely Hill 734 on map at: www.nexus. net/~911gfx/vietnam/maps/nd48-12/d48_12d. jpg. HQ Bty and SVC Bty/7th/15th Arty here, Apr-Oct71. Grid in 4th Div rpt per Jim Claeys. Also listed at ZA 2274-5355 per Craig Miller. Pleiku Pr, II Corps. [39]

Artillery Hill, LZ (BS 515-042?)
A.k.a. Arty Hill and Div Arty Hill. If grid correct, site was apx 4 km WSW Chu Lai AB, 2 km W QL-1, 7 km WNW Hoa Van, 36 km WNW Bong Son and 25 km WSW Thuan An. However, since XXIV Corps list shows it at same grid in "BT" UTM zone, listed grid is likely in error. Also listed at BT 434-039? Americal list. Binh Dinh Pr, II Corps.

Artillery Hill, LZ (BT 515-040)
A.k.a. Arty Hill and Div Arty Hill. If grid correct, site was apx 3.5 km WSW center of Chu Lai AB and 2 km W QL-1. Apr70 XXIV Corps grid per Don Armstrong. May or may not be same Artillery Hill as that listed at BT 434-090. Quang Tin Pr, I Corps.

Artillery Plateau (YD 063-547)
Original name of USMC firebase WSW Cam Lo that was later renamed Camp J. J. Carroll, 10Nov66. See Carroll, Cam, for location. Quang Tri Pr, I Corps.

Artillery Valley (n/a)
Apparently in 4th Div AO near Pleiku. II Corps.

Arty Hill (various)
See Artillery Hill. I/II Corps.

ARVN/US Laager Site (XT 614-226)
Vicinity of Trang Bao On and Truong Lap, apx 7 km NW to NNW Cu Chi Base and apx 2 km due N FSB Keene. Built 30Aug69, and used until at least 14Sep69 by 2d/14th Inf. Info/grid per Kirk Ramsey, 2/14/25th ID. 2d/14th Inf,

2d/49th ARVN Rgt here. Data per www.en.com/users/kramsey/ dragons.html. Binh Duong Pr, III Corps.

ARVN Adjutant General College (XS 8-9)
At Saigon. Gia Dinh Pr, III Corps.

ARVN Admin & Finance School (XT 91-01?)
At Thu Duc, NE Saigon. Gia Dinh Pr, III Corps.

ARVN Armor School (XT 92-00?)
NE Saigon. In difficult street fighting TF of students and faculty from this school defeated VC forces entrenched here during Tet '68. Binh Duong Pr, III Corps.

ARVN Army Social Training School (XS 8-9)
At Saigon. Gia Dinh Pr, III Corps.

ARVN Artillery School (BP 84-86?)
At Duc My. Khanh Hoa Pr, II Corps.

ARVN Band School (XS 922-997?)
At Thu Duc. Binh Duong Pr, III Corps.

ARVN Command & Staff College (BP 236-225?)
See Dalat Military Academy? Tuyen Duc Pr, II Corps.

ARVN Engineer School (XT 808-146)
At Phu Cuong17 km due N Tan Son Nhut AB. 5Apr68. Binh Duong Pr, III Corps.

ARVN Infantry School (XS 922-997?)
At Thu Duc. Binh Duong Pr, III Corps.

ARVN Junior Military Academy (YS)
At Vung Tau. Phuoc Tuy Pr, III Corps.

ARVN Logistics Management School (XS 8-9)
At Saigon. Gia Dinh Pr, III Corps.

ARVN Medical School (XS 8-9)
At Saigon. Gia Dinh Pr, III Corps.

ARVN Military Intelligence School (XS 8-9)
At Saigon. Gia Dinh Pr, III Corps.

ARVN Military Police School (YS 28-43?)
At Vung Tau. Phuoc Tuy Pr, III Corps.

ARVN Military Training Schools (n/a)
See Glossary.

ARVN National Defense College (XS 8-9)
At Saigon. Gia Dinh Pr, III Corps.

ARVN National Military Academy (BP 236-225)
See Dalat Military Academy. Tuyen Duc Pr, II Corps.

ARVN National NCO Academy (CP 04-55?)
At Nha Trang. Khanh Hoa Pr, II Corps.

ARVN Ordnance School (XS 8-9)
At Saigon. Gia Dinh Pr, III Corps.

ARVN Political Warfare College (BP 26-24?)
At Dalat. Tuyen Duc Pr, II Corps.

ARVN Quartermaster School (XS 8-9)
At Saigon. Gia Dinh Pr, III Corps.

ARVN Ranger Trng Center (XT 592-212)
See Trung Lap Trng Ctr. Hau Nghia Pr, III Corps.

ARVN Signal School (YS 28-43?)
At Vung Tau. Phuoc Tuy Pr, III Corps.

ARVN Transportation School (XS 8-9)
At Saigon. Gia Dinh Pr, III Corps.

Asan Point Refugee Camp (n/a)
On Island of Guam. See Operation New Life.

Ash, FSB (YS 366-823)
Apx 16 km NNW Nui Dat, 4 km due S FSB Dampier, 5 km SW FSB Coolah. On 1ATF NCO trng map per John Hollett. Phuoc Tuy Pr, III Corps.

Asheville, USS (n/a)
A.k.a. PG 84. Part of Coastal Flotilla 1. 165 ft long and capable of 37 knots. Armed with one 3-inch/.50-cal. gun forward, one 40mm gun aft, and four .50-cal. MGs. Op Market Time, SVN.

Ashland (n/a)
6Apr70, XXIV Corps future-use 5th Div FSB name.

Ashtabula, USS (n/a)
Aux Oiler, per Ralph Fries.

Asiatic Stamina, SS (n/a)
AO-51. Ocean Tug of MSC. See Evacuation of Da Nang, and Op Frequent Wind.

Askari, USS (n/a)
ARL-30. USN Landing Craft Repair Ship, a.k.a. ARL-30. SVN service with 9th Inf Div/MRF. See www.mrfa.org. See *YRBM-21*. III/IV Corps?

ASP 1 (AT/BT?)
Ammo Supply Point-1. III MAF's 1st Logistics ammo supply stg area adj Camp Hoover, below Freedom Hill and apx 3 km SW Da Nang AB. On 27Apr69, grass fire ignited portion of facility where defective/outdated munitions were stored. Resulting explosions triggered regular ordnance and massive explosions followed that some thought was nuclear blast. During next several days, over 40% of I Corps' ammo supply was destroyed, inc 38,000 short tons of munitions valued at over $75,000,000. Da Nang AB was closed for 24 hrs, while concussion, falling debris and related fires destroyed many buildings and much of nearby ville. 1 US KIA, 65 US WIA, with some 1,500 Viets left homeless. Took 4 months to restock reserve. Camp Hoover's 146 bldgs were almost completely destroyed. Discussion/photos in Oct2001 *Vietnam* Mag article, *Da Nang Seabee Base Destroyed*, pp 26-32, and in Apr91 *Leatherneck* Mag. Quang Nam Pr, I Corps.

ASP 340 (BR 450-455)
Ammo Supply Point 340? On QL-19, apx 2 km W An Khe. 30Apr68. Binh Dinh Pr, II Corps.

Aspen, FSB (AT 814-348?)
If grid correct, was apx 8 km SW Phuoc Binh, 14 km SSW An Hoa, 45 km SSW Da Nang and 6 km N Thach Bich. Americal List. Also listed at AT 014-348, which does not exist. Quang Nam Pr?, I Corps.

Aspen I, FSB (XT 745-840?)
Along Rte 245, apx 3 km SSW An Loc, 1.5 km SSW Xa Thanh Binh, 2.5 km N FSB Aspen II, 58 km NE Tay Ninh. FSBs Aspen I, Aspen II and Sidewinder sat in string along Rte 245, all within 8 km of An Loc protecting convoys and flank of city. 11th ACR here. Grid per Frank Penk, Jr. Also listed at XT 747-801, 12Aug68. Binh Long Pr, III Corps.

Aspen I, FSB (XT 748-801?)
If grid correct, was apx 7 km S An Loc and 1 km W QL-13. Also listed at XT 745-840. Binh Long Pr, III Corps.

Aspen II, FSB (XT 745-823)
A.k.a. Aspen 2. Along Rte 245, apx 6 km SSW An Loc, 3 km S Xa Thanh Binh, 2.5 km S FSB Aspen I, 57 km NE Tay Ninh. FSBs Aspen I, Aspen II and Sidewinder sat in string along Rte 245, all within 8 km of An Loc protecting convoys and that flank of city. 11th ACR here. Grid per Frank Penk, Jr. Also listed at XT 747-801, 12Aug68. Binh Long Pr, III Corps.

ASRAT Site (Dong Ha) (YD 24-59)
Also known as Waterboy Control. Call sign/cmpd for 620th Tac Control Ctr (TCS), Det 1, Dong Ha, Jun-Jul66. Recon Marine George Neville and his comrades quickly discovered this facility "...had nice beer garden with mixed drinks, in glass, with ice cubes." AF personnel there admitted to Neville that prior to Marine's arrival, "they watched the NVA march across the airstrip in formation. The unwritten rule was: they didn't shoot at NVA and NVA did not shoot at them!" Grid is est. Possibly also "Skyspot" radar bombing site. Quang Tri Pr, I Corps.
Assault, LZ (BR 292-363)
Apx 22 km SW An Khe, 8 km NE LZ Dauntless. '70. 4th Div op rpt grid per Jim Claeys. Binh Dinh Pr, II Corps.
Astor, LZ (XD 990-481)
Along QL-9, apx 34 km W Quang Tri, 16 km SW Cam Lo, and 10 km WSW Mai Loc. Apr70 XXIV Corps grid per Don Armstrong. Quang Tri Pr, I Corps.
Athena, LZ/FSB (AR 778-899)
At NE edge of Kontum and on or near Kontum's major AF. A Bty, 7th/15th Arty here, Apr-Oct71. 7th/15th Arty here at one time; Bty C/6th/14th Arty here 25Jan70, with two-175mm. Grid of AR 78-89 and arty info per Nolan Putman. 4th Div 1Jan70 arty grid per Jim Henderson. On map at: www.landscaper.net/chighmap.jpg. Kontum Pr, II Corps.
Athens, LZ (BR 640-590)
Apx 6 km WSW Vinh Thanh AF, 16 km NNE An Khe and 6 km ENE De Ponang. Likely a 1st Cav LZ, built apx 22Oct65. Binh Dinh Pr, II Corps.
Atiun (n/a)
Mapsheet name of L-7014-6540-4. SVN.
Atkinson, FSB (XT 005-775?)
Apx 7 km NW Dong Xoai AF and 75 km NNE Saigon. Also listed at XT 010-788 per 1st Cav ORLL, which puts it apx 1 km NNE of listed grid. Per Peter Cole, was named to honor Sp4 Gerald Atkinson, KIA 12Mar70. Occupied by B & E/2d/7th Cav, and B/2d/19th Arty, 1st Cav when attacked by Bn of NVA 95C Rgt, 15-16Apr70, with 7 US KIA, 25 WIA. Tay Ninh Pr, III Corps.
Atlanta, FSB (ZV 178-919)
Apx 6 km SW peak of Chu Don Mtn, 20 km WSW Phu Nhon AF, 4 km S Plei Bai and 55 km S to SSW Pleiku. Near Pleiku Pr, II Corps.
Atlantic City, Operation (n/a)
13-22Sep66. 173d Abn, Dau Tieng AF. 4th/503d and B Bty, 319th Arty provided security. III Corps.
Atlantic, LZ (XD 779-560)
Overlooked river valley (to W), apx 3 km SSW FSB Neville, 55 km W to WNW Quang Tri and 12 km NNW Ap La Vien. XXIV Corps grid per Don Armstrong. Quang Tri Pr, I Corps.
Atom, LZ (YD 295-522)
Apx 4 km SSW Quang Tri AF/QL-1, and 4 km WNW La Vang AF. Apr70 XXIV Corps grid per Don Armstrong. Quang Tri Pr, I Corps.
Atou Heliport (YC 516-495)
Apx 10 km from Laos, 30 km NW A Ro AF, 90 km WSW Da Nang and 65 km NW Kham Duc. Heliport #508, El. 3,740', at 15°49'N 107°22'E, per Feb73 TAD. Quang Nam Pr, I Corps.
ATSB Ben Keo (XT 23-43?)
See Ben Keo ATSB. Tay Ninh Pr, III Corps.
ATSB Hiep Hoa (XT 43-07?)
See Hiep Hoa ATSB. Hau Nghia Pr, III Corps.
ATSB Moc Hoa (XS 03-92?)
See Moc Hoa ATSB. Kien Tuong Pr, IV Corps.
ATSB Phuoc Xuyen (WS?)
See Phuoc Xuyen ATSB.
ATSB Sea Float (VQ?)
See Sea Float. Off An Xuyen Pr?, IV Corps.
ATSB Solid Anchor (VQ 988-674)
See Solid Anchor. An Xuyen Pr, IV Corps.
ATSB Tan An (XS 55-65)
See Tan An ATSB. Long An Pr?, III Corps.
ATSB Thuyen Nhon (n/a)
See Thuyen Nhon ATSB.
ATSB Tra Cu (XS 47-97)
See Tra Cu ATSB. Long An Pr, III Corps.
Attaboy, Camp (AR 695-544?)
If grid correct, was apx 6 km NNE Pleiku. Op rpt lists grid as AR 695-544, a grid which does not exist. Grid is guess, but AR 895-544 is possibility (14 km NW Pleiku). 1Jan66. Pleiku Pr, II Corps.
Atterbury East, Camp (YT 04-07)
Described as former Hawk Missile (LAAM) site outside Camp Frenzelle-Jones in Long Binh Post, per *Rangers at War*, p 225. HQ of only Natl Guard Inf unit deployed to SVN, Indiana Rangers of D/151st Inf (LRP). Listed grid is for Long Binh Post. Bien Hoa Pr, III Corps.
Attila, LZ (XD 880-585)
Apx 24 km due W Cam Lo and 45 km WNW Quang Tri. Apr70 XXIV Corps grid per Don Armstrong. Quang Tri Pr, I Corps.
Attleboro, Operation (n/a)
14Sep-24Nov66. Initially only 198th LIB involved but became largest US op in war to that date when after significant enemy presence was discovered 19Oct66, 1st Inf Div, 3d Bde/4th Div, 173d Abn, and several ARVN Bns were added to mix. 1,106 rptd NVA/VC KIA, per *Vietnam Order of Battle*, pp 9-14. 2/503d Inf and A Bty, 3d, 319th Arty moved by air for ops near Minh Thanh. War Zone C, Tay Ninh Pr, III Corps.
Attoopeu Airfield (XB 97-38)
A.k.a. Lima Site-10. CIA/SF Lima Site apx 565 km SE Vientiane, per Feb67 Natl Geo map. Grid *per Air Facilities Data-Laos*. El. 410'. Laos.
Attopeu SF Camp (XB 97-38?)
Apx 565 km SE Vientiane, per Feb67 Natl Geo map. SF camp/FOB in Laos when it declared neutrality (23Jul62). FTT 32 here then. Per *Special Forces at War*. MR4, Laos.
Auburn (n/a)
6Apr70, XXIV Corps future-use 5th Div FSB name.
Audie, FSB (YU 435-294)
Apx 13 km SE Djamap, 25 km due N Duc Phong, 10 km WSW FSB Libby and 34 km NE Song, apx 23 km from Cambodia. Built Feb70-Apr70, by B/8th Engr Bn, 1st Cav. [40] "FSBs Django and Joan closed on 23 and 25Feb70 respectively and 8th Abn Bn displaced to establish FSB Lolita (YU 369-261). As move N gained momentum and enemy activity increased, FSB's Candy, Loan, and Audie were established on 25, 26 and 27 Feb70 respectively...The

1st Abn Bn (-) moved to establish FSB Loan, leaving one rifle Co to secure FSB Judie."[41] Reopened 21Aug70, closed 31Aug70 by 5th/7th Cav. Reopened 13Sep70 by 2d/12th Cav, and closed 16Sep70 by 2d/5th Cav. Also apparently reopened 31Oct70. Grid per Peter Cole. Phuoc Long Pr, III Corps.[42]

Audrey, LZ (XD 990-612)
A.k.a. LZ Bob (XD 983-610)? Apx 34 km WNW Quang Tri, 3 km WNW Cam Lo and 5 km N QL-1. Apr70 XXIV Corps grid per Don Armstrong. Quang Tri Pr, I Corps.

August, FSB (XT 292-620)
Apx E TL-4, apx 3 km NE peak of Nui Ba Den and 13 km NNE Tay Ninh. 5Sep67. Tay Ninh Pr, III Corps.

Augusta, LZ (BR 801-727)
Apx 12 km due S Ha Tay, 30 km NNW Phu Cat AB, 10 km WSW Lac Son, 23 km SSW Bong Son and 11 km W QL-1. 4th Div AO, '70; Bty B/4th/42d and 1st/12th Inf here 19Aug70. 30 Apr70-31Oct70. Name/grid per Jim Claeys. Also listed at BR 797-727. Binh Dinh Pr, II Corps.

Ault, USS (n/a)
DD-698, per Ralph Fries.

Aurora I, Operation (n/a)
9-17 Jul66. 173d Abn, Long Khanh Pr. Search and Destroy ops in N Long Khanh Pr, III Corps.

Aurora II, Operation (n/a)
17 Jul-3Aug66. 173d Abn deployed 80 km NE Bien Hoa. Long Khanh, Binh Tuy and Lam Dong Pr. II and III Corps.

Aussie Log Supt Compound (YS 26-86)
A.k.a. ALSG and Camp Khuu-Ngoc-Tuoc. Australian Log Supt Cmpd at Vung Tau. On 29Feb72, was transferred to 3d ARVN Corps for use as ARVN R&R Ctr, and renamed Camp Khuu-Ngoc-Tuoc. At turnover, base was capable of suptg 1,500 personnel. Grid apx. Phuoc Tuy Pr, III Corps.

Austin, FSB (XT 369-315)
A.k.a. Patrol Base Austin. Apx 21 km SE Tay Ninh, 6 km SE Khiem Hanh and 11 km E FSB Mole City. Bty B/3d/13th Arty here fired over six-hundred 155mm rnds suptg 4th/9th Inf during Battle of Mole City, 22Dec68. Data per Manchu Assn website. Also listed at 364-313 and 370-314. 1Dec68-28Feb69. Tay Ninh Pr, III Corps.

Austin, LZ (YD 208-117)
NW the N end of A Shau Valley, apx 52 km WSW Hue, 8 km ESE Tou Rout, 7 km N Laotian border and 17 km SW Dong Ap Bia (Hamburger Hill). Apr70 XXIV Corps grid per Don Armstrong. Quang Tri Pr, I Corps.

Australian Army Force VN, HQ (XS 8-9)
A.k.a. HQ, AAFV. HQ was in Saigon suptg 1 Bn RAR (which was at Bien Hoa and attached to US 173d Abn). 25May65-2May66. 1 RAR rotated back to Aust in 66, and was replaced by 5 and 6 RAR/1ATF. Data per *SF Order of Battle*. See Australian Task Force HQ, AAAGV, AAFV HQ AATTV, and AFV in Major HQs Section. Gia Dinh/Bien Hoa Pr, III Corps.

Australian Army Training Team (n/a)
See Glossary.

Australian Forces (XT 98-13 and YS 43-67)
See Australian Task Force HQ, AAAGV, AAFV HQ AATTV, and AFV in Major HQs Section and Glossary. Bien Hoa/Phuoc Tuy Pr, III Corps.

Australian Forces VN, HQ (YS 43-67)
A.k.a. HQ, AFV. 3May66-15Mar72. See Australian Task Force HQ, AAAGV, AAFV HQ AATTV, and AFV in Major HQs Section. Phuoc Tuy Pr, III Corps.

Aux Buffle, Ile (CR 1-6)
A.k.a. Hon Trau Island. Binh Dinh Pr, II Corps.

Avalon (n/a)
6Apr70, XXIV Corps future-use III MAF FSB name.

Avenger, FSB (YS 455-846)
On W side of Rte-2, apx 15 km N Nui Dat, 5 km SE FSB Coolah and in Cu Bi Rubber Plantation. 161 Bty, RNZA (Hitching's Bty 14Apr68-18Mar69) set here 9-13Aug68 and 12-24Dec68. On 1ATF NCO trng map per John Hollett. Also listed at YS 45-83. Phuoc Tuy Pr, III Corps.

Ax, FSB/LZ (ZC 002-910)
Apx 20 km SE Phu Bai, 9 km W Phu Loc and 45 km NW Da Nang. Thua Thien Pr, I Corps.

Ax, LZ (XD 883-638)
Apx 24 km WNW Cam Lo, 46 km WNW Quang Tri and 6 km S Bo Ho Su and Ben Hai River (NVN). Apr70 XXIV Corps grid per Don Armstrong. Quang Tri Pr, I Corps.

Axe, LZ (BQ 9-7?)
A.k.a. Hill 258 (or 298?) NW Trung Luong, N Tuy Hoa, NNW LZ Eagle and due N LZ Apple. Involved in Battle of Dong Tre, during Op Nathan Hale, Jun66. Discussed at length in *The Fields of Bamboo*, pp 58, 65 et al. Phu Yen Pr, I Corps.

Ayers, FSB (XT 533-036)
Apx 30 km W to WNW Tan Son Nhut AB and 3 km S Khiem Cuong. In Mar69?, FSB Helgeson was turned over to ARVN by 2d/24th Inf, 25th Inf Div, and responsibility for FSB Ayers (XT 533-036) assumed by 2d Bde/25th Inf Div. FSB Keene and Ayers each held by rifle Co while Bn's remaining rifle Co was on continuous ops. Data per 15Mar69, QUARTEVAL Feeder Rpt, 2d Bde/25th Inf at: www.en.com/users/kramsey/ dragons.html. 224Feb68-15Mr69. Hau Nghia Pr, III Corps.

Aztec (n/a)
6Apr70, XXIV Corps future-use 5th Div FSB name.

BRAVO

Facility/Feature Name, Grid Coordinate, a.k.a. Name/History/Province/CTZ

Unless otherwise stated, 6-digit grid coordinates reference DMA L-7014, L-7015 or L-7016 series, 1:50,000 scale maps, while 2 and 4-digit coordinates reference AMS/DMA/NIMA 1:250,000, 1:500,000 and 1:1,000,000 scale maps. Unless otherwise stated, all heights are in meters. To convert meters to feet, multiply by 3.2808; feet to meters, multiply by .3048.

B-7 Compound (WS 84-10?)
At Can Tho, Oct63. US Army SF, Vietnam, Provisional B-Team Camp. Phong Dinh Pr, IV Corps.
B-32 Compound (XT 204-509?)
See Tay Ninh SF Camp. SF Det B-32 camp. Tay Ninh Pr, III Corps.
B-36 Compound (XT 204-509)
See Tay Ninh SF Camp. SF B-Team Camp, Tay Ninh. Tay Ninh Pr, III Corps.
B-36 Project Rapid Fire (n/a)
See Glossary.
B-50 Project (n/a)
See Glossary.
B-56 Project (n/a)
See Glossary.
B-130 Compound (ZA 240-501?)
Possibly at site of Pleiku SF Heliport, which was along QL-14 apx 3 km NNW Pleiku and 3 km W Pleiku/Cu Hanh AF. USARV Provisional B-Team Camp. Pleiku, Oct63. Pleiku Pr, II Corps.
B-320 Compound (BT 025-079?)
Possibly at Da Nang City SF Camp site, which was apx 2 km S to SE Da Nang AB. USARV, Provisional B-Team Camp. Da Nang, Oct63. Quang Nam Pr, I Corps.
B-410 Compound (XS 8-9)
USARV, Provisional B-Team Camp. Saigon, Oct63. Gia Dinh Pr, III Corps.
b, LZ (XT 513-904)
Apx 14 km NW Tonle Cham AF and 7 km due W tip of the Fishhook. 15-21Mar67. Tay Ninh Pr, III Corps.
b, LZ (XT 628-389)
Ap 15 km W Lai Khe and 16 km SE Dau Tieng. 16Sep66. Binh Duong Pr, III Corps.
b, LZ (YS 625-610)
Apx 14 km W Dat Do and 2 km W Xom Truong Qui/Rte 328. 6Apr66. Phuoc Tuy Pr, III Corps.
b, LZ (ZB 065-970)
Apx 11 km ESE Ngok Tavak AF and 1 km ESE Dak Rose. 30Dec63. Quang Tin Pr, I Corps.
B, FSB (YB 8-1?)
See Firebase B. Kontum Pr, II Corps.
B Battalion Training Area (n/a)
See Quang Trung Trng Ctr for detail.
B Dan Deung (n/a)
Mapsheet name of L-7014-6532-3. SVN.
B Du Damour (n/a)
Mapsheet name of L-7014-6733-3. SVN.
B Rdu (n/a)
Mapsheet name of L-7014-6432-2. SVN.
B Team (n/a)
See Glossary.
B. (name) (numerous)
Use of "B." as abbreviation for prefix "Ban" is common to Indochina maps, particularly those of Laos, Thailand and Cambodia. Its use is ubiquitous on Natl Geographic's excellent Feb67 Indochina map. Look in "Ban" beginning entries when seeking data for place names beginning with "B." (i.e., for B. Na, see Ban Na).
Ba, Mui (CQ 3-2)
Coastal point at 12°51'N-109°27'E. On ND49-13 JOG. Khanh Hoa Pr, II Corps.
Ba Bai SF Camp (WS 071-809)
A.k.a. FOB Tien Binh. Apx 7 km SW Chau Phu, 10 km W Chau Duc AF, 2 km due W Hill 230 (one of Seven Sisters) and only 3 km S Cambodia. 5th SF. Info/grid per *SF Order of Battle.* Chau Doc Pr, IV Corps.
Ba Be Lake (WK 6-7)
Apx 155 km N to NNE Hanoi. In Mtn/lake region known for its numerous rivers, waterfalls, deep valleys, caves and towering peaks. El. is 145 meters and surrounding peaks reach 1,745 meters. Ba Be is Vietnamese for "3 bays," and derived from S geography of this narrow, 7 km-long lake. Its N section (separated from Ba Be by a 300' wide channel edged with sheer chalk cliffs) is known as Be Kam. NVN.
Ba Bep Bridge (XT 781-133)
See Ba Dep Bridge. Binh Duong Pr, III Corps.
Ba Bien, Camp (YD 345-537)
On NE outskirts of Quang Tri, apx 3 km NNE La Vang AF. ARVN camp? Quang Tri Pr, I Corps.
Ba Bieu Relocation Ville (YD 345-537)
At Quang Tri. Sep67. Quang Tri Pr, I Corps.
Ba Chuc (n/a)
Mapsheet name of L-7014-5929-1. SVN.
Ba Chuc SF Camp (VS 905-595)
Apx 5 km from Cambodia, 8 km due W peak of Dop Chompa Mtn, 23 km SW Chau Duc AF and 4 km N Phum Khot Ramet. 5th SF. Moved to Ba Xoai. Info/grid per *SF Order of Battle.* Chau Doc Pr, IV Corps.
Ba Dai, Baie de (CP 1-1)
Bay at 11°55'N-109°16'E. Khanh Hoa Pr, II Corps.
Ba Dep Bridge (XT 781-133)
TL-8A bridge apx 3 km W Phu Cuong and about 19 km NNW Saigon. Along vital supply corridor between Cu Chi and Saigon-Long Binh-Tan Son Nhut area. 2d/34th Armor provided security here '68-69. See Phu Cuong Bridge.

Detailed story and photos of site in 23Sep68 issue of *Tropic Lightning News*, Vol. 3, No. 39, pp4-5. III Corps.

Ba Dinh District (WJ)
One of Hanoi's 4 districts (Quan): Hoan Kiem Dist (city center); Ba Dinh Dist (west area, inc Ho Chi Minh's Tomb); Hai Ba Trung Dist (on Red River, S Hoan Kiem Dist); and Dong Da Dist (SW area).

Ba Dong (n/a)
Mapsheet name of L-7014-6328-4. SVN.

Ba Dong (n/a)
Ville on Cau Mau Peninsula. An Xuyen Pr, IV Corps.

Ba Dong, Bai (BN 19-24)
See Bau Trang. Binh Thuan Pr, II Corps.

Ba Dua Heliport (XS 240-432)
Apx 25 km due W My Tho, 7 km S Cai Lay and about 4 km N northern channel of Mekong River. "Heliport #509, El. 7', earth. Don't stay on pad, VC will attack. At 10°21'N 106°08'E," per Feb73 TAD. Dinh Tuong Pr, IV Corps.

Ba Gi Airfield (BR 994-338)
About 1 km E QL-1, 15 km SE Phu Cat 1 AF and 15 km NW Qui Nhon AF. Per TPC K-10A. "Flight serv G3 Air, II Corps TOC ARVN 29Jul68, AF # VA2 189," in Aug69 TAD per Frank Penk, Jr. Not in Feb73 TAD. El. 39'. Binh Dinh Pr, II Corps.

Ba Gia (BS 58-79)
Apx 16 km WNW Quang Ngai and on N side of Song Tra Khuc River. Site of major battles in '65, during which apx 1,000 VC attacked 3 Bns ARVN Inf 29May65, driving them into panicked retreat. ARVN retook ville in Jun, but on 4Jul65, and in only 90 minutes, were again routed by VC. USMC was then deployed to retake ville. Americal List. Quang Ngai Pr, I Corps.

Ba Gia Airfield (BS 480-792)
Apx 15 km WNW Quang Ngai, 16 km S Tra Bong AF and 26 km SSW Chu Lai. Listed as "Abnd 28Jul67, AF # VA1-82," in Aug69 TAD per Frank Penk, Jr. Not in Feb73 TAD. Quang Ngai Pr, I Corps.

Ba Gia? SF Camp (AT 8148-3834)
If grid correct, was apx 7 km WSW Phuoc Binh AF and 12 km SW An Hoa. Listed in Quang Ngai Pr, which is not possible if grid correct? See Ba To (old). Info/grid per *SF Order of Battle*. Quang Nam Pr?, I Corps.

Ba Ho Falls (BP or CP)
Natural wonder and tourist attraction near Nha Trang. Apparently, 3 separate waterfalls tumble into 3 separate pools here. Khanh Hoa Pr, II Corps.

Ba Hon Airfield (VS 599-353)
See Cement Plant AF. Kien Giang Pr, IV Corps.

Ba Hon, Bai (VS 5-3)
A.k.a. Vinh Ba Hon. Bay at 10°14'N-104°35'E. On NC48-06 JOG. Kien Giang Pr, IV Corps.

Ba Hon, Baie de (VS 5-3)
A.k.a. Vinh Ba Hon. Bay at 10°14'N-104°35'E. On NC48-06 JOG. Kien Giang Pr, IV Corps.

Ba Hon, Vinh (VS 5-3)
Bay at 10°14'N-104°35'E. On NC48-06 JOG. Kien Giang Pr, IV Corps.

Ba Ke, Cape (YS 7-6)
See Cape Ba Ke. Phuoc Tuy Pr, III Corps.

Ba Kev Airfield (YA)
Apx 30 km NE Lumphat AF, and 30 km W SVN border. Per TPC K-10A. El. 984'. Cambodia.

Ba Kiem, Cape (YS 7-6)
See Cape Ba Kiem. Phuoc Tuy Pr, III Corps.

Ba Kiem, Mui (YS 7-6)
Coastal point at 10°31'N-107°31'E. On NC48-08 JOG. Phuoc Tuy Pr, III Corps.

Ba Lang An, Mui (BS 7-8)
A.k.a. Mui Batangan. Cape at 15°14'N-108°56'E. On ND49-01 JOG. Quang Ngai Pr, I Corps.

Ba Lang CAP (n/a)
CAP 3-3-5, 3rd CAG. Thua Thien Pr, I Corps.

Ba Loc, Ho (CR 02-23)
Freshwater lake apx 7 km due W Qui Nhon at 13°46'30"N 109°09'30"E. Binh Dinh or Phu Yen Pr, II Corps.

Ba Long (Thon Ha Vung) (n/a)
Mapsheet name of L-7014-6442-3. SVN.

Ba Long Airfield (YD 168-397)
Apx 21 km SW Quang Tri. "Insecure, abnd 30Jan67, AF # VA1-64," in Aug69 TAD per Frank Penk, Jr. Not in Feb73 TAD. Quang Tri Pr, I Corps.

Ba Long Heliport (YD 155-401)
Apx 20 km SW Quang Tri and 14 km SE Mai Loc in valley of a major tributary of Cua Viet River. Heliport #510, El. 65', at 16°37'30"N 107°01'30"E, per Feb73 TAD. Quang Tri Pr, I Corps.

Ba Long Radio Relay Site (YD 15-40?)
Apx 20 km SW Quang Tri and 14 km SE Mai Loc in valley of major tributary of Cua Viet River? 3d Recon radio relay site here '66-67. 12th Mar Arty '67, 6-105mm also here. Quang Tri Pr, I Corps.

Ba Long Valley (YD 1-4)
A.k.a. Song Thach Han River Valley or 556 Valley. Rte 556 ran along river's N bank from Ca Lu/QL-9 looping S to E in arc to Quang Tri. Area S of Mai Loc in valley was designated by USMC as Delta Five. Cited in *Combat Medic*, p 75. 3d Mar Div. Quang Tri Pr, I Corps.

Ba Long, FSB (YD 16-40?)
Apx 20 km SW Quang Tri and 14 km SE Mai Loc in valley of major tributary of Cua Viet River? 3d Recon radio relay site here '66-67. 12th Mar Arty '67, 6-105mm also here. Quang Tri Pr, I Corps.

Ba Lua Island (VS 4-2)
A.k.a. Balau Island, Ile Ba Lua and Quan Dao Bai Lao. In small Island grp, apx 20 to 30 km S Ha Tien. NIMA data. Kien Giang Pr, IV Corps.

Ba Lua, Ile (VS 4-2)
A.k.a. Balau Island and Quan Dao Bai Lao. NIMA data. Kien Giang Pr, IV Corps.

Ba Lum, Pointe de (CP 0-1)
See Pointe Ba Lum. Khanh Hoa Pr, II Corps.

Ba Luong Airfield (YD 168-397)
See Ba Long AF. Quang Tri Pr, I Corps.

Ba Mla Airfield (BQ 504-598)
See Phu Tuc AF. Phu Bon Pr, I Corps.

Ba Na Airfield (n/a)
Apx 300 km N Vientiane. Natl Geo map. El. 1,181'. Laos.

Ba Na Ku Airfield (n/a)
Apx 50 km S Sakon Nakhon (New) AF, 95 km SW NKP AB. Per ONC-J-11. El. 600'. N Cambodia.

Ba Na Mountain (ZC 206-704)
Apx 15-20 km W and WSW Da Nang, and N of Happy Valley. Apparently a.k.a. "R.C. Ba Na" or "Route Coloniale Ba Na" for road that spiraled up mtn? Strategic mtn mass that one time held French resort and later a USMC Auto Radio Re-transmission/OP/Radar Control site? Grid per G. Neville, 3d Recon Bn. See R.C. Ba Na and Hill 1467. Quang Nam Pr, I Corps.
Ba Na Muang Airfield (n/a)
Apx 12 km W the Mekong River and Laotian border, 80 km ENE Ubon AB. Per TPC K-10A. El. 620'. Thailand.
Ba Na Puong Airfield (n/a)
Feb67 Natl Geo map. El. 700'. Laos.
Ba Na Then Airfield (n/a)
70 km S Luang Prabang. Per ONC-J-11. El. 44'. Laos.
Ba Ngoi Airfield (BP 941-138)
Along coast apx 17 km SW Cam Ranh Bay's main airbase and 4 km N Xom Moi. "Abnd Pvt AF # VA2-83," in Aug69 TAD per Frank Penk, Jr. Not in Feb73 TAD. Khanh Hoa Pr, II Corps.
Ba Ngoi/Hane Cohe Airfield (CP 053-166?)
See Cam Ranh AF. Khanh Hoa Pr, II Corps.
Ba Ngoi/Trai Ca Airfield (BP 941-138)
See Ba Ngoi AF. Khanh Hoa Pr, II Corps.
Ba Non, Mui (XQ 7-5)
Coastal point on Con Son Island at 8°40'N-106°33'E. On NC48-11 JOG. South China Sea, SVN.
Ba Phu Lun Airfield (QC 22-83)
LS-136. CIA/SF, per *Air Facilities Data-Laos.*
Ba Quan, Mui (VF 8-7)
Coastal point at 18°46'N-104°49'E. NE48-06 JOG. NVN.
Ba Quau, Mui (VF 8-7)
A.k.a. Mui Ba Quan. Coastal point at 18°46'N-104°49'E. On NE48-06 JOG. NVN.
Ba Queo Receiver Station (XS 79-94)
See Phu Lam Signal Site. Gia Dinh Pr, III Corps.
Ba Rai, Rach (XS14)
See Rach Ba Rai River. Vinh Long Pr, IV Corps.
Ba Ren Bridge (BT 102-510)
QL-1 bridge over Song Chiem Son/Song Cau Lau Rivers apx 7 km S Da Nang and 7 km SW Marble Mtn. Also listed at BT 101-511. Americal List. Quang Nam Pr, I Corps.
Ba Ria (YS 43-67)
A.k.a. Xa Phuoc Le and Baria. Along Rte-2, apx 8 km SW Nui Dat and 22 km NE Vung. HQ 1ATF Arty/1st RAR, whose mission was to protect QL-15, in E portion of Rung Sat Special Zone (Forest of Assassins). Opcon US Army's IIFFV. MACV-SOG, USARV-UITG (Individual Trng Grp) Trng Bn here Mar71-Nov72, in 72 was renamed FANK (Forces Arm'ee Nationale Khmer Trng Cmd), redesignated Field Trng Cmd when FANK was taken over by 18th ARVN Div, Dec72. 161 Bty, RNZA (Kenning's Bty 13Jun65-13Jun66) set at listed grid, 23May-5Jun66. Also listed at YS 38-61. Capitol, Phuoc Tuy Pr, III Corps.
Ba Ria Airfield (YS 402-613)
Apx 20 km NE Vung Tau, on W edge of Phuoc Le, 7 km due W Dat Do and 8 km SSW Luscombe AF. El. 10', 1,400' laterite rwy. At 10°29'52"N-107°11'53"E. Phouc Tuy Pr, III Corps.
Ba Ria Base (YS 38-62)
A.k.a. Phuoc Le Base. In Xa Phuoc Le apx 20 km NNE Vung Tau and 8 km SW Nui Dat. 1st RAR. See Phuoc Le. Phuoc Tuy Pr, III Corps.
Ba Ria Heliport (YS 384-622)
In Phuoc Le, 20 km NE Vung Tau and 9 km SW Luscombe AF. "Heliport #511, El. 17', soccer field, Fuel-J4, Ammo-7.62, 2.75" rockets. Tower-124.7, 40.7." At 10°30'30"N-107°11'00"E, per Feb73 TAD. Phouc Tuy Pr, III Corps.
Ba Ria Signal Site (YS 36-86?)
Also Baria. Possibly on Hill 1654 at listed grid, which is 6 km NNW Phuoc Le (Ba Ria), 16 km SW Ngai Giao and 8 km WSW Nui Dat? Phuoc Tuy Pr, III Corps.
Ba Su Mountains (BT 1-0)
W of the Pineapple Forest and Barrier Island. Site of Base area 117, home of 2d NVA Div in Apr67. 196th LIB and 5th ARVN Div, swept during Op Frederick Hill?, Apr67. Ba Su Mtn in listed grid square. Quang Tin Pr, I Corps.
Ba Ta Ngane Airfield (n/a)
Apx 155 km SE NKP AB, and 80 km SE Savannakhet AF. Per ONC-J-11. El. 490' Laos.
Ba Thin, FSB (AN or BN?)
A.k.a. LZ Ba Thin or Ba Thinh. Possibly near Phan Thiet or Dong Ba Thin? Per *Currahee History, 1Feb69-31Dec69*, p 26, was built a Fwd CP for TF 3-506 during Op Double Eagle II, sometime between Nov68-Dec68. A, B, and C Cos/3d/506th Inf, 101st Abn plus 1st and 3d Bns/44th ARVN Rgt. Two 105mm Btys here per Jerry Berry. Dong Ba Thin is at CP 040-290, and may be related? Binh Thuan or Khanh Hoa Pr?, II Corps.
Ba Tien, Pointe de (CP 0-0)
See Pointe Ba Tien. Khanh Hoa Pr, II Corps.
Ba To (BS 555-325)
Apx 40 km SSW Quang Ngai, along headwaters of Song Tra Bong River and perhaps 3-4 km NE Ba To (New) SF Camp. CIDG Camp A-106 here, Mar65, then became ARVN Ranger camp, Sep70. During Op Double Eagle, Jan-Feb66, USMC Arty and Recon elements here suptg BLT 2/4 and 3/1. Also listed at BS 558-327, 565-318, 558-327 and 565-324. Americal, 1st Cav, SF camp, Det 9; 5th SF Det B-22, Oct65, A-106 Oct66. Map is L-7014-6738-4. See Ba To SF Camps. Quang Ngai Pr, I Corps.
Ba To (n/a)
Mapsheet name of L-7014-6738-4. Towns of this name also listed in grid squares: BS 6-5, BS 5-3, ZA 1-6. All are either in Quang Nam or Pleiku Pr, I or II Corps. SVN.
Ba To, LZ (BS 558-327)
At or adj to Ba To New AF, 28 km SW Mo Duc/Quang Hien, 3 km SW Ville of Ba To and 4 km ENE ville of Go Dien. Apr70 XXIV Corps grid per Don Armstrong. Quang Ngai Pr?, I Corps.
Ba To, Song (BS 5-3)
45 km SSW Quang Ngai. Quang Nam Pr, I Corps.
Ba To (new) SF Camp (BS 567-323)
Just S of Ba To, apx 40 km SSW Quang Ngai. SF camp/FOB converted to 69th ARVN Border Rangers. During Op Double Eagle, Jan-Feb66, USMC Arty Bty and Recon elements here suptg BLT 2/4 and 3/1. [43] Map is L-7014-6738-4. Info/grid per *SF Order of Battle*. Also listed at BS 558-327. Quang Ngai Pr, I Corps.

Ba To (old) SF Camp (AT 8148-3834)
Apx 3 km W Khuong Trung, 2 km SSW An Hoa and 42 km SSW Da Nang. 5th SF camp. Info/grid per *SF Order of Battle*. Moved to Gia Vuc. Quang Ngai Pr, I Corps.

Ba To Airfield (BS 565-324)
A.k.a. Ton Dung AF and Bao To AF. Apx 18 km ENE Gia Vuc AF, 27 km WSW Duc Pho and 42 km SSW Quang Ngai. "Abnd 28Jul67, AF # VA1-84," in Aug69 TAD per Frank Penk, Jr. Not in Feb73 TAD. Quang Ngai Pr, I Corps.

Ba To New Airfield (BS 557-320)
Apx 18 km ENE Gia Vuc AF, 27 km WSW Duc Pho AF, 20 km due S Minh Long AF and 42 km SSW Quang Ngai. Per TPC K-10A. El. 196', 2,300' steel-mat rwy. At 14°45'15"N-108°43'40"E. Map is L-7014-6738-4. Quang Ngai Pr, I Corps.

Ba Tri Airfield (XS 711-096)
See An Hiep AF. Long An Pr, III Corps.

Ba Tri Heliport (XS 461-030?)
Possible sp variant of Bao Tri? If grid correct, was apx 3 km N Phu Vinh, 4 km N Tra Vinh AF and 45 km due S My Tho. "Heliport #512, El. 10', earth. May also land on dusty road," per Feb73 TAD. Vinh Binh?, Pr, IV Corps.

Ba Tu, LZ (AQ 800-212)
See Batu. Darlac Pr, II Corps.

Ba Tu/My Hanh Corridor (XT/XS)
Saigon area infiltration route. III Corps.

Ba Vi Mountain (WJ 38-27)
A.k.a. Nui Ba Vi or Hill 1281. French positions on this mtn were involved in Battle for Hoa Binh, and abnd 6-10Jan52. Per *Street Without Joy*, p 54, on map at p 50. NVN.

Ba Xoai SF Camp (VS 9559-6279)
Apx 8 km from Cambodia, 4 km WNW peak of Dop Chompa Mtn, 7 km WSW That Son AF and 28 km SW Chau Duc AF. 5th SF Det 78, CIDG Det A-421, May66 (5th SF, Det A-429, Oct66?). Converted to ARVN 94th Border Rangers. Info/grid per *SF Order of Battle*. Chau Doc Pr, IV Corps.

Ba Xoai, Camp (VS 905-595)
See Ba Chuc. Chau Doc Pr, IV Corps.

Ba Xoi (VS?)
Likely sp variant of Ba Xoai. 5th SF, Det A-429 here, Oct66. Chau Doc Pr?, IV Corps.

Ba Xuyen Airfield (XR 070-62)
See Soc Trang AF. Ba Xuyen Pr, IV Corps.

Ba Xuyen Province (WR/WQ/XR)
One of 16 southern provs forming IV Corps.

Babylift, Operation (n/a)
Air evacuation program meant to evac 2,000 SVN orphans (many of Amerasian descent) during collapse of SVN in Apr-May75. Its very 1st effort ended in tragedy when C-5A carrying 314 orphans and crew crashed 4Apr75, just 14 minutes after takeoff from Tan Son Nhut (apparent VC sabotage) killing 138. Crash was only mishap of Babylift, that between 4Apr-9May75 evaced 2,678 Vietnamese and Cambodian orphans.

Bac Bo, Vinh (AC 8-1)
A.k.a. the Gulf of Tonkin. NVN/SVN.

Bac Giang Airfield (n/a)
Feb67 Natl Geo map. El. 50'. NVN.

Bac Ho (n/a)
See Glossary.

Bac Kan (n/a)
Mapsheet name of L-7014-6153-2. NVN only.

Bac Kan (WK 86-48)
Apx 130 km due N Hanoi and 30 km N Cho Moi. Vietminh HQs at Bac Kan, Ho Moi and Cho Don, were targets of French Para drops during Op Lea, 7Oct47. See map in *Street Without Joy*, p 31. NVN.

Bac Lac Airfield (ZT 084-773)
See Bao Loc Plantation. Lam Dong Pr, II Corps.

Bac Lieu (Vinh Loi) (n/a)
Mapsheet L-7014-6127-4. True name is: Vinh Loi (Bac Lieu). SVN.

Bac Lieu Airfield (WR 791-281)
On Cau Mau Peninsula at southern tip of SVN, 42 km SW Soc Trang major AF, 57 km SE Kien Long AF, 80 km Due S Can Tho and 185 km SW Saigon. 73d Avn "Bird Dog" Airstrip for FAC, observation and intel gathering May62. Per TPC K-10D. El. 10', 2,000' steel-mat rwy. At 09°18'04"N-105°43'13"E. Bac Lieu Pr, IV Corps.

Bac Lieu City (WR 80-27)
On Cau Mau Peninsula 42 km SW Soc Trang AF, 57 km SE Kien Long AF, 80 km Due S Can Tho and 185 km SW Saigon. 21st (ARVN) Inf Div Advsy Det, Advsy Team 51, HQ Mob. Adv Team #53. Capitol, Bac Lieu Pr, IV Corps.

Bac Lieu Province (WR/XR)
One of 16 southern provs forming IV Corps (IV CTZ).

Bac Mai (Hanoi) Airfield (WJ 89-21)
Major airport on S edge of Hanoi and 6 km SSW Gia Lam AF, the other major airfield of Hanoi area. Per ONC-J-11. El. 16'. NVN.

Bac Me (n/a)
Mapsheet name of L-7014-6054-2. NVN only.

Bac Ninh (n/a)
Mapsheet name of L-7014-6251-3. NVN only.

Bac Ninh (XJ 01-43)
See Bach Ninh. NVN.

Bac Quang (n/a)
Mapsheet name of L-7014-5953-1. NVN only.

Bac Si (n/a)
See Glossary.

Bac, Ile (CP 2-8)
A.k.a. Hon Do. Khanh Hoa Pr, II Corps.

Bach Dang (XT 202-789)
Apx 27 km due N Tay Ninh, 8 km WNW FSB Carolyn and 17 km SW Katum AF. Tay Ninh Pr, III Corps.

Bach Ho Bridge (YD 748-213)
QL-1 Bridge over Perfume River at SW corner of the Hue Citadel and 2 km S Citadel AF. XXIV Corps grid, 6Apr70. Thua Thien Pr, I Corps.

Bach Ma (n/a)
Mapsheet name of L-7014-6541-2. SVN.

Bach Ma Heliport (ZC 059-927)
At Bach Ma apx 9 km SW Phu Loc and 3.2 km NE peak Bach Ma Mtn (Hill 1408). "Heliport #514, El. 4,003', at 16°11'40"N-107°51'40"E." Thua Thien Pr, I Corps.

Bach Ma Mountain (ZC 040-900)
A.k.a. Hill 1408 or Dong Bach Ma. Major peak and large hill mass 65 km NW Da Nang, 3 km SW Bach Ma Resort,

42 km SE Hue and 12 km SW Q Phu Loc. Primary terrain feature in area. Nam Hoa Dist, Thua Thien Pr, I Corps.

Bach Ma Resort (ZC 060-925)
Old French resort apx 9 km due S Q Phu Loc, 3 km NE peak Nui Bach Ma, 45 km SE Hue and 1 to 2 km W of the Quang Nam Pr border. On 4,500' high plateau named "the White Horse" that overlooked coastal lowlands of Phu Loc District to NE and E, as well as Bach Ma massif to W and SW. Palatial French villas dotted area. "White Horse" name derived from legend about white clouds that often obscured its peaks. Resort area air-assaulted 13Jul69 by 1st/327th, 2d/502d Inf and 326th Engrs of 101st Abn, along with 54th ARVN Rgt, where they began const of FSB Sledge at ZC 067-920. Op ended 11Aug69 after enemy fled area. Over 80 LZs were also prepared for possible future use. FSB Sledge was apx 16 km SSW FSB Brick and 24 km E FSB Spear. It's const was hampered by winds that sometimes hit 100 mph! A.k.a. Hill 1408. Thua Thien Pr, I Corps.

Bach Ninh (XJ 01-43)
Also spelled Bac Ninh. On Road No. 18, apx 25 km NE Hanoi. Position held by French Foreign Legion Rgt during French War. See *Street Without Joy*, p 20 and Chp 2, map at p 46. NVN.

Bach Thach CAP (ZD 038-023)
See Thon Bach Thach CAP. 3d CAG, Phu Loc District, Thua Thien Pr, I Corps.

Bache, USS (n/a)
DD-470. 7th Flt Destroyer. See *Barry, USS*.

Backyard, The (YD)
Marine Recon nickname for general area between Dong Ha and Quang Tri. Per Tom Jacobs, the 3d Recon Bn, 3d Mar Div, always kept team or 2 in zone as early warning system. Recon teams were often trucked into "Backyard" and then walked to their RZs (Recon Zones). Quang Tri Pr, I Corps.

Bacon, LZ (XD 814-481)
In or overlooking river valley 9 km NNW Khe Sanh CB, 34 km WSW Cam Lo, 29 km W Mai Loc and 52 km W Quang Tri. Apr70 XXIV Corps grid per Don Armstrong. Quang Tri Pr, I Corps.

Bad Vibes Hill (XT 7-8?)
Terrain feature apparently N and within site of An Loc/Camp Alpha. Actions here described in *Father Soldier Son*, p 11 et al. Binh Long Pr, III Corps.

Badcoe Club (YS 28-43)
See Peter Badcoe Club. Phuoc Tuy Pr, III Corps.

Badger, LZ (BR 233-284)
Apx 29 km SW An Khe and 10 km SW LZ Assault. 4th Div AO, '70. 4th Div op rpt grid per Jim Claeys. Binh Dinh or Pleiku Pr, II Corps.

Badger, LZ (XD 950-636)
In Cam Lo? River Valley apx 27 km WNW Cam Lo, 50 km WNW Quang Tri and 23 km due N Khe Sanh CB. Apr70 XXIV Corps grid per Don Armstrong. Quang Tri Pr, I Corps.

Badger State, SS (n/a)
Merchant ship under govt contract, per Ralph Fries.

Badger Catch III, Operation (n/a)
See *Thomaston, USS*.

Bagdad, LZ (XD 899-623)
See Baghdad. Quang Tri Pr, I Corps.

Baghdad, LZ (XD 899-623)
Apx 36 km W Cam Lo, 54 km WNW Quang Tri and 21 km NNW Khe Sanh CB. Also spelled Bagdad. Apr70 XXIV Corps grid per Don Armstrong. Quang Tri Pr, I Corps.

Bagpipe, LZ (XD 692-443)
Overlooking Xe Banhiang River Valley approach from Laos, apx 16 km WNW Khe Sanh CB, 3 km E Lao border, 11 km NNE Sa Tiac and 65 km W To WSW Quang Tri. One of westernmost US FSBs in I Corps. Apr70 XXIV Corps grid per Don Armstrong. Quang Tri Pr, I Corps.

Bai Bung, Mui (VQ 70-50)
A.k.a. Mui Ca Mau. Cape Bai Bung, the southernmost tip of Cau Mau Peninsula and of SVN, some 320 km SW Saigon. At 8°38'N-104°44'E, On NC48-15 JOG. An Xuyen Pr, IV Corps.

Bai Chan, FSB? (YT 34-07)
Apx 12 km WSW Xuan Loc, 14 km NW Blackhorse Basecamp and 35 km SSE Bien Hoa. 2d/3d, 199th LIB here. Grid per 199th LIB Assn. Proper sp possibly "Boi Chanh?" Bien Hoa Pr, III Corps.

Bai Chuoampong (CP 1-6)
Coastal point at 12°23'N-109°20'E. On ND49-13 JOG. Khanh Hoa Pr, II Corps.

Bai de Fai Tsi Long (YJ 3-1)
NIMA data. NVN.

Bai des Cocotiers (YS 2-4)
Coconut Bay. Near Vung Tau. NIMA data. Bien Hoa/Phuoc Tuy Pr, III Corps.

Bai Khem, Mui (US 9-0)
Coastal point at 10°02'N-104°02'E. On NC48-05 JOG. Kien Giang Pr, IV Corps.

Bai Luei, Ile de (YS 3-5)
See Ile de Bai Luoi. Phuoc Tuy Pr, III Corps.

Bai Luoi (YS 30-50)
Bay apx 6 km NNE Vung Tau. Phuoc Tuy Pr, III Corps.

Bai Luoi Island (YS 30-51)
A.k.a. Ile de Bai Luei. Apx 7 km NNE Vung Tau. NIMA data. Phuoc Tuy Pr, III Corps.

Bai Luoi, Ile de (YS 3-5)
Ile de Bai Luei. Apx 7 km NNE Vung Tau. NIMA data. Phuoc Tuy Pr, III Corps.

Bai Ma Lieng Island (CQ 17-58)
In small island grp apx 14 km due N Tuy Hoa AB and within 4 km of coast. NIMA data. Phu Yen Pr, II Corps.

Bai Nhut (XQ 7-5)
A.k.a. Mui Ca Map. Coastal point at 8°38'N-106°37'E. On NC48-11 JOG. IV Corps.

Bai Nom, Mui (CP 0-0)
Coastal point at 11°49'N-109°14'E. On NC49-01 JOG. Khanh Hoa Pr, II Corps.

Bai Nom, Pointe (CP 0-0)
See Pointe Bai Nom. Khanh Hoa Pr, II Corps.

Bai Sao, Mui (US 9-1)
Coastal point at 10°04'N-104°03'E. On NC48-05 JOG. Kien Giang Pr, IV Corps.

Bai Sau, Pointe (CP 0-1)
See Pointe Bai Sau. Khanh Hoa Pr, II Corps.

Bai Thong, Mui (CP 1-2)
Coastal point at 11°56'30"N-109°16'36"E. On NC49-01 JOG. Khanh Hoa Pr, II Corps.
Bai Thuong (n/a)
Mapsheet name of L-7014-6048-1. NVN only.
Bai Thuong Airfield (n/a)
MIG base apx 35 km WNW Thanh Hoa and 130 km SSW Hanoi. Struck by Carrier TF-77 effort to blunt NVA Tet '68 Offensive. ONC-J-11. El. 73'. NVN.
Baie de la Pointe de Ca Mau (VQ 7-5)
A.k.a. Vung Mui Ca Mau. Coastal point at 8°38'N-104°44'E. NC48-15 JOG. An Xuyen Pr, IV Corps.
Baie des Pilotes (XH 8-8)
Bay of Pilots. NIMA data. NVN.
Bailey Compound (XT 98-13?)
HQ of118th Avn Co at Bien Hoa AB. Named to honor SSgt James E Bailey, US Army, KIA 4Sep64. Bien Hoa Pr, III Corps.
Bainbridge, USS (n/a)
CGN-25? With *USS Rogers* (DD 876), assisted *USS Enterprise* with its serious fire of 14Jan69. See *USS Enterprise*. Data per www.uss-salem.org/features/ fires/.
Bait, LZ (BR 401-647)
Apx 3 km WSW Kannack AF and 22 km NNW An Khe. 1st Cav, 9Dec65. Binh Dinh Pr, II Corps.
Bak Ri (YB)
Variant of "Dak Ri?" Per *Dak To*, p 138, was W of Ben Het, and ARVN outpost during battle for Dak To, 1Nov-1Dec67. Apparently an NVA Sgt named Vu Hong surrendered to ARVN here, 2Nov67, claiming to be arty specialist with 66th NVA Rgt. He also said that four Inf and one Arty NVA Rgts (66th from SW, 32d blocking to S, 24th blocking to NE, and 174th to NW, with 40th NVA Arty in supt) were planning attack of Dak To. That intel led to deployment of 173d Abn and eventually to Hill 875 battle. Kontum Pr, II Corps.
Bak To, SF Camp? (n/a)
Possible variant of "Ba To" or "Dak To?" Spelled as listed in DA Chief, Mil Hist records summary, which puts Det A-333 here '64, A-422 in '65 and A-224 in '66, Mike Forces 110-78 in '67, and closing in '68?
Bak-Bo Bay (AC 8-1)
A.k.a. Gulf of Tonkin.
Baker, FSB (YD 595-235)
Along N bank of and overlooking Song Bo River apx 14 km due W Hue and 7 km SSW An Lo Bridge. 101st Abn grid per Don Armstrong. Thua Thien Pr, I Corps.
Baker, LZ (BR 467-445)
Apx 2 to 3 km SW An Khe, 2 km SE An Tuc and 1 or 2 km S QL-19. 4th Div AO, '70. 4th Div op rpt grid per Jim Claeys. Binh Dinh Pr, II Corps.
Baker, LZ (BR 805-935)
On mtn apx 6 km SW Bong Son and overlooking Song An Lao Valley. 1stCav?, 30Oct66. Binh Dinh Pr, II Corps.
Bakwao, Mui (VF 8-7)
A.k.a. Mui Ba Quan. Coastal point at 18°46'N-104°49'E. On NE48-06 JOG. NVN.
Bald Hill (TJ 9-6)
In Muong Thanh Valley apx 290 km W Hanoi and immed S Eliane 2, due W main DBP complex and Position Junon, on E side of Nam Yum River at Dien Bien Phu during Op Castor, 20Nov53-7May54. NVN.
Baldie, LZ (YA 93-93?)
A.k.a. Baldy? Apparently within sight of LZ Mile High (YA 937-931), and if so, was roughly 34 km W to WNW Kontum. C/1st/35th Inf Div here. Kontum Pr, II Corps.
Baldie Mountain (YD 75-16?)
See Mount Baldy. Thua Thien Pr, I Corps.
Baldy, LZ (BT 133-453)
A.k.a. Hill 63 (also listed as Hill 55?) and FSB Baldy. Along W edge of QL-1 at its intersection with rte 535, some 12 km W of coast, 28 km NW Chu Lai, 16 km E FSB Ross and 33 km SSE Da Nang. CP for 196th LIB, Americal Div, until it became Rgtl HQ for 7th Marines, 1st Mar Div, Aug69. 1st, 2d and 3d Bns of 7th Mar rotated security among FSBs Ryder, Ross and Baldy. Also listed as BT 132-453, 135-305, 130-449, 136-455 and 139-455. Possibly named for its physical characteristics or to honor Col Paul A. Baldy, Sr., Adv to 25th ARVN Inf Div in early 60's. Americal, 5th and 7th Marines. Map is L-7014-6640-1? Quang Nam Pr, I Corps.
Baldy Airfield (BT 133-453)
A.k.a. LZ Baldy AF. W side of QL-1 some 12 km W the ocean, apx 28 km NW Chu Lai, 28 km E An Hoa, 14 km S Hoi An AF, and 33 km SSE Da Nang. Per ONC K-10. Also listed at BT 139-455 and as "Secure, hvy helo trfc, US Army, 4Feb69, AF # VA1-63," in Aug69 TAD per Frank Penk, Jr. Not in Feb73 TAD. See LZ Baldy AF. Quang Nam Pr, at Quang Tin Pr border, I Corps.
Baldy Mountain (YD 75-16?)
See Mount Baldy. Thua Thien Pr, I Corps.
Baletier, Joseph (n/a)
See *Peacock, USS*.
Balkan Outpost (n/a)
French Frontier outpost abnd in '50 as Vietminh gained strength. See Cao Bang. Northern Tonkin, NVN.
Balloon, LZ (YD 158-614)
Along QL-9 apx 5 km ENE Cam Lo and 20 km WNW Quang Tri. Apr70 XXIV Corps grid per Don Armstrong. Quang Tri Pr, I Corps.
Balmoral, FSPB (XT 930-330)
If grid correct, was apx 4.5 km NNW FSB Coral and 18 km NNW Bien Hoa CB. 3RAR (1ATF) FSB. See Coral, FSB, for detail. Binh Duong Pr, III Corps.
Baltic, LZ (YD 215-657)
Apx 3 km W QL-1, 19 km NW Quang Tri and 15 km W to WSW Cua Viet CB. Apr70 XXIV Corps grid per Don Armstrong. Quang Tri Pr, I Corps.
Bamboo Canal (XH 1-8)
The Song Luoc Canal des Bambous. NIMA data. NVN.
Bamboo Fence, The (AT 98-94)
Natural/enemy barrier on Charlie Ridge. Site of battle involving A/3d Recon Bn, '65, discussed in *Never Without Heroes*, pp 35-39. Grid is est. Quang Nam Pr, I Corps.
Bamboo Viper (n/a)
See Glossary.
Bamboo, LZ (XD 839-480)
Apx 5 km NE La Vien, 8 km due N Khe Sanh CB and 29 km WSW Cam Lo. Apr70 XXIV Corps grid per Don Armstrong. Quang Tri Pr, I Corps.

Bambous, Canal des (XH 1-8)
The Song Luoc Canal of Bamboo. NIMA data. NVN.
Ban A Ham Airfield (PB 8-0 or PB 9-1?)
Possibly Ban Don Tan AF? Apx 595 km N Bangkok per Feb67 Natl Geo map. El. 800'. Thailand.
Ban 'Y' Airfield (TJ 50-15)
LS-187. CIA/SF, per *Air Facilities Data-Laos.*
Ban An Airfield (TG 95-66)
A.k.a. L-110. CIA/SF, per *Air Facilities Data-Laos.*
Ban Ang (n/a)
Mapsheet name of L-7014-5851-4. NVN only.
Ban Ban (various)
Common Viet/Lao place-name. Sites inc: XK 0-7, UJ 8-8, UJ 9-7, UJ 8-7, UJ 9-5, VJ 9-1, WG 0-6, WG 0-5, and BQ 5-4. In Laos at: XD 0-2, UG 4-7, UG 1-5, TG 9-4, UG 4-7.
Ban Ban (UG 4-7?)
In Lao panhandle. On 31May52, French unit was cut off here during Laos counter-offensive. Discussed in *Street Without Joy*, p 107. In Mar70, F-105s trying to draw AA fire from an interdiction point on Rte 7 near Ban Ban drew barrage of 4 SAMs. Tactic apparently backfired on USAF when all air ops were banned in area thereby giving NVA unfettered access through zone of HCMT. Laos.
Ban Ban Airfield (n/a)
Apx 210 km NNE to NE Vientiane, per Feb67 Natl Geo map. El. 1,888'. Laos.
Ban Ban Airfield (UG 49-71)
LS-10. CIA/SF, per *Air Facilities Data-Laos.*
Ban Bang (n/a)
Mapsheet name of L-7014-6050-3. NVN only.
Ban Bat Camp (n/a)
See Bat Bat Camp. NVN.
Ban Beecher AF (TG 41-32)
LS-100. CIA/SF, per *Air Facilities Data-Laos.*
Ban Bek (XD?)
Small Lao ville near one of most successful HCMT interdiction missions of war when 20th TASS "Covey" FAC #281, flying out of Da Nang, discovered massive NVA truck park/ammo stg depot here night of 18Dec70. Near Delta-43, checkpoint on HCMT. O-2 Navigator of #281 used Starlight Scope to detect 12-truck convoy. 2 F-4s (call-sign Iceman) responded to Covey 281's call to "Moon Beam Control" and bombed area. To everyone's amazement, 28 secondary explosions and massive barrage of AA fire immed followed, suggesting much more significance to area than 1st thought. More strikes produced non-stop secondaries and, as result, airstrikes were initiated around clock for 10 days before mission terminated. Covey FACs flew 200 hours over site. 6,500 secondary explosions and 225 sustained fires were recorded. Detailed discussion in *Da Nang Diary*, pp 203-213. Laos.
Ban Bich Airfield (BQ 504-598)
See Phu Tuc AF. Phu Bon Pr, II Corps.
Ban Blech Airfield (BQ 004-597)
See Buon Blech AF. Phu Bon Pr, II Corps.
Ban Bo Han Airfield (MJ 2-9?)
On coast, apx 685 km SSW Bangkok and 155 km WNW Trang, per Feb67 Natl Geo map. El. 6'. Thailand.
Ban Bo Mei Airfield (QD 01-61)
LS-194. CIA/SF, per *Air Facilities Data-Laos.*
Ban Bonong AF (VE 56-84)
LS-12. CIA/SF, per *Air Facilities Data-Laos.*
Ban Boua Mu AF (TG 66-04)
LS-367. CIA/SF, per *Air Facilities Data-Laos.*
Ban Bouac AF (UG 59-32)
A.k.a. Lima Site-34. CIA/SF, per *Air Facilities Data-Laos.*
Ban Bouac Airfield, New (UG 58-31)
LS-116. CIA/SF, per *Air Facilities Data-Laos.*
Ban Brieng (AQ 95-55)
See Buon Brieng AF. Darlac Pr, II Corps.
Ban Buc (n/a)
Mapsheet name of L-7014-5951-4. NVN only.
Ban Bung Khla Airfield (UF 9-1)
Along Mekong River at Laotian border near 18°16'00"N-104°00'00"E, or apx 625 km NE Bangkok. Grid per (and listed as abnd, '66) 69 TAD. El. 600'. Thailand.
Ban Bungxang Airfield (WD 41-12)
LS-296. CIA/SF, per *Air Facilities Data-Laos.*
Ban Ca (YT 27-10)
Thought to be a misspelling of Bau Ca.
Ban Cao (n/a)
Mapsheet name of L-7014-6253-4. NVN only.
Ban Chai Buri Airfield (VE 4-5)
Along Mekong at Lao border, apx 600 km NE Bangkok per Feb67 Natl Geo map. Thailand.
Ban Chau (n/a)
Mapsheet name of L-7014-5951-1. NVN only.
Ban Chay (n/a)
Hamlet on Karst ridge overlooking Rte 92 near NVN border in Laos. Laos.
Ban Chiang Klang Airfield (PB 9-3)
Apx 620 km N Bangkok. Natl Geo map. El. 900'. Thailand.
Ban Chomhat Airfield (WD 52-72)
LS-295. CIA/SF, per *Air Facilities Data-Laos.*
Ban Chuang Airfield (n/a)
On Laotian border 30 km WNW Vientiane. Per ONC-J-11. El. 656'. Northern Cambodia.
Ban Chuk Chung Airfield (TJ 23-03)
LS-138. CIA/SF, per *Air Facilities Data-Laos.*
Ban Da Bom Airfield (XC 31-67)
LS-64. CIA/SF, per *Air Facilities Data-Laos.*
Ban Dan (n/a)
Mapsheet name of L-7014-6047-4. NVN only.
Ban Dan Airfield (n/a)
Feb67 Natl Geo map. El. 580'. Thailand.
Ban Dao Hon Gom (CQ 2-0)
The Hon Gom Peninsula. Khanh Hoa Pr, II Corps.
Ban Don (n/a)
Mapsheet name of L-7014-6534-1. SVN.
Ban Don (ZV 03-27)
On Tonle Srepok/Ea Krong River, 38 km NW Ban Me Thuot. 30 years after war, its domesticated Elephants are tourist attraction during dry season when roads are passable. 5th SF camp, Det. A-3 here, Dec64. See Ban Don AF. Darlac Pr, II Corps.
Ban Don Airfield (NL 3-0)
A.k.a. Surat Thani. Feb67 Natl Geo map. El. 15'. Thailand.
Ban Don Airfield (ZV 032-268)
A.k.a. Bandon AF. Along TL-1 and immed E the Da Krong (Ea Krong) River, 500 meters W Ban Don AF and 36 km NW Ban Me Thuot. 2,800' laterite/clay rwy. At

12°53'36"N-107°47'44"E. Photo with picture of sign reading: "*WELCOME TO BANDON International Airport, El. 184 meters, PLEASE WATCH FOR ELEPHANTS*," in *Vietnam Military Lore-Legends and Shadows*, p 801. Also listed at ZV 040-270. El. 607'. Darlac Pr, II Corps.

Ban Don SF Camp (ZV 025-267)
A.k.a. Camp Rose, Bandon, Trang Phuoc and Trang Phuc SF Camp. Along TL-1 and immed E the Da Krong (Ea Krong) River, 500 meters W Ban Don AF and 36 km NW Ban Me Thuot. 5th SF Det. A-3, Dec64. Renamed Camp Rose or Camp Gerald B. Rose to honor Sp5 Gerald Rose, KIA 22Feb65, in ambush on Mang Yang Pass. Chapter devoted to Rose in Ray Bows', *Vietnam Military Lore-Legends and Shadows*, p 799-808. See Ban Don AF. Info/grid per *SF Order of Battle*. Darlac Pr, II Corps.

Ban Don Tan Airfield (PB 8-0)
Possibly Ban A Ham AF? Apx 595 km N Bangkok per Feb67 Natl Geo map. El. 800'. Thailand.

Ban Done (East) Airfield (n/a)
Apx 190 km ENE Vientiane. El. 1,000'. Laos.

Ban Done (West) Airfield (SF 98-68?)
A.k.a. Lima Site-163 and Ban Done AF Apx 90 km NW Vientiane, per Feb67 Natl Geo map. El. 700'. Laos.

Ban Done Airfield (SF 98-68)
A.k.a. Lima Site-163 and Ban Done West AF. Apx 90 km NW Vientiane. CIA/SF, per *Air Facilities Data-Laos.*

Ban Dong (n/a)
A waypoint on Ho Chi Minh Trail along QL-9. NVN.

Ban Dong Airfield (VF 22-70)
LS-28. CIA/SF, per *Air Facilities Data-Laos.*

Ban Dong Hene Airfield (WD 30-47)
LS-54. CIA/SF, per *Air Facilities Data-Laos.*

Ban Dong Khan Khou Airfield (WD 10-27)
LS-304. CIA/SF, per *Air Facilities Data-Laos.*

Ban Donge Airfield (SF 98-68)
LS-163. CIA/SF, per *Air Facilities Data-Laos.*

Ban Drang (n/a)
Mapsheet name of L-7014-6635-3. SVN.

Ban Fang Lum Airfield (WB 4-7)
Possibly Chong Mek AF? Along Rte 16 at Lao border, apx 540 km ENE Bangkok. Natl Geo map. El. 570'. Thailand.

Ban Hae Don New Airfield (n/a)
Apx 90 km SSE Ubon AB and just N Cambodian border. Per ONC-K-10. El. 524'. Thailand.

Ban Hang Khang Airfield (n/a)
Possibly a.k.a. Ban Nam Kama AF? Apx 140 km NNE Vientiane, per Feb67 Natl Geo map. El. 3,800'. Laos.

Ban Hin Taek Airfield (NC 6-3)
At 20°15'00"N-99°38'00"E. NIMA data. Thailand.

Ban Ho Airfield (BQ 035-291)
See Buon Ho AF. Darlac Pr, II Corps.

Ban Hong Non Airfield (n/a)
Apx 300 km NE Vientiane. Natl Geo map. El. 4,600'. Laos.

Ban Hong Ten Airfield (n/a)
Along Mekong River at Laotian border, apx 560 km ENE Bangkok per Feb67 Natl Geo map. El. 600'. Thailand.

Ban Hong Thong Airfield (QQ 0-9)
At 13°29'00"N-100°54'00"E. NIMA grid. Thailand.

Ban Houana Airfield (VE 64-73)
LS-302. CIA/SF, per *Air Facilities Data-Laos.*

Ban Houaymun Airfield (WC 88-67)
LS-310. CIA/SF, per *Air Facilities Data-Laos.*

Ban Houei Dionne Airfield (TG 69-48)
LS-123. CIA/SF, per *Air Facilities Data-Laos.*

Ban Houei Keng Airfield (UH 87-14)
LS-226. CIA/SF, per *Air Facilities Data-Laos.*

Ban Houei Kong Airfield (XB 6-7)
Apx 520 km SE Vientiane, 215 km SW Da Nang SVN and 80 km E Pakse. Per Dec67 DMA TPC K-10A, and Feb67 Natl Geo map. El. 2,920'. Laos.

Ban Houei Lao Airfield (PB 59-86)
LS-147. CIA/SF, per *Air Facilities Data-Laos.*

Ban Houei Lung Airfield (n/a)
Apx 210 km NNE Vientiane. El. 4,800'. Laos.

Ban Houei Pamone Airfield (TF 59-94)
LS-272 and Ban Xon. CIA, per *Air Facilities Data-Laos.*

Ban Houei Sai Airfield (PC 51-41)
A.k.a. L-25. CIA/SF, per *Air Facilities Data-Laos.*

Ban Houei Sai Citadel Airfield (PC 51-41)
LS-283. CIA/SF, per *Air Facilities Data-Laos.*

Ban Houei Sai SF Camp (PC 4-4?)
SF camp when Lao neutrality declared, 23Jul62. FTT 2 here then. Per *Special Forces at War*. MR1, Laos.

Ban Houei Sane (XD 662-350?)
See Ban Houei Sane North AF. Laos.

Ban Houei Sane Airfield (XD 65-36)
LS-189. CIA/SF, per *Air Facilities Data-Laos.*

Ban Houei Sane North (XD 641-372)
Abnd French airstrip in Lao valley due W Khe Sanh and S the Se Pone River. USMC helos inserted Chinese Nung mercenaries here as part of Project Delta Ops in 66. Home of *Batallion Volontaire-33*, a Lao Army Post. See BV-33 for more interesting detail. Laos.

Ban Houei Sou Airfield (n/a)
Apx 530 km SE Vientiane. Natl Geo map. El. 2,900'. Laos.

Ban Hquaymun Airfield (XC)
Apx 40 km E Thai border in western Laos. Per TPC K-10A. El. 850'. Laos.

Ban Huai Kaeo Airfield (PS 6-6)
Apx 655 km NNW Bangkok per Feb67 Natl Geo map. El. 1,350'. Thailand.

Ban Huai Khi Nu Airfield (QS 0-6)
At 15°03'33"N-100°56'06"E. NIMA grid. Thailand.

Ban Huoei Kong SF Camp (XB 6-7 or TH6-7?)
SF camp when Lao neutrality declared, 23Jul62. FTT 18 and 42 here then. Per *Special Forces at War*. MR4, Laos.

Ban Huoi Heo (n/a)
Mapsheet name of L-7014-5848-3. NVN/Laos.

Ban In Thi Airfield (XB 7-3)
A.k.a. Ban Inthi. Apx 5 km due S Long Keo AF, 25 km N Cambodian border at southern end of Laos. Per TPC K-10A. El. 3,120'. Laos.

Ban Ka Long (n/a)
Mapsheet name of L-7014-6046-3. NVN/Laos.

Ban Kachong (n/a)
Places with this name are in grid squares VB 1-2, NJ 7-2, NU 9-8 and NJ 8-3. SF camp or AO per *SF Order of Battle.* Thailand.

Ban Kaeng Nang Airfield (VD 0-3 or VD 1-4)
Apx 60 km SSE Sakon Nakhon (New) AF, 90 km SW NKP AB. Per ONC-J-11. El. 820' Thailand.

Ban Kagnogtang Airfield (XB 8-7)
Apx 100 km E Pakse. Per TPC K-10A. Laos. El. 2,700'.
Ban Kapchoeng Airfield (UB 5-0?)
Apx 160 km SW Ubon AB and 7 km N Cambodian border. Per TPC K-10A. El. 720'. Thailand.
Ban Karai (n/a)
Mapsheet name of L-7014-6243-4. NVN/Laos.
Ban Karai Pass (XE 26-12)
On NVN/Laotian border, apx 60 km SW Dong Hoi (NVN) and 115 km NW Quang Tri. One of 3 major HCMT passes. See Mu Gia and Nape Passes. NVN/Laos.
Ban Keng Sai Airfield (UH 83-22)
LS-84. CIA/SF, per *Air Facilities Data-Laos.*
Ban Keng Tanga Airfield (WC 39-79)
LS-298. CIA/SF, per *Air Facilities Data-Laos.*
Ban Kengpe Airfield (WE 14-10)
LS-292. CIA/SF, per *Air Facilities Data-Laos.*
Ban Keun Airfield (TF 4-3?)
Apx 45 km due N Vientiane. Per ONC-J-11. Also on Feb67 Natl Geo map. El. 550'. Laos.
Ban Keun Airfield (TF 44-31)
LS-44. CIA/SF, per *Air Facilities Data-Laos.*
Ban Keun SF Camp (TF 4-3?)
SF camp when Lao neutrality declared, 23Jul62. FTT 47 here then. Per *Special Forces at War*. MR5, Laos.
Ban Kha (n/a)
Mapsheet name of L-7014-5651-2. NVN only.
Ban Kha Airfield (UG 57-28)
LS-94. CIA/SF, per *Air Facilities Data-Laos.*
Ban Khae Don New Airfield (WA 1-9)
Apx 95 km SSE Ubon AB and 14 km NW the Tri-border point where Laos, Cambodia and Thailand all meet. Per TPC K-10A. El. 524'. Thailand.
Ban Khami Airfield (UH 77-23)
LS-39. CIA/SF, per *Air Facilities Data-Laos.*
Ban Khemarat Airfield (WC 2-7)
On S bank of Mekong River and Laotian border, 70 km ESE Loeng Nok Tha airfield and 105 km NE Ubon AF. Per TPC K-10A. El. 400'. Thailand.
Ban Kho Airfield (n/a)
Apx 310 km NE Vientiane. Natl Geo map. El. 820'. Laos.
Ban Khoanag Airfield (QD 92-32)
A.k.a. L-41 and Moung Hai. CIA/SF base per *Air Facilities Data-Laos.*
Ban Khok Huai Airfield (TF 0-1)
At 18°10'00"N-102°10'00"E. NIMA data. Thailand.
Ban Khok Mai Airfield (XC 58-39)
LS-171. CIA/SF, per *Air Facilities Data-Laos.*
Ban Khok May Airfield (XC 5-3?)
80 km W SVN border, and 90 km E Thai border in Central Laos. Per TPC K-10A. El. 800'. Laos.
Ban Khok Tong Airfield (n/a)
Apx 270 km ESE Vientiane. Natl Geo map. El. 500'. Laos.
Ban Kia (n/a)
Mapsheet name of L-7014-6633-2. SVN.
Ban Kia Maa Airfield (UF 81-99)
LS-314. CIA/SF, per *Air Facilities Data-Laos.*
Ban Kol La (n/a)
Mapsheet name of L-7014-5753-4. NVN only.
Ban Kong Mi Airfield (YB 0-0)
A.k.a. Ban Kongmi. Apx 18 km N Cambodian border, 138 km ESE Pakse. Per TPC K-10A. El. 1,509'. Laos.
Ban Konghang Airfield (XB 8-4)
Apx 120 km WNW Dak To and 10 km NE Long Keo AF. Per ONC-K-10. El. 3,018'. Laos.
Ban Kongmi Airfield (YB 05-05)
LS-407. CIA/SF, per *Air Facilities Data-Laos.*
Ban Kop Airfield (VA 7-9)
At 14°27'00"N-104°44'00"E. NIMA data. Thailand.
Ban Kout Lamphong Airfield (WC 8-3)
Apx 20 km E Thai border in western Laos, per TPC K-10A. El. 500'. Laos.
Ban Koutlamphong Airfield (WC 88-43)
LS-447. CIA/SF, per *Air Facilities Data-Laos.*
Ban Kut Khae Don Airfield (VD 4-0)
At 16°17'00"N-104°27'00"E. NIMA data. Thailand.
Ban Kut Khaen Airfield (UE 0-9)
At 18°00'59"N-103°12'18"E. NIMA data. Thailand.
Ban Kut Kho Kan Airfield (TD 3-3 or TD 9-6)
Along Rte 27, apx 510 km NE Bangkok per Feb67 Natl Geo map. El. 549'. Thailand.
Ban La Tee Airfield (XB 91-68)
LS-190. CIA/SF, per *Air Facilities Data-Laos.* Apx 105 km E Pakse. Per TPC K-10A. El. 2,985'. Laos.
Ban Laboy Ford (XE 2-0)
A.k.a. Ban Loboy Pass. Apparently near 17°13'00"N-106°08'00"E. Heavily bombed interdiction choke point on HCMT in Laos. In Sep68, after 32 days of closure, NVA reopened fording point and, after renewed activity detected, site was targeted with between 50 to 100 USAF air sorties per day to re-close it. Data per *A Better War*, pp 82-83, and NIMA. NE48-11 JOG map. Laos.
Ban Lahanam Airfield (WC 24-98)
LS-301. CIA/SF, per *Air Facilities Data-Laos.*
Ban Lampang Luang Airfield (NA 2-0 or NA 4-1)
Possibly Ko Kha AF? along Wang River, apx 510 km NNW Bangkok per Feb67 Natl Geo map. El. 549'. Thailand.
Ban Lao Ngam Airfield (n/a)
Apx 465 km SE Vientiane. Natl Geo map. El. 1,750'. Laos.
Ban Laong Hwy Strip (WD 0-0?)
Apx 120 km SSE NKP AB (Cambodia). Per ONC-J-11map. El. 1,600'. Laos.
Ban Le (n/a)
Mapsheet name of L-7014-6054-1. NVN only.
Ban Le Kho Airfield (n/a)
Along Burmese border, apx 460 km NW Bangkok per Feb67 Natl Geo map. El. 600'. Thailand.
Ban Lee 2 Airfield (TG 52-60)
LS-253. CIA/SF, per *Air Facilities Data-Laos.*
Ban Lee Airfield (UH 10-13)
LS-233. CIA/SF, per *Air Facilities Data-Laos.*
Ban Liet SF Camp (YB 860-258)
Adj Ben Het/Ben Het AF, apx 16 km WNW Dak To 2 AF, 52 km NW Kontum. 5th SF. Info/grid per *SF Order of Battle*. A.k.a. FOB Dak To. Kontum Pr, II Corps.
Ban Loboy Ford (XE 2-0)
See Ban Laboy Ford. Laos
Ban Loi Airfield (VJ 01-46)
A.k.a. Na San AF. See Na San. NVN.

Ban Long (XS 33-45?)
Cluster of hamlets with this name apx 15 km due W My Tho and 6 km W Dong Tam. Described by trooper quoted in *Doc: Platoon Medic*, at p 153, as "Just another easily forgotten shit hole." Kien Hoa Pr, IV Corps.
Ban Long Airfield (YD 168-397)
See Ba Long AF. Quang Tri Pr, I Corps.
Ban Lot (n/a)
Mapsheet name of L-7014-5851-3. NVN only.
Ban Lou Airfield (UH 30-42)
LS-248. CIA/SF, per *Air Facilities Data-Laos*.
Ban Luu (n/a)
Mapsheet name of L-7014-5851-1. NVN only.
Ban M Gam (n/a)
Mapsheet name of L-7014-6734-4. SVN.
Ban M Trong (n/a)
Mapsheet name of L-7014-6734-3. SVN.
Ban M. (n/a)
Batallion de Marche. See *Batallion de Coree*.
Ban Mac (n/a)
Mapsheet name of L 701-5779-3. NVN/China.
Ban Mae Kon Ken Airfield (MU 4-2?)
Along Burmese border, apx 375 km NW Bangkok per Feb67 Natl Geo map. El. 550'. Thailand.
Ban Mae Lana Airfield (MB 1-6)
Listed as abnd in '66 NIMA data. At 19°35'00"N-98°13'00"E. On NE47-02 JOG. Thailand.
Ban Mae Sao Airfield (TH 0-2)
At 19°15'00"N-97°57'00"E, or apx 710 km NNW Bangkok and 10 km from Burmese border. NIMA data. Feb67 Natl Geo map. El. 712'. Thailand.
Ban Mae Tan Airfield (MV 1-0)
At 17°13'00"N-98°14'00"E. NIMA data. Thailand.
Ban Mae Thalop Airfield (n/a)
Along Fang River, apx 675 km NNW Bangkok. Natl Geo map. At 19°44'00"N, 99°10'00"E. El. 1,840'. Thailand.
Ban Maeo Thap Boek AF (QU 2-7)
At 16°55'00"N-101°08'00"E. NIMA data. Thailand.
Ban Mai Airfield (PV 8-6)
At 17°45'00"N-100°43'00"E. NIMA data. Thailand.
Ban Mai Airfield (WC 45-64)
LS-329. CIA/SF, per *Air Facilities Data-Laos*.
Ban Man SF Camp (WE 5-2 or UF 7-8?)
SF camp when Lao neutrality declared, 23Jul62. FTT 9 here then. Per *Special Forces at War*. MR2, Laos.
Ban Maya Airfield (TH 19-69)
LS-234. CIA/SF, per *Air Facilities Data-Laos*.
Ban Me Rang (n/a)
Mapsheet name of L-7014-5454-2. NVN/China.
Ban Me Thuot (AQ 793-026)
A.k.a. Lac Giao. Along QL-14 apx 50 km E Cambodia, 33 km NNW Lac Thien and 130 km WNW Nha Trang. Home of SF Det 32, the 23d ARVN Div, 5th SF Grp, Det. B-210, Dec64, B-23 (was B-430) '65, MACV-SOG, CCS, Nov67-Apr72. Per John Rochelle, the 2d/1st Cav (M-60 tank) unit was housed at N side of town and son of Gen Creighton Abrams (Capt. Abrams) served with that unit. Ban Me Thuot SF Camp was housed in large, rustic hunting lodge (a.k.a. the Grand Bungalow) used at one time by Emperor Bao Dai and for lodging by President Theodore Roosevelt during hunting trip in 1909 (per *Gone Native*, p 182, was beautiful Teak A-Frame bldg said to have burned down by cooking fire in late '68 or early '69). Was 1st CIDG camp opened in SVN ('61). A military area in city was at AQ 804-035 and listed grid is roughly at city center. On 30Jan68, NVA 33d Rgt and VC 301E LF Bn attacked 23d ARVN Div HQ, US MACV HQ, both AF's and many other targets. RF/PF and SF B-23 Det were only initial opposition. ARVN 8th Cav Sqdn and 45th Rgt were rushed in to reinforce later that day. On 1Feb68, ARVN 23d Ranger Bn was committed and next day, 1st/503d Inf, 173d Abn was also committed (from Pleiku). Although NVA threw 4 major attacks at BMT, US/ARVN forces pushed them out completely by 6Feb68, but apx 1/3 of city destroyed as result. Apparently 3 US Civilians were captured in fighting (head of USAID, Mike Benge, and 2 US missionaries, Betty Olsen and Henry Blood). [44] On 10Mar75, during Final Offensive, 3 NVA Divs (25,000 men) attacked 1,200 ARVN defending city, overwhelming them in matter of days and ending any hope of defending Kontum and Pleiku Prvs. On 14Mar75, Thieu ordered Pleiku and Kontum Provs abnd.[45] On L-7014-6634-3 map. Capitol, Darlac Pr, II Corps.
Ban Me Thuot (n/a)
Mapsheet name of L-7014-6634-3. SVN.
Ban Me Thuot City AF (AQ 800-038)
Along QL-14, apx 50 km E Cambodia, 33 km NNW Lac Thien and 130 km WNW Nha Trang. "Secure, hvy helo trfc ARVN 7Oct68, AF # VA2-86," in Aug69 TAD per Frank Penk, Jr. Not in Feb73 TAD. Darlac Pr, II Corps.
Ban Me Thuot City Airfield (AQ 800-038)
At NE edge of Ban Me Thuot, 8 km NW Ban Me Thuot East AF, 37 km SE Ban Don AF, 30 km W Buon Ea Yang AF. Per TPC K-10A. El. 1624', 3,500' asph rwy. Grid per TAD. Darlac Pr, II Corps. At 12°41'06"N-108°03'24"E. El. 1,624'. Darlac Pr, II Corps.
Ban Me Thuot East Airfield (AQ 799-023)
Apx 8 km SE Ban Me Thuot City AF, 22 km E Buon Ea Yang AF and 1. 5 km E QL-21. Also listed at AQ 755-995. Data per TPC K-10A. El. 1759'. 5,900' asph rwy. 1st grid per TAD, 2d from mapsheet L-7014-6634-3. At 12°39'55"N-108°07'27"E. Alt 1,759'. Darlac Pr, II Corps.
Ban Me Thuot East TACAN NDB (AQ 799-023?)
At Ban Me Thuot East AF, apx 7 km E Ban Me Thuot. Tac Air Nav and Non-Directional air nav Beacon site. Also listed at AQ 87-02. Darlac Pr, II Corps.
Ban Me Thuot East, FSB (AQ 883-018)
A.k.a. LZ Ban Me Thuot East or FSB Aquarius (AQ 889-016) or FSB Ban Me Thuot (885-012? At SE edge of Ban Me Thuot East AF, 9 km SE Ban Me Thuot AF, and near both FSBs Doris K and Aquarius. On map at www. landscaper.net/chighmap.jpg. See Ban Me Thuot East AF for possible location. B Bty, 2d/9th Arty here Dec69, and 7th/15th Arty elements here at one time also? Also listed at AQ 868-020? Darlac Pr, II Corps.
Ban Me Thuot Hunting Lodge (AQ 780-040)
See Grand Bungalow. Darlac Pr, II Corps.
Ban Me Thuot SF Camp (AQ 780-040)
A.k.a. Det 32, 5th SF camp. Housed in large, rustic, Teak A-Frame hunting lodge (a.k.a. The Grand Bungalow) used at one time by Emperor Bao Dai and for lodging by Pres. Theodore Roosevelt during 1909 hunting trip. Was 1st

CIDG camp opened in SVN ('61). Per John Rochelle, there was a "super" BX here and SF troops had best of everything. Grid *SF Order of Battle*. See Grand Bungalow. Darlac Pr, II Corps.

Ban Me Thuot West AF (AQ 868-020)
Apx 7 km E Ban Me Thuot, and 125 km WNW Nha Trang. "Flight serv G3 Air, II Corps TOC, hvy helo trfc, SVN Dir of Civ Avn, 23Mar68 US controllers but not AAF # (C-130, C-123, C-7), AF # VA2-12," in Aug69 TAD per Frank Penk, Jr. Not in Feb73 TAD. Darlac Pr, II Corps.

Ban Me Thuot, FSB (AQ 771-182)
Possibly a.k.a. Ban Me Thuot East FSB? Apx 7 km E Ban Me Thuot/Lac Giao, and at site that either was or later became BMT East AF. Grid per 4th Div op rpt courtesy Craig Miller, which also shows that 4th/42d Arty here mid-68. Darlac Pr, II Corps.

Ban Me Thuot, FSB (AQ 885-012)
At SE edge of Ban Me Thuot East AF, 9 km SE Ban Me Thuot AF, and near both FSBs Doris K and Aquarius. HQ & SVC Btys, 2d/17th Arty here, Nov70-Apr71. Grid and arty info per Nolan Putman. Darlac Pr, II Corps.

Ban Moung Airfield (PB 60-77)
LS-177. CIA/SF, per *Air Facilities Data-Laos.*

Ban Moung Ngan Airfield (UG 65-18)
LS-236. CIA/SF, per *Air Facilities Data-Laos.*

Ban Muang Chet Ton AF (QV 1-9)
At 18°04'00"N-101°04'00"E. NIMA data. Thailand.

Ban Muang Phrae Airfield (n/a)
On Laotian border, apx 420 km N to NNE Bangkok per Feb67 Natl Geo map. El. 1,600'. Thailand.

Ban Muang Pok Airfield (MB 5-7)
At 19°38'00"N-98°37'00"E. NIMA data. Thailand.

Ban Muong Lan (n/a)
Mapsheet name of L-7014-5651-1. NVN only.

Ban Muong Mo Airfield (n/a)
Apx 185 km NE Vientiane. Natl Geo map. El. 1,400'. Laos.

Ban Muong Ngat Airfield (n/a)
Apx 195 km NE Vientiane. Natl Geo map. El. 4,500'. Laos.

Ban Na Airfield (n/a)
Apx 155 km NNE Vientiane. El. 4,600'. Laos.

Ban Na Airfield (n/a)
Possibly Muong Ngoi AF? Apx 305 km due N Vientiane on Feb67 Natl Geo map. El. 1,181'. Laos.

Ban Na Airfield (TG 85-36)
LS-15. CIA/SF facility. See FSB Puncher. Data, per Kent Spalding. Laos.

Ban Na Ca (n/a)
Mapsheet name of L-7014-5947-1. NVN only.

Ban Na Kala Highway Strip (n/a)
Apx 320 km W Da Nang SVN. Per ONC-K-10. Laos.

Ban Na Khai 30 Airfield (n/a)
Apx 100 km ESE Luang Prabang. Per ONC-J-11. El. 3,800'. Laos.

Ban Na Khu Airfield (UD 9-5)
At 16°46'00"N-104°02'00"E, or apx 505 km NE Bangkok per Feb67 Natl Geo map. Grid per, and listed as abnd in, '66 NIMA Gaz. El. 596'. Thailand.

Ban Na Kouang Airfield (TG 49-01)
LS-281. CIA/SF, per *Air Facilities Data-Laos.*

Ban Na Luang Airfield (TF 69-92)
LS-66. CIA/SF, per *Air Facilities Data-Laos.*

Ban Na Phai (n/a)
Mapsheet name of L-7014-5651-3. NVN/Laos.

Ban Na Sun (n/a)
Mapsheet name of L-7014-5950-2. NVN only.

Ban Na Tai Airfield (TH 62-91)
A.k.a. L-50. CIA/SF, per *Air Facilities Data-Laos.*

Ban Na Tan Airfield (VE 81-85)
LS-237. CIA/SF, per *Air Facilities Data-Laos.*

Ban Na Tao Airfield (n/a)
Apx 120 km NW Vientiane. Natl Geo map. El. 850'. Laos.

Ban Na Then Airfield (TG 10-25)
LS-249. CIA/SF, per *Air Facilities Data-Laos.*

Ban Na Ti Airfield (TG 56-04)
A.k.a. LS-287 and Ban Naty. Per *Air Facilities Data-Laos.*

Ban Na To Airfield (n/a)
A.k.a. Sayaboury AF? Apx 165 km NNW Vientiane on Feb67 Natl Geo map. El. 1,070'. Laos.

Ban Na Tong (n/a)
Mapsheet name of L-7014-5852-3. NVN only.

Ban Na Wai Airfield (MB 9-7)
At 19°38'00"N-98°58'00"E. NIMA data. Thailand.

Ban Na Woua Airfield (PC 73-83)
LS-109. CIA/SF, per *Air Facilities Data-Laos.*

Ban Nachalit Airfield (VD 95-41)
LS-297. CIA/SF, per *Air Facilities Data-Laos.*

Ban Naeng Mut Airfield (UA 2-8)
A.k.a. Ban Naengmut. Apx 10 km N Cambode border and 175 km SW Ubon AB. Per TPC K-10A. El. 695'. Thailand.

Ban Nakay Neua Airfield (n/a)
Apx 10 km E Sam Neua AF, 180 km WSW Hanoi, 20 km from NVN border. Per ONC-J-11. El. 2,800'. Laos.

Ban Nakhua Airfield (n/a)
Apx 170 km W to WNW Vientiane. El. 250'. Laos.

Ban Nalay Airfield (WD 72-49)
LS-291. CIA/SF, per *Air Facilities Data-Laos.*

Ban Nam Bac Airfield (n/a)
Apx 290 km due N Vientiane. El. 1,148'. Laos.

Ban Nam Chuam Airfield (PC 66-59)
LS-290. CIA/SF, per *Air Facilities Data-Laos.*

Ban Nam Deng Airfield (TG 59-15)
LS-110. CIA/SF, per *Air Facilities Data-Laos.*

Ban Nam Dua Airfield (VF 18-12)
LS-143. CIA/SF, per *Air Facilities Data-Laos.*

Ban Nam Feng Airfield (UF 14-91)
LS-223. CIA/SF, per *Air Facilities Data-Laos.*

Ban Nam Hin Airfield (QB 50-15)
LS-104. CIA/SF, per *Air Facilities Data-Laos.*

Ban Nam Kama Airfield (n/a)
Possibly a.k.a. Ban Hang Khang AF? Apx 140 km NNE Vientiane, '67 Natl Geo map. El. 3,800'. Laos.

Ban Nam Keng Airfield (UG 79-18)
LS-108. CIA/SF, per *Air Facilities Data-Laos.*

Ban Nam Kueung Airfield (PC 32-55)
LS-150. CIA/SF, per *Air Facilities Data-Laos.*

Ban Nam Luang Airfield (TG 65-06)
LS-313. CIA/SF, per *Air Facilities Data-Laos.*

Ban Nam Muap Airfield (n/a)
Apx 515 km N Bangkok. Per Feb67 Natl Geo map. El. 1,000'. Thailand.

Ban Nam Na Airfield (TG 82-14)
A.k.a. LS 20A, LA30/98, Long Tieng AF, Long Tien AF, Ban Lontiang AF. Located apx 130 km NNE of Vientiane. On DMA L-1501 NE 48-01. El. 940'. See Long Tieng AF for more detail. Laos.
Ban Nam Nam (n/a)
Feb67 Natl Geo map. El. 656'. NVN.
Ban Nam Nen (n/a)
Mapsheet name of L-7014-5652-1. NVN only.
Ban Nam Nhion Airfield (n/a)
Apx 360 km NW Vientiane, 67 Natl Geo map. El? Laos.
Ban Nam Nhion Airfield (PC 39-56)
LS-149. CIA/SF, per *Air Facilities Data-Laos.*
Ban Nam Pao Airfield (n/a)
Apx 240 km NNE Vientiane. El. 2,100'. Laos.
Ban Nam Song Airfield (TG 44-13)
LS-363. CIA/SF, per *Air Facilities Data-Laos.*
Ban Nam Thao Airfield (TG 65-29)
LS-161. CIA/SF, per *Air Facilities Data-Laos.*
Ban Nam Thouei Airfield (PC 69-75)
LS-118. CIA/SF, per *Air Facilities Data-Laos.*
Ban Nam Tieng Airfield (XB 83-59)
LS-165. CIA/SF facility. Per *War in Laos*, p 24, was on E edge of Bolovens Plateau and consisted of 2 dirt AFs and French-style trenchworks in triangular shape. Laos.
Ban Nam Xao Airfield (UG 76-22)
LS-240. CIA/SF, per *Air Facilities Data-Laos.*
Ban Nam Xao Airfield (UG 77-18)
LS-208. CIA/SF, per *Air Facilities Data-Laos.*
Ban Nam Yon Nea Airfield (TF 78-96)
LS-307. CIA/SF, per *Air Facilities Data-Laos.*
Ban Nathom Airfield (UG 07-44)
LS-343. CIA/SF, per *Air Facilities Data-Laos.*
Ban Naty Airfield (TG 56-04)
LS-287 and Ban Na Ti. CIA/SF base per *Air Facilities Data-Laos.*
Ban Naty North Airfield (TG 56-05)
LS-327. CIA/SF, per *Air Facilities Data-Laos.*
Ban Ndoh (n/a)
Mapsheet name of L-7014-6533-2. SVN.
Ban Ngang Airfield (n/a)
Apx 430 km SE Vientiane. Natl Geo map. El. 560'. Laos.
Ban Nham (n/a)
Mapsheet name of L-7014-6834-1. SVN.
Ban Nham Airstrip (YU 35-65)
See O Rang AF and FSB David. Cambodia.
Ban Nong Bok Airfield (VD 79-88)
LS-183. CIALima Site apx 250 km E to ESE Vientiane on Natl Geo map. El. 640'. Grid per *Air Facilities Data-Laos.*
Ban Nong Boua Airfield (XC 67-33)
LS-134. CIA/SF facility apx 480 km SE Vientiane. Grid per *Air Facilities Data-Laos.* El. 700'. Laos.
Ban Nong Boua Airfield (XC)
In Central Laos, apx 100 km NE Pakse. El. 590'. Laos.
Ban Nong Bqua Airfield (n/a)
Apx 185 km WSW Da Nang SVN. El. 600'. Laos.
Ban Nong Dao Airfield (TF 70-14)
LS-83. CIA/SF, per *Air Facilities Data-Laos.*
Ban Nong Khan Yaeng AF (n/a)
Apx 4 km S Ban Samrong AF, 75 km NE Ubon AF and 5 km from Mekong River/Lao border. El. 465'. Thailand.
Ban Nong Lao Airfield (n/a)
Apx 205 km due E Vientiane. El. 1,100'. Laos.
Ban Nong Lom Hwy Airstrip (NA 4-2)
At 18°18'00"N-99°25'00"E. NIMA data. Thailand.
Ban Nong One Airfield (TG 65-32)
LS-101. CIA/SF, per *Air Facilities Data-Laos.*
Ban Nong Saeng (n/a)
Numerous villes (at least 44) bear this name in Thailand. SF Camp site and/or AO per *SF Order of Battle.* Thailand?
Ban Nong Saeng Airfield (n/a)
Possibly Buntharik AF? Apx 540 km ENE Bangkok and 5 km W of Laos, Feb67 Natl Geo map. El. 620'. Thailand.
Ban Nong Tong Airfield (QB 12-99)
LS-209. CIA/SF, per *Air Facilities Data-Laos.*
Ban Nong Vien Airfield (XB)
Apx 295 km SW Da Nang SVN, 30 km S Pakse, and 30 km E the Thai border. Per TPC K-10A. El. 300'. Laos.
Ban Nongla Airfield (UG 60-42)
LS-214. CIA/SF, per *Air Facilities Data-Laos.*
Ban Nongsa Airfield (WB 89-42)
LS-446. CIA/SF, per *Air Facilities Data-Laos.*
Ban Nou Kha Chok Airfield (PC 77-06)
LS-148. CIA/SF, per *Air Facilities Data-Laos.*
Ban Padou Airfield (XC 56-63)
LS-419. CIA/SF, per *Air Facilities Data-Laos.*
Ban Pak Chom Airfield (QV 9-8)
At 17°58'00"N-101°49'00"E. NIMA data. Thailand.
Ban Pak En Airfield (TG 56-20)
LS-97. CIA/SF, per *Air Facilities Data-Laos.*
Ban Pak Ham Airfield (RA 15-43)
LS-306. CIA/SF, per *Air Facilities Data-Laos.*
Ban Pak Mi Airfield (n/a)
Apx 95 km due W Vientiane. El. 900'. Laos.
Ban Pan (Thuan Chau) (n/a)
Mapsheet L-7014-5751-4. True name is: Thuan Chau (Ban Pan). NVN.
Ban Pang (n/a)
Mapsheet name of L-7014-6048-4. NVN only.
Ban Pawi Airfield (QC 53-78)
LS-285. CIA/SF, per *Air Facilities Data-Laos.*
Ban Peung Airfield (UG 44-22)
LS-95. CIA/SF, per *Air Facilities Data-Laos.*
Ban Pha Ka Airfield (UG 47-47)
LS-40. CIA/SF, per *Air Facilities Data-Laos.*
Ban Pha Kao Airfield (TG 24-66)
LS-308. CIA/SF, per *Air Facilities Data-Laos.*
Ban Pha Nop Airfield (n/a)
Apx 330 km ESE Vientiane. Natl Geo map. El. 558'. Laos.
Ban Pha Thong Airfield (TJ 33-07)
LS-169. CIA/SF, per *Air Facilities Data-Laos.*
Ban Pha Thong Airfield (TJ 34-09)
LS-247. CIA/SF, per *Air Facilities Data-Laos.*
Ban Phak Khagna Airfield (WD 37-64)
LS-303. CIA/SF, per *Air Facilities Data-Laos.*
Ban Pham Khao Airfield (n/a)
Apx 220 km NNE Vientiane. El. 4,300'. Laos.
Ban Phan Hop Airfield (WE 79-41)
L-53. CIA/SF, per *Air Facilities Data-Laos.*
Ban Phang Airfield (UG 16-22)
LS-239. CIA/SF, per *Air Facilities Data-Laos.*

Ban Phon Tin Mines (n/a)
DIA investigations into post-war allegations that US POWs were forced labor in these mines determined Caucasians working there were in fact French and Soviet employees. Discussed in *Prisoners of Hope*, p 208. Laos.
Ban Phone Sai Airfield (TF 94-03)
LS-309. CIA/SF, per *Air Facilities Data-Laos.*
Ban Phoungmay Airfield (UG 94-19)
LS-222. CIA/SF, per *Air Facilities Data-Laos.*
Ban Phumsaron Airfield (VA 6-8)
Apx 85 km SSW Ubon AB and 5 km N Cambodia per TPC K-10A. At 14°22'00"N-104°43'00"E. NIMA data. El. 600' or 656'. Thailand.
Ban Poeng Khloeng Airfield (MT 5-4)
At 15°48'00"N-98°35'00"E. NIMA data. Thailand.
Ban Pou Sung (n/a)
Mapsheet name of L-7014 5650-1. NVN/Laos.
Ban Poung Airfield (PC 66-54)
LS-324. CIA/SF, per *Air Facilities Data-Laos.*
Ban Pru Yai Airfield (n/a)
Apx 410 km ENE Bangkok per Feb67 Natl Geo map. El. 600'. Thailand.
Ban Pru Yai Airfield (VB 0-0)
Listed as abnd in '66 NIMA data. At 14°33'00"N-104°09'00"E. NIMA data. Thailand.
Ban Pu Kroy Airfield (n/a)
Near Cambodia/SVN border, apx 255 km ENE Phnom Penh and 15 km WNW Bu Krak SVN on Feb67 Natl Geo map. El. 2,250'. Cambodia.
Ban Pua Airfield (QB 0-2)
At 19°11'00"N-100°55'00"E. NIMA data. Thailand.
Ban Rosie Airfield (PC 62-33)
LS-250 and Tong Pa How. Per *Air Facilities Data-Laos.*
Ban Sa Lin (n/a)
Mapsheet name of L-7014-5554-3. NVN/China.
Ban Sa Noi Airfield (UG 53-39)
LS-119. CIA/SF, per *Air Facilities Data-Laos.*
Ban Sa Phout Airfield (QC 39-69)
LS-151. CIA/SF, per *Air Facilities Data-Laos.*
Ban Sak Ngoi Airfield (n/a)
Feb67 Natl Geo map. El. 500'. Thailand.
Ban Samet Airfield (QB 5-4?)
Apx 205 km N Vientiane. El. 4400'. Laos.
Ban Samrong Airfield (TB 2-8)
On S bank of Mekong River at Laotian border, 80 km NE Ubon AF, 55 km SE Ben Khemarat AF. Per TPC K-10A. El. 416'. Thailand.
Ban San Tiott Airfield (n/a)
Apx 175 km NNE Vientiane. El. 3,444'. Laos.
Ban San Tong Airfield (TG 7-2)
Apx 110 km SE Luang Prabang. El. 3,940'. Laos.
Ban Saphat Airfield (XC 0-3)
In western Laos, 40 km E Thailand. El. 400'. Laos.
Ban Saphat Airfield (XC 04-35)
LS-175. CIA/SF, per *Air Facilities Data-Laos.*
Ban Sapi Airfield (QB 40-48)
LS-60. CIA/SF, per *Air Facilities Data-Laos.*
Ban Se Airfield (TH 79-63)
LS-225. CIA/SF, per *Air Facilities Data-Laos.*
Ban Si Airfield (n/a)
Apx 160 km NNE Vientiane. El. 3,400'. Laos.
Ban Sing Keo Airfield (SG 98-99)
LS-332. CIA/SF, per *Air Facilities Data-Laos.*
Ban Siwilai Airfield (UF 6-1)
At 18°11'00"N-103°45'00"E. NIMA data. Thailand.
Ban Sok Airfield (XB 99-65)
LS-420. CIA/SF, per *Air Facilities Data-Laos.*
Ban Sok West Airfield (XB 9-6?)
Apx 115 km E Pakse. Per TPC K-10A. El. 1,600'. Laos.
Ban Song Airfield (UG 67-91)
LS-29. CIA/SF, per *Air Facilities Data-Laos.*
Ban Song Hac Airfield (n/a)
Apx 190 km NNE Vientiane. El. 3,500'. Laos.
Ban Song Khone Airfield (WE 20-90)
LS-77. CIA/SF facility apx 270 km due W Vientiane. Grid per *Air Facilities Data-Laos.* El. 1,000'. Laos.
Ban Sop Han Airfield (n/a)
Apx 560 km NNW Bangkok per Feb67 Natl Geo map. El. 1,330'. Thailand.
Ban Sop Siem Airfield (UH 23-12)
LS-269. CIA/SF, per *Air Facilities Data-Laos.*
Ban Soukhouma Airfield (WB 85-18)
L-45. CIA/SF, per *Air Facilities Data-Laos.*
Ban Suk Hdrah (n/a)
Mapsheet name of L-7014-6635-2. SVN.
Ban Sun Kang Airfield (UF 06-86)
LS-349. CIA/SF, per *Air Facilities Data-Laos.*
Ban Ta Viang Airfield (n/a)
Apx 140 km NE Vientiane. El. 1,300'. Laos.
Ban Tai (n/a)
Mapsheet name of L-7014-5946-1. NVN/Laos.
Ban Takhli Airbase (PS 3-8)
A.k.a. Ta Khli AB. At 15°16'00"N-100°18'00"E. NIMA data. Thailand.
Ban Talan Nua Airfield (XC 6-5)
Apx 70 km from SVN in central Laos. El. 2,953'. Laos.
Ban Tang Airfield (n/a)
Apx 210 km NE Vientiane. El. 4,300'. Laos.
Ban Tangvay Airfield (WD 70-14)
LS-299. CIA/SF, per *Air Facilities Data-Laos.*
Ban Tem (n/a)
Mapsheet name of L-7014-5847-2. NVN/Laos.
Ban Tha Airfield (n/a)
Apx 220 km NNE Vientiane. El. 3,800'. Laos.
Ban Tha Airfield (UG 52-83)
LS-52. CIA/SF, per *Air Facilities Data-Laos.*
Ban Tha Chang Airfield (n/a)
Along coast, apx 480 km SSW Bangkok per Feb67 Natl Geo map. El. 14'. Thailand.
Ban Tha Lang (n/a)
Mapsheet name of L-7014-5848-2. NVN/Laos.
Ban Tha Si Airfield (UF 76-84)
LS-61. CIA/SF, per *Air Facilities Data-Laos.*
Ban Tha Si Airfield (UF 7-8?)
A.k.a. Ban Thasi. Apx 160 km NE Vientiane on Feb67 Natl Geo map. El. 2,000'. Laos.
Ban Tha Ta Fang Airfield (LV 6-9)
A.k.a. Ban The Pang AF. At 18°04'05"N-97°41'43"E. NIMA data. Thailand.
Ban Tham Tat Airfield (UG 93-15)
LS-81. CIA/SF, per *Air Facilities Data-Laos.*

Ban Thamloup Airfield (n/a)
Apx 185 km NNE Vientiane. El. 4,600'. Laos.
Ban Than Lay Airfield (WE 07-11)
L-105. CIA/SF, per *Air Facilities Data-Laos.*
Ban Thang Airfield (TG 96-47)
LS-275. CIA/SF, per *Air Facilities Data-Laos.*
Ban Thang, Mui (CP 1-7)
Cape at 12°24'N-109°20'E. On ND49-13 JOG. Khanh Hoa Pr, II Corps.
Ban That Airfield (n/a)
Feb67 Natl Geo map. El. 550'. Thailand.
Ban Thateng SF Camp (WB 9-3?)
SF camp when Lao neutrality declared, 23Jul62. FTT 16 here then. Per *Special Forces at War*. MR4, Laos.
Ban The Pang Airfield (LV 6-9)
A.k.a. Ban Tha Ta Fang AF. At 18°04'05"N-97°41'43"E. NIMA data. Thailand.
Ban Ti Srenh (n/a)
Mapsheet name of L-7014-6634-2. SVN.
Ban Tieu, Plantation de (XS 9-8)
Plantation de Ban Tieu, a.k.a. Don Dien Ban Tieu. Gia Dinh Pr, III Corps.
Ban Tin Tok Airfield (QB 0-1)
At 19°08'00"N-100°56'00"E. NIMA data. Thailand.
Ban Ton Phung Airfield (PC 15-42)
LS-305. CIA/SF, per *Air Facilities Data-Laos.*
Ban Trap Airfield (AQ 851-236)
See Mewal AF. Darlac Pr, II Corps.
Ban Tsham (n/a)
Mapsheet name of L-7014-6635-4. SVN.
Ban Vieng Airfield (QC 18-89)
LS-135. CIA/SF, per *Air Facilities Data-Laos.*
Ban Vieng Airfield (UC 74-87)
LS-89. CIA/SF, per *Air Facilities Data-Laos.*
Ban Xani Airfield (WC 66-97)
LS-294. CIA/SF, per *Air Facilities Data-Laos.*
Ban Xen Con (n/a)
Mapsheet name of L-7014-5948-1. NVN/Laos.
Ban Xiang Khai Airfield (WD 11-88)
LS-293. CIA/SF, per *Air Facilities Data-Laos.*
Ban Xien Kok Airfield (n/a)
380 km NW Vientiane. Natl Geo map. El. 1,500'. Laos.
Ban Xieng Lip (n/a)
Mapsheet name of L-7014-5947-4. NVN only.
Ban Xieng Lom Airfield (PB 92-74)
LS-69. CIA/SF, per *Air Facilities Data-Laos.*
Ban Xon Airfield (n/a)
3,000' rwy, apx 110 km NNE Vientiane. El. 1,000'. Laos.
Ban Xon Airfield (TF 58-94)
LS-246. CIA/SF, per *Air Facilities Data-Laos.*
Ban Xon Airfield (TF 59-94)
LS-272 and Ban Houei Pamone. *Air Facilities Data-Laos.*
Ban Xot Airfield (VF 0-1?)
Apx 180 km N Vientiane. Natl Geo map. El. 4,600'. Laos.
Ban Y. Airfield (TJ 50-15)
LS-187. CIA/SF, per *Air Facilities Data-Laos.*
Ban Yot Don Chi Airfield (WB 2-8)
Listed as abnd in '66 NIMA data. At 15°13'00"N-105°15'00"E. NIMA data. Thailand.
Ban Yot Don Chi Airfield (WB 2-8)
Apx 40 km E Ubon AB, 25 km W Laos, 2 km S of the Mac Nam Mun (Upper Mekong) River, per TPC K-10A. Listed as abnd in '66 NIMA data. At 15°13'00"N-105°15'00"E. El. 550'. Thailand.
Banana, LZ (XD 839-488)
Apx 6 km NE La Vien, 9 km due N Khe Sanh CB and 29 km WSW Cam Lo. Apr70 XXIV Corps grid per Don Armstrong. Quang Tri Pr, I Corps.
Banana Island (BT 047-565)
In Song Thu Bon River, apx 21 km SSE Da Nang AB and 5 km due W QL-1 bridge. Quang Nam Pr, I Corps.
Banana Mountain (YD 750-086)
A.k.a. Nui Hoan Gay or Hill 434 (a.k.a. Mount Baldy or possibly LZ Apollo?). Significant terrain feature SW Hue, apx 13 km and about 4 km SE FSB Birmingham. Offered commanding view of Hue and used by all combatants as OP. Thua Thien Pr, I Corps.
Banana Quarry (YT 351-168)
Just S Song Dong Nai River, apx 37 km WNW Vo Dat AF, 13 km NNW Xa Binh Hoa and 43 km NE Bien Hoa AB. 169th Engrs/20th Engr Bde quarry for road work on QL20 Grid per Frank Penk, Jr. Also listed at YT 340-160. Binh Duong Pr, III Corps.
Bandit (n/a)
Apr70, XXIV Corps proposed 101st Abn FSB name.
Bandit, FSB (n/a)
A.k.a. Bandit Hill? 4th Div? See Bandit Hill. II or III Corps.
Bandit, FSB (n/a)
No data. 1st Cav and 11th ACR. III Corps.
Bandit, FSB/LZ (XT 862-362)
See Bandit Hill. Binh Duong Pr, III Corps.
Bandit Hill, FSB (XT 862-362)
A.k.a. LZ Bandit Hill. E of QL-13, apx 25 km NNW Bien Hoa AB, 17 km SW Phuoc Vinh AF, 6 km NW FSB Holiday Inn and 9 km ESE Lai Khe AF, immed S FSB Holiday Inn, WNW Luke's Castle and along western edge of War Zone D. Site on map in *Charlie Company,* p 6. 3d Sqdn, 11th ACR, Mar69. Grid per 14Mar69 *Summary of Combat Service Support to the 11th ACR*, signed by Maj. Harry W. Johnson Adjutant and courtesy Jim Cole. See FSB Bandit II and Holiday Inn. Also listed at XT 900-290 and 908-294. Binh Duong Pr, III Corps.
Bandit II, FSB (XT 908-294)
Apx 15 km SE Lai Khe AF and 7 km NNW Tan Uyen and 2 km W Xa Binh Co. 1st Cav and 11th ACR? Cited in *Vietnam: Reflexes and Reflections*. See Bandit and Bandit Hill. Binh Duong Pr, III Corps.
Bandit Net (n/a)
See Glossary.
Bandy, LZ (XD 894-633)
Apx 23 km WNW Cam Lo, 2 km? SE FSB 45 km WNW Quang Tri. Apr70 XXIV Corps grid per Don Armstrong. Quang Tri Pr, I Corps.
Bang Long (Long Phu) (n/a)
Mapsheet L-7014-6228-3. Full sheet name: Long Phu (Bang Long). SVN.

Bang (XD 8-9?)
In Quang Binh Pr. Disguised as state-run cattle farm in '59. One of very 1st sites that suptd opening of HCMT, per *The Blood Road*, p 14. NVN.

Bang, Mui (WG 8-4)
Coastal point at 19°24'N-105°48'E. NE48-03 JOG. NVN.

Bangkok (PR 7-3)
US Army Supt Cmd facility, Thailand. At various times occupied by 5th Med Field Hosp, 93d Psy Ops Co, 29th Sig Grp, Bangkok Sig Bn (Provisional), 302d and 325th Sig Bns, 167th, 334th and 347th Sig Cos, 313th Trans Co, 7th and 11th ASA Units. Thailand.

Bangkok, LZ (XD 999-639)
Near DMZ, apx 14 km WNW Cam Lo, 13 km ESE Bon Ho Su (NVN) and 36 km WNW Quang Tri. Apr70 XXIV Corps grid per Don Armstrong. Quang Tri Pr, I Corps.

Bangkok Airfield (n/a)
A.k.a. Krung Thep AF and Don Muang AF. Feb67 Natl Geo map. El. 12'. Thailand.

Bangkok Intl Airport (PR 7-3)
See Don Muang Airport. Apx 25 km NNE Bangkok proper, at 13°55'00"N-100°37'00"E. NIMA data. El. 12'. Thailand.

Bangkok SF Camp (PR 7-3)
A.k.a. Don Muang. Thailand. Apx 25 km NNE Bangkok proper? SF camp or AO per *SF Order of Battle.* Thailand.

Bangkok SF Liaison Det (PR 7-3?)
SF camp or AO per *SF Order of Battle.* Thailand.

Bangor, FSB (ZT 086-351)
A.k.a. LZ Bangor? Overlooked upper Song La Raa River apx 18 km ENE Tanh Linh, 12 km E Xa Huy Khiem, 38 km NW Phan Thiet, 33 km E Vo Dat and roughly 125 km ENE Saigon. Opened or reopened 9Sep70, closed 29Sep70 by 1st/5th Cav. Data per *1st Cav Div Op Rpt, ending 31Oct70*, courtesy Peter Cole. Binh Tuy Pr, III Corps.

Banh Lanh Village (BT-010-541 & BT 014-548)
Apx 11 km W Hoi An. Actually 2 separate hamlets apx 1 km apart at listed grids. Area N of river here controlled by US, area S of River VC controlled. NLF flag was being flown over easternmost ville when on 14Jan67, 12 CH-46s and 2 Cos of Marines were assigned to neutralize enemy and capture flag in what became known as "The River Raid." Quang Nam Pr, I Corps.

Banjo, LZ (XD 735-373)
Apx 4 km NE of Laos, apx 3 km NE Sa Tiac, 12 km WSW Khe Sanh CB and 62 km WSW Quang Tri. Apr70 XXIV Corps grid per Don Armstrong. Quang Tri Pr, I Corps.

Bannister, FSB (AN 918-213)
Apx 1.5 km SSW peak of Hill 386/Nui Ta Dom, 1 km E Ap Hoa Thanh (1), 1.4 km E QL-1 and 16 km NE Phan Thiet. 5th/22d Field Arty Op's site, Oct-Nov70. Grid and arty info per Nolan Putman. Binh Thuan Pr, II Corps.

Bantan, Cape (BT 6-0)
See Cape Bantan. Quang Tin Pr, I Corps.

Bantan, Mui (CP 1-7)
A.k.a. Mui Ban Thang. Cape at 12°24'N-109°20'E. On ND49-13 JOG. Khanh Hoa Pr, II Corps.

Banthan, Mui (CP 1-7)
A.k.a. Mui Ban Thang. Cape at 12°24'N-109°20'E. On ND49-13 JOG. Khanh Hoa Pr, II Corps.

Bao Bang (BT 16-46)
A.k.a. Bau Bang. Freshwater lake apx 2 to 3 km NE LZ Baldy, on E side of QL-1 apx 12 km S Hoi An Grid per TPC K-10A. Quang Nam Pr, I Corps.

Bao Chin Doan Trng School (n/a)
Vietnamese Natl Guard trng facility W of Haiphong on isle in Red River. Taught sabotage, anti-sabotage, mine and ambush detection. Per Bernard Fall, most of its students were former Vietminh troops already well-versed in such techniques. See *Street Without Joy*, p 184.

Bao Cong Outpost (YD 280-460)
Along Rte 566, apx 10 km SW Quang Tri. 16Oct66. Quang Tri Pr, I Corps.

Bao Chuc (WJ)
Apx 6 km NNW Vinh Yen and 40 km NW Hanoi. French Outpost of 1st Indochina War that was defended by 2, French G.M.s: the North African Groupement Mobile under Col Edon, and Mobile Grp 3 under Col Vauxem. Bao Chuc and Dao Tu were locations that were the focus of fighting during Giap's 13Jan51 offensive and battle of Vinh Yen. Elements of Vietminh 308 Div attacked this small outpost, and its 50 Sengalese and Viets fought to last man. See Chp 2 of *Street Without Joy*, and map on p 38. See Dao Tu and Vinh Yen. NVN.

Bao Don, FSB (XT 430-350)
Apx 25 km SE Tay Ninh, adj Bao Don SF Camp and a12 km SSW Dau Tieng. 20Apr67. Tay Ninh Pr, III Corps.

Bao Don SF Camp (XT 438-353)
Apx 25 km SE Tay Ninh, and 12 km SSW Dau Tieng. 5th SF Grp Det A-325, Oct66. Moved to Hiep Hoa. Info/grid per *SF Order of Battle*. Tay Ninh Pr, III Corps.

Bao Duc (n/a)
Mapsheet name of L-7014-6536-1. SVN.

Bao Ha (n/a)
Mapsheet name of L-7014-5853-2. NVN only.

Bao Ha (n/a)
Mapsheet name of L-7014-5953-2. NVN only.

Bao Lac (n/a)
Mapsheet name of L-7014-6154-4. NVN only.

Bao Loc (ZT 070-770)
Just N II Corps/III Corps border SE Nhon Co, NW Phan Thiet and roughly midway between the coast and Cambodian border and about 80 km SW Dalat. Capitol, Lam Dong Pr, II Corps.

Bao Loc, FSB? (ZT 09-78)
Actual name unknown. Along E edge of Bao Loc Plantation, apx 500 meters W Rte 335 and 2 km N QL-1. 3d/506th Inf. Grid per Jerry Berry. Lam Dong Pr, II Corps.

Bao Loc (Blao) (n/a)
Mapsheet name of L-7014-6532-2. SVN.

Bao Loc (new) SF Camp (ZT 085-870)
Apx 27 km WNW Di Linh, 3 km N Tan Phat AF, and 12 km N of Bao Loc Plantation AF/QL-20. 5th SF. Moved to Tan Rai. Info per *Order of Battle*, grid per TAD. *SF Order of Battle* lists ZT 650-792 as grid, but that appears to be in error because there is no such grid in ZT zone. Lam Dong Pr, II Corps.

Bao Loc (New) (ZT 065-792)
Apx 80 km SW Dalat, 3 km NW Bao Loc Plantation AF, 3 km N Bao Loc and 4 km WSW Tan Phat AF. SF camp here apparently moved to Tan Rai. Lam Dong Pr, II Corps.

Bao Loc (old) SF Camp (ZT 1340-8330)
Apx 75 km SW Dalat, 8 km NE Bao Loc, 3 km NE Tan Phat AF and 5 km NNE Bao Loc Plantation AF. Grid per *SF Order of Battle*. See Djral. Lam Dong Pr, II Corps.
Bao Loc (old) (ZT 084-833)
Apx 5 km NNE Bao Loc, immed NW Tan Phat AF and apx 80 km SW Dalat. 5th SF, Det A-232 (was 234) opened a camp here 30Sep65 and closed it Jan66. MACV Adv Team 38, Lam Dong Pr Advs also here. Grid per *SF Order of Battle*. Lam Dong Pr, II Corps.
Bao Loc Airfield (ZT 065-792)
Minor AF apx 79 km SW Dalat, 3 km W Tan Phat major AF and 3 km NW Bao Loc Plantation AF (minor). Per TPC K-10D. El. 2,822'. 3,500' steel-mat rwy. Grid per TAD. At 11°34'01"N-107°48'33"E. Lam Dong Pr, II Corps.
Bao Loc Airfield (ZT 084-773)
See Bao Loc Plant. AF. Lam Dong Pr, II Corps.
Bao Loc City Airfield (ZT 065-792)
See Bao Loc AF. Lam Dong Pr, II Corps.
Bao Loc New Airfield (ZT 065-792)
See Bao Loc AF. Lam Dong Pr, II Corps.
Bao Loc Plantation Airfield (ZT 084-773)
Minor AF apx 80 km SW Dalat, 3 km SW Tan Phat major AF and 3 km SE Bao Loc AF (minor). Per TPC K-10D. El. 2,733' 2,000' laterite rwy. Grid per TAD. At 11°32'30"N-107°49'40"E. Also spelled Bau Loc. See Bau Loc AF. Lam Dong Pr, II Corps.
Bao Loc/Di Linh (ZT 084-833)
MACV Adv. Team 38, Lam Dong Pr Advisors here. 5th SF, Det A-232 (was 234) here Oct65. Grid in *SF Order of Battle* indicates grid was ZT 840-833, but is in error since that grid does not exist. Capitol, Lam Dong Pr, II Corps.
Bao To Airfield (BS 565-324)
See Ba To AF. Quang Ngai Pr, I Corps.
Bao Trai (XT 52-04)
Apx 32 km WNW Tan Son Nhut AB/Saigon, and 2 km SW Khiem Cuong. 161 Bty, RNZA (Kenning's Bty 13Jun65-13Jun66) FSB set here 1-7Jan66. 3d/319th US Arty also here. Not same as Bao Tri. Hau Nghia Pr, III Corps.
Bao Trai, LZ (XT 545-048)
Apx 32 km WNW Tan Son Nhut AB/Saigon, and 3 km SW Khiem Cuong. Hau Nghia Pr, III Corps.
Bao Trai Airfield (XT 544-050)
A.k.a. Khiem Cuong AF. Apx 27 km WNW Tan Son Nhut AB/Saigon. Described as having been 5 km N LZ Wine (XS 535-967) in Plain of Reeds. 1st & 2d Bns/503rd Inf, 173d Abn, 1st Bn Royal Aust Army and Bty C/3d/19th Arty engaged 267th VC Bn and HQ of VC 506th Bn in Op Marauder here (1st US op in Mekong Delta, Jan66). Flight serv, contact G3 Air, III Corps "TOC ARVN(A) 13Sep68, AF # VA3-182," in Aug69 TAD per Frank Penk, Jr. Not in Feb73 TAD. Hau Nghia Pr, III Corps.
Bao Trai Basecamp (XT 544-050?)
A.k.a. Bao Tri or Khiem Cuong Basecamp? If grid correct, was apx 27 km WNW Tan Son Nhut AB/Saigon. Site of Belt Cmpd, MACV Adv Team 43, Bao Tri. See Belt Cmpd. Hau Nghia Pr, III Corps.
Bao Trai Heliport (XT 513-039)
Apx 32 km WNW Tan Son Nhut AB/Saigon, 2 km SW Khiem Cuong and 25 km NE the tip of Parrot's Beak. Heliport #515, El. 17', At 10°53'20"N-106°23'00"E, per Feb73 TAD. Hau Nghia Pr, III Corps.
Bao Trai Signal Site (XT 513-039?)
No data. Grid is est. Hau Nghia Pr, III Corps.
Bao Tri Airfield (XT 545-048)
See Bao Trai AF. Hau Nghia Pr, III Corps.
Bao Tri Basecamp (XT 544-050?)
See Bao Tri Basecamp. Hau Nghia Pr, III Corps.
Bar Room, LZ (XD 941-685)
See Barroom. Quang Tri Pr, I Corps.
Barataria, USCGC (n/a)
WHEC 381. 4May67-25Dec67. Sqdn 3 CGC, during Coast Guard's 1st deployment. SVN.
Baray Airfield (WU 0-7?)
Apx 90 km NNE Phnom Penh. Apparently not Baray Hwy Strip? El. 174'. Cambodia.
Baray Highway Strip (WU 0-7?)
Apx 90 km NNE Phnom Penh, 30 km NW Chamkar Leu AF, per TPC K-10A. Apparently different AF than Baray AF? El. 23' or 33'. Cambodia.
Barb, LZ (YA 604-494)
Apx 6 km NE Phum To Lay (Cambodia) and 64 km due E Pleiku. 11Jan66. Kontum Pr, II Corps.
Barb, FSB (YT 318-290)
See FSB Darb. Long Khanh Pr, III Corps.
Barbara, FSB (n/a)
Cambodian Incursion FSB. Location unknown, but possibly the LZ Barbara at XT 079-840 (apx 3 km NNW Thien Ngon AF)? B/2d/32d Arty with two-175mms here per *11th ACR Cambodia Invasion AAR, 1st Cav Div, May-Jun70*, courtesy Lou Rochat. [46] Tay Ninh Pr?, III Corps.
Barbara, FSB (YD 253-290)
A.k.a. Davis Hill and FSB Davis. Apx 28 km W Camp Evans and 50 km W to WNW Hue. 3d/187th Inf, 101st Abn here Feb-Apr69. Grid per 3d Bde 101st Abn ORLL of 13May69. Also listed at YD 328-336 and 362-370. Listed as "Davis" in Nov69-Jan70 rpts. See other LZ & FSB Barbara's in YD grid zone. Thua Thien Pr, I Corps.
Barbara, LZ (AR 760-268)
Apx 2 km W QL-14 and 10 km S Pleiku. Aug69. Pleiku Pr, II Corps.
Barbara, LZ (BP 668-670)
Remote site apx 38 km WNW Nha Trang12 km NNE Thach Trai. Apr67. See LZs Cora and Delores. Binh Dinh Pr, II Corps.
Barbara, LZ (XT 079-840)
Apx 3 km NNW Thien Ngon AF, and 5 km from Cambodia at closest point. 20Feb67. Possibly reopened for Cambodia Incursion, May 70? Tay Ninh Pr, III Corps.
Barbara, LZ (XS 117-598)
Apx 14 km NW Cai Lay, and 25 km SW Thuy Dong. 19Nov67. Dinh Tuong Pr, IV Corps.
Barbara, LZ/FSB (YD 329-337)
A.k.a. Doi 300 or Nui Cai Muong? Apx 42 km NW Hue, 15 km S Quang Tri and 22 km WNW Camp Evans. Likely built by 1st Cav, early to mid 68. 101st Abn also here. Also FSB Barbara listed at YD 253-290 and YD 330-337. Quang Tri/Thua Thien Pr border, I Corps.
Barbara, FSB/LZ (YD 362-370)
Apx 18 km WNW Camp Evans, 15 km SSE Quang Tri. Built by 1st Cav, early-mid 68. 101st Abn also here. Also

listed at YD 253-290 and YD 330-337. Quang Tri/Thua Thien Pr border, I Corps.

Barbara, FSB (YS 457-775)
On W side LTL-2, some 10 km NNE Nui Dat and 1 km N FSB Le Loi. On 1ATF NCO trng map per John Hollett. 1ATF AO. Phuoc Tuy Pr, III Corps.

Barbara, St. FSB (XT 273-679)
See St. Barbara, FSB. Tay Ninh Pr, III Corps.

Barbel, USS (n/a)
SS-580. US Submarine. In '66, and while in NVN waters, she struck and apparently sunk a surface ship rptd to have been "the largest transport in NVN inventory." *Barbel* herself was either damaged such that she could not leave the scene, or to avoid detection, had to remain submerged and inactive for a long period of time until an elaborate, and still top-secret, rescue plan was executed. Plan apparently involved intricate deception. Rumors suggest ship she sunk may not have been NVN vessel at all and/or that sinking may not have been accidental. Exact date and location of incident remain classified, as does true nature of incident. *Barbel* class was last USN conventional diesel-electric submarine designed featuring a "body-of-revolution, Albacore" hull. Sister subs *Barbel* (*SS-580*), *Blueback* (*SS-581*) and *Bonefish* (*SS-582*) were known as *The Lemon Sisters*. Was Decom Jan90, used as target, 30Jan2001, and sunk at 032°19'08.0"N-121°36'16.0"W (1,972 fathoms). [47] NVN.

Barbey, USS (n/a)
DE-1088. DD-Escort, per Ralph Fries.

Barbour County, USS (n/a)
LST 1195, Amphibious Ship. See Frequent Wind.

Baria (YS 43-67)
See Ba Ria. Phuoc Tuy Pr, III Corps.

Baria Heliport (YS 384-622)
In Phuoc Le, apx 20 km NE Vung Tau and 9 km SW Luscombe AF. "Heliport #511, El. 17', soccer field, Fuel-J4, Ammo-7.62, 2.75" rkts. Tower-124.7, 40.7. 10°30'30"N-107°11'00"E," Phuoc Tuy Pr, III Corps.

Barky Operations Center (YD 32-56?)
TOC for USAF TASS FACs (call-sign Barky) at Quang Tri and suptg 5th Mech Div in '70. MAC-SOG Mobile Launch Team-2 (MLT-2) HQ was 8 km W of the airfield. Quang Tri Pr, I Corps.

Barlow, FSB (XT 549-081)
Apx 5 km NE Khiem Cuong and 12 km SW Cu Chi. 28Feb69. Hau Nghia Pr, III Corps.

Barn BEQ (XS 8-9)
Billets for 53d Signal Co in Saigon. Data per *Vietnam Military Lore, 1959-1973*. Gia Dinh Pr, III Corps.

Barn, LZ (YD 130-670)
Near S edge of DMZ, apx 35 km NW Quang Tri, 14 km NW Cam Lo and 14 km due E Bon Ho Su. Apr70 XXIV Corps grid per Don Armstrong. Quang Tri Pr, I Corps.

Barnacle (n/a)
6Apr70, XXIV Corps future-use 5th Div FSB name.

Barnae Airfield (n/a)
Apx 240 km SW Ubon AB and 10 km NW Cambodia. Per ONC-K-10. El. 886'. Thailand.

Barnes, Camp (YD 24-59)
On QL-1 apx 12 km NW Quang Tri and 60 km NW Hue. USN Seabee camp at Dong Ha named to honor EOCS Donald J. Barnes, USN, Seabee Sr. Chief Equip Operator, NMCB-11, KIA 5Jun67, at Khe Sanh by 122mm rocket on 1st day of his 2d VN tour, during const activity at base. MCB-11 Seabees, 4May67-30Nov67. Grid apx. Data per *Vietnam Military lore 1959-1973*. Quang Tri Pr I Corps.

Barnett, FSB (YD 199-322)
Apx 24 km due W Camp Evans, 43 km WNW Hue and 20 km SSW Quang Tri. Appears to be in Quang Tri Pr just N its border with Thua Thien Pr. Quang Tri Pr, I Corps.

Barracuda, FSB (YD 894-988)
Near Thon Ben Tai, 16 km due S Phu Bai. 101st Abn grid per Don Armstrong. Thua Thien Pr, I Corps.

Barray Airfield (n/a)
Feb67 Natl Geo map. El. 174'. Cambodia.

Barrel Roll Operations (n/a)
Bombing of infiltration rtes and supt for Royal Lao Army in its fight with Communist Pathet Lao. "Lima Sites," small rudimentary airstrips for small transports were built throughout NE Laos for effort. US secret air ops in Laos were divided into 3 zones: Tiger Hound, Steel Tiger and Barrel Roll. On 28Feb65, Skyraiders and Skyhawks from *USS Coral Sea* carried out 1st Barrel Roll strikes on Mu Gia Pass. After USAF attack on critical Nape Pass early in Mar65, *USS Hancock* CVWs again hit Mu Gia. In both ops delayed-action bombs made travel risky for NVA By 23Mar65, half of eventual total of 43 Barrel Roll missions were completed. Totals were 134 strike, 28 flak suppression, 56 patrol, 32 aerial photo, and 25 escort sorties. See LS, Steel Tiger and Tiger Hound.

Barrier Island (BT 220-550?)
Apx 30-50 km S of Da Nang. 2d NVA Div staging area in coastal lowlands near Chu Lai. 1st/26th Marines conducted last of 62 SLF amphib assaults of war on 7Sep69 here during Op Defiant Stand (3d sweep of island in '69). Op was also 1st amphib assault conducted with Korean Marine Corps in SVN. USMC SLF air assaulted inland while Viet patrol craft cut off escape rtes. US 7th Fleet not used in amphib role again until Op Frequent Wind evacs of Spring '75. Quang Nam and Quang Tin Pr?, I Corps.

Barrier Reef (BT 220-550)
See Barrier Island. Gulf of Tonkin, II Corps.

Barroom, LZ (XD 941-685)
Listed grid puts site in DMZ and on bank of Rao Thanh River (which was NVN/SVN Demarcation line of Geneva Accords), apx 6 km E Bon Ho Su (NVN), 13 km NW the Rockpile (Thon Khe Tri) and 43 km WNW Quang Tri. Likely a temporary LZ as permanent FSB built in DMZ unlikely? Apr70 XXIV Corps grid per Don Armstrong. Quang Tri Pr, I Corps.

Barry, FSB (YU 170-331)
Within 5 km of Cambodia, apx 20 km ENE Bu Dop AF, 17 km WSW Djamap AF, 22 km N Song Be AF. Cambodian Incursion, May-Jun70. Phuoc Long Pr, III Corps.

Barry, USS (n/a)
A.k.a. DD-933. Flagship of DesRon 24, among 1st grp of Atlantic Fleet destroyers to deploy to RVN. Left Newport 29Sep65? with the *Samuel B. Roberts* (DD 823), *Charles S. Sperry* (DD 697), *Hawkins* (DD 873), *Vesole* (DD 878), and *Ingraham* (DD 594) on. *Harold E. Ellison* (DD 864) and *Bache* were joined by *Bainbridge* (DLGN 25).

Barsanti Affair, The (XT 98-13)
See Glossary.
Bartlett, LZ/FSB (AN 785-235)
A.k.a. Nui Tio Ha and Hill 349. Apx 8 km W and slightly S Thien Giao, 4 km N QL-1, and 18 km NW LZ Betty/Phan Thiet. On 3Mar68 elements of 3d-506th Inf here per www.currahee.org/pageb2.html. 5th/27th Arty (105s) here, per Jerry Berry. 3d/506th Inf/3d Bde/101st Abn. Info/grid per Jerry Berry. Binh Thuan Pr, II Corps.
Base, LZ (ZA 027-934?)
Apparent variant of Bass? See Bass, LZ. Spelled as listed in *Time Heals No Wounds*, p 137. Kontum Pr, II Corps.
Base 3 (XT 035-576)
Apx 18 km WNW Tay Ninh. Nature of site unknown. 25Apr66. Tay Ninh Pr, III Corps.
Base 4 (XT 280-670)
Along TL-4, apx 8 km due N peak of Nui Ba Den, and 17 km NNE Tay Ninh. Nature of site unknown. 7May66. Tay Ninh Pr, III Corps.
Base Area 100 (n/a)
In Quang Tin Pr, and neutralized by III MAF ops during '68. Quang Tin Pr, I Corps.
Base Area 101 (YD)
The Hai Lang Natl Forest, a rugged hill mass south of Quang Tri and base area of operations for 5th and 6th NVA Rgts in '67. See Hai Lang Forest. Quang Tri Pr, I Corps.
Base Area 112 (ZC or AT)
VC/NVA staging area SW An Hoa estimated to contain about 3,500 enemy troops in early '69, suptd by another 6,000 in nearby Que Son Mtns. Attacked by USMC Task Force Yankee in Dec68-Feb69. Quang Nam Pr, I Corps.
Base Area 114 (YD)
Staging area for 803d NVA Rgt. Thua Thien Pr, I Corps.
Base Area 116 (AT)
VC/NVA staging area apx 10 km SE An Hoa CB, neutralized by III MAF ops '68. 1st Mar Div, Quang Nam Pr, I Corps.
Base Area 117 (BT or BS?)
Coastal lowlands of Pineapple Forest, Barrier Island and Ba Su Mtns, 2d NVA Div staging area. I Corps.
Base Area 121 (BS)
NVA/VC staging area within striking distance of Quang Ngai. Quang Ngai Pr?, I Corps.
Base Area 202 (BR 130-307)
NVA/VC staging area apx 58 km ESE Pleiku and 40 km WSW An Khe. A.k.a. VC Valley and staging area for 95B NVA Rgt in Mid '69. 4th Div AO in '70. Grid per Jim Claeys. Pleiku Pr, II Corps.
Base Area 226 (BR 72-63)
NVA/VC staging area apx 10 km E Vinh Thanh and 30 km NE An Khe. 4th Div AO in '70. Grid per Jim Claeys. Binh Dinh Pr, II Corps.
Base Area 237 (n/a)
Staging area for E-301 Local Force VC Bn. II Corps.
Base Area 238 (AQ 780-740)
Home of 401st Local Force Bn (VC), in US 4th Div's AO. Kontum/Darlac Pr, II Corps.
Base Area 302 (YS)
E of QL-2, in Southern Long Khanh Pr, III Corps.
Base Area 303 (YS 3-7?)
A.k.a. Hat Dich Secret Zone. Southern III Corps.
Base Area 350 (XU)
Area in Cambodia along border just N the Fishhook and immed N Loc Ninh. Code-named "Dessert" during Op Menu, the secret bombing of Cambodia that began 18Mar69. At time, its civilian pop was est at under 130. 706 sorties flown and 20,157 tons of bombs dropped here.[48] Cambodia.
Base Area 351 (XU)
100 square km area in Fishhook, Cambodia. Code-named "Snack" during Op Menu, the secret bombing of Cambodia that began 18Mar69. At time, its civilian pop was est to be under 400. 885 sorties flown and 25,336 tons of bombs dropped here.[49] Cambodia.
Base Area 352 (XU)
Area in Fishhook of Cambodia code-name "Dinner" during Op Menu, the secret bombing of Cambodia that began 18Mar69. Its civilian pop was est at under 800 at time. 817 sorties flown and 23,391 tons of bombs dropped here.[50] Cambodia.
Base Area 353 (XU)
N of Tay Ninh along Cambodian border. 25 sq-km area in Cambodia near the Fishhook and supposed site of COSVN in '69. Sanctuary for 1st NVA Div code-named "Breakfast" during Op menu, the secret bombing of Cambodia that began 18Mar69. At time, its civilian pop was est at under 2,000. 228 sorties flown and 6,529 tons of bombs dropped here.[51] On map in *Rangers at War*, p 324, discussed at p 151. Tay Ninh Pr and Cambodia, III Corps.
Base Area 354 (XT)
An NVA/NLF Base area along Cambodian border N the Parrot's Beak and NE Tay Ninh. Was excluded from secret bombing program Op Menu, Mar69-May70, due to its large civilian pop. On map in *Rangers at War*, p 324, discussed at p 151. Tay Ninh Pr/Cambodia. III Corps.
Base Area 367 (XS)
NVA/NLF staging and base area in Cambodia consisting of S half of Parrot's Beak. Cambodia.
Base Area 483 (n/a)
NE portion of zone was in Chuong Thien Pr, S portion in An Xuyen Pr. Between Jun-Aug69, ARVNMC Bde A conducted pacification and reopening of QL-12, then returned beginning Sep69 with Bde B as part of TF 211 in sweeping 483 and U Minh Forest. IV Corps.
Base Area 604 (XD/YD)
NVA staging area along HCMT and centered around Tchepone. Base Areas 604, 610 and 611, along Lao border/A Shau Valley, were main source of NVA supply and troop infiltration into southern I Corps, per *A Better War*, p 142. Laos.
Base Area 609 (YB 74-25)
In general vicinity of listed grid. Tri-border area where Cambodian, Lao and SVN borders meet. Code-named "Lunch" during Op Menu, the secret bombing of Cambodia which began 18Mar69. Its civilian pop was est at under 200 at time. 992 sorties flown and 26,630 tons of bombs dropped here.[52] Staging area of B3 Front's 66th NVA Rgt, '68-71. See Op Quang Trung 22F. Adj Darlac and Kontum Prvs, II Corps.
Base Area 610 (XD/YD)
See Base Areas 604. Laos.

Base Area 611 (XD)
In Laos to W of A Shau Valley. Base area of 6th and 9th NVA Rgt in '68-69. See Base Areas 604. Laos.
Base Area 618 (XD/YD)
See Dawson River South. Quang Tri Pr, I Corps.
Base Area 701 (YV)
Staging area of 18B, 95C and 101D NVA Rgts of B3 Front in '68-69. Along border W Duc Lap and roughly halfway between Pleiku to NE and Ban Me Thuot to SE. 4th Div AO, adj Darlac Pr, II Corps.
Base Area 702 (YA 90-75 or ZA 09-75)
If in YA zone, was in Chu Pa Mtn Region apx 20 km NW Plei Mrong, 40 km WSW Kontum. If in ZA zone, was apx 20 km SW Kontum. Home of B3 Front HQ (apx 500 men), 66th NVA Inf Rgt (apx 2000 men), 101 D NVA Inf Rgt (apx 1800 men) and 24th NVA Rgt at various times. 4th Div list per Jim Claeys puts grid as YA 09-75, but that is apparent error as it is some 50 km W SVN in Cambodia. Kontum/Pleiku Prvs, II Corps.
Base Area 704 (VS/WT/VS/WS)
NVA/NLF Base area in Cambodia that straddled the Mekong River at border. Originally excluded from secret bombing program, Op Menu, Mar69-May70, due to large civilian pop, it was bombed nonetheless when MACV requests not to bomb were overruled at higher level. Cambodia.
Base Area 707 (n/a)
NVA/NLF Base area in Cambodia excluded from secret bombing program Op Menu, Mar69-May70, due to large civilian pop.
Base Area 740 (YU 750-790)
Code named "Supper" during Cambodian bombing campaign. In Cambodia and along SVN border SW Ban Me Thuot and W Duc Lap. Staging area for 1st NVA Inf Div (HQ), 320th, 95C NVA Rgts and K-394 NVA Bn in '69. 4th Div AO. 247 B-52 sorties flown and 6,780 tons of bombs dropped here.[53] Cambodia.
Base Area 'A' (YD 01-66)
See NVA Operational Area A. Quang Tri Pr, I Corps.
Base Area 'B' (YD 54-17)
See NVA Operational Area B. Thua Thien Pr, I Corps.
Base Area 'C' (AT 97-52)
See NVA Operational Area C. Quang Nam Pr, I Corps.
Base Area 'D' (BT 18-18)
See NVA Operational Area D. Quang Tin Pr, I Corps.
Base Area 'E' (BS 39-73)
See NVA Operational Area E. Quang Ngai Pr, I Corps.
Base Area 'F' (BS 70-57)
See NVA Operational Area F. Quang Ngai Pr, I Corps.
Base Camp (n/a)
See Camp in Glossary.
Base Camp 1 (XT 913-213)
A.k.a. Basecamp I. At Xom Ben Son, apx 10 km NW Bien Hoa AB. Basecamp s 1, 2 and 3 (and likely 4 & 5 too) were camps built by and for 1st US Engr Bn, 1st Inf Div Engrs during Op Rolling Stone, 10Feb-3Mar66, to facilitate construction of Route Orange. Camps were spread out along proposed path of Route Orange that ran from QL-13 just S Ben Cat, E to Rte 16, passing Tam Binh to its S. All were generally S to SE Lai Khe and were built near laterite pits used for mining materials needed for surfacing the road. See *Infantry in Vietnam*, pp 223-228, for discussion. Jul67. Also listed at XT 919-210. Bien Hoa Pr, III Corps.
Base Camp 2 (XT 930-270)
A.k.a. Basecamp II. Apx 15 km NNW Bien Hoa AB. See Basecamp 1. '67. Bien Hoa Pr, III Corps.
Base Camp 2 (XT 947-256)
A.k.a. Basecamp II. Apx 11 km NNW Bien Hoa AB. See Basecamp 1. '67. Bien Hoa Pr, III Corps.
Base Camp 3 (XT 911-252)
A.k.a. Basecamp III. Apx 13 km NW Bien Hoa AB. See Basecamp 1. '67. Binh Duong Pr?, III Corps.
Base Camp 4 (XT 796-210)
A.k.a. Basecamp IV. At intersection of TL-2A and QL-13, apx 22 km WNW Bien Hoa AB, 7 km NW Phu Loi. See Basecamp 1. Aug67. Binh Duong Pr, III Corps.
Base Camp 5 (XT 764-270)
A.k.a. Basecamp V. Apx 11 km SSE Ben Cat and 24 km WNW Bien Hoa AB. See Basecamp 1. Aug67. Binh Duong Pr, III Corps.
Base Camps I thru V (XT)
See Basecamp s I thru V. III Corps.
Base III (XT 660-580)
At road intersection, apx 11 km WSW Chon Thanh AF, 25 km NNW Lai Khe and 8 km SSE Minh Thanh AF. Nature of site unknown. 21Feb67. Binh Duong/Binh Long Pr border, III Corps.
Base IV (XT 760-610)
Apx 2 km SW Chon Thanh AF and 23 km due N Lai Khe. Nature of site unknown. 21Feb67. Binh Long Pr, III Corps.
Base Tay Ninh (XT 24-47)
Name used for Bde Trains Fwd, 199th LIB. See Tay Ninh. Tay Ninh Pr, III Corps.
Base Turnover Program (n/a)
See Glossary.
Base X (BR 896-412)
See Phu Cat AF. Binh Dinh Pr, II Corps.
Basilone, USS (n/a)
DD-824, per Ralph Fries.
Basis, LZ? (BQ 954-503)
4 km E Xuan Son (2) and 26 km NW Tuy Hoa AB/Hoa Thanh. Apparently 173d Abn LZ in '67. Data per Dan Gillotti, 15th Arty. Phu Yen Pr, II Corps.
Basin, The (ZD 105-002)
Per George Clancy, CAP 3-2-1's AO in '67-68 was from Cau Hai Bay to Loc Tri, an area they called "The Basin." Cau Hai was between FSB Tomahawk and 4 km SE FSB Roy (a FSB 2 km ENE Bac Thach and adj to Phuoc Tuong). CAP 3-2's HQ was at Cau Ha. Grid simply a point in basin. Thua Thien Pr, I Corps.
Basketball (n/a)
See Glossary.
Bass, FSB (YS 494-903)
On E edge of Courtenay Rubber Plantation, 23 km NNE Nui Dat, 4 km E Rte-2, 10 km NE FSB Coolah. In front yard of picturesque French planter's mansion. 161 Bty, RNZA (Hitching's Bty 14Apr68-18Mar69) FSB set here 12-22Oct68. On 1ATF NCO trng map per John Hollett. Also listed at YS 49-90. Long Khanh Pr, III Corps.
Bass, LZ (ZA 027-934)
A.k.a. FSB Polei Kleng? Apx 24 km WNW Kontum and just W Polei Kleng AF/SF Camp. Attack of 4Mar69 (in

which NVA used CS or similar gas) is described in *Time Heals No Wounds*, p 128 et seq. 4th Div, and 2d/9th and 1st/92d Arty elements here mid '68. Also listed at ZA 028-937 and 029-933 per Craig Miller. Photos/maps at http://1-14th.com/maps.html. Kontum Pr, II Corps [54]

Bassac Canal (WR 6-7)
A.k.a. Kinh Long My Den Hau Gian, and Kinh Togtoampu. Near 9°44'00"N-105°37'00"E. NC48-10. Chuong Thien Pr, IV Corps.

Bassac River (WS/XR)
A.k.a. Song Hau Giang. Tributary of Mekong River that small ships could navigate as far W as Chau Duc near Cambodian border. Can Tho, Binh Thuy, Long Xuyen and Chau Duc, Chau Phu are along its banks. IV Corps.

Bastard's Bridge (YD 128-671)
See C 2 Bridge. Quang Tri Pr, I Corps.

Bastogne, FSB (YD 620-095)
A.k.a. FOB Bastogne, and LZ Bastogne Apr68. Apx 15 km WSW Nam Hoa and 17 km SW Hue along N side of Hwy 547, some 8 km due W FSB Birmingham. Per Charles Dukes, initial const started late Mar/early Apr68, during Op Delaware, by 2d/502d Inf. [55]. Elements of 1st & 2d Bdes/101st Abn, inc 1st/502d Inf and 27th Engrs, also participated in const. N end of A Shau Valley was within 175mm range of site and 1st Bde/101st expanded base to accommodate 175's in prep for supt of 1st Cav/101st ops there during Op Delaware (Apr-May68). Was scene of heavy fighting and overrun/occupied by NVA during both '72 Easter and '75 Final Offensive.[56] 81mm, 105mm, 8", 175mm Btys of 321st and 11th Arty here, as well as 40mm Dusters, Trps of 3d/5th Cav. Per Russ Richardson, 1st/83d Arty was also here with its HQ at Camp Eagle. Hit by barrage of 122mm rockets apx 30Apr68, and resulting fire destroyed all 1st/502d Inf's records/daily journal entries for period 14Apr-30Apr68. XXIV Corps grid. Also listed at YD 620-094 and 625-095. Thua Thien Pr, I Corps.

Basswood, USCGS (n/a)
WLB 388. USCG Buoy Tender.

Bat, LZ (BS)
USMC LZ and fire supt position during Op Deckhouse IV. Existed only 26Feb67-3Mar67. HMM 263 landed troops here and 8 of 14 UH-34Ds in initial CA were hit by enemy fire, with 6 put out of action. Apx 1,500 meters inland from coast (8 km in another text) in N Duc Pho District, N Duc Pho and secured by 1st/5th Mar and 2 Btys of 1st/11th Arty. Quang Ngai Pr, I Corps.

Bat Bat Camp (n/a)
Sp variant of "Ban Bat" or "Ban Ban?" Neither NIMA nor NPIA Gaz lists such a name, but do list villes with name Ban Bat at XJ 9-8, VJ 0-7, and BQ 4-6. Numerous other places with the name Ban Ban (see Ban Ban entries) Former POW Bobby Garwood claimed to have seen 20 live US POWs at this NVN POW camp in Fall of '73, and another 22 planting vegetables there in Mar75. The Rock River flowed through or by this camp. Discussed in *Prisoners of Hope*, p 79. NVN.

Bat Nuoc Van (YS 1-5)
Mui Nuoampoc Van. Coastal point at 10°27'N-106°56'E. NC48-07 JOG. Gia Dinh Pr, III Corps.

Bat Nuoc Van (YS 1-5)
Gia Dinh Pr, III Corps.

Bataan, LZ (YD 173-521)
Apx 16 km due W Quang Tri, 8 km E Mai Loc and 10 km SE Cam Lo. Apr70 XXIV Corps grid per Don Armstrong. Quang Tri Pr, I Corps.

Bataillion de Marche Indochinois (n/a)
See Glossary.

Batallion de Coree (n/a)
See Glossary.

Batallion de Marche (n/a)
See Glossary.

Batallion Medical de Campagne (n/a)
See Glossary.

Batallion Volontaire-33 (n/a)
See BV-33. Laos.

Batangan Peninsula (BS 7-9 to 9 7-8)
A.k.a. Van Tuong Peninsula. Apx 20 km S Chu Lai and running roughly between BS 72-94-BS 78-85. Heavy fighting here 66-67, involving 1st Cav Div. [57] Huge op here also beginning 13Jan69 in which Americal. USMC, Navy and ARVN cordoned and swept entire 15 km neck of peninsula. 4th/3d Inf, 11th Inf Bde and 5th/46th, 198th LIB were at center of sweeping "hammer" forces. Was regarded as one of most heavily mined areas of country and most casualties here resulted from mines. During op, 210 VC were KIA and numerous prisoners and locals airlifted to CHIC (Combined Holding and Interrogation Ctr, Quang Ngai); over 12,000 people were displaced, 600 of whom were discovered to be VC soldiers or agents. My Lai-4, site of infamous My Lai massacre was at S end of peninsula, as were LZs Dottie and Uptight. Quang Ngai Pr, I Corps.

Batangan, Cap (BS 7-8)
A.k.a. Mui Ba Lang An. Cape at 15°14'N-108°56'E. On ND49-01 JOG. Quang Ngai Pr, I Corps.

Batangan, Mui (BS 7-8)
A.k.a. Mui Ba Lang An. Cape at 15°14'N-108°56'E. On ND49-01 JOG. Quang Ngai Pr, I Corps.

Batdambang Airfield (n/a)
Apx 240 km NW Phnom Penh per ONC-K-10. Spelled Battambang on DMA's TPC series and Feb67 Natl Geo maps. El. 59'. Cambodia.

Baton Rouge (1-10) (n/a)
Code name for intelligence control elements of Op Tiger Hound/Task Force Tally Ho flying FAC/intel missions into area immed adj to SVN which ran roughly from DMZ S to Cambodian border and about 100 km W into Laos. Dong Ha was Baton Rouge 10, for example. See Tiger Hound, Steel Tiger and Barrel Roll.

Baton Rouge Victory, SS (n/a)
In '66, this Merchant Marine-staffed cargo vessel was sunk in Saigon River (or possibly Song Nha Be River?) apx 20 km S or SE Saigon. 2 officers and five crew were KIA in blast. Data per www.fred.net/rphumm/info.html. [58]

Baton, FSB (YS 556-612)
Along LTL-23, apx 13 km ESE Nui Dat, 6.3 km ESE the Horseshoe and 2 km E FSB Serle. On 1ATF NCO trng map per John Hollett. Phuoc Tuy Pr, III Corps.

Battambang Airfield (UV 07-48)
Major AF, apx 240 km NW Phnom Penh and 72 km SW Siemreap AF, per Dec67 DMA TPC K-10A and Feb67 Natl Geo maps. El. 59'. Variant of Batdambang. Cambodia.

Battambang NDB (UV 07-48)
Non-Directional Air Nav Beacon site. At Battambang AF, Batdambang, Cambodia.
Battangan, Cape (BS 7-8)
A.k.a. Mui Ba Lang An/Cape Batangan. Cape at 15°14'N-108°56'E. On ND49-01 JOG. Quang Ngai Pr, I Corps.
Batterie, Pointe de la (CR 1-2)
See Pointe Batterie. Binh Dinh Pr, II Corps.
Battery Point (CR 1-2)
A.k.a. Pointe Sud. Coastal point at 13°46'N-109°15'E. On ND49-09. Binh Dinh Pr, II Corps.
Battle, LZ (BR 813-768)
Apx 19 km SSW Bong Son and 6 km SSE Ha Tay AF. 1st Cav?, 15Sep66. Binh Dinh Pr, II Corps.
Battle, LZ (XD 842-666)
Near DMZ, apx 6 km SW Bo Hu Su (NVN), 30 km WNW Cam Lo and 52 km WNW Quang Tri. Apr70 XXIV Corps grid per Don Armstrong. Quang Tri Pr, I Corps.
Battle Ax, FSB (ZC 091-302)
A.k.a. COB Battle-Ax. Apx 2 km NE peak of Hill 1143, 5 km SW FSB Dart, 9 km SE Saber, 8 km SSE LZ Javelin, and 26 km SW An Hoa. USMC base during assault on Base Area 112, Dec68-Feb69. On map in *US Marines in Vietnam-1969*, p 90. XXIV Corps grid. Also listed at ZC 11-30. Quang Nam Pr, I Corps.
Battle Creek BEQ (XS 813-918)
At Lot 24-26, Phu Tho Hoa St., Saigon, per *Vietnam Military Lore, 1959-1973*. Gia Dinh Pr, III Corps.
Battle For Hue, Operation (n/a)
31Jan-25Feb68. ARVN/USMC/1st Cav/101st Abn fight to retake Hue during Tet '68. Apx 5,113 NVA KIA, per *Vietnam Order of Battle*, pp 9-14. Thua Thien/Quang Tri Pr, I Corps.
Battle for Road No. 6 (WJ 3-0)
See Road No. 6, Battle for. NVN.
Battle for T'ai Hill Country (VJ)
See T'ai Hill Country, Battle for. NVN.
Battle Index, VHPA (n/a)
See Glossary.
Battle in the Alleys (AN 83-09?)
18-23 Feb68. At 0255 hours 18Feb68, VC 482nd LF Bn struck VN outpost near Phan Thiet soccer field, Quang Trung ARVN Camp, ARVN arty cmpd and RF site at school. Forced out by elements 3d/506th Inf in house -to-house fighting. Binh Thuan Pr, II Corps.
Battle of Hong Kong Hill, The (BR 452-469)
See Hong Kong Hill. Binh Dinh Pr, II Corps.
Battle of Grand, The (YS 28-43)
See Madame T's. Phuoc Tuy Pr, III Corps.
Battle of Slopes, The (YB 99-15)
See Hill 1338. Kontum Pr, II Corps.
Batu, LZ (AQ 800-212)
Possibly a.k.a. LZ Cacti or Cactu? Apx 16 km due N Ban Me Thuot City AF, and 6 km NW Quang Nhieu. 28Feb66. Darlac Pr, II Corps.
Bau Bang (BT 18-44)
Freshwater lake just W Thang Binh and 15 km SSE Hoi An, near 15°45N-108°22'E. Grid per DMA TPC K-10A. Quang Nam Pr, I Corps.
Bau Bang (XT 7-4)
See Ap Bau Bang. On 20Mar67 the 9th Inf Div fought major battle near this ville, involving 3/5th Cav and 273d VC Rgt. 4 US KIA and 67 WIA; 230 enemy KIA. Cited in *Doc: Platoon Medic*, p 15. Binh Duong Pr, III Corps.
Bau Ca, FSB (YT 27-10)
FSB a.k.a. Verna or Vema. On QL-1 apx 18 km W Xuan Loc, 29 km E to ESE Bien Hoa AB, 34 km NE Saigon, and 17 km NE Long Thanh North AF. 2d/3d and 5th/12th Inf, 199th LIB position likely in '68. Grid per 199th LIB Assn. Bien Hoa Pr, III Corps.
Bau Can Lo Than Island (CP 04-30)
In large, narrow lagoon N Cam Ranh Bay, and adj to Dong Ba Thin. Khanh Hoa Pr, II Corps.
Bau Co, FSB (XT 276-679)
A.k.a. Bau Company FSB, The French Fort and FSB St. Barbara. At Bau Co, apx 9 km due N Nui Ba Den, 18 km NE Tay Ninh West and perhaps 3 km W Hwy 4. Permanent base with four 175mm cannons of 1st/27th and 2d/3d Arty. Well established strongpoint by '68 that dated back to French War. Perimeter was high berm of compacted dirt with bunkers built into berm itself. Interior was crowded. Helo pad outside berm easily observed by VC. During Aug68 offensive, cut off for about 3 weeks and only re-supplied by helo lifts almost always accompanied by mortar attacks. Grid/Info per Butch Sincock. 25th Inf Div, Aug68. See St. Barbara. Tay Ninh, III Corps.
Bau Company FSB (XT 276-679)
See Bau Co, FSB. Tay Ninh Pr, III Corps.
Bau Dieu Outpost (XT 572-170)
Apx 7 km WNW Cu Chi. Hau Nghia Pr, III Corps.
Bau Don, Camp (XT 438-353)
See Bao Don SF Camp. Tay Ninh Pr, III Corps.
Bau Giang Refugee Camp (BS 670-694)
E of QL-1, apx 4 km SE Quang Ngai. Grid per NPIA. Quang Ngai Pr, I Corps.
Bau Loc Airfield (ZT 08-77 or 06-79?)
See Bao Loc AF. Lam Dong Pr, II Corps.
Bau Long Pond (XT 791-528?)
Along on QL-13, apx 15 km N Lai Khe and S of Ap Bau Long. Binh Duong Pr, III Corps.
Bau Ngua (YS 67-85)
Freshwater lake apx 33 km SE Xuan Loc, at 10°42N-107°27'E. On NC48-08 JOG. Phuoc Tuy Pr, III Corps.
Bau Rai Airfield (TU 3-8)
At 12°33'00"N-102°32'00"E. NIMA data. Thailand.
Bau Trang (BN 19-24)
Freshwater lake about 1 by 3 km in size apx 40 km NE Phan Thiet and 2 km from coast, at 11°04N-108°25'E. On NC49-01 JOG. Binh Thuan Pr, II Corps.
Bausell, USS (n/a)
DD-845, per Ralph Fries.
Baux Cape Varella (CN 0-9)
See Cape Baux Varella. Ninh Thuan Pr, II Corps.
Baxter, Camp (BT 03-77?)
A.k.a. 5th Transportation Terminal Cmd Cmpd. In E Da Nang, presumably along bank of Tourane River, near its mouth at Da Nang Bay (some say it was S of Da Nang?). Named to honor Larry Baxter, PFC USA, KIA 12May69. Baxter was driving 5,000 gallons gas truck when it was hit by an RPG. Instead of jumping clear to save himself

(which would have trapped convoy behind him), the badly wounded Baxter instead drove it through intense enemy fire, taking his truck over an embankment and off the road. He was awarded the Silver Star posthumously for that act. Base of Ops/HQ for 5th Trans Term Cmd, which loaded and off-loaded shallow-draft vessels, maintained own fleet of SKILACs and Y-type tankers, as well as medium trucks for hauling w/in 35 km radius. Also responsible for managing Camp Baxter and its activities. 5th's HHC was responsible for supervision of Deep Water Pier, bridge Ramp, and Tien Sha Ramp, controlling port ops through its Harbormaster's Office, and regulating entire harbor complex. NSA Hosp Da Nang here, as apparently was E(LRP)/50th Inf. Grid is est. Quang Nam Pr, I Corps. [59]

Baxter, LZ (BR 185-719)
Apx 17 km NNW Suoi Doi AF, 28 km SE Kontum and 9 km NE De Gir. 4th Div AO, '70; C Bty, 4th/42d Arty here Jun70. Name/grid per Jim Claeys. Also listed at BR 185-725 and BR 185-724. Kontum Pr, II Corps.

Bay, Dam (CP 1-4)
Bay at 12°11'N-109°18'E. On ND49-13 JOG. Khanh Hoa Pr, II Corps.

Bay, Dam (CP 2-4)
See Dam Bay. Khanh Hoa Pr, II Corps.

Bay, FSB (YT 27-10?)
Possibly a.k.a. FSB Gloria? Appears to have been along N side of QL-1, apx 18 km W to WNW Xuan Loc, and 28 km ESE Bien Hoa AB. 199th LIB position? Grid estimated from FSB map at www.redcatcher.org./Map5.html. Long Khanh Pr, III Corps.

Bayfield, USS (n/a)
A.k.a. APA-33. *Brown Water, Black Berets*, p 322.

Bayonet, LZ/FSB (BT 549-016)
Large basecamp in sandy flats just W QL-1 apx 5 km SSE Chu Lai AB and 4 km NNW LZ Gator. Positions/bunkers also lined a significant ridge that formed base's W perimeter and overlooked base. Incorporating ridge into edge of base rather than making ridge its center was unusual in FSB construction for VN. HQ 198th LIB, 1st/20th, 11th LIB here, '68-69. Americal List. Also listed at BT 550-015. Quang Tin Pr, I Corps.

Bayonet West, LZ/FSB (BT 547-000)
Immed SW LZ Bayonet, apx 7 km SSE Chu Lai AF and apx 2 km W QL-1. See Bayonet. Quang Tin Pr, I Corps.

Bazooka, LZ (XD 980-558)
Along QL-9 apx 13 km WSW Cam Lo and 34 km W Quang Tri. Apr70 XXIV Corps grid per Don Armstrong. Quang Tri Pr, I Corps.

BD Cranes (n/a)
See BD Cranes in Glossary and Big John in alpha index.

Be Duc Airfield (XS 478-450)
See Binh Duc AF. Dinh Tuong Pr, IV Corps.

Be Loung Heliport (YC 583-887)
At S end of A Shau Valley, apx 42 km SW Hue, 8 km ESE A Sap and 5 km N of Laos. Heliport #516, El. 1,904', at 16°10'00"N-107°25'00"E. 73 TAD. Thua Thien Pr, I Corps.

Be Luong (YC 584-885)
Remote site apx 1 km NW peak Dong Ong (Hill 831), 40 km SSW Hue, 15 km E the A Shau Valley and 7 km NNE Be Luong ville. Steep and rugged terrain surrounded site and its history is unknown. Thua Thien Pr, I Corps.

Be Nuoc Nhi (CP 1-6)
Bay at 12°22'48"N-109°20'00"E. On ND49-13 JOG. Khanh Hoa Pr, II Corps.

Beach, FSB (AT 875-988)
On coast just N Dam Lap An Lagoon, 5 km due E FSB Los Banos, 26 km NNW Da Nang AB, 9 km SE Thon Binh An and 3 km SE peak of Hill 334. XXIV Corps grid. Also listed at AT 870-980. Thua Thien Pr, I Corps.

Beagle, LZ (YD 239-039)
Near Laotian border, apx 33 km NW A Sap, 11 km NW Dong Ap Bia (FSB Destiny or Hamburger Hill) and 50 km WSW Hue. Apr70 XXIV Corps grid per Don Armstrong. Quang Tri Pr, I Corps.

Bear Cat (YS 14-98)
See Bearcat. Bien Hoa Pr, III Corps.

Bear, LZ (BN 160-610)
Apx 19 km NNW Song Mao, 60 km NE Phan Thiet and 11 km W LZ Ape. 2Mar67. Binh Thuan Pr, II Corps.

Bear, LZ (YD 134-412)
Just N of Laos, apx 8 km due S Tou Rout, 23 km WSW Hue and 21 km WNW Dong Ap Bia (FSB Destiny or Hamburger Hill). Apr70 XXIV Corps grid per Don Armstrong. Quang Tri Pr, I Corps.

Bearcat (n/a)
Apr70, XXIV Corps future-use 101st Abn FSB name.

Bearcat (YS 14-98)
A.k.a. Bear Cat and Camp Martin/Cox. Along E side of QL-15, apx 6 km SE Long Binh Post, 16 km SE Bien Hoa, 25 km ENE Saigon and 30 km WNW Blackhorse Basecamp. Originally French AF prior to WWII, then occupied by Japanese during WWII. At outset of US involvement, became SF Camp (Tri Quyet Thang). Named derived from radio call-sign of 1st SF unit sited here (which was boldly painted on roof of main bldg for easy aerial ID). Original 9th Inf Div main basecamp until it moved to Dong Tam in '67. Long Thanh North AF here. Royal Thai Army Expeditionary Force (Black Panthers), later renamed RTA Volunteer Force, arrived here in '68, and eventually built into entire 3 Bde Div consisting of 1st, 2d and 3d Bdes, 4 Bns RTA Div Arty, an Armored Cav Sqdn, supt Avn, MPs, Div HQ and a LRP Co. Also 9th US Inf Div, Royal Thai Bde here. Map is L-7014-6330-1, per Jim Stone, 2d/39th Inf. Bien Hoa Pr, III Corps.

Bearcat Base (YS 14-98)
Along E side of QL-15 apx 6 km SE Long Binh Post, 16 km SE Bien Hoa, 25 km ENE Saigon and 30 km WNW Blackhorse. 9th Inf, Royal Thai Bde. See Bearcat. Map is L-7014-6330-1, per Jim Stone. Bien Hoa Pr, III Corps.

Bearcat Heliport (YT 162-003)
Along E side of QL-15, apx 6 km SE Long Binh Post, 16 km SE Bien Hoa, 25 km ENE Saigon and 30 km WNW Blackhorse Basecamp. "Heliport #738, El. 164', 1,986' x 100' (CON/RC-3). Divided in 2 nearly equal heliports by bldg/woods. Arty advisory-Bien Hoa 290.0, 46.7." At 10°51'N 106°59'E, per Feb73 TAD. Map is L-7014-6330-1, per Jim Stone. Bien Hoa Pr, III Corps.

Bearcat Signal Site (YS/YT?)
No data. Bien Hoa Pr?, III Corps.

Bearcats (n/a)
See Glossary.

Beatrice (TJ 9-6)
"Between the Dominiques and Gabrielle a kind of yellow ridge appeared above the green. This was Beatrice, or rather its main earthwork…nearly four miles away...a very strong position, even said to be impregnable, and held by Legionnaires of Thirteenth Demi-Bde."[60] Apx 3.4 mi NNE Dien Bien Phu main CP, 1 mi N D3 and 3.1 mi due E A2. In Muong Thanh Valley apx 290 km W Hanoi. French strongpoint during Op Castor, 20Nov53-7May54, that was held by French Legion Bn. Commanded Rte 41 and had spectacular view of valley. 1st position overrun by Vietminh at start of their offensive/siege, 13Mar54. Of 750 Legionnaires there that day, only 200 survived. NVN.

Beau Geste SF Camp (ZV 105-946)
Apx 27 km WSW Phu Nhon AF, 18 km due E LZ X-Ray and 8 km S Plei Me. 5th SF. Info/grid per *SF Order of Battle*. See Ea Soup. Darlac Pr, II Corps.

Beauregard, FSB (n/a)
Built beginning 1Jan68, during Op Yellowstone, by 2d/14th Inf 25th ID. May or may not be same as FSB Beauregard at Bo Tuc? III Corps.

Beauregard, FSB (XT 380-855)
At Bo Tuc. Apx 7 km SE Katum, 38 km due W An Loc and 38 km NNE Tay Ninh. Per Larry Criteser, heavy action here involving the 4th/9th Inf Manchus, 25th Inf Div, several days before Christmas in '67. Grid apx. 67-68. Tay Ninh Pr, III Corps.

Beaver, LZ (BS 765-985)
See Beaver at BR 765-985. Binh Dinh Pr, II Corps.

Beaver, LZ/FSB (BR 766-982)
In or overlooking An Lo River Valley about 1 km E river, apx 9 km NW Bong Son, and 10 km W to WSW LZ English. Apparently 173d Abn and 4th Div FSB in '70. Cited in '70 Bn Annual Hist Supp of 3/503d Inf, 173d Abn, on net at www.gasparot.com/nammedic. Per 119th AHC website, on 27Aug70, elements of 2d/35th Arty and 1st/12th Inf were moved here from LZs Tape and Powder. C Bty, 4th/42d Arty here Dec69. 4th Div 31Jan70 ORLL grid per Jim Henderson. Also listed at BR 767-984, and at BS 765-985, but that grid is both in I Corps and the ocean. Binh Dinh Pr, II Corps.

Beaver, LZ (XD 73-62)
Apx 9 km NE FSB Neville, on S edge of DMZ, 27 km E Laos, and 24 km WNW Cam Lo. 3d Mar Div. Grid per map p 58, *US Marines in Vietnam-1969*. Quang Tri Pr, I Corps.

Beaver, LZ (XD 862-648)
At edge of DMZ apx 50 km WNW Quang Tri, 5 km SE Bo Hu Su and 29 km WNW Cam Lo. Apr70 XXIV Corps grid per Don Armstrong. Quang Tri Pr, I Corps.

Beavis, FSB (YS 256-781)
Apx 21 km NW Nui Dat, 2 km NE QL-15 and 1 km ESE FSB Dakota. Also listed at YS 280-780, 27Apr68, which is apx 2.5 km E of listed grid. On 1ATF NCO trng map per John Hollett. Bien Hoa Pr, III Corps.

Becky, FSB (XD 856-615)
Overlooking Cam Lo River Valley apx 26 km W and slightly N of Cam Lo, perhaps 2 km S the river and 48 km WNW Quang Tri. Apr70 XXIV Corps grid per Don Armstrong. Quang Tri Pr, I Corps.

Becky, LZ (BS 365-540)
In Song Re Valley, apx 7 km SSW Lang Re, 17 km WNW Minh Long AF and 34 km SE Quang Ngai. 1st Cav. Name/grid per Dan Gillotti. Quang Ngai Pr, I Corps.

Becky, LZ (XT 373-810?)
If grid is accurate, was apx 6 km SSW Bo Tuc, 10 km SSE Katum AF and 15 km S its closest point to Cambodia. Was also ENE LZ Carolyn, WSW LZ Julie and SE LZ Mustang. Per 1st Cav website, VC threw simultaneous attacks against many 1st Cav bases in III Corps on 12Aug69, inc Quan Lai (likely spelling variant of Quan Loi), LZ Becky, LZ Jon, LZ Kelly and LZ Caldwell. 2d/8th Cav, 1st Cav, Jul69, 2d/5th Cav '69. Also listed at XT 372-210 and XT 425-830? Tay Ninh Pr, III Corps. [61]

Becky, FSB (XT 372-210?)
If grid is accurate, was apx 4 km S Go Dau Ha13 km due N Duc Hue AF, 8 km NE the lower tip of the Angel's Wing and 7 km from Cambodia at closest point. Listed here Jul69. Also listed at XT 373-810 and XT 425-830? Tay Ninh Pr, III Corps.

Becky, FSB (XT 425-830?)
Apx 6 km SE Katum, 36 km NNE Tay Ninh City and 7 km S Cambodian border. 2d/8th Cav, 1st Cav, Jul-69, 2d/5th Cav, '69. Also listed at XT 372-210 and 373-810? Grid per Frank Penk, Jr. Tay Ninh Pr, III Corps.

Beechnut, LZ (XD 825-515)
Apx 27 km due W Mai Loc, 51 km due W Quang Tri and 10 km NNW Khe Sanh CB. Apr70 XXIV Corps grid per Don Armstrong. Quang Tri Pr, Corps.

Beehive Round (n/a)
See Canister Round in Glossary.

Bein Hoa Province (XT/YT)
See Bien Hoa Province. Misspelling of "Bien."

Belcher, FSB (YD 465-385)
Along QL-1, apx 18 km SE Quang Tri and 2 km SE My Chanh. Per *Into the Valley*, p 234, was built on 3 tiny knolls during Op Delaware, beginning 21Apr68, by 3d/21st Inf, 196th LIB while opcon to 3d Mar Div. One rpt puts site due W FSB Jeanne (YD 551-393). D/3d/82d Arty and 1st/6th Inf elements here too. Quang Tri Pr, I Corps.

Bell, LZ (XD 68-61)
Apx 35 km W Cam Lo, 56 km WNW Quang Tri, 4 km due N FSB Argonne, 6 km W FSB Greene, 14 km WNW FSB Neville and 8 km E Laos. 3d Mar Div, '69. Grid per map at p 58, *US Marines in Vietnam-1969. A*pparently differs from LZ Bell at YD 065-545? Quang Tri Pr, I Corps.

Bell, LZ (YD 065-545)
Apx 6 km NW Mai Loc, 10 km SW Cam Lo and 28 km W Quang Tri. Apr70 XXIV Corps grid per Don Armstrong. Either differs from LZ Bell at XD 68-61 or grid is in error? Quang Tri Pr, Corps.

Bell Tone (n/a)
Code name for USAF air defense detachment at Don Muang Royal Thai AFB, Thailand.

Bellatrix, USS (n/a)
AF-62. Aux Refrig, per Ralph Fries.

Belle Grove, USS (n/a)
LSD 2. USN Landing Ship, Dock. Suptd 9th Inf Div/MRF in '66-67, per MRF Assn at www.mrfa.org. III/IV Corps?

Belleau Woods, USS (n/a)
US Acft Carrier on loan to French Navy during WWII. Manned entirely by French naval personnel, it was one of only 2 carriers employed by French during 1st Indochina War. The 2carriers had total aircraft complement of 4 dive-bomber and fighter-bomber sqdns, consisting of US Bearcats, Corsairs, Hellcats and Helldivers. French also used US Catalina amphib acft for coastal surveillance. Data per *Street Without Joy*, pp 261.

Belt Compound (XT 513-039?)
At Bao Tri, apx 32 km WNW Tan Son Nhut AB and Saigon, 2 km SW Khiem Cuong and 25 km NE the tip of Parrot's Beak. Named to honor Sgt Marvin M. Belt, MACV Adv Team 43(?), WIA during mortar attack of Bao Trai, 18Dec65, died of wounds in Philippines, 26Dec65. Hau Nghia Pr, III Corps.

Bemis Compound (WS 8-4?)
A.k.a. Earl J. Bemis Cmpd. Possibly at or near Sa Dec, apx 28 km N Can Tho? Kien Van Subsector, Kien Phong Pr, HQ for Advsy Team #84 here. Named to honor Plt Ldr 2LT Earle J. Bemis, A/4th/39th Inf, 9th Div, KIA 1Jun69 while trying to rescue a second crew member of a downed helicopter after saving another in battle near Chau Doc. Dedicated 14Sep69. Data per *Vietnam Military Lore, 1959-1973*, p 222. Kien Phong Pr, IV Corps.

Ben, FSB (YS 598-759)
Apx 18 km NE Nui Dat, 4 km S FSB Raglan and 8 km NE FSB Rapier. On 1ATF NCO trng map per John Hollett. Phuoc Tuy Pr, III Corps.

Ben Cat (n/a)
Mapsheet name of L-7014-6331-3. SVN.

Ben Cat (XT 71-20)
Ville 7 km NE Cu Chi. Binh Duong Pr, III Corps.

Ben Cat (XT 78-32)
Along QL-13, between War Zones C and D, 6 km SSW Lai Khe, on east shore of Song Thi Thinh River, 50 km ESE Tay Ninh and 60 km due S An Loc. 161 Bty, RNZA (Kenning's Bty 13Jun65-13Jun66) FSB set here 4-16Sep65 and 19-23Feb66. 161 Bty was also set 2 km NW city 16-18Sep65, 10 km N city 18-23Sep65 and 6 km S city 8-14Oct65. Also a Ben Cat at XS 231-504. Binh Duong Pr, III Corps.

Ben Cat Airfield (XT 772-381)
See Lai Khe AF. Binh Duong Pr, III Corps.

Ben Cat Basecamp (XT 73-33)
Apx 25 km NNE Saigon, 18 km SSW Lai Khe and 7 km NE Cu Chi. 5th SF Det A-301 here. Battle of Ben Cat, took place 1Feb68, when US armored Cav Plts converged on VC controlled town from directions during night attack, driving enemy from town. HQ for elements of 1st Inf Div, 25th Inf Div at various times. Binh Duong Pr, III Corps.

Ben Cat Engineer Camp (XT 742-328)
At Ben Cat, apx 6 km SE Lai Khe AF, 5 km ENE Xom Rach Bap and 36 km NNW Tan Son Nhut AB. 554th Engr Bn here for road projects and Cambodian Incursion. Grid per Frank Penk, Jr. Binh Duong Pr, III Corps.

Ben Cat Heliport (XT 744-331)
Apx 25 km NNE Saigon, 18 km SSW Lai Khe and 7 km NE Cu Chi. "Heliport #517, El. 17', Fuel-J4 (J4 tanker avail) Ammo-7. 62, 2. 75" rockets, at 11°09'20"N-106°36'00"E," per Feb73 TAD. Binh Doung Pr, III Corps.

Ben Cat SF Camp (XT 737-320)
Apx 25 km NNE Saigon, 18 km SSW Lai Khe and 7 km NE Cu Chi. 5th SF Grp. Info/grid per *SF Order of Battle*. Det A-301 here, moved to Bien Hoa MSF. Binh Duong Pr, III Corps.

Ben Cau (XT 2-3)
Possibly 10-15 km due S Tay Ninh? ARVN and/or SF camp sometimes used by 25th Div Arty ground surveillance 5-man teams using TPS-25 ground scanning radar. See http://pacer.calpoly.edu/Tri/radar.html for detail. Grid est per NIMA. III Corps.

Ben Cui Hard Spot (XT 448-452)
Along Rte 239 at S corner of Ben Cui Rubber Plantation, apx 5 km WSW Dau Tieng AF, 18 km E Tay Ninh and 8 km ENE Checkpoint Tango/LTL-26. Consisted of 5' or 6' high dirt berm with closely spaced bunkers. Apparently had been a French fort/AF prior to 25th Div's occupation. By '67-68, the adj jungle had been Rome-plowed as far out as 1 km from perimeter. 2d/22 Inf (Mech) occupied site from about Dec68-Jun69 (replaced by ARVN). Absorbed several probes during period, and at least 2 significant ground attacks (one by 5th Bn, 95C VC Rgt on 21Feb69, with 28 VC KIA). Was also mortared frequently with little damage and few casualties. The 25th Div established a number of such "hard spots", small, strong positions designed to cover important terrain and lure VC/NVA into costly attacks. Each site could accommodate a full Mech Co, and these Cos were rotated each week. See Instant Patrol Base in Glossary. Grid/data per Bill Noyes, 2d/22d Inf (Mech) 25th Inf Div. Binh Duong Pr, III Corps.

Ben Cui Rubber Plantation (XT 44-45)
Roughly 8 x 4 km in size and generally 5 km WSW Dau Tieng, 22 km ESE Tay Ninh and 50 km NNW Cu Chi. Its E edge is apx 3 km W Dau Tieng, and 5 km W Michelin Plantation. Swept by 25th Inf Div/196th LIB elements Oct66, and heavy fighting here during battle for Tay Ninh, Aug-Sep68. Map/discussions of nearby battles in '68 in *The Infantry Brigade in Combat*. Binh Duong Pr, III Corps.

Ben Duc Airfield (XS 478-450)
See Binh Duc AF. Dinh Tuong Pr, IV Corps.

Ben Giang (n/a)
Mapsheet name of L-7014-6540-2. SVN.

Ben Giang Heliport (YC 976-366)
In valley apx 28 km due N Kham Duc, 26 km SW Ha Tan and 60 km SW Da Nang. Heliport #518, El. 558', at 15°41'30"N-107°46'30"E. TAD. Quang Nam Pr, I Corps.

Ben Goi Bay (CQ 20-15)
Very large, wide-mouthed bay apx 50 km NNE Nha Trang. 25 km wide at mouth and 27 km long. Hon Lon Island is on E side of bay. II Corps.

Ben Goi, Baie de (CQ 1-0)
Bay at 12°41'N-109°18'E. On ND49-13 JOG. Khanh Hoa Pr, II Corps.

Ben Hai Bridge (YD 19-81)
QL-1 bridge over Ben Hai River on border between N and S VN. Marker there today is inscribed ***20-7-54*** and ***30-4-75***; the day VN was partitioned by Geneva Convention and day it was reunited. Flagpole at S end that once held SVN flag was toppled in 1985 storm and never replaced. French Conc blockhouse on S end of bridge somehow survived

massive bombing, though original Ben Hai Bridge did not. I Corps in DMZ.

Ben Hai River (YD 26-83)
Official boundary between NVN and SVN. Roughly centered in demilitarized zone N of Quang Tri. Mouth of this river was apx 16 km NW mouth of Cua Viet River and US Naval/Marine base there. '72 Easter Offensive began with a heavy mortar, rocket and arty attack on every FSB in Quang Tri Pr followed by an armored assault across river along QL-1. Grid at river's mouth. Quang Tri Pr, I Corps.

Ben Het (YB 865-255)
Apx 13 km due E Tri-border meeting point, 15 km WNW Dak To, 16 km S Dak Seang AF and 53 km NW Kontum. Proximate to Ho Chi Minh Trail and considered strategic site. NVA used armor in attack on SF camp here, 30Mar69. 1st Bn 69th Armor, SF Advs, 3 SVN Inf Cos, two M-42 Dusters and Bty of US 175mm howitzers here for Battle of Ben Het that date, destroying 2 NVA PT-76 tanks and a troop carrier of 16th Co, 4th Bn, 202d NVA Armored Rgt. Besieged by 28th and 66th NVA Rgts May-Jun69. AF here. 5th SF Grp CIDG Det A-244, 5th SF CIDG Det A-244 '68. 4th Div and 173d Abn AO. Also listed at YB 872-252. Kontum Pr, II Corps.

Ben Het, FSB (YB 865-250)
15 km WNW Dak To, 16 km S Dak Seang AF. 30Apr68. Kontum Pr, II Corps.

Ben Het Airfield (YB 872-252)
Apx 15 km WNW Dak To AF, 15 km SSW Dak Seang AF, 14 km W Laos. Per ONC K-10 El. 2,198', 1,500' steel-mat rwy. Kontum Pr, II Corps.

Ben Het Heliport (YB 871-251)
At Ben Het AF, apx 15 km WNW Dak To 2 AF and 52 km NW Kontum. Grid per N. Putman. Kontum Pr, II Corps.

Ben Het Ranger Camp (YB 87-26)
A.k.a. Boch Ho ARVN Ranger Camp. At or near Ben Het AF, apx 15 km WNW Dak To 2 AF and 52 km NW Kontum. ARVN border ranger camp during Op Quang Trung 22F. Two US 155mm and four 175mm 7th/15th Arty pieces here Feb71. See Quang Trung Op. Kontum Pr, II Corps.

Ben Het SF Camp (YB 872-252)
Apx 15 km WNW Dak To AF, 15 km SSW Dak Seang AF, 14 km W Laos and 52 km NW Kontum. 5th SF Grp. Converted to ARVN 95th Border Rangers. Info/grid per *SF Order of Battle*. Kontum Pr, II Corps.

Ben Keo Heliport (XT 236-434)
Apx 13 km from Cambodian border above Parrot's Beak, immed S Ap Long My and 5 km S Tay Ninh. "Heliport #519, El. 33', soccer field, at 11°15'00"N-106°08'00"E," per Feb73 TAD. Tay Ninh Pr, III Corps.

Ben Keo Navy ATSB (XT 23-43?)
On Song Vam Co Dam River 5 km S Tay Ninh? USN Advanced Tactical Supt Base, '69-71. Per MRF Assn Website. Tay Ninh Pr, III Corps.

Ben Keo RF/PF Training Center (XT 235-476)
Apx 4 km due S Tay Ninh. Attacked 18Aug68 during Battle for Tay Ninh, and again night of 10-11Sep68. [62] Also listed at XT 231-435. Tay Ninh Pr, III Corps.

Ben Khe (BP 7-6)
Ville apx 25-30 km W Nha Trang. Khanh Hoa Pr, II Corps.

Ben Khe (BR 68-43)
See Binh Khe and LZ Tonto. Binh Dinh Pr, II Corps.

Ben Khemmarat Airfield (n/a)
A.k.a. Khemmarat AF. On Lao border, 555 km ENE Bangkok, and 20 km due S Ba Na Kala Highway (Laos) Airstrip. Per ONC-K-10. El. 400' (listed at 325' on 67Feb Natl Geo map). Thailand.

Ben Loi Airfield (WF 9-1 ?)
Apx 75 km SSE Vinh and 95 km NW Dong Hoi. Per ONC-J-11. El. 54'. NVN.

Ben Loi Bridge (XS 871-970)
A.k.a. Binh Loi Bridge. QL-1/QL-13 bridge over Song Saigon apx 4 km due E of E edge of Tan Son Nhut AB. Battle here 5May68 involving 6th VNMC Bn and VC 3d LF Bn with attached sapper unit. The "Green Door," a notorious brothel, sat nearby. Gia Dinh Pr, III Corps.

Ben Luc (XS 63-76)
Apx 14 km NNE Tan An, 34 km NNE My Tho and 17 km SW Saigon. Capitol of Ben Luc Dist (pop of apx 46,000). 2d/14th Inf, 25th Inf Div, basecamp here during Op Lanikai. Long An Pr, III Corps.

Ben Luc, FSB (XS 635-765)
Apx 14 km NNE Tan An, 34 km NNE My Tho and 17 km SW Saigon. Per Jim Stone, Ben Luc Bridge here. 6th/31st Inf, 9th Inf Div Arty Base in '70. Long An Pr, III Corps.

Ben Luc Basecamp (XS 623-763)
Apx 13 km NNE Tan An and 18 km SW Saigon. Long An Pr, III Corps.

Ben Luc Bridge (XS 618-748)
Over Song Vam Co Dong immed SW Ben Luc, 13 km NNE Tan An and 18 km SW Saigon. 150' span destroyed Jul68 by VC bomb, so US 15th Engrs built 1-lane pontoon bridge as temporary replacement, while 9th MP Co provided security. Long An/Gia Dinh Pr border, III Corps.

Ben Luc Heliport (XS 625-765)
Apx 13 km NNE Tan An and 18 km SW Saigon. "Heliport #766, El. 5', operates 2400-1200 daily, at 10°38'N 106°29'E," per Feb73 TAD. Long An Pr, III Corps.

Ben Luc NSB (XS 62-76?)
USN Supt Base, '68-71. Presumably at or near Ben Luc Bridge, on Song Vam Co Dong River, which was roughly13 km NNE Tan An and 33 km NNE My Tho. Name per MRF Assn Website. Long An Pr, III Corps.

Ben Nam Airfield (YT 300-254)
See Cay Gao AF. Long Khanh Pr, III Corps.

Ben Phuoc SF Camp (XS 47-56?)
Location unknown, however Tan Hiep is at listed grid, and apx 12 km NNW My Tho. 5th SF. See Tan Hiep? Info per *SF Order of Battle*. Dinh Tuong Pr, IV Corps.

Ben Phuoc? SF Camp (XT 443-065)
Along Song Vam Co Dong River apx 18 km NW Duc Hoa and 38 km WNW Tan Son Nhut AF and Saigon. 5th SF. See Hiep Hoa (old) SF Camp. Info/grid per *SF Order of Battle*. Long An Pr, III Corps.

Ben San Leprosarium (XT 907-213)
A.k.a. Xom Ben San Leprosarium. At Xom Ben San, apx 11 km NW Bien Hoa AB and 26 km NNE Tan Son Nhut AB. Bien Hoa, III Corps.

Ben Soi (XT 09-47)
Ville apx 8 km from Cambodian border, 14 km SW Tay Ninh and 37 km NW Duc Hue AF. Tay Ninh Pr, III Corps.

Ben Soi Engineer Camp (XT 089-470)
At Ben Soi, apx 10 km SW Tay Ninh West AF and 7 km from Cambodia at closest point. 588th Engr Bn camp here used for road projects and for Cambodian Incursion. Grid per Frank Penk, Jr. Tay Ninh Pr, III Corps.

Ben Soi SF Camp (XT 0923-4756)
At Cambodian border, 14 km SW Tay Ninh and 37 km NW Duc Hue AF. SF A-Team Camp, Det 59, 5th SF Grp CIDG Det A-321, Mar65. Info/grid per *SF Order of Battle*. Converted to A-120; ARVN 91st Border rangers. Also listed at XT 092-476. Tay Ninh Pr, III Corps.

Ben Soi SF CIDG Camp (XT 092-476)
Along Hwy 13, apx 13 km WSW Tay Ninh, 3 km S Ben Soi. Heavy fighting nearby, 22Aug68, and heavily attacked at 0005 Hrs 25Aug68 during Battle for Tay Ninh while defended by ARVN SF. Attacked again, 6Sep68 at 2315 hrs-7Sep68 at 0315 hrs. In all, was attacked 3 times during Sep68 without US personnel to assist, and ARVN losses were 37 KIA, 17 WIA. [63] Tay Ninh Pr, III Corps.

Ben Suc (XT 575-335)
Ville of 5,500 on Saigon River apx 20 km WSW Lai Khe and 43 km NW Tan Son Nhut AB. Considered heart of Iron Triangle (though it physically formed its NW corner), and VC controlled city for much of war. VC ousted ARVN here in 65 and held it until 8Jan67 when during Op Cedar Falls, all its inhabitants were moved to refugee camp at Pht Loi (near Phu Cuong) and then Rome plows completely flattened ville. Razing of Ben Suc drew outrage from US press. 1st Inf Div AO. Binh Duong, Tay Ninh and Hau Nghia Pr border, III Corps.

Ben Suc Heliport (XT 575-335)
Apx 20 km WSW Lai Khe and 43 km NW Tan Son Nhut AB/Saigon. Heliport #520, El.?," per Feb73 TAD. Binh Duong Pr?, III Corps.

Ben Tran (XS 4-5)
See Ben Tranh. Dinh Tuong Pr, IV Corps.

Ben Tranh Airfield (XS 463-523)
Apx 8 km NW My Tho, 45 km SW Saigon, 15 km SSW Long An AF (Tan An) 10 km NE Dong Tam AF. Per TPC K-10D. El. 16', 1,900' laterite rwy. At 10°25'20"N-10°20'10"E. Map is L-7014-6229-1, per Jim Stone. Dinh Tuong Pr, IV Corps.

Ben Tranh Heliport (XS 474-551)
Apx 8 km NW My Tho, 45 km SW Saigon, 1 km NE Ben Tranh AF and 10 km NE Dong Tam AF. "Heliport #710, El. 7', soccer field. Recommend S and SE approaches." At 10°27'30"N-106°21'00"E, per Feb73 TAD. Map is L-7014-6229-1, per Jim Stone. Dinh Tuong Pr, IV Corps.

Ben Tranh SF Camp (XS 474-551)
Apx 8 km NW My Tho, 45 km SW Saigon, 1 km NE Ben Tranh AF and 10 km NE Dong Tam AF. 5th SF. See Tan Hiep? Info/grid per *SF Order of Battle.* Map is L-7014-6229-1, per Jim Stone. Dinh Tuong Pr, IV Corps.

Ben Tre (XS 51-32)
A.k.a. Truc Giang. Apx 12 km S My Tho and 62 km SSW Saigon. Captured by VC during Tet '68, it was retaken only after massive bombing/Arty strikes that killed about 550 and wounded 1,200. Although typical battle, became famous due to remarks of American Maj who told news correspondent Peter Arnett that, "It became necessary to destroy the town in order to save it." Home of MACV Adv Team 96. NPIA Gaz also lists a Ben Tre at XS 720 610, and Ben Tre City at XS 504-317. Kien Hoa Pr, IV Corps.

Ben Tre (Truc Giang) (n/a)
Mapsheet L-7014-6229-2. Full sheet name: Truc Giang (Ben Tre). SVN.

Ben Tre Airfield (XS 480-347)
See Truc Giang AF. Kien Hoa Pr, IV Corps.

Ben Tre Base (XS 52-32)
A.k.a. Truc Giang Base. Apx 60 km SSW Saigon and 13 km S My Tho. 2d Bde/9th Inf and USN MRF basecamp, per Jim Stone, 2d/39th Inf. Kien Hoa Pr, IV Corps.

Ben Tre Heliport (XS 513-317)
A.k.a. Truc Giang Heliport? Apx 12 km S My Tho, 4 km SE Tuc Giang AF and at N edge of Truc Giang. "Heliport #521, El. 16' soccer field. Res for VIP only, at 10°14'15"N-106°23'00"E," per Feb73 TAD. Kien Hoa Pr, IV Corps.

Ben Tre Province (XS/XR)
In what later became known as IV Corps and absorbed into what became primarily Kien Hoa Pr?, Thought to have ceased existence shortly before or during early US presence in SVN? Dates of existence unknown.

Ben Tre SF Liaison Det? (XS 510-320)
Apx 12 km S My Tho, 4 km SE Tuc Giang AF and at N edge of Truc Giang. Dec68-Jan69. Kien Hoa Pr, IV Corps.

Ben Van River (BT 47-10)
W to NW Chu Lai. Quang Tin Pr, I Corps.

Bend (n/a)
6Apr70, XXIV Corps future-use 5th Div FSB name.

Benewah, USS (n/a)
A.k.a. APB-35. Self-propelled "barracks ship" built on class 542 LST hull. Launched May46, deployed to VN, 22Feb67, arriving Vung Tau on 22Apr67. Became Flagship of Cmdr, River Assault Flotilla One, MRF TF-117, and Cmdr, 2d Bde/9th Inf Div. Worked primarily in Mekong Delta and in Jun70, participated in Cambodian Incursion. Housed 1,150 men of MRF, inc. 160 crew. Per Nov70 *Stars & Stripes'* article re: ship's departure from VN, 16,800 helos landed on her deck during VN tour. '67 armament inc.: 2-quad-barreled 40 mms, two-3-inch/50's and twenty .50 and .30 cal. MGs. Carried 25 fiberglass assault boats. See *YRBM-21*. Data per MRF Assn website. III, IV Corps.

Bengal, LZ (YD 175-720)
Near FSB A-3, apx 4 km W QL-1/Gio Linh, and 24 km NNW Quang Tri. Apr70 XXIV Corps grid per Don Armstrong. Quang Tri Pr, Corps.

Bengal Mail, SS (n/a)
Merchant ship under govt contract, per Ralph Fries.

Bengali, Baie du (YH 0-9)
Bay at 20°44'N-107°00'E. On NF48-16 JOG. NVN.

Bengalie, Baie du (YH 0-9)
A.k.a. Bengali Bay. Bay at 20°44'N-107°00'E. On NF48-16 JOG. NVN.

Benjamin Chew, SS (n/a)
Merchant ship under govt contract, per Ralph Fries.

Benjamin Stoddert, USS (n/a)
DDG-22. Guided Missile

Bennington, LZ (YD 141-299)
Apx 39 km due W Camp Evans, 58 km WNW Hue and 29 km SW Quang Tri. Apr70 XXIV Corps grid per Don Armstrong. Quang Tri Pr, Corps.

Bennington, USS (n/a)
A.k.a. *The Benny Maru* and CVS-20. Deployed with VSG-59, 1May68 to 9Nov68; with CVSG-59, 20Feb64 to 11Aug64; with CVSG-59, 22Mar65 to 7Oct65; with CVSG-59, 4Nov66 to 23May67. During '61 crisis in Laos, *Bennington* took fourteen H-34 helos to Gulf of Siam for transfer to Lao forces fighting the Pathet Lao. During '62, *Hancock* carrier grp and *Bennington* submarine hunter-killer Grp moved near Da Nang. [64]

Benny Maru, USS (n/a)
Humorous nickname given aircraft carrier *Bennington* by its crew, per Chuck Matura. See *Bennington, USS*.

BEQ No. 1 (XS 845-924)
At 152 Yen Do St., Saigon. Data per *Vietnam Military Lore, 1959-1973*. Gia Dinh Pr, III Corps.

Berchtesgarden, FSB (YD 423-013)
A.k.a. Hill 1030, and Dong Ta Tach. Apx 5 km E Hwy 548/A Shau Valley, 34 km WSW Hue, and 26 km WSW FSB Birmingham. Described as having been, "on eastern lip of high ground overlooking A Shau Valley." Ground attack repulsed during Op Montgomery Rendezvous, 14Jun69, when at 0330 hrs, 96 NVA briefly overran it during 1 of 3 assaults, resulting in11 US KIA and 47 WIA, and 33 NVA KIA 3 POW (elements of 2d/327th Inf, and B/56th, B/2/319th and C/2d/11th Arty, hit by C2 & C3 Co's, K3 Bn, 6th NVA Rgt). 101st Abn 3d Bde FSB during '69. Apr70 XXIV Corps grid per Don Armstrong. Also listed at YD 435-011, 424-011, and 423-004. Thua Thien Pr, I Corps.

Berea Victory, SS (n/a)
Merchant ship under govt contract, per Ralph Fries.

Bering Strait, USCGC (n/a)
WHEC-382. 4May67-18Feb68, and 17May70-31Dec70. Sqdn 3 CGC, during CG's 2d and 6th deployments. Given to SVN Govt in Jan71, as CG left SVN following a 12-mo trng period roughly from Jan70-Jan71. Sister CGC *Yakutat W-380* also went through same process simultaneously. While trng a rotating cycle of 30-man Viet crews, it also provided MEDCAPS for Viets, as well as medical and fire supt for SF camp and USN 572d River Boat Sqdn in Song Ong Doc area (vic of VQ 80-99, offshore An Xuyen Pr). After turnover, renamed *Tran Quan Khai HQ-2*, which means Emperor's Dragon #2. Apparently after war, was involved in dispute with Chinese over oil rights and shot through bow but not sunk. An Xuyen Pr, IV Corps. [65]

Berkeley, USS (n/a)
DDG-15. Guided Missile DD. 1st deployed Mar64, and soon involved in Gulf of Tonkin Incident for which she became 1st DDG ever awarded Navy Unit Commendation. In 2d deployment, '66, she silenced shore batteries in rescue of F-4G and HU-16 Albatross between Hon Me Island and NVN coast. In '69-70, shot many NGS missions. On last deployment, beginning Apr72, she fired over 11,000 rnds (5"/54) and also assisted in mining of Haiphong Harbor (firing 280-5" rnds in 30 min while covering acft mining harbor, then departed at 32 knots!). Transferred to Greek Navy 30Sep92, and renamed *H.S. Themistokles* (DDG-221).

Berkett, FSB (XT 552-846)
See Burkett, FSB. Tay Ninh Pr, III Corps.

Berlin, LZ (BR 620-610)
Vinh Thanh Valley apx 21 km NE An Khe, on site of what became Vinh Thanh AF. 22Oct65. Binh Dinh Pr, II Corps.

Berryman, FSB (YS 390-860)
A.k.a. LZ Nathan. Apx 5 km SW Courtenay Rubber Plantation, 18 km NNW Nui Dat, 6 km W QL-2, 24 km SSW Xuan Loc and 12 km NW Binh Gia. 161 Bty, RNZA (Martin's Bty 13May67-14Apr68) FSB set here 11-21Jan68. 108 Bty RAA/B Bty 2d/35th US Arty here, Jan68. Phuoc Tuy Pr, III Corps.

Bess, FSB (XT 440-346)
Apx 12 km SSW Dau Tieng, 2 km SE Khiem Hanh, and 22 km ESE Tay Ninh. 22Jul67. Tay Ninh Pr, III Corps.

Bet My Tho (n/a)
Possibly at My Tho? In Mekong Delta and apparently near Pak Chong SF AF. My Tho is at XS 50-45, in Dinh Tuong Pr, IV Corps.

Beth, FSB (YS 604-679)
16 km ESE Nui Dat, 1 km W Rte-328, 12 km NE Dat Do and 5 km SSW Xuyen Moc. 161 Bty, RNZA (Master's Bty 6Sep70-8May71) FSB set here 29Mar-7Apr71. Apparently Bty US medium arty here also (35th?). On 1ATF NCO trng map per John Hollett. Also listed at YS 60-67. Phuoc Tuy Pr, III Corps.

Betsy LZ (AQ 800-060)
Apx 3 km N Lac Giao/Ban Me Thuot and immed NW Ban Me Thuot City AF. 173d Abn. Name/grid per Dan Gillotti. Darlac Pr, II Corps.

Betsy, LZ (BR 806-884)
Apparently a.k.a. or near site of LZ Andy (BR 797-895). Apx 6 km due N Ha Tay and 8 km SW Bong Son. 30Oct66. Binh Dinh Pr, II Corps.

Betty, FSB/LZ (various)
IV Corps apparently only CTZ not to have had a FSB or LZ named Betty. I, II and II Corps.

Betty, FSB/LZ (XT 450-263?)
Apparently within 5 km radius of listed grid (FSB Martha) and within 10 km of Go Dau Ha. Per Larry Criteser, FSBs Martha, Betty and Caroline were within 4 to 5 km of one another; with B/4th/9th at Betty, C/4th/9th at Caroline and A/4th/9th, 25th Div at Martha, '67. 1st Cav possibly here per *1st Cav. Op Rpt, May-Jul70*, pp 18, 38, courtesy Peter Cole. See LZ Betty listed at XT 408-390/487-388. Hau Nghia or Tay Ninh Pr, III Corps.

Betty, FSB (YT 114-370)
Apx 19 km SW Phuoc Vinh AF, and 27 km NNE Bien Hoa AB. Bien Hoa Pr, III Corps.

Betty, FSB (YT 14-08)
Apx 9 km SE Plantation AF, 4 km S QL-1, 50 km NW Nui Dat, 10 km due N Long Thanh AF and 15 km ESE Bien Hoa. 161 Bty, RNZA (Horsford's Bty 18Mar69-18Sep69) FSB set here 24-27Mar69. "Betty" was a common FSB name throughout SVN. Bien Hoa Pr?, III Corps.

Betty, FSB (YU 245-289)
Apx 10 km from Cambodia, apx 12 km SW Djamap, 21 km NNE Song Be/Phuoc Binh and 28 km due E Bu Dop. Closed 4Oct70. 1st/8th Cav Name/data per *1st Cav Div Op Rpt, ending 31Oct70*, courtesy Peter Cole. Phuoc Long Pr, III Corps.

Betty, LZ/FSB (AN 809-070)
A.k.a. Currahee Basecamp. Along coast apx 5 km S Phan Thiet and 2 km S QL-1. Home of 3d/506th Inf, 101st Abn. Per Jerry Berry, Betty housed 506th's TOC, US 105mm and ARVN 155mm Btys and was main FSB for 506th in '68-69. 3d/506th Inf, 3d Bde/101st Abn. AF C-130 capable. On 22Feb69, at 0200 hrs was hit by mortar, rocket and sapper attack w/perimeter breached at HHC & E/3d/506th positions. B-40 rocket detonated 4.2" ammo bunker. 3 US KIA, 29 WIA w/4.2" mortar and 1200 rounds of 4.2" ammo, and several bldgs destroyed/damaged. 21 NVA KIA, 1 POW, per www.currahee.org/pageb3.html. Per *Currahee History, 1Feb69 to 31Dec69*, Was mortared at least on following dates: 12Aug69, received 8-12 mortar rnds; 5Sep69, received 20-30 mortar rnds that destroyed several 500 gal fuel blivets; between 6-14Sep69, mortared several more times. Binh Thuan Pr, II Corps.

Betty, LZ (BP 355-722)
Remote site adj to Ban Khoueng, apx 60 km WNW Nha Trang. 3Apr67. Darlac Pr, II Corps.

Betty, LZ (XT 487-388?)
If grid correct, was 9 km S Dau Tieng and 28 km W Lai Khe. Listed at XT 487-388 and 408-390; unknown which is correct. 1st Cav possibly here per *1st Cav. Op Rpt, May-Jul70*, pp 18, 38, per Peter Cole. Tay Ninh Pr, III Corps.

Betty, LZ (XT 408-390?)
If grid correct, was 13 km SW Dau Tieng and 36 km W Lai Khe. Listed at XT 487-388 and 408-390; unknown which is correct. 1st Cav possibly here per *1st Cav. Op Rpt, May-Jul70*, pp 18, 38, per Peter Cole. Tay Ninh Pr, III Corps.

Betty, LZ (XT 686-654)
Apx 6 km E Minh Thanh AF and 7 km W Ql-13. 1st Cav. Name/grid per Dan Gillotti. III Corps.

Betty, LZ (YA 903-505)
Apx 34 km W to WNW Pleiku, 6 km SE Plei Djereng AF and 3 km SSW peak Hill 1005. Name/grid courtesy Dick Arnold as per Jan-Mar69 1st/35th Inf Bn daily logs. Also listed at YA 905-505. See LZ Lanetta. Pleiku Pr, II Corps.

Betty, LZ (YD 340-497)
See Betty-Sharon. Quang Tri Pr, I Corps.

Betty Beach, LZ (AN 82-07)
Adj to LZ Betty (AN 803-068), apx 4 km SW Phan Thiet. Section of beach cleared of mines and officially opened as recreation area for 3d/506th Inf, 101st Abn 1Sep69, even though they had already been at Betty for apx 1 year. Reason for delay is unknown. Binh Thuan Pr, II Corps.

Betty Lou, LZ (n/a)
Location unknown. Cited in *Dispatches*, p. 10. Michael Herr may have meant LZ Mary Lou, or perhaps one of any number of firebases named Betty?

Betty-Sharon, LZ/FSB (YD 340-497)
W of RR tracks and QL-1, apx 2 km S Quang Tri and 25 km NW Camp Evans. Betty and Sharon were initially separate perimeters built adj to one another. Per Mike Cohen, A/1st/8th Cav, '67-68, his Co helped in initial construction of Sharon (while other 1st Cav element built adj LZ Betty).as their 1st FSB after 1st/8th moved N from Bong Son area of II Corps, Dec67 or early Jan68. He recalls an old, French, tin-roofed, concrete army barracks that was incorporated into part of perimeter, as well as circular, French concrete observation tower also inside perimeter. One text describes site as somewhere in Khe Chau Valley of NE Quang Tri Pr and occupied by Army's 1st/11th Inf working with 3d/9th Marines during Op Montana Mauler, Mar-Jul69? Army's 5th/4th Arty suptd the 1st Bde/5th Mech Div from FSBs Sharon, Hai Lang and Nancy during '69. Elements of 4th/60th, E/71st and I/29th here late 67-Jan68 (Dusters, Quads, Searchlights);1st/44th Arty, per Paul Kopsick. Also listed at YD 335-495 and at YD 339-501. Quang Tri Pr, I Corps.

Beull, FSB (XT 213-532)
See Buell. Tay Ninh Pr, III Corps.

Bev, FSB (YT 26-09)
Apx 27 km ESE Bien Hoa AB, 40 km ENE Saigon and 20 km W Xuan Loc. 4th/12th Inf, 199th LIB here. Bien Hoa Pr, III Corps.

Beverley, FSB (YS 456-866)
See FSB Deverley. Phuoc Tuy Pr, III Corps.

Beverly, FSB (XT 334-894)
A.k.a. LZ Beverley, and FSB Bruiser. At Katum, apx 40 km NNE Tay Ninh, 7 km S Cambodian border, 7 km NW Bo Tuc and 105 km NNW Saigon. 11th ACR, 1st Cav with B Bty, 2d/32d Arty's two-175mms, and B Bty, 2d/19th Arty's six-105mms here at least May-Jun70. Grid and arty data per *11th ACR Cambodia Invasion AAR, 1st Cav Div, May-Jun70*, courtesy Lou Rochat. [66] Also listed at XT 331-899 and XT 330-900, 333-803 and 334-898 with 1st/5th Cav here '68, per Frank Penk, Jr. Tay Ninh Pr, III Corps.

Beverly, FSB (XT 333-802?)
Grid may be in error, but if correct, site was apx 9 km S Katum AF. Grid per Dan Gillotti. Tay Ninh Pr, III Corps.

Beverly II, FSB (YS)
Near Ham Tan, per John Mowat. 5th/2d or 5th/7th Arty Dusters here '70. Phuoc Tuy or Binh Tuy Pr, III Corps.

Bexar, USS (n/a)
APA-237. SVN

BG Bond KIA Site (YT 30-35?)
See Bond, BG KIA Site. Long Khanh Pr, III Corps.

Bhagdad, LZ (XD 899-623)
See Bagdad or Baghdad. Quang Tri Pr, I Corps.

Bi Doup Mountain (BP 460-373)
A.k.a. Hill 2,287 (7,503'). 24 km NE Dalat one of tallest peaks in S half of SVN. Tuyen Duc Pr, II Corps.

Bi Nhi (n/a)
AMS/DMA mapsheet L 701-6377-4. NVN/China.

Biah Yen (1) CAP HQ (BS 606-977 or BS 517-918)
See Binh Yen. Quang Ngai Pr, I Corps.

Bibb, USCGC (n/a)
WHEC 31. 4Jul68-28Feb69. Sqdn 3 CGC, during Coast Guard's 3d deployment.

Bible, FSB (XD 945-623)
Apx 18 km NW Vandegrift CB, 8 km WNW FSB Fuller and 40 km WNW Quang Tri. Quang Tri Pr, I Corps.

Bible, LZ (XD 946-624)
Apx 18 km WNW Cam Lo, 18 km NW Mai Loc and 29 km WNW Quang Tri. Apr70 XXIV Corps grid per Don Armstrong. Quang Tri Pr, I Corps.

Biddle, LZ (XD 997-467)
Along QL-9, apx 12 km SW Mai Loc and 34 km WSW Quang Tri. Apr70 XXIV Corps grid per Don Armstrong. Quang Tri Pr, I Corps.

Biddle, USS (n/a)
DLG-34, Guided Missile DD Ldr, Ralph Fries.
Bien Binh Quarry (ZB 081-172)
See Dien Binh Quarry. Kontum Pr, II Corps.
Bien Duc Airfield (XS 475-450)
See Binh Duc AF. Dinh Tuong Pr, IV Corps.
Bien Ho Lake (AR 772-545)
2 x 3 km lake immed NE Pleiku/Nansteph AF and apx 6 km N Pleiku. Pleiku Pr, II Corps.
Bien Hoa (n/a)
Mapsheet name of L-7014-6330-1. SVN.
Bien Hoa (XT 99-12)
A.k.a. Kampong-Sraka-Trey. Large city on bank of Song Dong Nai River, apx 22 km NE Saigon. In '66, its population was apx 60,000. In the 16th Century and while part of Cambodia, the city was known as Kampong-Sraka-Trey. Capitol of Bien Boa Pr, III Corps.
Bien Hoa (Spartan) Heliport (XT 990-105)
In Bien Hoa, apx 24 km NE Tan Son Nhut AB. "Heliport #522, El. 36', pads: 1 ea. 1,000' x 140' (PSP) and 6 ea. 900' x 120' (asph) lanes and others. J4. Caution-hvy tfc. Opr 2100-1500Z. Hazards-Con twr 84' to all ops from Lane #4. Microwave antenna 203' AGL 1/8 mi NNE Soccer Fld. (5). No fuel avail for tran acft. Traffic Pattern-no left tfc at main heliport when Lvg to S. (Left tfc only to soccer Fld). Commo-Spartan Tower-321.0, 121.4, 35.2, 2901.5, USB Opr 2100-1500Z, Ground Con-282.9. Arty advsy 290.0, 46.7, " per Feb73 TAD. Bien Hoa Pr, III Corps.
Bien Hoa, FSB (XU 357-003)
In Cambodia apx 12 km NNE Katum, 38 km WSW Loc Ninh, 20 km WNW tip of The Fishhook and just SE FSB X-Ray. Grid per *11th ACR Cambodia Invasion AAR, 1st Cav Div, May-Jun70*, courtesy Lou Rochat. [67] Cambodia.
Bien Hoa AFB Hospital (XT 988-129)
See USAF Hospitals. Bien Hoa Pr, III Corps.
Bien Hoa Airfield (XT 988-129)
Major US/RVNAF jet-capable AF apx 24 km NE Tan Son Nhut AB, 12 km E Phu Loi AF, 33 km E Cu Chi AF and 7 km NW Plantation AF. Had two 10,000' by 150' parallel conc rwys. In or nearby were sites of SF Det 60, Honour-Smith-Woodson Cmpd, Camp Train and Camp Zinn, 3d Combat Supt Grp. Comm passenger Jet capable AF that by '66 was 3d largest in SVN. On 2Nov64, VC attack inflicted 5 US KIA, 76 WIA, and destroyed six B-57 Canberra Bombers (another source says same attack took place 1Nov64, destroyed five B-57s, damaged 8 more, with 4 US KIA). On 16May65, twenty-four B-57s destroyed and many KIA by what was 1st thought to be caused by a VC attack, but later determined to have been accidental. [68] 10°58'26"N-106°49'21"E, El. 55'. Map is L-7014-6330-1, per Jim Stone. Bien Hoa Pr, III Corps.
Bien Hoa Base Camp (XT 99-12)
At Bien Hoa and apparently adj to or part of Bien Hoa AB. Apx 24 km Tan Son Nhut AB. Here were: SF Det 60, Honour-Smith-Woodson Cmpd, Camp Train and Camp Zinn, 3d ARVN Rangers Cmd MACV Advisors, HQ Australian Army Force (later the 1st ATF), VN (attached to 173d Abn, 65-66) 5th SF, Det C-3, MIKE Force A-302, Oct65, 3d/319th Arty. 101st Abn SERTS Trng Ctr here until it moved to Camp Evans in '70. 1st Cav replacement trng area also here at one time. 161 Bty, RNZA (Kenning's Bty 13Jun65-13Jun66) FSB set here when it arrived in VN. "Single Gun Ready" 15Jul65. 18Aug65, it was 6 km N Bien Hoa at XT 99-21, on 27 Aug65 it was 2.5 km N Bien Hoa. Map is L-7014-6330-1, per Jim Stone. See Camp Ray and SERTS. Bien Hoa Pr, III Corps.
Bien Hoa Heliport (YT 016-153)
See Lassiter Heliport. Bien Hoa Pr, III Corps.
Bien Hoa Province (XT/YT/XS)
One of 11 south-central provs forming III Corps (III CTZ). Sometimes spelled "Binh Hoa."
Bien Hoa RF Outpost (XT 344-179)
See Binh Hoa Outpost. Hau Nghia Pr, III Corps.
Bien Hoa SF Camp (MSF) (YT 007-124)
At NW corner of Bien Hoa, apx 3 km SE Bien Hoa AB. 5th SF. Grid in *SF Order of Battle* lists location as XT 007-124, however that is in Cambodia and grid zone should be "YT." Moved to Long Hai. Bien Hoa Pr, III Corps.
Bien Hoa SF Camp (YT 009-127)
At NW corner of Bien Hoa, apx 3 km SE Bien Hoa AB. 5th SF. Converted to HQ, USARV Individual Trng Grp. Info/grid per *SF Order of Battle*. Bien Hoa Pr, III Corps.
Bien Hoa-Saigon Hwy Bridge (XS 87-97?)
Normally referred to as the Saigon-Bien Hoa Hwy Bridge. Crosses Saigon River at NW corner of city apx 9 km W Tan Son Nhut AB and 4 km NE the Presidential Palace. heavy fighting here, Tet '68. Gia Dinh Pr, III Corps.
Bien Hoa TACAN NDB (XT 98-13)
Tactical Air Navigation and Non-Directional Air Nav Beacon site. At Bien Hoa AB. Bien Hoa Pr, III Corps.
Bien Hoa VFW Post (XT 98-13?)
See VFW Post 8316, Saigon. Bien Hoa Pr, III Corps.
Bien Hung, SF Camp (VQ 845-815?)
Listedspelling in DA Chief, Mil Hist records summary but not in other texts? Apparent variant of Binh Hung. See Binh Hung Camp. An Xuyen Pr?, IV Corps.
Bienville, USS? (n/a)
Hull #? *USS* or *USNS*? Possibly named *Bienville County* or *Parish*. Part of MSTS fleet, carried cargo stowed in easily handled containers. Was 1st such container vessel to reach SVN, when it arrived in Da Nang, 1Aug67.
Bier La Rue (n/a)
See Glossary.
Biet Dong Quan (n/a)
See Glossary.
Biet Hai (n/a)
See Glossary.
Biet Kichs (YD 868-188)
PF militia group led by legendary man named Chieu Tich Chung, who sported a black Khaki outfit complete with a pair of pearl-handled pistols. His HQ was in Luong Loc, apx 4k NW Hue/Phu Bai AF and on E bank of Song Loi Nong. Chung's aggressive and daring ops against the VC in area between Hue and Phu Bai were the stuff of legend, according to Marine CAP team members who knew or worked with him. Some data per www. capmarine.com. Thua Thien Pr, I Corps.
Big Blue (XT)
Acft/helo pilots nicknamed the Song Saigon and Song Thi Tinh, the Big and Little Blue. 25th and 1st US Inf Div AOs. Per *Low Level Hell*, p 58. III Corps.

Big Daddy (n/a)
SF A-Team code word transmitted to indicate they were under attack of unknown intensity. [69]

Big John (XS 890-935)
Nickname of US Army's floating crane at Newport Harbor. Used to lift items that ships' equip could not lift. Tanks, bulldozers, locomotives and other large vehicles or machinery and equip were its specialty. 8 Army heavy cranes served in VN. Their hulls were classified as "BD Cranes," and 4 of 8 were 100 ton cranes, while remaining 4 were 60 ton cranes. Data, photos, discussion at: http://academic.uofs.edu/faculty/gramborw/atav/4tc.htm.

Big Mamma (YB 957-998)
A.k.a. Chu Mom Ray (or Rai) Mtn or Hill 1773. See Hill 1773. Kontum Pr, II Corps.

Big Minh (n/a)
See Glossary.

Big Red, Operation (n/a)
7Sep65-8 Oct65. 173d Abn, at Ben Cat, Phuoc Vinh, Di An, and Phu Loc. 1/503d Inf destroyed two enemy hospitals, a signal school, and camps after airmobile assaults during this op. III Corps.

Big Rubber Plantation (XT 33-38)
Along NE side of QL-22, apx 10 km SE Tay Ninh, 17 km WSW Dau Tieng and just E the Song Vam Co Dong River. Map/discussions of nearby battles in '68 are in *The Infantry Brigade in Combat,* p 5 et al. Tay Ninh Pr, III Corps.

Big Springs, Operation (n/a)
30Jan-16Feb67. 173d Abn, War Zone D. 26 basecamp s found and destroyed including more than 1,000 bunkers, 78 huts, 24 tons of rice. 79 VC KIA.

Big Wind, LZ (BR 158-244)
See Big Windy. Pleiku Pr, II Corps.

Big Windy, LZ (BR 158-244)
A.k.a. LZ Big Wind. Along Dak Pihao River apx 45 km SE Pleiku and 47 km WSW An Khe. 4th Div AO, '70. Name/grid per Jim Claeys. See LZ Windy (BP 675-505). Pleiku Pr, II Corps.

Bigelow, USS (n/a)
A.k.a. DD 942. Accidental explosions in 5-inch/54-Caliber mounts of Destroyers *Manley* and *Bigelow* during Spring '67, reduced number of ships available for the NGS Unit.

Bigfoot Sightings(n/a)
See Glossary.

Biggerstaff Building (CP 04-55)
1st Field Force VN Arty HQ, in Ross Cmpd, Camp J. F. McDermott, Nha Trang. Named to honor Sp4 Henry C Biggerstaff, Quad .50 Cal. Gunner, E Bty, 41st Arty, KIA 10May68, while defending his position against massive VC ground attack. Grid apx only. Khanh Hoa Pr, II Corps.

Bill, LZ (XT 437-850)
See Billie. Tay Ninh Pr, III Corps.

Bill, FSB (XT 872-995)
See Bill at XU 870-000. Binh Long Pr, III Corps.

Bill, FSB (XU 706-178)
Apx 10 km NNW Loc Ninh and 6 km S border. Also listed at XT 872-995 and XU 870-000? Binh Long Pr, III Corps.

Bill, FSB (XU 870-000)
Apx 28 km WSW Song Be, and 16 km SE Loc Ninh. 1st/8th Cav, 1st Cav, '69, AO Commanche Warrior. Grid per Frank Penk, Jr. Possibly a 1st Cav base? FSB or LZ Bill is cited Shelby Stanton's *Anatomy of A Division*, per Peter Cole. Also listed at XT 872-995 and XU 706-178? Binh Long Pr, III Corps.

Bill, LZ/FSB (YV 920-954)
Apx 4.5 km E to ENE Hill 534, 7 km SSE peak Chu Pong Mtn, 60 km SSW Pleiku, 7 km E LZ George and 4 km SW LZ Ray. Opened by 1st/5th Cav, 1st Cav, Aug66, during Op Paul Revere II. Arty here thought to have suptg Battle for Hill 534, 14-15Aug66. Grid taken from map in article entitled *Paul Revere II*, 1st Cav '66 *Yearbook* courtesy Mr. Shutt. Also mentioned as 1st Cav base in Shelby Stanton's *Anatomy of A Division*, per Peter Cole. Pleiku Pr, II Corps.

Billie, LZ/FSB (XT 434-853)
A.k.a. Billy. Along Katum/An Loc road, apx 13 km ESE Katum, 33 km WSW An Loc, 15 km WSW tip of Fishhook, 6 km ESE Bo Tuc, 6 km S Cambodia and 40 km NE Tay Ninh. 1st Inf Div AO and occupied by 1st Cav in Oct-Nov68. HQ 7th Cav? Billy and Billie possibly same FSB; Billie listed at XT 435-853 and Billy at XT 437-843. Also listed at XT 427-840 in Nov68 per 3d Bde/1st Cav Journals for 1-2Nov68, which indicate base opened late Oct(30th?)68 and closed 17Nov68, courtesy J. W. Meara. Also listed at XT 437-863, and 445-845 Frank Penk, Jr. Tay Ninh Pr, III Corps.

Billings (n/a)
6Apr70, XXIV Corps future-use 5th Div FSB name.

Billings BEQ (XS 828-938)
At 32 Nguyen Minh Chieu St., Saigon. Data per *Vietnam Military Lore, 1959-1973.* Gia Dinh Pr, III Corps.

Billy Club (n/a)
6Apr70, XXIV Corps future-use III MAF FSB name.

Billy, FSB (XT 434-853)
See Billie, FSB. Tay Ninh Pr, III Corps.

Billy, FSB (XT 445-845)
See Billie, FSB. Tay Ninh Pr, III Corps.

Bin Hung Airfield (VQ 849-818)
See Binh Hung AF. An Xuyen Pr, IV Corps.

Bincang, Baie de (CP 0-7)
A.k.a. Dam Nha Phu. Bay at 12°25'N-109°13'E. On ND49-13 JOG. Khanh Hoa Pr, II Corps.

Bing Crosby (n/a)
See American Radio Service.

Bing Duong Airfield (XT 840-150)
See Lam Son AF. Binh Duong Pr?, III Corps.

Bing Hung Airfield (VQ 849-818)
See Binh Hung AF. An Xuyen Pr, IV Corps.

Bingo, LZ (ZA 015-860?)
Apx 4 km W Polei Trang, 8 km SSW Polei Kleng/LZ Bass, 6 km ESE FSB Brillo-Pad, 23 km W Kontum. Built and occupied by D/1st/14th Inf, 4th Div for about 2 weeks in Jun6. D Co suffered at least 3 KIA on this hill, among them William W. Boetje, son of owner of Boetje Mustard Co. Grid estimated per photos/maps at http://1-14th.com/maps.html. See LZs Alamo, Brillo-Pad, Bunker-Hill, and Hill 1124 and XYZ Pad. Kontum Pr, II Corps.

Binh An (YD 24-61)
13 km N Quang Tri along QL-1. Battle of Binh An here Jun68 inc 3d Sqd/5th Cav, and C and D Troops of 1st Sqd, 9th Cav, joined by C/1st/5th Cav and C/2d/5th Cav, 1st Cav against K-14 Bn, 812th NVA Rgt. Grid is rough estimate. Quang Tri Pr, I Corps.

Binh An CAP (YD 24-61)
See CAP 2-3-5. 2d CAG. Grid est. Quang Nam Pr, I Corps.

Binh Ba (YS 43-73)
On W edge of Binh Ba Rubber Plantation and along QL-2, apx 7 km NNW Nui Dat, 10 km WSW Ngai Giao and 35 km NNE Vung Tau. 161 Bty, RNZA (Kenning's Bty 13Jun65-13Jun66) FSB set here 2-8Apr66, also other elements of ANZAC 1ATF here at various times. Also listed at YS 45-74. Phuoc Tuy Pr, III Corps.

Binh Ba, Baie de (CP 0-1)
Bay at 11°52'N-109°13'E. On NC49-01 JOG. Khanh Hoa Pr, II Corps.

Binh Ba, Xa (n/a)
Mapsheet L-7014-6430-3. Sheet: Xa Binh Ba. SVN.

Binh Ba II Airfield (YS 443-744)
Along QL-2, apx 7 km NNW Nui Dat, 10 km WSW Ngai Giao and 35 km NNE Vung Tau. Listed as "Abnd, check security ARVN(A) 8Jul67, AF # VA3-118," in Aug69 TAD per Frank Penk, Jr. Not in Feb73 TAD. Phuoc Tuy Pr, III Corps.

Binh Ba Rubber Plantation (YS 43-73)
A French Rubber plantation straddling Rte-2 apx 6 km N Nui Dat and 6 km S Ngai Giao, NNE Vung Tau. See FSB Kylie for interesting note. Phuoc Tuy Pr, III Corps.

Binh Ba South Airfield (YS 443-744)
See Binh Ba II AF. Phuoc Tuy Pr, III Corps.

Binh Binh Province (n/a)
Spelling variant of Vinh Binh Pr. See Vinh Binh.

Binh Chanh, FSB (XS 71-78)
At Binh Chanh, along QL-4, apx 10 km SW Saigon and 12 km ENE Ben Luc. 3d/7th, 2d/3d, 4th/12th, 199th LIB, and also apparently 6th/31st Inf, 9th Inf Div basecamp, per Jim Stone, 2d/39th Inf. Long An Pr?, III Corps.

Binh Chanh Base (XS 720-790)
At Binh Chanh, along QL-4, apx 10 km SW Saigon and 12 km ENE Ben Luc. Joint Ops Ctr. Basecamp of 6th/31st Inf, 9th Div per Jim Stone, 2d/39th Inf. Long An Pr?, III Corps.

Binh Chanh Heliport (XS 761-784)
Apx 8 km SSW Saigon and 4 km due E Binh Chanh. Heliport #754, alt 10', PSP Pad outside cmpd. At 10°39'N 106°37'E, per Feb73 TAD. Gia Dinh Pr, III Corps.

Binh Chu SF Camp (VQ 83-81?)
A.k.a. FOB Binh Hung. Apparently at Binh Hung, apx 5 km from coast, 46 km SW Quan Long and 20 km NW Nam Can AF. 5th SF. Info/grid per *SF Order of Battle.* An Xuyen Pr, IV Corps.

Binh Dai (n/a)
Mapsheet name of L-7014-6329-3. SVN.

Binh Dai Airfield (XS 852-291)
On S bank of Mekong River, about 4 km NNW Binh Dai and 38 km WSW My Tho. "Abnd, overgrown 10Aug67, AF # VA4-184," in Aug69 TAD per Frank Penk, Jr. Not in Feb73 TAD. 4 km NNW Binh Dai, and 37 km ESE My Tho. Kien Hoa Pr, IV Corps.

Binh Dai Secret Zone (XS 86-26)
Near ville of Binh Dai, apx 40-45 km ESE My Tho. VC staging area attacked by 9th Inf MRF in conjunction with 34th Arty and naval DD gunfire in '69. Near 10°11'00"N-106°41'00"E. Binh Dai is in listed grid square. Data per MRF Assn website. Kien Hoa Pr, IV Corps. [70]

Binh Dia Heliport (XS 857-273)
Apx 3 km S the Mekong River near its mouth, apx 36 km E to ESE Truc Giang/Ben Tre, and 41 km ESE My Tho. "Heliport #523, alt 7' sod pad, wires on S, at 10°11'38"N-106°41'42"E," per Feb73 TAD. Kien Hoa Pr, IV Corps.

Binh Dien Bridge (XS 751-831)
Roughly 8 km SW Saigon's Cholon area, where QL-4 crossed the Rach Chu Dem River. Secured by 2d/34th Armor and 2d/14th Inf, 25th ID, during Op Toan Thang II. Hau Nghia Pr, III Corps.

Binh Dinh, FSB (XS 75-83)
Along QL-4 apx 5 km SW the SW corner of Saigon and 5 km NE Binh Chanh. 2d/3d, 199th LIB. Gia Dinh or Long An Pr, III Corps.

Binh Dinh, FSB (YD 567-053)
A.k.a. Hill 426. Along N edge of Hwy 547, apx 32 km WSW Phu Bai, 20 km SSW Ap Lai Bang, 2 km NW FSB Kim Qui, 2.5 km NE FSB Veghel, 7 km SW FSB Bastogne. Per Paul Shaffer, was built on 547 between Bastogne and Veghel, which grid confirms. Joint 1st/327th/101st Abn and 3d./54th ARVN Rgt FSB, Apr-May71. During Lam Son 720, beginning Apr '71, the 326th Eng built FSBs Co Pung, Binh Dinh and Kim Qui with 327th Inf/101st Abn providing security. Grid/data courtesy Cliff Snyder.[71] Also listed at YD 57-04. Thua Thien Pr, I Corps.

Binh Dinh Province (BS/BR/BQ/CP)
One of 12 north-central provs forming II Corps (II CTZ). Home of 18-B NVA Rgt and several VC Main Force Bns.

Binh Dong (XJ 7-1)
A typical French *de Lattre Line* Bunker position here, per *Street Without Joy*, p 177. NVN.

Binh Duc (XS 47-45)
On N edge of Mekong River in Mekong Delta 2 km W My Tho, 7 km E Dong Tam AF, 8 km S Ben Tranh AF and 50 km SW Saigon. 199th LIB position. Spelled "Binh Due" on 199th LIB Assn list? Dinh Tuong Pr, IV Corps.

Binh Duc Airfield (XS 478-450)
On N edge of Mekong River in Mekong Delta 2 km W My Tho, 7 km E Dong Tam AF, 8 km S Ben Tranh AF and 50 km SW Saigon, per TPC K-10D. El. 10', 2,300' steel-mat rwy. Dinh Tuong Pr, IV Corps.

Binh Due (XS 47-45)
Thought to be a misspelling of Binh Duc. See Binh Duc. Dinh Tuong Pr, IV Corps.

Binh Duong Airfield (XT 840-150)
See Lam Son AF. Binh Duong Pr, III Corps.

Binh Duong Province (XT)
One of 11 south-central provs forming III Corps (III CTZ).

Binh Gia (YS 50-78)
Town apx 12 km NE Nui Dat, 4 km E QL-2, 65 km E Saigon and 4 km SE Ngai Giao. Seized by 9th VC Div 28Dec64 in one of earliest major VC victories. Elements of ANZAC 1ATF here at various time. Name meant "peaceful house" in Viet, but Battle of Binh Gia, 28-31Dec64, resulted in over 60 ARVN dead among the 30th and 33d Ranger Bns and on 2d day when 4th ARVN Marine Bn was inserted and ambushed, of 326 men, 112 KIA and 71 WIA. During the ambush 29 of 4th's 35 officers were KIA. Also listed at YS 49-78. Phuoc Tuy Pr, III Corps.

Binh Gia Airfield (YS 465-780)
Apx 10 km NNE Luscombe AF/Nui Dat. Phuoc Tuy Pr, III Corps. El. 344', 2,000' PSP rwy. Phuoc Tuy Pr, III Corps.

Binh Gia Heliport (YS 490-777)
In Binh Gia, apx 31 km S to SSE Xuan Loc and 12 km NNE Nui Dat. "Heliport #524, alt 350', Church yard. At 10°38'30"N-107°16'45"E." Phuoc Tuy Pr, III Corps.

Binh Hiep SF Camp (XS 023-975)
A.k.a. FOB Moc Hoa. At Cambodian border, 7 km due N Muc Hoa AF and 30 km WNW tip of Parrot's Beak. 5th SF. *SF Order of Battle* lists grid as XS 023-975, but Muc Hoa AF is shown on several maps at apx XS 023-915? Unknown if site was different than Muc Hoa AF, or listed grid is slightly in error? Kien Tuong Pr. IV Corps.

Binh Hoa (YT 89-07)
Ville 13 km N Saigon, 10 km SE Phu Cuong and 7 km WNW Sanford AAF. Bien Hoa Pr, III Corps.

Binh Hoa Base (YT 42-27?)
Possible variation "Bien Hoa" or reference to base at Xa Binh Hoa (YT 42-27), which is apx 64 km NE Saigon and 44 km ENE Bien Hoa AB. Long Khanh Pr, III Corps.

Bien Hoa RF Outpost (XT 344-179)
In An Ninh Corridor at Ap Binh Hoa, apx 12 km W Trang Bang, and 4 km E Cambodian border/Angel's Wing. Cited in 18th Mil Hist Det, 25th Inf Div AAR of 19Nov69, which is at www.army.mil/cmh-pg/documents/vietnam/vni/232.htm. Tay Ninh Pr, III Corps.

Binh Hoa Province (XT/YT/XS)
See Bien Hoa Province. Villes of this name also common.

Binh Hung (various)
At least 3 SVN sites with this name. Grid squares inc: AN 8-1, XS 7-9 and VQ 84-81. III and IV Corps.

Binh Hung (VQ 84-81?)
See Binh Hung AF and Binh Hung SF Camp. An Xuyen Pr, IV Corps.

Binh Hung Airfield (VQ 845-815)
Apx 20 km NW Nam Can AF (southernmost AF in SVN), 50 km SW Quan Long, 130 km SSW Rach Gia, 105 km SW Bac Lieu AF, 290 km SW Saigon and 5 km E the coast some 32 km SSW Mui Bai Bung, tip of Cau Mau. Also listed at VQ 849-818. "Flight serv, contact G3 Air, IV Corps TOC MACV 26Jun68, AF # VA4-163," in Aug69 TAD per Frank Penk, Jr. Not in Feb73 TAD. El. 10'. An Xuyen Pr, IV Corps.

Binh Hung SF Camp (VQ 845-815)
See Binh Hung AF for location. Apparently 5th SF Det A-411 here (was Det 412), Oct65. Moved to Phu Quoc. Data per *SF Order of Battle.* An Xuyen Pr, IV Corps.

Binh Hung, Camp (VQ)
See Binh Hung SF Camp, Binh Chu, Nga Ba Dinh and Cai Do Van. IV Corps.

Binh Khe (Binh Lien) (n/a)
Mapsheet name of L-7014-6736-1. SVN.

Binh Khe Airfield (BR 765-683)
Along QL-19 at Binh Khe, apx 22 km ESE An Khe. "Abnd, AF # VA2-185," in Aug69 TAD per Frank Penk, Jr. Not in Feb73 TAD. Binh Dinh Pr, II Corps.

Binh Khe SF Camp (BR 657-447)
Along QL-19, apx 2 km NW Binh Khe, and 18 km due E An Khe. 5th SF. Info/grid per *SF Order of Battle.* Moved to Mai Linh. Binh Dinh Pr, II Corps.

Binh Khe, FSB (BR 683-429)
Near Song Con River, apx 1 to 2 km N Binh Khe/QL-19, some 22 km E An Khe and 21 km due W Phu Cat AB. 1st/92d and 3d/319th Arty here Apr68. Grid per Craig Miller as per 4th Div Op rpt. Binh Dinh Pr, II Corps.

Binh Koi, Baie de (CQ 1-0)
A.k.a. Goi, Ben. Bay at 12°41'N-109°18'E. On ND49-13 JOG. Khanh Hoa Pr, II Corps.

Binh Lien (Binh Khe) (n/a)
Mapsheet L-7014-6736-1. Full sheet name: Binh Khe (Binh Lien). SVN.

Binh Lien, FSB (BS 630-855)
A.k.a. LZ Dottie, Nui Dong De and Hill 102. Apx 12 km N Quang Ngai, and 1 km E QL-1. Apr70 XXIV Corps grid per Don Armstrong. Quang Ngai Pr, I Corps.

Binh Lieu (n/a)
Mapsheet name of L-7014-6452-2. NVN/China.

Binh Loc Airfield (YT 418-180)
Apx 4 km due W Xuan Loc AF. "Abnd, Pvt AF. AF # VA3-119," per Aug69 TAD, Frank Penk, Jr. Not in 73 TAD. Long Khanh Pr, III Corps.

Binh Loc, Plantation de (YT 4-1)
Plantation de Binh Loc a.k.a. Don Dien Binh Loch. Long Khanh and/or Bien Hoa Pr, III Corps.

Binh Loi (XS 923-893?)
See Compound Onc. Gia Dinh Pr, III Corps.

Binh Loi, Pointe du (XS 9-8)
See Pointe Binh Loi. Gia Dinh Pr?, III Corps.

Binh Loi Bridge (XS 871-970)
A.k.a. Ben Loi Bridge. QL-1/QL-13 bridge over Song Saigon apx 4 km E of E edge of Tan Son Nhut AB. Battle here 5May68 involving 6th VNMC Bn and VC 3d LF Bn with attached sapper unit. The "Green Door," a notorious brothel, sat nearby. Gia Dinh Pr, III Corps.

Binh Long (various)
Common Viet place-name. See grid squares BN 4-3, BR 8-5, WS 1-5 and XT 9-2 in SVN (others in NVN).

Binh Long (XT 76-88)
NVA name for An Loc. See An Loc and Easter Offensive. Binh Long Pr, III Corps.

Binh Long Airfield (XT 760-892)
See Hon Quan AF. Binh Long Pr, III Corps.

Binh Long Base (XS)
Author unable to determine location but possible sites inc Binh Long at: XS 406-427, on N bank Mekong, apx 10 km WSW My Tho (later site of Dong Tam); XS 474-505, near Truc Giang AF; XS 744-380, on N bank Mekong, apx 23 km ESE My Tho. Per Jim Stone, *Vietnam Order of Battle* lists this site as home of 4/39th Inf, 9th Div, Nov68-Feb69, and just before it moved to FSB Danger/Dickey. III Corps.

Binh Long Province (XT/XU)
One of 11 south-central provs forming III Corps (III CTZ).

Binh Nghia CAP Compound (BS?)
USMC CAP/PF cmpd a.k.a. Fort Page. Was 3 km-long and contained 6 hamlets. Large expanse of sand dunes bordered site to N, and wide river was to S. Fort consisted of single adobe bldg and large tent set back 200 meters from river. Was surrounded by moat lined with tall bamboo fence and punji stakes. Attacked by 21st VC Co (80 men) while only 6 Marines and 12 PFs were here (over half allied force was on ambush) 15Sep66, with 5 US KIA, but fort held. Again

attacked 16Sep and 18Sep66, but VC decimated.[72] Lima 6, 1st CAG per: www.capmarine.com. I Corps. Quang Ngai Pr, I Corps.

Binh Phuoc, FSB (XS 611-550?)
If grid correct, was apx 14 km NE My Tho and 12 km SE Tan An. 5th/60th and 2d/47th (Mech) Inf, 9th Inf Div base camp in '70, per Jim Stone, 2d/39th Inf. Grid is est. Map is L-7014-6229-1, per Jim Stone. Long An Pr, III Corps.

Binh Phuoc Base (XS 611-550?)
See Binh Phuoc, FSB. Long An Pr, III Corps.

Binh Phuoc Heliport (XS 611-550)
Apx 15 km NE My Tho, 13 km SSE Tan An. Heliport #525, alt 7', at 10°26'40"N-106°28'30"E, 73 TAD. Map is L-7014-6229-1, per Jim Stone. Dinh Tuong Pr, IV Corps.

Binh Son (BS 596-927?)
On QL-1 apx 16 km SSE Chu Lai, 20 km NNW Quang Ngai. Also listed at BS 612-933. Map is L-7014-6739-1. Quang Ngai Pr, I Corps.

Binh Son (n/a)
Mapsheet name of L-7014-6739-1. SVN.

Binh Son Airfield (BS 612-933)
On QL-1 apx 16 km SSE Chu Lai and 20 km NNW Quang Ngai. "Insecure, AF # VA1-230," in Aug69 TAD per Frank Penk, Jr. Not in Feb73 TAD. Quang Ngai Pr, I Corps.

Binh Son Airfield (YS 241-919)
Apx 26 km due E Saigon, 10 km due E Long Thanh AF and near Rte 320. "Unserviceable, Pvt AF, Avoid flying within a 1 nautical mile radius up to 4000' due to parachute jumping, AF # VA3-120," in Aug69 TAD per Frank Penk, Jr. Not in Feb73 TAD. Bien Hoa Pr, III Corps.

Binh Son CAP (BS 596-927?)
Along QL-1 apx 16 km SSE Chu Lai and 20 km NNW Quang Ngai. MTT 1-2, 1st CAG per Tim Duffie. Grid is est. Quang Ngai Pr, I Corps.

Binh Son Military District Compound (BS 601-922)
Apx 18 km NNW Quang Ngai and 2 km S the QL-1 Song Tra Bong bridge. ARVN/RF here attacked 3Dec67, by 2 Cos 48th VC Bn, 95th Sapper Co, P-31 Inf Co, and possibly C-21 Sapper Co. Suptg RVN troops were US Adv in cmpd, US 198th LIB's 1st/6th Inf, 1st/52d Inf, 1st/14th Arty, H Trp 17th Cav, 176th Avn Co, and ROK Marine Bde. Operation Binh Son Supt, 3-5Dec67, resulted in 34 VC KIA and 1 US KIA, 6 WIA. Data per Les Hines. Quang Ngai Pr, I Corps.

Binh Son Rubber Plantation (YS 24-94)
Apx 26 km due E Saigon, 10 km due E Long Thanh AF and straddling route 320. AO of 2d/39th and other 9th Div units who had their cmd posts here, per Jim Stone, 2d/39th Inf. Bien Hoa Pr, III Corps.

Binh Tan Heliport (XS 818-405)
Apx 7 km SSW Go Cong and 32 km ESE My Tho. "Heliport #711, alt 3' earth road, at 10°19'00"N-106°39' 30"E," per Feb73 TAD. Go Cong Pr, IV Corps.

Binh Tan Tan Heliport (WS 860-035)
Apx 8 km due S Can Tho and 7 km NE Thanh Hoa. "Heliport #712, alt 7' earth pad, obstructions S and W, dusty." At 09°59'30"N-105°47'00"E, per Feb73 TAD. Phong Dinh Pr, IV Corps.

Binh Tay (I to IV), Operation (n/a)
ARVN armored ops in II Corps, May-Jun69, run suptg Toan Thang 42. Area covered was from Kontum, S to Ban Me Thuot, and inc enemy base areas 701, 702 and 740. Binh Tay IV inc the largest aggregation of Armored forces ever assembled in II Corps, and was designed to augment the evac of Cambodians in Ops Cuu Long I-III. Kontum, Pleiku, Quang Duc and Darlac Prvs, II Corps.

Binh Thanh (WT?)
See Binh Thanh Thon SF Camp. Kien Tuong Pr, IV Corps.

Binh Thanh Thon (WT 86-04)
Apx 7 km from Cambodia, 6 km SW Long Khot AF, 35 km E Don Phuc AF, 22 km NW Muc Hoa AF and 95 km W Saigon. Kien Tuong Pr, IV Corps.

Binh Thanh Thon Airfield (WT 864-043)
Apx 7 km SW Cambodia, 6 km SW Long Khot AF, 35 km E Don Phuc AF, 22 km NW Muc IIoa AF and 95 km W Saigon. Per TPC K-10D. El. 20', 1,500' sod/clay rwy. At 10°53'45"N-105°47'10"E. Also listed at WT 861-033. Kien Tuong Pr, IV Corps.

Binh Thanh Thon SF Camp (WT 8618-0331)
Apx 8 km SW Cambodia, 7 km SW Long Khot AF, 22 km NW Muc Hoa and 94 km W Saigon. Det 70, 5th SF CIDG Det A-413, May65 (formerly Det 431). Oct65, Det A-413, Oct66, later converted to ARVN 86th Border Rangers. Info/grid per *SF Order of Battle.* Kien Tuong Pr, IV Corps.

Binh Thien Loampon, Bung (WT 00)
Freshwater lake at 10°55N-105°04'E. On NC48-06 JOG. Chau Doc, Pr, IV Corps.

Binh Thien, Bung (WT 0-0)
A.k.a. Bung Binh Thien Loampon. Freshwater lake at 10°55N-105°04'E. NC48-06 JOG. Chau Doc, Pr, IV Corps.

Binh Thuan Province (ZT/AN/BN)
One of 12 north-central provs forming II Corps (II CTZ).

Binh Thuy (WS 80-13?)
See Binh Thuy AF for location. 3rd Surgical Hosp here. Phong Dinh Pr, IV Corps.

Binh Thuy AFB Hospital (WS 80-13?)
See USAF Hospitals. Phong Dinh Pr, IV Corps.

Binh Thuy Airfield (WS 789-148)
Apx 1 km NW Navy Binh Thuy AF, 7 km NW Can Tho major AF, 65 km ENE Rach Gia and 30 km SW Vinh Long AF at western edge of Can Tho. Major AF on Mekong River and one of 3 AFs near Can Tho. Home of 632d Combat Supt Grp, USAF-USA-Viet joint control, Rwy made jet capable '65. El. 7', 6,000' asph rwy. At 10°05'03"N-105°43'05"E. Phong Dinh Pr, IV Corps.

Binh Thuy Airfield (Navy) (WS 80-13?)
Apx 7 km NW Can Tho 3 km NW Can Tho major AF, 1 km SE Binh Thuy major AF, 31 km SW Vinh Long AF and 70 km E Rach Gia. Minor AF on Mekong River and one of 3 AFs near Can Tho. El. 7' Phong Dinh Pr, IV Corps.

Binh Thuy Heliport (WS 830-l30)
Apx 2 km S Navy Binh Thuy AF and 8 km NW Can Tho. "Alt 9', 1900' x 100' (M8Al/ASP). Secure. Extensive copter tfc. No F/W acft. All tfc remain SE fld. No RON. Tran prk ltd to 3 acft. HAZARDS-Apch Rwy 21 over river, 20' bldg 300', 10' fence 150' NE thld. 76' lgtd twr 145' S the N end. 80' power poles 100' rgt and left of apch 150' prior to thld. Apch Rwy 03 over 40' poles 700', 20' bldg 300', 10' fence 125' SW thld. Periodic LST masts and crane barges on river. Traffic Pattern-Rgt tfc Rwy 03, left tfc Rwy 21. Tower-Contact Binh Thuy tower for advsy 312. 0, 118.1,

34. 2." At 10°04'00"N-105°44'00"E, per Feb73 TAD. Phong Dinh Pr, IV Corps.

Binh Thuy NSA Base (WS 78-15)
A.k.a. Binh Thuy Naval Supt Activity Base. Along S Bank of Bassac River near Can Tho. Apx 64 km by jeep from Long Xuyen AF. Photos/data at: http://hawley. interspeed. net/vietnam/Binhthuy.htm. Phong Dinh Pr, IV Corps.

Binh Thuy PBR Base (WS 80-15)
A.k.a. Binh Thuy/Can Tho PBR Base. On Bassac River, 8 km NW Can Tho. Mentioned on PBR Forces Assn website at www.pbr-fva.org/. River Div 51, TF-116, USN Gamewarden base here per MRF Assn at www.mrfa.org. Phong Dinh Pr, IV Corps.

Binh Thuy Signal Site (WS 8-I ?)
No data. IV Corps?

Binh Thuy TACAN NDB (WS 79-15)
Tactical Air Navigation and Non-Directional Air Nav Beacon site. At Binh Thuy AF, 8 km NW Can Tho and 6 km NW NDB Can Tho. Phong Dinh Pr, IV Corps.

Binh Thuy, Ap (XS 632-998?)
Ville apx 5 km NE Duc Hoa AF and 17 km WNW Tan Son Nhut AB (also listed at XT 632-998, which is apx 15 km SW Loc Ninh in Binh Long Pr?, but XT zone thought to be in error). A and C Cos 2d/14th Inf, 25th ID, here during Op Toan Thang II, '68. Hau Nghia Pr, III Corps.

Binh Tram (n/a)
See Glossary.

Binh Tram 8 (n/a)
Waypoint on HCMT. Vital MACV intel radio intercept site beginning early '68. Commo between this site and T-12 became a key intel resource. Data per *A Better War*, pp 48-52. See Binh Tram in Glossary.

Binh Tram 14 (n/a)
Waypoint on HCMT. Vital radio intercept site for MACV intel by May70. See Binh Tram in Glossary.

Binh Tram 18 (n/a)
Waypoint on HCMT. Vital radio intercept site for MACV intel by May70. See Binh Tram in Glossary.

Binh Tram 19 (n/a)
Waypoint on HCMT. Vital radio intercept site for MACV intel beginning early '68. See Binh Tram in Glossary.

Binh Tram 32 (n/a)
Waypoint on HCMT. Vital radio intercept site for MACV intel by May70. See Binh Tram in Glossary.

Binh Tram 33 (n/a)
Waypoint on HCMT in Base Area 604 near Tchepone. Vital radio intercept site for MACV intel by May70. See Binh Tram in Glossary. Laos.

Binh Tram 35 (n/a)
6th NVA Engr Bn secured this HCMT waypoint, per *A Better War*, p 100.

Binh Tuy Province (ZT/ZS/YT/YS)
One of 11 south-central provs forming III Corps (III CTZ). Ham Tan (ZS 03-79) was its Capital. III Corps.

Binh Yen (1) CAP HQ (BS 606-977 or BS 517-918)
Marine CAP HQ. Binh Yen (1) at both grids. If BS 606-977 correct, site was immed N Song Cap Da River, apx 10 km SW Chu Lai, 6 km due N Binh Son and 4 km E QL-1. If BS 517-918 site is correct, was apx 8 km WSW Binh Son and 14 km SSW Chu Lai AB? Quang Ngai Pr, I Corps.

Binhcang Bay (CP 0-7)
A.k.a. Dam Nha Phu. Bay at 12°25'N-109°13'E. On ND49-13 JOG. Khanh Hoa Pr, II Corps.

Binhcang, Baie de (CP 0-7)
A.k.a. Dam Nha Phu. Bay at 12°25'N-109°13'E. On ND49-13 JOG. Khanh Hoa Pr, II Corps.

Binkang Bay (CP 0-7)
A.k.a. Dam Nha Phu. Bay at 12°25'N-109°13'E. On ND49-13 JOG. Khanh Hoa Pr, II Corps.

Birch, LZ (YC 965-995)
Apx 13 km due W Phu Loc, 17 km SSE Phu Bai AF and 6 km due E Thon Ben Tau. 22Jul68. Thua Thien Pr, I Corps.

Bird, FSB (XD 956-599)
Just N Cam Lo River apx 17 km W Cam Lo and 16 km NW Mai Loc. 101st Abn inactive FSB grid per Don Armstrong. Quang Tri Pr, I Corps.

Bird, LZ (BR 726-809)
A.k.a. or near site of LZ Stewart (BR 731-803)? Just E Song Lon River, apx 16 km SW Bong Son, 10 km NW Ha Tay and 7 km NNE Nghia Nhon. A Bty, 2d/17th Arty here 27Nov66, suptg 2d/12th and 5th/7th Cav. Data per Jack Picciolo. Also listed at BR 732-805 and 735-811 (Feb-Oct66), and 743-817 (Dec66), and 726-809 and 795-840 (dates unknown)? Binh Dinh Pr, II Corps.

Bird, LZ/FSB (BR 743-817)
A.k.a. Hill 154. Just W Phu Huu 2, apx 8 km W LZ Pony, 15 km SW Phu Cat and in bend of Kim Son River. Was on gentle incline that rose from sandbars of Kim Son River to toe of narrow brush-covered ridge that overlooked base. T-bone shape, it was roughly 250 meters by avg of apx 80 meters in width. Considered a very poorly located and defended position. Initial assault to open base is described in *Chickenhawk*, pp 296-302, in which author makes note of a giant, 25-foot diameter water wheel located on far side of river from base that was used to raise water to a bamboo trough that then carried irrigation water to rice fields of Phu Huu 2. Major battle soon after opening is featured in *BIRD, The Christmastide Battle.* B/2d/19th (105mm) and C/6th/16th (155mm) Arty and C/2d/12th Cav, 1st Cav, were attacked by 22d NVA Rgt's 7th, 8th and 9th Bns on Christmas Day, '66, with 58 US KIA, 77 WIA. NVA lost 266 KIA. Map is L-7014-6737-1, per Ken Burrington. At listed grid 27Dec66. Also listed at BR 732-805 and 735-811 (Feb-Oct66), 726-809 and 795-840 (dates unknown)? Binh Dinh Pr, II Corps. [73]

Bird, LZ (BR 795-840)
If grid correct, was in Song Lon Valley and along LTL-3A, apx 2 km S Ha Tay and 14 km SW Bong Son. Binh Dinh Pr, I Corps.

Bird, LZ (YD)
Said to have been adj to Hill 154, and N of Dong Ha. Lima and Mike Cos, 3d/3d Marines, 3d Mar Div, attacked here 17Sep69, 13 US KIA, 23 WIA. 3d Mar Div, USMC, '69. Quang Tri Pr, I Corps.

Bird, LZ? (YA 646-492)
Just N Cambodian border, apx 21 km WSW Plei Djereng, and 59 km W Pleiku. Nature of site unknown, listed only as "Bird." 16Jan66. Kontum Pr, II Corps.

Birdie, LZ? (YA 974-003)
Apx 39 km W Phu Nhon, 10 km ESE peak of Chu Pong Mtn, and 14 km WSW Plei Me. Nature of site unknown,

listed only as "Birdie." Also listed at YA 973-106. 24Nov65. Pleiku Pr, II Corps.

Birmingham, FSB (YD 704-101)
A.k.a. Hill 90, Hue SW AF and B'ham. Apx some 12 km SSW Hue along Hwy 547, just N Song Huu Trach (W branch of Perfume River), apx 8 km E FSB Bastogne and 11 km W FSB Arsenal. Built by various units including 27th Engrs, 1st/502d Inf, and other 2d Bde/101st Abn elements during Op Jeb Stuart, Mar or Apr68? Named to honor PSG Edward A Birmingham, KIA 2Oct67, who drowned while trying to rescue man caught in middle of river crossing under fire. Per Timothy Carr, his brother Denny was KIA on B'ham 16Mar68, when a US or ARVN piloted B-57 (or unidentified acft) dropped 4 bombs (noted as D-4's, and apparently 500 pounders, 3 of which hit base) on B'ham during its 2d pass, killing apx 7 and wounding apx 20. Overrun and abnd in both '72 Offensive and '75 Final Offensive, while manned by ARVN forces. USMC Tac Air navigation unit, 326th and/or 27th Engrs(HQ?) here, as well as 81mm, 105mm, 8", 175mm Arty and 40mm M42 Dusters (of XXIV Corps 1st/44th Arty?). Per Russ Richardson, C Bty, 1st/83d Arty, elements of 1st/83d Arty were at Blaze, Bastogne and Birmingham, with HQ at Camp Eagle. Elements of 3d Bde/82d Abn also here '68 per Butch Sincock. Thua Thien Pr, I Corps.

Birmingham, LZ/FSB (BT)
Described as having been apx 24 km NW Chu Lai, which suggests it was relatively close to Tam Ky? Americal list. Quang Tin Pr, I Corps.

Birmingham, LZ/FSB (ZV 181-921)
Apx 5 km SW peak of Chu Don Mtn, 20 km WSW Phu Nhon AF and 54 km SSW Pleiku. Pleiku Pr, II Corps.

Bishop, LZ (YA 802-107)
Apx 7 km SSW Plei Ghao Kla, 13 km NW peak of Chu Pong Mtn, 57 km SW Pleiku, and within 2 km of Cambodia. Likely 1st Cav. 14Jan66. Pleiku Pr, II Corps.

Bishop, LZ (YD 263-632)
On W bank of Cua Viet River, apx 2 km E Thuong Nghia, 10 km SW Cua Viet Naval Base and 13 km NW Quang Tri. Apr70 XXIV Corps grid per Don Armstrong. Quang Tri Pr, I Corps.

Bison, LZ (XD 938-467)
On peak of or near Hill 691, apx 8 km ENE Khe Sanh CB, 17 km SW Mai Loc, 41 km WSW Quang Tri and 3 km N QL-9. 1st/9th Marines, 3dMar Div, '69. Grid per map at p 73, *US Marines in Vietnam-1969*. Apr70 XXIV Corps grid per Don Armstrong. Quang Tri Pr, I Corps.

Bison II, FSB (YA 895-357)
Immed N Plei Ya Kavn, 12 km SSE Plei Djereng AF, 36 km WSW Pleiku. Elements of Bty A/1st/92d Arty here Dec69. 10th Air Cav, 4th Div here, per Bob Patsfield. 4th ID 31Jan70 ORLL grid per Jim Claeys. Pleiku Pr, II Corps.

Bitrex (n/a)
See Glossary.

Black, LZ (BR 632-472)
Near intersection of QL-19 and TL-3A, apx 7 km NW Binh Khe and 16 km E to ENE An Khe. 6Dec65. Binh Dinh Pr, II Corps.

Black, LZ (BR 790-670)
Apx 2 km WSW Hoi San, 38 km NE An Khe, 20 km NE Vinh Thanh and 12 km due W Phu My. 30Oct66. Binh Dinh Pr, II Corps.

Black, LZ (YD 044-588)
Apx 11 km W Cam Lo, 3 km N QL-9 and 31 km WNW Quang Tri. Apr70 XXIV Corps grid per Don Armstrong. Quang Tri Pr, I Corps.

Black, McKinley, Moore Stg (CP 095-230)
A.k.a. Black, McKinley and Moore Ammo Stg Areas. At Cam Ranh Bay. See each individual named storage area for its history. Khanh Hoa Pr, II Corps.

Black, USS (n/a)
DD-666. *USS Black* and *Higbee* were dispatched from TF 71 to join Market Time following Vung Ro Incident in Mar65. See *Brown Water, Black Berets*, p 79. SVN.

Black Ammo Storage Area (CP 09-24)
On Cam Ranh Bay Peninsula, apx 3 km SW the S end of main AF rwy. Named to honor, Sp6 Lewis D Black, KIA while defusing ordnance 18Jul68. Formerly one of either Alpha, Alpha, Charlie and Yankee Ammo Stg areas at Cam Ranh renamed either Black, McKinley or Moore in ceremony, 12Jul69. Khanh Hoa Pr, II Corps.

Black and White Radio (n/a)
See Glossary.

Black Beach (YS 27-44)
Vung Tau R&R Ctr at Vung Tau and apx 60 km SE Saigon. Home of Beachcomber Club and various AAFES-V facilities. Phuoc Tuy Pr, III Corps.

Black Diamond Airfield (XT 935-140?)
Possibly a.k.a. Tan Ba Heliport? Grid is for Tan Ba Heliport and, if accurate, puts site was on W bank of Song Dong Nai, apx 6 km WNW Bien Hoa AB and 22 km NE Tan Son Nhut AB? Shown as AF or heliport N within 20 km of Saigon on map compiled by 517th Engrs Bn, in Aug '70. [74] Possibly a facility of 92d Engr Bn, which had a black diamond featured in its unit crest? The 92d apparently operated principally out of Long Binh Post and in that general area. Binh Duong or Bien Hoa Pr, III Corps.

Black Foot, LZ (YA 94-94?)
See Blackfoot, LZ. Kontum Pr, II Corps.

Black Jack (n/a)
See Blackjack.

Black Jack Mini-Pad (YT 062-115?)
See Blackjack Mini-Pad. Bien Hoa Pr, III Corps.

Black Jack, LZ (XD 984-640)
See Blackjack. Quang Tri Pr, I Corps.

Black Khmer, The (n/a)
See Glossary.

Black Panther Company (n/a)
See Hac Bo in Glossary.

Black Panthers (n/a)
See Thailand, Forces of in Major HQs Section.

Black Radios (n/a)
See Black and White Radio in Glossary.

Black River Salient, Battle for (n/a)
See Hoa Binh, Battle of. NVN.

Black River, The (WJ 35-35)
A.k.a. Song Hac Giang. Flows generally N, passing Hao Binh near WJ 33-06, and joins Red River near Viet Tri (vicinity WJ 50-45), some 55 km WNW Hanoi. NVN.

Black T'ai (n/a)
See Glossary.

Black Virgin Mountain (XT 283-583)
See Nui Ba Den, Nui Ba Den Signal Site, Tay Ninh and Retrans. Tay Ninh Pr, III Corps.

Blackfoot, FSB (XS 89-87)
On S bank of Song Saigon at SE corner of Saigon, 12 km SW Tan Son Nhut AB and 6 km due W Cat Lai. 5th/12th Inf, 199th LIB here. Gia Dinh Pr, III Corps.

Blackfoot, LZ (YA 94-94?)
A.k.a. Hill 1018 and Chu Kram Lo (or Chu Kan Lo) Mtn. Apx 8 km W Polei Kleng AF, and 30 km WNW Kontum. At 14°26'00"N-107°42'00"E. Kontum Pr, II Corps.

Blackfoot, LZ (YA 94-94?)
See Blackfoot. Kontum Pr, II Corps.

Blackhawk, FSB (BS 314-971)
Apx 23 km WSW Chu Lai, 19 km due S Tam Ky and 6 km NW peak of Nui Dong Tranh. Quang Tin Pr, I Corps.

Blackhawk, FSB (YU 243-194)
Apx 10 km NE Song Be City AF, 28 km ESE Bu Dop and 24 km NW Duc Phong. Phuoc Long Pr, III Corps.

Blackhawk, LZ (AR 98-99?)
Along QL-19 apx 19 km E Pleiku, on flat, tree-less plateau of boot-high grass, per *Time Heals No wounds* (p 75). Grid is very rough est based on rptd distance and bearing from Pleiku. 4th Div AO. Photos on internet at: www. landscaper.net/vietnam/ places.html. Pleiku Pr, II Corps.

Blackhawk, LZ/FSB (BR 035-535)
On N side of QL-19 near Plei Herel, apx 3 km SSW Suoi Doi AF, 25 km ENE Pleiku and 6 km NE Plei Kreh. 4th Div and then ARVN FSB in '70-71. Info/location per Tom Rethard, who described it as, "a good-sized FSB. Its firing battery area was in NW quadrant. The NE quadrant was used for arty quarters, and southern half was occupied by a US or ARVN Cav unit. The front gate was about 100 meters from road." 1st/10th Cav?, 1st/92d Arty and B/C Btys, 7th/15th Arty here. ARVN took over site in '71, and "leveled the place." Grid per Jim Claeys. Also listed at BR 039-539 per Nolan Putman. Pleiku Pr, II Corps.

Blackhaw, USCGS (n/a)
WLB 390. USCG Buoy Tender.

Blackhorse, LZ/FSB (YS 44-97)
A.k.a. LZ Black Horse. Along QL-2 apx 55 km due E Saigon, 12 km SSW Xuan Loc and 28 km due N Luscombe AF/Nui Dat. HQ 2d/3d, 199th LIB, 11th ACR HQ and also elements of 1ATF here. Long Khanh Pr, III Corps. See Blackhorse Basecamp and AF. III Corps.

Blackhorse Airfield (YS 437-963)
Apx 12 km S Xuan Loc AF, 28 km N Luscombe AF and 55 km due E Saigon, per TPC K-10D. El. 820', 2,300' asph rwy. Long Khanh Pr, III Corps.

Blackhorse Base Camp (YS 463-971)
A.k.a. LZ Blackhorse or Long Giao. Along QL-2 apx 55 km due E Saigon, 13 km SSW Xuan Loc and 28 km due N Luscombe AF/Nui Dat. Home of 11th Armored Cav Rgt, 11th ACR HQ, also HQ 2d/3d, 199th LIB. Per www. riverwolf.net/reflections/vietnam/, the service club here was 1 of 2 "model clubs" built in VN (see Freeworld Service Club), and was built "over a 5 year period, but open only 29 days before the base was closed." See Claymore Corner and Suoi Cat. Long Khanh Pr, III Corps.

Blackhorse Heliport (YT 062-122)
Apx 13 km SE Bien Hoa, 19 km NE Saigon, and 8 km WNW Long Thanh AF. Was some 38 km WNW Blackhorse Basecamp and apparently not related to it? "Heliport #763, alt 156', Arty advsy-Bien Hoa 290.0, 46.7. At 10°58'00"N-106°54'00"E," per Feb73 TAD. Bien Hoa Pr, III Corps.

Blackjack, LZ (XD 984-640)
Apx 16 km WNW Cam Lo and 36 km WNW Quan Tri. '70 XXIV Corps grid per D. Armstrong. Quang Tri Pr, I Corps.

Blackjack Mini-Pad (YT 062-115?)
Heliport adj to Plantation AF, apx 28 km NW Tan Son Nhut AB/Saigon. "L1 lighting avail. Remarks: Lctd 300 meters W twr. Appr Rwy 05, break left .25 mi for ldg 36 at Blackjack. Left tfc ldg Rwy 23, left base made N twr for ldg Rwy 23 at Blackjack. Hazards: 40' powerlines extending 120 meters parallel to Rwy 05 dep path, intersecting another 40' powerline running SE to twr. RED CARPET TOWER 322.8 67.2 Opr SR-SS Advsy, OT ctc Sanford Twr Arty Adv-Bien Hoa 290.0 46.7," per Apr72 TAD. Bien Hoa Pr, III Corps.

Blair House BOQ (XS 861-916)
A.k.a. White/Blair House. 93 Nguyen Du, Saigon, 7 rms. Named to honor Capt. Donald R. Blair, USA, Advisor, Long Hai Regional Force NCO Trng Ctr, KIA 8Jan66 in ambush of his RF unit. Data per *Vietnam Military Lore, 1959-1973*. Gia Dinh Pr, III Corps.

Blanchard, FSB (n/a)
Cited in *1st Cav Div Op Rpt, Feb-Apr70*, at p 12, per Peter Cole. 1st Cav in Tay Ninh, Phuoc Long and Hau Nghia Prvs, as well as Cambodia during period, and site likely in one of those areas. III Corps?

Blanco County, USS (n/a)
LST-344. Decom 15Sep74.

Blandy, USS (n/a)
DD-943, per Ralph Fries.

Blane (n/a)
6Apr70, XXIV Corps future-use 5th Div FSB name.

Blao (Bao Loc) (n/a)
Mapsheet name L-7014-6532-2. True name: Bao Loc (Blao) SVN.

Blao Hinh Da Airfield (ZT 084-773)
See Bao Loc Plant. AF. Lam Dong Pr, II Corps.

Blarney, LZ (YD 301-537)
Possibly a.k.a. LZ Boss (YD 301-548)? In the lowland plain apx 2.5 km SW QL-1, 4 km due W Quang Tri and 3 km SSW Quang Tri AF. Apr70 XXIV Corps grid per Don Armstrong. Quang Tri Pr, I Corps.

Blaster, FSB (XT 045-895?)
If grid correct, was apx 2 km inside Cambodia, 8 km NNW Thien Ngon AF and 27 km due W Katum. Possibly an Incursion FSB. If proper UTM zone was YT, it was 30 km due E An Loc? On 31Aug70 rpt. Cambodia.

Blaze, FSB (YD 538-022)
Roughly 5 km SW FSB Veghel, 20 km SW FSB Birmingham and 27 km SW Hue. Per Russ Richardson, elements of 1st/83d Arty were at FSB's Blaze, Bastogne and Birmingham, with HQ at Camp Eagle. Expanded to a FSP (forward supply point) for 3d Bde/101st Abn CP, 20Jul69. Also listed at YD 531-022, 542-030, 536-020, 535-020 and 539-023. 101st Abn. Thua Thien Pr, I Corps.

Bliss, FSB (XT 287-642)
At SE edge of Tay Ninh, apx 14 km SE Tay Ninh West AF and 21 km WSW Dau Tieng. Also listed at XT 291-631. Dec67-Sep68. Tay Ninh Pr, III Corps.

Bliss II, FSB (XT 284-616)
Along TL-4, at or near Ap Khe Doi, apx 3 km NNE peak of Nui Ba Den. 2d/32d Arty, 25th Div here. Name/grid per Dan Gillotti. Tay Ninh Pr, III Corps.

Blitz, FSB (YC 766-962)
A.k.a. Hill 861 and Dong Mang Chan. 25 km due S Hue, 23 km SW Phu Bai, 9 km WSW FSB Brick, 6 km NE FSB Spear. 2d Bde/101st Abn, '69-71. During Lam Son 720 beginning mid Jul71, 3d ARVN Rgt worked near FSB Nuts while 2d/11th and 2d/320th Arty fired in supt from FSBs Blitz and Normandy. Also during Lam Son 720 beginning in Apr '71, FSBs Fury, Kathryn, Maureen, Gladiator and later Eagle's Nest were all reopened by B/326th Engrs, while elements of 326th also rebuilt and enlarged FSBs Brick, Tennessee, Rendezvous and Rifle (including Rte 545, the road to FSB Rifle. Thua Thien Pr, I Corps.

Blondie, LZ (XD 901-680)
If grid correct, was in DMZ, apx 3 km ESE Bo Ho Su (NVN), and 46 km WNW Quang Tri. Seems unlikely a permanent base would have been in DMZ and this close to Ben Hai River? Apr70 XXIV Corps grid per Don Armstrong. Quang Tri Pr, I Corps.

Blondin, FSB (XT 013-732)
Apx 27 km NW Tay Ninh West AF, 13 km SW Thien Ngon, 7 km SW FSB Wainwright and about 5 km E Cambodia. Possibly named to honor Sp5 Michael A. Blondin, KIA 29Mar70? Also listed at XT 017-730 per 1st Cav, 30th Arty ORLLs. Tay Ninh Pr, III Corps.

Bloodstone, LZ (BR 913-630)
Apx 5 km SSE Phu My, 19 km N Phu Cat AB and 33 km SSE Bong Son. 2d/17th Arty here supt 1st Cav, 16Oct66. Data per Jack Picciolo. Binh Dinh Pr, II Corps.

Bloody Rice (YD 1-6?)
Apx 5 km NW Cam Lo, 20 km WNW Dong Ha, perhaps 1 km N "Fried Rice" and 6 km N QL-9. Significance of feature unknown. Noted on *Leatherneck* Mag map (date unknown) at: www.monboys.com. Quang Tri Pr, I Corps.

Bloody Ridge (YC 490-480)
Ridgeline including Dong A Tay (Hill 890?) and Dong A Tay Luat (Hill 801). Elements of 2d/327th Inf and 1st/502d Inf, 101st Abn fought NVA SW of FSB Veghel in running battle toward the A Shau Valley for 33 days in Mar-Apr69. NVA finally made stand on this ridge of Dong A Tay Mtn, resulting in 90 NVA KIA. Thua Thien Pr, I Corps.

Bludgeon (n/a)
6Apr70, XXIV Corps future-use III MAF FSB name.

Bludgeon, FSB (BT 342-007)
Apx 19 km WSW Chu Lai and 5 km N peak Nui Dong Tranh. 1st Cav and Americal Lists. Quang Tin Pr, I Corps.

Blue, LZ (AP 783-868)
Apx 13 km due S Ban Me Thuot and near LZ Deane (AP 812-950). Built Dec69, per John Linn (who helped construct it). At time, fire supt courtesy 4th Plt mortars of various Cos. John does not recall any 105mms here but presumes there were some. Montagnard ville apparently nearby. Darlac Pr, II Corps.

Blue, FSB (XT 258-290)
A.k.a. Patrol Base Blue. Apx 3 km N Cambodian border, 10 km W LZ Storm, 17 km due S Tay Ninh and 12 km WNW Go Dau Ha. Patrol base of 2d/22d Inf (Mech), 25th Inf Div, '70. Vice President (then SP5) Al Gore (nickname "Brother Buck") visited base week after it had been attacked (attack apparently took place 22Feb71) as reporter and wrote article about the attack for 20th Engr Bde newspaper, *The Laterite Lantern*. Also listed at XT 305-301, per Frank Penk. Tay Ninh Pr, III Corps.

Blue, FSB (XT 372-423)
Apx 13 km SW Dau Tieng and 16 km ESE Tay Ninh. Also listed at XT 370-420, and 307-484(likely error). Apr-Mar67. Tay Ninh Pr, III Corps.

Blue, LZ (XT 532-359)
Apx 3 km W Bung Binh, 24 km WSW Lai Khe. Feb66. Tay Ninh/Binh Duong Pr border, III Corps.

Blue, LZ (XT 668-985)
Apx 12 km SSW Loc Ninh AF13 km NNW An Loc. Jul67. Binh Long Pr, III Corps.

Blue, LZ (XT 781-729)
Apx 5 km NNW Xom Ruong, 16 km SSE An Loc and 3 km E QL-13. Aug66. Binh Long Pr, III Corps.

Blue, LZ (XT 940-300)
Apx 17 km NNW Bien Hoa AB and 7 km SW Khu Tru Mat. May67. Bien Hoa/Binh Duong Pr border III Corps.

Blue, LZ (BQ 919-337)
In valley apx 15 km ESE Cung Son AF. Oct66. Phu Yen Pr, II Corps.

Blue, LZ (BR 735-884)
Apx 9 km NW Ha Tay. Oct66-Jan67. Binh Dinh Pr, II Corps.

Blue, LZ (BS 56-82?)
Apparently just E of what had been LZ Alfa during Op Utah, and if so, was apx 15 km NW Quang Ngai. Landings here led to battles at nearby An Hoa (1). Used 9May66, during Op Montgomery. See Chau Ngai (4) for location. Per *Utter's Battalion*, pp 313-4. Quang Ngai Pr, I Corps.

Blue, LZ (BS 67-92?)
If grid correct, was on Batangan Peninsula, apx 17 km N Quang Ngai. Site of 1st major contact by US ground troops and also the 1st engagement involving US armored units in war, 17-19Aug65. 3d Marines, Op Starlite, 3 USMC BLT Bns, each suptd by Co of 3d Tank Bn. 573 enemy KIA vs. 46 US KIA rptd. Americal list. Quang Ngai Pr?, I Corps.

Blue, LZ (XD 73-27)
Apx 3 km W SVN border, 20 km SW Khe Sanh, 24 km SE Aloui (Laos) and 8 km due W FSB Saigon. ARVN Marine FSB in Laos during Lam Son 719. Good Lam Son 719 map at www.americal.org/174/map4.htm. Laos.

Blue, LZ (XT 258-290)
See FSB Blue. Tay Ninh Pr, III Corps.

Blue, LZ (YA 783-868)
Apx 15 km SE Cambodia, 44 km W Kontum, and 25 km WSW Polei Kleng. 1st/7th Cav 1st Cav CA'd here during Op Paul Revere and in battle here apx 2 Aug66. B Bty, 2d/9th Arty, 4th Div here, Dec69. Cited in article, *Paul Revere II*, 1st Cav '66 *Yearbook* courtesy Mr. Shutt. 4th Div 31Jan70 grid per Jim Henderson. Kontum Pr, II Corps.

Blue, LZ (YA 97-06)
Apx 48 km SSE Pleiku, 17 km E Cambodia and 12 km ENE peak Chu Pong Mtn. Possibly an LZ of 1st Cav's '65 Ia Drang campaign? Pleiku Pr, II Corps.
Blue, LZ (YA 985-248)
Apx 6 km E Duc Co AF, and 39 km SW Pleiku. 2d/17th Arty here 1Aug66, suptg 1st/12th Cav. Data per Jack Picciolo. Pleiku Pr, II Corps.
Blue, LZ (YD 068-606)
Apx 6 km WNW Cam Lo, 5 km N QL-9 and 27 km WNW Quang Tri. Quang Tri Pr, I Corps.
Blue, LZ (YS 670-670)
Apx 5 km W Xa Nhu Lam and 24 km E Nui Dat. Apr66. Phuoc Tuy Pr, III Corps.
Blue, LZ (YT 153-281)
A.k.a. FSBs Drennan, Charger, and Xom Cat AF. On N bank of Dong Nai River, apx 23 km NE Bien Hoa. Feb66. Bien Hoa Pr, III Corps.
Blue, USS (n/a)
DD-744, per Ralph Fries.
Blue Beach (BS 84-43)
Just N mouth of Tra Cau and Lo Bo Rivers apx 5 km NE Duc Pho and 17 km SE Mo Duc. USN designation for what the USMC called Red Beach, landing site of USMC TF Delta BLT 3/1 and 2/4, during Op Double Eagle, 28Jan66. See Red Beach. Quang Ngai Pr, I Corps.
Blue Beach (YD 299-749)
On coast roughly halfway between DMZ and mouth of Cau Viet River. USMC amphib landing area during Op Prairie, Sep66. Quang Tri Pr, I Corps.
Blue Ghost Airfield (BT 29-23?)
A.k.a. Watson Field and either Tam Key Alternate or Tam Ky AF. Either just NW or due S Tam Ky. If Tam Ky AF, grid is BT 31-19. Americal Div. See Watson Field. Quang Nam Pr, I Corps.
Blue Ridge, USS (n/a)
A.k.a. LCC 19. Acft Carrier flagship of TF 76.8, during Op Eagle Pull, and Op Frequent Wind. Frequently mentioned in *Tears Before the Rain.*
Blue Sector (XD 853-418)
Portion of northern perimeter of Khe Sanh CB. Was manned by C/1st/26th Marines during siege. See Khe Sanh entry for location. Quang Tri Pr, I Corps.
Blueberry, LZ (XD 755-485)
Apx 13 km NW Khe Sanh CB, 8 km NW Ap La Vien and 60 km W Quang Tri. Apr70 XXIV Corps grid per Don Armstrong. Quang Tri Pr, I Corps.
Bluebird, LZ (YD 241-589)
Near QL-1 railroad tracks and immed W Dong Ha, apx 12 km NW Quang Tri. Apr70 XXIV Corps grid per Don Armstrong. Quang Tri Pr, I Corps.
Bluebird, USS (n/a)
MSC-121. Minesweeper, Coastal, per Ralph Fries.
Blueridge, USS (n/a)
LCC-19. Amphib Attack Transport, per Ralph Fries.
Bluegill, USS (n/a)
SS-242, Submarine. Between '61-64, Viet sailors served short tours on 7th Fleet ships or with combined antisubmarine warfare exercises involving US subs *Bluegill* (SS 242), *Queenfish* (SS 393), and *Capitaine* (AGSS 336).
Bluejay, LZ (XS 937-587)
On E bank of Cua Soirap, just N Xom Ca Dah, apx 16 km NE Go Cong and 33 km SSE Saigon. Mar66. Gia Dinh Pr, III Corps.
Bn Gia Map (YU 344-375)
See Bu Gia Map. Phuoc Long Pr, III Corps.
Bna Nam Nhion Airfield (n/a)
Feb67 Natl Geo map. Laos.
B'Nom M' Hai Mtn (ZT 07-54)
A.k.a. Hill 1642 (or 5,387'). Apx 27 km S Bao Loc. Binh Tuy Pr?, III Corps.
Bo Bang CAP (YD?)
CAP 4-3-6, 4th CAG per Tim Duffie. Was also sited at Le Xuyen (YD 3-6). Quang Tri Pr, I Corps.
Bo Co, Mui (CP 1-5)
Coastal point at 12°14'00"N-109°16'12"E. On ND49-13 JOG. Khanh Hoa Pr, II Corps.
Bo Duc Base (XU 96-25)
On road between Bu Dop and An Loc, apx 5 km SSW Bu Dop, 7 km from Cambodian border and 32 km NE Loc Ninh. 1st CAV. Cambodian Invasion use, May-Jun70. Phuoc Long Pr, III Corps.
Bo Ho Su (XD 88-68)
NVA ville in DMZ and on N bank Ben Hai River apx 45 WNW Quang Tri and 24 km E Laos. NVN.
Bo Khoe Airfield (n/a)
A.k.a. Andaung Pech AF. Apx 345 km NE Phnom Penh and 85 km WSW Pleiku SVN. El. 984'. Cambodia.
Bo Loi Woods (XT 50-35)
See Boi Loi Woods. III Corps.
Bo Mua Airfield (XT 960-495)
See Phuoc Vinh AF. Phuoc Long Pr, III Corps.
Bo Tuc (Uyen Binh) (n/a)
Mapsheet name of L-7014-6232 2. SVN.
Bo Tuc, FSB (XT 38-86)
Apx 8 km SE Katum along road to An Loc, 48 km NE Tay Ninh and 6 km from Cambodia. According VHPA website, this FSB was attacked 22Dec67. Info per www.vhp.org/crash.htm. Tay Ninh Pr, III Corps.
Boa Loc New Airfield (ZT 100-810)
See Tan Phat AF. Lam Dong Pr, II Corps.
Boa, LZ (XD 997-383)
Apx 9 km due E Lang Kat, 15 km ESE Khe Sanh CB and 37 km WSW Quang Tri. Apr70 XXIV Corps grid per Don Armstrong. Quang Tri Pr, I Corps.
Boa, FSB (XT 561-323)
Apx 22 km WSW Lai Khe and 3 km SSE Bung Binh. Sep67. Tay Ninh Pr?, III Corps.
Boat (n/a)
6Apr70, XXIV Corps future-use 5th Div FSB name.
Bob, FSB (XT 245-437)
Apx 21 km SSE Tay Ninh W AF, and 15 km due S Tay Ninh. Feb67. Tay Ninh Pr, III Corps.
Bob, LZ (XD 983-610)
A.k.a. FSB Audrey (XD 990-612)? Apx 14 km WNW Cam Lo and 36 km WNW Quang Tri. Apr70 XXIV Corps grid per Don Armstrong. Quang Tri Pr, I Corps.
Bob, LZ (XT 262-916)
Apx 6 km WNW Katum and 6 km S Cambodia. Apr70. Tay Ninh Pr, III Corps.

Bobbie, LZ/FSB (ZA 061-738)
A.k.a. "Bobby" and spelled both ways in 1st/35th Inf logs. Apx 22 km SW Kontum, 10 km SSW LZ Patt and just W Krong Poko River. Cited in AAR at www.grunt.space.swri.edu/aarpt1.htm. Apparently near LZ Patt. 2d/8th Inf, 4th Div here at one point. Per Dick Arnold, grid was ZA 066-735 and spelled "Bobby" in Jan-Mar69 1st/35th Inf Bn daily logs. Also at ZA 097-834? Kontum Pr, II Corps.
Bobbie, LZ/FSB (ZA 097-834)
Listed at this grid per Dan Gillotti, which if correct, puts it apx 7 km due S Polei Krong AF and 16 km WSW Kontum. Also listed at ZA 061-738. Kontum Pr, II Corps.
Bobby, LZ (ZA 061-738)
See Bobbie. Kontum Pr, II Corps.
Bobcat, LZ (XD 944-654)
Apx 22 km WNW Cam Lo, 7 km SE Bon Ho Su (NVN) and 42 km WNW Quang Tri. Apr70 XXIV Corps grid per Don Armstrong. Quang Tri Pr, I Corps.
Boc Lo New Airfield (ZT 100-810)
See Tan Phat AF. Lam Dong Pr, II Corps.
Boch Ho (YB 87-26)
A.k.a. Ben Het ARVN Ranger Camp. See Ben Het. Kontum Pr, II Corps.
Bodner Field (BR 896-412)
See Bordner Field. Binh Dinh Pr, II Corps.
Boga Mountain (BR 727-534)
18 km WNW Phu Cat. Binh Dinh Pr, II Corps.
BOHICA, Operation (n/a)
See Glossary.
Boi Chan, FSB? (YT 34-07)
Apx 12 km WSW Xuan Loc AF, 14 km NW Blackhorse basecamp and 4 km S QL-1. 2d/3d Inf, 199th LIB position, likely in '68. Also spelled Bai Chan. Grid per 199th LIB Assn. Bien Hoa Pr, III Corps.
Boi Loi Woods (XT 50-35)
Apx 25 km NW Cu Chi, 15 km due N Tra Bang, 22 km W Ben Cat, 15 km NW Ho Bo Woods and W Thanh Dien Forestry Reserve. 25th Inf Div AO, swept during Op Cedar Falls, Jan-Feb67. Map in *Rangers At War,* pp 324-325. Tay Ninh, Binh Duong and Hau Nghia Prvs, III Corps.
Boise, FSB (YC 941-970)
Apx 20 km SSE Phu Bai, 15 km WSW Phu Loc and 13 km WNW Bach Ma. Bn CP for 2d/501st Inf, 18Feb70. Also listed at YC 945-968. Thua Thien Pr, I Corps.
Bolan, FSB (YS 963-974)
N of QL-1, apx 44 km WSW Phan Thiet, 15 km NNW Ham Tan AF, 115 km due E Saigon, and 13 km NE peak of Nui Be Mtn. Possibly named to honor Army MSgt Robert L. Bolan, KIA 24Jul70. Opened or reopened 9Sep70. 2d/11th ACR Data per *1st Cav Div Op Rpt, ending 31Oct70*, courtesy Peter Cole. Also listed at YS 983-968 in Feb71 rpt. Binh Tuy Pr, III Corps.
Bolling, Operation (n/a)
19Sep67-31Jan68. 1st Cav/173d Abn ops in Tuy Ho/Phu Hiep. 2/503d and A Bty, 3d/319th Arty returned to coastal area of II Corps. 715 rptd NVA/VC KIA, per *Vietnam Order of Battle*, pp 9-14. Phu Yen Pr, II Corps.
Bolo, FSB (ZC 082-272)
Apx 5 km SW COB Battle-Ax, 10 km SSE FSB Saber, 7 km ENE FSB Machete and 32 km SW An Hoa. USMC used during assault of Base Area 112, Dec68-Feb69. Apr70 XXIV Corps grid per Don Armstrong. On map in *US Marines in Vietnam-1969*, p 90. Quang Tin Pr, I Corps.
Bolovens Airfield (XB 65-80)
LS-55. CIA/SF, per *Air Facilities Data-Laos.*
Bolovens Plateau (XB 60-70)
Huge plateau in southern Laos that sloped up from Mekong River and then E some 120 km to rugged cliffs overlooking the Xe Kong River. Geographically dominated what was known as Laotian Military Region-4. Pakse was largest town in MR-IV. Grid roughly at center of mass. Laos.
Bols, LZ (BT 247-168)
A.k.a. Bowles? Apx 5 km SE Tam Ky, 10 km W Ql-1 and 28 km WNW Chu Lai. Also listed at BT 245-167. Americal list. Map is L-7014-6640-2. Quang Tin Pr, I Corps.
Bolster, USS (n/a)
ARS-38. Aux Ship, per Ralph Fries.
Bolt, FSB (XT 26-38)
A.k.a. FSBs Hull and Joyce. Apx 10 km S Tay Ninh, immed W Ap Van Long, and just E the Song Vam Co Dong River. 199th LIB. Tay Ninh Pr, III Corps.
Bolt, FSB (XT 047-821)
Apx 4 km due W Thien Ngon AF and 6 km S Cambodia. Mar67. Tay Ninh Pr, III Corps.
Bom Am Bla Airfield (BQ 504-598)
See Phu Tuc AF. Phu Bon Pr, II Corps.
Bomber, LZ (XD 890-220)
In Vietnam Salient, apx 2 km W Laotian border, 9 km SE Lang Chiem, 8 km SSW Lang Klung and 54 km SW of Quang Tri. Apr70 XXIV Corps grid per Don Armstrong. Quang Tri Pr, I Corps.
Bombing by NVA Air Force (n/a)
See Determined to Win in Glossary.
Bon Dak Ndrot (n/a)
Mapsheet name of L-7014-6534-3. SVN/Cambodia.
Bon Drang Phok (n/a)
Mapsheet name of L-7014-6534-4. SVN/Cambodia.
Bon Homme Richard, USS (n/a)
A.k.a. CVA-31. Deployed with CVW-5, 18Mar69-29Oct69; with CVW-5, 2Apr 70-12Nov70; with CVW-5, 27Jan68-10Oct68; with CVW-19, 28Jan64-21Nov64; with CVW-19, 21 Apr 65-13Jan66; with CVW-21, 26Jan67-25Aug67. In May65, planes from CVA 31 knocked out the Hanoi electrical power plant. [75]
Bon Sar Pa Airfield (YU 818-729)
See Duc Lap AF. Quang Duc Pr, II Corps.
Bon Sar Pa Outpost (YU 805-735)
Apx 11 km WSW Duc Lap (New) AF and 57 km SW Ban Me Thuot. Also listed at YU 818-729, Jan69. Quang Duc Pr, II Corps.
Bonanza, LZ (XD 935-679)
In DMZ apx 5 km WSW Bon Ho Su, and 45 km WNW Quang Tri. Apr70 XXIV Corps grid per Don Armstrong. Quang Tri Pr, I Corps.
Bond, BG William, KIA Site (YT 30-35?)
Apx 20 km ESE Phuoc Vinh AF and 32 km NNE Bien Hoa AF. Site where BGen William R. Bond was killed, 1 Apr70. Long Khanh Pr?, III Corps.
Bond, FSB (YS 625-647)
At intersection of Rte-23 and Rte 328, 4 km SSE FSB Discovery, 20 km ESE Nui Dat and 7 km N ocean. 161

Bty's deployment here part of Op Concrete, largest Australian military op to that point following WWII. Involved all 3 RAR Inf Bns, 1ATF HQ, a Field Rgt and suptg arms deployed to destroy HQ of D445 VC Rgt. 161 Bty, RNZA (Andrew's Bty 18Sep-6Sep70) FSB set here 20-26Apr70. [76] On 1ATF NCO trng map per John Hollett. Phuoc Tuy Pr, III Corps.

Bone Yard, The (YD 766-074)
NVA/VC massacre site along Khe Ke creek between Nui Ke Mtn on the S and Nui Hoan Gay (Banana Mtn) on N, 14 km due S Hue. 5 km SE FSB Birmingham, 7 km due S Pohl Bridge and 5 km SSW Nam Hoa District HQ, and 2 km N peak of Nui Ke. On 19Sep69, element of 1st/502d Inf, 101st Abn, found the remains of perhaps 2,000 Hue citizens massacred here after NVA kidnapped them from city during Battle for Hue, Tet '68. Bodies lined both sides of creek-bed for hundreds of yds under a 40' to 50' high canopy, and many had their hands bound behind their backs. Unknown if enemy originally intended to kill their prisoners or if it simply became a tactical necessity due to difficulty of moving such a large group without being detected coupled with huge logistical problems presented by feeding, clothing and moving them all. Grid per 1st/502d Inf, '69 Annual Hist Supp, 19Sep69 entry at p 27. Also listed at YD 756-074. Thua Thien Pr, I Corps.

Bong Da Thin (n/a)
Likely misspelling of Dong Ba Thin.

Bong Mieu (BT 26-05)
A.k.a. Mo Bong Mieu. Ville apx 18 km SE Tien Phuoc AF and 15 km SSE Tam Ky. Quang Tin Pr, I Corps.

Bong Ngu Airfield (WS 41-96)
Light-aircraft field on Hwy 30 just E the Mekong River, apx 30 km ENE Chau Duc AF, 10 km ESE Thuong Thoi AF and 150 km due W Saigon. Data per 517th Engr Det's IV *MR Major Road Net and AFs* map dated Sep70. Kien Tuong Pr, IV Corps.

Bong Son (BR 872-958)
A.k.a. Hoai Nhon. On QL-1 apx 75 km NNW Qui Nhon, 80 km SSE Quang Ngai, 8 km SSW LZ English and 52 km N Phu Cat AB. Bong Son and Qui Nhon, shared provincial capitol control of Binh Dinh Pr. Americal, 5th SF, Det A-321, Oct65, A-227 Oct66. See mapsheet L-7014-6837-4. Binh Dinh Pr, II Corps.

Bong Son (n/a)
Mapsheet name of L-7014-6837-4. SVN.

Bong Son Airfield (BR 846-947)
Apx 8 km SSW LZ English AF, 13 km NE Ha Tay AF, 52 km N Phu Cat 1 AF. On TPC K-10A. Listed as "Abnd Security Questionable 5Apr68, for security contact G3 Air, II Corps TOC, AF # VA2-87," in Aug69 TAD per Frank Penk, Jr. Not in Feb73 TAD. El. 100'. See mapsheet L-7014-6837-4. Binh Dinh Pr, II Corps.

Bong Son Bomber (n/a)
See Glossary.

Bong Son Bridges (BR 87-96)
3 bridges spanned the Song Lai Giang at Bong Son: 1) Iron-truss railroad bridge built by colonial French but blown in several places such that US Army Engrs converted it to vehicle bridge by spanning blown sections with wood planks. 2) Concrete-pier bridge that was the original QL-1 bridge, which also suffered numerous enemy attempts to destroy it. Its structural integrity was weakened such that Engrs built 3), a pontoon bridge for heavy truck/tank traffic immed SW of it. See mapsheet L-7014-6837-4. Binh Dinh Pr, II Corps.

Bong Son Plains (BR 880-970)
Binh Dinh Pr, II Corps.

Bong Son SF Camp (BR 848-948)
SW Bong Son AF, 18 km SSW LZ English, 12 km NNE Ha Tay AF and near My Duc. Was apparently on S side of An Lo River. 5th SF camp. Det A-321, Oct65, A-227 Oct66 and moved to Ha Tay. Grid per *SF Order of Battle.* Binh Dinh Pr, II Corps.

Bong Son Valley (BR 85-95)
Valley apx 80 km N Qui Nhon. Binh Dinh Pr, II Corps.

Bong Ton, Khinh (WS 3-5)
See Canal des Quatre Cantons. Chau Doc Pr?, IV Corps.

Bonneville, LZ (XD 847-223)
In center of Vietnam Salient, apx 10 km SW Lang Klung, 6 km SSE Lang Chiem, 6 km at closest point to Laotian border and 56 km SW of Quang Tri. Apr70 XXIV Corps grid per Don Armstrong. Quang Tri Pr, I Corps.

Boo Heung Pioneer, SS (n/a)
Korean-flag LST ship. See Evacuation of Da Nang.

Boo, FSB (YU 501-067)
Apx 7 km ENE Duc Phong AF, 33 km E Song Be and 28 km NE Bu Nard AF. Phuoc Long Pr, III Corps.

Books, Camp (AT 945-800)
A.k.a. Camp Red Beach and Camp J. K. Books (often referred to as Camp "Brooks" in error). At Da Nang and just S Red Beach, apx 8 km NW Da Nang AB and adj QL-1. Originally named Camp Red Beach but renamed to honor Cpl Jay K. Books, USMC, a data processor who volunteered for Marine CAC (pacification) team and was KIA 16Nov66, when 122mm rocket hit guard tower he was manning at Red Beach. HQ Force Logistics Cmd, USMC VN. Data per *Vietnam Military lore 1959-1973.* Quang Nam Pr, I Corps.

Boom Boom, FSB (n/a)
No data. 1st/12th Cav and 2d/19th Arty, 4th Div moved here after being opcon to 173d Abn during Battle of Dak To, 30Nov67. [77]

Boom-Boom Room, The (YD 625-095?)
At FSB Bastogne, along Hwy 547 apx 17 km SW Hue and 8 km W FSB Birmingham. Makeshift bunker/bar and rec room built by men of 321st Arty. Per Mike Gacek, entrance was lined with 105 mm shell casing hanging from its ceiling. The casings would ring clearly whenever anyone entering the room wearing a steel pot would bang into them (hence, the bunker's name), and rule was that the forgetful or uninitiated whose helmet "gonged" the casings would be obligated to buy a round of drinks for everyone in the bunker! Thua Thien Pr, I Corps.

Boonaroo, HMAS (n/a)
Logistics transport initially manned by civilians, but later commissioned into Royal Aussie Navy due to union bans. Was 1st ship to commission into RAN under Aussie White Ensign. *Sydney*, *Boonaroo* and *Jesparit* made total of 42 trips to VN carrying almost 200,000 DW tons of cargo, per www.navy.gov.au/4_history/vietnam.htm.

Boot, LZ (YU 501-067)
Apx 6 km E Duc Phong AF and 35 km E Song Be/Phuoc Binh. 1st Cav Div, '69? Name/grid per Dan Gillotti. Phuoc Long Pr, III Corps.

Boot, The (BR 860-760)
Hill mass apx 18 km S of Bong Son that resembled a boot. See Cuff. Tay Ninh Pr, III Corps.

Boots, LZ (BR 338-396)
Near or a.k.a. LZ Boots (BR 345-395), apx 15 km WSW An Khe. Oct65. Tay Ninh Pr, III Corps.

BOQ No. 1 (XS 816-938)
At 210 Vo Tanh St., Saigon. Data per *Vietnam Military Lore, 1959-1973.* Gia Dinh Pr, III Corps.

BOQ No. 2 (XS 827-939)
At 309-311 Cach Mang St., Saigon. Data per *Vietnam Military Lore, 1959-1973.* Gia Dinh Pr, III Corps.

BOQ No. 3 (XS 836-939)
At 189-193 Vo Tanh St., Saigon. Data per *Vietnam Military Lore, 1959-1973.* Gia Dinh Pr, III Corps.

Bordel Mobile de Campaigne (n/a)
See Glossary.

Bordelon, USS (n/a)
DD-881 per Ralph Fries.

Bordner Field (BR 896-412)
Informal name of Phu Cat AB. Named to honor LTC William Bordner, KIA when he stepped on a mine during initial survey for Phu Cat AB, 16Feb66. See Phu Cat AB and Bordner Hill. Binh Dinh Pr, II Corps.

Bordner Hill (BR 89-41)
Initial survey of Phu Cat AB took place 16Feb66, during which LTC William Bordner was KIA by mine. That site, Hill 151, was later named Bordner Hill in his honor. Original name for chosen site of Phu Cat was Base X. Near listed grid. Binh Dinh Pr, II Corps.

Borie, USS (n/a)
A.k.a. DD 215. On 19Jun68 replaced *USS Lowry* off Binh Thuan Pr. In supt D/3/506th, it fired on suspected VC positions near Cape Ke Ga. 2Aug68, was off Phan Thiet, per www.currahee.org/pageb2. Also spelled Broie?

Borikhane Airfield (UF 66-53)
A.k.a. LS-129. Apx 130 km NE Vientiane. CIA/SF facility. Grid per *Air Facilities Data-Laos.* El. 400'. Laos.

Borneo Design Battery (n/a)
See Glossary.

Boss, LZ (YD 301-548)
Possibly a.k.a. LZ Blarney (YD 301-534)? In lowland plain apx 2.5 km SW QL-1, 4 km due W Quang Tri and 3 km SSW Quang Tri AF. Apr70 XXIV Corps grid per Don Armstrong. Quang Tri Pr, I Corps.

Boston, USS (n/a)
A.k.a. CA-69 or CAG-1? This Heavy Cruiser along with Aussie warship HMAS *Hobart*, *USCGC Point Dume* and *PCF-12* were repeatedly attacked by unidentified acft, 16Aug66. Incident discussed in *Brown Water, Black Berets*, p 114. Market Time TF-115. NVN waters?

Bostos Cigarettes (n/a)
See Glossary.

Bouam Long Airfield (UG 26-86)
A.k.a. LS-32. Apx 125 km W Luang Prabang, per ONC-J-11. CIA/SF, per *Air Facilities Data-Laos.* El. 4,671'. Laos.

Bougainville, LZ (YD 025-376)
Apx 3 km SE LZ Bluebird, 35 km WSW Quang Tri and 12 km E Lang Kat. Apr70 XXIV Corps grid per Don Armstrong. Quang Tri Pr, I Corps.

Bouh Me Ga (BP 314-835)
S.L.A. Marshall's apparent misspelling of Boun Mi Ga SF Camp and Valley. See Buon Mi Ga. Darlac Pr, II Corps.

Boum Lao Airfield (QC 50-21)
LS-174. CIA/SF, per *Air Facilities Data-Laos.*

Boun Beng Heliport (BQ 235-820)
Apx 20 km due W Cheo Reo AF/Hou Bon, and 25 km SE Phu Nhon AF. Heliport #526, alt 623', at 13°23'40"N-108°26'30"E, per Feb73 TAD. Phu Bon Pr, II Corps.

Boun Loum Airfield (UG 26-86)
A.k.a. LS-88 and Buon Lom AF. CIA/SF, per *Air Facilities Data-Laos.*

Boun Mi Ga (BP 32-83)
See Buon Mi Ga. Darlac Pr, II Corps.

Boun Neua Airfield (RD 00-97)
A.k.a. L-30 and Buon Neua AF. CIA/SF, per *Air Facilities Data-Laos.*

Boundary Road (XT)
E to W road between Dau Tieng and QL-13 (Thunder Road), just S FSB Thunder II. Presumably so named because it formed the southern boundary of Michelin Rubber Plantation. Per *Low Level Hell's* 1st Div TAOR map. Binh Duong Pr?, III Corps.

Boung (generally)
See also Buong entries.

Boung Long Airfield (n/a)
Apx 330 km NE Phnom Penh on Feb67 Natl Geo map. Also spelled Buong Long. El. 1312'. Cambodia.

Boung Quioua, Cape (XE 6-8)
See Cape Boung Quioua. NVN.

Bourgery, Plantation de (AP 9-8)
A.k.a. Don Dien Bourgery. Darlac Pr, II Corps.

Bouton, Cape (WG 8-2)
See Cape Bouton. NVN.

Bow, LZ (XT 097-906)
Apx 3 km from Cambodia, 23 km due W Katum, and 43 km NNW Tay Ninh. May68. Tay Ninh Pr, III Corps.

Bowie, LZ (YD 313-723)
A.k.a. FSB C-4. Apx 17 km N Quang Tri, 2 km from ocean and 5 km NW Cua Viet Naval Base. Apr70 XXIV Corps grid per Don Armstrong. Quang Tri Pr, I Corps.

Bowles, LZ (BT 245-167)
A.k.a. LZ Bols? Apx 5 km SE Tam Ky, 28 km WNW Chu Lai and 10 km W Ql-1. Also listed at BT 247-168. Americal list. Quang Tin Pr, I Corps.

Bowling Alley Valley (ZD 17-03)
A.k.a. The Bowling Alley. Generally apx 12 km ENE Phu Loc and on N side of QL-1, ENE FSB Tomahawk. Thua Thien Pr, I Corps.

Bowman, LZ (BT 239-142)
Apx 10 km SW Tam Ky, 32 km WNW Chu Lai AB, 4 km SW LZ Bols and 5 km SE LZ Young. Apr70 XXIV Corps grid per Don Armstrong. Also listed at BT 238-140, BT 30-15 and BT 237-140. Quang Tri Pr, I Corps.

Boxer, FSB (BS 115-977)
Overlooking Song Tram River Valley apx 16 km due S Tien Phuoc, 27 km SW Tam Ky and 10 km ENE Hau Duc.

Base opened or reopened by Americal, 26Apr70. A FSB Boxer built 1Aug69 by 2d Bde/101st Abn while opcon Americal during Op Lamar Plain, but it is unknown if Boxer at BT 311-197 is a typo or different base? Boxer provided logistics, fire supt and C&C for SW AO of Lamar Plain. Apr70 XXIV Corps grid per Don Armstrong. Also listed at BS 112-976. Quang Tin Pr, I Corps.

Boxer, FSB (BS 311-197?)
If grid correct, this remote base would have been apx 11 km SW Gia Vuc AF and 55 km SW Duc Pho AF. Described as 101st Abn base, but author suspects this grid may be erroneous. Name/grid per Dan Gillotti, 15th Arty Assn. Kontum Pr, I Corps.

Boxer, USS (n/a)
A.k.a. CVA-21. As early as March, '50, 7th Fleet cmdr, with Destroyers *Stickell* (DD 888) and *Richard B. Anderson* (DD 786), visited Saigon as 60 acft from *Boxer* (CVA 21) over-flew city. In Oct53, 4 ships of Destroyer Div 30 conducted similar show at Saigon. See also *Stickell* and *Wasp*.

Boy, LZ (BR 753-473)
On S side of QL-19, apx 8 km SE Binh Khe, and 28 km ESE An Khe. Oct65. Binh Dinh Pr, II Corps.

Boy Youth Group (YT 04-07)
See Phanh Hanh Social Club. Bien Hoa Pr, III Corps.

Boyd, FSB (YD 740-133)
Along W side of Hwy 547 apx 8 km SSW Hue, 2 km SW Pohl (Nam Hoa) Bridge, 1 km W Ming Mang's Tomb, 4.5 km NW FSB Birmingham on hill apx 140 meters in height. Overlooked both bridge and tomb. Part of perimeter almost reached Hwy 547 not far from 1st/502d Inf road checkpoint built in '69. Apparently built by elements of 82d Abn in '68, and secured by 2d/505th Inf, 82d Abn in May68. Map of site in *All the Way-The 3d Bde, 82d Abn Div in Vietnam, 1968*, pp 21. Also listed at YD 735-134. Grid per Butch Sincock. Oct68-Nov69. Thua Thien Pr, I Corps.

Boyd Quarry (YD 743-137)
See Boyd, FSB. Thua Thien Pr, I Corps.

Boyd, USS (n/a)
DD-544. 7th Flt Destroyer, per Ralph Fries.

Bra, FSB (YU 324-496)
Remote site near Cambodia, apx 40 km NE Bu Dop, 14 km N Djamap AF/Bu Gia Map and 36 km due W Bu Prang. Opened 14May70? 11th ACR/1st Cav Cambodian Incursion FSB. Grid/some data per *11th ACR Cambodia Invasion AAR, 1st Cav Div, May-Jun70*, courtesy Lou Rochat.[78] Phuoc Long Pr, III Corps.

Bra, The (YB 66-21?)
If grid is accurate, was near Ban Phiadouang, apx 36 km due W Dak To 2 AF. Given name for "distinctive shape of a river where Hwy 110 split to meet the Ho Chi Minh Trail. Hwy 96 which crossed area was the main artery for supplies and troop movements for NVA." Binh Tram 37 here and area heavily fortified with AAA. Nickname for what was generally regarded as hottest and most feared operational area of southern Laos cross-border ops. For discussion, see www. specialoperations.com/MACVSOG/ tales_from_sog/The_Bra/Default.html. Laos

Brace, LZ (YA 815-873)
Apx 5 km SE Plei Trop, 44 km due W Kontum, 23 km WSW Polei Kleng AF and 7 km SW Polei Meo. 4th Div. Grid per Tom Lacombe. Kontum Pr, II Corps.

Brad, LZ (BR 864-767)
A.k.a. LZ Bradley? In 506 Valley, apx 8 km SE Ha Tay AF and 12 km NNW Phu My. Oct66 grid. Also listed at BR 813-819? Binh Dinh Pr, II Corps.

Bradley, LZ (BR 813-819)
A.k.a. LZ Brad (Nov66) and listed as LZ Brad at BR 864-767 in Oct66? Unknown which grid is accurate or if separate bases. If listed grid accurate, was in 506 Valley, apx 2 km SE Ha Tay AF and 18 km NNW Phu My. Binh Dinh Pr, II Corps.

Bradley, FSB (YD 278-119)
A.k.a. Hill 1021. Apx 44 km WSW Hue16 km E Tou Rout and 6 km WNW Co Pung Mtn. 101st Abn. Also listed as YD 278-122 and at YD 277-123. Thua Thien Pr, I Corps.

Bradley, FSB (YT 207-647)
Apx 18 km SSE Dong Xoai, 30 km NE Phuoc Vinh and 23 km SSW Bu Nard AF. Opened or reopened 1Aug70, closed 2Sep70. 2d/7th Cav. Data per *1st Cav Div Op Rpt, ending 31Oct70*, courtesy Peter Cole. Phuoc Long Pr, III Corps.

Bradley, USS (n/a)
Arrived 16Feb68 off Phan Thiet to replace *USS Cone* suptg TF 3d/506th Inf, per www.currahee.org/pageb2.html.

Bragg, FSB (XT 344-583)
A.k.a. Patrol Base Bragg. On N side of LTL 13, apx 15 km NE Tay Ninh, 6 km due E Nui Ba Den and 2 km NE Ap Phuoc Hoa. Nov68-Jan70. Elements of 4th/9th Inf, 3d/22d Inf, 4th/23d (Mech) Inf and 2d/34th Armor, 25th Div here at various times, as were elements of 7th/11th, 3d/13th and 1st 27th Arty. 163d RF Co here also. Also listed at XT 340-582. Tay Ninh Pr, III Corps.

Bragg II, FSB (XT 339 582)
Dec68 grid puts it on same site as original FSB Bragg. Perhaps so-named because it was 2d opening of site? Tay Ninh Pr, III Corps.

Bragg III, FSB (XT 350-580)
Sep69 grid puts it on virtually same site as original Bragg and Bragg II. Perhaps so named because it was 3d opening of site? Tay Ninh Pr, III Corps.

Brai An Mountain (AN 91-78)
See Braian Mtn. Lam Dong Pr, II Corps.

Braian Mountain (AN 91-78)
A.k.a. Hill 1874 (6,148') and Brai An Mtn. Apx 36 km due E Bao Loc. Lam Dong Pr, II Corps.

Brain, USS (n/a)
DD-630, per Ralph Fries.

Brandon, Baie du (WG 7-0)
A.k.a. Vung Phu Dien. Bay at 19°00'N-105°40'E. On NE48-03 JOG. NVN.

Brandy, LZ (XD 894-633)
See LZ Bandy. Quang Tri Pr, I Corps.

Brandywine, LZ (YD 029-653)
At southern boundary of DMZ, apx 7 km due N peak of Dong Ha Mtn, 18 km NNE Ca Lu, 10 km N QL-9 and 34 km WNW Quang Tri. Apr70 XXIV Corps grid per Don Armstrong. Quang Tri Pr, I Corps.

Brass, LZ (BR)
Siad to have overlooked the An Lao River Valley apx 20 km NNE Bong Son and roughly 3 km SE Nuoc Giao. Used during Op Masher/White Wing, 28Jan-6Mar66. Detailed

discussion of Masher/White Wing and this LZ in *A Contagion of War* vol of *Vietnam Experience* series, pp 32-48, with map at p 38. 2d/12th Cav, 1st Cav LZ. Binh Dinh Pr, II Corps.

Brass, LZ (BR 810-150)
Apx 9 km NNW Van Canh AF and 28 km WSW Qui Nhon. Apparent 1st Cav LZ. Name/grid per Dan Gillotti. Binh Dinh Pr, II Corps.

Bravo, FSB (XT 64-71?)
Apparently was apx 15 km SW An Loc, 7 km SE FSB C, 6 km SE Sroc Con Trang and at Rte 246 bridge crossing of Song Saigon. Grid only apx. Binh Long Pr, III Corps.

Bravo, LZ (XD 64-38)
Apx 22 km WSW Khe Sanh, 12 km E Aloui on QL-9. Laos, Lam Son 719, ARVN Abn. ARVN base during Lam Son 719. Good Lam Son 719 FSB map at www.americal.org/174/map4.htm. Laos.

Bravo, LZ (XT 278-102)
Under the Angel's Wing, apx 4 km from Cambodia and 5 km NW Duc Hue. Dec65. Hau Nghia Pr, III Corps.

Bravo, LZ (XT 512-904?)
Listed at both XT 512-904 and 521-904 in Mar67, and unknown which is correct. If at 512-904, was apx 3 km S Cambodia, 22 km due E Katum and 6 km due W tip of Fishhook. If at 521-904, was 1 km E of listed position. Tay Ninh Pr, III Corps.

Bravo, FSB (XT 623-815)
A.k.a. LZ Bravo. Apx 16 km SW An Loc and 10 km SSE tip of Fishhook. 67. Binh Long Pr?, III Corps.

Bravo, FSB (XT 720-997)
A.k.a. Allons I. Along QL-13, apx 12 km NNW An Loc and 8 km S Loc Ninh AF. Dec67. Binh Long Pr, III Corps.

Bravo, FSB (XT 960-300)
Apx 3 km S Khu Tru Mat and 16 km due N Bien Hoa AB. May67. Also listed at XT 980-322. Bien Hoa Pr, III Corps.

Bravo, FSB (YS 250-700)
Possibly a.k.a. FSB Stingray (YS 257-707) and/or FSB Hope (YS 253-704)? Along QL-15, apx 5 km due S Phu My and 19 km WNW Nui Dat/Luscombe AF. Dec67. Phuoc Tuy Pr, III Corps.

Bravo CAC (YD?)
See CAC listings. I Corps.

Bravo CAP (n/a)
See CAP Bravo listings.

Bravo Outpost (XD 85-41?)
On N side of Hill 558 road at S edge of Khe Sanh CB and outside main perimeter (1st/26th Mar sector), S of the "Rock Quarry "and N of Alpha Outpost. Outpost of 1st/9th Marines. Mislabeled map of position in *Valley of Decision,* p 388. Grid is rough estimate. Quang Tri Pr, I Corps.

Brawely (n/a)
6Apr70, XXIV Corps future-use 5th Inf FSB name.

Brazil Victory, SS (n/a)
Merchant ship under govt contract, per Ralph Fries.

Breaker Site (XD 756-532)
See Hill 665 for detail. Quang Tri Pr, I Corps.

Breakfast (n/a)
See Base Area 353. Cambodia.

Brenda, LZ (AQ 856-845)
Along QL-14, apx 15 km SSW Phu Nhon AF. Oct69. Pleiku Pr, II Corps.

Brennan, FSB? (YS 44-57)
Possible outpost of 8 RAR, 1ATF during Op Hammersley, Feb70. On northernmost slope of Long Hai Hills between Rte 44 and Rte 326, apx 4 km NNE FSB Isa, 3 km S Long Dien and 4 km SW Dat Do. Phuoc Tuy Pr, III Corps.

Brewer, FSB (n/a)
Possible misspelling Bruer or Bruiser? Per Peter Cole, is cited in *1st Cav Div Op* Rpt May-Jul70, at p 38. 1st Cav was in Tay Ninh, Phuoc Long, Hau Nghia Prvs, and Cambodia during period, and base likely in one of those areas. No data. III Corps?

Briarpatch, The (WJ)
Nicknamc for POW camp N or NW Son Tay POW camp, WNW Hanoi and along W side of Red River. On map at www.soft-vision.com/hanoi/ frame.html. NVN.

Brick, FSB (YC 835-995)
A.k.a. Hill 132. Apx 24 km S Hue, and 7 km E FSB Blitz. On 25-26May?68, 82d Abn's 3d Bde used Brick as staging area for attack on HQ of 5th NVA Rgt, on Hill 618 (Nui Ke), to NW. 1st/508th Inf assaulted Nui Ke and on successive days of battle, its B Co fixed bayonets and carried out 2 of very few bayonet charges of war, killing 13 NVA in 1st attack and 92 in 2d. In 2d Bde/101st Abn's AO, '69-71. During Lam Son 720, beginning in Apr '71, FSBs Fury, Kathryn, Maureen, Gladiator and later Eagle's Nest were all reopened by B/326th Eng, while elements of 326th also rebuilt and enlarged FSBs Brick, Tennessee, Rendezvous and Rifle (inc Rte 545, the road to FSB Rifle). Also listed at YC 834-966 per XXIV Corps index. Thua Thien Pr, I Corps.

Brick, LZ (XD 59-30)
Apx 6 km SE LZ Delta, 28 km SW Khe Sanh CB and 3 km SW LZ Lo Lo. LZ used by ARVN forces during Op Lam Son 719, Apr71. Good Lam Son 719 FSB map at www.americal.org/174/map4.htm. Laos.

Bridge #s (generally)
US employed 2, basic bridge numbering systems in VN. In some cases, system was based upon PK (Poste Kilometre) markers closest to bridge being numbered (QL-9 between Quang Tri and Khe Sanh, for example), where bridge was named for nearest PK marker along road which bridge carried (i.e., bridge near PK 9 became Bridge 9). In other cases, as with QL-19 between Pleiku and Qui Nhon, bridges were simply numbered in sequence as encountered and in reference to a given starting point. In case of QL-19, the 1st bridge on QL-19 west of its intersection with QL-1 (near Qui Nhon) was simply numbered "Bridge 1," and the next bridge to W of Bridge 1 was simply Bridge 2 (regardless of distance between bridges or relationship to PK markers).

Bridge 1 to Bridge 16 (BR/CR)
Numbered bridges along QL-19E between its intersection with QL-1, apx 15 km NW Qui Nhon, and W to Bridge 17 at Song Vuoi River and QL-19, E of Camp Radcliff and An Khe. All appear to be in Binh Dinh Pr, II Corps.

Bridge 2 (Dak To) (ZB 002-222)
On Rte 512, apx 4 km W Dak To 1 AF, 2 km WNW Dak To 2 AF and 7 km SE Dak To. Kontum Pr, II Corps. [79]

Bridge 3 (YB 952-239)
Apparently at site of Firebase 3, apx 7 km WNW Dak To 2 AF, 8 km ESE Ben Het and 46 km NW Kontum.

Name/grid per S-3 Daily Journals and Op rpts dated 31Jul-1Sep69, courtesy Bob Patsfield. Kontum Pr, II Corps.

Bridge 17 (BR)
QL-19E bridge at An Thuong (5), 2 km E Bridge 18 and 10 km E Camp Radcliff. Bridges 17 and 18 were in populated area not guarded by armor at night and attacked more frequently as result. Data per Ray Smith at www.rjsmith.com/ amp_radcliff_1.html. Binh Dinh Pr, II Corps.

Bridge 18 (BR 539-461)
QL-19E bridge over Suoi Voi River, 8 km E Camp Radcliff and 2 km W Bridge 18. Bridges 17 and 18 were in populated area not guarded by armor at night and attacked more frequently as result. Map is L-7014-6736-4, per Ken Burrington. Binh Dinh Pr, II Corps.

Bridge 19 (BR 522-462)
QL-19E bridge over Suoi Da Bang River, apx 5 km E Camp Radcliff. Binh Dinh Pr, II Corps.

Bridge 20 (BR 467-436)
QL-19E bridge over Song Ba River due S Camp Radcliff and just W An Tuc. In populated area that was not a free-fire zone. Binh Dinh Pr, II Corps.

Bridge 21 (BR 444-434)
QL-19E at Suoi Tani River. Was near populated area and in restricted fire zone thereby accommodating NVA/VC activities. Attacked and almost overrun, 14Jan68. Binh Dinh Pr, II Corps.

Bridge 22 (BR 401-448)
QL-19E bridge over Dak Jappur River apx 4 km E LZ Schueller. Per Ray Smith, was torrent during monsoon, trickle in dry season. Binh Dinh Pr, II Corps.

Bridge 23 (BR 375-458)
QL-19E bridge apx 1.5 km E LZ Schueller over ravine that carried water only during rainfall. Binh Dinh Pr, II Corps.

Bridge 24 (BR 366-459)
QL-19E bridge within 1 km? E LZ Schueller. Spanned Suoi Ca Tung River. Binh Dinh Pr, II Corps.

Bridge 25 (BR 307-457)
QL-19E bridge apx 6 km W LZ Schueller. Spanned Dak Ra River (described as raging torrent in monsoon but a trickle in dry season). At 13°58'15"N-108°30'25"E per www.rjsmith.com. Binh Dinh Pr, II Corps.

Bridge 26 (BR 288-454)
QL-19E bridge crossing the Dak Xa Wong River 3 km SW LZ Action. Binh Dinh or Pleiku Pr, II Corps.

Bridge 27 (BR 261-472)
QL-19E bridge at Plei Koo Jil, apx 500 meters W LZ Action, 1.3 km SSE Strongpoint 12 and crossing Dak Hattam River. Described as very secure when 1st/69th Armor was pulling security but attacked frequently when 1st/69th absent. Binh Dinh or Pleiku Pr, II Corps.

Bridge 36 (AR 862-481)
QL-19 bridge, apx 9 km ENE Pleiku. Pleiku Pr, II Corps.

Bridge 411, FSB? (BS 674-678)
Bridge security position and possibly a FSB on QL-1 apx 5 km SSE Quang Ngai. Apr70 XXIV Corps grid per Don Armstrong. Quang Ngai Pr, I Corps.

Bridge Ramp 1 (BT 04-82?)
At Camp Tien Sha(?), immed NE Da Nang. Attacked-destroyed apx 8Feb69. Grid is est. Quang Nam Pr, I Corps.

Bridge Site, Dak To (YB 957-242)
Between Ben Het and Dak To AF, apx 8 km E Ben Het and 7 km WNW Dak To 2 AF. A 173d Abn position during Battle of Dak To, 1 Nov-1Dec67. Elements of 503d Inf and 3d/319th Arty during battle. Also listed at YB 953-238. Kontum Pr, II Corps. [80]

Bridge Site, Tay Ninh (XT 270-458?)
Blocking position for A/B Cos, 4th/23d Inf, 25th Inf, per AAR, *Battle of Tay Ninh* (17Aug-27Sep68), HQ 25th ID, 2Feb69, p 14. Tay Ninh Pr, III Corps.

Bridge Site, The (XD 910-400)
Apx 1 km N Lang Khat, 6 km ESE Khe Sanh CB and 45 km WSW Quang Tri. Nickname Marines gave 1st bridge crossing swift Rao Quan River between Dong Ha and Khe Sanh CB. 3d Mar Div normally kept unit here, but bridge blown and site abnd Aug?67. Quang Tri Pr, I Corps.

Bridget, FSB (YS 51-53)
A.k.a. FSB Brigid. On coast at end of Rte-44, apx 1 km from ocean, 9 km NE Vung Tau, 17 km SSE Nui Dat and 9 km SSE FSB Horseshoe. Described in *Vietnam Gunners*, p 104, as very unpleasant location built on gray, metallic sand that was very hot underfoot and gave off an intense blinding glare. 161 Bty, RNZA, Andrew's Bty FSB set here 20-21Jun70 (right section); 21-31Aug70 (one tube?). Master's Bty here 22-30Sep70 for "Housekeeping." See Bridgid. Phuoc Tuy Pr, III Corps.

Bridget, USS (n/a)
DE-1024. DD-Escort, per Ralph Fries.

Bridgett, LZ (ZA 015-165)
See Brigit, LZ. Pleiku Pr, II Corps.

Bridgid, FSB (YS 517-542)
A.k.a. FSB Bridget. Apx 15.5 km SE Nui Dat and 8 km SSE FSB Horseshoe. On 1ATF NCO trng map per John Hollett. See Bridget. Phuoc Tuy Pr, III Corps.

Bridgett, LZ (ZA 015-164)
See Bridgit. Pleiku Pr, II Corps.

Bridgit, LZ (ZA 015-164)
Apx 15 km SW Oasis AF, 20 km SE Duc Co and 8 km SW Xuong Kuang. Also spelled Brigit, Bridgett and Bridget and proper spelling unknown. Per Don Blankin, his units were there May69, and it was, "a nasty place overlooking a big, wide valley." Apparently Arty Bty of 173rd or 101st had been overrun here prior to May69. Blankin also recalls that, "One side of LZ was a sheer drop to valley," and that "there was a village at one side set afire by .50 Cal. tracers during ground assault late May69. 2d/9th also lost howitzer here to direct hit from 75 RR in same time period." 10th Cav, 4th Div here, per Bob Patsfield. 4th Div AO, '68-70, and A Bty, 4th/42d Arty here Feb70. Grid per Jim Claeys. Pleiku Pr, II Corps.

Bridle (n/a)
6Apr70, XXIV Corps future-use 5th Div FSB name.

Brigadoon, LZ (BR 270-330)
Apx 23 km SW An Khe and 32 km SE Suoi Doi AF. 173d Abn. Name/grid per Dan Gillotti. Binh Dinh Pr, II Corps.

Bright, LZ (ZA 015-164)
Apparent misspelling, see Bridgit. Pleiku Pr, II Corps.

Bright Light Missions (n/a)
See Glossary.

Brigit, LZ (ZA 015-164)
See Bridgit. Pleiku Pr, II Corps.

Brillo Pad, FSB/LZ (YA 962-855)
Apx 10 km SW Polei Kleng SF Camp/AF, 15 km WSW Polei Krong AF, 6 WNW LZ Bingo, 28 km W to WSW Kontum, 36 km SSW Dak To 2 AF and 1.2 km SE OP Hill (a.k.a. Hill 1124). 16May68, mortar, RR, and B-40 fire resulted in 5 US KIA, 29 WIA (53 M-449 Firecracker rnds in addn to reg arty fired by elements of 1st/92d Arty). 25May68, 1st/12th Inf here recevied over 250 rnds of mortar and rocket fire with 4 US KIA, 35 WIA and 1 MIA. B Bty, 4th/42d Arty and C, 1st/12th, and B and D, 1st/14th Inf, 4th Div, here for 2 week siege in May-Jun68, followed by ground attack resulting in 41 NVA KIA; hill defended by 105s and 81mm mortars and also suptd by nearby FSB Mile High. Wounded here often 1st evaced to Polei Kleng SF Camp. CO of B Bty 4th/42d Arty, Capt. J. H. Binford Peay, later became 101st Abn CG in 90's, 4-star Gen JCS Vice Chair and CINC US Central Cmd. Reportedly named when someone said, "It's as tough as Brillo-Pad;" however Gen Peay (then CO of B Bty) did initial recon for base and said it was named Brillo-Pad because it looked like one. Grid per *4th Inf Div Op Rpt for period ending 31Jan69*. Also listed at YA 955-855 per Harry Dilkes, but according to Kevin Rafferty, B/1st/14th Inf, that puts it "on a hillside and YA 963 855 likely correct grid." Some data provide by Craig Miller per 4th Div Op rpts. Map is L-7014-6537-4. Photos/maps at http://1-14th.com/maps.html. Also listed at YA 955-859 & 962-855. See Alamo, Bunker-Hill, Bingo, Hill 1124, XYZ Pad & Chu Pa Mtn. Kontum Pr, II Corps.

Brink BOQ (XS 866-916)
Apx 800 meters ESE the US Embassy, Saigon. Named to honor, BGen Francis G Brink (see Brink Hotel). Data per *VN Military Lore, 1959-1973*. Gia Dinh Pr, III Corps.

Brink Hotel Annex (XS 86-91?)
At 5 Nguyen Sieu St., prior to Jul62-68, 47 rms, Saigon. Named to honor, Brink, BGen Francis G. Data per *Vietnam Military Lore, 1959-1973*. Gia Dinh Pr, III Corps.

Brink Hotel BOQ (XS 866-916?)
101 Hau Ba Trung (Brink Bar-Officers Club) prior to Jul62, 49 rms, Saigon. Named to honor BGen Francis G. Brink, the first MAAG Cmdr, who cautioned of inevitable escalation if US became too involved in VN. Became a suicide victim in Jul52, due to poor health. Data per *Vietnam Military Lore, 1959-1973*. Gia Dinh Pr, III Corps.

Brisbane, HMAS (n/a)
A.k.a. DDG-41 and "Steel Cat." 3d Aussie Guided Missile DD deployed to VN, with 2 tours of VN duty. Left Sydney, 20Mar69, and joined US 7th Flt from 31Mar69-14Sept69, serving from Mekong Delta to Haiphong, with 3 turns on gunline and one at Yankee Station. During 1st tour, fired 8000-5" rds at 649 targets, over all 4 CTZ's. Fired 1st shot at 2100 hrs, 15Apr69. On night of 6Jun69, fired 350 rnds over 3 hrs suptg US 3d Mar Div. On 22Jul69, her fwd gun suffered an in-bore explosion, wounding 1 sailor, but she still provided NGS for 15 more days, firing 21 missions with single gun before retiring to Subic Bay for repairs. "In 143 missions she damaged or destroyed 389 military structures, 313 bunkers, 14 sampans, 13 fighting holes and 900 metres of tunnel/trenches" Then joined *USS Constellation* and *Oriskany* as escort at Yankee Station. 2d tour was between 16Mar-15Oct71, stationed off Phouc Tuy Pr suptg 1 ATF until 21Apr71. During 2d tour, steamed 27,011 mi and fired 7,760 rnds. Left SVN 30Sep71. See *Perth*, and www.hmasperth.asn.au/. NVN/SVN.

Brister, USS (n/a)
DER-327. DD-Escort, Radar, per Ralph Fries.

Britton, FSB (XS 088-415)
Apx 31 km WSW My Tho and 6 km ESE Sung Hieu. Feb68. Dinh Tuong Pr, IV Corps.

Broadsword, FSB (ZC 054-393)
A.k.a. COB Broadsword. Apx 5 km WSW FSB Tomahawk, 8 km NW FSB Saber, 27 km WSW An Hoa and apx 65 km WSW Hoi An. Used during USMC assault on Base Area 112, Jan-Feb69. On map in *US Marines in Vietnam-1969*, p 90. Apr70 XXIV Corps grid per Don Armstrong. Quang Nam Pr, I Corps.

Brodt, Camp (AP 889-331)
SF Camp apx 16 km due S Duc Xuyen AF, 3 km N Phey Srunh AF, 8 km SE Romen, 6 km SE peak of Yook Nam Rmay Mtn (Hill 1442) and 115 km WSW Nha Trang. Named to honor SF Capt James H. Brodt, KIA 29Jan63. See Phey Srunh. Tuyen Duc Pr, II Corps.

Brodt-MacIver Compound (AR 783-500?)
At Pleiku but precise location unknown. Named to honor SF Capt James H. Brodt and PFC Neal MacIver, both KIA 29May63 in VC ambush in Central Highlands. Often incorrectly spelled "Brought-MacIver." See *Vietnam Military Lore, Legends, Shadows and Heroes*, p 516, for story of that ambush. Pleiku Pr, II Corps.

Brokenwing, Operation (n/a)
See Glossary.

Bronc, FSB (YA 766-371)
Apx 14 km SW Plei Djereng New AF, 8 km E Cambodia and 50 km WSW Pleiku. Per *Yearbook* Aug65-Dec69, p 82, courtesy Peter Cole. Jan66. Pleiku Pr, II Corps.

Bronco, FSB (BS 450-612)
A.k.a. LZ Cork? Apx 16 km WSW Nghia Hanh AF, 18 km SW Quang Ngai and 3 km SW peak Hill 1136. Also spelled "Broncho," though likely in error. Listed grid very closely matches that of LZ Cork? Quang Ngai Pr, I Corps.

Bronco, FSB (XU 815-510)
In Cambodia, apx 12 km WSW Phum Pu Tram Kraom, 13 km ESE FSB Anna, 43 km NNE Loc Ninh and 27 km NW Bu Dop AF. 1st Cav incursion base roughly 20 km from SVN border, May-Jun70. One acft shot down here and 5 hit by ground fire during Cav's extraction at closing, 24Jun70. Also spelled Bronc and Broncho, but this spelling used throughout *Airmobility, 1961-1971*, *Vietnam Studies* series, and thought to be correct. Cited in *1st Cav Op Rpt, May-Jul70*, p 26, 37, per Peter Cole. Grid per *11th ACR Cambodia Invasion AAR, 1st Cav Div, May-Jun70*, courtesy Lou Rochat. [81] Cambodia.

Bronco, FSB (ZC 123-650)
Apx 34 km WSW Da Nang AB, and 12 km NNW Ha Tan AF. Mar69. Quang Nam Pr, I Corps.

Bronco, LZ (BS 812-383)
Per Dick Arnold, Bronco was originally a USMC position known as LZ Montezuma. Adj to or at Duc Pho AF. Basecamp and HQ of 11th LIB at one point following USMC occupation. 1st/20th, 11th LIB, here '68-69. Also listed at BS 812-375 and BS 809-384. Base site shown clearly on map at http://all-media-inc.com/1bn14inf/maps.

html. Americal list. Base photos/maps at http://1-14th.com/maps.html. Quang Ngai Pr, I Corps.

Bronco Beach (BR 9-4 or CR 1-4?)
Name *Rites of Passage* author says 1st Cav called area around FSB Trains. See *Rites of Passage*, p 224. Binh Dinh Pr, II Corps.

Bronze, FSB (XT 388-627)
Near Song Saigon, apx 22 km ENE Nui Ba Den and 15 km WSW Minh Thanh AF. Mar67. Tay Ninh Pr, III Corps.

Brooke, USS (n/a)
DEG-1. DD-Escort, per Ralph Fries.

Brooks, Camp (AT 96-81?)
See Camp Books. Erroneous but common misspelling of Camp Books. No facility named "Brooks" was found in author's research. Quang Nam Pr, I Corps.

Brookville, SS (n/a)
Merchant ship under govt contract, per Ralph Fries.

Brother Buck (n/a)
See Glossary.

Brotherhood, Camp (AP 979-069)
A.k.a. Serignac Valley SF Camp and. Dam Pau SF Camp Apx 7 km NW Thanh Binh, 24 km SW Dalat and 7 km SSE Ngoc So. 5th SF. Info/grid per *SF Order of Battle.* See Dam Pau. Tuyen Duc Pr, II Corps.

Brought-MacIver Compound (AR 783-500?)
See Brodt-MacIver Cmpd. Pleiku Pr, II Corps.

Brown, Camp (YT 845-622)
Along QL-20, apx 30 km SW Bao Loc and 3 km W Da Hoa. Ap70-Oct71. Lam Dong Pr, II Corps.

Brown, FSB (XS)
Described as having been somewhere SW Saigon along QL-4. Name per James Cartmill. III Corps.

Brown, FSB (XS 094-612)
Apx 18 km NW Cai Lay, 23 km SW Thuy Dog AF, and 30 km SSE Moc Hoa. Grid per Cliff Snyder. Kien Tuong Pr, IV Corps.

Brown, FSB (XT 200-860)
A.k.a. FSB Foche? Apx 35 km N Tay Ninh and 13 km WSW Katum. UTM zone may instead be YS, as there is a FSB Brown listed at YS 210-800? Grid per Cliff Snyder. Tay Ninh Pr, III Corps.

Brown, FSB (YS 210-800)
S of QL-15, apx 36 km NW Vung Tau, 7 km NNW Phu My and 42 km ESE Tan Son Nhut AB Also listed at YS 225-804. Grids per Cliff Snyder. Bien Hoa Pr, III Corps.

Brown, FSB (YS 225-804)
Gird puts site apx 6 km NNW Phu My and 1.5 km E FSB Brown listed at YS 210-800. Grid per Cliff Snyder. Bien Hoa Pr, III Corps.

Brown, FSB (YS 664-580)
On coast just W Thuan Bien, 16 km E Dat Do, 40 km ENE Vung Tau and 10 km S Xuyen Moc AF. Also listed at YS 673-580, and YS 662-580. Grids per Cliff Snyder. Phuc Tuy Pr, III Corps.

Brown, FSB (YT 845-622)
Along QL-20, apx 3 km W Da Hoa, 27 km SW Bao Loc and 34 km NNE Vo Dat. Also listed at YT 843-621, and 846-625. Grids per Cliff Snyder. Lam Dong Pr, III Corps.

Brown, FSB (YU 03-37?)
If grid correct, was 3 km N the SVN border, 10 km NE Bu Dop AF, 4 km WSW Phum Leu 47 km E Snuol. Per 199th LIB Assn, Brown was at listed grid and 5th/12th Inf here during Cambodian Incursion, May70. Also listed at YU 064-387. Data per www.redcatcher.org/Cambodia. html. Cambodia.

Brown, FSB (YU 064-387)
In Cambodia, apx 6 km NE point where QL-14A crossed border, 10 km ESE Phum Chhaneng, 13 km NE Bu Dop, 28 km W Djamap/Bu Gia Map, and 14 km ESE FSB Ketter. Built slightly S FSB Myron, May70. Described in one text as, "a small brown scab about 100 meters in diameter scraped out of a lush, green field." Per Bernie Edelman, the Army unknowingly built Brown in what was actually a dry lake bed and, not long after a heavy NVA ground assault resulting in apx 54 NVA KIA (1 of only 2 US FSBs known to have suffered major ground assaults during incursion. FSB David apparently the other?), heavy rains followed filling the lake and inundating entire base. As result, Edelman says, Brown was isolated physically and without communication for several hours while troops found themselves bailing frantically with their helmets to survive. AO of 1st Cav, 11th ACR and 199th LIB. 5th/12th Inf, 199th LIB here at on point. Grid per *11th ACR Cambodia Invasion AAR, 1st Cav Div, May-Jun70*, courtesy Lou Rochat. [82] Also listed at YU 071-374 and YU 060-370, per Cliff Snyder. Cambodia.

Brown, LZ (XD 50-34)
1st ARVN Div FSB in Laos during Lam Son 719. Apx 5 km due W LZ Delta-1 and 35 km WSW Khe Sanh CB. See Lam Son 719 entry and Lam Son 719 map at www.americal.org/174/map4.htm. Laos.

Brown Beach (YS 664-580)
Apx 39 km ENE Ving Tau and 15 km ENE Long Phuoc Hai. Aug66. Also at YS 673-580. Phuoc Tuy Pr, III Corps.

Brown Eye, FSB (n/a)
Listed as 199th LIB FSB/patrol base on 199th LIB Assn website. No grid available. III Corps.

Brown-Graham (n/a)
See Camp Graham-Brown.

Bruce E. Webb, Camp (BT 53-07?)
3rd Bn 3rd Marine sector of Chu Lai CB. Named to honor Capt. Bruce Webb, CO I/3d/3d Marines, KIA 18Aug65, Van Tuong, during Op Starlight, by a VC casualty feigning death who tossed a grenade at Co CP group after it passed. Happened within minutes of his telling a Plt Sgt with the CP to stop shooting the already "dead" VC. Data per *Vietnam Military lore 1959-1973*. Quang Tin Pr, I Corps.

Brudenell White, HMAS (n/a)
AV-1353. Australian warship serving under US 7th Flt. Originally *USS LSM-319*, sold to Australia, '60, assigned to Australian Army Royal Engrs, 32 Small Ship Sqdn.

Bruer, FSB (n/a)
Possible misspelling Brewer or Bruiser? Per Peter Cole, is mentioned in 2d/7th Cav's Unit History '70-71, at p 2. 1st Cav in Tay Ninh, Phuoc Long, Hau Nghia Prvs, and Cambodia during period, and base likely in one of those areas. III Corps or Cambodia.

Bruiser, FSB (XT 334-896)
A.k.a. FSB Beverley. Immed SE Katum AF, 7 km S Cambodia and 40 km N to NNE Tay Ninh. Per Frank Penk, Jr., grid was XT 325-885 and was Cambodian Invasion

FSB, May-Jun70, with possibly 1st Cav, 25th Inf, 11th ACR or ARVN elements here. Tay Ninh Pr, III Corps.

Bruiser, FSB (YS 645-644)
3 km S Xuyen Moc, 18 km ESE Nui Dat, 5 km SE FSB Beth and 4 km SSW FSB Allisoun. Built on firm white sand that caused sandstorms when CH-47s arrived to re-supply. 161 Bty, RNZA (Master's Bty 22Sep70-29Mar71) FSB set here 14-21Oct70 and 2-28Jan71. On 1ATF NCO trng map, John Hollett. Also listed at YS 64-65. Phuoc Tuy Pr, III Corps.

Brule, USS (n/a)
AKL-28. SVN

Bruno (n/a)
6Apr70, XXIV Corps future-use 5th Div FSB name.

Bryant BEQ (XS 8-9)
At 104-106 Nguyen Huyh Duc St., Saigon. Named to honor SSgt Emmett J. Bryant, KIA 9Feb65, when Bu Dang Advsy Cmpd became 1st such cmpd overrun during war. Per *VN Military Lore, 1959-1973*. Gia Dinh Pr, III Corps.

Bryce Canyon, USS (n/a)
AD-36. Repair Ship, per Ralph Fries.

Bu Bang (Duc Phong) (n/a)
Mapsheet L-7014-6432-1. Name: Duc Phong (Bu Bang).

Bu Brang Airfield (YU 491-559)
See Bu Krak AF and do not confuse with Bu Prang AF. Quang Duc Pr, II Corps.

Bu Dang Advisory Compound (YU 458-065)
A.k.a. Holland Cmpd? Apx 2 km E Duc Phong AF, 3 km NE Vin Thien, 47 km NE Dong Xoai, 28 km E Song Be and about 125 km NNE Saigon. 1st US Advsy Cmpd overrun during war, 9Feb65. Phuoc Long Pr, III Corps.

Bu Dang Airfield (YU 440-047)
See Duc Phong AF. Phuoc Long Pr, III Corps.

Bu Dang Heliport (YU 458-065)
Apx 2 km E what became Duc Phong AF, 3 km NE Vin Thien, 47 km NE Dong Xoai, 28 km E Song Be and about 125 km NNE Saigon. "Heliport #527, alt 853', soccer field, trees border W side." At 11°49'00"N-107°15'00"E, per Feb73 TAD. Phuoc Long Pr, III Corps.

Bu Djamap Airfield (YU 340-368)
See Djamap AF. Phuoc Long Pr, III Corps.

Bu Djamap Heliport (YU 344-377)
See Bu Ja Mop AF. Phuoc Long Pr, III Corps.

Bu Dong Srei Airfield (YU 440-047)
See Duc Phong AF. Phuoc Long Pr, III Corps.

Bu Dop (XU 974-290)
Apx 7 km E, and 7 km S Cambodia, apx 32 km N An Loc, 42 km E Snuol Cambodia, 37 km WSW Djamap (Bu Gia Map), 74 km WSW Bu Prang. 5th SF, Det A-341 (was 311), Oct65, SF Det 46. 9th VC Div attacked this site in Nov-Dec67, and 1st Bde/1st Inf Div was moved to that AO in response. Phuoc Long Pr, III Corps.

Bu Dop Airfield (XU 975-291)
SW Bu Dop, 42 km E Snuol, 37 km WSW Djamap AF (Bu Gia Map), 74 km WSW Bu Prang AF, 7 km E and 7 km S Cambodia. Per TPC K-10A. El. 469', 2,900' laterite rwy. At 12°01'07"N-106°48'52"E. Phuoc Long Pr, III Corps.

Bu Dop Heliport (XU 975-225)
Apx 7 km S Bu Dop SF Camp/AF, 10 km from Cambodia and 25 km NW Song Be. "Heliport #528, alt 7'?, earth Pad," per Feb73 TAD. Phuoc Long Pr, III Corps.

Bu Dop SF Camp (XU 9745-2909)
Apx 33 km NE Loc Ninh, 28 km NW Song Be and 5 km from Cambodia. 5th SF. Transferred to ARVN 97th Border Rangers. Grid per *SF Order of Battle*. Phuoc Long Pr, III Corps.

Bu Ghia Heliport (YU 185-135)
Apx 26 km due W Duc Phong AF, 6 km SE Song Be AF and 6 km SE Phuoc Binh. Heliport #529, alt 565', at 11°52'30"N-107°00'00"E. Phuoc Long Pr, III Corps.

Bu Ghia Map (YU 344-375)
See Bu Gia Map. Phuoc Long Pr, III Corps.

Bu Ghia SF Camp (YU 185-205)
Apx 15 km NNE Song Be/Phuoc Binh, 22 km SW Djamap and 28 km NW Doc Phong AF. 5th SF. Moved to Bu Dop. Info/grid per *SF Order of Battle*. Phuoc Long Pr, III Corps.

Bu Ghia, Camp (YU 344-375)
See Bu Ghia Map SF Camp. III Corps.

Bu Gia Map (n/a)
Mapsheet name of L-7014-6433-3. SVN/Cambodia.

Bu Gia Map (YU 344-375)
A.k.a. Djamap (and sometimes spelled Djmap). Remote SF CIDG border surveillance camp and AF about 145 km NNE Saigon, 12 km from Cambodia, 35 km NE Song Be and 37 km WSW Bu Prang AF. Was supplied mostly by air. 5th SF Grp, Det. A-223, Dec64. Abnd in '65 due to imminent attack and thought to be on NVA invasion route. Reopened 6May66 by *502d Light Infantry Bde*, Col Hank Emerson's amusing name for a makeshift unit of one plt of 326th Engrs, a 17-man element from an RF Co from Bu Prang, 30 Montagnard porters, squad of VN Ntl Police who were interpreters, and Third Co, 4th Bn, 9th ARVN Rgt, its Recondo Plt, 30 Montagnard trackers (Apache Plt) and its US and US SF Advisors. Reopening discussed in *Battles in the Monsoon*, pp 228-229 (spelled Bn Gia Map there). Phuoc Long Pr, III Corps.

Bu Gia Map Airfield (YU 344-375)
A.k.a. Djamap AF. Apx 145 km NNE Saigon, 12 km SE Cambodia, 35 km NE Song Be and 37 km WSW Bu Prang AF. Per TPC K-10D. See Djamap AF. Phuoc Long Pr, III Corps.

Bu Gia Map SF Camp (YU 344-375)
A.k.a. FOB Bu Ghia and sometimes spelled Bu Ghia. At Bu Gia Map AF, apx 12 km SE Cambodia, 35 km NE Song Be and 37 km WSW Bu Prang AF. 5th SF. Sp variation is Bu Ghia Map in some texts. Info/grid per *SF Order of Battle*. Phuoc Long Pr, III Corps.

Bu Giao Airfield (YU 470-530)
See Bu Glao AF. Quang Duc Pr, II Corps.

Bu Giao SF Camp (YU 522-545)
See Bu Glao SF Camp. Quang Duc Pr, II Corps.

Bu Glao Airfield (YU 470-530)
A.k.a. Bu Krak South AF. Apx 22 km W to WNW Bu Prang AF, 36 km ENE Djamap AF, and 3 km SSW Bu Krak AF. "Abnd Overgrown, AF # VA2-270," in Aug69 TAD per Frank Penk, Jr. Not in Feb73 TAD. Quang Duc Pr, II Corps.

Bu Glao SF Camp (YU 522-545)
Apx 2 km SE Bu Krak AF, 26 km NE Djamap and 18 km WNW Bu Prang. 5th SF. Info/grid per *SF Order of Battle.* See Bu Prang (old). Quang Duc Pr, II Corps.

Bu Ja Map Airfield (YU 340-368)
See Djamap AF. Phuoc Long Pr, III Corps.
Bu Ja Mop Heliport (YU 344-377)
Near Bu Gia Map/Djamap AF, 37 km ENE Bu Dop AF, 35 km NE Song Be and 12 km from Cambodia. "Heliport #530, alt 1,260', NE end of airstrip, at 12°05'40"N-107°09'00"E," per Feb73 TAD. Phuoc Long Pr, III Corps.
Bu Krak Airfield (YU 491-559)
Apx 2 km SE Bu Krak, 3 km S Cambodia, 20 km WNW Bu Prang AF and 25 km NE Djamap AF. "Secure SF, US Army, 29Mar69, AF # VA2-176," in Aug69 TAD per Frank Penk, Jr. Not in Feb73 TAD. El. 2,789'. Quang Duc Pr, II Corps.
Bu Krak SF Camp (YU 4889-5610)
In mnts apx 2 km SE Bu Krak, 3 km S Cambodia, 20 km WNW Bu Prang AF and 25 km NE Djamap AF. 5th SF. Info/grid per *SF Order of Battle*. See Bu Prang (New). Quang Duc Pr, II Corps.
Bu Krak South Airfield (YU 470-530)
See Bu Glao AF. Quang Duc Pr, II Corps.
Bu Krak South SF Camp (YU 522-545)
Apx 2 km SE Bu Krak AF, 4 km S Cambodia and 18 km WNW Bu Prang AF. 5th SF. See Bu Prang (old). Data per *SF Order of Battle*. Quang Duc Pr, II Corps.
Bu Nard (YT 24-88)
Apx 23 km NE Dong Xoai, 24 km SE Song Be, 4 km SE QL-14, and 100 km NE Saigon. SF A-Team, SF Det 44, 5th SF CIDG Det A-344, Apr67. Phuoc Long Pr, III Corps.
Bu Nard Airfield (YT 273-887)
Apx 22 km SW Duc Phong AF, 25 km NE Dong Xoai AF and 22 km SE Song Be. El. 948', 2,600' laterite rwy. At 11°39'08"N-107°05'08"E. Phuoc Long Pr, III Corps.
Bu Nard SF Camp (YT 2701-8877)
Apx 22 km SW Duc Phong AF, 25 km NE Dong Xoai AF and 22 km SE Song Be. 5th SF camp. A-Team camp, SF Det 44, 5th SF Grp CIDG Det A-344, Apr67. Converted to ? ARVN Border Rangers. Grid per *SF Order of Battle.* Phuoc Long Pr, III Corps.
Bu Nard, FSB (YT 27 89?)
Also spelled Bunard. Likely near Bu Nard AF or that city. If that presumption is correct, site was in remote area along QL-14, apx 25 km NE Dong Xoai. HQ of 11th ACR here Summer of '69, under Col George S. Patton, III. Cited in *Low Level Hell*, p 128. Phuoc Long Pr?, III Corps.
Bu Prang (YU 52-54?)
If grid correct, was 3 km ESE Bu Krak AF, 19 km WNW Bu Prang New AF, 4 km S Cambodia and 24 km NE Djamap. RF Co here May-Jun66. Rumor that NVA planned to overrun outpost here led to Battle of Toumorong, Jun66. 5th SF Grp, Det. A-4, Dec64. See *Battles in The Monsoon*, pp 227-228. Quang Duc Pr, II Corps.
Bu Prang (new) SF Camp (YU 683-505?)
Apx 5 km S Cambodia and Tuy Duc, some 17 km ESE Bu Krak (old) SF camp/AF and 38 km NE Djamap AF. 5th SF camp constructed between Jan70 and early Aug70, by D/19th Engrs/35th Engr Grp/18th Engr Bde, as relocation of Bu Prang (old) SF camp. Most materials and prefab bunkers were airlifted 1st by C-130 from Cam Ranh to Nhon Co, then by CH-47 and CH-54 to site. Const material alone inc over 1.3 million board-feet (2,000 short tons) of lumber, and all facilities built underground. AF const began mid Feb70. Camp was moved to overcome vulnerability to standoff attacks, and its design and construction made it perhaps the most sophisticated SF camp of war. Det A-236 here 70. Converted to 89th Border Rangers. Also listed at YU 4889-5610? Info/grid per *SF Order of Battle*. Quang Duc Pr, II Corps. [83]
Bu Prang (old) SF Camp (YU 522-545)
Apx 4 km SE Bu Krak AF, 17 km WNW Bu Prang New AF, 4 km S Cambodia and 24 km NE Djamap. 5th SF. Det. A-4, Dec64. Info/grid per *SF Order of Battle.* Quang Duc Pr, II Corps.
Bu Prang Heliport (YU 522-545)
Apx 2 km SE Bu Krak AF, 19 km WNW Bu Prang New AF, 4 km S Cambodia and 24 km NE Djamap. Heliport #531, El. 2,882', per Feb73 TAD. Quang Duc Pr, II Corps.
Bu Prang New Airfield (YU 683-505)
Apx 5 km S Cambodia and Tuy Duc, some 19 km ESE Bu Krak (old) AF/SF Camp and 38 km NE Djamap AF. El. 2,900', 2,400' asph-treated crushed rock rwy. At 12°12'15"N-107°27'55"E. Quang Duc Pr, II Corps.
Buam Vang Airfield (UH 33-37)
A.k.a. LS-242. CIA/SF, per *Air Facilities Data-Laos.*
Buchanan, USS (n/a)
DDG-14. Guided Missile DD, per Ralph Fries.
Buck, Brother (n/a)
See Brother Buck in Glossary.
Buck, FSB (AT 806-320)
Apx 3 km N Thach Bich, 12 km SW Phuoc Binh and 46 km SSW Da Nang. Quang Nam Pr, I Corps.
Buck, LZ (BS 717-790)
Apx 9 km NE Quang Ngai and 7 km W QL-1. Said to have been 1st Cav, but more likely Americal? Name/grid per Dan Gillotti. Quang Tri Pr, I Corps.
Buck, LZ (YD 006-304)
At N end of Laotian Salient, apx 2 km NE Laos, 20 km SE Khe Sanh CB, 17 km due S Ca Lu AF and 2 km NW Lang Keri. Apr70 XXIV Corps grid per Don Armstrong. Quang Tri Pr, I Corps.
Buck, USS (n/a)
A.k.a. DD-761. Captured several NVA in routine boarding during Op Market Time, Jul66. Role discussed in *Brown Water, Black Berets*, p 94. Market Time TF-115. SVN.
Buckeye, LZ (BR 078-276)
Apx 8 km W LZ Big Windy, 20 km due E Plei Do Lim and 35 km SE Pleiku. 4th Div AO, '70. Name/grid per Jim Claeys. Pleiku Pr, II Corps.
Buckner, USNS (n/a)
MSTS troop transport originally in Atlantic but also possibly used to ferry troops to SVN?
Buckskin, FSB (AT 835-659)
A.k.a. Hill 502 or 512? 25 km SW Da Nang, 7 km ENE Stagecoach, 10 km SE of R.C. Ba Na. USMC position during Op Taut Bow. Apr70 XXIV Corps grid per Don Armstrong. Also listed at AT 830-658 and 823-659. Quang Nam Pr, I Corps.
Buddha, LZ (n/a)
Possibly Buddha Hill/Mtn? No data. Americal list, I Corps.
Buddha Mountain (BS 660-757)
A.k.a. Buddha Hill, Hill 101, Nui Thien An (Mtn of Heavenly Peace), and Little Round Top. Immed N Rte 521, apx 2.5 km NNE Quang Ngai and 2 km E QL-1. Named for

Buddhist Temple near its peak. CP for USMC TF Delta Op Utah, Mar66. Grid is est. Quang Ngai Pr, I Corps.

Buell, FSB (XT 213-532)

Apx 3.5 km N Tay Ninh, along Hwy 4 near Nui Ba Den, and within arty range of FSB Buell. Per 7Oct68 *Tropic Lightning News* (Vol. 3, No. 41), was attacked at least 3 separate times in less than 1 month in '68. Closed apx 10Aug68 and relocated as FSB Buell II to XT 227-568. 2d/22d and 3d/22d Inf, and B/2d/27th, 1st Bde/25th Inf Div here '68, as was C Bty, 2d/13th Arty, C Bty 3d/13th and 7th/11th Arty. 1st Cav. Also listed at XT 168-458, 212-533, 210-530, 219-535, 220-538, 222-564, 230-580, Jan69-Dec70, and at XT 220-546 per Frank Penk, Jr. On TL-7014-6231-4 map. Tay Ninh Pr, III Corps.

Buell II, FSB (XT 230-575)

Built astride hwy roughly 4 km NE FSB Buell (I), 4 km N Tay Ninh, 5 km due W Nui Ba Den Signal Site and 3. 8 km WNW The Rock Crusher site. Built apx 10Aug68 after original FSB Buell was closed. Cited in 7Oct68 *Tropic Lightning News* (Vol. 3, No. 41) and issue of 23Sep68 (vol. 3, No. 39) which states Buell II was apx 6 km N Tay Ninh. Suffered 4 separate major attacks during Battle for Tay Ninh, 17Aug-27Sep68. 1st attack was 18Sep68, when 2 Bns NVA followed 100 round mortar barrage in assault of 500 men defending the base (elements of 3d/22d, 4th/23d Inf, 2d/34th Armor, 3d/23th Arty) and repulsed only after employing supt of FSBs St. Barbara, Rawlins and heavy air strikes (US losses 1 KIA, 26 WIA). Attacked again morning of 22Aug68, with 3 US KIA and 18 WIA, again 10-11Sep68 with 17 US WIA and for 4th time 13Sep68, when hit by massive 1,000 rnds of 62mm/82mm mortars followed by human wave attack of 2 Bns 272d NVA/VC Rgt (Spooky and close air supt employed successfully and US forces suffered only 17 WIA). Had one Bty each of 155mm SP howitzers and 105s. Map/discussions of nearby '68 battles in *The Infantry Brigade in Combat*. Info/grid per Butch Sincock. On mapsheet TL-7014-6231-4 (Tay Ninh). Also listed at XT 220-560, Mar-Apr69. Tay Ninh Pr, III Corps.

Buell III, FSB (XT 210-530)

In same general location as Buell I & II, Apr-May69. Tay Ninh Pr, III Corps.

Buff, LZ (BS 539-824)

See Buff-Stinson, LZ. Quang Ngai Pr, I Corps.

Buff-Stinson, LZ (BS 539-824)

A.k.a. LZ Buff and LZ Stinson. On hilltop near Hau Duc, apx 13 km NW Quang Ngai, 5 km N the Song Tra Khuc River, 24 km due S Chu Lai, 5 km ENE ville of Xuan Hoa, 7 km NE Ba Gia AF and 9 km W QL-1. Prior to 21May69 was named LZ Buff, but on that date was renamed to also honor of LTC William Stinson, Jr, KIA on A/123d Avn Co. Helicopter #737, 3MAR69. Americal list. Map is L-7014-6739-3. Quang Ngai Pr, I Corps.

Buffalo (n/a)

In at least the 2d/7th Cav, 1st Cav ('65 and '66), "Buffalo" was 1st radio code word for a wounded soldier (WIA). Code for a KIA was "Elephant" Data per *Baptism*, p 256.

Buffalo, FSB (BR 27-48)

A.k.a. LZ Buffalo. Apx 5 km E Mang Yang Pass and on N side of QL-19 near confluence of 3 streams. Apx 3 km due E Plei Hauay, 3 km N LZ Action, 22 km WNW An Khe and 23 km ESE Suoi Doi AF. Was within 155mm arty range of FSB Schueller, with elements of 1st/92d arty and 1st/10th Cav here. Info per Tom Rethard. Photos of base on internet at: www.landscaper.net/vietnam/places.html. Binh Dinh or Pleiku Pr, II Corps.

Buffalo, FSB (YS 443-885)

A.k.a. LZ Buffalo. In Courtenay Rubber Plantation, along W side of Rte-2, 7 km due W FSB Flinders, 22 km due N Nui Dat and 8 km ESE FSB Wattle. 161 Bty, RNZA (Horsford's Bty 18Mar69-18Sep69) FSB set here 13-19Jul69 (one section). On 13Jul69, 161 fired its 1st "Chieu Hoi" mission using shells packed with Chieu Hoi leaflets and safe conduct passes for enemy. During Jul69, one of Bty's FO's radioed a legendary sit-rep while the RAR unit he was accompanying was in heavy battle, "Every time I put my fucking head up, it gets fucking well shot at, over." [84] On 1ATF NCO trng map per John Hollett. Also listed at YS 44-89. Phuoc Tuy Pr, III Corps.

Prvs, II/III Corps.

Buffalo, LZ (BR 483-448?)

See Buffalo, Rear Support Base. Binh Dinh Pr, II Corps.

Buffalo, Operation (n/a)

2-14Jul67. 3d Mar Div ops in DMZ that resulted in very heavy fighting and high US casualties in addition to 1,231 rptd NVA/VC KIA, per *Vietnam Order of Battle*, pp 9-14. Quang Tri Pr, I Corps.

Buffalo, Rear Support Base (BR 483-448?)

A.k.a. LZ Buffalo. Apparently a portion of An Khe/Camp Radcliff and home of HHC, 1st/10th Cav in '70-71 at least. Michael Belis tells us: "I was sent to An Khe [in '71] to help handle my Co's re-supply. There were never any more than 7 or 8 C/22d Inf men at Buffalo at any time during that mission. The place was known to us as 'Rear Support Base Buffalo,' not Firebase Buffalo, since there was no arty at all. It consisted of a perimeter paralleling the airstrip and river, with everything in cmpd located between the airstrip and river. HHC for 1st/10th Cav was there, and one or more of their maintenance units. There were Cobras, OH-58's and Hueys from Cav's D Trp here, and there was also a Field Hospital or some kind of Medical unit. I also saw a couple of wounded NVA brought there. On 4Apr71, I believe it was, sappers penetrated [the perimeter], killed a couple of Cav troopers, and blew up the chapel, some trucks and other stuff. I was there that night and it was not a good night." Binh Dinh Pr, II Corps.

Buffalo II, FSB (ZA or AR or BR?)

Presumed to have existed, but unable to substantiate. Likely a 4th Div base. Binh Dinh or Pleiku Pr, II Corps.

Buffalo III, FSB (ZA or AR or BR?)

10th Cav, 4th Div here, per Bob Patsfield. Binh Dinh or Pleiku Pr, II Corps.

Buffalo IV, FSB (ZA 003-411)

Apx 2 km S QL-19B, 8 km SW Ban Duc and apx 25 km WSW Pleiku. 10th Cav, 4th Div here per Bob Patsfield, who listed grid as 004-411 but w/out UTM. Listed grid per Dick Arnold. Pleiku Pr, II Corps.

Bui Chu Sector (XH 3-4)

At southern corner of Red River Delta and home of 2 Vietminh Rgts in 1st Indochina War. See TDKQ. NVN.

Bui Phat (XS)
Refugee settlement across river from French settlement in Saigon, and created by some of 900,000 Vietnamese displaced by Geneva Accords of 1954. During 300 day armistice created by those accords, citizens were allowed to move N or S to live in country of their choice. US 7th fleet carried many of 900,000 who left NVN from Catholic dioceses of Phat Diem and Bui Chu. Name of Tin-roofed ghetto was created by joining the names of those two dioceses. Gia Dinh Pr, III Corps.

Bui Vien BEQ (XS 854-903)
At 161 Bui Vien St., Jan 65, 24 rms, Saigon. Per R. Bows' *Vietnam Military Lore, 1959-1973.* Gia Dinh Pr, III Corps.

Buick, LZ (BR 562-501)
Grid puts site apx 35 km WNW Phu Cat AB and 10 km ENE An Khe. Oct65. Binh Dinh Pr, II Corps.

Buis BOQ (XS 833-893)
At 13 Yet Kieu St., prior to Jul62, 30 rms, Saigon. Named to honor, Maj. Dale R. Buis, Advisor to 7th ARVN Div and 1st American killed (along with MSgt Chester Ovnand) in VN War, KIA 8Jul59 while watching the movie *The Tattered Dress* starring Jeanne Crane in an old saw mill that had been converted to a mess hall at Bien Hoa. VC machine gunned the viewers when lights were turned on to change reels.(see Camp Davis). Data per R. Bows' *Vietnam Military Lore, 1959-1973.* Gia Dinh Pr, III Corps.

Bukrak (various)
See Bu Krak. Quang Duc Pr, II Corps.

Bull, LZ (BR 397-386)
Apx 11 km SE An Khe. 9Dec65. Binh Dinh Pr, II Corps.

Bulldog, LZ (BS 368-552?)
If grid correct, was roughly 28 km SW Quang Ngai, 17 km WNW Minh Long AF, 15 km S Ha Thanh AF and 6 km S Lang Re. XXIV Corps official grid for Bulldog is BS 637-552, so it may be that listed grid here is a transposition error. LZ Bulldogs are also listed at BS 368-552, 539-824, 637-552 and 730-528, and unknown if it was actually at all these grids? Grid per 10Mar70 Americal Div arty ORLL. Quang Ngai Pr, I Corps.

Bulldog, LZ (BS 637-552)
A.k.a. LZ Tiger, Nui Nham and Hill 513. Apx 18 km due S Quang Ngai and 7 km due W Quang Hien/Mo Duc AF. XXIV Corps grid per Don Armstrong. Quang Ngai Pr, I Corps.

Bulldog, LZ (BS 730-528)
Apx 1 to 2 km SSW Mo Duc AF, just W the N/S Rail line, 3 km W QL-1 and perhaps 23 km SE Quang Ngai. Americal list. Quang Ngai Pr, I Corps.

Bulldog, LZ? (BS 539-824?)
If grid correct, is same as that of LZ Buff-Stinson, apx 13 km NW Quang Ngai, 5 km N the Song Tra Khuc River and 24 km due S Chu Lai. Quang Ngai Pr, I Corps.

Bulldog, PZ (BR 581-449)
Along QL-19, apx 12 km due E An Khe and 8 km W Binh Khe. 14Dec65. Binh Dinh Pr, II Corps.

Bulldog II, LZ (BS 645-559)
Apx 16 km due S Quang Ngai and 7 km WNW Quang Hien/QL-1/Mo Duc AF. Americal. Name/grid per Dan Gillotti. Quang Ngai Pr, I Corps.

Buller (n/a)
See Glossary.

Bullet, FSB (BR? 497-564)
If grid correct, was apx 10 km NNE An Khe, 13 km SE Kannack AF and 14 km SW Vinh Thanh AF. 10th Cav, 4th Div here. Grid listed simply as 497-564, and presumed to have been in the BR grid zone. Name/grid per Bob Patsfield. Binh Dinh Pr, II Corps.

Bullet, FSB (YD 490-143)
Apx 3 km SSE Dong Ca Puy, 25 km WSW Hue and 6 km S FSB Rakkasan. Thua Thien Pr, I Corps.

Bulloch County, USS (n/a)
LST-509. Sent to VN, 1Apr70. SVN.

Bullshit Bombers (n/a)
See Glossary.

Bullshit Net, The (n/a)
See Glossary.

Bullwhip (n/a)
6Apr70, XXIV Corps future-use III MAF FSB name.

Bullwhip, FSB (ZC 056-664)
Apx 20 km SW R.C. Ba Na, 8 km W LZ Robin, 7 km NW Rattlesnake and 45 km SW Da Nang. Grid computed from map on page 109, *US Marines in Vietnam-1969*. Mar-May69. Quang Nam Pr, I Corps.

Bulsan, FSB (YS 210-932)
Apx 1 km SSW Ap Binh Son, 6 km E Long Thanh AF, 23 km WSW Blackhorse AF, 7 km W FSB Tanee, 10 km SW FSB Hunt and 9 km NW FSB Digger's Rest. On 1ATF NCO trng map per John Hollett. Bien Hoa Pr, III Corps.

Bun Son Airfield (BN 772-862)
See Phan Rang AF. Ninh Thuan Pr, II Corps.

Bun Taio Airfield (RD 09-68)
A.k.a. L-20 and Puntai. CIA/SF base per *Air Facilities Data-Laos.*

Bunard (YT)
See Bu Nard. Phuoc Long Pr, III Corps..

Bunard SF Camp (YT 2701-8877)
See Bu Nard SF Camp. Phuoc Long Pr, III Corps.

Bunard, FSB (YT 27 89)
See Bu Nard, FSB. Phuoc Long Pr, III Corps.

Bunds (n/a)
See Glossary.

Bung Bung Airfield (XT 960-495)
See Phuoc Vinh AF. Phuoc Long Pr, III Corps.

Bung Kan Airfield (n/a)
Along Mekong River at Laotian border, apx 610 km NNE Bangkok, 120 km ENE Vientiane, and 140 km NE Udorn AB. El. 700' (500' on ONC-J-11?). Thailand.

Bung Dau POW Camp (XT 495-096)
Apx 5 km NW Khiem Cuong and 34 km WNW Tan Son Nhut AB. Sep67. Hau Nghia Pr, III Corps.

Bung Kioua, Cape (XE 6-8)
See Cape Bung Kioua. NVN.

Bunker Hill, FSB (YT 143-233)
A.k.a. or near FSB Green/Hieu Liem Heliport, apx 20 km NE Bien Hoa, 6 km ENE Ap Mot, 13 km NE Plantation AF. Bien Hoa Pr, III Corps.

Bunker Hill, LZ (YA 995-826)
Apx 12 km SSW Polei Krong AF, 25 km WSW Kontum and perhaps 18 km SE FSB Brillo Pad. Occupied by B/1st/12th Inf and C/1st/14th Inf, 4th Div in '68. B Bty, 1st/92d Arty and 6th/29th Arty here Apr68. See LZs Alamo, Brillo-Pad, Bunker-Hill, Bingo, XYZ Pad and Hill

1124. Grid per Harry Dilkes, and also listed at YA 997-829 and 996-825. Map is L-7014-6537-4? Kontum Pr, II Corps.

Bunker Hill 10 (YT 025-160?)
Large concrete bunker at E end of main Bien Hoa AB rwy. Site of Battle of Bunker Hill 10, night of 30-31Jan68, and opening day of Tet '68, when apx 30 men holding site came under heavy VC attack from 3 sides. USAF SSgt Piazza drove truck loaded with ammo through heavy fire to relieve position, and later took cmd when officer there KIA. He was awarded SS, and he and his small band are credited with saving many lives and $100's of millions in acft. Grid is est. Bien Hoa Pr, III Corps. [85]

Bunn, FSB (AN?)
A.k.a. LZ Bunn. Apparently in vicinity of Phan Thiet. Elements of TF 3d-506th Inf, 101st Abn here 7Mar68 per www.currahee.org/pageb2.html. Binh Thuan Pr, II Corps.

Buntharik Airfield (n/a)
Possibly Ban Nong Saeng AF? Apx 5 km W Laotian border, 540 km ENE Bangkok per Feb67 Natl Geo map. El. 620'. Thailand.

Bunting, Camp (XS 80-45 or 63-76?)
A.k.a. Bunting Engineer Support Base? Possibly at My Tho although Bunting Engineer Support Base is listed at Ben Luc in Long An Pr? HQ 86th Combat Engr Bn. Named to honor Maj. Burtrum Bunting, KIA 12Feb68. Binh Tuong Pr?, IV Corps.

Bunting, Engr Supt Base (XS 63-76 or 80-45?)
A.k.a. Camp Bunting? Said to have been at Ben Luc, which is along QL-4 apx 26 km SW Tan Son Nhut AB. However Camp Bunting said to have been at My Tho? 86th Combat Engr Bn Cmpd. Named to honor Maj Burtrum Bunting, KIA 12Feb68. Data per Ray Bows, who lists it in Dinh Tuong Pr; however, Ben Luc is in Long An Pr? IV Corps.

Buon Ba Mia Airfield (BQ 504-598)
See Phu Tuc AF. Phu Bon Pr, II Corps.

Buon Beng SF Camp (BQ 214-849)
Apx 4 km NW Cheo Reo AF and Hou Bon, at or very near Ban Oi Ly, 35 km SE Phu Nhon AF in valley of Ba Ayun/Song Ba/Ea Pa Rivers. Info/grid per *SF Order of Battle.* 5thSF Grp, Det. A-431, A-432, Dec64. Moved to Phu Tuc. Phu Bon Pr, II Corps.

Buon Blech Airfield (BQ 004-597)
Apx 8 km NE Buon Brieng AF, 32 km SW Cheo Reo AF, 48 km due E Tieu Atar AF. El. 2,100', 3,100' steel-mat rwy. At 13°11'26"N-108°14'03"E. Phu Bon Pr, II Corps.

Buon Blech SF Camp (BQ 0078-5942)
On E side of Buon Blech AF, 8 km NE Buon Brieng AF, 32 km SW Cheo Reo AF, 48 km due E Tieu Atar AF. 5th SF Det 30, Det A-238, Oct66. Converted to RF/PF. Phu Bon Pr, II Corps.

Buon Bon Bla Airfield (BQ 504-598)
See Phu Tuc AF. Phu Bon Pr, II Corps.

Buon Brieng Airfield (AQ 951-550)
A.k.a. Ban Brieng AF. Apx 8 km SW Buon Blech AF, 55 km NNE Ban Me Thuot and 38 km SW Cheo Reo AF. "Abnd (C-123), ARVN, AF # VA2-188," in Aug69 TAD per Frank Penk, Jr. Not in Feb73 TAD. Also listed at AQ 929-568, which is site of an SF camp. Darlac Pr, II Corps.

Buon Brieng New Airfield (BQ 504-598)
See Phu Tuc AF. Phu Bon Pr, II Corps.

Buon Brieng SF Camp (AQ 929-568)
Apx 10 km SW Buon Blech AF, and 55 km NNE Ban Me Thuot. 5th SF Grp, Det. A-312, Dec64. Moved to Bao Loc. Info/grid per *SF Order of Battle.* Darlac Pr, II Corps.

Buon Dan Bak SF Camp (AP 978-760?)
Possibly Buon Dong Bak or Buon Dan Kang (BQ 12-01)? If listed grid correct, was just NE Lac Thien AF and 34 km SE Ban Me Thuot? 5th SF per *SF Order of Battle.* Darlac Pr, II Corps.

Buon Dong Bak (n/a)
Mapsheet name of L-7014-6633-4. SVN.

Buon Dong Bak SF Camp? (AP 978-760?)
See Buon Dan Bak SF Camp. Darlac Pr, II Corps.

Buon Ea Ana SF Camp (ZU 218-968?)
If grid correct, was along QL-14, apx 9 km SW Ban Me Thuot and 2 km E Xa Tho Thanh. 5th SF, per *SF Order of Battle.* Moved to ? Darlac Pr, II Corps.

Buon Ea Soup SF Camp (ZV 105-946)
Apx 6 km due W Plei Bai, 26 km WSW Phu Nhon AF and 53 km SSW Pleiku. 5th SF. Info/grid per *SF Order of Battle.* See Ea Soup. Darlac Pr, II Corps.

Buon Ea Thi (n/a)
Mapsheet name of L-7014-6734-2. SVN.

Buon Ea Yang (BQ 09-03)
Village apx 4 km NW Ban Knier and 28 km due E Ban Me Thuot. Darlac Pr, II Corps.

Buon Ea Yang 2 Airfield (BQ 100-030)
See Buon Ea Yang AF. Darlac Pr, II Corps.

Buon Ea Yang Airfield (BQ 094-033)
Apx 28 km E Ban Me Thuot East AF, 47 km W Khanh Duong New AF and 32 km NNE Lac Thien AF. "Contact SF for Security, US Army 22Dec66, AF # VA2-190," in Aug69 TAD per Frank Penk, Jr. Not in Feb73 TAD. Also listed at BQ 100-030. El. 1542'. Darlac Pr, II Corps.

Buon Ea Yang SF Camp (BQ 094-033)
See Buon Ea Yang AF for location. 5th SF. Info/grid per *SF Order of Battle.* Det A-233, Oct65. Moved to Trang Phuc. Darlac Pr, II Corps.

Buon Enao SF Camp (AQ 838-502?)
If grid correct, was apx 45 km N Ban Me Thuot, 13 km WSW Buon Brieng and 35 km SE Tieu Atar? 5th SF. Grid per *SF Order of Battle.* NIMA puts ville of that name in grid square AQ 8-0. Darlac Pr, II Corps.

Buon Enao, FSB (AQ 838-502?)
Possibly at or near Buon Enao SF Camp, or in grid square AQ 8-0? See Buon Enao SF Camp for more info. Darlac Pr, II Corps.

Buon Ha Airfield (BQ 757-143)
Apx 21 km ENE Khanh Duong AF/Ban M'Drak, 30 km SSW Cung Son AF/Son Ha and 39 km NW Ninh Hoa. Listed as "Abnd, AF # VA2-88," in Aug69 TAD per Frank Penk, Jr. Not in Feb73 TAD. Khanh Hoa Pr, II Corps.

Buon Hai Airfield (BQ 757-143)
See Buon Ha AF. Khanh Hoa Pr, II Corps.

Buon Ho (various) (AQ/BQ)
Common Viet place-name. See squares AQ 9-1, BQ 0-2, BQ 0-3 and BQ 1-2. All in II Corps.

Buon Ho (n/a)
Mapsheet name of L-7014-6634-1. SVN.

Buon Ho (BQ 03-29)
Village along QL-14, apx 37 km NE Ban Me Thuot. Darlac Pr, II Corps.

Buon Ho, FSB (BQ 033-288)
Along QL-14 at Buon Ho AF, apx 35 km NE Ban Me Thuot. 2d/17th Arty here, '70. Data per Jack Picciolo. Darlac Pr, II Corps.

Buon Ho Airfield (BQ 035-291)
Apx 36 km NE Ban Me Thuot, 28 km SSE Buon Brieng AF and 50 km due E Ban Don AF, per TPC K-10A. "Flight serv, contact 5th SF Nha Trang ARVN, 29Dec68, AF # VA2-85," in Aug69 TAD per Frank Penk, Jr. Not in Feb73 TAD. El. 2363' Darlac Pr, II Corps.

Buon Ho SF Camp (BQ 035-291)
At Buon Ho AF, apx 36 km NE Ban Me Thuot, 28 km SSE Buon Brieng AF and 50 km due E Ban Don AF. 5th SF. Moved to Buon Mi Ga. Info/grid per *SF Order of Battle.* Darlac Pr, II Corps.

Buon Ja Ea Kuat (n/a)
Mapsheet name of L-7014-6633-1. SVN.

Buon Konho(?) SF Camp (YU 9745-2909)
Along QL-14, apx 5 km E Gia Nghia AF, 58 km ENE Duc Phong AF/SF Camp and 2 km W Buon Konho. Also listed as Song Be SF Camp, but that is likely an error. Possibly a.k.a. either Buon Konho or Gia Nghia SF Camp? Phuoc Long Pr, III Corps.

Buon Krong SF Camp (AP 916-497)
In valley of Ea Krong Kno River (ZU 2-8), apx 4 km NE Duc Xuyen AF, immed S Buon Rocat and 110 km due W Nha Trang. 5th SF. Info/grid per *SF Order of Battle.* See Krong Kno. Darlac Pr, II Corps.

Buon Loum Airfield (UG 26-86)
LS-88 and Boun Lom AF. Per *Air Facilities Data-Laos.*

Buon Mi Ga Airfield (BP 307-835)
A.k.a. Buon Mi Ga Airstrip. Apx 52 km ESE Ban Me Thuot and 34 km ENE Lac Thien AF. "Insecure abnd 20Mar67, AF # VA2-55," in Aug69 TAD per Frank Penk, Jr. Not in Feb73 TAD. Also listed at BP 314-835. Darlac Pr, II Corps.

Buon Mi Ga SF Camp (BP 314-835)
Apx 54 km ESE Ban Me Thuot and 34 km ENE Lac Thien AF. 5th SF camp and airstrip in '65, per S.L.A. Marshall's description in *Ambush*, p228. Info/grid per *SF Order of Battle.* Det. A-2, Dec64. Moved to Buon Ea Yang. Darlac Pr, II Corps.

Buon Mi Ga Valley (BP 32-83)
Generally 55 km ESE Ban Me Thuot. Cited in *Ambush*, pp 228-230. Darlac Pr, II Corps.

Buon Neua Airfield (RD 00-97)
A.k.a. L-30 and Boun Neua AF. Apx 410 km NNW Vientiane on Feb67 Natl Geo map. El.? CIA/SF, per *Air Facilities Data-Laos.*

Buon Sar Pa SF Camp (YU 839-721)
Apx 6 km SE Cambodia, 8 km SW Duc Lap AF, just W Duc Lap and 55 km SW Ban Me Thuot. 5th SF. Grid *SF Order of Battle.* Converted to Eagle Flight. Quang Duc or Darlac Pr, II Corps.

Buon Tan Mo SF Camp (AQ 905-190)
Apparently a.k.a. Buon Tha SF Camp? Some 17 km NE Ban Me Thuot AF, 6 km ENE Quang Nhieu and 10 km due N Dat Ly. 5th SF. Moved to Buon Uing/Buon Yum. Grid per *SF Order of Battle.* Darlac Pr, II Corps.

Buon Tha SF Camp (AQ 905-190)
Apparently a.k.a. Buon Tan Mo SF Camp? Apx 17 km NE Ban Me Thuot AF, 6 km ENE Quang Nhieu and 10 km due N Dat Ly. 5th SF. See Buon Tan Mo. Grid per *SF Order of Battle.* Darlac Pr, II Corps.

Buon Thach Trai (n/a)
Mapsheet name of L-7014-6733-1. SVN.

Buon Thoat (n/a)
Mapsheet name of L-7014-6735-4. SVN.

Buon Trap (n/a)
Mapsheet name of L-7014-6634-4. SVN.

Buon Tsuke Airfield (ZU 235-613)
Apx 36 km SE Duc Lap AF, 42 km SSW Ban Me Thuot, and 22 km NW Duc Xuyen AF. 1,800' sod/dirt rwy. At 12°17'58"N-107°58'28"E. El, 440' Darlac Pr, II Corps.

Buon Uing SF Camp (AQ 821-376)
A.k.a. Buon Wing. Apx 35 km N Ban Me Thuot, and 4 km E Buon Yum SF Camp. 5th SF. Moved to Buon Brieng. Info/grid per *SF Order of Battle.* Darlac Pr, II Corps.

Buon Wing SF Camp (AQ 821-376)
See Buon Uing SF camp. Darlac Pr, II Corps.

Buon Ya Soup (n/a)
Mapsheet name of L-7014-6535-2. SVN.

Buon Yum SF Camp (AQ 879-387)
Apx 4 km W Buon Uing SF Camp, and 35 km due N Ban Me Thuot. 5th SF. Moved to Buon Brieng. Info/grid per *SF Order of Battle.* Darlac Pr, II Corps.

Buong (generally)
See also Boung entries.

Buong Incident, The (n/a)
See Glossary.

Buong Long Airfield (n/a)
See Boung Long AF. Cambodia.

Buon-Ho Tea Plantation (BQ 06-32?)
Apx 40 km E Ban Me Thuot. Hacked out of dense woods and an assembly point/bivouac for *Groupement Mobile 100*, 10Dec53-1Jan54, and just before its move to Cheo Reo. Darlac Pr, II Corps.

Buprang (various)
See Bu Prang. Quang Duc Pr, II Corps.

Burbank, FSB (XT 720-850)
Apx 4 km SW An Loc and 5 km W QL-13. 1st Cav. Name/grid per Dan Gillotti. Binh Long Pr, III Corps.

Burgess, LZ (YA 901-386)
Apx 3 km due W Plei Dauk Kla, 9 km SSE Plei Djereng New AF and 38 km WSW Pleiku. 4th Div AO, '70. Name/grid per Jim Claeys. Pleiku Pr, II Corps.

Buriram Airfield (TH 2-8)
Apx 310 km ENE Bangkok per Feb67 Natl Geo map. El. 560'. Thailand.

Burke, FSB (YS 302-932)
Apx 29 km NW Nui Dat, 6 km WNW FSB Wattle, 2.5 km ESE FSB Tanee, 9 km due E FSB Bulsan and 4 km NNE FSB Cedar. On 1ATF NCO trng map per John Hollett. Bien Hoa Pr, III Corps.

Burkett, FSB (XT 552-846)
A.k.a. FSB Berkett and Laager Burkett. Apx 24 km ESE Katum, 7 km SSW tip of Fishhook, 5 km WNW LZ Dot, 8 km ENE LZ Rita and 3 km E Fort Defiance, astride Hwy

246. Originally opened by 2d/11th ACR mid Apr70, and named Laager Burkett at that time. During Cambodian invasion, 2d/11th Arty w/six-155s, A Bty, 6th/27th Arty, w/two-8", B Bty, 2d/32d Arty w/two-8", C Bty, 2d/12th Arty w/six-155mm howitzers all here per *11th ACR Cambodia Invasion AAR, 1st Cav Div, May-Jun70*, courtesy Lou Rochat. [86] Also listed at XT 552-844 and 555-841. Tay Ninh Pr, III Corps.

Burlington Trail, Operation (n/a)
8Apr-11Nov68. Americal Div op. 1,931 rptd NVA/VC KIA, per *Vietnam Order of Battle*, pp 9-14. Quang Tin/Quang Nam Pr border, I Corps.

Burns Hall (XT 491-472?)
Dau Tieng Basecamp NCO Club. Named to honor Cpl John D. Burns, C Bty, 2d/77th Arty, who was KIA 11Jan67, by mortar fire. Grid is for Dau Tieng AF. Binh Duong Pr, III Corps.

Burt, FSB (XT 499-806)
Apx 40 km NE Tay Ninh, near Suoi Cut. Major battle here involving 2d/22d and 3d/22d Inf, 25th Inf Div, 1Jan68, during Op Yellowstone. 4th/9th Inf Manchus reinforced those elements on 2Jan68. Hit at midnight, 1Jan68, by 271st and 272d VC Rgts. Savage and desperate fighting lasted throughout night while Beehive rounds and close-in aerial napalm strikes were employed to repel enemy. Many APCs and Dusters hit and burned. All US reserves practically exhausted when enemy finally withdrew at dawn. Known as Battle of Suoi Cut or Battle of FSB Burt and discussed in detail in *Platoon Bravo Company*, Chp 4. Grid/data per Larry Mitchell. Also listed at XT 490-800 and 500-807, Dec67-Jan68. See 242d ASHC webpage at: www.vhpa.org/crash.htm Tay Ninh Pr, III Corps.

Bushmasters (n/a)
See Glossary.

Bushwack, FSB (BT 016-464)
A.k.a. LZ Bushwack. On ridge apx 17 km SW Hoi An and 28 km due S Da Nang AB. Apr70 XXIV Corps grid per Don Armstrong. Quang Nam Pr, I Corps.

Butcher, LZ (XD 846-393)
Overlooked QL-9, apx 3 km due S Khe Sanh CB, 2 km W intersection of Hwy 508/QL-9, and 2 km NNE Khe Sanh ville. Apr70 XXIV Corps grid per Don Armstrong. Quang Tri Pr, I Corps.

Butler, Camp (AT/BT?)
Said to have been at or near Da Nang. No other data. Quang Nam Pr, I Corps.

Butler, Camp (n/a)
In Okinawa, not SVN. Supt/Evac Hospital for VN Casualties in-transit.

Butler II, FSB (XT 540-050)
Apx 2 km due E Khiem Cuong and 15 km SW Cu Chi. May69. Hau Nghia Pr, III Corps.

Butt, LZ (BR 853-779)
Along Rte 506, apx 7 km SE Ha Tay. Oct66. Binh Dinh Pr, II Corps.

Butte, LZ (YS 645-913)
Apx 24 km SE Duc Phong and 55 km WNW Bao Loc. Apr66. Phuoc Long Pr, III Corps.

Butte BEQ (XS 849-930)
443 Hai Ba Trung, Saigon. Data per *Vietnam Military Lore, 1959-1973*. Gia Dinh Pr, III Corps.

Butterfly, LZ (XD 843-619)
Apx 21 km NW Ca Lu AF and 21 km due N Khe Sanh CB, in Song Can Lo River Valley. Apr70 XXIV Corps grid per Don Armstrong. Quang Tri Pr, I Corps.

Butterworth Hospital (n/a)
See 3 RAAF Hosp. Malaysia

Buttons, FSB/LZ (YU 141-072)
A.k.a. FSB Song Be. At Song Be AF, 2 km SW Phuoc Binh (Song Be), 110 km NNE Saigon and 43 km NE An Loc. Large Basecamp hosting 1st/12th Cav at one time per Tom Skelly, and HQ 2d Bde/1st Cav, '70. Author of *Apache Sunrise*, p 209, tells us it was larger than Song Be and featured C-130 capable AF equipped to provide instrument approaches. Grid per 1st Cav ORLL. Also listed at YU 138-072, 140-070, 145-070, XU 143-073 (possible UTM error?), Jan69-Feb71. Phuoc Long Pr, III Corps.

Buttons, LZ (XT 629-652)
At or just S Minh Thanh AF, 32 km NNW Lai Khe. Feb69. Binh Long Pr, III Corps.

Buttons, FSB (XU 143-073?)
Grid presumed to be in error. Should be "YU" zone.

Buu Son Airfield (BN 772-862)
See Phan Rang AF. Ninh Thuan Pr, II Corps.

Buzzard, FSB (YT 993-335)
Apx 3 km N Xa Hieu Tin, 23 km due E Vo Dat, 9 km NE Tanh Linh AF and 115 km ENE Saigon. 199th LIB. Possibly named to honor Army PFC Lloyd L. Buzzard, KIA 19Jun69? Opened or reopened 7Sep70, closed 22Sep70. 2d/5th Cav Data per *1st Cav Div Op Rpt, ending 31Oct70*, courtesy Peter Cole. Binh Tuy Pr, III Corps.

Buzzard, LZ (YD 031-604)
Apx 11 km WNW Cam Lo, 14 km NNE Ca Lu AF and 32 km WNW Quang Tri. Apr70 XXIV Corps grid per Don Armstrong. Quang Tri Pr, I Corps.

BV-33 (n/a)
Batallion Volontaire-33, Royal Lao Army unit stationed at Ban Houei Sane in Laos. In early 60s, BV-33 cmdr gave periodic briefings and intel rpts that were attended by US SF officers. Cmdr and his family would also occasionally cross border on Rte 9 to visit ARVN and SF Camps near Khe Sanh, and one CO killed when his vehicle struck mine during journey. On night of 23-24Jan68, after otherwise leaving the site unmolested, NVA finally attacked site using armor for 1st time in American War, and overran position, securing it completely. 519 Lao troops and their 2,270 dependents fled to SF Camp at Lang Vei, and SF blew bridge on Rte 9 behind them to delay pursuit. Refugees were 1st disarmed, then re-armed and sent to man previously abnd Old Lang Vei CIDG camp. [87]

Byrd, Operation (n/a)
26Aug66-20Jan68. 1 and sometimes 2 Bns of 1st Cav used in an economy of force op. 849 rptd NVA/VC KIA, per *Vietnam Order of Battle*, pp 9-14. Binh Thuan Pr, II Corps.

CHARLIE

Facility/Feature Name, Grid Coordinate, a.k.a. Name/History/Province/CTZ

Unless otherwise stated, 6-digit grid coordinates reference DMA L-7014, L-7015 or L-7016 series, 1:50,000 scale maps, while 2 and 4-digit coordinates reference AMS/DMA/NIMA 1:250,000, 1:500,000 and 1:1,000,000 scale maps. Unless otherwise stated, all heights are in meters. To convert meters to feet, multiply by 3.2808; feet to meters, multiply by .3048.

C-1, FSB (YD 213-672)
A.k.a. Charlie-1. Along QL-1, apx 6.5 km NW Dong Ha. ARVN and USMC. On map at p 90, *US Marines in Vietnam, Fighting the North Vietnamese, 1967*. Map is L-7014-6442-4, per Ken Burrington. Quang Tri Pr, I Corps.

C-1, Strong Point (YD 213-674)
See C-1, FSB. Quang Tri Pr, I Corps.

C-1, Strongpoint (TJ 9-6)
Apx 1 mi due W Dien Bien Phu main CP and immed N C3. One of the 5 Claudines; defensive positions at DBP, a.k.a. D1 thru D5. In Muong Thanh Valley apx 290 km W Hanoi. French strongpoint during Op Castor, 20Nov53-7May54. NVN.

C-2, FSB (YD 137-647)
A.k.a. Charlie-2. Apx 23 km NW Quang Tri, 12.5 km WNW Dong Ha and 6 km SSE Con Thien. USMC and ARVN. On map at p 90, *US Marines in Vietnam, Fighting the North Vietnamese, 1967*. Quang Tri Pr, I Corps.

C-2, Strong Point (YD 135-645)
See C-2, FSB. Quang Tri Pr, I Corps.

C-2, Strongpoint (TJ 9-6)
Apx 1.1 mi SSW Dien Bien Phu main CP, 6/10ths mi E C5, and immed W C3. One of 5 Claudines; defensive positions at DBP a.k.a. D1 thru D5. In Muong Thanh Valley apx 290 km W Hanoi. French strongpoint during Op Castor, 20Nov53-7May54. NVN.

C-2 Bridge (YD 128-671)
A.k.a. Bastards Bridge. Apx 3 km WNW Phu Phuong, 24 km NW Quang Tri and 9 km WSW Gio Linh. In apx Oct67, was built to N of FSB C-2 in order to maintain supply rte between C-2 and Con Thien. Defended first by BLT 2d Bn/3d Marines, and then 2d Bn/4th, who came under attack there 14Oct67. During fight, G Co's CO (Capt. Jack W Phillips), the Bn S-3 (Capt. J. W. McCarter, Jr.) and 3 newly-arrived Plt Ldrs were KIA and Sgt Paul A. Foster was awarded MOH. Attack also notable in that NVA employed Tear Gas. On15Oct67, while Gen Cushman and Gen Hochmuth were visiting battle site, they granted 2d/4th CO LTC Hammond's request that bridge be named "Bastard's Bridge" to honor the 21 KIA of 2d/4th Marines who died defending it (2d/4th's nickname was apparently the Magnificent Bastards?). Data per *US Marine in Vietnam, 1967*, pp 135-6. Quang Tri Pr, I Corps.

C-2 Bridge, Strong Point (YD 128-671)
Apx 3 km WNW Phu Phuong, 24 km NW Quang Tri and 9 km WSW Gio Linh. XXIV Corps grid. See C-2 Bridge. Quang Tri Pr, I Corps.

C-3, FSB (YD 143-611)
A.k.a. Charlie-3. On Hwy 561, apx 11.5 km due W Dong Ha, 9 km SSE Con Thien and 2.5 km N QL-9. USMC, ARVN. Also listed at YD 143-614. On map at p 90, *US Marines in Vietnam, Fighting the North Vietnamese, 1967*. Quang Tri Pr, I Corps.

C-3, Strong Point (YD 143-614)
See C-3, FSB. Quang Tri Pr, I Corps.

C-3, Strongpoint (TJ 9-6)
1 mi due S Dien Bien Phu main CP, immed E C2, 4/10ths mi W the White Thai position and 1 mi E C5. One of 5 Claudines, defensive positions at DBP a.k.a. D1 thru D5. In Muong Thanh Valley apx 290 km W Hanoi. French strongpoint during Op Castor, 20Nov53-7May54. NVN.

C-3 Bridge (YD 148-604)
A.k.a. Cam Lo Bridge. TL-8B bridge over Song Cam Lo, apx 3 km ENE Cam Lo and 21 km WNW Quang Tri. Quang Tri Pr, I Corps.

C-3 Compound (Bien Hoa) (XT 98-13?)
Just outside Bien Hoa. 3 Cos of mercenary troops (mostly Nung) and their US advisors HQ'd here as Mike Force unit (a.k.a. China Boy Bn). Moved to Nha Trang. Cited in *Ambush*, pp. 33-51. Gia Dinh Pr, III Corps.

C-3 Compound (Nha Trang) (CP 04-55?)
US Army SF, Vietnam, Provisional C-Team Camp. Nha Trang. Had cmd and control of SF units in SVN, Oct63. Relocated from Bien Hoa in 62? Khanh Hoa Pr, II Corps.

C-4, FSB (YD 313-725)
A.k.a. Charlie-4 and LZ Bowie. Adj to Giem Ha Trung, apx 17 km N Quang Tri, 2 km inland from ocean and 5 km NW Cua Viet Naval Base and mouth of that River. USMC, ARVN. Also listed at YD 314-724. On map at http://mcbride.space.swri.edu/visit/maps/cuamap.jpg. Quang Tri Pr, I Corps.

C-4 Hospital (XT 6-4?)
The C4 and C6 VC/NVA Hosp complexes were in SW corner of Thanh Dien Forest. Binh Duong Pr, III Corps.

C-4, Strong Point (YD 314-724)
See C-4, FSB. Quang Tri Pr, I Corps.

C-4, Strongpoint (TJ 9-6)
Somewhere to S or SW Dien Bien Phu main CP. One of 5 Claudines, defensive positions at DBP a.k.a. D1 thru D5. In Muong Thanh Valley apx 290 km W Hanoi. French strongpoint during Op Castor, 20Nov53-7May54. NVN.

C-5, Strongpoint (TJ 9-6)
Apx 1.5 mi SW Dien Bien Phu main CP, immed S C1 and .6 mi due W C2. One of 5 Claudines, defensive positions at DBP a.k.a. D1 thru D5. French strongpoint during Op Castor, 20Nov53-7May54. NVN.

C-6 Hospital (XT 6-4?)
The C4 and C6 VC/NVA Hosp complexes were in SW corner of Thanh Dien Forest. Binh Duong Pr, III Corps.

C-50 (YA/YB)
See Charlie 50. Cambodia.

C, FSB (XT 86-55?)
A.k.a. FSB Sroc Con Trang. Apx 10 km NE FSB Thrust, 12 km NW FSB Bravo, 20 km W An Loc, 5 km S Cambodia and just N Rte 246. See Sroc Con Trang. Tay Ninh Pr, III Corps.

c, LZ (XT 440-670)
Apx 17 km NE Nui Ba Den and 3 km E Ap Cha Do. 24May67. Tay Ninh Pr, III Corps.

c, LZ (XT 523-899)
Apx 13 km NW Tonle Cham AF and 6 km due W tip of the Fishhook. 15-21Mar67. Also listed at XT 520-900 Tay Ninh Pr, III Corps.

c, LZ (YS 595-605)
Apx 10 km E Dat Do, 3 km N the ocean and near Rach Song Cai River. 7Apr66. Phuoc Tuy Pr, III Corps.

C Med (AT/BT?)
A.k.a. Charlie Med. Marine Field Hosp near Da Nang. See Alpha Med. Quang Nam Pr, I Corps.

C Med (YD 541-318)
A.k.a. Charlie Med. At Camp Evans, apx 23 km NW Hue. 326th Med Bn cmpd, 101st Abn. Thua Thien Pr, I Corps.

C Med (XD 852-418)
A.k.a. Charlie Med. At Khe Sanh CB, immed E of Graves Registration, toward the W end of rwy and immed S the Acft parking apron. Quang Tri Pr, I Corps.

C Rations (n/a)
See Glossary.

C Rations, LZ (YU 180-098)
Apx 1 km S Song Be City AF and 5 km NE Song Be AF. Nov68. Phuoc Long Pr, III Corps.

C Team (CP 04-55?)
Highest level of Army SF unit hierarchy and 1st cmd and control element HQ'd at Nha Trang. See Glossary for detail. Khanh Hoa Pr, II Corps.

C Team Hospital (CP 04-55?)
Nha Trang. SF Hosp where all incoming SF Medics had to undergo training before deployment to an SF unit. Khanh Hoa Pr, II Corps.

C. Turner Joy, USS (n/a)
A.k.a. DD 951 and *Turner Joy*. See *Maddox, USS*.

C. E. Hosking Compound (XT 98-13)
A.k.a. C. E. "Snake" Hosking Cmpd. At or near Bien Hoa AB. Named to honor MSgt Charles E Hosking, USA, 5th SF Grp Mike Force, KIA 21Mar67, near Camp Cao Song Be, Don Luan Dist, when VC suspect grabbed a grenade from his belt and Hosking in turn grabbed the prisoner, preventing him from harming nearby comrades. For that act he was awarded the MOH. Data per *Vietnam Military Lore, 1959-1973.* Bien Hoa Pr, III Corps.

Ca Cau Hai CAP (ZD 090-007?)
See CAP 3-2-1. 3d CAG, Thua Thien Pr, I Corps.

Ca Lu (YD 012-455)
Ville W of Dong Toan Mtn, 10 km SW Mai Loc, 33 km WSW Quang Tri and apx 16 km SSE the Rockpile. Quang Tri Pr, I Corps.

Ca Lu, FSB (XD 980-540)
Along QL9 near Thon Son Lam, apx 11 km WNW Mai Loc, 36 km W Quang Tri and perhaps 3 km S the Rockpile. At this grid, Nov69. Also listed YD 012-455 and YD 013-449, Mar-Apr70. Quang Tri Pr, I Corps.

Ca Lu Airfield (XD 999-479)
Along QL-9, apx 10 km WSW Mai Loc and 34 km W Quang Tri. "Flight serv, contact Air Ops Officer III MAF Da Nang, USMC, 17Apr68, AF # VA1-181," in Aug69 but not Feb73 TAD, per Frank Penk, Jr. Quang Tri Pr, I Corps.

Ca Lu Combat Base/FSB (YD 012-455)
Apx 10 km SW Mai Loc, 33 km WSW Quang Tri and 16 km SSE the Rockpile. USMC 12th Arty had six 105mm howitzers here Nov67. Map is L-7014-6342-2, per Ken Burrington. Quang Tri Pr, I Corps.

Ca Lu Heliport (YD 244-597)
Possible mislabeling of Dong Ha Heliport? Along QL-1, immed SE Dong Ha and 12 km NW Quang Tri. "Heliport #532, alt 33'. Confined due to wires. Altn lndg area on soccer field 400 yds S, at 16°48'30"N-107°06'00"E," per Feb73 TAD. Quang Tri Pr, I Corps.

Ca Map (XQ 7-5)
Coastal point on Con Son Island at 8°38'N-106°37'E. On NC48-11 JOG. IV Corps.

Ca Mau (VQ 7-5)
Coastal point at 8°38'N-104°44'E. On NC48-15 JOG. An Xuyen Pr, IV Corps.

Ca Mau (WR 17-14)
A.k.a. Camau or Quan Long. Ville apx 64 km WSW Bac Lieu and 38 km SSW Kien Long AF. SF B-Team here in early 60's, also MAAG Intel. MACV contingent here '65. Described as, "…little more than an outpost at N edge of U Minh Forest," in *Baptism,* p 24. MACV's club here in a old, French tennis *sportif* known as The Club. See Camau (not same as Cua Mau). An Xuyen Pr, IV Corps.

Ca Mau, Baie de la (VQ 7-5)
A.k.a. Vung Mui Ca Mau. Bay at 8°36'N-104°45'E. On NC48-15 JOG. An Xuyen Pr, IV Corps.

Ca Mau, Pointe de (VQ 7-5)
See Pointe Ca Mau. An Xuyen Pr, IV Corps.

Ca Mau, Vung (VQ 7-5)
Bay at 8°36'N-104°45'E. On NC48-15 JOG. An Xuyen Pr, IV Corps.

Ca Mau (New) Airfield (WR 196-142)
See Quan Long AF. An Xuyen Pr, IV Corps.

Ca Mau (Quan Long) (n/a)
Mapsheet L-7014-6027-3. Full sheet name: Quan Long (Ca Mau). SVN.

Ca Mau Airfield (WR 196-142)
See Quan Long AF. An Xuyen Pr, IV Corps.

Ca Mau Moi Airfield (WR 196-142)
See Quan Long AF. An Xuyen Pr, IV Corps.

Ca Mau Old Airfield (WR 169-139)
See Quan Long City AF. An Xuyen Pr, IV Corps.

Ca Mau Province (VR/WR/VQ/WQ)
In what later became known as IV Corps and absorbed into what became primarily An Xuyen Pr. Thought to have ceased existence shortly before or during early US presence in SVN? Dates of existence not known.

Ca Na, Mui (BN 5-4)
Coastal point at 11°17'N-108°47'E. On NC49-01 JOG. Binh Thuan Pr, II Corps.

Ca Puy, Dong (YD 4-1)
Mtn at 16°25'00"N-107°19'00"E. Thua Thien Pr, I Corps.

Ca Tha, Mui (BN 5-4)
Mui Ca Nai. Coastal point at 11°17'N-108°47'E. On NC49-01 JOG. Binh Thuan Pr, II Corps.
Ca Tho, Baie (VS 53)
A.k.a. Vinh Ca Tho. Bay at 10°16'N-104°33'E. On NC48-06 JOG. Kien Giang Pr, IV Corps.
Ca Tho, Vinh (VS 5-3)
Bay at 10°16'N-104°33'E. On NC48-06 JOG. Kien Giang Pr, IV Corps.
Ca Tien, Mui (CP 0-0)
Coastal point at 11°49'N-109°12'E. On NC49-01 JOG. Khanh Hoa Pr, II Corps.
Cabbage, LZ (XD 993-684)
In DMZ, apx 1 km S the Ben Hai River, 11 km due W Bo Hu Su (NVN) and 37 km NW Quang Tri. Apr70 XXIV Corps grid per Don Armstrong. Quang Tri Pr, I Corps.
Cabildo, USS (n/a)
LSD-16. Lndg. Ship, Dock, per Ralph Fries.
Cable, LZ (XD 865-167)
At southern tip of Vietnam Salient, on Laotian border, apx 2 km due W Trouan (1), 3 km SSW peak Hill 556 (Co Van Mtn) and 25 km due S Khe Sanh CB. Apr70 XXIV Corps grid per Don Armstrong. Quang Tri Pr, I Corps.
CAC (n/a)
See Glossary.
CAC 3 (n/a)
USMC Combined Action Co. No data. I Corps.
CAC 3-1 (AT 944-701?)
See Tuy Loan. Thua Thien Pr, I Corps.
CAC 4 (n/a)
USMC Combined Action Co. No data. I Corps.
CAC 7 (n/a)
USMC Combined Action Co. Later became CAC Alpha 6 and CAC Alpha 9 per Tim Duffie's CAP Vets website. See CAP and CAC. I Corps.
CAC Alpha 1 (n/a)
USMC Combined Action Co. No data. I Corps.
CAC Alpha 2 (n/a)
USMC Combined Action Co. No data. I Corps.
CAC Alpha 3 (n/a)
USMC Combined Action Co. No data. I Corps.
CAC Alpha 6 (n/a)
USMC Combined Action Co. No data. I Corps.
CAC Alpha 9 (n/a)
USMC Combined Action Co. No data. I Corps.
CAC Alpha (n/a)
USMC Combined Action Co. No data. I Corps.
Cac Ba, Port de la (YH 1-9)
A.k.a. Baie d' Apowan. Bay at 20°43'N-107°02'E. On NF48-16 JOG. NVN.
Cac Ba, Port de la (YH 1-9)
A.k.a. Baie d' Apowan. Bay at 20°43'N-107°02'E. On NF48-16 JOG. NVN.
CAC Bravo (n/a)
USMC Combined Action Co. No data. I Corps.
CAC Delta (n/a)
USMC Combined Action Co. No data. I Corps.
CAC Echo (n/a)
USMC Combined Action Co. No data. I Corps.
CAC Foxtrot (n/a)
USMC Combined Action Co. No data. I Corps.
CAC Golf (n/a)
USMC Combined Action Co. No data. I Corps.
CAC Hotel (n/a)
USMC Combined Action Co. No data. I Corps.
CAC India (n/a)
USMC Combined Action Co. No data. I Corps.
CAC Oscar (XD)
USMC Combined Action Co at Khe Sanh ville, on S side of QL-9 apx 4 km due S what became Khe Sanh CB. HQ of CAP Oscar 1, 2 and 3 Plts, all of which were near Khe Sanh. Included 2 CAP Plts + 2 Plts 915th RF Co (SVN) and 4 US SF Det Advisors for total of apx 175 men when heavily attacked, 21Jan68. Elements later relocated to Khe Sanh CB during siege. See CAP 0-1 and 0-2 for more info. See CAP and CAC. Quang Tri Pr, I Corps. [88]
CAC Papa (YD 13-59)
Apparently 1st USMC CAC/CAP unit established N of Da Nang. CAC Papa HQ was at Cam Lo and set up inside an ARVN cmpd just outside Camp Carroll along QL-9 about 8 km W Cam Hu. CO's call-sign was Tiger Papa, and its two 15-man plts had call-signs of Tiger Papa 2, and Tiger Papa 3. TP-3 was at Cam Hu. Discussed in *A Voice of Hope*. Quang Tri Pr, I Corps.
CAC Papa 3 (YD 21-63)
At Cam Hu, apx 8 km E Cam Lo and 100 meters N QL-9. Fifteen-man Plt's call-sign was Tiger Papa 3. *A Voice of Hope* chronicles a tour with CAC Papa 3, the 1st CAC unit placed N Da Nang. Apparently overrun at least twice, 3May67 and ? See Tiger Papa 3, CAC Papa, CAP Papa. 4th CAG per Tim Duffie's CAP Vets website. Grid apx. Quang Tri Pr, I Corps.
CAC Quebec (n/a)
USMC Combined Action Co. I Corps.
CAC Romeo (n/a)
USMC Combined Action Co. I Corps.
CAC Sierra (n/a)
USMC Combined Action Co. I Corps.
Cache, USS (n/a)
T-AO 67. 140,000-barrel capacity MSTS Fuel Tanker.
Cachu Forest Reserve (XT 530-325)
Immed N Xa Trang Co, apx 40 km NW Saigon and 24 km W Lai Khe. Cited in *Cedar Falls-Junction City* as Cachua Reserve. Tay Ninh Pr?, III Corps.
Cachu, Reserve Forestiere de (XT 5-3)
A.k.a. Reserve Forestiere de Cachu. At Trang Co. NIMA data. Tay Ninh Pr?, III Corps.
Cachua Reserve (XT 5-3)
See Cachu. Forest III Corps.
CACO (n/a)
See Glossary.
CACO 2 (n/a)
2d CAG, Dist. III per T. Duffie CAP Website. Quang Nam Pr, I Corps.
CACO 2-1 (n/a)
2d CAG per CAP Website. Hieu Duc District, Quang Nam Pr, I Corps.
CACO 2-2 (n/a)
2d CAG per CAP Website. Dai Loc District, Quang Nam Pr, I Corps.

CACO 2-3 (n/a)
2d CAG per CAP Website. Dien Ban District, Quang Nam Pr, I Corps.
CACO 2-4 (n/a)
2d CAG per CAP Website. Hieu Nhon District, Quang Nam Pr, I Corps.
CACO 2-5 (n/a)
2d CAG per CAP Website. Hoa Vang District, Quang Nam Pr, I Corps.
CACO 2-7 (n/a)
2d CAG CAP Website. Hoa Vang District, Quang Nam Pr, I Corps.
CACO 2-8 (n/a)
2d CAG per CAP Website. Hoa Vang District, Quang Nam Pr, I Corps.
CACO 2-9 (n/a)
2d CAG per CAP Website. CAP 2-9-1 attacked by 2 reinforced Cos of NVA 21Nov68 at 2315hrs. Initial attack was against 5th Marine positions but then shifted to CAP cmpd. Recommended for Meritorious Unit citation for battle. [89] Duc Duc District, Quang Nam Pr, I Corps.
Cacti, LZ (BT 058-471)
Apx 8 km W LZ Baldy, 32 km S Da Nang and apx 10 km W QL-1. Named to honor a TF Oregon 4th Div Rgt nicknamed the "Blue Cacti." 2d Bde/4th Div here Apr69 (per *Time Heals No Wounds*, p 183, 1st/12th Inf Radio Log excerpt). Apr70 XXIV Corps grid per Don Armstrong. Also listed at BT 059-479, 060-473 and 063-470. Near Quang Nam/Quang Tin Pr border, I Corps.
Cactu, LZ (AQ 820-230)
Apparent misspelling of Cacti, or of Batu or Ba Tu. Grid puts site apx 18 km due N Ban Me Thuot City AF. Feb66. Darlac Pr, II Corps.
Caddo County* (*or Caddo Parish?*), *USS (n/a)
LST-515. SVN.
Cadet, LZ (BS 562-244)
Apx 8 km due S Ba To New AF, 30 km SW Duc Pho and 18 km E Gia Vuc AF. Set up 5Jul70 per Americal list. Near Quang Ngai/Binh Dinh Pr border, I Corps.
CAG (n/a)
Combined Action Grp. See Glossary.
CAG (n/a)
Guided Missile Heavy Cruiser (USN term).
CAG, 1st (n/a)
See 1st CAG.
CAG, 2d (n/a)
See 2d CAG.
CAG, 3d (n/a)
See 3d CAG.
CAG, 4th (n/a)
See 4th CAG.
Cah Noi (n/a)
Mapsheet name of L-7014-6244-3. NVN only.
Cai Ban, Baie de (CP 1-7)
A.k.a. Vung Cay Ban. Bay at 12°27'N-109°18'E. On ND49-13 JOG. Khanh Hoa Pr, II Corps.
Cai Ban, Mui (VS 6-2 (Cape at 10°08'N-104°39'E. On NC48-06 JOG. Kien Giang Pr, IV Corps.
Cai Be (XS 14-42)
A.k.a. Sung Hieu. Along N bank of Mekong River, 37 km due W My Tho. Several nearby FSBs suptd 2d/39th Inf and 4th/39th Inf of 9th Inf Div, per Jim Stone, 2d/39th Inf. Dinh Tuong Pr, IV Corps.
Cai Be, FSB (WS 97-40)
A.k.a. FSB Dickey and FSB Danger. On QL-4 apx 42 km due W Dong Tam and 14 km ENE Sa Dec, at 10°19'00"N-105°54'00"E. See FSB Danger. Dinh Tuong Pr, IV Corps.
Cai Be Heliport (XS 134-424)
At Sung Hieu, along N bank of Mekong River, 37 km due W My Tho. "Heliport #533, alt 7', earth pad, end of F/W strip at cmpd." At 10°20'00"N-106°02'00"E, per Feb73 TAD. Dinh Tuong Pr, IV Corps.
Cai Bi (Hai Phong) Airfield (XJ 80-03)
Major AF apx 95 km ESE Hanoi and 5 km SE Hai Phong. One of 2 major fields near port of Hai Phong. Per ONC-J-11. El. 15'. NVN.
Cai Cai Airfield (WT 559-072)
Apx 5 km S Cambodia some 6 km NE Don Phuc AF and 25 km W Binh Than Thon AF. El. 7', 1,500' clay rwy. At 10°55'12"N-105°30'40"E. Kien Phong Pr, IV Corps.
Cai Cai Heliport (WT 620-000)
Apx 10 km S Cambodia, 8 km E Don Phuoc AF and 125 km NE Ha Tien. "Heliport #534, alt 13' sod, at 10°51'30"N-105°33'30"E," per Feb73 TAD. Chau Doc Pr?, IV Corps.
Cai Cai SF Camp (WT 5616-0750)
A.k.a. FOB An Long. Apx 3 km S Cambodian border, 8 km NE Don Phuc AF and 30 km WNW Binh Thanh Thon AF 5th SF. Det A-412, Oct66, and Det 73. Converted to 76th ARVN Rangers. A.k.a. FOB An Long. Grid per *SF Order of Battle.* Kien Thuong Pr, IV Corps.
Cai CAP (n/a)
No data. I Corps.
Cai Do Van SF Camp (VQ 859-851)
A.k.a. FOB Binh Hung. Apx 13 km ENE Binh Hung, 43 km NE tip of Cau Mau Peninsula and 37 km SW Quan Long AF. 5th SF camp. Grid per *SF Order of Battle.* An Xuyen Pr, IV Corps.
Cai Doi SF Camp (WS 983-952)
A.k.a. FOB Moc Hoa. Apx 5 km NE Moc Hoa and 80 km due W Saigon. 5th SF. Grid per *SF Order of Battle.* Kien Tuong Pr, IV Corps.
Cai Doi Van Airfield (VQ 849-818)
See Binh Hung AF. An Xuyen Pr, IV Corps.
Cai Kit SF Camp (VS 995-764)
Apparently a.k.a. Nhan Hung SF Camp. Apx 3 km from Cambodia, 17 km WSW Chau Duc AF, 13 km N That Son and 63 km ENE Ha Tien. Data per *SF Order of Battle.* See Nhan Hung; FOB Tien Binh. Chau Doc Pr, IV Corps.
Cai Lap, Mui (US 8-2)
Coastal point at 10°11'N-103°58'E. On NC48-05 JOG. Kien Giang Pr, IV Corps.
Cai Lap, Pointe (US 8-2)
See Pointe Cai Lap. Kien Giang Pr, IV Corps.
Cai Lay (XS 22-50)
Along QL-4, apx 27 km WNW My Tho. Several FSBs supt 2d/39th Inf and other 9th Inf Div near this ville FSBs Moore and Cleopatra, among them), per Jim Stone, 2d/39th Inf. Dinh Tuong Pr, IV Corps.
Cai Lay (Khiem Ich) (n/a)
Mapsheet L-7014-6229-4. Full sheet name: Khiem Ich (Cai Lay). SVN.

Cai Lay Heliport (XS 228-504)
Along QL-4, apx 14 km NNW Vinh Long, 27 km WNW My Tho and 85 km SW Saigon. "Heliport #535, alt 7' soccer field," per Feb73 TAD. Dinh Tuong Pr, IV Corps.

Cai Mon Heliport (XS 338-285)
Apx 70 km SSW Saigon and 23 km SW My Tho. "Heliport #536, alt 7' sod, very confined, at 10°12'40"N-106°13'15" E," per Feb73 TAD. Kien Hoa Pr, IV Corps.

Cai Nhum Heliport (XS 220-245)
Apx 82 km SW Saigon and 34 km SW My Tho. "Heliport #537, alt 7' sod, soccer Field. Landing on road next to district house, at 10°10'00"N-105°00'00"E," per Feb73 TAD. Vinh Long Pr, IV Corps.

Cai Nuoc (n/a)
Mapsheet name of L-7014-6026-4. SVN.

Cai Nuoc (various)
Common Viet place-name. See grid squares WR 1-7 WR 1-8, WQ 1-9 and VQ 84-81. All in IV Corps.

Cai Nuoc (WR 1-8)
A.k.a. Xom Cai Nuoampoc. S Rach Gia and near 9°48'00"N-105°06'00"E. Kien Giang Pr, IV Corps.

Cai Nuoc (WR 1-8?)
A.k.a. Dam Chung and Xom Cai Nuoampoc? Near 9°48'00"N-105°06'00"E. Also possibly in UTM WQ 1-9 or WR 1-7? An Xuyen Pr, IV Corps.

Cai Nuoc Heliport (VQ 849-818)
On Cau Mau Peninsula, 5 km NNE Binh Hung AF, 40 km NNE tip of Cau Mau, 22 km NW Nam Can AF "Heliport #538, alt 7' earth road. Houses on side." At 08°53'N 104°52'E, per Feb73 TAD. An Xuyen Pr, IV Corps.

Cai Nvoc Airfield (VQ 849-818)
See Cai Nuoc AF. An Xuyen Pr, IV Corps.

Cai Sung, Baie (CP 1-6)
Bay at 12°22'N-109°19'E. Khanh Hoa Pr, II Corps.

Cai Sung, Baie (CP 1-6)
Bay at 12°22'N-109°19'E. Khanh Hoa Pr, II Corps.

Cai Tang (n/a)
See Glossary.

Caiban Bay (CP 1-7)
A.k.a. Vung Cay Ban. Bay at 12°27'N-109°18'E. On ND49-13 JOG. Khanh Hoa Pr, II Corps.

Caisson 1 thru 7 (XT)
See Caisson I thru VII, and FSB Thunder series. Binh Duong/Binh Long Prvs, III Corps.

Caisson I, FSB (XT 756-887)
On NW edge of An Loc, 20 km S Loc Ninh AF. Jul67. Also listed at XT 750-870 Aug67, and 792-446, Nov67. See FSB Thunder series. Binh Long Pr, III Corps.

Caisson I, FSB/LZ (XT 792-446?)
If grid correct, was 7 km NNE Lai Khe. Nov67. See FSB Thunder series. Binh Duong Pr, III Corps.

Caisson II, FSB (XT 731-818)
Apx 3 km WNW An Loc. Jul67. See FSB Thunder series. Binh Long Pr, III Corps.

Caisson II, FSB/LZ (XT 788-515)
Along QL-13, 14 km N Lai Khe. Nov67. Also listed at XT 792-513, Sep67. See FSB Thunder series. Binh Duong Pr, III Corps.

Caisson III, FSB/LZ (XT 768-613)
Apx 3 km W QL-13 and Ap Bau Bang, apx 7 km due N Lai Khe. Also listed at XT 760-610. Jul67. See FSB Thunder series. Binh Long Pr, III Corps.

Caisson III North, FSB (XT 767-607)
Along QL-13, immed S Chon Thanh AF. Nov67. See FSB Thunder series. Binh Long Pr, III Corps.

Caisson III South, FSB (XT 788-556)
Apx 7 km SSE Chon Than AF and 1 km E QL-13. Sep-Oct67. Also listed at XT 790-444 and XT 790-555. Binh Long Pr?, III Corps.

Caisson IV, FSB (XT 778-546)
Apx 6 km S An Loc in Xa Cat Rubber Plantation. Site of Battle of Xa Cat, 10Dec67. See Xa Cat. Aug-Dec67. See FSB Thunder series. Binh Long Pr, III Corps.

Caisson V, FSB (XT 736-540)
Apx 16 km NNW Lai Khe and 6 km W QL-13. Oct-Nov67. See FSB Thunder series. Binh Long Pr?, III Corps.

Caisson VI, FSB (XT 745-817)
Apx 6 km SSW An Loc and 2 km W QL-13. Nov-Dec67. See FSB Thunder series. Binh Long Pr, III Corps.

Caisson VII, FSB/LZ (XT 764-894)
Along QL-13 at N edge of AN Loc. Nov-Dec67. See FSB Thunder series. Binh Long Pr, III Corps.

Caisung Bay (CP 1-6)
A.k.a. Baie Cai Sung. Bay at 12°22'N-109°19'E. On ND49-13 JOG. Khanh Hoa Pr, II Corps.

Cajun, LZ (BR 372-921)
S of Dak Som River, 13 km E Kon Lok, 27 km NNW Kannack AF and 37 km SE Plateau Gi. 4th Div AO, '70. Binh Dinh Pr, II Corps.

Caldera, LZ (BR 235-266)
Apx 33 km SW An Khe and 4 km S LZ Badger. 4th Div AO, '70. 4th Div op rpt grid per Jim Claeys. Binh Dinh or Pleiku Pr, II Corps.

Caldwell, LZ/FSB (YU 439-049)
Immed S Duc Phong AF, near Vinh Thien, 28 km ESE Song Be, 4 km S QL-14 and 45 km NE Dong Xoai. 2d/12th Cav, 1st Cav, Jul-69. On 12Aug69, VC threw simultaneous attacks against many 1st Cav bases in III Corps, including Quan Loi, LZ Becky, LZ Jon, LZ Kelly and LZ Caldwell. Grid per 1st Cav Arty ORLL. Also listed at YU 440-050. Phuoc Long Pr, III Corps.

Caliente, USS (n/a)
AO-53. SVN

Cam Le Bridge (BT 015-716)
QL-1 bridge across Da Nang River apx 4 km due S Da Nang AB. Apr70 XXIV Corps grid per Don Armstrong. Quang Nam Pr, I Corps.

Cam Le Bridge (XT 722-972)
QL-13 bridge apx 12 km S Loc Ninh AF. Binh Long Pr, III Corps.

Cam Le River (AT 95-70)
A.k.a. the Da Nang River? W to E running stream that drained valley to N Ba Na, then passing Hoa Vang and southern edge of Da Nang before turning abruptly N and emptying into Da Nang Bay. Quang Nam Pr, I Corps.

Cam Linh Peninsula (CP 20-10)
Peninsula forming E edge of Cam Ranh Bay. AO, Korean 2d Marine Corps "Blue Dragons" Bde, '65, before moving to Hoi An area in '66. Khanh Hoa Pr, I Corps.

Cam Linh, Mui (CP 1-1)
Coastal point at 11°53'N-109°17'E. On NC49-01 JOG. Khanh Hoa Pr, II Corps.
Cam Linh, Pointe de (CP 1-1)
See Pointe Cam Linh. Khanh Hoa Pr, II Corps.
Cam Lo (n/a)
Mapsheet name of L-7014-6342-1. SVN/NVN/DMZ.
Cam Lo (YD 125-595)
Apx 23 km WNW Quang Tri, 15 km ENE the Rockpile and 11 km due E peak of Dong Ha Mtn. Apr70 XXIV Corps grid per Don Armstrong. Quang Tri Pr, I Corps.
Cam Lo Airfield (YD 12-59?)
Apparently near Cam Lo, which, puts it roughly 20 km WNW Quang Tri. In '69 TAD, but not Feb73 TAD. AF # VA1-98. Data per Frank Penk, Jr. Quang Tri Pr, I Corps.
Cam Lo Base Camp (YD 130-593)
A.k.a. Hill 37. 3d Mar Div Basecamp on QL-9, apx 15 km W Dong Ha, 23 km WNW Quang Tri and on S bank Mieu Giang River. Area renowned for "sweet water" that dripped from trees in area (whether that is a reference to a sap of some kind or what, is not known). 3d Mar Div, 12th Marine Arty '67, w/two 155mm. Quang Tri Pr, I Corps.
Cam Lo Bridge (YD 149-604)
See C-3 Bridge. Quang Tri Pr, I Corps.
Cam Lo CAC (YD 13-59?)
Papa CACO and CAP Papa 1, 4th CAG, Cam Lo District per CAP Website. Papa HQ here, call-sign Tiger Papa. Grid only apx. Quang Tri Pr, I Corps.
Cam Lo City (YD 128-595)
Apx 23 km WNW Quang Tri, 15 km ENE the Rockpile and 11 km due E Peak of Dong Ha Mtn. Quang Tri Pr, I Corps.
Cam Lo CP (YD 132-593)
Apx 23 km WNW Quang Tri, 15 km ENE the Rockpile. Marine cmd post, Aug66. Quang Tri Pr, I Corps.
Cam Lo River Valley (YD)
Large valley W of Quang Tri that contained Cam Lo, QL-9 and the Rockpile. Quang Tri Pr, I Corps.
Cam Ly Airfield (BP 185-220)
See Dalat/Cam Ly AF. Tuyen Duc Pr, II Corps.
Cam Ne (AT 96-68?)
Grid is for Cam Ne (4), a ville along E bank of Song Yen River, apx 8 km SW Da Nang AB and 5 km W QL-1. Per *Bloods, Reginald Edwards* Chp, p 1, it was here that CBS News correspondent Morely Safer filmed 1st infamous footage of US Marines burning down huts by igniting them with Zippo cigarette lighters (a.k.a. Zippo Raid). Said to have taken place, 5Aug65. Quang Nam Pr, I Corps.
Cam Ne CAP (AT 96-68?)
Apparently USMC CAP Team here per *Bamboo Brigades*. Cam Ne (4) is apx 8 km SW Da Nang AB and 5 km W QL-1. See T. Duffie's CAP Vets website. NIMA data. Quang Nam Pr, I Corps.
Cam Ngoc (n/a)
Mapsheet name of L-7014-6046-1. NVN only.
Cam Pha (n/a)
Mapsheet name of L-7014-6451-2. NVN only.
Cam Pha (YJ 4-2?)
In Sept65, attack sqdns from Carriers *Oriskany*, *Constellation*, *Coral Sea*, and *Intrepid* hit previously off-limit areas in port of Haiphong and smaller ports of Hon Gai and Cam Pha. During Tet '68, power plants, rail yards, naval facilities, barracks, and heavy industrial plants here struck by Carrier TF-77 attempts to blunt NVA Tet '68 offensive. At 21°01'00"N-107°19'00"E. NVN.
Cam Ranh (BP 99-17)
City apx 190 km NNE Saigon and on western edge of Cam Ranh Bay. Khanh Hoa Pr, II Corps.
Cam Ranh (n/a)
Mapsheet name of L-7014-6832-4. SVN.
Cam Ranh AAF (CP 053-166)
A.k.a. Cam Ranh Army Airfield and Dong Ba Thin AF. Along QL-1 on W side of bay, apx 4 km NW the main AB. Cam Ranh AF. Khanh Hoa Pr, II Corps.
Cam Ranh AF Cantonment (CP 060-310)
Along coast, apx 2 km NNW the N end of main rwy at Cam Ranh Bay AB. Khanh Hoa Pr, II Corps.
Cam Ranh AFB Hospital (CP 07-27)
See USAF Hospitals. Khanh Hoa Pr, II Corps.
Cam Ranh Airfield (CP 053-166)
A.k.a. 14th Aerial Port. Minor AF on E side of Cam Ranh Bay, apx 7 km due S Cam Ranh Bay AB and 40 km NE Phan Rang's major AF, per TPC K-10D. El. 20', 2,600' steel-mat rwy. At 11°54'25"N-109°12'43"E. See Cam Ranh Bay AB. Khanh Hoa Pr, II Corps.
Cam Ranh Army Cantonment (CP 053-166)
Adj Cam Ranh Army AF (Dong Ba Thin), along QL-1 and W side of bay, apx 4 km NW the main AB. Cam Ranh AF. Khanh Hoa Pr, II Corps.
Cam Ranh Army Logistics Area (CP 085-175)
On the Cam Ranh Peninsula, apx 7 km NW Howell (South Beach) and 8 km S main AB. Khanh Hoa Pr, II Corps.
Cam Ranh Bay (CP 00-15)
Apx 180 mi NE Saigon and 32 km S Nha Trang. Site of major USN port facility, a major USAF airport (along with Tan Son Nhut, the two primary points of entry for men and material during war) and a US Army complex. Initial const was by 39th Engr Bn under LTC Ernest E Lane Jr., Cmdr, 39th Engr Supt Bn, KIA 18May66. Const of facilities began Dec 65. On 23May70, Viet Cong sappers breached perimeter and destroyed large stocks of avn fuel here. Historically, the site was a strategic port and used by French in 19th Century, by Russian Fleet during Russo-Japanese War in 1905, by Japanese Southwestern Fleet in WWII, and by Soviets after NVN victory in '75. French began building the original colonial military and port facilities here in 1939, inc 8" and 6"-gun coastal batteries (8 mi range) on peak of main island that were apparently connected by underground rail lines. On 12Jan45, Acft from Halsey's strike force attempting to trap the Japanese fleet here instead found it had departed, but did destroy 20 Japanese seaplanes in harbor. In 1951, Chiang Kai Shek sent 30,000 troops to VN, of which 6,000 went to Cam Ranh only to be put in detention by French until sent home in '52. Between '54 and Jul56, was used as principal debarkation port for French forces. Per Mar98 issue of *Army* Magazine, the former US military and airbase facilities here are still being used by Vietnamese military forces. [90] One of the six autonomous municipalities of SVN. See also Powell's Ape and Map #28. Khanh Hoa Pr, II Corps. [91] [92]

Cam Ranh Bay (Army) Seaport (CP 050-155)
Apx 10 km due S main Cam Ranh AF and on W side of Cam Ranh peninsula. Berthing Feet: 6,500 lineal feet, Draft Max: 34, Cargo Capacity: 8,300 tons/day, Storage Covered w/in 5 km: 881,000 ft^2, Storage Uncov, w/in 5 km:377,000 yd^2. Khanh Hoa Pr, II Corps.

Cam Ranh Bay Airbase (CR 066-261)
At N end of Cam Ranh Bay, 10 km NNE Cam Ranh AF, 4 km SE Dong Ba Thin minor AF, and about 26 km due S Nha Trang's major AF, per TPC K-10A. Major, US AF capable of handling commercial jet liners, and along with Tan Son Nhut AFB, one of the 2 primary points of entry for men and material during war. Cam Ranh USAF Cantonment was co-located with USN Naval Air Facility. Host cmd was first the 483d Tactical Airlift Wing, 504th Tac Air Supt Grp here also. Road sign on E side of base read: "*DRIVE CAREFULLY - Don't Kill or Maim Your Replacement*." 10,000' conc rwy, El. 47'. At 11°59'37"N-109°13'23"E. Per Mar98 issue of *Army* Magazine, the former US military facilities here still in use by Vietnamese military. [93] Khanh Hoa Pr, II Corps.

Cam Ranh Bay Ammo Docks (CP 030-187)
Apx 6 km SSW main AF, 5 km NE the Port Facilities and 3 km NW the Army Port. Khanh Hoa Pr, II Corps.

Cam Ranh Bay Army Complex (CP 06-30)
Near listed grid. Consisted of main Army cantonment (CP 055-320), apx 3 km N main AF), Camp Thompson, Black McKinley and Moore ammo Stg Area (CP 095-230), apx 3 km SE main AF) Pugh Amphitheater, Howell Beach (CP 130-120), at SE corner of peninsula (and a.k.a. South Beach), the 22d Replacement Bn (one of Army's 2 major personnel replacement depots (other being 90th Rep depot at Long Binh), the Army Logistics area (CP 085-175) 8 km S the main AF and apx 8 km NNW Howell Beach) and Army Port (CP 050-155). Per Mar98 issue of Army Magazine, the former US military facilities here still in use by Vietnamese military. Khanh Hoa Pr, II Corps.

Cam Ranh Bay Beach (CP 130-120)
See Howell Beach/South Beach. Khanh Hoa Pr, II Corps.

Cam Ranh Bay Convalescent Hospital (CP 06-31)
On coast, apx 1 km SE the replacement center, 4 km ENE the main AB and 3 km NE Dong Ba Thin AF. Khanh Hoa Pr, II Corps.

Cam Ranh Bay Market Time Facility (CP 0-1?)
Cam Ranh Bay, Khanh Hoa Pr, joint USN/US Coast Guard/VN Navy off shore patrol facility, responsible for controlling NVA water based infiltration into SVN. Khanh Hoa Pr, II Corps.

Cam Ranh Bay Replacement Center (CP 05-32)
Immed NW of the convalescent center, apx 5 km NNW the main AB and 3 km NE Dong Ba Thin AF. Along with 90th Replacement Depot at Bien Hoa, one of the 2 largest such depots in VN. Khanh Hoa Pr, II Corps.

Cam Ranh Bay Navy Base (BP 980-153?)
USN Base, '65-71. Khanh Hoa Pr, II Corps.

Cam Ranh Bay USAF Cantonment (CP 060-305)
Immed N the main AF and immed S the Cam Ranh Bay Army Complex. Khanh Hoa Pr, II Corps.

Cam Ranh Bay VFW Post (CP 0-3)
See VFW Post 8316, Saigon. Khanh Hoa Pr, II Corps.

Cam Ranh Beach (CP 130-120)
See Howell Beach/South Beach. Khanh Hoa Pr, II Corps.

Cam Ranh Naval Air Facility (CR 066-261)
A.k.a. NAF Cam Ranh. Co-located with Cam Ranh USAF AB. Khanh Hoa Pr, II Corps.

Cam Ranh Port Facilities (BP 980-153)
11 km SSW the main airbase and on W side of bay directly opposite the Army Port and apx 6.5 km from it. Khanh Hoa Pr, II Corps. [94]

Cam Ranh RMK-BRJ Depot (CP 055-212)
On W side of Cam Ranh peninsula, due S the S end of main Cam Ranh AB rwy and apx 3 km NNE ammo unloading docks. Khanh Hoa Pr, II Corps.

Cam Ranh South Beach (CP 130-120)
See South Beach. Khanh Hoa Pr, II Corps.

Cam Ranh, Baie de (CP 0-1)
A.k.a. Vinh Cam Ranh. Bay at 11°53'N-109°10'E. On NC49-01 JOG. Khanh Hoa Pr, II Corps.

Cam Ranh, Pointe de (CP 1-1)
See Pointe Cam Ranh. Khanh Hoa Pr, II Corps.

Cam Ranh, Vinh (CP 0-1)
Bay at 11°53'N-109°10'E. On NC49-01 JOG. Khanh Hoa Pr, II Corps.

Cam Son Secret Zone (XS 2-4)
Generally 15 km W and WNW Dong Tam. VC staging area swept by 9th Inf Div during Op Coronado-V, Sep67. AAR at www.mrfa.org/ ctg117.htm. Dinh Tuong Pr, IV Corps.

Cam Son, Battle of (XS 1-4?)
During Op Coronado V, 15-16Sep67. 2d, 3d, and 5th/60th plus the 3/47th Inf Bn from MRF, 9th Inf Div fight a two-day battle along Rach Ba Rai, 2-4 miles NE Cai Be against the VC's 263d MF and 514th LF Bns. Met heavy VC resistance resulting in 16 US KIA, and 146 WIA as well as 213 VC KIA. Dinh Tuong Pr, IV Corps.

Cam Tam, FSB (YS 37-99)
Apx 8 km WNW Blackhorse Basecamp, 50 km ENE Saigon and 13 km SW Xuan Loc. 2d/3d Inf, 199th LIB here. Long Khanh Pr, III Corps.

Cam, LZ (BS 392-505)
Apx 14 km W Minh Long AF, 33 km SW Quang Ngai, 10 km NE Lang Baout and perhaps 44 km WNW Duc Pho/LZ Bronco. Also listed at BS 393-502. Americal List. Quang Ngai Pr, I Corps.

Camargue, Operation (YD 59-41 to YD 38-64)
Jul53 French op in area of Street Without Joy, coast of N Quang Tri Pr. Involved amphib landings coupled with 2 coordinated armored assaults (with Abn units as ready-reaction reserve) in effort to clear Vietminh 95 Rgt from coastal plains between QL-1, the coast, Quang Tri and Lai Ha (Lai Ha was NW Hue). 10 Inf Rgts, 2 Abn Bns and bulk of 3 armored Rgts, one armored train, 4 Arty Bns, 34 air-transports, 6 recon acft, 22 fighter-bombers and 12 naval vessels were assembled for attack into 6 TFs: 2 amphib, 3 land-borne groupements and 1 Abn force all under Gen LeBlanc. Began 28Jul53 and ended 4Aug53. Results were 17 French KIA, 100 WIA with enemy losses at 182 KIA, and 387 POWs. Most enemy evaded attack or slipped through cordon and, by Spring '54, 95 Rgt was back in area; pattern that would repeat itself throughout both Indochina Wars. Quang Tri Pr, I Corps. [95]

Camau (WR 17-15?)
A.k.a. Ca Mau or Quan Long and also spelled Ca Mau. Apx 26 km S Tan Phu SF Camp, 64 km WSW Bac Lieu and 38 km SSW Kien Long AF. SF B-Team here early 60's, also MAAG Intel element. MACV contingent here '65. In *Baptism,* p 24, described as "little more than an outpost at N edge of U Minh Forest." MACV's club here was in an old, French tennis *sportif.* MACV's club here was in an old, French tennis *sportif* known as The Club. Not same as Cua Mau. An Xuyen Pr, IV Corps.
Camau, Cape (VQ 7-5)
A.k.a. Mui Ca Mau. Cape at 8°36'N-104°45'E. On NC48-15 JOG. An Xuyen Pr, IV Corps.
Cambod III, FSB? (XU?)
No data. 7th/8th Arty here, May70. Name per Dan Gillotti, 15th Arty Assn. Cambodia.
Cambodia, Point (VQ 7-5)
Mui Ca Mau. Coastal point at 8°38'N-104°44'E. On NC48-15 JOG. An Xuyen Pr, IV Corps.
Cambodian Incursion (n/a)
See Glossary.
Cambodian Incursion, Operation (n/a)
29Apr-30Jun70. 13 major combat ops conducted, only 2 of which involved US ground forces (US Advs and US air supt were in all ops, however). Supplies and weapons capable of equipping 55 full strength VC Inf Bns and enough crew-served weapons to equip 82 to 90 VC Bns captured. Also captured was ammo sufficient to provide basic load for 52,000 NVA troops. Op also apparently forestalled NVA counteroffensive against Lon Nol govt. Lasted 63 days and 10,000+ NVA/VC were rptd KIA, per *Vietnam Order of Battle*, pp 9-14. Cambodia.
Cambodian Liberation Army (n/a)
A.k.a. CLA. See *Agence France Presse* in Glossary.
Camden, USS (n/a)
AOE-2. Aux Oiler, per Ralph Fries.
Camel, LZ (XD 989-668)
At DMZ's edge, apx 13 km NNE Ca Lu, 16 km NW Cam Lo and 36 km NW Quang Tri. Many other FSBs nearby including: LZs Bazooka (XD 980-558), Champ (XD 989-629), Deacon (XD 986-670), Hackney (XD 987-321), Parakeet (XD 987-343), Amber (XD 987-589), Tarzan (XD 987-645) and FSB Toledo (XD 988-481). Apr70 XXIV Corps grid per Don Armstrong. Quang Tri Pr, I Corps.
Camelot, FSB (XU 720-506)
Apx 3 km ESE FSB Anna and 10 km due W FSB Bronco, roughly 23 km NE Snuol, 64 km WNW Djamap, 42 km N Loc Ninh and 27 km due N the SVN border. Grid per *11th ACR Cambodia Invasion AAR, 1st Cav Div, May-Jun70,* courtesy Lou Rochat.[96] Cambodia.
Camerone Day (n/a)
See Glossary.
Camh Sat (n/a)
See Glossary.
Camile, LZ? (XT or XU?)
See Cara Camile. III Corps.
Camp (defined) (n/a)
See Glossary.
Camp (place name) (various)
Camps are listed alphabetically by name with last-name first, followed by a comma and then the word Camp, as in "Eagle, Camp."
Camp, USS (n/a)
A.k.a. DER-251. Participated in defense of Coastal Grp 16 base (apx 110 km S Da Nang), when attacked by 2 Bns of VC. Also providing offshore gunfire were *PCFs, 15, 20, 54, 75*, the *USS Gallup* and a C-47 Gunship. Role discussed in *Brown Water, Black Berets*, p 121. SVN.
Campbell, Camp (YD 82-33)
On beach apx 12 km NNE of Hue Citadel. Possibly original name of what became Eagle Beach, or was the Seabee/POL cmpd on opposite side of isthmus from Eagle Beach at Tan My? Named to honor SWF3 Stanley C. Campbell, USN, a Seabee with NMCB-7, KIA 25Aug66, shot by guard who had just arrived in-country, dedicated 30Oct66. Data per Ray Bows' *Vietnam Military Lore-1959-1973*. Grid only apx. Thua Thien Pr, I Corps.
Campbell, USS (n/a)
WHEC 32. 14Dec67-12Aug68. Sqdn 3 CGC, during Coast Guard's 2d deployment. On 13Mar69, replaced *USS Prichett* off Phan Thiet suptg TF 3d/506th Inf per www.currahee.org/ pageb3.html. Per Lt Kend Linderholm, who served on the *Campbell* stateside, "There were leftover plaques etc. [from her VN service], and even after a refit; rust. It was very noticeable when we went to Cuba for training. We closed up the 6" mount for simulated atomic attack and the rust holes in the mount [let light through] very nicely. The gun had not been replaced since the Vietnam trip, so I was a little nervous sitting next to it when it was fired." SVN.
Can Bau, FSB (YT 59-06)
A.k.a. FSB Can Ba. Apx 15 km SE Xuan Loc, 10 km due S peak Nui Chua Chan Mtn, 17 km ENE Blackhorse basecamp and 2 to 3 km WNW Hill 324. 2d/3d, 199th LIB here. Long Khanh Pr, III Corps.
Can Bo (n/a)
See Glossary.
Can Bo Platoons (n/a)
See Glossary.
Can Dot Airfield (XS 524-656)
See Long An AF. Dinh Thuong? Pr, IV Corps.
Can Duoc Bridge (XS 760-613)
LTL-5A bridge apx 23 km WSW Tan An and 26 km due S Saigon. Long An Pr, III Corps.
Can Duoc Heliport (XS 758-609)
Along LTL-5A, apx 23 km WSW Tan An and 26 km due S Saigon. Heliport #540, alt 5', conc pad, at 10°29'45"N-106°36'30"E, per Feb73 TAD. Long An Pr, III Corps.
Can Giay, Mui (AN 9-1)
A.k.a. Mui Da. Coastal point at 10°56'N-108°11'E. On NC48-08 JOG. Binh Thuan Pr, II Corps.
Can Gio (n/a)
Mapsheet name of L-7014-6329-1. SVN.
Can Gio Heliport (YS 165-518)
In Rung Sat Special Zone and on coast, apx 13 km WNW Vung Tau, and 48 km SE Saigon. Heliport #541, alt 5', conc, at 10°24'40"N-106°58'30"E, per Feb73 TAD. Gia Dinh Pr, III Corps.
Can Gio, Pointe (YS 1-5)
A.k.a. Mui Ganh Rai. Cape at 10°24'N-106°58'E. On NC48-07 JOG. Gia Dinh Pr?, IV Corps.

Can Giuoc (n/a)
Mapsheet name of L-7014-6330-3. SVN.
Can Giuoc Base (XS 825-711)
On LTL-5A, apx 23 km due S Tan Son Nhut AB. 9th ID base here. 3rd/39th, 5th/60th and 6th/31st Inf basecamp, per Jim Stone, 2d/39th Inf. Long An Pr, III Corps.
Can Giuoc District HQ (XS 84-73)
Along LTL-5A, apx 23 km due S Tan Son Nhut AB. HQ of 3d/47th ARVN Rgt in '68. Long An Pr, III Corps.
Can Giuoc Heliport (XS 831-730)
On W bank of Song Rach Cac apx 23 km due S Tan Son Nhut AB and adj to LTL 5-A. Heliport #542, alt 5', per Feb73 TAD. Long An Pr, III Corps.
Can Hoa (n/a)
See Glossary.
Can Lo Than, Bau (CP 0-3)
Lagoon at 12°03'N-109°11'E. On ND49-13 JOG. Khanh Hoa Pr, II Corps.
Can Tach Tria Airfield (BP 185-220)
See Dalat/Cam Ly AF. Tuyen Duc Pr, II Corps.
Can Tho (n/a)
Mapsheet name of L-7014-6129-2. SVN.
Can Tho (WS 84-10)
Apx 100 km SW Saigon. Largest population center (apx 154,000 in '68) of Mekong and center of all US Ops in Mekong Delta/IV Corps area. Site of SF Det 84, Can Tho Army AF, the Dempsey Cmpd, the Eakin Cmpd, 9th Inf Div elements, CORDS IV, Civ Org/Development Supt, MARS Station AB8AN, Adv Team 96 and 97, IV Corps (ARVN) Advsy Det, 5th SF Grp, Det. B-130, Dec64, C-4, Oct 65 Loc, A-424 Oct66. US Base at Can Tho was overrun by VC, 13Jan69, and in one bunker alone, killed 16 US personnel.[97] Capitol, Phong Dinh Pr, IV Corps.
Can Tho (B-40) SF Camp (WS 843-103)
At Can Tho, apx 125 km SW Saigon and immed SE Can Tho AF. 5th SF. Info/grid per *SF Order of Battle.* Phong Dinh Pr, IV Corps.
Can Tho (B-43) SF Camp (WS 843-103)
At Can Tho, apx 125 km SW Saigon and immed SE Can Tho AF. 5th SF. Redesignated B-40 and later RF/PF base. Also listed at WS 8430-1160. Info/grid per *SF Order of Battle* (see Append. H, Phong Dinh Pr, IV Corps.)
Can Tho (Old) Airfield (WS 840-108?)
See Can Tho AF. Phong Dinh Pr, IV Corps.
Can Tho, Camp (WS 865-0900)
SF Camp. At N edge of Can Tho city, apx 2 km SE Can Tho AF, 7 km SE Binh Thuy AF and not far from bank of Mekong. Phong Dinh Pr, IV Corps.
Can Tho Airfield (WS 840-108)
Apx 3 km NW Can Tho and 6 km SE Binh Thuy AF. See Binh Thuy AF & Can Tho AAF. Phong Dinh Pr, IV Corps.
Can Tho Army Airfield (WS 840-108)
One of 2 major and 1 minor AFs near Can Tho. Along Mekong River, apx 3 km NW Can Tho, 3 km SE Navy Binh Thuy minor AF, 7 km SE Binh Thuy major AF, 72 km SW My Tho, 65 km SW Dong Tam, 125 km SW Saigon and 30 km SE Vinh Long AF, per TPC K-10D. Built by French and improved by Japanese in WWII. 3,900' asph rwy. Home of Army's 13th Avn Bn (Combat). Also listed at WS 843-103. El. 7'. Phong Dinh Pr, IV Corps.
Can Tho Base (WS 8-1?)
Along Mekong River, apx 72 km SW My Tho, 65 km SW Dong Tam, 125 km SW Saigon and 30 km SE Vinh Long major AF. 2d Bde 9th Inf and USN MRF basecamp, per Jim Stone, 2d/39th Inf. Phong Dinh Pr, IV Corps.
Can Tho NDB (WS 83-12)
Non-Directional Air Nav Beacon site. Apx 3 km NW Can Tho and 6 km SE TACAN NDB Binh Thuy. Phong Dinh Pr, IV Corps.
Can Tho New Airfield (WS 789-148)
See Binh Thuy AF. Phong Dinh Pr, IV Corps.
Can Tho NSA (WS 8-1)
Along Mekong River, apx 72 km SW My Tho, 65 km SW Dong Tam, 125 km SW Saigon and 30 km SE Vinh Long major AF. 2d Bde 9th Inf and USN MRF basecamp. USN Supt Activity, '66-72, per MRF Assn Website. Phong Dinh Pr, IV Corps.
Can Tho PBR Base (WS 8-1)
A.k.a. Binh Thuy/Can Tho PBR Base. River Div 51, TF-116, USN Gamewarden base here per MRF Assn website at www.mrfa.org. Phong Dinh Pr, IV Corps.
Can Tho Province (WR)
In what later became IV Corps and absorbed into what later became primarily Chuong Thien Pr. Thought to have ceased existence shortly before or during early US presence in SVN? Actual dates of existence unknown. IV Corps.
Can Tho Seaport (WS 84-10)
Berthing Feet: 300 lineal feet, Draft Max: 8', Cargo Capacity: 800 tons/day, Storage Covered w/in 5 km: 32,000 ft^2, Storage Uncov, w/in 5 km: 28,000 yd^2. Phong Dinh Pr, IV Corps.[98]
Can Tho SF Camp (WS 843 116)
At N edge of Can Tho, apx 125 km SW Saigon and immed SE Can Tho AF. IV Corps HQ of 5th SF Grp. In *Team Sergeant*, author describes it as being next to Can Tho and C-130 capable AF. He also said, "The permanent bldgs were arranged in square-shaped perimeter," apx 100 yds square. "This setup would keep the 23 man B-Det busy supplying the five A-Det's."[99] Grid *SF Order of Battle.* Phong Dinh Pr, IV Corps.
Can Tho SF Camp (WS 865-0900)
In Can Tho, apx 3 km SE Can Tho AF. 5th SF Grp B-Team here early 60's. Later relocated. Grid *SF Order of Battle.* Phong Dinh Pr, IV Corps.
Canada, FSB (XT 581-502)
Apx 6 km NE Dau Tieng AF. Aug69. Binh Duong Pr, III Corps.
Canada, LZ (XD 945-685)
In DMZ, along S edge of Hwy 102, apx 6 km due W Bon Ho Su, and 42 km WNW of Quang Tri. Apr70 XXIV Corps grid per Don Armstrong. Quang Tri Pr, I Corps.
Canal des Bambous (XH 1-8)
Canal of Bamboo, Song Luoc. NIMA data. NVN.
Canal des Quatre Cantons (WS 3-5)
NIMA data. An Giang or Chau Doc Pr, IV Corps.
Canal de Rapides (XJ 3-3)
NW Hanoi? NVN.
Canal des Rapides Bridge (XJ 3-3?)
NW Hanoi and Op Linebacker target, Dec72. NVN.

Canary, LZ (BR 698-654)
Apx 9 km NE Vinh Thanh AF and 30 km NE An Khe. Oct66. Binh Dinh Pr, II Corps.
Canary/Duck, Operation (n/a)
7Dec66-5Jan67. 173d Abn, Phu My/Bearcat. Bde conducted 2-phase road security op along QL-15 between Phu My and Long Binh, and from Phu My to Bearcat in supt 199th LIB and 9th Inf Div.
***Canberra*, USS** (n/a)
A.k.a. CAG 2. In Feb68, *Canberra*, Heavy Cruiser *Providence*, and 7 other ships poured thousands of shells into NVA targets in Hue, inc the Citadel, suptg USMC ground units. Its place in history also includes following, rather odd story: On night of 6Apr67, sailor (Doug Hegdahl, 19) aboard this guided missile cruiser was awakened by sounds of a night bombardment of NVN coast and, eager to see the fireworks, went topside. There he was blown overboard by concussion of ship's guns and rescued by NVN fishermen after treading water for 10 hours without a life vest! He was then imprisoned at Hanoi Hilton under suspicion of being a sophisticated spy. Per *Prisoners of Hope*, Hegdahl was very intelligent and gifted with a photographic memory, but he played the role of village idiot for 2 1/2 years to convince his captors he was not a "super spy" and had instead been thrown overboard by his shipmates due to his quirky behavior. His strange antics while in captivity so annoyed his captors that he was offered an early release. At 1st he refused, but then later accepted after POW leader Richard Stratton realized that Hegdahl had memorized the names of all 250 POWs there, and ordered him to accept release and pass on names to US authorities (Hegdahl's memory device involved inserting the names of 250 POWs into tune of *Old MacDonald had a Farm*). At time of his release, NVN claimed to have only 59 US POWs and Hegdahl's info was not only a major intel coup, but served to save the lives of many of those 250 men. Discussed in *Prisoners of Hope*, pp 17-19.
Candle Stick Operations (n/a)
See Glossary.
Candy, FSB (YU 183-233)
Apx 22 km SW Djamap AF and 13 km due N Song Be City AF. Built Feb70-Apr70, B/8th Engr Bn, 1st Cav. [100] "FSBs Django and Joan closed on 23 and 25Feb70 respectively and 8th Abn Bn displaced to establish FSB Lolita(YU 369-261). As move N gained momentum and enemy activity increased, FSB's Candy, Loan, and Audie were established 25, 26 and 27 Feb70 respectively...The 1st Abn Bn (minus) moved to establish FSB Loan, leaving one rifle Co to secure FSB Judie." [101] Phuoc Long Pr, III Corps. [102]
Candy Stripe Highway (YD 777-250)
A.k.a. Hwy 552. Ran E to W from NE corner of Hue to area known as Phu My at YD 825-245. Road that provided access to POL facilities at Tan My/Eagle Beach on Vinh Loc Island. Thua Thien Pr, I Corps.
Canh Lo (BR 7-0)
WNW Binh Thanh, at 13°34'00"N-108°54'00"E. On mapsheet ND49-09. Binh Dinh Pr, II Corps.
Canh Tien (n/a)
Mapsheet name of L-7014-6736-2. SVN.
Canh Van Airfield (BR 948-209)
See ROK Strip/ROK AAF. Binh Dinh Pr, II Corps.
Canister Rounds (n/a)
See Glossary.
Cannister, LZ (BS 624-223)
Apx 12 km SE Ba To New AF. Jul67. Possible misspelling of Canister? Binh Dinh Pr, II Corps.
Cannon, FSB (YD 473-029)
Apx 2 km E Hwy 547, 33 km SW Hue, 10 km E FSB Eagle's Nest and 25 km WSW FSB Birmingham. XXIV Corps grid per Don Armstrong. Also listed at YD 475-028, 472-029 and 430-070(?). Thua Thien Pr, I Corps.
Cannon Ball, LZ (n/a)
Location unknown. 8th/4th Arty here, '68. Name/data per Dan Gillotti, 15th Arty Assn. I Corps.
Canons, Cole de (YD 1-5)
Pass of the Cannons. NIMA data. Quang Tri Pr, I Corps.
Canteen, LZ (BR 888-726)
Along Rte 506, apx 5 km NNW Phu My, 23 km SSE Bong Son and 3 km W QL-1. Oct66. Binh Dinh Pr, II Corps.
Canter, Camp (n/a)
No data. Quite possibly variant of Camp Carter, near Marble Mtn? Listed in Dec2001 *VETERAN* Mag, p 39.
Cantigny I, FSB (XT?)
Presumed to have existed, but location unknown. III Corps.
Cantigny II, FSB (XT 525-377)
Apx 13 km SSE Dau Tieng, 26 km due W Lai Khe. Jul69. Binh Duong/Tay Ninh Pr border, III Corps.
Cantons, Canal des Quatre (WS 3-5)
A.k.a. Khinh Bong Ton? NIMA data. An Giang or Chau Doc Pr, IV Corps.
Cao Bang (n/a)
Mapsheet name of L-7014-6254-2. NVN only.
Cao Bang (XL 30-17)
Capitol of Cao Bang Pr, apx 190 km NNE Hanoi, 48 km NW That Khe and 102 km NW Lang Son. Known for beauty of its waterfalls and grottos. Tho, Nung, Dao, and Meo minorities are principal residents. Region's products inc zinc, lumber, beef, sheep and pigs. NVN.
Cao Bang Airfield (XL 30-07)
Apx 188 km NNE Hanoi. 67 Natl Geo map. El. 750'. NVN.
Cao Bang Outpost (XL 30-17)
Apx 190 km NNE Hanoi, 48 km NW That Khe, 102 km NW Lang Son near Chinese border, and 40 km ENE Nguyen Binh. Major French frontier outpost of 1st Indochina War. Involved in Op Lea, Oct47, and later heavily contested by Vietminh in Fall, 1950. Supplied only by air after enemy forced end to convoys along R.C. 4. Under cmd of Col Charton when, in Sep50, French decided to abandon attempts to keep open the enemy-controlled 35 km stretch of R.C. 4 between Cao Bang and That Khe. At same time, they decided to abandon most Northern Frontier outposts (Nguyen Binh, Balkan and etc.) but to keep Cao Bang and Dong Khe even though defense and re-supply was very difficult. Retreat was response to Gen Giap's growing Divs, who had been building hard-surface roads toward Cao Bang, Lao Kay, Monkay and Lang Son and training in upper Red River (Song Coi) Valley (1st test of units had overrun Pho Lu in Spring '50). As 1950 began, Giap had built or was building the 304th, 308th, 312th, 316th and 320th Divs, each containing some 10,000 troops,

many of whom had received training in China. On map in *Street Without Joy*, p 31. NVN.

Cao Bien SF Camp (XT 977-497)
Apx 2 km E Phuoc Vinh AF and 36 km due N Bien Hoa AB. 5th SF Det A-312 (was 321), Oct65, See Phuoc Vinh. Info/grid per *SF Order of Battle*. Binh Duong Pr, III Corps.

Cao Dai (XT)
See Glossary.

Cao Dai 'A' Refugee Camp (BS 666-694)
E of QL-1, apx 4 km SE Quang Ngai. Grid per NPIA. Quang Ngai Pr, I Corps.

Cao Dai 'B' Refugee Camp (BS 666-693)
E of QL-1, apx 4 km SE Quang Ngai. Grid per NPIA. Quang Ngai Pr, I Corps.

Cao Dai 'C' Refugee Camp (BS 670-694)
E of QL-1, apx 4 km SE Quang Ngai. Grid per NPIA. Quang Ngai Pr, I Corps.

Cao Dai Church (XT 241-496)
Downtown Tay Ninh, apx 6 ESE Tay Ninh W AF. Tay Ninh Pr, III Corps.

Cao Dai CP (ZD 056-028)
Along QL-1 apx 5 km WNW Phu Loc. Some sort of cmd post near Cao Dai Tunnel, Apr68. Tay Ninh Pr, III Corps.

Cao Dai Temple (XT 241-496)
See Temple of Holy See. Tay Ninh Pr, III Corps.

Cao Dai Tunnel (ZD 054-026)
QL-1 or RR tunnel (?) apx 5 km WNW Phu Loc. Thua Thien Pr, I Corps.

Cao Do Bridge (BT 3-2?)
Apparently along QL-1, near Tam Ky. Built (or rebuilt) by USN Seabees in '70. Dedication plaque etched in concrete abutment of this bridge reads: *Cao Do Bridge, Built by MCB 49, 'Can Do More' 1970*. Photo of this etching as of 1999 is at: www.deltaforce.net/aircav/tamkybt.html. Possibly A.k.a. Cau Do Bridge, and if so, QL-1 crossed the Cau Do River just south of Da Nang at apx BT 02-72? Quang Nam or Quang Tin Pr, I Corps.

Cao Do River (BT 0-7)
A.k.a. Cau Do River. Formed W edge of Marble Mtn AB SE of Da Nang. The Cau Do, Yen, Tuy Loan La Tho, Thanh Quyt, Vu Gia, Cau Lau and Thu Bon Rivers all formed part of drainage that became the Da Nang River. All were S or SW Da Nang. Quang Nam Pr, I Corps.

Cao Lanh (n/a)
Mapsheet name of L-7014-6129-4. SVN.

Cao Lanh (WS 69-56)
Apx 4 km E the Mekong River, 22 km ENE Long Xuyen, 22 km NNW Sa Dec and 48 km NNW Can Tho. 5th SF Grp CIDG Det B-43, Feb67, and also Det 50 and 83. SF Det 50 cmpd here was renamed Camp Drum in '68. Kien Phong Pr, IV Corps.

Cao Lanh Airfield (WS 705-532)
Apx 3 km S Cao Lanh, 1 km N the Mekong River 47 km NNW Can Tho, 40 km NW Vinh Long AF, 22 km NE Long Xuyen AF, 105 km SW Saigon, and 80 km W My Tho. Originally an Army Caribou strip that was only 55' wide (Caribou's wheels were 26' apart), leaving little room for error. TPC K-10D map. El. 13', 1,400' asph rwy. At 10°25'32"N-105°38'41"E. Kien Phong Pr, IV Corps.

Cao Lanh City (WS 69-70)
Capitol, Kien Phong, IV Corps.

Cao Lanh Heliport (WS 697-558)
Apx 5 km N the Mekong River, 24 km ENE Long Xuyen, 23 km NW Sa Dec and 48 km NNW Can Tho. "Heliport #543, alt 10', PSP, Fuel-A+J4. Ammo-7.62, 2.75" rockets, Ltd Landing at sod Monument Pad is prohibited," per Feb73 TAD. Kien Phong Pr, IV Corps.

Cao Lanh RFTC (WS 7-5)
RVN Regional Force Trng Ctr. Kien Phong Pr, IV Corps.

Cao Lanh SF Camp (MSF) (WS 6951-5616)
Apx 4 km E the Mekong River, 22 km ENE Long Xuyen, 22 km NNW Sa Dec and 48 km NNW Can Tho. 5th SF CIDG Det B-43, Feb67, and also Det 50 and 83. Det 50 cmpd here renamed Camp Drum in '68, per *SF Order of Battle*. Also at WS 659-560. Kien Phong Pr, IV Corps.

Cao Lanh SF Camp (old) (WS 6951-5616)
Shares same grid as Cao Lanh MSF SF Camp, so the purpose of calling one old and other new is a puzzle. Assets moved to Chi Lang. Also listed at WS 6590-5600. Grid per *SF Order of Battle*. Kien Phong Pr, IV Corps.

Cao Linh Airfield (WS 705-532?)
See Cao Lanh AF. Kien Phong Pr?, IV Corps.

Cao Song Be Airfield (XT 914-734)
See Chi Linh AF. Phuoc Long Pr, III Corps.

Cao Thang (XT 164-922)
A.k.a. FSB Victor. Apx 7 km SE Cambodia, 17 km WNW Katum, 13 km NE Thien Ngon AF and 38 km due N Tay Ninh West AF. Tay Ninh Pr, III Corps.

CAP (n/a)
Combined Action Plt. See Glossary.

CAP 1 (AT/BT)
A.k.a. Mot CAP. Apparently positioned near Chu Lai AF in 67. History of this CAP team discussed in *Mot CAP*. Quang Tin and Quang Nam Pr, I Corps.

CAP 1-1-2 (n/a)
1st CAG, Quang Ngai or Quang Tin Pr, I Corps.

CAP 1-1-3 (n/a)
1st CAG, Quang Ngai or Quang Tin Pr, I Corps.

CAP 1-1-4 (n/a)
1st CAG, Quang Ngai or Quang Tin Pr, I Corps.

CAP 1-2-7 (BT 454-053)
Ky Sanh CAP. Apx 8 km due W Chu Lai and 20 km SE Tam Ky. CAP 1-2-7 here Aug-Nov68, per HM3 Richard Groulx (medic). 1st CAG, Quang Tin Pr, I Corps.

CAP 1-3-2 (n/a)
1st CAG, Quang Ngai or Quang Tin Pr, I Corps.

CAP 1-3-5 (BS 712-972)
A.k.a. CAP Phuoc Thuan. On coast at Phuoc Thuan 1, apx 10 km N Pinkville, 800 meters E LZ Paradise, 18 km SE Chu Lai. Heavily attacked 23Apr68 by est 200 VC, inc. 65 who made amphib assault using large, round wicker-baskets. Defending CAP 1-3-5 and RFs lost 3 KIA, 11 WIA, while VC lost at least 100 KIA. CAP 1-3-5 awarded Navy Meritorious Commendation for its performance. Radio log of attack and much CAP info available at: www.capmarine.com/cap1-3-5/1-3-5log.htm. 1st CAG. Quang Ngai Pr, I Corps.

CAP 1-3-9 (BS 715-608?)
Combined Action Plt at An Phong (I). Awarded Navy Meritorious Unit Commendation for action of 13Sep69, when CAP 1-3-9 and its PF forces engaged an estimated NVA Bn. Part of its element assigned to OP George, which

overlooked An Phong (I), was also attacked. In hand-to-hand fighting, NVA were finally forced to withdraw. Part of 1st CAG, III MAF. Quang Ngai Pr?, I Corps.

CAP 2-1-2 (n/a)
2d CAG per CAP Website. Hieu Duc District, Quang Nam Pr, I Corps.

CAP 2-1-5 (n/a)
2d CAG per CAP Website. Hieu Duc District, Quang Nam Pr, I Corps.

CAP 2-2-2 (n/a)
2d CAG per CAP Website. Dai Loc District, Quang Nam Pr, I Corps.

CAP 2-2-2 (n/a)
2d CAG, Quang Nam Pr, I Corps.

CAP 2-3-10 (n/a)
The Nhon. Per John Sallinger. 2d CAG, Quang Nam Pr, I Corps.

CAP 2-3-2 (n/a)
Quang Loc Dong 1 and 2, Binh Minh 1 (BT 024-790?), Tan My (BT 013-784?). Per John Sallinger. 2d CAG, Dien Ban District, Quang Nam Pr, I Corps.

CAP 2-3-3 (n/a)
Quang Loc Tay 1 and 2, Dong Ban An 3 (BS 801-394?), Dong Cau Nhi 1 and 2 (BT 048-574?), Dong Luy Tay 1 (BT 0-5, per NIMA). Per John Sallinger. 2d CAG, Quang Nam Pr, I Corps.

CAP 2-3-4 (BT 090-575?)
Triem Trung 1. Per John Sallinger. 2d CAG, Dien Ban Dist, Quang Nam Pr, I Corps.

CAP 2-3-5 (n/a)
At Binh An. Per John Sallinger. 2d CAG, Quang Nam Pr, I Corps.

CAP 2-3-6 (n/a)
Quang Loc Tay. Per John Sallinger. 2d CAG, Dien Ban District, Quang Nam Pr, I Corps.

CAP 2-3-7 (BT 042-617?)
Phong Ngu 2. Apx Feb71, 7th Co took over its AO, and Phong Ngu 2 later became CAP 2-7-6. Per John Sallinger. 2d CAG, Dien Ban District, Quang Nam Pr, I Corps.

CAP 2-3-8 (BT 042-617?)
Phong Ngu 1. In Feb71, area became part of 7th Co AO? and possibly 2-7-5? Per John Sallinger. 2d CAG, Dien Ban District, Quang Nam Pr, I Corps.

CAP 2-3-9 (n/a)
Long Chau 1 and 2, Gia Tinh Hoa Nhan, Trieu Chau 2. Per John Sallinger. 2d CAG, Quang Nam Pr, I Corps.

CAP 2-4-3 (BT 169-578)
2d CAG. On NE outskirts of Hoi An roughly 2 km ENE the main city per Tim Duffie's CAP Vets website. 2d CAG HQ was at BT 161-572, apx 1 km SW CAP 2-4-3. Portion of L-7014 series, 1:50,000 scale map of Cap 2-4-3 and 2d CAG HQ AOs on same website under address extension: /cap2-4-3/pcktmap.htm. Richard Clark, former team member who revisited the area in May97, notes that name of ville has been changed from "Thanh Taxy" to "Thanh Tay." Quang Nam Pr, I Corps.

CAP 2-7-1 (BT 030-637)
Apx Along QL-1, apx 11 km SSE Da Nang AB. Combined Action Plt at Viem Tay (3), and 800 meters N CAP 2-7-2. Overrun night of 9May70, with nearly every Marine KIA or WIA. In brief recounting entitled *Death of 2-7-1,* Rich Thorton recalls that when his CAP 2-7-2 relief team reached the unit, only one man was left standing out of 14 Marines. [103] Also listed at BT 061-030, but grid is in ocean. Listed grid per NPIA. 2d CAG. Quang Nam Pr, I Corps.

CAP 2-7-2 (BT 030-627?)
At Thanh Quyt 1 and apparently 800 meters S Viem Tay (3). Combined Action Plt here, per John Sallinger. 2d CAG, Quang Nam Pr, I Corps.

CAP 2-7-3 (n/a)
Main location was Than Quyt (1) just E QL-1. See CAP 2-1-7. 2d CAG. Dien Ban Dist, Quang Nam Pr, I Corps.

CAP 2-7-4 (n/a)
At Thanh Quyt 2 and 5. Combined Action Plt. Per John Sallinger. Quang Nam Pr, I Corps.

CAP 2-7-5 (n/a)
Combined Action Plt. 2d CAG, Quang Nam Pr, I Corps.

CAP 2-7-10 (BT 030-637?)
At Viem Tay 1. Combined Action Plt, per John Sallinger. 2d CAG, Quang Nam Pr, I Corps.

CAP 2-8-3 (n/a)
2d CAG per CAP Website. Hoa Vang District, 2d CAG, Quang Nam Pr, I Corps.

CAP 2-9-1 (n/a)
CAP 2-9-1, 2d CAG. Per Tim Duffie. I Corps.

CAP 2-9-1 (n/a)
Combined Action Plt 2-9-1 was attacked by 2 reinforced Cos of NVA at 2315hrs 21Nov68. Initial attack was against 5th Marine positions but then shifted to CAP cmpd. Unit recommended for Meritorious Unit citation. [104] 2d CAG, Duc Duc District, Quang Nam Pr, I Corps.

CAP 3-1 (AT 944-701?)
See Tuy Loan. Thua Thien Pr, I Corps.

CAP 3-2 (ZD 083-005?)
Per George Clancy, former 3-2 member, CAP 3-2 was along QL-1 apx 24-32 km SE Phu Bai. Grid is for Cho Cau Hai ville in Phu Loc. Ca Cau Hai is at ZD 090-007 and thought to be site of CAP 3-2-1, but locations may be reversed? 3d CAG, Thua Thien Pr, I Corps.

CAP 3-2-1 (ZD 090-007?)
Per George Clancy, former 3-2 member, CAP 3-2-1 was at Cau Hai (Ca Cau Hai), on QL-1 along S edge of very large and picturesque Cau Hai Bay. Apx 30 km SE Phu Bai and 1.5 km due W FSB Tomahawk. AO was from Cau Hai Bay to Loc Tri, an area they called The Basin. Cau Hai was between FSB Tomahawk and 4 km SE FSB Roy (FSB 2 km ENE Bac Thach and adj to Phuoc Tuong). CAP 3-2's HQ was at Cau Ha. Grid is for Ca Cau Hai ville ENE Phu Loc. Cho Cau Hai is at ZD 090-007 (in Phu Loc) and thought to be site of CAP 3-2 HQ, but locations may be reversed? 3d CAG, Thua Thien Pr, I Corps. [105]

CAP 3-4-3 (n/a)
Combined Action Plt. 3d CAG, Thua Thien Pr, I Corps.

CAP 3-5-1 (YD 921-111?)
Per Ed Saragoza, with unit '70-71, was apx 4 km SE Phu Bai CB along QL-1, among a group of villes known collectively as Loc Son. On 4Jun70, the team ambushed and killed 14 VC. Est grid. Thua Thien Pr, I Corps.

CAP 4-1-3 (YD or XD?)
Combined Action Plt. 4th CAG, Quang Tri Pr, I Corps.

CAP Alpha 1 (YD 882-172)
A.k.a. CAC One or Phu Bai One. Apx 2 km N Phu Bai AF and 1 km S Song Loi Nong River in area known as Thuy Long. This USMC Combined Action Plt/PF cmpd served Luong Van, which contained 4 separate hamlets. Thua Thien Pr, I Corps.

CAP Alpha 2 (YD 916-157)
A.k.a. Phu Bai 2. Marine CAP Team cmpd apx 2 km due W the W end of Hue/Phu Bai airfield's main rwy, 1.5 km SW the Song Dai Giang River and, 2.3 km NE QL-1 and roughly midway between Thon Tan To and Thon To Da. Thua Thien Pr, I Corps.

CAP Alpha (YD)
Combined Action Plt Alpha. 1st CAP Teams in VN. Initiated apx 1Aug65, and by '68, consisted of several units spread around Phu Bai complex, the RR tracks that paralleled QL-1 nearby, and QL-1 itself, between Hue and Phu Bai. Most set in low-lying sites along rivers and in rice-growing areas several km inland from coast and up to base of Nam Hoa Mtns. Thua Thien Pr, I Corps.

CAP Bravo 3 (n/a)
3rd CAG per CAP Website. Quang Nam Pr, I Corps.

CAP Bravo 4 (n/a)
3rd CAG per CAP Website. Quang Nam Pr, I Corps.

CAP Bravo (n/a)
Combined Action Plt. I Corps.

CAP Delta (n/a)
Combined Action Plt. See www.capmarine.com. I Corps.

Cap des Hirondelles (CR 1-2)
A.k.a. Mui Yen. Binh Dinh or Phu Yen Pr, II Corps.

CAP Echo 2 (ZC 02-44?)
Combined Action Plt at Hoa Hiep. Listed on CAP Website at http://w3.one.net/~timd/cap. Photo of site on p 63, *A Contagion of War* vol, *Vietnam Experience* series. Quang Nam Pr, I Corps.

CAP Echo 3 (n/a)
Combined Action Plt. See www.capmarine.com. I Corps.

CAP Echo 4 (n/a)
Combined Action Plt. See www.capmarine.com. I Corps.

CAP Echo (n/a)
Combined Action Plt. See www.capmarine.com. I Corps.

CAP Hotel 1 (n/a)
Combined Action Plt. See www.capmarine.com. I Corps.

CAP Hotel 8 (n/a)
3rd CAG per CAP Website. Thua Thien Pr, I Corps.

CAP India 2 (n/a)
Combined Action Plt. I Corps.

CAP Khe Sanh (XD)
See CAP 0-3. Quang Tri Pr, I Corps.

CAP Ky Hoa (n/a)
See Ky Hoa CAP. Quang Tin Pr, I Corps.

CAP One (AT/BT)
See CAP 1. Quang Tin and Quang Nam Pr, I Corps.

CAP Oscar 1 (XD 856-886)
At Huong Hoa District HQ, apx 600 meters NW the Old French Fort, 3 km due S Khe Sanh CB and in Khe Sanh ville. 4th CAG per CAP Website. Quang Tri Pr, I Corps.

CAP Oscar 2 (XD 856-386)
Combined Action Plt at Huong Hoa District HQ, apx 600 meters NW the Old French Fort, 3 km due S Khe Sanh CB and in Khe Sanh. Per Jim Taylor, team worked with Bru tribesman from Vil Bu, Vil Ch'eng, Vil Tacun and Vil C'on. When CAC Oscar withdrew to Khe Sanh CB after initial attacks against their vulnerable positions outside base during Tet '68, the Marines did not want to accept O-2's Bru comrades, so CAC Oscar asked for and received a spot in defensive perimeter of SF's FOB-3 along Khe Sanh CB's southern edge and along QL-9. 4th CAG per Tim Duffie's CAP Vets website. Quang Tri Pr, I Corps.

CAP Oscar 3 (XD 842-410)
A.k.a. CAP O-3. At both XD 842-410 and XD 843-414. Combined Action Plt assigned to Ta Cong. in Khe Sanh Valley. Originally on S side of QL-9 apx 800 meters S the W end of main Khe Sanh AF but its 11 Marines and 30 Bru evacuated that site 21Jan68 and blew up position as they left. During siege, its elements held part of S perimeter perpendicular to and N of QL-9, and apx 300 meters N its original position. Mislabeled but detailed map of both positions at p 344 *of Valley of Decision*. See CAC Oscar. Quang Tri Pr, I Corps.

CAP Oscar HQ (XD 856-386)
At Huong Hoa District HQ, apx 600 meters NW the Old French Fort, 3 km due S Khe Sanh CB and in Khe Sanh ville. Per Jim Taylor, Oscar Co/III MAF was originally designated as "SU-7." Detailed accounting of CAP Oscar units at Khe Sanh can be found in *Valley of Decision*, and on map, p 27. See CAC Oscar and CAP Oscar 2 for interesting detail. Quang Tri Pr, I Corps. [106]

CAP Papa (YD 13-59)
Apparently among 1st CAC/CAP units established N of Da Nang in Feb '67. CAC Papa HQ was set-up in Cam Lo along QL-9 about 8 km W Cam Hu. CO's call-sign was Tiger Papa, and its two 15-man plts had call-signs of Tiger Papa 2 and Tiger Papa 3. TP-3 was at Cam Hu. Discussed in *A Voice of Hope*. Quang Tri Pr, I Corps.

CAP Papa 2 (n/a)
See CAC Papa. Combined Action Plt. I Corps.

CAP Papa 3 (YD 21-63)
See CAC Papa 3. Quang Tri Pr, I Corps.

CAP Papa 6 (YD 0-5)
Danny Hatch, E/2d/9th 67-68, tells us he was transferred to 3d CAG, CAP Papa 6 Jan68, and that it was between Cam Lo and Camp Carroll in a large, tin refugee ville right on QL-9. Quang Tri Pr, I Corps.

CAP Phuoc Thuan (BS 712-972)
See CAP 1-3-5. Quang Ngai Pr, I Corps.

CAP Phuoc Thuan (BS 712-972)
See CAP 1-3-5. Quang Ngai Pr, I Corps.

CAP Romeo 1 (n/a)
1st CAG per CAP Website. I Corps.

Cap Saint Jacques (Xa Vung Tau) (n/a)
Mapsheet L-7014-6429-4. Sheet name: Xa Vung Tau (Cap Saint Jacques). SVN.

Cap St. Jacques Airfield (YS 300-473)
See Vung Tau AF. Phuoc Tuy Pr, III Corps.

CAP SU-7 (n/a)
Per Jim Taylor, Oscar Co/III MAF was originally designated as SU-7. Detailed accounting of CAP Oscar units at Khe Sanh can be found in *Valley of Decision*. See CAC Oscar. Quang Tri Pr, I Corps.

CAP Ta Chong (XD)
See CAP 0-3. Quang Tri Pr, I Corps.

CAP Teams (US Army) (n/a)
See Glossary.
CAP Teams (USMC) (n/a)
See Glossary.
CAP, Mobile Teams (n/a)
See Glossary.
Cape, FSB (YS 307-818)
Apx 19 km NW Nui Dat, 1.5 km NW FSB Colorado and 6 km SSE FSB Digger's Rest. RAR, RNZA or US FSB with one 105 Bty of RAA here Oct69. On 1ATF NCO trng map per John Hollett. Bien Hoa Pr, III Corps.
Cape An Hoa (BT 5-1)
Mui An Hoa. Coastal point at 15°31'N-108°41'E. On ND49-01 JOG. Quang Tin Pr, I Corps.
Cape An Hou (BT 5-1)
Mui An Hoa. Coastal point at 15°31'N-108°41'E. On ND49-01 JOG. Quang Tin Pr, I Corps.
Cape Ba Ke (YS 7-6)
Mui Ba Kiem. Coastal point at 10°31'N-107°31'E. On NC48-08 JOG. Phuoc Tuy Pr, III Corps.
Cape Ba Kiem (YS 7-6)
Mui Ba Kiem. Coastal point at 10°31'N-107°31'E. On NC48-08 JOG. Phuoc Tuy Pr, III Corps.
Cape Bantan (BT 6-0)
Mui Nam Tram. Coastal point at 15°25'N-108°50'E. On ND49-01 JOG. Quang Tin Pr, I Corps.
Cape Boung Quioua (XE 6-8)
A.k.a. Mui Ong. Coastal point at 17°57'N-106°31'E. On NE48-12 JOG. NVN.
Cape Bouton (WG 8-2)
A.k.a. Da Ong Coc. Coastal point at 19°13'N-105°46'E. On NE48-03 JOG. NVN.
Cape Bung Kioua (XE 6-8)
A.k.a. Mui Ongi. Coastal point at 17°57'N-106°31'E. On NE48-12 JOG. NVN.
Cape Chao (WG 9-8)
Coastal point at 19°44'N-105°52'E. NE48-03 map. NVN.
Cape Choa (WG 9-8)
A.k.a. Cape Chaoe. Coastal point at 19°44'N-105°52'E. On NE48-03 JOG. NVN.
Cape Chon May Ouest (ZD 1-0)
A.k.a. Mui Chon May Tay. Coastal point at 16°21'N-107°57'E. NE48-16. Thua Thien Pr, I Corps.
Cape Chumai West (ZD 1-0)
Mui Chon May Tay. Coastal point at 16°21'N-107°57'E. NE48-16 JOG. Thua Thien Pr, I Corps.
Cape de Hirondelles (CR 1-2)
A.k.a. Mui Yen. Coastal point at 13°45'N-109°18'E. On ND49-09 JOG. Binh Dinh Pr, II Corps.
Cape Falaise (WG 7-1)
A.k.a. Da Dau Rong. Coastal point at 19°06'N-105°45'E. On NE48-03 JOG. NVN.
Cape Kamao (VQ 7-5)
Mui Ca Mau. Coastal point at 8°38'N-104°44'E. On NC48-15 JOG. An Xuyen Pr, IV Corps.
Cape Koan Lan (YJ 5-0)
A.k.a. Cape Quan Lan. Coastal point at 20°48'N-107°28'E. On NF48-16 JOG. NVN.
Cape Kwala (US 9-5)
Mui Kwala. Coastal point at 10°27'N-104°00'E. On NC48-05 JOG. Kien Giang Pr, IV Corps.
Cape Lai (YD 2-9)
A.k.a. Mui Lai. Coastal point at 17°07'N-107°07'E. On NE48-12 JOG. NVN.
Cape Lay (YD 2-8)
A.k.a. Mui Lay. Coastal point at 17°05'N-107°07'E. On NE48-12 JOG. NVN?
Cape Mia (BS 8-4)
Coastal point at 14°50'N-109°00'E. On ND49-05 JOG. Quang Ngai Pr, I Corps.
Cape Mui Dinh Lighthouse (BN 84-57)
Apx 10 km ESE peak of Nui Ba Dec Mtn, and 22 km due S Phan Rang. Ninh Thuan Pr, II Corps.
Cape Mui Dong (XF 5-0)
A.k.a. Mui Ron. Coastal point at 18°07'N-106°27'E. On NE48-07 JOG. NVN.
Cape Mui Duong (XF 5-0)
A.k.a. Mui Ron. Coastal point at 18°07'N-106°27'E. On NE48-07 JOG. NVN.
Cape Mui Nai Lighthouse (VS 39-46)
Apx 5 km WSW Ha Tien. Kien Gang Pr, IV Corps.
Cape Muy Ang (XE 6-8)
A.k.a. Mui Ong. Coastal point at 17°57'N-106°31'E. On NE48-12 JOG. NVN.
Cape Nam Tram (BT 6-0)
Mui Nam Tram. Coastal point at 15°25'N-108°50'E. On ND49-01 JOG. Quang Tin Pr, I Corps.
Cape Quan Lan (YJ 5-0)
Coastal point at 20°48'N-107°28'E. NF48-16 map. NVN.
Cape Ron (XF 5-0)
A.k.a. Mui Ron and Mui Duong. Coastal point at 18°07'N-106°27'E. On NE48-07 JOG. NVN.
Cape Sainte Anne (WF 7-8)
A.k.a. Mui Ga. Coastal point at 18°50'N-105°43'E. On NE48-07 JOG. NVN.
Cape San Ho (CR 1-2)
A.k.a. Mui Yen. Coastal point at 13°45'N-109°18'E. On ND49-09 JOG. Binh Dinh Pr, II Corps.
Cape Sec (CP 1-6)
A.k.a. Mui Bai Chuoampong. Coastal point at 12°23'N-109°20'E. On ND49-13 JOG.
Cape Sot (XF 0-4)
A.k.a. Mui Sot. Coastal point at 18°28'N-105°57'E. On NE48-07 JOG. NVN.
Cape St. Jacques (YS 38-44)
A.k.a. Vung Tau Peninsula, Cape Vung Tau, and Mui Vung Tau. Apx 65 km SW Saigon and site of major Vung Tau R&R complex, 1ATF ANZAC facilities, seaport and C-130 capable airfield. Noted for its extreme beauty and sparkling beaches. For many centuries a prime Vietnamese vacation site. See Vung Tau for more detailed descriptions and facilities. At 10°19'N-107°05'E, per NC48-07. Phuoc Tuy Pr, III Corps.
Cape Ta Lus (WG 8-3)
A.k.a. Mui Ta Lus. Coastal point at 19°16'N-105°47'E. On NE48-03 JOG. NVN.
Cape Ti Oan (YS 4-4)
Mui Ky Van. Coastal point at 10°23'N-107°16'E. On NC48-08 JOG. Phuoc Tuy Pr, III Corps.
Cape Tiwan (YS 4-4)
Mui Ky Van. Coastal point at 10°23'N-107°16'E. On NC48-08 JOG. Phuoc Tuy Pr, III Corps.

Cape Tuoan (YS 4-4)
Mui Ky Van. Coastal point at 10°23'N-107°16'E. On NC48-08 JOG. Phuoc Tuy Pr, III Corps.
Cape Varalla (CQ 3-2)
A.k.a. Mui Ke Ga and Cape Varella. See Varella Khanh Hoa Pr, II Corps.
Cape Varella Lighthouse (CQ 32-26)
Apx 20 km SE Tuy Hoa AF. Phu Yen Pr, II Corps.
Cape Varella (CQ 35-25)
A.k.a. Mui Ke Ga and Cape Varalla. Easternmost point of SVN. Apx 30 km SSE Tuy Hoa and 75 km NNE Nha Trang, and at 12°53'N-109°28'E. On JOG map ND49-13. Phu Yen Pr, II Corps.
Cape Varella, False (CN 0-9)
Mui Da Vach. Coastal point at 11°43'N-109°14'E. On NC49-01 JOG. Ninh Thuan Pr, II Corps.
Cape Varella, Faux (CN 0-9)
Mui Da Vach. Coastal point at 11°43'N-109°14'E. On NC49-01 JOG. Ninh Thuan Pr, II Corps.
Cape Vungchua (XE 6-8)
A.k.a. Mui Ong. Coastal point at 17°57'N-106°31'E. On NE48-12 JOG. NVN.
Capital Military Zone (XS/XT)
Properly known as "Special Capital Zone" A Combat Tactical Zone inc Saigon and much of Gia Dinh Pr. One of five CTZs in SVN, others being I, II, III and IV Corps.
Capital Regiment, The (n/a)
See Glossary.
Capitol BEQ (XS 828-887)
At 107 Dong Khanh St., Cholon, (Capitol Enlisted Open Mess), Apr 63, 95 rms, Saigon. Data per *Vietnam Military Lore, 1959-1973*. Gia Dinh Pr, III Corps.
Caprice (n/a)
6Apr70, XXIV Corps proposed III MAF FSB name.
Capitaine, USS (n/a)
AGSS-336. Submarine, per Ralph Fries.
Cara, LZ? (XT or XU?)
See Cara Camile. III Corps.
Cara Camile, LZ? (XT or XU?)
Location unknown. 1st Cav Div. Name per Dan Gillotti, 15th Arty Assn. III Corps.
Caravelle (n/a)
See Glossary.
Caravelle, The Hotel (XS 865-914)
Saigon hotel where in Apr63, 18 very prominent Viets denounced Diem Regime because its policies were forcing peasants into arms of communists. Per *Twenty Years and Twenty Days*, p 27.
Carbine, LZ (BR 762-968)
In An Lo River Valley, apx 12 km WSW LZ English. Oct66. Binh Dinh Pr, II Corps.
Card, USNS (n/a)
A.k.a. T-AKV 40, Aircraft Ferry. Also listed as *USS Card*? In '64, the MSTS's Acft Carrier *USNS Card* (civil service crew aboard) was sunk by mine in Saigon harbor. Data per www.fred.net/rphumm/info.html.
Cardamon Mountains (n/a)
Mtn range along N border of Cambodia that was controlled by communist forces during 1st Indochina War. See map in *Street Without Joy*, p 277.
Cardinal, LZ (BT 128-388)
Apx 5 km S LZ Baldy and 38 km SSW Da Nang AB. May67. Quang Nam Pr, I Corps.
Cardinal, LZ (XD 939-611)
Apx 20 km WNW Cam Lo, 42 km WNW Quang Tri, 5 km WNW FSB Fuller and 4 km S of DMZ. 3d Mar Div, '69. Also listed at XD 938-612. Apr70 XXIV Corps grid per Don Armstrong. Quang Tri Pr, I Corps.
Carenten, LZ (BS 843-371)
A.k.a. Carenten Basecamp. Apx 8 km due W Duc Pho AF/LZ Bronco, 38 km ESE Quang Ngai and 7 km W QL-1. Trng area for 11th LIB, when they 1st arrived in '67. Per *Mad Minutes*, p 360, built as Carenten Basecamp in Jan66 by elements of 2/502d/101st Abn. Apparently located in part of abnd ville. Americal list. Quang Ngai Pr, I Corps.
Carentan II, Operation (n/a)
1Apr-31May68. 101st Abn/82d Abn's 3d Bde/ARVN 1st Div op. 2,100 rptd NVA/VC KIA, per *Vietnam Order of Battle*, pp 9-14. Thua Thien/Quang Tri Prvs, I Corps.
Carenton Basecamp (BS 842-372)
See Carentan. Quang Ngai Pr, I Corps.
Caribou, LZ (XD 854-216)
At S end Vietnam Salient, apx 2 km NE Lang Lio, 20 km due S Khe Sanh CB, SSE FSB Saigon, SW FSB Torch and 60 km SW Quang Tri. Apr70 XXIV Corps grid per Don Armstrong. Quang Tri Pr, I Corps.
Caridon, FSB (n/a)
Reported as 101st Abn FSB. No data.
Carlson, FSB (XU 504-186)
In Cambodia apx 5 km SW tip of Angel's Wing, 5 km W the SVN border, 25 km NW Memot, 16 km SSW Snuol and 26 km NW Loc Ninh. Grid per *11th ACR Cambodia Invasion AAR, 1st Cav Div, May-Jun70*, courtesy Lou Rochat.[107] Cambodia.
Carmen, FSB (YS 438-588)
Apx 8.5 km due S Nui Dat, 5.5 km due N FSB Isa and 6.5 km SW FSB Horseshoe. On 1ATF NCO trng map per John Hollett. Phuoc Tuy Pr, III Corps.
Carmen, LZ? (BS 650-356)
In river valley, apx 17 km W Duc Pho/QL-1 and 7 km E Ba To. 1st Cav Div or Americal? Name/grid per Dan Gillotti. Quang Ngai Pr, I Corps.
Carmen, LZ/FSB (ZA 181-774)
A.k.a. Hill 865 (or Hill 727?). E of TL-3B, apx 12 to 13 km SW Kontum and 13 km NE Plei Mrong. Per Dick Arnold, in 1st/35th Inf Bn logs, A Co built Carmen on Hill 865, beginning 10Sep68, at ZA 181-774. Cited in *Time Heals No Wounds*, p 207, where described as follows: "The hilltop had no trees, just large rocks on one side and a large boulder in center." 4th Div AO. Kontum Pr, II Corps.
Carnot, Ft. Airfield (n/a)
On NW border of Laos, apx 340 km NW Vientiane on Feb67 Natl Geo map. El. 1,200'. Laos.
Carol, FSB (YD 343-194) '
See LZ Carrol and FSB Ripcord. Thua Thien Pr, I Corps.
Carol, FSB/LZ (YT 058-888)
Apx 1 km W LTL-1A, apx 5 km N Ap Thuan Hoa, 42 km NNE Phuoc Vinh AF, 14 km N Dong Xoai and 28 km due E An Loc. Per Tom Skelly, base had large living area built upon and with PSP that in some places was 3 and 4 stories high, with one or two stories extending below ground.

1st/12th Cav followed 2d/12th Cav here. 2d/7th. 1st/12th Cav, 1st Cav, '69, AO Commanche Warrior. Peter Cole credits this grid to *1st Cav Div Op Rpts of Nov68-Jan69* and *Feb-Apr69*. See FSB Carol at YT 047-895. Phuoc Long, III Corps.

Carol, FSB/LZ (YT 290-100)
Along QL-1, apx 17 km W Xuan Loc. Mar71. Bien Hoa Pr, III Corps.

Carol, LZ (BR 693-729)
At or near Nghia Dien, apx 28 km SW Bong Song and 10 km SSW Phu Xuan. 173d Abn. Name/grid per Dan Gillotti, 15th Arty Assn. Binh Dinh Pr, II Corps.

Carol, LZ (BR 927-787)
Apx 33 km WSW Kontum, 2 km NE Polei Ya Dip Ya Rac, and 23 km NW Plei Mrong. A Bty, 2d/17th Arty here 11Nov66, suptg 1st/9th and 2d/12th Cav. Data per Jack Picciolo. Binh Dinh Pr, II Corps.

Carol, LZ (XT 958-888)
Apx 17 km NNW Dong Xoai and 20 km E An Loc. Jan69. Phuoc Long Pr?, III Corps.

Carol, LZ (YA 596-494)
On Cambodian border at S entrance to Plei Trap Valley, 5 km NE Phum To Lay (Cambodia) and 64 km W Pleiku. Jan66. Pleiku Pr, II Corps.

Carol, LZ (YD 342-192)
See Carroll at grid. Thua Thien Pr, I Corps.

Carolina, LZ (YD 056-619)
Apx 8 km WNW Cam Lo, 5 km N QL-9 and 29 km WNW Quang Tri. Apr70 XXIV Corps grid per Don Armstrong. Quang Tri Pr, I Corps.

Caroline County, USS (n/a)
LST-525. MRF Base Ship. Decom 15Sep74. III/IV Corps.

Caroline, FSB (XT 273-768?)
See Carolyn at grid. Tay Ninh Pr, III Corps.

Caroline, FSB (XT 276-788)
See Carolyn at grid. Tay Ninh Pr, III Corps.

Caroline, FSB (XT 305-498)
Apx 13 km ESE Tay Ninh W AF and 18 km W to WNW Dau Tieng. Per Larry Criteser, FSBs Martha, Betty and Caroline were within 4 to 5 km of one another; with B/4/9 at Betty, C/4/9 at Caroline and A/4/9 Manchus, 25th Inf Div here and at Martha in '67. Base listed concurrently with Nui Ba Den in USAF Herbicide gallonage rpt that also indicates total gallonages of following agents were sprayed within an 8 km radius of those two features: Orange, 50020; White, 66500; Blue, 2100. Also listed at XT 300-490. Hau Nghia/Tay Ninh Pr border, III Corps.

Carolyn (n/a)
6Apr70, XXIV Corps proposed Americal FSB name.

Carolyn, FSB (BS 300-970)
Apx 25 km WSW Chu Lai, 22 km due S Tam Ky's major AF and about 5 km S FSB Hustler. Americal List. Quang Tin Pr, I Corps.

Carolyn, FSB (XT?)
Possibly in XT UTM. Cited in *11th ACR Cambodia Invasion AAR, 1st Cav Div, May-Jun70*, courtesy Lou Rochat. III Corps.[108]

Carolyn, FSB/LZ (XT 265-786)
Apx 13 km SW Katum AF. Also listed at XT 360-780 Apr-May69, and 278-788, Jul70. Tay Ninh Pr, III Corps.

Carolyn, FSB (XT 273-768?)
A.k.a. LZ Caroline. This Americal Assn website grid is in dispute (see Carolyn at XT 276-788 for discussion). Apx 2 km E Rte 4 and 18 km due N Nui Ba Den. Was also NW LZ Ike, SW LZ Becky and NNE FSB St. Barbara. Major NVA attack by NVA 95C Rgt, 6May69, as part of plan to attack Tay Ninh.[109] 2d/19th Arty, 2d/8th Cav, 1st Cav here then. Also listed at XT 278-788 per Peter Cole. Tay Ninh Pr, III Corps.

Carolyn, FSB (XT 276-788)
A.k.a. LZ Caroline. Per Frank Penk Jr., the Americal Assn website grid for this base (XT 273-768) is definitely incorrect. Penk says, "Carolyn was at Prek Klok, and at very N end of PSP airstrip on east side of TL-4." Apx 21 km due N Nui Ba Den, 29 km NNE Tay Ninh city and 13 km SSW Katum. Also listed at XT 278-788, per Peter Cole. Tay Ninh Pr, III Corps.

Caron, USS (n/a)
DD-970. SVN

Carp, LZ (BT 509-052)
Inside USMC complex at Chu Lai, immed W QL-1 and 3 km due W the N end of the Chu Lai AB main rwy. 2d/7th Marines lifted out of this LZ, 21Apr66, at start of Op Hot Springs. See *Utter's Battalion*, p 310. Mar-Apr69. Quang Tin Pr, I Corps.

Carpenter's Hill (ZB 1-5?)
A.k.a. Carpenter's Mtn or OK Corral Hill. Apx 2 km N Toumorong Outpost, 1 km NE Dak Konong and Hill 1073, and 3 km NE LZ Lima Zulu. The Hill upon which William S. Carpenter, Jr. (famous West Point football player known as "The Lonesome End") was awarded MOH during Battle of Toumorong. During fight, he called for acft to drop Napalm on his own position when he felt his Co was being overrun, 8-9Jun66. See *Battles in the Monsoon*, pp 359-384. Kontum Pr, II Corps.

Carrol, LZ (YD 343-194)
A.k.a. Hill 927, Cheeseburger Hill, and FSB Ripcord. Apx 38 km due W Hue, 12 km NE the N end of A Shau Valley, 12 km NW FSB Maureen, 12 km SSE FSB O'Reilly, 5 km WNW FSB Granite, 2 km WNW Hill 805 and 1 km E Hill 1000. Apparently built by 1st Cav as FSB Carol in '68. Occupied by elements of 2d/506th Inf, 101st Abn and 2d/1st ARVN Rgt in Jan69, during Op Ohio Rapids. 2d/506th, again reopened it as FSB Ripcord by ground assault, 11Apr70, during Op Chicago Peak. See FSB Ripcord. Thua Thien Pr, I Corps.

Carroll, Camp (YD 063-547)
A.k.a. Artillery Plateau, Camp J. J. Carroll and FSB Tan Lam. S of QL-9, apx 1 km SW peak Nui Kiem (Hill 250), 7 km SW Cam Lo, 5 km NW Mai Loc, 8 km E to ESE the Rockpile, 26 km W to WNW Quang Tri. Originally named Artillery Plateau, but renamed 10Nov66, to honor Capt. James J. Carroll, USMC, CO K/3d/4th Marines, KIA 27Sep66 by friendly fire (improperly registered tank rounds) on Hill 400 while he was directing fire supt for attack on Hill 484. By Lam Son 719, was under ARVN control as FSB Tan Lam (2d ARVN Inf Rgt) per HQ 3d Bde/101st Abn Op Rpt of 30Apr71. 12th Marine Arty '67, including four-155s, six-105s here and then, in late Sep67, four-175s of Army's 6th/27th Arty were added for long range supt of Khe Sanh (175mm total later increase to six

tubes).[110] 2d/2d ARVN Inf Div dismantled Vandegrift CB in Oct69, and left over materials were used at Camp Carroll. Also listed at YD 063-544. Quang Tri Pr, I Corps.

Carroll, FSB (YD 062-548)
See Camp Carroll. Jul70. Quang Tri Pr, I Corps.

Carroll, FSB (YD 348-193)
A.k.a. FSB Ripcord (also Carol). Aug69 Also listed at YD 342-192 and 344-195, Jan-Aug68. Thua Thien Pr, I Corps.

Carroll, J. J. Camp (YD 063-547)
See Carroll, Camp. Quang Tri Pr, I Corps.

Carronade (n/a)
6Apr70, XXIV Corps proposed III MAF FSB name.

Carronade, USS (n/a)
A.k.a. IFS 1. In Apr66, rocket firing platforms of *USS Carronade* (IFS 1) and *St. Francis River* (LSMR 525) reinforced the Naval Gunfire Supt Unit off I Corps. In May67, *USS Clarion River* (LSMR 409) and *White River* (LSMR 536) were added. SVN.

Carrow, Camp (n/a)
A.k.a. Trang SF camp, per *SF Order of Battle*. Thailand.

Carry, FSB (YT 15-13)
Apx 6 km ESE Bien Hoa AB and immed NW Plantation AF about 26 km NE Saigon. Per Frank Penk, Jr., it was, "Marked on my map as an Australian FSB. IIFFV FSB? Near Bien Hoa AB. Grid/data per Frank Penk, Jr. Bien Hoa Pr, III Corps.

Carter, Camp (BT 06-73?)
Near Marble Mtn AF, SE of Da Nang. HQ 3d Marine Rgt and named to honor PFC Bruce W Carter, USMC, RTO, H/2d/3d Mar, 3d Mar Div, KIA 7Aug69, during Op Idaho Canyon, awarded MOH for throwing himself on grenade to save lives of men in his squad. Quang Nam Pr, I Corps.[111]

Carter Hall, USS (n/a)
LSD-3. Lndg. Ship, Dock, per Ralph Fries.

Cascade d' Argent (n/a)
The Silver Cascade. See Tam Do. NVN.

Casevac'd (n/a)
See Glossary.

Cash, LZ (YD 029-479)
Apx 4 km NE Ca Lu AF, 2 km Thon Hung Cat and 7 km WSW Mai Loc. Apr70 XXIV Corps grid per Don Armstrong. Quang Tri Pr, I Corps.

Casper, LZ (XD 847-646)
A.k.a. LZ Catalina, or built nearby. At S boundary DMZ, apx 1 km W Hill 696, 23 km due N Khe Sanh CB and 60 km WNW Quang Tri. Apr70 XXIV Corps grid per Don Armstrong. Quang Tri Pr, I Corps.

Cass Park I and II, Operations (AT)
See Vuong River Valley entry. Quang Nam Pr, I Corps.

Castan, Sam (BR 64-62?)
See Glossary.

Caster, LZ (BR 162-334)
Apx 34 km WSW An Khe. Sep69. Pleiku Pr, II Corps.

Castle, Camp (YS 140-980)
At or near Long Thanh North AF. Oct67-Apr68. Bien Hoa Pr, III Corps.

Castle, LZ? (YA 841-091)
Apx 5 km from Cambodia, 10 km NNW peak of Chu Pong Mtn and 53 km SW Pleiku. Nature of site unknown. Jan66. Pleiku Pr, II Corps.

Castle Army Airfield (YT 016-153)
A.k.a. Castle Field and/or Castle Heliport. At Bien Hoa AB. See Bien Hoa listings. Bien Hoa Pr, III Corps.

Castle Compound (YT 016-153)
Army base along N edge of Bien Hoa AB. The base or a cmpd within it apparently had this name, and apparently airstrip here also named Castle. 101st Abn, 1st Cav and HQ of 20th Engr Bde here at various times. Data per Frank Penk, Jr. Gia Dinh Pr, III Corps.

Castle Courier (n/a)
See Glossary.

Castle Heliport (YT 016-153)
Heliport in Army cmpd along N edge of Bien Hoa AB. 101st Abn, 1st Cav and HQ of 20th Engr Bde here at various times. Grid/name from '69 TAD per Frank Penk, Jr; not in '73 TAD. Bien Hoa Pr, III Corps.

Castle Rock, USCGC (n/a)
WHEC 383. 9Jul71-21Dec71. Sqdn 3 CGC, during CG's 8th deployment. Given to SVN Govt as CG left SVN.

Castle, OP (YD 663-225)
See OP Castle. Thua Thien Pr, I Corps.

Castor, Operation (TJ 94-67)
Op to secure Dien Bien Phu Valley (Viet for "Seat of Border Administration") along Nam Yum River about 290 km W Hanoi. Led to carefully planned and massive Vietminh siege/assault of French forces here and, ultimately, the end of the 1st Indochina War. Op began with para assault at 10:30 a.m., 20Nov53, and ended in total defeat and surrender of DBP's French forces at 5 p.m., 7May54. See Dien Bien Phu. Tonkin, NVN.

Castor, USS (n/a)
AKS-1. Amphib Attack. Cargo.

Castro, LZ/FSB (BR 728-774)
In valley apx 7 km SW Ha Tay AF. Oct66-Jan67. Cited in 1st Cav VN *Yearbook* Aug65-Dec69, at p 89, per Peter Cole. Binh Dinh Pr, II Corps.

Casualty Landmarks (n/a)
See Glossary.

Cat, LZ (BN 218-538)
Apx 11 km NNW Song Mao AF. Mar67. Binh Thuan Pr, II Corps.

Cat, LZ (YA 947-896?)
Apx 1 km N LZ Alamo (Hill 1124), 8 km SW Polei Kleng and 28 km due W Kontum. 2d/17th Arty here supt 1st Cav, 8Aug66. Per Jack Picciolo. Kontum Pr, II Corps.

Cat Airfield, LZ (YV 944-896)
A.k.a. Cat AF. Apx 12 km E Cambodian border, 27 km NNW Tieu Atar AF, 43 km WSW Phu Nhon AF and 64 km SSW Pleiku. "Check security, abnd, field mortared, Active Drop Zone, AF # VA2-266," in Aug69 TAD per Frank Penk, Jr. Not in Feb73 TAD. Pleiku Pr, II Corps.

Cat Ba (n/a)
Mapsheet name of L-7014-6450-3. NVN only.

Cat Ba National Park (YJ 10-00)
On Cat Ba Island, an 18 x 12 km isle in South Chin Sea, apx 25 km due E Haiphong. Considered by many as Vietnam's most beautiful national park. Numerous lakes, waterfalls and grottoes are found among its limestone hills (highest is 331 meters). Virtually all its surface streams are seasonal and flow into caves, becoming underground streams before emptying into sea. As a result, there are few

permanent lakes, largest of which, Ech Lake, is 3 hectares in size. High winds also limit vegetation. NVN.

Cat Bi (XJ 7-0?)
A.k.a. Catbai. AFs here struck by Carrier TF-77 attempts to blunt NVA Tet '68 Offensive. NVN.

Cat Fours (n/a)
A.k.a. Category Four Enlistees. See Project 100,000.

Cat Lai (XS 95-89)
On N shore of Song Dong Nai River, apx 5 km E its confluence with the Saigon River, 10 km W Saigon and just NW Dog Bone Island. Cat Lai was the stream "lighterage" area where munitions were transferred from ship to barge en route Long Binh Depot (see Cogido). Gia Dinh or Bien Hoa Pr, HQ, 199th LIB, III Corps. [112]

Cat Lai Navy ISB (XS 95-89?)
USN Intermediate Supt Base, '65-7, per MRF Assn Website. Cat Lai was the stream "lighterage" area where munitions were transferred from ship to barge en route Long Binh Depot (see Cogido). Gia Dinh or Bien Hoa Pr, III Corps. [113]

Cat Lai Terminal (XS 950-890)
In old fort on N bank of Dong Nai River, apx 15 km ESE Tan Son Nhut AB and 1.5 km W of LTL-25. Built by French prior to WWII. Home to 11th Trans Bn. NCO club here reputedly haunted by ghosts of seven French Officers entombed alive in wine cellar by Japanese during WWII. Cat Lai also listed at XS 963-850 in Bien Hoa Pr. Gia Dinh Pr, III Corps.

Cat Lo Navy Base (YS 360-520?)
If grid is correct, site was on coast W of QL-15, apx 12 km NE Vung Tau. USN Combat and Logistics Base, '65-71. Per MRF Assn Website.

Cat Lo Signal Site (YS 360-520)
Along QL-15, apx 12 km NE Vung Tau. Phuoc Tuy Pr, III Corps.

Catalina, LZ (XD 849-648)
Apparently a.k.a. or near LZ Casper. At southern edge of DMZ, apx 1 km W Hill 696, 23 km due N Khe Sanh CB and 60 km WNW Quang Tri. Apr70 XXIV Corps grid per Don Armstrong. Quang Tri Pr, I Corps.

Catamount, USS (n/a)
LSD-17. Lndg. Ship, Dock, per Ralph Fries.

Catapult, LZ/FSB (XD 826-616)
Apx 30 km W Cam Lo, 3 km due N FSB Neville, 8 km E FSB Greene, 7 km SW FSB Beaver and 4 km S the DMZ. Dominated upper Cam Lo Valley. Occupied by G/2d/4th Marines, 3d Mar Div, 9Mar69. XXIV Corps grid per Don Armstrong. On map at p 58, *US Marines in Vietnam-1969*. Quang Tri Pr, I Corps.

Catawba Victory, SS (n/a)
Merchant ship under govt contract, per Ralph Fries.

Catcher's Mitt (YT 00-30)
Baseball catcher's-mitt shaped terrain feature apx 15 x 20 km in size, due N Long Binh. Southernmost point was apx 8 km N Long Binh and 8 km NE Bien Hoa AB. Controlled by VC throughout war. 1st Div's AO, and described in one text as being a "...wooded ridge far to the E of Thunder Road." 1st Div Op Rpt of 15May69 mentions feature and that 11th ACR (opcon to them) and C/1st/18th Inf had significant contacts there, 3Feb69 and 14Feb69. Map in *Rangers at War*, Appendix I, p 325. Also listed at XT 988-322. Listed grid is apx center of mass. Phuoc Thanh/Phuoc Long and Bien Hoa Prvs, III Corps.

Catecka, FSB? (ZA 206-341)
At what later became Catecka AF, apx 13 km SSW Pleiku. 2d/17th Arty here supt 1st Cav, 23Oct65-11Nov65, during Ops Long Reach and Genevieve. Data per Jack Picciolo. Also listed at ZA 202-341. Pleiku Pr, II Corps.

Catecka 1 (ZA 18-35)
Ville apx 2 km W Catecka AF. Pleiku Pr, II Corps.

Catecka 2 (ZA 19-29)
Ville apx 6 km SSW Catecka AF. Pleiku Pr, II Corps.

Catecka Airfield (ZA 202-341)
Apx 9 km due W Hensel AF, 12 km SSW Pleiku, 12 km NE the Oasis AF and 35 km ESE Plei Djereng New AF, per TPC K-10A. El. 2,385'. "Abnd, Insecure ARVN US Army on airfield, AF # VA2-90," in Aug69 TAD per Frank Penk, Jr. Not in Feb73 TAD. Pleiku Pr, II Corps.

Catecka Base Camp (ZA 21-35)
Adj Catecka Tea Plantation, a.k.a. "The Stadium," and astride QL-19 about 5 km W its intersection with QL-14 and 12 km SSW Pleiku. Became HQ of 1st Bde/1st Cav during siege of Plei Me, Oct65. On 26Oct65, 1st Bde/1st Cav HQ moved to LZ Homecoming during siege in order to coordinate final effort to relieve Plei Me SF Camp. However, when Bde CO realized site was not appropriate for Bde HQ, it was moved to what became known as "The Stadium," at NW corner of plantation. When 3d Bde/1st Cav took over in Nov65, they began calling the Stadium, "Catecka." See Tea Plantation Camp and Turkey Farm. Pleiku Pr, II Corps.

Catecka Plantation, FSB? (ZA 109-271)
At what later became Oasis AF/basecamp apx 24 km SW Pleiku. 2d/17th Arty here supt 1st Cav, 31May66. Per Jack Picciolo. Pleiku Pr, II Corps.

Catecka Tea Plantation (ZA 18-33)
Large tea plantation adj 1st Cav's "Stadium," on QL-19, apx 5 km W its intersection with QL-14. Became HQ of 1st Cav 1st Bde during siege of Plei Me in Oct65 and was named "the Stadium" by Bde CO. Pleiku Pr, II Corps.

Category Four Enlistee (n/a)
See Glossary.

Cates, LZ/FSB (XD 926-443)
A.k.a. Hill 950. Apx 7 km ENE Khe Sanh CB, 35 km SW Dong Ha, 4 km SSW FSB Bison, 8 km SW Vandegrift CB and 2 km N Ql-1. 5th/7th Cav, 1st Cav air assaulted here during Op Pegasus, 1-8Apr68. 1st/9th Marines, Jun69. On various maps in *US Marines in Vietnam-1969*. Also listed at XD 927-437 and 932-432. Quang Tri Pr, I Corps.

Catherine, FSB (YD 466-112)
See FSB Kathryn. Thua Thien Pr, I Corps.

Catherine, FSB (YS 363-714)
Apx 8 km NW Nui Dat, 500 meters ESE FSB Thornton and 7 km W FSB Dagger. On 1ATF NCO trng map per John Hollett. Phuoc Tuy Pr, III Corps.

Catholic Relocation Camp (BR 869-964)
Apx 3 km E Bong Son AF, and S of the Song An Lao River. Jul68. Binh Dinh Pr, II Corps.

Cathryn, FSB (YD 466-112)
See FSB Kathryn. Thua Thien Pr, I Corps.

Cathy, FSB (BR? 966-703)
If UTM grid zone accurate, then site was apx 21 km SSE Bong Son, 17 km ESE Ha Tay AF and 3 km E QL-1. 10th Cav, 4th Div here. Presumed to have been in BR UTM. Name/grid per Bob Patsfield. Binh Dinh Pr, II Corps.
Cathy, FSB (YD 583-231)
Along N bank of Song Bo River, apx 14 km due W Hue and 12 km SSE Camp Evans. XXIV Corps grid per Don Armstrong. 101st Abn, Apr70. Quang Tri Pr, I Corps.
Cathy, LZ/FSB (YA 966-703)
Overlooked Ya Krong Bolah Valley apx 6 km ENE Plei Dei Go, 34 km SW Kontum, 16 km WNW Plei Mrong and 36 km NW Pleiku. Per John Grocki, B/1st/35th Inf /4th Div reoccupied this abnd site briefly in Sep or Oct69. He adds, "I got to spend a night up there, and it wasn't very big. Just enough room for a platoon and a mortar squad." Grid per S-3 Daily Journals/Op rpts of 31Jul-1Sep69, courtesy Bob Patsfield. Pleiku Pr, II Corps.
Cathy, LZ (ZA 048-489)
On mtn top slightly N Pleiku, apx 19 km W and 5 km NW Ban Duc. Elements of 4th Div here '68 or '69? Cathy, Helga, Phyllis and Ruby were apparently mutually suptg firebases. Name/grid per Dick Arnold. Pleiku Pr, II Corps.
Catigny, FSB (XT 70-33?)
In center of Iron Triangle, apx 5 km NE FSB Aachen, 8 km WSW Lai Khc and 22 km SE Dau Tieng, 25 km WNW FSB Holiday Inn and10 km W Ql-13, per *Low Level Hell's* 1st Div TAOR map. 1st Inf Div FSB named for WWII battle site. Built Nov68 by elements of 2d/28th/1st Inf Div, and heavily attacked 1st night of existence. Its const and battles are discussed in *Charlie Company*, at pp 68-76 et al. 1st Inf Div, '68-69. Grid apx. Tay Ninh Pr, III Corps.
Catigny 1, FSB (XT 652-336)
Apx 13 km WSW Lai Khe AF and 8 km W Ben Cat/QL-13. 3d Bde, 1st Inf Div, '68. Name/grid per Dan Gillotti, 15th Arty Assn. Tay Ninh Pr, III Corps.
Catskill, USS (n/a)
MCS-1. Coastal Minesweeper, per Ralph Fries.
Cau Ba, FSB (YT 59-06)
A.k.a. FSB Can Ba. Apx 15 km SE Xuan Loc, 10 km due S peak Nui Chua Chan Mtn, 17 km ENE Blackhorse basecamp and 2 to 3 km WNW Hill 324. 2d/3d, 199th LIB. Long Khanh Pr, III Corps.
Cau Baa (YT 59-06)
See Cau Ba. Long Khanh Pr, III Corps.
Cau Bong Bridge (XT 712-071)
Apx 13 km NW Tan Son Nhut AB and 3 km SE Tan Phu. Hau Nghia Pr, III Corps.
Cau Cay Airfield (YT 207-543)
See Rang Rang AF. Binh Tuy Pr, III Corps.
Cau Cay, Ap (n/a)
Mapsheet L-7014-6431-4. Sheet: Ap Cau Cay. SVN.
Cau Chim Bridge (AT 866-573)
Crossed Song Thu Bon apx 4 km NE An Hoa and just SE ville of Giang Hoa. Apr70 XXIV Corps grid per Don Armstrong. Possibly a security position or FSB here. Quang Nam Pr, I Corps.
Cau Dai Beach CAP (BT1-5?)
Misspelling of Cua Dai? A Song "Cua Dai" is in listed UTM grid square, which suggests site was near Hoi An, SE Da Nang. River with listed spelling is in BR 9-4 grid square, but that was not a USMC AO. CAP 2-4-4 per Tim Duffie. Quang Nam Pr?, I Corps.
Cau Dinh Jungle (XT 7-2)
Along Song Thi Thin River, apx 18 km ESE Ho Bo Woods, 17 km NE Cu Chi, 5 km NE Phu Hoa Dong/Filhol Rubber Plantation, 10 km NNW Phu Cuong, between QL-13 and river. 1st/503d Inf, 173d Abn elements here during Op Cedar Falls, Jan-Fe b67, in War Zone C, III Corps.
Cau Do Bridge (AT 999-705)
Apparently both a rail and vehicle bridge over Song Cau Do apx 4 km SSW Da Nang AB and 2 km West Ql-1. Secured by 1st Marines/1st Mar Div, '69. Apr70 XXIV Corps grid per Don Armstrong. Quang Nam Pr, I Corps.
Cau Do Bridge (BT 02-72?)
QL-1 bridge over Song Cau Do, apx 4 km S Da Nang AB. See Cao Do Bridge. Quang Nam Pr, I Corps.
Cau Do River (BT 0-7)
A.k.a. Cao Do River. The Cau Do, Yen, Tuy Loan La Tho, Thanh Quyt, Vu Gia, Cau Lau and Thu Bon Rivers all formed part of drainage that became the Da Nang River. All were S or SW Da Nang. Quang Nam Pr, I Corps.
Cau Ha CAP (BT 06-63?)
See CAP 3-2 HQ. Thua Thien Pr, I Corps.
Cau Ha Combat Base (BT 066-638)
Possibly a.k.a. FSB Cau Ha or LZ 413? Linked by road to Marble Mtn AB and along inland hwy between Hoi An and Da Nang, apx 14 km SSE Da Nang, 11 km NW Hoi An, 10 km S Marble Mtn AF, and 5 km SW "The Leprosarium." Aerial view of triangular-shaped cmpd as it was in Dec69 at: www.lbjlib.utexas.edu/shwv/images/a_ground.htm. Apparently home of 2d/1st Marines at some point. Data per Bob Lindgren. Quang Nam Pr, I Corps.
Cau Ha, FSB (BT 075-655)
A.k.a. LZ 413. Apx 8 km S Marble Mtn AB, 3 km W the coast and 11 km NW Hoi An. May or may not have been same facility as Cau Ha Combat Base. Apr70 XXIV Corps grid per Don Armstrong. Quang Nam Pr, I Corps.
Cau Hai Bay (AT 85-07)
Apx 25 km NW Da Nang and 55 km WSW Hue. See Lang Co Bridge. Thua Thien Pr, I Corps.
Cau Hai CAP (ZD 090-007?)
See CAP 3-2-1. 3d CAG, Thua Thien Pr, I Corps.
Cau Hai Lagoon (ZD 05-05)
See Dam Cau Hai. Thua Thien Pr, I Corps.
Cau Hai, Dam (ZD 0-0)
Lagoon at 16°20'N-107°52'E. Thua Thien Pr, I Corps.
Cau Hai, Lagune de (ZD 0-0)
Dam Cau Hai. Lagoon at 16°20'N-107°52'E. On NE48-16 JOG. Thua Thien Pr, I Corps.
Cau Ke (n/a)
Mapsheet name of L-7014-6228-4. SVN.
Cau Ke (XR 16-92)
Town apx 17 km SE Tra On AF, 30 km WSW Tra Vinh AF and 7 km NE the Mekong River. The Song Cau Ke River is in grid square AN 8-1. Vinh Binh Pr, IV Corps.
Cau Ke Heliport (XR 160-913)
Apx 2 km N the Mekong, 35 km WSW Tra Vinh AF/Phu Vinh, and 30 km N Khanh Hung/Soc Trang AF. "Heliport #544, alt 7', soccer field, at 09°52'30"N-106°03'40"E," per Feb73 TAD. Vinh Binh Pr, IV Corps.

Cau Khoi Rubber Plantation (XT 32-40)
Apx 8-10 km SE Tay Ninh and 70 km NW Saigon. Used as NVA/VC staging area for 275th NVA/VC Bn and D-14 Local Force Bn during Battle for Tay Ninh, 17Aug-27Sep68, per AAR, Battle of Tay Ninh (17Aug-27Sep68), HQ 25th ID, 2Feb69, p 13. Tay Ninh Pr, III Corps.

Cau Khoi, Plantation de (XT 32-40)
A.k.a. Don Dien Cau Khoi. Tay Ninh Pr, III Corps.

Cau Lanh (WS 69-70?)
See Cao Lanh. Kien Phong Pr?, IV Corps.

Cau Lau River (AT/BT)
The Cau Do, Yen, Tuy Loan La Tho, Thanh Quyt, Vu Gia, Cau Lau and Thu Bon Rivers all formed part of drainage that became the Da Nang River. All were S or SW Da Nang. Quang Nam Pr, I Corps.

Cau Lay Airfield (YT 207-543)
See Rang Rang AF. Long Khanh Pr, III Corps.

Cau Mau Peninsula (VQ 70-50)
At southern tip of SVN, and site of U Minh Forest, an extensive inundated region along its western coast, generally inaccessible by land and haven for VC. An Xuyen Pr, IV Corps.

Cau Mau SF Camp (WR 196-142?)
Possibly a.k.a. Camau or Quan Long SF Camp? No data for location. Listed grid is for Quan Long AF and may or may not be site of camp. Ca Mau Peninsula, Advsy Team 80. An Xuyen Pr, IV Corps.

Cau Muong Chuoi Bridge (XS 893-800)
Rte 260 bridge apx 4 km SSW Nha Be and 10 km NE Can Giuoc. Gia Dinh Pr, III Corps.

Cau Ngang Heliport (XR 594-826)
Apx 18 km SE Tra Vinh AF/Phu Vinh, and 56 km ENE Soc Trang AF/Khanh Hung. "Heliport #545, alt 10', sod. Field next to arty pieces or behind troop housing north of town. At 09°47'40"N-106°27'30"E," per Feb73 TAD. Vinh Binh Pr, IV Corps.

Cau Nguyen Di Linh Mountains (YT 9-0 to BN 1-7)
Mtn chain NE Vung Tau, running generally from YT 90-00 to BN 10-70, and parallel to coast apx 20-30 km inland from it. Highest peak appears to be Braian mtn at AN 91-78. Primarily in Binh Thuan Pr, II Corps.

Cau Noi Ferry Landing (XS 786-568)
LTL-5A ferry point across Song Vam Co Tay, apx 25 km ESE Tan An. 67-68. Connected Long An and Go Cong Prvs, III Corps.

Cau Rung Mountain (BT 07-10)
See Cua Rung Mtns. Quang Tin Pr, I Corps.

Cau Soi Heliport (ZC 038-310)
In valley of Song Cai River, apx 32 km SW An Hoa, 60 km SW Da Nang and 23 km NNE Kham Duc. Heliport #546, alt 262', per Feb73 TAD. Quang Nam Pr, I Corps.

Cau Soi Rap (XS 95-53)
Major waterway formed by confluence of Song Nha Be and Song Vam Co Dam Rivers apx 35 km S Saigon and 20 km N the northern mouth of Mekong. Meets South China Sea at YS 00-50, and its mouth is apx 3 km wide. Forms portion of Go Cong/Gia Dinh Provinces and III/IV Corps boundaries.

Cau Song Bay Hap (VQ 85-67)
Large bay apx 15 km NE Mui Bai Bung, southernmost tip of Cau Mau Peninsula. An Xuyen Pr, IV Corps.

Cau Tieu (XS 92-35)
Bay at mouth of My Tho River. Mouth at listed grid, apx 42 km ESE My Tho. Go Cong Pr, IV Corps.

Cau Tram Bridge (XS 740-760)
TL-18 Bridge at Cau Tram, apx 4 km SSE Binh Chau and 10 km NW Can Giuoc. Long An Pr, III Corps.

Cau Viet (YD 3-7)
See Cua Viet. Quang Tri Pr, I Corps.

Cav Hill (YA 922-270)
Apx 8 km ENE Duc Co AF and 37 km WSW Pleiku. Significance of site unknown. Feb68. Pleiku Pr, II Corps.

Cavalair, LZ (YA 974-036)
A.k.a. LZ Columbus. Apx 5 km ENE LZ X-Ray, 3 km ESE LZ Albany, 4 km due E LZ Falcon, 50 km SW Pleiku, 16 km W Plei Me, and 3 km NE Anta village. Bty A/2d/19th Arty, 1st Cav here. Originally opened apx 4Nov65, then on 5Nov65 was moved 2 km due W to new site called LZ Falcon (near NVA hospital fight of 1Nov65) closer to Chu Pong Mtn. Reopened 15Nov65 and renamed LZ Columbus. In use during 1st Battle of Ia Drang Valley, Grid per LtGen Hal Moore. Pleiku Pr, II Corps.

Cavalier, FSB (n/a)
See LZ Cavalair.

Cavalry Hill (YA 922-270)
See Cav Hill. Pleiku Pr, II Corps.

Cay Ban, Bai (CP 1-6)
A.k.a. Baie Cai Sung. Bay at 12°22'N-109°19'E. On ND49-13 JOG. Khanh Hoa Pr, II Corps.

Cay Ban, Baie de (CP 1-7)
A.k.a. Vung Cay Ban. Bay at 12°27'N-109°18'E. On ND49-13 JOG. Khanh Hoa Pr, II Corps.

Cay Bua Bridge (BS 692-648)
QL-1 bridge over the Song Ve River, 12 km SSE Quang Ngai and 10 km NNW Mo Duc AF. Americal List. Quang Ngai Pr, I Corps.

Cay Duong, Baie de (VS 7-2)
A.k.a. Vinh Cay Duong. Bay at 10°10'N-104°45'E. On NC48-06 JOG. Kien Giang Pr, IV Corps.

Cay Duong, Vinh (VS 7-2)
Bay at 10°10'N-104°45'E. On NC48-06 JOG. Kien Giang Pr, IV Corps.

Cay Ga, Mui (CP 0-6)
Coastal point at 12°18'N-109°15'E. On ND49-13 JOG. Khanh Hoa Pr, II Corps.

Cay Gao Airfield (YT 300-254)
Apx 10 km SE Bong Son, 46 km N Phu Cat and 4 km E QL-1. "Insecure, abnd, overgrown, Pvt AF, 8Jul67, AF # VA3-125," in Aug69 TAD per Frank Penk, Jr. Not in Feb73 TAD. Long Khanh Pr, III Corps.

Cay Giep Mountain (BR 920-880)
A.k.a. Hill 641. Binh Dinh Pr, II Corps.

Cay Giep Mountains (BR 920-880)
Generally 5 to 15 km E and SE Bong Son. On NW 1/4 of mapsheet L-7014-6837-4, per Ken Burrington. See Dam Tra O Lake. Binh Dinh Pr, II Corps.

Cayalya, FSB (XT 275-786)
A.k.a. Prek Klok. Along TL-4, apx 11 km SSW Katum AF and 20 km ESE Thien Ngon AF. ARVN FSB. Name/grid per Dan Gillotti. Tay Ninh Pr, I Corps.

Cayuga County, USS (n/a)
LST-1186. Lndg. Ship, Tank, per Ralph Fries.

CCC (ZA 236-863)
Along QL-14, apx 6 km S Kontum. MACV-SOG Command & Control Central. See FOB 2, Prairie Fire and MLT-2. Kontum Pr, II Corps.

CCC (AR 780-880)
At Kontum AF, along E edge of Kontum. MACV-SOG Command & Control Central. Oct69. See FOB 2, Prairie Fire and MLT-2. Kontum Pr, II Corps.

CCN (YD 887-148? & YD 328-526?)
MACV-SOG Command & Control North operated two permanent sites controlling its operations in Laos, the DMZ and NVN (Prairie Fire, et al). MLT-2 was at Quang Tri (in a cmpd apx 8 km W the Quang Tri AF), MLT-1 was at Phu Bai. See Prairie Fire, FOB 1 and MLT-1. Quang Tri and Thua Thien Prvs, I Corps.

CCS (AP 882-010?)
A.k.a. FOB 6(?). Apparently at or just S of Ban Me Thuot East AF, apx 5 km E to ESE of Ban Me Thuot/Lac Giao. Per *LRRP Company Command*, p 52, was at Ban Me Thuot in '68. Per Steve Sherman, The Hill (CCS's Radio relay site at AP 882-990), was 2 km S SOG CCS HQ, and listed grid est from that description. Was SOG's Command & Control South. See also MLT-1, MLT-2 and MAC-SOG HQ. Darlac Pr, II Corps.

Cecil, LZ (BR 290-840)
Remote site on plain apx 40 km NNW An Khe and 5 km SW peak of Hill 1164. Sep-Oct69. Binh Dinh Pr, II Corps.

Cecile, LZ/FSB (YC 385-980)
Near Tre Lit, just W Hwy 538 in A Shau Valley and apx 40 km SW Hue. Also spelled Cecille? Apr70 XXIV Corps grid per Don Armstrong. Also listed on Inactive Asset 101st Abn FSB list of 1Feb70 at same grid. One 1st Cav list has it at YD 379-981, but that point is well out to sea. Thua Thien Pr, I Corps.[114]

Cecile, LZ/FSB (YD 379-981)
See Cecile at YC 385-980. Thua Thien Pr, I Corps.

Cedar, FSB (YS 289-890)
Apx 25 km NW Nui Dat, 3 km NE FSB Digger's Rest and 17 km W Courtenay Rubber Plantation. Described in *Vietnam Gunners*, p 79, as a, "…tight and dirty location where 161 was put back-to-back with an Australian Bty, separated by a fallen windrow of trees." 161 Bty, RNZA (Hitching's Bty 14Apr68-18Mar69) FSB set here 28Sep-12Oct68. Also listed at YS 29-89. On 1ATF NCO trng map per John Hollett. Bien Hoa Pr, III Corps.

Cedar, LZ (ZD 070-102)
Apx 8 km W Phu Loc, 17 km SE Phu Bai. Jul68. Thua Thien Pr, I Corps.

Cedar Falls/Niagara, Operation (n/a)
See Niagara/Cedar Falls, Op.

Cedar Falls, Operation (n/a)
8-26Jan67. 1st Inf, 25th Inf Divs, 173d Abn, 11th ACR and ARVN units in search of VC MR 4 HQ in Iron Triangle. 720 rptd NVA KIA, per *VN Order of Battle*, pp 9-14. See Niagara/Cedar Falls. Binh Duong Pr, III Corps.

Cedar Mountain, LZ (BS 582-660)
Apx 2 km W Song Phuoc Giang, 4 km NW Nghia Hanh AF, 6 km SSW Quang Ngai AF and 10 km W QL-1. Also listed at BS 580-655. Quang Ngai Pr, I Corps.

Ceinture, Operation (WJ?)
20Nov47-22Dec47. Month-long French op meant to crush Vietminh in quadrangle NW Hanoi that abutted Thai Nguyen and Tuyen Quang. Involved some 18 Bns, 18 navy LC's and French Paras against Vietminh Rgt 112 (a.k.a. The Capital Rgt) which later became 304th Div and Bde Doc-Lap (Independence Bde, later became 308th Div). Literal translation of *ceinture* is belt. Data per *Street Without Joy*, p 30. NVN.

Celeb, LZ (AQ 832-213)
Apx 4 km due N Quang Nhieu and 16 km N ban Me Thuot City AF. Feb66. Darlac Pr, II Corps.

Cement Plant Airfield (VS 599-353)
Apx 20 km SE Ha Tien, 6 km N the coast, 50 km SW That Son AF, 230 km WSW Saigon and 58 km NW Rach Gia. Per TPC K-10D. El. 7'. 1,600' laterite rwy. At 10°16'18"N-104°38'03"E. Kien Giang Pr, IV Corps.

Cemetery Hill (CQ 152-482)
W of QL-1, apx 8 km NW Tuy Hoa major AF, 1 km NW Tuy Hoa, 19 km S Tuy An AF and 3 km from coast. At 0200, 31Jan68, 5th/95th NVA Rgt attacked Tuy Hoa, its prison (Phu Yen Rehabilitation Ctr, just S 6th/32d Arty position) and US arty positions. C Bty/6th/32d Arty (8" and 175mm Bty) at Tuy Hoa North AF was inc. At 0700, 4th/503rd Inf, 173rd with Bn of Korean 28th Regt was sent to reinforce 6th/32d, and together pushed NVA from cmpd. Through night, NVA suffered heavy casualties and survivors fled to hamlet immed S prison and at base of hill nicknamed "Cemetery Hill." 32d Arty Bn CO, LTC Robert Whitbeck was KIA in fight. 4/503rd CO later personally led charge on NVA positions in ville (19 US KIA, 39 WIA) followed by air strikes from Tuy Hoa jets, which ended battle. Few NVA survived and hill either named for that result, or because a Viet cemetery was on hill? Grid Per 15Feb68 AAR courtesy Chris Taylor, A/4th/503d Inf, 173d Abn. Tuy Hao North AF at CQ-154. Phu Yen Pr, II Corps.

Centenary, FSB (YS 662-698)
Along LTL-23, apx 22.5 km ENE Nui Dat, 18 km NE FSB Horseshoe, 500-meters SE FSB Rapier, 500 meters NE FSB Wells and 1 km SE FSB Scoobie. On 1ATF NCO trng map per John Hollett. Phuoc Tuy Pr, III Corps.

Center, LZ/FSB (BT 050-250)
A.k.a. Hill 348. Apx 14 km E Hiep Duc, 1.5 km NE Vinh Dong Hill, 7 km ESE Phuoc Tuy, 19 km SW Hawk Hill, 7 km SE LZ Ross and 7 km ESE LZ West. Apparently opened in '67 by 196th LIB. Likely named LZ Center because it was centered roughly halfway between LZs East and West. Abnd 11Aug69, by 3d/21st Inf, 196th LIB. 1st/6th Inf also here. Map is L-7014-6640-2. Also listed at BT 052-253 and 059-351. Quang Tin Pr, I Corps.

Center, LZ/FSB (XU 462-009)
A.k.a. LZ/FSB Centre. At NW end of Fishhook, apx 7 km E SVN border at its closest point, 4 km W Phum Dong (Cambodia), 17 km NE Katum and 28 km WSW Loc Ninh. LZ prepared by a 15,000 lb. Daisy Cutter. Apparently, Bn of 5th ARVN Abn air assaulted here at opening of Incursion, 1May70, suffering over 100 KIA when engaged as they landed. 42 helos and 22 gunship escorts used in airlift. 22 ARA Cobras attacked estimated 200-man NVA assault force. B Bty/1st/5th ARVN Arty here with six-105mms, and three-155mms. Possibly 1st Cav/25th Inf

11th ACR elements here also. Some data per *11th ACR Cambodia Invasion AAR, 1st Cav Div, May-Jun70*, courtesy Lou Rochat. [115] Grid and other data per Frank Penk, Jr. Also listed at XU 474-011. Cambodia.

Centipedes (n/a)
See Glossary.

Central Highlands (n/a)
Known to French as *Plateaux Montagnards*. 20,000 sq mile plateau along S edge of Truong Son Mtns. Ran roughly from Ban Me Thuot (Darlac Pr) N, to I Corps border (Thua Thien/Quang Nam Pr). Of strategic importance, it contained a population of about 1 million mostly Montagnard. Tea, Coffee and vegetables were its primary products. 1st Cav, 4th Div, 173rd Abn Bde and 1st Bde/101st Abn worked highlands during much of war.

Centre, FSB/LZ (XU 462-009)
See LZ Center at listed grid. Cambodia.

Cercle Hippique (XS 855-911)
Hotel/restaurant apx 700 meters SW Independence palace in Saigon. Gia Dinh Pr, III Corps.

Cercle Sportif (WJ 8-2)
In Hanoi. Sporting country club-like facility popular with correspondents and French. Author Zalin Grant describes it as center of colonial society during French rule, noting that it had, "…a big ballroom opening onto a terrace overlooking the swimming pool, and swimming became the prime social activity in Hanoi" while tennis took secondary role (reverse was true at Saigon Sportif). NVN. [116]

Cercle Sportif (XS 855-915)
Sporting and country club-like facility perhaps 200 meters W of Independence Palace, Saigon. Per Zalin Grant, Saigon's Cercle Sportif varied from Hanoi Sportif in that its terrace overlooked tennis courts and tennis was focus in Saigon with swimming its secondary activity (reverse was true at Hanoi Sportif). Gia Dinh Pr, III Corps. [117]

Ceti Indigene (n/a)
French name for Old Quarter of Hanoi, N Hoan Kiem Lake and city center. NVN.

Cha Da, Mui (CP 0-1)
Coastal point at 11°51'N-109°15'E. On NC49-01 JOG. Khanh Hoa Pr, II Corps.

Cha La (XS 1-6?)
A.k.a. Dam Dui. An Xuyen Pr, IV Corps.

Cha La Outpost (XT 294-500)
Along LTL-26, 6 km E Tay Ninh and 19 km W Dau Tieng. Feb68. Tay Ninh Pr, II Corps.

Cha Nam Kaa Mountain (AP 811-608)
A.k.a. Hill 1294. Darlac Pr, II Corps.

Cha Pa Mountain (UK 74-67)
A.k.a. Fan Si Pan Mtn. Apx 260 km NW Hanoi and tallest peak in Vietnam at 10,308' or 3,142 meters elevation. Also listed at 3,143 meters or 10,312'? NVN.

Cha Rang Valley (BR 937-318)
Large coastal valley generally 20-25 km NW Qui Nhon and W QL-1. Binh Dinh Pr, II Corps.

Chaigar (n/a)
See Glossary.

Chainat Airfield (n/a)
Along Chao Phraya River, apx 165 km NNW Bangkok per Feb67 Natl Geo map. Thailand.

Chaiyaphum Airfield (SC 8-4)
At 15°48'00"N-102°02'00"E, apx 280 km NE Bangkok per Feb67 Natl Geo map. Sometimes spelled Chiayaphum. NIMA data. El. 500'. Thailand.

Challenge, LZ (BR 628-822)
Apx 17 km W Ha Tay AF, 32 km SW LZ English and 21 km N Vinh Thanh AF. 4th Div AO, '70. Name/grid per Jim Claeys. Was fwd FSB and B/2d/35th Inf, here Mar-Apr70 per John Linn. Binh Dinh Pr, II Corps.

Challenge, LZ (YA 432-631)
Cambodian Incursion LZ apx 12 km NNE Phum Choy and 10 km from SVN border. Cambodia.

Cham (n/a)
See Glossary.

Chamber Pot, The (TJ 94-66)
French Pilots' nickname for Muong Thanh Valley, site of Dien Bien Phu. NVN.

Chamberlain, FSB (XS 552-984)
Along TL-10 at Ap Tho Mo (1), apx 4 km WNW Duc Hoa and 15 km SW Cu Chi. Don Koch describes it as "mudhole outside of Cu Chi." Fwd FSB of 9th Inf Div. B Bty/5th/2d here Jun69-Dec69, 6th/31st Inf here 70. Grid per Lee Pittman, E/6/31. Hau Nghia Pr, III Corps.

Chamkar Leu Airfield (WU)
5,900' rwy, apx 80 km NNE Phnom Penh, 30 km SE Baray Hwy Strip, and 25 km NNW Kampong Cham major AF, per TPC K-10D/TPC K-10A maps. El. 397'. Cambodia.

Champ, LZ (XD 989-629)
Appears to have been apx 6 km NW FSB Fuller, 12 km NW Cam Lo and 3 km S the DMZ. On map at p 58, *US Marines in Vietnam-1969*. 3d Mar Div, USMC, '69. Apr70 XXIV Corps grid per Don Armstrong. Also listed at XD 98-64. Quang Tri Pr, I Corps.

Champa (n/a)
See Glossary.

Champagne, LZ/FSB (AT 81-48)
Apx 8 km W An Hoa, 7 km NE FSB Pike and 9 km N Lance, TF Yankee, '69, USMC. Grid per map in *US Marines in Vietnam-1969*, p 90. Quang Nam Pr, I Corps.

Champassak Airfield (WB 91-42)
A.k.a. L-107 and Wat Phu. Apx 430 km SE Vientiane on Feb67 Natl Geo map. CIA/SF, per *Air Facilities Data-Laos*. El. 400'. Laos.

Chan May Dong, Mui (AU 8-0)
Cape at 16°21'N-108°01'E. Thua Thien Pr, I Corps.

Chan May Tay (ZD 1-0)
A.k.a. Mui Chon May Tay. Coastal point at 16°21'N-107°57'E. NE48-16 JOG. Thua Thien Pr, I Corps.

Chan May Tay (ZD 1-0)
Thua Thien Pr, I Corps.

Chan Muong Gorge (WJ 20-84)
Apx 95 km NW Hanoi. NW to SE running gorge SSE the confluence of Chay and Clear Rivers. The road between Phu Doan and Phu Tho passed trough this gorge. A 4 km depression lined with steep, jungle-covered walls that offered good ambush potential. Chan Muong was at its N end and Thai Binh at its S end. On its attack N toward Phu Doan, Op Lorraine crushed Vietminh roadblock here and later found large supply depot at Phu Hien. However, as French withdrew back S along same route 17Nov52, Rgt 36 ambushed and decimated a 2 mile-long convoy during

18-hour battle initiated at middle of the gorge as head of column reached Thai Binh (S end of gorge). Hand-to-hand fighting and bayonet charges marked the desperate melee. Cost 56 French KIA, 126 WIA, 133 MIA, 1 tank, 6 half-tracks and 5 other vehicles. See *Street Without Joy*, pp 96-104, maps at pp 98, 104. NVN.

Chan Thanh (XT 767-623)
See Chon Thanh. Binh Long Pr, III Corps.

Chandler, Theodore E., USS (n/a)
DD-717. 7th Flt Destroyer, per Ralph Fries.

Changwat Udon Thani, Sanam Bin AF (TE 6-2)
A.k.a. Sanam Bin Changwat Udon Thani. At 17°23'00"N-102°47'00"E. NIMA data. Thailand.

Chanh Hoa (XE 6-3?)
Port attacked by US carrier and Da Nang based US and VNAF acft during Flaming Dart II, 11Feb65. See Flaming Dart II. NVN.

Chanh Long (XT 860-230)
See Dog Leg Village. Binh Duong Pr, III Corps.

Chanh Luu (XT?)
Op Cedar Falls Joint US/ARVN assault here involving 2d/28th Inf Div here 23Jan67. Tay Ninh Pr?, III Corps.

Chanson, Camp (n/a)
French base of '50's. Location unknown.

Chantanaburi (SV 9-2 or SU 9-9?)
SF camp location per *SF Order of Battle.* Thailand.

Chanthaburi Airfield (SV 9-2 or SU 9-9?)
Apx 205 km ESE Bangkok per Feb67 Natl Geo map. El. 120'. Thailand.

Chantrea (XT 18-02)
Cambodian ville in Parrot's Beak, apx 18 km NE Moc Hoa and slightly SE Phum Tnaot. Battle of Chantrea here, involving 6th/31st Inf, 9th Div during Cambodian Incursion, 8May70. 2 days latter, some of same 6th/31st elements were in Battle for Phum Tnaot. Cambodia.

Chao Doc SF Camp (WS 131-842)
At Chau Phu, near Mekong River and apx 4 km NW Chau Doc AF. 5th SF Grp, Det. B-42 (was B-130), here Oct65. SF Det 76 also here. Transferred to RF/PF. Likely same as Chau Duc SF Camp. Info/grid per *SF Order of Battle.* Chau Doc Pr, IV Corps.

Chao Phya Hotel (PR 7-3?)
US Military run hotel/Officer's Club in Bangkok, Directly across street from privately run and infamous Florida Hotel. Thailand.

Chao, Cape (WG 9-8)
See Cape Chao. NVN.

Chao, Vung (CQ 1-7)
Bay at 13°21'N-109°18'E. On ND49-09 JOG. Phu Yen Pr, II Corps.

Chap Le (YD 0-9)
Port attacked by US carrier and Da Nang based US and VNAF acft during Flaming Dart II, 11Feb65. See Flaming Dart II. NVN.

Chaparral, LZ (XD 993-477)
Along QL-9, apx 12 km SW Mai Loc, 3 km S Ca Lu and 35 km WSW Quang Tri. Apr70 XXIV Corps grid per Don Armstrong. Quang Tri Pr, I Corps.

Chapelle Dispensary (BT 53-05?)
At New Life Village near Chu Lai. Named to honor Dickey Chapelle, female photographer/news correspondent, KIA in 65. Quang Tin Pr, I Corps.

Chaps (n/a)
6Apr70, XXIV Corps future-use III MAF FSB name.

Chapultapec, FSB (XD 820-564)
Apx 14 km NNW Khe Sanh CB, 2 km NW peak of Hill 1739 and 52 km W Quang Tri. Apr70 XXIV Corps grid per Don Armstrong. Quang Tri Pr, I Corps.

Chapultepec, FSB (YT 04-35)
A.k.a. FSB Mosby (YT 043-358)? Apx 22 km NNE Bien Hoa AB, 16 km SSE Phuoc Vinh and 27 km E to ESE Lai Khe. FSB of 3d/7th Inf, and 5th/12th Inf, 199th LIB. Binh Duong Pr, III Corps.

Charamaine, LZ (YA 998-217)
See Charmaine. Pleiku Pr, II Corps.

Charamine, LZ (YA 999-219)
See Charmaine. Pleiku Pr, II Corps.

Charger (n/a)
6Apr70, XXIV Corps future-use 5th Div FSB name.

Charger City (YA 955-245?)
A.k.a. FSB/LZ Charger? Apx 37 km SW Pleiku and 11 km due E Duc Co AF. Oct65. Also listed at ZA 958-245, but grid erroneous. Pleiku Pr, II Corps.

Charger City (ZA 958-245)
No such grid exists. See Charger City at YA 958-245. Pleiku Pr, II Corps.

Charger Hill, LZ (BT 443-732)
A.k.a. Fat City, FSB Charger Hill, Hill 29 (or Hill 35?) or Hawk Hill? Apx 10 km W Chu Lai, 4 km W Khuong Quang and 3 to 4 km W QL-1, near Que Son Valley. USMC, 4th 31st Inf, 196th LIB. Also listed at BT 440-077 and BT 435-079. Americal List. Quang Tin Pr, I Corps.

Charger Hotel (BT 54-05?)
At Chu Lai. Americal Div's stand-down billet. Quang Tin Pr, I Corps.

Charger, Camp (AT 96-76?)
a.k.a. Camp Hoa-My. Apx 5 km W Da Nang AB. Transferred to 3d ARVN Div 23Jun72. At transfer, could house 1,600 personnel. 196th LIB and FWMAF here. Turnover inspection by MACV/JGS IG Team, 27-28Jun72. Apparently renamed Camp Hoa-My after release to ARVN/RVNAF. Grid only apx. Quang Nam Pr, I Corps.

Charger, FSB (YT 154-288)
A.k.a. LZ Charger, LZ Blue, FSB Drennan and Xom Cat AF. Just N the Song Dong Nai River near its confluence with the Song Be River(?), apx 22 km NE Bien Hoa AB, 1 km NE Xom Cat, and 28 km SSE Phuoc Vinh AF. Grid per Peter Cole. Bien Hoa Pr, III Corps.

Chariot, FSB (YD 808-237)
In coastal sands apx 13 km NW Phu Bai AF and 6 km E Hue Citadel AF, on eastern outskirts of Hue. Apr70 XXIV Corps grid per Don Armstrong. Thua Thien Pr, I Corps.

Charles, FSB (BR 432-498)
Apx 7 km NW An Khe AF, 6 km NE An Dinh and 5 km S Plei Kon Go. Grid per Peter Cole. Binh Dinh Pr, II corps.

Charles, LZ (YT 408-647)
Apx 36 km ESE Dong Xoai AF and 27 km SSE Bunard AF. Mar71. Long Khanh Pr, III Corps.

Charles-Marie David de Mayréna (n/a)
See Kingdom of Sedang in Glossary.

Charles Berry, USS (n/a)
DE-1035. DD-Escort, per Ralph Fries.
Charles R. Ware, USS (n/a)
DD-865, per Ralph Fries.
Charles S. Sperry, USS (n/a)
A.k.a. DD 697. See Barry (DD 933).
Charleston, FSB (ZV 195-912)
Apx 6 km SE Plei Bar, 4 km SW peak Chu Don Mtn, 55 km S Pleiku, 2 km ESE FSB Atlanta and 18 km WSW Phu Nhon AF. Grid per Peter Cole, 1st Cav. Pleiku Pr, II Corps.
Charley Sites (n/a)
See Charlie Sites in Glossary.
Charlie 50 (YA/YB)
SOG op zone that covered NE tip of Cambodia bordering SVN and Laos, per Don Lewis, 170th AHC. Cambodia.
Charlie, Camp (XS 8-9)
Originally Tent City Charlie. Built in area known as "The Fish Market," on outskirts of Saigon at edge of Saigon Port. Erected by US Army QM Depot from Ft Bragg, NC. Administered by 543d QM Grp beginning in 65. In 66, renamed Camp Charlie and then Camp Davies which housed 506th Field Depot, largest Field Depot in World. When 506th moved to Long Binh, 4th and 125th Trans Cmds took over Camp Davies. Gia Dinh Pr, III Corps.
Charlie, Drop Zone (XT 349-925)
Apx 2 km NE Katum AF. Tay Ninh Pr, III Corps.
Charlie, FSB (XT 010-720)
Apx 28 km NW Tay Ninh AF, 5 km E Cambodia and 13 km SW Thien Ngon AF. 196th LIB here during Op Gadsden (Junction City), 1-21Feb67, with Bde Fwd CP at XT 12-63. Tay Ninh Pr, III Corps.
Charlie, FSB (XT 567-853)
Apx 6 km SW Minh Thanh AF. Mar-Apr67. Also listed at XT 560-850. Tay Ninh Pr, III Corps.
Charlie, FSB (XT 900-170)
Apx 4 km ENE Phu Loi AF. May67. Binh Duong Pr, III Corps.
Charlie, FSB (YS 290-620)
Described as "crab-covered seaside position" on Rte 15, apx 20 km due N Vung Tau, 9 km W Ba Ria, and 15 km WSW Nui Dat. 161 Bty, RNZA (Martin's Bty 13May67-14Apr68) FSB set here 16Dec67 and other days in Dec67. Phuoc Tuy Pr, III Corps.
Charlie, FSB (ZB 02-11?)
Apx 17 km SSW Dak To 2 AF, 32 km NW Kontum and 6 km NE FSB Delta, per map in *A Bright Shining Lie*. Also mentioned at pp 761, 765. Overrun and lost to NVA while an ARVN FSB, 14Apr72. Grid is rough approximation. Kontum Pr, II Corps.
Charlie, LZ (BR 805-925)
Apx 6 km WSW Bong Son AF. Oct66-Apr67. Binh Dinh Pr, II Corps.
Charlie, LZ (BT 098-245)
Apx 20 km W Tam Ky. Nov67. Quang Tin Pr, I Corps.
Charlie, LZ (XT 312-021)
Apx 8 km SSW Duc Hue AF, 2 km from Cambodia and 7 km due N the tip of Parrot's Beak. Dec65. Hau Nghia Pr, III Corps.
Charlie, LZ (XT 524-900)
Apx 19 km due E Katum AF, 3 km S Cambodia and 6 km W tip of Fishhook. Mar67. Tay Ninh Pr, III Corps.
Charlie, LZ (XU 629-308?)
Grid thought to be in error. May66. Cambodia.
Charlie, LZ ? (XT 635-305)
Apx 16 km ENE Dau Tieng. Nature of site unknown. Jun66. Binh Duong Pr, III Corps.
Charlie, LZ (YD 011-615)
In lowland plain apx 14 km W Dong Ha, 3 km NNW Cam Lo and 34 km WNW Quang Tri. Apr70 XXIV Corps grid per Don Armstrong. Quang Tri Pr, I Corps.
Charlie, LZ (YT 408-647)
See Charles. Long Khanh Pr, III Corps.
Charlie, LZ (YU 629-308?)
If grid correct, was apx 4 km SSW Bon Dung and 22 km SSW Bu Prang New AF. May66.
Charlie, Operation (XD 85-41)
The deconstruction of Khe Sanh CB by 3d/9th Marines, 17Jun-6Jul68. Quang Tri Pr, I Corps.
Charlie 1, FSB (YD 213-672)
Map is L-7014-6442-4, per Ken Burrington.
Charlie 2 Bridge (YD)
See C-2 Bridge. Quang Tri Pr, I Corps.
Charlie 2, FSB (YD 137-647)
See C-2. Quang Tri Pr, I Corps.
Charlie 3, FSB (YD 143-611)
See C-3. Quang Tri Pr, I Corps.
Charlie 4, FSB (YD 313-725)
See C-4. Quang Tri Pr, I Corps.
Charlie Ammo Storage Area (CP 09-17?)
One of 3 ammo stg areas at Cam Ranh Bay renamed 12Jul69 for 3 KIA EOD personnel. See Black, McKinley or Moore Ammo Stg Areas.
Charlie Brown, LZ (BS 932-222)
A.k.a. FSB Charlie Brown. At mouth of Dam Nuoc Man bay, on southern tip of an isthmus/peninsula, apx 11 km NNE Gia An, 29 km SSE Duc Pho AF, 28 km NNE Bong Son and 500 meters E QL-1. Described as virtually an island since it was nearly surrounded by water. Also listed at BS 935-224 and BS 928-220. Built near USN-built Naval port of Sa Huynh (sometimes spelled Sa-Hynh). D/1st/14th Inf, 4th Div here Dec 67. 1st/20th, 11th LIB, here '68-69. Americal list. Photos/maps of base at http://1-14th.com/maps.html. Apr70 XXIV Corps grid per Don Armstrong. Quang Ngai Pr, I Corps.
Charlie Med (BT?)
A.k.a. C-Med. Marine Field Hosp at or near Da Nang. Quang Nam Pr, I Corps.
Charlie Med (YD 541-318)
A.k.a. C Med. At Camp Evans, apx 23 km NW Hue. 326th Med Bn cmpd, 101st Abn. Thua Thien Pr, I Corps.
Charlie Med (XD 852-418)
At Khe Sanh CB, immed E of Graves Registration, toward the W end of rwy and immed S the Aircraft parking apron. Quang Tri Pr, I Corps.
Charlie Ridge (AT 89-64)
Large mtn mass running W to N roughly 20-25 km SW Da Nang, immed S Worth Ridge area and S Happy Valley. Haven for NVA/VC who used it frequently as staging area for attacks on Da Nang, An Hoa, Hoi An and Arizona territories. Characterized by high, narrow hills cut by numerous steep-sided valleys, ravines, gorges and covered with double, triple and single canopy jungle and dense

undergrowth. In *Never Without Heroes,* Larry Vetter offered this description: "The east end of the ridge ascended only gradually and was covered primarily by brush lands [that] ended at about the 300-meter level. At that point there was an abrupt 500 meter climb to approximately 2,625 feet above sea level. That was a grade of about 36%. The jungle began at about the 800-meter level, staring down at Marines like a 100-foot high wall." [118] Despite numerous attempts, enemy was never completely removed from area. Quang Nam Pr, I Corps.

Charlie Sites (n/a)
See Glossary.

Charmaine, LZ (YA 999-219)
Sometimes spelled "Charamine." Apx 12 km SW Oasis AF, 9 km W Xuong Kuang, 15 km ESE Duc Co AF and 35 km SW Pleiku. 1st/35th Inf fwd FSB, 24Jan69 to 7Feb-69. Per *Time Heals No Wounds*, a UFO was spotted from LZ by 2d/9th Arty, [119] and later also rptd circling at ZA 100-271, ZA 079-222 and ZA 009-231, and as having a red light but no sound. At 0500, it landed at YA 975-267 and arty was fired at it. It moved to YA 964-276 and more arty fired. Subsequent sweep found nothing. On 31Jan, 4 more UFOs with one blinking white beacon were spotted. 4th Div ORLL speculates there were other specific sightings of Soviet K-18 (Hog) and Yak-24 helos and Czech HC-2 Trainer and that these UFOs possibly were enemy acft of that nature. UFO's weren't the only strange happenings at this LZ. Per Dick Arnold, on night of 30Jan69, C/1st/35th had a tiger enter perimeter and try to drag-off sleeping trooper who, understandably, screamed loudly. The Tiger retreated and LP called to say, "We hear the mother growlin' and movin-around, give us some illum and we will zap his ass," probably intending to blow their Claymores on him. Illum was fired, but in meantime tiger gets between perimeter and LP, and perimeter lights-up the Tiger, along with the LP, and one US WIA (minor) results. Tiger was found dead in a.m.(400-500 lb) For additional Tiger attack info, see Tiger Attacks entry. Some data per Dick Arnold as per Jan, Feb, Mar69 1st/35th Inf Bn daily logs, which list grid as YA 998-217. Pleiku Pr, II Corps.

Chase, LZ (BP 866-654)
Apx 14 km SE La Thien AF and 24 km NE Duc Xuyen AF. Apr67. Khanh Hoa Pr, II Corps.

Chase, USCGC (n/a)
WHEC 718. 6Dec69-28May70. Sqdn 3 CGC, during Coast Guard's 5th deployment.

Chase County, USS (n/a)
LST-532 and *USNS Chase County*. MSTS Service Tank-Landing Ship. Ex-navy vessel manned by a Korean crew in '68. Per *Rangers At War*, p 48, on about 30Oct68, the Recon/LRRP elements of 1st Cav boarded her at Tan My (just E Hue in I Corps) for shipment to Saigon's Newport in III Corps, arriving 5Nov68. In doing so, they became only Army Recon unit to transfer by sea between two Military regions during entire war.

Chasseur Laottiens (n/a)
See Glossary.

Chasseurs Blindes (n/a)
See Glossary.

Chat and Gravel (n/a)
See Glossary.

Chateau, Camp (XT 2-4?)
Location unknown. Apparently was in or near Tay Ninh or Tay Ninh West AF (Tay Ninh SF camp was at XT 204-509). Possibly a 5th SF camp. Might also have been a nickname for the Grand Bungalow at Ban Me Thuot? See Tay Ninh and Grand Bungalow. Tay Ninh Pr, III Corps.

Chattahoochee, USNS (n/a)
T-AOG 82. Fuel Tanker of MSTS fleet that was used for storage and shuttle service in-country.

Chau Chan Airfield (YT 638-136)
Spelling variant of Chua Chan. See Gia Ray AF. Long Khanh Pr, III Corps.

Chau Chan, Nui (YT 61-11)
See Nui Chua Chan. Long Khanh Pr, III Corps.

Chau Doc (Chau Phu) (n/a)
Mapsheet L-7014-6030-3. Sheet name: Chau Phu (Chau Doc). SVN/Cambodia.

Chau Doc Airfield (WS 153-814)
See Chau Duc AF. Chau Doc Pr, IV Corps.

Chau Doc Heliport (WS 136-830)
Along S bank of Mekong, at SE edge of Chau Phu, 23 km NNE That Son, and apx 2 km WNW Chau Duc AF. Heliport #548, alt 10', soccer field, Fuel-J4. At 10°42'00"N-105°06'40"E, per Feb73 TAD. Chau Doc Pr, IV Corps.

Chau Doc Signal Site (WS)
Location unknown. Possibly atop one of Seven Sisters (Dop Chompa or Nui Co To?). Chau Doc Pr?, IV Corps.

Chau Duc (WS 16-82)
Spelling variant of Chau Doc, and also ville located a few km SE Chau Phu. See Chau Doc. Chau Doc Pr, IV Corps.

Chau Duc Airfield (WS 153-814)
Apx 7 km SE Cambodia, 3 km SW Chau Phu, on a branch of Mekong River, 80 km NE Ha Tien, 40 km SW Don Phuc AF, 100 km NW Can Tho, 53 km NW Long Xuyen AF and 165 km due W Saigon. Per TPC K-10D. El. 10', 1,600' sand/clay rwy. At 10°41'30"N-105°08'50"E. Chau Doc Pr, IV Corps.

Chau Duc City (WS 16-82)
Capitol, Chau Doc Pr. IV Corps.

Chau Duc Province (WS)
One of 16 southern provs forming IV Corps (IV CTZ)

Chau Duc SF Camp (WS 131-842)
See Chao Doc SF Camp. Chau Doc Pr, IV Corps.

Chau Duc Signal Site (WS)
Possibly a.k.a. Chau Doc Signal Site, and possibly at or near Chau Duc AF. Chau Doc Pr, IV Corps.

Chau Lang Airfield (VS 970-557)
Apx 55 km E to ENE Ha Tien, 5 km NW Tri Ton and nestled among the Seven Sisters about 5 km S peak of Dop Chompa Mtn. "Abnd, unserviceable at present 2Jun67, AF # VA4-164," in Aug69 TAD per Frank Penk, Jr. Not in Feb73 TAD. Chau Doc Pr, IV Corps.

Chau Lang SF Camp (VS 968-588)
Apx 55 km E to ENE Ha Tien, 5 km NW Tri Ton and among the Seven Sisters about 5 km S peak of Dop Chompa Mtn. 5th SF. Moved to Tien Binh. Apparently referred to as fictional "Chau Lu" in Robin Moore's *The Green Berets*. CIDG Det B-43, Apr69. Info/grid per *SF Order of Battle.* Chau Doc Pr, IV Corps.

Chau Ngai (4) (BS 560-823)
Apx 15 km NW Quang Ngai and 8 km W QL-1. Site of LZ Alfa during Op Utah, 4-7Mar66. CA here by 2d/7th Marines, 4Mar66, met by heavy fire and major fight ensued. Nearby Hills 85 and 97 (2 km WSW and 2 km W Chau Ngai, respectively) overlooked LZ, were heavily fortified by VC, and became sites of heavy fighting immed after CA. 2d/7th and suptg units lost 45 KIA and 120 WIA (25% of force). See *Utter's Battalion*, pp 248-260, for detailed account. Quang Ngai Pr, I Corps.
Chau Phu (Chau Doc) (n/a)
Mapsheet name of L-7014-6030-3. SVN/Cambodia.
Chau Phu Airfield (WS)
See Chau Duc AF. Chau Doc Pr, IV Corps.
Chau Phu Base Camp (WS 13-84?)
A.k.a. Camp Arnn. On S bank of Song Hau Giang at Chau Phu, apx 2 km E Cambodia, 3 km NW Chau Doc AF and 75 km NE Ha Tien. HQ of Det B-42. Renamed Camp Arnn to honor its CO, Maj. John O. Arnn, US SF, KIA 26Dec65. Shot by VC snipers while leading unit run (units Ops Sgt also KIA on that run). Chau Doc Pr, IV Corps.
Chau Son (n/a)
Mapsheet name of L-7014-6451-4. NVN only.
Chau Thanh (n/a)
Mapsheet name of L-7014-6028-4. SVN.
Chau Thanh (various)
Towns of this name listed in grid squares CQ 1-4 (Tuy Hoa), BS 6-7, BR 9-4, XS 4-4 and WS 8-0 (Cai Rang).
Chau Thanh (XS 4-4)
Near Dong Tam/My Tho. Site of James N. Crocker Cmpd? Dinh Tuong Pr, IV Corps.
Chau Thanh (Tuy Hoa) (n/a)
Mapsheet L-7014-6835-2. Sheet name: Tuy Hoa (Chau Thanh). SVN.
Chavane (YB 2-9?)
A.k.a. Chavan. Apx 550 km SE Vientiane. Ville in Laos near Dog's Head, described in *Da Nang Diary* as "a wide spot in road. Short on looks but long on history." Had been a WWII Japanese fighter base but in '70 was only a deserted grass field. Laos.
Chavane Airfield (YB 2-9?)
Apx 550 km SE Vientiane. El. 3,000'. Laos.
Chaw Chaw (Khorat?) (n/a)
SF camp or AO per *SF Order of Battle.* Thailand.
Chay River (WJ 19-93)
River of NW Tonkin that joins the Clear River (Song Lo) near Phu Doan at listed grid, apx 95 km NW Hanoi. Was Vietminh supply route from China with stg point at Phu Doan (objective of Op Lorraine). NVN.
Che Ket Mountain (BN 31-60)
A.k.a. Hill 1017 (3,337'). 15 km ENE Song Mao AF. Binh Thuan Pr, II Corps.
Che Tay (n/a)
Site of a 9th Inf Div Ground Radar Array Facility in '70. Cited in *Rangers At War*, p 128. III Corps?
Checker, LZ (BS 437-337)
Apx 12 km W Ba To New AF, 8 km NE Gia Vuc AF, 8 km W Go Dien and 38 km WSW Duc Pho/LZ Bronco. Americal list. Quang Ngai Pr, I Corps.
Checkmate (n/a)
Apr70, XXIV Corps future-use 101st Abn FSB name.
Checkmate, FSB (YD 633-083)
A.k.a. OP Checkmate and Hill 342. On S side Hwy 547 apx 1.5 km SSE FSB Bastogne, 5 km and NW FSB Normandy and 15 km SW Hue. Apparently used primarily as radio relay site and/or observation point? By early May72, during Easter Offensive, FSB's Bastogne and Checkmate had fallen after what Gen Abrams considered an admirably stubborn defense by ARVN. In 2d Bde/101st Abn AO, 68-72. Thua Thien Pr, I Corps.
Checkmate, OP (YD 633-083)
See Checkmate, FSB. Thua Thien Pr, I Corps.
Checkpoint 6 (YD 476-376)
Described as being at bridge site on QL-1 apx 7 km NNE Camp Evans and 5 km SSE Thon My Chan. Map is L-7014-6442-2, per Ken Burrington. Thau Thien or Quang Tri Pr, I Corps.
Checkpoint 8 (YD 519-348)
Apparently at QL-1 bridge apx 4 km NNW Camp Evans, 7 km SE Thon My Chan and 25 km NW Hue. Map is L-7014-6442-2, per Ken Burrington. Thua Thien Pr, I Corps.
Checkpoint D (YD 437-434)
Described as being at QL-1 bridge site over Song O Khe River; 14 km SE Quang Tri, and 4 km NNW Thon My. Map is L-7014-6442-2, per Ken Burrington. Quang Tri Pr, I Corps.
Checkpoint F (YD 460-400)
QL-1 bridge over Song Thac Ma River at Thon My Chan, apx 17 km SE Quang Tri. Map: L-7014-6442-2, per Ken Burrington. Quang Tri Pr?, I Corps.
Checkpoint Tango (XT 371-423)
A.k.a. FSB Hunter. Defended checkpoint on LTL-26 at intersection with Rte 239 (roads joining Tay Ninh and Dau Tieng), apx 3 km SE Ap Nam Ngon, 13 km WSW Dau Tieng and 11 km SE FSB Rawlins II. Occupied by Recon Plt, 3d Sqdn, 4th Arm Cav, '68, which both patrolled and acted as reaction force for convoys along LTL-26/Rte 239. Tay Ninh Pr, III Corps.
Cheeseburger Hill (YD 343-194)
A.k.a. FSB Ripcord. Nickname given base by men of 1st/506th Inf, 101st Abn, during siege of May-Jul70. Highlighted the many parallels between Battle for Ripcord and that of infamous, May69 Battle for Hamburger Hill. Hamburger Hill was also only about 27 km S Ripcord. Data per *Ripcord*, p 84. See Ripcord, FSB, for location and more detail. Thua Thien Pr, I Corps.
Cheetah, LZ (XD 878-576)
A.k.a. LZ Cheeta? Apx 16 km NW Ca Lu, 24 km WSW Cam Lo and 46 km W of Quang Tri. Apr70 XXIV Corps grid per Don Armstrong. Quang Tri Pr, I Corps.
Chenal du Lynx (YJ 5-2)
A.k.a. Lynx Channel. Channel near 21°03'N-107°28'E. On NF48-12 JOG.
Cheo Reo (BQ 21-85)
A.k.a. Hau Bon or Hou Bon. Immed SW Hou Bon, 40 km SE Phu Nhon AF, 90 km SW Phu Cat, 32 km NE Buon Blech. HQ of 1st Bde of 101st Abn May-Jun66, during Battle of Toumorong, and discussed in *Battles in the Monsoon*, pp 274, 302. 3d Bn/506th Inf/101st Abn HQ here Apr70-Sep70, while attached first to 4th Div and then IFFV during Invasion of Cambodia. Phu Bon Pr, II Corps.

Cheo Reo (Hau Bon) (n/a)
Mapsheet name of L-7014-6635-1. SVN.
Cheo Reo Airfield (BQ 233-818)
Apx 40 km SE Phu Nhon AF, immed SW Hou Bon, 90 km SW Phu Cat, 32 km NE Buon Blech AF, per TPC K-10A. El. 525', 4,100' steel-mat/asph rwy. Also listed at BQ 214-849. Phu Bon Pr, II Corps.
Cheo Reo SF Camp (BQ 214-849)
Nerar Ban Oi Ly, apx 5 km NW Cheo Reo AF/Hou Bon city. 5th SF. Info/grid per *SF Order of Battle.* See Buon Beng. Phu Bon Pr, II Corps.
Cheo Reo Signal Site (BQ 23-82?)
Possibly at Cheo Reo AF? Listed grid is for AF. Phu Bon Pr, II Corps.
Cheom Ksan Airfield (n/a)
Apx 300 km due N Phnom Penh. El. 247'. Cambodia.
Cherie, FSB (YS 455-909)
Along LTL-23, apx 300 meters N FSB Garth, 23 km N Nui Dat, and 4 km NE FSB Kate. On 1ATF NCO trng map per John Hollett. Long Khanh Pr, III Corps.
Cherokee, LZ (BS 864-207)
In narrow valley apx 8 km NW Gia An and 18 km SSE Duc Pho AF. Feb67. Binh Dinh Pr, II Corps.
Cherokee, LZ (XD 831-495)
Apx 27 km due W Mai Loc, 31 km WSW Cam Lo and 50 km W Quang Tri. Apr70 XXIV Corps grid per Don Armstrong. Quang Tri Pr, I Corps.
Cherokee, LZ (XU 742-062)
A.k.a. FSB Dick. Along QL-13, apx 4 km SSE Loc Ninh AF. Aug66. Binh Long Pr, III Corps.
Cherokee, LZ? (XS 927-971)
Apx 12 km ENE Tan Son Nhut AB and 9 km SSE Di An AF. Dec68-Feb69. Gia Dinh Pr, III Corps.
Cherry (n/a)
See Glossary.
Cherry, LZ (XD 771-551)
Apx 36 km WSW Cam Lo, 16 km NNW Khe Sanh CB and 56 km W Quang Tri. Apr70 XXIV Corps grid per Don Armstrong. Quang Tri Pr, I Corps.
Cheryl, FSB (YT 861-173)
Apx 13 km SW Tan Linh AF. '71. Binh Tuy Pr, III Corps.
Cheryl, LZ (BT 302-192)
A.k.a. LZ Sheryl. At or near Tam Ky's Major AF, 4 km SW QL-1, 4 km due S Tam Ky and 12 km NW Diem Pho. Sheryl on Americal list? Quang Tin Pr, I Corps.
Chesapeake, LZ (YD 034-663)
Apx 14 km NW Cam Lo and 15 km ESE Bon Ho Su (NVN) and 34 km WNW Quang Tri. Apr70 XXIV Corps grid per Don Armstrong. Quang Tri Pr, I Corps.
Chestnut, FSB (YS 231-801)
Along QL-15, apx 17 km SSE Long Thanh AF, 6 km NNW Phu My and 24 km NW Nui Dat. On 1ATF NCO trng map per John Hollett. 1ATF. Bien Hoa Pr, III Corps.
Chesterfield County, USS (n/a)
LST-551. With TF 115, 116, or 117. Decom 1Jun70.
Cheu Lang Chanh (XD 840-408)
See Lang Chen. Quang Tri Pr, I Corps.
Chevy, LZ (BS 429-718)
Apx 4 km E Ha Thanh, 6 km ENE Ha Thanh AF, 22 km W Quang Ngai and overlooking the Song Tra Khuc Valley. Also listed at BS 428-714 and BS 428-719. Map is L-7014-6739-3. Americal List. Quang Ngai Pr, I Corps.
Chevalier, USS (n/a)
DD-805, per Ralph Fries.
Cheyenne, LZ (BR 103-732)
Apx 40 km NE Pleiku, 46 km NW An Khe and 36 km ESE Kontum. B Bty, 4th/42d Arty here Jun70. 4th Div 31Jan70 ORLL grid per Jim Henderson. Kontum Pr, II Corps.
Cheyenne, LZ (BR 782-949)
Just S the Song An Lao River, apx 6 km W Bong Son AF. Oct66. Binh Dinh Pr, II Corps.
Cheyenne, LZ (YD 211-739)
A.k.a. FSB A-2 (YD 214-738)? Just W QL-1 about 25 km NW Quang Tri, 3 km SE Kinh Mon and 10 km SSW mouth of Ben Hai River/NVN border. One of northernmost FSBs in SVN. Apr70 XXIV Corps grid per Don Armstrong. Quang Tri Pr, I Corps.
Cheyenne, LZ ? (YT 928-536)
Apx 26 km due N Tan Linh AF. Nature of site unknown. Oct70. Binh Tuy Pr, III Corps.
Cheyenne, LZ (YA 679-403)
Just E the Ya Krong Bolah River, 3 km E Cambodia and 55 km W Pleiku. Jan66. Pleiku Pr, II Corps.
Chhep Airfield (n/a)
Apx 250 km NNE Phnom Penh. Cambodia.
Chi Hodrong Mtn (AR 777-368)
A.k.a. Dragon Mtn, Titty Mtn and Hill 1028. On E side of QL-19 approximately 1.5 km NW 4th Div's Camp Enari and apx 12 km SSE Pleiku, near intersection where QL19W left QL14S (QL19 then ran SW to Catecka/Oasis). Per Ray Smith, the name Chi Nu Drong was Anglicized to "Dragon" and hence mtn's nickname of Dragon Mtn. Dragon Mtn Signal Site here. Pleiku Pr, II Corps.
Chi Lang (AQ 755-995)
Ville just W Ban Me Thuot (and not the same Chi Lang as that in Chau Doc Pr, IV Corps). Darlac Pr, II Corps.
Chi Lang NTC (WS 0-6?)
RVNAF Natl Trng Ctr. Chau Doc Pr, IV Corps.
Chi Lang SF Camp (WS 027-636)
At or near That Son AF, apx 60 km ENE Ha Tien and 6 km NE peak Dop Chompa Mtn. Adv Team 61, MACV Ranger Cmd Adv Det, 5th SF Grp CIDG Det A-432, Sep70, MACV-SOG, USARV-UITG (Individual Trng Grp) Trng Bn, Nov70-Sep71, in 72 was renamed the FANK (Forces Arm'ee Nationale Khmer Trng Cmd). Transferred to Chi Lang Trng Ctr, USARV Individual Trng Grp, and later to 85th Border Rangers. Grid/data per *SF Order of Battle.* Chau Doc Pr, IV Corps.
Chi Lang Signal Site (VS 98-60?)
Possibly at That Son (a.k.a. Chi Lang) AF (WS 027-636), but more likely atop Dop Chompa Mtn. Grid is mtn's peak. Chau Doc Pr, IV Corps?
Chi Lang Trng Center AF (WS 027-635)
See That Son AF. Chau Doc Pr, IV Corps.
Chi Linh (XT 91-73?)
Ville on LTL-13, apx 16 km W Dong Xoai and 76 km due N Saigon. Binh Long Pr, III Corps.
Chi Linh Airfield (XT 914-734)
Along LTL-13, apx 16 km W Dong Xoai and 76 km due N Saigon. "SF, (C-130, C-123, C-7) ARVN (US Army also

on field) 13Feb69, USAF # VA3-286," in Aug69 TAD per Frank Penk. Not in Feb73 TAD. Binh Long Pr, III Corps.

Chi Linh SF Camp (XT 916-735)
Along Rte LTL-13, and adj to Chi Linh AF, apx 16 km W Dong Xoia and 76 km due N Saigon? SF Det 48, 5th SF CIDG Det A-333, here Jan67. Transferred to 1st Cav Div? Info/grid per *SF Order of Battle.* Binh Long Pr, III Corps.

Chi, LZ (BR 697-735)
In narrow river valley apx 14 km N Vinh Thanh AF, 32 km NNE An Khe. Jan67. Cited in 1st Cav. *Yearbook* Aug65-Dec69, p 89, per Peter Cole. Binh Dinh Pr, II Corps.

Chiang Kai-Shek (n/a)
See Glossary.

Chiang Kham Airfield (PB 3-5)
At 19°30'00"N-100°17'00"E, or apx 585 km N Bangkok. NIMA data. Feb67 Natl Geo map. El. 1,300'. Thailand.

Chiang Khan Airfield (QV 8-8)
At 17°54'00"N-101°41'00"E. NIMA data. Feb67 Natl Geo map. El. 400'. Thailand.

Chiang Khong Airfield (PC 4-3)
Apx 730 km N Bangkok, along rte 3 at Laotian border. Feb67 Natl Geo map. Listed abnd in '66. At 20°11'00"N-100°24'00"E. NIMA data. El. 1,200'. Thailand.

Chiang Mai (MA 9-7)
Apx 575 km NNW Bangkok. SF camp or AO per *SF Order of Battle.* Thailand.

Chiang Mai Airfield (MA 9-7)
Apx 550 km NNW Bangkok, at 18°46'00"N-98°58'00"E. NIMA data. Feb67 Natl Geo map. El. 1,062'. Thailand.

Chiang Rai (NB 8-9)
Apx 680 km due N Bangkok. SF camp or AO per *SF Order of Battle.* Thailand.

Chiang Rai Airfield (NB 8-9)
Apx 680 km due N Bangkok at 19°53'00"N-99°49'00"E. NIMA data. Feb67 Natl Geo map. El. 1,365'. Thailand.

Chiang Saen Airfield (n/a)
Near tri-border area of Burma, Laos and Cambodia, apx 725 km due N Bangkok. El. 1,500'. Thailand.

Chiayaphum Airfield (SC 8-4)
Spelling variant of Chaiyaphum AF. Thailand

Chic, LZ (BS)
Somewhere N of Quang Ngai and near refugee camp along river that housed 11,000 civilians during sweep of VC from Batangan Peninsula. Also housed an ARVN/SVN Govt combined Holding and Interrogation Ctr. Americal List. Quang Ngai Pr, I Corps.

Chicago, USS (n/a)
CG-11. Cruiser, per Ralph Fries.

Chicago Peak, Operation (YD 33-10)
Apr70 101st Abn Op focused on 2 NVA Rgts operating in slopes of Co Pung Mtn hill mass, in area known as The Warehouse. See Co Pung Mtn and FSB Ripcord. Thua Thien Pr, I Corps.

Chicken, LZ (YD 692-158)
A.k.a. OP Viper, OP Tiger and OP Ngoc Ho. Apx 6 km SW Hue, 7 km due N FSB Birmingham. Apr70 XXIV Corps grid per Don Armstrong. Thua Thien Pr, I Corps.

Chicken of the Sea (n/a)
See *Helgoland.* SVN.

Chickie Pie, OP (AT 8-4?)
See OP Chickie Pie. Quang Nam Pr, I Corps.

Chicksaw, LZ (BS 840-149)
Apx 5 km WNW Gia An and 15 km NNE LZ English. Feb67. Binh Dinh Pr, II Corps.

Chief, LZ (YD 035-361)
In river valley apx 34 km WSW Quang Tri, 1 km N LZ Dedham and 14 km NE Lang Klung. Apr70 XXIV Corps grid per Don Armstrong. Quang Tri Pr, I Corps.

Chiem Hoa (n/a)
Mapsheet name of L-7014-6053-2. NVN only.

Chiem Hoa (WK 2-4)
Apx 140 km NNW Hanoi and 30 km N Tuyen Quang. Involved in French Op Lea, Oct47. On map in *Street Without Joy*, p 31. NVN.

Chieu Hoi Center (XT 204-501)
At NW edge of Tay Ninh, apx 4 km ESE Tay Ninh West AF and near intersection of QL-22 and LTL-13. Aug67. Tay Ninh Pr, III Corps.

Chieu Hoi Program (n/a)
See Glossary.

Chieu Tich Chung (n/a)
See Biet Kichs.

Chim Chim, Mui (XQ 8-6)
Coastal point, 8°41'N-106°39'E. NC48-11 JOG. IV Corps.

Chin Si (n/a)
See Glossary.

Chin Sung (BT?)
SW Tam Ky. Americal list. Quang Tin Pr?, I Corps.

China, Forces of (Communist) (n/a)
See Chinese Communist Forces in Major HQs Section.

China, Republic of, Forces (n/a)
See Taiwan, Forces of, in Major HQs Section.

China Beach (BT 07-78)
A.k.a. My Khe. US in-country R&R center on ocean side of Tien Sha Peninsula between Monkey Mtn and Marble Mtn. Subject of popular 80's US TV Series of same name (show bore little resemblance to real place and what went on there). Da Nang, Quang Nam Pr, I Corps.

China Beach Public Works Cmpd (BT 06-77?)
See White Elephant. Quang Nam Pr, I Corps.

China Boy Battalion (n/a)
See Glossary and C-3 Cmpd.

Chinaimo Airfield (TE 49-81)
LS-279. Apx 10 km SE Vientiane, per ONC-J-11. CIA/SF, per *Air Facilities Data-Laos.* El. 570'. Laos.

Chinese Arroyo, The (XS 85-89)
Series of canals along S edge of Saigon, immed E Cholon and immed S of the Lycee. Gia Dinh Pr, III Corps.

Chinese Communist Forces (n/a)
See China, Communist Forces of in Major HQs Section.

Chinh Duc, FSB (YT 68-36)
Apx 6 km NW Vo Dat. 161 Bty, RNZA (Kenning's Bty 13Jun65-13Jun66) FSB set here 25-29Nov65. Grid is est. Long Khanh Pr, III Corps.

Chipola, USS (n/a)
AO-63. SVN

Chippewa, LZ (BS 485-967)
Apx 11 km SSW Chu Lai, 26 km NNW Quang Ngai and 10 km W QL-1. Also listed by arty ORLL at BS 485-968. Americal list. Quang Ngai Pr, I Corps.

Chitose Maru, SS (n/a)
Ocean Tug of MSC, under contract to DOD. See Evacuation of Da Nang, and Op Frequent Wind.

Chloe (n/a)
6Apr70, XXIV Corps future-use Americal FSB name.

Chloe, FSB (AT 938-476)
W of a long, narrow lake, apx 8 km ENE An Hoa AF, 26 km WSW Hoi An, and 28 km SSW Da Nang AB. Americal list. Quang Nam Pr, I Corps.

Cho (n/a)
See Glossary.

Cho Ben (YS 43-57)
Ville NE Vung Tau near 10°28'00"N-107°13'00"E. On NC48-07 JOG. Phuoc Tuy Pr, III Corps.

Cho Bo (n/a)
Mapsheet name of L-7014-6050-4. NVN only.

Cho Cau Ha CAP (ZD 083-005?)
See CAP 3-2 HQ. Thua Thien Pr, I Corps.

Cho Chu (n/a)
Mapsheet name of L-7014-6152-4. NVN only.

Cho Don (n/a)
Mapsheet name of L-7014-6153-3. NVN only.

Cho Don (WK 6-5)
Apx 130 km NNW Hanoi, 40 km NNW Cho Moi. Vietminh HQ, Bac Kan, Ho Moi and Cho Don were targets of French Para drops during Op Lea, 7Oct47. See map in *Street Without Joy*, p 31. NVN.

Cho Gao Heliport (XS 605-441)
Along Rte TL-25, apx 10 km due E My Tho, and 45 km SSW Saigon. "Heliport #549, alt 7' sod, very confined, wires, antennas, buildings." At 10°21'00"N-106°28'00"E, per Feb73 TAD. Go Cong Pr, IV Corps.

Cho Giat (n/a)
Mapsheet name of L-7014-6147-3. NVN only.

Cho Lach Heliport (XS 229-342)
Along Rte TL-30, on island in Mekong River, apx 28 km WSW My Tho and 16 km E Vinh Long. "Heliport #550, alt 7', soccer field." At 10°16'00"N-106°06'30"E, per 73 TAD. Kien Hoa Pr, IV Corps.

Cho Moi (BS 76-83?)
NE Quang Ngai, near coast and on southern end of Batangan Peninsula. Quang Ngai Pr, I Corps.

Cho Moi (n/a)
Mapsheet name of L-7014-6152-1. NVN only.

Cho Moi (UK 9-8)
Apx 90 km due N Hanoi, 40 km SSE Cho Don. Vietminh HQ Bac Kan, Ho Moi and Cho Don, were targets of French Para drops during Op Lea, 7Oct47. See map in *Street Without Joy*, p 31. NVN.

Cho Moi Navy Base (BS 76-83?)
If grid correct, was near Dong Xuan (2), apx 15 km NE Quang Ngai and at southern end of Batangan Peninsula. USN Logistics Installation, '69-71. Per MRF Assn Website. Quang Ngai Pr?, I Corps.

Cho Phuoc Hai (n/a)
Mapsheet name of L-7014-6429-1. SVN.

Cho Ra (n/a)
Mapsheet name of L-7014-6153-4. NVN only.

Cho River (BT 42-14)
Grid apx 15 km NW Chu Lai AF. Quang Tin Pr, I Corps.

Cho Thon, Camp (XT 7-6?)
Likely variant of "Chon Thanh." Listed spelling only in DA Chief, Mil Hist records summary, which also shows that Det A-332B (a.k.a. 325A) here '65, and A-33 in '66. See Chon Thanh SF Camp. Binh Long Pr?, III Corps.

Choa, Cape (WG 9-8)
See Cape Choa. NVN.

Choam Khsan Airfield (WA)
Apx 115 km due S Ubon AB, 90 km WNW Kampong Sralau AF, 10 km from Thai border and 30 km from Lao border, per TPC K-10A. El. 247'. Cambodia.

Choctaw, FSB (YT 02-22)
On E bank of Song Dong Nai, immed SW Xon Lon, 8 km NNE Bien Hoa AB and about 18 km W FSB New Orleans. 5th/12th and 3d/7th Inf, 199th LIB. Bien Hoa Pr, III Corps.

Choke Point Bombing (n/a)
See Glossary.

Cholon (XS 82-88)
Major suburb of Saigon, generally along the S to SW edge of city just E of what was known as "The Chinese Arroyo." Apparently 90% Chinese during war. See Saigon and Precinct Five. Gia Dinh Pr, III Corps. [120]

Cholon BOQ (XS 8-9)
US Officers billet, Oct 65-68, 16 rms, Saigon. Data per *Vietnam Military Lore, 1959-1973*. Gia Dinh Pr, III Corps.

Chom Chang (n/a)
Mapsheet name of L-7014-5753-2. NVN only.

Chon May Dong, Cape (AU 83-08)
See Chon May Dong. Thua Thien Pr, I Corps.

Chon May Dong, Mui (AU 83-08)
A.k.a. the Parrot's Beak and Mui Chan May Dong, per Ed Escoffier. Apx 35 km W to WSW Phu Bai, 3 km NNW Hill 88 and 37 km NNW Da Nang AB. Site of FSB Hill 88. At 16°21'N-108°01'E. Thua Thien Pr, I Corps.

Chon May Est, Cap (AU 8-0)
A.k.a. Mui Chan May Dong. Cape at 16°21'N-108°01'E. On ND49-01 JOG. Thua Thien Pr, I Corps.

Chon May Ouest, Cape (ZD 1-0)
See Cape Chon May Quest. Thua Thien Pr, I Corps.

Chon May Tay, Mui (ZD 1-0)
Cape Chon May Tay. Coastal point at 16°21'N-107°57'E. NE48-16. Thua Thien Pr, I Corps.

Chon May, Cap (AU 8-0)
Mui Chan May Dong. Cape at 16°21'N-108°01'E. On ND49-01 JOG. Thua Thien Pr, I Corps.

Chon May, Mui (AU 8-0)
A.k.a. Mui Chan May Dong. Cape at 16°21'N-108°01'E. On ND49-01 JOG. Thua Thien Pr, I Corps.

Chon May, Mui (ZD 1-0)
Mui Chon May Tay. Coastal point at 16°21'N-107°57'E. NE48-16 JOG. Thua Thien Pr, I Corps.

Chon May, Vung (AU 7-0)
Bay at 16°20'N-108°00'E. On ND49-01 JOG. Thua Thien Pr, I Corps.

Chon Thanh (XT 76-61)
Ville on Thunder Road (QL-13) at its intersection with LTL-13. Apx 25 km S An Loc, 15 km SE Minh Thanh AF, 33 km SW Dong Xoai AF and 24 km due N Lai Khe. Binh Long Pr, III Corps.

Chon Thanh Airfield (XT 767-610)
Apx 25 km S An Loc, 15 km SE Minh Thanh AF, 33 km SW Dong Xoai AF and 24 km due N Lai Khe AF, per TPC K-10D. El. 250', 3,600' steel-mat/ laterite rwy. 11°25'10"N-106°37'10"E. Binh Long Pr, III Corps.
Chon Thanh Heliport (XT 767-623)
Apx 25 km S An Loc, 15 km SE Minh Thanh AF, 33 km SW Dong Xoai AF and 24 km due N Lai Khe. "Heliport #551, alt 118', vacant lot." At 11°24'00"N-106°37'15"E, per 73 TAD. Binh Long Pr, III Corps.
Chon Thanh Hwy Strip AF (XT 767-610)
See Chon Thanh AF. Binh Long Pr, III Corps.
Chon Thanh SF Camp (XT 767-618)
Apx 25 km S An Loc, 15 km SE Minh Thanh AF, 33 km SW Dong Xoai AF and 24 km due N Lai Khe. 5th SF, Det A-325A (was 332-B), Oct65, A-333, Oct66 Moved to Chi Linh. Listed as Chon Thon SF Camp in Sherman's list, but likely same as Chon Thanh. Grid per *SF Order of Battle.* Binh Long Pr, III Corps.
Chon Thon SF Camp (XT 767-618?)
Likely variant of "Chon Thanh." Binh Long Pr?, III Corps.
Chonburi (n/a)
Thailand. SF camp or AO per *SF Order of Battle.*
Chong Ha Airfield (UH 28-17)
LS-48. CIA/SF, per *Air Facilities Data-Laos.*
Chong Mek Airfield (n/a)
Possibly Ban Fang Lum AF? Along Rte 16 at Laotian border, apx 540 km ENE Bangkok per Feb67 Natl Geo map. El. 570'. Thailand.
Choo Choo Train Insert (n/a)
See Glossary.
Chopper (n/a)
Apr70, XXIV Corps future-use 101st Abn FSB name.
Chord, LZ (XT 025-785)
Apx 7 km WSW Thien Ngon AF. Apr66. Tay Ninh Pr, III Corps.
Chowanoc, USS (n/a)
ATF-100. Aux Ship, per Ralph Fries.
Chris, FSB (n/a)
199th LIB FSB/patrol base on 199th Assn's website. No grid. Quite possibly Chris at YT 452-900? III Corps.
Chris, FSB/LZ (YT 452-900)
Appears to have overlooked Song Dong Nai River Valley, apx 70 km due W An Loc, 16 km E Bunard AF and 16 km S Duc Phong. Opened or reopened 13Aug70, closed 23Aug70. 2d/12th Cav Data per *1st Cav Div Op Rpt, ending 31Oct70*, courtesy Peter Cole. Arty ORLL grid. Phuoc Long Pr, III Corps.
Chris, LZ (BR 692-613)
A.k.a. Hill 975/Vinh Thanh Mtn. Apx 8 km E Vinh Thanh AF and 26 km NE An Khe. Oct69. Binh Dinh Pr, II Corps.
Christina, FSB (XT 308-855)
A.k.a. Christine and Kristine. Along TL-4, apx 5 km SSW Katum and 8 km due W Bo Tuc. Tay Ninh Pr, III Corps.
Christine, FSB (XT 308-855)
See Christina. Tay Ninh Pr, III Corps.
Christmas Bombing, The (n/a)
See Glossary.
Christopher, FSB (YT 735-492)
Along QL-20, apx 17 km due N Vo Dat. Jan71. Long Khanh Pr, III Corps.
Christy, LZ (YA 805-472)
Apx 24 km due W Pleiku. Jan66. Pleiku Pr, II Corps.
Chu (n/a)
Mapsheet name of L-7014-6351-4. NVN only.
Chu Amung Mountain (ZV 231-644)
A.k.a. Hill 589. Apx 25 km WNW Buon Brieng AF, 36 km SSW Phu Nhon, & 21 km E Tieu Atar. Darlac Pr, II Corps.
Chu Bak Mountain (YA 885-335)
See Hill 577. Pleiku Pr, II Corps.
Chu Don Mountain (ZV 23-94)
A.k.a. Hill 826. Apx 30 km ENE Chu Pong Mtn, 45 km S Pleiku, near Cambodian border. AO of NVA 32d and 33d Rgts in '65. Object "Cherry" for 1st Cav during effort to relieve the siege of Plei Me in Oct65. Pleiku Pr, II Corps.
Chu Dreh Mountain (AQ 903-625)
A.k.a. Hill 826. Pleiku Pr, II Corps.
Chu Dreh Pass (AQ 93-67?)
G.M. 100 heavily ambushed here 17Jul54. See Op Forget-Me-Not. Pleiku Pr, II Corps.
Chu Dron Airfield (YA 843-255)
See Duc Co AF. Pleiku Pr, II Corps.
Chu Dron SF Camp (YA 8460-2493)
A.k.a. Duc Co SF Camp. Adj Duc Co AF, apx 45 km SW Pleiku and 10 km from Cambodia. 5th SF. See Duc Co. Info/grid per *SF Order of Battle.* Pleiku Pr, II Corps.
Chu Drou Mountains (BR 1-4?)
Bordering Dak Payou (VC Valley) and Dak Doa Valleys, E LZ Blackhawk and above the Mang Yang Pass. Object of Task Force Winner Dec68?, inc elements of 2d Bde/4th Div, ARVN and a Mobile Strike Force. Discussed in *Time Heals No Wounds*, pp 76-77. Kontum Pr, II Corps.
Chu Goll Mountain (YA 92-53)
A.k.a. Hill 1005. Large hill mass apx 33 km W Pleiku, 7 km E Plei Djereng AF and overlooking Hwy 509. See Hill 1005 for more detail. Pleiku Pr, II Corps.
Chu Goungot Mountains (n/a)
Generally W of QL-14B and N of Duc Co. A/3d/12th Inf, 4th Div suffered NVA attack in these hills, 1May67, and as a result, the 4th Div began building bases and operating in that area. On 18May67, B/1st/8th Inf lost 21 KIA and 7 WIA out of one plt of 29 men; on 20May67, 1st/8th lost 16 KIA; and 66 WIA and, on 22May67, while 3d/12th Inf was moving to reinforce the 1st/8th, it suffered 10 KIA and 67 WIA. Battle data per *Dak To*, p 47. Op Francis Marion. Pleiku Pr?, II Corps.
Chu Grock Mountain (YA 810-690)
Hill 1438. See Sledge Hammer. Kontum Pr, II Corps.
Chu Kan Lo (n/a)
Likely variant of "Chu Kram Lo," a.k.a. Hill 1018 and LZ Blackfoot. In 4th Div AO, WNW Kontum and due S the Plei Trap Valley. See Chu Kram Lo. Kontum Pr?, II Corps.
Chu Kan Yan Mountain (YA 932-483)
See Hill 864. 18Jun66. Pleiku Pr, II Corps.
Chu Kbang Mountain (ZV 24-58)
A.k.a. Hill 541. Apx 28 km due W and WNW Buon Blech AF and 55 km N Ban Me Thuot. Darlac Pr, II Corps.
Chu Krah Mountain (AQ 83-83)
A.k.a. Hill 508. 17 km SSW Phu Nhon. Pleiku Pr, II Corps.
Chu Kram Lo Mountain (YA 9-9)
FSB a.k.a. Hill 1018. Apx 15 km E Cambodia and 12 km NW Polei Kleng. Large rock wall visible from this base

and about 500 meters NE of it gave enemy good observation and mortar position. Elements of 1st and 2d Bdes/4th Div here early '69, inc. 1st/12th and 1st/8th Inf. Described in *Time Heals No Wounds*, p 115-122. Near 14°26'00"N-107°42'00"E. Pleiku Pr, II Corps.

Chu Ktey Mountain (AQ 810-546)
See Hill 654. Darlac Pr, II Corps.

Chu Kuk, LZ (BQ 225-167)
A.k.a. FSB Chu Kuk. Apx 6 km WSW Ban Mrong and 41 km ENE Ban Me Thuot. FSB of Task Force 3-506, built Nov69, by elements of 3d/506th Inf, 101st Abn, while opcon to 1st Bde/4th Div to supt clearing ops along QL-21, E Ban Me Thuot, per *Currahee History, 1Feb69 to 31Dec69*, p 47. 2d/17th Arty here supt IFFV, '70. Grid and some data per Jack Picciolo. Darlac Pr, II Corps.

Chu Lai (BT 555-035)
Apx 55 air mi (88 km) SE Da Nang, 28 km SE Tam Ky, 565 km N Saigon and 3 km E QL-1. Bounded by An Tan River on N, QL-1 to W, and ocean to E. Originally a grp of coastal villes that later became a major US military complex/AF. "Chu Lai" is not Viet name, rather, Marine Gen Krulak named it per Chinese Mandarin pronunciation of his initials. Home to numerous USMC and Americal Div elements, inc 3d Mar Div FMF HQ, May 65-Jun69; HQ 23d Inf Div (Americal Div, originally Task Force Oregon). Defense Secty McNamara secured approval to build base in Mar-Apr65. On 1Jun65, VMA-225 (A-4 Skyhawks) flew 1st combat missions from its AF. Also home for Det B-11, 5th SF. 1st MAW, 1st Mar Div, FMF HQ (and at Da Nang). Also listed at BT 537-062. For map, see DMA L-7014-6739-4, 1:50,000 scale. Americal list. See Ky Ha AF. Quang Tin Pr, I Corps. [121]

Chu Lai, Old (BT 535-070)
The original PSP rwy at Chu Lai became known as Old Chu Lai while the adj 2, new rwys were under const, Sep-Oct65. Likely the N/S rwy later known as Ky Ha AF? BLT 2d/7th Marines provided security here, Oct65, after move N from Qui Nhon. Data per *Utter's Battalion*, p 167. Quang Tin Pr, I Corps.

Chu Lai Airfield (BT 537-062)
Apx 28 km SE Tam Ky AF, 36 km NNW Quang Ngai and 88 km SSE Da Nang. Built in Summer '65. El. 25', 10,000' conc and 6,000' alum-mat rwy. Quang Tin Pr. At 15°25'20"N-108°42'14"E. Quang Tin Pr, I Corps.

Chu Lai LAAM Sites (BT 53-06)
B and C Bty, 2d LAAM here '66. One at each end of Chu Lai AB rwy. C Bty later moved to Hill 141 on coast. See LAAM Sites. Quang Nam Pr, I Corps.

Chu Lai Main Gate (BT 520-044)
Americal list. Quang Tin Pr, I Corps.

Chu Lai NSA (BT 53-06?)
USN Supt Activity, '64-71. Per MRF Assn Website. Quang Tin Pr, I Corps.

Chu Lai NSA (BT 53-06?)
USN Supt Activity, '64-71. Per MRF Assn Website. Quang Tin Pr, I Corps.

Chu Lai Rai Island (BT 474-146)
Small Island in large lagoon apx 9 km NW Chu Lai AB. Quang Tin Pr, I Corps.

Chu Lai SF Camp (BT 55-03?)
Presumably near Chu Lai basecamp. 5th SF. Info/grid per *SF Order of Battle.* Quang Tin Pr, I Corps.

Chu Lai TOC (BT 562-045)
At SE end of Chu Lai AB. Tactical Ops Ctr at Chu Lai, Nov67. Quang Tin Pr, I Corps.

Chu Luc (n/a)
See Du Kich in Glossary.

Chu Ma (n/a)
Mapsheet sheet L 701-6476-3. NVN/China.

Chu Mom Rai (YB 957-998)
See Chu Mom Ray. Kontum Pr, II Corps.

Chu Mom Ray Mountain (YB 957-998)
A.k.a. Hill 1773, Chu Mom Rai and Big Mamma. See Hill 1773. Kontum Pr, II Corps.

Chu Pa, LZ (YA 952-678)
A.k.a. Hill 1485. On Chu Pa Mtn, apx 36 km SW Kontum. Opened 13Feb69, by elements of 1st/14th and 1st/12th Inf, 4th Div, suptg B/1st/14th, which had made heavy contact at YA 934-683, and completely engaged from 11-15Feb69, per AAR of 25Feb69, HQ 1st/14th Inf, posted with map at: http://1-14th.com/chupaaar.htm. Pleiku Pr, II Corps.

Chu Pa Mountain (YA 950-680)
A.k.a. Hill 1485 (4,872'). Apx 36 km SW Kontum, 36 km NW to WNW Pleiku, 8 km E the Se San River and 16 km due W Plei Mrong. This mtn and its hill-mass were carpet-bombed by B-52 strikes at 0630, 1Jun68, to help relieve siege of FSB Brillo-Pad. 4th Div AO. Pleiku Pr, II Corps.

Chu Pa Mountains (YA 95-68)
Generally 16 km due W Plei Mrong AF, 35 km NW Pleiku and 37 km SW Kontum. Grid per Jim Claeys' list. Kontum or Pleiku Pr, II Corps.

Chu Pao Pass (ZA 23-77?)
Along QL-14, apx 12 km S of Kontum. Site of bitter armored fights between T-54 and PT-76 Tanks of NVA and ARVN 3d Armored Cav, 26May-19Jun72. See John Paul Vann in Glossary. Kontum Pr, II Corps.

Chu Pong (YA 880-020)
A.k.a. Hill 732. Apx 30 km W Plei Me, 58 km SW Pleiku and 170 km WSW Qui Nhon. Also spelled Chu Prong. Also listed at YV 890-980. See Chu Prong Chu Pong Massif and LZs X-Ray and Albany. Pleiku Pr, II Corps.

Chu Pong Mountain/Massif (YA 880-020)
Hill mass of Hill 732. Apx 30 km W Plei Me and 60 km SW Pleiku. 1st Cav's 1st major battle site of war, 14-16 Nov 65. Involved 1st/7th, 2d/7th Cav and 2d/5th Cav, and a.k.a. Battle of Ia Drang Valley. See LZ X-Ray and LZ Albany. Often spelled "Chu Prong." Pleiku Pr, II Corps.

Chu Prong Mountain (various)
Common Vietnamese name for mtn peaks. Sites inc: ZA 0-7, AR 7-6, ZA 0-5, YA 8-0, BQ 6-7, BQ 1-7, BQ 4-0. Chu Pong Mtn, site of LZ X-Ray battle is listed on some maps as "Chu Prong" and others as "Chu Pong."

Chu Prong Mountain (AR 765-680)
A.k.a. Hill 1478? Apx 16 km NNE Pleiku. Not Chu Pong Mtn of LZ X-Ray fame. Cited in *Time Heals No Wounds*, p 118. Grid per 4th Div ORLL for 30Apr69. During Feb-Mar69, 2d/35th Inf, 4th Div sent here to neutralize 24th NVA Rgt and engaged in heavy fighting. Pleiku/Kontum Pr border, II Corps.

Chu Prong Mountain (ZA 000-490)
A.k.a. Hill 927. Apx 26 km W Pleiku. Pleiku Pr, II Corps.
Chu Prong Mountain (YA 88-02)
See Chu Pong Mtn at grid. Pleiku Pr, II Corps.
Chu Prong Mountains (AR 80-68)
Generally 20 km NNE Pleiku. Pleiku Pr, II Corps.
Chu Rpan (or Chu Rran)? (n/a)
Mapsheet name of L-7014-6636-1. SVN.
Chu Rran Mountain (BR 12-43)
A.k.a. Hill 1551. A 5,089' mtn apx 33 km E Pleiku and 37 km W An Khe/Camp Radcliff. Tallest and perhaps most significant terrain feature of area. 4th Div AO, '70. Pleiku Pr, II Corps.
Chu Thoi Mountain (ZA 22-75)
A.k.a. Hill 953. Apx 11 km SSW Kontum and 3 km W QL-14. LZ Highlander Heights here. Kontum Pr, II Corps.
Chu Ya Bruh Mountain (YB 869-889)
See Hill 611. Kontum Pr, II Corps.
Chu Yach Mountain (YB 928-137)
See Hill 865. Kontum Pr, II Corps.
Chua Chan Airfield (YT 638-136)
See Gia Ray AF. Long Khanh Pr, III Corps.
Chua Hoi SF Camp (WS 952-973)
A.k.a. FOB Moc Hoa. Was within 3 km of Cambodia, apx 10 km NW Moc Hoa/Muc Hoa AF and 85 km due W Saigon. 5th SF. Info/grid per *SF Order of Battle*. Kien Tuong Pr, IV Corps.
Chua Luu CAP (AT or BT?)
2d CAG per Tim Duffie. Quang Nam Pr, I Corps.
Chua, Mui (US 9-1)
Coastal point at 10°05'N-104°02'E. On NC48-05 JOG. Kien Giang Pr, IV Corps.
Chua, Vung (CQ 1-8)
Bay at 13°25'N-109°16'E. ND49-01. Phu Yen Pr, II Corps.
Chua, Vung (XE 6-8)
Bay at 17°56'N-106°31'E. On NE48-12 JOG. NVN.
Chuckwagon, LZ (ZC 175-553)
Apx 4 km ENE Ha Tan AF/SF Camp, 33 km SW Da Nang AB and 12 km NW An Hoa. XXIV Corps grid. Quang Nam Pr, I Corps.
Chudron Airfield (YA 843-255)
See Duc Co AF. Pleiku Pr, II Corps.
Chumai East Cape (AU 8-0)
A.k.a. Mui Chan May Dong. Cape at 16°21'N-108°01'E. ND49-01 JOG. Thua Thien Pr, I Corps.
Chumai West Cape (ZD 1-0)
See Cape Chumai West. Thua Thien Pr, I Corps.
Chumphon Airfield (n/a)
Near coast, apx 385 km SSW Bangkok per Feb67 Natl Geo map. El. 35'. Thailand.
Chuoampong, Bai (CP 1-6)
See Bai Chuoampong. Khanh Hoa Pr, II Corps.
Chuong Duong Bridge (WJ 9-0?)
One of two major bridges in Hanoi: the old Long Bien Bridge and new Chuong Duong Bridge respectively connected N and S parts of city across Red River. NVN.
Chuong Nghia (n/a)
Mapsheet name of L-7014-6638-2. SVN.
Chuong Nghia Airfield (BS 081-145)
See Plateau Gi AF. Kontum Pr, II Corps.
Chuong Thien Province (WR)
One of 16 southern provs forming IV Corps (IV CTZ). Possibly created shortly after or during early US presence in SVN. Actual dates of existence unknown. In Cau Mau area and in same relative position as what was earlier(?) known as Can Tho Pr, immed N Bac Lieu/Ba Xuyen Provs and E Kien Giang Pr, IV Corps.
Chup Plantation (WU 70-25)
Immed NW Phum Suong and 85 km WSW Snuol. 11°57'00"N-105°39'00"E, NC48-03 JOG. Cambodia.
Chup Plantation Airfield? (WU 63-18?)
Possible alternate name for "Phum Chup AF?" Apx 85 km ENE Phnom Penh. El. 82'. Grid est. Cambodia.
Church of Christ Orphanage (AT 945-683)
Along Rte 540, apx 10 km SW Da Nang AB. Oct68. Quang Nam Pr, I Corps.
Churchville, Battle of (YD 48-43)
Apx 5 km NE Thon My Chanh/QL-1, and 17 km SE Quang Tri. Took place 28Feb-4Mar68. Map is L-7014-6442-2, per Ken Burrington.
Chut, Mui (CP 0-5)
Coastal point at 12°13'N-109°13'E. On ND49-13 JOG. Khanh Hoa Pr, II Corps.
CIA Station Saigon (XS 863-922)
See Saigon CIA. Gia Dinh Pr, III Corps.
Cider, LZ (YA 829-891)
Apx 26 km SW Polei Kleng, 4 km NW peak of Hill 1528 (5,013'), 42 km WSW Kontum and 22 km E Cambodian border. Grid per 4thDiv ORLL for period ending 30Apr69, and printed in *Time Heals No Wounds*, at p 169. Also listed at YA 828-798. Kontum Pr, II Corps.
CIDG Camps (generally)
See formal name followed by comma and "CIDG," as in "A-102 CIDG Camp."
Cinch (n/a)
6Apr70, XXIV Corps future-use 5th Div FSB name.
Cinch, LZ (BR 983-692)
In small hill mass, apx 29 km SSE Bong Son, 8 km E QL-1 and 6 km from coast. Oct66. Binh Dinh Pr, II Corps.
Cincinnati, Operation (n/a)
17-23May67. 173d Abn, Bien Hoa/Long Binh AO. Bien Hoa Pr, III Corps.
Cindy, FSB (BS 345-883)
See Cindy, LZ. Quang Tin Pr?, I Corps.
Cindy, FSB (XT 384-815)
Apx 12 km SE Katum, 5 km S Bo Tuc and 25 km NNE Nui Ba Den. Per Arty ORLL grid. Tay Ninh Pr, III Corps.
Cindy, FSB/LZ (YD 192-411)
A.k.a. FSB Hooker. Apx 17 km WSW Quang Tri, and 12 km SE Mai Loc. Per Kevan Mynderup, Cindy was built by 1st/8th Cav, 1st Cav, beginning 29Aug68, and was hit by a typhoon during its construction. Grid per map courtesy Wm. Robert Stanley. 1st/5th Cav here per Frank Penk. Also listed at YD 198-403, 197-307, and 213-427. Quang Tri Pr, I Corps.
Cindy, FSB (YT 014-305)
Apx 17 km N to NNE Bien Hoa AB, 3 km SE Khu Tru Mat Mar69. Bien Hoa Pr, III Corps.
Cindy, FSB/LZ (YT 135-328)
Along a tributary of Song Dong Nai River, apx 4 km N the Dong Nai, 22 km NE Bien Hoa AB, 44 km NE Saigon, 25

km SE Phuoc Vinh AF and 12 km WSW FSB Liz. Built by 1st/12th Cav, 1st Cav, Feb-69. 1st/7th Cav, 1st Cav here May-69, during Op Cheyenne Saber. Grid per Frank Penk, Jr. Also at YT 139-313 per Peter Cole and XT 7-0 per Tom Skelly? Bien Hoa/Binh Duong Pr border, III Corps.

Cindy, FSB/LZ (XT 382-797)
Apx 6 km E Katum AF, 20 km W tip of Fishhook and 4 km from Cambodia at closest point. 1st Cav, '69? Name/grid per Dan Gillotti, 15th Arty Assn. Also listed at XT 384-815. Tay Ninh Pr, III Corps.

Cindy, FSB? (XT 7-0?)
Per Tom Skelly, was apx 13-15 km NW Saigon. He says base "had a decent sized hill in middle and was built along river." Apparently constructed by 1st/12th Cav, 1st Cav. Gia Dinh Pr?, III Corps.

Cindy, LZ/FSB (BS 343-882)
A.k.a. FSB Tra Bong. Near Cinnamon Forest, apx 2 km E Tra Bong, 27 km SW Chu Lai, 35 km WNW Quang Ngai, 8 km due S peak of Nui Dong Tranh (Hill 1362) and in Song Tra Bong Valley. Army 155 and 175mm arty units here. Major battle here Aug69. Also listed by arty ORLL at BS 342-883 and at BS 345-883. XXIV Corps grid per Don Armstrong. Americal list. Quang Ngai Pr, I Corps.

Cinnamon Forest (BS 3-8?)
Area near LZ Cindy at BS 343-882 or BS 342-883. Americal list. Quang Ngai Pr, I Corps.

Cinnamon General, The (n/a)
See Glossary.

Circle 3-4 BOQ (XS 8-9)
Officers billets for 34th Gen Supt Grp, Saigon. Data per *Vietnam Military Lore, 1959-1973*. Gia Dinh Pr, III Corps.

Circle Sportif (n/a)
See Cercle Sportif. NVN & SVN.

Cirlao Da Srang (n/a)
Mapsheet name of L-7014-6531-1. SVN.

Citadel, Hue (YD 75-23)
Large (apx 5.2 sq-km, or 1,300 acres), walled-city built on N bank of Song Huong (Perfume) River in Hue and interlaced with moats and thick fortress walls. Though often referred to as ancient, const actually began in 1804 under Emperor Nguyen Anh (a.k.a. Gia Long and 1st Nguyen emperor). Access to US military was generally restricted to tourism until NVA entrenched itself in this historic, beautiful and formidable structure during Tet '68. When all reasonable efforts to evict NVA failed, air and arty strikes were reluctantly authorized within the Citadel itself. It suffered heavy damage as result. See Hue entry. Thua Thien Pr, I Corps.

City, The (XU 52-21/52-23)
Listed grid is for building complex portion of this 3 by 5 km NVA supply depot and indicates it was apx 14 km SSW Snuol, 2 km E Rte 7, 25 km NW Loc Ninh, 4 km SW tip of Angel's Wing 11 km S Phum Rohar. Weapons stg area said to have been at XU 52-23, to N of bldg complex. Huge NVA/VC basecamp that was destroyed by US forces during May70 Cambodian Invasion. An estimated 11,700 bunkers and huge supply and ammo stores were also destroyed there. Nicknamed "The City" by US troops because of its incredible size. Grid apx. Cambodia.

Civil Air Transport Company (n/a)
See Glossary.

Claire, FSB (YT 820-455)
Apx 21 km NNW Tan Linh AF and 5 km W Mepu. Jan71. Binh Tuy Pr, III Corps.

Clara, FSB (XS 415-979)
Apx 5 km W the FSB Clara listed at XS 454-976, and about 14 km SE Duc Hue AF and 40 km W Tan Son Nhut AB. Grid per Peter Cole, 1st Cav. Also listed at XT 41-98, and likely UTM grid zone error? Hau Nghia Pr, III Corps.

Clara, FSB (XS 454-976?)
If grid correct, was apx 36 km W to WNW Tan Son Nhut AB, 10 km SW Khiem Cuong, and 15 km WNW Duc Hoa AF. 1st/7th Cav, 1st Cav, Jan-69. Grid per Frank Penk, Jr. On Americal list, a Clara is listed at XT 41-??, and on another list at XS 415-976? Hau Nghia Pr, III Corps.

Clara, FSB (XT 41-98?)
If grid correct, was in Cambodia, apx 13 km NE Katum? Clara also listed XS 454-976 and XS 415-979, which are likely all same base. Unknown which grid is correct; however, it is doubtful listed grid is correct? Cambodia?

Clare, FSB (n/a)
Possibly Clara or Claire? Cited in *1st Cav Div Op Rpt of Nov68-Apr69*, at p 3, per Peter Cole. During period, Cav was in III Corps.

Clare, FSB (YS 208-833)
On QL-15 apx 28 km NW Nui Dat, 2.5 km NW FSB Julia and 1.5 km S FSB Margaret. On 1ATF NCO trng map per John Hollett. 1ATF. Bien Hoa Pr, III Corps.

Clarion River, USS (n/a)
LSMR 409. In Apr66, the Rocket firing platforms of *USS Carronade* (IFS 1) and *St. Francis River* (LSMR 525) reinforced the Naval Gunfire Supt Unit off I Corps in May67, *USS Clarion River* (LSMR 409) and *White River* (LSMR 536) were added.

Clarke County, USS (n/a)
LST-601. SVN.

Clark Air Force Base Hospital (n/a)
A.k.a. Salamat-Po? Used extensively for treatment of Vietnam War casualties, particularly in early years of war and in later years as US forces were withdrawn. Navy and Marine casualties were sent here almost exclusively while Army casualties normally found their way to Camp Zama Japan's 249th Gen Hosp. At end of war, American POWs released by NVA were processed through this facility before returning home. See Clark Air Force Base, 249th Gen, US Army Hosp and USAF Hosp.

Clark Air Force Base (n/a)
Apx 5 km E Sapangbato, 8 km NW Angeles and 10 km SSW Bamban, the Philippines. Volcano Mt. Pinatubo was apx 11 nautical miles WSW Clark (its eruption in '95 or '96 led to permanent closure of base), 25 nautical mi E ocean and 55 nautical mi W Dingaln Bay. Bombing and surveillance missions over VN were flown from this base, as were many re-supply and personnel replacement flights. USAF hospital here was used extensively to treat VN casualties, particularly early in war. At outset of US involvement, B-57 bombers flew many missions from this field. Test pilot Chuck Yeager (1st man to break the speed of sound) was a wing cmdr(?) here and flew over 100 bombing missions over VN in early 60's. Philippines.

Clarksburg Victory, SS (n/a)
Merchant ship under govt contract, per Ralph Fries.

Class Six Store (n/a)
See Glossary.
Clateau, Baie (XH 8-8)
Bay at 20°41'N-106°48'E. On NF48-16 JOG. NVN.
Claude Jones, USS (n/a)
DD-1033 per Ralph Fries.
Claudette, FSB (XS 671-923)
Apx 15 km WNW Tan Son Nhut AB and on S side of QL-1. 199th LIB position. Near Hau Nghia/Gia Dinh Pr border, III Corps.
Claudine (TJ)
The Claudines were five defensive positions (known as D1 thru D5) forming the S and SW perimeter of main Dien Bien Phu complex at TJ 9-6 and situated in Muong Thanh Valley apx 290 km W Hanoi. French strongpoint during Op Castor, 20Nov53-7May54. NVN.
Claus, LZ (BR 838-652)
In mtns, apx 31 km S Bong Son and 7 km SW Phu My. Oct66. Binh Dinh Pr, II Corps.
Claw, FSB (XS 600-290)
See FSB Klaw. Kien Hoa Pr, IV Corps.
Claw II, FSB (XS 600-270)
See Klaw II. Kien Hoa Pr, IV Corps.
Claymore Corner (YT 63-08?)
Possibly the intersection of QL-1 and Rte 333? Between Suoi Cat and Gia Ray, apx 80 km ENE Saigon and 5 km S Gia Ray. Battle of Suoi Cat began in ambush of 1st Sqdn, 11th ACR here 2Dec66. 1st major engagement of war for US 11th ACR. Cav's successful tactics here helped establish SOP for many US armor units in war. III Corps.
Claymore Corners (XT 888-367)
Apx 12 km due E Lai Khe AF. On map in *Low Level Hell.* Binh Duong Pr, III Corps.
CLD SF Camp (XS 853-9295)
A.k.a. SF Cmd Liaison Det camp. Apx 7 km SW Tan Son Nhut AB and 16 km ESE Duc Hoa AF. CLD, 5th SF. Info/grid per *SF Order of Battle.* Gia Dinh Pr, III Corps.
Clear River (WJ 45-75)
A.k.a. the Song Lo. N to S flowing river in northern Tonkin, joining the Red River at Viet Tri, apx 45 km WNW Hanoi. 2 Inf Bns of French riverborne troops (Groupement C under LTC Communal) were sent up the Clear on LCT's beginning 9Oct47, during Op Lea. Data per *Street Without Joy*, p 29. NVN.
Cleaver (n/a)
6Apr70, XXIV Corps future-use III MAF FSB name.
Clemson, LZ (BS 480-828)
Apparently a.k.a. LZ Paris, as grids are identical. Apx 3 km N Ba Gia AF, 3 km NW Xuan Hoa, and 18 km NW Quang Ngai. Map is L-7014-6739-3. Americal list. Quang Ngai Pr, I Corps.
Cleopatra, FSB (XS 1-5?)
W of Cai Be along QL 4 and in Giao Duc District. 9th Inf FSB built in '68. Apparently closed Jan69, and occupants sent to FSB Dirk (a.k.a. FSB Schroeder). On map L-7014-6129-1 (Sa Dec). Data per Jim Stone, 2d/39th Inf. Dinh Tuong Pr, IV Corps.
Cleveland, USS (n/a)
LPD-7. Lndg. Platform, Dock, See Op End Sweep.
Clifford, LZ (BT 258-103)
Apx 10 km SSW Tam Ky AF, 15 km E FSB Boxer and 16 km ESE Tien Phuoc AF. Also listed at BT 259-104 by arty ORLL and at BT 260-135. Apr70 XXIV Corps grid per Don Armstrong. Americal list. Also listed at BT 260-135 which is apx 3 km N listed grid. Quang Tin Pr, I Corps.
Clipper, LZ (XD 856-650)
Apx 28 km WNW Cam Lo, 25 km N Khe Sanh CD and 50 km WNW Quang Tri. Apr70 XXIV Corps grid per Don Armstrong. Quang Tri Pr, I Corps.
Clive Steel, HMAS (n/a)
AV-1356. Australian warship serving under US 7th Flt. Originally *USS LSM-547,* sold to Australia, '60, assigned to Australian Army Royal Engrs, 32 Small Ship Sqdn.
Cloud (n/a)
XXIV Corps future-use 5th Div FSB name. Never built?
Cloud 9 (YA 810-690)
See Sledge Hammer. Kontum Pr, II Corps.
Clouds, Pass of (AT 9-9)
A.k.a. Hai Van Pass, Deo Hai Van and Deo Des Nuages. NIMA data. Thua Thien Pr, I Corps.
Clovis (n/a)
6Apr70, XXIV Corps future-use 5th Div FSB name.
Clowes, FSB (YS 385-636)
Apx 5.5 km SW Nui Dat, 800 meters N LTL-2 and 10 km WNW FSB Horseshoe. On 1ATF NCO trng map per John Hollett. 1ATF. Phuoc Tuy Pr, III Corps.
Club, LZ (YD 167-503)
In lowland area apx 16 km W Quang Tri and 8 km E Mai Loc. Apr70 XXIV Corps grid per Don Armstrong. Quang Tri Pr, I Corps.
Clubs, LZ (BS 441-028)
Remote site was apx 31 km WSW Thuan An and 43 km due W LZ English. Mar66. Binh Dinh Pr, II Corps.
Club Car, Operation (n/a)
1st Force Recon mission during which USMC Corpsman, "Doc" Michael L. LaPorte, allegedly defected to enemy. Per *Prisoners of Hope*, pp 67-68.
Club Montgomery (XS 8-9)
At 11 Dang Duc Sieu St., Saigon. Named to honor Sp4 William J. Montgomery, USA, KIA 4May64, when a C-7 Caribou in which he was a passenger crashed near Tan Hiep. Apparently 11th US soldier to die in SVN, and club became 1st mess hall in war to be named to honor a fallen SF soldier. Data per *Vietnam Military Lore, Legends, Shadows, and Heroes*, p 601-2. Gia Dinh Pr, III Corps.
Club Newbern (XT 958-001?)
In Camp Ho Ngoc Tau, apx 3 km E Thu Duc, apx 13 km S Bien Hoa AB and 16 km ENE Tan Son Nhut AB. Named to honor SSgt Michael Newbern, USA, Team 5, Det B-56 (Project Sigma), 5th SF, KIA 21Oct66, in VC ambush of his patrol during Op Fond Du Lac. 1st Det B-56 member to die in VN. Gia Dinh Pr, III Corps.
CN Gas (n/a)
A.k.a. Tear Gas. See M-79 Grenade Launcher, E-158 Canister, CS Gas Incident; all in Glossary.
Co A Nong Mountain (YD 239-118)
A.k.a. Tiger Mtn, or Hill 1228. Apx 50 km WSW Hue, 12 km Tou Rout. Quang Tri Pr, I Corps.

Co A Nong Mountain (YD 253-090)
See Hill 1228, and FSBs Tiger and Turnage. Thua Thien Pr, I Corps.

Co Co, Lach (CP 2-9)
Channel near 12°38'N-109°21'E. On ND49-13 JOG. Khanh Hoa Pr, II Corps.

Co Co, Mui (CQ 1-0)
Coastal point at 12°40'N-109°20'E. On ND49-13 JOG. Khanh Hoa Pr, II Corps.

Co Do (n/a)
Mapsheet name of L-7014-6029-2. SVN.

Co Ka Vu (YD 183-140)
A.k.a. Hill 672. SW Quang Tri Pr overlooking the Da Krong River Valley to its S and W. Quang Tri Pr, I Corps.

Co Kay Leuye (YD 12-07)
A.k.a. Hill 1175 and also spelled Co Cay Leuye and Co Ka Leuye. At Lao border, apx 65 km WSW Hue, 7 km due S LZ Dallas, 9 km SW FSB Cunningham. On map at p 32, *US Marines in Vietnam-1969*. Quang Tri Pr, I Corps.

Co Loa, FSB? (XU 475-010)
Either ville in Cambodia near FSB Center, or Cambodian Invasion FSB of 11th ACR/1st Cav TF. Apx 6 km W the SVN border, 15 km NW tip of Fishhook, 2 km NE FSB Center, 20 km NE Katum and 26 km WSW Loc Ninh. Grid per *11th ACR Cambodia Invasion AAR, 1st Cav Div, May-Jun70*, courtesy Lou Rochat. [122] Cambodia.

Co May Causeway (YS 370-540)
QL-15 causeway across tidal flats that connected Phuoc Le with Vung Tau. Nov67. Phuoc Tuy Pr, III Corps.

Co Pung, FSB (YD 336-107)
A.k.a. Co Pung Mtn, Hill 1615 and FSB An Duong Vuong. Built Apr71, at N end of A Shau Valley, apx 12 km due N FSB Destiny (Dong Ap Bia/Hamburger Hill), 11 km NNW A Luoi AF and perhaps 40 km due W Hue. Described in *Rendezvous With Destiny*, Fall '71, at p 38, as highest peak in N end of A Shau (nearby Dong Ngai was actually 100 meters taller). Apparently became FSB An Duong Vuong, when reopened, 9May71. Phase 1 of Lam Son 720 began with, among other things, 2d/502d Inf, 101st Abn assaulting this site apx 14Apr71, and securing it while A/326th Engrs built FSB here that was taken over by ARVN for balance of op and remained key OP/FSB throughout Summer. Thua Thien Pr, I Corps.

Co Pung Mountain (YD 335-107)
A.k.a. Hill 1615, FSB Co Pung and The Warehouse. Apx 43 km WSW Hue, 5 km NW Dong Ngai Mtn, 3.5 km NE La Dut (1), 4 km E the N end of A Shau Valley and 9 km due S FSB Ripcord. Hill mass known as "The Warehouse" by 101st Abn because it served as huge supply complex for NVA's 29th and 803d Rgts, 324B Div. Complex was objective of Op Chicago Peak, Apr70, and soon after that, Op Texas Star, which led to siege of FSB Ripcord. Ripcord was built early 70, as arty, Tac Air and B-52 airstrike FO platform for campaign to interdict NVA who'd been unmolested in Warehouse area for 2 years. See Ripcord. Thua Thien Pr, I Corps.

Co Put (XD 8-3 or 8-4?)
Along QL-9, N Lang Vei and W Khe Sanh. Home of 3d Bn, 101st Rgt, 325C NVA Div during siege of Khe Sanh. Quang Tri Pr, I Corps.

Co Roc Mountain (XD 741-317)
Main peak of range in Laos apx 15 km SW Khe Sanh, 7 km SW Lang Vei, and from which NVA rained 130 and 152mm arty shells on Khe Sanh CB during 67-68 siege. NVA arty kept inside caves and only brought out to fire and, despite heavy bombing and counter battery fire, was never silenced. Noted for its spectacular, rugged beauty and sheer cliffs. Good photo of it as seen from Hill 861 follows p 168 of *Valley of Decision*. Laos.

Co Roc Ridge (XD 7-2)
Ran apx from XD 725-350 to XD 770-310. In *Da Nang Diary* (p 108), author describes this ridge as "amoebae-shaped formation" that rose 1,200' above the Se Pone River in eastern Laos, just across border from SVN. It also reminded him of miniature version of 1/2 of the Grand Canyon. "Scrub jungle covered the top of this 8 km-long ridgeline, which ran roughly N/S on its axis. Its southern end sloped down gently to W before flattening into a large plain." Good photo of ridge as seen from Hill 861 is in pictorial following p 168 of *Valley of Decision*. Laos.

Co Trang (n/a)
Mapsheet name of L-7014-6243-1. NVN/Laos.

Coal Mines (various)
See An Hoa Industrial Complex, Mao Khe and Nong Son.

Coast Guard Division 11 (US 93-07?)
At An Thoi, Kien Giang Pr, IV Corps.

Coast Guard Division 12 (BT 0-1)
At Da Nang. Quang Nam Pr, I Corps.

Coast Guard Division 13 (CP 0-5 or YS 36-52?)
Stationed at Cat Lo. Cat Lo Navy Base was near YS 36-52? Khanh Hoa or Phuoc Tuy Pr?, II Corps.

Coastal Surveillance Force (n/a)
See Glossary.

Coat, LZ (BR 870-770)
On mtn apx 18 km SSE Bong Son, 6 km W QL-1 and 3 km NNE Lac Son. Feb66. Binh Dinh Pr, II Corps.

COB Battle Ax (ZC 11-30)
See Battle Ax. Quang Nam/Quang Tin Pr border, I Corps.

COB Dart (ZC 14-31)
See Dart, FSB. Quang Nam/Quang Tin border. I Corps.

COB Javelin (ZC 08-37)
See Javelin. Quang Nam Pr, I Corps.

Cobalt, LZ (YD 235-355)
Apx 20 km SW Quang Tri, 31 km WNW Camp Evans and 9 km ESE Ba Long. Apr70 XXIV Corps grid per Don Armstrong. Quang Tri Pr, I Corps.

Cobb Bridge (AT 945-704)
Bridge where hwy 540 crossed Da Nang River, apx 8 km SW Da Nang AB and 7 km due W Ql-1. Secured by USMC, with possible FSB here? Apr70 XXIV Corps grid per Don Armstrong. Quang Nam Pr, I Corps.

Cobra, LZ (BR 62-57)
In Vinh Thanh (Happy) Valley on W side Rte 3A and Song Con River, apx 20 km NE An Khe, 2.5 km due S the Old French (CIDG) Fort and 1 km due W Vinh Than. Discussed in *Battles in the Monsoon*, pp 82, 128, et al. 17th and 19th Arty (155mm) elements here suptg LZ Hereford during Op Benning/Crazy Horse, May66. Grid is est. Binh Dinh Pr, II Corps.

Cobra, LZ (BT 002-371)
Apx 13 km ESE Phuoc Binh AF, 10 km NW Binh Son and 34 km due S Da Nang AB. Americal. Grid per Dan Gillotti, 15th Arty Assn. Map is L-7014-6640-3. Quang Nam/Quang Tin Pr border, I Corps.
Cobra, LZ (BT 15-55?)
On wedge-shaped Barrier Island, straddling the Quang Nam-Quang Tin Pr border, and along coast of SVN due S Hoi An. Blue Beach, LZs Cobra, Krait and Rattler were used by ship-based Amphibious Ready Grp, BLT 1st/26th Marines, during Op Bold Pursuit, Jun-Jul69, 1st Mar Div, Americal. Grid estimated. Map is L-7014-6640-3. Quang Nam/Quang Tin Pr border, I Corps.
Cobra, LZ (XD 882-584)
Apx 45 km WNW Quang Tri, 24 km due W Cam Lo and 18 km NNE Khe Sanh CB. XXIV Corps grid per Don Armstrong. Quang Tri Pr, I Corps.
Cobra, LZ (XS 8-5?)
Apparently about 7 km NW Go Cong. 9th Inf Div LZ during Op Coronado, 4-7Jul67. See Go Cong, Battle of. Go Cong Pr, IV Corps.
Coc Leu (VM 1-9)
Near point where Red River enters NVN from China, apx 240 km NW Hanoi. French counter-attacked here during Battle for T'ai Highlands, Oct-Dec52. NVN.
Coc Muen Mountain (YD 318-180)
A.k.a. Hill 1298. Apx 3 km WSW FSB Ripcord, and 44 km WSW Hue. Thua Thien Pr, I Corps.
Cochin China (n/a)
See Glossary.
Cochise, LZ (BS 855-223)
Apx 11 km NNW Gia An, 17 km SSE Duc Pho. Feb67. Binh Dinh Pr, II Corps.
Cochise, Operation (BR)
30Mar68-31Jan69. Bong Son AO. Binh Dinh Pr, II Corps.
Cochise Green, Operation (BR)
30Mar68-31Jan69. 173d Abn op. 929 rptd NVA/VC KIA, per *VN Order of Battle*, pp 9-14. Binh Dinh Pr, II Corps.
Cochrane, USS (n/a)
A.k.a. DDG 21, Guided Missile Destroyer. Part of TF 76.8, During Op Eagle Pull.
Coco Club Annex (XS)
Somewhere in Saigon. Gia Dinh Pr, III Corps.
Cocoa Beach (YD 845-321)
A.k.a. Col Co Beach and Eagle Beach, 10 km NE Hue and near Tan My, Navy fuel tank farm and POL pipeline facility adj to and inc Eagle Beach R&R center built later. See Eagle Beach. Thua Thien Pr, I Corps.
Coconino County, USS (n/a)
A.k.a. LST-603 and "Lucky Coco." 1st major USN vessel of war damaged by mines planted by enemy frogmen. On 29Jun67, while docked at Cua Viet NSA, mine caused moderate damage and vessel was towed to Guam for repairs. Returned to VN 4Apr69. See also *Hyde*.
Coconut Bay (YS 2-4)
Baie des Cocotiers. Bay at 10°21'N-107°04'E. On NC48-07 JOG. Phuoc Tuy Pr, III Corps.
Coconut, LZ (YD 091-299)
Apx 17 km due E Lang Klung, 17 km NNW Tou Rout and 33 km SW Quang Tri. Apr70 XXIV Corps grid per Don Armstrong. Quang Tri Pr, I Corps.
Cocotiers, Baie des (YS 2-4)
See Coconut Bay. Phuoc Tuy Pr, III Corps.
CODIGO (YT 02-07)
See COGIDO. Bien Hoa Pr?, III Corps.
Cofat Air (XS 830-895)
See Air Cofat and Cofat Cmpd. Gia Dinh Pr, III Corps.
Cofat Compound (XS 830-895)
At Saigon, and apx 1.5 km SE of Phu Tho Racetrack. Prior to '63, site of Cofat Cigarette Mfg Co, which in '63 became site of HACOM (Headquarters Area Cmd), the HQ responsible for managing, among other things, Saigon area military mess facilities, billets and clubs. That responsibility was assumed by USN HEDSUPPACT (HQ Supt Activity) in Sep 62, but regained by HACOM in Dec 65. Gia Dinh Pr, III Corps.
Coffee, LZ (XD 813-518)
Apx 15 km NNW Khe Sanh CB, 30 km WNW Mai Loc and 54 km due Quang Tri. Apr70 XXIV Corps grid per Don Armstrong. Quang Tri Pr, I Corps.
Coffman, FSB (XT 027-684)
Apx 5 km E Cambodia, 16 km SSW Thien Ngon AF and 26 km NW Tay Ninh. Tay Ninh Pr, III Corps.
COGIDO or Cogido (YT 02-07)
On E bank of Song Dong Nai (or Song Nha Be?) at or near Rte 316 (Cogido) bridge, apx 23 km ENE Tan Son Nhut AB, 8 km SSE Bien Hoa AB and just W the Long Binh Depot. This base was an ammo and munitions barge-to-truck transfer point for ammo en route to Long Binh Depot for subsequent distribution throughout III Corps. Cat Lai was the stream "lighterage" area where munitions were transferred from ship to barge en route Long Binh. Origin of name unknown. Bien Hoa Pr, III Corps. [123]
Cogswell, USS (n/a)
DD-651, per Ralph Fries.
Cohe Airfield (CP)
See Cam Ranh AF. Khanh Hoa Pr, II Corps.
Cohoes, USS (n/a)
AN 78. 9th Div MRF base ship. IV Corps.
Cokawa, LZ (YD?)
Somewhere N of FSB Cates. 3d/2d ARVN Rgt here Jun69, 1st Mar Div '69. Quang Tri Pr, I Corps.
Col Co Beach (YD 845-321)
A.k.a. Cocoa and Eagle Beach. Apx 10 km ENE Hue and near Tan My Navy fuel tank farm and POL pipeline facility adj to and inc Eagle Beach. Eagle Beach R&R center built later. See Cocoa Beach, Eagle Beach and Tan My. Also listed at YD 83-33. Thua Thien Pr, I Corps.
Col de Canons (YD 1-5)
Pass of Cannons. Quang Tri Pr, I Corps.
Col de Da Troun (AN 7-6)
Mtn pass near Di Linh. 11°28'00"N-108°04'00"E. On map NC49-01. Lam Dong Pr?, II Corps.
Col des Mans (VK 8-7)
Mtn pass. NIMA data. NVN.
Col des Mans (XL 1-2)
Mtn pass. NIMA data. NVN.
Col des Partesans (WL 0-5)
Pass of the Partisans. NIMA data. NVN.
Col des Partisans (UK 0-1)
Deo Partisans or Partisan Pass. NIMA data. NVN.

Col des Vents (WK 9-7)
A.k.a. Deo Vents. Mtn pass. NIMA data. NVN.
Cold, FSB (BR?)
No data. 10th Cav, 4th Div here. Name/data per Bob Patsfield. Possibly Binh Dinh Pr, II Corps.
Cold, LZ (YD 304-429)
Apx 26 km NW Camp Evans, 10 km SSW Quang Tri and 3 km NNE LZ Anne. Name/grid per Kevan Mynderup, as per Daily Staff Journal of 1st/8th Cav. Quang Tri Pr, I Corps.
Coldy, FSB (XT 432-857)
Apx 5 km S Cambodia, 5 km due E Bo Tuc, 12 km ESE Katum and 40 km NNE Tay Ninh. Also listed at XT 328-57? per 30th Arty ORLLs. Tay Ninh Pr, III Corps.
Cole des Nuages (AT 9-9)
A.k.a. Hai Van Pass, Deo Hai Van and Deo Des Nuages. NIMA data. Thua Thien Pr, I Corps.
Colgan, FSB/LZ (BP 219-192?)
On southern edge of Dalat at point where secondary road that paralleled QL-20 S to join QL-1 exited city. B Bty, 2d/17th Arty here, Nov70-Apr71. Quite possibly named to honor Army Capt. George B Colgan III, KIA 1Dec69. Grid and data per Nolan Putman. Also listed at BP 154-008? Darlac Pr, II Corps.
Colgan, LZ (BP 154-008?)
At or near Dalat/Lien Khuong AF, apx 2 km S Duc Trong and 11 km ESE Thanh Binh. 2d/17th Arty here supt 1st Cav '70. Data per Jack Picciolo. Also listed at BP 219-192? Tuyen Duc Pr, II Corps.
Coliseum, The (XT)
Apx 3 km SW FSB El Paso, 18 km W Lai Khe and 15 km SE Dau Tieng, 1st Inf Div. 1st Inf Div, '69. Per *Low Level Hell's* 1st Div TAOR map. III Corps.
Colleton, USS (n/a)
A.k.a. APB-36. Launched 30Jul45 and left for VN, 8Mar67, to join MRF, the *USS Benewah* and *Asarki*. Armed with:8-.50 cal. and twelve 7.62mm MGs and armor plate. 3 ammo pontoons were attached and used for mooring MRF RAG small-craft. Also had several surgical operating and recovery rooms. Suptd MRF, TF 117 in Mekong Delta, Dong Tam, Nha Be, Sa Dec, Vinh Long, Song Ham Long, Song Soi Rap, Song Co Chien and Vung Tau during VN tour. Returned to US in '69 and later sold for scrap. Data per MRF Assn at www.mrfa.org navy_index.htm. III, IV Corps.
Collett, USS (n/a)
DD-730, per Ralph Fries.
Collie, LZ (YD 251-349)
Apx 29 km WNW Camp Evans, 18 km SW Quang Tri and 12 km ESE Ba Long. Apr70 XXIV Corps grid per Don Armstrong. Quang Tri Pr, I Corps.
Collins, LZ (BR)
Apparently near An Khe, and possibly near Crow's Foot. Short-term 1st Cav patrol base that may have existed for only day or two. Named to honor performance of brash and colorful B/1st/12th Cav FO Lt Brien T. "BT" Collins, who was very much alive at time and led a remarkable political life after the war. Collins lost an arm and leg during his second tour (5th SF), and later became Chief of Staff for California Governor, Jerry Brown, Jr., as well as head of several state agencies. Collins' exploits are featured in *Battles in the Monsoon*. Binh Dinh Pr?, II Corps. [124]

Coloa, FSB (XU 475-010)
See Co Lao, FSB. Cambodia.
Colonial, USS (n/a)
LSD-18. Lndg. Ship, Dock, per Ralph Fries.
Colorado BOQ (XS 8-9)
At 10 Nguyen Canh Chan St., Saigon. Data per *Vietnam Military Lore, 1959-1973*. Gia Dinh Pr, III Corps.
Colorado, FSB (XU 425-075)
Grid is in Cambodia and on border apx 20 km SE Memot, 8 km E Katum and 17 km W tip of Fishhook. Cambodian Invasion FSB, May and/or Jun70. Possibly 2d Bde/25th Inf Div HQ prior to May70? 1st/11th Armored Cav here during Cambodian Invasion. Possibly also 1st Cav, and ARVN elements here at various times? Also listed at XU 434-127. Data per Frank Penk, Jr. Cambodia.
Colorado, FSB (YS 316-804)
Apx 18 km NW Nui Dat, 36 km N to NNE Vung Tau, 1.5 km WNW FSB Pine and 1.5 km SE FSB Cape. Possibly 25th Inf Div 2d Bde HQ prior to May70? On 1ATF NCO trng map per John Hollett. 1ATF. Bien Hoa Pr, III Corps.
Colorado, LZ (XD 798-640)
Apx 10 km SW Bo Ho Su (NVN), 23 km NNW Khe Sanh CB and 55 km WNW Quang Tri. Apr70 XXIV Corps grid per Don Armstrong. Quang Tri Pr, I Corps.
Colorado, Operation (YD)
6Aug66. USMC assault into the "Street Without Joy." Quang Tri Pr, I Corps.
Colorado/Lien Ket 52, Operation (YD)
6-21Aug66. USMC/ARVN op. 674 rptd VC/NVA KIA, per *Vietnam Order of Battle*, pp 9-14. Quang Nam/Quang Tin Prvs, I Corps.
Colt, LZ (BR 681-911)
At N end of Crow's foot, apx 14 km NW Ha Tay and 50 km ENE An Khe. ROK Army elements fought here while opcon to 1st Cav during Op Crazy Horse, May66. See *Battles in the Monsoon*, pp 205, 215. Used during Op Masher/White Wing, 28Jan-6Mar66. Detailed discussion of that Op and this LZ in *A Contagion of War* vol, *Vietnam Experience* series, pp 32-48, with map showing this site at p 38. Binh Dinh Pr, II Corps.
Colt, LZ (BR 745-517)
If grid correct, was apx 14 km NW Phu Cat AB and 30 km ENE An Khe. 1st Cav, 65-68. Name/grid per Dan Gillotti, 15th Arty Assn. Binh Dinh Pr, II Corps.
Colt, LZ (BR 768-957)
A.k.a. LZ Mustang? Apx 12 km SSE Thuan An and 9 km NW Bong Son. Oct66. Binh Dinh Pr, II Corps.
Colt, LZ (BS 115-731)
Remote site is apx 4 km W Mang Xim and 54 km due W Quang Ngai. Jan-Apr68. Binh Dinh Pr, II Corps.
Colt, LZ (BT 114-371)
A.k.a. LZ Ordway. W of Hwy 543, apx 8 km W QL-1, some 5 km WSW Quy Thanh, 9 km SSW LZ Baldy, 26 km NW Tam Ky, 5 km ENE Cang Dong and 10 km W QL-1. Also listed at BT 113-327, 002-371 and 115-371. Map is L-7014-6640-2. Americal List. Photos/maps of base at http://1-14th.com/maps.html. Quang Tin/Quang Nam Pr border, I Corps. [125]
Colt, LZ (YD 011-454)
Along QL-9, apx 3 to 4 km S Ca Lu, 12 km WSW Mai Loc

and 34 km WSW Quang Tri. Apr70 XXIV Corps grid per Don Armstrong. Quang Tri Pr, I Corps.

Colt 45, FSB (BS 296-807)
Apx 9 km SW Tra Bong AF, 13 km NW Ha Thanh AF, 17 km W Ba Gia, and 36 km WNW Quang Ngai. Americal list. Quang Ngai Pr, I Corps.

Colton (n/a)
6Apr70, XXIV Corps 5th Div proposed FSB name.

Columbia BEQ (XS 822-940)
US enlisted billet in Saigon prior to '68. Name per *Vietnam Military Lore, 1959-1973*. Gia Dinh Pr, III Corps.

Columbia Eagle (n/a)
US munitions freighter hijacked in Mar70 by 2 of its crew who fancied themselves Marxist revolutionaries. Civilians Clyde McKay and Alvin Glatowski, forced ship to dock in Cambodian Port of Kompong Son, where they then claimed asylum but were instead imprisoned. In Oct70, they escaped from their guards along with Army Deserter named Larry Humphrey. Humphrey and McKay abandoned Glatowski and joined the Khmer Rouge. Glatowski failed to gain asylum in Russia or Sweden, turned himself in to US embassy in Phnom Penh and later served 5 years in US prison for hijacking. Data per *Prisoners of Hope*, pp 65-66.

Columbus, LZ (AR 802-446?)
Apx 12 km ESE Pleiku, 4 km S QL-19 and 12 km NE Cam Enari. 2d/17th Arty here supt 1st Cav. Data per Jack Picciolo. Pleiku Pr, II Corps.

Columbus, LZ (YA 974-036)
A.k.a. LZ Cavalair. Apx 5 km ENE LZ X-Ray, 3 km ESE LZ Albany, 4 km due E LZ Falcon, 16 km W Plei Me, and 50 km SW Pleiku. Original name was LZ Cavalair on 1Nov65, but changed to Columbus on 2d day of LZ X-Ray Battle, 15Nov65. Both LZ Columbus and LZ Falcon were used by 1st Cav 105 Btys to supt 1st/7th Cav during 1st Ia Drang Battle at LZ X-Ray. B/1st/12th Inf, B, 1st/21st Arty and C 2/17th Arty. See Cavalair. Grid per LtGen Hal Moore. Pleiku Pr, western II Corps.

Columbus, LZ (YD 186-401)
Along road between Ba Long and Quang Tri, apx 3 km E Ba Long and 19 km SW Quang Tri. Apr70 XXIV Corps grid per Don Armstrong. Quang Tri Pr, I Corps.

Columbus North, LZ (YA 652-871)
Along W edge of Plei Trap Valley, apx 50 km due W Kontum, 4 km from Lao border and 800 meters N of LZ Columbus South. Mar66. Kontum Pr, II Corps.

Columbus South, LZ (YA 651-863)
Along W edge of Plei Trap Valley, apx 50 km due W Kontum, 4 km from Lao border and 800 meters S of LZ Columbus North. Mar66. Kontum Pr, II Corps.

Com Thieu, Mui (YS 4-4)
Coastal point at 10°23'N-107°15'E. On NC48-08 JOG. Phuoc Tuy Pr, III Corps.

Com Thiu, Mui (YS 4-4)
Mui Com Thieu. Coastal point at 10°23'N-107°15'E. On NC48-08 JOG. Phuoc Tuy Pr, III Corps.

Combat Skyspot (UH 68-60)
See Lima Site 85. Laos.

Combat Trap (n/a)
See Glossary.

Combat Zone, The Vietnam (n/a)
See Vietnam Combat Zone for definition and text of Executive order 11216, dated 24Apr65.

Combined Action Groups (n/a)
See Glossary.

Combined Action School (YD 885-149)
At Phu Bai CB, '67. Precise location unknown, though was apparently near 3d Mar Div HQ. Trng area of USMC CAG, CAC, CAP and CUPP personnel. See CAG, CAC, CAP and CUPP. Grid is for Phu Bai AF. Discussed in *A Voice of Hope*. Thua Thien Pr, I Corps.

Combined Ammo Hill (YA 898-381)
See Combined Arms Hill. Pleiku Pr, II Corps.

Combined Arms Hill (YA 893-376)
Apx 35 km WSW Pleiku and 8 km SSE Plei Djereng new AF. Jul67. Pleiku Pr, II Corps.

Combined Holding & Interrogation Ctr (BT?)
See Long Dong. SE Quang Nam or possibly NE Quang Tin Pr?, I Corps.

Combined Recreation Compound (XS 863-918)
On US Embassy grounds in Saigon, and fronting on Hong Thap Tu St. Site of swimming pool facilities. Discussed in *Tears Before the Rain*, p 203.

Comet, LZ (YD 058-668)
Apx 7 km SW Con Thien, 12 km NW Cam Lo, 31 km NW Quang Tri and 3 km due N FSB Ironside. On map, p 58, *US Marines in Vietnam-1969*. Grid per Apr70 XXIV Corps grid per D. Armstrong. Quang Tri Pr, I Corps.

Comet (n/a)
A.k.a. RO-RO1. See *Lt Col John U. D. Page* for detail.

Comet, USNS (n/a)
TAKR-7 and possibly RO-RO1? MSTS Transport, per Ralph Fries. See *Lt Col John U. D. Page.*

Commanche (n/a)
6Apr70, XXIV Corps proposed 5th Div FSB name.

Commanche, LZ (YA 432-631)
Cambodian Incursion FSB in valley of Stoeng Ta Pak River, apx 10 km W SVN, 68 km W Plei Mrong and 82 km WNW Pleiku. Name/grid per Jim Claeys. B Bty, 4th/42d Arty here, May70. Cambodia.

Command Liaison Det SF Camp (XS 853-9295)
See CLD SF Camp at grid. Gia Dinh Pr, III Corps.

Commando Bergerol (n/a)
See Glossary.

Commando Club (UH 68-60)
Code for Site 85, TSQ-81 Radar controlled bombing missions in N Laos and NVN. See Lima Site 85 for detail.

Commando Hunt Operation (n/a)
See Glossary.

Commando Sabre (n/a)
See Glossary.

Commando Units, French (n/a)
See Glossary.

Commando Vault (n/a)
See Glossary.

Committee of National Leadership (n/a)
See Glossary.

Communal Routes (n/a)
See Glossary.

Compound One (XS 923-893?)
At Binh Loi. If grid correct, was along Song Saigon apx 12 km SE of Tan Son Nhut AB. Home of 149th Military Intel Grp, US Army Cmd and Coordination. NPIA grid; however, there are also Binh Loi villes at XS 660-615, 673-598 and 708-594. Gia Dinh Pr, III Corps.

Compton, FSB/LZ (XU 683-256)
Apx 3 km N the SVN border and point where QL-13 meets it. 18 km NNW Loc Ninh, SVN, and 15 km SE Snuol. Grid per *11th ACR Cambodia Invasion AAR, 1st Cav Div, May-Jun70*, courtesy Lou Rochat. [126] Cambodia.

Compton, FSB/LZ (YT 052-150)
UTM grid zone may be in error. See Fort Compton at YU 054-150 (which is apx 13 km NW Song Be AF in Phuoc Long Pr). If listed grid accurate (which is doubtful), was apx 7 km ENE Bien Hoa AB, 6 km SW Ap Moi and 5 km NNE Plantation AF. Bien Hoa Pr, III Corps.

Compton, FSB (YU 054-150)
A.k.a. Fort Compton. Apx 13 km NW Song Be AF. See Fort Compton. Per Peter Cole, is mentioned in *1st Cav Div Op Rpt, Feb70/Apr70*, at p 33. Phuoc Long Pr, III Corps.

Comstock, USS (n/a)
LSD-19. USN Landing Ship, Dock. Supt 9th Inf Div MRF in '66-67, per MRF Assn website at www.mrfa.org. Also moved 159th Trans Bn to open Utah Beach (later Wonder or Wunder Beach), 2Mar68. All CTZs.

Con, LZ (YA or ZA)
Ia Drang Campaign LZ, Oct-Nov65. Per *Pleiku*, was in "Search Area Jim" (which was in Valley of Ia Drang River, NE Chu Pong Mtn, and on map in that book at pp 88 and 116. Center of mass at apx ZA 00-13). Opened late Oct69(?), a by 2d/8th Cav, 1st Cav and 2 Btys of 105s suptg 2d/8th and 1st/12th Cav. LZs Punt and Homecoming were closed in conjunction with opening of LZ Con. Data per J. D. Coleman's *Pleiku,* p 106, thanks to Peter Cole. Pleiku Pr, II Corps.

Con Chim, Pointe (XQ 8-6)
See Pointe Con Chim. IV Corps.

Con Cuong (n/a)
Mapsheet name of L-7014-5947-2. NVN only.

Con Dao (XQ 7-5)
A.k.a. Vinh Con Son. Bay on Con Son Island at 8°40'N-106°38'E. On NC48-11 JOG. IV Corps.

Con Gia, FSB (ZT 07-00)
Along QL-1, apx 18 km NNE Ham Tan AF and 16 km ENE Ap Dai Mai. 199th LIB. Binh Tuy Pr, III Corps.

Con Ke, Mui (CP 0-1)
Coastal point at 11°56'N-109°11'E. On NC49-01 JOG. Khanh Hoa Pr, II Corps.

Con Khoai Refugee Center? (YD 538-338)
Along QL-1, apx 23 km NW Hue and 3 km N Camp Evans. Listed as Con Khoai R.C. Relocation Camp? NPIA data. Thua Thien Pr, I Corps.

Con Son (n/a)
Mapsheet name of L-7014-6328-3. SVN.

Con Son Correctional Center (XQ 77-63)
On Con Son Island. Infamous political prison notorious for its Tiger Cage underground cells and apparent inhumane treatment. See Con Son Island for detail.

Con Son Island (XQ 77-63)
A.k.a. Poulo Condore Island. 5 island group in South China Sea, 85 km from SVN coast at their closest point, and 200 km due E the westernmost tip of Mui Bai Bung (Cau Mau Peninsula). Consisting of: Con Son, largest by far at 16 km by avg of apx 6 km ; Hon Ba, 2d largest; Hon Bai Canh, 3d largest; Hon Cau, 4th largest and Hon Tre Lon, the smallest. As part of 1862 treaty between French and Emperor Tu Duc, France gained control of island and constructed infamous prison to house political prisoners and nationalists. Many now famous Vietnamese, Pham Van Dong and Le Duc Tho among them, were imprisoned here, spending years in underground cells, suffering terrible conditions and mistreatment. SVN govt used it for similar purposes after expelling French. Again became infamous in '70 when US press exposed its "Tiger Cages" (the cells of Con Son Correctional Ctr) and inhumane conditions.

Con Son Island Airfield (XQ 798-657)
In ocean apx 235 km due S Saigon and apx 85 km from mainland at its closest point. El. 20', 3,800' asph rwy that began at ocean's edge and perpendicular to coast. At 08°43'52"N-106°38'00"E. See Con Son Island.

Con Son Islands (XQ 80-60)
Large island grp apx 115 km SE Soc Trang AF and 85 km from mainland. Includes main isle of Con Son (XQ 77-62), as well as Hon Trung (XQ 89-71), Hon Cau (XQ 92-61), Hon Bai Canh (XQ 86-58), Hon Tai (XQ 80-55) Hon Ba (XQ 73-56) and Hon Tre Lon (XQ 70-63).

Con Son, Vung (XQ 7-5)
A.k.a. Vinh Con Son. Bay on Con Son Island at 8°40'N-106°38'E. On NC48-11 JOG. IV Corps.

Con Tach Tria Airfield (BP 185-220)
See Dalat Cam Ly AF. Tuyen Duc Pr, II Corps.

Con Thanh Airfield (XT 767-610)
See Chonh Thanh AF. Binh Long Pr, III Corps.

Con Thien Combat Base (YD 113-703)
A.k.a. The Hill of Angels, FSB A-4, Nui Con Thien and Hill 158. Apx 10 km W Gio Linh CB, 7 km WSW FSB A-3, and 28 km NW Quang Tri. From it, observation was unfettered for 15 km to coast in E, the Annamite mtns to W and DMZ to N. Strategically important but extremely vulnerable site because NVA arty (130 and 152mm cannons) across DMZ had greater range than US arty and was immune to counter-battery fire. Scene of heavy fighting and NVA bombardment in 67 generally, and heavily attacked 8May67 (anniversary of fall of Dien Bien Phu) when 2 Bns of NVA, with flame-throwers, breached wire and hand-to-hand combat ensued. USMC held position at great cost to friend and foe. 3d Bn/9th Marines here '67. Helo lndg zone here known as Death Valley. After American War ended, Viet govt built what is known as Trung Son Cemetery nearby. It contains 10,000 graves and remains of NVA soldiers who died or were MIA in Quang Tri area. Also listed at YD 116-700. Map is L-7014-6342-1, per Ken Burrington. Quang Tri Pr, I Corps.

Con Thien SF Camp (YD 117-701)
Apx 500 meters E Con Thien CB grid and apparently within that cmpd? Apx 10 km W Gio Linh. 5th SF. Info/grid per *SF Order of Battle.* Transferred to III MAF, to Da Nang MSF? Quang Tri Pr, I Corps.

Conch, LZ (YD 280-667)
Apx 1 km W Vinh Quan Ha, 8 km NNE Dong Ha and 15 km NNW Quang Tri. Apr70 XXIV Corps grid per Don Armstrong. Quang Tri Pr, I Corps.
Concord, FSB/Basecamp (YT 030-181)
Just S Song Dong Nai River, apx 7 km NNE Bien Hoa AB and 28 km NE Saigon. 2d/3d, Inf 199th LIB here. Grid per Frank Penk, Jr. Also listed at YT 034-174 and 010-020. Bien Hoa Pr, III Corps.
Concord, LZ (XD 759-610)
Apx 23 km NNE Khe Sanh CB and 57 km WNW Quang Tri. Apr70 XXIV Corps grid per Don Armstrong. Quang Tri Pr, I Corps.
Concord, FSB (YT 010-120)
Grid may be incorrect, but if accurate, site was just S the Song Dong Nai River and 6 km NNE Bien Hoa AB. Jan69. Bien Hoa Pr, III Corps.
Concrete, Operation (YS)
Largest Australian op up to that point following WWII, involving all 3 Inf RAR Bns, TF HQ, a Field Rgt and suptg arms, deployed to destroy HQ of D445 VC Rgt. Phuoc Tuy Pr, III Corps.
Condor, LZ (XD 908-400)
Along QL-9, apx 2 km N Lang Kat and 44 km WSW Quang Tri. Apr70 XXIV Corps grid per Don Armstrong. Quang Tri Pr, I Corps.
Cone, USS (n/a)
A.k.a. DD 866. Arrived off Phan Thiet 14Feb68 to replace *USS* Campbell suptg TF 3d/506th Inf, per www.currahee.org/pageb2.html. SVN.
Cone Victory, SS (n/a)
Merchant ship under govt contract, per Ralph Fries.
Conein, Lou (WJ 88-25)
See Patti Mission, The. NVN.
Conex Affair, The (XT 98-13)
See Barsanti Affair in Glossary.
Conflict, USS (n/a)
MSO-426. Minesweeper, Ocean, per Ralph Fries.
Cong Ba Ky Canal (XS 29-55?)
Apx 65 km SE Saigon. Key terrain feature during 1st Battle of Ap Bac, 2Jan63.
Cong Cam Son Secret Zone (n/a)
Patrolled by 2d Bde/9th Inf Div and 9th Div LRPD during Op Coronado, late '67. III or IV Corps.
Cong Hoa General Hospital (XS 8-9?)
Presumably in or near Saigon or Long Binh Post. Provided marginal medical care for wounded and sick members of 3d ARVN Ranger Grp and its families. Cited in *Rangers At War*, at p 263. Gia Dinh Pr, III Corps.
Cong Hoang Quoc Gia Ntl Forest Reserve (XD)
Natl Forest immed S of Mutter's Ridge and the S edge of DMZ, roughly at mid-point between the coast and Laotian border. Quang Tri Pr, I Corps.
Cong Ly (barracks?) (XS 8-9)
At 203 Cong Ly St. (pre '68), Saigon. Per *Vietnam Military Lore, 1959-1973.* Gia Dinh Pr, III Corps.
Congai (n/a)
See Glossary.
Congrints (n/a)
See Glossary.
Conn Hill (BT 55-03)
At Chu Lai CB. Named to honor PFC David B Conn, USMC, KIA 19Dec66 along Ben Song River near Chu Lai. He had but 4 days left in-country when shot by newly arrived trooper whom he was relieving from guard duty. Data per Ray Bows. Quang Tin Pr, I Corps.
Connecticut BOQ (XS 837-939)
At 123A Vo Tanh St., Saigon. Per *Vietnam Military Lore, 1959-1973.* Gia Dinh Pr, III Corps.
Connel, FSB (YT 315-628)
Remote site apx 27 km SE Dong Xoai, 37 km ENE Phuoc Vinh AF and 78 km NE Saigon. Quite possibly named to honor Army SSgt David A. Connel, KIA 9Oct70 (only Connel listed as casualty). Opened or reopened 14Oct70. 1st/7th Cav Name/data per *1st Cav Div Op Rpt, ending 31Oct70*, courtesy Peter Cole. Long Khanh Pr, III Corps.
Connell Quarry (AR 833-567)
A.k.a. Waterman Quarry. Apx 9 km NE Pleiku, 4 km W Plei Neh. Mar-Apr67. Pleiku Pr, II Corps.
Conner, LZ (AT 935-243?)
If grid correct, was apx 1 km NE LZ Karen, 5.5 km WSW Nui Liet Kiem/LZ West, 37 km W Tam Ky and 10 km SW LZ Dragon Base/Hill 270. Grid per map courtesy Bob Shrake, 4th/31st Inf, 196th LIB. Quang Tin Pr, I Corps.
Connie, LZ (BS 333-540)
Along LTL-5, apx 21 km WNW Minh Long AF and 7 km SW Lang Re. 1st Cav Div. Name/grid per Dan Gillotti. Quang Ngai Pr, I Corps.
Connie Francis Snake (n/a)
See Glossary.
Conquer, LZ (YA 600-400)
See Conquest. Cambodia.
Conqueror, SS (n/a)
Merchant ship under govt contract, per Ralph Fries.
Conquest, LZ (YA 601-401)
Incursion FSB also listed as LZ Conquer. Apx 65 km W Pleiku, 28 km SW Plei Djereng AF and 6 km W SVN. 4th Div, '70. Per John Linn, B/2d/35th Inf was here 7-13May70. B/4th/42d Arty here May70. 4th Div Jul70. Name/grid per Jim Claeys. Cambodia.
Conquest, USS (n/a)
MSO-488. Minesweeper, Ocean, per Ralph Fries.
Conroy, Camp (ZC 006-081)
At Kham Duc SF Camp apx 20 km W Laos, 55 km W to WSW Tien Phuoc, and 80 km SSW Da Nang. Described as the "Nung Cmpd." there. Named to honor SFC Paul A. Conroy, KIA 23Mar67. Data per Ray Bows. See Kham Duc. Quang Tin Pr, I Corps.
Consession de Don Dien Halle (XT 8-4)
Don Dien Halle Concession (also spelled Hallet). Plantation in Binh Duong Pr, III Corps.
Consolidated RVNAF Improvement/Modernization
See CRIMP in Glossary.
Constant, USS (n/a)
MSO-427. Minesweeper, Ocean, per Ralph Fries.
Constellation, LZ (YD 037-632)
Apx 11 km WNW Cam Lo, 31 km WNW Quang Tri. '70 XXIV Corps grid per D. Armstrong. Quang Tri Pr, I Corps.
Constellation, USS (n/a)
A.k.a. CVA-64. Deployed with CVW-14, 11Aug69-8May70; with CVW-14, 29May68-31Jan69; with CVW-9,

1Oct71-30 Jun72; with CVW-9, 21Jun74-22Dec74; with CVW-9, 5Jan73-11Oct73; with CVW-14, 5May64-1FEB65; with CVW-14, 29Apr67-4Dec67; with CVW-15, 12May66-3Dec66. With *Ticonderoga*, suptd destroyers *Maddox* and *Turner Joy* during Gulf of Tonkin Incident. On 1Jul66, F4-Bs saw 3 NVA PT boats headed for *Coontz* and destroyer *Rogers* (DD 876). US ships made for North SAR Station, 90 km E Haiphong, and within 30 min, F-4s from *Constellation* attacked the NVA craft. In Sept65 attack sqdns from Carriers *Oriskany*, *Constellation*, *Coral Sea*, and *Intrepid* hit previously off-limits areas in Haiphong and smaller ports of Hon Gai and Cam Pha. [127]

Constitution, LZ (YD 018-367)
Overlooked river valley apx 11 km NE Lang Klung, 12 km due S Ca Lu and 36 km WSW Quang Tri. XXIV Corps grid per Don Armstrong. Quang Tri Pr, I Corps.

Constitution, USS (BT 0-8)
Between 1844-1846, the *Constitution* circumnavigated the globe under Capt. John "Mad Jack"[128] Percival as part of US "East Indian Squadron," sailing 52,279 miles in 495 days. In May 1845, and while en route from Canton to Manila Bay, it anchored off what we know as Da Nang. While there, a plea to help a French Missionary named Monsignor Leferve (imprisoned in Hue by Emperor Thieu Tri) came while several Viet mandarins were aboard. In response, Percival took the mandarins hostage and sought to exchange them for the Monsignor. Some 50 Blue Jackets were then apparently sent overland to Hue to secure the man's release (thus becoming 1st US ground troops in combat role there and arguably the 1st US Vietnam veterans!). However, the Emperor refused the US effort and, finally, the frustrated Percival released his hostages and impetuously fired his cannons into Tourane (Da Nang) as *Constitution* set sail for Manila. That act was 1st-ever US shelling of Vietnam and killed/wounded some Viets in process, thus causing 1st-ever Viet casualties of formal US hostility. In Aug, 1849, US President Andrew Jackson sent a letter of apology via US "Minister of Southeastern Asia," Joseph Baletier, addressing it to "His majesty the magnificent King of Anam." Jackson wrote he'd sent the letter "...in order the you may understand how greatly I have grieved to hear it said, four years ago (which I have only heard lately, for first time because your country is so far from mine) Captain Percival by lndg troops in Toorong Bay and firing on your people [had killed/wounded some]." Jackson also included a warning that the incident "...ought to be forgotten and forgiven after my letter has come into your hand."! Author Ray Bows also notes that, "A ship's Musician named Cooke died at sea [May 11, 1845] and was buried at the foot of Monkey Mtn in Da Nang. The Vietnamese take care of his grave now." [129] Note: 1st US ship/Americans to visit VN are thought to have been Capt. John White and crew of ship *Franklin*, 1820. 1st USN ship to visit VN was *USS Peacock*, 1832. See *Peacock,* and First American Diplomat to VN in Glossary. Quang Nam Pr, I Corps. [130] [131]

Contigny II, FSB (XT 535-378)
See FSB Cantigny. Binh Duong Pr, III Corps.

Continental Air Services (n/a)
See Glossary.

Continental Hotel (XS 865-914)
Saigon. Gia Dinh Pr, III Corps.

Continental Palace BOQ (XS 865-914?)
At 132 Tu Do St., Saigon, Oct 64-68, 19 rms. Per *Vietnam Military Lore, 1959-1973.* Gia Dinh Pr, III Corps.

Convict (n/a)
Apr70, XXIV Corps future-use 101st Abn FSB name.

Conway, USS (n/a)
DD-507, per Ralph Fries.

Cony, USS (n/a)
DD-508, per Ralph Fries.

Coogee, FSB (XT 890-290)
1ATF FSB 4.5 km WNW FSB Coral and Just outside the western edge of War Zone D, 22 km NW Bien Hoa, 12 km E Ben Cat and sited equidistant between LTL-1A and LTL-16 apx 7.5 km due S their intersection. FSBs Coral and Coogee were the site of Battle for Coral, a major ANZAC battle described in *Vietnam Gunners* (see Append. H). 3RAR (1ATF), also 161 Bty, RNZA (Hitching's Bty 14Apr68-18Mar69) FSB set here 13-24May68. Binh Duong Pr, III Corps.

Cook, FSB (YS 296-627)
Along QL-2, apx 16 km SW Nui Dat, 18 km N Vung Tau, 5 km NNE FSB Andrea and 8 km SW Nui Thi. Author of *Vietnam Gunners* wrote that it was in "...flat, sandy covered with grass and fringed mangrove-like swamps of a tropical river delta." with 161 Bty, RNZA Master's Bty 6Sep70-8May71) FSB set here 27Nov-2Dec70. Bty here 27Nov70 to fire suptg a 2 ANZAC op on W slopes of Nui Dinh Mtns. On 1ATF NCO trng map per John Hollett. 1ATF. Also listed at YS 29-62. Phuoc Tuy Pr, III Corps.

Cook, USS (n/a)
High-Speed Transport, a.k.a. APD 130. In Jan62, she conducted beach surveys along SVN coast from Quang Tri to Vung Tau. In Feb-Mar63, *USS Weiss* (APD 135) did same thing. VC fired on shore parties from *Weiss*. [132]

Cook Inlet, USCGC (n/a)
WHEC 384. 2Jul71-21Dec71. Sqdn 3 CGC, during Cooast Guard's 8th deployment. Given to SVN Govt as CG left SVN. Role discussed in *Brown Water, Black Berets*, p 90. Market Time TF-115. SVN.

Cooke, Able Seaman (BT 0-8)
See *Constitution, USS*. Quang Nam Pr, I Corps.

Coolah, FSB (YS 398-861)
In jungle clearing covered with head-high grasses at S end of Courtenay Rubber Plantation, 20 km NNW Nui Dat 4 km W Rte-2, 5 km NW FSB Avenger. 161 Bty, RNZA (Hitching's Bty 14Apr68-18Mar69) FSB set here 2-9Aug68. On 1ATF NCO trng map per John Hollett. 1ATF. Also listed at YS 39-86. Phuoc Tuy Pr, III Corps.

Coong Bay (XQ 8-6)
A.k.a. Vinh Dong Bac. Bay on Con Son Island at 8°43'N-106°39'E. On NC48-11 JOG. IV Corps.

Coontz, USS (n/a)
A.k.a. DLG 8, Guided Missile Frigate. On 1Jul66, F4-Bs saw 3 NVA PT boats headed for *Coontz* and destroyer *Rogers* (DD 876). US ships then made for North SAR Station, 90 km E Haiphong. Within 30 min, F-4s from *USS Constellation* attacked the NVA craft.

Cooper (n/a)
6Apr70, XXIV Corps proposed 5th Div FSB name.

Cooper-Church Amendment (n/a)
See Glossary.
Coors, LZ (XD 875-590)
Apx 25 km due W Cam Lo, 18 km NNE Khe Sanh CB and 46 km WNW Quang Tri. Apr70 XXIV Corps grid per Don Armstrong. Quang Tri Pr, I Corps.
Copper, LZ (BR)
At N end of An Lao River valley apx 20 km NW Bong Son and 17 km WNW LZ Dog. Used during Op Masher/White Wing, 28Jan-6Mar66. Detailed discussion of Ops Masher/White Wing and this LZ in *A Contagion of War* vol, *Vietnam Experience* series, pp 32-48, with map showing this site at p 38. 1st/5th Cav, 1st Cav LZ. Binh Dinh Pr, II Corps.
Copper, LZ (XD 705-445)
Apx 15 km WNW Khe Sanh CB and 7 km due W Lang Ruon. Apr70 XXIV Corps grid per Don Armstrong. Quang Tri Pr, I Corps.
Copper State, SS (n/a)
Merchant ship under govt contract, per Ralph Fries.
Copperhead, FSB (XT 808-027)
Just N Tan Thoi Hiep on E side of Rte TL-16, apx 6 km due N Tan Son Nhut AB, 5 km NNW Camp Red Ball, 7 km ENE FSB All-American, 7.5 km ESE FSB Harrison and 10 km WSW Di An basecamp. Built by 2d/321st Arty on "abandoned missile site" (no explanation for phrase provided in 3d Bde's history) in Sep or Oct68, during Op Toan Than II. Grid/Info per Butch Sincock. Home of 2d/321st Arty, suptg 3d Bde/82d Abn and attached units of 1st/27th Inf (25th ID) and 11th ACR until the entire Bde finished its move from I Corps. 82d Abn base Oct68-Mar69. Gia Dinh Pr, III Corps.
Copperhead, LZ (XD 817-504)
At base of and apx 5 km SSW peak Dong Voi Mep, 2 km NE Rte 6081, and 9 km NNW Khe Sanh CB. Apr70 XXIV Corps grid per Don Armstrong. Quang Tri Pr, I Corps.
Cora, LZ (XS 116-570)
Apx 13 km NW Cai Lay and 25 km SW Thuy Dong AF. '67. See Barbara and Delores. Dinh Tuong Pr, IV Corps.
Coral Outpost (n/a)
Possibly 1ATF's FSB Coral? No data.
Coral, FSPB (XT 926-284)
A.k.a. LZ Coral and also listed at XT 934-292. ANZAC FSB of 1RAR/3RAR and 161 Bty RNZA (1ATF) Intentionally sited on a major enemy trail just inside the western edge of War Zone D, 20 km NNW Bien Hoa, 4.5 km due E FSB Coogee, 22 km ESE Ben Cat, 6 km WSW Khu Tru Mat and some 20 km S Phuoc Vinh. FSBs Balmoral, Coral and Coogee were the site of Battle for Coral, a series of 4 separate major engagements, 12May, 13May 26 May and 28May68 described in book of same name. 161 Bty, RNZA (Hitching's Bty 14Apr68-18Mar69) FSB set here 12-13May68 and 24May-6Jun68. Abnd 6Jun68. Battles here discussed in detail in *The Battle of Coral*. Grid per Dave Aitchison. Also listed at XT 933-338 and 930-290, May-Jun66. Bien Hoa Pr, III Corps.
Coral, LZ (BT?)
Per *Rites of Passage*, pp 283, 295, 1st/14th Inf/25th Div here '67, and built on highest mtn in area and had "wonderful view." I or II Corps.
Coral, LZ (YD 306-544)
Apx 7 km E Dong Ha and 8 km NNW Quang Tri. XXIV Corps grid per Don Armstrong. Quang Tri Pr, I Corps.
Coral Sea, USS (n/a)
CVA-43. Deployed with CVW-15, 12No 71-17Jul72; with CVW-15, 23Sep69-Jul 70; with CVW-15, 5Dec74-2Jul75; with CVW-15, 9Mar73-8Nov73; with CVW-15, 26Jul67-6Apr68; with CVW-15, 7Dec64-1 Nov65; with CVW-15, 7Sep68-18Apr69; with CVW-2, 29Jul66-23Feb67. In Spring '61 when Royal Laotian Army appeared to be on verge of defeat by communist forces, US fleet was sent to SEA as show of force. By end of Apr61 most of 7th fleet was deployed off Vietnam and ready for ops in Laos. TF inc *USS Coral Sea* (CVA 43) and *USS Midway* (CVA 41) carrier battle grps, anti-sub carrier *Kearsarge* (CVS 33), 1 helo carrier, 3 amphib grps, two subs, and 3 Marine BLTs. On 7Feb65, *Coral Sea's* CVW-15 and *Hancock's* CVW-21 flew Flaming Dart I, a one-time strike at NVA barracks at Dong Hoi. On 28Feb65, acft from *Coral Sea* carried out 1st Barrel Roll strikes on Mu Gia Pass. In Sept65 attack sqdns from Carriers *Oriskany*, *Constellation*, *Coral Sea*, and *Intrepid* hit previously off-limit areas in Haiphong and smaller ports of Hon Gai and Cam Pha. [133]
CORDS, Da Nang (BT)
Dan Nang, Civil Operations and Revolutionary Development unit, joint civilian/military agency aimed at winning the hearts and minds of Viet people. Quang Nam Pr, I Corps.
CORDS Club & 1st FFV Headquarters (CP 0-5)
In Nha Trang, CORDS 9 (Civil Operations and Revolutionary Development unit), joint civilian/military agency was aimed at winning the hearts and minds of Viet people. See Nha Trang. Khanh Hoa Pr, II Corps.
CORDS IV (n/a)
See Can Tho. IV Corps.
Core, USS (n/a)
T-AKV 13, Aircraft Ferry. On 11Dec61, Aircraft Ferry *USS Core*, USN MSTS, arrived in Saigon and off-loaded two Army helo transportation Cos. [134]
Cork, LZ (BS 449-611)
Apparently a.k.a. FSB Bronco (BS 450-612)? Apx 16 km WSW Nghia Hanh AF, 18 km SW Chu Lai, 42 km NW Duc Pho and apx 3 km SW peak Hill 1136. Described as " way up in mtns, per Tommy Acosta, 11th LIB, and high altitude affected helos lndg here with strong down-drafts making it difficult to reach by air during monsoon. Apparently built to supt Vernon Lake II and Iron Mtn Ops. Sign here read: *Welcome to LZ Cork, Home of the 11th LIB; Former Home of the 3rd NVA Div*, per Carl Caputo (courtesy Richard White) with photo of sign at www.hill4-11.org/photos/caputophotos/caputophotos-1.html. Map is L-7014-6739-3. XXIV Corps grid per Don Armstrong. Also listed at BS 450-612 and BS 448-612. See FSB Bronco. Americal list. Quang Ngai Pr, I Corps.
Coronado, LZ (YD 097-378?)
If grid correct, was on Hill 813, apx 7 km WSW Ba Long and 28 km SW Quang Tri. Listed at XD 097-378 per XXIV Corps index; however, that grid is deep in Laos and thought to be in error? Quang Tri Pr, I Corps.

Coronado, Operation (XS 9-6)
See FSBs X-Ray and Tango. US 9th Div elements, 3d Bn VNMC and 3d/47th ARVN in Rung Sat Special Zone, Jul67. Est 478 VC KIA. Long An/Gia Dinh Pr, III Corps.

Corps (n/a)
See Glossary.

Corps, LZ (XD 978-333)
Along Hwy 616, apx 42 km SW Quang Tri, 16 km SSW Ca Lu and 16 km SE Khe Sanh CB. Apr70 XXIV Corps grid per Don Armstrong. Quang Tri Pr, I Corps.

Corpus Christi Bay Heliport (CP/YS)
A.k.a. T-ARVH-1 and in previous life as *USS Albemerle* AV-5. *USNS Corpus Christi Bay* was mobile, sea-borne helicopter repair ship. In '66, was in Cam Ranh Bay (at apx CP 03-17) per map at: www.vietvet.org/visit/maps/camrasmall.jpg. At another time, apparently in Vinh Ganh Rai Bay about 2 to 3 km W Vung Tau, at YS 245-455. "Heliport #742, alt 47', 66' x 77' (Steel Deck), J 4 PPR, call Corpus Christi Bay via Vung Tau apr and state business and ETA. Apr strobes available on acft copter pad in emerg. Flat Top Control-68.05. Tower-285.9, 63.0. Opr 0001-0900Z except Sun. Flt flw svc. Arty advsy-Phuoc Tuy 369.6, 40.7. Radio/Nav Remarks-Available H24 in emerg, 10°21'N 107°03'E," per Feb73 TAD. Khanh Hoa Pr, II Corps, and Phuoc Tuy Pr, II/III Corps. [135]

Corpus Christi Bay, USS (n/a)
A.k.a. T-ARVH 1, former seaplane tender. See Corpus Christi Bay Heliport.

Corral, FSB (XU 930-537)
Apx 27 km NE Snuol, 45 km due N Loc Ninh and 9 km WNW FSB Bronco. Cited in *1st Cav Div Op Rpt, May-Jul70*, pp 37, 38, per Peter Cole. Grid per *11th ACR Cambodia Invasion AAR, 1st Cav Div, May-Jun70*, courtesy Lou Rochat. [136] Cambodia.

Corral, LZ (BR 414-308)
Remote location apx 17 km SSW An Khe. Likely 1st Cav. Dec65. Binh Dinh Pr, II Corps.

Corral, LZ (BR 734--700)
Roughly 8 km NNE LZ Horse, 16 km NNE Vinh Thanh, and 35 km NE An Khe. Discussed in *Battles in the Monsoon*, pp 152-158 and 172 where described as least likely location for FSB one could imagine. On hogback ridge barren except for Elephant Grass with much higher ridges to N, S and W. C Bty/2d/19th Arty here as was 1st/8th Cav, 1st Cav CP during part of Op Benning-Crazy Horse, NE An Khe, May66. Also listed at BR 754-718. Binh Dinh Pr, II Corps.

Corral, LZ (BR 754--718)
If grid correct, was apx 20 km NNE Vinh Thanh and 39 km NE An Khe. Likely same Corral as that listed at BR 734-700, and is apx 4 km ENE position listed for BR 734-700. Binh Dinh Pr, II Corps.

Corral, LZ? (ZA 140-160?)
If grid correct, site was 5 km SE Plei Ya Meur and 32 km SSW Pleiku. Nature of site unknown. Dec65. Actually listed in YA UTM, which is in Cambodia and in error for '65. Pleiku Pr, II Corps.

Corral, Operation (YA/YB)
See Glossary.

Corral Program (YA/YB)
See Glossary.

Corregidor, LZ (YD 173-537)
Near intersection of Hwys 559 and 569, apx 16 km due W Quang Tri, 9 km ENE Mai Loc and 2 km ENE Xom Rao Vinh. Apr70 XXIV Corps grid per Don Armstrong. Quang Tri Pr, I Corps.

Corregidor, LZ (BR?)
A.k.a. LZ Donahue/Corregidor. Apparently somewhere near LZ English and/or LZ Uplift? Cited in excerpt of '70 Bn Annual Historical supplement of 3d/503d Inf on net at www.gasparot.com/nammedic. Binh Dinh Pr?, II Corps.

Corregidor Hook Pad (YD 173-537?)
Apparently a CH-47 log pad a.k.a. LZ Corregidor (YD 173-537) or possibly at Camp Eagle or ? Cited in 101st Abn ORLL for period ending 31Jul69, p 25, online at: http://carlisle-www.army.mil/usamhi/DL/chron.htm#AVietnamWar19601973. Thua Thien Pr, I Corps.

Corry, USS (n/a)
DD-817, per Ralph Fries.

Corvette (n/a)
6Apr70, XXIV Corps proposed 5th Div FSB name.

Coryell Compound (AQ 81-06?)
A.k.a. Camp Coryell. Just NW Ban Me Thuot. Named to honor WO1 Michael N Coryell, USA, 155th AHC, 52d Avn Bn, KIA 27Oct67. Shot down while flying supt for 4th Div units under heavy attack at Plei Djereng. Det B-23, 5th SF Grp. See Coryell, Camp. Darlac Pr, II Corps.

Coryell, Camp (AQ 81-06?)
A.k.a. Coryell Cmpd. Just NW Ban Me Thuot AF and at NW side of Ban Me Thuot. Named to honor WO1 Michael N Coryell, (and his crew) USA, 155th AHC, 52d Avn Bn, KIA 30Oct66, shot down while flying suptg 4th Div units under heavy attack at Plei Djereng. Det B 23, 5th SF Grp. Was dedicated(?) 4Feb67. 1st known use of 122mm rockets against Camp was 15May68? Site also of infamous "Rocket Party of '69." Darlac Pr, II Corps.

Cossack, LZ (XD 895-202)
On SE edge of Vietnam Salient at Lao border, apx 3 km ENE peak Co Van Mtn (Hill 656), 1 km S Hwy 615, 23 km SSE Khe Sanh CB and 54 km SW Quang Tri. Apr70 XXIV Corps grid per Don Armstrong. Quang Tri Pr, I Corps.

COSVN Directive 38 (n/a)
See Glossary.

COSVN Resolution Nine (n/a)
See Glossary.

COSVN Guy, The (n/a)
See Glossary.

Cotton, FSB (XD 849-419)
Just S old Khe Sanh CB, and adj to connecting road that ran S to QL-9. Apr70 XXIV Corps grid per Don Armstrong. Quang Tri Pr, I Corps.

Cotton, LZ (BR 465-352)
Apx 10 km S to SSW An Khe. Likely 1st Cav. Dec65. Binh Dinh Pr, II Corps.

Cougar, FSB (XT 150-970)
Apx 4 km from Cambodia and 19 km NW Katum AF. Mar67. Tay Ninh Pr, III Corps.

Cougar, FSB (YS 501-715)
Apx 7 km NE Nui Dat, 6 km E FSB Dagger and 5.5 km SW FSB Longreach. On 1ATF NCO trng map per John Hollett. 1ATF. Phuoc Tuy Pr, III Corps.

Cougar, FSB (YT 735-000)
Along QL-1, apx 28 km WSW Xuan Loc and 17 km SE Nui Chua Chan. Jan68. Long Khanh Pr, III Corps.
Cougar, LZ (XD 853-593)
In mtns apx 19 km N Khe Sanh CB, 6 km NNE peak Dong Voi Mep (Hill 1739), 27 km W Cam Lo. Apr70 XXIV Corps grid per Don Armstrong. Quang Tri Pr, I Corps.
Cougar, LZ (XD)
Near Nui Tia Pong, apx 9 km NW Vandegrift CB, 6 km NW LZ Uranus, 3d Mar Div, '69. Quang Tri Pr, I Corps.
Cougar, Platoon Patrol Base (XS 3-4?)
Near Dong Tam (AO Kudzo) and described by Daniel Evans as, "a mini-frontier fort about two miles from Vinh Kim." Vinh Kim is at XS 3-4, apx 1 km up secondary road that branched off Widow-Maker Alley. Was no more than 100' wide and formed by "3-mud and sand reinforced berms surrounded by concertina wire." Had central Cmd bunker and bunker at each of its 3 corners. Built as OP/LP protecting Dong Tam basecamp. 4th/39th Inf, 9th Inf Div here Dec68. Cited in *Doc: Platoon Medic*, pp 65-66. Dinh Tuong Pr, IV Corps.
Country Club, The (AR 80-47)
A.k.a. Camp Holloway. Apx 3 km E Pleiku. Originally known as Old Pleiku, then as *The Country Club* and later renamed Camp Holloway to honor CWO Charles E Holloway, USA, 81st Trans Co, CH-21 pilot, KIA 22Dec62, during ARVN insertion. Pleiku Pr, II Corps.
Coup, LZ (BN 560-514)
Along QL-1 at or near Ap Vinh Hao and FSB Grace (BN 567-508), 31 km ENE Song Mao AF/Hai Ninh and 38 km SW Phan Rang. Mar67. Binh Thuan Pr, II Corps.
Coup Troops (n/a)
See Glossary.
Courage, LZ (CR 023-725)
Apx 4 km W the Gulf of Tonkin, 11 km NE Vinh Loi, 10 km E Ql-1, 27 km SE Bong Son and 33 km NNE Phu Cat AB. 4th Div AO, '70. Name/grid per Jim Claeys. Binh Dinh Pr, II Corps.
Court, LZ (BP 880-665)
In mtns apx 19 km NW Nha Trang and 8 km ENE Bien My. Apr67. Khanh Hoa Pr, II Corps.
Courtenay, Plantation de (YS 4-9)
See Courtenay Rubber Plantation. Phuoc Tuy/Long Khanh Pr border, III Corps.
Courtenay Airfield (YS 455-916)
At or adj to or a.k.a. Xuan Loc AF, apx 60 km ENE Saigon. "Insecure, abnd, pvt AF, 16Jun68, AF # VA3-127," in Aug69 TAD per Frank Penk, Jr. Not in Feb73 TAD. Phuoc Tuy/Long Khanh Pr border, III Corps.
Courtenay Hill (YS 47-96?)
1,000' hill along Rte 2 (LTL-2), apx 750 meters N of the Long Khanh/Phuoc Tuy Pr border. Closest ville was Xa Cam My. 1ATF, D and E Plts, HQ Co at this location in 71. Presumably in very general vicinity of Courtenay Rubber Plantation and Xuan Loc. Thus named because, "The name printed on the map we were on was 'Don Dien de Courtenay', so we named the hill 'Courtenay.' "[137] Grid is that for 820' hill apx 4 km Due E FSB Blackhorse AF/Basecamp and est to be likely location of this base. Long Khanh Pr, III Corps.
Courtenay Rubber Plantation (YS 4-9)
A.k.a. Don Dien Courtenay. N of Blackhorse Basecamp and along QL-2, straddling the Phuoc Tuy and Long Khanh Pr border apx 60 km ENE Saigon, 25 km SSW Vo Dat, 20 km N Nui Dat and S Xuan Loc. Phuoc Tuy/Long Khanh Pr border, III Corps.
Courtney, Camp (n/a)
On Okinawa, not in Vietnam.
Covey (n/a)
See Glossary.
Covey Mess Hall (BT 0-7)
Mess for 20th TASS FACs stationed at Da Nang AB. At page 112, *Da Nang Diary*, former Covey FAC pilot describes facility and notes that in '70, meals there were excellent and priced reasonably: Breakfast 25¢, Lunch 65¢, Dinner 55¢. Quang Nam Pr, I Corps.
Cox, Camp (YT 165-001)
See Martin Cox, Camp. Bien Hoa Pr, III Corps.
Coxha Gorge (XK 3-8?)
Dismal, waterless gorge of northern Tonkin frontier known as Gorge of Coxha. In Sep50, pursuing Vietminh trapped Col LePage's relief column from Lang Son as it tried desperately to join Col Charton's fleeing Cao Bang garrison following abandonment of Cao Bang frontier outpost. Col Charton's exhausted and battered men were holding a ridge on edge of gorge after a terrible ordeal along Quangliet (Quang Liet) Track. At 3 am one night, LePage's trapped and greatly outnumbered force made a do-or-die bid to escape by attacking upslope toward Charton's positions. Only small number reached Charton's ragged survivors, all of whom then fled along ridge in futile effort to escape Vietminh hordes who overwhelmed and slaughtered remnants. Though shot 4 times, Charton was taken prisoner and survived. Of the 100 BEP troops who managed to escape the noose, only 23 survived. See Cao Bang, Lang Son, Quanqliet Track and Namnang. NVN.[138]
Coyote, FSB (AT 902-718)
Apx 12 km WSW Da Nang AB, 4 km SE peak of Hill 324 and 4 km WNW Cobb Bridge (Hwy 540). Apr70 XXIV Corps grid per Don Armstrong. Quang Nam Pr, I Corps.
CP Red Devil (YD 284-538)
Apx 3 km SE QL-1/Quang Tri AF, 6 km NW La Vang AF and8 km NNW Thon Nhu Le. XXIV Corps grid. Quang Tri Pr, I Corps.
Crab, LZ (YD 012-455)
In wide valley along QL-9, apx 3 km due S Ca Lu and 34 km WSW Quang Tri. Apr70 XXIV Corps grid per Don Armstrong. Quang Tri Pr, I Corps.
Crabes, Pointe aux (YJ 0-1)
See Pointe Crabes. NVN.
Crane, LZ (XD 866-176)
At southern tip of Vietnam Salient, apx 2 km ESE Lang Tenouo, and 57 km SW Quang Tri. Apr70 XXIV Corps grid per Don Armstrong. Quang Tri Pr, I Corps.
Cranes, BD (n/a)
See BD Cranes in Glossary and Big John in alpha index.
Crapaud, Rade du (YJ 1-0)
Anchorage at 20°49'N-107°06'E. On NF48-16 JOG. NVN.
Crash at Marble Mountain 'O' Club (BT)
See Glossary.

Craterville (BT 15-28)
Apx 3 km WNW of Hoi An AF and 20 km SSE Da Nang AB. Apparently either the nickname of ville in Americal AO, or possibly a FSB name? Quang Nam Pr, I Corps.
Craw, FSB (YT 89-45)
See Crow, FSB. Binh Tuy Pr, III Corps.
Crescent (XT 420-570)
Unknown if this is a terrain feature or LZ? Site is apx 6 km WSW Dau Tieng. Also listed at XT 440-510. Apr69-Apr70. Tay Ninh Pr, III Corps.
Crescent, The (BR 8-9)
A 15 km long crescent-shaped ridgeline in area directly S Bong Son and parallel to and W of QL-1 between 2 and 5 km. On map in *Bird*, p. 18. Binh Dinh Pr, II Corps.
Crescent, The (XU 94-28?)
Crescent-shaped dry lake bed apx 3 km W FSB Ruth and 4 km WSW Bu Dop. Opening in otherwise dense jungle and on 20Jan70 was site of Battle of The Crescent, a 14 hour battle involving 2d Sqdn, 11th ACR (opcon to 1st Inf Div) whose overland attack surprised 65th NVA Rgt (plus part of anti-aircraft Rgt) who were poised to ambush aerial assault of clearing. Grid is est. Phuoc Long Pr, III Corps.
Crest, FSB (BS 816-379?)
If grid correct, then site was at or near Duc Pho AF, perhaps 1 km E QL-1 and An Tho, some 37 km SSE Quang Ngai. Americal List states grid is "BT" 816-379, which cannot be correct since that point is well out to sea. Proper grid zone likely BS as is said to have been an Americal base. Quang Ngai Pr?, I Corps.
Crest, LZ (XD 84-54)
On Dong Voi Mep (Hill 1739), apx 15 km due N Khe Sanh CB, 20 km W Laos and 15 km S the DMZ. In Jun64, radio intel units of ASA under cover name "Advsy Team One" had 2 LZs built on Hill 1739 (Tiger Tooth Mtn) to provide observation and radio monitoring capabilities. One LZ was built on crest of Hill and other on slope of hill and simply named LZs "Crest" and "Hill." ARVN and USMC troops were employed to build and secure lofty site. High winds and down drafts made landings here difficult. By 22Jun64, 100 ARVN and 73 Marines manned Advsy Team One site. See Dong Voi Mep SESU. Quang Tri Pr, I Corps. [139]
Cricket (n/a)
6Apr70, XXIV Corps proposed 5th Div FSB name.
Crimp, Operation (XT?)
8-14Jan66. 173d Abn, Binh Duong Pr, conducted generally W of the Hobo Woods. 1sATF, RAR made initial contact, then 173d discovered large bunker complex. 128 VC KIA, 91 POWs. III Corps.
Crocker Compound (XS 4-4?)
See James N. Crocker Cmpd. Dinh Tuong Pr?, IV Corps.
Crocker, Camp (XT 82-17?)
At Phu Cuong and about 32 km N Saigon. Home of MACV Advsy Team 70 and/or 91 (also at Thu Dat Mot in Binh Dinh Pr?). Binh Duong Pr, III Corps.
Crockett, FSB/PB (XT 742-165)
A.k.a. Basecamp or Patrol Base Crockett. Along LTL-8A, apx 6 km W Phu Cuong and 10 km E Cu Chi. Feb68-Mar69 at listed grid and also listed at XT 733-149, Jan68, so it seems permanent site was moved apx 1 km W the initial patrol base of this name. Binh Duong Pr, III Corps.
Crockett II, FSB (XT 746-162)
See Crockett, FSB, for location. Built or rebuilt beginning 20Ju69, and HQ, during Op Toan Thang II. Jan-Apr69. Binh Duong Pr, III Corps.
Crockett, USS (n/a)
A.k.a. PG 88. Part of Coastal Flotilla 1. 165' long and capable of 37 knots. Armed with one 3"/.50-cal. gun forward, one 40mm gun aft, and four .50-cal. MGs. Market Time, SVN.
Crocodiles in Vietnam (n/a)
See Glossary.
Cronin Army Museum (YS 17-98)
At Camp Martin-Cox, Bearcat, apx 33 km ENE Tan Son Nhut AB. Named to honor LTC William B Cronin, CO 2d/47th Inf, 9th Inf Div, KIA 27Apr67, Dinh Thuong Pr, during Op Palm Beach, when Bde cmd group ambushed as it walked down trail toward an LZ. Bien Hoa Pr, III Corps.
Crook, Edward, 1st Sgt (n/a)
See Glossary.
Crook, FSB (XT 060-593)
In flat, forested area along QL-13 near point where it crossed Suoi Ber Da River, apx 18 km NW Tay Ninh, 13 km NE Tay Ninh West AF and 10 km E Cambodia. Hit by series of attacks 5-7Jun69, while occupied by elements of 3d/22d Inf and 7th/11th Arty. Possibly also 1st Cav base in '69. In 3-day Battle of FSB Crook, enemy was 1st detected by border sensors and base radar5Jun69, then at 0300, heavy rocket/mortar attack was followed by 272d NVA Rgt charging from S and E. 16 NVA managed to breach wire. AC-47 and AC-119 gunships plus ARA and jets halted 1st night's attack. 2d night was repeat of 1st night when at 0200 a 25th Avn Night Hawk detected movement and arty was placed on NVA units. At 0300, a 90 minute barrage of 150 rocket and mortar shells per minute rained in and then followed by 2 Bns of 88th NVA Rgt attacking from N. NVA decimated by ARA/AC-119 fire and, by 0530 of 2d night, battle was over. On 3d night, an arty recon by fire in same area of earlier attacks triggered 3d, half-hearted attack that was quickly stopped. Grid per Peter Cole. Also listed at XT 055-595. Tay Ninh Pr, III Corps.
Crook, LZ (YA 87-02?)
See Crooks, LZ. Pleiku Pr, II Corps.
Crooks, FSB (XT 060-593)
See Crook, FSB. Tay Ninh Pr, III Corps.
Crooks, LZ (YA 875-125)
Possibly a.k.a. Hill 222 and LZ "Crook." In Ia Drang Valley apx 50 km WNW Phu Nhon, 50 km SW Pleiku and 10 km N peak of Chu Pong Mtn. 1st Cav LZ during 1st Ia Drang campaign. 2d/17th Arty here, 23Nov66, 23Oct65-11Nov65, during Op Long Reach. Name, and some data per Jack Picciolo. Also listed at YA 974-035, but that is grid for LZ Columbus/Cavalair? On, map in *Pleiku*, p 252, cited at pp 252-258. Pleiku Pr, II Corps.
Crosby (n/a)
6Apr70, XXIV Corps proposed 5th Div FSB name.
Crosby, Bing (n/a)
See Glossary.
Cross Bow, LZ (XD 865-591)
Apx 18 km NW Ca Lu, 36 km due W Dong Ha and 6 km NE peak of Dong Voi Mep (hill 1739). Apr70 XXIV Corps grid per Don Armstrong. Quang Tri Pr, I Corps.

Crossbow, LZ (XD 865-591)
See Crossbow. Quang Tri Pr, I Corps.

Crossroads, FSB (BQ 071-715)
See Area Crossroads. Phu Bon Pr, II Corps.

Crossroads, The (XS 5-3?)
Nickname of large canal network in AO of 9th Div MRF. In article entitled, *The crossroads of the Mekong*, pp 20-21, May 2000 issue of *Military* Magazine, Charlie Palek describes major action here 4Apr68, involving 3d/47th Inf, in which 32 US were KIA, 56 WIA and 10 MIA. Grid is est. Dinh Tuong or Kien Hoa Pr, IV Corps.

Crossroads Airfield (VC 5-8)
A.k.a. Loeng Nok Tha AF. At 16°10'00"N-104°36'00"E. NIMA data. Thailand.

Crouching Beast, Mountain of (YC 328-981)
See Dong Ap Bia/Hamburger Hill. Thua Thien Pr, I Corps.

Crow, FSB (YT 89-45)
Apx 12 km NNE Vo Dat, 15 km NNE Vo Dat AF, 5 km NW FSB Warrior, 48 km NE Xuan Loc and 24 km NW Tanh Linh AF. 4th/12th Inf, 199th LIB position. Spelled Craw on one list but that is thought to be error. Binh Tuy Pr, III Corps.

Crow, LZ (AT 900-866)
Apx 6 km NW Red Breach AF, 16 km NNE Da Nang AB and 2.5 km W Ap Kim Lien/QL-1, overlooking Song Cu De Valley to S and ocean to E. Likely had spectacular view. Apr70 XXIV Corps grid per Don Armstrong. Thua Thien Pr?, I Corps.

Crow, LZ (XD 827-479?)
In shadow of Hill 632, apx 3 km NNW Hill 950 and 6.5 km N Khe Sanh CB. LZ for C and D Cos, 3d/26th Marines, 26Dec67. Grid apx. Quang Tri Pr, I Corps.

Crow, LZ (XS 963-703)
Apparently a.k.a. FSB Tango (XS 96-71). Along E Bank of Song Nha Be River, apx 32 km SE Tan Son Nhut AB, 14 km SSE Nha Be and 14 km E to ESE Can Giuoc. Mar66. Gia Dinh Pr, III Corps.

Crow, LZ (YD 038-649)
In Song Ngan Valley, apx 20 km WNW Dong Ha, 3 km S southern edge of DMZ, and 11 km NE The Rockpile. 1st LZ used for lndg 3d/4th Marines during Op Hastings, 15Jul66. CH-46s of HMM-164 and HMM-265 made the insertions. Five CH-46 helos were lost on LZ that day. Two were hit by ground fire and crashed, one hit tree and two others collided; apx 15 KIA, 7 WIA. As a result, this area of Song Nang Valley became known as Helicopter Valley forever after.[140] Quang Tri Pr, I Corps.

Crow Hall (CP 03-52)
At Camp John McDermott, Nha Trang. Data per Ray Bows. Khanh Hoa Pr, II Corps.

Crow's Foot (BR 740-800)
A.k.a. Eagle's Claw. Terrain feature apx 40 km NNW Phu Cat, 18 km SW Bong Son and 20 km W QL-1 that from above resemble a bird's foot where mtns taper out and lower ridge fingers reach toward the ocean. *Chickenhawk* author described it as "seven intersecting valleys, 12 miles south of Bong Son." General AO during Op Crazy Horse, 1st Cav, May66, as per *Battles in the Monsoon*, p 96. On SE Quarter of L-7014-6737-1 map, per Ken Burrington. Binh Dinh Pr, II Corps.

Crow's Nest (BT 06-73?)
Apparently a Marine OP situated on one of the Marble Mtns. Described as 40-meter high marble outcropping apx 100 meters W of the Army SF Camp at base of largest of 4, Marble Mtn peaks. On 23Aug68, site was hit by apx 10-15 NVA while manned by 8 men of 3d/7th Marines, in an attack coordinated with another on the SF camp. Discussed on USMC Amtrac site at www.stealth.net/~stan/nva/nva.htm. Near listed grid. Quang Nam Pr, I Corps.

Crow's Nest (YT 00-00)
Feature defined by Cambodian border apx 30 km W the tip of Parrot's Beak, 85 km W Saigon and at intersection of UTM grid zones WT, XT VS and YS. Moc Hoa and Long Khot AF's were nearby. Invaded by ARVN 4th Armored Bde, 20Apr70, 3 Cav Rgts, 3 Ranger Bns in 3-day attack. On 28Apr70, ARVN 2d and 6th Armored Cav Rgts hit same area (sans US advisors). Kien Tuong Pr, IV Corps.

Cruickshank Field (XS 937-798)
Heliport apparently on tip of point in Song Nha Be River and adj to Nhe Be Tank Farm/Navy facility, apx 11 km SE Saigon and 5 km SE Nha Be. Likely named to honor William R. Cruickshank, ABF2 USN, KIA 10Mar69. Name/grid from a '69 TAD per Frank Penk, Jr; not in '73 TAD. Gia Dinh Pr, III Corps.

Crum Compound (WS 71-54?)
Advsy Team 50 Cmpd at Cao Lanh. Possibly 4 km N the Mekong River and 3 km SSE Cao Lanh. Named to honor Maj. Edward W Crum, USA, Adv Team 50, KIA 7Feb68, by mortar fire while trying to rescue a comrade wounded in attack on Team's cmpd. Data per *Vietnam Military Lore, 1959-1973*. Kien Phong Pr, IV Corps.

Crunch, FSB (BS 534-516)
A.k.a. Minh Long and LZ Crunch. At or just S Minh Long AF, apx 19 km W Mo Duc, 24 km SSW Quang Ngai, 3 km NE Con Loan and in valley of headwaters of Song Phuoc Giang River. Apr70 XXIV Corps grid per Don Armstrong. Quang Ngai or Quang Tin Pr, I Corps.

Crusader, LZ (YA 8-4?)
Appears to have been near Plei Toun Breng, apx 44 km due W Pleiku. 7th/15th Arty here. Pleiku Pr, II Corps.

Crystal, FSB (YS 30-97)
Apx 45 km due E Saigon, 14 km due W Blackhorse Basecamp and 16 km ENE Long Thanh AF. 2d/3d Inf, 199th LIB. Long Khanh Pr, III Corps.

Crystal, LZ (BR 892-659)
Just W QL-1, apx 23 km due N Phu Cat AB and 3 km SSW Phu My. 2d/17th Arty here Oct66, suptg 1/7th Cav, per Jack Picciolo, who puts grid at BR 8926-6614. A Bty, 5th/16th Arty here Aug70, supt 4th Div. Grid per Jim Claeys. Also listed at BR 85-95 and BR 982-348? Binh Dinh Pr, II Corps.

Crystal, LZ (BR 982-348?)
If grid correct, was at or near Ba Gi AF. This grid thought to be in error. Also listed at BR 85-95 and BR 892-659? Binh Dinh Pr, II Corps.

Crystal, LZ (XD 754-368)
On small hill, apx 3 km due E Lao Bao, 4 km W Lang Vei (2), 3 km N Laos, 11 km WSW Khe Sanh CB and2 km N QL-9. Apr70 XXIV Corps grid per Don Armstrong. Quang Tri Pr, I Corps.

Crystal Airfield (BR 894-658)
Along Ql-1, apx 12 km N LZ Hammond AF, 35 km S LZ English, 28 km S Bong Son AF, 47 km NE An Khe and 18 km from coast. Minor US airfield here per TPC K-10A and TPC K-10B. Listed as "Secure ARVN(MACV) 15Oct68, AF # VA2-296," in Aug69 TAD, per Frank Penk, Jr. Not in Feb73 TAD. El. 85'. Binh Dinh Pr, II Corps.

Crystal Airfield, LZ (BR 894-658)
See Crystal AF. Binh Dinh Pr, II Corps

CS Gas (n/a)
See M-79 Grenade Launcher, E-158 Canister, CS Gas Incident; all in Glossary.

CS Gas Incident (n/a)
See Glossary.

Cu Bi Rubber Plantation (YS 45-85)
Apx 15 km due N Nui Dat, 7 km NW Ngai Giao and 6 km S the Courtenay Rubber Plantation. Site of Battle of Cu Bi Rubber Plantation, 8Jan70, when Aussie 8RAR engaged a large VC force near FSB Peggy. Phuoc Tuy Pr, III Corps.

Cu Chi, FSB (XT 650-160)
Along N side of TL-8A, apx 5 km NE Cu Chi and 25 km NW Tan Son Nhut AB. Listed as FSB in Sep69 rpt and unknown if it was separate from Cu Chi CB. Hau Nghia Pr, III Corps.

Cu Chi Airfield (XT 63-14)
Apx 25 km NW Saigon, 22 km due W Phu Loi AF and 20 km NNE Duc Hoa AF. Per TPC K-10D. El. 39'. Hau Nghia Pr, III Corps.

Cu Chi Army Airfield (XT 650-145)
Apx 25 km NW Saigon, 22 km due W Phu Loi AF and 20 km NNE Duc Hoa AF, per TPC K-10D. El. 39', 2,900' asph rwy. 10°59'15"N-106°30'45"E. Hau Nghia Pr, III Corps.

Cu Chi Base Camp (XT 65-14)
A.k.a. Dong Zu, Dong Xu, Xon Hue or Xom Xu? Apx 5 km NE Cu Chi ville and along N side of TL-8A, 25 km NW Tan Son Nhut AB, 36 km SSE Dau Tieng, 50 km SE Tay Ninh and 4 km N QL-1. Just S of Iron Triangle. Major US basecamp and home of 25th Inf Div throughout most of war. When US 25th went home in '70, the 25th ARVN Div, formerly at Duc Hoa, took over base. Immense VC tunnel complexes throughout the area are alleged to have even under the base. Noted for its dust ("only place on earth you can stand up to your ass in mud and still get dust in your eyes" was common description of it.) Elements of 199th LIB here, Spring '68. 7th/11th Arty and 1st Bde/101st Div also here. Also 2d home of MACV Adv Team 99. Also listed at XT 63-14. Hau Nghia Pr, III Corps.

Cu Chi Hamlet String (XT 1-4 to XT 1-5)
Ran roughly from XT 19-45 to XT 19-50. Attacked by elements of 271st NVA/VC Bn on night of 17-18Aug68, as diversionary action for main assault on Tay Ninh. Again heavily attacked and occupied by Bn size force during night of 10-11Sep68. Data per AAR, Battle of Tay Ninh (17Aug-27Sep68), HQ 25th ID, 2Feb69, pp 13, 23. Tay Ninh Pr, III Corps.

Cu Chi Heliport (XT 628-125)
Just S Rte TL-8A, apx 2 to 3 km SSW Cu Chi AF, and 5 km NW Tan Phu. "Heliport #552, alt 32', soccer field. Call Cu Chi Ops on 43. 1 for pax or cargo info. Contact "Oblong Reels 56" on 44.1 prior to Ldg. Arty advsy-Hau Nghia 228.1, 46.8. At 10°58'00"N-106°29'15"E," per Feb73 TAD. Hau Nghia Pr, III Corps.

Cu Chi Hilton (XT 63-14?)
During lull in Nov-Dec68, 1st/14th Inf, 25th Inf rotated each line Co to Cu Chi CB for 3-day stand-down at what became known as "Cu Chi Hilton." 1st established during Sep68, so 2d Bde/25th Div troops would have place for R&R/reorganization. Refresher courses on patrolling, combat ops and stood equip/weapon inspections offered. In evening, troops entertained by bands whose female dancers were much appreciated. Hau Nghia Pr, III Corps.

Cu Chi Laager Site (XT 614-226)
See US/ARVN Laager Site. Binh Duong Pr, III Corps.

Cu Chi Signal Site (XT 6-1?)
No data. Hau Nghia Pr, III Corps.

Cu Chi University (XT 63-14?)
Cu Chi U was the Army Education Ctr at 25th Inf's Cu Chi CB, apx 25 km NW Saigon. Advertised on AFVN (Armed Forces Radio) in at least '70, offering courses in Principles of Accounting, Introduction to Business, Data Processing, Beginning French, Criminology, Real Estate, History of Western Civilization, Principles of Speech, and American Negro History. Each class was worth 3 Semester Credits and required a minimum of 10 students to schedule. CCU was sponsored by US Armed Forces Institute. Radio ads for it used phrase, "Don't you be drop out, drop in to Cu Chi U, or give 'em a call in Cu Chi at 5143 for more details." University of Maryland extension courses were also apparently available through many of US military installations in SVN. Hau Nghia Pr, III Corps. [141]

Cu Duc SF Camp (VS 472-497)
At NE edge of Ha Tien's Nouc Man Lagoon, apx 3 km from Cambodian border, 5 km ENE Ha Tien and 5 km NE Ha Tien South AF. 5th SF. Info/grid per *SF Order of Battle*. A.k.a. FOB Ha Tien. Listed at VB 472-497 but VB zone likely in error. Kien Giang Pr, IV Corps.

Cu Grock Mountain (YA 810-690)
See Sledge Hammer. Kontum Pr, II Corps.

Cu Hanh Airfield (AR 783-500)
See Pleiku/Cu Hanh AF. Pleiku Pr, II Corps.

Cu Ki Tem Dar Mountain (YA 84-77)
A.k.a. Hill 1528. Apx 28 km WNW Plei Mrong. See Sledge Hammer. Kontum Pr, II Corps.

Cu La Re Island (BT 98-02)
See Cu Lao Re Island and Airfield. Quang Tin or Quang Ngai Pr, I Corps.

Cu Lao Binh Chanh Island (XT 965-202)
In the Song Dong Nai, apx 6 km N Bien Hoa AB. Bien Hoa Pr, III Corps.

Cu Lao Binh Thuy (WS 86-12)
Island in Mekong River, immed N Can Tho and E Can Tho AF. Phong Dinh Pr?, IV Corps.

Cu Lao Cham (n/a)
Mapsheet name of L-7014-6740-4. SVN.

Cu Lao Cham Island (BT 35-65)
Apx 35 km SE Da Nang and 15 km ENE mouth of Song Thu Bon River near Hoi An. Much smaller Hon Ta and Hon Gia Islands are also in this three-island group. Quang Nam Pr, I Corps.

Cu Lao Hon Island (BN 63-42)
See 30-Minute Island. Binh Thuan Pr, II Corps.

Cu Lao Hon Island (BM 75-65)
A 4 by 7 km island apx 100 km ESE Phan Thiet and 115 km due S Phan Rang. Had two smaller islands off its N end and two off its S end as well (one of which was Il Du Sud Island. South China Sea.
Cu Lao Ma Nha Isle (CQ 20-68)
Island apx 10 km E Tuy An AF and 5 km E Dam O Lam Bay. Phu Yen Pr, II Corps.
Cu Lao Re Island Airfield (CT 003-012)
In Gulf of Tonkin, apx 33 km E Chu Lai. Minor AF here per TPC K-10B. Nature of US presence here otherwise unknown. El. 16', 2,500' sod/clay rwy. 15°22'52"N-109°08'22"E. Also listed at BT 99-02. I Corps.
Cu Lao Re Island (BT 987-020)
Described as beautiful island in Gulf of Tonkin, apx 32 km ESE Chu Lai and at intersection of grid zones BT, BS, CT and CS. Most of island is in BT zone. Apx 2 by 6 km in size and surrounded by coral reef. AF also here. Sometimes spelled "Cu La Re." Also listed at CT 000-020. I Corps.
Cu Lao Re Lighthouse (CT 02-03)
On Cu Lao Re Island, apx 47 km ESE Chu Lai. I Corps.
Cu Lao Xanh Island (CR 23-05)
Apx 23 km SE Qui Nhon. Binh Dinh Pr, II Corps.
Cu Lao Xanh Lighthouse (CR 22-06)
Apx 23 km SE Qui Nhon. Binh Dinh Pr, II Corps.
Cu Mong, Baie de (CR 1-0)
A.k.a. Dam Cu Mong. Bay at 13°34'N-109°15'E. On ND49-09 JOG. Phu Yen Pr, II Corps.
Cu Mong, Dam (CR 1-0)
Bay at 13°34'N-109°15'E. Phu Yen Pr, II Corps.
Cu Mong Mountain (YD 580-010)
A.k.a. Dong Cu Mung. Apx 10 km SSW FSB Bastogne, 4 km SE FSB Veghel and 25 SW Hue. On 5Mar72, ARVN 1st Inf Div launched Op Lam Son 45-72 on nearby suspected NVA logistical base. Thua Thien Pr, I Corps.
Cu Mong Pass (CR 030-130)
QL-1 pass, apx 11 km SSW Qui Nhon. Phu Yen/Binh Dinh Pr border, II Corps.
Cu Rao (n/a)
Mapsheet name of L-7014-5847-1. NVN only.
Cua (n/a)
Vietnamese for "estuary" or "river mouth."
Cua Be (CP 0-1)
A.k.a. Petite Passe. Channel near 11°51'N-109°15'E. On NC49-01 JOG. Khanh Hoa Pr, II Corps.
Cua Be, Lach (CP 2-9)
See Lach Cua Be. Khanh Hoa Pr, II Corps.
Cua Cung Hau River (XR 7-8)
Exits to South China Sea apx 110 km S Saigon, near 9°46'00"N-106°34'00"E. Vinh Binh Pr, IV Corps.
Cua Dai Beach CAP (BT 1-5?)
Spelled "Cau Dai" in CAP website listing? A Song Cua Dai is in listed UTM grid square, which suggests site was near Hoi An, SE Da Nang. CAP 2-4-4 here per Tim Duffie. Quang Nam Pr, I Corps.
Cua Dai, Pointe de (BT 1-5)
See Pointe Cua Dai. Quang Nam Pr, I Corps.
Cua Day (n/a)
Mapsheet name of L-7014-6248-4. NVN only.
Cua Gia (CQ 0-0)
Channel near 12°40'N-109°13'E. On ND49-13 JOG. Khanh Hoa Pr, II Corps.
Cua Ho LST Ramp (BT 52-13)
At mouth of Truong Giang Estuary, along S bank, apx 5 km NNW Chu Lai AB and 1 km SE Dong Tuan. On map in *The Marines in Vietnam 1954-1973*, p 234. Also spelled Cus Ho? Quang Tin Pr, I Corps.
Cua Ho VNN Junk Base (BT 52-13)
At mouth of Truong Giang Estuary, along its S bank, apx 5 km NNW Chu Lai AB and 1 km SE Dong Tuan. On map in *The Marines in Vietnam 1954-1973*, p 234. Also spelled Cus Ho? Quang Tin Pr, I Corps.
Cua Rung Mountain (BT 07-10)
Apx 6 km SW of and overlooking Tien Phuoc SF Camp. Quang Tin Pr, I Corps.
Cua Tam (AD 8-6)
Channel near 21°24'N-108°00'E. On NF49-09 JOG. NVN.
Cua Tra Ly (n/a)
Mapsheet name of L-7014-6349-4. NVN only.
Cua Tung (YD 25-82)
The mouth of Ben Hai River. NVN.
Cua Valley (YD 080-511)
Mai Loc AF is in this valley, apx 25 km W Quang Tri. Quang Tri Pr, I Corps.
Cua Viet (YD 3-7)
Mouth of Dong Ha River, apx 15 km due N Quang Tri. Quang Tri Pr, I Corps.
Cua Viet Combat Base (YD 220-590?)
Likely grid is erroneous; however, if correct, site was along QL-1, apx 21 km NW Quang Tri and 15 km WNW Cua Viet Naval facility. Nov69. Quang Tri Pr, I Corps.
Cua Viet Combat Base (YD 320-590)
Along N bank of Cua Viet River, apx 3 km NW Ha Tay, 16 km due N Quang Tri and 2 km W ocean. Also listed at YD 220-590, which is likely error. Quang Tri Pr, I Corps.
Cua Viet Heliport (YD 332-692)
At mouth of Dong Ha River, apx 15 km due N. Heliport #547, alt 13', at 16°54'00"N-107°11'30"E, per Feb73 TAD. Quang Tri Pr, I Corps.
Cua Viet Marine Amtrac Bn (YD 343-698)
A.k.a. Camp Kistler. Apx 16 km N Quang Tri, where Cua Viet River enters Gulf of Tonkin. Here Amtrac Bn Cmpd was co-located with large USN facility. Described as follows in *Combat Medic*, pp 88-89: "Overlooking the Dong Ha River, the cmpd was a dug-in installation set up in defensive posture with watchtowers, concertina wire, trenches and bunkers. These bunkers weren't [your typical] sandbagged-holes, but the best bunkers in country; buried, derelict Amtracs capable of withstanding direct hits from just about anything the gooks had to throw at them." Facility seized by NVA immed after signing of Paris Peace Accords, Mar73. XXIV Corps grid. On map at: http://wmcbride.space. swri.edu/visit/maps/cuamap.jpg. Also listed at YD 345-695. Quang Tri Pr, I Corps.
Cua Viet NSAD (YD 33-69)
Apx 16 km N Quang Tri at mouth of Cua Viet River. USN Supt Activity, '67-70. Per MRF Assn Website.
Cua Viet Port Facility (YD 342-698)
Apx 16 km N Quang Tri at mouth of Cua Viet River. 12th Mar Arty here in'67, with six 105mm howitzers, along

with USN Seabees/small craft personnel. Quang Tri Pr, I Corps.

Cua Viet R&R Center (YD 33-69)
likely near mouth of Cua Viet River and Cua Viet NSAD. In-country Marine R&R center and Standdown area for 3d Mar Div. Quang Tri Pr, I Corps.

Cua Viet River (YD 33-69)
Running W to E from Cam Lo and Dong Ha, then emptying into ocean 16 km N of Quan Tri. Formed by confluence of Mieu Giang, Thach Han and Vinh Phuoc Rivers. Used extensively for US and VC/NVA ops. Quang Tri Pr, I Corps.

Cua Viet USN/USMC Base (YD 343-698)
On coast where the Dong Ha/Cua Viet River emptied into Gulf of Tonkin, apx 16 km due N of Quang Tri. PBRs, landing craft, water-borne medevac, as well as other, larger LS-type and coastal patrol vessels operated out of this facility. Marine Amtrac Bn also based here, as was HQ of TF Clearwater (River Security Grp, I Corps). Seized by NVA immed after signing of Paris Peace Accords, Mar73. Quang Tri Pr, I Corps.

Cua, Mui (CP 0-1)
Coastal point at 11°51'N-109°15'E. On NC49-01 JOG. Khanh Hoa Pr, II Corps.

Cuc Den, Nui (XF 0-0)
Mtn range at 18°09'N-106°01'E. NE48-07 JOG. NVN.

Cuc Den, Nui (XF 0-0)
Mtn range at 18°09'N-106°01'E. NE48-07 JOG. NVN.

Cudgel, FSB (ZC 193-450)
Apx 12 km SSW Ha Tan AF and 17 km W to WSW An Hoa CB and 7 km SSW Linh Hep. Apr70 XXIV Corps grid per Don Armstrong. Quang Nam Pr, I Corps.

Cudgle, FSB (XS 085-520)
Apx 14 km W Cai Lay and 18 km N Vinh Long. Nov67. Dinh Tuong Pr, IV Corps.

Cuff, LZ? (BR 849-814)
Either an LZ or name of hill-mass that forms the "Cuff" of another hill mass known as "The Boot"? Site is apx 14 km S Bong Son. In Feb66 rpt. Binh Dinh Pr, II Corps.

Culvert, LZ? (XT 524-407)
Apx 6 km NE Dau Tieng. Nature of site unknown. Binh Duong Pr, III Corps.

Cung Son (new) SF Camp (BQ 803-434)
On N side Song Bra River near Cung Son AF, apx 30 km SSW Dong Tre, 46 km NW Van Ninh, 4 km due E Son Hoa and 35 km W Tuy Hoa. Also about 4 km ESE site of Cung Son (old) SF Camp. 5th SF. Info/grid per *SF Order of Battle.* SF Det 28, 2d Bn 13th Arty; and Det A-221, here Oct66. 2d/17th Arty here 65 or 66. Transferred to RF/PF. Also listed at BQ 807-432. Phu Yen Pr, II Corps.

Cung Son (old) SF Camp (BQ 781-445)
On N side Song Bra River, apx 2 km NE Son Hoa, 30 km SSW Dong Tre, 4 and 38 km W Tuy Hoa. Also about 4 km WNW site of Cung Son (new) SF Camp. 5th SF. Info/grid per *SF Order of Battle.* Det 28; 2d Bn 13th Arty; Det A-221, Oct66. Moved to Dong Tre. Phu Yen Pr, II Corps.

Cung Son (Son Ha) (n/a)
Mapsheet L-7014-6735-2. Full sheet name: Son Ha (Cung Son). SVN.

Cung Son Airfield (BQ 808-422)
Apx 30 km SSW Dong Tre AF, 35 km SE Phu Tuc AF, on Song Bra/Song Darang River 3 km E Son Hoa, per TPC K-10A. El. 108', 2,600' steel-mat rwy. At 13°02'20"N-108°58'46"E. Phu Yen Pr, II Corps.

Cung Son/Dong Tre (BS 7-1?)
See Le Hai. II Corps.

Cung Son/Dong Tre, Camp (BS 7-1?)
See Le Hai. II Corps.

Cung Song AF (BQ 808-422)
See Cung Son AF. Phu Yen Pr, II Corps.

Cung Sung AF (BQ 808-422)
See Cung Son AF. Phu Yen Pr, II Corps.

Cunningham, FSB (YD 185-134)
FSB a.k.a. Hill 815? Apx 1 km N Rte 922 and overlooking Song Da Krong River Valley, apx 6 km SE FSB Razor, 38 km SE Vandegrift CB, 22 km E Khe Sanh and 10 km from Laos. A large combat base which hosted 9th Mar CP, several arty btys and fwd logistics supt for several Inf Cos. FSBs Erskine, Razor, and Cunningham plus LZ Dallas were built during Op Dawson River South, Jan22-10Feb69, to facilitate attack on Base Area 618. On map at p 32, *US Marines in Vietnam-1969*. Also listed at YD 184-131. Quang Tri Pr, I Corps.

Cunningham, LZ/FSB (ZA 148-482)
Apx 8 km W to WNW Pleiku, 9 km SW Pleiku Nansteph AF and 6 km SE Plei Blo O'Dung. A Bty, 5th/16th Arty here May70. 4th Div 31Jul70 ORLL grid, per Jim Henderson. Pleiku Pr, II Corps.

CUPP An On 1 and 4 (BT 02-74)
See An On CUPP. Quang Nam Pr, I Corps.

Curahee, LZ (various)
See Currahee.

Curless, Outpost (YC 905-947)
Apx 19 km WSW Phu Loc, 4 km WSW FSB Boise and 20 km due S Phu Bai. Possibly named to honor 1Lt Eugene J. Curless, Jr., KIA 25Mar68. Cited in 2d/501st Inf op rpt, for period 1Jan-1Jul71. Thua Thien Pr, I Corps.

Currahee, FSB (BN)
A.k.a. LZ Currahee. Per *Currahee History, 1Feb69 to 31Dec69*, p 47, was built by TF 3-506, sometime in Oct69(?). Apart from suptg the Cos of 3d/506th Inf, 101st Abn, it also suptd joint US/ARVN 44th Rgt recon ops in Song Mao Mtns. NE Binh Thuan Pr, II Corps.

Currahee, FSB (YC 398-949)
Apx 14 km NNW A Sap, 43 km SW Hue and 35 km WSW FSB Birmingham. Built on floor of A Shau Valley in early '69. Ground attack repulsed during Op Montgomery Rendezvous,16Jun69, resulting in 7 US WIA, and 51 NVA KIA, 3 POWs (elements of B & E/2/502d Inf, A/2/319th, B/2/11th Arty and ARVN arty involved). 101st Abn inactive FSB grid per Don Armstrong. Also listed at YC 399-949 and 402-948. Thua Thien Pr, I Corps. [142]

Currahee, FSB (YV 5-7?)
Built by TF 3d/506 (3d/506th Inf, 101st Abn while opcon 4th Div) in mid-May 70. 3d/506th Inf with HHC/326th Engrs, air-assault to swampy lowlands of Prek Drang River, during Cambodian incursion and built this base in area that was home to NVA B-3 Front. When ready, six 105mm howitzers of D Bty, 2d/320th Arty were ferried

into site. Article about the TF can be found in *Rendezvous With Destiny*, Summer '70, pp 2-6. Prek Drang, Cambodia.

Currahee, FSB (YA 404-547?)
In valley apx 3 km NE Phum Choy, 82 km W to WNW Pleiku, 15 km W SVN border and 3 km NE the Tonle San River. Opened 5May70, as HQ of TF 3-506th Inf. Grid and Data per op rpt at http://currahee.hispeed.com/officialDocuments/official.html Also listed at YA 427-547 and YA 415-538? Cambodia.

Currahee, LZ (YA 427-525)
Apx 13 km W SVN, 6 km ENE Phum Choy, 5 km NE Tonle San River, 80 km W Pleiku. 4th Div Cambodian Incursion FSB, '70. Name/grid per Jim Claeys. Also listed at YA 404-547 in 1st/506th Op Rpt, and at YA 415-538 per 4th Div 31Jul70 ORLL grid per Jim Henderson. Cambodia.

Currahee Base Camp (AN 809-070)
Nickname of 3d/506th Inf, 101st Abn's LZ Betty at Phan Thiet. See Betty, LZ, for detail. Binh Thuan Pr, II Corps.

***Currituck*, USS** (n/a)
AV-7. Between May65-Apr67, Seaplane Tenders *Currituck*, *Salisbury Sound* and *Pine Island* provided supt for Marlin P-5 Seaplanes while variously anchored at Cham Island, Condore Island and Cam Ranh Bay, as part of Op Market Time. Role discussed in *Brown Water, Black Berets*, p 92. SVN.

Cus Ho LST Ramp (BT 52-13)
See Cua Ho LST Ramp. Quang Tin Pr, I Corps.

Cus Ho VNN Junk Base (BT 52-13)
See Cua Ho VNN Junk Base. Quang Tin Pr, I Corps.

***Cushing*, USS** (n/a)
DD-729, per Ralph Fries.

Cusseta, LZ (BR 628-89?)
Apx 24 km WSW Bong Son, 19 km WNW Ha Tay AF and 46 km NNE An Khe. Mar66. Binh Dinh Pr, II Corps.

Custer (n/a)
See Glossary.

Custer (n/a)
6Apr70, XXIV Corps future-use III MAF FSB name.

Custer, FSB (XT 333-896)
At Katum AF, apx 42 km NNE Tay Ninh. Dec67-Jan68. Tay Ninh Pr, III Corps.

Custer, FSB (YT 025-348)
Apx 20 km due N Bien Hoa, 16 km SW FSB Pershing, 17 km SSE Phuoc Vinh and 4 km NE Khu Tru Mat. Cited in 2d/7th Cav Unit History '70-71, p 7, per Peter Cole. Arty ORLL grid. Bien Hoa Pr?, III Corps.

Custer, LZ (BS 513-657)
Apx 7 km due W LZ Cedar Mtn, 12 km SW Quang Ngai AF, 10 km WNW Nghia Hanh AF, 17 km W QL-1 and overlooking Song Phuoc Giang River Valley. Americal List. Quang Ngai Pr, I Corps.

Cut, Phu (VK 6-6)
Mtn range at 22°15'N-104°41'E. Grid per DMA L-1501 map NF48-06.

Cutlass, FSB (ZC 003-910)
Apx 27 km SSE Phu Bai, 13 km SW Phu Loc, 6 km WSW Bach Ma Resort and 9 km W FSB Musket. Apr70 XXIV Corps grid per Don Armstrong. Thua Thien Pr, I Corps.

Cutlass, FSB (ZC 13-36)
A.k.a. Hill 551. Apx 5 km N FSB Dart, 3 km SW FSB Mace, 26 km SW An Hoa. TF Yankee, USMC, Dec68-Feb69. Grid per map in *US Marines in Vietnam-1969*, p 90. Quang Nam Pr, I Corps.

Cutlass, LZ (YS 109-872)
At edge of plantation apx 8 km SSW Long Thanh AF, 31 km ESE Tan Son Nhut AB and5 km W QL-15. Apr66. Bien Hoa Pr, III Corps.

Cutlass, Outpost (YD)
Apparently an ARVN outpost in FSB Brick AO. Thua Thien Pr, I Corps.

Cuu Long (I-III), Operation (n/a)
Successful ARVN armored ops in Cambodia, 9May70-30Jun70. Objective was to secure the Mekong River corridor to Phnom Penh so that it could be used by some 41 ships to evacuate that Cambodian Capitol. Began with ARVN air assault using US Army's 164th Avn Grp in what was largest air Armada ever assembled in IV Corps. Over 8,500 people, 3,880 of whom were military, and over 200 vehicles were evacuated. IV Corps.

Cuu Long Navy Yard (XS 8-9)
On estuary near Saigon. HQ VNMC in 1958 (2 Bns at that time), the 1st regular SVN govt units committed to counter-guerrilla ops. US MAAG LTC Frank Wilkinson, USMC, maintained office here. Gia Dinh Pr, III Corps.

Cuu Long Son (XH 8-9?)
A.k.a. The Nine Dragons and Presqu'ile de Do Son. 4 km-long peninsula at Don Son that was named for nine hills that formed its spine. See Do Son Beach. NVN.

DELTA

Facility/Feature Name, Grid Coordinate, a.k.a. Name/History/Province/CTZ

Unless otherwise stated, 6-digit grid coordinates reference DMA L-7014, L-7015 or L-7016 series, 1:50,000 scale maps, while 2 and 4-digit coordinates reference AMS/DMA/NIMA 1:250,000, 1:500,000 and 1:1,000,000 scale maps. Unless otherwise stated, all heights are in meters. To convert meters to feet, multiply by 3.2808; feet to meters, multiply by .3048.

D, Checkpoint (YD 437-434)
See Checkpoint D. Thua Thien Pr?, I Corps.

D, OP (XT 628-304)
See OP D. Binh Duong Pr, III Corps.

d, LZ (YS 585-593)
Apx 8 km E Dat Do, 2 km N the ocean and 1 km W the Rach Song Cai River. 7Apr66. Phuoc Tuy Pr, III Corps.

D 1 POW Camp (WJ)
US POW nickname for POW camp in NVN. Map at www.soft-vision.com/hanoi/frame.html, indicates it was S to SSE Hanoi and W the Red River. NVN.

D 1, Strongpoint (TJ 9-6)
Apx 1/2 mi due N of D2, 1/2 mi NW D3 and 2.5 mi NNE the Dien Bien Phu main CP. In Muong Thanh Valley, apx 290 km W Hanoi. French strongpoint during Op Castor, 20Nov53-7May54. NVN.

D 2, Strongpoint (TJ 9-6)
Apx 1/2 mi SW D3, 1/2 mi due S D1 and 1.8 mi NNE the Dien Bien Phu main CP. In Muong Thanh Valley, apx 290 km W Hanoi. French strongpoint during Op Castor, 20Nov53-7May54. NVN.

D 3, Strongpoint (TJ 9-6)
A.k.a. Dominique-3. A.k.a. D3. Apx 2.2 mi NE the Dien Bien Phu main CP, NE D2 and .5 mi SE D1. In Muong Thanh Valley apx 290 km W Hanoi. French strongpoint during Op Castor, 20Nov53-7May54. Fell to Vietminh, 2May54. NVN.

D 5, LZ? (YD 095-515)
Apx 5 km S of Mai Loc AF and 25 km WSW Quang Tri. Possibly a firebase, but true nature of site unknown. Nov67. Quang Tri Pr, I Corps.

D Go Kram (n/a)
Mapsheet name of L-7014-6539-3. Laos.

D Handle, LZ (YA 821-853)
In Plei Trap Valley, apx 8 km SSE Plei Trop, 43 km W Kontum and 23 km WSW Polei Kleng AF. Per Patrick Dudney, was named to honor the D-Handle entrenching tool that was responsible for most of its construction. Overrun, 30Mar69. 4th Div. Kontum Pr, II Corps.

Da, Mui (AN 9-1)
Coastal point at 10°56'N-108°11'E. On NC48-08 JOG. Binh Thuan Pr, II Corps.

Da Bac Heliport (ZD 055-021)
On S edge of QL-1, apx 3 km WNW Phu Loc, 5 km WNW FSB Tomahawk and 34 km SE Hue. Heliport #553, alt 131', at 16°17'00"N-107°51'30"E, per Feb73 TAD. Thua Thien Pr, I Corps.

Da Bac, Mui (AN 9-1)
Coastal point at 10°26'N-103°58'E. On NC48-05 JOG. Binh Thuan Pr, II Corps.

Da Bac, Mui (US 9-2)
Coastal point at 10°13'N-104°04'E. On NC48-05 JOG. Kien Giang Pr, IV Corps.

Da Bach River (XJ 8-1)
During Battle of Mao Khe, 27-28Mar51, the deep channels and bays of this river allowed French to move 3 destroyers and 2 LST's up the Da Bach River, and their gunfire helped end attack on beleaguered garrison at Mao Khe and Mao Khe Coal Mine. NVN.

Da Ban Heliport (XD 962-328)
Apx 15 km SSW Vandegrift CB, 4 km NE Hill 908 and 22 km WSW Ba Long AF. Heliport #554, alt 1,280', at 16°34'30"N-106°50'30"E, per Feb73 TAD. Sometimes sp "Da Dan;" however, listed sp thought to be correct. Quang Tri Pr, I Corps.

Da Bao, Mui (US 8-5)
Mui Da Bac. Coastal point at 10°26'N-103°58'E. On NC48-05 JOG. Kien Giang Pr, IV Corps.

Da Cho, Mui (CQ 3-0)
Mui Da Chon. Coastal point at 12°40'N-109°28'E. On ND49-13 JOG. Khanh Hoa Pr, II Corps.

Da Chon, Mui (CP 1-6)
Coastal point at 12°21'N-109°18'E. On ND49-13 JOG. Khanh Hoa Pr, II Corps.

Da Chon, Mui (CQ 3-0)
Coastal point at 12°40'N-109°28'E. On ND49-13 JOG. Khanh Hoa Pr, II Corps.

Da Chong, Mui (US 9-4)
Coastal point at 10°21'N-104°05'E. On NC48-05 JOG. Kien Giang Pr, IV Corps.

Da Chong, Pointe (US 9-4)
See Pointe Da Chong. Kien Giang Pr, IV Corps.

Da Con Do Island (YD 49-98)
See Tiger Island at grid. NVN.

Da Dan (XD)
See Da Ban. Quang Tri Pr, I Corps.

Da Dau Rong (WG 7-1)
Coastal point at 19°06'N-105°45'E. NE48-03 JOG. NVN.

Da Ha Mieng, Mui (CP 0-1)
Coastal point at 11°52'N-109°11'E. On NC49-01 JOG. Khanh Hoa Pr, II Corps.

Da Kir, Plantation de (YU 0-1)
Plantation de Da Kir a.k.a. Don Dien Da Kir and Don Dien Xa Da Kir. Phuoc Long Pr, III Corps.

Da Krong Bridge (XD 9-3?)
On QL-9(?) at the Da Krong River, apx 65 km N A Luoi. Near intersection with road that goes due S to A Shau Valley. Today there is a monument to Ho Chi Minh Trail at S end of this bridge that informs visitor entire road is itself the monument. Quang Tri Pr, I Corps.

Da Krong Valley (XD 9-4)
Valley providing a SE approach to Khe Sanh Valley near Laotian border. Quang Tri Pr, I Corps.

Da Krong Valley (YD 048-258)
Grid is apx 38 km SW Quang Tri and 3 km E Laotian Salient. Quang Tri Pr, I Corps.

Da Lat (BP 23-24)
See Dalat. Tuyen Duc Pr, II Corps.

Da Lat (n/a)
A.k.a. Dalat. Mapsheet name of L-7014-6632-1. SVN.

Da Mai, Ap (YS 93-98)
Ville apx 14 km NNW Ham Tan and 43 km WSW Phan Thiet. Binh Tuy Pr, III Corps.

Da Mai, FSB? (YS 99-96)
Apx 12 km N Ham Tan, 40 km WSW Phan Thiet and 7 km ESE Ap Da Mai (YS 93-98). Apparently 199th LIB position. Possibly a FSB? Binh Tuy Pr, III Corps.

Da Nahi, Pointe (XE 5-5)
See Pointe Da Nahi. NVN.

Da Nang (BT 03-78)
A.k.a. Touron and Tourane. Along coast, apx 610 km N Saigon, 88 air km from Chu Lai AB and 80 km S Hue. Northern commerce center and 2d largest city in SVN. Dominated by Monkey and Son Tra Mtn on Tien Sha Peninsula to NE. One of six autonomous municipalities of SVN; population apx 450,000 in '70. In 1845, *USS Constitution* sailed into Tourane Bay, attempted unsuccessfully to rescue a French Monsignor imprisoned in Hue and then shelled the city upon leaving; the 1st US shelling of Vietnam and producing 1st US inflicted Viet casualties! [143] [144] Site of Camp Books, CORDS-Da Nang, Da Nang Area Cmd, Da Nang Army Depot, Da Nang AB, USMC Air Facility, HQ USMC III MAF, USN NVASUPPACT, HQ Force Logistics Cmd, Camp Tien Sha, Camp E. E. Monahan, Camp Fay, Red Beach and Blue Beach, MCAF-Camp Books, 5th SF Det 2, 5th SF Grp, Det. C-1, Dec64, MIKE Force Det A-113, Oct65, 1st Mar Div, MACV-SOG, Command & Control North (CCN), Nov67-Apr72, FMF headquartered here and at Chu Lai. Also element of 173d Abn here, '68-69. Map is L-7014-6641-3. Excellent map image at www.ptfnasty.com/ptfDanang.html. See *Constitution*, *USS* and ASP-1. Quang Nam Pr, I Corps. [145] [146]

Da Nang (Mapsheet) (n/a)
L-7014-6641-3. Covers Da Nang city and areas to W and NW city. Most of the Tien Sha Peninsula not covered. Quang Nam Pr, I Corps.

Da Nang, Camp (BT 025-790)
See Da Nang SF Camp. Quang Nam Pr, I Corps.

Da Nang, Evacuation of (BT)
See Glossary.

Da Nang, Mui (BT 1-8)
Cape at 16°07'N-108°19'E. On ND49-01 JOG. Quang Nam Pr, I Corps.

Da Nang, Vinh (AT 9-8)
Bay at 16°08'N-108°11'E. On ND49-01 JOG. Quang Nam Pr, I Corps.

Da Nang, Vung (AT 9-8)
A.k.a. Vinh Da Nang. Bay at 16°08'N-108°11'E. On ND49-01 JOG. Quang Nam Pr, I Corps.

Da Nang/Marble Mountain Airfield (BT 065-738)
See Marble Mountain AF. Quang Nam Pr, I Corps.

Da Nang AFB Hospital (BT 01-7)
See USAF Hospitals. Quang Nam Pr, I Corps.

Da Nang Airbase (BT 008-754)
A.k.a. Tourane AF. In SW Da Nang, 6 km NW Marble Mtn AF, 8 km SE Red Beach AF and 60 km NNW Tam Ky. Originally a French built airbase with 10,000' asph rwy made jet capable in apx '65. On 15Jul67 it was hit with a massive 122mm rocket attack that lasted 45 minutes and destroyed six F-4 fighters, two F-8 Fighters, three C-130s. During attack, one ammo dump exploded with a roar that was heard at Hill 55. USMC, USN and USAF facility. El. 30', two 10,000' parallel asph/conc rwys. Map is L-7014-6641-3 Quang Nam Pr, I Corps.

Da Nang Ammo Supply Point-1 (BT 01-74)
See ASP-1 for location and history of massive 27Apr69 explosion here. III MAF, 1st Logistics ammo supply depot. Near listed grid. Quang Nam Pr, I Corps.

Da Nang Anti-Infiltration System (AT/BT)
See Glossary.

Da Nang Army Depot (BT 01-76?)
Home of 80th Gen Supt Grp. Quang Nam Pr, I Corps.

Da Nang Barrier (AT/BT)
See Da Nang Anti-Infiltration System in Glossary.

Da Nang Bridge Cargo Ramp (BT 03-75)
On Han (Da Nang) River apx 2 km due E Da Nang AB and 1 km S the Museum Ramp. On map in *The Marines in Vietnam 1954-1973*, p 238.

Da Nang City SF Camp (BT 025-079)
Apx 2 km S to SE Da Nang AB. 5th SF. Info/grid per *SF Order of Battle.* Moved to Hue? Quang Nam Pr, I Corps.

Da Nang East Airfield (BT 065-738)
See Marble Mountain AF. Quang Nam Pr, I Corps.

Da Nang East SF Camp (BT 0752-7193)
On coast at SE end of Marble Mtn Air Facility and near base of Marble Mtns, apx 7 km SE Da Nang AB. 5th SF FOB. Info/grid per *SF Order of Battle.* See McBride, Camp. Quang Nam Pr, I Corps.

Da Nang Ferry Ramp (BT 0-7)
USN small-craft docking facility across from Da Nang Hotel. Quang Nam Pr, I Corps.

Da Nang Harbor (BT 03-85)
Harbor facilities were situated at various points along W edge of Tien Sha Peninsula, in the Han river and its course through the city, as well as along city's N edge. Several othe munitions and other ships' anchorages scattered throughout Da Nang Bay. Excellent map/detail at www.ptfnasty.com/ptfDanang.html. Quang Nam Pr, I Corps.

Da Nang Heliport (BT 01-75)
Apparently at or near Da Nang AB. "Heliport #513, alt 33' (asph Heli portion is 500'. Approach to A/D: traffic will not operate below 2,000' within a 60° cone, 30° either side of centerline, extending from Rwy 17-35 for 5 nautical miles.

Heli Ops-372.0. At 16°02'30"N-108°12'12"E," per Feb73 TAD. Quang Nam Pr, I Corps.

Da Nang Market Time Base (BT 03-83)
At W end of Tien Sha Peninsula and immed N the Thong Nhat Piers, apx 7 km WNW Red Beach and 7 km NNE Da Nang AB. On map in *The Marines in Vietnam 1954-1973*, p 238. Quang Nam Pr, I Corps.

Da Nang Museum Ramp (BT 03-76)
On Han (Da Nang) River apx 2 km E Da Nang AB and 1 km N Bridge Cargo Ramp. On map in *The Marines in Vietnam 1954-1973*, p 238. Apparently Museum Beach (a.k.a. "Shit Beach?") nearby. Quang Nam Pr, I Corps.

Da Nang Naval Hospital (BT 01-76)
Open 66-70. Da Nang, Quang Nam Pr, I Corps.

Da Nang Naval Support Facility (BT)
A.k.a. Da Nang NSA. For excellent map/detail, visit www.ptfnasty.com/ptfDanang.html. Quang Nam Pr, I Corps.

Da Nang NDB (BT 01-63)
Non-Directional Nav Beacon site. Apx 4 km S Da Nang AB. See VOR DME Da Nang. Quang Nam Pr, I Corps.

Da Nang Northern Arty Cantonment (AT 921-799)
Apx 10 km NW Da Nang AB and 4 km WSW Red Beach AF. Nov-Dec69. Quang Nam Pr, I Corps.

Da Nang NSA (BT 0-7)
USN Supt Activity, Da Nang. '64-73, per MRF Assn Website. Quang Nam Pr, I Corps.

Da Nang PBR Base (BT 0-8)
River Div 55, TF-116, USN Gamewarden base here per MRF Assn at www.mrfa.org. Quang Nam Pr, I Corps.

Da Nang River (BT 02-72)
The Han, or Song Ha River or possibly the Cam Le River? A.k.a. the Tourane River. Quang Nam Pr, I Corps.

Da Nang Seaport (BT 03-80)
Berthing Feet: 7,100 lineal feet, Draft Max: 34', Cargo Capacity; 10,700 tons/day, Storage Covered w/in 5 km: 21,000 ft^2, Storage Uncov, w/in 5 km: 89,000 yd^2. Quang Nam Pr, I Corps. [147]

Da Nang SF Camp (BT 025-790)
A.k.a. Da Nang City SF Camp. W of QL-1, apx 5 km S Da Nang AB, 2 km W Lo Giang and 7 km SE Marble Mtn AF. Renamed Camp McBride, to honor SSgt Claude "Mickey" McBride, KIA 23Aug63 by sniper after breaking up an ambush of his patrol near An Diem. 5th SF, Det C-1. Grid per *SF Order of Battle.* Quang Nam Pr. Moved to Da Nang East. See Da Nang East and Da Nang City SF Camps. Quang Nam Pr, I Corps.

Da Nang VFW Post (BT 03-80?)
See VFW Post 8316, Saigon. Quang Nam Pr, I Corps.

Da Nang Vital Area (AT/BT)
See Glossary.

Da Nang VOR DME (BT 02-75)
Very high frequency Omnidirectional Radio ranging and Directional Measuring Equipment beacon site. A.k.a. Da Nang TACAN DME and VOR TACAN NDB Da Nang At Da Nang AB. Quang Nam Pr, I Corps.

Da Nang VOR TACAN NDB (BT)
Very high frequency Omnidirectional Radio Ranging, Tactical Air Navigation and Non-Directional Air Navigation Beacon site. Grid is BT 02-75. A.k.a. Da Nang TACAN DME and VOR TACAN NDB Da Nang At Da Nang AB. Quang Nam Pr, I Corps.

Da Nhai, Pointe (XE 5-5)
See Pointe Da Nhai. NVN.

Da Nhim, Dap Dam (BP 40-12)
A Dam on Ho Don Duong Lake20 km SE Dalat, near 11°51'N-108°37'E. On NC49-01 JOG. Tuyen Duc or Ninh Thuan Pr, II Corps.

Da Ong Coc (WG 8-2)
Coastal point at 19°13'N-105°46'E. NE48-03 JOG. NVN.

Da Phuoc, FSB? (XS 815-795)
A.k.a. Da Puoampoc. Grid is for Da Phuoc, on LTL-5A apx 9 km due S Saigon, 8 km E Binh Chanh, 7 km NNW Can Giuoc Heliport and 3 km due S Xom Tan Liem. Apparently 199th LIB position. Also listed at XS 81-80 on 199th LIB Assn list. 2d/3d Inf, '69. Gia Dinh Pr, III Corps.

Da Rode (ZB 000-227)
See Dak Rode. Kontum Pr, II Corps. [148]

Da Son, Mui (CQ 2-0)
Coastal point at 12°42'N-109°21'E. On ND49-13 JOG. Khanh Hoa Pr, II Corps.

Da Te River (YT 80-80)
Apx 120 km NE Saigon. Lam Dong Pr, II Corps.

Da Thay, Mui (US 7-4)
A.k.a. Mui Da Trai. Cape on Phu Quoc Island at 10°22'N-103°50'E. On NC48-05 JOG. Kien Giang Pr, IV Corps.

Da Trai, Cap (US 7-4)
A.k.a. Mui Da Trai. Cape on Phu Quoc Island at 10°22'N-103°50'E. On NC48-05 JOG. Kien Giang Pr, IV Corps.

Da Trai, Mui (US 7-4)
Cape on Phu Quoc Island at 10°22'N-103°50'E. On NC48-05 JOG. Kien Giang Pr, IV Corps.

Da Troun Pass (AN 7-6)
See Col de Da Troun. Lam Dong Pr?, II Corps.

Da Vach, Mui (CN 0-9)
Coastal point at 11°43'N-109°14'E. On NC49-01 JOG. Ninh Thuan Pr, II Corps.

Da Vaich, La Pointe (CN 0-9)
See Pointe Da Vaich. Ninh Thuan Pr, II Corps.

Da Vaich, Mui (CN 0-9)
Mui Da Vach. Coastal point at 11°43'N-109°14'E. On NC49-01 JOG. Ninh Thuan Pr, II Corps.

Dacas, FSB (YT 202-570)
See Dacus. Phuoc Long Pr, III Corps.

Dacus, FSB (YT 202-570)
Apx 25 km ENE Phuoc Vinh AF and 4 km NW Rang Rang. Jan71. Likely named to honor SSgt Freddie L. Dacus, KIA 12Nov70, or Sp4 William F. Dacus, KIA 25Apr70. 7th/8th Arty here. Phuoc Long Pr, III Corps.

Dac Cong (n/a)
See Glossary.

Dagger, FSB (YC 900-902)
A.k.a. FSB Pistol. Apx 47 km WNW Da Nang. Jan-Apr69. Thua Thien Pr, I Corps.

Dagger, FSB (YS 438-718)
1 km W LTL-2 apx 4 km due N Nui Dat and 10 km SW FSB Longreach. On 1ATF NCO trng map per John Hollett. 1ATF. Phuoc Tuy Pr, III Corps.

Dagger, LZ (ZC 144-410)
On Hill 1031 or 1050, apx 14 km WSW An Hoa AF, 46 km SW Da Nang AB, 6 km SW FSB Pike, 7 km SE FSB Maxwell, and 8 km NE Javelin. Task Force Yankee USMC FSB, Dec68-Feb69. On map in *US Marines in Vietnam-*

1969, p 90. Apr70 XXIV Corps grid per Don Armstrong. Also listed at ZC 15-41. Quang Nam Pr, I Corps.

Dagger, Patrol Base (XS 800-620)
Apx 16 km NNW Go Cong AF and 4 km NE Can Duoc. Apr68. Long An Pr, III Corps.

Dai An Airfield (ZC 152-540)
See Ha Tan AF. Quang Nam Pr, I Corps.

Dai Bao, Mui (US 8-5)
A.k.a. Mui Da Bac. Coastal point at 10°26'N-103°58'E. Kien Giang Pr, IV Corps.

Dai Dien Heliport (XS 591-058)
Apx 15 km ENE Tra Vinh AF/Phu Vinh, and 28 km SSE Truc Giang/Ben Tre. "Heliport #715, alt 7', road, at 10°01'N 106°27'E," Feb73 TAD. Kien Hoa Pr, IV Corps.

Dai Do, Battle of (YD 255-639)
Roughly 14 km NW Quang Tri and 3 km E QL-1. Took place-30Apr-2May68. Also listed at YD 272-703 and YD 254-628? See Nhi Ha. Map is L-7014-6442-4, per Ken Burrington. Quang Tri Pr, I Corps.

Dai Doi Du-Kich (n/a)
See Glossary.

Dai Doi Phong Khong (n/a)
See Glossary.

Dai Dong (various)
Numerous villes of this name. Sites inc: BT 180-220, BS 905-075, AT 9-5, AT 8-5. NVN/SVN.

Dai Dong (1) (BS 905-075)
Apx 5 km S Gia An, 7 km NNE LZ English and 1 km E Ql-1. Involved in portion of Battle of Tam Quan and A/1st/8th Cav, 1st Cav, 7Dec 67. Per Mike Cohen, ville was built against ocean and in wide-open area. Apparently his unit was unaware of fact an NVA Bn had moved into ville (presumably in preparation for Tet '68) and Cav troops were caught unaware and in open as they walked toward it. Cohen says his CO pulled back troops and called TOT arty and air strikes, reducing it to rubble. When assault resumed under presumption enemy were defeated, surviving NVA inflicted high casualties (23 KIA?). Cohen remembers vividly that it was Pearl Harbor Day when battle started and that he lost several friends here. Map is L-7014-6838-3, per Ken Burrington. Binh Dinh Pr, II Corps.

Dai Hoa-Xuan Phong, Battle of (AN 81-11)
Took place near Dai Hoa New life hamlet, apx 2 to 3 km NNW Phan Thiet and just N QL-1, 25-26Jul68, during Op VC Contact. 2 RF co's made initial contact, then 3d/505th CA'd to cordon area along with Tank Plt of A/1st/69th Armor, ARVN 4-8th APC Trp, and 3rd and 4th Bns, 44th ARVN Rgt. Result was 24 VC KIA, 22 POW; 1 US KIA, 14 WIA; 5 ARVN KIA, 41 WIA, per www.currahee.org/pageb2.html. Binh Thuan Pr, II Corps.

Dai La Pass (AT 940-753)
Apx 7 km WNW Da Nang AB, 3 km NE Ap Dai La and 3 km W QL-1. Described as being "N of Rumor Valley" and site of a USN Seabee rock crusher. Possible FSB or other USMC position here. XXIV Corps grid, per Don Armstong. Quang Nam Pr, I Corps.

Dai La Pass Rock Crusher (AT 94-75?)
Near Dai La Pass. Briefly HQ of 7th Mar/1st Mar Div before it moved to Hill 10, Aug69. Quang Nam Pr, I Corps.

Dai Loc (n/a)
Mapsheet name of L-7014-6640-4. SVN.

Dai Loc Bridge (AT 911 576)
LTL-4 bridge apx 21 km SSW Da Nang AB. Quang Nam Pr, I Corps.

Dai Loc CAP (AT 9 5?)
CAP 2-2-1, 2d CAG. Quang Nam Pr, I Corps.

Dai Loc District HQ (AT 925-575)
Near intersection of LTL-4 and Hwy 540, apx 16 km SSW Da Nang, 5 km SW Hill 55 and about 14 km W LTL-4's intersection with QL-1. Possibly USMC arty or CAP team position at one time? Also listed at AT 910-570, Feb68. Quang Nam Pr, I Corps.

Dai Loc Outpost (YD 6-4?)
ARVN pentagonal outpost NW Huong Dien District HQ. 1st Cav Liaison here Oct-Nov68. Built apx Oct68. Thua Thien Pr, I Corps.

Dai Loc, FSB (AT 916-583)
A.k.a. Hill 37 and LZ 432. Apx 21 km SSW Da Nang, 13 km NNE An Hoa6 km WSW Hill 55. Possibly a FSB or other USMC position? Apr70 XXIV Corps grid per Don Armstrong. Quang Nam Pr, I Corps.

Dai Loc, FSB? (BT 018-628?)
A.k.a. Whiskey Tower, Camp Middlesworth and possibly FSBs Phong Luc I and II (BT 015-625). Apx 13 km S Da Nang, 6 km ENE Hill 55, immed N Atu (2), S Phong Luc 2 and N Phong Luc 3, and 2 km W QL-1. In '69, home of Alpha Battery, 1st/11th Marine Arty. Map is L-7014-6640-4. Data per Ex-PFC John Middlesworth. Dai Loc District. Quang Nam Pr, I Corps.

Dai Mui, Pointe (XQ 8-6)
See Pointe Dai Mui. IV Corps.

Dai Nam BEQ (XS 858-905)
At 79 Tran Hung Dao St., Nov 65, 33 rms, Saigon. Per *Vietnam Military Lore, 1959-1973.* Gia Dinh Pr, III Corps.

Dai Ngai, Kinh (XR 15-76)
Canal a.k.a. Kinh Soc Trang Dai Ngai. Ba Xuyen or Phong Dinh Pr, IV Corps.

Dai Ninh (n/a)
Mapsheet name of L-7014-6632-2. SVN.

Dai Phong (n/a)
See Du Kich in Glossary.

Dai Phong Airfield (AT 879-396)
See Phouc Binh AF. Quang Nam Pr, I Corps.

Dai Tu (n/a)
Mapsheet name of L-7014-6152-3. NVN only.

Daisy Cutter (n/a)
See Glossary.

Dak (n/a)
Vietnamese word for stream.

Dak Ayunh River (AR 95-28)
A.k.a. the Ia Ayun River. Grid is on river at point apx 25 km SSE Pleiku and 6 km E Plei Do Lim AF. River's valley was staging area for H-15 VC Local Force Bn. QL-19 bridge over the Ayun was at BR 144-534. 4th Div AO. See Dak Ya-Ayun. Pleiku Pr, II Corps.

Dak Cvor Bong River (BR 58-90)
S.L.A. Marshall's apparent misspelling of Dak Kon Bong River. Binh Dinh Pr, II Corps.

Dak Da River (BR 307-457)
Bridge 25 on QL-19E crossed river near listed grid. Binh Dinh Pr, II Corps.

Dak Dam Airfield (YU 6-5)
A.k.a. Camp Rolland AF. On Cambodian border apx 280 km ENE Phnom Penh and 10 km NNW Bu Prang on Feb67 Natl Geo map. El. 3,000'. Cambodia.

Dak Dao (AR 90-67?)
See Dak Doa. Kontum Pr, II Corps.

Dak Djram (ZB 0-3)
Creek apx 3 km SW and W Toumorong Outpost that featured prominently in Battle of Toumorong, Jun66. See *Battles in the Monsoon*, pp 276-277. Kontum Pr, II Corps.

Dak Doa (AR 90-67?)
Apx 28 km SE Kontum. French garrison and G.M. 100 position attacked here by 803d Vietminh Rgt, 2Feb54 and again on 11Feb54. Also "Dak Dao." Kontum Pr, II Corps.

Dak Doa Heliport (AR 909-675)
Along TL-6D, apx 23 km NNE Pleiku, 23 km SSE Kontum and 3 km due W De Gir. Heliport #555, alt 2,231', 14°10'00"N-108°08'00"E per 73 TAD. Pleiku Pr, II Corps.

Dak Doa Valley (AR 90-68?)
Generally E LZ Blackhawk and bordered by Chu Drou Mtns. Home of NVA 408th Sapper Bn. 4th Div AO and object of Task Force Winner Dec68?, Op inc elements of 2d Bde/4th Div, ARVN and a Mobile Strike Force. Discussed in *Time Heals No Wounds*, pp 76-77. See Dak Payou Valley. Kontum Pr, II Corps.

Dak Hanjro (ZB 11-37)
A.k.a. Dak Honiro. Hamlet apx 2 km NW Toumorong Outpost and 17 km NNE Dak To 2 AF. See *Battles in the Monsoon*, pp 304, 306-307 et al. Kontum Pr, II Corps.

Dak Hattam River (BR 261-472)
Bridge 27 crossed this river at listed grid. On QL-19E apx 500 meters W of LZ Action, 1.3 km SSE Strongpoint 12. Binh Dinh Pr, II Corps.

Dak Honiang River Valley (YB 85-23)
S of Ben Het and at N end of Ngok Kom Leat Mtn Range. Terrain feature of Battle for Dak To, crossed by 4th/503d Inf, 173d Abn, 4-5Nov67. Cited in *Dak To*, p 141. A.k.a. Dak Heuntang River. Kontum Pr, II Corps.

Dak Honiro (ZB 11-37)
See Dak Hanjro. Kontum Pr, II Corps.

Dak Jappau River (BR 4-3)
See Dak Jappau Tea Plantation. Adj to plantation at PK 8 on QL-19, W of An Khe. Binh Dinh Pr, II Corps.

Dak Jappau Tea Plantation (BR 405-445?)
Astride QL-19E, 4 km E FSB Schueller and 8 km W of An Khe (at PK-8) near Bridge 22. *Groupement Mobile 100* encountered resistance here 24Jun54, before its annihilation at Mang Yang Pass apx 15 km further W. Cited in Bernard Fall's Street Without Joy. [149] II Corps.

Dak Kal River (YB 88-21)
S of Ben Het and 13 km W of Dak To 2 AF, at SE edge of Ngok Kom Leat Mtn mass. Terrain feature of Battle for Dak To, crossed by elements of 4th/503d Inf, 173d Abn, 6Nov67, in move toward Hill 823. Cited in *Dak To*, p 142. Kontum Pr, II Corps.

Dak Kir (YU 05-14?)
See Dakkir. Phuoc Long Pr, III Corps.

Dak Kon Bong River (BR 58-90)
Drains into Happy Valley (Vinh Thanh Valley) just N Vinh Thanh and apx 40 km N An Khe. CIDG Camp at Old French Fort there. Op Crazy Horse AO, May66. Apparently misspelled in *Battles in the Monsoon* as Dak Cvor Bong. 1st Cav. Binh Dinh Pr, II Corps.

Dak Kron Bung River (BR 48-96)
A.k.a. the Suoi Kon. Binh Dinh Pr, II Corps.

Dak Lak Lake (AP 93-73)
A.k.a. Dak Lac Lake. Apx 35 km SSE Ban Me Thuot. Lakeside palace here built by Emperor Bao Dai as retreat. Darlac Pr, II Corps.

Dak Lak Province (various)
Overlapped by UTM zones YV/ZV/ZU/AQ/AP/BQ/BP. In what later became known as II Corps and absorbed into what became primarily Darlac Pr. Thought to have ceased existence shortly before/during early US presence in SVN? Actual dates of existence unknown. II Corps.

Dak Lane Airfield (YC 968-013)
See Ngok Tavak AF. Quang Tin Pr, I Corps.

Dak Mil SF Camp (AP 930-730)
Apparently a.k.a. Lac Thien (old) SF Camp. At Lac Thien, apx 5 km WSW Lac Thien AF and 32 km SSE Ban Me Thuot. 5th SF. Info/grid per *SF Order of Battle.* See Lac Thien (old) SF Camp? Darlac Pr, II Corps.

Dak Mot Lap (n/a)
Sheet name, L-7014-6538-3. SVN/Laos/Cambodia.

Dak Mot, FSB? YB 957-238)
Apx 4 km WNW Dak To 2 AF and along road to Ben Het. FSB here? Grid per Nolan Putman. Kontum Pr, II Corps.

Dak Nhe Airfield (ZC 01-08)
See Kham Duc AF. Quang Tin Pr, I Corps.

Dak Ninh Kola (n/a)
Mapsheet name of L-7014-6638-1. SVN.

Dak Payou Valley (BR 130-390)
A.k.a. VC Valley and possibly Dak Pihao Valley (which runs generally from BR 15-45, S to BR 23-06). Was SE of LZ Blackhawk and bordered by Chu Drou Mtns. In NVA/VC Base Area 202. NVA 95B Div and US 4th Div AO. Object of Task Force Winner Dec68?, inc elements of 2d Bde/4th Div, ARVN and a Mobile Strike Force. See in *Time Heals No Wounds*, pp 76-77. Pleiku Pr, II Corps.

Dak Pek (YB 96-68)
Ville apx 40 km due S Kham Duc, 85 km NNW Kontum and 45 km NNW Dak To 2 AF. 4th Div AO grid per Jim Claeys' list (where grid was erroneously transposed as YB 68-96). Sometimes sp Dal Pek. Kontum Pr, II Corps.

Dak Pek Airfield (YB 952-683)
Apx 40 km due S Kham Duc, 14 km E Laos, 27 km N Dak Seang AF. Site of FOB #2 alternate launch site. 57th AHC suptg 4th ID here. El. 2,297', 1,500' laterite rwy. 15°04'27"N-107°44'42"E. Also listed at YB 948-682. Kontum Pr, II Corps.

Dak Pek SF Camp (YB 9497-6842)
Apx 40 km due S Kham Duc, 14 km E Laos, 27 km N Dak Seang AF. 5th SF camp/FOB, a.k.a. Dal Pek. Det 12, 5th SF Grp, Det. A-5 Dec64, A-242 Oct66, also tactical AF here. Per George "Sonny" Hoffman, "was an unusual SF camp in that it sat on seven hills surrounded by mountains [with Americans on 1 of the 7 hills]." Transferred to 88th

ARVN Border Rangers. Site of FOB #2 alternate launch site. Grid per *SF Order of Battle.* Kontum Pr, II Corps.

Dak Pek, FSB (YB9456-6849)
At or adj to Dak Pek SF Camp, apx 85 km NNW Kontum, 40 km due S Kham Duc and 27 km N Dak Seang AF. Elements of 1st/92d and 6th/29th Arty here 25Apr68. Data per 1st/92d Arty Op Rpt for period ending 30Apr68, courtesy Craig Miller. Kontum Pr, II Corps.

Dak Pihao Valley (BR 23-15)
A.k.a. Dak Payou or VC Valley. The Dak Pihao River runs generally from BR 15-45, S to BR 23-06. See Dak Payou Valley. Pleiku Pr, II Corps.

Dak Po Culvert (BR 363-461)
Culvert on QL-19E at the Dak Po River, and near LZ Schueller. Destroyed by large cmd-detonated mine as an M-113 APC crossed over it, 24Nov68. 7 WIA resulted and vehicle was destroyed. Binh Dinh Pr, II Corps.

Dak Poko River (YB 95-24)
Grid is at point river crosses Rte 512, apx 6 km WNW Dak To AF. The Dak Psi and Dak Poko Rivers were main drainage for Battle of Dak To AO, 1Nov-1Dec67. The Dak Psi formed AO's E boundary and Dak Poko its W. Both ran generally N/S. Kontum Pr, II Corps. [150]

Dak Psi River (ZB 10-25)
The Dak Psi and Dak Poko Rivers were main drainage system for Battle of Dak To AO, 1Nov-1Dec67. The Dak Psi formed AO's E boundary and Dak Poko its W. Both ran generally N/S. Kontum Pr, II Corps. [151]

Dak Ri (YB 977-220)
On S bank of Dak Poko River, apx 500 meters S of Rte 512 and 4 km WNW Dak To 2 AF. On 2Nov67, NVA Hoi Chanh from this ville alerted 173d Abn and 4th Div intel to plans for imminent attack on Dak To SF Camp and Dak To Dist HQ by elements of 32d and 66th NVA Rgts (174th NVA Rgt also later confirmed), 40th NVA Arty Rgt (inc. 200th arty Bn). This info in part led to Battle of Dak To, 1Nov67-1Dec67. See Dak To, Battle of and Hill 875. Kontum Pr, II Corps. [152]

Dak Rode (ZB 000-227)
Along Rte 512, apx 2 km W Dak To3 AF. On 21Mar68, CIA civilian agent "X" rptd large enemy force entering this ville. On 22Mar68 at midnight, 4th Div elements reacted with H&I arty/MG fire along ZB 997 line to disrupt NVA attack. Tac Air Cmd also employed "Fortify Elm" procedure that night. 4th Div news release lists grid as YB 000-227, but that point is deep in Laos and incorrect. Kontum Pr, II Corps. [153]

Dak Rode Heliport (YB 948-077)
Apx 15 km SSW Dak To 2 AF, 19 km SSE Ben Het and 36 km NW Kontum. Listed in '69 TAD as "insecure, abnd," but not in '73 TAD. Name/grid per Frank Penk, Jr. Kontum Pr, II Corps.

Dak Rose, FSB (YB 864-989)
Likely variant of "Dak Rode" In very remote/mountainous area apxt 5 km from Lao border, 18 km SE Kham Duc, 10 km WSW Ngok Tavak AF and 115 km due W Chu Lai. Built apx 19Jul70. Americal list. Quang Tin Pr, I Corps.

Dak Sak Airfield (YU 906-752)
See Duc Lap #2 AF. Quang Duc Pr, II Corps.

Dak Seang Airfield (YB 895-406)
Apx 27 km S Dak Pek AF, 14 km W Laos 23 km NW Dak To AF. El. 2,156', 1,400' clay rwy. At 14°49'33"N-107°41'23"E. Kontum Pr, II Corps.

Dak Seang SF Camp (YB 896-405)
Along river of same name (translates as "The River of Blood"), apx 10-15 km E Cambodia, 64 km NW to NNW Kontum, and 16 km NNE Ben Bet. Sat in valley in Tri-border area. Regarded by some as most vulnerable SF camp in SVN. Det 13, 5th SF, Det A-245, Oct66. "Anyone looking at it tactically," wrote Gary Beikirch (awarded the MOH for battle here 1Apr70), "could see that it appeared to have been designed by Custer and was quite reminiscent of Dien Bien Phu…" Also heavily attacked, 18Aug68 by 40th NVA Arty and 101D NVA Rgt. [154] Grid per *SF Order of Battle.* Transferred to 90th Border Rangers. Also listed at YB 872-256 and 902-409. Kontum Pr, II Corps.

Dak Sut (n/a)
Mapsheet name of L-7014-6538-4. SVN/Laos.

Dak Sut (various)
Common Viet place-name in Kontum Pr. Numerous sites of this name in YB 9-6 and ZB 0-7 grid squares.

Dak Sut (YB 924-498)
Roughly 28 km NNW Dak To and 10 km NNE Dak Seang. Apparently besieged allied CIDG or French camp here said to have been overrun in one text but without attribution. See Dak Sut SF Camp. Kontum Pr, II Corps.

Dak Sut Heliport (YB 925-582)
Apx 2 km N Lang Dak Gor Kla, 17 km N to NNE Dak Seang AF and 37 km NNW Dak To 2 AF. Listed in '69 TAD as "insecure, abnd," but not in '73 TAD. Name/grid per Frank Penk, Jr. Kontum Pr, II Corps.

Dak Sut SF Camp (YB 924-498)
Along W bank of Dak Poko River, apx 10 km NNE Dak Seang AF and 68 km NNW Kontum. 5th SF. Overrun and moved to Trung Dung. Info/grid per *SF Order of Battle.* Kontum Pr, II Corps.

Dak Tan Kan Valley (AS 80-13?)
Remote valley roughly 20 km due N Kontum. SF CIDG outpost at Toumorong overlooked valley and area was scene of heavy fighting for elements of 2d/502d, 1st/327th Inf, 101st Abn and NVA 24th Rgt during Op Hawthorne in Jun66, a portion of Battle for Dak To. See Toumorong and LZ Jenny. Kontum Pr, II Corps.

Dak To (ZB)
Mapsheet name of L-7014-6538-2. SVN.

Dak To (ZB 043-225)
Apx 42 km NW Kontum, 17 km ESE Ben Het and 23 km SSE Dak Seang AF. In Bahnar (Montagnard language), name literally means "hot water," where "Dak" is water and "To" is hot. [155] Name derived from nearby hot springs. Major 4th Inf and 173d Abn basecamp was nearby at Dak To 2 AF. SF 1st established border-monitoring outpost here in '62, but Montagnard militia could not hold it. In Aug65, SF built basecamp here. In May 67, presence of NVA 24th Rgt brought in US 173d Abn and 4th Div. Ensuing Battle of Dak To, May-Nov67 was extremely costly to both sides. In Nov67?, 4th Div's ammo dump exploded and virtually leveled the base but it was reconstructed in Dec67. Original SF camp was apparently overrun in '65. Also here: SF Det 14, Det. A-333, Dec64, A-211 '65, A-244 Oct66, and

4th/60th Arty. Elements of 1st Bn/69th Armor spearheaded drive to relieve SF camp when it was besieged by NVA during Tet '68. See Hill 875 and footnote to Engineer Hill. Kontum Pr, II Corps.

Dak To (Airfield #1) (ZB 040-230)
See Dak To 1 AF. Kontum Pr, II Corps.

Dak To (Airfield #2) (ZB 016-218)
See Dak To 2 AF. Kontum Pr, II Corps.

Dak To, Battle of (YB/ZB)
1Nov67-1Dec 67. Involved 173d Abn and 4th Div elements engaging NVA 24th, 32d, 66th and 174th Rgts and 40th NVA Arty of 1st NVA Div in Tri-border area NE, W and SW Dak To and Tanh Canh, and in Ngok Kom Leat Mtns S and SW Ben Het. Major battle sites and significant features were Hills 530, 724, 823, 875, 882, 1030, 1262, 1338 and 1416. The 5-day battle for Hill 875, 19-23Nov67, was one of bloodiest and most fierce of war. On 2Nov67, NVA Hoi Chanh from Dak Ri ville alerted 173d Abn and 4th Div intel to plans for imminent attack on Dak To SF Camp and Dak To Dist HQ by above listed NVA elements. This info in part led to battle in which 170,000 arty rounds, 2,100 tac airstrikes, 300 B-52 sorties and apx 900,000 gallons of acft fuel were exhausted by US forces. Enemy dead were est at between 1,200 and 1,644, while US suffered 191 KIA, 15 MIA and 642 WIA (another source rpts 289 US KIA?). ARVN lost 73 KIA. One US correspondent said, "With victories like this, who needs defeats?" [156] US elements inc: 1st, 2d, 4th 503d Inf, 173d Abn (Sep), 1st/12th Inf, 4th Div, 2d/19th Arty(105mm), 3d/319th Arty (105mm), 6th/14th Arty (175mm), 5th/16th Arty (155mm), 3d/18th Arty (175mm), 4th/42d Arty (105mm), 1st/92d Arty(155mm), SF Mike Cos #26 and #23, 173d Engrs, 1st/12th Cav, E-17th Cav, 1st/69th Armor, 173d Sup Bn, 335th AHC, 52d Avn Bn, 4th Avn Bn, 1st Cav Avn, 172 MI Det, 404th RRU Det, 51st Chemical Det, 46th PI Det, TACP (USAF), 24th Med HQ Det. See also Hill 875. Kontum Pr, II Corps. [157]

Dak To, Camp (YB 860-258)
See Ban Liet. II Corps.

Dak To, Camp (ZB 043-224)
See Tan Canh. II Corps.

Dak To, FSB (ZB 007-216)
At site of Dak To 2 AF. Apr-Oct68. Kontum Pr, II Corps.

Dak To/Tan Canh Airfield (ZB 044-024)
See Dak To 1 AF. Kontum Pr, II Corps.

Dak To 1 Airfield (ZB 044-024)
Apx 41 km NW Kontum AF, 30 km N Polei Kleng AF and 3 km NE and smaller than Dak To 1 AF. Per TPC K-10A. El. 2,165', 2,300' earth rwy. At 14°39'35"N-107°49'30"E. Also listed at ZB 040-230. Kontum Pr, II Corps.

Dak To 2 Airfield (ZB 012-216)
Apx 40 km NW Kontum AF, 28 km N Polei Kleng AF and 3 km SW and larger than Dak To 1 AF. TPC K-10A. El. 1,975', 4,200' asph rwy. At 14°39'09"N-107°47'47"E. Also listed at ZB 016-218. Kontum Pr, II Corps.

Dak To Bridge #2 (ZB 002-222)
See Bridge Site, Dak To. Kontum Pr, II Corps.

Dak To Bridge Site (YB 952-238)
See Bridge Site, Dak To. Also listed at YB 957-242 Kontum Pr, II Corps.

Dak To II (ZB 008-216)
Evidently the 2d location for Dak To CB, SW Dak To on hwy linking Ben Het to W with Tan Canh apx 5 km to E. 4th Div Bde HQ and principal FSB. Also listed at ZB 012-216. Kontum Pr, II Corps.

Dak To SF Camp (new) (ZB 043-225)
Apx 3 km ENE Dak To 2 AF, 4 km SSW Dak To Ville and 38 km NNW Kontum. 5th SF. Info/grid per *SF Order of Battle.* Moved to Ben Het. Kontum Pr, II Corps.

Dak To SF Camp (old) (ZB 05-26?)
If grid correct, site was adj Dak To ville, apx 7 km NE Dak To 2 AF and 43 km NNW Kontum. Also listed at ZB 043-225, which is same location as Dak To New SF Camp? 5th SF. Info/grid per *SF Order of Battle.* Moved to Plateau Gi. Elements of 1st Bn/69th Armor spearheaded a drive to relieve this camp when it was besieged by NVA during Tet '68. Per *Dak To*, p 53, on 15-16Jun67 a 10-man CIDG/US SF patrol was annihilated by 24th NVA Rgt, apx 1.4 km SW camp, signaling beginning of Battle for Dak To. On 17Jun67, camp was hit by hvy mortar barrage, as was ARVN 42d Rgt HQ at Tan Canh. Chief, Mil Hist records summary lists site as "Bak To" puts Det A-333 here '64, A-422 in '65, A-224 in '66, and Mike Forces 110-78 in '67, saying site closed in '68? Kontum Pr, II Corps.

Dak To Signal Site (ZB?)
No data. Kontum Pr, II Corps.

Dak Ya-Ayun (BR 096-551)
Along QL-19, apx 12 km W Phu Yen and 22 km W Mang Yang Pass. At bridge here on 27Jun54, the 803d Vietminh Rgt ambushed 1st Korea Bn of G.M. 42 as it was escaping W toward Pleiku with survivors of G.M. 100. The 1st Korea broke through with help of some tanks and camped at bridge that night after losing 59 KIA. On 28Jun54, column was again heavily ambushed at PK 3 (Ambush at Kilometer 3) by 108th VM Rgt, reinforced by elite 30th Independent Bn, where it lost 42 more KIA. When it finally reached Pleiku, 1st Korea Bn had lost more dead in 5-days along QL-19 than during its entire 3 years in Korea. See PK 3, Ambush. Data per *Street Without Joy*, pp 222-235, maps at pp 223, 233. Pleiku Pr, II Corps.

Dakkir (YU 05-14?)
A.k.a. Dak Kir. Roughly 12 km NW Phuoc Binh, 12 km NW Song Be AF and 33 km ENE Loc Ninh. 161 Bty, RNZA (Kenning's Bty 13Jul65-13Jun66) FSB set here 13-15Apr66, and on 16 Apr66, they were set 15 km S Dakkir (apx 7 km SE Song Be). Also a Plantation de Da Kir in YU 0-1. Phuoc Long Pr, III Corps.

Dakkir Airfield (YU 052-146)
Along E edge of plantation, apx 12 km NW Phuoc Binh, 12 km NW Song Be AF and 33 km ENE Loc Ninh. "Insecure, abnd, pvt AF, 2Jul67, AF # VA3-128," in Aug69 TAD per Frank Penk. Not in Feb73 TAD. Phuoc Long Pr, III Corps.

Dakota, FSB (YD 067-574)
On N side of QL-9 perhaps 4 km WSW Cam Lo, 26 km WNW Quang Tri. Apr70 XXIV Corps grid per Don Armstrong. Quang Tri Pr, I Corps.

Dakota, FSB (YS 245-784)
Apx 22 km NW Nui Dat, 3 km NW FSB Martine and 1 km E QL-15. On 1ATF NCO trng map per John Hollett. 1ATF. See FSBs North and South Dakota. Also listed at YS 244-777 per Dan Gillotti. Bien Hoa Pr, III Corps.

Dal Pek Airfield (YB 952-683)
See Dak Pek AF. Kontum Pr, II Corps.
Dalat (BP 23-24)
Apx 130 km NW Saigon and 80 km due W Cam Ranh Bay. Pine-covered mtn resort at 5,000'. One of the 6 autonomous municipalities of SVN, with '70 population of apx 60,000. Generally milder and cooler climate than lowland VN. Known for 1,500 varieties of orchids grown in area and for its pine trees, it was at one time home to Natl Military Academy of VN (equiv to US Military Academy) and VN Geographical Institute. Was creation of French, who thought its cool, clear mtn air would serve well as retreat from lowland heat and as a sanitarium for Tuberculosis patients. Designed by French architect Ernest Hebard, well-known urban planner, who saw it as a sanitarium and also noted its potential as provincial admin center. Colonial residents generally ignored Hebard's symmetrical plan and instead built "a rambling town of nostalgic cottages modeled after those of Alps and Alsace." [158] During American War, was HQ of 362d Signal Co and 362d Cmpd. See Tam Dao, the "Dalat of NVN." Capitol, Tuyen Duc Pr, II Corps.
Dalat (BP)
Mapsheet name of L-7014-6632-1. True sheet name is "Da Lat." SVN.
Dalat, FSB (BP 223-193)
Actual name unknown. Along QL-20 at Ap Tan Lac, apx 2 km SE central Dalat and 1.5 km S Ho Xuan Luong Lake. Tuyen Duc Pr, II Corps.
Dalat/Cam Ly Airfield (BP 185-220)
On W edge Dalat, apx 40 km SE Duc Xuyen AF, 86 km due W Cam Ranh Bay, 68 km NW Phan Rang AF, 22 km NNE Dalat Kien Kuong AF. Larger of 2 Dalat are AFs. El. 4,931', had two 4,400' parallel asph rwys. 11°56'54"N-108°24'50"E. Tuyen Duc Pr, II Corps.
Dalat/Lien Khuong Airfield (BP 142-001)
Between Cao Bac Lang and Duc Trong, apx 22 km SSW Dalat Cam Ly and Dalat. Smaller of 2 Dalat area AFs. El. 3,655', 4,800' asph rwy. 11°44'59"N-108°24'50"E. Tuyen Duc Pr, II Corps.
Dalat Coal(?) Mine (BP 28-22)
Just E of Dalat on N side QL-11. Tuyen Duc Pr, II Corps.
Dalat Military Academy (BP 236-225)
Vietnamese academy at NE edge Dalat, immed NE Ho Xuan Huong Lake and 1 km NW Khu Chi Lang. Tuyen Duc Pr, II Corps.
Dalat NDB (BN 14-99)
Non-Directional Air Nav Beacon site. At Dalat/Lien Khuong AF. Tuyen Duc Pr, II Corps.
Dalat of the North (WJ 6-7)
See Tam Dao. NVN.
Dalat Palace Hotel (BP 23-24?)
Built in 1922, it overlooks town lake. Was advertised by Air France as best place to stay while hunting Tigers in highlands. By 1990's hotel had been neglected for nearly 50 years and was described as gloomy, rat-infested and uncomfortable. In apx 1990, American millionaire Larry Hillbloom fell in love with it and invested some $40 million in renovations. One week after it was reopened in 1995, Hillbloom died in plane crash, and it has apparently not done well since. Architecture of area was French colonial and Swiss chalet in design. Oldest golf course in Vietnam is near hotel. Tuyen Duc Pr, II Corps.
Dallas, FSB (XT 545-847)
Apx 8 km SW tip of Fishhook, 46 km NE Tay Ninh, 23 km W to WSW An Loc and 16 km E Bo Tuc. Arty ORLL grid. No data. Tay Ninh Pr, III Corps.
Dallas, LZ (YD 104-144)
In mtns on W edge of A Shau Valley and within 7 km of Laos, apx 3 km NW Tou Rout, 6 km due W FSB Cunningham, 5 km SSW FSB Razor and 34 km SSE Vandegrift CB. FSBs Erskine, Razor, and Cunningham plus LZ Dallas were built during Op Dawson River South, Jan22-10Feb69, to facilitate Base Area 618 attack. On map at p 32, *US Marines in Vietnam-1969*. Also listed at YD 12-15 and YD 104-146. Quang Tri Pr, I Corps.
Dallas, Patrol Base (XT 291-282)
At road intersection along Rte 251, apx 3 km from Cambodia, 10 km WNW Go Dau Ha and 25 km SSE Tay Ninh City AF. Apr69. Also listed at XT 294-281. Tay Ninh Pr, III Corps.
Dallas, USCGC (n/a)
WHEC 716. 3Nov69-19Jun70. Sqdn 3 CGC, during Coast Guard's 5th deployment.
Dalphine, FSB (XD 770-535)
Apx 14 km NE Khe Sanh CB, 33 km W Mai Loc and 6 km WSW peak of Hill 1739. Apr70 XXIV Corps grid per Don Armstrong. Quang Tri Pr, I Corps.
Dam (n/a)
Vietnamese word for lagoon or bay (also Bau)
Dam An Khe (BS 92-28)
See Dam An Khe. Quang Ngai Pr, I Corps.
Dam Bay (CP 2-4)
Coastal point at 12°11'36"N-109°20'48"E. On ND49-13 JOG. Khanh Hoa Pr, II Corps.
Dam Cau Hai Bay (AT 85-07)
Very large tidal bay on E side of QL-1 and immed NW Hai Van Pass, apx 25 km NW Da Nang and 55 km WSW Hue. Apx 20 by 15 km in size. 2 narrow and very long tidal bays (between coast and Hue) fed Dam Cau Hai and they were the Pha Tam Giang (25 km by 3 km) on NE and Dam Thuy Tu (28 km by 1.5 km) to SE. Thua Thien Pr, I Corps.
Dam Chinh, Vung (CP 2-4)
See Vung Dam Chin. Khanh Hoa Pr, II Corps.
Dam Doi Heliport (WQ 12-91)
Apx 23 km ENE Binh Hung AF, 12 km WSW Xom Tan Long and 26 km S to SSW Quan Long. Heliport #558, alt 7', insecure. At 08°58'N 104°50'E, per Feb73 TAD. An Xuyen Pr, IV Corps.
Dam Dong (YD 9-1)
A.k.a. Dam Thuy Tu. Lagoon at 16°26'N-107°46'E. On NE48-16 JOG. Thua Thien Pr, I Corps.
Dam Dui (n/a)
A.k.a. Cha La. An Xuyen Pr, IV Corps.
Dam Ha (n/a)
Mapsheet name of L-7014-6551-4. NVN only.
Dam Lam Binh (BS 850-340)
Freshwater lake at 14°46N-109°01'E. On ND49-05 JOG. Quang Ngai Pr, I Corps.
Dam Nha Phu Bay (CP 10-65)
Large bay immed N Nha Trang, with Ninh Hoa at its NW

end. Roughly 18 km-long and 17 km-wide at its mouth. Khanh Hoa Pr, II Corps.

Dam Nha Phu Island (CP 10-65)
Apx 40 km N Cam Ranh Bay. Khanh Hoa Pr, II Corps.

Dam Nuoc Ngot CR 04-65)
Large, coastal lagoon apx 35 km SSE Bong Son. Apx 5 by 10 km in size. Binh Dinh Pr, II Corps.

Dam O Loan (CQ 13-66)
Bay 55 km S of Qui Nhon and adj to Tuy An AF. Phu Yen Pr, II Corps.

Dam Pau Airfield (AP 984-063)
Apx 6 km NW Riong Sereigne, 24 km WSW Dalat, and 88 km WNW Phan Rang. "Insecure, abnd, Overgrown 8Feb67, AF # VA2-49," in Aug69 TAD per Frank Penk, Jr. Not in Feb73 TAD. Tuyen Duc Pr, II Corps.

Dam Pau SF Camp (AP 979-069)
A.k.a. Serignac Valley SF Camp and Camp Brotherhood. Apx 7 km NW Riong Sereigne, 24 km WSW Dalat, and 88 km WNW Phan Rang. 5th SF. Relocated to Phey Srunh. Info/grid per *SF Order of Battle.* Tuyen Duc Pr, II Corps.

Dam Sam (YD 85-28)
Lagoon adj to Vinh Loc Island at Tan My NSA, and apx 8 km NE Hue. Early in war, the USN planned to build a major port here but projected high cost ended plan. Col Co naval facility was built instead. Thua Thien Pr, I Corps.

Dam Tay (YD 7-3)
A.k.a. Pha Tam Giang. Lagoon at 16°36'N-107°32'E. On NE48-16 JOG. Thua Thien Pr, I Corps.

Dam Thuy Tu (YD 90-26)
Long, narrow tidal bay SE Hue and between Hue and Ocean. Roughly 25 km by 3 km in size. Eagle Beach was on isthmus that formed the E side of this bay. See Eagle Beach, Tan My, Dam Cau Hai Bay and Pha Tam Giang Bay. Thua Thien Pr, I Corps.

Dam Tra (BR 97-84)
See Dam Tra O Lake. Binh Dinh Pr, II Corps.

Dam Tra (BR 98-83)
Coastal lagoon apx 17 km SE Bong Son, and 4 km from coast. Roughly 4 by 8 km in size. Binh Dinh Pr, II Corps.

Dam Tra O, Battle of (BR 983-837)
A.k.a. Battle of An Quang. Took place 28-29 Jun 67. Map is L-7014-6837-4.

Dam Tra-O Lake (BR 97-84)
A.k.a. Dam Tra. Apx 16 km SE Bong Son and 60 km NNW Qui Nhon. Large body of freshwater, apx 8 by 4 km, that emptied into Gulf of Tonkin near Phu Ha. 1Nov66 the 1st Sqdn/9th Cav and 5th/7th Cav engaged 93rd Bn, 2d VC Rgt near QL-1 and lake, S of the Gay Giep Mtns, during Op Thayer-II. On L-7014-6837-4 map at www.rjsmith.com/6837-4-2.htm#arvns. Binh Dinh Pr, II Corps.

Dam Tre, Baie de (XQ 8-6)
A.k.a. Vinh Dam Tre. Bay on Con Son Island at 8°44'N-106°40'E. On NC48-11 JOG. South China Sea.

Dam Tre, Vinh (XQ 8-6)
Bay on Con Son Island at 8°44'N-106°40'E. On NC48-11 JOG. South China Sea.

Dam, Baie de (US 9-1)
A.k.a. Vinh Dam. Bay on Phu Quoc island at 10°05'N-104°02'E. On NC48-05 JOG. Kien Giang Pr?, IV Corps.

Dam, Ben (XQ 7-5)
Bay of Con Son Island at 8°39'N-106°34'E. On NC48-11 JOG. South China Sea.

Dam, Vinh (US 9-1)
Bay on Phu Quoc island at 10°05'N-104°02'E. On NC48-05 JOG. Gulf of Thailand.

Dam, Vung (US 9-1)
A.k.a. Vinh Dam. Bay on Phu Quoc island at 10°05'N-104°02'E. On NC48-05 JOG. Gulf of Thailand.

Damato, USS (n/a)
DD-871, per Ralph Fries.

Dampier, FSB (YS 365-866)
Apx 3 km SE FSB Tasman, 6 km S FSB Wattle, 8 km W Rte-2 and 20 km NNW Nui Dat. During Jun70 (after 14Jun), 161 Bty had its biggest shoot of war, during which 184 "serials" pounded area around FSB Dampier.[159] 161 Bty, RNZA (Horsford's Bty 18Mar69-18Sep69) FSB set here 18-31Jul69 (right section), 19-31Jul69 (left section). On 1ATF NCO trng map per John Hollett. 1ATF. Phuoc Tuy Pr, III Corps.

Dan, FSB ? (XT 160-307)
Apx 2 km from Cambodia, 22 km due S Tay Ninh West AF and 5 km SSW Ap Van Long. True nature of site unknown. Mar66. Tay Ninh Pr, III Corps.

Dan, FSB (YT 590-579)
On plain. apx 2 km E Song Dong Nai River, 9 km NW Trai Lam Kay/QL-20, 35 km NW Xa Vo Dat, 10 km due N FSB Jupiter and 16 km NNE Dinh Quan. Opened 20Jul70, unit unknown, closed 2Aug70 by 1st/5th Cav, per *1st Cav Div Op Rpt, ending 31Oct70*, and also mentioned in *May-Jul70 Op Rpt* at p 38; per Peter Cole. Also listed at YT 585-582. Long Khanh Pr, III Corps.

Dan An SF Camp (WT 8618-0331)
A.k.a. Binh Thanh Thon SF camp. Just S Binh Than Thon AF, apx 10 km from Cambodia and 95 km W Saigon. 5th SF. See Binh Thanh Thon. Info/grid per *SF Order of Battle.* Kien Tuong Pr, IV Corps.

Dan Chu SF Camp (WT 5616-0750)
A.k.a. Cai Cai SF Camp. Apx 4 km S Cambodia, 30 km WNW Binh Thanh Thon and 125 km W to WNW Saigon. 5th SF Grp, Det. A-412 (was 313), Oct65. See Cai Cai. Grid per *SF Order of Battle.* Kien Tuong Pr, IV Corps.

Dan Cuong SF Camp (XS 028-899)
A.k.a. Moc Hoa SF Camp. At S edge of Moc Hoa AF, apx 8 km S Cambodia and 77 km W Saigon. See Moc Hoa. Data per *SF Order of Battle.* Kien Tuong Pr, IV Corps.

Dan Me Thuo East Airfield (AQ 799-023)
See Ban Me Thuot East AF. Sp variant of Ban Me Thuot East AF on DMA's ONC K-10. Darlac Pr, II Corps.

Dan Nam SF Camp (WS 105-945)
A.k.a. An Phu SF Camp. Along W bank of Song Ha Giang River, apx 4 km from Cambodia, 12 km NNW Chau Phu, 15 km NNW Chau Doc AF, and 82 km NE Ha Tien. 5th SF. See An Phu. Info/grid per *SF Order of Battle.* Chau Doc Pr, IV Corps.

Dan Phuc Airfield (WT 513-010)
See Don Phuoc AF. Kien Phong Pr, IV Corps.

Dan Quyen 38, Operation (n/a)
15May-7June69. 42d ARVN Rgt/22d ARVN Ranger Grp Op People"s Rights near Dak To/Ben Het. 945 NVA KIA, per *VN Order of Battle*, pp 9-14. Kontum Pr, II Corps.

Dan Sinh SF Camp (XS 2787-7758)
A.k.a. Tuyen Nhon or Thuy Dong SF Camp. At or near Thuy Dong AF, apx 54 km SW Tan Son Nhut AB and 26 km WNW Long An. 5th SF. See Tuyen Nhon. Info/grid per *SF Order of Battle.* Kien Tuong Pr, IV Corps.
Dan Tam SF Camp (US 867-295)
A.k.a. Phu Quoc or Duong Dong SF Camp. At S edge of Duong Dong AF and just N Duong Dong, on Phu Quoc Island. 5th SF. See Phu Quoc. Info/grid per *SF Order of Battle.* Gulf of Thailand.
Dan Thang 61, Operation (n/a)
See Hawthorne/Dan Thang 61.
Dan Thang 69, Operation (n/a)
18Apr-31Dec69. 22d ARVN Div op. 507 rptd NVA/VC KIA, per *Vietnam Order of Battle*, pp 9-14. Binh Dinh Pr, II Corps.
Dan Thanh SF Camp (WS 520-430)
A.k.a. Long Xuyen SF Camp. On W bank of Mekong just NW Long Xuyen AF, apx 47 km NW Can Tho. 5th SF. See Long Xuyen. Info/grid per *SF Order of Battle.* Chau Doc Pr, IV Corps.
Dan Thinh SF Camp (WS 9765-7585)
A.k.a. Kinh Quan II SF Camp. Apx 4 km N Kinh Quan SF Camp, 13 km SSE Moc Hoa AF and 80 km W to WSW Saigon. 5th SF. See Kinh Quan II. Info/grid per S*pecial Forces Order of Battle*. Kien Tuong Pr, IV Corps.
Dan Tien 33D, Operation (n/a)
1Nov-28Dec69. 23d ARVN Div op. 746 rptd NVA/VC KIA, per *Vietnam Order of Battle*, pp 9-14. Quang Duc Pr, II Corps.
Dan Tien 40, Operation (n/a)
12Nov-28Dec69. 23d ARVN Div op. 1,012 rptd NVA/VC KIA, per *Vietnam Order of Battle*, pp 9-14. Quang Duc Pr, II Corps.
Dan Tien SF Camp (**VS** 7622-6090)
A.k.a. Vinh Gia SF Camp. Within 3 km of Cambodia, apx 34 km ENE Ha Tien. 5th SF. See Vinh Gia. Info/grid per *SF Order of Battle.* Chau Doc Pr, IV Corps.
Dan Tri SF Camp (WS 3140-9565)
A.k.a. Thuong Thoi SF Camp. On N bank of Mekong, apx 7 km from Cambodia and 22 km NE Chau Phu/Chau Doc AF. 5th SF. See Thuong Thoi. Info/grid per *SF Order of Battle.* Kien Tuong Pr, IV Corps.
Dan Vang Quang, General (n/a)
See Glossary.
Dan Ve (n/a)
See Glossary.
Dan Viet SF Camp (**VS** 438-448)
A.k.a. Ha Tien (New SF Camp). Near coast, apx 3 km SSE Ha Tien city. 5th SF. See Ha Tien (new) SF camp. Info/grid per *SF Order of Battle.* Kien Giang Pr, IV Corps.
Dan Xay, Mui (US 7-4)
Coastal point at 10°23'N-103°51'E. On NC48-05 JOG. Kien Giang Pr, IV Corps.
Danang (AT/BT)
See Da Nang. Quang Nam Pr, I Corps.
Danang Airfield (BT 008-754)
See Da Nang AB. Quang Nam Pr, I Corps.
Danang PBR Base (BT)
See Da Nang PBR Base. Quang Nam Pr, I Corps.
Dancer, LZ (BS 682-402)
Apx 14 km WNW Duc Pho, 5 km ENE FSB San Juan Hill and 14 km SSW Mo Duc/Quang Hien. Americal list. Quang Ngai Pr, I Corps.
Dandy, LZ (XD 879-313)
At top of Vietnam Salient, apx 11 km SSE Khe Sanh, 7 km E Lang Tram 2 & 29 km WSW Ba Long AF. Apr70 XXIV Corps grid per Don Armstrong. Quang Tri Pr, I Corps.
Danford, FSB (YU 182-338)
Apx 4 km from Cambodia, 15 km WSW Djamap AF and 22 km ENE Bu Dop AF. Jan68. Phuoc Long Pr, III Corps.
Dang S'Ruin Mountain (ZT 053-256)
A.k.a. Nui Ong, Hill 1302 and 1304 (4,277'). Apx 12 km due E Tanh Linh AF. Binh Tuy Pr?, III Corps.
Dang Son Airfield (n/a)
3,600' rwy apx 130 km NE Hanoi, 110 km N Hai Phong and 20 km S China border. ONC-J-11. El. 840'. NVN.
Danger, FSB (WS 97-40)
A.k.a. FSB Cai Be and FSB Dickey. Off QL-4, apx 42 km due W Dong Tam and 14 km ENE Sa Dec. Built by elements of 2d/39th Inf as FSB Cai Be in late '68, then renamed FSB Dickey, and later FSB Danger. Per Daniel Evans, was built in "flat, muddy rice field" near Giao Duc (a.k.a. An Tri) by elements of 4th/39th Inf, 9th Div, sometime in early-mid '69. "Was a four-sided mud fort with fighting bunkers cut into berm walls all the way around." 6-tube arty bty set in middle of base with OPs built and manned day and night at all four corners. Soon after being built and given "Dickey" name, incoming Bn CO Col David Hackworth (4th/39th Inf) insisted name was appropriate for his "Hardcore" troops, and had it renamed "Danger." 2d/39th Inf and 4th/39th Inf in Cai Be AO. On map L-7014-6229-4 (Khiem Ich/Cai-Lay). Some data per *Doc: Platoon Medic*, pp 164-5, and Jim Stone, 2d/39th Inf. Dinh Tuong Pr, IV Corps.
Dangrek Mountains (n/a)
Mtn range along W border of Cambodia that was controlled by communist forces during 1st Indochina War. See map in *Street Without Joy*, p 277.
Dani, FSB (YS 622-648)
Apx 18 km ESE Nui Dat, 300 meters W FSB Bond and 13 km ENE FSB Horseshoe. On 1ATF NCO trng map per John Hollett. 1ATF. Phuoc Tuy Pr, III Corps.
Daniel Boone Operations (n/a)
See Glossary.
Daniel, FSB/LZ (BN)
Per *Currahee History, 1Feb69-31Dec69*, p 26, was built NW Song Mao by Task Force 3-506 during Op Double Eagle III, Phase I, around 17Dec68. 105-mm Bty here. 3d/506th Inf, 101st Abn AO per Jerry Berry. Likely Binh Thuan Pr, II Corps.
Danish (n/a)
6Apr70, XXIV Corps proposed 5th Div FSB name.
Danner Quarry (ZA 075-311)
Apx 23 km SW Pleiku and 6 km NW Oasis AF. Aug-Oct67. Pleiku Pr, II Corps.
dans le Baton (n/a)
See Glossary.
Dao Duc Doan Refugee Center? (BS 668-688)
E of QL-1, apx 5 km SE Quang Ngai. Listed as Dao Duc Doan R.C. NPIA data. Quang Ngai Pr, I Corps.

Dao Phu Quoc Island (US 90-40)
A.k.a. Phu Quoc Island. Apx 45 km W of SVN coast in Gulf of Thailand, and 45 km due W Ha Tien at point where Cambodia/SVN border meets ocean. By far largest Island in SVN territorial waters; some 50 km in length and 27 km at its widest (31 by 16.8 miles). Hill 565 at US 96-47 was tallest peak. Kien Giang Pr, IV Corps.

Dao Tu (XJ 7-2)
Along road between Bao Chuc and Vinh Yen, apx 40 km NW Hanoi. Here on 13Jan51, a Groupement Mobile under French Col Vanuxem, rushing from Vinh Yen to aid the small outpost of Bao Chuc, was heavily ambushed by Vietminh of 308th Div. Nearly an entire Sengalese Bn and much of 8th Algerian Saphis were lost in attack and survivors fled back to Vinh Yen. See Chp 2 of *Street Without Joy* and its map at p 38. See Vinh Yen. NVN.

Dao, FSB (YS 63-99)
Apx 20 km ENE Blackhorse CB, 17 km ESE Xuan Loc and atop or at E base of Hill 324. 4th/12th Inf, 3d/7th Inf, 199th LIB. Long Khanh Pr, III Corps.

Dao, Mui (XE 5-8)
Coastal point at 17°59'N-106°28'E. NE48-11 JOG. NVN.

Dap Dam Da Nhim (BP 40-12)
See Da Nhim. Tuyen Duc or Ninh Thuan Pr, II Corps.

Darb, FSB (YT 318-290)
See Darby. Long Khanh Pr, III Corps.

Darby, FSB (YT 318-290)
On W bank of Song Dong Nai River, apx 26 km NNW Xuan Loc, 36 km ENE Bien Hoa AB and 6 km NNE Ap Thanh Dang. Arty ORLL grid. Also listed at YT 321-290, Jan71. Long Khanh Pr, III Corps.

Darby, USNS (n/a)
MSTS Transport, per Ralph Fries.

Darby Crest, Operation (BR)
1Feb-15Apr69. 173d Abn. Crescent of Hoai An District.

Darby Mar I, Operation (CQ/BQ?)
Feb-6Mar69. 173d Abn. Tuy Hoa. Phu Yen Pr, II Corps.

Darby Punch II, Operation (BR)
10Mar-24May69. 173d Abn. An Khe. Binh Dinh Pr, II Corps.

Darby Trail, Operation (BR)
1-16Feb69. 173d Abn. Bong Son area. Binh Dinh Pr, II Corps.

Dark, LZ (AT 901-926)
Apx 2 km S Hill 1413, 26 km NW Da Nang AB, 14 km W the Hai Van Pass and 16 km SE Q Phu Loc. Apr70 XXIV Corps grid per Don Armstrong. Quang Nam Pr, I Corps.

Dark, LZ (XD 928-233)
Apx 4 km ESE Lang Haren, 12 km SE Khe Sanh CB and 15 km WSW Ba Long AF. Apr70 XXIV Corps grid per Don Armstrong. Quang Tri Pr, I Corps.

Darkhorse Base (XT 862-158)
Phu Loi Army AF, apx 7 km ENE Phu Cuong, 2 km W Phu Loi, 20 km N Saigon, 2 km N Lam Son and 4 km W FSB Venable Heights. 1st Inf Div, '69. Per *Low Level Hell's* TAOR map. III Corps.

Darlac Province (BQ/BP, et all)
One of 12 north-central provs forming II Corps (II CTZ).

Darn, FSB (XT 088-768)
Apx 16 km NNW Tay Ninh West AF and 16 km due S Thien Ngon AF. May70. Tay Ninh Pr, III Corps.

Dart, FSB (ZC148-281)
A.k.a. COB Dart. Apx 27 km SW An Hoa, 6 km NE FSB Battle-Ax, 6 km S FSB Cutlass and 11 km SE Saber. Task Force Yankee, USMC, Dec68-Feb69. On map in *US Marines in Vietnam-1969*, p 90. Apr70 XXIV Corps grid per Don Armstrong. Quang Nam Pr, I Corps.

Dat, FSB (YT 73-33)
Possibly FSB Vo Dat? At Vo Dat AF, near SW corner of Xa Vo Dat, 35 km NE Xuan Loc, 75 km ENE Bien Hoa AB and 21 km WNW Tanh Linh AF. 4th/12th Inf, '69. Name/grid per 199th LIB Assn. Long Khanh Pr, III Corps.

Dat, Mui (US 9-1)
Mui Dat Do. Coastal point at 10°03'N-104°00'E. On NC48-05 JOG. Kien Giang Pr, IV Corps.

Dat, Nui (YS 44-68)
See Nui Dat and Luscombe AF. Phuoc Tuy Pr, III Corps.

Dat Da Nang, Mui (BT 1-8)
A.k.a. Mui Da Nang. Cape at 16°07'N-108°19'E. On ND49-01 JOG. Quang Nam Pr, I Corps.

Dat Do (YS 48-60)
Apx 25 km NE Vung Tau, 10 km SE Nui Dat, 3 km S the Horseshoe, 6 km from ocean and apx 70 km ESE Saigon. Apparently substantial US/ANZAC presence here. *Vietnam Gunners* points out that there US Bty's of 8", 155mm and 175mm Arty suptg ANZAC and 1st Bde/9th Inf Div ops here at various times. Phuoc Tuy Pr, III Corps.

Dat Do, Mui (US -91)
Coastal point at 10°03'N 104°00'E. On NC48-05 JOG. Kien Giang Pr, IV Corps.

Dat Do Airfield (YS 48-60?)
A.k.a. Phuoc Tho AF. Presumably at Dat Do, and if so, was roughly 10 km SW Nui Dat/Luscombe AF, 70 km ESE Saigon and 25 km NE Vung Tau. AF # VA3-196. In Aug69 TAD but not Feb73 TAD. Data per Frank Penk, Jr. Phuoc Tuy Pr, III Corps.

Dat Vian Ka, Mui (BT 6-0)
Coastal point at 15°25'N-108°48'E. On ND49-01 JOG. Quang Tin Pr, I Corps.

Datrai, Cape (US 7-4)
A.k.a. Mui Da Trai. Cape on Phu Quoc Island at 10°22'N-103°50'E. On NC48-05 JOG. Kien Giang Pr, IV Corps.

Dau Mau Base (YD or XD?)
Per Garry Adams, was S of QL-9 somewhere between Dong Ha and Lao border. Likely ARVN position, and its name appears to be of NVA or ARVN origin. Per Hoang Nguyen, could mean any of following: "Bloody Head, Head of a Machete, or Blood Mark." While a tourist there after the war, Adams took picture of mtn that matches perfectly with famous NVA combat action photo (found on standard postcard in today's Vietnam) which shows NVA troops overrunning position in either 1972 or 1975, and lists it Dau Mau Base. No ville by this name in NPIA or NIMA. Quang Tri Pr, I Corps.

Dau Rong, Da (WG 7-1)
See Da Dau Rong. NVN.

Dau Tieng (XT 485-475)
Along QL-14 at N edge of Tri Tam, apx 59 km NNW Tan Son Nhut AB, 32 km WNW Lai Khe and 24 km E Tay Ninh. Apparently originally named LZ Dau Tieng in Feb66. 25th Inf Div major basecamp and AAF here. B & D Cos, 229th AHB, plus other supt units here Nov-68.

Possibly also used by 1st Div, 4th Div and 1st Cav. Binh Duong Pr, III Corps.

Dau Tieng, FSB (XT?)
No data available and unknown if this was different site than base camp at Dau Tieng. Binh Duong Pr?, III Corps.

Dau Tieng, LZ (XT 495-490)
See Dau Tieng Basecamp. Binh Duong Pr?, III Corps.

Dau Tieng, Quan (Tri Tam) (n/a)
Mapsheet L-7014-6231-1. Full sheet name: Tri Tam (Quan Dau Tieng). SVN.

Dau Tieng Airfield (XT 491-472)
At N edge of Tri Tam, apx 25 km ESE Tay Ninh, 23 km SW Minh Thanh AF and 32 km WNW Lai Khe AF. El. 76', 2,500' laterite rwy. Binh Duong Pr, III Corps.

Dau Tieng Base Camp (XT 495-470)
In War Zone C along E bank of Song Saigon River, roughly midway between Michelin and Ben Cui Rubber Plantations. Straddled Rte 14 at N end of Tri Tam, apx 27 km WNW Ben Cat, 3 km E the NE edge of Ben Cui Rubber Plantation and 35 km NNW Cu Chi. Apparently originally named LZ Dau Tieng in Feb66. Home of Camp Rainier, the permanent basecamp of 3d Bde/25th Inf Div, including 2d Bn 27th Inf "Wolfhounds", also elements of 4th Div and 1st CAV Div at various times. B & D Cos, 229th AHB, 1st Cav, plus other supt units here Nov-68. Good map of area in *The Infantry Brigade in Combat*. Binh Duong Pr, III Corps.

Dau Tieng Bridge (XT 484-468)
Rte 239 bridge over the Song Saigon, apx 1 km W Dau Tieng Basecamp. Binh Duong Pr, III Corps.

Dau Tran Strategies (n/a)
See Glossary.

Dauntless, LZ (BR 241-278)
Apx 28 km SW An Khe, 33 km SE Suoi Doi AF and 8 km SW LZ Assault. 4th Div, '70. Also listed at BR 240-279. 4th Div op rpt grid per Jim Claeys. Binh Dinh Pr, II Corps.

Davaich Head (CN 0-9)
Mui Da Vach. Coastal point at 11°43'N-109°14'E. On NC49-01 JOG. Ninh Thuan Pr, II Corps.

Davan Compound (CP 04-53?)
A.k.a. SF Det B-55 cmpd. In Nha Trang military complex. Named to honor SSgt Benedict M. Davan, USA, 521st MSF, 5th SF, KIA 17Mar69, during battle for Tuk Chup Knoll (Million Dollar Knoll) on Nui Coto Mtn and against 510th VC Bn. Benedict was awarded the DSC. Camp dedicated 11Se69. Data per *Vietnam Military Lore, 1959-1973*. Khanh Hoa Pr, II Corps.

Dave, FSB (XT 980-320)
Apx 2 km S Khu Tru Mat and 17 km due N Bien Hoa AB. Feb67. Bien Hoa Pr, III Corps.

David, Camp (CP 0-5)
See White House, The. Khanh Hoa Pr, II Corps.

David, FSB (XS 6-2?)
Apparently in central Giong Trom Dist and possibly a.k.a. FSB Giong Trom? Giong Trom is roughly 15 km SE Truc Giang and near 10°09'00"N-106°30'00"E? Built Sep68 by 2d Bde/9th Inf, when Bty C, 34th Arty was lifted off barges in early Oct69 and set here. Bty A, 34th Arty also here. Data per MRF Assn website. Kien Hoa Pr, IV Corps.

David, FSB/LZ (YU 346-653)
Cambodian Incursion FSB, May70. Immed NW of O Rang AF, apx 18 km NW Bu Krak, 28 km due N Djamap and 8 km NNW FSB Exodus. Detailed map at p 323 of *Rangers At War* shows it being apx 8 km NNE SVN border, 1 km N Ban Nham Airstrip (likely O Rang AF), 1 km SE Phu Pu Cham and apx 3.5 km NW O Rang. In *Apache Sunrise*, p 178, author says it was built atop a grass-covered rolling hill at elevation of 2,500', 8 km N the border and just N O Rang. Described in *Vietnam Reflexes and Reflections*, p 53, as being the 1st Cav's most remote invasion outpost. AO of 1st Cav, 11th ACR and 199th LIB. 1st/50th Cav, 1st Cav here. Cited in *Anatomy of A Division* and *Incursion*, and also 1st Cav. Op Rpt, May-Jul70, p 37, 38, per Peter Cole. Also listed at YU 345-533, which just inside SVN and 15 km W Bu Krak AF, Phuoc Long Pr?, Cambodia.

David, FSB (BQ 240-430)
Remote site apx 25 km NE Buon Ho AF and 58 km NW Ban Me Thuout. Name/grid per Dan Gillotti, 15th Arty Assn. Phu Bon Pr, II Corps.

David, FSB (XT 270-010)
Apx 8 km E Chantrea, 2 km W SVN border, and 8 km NNW tip of Parrot's Beak. Name/grid per Dan Gillette, 15th Arty Assn. Cambodia.

David, LZ (XT 713-484)
Apx 35 km due W Phuoc Vinh AF. Sep-Oct67. Binh Duong Pr, III Corps.

David Marion Lewis Tank Farm (BT 065-738)
At Marble Mtn NAS, apx 6 km SE Da Nang. Named to honor David Lewis, KIA 22Oct67, 1st USNAVSUPPACT KIA. Dedicated Jul68. Data per *Vietnam Military Lore, 1959-1973*. Quang Nam Pr, I Corps.

David Widder, Camp (XS 66-93?)
See Widder, Camp. An Long or Gia Dinh Pr, III Corps.

Davidson (n/a)
DOD contract Dredge, per Ralph Fries.

Davies, Camp (XS 87-92?)
A.k.a. Tent City Charlie or Camp Charlie. In Saigon Port area known as The Fish Market. Named to honor Capt. David M. Davies, Night Chief of Stg, 506th Field Depot (largest in world), KIA 2Apr66, by VC terrorist bombing of Victoria BOQ, 1st KIA of 506th Depot. When 506th Depot moved to Long Binh, the 4th and 125th Trans Cmds took over Camp Davies. Data per Ray Bows' *Vietnam Military Lore-1959-1973*. Gia Dinh Pr, III Corps.

Davis, Camp (XS 83-97)
A.k.a. Davis Station. The 3d Radio Research facility at Tan Son Nhut AB, originally named Davis Station. When Army Security Agency moved out in '72, was renamed Camp Davis. In '75, was Joint Military Commission facility. Named to honor Sp4 James T. Davis, US Army, 3d Radio Research Unit, 1st American to lose his life in open battle in VN War (see Buis), when KIA in ambush of ARVN truck near Saigon, 22Dec61. Also home of 509th Radio Research Grp, HQ. Radio Research units were often covers for ASA Secret Ops. Cited in *Tears Before the Rain*, p54. Gia Dinh Pr, III Corps.

Davis, LZ/FSB (YD 252-291)
A.k.a. Davis Hill and FSB Barbara. Apx 19 km W Camp Evans, 37 km WNW Hue, 28 km W Camp Evans and 25 km SSW Quang Tri. 2d/2d ARVN secured for US Arty

here Feb or Mar68, per 3d Bde 101st Abn ORLL of 13May68. Also listed at YD 253-290. See FSB Barbara. Thua Thien Pr, I Corps.

Davis Hill (YD 250-290)
See Davis, LZ/FSB at grid. Thua Thien Pr, I Corps.

Davis, USS (n/a)
DD-937, per Ralph Fries.

Davis Hill (YD 253-292)
A.k.a. LZ/FSB Davis. Apx 19 km W Camp Evans and 37 km WNW Hue. 1st Cav apparently here '68. Name per Frank Penk, Jr. Thua Thien Pr, I Corps.

Davis Station (XS 82-97)
See Davis, Camp. Gia Dinh Pr, III Corps.

Dawson River South, Op (XD)
During Op Dawson River South, USMC built FSBs Erskine, Razor, Cunningham and LZ Dallas between Jan22-10Feb69, in order to facilitate attacks of NVA/VC Base Area 618. Cunningham was a large combat base which hosted 9th Marine CP, several arty btys, and fwd logistics supt for several Inf Cos. Quang Tri Pr, I Corps.

Day Duong Dong Mtns (US 8-2)
On Phu Quoc Island. Mtn range at 10°11'N-103°58'E. On NC48-05 JOG. Gulf of Thailand.

Day River (WJ 75-15)
Tributary of Red River that runs roughly parallel to QL-1, leaving the Red River at point apx 30 km NW Hanoi, then running SE through Phu Ly, Ninh Binh and Phat Diem, and joining ocean at point apx 120 km SSE Hanoi. See Battle of Day River. NVN.

Day River, Battle of (n/a)
Took place 29May-18Jun51. Vietminh forces that infiltrated Red River Delta emerged in series of attacks against French garrisons in/near cities along the Day River and QL-1 (Phu Ly, Ninh Binh, Yen Cu Ha, Phat Diem, Nam Dinh and Thai Binh). Most fighting focused in area 60 km SSE Hanoi, and in an arc from QL-1 swinging to NE about 90 km from Hanoi. See *Street Without Joy*, Chp 2, with map at p 46. NVN.

Dayot, Cua (CP 2-9)
A.k.a. Cua Van. Bay at 12°39'N-109°23'E. On ND49-13 JOG. Khanh Hoa Pr, II Corps.

Dayot, Port (CP 2-9)
A.k.a. Cua Van. Port at 12°39'N-109°23'E. On ND49-13 JOG. Khanh Hoa Pr, II Corps.

Dayton, LZ (YD 201-155)
Near Rte 616, apx 8 km ENE Tou Rout, 53 km W to WSW Hue and 4 km due N LZ Austin. Apr70 XXIV Corps grid per Don Armstrong. Quang Tri Pr, I Corps.

Dayton, Operation (n/a)
5-17May67. 173d Abn. Phuoc Tuy Pr.

Daytona, FSB (YD 133-467)
Apx 6 km SE Mai Loc AF and 21 km WSW Quang Tri. Aug70. Quang Tri Pr, I Corps.

DBP (n/a)
See Dien Bien Phu. NVN.

De (n/a)
Vietnamese word for dike.

De Bodral Plantation (AR 92-62?)
Appears to be apx 20-25 km NE Pleiku. Site of ops involving A/7th/17th Cav suptg TF Powerhouse, 173d Abn, 27-31Dec67. Occupied by elements of NVA 95-B Regt and 280 Recon Co. Pleiku Pr, II Corps.

De Duc (BR 865-985?)
If correct De Duc, was just SE of LZ English, apx 4 km N Bong Son and 2 km W of QL-1. Recon courses for 23d ARVN taught here '68, per *Rangers At War*, at p 204. Binh Dinh Pr, II Corps.

De Duc Airfield (BS 879-005)
See English AF. Binh Dinh Pr, II Corps.

De Groi Outpost (AR 939-347)
Apx 22 km SE Pleiku. Jan68. Pleiku Pr, II Corps.

de Lattre Line (WJ/YJ/XJ/WH/XH)
See Glossary.

***de Lattre Line* Bunkers** (n/a)
See Glossary.

de Maries, Camp (n/a)
See Glossary.

De Shurley, Camp (ZD 027-024)
Along base of Hill 494 and 1.5 km NE its peak, apx 34 km SE Hue, 6 km WNW Phu Loc and immed S of and overlooking QL-1/Dam Cau Hai Bay. Seabee cantonment at the Phu Loc Rock Crusher, originally known as NMCB 9 Detachment Echo and later renamed to honor BU3 George De Shurley, KIA 31Mar68, along with 4 other Seabee mortarmen. Site was dedicated 6Apr68. Some data per Dave Schilling. Thua Thien Pr, I Corps.

Deacon, LZ (XD 986-670)
In DMZ, apx 36 km WNW Dong Ha, 25 km NNE Khe Sanh CB and 11 km ESE Bon Ho Su (NVN). Apr70 XXIV Corps grid per Don Armstrong. Quang Tri Pr, I Corps.

Dead Man, The (XT)
Apx 12 km due E the Michelin Plantation, 8 km W Thunder Road (QL-13), 15 km NNW Lai Khe and 5 km E FSB Picardy. Terrain feature resembling figure of person lying on ground in NW to SE posture, with the head at NW. 1st Inf Div, '69. Per *Low Level Hell's* 1st Div TAOR map. Dinh Tuong Pr?, III Corps.

Dead Man's Hill, FSB (YU 809-725)
A.k.a. LZ Lem. Apx 3 km due S Duc Lap AF, 7 km E Duc Lap, 48 km SW Ban Me Thuot and 12 km E Cambodia. 2d/17th Arty here supt Op Rome Plow, 16Feb70. Data per Jack Picciolo. Quang Duc Pr, II Corps.

Dead Man's Zone (XD/YD)
Sardonic nickname for the DMZ. See DMZ.

Deal, LZ (YD 148-472)
Apx 1 km N Hwy 557, 7.5 km NNW Ba Long AF, 5 km WSW Chau Lang and 7 km SE Mai Loc AF. Apr70 XXIV Corps grid per Don Armstrong. Quang Tri Pr, I Corps.

Dean, LZ (AP 812-950)
See Deane, LZ. Darlac Pr, II Corps.

Dean, LZ (BN 740-564)
Apx 23 km SSW Phan Rang and 3 km S peak of Nui Da Bac. Mar67. Ninh Thuan Pr, II Corps.

Dean's Strip Airfield (n/a)
Apx 80 km due S Ubon AF and 7 km N Cambodia. Per TPC K-10A. El. 500'. Thailand.

Deane, LZ (AP 812-950)
A.k.a. LZ Dean, but spelled this way in 4th Div 31Jan70 ORLL per Jim Henderson. Apx 8 km SSE Ban Me Thuot, 10 km SE Ban Me Thuot East AF and 9 km due W Trung Hoa. Per John Linn, was Bn fwd FSB with, B/2d/35th Inf,

4th Div here Nov-Dec69. Had 81mm and 4.2" mortars as well as 105mm Btys. B Bty, 2d/9th Arty here Dec69. Grid per Jim Claeys. Darlac Pr, II Corps.

Death Valley (AT 90-25)
A.k.a. Hiep Duc Valley. Generally 35-40 km W Tam Ky, 48 km S Da Nang, 56 km NW Chu Lai. Hiep Duc Valley was also known as Hiep Duc, Nui Loc Son Basin or Phuoc Valley. Americal List. Quang Nam Pr, I Corps.

Death Valley (BT?)
See *Rites of Passage*, p 394. Quang Ngai Pr?, I Corps.

Death Valley (BT 05-35)
Per Tom Brizendine, was variously known as Hiep Duc Valley, Dragon Valley and Que Son Valley (Hiep Duc Valley is near AT 95-26)? Home of 2d NVA Rgt. During Tet '69 and 1st/6th Inf made heavy contact with this unit. During 3-day battle the 16-inch guns of Battleship *New Jersey* were employed. Quang Nam Pr, I Corps.

Death Valley (n/a)
6Apr70, XXIV Corps future-use III MAF FSB name. Apparently never built.

Death Valley (YD 113-703)
Marine helo pilots' nickname for helicopter lndg area at Con Thien CB. Quang Tri Pr, I Corps.

Death Volunteers (n/a)
See Glossary.

Deb, FSB (XU 840-130)
See Debbie at grid. Binh Long Pr, III Corps.

Debbie, LZ/FSB (BS 872-324)
A.k.a. LZ Debbie-Thunder or LZ Thunder. On hill apx 9 km SE Duc Pho AF, 2 km N QL-1 and 3 km W the coast. Must have had a spectacular view of ocean and sizable lake to its NW apx 2 km. Overlooked area known as The Rice Bowl. Also listed at BS 882-036, 869-319 871-325 and 824-347. Americal list. Quang Ngai Pr, I Corps.

Debbie, FSB (XU 840-135)
A.k.a. LZ Deb. Apx 12 km ENE Loc Ninh AF and 21 km SW Bu Dop. Also listed at XU 904-135? Cited as Deb in 1st Cav. VN *Yearbook* Aug65-Dec69, p 290, per Peter Cole. Binh Long Pr, III Corps.

Debbie, FSB (XU 904-196)
Apx 18 km ESE Loc Ninh, 24 km WSW Song Be AF and 28 km SSW Bu Dop. 1st/5th, 1st/11th Cav, 1st Cav, '69. Grid per Frank Penk, Jr. Also listed at XU 840-135? Phuoc Long Pr, III Corps.

Debbie, FSB (YS 443-894)
Apx 1.5 km W LTL-2, some 22 km N Nui Dat and 8 km W FSB Flinders. On 1ATF NCO trng map per John Hollett. Phuoc Tuy Pr, III Corps.

Debbie, LZ (BS 824-347)
If grid correct, was apx 4 km S Duc Pho AF? Oct67. Quang Ngai Pr, I Corps.

Debbie, LZ (BS 872-324)
See Debbie-Thunder. Quang Tin Pr, I Corps.

Debbie, LZ (YA 815-440)
See Debby, LZ. Pleiku Pr, II Corps.

Debbie-Thunder, LZ (BS 872-325)
A.k.a. LZ Debbie, LZ Thunder and LZ Thunder Mtn. On hill apx 3 km W the coast, some 8 km SE Duc Pho and 20 km NNW Gia An. Was "hell of a hill to climb after a day-long patrol," says Tommy Acosta, 1st/20th, 11th LIB, '68-69. Americal, 173d Abn, '68-69. Elements of 4th Div apparently also here '70? Also listed at BS 868-318, 869-319, 874-325, 870-325 and by arty ORLL BS 870-321. Map is L-7014-6838-4 (Phuoc Dien), per Ray Smith, 1st/69th Armor. See also other LZ Debbie and FSB Thunder entries. Photos/maps of base at http://1-14th.com/maps.html. Quang Ngai, I Corps.

Debby, LZ (YA 815-440)
Apx 8 km SE Plei Djereng New AF and 33 km WSW Pleiku. Jan66. Pleiku Pr, II Corps.

Deckhouse II, Operation (n/a)
See Hastings/Deckhouse II, Op.

Deckhouse III, IV and V, Operations (n/a)
See *Thomaston, USS.*

Declination (n/a)
See Glossary.

Dedham, LZ (YD 035-351)
In river valley apx 34 km WSW Quang Tri, 1 km S LZ Chief and 14 km NE Lang Klung. Quang Tri Pr, I Corps.

Dee, LZ? (YA 655-469)
Possible LZ? On Cambodian border, 20 km due W Plei Djereng New AF. True nature of site unknown. Jan66. Kontum Pr, II Corps.

Deeble, FSB (YT 95-26)
Apx 2 km SE Tanh Linh, just SE Tanh Linh AF and 45 km NW Phan Thiet. 3d/7th Inf, 5th/12th Inf, 199th LIB here. Binh Tuy Pr, III Corps.

Deer Mission, The (n/a)
See Glossary.

Dees, Patrol Base (XT 551-224)
Apx 12 km NW Cu Chi and 6 km SW Xom Rung Cay. Aug69. Possibly named to honor either SFC Curtis C. Dees, KIA 5May69, or PFC Jerry R. Dees, KIA27Jul69. Hau Nghia Pr, III Corps.

Defiance, Fort (XT 503-833)
See Fort Defiance. Tay Ninh Pr, III Corps.

Defiant (n/a)
6Apr70, XXIV Corps proposed III MAF FSB name.

Defiant, LZ (XT 955-726)
Along LTL 13, apx 11 km WSW Dong Xoai. Jun67. Phuoc Long Pr, III Corps.

DeHaven, USS (n/a)
DD-727, per Ralph Fries.

Delaware, LZ (YB 913-001)
A.k.a. Hill 1483. Overlooking Plei Trap Valley, apx 24 km SSW Dak To 2 AF and 2 km SE LZ Ouachita (Hill 1274). 2d Bde/4th Inf Div here, early '69. Cited in *Time Heals No Wounds*, p 172. Kontum Pr?, II Corps.

Delaware/Lam Son 218, Operation (n/a)
19Apr-17May68. 1st Cav/101st Abn/199th LIB plus ARVN 1st Div/ARVN Abn TF Bravo in A Shau Valley. Op to preempt NVA attack of Hue. 869 rptd NVA/VC KIA. Thua Thien Pr, I Corps.

Dell, Camp (YT 932-258)
At or near Tanh Linh AF, apx 110 km ENE Saigon. Oct70. Binh Tuy Pr, III Corps.

DeLong Floating Piers (n/a)
See Glossary.

DeLong Pier, Cam Ranh (CR 110-238)
Cam Ranh Bay Pier. Khan Hoa Pr, II Corps.

Delores, LZ (XS 123-584)
15 km NW Cai Lay and 25 km SW Thuy Dong AF, near FSBs Barbara/Cora. Nov67. Dinh Tuong Pr, IV Corps.
Delta 43 (n/a)
Reference point on HCMT in Laos near Ban Bek, used by 20th TASS "Covey" and other FACs flying that area. See Ban Bek for detail. Laos.
Delta, FSB (XT 036-649)
Apx 18 km NW Tay Ninh West AF, 18 km SSW Thien Ngon AF and 5 km E Cambodia. 196th LIB here during Op Gadsden (Junction City), 1-21Feb67, with Bde Fwd CP at XT 12-63 (per Les Hines). 25th Inf Div patrol base, '69. Described in *Suicide Charlie*, as desolate place so close to border that lights of NVA trucks could be seen moving on HCMT, and B-52 strikes in Cambodia would bounce the men around on their air-mattresses…as if we were floating on choppy water." Dust storms caused by lndg choppers forced troops to flee every lndg/departure, and hit almost daily by mortar fire and, on one occasion, CS gas. Tay Ninh Pr, III Corps [161]
Delta, FSB (XT 328-078)
At or near Duc Hue AF. Dec65. Hau Nghia Pr, III Corps.
Delta, FSB (YA 835-747)
A.k.a. FSB Impossible (by Apr69). Remote site apx 44 km WSW Kontum, 3 km due S peak Hill 1528, and 28 km WNW Plei Mrong. 4th Div and 1st/92d Arty here Apr69. 1st/92d Arty opcon 6th/14th Arty here Jan69. Name/grid per Craig Miller. See LZ Delta (YA 935-585) entry. Kontum Pr, II Corps.
Delta, FSB (ZB 0-0?)
Roughly 20 km due S Dak To 2 AF, 25 km NW Kontum and 6 km SW FSB Charlie per map at front of *A Bright Shining Lie*. Also mentioned at pp 756-759, 765-766, 769 of same book. Described as strongest ARVN position along rocket ridge and bottom hinge of string of ARVN FSBs running along ridge between YB 99-15 to ZA 08-95, during '72 Offensive. Heavily attacked 3Apr72 and nearly overrun. Finally overrun and lost to NVA, 21Apr72. Grid only apx. Kontum Pr, II Corps.
Delta, LZ (XD 64-31)
Apx 16 km WSW Lang Vei, 8 km due S FSB Bravo, and 14 km ESE LZ Delta 1. ARVNMC base opened 9Feb71 by 1st ARVN Inf Div CA during Lam Son 719. Good map of Lam Son 719 at www.americal.org/174/ map4.htm. Laos.
Delta, LZ/FSB (YA 935-585)
Apx 34 km WNW Pleiku, 11 km NE Plei Djereng (old) AF. Oct69-Jan70. See FSB Delta (YA 835-747) entry. Pleiku Pr, II Corps.
Delta 1, LZ (XD 56-33)
Apx 8 km SE Aloui, 14 km WNW LZ Delta. 1st ARVN Div, Lam Son 719, '71. Good map of Lam Son 719 at www.americal.org/174/map4.htm. Laos.
Delta, Project (n/a)
See Project Delta in Glossary.
Delta CAC (YD?)
See CAC Listings. I Corps.
Delta CAP (n/a)
See CAP Delta listings. I Corps.
Delta Five (YD 1-4)
USMC's designation for combat zone S of Mai Loc in the Ba Long Valley. 3d Mar Div. Quang Tri Pr, I Corps.
Delta Force, Private (n/a)
See Private Delta Force in Glossary.
Delta Hilton (n/a)
A.k.a. "the best dining spot in Chau Doc Province." See YRBM-20. IV Corps.
Delta Junction (YD 526-035)
Apparently reference to junction of Rao Nui and Rao Nho Rivers, apx 28 km SW Hue, and 5 km SW FSB Veghel. May68. On map, river junction in concert with Hwy 547 forms the letter "D." Thua Thien Pr, I Corps.
Delta Med (YD)
Thought to be at Dong Ha or at staging area for Op Hastings SE Gio Linh? A Marine medical facility set-up to serve Op Hastings, 15Jul-3Aug67, and then expanded into a permanent facility thereafter. Quang Tri Pr, I Corps.
Delta Tangos (n/a)
See Delta Tango and Tin Trunk in Glossary.
Demilitarized Zone, The (DMZ) (XD/YD)
Created by UN's partitioning of Vietnam into two countries in 1954. Was an 8-km wide zone that followed course of Song Ben Hai River from its mouth on N of Quang Tri, to Bo Ho Su. From that point course was a straight line due W to Laotian border. Roughly coincided with 17th Parallel. See DMZ. Quang Tri Pr, I Corps.
Demise, LZ/FSB (BR 520-512)
See Denise. Binh Dinh Pr, II Corps.
Demon, LZ (YD 017-398)
On Dong Cho hill mass or its peak, overlooking the Song Thach Han River Valley, apx 9 km SSE Ca Lu, 15 km due W Ba Long AF and 34 km WSW Quang Tri. Apr70 XXIV Corps grid per Don Armstrong. Quang Tri Pr, I Corps.
Dempsey Compound (WS 84-02)
Cmpd adj to Can Tho AF, apx 120 km SW Saigon. Named to honor Col Jack T. Dempsey, USA, CO 13th Avn Bn, KIA 26Mar67, when his gunship was shot down near Can Tho while covering 2 other downed helicopter crews. Co D, Det C-4, 5th SF Grp here. Phong Dinh Pr, IV Corps.
Den Khach, Mui (US 9-1)
Mui Den Phach. Coastal point at 10°07'N-104°02'E. On NC48-05 JOG. Kien Giang Pr, IV Corps.
Den Phach, Mui (US 9-1)
Coastal point at 10°07'N-104°02'E. On NC48-05 JOG. Kien Giang Pr, IV Corps.
Den Phach, Pointe (US 9-1)
See Pointe Den Phach. Kien Giang Pr, IV Corps.
Den, FSB (YT 61-37)
Apx 13 km NW Vo Dat AF/Xa Vo Dat, 32 km NE Xuan Loc, 15 km SW Xa Phuong Lam and 8 km WNW FSB Chin Duc. 199th LIB elements attacked here Apr or May70, resulting in 23 enemy KIA.[162] 4th/12th and 3d/7th Inf, 199th LIB, also elements of 2d/40th Arty and 155mm howitzers of 2d/35th Arty. Long Khanh Pr, III Corps.
Denbigh BEQ (XS 843-943)
At 44 Thai Lap Thanh St., Saigon. Per R. Bows' *Vietnam Military Lore, 1959-1973.* Gia Dinh Pr, III Corps.
Denise, LZ/FSB (BR 520-512)
Apx 6 km NNE An Khe's major AF, 13 km WSW Vinh Thanh, 20 km WNW Binh Khe, 38 km WNW Phu Cat AB and 17 km SE Kannack. Also spelled Dennis and Demise, but Denise likely correct. 4th Div AO, '70, C Bty, 2d/9th

Arty here Feb70. Name/grid per Jim Claeys. Aug69-Oct70. Binh Dinh Pr, II Corps.

Dennis, LZ (BR 520-512)
See LZ Denise, LZ. This name/grid inS-3 Daily Journals and Op rpts dated 31Jul-1Sep69, courtesy Bob Patsfield. Binh Dinh Pr, II Corps.

Dennis C. Kidd Farm (XT 63-66?)
At Minh Thanh, apx 33 km NNW Lai Khe AF, 16 km WNW Chon Thanh AF and 70 km NNW Saigon. Built adj to Camp Irving R. Self. Named to honor MSgt Dennis C Kidd, US Army, KIA 4Aug64. Sgt Kidd built the farm to aid local populace and was targeted for murder by VC for that act. Data per *Vietnam Military Lore, 1959-1973*. Binh Long Pr, III Corps.

Denny, FSB (XT?)
Location unknown. Home of 25th Inf's 2d/12th and 2d/14th Inf for 3 weeks beginning late Aug70, per David Argabright. III Corps.

Dental BOQ (XS 8-9)
See Retro Molar Pad BOQ. Gia Dinh Pr, III Corps.

Denver BEQ (XS 8-9)
At 168 Nguyen Cu Trinh St., Saigon. Per R. Bows' *Vietnam Military Lore, 1959-1973.* Gia Dinh Pr, III Corps.

Denver, Operation (n/a)
10-25 Apr66. 173d Abn, Song Be, Phuoc Long Pr. Bde TF captured some 34 tons of rice and 2,167 documents.

Denver, USS (n/a)
LPD 9. See Frequent Wind, Op.

Deo (n/a)
Vietnamese word for "mountain pass."

Deo Dea Nuages (AT 9-9)
See Hai Van Pass. Thua Thien Pr, I Corps.

Deo Hai Van (AT 9-9)
A.k.a. Hai Van Pass, "Pass of Ocean Clouds," and Deo Des Nuages. See Hai Van Pass. Thua Thien Pr, I Corps.

Deo Hieng, Nui (YJ 5-3)
Mtn range at 21°07'N-107°29'E. Grid per DMA L-1501 map NF48-12. NVN.

Deo Mang Pass (BR 578-450)
Between Camp Radcliff and Qui Nhon on QL-19, and E Mang Yang Pass. See Mang Yang Pass and *Battles in the Monsoon*, pp 41, 197. Binh Dinh Pr, II Corps.

Deo Partisans (UK 0-1)
Col des Partisans or Partisan Pass. See Col des Partesans (WL 0-5). NIMA data. NVN.

Deo Van Long (n/a)
See Glossary.

Deo Vents (WK 9-7)
A.k.a. Col des Vents or Pass of Vents. NIMA data. NVN.

DEPCORDS (XT 99-09?)
Presumably supply depot or HQ for CORDS? Bien Hoa Pr?, III Corps.

DEPCORDS Trac Heliport (XT 999-098)
In Bien Hoa, along N bank of Song Dong Nai River, apx 4 to 5 km S to SSE Bien Hoa AB. "Heliport #767, alt 12', Acft Ldg-departing ctc Spartan Tower for tfc advsy. Hazards-10' fence on final app. 100' high wires W end of pad. Helipad surrounded by fence 4' to 12' high. Recommend Ldg hdg 270°, dep hdg 090°. Spartan Tower-321.0, 121.4, 35.2, 2901.5 USB Opr 2100-1500Z. Arty Adv-Bien Hoa 290.0 46.7." At 10°56'50"N-106°49'50"E, per Feb73 TAD. Bien Hoa Pr, III Corps.

Deperio, Patrol Base (XS 430-450)
Apx 3 km NE Dong Tam and 6 km W My Tho. Jan69. Dinh Tuong Pr, IV Corps.

DEROS, Patrol Base (XS 360-440)
Near intersection of of Rtes 210 and 212, apx 6 km NW Dong Tam. Jan69. Dinh Tuong Pr, IV Corps.

DEROS Hill (BN 692-872)
Apx 8 km W Phan Rang AB and 16 km WNW Phan Rang city. Oct69. Ninh Thuan Pr, II Corps.

Derwent (n/a)
Australian Escort ship serving under US 7th Flt.

Deshayes Airfield (n/a)
A.k.a. Postes Deshayes AF. Apx 275 km NE to ENE Phnom Penh and 40 km W the SVN border. Feb67 Natl Geo map. El. 900'. Cambodia.

DeShurley, Camp (ZD 084-004?)
See De Shurley, Camp. Thua Thien Pr, I Corps.

Desire, LZ (XT 632-458)
Apx 16 km NW Lai Khe and 15 km due E Dau Tieng/Tri Tam. May66. Binh Duong Pr, III Corps.

DeSoto County, USS (n/a)
LST-1171. SVN.

Desoto Missions (n/a)
See Glossary.

Desoto Patrols (n/a)
See Glossary.

Dessert (n/a)
Code name for Enemy Base Area 350 in Cambodia. See Base Area 350.

Destiny, FSB (YC 328-981)
A.k.a. Hill 937, Hamburger Hill or Dong Ap Bia. See Hamburger Hill for detail. Thua Thien Pr, I Corps.

Destroyer (n/a)
Apr70, XXIV Corps proposed 101st Abn FSB name.

Detachment Echo (ZD 084-004?)
See Camp De Shurley. Thua Thien Pr, I Corps.

Determined to Win, Op (n/a)
See Glossary.

Detroit, LZ (YA 935-050)
Very close to site of LZ Albany, and apx 51 km SW Pleiku, 22 km E Plei Me and 6 km NE peak Chu Pong. 2d/17th Arty here 21Aug66, suptg 8th Bn, 3rd Bde/1st Cav. Data per Jack Picciolo. Pleiku Pr, Pleiku Pr, II Corps.

Detroit, LZ (YD 782-269)
On E edge of Hue, apx 5 km due E Hue Citadel AF, 5 km NE QL-1 and 14 km NW Phu Bai AF. Apr70 XXIV Corps grid per Don Armstrong. Thua Thien Pr, I Corps.

Detroit BEQ (XS 8-9)
On Lot 34, Phu Tho Hoa St., Saigon. Data per *Vietnam Military Lore, 1959-1973*. Gia Dinh Pr, III Corps.

Deux Freres, Ile de (XJ 7-5)
Island of Two Monks (or Two Friars). NIMA data. NVN.

Deux Songs, Ile des (XJ 7-2)
Two Songs Island. NIMA data. NVN.

Deuxime Bureau (YS 278-427?)
See Ghost Mountain at grid. Phuoc Tuy Pr, III Corps.

Deverley, FSB (YS 456-866)
Along E side of LTL-2, 19 km N Nui Dat, 1 km S FSB Mary, 2 km N FSBs Avenger and Kylie. On 1ATF NCO trng map per John Hollett. Phuoc Tuy Pr, III Corps.
Devil, LZ (XD 822-666)
In DMZ, apx 24 km WNW Cam Lo and 5 km SE Bo Hu Su (NVN). Apr70 XXIV Corps grid per Don Armstrong. Quang Tri Pr, I Corps.
Devil's Backbone (n/a)
A 700-meter long ridge roughly 7.5 km from Laos in either I or II Corps. Apparently there was a FSB on this ridge at some time. I or II Corps?
Devil's Island (XT 503-014)
Island apparently formed by Song Vam Co Dam River apx 7 km SW Khiem Cuong and 35 km W to WNW Tan Son Nhut AB. Jan69. Hau Nghia Pr, III Corps.
Devin, FSB (XT 551-177)
See Devins. Hau Nghia Pr, III Corps.
Devins, FSB (XT 551-178)
A.k.a. FSB Kathy. Apx 2 km NE Xa An Duc and QL-1, 6 km due W Trang Bang, 10 km WNW Cu Chi and 32 km NW Saigon. FSB/Laager site of 25th Inf Div, secured by 1st/5th Mech. Photos at: www.users.uswest.net/~huffpapa/vietnam.html show it to have been circular and very muddy. One photo shows sign which reads, "*No Swimming, Fishing or Skiing after 6:30 PM.*" Possibly named to honor SP4 Richard C Devins, KIA 28Nov68. Also listed at XT 540-170 and 547-178, Nov69. Data/grid per Doug Huffman. Hau Nghia Pr, III Corps.
Dewey, USS (n/a)
DLG-14. Guided-Missile DD Ldr, per Ralph Fries.
Dewey Canyon, Operation (XD)
9th Marines op in Da Krong River Valley of W Quang Tri Pr. Took place 22Jan-18Mar69. By Jan69, the NVA were moving as much as 1,000 vehicles into SVN along Rte 922. XXIV Corps responded with several multi-Bde ops into Lao border area N of the A Shau Valley in order to interdict movement, destroy supply depots and engage NVA. During op, USMC captured dozen 122mm arty pieces (1st time they'd been found inside SVN) and destroyed some 525 tons of munitions and supplies, including more rockets/mortar rnds than enemy used during all of Tet '69 Offensive. Gen Abrams est that elimination of those resources saved allies between 5,000 and 6,000 casualties. Est 1,335 NVA KIA. Quang Tri Pr, I Corps.
Dewey Canyon II, Operation (XD/YD)
Phase I of Lam Son 719 and last major US op of war. Also and last major op for 101st Abn and 5th Inf (Mech) Divs. Was in supt of Lam Son 719 (ARVN Invasion of Laos) (began 29Jan71) in defensive rather than offensive role. Mission was to open QL-9 from Dong Ha to border as supply route for ARVN units heading W. 5th Mech cleared Rte 9 to, and secured reopening of, abnd Khe Sanh CB. Per *Da Nang Diary*, pp 229-230, Prairie Fire SF troops out of MLT-2, Quang Tri, flew ahead of armored column and planted a sign on deserted Khe Sanh airstrip as practical joke. It read: "*Welcome to CCN Country!*" See Lam Son 719 for more info. Some data per *Vietnam Order of Battle,* pp 9-14. Quang Tri Pr, I Corps.
Dexter, Camp (BN 77-87)
At Phan Rang AB, apx 9 km NNW Phan Rang. Named to honor Maj Herbert Dexter, KIA 18Sep65. Turned-over to SVN govt 23-24Mar72. Data per Ray Bows. Ninh Thuan Pr, II Corps.
Dexter, Operation (n/a)
4-6 May66. 173d Abn, Tan Uyen. 3-day op in NW portion of Bien Hoa Pr, III Corps.
Di An (XT 93-06)
Ville apx 10 km SSW Bien Hoa AF, 6 km SW Bien Hoa, 3 km E to ENE Di An AF/CB, and 15 km NE Tan Son Nhut AB. Pronounced "Zee-On", and often misspelled as Dian or Zeon or Xeon. Bien Hoa Pr, III Corps.
Di An AAF Airfield (XT 930-060)
Apx 10 km SSW Bien Hoa AF, 6 km SW Bien Hoa, 3 km E to ENE Di An AF and 15 km NE Tan Son Nhut AB. Listed as "Secure, hvy helo trfc (C-123) (C-7), US Army,7Jul69, AF # VA3-278," in Aug69 TAD per Frank Penk, Jr. Not in Feb73 TAD. Bien Hoa Pr, III Corps.
Di An Airfield (XT 909-055)
Tactical airfield apx 12 km NE Tan Son Nhut AB. TPC K-10D. El. 108', 2,800' laterite rwy Also listed at XT 95-05. Bien Hoa Pr, III Corps.
Di An Base Camp (XT 905-055)
A few km to W of Di An city, apx 13 km NE Tan Son Nhut AB, 12 km SW Bien Hoa AB and 27 km ESE Cu Chi. Major basecamp and HQ of US 1st Inf (Big Red One) Div. Pronounced "Zee-On" and often misspelled as Dian or Zeon or Xeon. Also listed at XT 895-065, Aug67, and XT 917-078, Mar67. Bien Hoa Pr, III Corps.
Di An Heliport (XT 901-062)
See Sabre Heliport. Bien Hoa Pr, III Corps.
Di An Signal Site (XT 9-0?)
No data. Bien Hoa Pr, III Corps.
Di Linh (n/a)
Mapsheet name of L-7014-6632-3. SVN.
Di Linh Airfield (AN 849-792)
See Djiring AF. Lam Dong Pr, II Corps.
Di Linh/Bao Loc (ZT 07-77?)
Apx 36 km WSW Dalat and 26 km E Tan Phat AF/Bao Loc. Home of MACV Adv. Team 38, Lam Dong Pr Advisors. 5th SF, Det A-232 (was 234) here Oct65. Grid per *SF Order of Battle*. Capitol, Lam Dong Pr, II Corps.
Di Santis, FSB (XT 024-763)
A.k.a. and commonly spelled "Disantis." On LTL-20, apx 5 km from Cambodia, 8 km SW Thien Ngon AF and 35 km NNW Tay Ninh. Honor Cpl William R. Di Santis, KIA 15Apr70. Data per Peter Cole. Tay Ninh Pr, III Corps.
Dia Diem Bunard (n/a)
Mapsheet name of L-7014-6432-3. SVN.
Dia Loc Pass (n/a)
No data. Variant of "Dai Loc?" I Corps.
Dia Phong (n/a)
See Du Kich in Glossary.
Diablo, FSB (XS or YS)
Somewhere SE Saigon. Apparently built by 1st/508th Inf, 82d Abn, apx 12Nov68, during ops SE Saigon that were vacated by 9th Inf Div (which was on ops in Phuoc Tuy/Long Khanh Pr?). Used to centralize Bn's 4.2" mortars for added fire supt for main Bn FSB at Lucifer. Lucifer

apparently built nearby and by same Bn. 3d Bde/82d Abn. Info per Butch Sincock. Pr?, III Corps.

Diamond, FSB (XT 334-211)
See Diamond I, FSB. Tay Ninh Pr, III Corps.

Diamond, LZ (BS 456-011)
Apx 53 km WNW LZ English, 30 km due W Thuan An and 18 km SSE Gia Vuc. Mar66. Binh Dinh Pr, II Corps.

Diamond, LZ (XD 825-484)
Apx 8 km NNE Khe Sanh CB and 18 km W Cam Lo. Apr70 XXIV Corps grid per Don Armstrong. Quang Tri Pr, I Corps.

Diamond, Patrol Base/FSB (XT 321-223)
A.k.a. FSB Diamond I? Apx 7 km WSW Go Dau Ha, 3 km E Cambodia at Angel's Wing, 25 km SSE Tay Ninh and 13 km due N Duc Hue AF. Also listed at XT 327-215, 330-180, 330-210, 334-210, 337-187. Feb-May67. Tay Ninh Pr, III Corps.

Diamond City (XT?)
242d ASHC pilots' nickname for a Vietnamese ville on Cambodian border. Mentioned on unit's webpage at: www.vhpa.org/crash.htm. No other data. III Corps.

Diamond Head, LZ (BR 686-420)
A.k.a. Diamondhead. Per Dave Holdorf and 15th Arty Rgt Assn, was along QL-19E, at or near Binh Khe, apx 22 km ESE An Khe/Camp Radcliff. C Bty, 7th/15th Arty here at one time. Grid apx. Binh Dinh Pr, II Corps.

Diamond I, FSB (XT 334-211)
A.k.a. Patrol Base Diamond I. Apx 3 km E Cambodia, 25 km SSE Tay Ninh and 8 km WSW Go Dau Ha. Built as part of Gen Ellis Williamson's "Force Fed Fire Supt System," in late '68 or early '69. Overrun in Battle of Patrol Base Diamond, 23Feb69, while defended by 2d/27th Inf, 25th Inf Div. After 10 minute mortar attack, base was hit with massive ground assault. Despite heavy arty and ARA, NVA breached perimeter and took 3 bunkers. Direct arty fire from tubes within camp finally broke assault. Apparently took 10 hrs to push NVA out See Force Fed Fire Supt System in Glossary. Tay Ninh Pr, III Corps. [163]

Diamond II, Patrol Base (XT 341-156)
At road intersection 4 km E Cambodia, 8 km NNE Duc Hue and 10 km SSW Go Dau Ha. Apparently built after Diamond I was overrun on 23Feb69. Diamond II assaulted by NVA 5Apr69, in Battle of Patrol Base Diamond II. [164] 2/27th Inf, 25th Inf Div. See Diamond I. Apr-May69. Tay Ninh Pr, III Corps.

Diamond III, FSB (XT 3-2?)
Apx 32 km SW Tay Ninh and likely built near FSBs Diamond I and II sometime in Spring or Summer of '69. Attacked 15Apr69, by 2 NVA Bns attacking elements of 2/27th Inf, 25 Inf Div here during Op Toan Thang III. 13 US KIA and est 190 enemy KIA. [165] See Diamond I and Diamond II. Tay Ninh Pr, III Corps.

Diamondhead, LZ (BR 69-43)
See Diamond Head. Binh Dinh Pr, II Corps.

Dian Basecamp (XT 95-05)
See Di An. Bien Hoa Pr, III Corps.

Diana, FSB (XT 424-830)
Apx 10 km S Cambodia, 13 km SE Katum, 35 km WSW An Loc and 27 km NNE Nui Ba Den Mtn. 1st Cav, '69. Grid per Frank Penk, Jr. FSBs Diana also listed at XT 425-168, 550-050 and 526-798? Tay Ninh Pr, III Corps.

Diana, FSB (XT 425-168)
Apx 9 km SSE Go Dau Ha, 23 km due W Cu Chi. 11Sep67. FSBs Diana also listed at XT 550-050, 528-800 and 424-830? Hau Nghia Pr, III Corps.

Diana, FSB (XT 528-800)
A.k.a. FSB Dianna. Apx 23 km ESE Katum and 12 km SSW tip of Fishhook. Jan70. Also listed at XT 526-798 as FSB Dianna. Tay Ninh Pr, III Corps.

Diana, FSB (XT 550-050)
Apx 3 km E Khiem Cuong 15 km SW Cu Chi. 9Sep67. FSBs Diana also listed at XT 528-800, 435-168 and 424-830? Hau Nghia Pr, III Corps.

Diane, FSB (YT 730-260)
Apx 7 km SSE Vo Dat AF and 17 km W Tanh Linh AF. Nov69-Jan70. Binh Tuy Pr, III Corps.

Diane, FSB (BR? 255-845)
If grid correct, was apx 46 km NNW An Khe, 46 km E Kontum and 9 km due S Kon Lok. 10th Cav, 4th Div here. BR grid zone presumed. Data per Bob Patsfield. Binh Dinh Pr, II Corps.

Diane, LZ/FSB (YA 855-199)
At crossroads apx 3 km ENE Plei Girao Kla, 10 km E Cambodia, 47 km SW Pleiku, 4 km S FSB Joan and 6 km SSE Duc Co AF. Apparently a 4th Div FSB. Name/grid per S-3 Daily Journal/Op rpts dated 31Jul-1Sep69, courtesy Bob Patsfield. Pleiku Pr, II Corps.

Dianna, FSB (XT 526-798)
A.k.a. FSB Diana. Apx 4 km NNE Bau Tram, 25 km WSW An Loc and 24 km ESE Katum. Also listed at XT 528-800 as FSB Diana. Tay Ninh Pr, III Corps.

Diaper, LZ (XD 936-241)
Along W edge of Vietnam Salient, apx 11 km ESE Lang Chei, 6 km SSE Lang Klung and 24 km SSW Ca Lu. Apr70 XXIV Corps grid per Don Armstrong. Quang Tri Pr, I Corps.

Dich Board (n/a)
See Glossary.

Dick, FSB (XU 740-060)
A.k.a. LZ Cherokee. Along QL-13, apx 4 km S Loc Ninh AF and 17 km due N An Loc. Binh Long Pr, III Corps.

Dick, FSB (YD 144-335)
Apx 27 km SW Quang Tri, 18 km SSE Mai Loc and 16 km WSW FSB Anne. XXIV grid per Don Armstrong. Also listed at YD 142-333. Quang Tri Pr, I Corps.

Dickey, FSB (WS 97-40)
A.k.a. FSB Cai Be and FSB Danger. On QL-4 apx 42 km due W Dong Tam and 14 km ENE Sa Dec, at 10°19'00"N-105°54'00"E. See FSB Danger. Dinh Tuong Pr, IV Corps.

Dickey Chapelle Dispensary (BT?)
40 patient civilian dispensary built in "New Life Village" refugee camp near Chu Lai, by 9th Engr Bn, 1st Mar Div. Named to honor female photo journalist Dickey Chapelle, KIA Nov 65(?), by VC booby trap while on Natl Geographic assignment in field with USMC unit during Op Black Ferret near Chu Lai. Quang Tin Pr, I Corps.

Diem Truong Heliport (ZD 027-143)
Apx 5.5 km W to WNW Phu Loc, 1 km S QL-1, and 31 km SE Hue. Heliport #559, alt 7', at 16°23'30"N-107°50'00"E, per 73 TAD. Thua Thien Pr, I Corps.

Dien Ban (BT 06-58)
Ville apx 17 km SSE Da Nang and birthplace of Nguyen Van Troi, celebrated Viet hero of war. Troi was an electrician who planted a cmd-detonated bomb on route of US Secty of Def Robert McNamara's motorcade. The bomb was discovered and Troi was executed, but his last words brought Dien everlasting respect. He said: "Long live Vietnam. Long live Ho Chi Minh," just before firing squad ended his days as an electrician. Many towns, streets and bldgs now bear his name. See also Han River Bridge. Quang Nam Pr, I Corps. [166]

Dien Ban Bridge (BT 057-588)
QL-1 bridge apx 8 km W Hoi An and 17 km SSE Da Nang AB. Quang Nam Pr, I Corps.

Dien Bien Phu (n/a)
Mapsheet name of L-7014-5651-4. NVN only.

Dien Bien Phu (TJ 94-66)
A.k.a. "The Chamber Pot" (French Pilots' nickname) and as Tran Dinh to Vietminh. In heart-shaped, Muong Thanh Valley of Nam Yum River, along far SW border of NVN (Tonkin), apx 290 km due W Hanoi, 75 km SW Lai Chau and 16 km E Laos. Small, 100-structure hamlet sat in this remote, 7 x 20 km valley which became site of Vietminh's epic siege and defeat of French Army in May54. Their stunning and overwhelming Viet victory there led to end of 1st Indochina War and France's eventual withdrawal from Vietnam. 1st occupied by French in 1887, under Gov Auguste Pavie (who gave his name to Pavie Trail). DBP translates as "Seat of Border Administration," and town was capital of Dien Bien Dist, Lai Chau Pr. Hill-tribes, including Thai and Hmong, were/are its primary residents, while today ethnic Vietnamese make up only about 1/3d of valley's 60,000 pop. At 21°23'00N-103°01'00E. NVN.

Dien Bien Phu (Airfield) (TJ 94-67)
Apx 5 km N Dien Bien Phu, 17 km N Ban Cong Den, 10 km E Laotian border and 290 km WNW Hanoi. In Muong Thanh Valley. Per ONC-J-11. El. 1821'. NVN.

Dien Bien Phu (Layout) (TJ 94-67)
View of surrounding positions from First Aid Post No. 29 (adj main Cmd Post on W bank of Nam Yum River) is described in *Doctor at Dienbienphu*, pp 19-20 as follows: "To the E, two-thirds of a mile beyond the river, rose a series of hills stretching north and south, the Elianes with their central peak, Eliane 2, and Dominiques with their central peak, Dominique 3, held by Moroccans and dominating the airfield. To N, and beyond end of rwy, rose Gabrielle, held by Fourth Bn, Seventh Algerian Rifles. Much farther to NE, over three miles away, three little hills stood out at foot of a high mtn; this position had the name of Anne-Marie and was held by Thai of Third Thai Bn. Between the Dominiques and Gabrielle a kind of yellow ridge appeared above the green. This was Beatrice, or rather its main earthwork…nearly four miles away...a very strong position, even said to be impregnable, and held by Legionnaires of Thirteenth Demi-Bde. To S and W stretched the plain, earthy at first, covered with shelters and bristling with radio aerials, beyond which it swiftly changed into a thick network of barbed-wire entanglements. Then the plain became green and overgrown, bounded far off by mountains, real mountains, like the nearer one behind the dark and forbidding Dominique." NVN.

Dien Bien Phu (Main Complex) (TJ 94-67)
A.k.a. The Metro. Along W bank of Nam Yum River in Muong Thanh Valley, immed S main rwy and apx 290 km W Hanoi. Main CP and defensive position of French during Op Castor, 20Nov53-7May54. Main position held ops CP, Foreign Legion Paras, 8th and 9th Paras, a Commando unit, the 1st Grp, some French Regular Inf, an aid station, a hospital, twelve 105 and four 155 howitzers, 24-120mm mortars, 4-Quad .50 Caliber and Bn of 82mm mortars. NVN.

Dien Bien Phu (Strongpoints) (TJ 94-67)
These were: the Ann-Maries (A1 to A5), Bald Hill, Beatrice, Claudines (C1 to C-5), Dominiques (D1 to D3), Elianes (E1 to E4), Gabrielle, Huguettes (H1 to H6), Junon, Isabelle, 2d Thai, The Five Hills, White Thai. See Dien Bien Phu (layout), Dien Bien Phu (Battle of). NVN.

Dien Bien Phu, 1st Battle of (TJ 94-67)
Took place 30Nov52. Defended by weak Laotian Inf unit, garrison first fell to Vietminh, 30Nov52.

Dien Bien Phu, Battle of (TJ 94-67)
20Nov53 to 7May54 - DBP was focus of Op Castor, French occupation and buildup of fortifications in Muong Thanh Valley and DBP (Vietnamese for "Seat of Border Administration"). Valley was along Nam Yum River, about 290 km due W Hanoi and only a few km E Laos. Buildup led to carefully-planned, massive Vietminh siege/assault of garrison; and ultimately to exit of French from VN.

Gen Navarre's purpose in opening DBP was unclear even to officers in charge but presumably it was meant to defend northern Laos. Giap countered by moving the 308th, 312th Inf Div and 351st Heavy Div to area, and later, an Independent Rgt. The 351st had (24) 105mm and lighter howitzers, plus (40) 82mm mortars, (20) 120mm heavy, 37mm and .50 Cal AA weapons, and from 12 to 16 Katyusha Rocket Launchers (a.k.a. Stalin Organs).

Although 17 Bns under French fought at DBP, there were never more than 10 Bns in valley at any one time.

Under overall cmd of Gen Navarre, Op Castor began 20Nov53, when 65 C-47 and C-119 acft out of Gia-Lam and Bac Mai AFs dropped 6th BCP (Para Assault Bn), 6th Colonial Paras (under Maj. Marcel Bigeard), and II/1 RCP (2d Bn, 1st Parachute Light Inf under Maj. Jean Brechignal) into DBP using 3 DZs. 1st stick arrived at 10:30 am, catching Vietminh totally by surprise.

For about one year, DBP had been home and training base of Vietminh Independent Rgt 148, with 3 Bns along Thai border and Bn 910 (with 3 extra Cos) in the valley the Friday French landed. Bn 910 was training in "Drop Zone Natasha" when 6th BCP landed. Those Vietminh took the parachutists under fire, killing several before they landed, but French soon rallied and drove Viets from field. By afternoon, 2,000 French troops had been inserted. Casualties for 1st day were 11 French KIA, 52 WIA, and roughly 100 Vietminh KIA.

On 2d day, Gen Jean Gilles, CO of op (his glass eye buttoned in breast pocket), dropped in with LTC Pierre Langlais (a.k.a. GAP-2) as well as 8th BPC and 5th BPVN (a Viet Para Bn along with photographer Brigitte Friang (her 6th combat jump). Over next weeks and months, North

African Troops and Legionnaires gradually replaced Para units until 12 Bns filled valley floor.

On 25Nov53, the 1st C-47 landed at DBP's newly constructed main AF. By 28Nov53, Gen Navarre had accurate intel of Giap's forces and their destination but did not believe them able to deliver sufficient arty or re-supply to threaten the DBP garrison. On 5Dec53, French Paras found Vietminh of 316th Div on Rte 41 and 5 km N from DBP's main complex. On 12Dec53, Gen de Castries (full name: Christian Marie Ferdinand de La Croix de Castries) replaced Col Gilles as CO of DBP.

On last day of Jan54, Giap had completed moving his heavy weapons into hillside caves dug within range of DBP (virtually undetected) and gave Arty and mortars order to open fire; the siege had begun. The Vietminh also began digging tunnels and trenches toward strongpoints Eliane and Dominique that day, and AA flak began reaching French air supt. Bombardment continued on daily basis but it was not until 13Mar54 that 1st major ground assaults were launched, overrunning Strongpoint Beatrice on 13Mar54, and Gabrielle on 14-15Mar54.

On 16Mar54, Bigeard's 6th Colonial Paras were dropped in. During next four months, positions throughout valley would be overrun and then taken back repeatedly in desperate hand-to-hand fighting. At one point during siege, a C-47 landed to medevac wounded and after loading was destroyed by arty leaving Genevieve de Galard-Jerraube, a nurse, stranded at base. She stayed on through battle caring for wounded and was captured at its end, earning title "The Angel of DBP" and later a Croix de Guerre and Knight's Cross of Legion of Honor (overall she had flown over 149 medevac missions, including 40 to DBP).

On 18Mar54, Capt. Bizard led survivors of H-6 as they abnd it in foot race to H-2, catching Vietminh off-guard.

On 9Apr54, elements of French 2d Bde jumped into valley. On 14 Apr54, a massive fire destroyed garrison's ration supply point. H-1 fell 23Apr, and 72 volunteers jumped in 24Apr54. H-5 was attacked on 1May.

On 2May54, Dominique-3 fell as did remaining H's, E-1 and D-3, leaving only E-2, E-4 and H-4 holding on. After the Elianes and Dominiques fell, 2d Para Light Inf (II/1RCP) was dropped in. On 5May54 H-4 fell, and on 6May54, 91 paratroopers jumped in along with big re-supply; the last reinforcement of garrison.

By end of battle, over 4,300 reinforcements had parachuted into DBP, including 681 untrained volunteers (curious side note: jump injury rate for untrained and para-qualified troops was same).

At 1700 hours on 7May54, Gen Christian de Castries radioed Hanoi with garrison's final radio message: "Au revior mon General; au revior mes camerades." As Vietminh entered the CP complex, "C'est Fini?" asked one of a French officer there. "Oui, c'est fini," came his weary reply, and battle for DBP was over.

In the end, the French had suffered 9,000 casualties, 7,000 of their troops had been captured, and a total of 62 transports, fighters and helos had been shot down. After surrender, Vietminh initially allowed French to air evac its wounded but soon balked and insisted both wounded and healthy walk back to Hanoi; a trek of some 290 km (and only about 20% survived tortuous journey). Vietminh losses at DBP possibly as high as 100,000. NVN.

Dien Bien Phu, Little (WS 005-515)
See Phan Chau (old). Chau Doc Pr, IV Corps.

Dien Binh (ZA 090-180)
Lightly defended ville along Hwy 14, apx 9 km ESE Dak To 3 AF and 32 km NNW Kontum. Attacked during Feb-Mar69. Cited in *Time Heals No Wounds*, p 117. Kontum Pr, II Corps.

Dien Binh Quarry (ZB 081-172)
Along QL-14, apx 33 km NNE Kontum and 8 km SE Dak To 2 AF. Oct68. Kontum Pr, II Corps.

Dien Chau (WF 6-9)
Apx 100 km S Thanh Hoa. Used as NVA waypoint along HCMT. Branch in road here headed NW toward Laos along Rte 75 (dirt) and was one of arteries leading to Truong Son Mtn passes of HCMT. NVN.

Dien Hong, FSB? (n/a)
Cited in *1st Cav Op Rpt, Feb70/Apr70*, p 14, per Peter Cole. During period, Cav was in NW III Corp. There is a Dien Hieu in XT 6-5, per NIMA Gaz. III Corps.

Dien Khanh (BP 93-55)
Apx 10 km due W Nha Trang. Site of Trung Dung SF/Dien Khanh Camps. Khanh Hoa Pr, II Corps.

Dien Khanh Bridge (BP 939-557)
Apx 10 km W Nha Trang. Khanh Hoa Pr, II Corps.

Dien Khanh SF Camp (BP 9370-5571)
A.k.a. Trung Dung SF Camp? Apx 10 km due W Nha Trang. Det A-502 (was 323). Oct65. See Trung Dung. Grid per *SF Order of Battle.* Khanh Hoa Pr, II Corps.

Dieu, Mui (CQ 3-2)
Mui Ke Ga. Coastal point at 12°53'N-109°28'E. On ND49-13 JOG. Khanh Hoa Pr, II Corps.

Digger, LZ (BR 775-638)
Apx 36 km NE to ENE An Khe, 12 km W QL-1 and 6 km NE LZ Football. 4th Div AO, '70. 4th Div op rpt grid per Jim Claeys. Binh Dinh Pr, II Corps.

Digger's Rest, FSB (YS 270-808)
Apx 27 km NW Nui Dat, 3 km SW FSB Cedar, 3 km NE FSB Hawk, 16 km W FSB Coolah and 8 km NE QL-15. Author of *Vietnam Gunners*, at p 82, writes that it was built by 9 RAR beginning 1Jan69, as a complete, state-of-the-art FSB: "A fortress of sandbags, bunds, culverts, barbed wire, [PSP] gun platforms, [MG] posts and dug-in [CP]." 161 Bty RNZA (Hitching's Bty 14Apr68-18Mar69) FSB set here 31Dec68 (left section), and both sections 1-29Jan69. When sent here 29 Sep-1Nov69, Andrew's Bty found site of old Digger's rest was under water and moved it apx 800 meters to N. On 1ATF NCO trng map per John Hollett. Also listed at YS 27-87. Bien Hoa Pr, III Corps.

Digger's Rest, FSB (YS 27-87)
Relocated site of this FSB. See Digger's Rest listed at YS 270-808 for detail. Bien Hoa Pr, III Corps.

Dillard, Camp (AN 968-862)
See Dillard Industrial Complex. Lam Dong Pr, II Corps.

Dillard Industrial Complex (AN 968-862)
Along QL-20 at or near Hip Thuan, apx 22 km SW Dalat/Lien Khuong AF, 6 km ESE Phu Hiep and 42 km SW Dalat. Apparently rock quarry and Engr facility here. Named to honor MGen John A. B. Dillard, Cmdr, US Army Engr Cmd VN, KIA, when helo shot down,

12May70. Also Listed at AN 981-858? See http://members.sitegadgets.com/kolsun/story. html. See Camp Dillard. Lam Dong Pr, II Corps.

Dillard Quarry (AN 968-862)
A.k.a. Gowers-Hansen Quarry? See Dillard Industrial Complex. Lam Dong Pr, II Corps.

Dinassaut (n/a)
See Glossary.

Dinh (n/a)
The community house in a Vietnamese village.

Dinh II, FSB (YT 818-368)
Apx 3 km W Quy Can and 14 km ENE Vo Dat AF. Apr70. Binh Tuy Pr, III Corps.

Dinh Ba, Ap (n/a)
Mapsheet L-7014-6530-1. Full name: Ap Dinh Ba. SVN.

Dinh Binh (BR 612-594?)
In Vinh Than Valley, apx 20 km NE An Kke and immed S Vinh Thanh AF. Involved in Op Horse. Discussed in *Battles in the Monsoon*. Binh Dinh Pr, II Corps.

Dinh Dien Ag Development Center (YD 090-693)
Apx 12 km N Cam Lo and 16 km NW Gio Linh. See Quang Tri Ag Dev Ctr. Quang Tri Pr, I Corps.

Dinh Lap (n/a)
Mapsheet name of L-7014-6452-3. NVN/China.

Dinh Quan (n/a)
Mapsheet name of L-7014-6431-2. SVN.

Dinh Quan Airfield (YT 579-391)
Just S QL 1 apx 16 km W Vo Dat AF. Per ONC K-10. El. 426', 1,400' laterite rwy. At 11°11'29"N-107°21'20"E. Long Khanh Pr, III Corps.

Dinh Quang (BR 628-545?)
Hamlet in Vinh Thanh (Happy) Valley, 2 km E Rte 3a, 2 km SE Vinh Thanh and on branch of Song Con River SE the Old French Fort. Involved in Crazy Horse battles, May66, 1st Cav. A Dinh Quang (B) is listed at BR 657-445. Binh Dinh Pr, II Corps.

Dinh Thanh Airfield (XT 491-472)
See Dau Tieng AF. Binh Duong Pr, III Corps.

Dinh Thanh Heliport (WR 295-945)
Apx 7 km ESE Kien Giang AF, 22 km SE Rach Gia and 14 km NNW Ap Luc. Heliport #560, alt 7', at 09°54'30"N-105°16'00"E, per Feb73 TAD. Kien Giang Pr, IV Corps.

Dinh Thanh North Airfield (XT 491-472)
See Dau Tieng AF. Dinh Tuong Pr, IV Corps.

Dinh Tuong PFTC (WS)
RVNAF Popular Force Trng Ctr. Near Duc Hoa? Dinh Tuong Pr, IV Corps.

Dinh Tuong Province (WS/XS)
One of 16 southern provs forming IV Corps (IV CTZ)

Dinh, FSB (YT 87-13)
Apx 3 km SSW Xa Suoi Kiet, 15 km SSW Tanh Linh City/AF and 48 km W to WNW Phan Thiet. 3d/7th Inf, 4th/12th Inf, 199th LIB. Binh Tuy Pr, III Corps.

Dinh, Mui (BN 8-5)
Cape at 11°22'N-109°01'E. On NC49-01 JOG. Ninh Thuan Pr, II Corps.

Dinner (n/a)
Code name of Base Area 352 in Cambodia. See Base Area 352. Cambodia.

Diodon, USS (n/a)
SS-398. Submarine, per Ralph Fries.

Diplomat and Warrior (n/a)
See Glossary.

Directives, COSVN (n/a)
See COSVN Directives in Glossary.

Dirk, FSB (AT 875-355)
Apx 14 km due S An Hoa, 5 km due S Phuoc Binh and 5 km NNW peak of Hill 944. Apr70 XXIV Corps grid per Don Armstrong. Quang Nam or Quang Tin Pr, I Corps.

Dirk, FSB (XS 140-480)
A.k.a. FSB Schroeder. Along QL 4, apx 8 km WSW Cai Lay and 18 km NNE Vinh Long. 9th Inf. Built as FSB Dirk in Jan69, after FSB Cleopatra closed and its occupants moved here. Later in '69, renamed Schroeder, to honor LTC Donald B. Schroeder, Bn CO, 2d/39th, KIA Mar69. On map L-7014-6129-1 (Sa Dec). Data per Jim Stone, 2d/39th Inf. Dinh Tuong Pr, IV Corps.

Dirty Bird (WJ 8-2?)
A.k.a. the Yen Phu Power Plant. Nickname of US POW Camp. NVN.

Disantis, FSB (XT 024-763)
A.k.a. FSB Di Santis. On LTL-20, apx 5 km from Cambodia, 8 km SW Thien Ngon AF and 35 km NNW Tay Ninh. Honor Cpl William R. Di Santis, KIA 15Apr70. Data per Peter Cole. Tay Ninh Pr, III Corps.

Discovery, FSB (YS 60-68)
On Rte 328, apx n18 km due E Nui Dat, 5 km NNW FSB Bond, 13 km NE Dat Do, 5 km W Xuyen Moc, and 14 km NE FSB Horseshoe. Placed in position to provide supt for 8 RAR's blockade of VC escape rtes from Long Hai Hills during ops there in '70. 161 Bty, RNZA (Andrew's Bty 18Sep69-6Sep 70) FSB set here 3-22Mar70 (left sect.), 11-24Mar70 (right sect.). Pr, III Corps.

Ditch (n/a)
6Apr70, XXIV Corps proposed 5th Div FSB name.

Div Arty Hill, LZ (BT 5158-0399)
See Artillery Hill. Quang Tin Pr, I Corps.

Div Trains (82d Abn) (XS 798-862)
See Division Trains. Gia Dinh Pr, III Corps.

Diver, LZ (XD 903-237)
In Vietnam Salient, apx 7 km ESE Lang Chei and 51 km SW Quang Tri. Apr70 XXIV Corps grid per Don Armstrong. Quang Tri Pr, I Corps.

Division Hill (AT 97-74)
See Division Ridge. Quang Nam Pr, I Corps.

Division Ridge (AT 97-74)
A.k.a. Division Hill and Hill 327. On Ridge apx 3 km W Da Nang, 4 km WSW Da Nang AB, 2 km NW Hwy 587 and 3.5 km NE Ap Thach Nham. HQ, 1st Mar Div here. Map is L-7014-6641-3. Quang Nam Pr, I Corps.

Division Trains (82d Abn) (XS 798-862)
Initial FSE (Forward Supply Element) supt cmpd of 3d Bde/82d Abn at Tan Son Nhut AB, when it moved S from I Corps in Sep-Oct68. This site also became site of all Bn HQ and Co rear areas of 3d Bde/82d Abn. In Fall of '68, initial fwd cmd post for 3d Bde/82d Abn was at "Tent City" in Bien Hoa Basecamp when Bde moved S from I Corps (Hue AO) beginning in Sep-Oct68 to take up its new AO covering the W and NW approaches to Saigon. It immed became apparent fwd Bde HQ needed to be closer to its actual AO, so a site was found at Camp Red Ball (XS 832-984) along N edge of Tan Son Nhut AB. Construction

of Bde's TOC at Camp Red Ball began 1Oct68 and it was operational by 16Oct68. During same period, new basecamp for Bde was built at Phu Loi Post (XT 860-155), and occupied on 20Oct68. [167] Gia Dinh Pr, III Corps.

Divisions navales d'assuaut (n/a)
See Glossary.

Divorce, FSB (n/a)
Location unknown. 7th/8th Arty here, 70. Name per Dan Gillotti, 15th Arty Assn. III Corps.

Dixie, LZ (AT 9-5?)
Somewhere in general vic of An Hoa Industrial Complex, SW of Da Nang (AT 92-53). During Op MACON, LZ and on 6Jul66, 2 full Bns were inserted at both LZ Dixie and LZ Savannah. At end of op, 10Jul66, 8 US were KIA and 33 WIA, with 87 rptd NVA KIA. Quang Nam Pr, I Corps.

Dixie Pete, LZ (XD 97-68?)
Said to have been 1 km N FSB Pete (XD 977-585) and occupied by G/2d/3d Marines, 3d Mar Div. On 21Sep69, those elements were attacked here, suffering 2 KIA and 59 WIA, in what was one of last attacks on 3d Mar Div before it went home in late '69. Grid is est based on grid of LZ Pete. Quang Tri Pr, I Corps.

Dixie Station (n/a)
Staging area in South China Sea for 7th Fleet's Task Force 77 Carrier Strike Grp in '65-66 operating in southern part of VN AO. Was at 11°N, 110°E, a point apx 130 km SE of Cam Ranh Bay. On map at: www.history.navy.mil/seairland/ch67big.gif. See Yankee Station. SVN.

Dizzy, FSB (ES? 480-840?)
Grid listed in ES grid zone, but no such grid zone exists? Listed as being at this grid in Jan69, while FSB Dizzy is also listed at WS 990-560 and 990-550 in Jan69? If grid were BS 480-840, site was apx 20 km NW Quang Ngai and 4 km due N Ba Gi AF in Quang Ngai Pr, I Corps?

Dizzy, FSB (WS 990-560)
Apx 14 km WNW Cai Lay and 23 km N Vinh Long. Also listed at WS 990-550. Jan69. Dinh Tuong Pr, IV Corps.

Djamap Airfield (YU 340-368)
A.k.a. Ap Bu Gia Map and Bu Ja Map AF. Apx 1 km SW Bu Gia Map, 37 km ENE Bu Dop AF, 25 km SW Bu Krak AF, 38 km WSW Bu Prang AF and 10 km from Cambodia. El. 1,260', 3,700' laterite rwy. At 12°05'13"N-107°08'55"E. Phuoc Long Pr, III Corps.

Djamap Heliport (YU 344-377)
See Bu Ja Mop AF. Phuoc Long Pr, III Corps.

Djamap SF Camp (YU 344-375)
Apparently a.k.a. Bu Ghia Map SF Camp. At or near Djamap AF, apx 12 km from Cambodia, 67 km NE Loc Ninh and 145 km NNE Saigon. 5th SF. See Bu Gia Map and Bu Ghia Map. Info/grid per *SF Order of Battle.* Phuoc Long Pr, III Corps.

Django, FSB (YU 3-1?)
Apparently in vic of FSB Joan (YU 335-108)? "FSBs Django and Joan closed on 23 and 25Feb70 respectively and 8th Abn Bn displaced to establish FSB Lolita (YU 369-261). As move N gained momentum and enemy activity increased, FSB's Candy, Loan, and Audie were established on 25, 26 and 27 Feb70 respectively...The 1st Abn Bn (-) moved to establish FSB Loan, leaving one rifle Co to secure FSB Judie." [168] Phuoc Long Pr?, III Corps.

Djarl SF Camp (ZT 084-833)
A few km N Tan Phat AF, apx 6 km NNE Bao Loc and 75 km SW Dalat. 5th SF. Relocated to Go Dau Ha. Info/grid per *SF Order of Battle.* Lam Dong Pr, II Corps.

Djiring Airfield (AN 849-792)
Apx 4 km ESE Di Linh, 6 km WNW peak Brai An Mtn, and 31 km due E Bao Loc. "Insecure, abnd, Mines suspected on field, AF # VA2-48," in Aug69 TAD per Frank Penk, Jr. Not in Feb73 TAD. Lam Dong Pr, II Corps.

Djmap (YU 34-37)
See Djamap. Phuoc Long Pr, III Corps.

Djran, Rapides de Lierg (YT 5-5)
River rapids on Song Dong Nai River, within 10 km SSW Loi Tan and roughly 20 km NW Vo Dat. NIMA data. Long Khanh Pr, III Corps.

DMZ (XD/YD)
The Demilitarized Zone. Sardonically nicknamed the "Dead Man's Zone." Dividing line between NVN and SVN, along 17th Parallel, established by Geneva Convention in 1954. Apx 30 km wide, it was abused to shelter NVA infiltration into SVN and was site of heavy fighting between USMC and NVA at various times. Its purported demilitarized status was generally ignored by both opposing forces as matter of necessity. Ben Hai River formed actual dividing line between the two countries and the boundaries of DMZ conformed to its course for apx 2/3ds of border's width. Quang Tri Pr, I Corps.

Do, Hon (BN 9-7)
See Hon Do. Ninh Thuan Pr, II Corps.

Do, Mui (XQ 7-5)
A.k.a. Mui Ca Map. Coastal point at 8°38'N-106°37'E. On NC48-11 JOG. IV Corps.

Do Ke Giai, General (n/a)
See Glossary.

Do Khe Airfield (n/a)
Apx 80 km S Vinh. Per map in *Vietnam Experience* Series, *Rain of Fire* vol, p. 11. NVN.

Do Son (n/a)
Mapsheet name of L-7014-6350-2. NVN only.

Do Son Beach (XH 8-9?)
Palm-lined beach at Do Son, apx 21 km SE of Hai Phong. Regarded as most popular seaside resort in northern part of Vietnam. 4 km-long peninsula there ends with string of small islands. 9 hills that line the peninsula are called the Cuu Long Son (the Nine Dragons). Do Son is well-known for its Water Buffalo fights, held annually on 10th day of each 8th lunar month (the date on which a celebrated 18th century peasant rebel leader was killed). NVN.

Do Son Peninsula (XH 8-9)
Controlled access to Haiphong Harbor. See *Newport News, USS*, and *Oklahoma City, USS.* NVN.

Do Son, Pointe (XH 8-9)
See Pointe Do Son. NVN.

Do Son, Presqu'ile de (XH 8-9)
Peninsula at 20°43'N-106°46'E. On NF48-16 JOG. NVN.

Do Xa (various)
Common Viet place name. NIMA Gaz lists sites at: XJ 4-3, XJ 1-0, WH 9-9, WG 6-9, all of which are in NVN. It lists none in SVN.

Do Xa Base Area (AS 86-80)
On western edge of I Corps/II Corps border generally surrounding point where Quang Tin and Quang Ngai Provs met Lao border, apx 55 km SW Tam Ky. Enemy stronghold in rugged mtns that had been under communist control since early stages of war until 1st attacked by allied forces during VNMC Op Bach Phoung XI, in '63. In ancient Vietnamese history area was used to hide from invading Chinese armies. On map at p 104 of *US Marines in Vietnam, 1967*. Quang Tin/Quang Ngai Prvs, I & II Corps.

Do Xa SF Camp (XS 10-41?)
Apparently an SF Camp here. If listed grid accurate, was apx 40 km due W My Tho, and on N bank of the Mekong River. Author has little confidence in listed grid. Dinh Tuong Pr?, IV Corps?

Doan (n/a)
See Glossary.

Doan Hung (n/a)
Mapsheet name of L-7014-6052-3. NVN only.

Doan Van, Ap (n/a)
Mapsheet L-7014-6433-2. Full sheet name: Ap Doan Van. SVN/Cambodia.

Doc Kinh CAP (n/a)
Papa 5, 4th CAG per T. Duffie's CAP Vets website at www.capmarine.com. Quang Tri Pr, I Corps.

Doc Kinh, Thon (n/a)
Mapsheet L-7014-6342-2. Full sheet name: Thon Doc Kinh. SVN/Laos.

Doc Lap Brigade (n/a)
See Glossary.

Doc Lop BOQ (CP 035-049?)
In downtown Han Trang, apx 2 km NNE the NW end of the Nha Trang AF main rwy and 1.2 km NE IFFV HQ. Khanh Hoa Pr, II Corps.

Doc, Mui (XE 5-8)
Coastal point at 17°58'N-106°30'E. NE48-12 JOG. NVN.

Dodge, LZ (XD 911-641)
On S edge of DMZ, apx 22 km WNW Cam Lo, 18 km NNW Ca Lu and 7 km NNW FSB Cunningham. On map at p 58, *US Marines in Vietnam-1969*. 3d Mar Div, '69. Apr70 XXIV Corps grid per Don Armstrong. Also listed at XD 94-65? Quang Tri Pr, I Corps.

Dodge City BEQ & Mess (XS 829-925)
In the MACV Annex, at Tan Son Nhut AB, Saigon, and just E the MACV HQ Cmpd. Gia Dinh Pr, III Corps.

Dodge City (BT 14-57)
VC infested area generally16 km due S Da Nang and on W side of QL-1. Go Noi Island formed its southern border. Named to reflect its "wild-west" character and ubiquitous booby-traps, mines and frequent enemy contact. A dangerous area at any time of war. Quang Nam Pr, I Corps.

Dodge City/Go Noi Island (BT 14-57/02-54)
USMC nickname for area of ops S of Da Nang. These were contiguous areas, with Dodge City covering roughly the N 1/2 and Go Noi the S 1/2 of a roughly rectangular area S of Da Nang from 10-20 km, bordering on and to W of QL-1, and from 6 to 20 km W of Hoi An. Area was apx 10 x 20 km and inc W portion of Dien Ban Dist, E 1/2 of Dai Loc Dist, and some 19 hamlets. Bordered on W by Song Vu Gia River; on N by Song Ai Nghia, Song Lo Tho and Song Than Quit Rivers; on E by QL-1; and on S by Song Thu Bon, Song Ba Ren and Song Chiem Son Rivers. Meandering course of Song Thu Bon separated Dodge City on N from Go Noi Island on S. Characterized by semi-open terrain covered with many rice fields, burial mounds, expanses of elephant grass, all interlaced with hedgerows and brushy areas. Both were VC havens throughout war and noted for booby-traps, mines and frequent ambushes. Quang Nam Pr, I Corps. [169]

Dodge City (BR 477-435)
See Sin City at listed grid. Binh Dinh Pr, II Corps.

Doe (n/a)
6Apr70, XXIV Corps proposed 5th Div FSB name.

Doezema Compound (YD 767-218?)
See Frank Doezema Cmpd and Hue MACV Cmpd. Thua Thien Pr, I Corps.

Dog, AO (BT?)
A.k.a. Sniper Valley, per *Rites of Passage*, pp 394, 449. Quang Ngai Pr, I Corps.

Dog, FSB/LZ (BS 88-01?)
A.k.a. LZ English, see English, LZ. Binh Dinh Pr, II Corps.

Dog, FSB (XT 617-521)
Apx 22 km NW Lai Khe, 15 km ENE Dau Tieng/Tri Tam. Mar-Apr67. Binh Duong/Binh Long Pr border, III Corps.

Dog, LZ (BN 178-541)
Apx 12 km NW Song Mao AF and 3 km WSW LZ Cat. Mar67. Binh Thuan Pr, II Corps.

Dog, LZ (BP 961-635?)
If grid correct, was apx 15 km NNW Nha Trang AF and 16 km S Ninh Hoa 28Apr67. Also listed at BP 988-645, same date? Khanh Hoa Pr, II Corps.

Dog, LZ (BP 988-645?)
If grid correct, was apx 13 km NNW Nha Trang AF and 16 km S Ninh Hoa. 28Apr67. Also listed at BP 961-635, same date? Khanh Hoa Pr, II Corps.

Dog, LZ (BR 695-684?)
If grid correct, was apx 11 km W Hoi San and 32 km NW An Khe. 10Oct67. Also listed at BR 782-908 on same rpt? Binh Dinh Pr, II Corps.

Dog, LZ (BR 782-908?)
If grid correct, was apx 8 km NNW Ha Tay and 9 km SW Bong Son. 10Oct67. Also listed at BR 695-684 on same rpt? Binh Dinh Pr, II Corps.

Dog, LZ (BS 881-005)
Apparently original site of what became LZ English. In Bong Son plain just W of QL-1, apx 7 km NNE Bong Son and 70 km NNE An Khe. Per *Chickenhawk*, p 268, LZ was in ancient Vietnamese burial ground surrounded by VC controlled villes. In initial assault to secure site (early '66, during Op Masher/White Wing and following naval and arty bombardment), among the forty 1st Cav helos involved in CA, 20 were damaged and 5 shot down, killing 2 pilots and 2 gunners (possibly 227th AHC). See An Lao Valley. Map is L-7014-6737-4, per Ken Burrington. Binh Dinh Pr, II Corps. [170]

Dog, LZ (BS 881-996?)
15th Arty Assn grid; however, puts this site in ocean and grid is in error. II Corps.

Dog, The (n/a)
See Glossary.

Dog Airfield, LZ (BS 879-010)
See English AF. Binh Dinh Pr, II Corps.
Dog Bone Island (XS/YS)
Island in Dong Nai River roughly shape of a dog biscuit. 15 km E Saigon, 4 km SW VC Island, 2 km E Cat Lai, and perhaps 7 km ENE confluence of Dong Nai and Saigon Rivers. 1st Inf Div, '69. Per *Low Level Hell's* 1st Inf Div TAOR map. III Corps.
Dog Bone, LZ (YB 911-121)
Apx 14 km SSE Ben Het, 17 km E Laos, 15 km SW Dak To 2 AF, 8 km SE Dak Wang Kram and 41 km NW Kontum. 1st/35th Inf/4th Div fwd base, early May68, per Dick Arnold. Grid per Phil Landis. Kontum Pr, II Corps.
Dog Leg Village (XT 860-230)
A.k.a. Chanh Long. Ville shaped like a dog's leg stretched-out along Rte 1A, apx 10 km NNE Phu Cuong, 4 km N Phu Loi AF and 25 km N Saigon. 1st Inf Div. Per *Low Level Hell's* 1st Div TAOR map. Binh Duong Pr, III Corps.
Dog Patch, The (AT 985-774)
See Dogpatch. Quang Nam Pr, I Corps.
Dog's Face (WT 95-85)
A.k.a. Dog's Head. Cambodian border feature along Tay Ninh Pr, apx 48 km S the Fishhook and perhaps 70 km W Saigon. Border here resembled that of a Boxer dog's head facing E. Invaded 2d week of May70 by elements of 9th, 25th Inf and various ARVN Divs during Cambodian Incursion. FSB Illingworth was at eye of dog's face and FSB Jay was to S where its collar would be, both being inside SVN. Tay Ninh Pr, III Corps.
Dog's Head (WT 95-85)
See Dog's Face. Tay Ninh Pr, III Corps.
Dogbone, The (n/a)
Apparently a geographical feature at or near Khe Sanh CB. Quang Tri Pr, I Corps.
Dogpatch, The (AT 958-773)
Generally W Da Nang AB. Area of dilapidated homes, bars and restaurants on road between Da Nang and Hill 327. Also listed at AT 990-740. Quang Nam Pr, I Corps.
Dogpatch POW Camp, The (n/a)
Inmate nickname for POW camp near Hanoi. See: www.soft-vision.com/hanoi/frame.html. NVN.
Dogtoampua, Mui (VR 8-3)
Coastal point at 9°20'N-104°50'E. On NC48-10 JOG. An Xuyen Pr, IV Corps.
Doi, Mui (CP 3-9)
Coastal point at 12°39'N-109°28'E. On ND49-13 JOG. Khanh Hoa Pr, II Corps.
Doi 300, FSB (YD 327-337)
See FSB Barbara. Thua Thien Pr, I Corp.
Doi Ma Creek, Battle of (XS 670-690)
Grid is in Rach Doi Ma, apx 12 km ENE Tan An and 1 km N Ap Ben Do and Song Vam Co Dong River. Took place 16-17Apr67, during Op Enterprise, 5/60th, C/3/60th and C/3/39th Inf of 3rd Bde/9th Inf Div engaged enemy near Ap Ray (644-702) and Ap Ben Do (adj villes with this name at XS 658-691 and 668-677), resulting in 73 VC KIA, 11 US casualties. Long An Pr, III Corps.
Doi Seang Airfield (RD 09-35)
LS-160. CIA/SF, per *Air Facilities Data-Laos.*
Doll, FSB (YT)
Possibly FSB Dolly? No data.
Dollar (n/a)
6Apr70, XXIV Corps proposed 5th Div FSB name.
Dollar, LZ (BR 874-845)
Apx 5 km W Van AN and QL-1, 11 km SSE Bong Son. Oct66. Binh Dinh Pr, II Corps.
Dolly, LZ (XT 522-588)
A.k.a. FSB Doll or Dolly? At N end of Razorback Ridge, on or immed N of Hill 284, apx 13 km NNE Dau Tieng, 25 km due E Nui Ba Den and 14 km SW Minh Thanh AF. Agent Orange map courtesy Ed Regan indicates site was roughly due S LZ Joe, perhaps 40 km WNW Phuoc Vinh, 15 km NE Dau Tieng and due E LZ White. Per Rod Barber, D/229th AHC, '69-70, who landed here many times, it "was on top of the Razorbacks just N of Dau Tieng." 1st/5th Cav, 1st Cav, '69, 2d/12th Cav, 1st Cav, Jul-69. Grid per Frank Penk, Jr. Binh Duong Pr, III Corps.
Dolphin (n/a)
6Apr70, XXIV Corps proposed 5th Div FSB name.
Dominate, FSB (XT 707-441)
Apx 9 km NW Lai Khe AF and 8 km WSW Ap Bau Bang. Oct69. Binh Duong Pr, III Corps.
Dominique (TJ 9-6)
One of series of at least 3 defensive positions at Dien Bien Phu, a.k.a. D1, D2 and D3, and "The Dominiques." Generally NE Main CP at DBP, "To the east, two-thirds of a mile beyond the river, rose a series of hills stretching north and south, the Elianes with their central peak, Eliane 2, and Dominiques with their central peak, Dominique 3, held by Moroccans and dominating the airfield."[171] In Muong Thanh Valley apx 290 km W Hanoi. French strongpoint during Op Castor, 20Nov53-7May54. Fell to Vietminh 2May54. NVN.
Domino, LZ (XD 865-171)
If grid correct, was at S tip of Vietnam Salient, apx 12 km SSE Lang Cei and 34 km SSW Ca Lu. Apr70 XXIV Corps grid per Don Armstrong. Also listed at XD 822-278? Quang Tri Pr, I Corps.
Domino, LZ (XD 822-278)
If grid correct, was at N end of Vietnam Salient, apx 3 km NW Lang Chie and 56 km WSW Quang Tri. Mar69. Also listed at XD 865-121? Quang Tri Pr, I Corps.
Domino Theory (n/a)
See Glossary.
Don, FSB (YT 162-108)
Apx 31 km due W Xuan Loc, 10 km E Plantation AF and 16 km ESE Bien Hoa AB. Bien Hoa Pr, III Corps.
Don, FSB (YU 161-110)
Apx 4 km due W Song Be City AF, 5 km due W Phuoc Binh, 5 km NNE Song Be AF and 115 km NNE Saigon. 2d/12th Cav, 1st Cav, '69. Grid per Frank Penk, Jr. Cited in 1st Cav VN *Yearbook* Aug65-Dec69, p 185, 278, per Peter Cole. Phuoc Long Pr, III Corps.
Don, LZ (BR 728-455)
Apx 5 km ENE Binh Khe and 25 km due E An Khe. Oct65. Binh Dinh Pr, II Corps.
Don, LZ (BS 761-278)
Near FSB Tempest, apx 13 km SSW Duc Pho AF, 19 km ESE Ba To and 21 km NE Gia An. Also listed at BS 764-277 per arty ORLL and per XXIV Corps facility index. Americal list. Binh Dinh Pr, II Corps.

Don, LZ (XD 63-27)
Apx 28 km SW Khe Sanh, 20 km SW Lang Vei and 18 km SE A Loui. ARVN LZ in Laos, Lam Son 719, Apr71, 1st ARVN Div. Good Lam Son 719 FSB map at www.americal.org/174/map4.htm. Laos.
Don Dien An Loc (YT 42-11)
Plantation de An Loc. Apx 5 km NE Xuan Loc. Long Khanh Pr, III Corps.
Don Dien An Vieng (YS 2-9)
Plantation de An Vieng. Bien Hoa/Gia Dinh Pr, III Corps.
Don Dien Ban Tieu (XS 9-8)
Plantation de Ban Tieu. Gia Dinh Pr, III Corps.
Don Dien Binh Loc (YT 4-1)
Plantation de Binh Loc. Long Khanh Pr, III Corps.
Don Dien Bourgery (AP 9-8)
Plantation de Bourgery. Darlac Pr, II Corps.
Don Dien Cau Khoi (XT 3-4)
Plantation de Cau Khoi and a.k.a. Don Dien Cau Khoi. Tay Ninh Pr, III Corps.
Don Dien Courtenay (YS 4-9)
Plantation de Courtenay. The Courtenay Rubber Plantation. Long Khanh/Phuoc Tuy Pr, III Corps.
Don Dien Da Kir (YU 0-1)
A.k.a. Plantation Xa Da Kir. Phuoc Long Pr, III Corps.
Don Dien Halle Concession (XT 8-4)
Plantation de Halle Concession (also spelled Hallet). Binh Duong or Phuoc Long Pr, III Corps.
Don Dien Long Thanh (YS 2-9)
Plantation de Long Thanh. Site of *Societe Terras Rouge,* Society of the Red Earth (or Terrace or Plains?). Bien Hoa and/or Gia Dinh Pr, III Corps.
Don Dien Michelin Plantation (XT 54-50)
Immed to NE Dau Tieng, apx 25 km due E Tay Ninh, 25 km ESE Nui Ba Den, 55 km NW Cu Chi, 15 km N Ben Suc, intersected by Rtes 244 and 239 with QL-14 forming its western border, 10 km SW Minh Than Rubber Plantation and 20 km due W Ap Bau Bang. Roughly 12 x 18 km in size. Site of Op Attleboro, 196th LIB and later elements of 4th Div, 25th Inf Div and 173d Abn along with ARVN elements totaling over 22,000 allied troops (largest op in war to that point) and battling 271st, 272d, 273d and 101st VC Rgts, 9th VC Div, Sep-Nov66. War Zone C, Binh Duong Pr, III Corps.
Don Dien Nguyen Dinh Quat (XT 8-4)
Plantation de Nguyen Dinh Quat. Binh Duong or Phuoc Long Pr, III Corps.
Don Dien Ong Que (YS 3-9)
Plantation de Ong Que. Long Khanh Pr, III Corps.
Don Dien Peysson (YT 4-0)
Plantation de Peysson. Long Khanh Pr, III Corps.
Don Dien Phu Reng (YT 1-9)
Plantation de Phu Reng. Phuoc Long Pr, III Corps.
Don Dien Phu Rieng (YT 1-9)
Plantation de Phu Rieng. Phuoc Long Pr, III Corps.
Don Dien Sauveterre (YS 4-9)
Plantation de Sauveterre. Long Khanh Pr, III Corps.
Don Dien Souchere (YS 4-9)
Plantation de Souchere. Long Khanh Pr?, III Corps.
Don Dien Suzzanah (YT 3-1)
Plantation de Suzzannah. Bien Hoa Pr, III Corps.
Don Dien Thies (XT 3-4)
Plantation de Thies and a.k.a. Don Dien Cau Khoi. Tay Ninh Pr, III Corps.
Don Dien Thuan Loi (YT 0-8)
Plantation de Thuan Loi. Bien Hoa/Gia Dinh Pr, III Corps.
Don Dien Ven Ven (XT 35-32)
Plantation de Ven Ven. Tay Ninh Pr, III Corps.
Don Dien Xuan Loc (YT 4-0)
Plantation de Xuan Loc. Long Khanh Pr, III Corps.
Don Duong (BP 3-1)
A.k.a. Dran. Near 11°51'00"N-108°35'00"E, within 20 km NE Dalat (also a Ho Don Duong at BP 4-1?). Tuyen Duc Pr, II Corps.
Don Duong (n/a)
Mapsheet name of L-7014-6732-4. SVN.
Don Duong Dam (BP 395-122)
Freshwater Dam along QL-11 apx 20 km SE Dalat. Tuyen Duc Pr, II Corps.
Don Luan Airfield (YT 062-753)
See Dong Xoai AF. Phuoc Long Pr, III Corps.
Don Muang, Tha Akatsayan (PR 7-3)
See Don Muang International Airport and Bangkok International Airport. Thailand.
Don Muang Air Force Base (PR 7-3)
A.k.a. Bangkok Intl. Airport. Apx 25 km NNE Bangkok proper? See Don Muang AB. Thailand.
Don Muang Airbase (PR 7-3)
A.k.a. Bangkok Intl Airport and Tha Akatsayan Don Muang Airport. Perhaps 25 km NNE Bangkok, 130 km SSE Takhli AB, 215 km SW Khorat AB, 730 km NW Saigon and about 50 km N the ocean. Major US bomber and fighter-bomber airbase in Thailand. See map in *Vietnam Experience* Series, *Rain of Fire* vol, p. 11. Bell Tone (code name for USAF air defense det) here. At 13°54'00"N-100°38'00"E. NIMA data. El. 12'. Thailand.
Don Muang Airfield (PR 7-3)
At Bangkok. SF Camp location possibly here per *SF Order of Battle*. El. 12'. Thailand.
Don Muang SF Camp (PR 7-3)
At Bangkok Intl. Airport, Thailand? SF camp or AO per *SF Order of Battle*. Thailand.
Don Nhon District (XS 6-2)
See Dong Nhon District. Kien Hoa Pr, IV Corps.
Don Phuoc Airfield (WT 516-010)
Apx 10 km from Cambodia, 35 km W Binh Than Thon AF, 41 km NE Chau Duc AF, 50 km NNW Cau Lanh AF 135 km due W Saigon. Per TPC K-10D. El. 12', 2,000' sod/clay rwy. 10°51'45"N-105°28'30"E. Kien Phong Pr, IV Corps.
Don Phuoc SF Camp (WT 513-010)
See Don Phuoc (New) SF Camp. Kien Phong Pr, IV Corps.
Don Phuoc (New) SF Camp (WT 513-010)
A.k.a. Don Phuoc SF Camp. Adj to Do Phuoc AF apx 10 km from Cambodia, 35 km W Binh Than Thon AF, 41 km NE Chau Duc AF, 135 km due W Saigon. SF Det 74, 5th SF Grp, Det. A-211, Dec64, A-430 Mike Force, Oct66. Transferred to RF/PF. Grid per *SF Order of Battle*. Kien Phong Pr, IV Corps.
Don Quan (n/a)
Mapsheet name of L-7014-6352-2. NVN only.

Don Son Peninsula (XH 8-9)
A.k.a. Do Son, Presqu'ile de. Peninsula at 20°43'N-106°46'E. On NF48-16 JOG. NVN.

Don Xoai (n/a)
Mapsheet name of L-7014-6332-2. SVN.

Don's Strip Airfield (UH 23-03)
LS-219. CIA/SF, per *Air Facilities Data-Laos.*

Donahue, LZ (BR?)
A.k.a. LZ Donahue/Corregidor. Apparently near LZ English and/or LZ Uplift? Cited in excerpt of '70 Bn Annual Historical supplement of 3d/503d Inf at www. gasparot.com/ nammedic. Binh Dinh Pr?, II Corps.

Donahue/Corregidor, LZ (BR?)
See Donahue or Corregidor. Binh Dinh Pr?, II Corps.

Doner, LZ (AT 934-242)
See LZ Donner. Quang Tin Pr, I Corps.

Dong (n/a)
Vietnamese for "East" when used <u>following</u> a place name. When used <u>before</u> a place name, such as "Dong Ha," means "Mountain" Ha or Mountain of Ha. Dong also means "village," and the "Dong" was also a unit of SVN currency.

Dong, Dam (YD 9-1)
A.k.a. Dam Thuy Tu. Lagoon at 16°26'N-107°46'E. On NE48-16 JOG. Thua Thien Pr, I Corps.

Dong A Tay (YC 490-980)
A.k.a. Bloody Ridge or Hill 890? Apx 36 km SW Hue, 3.5 km SSE FSB Zon, 17 km SW FSB Bastogne, SW FSBs Veghel and Blaze, and SE FSB Rendezvous. Elements of 2d/327th Inf and 1st/502d Inf, 101st Abn pushed NVA W of FSB Veghel toward the A Shau for 33 days in Mar-Apr69, until NVA made stand on ridge of Dong A Tay Mtn resulting in 90 NVA KIA. Thua Thien Pr, I Corps.

Dong A Tay Luat (YC 497-995)
A.k.a. Hill 809. See Dong A Tay, Bloody Ridge and Hill 890. Thua Thien Pr, I Corps.

Dong An, FSB (BS 7-7?)
A.k.a. FSB Ap Dong An. Located along Rte 521. Rte 521 runs from coast near My Lai to QL-1, apx 3 km N of Quang Ngia. No other data. Quang Ngia Pr?, I Corps.

Dong Ap Bia (YC 328-981)
A.k.a. Dong Ap Bia, Hamburger Hill, FSB Destiny and known to local Montagnard as The Mountain of Crouching Beast. At NW end of A Shau Valley, apx 45 km WSW Hue, 22 km NW the A Sap/A Shau AF, SF camp/ville complex, 9 km NW Ta Bat, 3 km E Laos and 25 km SE Tou Rout. See Hamburger Hill. Thua Thien Pr, I Corps.

Dong Ba, Mui (CP 0-4)
Coastal point at 12°08'N-109°13'E. On ND49-13 JOG. Khanh Hoa Pr, II Corps.

Dong Ba Canal (YD 7-2)
Murkey channel of Perfume River near Hue's central marketplace. Thua Thien Pr, I Corps.

Dong Ba Gate (YD 75-23?)
See Dong Ba Tower. Thua Thien Pr, I Corps.

Dong Ba Le Mountain (YD 187-274)
A.k.a. FSB Jerome and Hill 1102. Apx 13 km SSE Ba Long AF and 27 km SW Quang Tri. Quang Tri Pr, I Corps.

Dong Ba Point (CP 0-4)
See Point Dong Ba. Khanh Hoa Pr, II Corps.

Dong Ba Thin (CP 040-290)
Along QL-1, apx 5 km NW Cam Ranh Bay AB. Site of Flanders AF. 5th SF Grp SFOB, HQ 18th Engr Bde; 14th Engr Bn; MACV-SOG, USARV-UITG (Individual Trng Grp) Trng Bn, Nov70-Feb73, in 72 was renamed the FANK (Forces Arm'ee Nationale Khmer Trng Cmd), redesignated the Field Trng Cmd when FANK was taken over by 18th ARVN Div, Dec72. AO of Korean 2d MC Blue Dragons Bde in '65, before it moved to Hoi An area in I Corps in '66. See Flanders Field for more detail. Khanh Hoa Pr, II Corps.

Dong Ba Thin Airfield (CP 032-295)
Apx 22 km due S Nha Trang's major AF, on coast just E QL-1 and only 4 km NW Cam Ranh Bay's major airport, per TPC K-10A. El. 6', 2,300' asph rwy. At 12°01'18"N-109°11'42"E. CP 040-290. Khanh Hoa Pr, II Corps.

Dong Ba Thin Basecamp (CP 041-256)
Along QL-1, just S Xom My Cao near intersect of QL-1 and road that went E to Cam Ranh Bay AF complex, apx 4 km SW the center of Cam Ranh Bay's main rwy. Jan66. Khanh Hoa Pr, II Corps.

Dong Ba Thin Heliport (CP 027-295)
A.k.a. Flanders Army Heliport. Apparently on W side of Dong Ba Thin AF, apx 23 km due S Nha Trang AF, just SE Thon Tan Thanh and 4 km NE Cam Ranh Bay AB. "Heliport #739, alt 33', 600' x 400' (RC-3) Abnd. Arty positions along QL-1 for apx 10 mi N to 10 mi S. Max ordnance up to 15,000' firing to W. See Dong Ba Thin A/D Rmk," per Feb73 TAD. Khanh Hoa Pr, II Corps.

Dong Ba Thin SF Camp (CP 040-290)
E of Dong Ba Thin AF, and apx 5 km NNW Cam Ranh Bay AB. Major 5th SF camp. SF Det 37, Det B-51, 5th SF Grp, 5th SF Grp SFOB, Det. A-132, Det B-1, Dec64, Det B-51 (was B-1), Project Delta Det A-521 was 411), Oct65. Info/grid per *SF Order of Battle.* Transferred to DBTTC Unit. See Dong Ba Thin. Khanh Hoa Pr, II Corps.

Dong Ba Tower (YD 75-23?)
Guard tower at Dong Ba Gate of Imperial Palace in Hue. Along Mai Thuc Loan St. and within the Citadel. Major NVA strongpoint during Battle for Hue, Tet '68. Data per John Middlesworth. Thua Thien Pr, I Corps.

Dong Bac, Mui (XQ 8-6)
Coastal point on Con Son Island at 8°45'N-106°40'E. NC48-11 JOG. South China Sea.

Dong Bac, Vinh (XQ 8-6)
Bay on Con Son Island at 8°43'N-106°39'E. On NC48-11 JOG. South China Sea.

Dong Bac, Vung (XQ 8-6)
See Dong Bac, Vinh. South China Sea.

Dong Ban An 3 CAP (n/a)
See CAP 2-3-3. 2d CAG. Quang Nam Pr?, I Corps.

Dong Bo (YT 42-48)
A.k.a. Hill 182. Apx 75 km NE Saigon and 38 km WNW Vo Dat. Long Khanh Pr, III Corps.

Dong Bo Airfield (YT 369-487)
Apx 2 km W peak Dong Bo Mtn, 45 km due E Phuoc Vinh AF, 36 km WNW Vo Dat and 75 km NE Saigon. Listed as "Abnd, overgrown, unserviceable, AF # VA3-138," in Aug69 TAD per Frank Penk, Jr. Not in Feb73 TAD. Long Khanh Pr, III Corps.

Dong Bo Woods (CP 000-450)
Generally 7 km SW Cam Ranh Bay AB and 3 km ENE peak of Hong Rong Mtn. Khanh Hoa Pr, II Corps.

Dong Ca Puy (YD 479-168)
Apx 2.5 km NNW FSB Bullet and 26 km WSW Hue. Thua Thien Pr, I Corps.

Dong Cam (n/a)
Mapsheet name of L-7014-6835-3. SVN.

Dong Cam (YD)
Ville in DMZ along Rte 102, apx 2 km N the Ben Hai River, 6 km ENE Bo Ho Su and 27 km W Gio Linh. NVN.

Dong Cau Nhi 1 & 2 CAP (n/a)
See CAP 2-3-3. 2d CAG. A Cau Nhi is also listed in Thua Thien Pr at YD 4-4? Quang Nam Pr?, I Corps.

Dong Cha Pa Mountain (UK 74-67)
See Fan Si Pan. NVN.

Dong Che Dien Ridge (XD 846-393)
Hill 471 was at southern tip of this ridge, apx 2.5 km SW Khe Sanh CB. Held strategic value in its commanding view of Khe Sanh CB/plateau and was assaulted by 2d/26th Marines 4Apr68, during Op Pegasus. Attacked 5Apr68, with rptd 122 NVA KIA. Quang Tri Pr, I Corps.

Dong Cho Mountain (YD 019-397)
A.k.a. Hill 824. Apx 17 km E to ESE of Khe Sanh CB and 14 km SE Mai Loc. Apparently scene of heavy fighting for 3d/9th Marines, 5-18Jun69. Quang Tri Pr?, I Corps.

Dong Cho Mountain (YC 510-883)
A.k.a. Hill 820 or 824. Along ridge mass forming E side of A Shau Valley, 5 km due N of A Shau AF, 1 km NE Hill 787 (peak on same ridgeline) and 8 km due W the Be Luong Heliport. Thua Thien Pr, I Corps.

Dong Cung Cap (YD 490-198)
A.k.a. FSB Rakkasan. Apx 26 km W to WSW Hue Citadel AF and 14 km SSE Camp Evans. Thua Thien Pr, I Corps.

Dong Da, FSB? (n/a)
Cited in *1st Cav Op Rpt*, Feb70/Apr70, p 14, per Peter Cole. During that period, Cav was in NW III Corps. There is a Nui Da listed at ZT 08-17 and another at ZT 17-22? Likely III Corps.

Dong Da District (WJ)
One of Hanoi's 4 districts (Quan): Hoan Kiem Dist (city center); Ba Dinh Dist (west area, inc Ho Chi Minh's Tomb); Hai Ba Trung Dist (on Red River, S Hoan Kiem Dist); and Dong Da Dist (SW area).

Dong Da NTC (YD 88-14?)
See Dong Da Natl Trng Ctr. Thua Thien Pr, I Corps.

Dong Da National Training Center (YD 88-14?)
A.k.a. Dong Da NTC. RVNAF Natl Trng Ctr. Apparently an ARVN Basic Trng facility at or near Phu Bai. Near listed grid? Thua Thien Pr, I Corps.

Dong Dang (n/a)
Mapsheet name of L-7014-6352-4. NVN/China.

Dong Dang (XD 802-409)
A.k.a. Hill 689. Apx 4 km WSW Khe Sanh CB, 2 km WNW Hill 552 and 3 km due S Hill 881-S. 1st taken, during Battle for Hill 689, by I/3d/26th Marines 28-29Jun67. 2d battle for hill took place 16-19Apr68, when 1st/9th Marines were heavily engaged while sweeping it. US losses were set at 9 KIA, 46 WIA, 36 MIA and 12 non-battle casualties. Quang Tri Pr, I Corps. [172]

Dong Dang Ridge (XD 809-407)
Near listed grid and apx 3 km W Khe Sanh CB. Possible home of 2d Bn, 101st Rgt, 325(C) NVA Div during siege of that base. Possible sp variant of Dong Dan? Quang Tri Pr, I Corps.

Dong Den (AT 837-827)
A.k.a. Hill 868 (2,847') and LZ/OP Dong Den. Major strategic terrain feature apx 18 km WNW Da Nang AB, and overlooking the Song Cu De River Valley (a.k.a. Elephant Valley) to N, and Red Beach/Da Nang to E and SE. 3d Mar Div OP/LZ/Radio Relay site created by blowing top off the mtn. Initially manned by elements of 3d Recon Bn/3d Mar Div, a radio relay team and a naval gunfire fwd observation team. Site of infamous "Battle of Dong Den," Mar or Feb 66, when elements of A/3rd Recon Bn were overrun by several hundred Rock Apes. Sgt Maj. Fred Murray and Cpl Doug Durham distinguished themselves in the attack, though rumors persist they may have also "soiled themselves" in battle's ferocious opening assault. Battle ended with an unknown number of ape KIA and a significant laundry bill for the startled Marines. Grid per George Neville. Quang Nam Pr, I Corps.

Dong Den, LZ (AT 873-828)
A.k.a. Hill 868 and OP Dong Den. Major strategic terrain feature apx 18 km WNW Da Nang AB, and overlooking the Song Cu De River Valley (Elephant Valley) to N, and Red Beach/Da Nang to E and SE. '70 XXIV Corps grid per Don Armstrong. See Dong Den. Quang Nam Pr, I Corps.

Dong Den Outpost (AT 837-827)
See Dong Den Radio Relay Site. Quang Nam Pr, I Corps.

Dong Den Radio Relay Site (AT 837-827)
Radio relay site/OP manned and secured by elements of 3d Recon Bn, 3d Mar Div in '66-67. See Dong Den for location. Quang Nam Pr, I Corps.

Dong Ha (YD 245-599)
Along the Song Mieu Giang and at intersection of QL-1 and QL-9, apx 13 km NW Quang Tri. 1st major town on QL-1 S of the Ben Hai River. Site of Dong Ha CB. Quang Tri Pr, I Corps.

Dong Ha, FSB (YD 260-600)
Along QL-1 immed SE Dong Ha, 6 km NW Quang Tri AF and 3 km E Dong Ha AF. Apr69. Quang Tri Pr, I Corps.

Dong Ha Airfield (YD 243-597)
Apx 76 km NW Phu Bai, and 13 km NW Quang Tri per ONC J-11. El. 82'. 3,700' alum-mat rwy. At 16°48'44"N-107°06'15"E. Quang Tri Pr, I Corps.

Dong Ha Bridge (YD 242-611)
QL-1 bridge over the Song Mieu Giang, apx 9 km NW Quang Tri AF. Quang Tri Pr, I Corps.

Dong Ha Combat Base (YD 243-597)
On S edge of Dong Ha, apx 13 km NW Quang Tri, 14 km E Cam Lo, 63 km NW Hue. Site of Camp Spillman (?) Seabee and USMC 3d Mar Div base. Army 175mm cannon units here at various times and 1st Cav Div was here in '68. On 3Sep67, base ammo dump was hit by rockets and exploded. Blast ignited fuel bladders in nearby bulk fuel stg area and heavily damage s17 helos of HMM 361. Also site of Battle of Dong Ha, Apr-May68, in which the 8,000 man NVA 320th Div attacked city and its 5,000 USMC defenders; 68 US KIA, apx 865 NVA KIA. Map is L-7014-

6442-4, per Ken Burrington. Also listed at YD 205-605 in Sep70. Quang Tri Pr, I Corps.

Dong Ha Heliport? (YD 244-597)
Listed as Ca Lu Heliport in Feb73 TAD, but that may be an error? Along QL-1, immed SE Dong Ha and 12 km NW Quang Tri. "Heliport #532, alt 33'. Confined due to wires. Altn lndg area on soccer field 400 yds S, at 16°48'30"N-107°06'00"E," per Feb73 TAD. Quang Tri Pr, I Corps.

Dong Ha LCU Ramp (YD 23-62)
On S bank of Song Mieu Giang River, immed W the QL-1 bridge. USN naval river facility suptg USMC 3d Mar Div. On map in *The Marines in Vietnam 1954-1973*, p 241. Quang Tri Pr, I Corps.

Dong Ha Mountain (YD 019-593)
A.k.a. Hill 544, Hill 549 and FSB Fuller. On N side of Cam Lo River apx 22 km due W Dong Ha, 9 km due W Cam Lo, 12 km NNE Vandegrift, 4 km ESE Mutter's Ridge and 3 km N QL-9. See FSB Fuller. Quang Tri Pr, I Corps.

Dong Ha NSA (YD 24-59?)
USN Supt Activity '67-70. Per MRF Assn Website. Quang Tri Pr, I Corps.

Dong Ha Ramp (YD)
See Dong Ha LCU Ramp. Quang Tri Pr, I Corps.

Dong Ha Security Group (YD 320-590?)
HQ of TF Clearwater at Cua Viet Base. Portion of River Security Grp, I Corps. Brown Water Navy units at Cua Viet from Feb68 until TF terminated. TF was Broken into two groups, Dong Ha River Security Grp and Hue River Security Grp (Tan My?/Eagle Beach?). Per *Brown Water, Black Berets*, p 278. Quang Tri Pr, I Corps.

Dong Ha West, FSB (YD 205-605)
Apx 5 km WNW Dong Ha, 16 km WNW Quang Tri and 2 km N QL-9. Apr70 XXIV Corps grid per Don Armstrong. Also listed at YD 204-593. Quang Tri Pr, I Corps.

Dong Hene Airfield (n/a)
Apx 310 km SE Vientiane. El. 500'. Laos.

Dong Hene SF Camp (n/a)
Apx 310 km SE Vientiane. SF camp when Lao neutrality declared, 23Jul62. FTT 7 and 38 here then. Per *Special Forces at War*. MR3, Laos.

Dong Hoa (n/a)
Mapsheet name of L-7014-6028-3. SVN.

Dong Hoa Heliport (YS 063-478)
In Rung Sat Special Zone, right on coast of Cua Soi Rap, apx 21 km W to WNW Vung Tau, 5 km SW Thanh Tho and 47 km SE Saigon. "Heliport #757, alt 7', Cement Pad outside cmpd. Arty advsy-Nha Be 285.0 40.9." At 10°23' N 106°53' E, per Feb73 TAD. Gia Dinh Pr, III Corps.

Dong Hoi (n/a)
Mapsheet name of L-7014-6343-4. NVN only.

Dong Hoi (XE 74-31)
Coastal ville and port apx 165 km SE Vinh. Used as waypoint for NVA troops moving S to Ho Chi Minh Trail. Port and MIG base here attacked by USN acft carriers and Da Nang based US and VNAF acft during Flaming Dart I, 7-8Feb65. On 7Feb65. LBJ ordered a one-time reprisal strike on enemy barracks in NVN. *USS Coral Sea's* CVW-15 and *Hancock's* CVW-21 flew Flaming Dart I, a major attack on Dong Hoi. See Flaming Dart I. NVN.

Dong Hoi Airfield (XE 70-37)
MIG base on coast and 165 km SE Vinh. Per ONC-J-11. El. 59'. NVN.

Dong Hung (n/a)
Mapsheet name of L-7014-5928-2. SVN.

Dong Khe Outpost (n/a)
French frontier outpost along R.C. 4 between Cao Bang and Lang Son in NE Tonkin. Used as regular stopping point for embattled French convoys. It lay in remote valley surrounded by ubiquitous limestone hills and was re-supplied only by air after French discontinued convoys between That Khe and Cao Bang in 1950. During heavy weather that prevented re-supply/reinforcement, was overrun by Giap's newly formed 308th Div on 28May50. Began at 3 a.m. following barrage by arty/mortars Giap's men had manhandled onto surrounding ridges. On 2d day when weather broke, 30 Junker Tri-Motor acft dropped French 3d Colonial Para Bn, who surprised the looting and celebrating Viets (killing over 300) and took post back in 90 minute battle. Among ruins, 3d Par found a notebook outlining Giap's plans to take entire frontier, but warning apparently went unheeded. Monsoons halted further attacks, so Vietminh retired to focus on training, during which they built full scale models of Dong Khe and other frontier outposts and endlessly rehearsed attacks on them. In Sep50, they returned and again battered the post with arty from high ground. After 60 hours of desperate fighting, French lost it forever. The Battle of Dong Khe was in many respects the precursor of Dien Bien Phu battle because terrain, defenses and tactics were almost identical in miniature. See Pho Lu. NVN.[173]

Dong Khet SF Camp (AP 916-497)
Apparently a.k.a. Krong Kno SF Camp. At or adj to Buon Rocat, apx 4 km ENE Duc Xuyen AF and 40 km NW Dalat. 5th SF. Info/grid per *SF Order of Battle.* See Krong Kno. Darlac Pr, II Corps.

Dong La Ruong Mtn (XD 854-513)
A.k.a. Hill 1123. Large hill mass 6 km due N Dong Tri and 9 km NNE Khe Sanh CB. Quang Tri Pr, I Corps.

Dong Li Hi Cliffs (YC 85-97?)
The sheer cliffs of Dong Li Hi Mtn, along Song Ta Trach River apx 30 km S Phu Bai and a few miles N Ruong Ruong Valley. Cited in *Bonnie-Sue*, pp 241-246. Grid is guess. Thua Thien Pr, I Corps.

Dong Luy Tay 1 CAP (BT 0-5)
See CAP 2-3-3. At 15°53'00"N-108°15'00"E, per NIMA. 2d CAG, Quang Nam Pr, I Corps.

Dong Ma (YD 044-585)
A.k.a. Hill 328. Overlooked QL-9 apx 1.5 km N of that road, and was 2.8 km ESE peak Dong Ha and 8 km W Cam Lo. Quang Tri Pr, I Corps.

Dong Mang Chan (YC 766-962)
See FSB Blitz. Thua Thien Pr, I Corps.

Dong Nai River (YT)
See Song Dong Nai River. III Corps.

Dong Nai River Bridge (YT 015-055)
Rte 316 bridge over Song Dong Nai 7 km S Bien Hoa AB, 11 km NE Thu Duc. Bien Hoa Pr, III Corps.

Dong Nam Chan (YC 98-92)
A.k.a. Hill 1208. Apx 38 km SE Hue, 13 km SE Phu Loc and 6 km E FSB Pistol. Thua Thien Pr, I Corps.

Dong Ngai Mountain (YD 381-083)
A.k.a. Hills 1771 and 1774. Twin-peak mtn apx 12 km from Laos, 36 km WSW Hue and 5 km from north end of A Shau Valley. Thua Thien Pr, I Corps.

Dong Nghe (AT 87-65)
Ville just N the tip of Charlie Ridge, apx 6 km W Rte 540 and 15 km SW the southern edge of Da Nang AB. Quang Nam Pr, I Corps.

Dong Nhon District (XS 6-2?)
VC controlled area invaded by 9th Inf/MRF and 3d/34th Arty in Dec68. Cited in Annual Hist Rpt of 3d/34th Arty, for period 1Apr68-31Jan69, on MRF Assn Website at: www.mrfa.org 3_34th.htm. Ville of Dong Nhon is at 10°12'00"N-106°28'00"E. Kien Hoa Pr, IV Corps.

Dong Nhut (ZD 143-049)
A.k.a. Hill 592. Part of prominent hill mass on W edge of Dam Cau Hai Bay and N of Hai Van Pass. Hill 482, Nui Vinh Phong, was other major peak of this hill mass. Both overlooked FSBs Roy, Tomahawk and ocean. 101st Abn AO, '69-71. Thua Thien Pr, I Corps.

Dong Nom Mountain (YC 984-908)
See Hill 1208. Thua Thien Pr, I Corps.

Dong On Do (YD 290-402)
See Anne, FSB. Quang Tri Pr border, I Corps.

Dong Ong Do Mountain (YD 290-402)
See Hill 275 and LZ June. Quang Tri Pr, I Corps.

Dong Ong (YC 58-87)
A.k.a. Hill 831. Apx 15 km E the A Shau Valley, 6 km NNE Be Luong and 1 km S Be Luong Heliport. Thua Thien Pr, I Corps.

Dong Pa Thien (XD 8-5)
See Ghost Mountain. Quang Tri Pr, I Corps.

Dong Phong (n/a)
Rail and vehicle bridges here struck by Carrier TF-77 attempts to blunt NVA Tet '68 offensive. NVN.

Dong Phuc SF Camp (WT 5130-0100)
A.k.a. Don Phuoc SF Camp. Apx 41 km NE Chau Doc and 12 km from Cambodia, 16 km NE Mekong River and 35 km WSW Binh Thanh Thon. Det A-401 here Oct67. 251 MSF troops that were mixture of VN, ethnic Chinese and Cambodians tribes. Found on Dept of Army lists in this sp variation. Kien Phong Pr, IV Corps.

Dong Phuoc Airfield (WT 516-010)
See Don Phuoc AF. Kien Phong Pr, IV Corps.

Dong Re Lao (YD 406-036)
See Eagle's Nest, FSB. Thua Thien Pr, I Corps.

Dong Riang Tuan (XD 94-37)
See Hill 605. Quang Tri Pr, I Corps.

Dong Sa Mui (XD 8-5?)
A.k.a. Hill 1613. At extreme NW corner of Quang Tri Pr, roughly 8 km E Laos and 8 km S the DMZ. See Ghost Mtn. Quang Tri Pr, I Corps.

Dong So Mountain (YD 338-027)
A.k.a. Hill 1120. 4 km N Dong Ap Bia (Hamburger Hill) and 8 km NW A Luoi 1 AF (LZ Stallion) and on W edge of northern A Shau Valley. Thua Thien Pr, I Corps.

Dong Sre Viet (n/a)
Mapsheet name of L-7014-6432-4. SVN.

Dong Suong Airfield (n/a)
Apx 25 km SW Hanoi, per ONC-J-11. El. 81'. NVN.

Dong Ta Bang Mountain (XD 8-5)
N of Lang Phu Trang ridge (Ridge at XD 758-534). See Ghost Mtn. Quang Tri Pr, I Corps.

Dong Ta Tach (YD 42-01?)
A.k.a. FSB Berchtesgarden(?) or Hill 1000 or Hill 1030? See Berchtesgarden. Thua Thien Pr, I Corps.

Dong Tam Airfield (XS 408-453)
Along Mekong River, apx 55 km SW Saigon, 10 km due W My Tho, 7 km W Binh Duc AF, 10 km NW Truc Giang AF and 10 km SW Ben Tranh AF. Per TPC K-10D. El. 5', 2,300' asph rwy. At 10°20'35"N-106°17'23"E. Map is L-7014-6229-1, per Jim Stone. Dinh Tuong Pr, IV Corps.

Dong Tam Basecamp (XS 415-448)
Along N bank Mekong River, apx 7 km WSW My Tho, 10 km SW Ben Tranh AF, 16 km NW Truc Giang and 55 km SW Saigon. 600 acre island created among rice fields by dredging Mekong. Was main 9th Inf Div basecamp Aug68-Aug69, after Div moved from Bearcat (Dec66-Jul68). Base named by Viet Army Chief of Staff, Cao Van Bien at Gen Westmoreland's behest. Westy asked him for name that would represent "the spirit of cooperation between the US and SVN," and Cao said simply, "Dong Tam," which per Ex-PFC John Middlesworth, translates literally as "United Hearts and Minds." A Bde of 9th joined with Navy Seals, USN LST and River Patrol Boat units, SVNMC and elements of 7th ARVN Inf Div to form the MRF here. From May-31Jan69, HQ & Serv Bty 34th Arty constructed mess hall, 3 troop billets, a BOQ a BEQ, HQ, S-4 shop, 2 personnel bunkers and aid station. Map is L-7014-6229-1, per Jim Stone. Dinh Tuong Pr, IV Corps. [174]

Dong Tam Hanh (YD 429-122)
A.k.a. Hill 980 and FSB Maureen. See Maureen, FSB. Thua Thien Pr, I Corps.

Dong Tam Heliport (XS 415-448)
On N side of Dong Tam AF, apx 8 km W to WSW My Tho and 55 km SSW Saigon. "Heliport #752, alt 7', 4000' x 100' asph, 09-27-Uncontrolled. Lctd N side of Dong Tam Afld. Std tfc pattern N heliport 500'. F/W tkof and Ldg W side of heliport. Refuel on N cntr pads, rearm NW pads. HAZARDS-Appr Rwy 09 over Arty site and tfc pattern for Rwy 17 at Dong Tam, VA4-295. Two 220' towers 2000' S. 202' and 180' tower lgt off. Fuel-J4. Ammo-2.75" rockets, 7.62, 40mm. Arty advsy-Dong Tam 222.7, 42.6." At 10°21'N 106°18'E," per Feb73 TAD. Map is L-7014-6229-1, per Jim Stone. Dinh Tuong Pr, IV Corps.

Dong Tam NSA (XS 41-44)
Apx 8 km W to WSW My Tho and 55 km SSW Saigon. USN Supt base, '66-71, per MRF Assn Website. Map is L-7014-6229-1, per Jim Stone. Dinh Tuong Pr, IV Corps.

Dong Tam Seaport (XS 415-448?)
In Mekong River, apx 8 km W to WSW My Tho and 55 km SSW Saigon. Berthing Feet: 800 lineal feet, Draft Max: 15', Cargo Capacity: 1,200 tons/day, Storage Covered w/in 5 km: 89,000 ft^2, Storage Uncov, w/in 5 km: 11,000 yd^2. Grid is for Dong Tam Basecamp. Map is L-7014-6229-1, per Jim Stone. Dinh Tuong Pr, IV Corps. [175]

Dong Tam Supply Point (XS 420-430)
Nov67. Dinh Tuong Pr, IV Corps.

Dong Tam Va (XD 757-469)
A.k.a. Hill 778. 10 km WNW Khe Sanh CB and 2.5 km NW Hill 881-N. On 9May67, 24 Marines were KIA and 19 WIA in battle here. Quang Tri Pr, I Corps.

Dong Tau (n/a)
Mapsheet name of L-7014-6048-2. NVN only.

Dong Thai (n/a)
Mapsheet name of L-7014-5928-1. SVN.

Dong Thap Muoi (XS 0-7)
A.k.a. Plain of Reeds. See Plain of Reeds. III and IV Corps.

Dong Thuong Bridge (n/a)
Reportedly 65 miles S Hanoi. Attacked by US acft, 3Apr65; same day Ham Rong Bridge was attacked. NVN.

Dong Tien (n/a)
See Glossary.

Dong Tien Cong Mountain (YD 324-078)
See FSB Goodman. Thua Thien Pr, I Corps.

Dong Tien Patrol Base (XT 609-247)
A.k.a. Combined Patrol Base Dong Tien. In S portion of Ho Bo Woods and N FSB Patton II, apx 22 km SW Lai Khe. Cited in 3Sep69, AAA of 2d/14th Inf (Golden Dragons), 25th Inf Div, at: www.en.com/users/kramsey/vnr102.html#. Binh Duong Pr, III Corps.

Dong Toan, LZ (YD 029-478)
A.k.a. LZ Sarge, Xa'c, Nui Dong Toan and possibly Nui Ba Ho? May have also been known as OP Sarge at one point. Apx 5 km SW Vandegrift CB, 25 km W Quang Tri, 3 km due E Ca Lu and 6 km WSW Mai Loc. Was overrun by large NVA force and lost to enemy on 30Mar72 during Easter Offensive, while manned by ARVN and US Adv. Also listed at YD 038-478. Apr70 XXIV Corps grid per Don Armstrong. Quang Tri Pr, I Corps.

Dong Toc Airfield (CQ 154-481?)
See Tuy Hoa AF. Phu Yen Pr, II Corps.

Dong Tou Trouein (YD 142-185)
A.k.a. FSB Razor? Apx 58 km due W Hue. See FSB Ranger. Thua Thien Pr, I Corps.

Dong Tranh River (YS 0-4)
A.k.a. Long Tau Channel. Flows through Rung Sat Zone SE Saigon, and to W of the Nha Hai River and to E of the Nha Be (Saigon) River. Gia Dinh Pr, III Corps.

Dong Tranh, Cap de (YS 0-4)
A.k.a. Mui Dong Tranh. Cape at 10°23'N-106°52'E. On NC48-07 JOG. Phuoc Tuy Pr, III Corps.

Dong Tranh, Mui (YS 0-4)
Cape at 10°23'N-106°52'E. On NC48-07 JOG. Phuoc Tuy Pr, III Corps.

Dong Tre (BQ 91-70)
Apx 33 km NW Tuy Hoa, and 10 km SSW HA Bang/QL-1. "Dong Tre" translates literally as "Bamboo Field." SF Camp here attacked Jun66, in what was known as Battle of Dong Tre, during Op Nathan Hale. Battle discussed at length in *The Fields of Bamboo*. SF Det 29, 5th SF Grp, Det. A-233, Dec64, A-222 Oct66. Phu Yen Pr, II Corps.

Dong Tre/Cung Son, Camp (BS 7-1?)
See Le Hai. II Corps.

Dong Tre Airfield (BQ 910-705)
Apx 20 km WNW Tuy An AF, 35 km NW Tuy Hoa, 55 km SSW Qui Nhon AF, 26 km SW Song Cau AF and 68 km ESE Cheo Reo AF, per TPC K-10A. El. 60', 2,500' steel-mat rwy. At 13°17'50"N-109°04'16"E. Also listed at BQ 909-704. Phu Yen Pr, II Corps.

Dong Tre Gong Mountain (YC 608-827)
A.k.a. Hill 1030. Apx 40 km SSW Hue and 4 km W Be Loung (A Shau Valley). Thua Thien Pr, I Corps.

Dong Tre Heliport (BQ 909-704)
In valley at Dong Tre SF Camp, apx 26 km SW Song Cau AF, 30 km NNE Son Hoa/Cung Son AF and 33 km NW Tuy Hoa. "Heliport #561, alt 66'. Houses SE side, hill SW side", per Feb73 TAD. Phu Yen Pr, II Corps.

Dong Tre SF Camp (BQ 909-704)
In valley apx 26 km SW Song Cau AF, 30 km NNE Son Hoa/Cung Son AF and 33 km NW Tuy Hoa. 5th SF. Info/grid per *SF Order of Battle.* Converted to RF/PF. Phu Yen Pr, II Corps.

Dong Tri Mountain (XD 855-454)
A.k.a. Hill 1015. Dominates Khe Sanh Valley NE Lang Vie and WNW Khe Sanh AF. Used as OP by both sides at various times during siege of Khe Sanh CB. Also spelled Dong Tre. Map is L-7014-6342-3, per Ken Burrington. Quang Tri Pr, I Corps.

Dong Trieu (n/a)
Mapsheet name of L-7014-6351-3. NVN only.

Dong Trieu (XJ 57-32)
Coal Mining area NW Haiphong and within arty range of Mao Khe. French garrison here participated in Battle of Mao Khe, Mar51. Vietminh from this region were enlisted to dig the miles of trenches/tunnels used at Dien Bien Phu. Their work was particularly effective in digging tunnel under Strongpoint E2, in which massive explosive charge was detonated at 11pm, 6May54. In the huge blast, Capt. Come's 2d Co of 1st BCP completely disappeared. Gaping hole it produced can still be seen today. NVN.

Dong Trieu Mountains (XJ 5-3)
NW Haiphong. Following his stunning defeat at Battle of Vinh Yen, 13-17Jan51, Gen. Giap turned his focus toward this sensitive area. It controlled approaches to coal mines around Mao Khe and was within 30 km of Haiphong. The 308, 312th and 316th Vietminh Div began ops here with an opening attack toward Mao Khe, night of 23-24Mar51. See Chp 2 of *Street Without Joy*, p 41. NVN.

Dong Truoi (YC 9-9)
A.k.a. Hill 1170. Apx 12 km WSW of Phu Loc and 10 km ESE FSB Rifle? NIMA Gaz indicates site was near 16°14'00"N-107°45'00"E. Thua Thien Pr, I Corps.

Dong Van (n/a)
AMS/DMA mapsheet L 701-6080-2. NVN/China.

Dong Voi Mep (XD 84-54)
A.k.a. Hill 1739 or Tiger Tooth Mtn (sometimes also Hill 1701?). Apx 10 km NW Khe Sanh CB, 15 km SE Dong Sa Mui (Hill 1613), 15 km S the DMZ and 20 km W Laos. See LZ Crest, LZ Hill, Advisory Team One and SESU. Apparently highest terrain feature in Quang Tri Pr, I Corps.

Dong Xoai (YT 08-70)
At junction of QL-14 and LTL-13, apx 80 km NNE Saigon. District Capital and home of SF A-Team Camp. Site of Battle of Dong Xoai, 10Jun65 to 12Jun65. Heavy fighting in this area, Apr75, during NVA's Final Offensive. FSB Odessa (2d/505th Inf, 82d Abn) here. See Dong Xoai SF Camp. Phuoc Long Pr, III Corps.

Dong Xoai Airfield (YT 062-753)
Apx 35 km SE An Loc, 28 km NNE Phuoc Vinh AF, 32 km S Song Be and 80 km NNE Saigon. Per TPC K-10D. El. 282', 3,000' laterite rwy. At 11°32'51"N-106°53'26"E. Also listed at YT 076-759. Phuoc Long Pr, III Corps.

Dong Xoai Heliport (YT 075-755)
Along QL-14 at Dong Xoai SF Camp, apx 48 km SW Duc Phong, 12 km ESE Son Duoc and 80 km NNE Saigon. "Heliport #562, alt 280', Soccer Field, at 11°32'00"N-106°54'15"E," per Feb73 TAD. Phuoc Long Pr, III Corps.

Dong Xoai SF Camp (YT 0764-7597)
Along QL-14, apx 2 km W Dong Xoai, 48 km SW Duc Phong, 12 km ESE Son Duoc and 80 km NNE Saigon. Battle of Dong Xoai here, 10Jun65 to 12Jun65, in which apx 1,500 VC attacked 400 CIDG Montagnard and 24 US Seabees, resulting in 20 US KIA, 200 other allied casualties and 700 VC dead. ARVN 42d Ranger Bn reinforced and was itself attacked and routed, with many of its troops deserting in panic (giving MACV hint of things to expect from ARVN in future). 5th SF Grp SF A-Team Camp, Det A-342, Oct66, SF Det 45. Grid per *SF Order of Battle.* Transferred to RF/PF. Phuoc Long Pr, III Corps.

Dong Xuan (n/a)
Mapsheet name of L-7014-6835-4. SVN.

Dong Xuan District HQ (BQ 957-807)
Apx 2 km N Phuoc Long and 11 km NNE Dong Tre AF. Mar69. Phu Yen Pr, II Corps.

Dong Xuan SF Camp (BQ 952-797)
See La Hai SF Camp. Phu Yen Pr, II Corps.

Dong Xuyen (YD 7-2)
Ville apx 5 km N of Hue. Cordoned by 1st/501st Inf, 101st Abn during Op Carentan II, Apr68. 53 confirmed NVA KIA. Thua Thien Pr, I Corps.

Dong Zu (XT 65-14)
Possible anglicized sp of Xom Xu, Xom Hue (XT 635-110), or Dong Xu? Apparently site where US 25th Inf Div later built Cu Chi Basecamp. Shown on '67, 25th Inf Div-produced maps with this spelling? Hau Nghia Pr, III Corps.

Donner, LZ (AT 934-242)
Between LZ West and LZ Siberia, apx 4 km SE Hiep Duc and 37 km due W Tam Ky. Americal list. Map is L-7014-6640-3. Quang Tin Pr, I Corps.

Doody, FSB (YS 237-772)
On W side QL-15 apx 30 km NW Nui Dat, 2 km NNE FSB North Dakota and 6.5 km SSE FSB Clare. On 1ATF NCO trng map per John Hollett. Phuoc Tuy Pr, III Corps.

Doomsday I, FSB? (XT 770-810)
E of QL-13, apx 7 km S An Loc, 20 km N Chon Thanh AF. Jul70. Possible FSB? Binh Long Pr, III Corps.

Doomsday II, FSB? (XU 720-180)
Along QL-13, apx 13 km NNW An Loc, 7 km SSW Loc Ninh AF. Possible FSB? Binh Long Pr, III Corps.

Door of Death, The (WE 82-53)
NVA name for mouth of Mu Gia Pass. NVA soldiers en route the Ho Chi Minh Trail had to cross Truong Son Mtns through the few available passes, with Mu Gia the primary pass. As result, US focused round-the-clock bombing campaign on passes throughout war, making them much feared and very dangerous areas to traverse. Upon reaching pass from either end, "Already exhausted from climb, heavily laden soldiers broke into a run at Mu Gia. Truck drivers floored it. Anything to get through the 'Door of Death'." NVN. [176]

Dop Chompa Mountain (VS 98-60)
One of 7-peak grp rising from, mangrove plain generally E Ha Tien and N Rach Gia and collectively known as the Seven Sisters. Included Hue Duc Mtn (Hill 220), Nui Co To (Hill 61, just S Tri Tron), Dop Chompa (double-peak, tallest of which is 710 meters, SW That Son AF), Hill 232 (near Chau Phu) and Hill 296 (5 km from Cambodia and 10 km N That Son). IV Corps.

Dorie, FSB (YU 991-851)
See Dorrie. Quang Duc Pr, II Corps.

Doris, LZ (BR 061-342)
Apx 43 km WSW An Khe, 20 km Suoi Doi and 17 km ENE Plei Do Lim. 4th Div AO, '70; B Bty, 6th/29th Arty here May70. Also 173d Abn? Name/grid per Jim Claeys. Also listed at BR 057-343. Pleiku Pr, II Corps.

Doris K, FSB (AQ 881-012)
Possibly a.k.a. Ban Me Thuot East FSB. Along S edge of Ban Me Thuot East AF, 9 km ESE Ban Me Thuot and close to LZ Aquarius (AQ 889-016). C Bty, 2d/17th Arty here, Nov70-Apr71. Grid and arty info per Nolan Putman. Also listed at AQ 887-011. Darlac Pr, II Corps.

Dorn, FSB (XT 088-768)
Apx 7 km S Thien Ngon AF and 24 km NNW Tay Ninh West AF. Cambodian Incursion FSB, '70. Tay Ninh Pr, III Corps.

Dorothy, LZ (AS 827-183)
Apx 7 km NE Kon Tongang, 27 km E to ESE Dak To 2 AF and 31 km NNE Kontum. 1st/35th Inf, 4th ID here Apr-May69. Name/grid per Dick Arnold. Kontum Pr, II Corps.

Dorothy, LZ (YD 039-606)
Several km NE peak Dong Ha Mtn, apx 8 km WNW Cam Lo and 20 km due W Dong Ha. Apr70 XXIV Corps grid per Don Armstrong. Quang Tri Pr, I Corps.

Dorrie, FSB (YU 991-851)
Apx 13 km NE Duc Lap, 5 km SW Buon Dak Gang and 35 km SW Ban Me Thuot. Oct69. Quang Duc Pr, II Corps.

Dorris, LZ (various)
See Doris.

Doson Peninsula (XH 8-9)
A.k.a. Do Son, Presqu'ile de. Peninsula at 20°43'N-106°46'E. On NF48-16 JOG. NVN.

Dot, LZ (n/a)
Listed as 4th Div FSB. Possibly the LZ Dot at either BS 930-253 or at BS 630-855? No other data. II Corps.

Dot, LZ (BS 370-342)
In river valley apx 6 km N Gia Vuc AF and 4 km SSE Tanoat. Quang Ngai Pr, I Corps.

Dot, LZ (BS 930-253)
Along QL-1, apx 18 km SE Duc Pho and 12 km NNE Gia An. Quang Ngai Pr, I Corps.

Dot, LZ (XT 330-898?)
Per Bobby Jackson, was adj to or near Katum SF Camp. Listed grid is for SF camp. Grid may be typo of LZ Dots listed at either XT 566-849 or XT 527-847? 1st/7th Cav, 1st Cav. Tay Ninh Pr, III Corps.

Dot, LZ (XT 527-847)
If grid correct, was apx 5 km S Katum AF, 6 km WSW Bo Tuc. Jan69. Binh Duong Pr, III Corps.

Dot, LZ (XT 566-849)
Along Katum/An Loc Road (Rte 246), apx 25 km ESE Katum, 17 km E Bo Tuc, 7 km SW tip of Fishhook and 18 km WSW An Loc. Described as being S of the tip of Fishhook and 48 km NW Phuoc Vinh per 2Dec68 *Army Reporter* (vol. 4, no. 48). Heavily attacked by estimated 2,000 NVA in mid Nov68, while manned by 3d/36th ARVN Rgt and suptd by 1st Cav's 2d Bde Aerial Scouts, ARA and US 20th Arty. During battle, D Bty, 1st/5th Arty lowered their 105's muzzles and fired 900 rnds point-blank into attacking enemy, while US Arty at LZs Rita and Jake fired 1,200 rnds in supt. 287 NVA rptd KIA. Cited in *Time Heals No Wounds*, at p 165. Apparently 4th Div and 1st Cav here. Listed grid per Frank Penk, Jr. Also listed at XT 562-854, per Peter Cole. Tay Ninh Pr, III Corps.

Dottie, FSB (YT 200-537)
See Dotty, LZ. Long Khanh Pr, III Corps.

Dottie, LZ/FSB (BS 630-855)
A.k.a. FSB Binh Lien, Nui Dong De and Hill 102. Apx 12 km N Quang Ngai, 23 km SSE Chu Lai, N the Ham Giang River and 1.5 km E QL-1. 1st/20th, 11th LIB here '68-69. Also listed at BS 630-856. Apr70 XXIV Corps grid per Don Armstrong. Apr68-Sep70. Also listed at BS 727-854, 632-853, 672-856 (transposition error?) and 714-876 during same period. Quang Ngai Pr, I Corps.

Dotty, LZ (various)
See Dottie and Dot.

Dotty, FSB (YT 209-541)
A.k.a. FSB Garry Owen (YT 205-546). Apx 2 km W Rang Rang, 65 km NW Saigon, 6 km ENE Phuoc Vinh AF and 25 km SSE Dong Xoai. 1st/12th Cav, 1st Cav, Feb-69 AO, Op Cheyenne Saber. Grid per Frank Penk, Jr. Also listed at YT 200-537. Long Khanh Pr, III Corps.

Double Alpha, LZ ()
See LZ Alpha-Alpha. Binh Dinh Pr, II Corps.

Douche Boats (n/a)
See Glossary.

Doumer Bridge (WJ 89-27)
See Paul Doumer Bridge. NVN.

Doung Da National Training Center (YD 8-1)
Near Phu Bai and close to Camp Eagle? Apparently an ARVN or RF/PF trng facility. Data per Ray Bows. Thua Thien Pr, I Corps.

Dove, LZ (BR 666-882?)
If grid correct, was apx 14 km WNW Hat Tay AF and 18 km WSW Bong Son. Mar66. Also listed at BR 670-823? Binh Dinh Pr, II Corps.

Dove, LZ (XD 847-192)
At S-central end of Vietnam Salient, apx 1.5 km N Lang Tcnouo (2) (at Lao border), 4 km WNW Ban Se Re, 22 km due S Khe Sanh CB. XXIV Corps grid, Don Armstrong. Quang Tri Pr, I Corps.

Dove, LZ (XD or YD?)
Somewhere in hills of Hai Lang Forest (YD 4-4). On 11Oct67, 2 Bns of 1st Mar Regt landed here to begin Op Medina. Marine Arty here in supt. Photos of LZ and other material at www.usmcfew.com/0311/medina.html. Quang Tri Pr, I Corps.

Dove, LZ (YD 085-655)
Apx 27 km NW Quang Tri, 16 km due N Mai Loc and 7 km NNW Cam Lo/QL-9. Apparently at E end of Song Nang Valley (Helicopter Valley) and used during Op Hastings 16Jul66. See LZ Crow and Helicopter Valley. Quang Tri Pr, I Corps.

Dozier Airfield (XT 772-381)
See Dozier Army AF. Binh Duong Pr, III Corps.

Dozier Army Airfield (XT 772-381)
A.k.a. Dozier Field and Lai Khe AF. At Lai Khe Basecamp, and named to honor SFC Jerald Dozier, A/2d/28th Inf, 3d Bde/1st Div, KIA 13Oct65, near Ap Lai Khe. Dozier was 1st VN War casualty of 1st Div's 3d Bde. AF built at site where he was KIA, and dedicated, 20Jul66, per *Vietnam Military Lore, 1959-1973*. Binh Duong Pr, III Corps.

Drac, FSB (XT 902-610)
Apx 13 km NNW Phuoc Vinh AF and 14 km due E Chonh Thanh AF. Phuoc Long Pr, III Corps.

Dragon, FSB (XT 636-286)
A.k.a. Patrol Base Dragon and possibly Dragon Head? Apx 18 km WNW Phu Cuong and 8 km due N Cu Chi. Opened Apr69 and closed 16Jul69. Had two-105 howitzers and 14 fighting bunkers. 2d/14th Inf, 25th Inf and 2d/49th ARVN Rgt here. Per Kirk Ramsey, was built in Ho Bo Woods: "A patrol base gouged in one day out of the soil of peaceful-looking meadows where we had landed that morning and which we would leave just as quickly four weeks later. Was not elegant, but it was functional." Chinook brought in dozer and crew that were soon piling dirt into rough circular wall apx 3' high and unusual in that respect. Site overlooked large plateau and in clearing apx 1 km in diameter. Beyond clearing was thick brush and forest. On 2 sides of plateau, ground sloped gently to swampy streams whose banks were covered with tall trees. Sandy to loam soil of base had some patches of sand w/beach-type grass. Data per Kirk Ramsey, *Tales of a War Far Away*, illustrated memoir at: www.en.com/users/kramsey/default.html. Binh Duong Pr, III Corps.

Dragon, FSB/LZ (ZA 225-522)
See FSB Kelly at grid. Pleiku Pr, II Corps.

Dragon, LZ (BS 731-523)
Immed S to SE Mo Duc AF, and just W QL-1, roughly 23 km SSE Quang Ngai. 1st/1st Cav here '70. Apr70 XXIV Corps grid per Don Armstrong. Also listed at BS 730-529, 725-538 and 731-528. Quang Ngai Pr, I Corps.

Dragon, LZ (YA 430-591)
If grid correct, was apx 44 km N to NNE Ba Kev AF, 10 km W SVN, 80 km W Pleiku. 4th Div, '70. Jim Claeys lists grid as YA 443-059 (see alternate listing for that location); however, it is thought listed grid is correct? 4th Div 31Jul70 ORLL grid, per Jim Henderson. Incursion FSB. Cambodia.

Dragon, LZ (YA 443-059?)
If grid correct, was apx 12 km SE Ba Kev AF, 35 km W SVN, 87 km SW Pleiku, 33 km ENE Lumphat AF and 15 km NNW Phum Dok Yong. 4th Div, '70. Name/grid per Jim Claeys. Also listed at YA 430-591, per 4th Div Arty ORLL of 31Jul70, courtesy Jim Henderson (see alternate listing). Incursion FSB. Cambodia.

Dragon, LZ (YT 687-964)
See Dragon Head, FSB. Lam Dong Pr, II Corps.

Dragon, Patrol Base (XT 636-286)
See Dragon, FSB. Binh Duong Pr, III Corps.

Dragon Base, LZ (AT 999-315)
A.k.a. Hill 270, LZ Round Up and possibly FSB Dragon Head? Overlooked Que Son Valley, apx 4 km SW Que Son, 45 km due S Da Nang AB, 7 km SW Gang Dong, 35 km WNW Tam Ky and 25 km W QL-1. Map is L-7014-6640-3. Americal list. Quang Nam Pr, I Corps.
Dragon Crater, Battle of (YA)
See Dragon Crater, LZ. Pleiku or Kontum Pr, II Corps.
Dragon Crater, LZ (YA)
Somewhere near Plei Djereng. Built on edge of large bomb crater adj to large NVA bunker complex. CIDG battle here 10Nov66 led 1st to B-52 strike (and crater), and then to Battle of Dragon Crater, 19Nov66, when 1st/14th Inf/Eng and same CIDG elements doing BDA and destroying remaining bunkers were hit by returning NVA. See *Rites of Passage*, p 99, 100, 123. Pleiku or Kontum Pr, II Corps.
Dragon Fire, Operation (n/a)
5Sep-30Oct67. ROK 2d Marine Bde op. 541 rptd NVA/VC KIA, per *Vietnam Order of Battle*, pp 9-14. Quang Ngai Pr, I Corps.
Dragon Head, FSB (n/a)
Per John Alejandro, was a.k.a. Dragon Head. Unknown which LZ/FSB Dragon was being referenced by John, but likely the FSB Dragon Head at YT 687-964?
Dragon Head, FSB/LZ (YT 687-964)
A.k.a. FSB/LZ Dragon. Remote site at or near peak of Hill 659, apx 27 km ESE Duc Phong AF, and 43 km WNW Tan Phat AF/Bao Loc. Opened or reopened 28Oct70. 5th/7th Cav Data per *1st Cav Div Op Rpt, ending 31Oct70*, per Peter Cole. Also listed at XT 687-694, which is 7 km NE Minh Thanh AF? Lam Dong Pr, II Corps.
Dragon House Patrol Base (XT 9-0?)
Described in *Father Soldier Son*, at pp 129 et al, as patrol base of 1st/28th Inf, 1st Inf Div (Black Lions), and as having been near Di An. Was apparently set up around shell-pocked pagoda. Named "Dragon House" as result of pagoda's large lizard population. Bien Hoa Pr, III Corps.
Dragon Lady (n/a)
See U-2 Spy Plane and Madame Ngu, both in Glossary.
Dragon Mountain (AR 777-368)
A.k.a. Hill 1028, Titty Mtn and Chi Hodrong Mtn. On E side of QL-14/19 at NW corner of 4th Div's Camp Enari and apx 12 km SSE Pleiku. Was at intersection where QL19 W left QL14 S (QL19 then ran SW to Catecka Tea Plantation). Mtn had distinctive horseshoe shape. Name apparently evolved from anglicized pronunciation of its Vietnamese name. Per Tom Rethard, "the road to the front gate of Enari was just N of the mtn and bulk of encampment was E and NE of it." Per Richard Weaver, Jr, the 362d Signal Co (and possibly the 124th Sig Corps as well) maintained "Troposcatter" signal site here that inc 2, large, round Tropospheric antennas pointed toward Ban Me Thuot. [177] See Tropo Hill. Pleiku Pr, II Corps. [178]
Dragon Mountain Base Camp (AR 802-350)
See Enari, Camp. Pleiku Pr, II Corps.
Dragon Mountain Signal Site (AR 777-368)
A.k.a. Dragon Mtn Troposcatter Signal Site. See Dragon Mtn. Pleiku Pr, II Corps.
Dragon Mountain. Airfield (AR 803-339)
See Hensel AF. Pleiku Pr, II Corps.
Dragon Patrol Base (XT 636-286)
See FSB Dragon at grid. Binh Duong Pr, III Corps.
Dragon Valley (AT 84-34)
A.k.a. Antenna Valley? Generally W LZ Ross, apx 30-40 km SSW Da Nang and generally S and SSW Phuoc Binh and An Hoa. Per Tom Brizendine, Dragon Valley, Death Valley or Que Son Valley were all same valley. During Tet '69, 1st/6th Inf made heavy contact with 2d NVA Rgt and, during 3-day battle, employed the 16-inch guns of Battleship New Jersey. [179] Also listed at AT 91-37 and AT 90-36. Americal list, USMC, I Corps.
Dragon Valley (YA 95-83?)
See Punch Bowl Valley. Kontum Pr, II Corps.
Dragon's Head, FSB (YT 687-964)
See Dragon Head, FSB. Lam Dong Pr, II Corps.
Dragon's Jaw (WG 83-93)
A.k.a. the Thanh Hoa RR and Hwy Bridge, or Ham Rong Bridge. See Thanh Hoa Bridge for detail and bombing history. NVN.
Dragon's Lair (BT 397-145)
Per *Rites of Passage*, p 381, was EM Club of 1st/14th Inf, 25th Div at Hill 54, Summer '67. Quang Tin Pr, I Corps.
Dragonfly, LZ (XD 835-474)
Apx 3 km NNE KSCB, and 17 km WSW Ca Lu. Apr70 XXIV Corps grid per D. Armstrong. Quang Tri Pr, I Corps.
Dragoon, FSB (n/a)
No data. Cited in *1st Cav O Rpt, Feb70/Apr70*, p 14, per Peter Cole. At time, Cav was in NW III Corps?
Dragoons, LZ (BR 03-55?)
If this was an LZ, it appears to have been along QL-19 at or near Suoi Da AF. C Bty, 7th/15th Arty here in 68 or 69? On map at http://www.landscaper.net/images/7-15AO.gif. Pleiku Pr, II Corps.
Drake, Camp (n/a)
In Japan, not Vietnam.
Drake, LZ (ZA 07-12?)
A.k.a. FSB Drake. Apx 9 km NNW Plei Me SF Camp, 28 km ESE Duc Co SF Camp and 22 km NE LZ X-Ray. On *Ia Drang Valley* map in *The Rise and Fall of the American Army*, pp 368-9. Grid is est. 1st Cav. Pleiku Pr, II Corps.
Drango, LZ (AQ 812-208)
Near Mewal Plantation, 4 km NW Quang Nhieu and 16 km N Ban Me Thuot City AF. Feb66. Darlac Pr, II Corps.
Dreamer, FSB (ZT 02-25)
A.k.a. Hill 824 (ZT 027-232)? Apx 3 km SW peak of Nui Ong (Dang S'Ruin Mtn), 9 km E Tanh Linh AF and 5 km SSE Xa Hieu Tin. 199th LIB. Binh Tuy Pr, III Corps.
Dredge *Hyde* (n/a)
See *Hyde*, Dredge.
Drennen, FSB (YT 154-288)
A.k.a. FSB Charger, LZ Blue and Xom Cat AF (and Drinnon?). Just N the Song Dong Nai near its confluence with Song Be River, apx 22 km NE Bien Hoa AB, 1 km NE Xom Cat, and 28 km SSE Phuoc Vinh AF. Grid per Peter Cole. See also Drinnon. Bien Hoa Pr, III Corps.
Drinnon, FSB (YT 154-288?)
Possibly the proper sp of FSB Drennen? See Drennen for location. 1st Cav, 72, and likely named to honor Sgt Bedford L. Drinnon, KIA 3Jan72. Name per Dan Gillotti. Bien Hoa Pr, III Corps.

Drone, LZ (XD 973-616)
Apx 15 km WNW Cam Lo, 5 km S southern edge of DMZ and 27 km W Dong Ha. Apr70 XXIV Corps grid per Don Armstrong. Quang Tri Pr, I Corps.

Drop Zone Donna AF (ZA 163-057)
See Plei Me AF. II Corps.

Drop Zone Kent AF (BQ 910-705)
See Dong Tre AF. II Corps.

Drop Zone Natasha (TJ 9-6)
See DZ Natasha. NVN.

Drug Abuse (n/a)
See Glossary.

Drum, FSB (XT 202-867)
A.k.a. Old FSB Drum, and FSB Le Loi. Apx 15 km SW Katum, 13 km ESE Thien Ngon AF, 24 km NNW Nui Ba Den and 30 km due N Tay Ninh. Existed 13-17Mar70, as 1 of 7 FSBs opened and closed in as many weeks by 2d/8th Cav, 1st Cav, prior to Cambodian Incursion (7 were: Jamie, Mary Gwen, Heather, Victor, Flashner, Drum and Illingworth). Tay Ninh Pr, III Corps.

Dry, FSB (XT 044-796?)
Possibly a.k.a. FSB Wood? Apparently between Tay Ninh and Cu Chi and, if a.k.a. FSB Wood, then was apx 5 km E Cambodia, 4 km SW Thien Ngon AF and 34 km NW Tay Ninh, and built by 5th/7th Cav, May70, and holding B/1st/77th Arty after move from FSB Illingworth, 4Apr70, immed prior Cambodian Incursion. Arty ORLL grid. Photo/remarks at www.megsinet.com/randyjk/fsb1.htm. Tay Ninh Pr?, III Corps.

Dry Gulch, LZ (ZC 0-6?)
Used to land security elements for building of nearby FSB Bullwhip (ZC 056-664) during Op Oklahoma Hills, Mar-May69. Apparently W of Happy Valley, 1st Mar Div USMC, '69. Quang Nam Pr, I Corps.

Dry Lake (YA 749-234)
Apx 3 km E Cambodia, 9 km WSW Duc Co and 55 km SW Pleiku. Aug66. Pleiku Pr, II Corps.

Du Bop SF Camp (XU 974-291?)
Likely transposition of Bu Dop. See Bu Dop SF Camp. Phuoc Long Pr, III Corps.

Du Kich (n/a)
See Glossary.

Du Tho SF Camp (XR 060-507)
Apx 8 km due S Soc Trang AF, 12 km S Khanh Hung and 62 km SSW Tra Vinh AF. 5th SF. Info/grid per *SF Order of Battle.* Ba Xuyen Pr, IV Corps.

Duan Loc Airfield (YT 418-180)
See Binh Loc AF. Long Khanh Pr, III Corps.

Duane, USCGC (n/a)
WHEC 33. 4Dec67-28Jul68. Sqdn 3 CGC, during Coast Guard's 2d deployment. On 12Apr68, shelled VC positions near Phan Thiet. Credited with 9 VC KIA and 22 WIA, per www.currahee.org/pageb2.html.

Duang Hoa Thuang AF (BS 016-970)
See Hua Duc AF. Quang Ngai Pr, I Corps.

Dubuque, USS (n/a)
LPD 8, Amphibious Ship. See End Sweep, Op.

Duc Boa Base (XS 59-97)
See Duc Hoa. Hau Nghia Pr, III Corps.

Duc Co Airfield (YA 843-255) Apx 27 km due W The Oasis, 14 km from Laos, 20 km due S Plei Djereng New AF, per TPC K-10D. El. 1,247', 3,700' steel-mat rwy. At 13°47'08"N-107°38'00"E. Also listed at YA 846-249. Pleiku Pr, II Corps.

Duc Co SF Camp (YA 8460-2493)
A.k.a. Chu Dron SF Camp. Along QL-19, apx 13 km from Cambodian border and 55 km W Pleiku. FOB 5 here? 5th SF Grp Det 20, Det. A-215 in '67, and A-224, Dec64, A-253 Oct66. Transferred to 81st Border Rangers. Grid per *SF Order of Battle.* Pleiku Pr, II Corps.

Duc Co, FSB (YA 84-25?)
A position of 4th Div presumably at or near Duc Co AF or Duc Co SF Camp. C Bty, 7th/15th Arty here at one time. Pleiku Pr, II Corps.

Duc Duc ARVN HQ (AT 87-48?)
Sprawling ARVN HQ at An Hoa Industrial Complex, 33 km SSW Da Nang? Quang Nam Pr, I Corps.

Duc Duc District HQ (AT 867-477)
33 km SSW Da Nang. '66. Quang Nam Pr, I Corps.

Duc Hai Refugee Camp (BS 667-689)
E of QL-1, apx 5 km SE Quang Ngai. Grid per NPIA data. Quang Ngai Pr, I Corps.

Duc Hanh Combat Base (XT 573-075)
Apx 26 km WNW Tan Son Nhut AB and 6 km NE Khiem Cuong. Nov66. Hau Nghia Pr, III Corps.

Duc Hoa (n/a)
Mapsheet name of L-7014-6230-1. SVN.

Duc Hoa (XS 600-962)
Apx 23 km due W Tan Son Nhut AB/Saigon, and 12 km SE Kiem Cuong. 2d/14th Inf Bn CRIP (Combined Recon and Intel Plt) here with elements of 49th ARVN Rgt in Mar69, per 15Mar69, QUARTEVAL Feeder Rpt of 2d Bde/25th Inf Div at www.en.com/users/kramsey/dragons.html. Hau Nghia Pr, III Corps.

Duc Hoa Airfield (XS 594-968)
Apx 20 km SSW Cu Chi, 22 km W Saigon and 38 km NE Thuy Dong AF, per TPC K-10D. El. 7', 2,100' laterite rwy. At 10°49'27"N-106°27'29"E. Hau Nghia Pr, III Corps.

Duc Hoa Base Camp (XS 59-97)
Apx 23 km due W Tan Son Nhut AB/Saigon, and 12 km SE Kiem Cuong. HQ of 25th ARVN Inf Div until '70, when HQ moved to Cu Chi after US 25th Inf Div went home. 5th SF Det, Team 99 and 82d Abn here. Hau Nghia Pr, III Corps.

Duc Hoa Heliport (XS 598-968)
At Duc Hoa, apx 23 km due W Tan Son Nhut AB/Saigon, and 12 km SE Kiem Cuong. "Heliport #563, alt 10', Soccer Field, at 10°49'N 106°28'E," per Feb73 TAD. Hau Nghia Pr, III Corps.

Duc Hoa SF Camp (XS 6000-9625)
Immed N Duc Hoa, apx 22 km due W Tan Son Nhut AB and 10 km SE Kiem Cuong. 5th SF. Info/grid per *SF Order of Battle.* SF A-Team Camp also listed at XS 59-97. See Du Hue. Hau Nghia Pr, III Corps.

Duc Hue (n/a)
Mapsheet name of L-7014-6230-4. SVN/Cambodia.

Duc Hue (XT 321-088)
A.k.a. Khu Tru Mat. Apx 5 km from Cambodia, 52 km WNW Tan Son Nhut AB/Saigon, and 37 km SSE Tay Ninh. SF camp/AF here. Hau Nghia Pr, III Corps.

Duc Hue, Camp (XS 6000-9625)
SF Camp. At N edge of plantation, apx 18 km W Tan Son Nhut AB, 6 km NE Duc Hoa AF and 20 km S Cu Chi. Also listed at XT 3200-0900? Hau Nghia Pr, III Corps.
Duc Hue, Fort (XT 326-079)
Apx 5 km from Cambodia, 52 km WNW Saigon, and 37 km SSE Tay Ninh. Hau Nghia Pr, III Corps.
Duc Hue Airfield (XT 319-082)
Apx 6 km E Cambodia, 33 km WSW Cu Chi, 31 km N Thuy Dong AF and 50 km WNW Tan Son Nhut AB/ Saigon, per TPC K-10D. El. 7', 1,500' laterite rwy. Hau Nghia Pr, III Corps.
Duc Hue Engineer Camp (XT 322-090)
At or near Duc Hue AF/SF Camp, apx 52 km WNW Tan Son Nhut AB, 17 km N tip of Parrot's Beak and within 5 km at its closest point to Cambodian border. 92d Engr Bn camp here were used for road projects and for Cambodian Incursion. Grid per Frank Penk, Jr, who adds, "From my SOI notebook: Duc Hue, (Navy) PBR, Call-sign Remittance. This was during period Cav was at FSBs Elrod, Clara (etc.) and worked with the Navy." Hau Nghia Pr, III Corps.
Duc Hue PBR Base? (XT 32-08?)
Presumably at Duc Hue, but no grid data. Frank Penk, Jr. notes, "From my SOI notebook: Duc Hue, (Navy) PBR, Call-sign Remittance. This was during period Cav was at FSBs Elrod and Clara, and worked with the Navy." Hau Nghia Pr, III Corps.
Duc Hue SF Camp (XT3200-0900)
Apx 6 km E Cambodia, 33 km WSW Cu Chi, 31 km N Thuy Dong AF and 50 km WNW Tan Son Nhut AB/Saigon. 5th SF camp, CIDG Det A-325, SF A-Team Camp Transferred to 83rd Border Rangers. Grid per *SF Order of Battle.* Hau Nghia Pr, III Corps.
Duc Lap (YU 87-56)
Village, not the AF. Apx 12 km E Laos and 55 km SW Ban Me Thuot. Grid per Jim Claeys. Quang Duc Pr, II Corps.
Duc Lap (YU 913-751)
Apx 12 km E Laos, 50 km SW Ban Me Thuot and 47 km due N Gia Nghia AF. 5th SF camp, Det A-239, Oct66, SF Det 38. Quang Duc Pr, II Corps.
Duc Lap, FSB (XT 575-033)
Apx 6 km ESE Khiem Cuong and 23 km WNW Tan Son Nhut. Jan67. Hau Nghia Pr, III Corps.
Duc Lap Airfield (YU 819-725?)
If grid correct, was apx 36 km ESE Duc Phong AF. "Abnd 2Oct66, AF # VA2-95," in Aug69 TAD per Frank Penk, Jr. Not in Feb73 TAD. Quang Duc Pr, II Corps.
Duc Lap Airfield (YU 906-752)
A.k.a. Duc Lap 2 or Dak Sak AF. Apx 12 km E Laos, 50 km SW Ban Me Thuot, 60 km W Lac Thien AF and 47 km due N Gia Nghia AF. Per TPC K-10A. El. 2,264', 3,300' asph-treated crushed rock rwy. Also listed at YU 913-751. Quang Duc Pr, II Corps.
Duc Lap 2 Airfield (YU 906-752)
Apx 12 km E Cambodia, 48 km WSW Ban Me Thuot and 34 km NE Bu Prang New AF. "Flight serv chk 5th SF Pleiku (C-7) ARVN(A) 24Apr69, AF # VA2-293," Aug69 TAD, per Frank Penk, Jr. Not in Feb73 TAD. II Corps.
Duc Lap 2 Airfield (YU 906-752)
See Duc Lap AF. Quang Duc Pr, II Corps.
Duc Lap SF Camp (YU 9132-7513)
Apx 12 km E Laos, 50 km SW Ban Me Thuot and 47 km due N Gia Nghia AF. 5th SF. Det A-239, Oct66, SF Det 38 here. Grid per *SF Order of Battle.* Transferred to 96th ARVN Border Rangers. Quang Duc Pr, II Corps.
Duc Lap, LZ (YU 906-752?)
Apx 12 km E Laos, 50 km SW Ban Me Thuot and 60 km W Lac Thien AF. 1st/35th Inf, 4th Div here. Grid is for Duc Lap AF. Quang Duc Pr, II Corps.
Duc Long (WR 52-83)
See Vi Thanh. Chuong Thien Pr, IV Corps.
Duc Long (Vi Thanh) (n/a)
Mapsheet name of L-7014-6028-1. SVN.
Duc Long Heliport (WR 590-779)
Along Rte LTL-31, apx 12 km NW Long My and 45 km SW Can Tho. Heliport #716, alt 82', at 09°47'00"N-105°27'00"E, per Feb73 TAD. Chuong Thien Pr, IV Corps.
Duc Minh (n/a)
Mapsheet name of L-7014-6533-4. SVN/Cambodia.
Duc My Adv Camp (BP 83-84?)
If grid correct, was apx 40 km NNW Nha Trang AF and 28 km SW Van Ninh AF. Duc My Subsector, Adv Team 40. Khanh Hoa Pr, II Corps.
Duc My Airfield (BP 842-865)
Apx 40 km NNW Nha Trang AF and 30 km SW Van Ninh AF. "Secure, contact as per HQ II Corps MACV Sig Op Instructions ARVN(A), AF # VA2-96," in Aug69 TAD per Frank Penk, Jr, not in 73 TAD. Also listed at BP 835-845. Khanh Hoa Pr, II Corps.
Duc My Airfield (BP 835-845)
Major AF apx 40 km NNW Nha Trang AF, 30 km SW Van Ninh AF, 14 km from Ninh Hoa and on W edge of Tan Khan, per TPC K-10A/ONC K-10. El. 98', 3,200' asph rwy. At 12°32'10"N-109°00'45"E. Also listed at BP 842-865. Khanh Hoa Pr, II Corps.
Duc My Ranger Training Center (BP 8-8)
Apx 14 km WNW Ninh Hoa and near Duc My AF/SF Camp. ARVN long range patrol trng center in at least '68, per *Rangers At War*, at p 204. Also discussed in *Gone Native,* p 261. Khanh Hoa Pr, II Corps.
Duc My RTC (BP 8-8?)
RVNAF Regional Trng Ctr. Khanh Hoa Pr, II Corps.
Duc Pho (BS 81-38)
Apx 37 km SSE Quang Ngai and along QL-1 in area known as the Rice Bowl. HQ 1st Bde/101st Abn while it operated out of Duc Pho and Phan Rang, until Nov67 when balance of Div arrived in VN. Div (minus 3rd/506th Inf) moved to I Corps at that point. On 21Jun67, massive explosion destroyed Duc Pho ammo supply point (see Nelson Inn). Site of LZ Bronco. USMC's Op Desoto in this area. 18th Engr Bde elements here 67-68. Map is L-7014-6738-1, per Ken Burrington. Capitol, Duc Pho Dist, Quang Ngai Pr, I Corps.
Duc Pho Airfield (BS 809-384)
Along QL-1, apx 27 km ENE Ba To New AF, 40 km SSE Quang Ngai 38 km due N LZ English, per TPC K-10A. El. 36', 3,600' alum-mat rwy. Quang Ngai Pr, I Corps.
Duc Pho Heliport (BS 810-385)
Apparently at or near Duc Pho AF, along QL-1, apx 27 km ENE Ba To New AF, 40 km SSE Quang Ngai 38 km due N

LZ English. Heliport #564, alt 66', per Feb73 TAD. Also listed at BS 807-378. Quang Ngai Pr, I Corps.

Duc Pho-LZ Bronco (BS 81-38?)
Possible grid estimated per heliport grid. Apx 38 km SSE Quang Ngai on QL-1. Americal list. See LZ Bronco. Quang Ngai Pr, I Corps.

Duc Phong (YU 437-049)
Apx 30 km due E Song Be, 22 km NE Bunard AF and 48 km NE Dong Xoai AF SF Det 43, also spelled Duc Phuong? Phuoc Long Pr, III Corps.

Duc Phong (Bu Bang) (n/a)
Mapsheet name of L-7014-6432-1. SVN.

Duc Phong Airfield (YU 440-047)
Apx 30 km due E Song Be, 22 km NE Bunard AF and 48 km NE Dong Xoai AF per TPC K-10D. El. 919', 3,000' laterite/steel-mat rwy. At 11°47'41"N-107°14'22"E. Also listed at YU 437-049. Phuoc Long Pr, III Corps.

Duc Phong SF Camp (YU 4375-0495)
Apx 30 km due E Song Be, 22 km NE Bunard, 48 km NE Dong Xoai. 5th SF Grp Det A-343?, Oct66; also Det 43 here. 1st MGF, Det A-303 under Capt Bo Gritz here late 66-early67, per *Mobile Guerrilla Force*, pp 2-4, which states it was at N edge War Zone D, and perimeter the shape of a 5-point star. At p 73, it adds, "A few [km] NE of the camp, the town of Duc Phong straddled [QL-14], populated by 7,000 Vietnamese, Montagnard and Cambodians. The jungle surrounding the town was inhabited by elephants, tigers, wild boar, and leopards; before the war, hunters traveled from around the world to hunt its game." Also sp Duc Phuong? Grid per *SF Order of Battle.* Later became RF/PF. Phuoc Long Pr, III Corps.

Duc Phuong (YU 437-049?)
See Duc Phong. Phuoc Long Pr, III Corps.

Duc Phuong Airfield (YU 440-047)
See Duc Phong AF. Phuoc Long Pr, III Corps.

Duc Tanh (YS 45-78)
Fortified ville On Rte-2, apx 2 km W Ngai Giao, 9 km N Nui Dat and 7 km W FSB Longreach. 161 Bty, RNZA (Horsford's Bty 18Mar69-18Sep69) FSB set here 7-14Jun69. Also 108 Bty RAA and A Bty 2d/35th US Arty here '67. Phuoc Tuy Pr, III Corps.

Duc Trong, FSB (BP 149-007)
See Apollo, FSB. Tuyen Duc Pr, II Corps.

Duc Xuyen Airfield (AP 882-478)
Apx 55 km SSE Ban Me Thuot, 22 km SE Buon Tsuke AF, 52 km ENE Gia Nghia AF. Per TPC K-10A. El. 1,620', 1,300' steel-mat/PSP rwy. 12°10'45"N-108°08'05"E. Also listed at AP 916-497. Tuyen Duc Pr, II Corps.

Duc Xuyen SF Camp (AP 916-497)
Apparently a.k.a. Krong Kno SF Camp. Just E Duc Xuyen AF, apx 55 km SSE Ban Me Thuot. 5th SF. Info/grid per *SF Order of Battle.* See Krong Kno. Darlac Pr, II Corps.

Duc Xuyen (n/a)
Mapsheet name of L-7014-6533-1. SVN.

Duchess (n/a)
Australian Escort ship serving under US 7th Flt.

Duck, LZ (BR 670-919)
Apx 16 km NW Ha Tay and 18 km WSW Bong Son. Mar66. Binh Dinh Pr, II Corps.

Duck, LZ (BR 804-882)
Apx 9 km SW Bong Son, and 6 km N Ha Tay. 2d/17th Arty here supt 1st Cav, 11Jul66. Data per Jack Picciolo. Binh Dinh Pr, II Corps.

Duck, LZ (YD 223-153)
Overlooking Da Krong River Valley apx 25 km SSE Ba Long AF and 38 km SSW Quang Tri. Apr70 XXIV Corps grid per Don Armstrong. Quang Tri Pr, I Corps.

Duck/Canary, Operation (n/a)
See Canary/Duck, Operation.

Duck Early Warning System (n/a)
See DEWS in Glossary.

Duck Butt (n/a)
See Glossary.

Duckbutt (n/a)
See Glossary.

Dude, LZ (BR 986-740)
Apx 11 km NE Phu My, 26 km SE Bong Son and 6 km from coast. Oct66. Binh Dinh Pr, II Corps.

Duffel Bag Team (BR)
See Glossary.

Duffy, FSB (XU 676-216)
At Angel's Wing, apx 3 km S Cambodian border, 14 km NNW Loc Ninh AF and 30 km WSW Bu Dop. 1st Cav. Also listed at ZU 676-216, but grid does not exist and XU grid zone likely correct. Binh Long Pr, III Corps.

Duke, FSB (BS 240-855)
Apx 12 km WSW Tra Bong AF, 20 km NW Ha Thanh and 45 km SW Chu Lai. Quang Ngai Pr, I Corps.

Duke, LZ (ZA 235-762)
Along QL-14, apx 14 km S Kontum and 14 km NE Plei Mrong AF. Sep69. Kontum Pr, II Corps.

Duke Victory, SS (n/a)
Merchant ship under govt contract, per Ralph Fries.

Duluth, USS (n/a)
LPD 6. See Frequent Wind, Op.

Dume, Point, USCGC (n/a)
See *Point Dume*.

Dumfries, LZ (YD 096-334)
In valley of Khe Ta Laou River, apx 18 km SSE Ca Lu, 1.5 km NE Ta Laou and 9 km SW Ba Long AF. Apr70 XXIV Corps grid per Don Armstrong. Quang Tri Pr, I Corps.

Dunbar County Lima (XD 840-420)
3d/26th Marines fixed Listening Post (LP) set apx 400 meters from W end of Khe Sanh AF Runway during siege of Khe Sanh. Likely named for LP's call-sign. Grid estimated. Quang Tri Pr, I Corps.

Duncan, LZ (XT 134-385)
Apx 3 km from Cambodia and 15 km SSW Tay Ninh West AF. Mar66. Tay Ninh Pr, III Corps.

Duncan, USS (n/a)
DDR-874, per Ralph Fries.

Dung, Madame (n/a)
See Glossary.

Dung Long Heliport (YD 032-452)
Apx 5 km SE Vandegrift CB and 30 km WSW Quang Tri. Heliport #565, alt 82', 16°41'00"N-106°54'30"E, per Feb73 TAD. Quang Tri Pr, I Corps.

Dung Quat Bay (BT 60-05)
Bay immed E Chu Lai/Ky Ha. Quang Tin Pr, I Corps.

Dung Quat, Baie de (BT 5-0)
A.k.a. Vung Dung Quat. Bay at 15°24'N-108°45'E. On ND49-01 JOG. Quang Tin Pr, I Corps.
Dunkirk, LZ (YD 268-278)
Apx 16 km SW Ba Long AF and 23 km SSW Quang Tri. Apr70 XXIV Corps grid per Don Armstrong. Quang Tri Pr, I Corps.
Duong Cua Dan, Operation (n/a)
17Mar-30Jul68. A.k.a. People's Road Op. 9th Inf Div securing road work on QL-4. On 21 May68, was combined with Op Truong Cong Dinh. These joint ops resulted in 1,251 rptd NVA/VC KIA, per *Vietnam Order of Battle*, pp 9-14. Dinh Tuong and Kien Tuong Prvs, IV Corps.
Duong Da National Training Center (YD 8-1)
See Doung Da Ntl Trng Ctr. Thua Thien Pr, I Corps.
Duong Dong (n/a)
Mapsheet name of L-7014-5729-2. SVN/Cambodia.
Duong Dong Airfield (US 870-310)
Westernmost AF in SVN and the major AF on Dao Phu Quoc Island. Was just N Duong Dong, apx 60 km WSW Ha Tien AF and 25 km NNW An Thoi AF. Apparently originally built by Japanese during WWII, per Ben Youmans. On TPC K-10D. El. 23', 3,300' asph rwy, C-130 capable. At 10°31'36"N-103°57'58"E. Phu Quoc Island, Gulf of Thailand, IV Corps.
Duong Dong NDB (US 86-31)
On coast of Phu Quoc Island at Duong Dong AF. Kien Giang Pr, IV Corps.
Duong Dong SF Camp (US 87-31?)
See Xom Dong Duong SF Camp. IV Corps.
Duong Keo (n/a)
Mapsheet name of L-7014-6026-3. SVN.
Duong Uoi, OP (BT 148-122)
See Op Duong Uoi. Quang Tin Pr, I Corps.
Duong, Mui...(XF 5-0)
A.k.a. Mui Ron. Coastal point at 18°07'N-106°27'E. On NE48-07 JOG. NVN.
Duonh Uoi, OP (BT 148-122)
See OP Duong Uoi. Quang Tin Pr, I Corps.
DuPont, USS (n/a)
DD 941. On 29Aug67, lost 1 sailor KIA and 9 WIA when one of 40 shells fired by NVA Btys near DMZ hit the ship.
Durham, OP (AT 988-508)
See OP Durham. Quang Nam Pr, I Corps.
Durham, USS (n/a)
LKA 114. Part of TF 76.8, During Op Eagle Pull.
Duster Compound (YT 128-114)
Apx 6 km E Plantation AF and 14 km WSW Bien Hoa AB. Oct69-Oct70. Bien Hoa Pr, III Corps.
Duster Hill, FSB (BR 932-745)
A.k.a. Hill 198. Apx 1 km SE LZ Uplift, 8 km NNE Phu My and on E side of QL-1. Overlooked Uplift and C Bty, 4th/60th Arty kept a Duster Bty (track-mounted twin-40mm cannons) here as defense for Uplift. Map is L-7014-6837-3, per Ken Burrington. Binh Dinh Pr, II Corps.
Duster, LZ (XD 970-682)
Apx 6 km NW Cam Lo and 16 km WNW Dong Ha. Apr70 XXIV Corps grid per Don Armstrong. Quang Tri Pr, I Corps.
Dusty, FSB (XS 130-440)
Along QL-4, apx 16 km NE Vinh Long, 11 km SW Cai Lay. Jan69. Dinh Tuong Pr, IV Corps.
Dusty, LZ (XT 662-583)
A.k.a. FSB Gafsa or Gaf Sa (XT 660-579). Apx 12 km WSW Chonh Thanh AF and 23 km NNW Lai Khe. May66. Binh Long Pr, III Corps.
Dusty End, LZ (YT 470-330)
Apx 6 km SW Ap 107, 25 km due W Vo Dat AF and 26 km N Xuan Loc. May69. Long Khanh Pr, III Corps.
Dusty's Pub (CQ 200-428)
Per J. D. Wetterling (F-100 pilot '68), was his sqdn's recreation lounge at Tuy Hoa AB. Phu Yen Pr, II Corps.
DUTCH MILL (n/a)
See Glossary.
Dutchman, FSB (XT 700-810)
Apx 8 km SW An Loc, 8 km NW Tan Khai and 6 km W QL-13. May67. Binh Long Pr, III Corps.
Dutchman's House (XT 740-800)
Apx 6 km SSW An Loc, 5 km NNW Tan Khai and 2 km W QL-13. Binh Long Pr, III Corps.
Duz, LZ (BR 779-718)
Apx 5 km NNW Hoi San, 26 km SSW Bong Son, 13 km S to SSW Ha Tay, 13 km WNW Phu My/QL-1) and 41 km NE An Khe. 2d/17th Arty here suptg 1st Cav, Oct 66. Cited in 1st Cav VN *Yearbook* Aug65-Dec69, p 176, per Peter Cole. Grid/data per Jack Picciolo. Also listed at BR 785-713, Sep66. Binh Dinh Pr, II Corps.
Dwarf, FSB (BS 731-328)
Apx 10 km SW Duc Pho, 18 km due E Ba To New AF and 6 km NE Con Doc. Americal list. Quang Ngai Pr, I Corps.
Dyess, USS (n/a)
DD-880, per Ralph Fries.
Dyke, FSB (YS 276-808)
Apx 22 km NW Nui Dat, 7 km NNE FSB Nelson, 7 km due S FSB Cedar. 161 Bty, RNZA (Hitching's Bty 14Apr68-18Mar69) FSB set here 23-25Apr68. On 1ATF NCO trng map per John Hollett. Also listed at YS 27-80. Bien Hoa Pr, III Corps.
Dynamic, USS (n/a)
MSO-432 (also sp *Dymanic*?). Mine Sweeper, Ocean. SVN
Dynamo, LZ (XD 892-639)
On S edge of DMZ, apx 23 km WNW Cam Lo and 35 km WNW Dong Ha. Apr70 XXIV Corps grid per Don Armstrong. Quang Tri Pr, I Corps.
Dynasty Club & Grill (YS 28-42?)
At Vung Tau and visible from Vung Tau Lighthouse. Cited in *Team Sergeant*, p 43. Phuoc Tuy Pr, III Corps.
DZ Donna Airfield (ZA 163-057)
See Plei Me AF. Pleiku Pr, II Corps.
DZ Kent Airfield (BQ 910-705)
See Dong Tre AF. Phu Yen Pr, II Corps.
DZ Natasha (TJ 9-6)
Apx 290 km WNW Hanoi. One of 3 drop zones of French Paras at Dien Bien Phu during 1st day of Op Castor. Op began 20Nov53, when 65 C-47 and C-119 acft out of Hanoi's Gia-Lam and Bac Mai AFs dropped 6th BCP (Para Assault Bn), 6th Colonial Paras (under Maj. Marcel Bigeard), and II/1 RCP (2d Bn/1st Para Light Inf under Maj. Jean Brechignal) into Muong Thanh Valley. 1st stick arrived at 10:30 am, catching Vietminh totally by surprise. For apx 1 year, DBP had been home and trng

base of Vietminh Independent Rgt 148, with 3 Bns along Thai border and Bn 910 (with 3 extra Cos) in valley on day French landed. By coincidence, Bn 910 was trng in DZ Natasha when 6th BCP parachuted in. Bn 910 took the paras under fire, killing several before they landed, but French soon rallied and drove Viets from field. By afternoon, 2,000 French had been inserted. Casualties for 1st day were 11 French KIA, 52 WIA, and roughly 100 Viet Minh KIA. NVN.

ECHO

Facility/Feature Name, Grid Coordinate, a.k.a. Name/History/Province/CTZ

Unless otherwise stated, 6-digit grid coordinates reference DMA L-7014, L-7015 or L-7016 series, 1:50,000 scale maps, while 2 and 4-digit coordinates reference AMS/DMA/NIMA 1:250,000, 1:500,000 and 1:1,000,000 scale maps. Unless otherwise stated, all heights are in meters. To convert meters to feet, multiply by 3.2808; feet to meters, multiply by .3048.

E-1, Strongpoint (TJ 9-6)
Apx 1.7 mi NE the Dien Bien Phu main CP, .75 mi due S D3, .8 mi N of E2 and about .5 mi NE the 2d Thai position. One of 4 defensive positions (E1 thru E4) known as "Elianes." In Muong Thanh Valley apx 290 km W Hanoi. French strongpoint during Op Castor, 20Nov53-7May54. On 10Apr54, Bigeard counter-attacked Vietminh who had overrun E1 and, after taking terrible losses, pushed the Vietnamese out and held it for 20 more days. E-1 again fell to Vietminh, 2May54. NVN.

E-2, Strongpoint (TJ 9-6)
Apx 1.4 mi due E the Dien Bien Phu main CP, .7 mi N Bald Hill, and .7 mi NE E3. One of 4 defensive positions (E1 thru E4) at DBP known as "Elianes." In Muong Thanh Valley apx 290 km W Hanoi. French strongpoint during Op Castor, 20Nov53-7May54. Attempts by Vietminh to overrun E2 with frontal assaults were abnd 4Apr54. As alternative, Vietminh from coal mining area of Dong Trieu were enlisted to dig tunnel under position in which massive charge was placed and detonated at 11pm on 6May54. In that huge blast, Capt. Come's 2d Co of 1st BCP completely disappeared. Gaping hole it produced can still be seen today. E-2 was one of last positions to fall before the general surrender of 7May54. NVN.

E-3, Strongpoint (TJ 9-6)
On E Bank of Nam Yum River apx 1 km due E Dien Bien Phu main CP, .7 mi SW of E2 and immed S 2d Thai position. One of 4 defensive positions (E1 thru E4) at DBP known as "Elianes." In Muong Thanh Valley apx 290 km W Hanoi. Op Castor, 20Nov53-7May54. NVN.

E-4, Strongpoint (TJ 9-6)
Somewhere to E Dien Bien Phu main CP. One of 4 defensive positions (E1 thru E4) at DBP known as "Elianes." In Muong Thanh Valley apx 290 km W Hanoi. E-4 was one of last positions to fall during battle, lasting until the general surrender of 7May54. NVN.

E-5, Camp (WH 3-2?)
In jungle near Ngoc Lac, NVN, and apx 80 km from Camp 70. Vietminh POW Camp for French POWs in early 1950's. In Summer of '52, some 201 of 272 inmates held here died from drinking contaminated water. Discussed in *Prisoners of Hope*, p 7. NVN.

E, LZ (XT 500-890)
Apx 13 km NW Tonle Cham AF and 8 km WSW tip of the Fishhook. 23Mar67. Tay Ninh Pr, III Corps.

E. E. Monahan, Camp (AT/BT?)
See Camp E. J. Monahan. Quang Nam Pr, I Corps.

E Lam Thuong (n/a)
Mapsheet name of L-7014-6733-2. SVN.

E. J. Monahan, Camp (AT/BT?)
At Da Nang. 1st Mar Div, 1st FSG. Likely named to honor E. J. Monahan, Jr, Cpl USMC, KIA 24Aug65. Also listed as Camp E. E. Monohan? Quang Nam Pr, I Corps.

Ea Barr River (BP 3-8)
A.k.a. Ea Bar. Apx 35 km ENE Lac Thien and near 12°30'00"N-108°33'00"E. Site of VC/NVA basecamp discussed in *Ambush*, p 219. May be in Bauh Me Ga (a.k.a. Boun Mi Ga) Valley. Darlac Pr, II Corps.

Ea Bien Lam (BP 1-8)
Freshwater lake at 12°33N-108°20'E. See Krong Ana, Ea. Darlac Pr, II Corps.

Ea Dien (BP 1-9)
Freshwater lake at 12°36N-108°24'E. On ND49-13 JOG. Darlac Pr, II Corps.

Ea Hleo (AQ 9-6?)
See Forget-Me-Not, Op. Pleiku or Darlac Pr, II Corps.

Ea Hok River (AQ 84-78)
Apx 22 km SSW Phu Nhon. Pleiku Pr, II Corps.

Ea Hu (**AP 9-8**)
Freshwater lake at 12°33N-108°14'E. On ND49-13 JOG. Darlac Pr, II Corps.

Ea Kmok River (AQ 75-81)
Apx 22 km SE Phu Nhon. Pleiku Pr, II Corps.

Ea Knu San (BP 0-8)
Freshwater lake at 12°33N-108°18'E. See Krong Ana, Ea. Darlac Pr, II Corps.

Ea Krong Ana (BP 08-90)
One of a group of freshwater lakes roughly 30 km SE Ban Me Thuot, 5-15 km NW and WNW Ban Ti Sren and 15-20 km NE Lac Thien. Lakes were: Ea Knu San, Ea Krong Ana, Ea Ksautch and Ea Ka Nao. Darlac Pr, II Corps.
Ea Krong Bolah River (YA 86-60)
See Ya Krong. Pleiku Prvs, II Corps.
Ea Krong Bolah River (YA 86-60)
See Ya Krong. Pleiku Pr, II Corps.
Ea Krong Bolah Valley (YA 86-60)
See Ya Krong. Pleiku Prvs, II Corps.
Ea Krong Buong River (BP 3-8?)
In Boun Mi Ga Valley, within 50 km of An Loc. Cited in *Ambush*, p 212 (and sp Bouh Me Ga). Darlac Pr, II Corps.
Ea Krong Kno River (ZU 2-8)
Generally 110 km due W Nha Trang. See Buon Krong SF Camp. Darlac Pr, II Corps.
Ea Ksautch (BP 0-8)
Freshwater lake at 12°32N-108°17'E. See Krong Ana, Ea. Darlac Pr, II Corps
Ea Nhiae Coffee Plantation
(AQ 965-055) On QL-21, 18 km ENE Ban Me Thuot. Darlac Pr, II Corps.
Ea Ok River (AQ 80-78)
Apx 22 km SSW Phu Nhon. Pleiku Pr, II Corps.
Ea Soup SF Camp (ZV 105-946)
Apx 26 km WSW Phu Nhon and 7 km W Plei Bai. 5th SF. Info/grid per *SF Order of Battle.* Moved to Buon Brieng. Darlac Pr, II Corps.
Eager Yankee, Operation (n/a)
See *Thomaston, USS.*
Eagle, Camp (YD 827-137)
Built along Rte 546, apx 7 km SSE Hue, 9 km due W Phu Bai and 3 km W QL-1. Originally LZ Tombstone [180], then LZ El Paso, [181] and 1st established on apx 17Jan68 by 1st Cav Div, following its re-deployment to I Corps from LZ Two Bits in III Corps. Was briefly CP of 1st Bde/1st Cav until it re-deployed to Quang Tri later in Jan68. 1st/502d Inf arrived here 10Jan68 and was opcon to 1st Cav. Renamed Camp Eagle 10Mar69, when 101st Abn HQ moved here and began expanding it into large basecamp. Built partly on old graveyard. Only known significant ground action against Eagle occurred at 0030 hrs on 21May68, during Op Nevada Eagle, when an NVA Bn supplemented by VC Sapper Bn struck SW edge of base under cover of over 400 rnds of 122mm rocket, 81mm mortar and RPG into Div HQ area (5 US KIA and 34 WIA and 57 NVA KIA resulted). On 10Jun69, it was hit by 40-50 RPGs. [182] Elements of 3d Bde/82d Abn held portion of perimeter here '68, and called their section of the camp "Camp Rodriguez." Per Russ Richardson (C Bty), elements of 1st/83d Arty were at FSB's Blaze, Bastogne and Birmingham, with HQ'd here. Per Mar98 *Army* Mag, portions of base are in use by Viets today (Oct96). [183] XXIV Corps grid. Also listed at YD 827-173, 806-161, 812-154, 808-162 and 805-162. Map is L-7014-6541-4, per Ken Burrington. See Eagle Entertainment Bowl, and Eagle/Rodriguez. Thua Thien Pr, I Corps. [184] [185]
Eagle, FSB (XS 522-955)
Apx 8 km WSW Duc Hoa AF. Jan68. Also listed at XS 522-755, which if correct is 20 km due S of listed grid and apx 22 km SSW Duc Hoa AF. Hau Nghia Pr, III Corps.
Eagle, FSB (YB?)
Apparently near Dak To. Bde Forward CP for 173d Abn during Battle of Dak To, 1Nov-1Dec67. Kontum Pr, II Corps. [186]
Eagle, FSB (YT 778-389)
Apx 12 km NW of Vo Dat AF. Jul-Oct70. Also at YT 781-384. Binh Tuy Pr, III Corps.
Eagle, LZ (AT 832-659)
Apx 19 km WSW Da Nang AB and 16 km NE Ha Tan AF. Sep-Oct68. Quang Nam Pr, I Corps.
Eagle, LZ (AT 869-605)
Apx 17 km ENE Ha Tan AF and 20 km SW Da Nang AB. Mar68. Quang Nam Pr, I Corps.
Eagle, LZ (BQ 9-6?)
N of Tuy Hoa, WSW Trung Luong, SSE LZ Axe and NE LZ Apple. Involved in Battle of Dong Tre, during Op Nathan Hale, Jun66. Discussed at length in *The Fields of Bamboo*, pp 149, 152-156 et al. Phu Yen Pr, II Corps.
Eagle, LZ (BR 455-973)
Apx 38 km WNW Ha Tay AF and 41 km W Bong Son. Mar66. Binh Dinh Pr, II Corps.
Eagle, LZ (BT 335-182)
Apx 4 km due E Tam Ky AF and 5 km SE Tam Ky. Apr66. Quang Tin Pr, I Corps.
Eagle, LZ (YD 837-145)
See Eagle, Camp. Apr68. Thua Thien Pr, I Corps.
Eagle, LZ (YS 829-714)
On coast, apx 7 km WSW Pho Tri and 20 km SW Ha Tan AF. Aug66. Phuoc Tuy Pr, III Corps.
Eagle, LZ (n/a)
Apparently an ARVN LZ during their Cambodian Incursion. Cambodia.
Eagle, LZ (ZC 122-578)
Apx 3 km NW Thuong Duc CIDG Camp, 4 km WNW LZ Hawk and 37 km SW Da Nang. 7th Marine Rgt used Eagle in searching 10 sq-km area S of Hill 55, between Rte 4 and Song Thu Bon River, during Op Linn River, 1st/7th and 2/26th Marines, 28-29Jan69, 3d Bn 51st ARVN Rgt here Mar69. On map at p 109, *US Marines in Vietnam-1969.* 1st Mar Div. Quang Nam Pr, I Corps.
Eagle/Rodriguez, Camp (YD 815-148)
A.k.a. Camp Eagle and/or Camp Rodriguez. Along Rte 546, apx 7 km SW Hue and 3 km W QL-1. Built apx 500-1,000 meters SE Camp Eagle beginning 4Mar68, by C/307th Engrs/82d Abn. Named to honor 3d Bde/82d Abn's 1st VN casualty, SSG Joe S. Rodriguez, C/1st/505th Inf, KIA 29Feb68. Later its positions were likely blended into those of Eagle as it grew and 82d departed. Discussion of its construction, map, photo and its sign can be found in *All The Way-The 3d Bde, 82d Abn Div in Vietnam, 1968*, pp 6-8, which show the 2 bases as separate sites; however, one 82d vet tells us it was one big camp with 82d covering portion of perimeter. Grid/Info per Butch Sincock. 3rd Bde/82d Abn. See Camp Eagle. Thua Thien Pr, I Corps.
Eagle Base Camp (XT 960-495)
Apx 54 km NNE Saigon and 28 km SSW Dong Xoai. Nickname of 101st Div basecamp at Phuoc Vinh. Phuoc Long Pr, III Corps.

Eagle Bay Heliport (YS 442-673)
See Eagle Farm Heliport. Per Frank Penk, Jr, listed by this name in '69 TAD; however, called "Eagle Farm" in Feb73 TAD. Phuoc Tuy Pr, III Corps.

Eagle Beach (YD 830-330)
Slightly N Tan My and apx 10 km NE Hue. Formally opened as 101st Abn rest area by men of D/1st/506th Inf, 101st Abn, 1May69, who were greeted by a giant layer cake, huge outdoor buffet and Gen. Melvin Zais, the Div CG. Was equipped with miniature golf, USO stage, enlisted and officer/NCO clubs, water ski boats, surf boards, a PX, a massage parlor, pool tables, basketball courts and a dental clinic. Built as addition to Cocoa Beach (a.k.a. Col Co Beach) Navy POL Tank Farm. 101st Div ORLL for period ending 31Jul69, at p 24 states that it could accommodate 160 men for Standdown (overnight stays) and beach itself, 1,000 men during day. Same rpt states that salt water had therapeutic effect for healing jungle rot/cuts otherwise difficult to heal in the field. Also listed as 845-321. See Cocoa Beach. Thua Thien Pr, I Corps. [187]

Eagle Dustoff (n/a)
See Glossary.

Eagle Entertainment Bowl (YD 805-162)
Huge outdoor auditorium at Camp Eagle built by 326th Engrs. On Christmas Day, '69, 16,000 troops saw Bob Hope's USO show at this facility. See Camp Eagle. Thua Thien Pr, I Corps.

Eagle Eye, LZ (AT 846-846)
S of and overlooking Song Cu De River and Hwy 545, apx 10 km WNW Red Beach and 19 km NW Da Nang AB. Apr70 XXIV Corps grid per Don Armstrong. Thua Thien or Quang Nam Pr, I Corps.

Eagle Farm Heliport (YS 442-673)
In or near Luscombe AF at Nui Dat (1st ATF, RAR), apx 30 km NE Vung Tau and 42 km S Xuan Loc. Heliport #743, alt 180', 300' x 300' pad, grass. "Uncontrolled. Five-150' antennas, 600 meters S Pad, obstruction Lts O/R to Phuoc Tuy Arty. CAUTION-Pad within 1000 meters of Luscombe Afld, extv F/W OPS. Road carrying hvy tfc crosses W side of LZ. Arty advsy-Phuoc Tuy 369.6 40.7" per 73 TAD. At 10°33'N 107°14'E, per Feb73 TAD. Phuoc Tuy Pr, III Corps.

Eagle Flight SF Camp (AR 804-470)
Along QL-19, apx 3 km E Pleiku and in or adj to Pleiku AF/Camp Holloway. 5th SF camp that was a prototype of Mike Force concept. Info/grid per *SF Order of Battle*. Pleiku Pr, II Corps.

Eagle Heliport, Camp (YD 810-149)
Apx 9 km due W Phu Bai and 7 km SSE Hue. "Heliport #751, alt 104', seven pads vary in size. Eagle Intl pad reserved for Code 6 or above, PPR tel 956-5225 or 956-5446, marked by 100' x 100' insignia-pointed panel. Acft up thru UH-l may land at Bravo visitors. Larger acft should land at Eagle POL or APO. Commo-Hue Approach Con-274.1 125.5. Arty advsy-HN 67.85 59.50." At 16°24'N 107°38'E, per Feb73 TAD. Thua Thien Pr, I Corps.

Eagle I, FSB (XT 687-928)
Apx 7 km NW An Loc, 13 km WNW Quan Loi, 6 km WSW FSB Eagle II, 10 km ENE tip of Fishhook and 16 km SSW Loc Ninh. Per diary of "Frenchy" Torres, was built beginning 12Aug69. 1st/5th Cav here '69. During Cambodian Incursion, May-Jun70, BtyA/6th/27th Arty, with two-175s, and Bty C/6th/27th Arty, with two-175s here per *11th ACR Cambodia Invasion AAR, 1st Cav Div, May-Jun70*, courtesy Lou Rochat. [188] Grid per Frank Penk, Jr. Also listed at XT 695-927. Binh Long Pr, III Corps.

Eagle II, FSB (XT 741-951)
Apx 6 km ENE FSB Eagle I, 6 km N An Loc, 10 km NW Quan Loi and 14 km due S Loc Ninh. 1st/5th Cav, 1st Cav, '69. Grid per Frank Penk, Jr. Also listed at XT 746-528 per 1st Cav Arty ORLL, but that grid may be a transcription error. Binh Long Pr?, III Corps.

Eagle II, FSB? (XT 746-528?)
Apx 14 km NNW Lai Khe, 10 km SSW Chon Thanh AF and 52 km due N Saigon. Grid may not be accurate given listed position of Eagle I and fact it is also listed at XT 741-951, a point 10 km NW Quan Loi and 6 km N An Loc. Binh Duong Pr?, III Corps.

Eagle III, FSB (XT 746-528?)
Listed at XT 746-928, but that is thought to be in error. Binh Duong Pr?, III Corps.

Eagle Pull, Operation (n/a)
When it was apparent Cambodia had been lost to Khmer Rouge, a plan to evac US and allied personnel from Phnom Penh was initiated. Mission was dubbed Op Eagle Pull. On 3Mar75, Amphibious Ready Grp Alpha (TG 76.4), and 31st Marine Amphib Unit (TG 79.4) arrived off Kompong Som (Sihanoukville) in Gulf of Siam. By 11Apr75, force inc amphib ships *Okinawa*, *Vancouver*, and *Thomaston* (LSD 28), escorted by *Edson* (DD 946), *Henry B. Wilson* (DDG 7), *Knox* (DE 1052), *Kirk* (DE 1087) and Carrier *Hancock*. Gulf of Siam/Cambodia. [189]

Eagle's Beak (XS 585-775)
Apx 30 km SW Tan Son Nhut AB and 5 km W Ben Luc. Terrain feature resembling Eagle's beak, formed by channel of Song Vam Co Dong River. Long An Pr, III Corps.

Eagle's Claw (BR 740-800)
A.k.a. Crow's Foot. Terrain feature apx 40 km NNW Phu Cat, 20 km W QL-1 and 18 km SW Bong Son. From air resembled bird's foot where lower ridge fingers reach toward the ocean. In *Chickenhawk*, described as "seven intersecting valleys, 12 miles south of Bong Son." Gen location of LZs Bird, Horse and Hereford during Op Crazy Horse, 1st Cav, May66. Discussed in *Battles in the Monsoon*, p 96. On SE Quarter of L-7014-6737-1 map per Ken Burrington. Binh Dinh Pr, II Corps.

Eagle's Eye, OP (AT 9-8?)
See OP Eagle's Eye. Quang Nam Pr, I Corps.

Eagle's Gate (YD 803-146)
Apparent location of front gate to Camp Eagle. See Eagle, Camp. Apr-Aug70. Thau Thien Pr, I Corps.

Eagle's Nest (YB 604-355)
See Leghorn. Cambodia.

Eagle's Nest, FSB (YD 406-036)
A.k.a. Dong Re Lao, Hill 1487, Signal Hill, Signal Mtn and A Luoi Mtn. On E edge of A Shau Valley toward its northern end, apx 35 km WSW Hue, 1.5 km WNW FSB Georgia, 14 km due W FSB Veghel, perhaps 15 km E FSB Goodman and 10 km W FSB Cannon. Built in '68 by elements of 1st/502d Inf (opcon to 1st Bde/101st Div) and

101st Abn Engrs. Originally known as Signal Hill for a few days before being given its FSB name, when 1st opened 14Apr68, by LRRP, 8th Eng and 13th Sig Bn elements of 1st Cav during Op Delaware (who called it Signal Mtn, according to *LRRP Company Command*, p 3). Some '68 101st Abn rpts refer to it as Signal Hill. During Lam Son 720, beginning in Apr '71, FSBs Fury, Kathryn, Maureen, Gladiator and later Eagle's Nest were all reopened by B/326th Engrs with 3d Bde/101st Abn providing security. FSBs Co Pung, Binh Dinh and Kim Qui were built during same op as well. 101st Abn. Thua Thien Pr, I Corps. [190]

Eagle's Roost (BN 772-862?)
Nickname of Phan Rang basecamp of 506th Inf, 101st Abn, in Oct67, per www.currahee.org/pageb1.html.

Eakin Compound (WS 789-148?)
Apparently at or near Can Tho and possibly at Binh Thuy AF. Home of IV Corps ARVN Adv Grp. Named to honor Capt. Howard M. Eakin, Jr, USA, KIA 3Jun63, by gunfire while guiding a CH-21 medevac flight near Cau Mau, in An Xuyen Pr. Phong Dinh Pr, IV Corps.

Earl J. Bemis Compound (WS)
See Bemis Cmpd. Kien Phong Pr, IV Corps.

Earl McGovern (n/a)
See Glossary.

Earth, LZ (XD 913-520)
Apx 10 km NW Ca Lu, 12 km NE Khe Sanh CB and 34 km WSW Dong Ha. Apr70 XXIV Corps grid per Don Armstrong. Quang Tri Pr, I Corps.

Earthquake McGoon (n/a)
See Glossary.

Earthquake (n/a)
Apr70, XXIV Corps proposed 101st Abn FSB name.

East, LZ (BT 1310-2025)
A.k.a. FSB East, LZ Mary Lou, Nui VU, LZ 2, Hill 488 and Howard's Hill. On peak of Hill 488, apx 17 km due W Tam Ky, 7 km NNE Tien Phuoc and 10 km ESE LZ Center. Apparently opened '67 by 196th LIB. LZs Center, East and West were all 196th LIB bases of period, and built in line from E to W, spaced roughly 7 km apart. Center was likely so named because it was roughly centered between LZs East and West. Apr70 XXIV Corps grid per Don Armstrong. 1st Cav and Americal Lists. See Howard's Hill. Quang Tin Pr, I Corps.

East, LZ (n/a)
Cambodian Incursion LZ, May-Jun70. Clearing for base was created 1May70 at 0630 hrs by USAF drop of 15,000 lb. bomb (Daisy Cutter or Commando Vault) in order to provide LZ for ARVN Abn initial assault into Cambodia. LZ Terry Lynn also blown by a Daisy Cutter at same time and for same reason. Cambodia.

East 1, FSB (XU 536-008?)
If grid correct, was at Cambodian border, apx 21 km SW Loc Ninh, 11 km NNW tip of Fishhook and 24 km ENE Katum. Incursion FSB, May-Jun70. Data per Frank Penk, Jr. Also listed at XU 596-055 and 562-005? Cambodia or Binh Long Pr, III Corps.

East 1, FSB (XU 596-055?)
If grid correct, was apx 3 km E Cambodia, 15 km WSW Loc Ninh, 32 km NE Katum and 16 km due N tip of Fishhook, roughly halfway between the Fishhook and Angle's Wing. Cambodian Invasion FSB, May-Jun70. Data per Frank Penk, Jr. Also listed at XU 536-008 and XU 562-005? Binh Long Pr, III Corps.

East 2, FSB (XT 592-982)
Apx 16 km SW Loc Ninh, 9 km due N tip of Fishhook and 4 km E Cambodia. Cambodian Invasion FSB, May and/or Jun70. Possibly 1st Cav, 25th Inf, 11th ACR or ARVN elements here. Data per Frank Penk, Jr. Cambodia.

East I, FSB (XU 562-005)
Just inside SVN apx 26 km ENE Katum, 12 km NNW tip of Fishhook, 2 km E Cambodia and 20 km WSW Loc Ninh. Opened 1May70, with LZ prepared by 15,000 Lb. Daisy Cutter. B Bty, 3d ARVN, six-105mms. US 1st/9th Cav also here. 5 NVA KIA and 2 1/2Ton Trucks destroyed. A Bty, 46th ARVN, 3-155s. Cited in *Incursion*, per Peter Cole. Grid and some data per *11th ACR Cambodia Invasion AAR, 1st Cav Div, May-Jun70*, courtesy Lou Rochat. [191] Also listed at XU 596-055 and XU 536-008? Binh Long Pr, III Corps.

East Point (XQ 8-6)
See Point East. IV Corps.

East Ridge Mountain (AT 967-746)
Small hill mass apx 5 km due W Da Nang AB. Major USMC HQ facility built on Hill 327 of this mass. Quang Nam Pr, I Corps.

Easter Egg, The (XT 70-45?)
Egg-shaped terrain feature and aerial landmark discussed in *Low Level Hell,* and shown on 1st Div TAOR map on its inside cover. Apparently apx 10 km NW Lai Khe 7 km SE FSB El Paso and 48 km NNW Saigon. 1st Inf Div AO, '69. Also on map in *Rangers at War*, Appendix I, p 325. Binh Duong Pr, III Corps.

Easter Offensive (n/a)
See Glossary

Easton (n/a)
6Apr70, XXIV Corps proposed 5th Div FSB name.

Easton, LZ (BR 873-953?)
At S end of Bong Son/QL-1 Bridge (over Song Lai Giang), E of QL-1 and immed S Bong Son. 69th Armor website states it was named to honor Lt John Easton, 1st/69th Armor, KIA, 25Sep68, in Happy Valley (Suoi Ca Valley), apx 20 km S this location. Binh Dinh Pr, II Corps.

Easy, LZ (BR 810-914)
Apx 6 km SW Bong Son and 8 km due N Ha Tay AF. Oct66. Binh Dinh Pr, II Corps.

Ebbie, LZ (YA 814-460)
Apx 5 km WSW Plei Djereng New AF and 43 km W Pleiku. Jan66. Sometimes sp Eddie. Pleiku Pr, II Corps.

Ebony, LZ (CR 016-724)
Apx 27 km SW Bong Son, 4 km W the coast and 12 km ENE Phu My/QL-1. Oct66. Possibly same LZ Ebony cited in 1st Cav VN *Yearbook* Aug65-Dec69, p 88, per Peter Cole? Binh Dinh Pr, II Corps.

Ebony, LZ (YD 063-544)
Apx 1 km SE Than Dang Son, 5 km NW Mai Loc and 6 km SW Cam Lo. Cited in 1st Cav VN *Yearbook* Aug65-Dec69, p 88, per Peter Cole. XXIV Corps grid, provide by Don Armstrong. Quang Tri Pr, I Corps.

Echo CAC (YD?)
See CAC Listings. I Corps.

Echo CAP (n/a)
See CAP Echo listings. I Corps.

Echo, FSB (YT 029-155)
Apx 4 km NE Bien Hoa AB, 6 km NW Plantation AF and 25 km NNE Saigon. IIFFV FSB? Vicinity of Bien Hoa AB. Grid per Frank Penk, Jr. Bien Hoa Pr, III Corps.
Echo, LZ (BR 653-746)
Apx 4 km NW Nghia Dien, 15 km NNE Vinh Thanh AF and 27 km SW Bong Son. Near LZ Colt and in ROK AO. Heavy fighting here during Op Crazy Horse. See *Battles in the Monsoon*, pp 212-213. Binh Dinh Pr, II Corps.
Echo, LZ (XT 503-887)
Apx 18 km due E Katum AF, 8 km WSW tip of Fishhook and 5 km S Cambodia. Mar67. Tay Ninh Pr, III Corps.
Echo, LZ (XT 660-260)
Apx 1 km W the Song Saigon, 9 km NNE Cu Chi and 12 km SW Ben Cat. Jun66. Binh Duong Pr, III Corps.
Ed, LZ (XD 994-615)
On Mutter's Ridge, apx 12 km WNW Cam Lo, 14 km due W Dong Ha and 6 km S of S edge of DMZ. Apr70 XXIV Corps grid per Don Armstrong. Quang Tri Pr, I Corps.
Ed, LZ (XT 766-754)
Near Ap Tau O, apx 10 km S An Loc and 16 km due N Chonh Thanh AF. Jul67. Binh Long Pr, III Corps.
Edap Enang (ZA 035-312)
Apx 26 km SW Pleiku, 16 km WSW Catecka, and 8 km WNW the Oasis. Apparently a resettlement ville in 4th Div AO, '68. Pleiku Pr, II Corps.
Edap Enang, LZ (ZA 035-312)
In or adj to Edap Enang, apx 26 km SW Pleiku, 16 km WSW Catecka, and 8 km WNW the Oasis. B Bty, 5th/16th Arty here Dec69. 4th Div 31Jan70 ORLL grid per Jim Henderson. Pleiku Pr, II Corps.
Eddie, LZ (YA 814-460)
See Ebbie. Pleiku Pr, II Corps.
Eddy, LZ (BR 615-606)
At site of Vinh Thanh AF, 21 km NNE An Khe and 5 km NNW Vinh Thanh. Mar66. Binh Dinh Pr, II Corps.
Eden, LZ/FSB (YD 037-385)
A.k.a. FSB Eden. Apx 13 km ENE Lang Klung, 35 km SW Quang Tri and 17 km SSW Mai Loc. Apr70 XXIV Corps grid per Don Armstrong. Also listed at YD 035-385. Quang Tri Pr, I Corps.
Edith, FSB (XT 287-977)
On Cambodian border, apx 10 km NNW Katum and 1 km SE Phun Chitiev. Cambodian Incursion FSB May-Jun70. Tay Ninh Pr, III Corps.
Edna, LZ (YA 648-521)
At S end of Plei Trap Valley, apx 60 km due W Pleiku, 19 km W Plei Djereng New AF and 4 km from Cambodian. Aug70. Kontum Pr, II Corps.
Edson, USS (n/a)
DD 946. See Op Eagle Pull.
Edwards, Camp (AT/BT?)
At Da Nang, but precise location unknown. HQ USMC 1st Engr Bn. Quang Nam Pr, I Corps.
Edwards, Richard S., USS (n/a)
DD 950. See *Morton, USS*.
Egg, LZ (XT 068-875?)
Within 2 km of Cambodia, W QL-22, apx 7 km NNW Thien Ngon AF and 2 km SW Xa Mat. Feb67. Also listed at XT 086-825 same date? Tay Ninh Pr, III Corps.
Egg, LZ (XT 086-825?)
On QL-22 at Thien Ngon AF, apx 9 km S Cambodia. Feb67. Also listed at XT 068-875 same date, though author thinks this is most likely site. Tay Ninh Pr, III Corps.
Ehart, Camp (n/a)
Thought to be misspelling of Camp Enari. Listed in Oct/Nov 2000 *Veteran* Magazine, p 40, as 4th Div FSB. Apparently B/124th Sig Bn here, '68-70. See Enari. Pleiku Pr?, II Corps.
Eight-Inch Hill (BR 88-03?)
Apparently an 8" howitzer Bty or Bn position described as having been 500 meters N of LZ Uplift. 173d Abn, '70. Binh Dinh Pr, II Corps.
Eight-Klickville (YD 7-2? or YD 7-3?)
Greg Mills describes it as hamlet in white coastal sands apparently just N or NW Hue. Was both a terrain feature and in AO of 1st/502d Inf, 101st Abn in Spring/Summer of '68. Named in reference to its distance from another point no doubt (possibly An Lo Bridge or Quang Dien?), but precise location unknown. Thua Thien Pr, I Corps.
Eileen, LZ (ZA 03-93?)
At or in close proximity to Polei Kleng. Grid apx. 7th/15th Arty Bty here at one time. On map at 15th Arty website at www.landscaper.net/chighmap.jpg. Kontum Pr, II Corps.
Eisenhower, FSB (YT 244-373)
Along provincial road apx 11 km N the Song Dong Nai River/LTL24, some 35 km NE Bien Hoa AB and 28 km ESE Phuoc Vinh AF. Also listed at YT 239-331, which puts the site apx 4 km S listed grid, and near site of LZ Liz (YT 241-345), which is 32 km NE Bien Hoa, 6 km N the Song Dong Nai/LTL-24 and 33 km SE Phuoc Vinh. If 2d grid correct, base may have also been known as LZ Liz? Opened or reopened 2Aug70, closed 18Aug70. 2d/7th Cav, closed by 1st/12th Cav, per *1st Cav Div Op Rpt, ending 31Oct70*, courtesy Peter Cole. Long Khanh Pr, III Corps. Gia Dinh Pr, III Corps.
El Paso, FSB (XT 559-047)
If grid correct, was apx 2 km E Khiem Cuong and 15 km SW Cu Chi. Name/grid per Dan Gillotti, 15th Arty Assn. Binh Duong Pr, III Corp.
El Paso, FSB (XT 638-408)
Apx 5 km SE FSB Gela, 15 km ESE Dau Tieng and 17 km NW Ben Cat. On *Low Level Hell's* 1st Div TAOR map. Binh Duong Pr, III Corp.
El Paso, LZ (YD 805-162)
A.k.a. FSB El Paso. See Camp Eagle for location. Originally 1st Cav's 1st Bde HQ and basecamp in early '68. 1st/502d Inf, 101st Abn here Jan68, Site later renamed Camp Eagle, 10Mar69, when 101st Abn HQ moved-in and quickly expanded it into a very large basecamp. Built partly on old graveyard NW Phu Bai Airport, and W QL-1. Map is L-7014-6541-4, per Ken Burrington. Also listed at YD 808-162. See Eagle, Camp. Thua Thien Pr, I Corps.
El Paso II, Operation (n/a)
2Jun-13Jul66. 1st Inf Div and ARVN 5th Inf Div in search of VC's 9th Main Force Div. 855 NVA/VC KIA, per *Vietnam Order of Battle*, pp 9-14. Binh Long Pr, III Corps.
El Paso BEQ (XS 8-9)
Saigon. Data per *Vietnam Military Lore, 1959-1973*. Gia Dinh Pr, III Corps.

Elaine, FSB (XT 559-047)
Apx 7 km ESE Khiem Cuong and 23 km WNW Tan Son Nhut. Aug69-Jan70. Hau Nghia Pr, III Corps.

Elaine, FSB (YS 719-672)
Apx 8 km due E Nui Dat, 1 km SE FSB Feathers, 12.5 km S FSB Toby and 5.5 km N the ocean. On 1ATF NCO trng map per John Hollett. Phuoc Tuy Pr, III Corps.

Elaine, FSB (YU 595-180)
Apx 22 km NE Duc Phong AF/SF Camp and 8 km WSW Bu Binh. Built Feb70-Apr70, B/8th Engr Bn, 1st Cav. [192] Phuoc Long Pr, III Corps.

Elaine, LZ/FSB (YA 863-265)
Along QL-19B apx 2 km NE Duc Co AF/SF Camp, 44 km SW Pleiku and 26 km due W the Oasis AF. A/1st/92d Arty opcon to 3d/6th Arty suptg 1st/10th Cav here mid-69. Grid per 4th Div op rpt for period ending 31Jul69. Name/data/grid per Craig Miller. Pleiku Pr, II Corps.

Elaine, Strongpoint (TJ 9-6)
See Eliane. NVN.

Elbow, The (XD 96-43?)
Terrain feature along QL-9 E, roughly 1 to 2 km E to ENE the Da Krong Bridge, and 17 km ENE Khe Sanh. Apx location on *Leatherneck* Mag map at: www.monboys.com. Grid is est. Quang Tri Pr, I Corps.

Eldest Son, Operation (n/a)
On 23Feb70, the JCS ordered MACV-SOG to cease top secret Ops Eldest Son, Italian Green, and Pole Bean. In these ops, SF teams contaminated the NVA munitions supplies with faulty and rigged ammo throughout SEA theater. Sabotaged ammo and munitions were designed to explode or jam when fired, and reports indicate they were quite successful. Per *Green Berets at War*, p 234.

Eleanor, FSB (XT 916-736)
At or just N Chi Linh, apx 14 km WSW Dong Xoai, 22 km SE An Loc, 23 km N Phuoc Vinh, 6 km SSW Son Duoc and 19 km SSW FSB Jill. Per *LRRP Company Commander*, p 62, FSBs Carolyn Eleanor and Grant were intentionally built on enemy infiltration corridors, with FSBs Billy, Buttons, Dot, Ike, Jamie and Mud firing in supt of them. 2d/505th Inf, and Bty B 2/321st Arty, 82d Abn airlifted to Eleanor apx 8Jan69, in order to block elements of 5th VC Div, and on 14 Jan69, the Bn shifted to FSB Jill. Apparent 1st Cav base during late '68 and '69 (1st/5th Cav, '68). Also listed at XT 900-736, 916-736 and 913-727. Binh Long Pr, III Corps.

Eleanor, FSB (XU 934-026)
If grid correct, was 25 km WSW Song Be, 18 km NE An Loc and 22 km ESE Loc Ninh. Binh Long/Phuoc Long Pr border, III Corps.

Electric Bunker, The (YD 343-194)
Chuck Hawkins tells us this was a legendary, show-case bunker on FSB Ripcord that sported over 20 Claymore Mines and 3 Phougas barrels (all of which could be detonated from one switchboard). The bunker was also completely wired for light using power stolen from base's generators. See FSB Ripcord. Thua Thien Pr, I Corps.

Elenor, FSB (XT 918-732)
See FSB Eleanor. Binh Long Pr, III Corps.

Elephant (n/a)
6Apr70, XXIV Corps proposed 5th Div FSB name.

Elephant (n/a)
See Glossary.

Elephant, LZ (YA 805-610)
Apx 8 km NNW Plei Djereng Old AF and 46 km WNW Pleiku. Jan66. Kontum Pr, II Corps.

Elephant Valley (AT 850-856)
Due E Red Beach and the Nam O Bridge. Apparently named for its trumpeting wild elephants there in '65-66, by 1st and 3d Recon Bn elements. It is unlikely the animals survived long after that period because their value to enemy as pack animals made them fair game for extinction. Entry into this area was almost always heavily contested, forcing Marine units to approach it from more rugged surrounding peaks rather than from Valley's east entrance. See Elephant Valley (Thua Thien Pr). 1st Mar Div. Grid per G. Neville. Quang Nam Pr, I Corps.

Elephant Valley (YC 950-865)
A.k.a. Karam Barum River Valley and Hwy 545 Valley. Apx 10 km SW Bach Ma and 47 km WNW Da Nang AB. Thua Thien Pr, I Corps.

Elephant Valley (YD 35-04)
Apparently at one time name given northernmost, and very narrow tip of the A Shau Valley. FSBs Goodman, Airborne and Pepper lined its W side, with Eagle's Nest on E side at its S end. A Luoi here. Map on inside cover of *The Thirteenth Valley* shows location and many I Corps FSBs. 101st Abn, 1st Cav, USMC. Thua Thien Pr, I Corps.

Elephant's Ear, Little (XT 05-88)
See Little Elephant's Ear. Tay Ninh Pr, III Corps.

Eleven Bravo, FSB (YU 328-503)
A.k.a. FSB 11-Bravo. Cambodian Invasion FSB, May70. Described as having been just inside SVN near Cambodian border apx 14 km N Djamap AF/Bu Ghia Map, SW of FSB Exodus, and 12 km Duc E FSB Shakey's Hill. AO of 1st Cav, 11th ACR and 199th LIB. Also listed at "YT" 328-503, which is believed to be in error. Grid per *11th ACR Cambodia Invasion AAR, 1st Cav Div, May-Jun70*, courtesy Lou Rochat. [193] Phuoc Long Pr, III Corps.

Eleven-Alpha, LZ (YA)
See 10-Alpha, LZ. Pleiku Pr, II Corps.

Eliane (TJ 9-6)
Series of 4 defensive positions at Dien Bien Phu a.k.a. E1, E2, E3 and E4. "To the east, two-thirds of a mile beyond the river, rose a series of hills stretching north and south, the Elianes with their central peak, Eliane 2..."[194] In Muong Thanh Valley apx 290 km W Hanoi. French strongpoints at Dien Bien Phu, Op Castor, 20Nov53-7May54. NVN.

Elkhorn, USS (n/a)
AOG-7. Aux Oiler, per Ralph Fries.

Elle, LZ (XS 150-603)
Apx 15 km NNW Cai Lay and 19 km SW Thuy Dong AF. Nov67. Dinh Tuong Pr, IV Corps.

Elledge, LZ (ZB 165-065)
Apx 3 km SW Kon Dak Dem, 4 km NE Tri Dao and 21 km NNW Kontum. Likely named to honor 1Lt Michael S. Elledge, KIA 24Jul68, or PFC Wayne C., KIA 13Oct68. Sep69-Jan70. Kontum Pr, II Corps.

Ellen, FSB (YU 035-064)
A.k.a. LZ Ellen. Apx 10 km W to WSW Song Be AF, 15 km WSW Song Be AF/Phuoc Binh and 32 km E to ESE Loc Ninh. 1st/12th, 5th/7th Cav, 1st Cav, '68, 1st/8th Cav,

Oct-69, D/1st/7th Cav here Nov69, per "Frenchy" Torres. Grid per Frank Penk, Jr. Also listed at YU 036-067 and YT(?) 035-062 per Arty ORLLs. Phuoc Long Pr, III Corps.

Ellie, LZ (BS 925-271)
On coast apx 15 km SE Duc Pho and 15 km NNE Gia An. May67. Quang Ngai Pr, I Corps.

Ellingsworth, (XT 033-788)
See FSB Illingworth. Tay Ninh Pr, III Corps.

Elliott, LZ (XD 982-558)
See Elliott Combat Base. Quang Tri Pr, I Corps.

Elliott Combat Base (XD 982-542)
A.k.a. FSB/LZ Elliott. If grid correct, was on S and E of QL-9, apx 3 km SE the Rockpile, 13 km WSW Cam Lo and 2 km S of Thon Son Lam. Also listed at XD 990-540, 998-558, 975-613, Dec68-Jan70. Major USMC base. Quang Tri Pr, I Corps.

Elliott, USS (n/a)
A.k.a. DD-967. The destroyers *Elliott* and *Peterson* were named to honor USN Lt Cmdrs who were KIA on Song Vam Co Dong River during Op Giant Slingshot. See *Brown Water, Black Berets*, p 334. Apparently this craft never served in SVN.

Ellis, LZ (YD 018-594)
Apx 2 km W to WNW Mai Loc, 8 km SW Cam Lo and 8 km ENE to NE Ca Lu. Apr70 XXIV Corps grid per Don Armstrong. Quang Tri Pr, I Corps.

Ellison, Harold E., USS (n/a)
A.k.a. DD 864. See *Barry* (DD 933).

Elm, FSB (XT 274-700)
On TL-4, apx 12 km due N peak of Nui Ba Den and 21 km SSW Katum. '67. Tay Ninh Pr, III Corps.

Elois, FSB (XT 534-811)
Apx 3 km W the Song Vam Co Dong River, 9 km due N Thu Thua, 17 km SSW Duc Hoa, and 32 km SW Tan Son Nhut AB. Per David Argabright, was built by 2d/60th Inf beginning 8Jul70, and, "Elois was never spelled ending with an "e" in 3 months of S-3 Journal entries," so presumably "Elois" is correct sp. Name & Grid per David Argabright. Long An Pr, III Corps. [195]

Eloise, FSB (XT 534-811)
See Elois, FSB. Long An Pr, III Corps.

Elrod, FSB/LZ (XT 339-846)
Apx 4 km SW Bo Tuc, 34 km NNE Tay Ninh and 7 km SSE Katum. 1st/8th Cav, 1st Cav here, Jan-69, per Frank Penk, Jr. Also listed at "XS" 337-845, but that is thought to be incorrect grid zone. Tay Ninh Pr, III Corps.

Elsenberg, FSB (XT 113-494)
A.k.a. FSB Ap Cao Xa 3. At Ap Cao Xa, apx 6 km SW Tay Ninh West AF and 3 km NE Ben Soi. Oct70. Likely named to honor Willie E. Elsenberg, KIA 27May70. Tay Ninh Pr, III Corps.

Eltenge, Leroy (n/a)
MSTS or *USNS* troop transport that carried the 1st Bde of 101st Abn to Vietnam in '65.

Elvira, FSB (XS)
A.k.a. FSB Elvyra? 199th LIB FSB/patrol base per 199th LIB Assn list. 15Jun69 RedCatcher newspaper excerpt at www.redcatcher.org/Sum-06-15-69.html states, "arty and mortar fire from fire support base "Elvira" were called into the area nine miles SW of Saigon." Presumably base was within 20 km SW of Saigon. Gia Dinh Pr, III Corps.

Elvyra, FSB (n/a)
See Elvira. III Corps.

Elwood, LZ (AR 927-572)
Apx 19 km NE Pleiku and 5 km ENE Plei Neh. Apr66. Pleiku Pr, II Corps.

Ely (n/a)
6Apr70, XXIV Corps proposed 5th Div FSB name.

Em, FSB (YS 07-87)
On N side of LTL-25, apx 20 km due E Saigon, 8 km SW Long Thanh AF and 12 km ESE Cat Lai. 2d/3d Inf, 199th LIB here. Bien Hoa Pr, III Corps.

Embassy (US) Heliport (XS 863-922)
Heliport atop US Embassy in downtown Saigon. Was apx 6 km SE Tan Son Nhut AB and under 1 km W the Saigon River. "Heliport # 749, alt 129', 49' x 74' pad on rooftop, marked with white 'H', Offl Bus Only: PPR Tel 923-3410 or 927-7405, after normal duty hrs 927-7327. On roof of Embassy bldg. Contact Saigon Heliport H-3 for traffic advsy on 281.1 or 35.5. Contact Embassy Con 40.0 for ldng clearance. Arty advsy-Saigon 239.0, 34.9 46.0." At 10°49'N 106°42'E, per Feb73 TAD. Gia Dinh Pr, III Corps.

Emelia, LZ (BR 477-595)
A.k.a. LZ Amelia and Emilia. Along road between An Khe and Kannack, at or near Plei Ko Re, apx 15 km N An Khe. Was also close to LZ/FSB Aquarius and 7 km SE Kannack AF. 1st/92d Arty attached to 17th Arty here supt 1st/4th Inf, 12Dec69, per Jack Picciolo. Name/grid per Jim Claeys. Also listed at BR 472-596. Binh Dinh Pr, II Corps.

Emerald Buddha (PR 7-3?)
R&R tourist spot in Bangkok, Thailand.

Emery, FSB (XT 702-145)
See Emory. Binh Duong Pr, III Corps.

Emery, LZ (YA 902-658)
A.k.a. LZ Emory? On ridgeline apx 5 km SW Chu Pa Mtn, 3 km E the Ya Krong Bolah River and 22 km W Plei Mrong. Built by 1st/12th Inf, 4th Div in late Jan or early Feb69. Near listed grid. Kontum or Pleiku Pr, II Corps.

Emilia, LZ (BR 472-596)
See Emelia. Binh Dinh Pr, II Corps.

Emory, FSB (XT 702-145)
Along N side of Rte TL-8A (road linking Cu Chi with Phu Cuong/Lam Son), apx 4 km E Cu Chi, and in or near Tin Hoa. Units of 2d/14th Inf and 1st/5th (Mech) Inf, 25th Div here '68-69. 2d/14th Inf, 2d/49th ARVN Rgt elements here 8Aug69. Cited in 3Sep69, AAR/Quarteval Feeder rpts of 2d/14th Inf at: www.en.com/users/kramsey/ vnr102.html#. Info/grid per Doug Huffman, Kirk Ramsey and Butch Sincock. Binh Duong Pr, III Corps. [196] [197]

Empire State, SS (n/a)
Merchant ship under govt contract, per Ralph Fries.

Empress Baltimore, SS (n/a)
Merchant ship under govt contract, per Ralph Fries.

En, Mui (CR 1-2)
A.k.a. Mui Yen. Coastal point at 13°45'N-109°18'E. On ND49-09 JOG. Binh Dinh Pr, II Corps.

Enari, Camp (AR 802-350)
Originally Dragon Mtn Basecamp. Apx 12-14 km SSE Pleiku, 2 km SE QL-14/19, 10 km ENE Catecka AF, immed N of and including Hensel AF, 11 km due S Pleiku Area AF, 18 km ENE the Oasis and generally 2 to 3 km SE Dragon Mtn. Its NW corner was roughly 2 km SE QL-19

and 1.5 km E QL-14 at closest point. Basecamp and HQ of 4th Div. Named to honor, 1Lt Mark N Enari, USA, Plt Ldr in A/1st/12th Inf, 4th Div, KIA 2Dec66, while assaulting MG nest in order to protect 5 wounded men under its fire. Received first 4th Div posthumous Silver Star of VN War (camp named 14May67). Per Tom Rethard, "the road to 'front gate' of Enari was just N of [Dragon Mtn.] and bulk of the encampment was E and SE of it." Per Gus Reynolds, it was "amazing how many changes that place went through. Got there in Mar69 and moved off in Nov69. Went back in Mar70 and it was half the size it had been in Nov69 although it was never really very big." In Aug-Oct '71, base was HQ for ARVN 47th Rgt. 4th Avn Bn HQ'd here also. Elements here also provided security for 362d and 124th Sig Co's Troposcatter signal site on nearby Dragon Mtn. Signal Mtn (much smaller than Dragon) appears to have been along S edge of base and it was also apparently covered with commo antennas. FSB Merry (possibly also FSB Enari?) was name of 7th/15th arty position inside base in '71, per 1Nov71 ORLL courtesy Nolan Puttman. Grid is at center of mass and N Hensel AF on mapsheet L-7014-6636-4. On map, base is a rectangle, 1.3 km wide E to W and 2.5 km tall on its N to S axis, with Hensel AF definitely within its perimeter. Per *Dak To*, p 45, was built by 2d Bde/4th Div, when Bn was 1st sent to central highlands. Some data per Ray Bows' *Vietnam Military Lore, 1959-1973*. L-7014 map excerpt showing of site at: www.rjsmith.com/camp-enari-sm-nf.html#map-edge. See footnote to Engineer Hill. Pleiku Pr, II Corps. [198]

Enari, FSB (AR 80-35?)
A.k.a. FSB Merry? Per Nolan Puttman, here Oct71, site was "just outside Pleiku at old 4th Div base area." Apparently built within Enari's old perimeter after camp closed as US facility? C Bty/7th/15th Arty here. Also spelled "Anari." Pleiku Pr, II Corps.
Arty here. Pleiku Pr, II Corps.

Enari Airfield, Camp (AR 803-339)
See Hensel AF. Pleiku Pr, II Corps.

Enari Refugee Center (AR 800-350)
Immed S Camp Enari. NPIA data. Pleiku Pr, II Corps.

Enau, Camp (AR 801-339)
Apparent misspelling of Camp Enari? Pleiku Pr, II Corps.

End Sweep, Operation (NVN)
Clearing of mines from NVN waters at end of war. As part of Paris Peace Accords, on 6Feb73, one day after Cmdr TF 78 met with NVA Col Hoang Huu Thai, the 6-month op began. Ocean Minesweepers *Engage* (MSO 433), *Force* (MSO) 445), *Fortify* (MSO 446), and *Impervious* (MSO 449) swept areas off near Haiphong while escorted by Frigate *Worden* (DLG 18) and destroyer *Epperson* (DD 719). Later, amphib ships *New Orleans* (LPH 11), *Dubuque* (LPD 8), *Ogdon* (LPD 5), *Cleveland* (LPD 7), and *Inchon* (LPH 12) joined Op. Force carried 31 CH-53s from USN Helicopter Mine Countermeasures Sqdn 12 and from USMC Helo sqdns HMM-165 and HMH-463. Helos towed minesweeping sleds and etc., along waterways and port areas. Total of 10 ocean minesweepers, 9 amphib ships, 6 fleet tugs, 3 salvage ships, and 19 destroyer types served with TF 78. After week of clearing, Adm McCauley declared approaches to harbors of Haiphong, Hon Gai and Cam Pha free of mines. Flotilla then worked area off Vinh, and on 18Jul73, op ended and US 7th Fleet departed NVN territorial waters for last time in war. NVN. [199 200]

Endurance, USS (n/a)
MSO-434. Minesweeper, Ocean, per Ralph Fries.

Engage, USS (n/a)
MSO 433. See End Sweep, OP.

Energy, USS (n/a)
MSO-436. Minesweeper, Ocean, per Ralph Fries.

Engage, USS (n/a)
MSO-433. Minesweeper, Ocean, per Ralph Fries.

Engineer Base (XT 690-870)
Apx 6 km W An Loc and 10 km ESE tip of Fishhook. Apr67. Binh Long Pr, III Corps.

Engineer Hill (AR 795-525)
A.k.a. Pleiku North? Immed NE Pleiku/Cu Hanh AF and 5 km NNW Pleiku AF/Camp Holloway. Home of 330th Radio Research Co, as well as elements of 815th Engr Bn and 584th Engr Co, among others. Pleiku Pr, II Corps. [201]

Engineer LZs (various)
See Glossary.

English, LZ (BS 879-005)
Originally known as Area Dog and LZ Dog. Along W side of QL-1, apx 3 km NE An Lo River, 75 km SSE Quang Ngai, 82 km NNW Qui Nhon, 12 km SSW Gia An, 12 km due S Hammond AF, 5 km NNE Bong Son/Hoai Nhon, 7 km NE Bong Son AF, and 7 km W of the ocean. 173rd Abn and 1st Cav Bde-sized basecamp with C-130 capable AF. During Aug-Oct68, 19th Engr Bn upgraded LZ English AF rwy to C-130-capable asphaltic surface. [202] Site named LZ Dog when opened in early '66 by 1st Cav assault described in *Chickenhawk*, pp 265-268. Origin of name unknown. USMC, Americal, 2d/503d Inf 173d Abn (68-69), and 1st Cav elements here at various times. B Bty 2d/17th Arty here Aug67 (BS 8871-0091) per Jack Picciolo. Also listed at BS 875-010, 879-000, 877-077 and 877-013. Map is L-7014-6838-3 (Tam Quan). See LZs Dog and North English. Binh Dinh Pr, II Corps. [203]

English Airfield (BS 879-010)
Originally LZ Dog. Major C-130 capable AF on W side of QL-1, apx 12 km SSW Gia An, 12 km due S Hammond AF, 5 km NNE Bong Son/Hoai Nhon, 7 km NE Bong Son AF, and 7 km W mouth of An Lo River. During Aug-Oct68, 19th Engr Bn upgraded LZ English AF's rwy to C-130-capable asphaltic surface. [204] El. 98', 3,600' rwy. 14°28'19"N-109°02'05"E. Binh Dinh Pr, II Corps.

English North, LZ (BS 883-056)
See North English, LZ. Binh Dinh Pr, II Corps.

English, Camp (BS 879-005)
See LZ English. Binh Dinh Pr, II Corps.

Enhance, Project (n/a)
See Project Enhance in Glossary.

Enhance Plus, Project (n/a)
See Project Enhance Plus in Glossary.

Enid Victory, SS (n/a)
Merchant ship under govt contract, per Ralph Fries.

Enterprise, LZ (XD 885-361)
At N end of Vietnam Salient, apx 18 km SW Ca Lu, 47 km WSW Quang Tri and 6 km NW Lang Klung. XXIV Corps grid per Don Armstrong. Quang Tri Pr, I Corps.

Enterprise, Operation (n/a)
13Feb67-11Mar68. 9th Inf Div/ARVN/RF-PF op. 2,107 rptd NVA/VC KIA, per *Vietnam Order of Battle*, pp 9-14. Long An Pr, III Corps.

Enterprise, USS (n/a)
A.k.a. CVAN-65. Deployed with CVW-14 11Jun71-12FEB72; with CVW-14 12Sep72-12Jun73; with CVW-14 17Sep74-20May75; with CVW-9 3Jan68-18Jul68; with CVW-9 6Jan69-2Jul69; with CVW-9 19Nov66-6Jul67; with CVW-9 26Oct65-21Jun66. Suffered serious fire 14Jan69, while operating near Hawaii (similar to *Forrestal* fire. Apparently a rocket cooked off by flight deck exhausts and, as in *Forrestal's* Fire (29Jul67), hit another acft and started 4-hour disaster which, though less serious than 29Jul67 incident, was still substantial. *USS Bainbridge* raced to assist, and then escorted her into Pearl Harbor the next day. *USS Rogers* (DD 876), also assisted in dousing fires. Data per www.uss-salem.org/ features/fires/. [205]

Entrance Valley (YS 47-52)
Entrance to Minh Dam Secret Zone apx 4 km SE FSB Isa, 2 km N Hon Vung Mtn, 20 km ENE Vung Tau and roughly half way between Hill 327 (Hon Vung) and Hill 312. 1ATF, ANZAC AO. Phuoc Tuy Pr, III Corps.

Epperson, USS (n/a)
DD 719. On 8Jul68, replaced *USS Borie* off Binh Thuan Pr suptg TF 3d/506th Inf. On 13Jul68, shelled VC basecamp near Phan Thiet w/164-rnds of HE and WP. Credited w/16 VC KIA and 2 mortars KIA per www.currahee.org/pageb2.html. See End Sweep for more data.

Epping Forest, USS (n/a)
LSD-4/MCS-7. Minesweeper, Coastal. Crew member Ralph Fries tells us, "On 4Aug64 when the *Turner Joy* and *Maddox* thing happened, [we were] 200 miles SSE. We'd just left Nha Trang headed for Subic Bay after [surveying] all the harbors and coast line so we'd have accurate charts. French Charts would leave you high and dry."

Erawan, Camp (PS 7-3)
At Lopburi(Lop Buri), Thailand. Home of Royal Thai Army Abn Ranger School. Cited in *Rangers at War*, pp 272-3. Lop Buri Pr, Thailand.

Erhart, Camp (n/a)
Apparent misspelling of Camp Enari. See Enari.

Erie, LZ (XD 785-375)
At extreme NW edge of Vietnam Salient, apx 1 km from Laos, 9 km NNW Lang Chei, 24 km SW Ca Lu, 9 km SW Khe Sanh CB and 56 km WSW Quang Tri. Apr70 XXIV Corps grid per Don Armstrong. Quang Tri Pr, I Corps.

Ernest G. Small, USS (n/a)
DDR-838, per Ralph Fries.

Ernie, LZ (XT 300-286)
Apx 18 km SW Tay Ninh and 10 km WNW Go Dau Ha. Mar66. Tay Ninh Pr, III Corps.

Erskine, FSB (YD 164-107)
Remote site overlooking Song Da Krong River Valley apx 3 km SW FSB Cunningham, 18 km NW Dong Ap Bia (Hamburger Hill), 7 km NNE Co Cay Leuye and 7 km from Laotian border. 2d/3d Marines began const 1Feb69. FSBs Erskine, Razor, and Cunningham plus LZ Dallas were built during Op Dawson River South, Jan22-10Feb69, to facilitate attack on Base Area 618. See map at p 73, *US Marines in Vietnam-1969*. XXIV Corps grid per Don Armstrong. Quang Tri Pr, I Corps.

Erskine, FSB (YD 583-231?)
Grid is that of FSB Cathy and likely error? If correct, was apx 12 km SE Camp Evans and 16 km W Hue Citadel AF. Thua Thien Pr, I Corps.

Eskimo (n/a)
6Apr70, XXIV Corps future-use 5th Div FSB name.

Esquire, LZ/FSB (BR 976-747)
Apx 25 km SE Bong Son, 10 km NE Phu My and 6 km E QL-1 Cited in 1st Cav VN *Yearbook* Aug65-Dec69, p 88, per Peter Cole. Oct66. Binh Dinh Pr, II Corps.

Essex, LZ (YD 228-301)
Apx 32 km W Camp Evans, 25 km SSW Quang Tri and 21 km NNE Tou Rout. Apr70 XXIV Corps grid per Don Armstrong. Quang Tri Pr, I Corps.

Essex, USS (n/a)
A.k.a. CVA 9. See *Wasp, USS* for detail.

Esso, Camp (n/a)
Location unknown, though apparently in I Corps. There were several Esso, VinaTexaco and other oil refinery/stg facilities in SVN, with one site I Corps site N of Red Beach AF near Da Nang, and another at Tan My E of Hue. Listed in USAF Herbicide gallonage rpt that also indicates following agents were sprayed within an 8 km radius of this facility: Orange, 53410; White, 5600; Blue, 5500. I Corps.

Esso, LZ (BT 368-060)
Apx 18 km SSE Tam Ky, 2 km NW FSB Pearl and 16 km due W Chu Lai. Elements of 2d/1st Inf, 196th LIB here 14Aug67 during Op Benton. Name/grid per Les Hines. Quang Tin Pr, I Corps.

ESSO POL Terminal (AT 938-867)
Along QL-1 at coast, and apx 2 km NE Ap Kim Kien and 13 km NNW Da Nang AB. Quang Nam Pr, I Corps.

Est, Baie de l' (XQ 7-5)
A.k.a. Vinh Con Son. Bay of Con Son Island at 8°40'N-106°38'E. On NC48-11 JOG. IV Corps.

Est, Lagune de l' (YD 91)
A.k.a. Dam Thuy Tu. Lagoon at 16°26'N-107°46'E. On NE48-16 JOG. Thua Thien Pr, I Corps.

Est, Pointe del (XS 7-9)
See Pointe Est. Gia Dinh Pr?, III Corps.

Esteem, USS (n/a)
MSO-438. Minesweeper, Ocean, per Ralph Fries.

Ester, FSB (n/a)
A.k.a. Esther. No data. Possibly a 4th Div FSB in II Corps?

Esther, FSB (n/a)
A.k.a. Ester. No data. Possibly a 4th Div FSB in II Corps?

Eugene Lykes, SS (n/a)
Merchant ship under govt contract, per Ralph Fries.

Eunice, Camp (XU 896-188?)
If same as FSB Eunice, then was along QL 14A (linked Bu Dop and Loc Ninh), apx 13 km SW Bu Dop, 20 km NE Loc Ninh and 5 km S Cambodia (FSB Eunice also listed at XU 877-185, apx 2 km W listed grid).1st Inf Div rpt indicates Eunice was apx 85 mi (140 km) N Saigon, and FSB Eunice was apx 85 mi NNE Saigon, so likely same facility. Name per Bill Middlesworth. Phuoc Long Pr/Binh Long Pr border, III Corps.

Eunice, FSB (XU 877-184)
If grid correct, was apx 4 km NE Phu Loi AF and 12 km NW Bien Hoa AF. Listed at this grid and as 1st Cav, per 15th Arty Assn. Binh Duong Pr, III Corps.

Eunice, FSB (XU 896-188)
A.k.a. Camp Eunice? Along QL 14A (linked Bu Dop and Loc Ninh), apx 13 km SW Bu Dop, 20 km NE Loc Ninh and 5 km S Cambodia. Also listed at XU 877-185, apx 2 km W listed grid? Cited in *1st Cav Op Rpt, May-Jul70*, p 28, 38, per Peter Cole. Also listed at XU 877-185? Phuoc Long/Binh Long Pr border, III Corps.

Evacuation of Da Nang (BT)
See Da Nang, Evacuation of, in Glossary.

Evans, Camp (YD 541-318)
A.k.a. LZ Evans. Along Rte 601, apx 2.5 km SSE Phong Dien, 11 km WNW LZ Sally, 24 km NW Hue and perhaps 800 meters W QL 1. Initially USMC position, then 1st Cav HQ, followed by 101st Abn Bde HQ, '68-72. Per one rpt, was named to honor Marine named "Paul D. Evans," but no one with that middle initial was KIA. Same rpt implied Paul was with I/3d/26th Marines during Op Chinook (I, II, and/or III 3) in '66 or 67. If that rpt is otherwise correct, then base was likely named to honor Paul O. Evans, a USMC LCpl KIA 22Dec66. [206] In '70, 101st Abn moved its in-country trng facility (1 week "P" or "SERTs" Trng, for replacements) here from Bien Hoa AB. 101st Combat Leadership School (CLC) also here. 1st Cav HQ moved here from An Khe, early '68. Per Mar98 *Army* Magazine, Evans is now being farmed and no trace of it remains. [207] Per Ray Bows in his epic, *Vietnam Military Lore, Legends and Shadows*, Evans was opened by USMC and later occupied by 1st Cav, then 101st Abn units. Bows thinks it was named for one of 3 Marines: Cpl Paul O. Evans, Cpl Eric W. Evans, but most likely for PFC Sammy G. Evans, KIA 21Apr67, when bunker he was building there collapsed. Per Bob Witt, on 19May68, the birthday of Ho Chi Minh, an enemy mortar rnd found Evans' ammo dump, setting off fire/blasts that lasted 36 hrs and destroyed some 200 helos. [208] Also listed at YD 535-314. Map is L-7014-6442-2, per Ken Burrington. Thua Thien Pr, I Corps. [209]

Evans, FSB (XU 485-166)
In Cambodia apx 8 km W SVN border, 19 km SSW Snuol, 22 km NE Memot and 26 km WNW Loc Ninh, 1st Cav FSB during Cambodia Incursion, May70. Opened 4May70? Cited in *1st Cav Div Op Rpt for period May-Jul70*, pp 36, 38, per Peter Cole. Grid and some data per *11th ACR Cambodia Invasion AAR, 1st Cav Div, May-Jun70*, courtesy Lou Rochat. [210] Cambodia.

Evans, FSB (YT 223-060)
FSB that "sat firmly astride a known VC trail to and from Saigon," 7.5 km SSE FSB Anderson, 23 km WSW Xuan Loc, 8 km W FSB Sally, 4 km S QL-1 and 22 km E Bien Hoa. 161 Bty, RNZA (Hitching's Bty 14Apr68-18Mar69) FSB set here 25Apr-3May68. On 1ATF NCO trng map per John Hollett. Bien Hoa Pr, III Corps.

Evans, LZ (YD 426-478)
Apparently original site of Camp Evans. See Evans, Camp, for location. Also listed at YD 529-320 and YD 544-323 in Apr68 as well? Apr-Aug68. Thua Thien Pr, I Corps.

Evans, USS (n/a)
Arrived off Phan Thiet 3Feb68 to supt TF 3d/506 Inf, per www.currahee.org/pageb2.html.

Evans Airfield, Camp (YD 540-321)
A.k.a. Phong Dien AF. Apx 26 km SE Quang Tri, per ONC K-10 and ONC J-11. El. 63', 2,900' alum-mat rwy. At 16°33'31"N-107°22'48"E. Thua Thien Pr, I Corps.

Evans Army Airfield (YS 437-963)
At Blackhorse Basecamp, Long Giao, apx 57 km due E Saigon. Named to honor WO1 Thomas J. Jr Evans, Air Trp, 11th ARC, WIA 28Feb67 and died of wounds 1Mar67, after being shot down while engaging VC with his helicopter gunship near Tay Ninh. Data per *Vietnam Military Lore, 1959-1973*. Long Khanh Pr, III Corps.

Everett F. Larsen, USS (n/a)
DD-830, per Ralph Fries.

Eversole, USS (n/a)
DD-789, per Ralph Fries.

Excedrin, FSB (AT 015-347)
In Que Son Valley apx 40 km due S Da Nang AB, 4 km NNE Hill 270, 2 km W Que Son and 31 km WNW Tam Ky. Americal list. Quang Nam Pr, I Corps.

Excel, USS (n/a)
MSO 439. On 27Aug61, Cmdr Mine Div 93, with ocean minesweepers *Leader* (MSO 490) and *Excel* (MSO 439), made 1st official visit by ships of USN to Phnom Penh, the capital of Cambodia. [211]

Execute (n/a)
Apr70, XXIV Corps proposed 101st Abn FSB name.

Executive (n/a)
Apr70, XXIV Corps proposed 101st Abn FSB name.

Executive order 10977 (n/a)
See Glossary.

Executive Order 11216 (n/a)
See Glossary.

Executive Order 11231 (n/a)
See Glossary.

Exhibitor, SS (n/a)
Merchant ship under govt contract, per Ralph Fries.

Exodus, FSB (YT 365-572?)
YT grid zone possibly incorrect, but if accurate, was apx 80 km NW Saigon, 24 km W Loi Tan and 41 km ENE Phuoc Vinh AF. Described as Cambodian Incursion FSB. Long Khanh Pr?, III Corps.

Exodus, FSB (YU 365-572?)
If grid correct, was just inside SVN, apx 13 km due W Bu Krak, 14 km WNW Bu Krak AF, 22 km NNE Djamap AF/Bu Gia Map. In AO of 1st Cav, 11th ACR and 199th LIB. Also listed at YT 365-572; however, that grid would put base 36 km SE Dong Xoai, 44 km NW Vo Dat and some 80 km from Cambodia, and is thought to be erroneous. Also listed at YU 375-564, a site apx 1 km E listed grid. Cambodian Incursion FSB, May70. Phuoc Long Pr, III Corps. [212]

Exodus, FSB (YU 375-564)
Just inside SVN border, apx 12 km due W Bu Krak, 14 km WNW Bu Krak AF, 22 km NNE Djamap AF/Bu Gia Map. Grid in*11th ACR Cambodia Invasion AAR, 1st Cav Div, May-Jun70*, per Lou Rochat. [213] Also listed at YU 365-572, a point 10 km W of listed grid? Phuoc Long Pr, III Corps.

Exodus, LZ (YA 791-238)
At SW edge of Thanh Duc, apx 6 km SW Duc Co, 6 km W to WSW LZ Joan, and 50 km SW Pleiku. A Bty, 7th/15th (with two-8" Howitzers), A Bty 6th/14th (two-175s) and A Bty 7th/13th Arty here, Jun70. 4th Div 31Jul70 ORLL grid, per Jim Henderson. Pleiku Pr, II Corps.

FOXTROT

Facility/Feature Name, Grid Coordinate, a.k.a. Name/History/Province/CTZ

Unless otherwise stated, 6-digit grid coordinates reference DMA L-7014, L-7015 or L-7016 series, 1:50,000 scale maps, while 2- and 4-digit coordinates reference AMS/DMA/NIMA 1:250,000, 1:500,000 and 1:1,000,000 scale maps. Unless otherwise stated, all heights are in meters. To convert meters to feet, multiply by 3.2808; feet to meters, multiply by .3048.

F-1 (YB 822-226)
See Firebase 1. 15 Jun66. Kontum Pr, II Corps.
F-2 (YB 875-209)
See Firebase 2. 15 Jun66. Kontum Pr, II Corps.
F-3 (YB 894-186)
See Firebase 3. 15 Jun66. Kontum Pr, II Corps.
F-4 (YB 869-186)
See Firebase 4. 15 Jun66. Kontum Pr, II Corps.
F-5 (YB 898-188)
See Firebase 5. 15 Jun66. Kontum Pr, II Corps.
F-6 (YB 905-186)
See Firebase 6. 15 Jun66. Kontum Pr, II Corps.
F-7 (YB 865-187)
See Firebase 7. 15 Jun66. Kontum Pr, II Corps.
F-8 (YB 917-193)
See Firebase 8. 15 Jun66. Kontum Pr, II Corps.
F, Checkpoint (YD 460-400)
See Checkpoint F. Quang Tri Pr?, I Corps.
F, FSB (New) (YB 823-080)
See Firebase F. Kontum Pr, II Corps.
F, FSB (Old) (YB 821-078)
See Firebase F, Old. Kontum Pr, II Corps.
F, LZ (XT 970-200)
On Cu Lao Binh Chanh Island in the Song Dong Nai, apx 1 km WNW Ap Tan Trach and 6 km NNW Bien Hoa AB. 12Jun67. Bien Hoa Pr, III Corps.
F, Valley (CR 0-1?)
See Valley F. Binh Dinh Pr, II Corps.
F.O.M. Rations (n/a)
See Glossary.
Fac Ta (n/a)
Mapsheet name of L-7014-6253-2. NVN only.
Fai Tsi Long, Archipel (YH 5-9)
Long Chau Island grp. NIMA data. NVN.
Faifo (BT 146-517)
A.k.a. Hoi An. Apx 22 km SSE Da Nang AB. Portuguese colony trading post established in 1600's. Capitol, Quang Nam Pr, I Corps.
Fairfax, Operation (n/a)
30Nov66-14Dec67. Search and clear op around Saigon initially involving simply one Bn each from 1st, 4th, and 25th US Inf Divs. These were relieved by arrival of 199th LIB, Jan67. ARVN 5th Ranger grp later assumed defense of Saigon. 1,043 NVA/VC KIA, per *Vietnam Order of Battle*, pp 9-14. Gia Dinh and other Prvs, III Corps.
Fairport, SS (n/a)
Merchant ship under contract to MSTS. Apparently routinely carried 8,000 tons of ammo to Da Nang in at least '69. See www.war-stories.com/RedSky.htm.
Faith POW Camp (WJ)
US POW nickname for POW camp S or W the Red River, just N or NW Hanoi. On map at www.soft-vision.com/hanoi/frame.html. NVN.
Faitsilong Bay (YJ 3-1)
A.k.a. Baie de Fai Tsi Long. Bay at 20°55'N-107°15'E. On NF48-16 JOG. NVN.
Fake Hill, The (XD 9-6)
Apparently on or near Mutter's Ridge, and involved in Battle for Mutter's Ridge, Sep-Oct66. Named by I/3d/4th Marines because it was not specifically marked on their maps. Cited in *US Marines in Vietnam, 1966*, p 193. Quang Tri Pr, I Corps.
Falaise, Cape (WG 7-1)
See Cape Falaise. NVN.
Falcon (n/a)
Apr70, XXIV Corps proposed 101st Abn FSB name.
Falcon, FSB (YC 788-987)
Apx 21 km due S Hue, 14 km SE FSB Birmingham, 6 km SSE Nui Ke (Hill 618) and 18 km SW to SSW Phu Bai. Apr70 XXIV Corps grid per Don Armstrong. Thua Thien Pr, I Corps.
Falcon, LZ (AT 874-476)
At or adj to An Hoa AF, apx 32 km SSW Da Nang AB7 km due N Phuoc Binh AF. Nov66. Quang Nam Pr, I Corps.
Falcon, LZ (XT 943-238)
Apx 4 km ENE Xom Ben Son and 11 km NNW Bien Hoa AB. Jan66. Bien Hoa Pr, III Corps.
Falcon, LZ (ZA 026-033)
Between the Ia Tae and Ia Meur Rivers in the Ia Drang Valley, apx 9 km ENE LZ X-Ray, 9 km W Plei Me, 5 km E LZ Columbus (a.k.a. Cavalair). Opened during 1st Battle of Ia Drang Valley, Nov65. Elements of 2d/19th Arty and 1st Cav moved here after closing LZ Cavalair (5 km to E), 5Nov65. Was used in evacuation of casualties from and

105mm fire supt for big battle at X-Ray, 14-17Nov67. Also listed at ZA 021-031. Pleiku Pr, II Corps.

Falcon, LZ (ZB 133-212)
Apx 12 km E Dak To 2 AF, 5 km NE Dien Binh/QL-14, and 34 km NNW Kontum. Nov67. Kontum Pr, II Corps.

Falgout, USS (n/a)
DER-324. DD-Escort, Radar, per Ralph Fries.

Fall of Saigon (n/a)
See Operation Frequent Wind in main alpha listing, and Buong Incident, Evacuation of Da Nang, Final Offensive and American Radio Service in Glossary.

Fall, Bernard (YD)
See Glossary.

False Cape Varella (CN 0-9)
See Cape Varella, False. Ninh Thuan Pr, II Corps.

False Varela (CN 0-9)
See False Cape Varella. Ninh Thuan Pr, II Corps.

Fami Point (XS 9-7)
A.k.a. Pointe Phami. Coastal point at 10°40'N-106°46'E. On NC48-07 JOG. Gia Dinh Pr?, III Corps.

Famous Fighting Fourth (n/a)
See Glossary.

Fan Rang Bay (BN 8-7)
A.k.a. Vung Phan Rang. Bay at 11°34'N-109°04'E. On NC49-01 JOG. Ninh Thuan Pr, II Corps.

Fan Si Pan Mountain (UK 74-67)
A.k.a. Hill 3134, Fansipan Mtn and Dong Cha Pa. In Hoang Lien Mtns of NW NVN, apx 260 km NW Hanoi. At 10,312', tallest Mtn in all of Vietnam (on some maps listed at 10,308' and 10,310'). NVN.

Fan Song (n/a)
See Glossary.

Fang, LZ (XD 802-409)
A.k.a. Hill 689 or Chau Lang Chanh Mtn. Apx 4 km WSW Khe Sanh CB, 5.5 km NW Khe Sanh ville/QL-9, and 54 km WSW Quang Tri. Apr70 XXIV Corps grid per Don Armstrong. Quang Tri Pr, I Corps.

Fang, The (YS 29-47)
See Vung Tau Army AF. Phuoc Tuy Pr, III Corps.

Fanning, FSB (n/a)
No data. Apparently somewhere along QL1.

Fanri Bay (BN 3-3)
A.k.a. Vung Phan Ri. Bay at 11°09'N-108°35'E. On NC49-01 JOG. Binh Thuan Pr, II Corps.

Fansipan Mountain (UK 74-67)
See Fan Si Pan Mountain. NVN.

Fanthit Bay (AN 8-0)
A.k.a. Vinh Phan Thiet. Bay at 10°53'N-108°05'E. On NC48-08 JOG. Binh Thuan Pr, II Corps.

Fargo, LZ (YD 228-587)
Apx 4 km ESE Chau Lang and 11 km WSW Quang Tri. Apr70 XXIV Corps grid per Don Armstrong. Quang Tri Pr, I Corps.

Farley Field (YU 1-0)
Sign with this name was at 1 of Song Be's 3 AF's: Song Be AF or Song Be City AF or Song Be Heliport, roughly 115-120 km NNE Saigon. Sign read: *FARLEY FIELD, Song Be RVN, In Memory of Sp4 Gary L. Farley, D 168[?] Engineer Combat Bn.* Farley was KIA 12Nov67. Name/info per Jim Claeys. Phuoc Long, III Corps.

Farm Gate (XT 98-13)
See Glossary.

Farragut (n/a)
6Apr70, XXIV Corps proposed III MAF FSB name.

Farrell, FSB (YT 299-252)
Along LTL-24 near Ap Thanh Dang, apx 34 km ENE Bien Hoa AB, 12 km W to WSW Xa Binh Hoa, and perhaps 2 km S Song Dong Nai River. 4th/12th Inf, 199th LIB. Jan69. Long Khanh Pr, III Corps.

Fashner, FSB (XT 225-926)
See FSB Flashner. Tay Ninh Pr, III Corps.

Fat City, LZ/FSB (BT 429-089)
A.k.a. Charger Hill(?), Hill 29 and/or Hill 35? Apx 12 km WNW Chu Lai, 3 km WNW Khuong Quang, 16 km SE Tam Ky, and p3 to 4 km W QL-1, near Que Son Valley. USMC, 4th 31st Inf, 196th LIB, 1st/6th Inf, 198thLIB. Also listed at BT 470-070, 440-077, 439-075, 435-079 and 439-075. Americal List. Quang Tin Pr, I Corps.

Fat City Heliport (BT 470-070)
See Hill 69 Heliport. Quang Tin Pr, I Corps.

Father & Son Combinations (n/a)
See Glossary.

Fatherland Front, The (n/a)
See Glossary.

Fathom, FSB (XD 997-468)
On W side of QL-9 apx 11 km WSW Mai Loc, 1 km S of LZ Chaparral and 19 km SW Cam Lo. Apr70 XXIV Corps grid per Don Armstrong. Quang Tri Pr, I Corps.

Faulkner, Camp (BT 07-73)
At Da Nang East, just SE Camp Adenir and immed S Marble Mtn AF. Seabee cmpd named to honor Arnold Faulkner, EOH3, NMCB 4, KIA 22Mar66. F Trp, 2d/17th Cav here 71-72. Quang Nam Pr, I Corps.

Faux Cape Varella (CN 0-9)
A.k.a. Mui Da Vach. Coastal point at 11°43'N-109°14'E. On NC49-01 JOG. Ninh Thuan Pr, II Corps.

Fay, Camp (BT 063-826)
On Tien Sha Peninsula, and adj Camp Tien Sha, apx 8 km NNE Da Nang AB and 4 km WSW peak Son Tra Mtn. Often erroneously listed as Camp Shay or Fey. MACV-SOG camp. Per Steve Sherman, was spelled Fay, and named to honor Section Chief OP 37, USN Cmdr Robert J. Fay, KIA28Oct65, the 1st MAC-SOG lost in war. Spelled "Shay" on map at www.ptfnasty.com/ images/jpg/ ptfdanang1a.jpg, and "Fey" in Oct2001 *VIETNAM* Mag article: *Da Nang Seabee Base Destroyed*, pp 26-32. Quang Nam Pr, I Corps.

FDRD Navigation System (n/a)
See Glossary.

Feathers, FSB (YS 712-676)
Apx 8 km N the coast, 28 km E Nui Dat, 14 km S FSB Toby, 6 km E Xuyen Moc and 23 km ENE Dat Do. 161 Bty, RNZA (Master's Bty 6Sep70-8May71) FSB set here 9-13Dec70 and suptg B and Supt Cos, 7 RAR. On 1ATF NCO trng map per John Hollett. Also listed at YS 71-67. Phuoc Tuy Pr, III Corps.

February, LZ (XT 633-308)
Apx 16 km SW Lai Khe, 2 km W the Song Saigon and 15 km N Cu Chi. Jan66. Binh Duong Pr, III Corps.

Fechteler, USS (n/a)
DD-870, per Ralph Fries.

Federal (n/a)
Apr70, XXIV Corps future-use 101st Abn FSB name.

Feet Dry (n/a)
See Glossary.

Feet Wet (n/a)
See Glossary.

Fells, FSB (XS 273-498)
See FSB Fels. Dinh Tuong Pr, IV Corps.

Fels, FSB (XS 273-498)
A.k.a. FSB Fells (proper sp unknown). Along S side of QL-4, apx 5 km E Cai Lay, 25 km WNW My Tho, 1 km SE FSB Moore and W FSB Jaeger. Built in early '68 (Mar?) as 1st FSB of 2d/39th, 9th Inf Div to E Cai Lay, and then abnd in Apr68 (and apparently never reused), when FSB Moore was built to replace it. On map L-7014-6229-4 9 Khiem Ich/Cai-Lay). Data per Jim Stone, 2d/39th Inf. Dinh Tuong Pr, IV Corps.

Fence, The (n/a)
See Glossary.

Fennell, Camp (ZT 064-793)
At Bao Loc AF, apx 5 km WSW Tan Phat AF and 31 km W Di Linh. Oct71. Possibly named in honor of Capt. Robert H. Fennell, KIA 31Mar70. Lam Dong Pr, II Corps.

Ferdinand, FSB (n/a)
Said to have been an Army FSB besieged during Tet '70, and relieved by Marine close air supt. Data per DC Lukoskie; however, no other data regarding base discovered? I Corps?

Fern, FSB (XD 929-625)
Due N Mutter's Ridge and just S the southern border of DMZ. 45 km NW Quang Tri, 25 km NW CB Vandegrift. Quang Tri, Pr, I Corps.

Fern, LZ/FSB (XD 928-625)
A.k.a. Dong Tiou and LZ Fig? At W end of Mutter's Ridge, apx 3 km S southern edge of DMZ, 19 km WNW Cam Lo and 31 km W to WNW Dong Ha. Apr70 XXIV Corps grid per Don Armstrong. Quang Tri Pr, I Corps.

Ferry Ramp (BT)
See Da Nang Ferry Ramp. Quang Nam Pr, I Corps.

Fester, Lake (WJ 8-2?)
See Lake Fester. NVN.

Feu Rouge, Pointe du (XS 9-8)
See Pointe Feu Rouge. Gia Dinh Pr?, III Corps.

Fey, Camp (BT 063-826)
See Fay, Camp. Quang Nam Pr, I Corps.

Fiddler's Green, LZ/FSB (BT 215-437)
Apx 7 km E to ESE LZ Baldy, 2 km WSW Thang Binh, 5 km W the ocean, 15 km SSE Hoi An and 24 km NNW Tam Ky. Named to honor 1st/1st Cav's regimental song (of Civil War origin). Turned over to ARVN troops, then lost by ARVN and then re-taken by US troops several times during war. Built in Jan69 as part of Op Hardin Falls. Also listed at BT 216-436 per XXIV Corps facility index. Americal list. Quang Tin Pr, I Corps.

Fidel, Camp (BR 915-433)
Along S edge of Phu Cat AB, and 27 km NNW Qui Nhon. Was 7th/15th Arty/4th Div AO, and C Bty, 1st/9th Arty here, Feb70. Named to honor 1Lt Honorio M. Fidel., Jr, KIA 9Aug67, shortly after his death. Was concurrently dismantled and transferred to ARVN in Nov71. Name provide by Dave Holdorf and 7th/15th Arty Assn. Turnover data courtesy Ray Bows. On map at 15th Arty website at: www.landscaper.net/chighmap.jpg. 4th Div ORLL grid per Jim Henderson. Binh Dinh Pr, II Corps.

Field, FSB (ZA 238-255)
See Field Goal. Pleiku Pr, II Corps.

Field Clerk Whiskey (XD 979-559)
Call sign for 3d Recon Bn-manned radio relay site atop Rockpile during Op Hastings, Fall '66. See Rockpile Radio Relay Site. Quang Tri Pr, I Corps.

Field Force (n/a)
See Glossary.

Field Goal, LZ (ZA 238-255)
On Rte 5 near intersection of TL-6C and QL-14, apx 18 km NNE Plei Me SF Camp, 12 km due S Catecka and 5 km from QL-14. 1st Cav here suptg ARVN relief of Plei Me (32d and 33d NVA Rgt's Oct65 siege). 2/12th Cav, moved here 24Oct65. Map in *Pleiku*, p 88. Pleiku Pr, II Corps.

Field Goal South, LZ (ZA 202-207)
Apx 27 km SSW Pleiku, 8 km SSW LZ Field Goal and 16 km NNE Plei Me. 1st Cav, Oct65. Pleiku Pr, II Corps.

Fifth Precinct (XS 8-9)
See Precinct Five. Gia Dinh Pr, III Corps.

Fig, LZ (XD 924-625)
A.k.a. LZ Fern and Dong Tiou. At W end of Mutter's Ridge, apx 3 km S southern edge of DMZ, 20 km WNW Cam Lo and 32 km W to WNW Dong Ha. Apr70 XXIV Corps grid per Don Armstrong. Quang Tri Pr, I Corps.

Fig, LZ (ZA 083-231)
At Xuong Kuang, apx 30 km SSW Pleiku. Jan66. Pleiku Pr, II Corps.

File, LZ (BR 625-825)
A.k.a. FSB Phoenix City. Apx 18 km due W Ha Tay, 40 km NNE An Khe. Mar66. Binh Dinh Pr, II Corps.

File, LZ (YD 215-110)
Apx 2.5 km ESE FSB Cunningham, 29 km SSE Ba Long and 41 km SSW Quang Tri. Apr70 XXIV Corps grid per Don Armstrong. Quang Tri Pr, I Corps.

Filhol Rubber Plantation (XT 650-215)
Apx 10 km S the Iron Triangle, immed W Phui Hoa Dong, 7 km N Cu Chi, 15 km SSW Ben Cat, 8 km SE Ho Bo Woods, 12 km S Thanh Dien Forestry Reserve and 7 km WSW Chau Dinh Jungle, 25th Inf Div AO and involved in Op Cedar Falls, Jan-Feb67. Elements of 1st Inf, 25th Inf, 173rd Abn Bde, and 196th LIB here Jan67. On map 1 in *Rangers At War*, p 324. Binh Duong Pr, III Corps.

Fimnon Airfield (BP 142-001)
See Dalat/Lien Khuong. Tuyen Duc Pr, II Corps.

Fin, LZ (XD 983-686)
In DMZ and only 1 km S of the Ben Hai River/NVN border, apx 17 km NW Cam Lo and 27 km WNW Dong Ha. Apr70 XXIV Corps grid per Don Armstrong. Quang Tri Pr, I Corps.

Final Offensive, The (n/a)
See Operation Frequent Wind in main alpha listing, and Buong Incident, Evacuation of Da Nang, Final Offensive and American Radio Service in Glossary.

Finch, LZ (AT 86-86?)
Name of helo pad area at Camp Reasoner. See Reasoner for location. Quang Nam Pr, I Corps.

Finch, LZ (BR 385-995)
Apx 47 km WNW Bong Son, 27 km due S Gia Vuc AF and 36 km N Kannack AF. Mar66. Binh Dinh Pr, II Corps.
Finch, LZ (YD 53-50?)
Described as having been apx 3 km inland and along Quang Tri/Thua Thien Pr border near Thon Trung An and Thon Tham Khe. 105s of USMC's 3d/12th Arty Plt and Bty of 1st/11th Arty suptd elements of 1st Marine Rgt from this LZ during Op Badger Tooth, 26Dec-2Jan68. Thua Thien/Quang Tri Pr, I Corps.
Finch, USS (n/a)
DER-328. DD-Escort, Radar, per Ralph Fries.
Finger (n/a)
6Apr70, XXIV Corps proposed 5th Div FSB name.
Finger Lake (BT 02-74)
Along QL-1, apx 3 km S Da Nang near Marble Mtn. Grid est based on rptd location. Quang Nam Pr, I Corps.
Fire Support Base (defined) (n/a)
See Glossary.
Firebase (defined) (n/a)
See Fire Support Base in Glossary.
Firebase (name) (numerous)
Firebases are listed alphabetically by name with last name first, followed by a comma and then the acronyms "FSB" or "LZ," as in "Arsenal, FSB," "Bird, LZ." Numbered and lettered firebases are an exception, and they are listed first with the word "Firebase" followed by its numeric or alpha designation, as in Firebase 6 or Firebase C.
Firebase 0 (XT 185-765)
A.k.a. Firebase Zero. Along Rte 247, near Soc Ky and Suoi Ky River, apx 18 km SSE Thien Ngon AF and 15 km N Tay Ninh West AF. Opened 24Nov66. Also listed at XT 19-77. Bty B/1st/8th Arty. Per 25th Inf Div ORLL of 23Ap67, Op Attleborro, courtesy Les Hines. Tay Ninh Pr, III Corps.
Firebase 1 (XT 73-35?)
See Artillery Base I. Binh Long Pr, III Corps.
Firebase 1 (XT 270-680)
Apx 11 km NNW peak of Nui Ba Den. Mar67. Tay Ninh Pr, III Corps.
Firebase 1 (XT 276-785)
Along TL-4, apx 12 km SSW Katum AF and 21 km N Nui Ba Den. Bty A, 2d/77th and 1st/8th Arty suptg 2d/22d Inf. Opened 12Nov66, by 1st/5th Inf and later called FSB 1. Per 25th Inf Div ORLL of 23Ap67, Op Attleborro, courtesy Les Hines. Also listed at XT 275-790. Tay Ninh Pr, III Corps.
Firebase 1 (YB 805-215?)
If grid correct, was apx 8 km SW Ben Het, 21 km due W Dak To 2 AF and 8 km N Hill 875. Also listed at ZB 004-215, which is thought to be proper location or perhaps a different FSB 1? Also possibly incorrectly numbered (i.e., actually FSB 11)? Kontum Pr, II Corps.
Firebase 1 (YB 822-226)
A.k.a. F-1. Apx 6 km SW Ben Het. Also listed at ZB 004-215, which is perhaps a different FSB 1? 15Jun66. Kontum Pr, II Corps.
Firebase 1 (ZB 004-215)
Just SW Dak To 2 AF, apx 40 km NW Kontum and 16 km ESE Ben Het. HQ 1st/92d Arty and 6th/29th Arty (Jun68) here at times. Also listed at ZB 001-214 (and at YB 805-215 on 4th Div Bn Daily Journal per Phil Landis?). Grid per Craig Miller as per 4th Div Op Rpts which consistently list base near this point. Also listed at ZB 004-116, Oct68-Oct69. Kontum Pr, II Corps.
Firebase 2 (XT 270-780)
A.k.a. Artillery Base II, FSB II and Patrol Base II. On Rte 4 at Prek Klok, apx 32 km NE Tay Ninh, near Prek Klok stream, 12 km SSW Katum, N the French Fort, 20 km N Nui Ba Den, 5 km SE Artillery Base I (FSB I) and 18 km S Cambodia. SF Camp and AF here built '67. Site of Battle of Prek Klok II, 10Mar67, during Op Junction City, when 2d/2d Inf (Mech), 2d/33d Arty and elements of 168th Engr Bn were attacked by 272d VC Rgt. At 2208 hrs, heavy mortar attack was answered with counter bty/recon by fire, then enemy grnd assault. Battle over by midnight. 3 US KIA, 38 WIA, 197 NVA KIA. Tay Ninh Pr, III Corps.
Firebase 2 (XT 270-865)
Apx 6 km SW Katum AF and 18 km ENE Thien Ngon AF. Opened 15Nov66 by 1st/5th Inf and the 2d/22d Inf. Per 25th Inf Div ORLL of 23Ap67, Op Attleborro, courtesy Les Hines. Tay Ninh Pr, III Corps.
Firebase 2 (YB 875-209)
A.k.a. F-2. Apx 6 km due S Ben Het. 15 Jun66. See Firebase 6. Kontum Pr, II Corps.
Firebase 2 (YS 46-83)
Along Rte-2, apx 15 km due N Nui Dat, 5 km N FSB Allanbroke and 7 km NW Ngai Giao. 161 Bty, RNZA (Martin's Bty 28Apr67-6Apr68) FSB set here 10-11Jan68. Phuoc Tuy Pr, III Corps.
Firebase 3 (BR 361-457)
Along QL-19, apx 13 km due W An Khe. Sep67. Binh Dinh Pr, II Corps.
Firebase 3 (YB 952-239)
Apx 7 km WNW Dak To 2 AF, 8 km ESE Ben Het and 46 km NW Kontum. Jun68-Nov69. Data per S-3 Daily Journ-and 31Jul-1Sep69 op rpts, per Bob Patsfield. See Firebase 6. Also listed at YB 894-186? Kontum Pr, II Corps.
Firebase 3 (YB 894-186)
A.k.a. F-3. At Polei Lang Lo Kram, apx 7 km SE Ben Het. 15 Jun66. Also listed at YB 952-239? Kontum Pr, II Corps.
Firebase 4 (YB 869-186)
A.k.a. F-4. Apx 8 km due S Ben Het. 15Jun66. Kontum Pr, II Corps.
Firebase 4 (YB 903-703)
Apx 4 km NW Dak Pek AF and 6 km from Laos. Grid per Dan Gillotti. Kontum Pr, II Corps.
Firebase 4 (YB 94-18?)
A.k.a. Hill 664. Apx 11 km WSW Dak To 2 AF. Built beginning 4Jul67, by 4th/503d Inf, 173d Abn and B Bty, 3d/319th Arty, per *Dak To*, p 91. See Firebase 6. Kontum Pr, II Corps.
Firebase 4 (YS 410-870)
See Artillery Base 4. Long Khanh Pr?, III Corps.
Firebase 4-11 (BS 538-731)
See 4-11, FSB. Quang Ngai Pr, I Corps.
Firebase 5 (YB 898-188)
A.k.a. F-5. Apx 7 km SSE Ben Het. 15 Jun66. Kontum Pr, II Corps.
Firebase 5 (YB 990-153)
Per Tom Rethard, was ARVN FSB at N end of Rocket Ridge, apx 7 km SE FSB 6 and 7 km SSW Dak To 2 AF. Was on same hill mass as, and just E peak of Hill 1338 (FSB Flint). Per Ben Youmans, FSBs 5 and 6 were ARVN

bases in '70, and due W Tan Canh near Dak To? During Battle of Dak To, early Nov67, elements of 2d/503d Inf, 173d Abn worked around and from this position. Also involved in Op Quang Trung 22F, per 19May71 SRAG AAR. [214] See Firebase 6. Kontum Pr, II Corps.

Firebase 6 (YB 935-188)
A.k.a. Hill 1001. Apx 14 km WSW Tanh Canh (Kon Hojao), 8 km WSW Dak To 2 AF, 7 km NW Hill 1338, 7 km SE Ben Het and 8 km NW FSB 5 near NW end of Rocket Ridge. 6th/29th Arty here Jul68. Per Ben Youmans, FSBs 5 and 6 were ARVN occupied in '70. ARVN FSB's 1, 2, 3, 4, 5, 6, 7, Charlie and Delta were distributed along ridge known as Rocket Ridge. B Bty, 1st/92d Arty here suptg US 4th Div. Mentioned on internet at: www.thuntek.net/~asper/firebase.html. Per Tom Rethart, was turned over to 42d ARVN Rgt in late '70 or early '71, with four 105 howitzers and a US manned arty IOS (Improved Observation System) crew and, soon after, completely overrun early in '71, with 7 US KIA and 2 US MIA. Retaken in later op. Rethard describes base as having been, "within range of 175mm at Tanh Kanh [Tanh Canh] and very steep on both E and W faces, with ridge running to S. Had a view of a relatively flat area to W, with a lower ridgeline running a few km." He adds, "Shortly after I arrived at Dak To, the bodies of some MACV advisors were found downhill from FSB 6. One of them, who had been shot a couple of times, apparently lived for several days after the attack. Turns out he kept a journal even after he fell (it was found under his body). While he was still alive, the ARVNs swept the area and a lone ARVN took his watch and rings, leaving him to die. Needless to say, the advisors to Rgt I was with were not happy." Grid provide by Nolan Putman, 7th/15th Arty and Stan Lyman, B/1/92d Arty. On map in *A Bright Shining Lie*. Also listed at YA 933-188 and 988-135 (May65). See Firebase A and Polei Kleng Ranger Camp. Kontum Pr, II Corps. [215]

Firebase 6 (YB 988-135)
Apx 10 km SSW Dak To 2 AF. May68. Kontum Pr, II Corps.

Firebase 6 (YB 905-186)
A.k.a. F-6. Apx 16 km SSE Ben Het. 15Jun66. Kontum Pr, II Corps.

Firebase 7 (YB 865-187)
A.k.a. F-7. Apx 8 km due S Ben Het. 15Jun66. Kontum Pr, II Corps.

Firebase 7 (ZA 025-933)
Apx 3 km SW Polei Kleng AF and 8 km W Polei Krong AF. Mar68. Americal list. Kontum Pr, II Corps.

Firebase 7 (ZB 060-267)
Along QL-14, apx 5 km ENE Dak To 2 AF, and 38 km NNW Kontum and 6 km S Dak to Hamlet? 4th Div and 1st/92d Arty. Grid per Craig Miller. Kontum Pr, II Corps.

Firebase 8 (YB 917-193)
A.k.a. F-8. Apx 8 km SE Ben Het. 15 Jun66. Kontum Pr, II Corps.

Firebase 9 (YB 813-157)
Apx 22 km WSW Dak To 2 AF. Oct67. Kontum Pr, II Corps.

Firebase 10 (n/a)
Presumed to have existed, location unknown. II Corps.

Firebase 11 (CQ 124-437)
Apx 5 km SW Tuy Hoa N AF7 km WNW Tuy Hoa AF. Feb68. Pr, II Corps.

Firebase 11 (XT 300-490)
Apx 18 km WNW Dau Tieng and 13 km ESE Tay Ninh W AF. May67. Tay Ninh Pr, III Corps.

Firebase 12 (YB 874-256)
On Rte 512, apx 2 km due E Ben Het AF, 2 km W FSB 13, 18 km due W Dak To and 14 km WNW Dak To 2 AF. Built apx 2 Nov67 by elements of 173d Abn (opcon 1st Bde/4th Div) which had just moved to Dak To from Tuy Hoa. 173d Abn here during Battle of Dak To, 1 Nov-1Dec67. Elements of 503d Inf and 3d/319th Arty here '67. Also listed at YB 869-256 and 827-247? (Nov67-Jul69). On map at front of, and some data from, *Dak To*, p 139. Kontum Pr, II Corps. [216]

Firebase 13 (YB 916-259)
Apx 4 km E Ben Het AF, 2 km E FSB 12, 12 km WNW Dak To 2 AF and 16 km due W Dak To Ville. 173d Abn base during Battle of Dak To, 1 Nov-1Dec67. Elements of 503d Inf and 3d/319th Arty here '67. Oct67-Apr69. Also listed at YB 906-323. Kontum Pr, II Corps. [217]

Firebase 14 (YA 939-912)
A.k.a. Patrol Base 14 and LZ Incoming. Apx 9 km WSW Polei Kleng and 31 km W to WNW Kontum. Craig Miller, 1st/92d Arty confirms base was overrun 26Mar68, during night action in which NVA employed flame-throwers and tear gas to breech wire. 2 arty pieces were captured and used them to fire Beehive rnds at Arty positions still held by US troops. Name per Phil Landis, grid per Craig Miller. Elements of 1st/92d Arty and 2d/9th Arty here 12-16Apr68. 4th Div. Kontum Pr, II Corps.

Firebase 15 (YB 855-185)
A.k.a. Hill 823. Apx 6 km NE FSB 16, 7 km SSW Ben Het AF and 16 km WSW Dak To 2 AF. 173d Abn base during Battle of Dak To, 1 Nov-1Dec67. Elements of 503d Inf and 3d/319th Arty here '67. Photos/maps of site at http://1-14th.com/maps.html. Also listed at YB 853-186. Jan67-Dec68. Kontum Pr, II Corps. [218]

Firebase 16 (YB 815-151)
Apx 3 km NE Hill 875, 13 km SSW Ben Het, 6 km SW FSB 15 and 21 km WSW Dak To 2 AF. Described in Dak To, p 213, as being on a twin-peaked hill apx 5 km SW Hill 823 and 2 km SE Hill 882, and sitting on W edge of Dak Klong River, about 7 km E Cambodia. Built beginning 11Nov67 by elements of 2d/503d Inf, 173d Abn during Battle for Dak To. 503d Inf and 3d/319th Arty heavily attacked here, 12Nov67, in Battle of FSB 16, with 4 KIA and 43 WIA. On 13-14Nov67, another battle erupted involving B/2d/503d, on ridge apx 400 meters from FSB 16, resulting in 21 KIA and 17 WIA. Battles detailed in *Dak To*, pp 212-231. Also listed at YB 815-148. Oct67-Jan68. Kontum Pr, II Corps. [219]

Firebase 17 (ZB 088-347)
Apx 16 km NNE Dak To 2 AF. Nov-Dec67. Kontum Pr, II Corps.

Firebase 18 (YB 850-310)
Apx 6 km NNW Ben Het. Jun68. 6 km NNW Ben Het. Kontum Pr, II Corps.

Firebase 19 (YB 839-223)
Apx 5 km SW Ben Het. Jan69. Kontum Pr, II Corps.

Firebase 20 (XT 78-48)
A.k.a. FSB Ap Bau Bang. In flat area 1.5 km N Ap Bau Bang, on E side of QL-13. To its S was a rubber plantation, with wooded areas prominent to N and W. Abnd RR track ran parallel to and 30 meters E of QL-13. Site of Battle of Ap Bau Bang II, 19Mar67, when A Trp, 3d Sqdn, 5th Cav, 1st Bde 9th Inf Div (opcon 1st Inf Div) and Bty B, 2d/9th Arty were hit by 2d and 3d Bns, 273d Rgt, 9th VC Div. US battle losses were 3 US KIA, 63 WIA. Also resulted in 227 known VC KIA, 3 POWs, and capture of much equip and weapons. 29 air strikes delivered 29 tons of ordnance, and arty fired nearly 3,000 rounds in supt. Data per *Cedar Falls-Junction City*. 1st Bde/9th Inf Div was responsible for keeping Rte 13 open from Lai Khe to Quan Loi, and for defending FSBs that AO during Op Junction City. Grid apx. Binh Duong Pr, III Corps.
Firebase 20 (YB 823-082)
Apx 9 km E Cambodia, 47 km WNW Kontum, 24 km SSW Ben Het and 6 km SSE Hill 875. 4th Div and 1st/92d Arty here. Name/grid per Craig Miller. Kontum Pr, II Corps.
Firebase 21 (n/a)
Presumed to have existed. No data. II Corps?
Firebase 22 (XS 83-86)
A.k.a. FSB Twenty-Two. Apx 5 km S Saigon, along E edge of main N/S hwy, apx 8 km N Ap Phuoc Khanh and 8 km NNW Nha Be. 5th/12th Inf, 3d/7th Inf, 199th LIB. Gia Dinh Pr?, III Corps.
Firebase 23 (n/a)
Presumed to have existed. No data. II Corps?
Firebase 24 (YB 90-12?)
If grid correct, was apx 42 km NW Kontum, 15 km SW Dak To 2 AF, and 14 km SSE Ben Het. Dick Arnold extracted following grids of nearby patrol/ambush positions: YB 905-123, 907-118, 909-124. Listed grid est from this data. 1st/35th Inf, 4th Div FSB here May68, and likely ARVN FSB for most of war. Kontum Pr, II Corps.
Firebase 25 (YB 887-291)
Apx 15 km NW Dak To. 4th Div, 1st/92d Arty and 6th/29th Arty here at least Nov68, per Craig Miller. Kontum Pr, II Corps.
Firebase 26 (n/a)
Presumed to have existed. No data. II Corps.
Firebase 27 (n/a)
Presumed to have existed. No data. II Corps.
Firebase 28 (YB 86-14?)
If grid correct, was 3 km SE Dak Wang Kram, 13 km SSE Ben Het, 6 km E Hill 875 and 18 km SW Dak To 2 AF. Dick Arnold extracted following grids from patrol/ambush positions near base but without grid for base mentioned: YB 859-141, 861-139, 857-139, 853-137. Listed grid est from this data. 1st/35th Inf here May68, and likely an ARVN FSB for most of war. Kontum Pr, II Corps.
Firebase 29 (YB 839-223)
FSB apx 5 km SSW Ben Het and 17 km due W Dak To 2 AF. 25May68, 1st/8th Inf and 1st92d Arty hit by 2 NVA Bns that penetrated wire, occupied 6 US bunkers, captured and turned 2 of base's own arty pieces on its defenders, resulting in 14 US KIA, 54 WIA, 2 MIA and 125+ NVA KIA. This base and Ben Het SF Camp also attacked several times during 1st two weeks of Nov68, involving 100mm and 105mm arty fired from tri-border area, forcing its abandonment. [220] 4th Div here '68. Grid per 4th Div Ops Report for period ending 31Jan69. Some data courtesy Craig Miller, who was in 25May68 attack. May68-Nov69. Kontum Pr, II Corps.
Firebase 30 (XD 58-46)
See 30, LZ. Laos.
Firebase 30 (YB 971-267)
Apx 12 km E Ben Het, 8 km W Dak To and 6 km NNW Dak To 2 AF. Grid per Dick Arnold and taken from Jan, Feb, Mar69 1st/35th Inf Bn Daily Logs. May68-Mar69. Kontum Pr, II Corps.
Firebase 31 (XD 51-46)
See 31, LZ. Laos.
Firebase 31 (YB 895-443)
Apx 3 km due N Dak Seang AF, 10 km E Laos, 20 km WSW Tou Morong, 27 km NNW Dak To and 65 km NW Kontum. Grid per Phil Landis and 4th Div Daily Journal of May '68. 4th Div. Kontum Pr, II Corps.
Firebase 32 (YA?)
Possibly near LZ Karen (YA 815-309)? Per Ron Flint, C/1st/14th Inf, 4th Div here apx Sep-Nov68. Also likely an ARVN FSB at one time. Pleiku Pr?, II Corps.
Firebase 33 (YA?)
Presumed to have existed. No data. II Corps?
Firebase 34 (YB 924-227)
Apx 6 km ESE Ben Het, 9 km W Dak To 2 AF and 47 km NW Kontum. Per Ron Flint C/1st/14thIn was here apx Sep-Nov68. 4th/42d Arty here 11Apr69 per 4th Div Op rpt courtesy Craig Miller. Also likely an ARVN FSB at one time. Grid per Jan, Feb, Mar69 1st/35th Inf Bn Daily Logs. Kontum Pr, II Corps.
Firebase 40 (XT 760-770)
W of QL-13, apx 16 km N Chon Thanh AF and 2 km NW Xa Tan Khai. '67. Binh Long Pr, III Corps.
Firebase 101 (YB 858-183)
A.k.a. Hill 830. Apx 7 km due E Hill 875, 16 km SW Dak To 2 AF, 4 km SE Dak Wang Kram, 6 km NE FSB F and 13 km due S Ben Het. Built during Op Quang Trung 22F, 2Mar71, to provide security for FSB 202 and troops operating near 202. Elements of 42d ARVN Rgt and two-105mm howitzers emplaced here that day. Evacuated 5Mar71 under NVA overran several Bns of 42d ARVN and 22d Border Rangers nearby and also forced evac of FSB 202. Also listed at YB 858-139, which is apx 5 km S listed grid position? Kontum Pr, II Corps. [221]
Firebase 173 (n/a)
See Glossary.
Firebase 202 (YB 821-078)
A.k.a. FSB Foxtrot. On site of what was known as Old Firebase F (FSB F moved to YB 823-080), apx 23 km SW Dak To 2 AF, 6 km SSE Hill 875 and 6 km SW FSB 101. Elements of 42d ARVN Rgt here during Op Quang Trung 22F, Feb-Mar71. FSB 101 was built 2Mar71 in order to provide security for FSB 202 and troops operating in valley near 202. Evacuated under heavy NVA pressure, 4Mar71, with its elements moving overland to FSB 101, after destroying three-105mm howitzers with Thermite Grenades. See Foxtrot, FSB. Kontum Pr, II Corps. [222]
Firebase 411 (BS 539-732)
See 411, LZ/FSB. Quang Ngai Pr, I Corps.

Firebase 412 (BT 016-630)
See 412, LZ. Quang Nam Pr, I Corps.
Firebase 413 (BT 075-655)
See 413, LZ. Quang Nam Pr, I Corps.
Firebase 432 (AT 916-583)
See 432, LZ. Quang Nam Pr, I Corps.
Firebase 497 (BT 189-047)
A.k.a. Hill 497 or 593? Possibly named for its site's elevation; however, grid puts it on Hill 593? Apx 18 km SW Tam Ky AF and 12 km SE Tien Phuoc AF. 196th LIB, apparently opened 21Jan70, per Americal list. Quang Ngai Pr, I Corps.
Firebase 707 (n/a)
See 707, LZ. I Corps.
Firebase A (XT 255-250)
Grid puts site just inside Cambodia, apx 13 km due W Go Dau Ha, 3 km NE Phum Bavet, 22 km due S Tay Ninh and 2 km N QL-1. Cambodia.
Firebase A (XT 770-810)
Along E side of QL-13, apx 8 km SSE An Loc. Apr67. Binh Long Pr, III Corps.
Firebase A (XT 950-250)
Apx 13 km NNW Bien Hoa AB. May67. Bien Hoa Pr, III Corps.
Firebase A (YB 8-1?)
Generally W Dak To 2 AF. Built in conjunction w/FSB B, by elements of 42d ARVN Rgt during Phase I of Op Quang Trung 22F/04, beginning 14Feb71. Initial occupants were 2 ARVN Ranger Cos suptd by four 105s. On 12-13Feb71, 3 Bns of 42d CA'd into LZs W and SW FSBs A and B to begin ops under their fire supt. Op was response to NVA buildup near Ngok Toba Mtn (YB 82-10). FSB A was shifted N of its original position apx 17Feb71, to vic of FSB R. Closed 21Feb 71 and forces and 105s moved to Firebase F. See Firebase F. Kontum Pr, II Corps. [223]
Firebase A (YS 390-740)
See FSB Alpha. Phuoc Tuy Pr, III Corps.
Firebase B (XT 620-810)
Immed S Tonle Cham AF, apx 16 km SW An Loc and 10 SSE the tip of Fishhook. Mar-Apr67. Binh Long/Tay Ninh Pr border, III Corps.
Firebase B (XT 980-320)
Just S Khu Tru Mat and apx 16 km due N Bien Hoa AB. May67. Also listed at XT 990-330. Bien Hoa Pr, III Corps.
Firebase B (YB 8-1?)
Generally W Dak To 2 AF. Built in conjunction w/ FSB A, by elements of 42d ARVN Rgt during Phase I of Op Quang Trung 22F/04 beginning 14Feb71. 1st occupants were 2 ARVN Ranger Cos suptd by four105s and 42d ARVN Rgt TAC CP. On 15 and 16Feb71, 3 Bns of 42d CA'd into LZs W and SW FSBs A and B to begin ops under their fire supt. Op was a response to NVA buildup near Ngok Toba Mtn (YB 82-10). FSB was closed 26Feb71 and all elements moved to Firebase 6. Kontum Pr, II Corps.[224]
Firebase B (YS 250-700)
See FSB Bravo. Phuoc Tuy Pr, III Corps.
Firebase C (XT 560 850)
See Sroc Con Trang, FSB. III Corps.
Firebase C (XT 909-170)
Apx 9 km WNW Bien Hoa AB. May67. Pr, III Corps.
Firebase C (YS 290-620)
Along QL-15, apx 15 km WSW Nui Dat. Dec67. Pr, III Corps.
Firebase D (XT 030-550)
Apx 14 km WNW Tay Ninh W AF. May67. Pr, III Corps.
Firebase E (XT 430-270)
Apx 5 km ENE Go Dau Ha and 20 km S to SSW Dau Tieng. May67. Tay Ninh Pr, III Corps.
Firebase F (New) (YB 823-080)
Apx 25 km SW Dak To and 7 km SSE Hill 875. Built by elements of ARVN 2d/2d/42d Inf Rgt and 2d/72d border Rangers 21-22Feb71, as part of Op Quang Trung 22F. With its construction, FSBs A and W were closed. Four-105s were emplaced by nightfall 22Feb71. At 1950 hrs on 1Mar71, NVA mortar fire set off 105mm powder and ammo in spectacular explosion that destroyed most of fortifications, 200 rnds of 105 ammo, two-105s and damaged remaining two-105s. Kontum Pr, II Corps. [225]
Firebase F (Old) (YB 821-078)
Roughly 23 km SW Dak To 2 AF, 6 km SSE Hill 875 and 5 km WSW FSB 101. Built before construction of FSB 202 on same site during Op Quang Trung 22F, Feb-Mar71. FSB F had been relocated to YB 823-080 on 21-22Feb71. See Op Quang Trung 22F. Kontum Pr, II Corps. [226]
Firebase I through VII (XT)
See Artillery Bases I thru VII. III Corps.
Firebase I & II (XT)
See Artillery Bases I & II. Binh Long Pr, III Corps.
Firebase N (XT 450-270)
Apx 7 km ENE Go Dau Ha and 18 km S Dau Tieng. May67. Also listed at XT 580-450, 5May67. Tay Ninh Pr?, III Corps.
Firebase N (XT 580-450)
Apx 10 km E to ESE Dau Tieng/Tri Tam. Here 5May67. Also listed at XT 450-270, 16May67. Binh Duong Pr, III Corps.
Firebase O (XT 926-286)
Apx 16 km NNW Bien Hoa AB. May67. Bien Hoa Pr, III Corps.
Firebase R (YB 8-1?)
Apparently W or SW Dak To. ARVN FSB. See Firebase A for detail. Kontum Pr, II Corps. [227]
Firebase U (XT 905-306)
Apx 17 km NNW Bien Hoa AB. May67. Bien Hoa Pr, III Corps.
Firebase Z (XT 912-429)
Apx 8 km SW Phuoc Vinh AF and 30 km NNW Bien Hoa AB. May67. Pr, III Corps.
Firecracker Rounds (n/a)
See Glossary.
Firedrake, USS (n/a)
Ammunition ship plying both NVN and SVN coastline supplying warships/acft carriers with ammo/missiles. Article re ship in Nov2001 *Military* Mag, pp 14-16.
Firefly (n/a)
See Glossary.
Firefly, LZ (BR 953-690)
In coastal lowlands, apx 19 km NNE Phu Cat AB, 7 km SE Phu My/QL-1 and 34 km SSE Bong Son. Oct66. Binh Dinh Pr, II Corps.

Firefly, LZ (YD 061-661)
Apx 5 km WSW Thon An Hoa, 2 km SE of DMZ, 10 km NW Cam Lo and 20 km WNW Dong Ha. Apr70 XXIV Corps grid per Don Armstrong. Quang Tri Pr, I Corps.
Firestone (n/a)
Apr70, XXIV Corps proposed 101st Abn FSB name.
Firestone Trail (YS)
NVA/VC infiltration and communication route in Phuoc Tuy Pr. So named because the Ho Chi Minh sandals worn by VC plying the trail were fabricated from automobile tire treads (such as the US brand, Firestone Tires). Phuoc Tuy Pr, III Corps.
First, FSB (YC 864-833)
Variant of FSB Fist? See Fist. Thua Thien Pr, I Corps.
First Americans to Visit Vietnam (n/a)
See Glossary.
First Artillery Rounds Fired (n/a)
See Glossary.
First CAP Team (USMC) (BT 5-1?)
See Ky Hoa Cap. Quang Tin Pr, I Corps.
First Helicopter Kill of Tank (XT 76-88?)
See An Loc, Battle of.
First Helicopter Kill of Fixed-Wing Afct (n/a)
See Glossary.
First Human Wave Attack by Vietminh (n/a)
See Vinh Yen, Battle of. NVN.
First in Vietnam (n/a)
See Glossary.
First Indochina War (n/a)
See Glossary.
First Mining of NVN Ports (n/a)
See Linebacker, Operation.
First Night Helicopter Assault (CQ 1-3?)
See My Phu, Battle of, Phu Yen Pr, II Corps.
First NVA Armor Attack in SVN (XD 848-417)
See Lang Vei (old) SF. Quang Tri Pr, I Corps.
First NVA Attack in SVN (BS 081-145)
See Vic Klum. Kontum Pr, II Corps.
First Offensive (n/a)
See Glossary.
First Proof NVA Supplying VC by Sea (CQ)
See Vung Rio Incident in Glossary.
First Tank-to-Tank Battle (XD 51-46?)
See Lam Son 719. Laos.
First US Armored Unit in VN (BT)
See Operation Starlight.
First US Diplomat to Vietnam (n/a)
See *Peacock*.
First US Inflicted Vietnamese Casualties (n/a)
See *Constitution, USS*.
First US Navy Ship to Visit Vietnam (n/a)
See *Peacock*.
First US Shelling of Vietnam (n/a)
See *Constitution, USS*.
First Use of Smart Bombs (n/a)
See Linebacker and Thanh Hoa RR/Hwy Bridge.
First Use of Tanks by US Forces (BT)
See Operation Starlight.
First USMC Independent Ground Unit in SVN
See SESU Site. Quang Tri Pr, I Corps.
First USMC Helo Unit in SVN (XR 058-591)
See Shufly, Op. Ba Xuyen Pr, IV Corps.
Ship Bombed by NVA Acft (n/a)
See *Higbee, USS*. SVN.
First Vietnam Veterans (n/a)
See *Constitution, USS*.
First Vietnamese Ambassador to US (n/a)
See Glossary.
First Vietnamese to Visit US (n/a)
See Glossary.
Fish Market, The (XS 8-9)
Near Song Saigon, at SE(?) edge of Saigon Port. Site of Tent City Charlie. See Tent City Charlie and Fishmarket Bridge. Gia Dinh Pr, III Corps.
Fish Market Bridge, The (XS 885-892)
At SE corner of Saigon, near point where LTL-15 turns S, apx 10 km SW Tan Son Nhut and 4 km NE Phu My Tay. Jan67. Gia Dinh Pr, III Corps.
Fishbed (n/a)
See Glossary.
Fisher, FSB/LZ (YD 037-281)
On mtn peak apx 69 km WNW Hue, 4 km from Laos, 17 km NNW Tou Rout, 17 km E Lang Klung and 23 km SE Khe Sanh CB. Nov68. Used during Op Maine Crag, Mar-May69, 3d Mar Div, USMC, '69. Grid per map on p 65, *US marines in Vietnam-1969*. Quang Tri Pr, I Corps.
Fisherman's Island (CP 1-3)
Iles de Pechures. NIMA data. Khanh Hoa Pr, II Corps.
Fishhook, Highland (BS 00-47?)
See Highland Fishhook. I/II Corps.
Fishhook, The (XT 58-90)
Terrain feature roughly resembling shape of a fishhook-as defined by Cambodian border apx 80 km NW Saigon and 48 km N the Dog's Head. Extended from flat plains adj Memot, NE to E to O Rang. Long suspected as location of COSVN HQ. Invaded 1May70 during '70 Cambodian Incursion by elements of US 1st Cav, 9th Inf, 25th and 101st Abn, along with the 11th Armored Cav Rgt and several ARVN Divs. Tay Ninh/Binh Long Prvs, III Corps.
Fishmarket, The (XS 8-9)
See Fish Market. Gia Dinh Pr, III Corps.
Fishmarket Bridge (XS 885-892)
See Fish Market Bridge. Gia Dinh Pr, III Corps.
Fishnet, FSB (XS 77-87)
A.k.a. FSB Horseshoe Bend. Apparently built near site of a Fishnet Factory on SW edge of Saigon, apx 9 km SSW Tan Son Nhut AB, 12 km NNE Binh Chanh and 11 km due W FSB Blackfoot. 199th LIB Bde Fwd HQ, '68-69. Grid per 199th LIB Assn. Gia Dinh Pr, III Corps.
Fiske, USS (n/a)
DD-842, per Ralph Fries.
Fist, FSB (YC 866-836)
In valley along "Yellow Brick Road" and just W Nam Dong, apx 31 km S Hue, 46 km WNW Dan Nang AB and 28 km WSW Phu Loc. Apr-Nov69. 101st Abn inactive FSB grid per Don Armstrong. Also spelled "First?" Also listed at YC 880-840. Thua Thien Pr, I Corps.
Five, LZ (BP 552-865)
Remote site apx 2 km E Ea Krong Pach River, 28 km due W Duc My AF and 23 km S Khan Duong New AF. Apr67. Khanh Hoa Pr, II Corps.

Five Cents (YC 865-838)
See Nam Dong SF Camp. Nickname of camp/AF, derived from literal translation of Nam Dong, i.e. five dong. The Dong was Viet monetary unit roughly equivalent to US cent; hence, 5 cents. Thua Thien Pr, I Corps.
Five Fingers, FSB (n/a)
A.k.a. LZ Five Fingers. Name courtesy Jim Marsh, Gambler 19, 4th Avn Guns. Thought to be in either Pleiku or Binh Dinh Pr, II Corps.
Five Hills, The (TJ)
Key terrain feature of DBP battleground during Op Castor, 20Nov53-7May54. In Muong Thanh Valley apx 290 km W Hanoi. See Dien Bien Phu (Layout). NVN.
Five Mountains, The (BT 065-738)
The 5 peaks of the Marble Mtns. Quang Nam Pr, I Corps.
Five Oceans BOQ (XS 833-895)
At 49 Yet Kie St. prior to Jul62, 77 rms, Saigon. Data per *Vietnam Military Lore, 1959-1973*. Gia Dinh Pr, III Corps.
Flag (n/a)
6Apr70, XXIV Corps proposed 5th Div FSB name.
Flagstaff, USS (CP 0-2)
A.k.a. PGH-1, hydrofoil gunboat. With Coastal Sqdn 3 out of Cam Ranh Bay, and later Coastal Flotilla 1. Arrived SVN 30Apr67. Discussed in *Brown Water, Black Berets*, p 91. Market Time TF-115. Khanh Hoa Pr, II Corps.
Flak Alley (XD 90-43)
Nickname of instrument glideslope into Khe Sanh CB AF. NVA AA weapons set up in Valley E of Khe Sanh were placed to take advantage of only flight path available during IFR weather conditions. As result, AAA positions were able to engage and hit US acft, even when not visible, simply by firing at sound of planes along known glidepath. IFR approaches to base were avoided at all costs for that reason. Grid is apx. Quang Tri Pr, I Corps.
Flame Bath (n/a)
See Glossary.
Flame Drop (n/a)
See Glossary.
Flame Platoon (n/a)
See Glossary.
Flame Tanks (n/a)
See Glossary.
Flame Tracks (n/a)
See Glossary.
Flaming Arrow (n/a)
See Glossary.
Flaming Dart I, Operation (n/a)
On 7Feb65. LBJ ordered one-time reprisal strike on enemy barracks in NVN. 7th Fleet and Da Nang based Marine and VNAF flew the op 7-8Feb65. Inc USN fighter-bomber acft from carriers *USS Ranger*, *USS Hancock* and *USS Coral Sea*, as well as from USMC's Marble Mtn Air Facility at Da Nang that struck coastal ports of Dong Hoi and Vinh Linh. See Op Flaming Dart II. NVN.
Flaming Dart II, Operation (n/a)
7th Fleet Navy and Da Nang based Marine and VNAF air attacks in NVN, 11Feb65. Launched from Acft Carriers *USS Constellation* and *Ticonderoga* against ports of Chanh Hoa and Chap Le. NVN.
Flanders AHP (CP 027-295)
See Dong Ba Thin Heliport. Khanh Hoa Pr, II Corps.
Flanders Field (CP 027-295)
At Dong Ba Thin. Named to honor 1Lt Leon D. Flanders, USA, 117th Avn Co, KIA 18Jun66 by friendly mortar round while standing in chow line. 10th Avn Bn here. See Dong Ba Thin Heliport. Khanh Hoa Pr, II Corps.
Flanders, LZ (YD 017-464)
Apx 7 km WSW Ca Lu, 27 km WSW Quang Tri and 5 km SSW Mai Loc. Apr70 XXIV Corps grid per Don Armstrong. Quang Tri Pr, I Corps.
Flash, LZ (XD 821-401)
Apx 2.5 km WSW Khe Sanh CB, 3 km NW Khe Sanh ville/QL-9 and 52 km WSW Quang Tri. Apr70 XXIV Corps grid per Don Armstrong. Quang Tri Pr, I Corps.
Flashner, FSB (XT 225-926)
Along Rte 246, apx 7 km WNW Katum, 6 km S Cambodia, 20 km NE Thien Ngon AF and 42 km due N Tay Ninh. Named to honor Cpl Kenneth M. Flashner, KIA 28Feb70. Existed 8-13Mar70, as 1 of 7 FSBs opened and closed in as many weeks by 2d/8th Cav, 1st Cav, prior to Cambodian Incursion (7 were: Jamie, Mary Gwen, Heather, Victor, Flashner, Drum and Illingworth). Also spelled Fashner. Cited in *1st Cav Op Rpt, Feb70/Apr70*, p 8, per Peter Cole. Tay Ninh Pr, III Corps.
Flat, FSB (YT 73-33)
Possibly variant of FSB Flay? At S edge of Xa Vo Dat, a few km E or SE Vo Dat AF and apx 36 km NE Xuan Loc. 4th/12th Inf, 199th LIB. Long Khanh Pr, III Corps.
Flatiron, The (XU 70-20?)
Clothes-iron shaped terrain area where Hwy 13 crosses SVN border SE of Snuol, Cambodia, and just due N Loc Ninh. Grid is apx. Binh Long Pr, III Corps.
Flay, FSB (YT 77-14)
Possibly variant of FSB Flat? Apx 32 km E Xuan Loc, 18 km E Nui Chua Chan and 20 km S rptd position of FSB Flat (at Xa Vo Dat). 4th/12th Inf, 199th LIB. Long Khanh Pr, III Corps.
Fleek, FSB (XT 498-048)
Apx 3 km W Khiem Cuong and 33 km WNW Tan Son Nhut. Aug-Oct69. Possibly named to honor Sgt Charles C. Fleek, KIA 27May69. Also listed at XT 868-368 (Nov69-Jan70). Hau Nghia Pr, III Corps.
Fleek, FSB (XT 868-368)
Apx 3 km S Phu Giao and 9 km due E Lai Khe. Here Nov69-Jan70. Possibly named in honor of Sgt Charles C. Fleek, KIA 27May69. Also listed at XT 498-048 (Aug-Oct69). Binh Duong Pr, III Corps.
Fleetwood Field (XT 270-780)
Along TL-4, near Prek Klok, apx 13 km SSW Katum and 21 km due N Nui Ba Den. Apr67. Tay Ninh Pr, III Corps.
Fletcher, USS (n/a)
DD-445, per Ralph Fries.
Flexer, LZ (BR 3-4?)
4th Div FSB on N side of QL-19(?) between An Khe and Mang Yang Pass. Per Patrick Dudney, was named to honor Louis Flexer, 3d/12th Inf, 4th Div, who survived the war. Pleiku or Binh Dinh Pr, II Corps.
Flinders, FSB (YS 526-889)
A.k.a. FSB Trish. Apx 7 km due E FSB Buffalo, 4 km N Hill 869, 30 km NNE Nui Dat and 18 km due N FSB Longreach. *Vietnam Gunners* author notes that it was beset with "atrocious conditions in small jungle clearing

crisscrossed by tracked and wheeled vehicles that turned the ground into a foot deep, muddy quagmire." 161 Bty, RNZA (Horsford's Bty 18Mar69-18Sep69) FSB set here 2-18Jul69 (right section), 13-19Jul69 (left section). Large base in small jungle clearing. B Bty 2d/35th US Arty and US Dusters here. On 1ATF NCO trng map per John Hollett. Also listed at YS 52-89. Phuoc Tuy Pr, III Corps.

Flint (n/a)
6Apr70, XXIV Corps proposed 5th Div FSB name.

Flint, FSB (YB 99-15)
A.k.a. Hill 1338. On small, steep mtn-top apx 10 km SW Dak To 1 AF, 6 km SW Dak To 2 AF, 16 km SW Ben Het and 10 km WSW Dien Binh Ville. Home of NVA 32d Rgt and one of many 4th Div and 173d Abn battle sites during Battle of Dak To, 1Nov-1Dec67. Hill was taken in 2-day fight by 3d/12th Inf. Picture of site in *Vietnam Experience* series, *A Contagion of War* vol., p 179. B Bty, 1st/92d Arty here suptg US 4th Div. Mentioned on internet at: www. thuntek.net/~asper/firebase.html. Possibly also 4th Div FSB and HQ 1st Bde/4th Div in early '69, with 3/12th Inf and 6th/29th Arty here? Kontum Pr, II Corps.

Flintlock, LZ (YD 058-232)
In lowland area near river, apx 5 km E of Laotian Salient, 20 km SSW Ba Long AF and 25 km SSE Ca Lu. Apr70 XXIV Corps grid per Don Armstrong. Quang Tri Pr, I Corps.

Flora, LZ (XS 137-595)
Apx 13 km NW Cai Lay and 22 km SW Thuy Dong AF. Nov67. Dinh Tuong Pr, IV Corps.

Florida, FSB/FSPB (XS 990-551)
Apx 30 km WNW Vung Tau, 4 km E Cua Soirap River, 6 km SE Xom Ca Dah and 37 km SSE Saigon. Jan-Feb68. Also listed at "WS" 987-554 (23 km NNW Vinh Long), which is thought to be error ? Gia Dinh Pr, III Corps.

Florida, LZ (YD 065-654)
Apx 2 km S southern edge of DMZ, 10 km NW Cam Lo and 4 km WSW Thon An Hoa. Apr70 XXIV Corps grid per Don Armstrong. Quang Tri Pr, I Corps.

Florida, FSB? (YT 018-329)
Apx 3 km E Khu Tru Mat and 20 km NNE Bien Hoa AB. Oct69. Nature of site unknown, but likely FSB. Bien Hoa Pr, III Corps.

Florida BOQ (XS 813-925)
At 216 Nguyen Van Thoai St. (Florida Bar Officers Club), Saigon. Data per *Vietnam Military Lore, 1959-1973*. Gia Dinh Pr, III Corps.

Florida Hotel (PR 7-3)
Notorious US Servicemans' R&R hotel in Bangkok, Thailand. Directly across street from Chao Phya Hotel (US Military run hotel/Officers Club). The Bora-Bora Room was bar atop this structure. Thailand.

Flower, FSB (ZS 00-98)
Along N side of QL-1, apx 15 km N Ham Tan AF, 40 km WSW Phan Thiet and 6 km E Ap Da Mai. 199th LIB. 7th/8th Arty here, '70. Binh Tuy Pr, III Corps.

Floyd County, USS (n/a)
LST-762. USN Landing Ship, Tank. Suptd 9th Inf Div/MRF in '66, per MRF Assn website at www.mrfa.org. Decom 1Apr75. III/IV Corps?

Floyd, FSB/LZ/FSSB (BR 83-86?)
Apparently somewhere near Bong Son. If grid is reasonably accurate, was on S edge of large valley apx 4 km NE Ha Tay AF and 9 km SSW Bong Son. 173d Abn FSB in at least mid/late '70. Cited in excerpt of '70 Bn Annual Hist Supplement of 3d/503d Inf at www.gasparot.com/ nammedic. Grid based on nearby sensor-reading location and only very apx. Binh Dinh Pr, II Corps.

Flying Horse SF Camp (BN 3267-0387)
See Phi Ma SF Camp. Binh Thuan Pr, II Corps.

Flying Tiger Airlines (n/a)
See Glossary.

Flying Tiger SF Camp (BN 264-415)
See Phi Ho SF Camp. Binh Thuan Pr, II Corps.

Flying Tiger Site (BN 264-415)
See Phi Ho SF Camp. Binh Thuan Pr, II Corps.

FOB 1 (ZC & YD)
A.k.a. CCN and MLT-1. At Kham Duc (ZC 006-081) in 65-66, Khe Sanh (YD 09-52) in 66, Phu Bai (YD 86-16) from 66-Nov68, and Mai Loc (YD 086-508) in 67? Forward Operating Base of 5th SF Grp, MAC-SOG. Apx 100 SF troops at Mai Loc in 67, portion of which were split off to form FOB-3 at Khe Sanh. Per John Meyers, sat along QL-1, apx 10 km SE Hue, 1 km NW Phu Bai AF on N side of ARVN trng cmpd, just S Phu Luong. See Prairie Fire. Quang Tri, Thua Thien and Quang Nam Prvs, I Corps.

FOB 2 (AR 780-880)
At Kontum AF, along E edge of Kontum City. Oct69. Kontum Pr, II Corps.

FOB 2 (Kontum) (ZA 236-863)
A.k.a. CCC, MLT-2, and Camp Reno. Along QL 14, apx 6 km S Kontum. SF FOB and SOG CCC HQ. 5th SF Grp B-Team CIDG base, here 66-Nov68. Primarily manned by Bru tribesmen in '68. Camp was split by QL-14 (E side lower, more southerly than W side); Ops was on one side and Mess/Theater tents on other. J. P. Martin tells us that to N(?) and just outside main gate was Hazel's Whorehouse. "Hazel was an NVA spy and we had a .50 aimed her place; any attack she was first to go." The Nung were apparently inclined to shoot anyone other than CCC people who tried to enter gate facing Hazel's. There was also a pad on W(?) side used for rigging parachute, strings and ladders. On E(?) side of cmpd was the Reno Bar. Recon orderly room bldg was known as Snowden Hall. One SF trooper there in '68 recalls that Bru were initially invited to skin-flicks occasionally shown in theater; however, to great dismay of their SF advisors, the tribesman began masturbating one another during showings and invitation was terminated thereafter! [228] Grid per Barry Toll. See Prairie Fire. Kontum Pr, II Corps.

FOB 3 (XD 849-410? & YD 094-444)
SF Forward Operating Base at Khe Sanh, 67-May68, and Mai Loc May68-Nov68. At Khe Sanh, was along N edge of Rte 9 apx 500 meters SW the main rwy at Khe Sanh CB, immed W the CAP 0-3 position, and just S what became B/1st/26th Marines portion of Khe Sanh CB perimeter. Mislabeled map of this position is at page 344 of *Valley of Decision*. Quang Tri Pr, I Corps. [229]

FOB 4 (BT 07-71)
Per Frank Penk Jr., was SE of Da Nang on N side of Marble Mtn at mtn's base, and S of Marble Mtn AB. Here, 67-Nov68. 1st Cav provided supt acft to Sneaky Petes based at this site. Grid is est. Quang Nam Pr, I Corps.
FOB 4 - Marble Mountain, Da Nang
FOB 5 (YA 846-249)
Along QL-19, apx 13 km from Cambodian border and 55 km W Pleiku. Mike Boster tells us he helped establish FOB 5 at Duc Co's SF A Camp in '68. Also said to have been at Ban Me Thuot, 67-Nov68? Pleiku Pr, II Corps.
FOB 5 (AQ 780-040?)
Grid is for Ban Me Thuot SF Camp. Here 67-Nov68, according to MACV-SOG website. Also said to have been at Duc Co? Darlac Pr, II Corps.
FOB 6 (XT 958-001)
Apparently at or near Ho Ngoc Tao, 67-Nov68. Grid is along S bank of Song Dong Nai River at Thu Duc, apx 5 km SW Bien Hoa AB and 20 km NE Tan Son Nhut AB. See Ho Ngoc Tao. Binh Duong Pr, III Corps.
FOB A Shau (YC 388-992)
See A Luoi SF Camp. Quang Tri Pr, I Corps.
FOB An Long (WS 5616-0750)
See Cai Cai SF Camp. IV Corps.
FOB An Long (XS 030-912)
See Moc Hoa SF Camp. IV Corps.
FOB An Phu (WT 143-052)
See Phu Hiep SF Camp. IV Corps.
FOB Ba Xoai (VS 905-595)
See Ba Chuc SF Camp. IV Corps.
FOB Binh Hung (VQ 845-815?)
See Binh Chu, Nga Ba Dinh and Cai Do Van SF Camps. IV Corps.
FOB Bu Ghia (YU 344-375)
See Bu Ghia Map SF Camp. III Corps.
FOB Cung Son/Dong Tre (BQ 909-704?)
See Le Hai SF Camp. Phu Yen II Corps.
FOB Dak To (YB 860-258)
See Ban Liet SF Camp. II Corps.
FOB Dak To (ZB 043-224)
See Tan Canh SF Camp. II Corps.
FOB Dong Tre/Cung Son (BQ 909-704?)
See Le Hai SF Camp. Phu Yen II Corps.
FOB Four (BT 07-72?)
See FOB 4. Quang Nam Pr, I Corps.
FOB Five (YA 846-249?)
See FOB 5. Pleiku Pr, II Corps.
FOB Ha Tien (new) (VS 533-551)
See Tra Phu SF Camp. IV Corps.
FOB Ha Tien (VS 472-497)
See Cu Duc SF Camp. IV Corps.
FOB Kham Duc (YC 9640-0091)
See Ngok Tavak SF Camp. Quang Tin Pr, I Corps.
FOB Long Phu (WS 061-601)
See Luong Tan SF Camp. IV Corps.
FOB Mai Linh (BQ 0-9?)
See Phu Thien SF Camp. Phu Yen Pr?, II Corps.
FOB Moc Hoa (WS 983-952)
See Cai Doi, Binh Hiep, Minh Chau, Thanh Tri and Chua Hoi SF Camps. IV Corps.
FOB MR1 MSF (BS 9159-2630)
See Sa Huynh SF Camp. Quang Ngai Pr, I Corps.
FOB My Dien II (VS 995-7640)
See Nhan Hung SF Camp.
FOB Ngok Tavak (YC 9640-0091)
Old French Fort, apx 5 km SW Kham Duc. SF Camp here known as FOG Ngok Tavak (Forward Operating Grp). Overrun May68. Americal list. Quang Tin Pr, I Corps.
FOB Song Mao (AN 965-304)
See Phi Long, and Phi Ma (Flying Horse) SF Camps. Binh Thuan Pr, II Corps.
FOB Song Mau (BN 264-415)
See Phi Ho (Flying Tiger) and Phi Ma (Flying Horse) SF Camps. Binh Thuan Pr, II Corps.
FOB Ta Bat (old) (YC 499-837)
See A Shau FOB. Thua Thien Pr, I Corps.
FOB Tan An (WS 203-058)
See Vinh Xuong SF Camp. IV Corps.
FOB Three (XD 849-410?)
See FOB 3. Quang Tri Pr, I Corps.
FOB Thuong Duc (ZC 152-540)
A.k.a. Hill 52. At or adj to Ha Tan AF, apx 36 km SW Da Nang. 5th SF. Info/grid per *SF Order of Battle.* Quang Nam Pr, I Corps.
FOB Tien Binh (WS 071-809)
See Ba Bai SF Camp. IV Corps.
FOB To Chau (VS 419-495)
See To Chau (FOB). IV Corps.
FOB Trang Sup (XT 395-247)
See Go Dau Ho SF Camp. III Corps.
FOB Tuyen Nhon (XS 200-825)
See Hoi Dong Chieu SF Camp. IV Corps.
FOB Two (ZA 236 863)
See FOB 2. Kontum Pr, II Corps.
FOB Vinh Gia (VS 564-639)
See Gian Thanh SF Camp. IV Corps.
Foche, FSB (XT 203-865)
A.k.a. FSB Brown? Apx 13 km WSW Katum. Also listed at XT 190-860. Feb67. Tay Ninh Pr, III Corps.
Fog Factory, The (XD 852-418)
Less-than-affectionate USAF/Army pilots' nickname for oft fog-bound Khe Sanh AF and Plateau. Discussed in *Valley of Decision*, pp 33-35 et al. See Khe Sanh SF Camp and AF for more info. Quang Tri Pr, I Corps.
Foil, FSB (ZC 023-345)
In the valley of Song Cai River, 6k SE Ben Giang, 10 km WNW FSB Battle-Ax, 26 km due N Kham Duc and 60 km SE Da Nang. Apr70 XXIV Corps grid per Don Armstrong. Quang Nam Pr, I Corps.
Football Island (BT)
Near Go Noi Island and S Da Nang. Enemy staging area throughout war. 1st Mar Div AO. Quang Nam Pr, I Corps.
Football, LZ (BR 746 584)
Perhaps 30 km NE An Khe, 13 km E to ESE Vinh Thanh AF, 3 km SE LZ Arnold's Trail and 21 km NW Phu Cat AB. Also listed at BR 745-589. Per Jim Claeys, was built in apx Sep70, and within triangle formed by LZs Augusta, Arnold's Trail and John Henry. Described as being a "remote hilltop LZ." Claeys also remembers it as "sort of on an elongated hill, not a round hilltop, and built on down

slope rather than its peak." 4th Div AO, '70. Grid per Jim Claeys. Binh Dinh Pr, II Corps.

Force Fed Fire Support System (n/a)
See Glossary.

Force, USS (n/a)
MSO 445. See End Sweep, Op.

Ford, LZ ? (XT 570-570)
Simply listed as "Ford?" Was near Rte 245, at N edge of Michelin Plantation, apx 14 km NE Dau Tieng. Mar69. Binh Duong/Binh Long Pr border, III Corps.

Ford, Tennessee Ernie (n/a)
See Glossary.

Foreign Legion, French (n/a)
See Glossary.

Forest, FSB? (n/a)
See Forrest. III Corps.

Forest Fire, USS (n/a)
See *Forrestal, USS*.

Forest of Assassins (YS 05-65)
Vietnamese nickname for the Rung Sat Special Zone. See Rung Sat. Gia Dinh Pr, III Corps.

Forest People Sightings (n/a)
Vietnamese Yeti. See Nguoi Rung in Glossary.

Forest Royal, USS (n/a)
DD-872, per Ralph Fries.

Forge, LZ (XD 945-496)
Apx 12 km NE Khe Sanh CB, 4 km W QL-9, 5 km WNW Ca Lu and 38 km W of Quang Tri. Apr70 XXIV Corps grid per Don Armstrong. Quang Tri Pr, I Corps.

Forget-Me-Not, Operation (AQ 9-6?)
Last French Op of 1st Indochina War. Conducted while Geneva Peace Accords were being adopted and also <u>after</u> French Premier Pierre Mendes-France had promised (on 20Jun54) a cease fire within a month or he would resign his govt. Scraped together from shell-shocked remnants of G.M. 100 within weeks of its destruction at Mang Yang Pass, the op was launched 14Jul54. Force inc G.M. 100 survivors bolstered by G.M. 42, with 4th Vietnamese Arty, 1st Korea Bn and 3d/5th (Royal Poland) Armored Cav. Its ill-advised purpose was to mop-up Vietminh threatening QL-14 between Pleiku and Ban Me Thuot, and it 1st objective was Ea Hleo (then held by 1 Mountaineer Co and 30 local guerrillas), apx 85 km S Pleiku. At Ea Hleo, it was to disburse into Chu Dreh Mtns to seek enemy. On 17Jul54, it reached Ban Ea Teu, 2 km N Chu Dreh Pass, and at 12:15 pm, as its lead elements emerged from pass, unit was heavily ambushed. 1st Korea Bn, which had suffered so greatly at Mang Yang, was again severely bled with only 107 survivors (53 of whom were hospitalized). Ironically, the Armistice was signed, 20Jul54, 3 days later. See *Street Without Joy*, p 235-240.

Forget-Me-Not Ridge (YA 903-992)
On Hill 994. See Hill 994 for location. Per *Time Heals No Wounds*, p 167, this name was given to the ridge by Eddie Medors (1st/12th Inf, 4th Div), who was in Battle of Hill 994, Mar69. 4th Div AO, Kontum or Pleiku Pr, II Corps.

Forrest, FSB? (n/a)
Location unknown. 1st/8th Arty, 25th Inf Div here, 68. Name per Dan Gillotti. III Corps.

Forrestal, USS (n/a)
A.k.a. CVA-59 and *USS Forest Fire*. Deployed with CVW-17 6Jun67-15Sep67. Serious fire off Vietnam, 29Jul67, when Zuni Rocket was accidentally fired by electrical problem, hitting and igniting drop-tank of a parked A-4. Fire spread to other acft, detonating their bombs loads and blowing 7 major holes in deck. Blast and fire killed 134 men and lasted 13 hrs. 21 acft destroyed (inc some pushed overboard before becoming engulfed). Repair required complete removal/reconstruction of aft section down to hangar floor. Considered worst carrier fire of post WWII years. As result, *USS Forrest Fire* became her nickname. Data per www.uss-salem.org/features/fires/. [230]

Forster, USS (n/a)
DER-334. DD-Escort, Radar, per Ralph Fries.

Forsyth, FSB? (XT 278-101)
On Cambodian border, apx 10 km SSW Duc Hue AF and 8 km NNW tip of Parrot's Beak. Nature of site unknown. Aug68. Hau Nghia Pr, III Corps.

Fort (XR 13-97)
Apx 12 km ESE Tra On AF. Kien Hoa Prov, IV Corps.

Fort (XR 57-97)
Apx 12 km due E Tra Vinh AF. Kien Hoa Prov, IV Corps.

Fort (XR 74-96)
Apx 27 km ESE Tra Vinh AF. Kien Hoa Prov, IV Corps.

Fort (XS 06-18)
Apx 16 km due S Vinh Long and 5 km NE Khu Tru Mat. Vinh Long Prov, IV Corps.

Fort (XS 31-42)
Apx 12 km WSW Dong Tam and 20 km WSW My Tho. Dinh Tuong Prov?, IV Corps.

Fort (XS 63-89)
Apx 17 km due W Saigon, 7 km SE Duc Hoa. TPC K-10D. Hau Nghia Prov, III Corps.

Fort (XS 66-45)
Apx 16 km due E My Tho and 7 km W Vinh Binh. Dinh Tuong Prov?, IV Corps.

Fort (YS 03-66)
On N bank of Song Dong Tranh, apx 30 km SE Saigon and 33 km NE Vung Tau. Gia Dinh Prov, III Corps.

Fort, LZ (XD 854-593)
Apx 8 km NNE Khe Sanh CB, 14 km WNW Ca Lu. Apr70 XXIV Corps grid per D. Armstrong. Quang Tri Pr, I Corps.

Fort (An Tri) (WS 97-42)
Apx 12 km NW Vinh Long AF, near Ap An Tri. Dinh Tuong Prov?, IV Corps.

Fort (Ap An Dien) (XR 69-96)
At An Thien, 4 km SE Thanh Phu. TPC K-10D. Kien Hoa Prov?, IV Corps.

Fort Apache (AT 987-643)
Immed SW the Ha Dong RR Station, apx 500 meters NE the Ha Dong RR Bridge (over Song Bau Xau), 4. 5 km W QL-1, and 13 km S to SSW Da Nang AB. Apparently a 1st/1st Marines position. On map at http://1stbn1stmarines. org/hs/images/MarkedDaiLocMap. jpg. Data per John Middlesworth. Quang Nam Pr, I Corps.

Fort Apache (WE-4-3)
Apparently 3.5 km WSW Banneden, 2.7 km NE Ban Tuan and 2.8 km SE Ban Phonkeo. Alleged, Lao post-war POW camp for US VN POWs. Reported to US authorities in late 70's, it was investigated and dismissed. Subsequently

became object of privately-funded POW rescue mission organized by Bo Gritz. Discussed in *Prisoners of Hope*, pp 131-136 (sketch of base showing relative position is in photo its section). See Velvet Hammer, Op. Laos.

Fort Apache, FSB (XS or XT?)
Described as having been on edge of a rice paddy N of Saigon, and a few km N Ben Loi (or Binh Loi) Bridge along QL-13 (a Binh Loi is at XS 923-893). Apart from bunkers, site contained three-50' corrugated metal bldgs. An old ARVN or French NDP site occupied by 2d/18th Inf, 2d Bde/1st Inf Div in '68-69. No arty here, only mortar Plt. See www.ionet.net/~uheller/vnintro.html. III Corps.

Fort Carnot Airfield (TF 55-94)
A.k.a. Houei Sai AF. On NW border of Laos, apx 340 km NW Vientiane on Feb67 Natl Geo map. El. 1,200'. Laos.

Fort Compton (YT 052-150??)
A.k.a. FSB Compton. Grid zone may incorrect? See Fort Compton at YU 054-150 in Phuoc Long Pr. If grid correct, was apx 7 km ENE Bien Hoa AB, 6 km SW Ap Moi and 5 km NNE Plantation AF. Bien Hoa Pr, III Corps.

Fort Compton, FSB (YU 054-150)
In plantation apx 13 km NW Song Be AF, 12 km SW Phuoc Binh, 3 km SSE Xa Dak Kia, 32 km ENE Loc Ninh, 39 km due N Dong Xoai and 10 km S of Ft. Dillon. 1st/7th Cav/1st Cav, '69, AO Commanche Warrior. Grid per Frank Penk, Jr. Also listed at YT 052-150, per arty ORLL, which is 7 km ENE Bien Hoa AB in Bien Hoa Pr, but YT grid zone thought to be in error? In *1st Cav Div Op Rpt, Feb70-Apr70*, at p 33, per Peter Cole. Phuoc Long Pr, III Corps.

Fort Defiance, FSB (XT 503-833)
Apx 19 km ESE Katum, 12 km SW tip of Fishhook and 26 km WSW An Loc. 1st Cav? Apr70. Tay Ninh Pr, III Corps.

Fort Dent (XS 297-502)
A.k.a. FSB or OP Dent. Along N side of QL-4 at its intersection with Rte 211, apx 22 km WNW My Tho, 7 km E Cai Lay, 3 km E to ESE FSB Moore, and 2 km E FSB Fels. Ft. Dent was unofficial name given this outpost, secured during daylight hours by only 2 Plts of E/2d/39th Inf, Mar-Apr68. Named after E Co's CO, Capt Norman Dent, said to have been WWII 82d Abn vet. Data per Jim Stone, 2d/39th Inf. Dinh Tuong Pr, IV Corps.

Fort DeRussy R&R Center (n/a)
US Military-run R&R hotel on Waikiki Beach in Honolulu, Hawaii. Low room rates and beach-side location made it a desirable destination. For most part, only married soldiers were allowed to take their R&R leave in Hawaii. DOD was concerned that R&R on US soil might lead to higher desertion/AWOL rates, so Hawaii was restricted to married troops on theory they were a lower risk.

Fort Dillon, FSB (YU 045-260)
Along Song Be River, apx 11 km S Cambodia, 10 km SE Bu Dop, 20 km NNW Phuoc Binh/Song Be AF, 35 km ENE Loc Ninh and 10 km N Ft. Compton. 1st/7th Cav, 1st Cav, '69, AO Commanche Warrior. Grid per Frank Penk, Jr. Phuoc Long Pr, III Corps.

Fort Don Dak Namla (YV 806-981)
A.k.a. Fort Don Dak Nam. Along LTL-6, immed E Cambodian Border. 12°44'00"N-107°35'00"E. ND48-16 JOG. Darlac Pr, II Corps.

Fort Don Dasar (BP 2-3)
A.k.a. Fort Don Da Sa. At 12°02'00"N-108°30'00"E. ND49-13 JOG. Tuyen Duc Pr, II Corps.

Fort Granite, FSB (XU 929-081)
A.k.a. FSB Terry Ann and FSB Granite? Along Song Be River, apx 20 km due E Loc Ninh, 23 km W Song Be AF/Phuoc Binh and 20 km NE An Loc. FSBs Debbie and Eleanor were within 3 km. 1st/8th, 1st/12th Cav, 1st Cav, '69, AO Commanche Warrior. Grid per Frank Penk, Jr. Also listed at XU 927-083. Phuoc Long Pr, III Corps.

Fort Lane (CQ 275-229)
See Port Lane. Long Khanh Pr, II Corps.

Fort Mara (BN 030-730)
Remote site apx 37 km NW Song Mao AF, 30 km SSW Dalat/Lien Khuong AF and 16 km SE Phu Hiep/QL-20. Nov67. Lam Dong/Binh Thuan Pr border, II Corps.

Fort Marion, USS (n/a)
LSD-22. Lndg. Ship, Dock, per Ralph Fries.

Fort (Moc Hoa) (VS 97-88)
Apx 6 km SW Moc Hoa AF. Chau Doc Prov, IV Corps.

Fort Narai (SU 9-9?)
SF camp per *SF Order of Battle*. Thailand.

Fort (Ninh Ma) (CQ 22-16)
Apx 2 km NE Ninh Ma. Khanh Hoa Prov, II Corps.

Fort Nora (AN 958-297)
Apx 1 km S QL-1 at Ap Long Hoa, 23 km NNE Phan Thiet and 7 km SW Ap Long Lam. Oct67. Also listed at AN 963-297, per Jerry Berry. Binh Thuan Pr, II Corps.

Fort of the Three Frontiers (YU 6-5)
A.k.a. Poste de Trois Frontieres and Don Tuy Duc. Vicinity of Bu Prang New AF. At 12°17'00"N-107°27'00"E. ND48-16 JOG. Quang Duc Pr, II Corps.

Fort Page (BS?)
Marine CAP position at Binh Nghia. C/7th Marines here. See Binh Nghia CAP Cmpd. Quang Ngai Pr, I Corps.

Fort (Phum Veal Sre Teno) (XU 61-12)
Apx 13 km SW Loc Ninh AF. Binh Long, Pr, III Corps.

Fort Rach Cat (XS 8-6)
A.k.a. Don Rach Cat and Fort de Rach Cat. 10°30'00"N-106°43'00"E. NC48-07 JOG. Long An Pr, III Corps.

Fort Scott, FSB (XU 685-255)
In Cambodia, apx 2 km SE FSB Compton, 3 km N the point where QL-13 crossed SVN border, some 17 km NNW Loc Ninh and 17 km SE Snuol. Grid per *11th ACR Cambodia Invasion AAR, 1st Cav Div, May-Jun70*, courtesy Lou Rochat. [231] Cambodia.

Fort Statsenburg (n/a)
On Clark AFB the Philippines, not in Vietnam.

Fort Thanh Tho (YS 12-50)
At Thanh Tho, apx 2 km from ocean and 17 km WNW Vung Tau. Gia Dinh Prov?, III Corps.

Fort Three Frontiers (YU 6-5)
See Fort of the Three Frontiers. Quang Duc Pr, II Corps.

Fort Tuy Duc (YU 6-5)
See Fort of the Three Frontiers. Quang Duc Pr, II Corps.

Fort Wayne, Operation (XT)
1-4May67. 173d Abn, War Zone D. III Corps.

Fortify Elm (n/a)
See Glossary.

Fortify, USS (n/a)
MSO 446. See End Sweep, Op.

Fortress, The (XT)
See French Fort (Nui Ba Den). Tay Ninh Pr, III Corps.
Fortress, The (ZB 92-28?)
Apx 10 km NE Dak To, 10 km NE Prospectors' Camp and 45 km NNW Kontum. Discussed in *Chickenhawk* and shown on map at book's front. Possibly an old French fort and/or ARVN, or 1st Bde/101st Div position? Grid is est. Kontum Pr, II Corps.
Forward Operating Base 1 (YD 88-14?)
See FOB 1. Thua Thien Pr, I Corps.
Forward Operating Base 2 (ZA 236 863)
See FOB 2. Kontum, Kontum Pr, II Corps.
Forward Operating Base 3 (XD 849-410?)
See FOB-3. Quang Tri Pr, I Corps.
Forward Operating Base (n/a)
See FOB for listings.
Forward, FSB (YD 868-278)
A.k.a. FSB Sabre. Apx 9 km E Phu Vang and 9 km ENE Hue on triangular promontory in a lagoon. Built beginning apx 23May68. Night location beginning 18May68, for what was known as TF Sabre, 2/17th Cav elements att to 2d Bde/101st Abn. Converted to FSB when 2d/17th was assigned own arty w/addition of C/6th/33d Arty, and it operated out of this site for apx 2 months. Also listed at YD 867-272. Thua Thien Pr, I Corps.
Forward Supply Point Minh Long (BS 529-508)
See Minh Long (old) SF Camp. Data per Hank Anthony, 176th Avn Co. Quang Ngai Pr, I Corps.
Fou Loi (XT 86-16)
Likely misspelling of Phu Loi. Sp this way in *Ambush*, where at p 174 author indicates 1st/26th/1st Inf Div here, '66-67. Binh Duong Pr, III Corps.
Fougas or Fougasse (n/a)
See Glossary.
Fountaine, FSB? (YS 804-953)
Apx 22 km NW Ham Tan and 13 km WSW Ap Da Mai. Nature of site unknown. Feb71. Binh Tuy Pr, III Corps.
Fountainebleau Conference (n/a)
See Glossary.
Four Noes, The (n/a)
See Glossary.
Four-Twelve, LZ (BT 016-630)
See 412, LZ. Quang Nam Pr, I Corps.
Fox, LZ (BN 211-513)
Apx 7 km NW Soang Mao AF. Mar67. Binh Thuan Pr, II Corps.
Fox, LZ (BS 80-16)
Apx 4 km NW Gia An, 15 km due N LZ English, 24 km SSE Duc Pho and 3 km E of QL-1. Photos/maps at http://1-14th. com/maps.html. Quang Ngai/Binh Dinh Pr border, I or II Corps.
Fox, LZ (XD 927-546)
Overlooked Khe Trinh Hin River, apx 10 km NW Ca Lu, 16 km WNW Mai Loc and 32 km WSW Dong Ha. Apr70 XXIV Corps grid per D. Armstrong. Quang Tri Pr, I Corps.
Fox, Mini-Base (AT 96-47)
Apx 27 km SSW Da Nang, 8 km E An Hoa AF, 4 km SW LZ Hardcore, 3 km SW Phu Loc 1, 4 km WSW Phu Son Chinh, and 6 km NNW peak Nui Mat Rang. 1st/14th Inf, 4th Div apparently here. Grid est from photos/maps at http://1-14th.com/maps.html. Quang Nam Pr, I Corps.
Fox, USS (n/a)
DLG-33. Guided-Missile DD Ldr, per Ralph Fries.
Fox 1, LZ (n/a)
No data. 173d Abn here, '68-69. II Corps?
Fox Ridge (XD 873-383)
See Foxtrot Ridge. Quang Tri Pr, II Corps.
Foxtrot, FSB (XT 110-600)
Apx 10 km NNW Tay Ninh West AF and 17 km W Nui Ba Den. 196th LIB here during Op Gadsden (Junction City), 1-21Feb67, with Bde Fwd CP at XT 12-63, per Les Hines. Tay Ninh Pr, III Corps.
Foxtrot, FSB (YB 821-078)
A.k.a. FSB 202 and Hill 1000. Apx 24 km SW Dak To 2 AF, 5 km SSE Hill 875, 18 km SSW Ben Het and 26 km NW Polei Kleng. Originally named FSB 202. A.k.a. name info per Nolan Putman,7th/15th Arty. Kontum Pr, II Corps.
Foxtrot, FSB (ZB 054-118)
Apx 30 km NNW Kontum, 12 km SSE Dak To 2 AF and 8 km SSW Bien Binh. 4th Div 12Mar70 ORLL grid per Jim Henderson. Kontum Pr, II Corps.
Foxtrot, LZ? (XT 655-274)
Along Song Saigon, apx 15 km SW Lai Khe. Jun66. Nature of site unknown. Binh Duong Pr, III Corps.
Foxtrot, LZ (XT 972-623)
Apx 13 km NNE Phuoc Vinh AF. Jun67. Binh Long Pr, III Corps.
Foxtrot CAC (YD?)
See CAC Listings. I Corps.
Foxtrot Owl (YD 23-60?)
Call Sign for Dong Ha AF Control.
Foxtrot Ridge (XD 874-383)
A.k.a. Fox Ridge. Apx 8 km SSE Khe Sanh CB. Attack here 28May68 resulted in 13 US KIA, 44 WIA of F/2d/3d Marines, and 174 confirmed NVA KIA. On 19Jun68, C/1st/4th Marines was shelled and attacked here (XD 875-385) resulting in 7 US KIA and 35 WIA. 212 NVA also KIA in that battle. Grid/info per *The Final Formation*, p114. Quang Tri Pr, I Corps.
Foxy, LZ (YC 405-975?)
A.k.a. FSB Fox? If grid correct, was along E edge of A Shau Valley apx 38 km SW Hue, 18 km NNW A Sap, 33 km WSW FSB Birmingham. 101st Abn LZ on Rte 548. Also described as being S of A Luoi, N Currahee and Ta Bat AF. C-7A Caribou AF built here, 6-13Jun69. Used during Ops Massachusetts Striker, Apache Snow and Montgomery Rendezvous, May-Aug69. Grid is that of FSB Fox and may not be correct? Also an FSB/LZ Fox at XD 927-546. Thua Thien Pr, I Corps. [232]
Foxy Airstrip (YC 405-975?)
C-7A Caribou strip in A Shau Valley. See Foxy, LZ, for detail. Thua Thien Pr, I Corps.
Frag (n/a)
See Glossary.
Frag Order 11Jan65, 7Jun65-2Aug65, Op (n/a)
173d Abn, Bien Hoa Area. 1st joint US-ARVN op of war. Nine Bns penetrated deep into western Tan Uyen area of War Zone D. Some 400 VC (an entire Main Force VC Bn) were rptd killed in this 1st major engagement between VC and 173d Abn. Bien Hoa Pr?, III Corps.
Fragging (n/a)
See Glossary.

Fragging, French v. US (n/a)
See Glossary.
Fran, LZ (AR 892-249)
Near road intersection, apx 3 km due S Plei Do Lim AF, 8 km NE QL-14 and 26 km SSE Pleiku. Bty A/5th/16th Arty here Dec69. 4th Div 31Jan70 ORLL grid per Jim Henderson. Pleiku Pr, II Corps.
Frances, FSB (XT 573-758)
Apx 16 km due S tip of Fishhook, 7 km SSW Tonle Cham AF, 2 km ENE Srok Cay Son, 2 km S the Song Saigon, 11 km NNW Minh Thanh AF and 42 km NE Tay Ninh. 2d/60th(?), 9th Div here early Aug 70, per David Argabright. Binh Long Pr?, III Corps.
Francis Marion, Operation (n/a)
5Apr-12Oct67. 4th Div op. 1,203 rptd NVA/VC KIA, per *Vietnam Order of Battle*, pp 9-14. Pleiku Pr, II Corps.
Francis, FSB (XT 573-758?)
Sp variant of Frances? See Frances. Cited in *11th ACR Cambodia Invasion AAR, 1st Cav Div, May-Jun70*, courtesy Lou Rochat. [233] Binh Long Pr or Cambodia?
Frank, LZ (XT 485-194)
Along QL-1, apx 16 km WNW Cu Chi and 12 km ESE Go Dau Ha. Mar66. Hau Nghia Pr, III Corps.
Frank B. Evans, USS (n/a)
DD-754, per Ralph Fries.
Frank Doezema Compound (YD 767-218?)
A.k.a. the Hue MACV Cmpd. See Hue MACV Cmpd for location. Named to honor Sp4 Frank Doezema, Jr. (KIA 31Jan68; awarded DSC) on 4Jul68, at 11:15hrs, per *Stars & Stripes* article (unknown issue) entitled *Hue Memorial Erected, Honors Valorous G.I.*, courtesy Dennis Williams. Thua Thien Pr, I Corps.
Frank Knox, USS (n/a)
DD-742. At one point was grounded and freed by harbor tugs/salvage vessels of Harbor Clearance Unit 1. [234]
***Franklin* (Vessel)** (n/a)
See First Americans to Visit Vietnam.
Franklin D. Roosevelt, USS (n/a)
CVA-42. Deployed with CVW-l, 21Jun66-21Feb67.
Franks, FSB (XU)
Described as having been in Cambodia and SE Snuol. 11th ACR/1st Cav, May-Jun70. Cited in *11th ACR Cambodia Invasion AAR, 1st Cav Div, May-Jun70*, courtesy Lou Rochat. [235] Cambodia?
Fred Morris, SS (n/a)
Merchant ship under govt contract, per Ralph Fries.
Fred T. Berry, USS (n/a)
DD-858, per Ralph Fries.
Freda, FSB (XT 588-333)
A.k.a. or near FSB Gordon, apx 19 km WSW Lai Khe, 4 km NW Xa Duoc. Aug69. Binh Duong Pr, III Corps.
Freddie, LZ (BS 229-578)
In valley of tributary of Dak Drinh River, apx 33 km WNW Minh Long AF, 16 km W Lang Re and 41 km WSW Quang Ngai. Americal list. Quang Ngai Pr, I Corps.
Frederick Hill, LZ (n/a)
See Fredrick Hill. I Corps.
Frederick County, USS (n/a)
LST 1184. Part of T Grp 76.8, During Op Eagle Pull.
Fredrick Hill, LZ (n/a)
Location unknown. Apparent USMC 9th Mar Engr base? Quang Tri Pr?, I Corps.
Free, LZ (XT 032-710)
Apx 13 km SSW Thien Ngon AF and 8 km E Cambodia. Tay Ninh Pr, III Corps.
Free Fire Zone (n/a)
See Glossary.
Free World Heliport (XS 835-912)
In Saigon, apx 1 km NW the US Embassy. "Heliport #750, alt 30', 350' x 160', Laterite. Official Business Only. 500' traffic pattern, left traffic lndg W. Tfc from S rpt 5 mi S heliport; traffic from NE rpt over Newport Bridge. Do not overfly HQ CMAC, 1/4 mi NE. See Saigon Heliport Procedures. HAZARDS-150' sig twr SW corner, water twr 80' NW corner, guard twr 20' NE corner, 9' fence N and E, bldg SW corner. Peneprimed. Saigon (Hotel-3) Heliport Tower-281.1 120.4 35.5 Advsy only. Arty advsy-Saigon 239.0 46.0," per Feb73 TAD. Gia Dinh Pr, III Corps.
Free World Service Club (XT 175-517)
See Freeworld. Tay Ninh Pr, III Corps.
Freedom Hill (BT 97-73?)
At Da Nang, overlooking Camp Hoover and ASP-1, Said to have been in Camp Laurer? Included large PX, snack bar and transient barracks for troops in-transit on R&R, DEROS or replacement. See mapsheet L-7014-6641-3. Quang Nam Pr, I Corps.
Freedom Train, Operation (n/a)
Initial US air supt campaign triggered by '72 NVA Easter Offensive. Its 2d phase was Op Linebacker.
Freedom Village (BQ 045-289)
Apx 2 km E Buon Ho AF and 2 km N Buon Tring. Dec68. Darlac Pr, II Corps.
Freeman BEQ (XS 8-9)
US enlisted billet, Sep65-68, 41 rms, Saigon. Data per *Vietnam Military Lore, 1959-1973*. Gia Dinh Pr, III Corps.
Freeman Enlisted Area (AR 7-8?)
Advsy Team #22 Cmpd at Kontum. Named to honor MSgt Rube A Freeman, KIA 26Apr63. Kontum Pr, III Corps.
Freeman Hall BEQ (XS 8-9)
At 94-98 Nguyen Huyen Duc St., Cholon, Saigon. Named to honor MSgt Rube A. Freeman, KIA 26Apr63. Data per *Vietnam Military Lore, 1959-1973*. Gia Dinh Pr, III Corps.
Freeman-Anderson Compound (XR 05-59)
At Soc Trang. HQ for Adv Team # 71, and named to honor SFC Jimmy G. Freeman and Darrell E. Anderson, both KIA 24Mar69, when overrun at Tam Soc Op Base, Mobile Adv Team 71. Data per Ray Bows. Ba Xuyen Pr, IV Corps.
Freeworld Service Club (XT 175-517)
Per www.riverwolf.net/reflections/vietnam/, was service club at Tay Ninh West complex, "rebuilt by US and PHILCAG troops after the original club burned. Near [it], base cmdrs built small "stand down" cottages (HoJo Village), reserved strictly for returning LRRP and RECON patrols. 25 years after the withdrawal of US troops from SVN, the club was featured in a commemorative TV program as a "popular resort facility" for Vietnamese dignitaries." Same website says it was 1 of 2 model clubs built in SVN (see Blackhorse). Grid is for PHILCAG Cmpd. Tay Ninh Pr, III Corps.

French Airfield (An Khe) (BR 47-45?)
Abnd AF built by colonial French along QL-19 near An Khe. Later became major AF at An Khe under US forces? Apparently also departure point of G.M. 100, on morning of 24Jun54. By 6 p.m. that night, column virtually ceased to exist after 803d Vietminh Rgt ambush along E approach to Mang Yang Pass. Binh Dinh or Pleiku Pr?, II Corps.

French Casualties, 1st Indochina War (n/a)
See Glossary.

French Cemetery, Saigon (XS 810-940)
At W edge of city, 2 km S Tan Son Nhut AB, Saigon. Gia Dinh Pr, III Corps.

French Cemetery, Mang Yang (BR 227-529?)
Along QL-19E at its summit in the Mang Yang Pass. On 25Jun54, G.M. 100, a French armored column that was ambushed and annihilated by 803d Vietminh Rgt between what was later known as Bridge 25 and Strongpoint 5, apx 15 km from An Khe AF. Bodies of French KIA were then buried atop Man Yang Pass and white crosses used could apparently be seen a great distance from burial site. [236] Photos of site on webpage of Fred Lohr at: www.sirinet.net/~flohr/photo.htm. Pleiku Pr, II Corps.

French Civilians in Vietnam (n/a)
See Glossary.

French Factory, The (XT 35-32)
Along QL-2 near LZ Storm, apx 20 km SE Tay Ninh, perhaps 6 km NNW Go Dau Ha. Grid per 2-6Apr70 AAR of HQ 3d Bde/25th Inf Div. Tay Ninh Pr, III Corps.

French Far Eastern Air Force (n/a)
See Glossary.

French Foreign Legion (n/a)
See Glossary.

French Fort, The Old (AT?)
SW or near Da Nang? ARVN/US prisoner interrogation facility? Quang Nam Pr, I Corps?

French Fort, The Old (AT 916-582)
See Hill 37. Quang Nam Pr, I Corps.

French Fort, The (Vinh Thanh) (BR)
At head of Vinh Thanh Valley (a.k.a. Happy Valley), and along Song Con Creek, apx 2.5 km NW Vinh Than, 22 km NE An Khe. CIDG base in this crumbling, old fort involved in Op Crazy Horse, May66. See *Battles in the Monsoon*. W Suoi Ca Valley. 1st Cav. Binh Dinh Pr, II Corps.

French Fort, The (Khe Sanh) (XD 858-387)
See Khe Sanh SF Camp. A.k.a. New French Fort? L-7014-6342-3 map per Ken Burrington. Quang Tri Pr, I Corps.

French Fort, The (XS 338-845)
Near Long An/Kien Tuong Pr/III/IV Corps border, apx 32 km ESE Moc Hoa, 8 km NE Tuyen Nhon, and 8 km SSE tip of Parrot's Beak. Built on small, trapezoid-shaped island cut into canal. E/2d/39th here, 1Jun68, per Jim Stone. Stone reflects: "Why did we call that place "French Fort"? Was very bizarre, out in middle of nowhere. Just a mound of dirt alongside a not-too-wide canal. It had concrete pads for artillery emplacements. Strewn around on ground were old shell casings from AK-47, M-16, .30 cal and .50 cal weapons, some so corroded that it seemed they'd been there many, many years. It had the feel of a place that had been fought over, time and again for ages! Some thought that surely the French must have built it." Map is L7014-6230-3. Kien Tuong Pr, IV Corps.

French Fort, The (Rach Cat) (XS 8-6)
A.k.a. Fort de Rach Cat. At 10°30'00"N-106°43'00"E Perhaps 20 to 25 km due S Saigon? Apparently old French Fort here. Long An or Go Cong Pr, III or IV Corps.

French Fort, The (Cat Lai) (XS 950-890)
See Cat Lai Terminal. Gia Dinh Pr, III Corps.

French Fort, The (Ap Long Ninh) (XS 895-616)
A.k.a. FSB X-Ray. On island along Cua Soirap just E Ap Long Ninh, 13 km due E Can Giuoc, 17 km NNE Go Cong, and 30 km S Saigon. 2d/35th Arty here when it was known as "X-Ray" during Op Coronado, 20-21-Jul67, in supt 3d and 4th/47th Inf, US 9th Div (as well as 3d Bn VNMC and 3d/46th ARVN). Grid est from map on 199th LIB Assn website. Long An Pr, III Corps. [237]

French Fort, The (Nui Ba Den) (XT 273-679)
A.k.a. FSB St. Barbara and FSB Bau Co. Apparently at Bau Co, apx 9 km due N Nui Ba Den, 18 km NE Tay Ninh West and perhaps 3 km W Hwy 4. Per Butch Sincock, its perimeter was a high berm of compacted dirt with bunkers built into sides of berm. Its helo pad was built outside the berm and open to VC observation/attack. Four 175mm cannons plus 155 and 105 batteries sited here, per *Suicide Charlie*, p 117. 25th ID and 1st Cav. Fired supt during major attack on FSB Carolyn, 2Jun69. Also listed at XT 274-680 and XT 276-679. Tay Ninh Pr, III Corps.

French Fort, The (Ben Chau) (XT 28-68?)
Just outside Ben Chau, 10 km due S Prek Klok, 10 km N Nui Ba Den on Rte 4 in War Zone C. Arty base here, as were elements of 3d Bde 1st Inf Div, 2d/3d 199th LIB, 25th Inf Div at various times. Discussed in *Charlie Company*, pp 145 et al. III Corps.

French Fort, The (Dau Tieng) (XT 43-46?)
See Old French Fort (Dau Tieng). Tay Ninh Pr, III Corps.

French Fort, The (Ben Cat) (XT 75-34?)
See Artillery Base I. Binh Duong Pr, III Corps.

French Fort, The (Ngok Tavak) (YC 9640-0091)
A.k.a. Ngok Tavak, apx 5 km SW Kham Duc and used as SF Camp, known as FOG Ngok Tavak (Forward Operating Grp). See Ngok Tavak. Quang Tin Pr, I Corps.

French Fort, The (Ap Lai Bang) (YD 633-248)
Apx 2 km E Ap Lai Bang/Song Bo River, 1 km NE Hwy 598, 1 km W Thon Thuong, 2.5 km SSW LZ Sally, 3.3 km SW QL-1 and 8 km W Hue. Thua Thien Pr, I Corps.

French Fort, The (Ap Tay) (YS 39-62)
FSB near Ap Tay and on W side of Rte-2, 6 km S Nui Dat, 6 km E Nui Thi and 20 km NNE Vung Tau. 161 Bty, RNZA (Honner's Bty 13May66-13May67) FSB set here 8-24Sep66, and 10-11Dec66. Dilapidated conc-block French colonial era house here. Phuoc Tuy Pr, III Corps.

French Fort Basecamp (XT 275-682)
See French Fort, The, at grid. Tay Ninh Pr, III Corps.

French Fort Design (n/a)
See Glossary.

French Tank, The (BR 340-461)
Burned-out tank that was remnant of annihilation of G.M. 100, along QL-19E. Apparently hulk was later towed to LZ Schueller and placed at its entrance. [238]

French Union Forces (n/a)
See Glossary.

Frenchy's (BT 7-0?)
Civilian bar on QL-1, just S of Da Nang, and notorious among US troops for its VC-controlled drug trafficking and paraphernalia. Info courtesy Ex-PFC J. Middlesworth, A Bty, 1st/11th Arty, 1st Mar Div. Quang Nam Pr, I Corps.
Frenchman's Flat Quarry (XT 906-082)
Along W bank of Song Saigon, apx 12 km N Tan Son Nhut AB, near Ap Binh Hoa. Apr67. Binh Duong Pr, III Corps.
Frenchman's Pit (XT 689-082)
Along QL-1 near Ap Cho, apx 16 km NW Tan Son Nhut AB. Quarry. Oct66. Hau Nghia Pr, III Corps.
Frendling Hill (YD)
Apparently either Dong Ap Tay or Nui Ke (YD 490-980 or YD 760-055) were called Frendling Hill to honor Edward J. Frendling, D/1st/502d Inf, 101st Abn, KIA 31Mar69. Thua Thien Pr, I Corps.
Frenzell, Camp (YT 076-122)
See Camp Frenzell-Jones. Bien Hoa Pr, III Corps.
Frenzell-Jones, Camp (YT 076-122)
At or near Plantation AF/Long Binh Post. 199th LIB basecamp. Named to honor PFC Herbert Frenzell, USA, and Sp4 Billy C. Jones, both KIA 21Jan66, during VC ambush of 2d Plt, A/4th/12th Inf, 199th LIB. Frenzell exposed himself to draw enemy fire away from pinned-down element and was shot in the chest. His close friend, Billy Jones, then braved heavy fire to recover Frenzell's body and carried it for 2 hours while VC pursued survivors of attack. As rescue choppers finally arrived, Jones again exposed himself to heavy fire in effort to aid yet another wounded man. His last words as he lay dying, were: "I tried. I did all I could. I can't do any more." They may have been 1st KIA of 199th. Camp dedicated 28Sep67. Bien Hoa Pr, III Corps. [239]
Frequent Wind, Operation (n/a)
Code Name for US Naval evacuation of Saigon, Apr75. Original name of Op was "Talon Vise." 7th Fleet gathered WESTPAC resources as it became apparent fall of Saigon was imminent. Between 18-24Apry75, the USN concentrated a vast flotilla off Vung Tau and under Cmdr TF 76, with *USS Blue Ridge* as flagship. Flotilla was divided into Task Grp 76.4-Movement Transport Grp Alpha (inc *USS Okinawa*, *Vancouver*, *Thomaston* and LST 1183 *Peoria*); Task Grp 76.5-Movement Transport Grp Bravo (inc the *USS Dubuque*, *Durham* and *Frederick*); and Task Grp 76.9-Movement Transport Grp Charlie (inc the *Anchorage* (LSD 36), *Denver* (LPD 9), *Duluth* (LPD 6) and *Mobile* (LKA 115). The TF was joined by carriers *Hancock* and *Midway*, carrying numerous helos; 7th Fleet flagship *Oklahoma City*; amphib ships *Mount Vernon* (LSD 39), *Barbour County* (LST 1195), and *Tuscaloosa* (LST 1187); and eight destroyer types for naval gunfire, escort, and area defense. *Enterprise* and *Coral Sea* air wings of TF 77 provided air cover while TF 73 gave logistic supt. USMC Evac contingent (9th Mar Amphib Bde, a.k.a. Task Grp 79.1), inc 2 BLTs, 4 helo sqdns, supt and security Dets. At 1108 hrs 29Apr75, Task Grp 76.4 received order to execute Op. Mission was to evac all US personnel, and any Viets who were at risk for past cooperation with US. At 1244 hrs, from point 17 nautical mi from Vung Tau Peninsula, *USS Hancock* launched 1st helo wave of Op and 2 hours later, they landed at US. Defense Attaché Office cmpd in Saigon (primary LZ). 2d/4th Marines provided defensive cordon, and once in place, Task Grp 76.4 began lift. By 2100 hrs apx 5,000 evacuees and 2d/4th Marines had been transferred to fleet. Meanwhile, Ocean Tugs *Harumi*, *Chitose Maru*, *Osceola*, *Shibaura Maru*, and *Asiatic Stamina* began pulling barges filled with evacuees from Saigon Port out to flotilla. There, the refugees were registered, inspected for weapons and given medical exam. Flotilla of 26 VN Navy and other vessels also arrived at and concentrated off Son Island carrying some 30,000 evacuees. On 30-31Apr75, Task Grp 76.4 and the VN flotilla moved away from coast, still picking up morc seaborne refugees as they went. Also arriving over fleet came an unexpected armada of hundreds of VN Helos carrying panicked troops and their families. The very surprised *Hancock* and *Midway* had no choice but to allow them to land, and helos were pushed overboard to allow next wave aboard. On morning of 30Apr75, to utter shock of ship's crew, a fixed wing acft also made a safe lndg on *Midway* (see Buong Incident in Glossary). On evening of 2May76. bulk of op was complete and Task Grp 76.4 (with 6,000 evacuees) and MSC group of *USS Sgt Truman Kimbro*, *Sgt Andrew Miller*, *Greenville Victory*, *Pioneer Contender*, *Pioneer Commander*, *Green Forest*, *Green Port*, *American Challenger*, and *Boo Heung Pioneer* (with 44,000 refugees); and VNN group of 30,000 evacuees, set sail for reception centers in Philippines and Guam. Thus ended USN's 25-year role of supt to SVN govt. [240]
Fried Rice (YD 1-6?)
Area roughly 4 km NW Cam Lo, 1 km S "Bloody Rice" and 5 km N QL-9. Significance of site unknown. Apx location on *Leatherneck* Magazine map (date unknown) posted on net at: www.monboys.com. Quang Tri Pr, I Corps.
Friendling Hill (YD)
See Frendling Hill. Thua Thien Pr, I Corps.
Friendship, FSB (YS 533-786)
Apx 14.5 km NE Nui Dat, 2 km NNE FSB Longreach and 7 km WSW FSB Raglan. On 1ATF NCO trng map per John Hollett. Phuoc Tuy Pr, III Corps.
Fresno County, USS (n/a)
LST-1182. Lndg. Ship, Tank, per Ralph Fries.
Frodo, LZ (BR 165-435)
Apparently renamed FSB/LZ Yacht after only very short period as Frodo. Apx 33 km due W An Khe, 18 km SE Suoi Doi AF, 6 km ESE peak of Chu Rran Mtn and 10 km S QL-19. 3d/8th Inf, 4th Div here 7-13Jun70. Name/grid per Jim Claeys. Binh Dinh/Pleiku Pr border, II Corps.
Frog, LZ (YD 057-665)
Just S the Song Ngan River, apx 4.5 km WSW Thon An Hoa, 19 km WSW Dong Ha. Apr70 XXIV Corps grid per Don Armstrong. Quang Tri Pr, I Corps.
Frontier, LZ (XD 909-234)
In valley along eastern edge of Vietnam Salient, apx 1 km from Lao border, 7 km SSW Lang Klung, 20 km SSE Khe Sanh CB and 52 km SW Quang Tri. Apr70 XXIV Corps grid per Don Armstrong. Quang Tri Pr, I Corps.
Frontier City, FSB/PB (XT 203-298)
Apx 3 km E Cambodian border, 2 km W Ap Cai Tac and 19 km S Tay Ninh. Built during Toan Thang II by C Co 4th/9th Inf, as "instant patrol base." Constructed in 1 day

when CH-54 brought in 1 bulldozer and another was rafted down the Vam Co River/Rach Bao Canal then driven to site, followed by procedure outlined in "Instant Patrol Base" entry in Glossary. Manchus were apparently under mortar fire from moment they landed to build base. Ground was hardpan "so tough you couldn't drive a spike into it with a sledgehammer," and "was devoid of vegetation other than some stunted grass and a few parched shrubs." Heavily attacked by NVA 272d Rgt in what became Battle of Frontier City, 26-27Apr69, beginning on night of only 2d day of its existence. When observation tower detected movement to SW, defenders were told to act naturally and turn up their radios to feign ignorance. The song *Harry the Hairy Ap,e* by Ray Stevens was playing on AFVN Radio at that moment. A barrage of mortars, RPGs and AA fire then hit base, followed by a Bn of 271st NVA while 3 Spooky and 1 Shadow, 22 Cobra/Huey gunships and 4 jets blasted avenues of approach. Only 11 NVA reached perimeter where Claymores, 90mm RR and MG fire stopped them. 213 NVA KIA and 9 US WIA resulted. Name courtesy Mike Smith. Tay Ninh Pr, III Corps. [241]

Frost, LZ (XD 984-687)
In DMZ, apx 1.5 km S the Ben Hai River, 17 km NW Cam Lo and 17 km WNW Dong Ha. Apr70 XXIV Corps grid per Don Armstrong. Quang Tri Pr, I Corps.

Frustration, LZ (BR 273-462)
Apx 3 km SE LZ Action, 22 km due W An Khe, 3 km S QL-19 and 26 km ESE Suoi Doi AF. 4th Div '70. Data per Jim Claeys. Pleiku or Binh Dinh Pr, II Corps.

FSA MacDonald (YD 812-154)
See MacDonald, FSA. Thua Thien Pr, I Corps.

FSB (defined) (n/a)
See Fire Support Base in Glossary.

FSB (name) (various)
See name of base in its appropriate alphabetical order. For example, "Birmingham, FSB."

FSPB (name) (various)
See formal name of base in its appropriate alphabetical order. For example, "Coogee, FSPB."

Ft. Apache (AT 987-643)
See Fort Apache. Quang Nam Pr, I Corps.

Ft. Apache, FSB (WE-4-3)
See Fort Apache. Laos.

Ft. Apache, FSB (XT?)
See Fort Apache. III Corps.

Ft. Carnot Airfield (TF 55-94)
A.k.a. Houei Sai AF. See Fort Carnot AF. Laos.

Ft. Compton, FSB (YT 052-150?)
See Fort Compton at YU 054-150. Grid error.

Ft. Compton, FSB (YU 054-150)
See Fort Compton, FSB. Phuoc Long Pr, III Corps.

Ft. Defiance, FSB (XT 503-833)
See Fort Defiance.

Ft. Dent (XS 297-502)
See Fort Dent. Dinh Tuong Pr, IV Corps.

Ft. DeRussy (n/a)
See Fort DeRussy. Hawaii.

Ft. Dillon, FSB (YU 045-260)
See Fort Dillon, FSB. Phuoc Long Pr, III Corps.

Ft. Granite, FSB (XU 929-081)
See Fort Granite. Phuoc Long Pr, III Corps.

Ft. Lane (CQ 275-229)
See Port Lane. Phu Yen Pr, II Corps.

Ft. Mara (BN 030-730)
See Fort Mara. Lam Dong/Binh Thuan Pr border, II Corps.

Ft. Marion, USS (n/a)
LSD-22. Lndg. Ship, Dock, per Ralph Fries.

Ft. Narai (SU 9-9?)
See Fort Naria. Thailand.

Ft. Page (BS?)
See Fort Page. Quang Ngai Pr, I Corps.

Ft. Scott, FSB (XU 685-255)
See Fort Scott. Cambodia.

Ft. Statsenburg (n/a)
See Fort Statsenburg. Philippines.

Ft. Wayne, Operation (n/a)
1-4May67. 173d Abn, War Zone D. III Corps.

Fu Ya Lagoon (AT 8-9)
A.k.a. Dam Lap An. Lagoon at 16°14'N-108°04'E. On ND49-01 JOG. Quang Nam Pr, I Corps.

Fullbright-Aiken Amendment (n/a)
See Glossary.

Fuller, FSB (YD 014-592)
A.k.a. Dong Ha Mtn or Hill 544 (Hill 549 in some rpts). Apx 9 km due W Cam Lo, 33 km WNW Quang Tri, 5 km NE Elliott CB, 12 km NNE Vandegrift, 4 km due E FSB Pete and 3 km N QL-9. Battle for FSB Fuller took place beginning 24Jun71, when base was hit with 500 rounds of NVA arty, followed by an 800 round barrage soon after, and then, over a 30 period, some 5,400 rounds before it was evacuated by ARVN. Was later recaptured after heavy B-52 strikes reduced the height of mtn to what Richard White (3d/5th Cav) thinks was closer to 500 meters than 549 meters! [242] Also listed at YD 019-593. On map at p 58, *US Marines in Vietnam-1969*. Aerial photo of base at: http://members.odyessy1.net/scummin/. Some data per *A Better War*, p 284. NE48-16 JOG map indicates 544-meter height. Quang Tri Pr, I Corps.

Fuokmai Peninsula (CR 1-3)
A.k.a. Phuoampoc Mai, Ban Dao. Peninsula at 13°53'N-109°16'E. On ND49-09 JOG. Binh Dinh Pr, II Corps.

Funnel, The or LZ? (YT 080-440)
Terrain feature or FSB? Apx 14 km ESE Phuoc Vinh AF and 2 km W Phung. Apr69. Phuoc Long Pr?, III Corps.

Furr, LZ/FSB (XT?)
Possibly near FSB Mace/LZ Green? A Co/1st/7th Cav, here 70-71. Per Jerry Wood, was named to honor SFC William R. Furr, KIA 9Apr71. Wood says it was very small LZ and existed for only short time. III Corps?

Furse, USS (n/a)
DD 882. In Aug68, replaced *USS St. Francis River* off Binh Thuan Pr, suptg TF 3d/506th Inf. On 29Aug68, it shelled VC company near Phan Thiet, killing w/19 VC KIA, 6 WIA, per www.currahee.org/pageb2.html.

Fury, FSB (BT 151-264)
Apx 15 km WNW Tam Ky and 3 km S Duc An. Americal list. USMC and Americal. Quang Nam Pr, I Corps.

Fury, FSB (YC 534-846)
At S end of A Shau Valley, apx 42 km SW Hue, and 10 km ESE A Sap. FSB's Fury, Pike, Shield, Whip and Thor were originally built during Op Massachusetts Striker, 22Mar-8May69, using Combat Trap 10,000 lb. bombs (if

available) to initiate construction until hilltop "was clear enough for rappelling." [243] Phase one of Lam Son 720 began 14Apr71 with arty raid fired from Fury, while 1st/327th Inf secured base. Thua Thien Pr, I Corps.

GOLF

Facility/Feature Name, Grid Coordinate, a.k.a. Name/History/Province/CTZ

Unless otherwise stated, 6-digit grid coordinates reference DMA L-7014, L-7015 or L-7016 series, 1:50,000 scale maps, while 2- and 4-digit coordinates reference AMS/DMA/NIMA 1:250,000, 1:500,000 and 1:1,000,000 scale maps. Unless otherwise stated, all heights are in meters. To convert meters to feet, multiply by 3.2808; feet to meters, multiply by .3048.

G-4 NSA Hospital (BT 03-76?)
See USN/USMC Hosp, Da Nang. Quang Nam Pr, I Corps.

G, LZ (XT 930-570)
Apx 1 km ESE Sra Diop and 9 km NNW Phuoc Vinh AF. 9Jun67. 12Jun67. Binh Duong Pr, III Corps.

G. M. 100 (n/a)
See Glossary.

G Rieng (n/a)
Mapsheet name of L-7014-6539-2. SVN.

Ga, Mui (WF 7-8)
Coastal point at 18°50'N-105°43'E. NE48-07 JOG. NVN.

Ga La Hai SF Camp (BQ 952-797)
See La Hai SF Camp. Phu Yen Pr, II Corps.

Gabo, FSB (YS 463-826)
On E side of LTL-2, apx 15 km NNE Nui Dat and 4 km N FSB Alanbrooke. On 1ATF NCO trng map per John Hollett. Phuoc Tuy Pr, III Corps.

Gabrielle (TJ 9-6)
Apx 3.8 mi NNW Dien Bien Phu main CP, .5 mi NE A2 and .75 mi due N A4, and directly in line with main rwy. "To the N, beyond the end of rwy, rose Gabrielle, held by 4th Bn, 7th Algerian Rifles"[244] In Muong Thanh Valley apx 290 km W Hanoi. French strongpoint during Op Castor, 20Nov53 to 7May54. Held by 4th Bn, 7th Algerian Rgt and roughly 500 meters by 200 meters in size. Though very well built, was overrun night of 14-15Mar56, during 2d day of Vietminh offensive. NVN.

Gadsden, Operation (XT 12-63)
Per Les Hines, Apparently name of 196th LIB's portion of Op Junction City, 1-21Feb67. It's Bde CP was at listed grid. See FSBs Charlie, Delta and Foxtrot. Tay Ninh Pr, III Corps.

Gaf Sa, FSB? (XT 660-579)
See Gafsa. Binh Long Pr, III Corps.

Gafsa, FSB (XT 660-579)
A.k.a. FSB Dusty. Apx 12 km WSW Chonh Than AF. Also sp FSB Gaf Sa? Apr69. Binh Long Pr, III Corps.

Gail, LZ (BS 624-338)
Apx 6 km ENE Ba To New AF and 21 km WSW Duc Pho/QL-1. 1st Cav. Name/grid per Dan Gillotti. Quang Ngia Pr, I Corps.

Gail, FSB (YS 251-722)
On W side of QL-15, apx 3 km S Phu My and FSB North Dakota, 18 km WNW Nui Dat and 2 km NNW FSB Stingray. On 1ATF NCO trng map per John Hollett. Phuoc Tuy Pr, III Corps.

Gaiser, FSB (BN 269-548)
Apx 8 km due N Song Mao, 62 km NE Phan Thiet and 60 km WSW Phan Rang. B Bty, 5th/22d Arty here Oct-Nov70. Likely named after one of 2 men, both of whom were US Army. Interestingly, both were also 1Lts: James A. Gaiser, KIA 7Nov69, and Lewis B., KIA 27Jun67. Grid and arty info per Nolan Putman. Binh Thuan Pr, II Corps.

Galard-Jerraube, Genevieve de (n/a)
See Glossary.

Gallop (n/a)
6Apr70, XXIV Corps proposed 5th Div FSB name.

Gallup, USS (CP 0-2)
A.k.a. PG-85. Arrived off SVN 30Apr67, to join Coastal Sqdn 3 out of Cam Ranh Bay (later Coastal Flotilla 1). Was one of new *Asheville-class* patrol gunboats at time. 165' long, 37 knots top speed and armed with 3-inch/50 gun in front mount, 40mm gun aft, 2-.50 cal. MGs and 81mm mortar tube. Role discussed in *Brown Water, Black Berets*, p 91. Market Time TF-115. See *Wilhoite, USS,* for info on incident of 15Ju67. Khanh Hoa Pr, II Corps.

Galore, LZ (ZA 145-755)
Apx 16 km SW Kontum and 9 km NNE Plei Mrong. Nov67. Kontum Pr, II Corps.

Galveston, USS (n/a)
CLG 3. In Aug 65, guided missile cruiser *Galveston* (CLG 3) and destroyers *Prichett* (DD 561) and *Orleck* (DD 886) joined Op Starlight. On one fire mission, they were credited with over 100 VC KIA caught in open on beach.

Game Warden, Operation (n/a)
See Glossary.

Game Warden Supt Facility (XS 9-8?)
Apx 16 km SE Saigon and along bank of Song Nha Be River. Op Game Warden Supt Facility at Nha Be, home of Game Warden Ops, NSA Det. "Game Warden" was code name given allied river patrol Ops of Mekong Delta waterways, a combined USN/Army 9th Inf Div op primarily in IV Corps. Petroleum refinery here was partially destroyed by VC sabotage. Gia Dinh Pr, III Corps.

Gang Sa Ni Airfield (VF 19-89)
L-45. CIA/SF, per *Air Facilities Data-Laos.*

Ganh Daee Point (US 7-4)
See Point Ganh Daee. Kien Giang Pr, IV Corps.

Ganh Daee, Pointe (US 7-4)
See Pointe Ganh Daee. Kien Giang Pr, IV Corps.

Ganh Dau, Mui (US 7-4)
A.k.a. Mui Ganh Dau. Coastal point at 10°22'N-103°50'E. On NC48-05 JOG. Kien Giang Pr, IV Corps.
Ganh Dau, Mui (US 9-3)
Mui Ganh Giao. Coastal point at 10°15'N-104°05'E. On NC48-05 JOG. Kien Giang Pr, IV Corps.
Ganh Den, Mui (CQ 1-7)
Coastal point at 13°22'N-109°18'E. On ND49-09 JOG. Phu Yen Pr, II Corps.
Ganh Giao, Mui (US 9-3)
Coastal point at 10°15'N-104°05'E. On NC48-05 JOG. Kien Giang Pr, IV Corps.
Ganh Lon, Mui (US 8-3)
Coastal point at 10°16'N-103°56'E. On NC48-05 JOG. Kien Giang Pr, IV Corps.
Ganh Rai, Baie de (YS 20-54)
A.k.a. Vung Ganh Rai and Vinh Ganh Rai. Bay, immed NW the Vung Tau Peninsula, at 10°25'N-107°01'E. On NC48-07 JOG. Phuoc Tuy Pr, III Corps.
Ganh Rai, Mui (YS 1-5)
Cape at 10°24'N-106°58'E. On NC48-07 JOG. Gia Dinh Pr, III Corps.
Ganh Rai, Pointe (YS 2-4)
See Pointe Ganh Rai. Phuoc Tuy Pr, III Corps.
Ganh Rai, Vinh (YS 2-5)
See Ganh Rai, Baie de. Phuoc Tuy Pr, III Corps.
Ganh Tuong, Mui (CQ 1-8)
Coastal point at 13°24'30"N-109°16'30"E. On ND49-09 JOG. Phu Yen Pr, II Corps.
Ganh, Mui (CP 2-8)
Coastal point at 12°34'N-109°26'E. On ND49-13 JOG. Khanh Hoa Pr, II Corps.
Ganhrai Bay (YS 2-5)
A.k.a. Vung Ganh Rai. Bay at 10°25'N-107°01'E. On NC48-07 JOG. Phuoc Tuy Pr, III Corps.
Gannet, USS (n/a)
MSC-290. Minesweeper, Coastal, per Ralph Fries.
Gap-2 (n/a)
See Glossary.
Garden of Eden, The (YC 818-845)
Valley apx 4 km W Elephant Valley, E Ruong Ruong and 3 km NW Dong Den. Grid per George Neville, 3d Recon Bn/3d Mar Div. Also listed at "AT" 818-845, but YC zone thought to be correct. Quang Nam Pr, I Corps.
Garnet, FSB (BS 595-165)
Apx 30 km W Gia An, 18 km SSE Ba To New AF and 33 km WNW LZ English. Was also roughly within 5 km of FSBs Iron, Steel and Powder. Binh Dinh Pr, II Corps.
Garnet, LZ (BR 964-648)
Apx 7 km ESE Phu My (QL-1), 7 km WSW LZ Crystal and 33 km SSE Bong Son. 2d/17th Arty here supt 1st Cav. Data per Jack Picciolo. Oct66. Binh Dinh Pr, II Corps.
Garrett County, USS (n/a)
LST-786. USN Landing Ship, Tank. In '71, reconfigured as Small Craft Tender and returned to VN 24Apr71. Suptd 9th Inf Div/MRF in '67-68, per MRF Assn website at www.mrfa.org. III/IV Corps?
Garry Owen, FSB (XT 201-548?)
If grid correct, was just SE Ap Long My, apx 3 km S Tay Ninh, 8 km SSE Tay Ninh West AF and 76 km NW Tan Son Nhut AB. Also listed at "YT" 205-546, but unknown which grid zone is correct. Tay Ninh Pr?, III Corps.
Garry Owen, FSB (YT 205-546?)
A.k.a. FSB Dotty or Dottie (YT 209-541)? Apx 3 km SW Rang Rang, 27 km SE Dong Xoai and 45 km NNE Bien Hoa AB. Also listed at "XT" 201-548, but unknown which grid zone is correct. Phuoc Long Pr?, III Corps.
Garth, FSB (YS 455-905)
Along W side of LTL-2 apx 23 km N Nui Dat, 500 meters S FSB Cherie, 4 km NE FSB Kate and 7 km WNW FSB Flinders. On 1ATF NCO trng map per John Hollett. Long Khanh Pr, III Corps.
Gary Owen, FSB (XT or YT)
See Garry Owen. III Corps.
GATAC Central (n/a)
See GATAC in Glossary.
GATAC Laos (n/a)
See GATAC in Glossary.
GATAC North (n/a)
See GATAC in Glossary.
GATAC South (n/a)
See GATAC in Glossary.
Gator, LZ (BR 435-312)
Apx 15 km SSW An Khe. Dec65. Binh Dinh Pr, II Corps.
Gator, LZ/FSB (BS 578-961)
Near QL-1, apx 13 km SSE Chu Lai, 23 km NNW Quang Ngai, 12 km NNE LZ Dottie, 13 km SE LZ Fat City and 18 km due N FSB Stinson. Also listed at BS 571-963 and 572-965. HQ for 5/46th Inf, 198th LIB at one time. Americal list. Quang Ngai Pr, I Corps.
Gauge, LZ (XD 996-403)
Along QL-9, apx 6 km ESE Khe Sanh CB, 6 km ENE Khe Sanh and 13 km SW Ca Lu. Apr70 XXIV Corps grid per Don Armstrong. Quang Tri Pr, I Corps.
Gauloise Troupe (n/a)
See Glossary.
Gauvin Airfield (XS 040-331)
See Vinh Long AF. Vinh Long Pr, IV Corps.
Gauvin-Upton Airfield (XS 040-331)
See Vinh Long Army AF. Vinh Long Pr, IV Corps.
Gavin, LZ (BR 814-636)
Apx 38 km NW An Khe, 8 km NW Van Tien and 6 km SSE Hoi San. Oct66. Binh Dinh Pr, II Corps.
Gay Giep Mountain (BR 920-880)
See Cay Giep and Dam Tra O. Binh Dinh Pr, II Corps.
Gaylor, Camp (XS 82-97)
Tan Son Nhut AB, Saigon. Named to honor SSgt Gerald H. Gaylor, USA, Ops Sgt of 593d Signal Co, 69th Sig Bn, KIA 22Jan66, by terrorist bomb. 1st member of 69th Sig Bn to be killed by hostile action. Formerly the 39th Bn Cmpd prior to 39th Sig Bn's move to Vung Tau. Data per *Vietnam Military Lore, 1959-1973*. Gia Dinh Pr, III Corps.
Gaza Coastal Strip (BS 80-49)
About 2 km W the ocean, 7 km SE Mo Duc AF/Quang Hien and 11 km N Duc Pho. Americal list. Unknown if "strip" means terrain feature or airfield. Also listed at BT 240-450? Quang Ngai Pr, I Corps.
Gaza Strip (BT 240-450)
Nature of site unknown, but likely a terrain feature of sand dunes along coast apx 16 km SSE Hoi An, 24 km NNW

Tam Ky and 10 km due E LZ Baldy. Jan70. Also listed at BS 80-49? Quang Tin Pr, I Corps.

Gazelle, LZ (XD 872-536)
Apx 4 km ESE peak Dong Voi Mep (Hill 1739), 12 km NNE Khe Sanh and 15 km WSW Cam Lo. Apr70 XXIV Corps grid per Don Armstrong. Quang Tri Pr, I Corps.

Ge La, FSB (XT 604-422?)
See FSB Gela. Binh Duong Pr?, III Corps.

Geiger, FSB (XD 745-442)
Apparently a.k.a. LZ Unicorn (XD 745-439). Apx 7 km E Laotian border, 12 km WNW Khe Sanh CB, 7 km WSW Ap La Vien and 36 km WSW Mai Loc AF. 2/12th Arty here, and on FSB Smith, fired supt for 3d Recon Bn, and 2d and 3d Bns, 9th Marines during Op Dawson River West, USMC, Jan69. 101st Abn inactive FSB grid per Don Armstrong. Quang Tri Pr, I Corps.

Geiger, USNS (n/a)
TAP-197. MSTS Transport, per Ralph Fries.

Geisha, LZ (YT 063-754)
A.k.a. FSB Gunner II and also spelled Giessa? Just S Dong Xoai AF and 3 km WSW Dong Xoai. Jan69. Phuoc Long Pr, III Corps.

Gela, FSB (XT 604-422)
A.k.a. Patrol Base Gela and FSB Ge La. E of "The Onion," apx 13 km ESE Dau Tieng, 48 km NNW Tan Son Nhut AB/Saigon and 17 km WNW Lai Khe. 1st/28th Inf, 1st Inf Div, heavily attacked here by 165th Inf, 7th NVA Div with mortars, rockets and sappers at 0143 hrs, 13May69. 3 US KIA, 20 WIA and 39 NVA KIA. Described in *Low Level Hell* at pp 110-112, as looking "like a deputy's five-pointed star lying on ground with a wreath of 3 strands of concertina wire around it." 1st Inf Div, 8th/6th Arty here '69, and cited as Ge La in *Vietnam: Reflexes and Reflections*, p 126. Binh Duong Pr, III Corps.

Gela, FSB (XT 652-202?)
If grid correct, was apx 5 km NNE Cu Chi CB and 21 km SW Lai Khe. Grid per Dan Gillotti, 15th Arty Assn. Hau Nghia Pr, III Corps.

Gem, FSB (XT 528-545)
Apx 9 km NE Dau Tieng and 16 km SW Minh Thanh AF. Mar-Apr67. Binh Duong Pr, III Corps.

Gem, FSB (XT?)
Possibly same at Gem at XT 528-545? Said to have been HQ of 1st Cav per www2.okstate.edu/wcross/memoirs.html. III Corps.

Gen. Maurice Rose, USS (n/a)
See *Maurice Rose, Gen., USNS.*

Gen. Patch, USNS (n/a)
MSTS Transport, per Ralph Fries.

Gen. William Weigel, USNS (n/a)
Carried 3/506th Inf, 101st Abn to VN, Oct67, arriving at Cam Ranh Bay, 26Oct67. USO "Donut Dollies" were on hand to give the arriving Currahees refreshments. Bn then moved by truck to Phan Rang basecamp, a.k.a. "Eagle's Roost" per www.currahee.org/pageb1.html.

General Mobilization Act (n/a)
See Glossary.

Genesee, USS (n/a)
AOG-8. SVN.

Genevieve de Galard-Jerraube (n/a)
See Angel of DBP in Glossary.

George, LZ (BR 9-8)
Just E QL-1, apx 10 km SSE Bong Son, 7 km W the ocean and 18 km ENE LZ Bird. Used during Op Masher/White Wing, 28Jan-6Mar66. Detailed discussion of Ops Masher/White Wing and this LZ in *A Contagion of War* vol, *Vietnam Experience* series, pp 32-48, with map at p 38. 1st Cav LZ. Binh Dinh Pr, II Corps.

George, LZ (BS 478-859)
Apx 15 km ESE Tra Bong AF, 7 km N Ba Gi AF, 5 km SW Ngoc Tri and 21 km NW Quang Ngai. Also listed by arty ORLL at BS 470-867. Per Les Hines, on map TL-7014-6740-3 (Son Ha). Americal list. Quang Ngai Pr, I Corps.

George, LZ (XT 428-847)
Apx 5 km ESE Bo Tuc, just N Rte 246, 2 km W Ap Gu and 10 km SE Katum. Terrain consisted of open fields covered with tall, meadow grass, surrounded by medium to heavy jungle. Site of Battle of Ap Gu, 31Mar-1Apr67, involving 1st/26th Inf (the *Blue Spaders*) att 2d Bde/1st Div, later reinforced by 1st/16th Inf, 1st Div, being attacked by 1st, 2d and 3d Bns, 271st Rgt, 9th VC Div. FSB Thrust and FSB C fired in supt. Resulted in 17 US KIA and 102 WIA. The 3 Bns of 271st Rgt, 9th VC Div (and elements of 70th Guard Rgt) lost 609 KIA, 5 POW. Event is also notable in that CO of 1st/26th Inf was LTC Alexander Haig. Haig promoted to Col and given Cmd of 2de Bde/1st Inf Div, when Bde CO was WIA at nearby FSB C on last day of battle, 1Apr67. In late '68, Haig became Henry Kissinger's White House military advisor and by '70, was confidant to President Nixon. On 7Sep72, Nixon gave him rank of 4-Star Gen and made him Army's Vice Chief of Staff. Some data per *Cedar Falls-Junction City*. Also listed at XT 430-840. Tay Ninh Pr, III Corps.

George, LZ (XU 773-139)
Apx 6 km SE Loc Ninh AF, 15 km N An Loc and 8 km WSW Srok Proai. Binh Long Pr, III Corps.

George, LZ (YV 835-949)
Apx 3 km due W Hill 534, 700 meters E Cambodia, and apx 66 km SW Pleiku. Opened 12Aug66 by elements of 5th Cav, 1st Cav Div, during Op Paul Revere II. Arty here fired supt for Battle for Hill 534, 14-15Aug66. May have only existed for about 1 week. Grid taken from map in article entitled *Paul Revere II*, 1st Cav '66 *Yearbook* courtesy Mr. Shutt. Pleiku Pr, II Corps.

George, OP (n/a)
See OP George. Quang Tin or Quang Ngai Pr, I Corps.

George II, LZ (BS?)
Exact location unknown, however site is said to be on mapsheet L-7014-6739-3. Quang Ngai Pr?, I Corps.

George K. Mackenzle, USS (n/a)
DD 836. Destroyers *Rupertus* (DD 851), *Samuel N. Moore* (DD 747) and *Mackenzie* fought catastrophic Jul67 fire aboard carrier *Forrestal* at Yankee Station, in which 15 were killed and 63 injured.

Georgia BOQ (XS 8-9)
At 335 Cong Ly St., Saigon. Data per *Vietnam Military Lore, 1959-1973*. Gia Dinh Pr, III Corps.

Georgia, FSB (XS 065-616)
A.k.a. LZ Mace. Apx 22 km WNW Cai Lay, 28 km due N Vinh Long and 76 km WSW Saigon. Jan68. Dinh Tuong Pr, IV Corps.

Georgia, FSB (YD 420-033)
A.k.a. Hill 1242 (4,074'). Apx 36 km WSW Hue, 1 km N FSB Berchtesgarden and 1.5 km SE FSB Eagle's Nest, along NE edge of A Shau Valley. Built by elements of 1st Bde/101st Abn in Aug68 (D/1st 502d Inf assisting while opcon to 1st Bde), 11-21Aug68. Greg Mills, CO, D/1st/502 at time, adds this recollection: "We began building FSB Eagle's Nest one day, but the very next, someone didn't like the location, so we moved down the ridge apx two clicks and built FSB Georgia. There were NVA vehicle convoys in valley below running at night with lights on. We were out of arty range except for 175mm at FSB Bastogne for first 2 days, so we hid until the site was finalized and construction began." Also listed at YD 418-032 and YD 419-029. Thua Thien Pr, I Corps. [245]
Gerald B Rose, Camp (ZV 052-265?)
See Rose, Camp. Darlac Pr, II Corps?
Gerberas Airfield (YC 38-97)
Apparently FSB and AF here. In A Shau Valley roughly halfway between A Loui and Ta Bat AFs, apx 4.5 km NE A Loui and 8 km NNW Ta Bat. Origin of name unknown (no casualties of this name in CACF). On map at www.americal.org/ 174/ashau.htm. Listed as DMA AF VA-1, #66, alt 1,900'. Thua Thien Pr, I Corps.
Gerberas, FSB? (YC 38-97)
See Gerberas AF. Thua Thien Pr, I Corps.
German Red Cross Hospital Ship (n/a)
See *Helgoland*. SVN.
Geronimo, FSB (YD 691-201)
About 3 km W Hue, 2 km N the Perfume River and 10 km NNW Pohl (Nam Hoa) Bridge. 2d/501st/101st Abn, Spring '68, also 1st Cav. Also listed at YD 690-204 per 101st Abn rpt courtesy Don Armstrong. 15th Arty Assn lists at YD 652-202, which is grid for FSB T-Bone, and thought to be in error here. Thua Thien Pr, I Corps.
Geronimo, LZ (BS 878-170)
About 5 km NW Gia An, 3 km E QL-1, 1 km NE LZ Fox, 16 km due N LZ English, 5 km N Mahoney AF, and 23 km SSE Duc Pho. Photos/maps of base at http://1-14th.com/maps.html. Also listed at BS 880-174, Apr68. Binh Dinh Pr, II Corps.
Gerry, Camp (YT 04-07)
At Long Binh CB. Named to honor PFC Ronald L. Gerry, USA, 69th Signal Bn, accidentally killed 5Jan66 by an instructor's stray round, fist member of 69th Sig Bn to die in VN. Data per Ray Bows. Bien Hoa Pr, III Corps.
Gerry?, LZ (n/a)
Likely sp variant of FSB Jerry or Jerri? Frenchy Torres, tells us he thinks it was built near a red ball (main hwy) and possibly opened in '69. FSBs/LZs Jerri and Jerry are listed at both XU/YU 965-225, and also at BN 782-612. See also Jerri. III Corps.
Gettysburg, FSB (XS 358-876)
Along Kinh Gay Canal, apx 7 km SE tip of Parrot's Beak, 1 km SW Long Thanh Tay, 45 km due W Saigon, and 13 km NE Thuy Dong AF. Per Lee Pittman, 6th/31st Inf, was a dry-season only base of 3d Bde/9th Inf Div and, "was at end of a canal on its S side. The Bn CO slept in tent alongside the canal, with a foxhole next to it. During monsoon season, it was submerged and unusable." Per Dempsey B., "Before our STAB boats arrived in-country, my buddy and I were loaned to "Dufflebag Team" at Tuyen Nhon. Went out on an Army PACV to plant some sensors right across border on Parrot's Beak [near Gettysburg]. Army had a couple of 105s and some recon troops to supt UDT team there. The UDT team was making a canal using Det-Cord that would join the Vam Co Tay and Vam Co Dong Rivers." Elements of 2d/60th(?) here beginning Dec69, per David Argabright. Just inside Hau Nghia Pr at meeting point of Long An, Kien Tuong and Hau Nghia Pr borders, III Corps.
Gherardini, Camp (CR 06-21?)
Along QL-1 in Pioneer Valley, at Phu Tai. Possibly apx 8 km SW Qui Nhon? Cmpd of 66th MP Co until '70. Named to honor a Sp4 Sergio J. Gherardino, KIA 31Jan68. Data per Ray Bows. Binh Dinh Pr, II Corps.
Ghost Mountain (n/a)
Apparently USMC or SOG radio relay site somewhere in I Corps or Laos. May actually reference Tiger Tooth Mtn, or Hickory Hill, or Leghorn, or Sledge Hammer, or possibly Dong Den, all of which were OPs/radio relay sites. Per Robert LeFreniere, "Hill 1701 [a.k.a. Hill 1739], Dong Voi Mep, or Tiger or Tiger Tooth Mtn could well be it...that peak and 3 others (Dong Pa Thien, Dong Ta Bang and Dong Sa Mui) formed a rough horseshoe [that were the N and E] borders of Bru tribal land. I think they considered them 'ghostly' in sense of home to benevolent creation spirits rather than in more threatening sense of word. 'Ghost' or 'Haunted' Mtn could refer to a lot of places. The Bru thought 'wandering souls' inhabited about half the peaks in AO." No other data available. I Corps?
Ghost Mountain (n/a)
2nd highest peak in Cardamom mtn range of Cambodia, deep in SW Cambodia. Range was a refuge for Khmer Rouge from '75-79. Mentioned at www.phnompenhdaily.com/21-04-00.htm. Cambodia.
Ghost Mountain (YS 269 465 or 279-427?)
Apparently on Vung Tau Peninsula and one of the 4 peaks of either Nui Lon or Nui Nho (Hills236 and 245 on Lon, or Hills 136 and Hill(?) on Nho). Its Viet name is said to have translated as "Smaller Mountain." During French rule, fort ruins on mtn were known as the Deuxime Bureau (2d Office) of French Secret Police. Many Vietminh and sympathizers were tortured and killed here, and their ghosts are said to still haunt the ruins, along with ghosts from earlier centuries. Per www. hawaiian.net/~dsparks/vnch9-12.html. Phuoc Tuy Pr, III Corps.
Ghost Ship, The (n/a)
See Glossary.
Ghost Town Trail (XT)
Legendary enemy infiltration route from Cambodia, part of which was apx 5 km W and NW Dau Tieng. Apparently intersected QL-1 at some point. Battle of Ghost Town Trail was fought along trail, 3Nov66. C/1st/27th Inf, 25th Inf Div ambushed after lndg at LZ in mouth of a horseshoe-shaped clearing and badly mauled by well-entrenched unit. B & C/2d/1st, C/2d/27th, A/1/27th and C/3d/21st Inf all brought in to reinforce/rescue C/1st/27th here, during Op Attleboro. See *Ambush*, pp 10-32. Tay Ninh Pr, III Corps.
Gi Lang (n/a)
Mapsheet name of L-7014-6639-2. SVN.

Gi Ti Tree Plantation (AQ 855-035)
Extending between 5 and 10 km E of Ban Me Thuot and generally S and E the intersection where QL-21 splits into its E and S branches. Darlac Pr, II Corps.
Gia, Cua (CQ 0-0)
Channel near 12°40'N-109°13'E. On ND49-13 JOG. Khanh Hoa Pr, II Corps.
Gia, Pointe de (CR 1-2)
See Pointe Gia. Binh Dinh Pr, II Corps.
Gia Bac, Ap (n/a)
Mapsheet L-7014-6631-4. Sheet: Ap Gia-Bac. SVN.
Gia Binh (YD 1-7)
Roughly 15 km NW Con Thien. 90th NVA Rgt attacked by 2d/4th Marines nearby on 8Sep66. NVA had posted a sign in English at entrance to ville that read, "*We Will Fight To The Last Man*." It took a full week of fighting to evict them. At 16°56'00"N-107°01'00"E. Quang Tri Pr, I Corps.
Gia Dinh (XS 8-9)
Near or in Saigon (XS 87-95?). Original home of *Groupement Mobile 100*. Activated there 14Nov-29Nov53, before heading N along QL-14 and QL-19, through a string of ambushes and its ultimate destruction at Mang Yang Pass, 24Jun54. Gia Dinh Pr, III Corps.
Gia Dinh City (XS 87-95)
Apparent suburb of Saigon. Was along W edge of that city. Capitol, Gia Dinh Pr, III Corps.
Gia Dinh CORDS Rooftop Helipad (XS 859-945)
In Saigon, apx 5 km due E Tan Son Nhut AB and 2.5 km W the Saigon River. Heliport #756, alt 95'. "Roof Top Pad marked with yellow 'H.' Trees W and NE. Pad time 1 minute. Arty Adv-Saigon 239.0 234.9 40.6." At 10°48'N 106°42'E, per Feb73 TAD. Gia Dinh Pr, III Corps.
Gia Dinh Province (XS/XT/YS)
One of 11 south-central provs forming III Corps (III CTZ).
Gia Hoi (VK 37-03)
Apx 20 km NW Nghia Lo, 160 km NW Hanoi and 12 km SE Tu Le. French garrison here '52. See Tu Le. NVN.
Gia Kiem, Xa (n/a)
Mapsheet L-7014-6431-3. Sheet: Xa Gia Kiem. SVN.
Gia Lai Province (YA/ZA/AR)
In what later became known as II Corps. Appears to have been roughly the same size as, and absorbed into, Pleiku Pr. Thought to have ceased existence shortly before or during early US presence in SVN? II Corps.
Gia Lam (Hanoi) Airfield (WJ 92-26)
One of 2 major AFs near Hanoi, the other being Bac Mai. On N side of Red River (Song Hong), 5 km NE Hanoi and 8 km NE Bac Mai AF, per ONC-J-11. El. 25'. NVN.
Gia Le (YD 829-151)
Ville apx 7 km due W Phu Bai AP and 2 km SE Camp Eagle. Apr70 XXIV Corps grid per Don Armstrong. Thau Thien Pr, I Corps.
Gia Le, Camp (YD 514-318?)
If grid correct, was apx 3 km due W Camp Evans and 25 km NW Hue. Author suspects grid is a transcription or transposition error. 11Nov69. Thua Thien Pr, I Corps.
Gia Le, Camp (YD 830-150?)
A.k.a. Camp Wilkinson? Apx 7 km due W Phu Bai AF, 2 km SE Camp Eagle and 2.5 km SW QL-1. Navy Seabee camp, Mar68, when 3d Bde 82d Abn arrived to provide security for area S of Hue. Some 82d elements here during const of Camp Rodriguez, a few km to W. Discussed in *All The Way, 3d Brigade, 82d Airborne in Vietnam, 1968*, p 6, courtesy Butch Sincock. Possible alternate grids: YD 823-152, 829-149 and 836-153. Thua Thien Pr, I Corps.
Gia Le, FSB (YD 829-151)
A.k.a. Camp Wilkinson? Apx 7 km due W Phu Bai AF and 2 km SE Camp Eagle. Listed at above grid 30Apr70, and at YD 836-152, 31Jan69. Thua Thien Pr, I Corps.
Gia Le Combat Base (YD 823-162)
A.k.a. Camp Wilkinson and FSB Gia Le? Apx 12 km SE Hue Citadel AF, 7 km due W Phu Bai AF, 1 km SE Camp Eagle and 2.5 km SW QL-1. Apr68. Also listed at YD 829-149, Feb68, and YD 830-150, Nov69, and 833-152, Aug69. Thua Thien Pr, I Corps.
Gia Le CAP (YD 821-183)
Along QL-1 apx 7 km WNW Phu Bai Airport. Hotel 1, 3rd CAG and Alpha 6 and 9, 3rd CAG. Thua Thien Pr, I Corps. Hotel 3 was at Gia Le, along QL-1 and roughly midway between Hue and Phu Bai.
Gia Le Seabee Base Camp (YD 830-144)
A.k.a. Camp Wilkinson. Apx 5 km due W Phu Bai AF, 2 km SE Camp Eagle, 3 km NW Hill 80 and 9 km SE Hue. See Camp Wilkinson. Thua Thien Pr, I Corps.
Gia Long, FSB? (n/a)
No data. Cited in 1st Cav Op Rpt, Feb70/Apr70, p 15, per Peter Cole, and during that period, Cav was in NW III Corps. NPIA lists villes with this name at CP 033-533, and WR 809-265? III Corps?
Gia Nghia (YU 94-26)
Capitol, Quang Duc Pr, II Corps.
Gia Nghia(?) SF Camp (YU 9745-2909)
Along QL-14, apx 5 km E Gia Nghia AF, 58 km ENE Duc Phong AF/SF Camp and 2 km W Buon Konho. Possibly a.k.a. either Buon Konho or Gia Nghia SF Camp? Listed as Song Be SF Camp, but that may be error. If grid were XU, would be at Bu Dop AF. Phuoc Long Pr, III Corps.
Gia Nghia (Nghia Duc) (n/a)
Mapsheet name of L-7014-6532-4. SVN.
Gia Nghia Airfield (YU 925-289)
Apx 47 km due S Duc Lap AF, 32 km SE Bu Prang AF, 45 km SW Buon Tsuke AF and 80 km SW Ban Me Thuot, per TPC K-10A. El. 2,136', 2,100' laterite rwy. 12°00'35"N-107°41'17"E. Quang Duc Pr, II Corps.
Gia Rai (n/a)
Mapsheet name of L-7014-6027-2. SVN.
Gia Rai (WR 51-22)
Along QL-4 on Cau Mau Peninsula, apx 27 km ENE Quan Long. Bac Lieu Pr, IV Corps.
Gia Rav (YT 63-13)
See Gia Ray. Long Khanh Pr, III Corps.
Gia Ray Airfield (YT 638-136)
Along NE base of Nui Chua Chan Mtn, apx 18 km ENE Xuan Loc. Per ONC K-10. El. 492', 1,500' laterite-earth-clay rwy. Spelled Gia Rav on some maps. At 10°58'10"N-107°24'50"E. Long Khanh Pr, III Corps.
Gia Ray Heliport (YT 636-126)
At western base of Nui Chua Chan Mtn, apx 17 km WNW Xuan Loc and 3 km N QL-1. Heliport #566, alt 466'. 'Mace Tower' 43.0," per Feb73 TAD. Long Khanh Pr, III Corps.

Gia Ray Rock Quarry (YT 630-100)
Apx 1 km S Gia Ray, 25 km road distance NE Blackhorse Basecamp, 7 km NE Suoi Cat and 1 km N QL-1. 94th Engr Det worked this quarry in 67-68. Also listed at YT 620-110, Apr68, 630-090, May67 and 630-120, Dec66. On rpts from Dec66-Oct69. Long Khanh Pr, III Corps.
Gia Ria Heliport (WR 513-213)
On QL-4, apx 34 km ENE Quan Long AF and 30 km WSW Bac Lieu. "Heliport #567, alt 7', sod. Houses N and E. At 09°14'40"N-105°28'00"E," per Feb73 TAD. Bac Lieu Pr, IV Corps.
Gia Tinh Hoa Nhan CAP (n/a)
See CAP 2-3-9. 2d CAG, Quang Nam Pr, I Corps.
Gia Vuc (n/a)
Mapsheet name of L-7014-6738-3. SVN.
Gia Vuc Airfield (BS 375-270)
Apx 18 km WSW Ba To New AF, 56 km NW LZ English and 32 km ENE Plateau Gi AF. El. 443', 3,200' sod rwy. Also listed at BS 377-270. At 14°42'17"N-108°33'45"E. Map is L-7014-6738-3. Quang Ngai Pr, I Corps.
Gia Vuc SF Camp (BS 372-275)
Apx 18 km WSW Ba To New AF, 56 km NW LZ English and 32 km ENE Plateau Gi AF. 5th SF Grp, Det. A-112, Dec64, Det A-103, Oct65 (also listed Feb62-Feb69), SF Det 10, became ARVN SF, Feb69. Also listed at BS 379 270, 376-271 and by Arty ORLL at 377-265. Americal list, Map is L-7014-6738-3. Quang Ngai Pr, I Corps.
Gia Vuc SF Camp (BS 3775-2710)
Apx 18 km WSW Ba To New AF, 56 km NW LZ English and 32 km ENE Plateau Gi AF. 5th SF Grp, Det. A-112, Dec64, Det A-103, Oct65 (dates also listed as Feb62-Feb69, SF Det 10, turned over to ARVN SF, Feb69. Grid per *SF Order of Battle*. Transferred to VNSF, 70th Border Rangers. Map is L-7014-6738-3. Quang Ngai Pr, I Corps.
Gia Vuc, LZ (BS 372-270)
Apx 18 km WSW Ba To New AF, 56 km NW LZ English and 32 km ENE Plateau Gi AF. XXIV Corps grid per Don Armstrong. Quang Ngai Pr, I Corps.
Giai Manh, Mui (CP 1-2)
Mui Giai Nanh. Coastal point at 11°58'N-109°17'E. On NC49-01 JOG. Khanh Hoa Pr, II Corps.
Giai Nanh, Mui (CP 1-2)
Coastal point at 11°58'N-109°17'E. On NC49-01 JOG. Khanh Hoa Pr, II Corps.
Gian Thanh, Camp (VS 564-639)
See FOB Vinh Gia. Chau Doc Pr, IV Corps.
Giang Mung Pho (n/a)
Mapsheet name of L-7014-5453-1. NVN/China.
Giang River (YD 48-42)
A.k.a. My Chanh River. Map is L-7014-6442-2, per Ken Burrington. Thua Thien Pr, I Corps.
Giang Tay Airfield (BN 124-379)
Along QL-1, apx 2 km W Ap Luong Tay, 16 km WSW Song Mao AF/Hai Ninh. "Abnd, AF # VA2-233," in Aug69 TAD per Frank Penk, Jr. Not in Feb73 TAD. Binh Thuan Pr, II Corps.
Giang Thanh SF Camp (VS 564-639)
A.k.a. FOB Vinh Gia. At Cambodian border, apx 20 km NE Ha Tien and 29 km WNW Vinh Gia Heliport. 5th SF. Info/grid per *SF Order of Battle.* Chau Doc Pr, IV Corps.
Giang Thanh (VS 5-6)
Ville roughly 20 km NE Ha Tien and adj to Cambodian border. Kien Giang Pr, IV Corps.
Giant Slingshot, Operation (n/a)
See Douche Boats and Squeeze-Bore .50 Cal in Glossary.
Giant, LZ (XD 876-258)
In Vietnam Salient, apx 6 km SW Lang Klung, 16 km SSE Khe Sanh CB and 52 km SW Quang Tri. Apr70 XXIV Corps grid per Don Armstrong. Quang Tri Pr, I Corps.
Giao Duc (WS 97-40)
A.k.a. Ap An Tri, and site of FSB Danger (a.k.a. FSB Dickey). Apx 42 km due W Dong Tam and 14 km ENE Sa Dec, at 10°19'00"N-105°54'00"E. On map NC48-07. Dinh Tuong Pr, IV Corps.
Giao Duc Heliport (WS 978-403)
A.k.a. An Tri Heliport. Apx 42 km due W Dong Tam and 14 km ENE Sa Dec. "Heliport #568, alt 7', sod. Antenna on E side," per Feb73 TAD. Dinh Tuong Pr, IV Corps.
Giao Tri 3, Patrol Base (AT 888-703)
Apx 9 km SW Da Nang AB and 2 km E Hoi Vuc. USMC, Aug65. Quang Nam Pr, I Corps.
Gibraltar (YB 604-355)
See Leghorn MSS. Laos.
Gibraltar, FSB (YT 253-279)
Just S Song Dong Nai River, apx 30 km NE Bien Hoa AB and 16 km due W Xa Binh Hoa. Bien Hoa Pr, III Corps.
Giessa, LZ (YT 063-754)
See Geisha. Phuoc Long Pr, III Corps.
Gigi, LZ (BR 970-719)
On small mtn mass, apx 27 km SSE Bong Son, 7 km NE Phu My, 25 km NNE Phu Cat AF and 6 km W QL-1. Oct66. Binh Dinh Pr, II Corps.
Gll Ang (BS 0-9?)
Ville. If sp correct, is very atypical name for Vietnamese place (possible variant of Gi Lang?). On L-7014-6639-4. Quang Tin Pr, I Corps.
Gila, LZ (YD 346-696)
Near Cua Viet River and in close proximity to Cua Viet Naval Base, apx 16 km due N Quang Tri. Apr70 XXIV Corps grid per Don Armstrong. Quang Tri Pr, I Corps.
Gilaer, LZ (YD 333-314)
Apx 10 km SSE Dong Ong Do (Hill 275), 18 km WSW Ba Long AF and 11 km due S of Quang Tri. Apr70 XXIV Corps grid per Don Armstrong. Thua Thien Pr, I Corps.
Gimlet, FSB (YS 346-712)
10 km WNW Nui Dat, 500 meters NNE FSB Nola, 12.5 km SE FSB Le Loi and 2 km W FSB Catherine. On 1ATF NCO trng map per John Hollett. Phuoc Tuy Pr, III Corps.
Gimlet, LZ (AT 858-230)
In the Song Chang Valley apx 7 km SW Hiep Duc, 34 km W Tam Ky and 18 km NW Tien Phuoc AF. Also listed at AT 855-232, per XXIV Corps facility index. Map is L-7014-6640-3. Americal list. Quang Tin Pr, I Corps.
Ginger (n/a)
Apr70, XXIV Corps proposed 101st Abn FSB name.
Ginger, LZ (BR 542-578)
Apx 8 km WNW Vinh Thanh, 6 km WSW Vinh Thanh AF and 15 km NNE An Khe. Dec65. Binh Dinh Pr, II Corps.
Ginny (n/a)
6Apr70, XXIV Corps proposed Americal FSB name.

Gio Linh (YD 22-72)
Along QL-1, apx 22 km NNW Quang Tri, 6 km SSE Ben Hai River/NVN border, immed S the S edge of DMZ and 12 km NNW Dong Ha. Ville and USMC/5th Mech combat base location. Quang Tri Pr, I Corps.
Gio Linh, FSB (YD 218-732)
A.k.a. FSB A-2, Alpha 2, Camp Hill, The Alamo and possibly LZ Cheyenne. On E Side QL-1 apx 13 km N Dong Ha, 23 km NNW Quang Tri, 6 km SSE Ben Hai River/NVN border, immed S the S edge of DMZ and 3 km SE FSB A-2. *1968 Yearbook* of *Encyclopedia Britannica* has photo of sign here which reads, "*Camp Hill, Gio Linh, The Alamo of Vietnam*." Named to honor PFC Lamont D. Hill, USMC, 3d Plt/I/3d/4th Marines, 3d Mar Div, KIA 6Mar67 near Tan Lich, Quang Tri Pr, while providing M-60 covering fire though mortally wounded. 1st/12th Mar Arty here '67; four-175mm (US Army, attached), six-105mms (12th Marine Arty?) and secured by 3d Mar Div elements. Gio Linh ville was adj base and source of its common name. In '67, Marines built huge underground FDC bunker here and roof consisted multiple layers of massive 12" square timbers themselves covered with 8' of dirt and 10 layers of sandbags. Mongrel mascot named "Hardcore," became bases' early warning system because it could hear incoming long before humans, and whenever it would tuck-tail and run for cover, US troops ran for cover as well. [246] Also listed at YD 213-732. Map is L-7014-6442-4, per Ken Burrington. Quang Tri Pr, I Corps.
Gio Linh Airfield (YD 209-740)
Along QL-1, apx 24 km NNW Quang Tri. "Abnd, AF # VA1-67," in Aug69 TAD per Frank Penk, Jr. Not in Feb73 TAD. I Corps.
Gio Linh CAP (n/a)
4th CAG, Quang Tri Pr, I Corps.
Gio Linh Outpost (YD 214-710)
Apx 1 km S Gio Linh and 11 km NNW Dong Ha. Also at YD 220-740. USMC, May66. Quang Tri Pr, I Corps.
Gio Linh SF Camp (YD 209-740)
5th SF Grp "proposed" Camp/FOB site along QL-1, apx 24 km NNW Quang Tri. Info/grid per *SF Order of Battle. Const w*as proposed but apparently canceled by III MAF? Location would have been W QL-1 and slightly NW Gio Linh, apx 25 km NNW Quang Tri. Quang Tri Pr, I Corps.
Gio Mon Airstrip (YD 220-750)
E QL-1 near Gia Mon, apx 14 km N Dong Ha. Jan67. Quang Tri Pr, I Corps.
Giong Giua (n/a)
Mapsheet name of L-7014-6127-2. SVN.
Giong Trom (XS 66-21)
Along TL-26, apx 18 km SE Truc Giang/ Ben Tre. 9th Inf MRF AO. Possible FSB site of 3d/34th Arty. Cited in Annual Hist Rpt, 3d/34th Arty, for period 1Apr68-31Jan69, on MRF Assn at: www.mrfa.org3_34th.htm. Kien See Split Battery Echelon in Glossary. Kien Hoa Pr, IV Corps.
Giong Trom Heliport (XS 656-219)
Along Rte 174, apx 19 km SE Truc Giang/Ben Tre. "Heliport #569, alt 7', sod, small area." At 10°09'00"N-106°31'00"E, per Feb73 TAD. Kien Hoa Pr, IV Corps.
Giong Trom Pagoda (XS 65-21?)
Presumably near Giong Trom, along Rte 174, apx 19 km SE Truc Giang/Ben Tre. Built in '68 or '69 in part with materials/labor courtesy 3d/34rth Arty, 9th MRF, who also conducted 30 MEDCAPS and 20 ICAPS, treating 4,534 patients and dist supplies to 5 times that number. The Bn also provided materials for const of this Pagoda in Giong Trom Dist, as well as school and church in Ham Luong Dist. C Bty made also $90 monthly contributions to My Tho Leper Colony. Kien Hoa Pr, IV Corps.
Giong Trom, FSB (XS 6-2?)
A.k.a. FSB David? Giong Trom is roughly 18 km SE Truc Giang/Ben Tre. Built Sep68 by 2d Bde/9th Inf when Bty C, 34th Arty lifted off barges in early Oct69 and set here. Bty A, 34th Arty also here. Data per MRF Assn website. Kien Hoa Pr, IV Corps. [247]
Girl Youth Group Center (YT 04-07)
See Phanh Hanh Social Club. Bien Hoa Pr, III Corps.
Glacier (n/a)
Apr70, XXIV Corps proposed 101st Abn FSB name.
Gladiator, FSB (YD 416-211)
A.k.a. Hill 316. Apx 32 km due W Hue, 8 km ENE FSB Ripcord and 15 km NW FSB Rakkasan. Originally constructed 29Mar70, by 101st Abn Engrs, C/2d/506th Inf and B/2d/319th Arty, as part of Op Chicago Peak suptg const/defense of FSB Ripcord. During Lam Son 720, beginning in Apr '71, FSBs Fury, Kathryn, Maureen, Gladiator and later Eagle's Nest were all reopened by B/326th Eng for 101st Abn. FSBs Co Pung, Binh Dinh and Kim Qui also built during op as well. Also listed at YD 415-212. See FSB Ripcord. Thua Thien Pr, I Corps.
Gladis, FSB (XT 530-037)
See Gladys. Hau Nghia Pr, III Corps.
Gladstone, FSB (YS 265-733)
Apx 1 km E QL-15 apx 18 km WNW Nui Dat, 2 km NE FSB Gail and 3 km SE FSB North Dakota. On 1ATF NCO trng map per John Hollett. Phuoc Tuy Pr, III Corps.
Gladys, FSB (YT 25-27)
Near Song Dong Nai River, apx 16 km W Xa Binh Hoa and 30 km NE Bien Hoa AB. 5th/12th, 199th LIB here. Long Khanh Pr, III Corps.
Gladys, FSB (XT 530-037)
Apx 1 km SE Khiem Cuong, 16 km SW Cu Chi and 28 km WNW Tanh Son Nhut AB. '67. Hau Nghia Pr, III Corps.
Glass, LZ (XD 902-285)
In Vietnam Salient apx 2 km SW Lang Klung, 15 km SSE Khe Sanh CB and 21 km SSW Ca Lu. Apr70 XXIV Corps grid per Don Armstrong. Quang Tri Pr, I Corps.
Glen, LZ (BS 629-276)
See Glenn. Quang Ngai Pr, I Corps.
Glenn, LZ/FSB (BS 629-276)
Possibly a.k.a. Hill 763 and also sp Glen. Near I Corps/II Corps border, apx 22 km SW Duc Pho and 9 km SE Ba To New AF. Said to have been in the "tri-border area(?)" and 1st Cav Div here May67, according to *11-Charlie, Delta Company* article by Jim Breen in Jan2002 *Military* Mag, pp20-21. Cited in *2d/7th Cav Unit History* '70-71, p 2, per Peter Cole. Quang Ngai Pr, I Corps?
Glennon, USS (n/a)
DD-840, per Ralph Fries.
Glider (n/a)
6Apr70, XXIV Corps proposed 5th Div FSB name.

Gloria, FSB (YT 274-102)
Possibly a.k.a. FSB Bay? Along QL-1, apx 18 km W Xuan Loc and 28 km ESE Bien Hoa AB. Aug69. Long Khanh, III Corps.

Gloria Ann, LZ (ZA 096-745)
Apx 11 km W QL-14, 20 km SW Kontum and 5 km SE Polei Tum. B Bty/6th/29th Arty here De69. 4th Div 31Jan70 grid per Jim Henderson. Kontum Pr, II Corps.

Glove, LZ? (BR 859-782)
Along Hwy 506 in 506 Valley, apx 8 km SE Ha Tay AF and 16 km due S Bong Son AF. True nature of site unknown. Feb66. Binh Dinh Pr, II Corps.

Go Bac Chien Airfield (XS 029-902)
See Moc Hoa AF. Kien Tuong Pr, IV Corps.

Go Cong (n/a)
Mapsheet name of L-7014-6329-4. SVN.

Go Cong (XS 83-46)
Apx 40 km due S Saigon. Map is L-7014-6329-4, per Jim Stone. Capitol, Go Cong Pr, IV Corps.

Go Cong (YS 00-98)
City apx 9 km SE Di An, 17 km ENE Tan Son Nhut AB and 15 km due S Bien Hoa AB. Gia Dinh Pr, III Corps.

Go Cong, Battle of (XS 7-4?)
Took place 4-7Jul67, during Op Coronado I. 9th Inf Div MRF attacked enemy base area about 7 km NW Go Cong. Riverine FSB was set up and the MRF moved down the Vam Co to Rach Go Cong River, and inserted 3d/47 and 4th/47th Inf onto 7 beaches, while another Co CA'd onto LZ Cobra. Go Cong Pr, IV Corps.

Go Cong Airfield (XS 853-462)
In Mekong Delta apx 42 km due S Saigon, 10 km from Coast, 35 km due E My Tho, and 2 km E Go Cong, per TPC K-10D. El. 10', 1,800' soft asph rwy. At 10°21'50"N-106°41'27"E. Also listed at XS 840-469. Map is L-7014-6329-4, per Jim Stone. Go Cong Pr, IV Corps.

Go Cong Heliport (XS 840-460)
Apx 40 km due S Saigon, 34 km E My Tho, and 12 km ENE Vinh Binh. "Heliport #570, alt 10', Soccer Field. Fuel-A+ Ammo-7.62/2.75", at 10°22'00"N-106°41'00"E," per Feb73 TAD. Map is L-7014-6329-4, per Jim Stone. Go Cong Pr, IV Corps.

Go Cong Province (XS)
One of 16 southern provs forming IV Corps.

Go Cong SF Camp (XS 840-469)
Apx 40 km due S Saigon, 34 km E My Tho, and 12 km ENE Vinh Binh. 5th SF. Info/grid per *SF Order of Battle.* Moved to Ben Cat. Map is L-7014-6329-4, per Jim Stone. Go Cong Pr, IV Corps.

Go Da Ha Heliport (XT 390-250)
See Go Dau Ha Heliport. Tay Ninh Pr, III Corps.

Go Dau Ha (XT 39-24?)
Near intersection of QL-1 and QL-22, apx 26 km SE Tay Ninh and 28 km WNW Cu Chi. ARVN and/or SF Camp sometimes site of 25th Div Arty ground surveillance units (5-man teams using TPS-25 ground scanning radar. See http://pacer.calpoly.edu/Tri/ radar.html for detail). 5th SF, Det A-326, here Oct66. III Corps. Likely sp variant of Dau Ho. See Dau Ho SF Camp. Tay Ninh Pr?, III Corps.

Go Dau Ha (Hieu Thien) (n/a)
Mapsheet L-7014-6231-2. Full sheet name: Hieu Thien (Go Dau Ha).

Go Dau Ha Airfield (XT 412-242)
Apx 26 km SE Tay Ninh and 28 km WNW Cu Chi. "Unserviceable, AF # VA3-299," in Aug69 TAD per Frank Penk, Jr. Not in Feb73 TAD. III Corps.

Go Dau Ha Heliport (XT 390-250)
Near intersection of QL-1 and QL-22, apx 26 km SE Tay Ninh and 28 km WNW Cu Chi. Heliport #571, alt 30', Soccer Field, at 11°04'40"N-106°16'15"E, per Feb73 TAD. Tay Ninh Pr, III Corps.

Go Dau Ha Navy Base (XT 38-26?)
On Song Vam Co Don River, apx 25 km SE Tay Ninh. USN Advance Base, '69-71. Per MRF Assn Website. Tay Ninh Pr?, III Corps.

Go Dau Ha SF Camp (XT 395-247)
A.k.a. FOB Trang Sup. Near intersection of QL-1 and QL-22, apx 26 km SE Tay Ninh and 28 km WNW Cu Chi. 5th SF. Info/grid per *SF Order of Battle.* Also listed at XT 387-252. Tay Ninh Pr, III Corps.

Go Do Airfield (WS 477-155)
See Thoi Hoa AF. Phong Dinh Pr, IV Corps.

Go Kha, FSB? (AT 943-663)
A.k.a. Hill 41. USMC position? Along Rte 540 just E foot of Charlie Ridge. apx 11 km SW Da Nang AB. '70 XXIV Corps grid per Don Armstrong. Quang Nam Pr, I Corps.

Go Nhan, Pointe de (BS 7-9)
See Pointe Go Nhan. Quang Ngai Pr, I Corps.

Go Noi Island/Dodge City (BT 02-54)
Area W of QL-1 and roughly 28 km S Da Nang. Apx 55 sq km in size and immed S Dodge City. Described as island because it was surrounded by channels of Hoi An River. Americal, USMC, I Corps. See Dodge City for detailed description. Quang Tin Pr?, I Corps.

Go Noi, FSB (BT?)
Temporary 11th Marine Arty FSB on S edge of Go Noi Island at start of Op Durham Peak. Btys B and F, 11th Mar Arty 105mm howitzers moved here on 19Jul69 and trained muzzles N in order to deceive enemy about the direction 7th Marines would be moving (S to Que Son Mtns). Actual name, if any, unknown. Quang Nam Pr, I Corps.

Go Phu Refugee Camp (BS 645-723)
Immed S Quang Ngai. NPIA data. Quang Ngai Pr, I Corps.

Go Quao (Kien Hung) (n/a)
Mapsheet L-7014-6028-2. Full sheet name: Kien Hung (Go Quao). SVN.

Go Quao Heliport (WR 306-749)
Along N bank of Song Cai Long River, apx 6 km SW Ap Luc and 36 km SE Rach Gia. Heliport #717, alt 7', at 09°48'30"N-105°17'30"E, per Feb73 TAD. Chuong Thien Pr, IV Corps.

Go Song (BR 735-823)
Ville near LZ Bird and 7 km W Ha Tay used by 22d NVA Rgt as staging area for its Christmas Day attack of LZ Bird, 25-26Dec66. Binh Dinh Pr, II Corps.

Goc Chang (XT 645-236)
Apx 6 km due N Cu Chi CB. 2d/14th Inf, 2d/49th ARVN Rgt, joint ops here Summer '69. Hau Nghia Pr, III Corps.

Going Over The Fence (n/a)
See Glossary.

Gold, FSB (n/a)
Location unknown, though possibly at site of old FSB Gold, near Suoi Tre (XT 3-6)? Cited in *1st Cav Op Rpt,*

May-Jul70, p 37, per Peter Cole, and during period, Cav was in NW III Corps/Cambodia.

Gold, FSB/LZ (XT 385-705)
Apparently later the site of FSB Hood (XT 389-702, Dec67). Near Suoi Tre, apx 42 km WSW An Loc, 20 km S Cambodia, 16 km NE Nui Ba Den and 95 km NNW Saigon. Built beginning 19Mar67, in area surrounded by tree-line of sparse woodlands blighted by defoliants. Secured by 3d/22d Inf and 2d/77th Arty (opcon 3d Bde/4th Div) during phase II of Op Junction City. Site of Battle of Suoi Tre, 21Mar67, involving 3d/22d Inf, 2d/12th Inf, 2d/77th Arty and 272d VC Rgt. 15 US KIA, 28 WIA day one, 31 US KIA, 109 WIA on day two. 1st/502d Inf, 101st Abn here 14-19Jan68. Data per *Cedar Falls-Junction City*, p 136. Tay Ninh Pr, III Corps.

Gold, FSB (XT 657-386?)
If grid correct, was apx 13 km WNW Lai Khe AF and 19 km SE Dau Tieng AF. Name/grid per Dan Gillotti, 15th Arty Assn. Binh Duong Pr, III Corps.

Gold, LZ (BQ 755-352)
Apx 8 km SW Cung Son AF, 6 km NE Bau Ruk and 48 km NNW Duc My AF. Oct66. Phu Yen Pr, II Corps.

Gold, LZ (BS 84-14?)
Roughly 18 km due N Bong Son, 5 km W QL-1 and 6 km ESE LZ Brass. Used during Op Masher/White Wing, 28Jan-6Mar66. Discussion of Ops Masher/White Wing and this LZ in *A Contagion of War* vol, *Vietnam Experience* series, pp 32-48, with map showing site at p 38. 1st and 2d/5th Cav, 1st Cav Div. Binh Dinh Pr, II Corps.

Gold, LZ (BR 364-596)
Apx 8 km SW Kannack AF, 3 km SW Plei Ko Ri and 19 km NW An Khe. Mar66. Binh Dinh Pr, II Corps.

Gold, LZ (XT 705-345)
Apx 5 km WNW Ben Cat, 7 km SW Lai Khe. Dec65-Jan66. Binh Duong Pr, III Corps.

Gold, LZ (YA 624-494)
On Cambodian border at S end of Plei Trap Valley, apx 61 km due W Pleiku and 23 km ESE Phum Choy Cambodia. Jan66. Kontum Pr, II Corps.

Gold, LZ (YD 173-289)
Apx 10 km due S Ba Long AF, 4 km WNW Hill 1102 (Dong Ba Le), and 28 km SW of Quang Tri. Apr70 XXIV Corps grid per Don Armstrong. Quang Tri Pr, I Corps.

Goldberg, Camp (CR 082-225)
At Qui Nhon AF, apx 240 mi NE Saigon, 28 km SE Phu Cat, 64 km ESE An Khe and just off QL-1 on flat peninsula jutting into a small bay. Binh Dinh Pr, II Corps.

Golden BB, The (n/a)
See Glossary.

Golden Fleece, Operation (n/a)
Prgm apparently the forerunner of USMC CAC program.

Golden Gate Bridge (AT 927-531)
Bridge across Song Thu Bon River, apx 22 km WSW Hoi An and 24 km SSW Da Nang AB. USMC, Aug66. Quang Nam Pr, I Corps.

Golden Gate Bridge (XT 722-973)
QL-13 bridge apx 12 km due S Loc Ninh AF and 10 km NNW An Loc. Aug67. Binh Long Pr, III Corps.

Golden Rose, LZ (BT 231-315)
A.k.a. Hawk Hill, LZ Hawk Hill, and Hill 29. Apx 2 km W QL-1, 12 km NW Tam Ky, 13 km ESE LZ Colt/Ordway. Apparently given name while a 4th Div LZ, and 1st/14th Inf here. Grid est based on photos/maps of base online at http://1-14th.com/maps.html. Quang Tin Pr, I Corps.

Goldie, LZ (BS 680-658)
Along W side of QL-1, apx 8 km SSE Quang Ngai and 13 km NNE Quang Hien/Mo Duc AF. Apr70 XXIV Corps grid per Don Armstrong. Quang Ngai Pr, I Corps.

Goldsborough, USS (n/a)
DDG-20. Guided-Missile DD, per Ralph Fries.

Golf, LZ (XT 423-182)
Apx 10 km ENE Duc Hue AF and just E Song Vam Co Dong River. Jan66. Binh Duong Pr, III Corps.

Golf, LZ (XT 616-285)
Apx 2 km SW Xa Duoc and 18 km WSW Lai Khe. Jun66. Binh Duong Pr, III Corps.

Golf, LZ (XT 938-576)
Apx 9 km NNE Phuoc Vinh AF and 20 km SSW Dong Xoai. Jun67. Binh Duong Pr, III Corps.

Golf, LZ (YA 841-094)
Apx 17 km due S Duc Co SF Camp, 10 km NNW Chu Pong Mtn, 10 km E Cambodia. 1st Cav. On map in *The Rise and Fall of the American Army,* pp 368-9. Cited in *Pleiku*, p 252 (map), 256, 257, 258, per Peter Cole. Nov65. Pleiku Pr, II Corps.

Golf 5 (YB 604-355)
See Leghorn MSS. Laos.

Golf 6 (YC 25-90?)
NVA base area in Laos just across border from N end of the A Shau Valley. President Johnson approved secret MACV-SOG op here in Feb?67. Size of op forced SOG to request Marine Recon troops to bolster their Prairie Fire Team strength. Marines balked at participation in what they thought was "off-limits" area until shown teletyped order directly from White House. Grid is est. Laos. [248]

Golf CAC (YD?)
See CAC Listings. I Corps.

Golf Course, The (BR 470-480)
A.k.a. An Khe/Golf Course AF. Huge helicopter LZ at 1st Cav's An Khe basecamp, a.k.a. Camp Radcliff. Named "The Golf Course" after 1st Cav's Gen Wright selected site in Aug65, and told the advance team to "cut brush until we have a Golf Course." Per *Chickenhawk*, p 107, it was apx 3,000' x 4,000' in size when first completed. In *Baptism*, p 77, it is described in '65 as, "a huge helicopter pad, just an open grass-covered, stump-riddled field. At any one time, on it sat hundreds of helicopters." The original clearing was cut by elements of 1st Bde/101st Abn, which secured site for arrival of 1st Cav in Sep-Oct65. See Camp Radcliff, An Khe, and An Khe/Golf Course AF. Binh Dinh Pr, II Corps.

Golf Courses (n/a)
See Nui Dat Basecamp, An Khe and Dalat.

Goliath, LZ (XT 701-444)
A.k.a. FSB Domino. Apx 8 km WSW Ap Bau Bang and 9 km WNW Lai Khe. Aug-Oct67. Binh Duong Pr, III Corps.

Gonder, FSB (XU 807-383)
Apx 1 km N Cambodian border, 26 km ESE Snuol, 19 km NNE Loch Ninh and 17 km WSW Bu Dop. Likely named to honor Army Cpl Kenneth W. Gonder, KIA 19May70. Also misspelled Gandor. Listed in *11th ACR Cambodia*

Invasion AAR, 1st Cav Div, May-Jun70, courtesy Lou Rochat. [249] Cambodia.

Gonzales, FSB (XS or XT?)
Reconstructed by men of 2d/505th Inf, 3d Bde/82d Abn beginning 21Oct68, during Op Toan Thang. Later the Bn moved to FSB Harrison. FSB Harrison was at XT 738-051, and likely Gonzales was not more than a few km from Harrison. Original occupants and construction date is unknown, as is precise location. Info per Butch Sincock and '68 history of 3de Bde. [250] Gia Dinh or Binh Duong Pr, III Corps.

Good Neighbor Program (n/a)
See Glossary.

Good View Pass (BP 507-075)
Along QL-11, apx 27 km ESE Dalat. Apr70. Ninh Thuan Pr, II Corps.

Goodman, Camp (XS 853-929)
Apx 5 km NE Tan Son Nhut AB, Saigon. SF Cmd Liaison Det Cmpd, Saigon. Named to honor MSgt Jack L. Goodman, Operations NCO, Det A-18, 5th SF, KIA 17Jul63, during ambush of jeep while orienting replacements from Det A-22 along dirt road between Loch Ninh SF Camp and Xom Bung. Detailed description of site in *Gone Native*, pp 49-51. Data per Ray Bows' *Vietnam Military Lore, 1959-1973*. Gia Dinh Pr, III Corps.

Goodman, FSB (YD 324-078)
On Dong Tien Cong Mtn, apx 5 km NW FSB Airborne, 15 km W FSB Eagle and 42 km WSW Hue. 1st Cav here '68, and 101st Abn here after Cav. Also listed at YD 325-078 and 320-071. Cited in *Anatomy of A Division*, per Peter Cole. Thua Thien Pr, I Corps.

Goodman, J. L., Camp (XS 853-929)
See J. L. Goodman. Gia Dinh Pr, III Corps.

Goodsell Heliport (BT 013-752?)
A.k.a. LZ-11 and Goodsell Memorial Heliport. Described as having been adj to the LSI Cmpd (Lear-Siegler, Inc.) along W edge of Da Nang AB, per LTC R. H. Esau, Jr. in article entitled *Da Nang After The Armistice* reprinted in *The USMC in Vietnam, An Anthology and Annotated Bibliography*, p. 201. In Aug73, Esau found a plaque still on the LZ that read: LZ-11, *Goodsell Memorial Heliport, In Memory of Major William J. Goodsell USMCR, C.O. Marine Observation Squadron 6, KIA 6Jun66, Marine Air Group 36, First Marine Air Wing*. Quang Nam Pr, I Corps.

Goose, LZ (BT 504-035)
Apx 5 km SW Chu Lai and 3 km SW QL-1. Mar66. Quang Tin Pr, I Corps.

Goose, LZ (YD 3-6?)
Apx 1.5 km S Ben Hai River in DMZ and not far from coast? USMC here clearing NVA from DMZ during Op Hickory/Beau Charger, 18May67. Quang Tri Pr, I Corps.

Goose Early Warning System (n/a)
See DEWS in Glossary.

Gopher, LZ (XD 752-528)
Apx 4 km WNW Lang Buat, 9 km WSW peak of Hill 1739 (Dong Voi Mep), 14 km NW Khe Sanh CB and 38 km WSW Cam Lo. Apr70 XXIV Corps grid per Don Armstrong. Quang Tri Pr, I Corps.

Gophers (n/a)
See Glossary.

Gordon, FSB (XT 586-303)
A.k.a. FSB Freda? Along Song Saigon River, apx 18 km WSW Lai Khe and 4 km NW Xa Duoc. Oct68. Also cited in *1st Cav Op Rpt, May-Jul70*, p 37, per Peter Cole. Binh Duong Pr, III Corps.

Gordon, USS (n/a)
Troop transport that carried initial elements of 2d Bde/1st Inf Div to Vietnam after unit left Fort Riley Kansas, 14Jul65. Also delivered elements of 11th LIB to Duc Pho area, Dec67. Info per Sep99 *Military* Mag, p 26, and Jun-Jul 2000 *VETERAN* Magazine Locator section, p 40.

Gorge of Coxha (n/a)
See Coxha Gorge. NVN.

Gorvad, Camp (XT 966-492)
A.k.a. FSB Gorvad. At Phuoc Vinh, apx 54 km NNE Saigon, 22 km ENE Lai Khe and 70 km due E Tay Ninh. 1st Cav Basecamp. Named to honor LTC Peter L. Gorvad, CO, 2d/12th Cav, 1st Cav, KIA 8Mar69, by 122mm Rockets that hit cmd bunker of FSB Grant during attack by NVA 95C Rgt. Binh Duong Pr, III Corps.

Gosney Compound (XT 8-1)
US Adv Cmpd, Lam Son/Phu Loi. Named to honor Maj. Durward D. "Dean" Gosney, KIA 7Oct64, when his helicopter was shot down while suptg 5th ARVN Div. Home of 5th (ARVN) Inf Div Adv Detachment, Team 70. Data per *Vietnam Military Lore, 1959-1973*, pp 80-81, Binh Duong Pr, III Corps.

Government Mafia (n/a)
See Peoples' Anti-Corruption Movement in Glossary.

Gowers-Hansen Quarry Site (AN 968-862?)
A.k.a. Dillard Quarry? See Dillard Industrial Complex. Tuyen Duc Pr, II Corps.

Grace, LZ (BN 567-508)
Along QL-1 near Ap Vinh Hao and FSB Coup (BN 560-514), apx 11 km NNE Tuy Phong, 2 km from coast and 32 km ENE Song Mao AF. Mar67. Binh Thuan Pr, II Corps.

Graham Report (n/a)
See Glossary.

Graham's Folly (YS)
See Glossary.

Graham-Browne, Camp (XT 760-892?)
At Hon Quan, along QL-13 and immed N of An Loc? HQ for MACV Adv Team 47. Named to honor 1Lts Terry D. Graham and Fred Browne, both KIA 28Mar69. Data per Ray Bows. Binh Long Pr, III Corps.

Grand Bungalow, The (AQ 793-026)
A.k.a. Ban Me Thuot SF Camp. Along QL-14 at SE edge Ban Me Thuot/Lac Giao, apx 1 km SSW the SW end of BMT City AF rwy and 1 km NNE Ban Ale(2). SF unit housed in large, rustic hunting lodge (a.k.a. the Grand Bungalow) used at one time by Emperor Bao Dai, and by President Theodore Roosevelt for lodging during hunting trip in 1909. Apparently very 1st CIDG camp opened in SVN here in '61. Per John Rochelle, lodge had sign over entrance that read *Grand Bungalow*. He adds that there was a "super" BX here and that SF troops had best of everything. Per *Gone Native*, p 182, was beautiful Teak A-Frame bldg said to have been burned-down by cooking fire in late '68 or early '69. Taken over by SF Det 32 for HQ at some point. Darlac Pr, II Corps.

Grand Can, FSB? (n/a)
See Grand Canal, FSB. IV Corps.

Grand Canal, The (WS 81-82 et al)
See Phuoc Xuyen ATSB. Per John Caughran, "the 'Grand Canal' ran from Mekong River NE to Vam Co Dong or Vam Co Ta River at Moc Hoa." NIMA Gaz has listings for Grand Canal as a.k.a. Kinh Tong Doc Loc, at WS 9-4; as Kinh Togtoampu Phung Hiep den Hau Giang, at WR 9-8; as Grand Canal de Cai Con, at WR 6-7; and as Kinh Togtoampu Long My den Hau Giang, at WR 6-7.

Grand Canal de Cai Con (WR 6-7)
See Grand Canal, The, and Phuoc Xuyen.

Grand Canal?, FSB? (n/a)
No data. Listed as "FSB Grand Can" in herbicide spray listing and possible misspelling of Grand Canal or Grand Canyon? USAF Herbicide gallonage rpt with this listing indicates total gallonages of following agents were sprayed within an 8 km radius of facility: Orange, zero; White, 1540; Blue, zero. IV Corps.

Grand Eagle, Operation (n/a)
See Glossary.

Grand Hotel (CP 043-535)
On Rte 419 and overlooking beach at city center and apx 1 km NE Nha Trang AF perimeter. Per Don Truitt, IFFV HQ was in this Hotel at Nha Trang, '68-69, and CG at time was Lt Gen Peers. Khanh Hoa Pr, II Corps.

Grand Palace (PR 7-3)
R&R tourist spot in Bangkok, Thailand.

Grand Sommet des Mines (YJ 4-3)
A.k.a. Nui Khe Thut. NIMA data. NVN.

Grand Sommet Mountain (BP 985-450)
A.k.a. Hill 978 and Nui Cau Hai. Apx 8 km SW Nha Trang AF. Khanh Hoa Pr, II Corps.

Grand, LZ (YD 133-390)
Overlooked Song Thach Han River, apx 2.5 km WSW Ba Long AF and 22 km SW Quang Tri. Apr70 XXIV Corps grid per Don Armstrong. Quang Tri Pr, I Corps.

Granite (n/a)
Apr70, XXIV Corps proposed 101st Abn FSB name.

Granite, Camp (CR 066-208)
Along E side QL-1, immed S of Phu Tai (1), apx 2 km S Ho Ba Lake and 6 km due W Qui Nhon AF. Duane Good tells us it was at base of Vung Chua Mtn (from entrance, mtn was to right and 4 km to SE), and across road from ARVN Basecamp. Graveyard surrounded apx half of camp. Main gate was off QL-1 and there was an open field to E of base. US Signal site sat atop Vung Chau, but VC held ground between it and Granite. "Shit Beach" was at Junction of 440 and 441 S of AB? Immed after that was R&R area/beach that was probably most beautiful beach he ever saw. "If you gave the Viet guard a pack of US cigs, you'd get in to watch Koreans and medical people being dropped off by helo while Navy guns were pounding the mountains nearby…what a show! A Leper Colony was on coast nearby, though VC controlled area." Per Duane Good. site "was small. Consisted of Provost Marshal's Office (PMO, a.k.a. MP Station), 3 barracks bldgs for MP's, a motor pool, MP club, Sig Co barracks, MP Sentry dog-pen, with latrine at one end and showers (not real showers) at other. Probably less than 500 people there." Jim Claeys spent night here Dec70, and recalls some cliffs nearby and bunker line firing mad minutes into cemetery just outside wire. Grid apx. See Qui Nhon and Vung Chau Signal Site. Binh Dinh Pr, II Corps.

Granite, Fort (XU 929-081)
See Fort Granite & FSB Granite. Phuoc Long Pr, III Corps.

Granite, FSB (XU 927-083)
A.k.a. FSB Fort Granite and FSB Terry Ann? along Song Be River apx 20 km due E Loc Ninh AF, 6 km NW Bu R'Dang, 23 km due W Song Be. Also listed at XU 928-073 and 929-081. Binh Long Pr, III Corps.

Granite, FSB (YD 437-190)
Apx 28 km due W Hue, 15 km SW Camp Evans and 10 km due N FSB Maureen. Possibly built shortly after 1Feb70. 101st Abn FSB, with 2d/501st Inf here Apr70. Apparently penetrated by sappers in Feb or Mar70, and again on night of 29Apr70, when sappers led the way for 2 Inf Bns but the NVA Inf never got rolling because pre-planned arty fire decimated the units as they waited at base of hill for assault to begin. 2d attack resulted in 7 US KIA, 1 MIA, 7 WIA, 18 NVA KIA. Some data per *Ripcord*, p 90. Also listed as 432-197 and YD 439-189. Thua Thien Pr, I Corps.

Granite, FSB (YU 926-080?)
Apparent UTM zone error. See Granite at "XU" 928-072.

Grant, FSB/LZ (XT 389-626)
Apx 11 km ENE Nui Ba Den, 5 km NE FSB Bragg, 23 km NE Tay Ninh West and due S LZ Ike. Per *LRRP Company Commander*, p 62, FSBs Carolyn Eleanor and Grant were intentionally built on enemy infiltration corridors, with FSBs Billy, Buttons, Dot, Ike, Jamie and Mud firing in supt of them. Per Ray Bows, was named to honor Capt Joseph X. Grant, KIA 13Nov66. Per Tom Skelly, had great view of Nui Ba Den and there was a river to rear of base. Major attack by NVA 95C Rgt, 8Mar69, during Op Sheridan Sabre, and during which LTC Peter L. Gorvad, CO, 2d/12th Cav, 1st Cav, was KIA by 122mm Rockets that hit cmd bunker in opening salvo of battle (See Camp Gorvad). 13 US KIA and 39 WIA; 157 NVA/VC KIA. Also attacked by 95C Rgt, Jun69 (along with FSBs Barbara, Jamie and Phyllis) as part of planned attack of Tay Ninh. Sign at entrance read: *WELCOME TO LZ GRANT 1ST BN, 12TH, CAV. YOU'VE SEEN THE REST NOW LOOK AT THE BEST*, per photo courtesy Terry McGee. 1st/8th, 1st and 2d/12th Cav, 1st Cav here in '68-69. Also listed at XT 380-620 (Dec67-Feb69), 370-630 (Jan69) and 387-624 (Fe69). Tay Ninh Pr, III Corps.

Grant, LZ (YD 024-615)
On southern edge of DMZ, apx 12 km NW Cam Lo and 22 km WNW Dong Ha. Apr70 XXIV Corps grid per Don Armstrong. Quang Tri Pr, I Corps.

Grape, LZ (XD 903-637)
On S edge of DMZ, apx 22 km WNW Cam Lo and 34 km WNW Dong Ha. Apr70 XXIV Corps grid per Don Armstrong. Quang Tri Pr, I Corps.

Grapple, USS (n/a)
ARS-7. Aux Ship, per Ralph Fries.

Grass, LZ (XD 69-14)
Apx 32 km SSW Khe Sanh CB, 9 km SE LZ Green and 12 km SW FSB Passport. ARVN LZ during Lam Son 719. Good Lam Son 719 map at www.americal.org/174/map4.htm. Laos.

Gravel Mines (n/a)
See Glossary.
Gray, FSB (YS 207-933)
See FSB Grey. Bien Hoa Pr, III Corps.
Gray, LZ (AQ 88-99)
Originally FSB Phu Nhon. Apx 50 km SSE Pleiku. Renamed to honor 1Lt Richard J. Gray, WIA along with 11 other men by rocket fire 12Jun71, and who died 13Jun71. Per Tom Rethard, Arty Liaison with Gray's unit, the LZ "was a few hundred meters to E QL 14, level with Phu Nhon to its W. We spent a good portion of rainy season there. Gray was killed by a rocket fired from W side of Hill 415 at sunset (1st of 25+ rockets that evening). 23rd ARVN Div and 45th ARVN Rgt had their 'forward' HQ [Hill 415?] there to our N for a few weeks as well." Gray was hit by a fragment from 1st rocket of barrage, which landed in unit's only running 5-ton truck, "and my only Mack. Part of truck bed got him while he was playing horseshoes. For reasons we didn't understand, the NVA [95B Rgt] then shifted their rather accurate fire to ARVN 23d Div HQ, 100 meters N of us. By time we finished with them the next morning, there were no more rocket attacks in our AO." Gray stands out in Rethard's memory because every few weeks Gray's Grandmother would mail Gray a US $5 bill, which repeatedly had him explaining to authorities why he was in possession of US greenbacks when MPC was only legal in-country currency! 1Nov71 7th/15th Arty ORLL courtesy Nolan Puttman confirms renaming scenario. Home of ARVN 23rd Div HQ. Pleiku Pr, II Corps.
Gray, USS (n/a)
DE-1054. DD-Escort, per Ralph Fries.
Grayback, USS (n/a)
A.k.a. LPSS 574, Transport Submarine. Part of Logistic Supt Force 73. Carried USN/VNN UDTs, SEALs and VNMC to scout proposed lndg beaches in NVN.
Great Bay (XQ 7-5)
Bay a.k.a. Vinh Con Son. Con Song Island bay at 8°40'N-106°38'E. G rid per NC48-11. IV Corps.
Great Holy Dog, The (n/a)
See Meo Tribes.
Great Temple of Holy See (XT 241-496)
See Temple of Holy See. Tay Ninh Pr, III Corps.
Greater Wheel, The (n/a)
See Glossary.
Greek, LZ (YD 761-055)
A.k.a. Nui Ke, Hill 618, LZ Satan II, and OP Satan II. On Hill 618, at or near its peak, apx 15 km due S Hue, 16 km WSW Phu Bai. Apr70 XXIV Corps grid per Don Armstrong. See Nui Ke for detail. Thua Thien Pr, I Corps.
Greeley, Operation (n/a)
18Jun-14Oct67. 173d Abn, Dak To/Kontum. 4th/503d Inf deployed to Dak To AO following Battle of Slopes, and on 10Jul67, its A Co was heavily engaged by NVA while climbing Hill 830. Hill finally taken 12 Jul67, where network of 60 mutually suptg bunkers was found, as were 2 other bunker complexes.
Green, FSB (YS 200-835)
Along QL-15, apx 28 km NW Nui Dat and 12 km SSE Long Thanh AF. Jan68. Bien Hoa Pr, III Corps.
Green, FSB (YT 334-745)
Apx 90 km NNE Saigon, 15 km SSE Bunard AF, 26 km due E Dong Xoai and 45 km NE Phuoc Vinh. Opened or reopened 11Aug70. 1st/7th Cav. Data per *1st Cav Div Op Rpt, ending 31Oct70*, courtesy Peter Cole. Also listed at YT 331-752 (center of Bty) per Mike Paultry, 1st/21st Arty. Aug70-Jan71. Also listed at YT 331-752. Phuoc Long Pr, III Corps.
Green, LZ (BQ 923-365)
Apx 3 km WSW Lac Dien, 13 km ESE Cung Son AF and 16 km ESE Son Ha. Oct66. Phu Yen Pr, II Corps.
Green, LZ (XD 63-19)
Apx 32 km SW Khe Sanh, 20 km SE Sophia-2, 8 km SW LZ Green H-2 and 18 km WSW FSB Passport. ARVN LZ during Lam Son 719. Good Lam Son 719 map at www.americal.org/174/map4.htm. Laos.
Green, LZ (XT 616-995)
Apx 16 km SW Loc Ninh and 10 km NNE tip of Fishhook. Jul66. Binh Long Pr, III Corps.
Green, LZ (YS 300-730)
Apx 14 km WNW Nui Dat and 6 km ESE Phu My/QL-15. Dec67. Phuoc Tuy Pr, III Corps.
Green, LZ (YS 740-650)
Apx 4 km from coast, 3 km ESE Xa Nhu Lam and 26 km ENE Dat Do. Apr66. Phuoc Tuy Pr, III Corps.
Green, LZ (YT 147-287)
A.k.a. Hieu Liem Heliport and possibly FSB Bunker Hill. On N bank of Song Dong Nai, apx 23 km NE Bien Hoa AB. Feb66. Bien Hoa Pr?, III Corps.
Green Bay, SS (n/a)
Merchant ship under govt contract, per Ralph Fries.
Green Beach (BS 718-924)
At An Cuong, apx 21 km NNE Quang Ngai. Aug65. Quang Ngai Pr, I Corps.
Green Beach (YD 275-780)
5 km SE mouth of Ben Hai River, 12 km NW Cua Viet and 26 km NNW Quang Tri. May67. Quang Tri Pr, I Corps.
Green Door, The (XS 87-97)
Well-known brothel said to have been adj Ben Loi or Binh Loi, apx 4 km due E of Tan Son Nhut AB. Grid apx. Gia Dinh Pr, III Corps.
Green Dragons (n/a)
See Glossary.
Green Forest, SS (n/a)
Merchant vessel under contract to US govt. See Evacuation of Da Nang.
Green H-2, LZ (XD 69-22)
Apx 26 km SW Khe Sanh, 8 km NE LZ Green, 10 km due W FSB Passport and 23 km SE Aloui (Laos). ARVN LZ during Lam Son 719. Good Lam Son 719 map at www.americal.org/174/map4.htm. Laos.
Green Hill Signal Site (PR 7-3?)
Apparently at or near Bangkok? Data per Josef Rokus at http://phulam. com/history.htm. Thailand.
Green Wave, SS (n/a)
Merchant ship under govt contract, per Ralph Fries.
Green Line, The (BR 470-480)
The outer perimeter of 1st Cav Div's home basecamp at An Khe/Camp Radcliff when base 1st built in '65. Initially Hon Cong Mtn was outside the Green Line, but perimeter was later expanded to inc it. Binh Dinh Pr, II Corps.

Green Port, SS (n/a)
Commercial Transport under DOD contract. See Evacuation of Da Nang.

Green Storm, Operation (n/a)
See Greene Storm.

Green Sure 17, Operation (n/a)
See Greene Sure 17.

Green Wave, USS (n/a)
See Da Nang Evacuation of, in Glossary.

Greene Lightning, Operation (n/a)
1Jan-21Apr71. 173d Abn. Binh Dinh Pr, II Corps.

Greene Storm, Operation (n/a)
5Feb-15Mar71. 173d Abn. Binh Dinh Pr, II Corps.

Greene Sure 17, Operation (n/a)
Mar-21Apr71. 173d Abn. Binh Dinh Pr, II Corps.

Greene, FSB (XD 754-607)
Apx 10 km E Laos, 38 km W Cam Lo, 6 km NE FSB Argonne, 7 km E LZ Bell, 30 km NW FSB Elliott CB and 4 km S southern edge of DMZ. On map, p 58, *US Marines in Vietnam-1969*. 101st Abn inactive FSB grid per Don Armstrong. Also listed at XD 73-62. Quang Tri Pr, I Corps.

Greenville Victory, USNS (n/a)
See Da Nang, Evacuation of, in Glossary.

Greer, FSB (YD 989-041)
A.k.a. Hill 162 and possibly FSB Rock Crusher? About 1 km from shore of Dam Cau Hai bay, 10 km WNW Phu Loc, 16 km SE Phu Bai and 600 meters SW QL-1. 101st Abn inactive FSB grid per Don Armstrong. See FSB Rock Crusher. Feb69. Thua Thien Pr, I Corps.

Gregory, LZ (YD 350-422)
Apx 9 km S Quang Tri, 11 km SW Hai Lang and 22 km NW Camp Evans. Apr70 XXIV Corps grid per Don Armstrong. Thua Thien Pr, I Corps.

Gresham, USCGC (n/a)
WHEC 387. 4May67-28Jan68. Sqdn 3 CGC, during Coast Guard's 1st deployment.

Grey, FSB (YS 207-933)
At the Binh Son Rubber Plantation just S of Ap Binh Son, apx 6 km SE Long Thanh North AF and 27 km WSW Xuan Loc. Per Richard Shand, was operated by Royal Thai Army and had a section of 105 Howitzers. Jan68-Nov69. Also listed at YS 200-930. Bien Hoa Pr, III Corps.

Greyhound (n/a)
6Apr70, XXIV Corps future-use 5th Div FSB name.

Gridley, USS (n/a)
DLG-21. Guided-Missile DD Ldr, per Ralph Fries.

Grizzly (n/a)
6Apr70, XXIV Corps future-use 5th Div FSB name.

Groovy, LZ (AQ?)
Said to have been near Ban Me Thuot. 3d Bn/503d Inf 173d Abn, '68-69. Darlac Pr?, II Corps.

Groucho Marx Battle (XD 986-599)
Apx 12 km W Cam Lo and 3 km SW peak Dong Ha Mtn. Rescue mission of heavily engaged Groucho Marx 1st Force Recon Team in Razorback Valley, 8Aug66. Involved elements of HMM-161 and Echo/2d/4th Marines. Half of team was extracted when ground fire forced an abort, leaving 23 men on ground inc HMM-161 helicopter crew members from downed acft. Extraction was completed following day. 5 US KIA, 27 WIA. Quang Tri Pr, I Corps.

Groupement Blinde (n/a)
See Glossary.

Groupement de Commandos Mixtes (n/a)
See Glossary.

Groupement Mixtes d'Intervention (n/a)
See Glossary.

Groupement Mobile 100 (BR, et al)
See Glossary.

Groupement Operationne du Nord-Ouest
See GONO in Glossary.

Grouse, LZ (XD 955-594)
Apx 17 km W Cam Lo, 6 km NW Thon Son Lam and 29 km due W Dong Ha. XXIV Corps grid per Don Armstrong. Quang Tri Pr, I Corps.

Grove Jones Airfield (VE 48-64)
LS-141. CIA/SF, per *Air Facilities Data-Laos*.

Grove Jones 2 Airfield (VE 27-94)
LS-141A. Apx 180 km due E Vientiane, 80 km NNW NKP AB, 100 km W SVN border and 15 km E Cambodia, per ONC-J-11. CIA/SF facility. Grid per *Air Facilities Data-Laos*. El. 492'. Laos.

Grunt, FSB/LZ (n/a)
Per Peter Cole, was listed by W. Stan Tyson (CO 1st/12th Cav Sep71-Jun72). If Tyson was referring to his time frame as CO, Cav was in western III Corps. See LZ Grunt (AT 957-112). Likely III Corps?

Grunt, LZ (AT 957-112)
At or adj to Ton Ban, apx 16 km WSW Tien Phuoc AF, 39 km E Kham Duc and 37 km WSW Tam Ky. Americal list. Quang Tin Pr, I Corps.

Guadalcanal, LZ (BS 863-377)
On coast, apx 5 km E Duc Pho AF, 5 km E QL-1 and 40 km SE Quang Ngai. Apr-May67. Quang Ngai Pr, I Corps.

Guadalcanal, LZ (YD 266-332)
Apx 12 km SW Ba Long AF and 18 km SSW of Quang Tri. Apr70 XXIV Corps grid per Don Armstrong. Quang Tri Pr, I Corps.

Guadalupe, USS (n/a)
AO-32. Aux Oiler, per Ralph Fries.

Guang Khe (n/a)
Mapsheet name of L-7014-6244-2. NVN only.

Guard Channel (n/a)
See Glossary.

Gueao, Mui (CP 1-5)
Cape at 12°13'N-109°20'E. On ND49-13 JOG. Khanh Hoa Pr, II Corps.

Guerra Bridge (CQ 06-73?)
QL-1 bridge between Tuy Hoa and Song Cau. If listed grid correct, was immed NW Ha Yen, apx 17 km S of Song Cau. Named to honor Sp5 Jerry Guerra, KIA 28Aug67. Data per Ray Bows. Binh Dinh Pr, II Corps.

Guin, FSB (ZT 100-190)
Possibly FSB Guinn? Apx 31 km WNW Phan Thiet, 36 km NNE Ham Tan AF, 9 km SE peak Dang S'Ruin Mtn, 16 km due S FSB Bangor and 125 km ENE Saigon. If Guinn was proper sp, then site possibly named to honor Army Sp4 Robert G. Guinn, KIA 4Jun70. Opened by 199th LIB, closed 26Oct70, by 2d/8th Cav. Data per *1st Cav Div Op Rpt, ending 31Oct70*, courtesy Peter Cole. 3d/7th Inf, 199th LIB here. Binh Tuy Pr, III Corps.

Guinn, FSB (ZT 100-190)
See Guin. Binh Tuy Pr, III Corps.
Guio, Pointe (BN 2-2)
See Pointe Guio. Binh Thuan Pr, II Corps.
Gulf of Tonkin Incident (n/a)
See Glossary.
Gulf of Tonkin (C 8-1)
A.k.a. Vinh Bac Bo and Vinh Bac Phan. Anglo and French name for Vinh Bac Phan, the gulf of South China Sea formed by coast of NVN, northern SVN and southern China. NVN/SVN.
Gulf, LZ (YD 198-305)
Apparently a.k.a. LZ Monterey (YD 199-305). Apx 11 km ESE Ta Laou, 10 km SSE Ba Long AF and 24 km SW Quang Tri. Apr70 XXIV Corps grid per Don Armstrong. Quang Tri Pr, I Corps.
Gunfighter (n/a)
6Apr70, XXIV Corps future-use III MAF FSB name.
Gunfighter Village (BT 008-754)
Home of 8th(?) Tactical fighter Wing TFW) at Da Nang. Grid is for AB. Quang Nam Pr, I Corps.
Gunflint (n/a)
See Glossary.
Gunner, LZ (XD 891-261)
In Vietnam Salient, apx 5 km SW Lang Klung, 17 km SSE Khe Sanh CB and 21 km SW Ba Long AF. Apr70 XXIV Corps grid per Don Armstrong. Also listed at XD 977-313. Quang Tri Pr, I Corps.
Gunner, LZ (XD 977-313)
Apx 2 km from Laos, 43 km SW Quang Tri and 6 km ENE Lang Klung. USMC, Nov68. Also listed at XD 891-261, Apr670? Quang Tri Pr, I Corps.
Gunner I, FSB (XT 970-200)
On Island in Song Dong Nai, apx 6 km N Bien Hao AB. 12Jun67. Bien Hoa Pr, III Corps.
Gunner II, FSB (XT 917-734)
At or near Chi Linh AF. Apx 16 km WSW Dong Xoai. 11Jun67. Also XT 915-735? Binh Long Pr, III Corps.
Gunner III, FSB (YT 062-754)
A.k.a. FSB Geisha/Giessa. Immed S Dong Xoai AF and apx 27 km NNE Phuoc Vinh AF. 19Jun67. Phuoc Long Pr, III Corps.
Gunners' Day (YS 4-5)
26May. Anniversary of birth of 161 Royal New Zealand Arty. On 26May69, the 253rd birthday of the Rgt, 161 Bty fired a white phosphorus mission into Long Hai hills such that impacts formed the burning numerals "161." Per *Vietnam Gunners,* p 89. Phuoc Tuy Pr, III Corps.
Gunnison (n/a)
6Apr70, XXIV Corps future-use 5th Div FSB name.
Guns Base Camp (AR 809-354)
At Camp Enari/Hensel AF, apx 14 km SSE Pleiku. Sep69. Pleiku Pr, II Corps.
Gurhka, FSB (XD 826-482)
Just S of Ap La Vien, 4 km NE Khe Sanh CB and 28 km WSW Mai Loc. 101st Abn inactive FSB grid per Don Armstrong. Quang Tri Pr, I Corps.
Gurke, USS (n/a)
DD-783, per Ralph Fries.
Guy Fawkes Night (n/a)
See Glossary.
Gwen, LZ (XT 526-796)
See Mary Gwen. Tay Ninh Pr, III Corps.
Gwyn, FSB (XT 85-86)
Apx 7 km SSE Quan Loi, 10 km ESE An Loc and 23 km WNW Dong Xoai. 11th ACR here. Grid per Frank Penk, Jr. Binh Long Pr, III Corps.
Gypsy, LZ (ZA 062-447)
Just N of QL-19B, apx 3 km W Ban Duc, 19 km W Pleiku, and within 1 km of site of LZ Cathy. Per Bud Harton, was 4th Div FSB, Jan69. John Grocki says B/1st/35th Inf here '68 or '69, and describes it as having been in valley adj to mtn with flat spot on top that was site of abnd LZ "Cathy" (YA 966-703) but possibly he meant LZ Jane, which nearby at ZA 057-436). Grocki adds that Gypsy was "a rat hole. B 1st/35th lifted out of the Oasis and flew to this small, abnd base in Sep or Oct69. Just some remnants of sand bag bunkers when we got there. After we secured the perimeter, people started coming from everywhere and, 2 days later, we had a bunker line and perimeter wire. We slept in mud and ate C's while there was a mess tent set up for arty guys. One or two rounds of mortar fire blew up that mess tent one day!" Per Wayne Gass, it "was very near Cambodian border, and a very <u>big</u> FSB. Months after we left, the Engrs tore it down and in one of bunkers found an 18 foot Python. We always wondered why we never saw any rats!" Grid per Dick Arnold, who adds that 1st/35th Inf here Jul69. Pleiku Pr, II Corps.
GYROJET Pistol (n/a)
See Glossary.

HOTEL

Facility/Feature Name, Grid Coordinate, a.k.a. Name/History/Province/CTZ

Unless otherwise stated, 6-digit grid coordinates reference DMA L-7014, L-7015 or L-7016 series, 1:50,000 scale maps, while 2- and 4-digit coordinates reference AMS/DMA/NIMA 1:250,000, 1:500,000 and 1:1,000,000 scale maps. Unless otherwise stated, all heights are in meters. To convert meters to feet, multiply by 3.2808; feet to meters, multiply by .3048.

H-1 (TJ 9-6)
A.k.a. Huguette 1. Apx 2 km NW Dien Bien Phu main CP, immed N of C1 and 1 mi due S H6. One of the 6 Huguettes (a.k.a. H1 thru H6), defensive positions at DBP. In Muong Thanh Valley, apx 290 km W Hanoi. French strongpoint, Op Castor, 20Nov53-7May54. Fell to Vietminh 23Apr54. NVN.

H-2 (TJ 9-6)
A.k.a. Huguette 2. Somewhere NW Dien Bien Phu main CP. One of the 6 "Huguettes" (a.k.a. H1 thru H6), defensive positions at DBP. Muong Thanh Valley, apx 290 km W Hanoi. French strongpoint, Op Castor, 20Nov53-7May54. On 18Mar54 and under heavy pressure from Vietminh, Capt. Bizard's men holding H-6 abandoned it in dead run to H-2, catching Vietminh completely off-guard. H-2 fell to Vietminh 2May54. NVN.

H-3 (TJ 9-6)
A.k.a. Huguette 3. Somewhere NW Dien Bien Phu main CP. One of 6 Huguettes (a.k.a. H1 thru H6), defensive positions at DBP. In Muong Thanh Valley, apx 290 km W Hanoi. French strongpoint, Op Castor, 20Nov53-7May54. Fell to Vietminh 18Mar54. Under heavy pressure from enemy, the men under Capt. Bizard holding H-6 abnd it and ran to H-2, catching the Vietminh completely off-guard (H-2 fell 2May54). NVN.

H-4 (TJ 9-6)
A.k.a. Huguette 4. Apx 2.1 mi NW Dien Bien Phu main CP, .6 mi SW H6 and .75 mi NNW H1. One of the 6 Huguettes (a.k.a. H1 thru H6), defensive positions at DBP, situated in Muong Thanh Valley apx 290 km W Hanoi. French strongpoint during Op Castor, 20Nov53-7May54. H-4 fell to Vietminh on 4May54, the last French position to be overrun prior to general surrender of 7May54. NVN.

H-5 (TJ 9-6)
A.k.a. Huguette 5. Somewhere to NW Dien Bien Phu main CP. One of the 6 Huguettes (a.k.a. H1 thru H6) defensive positions at DBP. In Muong Thanh Valley apx 290 km W Hanoi. French strongpoint during Op Castor, 20Nov53-7May54. Heavily attacked 1May54 and overrun 2May.

H-6 (TJ 9-6)
A.k.a. Huguette 6. Apx 2 mi NNW Dien Bien Phu main CP, 1 mi N H1 and .6 mi NE H4. One of the 6 Huguettes (a.k.a. H1 thru H6), defensive positions at DBP. In Muong Thanh Valley, apx 290 km W Hanoi. Fell to Vietminh 2May54. NVN.

H-9 (YA/YB?)
See Hotel 9.

Ha Binh (BT 24-45)
Near listed grid and apparently on what was known as Barrier Island, a 2d NVA Div staging area in coastal lowlands near Chu Lai. Americal list AO, I Corps.

Ha Coi (n/a)
Mapsheet name of L-7014-6551-1. NVN only.

Ha Dong (n/a)
Mapsheet name of L-7014-6150-1. NVN only.

Ha Dong Bridge (AT 991-641)
Railroad Bridge over Song Bau Xau, apx 13 km SSW Da Nang AB, 500 meters SE Ft. Apache, and 4 km W QL-1. AO of 7th Marine Rgt, '69, which was S flank of 1st Mar Div (and which abutted Americal's N flank). XXIV Corps grid. On map at http://1stbn1stmarines.org/hs/images/MarkedDaiLocMap.jpg. Data per John Middlesworth. Also listed at AT 995-688. Quang Nam Pr, I Corps.

Ha Giang (n/a)
Mapsheet name of L-7014-5954-1. NVN only.

Ha Giang Airfield (n/a)
Feb67 Natl Geo map. El.? NVN.

Ha Hiat Massif, du (YJ 5-3)
A.k.a. Nui Deo Hieng Mtns. Mtn range at 21°07'N-107°29'E. Grid per DMA L-1501 map NF48-12.

Ha Lo Prison (WJ 9-2)
The Hanoi Hilton. US POW prison in Hanoi. NVN.

Ha Long Bay (YJ 1-1)
Just SW NVN's border with China, WNW Haiphong and perhaps the most famous natural feature of VN. Magnificent natural wonder including some 3,000 islands that rise sharply from clear, emerald waters of the Gulf of Tonkin. Likely also most photographed geographical feature of country. "Ha Long" translates as *Where the Dragon Descends into the Sea.* At 20°55'00"N-107°05'00"E. NVN.

Ha Long, Vinh (YJ 1-1)
Bay at 20°55'N-107°05'E. On NF48-16 JOG. NVN.

Ha Nha Hill (AT 787-553)
A.k.a. Hill 52. Apx 6 km E Ha Tan, 29 km SW Da Nang AB. XXIV Corps grid. Possible USMC position. Quang Nam Pr, I Corps.

Ha Noi (Hanoi) (WJ 88-25)
Mapsheet name of L-7014-6151-2. NVN only.

Ha Noi (WJ 88-25)
See Hanoi. NVN.

Ha Tan (ZC 162-480)
Apx 35 km SW Da Nang and 22 km NW Phuoc Binh AF. Dist HQ and AF here. USMC Quang Nam Pr, I Corps.

Ha Tan (Thuong Duc) (n/a)
Map is L-7014-6540-1. Sheet name: Thuong Duc (Ha Tan). SVN.
Ha Tan Airfield (ZC 152-540)
Apx 35 km SW Da Nang and 22 km NW Phuoc Binh AF, per TPC K-10A. El. 66', 2,300' sod/clay/rock rwy. At 15°51'50"N-107°56'31"E. Quang Nam Pr, I Corps.
Ha Tat (BR 799-820?)
Likely sp variant of Ha Tay. See Ha Tay SF Camp and AF. SF Det 53 said to have been here. Binh Dinh Pr, II Corps.
Ha Tay (BR 80-82)
Apx 6 km ENE Phu Xuan, 66 km NNW Qui Nhon, 15 km SSW Bong Son/Hoai Nhon and 19 km NNW Phu My-QL-1. AF, SF Camp and LZ Pony here. Binh Dinh Pr, II Corps.
Ha Tay (2) (BR 798-833)
Roughly 66 km NNW Qui Nhon, 6 km ENE Phu Xuan, 15 km SSW Bong Son/Hoai Nhon and 19 km NNW Phu My-QL-1. Hay Tay (2)? SF Camp a.k.a. LZ Pony. See Ha Tay. Map is L-7014-6737-1 (Hoai An). Grid/map info per Ray Smith. Binh Dinh Pr, II Corps.
Ha Tay, FSB? (BR 803-837)
At Ha Tay AF/SF Camp, 21 km SSW Bong Son. 2d/17th Arty here 20-23Oct65, during Op Claudine suptg 1st/8th Cav. Data per Jack Picciolo. Binh Dinh Pr, II Corps.
Ha Tay Airfield (BR 799-829)
Apx 66 km NNW Qui Nhon, 6 km ENE Phu Xuan, 15 km SSW Bong Son/Hoai Nhon and 19 km NNW Phu My (QL-1). "Security ck SF Pleiku (C-7), US Army, 11Apr69, Arty site near western edge, AF # VA2-300," in Aug69 TAD per Frank Penk, Jr. Not in Feb73 TAD. Binh Dinh Pr, II Corps.
Ha Tay SF Camp (BR 799-820)
A.k.a. Hay Tay (2) and LZ Pony? Apx 66 km NNW Qui Nhon, 6 km ENE Phu Xuan, 15 km SSW Bong Son/Hoai Nhon and 19 km NNW Phu My (QL-1). 5th SF camp, Det A-227 (and Det 53?). Grid per *SF Order of Battle.* Transferred to RF/PF. Also listed at BR 798-833. Map is L-7014-6737-1. Binh Dinh Pr, II Corps.
Ha Thanh (BS 395-705)
Ville along LTL-5B, apx 27 km S Tra Bong AF and 25 km due W Quang Ngai. LZ Shirley and CIDG Camp were apx 2 km SW ville. Also listed at 428-718? Americal list. Quang Ngai Pr, I Corps.
Ha Thanh (2) (BS 390-701)
SF Camp? Quang Ngai Pr, I Corps.
Ha Thanh, LZ (BS 386-704)
E of LTL-5B, apx 28 km S Tra Bong AF, and 27 km due W Quang Ngai. Apr70 XXIV Corps grid per Don Armstrong. Quang Ngai Pr, I Corps.
Ha Thanh, Old (BS 39-70?)
See Son Ha. Quang Ngai Pr, I Corps.
Ha Thanh Airfield (BS 390-700)
Along LTL-5B, apx 18 km S Tra Bong AF and 27 km W Quang Ngai. El. 131', 1,300' steel-mat rwy. At 15°05'38"N-108°33'51"E. Quang Ngai Pr, I Corps.
Ha Thanh Relocation Camp (YD 220-680)
Along QL-1, apx 22 km NW Quang Tri and 10 km NNW Dong Ha. Oct68. Quang Tri Pr, I Corps.
Ha Thanh SF Camp (BS 3867-7005)
CIDG Camp apx 28 km S Tra Bong AF, and 27 km W Quang Ngai. A-104 SF Camp, opened 28 Apr 65-Aug 70, then converted to ARVN 87th Border Rangers (Old Ha Thanh was apparently a.k.a. Son Ha). LZ Shirley here? Grid per *Special Forces of Battle.* Quang Ngai Pr, I Corps.
Ha Tien (VS 44-47)
Capitol, Kien Giang Pr, IV Corps.
Ha Tien (new) SF Camp (VS 438-484)
Apx 3km E Ha Tien North AF, 6 km ESE point where the Cambodian and SVN border meet Gulf of Thailand. Likely the westernmost SF camp on mainland SVN. 5th SF Grp, Det. A-421 (was 311), Oct65. SF Det 80. Grid per *SF Order of Battle.* Became RF/PF. Kien Giang Pr, IV Corps.
Ha Tien (new), Camp (VS 533-551)
See Tra Phu. IV Corps.
Ha Tien (old) SF Camp (VS 419-495)
At Ha Tien N AF, apx 3 km SE point where Cambodian and SVN border meet Gulf of Thailand. 5th SF Grp, Det. A-421 (was 311), Oct65. SF Det 80? Data per *SF Order of Battle.* Moved to Ha Tien (new). Kien Giang Pr, IV Corps.
Ha Tien, Camp (VS 472-497)
See Cu Duc. IV Corps.
Ha Tien Lighthouse (VS 44-47)
On coastal point apx 6 km due S point where Cambodian and SVN borders meet ocean, and 5 km WSW Ha Tien. Kien Giang Pr, IV Corps.
Ha Tien North Airfield (VS 419-495)
Apx 3 km SE point where Cambodian-SVN border meets Gulf of Thailand, 245 km WSW Saigon, 4 km NW Ha Tien and 7 km NW Ha Tien South AF. One of 2 minor AFs near Ha Tien and westernmost mainland airfield in SVN. Per TPC K-10D. El. 10', 1,800' laterite rwy. At 10°23'58"N-104°27'55"E. Kien Giang Pr, IV Corps.
Ha Tien PBR Base (VS 44-47?)
USN River Patrol Boat Staging Area, '68-70, per MRF Assn Website. Kien Giang Pr, IV Corps.
Ha Tien South Airfield (VS 457-455)
Apx 1 km from coast, 9 km SE point where SVN and Cambodia borders meet ocean, apx 245 km WSW Saigon, 3 km SE Ha Tien and 7 km SE Ha Tien AF. One of 2 minor AFs here, per TPC K-10D. El. 10', 1,300' sod-gravel rwy. 10°21'45"N-104°30'10"E. Kien Giang Pr, IV Corps.
Ha Tinh (n/a)
Mapsheet name of L-7014-6145-1. NVN only.
Ha Tinh (WF 81-04)
Apx 72 km SSW Vinh, 50 km N Mu Gia Pass and 220 km NW Quang Tri. Ville used as waypoint for NVA troops moving S to Ho Chi Minh Trail. NVN.
Ha Tinh Airfield (WF 81-04)
Apx 72 km SSW Vinh, 50 km N Mu Gia Pass and 220 km NW Quang Tri. El. 98'. NVN.
Ha Trung Lagoon (YD 9-2)
A.k.a. Lagune Ha Trung and Dam Ha Trung. Lagoon at 16°29'00"N-107°44'00"E. On NE48-16 JOG. Thua Thien Pr, I Corps.
Ha Trung, Dam (YD 9-2)
Lagoon at 16°29'N-107°44'E. On NE48-16 JOG. Thua Thien Pr, I Corps.
Ha Vung, Thon (Ba Long) (n/a)
Mapsheet L-7014-6442-3. True sheet name: Ba Long (Thon Ha Vung). SVN.
Ha Yen Cross (CQ 065-735)
Apx 4 km NW Ha Yen, 10 km NNW Tuy An AF, 2 km W QL-1 and 15 km ENE Dong Tre. Phu Yen Pr, II Corps.

Habans, Plateau des (AR 8-4)
Plateau de Kontum. Pleiku Pr, II Corps.
Hac Bo (n/a)
See Glossary.
Hackney, LZ (XD 987-321)
Apx 16 km SE Khe Sanh CB, 19 km WSW Ba Long AF and 16 km S Ca Lu. Possibly named to honor either SP4 Donnie L. Hackney, KIA 19Aug69, or SSgt Tate T. Hackney, KIA 22Jun68, both US Army. Apr70 XXIV Corps grid per Don Armstrong. Quang Tri Pr, I Corps.
HACOM, US ARMY (XS 830-895)
In Cofat Cmpd, Saigon. Army HQ Area Cmd (HACOM), unit responsible for managing, among other things, Saigon area military mess halls, billets and clubs. In Sep62 Responsibility shifted to USN HEDSUPPACT (HQ Supt Activity), but regained by HACOM, Dec 65. Prior to '63, was site of Cofat Cigarette Mfg Co. Gia Dinh Pr, III Corps.
Haeng Ho 6, Operation (n/a)
23Sep-9Nov66. ROK Capital Div op. 1,161 rptd VC KIA, per *VN Order of Battle*, pp 9-14. Binh Dinh Pr, II Corps.
Hai Ba Trung District (n/a)
One of Hanoi's 4 districts (Quan): Hoan Kiem Dist (city center); Ba Dinh Dist (west area, inc Ho Chi Minh's Tomb); Hai Ba Trung Dist (on Red River, S Hoan Kiem Dist); and Dong Da Dist (SW area).
Hai Dong (n/a)
Mapsheet name of L-7014-6836-1. SVN.
Hai Duong (XJ)
Mapsheet name of L-7014-6250-1. NVN only.
Hai Duong (XJ 38-15)
Roughly halfway between Haiphong and Hanoi. Railroad junction and canal network here led to southern Red River Delta. French position during French War. Cited in *Street Without Joy*, p 114. Power plants, rail yards, naval facilities, barracks, and industrial plants here hit by Carrier TF-77 attempt to blunt NVA Tet '68 offensive. NVN.
Hai Duong Bridge (XJ 38-15)
In SW portion of Haiphong. RR bridge hit by Carrier TF-77 attempt to blunt NVA Tet '68 offensive. NVN.
Hai Lang (YD 416-479)
At NE corner of intersection of Rte 602 and QL-1, apx 9 km SE of Quang Tri. Quang Tri Pr, I Corps.
Hai Lang, FSB (YD 415-479)
Apx 9 km SE Quang Tri and 500 meters E QL-1, in coastal lowlands. Army's 5th/4th Arty suptd 1st Bde/5th Mech Div from FSBs Sharon, Hai Lang and Nancy during '69. Quang Tri Pr, I Corps.
Hai Lang (Thon Dien Sanh) (n/a)
Mapsheet name of L-7014-6442-2. SVN.
Hai Lang District HQ (YD 416-479)
Along QL-1, apx 8 km SE Quang Tri and 40 km NW Hue. Map is L-7014-6442-2. Quang Tri Pr, I Corps.
Hai Lang Heliport (YD 415-482)
At Hai Lang, along QL-1, apx 8 km SE Quang Tri and 40 km NW Hue. Heliport #573, alt 33', at 16°42'30"N-107°16'00"E, per Feb73 TAD. Quang Tri Pr, I Corps.
Hai Lang National Forest (YD 3-3 and 4-4?)
A.k.a. NVA Base Area 101. Rugged hill mass S Quang Tri. Site of Ops Medina and Bastion Hill (Lam Son 138), 3d Mar Div effort to push 5th and 6th NVA Rgts out of area 11-15Oct67. On NE 1/4 of mapsheet L-7014-6442-3. Quang Tri Pr, I Corps.
Hai Long (Ap Long Linh) (n/a)
Mapsheet name of L-7014-6630-1. SVN.
Hai Ninh (n/a)
Mapsheet name of L-7014-6731-4. SVN.
Hai Phong (Haiphong) (XJ 75-07)
Mapsheet name of L-7014-6350-4. NVN only.
Hai Phong (XJ 75-07)
See Haiphong. NVN.
Hai Quan (n/a)
See Glossary.
Hai Van Bridge (AT 93-91)
Ql-1 bridge S of Hai Van Pass, apx 8 km due N Red Beach AF and 16 km NNW Da Nang AB. XXIV Corps grid. Quang Nam Pr, I Corps.
Hai Van Heliport (AT 933-915)
In the Hai Van Pass along QL-1, apx 17 km NNW Dan Nang AB, 2 km W FSB Moccasin and 4 km due N Ap Kim Liem. Heliport #622, alt 1,969', at: 16°11'30"N-108°07'45"E, per Feb73 TAD. TAD lists name as Nai Van, but that is apparent typo. Thua Thien Pr, I Corps.
Hai Van LAAM Site (AT 944-917)
See LAAM Sites. 1st LAAM Bn (479 men) had Bty A on Hill 724, N Hai Van Pass in Aug66. Per Ed Escoffier, 44th Arty, USN personnel at Hai Van site offered the "Best chow in Vietnam!" Quang Nam Pr?, I Corps.
Hai Van Pass (AT 94-93)
A.k.a. Deo Hai Van, Deo Dea Nuages or Pass of the Ocean Clouds. Famous QL-1 mtn pass overlooking the ocean apx 17 km NNW Da Nang AB. Noted for beautiful vistas and prime opportunity its terrain offered for NVA/VC ambush. Thua Thien/Quan Nam Prvs, I Corps.
Hai Van Peninsula (AT 98-94)
Apx 17 km due N of Da Nang AB, where steep mtns plunge into Gulf of Tonkin. Thua Tien Pr, I Corps.
Hai Van, FSB (AT 944-920)
Apx 27 km WSW Phu Loc, 16 km NNW Da Nang and 1 km E QL-1. XXIV Corps grid. Thua Thien Pr, I Corps.
Hai Yen Airfield (VQ 849-818)
See Binh Hung AF. An Xuyen Pr, IV Corps.
Hai Yen SF Camp (VQ 845-815)
At or near Binh Hung AF, apx 47 km SW Quan Long. 5th SF. Info/grid per *SF Order of Battle.* See Binh Hung. An Xuyen Pr, IV Corps.
Haines, Camp (YD 77-14?)
Seabee Camp said to have been S of the main USMC CB at Phu Bai and also said to have been at Hue? Named to honor EOC John C. Jr, Haines, USN, NMCB-4, KIA 7Mar67, when his jeep hit mine between An Hoa and Da Nang, NMCB-11, 28Jun69-18Nov69. Beginning Feb68, NMCB-4 elements here responsible for many major facilities of and around Phu Bai AF, and on 3Jun68, a Det from Haines began major expansion of Camp Evans, erecting apx 1000 wooden bldgs, resurfacing-matting 2,900-ft rwy, and building 23-mile, 8" Petro line to the Army's camp. Thua Thien Pr, I Corps. [251]
Haiphong (XJ 75-07)
A.k.a. Hai Phong. Apx 70 km SE Hanoi, and the major seaport of NVN. Because it was port to Soviet-bloc ships supplying NVA, bombing here was restricted for fear it

might damage those ships and give China or Russia excuse to enter war. 1st bombed 20Apr67, and in '68, but not again until '72, when it was also mined for 1st time (along with other NVN ports/waterways) in response to NVA Easter Offensive. On 24Sep40, Japanese planes bombed Haiphong and landed troops there that night. In Nov46, fight broke out between French troops and resentful Vietminh and, in response, a French vessel opened fire on city. In resulting panic and gunfire, some 6,000 Vietnamese were killed; an event that helped precipitate 1st Indochina War (see Hanoi entry for 19Dec46 incident). At 1,515 sq-km, today is VN's 3d largest city and main industrial city of N. Although a major port, it apparently has little street traffic. 2 major RR stations here: Thuong Li Station in far W, and Hai Phong Station in city center. NVN.

Haiphong (Hai Phong) (XJ 75-07)
Mapsheet L-7014-6350-4. Sheet name: Hai Phong (Haiphong). NVN only.

Haiphong Airfield (XJ-68-02)
Apx 80 km ESE Hanoi and 8 km SW that city. NVN.

Haiphong Station (XJ 75-07?)
One of 2 major RR stations within Haiphong's city limits: The Thuong Li Station (far W part of city), and Hai Phong Station (in city center). Presumably bombed heavily at times. See Haiphong. NVN.

Hair Pin, The (XD 92-40)
See Hairpin. Quang Tri Pr, I Corps.

Hairpin, The (XD 92-40)
Terrain feature on QL-9 E, roughly 7 km WSW Da Krong Bridge, and 9 km ESE Khe Sanh. Apx location on *Leatherneck* Magazine map at: www.monboys.com. Grid is est. Quang Tri Pr, I Corps.

Hairpin Curve, The (BR 582-438)
On QL-19E, apx 10 km E An Khe/Radcliff and 12 km W Binh Khe. Data per Jim Claeys. Binh Dinh Pr, II Corps.

Hal, LZ (XT 510-220)
Apx 5 km NNE Dau Tieng. Also listed at XT 500-290. Feb66. Hau Nghia Pr, III Corps.

Half Moon, USCGC (n/a)
WHEC 378. 4May67-29Dec67. Sqdn 3 CGC, during Coast Guard's 1st deployment.

Half Way Quarry (YT 985-700)
On QL-20, apx 10 km SW Bao Loc, 16 km NE Da Hoa and 110 km NE Bien Hoa AB. Oct71. Lam Dong Pr, II Corps.

Hall, FSB? (n/a)
Location unknown. 7th/8th Arty here '70. Name per Dan Gillotti, 15th Arty. III Corps.

Halle Concession, Plantation de (XT 8-4)
Plantation de Halle Concession (also spelled Hallet), a.k.a. Don Dien Halle. Binh Duong Pr, III Corps.

Halong, Baie d' (YJ 1-1)
A.k.a. Vinh Ha Long. Bay at 20°55'N-107°05'E. On NF48-16 JOG. NVN.

Halsey, LZ (BT 011-442)
In Que Son Mtns, apx 32 km due S Da Nang AB, 18 km SW Hoi An and 14 km W LZ Baldy. XXIV Corps grid. Quang Nam Pr, I Corps.

Halsey, USS (n/a)
DLG-23. Guided-Missile DD Ldr, per Ralph Fries.

Halvorson BEQ (XS 8-9)
At 72 Tran Tan Phat St., May 6568, 76 rms, Saigon. Named to honor SSgt Ernest J. Halvorson, C-123 Loadmaster, KIA 24Oct64, suptg SF border surveillance Camp at Bu Ghia Map (95 mi NNE Saigon), when his C-123 hit by ground fire and crashed in Cambodia. Data per *Vietnam Military Lore, 1959-197.3.* Gia Dinh Pr, III Corps.

Ham and Motherfuckers (n/a)
See Glossary.

Ham Long (XS 36-35)
Ville on Cu Lao Ban Island apx 10 km SW Dong Tam and 14 km WNW Truc Giang/Ben Tre. Kien Hoa Pr, IV Corps.

Ham Long Heliport (XS 367-354)
Along TL-30, apx 3 km N Mekong River, 10 km SW Dong Tam, 14 km WNW Truc Giang/Ben Tre, and 4 km WSW Ap An Thanh. "Heliport #574, alt 7', Soccer Field. Fly low level from river to S and depart same way, at 10°16'30"N-106°15'00"E," per Feb73 TAD. Kien Hoa Pr, IV Corps.

Ham Long River (XS 7-0)
See Ham Luong River. Kien Hoa Pr, IV Corps.

Ham Luong River (XS 7-0)
Generally 35 km SE Truc Giang/Ben Tre and 28 km ENE Tra Vinh, near mouth of one branch of Mekong. In Sep68, focus of 9th Inf/MRF ops. Also sp Ham Long. Data per MRF Assn website. Kien Hoa Pr, IV Corps. [252]

Ham Nghi BOQ (XS 8-9)
At 171 Ham Nghi St., prior to Jul 62-68, 19 rms, Saigon. Per R. Bows' *Vietnam Military Lore, 1959-1973.* Gia Dinh Pr, III Corps.

Ham Rong Bridge (n/a)
Apx 150 km S Hanoi. Bridge crossing river at North edge of Thanh Hoa. For many NVA troops, represented the beginning of Ho Chi Minh Trail. Very heavily bombed (approaches to it remain severely cratered) and finally, after years of unsuccessful attempts, was destroyed by Smart Bombs, 13May72, during Op Linebacker. NVN.

Ham Rong Mountain (AR?)
A.k.a. Hill 1162? Pleiku Pr?, II Corps.

Ham Rong Mountain (US 868-488)
A.k.a. Hill 365. Phu Quoc Island, IV Corps.

Ham Tam (ZS?)
See Ham Tan. Binh Tuy Pr, III Corps.

Ham Tan (n/a)
Mapsheet name of L-7014-6530-2.

Ham Tan (ZS 020-825)
Along LTL-23, apx 45 km SW Phan Thiet, 82 km ENE Vung Tau and 5 km from and La Gi and the ocean. Also sp Ham Tam in some texts. Capitol, Binh Tuy Pr, III Corps.

Ham Tan (MAAG) Heliport (ZS 045-800)
On ocean, at E edge of La Gi, 8 km SE Ham Tan AF and 40 km SW Phan Thiet. Heliport #575, alt 16', 10°39'45"N-107°47'30"E, per Feb73 TAD. Binh Tuy Pr, III Corps.

Ham Tan Airfield (YS 988-841)
Apx 5 km NW Ham Tan, 45 km WSW Phan Thiet AF and 70 km ENE Vung Tau. Per TPC K-10A. El. 34', 3,400' laterite rwy. Binh Tuy Pr, III Corps. At 10°41'50"N-107°43'58"E.

Ham Tan Signal Site (ZS?)
No data. Possibly a.k.a. Ham Tan Station (ZS 03-79), or at or near Ham Tan AF? Binh Tuy Pr?, III Corps.

Ham Tan Station (ZS 03-79)
On coast, at W side of La Gi, 6 km SE Ham Tan AF and 43 km SW Phan Thiet. Adv Team 87, 2d Corps Adv Grp possibly here. Binh Tuy Pr, III Corps.
Ham Tan, FSB (YS 98-84)
A.k.a. FSB Riviera or Old Ham. Apx 5 km NW Ham Tan, 45 km WSW Phan Thiet AF and 70 km ENE Vung Tau. John Driscoll, D Bty, 5th/2d Arty, thinks he recalls small AF (used almost exclusively by Air America), small Seabee cmpd and well-appointed (had running water, and bar) MACV cmpd apx 8 km from FSB (unclear if description relative to FSB Sylvia or Ham Tan?). Adv Team 48, also 2d/3d, 3d/7th, 199th LIB. Capitol, Binh Tuy Pr, III Corps.
Ham Thuan Bac (n/a)
Mapsheet name of L-7014-6631-3. SVN.
Ham Thuan District HQ (AN 8-1?)
On 19Sep69, 3d/506th Inf established Liaison team at this facility, inc 1 US officer and 1 NCO. Data per *Currahee History, 1Feb69-31Dec69*, p 43. Binh Thuan Pr, II Corps.
Hamburger Hill (YC 328-981)
A.k.a. Dong Ap Bia, Hill 937, FSB Destiny, and to local Montagnard as The Mountain if the Crouching Beast. At NW end of A Shau Valley, apx 45 km WSW Hue, 22 km NW the A Sap/A Shau AF, SF Camp/ville complex, 9 km NW Ta Bat, 3 km E Laos and 25 km SE Tou Rout. Site of one of last major hill fights of war, 10-20May69. During Op Apache Snow, elements of 101st Abn's 2d Bde and 1st ARVN Div suffered heavy (and very controversial) losses taking hill from 29th NVA Rgt. 3d/187th Inf, 101st Abn started the battle on 10May69. On 11May69, they assaulted to within 25 meters of its crest and might have taken it except a heavy rainstorm intervened, making the slopes a muddy quagmire. Elements of 1st/506th, 2d/506th and 2d of 501st Inf reinforced with 2d/3d Inf/1st ARVN Div all moved into position on 18-19May, then launched coordinated final assault on 20May. 56 US KIA and about 400 WIA resulted, as well as 630 enemy KIA, 3 POWs and 40 crew served weapons captured. Became very controversial in press and led to drastic reductions in aggressiveness of US ops that followed. Thua Thien Pr, I Corps.
Hamilton, FSB (XT?)
25th Inf Div FSB said to have been within arty range of FSB Jackson (XT 425-168). Apparently took friendly fire from Jackson in '70. 2d/27th (Wolfhounds) Inf here early 70. Tay Ninh Pr?, III Corps.
Hamilton, FSB (YT 003-613)
Along QL-14 between FSBs Remagen 3 and 4, apx 17 km SSW Dong Xoai, 14 km NNE Phuoc Vinh and 65 km NNE Saigon. Opened or reopened 3Aug70, closed 3Sep70. 1st/7th Cav. Data per *1st Cav Div Op Rpt, ending 31Oct70*, courtesy Peter Cole. Phuoc Long Pr, III Corps.
Hamilton, USCGC (n/a)
WHEC 715. 1Nov69-25May70. Sqdn 3 CGC, during Coast Guard's 5th deployment.
Hamlet 3 (YS 4-7?)
See Slope 30. Phuoc Tuy Pr, III Corps.
Hamlet Evaluation System (n/a)
See Glossary.
Hamlet, LZ (YD 281-662)
Apparently on island in Cua Viet River, apx 7 km SW Cua Viet CB, 13 km NNW Quang Tri and 1 km SE Vinh Quan Ha. Apr70 XXIV Corps grid per Don Armstrong. Quang Tri Pr, I Corps.
Hamlin (n/a)
6Apr70, XXIV Corps proposed 5th Div FSB name.
Hammer, FSB (BN 240-740)
Apx 28 km due N Song Mao AF and 7 km SSW Karang Go. Mar67. Tuyen Duc Pr, II Corps.
Hammer, FSB (ZC 018-942)
A.k.a. LZ Hammer. Apx 9 km SW Phu Loc, 6 km WNW Bach Ma Resort and 25 km SE Phu Bai. XXIV Corps grid. Thua Thien Pr, I Corps.
Hammer, LZ (BR 963-966)
Apx 8 km W Bong Son and 7 km SE LZ English. 1st Cav. Name/grid per Dan Gillotti. Binh Dinh Pr, II Corps.
Hammer, LZ (YS 103-784)
Apx 14 km due S Long Thanh AF and 34 km SW Tan Son Nhut AB. Jan66. Bien Hoa Pr, III Corps.
Hammer, LZ (YS 267-872)
Apx 15 km ESE Long Thanh AF and 9 km SE Ap Binh Son. Jan68. Bien Hoa Pr, III Corps.
Hammerstone, FSB (XU 500-397)
Apx 8 km NW Snuol, 11 km E Phum Sre Thom and 40 km NW Loc Ninh. Grid per *11th ACR Cambodia Invasion AAR, 1st Cav Div, May-Jun70*, courtesy Lou Rochat. [253] Also listed at XU 500-930, but likely in error Cambodia.
Hammond, LZ/FSB (BR 888-570)
On W side of QL-1 apx 10 km NNW Phu Cat AB, 20 km from coast and 12 km due S LZ Crystal. 1st Cav Bde FSB in '66, and tactical Army AF. Attacked by NVA 23Sep66 in move to ease pressure on enemy forces under attack in Kim Son and 506 Valleys during Op Thayer I. Also listed at BR 883-570 and 8775-5450 per 2d/17th Arty ORLLs courtesy Jack Picciolo. Map is L-7014-6837-3, per Ken Burrington. Binh Dinh Pr, II Corps.
Hammond Airfield (BR 881-540)
A.k.a. LZ Hammond. On W side of QL-1 about 10 km NNW Phu Cat, 20 km from coast and 12 km due S LZ Crystal. Minor US AF here per TPC K-10B. El. 66'. C-130-capable tac AF. Listed as "Abnd, security questionable 12Jan68, AF # VA2-234," in Aug69 TAD per Frank Penk, Jr. Not in Feb73 TAD. Binh Dinh Pr, II Corps.
Hamner, USS (n/a)
DD-718, per Ralph Fries.
Hampshire County, USS (n/a)
LST-819. Lndg. Ship, Tank, per Ralph Fries.
Hampton, FSB (XT 417-238)
Along QL-1, apx 3 km ESE Go Dau Ha and 25 km WNW Cu Chi. 25th Inf Div AO. Also listed at XT 410-230 and 434-241. Jul68-Jan70. Tay Ninh Pr, III Corps.
Hampton III, FSB (XT?)
Location unknown. 7th/11th Arty, 25th Div here 68. Name per Dan Gillotti, 15th Arty. Tay Ninh Pr?, III Corps.
Hamster (n/a)
6Apr70, XXIV Corps proposed 5th Div FSB name.
Han River Bridge (BT 04-76?)
In Da Nang. If grid identifies correct bridge, it connected E Da Nang with the Tien Sha Peninsula. Renamed the

Nguyen Van Troi Bridge after the war. See Nguyen Van Troi for interesting history. Quang Nam Pr, I Corps.

Han, Vung (XF 4-0)
Bay at 18°07'N-106°24'E. On NE48-07 JOG. NVN.

Hancock, USS (n/a)
CV-19, Acft Carrier. Deployed with CVW-21 18Mar75-20Oct75; with CVW-21 18Jul68-3Mar69; with CVW-21, 2Aug69-1 Apr 70; with CVW-21, 22Oct70-3 Jun 71; with CVW-21, 7Jan72-3Oct 72; with CVW-21, 8May73-8Jan 74; with CVW-21, 10Nov65-1 Aug 66; with CVW-21, 21Oct64-29May65; with CVW-5, 5Jan67-22Jul67. For assigned units, see Carrier Deployment Section. During Laotian crisis in '62, *Hancock* carrier grp and *Bennington* (CVS-20) submarine hunter-killer grp moved near Da Nang. On 7Feb65, *Coral Sea's* CVW-15 and *Hancock's* CVW-21 flew Flaming Dart I, a one-time strike at NVA barracks at Dong Hoi. 2d Rolling Thunder op took place15Mar65, as USN sent 64 Skyhawks and Skyraiders + 30 supt acft from *Hancock* and *USS Ranger* to hit Phu Qui ammo depot. See Op Eagle Pull. [254]

Hane Cohe/Ba Ngoi Airfield (CP 053-166)
See Cam Ranh AF. Khanh Hoa Pr, II Corps.

Hangi (n/a)
See Glossary.

Hanh, Mui (US 9-0)
Coastal point at 10°00'N-104°01'E. On NC48-05 JOG. Kien Giang Pr, IV Corps.

Hank, FSB (YC 910-880)
In Ruong Ruong Valley, apx 54 km WNW Da Nang AB and 22 km SW Phu Loc. '69. Thua Thien Pr, I Corps.

Hank, LZ (BR 730-570)
Apx 28 km ENE An Khe and 11 km E Vinh Thanh ville. Dec65. Binh Dinh Pr, II Corps.

Hann, FSB (n/a)
Location unknown. 2d/32d Arty, 23d Grp here 70. Name per Dan Gillotti, 15th Arty. Tay Ninh Pr?, III Corps.

Hanna, FSB (XT 032-719)
See Hannas. Mar-Apr70. Tay Ninh Pr, III Corps.

Hannas, FSB (XT 032-719)
Apx 24 km NW Tay Ninh AF, 30 km NW Tay Ninh, 12 km SSW Thien Ngon and about 6 km E Cambodia. Also listed at XT 347-717, which would put site 15 km NNE Nui Ba Den, but is thought to be in error. Cited in *Apache Sunrise*, p 78, 86 and 94, where author indicates it being named for CO of similar FSB who lost both legs when that base was overrun. He also states it was "within a half mile of river that acted as border between Cambodia and Vietnam," and described it as giant keyhole from air, running E/W, with thick jungle as keyhole's border. Base was in large circular portion of keyhole at E end, with narrow portion pointing at Cambodia. Tay Ninh Pr, III Corps.

Hanoi (WJ 88-25)
A.k.a. Ha Noi and Ha-Noi. Along Red River (Song Hong), apx 900 km N Saigon and 80 km WNW Haiphong. Capital of NVN during war, and today capital of united Vietnam. Population in '70, apx 1.1 million. In Nov46, following end of WWII and while French were reasserting their authority in VN, some 6,000 Viets died when French vessel opened fire on city during rioting here. That event signaled end to uneasy truce between the 2 powers. On 19Dec46, Vietminh cut-off power and water to Hanoi, then launched series of attacks on French positions, to which French responded with counter-attacks that recaptured all areas taken by Vietminh. As a result, Ho Chi Minh and his staff fled city for jungle where they would remain until French defeated in 1945. Events at Hanoi and Haiphong in Nov-Dec46 marked beginning of French War. HQ of Fr *1st Chasseurs Blindes* (Armored Cav), and Abn Group 1, among other Fr units. Portions of city heavily bombed by Guam-based B-52s and carrier-based acft during American War. City dotted with lakes, shaded boulevards and luxuriant parks, and foreigners often think it a slow-paced and pleasant locale. Today Hanoi is preferred by some tourists over HCMC because it has less traffic, less pollution, more trees and more open space. City's center is also regarded as architectural masterpiece, featuring many blocks retaining air of 1930's provincial French town. 2 bridges, the old Long Bien Bridge and new Chuong Duong Bridge, connect N and S parts of city. Hanoi has 4 districts or Quan. Hoan Kiem (its center); Ba Dinh District (W area that includes Ho Chi Minh's Mausoleum); Hai Ba Trung (along river S Hoan Kiem District); and Dong Da (SW area). NVN. [255]

Hanoi (Ha Noi) (n/a)
Mapsheet L-7014-6151-2. Sheet: Ha Noi (Hanoi). NVN.

Hanoi, LZ (XD 802-310)
At NW corner Vietnam Salient, apx 10 km SE Lao Bao, 12 km SSW Khe Sanh and 58 km WSW Quang Tri. '70 XXIV Corps grid per Don Armstrong. Quang Tri Pr, I Corps.

Hanoi Airfield (WJ 82-26)
See Gia Lam (Hanoi) AF. NVN.

Hanoi Army Museum (WJ 8-2)
On Dien Bien Phu St. in Hanoi. Modern day museum featuring captured US war materials, vehicles, armor and debris from acft shot down over NVN (B-52 wreckage inc). Also includes a very detailed map of maze of roadway and paths that formed the Ho Chi Minh Trail. [256]

Hanoi Hannah (n/a)
See Glossary.

Hanoi Hilton (WJ 8-2)
The Ha Lo Prison. US POW prison, Hanoi. NVN.

Hanoi Power Plant (WJ 8-2)
Knocked out by acft from *Bon Homme Richard* (CVA 31), May65. NVN.

Hansard, Patrol Base (XT 192-544)
Apx 3 km NE Tay Ninh W AF and 9 km SW Nui Ba Den. Mar69. Possibly named in honor of Capt James B. Hansard, KIA 23Oct68. Tay Ninh Pr, III Corps.

Hansen-Gowers Quarry (AN 968-862?)
In Dillard Industrial Complex, which was along QL-20 near Hip Thuan, apx 22 km SW Dalat/Lien Khuong AF, 6 km ESE Phu Hiep and 42 km SW Dalat. Named to honor Sp5 Stanley R. Hansen, USA, 102d Engr Co, and Sp4 Thomas A. Gowers, USA, 815th Engr Bn, KIA 21May70 when their convoy ambushed on Hwy 20, 32 km from Duc Trang, while en route Dalat. Tuyen Duc Pr, II Corps.

Hanson, USS (n/a)
DD-832, per Ralph Fries.

Hant, Pointe (US 9-0)
See Pointe Hant. Kien Giang Pr, IV Corps.

Hao Chu Hi Mountain (BP 82-04)
A.k.a. Hill 1451 (or 4,761'). Apx 18 km ENE Phan Rang AF. Ninh Thuan Pr?, II Corps.
Haong Su Phi (n/a)
Mapsheet name of L-7014-5954-3. NVN only.
Hap, LZ (BS 917-268)
Near coast, apx 32 km NNE Bong Son, 16 km SE Duc Pho AF and 2 km E QL-1. May67. Possibly named to honor 1Lt Edward F. Hap, KIA 20Jul66. Quang Ngai Pr, I Corps.
Hapoix, Pointe (BT 5-1)
See Pointe Hapoix. Quang Tin Pr, I Corps.
Happy, LZ (XD 774-583)
Apx 2 km N Lang Ha, 19 km NNW Khe Sanh CB and 47 km W to WSW Dong Ha. Apr70 XXIV Corps grid per Don Armstrong. Quang Tri Pr, I Corps.
Happy Valley (BP 300-800)
Generally about 65 km WSW Nha Trang? Also listed at BP 400-650, which is not a valley? Tuyen Duc Pr, II Corps.
Happy Valley (BR 625-556)
A.k.a. Vinh Thanh Valley or Suoi Cai Valley (also sp Soui Cai). Apx 28 km WNW Phu Cat and 20 km NW An Khe. 22d NVA Rgt (among other units) infiltration route to that area of northern II Corps coastal plains. Described at 69th Armor website as place Lt John Easton was KIA, 25Sep68. LZ Easton, 20 km to N, was named in his honor. Discussed in *Chickenhawk*, p 95. Map is L-7014-6739-3 and SW 1/4 of L-7014-6737-2. Binh Dinh Pr, II Corps.
Happy Valley (BS 410-079?)
Generally S of R.C. Ba Na, with Worth Ridge to its N and Charlie Ridge to its S. FSBs Rattlesnake and Bullwhip were at its W edge, and hills 40 and 55 (Camp Muir) were to its E. In area known as Do Xa, that in ancient past was hiding place from invading Chinese. VC stronghold and staging area SW Da Nang for VC/NVA 122mm Rocket units. USMC and Americal list. On SW 1/4 of map is L-7014-6737-2, per Ken Burrington. Quang Nam Pr, I Corps.
Happy's Strip Airfield (QB 46-24)
LS-264. CIA/SF, per *Air Facilities Data-Laos.*
Har Due Airfield (TF 36-56)
LS-366. CIA/SF, per *Air Facilities Data-Laos.*
Harbor Clearance Unit 1 (n/a)
See Glossary.
Harbor Defense and Surveillance Units (n/a)
Units HQ'd at ports of Vung Tau, Cam Ranh Bay, Qui Nhon, Nha Trang, and Vung Ro. SVN.
Harbor Entrance Control Post (CR 12-23?)
See Hill, The. Qui Nhon. Binh Dinh Pr, II Corps.
Hard Core, FSB (YD 449-511)
See Hardcore. Quang Tri Pr, I Corps.
Hard Core, LZ (AT 977-501)
See Hardcore. Quang Nam Pr, I Corps.
Hard Rice (n/a)
See Glossary.
Hard Spots (n/a)
See Glossary.
Hard Times, LZ (BR 613-607)
A.k.a. Hardtimes. In the Vinh Thanh Valley immed SW Vinh Thanh AF and apx 20 km NE An Khe/Camp Radcliff, 4 km NNW Vinh Thanh and 33 km NW Phu Cat AB. 4th Div AO, '70. Name/grid per Jim Claeys. Map is sheet L-7014-6737-2 (Tien Thuan), per Ray Smith. Also 2d/17th Arty here 9-21Sep67, and listed at BR 616-606, per Jack Picciolo. Binh Dinh Pr, II Corps.
Hard, Camp (AR 885-279)
SF camp at or near Plei Do Lim AF, apx 22 km SE Pleiku. 5th SF. Info/grid per *SF Order of Battle.* See Plei Do Lim. Pleiku Pr, II Corps.
Hardcore, FSB (AT 977-502)
See Hardcore, LZ, at grid. Quang Nam Pr, I Corps.
Hardcore, FSB (XS 752-933)
Apx 4 km WSW Tan Son Nhut AB, 7 km S FSB All-American, 2 km E Vinh Binh pacification hamlet. Built in southern portion of 82d Abn's new AO during Sep or Oct68 by men of 1st/508th Inf, 82d Abn, following the shift of 3d Bde from I Corps and as part of Op Toan Than. Data per Butch Sincock. Home of 1st/508th Inf, 3d Bde/82d Abn, Oct68-Mar69. Gia Dinh Pr, III Corps.
Hardcore, FSB/LZ (YD 448-288)
Along Street Without Joy and Song Vinh Dinh River, apx 6 km NNE Hai Lang, 11 km due W Quang Tri and 7 km SW Wunder Beach. Also listed at YD 448-395 per Robert Stanley, B/229th AHB, '68-69, and at YD 460-512 and 493-563? Quang Tri Pr, I Corps.
Hardcore, FSB (YD 493-563?)
Adj Utah Beach (later renamed Wunder Beach), 1st Cav and 2d Bde 101st Abn, '68. Grid per Gen Cushman, 2d Bde CO in 67-68, however most data suggests it is either incorrect or site was moved at some point? Also listed at YD 450-509 and YD 448-395, YD 449-511 and YD 450-509. Map is L-7014-6442-2. Quang Tri Pr, I Corps.
Hardcore, LZ/FSB (AT 977-501)
A.k.a. LZ Hawk. On hill overlooking valley of Song Thu Bon River apx 2 km SE Thon Bon, 17 km WSW Hoi An, 12 km ENE An Hoa, 13 km W QL-1 and 23 km due S Da Nang AB. Photos and maps of site are at http://1-14th.com/maps.html. Americal list. Quang Nam Pr, I Corps.
Hardcore, LZ (BR 627-472)
Along QL-19, apx 14 km due E An Khe and 8 km WNW Binh Khe. Apr-Sep70. Binh Dinh Pr, II Corps.
Hardcore, LZ/FSB (YD 460-512)
If grid correct, was in coastal sands apx 12 km ENE Quang Tri and 5 km W Wunder Beach. Aug-Nov68. Also listed at YD 448-288 and 448-395? Quang Tri Pr, I Corps.
Hardihood, Operation (n/a)
16 May-8 Jun66. 173d Abn, Phuoc Tuy Pr. On 19May66 the 1/503d Inf engaged est 50 VC, 20 VC KIA. III Corps.
Hardin (n/a)
6Apr70, XXIV Corps proposed 5th Div FSB name.
Hardspots (n/a)
See Hard Spots in Glossary.
Hardtimes, LZ (BR 613-607)
See Hard Times. Binh Dinh Pr, II Corps.
Hardtop (n/a)
6Apr70, XXIV Corps proposed 5th Div FSB name.
Hardtop, FSB (YD 01-29)
Apx 40 km SW Quang Tri, 2 km from Laos, 4 km SE FSB Whisman, 16 km due S Vandegrift CB and 3 km NW FSB Fisher. USMC, '69, 1st Cav. Grid per map on p 65, *US Marines in Vietnam-1969*. Quang Tri Pr, I Corps.
Hardwick, LZ (XD 764-459)
Along Rte 6082, apx 10 km WNW Khe Sanh CB, 5 km due

W Ap La Vien and 23 km WSW Ca Lu. Apr70 XXIV Corps grid per Don Armstrong. Quang Tri Pr, I Corps.

Hardy, Camp (AR 885-279?)
A.k.a. Plei Do Lim SF Camp. Roughly 28 km due E the Oasis AF, 22 km SSW Pleiku and 29 km due N Phu Nhon AF. Named to honor Capt Herbert Hardy, KIA 4Mar63, in Phu Bon Pr. Data per *Vietnam Military Lore, Legends, Shadows, and Heroes*, p 529-532. Pleiku Pr, II Corps.

Hardy, Camp (n/a)
On Okinawa, not in Vietnam. Named for Capt. Herbert F. Hardy, Jr, US Army KIA, RVN, 4Mar64.

Harley (n/a)
6Apr70, XXIV Corps proposed 5th Div FSB name.

Harnett County, USS (n/a)
LST-821. USN Landing Ship, Tank. Suptd 9th Inf Div/MRF in '67-68, per MRF Assn at www.mrfa.org. Returned to VN 12Oct70? III/IV Corps?

Harold E. Ellison, USS (n/a)
A.k.a. DD 864. See *Barry* (DD 933).

Harold E. Holt, USS (n/a)
DE-1074. DD-Escort, per Ralph Fries.

Harold Holt Memorial Swimming Pool (YS 28-43)
Eddie Tricker tells us this was a large, modern pool near 1ATF's Peter Badcoe Club in Vung Tau. He adds, "poor old Harold had just about every swimming pool built at time named after him, following his mysterious death at Cheviot Beach in Victoria." See Peter Badcoe Club. Phuoc Tuy Pr, III Corps.

Harper, FSB (YD 898-200)
A.k.a. FSB Lanyard. In coastal sands along Rte 552, apx 6 km due N Phu Bai AF and 1 km NNW Thon Hoa Da Tay. Jan70. Thua Thien Pr, I Corps.

Harper's Ferry, FSB (XT 912-303)
Apx 8 km WSW Khu Tru Mat and 17 km NNW Bien Hoa AB. Dec68-Jan69. Binh Duong Pr, III Corps.

Harris, Patrol Base (XT 417-126)
A.k.a. FSB Harris. In An Ninh Corridor on E side of Song Vam Co Dong, apx 9 km due E southern tip of Angel's Wing and 23 km WSW Cu Chi. Hau Nghia Pr, III Corps.

Harrison, FSB (XT 738-051)
In Tan Hiep, apx 11 km NW Tan Son Nhut AB, 16 km SW Phu Loi Post, 16 km SE Cu Chi and 16 km W Di An Basecamp. After 2d/505th Inf reconstructed FSB Gonzales,21Oct68 during Op Toan Thang, it moved to Harrison. Unknown if base existed prior to their arrival. 2d/505th was responsible for center of 3d Bde/82d Abn's AO, NW Saigon. Grid/info per Butch Sincock and '68 history of 3de Bde. [257] Home of 2d/505th Inf, 3d Bde/82d Abn, Oct68-Mar69. Gia Dinh Pr, III Corps.

Harrison, FSB (YT 167-172)
Apx 17 km ENE Bien Hoa, 8 km N QL-1 and 55 km NW Nui Dat. 161 Bty, RNZA (Martin's Bty 13May67-14Apr68) FSB set here 11-13Feb68. Also listed at YT 160-170 and 170-160. Bien Hoa, III Corps.

Harry, FSB (XU 730-085)
W of QL-13 near Loc Ninh AF, and apx 75 km NE Tay Ninh. Dec67-Jan68. Binh Long Pr, III Corps.

Harry E. Hubbard, USS (n/a)
DD-748, per Ralph Fries.

Harry Chauvel, HMAS (n/a)
AV-1354. Australian LSM serving under US 7th Flt. Originally *USS LSM-47,* sold to Australia, '60, assigned to Australian Army Royal Engrs, 32 Small Ship Sqdn.

Hart, LZ (ZA or AR)
Per George Critter, 1st/10th Cav, was on QL-19 (or QL-14?) between "Basecamp " (Enari or Pleiku?) and Oasis. Description suggest site was in ZA 2-3, AR 7-3 or AR 7-4. Also states it was named for Phillip D. Hart, a 4th Div replacement, who in Jul or Aug66 was KIA when he walked into helo tail rotor. No Hart by that first name or second name is listed in the CACF, nor is an Army Hart KIAs listed for either month? Pleiku Pr, II Corps.

Hartman, FSB (XT 759-739)
Along QL-13, apx 15 km S An Loc, and 3 km S Xa Tan Kai. 1st/8th Arty, 25th Div here '69. Name/grid per Dan Gillotti, 15th Arty. Tay Ninh Pr?, III Corps.

Hartone?, LZ (YB or ZB?)
Apparently near Dak To or Kontum. 1st/92d Arty Op Rpt for period ending 30Apr68, has entry which states: "B/1/92 was airlifted from LZ Hartone ["r" is partially obscured and might be an "n" or "v" or ?] to Dak To and then returned by road [to Pleiku]." Kontum Pr?, II Corps.

Harumi, SS (n/a)
Ocean Tug of MSC. See Frequent Wind.

Harvest Moon, Op (BT)
8-20Dec65. BLT 2d/7th Marines working in Song Chang Valley and Que Son Mtns. 2d/7th alone lost 20 KIA and 95 WIA (and heavy non-battle losses (51 on a single day) to Immersion-Foot, disease, accidents, shell-shock and etc.). Data per account of Op's heavy fighting in *Utter's Battalion*, pp 177-216. Quang Tin/Quang Nam Pr, I Corps.

Harwood, USS (n/a)
DD-861, per Ralph Fries.

Haskins, Camp (AT 94-83)
Apx 8 km NW Da Nang AB at Red Beach, and N of Camp Books. Camp and stg area for 30th Naval Const Rgt. Per John Doherty, here 69-70, "The S boundary of Camp Viking was the N boundary of Camp Haskins. Camp Haskins was a Navy Seabee base until late 70 or early 71, when an Army Engr Bn moved in. On the other side of QL-1 by Haskins was the USMC FLC. These were the only cmpds close by." Named to honor BUL2 Donald D Haskins, Seabee with C Co, NMCB-9, KIA 31Oct65, split into Camp Haskins North and South after arrival of III MAF, which was sited in Haskins South. See Camp Adenir for more detail. Either a.k.a. or adj to Camps Viking North and South? Quang Nam Pr, I Corps.

Haskins North, Camp (AT 94-83)
At Red Beach, apx 8 km NW Da Nang AB and N Camp Books. Camp/stg area for 30th Naval Const Rgt. See Haskins for name origin/detail and also Camp Adenir. Immed S of Camps Viking? Quang Nam Pr, I Corps.

Haskins South, Camp (AT 94-82)
At Red Beach, apx 8 km NW Da Nang AB and N of Camp Books. HQ USMC III MAF. See Camp Haskins for detail and also Camp Adenir. Quang Nam Pr, I Corps.

Hassayampa, USS (n/a)
AO-145. Aux Oiler, per Ralph Fries.

Hastings, LZ (YD 177-328)
On ridge of Nui Da Ban Mtn, apx 26 km SW Quang Tri, 7 km SSE Ba Long AF, 7 km due S Thon Thanh Tra, 7 km NNW peak of Dong Ba Le Mtn (a.k.a. Hill 1102 or 1110), and overlooking valley of Khe Ta Laou River to SW, and Khe Ba Dang River Valley to N. Apr70 XXIV Corps grid per Don Armstrong. Quang Tri Pr, I Corps.
Hastings, Operation (YD/XD)
Assault of 324-B NVA Div elements in Song Nang Valley and Hill 208 areas, Jul-Aug66. Designed to spoil planned attack of Hue by 341st NVA Div, at time staged just below DMZ and Razorback (Mutter's) Ridge. Began 15Jul66, ended 3Aug66. 126 USMC KIA, 448 WIA. 882 NVA KIA, per *Vietnam Order of Battle*, pp 9-14. See Hill 208, Helicopter Valley and LZ Crow. Quang Tri Pr, I Corps.
Hastings/Deckhouse II, Operation (XD/YD)
7Jul-3Aug66. USMC/ARVN/VNMC op to find and destroy NVA 324B Div in DMZ; however, NVA inflicted heavy casualties on Marines. Quang Tri Pr, I Corps.
Hat, LZ (BR 840-740)
Apx 9 km NW Phu My, 6 km NNE Hoi San and 22 km due S Bong Son. Feb66. Binh Dinh Pr, II Corps.
Hatty, LZ (CR 009-685)
Apx 9 km NW Vinh Loi and 30 km SSE Bong Son. Oct66. Binh Dinh Pr, II Corps.
Hat Dic Area (YS 3-7?)
See Hat Dich Zone. III Corps.
Hat Dich Special Zone (YS 3-7)
A.k.a. Base Area 303. Generally 10 km NW Nui Dat, 10 km N Nui Thi and 50 km ESE Saigon. Region adjoining Phuoc Tuy and Long Khanh Pr borders assaulted by 1st ATF and 1st Bde/9th US Inf Div during Op Duntroon, 10-21Jan68, against 274th VC Main Force Rgt. Also area of Op Silver Lake, 9Jan-19Jan67, involving newly arrived 3/39th, 2/60th, and 5/60th Inf Bns under control of 3d Bde/9th Inf Div also fighting 274th Rgt. III Corps.
Hat Khon Airfield (TG 86-93)
LS-271. CIA/SF, per *Air Facilities Data-Laos.*
Hat Yai International Airfield (PH 5-6)
At 6°56'00"N-100°26'00"E. NIMA data. Thailand.
Hatchet, LZ (ZC 017-418)
Apx 7 km NE Ben Giang, 19 km SW Ha Tan AF and 55 km SW Da Nang AB. Apr70 XXIV Corps grid per Don Armstrong. Quang Nam Pr, I Corps.
Hau Bon (BQ 24-82)
A.k.a. Hou Bon. Apx 80 km SE Pleiku and 34 km NW Phu Tuc AF. Hau Bon Subsector Adv Team 31 at Cheo Reo. Phu Bon or Pleiku Pr, II Corps.
Hau Bon (Cheo Reo) (n/a)
Mapsheet L-7014-6635-1. Sheet: Cheo Reo (Hau Bon).
Hau Bon Airfield (BQ 24-82?)
A.k.a. Cheo Reo AF? At Hou Bon, apx 80 km SE Pleiku and 34 km NW Phu Tuc. Phu Bon Pr, II Corps.
Hau Duc (BS 02-97)
On mapsheet L-7014-6639-4. Quang Tin Pr, I Corps.
Hua Duc, New (BT 073-064)
See New Hau Duc. Quang Tin Pr, I Corps.
Hau Duc (Tien Tra) (n/a)
Mapsheet name of L-7014-6639-4. SVN.
Hau Duc Airfield (BS 016-970)
Apx 52 km W to WSW Chu Lai, and 36 km SW Tam Ky. "Insecure, abnd, Overgrown 28Jul67, AF # VA1-81," in Aug69 TAD per Frank Penk, Jr. Not in Feb73 TAD. Quang Tin Pr, I Corps.
Hau Duc Relocation Camp (BT 033-037)
Apx 13 km SW Tien Phuoc AF and 33 km SW Tam Ky. Jul68 Quang Tin Pr, I Corps.
Hau Duc SF Camp (BT 02-98?)
Possibly at Old Hau Duc, apx 52 km W to WSW Chu Lai and 36 km SW Tam Ky. 5th SF camp. Info/grid per *SF Order of Battle.* See Tra My. Quang Tin Pr, I Corps.
Hau Duc, New (BT 070-062)
Apx 46 km due W Chu Lai, 28 km SW Tam Ky, 6 km NE Old Hau Duc, near LZ Mildred and apx 8 km E LZ Mary Ann. Americal list author's Huey was run off this base by mortars and saw ARVNs or CIDG actually using cross bows for weapons. Also listed at BT 073-063?, (Old Hau Duc listed by arty ORLL at BT 024-979), Americal AO, 1st Bde HQ, '69, also 1st Bn, 502d Inf, 101st Abn, opcon to Americal here mid '69. Quang Tin Pr, I Corps.
Hau Duc, Old (BS 024-979)
Apx 52 km W to WSW Chu Lai. Grid per ORLL. Ha Duc or New Hau Duc is at BT 048-043. Americal list. Quang Tin Pr, I Corps.
Hau Nghia Airfield (XT 544-050)
Adj to Khiem Cuong, apx 30 km WNW Tan Son Nhut AF and Saigon. El. 13', 1,300' rwy. At 10°53'55"N-106°24'40"E. Hau Nghia Pr, III Corps.
Hau Nghia Dist HQ (XT 524-054)
Apx 3 km S Kiem Cuong and 9 km NW Duc Hoa AF. Aug69. Hau Nghia Pr, III Corps.
Hau Nghia Province (XT/XS)
One of 11 south-central provs forming III Corps (III CTZ).
Haverfield, USS (n/a)
DER-393. See *Point Welcome.*
***Hawaii*, the Movie** (n/a)
See Shotgun, Operation.
Hawk, FSB (XD 907-401)
See Hawk, LZ, at grid. Quang Tri Pr, I Corps.
Hawk, FSB (XD 954-407)
If grid correct, was apx 40 km WSW km Quang Tri and 12 km W Khe Sanh CB. Nov68. Quang Tri Pr, I Corps.
Hawk, FSB? (XT 855-405)
Apx 8 km ENE Lai Khe AF, 30 km NNW Bien Hoa AB and 13 km SW Phuoc Vinh AF. Nature of site unknown. Jan69. Binh Duong Pr, I Corps.
Hawk, FSB (YS 254-858)
Apx 20 km WNW Nui Dat, 12 km SE FSB Archer and 30 km NNW Vung Tau. 161 Bty, RNZA (Hitching's Bty 14Apr68-18Mar69) FSB set here 21-24Jul68. On 1ATF NCO trng map per John Hollett. Also listed at YS 25-86. Bien Hoa Pr, III Corps.
Hawk, LZ (AT 817-471)
Apx 6 km W An Hoa AF. Nov67. Quang Nam Pr, I Corps.
Hawk, LZ (AT 875-615)
Along S edge of Charlie Ridge, apx 21 km SW Da Nang AB and 6 km NE Dai Loc. Mar68. Quang Nam Pr, I Corps.
Hawk, LZ (AT 978-501)
A.k.a. LZ/FSB Hardcore. Apx 26 km due S Da Nang AB. Apr68. Quang Nam Pr, I Corps.

Hawk, LZ (AT 998-538)
Near Ky Lan RR bridge, apx 14 km WSW Hoi An. Dec67. Quang Nam Pr, I Corps.
Hawk, LZ (BS 749-601)
In coastal lowland, apx 3 km from coast and 7 km NNE Mo Duc AF. Jun66. Quang Ngai Pr, I Corps.
Hawk, LZ (XD 907-401)
Apx 13 km SW Ca Lu and 46 km WSW Quang Tri. Jun68-Mar69. Also listed at XD 895-405. Quang Tri Pr, I Corps.
Hawk, LZ (XD 954-407)
See Hawk, FSB at grid. Quang Tri Pr, I Corps.
Hawk, LZ (YS 645-700)
Apx 2 km NW Xuyen Moc and 21 km E to ENE Nui Dat. Aug66. Phuoc Tuy Pr, III Corps.
Hawk, LZ (ZC 024-025)
Apx 6 km SSE Kham Duc and 6 km due E Ngok Tavak AF. Feb68. Quang Tin Pr, II Corps.
Hawk, LZ (ZC 175-553)
Apx 3 km ENE Ha Tay AF, 6 km NE Thuong Duc CIDG Camp and 35 km SW Da Nang. 7th Marine Rgt used it and LZ Eagle in searching 10 sq-km area S of Hill 55, between Rte 4 and Song Thu Bon River, during Op Linn River, 1st/7th and 2/26th Marines, 28-29Jan69. 2d Bn 51st ARVN Rgt here Mar69. On map p 109, *US Marines in Vietnam-1969*. Quang Nam Pr, I Corps.
Hawk Hill Heliport (BT 226-320)
A.k.a. Hill 29. Adj to Hawk Hill, apx 12 km NW Tam Ky, 16 km SE LZ Baldy. "Heliport #714, alt 94', Fuel-J4, Ammo: 7.62, 40mm, Rockets, Flares. Secure PSP pkg area. Windsock adj to pkg area. Peneprime treated, traffic pattern-normally left traffic lndg E, except optional right traffic lndg E is Dustoff pad. Arty advsy-VN 66.80 56.35. At 15°33'N 103'25'E," per Feb73 TAD. A.k.a. Hill 29. Map is L-7014-6640-2. Quang Tin Pr, I Corps.
Hawk Hill, FSB (BT 231-315)
A.k.a. Hawk Hill, LZ Hawk Hill, LZ Golden Rose and Hill 29. Apx 12 km NW Tam Ky, 16 km SE LZ Baldy, 3 km W QL-1 and just E the N-S railroad tracks. Apparently named Golden Rose while a 4th Div LZ and 1st/14th Inf here. Also listed at BT 230-315, 224-315 and 30-28? Americal list. Map is L-7014-6640-2. Quang Tin Pr, I Corps.
Hawk Missile (n/a)
See Glossary.
Hawk's Nest (BT 545-027)
At Chu Lai complex, apx 1 km WSW the S end of the main Chu Lai AF rwy, 1 km NW Hoa Van (1) and immed NE QL-1. Basecamp of the 1st/1st Cav here, '70. Data per Les Hines. Pr, II Corps.
Hawk's Nest (CR 07-76?)
Just off coast apx 2 km and 28 km SE Bong Son, 37 km NE Phu Cat AB. That or it was on coast opposite those islands near Lighthouse indicated on TPC K-10A. Map at www. landscaper.net/chighmap.jpg suggests site was on one of 2 islands near listed grid. Possibly an observation or Signal Site? Binh Dinh Pr, II Corps.
Hawkeye Teams (n/a)
See Glossary.
Hawkins, USS (n/a)
A.k.a. DD 873. See *Barry* (DD 933).
Hawks (n/a)
See Glossary.
Hawthorne/Dan Thang 61, Operation (n/a)
2-21Jun66. 1st Bde/101st Abn and ARVN op. 531 rptd NVA/VC KIA, per *Vietnam Order of Battle*, pp 9-14. Kontum Pr, II Corps.
Hay Tay (2) (BR 798-833)
See Ha Tay. Binh Dinh Pr, II Corps.
Haymaker, FSB (XU 685-228)
Apx 300 meters S Cambodia border near point where QL-13 crosses it, roughly 26 km NNE Loc Ninh AF. Per John Mowat, 71st Arty Quad .50's, was in Cambodia and possibly near Snuol. John Driscoll, 5th/2d Arty thinks it was just on border and was an ARVN base. His 8" guns were moved there in '70 to augment 175mms firing from FSB Wade suptg ARVN that were "getting their butts kicked" in Cambodia. '70-71. Binh Long Pr, III Corps.
Haynsworth, USS (n/a)
DD-700, per Ralph Fries.
Hazard, Camp/FSB/LZ (XT 078-840)
Apx 3 km NNW Thien Ngon AF, 5 km S Cambodia and about 38 km NNE Tay Ninh. Tay Ninh Pr, III Corps.
Hazard, FSB (XT 078-840)
See Hazard, Camp. Tay Ninh Pr, III Corps.
Hazel, FSB (n/a)
Precise No data. An 11th ACR/1st Cav Cambodian Incursion FSB, May-Jun70. 1st/11th Howitzers with six-155s, B Bty, 2d/32d Arty, with two-8" howitzers here May-Jun70, during Cambodian Invasion, per *11th ACR Cambodia Invasion AAR, 1st Cav Div, May-Jun70*, courtesy Lou Rochat. [258] Cambodia or III Corps.
Hazel, FSB (YS)
Apparently SSE Xuan Loc. Built on level ground with jungle and/or a rubber plantation nearby (likely Courtenay Rubber Plantation). Abnd ville was nearby. 105mm Bty (3 guns) and elements of 3d/22d Inf, 3d Bde/25th Inf Div here and '70 and/or '71. Recon Co elements of 3d/22d were rptd to have even used some patrols to hunt game that inc wild boar and apparently even a Peacock! Info courtesy Herb Artola, 3d/22d Inf. Phuoc Tuy Pr, III Corps.
Hazel's Whorehouse (ZA 236 863)
See FOB 2. Kontum Pr, II Corps.
HCMT (n/a)
See Ho Chi Min Trail in Glossary.
HE Bird (n/a)
See Glossary.
He Who Shines (n/a)
See Ho Chi Minh in Glossary.
Head Shed (YT 040-064)
See Headshed. Bien Hoa Pr, III Corps.
Headshed, The (YT 040-064)
Nickname for USARV HQ and its heliport at Long Binh Post. See USARV HQ for detailed history. Along S side of Hwy 319, apx 11 km SE Bien Hoa AB, 26 km WNW Tan Son Nhut AB and 13 km due E Di An. Per Frank Penk, Jr., USARV HQ here. Bien Hoa Pr, III Corps.
Heart-Shaped Woods, The (XT 950-220)
A 6 x 5 km, heart-shaped jungled area with tip pointing S. That tip about 6 km NE Bien Hoa AB, and the banks of Song Dong Nai River formed wood's E edge. Grid is at apx center of mass. On map in *Rangers At War*, p 234-5. Also XT 880-250. Tay Ninh/Binh Duong Pr, III Corps.

Hearts, LZ (BS 460-060)
Apx 3 km NNE LZ Clubs, 29 km WSW Thuan An and 24 km SSE Gia Vuc AF. Mar66. Binh Dinh Pr, II Corps.
Heather, FSB (XT 225-906)
If grid correct, was apx 10 km due W Katum AF, 7 km S Cambodian border. Mar70. Also listed at XT 225-906, which is 2 km N listed grid? Tay Ninh Pr, III Corps.
Heather, FSB (XT 255-926)
Apx 12 km WNW Katum, 16 km NE Thien Ngon AF and 7 km S Cambodia. Existed 2-5Mar70. 1 of 7 FSBs opened and closed in as many weeks by 2d/8th Cav, 1st Cav, prior to Cambodian Incursion (7 were: Jamie, Mary Gwen, Heather, Victor, Flashner, Drum and Illingworth. ORLL grid. Also listed at XT 225-906, which is apx 2 km S of listed grid? Tay Ninh Pr, III Corps.
Heaven Dragon, SS (n/a)
Merchant ship under govt contract, per Ralph Fries.
Heavy Drop (YA 810-690)
See Sledge Hammer. Kontum Pr, II Corps.
Hector, LZ (XD 994-690)
In DMZ, apx 1.5 km S the Song Ben Hai River, 16 km NW Cam Lo and 26 km WNW Dong Ha. Apr70 XXIV Corps grid per Don Armstrong. Quang Tri Pr, I Corps.
Hector, USS (n/a)
AR-7. Repair Ship.
Hedgehog, LZ (XD 855-386)
Just W intersection of QL-19 and Hwy 608, apx 3 km SSE Khe Sanh CB and 17 km WSW Ca Lu. Jun69. Quang Tri Pr, I Corps.
HEDSUPPACT, USN (XS 830-895)
At the Cofat Cmpd, Saigon. Originally site of US Army's HACOM (Headquarters Area Cmd); unit responsible for managing, among other things, Saigon area military mess facilities, billets and clubs. That responsibility assumed by USN's Headquarters Supt Activity (HEDSUPPACT) in Sep62, but returned to HACOM, Dec 65. Prior to '63, site was that of Cofat Cigarette Mfg Co. Gia Dinh Pr, III Corps.
Hegdahl, Doug (n/a)
See *Canberra, USS.*
Hegert BOQ (XS 855-916)
See Hergert. Gia Dinh Pr, III Corps.
Heidi, LZ/FSB (YD 275-275)
Apx 17 km SW Ba Long AF and 26 km SSW Quang Tri. Apr70 XXIV Corps grid per Don Armstrong. 1st/1st ARVN here Feb-Mar68 per 13May68, 3d Bde/101st Abn ORLL. Also listed at YD 274-273. Quang Tri Pr, I Corps.
Heilman Hall (CR 0-2)
At Qui Nhon and within 394th Trans Bn Cmpd. Binh Dinh Pr, II Corps.
Helen, FSB (YD 515-219)
A.k.a. Hill 674. On Rocket Ridge, apx 20 km due W Hue, 12 km SSW Camp Evans and 8 km E FSB Granite. Also listed at YD 515-220 and 516-219. Thua Thien Pr, I Corps.
Helen, FSB (YS 317-767)
Apx 15 km NE Nui Dat, 1.5 km ESE FSB Jill and 14 km due W FSB Le Loi. On 1ATF NCO trng map per John Hollett. Phuoc Tuy Pr, III Corps.
Helen, LZ (XS 533-389)
Apx 7 km SSE My Tho and 7 km NNE Ben Tre/Truc Giang. Mar66. Kien Hoa Pr, IV Corps.
Helen, LZ (XT 593-217)
Apx 7 km NW Cu Chi. Apr67. Hau Nghia Pr, III Corps.
Helen, LZ (YU 805-631)
Immed S Duk Song, apx 7 km E Cambodia, 16 km SW Duc Lap AF and 19 km NE Bu Prang AF. Oct69. Quang Duc Pr, II Corps.
Helena, LZ (YS 713-941)
Apx 16 km WNW Nui Be, 28 km NW Ham Tan AF and 29 km SE Xuan Loc. Apr66. Phuoc Tuy Pr, III Corps.
Helena BEQ (XS 843-941)
In Saigon, apx 3 km ESE Tan Son Nhut Airbase. Gia Dinh Pr, III Corps.
Helga, LZ (YA 964-497)
A.k.a. LZ Hilga. Apx 28 km W Pleiku, 6 km SE peak Hill 1005, and 11 km ENE Plei Djereng New AF. LZs Cathy, Helga, Phyllis and Ruby were apparently mutually suptg firebases? Name & grid per Dick Arnold as per Jan-Mar69 1st/35th Inf Bn daily logs. Pleiku Pr, II Corps.
Helgeson, Patrol Base (XT 629-978)
Apx 15 km SW Loc Ninh, 10 km NNE tip of Fishhook, 16 km NW An Loc and 7 km E Cambodia. In Mar69(?), turned over to 49th ARVN Rgt by 2d/14th Inf, 25th Inf Div and responsibility for FSB Ayers was assumed by that Bn. Likely named to honor Army Sgt Dale G Helgeson, KIA 1Mar69. Data per 15Mar69, QUARTEVAL Feeder Rpt, 2d Bde/25th Inf Div at: www.en.com/users/ kramsey/dragons. html. Binh Long Pr, III Corps.
Helgoland (n/a)
A.k.a. *Chicken of the Sea.* German Red Cross Hospital ship that worked coast between Quang Tri and Da Nang. Treated all wounded/seriously ill Viet civilian (inc VC) casualties. In Jun67, docked on Han River near III MAF HQ and, after ignoring warning of possible rocket attack, was bracketed by rockets. Thereafter, it moved into Da Nang Harbor whenever intel warned of possible attack (thereby gaining its nickname). Its moves became a warning sign to all that rocket attack was imminent. In VN at least-67-70. Cited in *Da Nang Diary*, p 103 and also in *Marines & Military Law in Vietnam*, p 63, with photo at p 62, per John Middlesworth. SVN.
Helicopter Bug (n/a)
See Glossary.
Helicopter Valley (YD 03-64)
A.k.a. the Song Ngan Valley. Rugged valley N Mutter's Ridge that ran parallel to and just S the southern edge of DMZ. Ran from point roughly due N the Rockpile until it turned N and joined the Ben Hai River in DMZ at point (YD 07-73) NNW Con Thien. Also 5 km S Hill 208 (CP for 324-B NVA Div), and staging area for 90th NVA Rgt (1,500 men). In '66 during Op Hastings, earned name when on 15Jul66, a Sqdn of CH-46 Medium Helos met disaster here. During 3d wave carrying 3d/4th Marines into valley at LZ Crow, 2 collided in mid-air and another crashed into jungle trying to avoid the mid-air crash. 4th CH-46 was shot down and, as its panic-stricken occupants tried to flee, many were killed by still rotating blades. 2 destroyed helos were from USMC's MAG 16 Sqdn HMM-265 (Marble Mtn) and others involved that day inc HMM-164 and HMM-163. Apx 15 KIA and 7 WIA. Highly detailed account of 15Jul66 actions at LZs Crow, Robin and Dove

that day is in *Bonnie-Sue-A Marine Helicopter Sqdn in VN*, pp 47-73. Quang Tri Pr, I Corps.

Helicopters, NVA (n/a)
See Glossary.

Helix FACs (BT 537-062)
TASS FACs flying out of Chu Lai and suptg Americal Div. Grid is for Chu Lai AF. Quang Tin Pr, I Corps.

Hell, LZ (YB 873-251)
Apx 2 km ESE Ben Het and 14 km WNW Dak To 2 AF. Jul70. Kontum Pr, III Corps.

Hell 2-11, FSB (BS)
A.k.a. Hell Two-Eleven and possibly Hill 211? Near Chu Lai, '66-67. 2d/11th Arty, 1st Mar Div nickname for FSB that was likely one of the USMC's Hill firebases otherwise unnamed except for Hill number. Quang Tin Pr?, I Corps.

Hell of Hoa Binh (WJ 34-05)
See Hoa Binh, Battle for. NVN.

Hell's Half Acre (CQ 26-38)
Nickname for Phu Hiep. Apx 7 km SE Tuy Hoa AF and 85 km NNE Nha Trang. 134th AHC and 268th Avn Bn here. See Phu Hiep AF. Phu Yen Pr, II Corps.

Hemp, LZ (YD 275-434)
Apx 11 km ENE Ba Long AF, 4 km SSW Thon Tan La and 12 km SW Quang Tri. Apr70 XXIV Corps grid per Don Armstrong. Quang Tri Pr, I Corps.

Henderson, FSB (YD 081-411)
A.k.a. Hill 654? Apx 12 km SE Vandegrift CB, 7 km due N FSB Tun Tavern, 10 km due W Ba Long. Re secured 11Jun69, by 2d/9th Marines and two Btys of 2d/12th Mar Arty, Op Apache Snow. Elements 2d/501st In, 101st Abn were attacked and overrun by est NVA Bn on19May70. Only 5 US troops out of 37 survived.[259] Also listed 085-408. On map at p 32, *US Marines in Vietnam-1969*. Quang Tri Pr, I Corps.

Henderson Hill, Operation (n/a)
24Oct-6Dec68. USMC 9th Marines. 700 rptd NVA/VC KIA, per *Vietnam Order of Battle*, pp 9-14. N central Quang Nam Pr, I Corps.

Henrico, USS (n/a)
APA 45. See *Vancouver, USS*.

Henry, FSB (YD 688-093)
Just N the Song Huu Trach and just S Hwy 547, apx 2 km WSW FSB Birmingham, 13 km SW Hue and 8 km SW Nam Hoa (Pohl) Bridge. Opened by D/1st/502d Inf to facilitate const of FSB Bastogne, Apr68. Per Peter Smith, Back-hoe came in and dug foxholes, then came back a few days later and filled them in when Bastogne completed. Old French or Viet fortifications were apx 200 meters to its SW. Also listed at YD 687-093. Thua Thien Pr, I Corps.

Henry, FSB (XU 460-390)
Apx 12 km SE Snuol AF and 6 km Phum Sre Thom. May70. Cambodia.

Henry B. Wilson, USS (n/a)
DDG 7. In May68, gunfire from *Wilson* in northern I Corps decimated NVA Bn, killing 82. See Op Eagle Pull.

Henry County, USS (n/a)
LST-824. SVN.

Henry R. Tucker, USS (n/a)
DD-875, per Ralph Fries.

Hensel Airfield (AR 803-339)
At Camp Enari, apx 14 km SSE Pleiku, 10 km due E Catecka AF, 13 km due S Pleiku Area AF and 9 km ENE the Oasis, per TPC K-10A and ONC K-10. 4th Div HQ and home of 4th Avn Bn. Named to honor WO-1 Ernest V Hensel, Huey gunship pilot in D Trp 1st Sqdn, 10th Cav, KIA 17Feb67, when shot down attacking a VC position. Prior to earning his wings, Hensel had been a disc jockey on Armed Forces Radio Korea. El. 2,529', 2,800' steel-mat rwy. At 13°51'38"N-108°02'26"E. Pleiku Pr, II Corps.

Hepatitis Tavern (WR 170-394)
The Tan Phu SF Camp mess hall. Was inside thatched roof hut and a.k.a. the Titis Tavern. See Tan Phu SF Camp. An Xuyen Pr, IV Corps.

Hepburn, USS (n/a)
DE-1055. DD-Escort, per Ralph Fries.

Hereford, LZ (BR 663-628)
On ridge of Hill 766(?), apx 6 km ENE Vinh Thanh AF, 7 km NNE Vinh Thanh ville, 5 km NE the old French (CIDG) Fort on Rte 3A and 26 km NE An Khe, Site of major fight at LZ and on adj hill 766 during Op Benning-Crazy Horse, May66, involving A/B Cos, 2d/8th Cav, C/1st/12th Cav, 1st/5th Cav and 2d/12th Cav, 1st Cav. *Look* Magazine correspondent Sam Castan was KIA when plt of C/1/12th Inf overrun here 22May66. See Castan, Sam in Glossary. Binh Dinh Pr, II Corps.[260]

Hergert BOQ (XS 855-916)
In Saigon apx 5 km SE Tan Son Nhut AB. Named to honor, Col Thomas M. "Bud" Hergert, USAF, KIA 8Mar64, shot down by ground fire while flying A-H-1 Skyraider as wingman to ARVNAF Skyraider, 32 km E Tay Ninh. Data per *Vietnam Military Lore, Legends, Shadows, and Heroes*, p 547 et al. Gia Dinh Pr, III Corps.

Hermitage, USS (n/a)
LSD-34. Lndg. Ship, Dock, per Ralph Fries.

Hero's Day (AR)
See Glossary.

Heroin Usage (n/a)
See Glossary.

Herring, FSB (YS 492-551)
Along Hwy 326, apx 7 km S Horseshoe FSB, 15 km SE Nui Dat, 3 km S Dat Do and 23 km ENE Vung Tau. In sandy wastes of what had once been a large, well-cultivated field. Sand blown by arriving/departing CH-47 and other acft caused numerous maintenance problems. 161 Bty, RNZA (Martin's Bty 13May67-14Apr68) FSB set here 17Mar-6Apr68. On 1ATF NCO trng map per John Hollett. Also listed at YS 49-55. Phuoc Tuy Pr, III Corps.

Hialeah BOQ (XS 813-915)
At 221-223 Nguyen Van Thoai St., Saigon. Per R. Bows' *Vietnam Military Lore, 1959-1973.* Gia Dinh Pr, III Corps.

Hickam AFB Hospital (n/a)
See USAF Hospitals.

Hickman County, USS (n/a)
LST-825. SVN.

Hickory Hill MSS Site (XD 844-456)
A.k.a. Hickory Hill radio relay, Lemon Hill, Dong Tri and Hill 950 (and 953?). Apx 3.5 km due N Khe Sanh CB, 1.2 km due W Hill 1015 (Dong Tre) and 2.5 km ENE Hill 558. 1st occupied by USMC in '67, and almost overrun that year. Per Barry Toll, was also radio relay site for SOG-35

ops (i.e., Ground Studies Div, cover name for cross border strategic recon ops). TF 1 Adv. Element (SOG's CCN) here 3Jun71, when NVA arty began battering site. On 4Jun71, 5 SF WIA and 10 indigenous commandos were medevaced, leaving SSgt Jon R. Caviani and Sgt John R. Jones along with 23 commandos to defend it. In early morning of 5Jun71, under cover of poor weather preventing air supt, NVA overran site. Jones is still MIA but Caviani was captured and later released, 27Mar73 (and awarded the MOH). May have also been a "White Radio" facility. In *The Final Formation,* at p 148, it's described as having been on both Hills 950 and 1015? On map p 89 in *War In The Shadows* vol., *Vietnam Experience* series. NIMA also lists a Dong Tri XD 7-7. Quang Tri Pr, I Corps.

Hickory Radio Relay Site (XD 844-456)
See Hickory Hill MSS site. Quang Tri Pr, I Corps.

Hickory, FSB (XD 86-46)
A.k.a. Hickory Radio Relay site? Apx 5 km N Khe Sanh CB, 15 km WSW Vandegrift CB and 48 km WSW Quang Tri. Used during Lam Son 719. Quang Tri Pr, I Corps.

Hidden Charm, LZ (YD?)
Location unknown. Marine helo pilots' nickname for LZ near Con Thien (possibly Gio Linh, Con Thien or Cam Lo?). Cited in *Bonnie-Sue*. Quang Tri Pr, I Corps.

Hien Loc (1) (BT 046-293)
ARVN outpost at E base of Hill 106 here, apx 15 km ENE Hiep Duc. Op Harvest Moon, 12Dec65. See *Utter's Battalion*, pp 197-8. Quang Tin Pr?, I Corps.

Hien Si Bridge (YD 610-278)
Apx 14 km WNW Citadel AF, 6 km NW LZ Sally and 7 km ESE Camp Evans. Apr69. Thua Thien Pr, I Corps.

Hiep Duc (AT 91-25)
In area known as Death Valley and Hiep Duc Valley, apx 48 km SSW Da Nang, 32 km NW Tam Ky and 56 NW Chu Lai. Quang Nam/Quang Tin Pr border, I Corps.

Hiep Duc (n/a)
Mapsheet name of L-7014-6640-3. SVN.

Hiep Duc District HQ (AT 910-240)
Apx 48 km SSW Da Nang and 32 km NW Tam Ky. Nov65. Quang Tin Pr, I Corps.

Hiep Duc Heliport (AT 912-246)
Apx 48 km SSW Da Nang and 32 km NW Tam Ky and apx 56 NW Chu Lai. Heliport #576, alt 66', at 15°35'00"N-108°07'1S"E, per Feb73 TAD. Map is L-7014-6640-3. Quang Nam Pr, I Corps.

Hiep Duc SF Camp (AT 910-250)
Along Rte 534 at Hiep Duc, apx 52 km SSW Da Nang and 38 km W Tam Ky. 5th SF. Info/grid per *SF Order of Battle*. Per *Through the Valley*, p 32, SF Det A-423 established camp here and at Phuoc Son, Apr63, and turned them over to SVN, Dec63, before returning to Okinawa. In Nov65, was overrun and held by VC. Map is L-7014-6640-3. See Phuoc Son. Quang Nam/Quang Tin Pr border, I Corps.

Hiep Duc Valley (AT 91-25)
A.k.a. Antenna and Death Valley? Apx 50 km SSW Da Nang, near Song Chang (AK) Valley, SW LZ Ross and N and NW LZ West. During Op Mississippi, late '66, civilians of valley relocated to My Loc (2). Heavy fighting throughout war, inc: 5th Marines/3d Mar Div, '66, 196th LIB, '68, 7th Marines/1st Mar Div, 21-29Aug69, and also Americal's 4th/31st Inf. See also LZ West and Antenna Valley. Quang Nam/Quang Tin Pr border, I Corps.

Hiep Hoa (various)
NIMA Gaz lists several villes by this name at: YT 0-0, XT 4-0 and YS 8-7. All locations in III Corps.

Hiep Hoa (XT 43-09?)
At edge of Sugar Cane Plantation apx 13 km ESE Duc Hue AF, 10 km WNW Khiem Cuong and 40 km WNW Saigon. 5th SF, Det A-351, A-352, A-353, A-354, B-35, Oct66, SF Det 65, SF A-Team Camp. Hau Nghia Pr, III Corps.

Hiep Hoa (B-Det) SF Camp (XT 430-037)
Apx 12 km SE Duc Hue AF, 11 km WSW Khiem Cuong and 42 km WNW Saigon. 5th SF. Grid per *SF Order of Battle.* Relocated to Duc Hoa. Hau Nghia Pr, III Corps.

Hiep Hoa (New) SF Camp (XT 430-072)
In Sugar Cane Plantation, 12 km ESE Duc Hue AF, 19 km NW Duc Hoa AF, 10 km WNW Khiem Cuong and 40 km WNW Saigon. 5th SF, Det A-351, A-352, A-353, A-354, B-35 here Oct66, SF Det 65, SF A-Team. Moved to Duc Hue. Grid per *SF Order of Battle.* Hau Nghia Pr, III Corps.

Hiep Hoa (Old) SF Camp (XT 443-065)
Apx 2 km SE Hiep Hoa (New) SF Camp, and 14 km ESE Duc Hue. 5th SF, Det A-21, A-351, A-352, A-353, A-354, B-35, Oct66, SF Det 65, SF A-Team Camp. A-21 overrun Thanksgiving '63, with 4 US MIA resulting.[261] Grid per *Special Forces Order of Battle.* Moved to Muc Hoa. Long An Pr, III Corps.

Hiep Hoa (TC) SF Camp (XT 430-072)
Apx 12 km ESE Duc Hue AF, 10 km WNW Khiem Cuong and 40 km WNW Saigon. Meaning of (TC) unknown. 5th SF. Info/grid per *SF Order of Battle.* Moved to Tra Cu. Hau Nghia Pr, III Corps.

Hiep Hoa Airfield (XT 437-071)
Apx 12 km ESE Duc Hue AF, 10 km WNW Khiem Cuong and 40 km WNW Saigon. Possibly abnd early in war? On NC 48-07 JOG. Listed as "Insecure, abnd, rwy is used as road 10Aug67, AF # VA3-267," in Aug69 TAD per Frank Penk, Jr. Not in Feb73 TAD. Hau Nghia Pr, III Corps.

Hiep Hoa Navy ATSB (XT 43-07?)
On Song Vam Co Dong, apx 46 km SSE Tay Ninh. USN Advanced Tactical Supt Base, '69. Grid may not be accurate. Data per MRF Assn. Hau Nghia Pr, III Corps.

Hiep Khanh Airfield (YD 639-275)
See Van Xa AF. Thua Thien Pr, I Corps.

Hieu Duc Heliport (AT 929-712)
Apx 9 km WSW Da Nang AB and 8 km W QL-1. One of 2 heliports in this area. Heliport #577, alt 33', 16°00'30"N-103°07'40"E, per Feb73 TAD. Quang Nam Pr, I Corps.

Hieu Duc Heliport (AT 935-688)
Along Rte 540, apx 10 km SW Da Nang AB and 7 km W QL-1. One of 2 heliports in this area. Heliport #578, alt 33' 15°59'00"N-108°08'00"E. Quang Nam Pr, I Corps.

Hieu Liem Heliport (YT 149-285)
A.k.a. or near FSBs Bunker Hill and Green. Along N bank of Song Dong Nai River, apx 23 km NE Bien Hoa AB. Heliport #575, alt 62', 11°06'30"N-106°58'00"E, per Feb73 TAD. Bien Hoa/Long Khanh Pr border, III Corps.

Hieu Thien (Go Dau Ha) (n/a)
Mapsheet name of L-7014-6231-2. SVN.

Higbee, USS (n/a)
A.k.a. DD 806. 1st USN vessel attacked by NVA MIGs during War. One dropped bomb on its stern, wounding 4. Role discussed in *Brown Water, Black Berets*, p 79. SVN.
High Clerical Association (n/a)
See Glossary.
Highboy, FSB (BS 915-137)
Along QL-1 just NE Gia An, apx 20 km NNE Bong Son, 5 km NE Mahoney AF, and 25 km SSE Duc Pho. Also near LZ Lowboy (BS 913-147). XXIV Corps grid. Also listed at BS 913-145. Binh Dinh or Quang Ngai Pr, I Corps.
Highland Fishhook (BS 00-47?)
Terrain feature formed by I Corps-II Corps, Quang Ngai-Binh Dinh Pr borders, roughly 35 km NW Bong Son. On map in *Rangers at War*, p 328. Grid est. I/II Corps.
Highlander Heights, LZ/FSB (ZA 20-73?)
A.k.a. Hill 953 or Chu Thoi Mtn? Between Pleiku and Kontum, along W side QL-14, about16 km S Kontum and apx 5 km E point where Kontum River makes a 90 degree turn from S to W. Apparently 2d Bde/4thInf Div Log supt base. Also listed at ZA 23-78. Kontum Pr, II Corps.
Highway (generally) (n/a)
See Glossary.
Highway 1 (various)
See QL-1. I, II/III Corps.
Highway 1A (BR?)
See QL-1A.
Highway 2 (YS)
See QL-2. III Corps.
Highway 3A (BR?)
See QL-3A. II Corps.
Highway 4 (XS/WS/WR/XR)
See QL-4. III/IV Corps.
Highway 9 (XD/YD)
See QL-9. Quang Tri Pr, I Corps.
Highway 13 (XT)
See QL-13 or Thunder Road. III Corps.
Highway 14 (AR)
See QL-14. I/II Corps.
Highway 19 (ZA/AR/BR)
See QL-19. II Corps.
Highway 92 (n/a)
A.k.a. Rte 92. Intersected Rte 9 E of Tchepone (after it left Quang Tri Pr near Khe Sanh). Laos.
Highway 401 (AN 900-105)
Coastal road originating at its intersection with QL-1, and running E from Phan Thiet to Hai Long on Hon Lao Peninsula. Binh Thuan Pr, II Corps.
Highway 533 (BT 24-18)
A.k.a. the Tien Phuoc Hwy? Ran from Tam Ky SW to Tien Phuoc. Quang Tin Pr, I Corps.
Highway 534 (BT 22-43)
A.k.a. the Old French Road. Ran generally ENE/WSW from Ha Binh (2) on coast, to QL-1 near Thang Binh, then WSW to Hiep Duc. Americal list. Quang Tin Pr, I Corps.
Highway 535 (AT/BT 08-40)
Listed as the Tien Phuoc Hwy, which is odd since Hwy 533 goes to Tien Phuoc, not 535? Ran SW from QL-1 near LZ Baldy, to Que Son. Quang Nam/Quang Tin Pr, I Corps.
Highway 540 (AT 82-57)
N/S route connected Da Nang and QL-1 with LTL Rte 4 at bridge crossing tributary of Song Thu Bon River apx 19 km SSW Da Nang and 15 km E QL-1's intersection with LTL-4. Grid is that of bridge. Quang Nam Pr, I Corps.
Highway 545 (YD 87-00?)
A.k.a. Rifle Road, An all-weather road linking FSB Rifle to QL-1, SE of Phu Bai. Beginning in Apr71, during Lam Son 720, 326th Engrs rebuilt/enlarged FSBs Brick, Tennessee, Rendezvous and Rifle. Also improved all-weather Rte 545, the FSB Rifle road, and the road to FSB Rakkasan. Grid apx. 101st Airborne Div, Thua Thien Pr, I Corps.
Highway 547 (YD 755-144)
Road running W from Hue (near Nam Hoa) to the A Shau Valley. Built by 101st Abn, '68. Grid is for Hwy 547 bridge over Perfume River. Thua Thien Pr, I Corps.
Highway 547 Bridge (YD 755-144)
A.k.a. Nam Hoa Bridge and Pohl Bridge. See Pohl Bridge for detail. Thua Thien Pr, I Corps.
Highway 548 (XD/YD/YC 48-98)
A.k.a. Rte 548. Parallels Lao border, then enters SVN S of the Da Krong Valley, becoming Rte 548 there and then turning E. Major infiltration route from Laos-Ho Chi Minh Trail reopened by NVA Engrs early '69. In Jan69, MACV counted over 1000 trucks/day using this conduit. As result, XXIV Corps launched Op Dewey Canyon, major multi-Bde, 9th Marine assault into Da Krong Valley area, beginning 18Jan69. During period, NVA employed 12.7mm, 25mm and 37mm AA fire with air bursts up to 16,000'. See Route 922. Quang Tri Pr, I Corps.
Highway 551 (YD 83-31)
Ran from NE corner of Hue, through Phu Vang (YD 783-YD 7826-269) to LCU Ramp at Tan My (YD 862-312). A POL line ran from Tank Farm on Vinh Loc Island near Eagle Beach (a.k.a. Tan My) along Hwy 551 to Hue. 101st Abn (as well as ARVN/RF/PF units) was responsible for security along line, its pumping stations, the LCU Ramp at Tan My and Hwy 551 itself. Thua Thien Pr, I Corps.
Highway 554 (YD 690-342)
Ran NE from its intersection with QL-1 at YD 623-304 (An Lo Bridge), to its terminus near Quang Dien at listed grid. Was only apx 8 km in length. See Quang Dien District HQ. Thua Thien Pr, I Corps.
Highway 559 (YD)
Left QL-9 E of Cam Lo running S, then E to join QL-1 below Dong Ha just north of QL-1/Vinh Phuoc Bridge. Quang Tri Pr, I Corps.
Highway 561 (YD)
N to S link in eastern Quang Tri Pr that was improved or built as part of McNamara's Wall. Quang Tri Pr, I Corps.
Highway 585 (BT 10-20)
In vicinity of Tien Phuoc AF. Quang Tin Pr, I Corps.
Highway 598 (YD 608-255)
Rural rte running from Hue W to Ap Lai Bang on E bank of Song Bo River, then resumed W and NW journey on E bank. Grid is for Ap Lai Bang. Thua Thien Pr, I Corps.
Highway 614 (YC/ZC/AT?)
A.k.a. The Yellow Brick Road and QL-614. Road leading to A Shau Valley from S. It became QL-548 in valley proper. Many enemy supply caches were found along road by 101st Abn in '69. Quang Nam/Thua Thien Pr, I Corps.

Highway 615 (YA?)
See Plei Trap Road. II Corps.
Highway 922 (XD?)
See Hwy 548.
Highway 966 (n/a)
A.k.a. Rte 966. W of Chu Lai in Laos.
Highway Orange (XT)
See Route Orange. III Corps.
Hilga, LZ (YA 964-497)
A.k.a. LZ Helga. Apx 28 km W Pleiku, 6 km SE peak Hill 1005, and 11 km ENE Plei Djereng New AF. LZs Cathy, Helga, Phyllis and Ruby were mutually suptg firebases? Name & grid per Dick Arnold as per Jan-Mar69 1st/35th Inf Bn daily logs. Pleiku Pr, II Corps.
Hill, Camp (YD 218-732)
A.k.a. FSB Gio Linh or The Alamo. On E Side QL-1 apx 13 km N Dong Ha, 23 km NNW Quang Tri and about 3 km SE FSB A-2. *1968 Yearbook* of *Encyclopedia Britannica* contains photo of a sign here which reads, "*Camp Hill, Gio Linh, The Alamo of Vietnam*." Named Camp Hill to honor PFC Lamont D. Hill, USMC, I/3d/4th Mar/3d Mar Div, KIA 6Mar67, near Tan Lich, Quang Tri Pr, while providing M-60 continuous covering fire though mortally wounded. 1st/12th Mar Arty here '67; four-175mms (US Army, attached), six-105mms, and secured by 3d Mar Div. Gio Linh was adj to base and source of its more common name. In '67, USMC built huge underground FDC bunker here. Its roof contained multiple layers of massive 12″ square timbers that were themselves covered with 8 feet of dirt and 10 layers of sandbags. Mascot dog named Hardcore became bases' early warning system because it could hear enemy incoming long before humans could. Whenever dog tucked his tail and ran for cover, troops grabbed their helmets and ran for cover as well. [262] NE Quang Tri Pr, I Corps.
Hill, LZ (YD 218-732)
See Hill, Camp, at grid. Quang Tri Pr, I Corps.
Hill, LZ (XD 84-54)
On Dong Voi Mep (Hill 1739/Tiger Tooth Mtn), apx 15 km due N Khe Sanh CB, 20 km W Laos and 15 km S the DMZ. In Jun64, radio intel units of ASA, under cover name "Advsy Team One," had 2 LZs built on Hill 1739 to provide observation-radio monitoring capabilities. One LZ was built on crest of hill and other on down slope, and named simply LZs "Crest" and "Hill." ARVN and USMC troops were employed to build/secure lofty site. High winds and downdrafts made landings here very difficult. By 22Jun64, 100 ARVN and 73 Marines manned site. See Dong Voi Mep and SESU. Quang Tri Pr, I Corps. [263]
Hill, OP (YA)
A.k.a. Hill 1124. See OP Hill. Kontum Pr, II Corps.
Hill, OP, 250 (AT or BT)
See Hill 250. Quang Tin Pr?, I Corps.
Hill, The (AP 822-990)
Apx 3 km due S Ban Me Thuot, 5 km S Ban Me Thuot City AF and 7 km WSW Ban Me Thuot East AF. Per SF expert Steve Sherman, "The Hill" was 2 km S of SOG CCS and site of SOG CCS's Radio Relay Site. Darlac Pr, II Corps.
Hill, The (CR 126-217
See Qui Nhon Harbor Entrance Control Post. Binh Dinh Pr, II Corps.
Hill 5 (BT 03-62)
Apx 6 km ESE Hill 55, 2 km W QL-1 and 14 km S At Da Nang. On map at p 98 of *US Marines in Vietnam-1969*. Quang Nam Pr, I Corps.
Hill 10 (AT 923-691)
Apx 5 km SW Hill 327, 15 km SW Da Nang, 10 km NW Hill 55 (Camp Muir), 4 km NW Hill 40 and 27 km NW Hoi An. HQ of 7th Mar/1st Mar Div after it moved from Dai La Pass Rock Crusher (FSB Stallion). 1st/11th Marine Arty here. 3d/7th Marines used site during Op. Oklahoma Hills, Mar-May69. 1st Mar Div, Grid per map on p 109, *US Marines in Vietnam-1969*. Map is L-7014-6640-4. Quang Nam Pr, I Corps.
Hill 10 (BS 583-722)
Immed W Quang Ngai AF. Quang Ngai Pr, I Corps.
Hill 10 (BT 200-390)
Along QL-1 apx 7 km SE LZ Baldy. 7th Marines, 1st Mar Div basecamp. Also Americal. Quang Tin Pr, I Corps.
Hill 10 Bridge (BT 208-375)
Along QL-1 apx 10 km SE LZ Baldy and 18 km NW Tam Ky. Apparently attacked or destroyed by VC, Apr70. Quang Tin Pr, I Corps.
Hill 14 (BT 286-190)
In lowland area along S side of Hwy 531, a few km NW Tam Ky's major AF, and 3 km SW Tam Ky. Americal list. Quang Tin Pr, I Corps.
Hill 21 (BT 322-334)
Apx 8 km due N Tam Ky. May66. Quang Ngai Pr, I Corps.
Hill 22 (AT 904-718)
Apx 11 km WSW Da Nang AB. USMC, Sep68-Mar69. Quang Nam Pr, I Corps.
Hill 22 (AT 953-667)
Apx 5 km NNW Hill 55, between La Chau (4) and La Chau (5). USMC position? On map at http://1stbn1stmarines.org/hs/images/MarkedaiLocMap.jpg. Quang Nam Pr, I Corps.
Hill 22 (BS 515-802)
Near Xuan Hoa, apx 16 km WNW Quang Ngai. Feb66. Quang Ngai Pr, I Corps.
Hill 22 (BS 715-924)
Near An Cuong, apx 20 km NNE Quang Ngai. Aug65. Quang Ngai Pr, I Corps.
Hill 22 (BT 423-091)
Apx 12 km WNW Chu Lai AB and 4 km S Diem Pho. USMC, Nov65. Quang Tin Pr, I Corps.
Hill 23 (BS 56-78?)
Apx 500 meters N Phuoc Loc 1, and 10 km WNW Quang Ngai. Secured by 3d/7th Mar during Op Texas, Mar66. Per *USMC in Vietnam, 1966*, p 126. Quang Ngai Pr, I Corps.
Hill 23 (BS 675-920)
Apx 7 km due E Binh Son/QL-1. USMC, Aug68. Listed at BT 675-920 in error. Quang Ngai Pr, I Corps.
Hill 24 (AT 871-989)
Apx 19 km ESE Phu Loc. Apr68. Quang Nam Pr, I Corps.
Hill 24 (AT 927-848)
Apx 4 km NNW Red Beach AF and `3 km NNE Da Nang AB. Apr68. Quang Nam Pr, I Corps.

Hill 25 (BT?)
Apparently USMC basecamp or FSB site. On mapsheet L-7014-6640-4, as are An Hoa, Liberty Bridge and Hills 10, 25, 52, 55, 65. Quang Nam Pr, I Corps.
Hill 26 (BS 771-616?)
Also listed by arty ORLL at BS 771-816; however; both grids are in ocean and both appear to be in error? Americal list. Quang Ngai Pr, I Corps.
Hill 26 (BT 316-338)
Apx 16 km SE Thang Binh/QL-1. Quang Tin Pr, I Corps.
Hill 27 (XT 752-330)
See Hill 29 at grid. Binh Duong Pr, III Corps.
Hill 28 (BT 257-234)
Apx 25 km WNW Tam Ky. Nov67. Quang Tin Pr, I Corps.
Hill 29 (BT 226-318)
See Hawk Hill. Quang Ngai Pr, I Corps.
Hill 29 (BT 235-315)
Apx 14 km NW Tam Ky, 1 km of QL-1 R&R tracks and 5 km W QL-1. 4th/12th Mar HQ 4th/11th Arty w/4-SP 155mm's here 18Jun66 during Op Kansas per *USMC in Vietnam, 1966*, p 135-6. Also listed at BT 234-315. Quang Tin Pr, I Corps.
Hill 29 (XT 752-330)
Listed as Hill 27, but is Hill 29. Apx 6 km SSW Lai Khe AF. May69. Binh Duong Pr, III Corps.
Hill 29 Heliport (BT 226-320)
See Hawk Hill Heliport. Quang Ngai Pr, I Corps.
Hill 30 (YD 140-610)
Apx 10 km W Dong Ha. Jul67. Quang Tri Pr, I Corps.
Hill 31 (YD 150-610)
Apx 8 km W Dong Ha. Jul67. Quang Tri Pr, I Corps.
Hill 31 (YD 269-732)
Apx 13 km NNE Dong Ha. Jul67. Quang Tri Pr, I Corps.
Hill 31 (XD 510-460)
See 31, LZ/FSB. Laos.
Hill 34 (AT 787-553)
A.k.a. Ha Nha Hill. Apx 6 km E Ha Tan, 29 km SW Da Nang AB. USMC basecamp or FSB site? XXIV Corps grid. Map is L-7014-6641-3. Quang Nam Pr, I Corps.
Hill 34 (AT 977-717)
Apx 5 km SW Da Nang AB. Quang Nam Pr, I Corps.
Hill 34 (AT 985-719)
Apx 5 km SSW Da Nang AB. Dec68-Aug69. Quang Nam Pr, I Corps.
Hill 35 (BT 437-077)
A.k.a. Fat City or Charger Hill. Near Que Son Valley, apx 10 km W Chu Lai, 4 km W Khuong Quang and 3 to 4 km W QL-1. USMC, 4th 31st Inf, 196th LIB, Americal. Also listed at BT 443-732, BT 440-077 and BT 435-079 and at Hill 29? Americal List. Quang Tin Pr, I Corps.
Hill 37 (AT 916-582)
A.k.a. Dai Loc, LZ 432 and apparently, The Old French Fort. Apx 5 km SW Hill 55 (Camp Muir), 25 km due W Hoi An and SE Charlie Ridge. USMC basecamp. Also listed at AT 94-59. On map in *US Marines in Vietnam-1969*, pp 98, 109. Quang Nam Pr, I Corps.
Hill 37 (YD 088-598)
Apx 3 km WNW Cam Lo. Jul67. Quang Tri Pr, I Corps.
Hill 37 (YD 130-593)
See Cam Lo. Quang Tri Pr, I Corps.
Hill 38 (BT 16-38?)
Apx 7 km SSE Hill 63 (LZ Baldy), 18 km due S Hoi An, 4 km W Ql-1 and 8 km SSE Baldy AF. Quang Nam/Quang Tin border area, I Corps.
Hill 38 (BT 279-222)
A.k.a. Nui Tac Huong? Apx 13 km Due W Tam Ky, 10 km NE Tien Phuoc. CAP Team 1-1-2 here, ‘68? XXIV Corps grid. Also listed at BT 282-225. Quang Tin Pr, I Corps.
Hill 40 (AT 94-66)
Apx 15 km SW Da Nang, 6 km NW Hill 55 and 8 km W QL-1. USMC position during Op Oklahoma Hills, 31Mar-29May69. Grid est per map on p 109, *US Marines in Vietnam-1969*. Quang Nam Pr, I Corps.
Hill 40 (BT 34-26)
Apx 5 km NE Tam Ky and 3 km W of the coast. Quang Tin Pr, I Corps.
Hill 40 Heliport (AT 915-692)
Apx 12 km SW Da Nang and N of Charlie Ridge. Heliport #580, alt 33', 15°59'30"N-108°07'00"E, per Feb73 TAD. Quang Nam Pr, I Corps.
Hill 41 (AT 943-663)
A.k.a. Go Kha. Possible USMC basecamp or FSB, apx 11 km SW Da Nang AB along Hwy 540, just E the foot of Charlie Ridge. XXIV Corps grid. Also listed at AT 930-660 and 935-663, Sep65-Sep69. Quang Nam Pr, I Corps.
Hill 42 (AT 98-51?)
Apx 2 km S My Loc 4, 13 km SSW Hill 55 and 5.5 km ENE An Hoa CB. L/3d/9th Mar CA’d here per during Op Macon 4-6Jul66 per *USMC in Vietnam, 1966*, p 202, 204. Quang Nam Pr, I Corps.
Hill 43 (BS 685-915)
Apx 24 km SE Chu Lai, 18 km NNE Quang Ngai, and 4 km WSW An Cuong/coast. Involved in Op Starlight, 1st major 3d Mar Div op of war, 8-19Aug65 (also 1st op to use US tanks in war). See Starlight. Quang Ngai Pr, I Corps.
Hill 43 (BT 113-327)
Apx 23 km NW Tam Ky, 6 km ENE Binh Son and 45 km SSE Da Nang AB. USMC. Also listed at BT 123-320, Dec65. Quang Tin Pr, I Corps.
Hill 44 (YD 0-6)
On N side of Hwy 547 between FSBs Birmingham and Bastogne. Scene of heavy contact by elements of both 82d and 101st Abn, ‘68 and ‘69, and also site of major battle during ‘72 Easters Offensive. Thua Thien Pr, I Corps.
Hill 45 (BS 721-938)
Apx 13 km ENE Binh Son/QL-1. Aug65. Listed at BT 721-938 in error. Quang Ngai Pr, I Corps.
Hill 46 (YD 810-060)
See Panther III. Thua Thien Pr, I Corps.
Hill 47 (WJ 6-5)
Roughly 35-40 km NW Hanoi and 3.5 mi NE Vinh Yen. Focus of fighting during battle of Vinh Yen, 13-17Jan51. See Vinh Yen. NVN.
Hill 48 (YD 114-734)
On edge of DMZ, apx 18 km NW Dong Ha. May-Sep67. Quang Tri Pr, I Corps.
Hill 48 (YD 670-050)
Apx 19 km SSW Hue Citadel AF. Jul68. Thau Thien Pr, I Corps.

Hill 49 (BT 338-238)
Apx 3 km NE Tam Ky, and in coastal plain some 4 km from ocean. Apr70 XXIV Corps grid per Don Armstrong. Quang Tin Pr, I Corps.
Hill 49 (BT 501-037)
Apx 6 km SW Chu Lai and 4 km W QL-1 1 near base of rocket ridge. 5th Marines position, Spring '66. See *Utter's Battalion*, p 282. Quang Tin Pr, I Corps.
Hill 50 (BS 55-84?)
Apx 1.5 km NE Hill 97, 1.5 km N Chau Ngai 1, 1 km SSE Khanh My 1 and 15 km NE Quang Ngai. Site of NVA CP and terrain feature of Op Utah, 4-7Jul66, per *USMC in Vietnam, 1966*, p 109-112, et al. Quang Ngai Pr, I Corps.
Hill 50 (BS 686-937?)
Listed at "BT" 686-939, but that grid puts it in ocean. Aug65. Quang Ngai Pr?, I Corps.
Hill 50 (BT 03-33)
Apx 4 km SSW Que Son, 3 km S FSB Ross and 3 km SE Son Tra. Apparently a position of 1st/7th Marines in '70. Discussed in detail in *Son Thang 4, An American War Crime*. Quang Nam Pr, I Corps.
Hill 51 (BT 025-343)
See LZ Ross. Quang Nam Pr, I Corps.
Hill 51 (YD 549-281)
Also listed at YD 540-280 and YD 552-284. Jun67-Jan68. Thua Thien Pr, I Corps.
Hill 52 (AT 788-552)
A.k.a. FSB Mustang. Along Rte 4, apx 19 km WSW Hill 55, 35 km W Hoi An, 10 km WSW Hill 65 and 33 km SW Da Nang. Built apx 21Mar69 by 1st/7th Marines in preparation for Op Oklahoma Hills. Mar69-Apr70. On mapsheet L-7014-6640-4. Grid est per map, p 109, *US Marines in Vietnam-1969*. Quang Nam Pr, I Corps.
Hill 52 (ZC 2161-5530)
See Hill 52 SF Camp. Quang Nam Pr, I Corps.
Hill 52, Camp (SF FOB) (ZC 2161-5530)
A.k.a. FOB Thuong Duc. In the Thuong Duc River Valley, apx 6 km E Ha Tan32 km SW Da Nang, 36 km W Hoi An and 12 km NW An Hoa. Info/grid per *SF Order of Battle.* Quang Nam Pr, I Corps.
Hill 54 (BT 396-145)
Apx 1 to 2 km W QL-1, some 3 km NNW Diem Pho, 16 km NW Chu Lai, and 11 km SE Tam Ky. Arty here suptd area N Chu Lai. CP 1st/5th Mar here Jun66, per *USMC in Vietnam, 1966*, p 131. Built and used during Op Burlington Trail? 196th LIB here '67. Per *Rites of Passage*, pp 379-80, was basecamp of 1st/14th Inf/25th Div, Summer '67. Americal list. Photos/maps at http://1-14th.com/maps.html. Also listed at BT 394-144. Quang Tin Pr, I Corps.
Hill 54, LZ (BT 396-145)
See Hill 54. Quang Tin Pr, I Corps.
Hill 55 (AT 965-615)
A.k.a. Camp Muir and Nui Bo Bo. Apx 18 km WNW Hoi An, 10 km NW Liberty Bridge, 6 km WSW Whiskey Tower, 25 km NW LZ Baldy, Due N Dodge City area, E Charlie Ridge and 20 km SW Da Nang. Apparently also used by French in 1st Indochina war, who reportedly lost an entire Bn in battle here during 1950's. HQ 1st/11th Marines Arty. Fwd CP for USMC forces HQ'd at Da Nang in '66. C Bty, 1st/11th Arty benchmark listed at AT 9611-6112, per John Middlesworth. See Camp Muir. On mapsheet L-7014-6640-4. Also listed at AT 970-620 and 967-617. Dai Loc Dist, Quang Nam Pr, I Corps.
Hill 55 (BT 01-33)
Apx 4 km SW Que Son, 3 km SE FSB Ross and 1.5 km NNE Hill 270. Possibly a position of 1st/7th Marines in '70. Discussed in *Son Thang 4, An American War Crime*. Quang Nam Pr, I Corps.
Hill 55 LAAM Site (AT 965-615)
See LAAM Sites. Assault Fire Unit of 15 Hawk missiles here 66. Quang Nam Pr, I Corps.
Hill 56 (YD 114-734?)
Apx 11 km due W Gio Linh. Also listed at YD 140-733? 114-734? May67. Quang Tri Pr, I Corps.
Hill 56 (YD 140-733?)
Apx 7 km due W Gio Linh. Also listed at YD 114-734? May67. Quang Tri Pr, I Corps.
Hill 56 (YD 578-282)
Apx 5 km SE Camp Evans, 3 km W song Bo River and 3 km ESE Ap Thuong An. Jun67. Thua Thien Pr, I Corps.
Hill 57 (YT 16-18)
A.k.a. Nui Ong Ta. Apx 9 km NE Plantation AF, 4 km N QL-1 and 34 km NE Saigon. Bien Hoa Pr, III Corps.
Hill 58 (YD 230-530)
Apx 11 km W Quang Tri. Jan68. Quang Tri Pr, I Corps.
Hill 59 Heliport (BT 164-233)
Apx 13 km due W Tam Ky and 12 km NW Tien Phuoc I Corps, heliport #581, alt 525', 15°35'00"N-108°21'00"E, per 73 TAD. Quang Tin Pr, I Corps.
Hill 59 (BT 165-233)
NW LZ East and overlooking Tam Ky River basin, apx 13 km due W Tam Ky and 12 km NW Tien Phuoc. Americal List. Quang Tin Pr, I Corps.
Hill 60 (AT 886-773)
Near Thon Tung Son, apx 11 km WNW Da Nang AB, and 2 km NW Rte 545. Sep68. Quang Nam Pr, I Corps.
Hill 60 Heliport (AT 831-578)
A.k.a. Hill 65 Heliport? Along S edge of Charlie Ridge, apx 24 km SW Da Nang AB and 12 km ENE Ha Tan AF. Heliport #582, alt 131', 15°53'00"N-108°05'00"E, per Feb73 TAD. Quang Nam Pr, I Corps.
Hill 61 (YD 516-311)
Apx 4 km SW Camp Evans and 25 km WNW Hue. Jan68. Thua Thien Pr, I Corps.
Hill 63 (BT 132-453)
A.k.a. FSB/LZ Baldy. Along W edge of QL-1 at its intersection with Rte 535, apx 12 km W ocean, 28 km NW Chu Lai, 16 km E FSB Ross and 33 km SSE Da Nang. 3d/11th Arty, 3d/11th Mar Arty suptg 7th Mar Rgt from this site in '69. Also listed at BT 136-448, 130-450, 135-452 and 132-454. Quang Nam Pr, I Corps.
Hill 63 (BT)
NVA occupied hill adj to Hill X. Attacked by 4th/31st, 3d/21st and 2d/1st Inf elements, 196th LIB, 23Nov67, 7 US KIA, 31 WIA. May be same Hill 63 that later became LZ Baldy? Quang Tin or Quang Nam Pr?, I Corps.
Hill 63 Airfield (BT 139-455)
A.k.a. Baldy AF. Along W edge of QL-1 at its intersection with Rte 535, some 12 km W ocean, 28 km NW Chu Lai and 33 km SSE Da Nang. "AF # VA1-63," in Aug69 TAD per Frank Penk, Jr. Not in Feb73 TAD. I Corps.

Hill 64 (XD 823-416)
Small Knob of hill in Khe Sanh Valley near the Rock Quarry and a few km WNW Khe Sanh CB. Used as OP. Scene of 1st NVA assault in immed vic of Khe Sanh CB, when at 0445hrs, on 8Feb68, 1st Plt/A/1st/9th Marines on OP duty were attacked by 101D Rgt, 325-C NVA Div. At least 24 US KIA and 29 WIA out of force of 65 men, with 150 NVA KIA. Of significant note during battle was tragic fact that most of newly introduced M-16 rifles jammed repeatedly. Some Marines spent much of fight simply clearing jams from M-16s so that others could use them. Many US dead found with cleaning rods in barrel of their weapon. Quang Tri Pr, I Corps.

Hill 65 (AT 879-578)
FSB a.k.a. Hill 65 and Nui Bo. Along Rte 4, 28 km SW Da Nang, 26 km W Hoi An, 8 km SE FSB Buckskin, 15 km E FSB Hawk and 10 km SW Hill 55 (Camp Muir). 11th Mar Arty Permanent OP (POP) built here '69, employing new IOD, and, with Hill 250, covering Thuong Duc Corridor approaches to Da Nang. Also listed at AT 882-578. 1st Mar Div. On mapsheet L-7014-6640-4. See IOD and POP. Quang Nam Pr, I Corps.

Hill 65 (BS 885-160)
Apx 2 km N Gia An, 16 km N LZ English and 2 km W QL-1. Feb66. Quang Ngai Pr, I Corps.

Hill 65 (XT or YT)
Apx 25 km N Bien Hoa and N of the Dong Nai River. Site of battle involving 1st/503d Inf and 3d/319th Arty, 173d Abn, and NVA regulars of Q-761 Rgt, 8Nov65, during Op Hump. One of earliest battles with NVA in SVN and one of few in which NVA choose to stand and fight. US casualties were 50 KIA, 82 WIA, while apx 110 NVA were KIA. War Zone D, Bien Hoa or Binh Duong Pr, III Corps.

Hill 65 Heliport (AT 831-578)
A.k.a. Hill 60 Heliport? Along S edge of Charlie Ridge, apx 24 km SW Da Nang AB and 12 km ENE Ha Tan AF. On 579th Engr Det (Terrain) map (dated Aug70) in same site as Hill 60 Heliport. Quang Nam Pr, I Corps.

Hill 68 (BS 708-608)
See Nui Dep. Quang Ngai Pr, I Corps.

Hill 68 (BT 316-131)
Apx 11 km S Tam Ky. Americal. Quang Tin Pr, I Corps.

Hill 69 (BT 436-073)
XT "436" may be transposition of 463, but if listed grid correct, was apx 11 km WNW Chu Lai. Americal list. Also listed at BS 462-072? Quang Tin Pr, I Corps.

Hill 69 (BT 462-072)
Apx 8 km WNW Chu Lai and within 2 km W QL-1. Americal list. Quang Tin Pr, I Corps.

Hill 69 Heliport (BT 470-070)
A.k.a. LZ Hill 69 and possibly Fat City Heliport. At or near Khuong Quang, apx 8 km WNW Chu Lai and within 2 km W QL-1. Heliport #583, alt 230', at 15°26'00"N-108°38'30"E, per Feb73 TAD. Quang Tin Pr, I Corps.

Hill 69, LZ (BT 462-072)
At or just W Khuong Quang, apx 7 km WNW Chu Lai AB, 22 km SE Tam Ky and 2 km W QL-1. Apr70 XXIV Corps grid per Don Armstrong. Quang Tin Pr, I Corps.

Hill 70 (AT 955-725)
In Da Nang and immed N Da Nang AB, apx 2 km S of coast. and Sep68. Quang Nam Pr, I Corps.

Hill 70 (BS 653-936?)
Also listed at BT 653-936, but that grid puts it in ocean. Aug65. Quang Ngai Pr?, Pr, I Corps.

Hill 70 (YD 076-673?)
A.k.a. Hill 72? Said to have been N of Cam Lo and W Camp Carroll. Hill 72 at listed grid may be same hill and, if so, was in the Song Ngan River Valley, apx 10 km NNW Cam Lo and 4 km WNW Thon Bai An. On 30Mar67, thirty-five men of a 3d/9th Marines Weapon Plt were heavily attacked here, resulting in 16 US KIA. Quang Tri Pr, I Corps.[264]

Hill 72 (YD 076-673)
A.k.a. Hill 70? In the Song Ngan River Valley, apx 10 km NNW Cam Lo and 4 km WNW Thon Bai An. Jul66. Quang Tri Pr, I Corps.

Hill 74 (BS 702-895?)
Listed at BT 702-895, but that puts it in ocean? Aug65. Quang Nam Pr, I Corps.

Hill 75 (WJ 6-5)
Roughly 35-40 km NW Hanoi and 3.8 mi ENE Vinh Yen. Focus of fighting during battle of Vinh Yen, 13-17Jan51. See Vinh Yen. NVN.

Hill 76 Heliport (BT 429-072)
Apx 12 km W to WNW Chu Lai, 3 km SW QL-1 and 18 km SE Tam Ky. Heliport #584, alt 6', at 15°26'00"N-108°36'00"E, per Feb73 TAD. Quang Tin Pr, I Corps.

Hill 76, FSB (BT 451-038)
Apx 8 km W and slightly S Chu Lai AB. Per Tom Brizendine, "was an actual firebase with 105s and I believe 175's." Cited in *Friendly Fire* as origin of "Friendly Fire" that hit Hill 707 on Rocket Ridge. Also listed at BT 452-039. Americal List. Quang Tin Pr, I Corps.

Hill 78 (YD 808-186)
See Three Sisters. Thua Thien Pr, I Corps.

Hill 82 (YS 494-620)
See FSB Horseshoe. Phuoc Tuy Pr, III Corps.

Hill 84 (BT 248-169)
See Nui Yon. Quang Tin Pr, I Corps.

Hill 84 (YD 091-609)
Apx 3 km NW Cam Lo. Jul66. Quang Tri Pr, I Corps.

Hill 84 (YS 26-58?)
A.k.a. FSB Andrea. On Long Son Island, apx 20 km SW Nui Dat, 13 km N Vung Tau. See Andrea for detailed history. Phuoc Tuy Pr, III Corps.

Hill 85 (BS 541-817)
Apx 1 km SW Chau Ngai (1), 14 km NE Quang Ngai and 1 km S Hill 97. Overlooked Chau Ngai complex, per *USMC in Vietnam, 1966*, p 109, 112. Secured by 2d/7th Mar during Op Utah, 4-7Mar66. See Chau Ngai (4). Quang Ngai Pr, I Corps.

Hill 88, FSB (AU 808-018)
A.k.a. Nui Trun. On coast at base of Mui Chon May Dong, apx 3 km SSE its tip, 35 km NNW Da Nang AB, 5 km N QL-1 and 36 km ESE Phu Bai. Per Ed Escoffier, a 155 Bty, and 44th Arty Duster and Searchlight unit here. Initially 155s were split-trails but later replaced with SP 155s of KY Ntl Guard. FSB built by 2d Howitzer Bn, 138th KY Ntl Guard (one of few ground combat Ntl Guard units sent to VN. Sent as reaction to Tet '68, the Bn 1st set up at Camp Eagle and then built/occupied 3 FSBs along QL-1, SE Hue and as far S as FSB Tomahawk Hill). FSB Los Banos was

just S Hill 88, in saddle of same Mtn. Also listed at AU 800-010, Oct68-Nov69. Thua Thien Pr, I Corps.

Hill 88 (YD 094-642)
Apx 6 km NNW Cam Lo. Sep67. Quang Tri Pr, I Corps.
Hill 88 (ZD)
See Hill 88 in AU UTM. Thua Thien Pr, I Corps.
Hill 93 (BT 248-169)
See Nui Yon. Quang Tin Pr, I Corps.
Hill 94 (BR 978-440)
Along Rte 502 at Chanh Liem, and 7 km E Phu Cat AB. Mar66. Binh Dinh Pr, II Corps.
Hill 97 (BS 538-825)
Apx 1 km N Hill 85, 1 km NW Chau Ngai (1), 14 km NE Quang Ngai, and overlooked Chau Ngai ville complex. 2d/7th Mar here during Op Utah, 4-7Mar66, per *USMC in Vietnam, 1966*, p 109, 112. See Chau Ngai (4). Quang Ngai Pr, I Corps.
Hill 100 (YD 06-65?)
Apx 13 km NE the Rockpile, 3 km ENE Hill 208, 2 km ESE Song Ngan River and 10 km NW Cam Lo. 2d/4th Mar objective/position during Op Hastings, 19Jul66, per *USMC in Vietnam, 1966*, p 169. Map 170. Quang Tri Pr, I Corps.
Hill 101 (BS 659-754)
See Buddha Mtn. Quang Ngai Pr, I Corps.
Hill 101 (WJ 6-5)
Roughly 35-40 km NW Hanoi and 2.5 mi NNE Vinh Yen. Focus of fighting during battle of Vinh Yen, 13-17Jan51. See Vinh Yen. NVN.
Hill 102 (AT 925-270)
A.k.a. Million Dollar Hill. Apx 8 km WNW Nui Liet Kiem/LZ West, 1 km NE Hill 108, 33 km WNW Tam Ky and 9 km SW LZ Dragon Base. See Million Dollar Hill. Quang Nam Pr, I Corps.
Hill 102 (BS 630-855)
A.k.a. LZ Dottie or Nui Dong De? Apx 12 miles S Chu Lai, E QL-1, and N Ham Giang River. Americal list. Quang Ngai Pr, I Corps.
Hill 105 (BS 702-601)
See Nui Vong. Quang Ngai Pr, I Corps.
Hill 108 (AT 922-258)
Apx 3 km NE Hiep Duc, 38 km W Tam Ky, 1 km S Hill 102, 10 km SW LZ Dragon Base and 7 km W to WNW Nui Liet Kiem/LZ West. Possible USMC and/or Americal Div position here. Grid per map courtesy Bob Shrake, 4th/31st Inf, 196th LIB. Quang Tin Pr, I Corps.
Hill 110 (AT 978-236)
Apx 2 km SW Nui Liet Kiem/LZ West, 31 km W Tam Ky and 8 km SSW LZ Dragon Base. Possible USMC and/or Americal Div position here. Grid per map courtesy Bob Shrake. Quang Tin Pr, I Corps.
Hill 110 (BS 729-849)
Apx 15 km NE Quang Ngai. Quang Ngai Pr, I Corps.
Hill 110 (BT 033-385)
Apx 17 km ESE An Hao AF. Quang Nam Pr, I Corps.
Hill 110 (BT 232-189)
Along Hwy 533, apx 9 km WSW Tam Ky and 12 km ENE Tien Phuoc. Near Young Heliport and E LZ East. Americal list. Quang Tin Pr, I Corps.
Hill 119 (AT 998-508)
Apx 13 km ENE An Hoa and 26 km due S Da Nang. 11th Marine Arty POP site here, with IOD covering Go Noi Island and Dodge City approaches to Da Nang. See IOD and POP. 1st Mar Div FSB also? Quang Nam Pr, I Corps.
Hill 123 (BT 055-370)
Apx 13 km WSW Thang Binh/QL-1. May67. Quang Nam Pr, I Corps.
Hill 124 (AT 870-780)
Apx 14 km WNW Da Nang AB. Quang Nam Pr, I Corps.
Hill 124 (YD 077-623)
Apx 6 km NW Cam Lo. Feb67. Quang Tri Pr, I Corps.
Hill 128 (BS 688-870)
Apx 24 km SE Chu Lai AF. Quang Ngai Pr, I Corps.
Hill 128 (XT 757-899)
Immed N An Loc and 500 meters W QL-13. Jul67. Binh Long Pr, III Corps.
Hill 132 (ZD 117-014)
See FSB Tomahawk. Also listed at ZD 108-009, May66. Thua Thien Pr, I Corps.
Hill 136 (YS 286-418)
See Nui Nho. Phuoc Tuy Pr, III Corps.
Hill 138 (AT 979-307)
See LZ Leslie at grid. Quang Nam Pr, I Corps.
Hill 140 (YD 810-080)
See FSBs Arsenal and Panther III. Thua Thien Pr, I Corps.
Hill 140? (YD 663-225)
See OP Castle. Thua Thien Pr, I Corps.
Hill 141 (BS 474-863)
A.k.a. An Hoa Outpost. Apx 15 km WSW Binh Son, 23 km NW Quang Ngai, 2 km S Rte 529 and overlooking Vinh Tuy Valley. Site of remote outpost of 936th RF Co overrun night of 18-19Mar66, with 31 KIA, 85 MIA and 30 survivors. Assaulted by 3d/7th Mar and 5th ARVN Abn Bn relief force, 19Mar66, during Op Texas. Info per *USMC in Vietnam, 1966*, p 120-21, 271. Quang Ngai Pr, I Corps.
Hill 141 (BT 66-05)
On Mui Nam Tram, apx 13 km due E Chu Lai AB and 2.5 km NE Tuyet Diem. Bty C, 2d USMC LAAM Bn Hawk AA missile site moved here late '66, to protect Chu Lai and Song Tra Bong Valley. See LAAM Sites for detail. Data, per *USMC in Vietnam, 1966*, p 271. Quang Tin Pr, I Corps.
Hill 141 LAAM Site (BT 66-05)
See LAAM Sites. C Bty, 2d LAAM moved here after initially being sited at S end of Chu Lai AF in '66. Quang Nam Pr, I Corps.
Hill 142 (CR 051-737)
A.k.a. Hill 142. On coast apx 16 km ENE Phu My/QL-1. Binh Dinh Pr, II Corps.
Hill 142 (VS 58-29)
See Nui Sai Voi, Battle of. Kien Giang Pr, IV Corps.
Hill 144 (BS 673-960)
Apx 16 km SE Chu Lai AF. Quang Ngai Pr, I Corps.
Hill 144 (XD 987-565)
A.k.a. the Little Rockpile. 1 km NE the taller Rockpile peak in Razorback Valley, 4 km SW peak Dong Ha Mtn and 14 km WSW Cam Lo. Quang Tri Pr, I Corps.
Hill 145 (VS 89-61)
See Nui Tuong. Chau Doc Pr, IV Corps.
Hill 150 (BS 818-382)
See Mt. Montezuma. Quang Ngai Pr, I Corps.

Hill 150 (BT 041-191)
Apx 14 km ESE Hiep Duc. Aug66. Quang Tin Pr, I Corps.
Hill 150 (XU 715-095)
Apx 2 km NW Loc Ninh AF. Binh Long Pr, III Corps.
Hill 151 (AT 938-476)
Apx 6 km due E An Hoa AF. Americal list. No data. Quang Nam Pr, I Corps.
Hill 151 (BR 89-41)
See Bordner Hill. Binh Dinh Pr, II Corps.
Hill 154 (BR 743-817)
See LZ Bird at listed grid. Binh Dinh Pr, II Corps.
Hill 155 (BT 045-214)
Apx 14 km E to ESE Hiep Duc. Quang Tin Pr, I Corps.
Hill 157 (WJ 6-5)
Roughly 35-40 km NW Hanoi and 3.5 mi ENE Vinh Yen. Focus of fighting during battle of Vinh Yen, 13-17Jan51. See Vinh Yen. NVN.
Hill 158 (YD 113-703)
A.k.a. Nui Con Thien, FSB Con Thien and Hill of Angel. From it, observation was unfettered for 15 km to coast in E, the Annamite mtns to W and DMZ to N. A strategically important but extremely vulnerable Marine base because NVA arty (130mm and 152mm cannons) across DMZ had greater range than the US arty and was immune to counter-battery fire. See Con Thien. Quang Tri Pr, I Corps.
Hill 159 (BT 280-158)
Apx 4 km SE Tam Ky AB, 17 km E Tien Phuoc and 13 km ESE Hill 37. XXIV Corps grid. Quang Tin Pr, I Corps.
Hill 160 (CP 034-568)
See Nha Trang Buddha. Khan Hoa Pr, II Corps.
Hill 162 (YD 070-636)
Apx 7 km NW Cam Lo. Mar69. Quang Tri Pr, I Corps.
Hill 162 (YD 97-03)
See FSB Rock Crusher. Thua Thien Pr, I Corps.
Hill 162 (YD 989-041)
See Greer, FSB. Thien Pr, I Corps.
Hill 163 (BS 872-328)
Apx 21 km SE Mo Duc, 4 km due E Duc Pho and 2.5 km SW mouth of Tra Cau/Lo Bo Rivers. Part of Nui Dau Hill mass. Overlooked Red Beach (assault beach of TF Delta BLT during Op Double Eagle), and recon OP, Jan-Feb66. Secured by Co of 2d/4th Mar & Co of 4th ARVN Rgt, 27Jan66, per *USMC in Vietnam, '66*, p 23, 27, map p 20. Quang Ngai Pr, I Corps.
Hill 164 (BS 873-324)
See Nui Dau. Quang Ngai Pr, I Corps.
Hill 165 (BT)
Near LZ Professional. Americal list. Quang Tin Pr, I Corps.
Hill 170 (AT 888-383)
Apx 9 km S An Hoa AF. Nov67. Quang Nam Pr, I Corps.
Hill 171 (BS 517-779)
Apx 12 km W Quang Ngai. Quang Ngai Pr, I Corps.
Hill 172, Battle of (XU 9-2 or 9-3?)
Near of Bo Duc. Several Bo Ducs listed in general vic of listed grid squares and Bu Dop AF, just S Cambodian border, apx 30 km NW Loc Ninh. After Srok Silamlite III, Bo Duc area was quiet until 8Dec67, when at 0100 a Medevac called to an NDP (1st/2d Inf and B/1st/5th Arty, 1st Inf Div) received fire from undetected VC force. Fire alerted NDP of impending attack and 2 ambush patrols were called -in as perimeter came under heavy fire. Direct arty was needed to blunt initial assault, which was soon followed by a 2d. By 0400, VC retreated, leaving behind 49 known KIA. Phuoc Long Pr?, III Corps.
Hill 173 (BT 16-24)
Roughly 15 km WNW Tam Ky. Americal list indicates it was near this grid. Quang Tin Pr, I Corps.
Hill 174 (YD 08-67?)
6 km SW Con Thien and site of last major battle of Op Hickory, 28-31May67. Grid is est. Quang Tri Pr, I Corps.
Hill 177 (XU 722-112)
Apx 3 km NNW Loc Ninh AF. Binh Long Pr, III Corps.
Hill 180 (YD 855-133)
Apx 3 km WSW Phu Bai AF, 2.5 km SW QL-1 and 13 km SE Hue. Prominent terrain feature, USMC position and OP in'66. Later believed to have been US Army signal site or OP. Thua Thien Pr, I Corps.
Hill 180 (BN 757-882)
See Nui Dat at grid. Ninh Thuan Pr, II Corps.
Hill 182 (BS 567-878)
See LZ Phoenix. Quang Ngai Pr, I Corps.
Hill 184 (CP 079-177)
Apx 7 km SSE the S end of Cam Ranh Bay AF rwy. Feb66. Khanh Hoa Pr, II Corps.
Hill 185 (BT 173-078)
See FSB Professional. Quang Tin Pr, I Corps.
Hill 188 (XD 987-593)
Apx 13 km NW Mai Loc AF. Quang Tri Pr, I Corps.
Hill 190 (AT?)
Apparently NW Da Nang. 11th Mar Arty Permanent OP (POP) employing Integrated Observation Devices (IOD), and covering Elephant Valley, Hai Van Pass and approaches to Da Nang. 1st Mar Div. See IOD and POP. Quang Nam Pr, I Corps.
Hill 190 (YD 068-593)
Apx 6 km WNW Cam Lo. Mar67. Quang Tri Pr, I Corps.
Hill 198 (BR 932-745)
A.k.a. Duster Hill. See Duster Hill for detail. II Corps.
Hill 200 (AT 795-527)
Apx 9 km NW An Hoa AF. Quang Nam Pr, I Corps.
Hill 200 (YD 0-6)
Apx 9.5 km NNE the Rockpile, 2 km WNW Hill 200, 1 km N Song Ngan River and 13 km WNW Cam Lo. Objective of 3d/4th Mar during Op Hastings 15-16Jul66, per *USMC in Vietnam, 1966*, p 166, map 170. Quang Tri Pr, I Corps.
Hill 203 (XU 700-090)
Apx 3 km WNW Loc Ninh AF. Binh Long Pr, III Corps.
Hill 208 (YD 042-644)
Overlooking the Song Nang Valley, apx 20 km W Don Ha 10 km NE the Rockpile, just S the Song Ngan River, 2.5 km WSW Hill 100 and 12 km WNW Cam Lo. During Op Hastings, was assaulted and taken by 2d/4th Marines 20Jul66 as suspected CP of the NVA 324B Div, but though heavily fortified, was only lightly defended. Op Hastings, 15Jul66-3Aug66, was effort to eliminate NVA here and in valley in order to spoil apparent planned attack of Hue by 341st NVA Div, then poised just below the DMZ for that mission. SW the hill and near the Rockpile were the 803d and 812th NVA Rgts, while the 90th Rgt of 324-B was in Song Nang Valley itself. Per *USMC in Vietnam, 1966*, p 163, 172, map 170. Quang Tri Pr, I Corps.

Hill 210 (WJ 6-5)
Roughly 35-40 km NW Hanoi and 2.5 mi N Vinh Yen. Focus of fighting during battle of Vinh Yen, 13-17Jan51. See Vinh Yen. NVN.
Hill 211, FSB (BS)
See Hell 2-11, FSB. Quang Tin Pr?, I Corps.
Hill 213 (BS 4-9?)
See Hill 707. Quang Tin Pr?, I Corps.
Hill 214 (ZC 190-450)
See FSB Pike. Quang Nam Pr, I Corps.
Hill 218 (BT 028-372)
Apx 18 km SE An Hao AF. Jan71. Quang Nam Pr, I Corps.
Hill 218 (YD 636-065)
Apx 26 km WSW Phu Bai and 13 km W to WNW Hill 618 (Nui Ke). USMC FSB? '67. Thua Thien Pr, I Corps.
Hill 220 (WS 17-33)
See Hue Duc Mountain. IV Corps.
Hill 221 (WS 17-33)
At SE edge of Hue Duc. Kien Giang Pr, IV Corps.
Hill 222 (WJ 20-80)
Overlooked Chan Muong Gorge. Old Chinese fort here dominated the area and was Vietminh position during ambush of Chan Muong Gorge, 17Nov52. See Chan Muong Gorge, and *Street Without Joy*, p 97, on map at p 98. Grid is est. NVN.
Hill 222 (XU 774-147)
Apx 7 km NE Loc Ninh AF. Binh Long Pr, III Corps.
Hill 222 (YA 87-02)
See Crooks. Pleiku Pr, II Corps.
Hill 222 (YD 03-06?)
Portion of Turkey Ridge and near listed grid. See Turkey Ridge. Quang Tri Pr, I Corps.
Hill 224 (ZC 118-535)
Apx 3 km WSW Ha Tan AF. Quang Nam Pr, I Corps.
Hill 227 (YD 03-06?)
See Marine Hill and Turkey Ridge. Quang Tri Pr, I Corps.
Hill 230 (BT 02-95)
On Hon Son Tra Island, apx 15 km N Da Nang, 11 km NNW Monkey Mtn. Thua Thien Pr?, I Corps.
Hill 230 (WS 09-80)
See Nui Sam. Chau Duc Pr, IV Corps.
Hill 232 (WS 09-80)
One of 7 peak grp collectively known as "Seven Sisters" and rising from flat, mangrove plain generally E Ha Tien and N Rach Gia. Included Hue Duc Mtn (Hill 220), Nui Co To (Hill 61, just S Tri Tron), Dop Chompa (actually two separate peaks, highest of which is 710 meters, SW That Son AF), Hill 232 (near Chau Phu) and Hill 296 (5 km from Cambodia and 10 km N That Son). Chau Doc/Kien Giang Prvs, IV Corps.
Hill 238 (AN 758-213)
See Nui Khinh. Binh Thuan Pr, II Corps.
Hill 241 (BS 476-812)
Apx 17 km NW Quang Ngai. Quang Ngai Pr, I Corps.
Hill 242 (BT 129-225)
Apx 17 km due W Tam Ky. Aug66. Quang Tin Pr, I Corps.
Hill 244 (AT 946-744)
Apx 6 km WSW Da Nang AB. Quang Nam Pr, I Corps.
Hill 245 (YS 269 465)
See Nui Lon. Phuoc Tuy Pr, III Corps.
Hill 246 (YD 625-144)
ARVN FSB apx 5 km N FSB Bastogne and apx 12 km SW Hue. Built Apr71. Thua Thien Pr, I Corps.
Hill 247 (XD 951-432)
To S of QL-9 and Song Thach Han River, apx 2 km WSW Lang Ruou, 10 km due E Khe Sanh CB. On 21Jul67, during ambush of convoy along QL-9, NVA fire from this position resulted in 3 USMC KIA. Data per *The Final Formation*, p 31. Quang Tri Pr, I Corps.
Hill 247 (YD 505-144)
See Rio, FSB. Thua Thien Pr, I Corps.
Hill 248 (XT 525-580)
Peak of hill mass apx 7 km ESE FSB White, 30 km ENE Tay Ninh and 24 km due E Nui Ba Den. Like Nui Ba Den, a major navigational feature in Tay Ninh Pr, III Corps.
Hill 248 (YC 902-913)
Apx 7 km NNE Ruong Ruong. Also listed at YC 913-894. Jan-Feb69. I Corps.
Hill 248 (XD 94-42?)
A.k.a. LZ Mike. Very roughly 8 km SW Ca Lu, 8 km S LZ Robin, 2 km S Rte 9, and 12 km E Khe Sanh CB. Surrounded on 3 sides by river and its tributaries. At opening of Op Pegasus (op to lift siege of Khe Sanh), the 1st/7th Cav CA'd to secured site and was immed followed by 2d/7th Cav. Quang Tri Pr, I Corps.
Hill 249 (YD 03-06?)
Portion of Turkey Ridge and near listed grid. See Turkey Ridge. Quang Tri Pr, I Corps.
Hill 250 (AT or BT)
A.k.a. OP Hill. 11th Mar Arty Permanent OP (POP) employing the Integrated Observation Devices (IOD) and, along with Hill 65, covering the Thuong Duc Corridor approach to Da Nang. 1st Mar Div. See IOD and POP. Quang Nam Pr, I Corps.
Hill 250 (YD 068-556?)
Grid is possible site, and if correct, was apx 5 km NNW Mai Loc AF. "Rainbelt Radio Relay" here per George Neville, 3d Recon Bn. Secured by elements of 3d Recon Bn, 3d Mar Div. Dec66-Aug67. Quang Tri Pr, I Corps.
Hill 251 (AN 898-291)
See Nui Xa To. Binh Thuan Pr, II Corps.
Hill 251 (BT 15-28)
Near Duc An, apx 17 km NW Tam Ky. Americal list. Quang Tin Pr, I Corps.
Hill 252 (YD 03-56?)
Apx 6.5 km WSW Cam Lo, 500 meters S QL-9 and 2 km due E the Rockpile. Described as hill of solid rock in which NVA had somehow carved bunkers in N Face. On 17-18Aug66, during Op Prairie, NVA halted 2d/4th Marines sweeping QL-9 at Khe Geo Bridge opposite hill, resulting in 2 KIA and 5 WIA US. Per *USMC in Vietnam, 1966*, p 181-2. Quang Tri Pr, I Corps.
Hill 253 (BT 181-205)
Apx 13 km due W Tam Ky. Aug66. Quang Tin Pr, I Corps.
Hill 258 (n/a)
Cited in 1st Cav VN *Yearbook* Aug65-Dec69, p 85, per Peter Cole. Apparently 1st Cav battle site or LZ? Possibly I Corps or II Corps.
Hill 258 (XU 9-2)
A.k.a. LZ Axe or Ax. See Axe. Vicinity of Dong Tre. Phu Yen Pr, II Corps.

Hill 259 (WS 05-64)
See Nui Cam Mountain. Chau Doc Pr, IV Corps.
Hill 259 (YU 137-052)
Immed S Rte 311, apx 2 km SSE Song Be AF. Jan68. Phuoc Long Pr, III Corps.
Hill 261 (WS 01-55)
A.k.a. Nui Ba Doi. Roughly midway between Nui Coto and Dop Chompa Mtn, apx 3 km N Tri Ton, 55 km E Ha Tien and 10 km SSW That Son AF. Chau Doc Pr?, IV Corps.
Hill 262 (YD 031-644)
Apx 10 km NW Cam Lo. Apr69. Quang Tri Pr, I Corps.
Hill 266 (VS 99-72)
See Nui Giai. Chau Doc Pr, IV Corps.
Hill 270 (AT 860-680?)
If correct Hill 270, was N of Charlie Ridge and apx 17 km SW Da Nang AB. Also listed at AT 865-682. 11th Mar Arty Permanent OP (POP) employing Integrated Observation Devices (IOD), and covering routes leading to Da Nang from Happy Valley, Mortar Valley, Sherwood Forest and Charlie Ridge. 1st Mar Div. See IOD and POP. Quang Nam Pr, I Corps.
Hill 270 (BT 196-114)
Apx 8 km ESE Tien Phuoc AB and 16 km SW Tam Ky. Jun69. On 21May69, during Op Lamar Plain, elements of 1st/501st Inf, 101st Abn (opcon to Americal Div) fought vicious battle here (or possibly Hill 270 at BT 420-048?), resulting in 25 enemy KIA. Quang Tin Pr, I Corps.
Hill 270 (BT 420-048)
Apx 12 km W Chu Lai AB, 20 km SSE Tam Ky and 6 km SW Khuong Quang. Americal list. A Hill 270 also at BT 196-114. Quang Tin Pr, I Corps.
Hill 270, LZ (BT 421-048)
Apx 12 km W Chu Lai AB, 20 km SSE Tam Ky and 6 km SW Khuong Quang. Apr70 XXIV Corps grid per Don Armstrong. Quang Tin Pr, I Corps.
Hill 270 (BT 435-019)
Apx 12 km WSW Chu Lai AB and 9 km NE peak of Nui Dong Tram. Feb71. Quang Tin Pr, I Corps.
Hill 271 (YA 622-516)
Along N edge of Rte 615, apx 25 km WNW Plei Djereng New AF and 3 km SE LZ Lane. Said to have also been S of LZ Lane. See *Rites of Passage*, p 81. Pleiku Pr, II Corps.
Hill 275 (YD 290-402)
A.k.a. Dong Ong Do Mountain and LZ June. Apx 12 km due W Ba Long AF and 13 km SSW Quang Tri. Quang Tri Pr, I Corps.
Hill 282 (AT 93-78)
Apx 6 km NW Hill 327 and 5 km W Da Nang. Map at p 98, *US Marines in Vietnam-1969*. Quang Nam Pr, I Corps.
Hill 282 (VS 94-68)
See Nui Ta Bac. Chau Doc Pr, IV Corps.
Hill 283 (YA 584-514)
Apx 2.5 km SSW LZ Lane, 28 km WNW Plei Djereng New AF and 4 km E Cambodia. 1st/14th Inf/25th Div here, Nov66. On 13Nov66, A/1st/14th Inf in big battle with 33d NVA Rgt apx 2 km from this hill, and was later reinforced by C Co. 15 US KIA and 38 WIA (13 of KIA and 37 of WIA were from A Co). See *Rites of Passage*, pp 63, 76. Pleiku Pr, II Corps.
Hill 284 (XT 53-58)
A.k.a. FSB Pine Ridge. Apx 12 km NNE Dau Tieng AF/Tri Tam. Tallest peak of the Nui Tha La hill mass (a.k.a. The Razorbacks). See Razorbacks and Pine Ridge. Binh Duong Pr, III Corps.
Hill 285 (BS 829 285)
Immed E Duc Pho, apx 3 km E QL-1 and 7 km SE Quang Hien. Also listed at BS 820-286 and by arty ORLL at BS 820-235. Americal list. Quang Ngai Pr?, I Corps.
Hill 285 (YD 629-223)
See OP Apache. Thua Thien Pr, I Corps.
Hill 296 (VS 98-73)
Apx 12 km N Dop Chompa and 10 km N That Son AF. One of 7 peak grp, collectively known as the "Seven Sisters," rising from flat, mangrove plain generally E Ha Tien and N Rach Gia. Included Hue Duc Mtn (Hill 220), Nui Co To (Hill 61, just S Tri Tron), Dop Chompa (actually two separate peaks, highest of which is 710 meters, SW That Son AF), Hill 232 (near Chau Phu) and Hill 296 (5 km from Cambodia and 10 km N That Son). See Dop Chompa Mtn. Chau Doc Pr, IV Corps.
Hill 296 (ZC 119-529)
Apx 4 km WSW Ha Tan AF/Thuong Duc. Oct68. Quang Nam Pr, I Corps.
Hill 300 (YT 437-038)
Immed E LTL-2, apx 6 km SW Xuan Loc. Jul67. Long Khanh Pr, III Corps.
Hill 301 (AT 863-665)
Also listed as Hill 310? Apx 16 km SW Da Nang AB. Apr69. Quang Nam Pr, I Corps.
Hill 302 (CQ 319-235)
See Nui Vung Ro. Phu Yen Pr, II Corps.
Hill 309 (YC 8-8)
In Ruong Ruong Valley and adj to French-built AF there. Cited in *Bonnie-Sue*, pp 241-246. Thua Thien Pr, I Corps.
Hill 309 (YD 652-202)
A.k.a. Nui Hon Vuon and FSB T-Bone. Visible from LZ Sally, apx 8 km WSW Hue Citadel AF and 7 km SSE LZ Sally/Van Xa. Scene of battle involving D/2d/501st Inf, 101st Abn, 20Mar68. Later site of FSB T-Bone. Had commanding view of Hue enjoyed by NVA during Tet '68. Thua Thien Pr, I Corps.
Hill 309 (YT 481-003)
Apx 8 km S Xuan Loc. Dec66. Long Khanh Pr, III Corps.
Hill 310 (AT 863-665)
Also listed as Hill 301? Apx 16 km SW Da Nang AB. Nov68. Quang Nam Pr, I Corps.
Hill 314 (BT 148-242)
Apx 16 km WNW Tam Ky. Quang Nam Pr, I Corps.
Hill 314 (YD 020-622)
Apx 10 km WNW Cam Lo. Aug66. Quang Tri Pr, I Corps.
Hill 316 (YD 416-211)
See FSB Gladiator. Thua Thien Pr, I Corps.
Hill 316 (YD 604-100)
A.k.a. Nui Mai Nha. Apx 18 km SW Hue Citadel AF and 11 km W FSB Birmingham. Jul67. Thau Thien Pr, I Corps.
Hill 324 (AT 884-742)
Apx 7 km WNW Hill 327 and 12 km W Da Nang. Map at p 98, *US Marines in Vietnam-1969*. Quang Nam Pr, I Corps.

Hill 324 (YS 63-99)
A.k.a. FSB Dao? Apx 20 km ENE Blackhorse Basecamp, 17 km ESE Xuan Loc. FSB Dao was either immed to E or atop this mtn. Long Khanh Pr, III Corps.
Hill 324 (YT 62-10)
A.k.a. FSB Mace? Prominent feature near Gia Ray, apx 10 km due S Nui Chua Chan, 16 km SE Xuan Loc. 3d/7th Inf, HQs 2d/3d Inf, 199th LIB. Binh Thuy Pr, III Corps.
Hill 327 (AT 978-743)
A.k.a. Division Ridge and Division Hill. On ridge 4 km WSW Da Nang AB, 2 km NW Hwy 587 and 3.5 km NE Ap Thach Nham. HQ, 1st Mar Div. See mapsheet L-7014-6641-3. Quang Nam Pr, I Corps.
Hill 327 (YS 58-51)
A.k.a. Hon Vung Mtn. Apx 21 km ENE Vung Tau and 2 km from ocean. Has spectacular view of coast and Vung Tau area to W. Phuoc Tuy Pr, III Corps.
Hill 327 LAAM Site (AT 97-74)
See LAAM Sites. Bty B/1st LAAM here in '66. Quang Nam Pr, I Corps.
Hill 333 (YD 546-049)
Apx 1.5 km NNW FSB Veghel. Thua Thien Pr, I Corps.
Hill 342 (YD 633-084)
See OP Checkmate. Thau Thien I Corps.
Hill 347 (YD 107-267)
See Shiloh, FSB. Quang Tri Pr, I Corps.
Hill 348 (BT 050-250)
See FSB Center. Quang Tin Pr, I Corps.
Hill 349 (AN 783-239)
See Nui Toi Ha and LZ Bartlett. Binh Thuan Pr, II Corps.
Hill 350 (AT 837-857)
On S side of Hwy 535, apx 19 km NW Da Nang AB and 11 km WNW Red Beach AF. Quang Nam Pr, I Corps.
Hill 352 (BT 075-225)
See Nui Hoac. Quang Tin Pr, I Corps.
Hill 356 (AN 912-438)
See Nui Dagai. Binh Thuan Pr, II Corps.
Hill 356 (BT 119-235)
Apx 17 km W Tam Ky. Aug66. Quang Tin Pr, I Corps.
Hill 358 (AT 932-885)
Apx 7 km NNW Red Beach AF. Quang Nam Pr, I Corps.
Hill 361 (CR 151-312)
See Nui Den. Apx 3.5 km WSW the S end of Qui Nhon AF rwy. Binh Dinh Pr, II Corps.
Hill 362 (YD 01-62?)
Apx 7 km NNE the Rockpile, 2 km S Song Ngan River, 4 km SW Hill 208 and 12 km WNW Cam Lo. I/2d/5th Mar radio relay site 24-25Jul66, during Op Hastings. Heavily assaulted by 6th/812th NVA Rgt night of 24-25Jul, the last large engagement of Op. 18 US KIA and 82 WIA, per *USMC in Vietnam, 1966*, p 173. Quang Tri Pr, I Corps.
Hill 362 (YD 011-617?)
Apx 12 km W Cam Lo and adj to Dong Ha Mtn. Attacked and cleared by USMC during Op Hastings, Aug66. Grid apx? Quang Tri Pr, I Corps.
Hill 364 (AT 94-76)
Apx 5 km due W Da Nang and 4 km NW Hill 327 (Division Hill). Quang Nam Pr, I Corps.
Hill 365 (US 868-488)
See Ham Rong Mtn. Phu Quoc Island, IV Corps.
Hill 375 (YT 62-11)
See FSB Mace. Quang Tri Pr, I Corps.
Hill 381 (AT 994-391)
Apx 14 km SE An Hoa AF. Jan71. Quang Nam Pr, I Corps.
Hill 385 (YD 118-432)
Apx 25 km WSW Quang Tri and 8 km SSE Mai Loc. Within view of Hill 819 Radio Relay Site. See India Relay. Quang Tri Pr, I Corps.
Hill 386 (AN 925-223)
See Nui Ta Dom. Binh Thuan Pr, II Corps.
Hill 390 (AT 88-75)
Apx 9 km W Hill 327, 4 km due N Hieu Duc and apx 10 km due W Da Nang. Quang Nam Pr, I Corps.
Hill 391 (YD 006-305)
Apx 16 km ESE Khe Sanh CB. Quang Tri Pr, I Corps.
Hill 396 (AT 884-747)
Apx 12 km due W Da Nang AB. Quang Nam Pr, I Corps.
Hill 396 (YT 389-125)
Apx 8 km NW Xuan Loc. Long Khanh Pr, III Corps.
Hill 400 (XD 992-516)
Part of Nui Cay Tre Ridge or Mutter's Ridge. Was dominated by Hills 400, 461 and 484. In Sep-Oct66, 3d/4th Marines took these hills and ridge during Op Prairie (ridgeline renamed using Bn's call-sign, "Mutter").Capt. J. J. Carroll was KIA near Hill 400 as part of op, and Camp Carroll later named for him. Description of Battle for Hill 400 in *Bonnie-Sue*, pp 176-183. Grid may be XD 998-614? See Mutter's Ridge. Quang Tri Pr, I Corps.
Hill 400 (ZC 113-522)
Apx 4 km WSW Ha Tan AF. Quang Nam Pr, I Corps.
Hill 401 (XD 973-333)
Apx 15 km SE Khe Sanh CB. Quang Tri Pr, I Corps.
Hill 405 (ZV 09-75)
See Tieu Atar Mtn. Pleiku Pr, II Corps.
Hill 406 (BT 14-22?)
Apx 2 km NE LZ East and 14 km W Tam Ky. Resembled narrow loaf of bread and scene of heaving fighting involving B & D Cos 3/21st Inf, 196th LIB, 6Jun68. See *Into the Valley*, Chp 31. Grid apx. Quang Tin Pr, I Corps.
Hill 407 (BT)
In Song Chang Valley. Battle site/FSB of 2d/1st, 2d/7th and 3/d3d Marines 10Dec65, during Op Harvest Moon. See *Utter's Battalion*, pp 192-200. Quang Tin Pr?, I Corps.
Hill 410 (BT 389-034)
Apx 15 km W to WSW Chu Lai, 20 km SSE Tam Ky, 9 km WSW Khuong Quang and 7 km NNE Nui Dong Tranh Mtn. Used intermittently in concert with need and weather (common of many FSBs). Les Hines also notes that it is mentioned in *Friendly Fire*. Also listed at BT 389-034. Americal list. Quang Tin Pr, I Corps.
Hill 411 (BS 540-730)
Apx 10 km W Quang Ngai, 16 km ENE Ha Thanh AF, and 10 km SE Ba Gia AF. Americal. Quang Ngai Pr, I Corps.
Hill 412 (XD 992-377)
Apx 16 km ESE Khe Sanh CBQuang Tri Pr, I Corps.
Hill 416 (YD 740-065)
See Nui Sa Truc. Thua Thien Pr, I Corps.
Hill 418 (YT 34-18)
See Nui Soc Lu. Bien Hoa Pr, III Corps.
Hill 422 (BS 732-840)
Apx 14 km NE Quang Ngai. Quang Ngai Pr, I Corps.

Hill 424 (YD 750-087)
See Nui Hoan Gay. Apx Jul67. Thua Thien Pr, I Corps.
Hill 426 (YA 922-269)
Along QL-19, apx 8 km ENE Duc Co AF. Jan68. Pleiku Pr, II Corps.
Hill 423 (YU 210-517)
See Shakey's Hill. Cambodia.
Hill 424 (YD 750-087)
Jul67. Thua Thien Pr, I Corps.
Hill 425 (n/a)
A.k.a. OP Sunrise. N Que Son Mtns and covering Phu Loc and An Hoa Basin approaches to Da Nang. Was E of Spider Lake, SE Phu Loc and SSW Phu Nam Tay. 11th Mar Arty Permanent OP (POP) employing Integrated Observation Devices (IOD). Secured by1st Marine Recon Bn, '70. Described as barren sliver of rock, splattered with sandbags and radio antenna overlooking a valley that ran SW to NE out of Thong Duc Mtns into the Arizona. Spider and Alligator lakes in this valley. 1st Mar Div. See IOD and POP. Quang Nam Pr, I Corps.
Hill 426 (YA 922-269)
Jan68. Pleiku Pr, II Corps.
Hill 426 (YD 567-053)
See FSB Binh Dinh. Thua Thien Pr, I Corps.
Hill 430 (CQ 258-221?)
Also listed at CQ 282-218? Correct grid unknown. Phu Yen Pr, II Corps.
Hill 430 (CQ 282-218?)
Also listed at CQ 258-221? Correct grid unknown. Phu Yen Pr, II Corps.
Hill 432 (AQ 84-93)
Apx 55 km SSE Pleiku, 7 km SSW Phu Nhon AF and 3 km W QL-14. Pleiku Pr, II Corps.
Hill 433 (YD 712-135)
A.k.a. Hon Dun Mtn. Apx 8 km SW Hue, and 3.5 km NNE FSB Birmingham. Thua Thien Pr, I Corps.
Hill 434 (YD 750-086)
A.k.a. Nui Hoan Gay, Banana Mtn (and possibly Mount Baldy or LZ Apollo?). Apx 12 km S Hue and 4 km SE FSB Birmingham. Thua Thien Pr, I Corps.
Hill 435 (ZC 03-25)
See FSB Machete. Quang Tin Pr?, I Corps.
Hill 440 (AT 925-238)
See Nui Liet Kiem and LZ West. Quang Tin Pr, I Corps.
Hill 444 (n/a)
USMC FSB in Happy Valley. Quang Nam Pr, I Corps.
Hill 445 (AT 990-251)
A.k.a. Nui Liet Kiem (Mtn of Leeches). See LZ West. Quang Tin, Pr, I Corps.
Hill 449 (ZC 202-652)
Apx 13 km NNE Ha Tan AF. Quang Nam Pr, I Corps.
Hill 450 (XD 978-480?)
Listed at YD 978-480; however, grid is in ocean. If XD is proper grid zone, site was apx 12 km WSW Mai Loc. Apr68. Quang Tri Pr?, I Corps.
Hill 457 (AT 8-4?)
See OP Chickie Pie. Quang Nam Pr, I Corps.
Hill 461 (XD 945-624)
A.k.a. FSB Sierra and part of Nui Cay Tre Ridge (Mutter's Ridge). Apx 7 km NNW the Rockpile and 8 km WNW peak Dong Ha Mtn. This peak and its hill mass formed W end of ridge, while Hill 484 (Nui Cay Tre) was at its center and Hill 400 at its E end. See Mutter's Ridge and Nui Cay Tre. Quang Tri Pr, I Corps.
Hill 462 (ZC 189-648)
Apx 12 km NNE Ha Tan AF. Quang Nam Pr, I Corps.
Hill 467 (YS 29-72)
A.k.a. Nui Thi Vai. Apx 14 km WNW Nui Dat, 5 km SE Phu My, 47 km SE Saigon, 4 km E QL-15 and 3 km WNW Nui Ong Trinh. One peak of a twin-peak monolith jutting out of plain SE Saigon. Phuoc Tuy Pr, III Corps.
Hill 471 (XD 846-393)
At S end of Dong Che Dien Ridge and 3 km SW Khe Sanh CB. Strategic value in its commanding view of Khe Sanh CB. Assaulted by 2d/26th Marines 4Apr68, during Op Pegasus. B/1st/9th Mar attacked here 5Apr68 with 10 US KIA, 56 WIA, and 122 NVA KIA. Quang Tri Pr, I Corps.
Hill 471 (ZV 058-820)
See Tieu Teo Mtn. Pleiku Pr, II Corps.
Hill 474 (YD?)
Apparently a 101st Abn position or FSB here. No data.
Hill 481 (YC 867-811)
Apx 3 km SSW Ruong RuongThua Thien Pr, I Corps.
Hill 482 (AT 875-175)
Apx 43 km W to WSW Tam Ky, and 7 km SSW Hiep Duc. Americal list. Quang Tin Pr, I Corps.
Hill 482 (ZD 150-067)
See Nui Vinh Phong, Thua Thien Pr, I Corps.
HIll 484 (XD 968-617)
A.k.a. Nui Cay Tre Mtn and part of. Mutter's Ridge. Apx 6 km due N the Rockpile and 5.5 km WNW peak Dong Ha Mtn. Ridge was dominated by Hills 400, 461 and 484. In Sep-Oct66, the 3d/4th Mar took these hills during Op Prairie and ridgeline was renamed in their honor by using the Bn's call-sign, "Mutter" for name. See Mutter's Ridge. Capt. J. J. Carroll was KIA near Hill 400 as part of op, and Camp Carroll later named for him. Also listed at XD 986-617? Quang Tri Pr, I Corps.
Hill 488 (BT 132-203)
A.k.a. FSB East, LZ Mary Lou, Nui Vu, LZ 2 and Howard's Hill. Apx 18 km W Tam Ky and 43 km WNW Chu Lai. Objective and FSB during Op Double Eagle, 20Feb66 (see *Utter's Battalion*, p 220). Named to honor SSgt Jimmie Howard, acting CO, 1st Plt/C/1st/5th Marines, 1st Mar Div who led an attack on this objective 13June66. Howard had been awarded 3 PHs and Silver Star in Korea, and for action in which hc was KIA, was awarded his 4th PH and recommended for MOH. From air, the hilltop "resembled the three blades on an airplane propeller," per *Small Unit Actions in Vietnam, 1966*, with detailed discussion of battle at p 30. Also listed at BT 1310-2025. Quang Tin Pr, I Corps.
Hill 494 (ZD 020-010)
Apx 34 km SE Hue and 1.5 km S QL-1/Dam Cau Hai Bay. See Camp De Shurley. Thua Thien Pr, I Corps.
Hill 495 (XT 504-833)
Apx 19 km ESE Katum AF and 12 km SW tip of the Fishhook. Jan68. Tay Ninh Pr, III Corps.
Hill 497 (BT 189-047)
A.k.a. FSB 497 and presumed to have been named for its height; however, listed grid pinpoints a Hill 593? 196th

LIB base apparently opened 21Jan70, per Americal list. Quang Tin Pr, I Corps.

Hill 502 (AT 830-658)
See FSB Buckskin (also a.k.a. Hill 512?). Also listed at AT 823-659 in Apr69, and AT 856-663 in Sep68. Quang Nam Pr, I Corps.

Hill 502 (XD 873-429)
Apx 3 km NE Khe Sanh CB. Quang Tri Pr, I Corps.

Hill 504 (YS 36-67)
See Nui Thi Mtn and Signal Site. Phuoc Tuy Pr, III Corps.

Hill 504 (XD 966-467)
Apx 13 km ENE Khe Sanh CB. Quang Tri Pr, I Corps.

Hill 506 (BR 492-506)
A.k.a. Hon Nui Dat. Overlooked Camp Radcliff. Map is L-7014-6737-3, per Ken Burrington. Binh Dinh Pr, II Corps.

Hill 508 (AQ 83-83)
See Chu Krah Mtn. Pleiku Pr, II Corps.

Hill 508 (BS 63-44?)
Between Ba To and Tra Cau Rivers, apx 18 km SW Mo Duc, 5 km E Ba To and 16 km W Duc Pho. E/2d/4th Mar CA'd here 31Jan66 to install radio relay commo plt. Per *USMC in Vietnam, 1966*, p 29, map p 20. Grid estimated but may be BS 61-42? Quang Ngai Pr, I Corps.

Hill 508 (ZC 10-45)
See FSB Maxwell. Quang Nam Pr, I Corps.

Hill 508 Radio Relay Site (BS 63-44?)
See Hill 508. Quang Ngai Pr, I Corps.

Hill 510 (AT 946-404)
Apparently a.k.a. LZ Ike and possibly LZ Yonkers? Apx 7 km E Phouc Binh, 12 km SW An Hoa AF, and 36 km SSW Da Nang AB. Americal list. Quang Nam Pr, I Corps.

Hill 512 (AT 835-659)
See FSB Buckskin. Quang Nam Pr, I Corps.

Hill 512 (XD 954-451)
Apx 12 km ENE Khe Sanh CB. Quang Tri Pr, I Corps.

Hill 513 (BS 638-552)
A.k.a. LZ/FSB Tiger, LZ Bulldog and Nui Nham. Overlooks Song Ve River Valley and coast, apx 8 km WNW Mo Duc AF and 18 km due S Quang Ngai. See LZ Tiger and LZ Bulldog. Quang Ngai Pr, I Corps.

Hill 515 (XQ 77-63)
Apx 100 km SW mouth of Mekong River. Hills 610 (2,001') and 515 (1,690') were 2 highest points on Con Son (Poulo Condore) Island. South China Sea.

Hill 516 (XD 799-459)
Apx 7 km NW Khe Sanh CB and 5 km due E Hickory Radio Relay site. B/1st/9th Marines made opening contact of what became "The Hill Fights" here, 24Apr67. 14 US KIA, 2 MIA, 18 WIA for B/1/9 here and nearby that day. Data per *The Final Formation*, p 15. Quang Tri Pr, I Corps.

Hill 522 (ZC 103-528)
Apx 5 km WSW Ha Tan AF. Quang Nam Pr, I Corps.

Hill 524 (CP 16-28)
A.k.a. Nui Hoc Nom Mtn. Apx 12 km SW Phu Hiep AF. Khanh Hoa Pr, II Corps.

Hill 527 (XD 792-384)
Apx 6 km SW Khe Sanh CB. Quang Tri Pr, I Corps.

Hill 530 (YB 84-02)
Apx 27 km SW Dak To 2 AF, 5 km ESE Hill 1030. See Dak To, Battle of. Grid apx. Kontum Pr, II Corps.

Hill 534 (YA 865-947)
Apx 64 km SW Pleiku, 3 km E Cambodia, 33 km SSE Duc Co, 9 km SW LZ X-Ray and 8 km S peak Chu Pong Mtn (Hill 732). Mtn at S end of Chu Pong Massif. Last engagement of Op Paul Revere II here 14-15Aug66, when A/1st/5th Cav, 1st Cav, walked into NVA basecamp and were joined by B/2d/5th Cav and another Bn. Battle ended morning of 15Aug. Apx 138 NVA KIA. Grid per map in *Paul Revere II*, 1st Cav '66 *Yearbook* courtesy Mr. Shutt. Pleiku Pr, II Corps. [265]

Hill 541 (ZV 24-58)
See Chu Kbang Mtn. Darlac Pr, II Corps.

Hill 542 (XD 809-392)
Apx 4 km SW Khe Sanh CB. Quang Tri Pr, I Corps.

Hill 544 (YD 014-593)
A.k.a. Dong Ha Mtn and Hill 549 (NE48-16 JOG lists it as Hill 544). On N side of Cam Lo River apx 9 km due W Cam Lo, 12 km NNE Vandegrift and 3 km N QL-9. See FSB Fuller. Quang Tri Pr, I Corps.

Hill 549 (VS 95-58)
See Nui Dai. Chau Doc Pr, IV Corps.

Hill 549 (YD 014-593)
See Hill 544. Quang Tri Pr, I Corps.

Hill 549 (XD 885-362)
Apx 6 km SSE Khe Sanh CB. Quang Tri Pr, I Corps.

Hill 551 (ZC 003-910)
See FSB Cutlass. Thua Thien Pr, I Corps.

Hill 552 (YD 029-479)
Apx 7 km WSW Mai Loc. Jan68. Quang Tri Pr, I Corps.

Hill 552 (XD 822-402)
Apx 3 km SW Khe Sanh CB, 4.7 km SSE Hill 861 and 2 km ESE Dong Dang (Hill 689). Good view of Khe Sanh CB to NE and Rte 9 to S. During Op Pegasus, Apr '68, the 1st/9th Marines in concert with 1st Cav took this hill. NVA did not resist or counterattack. [266] Quang Tri Pr, I Corps.

Hill 555 (AT 94-21)
Apx 35 km WSW Tam Ky, 15 km WNW Tien Phuoc SF Camp and 14 km SSW Nui Loc Son. 1st Recon Bn OP 13-14Jun66, during Op Kansas, per *USMC in Vietnam, 1966*, p 132, map on p 133. Quang Tin Pr, I Corps.

Hill 557 (XD 762-445)
Apx 10 km WNW Khe Sanh CB. Recon Team Seven-Up contact here mentioned in *The Final Formation* at p. 36. Quang Tri Pr, I Corps.

Hill 558 (XD 820-451)
Formed edge of Khe Sanh Plateau apx 4 km NW Khe Sanh CB, overlooking Rao Quan Valley, apx 1 km to its E. 2d/26th Marines here, as were CIDG? For some reason, position suffered only minor shelling and periodic probes during siege. Mislabeled map showing layout of position at p 316 of *Valley of Decision*, with photos at p 168. Quang Tri Pr, I Corps.

Hill 558 (YC 683-921)
A.k.a. FSB Spear. Apx 24 km W FSB Sledge and 19 km ESE FSB Tennessee, 101st Abn. Also listed at ZC 18-39? Thua Thien Pr, I Corps.

Hill 558 (ZC 18-39)
Apx 15 km SSE Ha Tan AF. Quang Nam Pr, I Corps.

Hill 589 (ZV 231-644)
See Chu Amung Mtn. Darlac Pr, II Corps.

Hill 562 (CR 050-203)
See Vung Chau Mountain. Binh Dinh Pr, II Corps.
Hill 565 (US 95-47)
Highest point (1,854') on Dao Phu Quoc Island. Kien Giang Pr, IV Corps.
Hill 567 (CP 18-98)
A.k.a. Nui Ba Lon Mtn. On Hon Lon Island, 45 km NNE Nha Trang. Khanh Hoa Pr, II Corps.
Hill 575 (AT 80-41)
See Lance, FSB. Quang Nam Pr, I Corps.
Hill 577 (YA 885-335)
A.k.a. Chu Bak Mtn. 9 km NE Duc Co. Pleiku Pr, II Corps.
Hill 579 (AT 952-355?)
A.k.a. FSB Ryder and Hon Chau Mtn? Apx 48 km W Tam Ky, 14 km NW FSB Ross and 7 km SE An Hoa CB. *Son Thang*, p 13, claims Ryder was on a Hill 579; however, other texts put it on Hill 675? See LZ Ryder and Hill 675. Quang Nam Pr, I Corps.
Hill 592 (BS 77-32?)
Apx 10 km SW Duc Pho and 22 km due S Mo Duc. Terrain feature of Op Double Eagle, Jan66. Map in *USMC in Vietnam, 1966*, p 20. Grid apx. Quang Ngai Pr, I Corps.
Hill 592 (ZD 143-049)
See Dong Nhut, Thua Thien Pr, I Corps.
Hill 593 (BT 189-047)
Apparently a.k.a. FSB 497? FSBs normally named for their elevation; however, listed grid shows a Hill 593? 196th LIB base apparently opened 21Jan70, per Americal list. Quang Tin Pr, I Corps.
Hill 600 (ZC 088 542)
Apx 6 km W Ha Tan AF. Oct68. Quang Nam Pr, I Corps.
Hill 602 (BR 97 73)
A.k.a. Nui Nhiao. Apx 8 km NE Phu My, 10 km NE Crystal AF and 21 km SE Bong Son and 6 km E QL-1. Binh Dinh Pr, II Corps.
Hill 605 (XD 94-37)
A.k.a. Dong Riang Tuan. Apx 12 km SSW Vandegrift CB and 7 km N Lao border. Grid per map at p 32, *US Marines in Vietnam-1969*. Quang Tri Pr, I Corps.
Hill 605 (YD 375-200)
Apx 3.3 km E to ENE FSB Ripcord and 32 km W Hue. Significant terrain feature during siege of FSB Ripcord, May-Jul70. 1:50,000 scale map image of site in *Ripcord, Screaming Eagles Under Siege, Vietnam 1970*, at p 206. See FSB Ripcord. Thua Thien Pr, I Corps.
Hill 606 (XD 882-496)
Apx 21 km W Mai Loc, 12 km WNW Ca Lu, 9 km NNE Khe Sanh CB and 44 km W Quang Tri. M/1st/3d Marines here 21Jul67, and made contact while moving from hill to its objective at XD 903-497, resulting in 6 US KIA. Data per *The Final Formation*, p 30. Also listed at XD 863-493, Jul67. Quang Tri Pr, I Corps.
Hill 609 (AQ 925-550)
Apx 10 km WSW Buon Blech AF. Darlac Pr, II Corps.
Hill 610 (XQ 74-58)
Apx 100 km SW mouth of Mekong River. Hills 610 (2,001') and 515 (1,690') were two highest points on Con Son (Poulo Condore) Island. South China Sea.
Hill 611 (YA 869-889)
A.k.a. Chu Ya Bruh Mtn. E Plei Trap Valley, apx 37 km due W Kontum. D and C Cos, 1st/12th Inf, 4th Div FSB apparently here in '69. Also listed at same grid in "YB" UTM zone, but that is thought to be an error. Map is L-7014-6537-4. Kontum Pr, II Corps.
Hill 613 (YD 059-328)
See Tun Tavern, FSB. Quang Tri Pr, I Corps.
Hill 614 (VS 99-47)
A.k.a. Nui Co To Mtn and Million Dollar Knoll. See Nui Co To. Chau Doc Pr, IV Corps.
Hill 618 (YD 760-055)
See Nui Ke. Thua Thien Pr, I Corps.
Hill 619 (BR 94-93)
Hon Cau Mtn. See Lo Dieu Beach. Binh Dinh Pr, II Corps.
Hill 621 (BT 08-86)
A.k.a. Monkey or Mon Ky Mtn, and site off Monkey Mtn (a.k.a. Onderko) Signal Site. One of 2 major hills (Son Tra/Hill 696 being the other) on the Tien Sha Peninsula overlooking Da Nang to SW. Quang Nam Pr, I Corps.
Hill 621 (YA 68-57)
On E side of Plei Trap Valley, apx 13 km E Cambodia, 55 km WNW Pleiku, 16 km WNW Plei Djereng AF, 10 km NW the San/Ya Krong Bolah, and 5 km E the Nam Sathay River. On 22Mar67, C/2d/35th Inf involved in big fight on slopes of this mtn, vicinity of YA 680-569, per Dick Arnold. Kontum Pr, II Corps.
Hill 630 (YC 808-878)
Apx 7 km WNW Ruong Ruong. Thau Thien Pr, I Corps.
Hill 632 (XD 826-482)
Apx 7 km NNE Khe Sanh CB, and 4 km NW Hill 1015 (Dong Tri). Quang Tri Pr, I Corps.
Hill 635 (YB 803-096)
Actually Hill 935. 66th NVA Rgtl forces mislabeled Hill 635 in cease fire proposal of 4-5Mar71 during Op Quang Trung 22F See Hill 935. Kontum Pr, II Corps.
Hill 636 (YC 847-803)
Apx 6 km SW Ruong Ruong. Thau Thien Pr, I Corps.
Hill 641 (BR 9-8)
A.k.a. Cay Giep Mtn. Apx 10 km SE Bong Son, 46 km N Phu Cat and 4 km E QL-1. Binh Dinh Pr, II Corps.
Hill 642 (YC 913-848)
Apx 4 km due E Ruong Ruong. Thau Thien Pr, I Corps.
Hill 642 (YD 584-036)
See FSB Kim Qui. Thua Thien Pr, I Corps.
Hill 644 (BN 74-58)
A.k.a. Nui Da Bac Mtn. Apx 22 km SSE Phan Rang. Ninh Thuan Pr?, II Corps.
Hill 647 (YD 52-23?)
See FSB Meredith. Thua Thien Pr, I Corps.
Hill 649 (BN 74-95)
See Nui Da Bac. Ninh Thuan Pr, II Corps.
Hill 654 (AQ 810-546)
A.k.a. Chu Ktey Mtn. Apx 19 km WSW Buon Blech AF. Darlac Pr, II Corps.
Hill 654 (YD 081-411)
See FSB Henderson. Quang Tri Pr, I Corps.
Hill 658 (XD 911-563)
Apx 7.5 km WNW Elliott CB, 11 km WSW FSB Fuller 21 km W Cam Lo. 3d Mar Div FSB? Quang Tri Pr, I Corps.
Hill 660 (YD 098-443)
See FSB Summer. Quang Tri Pr, I Corps.

Hill 662 (AT 82-43)
A.k.a. Nui Hoa Ngan. Apx 6 km NW Phuoc Binh and 38 km SW Da Nang. Quang Nam Pr, I Corps.
Hill 664 (YB 9-1?)
See Firebase 4. Kontum Pr, II Corps.
Hill 665 (XD 761-531)
A.k.a. FSB Alpine. Apx 1.7 km SW Nguon Rao, 8 km NW Hill 881-N, 25 km WNW Ca Lu, 14 km NW Khe Sanh CB and 57 km due W Quang Tri. 3d Recon Bn "Team Breaker" contact site (XD 756-532) and scene of at least 2 significant tiger attacks. On 9May67, an A/3rd Recon Bn, 7-man team inserted on BDA mission, after the opening battles for Khe Sanh. On morning of 10May67, they were hit by estimated 100 NVA. Several heroic rescue attempts made with heavy damage to acft and their crews (1 KIA) finally succeeded in extracting 3 survivors. Bodies of James Tycz, Sam Sharp, "Doc" Malcolm Miller and a Lt Heinz Alhmeyer were never recovered. Sgt Tycz and PFC Steven Lopez were awarded the Navy Cross for this action. Entire team was KIA or WIA. Emergency extract of Recon Team "Breaker" described in M. Sturkey's *Bonnie-Sue*, pp345-351. See FSB Alpine entry and Tiger Attacks (Glossary). Quang Tri Pr, I Corps. [267]
Hill 666 (BR 398-690)
Apx 5 km NNW Kannack AF, 6 km WNW Kon Creh, 42 km WSW Ha Tay, 57 km NW Phu Cat AB and overlooking Song Bo River Valley. 4th Div AO, '70. Name/grid per Jim Claeys. Also listed at BR 358-690? Binh Dinh Pr, II Corps.
Hill 671 (YA 51-52)
Sharp peak roughly 2 km ESE Phum Chuoy, 3 km W Phum Hay and 15 km WNW old Plei Djerang. Cambodia.
Hill 674 (YD 516-219)
A.k.a. Hill 2211 (in feet) and Whiskey Relay thought to have been here. Apx 6 km WSW Ap Thanh Tan, 11 km SSW Camp Evans and 22 km due W Hue. Radio relay site operated by 3d Recon Bn, 3d Mar Div in at least 66 and 67. Info per Steve Laktash. Also listed at YD 510-210 and 518-219, Oct67-Jan68. Quang Tri Pr, I Corps. [268]
Hill 674 (YD 571-217?)
Likely transposition of YD 517-217? See FSB Long. Thua Thien Pr, I Corps.
Hill 675 (AT 82-43)
A.k.a. Hon Chau Mtn and FSB Ryder. Apx 5 km ENE Phuoc Binh AF 7 km SE An Hoa AF and 35 km SSW Da Nang. In *Son Thang*, Ryder is said to have been on Hill 579? Quang Nam Pr, I Corps.
Hill 678 (XD 848-331)
Apx 2 km SE LZ Snapper, 9 km NNE Lang Chei and 7 km due S Khe Sanh CB. Map is L-7014-6342-3, per Ken Burrington. Quang Tri Pr, I Corps.
Hill 679 (XD 893-457)
Apx 6 km NE Khe Sanh CB. Jul68. Quang Tri Pr, I Corps.
Hill 681 (XD 803-443)
See Hill 861. Transposition. Quang Tri Pr, I Corps.
Hill 682 (BP 97-62)
A.k.a. Nui Chau Mtn. Apx 11 km WNW and overlooking Nha Trang. Khanh Hoa Pr, II Corps.
Hill 682 (BS 79-24?)
Apx 11 km WSW Tam Quan, 5 km SSW Hill 726 and 22 km SSW Du Pho. Significant terrain feature of Op Double Eagle, Jan66. Map in *USMC in Vietnam, 1966*, p 20. Grid may not be accurate. Binh Dinh Pr, II Corps.
Hill 686 (ZC 088-535)
Apx 6 km due W Ha Tan AF. Quang Nam Pr, I Corps.
Hill 689 (XD 802-409)
A.k.a. Dong Dang. Apx 5 km WSW Khe Sanh CB, 2 km WNW Hill 552 and 3.5 km due S Hill 881-S. 1st taken, during Battle for Hill 689, by I/3d/26th Marines, 28-29Jun67. 2d Battle for Hill 689 took place 16-19Apr68, when 1st/9th Marines were heavily engaged while sweeping Hill with 9 US KIA, 46 WIA, 36 MIA and 12 non-battle casualties. Quang Tri Pr, I Corps. [269]
Hill 691 (XD 926-443?)
Listed at YD 926-443; however, grid is in ocean. If XD is proper grid zone, site was apx 17 km WSW Mai Loc. Jul-Sep68. Quang Tri Pr?, I Corps.
Hill 694 (ZS 17-97)
See Nui Takou (2,277'). Binh Tuy Pr?, III Corps.
Hill 695 (XD 85-66)
See Lu Bu Mtn and Sierra North. Quang Tri Pr, I Corps.
Hill 696 (BT 10-84)
A.k.a. Son Tra Mtn. Apx 13 km NE Da Nang AB. Tallest of 2 peaks on Tien Sha Peninsula. Quang Nam Pr, I Corps.
Hill 700 (XD)
Lofty OP overlooking approaches to Hill 881-N and 881-S. Emergency extract of USMC Recon Team "Hawk" here described in *Bonnie-Sue*, pp 323-329. During action (24-25Apr67), crewman of USMC HMM-265. LCpl Daniel G. DuLude became only known member of US forces to be awarded Silver Star on 2 consecutive days. Severely wounded 16Oct67, he was finally medevaced to US. Quang Tri Pr, I Corps.
Hill 701 (AQ 910-310)
Apx 16 km NNE Quang Nhieu. Dec69. Darlac Pr, II Corps.
Hill 701 (BR 83-67)
A.k.a. Nui Xa Rong. Apx 7 km WSW Phu My and 29 km due S Bong Son. Binh Dinh Pr, II Corps.
Hill 704 (YS 740-720)
Apx 33 km ESE Xuan Loc. Binh Tuy Pr, III Corps.
Hill 705 (YA 764-326)
See FSB Mary. Pleiku Pr, II Corps.
Hill 706 (BR 453-468)
See Hon Cong Hill. Binh Dinh Pr, II Corps.
Hill 706 (CQ 276-260)
See Nui Ba Dai. Phu Yen Pr, II Corps.
Hill 707 (BS 418-998?)
Possibly a.k.a. LZ Hill 707? Per *Rangers At War*, p 33, Hills 213 and 707 were near Chu Lai and maintained as radio-relay outposts and OPs for "Burning Rope Patrollers" LRRP teams of 196th LIB during at least Jun67. See Hill 707, LZ. Quang Tin Pr?, I Corps.
Hill 707, LZ/FSB (BS 418-998)
Apx 14 km SW Chu Lai, 7 km NE peak of Nui Dong Tranh and 14 km NE Tra Bong AF. One of several hilltops forming Rocket Ridge W of Chu Lai. Per Tom Brizendine, was recipient of "Friendly Fire" incident featured in book *Friendly Fire,* and source of incoming was Hill 76, an Americal FSB holding 105s and possibly 175s. XXIV Corps grid. Also listed at BT 418-034 which is thought to be an error. Quang Tin Pr, I Corps.

Hill 710 (VS 98-60)
See Dop Chompa Mountain. Chau Doc Pr, IV Corps.
Hill 711 (ZV 115-820)
Apx 7 km E Tieu Teo Mtn. Pleiku Pr, II Corps.
Hill 722 (AT 840-613)
Apx 8 km NW Dai Loc. Apr69. Quang Nam Pr, I Corps.
Hill 723 (YU 184-068)
A.k.a. Nui Ba Ra Mtn and the White Virgin Mtn. Apx 5 km E Song Be (south) AF, and 5 km due S Song Be City (N) AF. See Nui Ba Ra entries. Phuoc Long Pr, III Corps.
Hill 724 (AT 944-916)
A.k.a. Nui A Van of Nui Hai Van? At the Hai Van Pass, apx 11 km due N Red Beach AF. Site of USMC A or B Bty 1st LAAM Hawk missile site, beginning Aug66, per *USMC in Vietnam, 1966*, p 270. Thua Thien Pr, I Corps.
Hill 724 (YB 90-15?)
Roughly 12 km SW Dak To 2 AF and 9 km W Hill 1338. On 10Nov67, A, B and D Cos, 3d/8th Inf, 4th Div heavily attacked while moving toward its summit. Fight lasted through to following day and resulted in 18 US KIA and apx 120 WIA, and 92 NVA KIA. At battle's end, one US Co had only 44 men standing, another had but 59, and only 79 were standing in third, per *Dak To*, p 180. See Dak To, Battle of. Grid apx only. Kontum Pr, II Corps.
Hill 726 (BS 92-29?)
Apx 18 km due S Duc Pho and 10 km NW Tam Quan. Per *USMC in Vietnam, 1966*, p 33, map p 20. Terrain feature of Op Double Eagle, Jan66. Grid may not be accurate. Binh Dinh Pr, II Corps.
Hill 727? (ZA 181-774)
See FSB/LZ Carmen. Kontum Pr, II Corps.
Hill 731 (YT 92-17)
See Nui Ba Dan (2,398'). Binh Tuy Pr, III Corps.
Hill 732 (YA 885-106)
A.k.a. Chu Pong Mtn. Apx 30 km W Plei Me, 58 km SW Pleiku and 170 km WSW Qui Nhon. Also spelled Chu Prong. See Chu Prong, Chu Pong Massif and LZ X-Ray. Nov65. Pleiku Pr, II Corps.
Hill 734? (ZA 23-48?)
See Artillery Hill. Pleiku Pr, II Corps.
Hill 736 (BR 535-929)
A.k.a. LZ Y. Remote site, apx 27 km SW Thuan An. 17Mar66. Binh Dinh Pr, II Corps.
Hill 744 (YB 738-023)
Along W side Plei Trap Valley, apx 47 km WNW Kontum and 10 km E Cambodia. B and C Cos, 1st/12th Inf, 4th Div apparently secured site in '69. Map is L-7014-6537-4. Kontum Pr, II Corps.
Hill 745 (YA 938-574)
A.k.a. or near LZ 504C? Apx 32 km WNW Pleiku and 11 km NW Chu Prong Mtn. Pleiku Pr, II Corps.
Hill 747 (BT42-00?)
Apx 13 km WSW Chu Lai? Just to NE Hill 707 and part of Rocket Ridge. Per Tom Brizendine, B/1st/6th Inf's CP and 81mm mortar section here. Grid est. Quang Tin Pr, I Corps.
Hill 748 (BR 186-516)
Apx 500-meters S Phu Yen (2)/QL-19, and 32 km WNW An Khe. Feb66. Pleiku Pr, II Corps.
Hill 749 (ZC 125-650)
See FSB Rattlesnake. Quang Nam Pr, I Corps.
Hill 750 (YC 994-944)
Apx 16 km NE Ruong Ruong. Thua Thien Pr, I Corps.
Hill 750 (ZC 003-910)
Apx 13 km SW Phu Loc. Feb69. Thua Thien Pr, I Corps.
Hill 758 (XD 783-423)
Apx 6.5 km due W Khe Sanh CB, 2 km SSE Hill 881-S and 3 km SW Hill 861. Quang Tri Pr, I Corps.
Hill 762 (YB 950-110)
Apx 12 km SSW Dak To 2 AF. Kontum Pr, II Corps.
Hill 763 (BS 629-276)
A.k.a. FSB Glen? Near I Corps/II Corps border and apx 22 km SW Duc Pho and 9 km SE Ba To New AF. 1st Cav? Quang Ngai Pr?, I Corps?
Hill 763 (YB 892-323)
Apx 9 km S Camp Dak Seang, 16 km NW Dak To 2 AF and 1.5 km ESE Hill 1043. After overland march, was secured by 23d ARVN Ranger Bn, 4Apr70. 28th NVA Rgt was entrenched on nearby Hill 1043 and, that afternoon, began mortaring ARVN here (killing ARVN CO and Senior US Adv in 1st barrage) and then kept the ARVN under heavy mortar/small arms fire for several days. In afternoon of 5Apr70, NVA probed perimeter and on morning of 6Apr70, mounted major assault that was repulsed. 2 days of heavy weapons and mortar fire followed failed assault. At apx 7 pm on 7Apr70, NVA mounted human wave attack that nearly overran ARVN as hand-to-hand combat ensued. At 10:30 am on 8Apr70, ARVN were ordered to withdraw overland to 22d ARVN Ranger Bn, crossing Dak Poko en route. Pursued by NVA and heavy mortar fire, the 23d also broke through 2 ambushes before reaching 22d Rangers. In battle, the 22d suffered 218 KIA/WIA and 19 MIA. Detailed discussion in *Rangers At War*, p 263-267. SF Advisor SFC Gary Littrell was awarded MOH for his substantial heroics during this action. Kontum Pr, II Corps.
Hill 766 (BR 66-65?)
See Almost Hill 766 and Hereford. Binh Dinh Pr, II Corps.
Hill 766, Almost (BR 66-65?)
See Almost Hill 766 and Hereford. Binh Dinh Pr, II Corps.
Hill 771 (BR 202-516)
Apx 1 km SW Phu Danh/QL-19 and 30 km WNW An Khe. Feb66. Pleiku Pr?, II Corps.
Hill 771 (CP 04-81)
A.k.a. Nui Tien Du Mtn. Apx 6 km E Ninh Hoa. Khanh Hoa Pr, II Corps.
Hill 778 (XD 757-469)
A.k.a. Dong Tam Va. Apx 10 km WNW Khe Sanh CB and 2.5 km NW Hill 881-N. On 9May67, 24 Marines were KIA and 19 WIA in battle here. Quang Tri Pr, I Corps.
Hill 783 (BR 188-503)
Apx 2 km S Phu Yen (2)/QL-19, and 32 km WNW An KheFeb66 Pleiku Pr, II Corps.
Hill 785 (AT 807-650)
Apx 23 km SW Da Nang AB. Quang Nam Pr, I Corps.
Hill 800 (XD 759-444)
Apx 9 km WNW Khe Sanh CB, 58 km WSW Quang Tri and 6 km WSW Ap La Vien. Cited in *The Final Formation*, p 27. Quang Tri Pr, I Corps.

Hill 800 (YA 817-839)
Apx 18 km WNW FSB Bunker Hill, 45 km WSW Kontum and 24 km SW Polei Kleng AF. 4th Div AO and possible FSB. Grid per Tom Lacombe. Kontum Pr, II Corps.
Hill 801 (AN 736-315)
See Nui Hop. Binh Thuan Pr, II Corps.
Hill 801 (YC 497-995)
A.k.a. Dong A Tay Luat. See Dong A Tay, Bloody Ridge and Hill 890. Thua Thien Pr, I Corps.
Hill 805 (YD 362-188)
Apx 1.5 to 2 km E to ESE FSB Ripcord and about 36 km due W Hue. Site of heavy fighting during *Battle of Hill 805*, 12-18Jul70, involving elements of 2d/501st and 2d/506th Inf, 101st Abn suptg FSB Ripcord battle. 1:50,000 scale map of site in *Ripcord, Screaming Eagles Under Siege, Vietnam 1970*, at p 206. See FSB Ripcord. Thua Thien Pr, I Corps.
Hill 809 (YD)
Overlooked Hwy 548 on E rim of the A Shau Valley. 101st Abn, L/75th Inf Ranger "Cubs Team" ambushed here and object of intense efforts to rescue them which resulted in several helos being shot down, many KIA/WIA and 2 MIA, 23-25Apr71. Heroic effort described in detail in *Rangers At War*, pp 170-173. Thua Thien Pr, I Corps.
Hill 810 (YB 973-248)
Apx 5 km NW Dak To 2 AF and 8 km WSW Dak To. Elements of 4th/503d Inf, 173d Abn worked hill, 27Nov67. Kontum Pr, II Corps.
Hill 814 (BR 588-477)
A.k.a. Hon Ong Binh Mtn and LZ 2. Apx 12 km ENE An Khe. 14Dec65. Binh Dinh Pr, II Corps.
Hill 815 (YD 185-134)
See FSB Cunningham. FSB Razor is also listed as Hill 815? Quang Tri Pr, I Corps.
Hill 816 (YB 88-02?)
Said to have been near listed grid. 4th Div patrol base or FSB, apx 37 km WNW Kontum, 24 km SW Dak To 2 AF, 3 km W LZ Delaware and LZ Ouachita, and about 3 km S Hill 994. Built apx 21Apr69 by B/1st/12th Inf and described in *Time Heals No Wounds*, p 172, as "surrounded by a thick forest of Mahogany and Teak trees, and large enough for [only one] helicopter to land." 4.2" mortar Plt here also. Also listed at YA 88-02, but "YA" grid zone is thought to be in error. Kontum Pr, II Corps.
Hill 819 (BR or BS)
Along Nui Luong River, NW LZ English. On 13Nov68, SSgt Laszlo Rabel, Team Delta, 74th Inf Det (Abn LRRP) gave his life on steep slope of this mtn to save his team members and later awarded MOH. Binh Dinh Pr, II Corps.
Hill 819 (YD 096-377)
Apx 15 km due S Mai Loc. Feb67. Quang Tri Pr, I Corps.
Hill 819 Radio Relay Site (YD 097-378)
See India Relay Site. Quang Tri Pr, I Corps.
Hill 821 (XD 763-443)
Apx 8 km WNW Khe Sanh CB. Quang Tri Pr, I Corps.
Hill 823 (YB 853-187)
A.k.a. FSB 15 and Hill 825? Apx 17 km WSW Dak To 2 AF and 8 km NE Hill 875. Assaulted by 4th/503d Inf, 6Nov67 (reinforced by C/1/503d, 7Nov), whose mission was to secure hill and build FSB 15. Heavy fighting resulted in 17 US KIA and 37 WIA, 6-7Nov67. See Dak To, Battle of and Hill 875. Also listed at YB 854-186, and at same grid as Hill 825? Kontum Pr, II Corps. [270]
Hill 824 (YD 019-397)
See Dong Cho Mtn. Jan68. Quang Tri Pr, I Corps.
Hill 824 (ZT 027-232)
A.k.a. FSB Dreamer? Apx 3 km SW peak of Nui Ong (Dang S'Ruin Mtn), 9 km E Tanh Linh AF and 5 km SSE Xa Hieu Tin. Binh Tuy Pr, III Corps.
Hill 825 (YB 853-187)
A.k.a. FSB 15 and Hill 823? Dec67. See Hill 823. Kontum Pr, II Corps.
Hill 826 (AQ 903-625)
See Chu Dreh Mountain. Pleiku Pr, II Corps.
Hill 826 (ZV 23-94)
See Chu Don Mtn. Darlac Pr?, II Corps.
Hill 829 (BS 53-37)
Apx 23 km SW Mo Duc, 4 km NW Ba To and 24 km due W Duc Pho. USMC 14-man recon team heavily attacked on this hill during Op Double Eagle, 21-22Jan66, resulting in two MIAs. Per *USMC in Vietnam, 1966*, p 24, map p 20.
Hill 830 (YB 858-139)
A.k.a. FSB 101. Per map in *Dak To*, was apx 14 km SW Dak To 2 AF, 10 km WSW Hill 1338 and 13 km S Ben Het. Site of battle involving 4th/503d Inf, 173d Abn, 10-12Jul67, in early stages of Battle for Dak To, during which Bn suffered 22 KIA and 62 WIA. Data per *Dak To*, Hill 830 Chp. See NE 48-08 JOG. Pleiku Pr, II Corps.
Hill 831 (YC 590-877)
A.k.a. Dong Ong. Apx 15 km E the A Shau Valley, 6 km NNE Be Luong and 1 km S Be Luong Heliport. Thua Thien Pr, I Corps.
Hill 832 (XD 873-445)
Apx 5 km NE Khe Sanh CB. Apx Khe Sanh CB. Jul67. Quang Tri Pr, I Corps.
Hill 837 (YT 605-101)
A.k.a. Nui Chua Chan Mtn. Apx 3 km SE Gia Ray, 4 km N Suoi Cat and about 70 km of Saigon. See Nui Chua Chan. Long Khanh Pr, III Corps.
Hill 842 (AR 797-348)
A.k.a. Artillery Hill or Signal Mtn? Within perimeter of Camp Enari, along its W central edge. See Artillery Hill. Pleiku Pr, II Corps.
Hill 842 (YB 796-084)
Apx 4 km due S Hill 875 and 24 km SW Dak To 2 AF. 4th Div AO and possible battle site. Grid per Nolan Putman. Kontum Pr, II Corps.
Hill 845 (AT 17-44)
See Nui Mat Rang. Quang Nam Pr, I Corps.
Hill 848 (ZA?)
See Plei de Cong, FSB. Pleiku Pr, II Corps.
Hill 851 (YB 9-1?)
Near Pleiku? 4th Div patrol base suptd by Arty from Hill 1338. Hill 1338 was apx 6 km SSW Dak To 2 AF at YB 989-152. II Corps.
Hill 854 (ZC 15-73)
Apx 27 km WSW Da Nang. On map at p 98 of *US Marines in Vietnam-1969*. Quang Nam Pr, I Corps.
Hill 854(?) (YD 343-194)
See FSB Ripcord. Thua Thien Pr, I Corps.

Hill 861 (XD 803-443)
Apx 3 km ENE Hill 881-S, 4 km SE Hill 881-N, and 8 km WNW Khe Sanh CB. Hills 881-S, 881N and 861 were sites of what were known as "the Hill Fights" Apr-May67, involving 2 USMC Bns against large NVA force committed to destroying Khe Sanh CB. E/2d/9th Marines lost 18 KIA, 59 WIA here 15-16Mar67. B Co lost 14 KIA (6 by friendly fire) and 18 WIA here 23Apr67. 2d/3d Marines took hill 28Apr67, following two B-52 strikes (382,700 lb. of ordnance 28Apr67 alone) [271]. After Hill Fights, Hills 881S and 861 became "outposts" occupied by 1st/26th and 2d/26th Marines as defensive positions for KSCB, early '68. Heavily attacked 20-21Jan68 with 4 US KIA, 30 WIA. Had a tunnel or tunnel system that apparently went clear through mtn that had great strategic value. Tunnel not discovered until Bru Huong Hoa Dpty Dist Chief asked why it was not being used by Americans to attack NVA rear near end of battle, Apr67. [272] Detailed discussions of '67-68 battles *in Valley of Decision.* Excellent topo maps of site in *The Final Formation*, pp 1-6. Map is DMA L-7014-6342-3. See Hill 1019, Hill Fights, and Hill 861-A. Quang Tri Pr, I Corps.

Hill 861-A (XD 806-445)
Apx 5 km NW Khe Sanh CB. Small knoll several hundred meters to NE of, and on same ridgeline as, main positions originally constructed on Hill 861. After NVA used the slightly higher knoll as avenue of approach and firing position during attack of 20-21Jan68, E/2d/26th Marines established separate, permanent outpost here that was not connected to perimeter of 861 proper. Good photos of site are in pictorial following p 168 in *Valley of Decision.* Excellent map of site in *The Final Formation,* first 6 pages. Map is L-7014-6342-3. Quang Tri Pr, I Corps.

Hill 862 (XD 717-447)
Apx 13 km WNW Khe Sanh CB Quang Tri Pr, I Corps.

Hill 864 (YA 932-483)
A.k.a. Chu Kan Yan Mtn. Apx 8 km NE Plei Djereng New AF. Pleiku Pr, II Corps.

Hill 865 (YB 928-137)
A.k.a. Chu Yach Mtn. Apx 12 km SW Dak To 2 AF and 1 km ESE Hill 882. Kontum Pr, II Corps.

Hill 865 (ZA 181-774)
See LZ Carmen. Kontum Pr, II Corps.

Hill 866 (AT 833-606)
See FSB Longhorn. Quang Nam Pr, I Corps.

Hill 868 (AT 838-828)
See Dong Den. Quang Nam Pr, I Corps.

Hill 872 (ZB 0-4)
See Toumorong. Apx 1 km E LZ Lima Zulu and apx 3 km W Toumorong Outpost. Battle for Toumorong here May-Jun66. 1st Bde/101st Abn. Kontum Pr, II Corps.

Hill 874 (YS 88-90)
A.k.a. Nui Be. See Nui Be.

Hill 875 (YB 797-134)
Roughly 7 km E Cambodia, 15 km SSW Ben Het, 23 km SW Dak To 2 AF and 30 km NW Polei Kleng. Battle here 19-23Nov67, one of bloodiest and most fierce of the Battle for Dak To, and of entire war itself as well. Involved 26th SF Mike Co, 2d/503d and 4th/503d Inf, 173d Abn as well as 1st/12th Inf, 4th Div, during Op MacCarthur. On 18Nov67, the 26th SF Mobile Reaction (Mike) Co ran into large NVA force entrenched on E slope of hill. The 174th NVA Rgt manned bunker complex which inc connecting tunnels built 3 to 6 months earlier so that jungle provided excellent camouflage. The Mike Co backed off and on 19Nov, 2/d/503d Inf was assigned to clear hill but met buzz-saw when C and D Cos, 2d/503d Inf suptd by 355th AHC, attacked up N slope. After 4 hours of heavy contact, NVA assaulted downhill in human wave. Co A (in reserve) was cutting an LZ at bottom of hill when waves of screaming NVA overran it, wiping-out 2 entire platoons. A Co's 6-man CP all died in hand-to-hand fighting. Later airstrike added to casualties when 500 lb bomb landed in crater filled with US wounded and medics, killing 42. Friendly arty also began hitting position and a desperate NCO searched frantically through the mangled radios until he found one that worked and, by some miracle found, the Redleg push and stopped the arty. Of 16 officers leading the ground charge, 8 were KIA; of 13 Bn medics, 11 were KIA. The 335th AHC lost six UH-1s that day as well. On 21Nov67, new LZ was finally cut and for 1st time, medevacs began extracting wounded of 19-20Nov while for 7 hours hill was hit with every arty and air asset available. At 1500 hrs on 21Nov, another US attack inched up the hill behind a rolling barrage of arty but soon came upon mutually suptg bunkers flush to ground featuring as much as 14' of overhead dirt/logs protection. Conventional weapons were useless against these defenses; however, 22 lb. satchel charges plus grenades used to ignite a napalm mixture poured into bunkers did prove effective. Despite US attack, an NVA probe also managed to flank the assault and hit US rear. After closing to within 250' of top of hill, US assault of 21No67 was halted. US troops withdrew and again deluged hill with arty and air strikes that lasted all night and all day of 22Nov. On 23Nov67, the 2/503d Inf, was able to sweep battlefield of prior day's action and found 76 US KIA. 4th/503d Inf was also reinforced with 2 Cos from 1st/12th Inf, 4th Div. Final attack on morning of 23d met only light resistance and, by 1155 hrs, summit was reached and Battle of Hill 875 was over. Map is TL-7014-6538-3. Grid/map data courtesy Chris Taylor. See Dak To, Battle of. Kontum Pr, II Corps.

Hill 881 North (XD 775-458)
Apx 8 km NW Khe Sanh CB and 2 km due N Hill 881-S. See Hill 881 S for a detailed history. During Op Pegasus (op to relieve siege of Khe Sanh), Hill 881-N was last enemy position threatening the base to be taken. On 14Apr68, elements of 3d Mar Div assaulted and took hill at bayonet point. Maps of area in *The Final Formation*, pp 1-6. Map is DMA L-7014-6342-3. Quang Tri Pr, I Corps.

Hill 881 South (XD 778-438)
Apx 7 WNW the Khe Sanh CB and 2 km due south of Hill 881N. Hills 881S, 881N and 861 were sites of what is known as "the Hill Fights," Apr-May67, involving 2 USMC Bns against large NVA force committed to destroying Khe Sanh. After the Hill Fights, Hills 881S and 861 became 'outposts' occupied by 1st/26th Marines and defensive positions during Siege of Khe Sanh, early '68. Map showing layout of position here at p 250 of *Valley of Decision*, with several photos in pictorial following p 168. Maps of area in *The Final Formation*, pp 1-6. Map is L-7014-6342-3. See Hill 1019. Quang Tri Pr, I Corps.

Hill 882 (YB 82-15?)
Roughly 18 km WSW Dak To 2 AF, 10 km S Ben Het, 2 km N Hill 875 and 3 km NW FSB 16. On 17-19Nov67, A/1st/503d Inf, 173d Abn engaged NVA near YB 805-161, during Battle of Hill 882, losing 6 US KIA and 29 WIA while killing 51 NVA. On map at front of *Dak To*. Grid apx. See Dak To, Battle of. Kontum Pr, II Corps. [273]

Hill 882 (YB 920-140)
A.k.a. Ngok Dorlang Mtn. Apx 12 km SW Dak To 2 AF. Kontum Pr, II Corps.

Hill 882? (YU 510-530?)
Possibly at listed grid, and if so, was apx 4 km SE Bu Krak AF. Apr71. Phuoc Long Pr, III Corps.

Hill 886 (AT 822-605)
Apx 10 km WNW Dai Loc. Quang Nam Pr, I Corps.

Hill 887 (YA 488-639)
See Phillips, FSB. Cambodia.

Hill 889 (YB 825-152)
Per map in *Dak To*, was apx 9 km SSW Ben Het, 4 km WSW FSB 15 (Hill 823) and 17 km WSW Dak To 2 AF. Prominent terrain feature of Battle for Dak To, May-Dec67. On NE 48-08 JOG. Pleiku Pr, II Corps.

Hill 890 (YC 490-980)
Part of Bloody Ridge or Dong A Tay. See Dong A Tay Luat and Hill 801. Thua Thien Pr, I Corps.

Hill 902 (YD 336-172)
Apx 2.3 km SSW FSB Ripcord, and 40 km W to WSW Hue. Scene of heavy fighting during Siege of FSB Ripcord, Mar-Jul70. See FSB Ripcord. Thua Thien Pr, I Corps.

Hill 903 (YA 921-548)
A.k.a. Chu Groll. Apx 3 km N Hill 1005, 6 km ENE Plei Djereng (old) AF and 11 km NNE Plei Djereng New AF. A/1st/14th Inf/25th Div here, Oct66. See *Rites of Passage*, pp 25-26. Pleiku Pr, II Corps.

Hill 903 (YB 790-446)
Ngok Lang Lo. 16 km SW Dak Sut. Kontum Pr, II Corps.

Hill 905 (YB 790-210)
Apx 23 km due W Dak To 2 AF. Kontum Pr, II Corps.

Hill 906 (AN 732-253)
See Nui Ong. Binh Thuan Pr, II Corps.

Hill 908 (XD 94-31)
Apx 3 km NW Laotian border, 17 km SSW Vandegrift CB and 3 km SW Da Ban Heliport. Grid per map, p 32, *US Marines in Vietnam-1969*. Quang Tri Pr, I Corps.

Hill 918 (XD 726-444)
Apx 5 km W Hill 881-S. Regarded as very dangerous site. Swept by 3d/26th Marines in late Dec67, but although strong evidence was found indicating NVA was there in force, only one man was KIA while retrieving his own booby trap. [274] Quang Tri Pr, I Corps.

Hill 923 (ZB 018-258)
See Mortar Mountain. Kontum Pr, II Corps.

Hill 927 (YD 343-194)
See FSB Ripcord. Thua Thien Pr, I Corps.

Hill 927 (ZA 000-429)
See Chu Prong Mtn. 26 km W Pleiku. Pleiku Pr, II Corps.

Hill 928 (BR 073-429)
Apx 30 km ESE Holloway AF and 4 km E Plei Klah. Aug66. Pleiku Pr?, II Corps.

Hill 929 (ZC 04-35)
See FSB Saber. Quang Nam Pr?, I Corps.

Hill 935 (YB 803-096)
Apx 3 km W Ngok Toba Mtn, 24 km SW Dak To 2 AF and 3 km S of Hill 875. Major here battle involving 42d ARVN Rgt and 66th NVA Rgt during Op Quang Trung 22F, 27-28Feb71. Was also proposed site for release of ARVN 42d Rgt WIA/POWs by elements of 66th NVA Rgt and NFLSV PLAF Cmd, Western Highland Front, scheduled for between 0800Hrs 4Mar71 and 1600 hrs 5Mar71. Cease fire within 10 km radius of Hill 635 (NVA called it 635 but analysis determined it to be Hill 935) and planned release were canceled when: no suitable LZ found, ARVN POWs could not be seen from air, and NVA heavily mortared 22d Ranger Bn on 4Mar71. [275] Kontum Pr, II Corps.

Hill 937 (YC 328-981)
A.k.a. Dong Ap Bia, Hamburger Hill and FSB Destiny. At NW end of A Shau Valley, apx 45 km WSW Hue, 22 km NW the A Sap/A Shau AF/SF Camp/ville complex, 9 km NW Ta Bat, 3 km E Laos and 25 km SE Tou Rout. See Hamburger Hill for more detail. Thua Thien Pr, I Corps.

Hill 943 (ZC 181-604)
Apx 7 km NE Ha Tan AF. Apr69. Quang Nam Pr, I Corps.

Hill 947 (YB 770-240)
Apx 25 km WNW Dak To 2 AF. Kontum Pr, II Corps.

Hill 950 (XD 844-456)
A.k.a. Dong Tri, Hill 959 and Hickory Hill Radio Relay/MSS site. Apx 3.5 km due N Khe Sanh CB, 1.2 km due W Hill 1015 (Dong Tre) and 2.5 km ENE Hill 558. Was Radio Relay and OP for Marine Recon in area during '67-69. Apparently Hickory Hill Relay here at one point, as well as on hill 1015? Heavily attacked and almost overrun in Summer '67. Overrun 4-5Jun71 by est NVA Bn-sized element with SGT Robert R Jones KIA and SSG Jon Cavaini awarded MOH, per www.specialoperations.com/MACVSOG/tales_from_sog/Co_Roc/Default.html. 105s here at some point? Photos of facility following p 168 of *Valley of Decision*. Also listed at XD 835-446. See Hickory Hill and Hill 959.Quang Tri Pr, I Corps.

Hill 951 (ZU 14-42)
See Yok Nam Lao Mtn (3,120'). Lam Dong Pr?, II Corps.

Hill 953 (AT 17-38)
Apx 37 km due S Da Nang. Quang Nam Pr, I Corps.

Hill 953 (BS 7-2?)
Apx 23 km SW Duc Pho and 21 km W Tam Quan. Map in *USMC in Vietnam, 1966*, p 20. Binh Dinh Pr, II Corps.

Hill 953 (XD 844-456)
See Hill 950 at grid. Quang Tri Pr, I Corps.

Hill 953 (ZA 22-75)
A.k.a. Chu Thoi Mtn. Apx 3 km W QL-14 and 11 km SSW Kontum. See LZ Highlander Heights. Kontum Pr, II Corps.

Hill 959 (XD 844-456)
See Hill 950 and Hickory Hill. Quang Tri Pr, I Corps.

Hill 963 (YB 790-100)
Apx 27 km SW Dak To 2 AF. Kontum Pr, II Corps.

Hill 975 (BR69-62)
See Vinh Thanh Mtn/LZ Chris. Binh Dinh Pr, II Corps.

Hill 976 (BP 98-46)
A.k.a. Nui Chau Hin. Apx 8 km SE and overlooking Nha Trang. Khanh Hoa Pr, II Corps.

Hill 976 (YB 790-446)
Nui Pon Mtn. 6 km ESE Dak Sut. Kontum Pr, II Corps.

Hill 978 (BP 985-450)
A.k.a. Grand Sommet Mtn. Apx 8 km SW Nha Trang AF. Khanh Hoa Pr, II Corps.
Hill 980 (YD 429-122)
A.k.a. Dong Tam Hanh and FSB Maureen. See Maureen. Thua Thien Pr, I Corps.
Hill 986 (XT 283-583)
See Nui Ba Den. Tay Ninh Pr, III Corps.
Hill 986 Signal Relay Site (XT 283-583)
See Nui Ba Den. Tay Ninh Pr, III Corps.
Hill 990 (YB 817-246)
Apx 6 km WSW Ben Het AF and 20 km due W Dak To 2 AF. 4th/503d Inf, 173d Abn worked this hill during Battle of Dak To, mid-Nov67. Kontum Pr, II Corps.
Hill 994 (YA 903-992)
A.k.a. Forget-Me-Not-Ridge. Apx 13 km NW Polei Kleng and in N end Plei Trap Valley. Battle for Hill 994, Mar69, involving 2de Bde/4th Div is described in *Time Heals No Wounds*, pp 145-168 and 170. Kontum Pr, II Corps.
Hill 1000 (YB 821-078)
See FSBs 202 and Foxtrot. Kontum Pr, II Corps.
Hill 1000 (YD 333-193)
Apx 1 km due W FSB Ripcord and 38 km W Hue. Assaulted by various elements 2d/501st and 2d/506th Inf, mid Jul70, as part of effort to relieve pressure on FSB Ripcord during siege of that base, 1-23Jul70. DMA 1:50,000 scale map image of site in *Ripcord*, at p 206. See FSB Ripcord. Thua Thien Pr, I Corps. [276]
Hill 1001 (YB 935-188)
See Firebase 6. Kontum Pr, II Corps.
Hill 1005 (YA 916-520)
Apx 3 km S Hill 903, 6 km E Plei Djereng (old) AF and 7 km NNE Plei Djereng New AF. B/1st/14th Inf/25th Div in battle here, 19 or 20Oct66. See *Rites of Passage*, pp 22-24. See Chu Goll Mountain. Pleiku Pr, II Corps.
Hill 1015 (XD 854-454)
A.k.a. Dong Tre Mtn, Hickory Radio Relay and possibly Hickory Hill. Apx 3.8 km NNE Khe Sanh CB, 1.2 km due E Hill 950 and 3.8 km E Hill 558. Overlooked Khe Sanh Valley to SW, and used as both US and NVA OP at various times during Siege of Khe Sanh CB, '67-68. On map in *The Final Formation*, pp 1-6. Quang Tri Pr, I Corps.
Hill 1017 (BN 31-60)
See Che Ket Mtn. Binh Thuan Pr, II Corps.
Hill 1018 (YA 94-94?)
A.k.a. LZ Blackfoot and Chu Kram Lo (or Chu Kan Lo) Mtn. Apx 8 km W Polei Kleng AF, and 30 km WNW Kontum. Kontum Pr, II Corps.
Hill 1019 (YA 925-579)
18 km NNE Plei Djereng New AF. Pleiku Pr, II Corps.
Hill 1025 (AT 807-627)
Apx 25 km SW Da Nang AB. Quang Nam Pr, I Corps.
Hill 1028 (AR 777-368)
A.k.a. Dragon Mtn and Chi Hodrong. See Dragon Mtn. Pleiku Pr, II Corps.
Hill 1030 (YB 822-081)
Roughly 23 km SW Dak To 2 AF, 47 km WNW Kontum. See Dak To, Battle. Grid apx. Kontum Pr, II Corps.
Hill 1030 (YC 608-827)
A.k.a. Dong Tre Gong Mtn. Apx 40 km SSW Hue and 4 km W Be Loung (A Shau Valley). Thua Thien Pr, I Corps.
Hill 1030 (YD 424-011)
A.k.a. Dong Ta Tach (?) or FSB Berchtesgarden. See Berchtesgarden. Thua Thien Pr, I Corps.
Hill 1031 (BN 59-77)
See Ya Bo Mtn. Ninh Thuan Pr?, II Corps.
Hill 1031 (ZB or YB?)
FSB apparently near Dak To. No data. If a.k.a. Hill 1030, was at YB 822-081 and apx 23 km SW Dak To 2 AF, 47 km WNW Kontum. Kontum Pr, II Corps.
Hill 1043 (YB 880-327)
Apx 17 km NW Dak to 2 AF and 1.5 km WNW Hill 763. 28th NVA Rgt position in Apr70. Also listed in Jun67 rpt. See Hill 763. Kontum Pr, II Corps.
Hill 1050 (ZC 15-41)
See FSB Dagger. Quang Nam Pr, I Corps.
Hill 1051 (YB 793-542)
Ngok Pong Der. 13 km W Dak Sut. Kontum Pr, II Corps.
Hill 1062 (YB or YA?)
Just S Dak To, per info supplied by Ben Youmans. 31Mar-5Apr68, C/2d/35th Inf, 4th Div, suffered hvy casualties here. Kontum Pr, II Corps.
Hill 1062 (ZC 200-604)
Apx 28 km SW Da Nang. Apr69. Quang Nam Pr, I Corps.
Hill 1064 (AT 86-04)
Apx 46 km WSW Tam Ky. Quang Tin Pr, I Corps.
Hill 1066 (ZC 143-623)
Apx 33 km WSW Da Nang. Quang Nam Pr, I Corps.
Hill 1073 (ZB or YB)
See Toumorong. NW Toumorong Outpost and immed S Dak Konong. Fighting here May-Jun66 during Battle for Toumorong. 1st Bde/101st Abn. Kontum Pr?, II Corps.
Hill 1094 (YC 826-787)
Apx 7 km SW Ruong Ruong. Thua Thien Pr, I Corps.
Hill 1102 (YD 187-274)
A.k.a. FSB Jerome and Dong Ba Le. Apx 13 km SSE Ba Long AF and 27 km SW Quang Tri. Quang Tri Pr, I Corps.
Hill 1103 (BS 53-18)
A.k.a. Nui Lang Ram. Apx 18 km SE Gia Vuc AF and 15 km S Ba To New AF. Quang Ngai Pr, I Corps.
Hill 1104 (BR 221-495)
Apx 1.5-2 km to S and SE and overlooking the Mang Yang pass and QL-19E. II Corps (on map L7014-6736-4).
Hill 1110 (189-283)
A.k.a. Hill 1102, FSB Jerome and Dong Bai Le? Apx 54 km WNW Hue, 34 km WSW Camp Evans and 25 km SSE Mai Loc. Quang Tri Pr, I Corps.
Hill 1112 (AT 78-78)
Apx 20 km due W Da Nang and 9 km N Hill 1478. Quang Nam Pr, I Corps.
Hill 1118 (BP 82-48)
See Nui Se Gai. Khanh Hoa Pr, II Corps.
Hill 1120 (YD 338-027)
A.k.a. Dong So Mtn. Apx 4 km N Dong Ap Bia (Hamburger Hill) and 8 km NW A Luoi 1 AF and on W edge of northern A Shau Valley. Thua Thien Pr, I Corps.
Hill 1123 (XD 854-513)
A.k.a. Dong La Ruong Mtn. Large hill mass apx 6 km due N Hill 1015 (Dong Tri) and 9.5 km NNE Khe Sanh CB. Quang Tri Pr, I Corps.

Hill 1124 (YA 956-859)
A.k.a. OP Hill. Apx 28 km W Kontum, 12 km SW Polei Kleng AF and 1.2 km NW LZ Brillo-Pad. Observation point used by 4th Div LRRPs in conjunction with Inf and Arty units on Brillo-Pad. Overrun night of 15May68, during an attack in which NVA used flame-throwers. Grid per Kevin Rafferty, B/1st/14th Inf, 4th Div. Map is L-7014-6537-4. See LZs Alamo, Bunker-Hill, Bingo, XYZ Pad and Brillo-Pad. Kontum Pr, II Corps.
Hill 1128 (YC 756-783)
Apx 13 km WSW Nong Truong Nam Dong and 12 km E Laos. May69. Thua Thien Pr, I Corps.
Hill 1162 (AR?)
A.k.a. Ham Rong Mountain? Pleiku Pr, II Corps.
Hill 1164 (BR 33-86)
Apx 44 km NNW An Khe. Binh Dinh Pr, II Corps.
Hill 1166 (ZC 142-623)
Apx 33 km WSW Da Nang AB. Quang Nam Pr, I Corps.
Hill 1170 (YC 9-9)
A.k.a. Dong Truoi. 12 km WSW of Phu Loc, 10 km ESE FSB Rifle? Thua Thien Pr, I Corps.
Hill 1175 (YD 107-098)
Apx 6 km SSE A Dang, 2 km E Laos and 4 km SE Tou Rout. Feb69. Quang Tri Pr, I Corps.
Hill 1178 (ZC 17-78)
Apx 24 km due E Da Nang. On map at p 98 of *US Marines in Vietnam-1969*. Quang Nam Pr, I Corps.
Hill 1188 (BR 215-580)
Listed as Hill 1198, but is Hill 1188. Apx 6 km NNE Phu Danh/QL-19 and 36 km NW An Khe. Pleiku Pr?, II Corps.
Hill 1198 (BR 215-580)
See Hill 1188. Pleiku Pr?, II Corps.
Hill 1198 (YA 937-931)
See Mile High. Kontum Pr, II Corps.
Hill 1208 (YC 984-908)
A.k.a. Dong Nam or Dong Nam Chan. Apx 14 km SW Phu Loc, 46 km W to WNW Da Nang, 6 km E FSB Pistol and 5 km NNE FSB Plum. Thua Thien Pr, I Corps.
Hill 1224 (YD 23-05)
Apx 12 km SE FSB Cunningham, 1 km Lao border and 36 km S Ba Long AF. Used by ARVN forces during Op Apache Snow, 10May-7Jun69. Grid per map, p 32, *US Marines in Vietnam-1969*. Thua Thien Pr, I Corps.
Hill 1228 (XD 813-515)
Apx 10 km NNW Khe Sanh CB, 7.5 km NW Dong Tri (Hill 1015) and 6.5 km N Hill 558. Quang Tri Pr, I Corps.
Hill 1228 (YD 253-090)
A.k.a. Co A Nong Mtn and FSBs Tiger and Turnage. Apx 10 km SE FSB Cunningham, 6 km N Laos, 5 km NE Hill 1224 and 32 km SSE Ba Long AF. Used by ARVN forces during Op Apache Snow, 10May-7Jun69. On map at p 32, *US Marines in Vietnam-1969*. Also 1st Cav and USMC. See FSB Tiger or Turnage. Thua Thien Pr, I Corps.
Hill 1235 (ZC 200-620)
Apx 8 km NNE Ha Tan AF. Quang Nam Pr, I Corps.
Hill 1242 (YD 420-033)
See FSB Georgia. Thua Thien Pr, I Corps.
Hill 1255 (YB 836-444)
Ngok Sie. 30 km NNW Dak To 2 AF. Kontum Pr, II Corps.
Hill 1262 (YB 975-149)
Apx 8 km SW Dak To 2 AF and 4 km WSW Hill 1338. See Dak To, Battle of. Grid apx only. Kontum Pr, II Corps.
Hill 1274 (YB 893-016)
Ngok Tahun Mtn. See LZ Ouachita. Kontum Pr, II Corps.
Hill 1281 (WJ 38-27)
See Ba Vi. NVN.
Hill 1294 (AP 811-608)
A.k.a. Cha Nam Kaa Mtn. Apx 14 km NNW Duc Xuyen AF. Darlac Pr, II Corps.
Hill 1298 (YD 318-180)
See Coc Muen Mtn. Thua Thien Pr, I Corps.
Hill 1302 (ZT 053-256)
See Hill 1304. Binh Tuy Pr, III Corps.
Hill 1304 (ZT 053-256)
See Dang S'Ruin Mtn. A.k.a. Hill 1302 and Nui Ong. Binh Tuy Pr, III Corps.
Hill 1308 (XD 676-573)
A.k.a. FSB Argonne. Apx 2 km E of Laos, 13 km S the southern edge of DMZ, 3 km SW Dong Sa Mui (Hill 1550) and 15 km due W FSB Neville. See FSB Argonne. Quang Tri Pr, I Corps.
Hill 1314 (YB 999-130)
See FSB Yankee/Artillery Hill. Kontum Pr, II Corps.
Hill 1315 (ZB 035-329)
Apx 12 km NNE Dak To 2 AF. Kontum Pr, II Corps.
Hill 1338 (YB 989-152)
A.k.a. Ngok Bor Beang Mtn and/or near FSB Flint. Apx 6 km SSW Dak to 2 AF. Prominent in Battle of Dak To, 1Nov-1Dec67. On 17May67, during Op Greely and in response to impending attacks on Dak To SF Camp and Tan Canh (42d ARVN Rgt), TF McQuarrie under 173d Abn Bde Dpty Cmdr Col Claude McQuarrie, deployed to Dak To. TF inc 1st/503d Inf, 2d/503d Inf, B Bty, 3d/319th Arty and suptg units. To deny NVA Hill 1338, it became 1st objective. On 18-20May67, A and C Cos, 2d/503d began ascent. On night of 21May67, and apx halfway to top, C Co met NVA in brief skirmish. On 22May67, A Co was engaged and overrun in "The Battle of Slopes." Of 137 men, A Co lost 76 KIA and 23 WIA. On 3Nov67, during Op MacArthur, B/3/12th, 4th Inf made heavy contact here, within 900 meters A/2d/503d's battle site. See FSB Flint and Dak To, Battle of. Kontum Pr, II Corps.
Hill 1361 (BP 88-72)
A.k.a. Hon Ba Mtn. Apx 22 km NW Nha Trang. Khanh Hoa Pr, II Corps.
Hill 1362 (BS 36-96)
A.k.a. Nui Dong Tranh or possibly LZ Pineapple. Major terrain feature apx 24 km S Tam Ky and overlooking the Batangan Peninsula 30 km to E. Quang Ngai Pr, I Corps.
Hill 1364 (BT?)
Assaulted by 1st/6th Inf, 198th LIB during '69, where large training site of 2d NVA Rgt was found and which Tom Brizendine describes as containing, "2-story hootches with running water funneled in by bamboo! VERY elaborate!" Quang Tin Pr?, I Corps.
Hill 1408 (ZC 040-900)
See Bach Ma Mtn and Bach Ma Resort for detailed history. Nam Hoa District, Thua Thien Pr, I Corps.

Hill 1416 (ZB 132-314)
A.k.a. Ngok Wan. Apx 14 km NE Dak To 2 AF and 10 km NNE Tan Canh. Site of major ARVN 3d & 9th Volunteer Bn's engagement with NVA 24th Rgt, during Battle of Dak To, 1Nov-1Dec67. Taken 20Nov after 4-day battle. Story-map at p 169, 178 *A Contagion of War* vol, *Vietnam Experience*. Also on map in *Dak To*. Kontum Pr, II Corps.
Hill 1438 (YA 810-690)
Cu Grock Mtn. See Sledge Hammer. Kontum Pr, II Corps.
Hill 1442 (AP 86-38)
See Youk Nam Ramay Mtn. Tuyen Duc Pr, II Corps.
Hill 1451 (BP 82-04)
See Hao Chu Hi Mtn. Ninh Thuan Pr?, II Corps.
Hill 1467 (ZC 20-61)
A.k.a. Ban Na or R.C. Ba Na Mtn. See Ban Na. Quang Nam Pr, I Corps.
Hill 1468 (ZC 08-93)
Vic of Bach Ma heliport, apx 6 km S Phu Loc and 40 km WNW Da Nang. On map at p 98 of *US Marines in Vietnam-1969*. Quang Nam Pr, I Corps.
Hill 1479 (ZB 134-363)
See Toumorong SF Camp. Kontum Pr, II Corps.
Hill 1483 (YB 913-001)
See LZ Delaware. Kontum Pr, II Corps.
Hill 1485 (YA 95-67)
See Chu Pa Mtn. Pleiku Pr, II Corps.
Hill 1487 (YD 406-036)
A.k.a. Dong Re Lao or FSB Eagle's Nest. See Eagle's Nest, FSB. Thua Thien Pr, I Corps.
Hill 1512 (YB 911-029)
Apx 10 km E Plei Trap Valley and 36 km WNW Kontum. Map is L-7014-6537-4. Kontum Pr, II Corps.
Hill 1528 (YA 84-77)
Cu Ki Tem Dar Mtn. Apx 28 km WNW Plei Mrong. See Sledge Hammer. Kontum Pr, II Corps.
Hill 1584 (BP 030-182?)
See Pra Lean Signal Site. Tuyen Duc Pr, II Corps.
Hill 1550 (XD 699-589)
Nui Sa Mui. Apx 3 km NE FSB Argonne, 34 km NW Khe Sanh CB and 4 km E Lao border. Quang Tri Pr, I Corps.
Hill 1551 (BR 12-43)
Chu Rran Mountain. Pleiku Pr, II Corps.
Hill 1152 (AR 811-801)
See Klondike. Kontum Pr, II Corps.
Hill 1570 (YB 911-028)
Ngok Ian Drang Mtn. Apx 20 km SSW Dak To 2 AF. 2d Bde/4th Div here '68-69, inc B/1st/12th Inf, 4th Div. Kontum Pr, II Corps.
Hill 1613 (XD)
See Dong Sa Mui. Quang Tri Pr, I Corps.
Hill 1615 (YD 335-107)
See Co Pung Mtn, and FSBs Co Pung and An Duong Vuong. Thua Thien Pr, I Corps.
Hill 1637 (BP 66-24)
See Nui Marrai (5,371'). Ninh Thuan Pr, II Corps.
Hill 1642 (ZT 07-54)
See B'Nom M' Hai Mtn. Binh Tuy Pr?, III Corps.
Hill 1654 (YS 36-86?)
See Ba Ria Signal Site. Phuoc Tuy Pr, III Corps.
Hill 1664 (AN 84-68)
See M'Neun Pantar Mtn. Lam Dong Pr, II Corps.
Hill 1701 (XD 84-54)
See Hill 1739. Quang Tri Pr, I Corps.
Hill 1712 (ZC 02-77)
A.k.a. Nui Mang. Highest peak in Quang Nam Pr. Apx 17 km due W Hai Van Pass, 42 km due W Da Nang and 52 km SE Hue. On map at p 98 of *US Marines in Vietnam-1969*. Quang Nam Pr, I Corps.
Hill 1714 (YD 354-071)
See Hill 1774. Thua Thien Pr, I Corps.
Hill 1731 (XD 84-54)
See Hill 1739. Quang Tri Pr, I Corps.
Hill 1739 (XD 84-54)
A.k.a. Dong Voi Mep and Tiger Tooth Mtn, Hill 1731 (and possibly Ghost Mtn?). 5,705' mtn apx 15 km due N Khe Sanh CB, 20 km W Laos and 15 km S DMZ. Tallest Mtn in I Corps? Good photo of mtn as seen from Hill 861 in pictorial following p 168 of *Valley of Decision*. Photo clearly indicates where mtn got its nickname. See Dong Voi Mep, LZ Crest, LZ Hill, Ghost Mtn, Advisory Team One and SESU. Quang Tri Pr, I Corps.
Hill 1748 (ZB 002-372)
Ngok Jrong. 16 km N Dak To 2 AF. Kontum Pr, II Corps.
Hill 1773 (YB 957-998)
A.k.a. Chu Mom Ray Mtn and Big Mamma. Major terrain feature apx 15 km E Plei Trap Valley and 32 km WNW Kontum. Map is L-7014-6537-4, and on map in *A Bright Shining Lie*. Kontum Pr, II Corps.
Hill 1773 (YD)
A.k.a. Dong Ca Pu. Apx 38 km WSW Hue. Reportedly highest point in Thua Thien Pr, however Dong Ngai Mtn at 1774 meters appears to be higher and is also in that Pr?, Thua Thien Pr, I Corps.
Hill 1774 (YD 382-082)
See Dong Ngai Mtn. Thua Thien Pr, I Corps.
Hill 1812 (BP 20-12)
See Quan Do Mtn. Tuyen Duc Pr, II Corps.
Hill 1865 (ZC 11-04)
Apx 13 km ESE Kham Duc. Quang Tin Pr, I Corps.
Hill 1874 (AN 91-78)
See Braian Mtn. Lam Dong Pr, II Corps.
Hill 1931 (WJ 46-26)
See Nui Vien Nam. NVN.
Hill 1982 (AP 78-13)
See Nui Ta Dung. Lam Dong Pr, II Corps.
Hill 1998 (AP 985-295)
A.k.a. Hon Nga Mtn. Apx 22 km WNW Dalat. Tuyen Duc Pr, II Corps.
Hill 2066 (AS 92-34)
See Ngok Krinh Mtn. Kontum Pr, II Corps.
Hill 2167 (BP 218-327)
See Lang Bian Signal Site. Tuyen Duc Pr, II Corps.
Hill 2287 (BP 460-373)
See Bi Doup Mtn. At 7,503', possibly tallest peak in southern 1/2 of SVN? Tuyen Duc Pr, II Corps.
Hill 2299 (AS 78-60)
Apx 72 km due N Kontum. Kontum Pr, II Corps.
Hill 2378 (ZB 12-54)
Apx 67 km NNW Kontum. Kontum Pr, II Corps.
Hill 2597 (ZB 21-68)
See Ngoc Linh Mtn. At 8,520', the tallest peak in SVN. Kontum Pr, II Corps.

Hill 3142 (UK 74-67)
A.k.a. Cha Pa Mtn (and Fan Si Pan Mtn?). Apx 260 km NW Hanoi. 10,308' elevation. NVN.
Hill 3143 (UK 74-67)
A.k.a. Fan Si Pan Mtn (and Cha Pa Mtn?). In Hoang Lien Mtns, apx 260 km WNW Hanoi. At 10,312', is tallest Mtn in Vietnam. See Hill 2597 and Hill 3280. NVN.
Hill 3280? (ZB 21-68)
Mtn at that grid is 2597, and apparently, no peak in SVN is taller. See Hill 2597. Kontum Pr, II Corps.
Hill Alpha (TJ 41-33)
Apx 300 meters SSW Hill Pi and 600 meters SE Muong Khoua. French position during Siege of Muong Khoua. See Muong Khoua for detail. Laos.
Hill Billy, FSB (n/a)
See Hillbilly, FSB. Cambodia or III Corps.
Hill Fights, The (XD)
Initial, legendary, bloody and brutal battles for Hills 861, 881-N and 881-S 27Apr67-5May67 (preceded Battle for Khe Sanh, Winter 67-68), involving 2d Bn/3d Marines, who took Hill 861 on 28Apr67 (hill held over 425 NVA bunkers/fighting positions). 881-S fell 2May67 to J, K and M Cos 2d/3d Marines (M Co had only 29 out of its 190 men left standing after assault, inc 43 KIA). Hill 881-N was last to fall at 1445hrs, 5May67, to E, G and H Cos, 2d/3d Marines. Quang Tri Pr, I Corps.
Hill of Angels (YD 113-703)
A.k.a. Hill 158 or Con Thien. See Con Thien and A-4. Quang Tri Pr, I Corps.
Hill Pi (TJ 41-33)
Apx 400 meters ESE Muong Khoua and 300 NNE Hill Alpha. French position here during Siege of Muong Khoua. See Muong Khoua. Laos.
Hill Radio Relay, The (AP 822-990)
See The Hill Radio Relay. Darlac Pr, II Corps.
Hill Top, FSB (XU 348-097)
See Hilltop, FSB. Cambodia.
Hill X (BT?)
NVA Occupied hill adj Hill 63, attacked by 4th/31st, 3d/21st and 2d/1st Inf elements, 196th LIB, 23Nov67. 7 US KIA, 31 WIA. Near Chu Lai? Quang Tin Pr?, I Corps.
Hillbilly, FSB (XT or XU?)
Per Peter Cole, is mentioned in 2d/7th Cav's Unit History for '70-71, p 2. During that period, Cav was in western III Corps or Cambodia.
Hilltop, FSB (XU 348-097)
In Cambodia, apx 6 km NE Memot, 33 km SW Snuol, 21 km N Katum, SVN, and 13 km N the SVN border. Elements of 2d/60th Inf (?) here, May-Jun70, per David Argabright. Grid in *11th ACR Cambodia Invasion AAR, 1st Cav Div, May-Jun70*, courtesy Lou Rochat. [277] Cambodia.
Hin Heup Airfield (TF 19-62)
LS-365. CIA/SF, per *Air Facilities Data-Laos.*
Hin Luk Airfield (MJ 2-9)
A.k.a. Phuket AF. At 8°07'00"N-98°18'00"E. Thailand.
Hinayana (n/a)
See Glossary.
Hippique, Cercle (XS 855-911)
Hotel/restaurant apx 700 meters SW Independence palace in Saigon. Gia Dinh Pr, III Corps.
Hipshoot, LZ (ZA 187-112)
At S edge of ville apx 35 km SSW Pleiku, 22 km NW Phu Nhon AF and 10 km NE Plei Me. 4th Div AO, '70. Name/grid per Jim Claeys. Pleiku Pr, II Corps.
Hiran, FSB (YS 214-854)
Apx 34 ESE Saigon 28 km NW Nui Dat, 1 km W FSB Jenny and 2 km NE QL-15. On 1ATF NCO trng map per John Hollett. Bien Hoa Pr, III Corps.
Hirondelles, Cap des (CR 1-2)
A.k.a. Mui Yen. Apx 5 km s due W Qui Nhon. NIMA data. Khanh Hoa Pr, II Corps.
Hirondelles, Cape des (CR 1-2)
See Cape Hirondelles. Binh Dinh Pr, II Corps.
Hissem, USS (n/a)
DER-400. In '66, *USS Ingraham* (DD-694) and *Hissem* intercepted trawler trying to infiltrate men/supplies from China and forced it to return. Role discussed in *Brown Water, Black Berets*, p 95. Market Time TF-115. SVN.
HL (road system) (n/a)
Designator for "communal" road system in SVN; the lowest quality road system in SVN. Normally two digits in diamond-shaped box. Connectors between smaller towns and hamlets. See QL, LTL, TL, Route, Highway, HL, R.C., *Route Colonial.*
HL-28 (WS 7-2)
Communal dirt road that ran in loop between Binh Thuy and Phong Phu in Phong Dinh Pr, IV Corps.
Ho (n/a)
One Vietnamese word for "Lake?"
Ho, LZ (BR 737-767)
Near site of LZ Castro, apx 8 km SW Ha Tay and 28 km SSW Bong Son. Cited in 1st Cav VN *Yearbook* Aug65-Dec69, p 89, per Peter Cole. May67. Also listed at BR 748-728, Oct66. Binh Dinh Pr, II Corps.
Ho, LZ (BR 748-728)
Apx 12 km SSW Ha Tay AF and 24 km SSW Bong Son. Cited in 1st Cav VN *Yearbook* Aug65-Dec69, p 89, per Peter Cole. Oct66. Also listed at BR 737-767, May67. Binh Dinh Pr, II Corps.
Ho Bo, FSB (XT 61-24)
SE edge of Hobo Woods, apx 3 km W Ql-1 and 18 km NW Saigon. 161 Bty, RNZA (Kenning's Bty 13Jun65-13Jun66) FSB set here 7-14Jan66. Hau Nghia Pr, III Corps.
Ho Bo Woods (XT 620-280)
Center of mass apx 25 km SSW Ben Cat and 35 km due W Bien Hoa. Densely jungled area and VC refuge apx 30 x 12 km in size. Straddled QL-1 at depth of about 5 km on either side starting apx 15 km NW Saigon, running to point about 30 km NW that city. Its N boundary was formed by Binh Duong/Gia Dinh Pr border. Legendary among 25th Inf Div and 196th LIB Troops and site of many battles in War Zone C, inc Op Cedar Falls Jan-Apr67. On map in *Vietnam Gunners*, p 62, and map in *Rangers At War,* pp 324-325. See Iron Triangle. Binh Duong Pr, III Corps.
Ho Chi Minh (n/a)
See Glossary.
Ho Chi Minh Campaign, The (n/a)
See Final Offensive in Glossary.
Ho Chi Minh City (XS 8-9)
Post-American War name for Saigon. See Saigon and Ly Tong. Gia Dinh Pr, III Corps.

Ho Chi Minh Sandals (n/a)
See Glossary.

Ho Chi Minh Trail (n/a)
See Glossary.

Ho Chi Minh, Thanh Pho (Saigon) (n/a)
Mapsheet L-7014-6330-4. True sheet name: Thanh Pho Ho Chi Minh (Ho Chi Minh City). SVN.

Ho Dan Kich Dam (BP 14-27)
Dam on Ho Dan Kich Lake, apx 7 km NW Dalat. Provided hydroelectric power for area. See Ho Dan Kich Lake. Tuyen Duc Pr, II Corps.

Ho Dan Kich Lake (BP 16-30)
Large lake apx 8 km NW Dalat. A.k.a. Lac Duong? Was about 5 km long and 2 km wide, and dammed to provided hydroelectric power for area. Tuyen Duc Pr, II Corps.

Ho Don Duong (BP 40-13)
A.k.a. Ho Dan Kich? Dam and lake apx 20 km SE Dalat providing power for Dalat area. Tuyen Duc Pr, II Corps.

Ho Don Duong (BP 4-1)
Freshwater lake at 11°52N-108°37'E. On NC49-01 JOG. Tuyen Duc Pr?, II Corps.

Ho Jo Village (XT 175-517)
See Freeworld Service Club. Tay Ninh Pr, III Corps.

Ho Nai Prison (YT 0-1 or YT 1-1?)
Possibly a.k.a. Hoa Nai prison? Apparently near Bien Hoa. POW camp for VC and NVA captured in that area. If Hoa Nai correct sp, then it was a.k.a. prison #508, Ho Nai Prison or Thanh Hoa Prison and in what is today Dong Nai Pr. Bien Hoa Pr?, III Corps.

Ho Ngoc Tau SF Camp (XT 958-001)
A.k.a. FOB 6. Along Rte 316, apx 3 km W Thu Duc, 16 km ENE Tan Son Nhut AB and 13 km S Bien Hoa AB. SF Det 61, and 5th SF, Det A 310 Oct65, A 303 Dec66, B 61 Oct66. Also sp No Ngoc Tau in document indicating Det A-314, a.k.a. Det 301, here '65, and B-56 Sigma here '66. 1st MGF (Det A-303) under Bo Gritz was trained here, Nov-Dec66. Grid per *SF Order of Battle.* Moved to Trang Sup, Project SIGMA. See Saigon Buddhist Pagoda. Gia Dinh Pr, III Corps.

Ho Ngoc Tau, Camp (XT 958-001)
See Ho Ngoc Tau SF Camp. Gia Dinh Pr, III Corps.

Ho Tram, Mui (YS 6-5)
Coastal point at 10°28'N-107°27'E. On NC48-08 JOG. Phuoc Tuy Pr, III Corps.

Ho Xa (Vinh Lo) (n/a)
Mapsheet L-7014-6443-3. Full sheet name is: Vinh Lo (Ho Xa). NVN only.

Ho Xuan Huong (BP 23-22)
Narrow freshwater lake at center of Dalat. At 11°56'N-108°27'E. On NC49-01 JOG. Tuyen Duc Pr, II Corps.

Ho Xuan Island (BT 43-16)
Center of mass apx 15 km NW Chu Lai AF, in tidal bay formed by Ben Van River. See Ky Xuan Isle. Quang Tin Pr, I Corps.

Ho Xaun Huong (BP 225-215)
Freshwater lake in City of Dalat. Tuyen Duc Pr, II Corps.

Hoa Binh (n/a)
Mapsheet name of L-7014-6050-1. NVN only.

Hoa Binh (WJ 34-05)
On Road No. 6 along N bank of Black River, apx 50 km SW Hanoi. French garrison here involved in heavy fighting during 1st Indochina War. Term "Hoa Binh" means "Peace." See Hoa Binh Salient and *Street Without Joy*, Chp 2, map at p 46. NVN.

Hoa Binh Airfield (WJ 34-05)
Presumably at Hoa Binh. Used by French during Battle for Hoa Binh, 14Nov51-24Feb52. NVN.

Hoa Binh Heliport (XS 787-384)
At Ap Binh, apx 1 km N the Song Cua Tieu branch of Mekong River, apx 8 km SW Go Cong and 30 km ESE My Tho. "Heliport #718, alt 5', Conc pad, wires, antennas and bldgs. Caution: very confined, per Feb73 TAD. Go Cong Pr, IV Corps.

Hoa Binh Salient (WJ 3-0)
On N bank of Black River apx 60 km SW Hanoi. Ran from Hao Binh up Road No. 6 ENE toward Hanoi. Kept open despite heavy pressure from Vietminh who surrounded area from W, S and NW, Nov51-Feb52. See Chp 2 of *Street Without Joy*, and map on p 50. NVN.

Hoa Binh, Battle of (WJ 34-05)
A.k.a. Battle for Road No. 6, the Hell of Hoa Binh, and Battle of the Black River Salient. Took place 14Nov51-24Feb52. This "meat grinder" op (Code name Lotus) was initiated as counterattack by French in response to Vietminh attack on Nghia Lo of 22Sep51. 3 Para Bns were dropped into Hoa Binh virtually unopposed on 14Nov51, while 15 Inf Bns, 7 Arty Bns, 2 armored grps and 2 Dinassauts began moving up the Black River Valley. In response and seeing an opportunity, Gen. Giap sent 304th, 308th Inf Divs (supported by arty, AAA and eng units), plus some "Regional Troops" (semi-regulars), to Hao Binh. Giap also ordered 316th and 320th Divs into lowlands between Hoa Binh and Hanoi in order to disrupt French supply lines to Hoa Binh. 1st major attack took place at Tu Vu, 9Dec51, when French Moroccan garrison overrun by 3 Rgts of Vietminh 308th and 312th Divs, who lost some 400 dead and withdrew the next morning. On 12Jan52, an entire river convoy ambushed S of Notre Dame Rock, severely damaging nearly every ship and sinking 4 patrol boats and one LSSL. Ambush ended French attempts to resupply Hoa Binh area by river. After that, Road No. 6 became main means of re-supply rte, with 10 strongpoints held by 1 Inf Bn, 1 Arty Bn, 2 Armored Bns and an Engr Grp along it. On 8Jan52, the strongpoint at Xom Pheo, with much of it overrun before VM withdrew leaving 700 of its own dead. On 9Jan52, VM destroyed almost an entire Mobile Bn, forcing closure of Road No. 6. An Abn TF under Col Gilles then spent 11 very costly days of fighting to reopen Road 6 from Day River to Hoa Binh Salient, committing 12 Inf Bns along the stretch just to keep it open. Gen. Salan, who succeeded the dying Gen. De Lattre in Jan52, then realized futility of effort and ordered a complete withdrawal, calling it Op Amaranth, (22-24Feb52).Battle proved as costly for French as 1950 border fort battles and later battle for Dien Bien Phu. Ironically, term "Hoa Binh" means "Peace" in Vietnamese. Data per *Street Without Joy*, Chp 2. NVN.

Hoa Cam Heliport (AT 977-729)
Apx 4 km SW Da Nang AB and 2 to 3 km W QL-1. Heliport #585, alt 115', at 16°01'20"N-108°10'30"E, per Feb73 TAD. Quang Nam Pr, I Corps.

Hoa Cam SF Camp (AT 976-767)
Apparently apx 4 km SW Da Nang AB and 2 to 3 km W QL-1. 5th SF camp. Info/grid per *SF Order of Battle.* Quang Nam Pr, I Corps.

Hoa Cam Training Center (AT 974-718)
Apx 4 km SW Da Nang AB and 2 to 3 km W QL-1. Possibly ARVN or RF/PF trng facility? 68-69. Also listed at AT 985-727. Quang Nam Pr, I Corps.

Hoa Do, Mui (CP 1-6)
A.k.a. Mui Bai Chuoampong. Coastal point at 12°23'N-109°20'E. ND49-13 JOG. Khanh Hoa Pr, II Corps.

Hoa Hiep (various) (various)
At least 4 Hoa Hiep NIMA Gaz listings. See grid squares: BR 6-3, BR 9-5, WT 9-7 and ZC 0-4. I, II and IV Corps.

Hoa Hiep CAP (ZC 02-44?)
Echo 2 ('67), 2d CAG and Quebec 4, 2d CAG, Hoa Vang District per Tim Duffie. Photo at p 63 of *A Contagion of War* vol, *VN Experience* series. Quang Nam Pr, I Corp.

Hoa Hiep Valley (BR 660-380)
Generally 18 km ESE An Khe, 6 km SW Binh Khe. Binh Dinh Pr, II Corps.

Hoa Hoi (CR 0-7)
N of Qui Nhon and apx 1,200 meters inland from ocean, just E QL-1. Was focus of Op Irving-Thayer Oct66. Battle here involving 1st/9th Cav and 1st/12th Cav, 1st Cav discussed at length in *The Fields of Bamboo*. Near 14°12'00"N-109°11'00"E. Binh Dinh Pr, II Corps.

Hoa Khanh CAP (AT 9-7?)
CAP-3 here per Tim Duffie. Quang Nam Pr, I Corps.

Hoa Lac Airfield (XJ 52-26)
Apx 35 km due W Hanoi. NVN.

Hoa Loi Woods (XT 880-260)
Apx 16 km NW Bien Hoa AB. Binh Duong Pr, III Corps.

Hoa Long (various)
Common Viet place-name. Sites inc: XS 701-484, WS 670-575, XS 571-379, WS 429-540, WR 665-848, WS 153-840, WS 727-368 and YS 49-62. III & IV Corps.

Hoa Long (YS 419-635)
Was at intersection of Rte 358 and LTL-53, apx 3 km SSW Nui Dat and 4 km NE Ba Ria. Apparently elements of ANZAC 1ATF here or was a significant terrain feature of their AO. See Hoa Long Dance in Glossary. Phuoc Tuy Pr, III Corps.

Hoa Long Dance, The (YS 42-63)
See Glossary.

Hoa Long Heliport (WS 727-370)
Apx 11 km due W Sa Dec and just N Ap Ba. "Heliport #586, alt 7', sod, yellow PSP, at 10°17'15"N-105°39'39"E," per Feb73 TAD. Sa Dec Pr, IV Corps.

Hoa Lu BEQ (XS 853-907)
At 60 Vo Tanh St. (Hoa Lu Enlisted Open Mess), Aug 64, 47 rms, Saigon. Per R. Bows' *Vietnam Military Lore, 1959-1973.* Gia Dinh Pr, III Corps.

Hoa Luong CAP (n/a)
CAP 2-1-5, 2d CAG. Quang Nam Pr, I Corps.

Hoa My, Camp (AT 96-76?)
Apx 5 km W Da Nang AB and a.k.a. Camp Charger. See Camp Charger. Grid is est. Quang Nam Pr, I Corps.

Hoa Nai Prison (YT 0-1 or YT 1-1?)
Possibly a.k.a. Ho Nai prison? Apparently near Bien Hoa. POW camp for VC and NVA captured in that area. If Hoa Nai correct, then it is a.k.a. prison #508, Ho Nai Prison or Thanh Hoa Prison, and in what today is Dong Nai Pr. Bien Hoa Pr?, III Corps.

Hoa Ngan Mountain (AT 82-43)
A.k.a. Hill 662. Apx 6 km NW Phuoc Binh and 38 km SW Da Nang. Quang Nam Pr, I Corps.

Hoa Phat Orphanage (BT 988-767)
NW Da Nang AB. Mar66. Quang Nam Pr, I Corps.

Hoa Phu CAP (AT 92-78 or 9-5?)
Bravo 1, 3rd CAG per Tim Duffie. Listed in Thua Thien Pr, but NIMA grid suggests it was in Quang Nam Pr?, I Corps.

Hoa Phu CAP (AT 92-78 or 9-5?)
CAP 3-2, 3rd CAG per Tim Duffie. Listed in Thua Thien Pr, but NIMA suggests it was in Quang Nam Pr?, I Corps.

Hoa Thanh CAP (AT 9-7)
CAP 2-5-7, 2d CAG. Hoa Vang, Quang Nam Pr, I Corps.

Hoa Thanh, Ap (AN 91-21)
Apx 20 km NE Phan Thiet and along QL-1. FSB Bannister was nearby. On TPC-K10A map. Binh Thuan Pr, II Corps.

Hoa Tho CAP (AT 9-7?)
No data. Per CAP Website.

Hoa Vang (BT 011-729)
Apx 4 km due S Da Nang AB. XXIV Corps grid. Quang Nam Pr, I Corps.

Hoa Vinh CAP (AT 9-7 or 9-8)
Noted in *Study In Counterinsurgency,* per CAP Website. Quang Nam Pr, I Corps.

Hoai An (n/a)
Mapsheet name of L-7014-6737-1. SVN.

Hoai An (BP 7-8?)
Near 14°21'00"N-108°57'00"E, just W Duc My. Khanh Hoa Pr, II Corps.

Hoai An (BR 81-79)
Along Tl-3A, apx 4 km due N Ha Tay AF and 8 km SW Bong Son AF. Binh Dinh Pr, II Corps.

Hoai An CIDG Camp (BR 803-839)
See Hoai An SF Camp. Binh Dinh Pr, II Corps.

Hoai An SF Camp (BR 803-839)
A.k.a. Hoai An CIDG Camp. Just N Ha Tay AF, apx 13 km SW Bong Son and 6 km ENE Phu Xuan. 5th SF Det A-223 here Oct65, converted to MAT #? Indexed in *Special Forces Order Battle.* 2d/17th Arty here supt 1st Cav, 11Feb66. Grid per Jack Picciolo. Binh Dinh Pr, II Corps.

Hoai Nhon (BR 85-96?)
A.k.a. Bong Son. Apx 3 km NE Bong Son AF, 10 km SSW LZ English and 50 km N Phu Cat. Binh Dinh Pr, II Corps.

Hoai Nhon (BR 87-96)
See Bong Son. Binh Dinh Pr, II Corps.

Hoai Nhon Airfield (BR 846-947)
See Bong Son AF. Binh Dinh Pr, II Corps.

Hoai Nhon Delta (BR 8-9)
Delta of Hoai Nhon River? General base area of NVA Sao Vang Div's 22d Rgt. Apparently near Bong Son. See *Bird*, Chp 1. Binh Dinh Pr, II Corps.

Hoan Kiem District (WJ 8-2)
One of Hanoi's 4 districts (Quan): Hoan Kiem Dist (city center); Ba Dinh Dist (west area, inc Ho Chi Minh's Tomb); Hai Ba Trung Dist (on Red River, S Hoan Kiem Dist); and Dong Da Dist (SW area). NVN.

Hoan Kiem Lake (WJ 8-2)
Hanoi. Hoan Kiem District includes city center and this lake. To N of Hoan Kiem Lake is Old Quarter of Hanoi, known to French as *Ceti Indigene*. NVN.

Hoang Hoa Tham Dependent Quarters (XS or XT)
Precise location unknown but apparently was in Gia Dinh or Bien Hoa Pr, and near Saigon or Long Binh Post. In '68, consisted of 103 houses for 3d ARVN Ranger Grp, 36th ARVN Ranger Bn's apx 145 families. Data per in *Rangers At War*, p 262. See Camp Phanh Hanh. III Corps.

Hoang Lien Mtns (UK 74-67)
Mtn range in NW NVN which is home to tallest peak in Vietnam (N or S), Fan Si Pan Mtn, which is some 3,143 meters or 10,312' in height. Grid is for that mtn. NVN.

Hoang Su Phi (n/a)
Mapsheet name of L 701-5979-3. NVN/China.

Hoang Xa (n/a)
Mapsheet name of L-7014-6051-2. NVN only.

Hobart, HMAS (n/a)
A.k.a. DDG-39. VN service, 67-72, first beginning in Mar68, adding heft to NGS Unit when losses to accidents and Op Sea Dragon reduced NGSA's effectiveness. On 17Jun68, was hit by US acft launched Sparrow missiles inflicting 2 KIA and 7 WIA (acft from *USS Enterprise*), while serving with US 7th Flt interdicting coastal traffic and providing NGS. At 0315 hrs, 17Jun68 she was a few km N of DMZ and near shore when one missile hit amidships, causing superstructure damage and another hit aft below main deck. *Enterprise* sent helo soon after the hit for 3 injured sailors who required hospitalization. Along with US Heavy Cruiser *Boston*, *USCGC Point Dume* and PCF-12 were repeatedly attacked by unidentified acft, 16Aug66. Incident discussed in *Brown Water, Black Berets*, p 114. Market Time TF-115. See *Point Welcome*, *Perth*, and www.hmasperth.asn.au/. NVN/SVN

Hobo Woods (XT 620-280)
See Ho Bo Woods. Binh Duong Pr, III Corps.

Hoc Mon, FSB (XT 707-080)
A.k.a. FSB Nhi Binh. Apx 16 km NW Tan Son Nhut, 1 km SE Tan Phu. Jan69. 11th ACR, 25th Div, 2d/3d, 4th/12th Inf '69. Info per 199th LIB Assn. Also listed at XT 74-04. Binh Duong Pr, III Corps.

Hoc Mon Base (XT 74-04)
Along TL-15, apx 8 km NW Tan Son Nhut AB, 17 km SE Cu Chi and 11 km SE Tan Phu. 25th Inf, 11th ACR, 199th LIB. Binh Duong or Gia Dinh Pr, III Corps.

Hoc Mon Bridge (XT 712-071)
Apx 15 km NW Saigon on QL-1. 1st Plt, D Trp, 3d/4th Cav was securing bridge at start of Tet '68. It then moved S to Tan Son Nhut battle, 31Jan68.[278] Also bridge at ville of Hoc Mon on TL-15, and 10 km NW Saigon (XT 745-040). Binh Duong Pr, III Corps.

Hoc Mon Canal (XT 680-010)
Apx 14 km WNW Tan Son Nhut AB. Oct68. Hau Nghia Pr, III Corps.

Hoc Mon Heliport (XT 755-039)
N side of QL-1, apx 8 km NW Tan Son Nhut, 17 km SE Cu Chi and 11 km SE Tan Phu. Heliport #587, alt 20', at 10°53'00"N-106°36'00"E. Gia Dinh Pr, III Corps.

Hoc Xan (XT)
AO of 268 VC Rgt, and object of 2d/14th Inf, 2d/49th ARVN Rgt, joint ops, Summer '69. Location unknown, but likely near Cu Chi. III Corps.

Hochmuth, Camp (YD 885-135)
On W side of QL-1, directly across hwy from Phu Bai AF at Phu Bai. Marine basecamp and HQ 3d Mar Div, VN. Named to honor USMC MGen Bruno A. Hochmuth, Cmd Gen, 3d Mar Div, KIA 14Nov67, when UH1-E carrying Hochmuth and 5 others was struck by enemy ground fire along QL-1 near Camp Evans (11 km N Hue), exploded in mid air and crashed into shallow pond drowning anyone not killed in explosion. In Apr70, the 101st Abn took over base and moved Div HQ here as 3d Mar Div departed VN. Thua Thien Pr, I Corps.

Hockmuth, Camp (YD 885-135)
See Hochmuth. Thua Thien Pr, I Corps.

Hog, FSB (YD 45-44?)
If grid correct, was just E QL-1, apx 3 km N Thon My Chanh, 14 km SE Quang Tri and 35 km NW Hue. Built by 1st/501st Inf, 29Feb68. A Bty 1st/321st Arty moved here from FSB Mogan at same time. Near Thua Thien/Quang Tri Pr border, I Corps.

Hoi An (BT 146-517)
Site of Portuguese colony of Ancient Faifo, a trading site established in 1600's. Heavily, VC, the area was assigned to 9th Marine Rgt until it left in '69. Home of Quang Nam Adv Team 15, and AO of Korean 2d Marine Corps 'Blue Dragons' Bde, after it left Cam Linh Peninsula-Dong Ba Thin area. Also listed at BT 142-576 per pilot's Guide. On 14Jul67 the Adv cmpd and Hoi An Province Prison were simultaneously attacked by several VC plts dressed in ARVN uniforms who released 1,196 prisoners, only 206 of whom were recaptured. On mapsheet L-7014-6640-1. Capitol, Quang Nam Pr, I Corps.

Hoi An (Hoian) (n/a)
Mapsheet L-7014-6640-1. Sheet name: Hoian. SVN.

Hoi An Advisor's Compound (BT 142-573?)
See Hoi An. Quang Nam Pr, I Corps.

Hoi An Airfield (BT 142-576)
Apx 22 km SE Da Nang, just N Hoi An and 2 km from ocean. Controlled by ROK army and MACV. Per TPC K-10A. El. 10', 1,900' PSP/steel-mat rwy. At 15°53'00"N-108°19'47"E. "Contact as per MACV I Corps Signal Operating Instructions (C-7) ARVN (ROK Army/MACV) 23Jan69, AF # VA1-206," in Aug69 TAD per Frank Penk, Jr. Not in Feb73 TAD. Quang Nam Pr, I Corps.

Hoi An CAP (BT 1-5?)
Likely in or near Hoi An, which was near coast apx 23 km SE Da Nang AB. Spelled Hoi Anh in one text. 2d CAG per CAP Website. Quang Nam Pr, I Corps.

Hoi An Catholic Orphanage (BT 144-574)
Near Hoi An Heliport, apx 2 km E Hoi An AF, 23 km SE Da Nang AB. Jul68. Quang Nam Pr, I Corps.

Hoi An Heliport (BT 146-573)
At N edge of Hoi An, apx 2 km E Hoi An AF and 23 km SE Da Nang AB. Heliport #588, alt 16', at 15°53'00"N-108°20'00"E, per Feb73 TAD. Quang Nam Pr, I Corps.

Hoi An PBR Base (BT 14-57?)
Apx 22 km SE Da Nang, and perhaps 2 km from ocean. USN Patrol Boat Base, '69-71, per MRF Assn website. Quang Nam Pr, I Corps.
Hoi An River (BT 1-5?)
Americal list. Quang Nam Pr, I Corps.
Hoi Anh CAP (BT 1-5?)
See Hoi An CAP. Quang Nam Pr, I Corps.
Hoi Binh, Pointe de (XR 3-4)
See Pointe Hoi Binh. Ba Xuyen Pr, IV Corps.
Hoi Chanh (n/a)
See Glossary.
Hoi Dong Chieu SF Camp (XS 200-825)
Along N side of Song Vam Co Tay River, 10 km WNW Thuy Dong AF, 15 km SW tip of Parrot's Beak and 62 km W Saigon. 5th SF. Info/grid per *SF Order of Battle.* A.k.a. FOB Tuyen Nhon. Kien Tuong Pr, IV Corps.
Hoi Hai CAP (n/a)
Apparently noted in *Velvet Glove*. 1/9 Marines here per CAP Website. Quang Nam Pr, I Corps.
Hoi Son 1, 3, 5 (BR 7-6?)
Generally 20 km NNW Phu Cat, N LZ Hotel and about 8 km W QL-1. Involved in battles during Op Thayer-Irving, Oct66. The focus of *The Fields of Bamboo*, pp 218-221. Also involved in battles during Op Crazy Horse, May66. Binh Dinh Pr, II Corps.
Hoi Son 5 (BR 7-6?)
On E bank of Soui Ca River 8 km W QL-1, 2.5 km N LZ Hotel, 18 km NNW Phu Cat, 11 km due E LZ Horse. In Op Crazy Horse AO, May66, and discussed in *Battles in the Monsoon*, pp 138-151. Also a focus of *The Fields of Bamboo*, pp218, 221. 1st Cav. Binh Dinh Pr, II Corps.
Hoi Van (BR 699-871)
Apx 11 km NW Ha Tay AF and W the Phu Cat/Bong Son coastal plain. Apparently near Song Nuoc Luong River. Cited in *Bird*, p 14. Binh Dinh Pr, II Corps.
Hoi Vuc (AT 874-713)
Apx 13 km WSW Da Nang AB. Grid per G. Neville, 3d Recon/3d Mar Div. Quang Nam Pr, I Corps.
Hoi Xuan (n/a)
Mapsheet name of L-7014-6049-4. NVN only.
Hoian (Hoi An) (n/a)
Mapsheet name of L-7014-6640-1. SVN.
HoJo Village (XT 175-517)
See Freeworld Service Club. Tay Ninh Pr, III Corps.
Hokmuth, Camp (YD 885-135)
See Hochmuth. Thua Thien Pr, I Corps.
Holcomb, Camp (YD or XD)
Said to have been somewhere in Quang Tri Pr. Apparently named to honor SSgt Melvin D. Holcomb, USMC, KIA 6Jul67. Quang Tri Pr, I Corps.
Holcomb, FSB (YD 118-431)
25 km WSW Quang Tri, 5 km SE FSB Summer and 10 km SSE Vandegrift CB. Also listed at YD 119-432 on XXIV Corps index (Don Armstrong). Quang Tri Pr, I Corps.
Hole, The (XT?)
1st Avn Bn pilot's nickname for a stovepipe-shaped hole cut in triple-canopy jungle by elements of 2d/28th Inf, 1st Inf Div, during Op Shenandoah II, Oct-Nov67 (battling the 271st VC Rgt). Used by helos of 1st Avn Bn to extract many US WIA/KIA. Initially all extractions were by hoist, but eventually clearing was widened to 100' diameter, and Hueys would actually hover down this narrow hole to land. Binh Duong or Binh Long Pr, III Corps.
Holiday Inn, FSB (XT 908-335)
Along Rte TL-16, apx 14 km ESE Lai Khe, 20 km NNW Bien Hoa AB, 6 km SE FSB Bandit Hill, 8 km due W Khu Tru Mat and along W edge of War Zone D. Map in *Charlie Company* at p 6 shows location. 2d Sqdn, 11th ACR, Mar69. Grid per 14Ma469 *Summary of Combat Service Support to the 11th ACR*, signed by Maj. Harry W. Johnson Adjutant, courtesy Jim Cole. See Bandit Hill. Binh Duong Pr, III Corps.
Holmes County, USS (n/a)
LST-836. SVN.
Holland Compound (YU 458-065?)
Possibly a.k.a. the Bu Dang Adv Cmpd? US Adv Cmpd at Van Kiep Natl Trng Ctr, Duc Phong, along QL-14, apx 105 km NNE Bien Hoa AB and 30 km E of Song Be. Named to honor Capt. Carlton J. Holland, USA, KIA 9Feb65, at Bu Dang, when 1st US Adv Cmpd was overrun. Data per *Vietnam Military Lore, 1959-1973*. Pr?, III Corps.
Hollandia, Operation (n/a)
9-17 Jun66. 173d Abn, Phuoc Tuy Pr. Bde deployed to Lon Hai Peninsula, E of Vung Tau, to find 274th and 275th VC Rgts and their HQ. III Corps.
Holloway, Camp (AR 802-472)
Along N side of QL-19, apx 3 km E Pleiku. Originally known as Old Pleiku, then *The Country Club* and later named Camp Holloway to honor CWO Charles E Holloway, 81st Trans Co, a CH-21 pilot, KIA 22Dec62, during an ARVN insertion. One of earliest named installations in VN. Home of 81st Trans Co (Light Helo), 43d Sig Bn, 52d Avn Bn and other 4th Div units inc 2d/320th Arty. Data per *Vietnam Military Lore, 1959-1973.* Pleiku Pr, II Corps.
Holloway, LZ/FSB? (YB 910-120)
Apx 15 km SSE Ben Het and 43 km NW Kontum. True nature of site unknown. Kontum Pr, III Corps.
Holloway Airfield (AR 804-470)
A.k.a. Pleiku Area AF. On N side of QL-19, apx 4 km due E Pleiku. Named to honor, CWO Charles E Holloway, US Army, 81st Trans Co, CH-21 pilot, KIA 22Dec62, during ARVN insertion (81st later renamed the 119th Avn Co) and it named their airfield for 1st member of that unit KIA in VN. 4th Div. El. 2,460', 4,100' PSP rwy. At 13°58'39"N-108°02'25"E. II Corps.
Holly (n/a)
6Apr70, XXIV Corps proposed 5th Div FSB name.
Hollywood, LZ/FSB (BR or BS)
Described as temporary FSB in An Lao Valley. 173d Abn. Binh Dinh Pr, II Corps.
Holt Swimming Pool (YS 28-43)
See Peter Badcoe Club. Phuoc Tuy Pr, III Corps.
Holy See, Temple of (XT 241-496)
See Temple of Holy See and also Temple of Holy See (2) at XT 265-463. Tay Ninh Pr, III Corps.
Homecoming, LZ (ZA 210-100)
Apx 6 km NE Plei Me SF Camp/AF, 3 km S LZ South and about 22 km due S Catecka. Initially occupied by 2 Btys of 2d/19th Arty suptg ARVN column moving to break 32d and 33d NVA Rgt's Oct65 siege of Plei Me. On 26Oct65,

1st Bde/1st Cav HQ moved here to coordinate final actions of effort to rescue Plei Me; however, when Bde CO realized site was not appropriate for Bde HQ, it was moved to "what became known as The Stadium, adj to sprawling Catecka Tea Plantation." On map in *Pleiku*, p 88. Grid is est. Pleiku Pr, II Corps.

Homecoming, Operation (NVN)
See Glossary.

Homestead (n/a)
Apr70, XXIV Corps proposed 101st Abn FSB name.

Hon (n/a)
Vietnamese word for mountain or hill or island.

Hon Ba Island (XQ 72-57)
Part of Con Son Island grp; 5 islands in South China Sea apx 85 km at their closest point to SVN coast and 200 km due E western-most tip of Cau Mau Peninsula. Consisting of Con Son, the largest (16 km-long and avg of 6 km-wide, Hon Ba, Hon Bai Canh, Hon Cau and Hon Tre Lon. See Con Son Island. South China Sea.

Hon Ba Mountain (BP 88-72)
A.k.a. Hill 1361. Apx 22 km NW Nha Trang. Khanh Hoa Pr, II Corps.

Hon Bai Canh (XQ 87-58)
See Hon Ba Island for location and data. See Con Son Island. South China Sea.

Hon Bai Canh Island (XQ 86-58)
See Con Son Islands. IV Corps.

Hon Cau Island (CP 23-57)
Apx 20 km ENE Nha Trang AF. Khanh Hoa Pr, II Corps.

Hon Cau Island (CR 1-3)
A.k.a. Ile Juan Prieto. Binh Dinh Pr, II Corps.

Hon Cau Island (XQ 92-61)
See Con Son Islands. IV Corps.

Hon Cau Island (XQ 92-61)
See Hon Ba Island for location and data. See Con Son Island. South China Sea.

Hon Cau Mountain (BR 94-93)
A.k.a. Hill 619. Apx 8 km WSW Bong Son. See Lo Dieu Beach. Binh Dinh Pr, II Corps.

Hon Cha La Island (CP 25-67)
Apx 26 km NE Nha Trang AF. Khanh Hoa Pr, II Corps.

Hon Chau Mountain (AT 82-43)
See Hill 675 and FSB Ryder. Quang Nam Pr, I Corps.

Hon Chong (n/a)
Mapsheet name of L-7014-5929-3. SVN.

Hon Chong, Mui (VS 6-2)
Coastal point at 10°08'N-104°39'E. On NC48-06 JOG. Kien Giang Pr, IV Corps.

Hon Chuoi Island (VQ 48-88)
Apx 30 km W of SVN coast of Ca Mau Peninsula, 37 km WNW Binh Hung AF. An Xuyen Pr, IV Corps.

Hon Chut, Mouillage de (CP 0-0)
Ship anchorage at 11°48'N-109°11'E. On NC49-01 JOG. Khanh Hoa Pr, II Corps.

Hon Cong Mountain (BR 453-468)
A.k.a. Hill 706, Hong Kong Mtn/Hill and Hon Kong Mtn; however "Hon Cong" is Vietnamese and map sp. Originally not inc within perimeter of what became Camp Radcliff, but after US signal site atop this mtn was overrun in late Feb66(?) the "Green Line" outer perimeter of huge base was enlarged to include it. Generally formed camp's W edge. Noted landmark also due to huge 1st Cav patch painted (on PSP, says one source) on S face of mtn in color. When 173d Abn took over An Khe following 1st Cav's moved to Quang Tri, Jan68, they also apparently built a huge replica of 173d's Div patch on face of mtn. Each was several stories in height and could be seen for many miles. Author of *Chickenhawk* claims that on New Year's Eve, '65-66, alcohol-impaired troops of 1st Cav began discharging their weapons into air in "celebration" that became known as The Battle of Hong Kong Hill. Much of the fire somehow became focused on Hong Kong Hill, and men occupying the radio-relay site on mtn then began returning the favor by firing back at camp. When firing stopped at apx 12:30 am, some 7 men were said to have been killed in maintenance area of camp and unknown number wounded (LtGen Hal Moore has no memory of this event and review of CACF does not supt claim; perhaps more myth than fact?). Mtn was also used as trng area for newly-arrived troops. Good map in *Infantry in Vietnam*, p 265. Map is L-7014-6736-4, per Ken Burrington. Binh Dinh Pr, II Corps. [279] [280] [281]

Hon Cong Mountain Signal Site (BR 452-469)
Atop Hon Cong Mtn at An Khe CB. Control/radio-relay site for 1st Cav commo and presumably for 173d Abn as well. In late Feb66(?)before 1st Cav's An Khe was enlarged to include mtn, VC sappers overran US Army signal site here, destroyed radio towers and killed most personnel. A/2d/7th Cav re-secured site with one-plt in night air-assault while another climbed mtn the next morning, capturing 1 VC and finding 1 KIA. Per *Baptism*, shortly after, base perimeter was expanded to include mtn and signal site was never attacked again. Map is L-7014-6736-4, per Ken Burrington. Binh Dinh Pr, II Corps. [282]

Hon Cong Valley (BR)
Just NE of Hon Cong Mtn at An Khe. Home of 5th SF Det B-22. Helped 1st Cav locate in that area during '65. Binh Dinh Pr, II Corps.

Hon Dau (VR 35-68)
See Hon Nam Du Island. Kien Giang Pr, IV Corps.

Hon Do (BN 9-7)
Coastal point at 11°34'N-109°08'E. On NC49-01 JOG. Ninh Thuan Pr, II Corps.

Hon Do Island (CP 22-78)
Apx 34 km NE Nha Trang AF. Khanh Hoa Pr, II Corps.

Hon Do Island (CP 2-8)
A.k.a. Ile Bac. Khanh Hoa Pr, II Corps.

Hon Dun Mtn (YD 712-135)
A.k.a. Hill 433. Apx 8 km SW Hue, 3.5 km NNE FSB Birmingham. Thua Thien Pr, I Corps.

Hon Dung (CP 2-5)
A.k.a. Pyramid Island. Khanh Hoa Pr, II Corps.

Hon Duoc Island (CQ 16-06)
In Ben Goi Bay. Khanh Hoa Pr, II Corps.

Hon Gai (YJ 1-1?)
In Sept65, attack sqdns from Carriers *Oriskany*, *Constellation, Coral Sea*, and *Intrepid* hit previously off-limits areas in port of Haiphong and smaller ports of Hon Gai and Cam Pha. Also hit during Pierce Arrow, 2-7Aug64. Additionally, power plants, rail yards, naval facilities, barracks, and heavy industrial plants here struck

by Carrier TF-77 attempts to blunt NVA Tet '68 offensive. At 20°57'00"N-107°05'00"E. See Pierce Arrow. NVN.

Hon Gian (VR 31-77)
Apx 90 km WSW Rach Gia and 45 km W the coast. Part of island grp that inc Hon Gian, Hon Truoc, Hon Dau, Hon Mau and largest, Hon Nam Du. Gulf of Thailand.

Hon Gom Peninsula (CQ 2-0)
A.k.a. Ban Dao Hon Gom. Just above Ninh Hoa. Khanh Hoa Pr, II Corps.

Hon Gom, Ban Dao (CQ 2-0)
Peninsula at 12°40'N-109°24'E. On ND49-13 JOG. Khanh Hoa Pr, II Corps.

Hon Gom, Presqu'ile (CQ 2-0)
A.k.a. Ban Dao Hon Gom. Peninsula. On ND49-13 JOG. Khanh Hoa Pr, II Corps.

Hon Heo Secret Zone (CP 05-33)
Coastal area apx 18 km S Nha Trang. See *Androscoggin*, CGC. Market Time TF-115. Khanh Hoa Pr, II Corps.

Hon Heo, Baie de (VS 4-3)
A.k.a. Vinh Hon Heo. Bay at 10°17'N-104°32'E. On NC48-06 JOG. Kien Giang Pr, IV Corps.

Hon Heo, Vinh (VS 4-3)
Bay at 10°17'N-104°32'E. Kien Giang Pr, IV Corps.

Hon Khanh Hoi Island (BN 8-8)
NE Phan Rang. Ninh Thuan Pr, II Corps.

Hon Khoai Island (VQ 8-3)
Apx 22 km SE the tip of Ca Mau Peninsula, 40 km SSW Nam Can AF and 14 km S of coast at closest point. An Xuyen Pr, IV Corps.

Hon Khoi, Baie de (CP 0-9)
A.k.a. Vung Hon Khoi. Bay at 12°35'N-109°12'E. On ND49-13 JOG. Khanh Hoa Pr, II Corps.

Hon Khoi, Pointe (CP 0-9)
See Pointe Hon Khoi. Khanh Hoa Pr, II Corps.

Hon Khoi, Vung (CP 0-9)
Bay at 12°35'N-109°12'E. On ND49-13 JOG. Khanh Hoa Pr, II Corps.

Hon Kong Hill, Battle of (BR 452-469)
See Hon Cong Hill, Battle of. Pleiku Pr, II Corps.

Hon Kong Mountain (BR 454-468)
A.k.a. Hong Kong Mtn and Hon Cong Mtn. See Hon Cong Mtn. Binh Dinh Pr, II Corps.

Hon Lan, Mui (CP 0-1)
A.k.a. Mui Hon Luong. Coastal point. On NC49-01 JOG. Khanh Hoa Pr, II Corps.

Hon Lan, Pointe (CP 0-1)
See Pointe Hon Lan. Khanh Hoa Pr, II Corps.

Hon Lao Island (BN 0-0)
See Tiger Island at grid. II Corps.

Hon Lon Island (CP 23-93)
A.k.a. Hon Loampon. Large Island on E side of Ben Goi Bay, just above Ninh Hoa, apx 40 km NNE Nha Trang. Roughly 12 by 5 km in size. Khanh Hoa Pr?, II Corps.

Hon Lon Lighthouse (CP 19-48)
On Hon Lon/Hon Tre Island, apx 17 km ESE Nha Trang, and 2 km NE Thon Bic Dam. Khanh Hoa Pr, II Corps.

Hon Luong, Mui (CP 01)
Coastal point at 11°53'N-109°12'E. On NC49-01 JOG. Khanh Hoa Pr, II Corps.

Hon Mau (VR 35-65)
See Hon Nam Du Island. Kien Giang Pr, IV Corps.

Hon Mieu Island (CP 07-47)
Apx 7 km SE Nha Trang AF. Khanh Hoa Pr, II Corps.

Hon Minh Hoa Island (VS 5-0)
Roughly 55 km due W Rach Gia. Kien Giang Pr, IV Corps.

Hon Mun Island (CP 16-46)
Apx 15 km SE Nha Trang AF, 3 km S Hon Tre Island. Khanh Hoa Pr, II Corps.

Hon Nai, Pointe (CP 1-2)
See Pointe Hon Nai. Khanh Hoa Pr, II Corps.

Hon Nam Du Island (VR 30-70)
Apx 90 km WSW Rach Gia and 45 km W the coast. Part of island grp that inc Hon Gian, Hon Truoc, Hon Dau, Hon Mau and largest, Hon Nam Du. Gulf of Thailand.

Hon Nei, Point (CP 1-2)
See Point Hon Nei. Khanh Hoa Pr, II Corps.

Hon Nga Mountain (AP 985-295)
See Hill 1998. Tuyen Duc Pr, II Corps.

Hon Ngang, Mui (CQ 2-0)
Coastal point at 12°42'N-109°25'E. On ND49-13 JOG. Khanh Hoa Pr, II Corps.

Hon Nieu (n/a)
Mapsheet name of L-7014-6146-1. NVN only.

Hon Noi Island (CP 18-32)
Apx 13 km NE Cam Ranh Bay. Khanh Hoa Pr, II Corps.

Hon Nui Dat (BR 492-506)
A.k.a. Hill 506. Overlooked Camp Radcliff. Map is L-7014-6737-3, per Ken Burrington.

Hon Nui Tau (AT 9-4)
Mtn in Que Son Mtns. On *Phuoc Ha-Que Son Valley* map in *The Rise and Fall of the American Army*, pp 368-9. Quang Nam Pr, I Corps.

Hon Ong Binh Mountain (BR 588-477)
A.k.a. Hill 814 and LZ 2. Apx 12 km ENE An Khe. 14Dec65. Binh Dinh Pr, II Corps.

Hon Quan (XT 75-87?)
Along QL-13 and N of An Loc. Binh Long Pr, III Corps.

Hon Quan (An Loc) (n/a)
Mapsheet L-7014-6332-3. Actual name is: An Loc (Hon Quan). SVN.

Hon Quan, LZ (XT 762-891)
Along QL-13 at N edge of An Loc, apx 95 km due N Saigon, 2 km NE Xa Thanh Binh and 20 km S Loc Ninh AF. Jul66. Binh Long Pr, III Corps.

Hon Quan Airfield (XT 760-892)
On N edge of An Loc and on QL-13, apx 95 km due N Saigon, 2 km NE Xa Thanh Binh and 20 km S Loc Ninh AF. El. 328', 1,500' laterite rwy. At 11°39'22"N-106°36'50"E. Binh Long Pr, III Corps.

Hon Quan Heliport (XT 760-892)
On northern outskirts of An Loc, apx 20 km S Loc Ninh AF. Heliport #589, alt 328', at 11°39'N 106°37'E, per Feb73 TAD. Binh Long Pr, III Corps.

Hon Quan SF Camp (XT 7576-8732)
At SW corner of An Loc, apx 22 km S Loc Ninh AF and 90 km due N Saigon. SF Det 50, 5th SF, Det B-33 (was B-11), Oct65, B-36 Oct66. Grid per *SF Order of Battle.* Also listed at XT 7580-8780, and XT 7385-8770. Moved to Loc Ninh. Binh Long Pr, III Corps.

Hon San Mountain (CP 034-568)
See Nha Trang Buddha. Khan Hoa Pr, II Corps.

Hon Shut Anchorage (CP 0-0)
A.k.a. Hon Chut, Mouillage de. An Anchorage at 11°48'N-109°11'E. On NC49-01 JOG. Khanh Hoa Pr, II Corps.
Hon Son Tra Island (BT 02-95)
A.k.a. Hill 230. Apx 15 km due N Da Nang, 11 km NNW Monkey Mtn. Thua Thien Pr?, I Corps.
Hon Tai Island (XQ 80-55)
Portion Con Son Island Grp. See Con Son. IV Corps.
Hon Tam Island (CP 09-46)
Apx 8 km SE Nha Trang AF. Khanh Hoa Pr, II Corps.
Hon Thi Island (CP 08-70)
Apx 18 km NNE Nha Trang AF, in Dam Nha Phu Bay. Khanh Hoa Pr, II Corps.
Hon Thi, Mui (CP 1-6)
A.k.a. Mui Da Chong. Coastal point at 12°21'N-109°18'E. On ND49-13 JOG. Khanh Hoa Pr, II Corps.
Hon Thom (n/a)
Mapsheet name of L-7014-5728-1. SVN.
Hon Trau Island (CR 1-6)
A.k.a. Ile Aux Buffle. NIMA data. Binh Dinh Pr, II Corps.
Hon Tre (n/a)
Mapsheet name of L-7014-6833-2. SVN.
Hon Tre Island (CP 15-50)
Large Island in S China Sea, apx 3 km E Nha Trang, and about 10 x 5 km in size. 5th SF Grp Det here. See Reich Trng Ctr. Khanh Hoa Pr, II Corps.
Hon Tre Island (VS 83-02)
A.k.a. Torture Island, and Ile Tortue or Tecksu Island. Apx 25 km WSW Rach Gia, near 9°58'00"N-104°50'00"E. On map NC48-10. Kien Giang Pr, IV Corps.
Hon Tre Lon Island (XQ 70-63)
In Con Son Island grp. See Con Son Islands. IV Corps
Hon Trung Island (XQ 89-71)
In Con Son Island grp. See Con Son Islands. IV Corps.
Hon Truoc (VR 34-71)
See Hon Nam Du Island. Kien Giang Pr, IV Corps.
Hon Vung Mountain (YS 58-51)
A.k.a. Hill 327. Apx 21 km ENE Vung Tau and 2 km from ocean. Had spectacular view of coast and Vung Tau area to W. Phuoc Tuy Pr, III Corps.
Hong, FSB (XT or XU?)
A.k.a. FSB Hung Voung? Apparently built Feb-Apr70, by 1st Cav, and mentioned in Feb-Apr70, 8th Engr Bn Op Rpt, at p 31, per Peter Cole. During period, Cav was in NW III Corps prior to Cambodian Incursion. Likely III Corps.
Hong Chong Airfield (VS 599-353)
See Cement Plant AF. Kien Giang Pr, IV Corps.
Hong Cong Hill (BR 452-469)
See Hon Cong Hill, Battle of. Pleiku Pr, II Corps.
Hong Gai (n/a)
Mapsheet name of L-7014-6450-4. NVN only.
Hong Ha, FSB (XU 844-138)
Apx 22 km ENE Loc Ninh, 27 km WNW Song Be/Phuoc Binh and 11 km S Cambodia. Closed 1May70, per *11th ACR Cambodia Invasion AAR, 1st Cav Div, May-Jun70*, courtesy Lou Rochat.[283] Also mentioned in *1st Cav Op Rpt, Feb70/Apr70*, p 15, per Peter Cole. Apr70. Binh Long Pr, III Corps.
Hong Kong BOQ (XS 827-886)
At 28-30 Ngo Quyen St. (Hong Kong Bar Officer's Club) Jan 63, 114 rms (The Hong Cong BOQ maintained an annex also on Ngo Quyen), Saigon. Data per R. Bows' *Vietnam Military Lore, 1959-1973.* Gia Dinh Pr, III Corps.
Hong Kong Hill (BR 453-468)
See Hon Cong Hill. Binh Dinh Pr, II Corps.
Hong Kong Hill, Battle of (BR 453-468)
See Hon Cong Hill, Battle of. Pleiku Pr, II Corps.
Hong Kong Signal Site (BR 452-469)
Variant of Hon Cong Signal Site. See Hon Cong Hill, Camp Radcliff. Binh Dinh Pr, II Corps.
Hong Lam (CP 0-5?)
Near Nha Trang. L-7014-6736-4. Khanh Hoa Pr, II Corps.
Hong Non Airfield (UH 82-57)
LS-86. CIA/SF, per *Air Facilities Data-Laos.*
Hong Non Airfield, New (UH 83-57)
LS-122. CIA/SF, per *Air Facilities Data-Laos.*
Hong Ngu (n/a)
Mapsheet name of L-7014-6030-1. SVN/Cambodia.
Hong Ngu (WS 37-94)
On E bank of Mekong River, apx 27 km ENE Tan Phu, 6 km S Cambodia and 96 km NW Can Tho. Soon after Paris Peace Accords were signed (Mar73), the NVA launched Div-sized attack on this city but ARVN 9th Div pushed them back into Cambodia. Kien Phong Pr, IV Corps.
Hong Ngu Heliport (WS 375-945)
Along E bank of Mekong River, apx 27 km ENE Tan Phu, 6 km S Cambodia and 96 km NW Can Tho. Heliport #590, alt 13', sod, soccer field. At 10°48'30"N-105°21'00"E, per Feb73 TAD. Kien Phong Pr, IV Corps.
Hong Quoy, Pointe (US 7-3)
See Pointe Hon Quoy. Kien Giang Pr, IV Corps.
Hong Sa Alternate Airfield (QB 44-71)
LS-62A. CIA/SF facility. Grid per *Air Facilities Data-Laos.* El. 2,000'. Laos.
Hong Sa Airfield (QB 45-81)
A.k.a. LS-62 and Hongsa AF. Apx 230 km NW Vientiane, per Feb67 Natl Geo Map. CIA/SF, per *Air Facilities Data-Laos.* El. 2,000'? Laos.
Hongam Peninsula (CQ 2-0)
A.k.a. Ban Dao Hon Gom. Peninsula at 12°40'N-109°24'E. Khanh Hoa Pr, II Corps.
Honghoi Bay (CP 0-9)
A.k.a. Vung Hon Khoi. Bay at 12°35'N-109°12'E. On ND49-13 JOG. Khanh Hoa Pr, II Corps.
Hongom Peninsula (CQ 2-0)
A.k.a. Ban Dao Hon Gom. Peninsula at 12°40'N-109°24'E. ND49-13 JOG. Khanh Hoa Pr, II Corps.
Hongsa Airfield (n/a)
See Hongsa AF. Laos.
Honkhoi Bay (CP 0-9)
A.k.a. Vung Hon Khoi. Bay at 12°35'N-109°12'E. On ND49-13 JOG. Khanh Hoa Pr, II Corps.
Honolulu Conference (n/a)
See Glossary.
Honour-Smith Compound (XT/YT)
A.k.a. Woodson Cmpd. Villa on Cong Ly St., Bien Hoa. Named to honor Col Charles M. Honour, and Capt. Albert M. Smith, 145th Avn Bn helicopter pilots KIA 18Feb65, when their Helo hit high tension wire and crashed. Prior to 145th Avn Bn move to cmpd in May '68, it had been named the Woodson Cmpd to honor Capt. Richard E Woodson, USAF, KIA 1Aug66. Bien Hoa Pr, III Corps.

Hood, FSB (XT 389-702)
See FSB Gold for detail. Dec67. Tay Ninh Pr, III Corps.

Hook, LZ ? (AT 935-057)
In Song Nanh River Valley, apx 6 km SSW Ton Bong and 19 km SW Tien Phuoc AF. Nature of site unknown. Quang Tin Pr, I Corps.

Hook, LZ (BN 187-664)
Apx 22 km NNW Song Mao, 43 km NW Tuy Phong. Mar67. Binh Thuan Pr, II Corps.

Hooker, FSB (XT 302-507)
At Angel's Wing's edge, apx 9 km WSW Go Dau Ha and 13 km due N Duc Hue AF. Apr68. Tay Ninh Pr, III Corps.

Hooker, FSB (XT 564-855)
Apx 3 km WSW tip of Fishhook, 24 km due E Katum and 20 km due W An loc. Mar70. Tay Ninh Pr, III Corps.

Hooker, FSB (YD 192-411)
A.k.a. FSB Cindy. Apx 17 km SW Quang Tri and 14 km SE Mai Loc. Apr70 XXIV Corps grid per Don Armstrong. Quang Tri Pr, I Corps.

Hooper, LZ (BS 483-074)
Apx 40 km due W LZ English, 7 km NW LZ Lewis and 32 km SSW Ba To New AF. 4th Div AO, '70. John Linn, 35th Inf, says it was Bn fwd FSB built from scratch, Feb-Mar70. Name/grid per Jim Claeys. Binh Dinh Pr, II Corps.

Hoosier (n/a)
6Apr70, XXIV Corps proposed 5th Div FSB name.

Hoover, Camp (AT 983-777?)
Apx 2 to 3 km NW the N end of Da Nang AB main rwy. Said to have been adj to ASP-1, across from in-country R&R center and just below Freedom Hill PX, which appears to put it further to W of the AB? Navy Seabee (NMCB-5) cmpd named to honor SWF2 William C, Hoover KIA 9Jun65, in attack of SF Camp at Dong Xoai. Hoover's 146 bldgs were almost completely destroyed when ASP-1 detonated 27Apr69. See ASP-1. Discussion/photos in Oct2001 *Vietnam* Mag article, *Da Nang Seabee Base Destroyed*, pp 26-32, and in Apr91 *Leatherneck* Mag. Grid per map *in Vietnam Military Lore, 1959-1973*, p 621. Quang Nam Pr, I Corps.

Hop Tac (n/a)
See Glossary.

Hope, FSB (YS 253-704)
Apparently a.k.a. FSB Bravo (YS 250-700) and FSB Stingray (YS 257-707). Along QL-15, apx 5 km due S Phu My, 25 km N Vung Tau and 18 km WNW Nui Dat. Nov69-Jan70. Phuoc Tuy Pr, III Corps.

Hope, LZ (XD 34-46 or XD 34-49)
ARVN invasion base N Tchepone, and roughly 50 km W to WNW Khe Sanh. Depending on which grid is more accurate. XD 34-46 puts it 18 km WNW Aloui, and XD 34-48 puts it 22 km NW Aloui. 2 ARVN Bns assaulted here 6Mar71, in an 65 km airlift involving 120 helos during Lam Son 719. 1st ARVN Div. Also listed at XD 34-49. See Lam Son 719 map at www.americal.org/174/ map4.htm. W of DMZ in Laos.

Hope, USS (XS)
A.k.a. AH-7. Hospital Ship. Docked at Saigon Harbor at one point. See *USS Repose* and *USS Sanctuary*.

Hopewell, USS (n/a)
DD-681, per Ralph Fries.

Hopper, LZ (BS 483-074)
See Hooper. Binh Dinh Pr, II Corps.

Horn, Camp (BT 04-75?)
Former French cmpd on E side of Da Nang River opposite Da Nang, I Corps HQ III MAF, Da Nang. Named to honor Col Charles H. Horn, USMC, Force Engr, III MAF, body found tangled in wreckage of VC destroyed Nam-O Bridge, Song Ca De River, 13Apr67. Actual cause of death remains mystery, although USMC records list him as drowning victim. Grid is est. Quang Nam Pr, I Corps.

Horn, FSB/LZ (XD 896-405)
A.k.a. LZ Horn. On QL-9 apx 2 km NW Lang Kat, 6 km ESE Khe Sanh CB and 45 km WSW Quang Tri. '70 XXIV Corps grid per Don Armstrong. Quang Tri Pr, I Corps.

Horn, LZ (BR 987-679)
Apx 8 km W coast, 8 km E Phu My/QL-1 and 30 km SSE Bong Son. Oct66. Binh Dinh Pr, II Corps.

Horn, LZ (XD 896-405)
See Horn, FSB. Quang Tri Pr, I Corps.

Horne, USS (n/a)
DLG-30. Guided-Missile DD Ldr, per Ralph Fries.

Hornet, FSB/LZ (YD 047-376)
Apx 11 km WSW Ba Long AF, 13 km SSW Mai Loc, 12 km SSE Ca Lu, 16 km E Lang Krat and 31 km WSW to SW of Quang Tri. Apr70 XXIV Corps grid per Don Armstrong. Quang Tri Pr, I Corps.

Hornet, USS (n/a)
A.k.a. CVS-12. Deployed with CVSG-57 30Sep68-13May69; with CVSG-57 12Aug65-23Mar66; with CVSG-57 27Mar67-28Oct67. [284]

Horse, LZ (BR 696-633)
On E side of Happy Valley, apx 3 km due E LZ Hereford, 9 km NE Vinh Thanh, 8 km WNW Vinh Thanh AF and 28 km NE An Khe. Op Crazy Horse FSB, Oct66. On map in *Battles in the Monsoon*, p 199. Cited in *Anatomy of A Division,* per Peter Cole. Binh Dinh Pr, II Corps.

Horseshoe, FSB (BT or BS?)
S Chu Lai? Americal list. Quang Tin Pr?, I Corps.

Horseshoe, FSB (YS 494-620)
A.k.a. Hill 82 and Horseshoe Hill. Small, steep, rock-strewn extinct volcano roughly 9 km SE Nui Dat, 1 km N Dat Do, 7 km due N FSB Herring and immed E Tl-52. Its depressed crater could comfortably hold one rifle co. Was impossible to dig here, so sand for sand bags and emplacements had to be trucked to site. Many tons of gravel were also trucked-in for use in constructing floors of gun emplacements. Used as permanent outpost by 1ATF (5, 6 and 7 RAR) to control rice-rich central district of Phuoc Tuy Pr. By late '70, position was enhanced with generators and nightly movies. US had 4.2" mortars here and RAR had 105s here at times. One RAR Infantryman wrote that during his tour, "Unfortunately two [US troops] walked into mine field and another shot himself." [285] 161 Bty, RNZA, Honner's Bty firebase 1st set here 22-24Mar67; Martin's Bty here 5-17Mar68. Hitching's Bty here: 5-17Mar68, 16-27Aug68, 5-8Dec68, left section 19-20Mar68. Andrew's Bty: alternate section: 1Nov69-5Dec69 and 10Jan-13Feb70, left section: 22Mar-4Apr70, 4-7May70, right section: 4-17Apr70, 30Apr-7May70. Master's Bty, left section: 1Feb-10Mar71, right section: 10Mar-23April. A mine field (Graham's Folly) was erected

outside that ran some 10 km to coast (see Graham's Folly). On 1ATF NCO trng map per John Hollett. Also listed at YS 49-63. Phuoc Tuy Pr, III Corps.

Horseshoe, The (YS 49-63)
See Horseshoe, FSB, for detail. Phuoc Tuy Pr, III Corps.

Horseshoe Area (BS 45-75)
Apx 32 km SSW Chu Lai. Described on Americal list as being along Song Tra Khuc River. Resembled inverted horseshoe. Map is L-7014-6739-3. Quang Ngai Pr, I Corps.

Horseshoe Basecamp (YS 514-613)
If grid correct, was apx 2 km ESE FSB Horseshoe/Hill 82, and along N side LTL-23, just W Ap Hong Hoa. See Horseshoe, FSB. '67. Phuoc Tuy Pr, III Corps.

Horseshoe Bend, FSB (XS 766-866)
Apparently near site of Fishnet Factory (FSB Fishnet), on SW edge of Saigon, apx 9 km SSW Tan Son Nhut AB, 12 km NNE Binh Chanh and 11 km due W FSB Blackfoot. 199th LIB Bde Fwd HQ. Gia Dinh Pr, III Corps.

Horseshoe Bend, The (XS 55-93)
Terrain feature formed by Song Vam Co Dong River apx 6 km SW Duc Hoa and 25 km due W Saigon. Map is L-7014-6230-1. Long An Pr, III Corps.

Horseshoe Hill/FSB (YS 490-620)
Hill 82. Steep, rock-strewn extinct volcano apx 9 km SE Nui Dat, 3 km N Dat Do and 1 km W Hwy 44. See Horseshoe, FSB. Phuoc Tuy Pr, III Corps.

Hosking Compound (XT 98-13?)
See C E Snake Hosking. Bien Hoa Pr, III Corps.

Hospital Fight, The (ZA 042-026)
In Ia Drang Valley, apx 45 km SW Pleiku. Battle of 1Nov65, involving 1st Cav elements that discovered large NVA hospital complex which had been suptg siege of Plei Me. Fight here was part of jigsaw puzzle of discovery that precipitated 1st major battle of American War, which took place at LZ X-Ray beginning 14Nov65, and was followed by terrible disaster at LZ Albany. Pleiku Pr, II Corps.

Hospital Ship *Helgoland* (n/a)
See *Helgoland*. SVN.

Hospital Ship *Hope* (n/a)
See *Hope, USS*. SVN.

Hospital Ship *Repose* (n/a)
See *Repose*. SVN.

Hospital Ship *Sanctuary* (n/a)
See *Sanctuary*. SVN.

Hot Chow, LZ (BR?)
Apparently near An Khe or Camp Holloway? Cited in query by Bill Beaird at http://wae.com/messages/msgs27211.html. No other data reference to it has been unearthed. 227th AHC apparently here. Binh Dinh or Pleiku Pr?, II Corps.

Hot Rocks Quarry (BQ 192-135)
Apx 42 km ENE Ban Me Thuot, 15 km NE Buon Ea Yang AF and 7 km SW Ban Mrong. 70. Darlac Pr, II Corps.

Hotel (n/a)
See Glossary.

Hotel, FSB (YT 102-207)
Apx 21 km NE Bien Hoa AB and 4 km NW Song Dong Nai River. Jan-Feb68. Bien Hoa Pr, III Corps.

Hotel, FSB ? (XT 655-288)
Apx 15 km SW Lai Khe and along Song Saigon River. Nature of site unknown. Possibly an LZ. Jun66. Binh Duong Pr, III Corps.

Hotel, LZ (BR 806-587)
Apx 2.5 km S Hoi Son 5, 8 km W QL-1, 17 km NNW Phu Cat and on W side Suoi Ca River. Used during Op Crazy Horse, May66. See *Battles in the Monsoon*, p 78-80, et al. Grid per Dan Gillotti. Binh Dinh Pr, II Corps.

Hotel, LZ (XD)
Lam Son 719, VNMC FSB. On map of Lam Son 719 at www.americal.org/174/map4.htm. Laos.

Hotel 3 Heliport (XS 810-946)
See Saigon Hotel-3 Heliport. Gia Dinh Pr, III Corps.

Hotel 6 (XS 83-89?)
Possibly at or near the Cofat Cmpd? Per Carl Reardon, was name of the CIA helipad in Saigon. Gia Dinh Pr, III Corps.

Hotel 9 (YA/YB?)
SOG op zone located just W of both SOG's Juliet 9 op zone and The Bra, per Don Lewis, 170th AHC.

Hotel Alpha (XT 98-13?)
Landing pad at Bien Hoa AB. Described as large open area surrounded by a chain link fence in *Low Level Hell*, p 34. Bien Hoa Pr, III Corps.

Hotel CAC (YD?)
See CAC Listings. I Corps.

Hotel CAP (n/a)
See CAP Hotel listings. Thua Thien Pr?, I Corps.

Hotel Caravelle (n/a)
See Caravelle, The Hotel. Saigon.

Hotel Metropole (WJ)
In Hanoi next to Bank of Indochina Bldg, and across street from French Governor's residence. Per *Street Without Joy*, p 252. NVN.

Hotfoot, Operation (n/a)
See Glossary.

Hotfoot/White Star (n/a)
See Glossary.

Hou Bon (BQ 24-82)
See Hau Bon and Cheo Reo. Phu Bon Pr, II Corps.

Houan Repou, Rapides De (YT 5-5)
A.k.a. the Thac Houan Repou. Long Khanh Pr?, III Corps.

Houei Hinsa Airfield (UH 50-56)
LS-215. CIA/SF, per *Air Facilities Data-Laos.*

Houei Hok Airfield (UH 65-61)
LS-198. CIA/SF, per *Air Facilities Data-Laos.*

Houei Hong Airfield (TG 55-68)
LS-200. CIA/SF, per *Air Facilities Data-Laos.*

Houei Kah Moun Airfield (UH 68-68)
LS-111. CIA/SF, per *Air Facilities Data-Laos.*

Houei Ki Nin Airfield (TG 82-47)
LS-38. CIA/SF, per *Air Facilities Data-Laos.*

Houei Kong Airfield (XB 65-73)
L-56. CIA/SF, per *Air Facilities Data-Laos*. On Feb67 Natl Geo Map. El. 2850'. Laos.

Houei Ma Airfield (UH 64-55)
LS-107. CIA/SF, per *Air Facilities Data-Laos.*

Houei Mai Airfield (TF 39-78)
LS-325. CIA/SF, per *Air Facilities Data-Laos.*

Houei Moun Airfield (UH 58-45)
LS-221. CIA/SF, per *Air Facilities Data-Laos.*

Houei Nam Om Airfield (TF 82-82)
LS-224. CIA/SF, per *Air Facilities Data-Laos.*
Houei Sa An Airfield (UG 39-93)
LS-23. CIA/SF, per *Air Facilities Data-Laos.*
Houei Sa An Airfield (UG 41-91)
LS-127. CIA/SF, per *Air Facilities Data-Laos.*
Houei Sai Airfield (TF 55-94)
LS-284 and Fort Carnot AF. On NW border of Laos, apx 340 km NW Vientiane on Feb67 Natl Geo Map. CIA/SF facility. Grid per *Air Facilities Data-Laos.* El. 1,200'. Laos.
Houei Sang Airfield (UG 81-92)
LS-206. CIA/SF, per *Air Facilities Data-Laos.*
Houei Soi Airfield (XB 68-53)
LS-164. CIA/SF, per *Air Facilities Data-Laos.*
Houei Thom Airfield (UH 53-12)
LS-27. CIA/SF, per *Air Facilities Data-Laos.*
Houei Tong Ko Airfield (UH 18-53)
LS-184. CIA/SF, per *Air Facilities Data-Laos.*
Hound, LZ (XD 818-264)
In Vietnam Salient, apx 16 km SSW Khe Sanh and 57 km SW Quang Tri. Mar69. Quang Tri Pr, I Corps.
Houng Dien (YD 629-428)
Ville and military cmpd at extreme N end Pha Tam Giang Bay, apx 22 km NW Hue and about 5 km from ocean. 1st Cav/101st Abn basecamp and possibly some naval facilities here '68 as well. Thua Thien or Quang Tri Pr, I Corps.
Houston, LZ (XD 694-452)
Apx 9 km NNW Lao Bao, 16 km WNW Khe Sanh CB and 31 km WSW Ca Lu. Apr70 XXIV Corps grid per Don Armstrong. Quang Tri Pr, I Corps.
Houston, FSB (XT 436-073)
At or near Tan Hoa AF/Hiep Hoa Navy Base/Hiep Hoa SF Camp, apx 14 km ESE Duc Hue AF and 23 km WSW Cu Chi. Nov68-Mar69. Also listed at XT 410-230 and 442-073. Hau Nghia Pr, III Corps.
Houston, Operation (n/a)
26Feb-12Sep68. 1st Mar Div. 702 rptd NVA/VC KIA, per *Vietnam Order of Battle*, pp 9-14. Thua Thien/Quang Nam Pr border, I Corps.
Houston, USS (n/a)
86 survivors from 28Feb42 sinking of this heavy cruiser during WWII were held as POWs by Japanese at Camp 5-E, on outskirts of Saigon. Data per *Vietnam Military Lore, Legends, Shadows, and Heroes*, p 11. See Project Embankment, and Camp 5-E.
Houston BEQ (XS 8-9)
At 1015-1021 Tran Hung Dao St., Saigon. Named to honor Sgt John L. Houston, SF Det A-726, Nam Dong CIDG Camp, KIA 6Jul64 in battle where Capt. R. C. Donlan became 1st recipient of MOH in VN. Data per *Vietnam Military Lore, 1959-1973.* Gia Dinh Pr, III Corps.
Howard Johnson's (XD 845-382)
Khe Sanh Marines' nickname for small Viet restaurant on N side QL-9 in Khe Sanh ville noted for it's delicious soups and noodle dishes; a welcome respite from C-Rations for US Troops. Discussion/map in *End of the Line, The Siege of Khe Sanh*, pp 79-80. Quang Tri Pr, I Corps.
Howard's Hill (BT 132-203)
A.k.a. Hill 488, Nui Vu, LZ 1, LZ 2, LZ East and LZ Mary Lou. Apx 43 km WNW Chu Lai, and 18 km W Tam Ky. From air, hilltop "resembled the three blades on an airplane propeller," per *Small Unit Actions in Vietnam, 1966* (has detailed discussion of battle, p 30 et seq.). Named to honor SSgt Jimmie Howard, acting 1st Plt Cmdr, 1st Recon Bn, 1st Mar Div, who led his unit to occupy this objective 13June66. Howard had been awarded 3 PHs and the Silver Star in Korea and, for an action here on 16Jun66, was awarded his 4th PH and the MOH. USMC. Quang Tin Pr, I Corps.
Howell Beach (CP)
A.k.a. Cam Ranh Beach. Named to honor CPL Sammie Howell, USA, 96th S&S Bn, who drowned 27Jan67, while trying to save lives of 3 men caught in undertow at Cam Ranh Beach. Khanh Hoa Pr, II Corps.
Howie, FSB (YS 96-89)
Apx 6 km NNW Ham Tan AF, 43 km WSW Phan Thiet, 9 km E peak Nui Be Mtn and 78 km NE Vung Tau. 2d/3d Inf, 199th LIB. Binh Tuy Pr, III Corps.
Hua Bon (BQ 24-83)
See Hau Bon. Phu Bon Pr, II Corps.
Hua Bon Airfield (BQ 233-818)
See Cheo Reo AF. Phu Bon Pr, II Corps.
Hua Duc (BT)
See Hau Duc (new and old). Quang Tin Pr, I Corps.
Hua Duc Airfield (BS 016-970)
See Hau Duc AF. Quang Tin Pr, I Corps.
Hua Hin (PP 0-9)
Along coast apx 140 km SSW Bangkok. SF camp or AO per *SF Order of Battle*. Thailand.
Hua Hin Airfield (PP 0-9)
Along coast at 12°37'00"N-99°58'00"E, or apx 140 km SSW Bangkok per Feb67 Natl Geo Map. NIMA data. El. 10'. Thailand.
Hua Moung Airfield (UH 63-30)
LS-58. Apx 260 km NNE Vientiane on Feb67 Natl Geo Map. Per *Air Facilities Data-Laos.* El. 2,700'. Laos.
Hua Nghia Airfield (XT 544-050)
See Hau Nghia AF or Bao Trai AF. Common misspelling of "Hau." Hau Nghia Pr, III Corps.
Hua Nghia Province (XT)
See Hau Nghia Province. Common misspelling.
Huai San Airfield (PC 4-0)
Listed as abnd in '66 NIMA data. At 19°58'00"N-100°26'00"E. NIMA data. Thailand.
Hub, The (BQ 95-55)
Roughly 27 km NW Tuy Hoa AB. Forested area nicknamed "The Hub" during Op Geronimo, by 101st Abn's 1st Bde elements. Discussed in *Mad Minutes and Vietnam Moments*, p 297. See Phong Cao. Phu Yen Pr, II Corps.
Huckleberry, LZ (YD 363-495)
Between or near QL-1 rail tracks and QL-1, apx 3 km SE Quang Tri, and apx 1 to 2 km SE La Vang AF. Name/grid per Kevan Mynderup, as per 1st/8th Cav Daily Staff Journal of 3Mar68. Quang Tri Pr, I Corps.
Hue (YD 76-22)
Apx 640 km N Saigon, 48 km SE Quang Tri, 75 km NW Da Nang and 16 km from ocean. Former Imperial Capitol of VN, and Capitol of VN until 1945. Built by Chinese in 1601 and modeled after Peking. Citadel moat surrounds what is known as "Interior City" (Than Noi) and another

surrounds the "Great Interior City" (Dai Noi). Was seized by NVA during Tet '68 and resulted in month-long battle in which thousands of NVA, ARVN, USMC, USA and civilian were killed/wounded. To S of city in area of rolling hills near confluence of S an W forks of Perfume River is area spotted with perhaps 1,000 elaborate Chinese dynasty tombs, including 6 major tombs (among which are massive tombs of Minh Mang and Tu Duc). In '45, Viet communists destroyed nearly 100 buildings in Great Interior City in effort to erase Vietnam's Chinese past, some of which were later restored by SVN Govt only to be destroyed again during Tet '68. Home of ARVN 1st Inf Div Adv Det, Adv Team 3-Hue Citadel, a MACV Cmpd and some naval supply LST lndg docks, but no major US military units/facilities within city itself. French architecture is very evident throughout city. Major university also here. Tet '68 attack was launched when 804th Bn, 4th NVA Rgt surprised US troops holding MACV cmpd on S side of river, 31Jan68 at 0340 hours. 800th and 802d Bns of 6th NVA Rgt reinforced by VC 12th Sapper Bn took Citadel itself, forcing ARVN Hac Bo Ranger Bn back to 1st ARVN Div HQ, while 806th and 810th Bns of 6th NVA Rgt took positions blockading QL-1 at N and S edges of city. In response, US 1st and 5th Marine Rgts attacked from S, and later, 3d Bde of 1st Cav, 1st/77th Arty Bn and elements of 101st Abn's 2d Bde attacked from NW, while ARVN Inf attacked from E and W. Ensuing battle lasted 23 days. See Bone Yard and Hue Massacre. Capitol, Thua Thien Pr, I Corps.

Hue (maps)
Maps sheets of interest: L7014-6541-4 (Hue), 1:50k coverage of FSBs Birmingham, Arsenal, Brick, Rifle, and mtns of Nui Ke, Nui Hoan Gay (Banana Mtn), Nui Mo Tau and etc. TPC J-11D for 1:500k scale, and 1:250k scale L-1501, NE4816 (Hue, Vietnam/Laos) JOG.

Hue (Citadel) Airfield (YD 748-230)
See Hue (Thanh Noi) AF. Thua Thien Pr, I Corps.

Hue (Thanh Noi) Airfield (YD 748-230)
A.k.a. Hue Citadel AF. Inside walls of the Hue Citadel, apx 1 km N the Perfume (Song Huong) River and 1 km E QL-1. Map is L7014-6541-4. El. 5', 2,400' crushed-rock rwy. Thua Thien Pr, I Corps.

Hue Airfield (YD 887-148)
See Hue/Phu Bai AF. Thua Thien Pr, I Corps.

Hue Citadel (YD 75-23)
A.k.a. the Imperial City, the Forbidden City and "the Great Within." Along N bank of Song Huong in heart of Hue. Surrounded by walls at places 20' thick, this fortress was interlaced with moats and covered some 1,300 acres (5.2 sq-km or apx 700 by 700 yds in size). Often referred to as "ancient;" however, was built in by Emperor Nguyen An (Gia Long) beginning in 1804. Seized by NVA during Tet 68. Though initially allied forces doggedly resisted using arty or airstrikes against the Citadel during 23-day battle to retake it, in the end the allies were forced to do so, destroying much of Citadel in process. At main gate, NVA raised their flag on flagpole known as "King's Knight," and much of fighting and press coverage focused on that flag. Thua Thien Pr, I Corps.

Hue Civilian Defense Corps (n/a)
See Glossary.

Hue Duc Mountain (WS 17-33)
A.k.a. Hill 221. One of 7 peak grp rising from flat, mangrove plain generally E Ha Tien and N Rach Gia and collectively known as "Seven Sisters." Included Hue Duc Mtn (Hill 220), Nui Co To (Hill 61, just S Tri Tron), Dop Chompa (actually two separate peaks, highest of which is 710 meters, SW That Son AF), Hill 232 (near Chau Phu) and Hill 296 (5 km from Cambodia and 10 km N That Son). Kien Giang Pr, IV Corps.

Hue LCM Ramp (YD 773-225)
See Hue LCU Ramp. Thua Thien Pr, I Corps.

Hue LCU Ramp (YD 773-225)
A.k.a. Hue LCM Ramp and South Hue LCU Ramp. On S bank of Song Huong River, 2.6 km E Citadel AF and about 700 meters ESE the SE corner of Citadel's outer wall. See Hue MACV Cmpd. Thua Thien Pr, I Corps.

Hue LCU Ramp North (YD 760-250)
At NE corner of Hue Citadel and along S bank of the Song Huong River, apx 2.3 km NE Hue Citadel AF. Thua Thien Pr, I Corps.

Hue MACV Compound (YD 767-218?)
A.k.a. the Frank Doezema cmpd. On S bank of Perfume River in heart of city and overlooking the Citadel on N bank. Named to honor Sp4 Frank Doezema, Jr. (KIA 31Jan68, awarded DSC) on 4Jul68, at 11:15hrs, per *Stars & Stripes* article (unknown issue) entitled *Hue Memorial Erected, Honors Valorous G.I.*, courtesy Dennis Williams. Under siege during Tet '68, and opening point of Hue Tet '68 attack when 804th Bn, 4th NVA Rgt surprised small contingent of US SF and MACV Advsy troops housed here. At apx 0340H 31Jan68, NVA surrounded cmpd. While defending an Aussie bunker here, 5 US pilots of 282d AHC were severely wounded, leaving only 1 healthy pilot in Det. An Aussie Advisor, Desi F. Ford, is credited with saving many lives for MG fire that denied NVA access to site. Medevacs were directed to LCM Ramp (YD 773-225), and then several very brave EMs of 282d AHC made 3 trips through enemy lines carrying WIA to Ramp.[286] SF, MACV (and CIA?) operatives/Advisors here. Grid is est. Thua Thien Pr, I Corps.

Hue Massacre site (YD 766-074)
See The Bone Yard. Thua Thien Pr, I Corps.

Hue NSAD (YD 785-230)
On S bank of Perfume River just opposite the SE corner of Citadel. On map in *The Marines in Vietnam 1954-1973*, p 243. Thua Thien Pr, I Corps.

Hue Security Group (YD)
Portion of River Security Group I Corps, at Tam My? Brown Water Navy units with HQ at Cua Viet. TF was Broken into 2 grps, Dong Ha River Security Group and Hue River Security Group (Tan My?). Per *Brown Water, Black Berets*, p 278. Quang Tri/Thua Thien Prvs, I Corps.

Hue SF Camp (YD 747-230)
Inside Hue Citadel, and immed adj to Hue Citadel AF. 5th SF. Data per *SF Order of Battle.* Thua Thien Pr, I Corps.

Hue Southwest Airfield (YD 707-105)
Immed E of FSB Birmingham/Hill 90, apx 15 km SSW Hue. Peneprimed field capable of holding large numbers of helos and perhaps also very light observation acft. Several large, rubber blivet fuel cells there as well. Uncontrolled. Per ONC J-11. El. 79'. Thua Thien Pr, I Corps.

Hue/Phu Bai Airfield (YD 887-148)
Along E edge of Hwy QL-1 at Phu Bai, apx 12 km SE Hue, 63 km NW Marble Mtn AB, and 76 km SE Dong Ha AF. HQ 3d Mar Div and later 101st Abn here. 85th Evac Hosp was at NW end of rwy. On 8Mar65, 3d Bn/9th Marines (1st US major ground force) landed on beach just S Nam O Bridge. Later that same day, another Bn was landed at Da Nang by C-130s via Okinawa. With H-34 helos of HMM-162 providing logistical supt, units formed 9th MEF. Purpose was to protect Da Nang and its AF from VC. Enclave at Phu Bai AF (15 km S Hue) soon followed, then another at Ky Ha, just S Tam Ky. 5,600' asph rwy serviced by Army, USAF and Viet civilian air controllers, provided combat Avn supt in Hue/Phu Bai AO. Per ONC J-11. El. 49', 5,500' and 5,560' x 150' wide asph rwys. At 16°23'57"N-107°42'12"E. Thua Thien Pr, I Corps.

Hue, Battle For, Operation (n/a)
See Battle for Hue, Operation.

Hue/Phu Bai Railroad (YD)
Narrow-gauge railroad line that ran along W edge of QL-1 between Hue and Phu Bai. The line actually paralleled QL-1 all the way from Hanoi to Saigon, but many stretches of it were unusable due to enemy activity and difficulties involved in securing it. Thua Thien Pr, I Corps.

Hue/Tan My/Phu Bai NSA (YD 82-33?)
At Tan My apx 12 km NNE Hue? USN Supt Activity, '65-70. Per MRF Assn Website. Thua Thien Pr, I Corps.

Huei Thong Airfield (TH 87-50)
LS-196. CIA/SF, per *Air Facilities Data-Laos.*

Huertgen, FSB (XT 692-325)
W of the Thi Thin River, apx 10 km SW Lai Khe, 5 km WSW Ben Cat, 38 km NNW Saigon. Named after the famous WWII 1st Inf Div battle site in the Huertgen Forest. 1st Inf Div, '69. Per *Low Level Hell's* 1st Div TAOR map. Dec68-Apr69. Binh Duong Pr, III Corps.

Huguette (TJ 9-6)
Series of 6 defensive positions a.k.a. Huguette 1 thru 6 (or H1 thru H6), situated in Muong Thanh Valley apx 290 km W Hanoi. The Huguettes formed NW perimeter of main DBP complex and were strung along PSP surfaced roadbed of Rte 41. French strongpoints during Op Castor, 20Nov53-7May54. On 5Apr54, this tiny garrison of only 88 Legionnaires under cmd of two Lts was heavily attacked, yet held against a much superior force. Later, additional reinforcements of 8th Assault SAS Co and 2 tanks were added to its defenses. NVN.

Hui Vien Nam (WJ 46-26)
Street Without Joy's misspelling of Nui Vien Nam. See Nui Vien Nam. NVN.

Hull, FSB (XT 263-380)
A.k.a. FSBs Bolt, Hull and Joyce. On QL-1, apx 25 km WSW Dau Tieng and 9 km SSE Tay Ninh. 25th Div AO. Dec68-Jan70. Tay Ninh Pr, III Corps.

Hull, USS (n/a)
DD-945, per Ralph Fries.

Human Sea Wave Attacks (n/a)
See Glossary.

Hump, LZ (BR 752-942)
Apx 10 km W Bong Son and 12 km NNW Ha Tay AF. Oct66-Feb67. Binh Dinh Pr, II Corps.

Hump, Operation (n/a)
5-9Nov65. 173d Abn, War Zone D. 1st/503d Inf fought large MF VC Rgt. The VC left cover and charged 173d Bde's positions, suffering estimated 403 KIA. III Corps.

Hundred P Alley (XS 82-96)
A.k.a. 100 Piaster Alley. Labyrinth of muddy alleys across from main gate at Tan Son Nhut AB. Dangerous area populated by military misfits, AWOLs and deserters. Gia Dinh Pr, III Corps.

Hung Dao BEQ (XS 854-902)
At 126-130 Tran Hung Dao St., Nov 65, 105 rms, Saigon, directly across street from Metropole BEQ. See Metropole for 4Dec65 bomb info. Per R. Bows' *Vietnam Military Lore, 1959-1973.* Gia Dinh Pr, III Corps.

Hung Dao, FSB? (XT 099-762)
Apx 7 km S Thien Ngon AF, 12 km due E Lo Go and 25 km NNW Tay Ninh West AF. Tay Ninh Pr, III Corps.

Hung Hoa (WJ 30-47)
Apx 55 km WNW Hanoi. During Op Lorraine, 29Oct8-Nov52, French forces moved to higher ground in this area. See *Street Without Joy*, Chp 3, map at p 80. NVN.

Hung Trung (n/a)
Mapsheet name of L-7014-6144-2. NVN only.

Hung Tuy District HQ (YD)
US Advisory cmpd here. Somewhere near Hue/Phu Bai. Thua Thien Pr, I Corps.

Hung Vuong, FSB? (XS)
See Hong, FSB? III Corps.

Hung Yen (n/a)
Mapsheet name of L-7014-6250-3. NVN only.

Hung Yen (XH 10-78)
Along Red River, apx 46 km SE Hanoi and at center of Red River Delta. Major French-held position of 1st Indochina War. Home of an entirely Vietnamese Mobile Group (French-trained), that was created in 1953. Per *Street Without Joy*, p 20. NVN.

Hungnam, LZ (XD 766-456)
Apx 9 km WNW Khe Sanh CB, 24 km WSW Ca Lu and 58 km WSW Quang Tri. Apr70 XXIV Corps grid per Don Armstrong. Quang Tri Pr, I Corps.

Hunsley, Patrol Base (XT 597-270)
A.k.a. Joint Patrol Base and FSB Hunsley. Apx 14 km NNW Cu Chi, 8 km NNW Patrol Base Dragon, and 13 km NE Trang Bang. Built apx 8Aug69. Likely named to honor Army 1Lt Dennis R. Hunsley, KIA 15Mar69. Constructed Aug69? by units of 2/14th Inf. Had two or three 105mm howitzers. Info/grid per Kirk Ramsey, 2/14/25th ID2d Bn, 49th ARVN Rgt and 2d/14th Inf, 25th Inf Div elements here. Binh Duong Pr, III Corps. [287]

Hunt, FSB (YT 261-021)
Apx 21 km WSW Xuan Loc, 6 km SW FSB Sally, 6 km SE FSB Evans and 14 km NW FSB Wattle. On 1ATF NCO trng map per John Hollett. Apr-Jun68. Also listed at YT 250-010. Bien Hoa Pr, III Corps.

Hunter, FSB (XT 371-422)
A.k.a. Checkpoint Tango. Along LTL-26, at its intersection with Rte 239, apx 3 km SE Ap Nam Ngon, 13 km WSW Dau Tieng and 23 km ESE Tay Ninh West AF. Jun69-Jan70. Tay Ninh Pr, III Corps.

Hunterdon County, USS (n/a)
LST/AGS-838. USN Landing Ship, Tank. Suptd 9th Inf Div/MRF in '67-68, per MRF Assn website at www.mrfa.org. See *YRBM-21*. III/IV Corps?
Hunter-Killer Team (n/a)
See Glossary.
Huong (n/a)
Vietnamese word for village.
Huong Dien District HQ (YD 68-41?)
Apx 20 km NNW Hue, 15 km NE Camp Evans and 16 km due N LZ Sally. MACV Adv Team, 1st Cav liaison and ARVN cmpd. Thua Thien Pr, I Corps.
Huong Hoa (n/a)
Mapsheet name of L-7014-6342-3. Laos.
Huong Hoa CAC/CAP (XD 858-386)
See CAP Oscar. Quang Tri Pr, I Corps.
Huong Hoa Dist HQ (XD 858-386)
At Khe Sanh ville. Forces here inc an Army SF Det, MACV Adv Team #4, Marine CAC and a SVN RF Co ('67). All apparently part of USMC CAC Oscar CP. Quang Tri Pr, I Corps.
Huong Hoa Village (XD860-375)
Vicinity Khe Sanh ville complex. Incident here 7May67, in which PFC Robert Todd was KIA is mentioned in *The Final Formation*, p 22. Quang Tri Pr, I Corps.
Huong Khe (n/a)
Mapsheet name of L-7014-6145-3. NVN/Laos.
Huong My (BT 242-403)
Apx 5 km E QL-1, 4 km from coast, 20 km SSE Hoi An, and 21 km NNE Tam Ky. Quang Tin Pr, I Corps.
Huong My Heliport (XS 542-070)
Apx 2 km E Cau Mong, 13 km NE Phu Vinh and 36 km SSE My Tho. Heliport #592, alt 7', sod (hard), at 10°00'45"N-106°24'20"E, 73 TAD. Kien Hoa Pr, IV Corps.
Huong Thuy (YD 846-173)
Town along QL-1, apx 7 km SE of Hue and 16 km NW Phu Bai. Map between pp 368-9 in *The Rise and Fall of the American Army*, has positions of Phu Bai and this ville reversed. Thua Thien Pr, I Corps.
Huong Thuy CAP (YD 84-17)
Hotel Co?, 3rd CAG per T. Duffie's CAP Vets website at www.capmarine.com. Thua Thien Pr, I Corps.
Huong Thuy Jungle (YD 840-040)
Generally 7 km SE Hue and 16 km NW Phu Bai. Thua Thien Pr, I Corps.
Huong Tra (YD 754-252)
Apx 2 km N Hue and 4 km NE QL-1. ARVN District HQ, '68. Thua Thien Pr, I Corps.
Huron (n/a)
6Apr70, XXIV Corps proposed 5th Div FSB name.
Hurricane, LZ (BT 529-077)
Immed W Chu Lai AF, apx 1 to 2 km E QL-1 and said to have been on or near Div Arty Hill. XXIV Corps grid; however, also listed at BT 537-033, and BT 515-040 by '70 arty ORLL on Americal list. Quang Tin Pr, I Corps.
Hurricane Forward (XS/XT/YT)
See Hurricane Forward in Glossary.
Hurt, Camp (VQ 98-67)
A.k.a. MACV Team 64 Cmpd. At ATSB Solid Anchor, vicinity of Nam Can, Cau Mau Peninsula. Image of sign at cmpd at: http://members.xoom.com/mdturner/vietnam.htm. Named to honor Capt. Ronald W Hurt, KIA 23Mar70, while with MACV Adv Team 64. Data per Mike Turner. See Solid Anchor. An Xuyen Pr, IV Corps.
Hurtegen, FSB (XT 692-325)
See Huertgen. Binh Duong Pr, III Corps.
Hurtgen, FSB (XT 692-325)
See Huertgen. Binh Duong Pr, III Corps.
Huskey, FSB (YT 46-08)
See Husky, FSB. Long Khanh Pr, III Corps.
Husky, FSB (YT 46-08)
Several km E of QL-1, at or near Xuan Loc AF, 13 km NNE Blackhorse Basecamp, 47 km ESE Bien Hoa AB and 40 km N Nui Dat. HQ, 199th LIB/hvy arty base. Grid apx and per 199th LIB Assn. Long Khanh Pr, III Corps.
Hussey Compound (XT 64-16?)
Advsy Team 90 Cmpd. At Cu Chi Basecamp. Named to honor Maj George E Hussey, Advisor to 1st Bn, 46th Inf Rgt, 25th ARVN Div, KIA 4May70, when his ARVN unit was ambushed in Cambodia. Data per Ray Bows. Hau Nghia Pr?, III Corps.
Huster, Camp (XS 82-96)
At Tan Son Nhut AB, Saigon. Named to honor Sp4 Robert R Huster, KIA 8Apr67. Data per Ray Bows. Gia Dinh Pr, III Corps.
Hustler, FSB/LZ (BT 298-030)
Apx 25 km WSW Chu Lai, 17 km due S Tam Ky AF. Americal list author indicates it was built 1Apr70, however, 1st/502d Inf, 101st Abn '69 Bn Annual Hist Supp indicates it was built by that Bn, May69, while opcon to Americal. Also listed at BT 299-028 per 1st/46th Inf AAR, and BT 296-031. Americal list. Quang Tin Pr, I Corps.
Huynh An CAP, Thonh (YD 882-172)
See CAP Alpha 1. Thua Thien Pr, I Corps.
Hyde, Dredge (n/a)
US Army Dredge. 1st vessel working for USN NSA to be damaged by enemy action in war. In unusual arrangement, this Army dredge was at sea working for USN on land. On 9May67, while dredging the Cua Viet Bar NNE Quang Tri, Limpet mines were placed by enemy swimmers on her port quarter and starboard bow. When the bow mine exploded (0400 hrs), her crew dropped its hopper of sand and beached the vessel on S bank of river. 2 hrs later the 2d charge went off. The dredge suffered major damage but was repaired. See *Coconino County, USS*.
Hydress Pass (YH 2-9)
Passe des Hydress. NIMA data. NVN.

INDIA

Facility/Feature Name, Grid Coordinate, a.k.a. Name/History/Province/CTZ

Unless otherwise stated, 6-digit grid coordinates reference DMA L-7014, L-7015 or L-7016 series, 1:50,000 scale maps, while 2- and 4-digit coordinates reference AMS/DMA/NIMA 1:250,000, 1:500,000 and 1:1,000,000 scale maps. Unless otherwise stated, all heights are in meters. To convert meters to feet, multiply by 3.2808; feet to meters, multiply by .3048.

I, Firebase (XT 75-34?)
See Artillery Base I/Firebase 1. Binh Duong Pr, III Corps.

I, Firebase (XT 73-85?)
See Firebase or Artillery Base 1. Binh Duong Pr, III Corps.

I, Firebase (ZB 005-215?)
See Firebase 1. Kontum Pr, II Corps.

I & I (n/a)
See Glossary.

I Corps (n/a)
A.k.a. I CTZ or Military Region 1 and pronounced "Eye Corps." Northernmost of the five CTZs in SVN. Consisted of following 5 Provs and island of Cu Lao Re: Quang Ngai, Quang Nam, Quang Tin, Quang Tri, Thua Thien and, at one time, Quang Da Provs.[288]

I CTZ MSF Camp (BT 065-733)
At or adj to Marble Mtn AF, apx 6 km SE Da Nang AB. 5th SF. Info/grid per *SF Order of Battle.* Transferred to ARVN Border Rangers Cmd. Quang Nam Pr, I Corps.

I V Long, Camp (YD)
See I. V. Long, Camp. Quang Tri Pr, I Corps.

I. V. Long, Camp (YD 243-597?)
At Dong Ha (or Camp Carroll?), Jan/Feb68. HQ 3d Bn, 3d Mar Rgt, 3d Mar Div. Named to honor Bn's legendary Sgt Maj, I. V. Long, "Old School" Marine who overcame Muscular Dystrophy as child and amazed all with his determination, stamina and devotion to the Corps.
Sometime in '68, he was transferred to Dong Ha as Bn Sgt Major and severely injured by fragging incident in which a grenade was tossed into his cot. Though badly injured, he insisted on walking to jeep that took him to the hospital. Quang Tri Pr, I Corps.[289]

I'm Dreaming of a White Christmas (n/a)
See American Radio Service in Glossary.

Ia Ayun River (AR 95-28)
A.k.a. the Dak Ayunh River. Apx 25 km SE Pleiku. Valley of this river was staging area of H-15 VC Local Force Bn. 4th Div's AO. Pleiku Pr, II Corps.

Ia Bang Lake (AR 825-362)
1 km diameter lake at NE corner of Camp Enari. On ND49-09 JOG. Pleiku Pr, II Corps.

Ia Drang River (YA 90-05)
Generally 40-50 km SW Pleiku. In what Vietnamese call The Valley of a Thousand Ghosts, their superstitious name for Ia Drang Valley. Belief is that the ghosts of the thousands of NVA/VC MIA in this area still wander the valley. Heavily bombed by B-52 Arc Light missions, particularly during and after 1st Ia Drang Battles at LZ X-Ray and LZ Albany, Nov65. Pleiku Pr, II Corps.

Ia Drang Valley (YA 90-05)
Ran generally from YA 80-07 E to YA 90-07, adj to Cambodian border apx 55 km SW Pleiku and 45 km WNW Phu Nhon AF. Site of battles for LZs X-Ray/Albany, the 1st major battles of US war involving 1st Cav helicopter assets and Airmobility concept. Map is L7014-6535-3. See LZ Albany and LZ X-Ray. Pleiku Pr, II Corps.

Ia Grouille River (YA 87-35)
Apx 10 km S Plei Djereng New AF. Pleiku Pr, II Corps.

Ia Lou (ZA 12-69?)
Freshwater lake apx 3 km NE Plei Mrong. 14°11N-107°53'E. ND48-08 JOG. Kontum or Pleiku Pr, II Corps.

Ia Meur River (YA 98-00)
Ran from NE to SW and roughly parallel to Cambodian border about 10 km E Chu Pong Mtn and LZ X-Ray, in the Valley of a Thousand Ghosts (Vietnamese superstitious name for Ia Drang Valley). Pleiku Pr, II Corps.

Ia Tae River (YA)
In Ia Drang Valley, near Ia Drang and Ia Meur Rivers, E Chu Pong Mtn and W Plei Me SF Camp. See Falcon. Pleiku Pr, II Corps.

Ianetta, LZ (YA 852-457)
See LZ Lanetta. Pleiku Pr, II Corps.

Iannetta, LZ (YA 852-457)
See LZ Lanetta. Pleiku Pr, II Corps.

Ichiban, LZ (BR 928-787)
In coastal plain apx 17 km SSE Bong Son, 12 km NNE Phu May, 14 km NNE Crystal AF, 5 km S Van An and 2 km W QL-1. Map is L-7014-6837-4 (Bong Son), per Ray Smith, or L-7014-6837-3 as per Ken Burrington? Binh Dinh Pr, II Corps.

ICS-64 (BT 060-840)
Integrated Communications Systems Site 64 on Monkey Mtn, Da Nang. Later renamed the Onderko ICS to honor Capt. John Onderko, KIA 4Feb68. See Monkey Mtn Signal Site. Quang Nam Pr, I Corps.

Idaho, LZ (YD 217-117)
Along Hwy 548, apx 53 km WSW Hue, 8 km ESE Tou Rout and 42 km SSW Quang Tri. XXIV Corps grid per Don Armstrong. Quang Tri Pr, I Corps.

Idaho Beach, Camp (AN 795-070)
At Phan Thiet AF/LZ Betty, apx 60 km SW Song Mao. Apr70. Binh Thuan Pr, II Corps.

Idaho BOQ (XS 812-924)
At 116 Phu Tho Hoa St. (Idaho Bar Officers Club), Saigon. Per R. Bows' *Vietnam Military Lore, 1959-1973.* Gia Dinh Pr, III Corps.

Idaho Canyon, Operation (n/a)
21Jul-25Sep69. 3d Mar op. 565 rptd NVA/VC KIA, per *Vietnam Order of Battle*, pp 9-14. Quang Tri Pr, I Corps.
IFFV HQ, Nha Trang (CP 042-534)
Overlooking beach, apx 2.4 km NE the NW end of Nha Trang AF main rwy. Per Don Truitt, was in Grand Hotel at Nha Trang, '68-69, and CG then was Lt Gen. Peers. Khanh Hoa Pr, II Corps.
IFFV HQ and CORDS Club (CP 03-52?)
IFFV (1st Field Force, Vietnam) Nha Trang. Per Don Truitt, was in Grand Hotel, '68-69, and CG was Lt Gen. Peers. See terms Field Force, and IFFV in Corps Level Command Section. Khanh Hoa Pr, II Corps.
Igloo White (n/a)
See Glossary.
II, FSB (XT 270-780)
See Artillery Base II. Tay Ninh Pr, III Corps.
II Corps (n/a)
A.k.a. II CTZ (Combat Tactical Zone) or MRII (Military Region II). Pronounced "Two Corps." 2d northernmost of the five CTZs in SVN. Consisted of following 12 Provs: Binh Dinh, Ninh Thuan, Binh Thuan, Phu Bon, Darlac, Phu Yen, Khan Hoa, Pleiku, Kontum, Quang Duc, Lam Dong, Tuyen Duc and, at any earlier time, (Gia Lai), (Thanh Hoa), and (Dak Lak) Provs. [290]:
II CTZ MSF Camp (AR 765-474)
In the heart of Pleiku. 5th SF. Info/grid per *SF Order of Battle.* Closed to Kontum MSF. Pleiku Pr, II Corps.
IIFFV HQ (YT 050-105)
2d Field Force, Vietnam HQ. Along S side of Hwy 317, roughly midway between Bien Hoa and Plantation AF's, apx 24 km NE Saigon and just N Long Binh Post. A.k.a. The Plantation CB or Long Binh North. Also listed at YT 048-106. See Plantation Cmpd and Red Carpet Heliport. Bien Hoa Pr, III Corps.
III, FSB (XT?)
See Artillery Base III. Tay Ninh Pr?, III Corps.
III Corps (n/a)
A.k.a. III CTZ (Combat Tactical Zone), commonly pronounced "Three Corps", 2d southernmost of the five CTZs in SVN. Consisted of following 11 Provs and a Special CTZ: Binh Duong, Long An, Bien Hoa, Long Khanh, Binh Long, Phuoc Long, Binh Tuy, Phuoc Tuy, Gia Dinh, Tay Ninh, Hau Nghia, Special Capital Zone and at other times, (Saigon) and (Phuoc Thanh) Provs. [291]
III Corps ARVN Adv Grp (XT 98-13?)
In the Train Cmpd, at Bien Hoa CB. Advsy Team 95 here. Bien Hoa Pr, III Corps.
III MAF, NSA, Da Nang (BT 03-80 & BT 06-77?)
A.k.a. the Wooden Elephant and White Elephant. Apparently near BT 03-80 and BT 06-77 in succession. The HQ of NSA (Naval Supt Activities), Da Nang. 1st in Da Nang, 15Aug69, in facility nicknamed "The White Elephant." Moved to China Beach Public Works Cmpd in E Da Nang and renamed "The Wooden Elephant." Quang Nam Pr, I Corps.
III Marine Amphibious Force (MAF) HQ (BT)
At Camp Horn and later, Camp Haskins, Da Nang. See Major HQs Section entry. Quang Nam Pr, I Corps.
Ike, LZ (AT 945-405)
A.k.a. Hill 510 and possibly FSB Yonkers? Apx 12 km SE An Hoa AF, 35 km SSW Da Nang and 20 km WSW LZ Baldy. Also listed at AT 938-396. Americal list. Map is L-7014-6640-3. Also listed at AT 646-405; however, no such grid exists. Quang Nam Pr, I Corps.
Ike, LZ (XT 344-716)
Apx 15 km NNE Nui Ba Den, 25 km NE Tay Ninh West AF and 8 km SE FSB Carolyn. Also N LZ Ryder and within arty range of FSBs Carolyn and Barbara. 2d/8th, 2d/5th Cav, 1st Cav here '69, per Frank Penk, Jr. Also listed at XT 338-742, XT 338-719, and XT 348-720. Arty ORLL grids. Tay Ninh Pr, III Corps.
Il Du Sud Island (BM 75-65)
Uninhabited? island, apx 1.5 x .5 km in size, and 110 km ESE Phan Thiet. Cu Lao Hon Island, 100 km ESE Phan Thiet, has 2 small islands off its N end and 2 off its S end, one of which is Il Du Sud. South China Sea.
Ile Aux Buffle (CR 1-6)
A.k.a. Hon Trau Island. Binh Dinh Pr, II Corps.
Ile Ba Lua (VS 4-2)
A.k.a. Balau Island and Quan Dao Bai Lao. NIMA data. Kien Giang Pr, IV Corps.
Ile Bac (CP 2-8)
A.k.a. Hon Do. NIMA data. Khanh Hoa Pr, II Corps.
Ile Bai Ma Lieng (CQ 1-5)
Island among grp of small islands apx 14 km due N Tuy Hoa AB, and 2 to 4 km off coast. Phu Yen Pr, II Corps.
Ile Cu X (n/a)
Mapsheet name of L-7014-6550-1. NVN only.
Ile d' An Thoi (US 95-05?)
See An Thoampoi island. Kien Giang Pr?, IV Corps.
Ile d' An Thomapoi (US 9-0)
See An Thomapoi Island. Kien Giang Pr, IV Corps.
Ile de Bai Luei (YS 3-5)
See Ile de Bai Luoi. Phuoc Tuy Pr, III Corps.
Ile de Bai Luoi (YS 3-5)
Ile de Bai Luei. Apx 7 km NNE Vung Tau. NIMA data. Phuoc Tuy Pr, III Corps.
Ile de Deux Freres (XJ 7-5)
Island of Two Monks (or Two Friars). NIMA data. NVN.
Ile De La Table (n/a)
Mapsheet name of L-7014-6550-4. NVN only.
Ile de Pirates (YJ 6-4)
Island of Pirates. NIMA data. NVN.
Ile de Pirates (YJ 6-4)
Island of Pirates. NIMA data. NVN.
Ile de Sangliers (YJ 6-1)
Island of Wild Boar. NIMA data. NVN.
Ile de Singes (YJ 8-5)
Island of Monkeys? NIMA data. NVN.
Ile de Sylphes (YJ 5-1)
Island of Sylphs. NIMA data. NVN.
Ile des Deux Songs (XJ 7-2)
Two Songs Island. NIMA data. NVN.
Ile des Merdeilles (YJ 0-1)
NIMA data. NVN.
Ile des Merveilles (YJ 0-1)
Island of Wonder? NIMA data. NVN.
Ile des Tres Sommets (YJ 1-0)
Island of Three Summits. NIMA data. NVN.

Ile Juan Prieto (CR 1-3)
A.k.a. Hon Cau Island. Binh Dinh Pr, II Corps.
Ile Longue (n/a)
Mapsheet name of L-7014-6450-1. NVN only.
Ile Pyramid (CP 2-5)
A.k.a. Pyramid Island or Hon Dung. NIMA data. Khanh Hoa Pr, II Corps.
Ile Tching Lan Xan (n/a)
Mapsheet name of L-7014-6551-2. NVN only.
Ile Tortue (VS 83-02)
See Hon Tre Island. Kien Giang Pr, IV Corps.
Iles de Pechures (CP 1-3)
Fishermens' Island. NIMA data. Khanh Hoa Pr, II Corps.
Illingworth, FSB (XT 033-788)
Along LTL-20, apx 4 km SW Thien Ngon AF, 8 km NE Cambodia and 35 km NW Tay Ninh. Possibly named to honor Cpl John J. Illingworth, KIA 14Mar70. Existed 17Mar-2Apr70, and 1 of 7 FSBs opened and closed in as many weeks by 2d/8th Cav, 1st Cav, prior to Cambodian Incursion (7 were: Jamie, Mary Gwen, Heather, Victor, Flashner, Drum and Illingworth). Withstood heavy ground assault by a Bn of 272d NVA Rgt, 1Apr70, with 24 US KIA, 54 US WIA. C/2d/8thCav, E/2d/8th Cav, and elements of A Trp, 11th ACR, B Bty 1st/77th Arty, A Bty 2d/32d Arty, B/5th/2d FA, 1/29th FA. Also listed at XT 039-793. Tay Ninh Pr, III Corps.
Illini (BR 784-667)
Apx 3 km W Hoi San and 16 km S Ha Tay AF. 2d/9th Arty, 4th Div here, '67. Per *Rites of Passage*, p 235, 1st/14th Inf/25th Div also here '67. Name/grid per Dan Gillotti, 15th Arty. Binh Dinh Pr, II Corps.
Impact Rock (YD 343-194)
Dominant terrain feature on FSB Ripcord. See FSB Ripcord. Thua Thien Pr, I Corps.
Impervious, USS (n/a)
MSO-449. Minesweeper, Ocean. See Op End Sweep.
Implicit, USS (n/a)
MSO-455. Minesweeper, Ocean, per Ralph Fries.
Impossible, FSB (YA 835-747)
A.k.a. FSB Delta (Jan69). Remote site apx 44 km WSW Kontum, 3 km due S peak Hill 1528, and 28 km WNW Plei Mrong. 4th Div and 1st/92d Arty here Apr69. 1st/92d Arty opcon 6th/14th Arty here Jan69. Name/grid per Craig Miller. Kontum Pr, II Corps.
In articulo mortis (n/a)
See Glossary.
Ina, FSB (XT 607-621)
A.k.a. FSB Lori (XT 605-624). Apx 8 km SSW Minh Thanh AF, 19 km NE Dau Tieng and 65 km NNW Saigon. 1st/7th Cav, 1st Cav here at one point per Frank Penk, Jr. Grid per Peter Cole. Binh Long Pr, III Corps.
Ina, LZ (BR 348-309)
See Yna. Binh Dinh Pr, II Corps.
Inca, LZ (YD 035-640)
On S edge of DMZ, apx 10 km WSW Thon An Hoa, 13 km NW Cam Lo and 35 km WNW Dong Ha. Apr70 XXIV Corps grid per Don Armstrong. Quang Tri Pr, I Corps.
Inchon, USS (n/a)
LPH 12, Amphibious Ship. See End Sweep, Op.
Incoming, LZ (YA 939-912)
Apparently a.k.a. FSB/PB 14 and Incoming Hill. Apx 9 km WSW Polei Kleng and 31 km W to WNW Kontum. Near LZs Virgin and Mile High, which were near end of long ridgeline overlooking N end of Plei Trap Valley. On same ridge to S was LZ Incoming. All were apx 25 km E Cambodia. Described as Bn HQ FSB occupied/built by 1st/14th Inf. Craig Miller confirms base was overrun 26Mar68, during night action in which NVA employed flame-throwers and tear gas to breech wire, capture 2 arty pieces and use them to fire Beehive rnds at Arty positions still held by US. Unit was "Death to Last Man" NVA 325C Div. Info per Ben Youmans, grid per Craig Miller. Also listed at YA 9390-9123. Kontum Pr, II Corps.
Incoming Hill (YA 939-912)
See Incoming, LZ. Kontum Pr, II Corps.
Independence, USS (n/a)
CVA-62. Deployed with CVW-7 10 May 65-13 Dec 65.
Independence Brigade (n/a)
See Glossary.
Independence Palace (XS 857-915)
A.k.a. the Norodom Palace and Presidential Palace. See Presidential Palace. Gia Dinh Pr, III Corps.
India, FSB (XT 260-780)
Apx 14 km SSW Katum, 2 km SW Prek Klok and 19 km N to NNW Nui Ba Den. Apr67. Tay Ninh Pr, III Corps.
India CAC (YD?)
See CAC Listings. I Corps.
India CAP (n/a)
See CAP India listings. I Corps.
India Relay (YD 097-378)
A.k.a. Hill 819 Radio Relay Site. OP and radio relay site built overlooking valleys of Song Quang Tri and Da Krong Rivers SE Vandegrift CB, apx 27 km SW Quang Tri and 14 km due S Mai Loc AF. Provided supt for 3rd Recon Bn ops and 3d Mar Div. Apparently built '68 or earlier. Had LZ built in saddle (YD 097-374) just outside perimeter wire and, on trail leading to it, was a poignant memorial, "a simple one, two recon bush hats sitting on a couple of pieces of metal in form of a crosses with a small wooden plaque" inscribed with the names of LCpl. Gerald McGinley and LCpl. Dennis Mickelson, A/3d Recon Bn, KIA 28Dec68. Call-sign "Colonial"(?) in May69? Described as having a deep, heavily sandbagged Commo bunker, a lightning/target rod antenna, and "an open-air two-holer on W side," May69. Defenses inc two M-60 MGs and one 81mm mortar. Data per Dennis Soldner at: www.3rdrecon.org/distlit1.htm (photos and maps at that website). Quang Tri Pr, I Corps.
Indian Country (n/a)
Enemy controlled areas.
Indiana Rangers (n/a)
See Glossary.
Indictment #1, Public (n/a)
See Glossary.
Indictment #2, Public (n/a)
See Glossary.
Indigo, FSB (YS 060-380)
See FSB New Indigo. Bien Hoa Pr, III Corps.

Indochinese Highlands, Battle for the (n/a)
Began 22Sep51-Feb52. Began with Vietminh attack on Nghia Lo, apx 210 WNW Hanoi. Battle sites inc: Nghia Lo, Hoa Binh, Tu Vu, Notre Dame Rock, Mt. Ba Vi, Nui Vien Nam (Bernard Fall spells it "Hui" Vien Nam), Kem and Xom Pheo (see also those entries). SVN/NVN.
Indochine-Sud-Est Asiatique (n/a)
See Glossary.
Indra, USS (n/a)
ARL-37. Repair Barge of MRF. Role discussed in *Brown Water, Black Berets*, p 251. SVN.
Infantry Route One (n/a)
See Glossary.
Inflict, USS (n/a)
MSO-456. Minesweeper, Ocean, per Ralph Fries.
Ingalls, FSB (YT 739-302)
Along Rte 334 just SE Vo Dat AF, apx 34 km NE Xuan Loc and 94 km ENE Saigon. Opened or reopened 8Oct70, closed 1Nov70. 2d/5th Cav. Data per *1st Cav Div Op Rpt, for period ending 31Oct70*, courtesy Peter Cole. Binh Tuy Pr, III Corps. [292]
Ingham, USCGC (n/a)
WHEC 35. 16Jul68-3Apr69. Sqdn 3 CGC, during Coast Guard's 3d deployment.
Ingraham, USS (n/a)
A.k.a. DD-694. See *Hissem, USS*. Role discussed in *Brown Water, Black Berets*, p 95. Market Time TF-115. SVN.
Ingrid, LZ (ZA 150-948)
Apx 11 km NW Kontum, 5 km NE Polei Breng and 5 km W QL-14. 4th Div AARs indicate LZs Muriel, Ingrid, Thunder and Irma Jay were built by 1st/14th Inf, early-mid Jul68, while LZ Bass was being demolished. Data per Dick Arnold. Kontum Pr, II Corps.
Insect Armies, The (n/a)
See Glossary.
Inshore Undersea Warfare Units (n/a)
See Glossary.
Instant Patrol Bases (n/a)
See Glossary.
Institute for Propagation of Buddhist Faith (n/a)
See High Clerical Association in Glossary.
Interieure, Point (BT 6-0)
See Point Interieure. Quang Tin Pr, I Corps.
International BEQ (XS 853-899)
At 289 Tran Hung Dao St., Nov 62, 96 rms, Saigon, per *Vietnam Military Lore, 1959-1973*. Gia Dinh Pr, III Corps.
International House, The (XS 866-911)
At 69 Nguyen Hue St., Saigon. Apx 300 meters W the Saigon River and 1.5 km SSE US Embassy. Operated by US Embassy for diplomatic and civilian personnel and also open to field grade officers (full Col and above), per *Vietnam Military Lore, 1959-1973*. Gia Dinh Pr, III Corps.
Interprovincial Routes (n/a)
See Glossary.
Interzone NAMBO (n/a)
The geographic HQ of NLF. Covered roughly the southern 1/4 of SVN, including the Mekong Delta in conjunction with Interzone V (HQ for northern 3/4s of SVN) which were combined into COSVN HQ, Mar62.
Interzone V (n/a)
A geographic HQ of NLF, and roughly the northern 3/4s of SVN in conjunction with the NAMBO Interzone (HQ for southern 1/4 of SVN inc the Mekong Delta) which were combined into COSVN, Mar62.
Intrepid, FSB (YT 923-089)
Near abnd railway line apx 2 km NW Song Dinh, 47 km due W Phan Thiet, 13 km NNW FSB Bolan, and 27 km NNW Ham Tan. Opened or reopened 29Sep70. 1st/5th Cav Name/data per *1st Cav Div Op Rpt, ending 31Oct70*, courtesy Peter Cole. Binh Tuy Pr, III Corps.
Intrepid, USS (n/a)
A.k.a. CVS-11. Deployed with CVW 10 4Jun68-8FEB69; with CVW-10 11May67-30Dec67; with CVW-10 4Apr66-21Nov66. In Sep65 attack sqdns from Carriers *Oriskany*, *Constellation*, *Coral Sea*, and *Intrepid* hit previously off-limits areas of Haiphong and smaller ports of Hon Gai and Cam Pha. [293]
***Intrepid* Four, The** (n./a)
See Glossary.
Invasion, LZ (YA 598-445)
Cambodian Incursion FSB apx 4 km N LZ Conquest, 6 km W SVN border, 23 km WNW Plei Beng and 63 km W Pleiku. 4th Div, '70. Name/grid per Jim Claeys. B Bty, 4th/42d Arty here May70. Cambodia.
IOS Linda ? (AT 865-681)
See Linda, IOS. Quang Nam Pr, I Corps.
Iowa BOQ (XS 823-937)
At 266 Truong Minh Ky St., Saigon. Per R. Bows' *Vietnam Military Lore, 1959-1973.* Gia Dinh Pr, III Corps.
Iowa, FSB (XU 516-235)
In Cambodia, apx 3 km due W tip of Angel's Wing/SVN border, 27 km NW Loc Ninh, 11 km SSW Snuol and 27 km NE Memot. Grid per *11th ACR Cambodia Invasion AAR, 1st Cav Div, May-Jun70*, courtesy Lou Rochat. [294] Cambodia.
Iredell County, USS (n/a)
LST-839. SVN.
Irene, LZ (BR 980-705)
Apx 28 km SSE Bong Son and 7 km NE Phu My/QL-1. Oct66. Binh Dinh Pr, II Corps.
Irene, FSB (ZC 108-125)
Apx 10 km ENE Kham Duc, 7 km due N Hill 1865 and 60 km WSW Tam Ky. Cited in 1st Cav VN *Yearbook* Aug65-Dec69, p 93, per Peter Cole. Quang Tin Pr, I Corps.
Iris, FSB (n/a)
10th Cav, 4th Div here, per Bob Patsfield. Possibly Binh Dinh or Pleiku Pr, II Corps.
Irma, LZ (n/a)
1st Cav FSB/LZ. No data. Pleiku or Kontum Pr?, II Corps?
Irma, LZ (ZA 151-924)
See Irma Jay. Kontum Pr, II Corps.
Irma J, LZ (ZA 151-924)
See Irma Jay. Kontum Pr, II Corps.
Irma Jay, LZ (ZA 151-924?)
Known variously as LZ Irma, LZ Irma J and LZ Irma Joy. About 2 km N Rte 511, some 10 km WNW Kontum, 3 km ENE Polei Breng, and 6 km E Polei Krong AF. Also listed at ZA 102-924, which if accurate, puts it at or near Polei Krong AF/SF Camp, apx 15 km WNW Kontum? Kevin Rafferty, B/1st/14th Inf, 4th Div has picture of 4'x8' sign

taken here that read: *WELCOME TO FB IRMA JAY, Golden Dragons 1/14 Inf.* Per Dick Arnold, 4thDiv AARs indicate LZ Bass was dismantled by 1st/14th in early Jul68, while they were also constructing LZs Muriel, Ingrid, Thunder and Irma Jay. Apparently built as Bn HQ. 2d/9th Arty and possibly 1st/92d Arty here, Jul68, per info courtesy Craig Miller. All three spellings appear in various 4th Div Op Rpts. Photos/maps of base at http://1-14th.com/maps.html. Kontum Pr, II Corps.

Irma Joy, LZ (ZA 151-924)
See Irma Jay. Kontum Pr, II Corps.

Iron, FSB (BS 560-164)
Apx 36 km SE Duc Pho, 18 km due S Ba To New and 35 km WNW LZ English. Near Quang Ngai/Binh Dinh Pr border, I or II Corps.

Iron, FSB (XT 623-664)
Apx 4 km due S Min Thanh AF and 21 km NE Dau Tieng. Name/grid per Dan Gillotti. Binh Long Pr, III Corps.

Iron Horse (n/a)
6Apr70, XXIV Corps proposed III MAF FSB name.

Iron Mountain? (n/a)
Unclear whether this is a FSB or an AO? Americal Assn list puts it W Duc Pho. Quang Ngai Pr?, I Corps.

Iron Mountain Operational Zone (n/a)
Mentioned but not defined in USMC '69 history vol. Possibly S Da Nang and W Duc Pho? I Corps.

Iron T (XT 72-28)
See Iron Triangle. Binh Duong Pr, III Corps.

Iron Triangle, The (XT 72-28)
A.k.a. the Iron T. A 320-square-km region generally about 30-40 km NNW Saigon. Triangle-shaped jungled area and VC refuge of great legend and scene of many US ops. Than Dien Forest, Song Saigon, and Song Thi Thinh Rivers (N Bien Hoa), formed its general boundaries. Also bounded at NE apex by Ben Cat, with Xom Rach Bap at its W apex and Xom Ben Co at its SE apex, and Song Saigon generally forming its SE to NW bottom edge. Area along Song Saigon in Triangle was known as Ann Margaret, with Ho Bo Woods to S. On maps in *Vietnam Gunners*, p 62, and *Rangers At War*, pp 324-325. Binh Duong Pr, III Corps.

Iron Triangle, Operation (n/a)
8-14 Oct65. 173d Abn, Ben Cat. CA following B-52 air strike (1st tactical use of B-52s suptg ground troops in VN War). 106 VC KIA. III Corps.

Ironwood, USCGS (n/a)
WLB 297. USCG Buoy Tender.

Ironsides, LZ (YD 03-65)
A.k.a. LZ Ironsides. Apx 3 km due S FSB Comet, 11 km SW Con Thien and 10 km NNW Cam Lo, per map at p 58, *US Marines in Vietnam-1969*. 1st Mar Div. Grid estimated from that map. Quang Tri Pr, I Corps.

Irsking, FSB (YD 164-107)
See Erskine, Quang Tri Pr, I Corps.

Irsking, FSB (YD 583-231)
See Erskine. Thua Thien Pr?, I Corps.

Irving, Operation (n/a)
2-24Oct68. 1st Cav, ARVN and ROK op. '681 rptd NVA/VC KIA, per *Vietnam Order of Battle*, pp 9-14. Binh Dinh Pr, II Corps.

Irving A. Self, Camp (XT 63-66)
A.k.a. Camp Self. At Minh Thanh, apx 33 km NNW Lai Khe AF, 16 km WNW Chon Thanh AF and 70 km NNW Saigon. Named to honor SSgt Irving A. Self, 5th SF, Det A-132, KIA 19May64. Binh Long Pr, III Corps.

Isa, FSB (YS 438-533)
On N edge of Long Hai Hills, 8 km SSE Long Dien, 3 km NNE Long Hai AF and 10 km SW Dat Do. 8 RAR FSB in Apr70, with 161 Bty RNZA firing supt from FSB Horseshoe. On 1ATF NCO trng map per John Hollett. Also listed at YS 44-54. Phuoc Tuy Pr, III Corps.

Isabelle (TJ 9-6)
French position apx 7 km S main complex and near No. 2 AF at Dien Bien Phu. Muong Thanh Valley apx 290 km W Hanoi. French strongpoint during Op Castor, 20Nov53-7May54. Held 1/4th of total French troop strength, some 105mm howitzers and a Plt of M-24 light tanks. NVN.

Isabelle, Pointe (AT 9-8)
See Pointe Isabelle. Quang Nam Pr, I Corps.

Island Tree (n/a)
See Glossary.

Italian Green, Operation (n/a)
See Eldest Son, Operation.

IV Corps (n/a)
A.k.a. IV CTZ (Combat Tactical Zone), commonly pronounced "Four Corps." Southernmost of five CTZs in SVN. Consisted of following 16 Provs plus islands of Con Son and Dao Phu Quoc: Kien Tuong, Go Cong, An Giang, Kien Giang, An Xuyen, Kien Hoa, Ba Xuyen, Kien Phong, Bac Lieu, Phong Dinh, Chau Doc, Sa Dec, Chuong Thien, Vinh Binh, Dinh Tuong and Vinh Long Prvs, and at various other times, (Can Tho), (Tra Vinh), (Rach Gia), (Soc Trang), (My Tho), (Ben Tre) and (Ca Mau) [295]

IV Long, Camp (YD)
See I. V. Long, Camp. Quang Tri Pr, I Corps.

Ivory Tower Bar (XS 8-9)
10/A Tran Hung Dao St., Saigon. Per Fragging expert George Lepre, on 30Jun69, SSG Calvin T. Yates was here drinking and talking to a Vietnamese woman when 3 Vietnamese Abn officers from 11th Abn Bn entered (LTC Nguyen Viet Can, Capt Do Ngoc Nuoi, and Capt Pham Van Bach) and threatened Yates with their weapons. Another American sneaked out and informed the MPs. MP's SGT Eugene T. Cox and James H. Workman responded and tried to convince Vietnamese to desist. They instead turned on the MP's, and LTC Viet Can shot and killed both Cox and Workman. Viet Ntl Police unit deftly avoided arresting the Viet paratroopers as they fled, but some Americans followed the trio into Meyerkord Housing Area. The 3 were arrested, stood trial and given 6-month suspended sentences. Gia Dinh Pr, III Corps.

Ivy, LZ (BR 890-630)
Apx 9 km NE Vinh Thanh and 28 km NE An Khe. 1st Cav. Name/grid per Dan Gillotti Binh Dinh Pr, II Corps.

Ivy Leaf (n/a)
See Glossary.

Iwo Jima, USS (n/a)
LPH 2. Lndg. Platform, Helo. Part of TF 76?

Juliet

Facility/Feature Name, Grid Coordinate, a.k.a. Name/History/Province/CTZ

Unless otherwise stated, 6-digit grid coordinates reference DMA L-7014, L-7015 or L-7016 series, 1:50,000 scale maps, while 2- and 4-digit coordinates reference AMS/DMA/NIMA 1:250,000, 1:500,000 and 1:1,000,000 scale maps. Unless otherwise stated, all heights are in meters. To convert meters to feet, multiply by 3.2808; feet to meters, multiply by .3048.

J, Patrol Base (XT 544-210)
Apx 11 km WNW Cu Chi CB and 2 km NE Rung Cay. 14Mar69. Hau Nghia Pr, III Corps.

J-9 (YA/YB?)
See Juliet 9.

J. F. McDermott AF, Camp (CP 039-520)
See Nha Trang AF. Khanh Hoa Pr, II Corps.

J. F. McDermott, Camp (CP 051-501)
See McDermott, Camp. Khanh Hoa Pr, II Corps.

J. J. Carroll, Camp (YD 063-547)
A.k.a. Camp Carroll and originally referred to as Artillery Plateau. Was apx 27 km W to WNW Quang Tri, 5 km NNW Mai Loc, 6 km SW of Cam Lo, and a few km S of or straddling QL-9. On 10Nov66, was named to honor Capt. James J. Carroll, USMC, CO K/3d/4th Mar, KIA 27Sep66, by friendly fire (improperly registered tank rounds) on Hill 400, while directing fire supt for attack on Hill 484. 3d Mar Div and 12th Mar Arty '67, with 4-155mm, 6-105mms and 6 US Army 175mms here. Quang Tri Pr, I Corps.

J. L. Goodman, Camp (XS 8-9)
In Saigon and possibly near MACV HQ on Tan Son Nhut AB? 5th SF Grp Cmd Liaison Det Cmpd. Named to honor MSgt Jack L. Goodman, Ops NCO, Det A-18, 5th SF, KIA 17Jul63, in ambush of jeep on dirt road between Loch Ninh SF Camp and Xom Bung, while orienting replacement from Det A-22. Monument to Goodman also erected at Loc Ninh, per *Vietnam Military Lore: 1959-1973*, which has photos of both the monument at Loc Ninh and sign at Camp Goodman. Gia Dinh Pr, III Corps.

Jack, LZ (BR 703-938)
Apx 15 km NW Ha Tay AF and 16 km WSW Bong Son. Oct66. Binh Dinh Pr, II Corps.

Jack, FSB (YD 498-282)
A.k.a. LZ Jack or Hill 50. Apx 10 km SW Camp Evans, 13 km SSW LZ Jeanie and heavily attacked during Tet '68, 101st Abn and 5th/7th/1st Cav. 175mms of 1st/83d Arty here '69. Mutual supt with LZ Jeannie. Also listed at YD 492-279 and YD 495-287. Thua Thien Pr, I Corps.

Jack, FSB (XT 987-326)
Apx 2 km SW Khu Tru Mat and 17 km due N Bien Hoa AB. Jul68-Jan69. Binh Duong Pr?, III Corps.

Jackal, LZ (XD 940-626)
Along Mutter's Ridge, apx 15 km NNW Ca Lu, and 18 km WNW Cam Lo. Apr70 XXIV Corps grid per Don Armstrong. Quang Tri Pr, I Corps.

Jackie (n/a)
6Apr70, XXIV Corps proposed Americal FSB name.

Jackie, FSB (XT 522-742)
Apx 3 km SE Bau Tram, 14 km NW Minh Thanh AF, 26 km SW An Loc and 28 km NE Nui Ba Den. 3d ARVN Abn Bn, 2d ARVN Abn Bde apparently here at one time. 1st Bde/1st Cav here, Fall '69, per Frank Penk, Jr. Cited in 1st Cav VN *Yearbook* Aug65-Dec69, p 259, per Peter Cole. Also listed at XT 525-780, some 4 km N listed grid. Tay Ninh Pr, III Corps.

Jackie, LZ (ZV 182-125)
Along Rte TL-1, apx 14 km NW Ban Me Thuot/Lac Giao, 23 km SE Ban Don, and 4 km ENE the Tonle Srepok River. 2d/35th Inf here, Sep68. Name/grid per Ben Youmans. Darlac Pr, II Corps.

Jackson, Camp (n/a)
Location unknown; however, Ray Bows has data putting it in Quang Nam Pr. May or may not be same Camp Jackson as that at ZC 0059-0810, and a.k.a. Kham Duc SF Camp, in Quang Duc Pr?, Named to honor SFC William E. Jackson, Intel NCO with SF Team A-732, WIA 19Jan64, who died wounds 5Feb64, per *Vietnam Military Lore, legends, Shadows, and Heroes*, p 441-452, photo of gate at p 450. Quang Nam Pr?, I Corps.

Jackson, Camp (ZC 0059-0810)
A.k.a. Kham Duc SF Camp. At Kham Duc AF, apx 80 km SW Da Nang and 8 km NNE Ngok Tavak AF. See Kham Duc. Quang Duc Pr, I Corps.

Jackson, FSB (BN?)
Apparent 3d/506th Inf FSB. Location unknown. Name per Jerry Berry. Binh Thuan Pr, II Corps?

Jackson, FSB (XT 427-168)
Roughly 2 km E Song Vam Co Dong River, apx 9 km SSE Go Dau Ha, 22 km due W Cu Chi and 33 km SE Tay Ninh. Was within arty range of FSB Hamilton. Friendly fire from Jackson apparently fell on Hamilton at one point in '70. 6th/31st Inf, 9th Div, 2d/27th Inf, 25th Inf and 1st Cav. 2d/5th Cav, 1st Cav here '69? Hau Nghia Pr, III Corps.

Jackson Bridge (XT 425-168)
See Jackson, FSB. Hau Nghia Pr, III Corps.

Jackson Hole, LZ (YA 902-315)
At or adj to Le Thanh, apx 4 km NNW LZ Meredith, 20 km WNW the Oasis and 42 km SW Pleiku. 4th Div AO, '70. Data per Jim Claeys. Also listed at YA 890-310 and 898-315, Jul67-Oct70. See Le Thanh. Pleiku Pr, II Corps.

Jager, FSB (XS 397-494)
See Jaeger. Kien Hoa Pr, IV Corps.

Jaeger, FSB (XS 397-494)
A.k.a. FSB Jager. Along S bank of Mekong River, apx 12 km WSW My Tho and 15 km NW Truc Giang/Ben Tre. Built early '68, by 5th/60th Inf (Mech), 1st Bde/9th Inf

Div, as patrol base. Per Jim Stone, "was overrun by VC during last dying days of '68 Tet Offensive in Mekong Delta (24-25Feb68)." Attack in Summer or Fall '68 resulted in 100 NVA/VC KIA. Cited in *Doc: Platoon Medic*, p 15. Kien Hoa Pr, IV Corps.

Jaguar (n/a)
6Apr70, XXIV Corps proposed 101st Abn FSB.

Jake, FSB/LZ (XT 622-809)
A.k.a. LZ Bravo. At or near Tonle Cham, apx 10 km due S tip of Fishhook, 16 km SW An Loc, 32 km ESE Katum and 6 km NNE Xom Bau Lang. Built near a "rocky river." 1st/12th Cav, 1st Cav here Apr69, per Frank Penk, Jr. 3d/11th Arty here from Lai Khe with six-155s; and from Quan Loi, C Bty, 6th/27th Arty, with two-175mms, A Bty, 2d/35th Arty with six-155s moved here to supt Cambodian Invasion, May-Jun70, per *11th ACR Cambodia Invasion AAR, 1st Cav Div, May-Jun70*, courtesy Lou Rochat. [296] Also at XT 625-813 and 619-825. Tay Ninh Pr, III Corps.

Jamaica Bay, Dredge (n/a)
During the war, one of world's largest dredges. Sunk by VC sappers 10Jan69, thereby temporarily halting efforts to build 9th Inf Div's new artificial island basecamp at Dong Tam. See Dong Tam. Dinh Tuong Pr, IV Corps.

Jame, LZ (BR 786-936)
Apx 7 km WSW Bong Son, 11 km due N Ha Tay AF and about 2 km S the Song An Lao. Possibly "James" or "Jamie?" Oct66. Binh Dinh Pr, II Corps.

James, LZ (BR 786-936)
See Jame. Binh Dinh Pr, II Corps.

James N. Crocker Compound (XS 4-4?)
At Chau Thanh, which was apparently near Dong Tam/My Tho, roughly 50 km SW Saigon? Named to honor Capt. James N Crocker, USA KIA 8Jul69, near Trung An, when his helicopter, loaded with wounded ARVN soldiers rescued in daring lndg, exploded in mid-air after receiving ground fire immed after lift-off. Dedicated 8Nov69. *Vietnam Military Lore, 1959-1973* lists Chau Thanh as being in Binh Duong Pr; however, data suggests it was in Dinh Tuong Pr, because Trung An is in listed grid square. Dinh Tuong Pr?, III Corps.

Jamestown, USS (n/a)
AGTR-3. Aux Ship, per Ralph Fries.

Jamie, LZ (BR 786-936)
See Jame. Binh Dinh Pr, II Corps.

Jamie, FSB/LZ (XT 482-715)
Apx 35 km NE Tay Ninh, 15 km NE FSB Grant, 18 km SW Bo Tuc. 2d/7th Cav here '68. Elements of 2d/60th(?) here early Jun70, per David Argabright. Attacked by NVA 95C RGT in early Jun69 (along with FSBs Barbara, Grant and Phyllis) as part of planned attack on Tay Ninh. Existed 11-25Feb70, as 1 of 7 FSBs opened and closed in as many weeks by 2d/8th Cav, 1st Cav, prior to Cambodian Incursion (7 were: Jamie, Mary Gwen, Heather, Victor, Flashner, Drum and Illingworth). Per Peter Cole, is mentioned in *1st Cav Op Rpt, Feb70/Apr70*, p 68, and 1st Cav *Yearbook* Aug65-Dec69, p 75, 185, 214, 250, 294, and in *Incursion*. Also listed at XT 478-713, 482-715 and 555-984(Aug70). Tay Ninh Pr, III Corps. [297]

Jamie, FSB (XT 555-984)
Apx 2 km from Cambodian border, 19 km SW Loc Ninh and 10 km NNE tip of Fishhook. Aug70. Also listed at XT 482-715, Apr69-May70. Binh Long Pr, III Corps.

Jan, FSB (n/a)
Cited in *1st Cav Op Rpt, Feb70/Apr70*, p 12, per Peter Cole. During that period, Cav was in NW III Corps. Likely III Corps.

Jane, FSB (YS 456-837)
On W side of LTL-2 apx 16.5 km NNE Nui Dat, 5 km N FSB Alanbrooke and 1 km S FSB Avenger. On 1ATF NCO trng map per John Hollett. Phuoc Tuy Pr, III Corps.

Jane, LZ (BS 660-758)
Overlooked Hwy 523, apx 1.5 km N the Song Tra Khuc River, 3.5 km NNE Quang Ngai and 2 km E QL-1. Americal List. Quang Ngai, I Corps.

Jane, LZ (XT 202-341)
Above the Angel's Wing, apx 6 km NE Cambodia, 18 km SSE Tay Ninh West AF and 27 km NNW Duc Hue. Mar66. Tay Ninh Pr, III Corps.

Jane, LZ (YA 583-590)
Apx 2 km from Cambodia, 26 km WSW Plei Djereng (old) AF, 6 km SE Phum Hay (C) and 65 km W Pleiku. Jan66. Kontum Pr, II Corps.

Jane, LZ (ZT 003-872)
Remote site apx 30 km WNW Tan Phat AF/Bao Loc, 26 km N Da Hoa and 110 km NE Bien Hoa AB. Feb67. Lam Dong Pr, II Corps.

Jane, LZ/FSB (YD 379-437)
Apx 11 km SSE Quang Tri and 6 km W QL-1. 1st Cav, '68. Elements of 4th/60th, E/71st and I,/29th here late 67-Jan68 (Dusters, Quads, Searchlights); AO of 1/44th Arty and others, per Paul Kopsick. Map is L-7014-6442-3, per Ken Burrington. Also listed at YD 373-429 per Gen J. Cushman, CO 2d Bde/101st Abn, as well as at YD 375-430, 379-430 and 380-425. Quang Tri Pr, Corps.

Jane, LZ (ZA 057-436)
S of Rte 509, apx 19 km WSW Pleiku, 3 km SW Ban Duc, 7 km ENE Plei Del, and 18 km NW Catecka AF. 1st Cav and/or 4th Div FSB. Data per Dick Arnold as per Jan-Mar69 1st/35th Inf Bn Daily Logs. Pleiku Pr, II Corps.

Jane Mansfield Mountains (BR 90-76)
See Miss America Mtns. Binh Dinh Pr, II Corps.

Janet, FSB (YS 258-679)
On W side of QL-15 apx 18 km due W Nui Dat, 1 km S FSB Penny and 2.5 km NW FSB South Dakota. On 1ATF NCO trng map per John Hollett. See Xuyen Moc, FSB. Phuoc Tuy Pr, III Corps.

Janet, FSB (YS 65-68)
A.k.a. FSB Xuyen Moc? Along Rte-23 at Xuyen Moc AF, apx 22 km due E Nui Dat, 12 km ENE Dat Do. 161 Bty, RNZA (Horsford's Bty 18Mar69-18Sep69) firebase here 24-31Aug69. Phuoc Tuy Pr, III Corps.

Janet, FSB (YU 122-085)
On Rte 311, apx 4 km NW Song Be AF, 38 km E Loc Ninh and 5 km WNW Phuoc Binh. 5th/7th Cav, 1st Cav, '69. Grid per Frank Penk, Jr. Also listed at YU 094-102 and YU 094-105 and unknown which grid is correct or if base was moved? Phuoc Long Pr, III Corps.

Janet, FSB (YU-094-102)
A.k.a. Janett. Along Rte 311, apx 6 km NW Song Be AF, 37 km E Loc Ninh and 7 km WNW Phuoc Binh. Also listed at YU 094-105 and 122-085 but unknown which grid is correct or if base moved? Phuoc Long Pr, III Corps.
Janet, LZ (BS 604-300)
See Janice. Quang Ngai Pr, I Corps.
Janet, LZ/FSB (XT 702-208)
Apx 6 km ENE Cu Chi, 11 km WNW Phu Cuong and 2 km S Ben Cat. Binh Duong Pr, III Corps.
Janet, LZ/FSB (YA 896-243)
Apx 41 km SW Pleiku, 4 km W Plei Luong and 6 km ESE Duc Co. 10th Cav, 4th Div here. Name per Bob Patsfield, grid per Dick Arnold as per Jan-Mar69 1st/35th Inf Bn daily logs. Pleiku Pr, II Corps.
Janet, LZ (YD 215-375)
Apx 7 km SE Ba Long AF and 20 km SW Quang Tri. XXIV Corps grid per D. Armstrong. Quang Tri Pr, I Corps.
Janet, LZ (YU 094-104)
See FSB Janet at grid. Phuoc Long Pr, III Corps.
Janett, LZ (YU 094-104)
See FSB Janet at grid. Phuoc Long Pr, III Corps.
Janie, FSB (XT 482-715)
Apx 26 km SE Katum, 25 km NE Nui Ba Den and 6 km SSW Bao Trai. Aug70. Tay Ninh Pr, III Corps.
Janice, LZ (BS 604-300)
Apx 4 km due E Can So and 6 km SE Ba To New AF. 1st Cav or Americal? Name/grid per Dan Gillotti, 15th Arty. Quang Ngai Pr, I Corps.
Japanese Invasion of Vietnam (n/a)
See Glossary.
Jarrett, FSB (XT 418-125)
Along Song Vam Co Dong River, apx 9 km ENE Duc Hue AF and 24 km WSW Cu Chi. Temporary base of 6th/31st Inf, 9th Inf Div. May70. Hau Nghia Pr, III Corps.
Jason, USS (n/a)
AR-8. Repair Ship. US 7th Flt or MRF? Per Ralph Fries.
Javelin, LZ (ZC 083-378)
A.k.a. COB Javelin or FSB Javelin. Apx 4 km NNW FSB Battle-Ax, 23 km WSW Phuoc Binh, 27 km NNE Kham Duc AF 7 km N FSB Bolo, 3 km SE FSB Broadsword, and 17 km SW An Hoa CB. 1st Mar Div during Task Force Yankee's assault of Base Area 112, Jan-Feb69. On map in *US Marines in Vietnam-1969*, p 90. Apr70 XXIV Corps grid per Don Armstrong. Quang Nam Pr, I Corps.
Jay, FSB (BS 714-293)
Apx 14 km SW Duc Pho and 4 km E Con So. 1st Cav. Name/grid per Dan Gillotti. Quang Ngai Pr, I Corps.
Jay, FSB (XT 039-750)
A.k.a. LZ Jay. Along Cambodian border in War Zone D, apx 45 km NW Nui Ba Den and 10 km S of FSB Illingworth. 2d/7th Cav, 1st Cav, attacked by Plt of 272d NVA Rgt, 29-30Mar70, resulting in 15 US KIA, 53 US WIA. Listed at both XT 039-750 and XT 387-510?, and at XT 03-75 per 18th Mil History Det, 25th Inf Div, rpt for 2-6Apr70. See FSB Jay listed at XT 387-510. Tay Ninh Pr, III Corps. [298]
Jay, FSB (XT 387-510?)
If grid correct, was 10 km WNW Dau Tieng, 15 km W Tay Ninh and 15 km SE Nui Ba Den. See FSB Jay listed at XT 039-750. Tay Ninh Pr, III Corps.
Jean, FSB (YA 806-233)
A.k.a. LZ Jean. Per Rodger Leffler, D/1/35th, it, "was 5 or 6 km west of Duc Co on a hill overlooking Rte 19." Listed grid however indicates it was actually along Rte 198 (not 19), apx 5 km SW Duc Co, and 49 km SW Pleiku. Apparently built Nov68 by 4th Div. C/D Cos, 1st/35th Inf, 4th Div attacked 13Nov68, with 1 US KIA, 3 WIA. Grid per 4th Div Ops Rpt for period ending 31Jan69; also listed at YA 808-233 in that rpt. Pleiku Pr, II Corps. [299]
Jeanne, FSB (YD 552-395)
See Jeanne, LZ, at grid. Thua Thien Pr, I Corps.
Jeanne, FSB (YU 558-178)
Apx 17 km NE Duc Phong, 4 km W FSB Elaine, 24 km WSW Nhon Co AF and 40 km ENE Song Be. Closed 30Aug70, by 2d/12th Cav. Reopened 31Oct70. Cited in *1st Cav Op Rpt, May-Jul70*, p 18, 38, and data per *1st Cav Div Op Rpt, ending 31Oct70*, courtesy Peter Cole. Phuoc Long Pr, III Corps.
Jeanne, LZ/FSB (YD 552-395)
A.k.a. LZ/FSB Jean and Jeannie. In coastal sands apx 8 km NNE Camp Evans, 25 km NW Hue, 4 km SW Ap Tay Hoang and 7 km NE QL-1. D/2d/7th Cav, 1st Cav and Bty of 1st/21st Arty here mid '68. Described as an "oasis in sand," with a huge green-nylon, cargo parachute at its center covering mess area that was landmark visible for miles. Suptd by LZ/FSB Jack. XXIV Corps 101st Abn inactive FSB grid per Don Armstrong. Also listed at YD 548-388. Thua Thien Pr, I Corps.
Jeannie, FSB (n/a)
199th LIB FSB/patrol base on 199th LIB Assn list. Grid unknown. III Corps.
Jeannie, LZ/FSB (YD 548-388)
See Jeanne, LZ, at grid. Thua Thien Pr, I Corps.
Jeb Stuart, Operation (n/a)
22Jan-31mar68. 1st Cav op. Followed Pershing. 3,268 rptd NVA/VC KIA, per *Vietnam Order of Battle*, pp 9-14. Quang Tri Pr, I Corps.
Jeb Stuart III, Operation (n/a)
17May-3Nov68. 1st Cav op. 2,114 rptd NVA/VC KIA, per *Vietnam Order of Battle*, pp 9-14. Quang Tri and Thua Thien Pr, I Corps.
Jeff, LZ (BS 688-328)
In mtns apx 24 km SSE Mo Duc/Quang Hien, 18 km due W FSB Debbie-Thunder, 14 km SW Duc Pho AF and SE FSB San Juan Hill. Apparently put into use 22Apr69 suptg southern Song Ve Valley ops. Americal list. Also listed at BS 689-323. Quang Ngai Pr, I Corps.
Jefferson, FSB (AN 831-520)
Apx 42 km due N Phan Thiet and 3 km SSE Ap Gia Bac. Jul68. Lam Dong Pr, II Corps.
Jefferson Glenn/Op Ord 13-70 (n/a)
5Sep70-6Apr71. Last offensive op of war for US ground forces. 101st Abn, SVN govt and 1st ARVN Inf Div ops. 2,026 rptd NVA/VC KIA, per *Vietnam Order of Battle*, pp 9-14. Thua Thien Pr, I Corps.
Jeffries, FSB (n/a)
No data. Name per W. Stan Tyson (CO 1st/12th Cav Sep71-Jun72), as related by Peter Cole. During that period, Cav was in NW III Corps.
Jennifer's Strip Airfield (PC 90-20)
LS-259. CIA/SF, per *Air Facilities Data-Laos.*

Jennings County, USS (n/a)
LST-846. USN Landing Ship, Tank. Suptd 9th Inf Div/MRF in '67-68, per MRF Assn website at www.mrfa.org. Decom 25Sep70. III/IV Corps?

Jenny, FSB (YS 49-62?)
If correct, apparently at or near FSB Horseshoe, apx 9 km SE Nui Dat. Map at p 74 of *Vietnam Gunners* shows FSB Jenny at both YS 22-85 in Bien Hoa Pr and at listed grid. On 1ATF NCO trng map per John Hollett also at YS 22-85. Phuoc Tuy Pr, III Corps.

Jenny, FSB (YS 224-857)
Apx 28 km NW Nui Dat, 4 km E QL-15, 4 km NE FSB Archer, 8 km NW FSB Dyke and 3 km W FSB Hawk. 161 Bty, RNZA (Hitching's Bty 14Apr68-18Mar69) FSB set here 29Jan17Feb69. On 1ATF NCO trng map per John Hollett. Map at p 74 of *Vietnam Gunners* shows FSB Jenny at both YS 49-63 (near FSB Horseshoe) in Phuoc Tuy Pr, and at listed grid. Bien Hoa Pr, III Corps.

Jenny, LZ (BR 851-550)
Apx 2 km NW Tan Hoa, 13 km SSW Phu My, 38 km ENE An Khe and 4 km W QL-1. C Bty, 7th/15th Arty here. Grid per Dan Gillotti/15th Arty Assn. Binh Dinh Pr, II Corps.

Jenny, LZ (YB or ZB)
Possibly at or near Dak Seang or Dak To? Built on abnd US Air strip and used by Col David Hackworth's 1/327th Inf, 101st Abn, during Battle of Toumorong, Op Hawthorne II, Jun66? Discussed in *Battles in the Monsoon*, p 278. Kontum Pr, II Corps.

Jerome, Camp (AQ 863-023?)
Listed at AQ 063-023, but no such grid exists. Instead may have been at AQ 863-023? If speculation correct, then site was apx 6 km SE Ban Me Thuot City AF and 3 km WSW Ban Me Thuot East AR. Jul70. Darlac Pr, II Corps.

Jerome, FSB (YD 187-274)
A.k.a. Dong Ba Le and Hill 1102. Apx 54 km WNW Hue, 34 km WSW Camp Evans and 25 km SSE Mai Loc. Also listed as 189-283 and 188-275. Quang Tri Pr, I Corps.

Jerome County, USS (n/a)
LST-848. USN Landing Ship, Tank. SVN service with 9th Inf Div/MRF. See www.mrfa.org. Sent to VN 1Apr70. III/IV Corps?

Jerraube, Genevieve de Galard-Jerraube (n/a)
See Angel of DBP in Glossary.

Jerri, FSB/LZ (XU 963-235)
A.k.a. Jerry. Apx 24 km ESE Loc Ninh, 19 km WSW Song Be AF and 4 km E the Song Be. 1st/7th Cav, Sep69 1st/8th Cav, Sep69, 1st/5th Cav, Nov69, 1st/12th Cav, Dec69. Also listed at XU 965-225, and "YU" 963-222 (error?). Grid per Frank Penk, Jr. Phuoc Long Pr, III Corps.

Jerry, LZ (BN 782-612)
Apx 4 km W of coast, 6 km WSW Thon Son Hai, 18 km SSW Phan Rang and 33 km NE Tuy Phong. Mar67. Ninh Thuan Pr, II Corps.

Jerry Guerra Bridge (CQ 06-73?)
See Guerra Bridge. Binh Dinh Pr, II Corps.

Jesparit, HMV (YS)
Logistical transport initially manned by civilians, but later commissioned into Royal Aussie Navy due to union bans. Per Eddie Tricker, *Jeparit* routinely off-loaded ANZAC supplies at Vung Tau (1ATF, HQ Nui Dat). *Sydney*, *Boonaroo* and *Jesparit* made total of 42 trips to VN carrying almost 200,000 DW tons of cargo, per www.navy.gov.au/4_history/ vietnam.htm. III Corps.

Jess, LZ/FSB (XT 188-719)
Apx 19 km due N Tay Ninh West, 24 km SW Katum AF and 16 km NW Nui Ba Den. 2d/5th Cav, 1st Cav here in'68, per Frank Penk, Jr. (1st Cav '68-70). Also listed at XT 188-717, per Peter Cole. Tay Ninh Pr, III Corps.

Jester, LZ/FSB (AN 793-436)
Apx 11 km NW Nui Ba, 20 km NNW Thien Giao and 30 km NNE Phan Thiet. D/2/320th Arty. 3d/506th/101st Abn AO. Info/grid per Jerry Berry. Binh Thuan Pr, II Corps.

Jewel, FSB (n/a)
See Jewell. III Corps?

Jewell, FSB (n/a)
A.k.a. Jewel. Location unknown, but was built Feb70-Apr70, by B/8th Engr Bn, 1st Cav.[300] Possibly named to honor one of following: SSgt David P., KIA 15Dec67; Cpl Philip L., KIA 21Nov69; or Sp4 Steven T., KIA 26Jan66. Cited in *1st Cav Op Rpt, Feb70/Apr70*, p 13, per Peter Cole. During period, Cav was in NW III Corps.

Jilian, FSB (YT 338-064)
Near intersection of Rtes 321 and 25, apx 5 km S QL-1, 48 km ENE Nui Dat, 15 km WNW FSB Wattle, and 20 km NW FSB Buffalo. 12 km WSW Xuan Loc, 4 km E FSB Sally, 14 km NW Blackhorse Basecamp and 12 km E FSB Evans. 161 Bty, RNZA (Horsford's Bty 18Mar69-18Sep69) FSB set here 27Mar-2Apr69. Named after Bty CO's wife. While suptg US units here 29Mar69, the "Yanks" radioed back rpt for one 161 Bty mission that went: "three elephants KIA."[301] On 1ATF NCO trng map per John Hollett. Sp Jillian *in Vietnam Gunners* and Jilian on 1ATF NCO Map? Long Khanh Pr, III Corps.

Jill, FSB (XT 952-941)
A.k.a. FSB Wescott. Apx 26 km SE Loc Ninh, 23 km SW Song Be AF and 6 km E Srok Phu Mieng. 2d/7th Cav, 1st Cav here '68 and reopened as FSB Wescott by 1st/8th Cav, Jul69. 1st/7th Cav, 1st Cav, Sep69. On 12Nov68, 2d/505th Inf, and Bty B 2/321st Arty, 82d Abn were airlifted to FSB Eleanor (XT 916-736) in order to block elements of 5th VC Div, and on 14 Jan69, Bn shifted to Jill. Grid per Frank Penk, Jr. 3d Bde/82d Abn also here per Butch Sincock. Also listed at XT 955-905, which is apx 4 km S listed grid and 21 km E and slightly N An Loc. Unknown if base moved or grid in error? Phuoc Long Pr, III Corps.

Jill, FSB (XT 955-905)
A.k.a. FSB Wescott. Along Song Be River, apx 21 km E and slightly N An Loc, 28 km SE Loc Ninh and 7 km SE Srok Phu Mieng. Listed at XT 988-902 and 952-941 (apx 4 km N listed grid), and unknown if base moved or grid in error? Also listed at "YT" 955-905, but that is thought to be an error. Phuoc Long Pr, III Corps.

Jill, FSB (YS 302-770)
Apx 16 km NW Nui Dat. On 1ATF NCO trng map per John Hollett. Phuoc Tuy Pr, III Corps.

Jill, FSB (YT 955-906?)
See Jill at XT 955-905. Also listed at XT 955-906, and said to have been a 1st Cav base in III Corps, so likely XT is correct grid zone. If YT correct, was apx 17 km NW Tan Phat AF/Bao Loc. Name/grid per Dan Gillotti, 15th Arty. Phouc Long Pr, II Corps**?**

Jillian, FSB (YT 338-064)
See Jilian. Long Khanh Pr, III Corps.
Jim, FSB (XT 882-382)
Apx 2 km SE Phu Giao and 12 km E Lai Khe. Dec68-Feb69. Also at XT 885-393. Binh Duong Pr, III Corps.
Jim, LZ (BR 738-463)
Apx 5 NE Binh Khe and 25 km due E An Khe. Oct65. Binh Dinh Pr, II Corps.
Jo Ann, FSB (ZS 137-954)
Along Song Phan River, apx 28 km WSW Phan Thiet, 19 km NE Ham Tan AF, 6 km NNW Xom Rey and 4 km W peak Nui Takou Mtn. Opened or reopened 18Sep70, closed 7Oct70. 2d/11th ACR. Reopened 29)ct70, by same unit, per *1st Cav Div Op Rpt, ending 31Oct70*, courtesy Peter Cole. Binh Tuy Pr, III Corps.
Jo Ann, LZ (BR 230-399)
Apx 27 km WSW An Khe and 23 km SE Suoi Doi AF. Sep69. Binh Dinh Pr, II Corps.
Joan, FSB (XD 939-601)
Near Cam Lo River20 km W and slightly N Cam Lo, 2 km W FSB Bird, 42 km WNW Quang Tri and 19 km NW Mai Loc. 101st Abn inactive FSB grid per Don Armstrong. Quang Tri Pr, I Corps.
Joan, FSB/LZ (YA 842-251)
At or immed SE of Duc Co AF, apx 45 km SW Pleiku. Nov68-Oct69. Also at YA 842-280. Pleiku Pr, II Corps.
Joan, FSB (YT 336-106)
Along QL-1 near its intersection with QL-20, apx 12 km due W Xuan Loc, 35 km WNW Bien Hoa AB and 10 km SSW Xa Gia Kiem. Long Khanh Pr, III Corps.
Joan, FSB (YU 335-108)
Remote site apx 12 km NW Duc Phong AF/SF camp and 16 km due E Song Be City AF. "FSBs Django and Joan closed on 23 and 25Feb70 respectively and 8th Abn Bn displaced to establish FSB Lolita (YU 369-261). As move N gained momentum and enemy activity increased, FSB's Candy, Loan, and Audie were established on 25, 26 and 27 Feb70 respectively...The 1st Abn Bn (-) moved to establish FSB Loan, leaving one rifle Co to secure FSB Judie." [302] Phuoc Long Pr, III Corps.
Joan, LZ/FSB (YA 842-280)
Apx 6 km NNE Plei Girao Kla, 3 km SSE Duc Co AF, 12 km E Cambodia and 45 km SW Pleiku. Apparently built Nov68 by 4th Div. Grid per 4th Div Ops Report for period ending 31Jan69. A Bty, 5th/16th Arty here Dec69. Also listed at YA 842-251 per 4th Div 31Jan70 ORLL courtesy Jim Henderson. Also listed at YA 884-280, but that is thought to be an error? Kontum Pr, II Corps. [303]
Joanie, LZ (BT 296-232)
At NW edge of Tam Ky at or near Tam Key Alternate AF, apx 1 km W QL-1 and 28 km NW Cu Lai. Apr-Sep70. Apparently moved to BT 426-089. Quang Tin Pr, I Corps.
Joanie, LZ (BT 426-089)
Apx 3 km W Ql-1, some 18 km SE Tam Ky, 4 km WNW Khuong Quang and 12 km NE Chu Lai. Oct70. Apparently moved here from BT 296-232? Quang Tin Pr, I Corps.
Joanie, FSB (XU or YU?)
Per John Mowat (D/71st Arty Quad .50's in '70) was near Loc Ninh. Possibly LZ Joan at YU 335-108? Binh Long or Phuoc Long Pr, III Corps.
Joann, FSB/LZ (various)
See Jo Ann, FSB/LZ.
Joe, FSB (XT 629-669)
Near Minh Thanh AF, apx 25 km WSW An Loc, 30 km WSW FSB Eleanor, 43 km ENE Tay Ninh and 24 km SSE tip of Fishhook. 2d/8th Cav, Oct-68, 5th/7th Cav, 1st Cav here in'68 per Frank Penk, Jr. 2d/505th Inf, 82d Abn moved here from FSB Odessa, 11Feb69, and stayed to 14Feb69. 3d Bde/82d Abn and 1st Cav lists. Also listed at XT 629-663 and XT 638-672. Binh Long Pr, III Corps.
Joe, FSB (YD 882-158)
Just W Hwy 595, on S edge of Thon My Luong, apx 1 km N the W end of Phu Bai AF rwy. 101st Abn inactive FSB grid per Don Armstrong. Thua Thien Pr, I Corps.
Joe, LZ (BR 635-510)
Overlooking Song Con River Valley, apx 2 km NW Tien Thuan and 16 km ENE An Khe. 1st Cav, Nov65. Binh Dinh Pr, II Corps.
Joe, LZ (XT 768-681)
Apx 4 km W Xom Ruong, 20 km S An Loc and 7 km due N Chon Thanh AF. Jul67. Binh Long Pr, III Corps.
Joe Log BOQ (XS 8-9)
At 574 Nguyen Trai St., Saigon, Mar65. Korean officers billeted here beginning Oct 65, pending completion of quarters to be supplied by SVN Government, per *Vietnam Military Lore, 1959-1973*. Gia Dinh Pr, III Corps.
JOG (n/a)
See Glossary.
John, FSB (BS 542-384)
Apx 27 km due W Duc Pho AF/QL-1. Grid per Americal Assn list arty ORLL. See FSB Jon. Quang Ngai Pr, I Corps.
John, LZ (BN 743-598)
Apx 22 km SSW Phan Rang. '67. Ninh Thuan Pr, II Corps.
John, LZ (BS 917-238)
Along QL-1, apx 9 km NNE Gia An and 18 km SE Duc Pho AF. May67. Listed in II Corps, but grid in I Corps? Quang Ngai Pr, I Corps.
John, LZ (XD 983-439)
Along QL-9, apx 5 km SSW Ca Lu and 35 km WSW Quang Tri. Apr68. Quang Tri Pr, I Corps.
John, LZ (XS 656-832)
Apx 20 km SW Tan Son Nhut AB and 6 km NW Ben Chanh. Feb66. Long An Pr, III Corps.
John, LZ (XT 641-115)
Apx 6 km N Cu Chi and 21 km SW Lai Khe. Mar66. Hau Nghia Pr, III Corps.
John A. Bole, USS (n/a)
DD-755, per Ralph Fries.
John Henry, LZ/FSB (BR 674-708)
In mtns along road between Vinh Thanh/Dinh Binh and Nghia Dinh, apx 4 km SW Nghia Dinh, 12 km NE Vinh Thanh, 32 km NE An Khe and 11 km SSE LZ Challenge. 4th Div AO, '70; B Bty, 6th/29th Arty here 21Aug70. Name/grid per Jim Claeys. Also mentioned on 129th AHC's webpage at www.vhfcn.org/129th/129thhist.htm. Binh Dinh Pr, II Corps.
John F. McDermott, Camp (CP 051-501)
See McDermott, Camp. Khanh Hoa Pr, II Corps.

John L. Houston BEQ (XS 8-9)
At 1015 Tran Hung Dao St., Apr 65, 66 rms, Saigon. Per *Vietnam Military Lore, 1959-1973*. Gia Dinh Pr, III Corps.
John Monash. HMAS (n/a)
AV-1351. Australian LSM serving under US 7th Flt. Likely purchased from US in '60.
John Page, Army Vessel (n/a)
See *Lt Col John U. D. Page*.
John Paul Jones, USS (n/a)
DDG-32. Guided-Missile DD, per Ralph Fries.
John Paul Vann Crash Site (ZA 20-68?)
Between 2 streams (the Khol and Drou) and on E side QL-14, apx 5 km S Chu Pao Pass, 20 km S Kontum, immed E QL-14 bridge over the Khol and just W Ro Uay. Grid is est based on map in *A Bright Shining Lie*, with data at p786. Pleiku or Kontum Pr, II Corps.
John R. Craig, USS (n/a)
DD 885. Authorized to patrol no closer than 4 mi off NVN coast, 25Fe-6Mar64, then joined by *USS Maddox*. See *Maddox, USS.*[304]
John S. McCain, USS (n/a)
DDG-35. Guided-Missile DD, per Ralph Fries.
John U. D. Page, Army Vessel (n/a)
See *Lt Col John U.D. Page*.
John W. Thomason, USS (n/a)
DD-760, per Ralph Fries.
John W. Weeks, USS (n/a)
DD-701, per Ralph Fries.
Johnson, LZ ? (ZA 013-242)
A.k.a. LZ Jones (ZA 004-242)? Apx 11 km WSW Oasis AF and 34 km SW Pleiku. Jan66. Also listed with name Jones, same date? Pleiku Pr, II Corps.
Johnson City Airfield (BS 83-43?)
See Johnson City. Quang Ngai Pr, I Corps.
Johnson City (BS 83-43?)
Apx 500 meters inland from Red Beach, just N mouth of Tra Cau and Lo Bo Rivers, apx 4 km NE Duc Pho and 17 km SE Mo Duc. Fwd Operating Base of MAG-36, Opened 30Jan66, during Op Double Eagle. Per *USMC in Vietnam, 1966*, p 29. had supply point, TF HQ MAG-36 Combat Ops Ctr, MAS Sqdn 2 DASC (Direct Air Supt Ctr) and an "expeditionary AF," complete with tower, rwy, lndg lights and TAFDS. See Red Beach. Quang Ngai Pr, I Corps.
Joint Army-Navy Intelligence Service (n/a)
See JANIS in Glossary.
Joint General Staff HQ (XS 825-945)
On S edge of Tan Son Nhut AB. Presumably joint ARVN/MACV staff here? Gia Dinh Pr, III Corps.
Joint Operations Graphics Map (n/a)
See Glossary.
Joint Patrol Base Hunsley (XT 597-270)
See Hunsley, Patrol Base. Binh Duong Pr, III Corps.
Joint, LZ (YD 005-511)
Apx 3 km due N Ca Lu, 3 km E QL-9 and 13 km SW Cam Lo. Apr70 XXIV Corps grid per Don Armstrong. Quang Tri Pr, I Corps.
Jolley Trail (YU/YT)
NVA/VC infiltration rte running generally S from Cambodian near YU 20-40/Djamap on meandering path along E edge of N/S mtn mass E of Song Be and Phuoc Long/Quang Duc/Lam Dong Pr border to Long Khanh, Phuoc Tuy and Bin Tuy Provs. On map in *Rangers at War*, p 325. Origin of name unknown. Phuoc Long Pr, III Corps.
Jolly Green Giant (n/a)
See Glossary.
Jom Mog Airfield (PD 86-27)
LS-345. CIA/SF, per *Air Facilities Data-Laos.*
Jon, LZ (XT?)
Location unknown. On 12Aug69, VC threw simultaneous attacks at many III Corps 1st Cav bases, inc Quan Loi, LZ Becky, LZ Jon, LZ Kelly and LZ Caldwell. III Corps.
Joncs, Plaine de (XS 0-7)
See Plain of Reeds. III and IV Corps.
Jones, Camp (YT 07-12)
See Frenzell-Jones, Camp. Bien Hoa Pr, III Corps.
Jones, LZ ? (ZA 004-242)
Apx 11 km WSW Oasis AF and 34 km SW Pleiku. Jan66. Also listed as "Johnson," same date? Pleiku Pr, II Corps.
Jones, Claude, Preble USS (n/a)
DD-1033, per Ralph Fries.
Jones Creek (YD 23-79 to YD 29-66)
Nickname for tributary of Cau Viet River that ran between Ben Hai and Cua Viet rivers joining the Cua Viet at YD 29-66. USMC or 196th LIB gave it this name. Used by NVA throughout war as corridor feeding units into villes along its course to engage 3d Mar Div, elements of 196th LIB (Apr68) and later, Army's 5th Mech Div. Heavy fighting common and took many US/NVA lives, inc Battle of Dai Do (YD 255-639). 196th LIB battle here discussed in *Into The Valley.* Quang Tri Pr, I Corps.
Jones/Frenzell, Camp (YT 076-122)
See Frenzell-Jones, Camp. Bien Hoa Pr, III Corps.
Jose, FSB (YD 533-185)
Apx 19 km due W Hue, 20 km NE FSB Birmingham and 7 km SSW Ap Than Tan. Also listed at YD 538-184 and 540-185. May68. Thua Thien Pr, I Corps.
Joseph, LZ (BR 766-854)
Apx 4 km NW Ha Tay AF and 14 km SW Bong Son. Oct66. Binh Dinh Pr, II Corps.
Joseph Strauss, US S (n/a)
DDG 16. On 5Apr72, during Easter Offensive, Destroyers *Strauss* and *Richard B. Anderson* fired on Ben Hai Bridge in northern half of DMZ.
Jouett, USS (n/a)
DLG-29, Guided Missile DD Ldr, Ralph Fries.
Joy, FSB (YT 6726-6926)
A.k.a. LZ Joy. Apx 46 km NNW Vo Dat AF and 42 km WSW Tan Phat AF/Bao Loc. Per Bobby Jackson, site named for his wife and, "Built, occupied and abandoned by 1st/7th Cav after about 3 weeks in Apr or May69. Sustained one heavy attack," a fact confirmed by diary of "Frenchy" Torres, which notes that NVA attempted overrun, 9Jun69. Grid per aerial photo courtesy Mr. Jackson. AO Commanche Warrior. 4th/12th Inf, 199th LIB, and 1st/7th Cav, 1st Cav in '69. Also listed at YT 68-68 per Peter Cole. Long Khanh Pr?, III Corps.
Joy, FSB/LZ (YT 684-254)
Apx 8 km SSW Vo Dat AF. Also listed at YT 676-692, which is 46 km NNW Vo Dat AF, and at YT 768-256, which is 9 km SSE Vo Dat AF? Unknown if base was in all locations or if some grids in error? 1st/7th Cav, Sep69 1st/8th Cav, Sep69, 1st/5th Inf, Nov69, 1st/12th Cav,

Dec69, AO Commanche Warrior, per Frank Penk, Jr. Per diary of "Frenchy" Torres, NVA attempted to overrun Joy, 9Jun69. See FSB Joy at YT 6726-6926 for more detail. Binh Tuy Pr, III Corps.

Joy, LZ (BP 280-855)
Remote site apx 31 km ENE Lac Thien AF and 15 km due E Ban Ti Shrenh. Apr67. Darlac Pr, II Corps.

Joy, LZ (BR 844-614)
Apx 9 km SSW Phu My, 20 km NNW Phu Cat AB and 5 km W QL-1. Oct66. Binh Dinh Pr, II Corps.

Joy, LZ (YT 676-692)
See Joy, FSB at YT 684-254. Long Khanh Pr, III Corps.

Joy, LZ (YT 768-256)
See Joy, FSB, at YT 684-254. Binh Tuy Pr, III Corps.

Joyce, LZ/FSB (XT 262-383)
A.k.a. FSBs Bolt and Hull. Along QL-1, apx 17 km SW Tay Ninh West AF and 25 km WSW Dau Tieng. Aug67. Tay Ninh Pr, III Corps.

Joyce, LZ (YD 018-618)
Apx 8 km WNW Mai Loc, 6 km NNE Ca Lu 3 km S QL-9 and 11 km WSW Cam Lo. Apr70 XXIV Corps grid per Don Armstrong. Quang Tri Pr, I Corps.

Joyce, LZ (ZA 195-685)
At bridge site along QL-14 apx 7 km ENE Plei Mrong AF 22 km NNW Pleiku and 22 km SSW Kontum. Per Tom Lacombe. 29Jun69 issue of 4th Div newspaper states that LZs Penny, Nicole and Joyce gave arty supt to B/1st/12th Inf in contact 8 km S Highlander Heights, and also for B 2d/35th. 4th Inf Div, '69. Cited in *Time Heals No Wounds*, p 299. Jun-Oct69. Pleiku/Kontum Pr border, II Corps.

Joyce Airfield (BR 912-707)
A.k.a. LZ Joyce AF, Litts AF and Camp Litts AF (Possibly named to honor PFC James G. Litts, KIA 4Oct66). Along QL-1, apx 4 km NNE Phu My, 6 km NNE Crystal AF, and 27 km SSE Bong Son. "Insecure, abnd 29Jul68, AF # VA2-152," in Aug69 TAD per Frank Penk, Jr. Not in Feb73 TAD. Binh Dinh Pr, II Corps.

Juan Prieto Island (CR 1-3)
A.k.a. Hon Cau Island. Binh Dinh Pr, II Corps.

Juan Prieto, Ile (CR 1-3)
A.k.a. Hon Cau Island. Binh Dinh Pr, II Corps.

Juanita, FSB (YS 226-776)
Apx 24 km WNW Nui Dat, 17 km SW FSB Dampier, 1 km W QL-15 and 40 km SE Bien Hoa. Built beginning 11Apr69. 161 Bty, RNZA (Horsford's Bty 18Mar69-18Sep69) FSB set here 11-16Apr69. On 1ATF NCO trng map per John Hollett. Also listed at YS 22-77. In Phuoc Tuy Pr at Bien Hoa Pr border, III Corps.

Jud, FSB (XT 196-730)
Apx 16 km SW Thien Ngon AF, 16 km NW Nui Ba Den and 23 SSW Katum AF. Jan70. Tay Ninh Pr, III Corps.

Judie, FSB (YU 253-145)
A.k.a. Judy. Apx 8 km ENE Song Be City AF and 20 km WNW Duc Phong AF. 2d/12th Cav, 1st Cav, Oct-69. "FSBs Django and Joan closed on 23 and 25Feb70 respectively and 8th Abn Bn displaced to establish FSB Lolita (YU 369-261). As move N gained momentum and enemy activity increased, FSB's Candy, Loan, and Audie were established on 25, 26 and 27 Feb70 respectively...The 1st Abn Bn moved to estab FSB Loan, leaving one rifle Co to secure FSB Judie." [305] Grid/unit data per Frank Penk, Jr., quote per Peter Cole. Apr70. Also listed at XU 258-143? Phuoc Long Pr, III Corps.

Judy (n/a)
6Apr70, XXIV Corps proposed Americal FSB name.

Judy, FSB (n/a)
No data. Apparently 10th Cav, 4th Div here. Name per Bob Patsfield. Possibly Binh Dinh or Pleiku Pr, II Corps.

Judy, FSB (AN 071-134?)
Listed at AT 271-134; however, no such grid exists? If grid listed grid variation correct, was apx 22 km WNW Phan Thiet. 3d/506th/101st Abn. Binh Thuan Pr, II Corps.

Judy, FSB (AT 014-863?)
No such grid exists and proper grid unknown. Name/grid per Dan Gillotti, 15th Arty Assn, who indicates it was a 196th LIB FSB. I Corps.

Judy, FSB (XU 258-143?)
A.k.a. LZ Judie. Cambodian Incursion LZ? If grid correct, was apx 10 km due N Memot AF, 33 km SW Snuol AF and 17 km N the SVN border. Also listed at "YU" 258-143, and that grid is thought to be proper grid? Cambodia.

Judy, FSB (ZT 272-136)
Apx 16 km WNW Phan Thiet, 1.5 km E Xa Muong Man/Rte 342 and 1 km E Hill. 212. 3d/506th Inf, 101st Abn AO. Housed 105mm Btys. 3d/506th Inf, 3d Bde/101st Abn. Data per Jerry Berry. Binh Thuan Pr, II Corps.

Judy, LZ (AT 865-014)
Apx 32 km ESE Kham Duc, 28 km WSW Tien Phuoc, 16 km WNW Hau Duc, 3 km S peak of Hill 1064 and 48 km WSW Tam Ky. Grid courtesy Tom Poppell as taken from L-7014-6639-4 map. Also listed at AT 861-015 and 961-015. Quang Tin Pr, I Corps.

Judy, LZ (CR 082-626)
A.k.a. Hill 168. At S end of Isthmus, overlooking ocean, apx 3 km SE Vinh Loi, 23 km NE Phu Cat AB and 40 km SSE Bong Son. Oct66. Binh Dinh Pr, II Corps.

Judy, LZ (YU 254-149)
See Judie. Phuoc Long Pr, III Corps.

Julia, FSB (YS 225-815)
A.k.a. Basecamp Julia. Along QL-15, apx 15 km SSE Long Thanh AF, 7 km NNW Phu My and 25 km WNW Nui Dat. Jan69. Bien Hoa Pr, III Corps.

Julian, LZ (WT 966-758)
On Cambodian border at base of Dog's Head, apx 14 km SW Thien Ngon AF. Mar67. Tay Ninh Pr, III Corps.

Julie, FSB/LZ (XT 520-890)
Apx 4 km S Cambodian border, 6 km due W tip of Fishhook, 20 km due E Katum AF, and 24 km due W An Loc. Built 18-19Oct68 by elements of 2d/28th Inf, 1st Inf Div (Black Lions). Major battle here began 25Oct68, just after midnight, when at least 4 NVA Bns assaulted the one Bn of 1st Inf Div defending Julie and resulting in 8 US KIA, 128 NVA KIA. Discussed in *Charlie Company*, pp 47-59, 111-116. 1st Cav and 1st Inf Div. Also listed at XT 510-914 and 524-898. Tay Ninh Pr, III Corps.

Julie, FSB (YS 111-831)
Along QL-15, apx 14 km SE Long Thanh AF and 10 km NNW Phu My. Jul-Aug70. Bien Hoa Pr, III Corps.

Julie, LZ (XT 524-892)
See FSB Julie at grid. Tay Ninh Pr, III Corps.

Juliet, LZ (BT 077-273)
Apx 23 km WNW Tam Ky and 5 km SE Binh Son. Americal Div, 68-71. Name/grid per Dan Gillotti. Quang Tin Pr, I Corps.

Juliet, LZ (YA 970-051)
In Ia Drang Valley, apx 48 km SW Pleiku, 38 km W Phu Nhon, 7 km ENE LZ X-Ray, 12 km ENE peak Chu Pong Mtn, 16 km E Cambodia and 17 km due W Plei Me SF Camp. 2d/17th Arty here suptg 1st Cav, Aug 66. Cited in 1st Cav VN *Yearbook* Aug65-Dec69, p 120, per Peter Cole. Grid/arty data per Jack Picciolo. Pleiku Pr, II Corps.

Juliet 9 (YA/YB?)
E of SOG's Hotel-9 op zone; SOG AO that inc the Bra, per Don Lewis, 170th AHC.

July, LZ (XT 651-268)
Apx 17 km SW Lai Khe, 11 km N Cu Chi and 1 to 2 km from Song Saigon River. Jan66. Binh Duong Pr, III Corps.

June, LZ/FSB (YT 137-788)
Along QL-14, apx 6 km NE Dong Xoai and 17 km SW Bunard AF. Jan-Feb69. Phuoc Long Pr, III Corps.

Junction City, FSB (XT 620-328)
N Saigon River, apx 16 km WSW Lai Khe, 42 km NNW Tan Son Nhut AB and 22 km SE Dau Tieng. 1st Inf Div, '69. On *Low Level Hell's* 1st Div TAOR map. Dec68-Jan69. Also listed at XT 635-506, which is apx 15 km ENE Dau Tieng? Binh Duong Pr, III Corps.

Junction City, FSB (XT 635-506)
See Junction City at XT 62-32. Binh Duong Pr, III Corps.

Junction City, Operation (n/a)
22Feb-14May67. Took place in area against Cambodian border, described as having its SE corner at Ben Cat, it S border on line from Ben Cat to Cambodian border just N Tay Ninh, with QL-13 its E boundary. ARVN, 1st, 4th, and US IIFFV 25th Inf Divs, 196th LIB, 11th ACR and 173d Abn (22 US and 4 ARVN Bns) in largest op of war to that date. 2,728 rptd NVA/VC KIA, per *Vietnam Order of Battle*, pp 9-14. During this op, the 2d/503d Inf with A Bty, 319th Arty, under BG John Deane, Jr., made only combat parachute jump of war. DZ was in War Zone C. Elements of US 1st, 25th, 4th, and 9th Inf Divs, 173d Abn, 199th LIB, 11th ACR and ARVN also involved. Mission was to find COSVN. COSVN HQ itself escaped, but its Public Info Office for Psychological Propaganda and a COSVN Signal site were destroyed. Tay Ninh (et al) Pr, III Corps.

Junction City II, Operation (n/a)
20Mar-13Apr67. Minh Thanh area. 2d phase of op began with building of several FSBs along QL-13 from Lai Khe to Quan Loi. A Trp/3d Sqdn/5th Cav attacked N of Bau Bang by VC 273d Rgt, swarming over ACAVs and tanks on SE perimeter. Arty Supt by A Bty, 3d, 319th Arty helped save day. 227 VC KIA, 3 US KIA.

June, FSB (XT 70-75?)
Per *All the Way-The 3d Bde, 82d Abn Div in Vietnam 1968*, at p 50, June was 22 km E FSB Eleanor, and listed grid est from that description. If correct, was 16 km SSW An Loc, 7 km W QL-13 and 10 km NE Minh Thanh AF. Built by 2d/505th Inf, 82d Abn, 26Jan68, then abnd several days later for move to FSB Odessa. Binh Long Pr?, III Corps.

June, FSB/LZ (YD 297-402)
A.k.a. Hill 275. Per map courtesy Wm. Robert Stanley, was on Dong Ong Do Mtn (Hill 275), apx 13 km SSW Quang Tri, 12 km due E Ba Long AF. Quang Tri Pr, I Corps.

June, FSB (YT 137-785)
A.k.a. LZ June. Along QL-14, apx 8 km ENE Dong Xoai AF, 6 km ENE Dong Xoai and 18 km SW Bunard AF. Also listed at YT 137-788 per Peter Cole. 1st/7th Cav, 1st Cav, and 82 Abn here '69, per Frank Penk, Jr., who also lists grid as YT 143-796. Phuoc Long Pr, III Corps/

Junior, LZ (YD 013-643)
Apx 15 km NNW Mai Loc, 5 km due N FSB Fuller, 20 km N Vandegrift CB, 3 km S the DMZ and 11 km NW Cam Lo. 3d Mar Div, '69. On map at p 58, *US Marines in Vietnam-1969*. Apr70 XXIV Corps grid per Don Armstrong. Quang Tri Pr, I Corps.

Junkies (n/a)
See Glossary.

Junkmen (n/a)
See Glossary.

Junon, Strongpoint (TJ 9-6)
French position at Dien Bien Phu, 1/2 mi SE Main CP on W bank of Nam Yum River, 1/3 mi W E3 and 1/2 mi N the White Thai position. In Muong Thanh Valley apx 290 km W Hanoi. Op Castor, 20Nov53-7May54.

Jupiter, FSB (YT 497-492)
Apx 28 km NW Vo Dat, 14 km SE Lot Tan and overlooking valley of Song La Nao River (or tributary) to S. Long Khanh Pr, III Corps.

Jupiter, LZ (BQ 616-285)
Apx 22 km SW Son Ha, 10 km W Bau Ruk, 10 km SE Ban Yo, and 24 km SW Cung Son AF. 2d/17th Arty here supt 1st Cav, 6Jul66. Phu Yen Pr, II Corps.

Jupiter, LZ (BR 616-606?)
If grid correct, was at site of Vinh Thanh AF, apx 20 km NE An Khe. Name/grid per Dan Gillotti, 15th Arty Assn. Binh Dinh Pr, II Corps.

Jupiter, LZ (YD 096-655)
See Jupitor. Quang Tri Pr, I Corps.

Jupitor, LZ (YD 096-655)
Also sp Jupiter? Apx 6 km N to NNE Cam Lo, 16 km WNW Dong Ha and 2 km S Thon An Hoa. Apr70 XXIV Corps grid per Don Armstrong. Quang Tri Pr, I Corps.

KILO

Facility/Feature Name, Grid Coordinate, a.k.a. Name/History/Province/CTZ

Unless otherwise stated, 6-digit grid coordinates reference DMA L-7014, L-7015 or L-7016 series, 1:50,000 scale maps, while 2- and 4-digit coordinates reference AMS/DMA/NIMA 1:250,000, 1:500,000 and 1:1,000,000 scale maps. Unless otherwise stated, all heights are in meters. To convert meters to feet, multiply by 3.2808; feet to meters, multiply by .3048.

K Intervals (n/a)
See Glossary.

Ka Nao, Ea (BP 0-8)
Freshwater lake at 12°31N-108°15'E. See Krong Ana, Ea. Darlac Pr, II Corps.

Kabin Buri Airfield (n/a)
Apx 130 km ENE Bangkok per Feb67 Natl Geo Map. El. 75'. Thailand.

Kadena AFB (n/a)
On Okinawa. Not in the Indochina theater.

Kadena AFB Hospital (n/a)
See USAF Hospitals.

Kaiduong Bay (VS 7-2)
A.k.a. Vinh Cay Duong. Bay at 10°10'N-104°45'E. On NC48-06 JOG. Kien Giang Pr, IV Corps.

Kailap Point (US 8-2)
See Point Kailap. Kien Giang Pr, IV Corps.

Kala Airfield (AN 849-792)
See Djiring AF. Lam Dong Pr, II Corps.

Kala, FSB/LZ (YC 988-094)
At or immed W Kham Duc AF/SF camp, apx 75 km WSW Tam Ky and 7 km NNE Ngok Tavak AF. Apparently built 12Jul70, per Americal website list. Also listed at YC 987-097 and 987-089. Quang Tin Pr, I Corps.

Kalasin Airfield (UD4-1)
Abnd, per '66 NIMA data. At 16°26'00"N-103°31'00"E. NIMA data. Thailand.

Kalsu, James Robert, Capt. (n/a)
See Glossary.

Kamao Point (VQ 75)
See Point Kamao. An Xuyen Pr, IV Corps.

Kamao, Cape (VQ 7-5)
Mui Ca Mau. Coastal point at 8°38'N-104°44'E. On NC48-15 JOG. An Xuyen Pr, IV Corps.

Kamphaeng Saen Airfield (NR 9-5)
At 14°06'00"N-99°55'00"E. NIMA data. Thailand.

Kampon Chhnang Airfield (n/a)
5,000 rwy, 75 km NNW Phnom Penh. El. 49'. Cambodia.

Kampone Spoe (VT 4-6)
See Kompong Speu. Cambodia.

Kampone Spoe Airfield (n/a)
45 km WSW Phnom Penh. El. 98'. Cambodia.

Kampong Cham Airfield (WU 48-30)
Major AF on N bank of Mekong River apx 75 km NE Phnom Penh, 25 km SSE Chamkar Leu AF, 58 km SE Baray Hwy Strip and 105 km due W Snuol, per TPC K-10D. El. 148'. Cambodia.

Kampong Cham NDB (WU 48-30)
Non-Directional Air Nav Beacon site. Just S Phum Kav Ramuol. Cambodia.

Kampong Chhnang Airfield (n/a)
50 km NNW Phnom Penh. Per ONC-K-10, DMA, 1:1 million scale map. El. 50'. Cambodia.

Kampong Soam Airfield (US 36-75)
A.k.a. Sihanoukville AF. On coast, 190 km SW Phnom Penh, 18 km W Ream Kampong AF and 90 km from SVN border. TPC El. 20' (but 3' on Natl Geo map). Cambodia.

Kampong Spoe (VT 4-6)
See Kompong Speu. Cambodia.

Kampong-Sraka-Trey (XT 99-12)
The 16th Century name of Bien Hoa. See Bien Hoa.

Kampong Sralu Airfield (WA)
On W side of Mekong River at Laotian border, apx 90 km ESE Choam Khsan and 8 km SW Khong AF. Per TPC K-10A. El. 250'. Cambodia.

Kampong Thum Airfield (VV)
Apx 12 km NNE Kampong Thum South AF and 8 km NE Kampong Thum Hwy AF. TPC K-10A. El. 39'. Cambodia.

Kampong Thum Hwy Strip (VV)
Apx 130 km N Phnom Penh, 8 km SSW Kampong Thum AF, and on N edge of that city, per Dec67 DMA TPC K-10A map. El. 33'. Cambodia.

Kampong Thum South Airfield (VV)
Major AF with 3,900' rwy, 4 km S Kampong Thum Highway Strip, 10 km SSW Kampong Thum (North) AF. Per TPC K-10A. El. 40'. Cambodia.

Kampot Airfield (n/a)
On coast apx 135 km SW Phnom Penh, 35 km W the SVN border, 25 km WNW Pong Toek AF and 40 km NW Ha Tien SVN, per TPC K-10D. El. 42'. Cambodia.

Kampot Airfield (n/a)
On Feb67 Natl Geo Map. El. 13'. Cambodia.

Kampuchea (n/a)
Formerly Cambodia. Apx 70,000 sq mi in size and population of 7 million in '70. Ethnic composition was about 85% Khmer, 9% Viet and 5% Chinese during war.

Kampuchea Krom (XS, XR, WR)
Ancient Cambodian name for the Mekong Delta. SVN.

Kam-Ranh Bay (CP 0-1)
A.k.a. Vinh Cam Ranh. Bay at 11°53'N-109°10'E. On NC49-01 JOG. Khanh Hoa Pr, II Corps.

Kan Nak (n/a)
Mapsheet name of L-7014-6737-3. SVN.

Kanchanaburi (NR 4-6)
Apx 110 km WNW Bangkok. US Army Supt Cmd facility, Thailand. At various times occupied by 91st and 561st

Engr Cos, 558th S&S Bn and 305th S&S Co. SF camp or AO per *SF Order of Battle.* Thailand.

Kanchanaburi Airfield (NR 4-6)
At 14°08'00"N-99°27'00"E, or apx 110 km WNW Bangkok per Feb67 Natl Geo Map. NIMA data. El. 100'. Thailand.

Kangaroo, LZ (XD 855-493)
On Hill 1015 overlooking the Khe Sanh Valley, apx 4 km N Khe Sanh CB, 15 km WSW Ca Lu and 49 km WSW Quang Tri. Apr70 XXIV Corps grid per Don Armstrong. Quang Tri Pr, I Corps.

Kangaroo Heliport (YS 434-670)
At or near Luscombe AF/Nui Dat, and apx 28 km NNE to NE Vung Tau. "Heliport #737, alt?, approach E to W depending on wind. CAUTION-Luscombe Afld 1000 meters from pad, F/W Ops. PSP prk area 1,000' x 300'. Arty advsy-Phuoc Tuy 369.6, 40.7." At 10°32'N 107°14'E, per Feb73 TAD. Phuoc Tuy Pr, III Corps.

Kannack (BR 42-63)
Apx 24 km W Vinh Thanh (Happy) Valley and 25 km due N An Khe/Camp Radcliff. On W bank of Song Ba River. See Kannack SF camp. Binh Dinh Pr, II Corps.

Kannack, FSB (BR 42-63?)
Mentioned at www3.servtech.com/vhpa/info /panel/battle in document 70010920.htm. Presumably at or near Kannack AF? 1st Cav and/or 4th Div FSB. Grid is est. Binh Dinh Pr, II Corps.

Kannack Airfield (BR 423-650)
Apx 20 km NNW An Khe, 65 km SE Kontum AF, 58 km SW LZ English, per TPC K-10A. El. 1,575'. Also listed at BR 419-648 and as "Insecure, abnd, AF # VA2-99," in Aug69 TAD per Frank Penk, Jr. Binh Dinh Pr, II Corps.

Kannack SF Camp (BR 423-629)
Apx 24 km W Vinh Thanh (Happy) Valley, 25 km due N An Khe/Camp Radcliff. On W bank of Song Ba River. The Son Hai Co made heroic and famous defense of SF CIDG Camp here in Aug65, despite fact that 90 man CIDG Co was outnumbered 10 to 1. 5th SF Grp, Det. A-231, Dec64, A-221 (was 112) Oct 6. Grid per *Special Order of Battle.* Moved to Cung Son. Also listed at BR 422-647, Mar66. Binh Dinh Pr, II Corps.

Kansas, LZ (YD 098-206)
Apx 20 km SSE Ba Long AF, 39 km SSW Quang Tri and 32 km SW Khe Sanh CB. Apr70 XXIV Corps grid per Don Armstrong. Quang Tri Pr, I Corps.

Kaoh Chan Island (XV 1-4)
See Ko Chan. Cambodian.

Kaoh Nhek Airfield (YV)
4,000' rwy, 32 km SSW Sre Mat AF, 50 km W SVN border, per TPC K-10A. El. 440'. Cambodia.

Kara, LZ (AQ 805-194)
Apx 4 km NW Quang Nhieu and 16 km due N Ban Me Thuot. Feb66. Darlac Pr, II Corps.

Karen, LZ (AT 915-238)
Along Hwy 535 and adj to Hiep Duc, apx 40 km due W Tam Ky and 53 km SSW Da Nang AB. Apr70 XXIV Corps grid per Don Armstrong. Americal site lists grid as AT 955-238, and is also listed at AT 924-236, 926-238 and 925-238. Unknown which is correct. Quang Tin Pr?, I Corps.

Karen, LZ (AT 925-238)
Apx 7 km WSW LZ West/Nui Liet Kiem Mtn, 2.5 km ENE LZ Siberia, 36 km W to WNW Tam Ky, 2 km ESE Hiep Duc and 54 km SSW Da Nang AB. Also listed at AT 924-236, 926-238 and 915-238 and 955-238. Map is L-7014-6640-3. Americal list. Quang Tin Pr?, I Corps.

Karen, LZ/FSB (YA-815-309)
Apx 7 km due W Le Thanh, 6 km NW Duc Co AF/SF Camp, and 46 km WSW Pleiku. Apparently built Nov68 by 4th Div. Grid per 4th Div Ops Rpt for period ending 31Jan69. Pleiku Pr, II Corps. [306]

Karen, FSB (YT 004-563)
A.k.a. FSB Remagen. Apx 8 km NNE Phuoc Vinh AF and 20 km SSW Dong Xoai. Aug69. Binh Duong Pr, III Corps.

Karl, LZ (XT 481-305)
Apx 22 km NW Cu Chi, 16 km due S Tri Tam/Dau Tieng AF. Feb66. Tay Ninh Pr, III Corps.

Karst (n/a)
See Glossary.

Karum Baran River (YC 95-86)
Paralleled the Yellow Brick Road in southern Thua Thien Pr. E to W flow drained into A Shau Valley and then into Laos. Thua Thien Pr, I Corps.

Kason Mai (n/a)
Mapsheet name of L-7014-6539-1. SVN.

Kate, FSB/LZ (XT-306-255)
Apx 2 km E Cambodian border, 8 km W Go Dau Ha and 23 km SSE Tay Ninh. 5th/7th Cav, 1st Cav here '69, per Frank Penk, Jr. Tay Ninh Pr, III Corps.

Kate, FSB (YD 433-150)
See Katy. Thua Thien Pr, I Corps.

Kate, FSB (YS 421-884)
Apx 21 km due N Nui Dat, 2 km W FSB Buffalo and 3 km NE FSB of Coolah. On 1ATF NCO trng map per John Hollett. Phuoc Tuy Pr, III Corps.

Kate, FSB (YT 125-497)
See Katie. Phuoc Long Pr, III Corps.

Kate, FSB/LZ (YT 300-255)
Along LTL-24, just N Ap Than Dang, apx 2 km S the Song Dong Nai River, 8 km WNW Xa Gia Kiem and 33 km ENE Bien Hoa AB. Per Frank Penk, Jr, this was small base used by SF-led 3rd Mike Force. Grid also per Frank Penk, Jr. Long Khanh Pr, III Corps.

Kate, LZ (n/a)
No data. Site of three day battle, 29, 30 and 31Oct69, involving 1st/92d Arty and elements of 4th Div? Quang Duc Pr, II Corps.

Kathleen, FSB (YT 050-990)
A.k.a. Kathy. On road connecting Song Be and An Loc LTL-1A), apx 32 km ENE An Loc, 12 km SW Song Be AF, and 7 km ENE Bu R'Drang. 1st/8th Cav, 1st Cav, here '69, per Frank Penk, Jr. Phuoc Long Pr, III Corps.

Katho Bay (VS 5-3)
Vinh Ca Tho. Bay at 10°16'N-104°33'E. On NC48-06 JOG. Kien Giang Pr, IV Corps.

Kathryn, FSB (YD 466-112)
A.k.a. Cathryn and Catherine. Apx 28 km WSW Hue, 23 km due W FSB Birmingham, S FSB Rakkassan and NW FSB Strike. During Lam Son 720, beginning in Apr '71, FSBs Fury, Kathryn, Maureen, Gladiator and later Eagle's Nest were all reopened by B/326th Engrs with 3d Bde

101st Abn providing security. FSBs Co Pung, Binh Dinh and Kim Qui were built during same op as well. 7th/11th Arty had 155s here during that op. Also listed at YD 47-11 and YD 476-111. 101st Abn. Thua Thien Pr, I Corps.

Kathy, FSB (XS 62-88)
A.k.a. Ly Van Manh. At or near site of old French Fort, apx 8 km SSE Duc Hoa AF, 20 km WSW Tan Son Nhut AB and 13 km due N Ben Luc. 4th/12th and 3d/7th Inf, 199th LIB here. Hau Nghia Pr, III Corps.

Kathy, FSB (XT 550-170)
A.k.a. Devins. Apx 10 km WNW Cu Chi and 11 km SE Xom Rung Cay. Hau Nghia Pr, III Corps.

Kathy, FSB (YT 054-993)
A.k.a. Kathleen. On road connecting Song Be/An Loc (LTL-1), apx 32 km ENE An Loc, 12 km SW Song Be AF, and 7 km ENE Bu R'Drang. 1st/8th Cav, 1st Cav, '69. Grid per Frank Penk, Jr. Phuoc Long Pr, III Corps.

Kathy, LZ (YD 587-234)
Apx 2 km W Song Bo, 6 km due W Hue Citadel AF and 10 km SE Camp Evans. Mar68. Thua Thien Pr, I Corps.

Katie, FSB (YT 125-497)
Apx 16 km due E Phuoc Vinh AF, 8 km NE Bao Phung and 37 km NNE Bien Hoa AB. Phuoc Long Pr, III Corps.

Katie, FSB (YD 433-150)
See Katy. Thua Thien Pr, I Corps.

Kato, FSB/LZ (n/a)
No data. Possible sp variant of "Kate"?

Katum (XT 330-900)
At intersection of Rtes 4 and 246, apx 12 km NNE Prek Klok, 5 km NW Bo Tuc, 42 km W An Loc, 5 km S Cambodia. 5th SF Grp CIDG Det A-32, 1st Cav. Also listed at XT 32-94. Map is L-7014-6232-3. See Katum Base, 173d Abn DZ and Beverly. Tay Ninh Pr, III Corps.

Katum Airfield (XT 331-901)
Apx 8 km S Cambodia, 22 km ENE Thien Ngon AF, 40 km NNE Tay Ninh, 43 km W An Loc. Per essay written by C-130 pilot Sam McGowan and entitled *KATUM*, this AF and that at Tonel Cham were 2 of most dreaded by C-130 crews during war. The rwys short and AF within arty range of Cambodia, so landings here could bring variety of arty and other AA fire directed at acft at or near base. Field was initially constructed during Op Junction City, early '67, and "was a place whose name on a mission frag order instantly put an airlift crew into a sober and somber mood, especially if the order read '*Bien Hoa-Katum, Shuttle X*' which meant 'Shuttle as required' between the two bases." [307] El. 133', 3,000' laterite rwy. Also listed at 330-900. See Katum Base, 173d Abn Drop Zone and FSB Beverly. Tay Ninh Pr, III Corps.

Katum, FSB (XU 332-898)
See Katum Base. Tay Ninh Pr, III Corps.

Katum Base (XT 330-900)
A.k.a. FSB Katum. Apx 8 km S Cambodia, 40 km NNE Tay Ninh, and 43 km W An Loc. 25th Inf Div, 173d Abn. Per Larry Mitchell, "Katum was larger than a typical FSB and fwd base for 1st Bde/25th Inf Div during Op Yellowstone (apx 8Dec67 to 22Feb68), good bit of arty and usually 2 Bn of Inf" inc 4th/9th Manchus. 2d/60th(?) here pre & post Cambodia, per David Argabright. Katum area was site of only US combat parachute jump of VN War when, during Op Junction City, 173d Abn jumped from C-130s in DZ along axis of XT 329-030 to XT 343-030. DZ was apx 300 meters wide running about 150 meters to either side of line between XT 329 to XT 343 and was 3 km N Katum. FSBs Beverly and Beauregard also near or at Katum. Also listed at XU 332-898. Map is L-7014-6232-3. Tay Ninh Pr, III Corps.

Katum SF Camp (XT 330-898)
At Katum AF, apx 6 km S Cambodia, 45 km WSW Loc Ninh and 42 km NNE Tay Ninh. On night of 25Sep68 at 0330 hrs, Co A 5th SF Grp received indirect fire inc apx twenty 122mm rockets, 150-82mm mortar mixed and over 100 rounds of RPG, followed by ground attack by D-5 local VC Bn. 141 VC were KIA and 7 were POW. [308] Grid per AAR, *Battle of Tay Ninh* (17Aug-27Sep68), HQ 25th ID, 2Feb69, courtesy Butch Sincock. *SF Order of Battle* lists grid as XT 3299-8977 and says site transferred to 84th ARVN Border Rangers. Tay Ninh Pr, III Corps.

Katy, FSB (YD 433-150)
On large plateau, apx 1 km N the Song Bo River, 7 km NW FSB Kathryn and 30 km WSW Hue. 101st Abn inactive FSB grid per Don Armstrong. Thua Thien Pr, I Corps.

Katy, FSB (YT 125-497)
See Katie. Phuoc Long Pr, III Corps.

Kau Hai Lagoon (ZD 0-0)
A.k.a. Dam Cau Hai. Lagoon at 16°20'N-107°52'E. On NE48-16 JOG. Thua Thien Pr, I Corps.

Kay, LZ (CR 030-686)
2 km from coast, 13 km ENE Phu My, 7 km NNW Vinh Loi and 28 km NNE Phu Cat. '66. Binh Dinh Pr, II Corps.

Kay, LZ (ZA 062-375)
Near Ia Bolang River, apx 21 km WSW Pleiku, 13 km WSW Plei Pao Xoi and 13 km WNW Catecka AF. 10th Cav, 4th Div here. Name per Bob Patsfield, grid per Dick Arnold as per Jan-Mar69 1st/35th Inf Bn daily logs. Also listed at ZA 061-378. Pleiku Pr, II Corps.

Ke Bon (n/a)
Mapsheet name of L-7014-6048-3. NVN only.

Ke Ga, Mui (CQ 3-2)
Coastal point at 12°53'N-109°28'E. On ND49-13 JOG. Khanh Hoa Pr, II Corps.

Ke Ga, Mui (CR 1-0)
Coastal point at 13°34'N-109°18'E. On ND49-09 JOG. Phu Yen Pr, II Corps.

Ke Ga, Mui (ZS 2-8)
Coastal point at 10°42'N-107°58'E. NC48-08 JOG. NVN.

Ke Ga, Pointe de (ZS 2-8)
See Pointe Ke Ga. Binh Thuan Pr, II Corps.

Kega Pointe de (CR 1-0)
See Point Ke Ga. Phu Yen Pr, II Corps.

Ke Sach Heliport (XR 085-798)
On island in Mekong River and adj Cu Lao Dung, apx 23 km NNE Soc Trang AF and 20 km NNE Khanh Hung. Heliport #719, alt 10', at 09°47'00"N-105°59'20"E, per Feb73 TAD. IV Corps.

Ke Sat (n/a)
Mapsheet name of L-7014-6250-4. NVN only.

Ke Sat (XJ 1-1)
Along Road No. 5, apx 32 km ESE Hanoi. AFs here struck by Carrier TF-77 attempts to blunt NVA Tet '68 offensive. Also French position of French War that Bernard Fall described as one of the "Rich Forts." See French Fort

Design in Glossary for explanation. Per *Street Without Joy*, p 176, map at p 46. NVN.

Keane, FSB (XT 614-017)
See Keene at grid. Hau Nghia Pr, III Corps.

Keane, FSB (YT 040-350)
A.k.a. FSB Keene or Kien (both in same genera area)? Apx 22 km NNE Bien Hoa AB. 2d/14th Inf, 25th Div here. Feb68. See FSB Kien (a.k.a. Mahone) and website of 242d AHC. Binh Duong Pr, III Corps.

Kearsarge, USS (n/a)
CVS-33. Acft Carrier. Deployed with CVSG-53 17 Aug 67 to 6 Apr '68; with CVSG-53, 29Mar69-4Sep69; with CVSG-53, 19Jun64-16Dec64; with CVSG-53, 9Jun66-20Dec66. See *Coral Sea, USS.* [309]

Keaton, Camp/FSB (XS 637-767)
Along QL-4 at Ben Luc, apx 18 km SW Saigon, 14 km NNE Tan An and 9 km WSW Binh Chanh. Basecamp of 6th/31st Inf, 3d Bde. Named to honor Capt. Everett D Keaton, USA, CO D/6th/31st Inf, 9th Div, KIA 20Jan70, by booby trap. Was CO of A/4th/49th Inf, 9th Div, when he first arrived in-country. Also listed at XS 635-757. Long An Pr, III Corps.

Keaton, FSB (XS 637-767)
See Keaton, Camp. Long An Pr, III Corps.

Keene, FSB (XT 614-017)
A.k.a. Patrol Base Keene, and apparently as Keene I, II & III (grids all similar so Keene may have been built and rebuilt several times in same general location; a common practice in III Corps). At My Hanh, Duc Hoa District, apx 9 km ESE Khiem Cuong, 21 km WNW Tan Son Nhut AB and 5 km NNE Duc Hoa AF. Built as 2d/14th Inf, 25th ID, Bn HQ near end of Aug68. FSBs Keene and Ayers were each held by rifle Co, while remaining rifle Co was on continuous ops nearby. 1st attacked at 0350 hrs, 30Oct-1Sep68, with VC/NVA. Hvy mortar fire from NE and SE allowed sappers cut into E and SE sides of perimeter using Bangalore torpedoes. One grp was discovered before penetrating inner-wire and annihilated with.50 Cal. fire, in seconds. Sappers breaching SE side survived only 15 min. As NVA withdrew to NE, 105 arty and 81 mortar fire from Keene dogged them. They also ran into an A Co ambush. By 0500 hrs, battle was over with 13 VC KIA, 5 VC POW. On 27Mar69, Task Force Satan (inc B/1st/508th Inf, Trp A, 1st/11th ACR and Bty C, 2d/321st Arty, all part of or opcon to 82d Abn) was deployed to this base (in AO Hades), 3d Bde/82d Abn. 82d Abn data per Butch Sincock. Info/grid per Kirk Ramsey. Also listed at XT 604-016. Nov68-Jun69. See ARVN/US Night Laager site (was due N of Keene). Hau Nghia Pr, III Corps. [310 311]

Keene, FSB (YT 040-350)
A.k.a. FSB Keane or Kien (both in same general area)? Apx 22 km NNE Bien Hoa AB. 2d/14th Inf, 25th Div here. See FSB Kien (a.k.a. Mahone) and website of 242d AHC. Feb68. Binh Duong Pr, III Corps. [312]
Mahone). Bien Hoa Pr, III Corps.

Keene I, FSB (XT 604-016)
See Keene, FSB at grid. Hau Nghia Pr, III Corps.

Keene II, FSB (XT 604-016?)
See Keene, FSB at grid. Presumed to have existed. Hau Nghia Pr, III Corps.

Keene III, FSB (XT 600-010)
Near My Hanh, apx 9 km ESE Khiem Cuong, 21 km WNW Tan Son Nhut AB and 5 km NNE Duc Hoa AF. 1st/8th Arty, 25th Div here. Apr69. Hau Nghia Pr, III Corps.

Kega Point (CR 1-0)
See Point Kega. Phu Yen Pr, II Corps.

Kega, Point (ZS 2-8)
See Point Kega. Binh Thuan Pr, II Corps.

Kein Giang Province (VR/VS/WR/WS)
See Kien Giang Province. Misspelling of "Kien."

Kein Hoa Province (XR/XS)
See Kien Hoa Province. Misspelling of "Kien."

Kein Phong Province (WS/WT?)
See Kien Phong Province. Misspelling of "Kien."

Kein Tuong Province (WS/WT/XS?)
See Kien Tuong Province. Misspelling of "Kien."

Kelley/McCoy, FSB (BS 539-732)
See FSB 4-11. Quang Ngai Pr, I Corps.

Kelley, LZ/FSB (YD 404-119)
A.k.a. Kelly. Apx 34 km WSW Hue, 25 km SSW Camp Evans, 17 km SSE FSB O'Reilly and 27 km E Tou Rout. Thua Thien Pr, I Corps.

Kelly, FSB (XT 813-558)
Apx 5 km SE Chon Thanh AF and 17 km WNW Phuoc Vinh AF. 1st Cav. Name/grid per Dan Gillotti, 15th Arty Assn. Binh Long Pr?, III Corps.

Kelly, FSB/LZ (ZA 228-533)
Apparently a.k.a Artillery Hill and FSB Dragon. Along W edge of QL-14, apx 5 km NNW Pleiku, 1 km SW Bien Ho Lake, 6 km WNW Pleiku/Cu Hanh AF and 5 km SSW Plei Mui. 1st/92d Arty here in '70, and preceded by 30th FA. Likely named to honor 1Lt George Thomas Kelly, an FO Adv assigned to an ARVN Rgt, KIA 23Apr70. Name /data per map provided by Patrick "O" Kelly (as per Ben Youmans), and other data per 1st/92d Arty website at www.bravecannons.org/stories/C_SO_DP_rktactk_1.html. Pleiku Pr, II Corps.

Kelly, LZ (XU 734-085)
A.k.a. Kelley. Along QL-13, at or adj to Loc Ninh AF, 20 km N An Loc and 75 km NW Tay Ninh. On 12Aug69, VC threw simultaneous attacks against many 1st Cav bases in III Corps, including Quan Lai, LZs Becky, Jon, Kelly and Caldwell. 1st/7th, 1st/8th, 2d/12th Cav/1st Cav here per Frank Penk, Jr. "Frenchy" Torres tells us D/1st/7th Cav here Aug69. Also listed at XU 730-090. Nov68-Jun69. Binh Long Pr, III Corps.

Kelly, LZ (YD 404-119)
See Kelley. Thua Thien Pr, I Corps.

Kem Pass (WJ 5-0?)
Along Road No. 6 apx 35 km WSW Hanoi. On 9Jan52, Vietminh ambushed/destroyed almost an entire Mobile Bn here, forcing closure of Road No. 6. Per *Street Without Joy*, Chp 2; map at p 50. NVN.

Kemper County, USS (n/a)
LST 854. MRF base ship. IV Corps.

Ken, FSB? (YC 98-62)
Possibly Ken or Kien Valley? This name appears to be imprinted on map at p 109, *US Marines in Vietnam-1969*. If in fact a FSB, it was roughly 8 km SW FSB Bullwhip, 14

km W FSB Rattlesnake, 17 km WNW LZ Hawk. Grid roughly estimated from that map. Quang Nam Pr, I Corps.

Ken, LZ (BR 793-465)
10 km WNW Phu Cat AB. Dec65. Binh Dinh Pr, II Corps.

Ken Thao Airfield (QV 53-64)
A.k.a. L-06 and possibly Kene Thao AF? If same as Kene Thao, was apx 125 km WSW Vientiane on Feb67 Natl Geo Map. El. 875'. CIA/SF, per *Air Facilities Data-Laos.*

Ken Valley (YC 97-63?)
SW FSB Bullwhip, apx 50 km WSW Da Nang. Main enemy arms/ammo stg area for Da Nang attacks. Target of Op Oklahoma Hills, Mar-May69. Quang Nam Pr, I Corps.

Kene Thao Airfield (QV 98-62?)
Variant of Ken Thao? If so, was L-06, and apx 125 km WSW Vientiane, per Feb67 Natl Geo Map. El. 875'. Laos.

Keng Ka Boa Airfield (VD 85-54)
See Keng Kaboa AF. Laos.

Keng Kaboa Airfield (n/a)
A.k.a. LS-235 and Keng Ka Boa AF. Apx 65 km SSE NKP AB (Thailand), per ONC-J-11. CIA/SF facility. 3,300' rwy, El. 550'. Grid per *Air Facilities Data-Laos.*

Keng Kok Airfield (WD 21-18)
LS-139. Apx 320 km SE Vientiane on Feb67 Natl Geo Map. El. 560'. CIA/SF, per *Air Facilities Data-Laos.*

Kent, FSB (n/a)
No data. 10th Cav, 4th Div here, per Bob Patsfield. Possibly Binh Dinh or Pleiku Pr, II Corps.

Kentucky, Operation (n/a)
1Nov67-28Feb69. 3d Mar Div. Con Thien/DMZ. 3,921 rptd NVA/VC KIA, per *Vietnam Order of Battle*, pp 9-14. Quang Tri Pr, I Corps.

Keo Sa Khai Neua Airfield (TF 76-94)
LS-331. CIA/SF, per *Air Facilities Data-Laos.*

Kep Airfield (XJ 31-66)
Apx 75 km NNE Hanoi per map in *Vietnam Experience* Series, *Rain of Fire* vol, p. 11. NVN.

Kep Airfield (VS 24-58)
On coast apx 135 km SSW Phnom Penh and 20 km NW Ha Tien (SVN) on Feb67 Natl Geo Map. El. 26'. Cambodia.

Kep Ha Airfield (XJ 67-65)
Apx 85 km NE Hanoi and 35 km ESE Kep AF on Feb67 Natl Geo Map. El. 60'. NVN.

Keppel Shipyards (n/a)
Ship repair facility in Singapore and under US contract during war. Not in VN.

Kerry Lou, FSB (YD?)
Unknown location, but apparently occupied or built by 2d/501st Inf after '70? Thua Thien Pr?, I Corps?

Kerry, FSB (YT 13-13)
Apx 13 km E to ESE Bien Hoa, 5 km ESE FSB Kiama, 30 km NE Saigon, 6 km E Plantation AF and 34 km W to WNW Xuan Loc. Described by *Vietnam Gunners* author as "a spectacular position sitting on a major terrain feature with a marvelous view of surrounding countryside." Overlooked converging on Saigon, which led to long delays for fire mission clearance due to friendly congestion in area. 161 Bty, RNZA (Hitching's Bty 14Apr68-18Mar69) FSB set here 17Feb-10Mar69. 12Feb69, HQ 1ATF, B Sqdn 1st Armored Rgt, A Sqdn 1, Cav Rgt, 9 RAR Bn HQ, and Supt Co here. Bien Hoa Pr, III Corps.

Ketter, FSB (XU 925-429)
In Cambodia apx 3 km WSW Phum Chhaneng, 37 km ENE Snuol, 13 km NNW Bu Dop and 43 km WNW Djamap/Bu Gia Map. Likely named to honor Capt. Terry L. Ketter, KIA 10May70. Grid per *11th ACR Cambodia Invasion AAR, 1st Cav Div, May-Jun70*, courtesy Lou Rochat. [313] Also listed at XU 928-427. Cambodia.

Kettle (n/a)
Apr70, XXIV Corps proposed 101st Abn FSB name.

Kevin Wheatley Stadium (YS 28-43)
Just N the Peter Badcoe club in 1ATF cmpd at Vung Tau. RAR scout Eddie Tricker describes it as huge facility, big enough to "hold a basketball game and its entire audience." He also says that it "…was used only for concert parties on my visits. I was present for 2, one a Noggie show complete with strippers, and other an Aussie concert party complete with dancing girls. Both filled the hall to capacity!" See Peter Badcoe Club. Vung Tau Peninsula, Phuoc Tuy Pr, III Corps. [314]

Kew, FSB (ZS 13-99?)
Apparent misspelling of FSB Kow? Binh Tuy Pr, III Corps.

Key, FSB (XS 510-310)
Just across river from and immed S Truc Giang/Ben Tre, apx 14 km S My Tho. Jan-Jul69. Kien Hoa Pr, IV Corps.

Keystone, LZ (XD 895-632)
Just S southern edge of DMZ, apx 22 km WNW Cam Lo and 34 km W to WNW Dong Ha. Apr70 XXIV Corps grid per Don Armstrong. Quang Tri Pr, I Corps.

Keystone Robin, Operation (n/a)
See Glossary.

Kha Phu Airfield (UG 42-27)
LS-35. CIA/SF, per *Air Facilities Data-Laos.*

Khai Minh BOQ (XS 849-927?)
In Saigon. Gia Dinh Pr, III Corps.

Khai Minh Hotel (XS 849-927)
In Saigon. Gia Dinh Pr, III Corps.

Khai Quang Heliport (WR 023-300)
Apx 24 km NW Quan Long AF and 3 km NW Ap Sau. "Heliport #593, alt 7', sod, building on N." At 09°19'15"N-105°01'00"E, per Feb73 TAD. An Xuyen Pr, IV Corps.

Khak Pha Airfield (n/a)
Near coast, apx 800 km S Bangkok and 75 km SE Songkhla AF. El. 30'. Thailand

Khaki, FSB (XS 560-270)
Apx 7 km ESE Truc Giang and 6 km WNW Ap Dong Nhon. Jan69. Kien Hoa Pr, IV Corps.

Kham Don SF Camp (n/a)
Fictional name representing an actual SF Camp visited by *The Green Berets* author Robin Moore during a 6-month visit to VN in '64 or '65. Mentioned at p 253, *The Green Berets*. Possibly Ban Don or Kham Duc?

Kham Duc (ZC 003-081)
In valley of Song Cai River, apx 20 km W Laos, 55 km W to WSW Tien Phuoc, 80 km SSW Da Nang and 70 km WSW Tam Ky. Overrun/evacuated under fire, 10-11May68. May68 air evac of site was chaotic and often heroic, resulting in C-130 with over 100 refugees aboard being shot down and numerous other acft being severely damaged. After evac, 3-man USAF air control team inadvertently left behind was rescued by C-130 pilot who landed on enemy-controlled rwy (earning MOH). Site

recaptured 12Jul70, by many of same Americal Div elements responsible for '68 evac. Among those units were 1st/82d Arty, 2d/1st Inf and apx 6,000 ARVN troops.[315] CIDG SF Det A-105 opened Sep63, overrun 12 May68. 5th SF Grp, Det. A-322, Dec64, Det A-105, Oct65, SF Det 5. Also listed at ZC 006-079. Quang Tin Pr, I Corps.

Kham Duc Airfield (ZC 003-081)
Apx 70 km W Tam K, and 10 km NNE Ngok Tavak AF. Per TPC K-10A. El. 1,115', 6,000' asph rwy. At 15°25'57"N-107°47'52"E. Quang Tin Pr, I Corps.

Kham Duc SF Camp (ZC 0059-0810)
At Kham Duc, apx 20 km W Laos, 55 km W to WSW Tien Phuoc, and 80 km SSW Da Nang. CIDG SF Det A-105 opened here Sep63, was overrun 12May68; 5th SF Grp, Det. A-322, Dec64; Det A-105, Oct65, SF Det 5. Grid per *Special Order of Battle*. Overrun and moved to Nong Son. Quang Tin Pr, I Corps.

Kham Duc, Camp (YC 9640-0091)
See Ngok Tavak. Quang Tin Pr, I Corps.

Khammouane Airfield (n/a)
A.k.a. Thakhek. On Feb67 Natl Geo Map. El. 450'? Laos.

Khan, FSB (XS 480-260)
On S bank of Ham Luong River, apx 7 km SSW Truc Giang/Ben Tre and 27 km due N Tra Vinh AF/Phu Vinh. Jan69. Kien Hoa Pr, IV Corps.

Khan Duc Airfield (ZC 003-081)
See Kham Duc AF. Quang Tin Pr, I Corps.

Khang Hong Airfield (UG 28-48)
LS-68. CIA/SF, per *Air Facilities Data-Laos.*

Khang Khai Airfield (UG 17-58)
LS-08. Apx 175 km NNE Vientiane on Feb67 Natl Geo Map. El. 3,600'. CIA/SF per *Air Facilities Data-Laos.*

Khang Kho Airfield (UG 05-24)
LS-204 and Khang Ko AF. Apx 150 km NNE Vientiane, per ONC-J-11. CIA/SF facility. El. 4,850'. Grid per *Air Facilities Data-Laos.*

Khang Ko Airfield (UG 05-24)
LS-204 and Khang Ko AF. Apx 150 km NNE Vientiane, per ONC-J-11. CIA/SF facility. El. 4,850'. Grid per *Air Facilities Data-Laos.*

Khang River (AT 05-20)
See Song Chang. Quang Nam Pr, I Corps.

Khanh Duong Airfield (BQ 554-098)
Apparently a.k.a. M'Drak AF. Apx 2 km NW Khanh Duong New AF, 2 km NW Ban M'Drak, and 46 km ENE Buon Ea Yang AF. "AF # VA2-235. Abnd, recommend use Khanh Dong New AF, 7Feb67," in Aug69 TAD per Frank Penk, Jr. Not in Feb73 TAD. Khanh Hoa Pr, II Corps.

Khanh Duong New Airfield (BQ 562-087)
Apx 47 km E Buon Ea Yang AF, 36 km NW Duc My AF, 42 km SW Cung Son AF and near Ban M'Drak, per TPC K-10A. El. 1,400', 3,500' steel-mat rwy. At 12°43'58"N-108°45'15"E. Khanh Hoa Pr, II Corps.

Khanh Hoa Province (BQ/CQ/BP/CP)
One of 12 north-central provs forming II Corps.

Khanh Hoi (BN 86-82?)
A.k.a. Hon Khanh Hoi and Thanh Hai? Apx 6 km NE Phan Rang. Ninh Thuan Pr, II Corps.

Khanh Hung (XR 117-604)
Perhaps 20 km NE Soc Trang. Villes of same name also at: XU 729-036, XR 075-617, XR 070-612, among many other locations. Ba Xuyen or Phong Dinh Pr, IV Corps.

Khanh Hung (Soc Trang) (n/a)
Mapsheet name of L-7014-6128-2. SVN.

Khanh Hung Airfield (XR 058-591)
See Soc Trang AF. Ba Xuyen Pr, IV Corps.

Khanh Hung City (XR 070-62)
A.k.a. Soc Trang. In heart of Mekong Delta, apx 160 km S Saigon with only 10' El. Site of Soc Trang AF (3 km SW Khanh Hung), originally a Japanese fighter base during WWII that inc hard-surface rwy and buildings built by both French and Vietnamese. 1st US unit here was Marine helo sqdn (one of few places outside I Corps where USMC operated) but Marines were quickly replaced by US Army's 93d Trans Co, Jan 62, which was then supplanted by 121st Avn Co. See Soc Trang for more detail. Capitol, Ba Xuyen Pr, IV Corps.

Khanh Van, FSB (XT 925-195)
Apx 11 km NW Bien Hoa AB and 6 km NE Phu Loi AF. Jan68. Bien Hoa Pr, III Corps.

Khao Saphan Nak Army AF (PS 7-5)
At 14°56'00"N-100°40'00"E. NIMA data. Thailand.

Khe Ba Le River (YD 17-22)
Roughly 32 km SW Quang Tri and a drainage of S side of Dong Ba Le (Hill 1102). Quang Tri Pr, I Corps.

Khe Bo (n/a)
Mapsheet name of L-7014-5947-3. NVN/Laos.

Khe Chau Valley (YD)
N of Dong Ha Mtn (FSB Fuller). One objective of Op Montana Mauler involving 3d/5th Cav, 1st/11th Inf and 3d/9th Marines, Mar-Jul69. Quang Tri Pr, I Corps.

Khe Ga Point (CP 0-6)
See Point Khe Ga. Khanh Hoa Pr, II Corps.

Khe Ga, Mui (CP 0-6)
Mui Cay Gai. Coastal point at 12°18'N-109°15'E. On ND49-13 JOG. Khanh Hoa Pr, II Corps.

Khe Gia Bridge (YD 027-561)
See Khe Gio Bridge. Quang Tri Pr, I Corps.

Khe Gio, FSB (YD 027-561)
On QL-9 at Khe Gio Bridge, apx 6.5 km WSW Cam Lo, 500 meters S QL-9 and 2 km due E the Rockpile. Apr67. Quang Tri Pr, I Corps.

Khe Gio Bridge (YD 026-561)
A.k.a. Khe Gia Bridge. On QL-9 in apx 6.5 km WSW Cam Lo, 2 km due E the Rockpile and 4 km SSE FSB Fuller. 3d Mar Div provided defense of bridge. Rock Face of Hill 252 overhung this site and NVA dug-into hill's solid rock ambushed 2d/4th Marines sweeping QL-9 at bridge opposite the hill, 17-18Aug66, during Op Prairie. Per *USMC in Vietnam, 1966*, p 181-2. Quang Tri Pr, I Corps.

Khe Ho (XD 99-81?)
Apx 20 km WSW Vinh Linh (YD 14-87) and 10 km N Ben Hai River? In '59, was main base of NVA's 301st Bn and one of very first sites suptg the opening of the HCMT. Per *The Blood Road*, p 14. NVN.

Khe Lo Moi Valley (YC 789-923)
Generally 64 km WNW Da Nang. Thua Thien Pr, I Corps.

Khe Phat Airfield (n/a)
45 km NW Dong Hoi and 135 km SSE Vinh. Per ONC-J-11. El. 60'. NVN.

Khe Sanh (XD 852-418)
N of QL-9, apx 44 km SW Dong Ha, 52 km WSW Quang Tri and just S the DMZ on large plain. Apx 6 km E Laotian border and 24 km S the DMZ. To its W was an Old French Fort, to N and E was steep precipice that dropped hundreds of feet to Rao Quan River. Described circa '66 in *Bonnie-Sue* as, "just an old French airstrip on a 457-meter high plateau, and nothing else." Was site of one of most controversial and well-known battles of war, the Siege of Khe Sanh. Apx 75 days in duration, the siege immed preceded, and lasted through, the Tet '68 Offensive. During period, base could only be supplied by air and was under almost continual NVA rocket/arty fire. On 29Feb68, units of NVA 304 Div launched perhaps only(?) significant ground attack of siege, were unable to breach wire, and suffered major casualties. Siege broken by Op Pegasus, beginning 1Apr68, involving Army's 1st Cav Div and 3d Mar Div elements. Shortly thereafter, base was abnd. In '71, was reopened by 101st Abn and 5th Mech Div suptg Lam Son 719, the disastrous ARVN invasion into Laos. Army SF CIDG camp was at Khe Sanh ville, 5th SF Grp, Det. A-323, Dec64, Det A-101, Oct65, 37th ARVN Ranger Bn, 26th Marine Rgt, 1st/13th Arty, Huong Hoa Dist HQ, USMC Combined Action Co, RF Co. 5,772 Marines, 228 Navy Corpsman and Doctors, 30 Army and two USAF Liaison personnel faced apx 38,500-43,000 NVA of 325-C Div on N, 364 Div on S, 324-B Div to E, another Div to W and SW, and yet another to SE. Good maps in *The Final Formation*, pp 1-6, and site map on Khe Sanh Vets website at: www. geocities.com/~khesanh/. Also listed at XD 853-418 per XXIV Corps index, 6Apr70. Quang Tri Pr, I Corps.

Khe Sanh, Camp (XD 840-385)
Unknown if this was separate from other Khe Sanh SF camps listed? Quang Tri Pr, I Corps.

Khe Sanh, FSB (XD 850-410)
Immed S former position of Khe Sanh CB. Nov69. Quang Tri Pr, I Corps.

Khe Sanh Air Strike Data (n/a)
See Glossary.

Khe Sanh Airfield (XD 852-418)
Nicknamed The Fog Factory by early USAF and Army pilots. 3,300' PSP or steel-mat rwy that was C-130 capable as early as '65. Discussed in *Valley of Decision*, pp 33-35 et al. Also listed at XD 849-418 in Aug69 TAD courtesy Frank Penk, Jr., which also states site was "Insecure, abnd, Probably Mined, AF # VA1-44." Not in Feb73 TAD. Map is L-7014-6342-3, per Ken Burrington. El. 1608', per ONC J-11. See other Khe Sanh entries. Quang Tri Pr, I Corps.

Khe Sanh Air Strike Data (XD 8-4)
See Glossary.

Khe Sanh Ammo Dump (XD 852-417)
Along S side of main rwy and roughly 300 meters due E the air control tower. At 5:30 a.m. 21Jan68, during opening arty and rocket attacks initiating Siege of Khe Sanh, was hit by incoming rockets and, as result, over 1,500 tons of munitions were destroyed in apocalyptic explosion that collapsed the post office and PX, buckled portions of rwy and flattened rwy lights and radio antennas. Spectacular fire with ammo cooking off regularly lasted several days.

Khe Sanh Battlefield (XD)
Geographical elements involved the Battle for Khe Sanh were: Hills 552, 558, 681, 881-S, 881-N, 950, 1015, Hickory Relay, CAP Team facilities of CAC Oscar, Khe Sanh Ville and Lang Vei. Units/ops controlled by or originating in Khe Sanh inc: SF Project Delta '66, Force and Bn Recon, BV-33 in Laos suptd by Marine Arty, Project Tigerhound surveillance acft, SOG, 26th Marines, 1st/12th Mar Arty, ARVN. Quang Tri Pr, I Corps.

Khe Sanh CAP (XD 85-41?)
See CAP Oscar-3. Quang Tri Pr, I Corps.

Khe Sanh Coffee Plantations (XD 858-390)
Plantations along W edge of Khe Sanh ville, owned by French families named Llinares, Eugene Poilane and Simard. In Feb63, French Dr. named Wolff was assassinated by Vietminh after leaving Llinares' house after professional call (Llinares apparently lost his fortune when communists took over NVN). Mr. Poilane was stopped and executed by Vietminh 20Apr64, while driving along Rte 9 en route Quang Tri (he had settled on KS Plateau in 1919 and had fathered 10 children, 5 of whom were born after he was 60). His son, Felix took over ops and added more colorful history (see *Le Petite Fleur* and Poilane). Khe Sanh Ville was originally settled by workers recruited for Poilane plantation. Also at XD 842-382. See Simard Coffee Plantation. Quang Tri Pr, I Corps. [316]

Khe Sanh Combat Base (XD 852-418)
A.k.a. KSCB. See Khe Sanh. Quang Tri Pr, I Corps.

Khe Sanh Front HQ (XD 38-63 to XD 50-70)
In Laos generally 16 km W Khe Sanh CB. NVA HQ for Khe Sanh offensive, '68, and objective of ARVN attempt to cut HCMT during Lam Son 719, '71. Laos.

Khe Sanh Heliport (XD 858-384)
At Thuong Van near old French fort, apx 3.5 km S Khe Sanh AF, 1 km E Khe Sanh Ville and 500 meters S QL-9. Heliport #594, alt 1,444', at 16°37'30"N-106°44'45"E, per 73 TAD. Quang Tri Pr, I Corps.

Khe Sanh Howard Johnson's (XD 845-382)
See Howard Johnson's. Quang Tri Pr, I Corps.

Khe Sanh Mike Force OP (XD 778-531)
Apx 14 km NNW Khe Sanh CB. SF CIDG OP during siege. Attacked/overrun 7Feb68. Grid per *The Final Formation*. Quang Tri Pr, I Corps.

Khe Sanh Military Post (XD 858-130)
Apx 3 km due S the Khe Sanh CB. Former French or ARVN fort? Quang Tri Pr, I Corps.

Khe Sanh Outpost (XD 849-418)
At what became Khe Sanh CB, apx 50 km WSW Quang Tri and 16 km WSW Ca Lu. May66. Quang Tri Pr, I Corps.

Khe Sanh Red Watch (n/a)
See Glossary.

Khe Sanh SF Camp (new) (XD 852-418)
1st US facility at what was later became Khe Sanh AF. Built by SF troops at nearby French Fort in preparation for specially trained SF A-Team that deployed from Ft Bragg while original SF camp site at Old French Fort (1st SF camp in area) was being abnd. Const began Mar65. Initial efforts made the 3,300' rwy C-130 capable, added concrete

bunkers and concrete structures on which SF troops mounted acft 2.75" rocket pods. Many Marines who came in '67-68 mistakenly thought ruins of old SF camp were French. Camp later moved to Lang Vei. Detailed discussion in *Valley of Decision*, pp 33-35. Also listed at XD 840-385 and XD 845-380?? Quang Tri Pr, I Corps.

Khe Sanh SF Camp (Old) (XD 858-385)
A.k.a. The Old French Fort, or The Alamo. Apx 4 km SSE Khe Sanh CB and just SW intersection of QL-9 and road N to Khe Sanh CB. SF A team 1st moved here '62 and took over old French military base (concrete, built '52). They nicknamed site The Alamo, though usually referred to as The Old French Fort. Khe Sanh SOG FOB-1 moved here when SF Camp assets moved to Lang Vei. SF FOB-3 moved here from Khe Sanh ville, Summer '67. Was occupied by NVA, Jan68 when, due to miscommunication, an assaulting allied force was unaware of NVA presence. As result, became scene of one of worst US-related debacles of war. On 21Jan68, US helos were mistakenly directed to insert an SVN RF Co adj to fort as part of effort to reinforce units beleaguered by 20Apr68 NVA offensive in Khe Sanh Plateau. Allies were under impression site was held by friendlies and landed in midst of dug-in NVA Bn. In slaughter that followed, 13 pilots, 14 crewmen and 74 RF troops were KIA.[317] In Apr68 during The Battle for Old French Fort, 1st/5th Cav, 1st Cav retook site after CA from LZ Wharton during Op Pegasus. See BV-33 and Alamo, The. Quang Tri Pr, I Corps.

Khe Sanh SF Camp (XD 795-360)
Per *The Final Formation*, p. 51, SF Det A-101, moved to this newly constructed facility shortly before 7Feb68. On 7Feb68, position was heavily attacked by NVA Inf assisted by tanks and then abnd with 6 US KIA. Also listed at Quang Tri Pr, I Corps.

Khe Sanh SOG (XD 858-385)
See SOG Khe Sanh. Quang Tri Pr, I Corps.

Khe Sanh Stamp (n/a)
See Glossary.

Khe Sanh Target Center (XD)
See Muscle Shoals, Dutch Mill and Spotlight.

Khe Sanh Village (XD 845-380)
Bru tribal ville on QL-9 about midway between Khe Sanh CB and Lang Vei and apx 3 km S Khe Sanh CB. Site of Army SF CDIG camp. 5th SF Grp, Det. A-323, Dec64, Det A-101, Oct65, Huong Hoa Dist HQ, USMC CAC, and SVN RF Co, overrun by NVA during major battle, 19-21Jan68. Quang Tri Pr, I Corps.

Khe Ta Laou River (YD 15-32)
Grid is point in river's valley, apx 7 km ESE Ta Laou and 27 km SW Quang Tri. Quang Tri Pr, I Corps.

Khe Tre Heliport (YC 91-89)
In E portion of Ruong Ruong Valley, apx 53 km WNW Da Nang AB and 20 km WSW Phu Loc. Heliport #595, alt 180', at 16°10'30"N-107°43'30"E, per Feb73 TAD. Thua Thien Pr, I Corps.

Khe Tri, Thonh (XD 979-559)
See Rockpile, The. Quang Tri Pr, I Corps.

Khe Trinh Hin River (XD 94-54)
Apx 40 km W Quang Tri. Quang Tri Pr, I Corps.

Khe Xa Ba River (XD 8-4)
See Khe Xa Bai River. Quang Tri Pr, I Corps.

Khe Xa Bai River (XD 8-4)
Provided NW avenue of approach to Khe Sanh CB. Also spelled Khe Xa Ba. Quang Tri Pr, I Corps.

Khemarak Phouminville AF (n/a)
Apx 210 km W Phnom Penh. El. 100'. Cambodia.

Khemmara Airfield (n/a)
A.k.a. Ben Khemmarat AF. Along Mekong River at Laotian border, apx 555 km ENE Bangkok and 20 km due S Ban Na Kala Hwy Strip (Laos) on Feb67 Natl Geo Map. El. 325' (400' on ONC K-10). Thailand.

Khi Trau Sightings(n/a)
See Glossary.

Khiem Cuong (XT 53 06)
A.k.a. Bao Trai. Apx 30 km WNW Tan Son Nhut AB, 17 km SW Cu Chi and 22 km ESE Duc Hue. Capitol, Hau Nghia Pr, III Corps.

Khiem Ich (Cai Lay) (n/a)
Mapsheet name of L-7014-6229-4. SVN.

Khieu Manang Airfield (UF 24-97)
LS-192. CIA/SF, per *Air Facilities Data-Laos.*

Khinh Bong Ton (WS 3-5)
See Canal des Quatre Cantons. An Giang Pr, IV Corps.

Khiri Khan, Prachuap AF (NP 8-0)
At 11°47'00"N-99°48'00"E. NIMA data. Thailand.

Khmer-Serei (n/a)
See Glossary.

Khlong Ngae, Sathani (PH 6-5)
A.k.a. Klong Ngae. SF camp or AO, per *SF Order of Battle.* Khlong Ngae, Sathani. At 6°47'00"N-100°27'00"E. NB47-07 JOG. Grid square is for RR Station. Thailand.

Khlong Yai Airfield (n/a)
On Feb67 Natl Geo Map. El. 10'. Cambodia.

Khoa Yoi (NQ 9-6)
A.k.a. Phetburi. SF camp or AO, per *SF Order of Battle.* At 13°14'00"N-99°50'00"E. ND47-11 JOG. Thailand.

Khok Krathiam Airfield (PS 8-4)
At 14°52'00"N-100°44'00"E. NIMA data. Thailand.

Khon Kaen (TD 6-2)
Apx 100 km due S Udorn AB, and 380 km NE Bangkok. US Army Supt Cmd Facility. 569th Trans Co. Thailand.

Khon Kaen Airfield (TD 6-2)
Major AF at 16°28'00"N-102°47'00"E, apx 100 km due S Udorn AB, and 380 km NE Bangkok, per Feb67 Natl Geo and ONC-J-11s. NIMA data. El. 750' or 629'. Thailand.

Khon Kaen SF Camp (n/a)
Apparently near Khon Kaaen AF, apx 100 km due S Udorn AB, and 380 km NE Bangkok. Thailand.

Khong Airfield (n/a)
On Cambodian border, apx 550 km SE Vientiane, and 360 km W Qui Nhon SVN, per ONC-K-10 and Feb67 Natl Geo map. El. 37'. Laos.

Khong Island Airfield (WA 89-60)
L-07. CIA/SF, per *Air Facilities Data-Laos.*

Khong Sedone Airfield (WC 85-24)
LS-289. Apx 20 km from Thai border and 50 km N Pakse, per TPC K-10A. CIA/SF base per *Air Facilities Data-Laos.* El. 427'. Laos.

Khorat (SB 8-5)
A.k.a. Chaw Chaw? Apx 220 km NE Bangkok. US Army Supt Cmd facility here. At various times occupied by 256th AG Co, 538th Engr Co, 593d Engr Co, 738th Engr Co, 9th

Log Cmd, 7th Maint Bn, 57th Maint Co, 597th Maint Co, 428th Med Bn H&H Det, 21st Med Depot, 31st Med Field Hosp, 13th, 40th and 219th MP Cos, 41st Ord, 55th, 207th and 442d Sig Bn, 331st, 558th and 590th SS Cos, 511th, Supply Co, 519th Trng Bn, 291st Trans Co, 501st Army Field Depot and SF Det? Thailand.

Khorat Airbase (SB 8-5)
A.k.a. Korat, Nakhon Ratchasima, Nakhon Rachasima, Camp Nasty, and Chaw Chaw? At Nagor Rjasima, apx 220 km NE Bangkok, 650 km NW Saigon, 259 km NNE U Tapao AB and 680 km due W Quang Ngai and 350 km SSW Vientiane. Major US fighter-bomber base 1st opened by eight F-105 Thunderchiefs of 36th TFS, 6Jun64. A tiny base at time, it consisted of rwy and a few dilapidated wooden shacks with rusty, tin roofs. This cluster of unpainted wooden slat-walled huts was quickly named "Camp Nasty" by 1st stunned aircrews here. US Army Supt Cmd facility here or nearby (see Khorat entry). At 14°56'00"N-102°05'00"E. NIMA data. El. 729'. Thailand.

Khorat Airfield (SB 7-4)
A.k.a. Korat and Nakhon Rachasima AF. At 14°54'00"N-102°01'00"E, or apx 220 km NE Bangkok. NIMA data. On Feb67 Natl Geo Map. El. 729'. Thailand.

Khorat Army Airfield (SB 8-6)
A.k.a. Korat Army AF. At 15°00'00"N-102°05'00"E. NIMA data. Thailand.

Khorat Plateau (n/a)
Large plateau on SE tip of Thailand and NW the Tri-border area where Cambodia, Laos and Thailand meet. Thailand.

Khu 6 District (BR)
NVA/VC stronghold and staging area. Boundaries described in 31Jan70 4th Div ORLL (per Jim Henderson) as having been BR 24-02 to AQ 87-98 to AR 80-47 to BR 26-47. Center of mass apx 35 km SE Pleiku, and grids describe a rectangle oriented N/S, with its NW corner near Pleiku and roughly 40 km wide by 45 km in height. Pleiku and Phu Bon Pr, II Corps.

Khu Pho Nam Tho (n/a)
Mapsheet name of L-7014-6641-2. SVN.

Khu Tru Mat (XT 321-088)
See Duc Hue. Hau Nghia Pr, III Corps.

Khun Yuam Airfield (LA 8-8)
At 18°49'10"N-97°56'17"E, or apx 625 km NNW Bangkok. NIMA data. El. 1,320'. Thailand.

Khun Yuam Airfield (n/a)
On Feb67 Natl Geo Map. El. 1320'. Thailand.

Khuu Ngoc Tuoc, Camp (YS 26-86)
Former 1ATF Logistical Supt Grp Cmpd (ALSG) at Vung Tau. Transferred to 3d ARVN Corps for use as R&R facility 29Feb72, and renamed Camp Khuu-Ngoc-Tuoc by SVN Govt. Grid apx. Phuoc Tuy Pr, III Corps.

Ki Tem Dar, Cu (YA 84-77)
See Cloud 9. Kontum Pr, II Corps.

Kiama, FSB (YT 09-14)
1ATF FSB apx 28 km NE Saigon, 10 km ENE Bien Hoa, 5 km WNW FSB Kerry, 2 km N QL-15 km NE Plantation AF. 161 Bty, RNZA (Hitching's Bty 14Apr68-18Mar69) FSB set here 3-18Jul68. Bien Hoa Pr, III Corps.

Kidd Farm (XT 63-66?)
A.k.a. Dennis C Kidd Farm. Next to Camp Self at Minh Thanh, apx 33 km NNW Lai Khe AF and 70 km NNW Saigon. Named to honor MSgt Dennis C Kidd, KIA 4Aug64. Sgt Kidd built farm to aid local populace and was targeted for murder by VC for that act. Grid apx. See Camp Self. Binh Duong Pr?, III Corps.

Kien, FSB (XT 519-418)
A.k.a. FSB Mahone and sometimes sp Keane or Keene. On edge of rubber plantation, apx 5 km SE Dau Tieng, 8 km W FSB Gela, 26 km WNW Lai Khe and 12 km NW FSB Tennessee, per *Low Level Hell's* 1st Div TAOR map. On 14Sep69, renamed FSB Kien to honor ARVN LTC Thien Ta Kien, KIA (circumstances unknown), per *Low Level Hell*, p 229. 2d/22d Mech Inf, 1st Inf Div AO, '69. Binh Duong Pr, III Corps.

Kien, FSB? (ZC 0-5)
Also spelled Ken? Apparently near An Diem, roughly 38 km SW to WSW Da Nang AB, and apx 8 km SW FSB Bullwhip (ZC 05-66), 14 km W FSB Rattlesnake (ZC 125-650), 17 km WNW LZ Hawk (ZC 16-56). USMC map annotation from which this name was taken may instead indicate Ken or Kien Valley? See Kien, FSB, at XT grid. Quang Nam Pr, I Corps.

Kien An (Hai Phong) Airfield (XJ 6-0)
A.k.a. Kien An Bomber Field. Apx 10 km SW Haiphong and 85 km ESE Hanoi. One of 2 major fields near port of Hai Phong. Struck by 7th Fleet Carrier TF-77 attempts to blunt NVA Tet '68 offensive. On ONC-J-11. El. 15'. NVN.

Kien An Bomber Field (XJ 6-0)
Apx 8 km SW Haiphong. Large French bomber base built here during 1st Indochina War. Process took $20 million, 2-years and thousands of Vietnamese to haul crushed rock from mtns to this marshy location. 1st acft to land buckled rwy and, per *Street Without Joy*, p 181, the project was abnd as total loss. Apparently the project was revived, because a Kien An AF was active in American War? NVN.

Kien An Navy Base (WS 41-68)
On Mekong River, apx 6 km NE Cho Moi and 28 km SE Chau Duc AF. Joint USN and RVNN Base, '69-70. Per MRF Assn Website. Sa Dec Pr?, IV Corps.

Kien Binh (XS/WR)
Hamlets of this name in: XS 1-7, near at Ap Bac, and WR 3-9, 26 km ESE Rach Gia. Kien Tuong Pr, IV Corps.

Kien Binh Heliport (WR 310-980)
Apx 17 km E to ESE Kien Giang AF, 3 km SW Ap Thanh An, and 23 km ESE Rach Gia. Heliport #596, alt 10', sod (hard). At 09°56'00"N-105°16'45"E, per Feb73 TAD. Kien Giang Pr, IV Corps.

Kien Giang Airfield (WS 149-004)
Major AF apx 8 km SE Rach Gia and 6 km SE Rach Gia City AF, 72 km W Can Tho, 195 km SW Saigon, and 85 km SE Ha Tien. Per TPC K-10D. El. 13', 3,700' asph rwy. At 09°57'15"N-105°08'09"E. Kien Giang Pr, IV Corps.

Kien Giang Province (VS/VR/WS/WR)
One of 16 southern provs forming IV Corps (IV CTZ).

Kien Giang SF Camp (VS 438-448)
Along coast, at or just S Ha Tien South AF, apx 3 km SE Ha Tien, within 10 km of Cambodia and 75 km NW Rach Gia. 5th SF. Grid per *SF Order of Battle.* See Ha Tien (new). Kien Giang Pr, IV Corps.

Kien Hoa Airfield (XS 51-32?)
See Ben Tre AF. Kien Hoa Pr, IV Corps.

Kien Hoa Province (XS/XR)
One of 16 southern provs forming IV Corps (IV CTZ).
Kien Hung (Go Quao) (n/a)
Mapsheet name of L-7014-6028-2. SVN.
Kien Long Airfield (WR 286-505)
At Kien Long, apx 37 km NNE Quan Long major AF, 58 km SSE Rach Gia, 82 km SE Can Tho and 76 km W Soc Trang AF. See TPC K-10D. El. 5', 1, 700' PSP rwy. At 09°30'00"N-105°15'30"E. Chuong Thien Pr, IV Corps.
Kien Luong (n/a)
Mapsheet name of L-7014-5929-4. SVN/Cambodia.
Kien Phong Province (WT/WS/XS)
One of 16 southern provs forming IV Corps (IV CTZ).
Kien Thien Heliport (WR 480-585)
See Kien Tien Heliport. Chuong Thien Pr, IV Corps.
Kien Tien Heliport (WR 480-585)
A.k.a. Kien Thien Heliport. Apx 23 km ENE Kien Long AF, 43 km NW Bac Lieu and 24 km S to SSW Vi Thanh. "Heliport #599, alt 10', graded. Bldg on N, at 09°34'00"N-105°26'00"E," per Feb73 TAD. TAD lists grid as WP 480-585, but that is an error. Chuong Thien Pr, IV Corps.
Kien Tuong Province (WT/WS/XS)
One of 16 southern provs forming IV Corps (IV CTZ).
Kien Vang (n/a)
A.k.a. PGM 603. VNN Motor gunboat.
Kieng Phuoc Heliport (XS 912-488)
7 km ENE Go Cong AF, 9 km ENE Go Cong, 4 km SW Xom Vam Lang. Heliport #598, alt 3', dirt road. 10°23'00"N-106°44'30"E, per TAD. Go Cong Pr, IV Corps.
Kikuik Bay (BT 5-0)
A.k.a. Vung Dung Quat. Bay at 15°24'N-108°45'E. On ND49-01 JOG. Quang Tin Pr, I Corps.
Kilda Heliport (YS 298-438)
See Saint Kilda Heliport. Phuoc Tuy Pr, III Corps.
Killer, LZ (YT 058-205)
A.k.a. FSB Strike. Apx 9 km NE Bien Hoa AB, 1 km N the Song Dong Nai River and 4 km W Ap Mot. Feb69. Bien Hoa Pr, III Corps.
Killer Teams (n/a)
See Glossary.
Kilo, FSB/LZ? (XT 595-265)
Apx 12 km NNE Cu Chi, 22 km SW Lai Khe and 10 km due E Xom Rung Cay. Jun66. Possible FSB? Binh Duong Pr, III Corps.
Kilo India Alpha (n/a)
See Glossary.
Kilometer 15, Ambush at (BR 223-520)
See *Groupement Mobile 100* in Glossary and Mang Yang Pass in main alpha listing.
Kilometer 3, Ambush at (AR 7-4)
See PK 3, Ambush at.
Kim, FSB (XT 570-762)
Apx 7 km due E Bau Tram, 23 km SW An Loc and 12 km NNW Minh Than AF. 36th ARVN Rangers here Apr69, opcon 1st Cav per Frank Penk, Jr. Binh Long Pr, III Corps.
Kim, LZ (BR 764-954)
Apx 9 km due W Bong Son. Oct66. Likely 1st Cav Div. Binh Dinh Pr, II Corps.
Kim Bong, Pointe de (BS 9-1)
See Pointe Kim Bong. Quang Ngai Pr?, I Corps.
Kimbro, Sgt Truman, USNS (n/a)
See Evacuation of Da Nang.
Kim Chau Coffee Plantation (AQ 920-890)
On QL-21, 18 km E Ban Me Thuot. Darlac Pr, II Corps.
Kim Doi, Thonh (YD 754-313)
See Thon Kim Doi. Thua Thien Pr, I Corps.
Kim Lien (various)
Common Vietnamese place name. Sites inc: WJ 8-2, WG 4-0, WF 3-8 and AT 9-8.
Kim Lien (WF 3-8?)
NVN ville that was birthplace of Ho Chi Minh. In Nghe An Province, near port of Vinh. NIMA location is 18°53'00"N-105°19'00"E, if listed grid square correct. NVN.
Kim Lien, Vung (AT 9-8)
Bay at 16°08'N-108°08'E. ND49-01 JOG. Quang Nam Pr, I Corps.
Kim Lu (WJ 8-2)
Suburb of Hanoi. Formerly a French base, in '59. Its blockhouse and other facilities were converted by NVA as primary warehouse for supplying building of HCMT. Data per *The Blood Road*, p 15. NVN.
Kim Lu Xa (n/a)
Mapsheet name of L-7014-6144-1. NVN only.
Kim Noi (n/a)
Mapsheet name of L-7014-5852-4. NVN only.
Kim Qui, FSB (YD 584-036)
A.k.a. Hill 642. Apx 21 km SSW Ap Lai Bang, 33 km WSW Phu Bai, 2 km SE FSB Binh Dinh, 3.5 km due E FSB Veghel, 7 km SW FSB Bastogne. Joint 1st/327th Inf/101st Abn and 3d/54th ARVN Rgt FSB, Apr-May71. Paul Shaffer recalls it was S of FSBs Bastogne and Veghel, which roughly matches grid. Paul Grandy describes it as having been 1 km W of YC 561-952, which is apx 4 km S FSB Veghel and 5 km SSW listed grid? Also spelled Quy, Quay and Quee, but Qui apparently correct. Per Bernie Davies (through Roger Ables), D Bty 2d/320th Arty moved here from Veghel, 5Jul71 (and still there in Sep when he left). On 1st night, a Typhoon "washed us out putting 5 of our 6 guns out of commission." Rain/mud fouled guns already in need of maintenance from hvy use and got most ammo wet. Ammo dump, "big pit [with] ammo stacked about 6' high by 10' long" filled with water, and "we had to ship every round out." During Lam Son 720, beginning Apr '71, 326th Eng built FSBs Co Pung, Binh Dinh and Kim Qui with 327th Inf providing security. Per Hoang Nguyen, Kim Qui means Golden Turtle, and adds, "The turtle is one of four revered animals in VN: Long (dragon), ly (unicorn-like animal), qui (turtle, and phu+o+.ng (phoenix)." Also listed at YD 58-03. Grid/data courtesy Cliff Snyder.[318] Thua Thien Pr, I Corps.
Kim Son River (BR 750-800)
Flowed NE from mtns through Bong Son. LZ Bird and Pony were along its course. On SE 1/4 of L-7014-6737-1 map, per Ken Burrington. See Kim Son Valley and LZ Bird. Binh Dinh Pr, II Corps.
Kim Son Valley (BR 740-800)
Grid roughly at center of mass, apx 10 km WSW Ha Tay. Valley of Kim Son River, generally 25 km SW Bong Son, 35-40 km NNW Phu Cat and site of Ha Tay AF. LZ Bird was along river and site of major attack by NVA 22d Rgt on Christmas Eve, '66. Discussed in both *Bird* and

Chickenhawk. On SE 1/4 of L-7014-6737-1 map, per Ken Burrington. See LZ Bird. Binh Dinh Pr, II Corps.

Kin (n/a)
Vietnamese word for "secret."

King, FSB (n/a)
Location unknown. Cited in 1st Cav Op Rpt, Feb70/Apr70, p 31, per Peter Cole. Likely III Corps.

King, LZ (BR 719-935)
Apx 15 km WSW Bong Son and 15 km NW Ha Tay AF. Oct66. Binh Dinh Pr, II Corps.

King, LZ (XS 564-947)
Just N Song Vam Co Dong River apx 3 km SW Duc Hoa AF. Mar66. Hau Nghia Pr, III Corps.

King, LZ (XU 659-048)
Apx 7 km SW Loc Ninh and 18 km NNW An Loc. Jun66. Binh Long Pr, III Corps.

King, LZ (YD 265-438)
Along Hwy 556, apx 11 km ENE Ba Long AF, 3 km SW Thon Tan La, 11 km SW Quang Tri. Apr70 XXIV Corps grid per Don Armstrong. Quang Tri Pr, I Corps.

King, USS (n/a)
DLG-10. Guided-Missile DD Ldr, per Ralph Fries.

King Duy Thant Hotel 1 (CP 042-543)
In Nha Trang and overlooking the ocean, apx 2.2 km NE the NW end of the AF's main rwy and 600 meters N IFFV HQ. Khanh Pr, II Corps.

King Khoai (n/a)
Mapsheet name of L-7014-5752-3. NVN only.

King Marie the First (n/a)
See Kingdom of Sedang in Glossary.

Kingdom of Sedang (n/a)
See Glossary.

Kingfisher, Operation (n/a)
16Jul-31)ct67. 3d Mar Div ops in DMZ. 1,117 rptd NVA/VC KIA, per *Vietnam Order of Battle*, pp 9-14. Quang Tri Pr, I Corps.

Kingman, LZ (YD 190-164)
Apx 1.5 km SSW Dong Ba Le (Hill 1102) and 28 km SW Quang Tri. Possibly named to honor 1Lt Barry D. Kingman, KIA 29Dec68? Apr70 XXIV Corps grid per Don Armstrong. Quang Tri Pr, I Corps.

Kings' Knight (YD 761-221)
Flagpole at main gate of Hue Citadel. Much of Tet '68 fighting and press coverage in Hue focused on NVA flag raised upon it. Thua Thien Pr, I Corps.

Kinh (n/a)
Viet place-name prefix meaning "canal."

Kinh Cung Heliport (WS 960-760)
Apx 34 km NE Cao Lanh, and 33 km W Thuy Dong AF. "Heliport #720, alt 7', earth pad. South of Canal, West of outpost. At 10°38'00"N-105°52'30"E," per Feb73 TAD. Kien Tuong Pr, IV Corps.

Kinh Cung SF Camp? (WS 9765-7585)
See Kinh Quan SF Camp. Kien Tuong Pr, IV Corps.

Kinh Do Movie Theater (XS 8-9)
Saigon. Site of terrorist bombing, 16Feb64, in which 2 US soldiers were KIA and 50 other Americans and their dependents wounded, during showing of *The List of Adrian Messenger*. Data per *Vietnam Military Lore, 1959-73*. Gia Dinh Pr, III Corps.

Kinh Duc (ZU 2-0)
Roughly 25 km NE Bao Loc/Tan Phat AF's and 78 km SW Dalat. Lam Dong Pr, II Corps.

Kinh Gay (XS 358-876)
Canal. See FSB Gettysburg. III/IV Corps.

Kinh Lagrange (XS 273-773)
Canal. See Tuyen Nhon ATSB. Kien Tuong Pr, IV Corps.

Kinh Mo Kay (XS 4-2)
Canal apx 12 km SW Truc Giang. Kien Hoa Pr, IV Corps.

Kinh Quan (WS 97-75?)
A.k.a. Kinh Cung? Apx 29 km W to WSW Thuy Dong AF and 16 km SSW Moc Hoa AF. Kien Tuong Pr, IV Corps.

Kinh Quan II SF Camp (WS 9765-7585)
A.k.a. Kinh Cung SF Camp? Along Kinh Cung Canal near its intersection with Kinh Bui Cu, in vic Ap Kinh Cung (3), apx 29 km W to WSW Thuy Dong AF and 16 km SSW Moc Hoa AF. SF Det 71, 5th SF, Det A-416, Oct66. Grid per *SF Order of Battle*. Converted to A-144; ?? ARVN Border Rangers. Kien Tuong Pr, IV Corps.

Kinh Song Canal (WR)
Possibly Kinh Son Canal? Ran from Thoi Binh (WR 10-33?) to Tan Phu (WR 170-394). An Xuyen Pr, IV Corps.

Kinh Te (XS 89-90)
Canal that emptied into Saigon River at Port of Saigon. On map at: http://home.epix.net/~gramborw/ saigon.htm. Gia Dinh Pr, III Corps.

Kinh Thu Thua (XS 43-72)
A.k.a. Kinh Moampoi or Song Thu Thua. Roughly 30-40 km WSW Saigon. See Thu Thua. Long An Pr, III Corps.

Kinh Togtoampu Long My Den Hau Giang
WR 6-7. See Grand Canal, The, and Phuoc Xuyen.

Kinh Togtoampu Phung Hiep Den Hau Giang
See Grand Canal, The, and Phuoc Xuyen.

Kinh Tong Doc Long (WS 9-4)
A.k.a. The Grand Canal. Terrain feature of 1st Battle of Ap Bac. See Grand Canal and Phuoc Xuyen. IV Corps.

Kinh Vinh Chau (WR 8-2)
Canal near Bac Lieu, SSW Soc Trang AF. Ville of Vinh Chau is at XR 0-3. Bac Lieu Pr, IV Corps.

Kinh Xang Canal (XS 400-390)
Runs NNW to SSE, joining the Song My Tho at Dong Tam. See *Doc: Platoon Medic*, p 82. Also listed at XS 630-890 in Hau Nghia Pr. Dinh Tuong Pr, IV Corps.

Kinnard, FSB/LZ (BN?)
In mtns of NE Binh Thuan Pr and generally N Phan Thiet. Named to honor 1Lt Dennis R. Kinnard, 3d/506th Inf Arty FO, KIA 23Jun68 on FSB Bartlett, per www.currahee.org/ pageb3.html. Cited in *Currahee History, 1Feb69-31Dec69*, p 25. 3/506th Inf, 44th ARVN Rgt and B Trp 7/17th Cav here. Per same rpt at p 46, was opened at 0645 hrs, 27Sep69, by elements of TF 3-506, during Op Hancock Flame. By 1300 hrs, commo was established between the new FSB and LZ Betty, and by 1500 hrs, B, C, and D Cos plus COBRAA Teams 41, 43 and 45 were in place; Hancock Flame AO. Binh Thuan Pr?, II Corps.

Kiou Ca Cham Airfield (TG 09-68)
See Kiou Cacham AF. Laos.

Kiou Cacham Airfield (TG 09-68)
LS-04 and Kiou Ca Cham AF. Apx 185 km NNW Vientiane. CIA/SF, per *Air Facilities Data-Laos.*

Kiou Cha Cham SF Camp (TG 09-68?)
A.k.a. LS-04? Apx 185 km NNW Vientiane. SF camp/FOB when neutrality declared (23Jul62). FTT 22 and 23 here then. Per *Special Forces at War*. MR1, Laos.

Kiowa, LZ/FSB (BR 337-657)
Apx 8 km due W Kannack AF, 25 km NW An Khe, 3 km SE Plei Kon Trang and 82 km NW Qui Nhon. Name/grid per Jim Claeys. Also mentioned on 129th AHC's webpage at vhfcn.org/129th/129thhist.htm. Binh Dinh?, Pr, II Corps.

Kiowa, LZ (XD 854-651)
On S edge of DMZ, apx 27 km WNW Cam Lo and 23 km due N Khe Sanh CB. Apr70 XXIV Corps grid per Don Armstrong. Quang Tri Pr, I Corps.

Kirk, USS (n/a)
DE 1087. See Op Eagle Pull.

Kistler, Camp (YD 345-695)
At Cua Viet CB, apx 16 km due N Quang Tri, and on S bank at mouth of Cua Viet River. Basecamp of 1st Amphibian Tractor (Amtrac) Bn, 3rd Mar Div. Named to honor Sgt Leroy J. Kistler, KIA 21Jun67. Photos, map and other data about Kistler at: http://wmcbride.space.swri.edu/visit/maps/maproom2.htm and http://wmcbride.space.swri.edu/visit/maps/cuamap.jpg. Grid per Don Armstrong. Some data per Ray Bows. Quang Tri Pr, I Corps.

Kitty, FSB (XT 532-284)
Apx 26 km WSW Lai Khe, 18 km NW Cu Chi and 5 km NE Xom Rung Kay. Sep67. Hau Nghia/Tay Ninh Pr border, III Corps.

Kitty Hawk, USS (n/a)
CV-63. Acft Carrier. Deployed with CVW-11, 21May75-15Dec75; with CVW-11, 18Nov67-28Jun68; with CVW-11, 23Nov73-9Jul74; with CVW,-11 6Nov70-17Jul71; with CVW-11, 30Dec68-4Sep69; with CVW-11, 17Oct63-20Jul64; with CVW-11, 17Feb72-28Nov72; with CVW-11, 19Oct65-13Jun66; with CVW-11, 5Nov66-19Jun 67. See Op Yankee. [319]

Kiwi, LZ (YD 243-585)
Along Song Vinh Phuoc River apx 11 km WNW Quang Tri and 4 km due S Dong Ha Apr70 XXIV Corps grid per Don Armstrong. Quang Tri Pr, I Corps.

Kiwi Club (YS 43-67)
At Nui Dat 1ATF basecamp. Apparently the EM/NCO club of 161Bty RNZ Arty. Phouc Tuy Pr, III Corps.

Klahan Airfield (XB 44-94)
LS-326. CIA/SF, per *Air Facilities Data-Laos.*

Klamath, USCGC (n/a)
WHEC 66. 7Jul69-3Apr70. Sqdn 3 CGC, during Coast Guard's 4th deployment. SVN.

Klaw, FSB (XS 600-290)
A.k.a. FSB Claw. Apx 10 km ESE Truc Giang/Ben Tre. Built Jan69? In early Nov69, Bty C, 34th Arty, MRF occupied firing platforms at this base, supt 3d/37th Inf patrol base construction prgm. Kien Hoa Pr, IV Corps. [320]

Klaw II, FSB (XS 600-270)
Apx 11 km SW Truc Giang/Ben Tre and 200 meters S site of original FSB Klaw. 31Jan69. Kien Hoa Pr, IV Corps.

Klet Gir (AQ 95-05)
Straddles QL-21, apx 15 km E of Ban Me Thuot. *Societe d' Exploitation Agricole du Darlac*, an Ag experimentation and trng facility/plantation here. Darlac Pr, II Corps.

Klondike, USS (n/a)
AR-22. Repair Ship.

Klondike MSS (AR 811-801)
At peak of Hill 1152, apx 9 km SSE Kontum AF, 6 km NW Kon Xolang, and 6 km E QL-14. Per Steve Sherman, was "E of the CCC Montagnard Camp," and replaced SOG CCC's Sledge Hammer MSS (closed Mar69). Sledge Hammer's assets moved here and reopened Apr69 as Klondike. Kontum Pr, II Corps.

Klong Ngae (PH 6-5)
See Khlong Ngae, Sathani. Thailand.

Knife, FSB (XU 884-185)
Apx 18 km NE Loc Ninh and 14 km SSW Bu Dop. Jan68. Binh Long Pr, III Corps.

Knight, FSB (YD 528-422)
In coastal sands between two narrow lakes apx 4 km NW FSB Jeanne, 5 km due W Ap Tay Hoang, 23 km SE Quang Tri, 26 km NW Hue and about 6 km NE QL-1. XXIV Corps grid per Don Armstrong. Thua Thien Pr?, I Corps.

Knox, FSB (XT 280-778)
Apx 13 km SSW Katum and 2 km E Prek Klok. Jan-Feb68. Tay Ninh Pr, III Corps.

Knox, USS (n/a)
DE 1052. See Op Eagle Pull.

Ko (n/a)
One of many Vietnamese words for mountain.

Ko Chang Island (QP 1-8 ?)
An Island (possibly Kaoh Chan Island in Cambodian waters at XV 1-4, or Ko Chang Klua Island at QP 1-8 in Thai waters?). On 14Jun41, an old French cruiser sank 1/3 of entire Thai Naval fleet in battle off this island. Per *Street Without Joy*, p 22. Thailand?

Ko Chang Klua Island (QP 1-8)
See Ko Chan. Thailand.

Ko Kha Airfield (n/a)
Possibly Ban Lampang AF? Along Wang River, apx 510 km NNW Bangkok per Natl Geo map. El. 549'. Thailand.

Ko Sien Mountain (CR 020-230)
A.k.a. Ko Sin Mtn and Hill 244? Apx 5 km due W Qui Nhon AF and 3 km E QL-1. Binh Dinh Pr, II Corps.

Ko Tang Island (TS 96-40)
See Koh Tang Island. Cambodia.

Koan Lan, Cape (YJ 5-0)
See Cape Koan Lan. NVN.

Koelper BEQ/BOQ (XS 8-9)
8 Nguyen Van Trang, May 65, 65 rms, 32 transient rms, Saigon. Likely named to honor Capt. Donald E Koelper, KIA 16Feb64 at Kinh Do Theater, after rushing in to warn patrons of VC bomb thrown into bldg (*The List of Adrian Messenger* playing). Gia Dinh Pr, III Corps.

Koelper Compound (XS 8-9)
At 8 Nguyen Van Trang St., Saigon, was MACV (Military Assistance Cmd Vietnam) Headquarters until MACV moved to MACV Cmpd #1 (Pentagon East) adj Tan Son Nhut AB. Named to honor Capt. Donald E Koelper, USMC, KIA 16Feb64 at Kinh Do Theater, after rushing in to warn patrons of VC bomb thrown into bldg (*The List of Adrian Messenger* was playing). Data per *Vietnam Military Lore, 1959-1973*. Gia Dinh Pr, III Corps.

Koh Kong Southeast Airfield (n/a)
Apx 210 km due W Phnom Penh, per TPC K-10D. 4,600' rwy, El. 20'. Cambodia.
Koh Tang Island (TS 96-40)
A.k.a. Poulo Wai. Apx 65 km SW Kampour Som (Sihanoukville), 30 km NE Poulo Wai Island, 125 km due W Dao Phu Quoc Island, 270 km SW Phnom Penh and 75 km S Koah Rong Island. Crew of US merchant ship *SS Mayaguez* (also frequently spelled *Mayquez*?) were thought to have been taken here following its capture by Cambodian gunboat, 12May75. Unknown to US, on 13May75, the 39 crew had been moved to mainland. On 14May70, 200 Marines air assaulted island under mistaken belief crew was being held here, while *USS Holt* seized deserted *SS Mayaguez*. Heavy resistance met and US could not advance beyond beach, suffering 15 KIA and 50 WIA, until withdrawn under naval gunfire,15May70. Ironically, crew was released same day and delivered to *USS Wilson* by fishing boat. US Dead were inc in casualty list of Vietnam War. Gulf of Thailand. Cambodia.
Koiner, USS (n/a)
DER-331. DD-Escort, Radar, per Ralph Fries.
Kok Kieng Airfield (TF 33-53)
LS-282. CIA/SF, per *Air Facilities Data-Laos.*
Kolby, FSB (YD 40-11)
Near listed grid, which suggests it was apx 5 km SW FSB Maureen and 40 km SSW Hue. 101st Abn AO, '69-71. Thua Thien Pr, I Corps.
Kole Kole, Operation (n/a)
14May-7Dec67. 25th Inf Div op. 645 rptd enemy KIA, per *Vietnam Order of Battle*, pp 9-14. Hau Nghia Pr, III Corps.
Kompong Chak Airfield (n/a)
Possibly a.k.a. Svay Rieng AF? Apx 60 km NW tip of Parrot's Beak, 15 km SW Cambodia/SVN border, 105 km ESE Phnom Penh and 35 km SE Tay Ninh, on Feb67 Natl Geo Map. El. 23'. Cambodia.
Kompong Cham Airfield (n/a)
Along Mekong River, apx 75 km NE Phnom Penh, on Feb67 Natl Geo Map. El. 68'. Cambodia.
Kompong Chhnang Airfield (n/a)
Along Tonle Sap River, apx 80 km NNW Phnom Penh, on Feb67 Natl Geo Map. El. 66'. Cambodia.
Kompong Speu (VT 4-6)
A.k.a. Kampong Spoe and site of Kampone Spoe AF. Arms depot on Sihanouk Trail and apx 40 km WSW Phnom Penh. Cited in *A Better War*, at p 102. At 11°27'00"N-104°32'00"E. On JOG map NC48-02. Cambodia.
Kompong Sralao Airfield (n/a)
Along Mekong River at Cambodia/Laos border, apx 295 km NNE Phnom Penh and 10 km WSW Khong, Laos, on Feb67 Natl Geo Map. El. 250'. Cambodia.
Kompong Thom Airfield (n/a)
Apx 130 km due N Phnom Penh. El.? Cambodia.
Kompong Trach Airfield (n/a)
NNW Parrot's Beak, apx 10 km from SVN border 95 km ESE Phnom Penh and 35 km WNW Tay Ninh. On Feb67 Natl Geo Map. El. 26'. Cambodia.
Kon Barr Road (BR 3-5)
Branch road off QL-19E to Kon Barr at PK-15, apx 15 km W An Khe. French *Groupement Mobile 100* was ambushed at this intersection, 24Jun54. Binh Dinh Pr?, II Corps.
Kon Bring Bridge (ZA 039-288)
Grid may not be accurate, but if correct, was apx 27 km SW Pleiku. Pleiku Pr, II Corps.
Kon Chara (AR 777-873)
Ville or terrain feature apx 10 km due S Kontum. Data per in 31Jan70 4th Div ORLL courtesy Jim Henderson. Significance not otherwise apparent. Also a Kon Chara (1) listed in NIMA in grid sq BR 1-5. Kontum Pr, II Corps.
Kon Giong (n/a)
Mapsheet name of L-7014-6737-4. SVN.
Kon Henong (Kon Honong) (n/a)
Mapsheet L-7014-6538-1. Full sheet name: Kon Honong (Kon Henong). SVN.
Kon Hojao (ZB 060-220)
See Tanh Canh. Kontum Pr, II Corps.
Kon Hojao Airfield (ZB 044-024)
See Dak To I AF. Kontum Pr, II Corps.
Kon Hojao West Airfield (ZB 012-216)
See Dak To 2 AF. Kontum Pr, II Corps.
Kon Hokong (ZB 143-149)
Lightly defended ville along Hwy 14 E of Dak To. Attacked Feb-Mar69. Cited in *Time Heals No Wounds*, p 117. Kontum Pr, II Corps.
Kon Honong (ZB 0-3?)
Hamlet apx 1 km N LZ Lima Zulu (ZB 14-47?) and 3 km due W Toumorong Outpost. Involved in battle for Toumorong, Jun66. Elements of 1st/327th Inf here then. See *Battles in the Monsoon*, pp 316, 354. 101st, 4th Inf and 1st Cav. Kontum Pr, II Corps.
Kon Honong (Kon Henong) (n/a)
Mapsheet name of L-7014-6538-1. SVN.
Kon Horing (ZB 125-160)
Lightly defended ville along Hwy 14 apx 31 km NNW Kontum and 12 km ESE Dak To 2 AF. Also sp Kon Noring. Attacked by 304th Local Force Bn 23-25Feb69 and defended by elements of 42d ARVN Rgt and US 4th Div gunships/air supt. 52 civilians killed, 36 wounded, 5 missing and 132 houses destroyed. Also attacked by at least Bn-sized element 21Mar69, where US 1st/92d Arty suptg ARVN lowered muzzles and fired directly into advancing enemy (Bty A suffered 4 WIA per 4th Div op rpt courtesy Craig Miller, which also lists grid as YB 121-162). Cited in *Time Heals No Wounds*, p 117. Kontum Pr, II Corps.
Kon Mahar (n/a)
Mapsheet name of L-7014-6637-1. SVN.
Kon Plong Airfield (BS 081-145)
See Plateau Gi AF. Kontum Pr, II Corps.
Kon Som Luh (AR 814-888)
Apx 13 km ENE Kontum, 3 km SE Polei Krong AF and 2 km SW Polei Breng. ARVN RF/PF outpost May68, in AO of 24th NVA Rgt and 304th VC Main Force Bn. On night of 13-14May68, it was attacked from 3 sides by NVA the 6th Bn/24th Rgt. Pre-planned arty fire and perfect adjustments by ARVN FO however saved the day. ARVN 155mms at Kontum coupled with US 8" and 175mms of C/6th/14th at Kontum were on way to target within 4 minutes of initial attack, and credited with 147 NVA KIA. The ARVN suffered only 3 WIA. Kontum Pr, II Corps. [321]
Kon Tum (various)
Common Viet place-name. NIMA Gaz lists villes of this

name at: ZA 1-9, AR 7-8, BR 6-7 (a Mtn), ZA 1-9 and ZA 2-9. See Kontum. All grids in II Corps.

Kona, LZ (AQ 818-172)
A.k.a. LZ Toba? Apx 2 km W Quang Nhieu and 13 km due N Ban Me Thuot City AF. Feb66. Darlac Pr, II Corps.

Kong Roman (n/a)
Mapsheet name of L-7014-6638-3. SVN.

Konshim, Mui (XQ 8-6)
A.k.a. Mui Ta Be. Coastal point at 8°42'N-106°40'E. On NC48-11 JOG. IV Corps.

Kontum (n/a)
Mapsheet name of L-7014-6637-4. SVN.

Kontum (Maps) (AR)
See DMA L-7014-6537-4 and L-7014-6637-4.

Kontum Airfield (AR 790-890)
Along NE edge of Kontum, apx 40 km SE Dak To AF, 15 km E Polei Krong AF and 37 km due N Pleiku AF. Per TPC K-10A. El. 1,804', 3,600' asph rwy. At 14°21'15"N-108°01'17"E. Kontum Pr, II Corps.

Kontum Bridge (AR 75-92?)
Apparently QL-14 bridge over Kontum River, some 6 km N Kontum? Cited in *Time Heals No Wounds*, p 299. 2d Bde/4th Div security here '69. Kontum Pr, II Corps.

Kontum City (AR 77-80)
Along QL-14, apx 35 km N Pleiku. SF Det 16, 5th SF, Det B-24 (Oct66), MACV-SOG, Command and Control Central (CCC), Nov67-Apr72. Occupied by NVA/VC forces during Tet '68. 1st Bn 69th Armor spearheaded drive to retake it. Satellite images of Kontum/Pleiku area at http://coombs.anu.edu.au/~vern/space.html. Capitol, Kontum Pr, II Corps.

Kontum Province (various)
YB/YA/ZB/ZA/BS/BR. One of 12 north-central provs forming II Corps (II CTZ). [322]

Kontum Quarry (ZA 230-875)
Apx 5 km SW Kontum AF and 1 km W QL-14. 584th Engrs, 20th Engr Bn worked quarry out of base called Wooly Bully. CSM Steve "Sapper 7" Walls recalls that Wooly-Bully was immed adj to SF Mike Force trng camp SW Kontum, with only concertina separating 2 camps. Says SF camp was overrun/evaced in late '68 or early '69, adding wryly that "the 1st notice of the evac came when SF troops blew Bangalore torpedoes buried under their camp during attack and debris and NVA bodies from blast started falling into Wooly Bully!" Kontum Pr, II Corps.

Kontum Relocation Camp (ZA 227-845)
A.k.a. Tan Phu R.C. Along QL-14, apx 3 km SW Kontum. NPIA data. Kontum Pr, II Corps.

Kontum SF (MSF) Camp (AR 810-890)
At NE edge of both Kontum city/AF. 5th SF. Per CSM Steve "Sapper 7" Walls, was immed adj to Wolly Bully Quarry, with only concertina separating 3 camps. Apparently overrun and evaced late '68 or early '69. See Wooly Bully for more detail. Grid per *SF Order of Battle.* See FOB-2. Kontum Pr, II Corps.

Kontum SF Camp (B-21) (AR 810-890)
Possibly a.k.a. FOB 2 (ZA 236 863)? At NE edge of both Kontum city/AF. 5th SF. Info/grid per *SF Order of Battle.* Moved to Song Be. See FOB-2. Kontum Pr, II Corps.

Kontum SF Camp (B-24) (ZA 2751-8891)
Along Dak Bla River, apx 6 km W Kontum and 6 km ESE Polei Breng. SF Det 16, 5th SF, Det B-24, Oct66. Grid per *SF Order of Battle*. See FOB-2. Kontum Pr, II Corps.

Kontum, Plateau de (AR 8-4)
A.k.a. Kontum Plateau or Plateau des Habans. II Corps.

Kool-Aid (n/a)
See Glossary.

Korat Airbase (SB 8-5)
See Khorat AB. Thailand.

Korat Airfield (SB 7-4)
See Khorat AF. Thailand.

Korat Army Airfield (SB 8-6)
See Khorat Army AF. Thailand.

Korat Plateau (n/a)
See Khorat Plateau. Thailand.

Kord, FSB (XS 410-340)
Apx 11 km W Truc Giang/Ben Tre and 16 km SW My Tho. Jan69. Kien Hoa Pr, IV Corps.

Korean Forces, Vietnam (n/a)
See Major HQs Section.

Korean Regiment, The (n/a)
See *Batallion de Coree.*

Koropey. FSB (XU 0-3?)
Cambodian Incursion FSB, '70. 3d/4th Cav operated out of this FSB and FSB Schultz, keeping Rte 7 between Memot and Snuol, Jun70. Cambodia.

Kotrc, Patrol Base/FSB (XT 358-148)
A.k.a. PB Rittgers. In An Ninh Corridor apx 4 km due E S tip of Angel's Wing, some 28 km due W Cu Chi, 34 km SSE Tay Ninh and 6 km WNW Patrol Base Harris. Originally named Patrol Base Rittgers. Likely named to honor Maj James C Kotrc, KIA 29Jul69, but origin of Rittger name unknown. Apparently built early Aug69. Attacked 12Aug69 with 57 enemy KIA, and again 5Sep69 with 17 enemy KIA. On night of 12-13Oct69, attacking force engaged by 2d/27th Inf patrolling out of base. Mentioned in AAR at www.army.mil/cmh-pg/documents/vietnam /vni/232.htm. Hau Nghia Pr, III Corps.

Kow, FSB (ZS 13-99)
A.k.a. FSB Kew? Apx 17 km ENE peak of Nui Be Mtn, 16 km NNE Ham Tan AF, 18 km due N Ham Tan, 54 km ESE Xuan Loc and 17 km ENE Nui Ta Kou Mtn. 3d/7th Inf, '70. Grid per 199th LIB Assn. Binh Tuy Pr, III Corps.

Krait, LZ (BT or BS)
On wedge-shaped Barrier Island, along coast due S Hoi An. Op Bold Pursuit, Jun-Jul69, in area. Blue Beach, LZs Cobra, Krait and Rattler were used by Amphib Ready Grp, BLT 1st/26th Marines, during op. 1st Mar Div, Americal list. Quang Nam/Quang Tin Pr border, I Corps.

Krakor Airfield (UU)
Apx 10 km S Tonle Sap Lake, 130 km NW Phnom Penh, 25 km due E Pouthisat, 105 km SSE Siemreap AF and 120 km SE Battambang AF, per Dec67 DMA TPC K-10A and Feb67 Natl Geo Map. El. 49'. Cambodia.

Kramer, FSB (XT 020-727)
A.k.a. Krammer? Apx 5 km E Cambodia, 31 km NW Tay Ninh, 12 km SSE Thien Ngon AF and 28 km WNW Nui Ba Den. Cited in *1st Cav Op Rpt, Feb-Apr70*, p 6, per Peter Cole, and *11th ACR Cambodia Invasion AAR, 1st Cav Div, May-Jun70*, per Lou Rochat. [323]. Tay Ninh Pr, III Corps.

Kramer Compound (BS 64-73)
A.k.a. the Quang Ngai MAAG Det Cmpd. At Quang Ngai city. Named to honor Capt Leon J. Kramer, USA, KIA 31Jan63, per *Vietnam Military Lore, legends, Shadows, and Heroes,* p 378. Quang Ngai Pr, I Corps.

Krammer, FSB? (n/a)
Possibly same as Kramer listed at XT 020-727? No one with last name Krammer in CACF, which suggests Kramer is sp? Mentioned with this sp in *11th ACR Cambodia Invasion AAR, 1st Cav Div, May-Jun70*, courtesy Lou Rochat. [324]. See FSB Kramer. III Corps or Cambodia?

Kratie Airfield (n/a)
Along Mekong River, apx 160 km due NE Phnom on Feb67 Natl Geo Map. El. 98'. Cambodia.

Kraus, LZ (ZA 132-471)
Near stream, apx 21 km due W Pleiku, and 6 km WNW Ban Duc. C Bty, 2d/9th Arty here Dec69. 4th Div 31Jan70 ORLL grid per Jim Henderson. Pleiku Pr, II Corps.

Krause Barracks (BP 23-24)
See Dalat entry for detail. Tuyen Duc Pr, II Corps.

Kretchner, USS (n/a)
DER-329. DD-Escort, Radar, per Ralph Fries.

Krishna, USS (n/a)
ARL-38. USN Landing Craft Repair Ship. Service with 9th Inf Div/MRF. See www.mrfa.org. III/IV Corps?

Kristine, FSB (XT 306-853)
See FSB Christina. Tay Ninh Pr, III Corps.

Kro Layu (n/a)
Mapsheet name of L-7014-6532-1. SVN.

Krong Kno Airfield (AP 882-478)
See Duc Xuyen AF. Tuyen Duc Pr, II Corps.

Krong Kno River (ZU 2 8)
A.k.a. Ea Krong Kno. Apx 110 km due W Nha Trang. See Buon Krong SF Camp. Darlac Pr, II Corps.

Krong Kno SF Camp (AP 916-497)
A.k.a. Krong No. Apx 11 km E to ENE Duc Xuyen AF, 7 km due E Buon Rocat and 56 km SSE Ban Me Thuot. 5th SF. Info/grid per *SF Order of Battle.* Moved to Bu Prang and Buon Sar Pa (split). Darlac Pr, II Corps.

Krong Kno Airfield (AP 882-478)
See Duc Xuyen AF. Darlac/Tuyen Duc/Quang Duc tri-border intersection, II Corps.

Krong No Airfield (AP 882-478)
See Duc Xuyen AF. Tuyen Duc Pr, II Corps.

Krong No SF Camp (AP 916-497)
See Krong Kno SF Camp. Darlac Pr, II Corps.

Krong Poko River (ZA 099-913)
Float bridge built by ARVN Engrs at listed grid 11-14May71, as part of Op Quang Trung 22F. Job was to take 1 day, but took 4. Kontum Pr, II Corps. [325]

Krung Thep (n/a)
As late as '67, Thai name for Bangkok? Thailand.

Krung Thep Airfield (n/a)
See Bangkok Intl Airport and Don Muang AF. On Feb67 Natl Geo Map. El. 12'. Thailand.

Krypton, LZ (XD 891-573)
Apx 16 km NNE Khe Sanh CB, 22 km W Cam Lo and 14 km NW Ca Lu. Apr70 XXIV Corps grid per Don Armstrong. Quang Tri Pr, I Corps.

Kua Be, Lach (CP 2-9) A.k.a. Lach Cua Be. Channel near 12°35'N-109°24'E. On ND49-13 JOG. Khanh Hoa Pr, II Corps.

Kuchinairai Airfield (n/a)
Apx 485 km NE Bangkok. Natl Geo Map. El.? Thailand.

Kue, Camp (n/a)
US Army and SF Camp on Okinawa and site of Camp Kue Army Hosp. Some VN casualties treated here. Okinawa.

Kue Army Hospital, Camp (n/a)
US Army Hosp on Okinawa. Some VN War casualties treated here. Cited in *Team Sergeant*, p 209. Okinawa.

Kue Hospital, Camp (n/a)
At Kadena AFB, Okinawa. Not in SVN.

Kukhan Airfield (VB 2-7?)
A.k.a. Khukhan AF. Apx 10 km SW Sisaket AF and 75 km WSW Ubon AB. Per TPC K-10A. El. 400', Thailand.

Kukhan Airfield (VB 2-7?)
See Kukhan AF. Thailand.

Kula Gulf, USS (n/a)
T-AKV 8, Converted Escort Carrier. Served as acft ferry for MSTS fleet. SVN.

Kum Sah (n/a)
See Glossary.

Kumong, Baie de (CR 1-0)
A.k.a. Dam Cu Mong. Bay at 13°34'N-109°15'E. On ND49-09 JOG. Phu Yen Pr?, II Corps.

Kwala Point (US 9-5)
See Point Kwala. Kien Giang Pr, IV Corps.

Kwala, Mui (US 9-5)
Coastal point at 10°27'N-104°00'E. On NC48-05 JOG. Kien Giang Pr, IV Corps.

Kwinhon Bay (CR 0-2)
A.k.a. Vung Qui Nhon. Bay at 13°50'N-109°14'E. On ND49-09 JOG. Binh Dinh Pr?, II Corps.

Ky Anh (n/a)
Mapsheet name of L-7014-6245-2. NVN only.

Ky Con, FSB (XT 506-936)
At Cambodian border, apx 8 km WNW tip of Fishhook, 17 km ENE Katum and 28 km SW Loc Ninh. Grid per *11th ACR Cambodia Invasion AAR, 1st Cav Div, May-Jun70*, courtesy Lou Rochat. [326]

Ky Dong, FSB? (XT 163-918)
A.k.a. FSB Victor and FSB Cao Thang? Apx 7 km SE Cambodia, 17 km W to WNW Katum, 13 km NE Thien Ngon AF and 43 km N to NNW Tay Ninh. C Bty, 1st ARVN Arty with six-105mms, A Bty, 46th ARVN arty with three-155s here during Cambodian Incursion, per *11th ACR Cambodia Invasion AAR, 1st Cav Div, May-Jun70*, courtesy Lou Rochat. [327] FSB Victor apparently only existed 5-8Mar70, as 1 of 7 FSBs opened/closed in as many weeks by 2d/8th Cav, 1st Cav, prior to Cambodian Incursion (7 were: Jamie, Mary Gwen, Heather, Victor, Flashner, Drum and Illingworth). Tay Ninh Pr, III Corps.

Ky Ha Heliport (BT 532-114)
A.k.a. Ky Ha Army Heliport. On isthmus apx 10 km NNW Chu Lai AB, 5 km NNE Ky Ha AF and 3 km N Dong Tuan. Listed in '69 TAD, not in 73 TAD. Grid per frank Penk, Jr. Quang Tin Pr, I Corps.

Ky Ha Marine Air Facility (BT 529-116)
Apx 2 km N the N end of Chu Lai AB rwy, and within 1 km of coast, 3.5 km NE Ql-1, 17 km NNW Binh Son and 4 km due E Ky Xuan Island. Helo facilities at both Ky Ha and Marble Mtn were built by 4 Seabee Bns of 30th Naval Const Rgt. At Ky Ha, Seabees, MAB Sqd 36 and Marine Engrs helped build AF. MAG-36 flew 1st mission from Ky Ha on 12Sep65. USMC 1st MAW, 123d Avn Bn HQ also here. On 8Mar65, 3d/9th Marines (1st major US ground force in VN) landed on beach just S Nam O Bridge. Later same day, C-130s landed another Bn at Da Nang via Okinawa. With H-34 helos of HMM-162 providing log supt, units formed 9th ME. Mission was to protect Da Nang/AF from VC. Enclave at Phu Bai AF (15 km S Hue) soon followed, then another at Ky ha, just S Tam Ky. Some data per HM2 William Kelley (author's brother), RVN 66-67. Americal list. Quang Tin Pr, I Corps.

Ky Hoa (BT 4-1)
Coastal ville SE Chu Lai. At 15°28'00"N-108°35'00"E per NIMA. See Ky Hoa CAP. Quang Tin Pr, I Corps.

Ky Hoa CAP (BT 5-1?)
At coastal fishing ville apx 6 km SE Chu Lai. 3d Plt, I/3d Bn/1st Marines here 14May66 when LtGen Victor Krulak secretly returned to VN against Gen Westmoreland's orders. That day, 14-man squad of 3d plt + 2 Corpsman and a mortar team was designated as 1st CAP team in Chu Lai area and separated from its Co completely. Krulak told them to remain at Ky Hoa indefinitely and not to join in ops with any other units, then he and India Co left them to fend for themselves. Team was one of very first 37 "semi-secret" CAP teams formed at end of '66, although "official" USMC records show no teams created before '67. [328] Quang Tin Pr?, I Corps.

Ky Hoa Island (BT 48-10)
A.k.a. Pork Chop Island? Apx 7 km NE Chu Lai. Large island in huge lagoon formed by confluence of Song Ben Vam and Vung An Hoa bay. Americal AO and within 122mm rocket range of An Tan. Quang Tin Pr, I Corps.

Ky Hoa Island CAP (BT 48-10?)
1st CAG per CAP Website. Quang Tin?, I Corps.

Ky Hoa Island LAAM Site (BT 48-10?)
See LAAM. A Bty/2d LAAM, '66. Quang Tin Pr, I Corps.

Ky Khuong (BT 42-13)
A.k.a. Camp Swann. Marine CAC cmpd at Ky Khuong, roughly 13 km NW Chu Lai and 14 km SE Tam Ky See Camp Swann for more detail. Near 15°28'00"N-108°35'00"E. Quang Tin Pr, I Corps. [329]

Ky Khuong CAP (BT 42-13)
CAP Kilo 1 per CAP Website. See Camp Swann. Quang Tin Pr, I Corps.

Ky Lan Bridge (AT 997-547)
Song Thu Bon River RR bridge, apx 21 km due S Da Nang AB, 14 km WSW Hoi Ana and 7 km W QL-1. XXIV Corps grid. Quang Nam Pr, I Corps.

Ky Lo Valley (BQ 950-800)
Apx 22 km NE Cung Son AF. Phu Yen Pr, II Corps.

Ky Luat (WH 1-4)
A.k.a. Ky Lua. Apx 3.5 km from Lang Son, and famous for its scenic caverns. NVN.

Ky My (BT 247-254)
Apx 6 km NW Tam Ky and 2.5 km W QL-1. RF outpost. Americal list. Quang Tin Pr, I Corps.

Ky Phu (various)
Fairly common Viet place name. Sites inc: WJ 6-8; Ky Phu (1) at BT 354-232 and BT 471-043; Ky Phu (2) at BT 344-231 and BT 480-049; and Ky Phu (3) at BT 350-227 and BT 487-053. NVN and SVN.

Ky Phu (BT 465-042?)
If grid correct, was 5 km W Chu Lai. Battles here during Op Harvest Moon and Double Eagle, Dec65 and Feb66. See *Utter's Battalion*, pp 208-228. Quang Tin Pr, I Corps.

Ky Sanh CAP (BT 454-053)
Apx 8 km due W Chu Lai and 20 km SE Tam Ky CAP 1-2-7 here at least Aug-Nov68, per HM3 Richard Groulx. Quang Tin Pr, I Corps.

Ky Sanh Valley (BT 45-05?)
NW LZ Bayonet and near Chu Lai. If grid correct, was apx 8 km W Chu Lai. Quang Tin Pr, I Corps.

Ky Son Annex BEQ (XS 855-901)
At 46-48 Nguyen Khac Nhu St., Sep 64, 57 rms, Saigon. Per *VN Military Lore, 1959-1973.* Gia Dinh Pr, III Corps.

Ky Son BEQ and EM Mess (XS 855-901)
At 247-249 Tran Hung Dao St., Nov 65, 106 rms, Saigon. Per V*N Military Lore, 1959-1973.* Gia Dinh Pr, III Corps.

Ky Tra (BT 316-089 or BT 19-01?)
Listed grid puts it apx 12 km due S Tam Ky; however, map at www.americal.org/174/map1a.htm shows Ky Tra lists it at BT 19-01, which is apx 14 km ESE LZ Professional, 25 km WSW Tam Ky and 16 km ENE Hau Duc? Also listed at BT 316-094. BT 313-097 and BT 303-095. Americal list. Quang Tin Pr, I Corps.

Ky Tra Relocation Camp (YD 250-661)
In coastal sands, apx 10 km WSW Cua Viet, 3 km E QL-1 and 17 km NNW Quang Tri. Apr68. Quang Tri Pr, I Corps.

Ky Van, Mui (YS 4-4)
Coastal point at 10°23'N-107°16'E. On NC48-08 JOG. Phuoc Tuy Pr, III Corps.

Ky Xuan Island (BT 48-10)
Center of mass apx 7 km NW Chu Lai AF, in tidal bay formed by the Song Ben Van. See Ho Xuan Island. Quang Tin Pr, I Corps.

Kylie, FSB (YS 456-847)
On W side of Rte-2, apx 3 km NNE FSB Peggy, 7 km N Duc Tanh and 17 km N Nui Dat. Initially built on small scale since it housed only a section of 161 Bty RNZA 30May70; however, later expanded significantly to accommodate new M2A2 Howitzers added to cover Binh Ba Rubber Plantation. 161 Bty, RNZA (Andrew's Bty 18Sep69-6Sep 70) FSB set here 30May-6Jun70 and 1-12Jul70 (right section); 29-30Jun70 (left section). On 1ATF NCO trng map per John Hollett. Also listed at YS 45-84. Phuoc Tuy Pr, III Corps.

LIMA

Facility/Feature Name, Grid Coordinate, a.k.a. Name/History/Province/CTZ

Unless otherwise stated, 6-digit grid coordinates reference DMA L-7014, L-7015 or L-7016 series, 1:50,000 scale maps, while 2- and 4-digit coordinates reference AMS/DMA/NIMA 1:250,000, 1:500,000 and 1:1,000,000 scale maps. Unless otherwise stated, all heights are in meters. To convert meters to feet, multiply by 3.2808; feet to meters, multiply by .3048.

L-Sites (numerous)
A.k.a. Lima Sites or Laos Sites. See LS entries for complete listing of all L and LS Lima Sites. See also Lima Sites, Charlie Sites, Victor Sites and PS Sites in Glossary.

L-509 Series Maps (n/a)
See Glossary.

L-1501 Series Maps (n/a)
See Glossary.

L-7014 Series Maps (n/a)
See Glossary.

L'asphyxie par le vide (n/a)
See Glossary.

L'homme Sauvage Sightings(n/a)
See Glossary.

La Chau CAP (BS or AT)
Possibly in either BS 6-6 or AT 9-6 grid squares? CAP 2-1-4, 2d CAG here per Tim Duffie. Hieu Duc District, Quang Nam Pr, I Corps.

La Chu CAP (YD 694-244?)
CAP 3-4-2, 3rd CAG here per Tim Duffie. Hieu Duc District, Quang Nam Pr, I Corps.

La Chu, Thonh (YD 694-244)
See Thonh La Chu. Thua Thien Pr, I Corps.

La Gi (ZS 04-79)
Coastal ville along LTL-23, apx 5 km SSE Ham Tan and 45 km SW Phan Thiet. Also spelled Lagi on DMA TPC K10-D map. Binh Tuy Pr, III Corps.

La Gieo (n/a)
Mapsheet name of L-7014-6252-4. NVN only.

La Ha Borrow Pit (BS 677-683)
See La Ha Quarry. Quang Ngai Pr, I Corps.

La Ha Quarry (BS 684-677)
Apx 6 km SE Quang Ngai and 2 km E QL-1. Mar69. Quang Ngai Pr, I Corps.

La Ha Refugee Camp (BS 671-686)
Apx 6 km SE Quang Ngai. Grid per NPIA data. Quang Ngai Pr, I Corps.

La Hai SF Camp (BQ 952-797?)
A.k.a. Ga La Hai or Dong Xuan SF Camp? Along LTL6B at Dong Xuan, apx 12 km NNE Dong Tre and 16 km SW Song Cau/QL-1. SF CIDG Camp here during Battle of Dong Tre, Op Nathan Hale, Jun66. Map in *The Fields of Bamboo*, p 13 et al. Phu Yen Pr, II Corps.

La Hierre Airfield (YC 497-834)
See A Shau AF. Thua Thien Pr, I Corps.

La Khong Pheng Airfield (WC 61-58)
LS-159. CIA/SF, per *Air Facilities Data-Laos.*

La PIT (AR?)
Plantation *Indochinoise de The*. Tea plantation in Central Highlands near Pleiku. Site of a major engagement of *Groupement Mobile 100*, May54. Pleiku Pr, II Corps. [330]

La Pointe Da Vaich (CN 0-9)
A.k.a. Mui Da Vach. Coastal point at 11°43'N-109°14'E. On NC49-01. Ninh Thuan Pr, II Corps.

La Pointe Sopt (CP 0-1)
A.k.a. Mui Sop. Coastal point at 11°53'N-109°12'E. On NC49-01 JOG. Khanh Hoa Pr, II Corps.

La Son, FSB (YD 934-072)
See Anzio, FSB. Thua Thien Pr, I Corps.

La Ta Sin Airfield (XB 73-64)
LS-130. CIA/SF, per *Air Facilities Data-Laos.*

La Van, Dam (BS 9-2)
Dam Nuoampoc Man. Lagoon at 14°41'N-109°04'E. On ND49-05 JOG. Binh Dinh Pr, II Corps.

La Vang (YD 344-510)
Village along QL-1 and immed S Quang Tri. Site of La Vang AF. Quang Tri Pr, I Corps.

La Vang, FSB (YD 345-496)
A.k.a. La Vang CB. See FSB Sharon, and La Vang CB. Quang Tri Pr, I Corps.

La Vang (Quang Tri City) Airfield (YD 309-556)
AF apx 10 km SW Quang Tri AF, per ONC J-11. El. 60'. Quang Tri Pr, I Corps.

La Vang Airfield (YD 343-509)
See Quang Tri/La Vang AF. Quang Tri Pr, I Corps.

La Vang Basilica (YD 34-50?)
Apx 6 km outside Quang Tri. Monument built in 1900 to celebrate alleged appearance of Virgin Mary to grp of persecuted Roman Catholics. Destroyed in '72 Easter Offensive, it had been a major pilgrimage site until then. Quang Tri Pr, I Corps.

La Vang Combat Base/FSB (YD 345-496)
W of QL-1, apx 2 km S Quang Tri, 9 km NW Hai Lang and 47 km NW Hue. Cited in 101st Abn ORLL for period ending 31Jul69, p 28, online at: http://carlisle-www.army.mil/usamhi/ DL/chron.htm#AVietnamWar19601973. XXIV Corps grid. See LZ Sharon. Quang Tri Pr, I Corps.

La, Mui (CQ 2-2)
Coastal point at 12°51'N-109°25'E. On ND49-13 JOG. Khanh Hoa Pr, II Corps.

La, Route (n/a)
Rail and vehicle bridges along this rte hit during Carrier TF-77 attacks to blunt NVA Tet '68 offensive. NVN.

LAAM Sites (AT and BT)
Light Anti-Aircraft Missile sites deploying Hawk AA Missile. Each LAAM Bty had 36 missiles mounted on 12 launchers holding 3 Hawks each. 1st and 2d Bns deployed

to SVN beginning in '65, with 1st Bn protecting Da Nang AB and 2d Bn Chu Lai AF. 1st LAAM Bn (479 men): Bty A was on Hill 724, N Hai Van Pass in Aug66 (according to Ed Escoffier, the USN at Hai Van site offered "Best chow in Vietnam!); Bty B was on Hill 327 (Division Hill) just W Da Nang; Bty C was on N end of Tien Sha Peninsula, E the USAF CRC; and Assault Fire Unit of 15 Hawks was put on Hill 55, SW Da Nang. 2d LAAM Bn (460 men): Bty A on Ky Hoa Island N Chu Lai; Bty B at N end of Chu Lai AF; Bty C at S end of Chu Lai AF (Bty C moved to Hill 141 further SE Chu Lai AF to better cover the Song Tra Bong Valley). To author's knowledge, no HAWK missiles were ever fired in anger, although two were fired accidentally in '66. Some data per *USMC in Vietnam, 1966*, p 271-72.

Labonte Airfield (BR 799-829)
See Ha Tay AF. Binh Dinh Pr, II Corps.

Laboy Ford (XE 2-0)
See Ban Loboy Pass. Laos.

Lac Giao (AQ 793-026)
Alternate name for Ban Me Thuot. See Ban Me Thuot. Darlac Pr, II Corps.

Lac Hoa (n/a)
Mapsheet name of L-7014-6227-4. SVN.

Lac Tanh, Xa (Tan Linh) (n/a)
Mapsheet L-7014-6531-3. Full sheet name: Tan Linh (Xa Lac Tanh). SVN.

Lac Thien (AP 93-73)
On SW edge of Lake Thien. 35 km SE Ban Me Thuot. 5th SF, Det A-236 in this area, Oct65. Darlac Pr, II Corps.

Lac Thien (AP 95-74)
Lake apx 35 km SE Ban Me Thuot. Was about 5 x 4 km in size. Darlac Pr, II Corps.

Lac Thien (new) SF Camp (AP 975-736)
Along Rte 422, apx 7 km NE Lac Thien City, 4 km due N Lac Thien AF and 30 km SSE Ban Me Thuot. 5th SF. Info/grid per *SF Order of Battle.* Transferred to RF/PF. Darlac Pr, II Corps.

Lac Thien (old) SF Camp (AP 930-730)
Apparently a.k.a. Dak Mil SF Camp. Along Rte 422, at Lac Thien City, 5 km due WSW Lac Thien AF, 7 km SW Lac Thien New SF Camp, and 32 km SSE Ban Me Thuot. 5th SF, Det A-236, Oct65. Grid per *SF Order of Battle.* Relocated to Buon Uing/Yum. Darlac Pr, II Corps.

Lac Thien Airfield (AP 975-736)
Along Rte 422, apx 5 km ENE Lac Thien, 2 km NE Buon Ma and 33 km SE Ban Me Thuot. "Flight serv, contact II Corps TOC Pleiku, MACV 24Apr69, AF # VA2-208," in Aug69 TAD per Frank Penk, Jr. Not in Feb73 TAD. El. 1,385'. Darlac Pr, II Corps.

Lac Trom Dong (n/a)
Mapsheet name of L-7014-6639-3. SVN.

Lac Trom Dong, FSB? (AS 9-6)
Possibly a FSB? Roughly 25 km N Mang Buk. On L-7014-6639-3 map. Kontum or Quang Ngai Pr, I or II Corps.

Lach Cua Ba Island (CP 38-90)
In channel between Hon Lon Island and Ben Goi Peninsula. Khanh Hoa Pr, II Corps.

Lach Cua Be (CP 2-9)
A.k.a. Petite Passe. Channel near 12°35'N-109°24'E. On ND49-13 JOG. Khanh Hoa Pr, II Corps.

Lady-Smith, FSB (XT 12-73)
Apx 20 km NNW Tay Ninh and 10 km SSE Thien Ngon AF. Also appears to have been near FSBs Moose, Jess, Hanna, Wainwright and Hung Dao. Tay Ninh Pr, III Corps.

Lady's Pagoda (WJ 8-2)
Near Great Lake of Hanoi. Per *Street Without Joy*, in footnote at p 131, there was a sign at this pagoda indicative of matter-of-fact way in which sex was dealt with in French Colonial Vietnam. It read: "*It is formally forbidden for lovers to bring their girlfriends into this temple to make whoopee on the premises. This is a holy place.*" NVN.

Lagan, Pointe (BN 4-3)
See Pointe Lagan. Binh Thuan Pr, II Corps.

Lagi (ZS 04-79)
See La Gi. Binh Tuy Pr, III Corps.

Lagrange, Kinh (XS 273-773)
Canal. See Tuyen Nhon ATSB. Kien Tuong Pr, IV Corps.

Lagune de Cau Hai (ZD-05-05)
See Dam Cau Hai. Thua Thien Pr, I Corps.

Lagune de Ha Trung (YD 9-2)
See Ha Trung Lagoon. Thua Thien Pr, I Corps.

Lagune De L'ouest (YD 7-3)
A.k.a. Pha Tam Giang Lagoon? Thua Thien Pr, I Corps.

Lahan Sai Airfield (n/a)
On Feb67 Natl Geo Map. El. 900'. Thailand.

Lai Bang, Ap (n/a)
Mapsheet L-7014-6441-1. Sheet: Ap Lai Bang. SVN.

Lai Bang, Ap (YD 608-255)
See Ap Lai Bang. Thua Thien Pr, I Corps.

Lai CAP (n/a)
1st CAG per CAP Website. Quang Tin Pr, I Corps.

Lai Chau (n/a)
Mapsheet name of L-7014-5653-3. NVN only.

Lai Chau (n/a)
Capitol of Thailand (Feudal Thai Federation) and last stronghold of French in NW Indochina in early '50's immed prior to Op Condor (opening of Dien Bien Phu in Nov53) and after Vietminh pressure pushed French out of Northern Tonkin frontiers in 1950. Apx 2,000 Thai partisan troops left Lai Chau for DBP on foot during siege in '54; but few arrived there. Thailand.

Lai Chau (UK 12-42)
At confluence of Black and another river, apx 320 km NW to WNW Hanoi, 110 km SW Lao Kay and 80 km NNE Dien Bien Phu. Home of ZANO (Autonomous Zone North West), the ill-fated Lai Chau airhead behind Viet Minh lines. French hastily built airheads at Lai Chau and Na San in order to supt Col Bigeard's 6th Paras as they retreated from Tu Le, Oct52. Became French strongpoint during communist Spring Offensive of '53. Per *Street Without Joy*, pp 20, 76, and Chp 5; maps at p 67 and 117. NVN.

Lai Chau Airfield (UK 12-42)
Apx 300 km WNW Saigon. El. 591'. NVN.

Lai Hai (YD 59-41)
Apx 25 km NW Hue. Ville was S limit of Op Carmargue, Jul53. Grid apx. See Op Carmargue. Quang Tri Pr, I Corps.

Lai Khe (XT 770-380)
On QL-13, apx 10 km S Ap Bau Bang, 50 km S An Loc and 60 km due E Tay Ninh. Binh Duong Pr, III Corps.

Lai Khe, FSB/LZ (XT 760-370)
See Lai Khe BC.Jul70. Binh Duong Pr, III Corps.
Lai Khe Airfield (XT 772-381)
Apx 6 km NNE Ben Cat and 40 km due N Tan Son Nhut AB, per TPC K-10D. El. 121', 3,500' alum-mat rwy. At 11°11'41"N-106°37'23"E. Binh Duong Pr, III Corps.
Lai Khe Artillery Base (XT 770-380?)
Cited in *Cedar Falls-Junction City*. Thought to be in same location as Lai Khe Basecamp. Binh Duong Pr, III Corps.
Lai Khe Base Camp (XT 770-380)
A.k.a. Lai Khe Arty Base. Apx 6 km NNE Ben Cat, 48 km SW Dong Xoai AF, 22 km SW Phuoc Vinh AF, 70 km due E Tay Ninh and 40 km due N Tan Son Nhut AB/Saigon. HQ/home of US 1st Inf Div, '66-69, and of ARVN 5th Inf Div. 6th/15th Arty; 8th/6th Arty, 1st Inf Div, Advsy Team 70 (District Civic Action Team), 2/28th Inf (Black Lions) here. Home of C/2d Bn/28th Inf 1st Inf Div, the focus of Goldman and Fuller's, *Charlie Company*. 161 Bty, RNZA (Kenning's Bty 13Jun65-13Jun66) FSB set here 27-28Sep65. Binh Duong Pr, III Corps.
Lai Khe SF Camp (XT 737-320)
Along QL-13, apx 7 km SSW Lai Khe AF, 2 km SSE Ben Cat and 35 km NNW Tan Son Nhut AB. 5th SF. See Lai Khe Basecamp for more detailed Info. Grid per *SF Order of Battle*. See Ben Cat. Binh Duong Pr, III Corps.
Lai, Cape (YD 2-9)
See Cape Lai. NVN.
Lai, Mui (YD 2-9)
Coastal point at 17°07'N-107°07'E. NE48-12 JOG. NVN.
Lak Ea Gam (n/a)
Mapsheet name of L-7014-6733-4. SVN.
Lak Sao Airfield (VF 98 11)
LS-49. Apx 250 km E to ENE Vientiane. CIA/SF facility. Grid per *Air Facilities Data-Laos*. El. 1,700'. Laos.
Lake Fester (WJ 8-2?)
Apparently a pond inside cmpd of either the Hanoi Hilton or The Zoo POW camps in Hanoi. NVN.
Lakhe Thon (n/a)
Mapsheet name of L-7014-6145-2. NVN only.
Lakhonpeng Airfield (n/a)
Apx 380 km SE Vientiane. El. 500'. Laos.
Lam, FSB (YT 73-49)
On QL-1 apx 18 km due N Vo Dat and NE Xa Phung Lam. ANZAC and/or 199th LIB? Long Khanh Pr, III Corps.
Lam City, LZ (BT 512-101)
Apx 5 km NNE Chu Lai, 3 km S Dong Tuan and 2 km NW Ky Ha. Apr70 XXIV Corps grid per Don Armstrong. Quang Tin Pr, I Corps.
Lam Dong Province (YT/ZT/AN)
One of 12 north-central provinces forming II Corps (II CTZ). Also UTM zones AP, BP, ZV and YU.
Lam Na Airfield (QU 0-1)
At 16°27'00"N-100°58'00"E. NIMA data. Thailand.
Lam Nam Chi River (n/a)
Thai name for upper Mekong River W of Ubon Ratchathani and before it becomes the Mac Num River toward W Thai border. See Mac Num. Thailand.
Lam Son (n/a)
Vietnamese phrase meaning "Blue Mountain."
Lam Son (n/a)
Small ville that was birthplace of Le Loi, the heroic nationalist who led defeat of invading Chinese in 1428. The name graced many ARVN ops in order to honor Le Loi and nationalist spirit. Literal translation is "Blue Mountain." Thanh Hoa Pr, NVN?
Lam Son (XT 840-150)
Apx 3 km SW Phu Loi and 15 km WNW Bien Hoa AB. Apparently HQ of ARVN 5th Inf Div, and home of 5th ARVN Inf Div Advsy Det, Advsy Team 70. Binh Duong Pr, III Corps.
Lam Son 45-72, Operation (n/a)
See Cu Mong Mountain.
Lam Son 207, Operation (XD)
See Pegasus/Lam Son 207, Op.
Lam Son 216 (XD/YD)
Apr68 invasion of A Shau Valley, and a.k.a. Op Delaware. 1st Cav. Thua Thien Pr, I Corps.
Lam Son 218, Operation (n/a)
See Delaware/Lam Son 218.
Lam Son 245, Operation (n/a)
2Aug68-24Apr69. ARVN 54th Rgt. 636 rptd NVA KIA, per *Vietnam Order of Battle*, pp 9-14. Thau Thien Pr, I Corps.
Lam Son 261, Operation (n/a)
11Sep68-24Apr69. 1st ARVN Rgt op. 724 rptd NVA/VC KIA, per *Vietnam Order of Battle*, pp 9-14. Quang Tri and Thua Thien Prvs, I Corps.
Lam Son 271, Operation (n/a)
16Oct68-24Apr69. ARVN 2d Rgt. 603 rptd NVA KIA, per *Vietnam Order of Battle*, pp 9-14. Quang Tri Pr, I Corps.
Lam Son 277, Operation (n/a)
22Apr-20Jun69. 2d ARVN Rgt. 541 rptd NVA KIA, per *Vietnam Order of Battle*, pp 9-14. Quang Tri Pr, I Corps.
Lam Son 719 (XD)
A.k.a. Op Blue Mountain 719. Disastrous ARVN invasion of Laos, Apr71. ARVN effort to cut Ho Chi Minh Trail, destroy supply depots and disrupt commo using major armored and aerial assault W along Rte 9 from Khe Sanh area to Tchepone. ARVN encountered heavy resistance after initial gains and was forced to flee in disorderly retreat. Alert to potential of an attack cross-border, the NVA put roughly 60,000 troops around Tchepone (Base Area 604), inc the 2d, 304th, 308th, 320th, 324th Divs, plus the 27th 7 28th Inf Rgts, 8 arty Rgts, 3 Engr Rgts, 6 anti-acft Rgts, 8 sapper Bns and other suptg units. US ground troops were prohibited from participating by Cooper-Church amendment, but US did provide helo assets, as well as B-52, Tac Air and long distance arty (inc 18-155mm, 16-175mm and eight-8" guns firing from positions at or near newly reopened Khe Sanh CB. Involved 1st major tank-on-tank battle of war near FSB 31, when ARVN 1st/11th Armored Cav performed "brilliantly" by destroying 16-PT-76 and 6-T-54s with no friendly losses. However, of 62 ARVN tanks that entered Laos, only 25 returned and, of 162 APCs involved, only 64 returned (most lost to breakdowns or lack of fuel and simply abnd by ARVN in its hasty retreat). NVA losses est at 16 of 33 maneuver Bns, 3,500 supt troops, 75 of 110 tanks, and overall total of 16,000 KIA. In fact, losses were so great that for rest of '71, NVA had to focus ops around the DMZ

while its losses were being replaced. US losses inc 107 helos destroyed, 544 damaged (mostly 101st Div, virtually every one of which was hit by grnd fire). Good Lam Son 719 map at www.americal.org/174/map4.htm. Some data per *A Better War*, pp 242-262. Laos.

Lam Son 719, (US) Operation (XD)
A.k.a. Op Blue Mountain 719. 30Jan-6Apr71. US 101st Abn and Americal Avn units suptd this massive invasion into Laos, while US ground forces of 101st Div and US 5th Div (Mech) secured positions along QL-9 (including the reopening of Khe Sanh CB). **Phase I** began 30Jan71 and ended 7Feb71. Was essentially US op known as Op Dewey Canyon II, during which armored Cav and Engr units of 1st Bde/5th Div (Mech) pushed from Vandegrift CB along QL-9 to Khe Sanh Plateau and reopened KSCB. **Phase II** began 8Feb69, when 6 ARVN Bns CA'd into Laos while ARVN Armored Bde pushed into Laos along QL-9. Although 19,360 NVA were rptd KIA in op, it is generally regarded as complete disaster for ARVN, who also suffered heavy casualties and eventually retreated in disarray to avoid complete annihilation. *Vietnam Order of Battle*, pp 9-14. Quang Tri Pr, I Corps and Laos.

Lam Son 720 (YD)
Apr-71. Mission was to build, rebuild and reoccupy a screen of FSBs W of Hue while ARVN/US forces were otherwise focused on Lam Son 719 Laos invasion. Attack never materialized because NVA took LS 719 assault on the HCMT very seriously (they're Achilles Heel), throwing in every available unit and their reserves to defend it (even to point of leaving but 1 or 2 Divs to guard all of NVN). During LS 720, FSBs Fury, Kathryn, Maureen, Gladiator and later Eagle's Nest were all reopened by B/326th Eng with 3d Bde/101st Abn providing security. FSBs Co Pung, Binh Dinh and Kim Qui were built during same op. See FSB Kathryn. Thua Thien Pr, I Corps.

Lam Son Airfield (XT 840-150)
Apx 18 km due E Cu Chi AF, 17 km due N Saigon and 2 km SW Phu Loi AF. El. 98', 2,300' laterite rwy. At 10°59'18"N-106°41'05"E. Binh Duong Pr, III Corps.

Lam Son NTC (CP 1-6)
RVNAF Natl Trng Ctr. At S tip of Ninh Hoa Peninsula, apx 20 km NNE Nha Trang? Khanh Hoa Pr, II Corps.

Lamar Plain, Operation (n/a)
16May-13Aug69. AMERICAL with opcon elements of 101st Abn ops SW Tam Ky. 524 rptd NVA/VC KIA, per *Vietnam Order of Battle*, pp 9-14. Quang Tin Pr, I Corps.

Lambert, FSB (XS 320-490)
Along S side of QL-4, apx 7 km E Cai Lay, 15 km WSW Ben Tranh and 11 km NW Dong Tam. James Cartmill recalls it was "hidden off the road, directly behind a village." Grid per Cliff Snyder. Dinh Tuong Pr, IV Corps.

Lametta, LZ (YA 852-457)
See Lanetta. Pleiku Pr, II Corps.

Lampang (NA 5-1)
SF camp or AO per *SF Order of Battle.* Thailand.

Lampang Airfield (NA 5-1)
At 18°16'00"N-99°31'00"E, apx 510 km NNW Bangkok. NIMA data. On Feb67 Natl Geo Map. El. 793'. Thailand.

Lan Co Bridge (ZC 887-960)
See Lang Co Bridge. Thua Thien Pr, I Corps.

Lan Ha, Baie de (YH 2-9)
Bay at 20°45'N-107°07'E. On NF48-16 JOG. NVN.

Lan Nga River (YS)
See Rice Bowl, The. Binh Tuy Pr, III Corps.

Lancaster II, Operation (n/a)
21Jan-21Nov68. 3d Mar Div ops 1,801 NVA/VC KIA, per *Vietnam Order of Battle*, pp 9-14.

Lance, FSB (AT 797-406)
FSB a.k.a. Hill 575. Apx 5 km NW FSB Spear, 15 km SW An Hoa, and 4 km ESE FSB Dagger. Built starting 11Dec68 in preparation for TF Yankee's assault on Base Area 112. Americal list, USMC, '69. On map in *US Marines in Vietnam-1969*, p 90. Apr70 XXIV Corps grid per Don Armstrong. Quang Nam Pr, I Corps.

Lance, LZ (BR 278-749)
Remote site, apx 18 km NW Kannack AF and 37 km NNW An Khe. Apr-Oct70. Binh Dinh Pr, II Corps.

Lancer, LZ (YA 660-410)
On Cambodian border at point where Ya Krong Bolah meets it, apx 56 km WSW Pleiku and 19 km WSW Plei Djereng New AF. Jan66. Kontum Pr, II Corps.

Lance, FSB (YS 515-645)
Apx 8 km SE Nui Dat, 3 km SE Long Tan and 4 km NNE Dat Do. 161 Bty, RNZA (Honner's Bty 13Jun66-13May67) FSB here 1-8Feb67. 1ATF NCO trng map per John Hollett. Also at YS 51-64. Phuoc Tuy Pr, III Corps.

Lance, LZ (BR 278-749)
Near Kong Poi and on Mtn overlooking Song Ba River Valley, apx 17 km NW Kannack AF, 58 km ENE Pleiku, 12 km NW Hill 666 and 35 km NW An Khe. 4th Div AO, '70. Per John Linn, A Bty/4th/42d Arty was here Jun70. Name/grid per Jim Claeys. Binh Dinh Pr, II Corps.

Lancer (n/a)
Apr70, XXIV Corps proposed 101st Abn FSB name.

Lancing (n/a)
Apr70, XXIV Corps proposed 101st Abn FSB name.

Land, Camp (n/a)
Likely in Da Nang near ASP-1 and W of the AB. Said to have been destroyed by ammo dump explosion in Apr69 (ASP-1 blew Apr69) and rebuilt by 15Mar70. Named to honor LCpl David A. Land, USMC dog-handler, KIA 7Jun67. Per *Vietnam Military Lore, Legends, Shadows, and Heroes*, p 497. Quang Nam Pr, I Corps.

Land of Big PX (n/a)
See Glossary.

Land to the Tiller Program (n/a)
See Glossary.

Landing Zone (defined) (n/a)
See Glossary.

Landing Zone (name) (various)
Landing Zones (LZs) are listed alphabetically by name with last name first, followed by a comma and then the letters "LZ," or "FSB," as in "Janet, LZ," or "Janet, FSB."

Landshark Bravo (n/a)
See Glossary.

Landslide (n/a)
See Glossary.

Lane, Camp (BR 948-266)
See Lane Army AF. Binh Dinh Pr, II Corps.

Lane, Fort (CQ 275-229)
See Port Lane. Long Khanh Pr, II Corps.
Lane, LZ (XD 932-255)
Along E edge of Vietnam Salient, apx 5 km SSE Lang Klung, apx 19 km SSE Khe Sanh CB and 49 km SW Quang Tri. Apr70 XXIV Corps grid per Don Armstrong. Also listed at YD 932-295, apx 4 km N position described above. Nov68. Quang Tri Pr, I Corps.
Lane, LZ (YA 600-530)
In the Plei Trap Valley apx 27 km WNW Plei Djereng New AF, 63 km WNW Pleiku, 4 km E Cambodia, 3 km NNE Hill 283 and 2 km W Rte 615. Built beginning apx 6Nov66 by 1st/14th Inf/25th Div (before it became part of 4th Div). Photos/maps at http://1-14th.com/ maps. html. See *Rites of Passage*, pp 50, 73. Kontum Pr, II Corps.
Lane, Port (CQ 287-233)
See Port Lane. Long Khanh Pr, II Corps.
Lane Army Airfield (BR 950-270)
A.k.a. An Son AF. Apx 14 km WNW Qui Nhon AF, 5 km due N the ROK Strip AF, 10 km SSW Ba Gi AF and 18 km SSE Phu Cat AB, per TPC K-10A. Named to honor Sp5 James E Lane, KIA 15Jul62, when CH-21 shot down. 7th Sqdn, 17th Cav here 71-72. El. 40'. Binh Dinh Pr, II Corps.
Lane Hospital Ward (BT 55-03)
In 312th Evac Hosp, Chu Lai. Named to honor 1Lt Sharon A. Lane, KIA by mortar fire, 8Jun69, only US female to die by enemy fire in VN War. Quang Tin Pr, I Corps.
Laneta, LZ (YA 852-457)
See Lanetta. Pleiku Pr, II Corps.
Lanetta, LZ (YA 852-457)
Along Rte 509 and just S Plei Djereng New AF, apx 38 km W Pleiku and 7 km NNE Plei Beng. Built Nov67 or late '68? Per Dick Arnold, was 1st/35th fwd FSB from 15Dec68-16Jan69, while Dave Fogg cites 2Dec68 *Daily Journal* entry stating, "E Co 1st/35th made C/A from LZ Joan to LZ Lanetta at YA 853-457 to secure Bty C 2d/29th Arty." Apparently mutually suptd by LZs Mary Etta and Betty, and described in 4th Div rpts as "night laager for 1st/35th" Inf units. 1 entry states: "two platoons are leaving Ianetta on foot to meet 1/69 element at junction of Rte. 509 & 14-B." Sp Lametta in *Time Heals No Wounds*, pp 104, but both Lanetta and Ianetta in other 4th Div rpts. 10th Cav here, per Bob Patsfield. Sp variously Ianetta, Iannetta, Laneta, Lannetta and Lametta; however, correct sp thought to be Lanetta. Grid per 4th Div ORLL referenced in *Time Heals No Wounds*, pp 101-107. Pleiku Pr, II Corps.
Lang (n/a)
See Glossary.
Lang, Mui (CQ 1-7)
A.k.a. Mui Lang. Coastal point at 13°20'N-109°18'E. On ND49-09 JOG. Phu Yen Pr, II Corps.
Lang Be (n/a)
Mapsheet name of L-7014-6049-1. NVN only.
Lang Bian Mountain (BP 230-330)
A.k.a. Hill 2167 (7,110') and Nui Lang Bian. 38 km ESE Duc Xuyen AF and 35 km due N Dalat. Major US signal and radio-relay site. Tuyen Duc Pr, II Corps.
Lang Bian Signal Site (BP 230-330)
A.k.a. Lang Bian Mtn Signal Cmpd. Apx 35 km due N Dalat. On 15Sep77, site was transferred from 566th Signal Co (US) to ARVN 3d Sig Cntr, 662d Sig Bn. At time of turnover, site consisted of 29 buildings, 2 antenna supt towers and could house 120 personnel. MACV-JGS IG conducted a Post-Turnover inspection was 10May72. Some data per Ray Bows. Tuyen Duc Pr, II Corps.
Lang Chan (Lang Chieng Trai) (n/a)
Mapsheet L-7014-6049-3. Sheet name: Lang Chan (Lang Chieng Trai). NVN only.
Lang Chen (XD 840-408)
A.k.a. Cheu Lang Chanh. Ville immed SW Khe Sanh CB. About 6,000 local Bru tribe members gathered here in hopes of escaping fighting at outset of Siege of Khe Sanh. Quang Tri Pr, I Corps.
Lang Chum (n/a)
Mapsheet name of L-7014-5950-1. NVN only.
Lang Co, FSB (AT 886-957)
Apx 23 km NNW Da Nang AB, 7 km WNW the Hai Van Pass and 58 km ESE Hue. Oct69. Listed at ZC 886-957; however, that is erroneous. Thua Thien Pr, I Corps.
Lang Co Bridge (AT 886-956)
A.k.a. Ga Lang Co Bridge and Station Lang Co. Apx 1 km N QL-1 at SW end of Dam Lap An Bay, 23 km NNW Da Nang AB, 7 km WNW the Hai Van Pass and 58 km ESE Hue. Per Ed Escoffier, 1 Duster of 44th Arty and Quad-50 plus Inf security here '68-69. Thua Thien Pr, I Corps.
Lang Co Station (AT 88-99?)
Apparent USMC/CAP team site at N edge of Lang Co, apx 23 km NNW Da Nang AB. Per Ed Escoffier, 44th Arty, apx dozen Marines occupied site. See Lang Co Bridge for location. Thua Thien Pr, I Corps.
Lang Dak Sang (YB 895-406)
See Dak Seang AF. Kontum Pr, II Corps.
Lang Dat (n/a)
Mapsheet name of L-7014-6053-4. NVN only.
Lang Dong Island (BT 161-535)
Apx 4 km SE Hoi An and 26 km SE Da Nang AB. 5 x 3 km Island formed by river channel of Song Thu Bon and other rivers. Quang Nam Pr, I Corps.
Lang Hoan Tap (XD 7-4)
Vicinity of Khe Sanh and possible home of 101st Rgt, 325(C) NVA Div during Siege of Khe Sanh. Near 16°39'00"N-106°39'00"E. Quang Tri Pr, I Corps.
Lang Mai Bay (CR 09-21)
On S side of Qui Nhon Peninsula and E to SE the main AF. Binh Dinh Pr, II Corps.
Lang Mai, Baie de (CR 0-2)
A.k.a. Vung Lang Mai. Bay at 13°45'N-109°14'E. On ND49-09 JOG. Binh Dinh Pr?, II Corps.
Lang Mai, Vung (CR 0-2)
See Lang Mai, Baie de. Binh Dinh Pr?, II Corps.
Lang Met (n/a)
Mapsheet name of L-7014-6252-2. NVN only.
Lang Miet Heliport, Xa (XD 818-486)
See Xa Miet Heliport. Quang Tri Pr, I Corps.
Lang Minh Mang (YD 748-133)
Apx 8 km S of Hue along Hwy 547, between FSB Birmingham and Pohl Bridge, 2 km WNW Nam Hoa and 1 km SW Pohl/Nam Hoa Bridge. Tomb of Chinese VN Emperor Minh Mang, and noted for its beautiful grounds, sculpture and buildings("Lang" is Viet word for "tomb"). Very large, walled cmpd of at least 50 acres. Was off limits to patrolling GIs. See Hue. Thua Thien Pr, I Corps. [331]

Lang Mo (n/a)
Mapsheet name of L-7014-6243-2. NVN/Laos.
Lang Phu Trang Ridge (XD 758-534)
6 km N of Hill 881-N, and 1 km W Nuen Rao. Quang Tri Pr, I Corps.
Lang Phuoc Hoa (YS 29-61)
On QL-15, apx 10 km WNW Ba Ria, 16 km WSW Nui Dat. Elements of ANZAC 1ATF here, or it was significant terrain feature of their AO. Phuoc Tuy Pr, III Corps.
Lang Rao (n/a)
Mapsheet name of L-7014-6047-3. NVN only.
Lang Son (n/a)
Mapsheet name of L-7014-6352-1. NVN/China.
Lang Son (XK 83-15)
Apx 140 km NE Hanoi and 100 km SE Cao Bang. Involved in French Op Lea, Oct47. Populated primarily by ethnic minorities of Tho, Nung, Man and Dao. Apx 3.5 km from caves of Ky Lua. Major attraction is history as an important trading post/crossing point to China. Today become boom-town in trade with China despite uneasy relations between the 2 countries and fact northern border region is still apparently heavily mined, fortified and guarded. NVN. Is Capitol of alpine Lang Son Pr, NVN.
Lang Son Airfield (XK 83-15)
Apx 135 km NE Hanoi. El.? NVN.
Lang Son Outpost (XK 83-15)
Major French outpost of 1st Indochina War. In frontier of NE Tonkin near Chinese border and at eastern terminus of R.C. 4, apx 130 km NE Hanoi, 53 km SE That Khe, 102 km SE Cao Bang and 15 km W the border. When abnd by French under heavy Vietminh pressure in late 1950, its CO, Col Constans, failed to destroy garrison's huge arsenal and thereby enriched the enemy greatly. NVN.
Lang Tam (n/a)
Mapsheet name of L-7014-6050-2. NVN only.
Lang Thuong (CQ 32-27)
15 km SE Phu Hiep. Khanh Hoa Pr, II Corps.
Lang Thuong Lighthouse (CQ 32-27)
NE of Vung Ro Bay and 2 km NE of Ninh Ma. Phu Yen Pr, II Corps.
Lang Troi (n/a)
Mapsheet name of L-7014-6451-3. NVN only.
Lang Tung (n/a)
Mapsheet name of L-7014-6049-2. NVN only.
Lang Vei (XD 788-370)
Ville that housed SF A Camp, apx 7 km SW Khe Sanh. See Lang Vei SF Camp entries. Quang Tri Pr, I Corps.
Lang Vei (new) SF Camp (XD 7844-3673)
Along S side of QL-9, apx 9 km SW Khe Sanh CB. Moved here from Old Lang Vei SF Camp, Nov67. 5th SF. Overrun and moved to Hill 52 (Quang Nam Pr). Map opposite p 1 of (and significant discussions of facilities and actions here in) *Valley of Decision*. Some info/grid per *SF Order of Battle*. Quang Tri Pr, I Corps.
Lang Vei (old) SF Camp (XD 848-417)
SF "A" Camp along S side of Rte 9, apx 8 km SW Khe Sanh CB. Moved to new site at XD 784-367 in Nov67, which was apx 1 km W this original site and 9 km SW Khe Sanh CB. 7Feb68 attack involved 1st use of armor by NVA in SVN. 11 PT-76 Amphibious Tanks were used in assault. SF Det 1. Grid per *SF Order of Battle*. Map opposite p 1 of (and significant discussions of facilities and actions here in) *Valley of Decision*. The Old Lang Vei was reopened and staffed by Lao troops (and their families) that fled BV-33 at Ban Houei Sane's BV-33, when overrun 23-24Jan68. See BV-33. Quang Tri Pr, I Corps.
Lang Vei SF Camp (XD 795-360)
Apx 3 km due S Khe Sanh CB. *The Final Formation* gives this grid for camp as of 4May67 (at p 22), and rpts it attacked by NVA Bn on 4May67. Quang Tri Pr, I Corps.
Lang Vei SF Camp (#1) (XD 794-362)
1st SF Camp location at Lang Vei. Map is L-7014-6342-3, per Ken Burrington. Quang Tri Pr, I Corps.
Lang Vei SF Camp (#2) (XD 783-358)
Second SF Camp location at Lang Vei. Map is L-7014-6342-3, per Ken Burrington. Quang Tri Pr, I Corps.
Lang Zoi (n/a)
Mapsheet name of L-7014-5954-2. NVN only.
Langely, LZ (YD 024-354)
Apx 15 km WSW Ba Long AF, 13 km SSE Ca Lu and 35 km SW Quang Tri. Apr70 XXIV Corps grid per Don Armstrong. Quang Tri Pr, I Corps.
Langley, FSB (YD 023-358)
Near Lang Roao, apx 36 km SW Quang Tri and 8 km S FSB Henderson. Quang Tri Pr, I Corps.
Lannetta, LZ (YA 852-457)
See Iannetta or Lanetta. Pleiku Pr, II Corps.
Lanyard, FSB (XT 075-892)
On Cambodian border at Xa Mat, near point where SVN Rte 22 crossed it to become Cambodian Rte 78, apx 8 km due N Thien Ngon AF, 26 km due W Katum AF and 42 km NNW Tay Ninh. Incursion FSB, May and/or Jun70. Possibly 1st Cav, 25th Inf, 11th ACR or ARVN elements here. Tay Ninh Pr/Cambodia, III Corps.
Lanyard, FSB (YD 897-198)
A.k.a. FSB Harper, Jan70. In coastal sands along Hwy 552, apx 5 km due N Phu Bai AF, 1 km NNW ville of Thon Hoa Da Tay, 3 km SW Dam Ha Trung Lagoon and 12 km W Hue. 101st Abn inactive FSB grid per Don Armstrong. Thua Thien Pr, I Corps.
Lao Bao, FSB (XD 70-37)
At Laotian border, apx 15 km WSW Khe Sanh, 18 km ESE Aloui and 10 km WNW Lang Vei. ARVN FSB during Lam Son 719. Good Lam Son 719 FSB map at www.americal.org/174/map4.htm. Quang Tri Pr, I Corps.
Lao Bao Airfield (XD 698-369)
At Laotian border, apx 17 km WSW Khe Sanh CB. Possibly in use during Lam Son 719. El. 690' (On Feb67 Natl Geo Map at 170'?). "Abnd 30Jan67, AF # VA1-71," in Aug69 TAD per Frank Penk, Jr. Not in Feb73 TAD. Quang Tri Pr, I Corps.
Lao Cai (UK 92-89)
Major Chinese border trading town noted for beautiful scenery. Possibly also Lao Khe and Lao Kay? At 22°29'00"N-103°57'00"E. NVN.
Lao Cai Airfield (UK 9-8)
Apx 260 km NW Hanoi. El. 295'. NVN.
Lao Kay (n/a)
Mapsheet name of L-7014-5753-1. NVN only.
Lao Kay (UK98)
A.k.a. Lao Cai. Apx 260 km NW Hanoi, where Red River

meets the Chinese border. French outpost here in '40's and '50's. NVN.

Lao Kay Outpost (UK 9-8?)
A.k.a. Lao Cai and Lao Khe? A French frontier outpost of 1st Indochina War in northern Tonkin. Sat in shadow of Yunnan Chinese border area along Red River (Song Coi) 30 km upstream from Pho Lu outpost. Was evacuated by French in late 1950, thus opening the immense NW reaches of Tonkin, Lai Chau and NE reaches of Thailand and Laos to Vietminh. After its fall, the French only retained control of Song Coi (Red River Delta). Likely sp variant of "Lao Cai." See Cao Bang. NVN.

Lao Na Airfield (QU 1-2)
At 16°29'00"N-100°59'00"E. NIMA data. Thailand.

Lao Ta Airfield (TJ 12-04)
LS-121. CIA/SF, per *Air Facilities Data-Laos.*

Laos (n/a)
Country of 92, 429 sq mi and apx 3 million population in '70. At time, was apx 75% ethnic Lao and 25% Thai tribal peoples who had migrated from Thailand. Formed portion of NW border of SVN. Border adj DMZ was invaded by ARVN, Feb71 (Lam Son 719), in op that became disastrous failure.

Laotian Corridor (n/a)
MACV's name for portion of HCMT passing through Laos. NVA rptd that by end of '71, supplies of the Binh Trams of 559th Grp (in charge of that portion) had risen to 6,000 tons each, which they estimated could supply 50,000 to 60,000 troops for 4 months. Another 30,000 tons of supplies were also stored along the Transportation Corridor (the HCMT). Data per *A Better War*, p 238. See Binh Tram and Ho Chi Minh Trail in Glossary. Laos.

Laotian Gateway (XD 66-37)
SF nickname for point where QL-9 crossed Laotian border just W Lang Vei. Cited in *Team Sergeant*, p 139. Quang Tri Pr, I Corps.

Laotian Military Regions (n/a)
See Glossary.

Laotian Salient (XD 97-23)
Geographical feature defined by Laotian border apx 40 km SW of Quang Tri. In *Da Nang Diary* (p 183-4) author wrote that Salient "resembled the business end of a hatchet roughly 5 miles wide and jutting 8 miles due N into Vietnam." Was immed E and adj to Vietnam Salient. Grid near center of mass. See Vietnam Salient. Laos.

Lap An, Dam (AT 8-9)
Lagoon at 16°14'N-108°04'E. On ND49-01 JOG. Quang Nam Pr, I Corps.

Laramie, LZ/FSB (BS 790-043)
Overlooking An Lao Valley, apx 9 km NW LZ English and 6 km SSE Thuan An. Cited in 1st Cav VN *Yearbook* Aug65-Dec69, p 116, 290, 291, per Peter Cole. USAF Herbicide rpt indicates total gallons of following agents were sprayed within 8 km radius of this facility: Orange, 68970; White, 490; Blue, 10570. Grid per Dan Gillotti. Binh Dinh Pr, II Corps.

Larry, LZ (BR 259-768)
Apx 40 km NW An Khe and 25 km NNE Kannack AF. On map (Enc #5) of 4th Div AO in ORLL of 31Jan70 per Jim Henderson, B/1st/22d Inf. Sep-Oct69. Grid per Dan Gillotti. Binh Dinh Pr, II Corps.

Larson Airfield (BT)
At Da Nang, but unknown which Da Nang area AF it references. Named to honor Cpl Jeffry A. Larson, 1st Cav, KIA 2Jan68. Quang Nam Pr, I Corps.

Lash, FSB (YC 673-668)
Apx 6 km from Laotian border some 74 km WSW Da Nang, 42 km due N A Ro AF, 48 km WNW Ha Tan AF and 12 km NW Ai Yinh Young. 1st/502d Inf, 101st Abn here Apr-May69, during Op Massachusetts Striker. Listed as closed (but re-openable) in 1Feb70 XXIV Corps 101st Abn FSB rpt. Also listed at YC 674-660. Near Thua Thien/Quang Nam Pr border, I Corps.

Lassiter Heliport (YT 016-153)
Apx 1 to 2 km SE Bien Hoa AB, and 26 km NE Tan Son Nhut AB. "Heliport #755, alt 125', Rwy-1200' x 200' (Peneprime) 09L-27R; CH-47, 1000' x 300' (Peneprime) 09C-27C. Operates 0001-1400Z. Closed to F/W acft. Acft entering traffic from SE must cross extended centerline of Bien Hoa active rwy 4 nautical miles E at 500' MSL or below. See Bien Hoa helicopter entry departure and transition routes, and VFR flight within Bien Hoa air traffic zone (ATZ). Commo-Saigon Appr Con 363.8, 134.1, Tower-264.9, 120.6, 65.55. Arty advsy-Bien Hoa 290.0, 46.7. Radio/Nav Remarks-Vietnamese controllers 2315-1100Z, US controllers 1100-2315Z. At 10°59'45"N-106°51'30"E, per Feb73 TAD. Bien Hoa Pr, III Corps.

Lat Houang Airfield (UG 09-44)
LS-09. CIA/SF, per *Air Facilities Data-Laos.*

Lat Khai Airfield (UG 04-34)
LS-280. CIA/SF, per *Air Facilities Data-Laos.*

Lat Sen Airfield (UG 03-38)
LS-276. CIA/SF, per *Air Facilities Data-Laos.*

Laterite (n/a)
See Laterite Soil in Glossary.

Laterite Lantern, The (n/a)
Bde newspaper of 20th Engr Bde. Vice President (then SP4) Al Gore (nickname "Brother Buck") worked as reporter for this paper. Bde was HQ'd at Bien Hoa. See FSB Blue. Bien Hoa Pr, III Corps.

Laterite Pit Quarry (XT 104-502)
Apx 7 km WSW Tay Ninh West AF and 4 km NE Ben Soi. Sep67. Tay Ninh Pr, III Corps.

Laterite Pit Quarry (XT 670-140)
Apx 3 km SE Cu Chi. Apr66. Hau Nghia Pro, III Corps.

Laterite Pit Quarry (XT 744-356)
Apx 3 km N Ben Cat and 5 km SW Lai Khe. Feb-Apr67. Also listed at XT 752-355. Binh Duong Pr, III Corps.

Lau Vuc (n/a)
Fictional name used to disguise actual or composite of SF camps visited by *The Green Berets* author Robin Moore during 6-month visit to VN in '64 or '65. In book, is described as being 50 miles across mountainous jungle from Da Nang and 5 km from Lao border; a description that closely fits Kham Duc. Moore also says shape was triangular, with perimeter walls made of sandbags and mud. At each of its 3 corners were big, tall bunkers, and each of perimeter walls had smaller bunkers sporting MG posts.[332]

Lauffer, FSB (n/a)
Cited in *1st Cav Op Rpt, May-Jul70*, p 29, per Peter Cole. Possibly named to honor PFC Billy A. Lauffer, KIA

21Sep66. During rpt period, the Cav was in western III Corps/Cambodia.

Laura, FSB (XT 225-888)
Apx 5 km SE Cambodia, 8 km NNE Thien Ngon AF, 4 km SW Ky Dong, 20 km due W Katum and 41 km NNW Tay Ninh. Tay Ninh Pr, III Corps.

Laura Kay, LZ (AR 953-396)
Apx 19 km ESE Pleiku, 18 km ENE Camp Enari, 12 km NW LZ Doris and 13 km NNE Plei Do Lim. 4th Div AO, '70. Name/grid per Jim Claeys. Pleiku Pr, II Corps.

Laurer, Camp (AT or BT)
One source claims Laurer was USMC camp at Marble Mtn, while another says it was location of Freedom Hill, and R&R transit barracks at Da Nang? Apparently named to honor Cpl Charles R. Laurer, 3d Amphib Track Co, KIA 18Jun67, while attempting rescue of wounded comrades. Some data per Ray Bows. Quang Nam Pr, I Corps.

Laurie, FSB (BN 036-280)
Apx 28 km NE Phan Thiet, 4 km E Ray Dau, and 13 km ENE Nui Ta Don (Hill 385). 3d/506th Inf, 101st Abn. Name/grid per Jerry Berry. Binh Thuan Pr, II Corps.

Laurio, LZ (BR 773-728)
Apx 41 km NE An Khe, 15 km WNW Phu My/QL-1 and 12 km SSW Ha Tay AF. Oct66. Binh Dinh Pr, II Corps.

LaVang, FSB (YD 34-50?)
See La Vang, FSB & Quang Tri AF. Quang Tri Pr, I Corps.

Lawrence, USS (n/a)
DDG-4. Guided-Missile DD, per Ralph Fries.

Lawton, LZ (XT 695-928)
Apx 6 km NW An Loc, 16 km SSW Loc Ninh and 4 km W QL-13. Jul69. Binh Long Pr, III Corps.

Laxoner, LZ ? (BR 510-380)
Apx 8 km SSE An Khe and 19 km WSW Binh Khe. Possible LZ. Dec65. Binh Dinh Pr, II Corps.

Lay, Mui (YD 2-8)
Coastal point at 17°05'N-107°07'E. NE48-12 JOG. NVN?

Layto, FSB (XT 060-770)
See Layton, FSB. Tay Ninh Pr, III Corps.

Layton, FSB (XT 060-770)
A.k.a. Laytons or Layto? Apx 9 km ENE Cambodian border just E Dog's Head, apx 6 km SSE Thien Ngon AF, 30 km WSW Katum, 28 km NNW Tay Ninh W AF and 33 km NNW Tay Ninh. 1st Cav. Tay Ninh Pr, III Corps.

Laytons, FSB (XT 060-770)
See Layton, FSB. Tay Ninh Pr, III Corps.

Lazaret, Pointe du (XS 9-7)
See Pointe Lazaret. Gia Dinh Pr?, III Corps.

Lazaret, Pointe du (YS 2-4)
See Pointe Lazaret. Phuoc Tuy Pr?, III Corps.

Lazarus, Operation (n/a)
See Glossary.

Lazarus Omega, Operation (n/a)
See Glossary.

LBJ (YT 04-07?)
Acronym of, and slang for infamous Long Binh Jail at Long binh Post, and alos the initials of President Lyndon Johnson. See Long Binh Jail. Bien Hoa Pr, III Corps.

LCM-6 (n/a)
USN Landing Craft, Mechanized/Medium. SVN

LCM-873 (n/a)
USN Landing Craft, Mechanized/Medium. SVN

LCU Ramp, Tan My (YD 826-312)
See Tan My LCU Ramp. Thua Thien Pr, I Corps.

Le asphyxie par le vide (n/a)
See L'asphyxie in Glossary.

Le Cambodge River (WT, WS, XS, XR)
See Mekong River. IV Corps.

Le Coeur (WR 1-3?)
Village NW Tan Phu SF Camp. An Xuyen Pr, IV Corps.

Le Guerre des Grandes Vides (n/a)
See Glossary.

Le Guerre sans fronts (n/a)
See Glossary.

Le Hai SF Camp (BQ 909-704?)
If grid correct, was just SW Dong Tre AF and near Phu Hoi, apx 21 km WNW Tuy An AF and 56 km SSW Qui Nhon. 5th SF. Info/grid per *SF Order of Battle.* FOB Dong Tre/Cung Son. Phu Yen Pr, II Corps.

***Le homme Sauvage* Sightings**(n/a)
See Glossary.

Le Hon Phong Forest (BN 30-57?)
A VC/NVA sanctuary in Song Mao Mtns, and AO of 3d/506th Inf, 101st Abn. Apparently roughly 10-15 km N to NE Song Mao in NE Binh Thuan Pr?, It also reportedly held a POW camp containing US and ARVN POWs, and in Sep69, was focus of joint 44th ARVN Rgt/US op to clear area of enemy and capture POW camp. 4 US and 3 ARVN Cos were committed to mission. On 3Sep69, D/3d/506th found major hospital complex; however, POW complex was apparently not found. Data per *Currahee History, 1Feb69-31Dec69*, pp 41-44, pub of 3d/506th Inf. See Song Mao Mtns. Binh Thuan Pr, II Corps.

Le Lac (BP 23-22?)
A.k.a. Ho Xuan Huong. A freshwater lake at 11°56N-108°27'E. On NC49-01 JOG. Tuyen Duc Pr, II Corps.

Le Lai Hotel (XS 8-9)
In Saigon, along Duong Le Lai St., at corner of Le Lai and Le Van Duyet (enlisted billets, 4th Trans Cmd), near central market. After '68 Tet Offensive, hotel acquired nickname "Old Ironsides" as reflection of voluminous and often indiscriminate small arms fire that poured from its various balconies! For a time, it housed HQ of 4th Trans Cmd. Gia Dinh Pr, III Corps.

Le Lai, FSB (n/a)
See Loan, FSB. Phuoc Long Pr?, III Corps.

Le Loi (XT 202-868)
Site of old FSB Drum, apx 15 km SW Katum, 13 km ESE Thien Ngon AF, 24 km NNW Nui Ba Den and 30 km due N Tay Ninh. FSB Drum existed 13-17Mar70, as 1 of 7 FSBs opened and closed in as many weeks by 2d/8th Cav, 1st Cav, prior to Cambodian Incursion (7 were: Jamie, Mary Gwen, Heather, Victor, Flashner, Drum and Illingworth). Tay Ninh Pr, III Corps.

Le Loi, FSB (YU 253-294)
A.k.a. LZ Betty. Apx 10 km from Cambodia, 12 km SW Djamap, 21 km NNE Song Be/Phuoc Binh and 28 km due E Bu Dop. Apr70. Phuoc Long Pr, III Corps.

Le Loi, FSB (YS 456-768)
On Rte-2, apx 7 km N Nui Dat, 4 km S Duc Tanh, and 3 km SW Ngai Giao. 161 Bty, RNZA, Andrew's Bty set here 27-30Apr70, 7May-7Jun70, 6-29Jun70 and 1-14Jul70 (left section), 14-20Jun70 (right section); Master's Bty,

22Oct70, 3-9Dec70. US 1st/8th Arty also here until Apr/May70, when it moved to supt Cambodian Incursion. While at Le Loi in 70, 8 RAR developed unusual ambush tactic in which squads would hide in upraised scoops of "earth scrapers" (earth-movers) that then dropped them off at ambush positions along Rte 2 without local VC operatives observing them leaving cmpd. [333] During Jun70 (after 14Jun), 161 Bty fired its biggest shoot of war, during which 184 "serials" pounded area around FSB Dampier. On 1ATF NCO trng map per John Hollett. Also listed at YS 45-76. Phuoc Tuy Pr, III Corps.

Le Loi I, Operation (n/a)
8Dec68-10Feb69. ARVN 1st Ranger Grp op. 695 rptd NVA/VC KIA, per *Vietnam Order of Battle*, pp 9-14. Quang Nam Pr, I Corps.

Le My (n/a)
Mapsheet name of L-7014-6052-2. NVN only.

Le My (AT 91-82)
Village complex apx 12 km NW Da Nang AB and 3 km W Red Beach. 2d/3d Mar set-up defensives here in mid-65 (later relieved by 1st/3d Mar), to provide security for pacification program in AO. Also a Le My, a.k.a. Ap Quan Nam (2), at AT 8-8. Quang Nam Pr, I Corps.

Le My CAP (AT 91-82?)
Apparently noted in *Study In Counterinsurgency* per CAP Website. Quang Nam Pr, I Corps.

Le Petite Fleur (XD 858-390)
Name given his Coffee plantation by Felix Poilane. See Poilane Coffee Plantation. Quang Tri Pr, I Corps.

Le Phuoc Duc (n/a)
USCG cutter transferred to VNN control. See *Point Garnet*, CGC.

Le Quy Don BOQ (XS 852-918)
A.k.a. Le Qui Don. At 23-25 Le Quy Don St., Jan 65, 29 rms, Saigon. Per R. Bows' *Vietnam Military Lore, 1959-1973.* Gia Dinh Pr, III Corps.

Le Thanh (ZA 110-270)
Near Oasis AF, apx 24 km SSW Pleiku. 73d Abn Bde Div basecamp Jackson Hole built here Apr or May66. After building it, 173d built string of smaller camps from Plei Djereng (Rte 509N) to Ia Drang Valley S QL-19. Data per *Dak To*, pp 46-47. See Jackson Hole. Pleiku Pr, II Corps.

Le Thanh (Thanh An) (n/a)
Mapsheet L-7014-6536-4. Full sheet name: Thanh An (Le Thanh). SVN.

Le Thanh Base (YA 829-251)
Apx 3 km WSW Duc Co and 47 km SW Pleiku. Apr67. Pleiku Pr, II Corps.

Le Thanh District HQ (ZA 246-245)
Along QL-14, apx 15 km WSW Plei Do Lim and 22 km due S Pleiku. Oct65. Pleiku Pr, II Corps.

Le Thant Airfield (ZA 104-274)
See Oasis AF. Pleiku Pr, II Corps.

Le Thuy (XE 9-0?)
Ville just N of DMZ. Heavily fortified with NVA radar-controlled AA sites. Cited in *Bonnie-Sue*, p 474. NVN.

Le Trapeze (CQ 1-6)
See The Trapeze. Phu Yen Pr, II Corps.

Le Trung (AR 930-470)
Ville on QL-19, apx 14 km E Pleiku, 15 km WSW Suoi Doi. 4th Div, '70. Data per Jim Claeys. Pleiku Pr, II Corps.

Le Trung Mountain (AR 920-470)
14 km E Pleiku and 1 km S QL-19. Pleiku Pr, II Corps.

Le Van Duyet Reloc. Camp (BS 802-395)
Along E side of QL-1, near Duc Pho AF, apx 36 km SSE Quang Ngai. Oct68. Quang Ngai Pr, I Corps.

Le Xuyen CAP (YD 3-6)
CAP 4-3-6, 4th CAG per Tim Duffie. Was also at Bo Bang. Quang Tri Pr, I Corps.

Lea, Operation (WK)
7Oct47-8Nov47. French op to capture communist leaders of Vietminh and ICP. Combined deep armor thrusts and para drops involving some 15,000 French troops (20 Bns), facing some 40,000 Vietminh in 100 x 100 x 100 mile triangle of Tonkin's most inaccessible jungle terrain. Vietminh HQ, Bac Kan, Ho Moi and Cho Don, were specific targets of para drops. Apparently op came very close capturing Ho Chi Minh and Gen Giap when grp of Japanese and Nazi instructors [334] were captured. So close were French on his trail, that Ho Chi Minh's mail was found waiting for his signature. [335] See map in *Street Without Joy*, p 31.

Lead, FSB (XT 624-444)
Apx 13 km ESE Dau Tieng/Tri Tam. 1st Inf Div. Name/grid per Dan Gillotti. Binh Duong Pr, III Corps.

Leach, Camp (n/a)
No data available.

Leader, USS (n/a)
MSO 490. Cmdr Mine Div 93, with minesweepers *Leader* (MSO 490) and *Excel* (MSO 439). On 27Aug61 made 1st official USN ship visit to Phnom Penh. Cambodia. [336]

League (n/a)
Apr70, XXIV Corps proposed 101st Abn FSB name.

Leahy, USS (n/a)
DLG-16. Guided-Missile DD Ldr, per Ralph Fries.

Leaning Tower of Pisa, The (YS 50-54)
RNZA and RAR nickname for 40' NOD tower at FSB Thrust. See FSB Thrust. Phuoc Tuy Pr, III Corps.

Leary, USS (n/a)
DD-879, per Ralph Fries.

Leatherneck, FSB/LZ (XD 948-312)
A.k.a. Hill 908. On Lao border near of Lang Sa Tram, at upper E edge of Vietnam Salient, apx 12 km due W FSB Tun Tavern and 15 km SW FSB Henderson. Also listed at YD 949-313. Listed as inactive in 1Feb70, XXIV Corps 101st Abn rpt. Also at XD 951-316. Quang Tri Pr, I Corps.

Leatherneck Square (YD 170-640)
Rectangular AO bounded by USMC positions at Dong Ha, Gio Linh, Con Thien and Cam Lo. Grid roughly center of mass. Quang Tri Pr, I Corps.

Lee, FSB (n/a)
Location unknown, but possibly Lee at YU 427-059 or BR 708-900? Cited in 1st Cav VN *Yearbook* Aug65-Dec69, p 260, and also in *Incursion*, per Peter Cole.

Lee, FSB (XT 082-798)
Apx 12 km SSE An Loc, 4 km E QL-13 and 27 km WNW Dong Xoai. Also listed at XT 070-790 and 085-800. Feb-Dec67. Tay Ninh Pr, III Corps.

Lee, FSB (XT 190-559)
Apx 8 km SW Nui Ba Den and 4 km NNE Tay Ninh West AF. Nov69-Jan70. Tay Ninh Pr, III Corps.

Lee, FSB (YU 427-059)
Apx 11 km W Duc Phong AF and 16 km ESE Phuoc Binh/Song Be City AF. Jan70. Phuoc Long Pr, III Corps.
Lee, LZ (BR 708-900)
Near Song Lon River, 17 km WSW Bong Son, 12 NW Ha Tay AF and 22 km SSW Thuan An. A Bty, 2d/17th FA here 29Nov65, supt 2d/12th and 5th/7th Cav. Arty data/grid per Jack Picciolo. Binh Dinh Pr, II Corps.
Lee, LZ/FSB (n/a)
Per Tom Skelly, was "in mtns near a substantial Montagnard population." Possibly FSB Lee at YU 427-059 or BR 708-900?
Lee, LZ (YS 761-680)
Apx 3 km ENE Xa Nhu Lam26 km ENE Dat Do6 km NW Binh Chau. Apr66. Phuoc Tuy Pr, III Corps.
Leech Island (YC 834-997)
A 4 x 1.5 km island in Song Ta Trach (S fork of Perfume) River, apx 22 SSE Hue and 26 km due W Q Phu Loc. FSB Rifle here, and to its SW was home of 5th NVA Rgt in '69. Possibly named for its shape or for its dense population of what troops called Dry-Land or Tree Leeches, that lived in trees and wet grasses, moving toward their prey when sensing heat in motion similar to that of the Inch Worm. Was smaller and more ubiquitous leech than its waterborne cousin, though both were equally dreaded by the troops in the field. Thua Thien Pr, I Corps.
Leech Mountain (AT 9-2)
See LZ West/Nui Liet Kiem Mtn. Quang Nam Pr, I Corps.
Leech Valley (AT 8-6)
Along Song Lo Dong River, apx 17 km SW Da Nang. Quang Nam Pr, I Corps.
Lefevre, Monsignor (BT 0-8)
See *Constitution, USS*. Quang Nam Pr, I Corps.
Leghorn MSS Site (YB 604-355)
A.k.a. Eagle's Nest, Gibraltar, and GOLF-5. Apx 10 km W SVN border at closest point, and apx 28 km W to WSW Dak Seang AF, 43 km WNW Dak To 2 AF, and 27 km WNW Ben Het. Hill was so steep and its peak so small that NVA could neither attack it by ground or hit it effectively with arty/mortar. Numerous ground assaults easily beaten off. Appears to have been in excess of 3,500' (1,070+ meters) in height. Per Barry Toll, was SOG MSS site used as radio relay for SOG-35 ops (i.e., Grnd Studies Div; cover name for cross border recon ops). Possibly a "White Radio" facility. Featured in John Plaster's *SOG*, which includes photo and map showing general location. 1st occupied 15Jan67, and credited with saving many lives among SOG/Recon teams in Laos. SOG's most secret site worked well as OP until NVA realized its potential and masked their movements. Though meant to be temporary, it was in continuous op for 5 yrs with small security Det and RTO's eventually replacing recon teams. Also used as testing pad for NSA commo equip used to intercept, manipulate and/or block NVA radio commo suptg SOG and unrelated ops. 1st Lt George Sisler found site, gave photos to Singlaub with proposal saying, "I am absolutely certain that I could stay on top of that rock indefinitely." Ambassador Sullivan didn't want SOG in Laos, but after much pressure finally allowed a small SOG team in, "provided they were armed with obsolete World War II-era weapons." Though forbidden, Singlaub visited site stripped of all ID, and in 70, so did Martha Raye, who sang, and kissed all the men before leaving. Some data per Jim Jones as gleaned from *SOG and The Secret War Against Hanoi.* On map at p 89, *War In The Shadows*, *Vietnam Experience* series. Good photo of site at www.170thahc.org/WarStories/WarStories.html. Grid per Steve Sherman. See Sledgehammer and Hickory Hill. Laos
Legionnaire, LZ (BT 15-25)
A.k.a. OP Legionnaire? In mtns apx 17 km WNW Tam Ky and 12 km ESE Binh Son. Quang Tin Pr, I Corps.
Legionnaire, LZ (n/a)
A.k.a. Op Legionnaire. Said to have been near Laotian border and OP used for surveillance of Ho Chi Minh Trail. Also an 82d Abn Bde arty base. Americal Assn list. See OP Legionnaire (BT 15-25). I or II Corps?
Lejuene, FSB (XD 968-534?)
See Lejune. Quang Tri Pr, I Corps.
Lejune, FSB (XD 959-936?)
On N side of Cam Lo River apx 15 km due W Cam Lo, 38 km WNW Quang Tri and 16 km NW Mai Loc. 101st Abn inactive FSB grid per Don Armstrong; however, also listed at XD 968-534, which is 6 km due S listed grid, and 17 km WSW Cam Lo, 14 km WNW Mai Loc? Unknown which grid is correct. Quang Tri Pr, I Corps.
Lem, LZ (YU 809-725)
A.k.a. Dead Man's Hill. Apx 3 km due S Duc Lap AF, 7 km E Duc Lap, 48 km SW Ban Me Thuot and 12 km E Cambodia. 2d/17th Arty here supt 23d ARVN Div, Op Binh Tay III, per Jack Picciolo. Quang Duc Pr, II Corps.
Lemon, LZ (YD 534-415)
In coastal sands apx 26 km SE Quang Tri, 2 km SSW Ap Tay Hoang, 18 km SE Hai Lang and 7 km NE QL-1. Jan68. Thua Thien Pr, I Corps.
Lemon Hill (XD 844-456)
See Hickory Hill MSS Site. Quang Tri Pr, I Corps.
Lemont, LZ (YD 057-675)
Apx 1.5 km S the southern edge of DMZ, 4 km WNW Thon An Hoa, 11 km NW Cam Lo and 20 km WNW Dong Ha. Apr70 XXIV Corps grid per Don Armstrong. Quang Tri Pr, I Corps.
Lenawee, USS (n/a)
APA 195. In 63, participated in Op People-to-People, carrying 10,000 lb of textbooks/medical supplies to SVN. On 7Nov64 she left US to join TF 76, carrying Marines in gulf from12Dec64-10Apr65. On 15Apr65, she landed elements of 3d Mar Div at Da Nang and, on apx 20Apr65, landed 4th Marines at Hue. On 7May64, delivered more 4th Marines to Chu Lai. On 9Aug65, she departed CA with BLT 1/1 on 1st nonstop voyage by an APA direct to Da Nang, arriving 28Aug65. On 28Oct65, returned to US. Last deployment was 4Sept66. [337]
Lenetta, FSB (YA 852-457)
See Lanetta. Pleiku Pr, II Corps.
Leo, FSB (YT 564-738)
Apx 8 km NE FSB Aries, 3 km W the Song Dong Nai River, 14 km NNW Loi Tan, 84 km NE Bien Hoa AB and 47 km E Dong Xoai. Opened or reopened 30Aug70, closed 9Sep70. 1st/5th Cav Data per *1st Cav Div Op Rpt, ending 31Oct70*, courtesy Peter Cole. See LZ Leo at XD grid. Long Khanh Pr, III Corps.

Leo, LZ (XD 906-553)
On edge of river valley, apx 15 km NNE Khe Sanh CB, 21 km W to WSW Cam Lo and 12 km NW Ca Lu. XXIV Corps grid per Don Armstrong. See LZ Leo at YT grid. Quang Tri Pr, I Corps.
Leon Nok Tha Airfield (VC 5-8)
See Loeng Nok Tha AF. Thailand.
Leonard F. Mason, USS (n/a)
DD-852, per Ralph Fries.
Leong Nok Tha Airfield (VC 5-8)
See Loeng Nok Tha AF. Thailand.
Leopard (n/a)
Apr70, XXIV Corps proposed 101st Abn FSB name.
Leopard, FSB (YS 447-747)
Apx 7 km NNE Nui Dat, 8 km WSW FSB Longreach and1 km W LTL-2. Per Herb Artora, there were rubber trees along N and E sides, jungle to W and ville to S with an arty Bty that had its own circular perimeter about 1-2 km distant. 105mm Bty and elements of 3d/22d Inf, 3d Bde/25th Inf Div here for several months and until it stood down in Apr71. Name may have originated from 3d/22d Inf's "Leopard" call-sign. Old (possibly French), dirt, fixed-wing acft airstrip here as well. On 1ATF NCO trng map per John Hollett. Phuoc Tuy Pr, III Corps.
Leprosarium, The (BT 08-67?)
Apparently nickname of USMC Co-sized patrol base apx 100 meters from ocean, 2 km S Marble Mtn and 5 km NE Cau Ha CB. Per Bob Lindgren, 2d/1st Marines corpsman, 2 elderly missionaries ran small Leper colony in cmpd until mid '60's, but were killed when boy tossed grenade into their jeep. Was thereafter abnd and later became USMC Co-sized cmd center. Occupied by elements of 1st and 9th Mar Rgts at various times. "I can still remember a few bodies lying to rot outside the wire and, man, did they stink," Bob added. Grid is est. Quang Nam Pr, I Corps.
Leroy Eltenge, MSTS? (n/a)
MSTS or *USNS* troop transport that carried 1st Bde of 101st Abn to Vietnam in '65.
Les Pieges (n/a)
A.k.a. The Traps. Nickname assigned to acft they flew by French pilots of 1st Indochina War.
Leslie, LZ (AT 979-307)
A.k.a. Hill 138. In or just SW the Que Son Valley, apx 2.5 km WSW LZ Dragon Base, 33 km WNW Tam Ky and 6 km NNW LZ West/Nui Liet Kiem. Americal, 196th LIB, 1st Cav, and USMC position. 2/12th Cav, 1st Cav here and at LZ Ross were heavily attacked on night of 2Jan68. Grid per map courtesy Bob Shrake, 4th/31st Inf, 196th LIB. Cited in 1st Cav VN *Yearbook* Aug65-Dec69, p 54, 121, 211, per Peter Cole. Quang Nam Pr, I Corps.
Lewis, LZ/FSB (BR 534-973)
A.k.a. LZ Louis and unknown if simply sp variant, or if distinctly different name? Apx 35 km W LZ English, 31 km NE Ha Tay AF, 54 km N An Khe and3 km SE Hill 1114. Per VHPA Battle index, was built apx 16Feb70. 199th AHC and 4th Div AO, '70. Grid per Jim Claeys. Also listed at BR 549-973. Binh Dinh Pr, II Corps.
Lewis Tank Farm (BT 06-73)
At Marble Mtn AF, apx 6 km ESE Da Nang AB. Named to honor David Marion Lewis, SN, USN, KIA 22Oct67, the 1st individual KIA from USNAVSUPPACT. Was dedicated Jul68. Quang Nam Pr, I Corps.
Lexington, LZ (XD 849-353)
Apx 8 km due S Khe Sanh CB, 4 km due S Khe Sanh ville and 9 km NW Lang Klung. Apr70 XXIV Corps grid per Don Armstrong. Quang Tri Pr, I Corps.
Lexington, USS (n/a)
CVA-16. Acft Carrier, per Ralph Fries. Dates and extent of involvement unknown?
Leyte, LZ (YD 043-213)
Apx 22 km SW Ba Long AF, 29 km SE Khe Sanh CB and 42 km SW Quang Tri. Apr70 XXIV Corps grid per Don Armstrong. Quang Tri Pr, I Corps.
Li Lich Airfield (YT 369-487)
See Dong Bo AF. Long Khanh Pr, III Corps.
Li Minh Forest (WR)
Forested region and NVA VC staging area in NE An Xuyen Pr, IV Corps.
Li Tinh Heliport (BT 477-081)
On large island in large lagoon formed by meeting of Song Ben Va River and Vung An Hoa Bay, Apx 5 km NW Chu Lai AF, 4 km SSW Dong Tuan and 23 km SE Tam Ky. Heliport #604, alt 7', at 15°26'30"N-108°39'00"E, per Feb73 TAD. Quang Tin Pr, I Corps.
Libby (n/a)
Apr70, XXIV Corps proposed 101st Abn FSB name.
Libby, FSB/LZ (YT 448-290)
Apx 1 km E of QL-20, some 4 km NE Xa Binh Hoa, 21 km due N Xuan Loc, 11 km NE Xa Gia Kiem and 48 NE Bien Hoa AB. 1st/7th Cav, 1st Cav, May69, AO Commanche Warrior. Cited in *1st Cav Div operational Rpt, May-Jul69*, p 13, per Peter Cole. Grid per Frank Penk, Jr. Possibly same LZ Libby listed at YT 426-060? Aug68-Jan70. Long Khanh Pr, III Corps.
Libby, FSB/LZ (YU 535-333)
Apx 20 km ESE Djamap/Bu Gia Map, 24 km SW Buprang New AF, 42 km NE Song Be/Phuoc Binh and 10 km ENE FSB Audie. Opened or reopened 7Oct70, closed 27Oct70. 2d/12th Cav Data per *1st Cav Div Op Rpt, ending 31Oct70*, courtesy Peter Cole. Quang Duc Pr, II Corps.
Libby, LZ (YT 426-060)
A.k.a. LZ Lizzy? Apx 5 km SW Xuan Loc and 4 km NNW Ap Tho Giao. 4th/12th Inf, 199th LIB, III and possibly an 1ATF Aussie base? Per diary of "Frenchy" Torres, the NVA attempted to over-run Libby, 20May69. Closed prior to Cambodian Incursion but reopened for it as staging area as 11tha ACR RedCatcher Rear and 5th/12th Cav and 199th LIB, in May70. One writer described it as being overrun with rats. [338] Possibly same Libby listed at YT 448-290? 1st Cav arty ORLL grid. Long Khanh Pr, III Corps.
Liberty Bridge (AT 924-530)
Rte 540 bridge over Song Thu Bon, apx 8 km NE An Hoa CB and 8 km SE Hill 55. 5th Marine Rgt AO. Site of FSB Phu Lac. Also listed at BS 962-648? On mapsheet L-7014-6640-4. See Phu Lac 6. Quang Nam Pr, I Corps.
Liberty Bridge (BS 692-648)
The QL-1 bridge over the Song Ve, apx 4 km SSE Quang Ngai? Unknown if bridge truly had this name? No other info available. Quang Ngai Pr, I Corps.

Liberty Canyon, Operation (n/a)
1st Cav's move from Camp Evans in I Corps to III Corps, Oct '68, the largest allied intra-theater combat deployment of 2d Indochina war. Move involved C-130s for most manpower deployment, but also LSTs transporting vehicles and equip by water down coast and then up the Nha Be and Song Saigon to Saigon for offloading.
Liberty City (n/a)
See Glossary.
Liberty Road (AT 88-52)
Rte 540 between Liberty Bridge and An Hoa. Connected Hill 55 with An Hoa. Built '66. Quang Nam Pr, I Corps.
Lien Chieu, Baie de (AT 9-8)
A.k.a. Vung Kim Lien. Bay at 16°08'N-108°08'E. On ND49-01 JOG. Quang Nam Pr, I Corps.
Lien Chieu Esso Plant (AT 937-867)
Along NW shore of Da Nang Bay, apx 12 km NNW Da Nang AB. Refinery and POL stg. Per *US Marines in Vietnam, 1965*, p 184, 5Aug65 VC attack on depot and its 2 RF Cos destroyed 2 JP-4 stg tanks and damaged 3 others with loss of 1,650,000 gal of avn fuel; most of I Corp's commercial supply. Quang Nam Pr, I Corps.
Lien Chieu Petroleum Depot (AT 937-867)
Quang Nam Pr, I Corps.
Lien Doi Nguoi Nhai (n/a)
See LDNN in Glossary.
Lien Ket 26, Operation (n/a)
See Utah/Lien Ket 26, Op.
Lien Ket 28, Operation (n/a)
See Texas/Lien Ket 28, Op.
Lien Ket 414, Operation (n/a)
25Aug-31Dec69. ARVN 4th Rgt op. 710 rptd NVA KIA, per *VN Order of Battle*, pp 9-14. Quang Ngai Pr, I Corps.
Lien Ket 52, Operation (n/a)
See Colorado/Lien Ket 52, Op.
Lien Ket 531, Operation (n/a)
26Aug-31Dec69. 5th ARVN Rgt op. 542 rptd NVA KIA, per *VN Order of Battle*, pp 9-14. Quang Tin Pr, I Corps.
Lien Ket 81, Operation (n/a)
17-22Feb67. ARVN 2d Div op. 813 rptd NVA KIA, per *Vietnam Order of Battle*, pp 9-14. Quang Ngai Pr, I Corps.
Lien Khuong Airfield (BP 142-001)
See Dalat/Lien Khuong. Tuyen Duc Pr, II Corps.
Lien So (n/a)
See Glossary.
Lien Thach (n/a)
Mapsheet name of L-7014-6834-4. SVN.
Lienchien Esso Depot (AT 94-88)
See Lieu Chieu Esso. Quang Nam Pr, I Corps.
Lieng Djran, Rapides de (YT 580-574)
Rapids on the Song Dong Nai apx 70 km NE Bien Hoa AB and 2 km S Loi Tan Mil. Camp. Long Khanh Pr, III Corps.
Lieu Cheou, Baie de (AT 9-8)
A.k.a. Vung Kim Lien. Bay at 16°08'N-108°08'E. On ND49-01 JOG. Quang Nam Pr, I Corps.
Lieu Chieu Esso Depot (AT 94-88)
A.k.a. Lienchien (or Lien Chien?) Esso Depot. 15 km NNW Da Nang and at southern foot of Hai Van Pass. Secured by 2d/26th Marines, '69. Quang Nam Pr, I Corps.
Life, LZ (CR 002-762)
Apx 5 km from coast, 26 km SE Bong Son and 14 km NE Phu My. Oct66. Binh Dinh Pr, II Corps.
Lifesaver, Operation (n/a)
During '70, the 101st Abn instituted prgm in which hundreds of preemptive LZs where cut along ridgelines and on hilltops throughout its AO at blitzkrieg rate of as many as 10 or more per day. Intent was to facilitate any future ops or emergency extractions that might develop as tactical need arose. 326th Engrs w/Inf Plt security were airlifted to sites and, as soon as LZ was cut or cleared, were extracted and flown to next site. No matter where men of 101st were, they could generally count on an LZ being nearby.
Lighthouses (various)
For lighthouse entries, see: Cape Varella (CQ 32-26), Cu Lao Re (CT 02-03), Cu Lao Xanh (CR 22-06), Ha Tien (VS 44-47), Hon Lon (CP 19-48), Lang Thuong (CQ 32-27), Mui Dinh (BN 84-57), Mui Khe Ga (ZS 27-84), Mui Nai (VS 39-46), Nha Trang (CP 01-51), Phuoc Chau (CR 23-06), Qui Nhon (N) (CR 13-24), Qui Nhon (S) (CR 12-22), Tan Phung (CR 05-76), Vung Tau (YS 278-427).
Lightning, LZ (YD 210-770)
Along QL-1, apx 2 km SE Ben Hai River, 16 km WNW Cua Viet and 28 km NNW Quang Tri, 3d Mar Div, Apr69. On map at p 73, *US Marines in Vietnam-1969*. See LZ Tornado. Quang Tri Pr, I Corps.
Lightning, LZ (XT 542-328)
Apx 3 km SW Xom Bung Binh and 25 km WSW Lai Khe. May66. Tay Ninh Pr, III Corps.
Lil, FSB (YT 212-128)
Along QL-1, apx 25 km WNW Xuan Loc, 15 km due E Plantation AF and 35 km ENE Saigon. 2d/7th Cav here Mar69, Op Cheyenne Saber, per Frank Penk, Jr., who also lists grid at YT 206-131. Bien Hoa Pr, III Corps.
Lillian, FSB (YC 496-856)
In A Shau Valley, apx 2 km N A Sap, 5 km WNW FSB Fury and 42 km SW Hue. 101st Abn inactive FSB grid per Don Armstrong. Also listed at YC 497-857 (and 439-868 which is error). Thua Thien Pr, I Corps.
Lillie, LZ (ZA 119-561)
Apx 14 km NW Pleiku, 7 km NE Plei Bek and 12 km WNW Pleiku/Nansteph AF. 1st/35th Inf fwd FSB from 12Feb69 until abnd and dismantled, 3Mar69. On 28Feb69, while C Co here, was hit by mortar/recoilless rifle fire, with 30 WIA but no KIA, per Feb69 1st/35th Inf Bn logs. Data per Dick Arnold. Pleiku Pr, II Corps.
Lima, LZ/FSB (BR 64-45?)
Apx 16 km E An Khe and E of An Khe Pass, immed S QL-19. Large, unsecured Laager site for 1st Cav helo units in 65-66, used to launch major ops in Happy Valley/Vinh Thanh Valley area. Grid is est. Binh Dinh Pr, II Corps.
Lima, LZ ? (XT 625-295)
Apx 18 km SW Lai Khe and 1 km S Xa Duoc. Nature of site unknown. Jun66. Binh Duong Pr, III Corps.
Lima Laager Site (BR 64-45?)
See LZ Lima at grid Binh Dinh Pr, II Corps.
Lima Lima (n/a)
See Glossary.
Lima Sites (generally)
Complete listing (with grids) of approximately 450 "L-Site" and "Lima Site" locations under "LS" entry. A.k.a. L

Sites, LS Sites, Laos Sites, and Listening Sites. Numerous, rudimentary STOL acft capable AF's were built throughout NE Laos for Op Barrel Roll (bombing of NVA infiltration rtes), for CIA ops and for suptg Royal Lao Army against Pathet Lao. Per Kent Spalding, in Air America lexicon, "L-Site" or "LS," or "Lima Site" stood for "Laos Site" (accordingly, "Charlie Sites" were in Cambodia, and "Victor Sites" were in VN). He says Air America did not run Lima sites; instead, they were run by USAF or Army SF operatives in concert with civilian/CIA personnel. Jim Henthorn has plotted (in red letters) location of all 400 Lima-Sites on L-1501 JOG map images he has installed at www.nexus.net/~911gfx/Laos.html. *Air Facilities Data-Laos* contains complete, hard-copy listing of "L," "LS," and Lima-Site AFs in Laos (cross-referenced with Lao name), See Charlie Sites, Victor Sites and PS Sites, Tiger Hound, Steel Tiger, Barrel Roll. Laos.

Lima-Site 20 SF Camp (TG 79-24 or RD 09-68?)
At either Sam Thong AF (TG 79-24) and known as LS 20, or at RD 09-68 as L-20 and a.k.a. Bun Taio AF or Puntai AF? SF/CIA site in Laos when neutrality declared (23Jul62). FTT 3, 14, 19, 33, 40 and 41 here then. Per *Special Forces at War*. See LS for complete listing of all L and LS Lima Sites. MR2, Laos.

Lima Site 36 (UH 41-10)
At Na Khang AF in northern Laos. LS 36 was staging area for SAR ops and resupply point for friendly guerrillas. Lost to enemy, Apr67. See LS for listing of all L and Lima Sites.

Lima Site-85 (UH 68-60)
A.k.a. Site 85, LS-85, Combat Skyspot and Phu Pha Thi Mtn. Originally a Meo guerrilla base apx 25 km from NVN border, 125 nautical miles W Hanoi, and 45 km W Sam Neua, in Laos. In '67, a "TSQ-81 facility" was added to existing USAF/CIA TACAN facility (built Aug66) atop steep 5,500' high ridge called Phou Pha Thi. Operational 1Nov67, and terminated 11Mar68. TSQ-81 was modified version of SAC's Radar Bomb Scoring (RBS) system, which predicted bomb impact points for simulated drops, while TSQ-81 guided and controlled bombers to targets, providing precise bomb release points under radar control. Similar systems established earlier in SVN (one also in Thailand) under code name "Combat Skyspot." TSQ-81 Site 85 equip differed from Skyspot equip in that it was designed as small packages that could be inserted by helo. Code name for Site 85 directed ops was "Commando Club." Was only facility of its kind in Laos and could provide ground-vectored radar bombing in both northern NVN and Laos. Though operated by US in "compliance" with '62 Geneva Accords, site and its purpose were ultra-secret and sensitive politically and militarily. On 11Mar67, at 0300 hrs, a force of 20 NVA sappers attacked site, killing or capturing 10 of 16 US troops there (another rpt says total US MIA/KIA was 12). Photos in *War In Laos*, pp 26, 29. See First Helo Kill of Fixed Wing acft in Glossary, and LS entries for listing of all L, LS & Lima Sites. Laos.

Lima Zulu (n/a)
See Glossary.

Lima Zulu, LZ (ZB 14-47?)
Apx 1 km S Kon Honong (or Honing?) and 5 km W Toumorong Outpost. Hill 827 was directly N of this LZ. 1st/327th Inf LZ secured by 1st or 2d/30th Arty and A/2d/502d Inf, 101st Abn suptg David Hackworth's 1st/327th at LZ Jenny during Battle of Toumorong (Op Hawthorne II). Heavily attacked and nearly overrun 5Jun66? See *Battles in the Monsoon*, pp 280, 294, 297, 316. Grid estimated. Kontum Pr, II Corps.

Limit, LZ (XD 932-287)
Apx 26 km WSW Ba Long, 16 km SE Khe Sanh CB and 21 km SSW Ca Lu. Apr70 XXIV Corps grid per Don Armstrong. Quang Tri Pr, I Corps.

Lin CAP (n/a)
1st CAG. Location unknown. I Corps.

Lincoln, LZ (BR 499-307)
Apx 15 km S An Khe, 22 km ESE LZ Assault, 3 km SW LZ Winnie and 23 km SW Binh Khe. 4th Div AO, '70. 4th ID op rpt grid per Jim Claeys. Binh Dinh Pr, II Corps.

Linda (n/a)
6Apr70, XXIV Corps proposed Americal FSB name.

Linda, FSB (XT 525-043)
Near Bao Trai Heliport, W of Khiem Cuong and QL-1, apx 32 km WNW Tan Son Nhut AB and 16 km SW Cu Chi. 1st/506th Inf, 101st Abn, Dec68. Hau Nghia Pr, III Corps.

Linda, IOS (AT 865-681)
A.k.a. FSB Linda? In lowlands apx 8 km SSW Da Nang AB, 5 km W QL-1 and perhaps 6 km NE tip of Charlie Ridge. Integrated Observation Site (see IOD)? Americal list. Quang Nam Pr, I Corps.

Linda, LZ (AT 865-681)
See Linda, IOS. Quang Nam Pr, I Corps.

Linda, LZ (BP 720-629)
Apx 35 km WNW Nha Trang and 22 km SW Duc My AF. Apr67. Khanh Hoa Pr, II Corps.

Linda, LZ (BR)
Map at www.landscaper.net/ indicates it was generally ENE An Khe, SW Hammond AF, NW Phu Cat and N or NW Camp Fidel. C Bty, 7th/15th Arty here for Hipshoot. Binh Dinh Pr, II Corps.

Linda, LZ (BR 935-467)
Apx 4 km ENE Phu Cat AB, immed SE Phu Cat (minor) AF and 3 km E QL-1. Grid per Dan Gillotti, 15th Arty Assn. Binh Dinh Pr, II Corps.

Linda Lynne, FSB (n/a)
A.k.a. Lindalynne. No data. 10th Cav, 4th Div FSB, per Bob Patsfield. Possibly Binh Dinh or Pleiku Pr, II Corps.

Lindy, FSB (YS 448-858)
Apx 18.5 km N Nui Dat, 5 km E FSB Coolah and 1 km W LTL-2. On 1ATF NCO trng map per John Hollett. Phuoc Tuy Pr, III Corps.

Line Bravo (BS 865-162)
In valley, apx 6 km NW LZ English and 11 km due N Bong Son. Nature of site unknown but likely an operational zone boundary or LOD? Feb67. Binh Dinh Pr, II Corps.

Linebacker, Operation (n/a)
2Apr72-22Oct72. 2d phase (Op Freedom Train being 1st) of US Air response to NVA's Easter, 72 Offensive. Full-scale resumption of bombing of NVN, 3 1/2 years after LBJ's Rolling Thunder bombing ops had ceased. Aimed at cutting off any means of resupply for attacking NVA forces, including land links to China, main supply points and road/rail/water access to SVN. Included air-mining of Haiphong Harbor for 1st time, and 1st use of "Smart

Bombs" to destroy key NVN targets and bridges (the Dragon's Jaw or Ham Rong Bridge, was finally destroyed by Smart Bombs on 13May72, after years of unsuccessful attempts). NVN.

Linebacker II, Operation (NVN)
18 and 26Dec72. A.k.a. The Christmas Bombings. B-52 strikes on Hanoi area designed to force NVN to negotiating table. Also resulted in heavy acft losses from Soviet SAMs once NVA AAA realized all B-52s were flying exact same pattern in (over Thud Ridge) and out (NNW up Red River Valley). As a result, USAF had to alter attack rtes into variety of patterns. Estimated that between 884 to 1,242 SAMs were fired and that 15 B-52's were downed in these raids. Maps and details in *Vietnam Experience*, *Rain of Fire* vol, pp 146-160. NVN.

Lion, FSB (WD or WC?)
In Summer '71, 3 Rgts of Hmong Lao (GM's 21, 22 and 23) under Vang Pao took control of Plain de Jars (PDJ) away from PAVN, then in Fall '71, built elaborate series of interlocking FSBs across middle of the PDJ. Among these base were those code-named "Lion," "Mustang" and "Puncher." Total built unknown. Mustang built Aug71, and Lion Nov71. In Dec71, PAVN counter-attacked and overran them all. Photos/discussion in *War In Laos*, pp 33, 43-48. See FSB Puncher. Laos.

Lion, LZ (BR)
Overlooking and on E side of An Lao River Valley apx 15 km NW Bong Son, 10 km WNW LZ 4, 6 km NE LZ Root and 15 km W ocean. Used during Op Masher/White Wing, 28Jan-6Mar66. Detailed discussion of Ops Masher/White Wing and this LZ in *A Contagion of War* vol, *Vietnam Experience* series, pp 32-48, with map showing site at p 38. 1st/12th Cav, 1st Cav LZ. Binh Dinh Pr, II Corps.

Lion, LZ (BS 715-300)
In mtns apx 3 km ENE Con Doc, 13 km SW Duc Pho AF and 26 km NW Gia An. Quang Ngai Pr, I Corps.

Lion, LZ (BT)
Near coast and center of Barrier Island, due S Hoi An, and 32 km S Da Nang. Red Beach, LZs Lion and Tiger were used by ship-based Amphibious Ready Group, BLT 1st/26th Marines, during Op Daring Rebel Bold Pursuit, an attack by C/1st/26th Marines against elements of 3d, 36th and 38th VC Rgts here, Jun-Jul69. 1st Mar Div, Americal list. Near Quang Nam/Quang Tin Pr border I Corps.

Lion, OP (YD 601-189)
See OP Lion. Thua Thien Pr, I Corps.

Lipan, USS (n/a)
A.k.a. ATF 85. Salvage Vessels such as Tug *Lipan* helped to free many grounded ships, inc DD *Frank Knox*, the *Terrell County* (LST 1157), and some NVA trawlers. [339]

List of Adrian Messenger, The (XS 8-9)
See Kinh Do Movie Theater. Gia Dinh Pr, III Corps.

Litchfield County, USS (n/a)
LST-901. Decom 6Dec69. SVN.

Little Blue (XT)
Acft/helo pilots nicknamed the Song Saigon and Song Thi Tinh Rivers, the Big and Little Blue. Per *Low Level Hell*, p 58. III Corps.

Little Dien Bien Phu (WS 005-515)
See Phan Chau (old) and Tri Ton SF camp (nickname of Tri Ton). Kien Giang Pr, IV Corps.

Little Elephant's Ear (XT 05-88)
Cambodian border feature immed N point where QL-22 crosses border, due W FSB Mustang, between Rte 246 and border about 35 km due W Katum. Tay Ninh Pr, III Corps.

Little Mesopotamia (WJ 25-85)
Low-lying, water-logged plain between Red and Clear Rivers. Vietminh Inf Rgt 36 (of 308th Div) and Rgt 176 (of 316th Div) were here Fall of '52, when French launched Op Lorraine at Vietminh supply points of Yen Bai and Thai Nguyen (and etch). Giap continued his T'ai Highland offense thrust to SW despite threat, but did send these 2 Rgts to Op Lorraine AO, ordering them to stop French at all costs. NVN.

Little Pass (CP 0-1)
A.k.a. Cua Be. Channel near 11°51'N-109°15'E. On NC49-01 JOG. Khanh Hoa Pr, II Corps.

Little Rock BEQ (XS 8-9)
73d Med Det NCO Club, Saigon. Gia Dinh Pr, III Corps.

Little Rockpile, The (XD 987-565)
A.k.a. Hill 144. Apx 1 km NE the Rockpile in Razorback Valley, 4 km SW peak Dong Ha Mtn and 14 km WSW Cam Lo. Quang Tri Pr, I Corps.

Little Rubber Plantation (XT 38-34)
Along E side of QL-22, apx 20 km SE Tay Ninh, 18 km SW Dau Tieng and just E the Song Vam Co Dong. Good map/discussions of nearby '68 battles in *The Infantry Brigade in Combat,* p 5 et al. Tay Ninh Pr, III Corps.

Litts, Camp (BR 908-704)
See Litts, LZ. Binh Dinh Pr, II Corps.

Litts, LZ (BR 908-704)
A.k.a. Joyce AF and Camp Litts AF. Along QL-1, apx 4 km NNE Phu My, 6 km NNE Crystal AF, and 27 km SSE Bong Son. Per *Rites of Passage*, pp 324-5, was large FSB with C-130 capable AF, and was 3de Bde/25th Div HQ here May67. Named to honor PFC James G. Litts, KIA 4Oct66. Apr67-Mar68. Also listed at BR 908-704. Binh Dinh Pr, II Corps.

Litts Airfield (BR 908-704)
See Litts AF, Camp. Binh Dinh Pr, II Corps.

Litts Airfield, Camp (BR 912-707)
See Litts, LZ. Binh Dinh Pr, II Corps.

Litz, LZ (YD or XD?)
Precise location unknown. Mapsheet designation suggests it was no less than 35 km WNW to NW Hue. Map is L-7014-6442-3, per Ken Burrington. Thua Thien or Quang Tri Pr, I Corps.

Livesaver, Operation (n/a)
See Lifesaver, Op.

Liz, FSB/LZ (BS 752-436)
On Nui Xuong, overlooking Song Tra Cau Delta apx 8 km NW Duc Pho, 1 km W QL-1 RR tracks and 3 km W QL-1 itself. Americal list author says for US helos, enemy ground fire was heavy in this area. 2d/35th Inf, 4th Div fwd FSB from 15Apr-15Dec67, per Dick Arnold. Also listed at BS 751-436, 757-432, and by arty ORLLs at BS 753-434 and 753-432. Oct67-Apr70. Photo of Liz online at www3.servtech.com/americal/174/liz69.htm. Apr70 XXIV Corps grid per Don Armstrong. Quang Ngai Pr, I Corps.

Liz, FSB (XU 728-033)
Along QL-13, apx 6 km S to SSW Loc Ninh and 14 km NNW An Loc. FSBs Allons I, II and Liz ran in string along

QL-13, all within 10 km of S Loc Ninh and all within 2 km of each other. 11th ACR here. Grid per Frank Penk, Jr. Binh Long Pr, III Corps.

Liz, FSB (YT 212-128)
Along QL-1, apx 25 km W Xuan Loc, 23 km ESE Bien Hoa AB and 15 km due E Plantation AF. 2d/7th Cav, 1st Cav, Feb69, In AO Apache during Op Cheyenne Saber. Grid per Frank Penk, Jr. See LZ Liz at YT 241-345. Bien Hoa Pr, III Corps.

Liz, FSB/LZ (YT 241-345)
On E side of main N/S hwy, 32 km NE Bien Hoa AB, 34 km NW Xuan Loc and 6 km N Song Dong Nai River. Feb69. See Liz at YT 212-128. Long Khanh Pr, III Corps.

Liz, LZ (BS 757-432)
See Liz, FSB/LZ at grid. Quang Ngai Pr, I Corps.

Liz, LZ (n/a)
No data. Described as having been near Pleiku? II Corps.

Liz, LZ (XD 37-39)
Apx 8 km SE Tchepone, 13 km WSW Aloui and 48 km W and slightly S of Khe Sanh. ARVN FSB in Laos during Lam Son 719, 1st ARVN Div. Good Lam Son 719 FSB map at www.americal. org/174/map4.htm. Laos.

Liz, LZ (YT 973-863)
Apx 15 km WNW Tan Phat AF/Bao Loc and 13 km NNW Ap Cong Hinh/QL-20. Feb67. Lam Dong Pr, II Corps.

Lloyd Thomas, USS (n/a)
DD-764, per Ralph Fries.

Lo Bo River (BS 82-37)
River that met QL-1 at listed grid, apx 2 km S Duc Pho AF, and 18 km SSE Mo Duc. Quang Ngai Pr, I Corps.

Lo Dieu Beach (BR 97-96)
On coast, apx 11 km SE LZ English, 12 km due E Bong Son and 4 km NE peak Hill 619 (Hon Cau Mtn). R&R beach and resort area for 173d Abn in at least '70. Binh Dinh Pr, II Corps.

Lo Ke (XT?)
Apparently near Iron Triangle. On 2Mar66, the 272d VC Rgt heavily attacked a Bn of 3d Bde/1st Inf Div near this ville. On 7Mar66, elements of 2d/503d Inf, and 1st Bde 1st Inf Div were also heavily attacked by 271st VC Rgt. War Zone D, III Corps.

Lo Lo, LZ (XD 43-36)
See LZ Lolo. Laos.

Lo Trung, LZ (AR 92-47)
See Trung, LZ. Pleiku Pr, II Corps.

Lo, Mui (XF 0-4)
Coastal point at 18°29'N-105°57'E. NE48-07 JOG. NVN.

Loampon, Mui (CQ 3-2)
Coastal point at 12°55'N-109°27'E. ND49-13 JOG. Khanh Hoa Pr, II Corps.

Loan, FSB (YU?)
A.k.a. FSB Le Lai. Location unknown, but apparently N FSB Judie (YU 0-1?)? Per Peter Cole, is mentioned in *1st Cav Div Op Rpt, Feb-Apr70,* pp12, 31. "FSBs Django and Joan closed on 23 and 25Feb70 respectively and 8th Abn Bn displaced to establish FSB Lolita (YU 369-261). As move N gained momentum and activity increased, FSB's Candy, Loan, and Audie were established on 25, 26 and 27 Feb70 respectively...The 1st Abn Bn (-) moved to establish FSB Loan, leaving 1 rifle Co to secure FSB Judie." [340] Phuoc Long Pr?, III Corps.

Lobo (n/a)
6Apr70, XXIV Corps proposed III MAF FSB name.

Lobo, FSB/LZ (BS 645-538)
On Nui Nham, apx 8 km WNW Mo Duc, 7 km due W Quang Dien and 17 km due S Quang Ngai. See LZs Tiger, Bulldog and Nui Nham. Quang Ngai Pr, I Corps.

Lobo, FSB (XT 868-368)
Apx 15 km SSW Phuoc Vinh AF and 10 km due E Lai Khe. Nov69-Feb70. Binh Duong Pr, III Corps.

Loboy Ford (XE 2-0)
See Ban Loboy Pass. Laos.

Loc An (various)
Common Viet ville name. Sites inc: XE 8-0, BS 8-3, YS 1-9 and BT 0-2. NVN/SVN.

Loc An CAP (BS 8-3 or BT 0-2?)
Hotel 3, 3rd CAG. Thua Thien Pr, I Corps.

Loc Ban CAP (n/a)
Alpha 3, 3rd CAG. Thua Thien Pr, I Corps.

Loc Ban CAP (n/a)
CAC 4, 3rd CAG. Thua Thien Pr, I Corps.

Loc Chau (WF 7-7?)
Port city attacked by USN carrier-based acft during Pierce Arrow, 2-7Aug64. See Pierce Arrow, Op. NVN.

Loc Dien CAP (n/a)
Hotel 8, 3rd CAG. Thua Thien Pr, I Corps.

Loc Giang (XT?)
Somewhere in Angel's Wing, Parrot Beak 25th Inf Div AO. ARVN Inf Camp, sometimes occupied by 25th Div Arty ground surveillance 5-man teams using the TPS-25 ground scanning radar. See http://pacer.calpoly.edu/Tri/radar.html for detail. Binh Long Pr, III Corps.

Loc Hoa SF Camp (n/a)
Possible sites inc: AT 925-771 (Quang Nam Pr), XS 816-923 (Gia Dinh Pr), XS 021-251 (Vinh Long Pr), XS 067-254 (Vinh Long Pr), XT 4-1 (Hau Nghia Pr NE the Parrot's Beak) and XU 7-2 (near Cambodian border N Loc Ninh)? SF Det 64 here. I, III or IV Corps.

Loc Minh, Camp? (n/a)
Apparent sp variant of Loc Ninh? Sp Loc Minh only in DA Chief, Mil Hist records summary. See Loc Ninh SF Camp.

Loc Ninh (n/a)
Mapsheet name of L-7014-6332-4. SVN/Cambodia.

Loc Ninh (XU 75-06)
On QL-13, apx 110 km due N Saigon, 15 km from Cambodia, 45 km due W Song Be and 42 km ENE Katum. Described in *Father Soldier Son*, as similar to An Loc, and as quaint French colonial town (off-limits to all but US SF up to '69?) with cobble-stone town square/fountain. Heavily attacked in Battle of Loc Ninh, 29Oct-7Nov67, by two Rgts of 9th VC Div. On 1Nov, besieged base was reinforced by ARVN and US 1st Bde/1st Inf Div. Battle ended 7Nov67, w/850 VC dead. Binh Long Pr, III Corps.

Loc Ninh (new) SF Camp (XU 7314-0823)
Along QL-13 at Loc Ninh AF, apx 500 meters N Old Loc Ninh SF Camp's position and 115 km N Saigon. SF Det 49, 5th SF Grp, Det. A-434, Dec64, Det A-331 (was 314), Oct65, A-331 Oct66. Grid per *SF Order of Battle.* Became 74th ARVN Border Ranger camp. Binh Long Pr, III Corps.

Loc Ninh (old) SF Camp (XU 733-088)
Along QL-13 at Loc Ninh AF, apx 500 meters S Loc Ninh

New SF Camp site and 115 km N Saigon. SF Det 49, 5th SF Grp, Det. A-434, Dec64, Det A-331 (was 314), Oct65, A-331 Oct66. Relocated. Grid per *SF Order of Battle.* Binh Long Pr, III Corps.

Loc Ninh Airfield (XU 733-084)
Apx 15 km both S and E Cambodia, 32 km SW Bu Dop AF, 45 km ENE Katum AF, 20 km due N An Loc and 45 km due W Song Be, per TPC K-10D. El. 492', 3,100' asph rwy. At 11°49'54"N-106°35'33"E. Also listed at XU 731-082. "Battle of Loc Ninh Airstrip" took place 31Oct67, during Op Shenandoah II, when elements of 6/15th Arty, 1st Inf Div killed 82 VC in 3d of 3 small battles prior to Srok Silamlite III. Binh Long Pr, III Corps.

Loc Ninh District HQ (XU 730-097)
Apx 14 km S Cambodia, 31 km SW Bu Dop AF and 19 km due N An Loc. Oct67. Binh Long Pr, III Corps.

Loc Ninh Heliport (XU 737-095)
E QL-13 and immed NE Loc Ninh AF, apx 22 km N An Loc. "Heliport #605, alt?, vacant lot." 11°50'40"N-106°35'30"E, per Feb73 TAD. Binh Long Pr, III Corps.

Loc Ninh Rubber Plantation (XU 68-93)
Large plantation that surrounded Loc Ninh to W, N and E. 1st Inf Div engaged 3 VC Rgts in and around plantation during Op Shenandoah II, Oct-Nov67, and in Battle of Loc Ninh. Binh Long Pr, III Corps.

Loc Son CAP (YD 921-111?)
See CAP 3-5-1. Grid is est. Thua Thien Pr, I Corps.

Loc Thien SF Camp (n/a)
SF Det 33. No data.

Local Force VC (n/a)
See Glossary.

Location Alpha (n/a)
No data available.

Location Coco (n/a)
No data available.

Locust, LZ (XD 968-368)
Apx 14 km SW Khe Sanh CB, 14 km SSW Ca Lu and 41 km WSW Quang Tri. Apr70 XXIV Corps grid per Don Armstrong. Quang Tri Pr, I Corps.

Loei Airfield (QV 9-2)
Along Loei River near 17°26'00"N-101°44'00"E, or apx 435 km NNE Bangkok. NIMA data. El. 800'. Thailand.

Loei Province (QV 6-2?)
SF camp AO per *SF Order of Battle.* Thailand.

Loeng Nok Tha Airfield (VC 5-8)
A.k.a. Crossroads AF. Apx 43 km W Lao border and 120 km NNW Ubon AB, 135 km S NKP, and 125 km SSE Sakhon Nakhon (New) AF. At 16°10'00"N-104°36'00"E. Listed as abnd in '66 NIMA data. Thailand.

Loftberg, USS (n/a)
DD-759, per Ralph Fries.

Log Base 1 (YS 440-740)
A.k.a. Logistical Base 1. Along LTL-2, apx 36 km S Xuan Loc, 6 km N Nui Dat and 6 km SSW Xa Binh Gia. Apr66. Phuoc Tuy Pr, III Corps.

Logan, Camp (XT 98-13)
At Bien Hoa. Apparently only Seabee camp outside I Corps and furthest from the ocean. Was also last Seabee camp in VN to be named for Seabee KIA. Home of NMCB-5. Named to honor UTC William Logan, killed in motor vehicle accident, 10Aug71. Facility dedicated, Fall 71. Grid apx. Data per Ray Bows. Bien Hoa Pr, III Corps.

Logan, LZ (BR 469-493)
Just NE An Khe Golf Course AF and 4 km N An Khe AF, just beyond perimeter of Camp Radcliff. Also listed at BR 467-467 in same rpt, which if accurate, indicates it was within perimeter of Camp Radcliff and apx 1 km E peak Hon Cong Mtn 2d grid may be in error, as it was atypical for FSB to be built within major base and separately named (though common to have separately named camps or cmpds within a large base). Binh Dinh Pr, II Corps. [341]

Logistics Support Unit Bravo (XD 847-417)
A.k.a. LSU Bravo. Immed SE the SE corner of main parking apron of Khe Sanh AF. Handled all supply needs for facility and surrounding hill positions. *Valley of Decision* has several good maps showing its location. Quang Tri Pr, I Corps.

Logo, LZ (XT 966-758)
Apx 11 km due W Dong Xoai and 20 km E QL-13. Also listed at XT 969-752. Mar67. Phuoc Long Pr, III Corps.

Loi Giang CAP (n/a)
CAP 2-5-1, 2d CAG. Quang Nam Pr, I Corps.

Loi Hong Canal (YD 81-20/87-18)
Runs from SE corner of Hue to estuary apx 5 km NW Phu Bai AF. Thua Thien Pr, I Corps.

Loi Tan (n/a)
Mapsheet name of L-7014-6431-1. SVN.

Lois, FSB (YT 04-24)
Apx 12 km NNW Bien Hoa AB. 3d/7th Inf and 4th/12th Inf, 199th LIB. A Lois is also listed at YT 129-230? Bien Hoa Pr, III Corps.

Lois, FSB (YT 129-229)
Just S Song Dong Nai River, apx 16 km NE Bien Hoa AB and 4 km NE Ap Mot. 1st Cav's 1st/7th Cav here Mar-69, D/1st/7th here 10Apr69, 1st/8th Cav here, May69. AO Apache, during Op Cheyenne Saber, per Frank Penk, Jr. Also Lois listed at YT 040-240? Bien Hoa Pr, III Corps.

Lois, LZ (AQ 845-145)
Midway between Ban Me Thuot and Ban Me Thuot East AFs, apx 3 km ESE Ban Me Thuot AF and 4 km E Lac Giao. A Bty, 2d/9th Arty here Dec69. 4th Div 31Jan70 ORLL grid per Jim Henderson. Darlac Pr, II Corps.

Lolita, FSB (YU 369-261)
A.k.a. FSB Nguyen Trai. Remote site along river apx 13 km S to SSE Djamap AF/Bu Gia Map, 27 km NE Song Be and 23 km NNW Duc Phong AF/SF Camp. Built Feb70-Apr70, by B/8th Engr Bn, 1st Cav. [342] "FSBs Django and Joan closed 23 and 25Feb70 respectively, and 8th Abn Bn displaced to establish FSB Lolita. As move N gained momentum and enemy activity increased, FSB's Candy, Loan, and Audie were built 25, 26 and 27Feb70 respectively...1st Abn Bn (-) moved to build FSB Loan, leaving one rifle Co to secure FSB Judie." [343] Also listed at YU 363-262 and 372-272. See Nguyen Trai. Phuoc Long Pr, III Corps.

Lolo, LZ (XD 43-36)
A.k.a. LZ Lo Lo. Overlooked Rte 9, apx 28 km W Khe Sanh, 15 km due E LZ Liz and 7 km WNW LZ Alpha. 1st ARVN Div assaulted here and at LZ Sophia West, 3-6Mar71, during Lam Son 719. See Lam Son 719 AO map at www.americal.org/174/map4.htm. W DMZ in Laos.

Lom Sak Airfield (QU 3-6)
A.k.a. Lomsak AF. At 16°49'00"N-101°15'00"E, or apx 345 km NNE Bangkok on Feb 67 Natl Geo map. NIMA data. El. 500'. Thailand.

Lom Sak SF Camp (QU 3-6)
A.k.a. Lomsak SF Camp. Apx 345 km NNE Bangkok. SF camp or AO per *SF Order of Battle.* Thailand.

Lomax, LZ (CR 015-677)
On mtn overlooking ocean and bay, apx 10 km NE Vinh Loi, 32 km SSE Bong Son and 9 km E of QL-1. Oct66. Binh Dinh Pr, II Corps.

Lombard, Pointe du (XS 7-7)
See Pointe Lombard. Long An Pr?, III Corps.

Lomphat Airfield (n/a)
Along Srepok River, apx 315 km NE Phnom Penh and 65 km W SVN border. Natl Geo Map. El. 200'. Cambodia.

Lomsak Airfield (QU 3-6)
See Lom Sak AF. Thailand.

Lomsak SF Camp (QU 3-6)
See Lom Sak SF Camp. Thailand.

Lon, Bung (WT 0-0)
A.k.a. Bung Binh Thien Loampon. Freshwater lake at 10°55N-105°04'E. NC48-06 JOG. Chau Doc Pr, IV Corps.

Lonely Boy, LZ (BT 070-062?)
A.k.a. New Hau Duc. Apx 10 km NNE Old Hau Duc, 27 km WSW Tam Ky and 10 km SSW Tien Phuoc AF. Quang Tin Pr, I Corps.

Lonely Summit (XT 283-583)
Call Sign for Nui Ba Den Provisional Co Radio Relay facility at peak of Nui Ba Den Mtn. See Nui Ba Den. Tay Ninh Pr, III Corps.

Lonely, LZ/FSB (AQ 868-994)
Possibly a.k.a. Hill 432. On W side of QL-14 apx 7 km SSW Phu Nhon, 48 km SSE Pleiku, 22 km S Weigt-Davis and 38 km WNW Cheo Reo. Was just N point where QL-14 crossed branch of Ia Drang River. Per Mike Young, occupied highest ground in area and downward slope was most pronounced to S and toward 20' wide stream with Bailey Bridge across it. Phu Nhon was visible to NE. There was depression between the 2 locations and both were within arty range of one another. Apart from Engrs, only 2 tubes of 1st/92d Arty 155s here (later increased to full Bty). B/20th Engrs, one arty section and ARVN armored cav unit here '70-71. Soon after const, VC dug in between Phu Nhon and Lonely, and then attacked Phu Nhon. Was Southernmost cmpd of 20th Engr Bn and had no other US Army supt except the arty. Tom Rethard adds: "In Apr71, C/7/15th Arty fired in supt during attack here, possibly after US units were evaced." An excerpt from his letter dated 7Apr71, states, "Lonely was overrun, with 2 KIA, 14 WIA and 2 guns destroyed. When reinforcements arrived, they caught the NVA unloading people and supplies from trucks [and killed apx 100]" 20th Engrs here only until 3d wk of Apr71, when US forces evaced after 12 days of shelling/siege by 95B NVA Rgt. Exit convoy described as comical because "we had to pile everything we had onto too few vehicles. All manner of trucks, road working equip and etc were used (with everything and everybody stuffed onto and into those vehicles). We looked more like a circus parade than a military convoy. I'll never forget watching Walter Cronkite tell the nation of ignominious defeat and withdrawal of Army from LZ Lonely. Since the word got out late, we had the luxury of hearing about our defeat while drinking gin and tonic in Officers Club [Pleiku]. Man, that was surreal!" Listed grid and other info per Mike Young and Nolan Putman. On map at www.landscaper.net/. Pleiku Pr, II Corps.

Long, Camp (XD or YD?)
See Camp I. V. Long.

Long, FSB (YD 571-217)
A.k.a. Hill 674? Apx 23 km W Hue, 6 km WSW Ap Thanh Tan and near FSB's Helen and Meredith (possibly earlier or later name of those same FSBs?). Also listed at YD 522-217, a site 5 km S listed grid. Apr70 XXIV Corps grid per Don Armstrong. Thua Thien Pr, I Corps.

Long, FSB (YD 522-217?)
See Long at YD 571-217. Thua Thien Pr, I Corps.

Long, FSB (YS 250-750)
Along QL-15 at Phu My, apx 30 km N Vung Tau and 19 km WNW Nui Dat. Apr68. Phuoc Tuy Pr, III Corps.

Long An (XS 55-65)
Capitol, Long An Pr, III Corps.

Long An Airfield (XS 524-656)
A.k.a. Tan An AF. Apx 35 km SW Saigon, 30 km SE Thuy Dong AF, 15 km NNE Ben Tranh AF and about 1 km W Tan An. 3rd Bde/9th Inf Div HQ from early Sep70 to departure, per David Argabright. El. 7', 1,500' asph rwy. At 10°32'35"N-106°23'36"E. Long An Pr, III Corps.

Long An Helipad (XS 547-647)
Apx 2 km SE Long An AF. Long An Pr, III Corps.

Long An Province (XT/XS/YS)
One of 11 south-central provs forming III Corps (III CTZ). Generally S and SW Saigon. Contained 6 districts and Tan An, apx 40 km SW Saigon, was its capital. Pop in '68 was apx 381,000. 25th Inf Div tactical base was at Ben Luc, capital of Ben Luc Dist (pop of apx 46,000). Main economy was agriculture, principal crop was rice. QL-4 and 5 were main arteries. III Corps.

Long An? SF Camp (MSF) (XS 5660-6395)
A.k.a. Tan An SF Camp or Moc Hoa SF Camp? Just SE Tan An, 32 km SW Saigon, 22 km NNE My Tho and 4 km ESE Long An AF. 5th SF. Later became RF/PF base. Named Moc Hoa SF Camp in *SF Order of Battle*, but may be error? See Moc Hoa. Long An Pr, III Corps.

Long Beach, USS (n/a)
CGN 9. Cruiser. TF 76.8, During Op Eagle Pull.

Long Bien Bridge (WJ 89-27)
A.k.a. Paul Doumer Bridge. 1 of 2 major bridges over Red River; the older Long Bien and newer Chuong Duong. See Paul Doumer Bridge. NVN.

Long Bien, FSB? (XT 263-888)
Apx 6 km due W Katum, 20 km ENE Thien Ngon AF and 39 km N Tay Ninh. A Bty, 2d/35th Arty with six-155s here Apr70? Closed 1May70, per *11th ACR Cambodia Invasion AAR, 1st Cav Div, May-Jun70*, courtesy Lou Rochat. [344] Tay Ninh Pr, III Corps.

Long Binh (Post) (YT 04-07)
A.k.a. Camp Ranger and 506th Field Depot? At intersection of QL-1 and QL-15, just NE the Song Cai River and 20 km NE Saigon. Largest military base in VN. The 2d Bde/1st Inf Div departed Ft. Riley Kansas, 14Jul65 (aboard *USS Gordon*), and once in VN immed began const

of "Camp Ranger," their basecamp at Long Binh; apparently initial phase of what later became Long Binh Post. At height of US involvement, it covered 18 sq mi and held over 100,000 of the 540,000 total US troops in VN. Major supt, maintenance and logistical facility which, beginning in '66, also housed the 90th Replacement Depot, the major personnel replacement center in VN (prior to that, 90th was at Camp Alpha in Tan Son Nhut AB). Also home to infamous Long Binh Jail, HQ US Army Vietnam (USARV), HQ 1st Logistical Cmd, 1st Avn Bde, 18th MP Bde, 44th Med Bde, 199th Lt Inf Bde, HQ of II ARVN Corps and 93rd Evac Hosp, Nov65-Apr71. Also home to or known as 506th Field Depot (originally at Camp Davies; moved here '67), and billed as largest Field Depot in world. Apparently, major ammo dumps here exploded 4Jan67? Per *ARMY* Mag, in Oct96 virtually no evidence of base remained and, now in its place a large industrial park where tennis shoes, bikes and clothing are produced has been built. [345] See Cogido, Camp Ranger and Cat Lai. Bien Hoa Pr, III Corps. [346]

Long Binh AAF Airfield (YT 074-067)
See Sanford and Plantation AFs. Bien Hoa Pr, III Corps.

Long Binh Ammo Supply Heliport (YT 04-07)
At Long Binh Post, apx 7 km SE Bien Hoa AB, 3 km SSW Plantation AF and 27 km NE Tan Son Nhut AB. At YT 059-085 was a 36' x 80' asph pad; and at YT 058-118, was a 46' x 82' asph pad. "Heliport #740, alt 131', Copter pad lighted from sunset to sunrise, 3 lights mark ea corner of pad. 5 ea Cargo, 1 ea VIP. Long Binh Ammo-230.9, 45.7 Advsy. Arty advsy-Bien Hoa 290.0, 46.7." At 10°56'N 106°52'E, per Feb73 TAD. See Cogido and Cat Lai. Bien Hoa Pr, III Corps.

Long Binh ASP (YT 048-093)
Long Binh ammo supply pt. Oct71. Bien Hoa Pr, III Corps.

Long Binh Depot Heliport (YT 085-101)
Apx 3 km ESE Plantation AF, 10 km ESE Bien Hoa AB and 3 km ENE Long Binh Ammo Supply heliport. "Alt 120', 100' x 50' PSP rwy. Offl Bus Only. Arty advsy-Bien Hoa 290.0, 46.7," per Feb73 TAD. Bien Hoa Pr, III Corps.

Long Binh Dustoff Pad (YT 048-088)
Apx 7 km SE Bien Hoa AB, 3 km SSW Plantation AF and 27 km NE Tan Son Nhut AB. The 93d Evac Hosp Dustoff pad at Long Binh Post in '69, per '69 TAD. Listed in '69 TAD, but not in '73 TAD. Data per Frank Penk, Jr. Bien Hoa Pr, III Corps.

Long Binh Hospital Heliport (YT 046-076)
A.k.a. the 24th Evac Hosp Heliport. "Alt 130', 340' x 180', asph. Hosp Offl Bus Only. No shutdown. Acft may park HQ USARV Heliport, mil taxis available. No overflight of Hosp. All acft carrying patients must coordinate their needs with 'Wide Minnow Con' at 62.05. Dust Off Advsy SVC-Wide Minnow 62.05. Arty advsy-Bien Hoa 290.0, 46.7," per Feb73 TAD. Bien Hoa Pr, III Corps.

Long Binh Jail (YT 04-07?)
A.k.a. LBJ. Somewhere within Long Binh Post, apx 20 km NE Saigon. Infamous US Army prison for moderately serious and felony crimes not requiring sentences of more than 6 months to a year(?). Long-term prisoners were sent to stateside military prisons. As disincentive for soldiers trying to escape combat by intentionally committing crimes, LBJ time was counted as "Bad Time," and did not diminish one's 365-day tour. Also holding facility for serious felons being sent to US. Bien Hoa Pr, III Corps.

Long Binh Navy Base (YT 0-1?)
USN River forces ops base, '69-70. Per MRF Assn Website. Bien Hoa Pr?, III Corps.

Long Binh North (YT 048-106)
See Plantation AF. Bien Hoa Pr, III Corps.

Long Binh Relocation Camp (BT 515-051)
Along QL-1, directly W Chu Lai military complex and AF. Nov69. Quang Tin Pr, I Corps.

Long Chau 1 and 2 CAP (n/a)
See CAP 2-3-9. 2d CAG. Quang Nam Pr, I Corps.

Long Chien Airfield (TG 82-14)
See Long Tieng AF. Laos.

Long Chien Lima Site (TG 82-14)
See Long Tieng Lima Site. Laos.

Long Dien (YS 43-59)
Town apx 22 km NE Vung Tau, 7 km S Nui Dat, 4 km W Dat Do. Scene of heavy fighting 3-6Feb68, during Tet '68, involving C and D Cos, 3 RAR. Phuoc Tuy Pr, III Corps.

Long Dinh Bridge (XS 380-497)
QL-4 bridge adj to Long Dinh Heliport, apx 13 km WNW My Tho. Dinh Tuong Pr, IV Corps.

Long Dinh Heliport (XS 381-496)
Along N side of QL-4, apx 13 km WNW My Tho. Heliport #606, alt 7', sod. Wires to S, at 10°24'00"N-106°16'00"E, per Feb73 TAD. Dinh Tuong Pr, IV Corps.

Long Dong (BT?)
Small Island NW Barrier Island. Site of ARVN Combined Enemy Holding and Interrogation Ctr. SE Quang Nam or possibly NE Quang Tin Pr?, I Corps.

Long Duc 2, FSB (XT 91-00)
Apx 5 km due S Di An Basecamp, 6 km SSW Di An, 5 km NE Saigon and 16 km SW Bien Hoa AB. Presumably near ville of Long Duc 2. 2d/3d Inf, '67. Grid per 199th LIB Assn. Gia Dinh Pr?, III Corps.

Long Giao (YS 43-97?)
Apx 12 km S Xuan Loc AF, 28 km N Luscombe AF and 55 km due E Saigon. Blackhorse Basecamp here, home of 11th Armored Cav Rgt and 7th Surgical Hosp (MASH) 67-69, Long Khanh Pr, III Corps.

Long Giao Airfield (YS 437-963)
See Blackhorse AF. Long Khanh Pr, III Corps.

Long Giao Basecamp (YS 435-970)
Apx 12 km S Xuan Loc AF, 28 km N Luscombe AF and 55 km due E Saigon. Jan67. Also listed at YS 440-960. Long Khanh Pr, III Corps.

Long Hai (YS-438-512)
On coast, apx 17 km NE Vung Tau, 17 km S Luscombe AF (Nui Dat), 66 km SE Saigon. NCO Trng Ctr here. 5th SF Det B-36 personally assigned here by President Diem to protect shrimping ops of his wealthy friends. Men of Det B-36, a.k.a. Shrimp Soldiers, formed Aug67 for recon in II/III Corps CTZs, and later became C &C for 3d MSF Nov70-Nov72, 1 of 3 MACV-SOG, USARV-UITG (Individ Trng Grp) Trng Bn sites in VN. In 72 was renamed the FANK (Forces Arm'ee Nationale Khmer Trng Cmd), and redesignated Field Trng Cmd when FANK was taken over by 18th ARVN Div, Dec72. Also home to ARVN's Long Hai Rgt. Phuoc Tuy Pr, III Corps.

Long Hai Airfield (YS 432-512)
On coast apx 17 km NE Vung Tau, 12 km ENE Vung Tau major AF, 17 km S Luscombe (Nui Dat) AF, 66 km SE Saigon and E Ap Phuoc Tinh. TPC K-10D. El. 7' steel-mat rwy. At 10°24'28"N-107°13'20"E. Also listed at YS-438-512. Phuoc Tuy Pr, III Corps.

Long Hai Heliport (YS 449-493)
On coast, apx 2 km ESE Long Hai AF and 18 km ENE Vung Tau. Heliport #607, alt 10', at 10°23'30"N-107°14'00"E, per Feb73 TAD. Phuoc Tuy Pr, III Corps.

Long Hai Mountains (YS 46-54)
Generally 20 km NE Vung Tau and 15 km due S Nui Dat. Rugged mtn chain rising from plain S Ba Ria, S Long Dien, and bordering coast. Part of Minh Dam Secret Zone, nerve center for VC ops in Phuoc Tuy Pr. Viet Nationalists used former Japanese fortifications and caves in these mtns to launch attacks on French, US and ANZAC forces working area. Long Hai AF was on coast at SW edge of this hill mass. See Gunners Day for interesting historical note. Phuoc Tuy Pr, III Corps.

Long Hai RF NCO Trng Center (YS 43-52?)
If grid at all accurate, was apx 16 km ENE Vung Tau? ARVN's Long Hai Regional Force NCO Trng Ctr. Phuoc Tuy Pr, III Corps.

Long Hai SF Camp (YS-4384-5122)
On coast apx 17 km NE Vung Tau, 17 km S Luscombe AF (Nui Dat), 66 km SE Saigon. 5th SF Det B-36 personally assigned here by President Diem to protect shrimping ops of his wealthy friends. Det B-36, a.k.a. "Shrimp Soldiers," was formed Aug67 for recon in II/III Corps CTZs, and later became C &C for 3d MSF. 1 of 3 MACV-SOG, USARV-UITG (Individ Trng Grp) Trng Bn sites in VN, Nov70-Nov72. In 72 was renamed FANK (Forces Arm'ee Nationale Khmer Trng Cmd), and later redesignated Field Trng Cmd when FANK taken over by 18th ARVN Div, Dec72. Also site of ARVN's Long Hai RF NCO Trng Ctr Grid per *SF Order of Battle.* Phuoc Tuy Pr, III Corps.

Long Hai, Camp (XS-4384-5122)
See Long Hai SF Camp. Phuoc Tuy Pr, III Corps.

Long Hoa (XT 248-470)
Ville apx 2 km S Tay Ninh, at its SE edge. Home of Great Temple of Holy See, main temple of Cao Dai sect. Attacked 18Aug68 during Battle for Tay Ninh, when est Co of NVA forced way into city center. By end of day, enemy occupied the E and S fingers of town. Data per AAR, *Battle for Tay Nin*h (17Aug-27Sep68), HQ 25th ID, 2Feb69, p 13. Tay Ninh Pr, III Corps.

Long Horn, FSB (AT 833-606)
A.k.a. Hill 866 and Longhorn. Atop Charlie Ridge, apx 23 km SW Da Nang and 13 km due W Hill 55. Const between 20-25Ap69, by USMC Engrs to supt Op Oklahoma Hills with 3d/7th Marines pulling security. XXIV Corps grid per Don Armstrong. Also listed at AT 823-605 and 824-666. Quang Nam Pr, I Corps.

Long Keo Airfield (XB 79-40)
LS-172. Apx 240 km WSW Quang Ngai, 130 km WNW Dak To SVN and 10 km SW Ban Konghang AF. CIA/SF, per *Air Facilities Data-Laos.* El. 3,250'. Laos.

Long Khanh (various)
Common Viet place-name. Villes with this name in grid squares: WS 3-9, XS 2-4, XT 2-3, XR 5-6, YT 0-0 and BS 7-0. II/III/IV Corps.

Long Khanh (BS 740-080)
Ville in An Lao Valley apx 16 km NW Bong Son, 2 km S Thuan An and 15 km NW LZ English. 7th Bn, 22d NVA Rgt staging area during Dec66 attack of LZ Bird. Cited in *Bird*, p 15. Binh Dinh Pr, II Corps.

Long Khanh Heliport (XR 590-610)
N of road TL-30, apx 55 km due E Soc Trang AF/Khanh Hung, and 40 km SSE Tra Vinh AF/Phu Vinh. "Heliport #608, alt 7', white corners. At 09°36'00"N-106°27'00"E," per Feb73 TAD. IV Corps.

Long Khanh Province (YS/YT)
One of 11 south-central provs forming III Corps (III CTZ).

Long Khanh SF Camp (XR-587-629)
Along Rte TL-30, apx 55 km due E Soc Trang AF/Khanh Hung, and 40 km SSE Tra Vinh AF/Phu Vinh. 5th SF. Info/grid per *SF Order of Battle.* Moved to Vinh Gia? Vinh Binh Pr, IV Corps.

Long Khanh SF Camp (YT-740-331)
At S edge of Xa Vo Dat, apx 35 km NE Xuan Loc. 5th SF. Info/grid per *SF Order of Battle.* See Tuc Trung. Long Khanh Pr, III Corps.

Long Khat SF Camp (WT 892-060)
A.k.a. Long Khot SF Camp. Apx 3 km SW Long Khot AF, 4 km S Cambodia, 53 km NNE Cao Lanh, and 4 km ENE Binh Thanh Thon AF. 5th SF. Info/grid per *SF Order of Battle.* Moved to Binh Than Thon; MACV AT#? Also listed at WT 892-360, which is in Cambodia and presumably an error. Kien Tuong Pr, IV Corps.

Long Khot (WT 93-06)
Just W the Crow's Nest, apx 21 km NE Moc Hoa, 1 km S Cambodia and 8 km ENE Binh Thanh Thon AF. Portion MACV Det 72 here Oct71-Sep72. Data per Bill Hunt. Kien Tuong Pr, IV Corps.

Long Khot 2 Airfield (WT 912-069)
On Cambodian border, 6 km NE Binh Thanh Thon AF, 21 km NW Muc Hoa AF and 93 km W Saigon, per TPC K-10D. El. 6', 1,200' clay rwy. At 10°55'10"N-105°50'19"E, per Feb73 TAD. Kien Tuong Pr, IV Corps.

Long Khot Airfield (WT 864-043)
See Binh Thanh Thon. Kien Tuong Pr, IV Corps.

Long Khot Heliport (WT 917-074)
On Cambodian border, roughly 6 km NE Binh Thanh Thon AF, 21 km NW Muc Hoa AF and 93 km W Saigon. "Heliport #609, alt 16', low level from Vinh Loi," per Feb73 TAD. Kien Tuong Pr, IV Corps.

Long Knot (WT 93-06)
See Long Khot. Kien Tuong Pr, IV Corps.

Long Lao River (BR)
Sp variant of Song Lao? Apparently W of Bong Son. Its valley provided an attack route for 9th Bn, 22d NVA Rgt in its part of attack of LZ Bird, Dec66. Cited in *Bird*, p. 14. Binh Dinh Pr, II Corps.

Long Le Airfield (YS 44-68?)
Built adj to Luscombe AF and 1st ATF ANZAC HQ at Nui Dat. 28 km due S Blackhorse AF, apx 60 km SE Saigon, 30 km NE Vung Tau. Const finished during Dec 66. ONC K-10. El. 366'. See Luscombe AF. Phuoc Tuy Pr, III Corps.

Long Lines North (CR 03-23?)
On Vung Chau Mtn, W of Qui Nhon. 1st Sig Bde, Long Lines Det. North, IWCS. Included 518th, 362d Sig Cos, AFVN and AFRTS. Data per Jerry Ault and Duane Good. See Camp Granite, and Phu Lam and Vung Chau Signal Sites. Binh Dinh Pr, II Corps.

Long Lines South (XS 78-89)
See Phu Lam Signal Site. Gia Dinh Pr, III Corps.

Long Loc Heliport (XR 645-630)
See Long Toan Heliport. Vinh Binh Pr, IV Corps.

Long My (n/a)
Mapsheet name of L-7014-6128-3. SVN.

Long My Depot (CR 0-2)
At Qui Nhon. Binh Dinh Pr, II Corps.

Long My Heliport (WR 631-697)
Along TL-42, apx 16 km SE Vi Thanh AF and 47 km SSW Can Tho. Heliport #722, alt 10', at: 09°41'30"N-105°38'5"E, per Feb73 TAD. Chuong Thien Pr, IV Corps.

Long My Marketplace (XT 236-472)
In heart of Tay Ninh city, apx 76 km NW Tan Son Nhut AB and Saigon. Scene of fighting 18Aug68, during Battle for Tay Ninh, 17Aug-27Sep68. Tay Ninh Pr, III Corps.

Long My Valley (CR 0-1?)
A.k.a. Valley F and site of 19th Engr Bn Log Depot. Apparently near Qui Nhon. Home of 19th Eng Bn after it moved from "Valley A." C/19th Engr Bn started new facility const in Mar67, building 30 acre cantonment that held apx 2,000 men. Prefab yard established to "construct tent frames, tent floors, latrines, shower facilities and mess hall area." B Co removed apx 74,000 cubic yds of laterite and 24,000 cubic yds of soil while building roads, Stg areas and drainage syst. Other attached units inc 544th Float Bridge Co and plt of 509th Panel Bridge Co. Data per article on internet at www.war-stories.com/Incoming.htm. Binh Dinh Pr, II Corps.

Long Ngoc (n/a)
Rail and vehicle bridges here struck by Carrier TF-77 attempts to blunt NVA Tet '68 offensive. NVN.

Long Nguyen Secret Zone (XT 73-54)
VC Staging area generally NE Michelin Plantation and between it and Minh Thanh Rubber Plantation, with Binh Duong/Binh Long Pr border splitting it roughly in half on E/W axis. Was N Boundary Road and W Thunder Road (QL-13), NE Dau Tieng and NW Lai Khe. An objective of 1st Div during Op Thoan Thang in '69. Per *Low Level Hell's* 1st Div TAOR map. Grid roughly center of mass, roughly 20 km NNE Lai Khe and 10 km W FSB Thunder II, per map in *Rangers at War*, Appendix I, p 324. Binh Duong/Binh Long Pr border, III Corps.

Long Phu (WR 7-6)
Ville perhaps 27 km SE Vi Thanh AF and 45 km SSE Can Tho. Chuong Thien Pr?, IV Corps.

Long Phu (Bang Long) (n/a)
Mapsheet name of L-7014-6228-3. SVN.

Long Phu Heliport (1) (WR 755-666)
Apx 5 km SW Phuong Phu, 27 km ESE Vi Thanh and 44 km SSW Can Tho. Heliport #610, alt 7', per Feb73 TAD. Chuong Thien Pr, IV Corps.

Long Phu Heliport (2) (XR 242-619)
Roughly 20 km E to ENE Soc Trang AF, 4 km SW Dai An, and 17 km due E Khanh Hung. Heliport #723, alt 7', per Feb73 TAD. Ba Xuyen Pr, IV Corps.

Long Phu Navy ISB (XR 2-5)
Apparently apx 20 km E Soc Trang AF on Mekong River? USN Intermediate Supt Base, '69-71. Per MRF Assn Website. Ba Xuyen Pr, IV Corps.

Long Phu SF Camp (WR 755-665)
A.k.a. Tra Lang SF Camp? Apx 32 km WNW Soc Trang, 45 km SSE Can Tho, 27 km SE Vi Thanh AF and at same grid as Tra Lang SF Camp. 5th SF. Info/grid per *SF Order of Battle.* Moved to Luong Tan. Ba Xuyen Pr, IV Corps.

Long Phu, Camp (WS 061-601)
See Luong Tan. IV Corps.

Long Phuoc (YS 43-66?)
VC hamlet apx 2 or 3 km SW Nui Dat that was completely evacuated, Jun66. Residents moved to Hoa Long, near Long Phuoc, so that they could maintain their rice fields. 6 RAR conducted sweep of ville during Op Enoggera, 21Jun-5Jul66, while suptd by 161 Bty, RNZA at Nui Dat. Phuoc Tuy Pr, III Corps.

Long Pot Airfield (TG 36-37)
LS-132. CIA/SF, per *Air Facilities Data-Laos.*

Long Reach, FSB (YS 526-767)
See Longreach. Phuoc Tuy Pr, III Corps.

Long Rhan (YT 46-08)
A.k.a. Xuan Loc. Apx 60 km WNW Saigon and 65 km NNE Vung Tau. Capitol, Long Khanh Pr, III Corps.

Long Son Island (YS 27-56)
In tidal marsh roughly 12 km N Vung Tau and 18 km SW Nui Dat. 161 Bty, RNZA (Andrew's Bty 18Sep-6Sep70) firebase called Andrea built here 4-17Apr70. See FSB Andrea. Phuoc Tuy Pr, III Corps.

Long Tan, FSB (YS 49-66)
N of route 52, apx 6 km ESE Nui Dat, 30 km NE Vung Tau and 5 km due N Dat Do. 161 Bty, RNZA (Honner's Bty 13Jun66-13May67) FSB set here 19-25Nov66. Site of Battle of Long Tan, 17Aug68, a major battles involving 1 ATF ANZAC forces, when D Co/6RAR was attacked by and est 1,500 VC of 275th MF Rgt. A and C Cos, 6RAR were added to fray by APCs of 3 Trp, 1APC Sqdn, and when fighting ended, Aussies had suffered 17 KIA and 21 WIA. Also listed at YS 48-67. Phuoc Tuy Pr, III Corps.

Long Tau Channel (YS 03-52)
A.k.a. Song Dong Tranh River. Ship channel running through Rung Sat Special Zone generally SSE from point on Song Nha Be River immed E Nha Be, joining ocean E of Xom Vam Lang and apx 5 km E the Cua Soirap entrance to Song Nhe Be/Song Saigon River complex. Was only deep-draft channel to port facilities of Saigon from sea. Grid is at river's mouth. Gia Dinh Pr, III Corps. [347]

Long Tau River (YS 0-6)
Ran through Rung Sat Special Zone, SE Saigon. Main ship channel to Saigon. Go Cong Pr, IV Corps.

Long Thanh (YS 135-935?)
Likely at or near Long Thanh AF. 5th SF Grp, Det. A-212, Dec64, Det B-53 (was A-412) MACV, 5th SF Operating Base (SFOB), Oct65. Bien Hoa Pr, III Corps.

Long Thanh Airfield (YS 135-935)
Apx 27 km E Saigon, 5 km S Long Thanh North, 25 km SE Bien Hoa AF and 36 km WSW Xuan Loc AF. Minor of the 2 Long Thanh AF's. El. 33', 1,800' laterite/grass rwy. At

10°47'48"N-106°57'10"E. Some security provided by Thai Adv-led ARVN Ranger recon units here, and near Bearcat. Long Thanh, Bien Hoa Pr, III Corps.

Long Thanh I Airfield (YS 135-935)
See Long Thanh AF. Bien Hoa Pr, III Corps.

Long Thanh II Airfield (YS 145-982)
See Long Thanh North AF. Bien Hoa Pr, III Corps.

Long Thanh North Airfield (YS 145-982)
A.k.a. Long Thanh North Army AF. Major AF and larger of 2 Long Thanh AF's. Apx 5 km N Long Thanh AF, 27 km ENE Saigon, 20 km SE Bien Hoa AF and 32 km WSW Xuan Loc AF. Home of 210th Avn Bn (Combat), El. 140', 5,000' asph rwy. At 10°50'10"N-106°57'50"E. Some security provided by Thai Adv-led ARVN Ranger recon units here and near Bearcat. Bien Hoa Pr, III Corps.

Long Thanh Outpost (YS 138-921)
At Long Thanh ville along QL-15, apx 2 km S Long Thanh AF and 25 km E Saigon. Jan68. Bien Hoa Pr, III Corps.

Long Thanh SF Training Center (YS 1-9?)
MACV-SOG training facility for ARVN Ranger units. Partial security provided by Thai Adv-led ARVN Ranger recon units here and near Bearcat. Cited in *Rangers At War*, at p 275. Bien Hoa Pr, III Corps.

Long Thanh South Airfield (YS 230-771)
See Phu My AF. Phuoc Tuy Pr, III Corps.

Long Thanh, Plantation de (YS 2-9)
A.k.a. Don Dien Long Thanh. Site of *Societe Terras Rouge;* the Society of Red Earth or Terrace or Plains(?). Bien Hoa and/or Gia Dinh Pr, III Corps.

Long Thun SOG Training Camp (XS 7-7 or CP 0-5?)
Possibly either at the Davan Cmpd (CP 04-53) at Nha Trang, or Long Thuong in Long An Pr (near XS 765-760). SOG-South B-55 trng camp here Jan 68, and that Det is listed as having been at the Davan Cmpd in Nha Trang? Discussed in *LRRP Company Command*, p 50-51. Khanh Hoa or Gia Dinh/Long An Pr?, II or III Corps.

Long Thuong SOG Trng Camp (CP 0-5 or XS 7-7?)
See Long Thun SOG Trng Camp. Khanh Hoa or Gia Dinh/Long An Pr?, II or III Corps.

Long Tien Airfield (TG 82-14)
See Long Tieng AF. Laos.

Long Tien Lima Site (TG 82-14)
See Long Tieng Lima Site. Laos.

Long Tieng Airfield (TG 82-14)
A.k.a. LS-30/LS-98, LS 20A(?), Long Tien AF, Long Chien AF, Ban Nam Na AF(?), and Ban Longtiang AF. Apx 130 km SE Luang Prabang, 135 km NNE Vientiane and 55 km ENE Vang Vieng AF. CIA/SF Lima Site. 5,000' rwy, El. 3,215'. See Long Tien Lima Site and Lima Site. Grid per *Air Facilities Data-Laos.* At 19°06'00"N-102°56'00"E, maps are NE48-01 & TPC J-11D. Laos.

Long Tieng Lima Site (TG 82-14)
A.k.a. LS-30/LS-98, LS 20A?, Long Tien, Long Chien, Ban Nam Na and Ban Longtiang. Apx 130 km SE Luang Prabang, 135 km NNE Vientiane and 55 km ENE Vang Vieng AF, per ONC-J-11. Apparently the main operating base for Lima Site "secret war" in Laos. Long Tieng Valley was virtually uninhabited when CIA built it in '62 as HQ for Vang Pao, leader of Hmong. Raven FACs here also. Complete listing of Lima Sites at "LS" entry. Near 19°06'00"N-102°56'00"E, map is NE48-01 or TPC J-11D. See Lima Sites in Glossary. Laos.

Long Toan Airfield (XR 649-669)
Apx 6 km WSW Ba Dong, 60 km ENE Soc Trang, 36 km SE Tra Vinh and 130 km SSW Saigon. Listed as "Abnd, Caution: rwy unsafe, SVN Directorate of Civ Avn. AF # VA4-168," in Aug69 TAD per Frank Penk, Jr. Not in Feb73 TAD. Vinh Binh Pr, IV Corps.

Long Toan Heliport (XR 645-630)
A.k.a. Long Loc Heliport. Apx 6 km WSW Ba Dong, 60 km ENE Soc Trang, 36 km SE Tra Vinh and 130 km SSW Saigon. "Heliport #611, alt 7', VC all sides." At 09°37'00"N-106°29'30"E, per Feb73 TAD. Maps are L-7014 6228-2 (Tra Cu), and/or L-7014 6328-3 (Ba Dong). Vinh Binh Pr, IV Corps.

Long Tre, Camp? (BQ or BR?)
Possible variant of Dong Tre and, if that is case, then was at BQ 909-704, apx 33 km NW Tuy Hoa. Listed as Long Tre in DA Chief, Mil Hist records summary which also indicates Det A-433 (a.k.a. 222) here '65. If not sp error, then possibly in grid square BR 8-0, near Van Canh? See Dong Tre, Long Tre/Van Canh, and Van Canh SF Camps. Phu Yen or Binh Dinh Pr, II Corps.

Long Tre/Van Canh SF Camp (BR?)
Possible misspelling of "Dong Tre?" If not misspelling, then possibly in grid square BR 8-0, which is site of Van Canh? 5th SF, Det A-222 (was 433) hereOct65. See Dong Tre and Van Canh SF Camps. Likely Binh Dinh or Phu Yen Pr, II Corps.

Long Van Airfield (CP 039-520)
See Nha Trang AF. Khanh Hoa Pr, II Corps.

Long Van Compound (CP 039-520?)
At Nha Trang. Army Avn units here, inc 17th Avn Grp (controlled Avn assets of IFFV/II Corps) and 8th Field Hosp. Khanh Hoa Pr, II Corps.

Long Vinh (XR54-62)
Along Rte 159, apx 14k km WSW Long Toan Heliport. Vinh Binh Pr, IV Corps.

Long Xuyen (n/a)
Mapsheet name of L-7014-6029-1. SVN.

Long Xuyen (WS 52-41)
Apx 56 km NW Can Tho and 135 km SW Saigon. MACV Adv Team 52, An Giang Sector here. Capitol, Chau Doc Pr, IV Corps.

Long Xuyen Airfield (WS 521-416)
In Mekong Delta, apx 46 km NW Can Tho, 56 km NE Rach Gia, 22 km SW Cau Lanh AF, 54 km ESE That Son AF and 140 km SW Saigon. El. 16', 3,400' rwy. At 10°19'38"N-105°28'43"E. Chau Doc Pr, IV Corps.

Long Xuyen Heliport (WS 485-457)
Apx 48 km NW Can Tho and about 140 km WSW Saigon. Heliport #612, alt 10', soccer field, at: 10°23'00"N-105°26'30"E, per Feb73 TAD. An Giang Pr, IV Corps.

Long Xuyen Navy ASB (WS 52-43?)
If grid correct, was along W bank of Mekong, apx 46 km NW Can Tho and 140 km SW Saigon. USN Advanced Supt Base, '66-71. Per MRF Assn Website. See Long Xuyen AF. An Giang Pr, IV Corps.

Long Xuyen SF Camp (WS 521-416)
In Mekong Delta, apx 46 km NW Can Tho, 56 km NE Rach Gia, 22 km SW Cau Lanh AF, 54 km ESE That Son

AF and 140 km SW Saigon. 5th SF. Info/grid per *SF Order of Battle.* Moved to Chao Doc. MACV Advsy Team 52, An Giang Sector here? An Giang Pr, IV Corps.

Long Xuyen Signal Site (WS?)
Possibly at Long Xuyen AF/Navy Base, apx 46 km NW Can Tho. ONC K-10D map shows tower symbol at that location. An Giang Pr?, IV Corps.

Longhorn, FSB (AT 833-606)
See Long Horn. Quang Nam Pr, I Corps.

Longreach, FSB (YS 526-767)
Apx 10 km NNE Nui Dat, 3 km W FSB Wilton, 1 km E Ngai Giao and 7 km E Rte-2. 161 Bty, RNZA (Hitching's Bty 14Apr68-18Mar69) FSB set here 28Aug-5Sep68. US Bty A/2d/35th Arty here. On 1ATF NCO trng map per John Hollett. Also at YS 52-76 Phuoc Tuy Pr, III Corps.

Loo Hong Phong Forest (BN 100-300)
Apx 35 km ENE Phan Thiet. Binh Thuan Pr, II Corps.

Loon, LZ/FSB (XD 876-334)
At N edge of and centered on the Vietnam Salient, apx 8 km SSE Khe Sanh CB, 50 km WSW Quang Tri, 8 km NE Lang Chie and 7 km SSW Lang Kat. Opened 2Jun68 by elements of 1st and 4th Marines, 3d Mar Div during Ops Robin North/Robin South, an op against 308th NVA Div's 88th and 102d Rgts. Apparently attacked very next morning, 3Jun68, by elements of 88th NVA Rgt. C/1st/4th Marines hit by 18 rnds 130mm arty fire from Co Roc Ridge on 5Jun68, resulting in 9 US KIA, 3 WIA. Attacked 5-6Jun68 by NVA Bn, with 24 USMC KIA and 37 WIA. CH-46 (#151940) crashed with 11 crew and passengers while evacuating 8 bodies.[348] Cited in *Dispatches*, p. 234, as metaphor for entire war. Apparently a very bad place. Fighting at and around Loon detailed in *After Tet*, pp 226-227. XXIV Corps grid. Quang Tri Pr, I Corps.

Lop Buri Airfield (PS 7-3)
A.k.a. Lopburi AF. Along Laotian border, apx 125 km N Bangkok per Feb67 Natl Geo Map. El. 98'. Thailand.

Lopburi (PS 7-3)
A.k.a. Lop Buri. Apparently at or near Lop Buri AF, apx 125 km N Bangkok. US Army Supt Cmd facility Thailand, here with HQ 46th Army SF Co, Oct66-Apr74. Thailand.

Loraine, FSB (various)
See Lorraine. SVN.

Lorene, FSB (XT 805-026)
Apx 6 km due N Tan Son Nhut AB and 11 km WSW Di An AF. Aug67. Gia Dinh Pr, III Corps.

Lori, FSB (XT 605-624)
A.k.a. Ina? Apx 6 km SSW Minh Thanh AF, 33 km E Nui Ba Den and 18 km NE Dau Tieng. Binh Long Pr, III Corps.

Lori, LZ (BR 929-756)
Near QL-1, apx 5 km E Lac Son, 21 km SSE Bong Son AF, 11 km NNE Crystal AF and 33 km N Phu Cat AB. 4th Div, '70. Data per Jim Claeys. Binh Dinh Pr, II Corps.

Lorinda, SS (n/a)
Merchant ship under govt contract, per Ralph Fries.

Lorraine, FSB (XT 709-409)
Apx 7 km NW Lai Khe and 55 km NNW Tan Son Nhut. Per *Low Level Hell's* 1st Div TAOR map. 1st Inf Div AO, '69. Also listed at XT 713-410, 708-433. Mar-Aug69. Binh Duong Pr, III Corps.

Lorraine, FSB (XT 805-026)
See Lorene. Gia Dinh Pr, III Corps.

Lorraine I, FSB (XT 708-433)
Apx 2 km N FSB Lorraine and 9 km NW Lai Khe. Also at XT 713-447. Sep-Nov67. Binh Duong Pr, III Corps.

Lorraine II, FSB (XT 683-483)
Apx 16 km NNW Lai Khe and 7 km NNW Lorraine I. Also listed at XT 685-496. Nov67. Binh Duong Pr, III Corps.

Lorraine, Operation (WJ)
29Oct-28Nov52. Apparently largest French Op to that point of French War, with over 30,000 men among 4 entire G.M.'s, 1 Abn Grp with 3 Para Bns, 5 commando units, 3 armored sub-grps, 2 tank-destroyer/Recon sqdns, 2 dinassauts, 2 arty Bns and 3 Engr Bns. Organized in desperate effort to save troops trapped in NW (T'ai) highlands by major Vietminh offensive (Battle for T'ai Hill Country), WNW and NW Hanoi in Fall of '53. Was last French thrust deep into Vietminh territory of 1st Indochina War. Had 4 stages: Stage 1: Oct29-8Nov52, an attack to open bridgehead on Red River toward Phu Tho. Stage 2: Bridgehead expanded to link with TF moving up Road No. 2 from Viet Tri, at which point combined force would push N to Phu Doan where an Abn Grp would drop in and a Dinassaut would move up to block any water escape. Stage 3: Supply depots and equip near Phu Doan would be destroyed in hopes of pulling VM in to defend. Stage 4: Possible further ops or building of permanent forts in area. VM supply points at Yen Bai and Thai Nguyen were targeted, but Giap continued T'ai Highland offense through SW Tonkin despite threat, though he did send Inf Rgt 36 (308th Div) and Rgt 176 (316th Div) from "Little Mesopotamia", to prevent French from reaching the supply points at any cost. The Rgts were unable to blunt Fr drive, however, and Lorraine was moderately successful around Phu Doan and Phu Hien. Gen. Salan ordered withdrawal after his forces had pushed as far north as Phu Yen Binh (145 km NW Hanoi) because op had not eased pressure of VM's T'ai Highland offensive as expected and VM had reached the Black River. Withdrawing Fr were badly mauled by ambush of 36th Rgt at Chan Muong Gorge. By 23Nov52, all elements reached narrow bridgehead at Viet Tri, anchored by forces at Phu Duc and Co Tich. On 214 Nov52, elements of 36th and 176th Rgts attacked Phu Duc and Co Tich, with Fr suffering 12 KIA, 40 WIA and 41 MIA. By 1Dec52, Fr had destroyed all its permanent fortifications N of Viet Tri and had lost nearly an entire Bn of men. See *Street Without Joy*, Chp 3, map at p 80. NVN.

Los Banos, FSB (AT 832-999)
On coast at base of Cape Mui Chon May Dong, apx 4 km SSE its tip, 34 km NNW Da Nang AB, 5 km N QL-1 and 37 km ESE Phu Bai. Per Mike Young, was just S Hill 88 and in saddle of Nui Trun Mtn. Overlooked Hai Van Pass and used by 101st Abn in '68-69, then closed. Dusters of 44th Arty here '68-69, says Ed Escoffier. Reopened by 1st/13th Arty, USMC, '69. Also listed at AU 84-00 and ZD 183-134? Apr70 XXIV Corps grid per Don Armstrong. Nov68-Sep70. See Hill 88. Thua Thien Pr, I Corps.

Los Banos, FSB (AU 830-000)
See Los Banos at AT 832-999. Thua Thien Pr, I Corps.

Los Banos, FSB (BT 525-105)
Apx 6 km NNW Chu Lai, 2 km S Dong Tuan and 5 km NE QL-1. Sep67. Quang Tin Pr, I Corps.

Lotus, LZ (YD 246-602)
Along QL-1, apx 1 km E Dong Ha AF and 11 km NW Quang Tri. Apr70 XXIV Corps grid per Don Armstrong. Quang Tri Pr, I Corps.
Lotus, Operation (WJ 3-0)
14Nov51-24Feb52. French counterattack on Hoa Binh in response to a Vietminh attack on Nghia Lo (22Sep51; opening attack of Battle for Indochinese Highlands). See Hoa Binh, Battle for. NVN.
Lou, LZ (BS 401-422)
Remote site was apx 35 km WSW Mo Duc AF/QL-1 and 18 km SW Minh Long AF. 1st Cav. Name/grid per Dan Gillotti. Quang Ngai Pr, II Corps.
Lou, LZ? (YA 581-498)
On Cambodian border at S end of Plei Trap Valley, apx 66 km due W Pleiku. Nature of site unknown. Jan66. Kontum Pr, II Corps.
Louis, LZ/FSB (BR 531-971)
A.k.a. LZ Lewis and unknown if simply sp variant, or if distinctly different name? Apx 35 km W LZ English, 31 km NE Ha Tay AF, 54 km N An Khe and3 km SE Hill 1114. Per VHPA Battle index, was built apx 16Feb70. 199th AHC and 4th Div AO, '70. Originally a 1st Cav FSB and later 4th Div. Also listed at BR 549-973. Grid per Jim Claeys. Apr-Oct70. Binh Dinh Pr, II Corps.
Louisiana, FSB (WS 977-404)
Apx 13 km NNW Vinh Long, 16 km ENE Sa Dec and 3 km N QL-4. Jan68. Dinh Tuong Pr?, IV Corps.
Love, Camp (BT or AT?)
USMC 7th Engr Bn Cmd post in Da Nang. 5th Mar Div, Dec68. Quang Nam Pr, I Corps.
Lowboy, LZ (BS 913-147)
Along QL-1 apx 2 km N of Gia An, 20 km NNE Bong Son and 4 km NE Mahoney AF and 13 km NNE LZ English. Map is L-7014-6838-3 (Tam Quan). Grid and map data per Ray Smith. See LZ Highboy. Quang Ngai/Binh Dinh Pr border, II Corps.
Lowe, USS (n/a)
DER-325. DD-Escort, Radar, per Ralph Fries.
Lower LZ Tiger (YD 25-09?)
See Tiger, FSB. Thua Thien Pr, I Corps.
Lowry, USS (n/a)
A.k.a. DD 704. On 27May68, replaced *USS Uhlmann* off Binh Thuan Prov suptg TF 3d/506th Inf, per www. currahee.org/pageb2.html.
Loyalty, USS (n/a)
MSO-457. Minesweeper, Ocean, per Ralph Fries.
LS Sites (numerous)
A.k.a. Lima Sites, L Sites, LS Sites, Laos Sites, and Listening Sites. Numerous, rudimentary STOL acft-capable AF's were built throughout NE Laos for Op Barrel Roll, the bombing of NVA infiltration rtes and suptg Royal Lao Army in fight with Communist Pathet Lao. Per Kent Spalding, in Air America lexicon, L-Site or LS, or Lima Site stood for "Laos Site" (additionally, Charlie Sites were in Cambodia, and Victor Sites were in VN). Spalding also tells us that Air America did not run Lima sites, instead, they were normally run by USAF or US Army SF operatives in concert with civilian personnel. Jim Henthorn has plotted (in red lettering) the location of all 400 Lima-Sites on 1:250,000 L-1501 JOG map images he has installed at www.nexus.net/~911gfx/Laos.html (a remarkable accomplishment). *Air Facilities Data-Laos* contains listing of all Air America/CIA & SF L, LS, and Lima-Site AFs in Laos (cross-referenced with Lao AF name), See Charlie Sites, Victor Sites, PS Sites, Tiger Hound, Steel Tiger, Barrel Roll. Complete listing of L & LS Lima Sites follows:
L-01 (TH 33-48)
Lima Site. See Moung Sung AF. Laos.
L-02 (QE 89-48)
Lima Site. See Moung Ou Tay AF. Laos.
L-03 (UG 27-40)
Lima Site. See Xieng Khouang Ville AF. Laos.
L-04 (VH 03-58)
Lima Site. See Sam Neua AF. Laos.
L-05 (XB 43-94)
Lima Site. See Paksong AF. Laos.
L-06 (QV 53-64)
Lima Site. See Ken Thao AF. Laos.
L-07 (WA 89-60)
Lima Site. See Khong Island AF. Laos.
L-08 (TE 43-88)
Lima Site. See Vientiane AF. Laos.
L-09 (QA 55-16)
Lima Site. See Paklay AF. Laos.
L-11 (WB 84-73)
Lima Site. See Pakse AF. Laos.
L-13 (UJ 98-03)
Lima Site. See Moung Het AF. Laos.
L-15 (TK 00-00)
Lima Site. See Phong Saly AF. Laos.
L-16 (TF 32-94)
Lima Site. See Vang Vieng AF. Laos.
L-17 (VH 43-73)
Lima Site. See Sop Hao AF. Laos.
L-19 (XD 60-10)
Lima Site. See Muong Nong AF. Laos.
L-20 (RD 09-68)
Lima Site. See Bun Taio AF and Puntai AF. Laos.
L-21 (UG 13-54)
Lima Site. See Phoung Savan AF. Laos.
L-22 (UG 06-51)
Lima Site. See Xieng Khouang AF. Laos.
L-23 (QB 86-30)
Lima Site. See Sayaboury AF. Laos.
L-25 (PC 51-41)
Lima Site. See Ban Houei Sai AF. Laos.
L-26 (QE 88-69)
Lima Site. See Ou Neua AF. Laos.
L-27 (RC 12-90)
Lima Site. See Moung Sai AF. Laos.
L-30 (RD 00-97)
Lima Site. See Boun Neua AF. Laos.
L-31 (UH 82-35)
Lima Site. See Moung Peun AF. Laos.
L-34 (QC 57-29)
Lima Site. See Moung Houn AF. Laos.
L-35 (UF 59-34)
Lima Site. See Paksane AF. Laos.

L-38 (XD 27-48)
Lima Site. See Tchepone AF. Laos.
L-39 (VD 75-30)
Lima Site. See Savannakhet AF. Laos.
L-40 (VE 85-21)
Lima Site. See Thakhet East AF. Laos.
L-40A (VE 81-24)
Lima Site. See Thakhet West AF. Laos.
L-41 (QD 92-32)
Lima Site. See Ban Khoanag AF and Moung Hai *AF*. Laos.
L-42 (QD 23-43)
Lima Site. See Moung Sing AF. Laos.
L-44 (XC 52-37)
Lima Site. See Saravane AF. Laos.
L-45 (VF 19-89)
Lima Site. See Gang Sa Ni AF. Laos.
L-45 (WB 85-18)
Lima Site. See Ban Soukhouma AF. Laos.
L-46 (VM 01-43)
Lima Site. See Seno AF. Laos.
L-46A (VM 01-43)
Lima Site. See Seno AF. Laos.
L-47 (VH 62-11)
Lima Site. See Xam Tai AF. Laos.
L-49 (QV 86-83)
Lima Site. See Sanakham AF. Laos.
L-50 (TH 62-91)
Lima Site. See Ban Na Tai AF. Laos.
L-52 (VH 05-81)
Lima Site. See Nong Khang AF. Laos.
L-53 (WE 79-41)
Lima Site. See Ban Phan Hop AF. Laos.
L-54 (TH 03-02)
Lima Site. See Luang Prabang AF. Laos.
L-56 (XB 65-73)
Lima Site. See Houei Kong AF. Laos.
L-57 (WE 21-25)
Lima Site. See Mahaxay AF. Laos.
L-59 (UH 28-62)
Lima Site. See Moung Son AF. Laos.
L-60 (VH 50-40)
Lima Site. See Moung Sol AF. Laos.
L-61 (WD 58-44)
Lima Site. See Moung Phalane AF. Laos.
L-61A (WD 52-29)
Lima Site. See Moung Phalane SW AF. Laos.
L-100 (QD 50-19)
Lima Site. See Nam Tha AF. Laos.
L-105 (WE 07-11)
Lima Site. See Ban Than Lay AF. Laos.
L-106 (TG 99-51)
Lima Site. See Moung Phanh AF. Laos.
L-107 (WB 91-42)
Lima Site. See Champassak AF and Wat Phu AF. Laos.
L-108 (TG 79-60)
Lima Site. See Moung Soui AF. Laos.
L-109 (UG 02-72)
Lima Site. See Moung Kheung AF. Laos.
L-110 (TG 95-66)
Lima Site. See Ban An AF. Laos.

LS-01 (VG 02-12)
Lima Site. See Moung Ngai AF. Laos.
LS-02 (UG 50-55)
Lima Site. See San Tiau AF. Laos.
LS-03 (UG 94-56)
Lima Site. See Nong Het AF. Laos.
LS-04 (TG 09-68)
Lima Site. See Kiou Cacham AF. Laos.
LS-05 (UG 02-12)
Lima Site. See Pa Doung AF. Laos.
LS-06 (UG 07-89)
Lima Site. See Phou Vieng AF. Laos.
LS-07 (UG 55-85)
Lima Site. See Nam Lan AF. Laos.
LS-08 (UG 17-58)
Lima Site. See Khang Khai AF. Laos.
LS-09 (UG 09-44)
Lima Site. See Lat Houang AF. Laos.
LS-10 (UG 49-71)
Lima Site. See Ban Ban AF. Laos.
LS-10 (XB 97-38)
Lima Site. See Attopeu AF. Laos.
LS-11 (UG 53-00)
Lima Site. See Tha Thom AF. Laos.
LS-12 (VE 56-84)
Lima Site. See Ban Bonong AF. Laos.
LS-13 (UG 32-04)
Lima Site. See Ta Viang AF. Laos.
LS-14 (TG 92-05)
Lima Site. See Pha Khao AF. Laos.
LS-15 (TG 85-36)
Lima Site. See Ban Na AF. Laos.
LS-16 (TG 70-74)
Lima Site. See Phou Fa AF. Laos.
LS-17 (TG 63-41)
Lima Site. See Nam Chong AF. Laos.
LS-18 (UG 34-51)
Lima Site. See Tha Lin Noi AF. Laos.
LS-19 (UG 19-37)
Lima Site. See Phou Khe AF. Laos.
LS-20 (TG 79-24)
See Lima Site 20 & Sam Thong AF. Laos
LS-21 (UG 38-22)
Lima Site. See Pha Peung AF and also PS-21. Laos.
LS-22 (UF 17-96)
Lima Site. See Moung Oum AF. Laos.
LS-23 (UG 39-93)
Lima Site. See Houei Sa An AF. Laos.
LS-24 (VG 22-07)
Lima Site. See Moung Sam AF. Laos.
LS-25 (SG 99-50)
Lima Site. See Phou Chai AF. Laos.
***LS-25** (SG 99-50)*
Lima Site. See Phou Chia AF. Laos.
LS-26 (TG 60-49)
Lima Site. See Xieng Dat AF. Laos.
LS-27 (UH 53-12)
Lima Site. See Houei Thom AF. Laos.
LS-28 (VF 22-70)
Lima Site. See Ban Dong AF. Laos.

LS-29 (UG 67-91)
Lima Site. See Ban Song AF. Laos.
LS-30/98 (TG 82-14)
Lima Site. See Long Tieng AF. Laos.
LS-31 (UG 73-93)
Lima Site. See Pien Lieu AF. Laos.
LS-32 (UG 26-86)
Lima Site. See Bouam Long AF. Laos.
LS-33 (UH 07-09)
Lima Site. See San Pa Ka AF. Laos.
LS-34 (UG 59-32)
Lima Site. See Ban Bouac AF. Laos.
LS-35 (UG 42-27)
Lima Site. See Kha Phu AF. Laos.
LS-36 (UH 41-10)
See Lima Site 36 & Na Khang AF. Laos.
LS-37 (TG 61-14)
Lima Site. See Moung Phun AF. Laos.
LS-38 (TG 82-47)
Lima Site. See Houei Ki Nin AF and also PS-38. Laos.
LS-39 (UH 77-23)
Lima Site. See Ban Khami AF and also PS-39. Laos.
LS-40 (UG 47-47)
Lima Site. See Ban Pha Ka AF. Laos.
LS-41 (TG 71-49)
Lima Site. See San Louang AF. Laos.
LS-42 (QB 48-49)
Lima Site. See Phou Khong AF. Laos.
LS-43 (WF 09-23)
Lima Site. See Nape AF. Laos.
LS-44 (TF 44-31)
Lima Site. See Ban Keun AF. Laos.
LS-46 (UF 95-94)
Lima Site. See Moung Moe AF. Laos.
LS-47 (VG 14-17)
Lima Site. See Nam Thom AF. Laos.
LS-48 (UH 28-17)
Lima Site. See Chong Ha AF. Laos.
LS-48A (UH 30-20)
Lima Site. See Moung Hiem AF. Laos.
LS-49 (VF 98-11)
Lima Site. See Lak Sao AF. Laos.
LS-50 (UH 03-01)
Lima Site. See Phu Cum AF. Laos.
LS-50A (UH 04-00)
Lima Site. See Phu Cum AF. Laos.
LS-51 (TG 63-17)
Lima Site. See Pa Ka AF. Laos.
LS-51 (TG 63-17)
Lima Site. See Pha Khe AF. Laos.
LS-52 (UG 52-83)
Lima Site. See Ban Tha AF. Laos.
LS-53 (TF 66-34)
Lima Site. See Ritaville AF. Laos.
LS-54 (WD 30-47)
Lima Site. See Ban Dong Hene AF. Laos.
LS-55 (XB 65-80)
Lima Site. See Bolovens AF. Laos.
LS-56 (TG 44-43)
Lima Site. See Moung Chim AF. Laos.
LS-57 (TG 81-74)
Lima Site. See Phou So AF. Laos.
LS-58 (UH 63-30)
Lima Site. See Hua Moung AF. Laos.
LS-59 (UH 85-25)
Lima Site. See Phou Kouk AF. Laos.
LS-60 (QB 40-48)
Lima Site. See Ban Sapi AF. Laos.
LS-61 (UF 76-84)
Lima Site. See Ban Tha Si AF. Laos.
LS-62 (QB 45-81)
Lima Site. See Hong Sa AF. Laos.
LS-62A (QB 44-71)
Lima Site. See Hong Sa AF. Laos.
LS-63 (UF 75-96)
Lima Site. See Moung Nham AF. Laos.
LS-64 (XC 31-67)
Lima Site. See Ban Da Bom AF. Laos.
LS-65 (UG 18-10)
Lima Site. See Pha Phai AF. Laos.
LS-66 (TF 69-92)
Lima Site. See Ban Na Luang AF. Laos.
LS-67 (QB 82-65)
Lima Site. See Phu Houei Mouei AF. Laos.
LS-67 (QB 82-65)
Lima Site. See Phu Hua Moui AF. Laos.
LS-68 (UG 28-48)
Lima Site. See Khang Hong AF. Laos.
LS-69 (PB 92-74)
Lima Site. See Ban Xieng Lom AF. Laos.
LS-70 (UG 40-47)
Lima Site. See Na Dao AF. Laos.
LS-71 (UG 58-55)
Lima Site. See Phou Nong AF. Laos.
LS-72 (TG 88-27)
Lima Site. See Tha Tam Bleung AF. Laos.
LS-73 (QB 83-14)
Lima Site. See Nam Tang AF. Laos.
LS-74 (TG 41-33)
Lima Site. See Tham Sorm AF. Laos.
LS-75 (TF 72-84)
Lima Site. See Sop Hien AF. Laos.
LS-76 (UH 36-53)
Lima Site. See Pha Bong AF. Laos.
LS-77 (WE 20-90)
Lima Site. See Ban Song Khone AF. Laos.
LS-78 (TG 55-48)
Lima Site. See Na Poung AF. Laos.
LS-79 (SG 95-35)
Lima Site. See Naw Nuen AF and also PS-79. Laos.
LS-80 (TG 85-87)
Lima Site. See Phu Sang Nao AF. Laos.
LS-81 (UG 93-15)
Lima Site. See Ban Tham Tat AF. Laos.
LS-82 (UG 74-80)
Lima Site. See Phu Se Bott AF. Laos.
LS-83 (TF 70-14)
Lima Site. See Ban Nong Dao AF. Laos.
LS-84 (UH 83-22)
Lima Site. See Ban Keng Sai AF. Laos.

LS-85 (UH 68-60)
See Lima Site 85 & Phu Pha Thi AF. Laos.
LS-86 (UH 82-57)
Lima Site. See Hong Non AF. Laos.
LS-87 (VH 00-70)
Lima Site. See Phia Khan AF. Laos.
LS-88 (UG 26-86)
Lima Site. See Boun Loum AF. Laos.
LS-89 (UG 74-87)
Lima Site. See Ban Vieng AF. Laos.
LS-90 (TG 50-20)
Lima Site. See Tin Bong AF. Laos.
LS-91 (VF 35-87)
Lima Site. See Moung Tiouen AF. Laos.
LS-92 (QB 26-92)
Lima Site. See Sing Ka AF. Laos.
LS-93 (PC 53-93)
Lima Site. See Moung Moungw AF. Laos.
LS-94 (UG 57-28)
Lima Site. See Ban Kha AF. Laos.
LS-95 (UG 44-22)
Lima Site. See Ban Peung AF. Laos.
LS-96 (QV 21-55)
Lima Site. See Phu Mieng Mane AF. Laos.
LS-97 (TG 56-20)
Lima Site. See Ban Pak En AF. Laos.
LS-98/30 (TG 82-14)
Lima Site. See Long Tieng AF. Laos.
LS-99 (TG 42-31)
Lima Site. See Phu Houot AF. Laos.
LS-100 (TG 41-32)
Lima Site. See Ban Beecher AF. Laos.
LS-101 (TG 65-32)
Lima Site. See Ban Nong One AF. Laos.
LS-102 (TG 65-70)
Lima Site. See Phu Fa Noi AF. Laos.
LS-103 (TG 52-43)
Lima Site. See Phou Da Pho AF. Laos.
LS-104 (QB 50-15)
Lima Site. See Ban Nam Hin AF. Laos.
LS-105 (QB 35-44)
Lima Site. See Phu De Me AF. Laos.
LS-106 (QB 55-33)
Lima Site. See Nong Sakhe AF. Laos.
LS-107 (UH 64-55)
Lima Site. See Houei Ma AF. Laos.
LS-108 (UG 79-18)
Lima Site. See Ban Nam Keng AF. Laos.
LS-109 (PC 73-83)
Lima Site. See Ban Na Woua AF. Laos.
LS-110 (TG 59-15)
Lima Site. See Ban Nam Deng AF. Laos.
LS-111 (UH 68-68)
Lima Site. See Houei Kah Moun AF. Laos.
LS-112 (TG 60-37)
Lima Site. See Sam Sen AF. Laos.
LS-113 (UF 00-91)
Lima Site. See Moung Cha AF. Laos.
LS-114 (UH 10-12)
Lima Site. See Phoung Sam AF. Laos.
LS-115 (UG 32-72)
Lima Site. See Phou Kheo AF. Laos.
LS-116 (UG 58-31)
Lima Site. See New Ban Bouac AF. Laos.
LS-117 (TG 63-51)
Lima Site. See New Xieng Dat AF. Laos.
LS-118 (PC 69-75)
Lima Site. See Ban Nam Thouei AF. Laos.
LS-118A (PC 65-75)
Lima Site. See Nam Lieu AF. Laos.
LS-118A (PC 65-75)
Lima Site. See Nam Yu AF. Laos.
LS-119 (UG 53-39)
Lima Site. See Ban Sa Noi AF. Laos.
LS-120 (TG 95-50)
Lima Site. See Pop's Field AF. Laos.
LS-121 (TJ 12-04)
Lima Site. See Lao Ta AF. Laos.
LS-122 (UH 83-57)
Lima Site. See New Hong Non AF. Laos.
LS-123 (TG 69-48)
Lima Site. See Ban Houei Dionne AF. Laos.
LS-124 (QB 66-07)
Lima Site. See Moung Phieng AF. Laos.
LS-125 (PD 99-08)
Lima Site. See Nam Bu AF. Laos.
LS-126 (VF 59-59)
Lima Site. See New Son Soak AF. Laos.
LS-127 (UG 41-91)
Lima Site. See Houei Sa An AF. Laos.
LS-128 (UG 42-89)
Lima Site. See Moung Khao AF. Laos.
LS-129 (UF 66-53)
Lima Site. See Borikhane AF. Laos.
LS-130 (XB 73-64)
Lima Site. See La Ta Sin AF. Laos.
LS-131 (TH 36-71)
Lima Site. See Mok Lok AF. Laos.
LS-132 (TG 36-37)
Lima Site. See Long Pot AF. Laos.
LS-133 (TF 27-47)
Lima Site. See Phong Hong AF. Laos.
LS-134 (XC 67-33)
Lima Site. See Ban Nong Boua AF. Laos.
LS-135 (QC 18-89)
Lima Site. See Ban Vieng AF. Laos.
LS-136 (QC 22-83)
Lima Site. See Ba Phu Lun AF. Laos.
LS-137 (TH 18-76)
Lima Site. See Mak Phout AF. Laos.
LS-138 (TJ 23-03)
Lima Site. See Ban Chuk Chung AF. Laos.
LS-139 (WD 21-18)
Lima Site. See Keng Kok AF. Laos.
LS-140 (UG 07-29)
Lima Site. See Phou Houang AF. Laos.
LS-141 (VE 48-64)
Lima Site. See Grove Jones AF. Laos.
LS-141A (VE 27-94)
Lima Site. See Grove Jones 2 AF. Laos.

LS-142 (QC 28-78)
Lima Site. See Phou Pang Sang AF. Laos.
LS-143 (VF 18-12)
Lima Site. See Ban Nam Dua AF. Laos.
LS-145 (QC 46-74)
Lima Site. See Tong Prang AF. Laos.
LS-146 (QB 54-06)
Lima Site. See Phou Nam Nhiou AF. Laos.
LS-147 (PB 59-86)
Lima Site. See Ban Houei Lao AF. Laos.
LS-148 (PC 77-06)
Lima Site. See Ban Nou Kha Chok AF. Laos.
LS-149 (PC 39-56)
Lima Site. See Ban Nam Nhion AF. Laos.
LS-150 (PC 32-55)
Lima Site. See Ban Nam Kueung AF. Laos.
LS-151 (QC 39-69)
Lima Site. See Ban Sa Phout AF. Laos.
LS-152 (QC 14-88)
Lima Site. See Vien Pou Kha AF. Laos.
LS-153 (TG 11-30)
Lima Site. See Moung Kassy AF. Laos.
LS-154 (SF 98-79)
Lima Site. See Nong Pet AF. Laos.
LS-155 (PB 87-62)
Lima Site. See Phia Chan AF. Laos.
LS-156 (TG 37-56)
Lima Site. See Phou Soung AF. Laos.
LS-157 (TF 49-73)
Lima Site. See Moang Soum AF. Laos.
LS-158 (RA 10-85)
Lima Site. See Moung Met AF. Laos.
LS-159 (WC 61-58)
Lima Site. See La Khong Pheng AF. Laos.
LS-160 (RD 09-35)
Lima Site. See Doi Seang AF. Laos.
LS-161 (TG 65-29)
Lima Site. See Ban Nam Thao AF. Laos.
LS-162 (QC 13-52)
Lima Site. See Sen Sai AF. Laos.
LS-163 (SF 98-68)
Lima Site. See Ban Done AF. Laos.
LS-163 (SF 98-68)
Lima Site. See Ban Donge AF. Laos.
LS-164 (XB 68-53)
Lima Site. See Houei Soi AF. Laos.
LS-165 (XB 83-59)
Lima Site. See Ban Nam Tieng AF. Laos.
LS-166 (XB 88-51)
Lima Site. See Phou Kahm Phouk AF. Laos.
LS-167 (XB 68-77)
Lima Site. See Tang Hung AF. Laos.
LS-168 (QC 15-78)
Lima Site. See Moung Ngeum AF. Laos.
LS-169 (TJ 33-07)
Lima Site. See Ban Pha Thong AF. Laos.
LS-170 (TG 29-67)
Lima Site. See Pha Langmou AF. Laos.
LS-171 (XC 58-39)
Lima Site. See Ban Khok Mai AF. Laos.
LS-172 (XB 79-40)
Lima Site. See Long Keo AF. Laos.
LS-173 (TF 91-83)
Lima Site. See Tong Hang AF. Laos.
LS-174 (QC 50-21)
Lima Site. See Boum Lao AF. Laos.
LS-175 (XC 04-35)
Lima Site. See Ban Saphat AF. Laos.
LS-176 (TH 25-68)
Lima Site. See Nam Thuam AF. Laos.
LS-177 (PB 60-77)
Lima Site. See Ban Moung AF. Laos.
LS-178 (TH 93-63)
Lima Site. See Phou Saly AF. Laos.
LS-179 (UH 67-43)
Lima Site. See Nhot Phat AF. Laos.
LS-180 (XB 33-77)
Lima Site. See New Paksong AF. Laos.
LS-181 (UG 53-48)
Lima Site. See Na Xieng AF. Laos.
LS-182 (UG 91-09)
Lima Site. See Moung Mo AF. Laos.
LS-183 (VD 79-88)
Lima Site. See Ban Nong Bok AF. Laos.
LS-184 (UH 18-53)
Lima Site. See Houei Tong Ko AF. Laos.
LS-185 (UH 43-64)
Lima Site. See Phou Tai AF. Laos.
LS-186 (TH 05-67)
Lima Site. See Tong Too AF. Laos.
LS-187 (TJ 50-15)
Lima Site. See Ban Y AF. Laos.
LS-189 (XD 65-36)
Lima Site. See Ban Houei Sane AF. Laos.
LS-190 (XB 91-68)
Lima Site. See Ban La Tee AF. Laos.
LS-192 (UF 24-97)
Lima Site. See Khieu Manang AF. Laos.
LS-193 (TH 18-89)
Lima Site. See Mok Plai AF. Laos.
LS-194 (QD 01-61)
Lima Site. See Ban Bo Mei AF. Laos.
LS-195 (UH 30-44)
Lima Site. See Muang Kout AF. Laos.
LS-196 (TH 87-50)
Lima Site. See Huei Thong AF. Laos.
LS-197 (TG 49-58)
Lima Site. See Phou Vieng AF. Laos.
LS-198 (UH 65-61)
Lima Site. See Houei Hok AF. Laos.
LS-199 (UG 76-21)
Lima Site. See Nam Song AF. Laos.
LS-200 (TG 55-68)
Lima Site. See Houei Hong AF. Laos.
LS-201 (UG 84-83)
Lima Site. See Sam Song Hong AF. Laos.
LS-202 (VF 00-95)
Lima Site. See Thung Peeut AF. Laos.
LS-203 (TH 35-83)
Lima Site. See Nam Bac AF. Laos.

LS-204 (UG 05-24)
Lima Site. See Khang Kho AF. Laos.
LS-205 (UH 75-46)
Lima Site. See Pha Hang AF. Laos.
LS-206 (UG 81-92)
Lima Site. See Houei Sang AF. Laos.
LS-207 (TF 82-87)
Lima Site. See Nam Moh AF. Laos.
LS-208 (UG 77-18)
Lima Site. See Ban Nam Xao AF. Laos.
LS-209 (QB 12-99)
Lima Site. See Ban Nong Tong AF. Laos.
LS-210 (XC 48-07)
Lima Site. See Thateng AF. Laos.
LS-211 (TF 62-99)
Lima Site. See Phone Sai AF. Laos.
LS-212 (UF 45-90)
Lima Site. See Phu Moun AF. Laos.
LS-213 (TG 43-74)
Lima Site. See Pha Hong AF. Laos.
LS-214 (UG 60-42)
Lima Site. See Ban Nongla AF. Laos.
LS-215 (UH 50-56)
Lima Site. See Houei Hinsa AF. Laos.
LS-216 (PC 97-61)
Lima Site. See Ta Fa AF. Laos.
LS-217 (TJ 44-21)
Lima Site. See Yung Tuia AF. Laos.
LS-218 (TF 80-96)
Lima Site. See Nam Pha Noi AF. Laos.
LS-219 (UH 23-03)
Lima Site. See Don’s Strip AF. Laos.
LS-220 (UH 61-16)
Lima Site. See Phou Pha Louom AF. Laos.
LS-221 (UH 58-45)
Lima Site. See Houei Moun AF. Laos.
LS-222 (UG 94-19)
Lima Site. See Ban Phoungmay AF. Laos.
LS-223 (UF 14-91)
Lima Site. See Ban Nam Feng AF. Laos.
LS-224 (TF 82-82)
Lima Site. See Houei Nam Om AF. Laos.
LS-225 (TH 79-63)
Lima Site. See Ban Se AF. Laos.
LS-226 (UH 87-14)
Lima Site. See Ban Houei Keng AF. Laos.
LS-227 (UF 07-81)
Lima Site. See Moung Ao Neua AF. Laos.
LS-228 (UH 92-15)
Lima Site. See Phou Pha Louom AF. Laos.
LS-229 (TG 73-04)
Lima Site. See Pong Ta AF. Laos.
LS-230 (UH 32-01)
Lima Site. See Pha Poun AF. Laos.
LS-231 (UG 82-91)
Lima Site. See Phou Sam Soun AF. Laos.
LS-232 (UG 74-26)
Lima Site. See Phou Ngieu AF. Laos.
LS-233 (UH 10-13)
Lima Site. See Ban Lee AF. Laos.
LS-234 (TH 19-69)
Lima Site. See Ban Maya AF. Laos.
LS-235 (VD 85-54)
Lima Site. See Keng Ka Boa AF. Laos.
LS-236 (UG 65-18)
Lima Site. See Ban Moung Ngan AF. Laos.
LS-237 (VE 81-85)
Lima Site. See Ban Na Tan AF. Laos.
LS-238 (TG 77-44)
Lima Site. See Than Heup AF. Laos.
LS-239 (UG 16-22)
Lima Site. See Ban Phang AF. Laos.
LS-240 (UG 76-22)
Lima Site. See Ban Nam Xao AF. Laos.
LS-241 (VF 42-76)
Lima Site. See Pha Hom AF. Laos.
LS-242 (UH 33-37)
Lima Site. See Buam Vang AF. Laos.
LS-243 (TJ 51-96)
Lima Site. See Nam Houn AF. Laos.
LS-244 (TF 71-95)
Lima Site. See Phu Sang Noi AF. Laos.
LS-245 (VF 38-96)
Lima Site. See Pha Ka AF. Laos.
LS-246 (TF 58-94)
Lima Site. See Ban Xon AF. Laos.
LS-247 (TJ 34-09)
Lima Site. See Ban Pha Thong AF. Laos.
LS-248 (UH 30-42)
Lima Site. See Ban Lou AF. Laos.
LS-249 (TG 10-25)
Lima Site. See Ban Na Then AF. Laos.
LS-250 (PC 62-33)
Lima Site. See Ban Rosie AF. Laos.
LS-250 (PC 62-33)
Lima Site. See Tong Pa How AF. Laos.
LS-251 (TF 77-82)
Lima Site. See Phu Khan Hua AF. Laos.
LS-252 (TF 71-91)
Lima Site. See New Na Luang AF. Laos.
LS-253 (TG 52-60)
Lima Site. See Ban Lee 2 AF. Laos.
LS-254 (RB 03-59)
Lima Site. See Muong Nane AF. Laos.
LS-255 (TF 93-77)
Lima Site. See Phu He AF. Laos.
LS-256 (SH 98-21)
Lima Site. See Phou Dam AF. Laos.
LS-258 (RA 02-53)
Lima Site. See Mary's Strip AF. Laos.
LS-259 (PC 90-20)
Lima Site. See Jennifer’s Strip AF. Laos.
LS-260 (TG 31-49)
Lima Site. See Sala Phou Koun AF. Laos.
LS-261 (TG 73-94)
Lima Site. See Muang You AF. Laos.
LS-262 (UF 99-96)
Lima Site. See Thung Peeut AF. Laos.
LS-263 (VF 53-72)
Lima Site. See Pha Du AF. Laos.

LS-264 (QB 46-24)
Lima Site. See Happy's Strip AF. Laos.
LS-265 (VF 63-56)
Lima Site. See Old San Soak AF. Laos.
LS-266 (TF 89-87)
Lima Site. See Thong Miang AF. Laos.
LS-267 (PC 16-51)
Lima Site. See Van Pak Len AF. Laos.
LS-268 (QB 61-04)
Lima Site. See Nam Tan AF. Laos.
LS-269 (UH 23-12)
Lima Site. See Ban Sop Siem AF. Laos.
LS-270 (UF 09-90)
Lima Site. See Ohu Sa Ngop AF. Laos.
LS-270 (UF 09-90)
Lima Site. See Phia Louang AF. Laos.
LS-271 (TG 86-93)
Lima Site. See Hat Khon AF. Laos.
LS-272 (TF 59-94)
Lima Site. See Ban Houei Pamone AF. Laos.
LS-272 (TF 59-94)
Lima Site. See Ban Xon AF. Laos.
LS-273 (TF 64-93)
Lima Site. See Pak Mouei AF. Laos.
LS-274 (PB 91-73)
Lima Site. See Xieng Lom AF. Laos.
LS-275 (TG 96-47)
Lima Site. See Ban Thang AF. Laos.
LS-276 (UG 03-38)
Lima Site. See Lat Sen AF. Laos.
LS-277 (UG 00-43)
Lima Site. See Si Siang Mai AF. Laos
LS-278 (UH 16-43)
Lima Site. See Nam Hang AF. Laos.
LS-279 (TE 49-81)
Lima Site. See Chinaimo AF. Laos.
LS-280 (UG 04-34)
Lima Site. See Lat Khai AF. Laos.
LS-281 (TG 49-01)
Lima Site. See Ban Na Kouang AF. Laos.
LS-282 (TF 33-53)
Lima Site. See Kok Kieng AF. Laos.
LS-283 (PC 51-41)
Lima Site. See Ban Houei Sai Citadel AF. Laos.
LS-284 (TF 55-94)
Lima Site. See Houei Sai AF. Laos.
LS-285 (QC 53-78)
Lima Site. See Ban Pawi AF. Laos.
LS-286 (QV 26-59)
Lima Site. See Na Lang AF. Laos.
LS-286 (QV 26-59)
Lima Site. See Na Leng AF. Laos.
LS-287 (TG 56-04)
Lima Site. See Ban Na Ti AF. Laos.
LS-287 (TG 56-04)
Lima Site. See Ban Naty AF. Laos.
LS-288 (TF 77-95)
Lima Site. See Nam Yon AF. Laos.
LS-288 (TF 77-95)
Lima Site. See Nam Yong AF. Laos.
LS-288 (TJ 63-24)
Lima Site. See Xing Than AF. Laos.
LS-289 (WC 85-24)
Lima Site. See Khong Sedone AF. Laos.
LS-290 (PC 66-59)
Lima Site. See Ban Nam Chuam AF. Laos.
LS-291 (WD 72-49)
Lima Site. See Ban Nalay AF. Laos.
LS-292 (WE 14-10)
Lima Site. See Ban Kengpe AF. Laos.
LS-293 (WD 11-88)
Lima Site. See Ban Xiang Khai AF. Laos.
LS-294 (WC 66-97)
Lima Site. See Ban Xani AF. Laos.
LS-295 (WD 52-72)
Lima Site. See Ban Chomhat AF. Laos.
LS-296 (WD 41-12)
Lima Site. See Ban Bungxang AF. Laos.
LS-297 (VD 95-41)
Lima Site. See Ban Nachalit AF. Laos.
LS-298 (WC 39-79)
Lima Site. See Ban Keng Tanga AF. Laos.
LS-299 (WD 70-14)
Lima Site. See Ban Tangvay AF. Laos.
LS-300 (XD 09-28)
Lima Site. See Muang Phine AF. Laos.
LS-301 (WC 24-98)
Lima Site. See Ban Lahanam AF. Laos.
LS-302 (VE 64-73)
Lima Site. See Ban Houana AF. Laos.
LS-303 (WD 37-64)
Lima Site. See Ban Phak Khagna AF. Laos.
LS-304 (WD 10-27)
Lima Site. See Ban Dong Khan Khou AF. Laos.
LS-305 (PC 15-42)
Lima Site. See Ban Ton Phung AF. Laos.
LS-306 (RA 15-43)
Lima Site. See Ban Pak Ham AF. Laos.
LS-307 (TF 78-96)
Lima Site. See Ban Nam Yon Nea AF. Laos.
LS-308 (TG 24-66)
Lima Site. See Ban Pha Kao AF. Laos.
LS-309 (TF 94-03)
Lima Site. See Ban Phone Sai AF. Laos.
LS-310 (WC 88-67)
Lima Site. See Ban Houaymun AF. Laos.
LS-311 (WD 01-16)
Lima Site. See Phowachedy AF. Laos.
LS-312 (TG 73-83)
Lima Site. See Phou Sai AF. Laos.
LS-313 (TG 65-06)
Lima Site. See Ban Nam Luang AF. Laos.
LS-314 (UF 81-99)
Lima Site. See Ban Kia Maa AF. Laos.
LS-315 (SG 94-95)
Lima Site. See Paseau AF. Laos.
LS-316 (UF 11-94)
Lima Site. See Tham Lo AF. Laos.
LS-317 (TF 95-90)
Lima Site. See Thong Khen AF. Laos.

LS-318 (TF 73-98)
Lima Site. See Song Lai AF. Laos.
LS-319 (TG 45-05)
Lima Site. See Moung Sao AF. Laos.
LS-320 (PC 59-98)
Lima Site. See Moung Lem AF. Laos.
LS-321 (TG 94-02)
Lima Site. See Nyot Mo AF. Laos.
LS-322 (QV 27-68)
Lima Site. See Nong Luang AF. Laos.
LS-323 (QB 58-63)
Lima Site. See Phou Leang AF. Laos.
LS-324 (PC 66-54)
Lima Site. See Ban Poung AF. Laos.
LS-325 (TF 39-78)
Lima Site. See Houei Mai AF. Laos.
LS-326 (XB 44-94)
Lima Site. See Klahan AF. Laos.
LS-327 (TG 56-05)
Lima Site. See Ban Naty North AF. Laos.
LS-328 (QC 08-54)
Lima Site. See Pha Poon AF. Laos.
LS-329 (WC 45-64)
Lima Site. See Ban Mai AF. Laos.
LS-330 (TF 94-83)
Lima Site. See Thong Noi AF. Laos.
LS-331 (TF 76-94)
Lima Site. See Keo Sa Khai Neua AF. Laos.
LS-332 (SG 98-99)
Lima Site. See Ban Sing Keo AF. Laos.
LS-333 (UF 08-93)
Lima Site. See Nong Kha AF. Laos.
LS-334 (TF 99-90)
Lima Site. See Toong Cha AF. Laos.
LS-335 (TF 72-95)
Lima Site. See Nam Ve AF. Laos.
LS-336 (TH 96-07)
Lima Site. See Phou San AF. Laos.
LS-337 (TG 73-09)
Lima Site. See Phou Kang Neua AF. Laos.
LS-338 (UG 07-34)
Lima Site. See Nong Kala AF. Laos.
LS-339 (UH 05-03)
Lima Site. See Shing Scha AF. Laos.
LS-340 (UF 06-89)
Lima Site. See Pa Doung Noi AF. Laos.
LS-341 (TG 73-03)
Lima Site. See Pha Deng AF. Laos.
LS-342 (PA 71-48)
Lima Site. See Moung Pa AF. Laos.
LS-343 (UG 07-44)
Lima Site. See Ban Nathom AF. Laos.
LS-344 (TF 98-87)
Lima Site. See Nam Poune AF. Laos.
LS-345 (PD 86-27)
Lima Site. See Jom Mog AF. Laos.
LS-349 (UF 06-86)
Lima Site. See Ban Sun Kang AF. Laos.
LS-354 (TG 04-87)
Lima Site. See Xieng Ngeun AF. Laos.
LS-361 (TG 51-31)
Lima Site. See Pong Hai AF. Laos.
LS-362 (TF 75-98)
Lima Site. See Phou San Nyai AF. Laos.
LS-363 (TG 44-13)
Lima Site. See Ban Nam Song AF. Laos.
LS-364 (TF 6000)
Lima Site. See PK 21 AF (Mil Res) AF. Laos.
LS-365 (TF 19-62)
Lima Site. See Hin Heup AF. Laos.
LS-366 (TF 36-56)
Lima Site. See Har Due AF. Laos.
LS-367 (TG 66-04)
Lima Site. See Ban Boua Mu AF. Laos.
LS-402 (XB 78-86)
Lima Site. See Phou Louang AF. Laos.
LS-407 (YB 05-05)
Lima Site. See Ban Kongmi AF. Laos.
LS-418 (WB 57-95)
Lima Site. See Phou Lat Seua AF. Laos.
LS-419 (XC 56-63)
Lima Site. See Ban Padou AF. Laos.
LS-420 (XB 99-65)
Lima Site. See Ban Sok AF. Laos.
LS-440 (XB 82-38)
Lima Site. See Phou Douak AF. Laos.
LS-446 (WB 89-42)
Lima Site. See Ban Nongsa AF. Laos.
LS-447 (WC 88-43)
Lima Site. See Ban Koutlamphong AF. Laos.
LS-449 (XB 37-81)
Lima Site. See Toong Set AF. Laos.
LS-450 (WB 74-69)
Lima Site. See Phone Thong AF. Laos.
LSI Compound (BT 013-752?)
Along W edge of Da Nang AB and immed adj to LZ-11/Goodsell Heliport. In cmpd of Lear-Siegler, Inc. (pvt contractor), Aug73. See Goodsell Heliport for more detail. Quang Nam Pr, I Corps.
LST-550, USNS (n/a)
MSTS Transport, per Ralph Fries.
LST Westchester County (n/a)
See Westchester County, LST.
LSU Bravo (XD 847-417)
A.k.a. Logistics Supt Unit Bravo. Immed SE the SE corner of main parking apron at Khe Sanh AF. Handled all supply needs for facility and surrounding hill positions. Good map in *Valley of Decision*. Quang Tri Pr, I Corps.
Lt Col John U. D. Page, US Army Vessel (n/a)
Largest vessel in US Army fleet. Transported supplies (primarily munitions) from Cam Ranh Bay along coast N to Chu Lai and S to Phan Thiet et al. "In conjunction with the *John Page*, Army developed 2 roll-on, roll-off freighters, the *Comet* (RO-RO1) and the *Sea Lift* (RO-RO2). These ships had stern ramps which were designed to be lowered onto deck of the *Page*." Data per Kerry Myers at http:// 134.198.33.115/myers/page.htm. SVN.
LTL (Road Type)
See Glossary.

LTL-4 (AU/BT/ZC)
Inter-Provincial Rte 4. E/W route joined Ha Tan and QL-1, Intersecting QL-1 apx 20 km SE Da Nang at Dien Ban. Ha Tan was apx 32 km W Dien Ban. Was N of and roughly paralleled Song Thu Bon River. Quang Nam Pr, I Corps.

LTL-5A (XS)
Inter-Provincial Rte 5A. N/S route connecting Saigon with Go Cong, apx 50 km due S Saigon. Can Duoc was along this road. III/IV Corps.

LTL-7A (XS/XR)
Inter-Provincial Rte 7A. NW/SE route ran along S bank of a branch of Mekong River and connected Vinh Long with Phu Vinh, apx 55 km SE Vinh Long. IV Corps.

LTL-7B (AR/BQ/CQ)
Inter-Provincial Rte 7B. This NW to SE route ran the course of a very long river valley that ran between Pleiku and Tuy Hoa, via a portion of QL-14. Left QL-14 apx 32 km SSE Pleiku and 4 km S My Thach. Hou Bon, Phu Tuc and Son Ha were along this route. Distance between Pleiku and Tuy Hoa via this road was roughly 180 km. II Corps.

LTL-8A (VS/WS/WT)
Inter-Provincial Rte 8A. This NE/SW route connected Rach Gia with Long Xuyen. Distance between 2 villes was apx 60 km. IV Corps.

LTL-8B (ZA/AR?)
Inter-Provincial Rte 88. NNW to SSE route connected Dao Thong/Dak Song (on QL-14) with Gia Nghia. Distance between 2 villes was apx 36 km. II Corps.

LTL-9 (WS)
Inter-Provincial Rte 9. NE/SW route connected the Ha Tien/Rach Gia road with LTL 10, the Chau Duc (Chau Phu)/Long Xuyen road. Joined the LTL 10 perhaps 40 km SE Chau Duc (Chau Phu). IV Corps.

LTL 10 (WS)
Inter-Provincial Rte 10. See LTL-27. IV Corps.

LTL-23 (YS/ZS)
Inter-Provincial Rte 27. WSW/ENE rte connected Nui Dat, Dat Do, and Ba Ria with Ham Tan, then ran NE from Ham Tan apx 20 km to QL-1. Distance between Ham Tan and Phuoc Le (Ba Ria) was about 65 km. Joined QL-2 and QL-15 at Ba Ria. Phuoc Tuy/Binh Tuy Prvs, III Corps.

LTL-27 (WS/WR/XR)
Inter-Provincial Rte 27. NW/SE route connected Long Xuyen with Can Tho. In concert with LTL-10, it ran NW to SE along Mekong River and connected Chau Duc (Chau Phu) with Can Tho. Intersected the Rach Gia road (LTL-8A) apx 50 km NW Can Tho, near Long Xuyen. IV Corps.

LTL-31 (WS/WR)
Inter-Provincial Rte 31. NE/SW running route connected Can Tho with Vi Thanh via portion of QL-4. Joined QL-4 perhaps 15 km S Can Tho. Distance between those villes was apx 60 km. IV Corps.

Lu Lu, LZ (XD 47-41)
See LZ Lulu. Laos.

Lu Bu Mountain (YD 85-66)
A.k.a. Hill 695 and LZ Sierra North. On S edge of DMZ and adj the Song Nang Valley, apx 24 km due N Khe Sanh CB. Quang Tri Pr, I Corps.

Luan Thanh Airfield (BN 772-862)
See Phan Rang AF. Ninh Thuan Pr, II Corps.

Luang Prabang Airfield (TH 03-02)
A.k.a. L-54. Major AF along Mekong River apx 410 km WSW Hanoi and 220 km NNW Vientiane. CIA/SF facility. Grid per *Air Facilities Data-Laos.* El. 978'. Laos.

Luang Prabang SF Camp (TH 03-02)
Along Mekong River apx 410 km WSW Hanoi and 220 km NNW Vientiane. SF camp when Lao neutrality declared, 23Jul62. Det BB, FTT 10, 24 and ATT 1 here then. Per *Special Forces at War*. MR1, Laos.

Luc An Chau (n/a)
Mapsheet name of L-7014-5953-3. NVN only.

Luc Luong Dac Biet (n/a)
See LLBD in Glossary.

Luc Nam (n/a)
Mapsheet name of L-7014-6251-1. NVN only.

Lucas, FSB (n/a)
No data available. Listed in photo gallery of Pike Military Research at www.militaryunits.com/namphotos.htm.

Lucifer, FSB (XS or YS)
SE Saigon. Apparently built by 1st/508th Inf, 82d Abn apx 12Nov68, during ops in area SE Saigon that had been vacated by 9th Inf Div. Used as main Bn CP. FSB Diablo was also apparently built nearby at same time by same Bn, and used to centralize Bn's 4.2" mortars for added fire supt. 3d Bde/82d Abn. Info per Butch Sincock. Pr?, III Corps.

Luciole (n/a)
See Glossary.

Lucky BOQ (XS 827-886)
At 34 Ngo Quyen St., Saigon. Per R. Bows' *Vietnam Military Lore, 1959-1973.* Gia Dinh Pr, III Corps.

Lucky Strike, LZ (ZT 255-378)
Remote site in valley apx 37 km NNW Phan Thiet and 26 km NE Tanh Linh. Feb67. Binh Tuy Pr, II Corps.

Lucrezia Borgia (n/a)
See Glossary.

Lucy, LZ (YC 424-944)
In the A Shau Valley, apx 13 km NW A Sap, 43 km SW Hue and 67 km S FSB Eagle's Nest. 3d ARVN Inf Div CA'd here 29Apr69(?), and became responsible for its security during Op Delaware. Also listed at YC 425-948. Thua Thien/Quang Tri Pr border, I Corps.

Ludwig, FSB (XS 420-760)
Apx 1 km W Song Vam Cotay River, 11 km NW Tan An, 8 km NW Long An AF, 7 km due W Thu Thua and 18 km ESE Thuy Dong AF. Jan69. Long An Pr, III Corps.

Luke The Gook (n/a)
See Glossary.

Luke's Castle, FSB (XT 958-208?)
If grid correct, was on island in Song Dong Nai River, apx 7 km NNE Bien Hoa AB, 23 km SE Lai Khe, 27 km NNE Saigon and 6 km SSW Luke's Castle. On map in *Charlie Company*, p 6, and *Low Level Hell's* 1st Div TAOR map. Grid per Frank Penk, Jr. Also listed at XT 987-260? Tay Ninh Pr, III Corps.

Luke's Castle (XT 987-260?)
If grid correct, was apx 12 km due N Bien Hoa AB, 25 km SE Lai Khe and 6 km NNE Luke's Castle listed at XT 958-208. Dec68-Jan69. Unknown if site moved or if one grid incorrect? Bien Hoa Pr, III Corps.

Lulu, LZ (XD 47-41)
Apx 4 km WNW Aloui in Laos. May be spelling variant of LZ Lolo (or Lo Lo), which is listed at XD 43-37 on map at www.americal.org/174/map4.html. Cited in *The Final Formation*, p 141. Laos.
Lumphat Airfield (YV)
Along Tonle Srepok River, apx 55 km SSE Viracheay AF, 30 km SW Ba Kev AF and 70 km W SVN border. Per TPC K-10A. 3,400' rwy, El. 328'. Cambodia.
Lunch (n/a)
See Base Area 609. Cambodia.
Luoi Cay, Mui (CQ 1-8)
Coastal point at 13°24'N-109°18'E. On ND49-09 JOG. Phu Yen Pr, II Corps.
Luong Hoa SF Camp (XT 594-968)
Apx 3 km from Cambodian border, 7 km N tip of Fishhook, and 18 km SW Loc Ninh. SF Det 62, 5th SF Grp CIDG Det A-353, May67. Grid per *Special Forces Order of Battle* is XS 594-968; however, proper grid zone thought to be XT). Later closed and moved to Duc Hue, 51st ARVN Ranger. Binh Long Pr, III Corps.
Luong Loc (YD 868-188)
Hamlet apx 4k NW Hue/Phu Bai AF, and on E bank of Song Loi Nong. Biet Kich PF/militia HQ of Chieu Tich Chung. See Biet Kich in Glossary. Thau Thien Pr, I Corps.
Luong Mang (n/a)
AMS/DMA mapsheet L 701-6180-3. NVN/China.
Luong Phai Pass (XK 4-7?)
Along R.C. 4, between That Khe and Dong Khe, and N Hanoi. Was major bottleneck exploited by Vietminh to ambush French convoys in early 50's. NVN.
Luong Son (n/a)
Mapsheet name of L-7014-6150-4. NVN only.
Luong Son (BN 125-385?)
Apx 16 km WSW Song Mao AF, 2 km W Ap Luong Tay and 38 km NE Phan Thiet. Binh Thuan Pr, II Corps.
Luong Son Airfield (BN 123-380)
Apx 16 km WSW Song Mao AF, 2 km W Ap Luong Tay and 38 km NE Phan Thiet. "Flt Serv ck 5th SF ARVN (and US Army on site) 1Aug68, AF # VA2-228," in Aug69 TAD per Frank Penk, Jr. Not in Feb73 TAD. II Corps.
Luong Son Compound (BN 125-385)
See Luong Son SF Camp. Binh Thuan Pr, II Corps.
Luong Son SF Camp (BN 125-385)
Apx 16 km WSW Song Mao AF, 2 km W Ap Luong Tay and 38 km NE Phan Thiet. SF Det 41, 5th SF, Det A-237, Oct66. Grid per *SF Order of Battle.* Transferred to RF/PF. Binh Thuan Pr, II Corps.
Luong Tan SF Camp (WS 061-601)
Apx 6 km SW That Son AF, 65 km ENE Ha Tien and 8 km due E peak Dop Chompa Mtn. 5th SF. Moved to An Phu. Info/grid per *SF Order of Battle.* Chau Doc Pr, IV Corps.
Luong Tay, Ap (n/a)
Mapsheet L-7014-6631-2. Sheet: Ap Luong Tay. SVN.
Luong Vien CAP (YD 9-2 or ZD 0-1?)
CAP 3-3-5, 3rd CAG. Villes of Luong Vien listed at both ZD 030-152 and YD 922-213? Thua Thien Pr, I Corps.
Lurch, LZ (AT 926-238)
Apx 3 km E Hiep Duc, 37 km W Tam Ky and 38 km SW Hoi An. Americal list. Quang Nam Pr, I Corps.
Luscombe Airfield (YS 437-681)
Near Long Le AF and adjacent 1st ATF ANZAC HQ at Nui Dat. 28 km due S Blackhorse AF, apx 60 km SE Saigon, 30 km NE Vung Tau. Construction finished during Dec 66. Per TPC K-10D. El. 115', 2,900' asph rwy. 10°33'32"N-107°13'43"E. Phuoc Tuy Pr, III Corps.
Lute, LZ (XD 996-677)
On S edge of DMZ, apx 11 km W Thon An Hoa, 14 km NW Cam Lo and 25 km WNW Dong Ha. Apr70 XXIV Corps grid per Don Armstrong. Quang Tri Pr, I Corps.
Luzerne County, USS (n/a)
LST-902. Decom 12Aug70. SVN.
Ly Ba So POW Camp (WG 82-90?)
Vietminh or Fr POW camp at Thanh Hoa, holding political prisoners until Geneva Accords were signed in 1954. NVN.
Ly Hoa (n/a)
Mapsheet name of L-7014-6344-3. NVN only.
Ly Ly River (BT 00-33)
See Song Ly Ly. Quang Nam Pr, I Corps.
Ly Son Airfield (CT 003-012)
See Cu Lao Re AF. Island E I Corps.
Ly Tong (n/a)
See Glossary.
Ly Van Manh, FSB (XS 62-88)
A.k.a. FSB Kathy. At or near Old French Fort, apx 8 km SSE Duc Hoa AF, 20 km WSW Tan Son Nhut AB and 13 km due N Ben Luc. 4th/12th and 3d/7th Inf, 199th LIB here. Hau Nghia Pr?, III Corps.
Lyman K. Swenson, USS (n/a)
DD-797, per Ralph Fries.
Lynch, Camp (YS 459-840)
Along LTL-2, apx 26 km due S Xuan Loc, 13 km S Blackhorse AF and 15 km NNE Nui Dat. Described as large base with many large tents, wooden walkways and lots of mud, per Herb Artola, 3d/22d Inf. 2d Bde/25th Inf Div here '70 and/or '71. On 6Sep71 1ATF NCO trng map, DMA L-607-6430, courtesy John Hollett. Also listed at YS 458-836 as FSB Lynch. Phuoc Tuy Pr, III Corps.
Lynch, FSB (YS 458-836)
See Lynch, Camp. Phuoc Tuy Pr, III Corps.
Lynette, FSB (YS 572-630)
On N side of LTL-23 apx 14.5 km ESE Nui Dat, 8 km ENE FSB Horseshoe and 2.5 km NE FSB Baton. On 1ATF NCO trng map per John Hollett. Phuoc Tuy Pr, III Corps.
Lynn, LZ (BR 778-640)
Apx 13 km WSW Phu My, 35 km NE An Khe, 20 km S Ha Tay AF and 12 km W QL-1. Binh Dinh Pr, II Corps.
Lynn, LZ (YA 866-133)
Apx 8 km E Cambodia, 50 km SW Pleiku, 14 km S to SSE Duc Co AF, and 6 km SE Plei Girao Kla. A Bty, 5th/16th Arty, 4th Div here Dec69. 4th Div 31Jan70 ORLL grid per Jim Henderson. Pleiku Pr, II Corps.
Lynne, LZ (YA 866-133)
See Lynn. Pleiku Pr, II Corps.
Lynnette, FSB (YS 572-630)
See Lynette at grid. Phuoc Tuy Pr, III Corps.
Lynx, Channel (YJ 5-2)
A.k.a. Chenal du Lynx. Channel near 21°03'N-107°28'E. On NF48-12 JOG. NVN.

Lynx, FSB (YS 75-82)
ANZAC FSB on Rte-329, apx 2 km S LTL-23, 35 km NE Nui Dat, 14 km ENE FSB Raglan, 8 km due S Hill 2310, 40 km SSE Juanita, 25 km ENE Xa Binh Gia, 22 km W to WSW Ham Tan AF, 14 km SW peak Nui Be Mtn and 33 km NE Dat. 161 Bty, RNZA (Master's Bty 6Sep70-8May71) FSB set here 31Jan-21Feb71 (right section). Phuoc Tuy Pr, III Corps.

Lynx, LZ (YD 249-593)
Immed E Dong Ha CB/AF, on W side of QL-1 and apx 11 km NW Quang Tri. Apr70 XXIV Corps grid per Don Armstrong. Quang Tri Pr, I Corps.

Lyon, FSB (YD 65-283?)
A.k.a. Hill 285? Near Thon An Van Thuong, apx 10 km E Hue and 5 km S LZ Sally. Thua Thien Pr, I Corps.

LZ (defined) (n/a)
Landing Zone, a.k.a. "Lima Zulu" See Landing Zone and Fire Support Base in Glossary.

LZ (name) (various)
LZs (Landing Zones) are listed alphabetically by name with last name first, followed by a comma and then the letters "LZ," or "FSB," as in "Janet, LZ," or "Janet, FSB."

LZ 11 Goodsell Heliport (BT 01-76?)
See Goodsell Heliport. Quang Nam Pr, I Corps.

MIKE

Facility/Feature Name, Grid Coordinate, a.k.a. Name/History/Province/CTZ

Unless otherwise stated, 6-digit grid coordinates reference DMA L-7014, L-7015 or L-7016 series, 1:50,000 scale maps, while 2- and 4-digit coordinates reference AMS/DMA/NIMA 1:250,000, 1:500,000 and 1:1,000,000 scale maps. Unless otherwise stated, all heights are in meters. To convert meters to feet, multiply by 3.2808; feet to meters, multiply by .3048.

M&M Piers (XS 8-9)
A.k.a. *Messageries Maritimes* Piers, Saigon. See 4th Transportation Cmd HQ, Saigon. Gia Dinh Pr, III Corps.

M'Drack Airfield (BQ 586-056)
Apparently a.k.a. Khanh Duong (old) AF. Along QL-21 just NW site of Khanh Duong New AF, apx 36 km NW Duc My AF/Tan Khanh, 54 km W Van Ninh AF, and 74 km NW Nha Trang. "Insecure, abnd, SVN Directorate of Civ Avn, 7Feb67, AF # VA2-100," Aug69 TAD per Frank Penk. Not in Feb73 TAD. Khanh Hoa Pr, II Corps.

M'Neun Pantar Mountain (AN 84-68)
A.k.a. Hill 1626 (5,459'). Apx 30 km ESE Bao Loc. Lam Dong Pr, II Corps.

Ma Noi (n/a)
Mapsheet name of L-7014-6732-3. SVN.

Ma Rem (n/a)
SF camp per *SF Order of Battle*? Thailand or Cambodia?

Ma River (VJ)
A.k.a. Nam Ma River. See Na San. NVN.

Ma Ty, Thon (n/a)
Mapsheet name of L-7014-6732-1. Actual name is: Thon Ma Ty. SVN.

Ma Xoa Mountain (YC 84-91)
N of the Ruong Ruong Valley, apx 25 km S Phu Bai and 14 km due W peak of Dong Nam. Cited in *Bonnie-Sue*, pp 241-246. Thua Thien Pr, I Corps.

MAAG Advisory Team #22 Compound (AR 7-8)
At Kontum. Kontum Pr, II Corps.

MAAG Det Compound, Quang Ngai (BS 64-73)
See Kramer Cmpd. Quang Ngai Pr, I Corps.

MAAG Det Compound, Tam Ky (BT 3-2)
See Payne Cmpd. Quang Tin Pr, I Corps.

Mabel, LZ (BR 765-615)
Apx 33 km NE An Khe, 13 km W QL-1 and 15 km ENE Vinh Thanh. Oct66. Binh Dinh Pr, II Corps.

Mac, LZ (BS 348-510)
A.k.a. LZ MacArther or MacArthur. Overlooking Song Re Valley, apx 18 km W Minh Long AF and 12 km S Lang Re. 1st Cav. Name/grid per Dan Gillotti, 15th Arty Assn. Quang Ngai Pr, I Corps.

Mac Nam Mun River (n/a)
Upper Mekong River as it approaches western Thai border at Ban Dan, and after passing Ubon Ratchathani (Ubon AB). See Lam Nam Chi River. Thailand.

Macao, LZ (XD 928-482)
Apx 10 km NE Khe Sanh CB, 8 km due W Ca Lu and 41 km W to WNW Quang Tri. Apr70 XXIV Corps grid per Don Armstrong. Quang Tri Pr, I Corps.
Macardale, LZ (XD 856-507)
Apx 9 km N to NNE Khe Sanh CB, 14 km WNW Ca Lu and 48 km due W of Quang Tri. Apr70 XXIV Corps grid per Don Armstrong. Quang Tri Pr, I Corps.
MacArthur, LZ (BS 348-510)
See Mac, LZ. Quang Ngai Pr, I Corps.
MacArthur, Operation (n/a)
1Nov-14Dec67 (also listed as 12Oct67-31Jan68.?). 173d Abn. On 6Nov67, S Ben Het, 2 Cos of 4th/503d Inf engaged NVA 66th Rgt in Ngok Kom Leat hill mass (7 US KIA). On 11Nov67, Task Force Black (elements of C/1st/503 Inf and 2 pltn/D/1st/503) were ambushed near Dak To, resulting in 20 KIA, 154 WIA, 2 MIA (A PFC Barnes awarded MOH in this fight). On 19Nov67, 2/503d Inf assaulted Hill 875. C and D Co's were heavily engaged w/small arms and RR fire when they reached 1st of 2 ridges. While A Co was securing rear, it came under intense attack (PFC Carlos Lozada awarded MOH in this action). Tragically, 42 US WIA were KIA by errant 500 lb. bomb in battle. On Thanksgiving Day '67, 4th/503d and remainder of 2d/503d Inf took Hill 875. Battle marked climax of Battle of Dak To. 2d/503d lost 107 KIA, 282 WIA and 10 MIA. See Hill 875 and Dak To Battle of. Kontum Pr, II Corps.
MacDonald FSA (YD 82-13)
Logistical Fwd Supt Area of 2d Bde/101st Abn situated at LZ El Paso (later renamed Camp Eagle), Jan-Feb68. See Eagle, Camp, for location. Thua Thien Pr, I Corps.
Mace, FSB (YT 628-125?)
If grid is accurate, was apx 3 km ENE peak of Nui Chua Chan, 17 km ENE Xuan Loc and 6 km ENE of FSB Mace listed at YT 595-080. Unknown if site moved or grid in error? Jul70-Feb71. See Mace also at YT 595-080. Long Khanh Pr, III Corps.
Mace, FSB (YT 595-080)
Per William Gaschler, was at southern base of Nui Chua Chan Mtn, apx 3 km SSW its peak and just N Ap Suoi Cat. Also apx 13 km due E Xuan Loc and 75 km ENE Saigon. Dirt road on N separated ville from FSB, and grassland (had to be cleared of mines) extended apx 500 meters to S and to that road. Top of Nui Chua Chan was signal site (313th Sig Co). Glascher adds that location was poor because 33d NVA Rgt had spotters on mtn adjusting rocket/mortar fire. Also listed at YT 628-125, apx 6 km ENE this site, while *Rangers At War,* at p 327, shows it apx 8 km ESE Nui Chua Chan and about same distance SSW Gia Ray? Unknown which location is correct or if site moved. 3d/7th Inf, HQs 2d/3d Inf, 199th LIB and 1st Cav. Long Khanh Pr, III Corps.
Mace, FSB (ZC 174-353)
A.k.a. Hill 375. Built on very narrow ridgeline 20 km SW An Hoa and 3 km NE FSB Cutlass. Initial const facilitated USAF Combat Trap, 10,000 lb. bomb drop. Used as part of USMC's Task Force Yankee's attack on Base Area 112, Dec68-Feb69. On map in *US Marines in Vietnam-1969*, p 90. Apr70 XXIV Corps grid per Don Armstrong. See Combat Trap in Glossary. Quang Nam Pr, I Corps.
Mace, LZ (XS 065-613)
A.k.a. FSB Georgia. Apx 21 km NW Cai Lay and 28 km N Vinh Long. Nov67. Kien Phong Pr, IV Corps.
Machete, FSB (XS 650-620)
Apx 30 km SSW Saigon, 10 km ESE Tan An and 24 km NW My Tho. Jul68. Phuoc Tuy Pr, III Corps.
Machete, FSB (ZC 023-204)
A.k.a. Hill 435. Apx 7 km WSW FSB Bolo, 10 km S FSB Saber and 38 km SW An Hoa, within 3 km of Quang Tin Pr. Used during '69 USMC assault on Base Area 112. See map in *US Marines in Vietnam-1969*, p 90. Apr70 XXIV Corps grid per Don Armstrong. Quang Nam Pr, I Corps.
Machine Gun Valley (YA or ZA?)
Somewhere SW Pleiku. So named because in Apr66, a 4-ship heliborne force of unknown origin flew over valley spraying it with all 8 door guns, apparently unaware that 2d/7th Cav, 1st Cav, was below them. Incident discussed in *Baptism*, Chp 22. Pleiku Pr, II Corps.
MacIver-Brodt Compound (AR 783-500?)
See Brodt-MacIver Cmpd. Pleiku Pr, II Corps.
Mack, LZ (XT 769-786)
Apx 18 km N Chonh Thanh AF, 2 km E QL-13 and 9 km SSE An Loc. Jul 67. Binh Long Pr, III Corps.
Mack, FSB/LZ (XD 969-617)
Apx 40 km WNW Quang Tri and 16 km WNW Cam Lo. Re-opened 1Mar69, by G/1st/4th and L/3d/4th Marines, 3d Mar Div, who were then attacked 2Mar69 by elements of 246th NVA Rgt. Was very unusual for normally patient and methodical NVA to mount attack within only 1 day of a FSB's opening. On map at p 58, *US Marines in Vietnam-1969.* 101st Abn inactive FSB grid per Don Armstrong. Also listed at XD 968-585. Quang Tri Pr, I Corps.
MacNamara's Wall (XD/YD)
See McNamara's Wall. Quang Tri Pr, I Corps.
Macon, LZ (YA 935-052)
Apx 23 km SSE Duc Co, 52 km SW Pleiku, 5 km due N LZ X-Ray and near Ia Drang River. Opened 15Nov65 by elements of 2d/7th Cav, 1st Cav and C 2d/17th and Bty of 21st Arty, during 2d day of 1st LZ X-Ray battle. However, when arty units found soil too soft, units then moved to LZ Columbus later that same day. Grid per Peter Cole. Also listed at YA 935-952 in error. Pleiku Pr, II Corps.
Macon, FSB (YA 935-952?)
See Macon at YA 935-052. II Corps.
Macon, Operation (n/a)
4Jul-27Oct66. USMC securing the proposed An Hoa industrial complex. 507 NVA/VC KIA, per *Vietnam Order of Battle*, pp 9-14. Quang Nam, Pr, I Corps.
MAC-SOG (n/a)
See Glossary.
MAC-SOG CCC (ZA 236-863)
See CCC and FOB 2.
MAC-SOG CCN (YD 887-148? & YD 328-526?)
See CCN, Prairie Fire and FOB 1.
MAC-SOG CCS (AP 882-010?)
See CCS.
MAC-SOG Operational Divisions (n/a)
See SOG-00 et seq. in Glossary.

MAC-SOG Radio Relay Site (YB 604-355?)
Likely "Leghorn." Described as radio relay site situated on 7,200' mtn top in Laos and operated by 5th SF Grp personnel assigned to MAC-SOG Prairie Fire and other "Over the Fence" Ops. Could intercept virtually any MAC-SOG Team's line-of-sight radio transmissions and relay them to CCN, MLT-1 or MLT-2. Its formal name or nickname was not cited in *Da Nang Diary* reference to it. See Leghorn, Hickory Hill, and Sledgehammer. Laos.
MACV 29 Signal Site (n/a)
No data available.
MACV Adv. Team 1 (BT 0-7)
At Hotel Da Nang. I Corps US Army Adv Grp, per Ray Bows. Quang Nam Pr, I Corps.
MACV Adv. Team 1 (BT 14-57?)
At Hoi An. Prov Adv to 2d ARVN Div, per Ray Bows. Quang Nam Pr, I Corps.
MACV Adv. Team 2 (BS 65-73)
In Quang Ngai City. Adv to both Quang Ngai and Quang Tin Pr. Data per Ray Bows. Quang Ngai Pr, I Corps.
MACV Adv. Team 3 (YD 748-230)
At Hue Citadel. Adv to 1st ARVN Inf Div. Data per Ray Bows. Thua Thien Pr, I Corps.
MACV Adv. Team 4 (YD 34-54)
Quang Tri Pr Advrs, per Ray Bows. Quang Tri Pr, I Corps.
MACV Adv. Team 5 (YD 8-1)
At Phu Bai or Doung Da Natl Trng Ctr near Phu Bai. Per Ray Bows. Thua Thien Pr, I Corps.
MACV Adv. Team 6 (BT 0-7)
At Da Nang. I Corps Area Log Cmd Advrs (also in Quang Ngai & Hue. Data per Ray Bows. Quang Nam Pr, I Corps.
MACV Adv. Team 6 (CR 09-23?)
At Qui Nhon. II Corps Area Log Cmd Det. Data per Ray Bows. Binh Dinh Pr, II Corps.
MACV Adv. Team 9 (XS 8-9)
In Cholon. III Corps Area Log Cmd Adv. Data per Ray Bows. Gia Dinh Pr, III Corps.
MACV Adv. Team 10 (WS 789-148?)
In the Eakin cmpd (co-located with MACV Team 96) at Can Tho. IV Corps ARVN Log Cmd Advrs. Data per Ray Bows. Vinh Long Pr, IV Corps.
MACV Adv. Team 11 (CP 04-55?)
At Nha Trang. ARVN V Corps area Log Cmd Advrs. Per Ray Bows. Khanh Hoa Pr, II Corps.
MACV Adv. Team 15 (BT 14-57?)
At Hoi An. Prov Advrs. Data per Ray Bows. Quang Nam Pr, I Corps.
MACV Adv. Team 21 (AR 80-47)
At Pyle Barracks in Pleiku. Pleiku Pr, Sector, Chieu Hoi, and RF/PF Advrs. Data per Ray Bows. Pleiku Pr, II Corps.
MACV Adv. Team 24 (AR 810-890?)
In Camp Mary Jane at Kontum. Per Chuck Schwiderski, served 3d ARVN Highland Scout Cos and elements of 42d ARVN Rgt. Grid is for AF. Kontum Pr, II Corps.
MACV Adv. Team 26 (BP 23-24?)
At Dalat. Sector Advrs. Tuyen Duc Pr, II Corps.
MACV Adv. Team 29 (BR 896-412?)
At Phu Cat AB. Quang Ngai Pr, I Corps.
MACV Adv. Team 31 (BQ 233-818?)
At Hau Bon (a.k.a. Cheo Reo). Hau Bon subsector Adv. Data per Ray Bows. Pleiku Pr, II Corps.
MACV Adv. Team 32 (YU 974-291?)
At Gia Nghia. Gia Nghia subsector Adv. Grid is for SF camp. Per Ray Bows. Quang Duc Pr, II Corps.
MACV Adv. Team 33 (AQ 780-040?)
At Ban Me Thuot. Data per Ray Bows. Darlac Pr, II Corps.
MACV Adv. Team 37 (AN 801-068?)
At Phan Thiet. Prov Adv. Data per Ray Bows. Grid is for SF. Binh Thuan Pr, II Corps.
MACV Adv. Team 38 (ZT 134-833?)
At Bao Loc. Data per Ray Bows. Lam Dong Pr, II Corps.
MACV Adv. Team 40 (BP 83-84?)
At Duc My. Subsector Adv. Data per Ray Bows. Khanh Hoa Pr, II Corps.
MACV Adv. Team 43 (XT 544-050?)
In Belt Cmpd at Bao Tri (Khiem Cuong). Subsector Adv. Data per Ray Bows. Hau Nghia Pr, III Corps.
MACV Adv. Team 44 (XS 87-95?)
At Gia Dinh city. Prov Advrs responsible for Binh Chan, Go Vap, Hoc Mon, Nha Be, Tan Binh and Thu Duc districts. Data per Ray Bows. Gia Dinh Pr, III Corps.
MACV Adv. Team 44 (XT 755-039?)
At Hoc Mon. Subsector Adv. Data per Ray Bows. Grid is for heliport. Gia Dinh Pr, III Corps.
MACV Adv. Team 46 (BP 95-55?)
Dien Khanh Dist, '68-69, per Jim Alkek. Dien Khanh listings also at BR 8-9 and CP 0-6. Grid is est. Khanh Hoa Pr?, II Corps?
MACV Adv. Team 47 (XT 730-877?)
Apparently at An Loc. Binh Long Sector Adv. Data per Ray Bows. Grid is SF camp. Binh Long Pr, III Corps.
MACV Adv. Team 48 (ZS 045-800?)
At Ham Tan. Data per Ray Bows. Grid is for MAAG heliport. Binh Tuy Pr, III Corps.
MACV Adv. Team 49 (YT 460-094?)
At Xuan Loc. Long Khanh sector Adv. Per Ray Bows. Grid is for heliport. Long Khanh Pr, III Corps.
MACV Adv. Team 50 (WS 71-54?)
In Crum Cmpd at Cao Lanh. 44th Special Tac Zone Adv. Don Armstrong tells us 44th STZ was general code name for Delta ops controlled out of Moc Hoa by team 50 using 21st and 7th ARVN Divs. 7th ARVN was further controlled by US Advsy team 75. Some data per Ray Bows. Grid is for old SF camp. Kien Phong Pr, IV Corps.
MACV Adv. Team 51 (WR 791-281)
At Bac Lieu AF. Adv Det to 21st ARVN Inf. Data per Ray Bows. Bac Lieu Pr, IV Corps.
MACV Adv. Team 52 (XS 040-331)
In Patch Cmpd at Vinh Long AF. Vinh Long sector Adv. Data per Ray Bows. Vinh Long Pr, IV Corps.
MACV Adv. Team 52 (WS 521-416)
At Long Xuyen. An Giang subsector Adv. Data per Ray Bows. An Giang Pr, IV Corps.
MACV Adv. Team 54 (WS 105-048?)
At Rach Gia. Rach Gia subsector and 4th ARVN Ranger Grp Adv. Data per Ray Bows. Grid is for old AF. Kien Giang Pr, IV Corps.
MACV Adv. Team 56 (WS 843-103?)
At Can Tho. Phong Dinh sector Adv. Data per Ray Bows. Phong Dinh Pr, IV Corps.

MACV Adv. Team 57 (XR 459-975?)
At Phu Vinh. Vinh Binh sector Adv. Per Ray Bows. Grid is for Tra Vinh AF. Vinh Binh Pr, IV Corps.

MACV Adv. Team 58 (WR 521-816?)
At Vi Thanh. Chuong Thien Adv. Data per Ray Bows. Grid is for old Vi Thanh AF. Chuong Thien Pr, IV Corps.

MACV Adv. Team 59 (WR 169-139?)
At Quan Long. An Xuyen sector Adv. Data per Ray Bows. Grid is for AF. An Xuyen Pr, IV Corps.

MACV Adv. Team 60 (WS 845-384?)
At Sa Dec city. 9th ARVN Inf Div Adv. Det. Data per Ray Bows. Sa Dec Pr, IV Corps.

MACV Adv. Team 61 (WS 027-636?)
At Chi Lang Ntl Trng Ctr, near That Son AF, apx 60 km ENE Ha Tien and 6 km NE Dop Chompa Mtn. ARVN Ranger Cmd Adv Det. Data per Ray Bows. Grid is for SF camp. See Teams 64 and 96. Pr, IV Corps.

MACV Adv. Team 63 (XR 058-591?)
At Khanh Hung (Soc Trang). Ba Xuyen Adv. Data per Ray Bows. Grid is for Soc Trang. Ba Xuyen Pr, IV Corps.

MACV Adv. Team 64 Compound (VQ 98-67)
See Camp Hurt. An Xuyen Pr, IV Corps.

MACV Adv. Team 64 (WS 153-814?)
At Chau Doc. Delta Military Assist Cmd/Chau Doc sector Adv. Included Province recon unit (Project Phoenix), a USN Seal Team and 9 USN patrol boats. Data per Ray Bows. Grid is for Chau Doc AF. See Teams 61 and 96. Chau Doc Pr, IV Corps.

MACV Adv. Team 65 (WS 845-384?)
At Sa Dec. Data per Ray Bows. Sa Dec Pr, IV Corps.

MACV Adv. Team 67 (XT 960-495?)
At Phuoc Vinh. Phuoc Long Adv to 31st ARVN Rangers, some ARVN arty and RF/PF units. Data per Ray Bows. Grid is for SF camp and AF. Phuoc Long Pr, III Corps.

MACV Adv. Team 67 (YU 19-11?)
At Song Be, per Rick Harris. Phuoc Long Pr, III Corps.

MACV Adv. Team 70 (XT 84-18?)
In Gosney Cmpd at Phu Loi. 5th ARVN Rangers Adv with staff at both Phu Loi and Lai Khe. Data per Ray Bows. Binh Duong Pr, III Corps.

MACV Adv. Team 70 (XT 862-158?)
At Thu Mau Mot. Thu Dau Mot subsector Adv. Data per Ray Bows. Grid is for Thu Dau Mot AF (a.k.a. Phu Loi AF). Binh Duong Pr, III Corps.

MACV Adv. Team 71 (XR 07-62?)
At Soc Trang (Khanh Hung) city. Ba Xuyen sector Adv. Data per Ray Bows. Ba Xuyen Pr, IV Corps.

MACV Adv. Team 72 (XR 459-975?)
At Tra Vinh. Tra Vinh subsector Adv. Data per Ray Bows. Vinh Binh Pr, IV Corps.

MACV Adv. Team 72 (XS 029-902?)
At Moc Hoa. Team member Bill Hunt tells us: "While a District Advisor in '72, it was so late in game we were just trying to keep old team houses open. I was in 3 districts. There were never more than 3 of us, even though we generally had bunks for 9 or so. In '72 it was just me and one of five DSA's." Kien Tuong Pr, IV Corps.

MACV Adv. Team 74 (XT 687-050?)
At Quang Trung Ntl Trng Cntr, apx 16 km NW Saigon. Data per Ray Bows. Gia Dinh Pr, III Corps.

MACV Adv. Team 75 (XS 49-45?)
At My Tho. Adv to 7th ARVN Inf Div and Dinh Tuong Pr, per Ray Bows. Grid is for AF. Dinh Tuong Pr, IV Corps.

MACV Adv. Team 78 (YU 458-065?)
In the Holland Cmpd at Duc Phong (possibly a.k.a. the Bu Dang Adv Cmpd?). Adv to Van Kiep Ntl Trng Cntr. Data per Ray Bows. Grid is for Bu Dang Adv Cmpd, apx 2 km E Duc Phong AF. Phuoc Long Pr, III Corps.

MACV Adv. Team 80 (WR 196-142?)
At Ca Mau (Quan Long). Ca Mau Peninsula and subsector Adv. Data per Ray Bows. Grid is for old Quan Long AF. An Xuyen Pr, IV Corps.

MACV Adv. Team 83 (XS 840-469?)
At Go Cong city. IV Corps CTZ and Go Cong sector Adv. Data per Ray Bows. Grid is for SF camp, See MACV Team 85. Go Cong Pr, IV Corps.

MACV Adv. Team 84 (WS 705-532?)
At Cao Lanh. Kien Phong Sector Adv, per Ray Bows. Grid is for Cao Lanh AF. Kien Phong Pr, IV Corps.

MACV Adv. Team 85 (XR 3-8?)
Tieu Can Dist, '72, per Bill Hunt. Vinh Binh Pr, IV Corps.

MACV Adv. Team 85 (XS 840-469?)
At Go Cong and co-located with H Bty, 29th Arty (searchlight). Go Cong Adv. Data per Ray Bows. Grid is for SF camp. See MACV Team 83. Go Cong Pr, IV Corps.

MACV Adv. Team 86 (XS 524-656?)
At Tan An. Long An sector Adv. Data per Ray Bows. Grid is for Tan An AF. Long An Pr, III Corps.

MACV Adv. Team 87 (YT 461-085?)
At Xuan Loc. 18th ARVN Inf Adv Det, per Ray Bows. Grid is for Xuan Loc SF camp. Long Khanh Pr, III Corps.

MACV Adv. Team 88 (WR 537-822?)
At Vi Thanh. Chuong Thien Adv. Data per Ray Bows. Grid is for Vi Thanh AF (old). Chuong Thien Pr, IV Corps.

MACV Adv. Team 89 (YS 402-613?)
At Ba Ria. Phuoc Tuy sector Adv. Data per Ray Bows. Grid is for Ba Ria AF (heliport at YS 384-622, also possible site). Phuoc Tuy Pr, III Corps.

MACV Adv. Team 90 (XT 202-508)
In the Wallace Cmpd at Tay Ninh East (Tay Ninh City AF), per Ray Bows. Tay Ninh Pr, III Corps.

MACV Adv. Team 91 (XT 862-158?)
At Phu Cuong (Phu Loi). Binh Duong sector and 5th ARVN Engr Adv. Data per Ray Bows. Grid is for Phu Loi AF. Binh Duong Pr, III Corps.

MACV Adv. Team 93 (XS 480-347?)
At Ben Tre (Truc Giang). Kien Hoa sector Adv, per Ray Bows. Grid is for AF. Kien Hoa Pr, IV Corps.

MACV Adv. Team 95 (XT 99-14?)
In Train cmpd at Bien Hoa. III Corps Adv. Co-located with Team 98? Data per Ray Bows. Bien Hoa Pr, III Corps.

MACV Adv. Team 96 (WS 789-148)
In Eakin cmpd (co-located with Team 10) at Can Tho. IV Corps Adv Grp. Advised the 63d ARVN Inf Bn at Binh Thuy AF. Data per Ray Bows. Vinh Long Pr, IV Corps.

MACV Adv. Team 96 (WS 153-814?)
At Chau Doc. IV Corps CTZ Adv. Det. Data per Ray Bows. Grid is for Chau Doc AF. See Teams 61 and 64. Chau Doc Pr, IV Corps.

MACV Adv. Team 96 (WS 840-108?)
At Can Tho. 65th ARVN Inf Bn Adv. Det. Data per Ray Bows. Grid is for Can Tho AF. Phong Dinh Pr, IV Corps.
MACV Adv. Team 98 (XT 99-14?)
In the Train cmpd at Bien Hoa AB. Bien Hoa sector Adv. Apparently co-located with Team 95. Data per Ray Bows. Bien Hoa Pr, III Corps.
MACV Adv. Team 99 (XS 600-962?)
At Duc Hoa. 25th ARVN Inf Div Adv. Det. Data per Ray Bows. Grid apx. Hau Nghia Pr, III Corps.
MACV Adv. Team 100 (XS 819-962?)
Apparently in Saigon and perhaps at JGS HQ on Tan Son Nhut AB? Capital Military Dist Adv. Det HQ Army (ARVN), and Adv to 61st ARVN Arty Bn, as well as 3d and 5th ARVN Ranger Grps. Data per Ray Bows. Grid is generic for Tan Son Nhut AB. Gia Dinh Pr, III Corps.
MACV Adv. Team 162 (XS 819-962?)
At Tan Son Nhut AB. ARVN Abn Div Adv. Det, with Adv assigned to 1st, 2d, 3d, 5th, 6th, 7th, 8th, and 9th Abn Bns, as well as 1st and 2d ARVN Arty Bns. Data per Ray Bows. Grid is for Tan Son Nhut AB. Gia Dinh Pr, III Corps.
MACV Adv. Team #? (CP 04-55?)
At Nha Trang. ARVN NCO Academy Adv. Data per Ray Bows. Khanh Hoa Pr, II Corps.
MACV Adv. Team #? (AQ 78-04?)
At Ban Me Thuot. 23d ARVN Inf Adv. Det. Data per Ray Bows. Darlac Pr, II Corps.
MACV Adv. Team #? (XT 772-381?)
At Ben Cat. Ben Cat subsector Adv. Data per Ray Bows. Grid is for AF. Binh Duong Pr, III Corps.
MACV Adv. Team #? (YT 411-104?)
At An Loc. Binh Long sector Adv. Data per Ray Bows. Grid is for AF. Binh Long Pr, III Corps.
MACV Adv. Team #? (ZT 065-792?)
At Bao Loc/Di Linh. Lam Dong Prov Adv. Data per Ray Bows. Grid is for AF. Lam Dong Pr, II Corps.
MACV Adv. Team #? (BQ 233-818?)
At Hua Bon (a.k.a. Cheo Reo). Phu Bon sector Adv. Data per Ray Bows. AF grid. Phu Bon Pr, II Corps.
MACV Adv. Team #? (YS 14-98?)
At Bearcat. Long Thanh subsector Adv. Data per Ray Bows. Bien Hoa Pr, III Corps.
MACV Adv. Team #? (AN 801-068?)
At Phan Thiet. Binh Thuan sector Adv. Data per Ray Bows. Grid is for AF. Binh Thuan Pr, II Corps.
MACV Adv. Team #? (BT 309-186?)
At Tam Ky. Quang Tin sector Adv. Data per Ray Bows. Grid is for AF. Quang Tin Pr, I Corps.
MACV Adv. Team #? (CR 08-23?)
At Qui Nhon. Binh Dinh sector Adv. Data per Ray Bows. Binh Dinh Pr, II Corps.
MACV Adv. Team #? (XS 87-95?)
At Thu Duc near Saigon. ARVN Inf School Adv. Data per Ray Bows. Gia Dinh Pr, III Corps.
MACV Adv. Team #? (XT 592-212?)
At Trung Lap. Trung Lap Advisors. Data per Ray Bows. Grid is for Trung Lap Trng Ctr. Hau Nghia Pr, III Corps.
MACV Adv. Team #? (CQ 154-481?)
At Tuy Hoa. Phu Yen sector Adv. Data per Ray Bows. Grid is for Tuy Hoa AF. Phu Yen Pr, II Corps.
MACV Adv. Team #? (WS 789-148?)
At Binh Thuy AF. ARVN 84th Ordnance Adv. Det. Data per Ray Bows. Phong Dinh Pr, IV Corps.
MACV Annex (XS 832-953)
At SE corner of Tan Son Nhut AB, Saigon, and just E the MACV HQ Cmpd. Gia Dinh Pr, III Corps.
MACV Annex 7th Finance (XS 831-954)
In MACV Annex, SE side of Tan Son Nhut, Saigon, just E MACV HQ Cmpd. Gia Dinh Pr, III Corps.
MACV Annex EM Club (XS 830-953)
In MACV Annex, SE side of Tan Son Nhut, Saigon, just E MACV HQ Cmpd. Gia Dinh Pr, III Corps.
MACV Annex Gym (XS 832-953)
In MACV Annex, SE side of Tan Son Nhut, Saigon, just E MACV HQ Cmpd. Gia Dinh Pr, III Corps.
MACV Annex NCO Club (XS 830-953)
In MACV Annex, SE side of Tan Son Nhut, Saigon, just E MACV HQ Cmpd. Gia Dinh Pr, III Corps.
MACV Annex Pool (XS 832-953)
In MACV Annex, SE side of Tan Son Nhut, Saigon, just E MACV HQ Cmpd. Gia Dinh Pr, III Corps.
MACV Annex PX/Barber (XS 832-951)
In MACV Annex, SE side of Tan Son Nhut, Saigon, just E MACV HQ Cmpd. Gia Dinh Pr, III Corps.
MACV Annex Tennis Court (XS 832-953)
In MACV Annex, SE side of Tan Son Nhut, Saigon, just E MACV HQ Cmpd. Gia Dinh Pr, III Corps.
MACV Annex Theater (XS 833-953)
In MACV Annex, SE side of Tan Son Nhut, Saigon, just E MACV HQ Cmpd. Gia Dinh Pr, III Corps.
MACV Compound # 1 (XS 825-958)
A.k.a. Pentagon East. Adj Tan Son Nhut AB, and 2d home of MACV HQ beginning '68, after originally having been in the Keopler Cmpd at 8 Nguyen Van Trang St. (or 137 Pasteur St.?), Saigon. Data per *Vietnam Military Lore, 1959-1973*. Gia Dinh Pr, III Corps.
MACV Compound # 1 (XS 854-922)
Pre '68, was at 137 Pasteur St. (or 8 Nguyen Van Trang St.?), Saigon, per *Vietnam Military Lore, 1959-1973*. Gia Dinh Pr, III Corps.
MACV Compound # 2 (XS 8-9)
At 606 Tran Hung Dao St. (pre '68), Saigon. Data per *Vietnam Military Lore, 1959-1973*. Gia Dinh Pr, III Corps.
MACV Compound # 3 (XS 8-9)
At 2 Tran Hoang Quan St., Saigon, per *Vietnam Military Lore, 1959-1973*. Gia Dinh Pr, III Corps.
MACV Compound, Hue (YD 767-218)
See Hue MACV Cmpd. Thua Thien Pr, I Corps.
MACV Forward (XS 8-9)
See Hurricane Forward. Gia Dinh Pr, III Corps.
MACV HQ (XS 825-953, et al)
Originally in the Keopler Cmpd at 8 Nguyen Van Trang St., Saigon. Was MACV HQ until it moved to MACV Cmpd #1 (Pentagon East) that was const adj to Tan Son Nhut AB as network of 2-story pre-fabricated bldgs that provided air-conditioned working space for 4,000 troops. In addition to utilities and cantonments, it inc mortar shelters, security fences and guard towers. MACV exercised C & C over all US units in VN, and Gens William Westmoreland and Creighton W. Abrams were simultaneously MACV and USARV Cmdrs during their

tours. Grid is just SE Main rwy at Tan Son Nhut and just W the MACV Annex. Gia Dinh Pr, III Corps.

MACV HQ Bank of America (XS 825-954)
In MACV HQ Cmpd at SE side of Tan Son Nhut AB, Saigon. Gia Dinh Pr, III Corps.

MACV HQ Compound (XS 825-955)
At SE corner of Tan Son Nhut AB, Saigon, and just W the MACV Annex. Gia Dinh Pr, III Corps.

MACV HQ Post Off (XS 825-954)
In MACV HQ Cmpd at SE side of Tan Son Nhut AB, Saigon. Gia Dinh Pr, III Corps.

MACV In Exile (VE 6-2)
See US Support Activities Group NE. Thailand.

MACV Objectives Plan (n/a)
See Glossary.

MACV Ranger Cmd Trng Center (WS 027-636)
At Chi Lang near That Son AF, apx 60 km ENE Ha Tien and 6 km NE peak Dop Chompa Mtn. ARVN Ranger Natl Trng Ctr, Adv Team 61, MACV Ranger Cmd Adv Det. Chau Doc, Pr, IV Corps.

MACV Recondo School (CP 03-52?)
At Nha Trang in the Project Delta Cmpd, apx 500 meters from Nha Trang SF camp. Per Paul Brubaker, school began life at order of Gen Westmoreland, 16Sep66, and under initial cmd of Maj. A. J. Baker. Westy also apparently coined term "Recondo" at same time. Detailed discussion of site as of Oct66 in *Gone Native*, Chp 4, which states it was under Project Delta and that Delta's cmpd was 500 meters outside SFOB's gate. Delta Cmpd inc 91st ARVN Abn Ranger Bn, ROK unit, Nung mercenaries and school. 3-wk course inc instruction and OJT in patrolling, recon, jungle combat and survival. To qualify, one had to be serving in LRP or LRRP related unit and have been in-country at least 6-months. Final exam was actual, supervised patrol known as "You Bet Your Life" FTX (Field Trng Exercise). Grads authorized to wear arrowhead-shaped patch on breast pocket that featured word "Recondo" across top and a "V" matching shape of the down-pointing arrowhead. School's motto was "Smart, Skillful, Tough, Courageous, Confident" (SSTCC). Khanh Hoa Pr, II Corps.

MACV-JGS IG BTI Teams (n/a)
See Glossary.

MACV-SOG (n/a)
See MAC-SOG.

MACV-SOG CCC (ZA 236-863)
See MAC-SOG CCC.

MACV-SOG CCN (YD 887-148? & YD 328-526?)
See MAC-SOG CCN.

MACV-SOG CCS (AP 882-010?)
See MAC-SOG CCS.

MACV-SOG Operational Divisions (n/a)
See SOG-00 et seq. in Glossary.

Mad Minute (n/a)
See Glossary.

Madagui (n/a)
Mapsheet name of L-7014-6531-4. SVN.

Madaket, SS (n/a)
Merchant ship under govt contract, per Ralph Fries.

Madame T's (YS 27-44)
Infamous bar in resort town of Vung Tau. Site of what became known as both "The Battle of Grand," and "The Punch-up at Madame T's." Took place apx 1Nov69, when 161 Bty RNZA had significant philosophical disagreement with RNZIR troops here and major brawl ensued. Reportedly, the "disagreement" ended in draw. Data per *Vietnam Gunner*. Phuoc Tuy Pr, III Corps.

Madame Nhu (n/a)
See Glossary.

Madden, FSB (YT 83-28?)
Apx 19 km NW Tan Linh AF and 45 km NE Xuan Loc. 4th/12th Inf, 199th LIB. Binh Tuy Pr, III Corps.

Maddox, USS (n/a)
DD 731. Capt, John J. Herrick, Cmdr Destroyer Div 192, was directed to obtain intel on coastal geography-hydrography, defensive installations, naval forces, and junk traffic, in vicinity of Hon Nieu, Hon Matt and Hon Me Islands and area near Vinh Son. Was to go no closer to shore than 4 mi. Apparent NVA PT boat attacks on *Maddox* and Destroyer *C. Turner Joy* in '64 led to *Gulf of Tonkin Resolution* and ultimate committal of ground forces in SVN. See Gulf of Tonkin Incident. [349]

Madeline, FSB (XS 82-71)
Just E LTL-5A, apx 16 km due S Saigon and 5 km NNE Ap Bac. 3d/7th Inf, 199th LIB here. Gia Dinh Pr, III Corps.

Madera County, USS (n/a)
LST-905. SVN.

Mae Hong Son Airfield (LB 8-2)
At 19°15'00"N-97°57'00"E or apx 660 km NNW Bangkok and 10 km from Burmese border. NIMA data. Feb67 Natl Geo map. El. 712'. Thailand.

Mae Rim Airfield (MA 9-8)
At 18°54'00"N-98°57'00"E. NIMA data. Thailand.

Mae Sai Airfield (n/a)
On Burmese border, apx 745 km N and slightly W Bangkok, per Feb67 Natl Geo map. Northernmost AF in this country. El. 1,500'. Thailand.

Mae Sariang Airfield (LA 8-1)
At 18°11'00"N-97°56'00"E. NIMA data. Thailand.

Mae Sot Airfield (n/a)
On Burmese border, apx 385 km NW Bangkok per Feb67 Natl Geo map. El. 689'. Thailand.

Mae Sot Airfield (MU 5-4)
A.k.a. Nds Mae Sot AF. At 16°42'00"N-98°33'00"E. NIMA data. Thailand.

Maeng Ho 9, Operation (n/a)
17Dec67-30Jan68. ROK Capitol Div op. 749 rptd NVA/VC KIA, per *Vietnam Order of Battle*, pp 9-14. Binh Dinh Pr, II Corps.

Maeng Ho 10, Operation (n/a)
16Feb-1Mar68. ROK Capitol Div op. 664 rptd NVA KIA, per *VN Order of Battle*, pp 9-14. Binh Dinh Pr, II Corps.

Magoffin, USS (n/a)
APA-199. Amphib Attk, Transport, per Ralph Fries.

Maha Sarakham Airfield (n/a)
Apx 400 km NE Bangkok per Feb67 Natl Geo map. El. 450'. Thailand.

Mahan, USS (n/a)
DLG 11, Guided Missile Cruiser. Apparently deployed in the vicinity of SVN, '62?

Mahaxay Airfield (WE 21-25)
A.k.a. L-57. Apx 280 km ESE Vientiane on Feb67 Natl Geo map. CIA per *Air Facilities Data-Laos.* El. 498'. Laos.
Mahayana (n/a)
See Glossary.
Mahnomen County, USS (n/a)
LST-912. In Dec66, she grounded off Chu Lai but all efforts to free her were fruitless and, after her 1,000 ton cargo of cement was off-loaded, she was cut-down to her 2d deck and abnd. Photo and story in *The Marines in Vietnam 1954-1973*, p 247. Decom 31Jul67. I Corps.
Mahone, FSB (XT 538-375)
A.k.a. FSB Kien and FSB Mahone I. At edge of rubber plantation apx 11 km SE Dau Tieng/Tri Tam, 23 km due W Lai Khe and 4 km N Ap Bung Binh. On 14Sep69, was renamed FSB Kien to honor KIA ARVN LTC Thien Ta Kien (reason for honor is unknown), per *Low Level Hell*, p 229. 2d/22d Inf, 1st Inf Div AO, '69. Also listed at XT 521-417. Oct68-Jun69. Binh Duong Pr, III Corps.
Mahone I, Patrol Base (XT 538-375)
See FSB Mahone. Binh Duong Pr, III Corps.
Mahone II, FSB (XT 521-417)
Apx 4 km NNW FSB Mahone I's position, 7 km SSE Dau Tieng/Tri Tam and 25 km WNW Lai Khe. Mar-Apr69. Binh Duong Pr, III Corps.
Mahone III, FSB (XT 520-410)
Apx 50 meters S position of FSB Mahone II, apx 8 km SSE Dau Tieng/Tri Tam and 24 km WNW Lai Khe. 69. Binh Duong Pr, III Corps.
Mahoney, FSB (BS 880-030)
Apx 10 km due N LZ English, 2 km SW Tan Quan and about 5 km from coast. Binh Dinh Pr, II Corps.
Mahoney Airfield (BS 875-117)
A.k.a. Mahoney Army AF. Apx 2 km SW Tan Quan, 12 km due N LZ English, 28 km SSE Duc Pho AF, 6 km from ocean and 2 km W QL-1, per TPC K-10A. El. 32'. Listed as "Insecure, US Army, 4Sep67, AF # VA2-282," in Aug69 TAD per Frank Penk, Jr. Not in Feb73 TAD. Also listed at BS 880-030. Binh Dinh Pr, II Corps.
Mai Cay Ga (CP 0-6)
A.k.a. Mui Cay Ga and Mui Ke. Coastal point at 12°18'N-109°15'E. On ND49-13 JOG. Khanh Hoa Pr, II Corps.
Mai Dang CAP (YD 3-4)
Vicinity of Hai Lang. Listed as Phon Mai Dang at CAP website but properly Thon Mai Dang or Mai Dang Phuong. CAP 4-2-8 here, per Tim Duffie. Quang Tri Pr, I Corps.
Mai Ke Ga (CP 0-6)
See Mui Cay Ga. Khanh Hoa Pr, II Corps.
Mai Linh SF Camp (BQ 245-929)
A.k.a. Mail Linh FOB, Cheo Reo or Hou Bon SF Camp? In valley of Ba Ayun River, apx 92 km SW Qui Nhon, 36 km NW Phu Tuc, 40 km ESE Phu Nhon and 125 km NW Nha Trang. 5th SF, Det 23. Transferred to RF/PF. Info per *SF Order of Battle.* Phu Bon Pr, II Corps.
Mai Linh, Camp (n/a)
See Phu Thien SF Camp. II Corps.
Mai Loc (YD 094-444)
Ville and SF Camp apx 25 km due W Quang Tri and 8 km SSW Cam Lo. Became fwd CP for 2 Bns of 101st Abn on 30Sep69. 1st and 2d Bn, 506th Inf landed at old USMC AF here 30-31Sep, to allow 3d Mar Div to re-deploy elsewhere in I Corps. In eight-Co CA next day, Currahees then built 2 FSBs, Scotch and Shrapnel. 101st left area on 31 Oct69 as Marines/1st ARVN Div returned. Attacked 10Apr70. Also at YD 094-518. Quang Tri Pr, I Corps.
Mai Loc Airfield (YD 092-516)
Apx 25 km due W Quang Tri and 8 km SSW Cam Lo. El. 348', 3,200' laterite rwy. At 16°44'17"N-106°57'43"E. Also listed at YD 086-508. Quang Tri Pr, I Corps.
Mai Loc SF Camp (YD 0865-5080)
Apx 25 km due W Quang Tri and 8 km SSW Cam Lo. 5th SF. Info per *SF Order of Battle.* Quang Tri Pr, I Corps.
Mai Loc, FSB (YD 094-518)
Apx 25 km due W Quang Tri, 8 km SSW Cam Lo. See Mai Loc. XXIV Corps grid. Sep70. Quang Tri Pr, I Corps.
Mai Son (n/a)
Mapsheet name of L-7014-5751-2. NVN only.
Mai Xa (n/a)
Mapsheet name of L-7014-6149-2. NVN only.
Mai Xa Chanh Command Post (YD 280-667)
Apx 6 km WSW mouth of Cua Viet River and 16 km NNW Quang Tri. May68. Quang Tri Pr, I Corps.
Mai Xa Thi (YD 280-666?)
A.k.a. Mai Xai Tai? On N bank of the Cua Viet River and km SW its mouth, some 6 km NE Dong Ha. USMC plt-sized basecamp in ruins of Catholic Church on bank of Dong Ha(?) River. Apparently near Cua Viet Naval cmpd. Patrols from base were run along river's edge and inland to free-fire zone between river and DMZ, per *Combat Medic*, p. 94 (sp Mai Xi Tai). Quang Tri Pr, I Corps.
Mai Xi Tai (YD 280-666?)
See Mai Xa Thi. Quang Tri Pr, I Corps.
Main Force VC Units (n/a)
See Glossary.
Main Office, The (XS 91-97?)
See RMK-BRJ Main Office. Gia Dinh Pr, III Corps.
Majestic, Hotel (XS 86-92?)
At 1 Tu Do St., Saigon. Gia Dinh Pr, III Corps.
Mak Phout Airfield (TH 18-76)
LS-137. CIA/SF, per *Air Facilities Data-Laos.*
Mallard, LZ (XD 779-438)
Apx 8 km WNW Khe Sanh CB and 1 km E Lang Ruon. 70 XXIV Corps grid per D. Armstrong. Quang Tri Pr, I Corps.
Mallet (n/a)
6Apr70, XXIV Corps proposed III MAF FSB name.
Mambo, LZ (BS 875-049)
Apx 4 km N LZ English, 9 km SSW Gia An and 2 km W QL-1. Mar67. Binh Dinh Pr, II Corps.
Mameluke Thrust, Operation (n/a)
18May-23Oct68. 1st Mar Div op. 2,278 rptd NVA KIA, per *VN Order of Battle*, pp 9-14. Quang Nam Pr, I Corps.
Man Lyr Base Area (Cambodia)
Apx 10 km W Duc Lap. NVA/VC staging area opposite 4th Div's AO and immed adj to Quang Duc Pr. Cambodia.
Man Tribes (n/a)
See Glossary.
Man's Head, The (WD or XD?)
Terrain feature of Xe Krong River in northern Laos. Cited in *Da Nang Diary*, at p 38. Laos.
Manasas, LZ (BS 555-679)
See Manassas, LZ. Quang Ngai Pr, I Corps.

Manassas, LZ (BS 551-663)
Apx 6 km NW Nghia Hanh AF and 12 km SW Quang Ngai. Also listed at BS 552-666 and BS 555-679. Map is L-7014-6739-3. Spelled Manasas on XXIV Corps facility index of 6Apr70. Americal list. Quang Ngai Pr, I Corps.

Manchester, LZ (BS 302-882)
In Song Tra Bong River Valley, apx 3 km W Tra Bong AF and 28 km SW Chu Lai. Grid per ORLL. Americal list. Quang Ngai/Quang Tin Pr border, I Corps.

Manchu International Airport (XT 450-263)
At or immed S Gia Binh and QL-1, apx 43 km NW Saigon and 20 km WNW Cu Chi CB. Humorous nickname for FSB Martha. Photo of sign at www.oregoncoast.com/willy/cp13.jpg reads: *Manchu International Airport, Use Gate 23 for Exit, Elevation 5'; Clear Weapons Before Entry-The Life You Save May be Your Replacement; Coffee Shop At XT 450-263;* (*two lines unreadable*); *KEEP UP THE FIRE.* Per Larry Criteser, Martha was built during Feb/April 67 by elements of 4th/9th Manchus. Aug '67, was in AO of 2d/12th?, 4th/9th Inf, 25th Inf Div and 187th AHC. Mentioned on at 187th's site at: www.kbi.org/187thahc/stories/bauman.htm. FSBs Martha, Betty and Caroline were apparently within apx 4 to 5 km of one another; with B/4/9 at Betty, C/4/9 at Caroline and A/4/9, 25th Inf at Martha in '67. Tay Ninh Pr?, III Corps.

Mang Buk (n/a)
Mapsheet name of L-7014-6638-4. SVN.

Mang Buk (new) SF Camp (AS 998-420)
Just E Mang Buk AF, apx 72 km WSW Quang Ngai and 28 km NNW Plateau Gi. 5th SF. Info/grid per *SF Order of Battle.* Transferred to RF/PF camp. Also listed at AS 9841-4180. Kontum Pr, II Corps.

Mang Buk (old) SF Camp (AS 998-420)
See Mang Buk (new) for location. 5th SF Grp CIDG Det A-246, Ju64 and SF Det 15. Grid per *SF Order of Battle.* Also listed at AS 9841-4180. Kontum Pr, II Corps.

Mang Buk Airfield (AS 983-417)
Apx 68 km SW Quang Ngai AF, 43 km NE Dak To AF, 30 km NNW Plateau Gi AF, per TPC K-10A. El. 4,068', 2,000' earth/PSP rwy. At 14°50'05"N-108°11'55"E. Also listed at AS 998-420. Kontum Pr, II Corps.

Mang Giang Pass (BR 223-520)
Viet spelling apparently Anglicized into "Mang Yang." See Mang Yang Pass. Pleiku Pr, II Corps.

Mang Yang Pass (BR 223-520)
Strategic mtn pass along QL-19E between An Khe and Pleiku, apx 26 km WNW An Khe and 36 km W of the Deo Mang Pass. Hwy 19E was main supply rte between Qui Nhon and Pleiku. 10" fuel pipeline and numerous pumping stations that ran road's entire length were the frequent target of VC/NVA attacks and sabotage. LZs Schueller and Action were among many bases used to keep it open. Pass itself became famous due to 1954 Viet Minh ambush of French Armored column, G.M. 100, in which entire force was annihilated. The white crosses of French graves could still be seen from below pass in US War, and were stark warning of potential danger (Viets may have removed crosses after '75?). Map at www.rjsmith.com/mang_yang.Html, and on L-7104-6637-2 map. Excellent photos of pass and FSBs in area on Fred Lohr's webpage at: www.sirinet.net/~flohr/photo.htm. See *Groupement Mobile 100* in Glossary. Pleiku Pr, II Corps.

Mang Yang Pass Cemetery (BR 227-529)
See French Cemetery, Mang Yang. Pleiku Pr, II Corps.

Mang Yang Pass, FSB? (BR 223-563)
Apx 18 km E Suoi Doi, 4 km N the Mang Yang Pass and 28 km WNW An Khe. 2d/17th Arty here supt 1st Cav, 12Jan66. Data per Jack Picciolo. Pleiku/Binh Dinh Pr border, II Corps.

Mang Yang, FSB ? (BR 121-549)
On S side QL-19 at Dinh Dien Dak Quon, apx 7 km E Suoi Doi and 35 km ENE Pleiku. 2d/17th Arty here supt 1st Cav, Jul66. Data per Jack Picciolo. Binh Dinh Pr, II Corps.

Mango, LZ (YC 957-834)
Apx 8 km ESE Ruong Ruong, 47 km WNW Da Nang AB. Apr70 XXIV Corps grid per Don Armstrong. Thua Thien Pr, I Corps.

Manitowac County, USS (n/a)
LST-1180. SVN.

Manley, USS (n/a)
DD 940. Accidental explosions in 5-inch/54-Caliber mounts of destroyers *Manley* and *Bigelow* (DD 942) during Spring '67, reduced the number of ships available for Naval Gunfire Supt Unit.

Mann, USNS (n/a)
MSTS Transport, per Ralph Fries.

Manor BOQ (XS 8-9)
At 31 Cao Thang St., prior to Jul 62, 16 rms, Saigon. Per *VN Military Lore, 1959-1973*. Gia Dinh Pr, III Corps.

Mans, Col des (VK 8-7)
Mtn pass. NIMA data. NVN.

Mans, Col des (XL 1-2)
Mtn pass. NIMA data. NVN.

Mansfield, USS (n/a)
DD 728. On 25Sep67, NVA fire near DMZ hit the Destroyer *Mansfield*; I KIA, 2 WIA USN sailors.

Mantle, LZ (BR 768-658)
Apx 4 km SW Hoi San, 36 km NE An Khe and 12 km W QL-1. Oct66. Binh Dinh Pr, II Corps.

Manua Kea, USS (n/a)
AE-22. Aux Explosive.

Manuna Loa, USS (n/a)
AE-8. Aux Explosive, per Ralph Fries.

Mao, LZ (BR 670-847)
Apx 1 km Nghia Nhon, 13 km WNW Ha Tay AF and 20 km WSW Bong Son. Jan67. Binh Dinh Pr, II Corps.

Mao Khe Coal Mine (XJ 4-3 or XJ 6-2)
Apx 1 km NW Mao Khe, 30 km NNW Haiphong and to N the Da Bach River. French position here overrun during battle of Mao Khe, 27-28Mar51. See Mao Khe, Battle of.

Mao Khe, Battle of (XJ 4-3 or XJ 6-2)
NVN Coal mining ville apx 30 km NNW Haiphong and just N the Da Bach River. Following his stunning defeat at Battle of Vinh Yen, 13-17Jan51, Gen. Giap turned his focus toward this sensitive area. The area controlled the approaches to coal mines around Mao Khe and was within 30 km of Haiphong Port. The 308, 312th and 316th Vietminh Div began ops here with an opening attack toward Mao Khe the night of 23-24Mar51. The French had 3 positions defending the town and nearby mine: 3 French

NCO's and 95 Tho Tribesman under a Viet Lt defended the mine itself; the RICM had an armored car plt defending Mao Khe, which straddled Road 18; and E the ville was a Co of 30th Composite Sengalese plus more Tho partisans. These 400 men became the focus of a 3 Div VM attack beginning at 0400, 27Mar51. The French were able to move 3 destroyers and 2 LST's up the Da Bach River and their gunfire plus bombing and strafing courtesy B-26's and Hellcats, as well as an attack by 6th French Paras from W, helped save the beleaguered garrison. The VM suffered over 400, while the French lost apx 40 KIA and 150 WIA. See Chp 2 of *Street Without Joy*, pp 41-43, w/map on p 42.

Mao Tao Secret Zone (YS)
A VC/NVA staging and basecamp area near Gia Ray and Nui Chua Chan Mtn. Was 173d Abn LRRP recon zone during Op Toledo, Aug66. Phuoc Tuy Pr, III Corps.

MAP (n/a)
Military Assistance Program. A US program that provided various acft to French during 1st Indochina war beginning in 1951.

Mara, Fort (BN 030-730)
See Fort Mara. Lam Dong/Binh Thuan Pr border, II Corps.

Maragaret, FSB (YU 270-240)
See Margaret. Phuoc Long Pr, III Corps.

Marauder, Operation (n/a)
1-8Jan66. 173d Abn. 1st/503d and 1/RAR conducted air assault to area along Oriental River in Plain of Reeds, in Mekong Delta. On 2Jan66, the 2/503d engaged fortified positions using air, extensive Arty and tear gas. Numerous VC KIA, 326 suspected VC captured. 267th VC Bn badly mauled. Hau Nghia Pr, III Corps.

Marble Mountain (BT 100-660)
See Marble Mountains. Quang Nam Pr, I Corps.

Marble Mountain Airfield (BT 065-738)
A.k.a. Marble Mtn Air facility. Apx 5 km SE Da Nang's major Airport, 15 km SE of Red Beach AF, 17 km NNW Hoi An, 60 km NNW Tam Ky. USMC jet and helicopter airbase, home to 16th Combat Avn Grp. Described as a desolate, even ugly facility. Folklore has it than when Vietnamese learned it would become a US airbase, they pulled the coniferous trees then covering the area out by their roots and denuded the area completely. The Cao Do River ran along E edge of base. The USMC established their main helicopter base here when USAF brought in their attack and fighter acft to Da Nang. Team C-1, 5th SF Grp; MAG 16 all here. El. 29' with 4,500' and 1,000' asph rwys. At 16°01'46"N-108°15'24"E. Quang Nam Pr, I Corps.

Marble Mountain SF Camp (BT 065-738?)
A.k.a. Camp Villa Rosa? Said to have been at base of largest of Marble Mtns. Apparently attacked, 23Aug68, by NVA Sapper force. Attack discussed in article on Internet at www.stealth. net/~stan/nva/nva.htm. See Camp Villa Rosa? Quang Nam Pr, I Corps.

Marble Mountains (BT 065-738)
A.k.a. Alpha-6. A series of four (some say five), rugged marble outcroppings of volcanic origin, apx 15 km S Monkey Mtn, and 6 to 8 km SE Da Nang AB. The outcroppings were honeycombed with a maze of tunnels and beautiful, cavernous grottos. While these hills were quarried for their marble, they were also of great religious and spiritual significance to Vietnamese. There remains also a famous Religious shrine hewn out of a huge cavern on one of hills that was off limits to US forces during war for religious reasons. Was later discovered the VC/NVA used that shrine as major hospital and sanctuary throughout conflict and apparently with impunity, even though it was only stone's throw from US forces. Ironically, US SF camp and USMC's MAG-16 facilities lay within few hundred meters of this VC refuge. Team C-1, 5th SF Grp, MMAF, Marble Mtn Air Facility, HQ 1st Marine Air Wing (1st MAW). Quang Nam Pr, I Corps.

Marbre, Montagnes de (BT 0-7)
A.k.a. the Marble Mountains. Mtn range at 16°00'N-108°16'E. On ND49-01 JOG. See Marble Mtns. Quang Nam Pr, I Corps.

March, LZ (XT 644-283)
2 km W Song Saigon, 16 km SW Lai Khe and 12 km due N Cu Chi. Apr66. Binh Duong Pr, III Corps.

Marcia, LZ (BR 032-399)
Apx 27 km ESE Pleiku, 16 km S Suoi Doi AF and 10 km SSE Plei Kreh. Aug69. Pleiku Pr, II Corps.

Mardi, FSB (YS 605-617)
Apx 5 km N the coast, 2 km S Rte-23, 18 km ESE Nui Dat and 11 km E Dat Do. 161 Bty, RNZA (Horsford's Bty 18Mar69-18Sep69) FSB set here 16-23Apr69. In rice paddy with 3 rivers fringing its perimeter. On 1ATF NCO trng map per John Hollett. Also listed at YS 60-61. Phuoc Tuy Pr, III Corps.

Mardy, LZ (BR 074-430)
See LZ Marty. Pleiku Pr, II Corps.

Mare, LZ (BQ 774-239)
Near Ea Krong Hin River, apx 2 km S Bun Duk, 20 km S Son Hoa/Cung Son AF and 26 km NE Khanh Duong New AF. Mar-Apr67. Phu Yen Pr, II Corps.

Marech Airfield (n/a)
Apx 115 km W Phnom Penh. El. 425'. Cambodia.

Marechaux d' Empire (n/a)
Marshal de Lattre's jaunty nickname for the grp of Colonels defending the Red River Valley and his "*de Lattre Line*," per *Street Without Joy*, p 60.

Margaret, FSB (YS 209-848)
On E side of QL-15, apx 28 km NW Nui Dat, 1 km NNW FSB Clare and 1.5 km SW FSB Hiran. On 1ATF NCO trng map per John Hollett. Bien Hoa Pr, III Corps.

Margaret, FSB (YU 270-240)
Apx 22 km NE Song Be, 25 km NW Duc Phong and 14 km SSW Djamap. Built Feb70-Apr70, by B/8th Engr Bn, 1st Cav. Also sp Maragaret? Phuoc Long Pr, III Corps. [350]

Margaret Brown, SS (n/a)
Merchant ship under govt contract, per Ralph Fries.

Marge (n/a)
6Apr70, XXIV Corps proposed Americal FSB name.

Marge, FSB (n/a)
FSB/patrol base of the199th LIB carried on 199th LIB Assn's FSB list. No grid available. III Corps.

Marge, FSB (XU 258-143)
If grid correct, was apx 10 km NNW Memot AF, 16 km N the SVN border and 64 km due N Tay Ninh. Cambodia.

Marge, FSB (XU 732-075)
Along QL-13 near Loc Ninh AF, apx 21 km N An Loc and 75 km NE Tay Ninh. 1st Cav, '69. Grid per Frank Penk, Jr. Also listed at XU 739-062. Binh Long Pr, III Corps.

Marge, LZ (BT)
Site described as having been N of Dragon Valley (BT 03-33 or AT 84-34), but Americal list grid at BT 185-674 is in ocean and cannot be correct? Likely somewhere generally W or NW of Tam Ky. 2d/1st Inf/196th LIB re-established this base 16Jan71. Quang Nam or Quang Tin Pr, I Corps.
Margo, FSB/LZ (XD 901-609)
In Valley of Cam Lo River apx 23 km due W Cam Lo and 45 km WNW Quang Tri. Built Sep68? G/2d/26th Mar Div apparently here at one point. 2d/26th Marines here '68 and/or '69. 101st Abn inactive FSB grid per Don Armstrong. Quang Tri Pr, I Corps.
Maria, FSB (XT 183-761)
19 km NNW Nui Ba Den, 24 km due N Tay Ninh West AF and 11 km NW FSB St. Barbara. Tay Ninh Pr, III Corps.
Marge, FSB (YS 578-779)
See FSB Marj. Phuoc Tuy Pr, III Corps.
Maria, FSB (YT 290-070)
Apx 42 km NNW Nui Dat, 16 km W to WSW Xuan Loc, 16 km ENE Long Thanh North AF, 3 km S QL-1 and 32 km ESE Bien Hoa AB. Grid/name per Eric Weil. 161 Bty, RNZA (Hitching's Bty 14Apr68-18Mar69) FSB set here 5-8Mar69 (right section). 1ATF. Long Khanh Pr, III Corps.
Maria, LZ (ZT 213-036)
Along QL-1, apx 3 km WSW Ap Phu Hung, 17 km WSW Phan Thiet and 15 km WSW Phan Thiet AF/LZ Betty. Oct70. Binh Tuy Pr, III Corps.
Marie, LZ (AQ 876-249)
E of a plantation, apx 16 km WSW Buon Ho AF, 7 km NNE Quang Nhieu, 20 km NNE Ban Me Thuot and 14 km W QL-14. A Bty, 2d/9th Arty here Dec69. 4th Div 31Jan70 ORLL grid per Jim Henderson. Darlac Pr, II Corps.
Marie-Rose M. (n/a)
See Glossary.
Marietta, LZ (YA 766-492)
A.k.a. Maryetta, and Mary Etta. Apx 9 km NW Plei Djereng New AF, 7 km SW Plei Djereng AF, 46 km due W Pleiku and 3 km S the Se San River. Per Dick Arnold, was built by 1st/35th Inf, 7Dec68, and named for wife of B Co 1st/35th's 1Sgt: "Was 1st listed in logs with 'Marietta' sp (town in Georgia), while all spellings afterwards are 'Mary Etta' or some convoluted variation! Logs also state that Top's wife was chosen, 'Because the Captain's girlfriend already has one named for her.' "10th Cav, 4th Div here, per Bob Patsfield. Per Dave Fogg, 6Dec68 Daily Journ says "B Co will make a C/A from their night location to grid YA 762-492 to build a new firebase…called Marietta" and Dave adds that Marietta was named for B/1/35 1Sgt's wife. Grid courtesy Dick Arnold as per Jan-Mar69 1st/35th Inf Bn daily logs. Also listed at YA 664-921, but that grid thought to be in error. Kontum Pr, II Corps.
Marijuana Dogs (n/a)
See Glossary.
Marijuana Usage (n/a)
See Drug Abuse in Glossary.
Marine Hill (YD 03-06?)
A.k.a. Hill 227or 222 or 249, and possibly Turkey Ridge? Per brother-in-law of Dennis Rees (5th Mech), Marine Hill was USMC battle site or position somewhere just E FSB Fuller (Dong Ha Mtn), N QL-9, WNW? of Cam Lo and apparently near Dong Ha CB. Described as Hill 227 or may have been (or inc) either Hills 222 or 249, that were part of Turkey Ridge? Quang Tri Pr, I Corps. [351]
Marine Unit, Vietnam (n/a)
See Glossary.
Marion, LZ (YD 115-173)
Just SE Pa Ling, apx 22 km SSW Ba Long AF and 41 km SW Quang Tri. Apr70 XXIV Corps grid per Don Armstrong. Quang Tri Pr, I Corps.
Marisa, FSB (YU 454-222)
Apx 16 km NNE Duc Phong, 21 km SE Djamap AF and 30 km SE Cambodia. Described as 1st Cav "Mini-firebase." Built Feb70-Apr70, B/8th Engrs, 1st Cav. [352] Cited in *11th ACR Cambodia Invasion AAR, 1st Cav Div, May-Jun70*, courtesy Lou Rochat. [353] Phuoc Long Pr, III Corps.
Marj, FSB (YS 578-779)
Apx 17 km NE Nui Dat, 5 km ENE FSB Longreach and 3 km SW FSB Raglan. On 1ATF NCO trng map per John Hollett. Phuoc Tuy Pr, III Corps.
Mark, LZ (BS 730-329)
Apx 10 km WSW Duc Pho AF and QL-1. 1st Cav. Name/grid per Dan Gillotti. Quang Ngai Pr, I Corps.
Mark, LZ (BR 827-816)
Apx 3 km SE Ha Tay and 13 km SSW Bong Son. Oct66. Binh Dinh Pr, II Corps.
Mark, LZ (XD 9-3?)
See Thor, LZ. Quang Tri Pr, I Corps. [354]
Mark, USS (n/a)
AKL-12. Amphib Attack. Cargo.
Mark Twain, LZ (BR 277-209)
Overlooked branch of Song Ba River, apx 32 km SW An Khe, 37 km NNE Cheo Reo AF, 15 km NE De Ping Djong, and 7 km SW LZ Caldera. A Bty, 6th/29th Arty here, Jun70. 4th Div 31Jul70 ORLL grid, per Jim Henderson. Binh Dinh Pr, II Corps.
Markab, USS (n/a)
AR 23. Repair and Maint Ship under NSA Saigon.
Market Time, Operation (n/a)
See Glossary.
Market Time Facility, Cam Ranh (CP 04-16?)
At Cam Ranh Bay. Joint USN/US Coast Guard/VN Navy off shore patrol facility, responsible for controlling NVA water based infiltration into SVN. Khanh Hoa Pr, II Corps.
Market Time Facility, Qui Nhon (CR 08-23?)
See Qui Nhon Market Time. Binh Dinh Pr, II Corps.
Marla, FSB (ZT 213-036)
Along QL-1, apx 18 km WSW Phan Thiet, 2 km NE Ap Phu Minh, 5 km SE Ap Hu Sung and 130 km E to ENE Saigon. Opened or reopened 7Oct70, closed 18Oct70. 2d/11th ACR Name/data per *1st Cav Div Op Rpt, ending 31Oct70*, courtesy Peter Cole. Binh Thuan Pr, II Corps.
Marla, LZ (YD 334-504)
See Mirla, LZ. Quang Tri Pr, I Corps.
Marlene, LZ (ZA 108-395)
Apx 15 km WSW Pleiku, 8 km W Plei Pao Xoi and 11 km WNW Catecka AF. C Bty, 2d/29th Arty here Dec69, and elements of 10th Air Cav here also. 4th Div 31Jan70 ORLL grid per Jim Henderson. Pleiku Pr, II Corps.
Marne, FSB (AT 843-419)
Apx 7 km SW An Hoa, 8 km SE FSB Champagne and 7 km ENE FSB Lance. Used during '69 USMC 1st Mar Div assault on base Area 112. On map in *US Marines in*

Vietnam-1969, p 90. Apr70 XXIV Corps grid per Don Armstrong. Quang Nam Pr, I Corps.

Mars, FSB (YT 102-344)
Apx 22 km SE Phuoc Vinh, 23 km NNE Bien Hoa AB and 10 km SSE Bao Phung. Opened or reopened 5Oct70, closed 24Oct70. 1st/12th Cav per *1st Cav Div Op Rpt, ending 31Oct70*, per Peter Cole. Bien Hoa Pr, III Corps.

Mars, LZ (XD 907-543)
On Nui Tia Pong Hill Mass, overlooking Khe Trinh Hin River Valley, apx 9 km WSW Thon Son Lam, 11 km NW Ca Lu and 33 km WSW Dong Ha. Apr70 XXIV Corps grid per Don Armstrong. Quang Tri Pr, I Corps.

Mars, USS (n/a)
AFS 1. Combat Stores Ship.

MARS Station AB8AN (WS 84-10?)
Military Amateur (or Affiliated?) Radio Service station at Can Tho. See Can Tho. Phong Dinh Pr, IV Corps.

Marsh, Camp (CQ 200-428)
At Tuy Hoa. Named to honor PFC Johnny Joe Marsh, B Bty, 5th Bn, 27th Arty, 101st Abn, KIA 6Mar66, by mortar fire during attack of newly formed Arty base at Tuy Hoa. Per Ray Bows, was dedicated 10May67. Grid is for AB. Phu Yen Pr, II Corps.

Marsha, FSB (n/a)
No data. 10th Cav, 4th Div here, per Bob Patsfield. Possibly Binh Dinh or Pleiku Pr?, II Corps.

Marsha, FSB (XT 597-822)
Apx 2 km SE tip of Fishhook, and 16 km W An Loc. Apparently 3d/11th Arty with Bty of 155s here during Cambodian Incursion(?), per *11th ACR Cambodia Invasion AAR, 1st Cav Div, May-Jun70*, courtesy Lou Rochat. [355] Grid per Dan Gillotti. Tay Ninh Pr?, III Corps.

Marston Matting (n/a)
See Glossary.

Martain, FSB (XT 703-147)
Apx 6 km due E Cu Chi, 11 km W Phu Cuong and 22 km NNE Tan Son Nhut AB. Sp both "Martain" and "Martian?" Aug68. Binh Duong Pr, III Corps.

Martha, Camp (XT 450-263)
See FSB Martha at grid. Hau Nghia Pr, III Corps.

Martha, FSB (XT 450-263)
A.k.a. Manchu Intl Airport. At or immed S Gia Binh and QL-1, apx 43 km NW Saigon and 20 km WNW Cu Chi CB. Photo of sign here reading "*Manchu International Airport, Use Gate 23 for Exit, Elevation 5', Clear Weapons Before Entry-The Life You Save May be Your Replacement, Coffee Shop At XT 450263,* (*two lines unreadable*), *KEEP UP THE FIRE,*" is at www.oregoncoast.com/willy/cp13.jpg. Per Larry Criteser, was built Feb/April 67 by 4th/9th Manchus. Aug '67. In AO of 2d/12th?, 4th/9th Inf, 25th Div, and 187th AHC. Mentioned on 187th AHC's website at: www.kbi.org/187thahc/stories/bauman.htm. FSBs Martha, Betty and Caroline were apparently all within about 4 to 5 km of one another; with B/4/9 at Betty, C/4/9 at Caroline and A/4/9, 25th Inf at Martha in '67. Also listed at XT 443-264, Sep67. Hau Nghia Pr, III Corps.

Martha Raye (n/a)
See Raye, Martha, in Glossary.

Martian, FSB? (XT 703-147)
See FSB Martain. Binh Duong Pr, III Corps.

Martin, Camp (YU 143-072)
At or just N Song Be AF, W Phuoc Binh, 23 km SE Bu Dop AF and 40 km due E Loc Ninh. Nov69-Jan70. Phuoc Long Pr, III Corps.

Martin, Camp (YS 140-980)
See Martin Cox. Bien Hoa Pr, III Corps.

Martin Cox, Camp (YS 140-980)
A.k.a. Bearcat. At Bearcat, adj to Long Thanh North AF and Tri Quyet Thang SF Camp. Originally a French AF prior to WWII, then Japanese AF, and French again at start of US involvement. Later SF Camp named to honor SFC Martin Cox, USA, B/1st Engr Bn, 1st Inf Div, KIA 6Apr66, when jeep hit land mine apx 32 km from Bearcat (brother-in-law was in same convoy). Original main base of 9th Inf Div until Mar67 or '68, and also home to Royal Thai Army HQ. Also listed at YS 170-990, 160-000, 175-995 and YT 165-001 (also correct though in different UTM zone). Bien Hoa Pr, III Corps.

Martine, FSB (YS 259-759)
On E side of QL-15 apx 20 km WNW Nui Dat, 11. 5 km NW FSB Weir and 4.5 km due W FSB Melissa. On 1ATF NCO trng map per John Hollett. Phuoc Tuy Pr, III Corps.

Marty, LZ (BR 074-430)
Apx 5 km W Chu Rran Mtn (a.k.a. Hill 1551), 12 km SSE Suoi Doi AF, 10 km N LZ Doris, 15 km S LZ Blackhawk, 30 km ESE Pleiku and 12 km SE Plei Kreh. 4th Div AO, '70. Name/grid per Jim Claeys. Pleiku Pr, II Corps.

Maruk Airfield (PQ 0-0)
At 12°42'00"N-99°58'00"E. NIMA data. Thailand.

Marvin the Arvin (n/a)
See Glossary.

Mary, FSB (YA 764-326)
A.k.a. Hill 705(?) and FSB Mary S. On Hill 705 (or its mass), apx 10 km SW Plei Beng, 12 km NW Duc Co and 49 km WSW Pleiku. Apparently built Nov68 by 4th Div. Grid per 4th Div Ops Report for period ending 31Jan69. Pleiku Pr, II Corps.

Mary, FSB (YS 456-875)
Along LTL-2, apx 20 km NNE Nui Dat and 7 km WSW FSB Flinders. On 1ATF NCO trng map per John Hollett. Phuoc Tuy Pr, III Corps.

Mary, LZ (BN 524-764)
Apx 6 km WSW peak Ya Bo Mtn, 29 km W Phan Rang, 27 km WSW Phan Rang AB and 18 km due W Thon Huu Duc. Jan67. Ninh Thuan Pr, II Corps.

Mary, LZ (BR 499-489)
Along Rte 508, apx 4 km NE main An Khe AF and 21 km WNW Binh Khe. Apr67. Binh Dinh Pr, II Corps.

Mary, LZ (BS 904-150)
Apx 2 km N Gia An, 14 km NNE LZ English and 1 km W QL-1. Feb67. Quang Ngai Pr, I Corps.

Mary, LZ (YA 586-483)
On Cambodian border at S entrance to Plei Trap Valley, apx 65 km due W Pleiku and 6 km SE Phum Hay. Jan66. Kontum Pr, II Corps.

Mary, LZ (YA 784-917)
A.k.a. LZ Mistress Mary. At N end of Plei Trap Valley and along its E edge, apx 3 km SE Plei Trop, 26 km due W Polei Kleng and 46 km WNW Kontum. 1st/35th Inf, 4th Div rptd here, 1340 hrs 6Mar69. On map at www.landscaper. net/chighmap.jpg. 7th/15th Arty here at

one point. Also listed at YA 789-917 and 764-236? Listed grid per Ben Youmans, David Fogg and Tom Lacombe. Kontum Pr, II Corps.

Mary, LZ (YA 82-09?)
If grid correct, was along Ia Drang River apx 12 km NW Chu Pong Mtn, 12 km WNW Anta Village, 35 km due W Plei Me, and only 2 km from Cambodia. Used in opening stages of 1st Ia Drang Battle. 3Nov65, was named to honor Mary Black, wife of reporter Charlie Black (who'd covered the 1st Cav from its birth as 11th Air Assault Div), by LTC John B. Stockton, CO 227th AHB, 1st Cav. Ambush sprung nearby by 1st Cav was Div's 1st successful ambush of war. Ambush also triggered 1st night helo reinforcement of a unit in war, and also helped 1st Cav perfect use of gunship ARA supt to within 50 meters of friendlies. [356] Mortar Plt of A/1st/8th Cav, 1st Cav was suptg. Cited in 1st Cav VN *Yearbook* Aug 65-Dec69, p 185, 239, 251, 294, and in *Pleiku,* p 137, 144, 145, 148, 152, 276, per peter Cole. Grid is est. Pleiku Pr, II Corps.

Mary, LZ (YT 265-999)
Apx 20 km WSW Duc Phong, 13 km SE Song Be/Phuoc Binh and 12 km NNW Bunard AF. 2d/8th Cav, 1st Cav here Sep-69, per Frank Penk, Jr. Phuoc Long Pr, III Corps.

Mary, LZ (YT 993-845)
Apx 11 km WNW Tan Phat AF, 8 km NW Bao Loc AF and 6 km SE LZ Liz. Feb67. Lam Dong Pr, II Corps.

Mary, LZ (YU 138-072)
NW Phuoc Binh/Song Be, apx 2 km due N Song Be AF and 5 km WSW Song Be City AF. 1st Cav. Name/grid per Dan Gillotti. Phuoc Long Pr, III Corps.

Mary, LZ (ZB 059-475?)
If listed grid zone correct, was apx 4 km W Tou Morong and 64 km NNW Kontum. Jun66. Actually listed at YB 059-475 in error as that grid puts site in Laos and 60 km W SVN border? Kontum Pr, II Corps.

Mary Ann, FSB/LZ (AS 962-998)
Apx 57 km W Chu Lai, 7 km WNW Hau Duc 40 km SW Tam Ky and 22 km SW Tien Phuoc AF. On remote hill that overlooked Song Tranh and Nam Nim River Valleys near their confluence. Attacked and overrun 28Mar71, with 30 US KIA and 78 WIA, but only 15 known NVA KIA. Drug use, poor discipline and poor leadership were cited as contributing factors to the defeat (see *Sappers in the Wire* for detailed account of battle). Possibly built in 2 locations of Americal AO? Const of '70 era Mary Ann began 19Feb70, when D/1st/46th Inf, assaulted into site, followed shortly by HQ, 2d and 3d Plts, A/26th Engrs at 1045hrs that same day. 1 hr later, a CH-46 brought in Case 450 bull-dozer and by 1400 hrs, 3 gun pits, the FDC and CP bunkers were complete. Then Engrs began removal of surrounding vegetation. Const continued thru 20Feb70 and on 21Feb70, two-105mm howitzers of B Bty, 3/82d Arty were brought in at 1140 hrs. Fire missions commenced and basic FSB was complete that day. Also listed at AS 962 999, AS 959-999 and AS 961-882. Listed grid/info per Tommy Poppell, B/1st/46th, 196th LIB/Americal. Quang Tin Pr, I Corps. [357] [358]

Mary Etta, LZ (YA 766-492)
A.k.a. Maryetta, and Marietta. Apx 9 km NW Plei Djereng New AF, 7 km SW Plei Djereng AF, 46 km due W Pleiku and 3 km S the Se San River. Per Dick Arnold, was built by 1st/35th Inf, 7Dec68, and named for wife of B Co 1st/35th's 1Sgt: "Was 1st listed in logs with 'Marietta ' sp (town in Georgia), while all spellings afterwards are 'Mary Etta' or some convoluted variation! Logs also state that Top's wife was chosen, 'Because the Captain's girlfriend already has one named for her.' "10th Cav, 4th Div here, per Bob Patsfield. Per Dave Fogg, 6Dec68 Daily Journ says "B Co will make a C/A from their night location to grid YA 762-492 to build a new firebase…called Marietta" and Dave adds that Marietta was named for B/1/35 1Sgt's wife. Grid courtesy Dick Arnold as per Jan-Mar69 1st/35th Inf Bn daily logs. Also listed at YA 664-921, but that grid thought to be in error. Kontum Pr, II Corps.

Mary Gwen, FSB (XT 526-796)
Apx 24 km WSW An Loc, 42 km NE Tay Ninh and 23 km ESE Katum. In use at least 25Feb-2Mar70. Was 1 of 7 FSBs opened and closed in as many weeks by 2d/8th Cav, 1st Cav, prior to Cambodian Incursion (7 were: Jamie, Mary Gwen, Heather, Victor, Flashner, Drum and Illingworth. Tay Ninh Pr, III Corps.

Mary Jane, Camp (AR 810-890?)
At Kontum. Home of Kontum sector MACV Advsy team. Possibly at SF camp or AF? Cited in *Vietnam Military Lore, 1959-1973*. Kontum Pr, II Corps.

Mary Lou, LZ (BT 132-203)
A.k.a. LZ Marylou, Nui Vu, LZ 2, Howard's Hill, LZ East and Hill 488. Apx 16 km W Tam Ky, 10 km SE LZ Center and 6 km NNE Tien Phuoc AF. Per Ben Youmans and Dick Arnold, was named for wife of LTC Robert G. Kimmel, Bn CO, 1st/35th Inf/3rd Bde/4th Div, who was shot down and killed while directly over A/1st/35th Inf, 14Nov67. Used by 1/35th while opcon to Americal Div, working area between Duc Pho and Da Nang. Grid per Americal list. Quang Tin Pr, I Corps.

Mary Lou, LZ/FSB (ZA 228-829)
A.k.a. Marylou, and FSE Mary Lou. Along E side(?) of QL-14, apx 7 km S Kontum and 33 km due N Pleiku. Dick Arnold reports it a fwd FSB of 1st/35th Inf, 4th Div, Oct67 to Nov67, during Op Wheeler. Per John Rochelle, it was "on the edge of a hill, rather than on its top." 10th Cav, and 1st/92d Arty, 4th Div here, among others. Battle here apx 14May69, per Eric Weil, 7th Cav, 1st Cav. 4th Div Op Rpt for period ending 31Jan69 (per Craig Miller) states that it was apparently rather large and provided many services: "Div Supt Cmd operates FSE Mary Lou suptg 2d Bde...[providing] Class I, II, III, IIIA and IV fast moving items and barrier material...1st Log Cmd ASP...provides graves registration service." Also listed at ZA 228-878, 228-838, 22-75 and 20-73? Grid per Craig Miller. Photos/maps of base at http://1-14th.com/maps.html. Kontum Pr, II Corps. [359].

Mary S, FSB (YA 764-326)
A.k.a. Hill 705(?) and simply FSB Mary. On Hill 705 (or its mass), apx 10 km SW Plei Beng, 12 km NW Duc Co and 49 km WSW Pleiku. Apparently built in Nov68 by 4th Div. Grid per 4th Div Ops Rpt for period ending 31Jan69. Pleiku Pr, II Corps.

Mary's Strip Airfield (RA 02-53)
LS-258. CIA/SF, per *Air Facilities Data-Laos.*

Maryetta, LZ (YA 766-492)
See LZ Mary Etta. Kontum Pr, II Corps.

Maryland BOQ (XS 8-9)
At 41 Nguyen Duy Duong St., Saigon. Per R. Bows' *Vietnam Military Lore, 1959-1973.* Gia Dinh Pr, III Corps.
Marylou, LZ (BT 132-203)
See Mary Lou at grid. Quang Tin Pr, I Corps.
Marylou, LZ (ZA 228-829)
See LZ Mary Lou at grid. Kontum Pr, II Corps.
Masher/White Wing, Operation (n/a)
A.k.a. Thang Phong II and later renamed White Wing. 24Jan-6Mar 66. 1st Cav, ROK and ARVN ROKs. Included 1st significant cross-CTZ-border op. USMC on Op Double Eagle moved S into Binh Dinh Pr, joining 1st Cav elements. 2,389 NVA/VC KIA, per *Vietnam Order of Battle*, pp 9-14. Soon after Op Masher was publicized on US TV, the Pentagon was told to change its name to something less graphic. Name then became "White Wing," but level of its violence was unfettered by switch. Quang Ngai/Binh Dinh Prvs, I/II Corps.
Massachusetts, LZ (YD 143-188)
A.k.a. LZ Missouri? Apx 3 km NE Pa Ling, 21 km S Ba Long AF and 38 km SSW of Quang Tri. Apr70 XXIV Corps grid per Don Armstrong. Quang Tri Pr, I Corps.
Massachusetts BOQ (XS 827-939)
At 1 Vo Tanh St., Saigon. Per R. Bows' *Vietnam Military Lore, 1959-1973.* Gia Dinh Pr, III Corps.
Massey, USS (n/a)
DD-778, per Ralph Fries.
Massey Harris, Operation (YS 6-6)
29Aug-20Sep70. 1ATF op to destroy gardens (of 84th VC Rear Services Grp) hidden under canopy in Binh Chau area, along lower Phuoc Tuy/Binh Tuy Pr border, SE Xuyen Moc. Data per Eddie Tricker's summary at www.diggerz.org. III Corps.
MAT Teams (n/a)
See Glossary.
Mat Tran To Quoc (n/a)
See Glossary.
Mat, FSB (ZT 018-055)
Apx 10 km ESE Song Dinh, 36 km W Phan Thiet, 22 km NNE Ham Tan AF and 6 km N QL-1. Opened or reopened 9Sep70. 2d/11th ACR Data per *1st Cav Div Op Rpt, ending 31Oct70*, courtesy Peter Cole. 5th/12th Inf, 3d/7th Inf, 199th LIB also here. Binh Tuy Pr, III Corps.
Mathew, LZ (BR 817-850)
See Matthew. Binh Dinh Pr, II Corps.
Mathews, USS (n/a)
AKA-96. Amphib. Attack. Cargo ship. Served in vicinity of Chu Lai in at least May-Jun65.
Mattaponi, USS (n/a)
AO-41. Aux Oiler.
Matthew, LZ (BR 817-850)
Apx 16 km SSW Bong Son, 4 km SSE Ha Tay AF, 6 km ESE Phu Xuan and 48 km NE An Khe. Oct66. Binh Dinh Pr, II Corps.
Mattie, LZ (BR 225-238)
Apx 30 km SW An Khe, 18 km NNE De Ping Djong, 21 km NW Plei Niang and 5 km NE Dak Pihao River. Possibly named to honor PFC Andrew M. Mattie, KIA 23Feb69 (only KIA with that last name). 1st/92d attached 17th Arty here supt 1st/10th Cav, 9Sep69. Name/grid per Jim Claeys. Binh Dinh or Phu Bon Pr, II Corps.
Mattie, LZ? (BR 421-820?)
Grid is either error or site was a.k.a. LZ Niagara? LZ Niagara consistently listed at this grid on same Jul70 date. See Niagara for location. Binh Dinh Pr, II Corps.
Matty, LZ (BR 225-238)
See Mattie. Binh Dinh/Phu Bon Pr, II Corps.
Maty, LZ (BR 225-238)
See Mattie. Binh Dinh/Phu Bon Pr, II Corps.
Mau Ca Heliport (BS 044-991)
Along Rte 531, apx 16 km SSW Tien Phuoc and 4 km NE Hau Duc. Heliport #613, alt?, at: 15°21'30"N-108°14'45"E, per Feb73 TAD. Quang Tin Pr, I Corps.
Mau Chanh CAP (AT 8-4?)
CAP 2-9-1 and 2-9-2, 2d CAG here per T. Duffie's website at www. capmarine.com. Quang Nam Pr, I Corps.
Maud, LZ (BT?)
A.k.a. LZ Maude? Americal Assn list indicates site was NW LZ Professional (BT 173-077), which suggests it may not be same Maude as that listed at AT 835-757. It also says initial site clearing made with 10,000 pound bomb (Combat Trap), apx Aug70, which also seems unlikely for the AT location of Maude? See Combat Trap and Daisy Cutter in Glossary. Quang Nam or Quang Tin Pr, I Corps.
Maud, LZ (AT 837-757)
See Maude. Quang Nam Pr, I Corps.
Maude, LZ (AT 835-757)
Apx 4 km WSW Thon Phuoc Son, 17 km due W Da Nang AB, 6 km NW Hieu Duc and 24 km NNE Ha Tan AF. May-Jul71. Americal list indicates an LZ Maud was NW LZ Professional; hence, may not be same as this Maude, and that initial site clearing made with 10,000 pound bomb apx Aug70. Americal list. Quang Nam Pr, I Corps.
Maumee, USS (n/a)
T-AO 149. 190,000-barrel Fuel Tanker, MSTS fleet.
Maurean, LZ ? (YD 281-122)
If grid correct, was apx 48 km WSW Hue and 16 km E Tou Rout. Nature of site unknown, but apparently not same as FSB Maureen at YD 428-121? Thua Thien Pr, I Corps.
Maureen, FSB/LZ (YD 429-122)
A.k.a. Hill 980 or Dong Tam Hanh. Apx 32 km WSW Hue, 5 km due S FSB Granite, 15 km ENE FSB Bradley and 10 km W FSB Kathryn. During Lam Son 720, beginning Apr '71, FSBs Fury, Kathryn, Maureen, Gladiator and later Eagle's Nest were all reopened by B/326th Engrs, with 3d Bde/101st Abn providing security. FSBs Co Pung, Binh Dinh and Kim Qui were also built during that op. 101st Abn FSB. Listed as an LZ, 22Jul68, and as a FSB, 28Jul69. Also listed at YD 428-119, 428-122 and YD 482-124 (likely transposition error). Thua Thien Pr, I Corps.
Maureen, FSB (YS 435-766)
Apx 9 km N Nui Dat, 3 km SW FSB Alanbrooke and 2 km W FSB Le Loi (at LTL-2). FSBs Maureen, Robin and Rhode Island all appear to have been near one another and may be succession of bases since it seems unlikely they would have coexisted. On 1ATF NCO trng map per John Hollett. Phuoc Tuy Pr, III Corps.
Maurice Rose, Gen., USS (n/a)
A.k.a. AP 126. MSTS or *USNS*? In '65, delivered some initial elements of 1st Cav to SVN, including 2d/7th Cav. Cited in *Baptism*.

Maury, FSB (XT?)
Location unknown. 7th/11th Arty, 25th Div here '68. Name/data per Dan Gillotti. III Corps.
Maury, USS (n/a)
AGS 16. Hydrographic Survey Ship. USN.
Maverick (n/a)
Apr70, XXIV Corps proposed 101st Abn FSB name.
Maverick, LZ (YA 686-414)
Apx 3 km E Ya Krong Bolah River and Cambodia, 16 km WSW Plei Djereng New AF and 53 km WSW Pleiku. Jan66. Kontum Pr, II Corps.
Maverick, FSB (ZC 145-533)
In Song Thu Bon River Valley either at, or immed N, Ha Tan AF/SF Camp, apx 35 km SW Da Nang AB. Apr70 XXIV Corps grid. Quang Nam Pr, I Corps.
Max, LZ (BS 756-469)
Along QL-1 near Thac Tru, apx 27 km SSE Quang Ngai, 7 km SE Mo Duc AF, 8 km SE Quang Hien and 10 km NNW Duc Pho. Apr70 XXIV Corps grid per Don Armstrong. Also listed at BS 763-472 per19th Engr Bn website at: http://home.earthlink.net/ ~engr19/dlaugoct68.htm. Also at BS 759-469 and 763-472 (Jul68-Apr70). Map is L-7014-6738-2 (An Lao), per Ray Smith. Quang Ngai Pr, I Corps.
Max, LZ (XT 700-755)
Apx 13 km NE Minh Thanh AF, 13 km SSW An Loc and 7 km W Tan Khai/Ql-13. Aug67. Binh Long Pr, III Corps.
Max Von Sydow (n/a)
See Shotgun, Operation.
Maxwell, FSB (ZC 098-418)
A.k.a. Hill 508? Apx 4 km W to WSW FSB Cudgel (ZC 193-450), on a plateau overlooking the valley of Song Cat River, 16 km SW Ha Tan AF, 26 km WSW An Hoa AF and 51 km SW Da Nang AB. Used by USMC Task Force Yankee Dec68-Feb69. On map in *US Marines in Vietnam-1969*, p 90, as being at roughly ZC 10-45, some 8 km ENE FSB Tomahawk (not same as 101st Abn FSB Tomahawk), 8 km SE LZ Javelin and 6 km SSE COB Scimitar. Quang Nam Pr, I Corps. Apr70 XXIV Corps grid per Don Armstrong. Quang Nam Pr, I Corps.
May Bay My, 4181 (n/a)
See Glossary.
May, LZ (XT 148-309)
On Cambodian border, apx 22 km SSW Tay Ninh and 25 km WNW Go Dau Ha. Mar66. Tay Ninh Pr, III Corps.
May, LZ (XT 625-288)
Apx 3 km SE Xa Douc, 16 km WSW to SW Lai Khe and 15 km NNW Cu Chi. Jan66. Binh Duong Pr, III Corps.
Mays, LZ (BR 753-698)
Apx 37 km NE An Khe, 6 km WNW Hoi San, 27 km SSW Bong Son and 14 km SSE Ha Tay AF. Oct66. Binh Dinh Pr, II Corps.
May Tao Secret Zone (YS)
VC Staging area in 1ATF's AO. 161 Bty, RNZA (Kenning's Bty 13Jul65-13Jun66) FSB set here 30Mar-3Apr66. Phuoc Tuy Pr, III Corps.
Mayaquez, SS (n/a)
Merchant ship under govt contract, per Ralph Fries.
Mayaguez Incident (TS 96-40)
12-15May75. See Koh Tang Island for history.
Mayréna, Charles-Marie David de (n/a)
See Kingdom of Sedang.
McCaffery, USS (n/a)
DD-860, per Ralph Fries.
McBride, Camp (BT 0752-7193)
Near coast, apx 8 km SE Da Nang AB and 3 km S Marble Mtn AB. 5th SF Det C-1 here. Named to honor SSgt Claude "Mickey" McBride, KIA 23Aug63, by sniper after breaking up ambush of his patrol near An Diem (see McBride BOQ), per *Vietnam Military Lore, 1959-1973*. Grid per *SF Order of Battle*. Quang Nam Pr, I Corps.
McBride BEQ (XS 8-9)
At Cholon, Feb66, and closed prior to '68, Saigon. Named to honor SF SSgt Claude "Mickey" McBride Det A-18, KIA 23Aug63 by sniper after breaking up ambush of his patrol near An Diem. Gia Dinh Pr, III Corps.
McCarthy BOQ (XS 8-9)
Oct 65-68, 56 rms, Saigon. Named to honor Capt Walter R. McCarthy, who was KIA 16Jun62, with 1LT William F. Train (see Train Cmpd), during ambush near Ben Cat Spec Forces Camp 34 km N Saigon. Gia Dinh Pr, III Corps.
McClellan, FSB ? (XT 286-686)
Apx 24 km SE Thien Ngon AF, 21 km S Katum AF and 11 km NNE Nui Ba Den. FSB? Jan68. Tay Ninh Pr, III Corps.
McClintock, FSB (YD 04-31)
Near or possibly on Nui Gia? Apx 37 km SW Quang Tri, 15 km SSE Vandegrift CB, 5 km ESE FSB Mink, 5 km NW FSB Fisher, 10 km ESE FSB Whisman. On 15Jan69, helicopter carrying Col Michael Spark, Rgt CO 3d Marines, LTC Ermil Whisman, CO 1st/12th Marines and 3d Rgt SgtMaj Ted McClintock was shot down near FSB Maxwell during TF Yankee, an attack on Base Area 112. FSBs were later named after all 3 men. USMC, '69. Grid per map at p 73, *US Marines in Vietnam-1969*. Quang Tri Pr, I Corps.
McCoy/Kelley, FSB (BS 539-732)
See FSB 4-11. Quang Ngai Pr, I Corps.
McDermott, Camp (CP 051-501)
A.k.a. Camp John F. McDermott and J. F. McDermott. In heart of Nha Trang, near S bank of Song Cai River and at its mouth, apx 3 km NNE Nha Trang AF. Named to honor Sp4 John F McDermott, US Army Supt Facility, KIA 18Nov65. Grid is for Heliport. Khanh Hoa Pr, II Corps.
McDermott Airfield, Camp (CP 039-520)
See Nha Trang AF. Khanh Hoa Pr, II Corps.
McDermott Heliport, Camp (CP 051-501)
Along S bank of the Song Cai River near its mouth, and within city of Nha Trang. "El. apx 16', peneprime, 1 hr PPR, Ctc Nha Trang Dust-Off Ops 46.9. High wires all quadrants. At 12°12'20"N-109°12'35"E," per Feb73 TAD. Khanh Hoa Pr, II Corps.
McDermott, J. F., Camp (CP 051-501)
See McDermott, Camp. Khanh Hoa Pr, II Corps.
McGuire Rigs (n/a)
See Glossary.
McKean, USS (n/a)
DD 784. On 5Aug65, deployed to SEA, and on 7Dec65, began coast supt duty. On night of 15Dec65, VC/NVA attacked SVN RF outpost at My Trang (Quang Ngai Pr), but within 20 min of battle's start, *McKean* began delivering WP, HE, and Illum over 5 hours. Gen. Huang Xauw Lam, CG 2d ARVN Inf, said, "Naval gunfire…was a major factor in defeating the enemy and making the

battlefield so untenable that he abandoned his dead and wounded as well as arms and equipment." Left SEA 20Dec65 and returned to 22 Dec66 for SAR duty in Gulf, serving as helo in-flight refueling ship and gun platform until 23Jan67, and again on gun-line from 23Feb-12Apr67 (firing some 4,090 rounds of 5").

McKinley Ammo Stg. Area (CP 095-230)
On Cam Ranh Bay Peninsula, apx 3 km SW the S end of main AF rwy. Named to honor Sp6 Paul B McKinley, KIA 22Nov67, when VC booby-trapped Jeep he and Sp5 Dean Moore were using N of Phan Thiet. Note: Alpha, Alpha, Charlie and Yankee Ammo Stg areas at Cam Ranh renamed either Black, McKinley or Moore in ceremony, 12Jul69. Khanh Hoa Pr, II Corps.

McLain, Operation (n/a)
20Jan68-31Jan69. 173d Abn recon-in-force pacification op. 1,042 NVA/VC KIA, per *Vietnam Order of Battle*, pp 9-14. Binh Thuan Pr, II Corps.

McMorris, USS (n/a)
DE-1036. DD-Escort, per Ralph Fries.

McNair, FSB (XT 454-270)
Apx 25 km NE Cu Chi and 19 km SSW Dau Tieng/Tri Tam. Possibly named to honor SSgt Willie C. McNair, KIA 19Devc67. Oct-Nov68. Tay Ninh Pr, III Corps.

McNamara's Wall (XD/YD)
An electro-mechanical barrier that was the brainchild of Secty of Defense Robert S. McNamara. Originally code named "Project Practice Nine" (later renamed "Project Illinois City"), this proposed 300 yard wide swath of land immed south of DMZ was to be cleared of vegetation (via Rome Plow) and filled with mines, electronic sensors and OPs. Cut was supposed to run from ocean to Lao border and was meant to stop NVA infiltration across DMZ. Though test portions were constructed, it was never implemented due to its extremely high cost and impracticability. Idea was generally viewed as naive, over-ambitious and as complete folly by both US troops and press. During the 1630's, the Nguyen Dynasty attempted to create an earlier version of McNamara's Wall in another unsuccessful effort to prevent invasions from N. These two 20' high walls were also built near the 17th Parallel. See Saigon Moat. Quang Tri Pr, I Corps.

McNerney, FSB (BR 023-522)
Along QL-19, apx 5 km SW Suoi Doi AF, 25 km ENE Pleiku and 47 WNW An Khe. Cited in *Brennan's War*, and described as having been between Mang Yang and Pleiku. No casualty by this name in CACF. Name/data per Jim Claeys. Apr69. Pleiku Pr, II Corps.

Me Ann Heliport (WS 933-630)
Apx 32 km ENE Cao Lanh AF, and either a.k.a. or just S of My An Heliport (WS 933-636). Heliport #614, alt 7', at: 10°31'30"N-105°51'45"E," per Feb73 TAD. Kien Phong Pr, IV Corps.

Me Linh (XT 276-785)
At or just N Prek Klok, apx 12 km SSW Katum, 30 km N to NNE Tay Ninh and 22 km due N Nui Ba Den. Tay Ninh Pr, III Corps.

Me Linh, FSB? (XT 276-785)
At or just N Prek Klok, apx 12 km SSW Katum, 30 km N to NNE Tay Ninh and 22 km due N Nui Ba Den. Either ville or FSB involved in Cambodian Incursion, May-Jun70, per *11th ACR Cambodia Invasion AAR, 1st Cav Div, May-Jun70*, courtesy Lou Rochat. [360]

Me Phuc Tay SF Camp (n/a)
SF Camp mentioned in Michael Herr's *Dispatches*, p. 257. Likely is My Phuoc Tay SF Camp at XS 201-598. See that entry. Dinh Tuong Pr, III Corps.

Meade, FSB (BR 805-724)
Apx 43 km NE An Khe and 11 km due S Ha Tay AF. Oct66-Feb67. Binh Dinh Pr, II Corps.

Meade, LZ (XT 605-112)
Apx 6 km SW Cu Chi. Jul68-May69. Also listed at XT 600-100 and 612-116. Hau Nghia Pr, III Corps.

Meat Market, The (CP 03-53?)
In Nha Trang. Apparent daily routine at main gate of 173d Abn cmpd (began at apx 1700 hrs during at least '70), during which hundreds of Lambretta Motor scooter-borne prostitutes would be dropped off into what John Rotundo, describes as a "holding pen." "American GIs would then select their 'dates' from the pen and escort them onto the post for a movie, ice cream or just plain screwing until they had to be picked up later in evening," per *Charlie Ranger*, p 213. Khanh Hoa Pr, II Corps.

Mecon or **Mecom River** (WT, WS, XS, XR)
See Mekong River. IV Corps.

Medregal, USS (n/a)
AGSS-480. SVN.

Meeker County, USS (n/a)
LST-980. Lndg. Ship, Tank, per Ralph Fries.

Meg, LZ (YA 560-545)
Along Cambodian border, apx 4 km NNE Phum Hay, 28 km due W Plei Djereng (old) AF and 67 km WNW Pleiku. Jan66. Kontum Pr, II Corps.

Megan, FSB (n/a)
No data available.

Mekong Delta (WT, WS, XS, XR)
Per Courtney Frobenius, the Mekong River Delta is in reality formed by three major river systems. 1st system consists of 3 rivers: the Dong Nai, Song Be, and Saigon, all of which originate within and drain S II and N III Corps. 2d system is formed by 2 rivers just S Saigon and N My Tho: the Vam Co Dong and Vam Co Tay, which originate in Cambodia and enter VN generally through the Parrot's Beak and Plain of Reeds. 3d system includes 2 rivers: the Mekong and Bassac, whose delta in geologic sense is the most recent and largest river delta on earth. Much of Mekong in VN is a tidal river that can rise and fall as much as 10' twice daily at peak tides. Roughly 26,000 sq mi in size, it also includes very complex and elaborate maze of canals, sloughs and channels. Its very fertile soil is excellent for growing rice and most SE Asia rice is harvested here. Delta also provided very difficult terrain in which to conduct military ops, and US 9th Inf Div/USN combined Inf and water-borne tactics to create MRF concentrated on ships and floating man-made bases throughout region in order to overcome those difficulties. Throughout war, its vast mangrove swamps remained largely a VC stronghold. IV Corps.

Mekong River (WT, WS, XS, XR)
A.k.a., the Mecon, Mecom, Mekong, le Cambodge, Tonle Thom and Song Lon. Originating in mtns of SW China, the mighty Mekong drains vast region of Asia and SE Asia

during its 2,800 mile journey to fertile delta SE of Saigon. On journey south, it passes through or borders Burma, Thailand, Laos, Cambodia and Vietnam. 1st explored by westerners in mid-to-late 19th century, the Mekong's origins remained unknown to western world until start of 20th Century. Much of Mekong in VN is tidal river that can rise and fall as much as 10' twice daily at peak tides. See Mekong Delta. IV Corps. [361]

Melanie, FSB (n/a)
No data. FSB listed by W. Stan Tyson (CO 1st/12th Cav, Sep71-Jun72) as related by Peter Cole. If Tyson was referring to base used during his period as CO, it was likely in W or central III Corps.

Melbourne (n/a)
Australian Escort ship serving under US 7th Flt.

Melia Jaune (n/a)
See Glossary.

Melinda, FSB (XT 167-366)
See FSB Molinda. Tay Ninh Pr, III Corps.

Melinda, FSB (YT 17-40)
If grid correct, was apx 33 km NE Bien Hoa AB and 27 km NW Xa Binh Hoa. 3d/7th Inf, 199th LIB. Long Khanh Pr, III Corps.

Melissa, FSB (YS 304-761)
Apx 16 km NW Nui Dat, 1 km S FSB Jill and 7.5 km ESE FSB Chestnut. On 1ATF NCO trng map per John Hollett. Phuoc Tuy Pr, III Corps.

Mello, LZ (AT 805-158)
Possibly a.k.a. LZ Mellon? Apx 32 km due W Tien Phuoc AF and 14 km SW Hiep Duc. Apr70 XXIV Corps grid. Quang Tin Pr, I Corps.

Mellon, LZ (AT 804-184)
Possibly a.k.a. LZ Mello? In Que Son Valley apx 50 km due W Tam Ky. Built to block NVA/VC infiltration rte from Kham Duc area to W. Also listed at AT 805-184, 805-183 and 803-181. Map is L-7014-6640-3. Americal list. Quang Tin Pr, I Corps.

Mellon, USCGC (n/a)
WHEC 717. 31Mar70-2Jul70. Sqdn 3 CGC, during Coast Guard's 5th deployment.

Melody, LZ (AR 995-196)
Apx 25 km NNE Phu Nhon AF, 17 km E My Thach/QL-14 and 24 km SE Camp Enari. Sep69. Pleiku Pr, II Corps.

Memot Airfield (XU 296-056)
Apx 8 km W the SVN border, 120 km NW Saigon SVN, 140 km ENE Phnom Penh, 35 km SW Snuol and 16 km N Katum SVN AF, per TPC K-10D. Sp Mimot on Feb67 Natl Geo map. Elements of 2d/60th(?) Inf here early Jun70, per David Argabright. 3,570' rwy, El. 262'. Cambodia.

Memphis, LZ (XD 877-355)
Apx 9 km SSE Khe Sanh and 20 km SW Ca Lu. '70 XXIV Corps grid per Don Armstrong. Quang Tri Pr, I Corps.

Mendota, USCGC (n/a)
WHEC 69. 28Feb69-3Nov69. Sqdn 3 CGC.

Meng Ho, Operation (n/a)
Common ARVN Op name. Meant "Fierce Tiger."

Menu, Operation (n/a)
Top secret and illegal B-52 bombing raids of NVA/NLF sanctuaries in Cambodia. Began 18Mar69 and continued until May70, when allied forces invaded Cambodia, at which time it was renamed Op Freedom Deal and expanded to targets all over Cambodia. On 15Aug73, the US Congress terminated its funding after some 16,527 sorties and dropping of 383,851 tons of munitions.

Meo Tribes (n/a)
See Glossary.

Mercer, USS (n/a)
APB-39. Originally APL-39, then reclassed as APB-39 in 1945. Was barracks ship built on a LST hull. Arrived at Vung Tau, 31Jul68, then moved to Mekong Delta as mobile base for river sqdns of MRF, TF-117. Data per MRF Assn website. III, IV Corps.

Mercury BEQ (XS 8-9)
At 190 Su Vanh Hanh St., Saigon. Per R. Bows' *Vietnam Military Lore, 1959-1973.* Gia Dinh Pr, III Corps.

Mercury, LZ (XD 872-533)
Apx 7 km SSE Khe Sanh CB and 19 km SW Ca Lu. Apr70 XXIV Corps grid per D. Armstrong. Quang Tri Pr, I Corps.

Merdeilles, Ile des (YJ 0-1)
NIMA data. NVN.

Mere Gook Rule (n/a)
See Glossary.

Meredith, FSB? (BR? 318-058?)
If "BR" grid zone correct, was just E Song Ba River, apx 16 km SW Plei Niang, 43 km SSW An Khe and 52 km due W Van Canh AF. 10th Cav, 4th Div here. Grid without UTM per Bob Patsfield. Binh Dinh Pr?, II Corps?

Meredith, FSB/LZ (YA 916-277)
Apx 3 km SE Le Thanh, 20 km W Oasis, 6 km NE Plei Luong Ya Rang, 38 km WSW Pleiku and 18 km E Cambodia. 3d/8th Dragoons, 4th Inf reopened this base during Cambodian Incursion. John Linn was extracted from Cambodian Incursion to this FSB, May70, then trucked to Camp Radcliff for stand down. May be same Meredith described as having been a 1st Cav FSB in Cambodia and W Plei Djereng? Grid per Jim Claeys. Pleiku Pr, II Corps.

Meredith, FSB (YA?)
Described as having been a 1st Cav FSB built on small crest of ridgeline in Cambodia and W Plei Djereng Description does not correspond with that of 4th Div FSB Meredith at YA 916-277, which is inside SVN and some 20 km SSE Plei Djereng? Cambodia or SVN?

Meredith, LZ/FSB (YD 474-207)
Apx 26 km due W Hue, 13 km SSW Camp Evans and 10 km WSW Thanh Tan. Apr70 XXIV Corps grid per Don Armstrong. May68. Thua Thien Pr, I Corps.

Meredith Victory, SS (n/a)
Merchant ship under govt contract, per Ralph Fries.

Merideth (n/a)
See Meredith. This sp in 1st Cav VN *Yearbook* Aug 65-Dec69, p 99, per Peter Cole.

Merrell, Camp (BT 555-035?)
At Chu Lai. Named to honor CPL Lowell, H. Merrell, USA, first KIA Marine of 1st Force Recon in VN, KIA 22Apr65 in ambush S the Tra Bong River. Camp built near site of his death. Data per *Vietnam Military Lore, 1959-1973*, p 90. Quang Tin Pr, I Corps.

Merrick, USS (n/a)
AKA 97. Amphib. Attack. Cargo. Served in vicinity of Chu Lai during at least May-Jun65.

Merrill D. Reich Training Area (CP 15-50)
On Hon Tre Island, apx 3 km E Nha Trang. Combat orientation trng center named to honor 1Lt Merrill D. Reich Jr, KIA 27May68, while training on same course. 5th SF Grp facility. Data per *Vietnam Military Lore, 1959-1973*. Khanh Hoa Pr, II Corps.

Merrimac, LZ (YD 123-321)
Near Khe Ta Laou River, apx 4 km due Ta Laou and 29 km SW Quang Tri. Apr70 XXIV Corps grid per Don Armstrong. Quang Tri Pr, I Corps.

Merry, FSB (AR 80-35)
Apx 12-14 km SSE Pleiku, 2 km SE QL-14/19, and about 10 km ENE Catecka AF. Arty site inside Camp Enari occupied by 7th/15th Arty, '71. 1Nov71 ORLL per Nolan Puttman. Pleiku Pr, II Corps.

Merveilles, Ile des (YJ 0-1)
Island of Wonder? NIMA data. NVN.

Mesopotamia, Little (WJ 25-85)
See Little Mesopotamia. NVN.

Messageries Mairitimes Piers (XS 8-9)
A.k.a. M&M Piers, Saigon. See 4th Transportation Cmd HQ, Saigon. Gia Dinh Pr, III Corps.

Metro, The (TJ 94-67)
French nickname for underground network of tunnels and bunkers at Dien Bien Phu. NVN.

Metro Station (n/a)
See Glossary

Metropole BEQ (XS 853-901)
At 148 Tran Hung Dao, Nov 65, Saigon. 106 rms across street from Hung Dao BEQ. Site of VC terrorist bombing, 4Dec65, causing 8 KIA and 160 WIA civilian, ARVN and US personnel. Data per R. Bows' *Vietnam Military Lore, 1959-1973*. Gia Dinh Pr, III Corps.

Mewal Airfield (AQ 851-236)
Apx 20 km NNE Ban Me Thuot, 6 km NNE Quang Nhieu and 17 km W QL-14. "Insecure, abnd, Pvt AF, 9Feb67, AF # VA2-101," in Aug69 TAD per Frank Penk, Jr. Not in Feb73 TAD. Darlac Pr, II Corps.

Mewal Plantation (AQ 855-235)
Center of mass apx 20 km NNE Ban Me Thuot, 5 km NNE Quang Nhieu and 16 km W QL-14. Staging area for E-301 VC Local Force Bn and in US 4th Div's AO. Also listed at AQ 866-222. Darlac Pr, II Corps.

Mewal Plantation SF Camp (AQ 905-190)
Apx 15 km NE Ban Me Thuot and 6 km NE Dat Ly, per *SF Order of Battle*. See Buon Tan Mo. Darlac Pr, II Corps.

Mexia (n/a)
Apr70, XXIV Corps proposed 101st Abn FSB name.

Mexico, FSB (YD 403-233)
Apx 34 km W Hue, 16 km SW Camp Evans and 16 km due W Ap Thanh Tan. 101st Abn inactive FSB grid per Don Armstrong. Thua Thien Pr, I Corps.

Meyerkord BOQ (XS 852-918)
At 89-91 Nguyen Du, Saigon, 1 block from Independence Palace. An officers R&R billet when it opened in '65, its address has also been listed as 113 Nguyen Du on later documents. Main PX was in same block? Named to honor LT Harold D Meyerkord, USN Advisor, River Assault Group 23, KIA 16Mar65, gunshot while on river patrol with RAG-23. Data per *Vietnam Military Lore, 1959-1973*. See *Meyerkord, USS*. Gia Dinh Pr, III Corps.

Meyerkord R & R Billet (n/a)
Named in memory of, Meyerkord, LT Harold D. No data.

Meyerkord, USS (n/a)
DE launched Oct65, and named to honor Lt Dale H. Meyerkord, USN, KIA 16Mar65; 1st American Naval officer to die in VN War. Meyerkord BOQ in Saigon also named for this officer Discussed in *Brown Water, Black Berets*, p 67. SVN.

Mia, Cape (BS 8-4)
See Cape Mai. Quang Ngai Pr, I Corps.

Mia Linh (various)
Villes with this name in grid squares: YD 3-4, YD 3-5 and YD 2-9. Quang Tri Pr, I Corps.

Mia Linh SF Camp (YD 3-4?)
Variant of Mai Linh SF Camp or My Linh? Grid may be in error, though a Mai Linh is in listed grid square. Also Mai Linh SF Camp at BQ 245-928. Quang Tri Pr, I Corps.

Mia Linh SF Camp (BQ 245-929)
A.k.a. Cheo Reo and/or Buon Beng SF Camp. Along Rte TL-2E, just W Cheo Reo AF and 2 km W Hou Bon, apx 78 km SE Pleiku. 5th SF, Det A-112, Oct65, A-226 Oct66. Phu Bon Pr, II Corps.

Miami, FSB (YD 153-337)
Apx 58 km WNW Hue, 26 km SW Quang Tri and 18 km SSE Mai Loc. Also listed at YD 155-336 per XXIV Corps index (Don Armstrong). Quang Tri Pr, I Corps.

Miami Beach (CQ 104-783)
At point where QL-1 runs along ocean, apx 10 km SSE Song Cau AF, 11 km N Tuy An. Apr69. Ken Williamson tells us B/84th Engrs where here. Possibly also recreation area? Phu Yen Pr, II Corps.

Miang Gang Pass (BR 245-506)
See Mang Yang Pass. Binh Dinh Pr?, II Corps.

Michael, FSB (XT 019-774)
Along LTL-20, apx 8 km SW Thien Ngon AF, 6 km from Cambodia and 35 km NNW Tay Ninh. 1st Cav, '68. Grid per Frank Penk, Jr. Also listed at XT 042-763, but unknown which grid is correct or if location moved? Tay Ninh Pr, III Corps.

Michael, FSB/LZ (XT 042-763)
Along LTL-20, apx 6 km SW Thien Ngon AF, 9 km E Cambodia, 35 km NNW Tay Ninh and 7 km ENE Lo Go. Also listed at XT 019-774, but unknown which grid is correct or if location moved? Tay Ninh Pr, III Corps.

Michael, SS (n/a)
Commercial contract tug, per Ralph Fries.

Michelin Rubber Plantation (XT 54-54)
A.k.a. Don Dien Michelin. Generally 25 km due E Tay Ninh, 25 km ESE Nui Ba Den, 35 km NW Cu Chi, and immed E and NE Dau Tien Intersected by Rtes 244 and 239 with QL-14 forming its western border, 10 km SW Minh Than Rubber Plantation and 20 km due W Ap Bau Bang. Roughly 12 x 18 km in size. Site of Op Attleboro: 196th LIB, and later elements of 4th Div, 25th Inf Div and 173d Abn along with ARVN elements totaling over 22,000 allied troops (largest op to that point in war), battling the 271st, 272d, and 273d and 101st VC Rgts (9th VC Div), Sep-Nov66. Shown on *Low Level Hell's* 1st Div TAOR map. Also good map/discussions of nearby battles in *The Infantry Brigade in Combat*. Listed grid is arbitrary pt. Was largest rubber plantation in SVN. It is said US forces were

required to pay owners for any Rubber Trees damaged or destroyed, thereby restricting ops within plantations. Binh Duong Pr, III Corps.

Michelle, LZ (YS 097-806)
Apx 14 km SSW Long Thanh AF and 33 km WSW Tan Son Nhut AB. Oct66. Bien Hoa Pr, III Corps.

Michelle, FSB (YT 285-098)
A.k.a. FSB Carol. Along QL-1, apx 30 km ESE Bien Hoa AB and 18 km W Xuan Locl km S QL-1. 69-70. Long Khanh Pr, III Corps.

Mickey, LZ (AQ 850-180)
Apx 3 km NE Quang Nhieu and 16 km NNE Ban Me Thuot City AF. Mar66. Darlac Pr, II Corps.

Middlesworth, Camp (BT 018-628)
A.k.a. FSB Dai Loc, FSB 412, Whiskey Tower and possibly FSBs Phong Luc I and/or II. Apx 9 km S Da Nang, 6 km ENE Hill 55, immed N An Tu 2, SE Phong Luc 2, N Phong Luc 3, and 2 km W QL-1. Unofficial nickname for this A Bty, 1st/11th Arty, 1st Mar Div FSB in '69. On map L-7014-6640-4. Named to honor a Bty Supply Cpl, who while impersonating a Marine Lt "liberated" very large and much-needed supply of socks for Bty from naval supply depot near Da Nang. The Cpl further distinguished himself during major NVA/VC ground and mosquito assault of Bty's position, Jul69, when he exposed himself repeatedly to enemy fire in order to deliver sorely need supply of mosquito repellent to the embattled bunker-line. Dai Loc District. Quang Nam Pr, I Corps.

Midway, USS (n/a)
CV-41. Acft Carrier. Deployed with CVW-5, 1Jan-31Dec75; with CVW-5, 1Jan-31Dec74; with CVW-5, 10Apr72-3Mar73; with CVW-5, 11Sep73-31Dec73; with CVW-5, 16Apr71-6Nov71; with CVW-2, 6Mar65-23Nov65. Was permanently home-ported in WESTPAC. See *Coral Sea, USS*. [362]

Miet Xa Heliport (XD 818-486?)
Apx 4 km N Ap La Vien, 9 km NW Khe Sanh CB and 53 km W of Quang Tri. Listed at ZD 818-486 in '69 TAD, but no such grid exists. However, NIMA lists a Xa Lang Miet in XD 7-4 and is likely location of Xa Miet. Not in '73 TAD. Data per Frank Penk, Jr. Quang Tri Pr, I Corps.

Mieu Giang Bridge (YD 2-6?)
A.k.a. Dong Ha Bridge. QL-1 bridge over the Mieu Giang River at Dong Ha. Quang Tri Pr, I Corps.

Mieu Giang River (YD 2-6?)
Cua Viet River is formed by confluence of Mieu Giang, Thach Han and Vinh Phuoc Rivers, all joining NW Quang Tri. Quang Tri Pr, I Corps.

Miguel, FSB (YD 484-206)
Apx 25 km due W Hue, 13 km SSW Camp Evans and 10 km NNE FSB Kathryn. 101st Abn inactive FSB grid per Don Armstrong. Also listed at YD 489-198. May-Nov68. Thua Thien Pr, I Corps.

Mike, FSB (XT 436-837)
Apx 14 km SE Katum, 6 km SE Bo Tuc and 37 km NNE Tay Ninh. 1st/7th Cav, 1st Cav here, per Frank Penk, Jr. Cited in *Anatomy of a Division*, and 2d/7th Cav Unit History '70-71, p 2, per Peter Cole. Tay Ninh Pr, III Corps.

Mike, LZ (AT 934-356)
Apx 8 km SE Phuoc Binh AF, 15 km SSE An Hoa CB and 5 km SW Ap Hai. Apr70 XXIV Corps grid per Don Armstrong. Quang Nam Pr?, I Corps.

Mike, LZ (BR 675-706)
Apx 3 km SSW Nghia Dien and 16 km NNE Vinh Thanh and 33 km NE An Khe. Sep-Oct66. Binh Dinh Pr, II Corps.

Mike, LZ (BS 930-258)
Near coast, apx 16 km NNE Gia An and 17 km SE Duc Pho AF. May67. Listed as in II Corps, but grid appears to be in I Corps? Quang Ngai Pr, I Corps.

Mike, LZ (XD 932-417)
Overlooking QL-9 to N and W, apx 9 km SW Ca Lu, 43 km WSW Quang Tri and 8 km E Khe Sanh CB. Surrounded on 3 sides by Quang Tri River and its tributaries. 1st/7th Cav CA'd to and secured site followed immed by 2d/7th Cav at opening of Op Pegasus. Quang Tri Pr, I Corps.

Mike, LZ (XS 521-979)
Apx 8 km WNW Duc Hoa AF and 7 km S Khiem Cuong. Mar66. Hau Nghia Pr, III Corps.

Mike, LZ (XT 407-179)
Just E Song Vam Co Dong River, apx 13 km NE Duc Hue AF, 7 km SSE Go Dau Ha and 25 km WNW Cu Chi. Jan66. Hau Nghia Pr, III Corps.

Mike Force (n/a)
See Mobile Strike Force Cmd.

Mike Force OP (XD 778-531)
Apx 14 km NNW Khe Sanh CB. CIDG OP during siege. Grid per *The Final Formation*. Quang Tri Pr, I Corps.

Mil, LZ (BS 392-501)
Apx 15 km W Minh Long AF and 11 km S Lang Re. 1st Cav. Name/grid per Dan Gillotti. Quang Ngai Pr, I Corps.

Mildred, FSB/LZ (BS 024-978?)
Apx 36 km SW Tam Ky, 3 km N Hau Duc and 18 km SSW Tien Phuoc. Also an LZ Mildred listed at BT 048-043, which is apx 5 km NE this site, and is possible they were same FSB? XXIV Corps grid. Quang Tin Pr, I Corps.

Mildred, LZ (BT 048-043?)
Apx 32 km SW Tam Ky, 7 km NE Old Hau Duc and 13 km SW Tien Phuoc AF. Also a FSB Mildred in XXIV Corps records at BS 024-978, which is apx 5 km SW this site. Possible they were same base? Quang Tin Pr, I Corps.

Mile, LZ (XD 993-516)
Apx 3 km N Ca Lu and 14 km SW Cam Lo. Apr70 XXIV Corps grid per Don Armstrong. Quang Tri Pr, I Corps.

Mile High, LZ/FSB (YA 937-931)
A.k.a. Hill 1198. Apx 8 km due W Polei Kleng and 32 km WNW Kontum. LZs Mile High, Incoming and Virgin were near N end of ridge overlooking N end of Plei Trap Valley. Had mutual suptg fire with FSB Brillo-Pad. 1st/35th Inf here Mar-Apr68, and possibly 173d Abn here, '67. HQ 1st/12th, 4th Div here early '69. 4th/4th Arty 105mm Bty and 4.2" mortar Bty here, '69. Per Phil Landis, from site he could look down on Brillo-Pad and watch incoming hit it. At p 83 of *Time Heals No Wounds*, author says it was not a typical LZ, "[Bn HQ] was in center of perimeter. In front was a pole, on it a human skull. Hair wrapped in plastic hung from pole. There was a sign shaped like a feather with '*RED WARRIORS*' printed on it." In late Apr68, 2 Cos of 1st/35th Inf left wire, moving across saddle on Hill 1198 to secure and clear a knob only 600 meters to N that was to become LZ Virgin. HQ of NVA 325C Div was there

when they arrived and, in vicious ambush, both Cos were badly mauled (per Ben Youmans). Tom Dilley says LZ called "Baldie" (possibly Virgin or Brillo Pad?) was nearby and within sight of Mile High. Also listed at YA 936-930. Grid per Phil Landis. Kontum Pr, II Corps.

Miles, FSB (XT 290-630)
Apx 3 km NNE peak Nui Ba Den, 17 km NE Tay Ninh West AF and 1 km E TL-4. Jul69. Tay Ninh Pr, III Corps.

Military Council, The (n/a)
See Glossary.

Military Operations (generally)
See Operation's name in main alpha listing. Entries are formatted name first, followed by a comma and then word Operation or Op. For example: Cedar Falls, Operation.

Military Police Billets, Saigon (XS 8-9)
At 96 Tran Hung Dao St., Saigon. Home of 560th MP Co until '66. Data per *Vietnam Military Lore, 1959-1973.* Gia Dinh Pr, III Corps.

Military Police Compound, Saigon (XS 8-9)
At 30 Petrus Ky St., Saigon. Home of 560th MP Co after '66, per *Vietnam Military Lore, 1959-1973.* Gia Dinh Pr, III Corps.

Military Regions (n/a)
See Glossary

Military Revolutionary Council (n/a)
See Glossary.

Military Schools (n/a)
See ARVN and RVNAF listings.

Miller, Camp (BT 55-03)
At Chu Lai. Was dedicated 9Jul67 to honor UTP2 James O. Miller, USN, 30th Naval Const Rgt, NMCB-8, KIA 6Feb67, during VC attack of Tam Ky's Payne Cmpd. Miller was 1st member of NMCB-8 to be KIA in VN. Data per Ray Bows. Quang Tin Pr, I Corps.

Miller, FSB (YD 973-361)
A.k.a. LZ Miller. Apx 3 km SW shore of Dam Cau Hai Bay, 14 km SE Phu Bai, 8 km due W FSB Roy, 2 km S QL-1 and about 1 km E Thon Ke Bang. 101st Abn AO. '69-70. Thua Thien Pr, I Corps.

Miller, FSB (YS 67-96)
A.k.a. LZ Miller. Apx 24 km ESE Xuan Loc, 24 km ENE Blackhorse Basecamp and 5 km S QL-1. 199th LIB. (Grid may also possibly be XS 67-96, which would put site 17 km E and slightly N Tan Son Nhut AB, in Gia Dinh Pr?) Long Khanh Pr, III Corps.

Miller, Patrol Base (XT 125-542)
Apx 5 km NW Tay Ninh West AF and 16 km WSW peak Nui Ba Den Mtn. Mar66-Mar69. Tay Ninh Pr, III Corps.

Miller, T.C. (AQ 870-998)
Along QL-14, at or near Phu Nhon AF. Nature of site and meaning of initials "T.C." unknown. 1st/92d Arty here '71, and PFC Thomas C. "TC" Miller was KIA 1Feb71, so possibly named in his honor? Pleiku Pr, II Corps.

Miller, Sgt Andrew, USNS (n/a)
See Evacuation of Da Nang.

Million Dollar Hill (AT 925-270)
A.k.a. Hill 102. Apx 8 km WNW Nui Liet Kiem/LZ West, 1 km NE Hill 108, 33 km WNW Tam Ky and 9 km SW LZ Dragon Base. Per Americal list, it was near Hiep Duc across "Old French Road" slightly N of LZ Karen, S Song Lau River and Nui Chom Mtn (SW Wedding Cake Hill?). Reportedly got its name from battle in which over a million dollars worth of helos were lost? See Million Dollar Hill or Knoll in II and IV Corps. Quang Nam Pr, I Corps.

Million Dollar Hill (VS 99-47)
A.k.a. Nui Coto or Nui Co To or Million Dollar Hill or Million Dollar Knoll. On Nui Coto Mtn and site of major battle against 510th VC Bn waged by 5th SF 521st MSF, 16-26Mar69. 1 of 7 peak grp rising from flat, mangrove plain generally E Ha Tien and N Rach Gia and collectively known as "Seven Sisters." Included Hue Duc Mtn (Hill 220), Nui Co To (Hill 61, just S Tri Tron), Dop Chompa (actually two separate peaks, highest of which is 710 meters, SW That Son AF), Hill 232 (near Chau Phu) and Hill 296 (5 km from Cambodia and 10 km N That Son). Chau Doc/Kien Giang Prvs, IV Corps.

Million Dollar Hill (YA?)
Near or in Plei Trap Valley. Per Tom Lacombe, who also says it was a.k.a. Silver Star Hill. Apparently not a FSB, but rather a battle site. Kontum Pr?, II Corps.

Million Fingers Massage Parlor (BR 47-45)
THE MILLION FINGERS MASSAGE PARLOR, LAUNDRY AND TANK WASH was printed on sign over a bar, brothel and laundry in Sin City near An Khe/Camp Radcliff. Sign proudly proclaiming its name also hung over entrance. When due to concerns for the morality and well-being of his troops, the 1st Cav's CG threatened to have it shut down, the sign was quickly replaced by another that read: *NO MORE WHOREHOUSE, LAUNDRY ONLY.* Data per *A Better War*, p 290. Binh Dinh Pr, II Corps.

Milt Reservation (XT 097-762)
Military Reservation? Possible ARVN base along W side QL-22, apx 8 km S Thien Ngon AF and 26 km SW Katum. Mar67. Nature of site unknown. Tay Ninh Pr, III Corps.

Milton, LZ (BR 6-6?)
Somewhere near LZs Horse and Hereford. Built suptg Op Crazy Horse, May66 and discussed in *Battles in the Monsoon*, p 88. 1st Cav. Binh Dinh Pr, II Corps.

Mimosa, LZ (ZC 180-134?)
If grid correct, was 10 km NE Kham Duc, 65 km WSW Tam Ky and 70 km SSW Da Nang AB. Grid rptd as ZC '1801344' and that typo may indicate it was either at 180-134, or 1801-344X?? If latter grid accurate, it was just a few km N FSB Javelin and 56 km SW Da Nang AB? Americal list. Quang Tin or Quang Nam Pr, I Corps.

Mimot (XU 296-056)
See Memot. Cambodia.

Mimot Airfield (XU 296-056)
See Memot AF. Cambodia

Min Rong Sakang Airfield (ZT 094-874)
See Xa Tan Rai AF. Lam Dong Pr, II Corps.

Minchac, Pointe (YJ 6-1)
See Pointe Mincha. NVN.

Minchao, Pointe (YJ 6-1)
See Pointe Minchao. NVN.

Mines, Grand Sommet des (YJ 4-3)
A.k.a. Nui Khe Thut. NIMA data. NVN.

Mines. Land (n/a)
See Glossary.

Mines, Pointe des (YJ 2-1)
See Pointe Mines. NVN.

Ming Hue Island (VS 5-0)
NIMA data. Kien Giang Pr, IV Corps.
Ming Mang's Tomb (YD 747-133)
See Minh Mang's Tomb. Thua Thien Pr, I Corps.
Ming Thanh Rubber Plant (XT 630-690)
See Minh Thanh Rubber. Binh Long Pr, III Corps.
Minh, LZ (BR 707-760)
Apx 7 km SSW Phu Xuan, 13 km SE Ha Tay AF and 37 km NE An Khe. Oct66-Jan67. Binh Dinh Pr, II Corps.
Minh Chau SF Camp (WS 929-993)
A.k.a. FOB Moc Hoa. S of Muc Hoa AF, 2 to 3 km S Moc Hoa and apx 78 km W Saigon. 5th SF. Info/grid per *SF Order of Battle.* Kien Tuong Pr, IV Corps.
Minh Dam Secret Zone (YS)
Area generally N of Vung Tau and SE Saigon. Nerve center for much VC activity. Long Dat District and villes of Long Dien and Dat Do were within zone. Vietminh/VC used former Japanese fortifications/caves in Long Hai Mtns to launch attacks on French, and the US and Australian forces who followed. On 18Feb70, 8 RAR engaged the 445D VC Bn here. Phuoc Tuy Pr, III Corps.
Minh Long, LZ (BS 541-525)
Near Minh Long AF, apx 24 km SSW Quang Ngai, and 15 km SSW Nghia Hanh AF. Apr70 XXIV Corps grid per Don Armstrong. Quang Ngai Pr, I Corps.
Minh Long (new) SF Camp (BS 5355-5099)
Apx 19 km due W Mo Duc AF and 21 km SSW Quang Ngai AF. Det A-108, 25Aug66. In Sep70, became 68th ARVN Border Ranger camp. Possibly a base before Aug66? Grid per *SF Order of Battle.* SW Quang Ngai. Quang Ngai Pr, I Corps.
Minh Long (old) SF Camp (BS 529-508)
SW Quang Ngai, apx 20 km due W Mo Duc AF, 22 km SSW Quang Ngai AF. Det A-108, 25Aug66. Relocated. Per Hank Anthony, site was also used as Forward Supply Point for 1st Bde/101st Abn during Op Malheur II, in '67. Elements of 1st/327, 2d/327th and 2/502d Inf here. Grid per *SF Order of Battle.* Quang Ngai Pr, I Corps.
Minh Long Airfield (BS 534-514)
Apx 19 km due W Mo Duc AF, 22 km SSW Quang Ngai AF, per TPC K-10A. El. 250', 2,000' rwy. At 14°55'42"N-108°42'31"E. Quang Ngai Pr, I Corps.
Minh Long Forward Supply Point (BS 529-508)
See Minh Long (old) SF Camp. Quang Ngai Pr, I Corps.
Minh Long Road (BS)
Routes 516 and 517. Quang Ngai Pr?, I Corps.
Minh Long, FSB (BS 536-511)
A.k.a. LZ Crunch. Apx 24 km SSW Quang Ngai, and 15 km SSW Nghia Hanh AF. Also listed at BS 458-466, 536-513 and 541-525. Americal List. Quang Ngai Pr, I Corps.
Minh Mang's Tomb (YD 747-133)
On S side Hwy 547 between FSB Birmingham and Pohl/Nam Hoa Bridge, apx 8 km S Hue. Tomb of Chinese VN Emperor Minh Mang. Noted for its beautiful grounds, sculpture and buildings, the tomb was/is large, walled cmpd of at least 50 acres. Was off limits to patrolling GIs. See Hue. Thua Thien Pr, I Corps.
Minh Thanh (XT 63-67)
Apx 43 km SSW Loc Ninh and 42 km NE Tay Ninh. During Op Junction City, Mar67, Minh Thanh was Fwd base for elements of 173d Abn. SF Camp, Army AF and rubber plantation also here. Binh Long Pr, III Corps.
Minh Thanh Airfield (XT 630-664)
Apx 43 km SSW Loc Ninh AF, 42 km NE Tay Ninh, 15 km WNW Chon Thanh AF and 45 km WSW Dong Xoai, per TPC K-10D. El. 164', 3,100' laterite rwy. At 11°27'10"N-106°29'47"E. Binh Long Pr, III Corps.
Minh Thanh Road (XT 70-75)
Road running between Minh Than and QL-13, joining QL-13 apx 2 km S An Loc. Battle of Minh Thanh Road took place beginning 9Jul66, during Op El Paso II, when 272d VC Rgt hit 1st/4th Cav, 1st Inf Div, in 3 separate ambushes along road between An Loc and Minh Thanh. Action notable in that it taught US forces how to use armor in breaking up convoy attacks. 238 VC KIA. As a result of this battle and actions at Ap Tau O and Srok Dong, the 1/4th Cav received the PUC. Binh Long Pr, III Corps.
Minh Thanh Rubber Plantation (XT 630-670)
Adj to Minh Thanh, apx 35 km NE Tay Ninh, 1 km W Rte 242 and 10 km NE Michelin Rubber Plantation. Binh Duong Pr, III Corps.
Minh Thanh SF Camp (XT 6435-6682)
N of LTL-13, apx 42 km ENE Tay Ninh and 73 km NNE Tan Son Nhut AB/Saigon. SF Det 51, 5th SF Grp; Det. A-9, Dec64, Det A-332 (was 332-A), Oct65, A-332 Oct66. Later an RF/PF camp. Grid per *SF Order of Battle.* Binh Long Pr, III Corps.
Minh, FSB? (n/a)
Cited in 1st Cav VN *Yearbook* Aug 65-Dec69, p 89, per Peter Cole. No data.
Mini, FSB (WT 9-4?)
Described as being E of Kampong Tasuos (WT 8-2) on bank of Rach Cai Bac at Cambodian border. Hastily built by A and C/2d(Mech)/22d Inf, and Tracks of 1st/5th (Mech), 25th Inf Div, 6May70. Here pontoon bridge was built for their entry into Cambodia, 7May70. Cambodia.
Mini-Base Fox (AT 96-47)
See Fox, Mini-Base. Quang Nam Pr, I Corps.
Mini-Tet (n/a)
See Glossary.
Mining of NVN Waters (n/a)
See Glossary.
Mink, FSB (XD 985-357)
Apx 8 km due S Khe Sanh CB and 7 km WSW Lang Kat, at top-center of Vietnam Salient. Built Nov68? Also listed at YD 985-355; however, that grid is in Thua Thien Pr near Dam Cau Hai, SE Phu Bai and presumed to be incorrect. 101st Abn inactive FSB grid per Don Armstrong. Quang Tri Pr, I Corps.
Mink, FSB (YD 01-33)
Apx 14 km due S Vandegrift CB, 4 km NE Laotian border and 18 km WSW Ba Long AF. Grid per map on p 65, *US Marines in Vietnam-1969*. Also listed at XD 985-355. Listed grid likely in error and XD 985-357 is likely site. Quang Tri Pr, I Corps.
Minnesota, LZ (YD 117-193)
Apx 2 km N Pa Ling, 39 km SW to SSW Quang Tri and 21 km SSW Ba Long AF. Apr70 XXIV Corps grid per Don Armstrong. Quang Tri Pr, I Corps.

Minnesota, LZ (XT 813-646)
Apx 3 km S Xom Ruong and 6 km NE Chon Than AF. 1st Inf Div. Name/grid per Dan Gillotti, 15th Arty Assn. Binh Long Pr, III Corps.

Minnetonka, USCGC (n/a)
WHEC 67. 5Jan68-29Sep68. Sqdn 3 CGC.

Mins (n/a)
See Glossary.

Minuteman, LZ (BS 779-846)
At southern tip of Batangan Peninsula, apx 11 km SSE An Cuong, 17 km NE Quang Ngai and 16 km W QL-1. Apr70 XXIV Corps grid per Don Armstrong. Americal Assn site lists grid as BS 786-857? Quang Ngai Pr, I Corps.

Minuteman, LZ (BS 786-857?)
Apx 24 km S Chu Lai, 6 km ENE Mo Duc AF and 17 km NNW LZ Bronco and on coast. Also listed at BS 779 846 (apx 1 km W this site) on XXIV Corps list of 6 Apr70? Americal list. Quang Ngai Pr, I Corps.

Minuteman Manor (BT 54-05?)
At Chu Lai AB? Home cmpd of 176th Avn Co and 176th AHC, apparently at Chu Lai while suptg Americal Div. Quang Tin Pr, I Corps.

Mirador, Pointe du (XS 9-3)
See Pointe Mirador. Go Cong Pr, IV Corps.

Mirla, LZ (YD 334-504)
Apx 2 km SSW Quang Tri, and roughly 2 km W La Vang AF/QL-1. Name/grid per Paul Kopsick, who also notes that elements of 4th/60th, E/71st and 1/29th here late 67-Jan68 (Dusters, Quads, Searchlights). 1st/44th Arty AO. Quang Tri Pr, I Corps.

Mispillion, USS (n/a)
AO-105. Aux Oiler, per Ralph Fries.

Miss America Mountains (BR 90-76)
A.k.a. the Jane Mansfield Mtns. Nickname of mtn range N and NW LZ Uplift. Apparently derived from fact Miss America once entertained troops on stage in area with the mtn range as her backdrop, per www.rjsmith.com/6837-iii.html#lzuplift. Generally 3-5 km NW LZ Uplift and 10 km N Phu My. II Corps.

Mississippi, LZ (ZA 060-155)
Apx 14 km NNW Plei Me, 24 km NE Chu Pong Mtn and 35 km SSW Pleiku. 1st/12th Cav, 1st Cav LZ during early stages of 1st Ia Drang Battle, Nov65. Near Plei Me SF Camp. Cited in *Pleiku*, p 134. Pleiku Pr, II Corps.

Mississippi BOQ (XS 8-9)
At 509B Vo Di Nguy St., Saigon. Per R. Bows' *Vietnam Military Lore, 1959-1973.* Gia Dinh Pr, III Corps.

Missouri, LZ (YD 146-189)
A.k.a. LZ Massachusetts? Apx 3 km NE Pa Ling, 21 km S Ba Long AF and 38 km SSW of Quang Tri. Apr70 XXIV Corps grid per Don Armstrong. Quang Tri Pr, I Corps.

Missouri BOQ (XS 823-933)
At 918 Thoai Ngic Hau S., Tan Son Nhut, Saigon. Per *Vietnam Military Lore, 1959-1973.* Gia Dinh Pr, III Corps.

Missy, FSB (XT 293-554)
Apx 5 km SSE peak Nui Ba Den and 13 km ENE Tay Ninh West AF. Name/grid per Dan Gillotti, 15th Arty Assn. Tay Ninh Pr, III Corps.

Mistress Mary, LZ (YA 784-917)
See LZ Mary at grid. Pleiku Pr, II Corps.

Mit, FSB/LZ (BS 733-358)
See Mitt. Quang Ngai Pr, I Corps.

Mitchel, FSB (XT 169-460)
See Mitchell. Tay Ninh Pr, III Corps.

Mitchell, FSB (XT 169-460)
Apx 3 km WSW Tay Ninh, 7 km due S Tay Ninh West AF and 2 km W Long My. Dec68-Apr69. Also listed at AT 160-450. Tay Ninh Pr, III Corps.

Mites (n/a)
See Glossary.

Mitt, LZ/FSB (BS 733-358)
A.k.a. LZ/FSB Mit. Apx 9 km WSW Duc Pho AF, 8 km NE FSB Jeff and overlooking Song Tra Cau River Valley to N. XXIV Corps grid per Don Armstrong. Also listed at BS 730-358. Quang Ngai Pr, I Corps.

MLS (n/a)
See Glossary.

MLT-1/MLT-2 (YD 887-148? & YD 328-526?)
Mobile Launch Team. MAC-SOG Command and Control North (CCN) operated two permanent sites controlling its operations in Laos, the DMZ and NVN (Prairie Fire, et al). MLT-2 was at Quang Tri (in a cmpd apx 8 km W the Quang Tri AF), MLT-1 was at Phu Bai. See Prairie Fire.

Mo, FSB (YU 259-429)
A.k.a. LZ/FSB Moe? Remote site apx 3 km from Cambodia, 10 km NW Djamap AF/Bu Gia Map, 43 km WSW Bu Prang and 32 km NE Bu Dop. Also listed at YU 276-414 per *11th ACR Cambodia Invasion AAR, 1st Cav Div, May-Jun70*, and in another list at YU 355-430. Opened or reopened 30Aug70, closed 11Sep70 by 5th/7th Cav grid/data per *1st Cav Div Op Rpt, ending 31Oct70*, courtesy Peter Cole. Phuoc Long Pr, III Corps.

Mo, FSB (YU 276-414)
Listed grid is apx 5 km from Cambodia, 7 km NW Djamap AF/Bu Gia Map, 41 km WSW Bu Prang and 33 km NE Bu Dop. Described as small 1st Cav FSB apx 2 km from Cambodian border with B Bty/1st/30th Arty (medium arty plt of three-155's and staffed by a plt Ldr, an XO, fire control officer, and 50 troopers) here '69. [363] Grid per *11th ACR Cambodia Invasion AAR, 1st Cav Div, May-Jun70*, courtesy Lou Rochat. [364] Also listed at YU 259-429 per 1st Cav Rpt, and at YU 355-429 on another list? Phuoc Long Pr, III Corps.

Mo, FSB (YU 355-429?)
A.k.a. LZ/FSB Moe? Listed grid is apx 5 km NNE Djamap, 13 km E Cambodia and 34 km WSW Bu Prang? Grid may not be correct (unless site was moved?) as official rpts list it as YU 259-429 and 276-414. Phuoc Long Pr, III Corps.

Mo, Vung (CQ 1-8)
A.k.a. Vung Mu. Bay at 13°27'N-109°20'E. On ND49-09 JOG. Phu Yen Pr, II Corps.

Mo Cay (XS 4-2)
Apx 11 km S to SSW Truc Giang. Kien Hoa Pr, IV Corps.

Mo Cay, FSB (XS 46-20?)
Presumably near Mo Cay, and apx 12 km S Truc Giang. 2d Bde/9th Div MRF TF basecamp, per Jim Stone, 2d/39th Inf, and mentioned in Hist Rpt of 3d/34th Arty, dated 14Apr69 for period 1Apr68-31Jan69, on MRF Website at: www.mrfa.org3_34th.htm. Kien Hoa Pr, IV Corps.

Mo Cay Base (XS 46-20?)
See Mo Cay, FSB. Kien Hoa Pr, IV Corps.
Mo Cay Heliport (XS 463-196)
Apx 11 km S to SSW Truc Giang. Heliport #616, alt 7', very confined, VC to N and E. Data per Feb73 TAD. Kien Hoa Pr, IV Corps.
Mo Duc (BS 733-543)
A.k.a. LZ Dragon. Dist Capital not far from, and S of Duc Pho. Also listed at BS 725-535. Americal list. On map L-7014-6738-1. Quang Ngai Pr, I Corps.
Mo Duc (n/a)
Mapsheet name of L-7014-6738-1. SVN.
Mo Duc Airfield (BS 733-543)
Along QL-1 just S Quang Hien, apx 19 km due E Minh Long AF, 22 km SSE Quang Ngai, per TPC K-10A. "Security Questionable, USMC, 16Sep68, contact as per HQ I Corps Adv Grp Signal Op Instructions, AF # VA1-209," in Aug69 TAD per Frank Penk, Jr. Not in Feb73 TAD. El. 131' Map is L-7014-6738-1. Also listed at BS 725-535. Quang Ngai Pr, I Corps.
Mo Duc Heliport (BS 711-625)
Also sp Mu Duc Heliport? Just W QL-1 apx 13 km SSE Quang Ngai, 2 km N LZ Snoopy and 8 km NNW Mo Duc/Quang Hien. Heliport #617, alt 16', at: 15°02'00"N-108°52'15"E, per Feb73 TAD. Quang Ngai Pr, I Corps.
Mo Duc Road (BS 7-5)
The 26th Engr Bn (et al) worked on this road and completed the project from BS 770-535 to ocean beach at BS 790-540, during Mar-Apr70. Quang Ngai Pr, I Corps.
Mo Duc/LZ Dragon (BS 733-543)
See Dragon, LZ. Americal list. Quang Ngai Pr, I Corps.
Mo O, Mui (CQ 1-8)
Mui Ong Dien. Coastal point at 13°28'N-109°20'E. On ND49-09 JOG. Phu Yen Pr, II Corps.
Mo O, Vung (CQ 1-8)
A.k.a. Vung Mu. Bay at 13°27'N-109°20'E. On ND49-09 JOG. Phu Yen Pr, II Corps.
Mo Trang (n/a)
Mapsheet name of L-7014-6252-3. NVN only.
Moang Soum Airfield (TF 49-73)
LS-157. CIA/SF, per *Air Facilities Data-Laos.*
Moat (n/a)
Apr70, XXIV Corps proposed 101st Abn FSB name.
Moberly, LZ (BS 558-321)
A.k.a. LZ Mobley? At Ba To New AF, apx 27 km WSW Duc Pho, and 3 km E Go Dien. 2d/17th Arty here supt 1st Cav 5Aug67, during Op Pershing. Data per Jack Picciolo. Quang Ngai Pr, I Corps.
Mobil, LZ (BT 310-020)
Apx 23 km WSW Chu Lai and 7 km WSW FSB Pearl. Elements of 2d/1st Inf, 196th LIB & Bn HQ here 14Aug67 during Op Benton. Name & grid per Les Hines. Quang Tin Pr, I Corps.
Mobile, USS (n/a)
LKA 115. See Frequent Wind.
Mobile CAP Teams (n/a)
See Glossary.
Mobile Launch Teams (n/a)
See Glossary.
Mobile Riverine Force (n/a)
See Glossary.
Mobile Strike Force Camps (n/a)
See 1st CTZ MSF Camp and 2d CTZ MSF.
Mobile Strike Force Commands (n/a)
See Glossary.
Mobilization Act of 1968 (n/a)
See Glossary.
Mobley, LZ (BS 558-321)
See Moberly. Quang Ngai Pr, I Corps.
Mobsy, FSB (YT 043-358)
Apx 16 km SSE Phuoc Vinh AF. Name/grid per Dan Gillotti. Binh Duong Pr, III Corps.
Moc Chau (Na Bo) (n/a)
Mapsheet name of L-7014-5950-4. NVN only.
Moc Chau (VJ 69-03)
Apx 122 km WSW Hanoi. Non-Directional Beacon site.
Moc Hoa (n/a)
Mapsheet name of L-7014-6130-1. SVN/Cambodia.
Moc Hoa (XS 03-91)
A.k.a. Muc Hoa. Apx 76 km due W Saigon. At various times and locations the site of SF Det 69, 5th SF Grp, Det. A-221 and A-424, Dec64, Det B-41, Oct65, A-414 (was 424), Oct66. Per Bill Hunt, Muc Hoa was also home of MACV Adv Team 72. See Moc Hoa SF Camps. Capitol, Kien Tuong Pr, IV Corps.
Moc Hoa, Camp (WS 983-952)
See Cai Doi, Binh Hiep, Minh Chau, Thanh Tri and Chua Hoi SF Camps. IV Corps.
Moc Hoa Airfield (XS 029-902)
Apx 78 km due W Saigon, 45 km SW Duc Hue AF and 20 km SE Binh Thanh Thon AF, per TPC K-10D. El. 10', 2,900' laterite rwy. At 10°46'05"N-105°56'20"E. Kien Tuong Pr, IV Corps.
Moc Hoa Navy ATSB (XS 03-92?)
On Song Vam Cotay River, apx 78 km due W Saigon? USN Advanced Tactical Supt Base, '68-71. Per MRF Assn Website. Kien Tuong Pr, IV Corps.
Moc Hoa SF Camp (B-Det) (XS 0305-9091)
Along Song Vam Cotay River, apx 77 km due W Saigon, 65 km NW My Tho, 7 km due S Cambodian border and 28 km WSW the tip of Parrot's Beak. 5th SF. Also listed at XS 030-912. Data per *SF Order of Battle.* See Moc Hoa for SF unit data. Kien Tuong Pr, IV Corps.
Moc Hoa SF Camp (CIDG) (XS 0282-8995)
Along Song Vam Cotay River, apx 78 km due W Saigon, 65 km NW My Tho, 7 km due S Cambodian border and 28 km WSW the tip of Parrot's Beak. 5th SF. Moved to Thanh Tri. See Moc Hoa for SF unit data. Info/grid per *SF Order of Battle.* Kien Tuong Pr, IV Corps.
Moc Hoa Signal Site (XS 03-91?)
No data. Kien Tuong Pr?, IV Corps.
Moc Hoa? SF Camp (MSF) (XS 5660-6395)
A.k.a. FOB An Long or Muc Hoa SF Camp? Just SE Tan An, 32 km SW Saigon, 22 km NNE My Tho and 4 km ESE Long An AF. Name may be in error? More likely Tan An or Long An SF Camp? 5th SF. Transferred to RF/PF base. Data per *SF Order of Battle*. Long An Pr, III Corps.
Moccasin, FSB (AT 941-918)
Overlooking ocean near Hai Van Pass apx 2 km E QL-1, 16 km NNW Da Nang and 2 km from coast. XXIV Corps grid. Thua Thien Pr, I Corps.

Mockingbird, LZ (YD 137-771)
Near the Ben Hai River, apx 33 km NW Quang Tri, 6 km WNW Kinh Mon and 13 km WSW mouth of Ben Ha River. May67. Quang Tri Pr, I Corps.

Moe, FSB/LZ (YU 259-429?)
A.k.a. LZ/FSB Mo (Mo without the "e" is thought to be correct sp). See Mo, FSB listings. Described as small 1st Cav FSB near Song Be, NW Saigon and apx 2 km from Cambodian border. B Bty, 1st/30th Arty (medium arty plt of three 155s and staffed by plt Ldr, an XO, fire control officer, and 50 troops), here '69. FSB Mo also listed at YU 355-429 and YU 276-414? Phuoc Long Pr, III Corps. [365]

Mogan, FSB (YD 5-5?)
E of Hai Lang covering the Street Without Joy and beachhead (later named Utah Beach). Named to honor CO of A/1st/327th Inf (per Gen Cushman), or may have been named to honor John E. Mogan, KIA 15Dec67. Built by 1st/501st Inf, 101st Abn, apx 19Feb68. A Bty 1st/321st Arty and a Seabee working party (14th Engr Bn) here also. Was relocated shortly after const due to poor security of initial site. Quang Tri Pr?, I Corps.

Mortensen Hospital (AP 864-485?)
At An Lac. Grid is for An Lac SF Camp (new), which was apx 5 km SSW Duc Xuyen AF, 32 km SSW Lac Thien and 10 km SW An Lac. Named to honor SF medic, Sgt Allan D Mortensen, KIA near Bien Hoa, 10Mar68. Data per Ray Bows. Darlac Pr, II Corps.

Mohawk, Camp (XS 265-499)
Along S side of QL-4, apx 750 meters S main gate to FSB Moore, 3 km E Cai Lay, 24 km WNW My Tho and 1 km WNW Ap Qui Trinh. 2d/39th Inf outpost secured by E/2d/39th Apr-Jun68. Opened Apr68, in conjunction with opening of FSB Moore. Unofficially named Mohawk as reference to Mohawk Indian-style haircuts worn by members of E/2d/39th Inf as inspired by their CO, Capt Norman Dent (said to have been 82d Abn WWII paratrooper who apparently sported haircut then and in VN). Consisted of 6 perimeter bunkers, prefab watchtower, CP and 2 CP bunkers. Data per Jim Stone. Dinh Tuong Pr, IV Corps.

Mohawk, FSB (BR 650-793)
Apx 17 km WSW Ha Tay AF. 173d Abn. Name/grid per Dan Gillotti. Binh Dinh Pr, II Corps.

Moi (n/a)
See Glossary.

Moi Loi Heliport (XS 800-563)
Apx 11 km NNW Go Cong and AF, 33 km ENE My Tho and 32 km due S Saigon. Heliport #709, alt 5', at: 10°27'N 106°38'E, per Feb73 TAD. Go Cong Pr, IV Corps.

Moinester, USS (n/a)
FF-1097. SVN.

Mok Lok Airfield (TH 36-71)
LS-131. CIA/SF, per *Air Facilities Data-Laos.*

Mok Plai Airfield (TH 18-89)
LS-193. CIA/SF, per *Air Facilities Data-Laos.*

Molala, USS (n/a)
A.k.a. ATF-106. ATFs provided towing, salvage and rescue ops. In '70 or'71, towed several Army harbor-tugs from Da Nang to Subic Bay. 205' long with crew of 90, and a sea-going vessel. Armed with 3-inch/50 Cal, rapid-fire gun mount just fwd of bridge. 3" mount could also fire tow/escape lines over bow or super-structure of ship in distress. Later sold (with ATF-107?) to Mexican Navy w/new names of *Kukulkan* (A-52) and *Otomi* (A-17). Data per http://members.xoom.com/mdturner/navy.htm.

Mole, FSB (XT 249-309)
See Mole City. Tay Ninh Pr, III Corps.

Mole, Patrol Base (XT 248-310)
See Mole City. 12Dec68. Tay Ninh Pr, III Corps.

Mole City, FSB (XT 249-309)
A.k.a. Patrol Base Mole City, FSB Mole, and later renamed FSB Sedgewick. Apx 15 km due S Tay Ninh, 3 km ENE Ap Cai Tac, 5 km from Cambodia and 14 km W FSB Austin. Built by A/65th Eng and 4th/9th Inf beginning 18Dec68. Sign at entrance to base read: "*WELCOME TO MOLE CITY, The Sandbag Capitol of the World.*" [366] Apparently given its name due to fact its bunkers were built deep into ground such that only the roofs and firing ports were no more than a few feet above ground level (an unusual feature for US FSBs). Battle of FSB Mole City described at www3.servtec.com/vhpa/info/panel/battle/68122200.htm (and erroneously listed in Quang Tri Pr). During Toan Thang II, base was attacked by 272d VC Rgt, 22Dec68, resulting in 17 US KIA, 34 US WIA and 103 VC KIA. On map in *Suicide Charlie*, where author appears to name 207th Rgt, 9th NVA as Dec68 attackers? In '69-70, 4/9th Inf, 25th Inf Div here per Manchu Mike Smith. See Manchu Assn website at www.manchu.org/mole_city for detail of battle. Aerial photo of base at www.manchu.org/mole_city/index13.htm. See Force Fed Fire Supt System in Glossary. Tay Ninh Pr, III Corps. [367] [368]

Mole City II, FSB (XT 240-310)
Rebuilding of (or built near) original FSB Mole City, apx 15 km S Tay Ninh. Built by C/4th/9th Inf, 25th Inf Div, Apr or May69. Described in *Suicide Charlie* as contrasting with its namesake in that bunkers were built above ground in more conventional manner than subterranean bunkers of original. This was apparently due to fact Mole City II was built during rainy season while original was built during dry season and flooded. Tay Ninh Pr, III Corps. [369]

Molinda, FSB (XT 167-366)
A.k.a. Melinda? Apx 2 km NW Ap Van Long, 12 km SE Tay Ninh, 16 km S Tay Ninh West AF and 6 km from Cambodia. Feb70. Tay Ninh Pr, III Corps.

Mon Dial BEQ (XS 8-9)
Possibly Mondail BEQ? At 265 Pham Ngu Lao St., Saigon. Per R. Bows' *Vietnam Military Lore, 1959-1973.* Gia Dinh Pr, III Corps.

Mon Kay (ZJ 09-85)
A.k.a. Mong Cai and Muong Cai. Within 10 km of ocean at point Chinese and NVN borders also meet ocean, apx 155 km ENE Haiphong and 240 km ENE Hanoi. NVN.

Mon Ky Mountain (BT 06-86)
A.k.a. Monkey Mtn. On the Tien Sha Peninsula apx 12 km NNE Da Nang AB and overlooking the city. Viet name for Hill 621, which US troops called Monkey Mtn. See also Monkey Mtn, *Constitution, USS*, and Da Nang entries. Quang Nam Pr, I Corps.

Monahan, Camp (AT/BT?)
A.k.a. Camp E. J. (or E. E.) Monahan. Somewhere in the Da Nang area. 1st Mar Div, 1st FSG. Likely named to

honor E. J. Monahan, Jr, Cpl USMC, KIA 24Aug65. Quang Nam Pr, I Corps.

Monastery Compound (XS 49-45)
See My Tho. Dinh Tuong Pr, IV Corps.

Mondial BEQ (XS 8-9)
See Mon Dial BEQ. Gia Dinh Pr, III Corps.

Mondol Kuri (YU 380-780)
A.k.a. Mondel Kiri. Apx 26 km NNW Bu Krak, 43 km N Djamap/Bu Gia Map, 100 km WSW Ban Me Thuot and 14 km NNE O Rang AF. Assaulted and secured by A/1st/9th Cav, 1st Cav during Cambodian Incursion. Grid/some data per *11th ACR Cambodia Invasion AAR, 1st Cav Div, May-Jun70*, courtesy Lou Rochat.[370] Cambodia.

Mondol Kiri City Airfield (YU 380-785)
Apx 100 km WSW Ban Me Thuot, 42 km NW Bu Prang AF, 45 km N Bu Gia Map, 14 km NNE O Rang AF and 18 km N of SVN border, per TPC K-10A. 4,300' rwy, El. 2,297'. Cambodia.

Mong Cai Airfield (n/a)
A.k.a. Mong Kay and Muong Cai AF. On S edge of Mong Cai and apx 5 km N the coast at China border in NW NVN, apx 224 km ENE Hanoi. Per ONC-J-11. El. 33'. NVN.

Mong Tay, Mui (US 7-3)
Coastal point at 10°18'N-103°52'E. On NC48-05 JOG. Kien Giang Pr, IV Corps.

Mongom, Pointe (XS 7-7)
See Pointe Mongom. Gia Dinh Pr?, III Corps.

Mongoose, LZ (YD 788-167?)
If grid correct, was apx 1 km WNW Camp Eagle, 6 km SE Hue, 1 km N FSB Panther I and 4 km NE Pohl Bridge. See discussion in Mongoose at YD 783-269 for addnl detail. Also listed at YD 783-269 and 789-271. Correct grid unknown. Thua Thien Pr, I Corps.

Mongoose, FSB (YD 783-269)
If grid correct, was near Hwy 551 apx 2 km from NE corner of Hue and Phu Vang's USMC Bn CP. 1st/501st and A/1/321 Arty, 15May68. Built by elements of 505th Inf, 3d Bde/82d Abn, '68. On map in *All the Way-The 3d Brigade, 82d Abn Division, Vietnam 1968*, p 8, which lists it as an LZ at YD 788-167, while XXIV Corps list puts grid at YD 789-271? Grid is for Phu Vang ville's center, not necessarily the FSB. Thua Thien Pr, I Corps.

Monica, LZ (ZA 112-678)
A.k.a. FSB Plei Mrong. At or just N Plei Mrong, apx 25 km NNW Pleiku and 24 km SW Kontum. 1st/92d Arty here 4Jan69, firing in supt ARVN Op Binh Tay. 1st/92d, 3d/6th and 2d/9th Arty here 18Jan69. Data on 4th Div, 1st/92d Arty op rpt per Craig Miller. Pleiku Pr, II Corps.

Monitor (n/a)
See Glossary.

Monitor, LZ (XD 868-353)
Apx 8 km SSE Khe Sanh CB and 20 km SW Ca Lu. Apr70 XXIV Corps grid per D. Armstrong. Quang Tri Pr, I Corps.

Monkay Outpost (n/a)
Likely sp variant of Mong Cai. French frontier outpost at extreme NE corner of Tonkin where Chinese and Viet borders meet the Tonkin Gulf, apx 230 km ENE Hanoi and apx 3 km from coast. French abnd its defense in 1950, as Vietminh were gaining strength. See Mong Cai and Cao Bang. NVN.

Monkey, LZ (BR 683-633)
Apx 7 km E Binh Dinh, 27 km NE An Khe, 5 km ENE LZ Hereford and 8 km NE Vinh Thanh. Roughly midway between LZs Hereford and Horse. Used during Op Crazy Horse, May66. Discussed in *Battles in the Monsoon*, pp 173, 175-176, 180-181 et al. Binh Dinh Pr, II Corps.

Monkey, LZ (XD 970-678)
In DMZ, apx 17 km NW Cam Lo, 28 km WNW Dong Ha and 12 km W Thon An Hoa. Apr70 XXIV Corps grid per Don Armstrong. Quang Tri Pr, I Corps.

Monkey Mountain (BT 06-86)
A.k.a. Hill 621 (2,037') and possibly Mon Ky Mtn. At W end of Tien Sha Peninsula, apx 12 km NNE Da Nang AB and 4 km WNW Hill 696/Son Tra Mtn. Name is said to have been an Anglicized version of Mon Ky (possibly Hill 621's Viet name), but also said to have been so-named because of the monkeys which inhabited it? Overlooked Da Nang (Tourane) to SW and Marble Mtn AF to S. Site of Monkey Mtn Signal site (a.k.a. Onderko Commo Site) and home of occasional VC snipers. Occupied by elements of 1st Sig Bde, 194th MPs, and USMC securing USAF 620th TC Sqdn (radar) facility. Map is L-7014-6641-3. See also Onderko, *Constitution, USS,* and Da Nang entries for addnl history. Quang Nam Pr, I Corps.

Monkey Mountain Signal Site (BT 06-84)
A.k.a. Onderko Commo Site, ICS-64, and Hill 621 (2,037'). On Tien Sha Peninsula, apx 12 km NE Da Nang AB, 4 km WNW Son Tra Mtn and 11 km NNE Marble Mtn AF. Apparently on ridge perhaps 2 km S of the peak of Hill 621 rather than at its top. Occupied by elements of 1st Sig Bde, 194th MPs, and also USMC securing USAF 620th TC Sqdn (radar). See Monkey Mtn, Onderko and *Constitution, USS*. Quang Nam Pr, I Corps.

Monkey Peninsula (US 9-0)
A.k.a. Presqu'ile aux Singes. Peninsula forming S end of Phu Quoc Island, near 10°01'N-104°03'E. On NC48-05 JOG. Kien Giang Pr, IV Corps.

Monmouth County, USS (n/a)
LST-1032. Decom 12Aug70. SVN.

Mons, NDP (XT 720-369)
A.k.a. Mons I? Along LTL-14, apx 6 km W to WSW Lai Khe and 6 km NNW Ben Cat. Evolved into FSB Mons series (II, III, IV, VI, XVI). No listing found for Mons I or V or VII etc., so number sequence possibly entire scheme? 4Apr69. Binh Duong Pr, III Corps.

Mons, FSB (XT 712-409)
Apx 7 km NW Lai Khe AF. 3d Bde/1st Inf Div. Grid per Dan Gillotti. Binh Duong Pr, III Corps.

Mons II, FSB (XT 726-413)
Apx 7 km NW Lai Khe 7 km SW Ap Bau Bang. 1May69. Binh Duong Pr, III Corps.

Mons III, FSB (XT 740-453)
Apx 8 km NNW Lai Khe and 5 km WSW Ap Bau Bang. 15May69. Binh Duong Pr, III Corps.

Mons IV, FSB (XT 734-434)
Apx 8 km NW Lai Khe and 6 km WSW Ap Bau Bang. 1Jun69. Binh Duong Pr, III Corps.

Mons V, FSB (XT)
May or may not have existed? Binh Duong Pr, III Corps.

Mons VI, FSB (XT 559-402)
Apx 22 km WNW Lai Khe and 11 km SE Dau Tieng/Tri Tam. 1Jul69. Binh Duong Pr, III Corps.
Mons VII? through XV?, FSB (XT)
May or may not have existed? Binh Duong Pr, III Corps.
Mons XVI, FSB (XT 630-356)
Apx 14 km WSW Lai Khe and 19 km SE Dau Tieng/Tri Tam. 15Nov69. Binh Duong Pr, III Corps.
Monsignor Lefevre (BT 0-8)
See *Constitution, USS*. Quang Nam Pr, I Corps.
Montagnard (n/a)
See Glossary.
Montagnard Camp (ZA 233-828?)
If grid correct, was apx 6 km SSW Kontum, W of QL-14. Grid actually listed as ZA 2337828, which is short one digit, and listed grid is est. Central Kontum Pr, II Corps.
Montana BEQ (XS 815-918)
Lot PS, on Phu Tho Hoa St., Saigon. Per R. Bows' *Vietnam Military Lore, 1959-1973.* Gia Dinh Pr, III Corps.
Montana, LZ (YD 200-114)
Near Rte 9222, apx 7 km due E Tou Rout, 1 km E FSB Cunningham and 42 km SSW Quang Tri. Apr70 XXIV Corps grid per Don Armstrong. Quang Tri Pr, I Corps.
Monterey BEQ (XS 8-9)
At 87 Nguyen Dinh Chieu St., Saigon. Data per *Vietnam Military Lore*, 1959-1973. Gia Dinh Pr, III Corps.
Monterey, LZ (YD 199-305)
A.k.a. LZ Gulf. Apx 11 km SSE Ba Long AF and 25 km SSW Quang Tri. XXIV Corps grid per Don Armstrong. Quang Tri Pr, I Corps.
Montezuma, LZ/FSB (BS 812-383)
A.k.a. LZ Bronco and Duc Pho AF. Adj to or at Duc Pho AF, apx 37 km SSE Quang Ngai. 1 of few bases to have a separate mtn within base perimeter (Mt. Montezuma/Hill 150 here). Originally built in '66 or early '67, by USMC and occupied by TF X-Ray, inc 3d/7th and 2d/5th Marines. As DMZ activities forced Marines to deploy X-Ray's assets there, 1st Cav was ordered to replace departing Marines, 1Apr67, and given 12 hours notice to land Bn (2d/5th Cav) at Montezuma/Duc Pho, and then expand it to Bde-size in only 36 hrs. In deference to USMC (their AO), op was named "Lejune" and LZs built during op also given historic USMC names. 8th Engr Bn, 1st Cav, built C7A Caribou strip here beginning 7Apr67, completing it's 1,500' long rwy 8Apr67. Rwy was soon expanded to service C-123s and, at peak, was handling over 1,000 landings/take-offs per day. Light, sandy soil resulted in perpetual dust clouds from acft traffic. Once Cav Bde was in place, an LST/LCM seaport (Razorback Beach) was built directly E Montezuma to facilitate Cav's resupply needs. Op Lejune ended 22Apr67, and 1st Cav was relieved by 3d/Bde/25th Inf Div (which soon became part of TF Oregon). Per Dick Arnold, base later became an Americal Div LZ renamed LZ Bronco. Also once basecamp/HQ of 11th LIB. History discussed in *VN Studies* vol, *Airmobility 1961-1971*. Also mentioned in *Bloods*, p 92, and in 1st Cav VN *Yearbook* Aug65-Dec69, p 110, per Peter Cole. Also listed at BS 812-375, 809-384 and 815-311. Apr67-Jan68. See Razorback Beach. Quang Ngai Pr, I Corps.[371]

Montezuma Airfield (BS 812-383)
See LZ Montezuma. Quang Ngai Pr, I Corps.
Montezuma Mountain (BS 818-382)
See Mt. Montezuma. Quang Ngai Pr, I Corps.
Monticello, USS (n/a)
LSD-35. Lndg. Ship, Dock, per Ralph Fries.
Montrose, USS (n/a)
APA-212. Amphib Attack, Transport, per Ralph Fries.
Monument Pad (WS 697-558)
Heliport pad near Cao Lanh Heliport, which was along LTL-30, apx 5 km N the Mekong, 23 km NW Sa Dec and 48 km NNW Can Tho. Kien Phong Pr, IV Corps.
Moon, FSB (YT 89-20)
Apx 8 km SW Tanh Linh, 51 km WNW Phan Thiet and 18 km SE Vo Dat. 3d/7th/199th LIB. Binh Thuy Pr, III Corps.
Moon, LZ (XD 899-516)
In the Khe Trinh Hin River Valley, 11 km WNW Ca Lu and 35 km WSW Dong Ha. Apr70 XXIV Corps grid per Don Armstrong. Quang Tri Pr, I Corps.
Moon, LZ (XD)
Lam Son 719 base of 1st ARVN Div. Good Lam Son 719 map at www.americal.org/174/map4.htm. Laos.
Moonbeam, LZ (BQ 788-483)
Apx 3 km S Tan Binh, 25 km SSW Dong Tre, 6 km NNE Son Hoa and 7 km NNW Cung Son AF. Oct66. Phu Yen Pr, II Corps.
Mooney, FSB (YD 446-195)
A.k.a. LZ Mooney. Apx 3 km SSE FSB Granite, 28 km due W Hue, 4 km NNE FSB Katy and 13 km WSW Ap Thanh Tan. 101st Abn inactive FSB grid per Don Armstrong. Also listed as YD 445-195, 445-190 and 446-196. Cited in 1st Cav VN *Yearbook* Aug65-Dec69, p 99, 184, per Peter Cole. Thua Thien Pr, I Corps.
Moonglow (n/a)
See Glossary.
Moore, FSB (XS 260-500)
A.k.a. FSPB Moore and possibly FSB Vanh Kim? Main gate was 500 meters N QL-4, apx 3 km E Cai Lay, 24 km WNW My Tho, 17 km WNW Dong Tam and 1 km NW FSB Fels. Built Apr68 to replace FSB Fels (or Fells, XS 273-498). Opened as Bn-sized basecamp but grew into a Bde-sized facility with permanent wood structures over time. Apparently turned-over to ARVN somewhere between Jul-Aug69, when US 9th Div departed this AO, and possibly renamed FSB Vinh Kim at that time. 2d/39th Inf and other 9th ID elements here. Per Don Armstrong, 9th Div Quarterly rpts for Oct68, show C and D Cos, 1st/84 Arty each had 2 tubes of 105mm at FSPB Moore. On map in *Rangers at War*, p 326, and mentioned in *Doc: Platoon Medic*, p 81. On map L-7014-6229-4 (Khiem Ich/Cai-Lay). Data per Jim Stone, 2d/39th Inf. Also listed at XS 250-500. Dinh Tuong Pr, IV Corps.
Moore, FSB (XS 770-800)
Just E Tan Nhiau, 6 km E Binh Chanh (and QL-4), 3 km W LTL-5A, 4 km WNW Ap Phuoc Khan, 13 km WSW Nha Be and 18 km SSW Tan Son Nhut AB. Grid per Don Armstrong. Gia Dinh Pr, III Corps.
Moore, FSPB (XS 26-50)
See FSB Moore at XS 266-505. Dinh Tuong Pr, IV Corps.

Moore, LZ/FSB (BS 431-985?)
If grid correct, was 13 km SW Chu Lai AB and 8 km ENE peak Nui Dong Tranh Mtn. Americal Assn lists grid in "BT" grid zone; however, that it in ocean and incorrect. Americal list. Quang Ngai Pr, I Corps.

Moore Ammo Storage Area (CP 095-230)
On Cam Ranh Bay Peninsula, apx 3 km SW the S end of main AF rwy. Named to honor Sp5 Dean Moore, KIA 22Nov67, when VC booby-trapped Jeep he and Sp6 Paul McKinley were using N Phan Thiet. Alpha, Charlie and Yankee Ammo Stg areas at Cam Ranh renamed either Black, McKinley or Moore in ceremony, 12Jul69. Data per *VN Military Lore, 1959-1973*. Khanh Hoa Pr, II Corps.

Moose, FSB (XT 130-716)
Apx 13 km SSE Thien Ngon AF, 20 km NW Nui Ba Den, 24 km NNW Tay Ninh and 3 km NE Ap Trai Bi. Tay Ninh Pr, III Corps.

Moose, FSB (YD 060-348)
In river valley apx 17 km SSW Mai Loc, 22 km ESE Khe Sanh and 11 km W FSB Miami. XXIV Corps grid per Don Armstrong. Quang Tri Pr, I Corps.

MOOSE, Operation (XS 8-9)
Humorous acronym for *Move Out Of Saigon Expeditiously*. Code name given organized withdrawal of US forces from Saigon in '72, following, or in anticipation of, signing of Paris Peace Accords. Gia Dinh Pr, III Corps.

More Flags Program (n/a)
See Glossary.

Moreau Bowl (CP 0-5)
See Nha Trang Cham Temple. Khanh Hoa Pr, II Corps.

Morgan, FSB (YD)
See FSB Mogan. Quang Tri Pr?, I Corps.

Morgenthau, USCGC (n/a)
WHEC 722. 6Dec70-31Jul71. Sqdn 3 CGC, during Coast Guard's 7th deployment.

Mortain, FSB (XT?)
Location unknown. 1st/7th Arty, 25th Inf Div here'69. Name per Dan Gillotti. III Corps.

Mortar Inn, The (XT 960-495?)
Team club of MACV Advsy Team 67 at Phuoc Vinh. Grid is for SF Camp and AF there. Phuoc Long Pr, III Corp.

Mortar Mountain (ZB 018-258)
A.k.a. Suim Ngok Tu Mtn and Hill 923. Apx 3 km due N Dak To 2 AF, 1 km SW Dak Rou, and 4 km ESE FSB 30. Likely so named because NVA could readily employ it to mortar virtually any position around Dak To. On map at http://1-14th.com/lzMortarMtn.html. Kontum Pr, II Corps.

Mortar Valley (AT/BT?)
In same general area as Happy Valley, Sherwood Forest and Charlie Ridge. Cited in *Combat Medic*, p 193. Quang Nam Pr?, I Corps.

Mortimer, LZ (BR 72-70?)
Apx 4 km SW LZ Corral, 7 km NE LZ Hereford, 35 km NE An Khe and 5 km N LZ Horse. Used during Op Crazy Horse, May66. See *Battles in the Monsoon*, p 197. Grid est from description. Binh Dinh Pr, II Corps.

Morton, USS (n/a)
DD 948. In Sep64, 1st Desoto Patrol following Gulf of Tonkin Incident was initiated and on 17-18Sep64, Destroyer *Morton* (DD 948) and *Richard S. Edwards* (DD 950) cruised within 20 mi of NVN. On night of 18Sep64, both fired on what they thought were high-speed vessels in attack. Later investigation left doubt of attack due to lack of firm evidence. Thereafter, Desoto Ops were discontinued in Gulf of Tonkin. [372]

Mosby, FSB (YT 043-358)
A.k.a. FSB Chapultapec (YT 04-35)? Apx 23 km NNE Bien Hoa AB, 6 km NE Khu Tru Mat and 16 km SSE Phuoc Vinh AF. 1Jan69. Name per Jim Claeys. Binh Duong Pr, III Corps.

Mot CAP (BT?)
Mot is Viet word for numeral 1; hence, Cap Mot translates as CAP 1. Apparently near Chu Lai AF, 67. History of this CAP team discussed in *Mot CAP*. Quang Tin and Quang Nam Pr, I Corps.

Motor Pool, LZ (BT 025-289)
A.k.a. Nui Loc Son and Nui Loc Son Base. Overlooking and along S edge of Song Chang River Valley apx 10 km NE Tien Phuoc SF Camp/AF, 27 km due W Tam Ky and 9 km SSE Phuoc Tuy. Originally a remote USMC position was used for several Ops circa '67, and later renamed LZ Motor Pool by its Americal Div occupants? Map is L-7014-6640-3. Grid per Les Hines. Quang Tin Pr, I Corps.

Mouillage de Hon Chut (CP 0-0)
See Hon Chut. Khanh Hoa Pr, II Corps.

Moung (various)
See also Muong entries.

Moung Ao Neua Airfield (UF 07-81)
LS-227. CIA/SF, per *Air Facilities Data-Laos.*

Moung Cha Airfield (UF 00-91)
LS-113. CIA/SF, per *Air Facilities Data-Laos.*

Moung Chim Airfield (TG 44-43)
LS-56. CIA/SF, per *Air Facilities Data-Laos.*

Moung Hai Airfield (QD 92-32)
A.k.a. L-41and Ban Khoanag AF. CIA/SF, per *Air Facilities Data-Laos.*

Moung Het Airfield (UJ 98-03)
L-13. CIA/SF, per *Air Facilities Data-Laos.*

Moung Hiem Airfield (UH 30-20)
LS-48A. CIA/SF, per *Air Facilities Data-Laos.*

Moung Houn Airfield (QC 57-29)
L-34. CIA/SF, per *Air Facilities Data-Laos.*

Moung Kassy Airfield (TG 11-30)
LS-153. CIA/SF, per *Air Facilities Data-Laos.*

Moung Kau/Pakse SF Camp (WB 8-6)
A.k.a. Moung Kao SF Camp. SF camp when Lao neutrality declared, 23Jul62. Det BD, ATT 2 and Provincial FTT 2 here then. Per *Special Forces at War*. MR4, Laos.

Moung Khao Airfield (UG 42-89)
LS-128. CIA/SF, per *Air Facilities Data-Laos.*

Moung Kheung Airfield (UG 02-72)
L-109. CIA/SF, per *Air Facilities Data-Laos.*

Moung Lem Airfield (PC 59-98)
LS-320. CIA/SF, per *Air Facilities Data-Laos.*

Moung Met Airfield (RA 10-85)
LS-158. CIA/SF, per *Air Facilities Data-Laos.*

Moung Mo Airfield (UG 91-09)
LS-182. CIA/SF, per *Air Facilities Data-Laos.*

Moung Moe Airfield (UF 95-94)
LS-46. CIA/SF, per *Air Facilities Data-Laos.*

Moung Mounge/T Airfield (PC 53-93)
LS-93. Meaning of "/T" is unknown. CIA/SF, per *Air Facilities Data-Laos.*
Moung Ngai Airfield (VG 02-12)
LS-01. CIA/SF, per *Air Facilities Data-Laos.*
Moung Ngeum Airfield (QC 15-78)
LS-168. CIA/SF, per *Air Facilities Data-Laos.*
Moung Nham Airfield (UF 75-96)
LS-63. CIA/SF, per *Air Facilities Data-Laos.*
Moung Ou Tay Airfield (QE 89-48)
L-02. CIA/SF, per *Air Facilities Data-Laos.*
Moung Oum Airfield (UF 17-96)
LS-22. CIA/SF, per *Air Facilities Data-Laos.*
Moung Pa Airfield (PA 71-48)
LS-342. CIA/SF, per *Air Facilities Data-Laos.*
Moung Peun Airfield (UH 82-35)
L-31. CIA/SF, per *Air Facilities Data-Laos.*
Moung Phalane Airfield (WD 58-44)
L-61. CIA/SF, per *Air Facilities Data-Laos.*
Moung Phalane SW Airfield (WD 52-29)
L-61A. CIA/SF, per *Air Facilities Data-Laos.*
Moung Phanh Airfield (TG 99-51)
L-106. CIA/SF, per *Air Facilities Data-Laos.*
Moung Phieng Airfield (QB 66-07)
LS-124. CIA/SF, per *Air Facilities Data-Laos.*
Moung Phun Airfield (TG 61-14)
LS-37. Apx 100 km SE Luang Prabang, per ONC-J-11. CIA/SF, per *Air Facilities Data-Laos.* El. 3,600'. Laos.
Moung Sai Airfield (RC 12-90)
L-27. Apx 305 km NNW Vientiane. CIA/SF, per *Air Facilities Data-Laos.* El. 1,804'. Laos.
Moung Sam Airfield (VG 22-07)
LS-24. CIA/SF, per *Air Facilities Data-Laos.*
Moung Sao Airfield (TG 45-05)
LS-319. CIA/SF, per *Air Facilities Data-Laos.*
Moung Sing Airfield (QD 23-43)
L-42. CIA/SF, per *Air Facilities Data-Laos.*
Moung Sol Airfield (VH 50-40)
L-60. CIA/SF, per *Air Facilities Data-Laos.*
Moung Son Airfield (UH 28-62)
L-59. CIA/SF, per *Air Facilities Data-Laos.*
Moung Soui Airfield (TG 79-60)
L-108. CIA/SF, per *Air Facilities Data-Laos.*
Moung Sung Airfield (TH 33-48)
L-01. CIA/SF, per *Air Facilities Data-Laos.*
Moung Tiouen Airfield (VF 35-87)
LS-91. CIA/SF, per *Air Facilities Data-Laos.*
Mount Baldy (YD 75-16?)
Possibly Banana Mtn (a.k.a. Nui Hoan Gay/Hill 434) or either Nui Sa Truc (Hill 416) 3 km SE FSB Birmingham, or Hill 378 which was 4.5 km due S Birmingham. Thua Thien Pr, I Corps.
Mount Dabney (XD 8-4?)
Hill near Khe Sanh CB? Quang Tri Pr, I Corps.
Mount Katmai, USS (n/a)
AE-16, Ammo Ship. Comm 21Jul45. Atlantic Flt 8Sep45-Oct45; Pacific, Oct45 to war's end. Korean war, 18Aug50 rearming TFs 77 & 95 to end of war. On 15May65 arrived Subic Bay for carrier grps/NGS rearm ops off VN to Nov65. Returned US, 16 Dec65, rejoining WESTPAC at Yankee Sation, Jul66. Returned to US, 12Jan67, rejoining WESTPAC. 30Aug67. Returned to US, 11Mar67, rejoining WESTPAC, 24Sep67, working off VN into '69. Sold to Maritime Admin, 5Apr74. Data per www.hazegray.org/danfs/auxil/ae16.txt.
Mount McKinley, USS (n/a)
AGC 7. See *Vancouver, USS.*
Mount Montezuma (BS 818-382)
Within perimeter of Duc Pho AF/ LZ Bronco. Peak was 1.5 km E QL-1 and perhaps 300 meters ESE the AF rwy. 6th Bn, 11th Arty (in supt 11th Inf Bde) Counter-Mortar Radar Unit here, Dec68. Quang Ngai Pr, I Corps.
Mount Vernon, USS (n/a)
LSD 39, Ldng Ship, Dock. See Op Frequent Wind.
Mountain of Leeches (AT 990-251)
A.k.a. Nui Liet Kiem and Hill 440. N of the Song Chang and S the Song Lau, apx 30 km W Tam Ky and 3 km S Quang Nam Pr border. Quang Tin Pr, I Corps.
Mountain of the Crouching Beast (YC 328-981)
See Dong Ap Bia/Hamburger Hill. Thua Thien Pr, I Corps.
Mouse Ears, The (XS 68-58)
Terrain feature resembling and upside-down Walt Disney Mouseketeer's hat formed by Song Vam Co Tay River 30 km SSW Saigon and 15 km SE Tan An. On map in *Rangers at War*, p 326. Long An Pr, III Corps.
Mousetrap, The (TJ 41-33)
Nickname of main French garrison of Muong Khoua. See Muong Khoua, Siege of. Laos.
Move Out Of Saigon Expeditiously (n/a)
See MOOSE, Operation.
Mowhawk, FSB (n/a)
See Mohawk.
MR1, MR2, MR3 and MR4 (n/a)
Military Regions in SVN that were known as I Corps through IV Corps until Jul70. On 1Jul70, the Corps CTZs were re-designated as Military Regions (MR's) 1 through 4, numbers that corresponded with the prior Corps numbering. No explanation of purpose of that change was unearthed during the research for this project. See Military Regions section for more detail.
MR1, MR2, MR3, MR4, MR5 (n/a)
See Laotian Military Regions in Glossary.
MRF (n/a)
Mobile Riverine Force.
MR-I MSF, Camp (BS 9159-2630)
See 1st CTZ MSF, and Sa Huynh. Quang Ngai Pr, I Corps.
MR-II MSF, Camp (AR 765-474)
See 2d CTZ MSF. Pleiku Pr, II Corps.
MSS (various)
Mission Support Site (MAC-SOG). For examples see Leghorn, Hickory Hill and Sledgehammer.
MSS 2 (n/a)
Decommissioned WWII LST converted to temporary minesweeping duties in VN. In early Apr73, after she was filled with foam and other shock absorbing materials, brave volunteers made 8 runs up the Haiphong channel to ensure that all the aerial mines had been cleared during Op End Sweep. See End Sweep. [373]
MSTS (Ship's name) (various)
See vessel's formal name in main alpha listings. For example: *Patch, MSTS.*

Mt. Ba Vi (WJ 38-27)
See Ba Vi. NVN.
Mt. Dabney (XD 8-4?)
See Mount Dabney. Quang Tri Pr, I Corps.
Mt. Hui Vien Nam (WJ 46-26)
Street Without Joy's apparent misspelling of "Nui Vien Nam." See Nui Vien Nam. NVN.
Mt. Katmai, USS (n/a)
See *Mount Katmai. USS.*
Mt. McKinley, USS (n/a)
See *Vancouver*, *USS.*
Mt. Montezuma (BS 818-382)
See Mount Montezuma. Quang Ngai Pr, I Corps.
Mt. Nui Vien Nam (WJ 46-26)
See Nui Vien Nam. NVN.
Mt. Pr'line Commo Site (BP 03-18?)
See Pra Lean Signal Site. Tuyen Duc Pr, II Corps?
Mu, Vung (CQ 1-8)
Bay at 13°27'N-109°20'E. On ND49-09 JOG map. Phu Yen Pr, II Corps.
Mu, Vung (CR 1-0)
Bay at 13°34'N-109°18'E. On ND49-09 JOG map. Phu Yen Pr, II Corps.
Mu Duc Heliport (BS 711-625)
Sp variant or a.k.a. Mo Duc Heliport? Apx 13 km SSE Quang Ngai, 2 km N LZ Snoopy, 8 km NNW Mo Duc/Quang Hien, W QL-1. Heliport #617, alt 16', per Feb73 TAD. Quang Ngai Pr, I Corps.
Mu Gia Pass (WE 82-53)
A.k.a. Deo Mu Gia and Door of Death. Apx 180 km NW Quang Tri, 110 km due S Vinh and 95 km WNW Dong Hoi, near 17°40'00"N-105°47'00"E. Most important and most heavily used passes of HCMT. Also perhaps most heavily bombed piece of real estate in history of planet. On 28Feb65, acft from *USS* Coral Sea carried out 1st Barrel Roll strikes here. Key part of strategic NVA supply and troop infiltration route known as Ho Chi Minh Trail. Also called The Door of Death by NVA soldiers seeking access to HCMT through the Truong Son Mtns. Mu Gia was one of few available passes and, as a result, was focus of round-the-clock bombing, making it and other passes much feared and incredibly dangerous areas to traverse. Upon reaching pass from either end, "Already exhausted from climb, heavily laden soldiers broke into a run at Mu Gia. Truck drivers floored it. Anything to get through the 'Door of Death.' "[374] See Ban Karai and Ban Raving and Nape passes. Truong Son Mtns, Quang Binh Pr. NVN.
Muang Bac (n/a)
Mapsheet name of L-7014-6540-3. SVN.
Muang Kay Airfield (n/a)
On Mekong River, 20 km SW Luang Prabang. Per ONC-J-11. El. 800'. Laos.
Muang Kout Airfield (UH 30-44)
LS-195. CIA/SF, per *Air Facilities Data-Laos.*
Muang Met Airfield (n/a)
120 km NW Vientiane, 115 km SSW Luang Prabang. Per ONC-J-11. Laos.
Muang Phine Airfield (XD 09-28)
LS-300. CIA/SF, per *Air Facilities Data-Laos.*
Muang Phon Savan Airfield (n/a)
120 km ESE Luang Prabang. ONC-J-11. El. 3,609'. Laos.
Muang You Airfield (TG 73-94)
LS-261. CIA/SF, per *Air Facilities Data-Laos.*
Muc Hoa (XS 03-91)
See Moc Hoa. Per Bill Hunt, was home of MACV Adv Team 72. Kien Tuong Pr, IV Corps.
Muc Hoa SF Camps (XS 03-91)
See Moc Hoa. Kien Tuong Pr, IV Corps.
Muc Tan (XT?)
Fictional name used by *The Green Berets* author to represent either an actual camp or composite of SF Camps visited during his 6-month visit to VN, '64 or '65, and noted on pp 80-82 of his book. Described as being on NE edge of a large rubber plantation, 10 mi E Cambodia and 50 mi from Saigon. Was apparently a "showcase" SF camp, with "…snow white block cement structures, perfectly aligned," that had pitched shingle roofs. The perimeter berm was straight, clean with circular concrete MG positions. Likely III or IV Corps A-Team site. Duc Hoa, Muc Hoa, Tay Ninh, An Loc, Song Be, and Minh Than may generally fit that description.
Mud, LZ (BR 639-587)
In Vinh Thanh/Happy Valley, apx 3 km NE Vinh Thanh, 3 km SE Vinh Thanh AF and 22 km NE An Khe. Oct65. Binh Dinh Pr, II Corps.
Mud, LZ (ZB 125-163)
A.k.a. FSB Pierson. Near QL-14, apx 13 km SE Dak To 2 AF, 2 km SE Dien Binh, 10 km SSE Tanh Canh and 28 km NNW Kontum. On map at www.landscaper.net/chighmap.jpg. Grid per Nolan Putman. Kontum Pr, II Corps.
Muff Diver's Lounge (BT 008-754)
Small lounge situated in Covey FAC (20th TASS) cmpd at Da Nang AB. Built in '70, it was site of frequent and very boisterous parties. Discussed in detail in *Da Nang Diary*. Listed grid is that of AB. Quang Nam Pr, I Corps.
Mui (n/a)
Vietnamese for Cape or point.
Mui (name) (various)
See name in its appropriate alphabetical listing. For example, to access Mui Bai Khem, see Bai Khe, Mui; for Mui Hon Ngang, see Hon Ngang, Mui.
Mui Dinh Lighthouse (BN 84-57)
Apx 10 km ESE peak of Nui Ba Dec Mtn, and 22 km due S Phan Rang. Ninh Thuan Pr, II Corps.
Mui Dinh, Baie de (BN 6-4)
A.k.a. Baie de Padaran. Bay at 11°15'N-108°50'E. On NC49-01 JOG. Binh Thuan Pr, II Corps.
Mui Khe Ga Lighthouse (ZS 27-84)
On very small island just off Mui Khe Ga Cape, 28 km SSW Phan Thiet. Binh Thuan Pr, II Corps.
Mui Lon, FSB (XT 604-109)
Apx 7 km SW Cu Chi CB. 67. Hau Nghia Pr, III Corps.
Mui Nai Lighthouse (VS 39-46)
Apx 5 km WSW Ha Tien. Kien Gang Pr, IV Corps.
Muir, Camp (AT 965-615)
On Hill 55, apx 16 km SSW Da Nang AB. 3d/3d Marines, HQ 1st/11th Marines Arty. Named to honor 3d/3d Mar Bn CO LTC Joseph E. Muir, KIA on Hill 55, 11Sep65; stepped on booby-trapped 155 shell. Forward CP for Marines HQ'd at Da Nang in '66. Used by French in 1st Indochina war, who reportedly lost entire Bn in battle here during 1950's. See Hill 55. Quang Nam Pr, I Corps.

Muir, FSB (AT 965-615)
A.k.a. Hill 55. See Camp Muir and Hill 55 for detail. XXIV Corps grid. Mar-Apr69. Quang Nam Pr, I Corps.

Mukdahan Airfield (VD 6-1)
Directly W across the Mekong River from Savannakhet (Laos), and 540 km NE Bangkok at 16°27'00"N-104°43'00"E. Feb67 Natl Geo map. Thailand.

Mule, LZ (XD 781-561)
Apx 2 km N Lang Ha, 18 km NNW Khe Sanh CB and 46 km W Dong Ha. Apr70 XXIV Corps grid per Don Armstrong. Quang Tri Pr, I Corps.

Mule Team (n/a)
See Glossary.

Mule Train (n/a)
6Apr70, XXIV Corps proposed III MAF FSB name.

Mullany, USS (n/a)
DD-538, per Ralph Fries.

Mullen, Patrol Base (XT 196-553)
A.k.a. FSB Lee (XT 190-559)? Apx 4 km NNE Tay Ninh West AF and 8 km WSW peak Nui Ba Den. Mar69. Tay Ninh Pr, III Corps.

Mullinix, USS (n/a)
DD-944. SVN.

Munsee, USS (n/a)
ATF-107, Fleet Ocean Tug. SVN

Muong (n/a)
See also Moung entries.

Muong Airfield (n/a)
Apx 205 km WNW Phnom Penh. El.? Cambodia.

Muong Ang (n/a)
Mapsheet name of L-7014-5652-3. NVN only.

Muong Boum (n/a)
Mapsheet name of L-7014-5553-1. NVN/China.

Muong Bu (VJ 0-6)
French outpost W of the Black River. Survivors (16 of 84 men) of Muong Chen battle fled here, upon which the heroic Sgt Peyrol took out a bottle of Champagne he'd been saving for his daughter's birthday. His small force had endured the might of entire 312tth Vietminh Div and had much to celebrate for simply being alive. NVN.

Muong Cai (ZJ 09-85)
A.k.a. Mon Kay and Mong Cai. Within 10 km of ocean at point Chinese and NVN borders also meet ocean, apx 155 km ENE Haiphong and 240 km ENE Hanoi. NVN.

Muong Cassy Airfield (n/a)
A.k.a. Muong Kassy AF. Apx 140 km NNW Vientiane on Feb67 Natl Geo map. El. 1,300'. Laos.

Muong Cha (n/a)
Mapsheet name of L-7014-5552-1. NVN/Laos.

Muong Cha (n/a)
Mapsheet name of L-7014-6054-4. NVN only.

Muong Cha Airfield (n/a)
115 km NNE Vientiane. Per ONC-J-11. El. 3,700'. Laos.

Muong Chen (n/a)
Mapsheet name of L-7014-5852-2. NVN only.

Muong Chen Outpost (VJ 24-94?)
Apx 33 km WNW Nghia Lo, 100 km ESE Dien Bien Phu and 175 km NW Hanoi.

Muong Chen Outpost (VJ 2-9)
French frontier outpost in northern Tonkin. Described as small, log post on Muong Chen Hill. In 1952, the 284th Local Supplitive Co of 50 Tai Partisans held this outpost under French Sgt Peyrol. In Fall of '52, Maj. Marcelle Bigeard's (later of Dien Bien Phu fame) 6th French Colonial Paras passed through post while under hot pursuit by 312th Vietminh Div. 6th Paras had been sent to engage the 312th in order to give the French outposts of region chance to escape rapidly expanding Vietminh control. The 312th was an hour behind Bigerad's column but he needed a 3-hour lead to effect an escape, so he asked Peyrol and his small garrison to hold a rear-guard action to buy those hours; a Div against 50 men! When the Vietminh reached Muong Chen, Peyrol's unit held for requested 3-hours, and then its 40 Tai and 3 French survivors bolted through the Vietminh's lines. For 16 days they were pursued across the NW corner of Tonkin until Peyrol and only 15 survivors finally reached the Black River and safety. Apparently near 21°40'00"N-104°16'00"E per NIMA Gaz. NVN.

Muong Et Airfield (n/a)
Apx 350 km NE Vientiane. Natl Geo map. El. 886'. Laos.

Muong Hai Airfield (n/a)
Apx 355 km NNW Vientiane. El. 2,789'. Laos.

Muong Han Airfield (n/a)
See Hongsa AF. Laos.

Muong Houn Airfield (n/a)
Apx 220 km NNW Vientiane. El. 1,600'. Laos.

Muong Hum (n/a)
Mapsheet name of L-7014-5754-3. NVN/China.

Muong Hung (n/a)
Mapsheet name of L-7014-5750-1. NVN/Laos.

Muong Kassy Airfield (n/a)
A.k.a. Muong Cassy AF. Apx 140 km NNW Vientiane on Feb67 Natl Geo map. El. 1,300'. Laos.

Muong Khao Airfield (n/a)
Apx 220 km NNE Vientiane. El. 3,600'. Laos.

Muong Khoa (n/a)
Mapsheet name of L-7014-5753-3. NVN only.

Muong Khoua, Siege of (TJ 41-33)
13Apr-18May53. A.k.a. Muang Khoua or The Mousetrap. Along W bank of confluence of Nam Pak and Nam Hou Rivers, apx 65 km SW Dien Bien Phu. French outpost here under Capt. Teullier became legend for enduring month-long siege by overwhelming Vietminh forces during 1953 Communist Spring Offensive. Hill Alpha and Hill Pi were positions within 600 meters of main fort in town. All 3 positions were held by a total force of 300 *Chasseur Laotiens* (Laotian Light Inf), a handful of French off and NCO's, three 81mm and two 60mm mortars, and 2 MGs facing the entire 910th Bn of 148th Regional Rgt, a mortar Co, and other elements of 316th Vietminh Div. On 12Apr53, an attempted escape by water down river 40 miles to Muong Ngoi was ambushed only 600 meters below town. Initial attack on base took place 13Apr53. On 3Apr53, Teullier had been ordered to hold position at all costs for at least 14 days to keep Vietminh engaged so other garrisons in area could escape. Hand-to-hand battles raged before hills fell. On27Ap53, French cmd parachuted in Legion of Honor for Capt. Teullier and enough *Croix de Guerre* for entire unit as honor for their heroic stand (Teullier waded across river under fire to hill positions and personally awarded each man their medals). Final assault took place 18May53, after 36 days of attacks. Only 4

among the 300 French are known to have survived. Per *Street Without Joy*, pp116-130, maps at pp 117, 120. Laos.

Muong Khuong (n/a)
AMS/DMA mapsheet L 701-5879-3. NVN/China.

Muong Lam (n/a)
Mapsheet name of L-7014-5751-3. NVN only.

Muong Lam (n/a)
Mapsheet name of L-7014-5948-3. NVN/Laos.

Muong Lat (n/a)
Mapsheet name of L-7014-5950-3. NVN/Laos.

Muong Mugne Airfield (n/a)
Apx 280 km NW Vientiane. El. 2,000'. Laos.

Muong Nane Airfield (RB 03-59)
LS-254. CIA/SF, per *Air Facilities Data-Laos.*

Muong Ngeun Airfield (n/a)
Apx 330 km NNW Vientiane. El. 2,300'. Laos.

Muong Ngoi (TJ)
Apx 45 km SSE Muong Khoua (65 km by water) and 85 km SSW Dien Bien Phu. Apparently a French garrison here '53. See Muong Khoua, Siege of. Laos.

Muong Ngoi Airfield (n/a)
Possibly Ban Na AF? Apx 305 km due N Vientiane on Feb67 Natl Geo map. El. 1,181'. Laos.

Muong No (n/a)
Mapsheet name of L-7014-5553-2. NVN only.

Muong Nong Airfield (XD 60-10)
A.k.a. L-19. Apx 445 km ESE Vientiane on Feb67 Natl Geo map. Per *Air Facilities Data-Laos.* El. 600'. Laos.

Muong Ou Tay Airfield (n/a)
Apx 470 km NNW Vientiane. El. 2,297'

Muong Peun Airfield (n/a)
Apx 230 km NE Vientiane. El. 3,932'. Laos.

Muong Phalane Airfield (WD 6-4)
Apx 340 km ESE Vientiane. El. 560'. Laos.

Muong Phalane SF Camp (WD 6-4)
A.k.a. Muong Phalan. SF camp when Lao neutrality declared, 23Jul62. FTT 26 and ATT 3 here then. Per *Special Forces at War*. MR3, Laos.

Muong Phalane TACAN Site (WD 6-4?)
1 of 4 USAF Op Bright Light TACAN sites in Laos and thinly disguised as an "Air America commo facility." Attacked by NVA, 25Dec67, in order to disrupt potential air war against NVA in central/SVN during planned '68 Tet Offensive. Was mortared and then overrun. Most structures were destroyed and 2 US Lockheed Corp. civilians were killed; however, the TACAN equipment had not been damaged when Lao Army recaptured site. Laos.

Muong Sai Airfield (n/a)
Apx 310 km NNW Vientiane. El. 1,804'. Laos.

Muong Sen (n/a)
Mapsheet name of L-7014-5847-4. NVN/Laos.

Muong Sing Airfield (n/a)
Apx 385 km NNW Vientiane. El. 2,231'. Laos.

Muong So (Phong Tho) (n/a)
Mapsheet L-7014-5654-2. Sheet name: Phong Tho (Muong So). NVN/China.

Muong Soi Airfield (n/a)
Apx 325 km NE Vientiane. El. 1,312'. Laos.

Muong Son Airfield (n/a)
Apx 285 km NNE Vientiane. El. 3,000'. Laos.

Muong Soui Airfield (n/a)
Apx 175 km N Vientiane. El. 3,600'. Laos.

Muong Soum Airfield (n/a)
Apx 90 km due N Vientiane, 70 km NNW Ritaville AF. Per ONC-J-11. El. 900'. Laos.

Muong Te (n/a)
Mapsheet name of L-7014-5553-4. NVN only.

Muong Thanh Valley (TJ 93-63)
Valley in which Dien Bien Phu was located. NVN.

Muong Tiouen Airfield (n/a)
Apx 210 km due ENE Vientiane. El. 1,300'. Laos.

Muong Tong (n/a)
Mapsheet name of L-7014-5553-3. NVN/Laos.

Muong Tong (n/a)
Mapsheet name of L-7014-5652-4. NVN only.

Muong Trai (n/a)
Mapsheet name of L-7014-5752-2. NVN only.

Muong, Mui (CP 1-8)
Coastal point at 12°30'N-109°19'E. On ND49-13 JOG. Khanh Hoa Pr, II Corps.

Muong/Nung (n/a)
See Glossary.

Muriel, FSB (ZA 137-913)
A.k.a. LZ Muriel. Just E Polei Breng, 4 km E Polei Krong AF and 11 km WNW Kontum. Per Dick Arnold, 4th Div AARs indicate LZs Muriel, Ingrid, Thunder and Irma Jay were built by 1st/14th Inf, early-mid Jul68, while LZ Bass was being demolished, and Muriel was dismantled 12Aug8 by 1st/14th Inf. 1st/92d and 2d/9th Arty here Jun-Jul68. Name/grid per Craig Miller. Also listed at ZA 141-912 Kontum Pr, II Corps.

Murray Field (YS 29-47?)
765th Trans Bn's baseball field at Vung Tau. Phuoc Tuy Pr, III Corps.

Murrel D Thomas Open Mess (XS 8-9)
Within Camp Jack L. Goodman, Saigon. Named to honor SSgt Murrel D Thomas, SF Det A-301, KIA, 22May65, near Ben Cat. Gia Dinh Pr, III Corps.

Muscara Compound (XS 8-9)
At 121 Chi Lang St., Saigon. Named to honor SFC Carrnen Muscara, KIA 28Apr68 after being shot down while flying as volunteer recon photographer with Maj. Morrison Cotnor, liaison to 28th "White Horse Rgt" of ROK 9th Inf Div. Their mission was to photograph caves and bunkers concealing VC anti-aircraft facilities near Tuy Hoa. Plane crashed in sea SE Tuy Hoa. Data per R. Bows' *Vietnam Military Lore, 1959-1973.* Gia Dinh Pr, III Corps.

Muscatine, Operation (n/a)
19Dec67-10Jun68. 1st Bde of Americal Div. 1,129 rptd NVA/VC KIA. Quang Ngai Pr, I Corps.

MUSCLE SHOALS System (XD)
See Glossary.

Museum Beach (BT 033-767)
Possibly a.k.a. "Shit Beach?" See Da Nang Museum. Quang Nam Pr, I Corps.

Museum Ramp (BT 033-767)
See Da Nang Museum. Quang Nam Pr, I Corps.

Mushroom, The (XT 58-32)
An upside-down mushroom-shaped terrain feature and aerial landmark formed by course of Song Saigon River, apx 45 km NW Saigon, 20 km WSW Lai Khe and 8 km

SSE Dau Tieng in area known as "The Trapezoid." FSB Tennessee was at point where stem joined cap of mushroom. Stem of Mushroom was major drop-off point along Saigon River for NVA/VC troops/supplies destined for Iron Triangle. Discussed in *Low Level Hell* and on its 1st Div TAOR map. Also on map in *Rangers at War*, Appendix I, p 324. Grid apx. Binh Duong Pr, III Corps.

Musket, FSB (ZC 094-937)
N the Hai Van Pass apx 30 km SSW Phu Bai, 9 km due S Phu Loc and QL-1. Photo easy re: '70 arty strike from this FSB is in *Vietnam Experience, Combat Photographer* vol, pp 36-37. Thua Thien Pr, I Corps.

Muskrat, FSB (XD 825-537)
Apx 2 km SW peak of Hill 1739, 14 km NNW Khe Sanh CB, 27 km W Mai Loc and 8 km N to NNE Ap La Vien. XXIV Corps grid. Quang Tri Pr, I Corps.

Mustang, FSB (AT 788-552)
A.k.a. Hill 52. Along Rte 4, apx 10 km WSW Hill 65, 7 km due E FSB Hawk, 19 km WSW Hill 55, 35 km W Hoi An and 33 km SW Da Nang. Built by 1st/7th Marines beginning apx 21Mar69, in prep for Op Oklahoma Hills. Map is L-7014-6640-4, and shown on *US Marines in Vietnam-1969* map, p 109. Apr70 XXIV Corps grid per Don Armstrong. Quang Nam Pr, I Corps.

Mustang, FSB (WD or WC?)
See FSB Lion. Laos.

Mustang, FSB (XT 090-910)
Along Rte 246, 2 km E Cambodia, 9 km N Thien Ngon AF, 24 km due W Katum, 3 km NE QL-22/Rte 246 junction. 3d/21st Inf, 196th LIB here, Op Junction City, 22Feb-17Mar67. 2d/1st Inf also here. Tay Ninh Pr, III Corps.

Mustang, FSB/LZ (XT 366-820)
Apx 9 km SSE Katum, 42 km WSW An Loc, 28 km due E Thien Ngon AF and 32 km NNE Tay Ninh. Also listed at XT 432-817 and 371-820, Jan69. Tay Ninh Pr, III Corps.

Mustang, LZ (BR 473-466)
At An Khe AF, 3 km SSE the Golf Course and 41 km W Phu Cat AB. Mar66. Binh Dinh Pr, II Corps.

Mustang, LZ (BR 770-980?)
Along An Lao River apx 10 km WNW Bong Son/Hoai Nhon, 13 km SSE Thuan An and 12 km WSW LZ English. Per Mike Cohen, A/1st/8th Cav, was built on small hill along E bank of river by his A Co during Nov67. He recalls this company-sized LZ being built with sandbags filled at river's edge and carried back up hill on "Mules" (see Mule in Glossary). Remains of old, bomb-destroyed and rusty steel bridge crossed river nearby. Hill was apx 150' high and featured quad .50 Cal MG mounted in fixed site along N edge of base. Each night, quad .50 would fire a few hundred rounds up An Lao Valley to test guns and put on a show. Helo lndg pad was built at NW edge and outside the wire, then peneprimed to minimize dusty landings. Binh Dinh Pr, II Corps.

Mustang II, LZ (AR 780-545)
Apx 4 km due N Pleiku-Cu Hanh AF, 4 km E Pleiku-Nansteph AF, 7 km N to NNE Pleiku and 5 km SE Plei Mui. 3Jan66. See Mustang III. Pleiku Pr, II Corps.

Mustang III, PZ (ZA 218-342)
Immed SE Catecka AF and 13 km SSW Pleiku and 7 km SSE Plei Pao Xoi. Apparently a PZ, 3Jan66. See Mustang II. Pleiku Pr, II Corps.

Mustangs, LZ (XT 320-397)
Apx 2 km NNW LZ Warhorse, 8 km SE Tay Ninh, 5 km NE Ap Van Long and 17 km WSW Dau Tieng. 1st Cav LZ. Name/grids per Kevan Mynderup. Tay Ninh Pr, III Corps.

Mutter's Ridge (XD 945-624 to XD 999-615)
Ran roughly E to W from XD 94-62 to XD 99-62 as part of major ridgeline a.k.a. Nui Cay Tre Ridge, and was dominated by Hills 461, 484 (Nui Cay Tre) and Hill 400. Portion of Nui Cay Tre Mtn range that included spiny series of hills running parallel to center of DMZ, apx 18 km due N Vandegrift CB, 4 km WNW to NW FSB Fuller and 5 km N the Rockpile. Roughly at center of Quang Tri Pr, between the coast and Laotian border. Ridge formed N end of what was known as Razorback Valley. Scene of heavy fighting for 3d Bn/4th Mar/3d Mar Div, Op Prairie, Aug-Oct66, during which K/3d/4th's CO, Capt. J. J. Carroll was KIA (see Camp Carroll). During op, 3d/4th Marines assaulted ridge for control of Hills 400 and 484, initiating Battle of Nui Cay Tre Ridge, 22Sep-5Oct66. Call sign of 3d/4th and its CO (Col William J. Masterpool) was "Mutter," and when Bn finally took hill 5Oct66, it was renamed "Mutter's Ridge" in their honor. Map is L-7014-6342-1 (Cam Lo). Quang Tri Pr, I Corps.

MUVN (n/a)
See Shufly.

Muy Ang, Cape (XE 6-8)
See Cape Muy Ang. NVN.

My An (n/a)
Mapsheet name of L-7014-6130-2. SVN.

My An (WS 92-62)
Along Rte 214, apx 29 km SSW Moc Hoa and 33 km NNW Vinh Long AF. Kien Tuong Pr, IV Corps.

My An Heliport (WS 933-636)
A.k.a. Me An Heliport. Apx 24 km ENE Cao Lanh AF. Heliport #708, alt 7', at: 10°31'N 105°51'E, per Feb73 TAD. Kien Phong Pr, IV Corps.

My An/My Da SF Camp (WS 9998-6205?)
If grid correct, was apx 6 km E My An, 30 km SSW Moc Hoa, 32 km NNW Vinh Long AF and 52 km WNW My Tho. However, it is possible proper grid is WS 933-620, as that is site of My An. SF Det 72, 5th SF Op Bases (SFOB); also Det A-426 (was A-433) and later an RF/PF base. Grid per *SF Order of Battle*. Kien Tuong Pr, IV Corps.

My Binh Base (XS 720-490)
Along W side of Dong So, apx 13 km WNW Go Cong and 22 km ENE My Tho. Apr70. Go Cong Pr, IV Corps.

My Ca Bridge (CP 0-2)
On Cam Ranh Peninsula between main AB(?) and 6th Convalescent Hosp. Khanh Hoa Pr, II Corps.

My Ca Monastery (CP 0-2)
A.k.a. Monastere de My Ca. At Xom My Ca, near 11°59'00"N-109°13'00"E. Khanh Hoa Pr, II Corps.

My Canh 2, Battle of (CQ 0-2?)
Near Tuy Hoa, Feb66. Apparently took place in Tuy Hoa Rice Bowl, and involved Tiger Force Recon elements of 101st Abn's 1st Bde. Discussed in *Rangers At War*, at p. 154. Phu Yen Pr, II Corps.

My Canh Floating Restaurant (XS 8-9)
Restaurant in Saigon River hit by terrorist bombing in '65? Gia Dinh Pr, III Corps.

My Chan Bridge, Thon (YD 460-400)
A.k.a. Song Thac Ma Bridge. See Thon My Chan Bridge. Quang Tri Pr at Thua Thien Pr border, I Corps.

My Chanh, FSB (YD 442-394)
See FSB Nancy. Quang Tri Pr, I Corps.

My Chanh Bridge (YD 460-400)
QL-1 bridge over Rao Tach Ma, apx 33 km NW Hue and 16 km SE Quang Tri. Quang Tri/Thua Thien Pr, I Corps.

My Chanh RR Bridge (YD 461-399)
See My Chanh Bridge. Quang Tri/Thua Thien Pr, I Corps.

My Chanh, Thon (YD 465-403)
Along QL-1 apx 35 km NW Hue, 18 km SE Quang Tri. Map is L-7014-6442-2, per Ken Burrington. Quang Tri Pr?, I Corps.

My Chanh Defensive Line (YD 4-3)
During '72 Easter Offensive, ARVN stopped NVA armor thrust S down QL-1 at a last-stand defensive line set-up along My Chanh River (formed Quang Tri/Thua Thien Pr border), roughly 35 km NW Hue. B-52 and naval gunfire then badly mauled static NVA and their extended supply lines, forcing start of their eventual retreat back to Ben Hai River. Thua Thien/Quang Tri Pr, I Corps.

My Chanh Heliport (YD 046-339)
In Da Krong River Valley apx 15 km SSE Vandegrift CB, 7 km SSE FSB Henderson and 14 km WSW Ba Long AF. Heliport #618, alt 1,440'. On map at p 32, *US Marines in Vietnam-1969*. Quang Tri Pr, I Corps.

My Chanh River (YD 48-42)
A.k.a. River Giang. Apx 35 km NW Hue, 18 km SE Quang Tri. Map is L-7014-6442-2, per Ken Burrington. Quang Tri or Thua Thien Pr, I Corps.

My Chanh Valley (YD 40-34)
Apx 16 km SSW Quang Tri, 35 km WNW Hue. VC base area swept by Op Liberty Canyon. Thua Thien Pr, I Corps.

My Da (BN 7-7)
A.k.a. Thon Togtoampu Tam. At 11°31'00"N-108°58'00"E, per NIMA. Ninh Thuan Pr, II Corps.

My Da (WS 999-620?)
See My An/My Da SF Camp. Kien Tuong Pr, IV Corps.

My Da/My An SF Camp (WS 9998-6205)
See My An/My Da SF Camp. Kien Tuong Pr, IV Corps.

My Dien (various)
Common Viet place-name. Sites inc: XJ 1-5, WH 9-0, CR 0-3 and CQ 1-3. NVN and II Corps.

My Dien II SF Camp (XS 365-605)
Apx 48 km SW Saigon, 18 km WSW Tan An and 22 km NW My Tho. 5th SF Grp CIDG Det A-416, Jan68. E/2d/39th here on 2Jun68, per Jim Stone, 2d/39th Inf. Also listed at VS 365-605; however, that grid is in Cambodia apx 15 km NNW Ha Tien SVN, and likely in error. Grid per *SF Order of Battle.* Also listed at VS 995-764 as Nhan Hung SF Camp? Kien Tuong Pr, IV Corps.

My Dien II, Camp (VS 995-764?)
See Nhan Hung. Chau Doc Pr, IV Corps.

My Duc (n/a)
Mapsheet name of L-7014-6343-3. NVN only.

My Hanh (XT 614-017)
Hamlet in Duc Hoa Dist apx 22 km WNW Tan Son Nhut AB and 9 km ESE Khiem Cuong. At end of Aug68, 2d/14th Inf 25th ID moved here to build FSB Keene as Bn HQ, during Op Toan Thang III. Data per Hist Supp, 1Jan-31Dec68, 2d/14th Inf on-line at www.en.com/users/kramsey/vnr102.html#. Hau Nghia Pr, III Corps.

My Hanh/Ba Tu Corridor (XT/XS)
Saigon area infiltration route. Hau Nghia Pr, III Corps.

My Khe (BT 07-78)
A.k.a. China Beach. US, in-country R&R center on Tien Sha Peninsula between Monkey Mtn and Marble Mtn. See China Beach for detail. Da Nang, Quang Nam Pr, I Corps.

My Lai 4 (BS 73-77)
Near LZ Pinkville, roughly 8 km S LZ Uptight (at BS 720-780) and 10 km SE LZ Dottie. One of 4 small hamlets integrated within Song My, inc: My Lai 1, 2, 3 and 4. My Lai 4 was site of 16Mar68 massacre of estimated 500 unarmed civilians by C/1st Bn, 20th Inf Rgt, 11th Inf Bde, 23d Inf (Americal) Div, under Cmd of Capt. Ernest Medina and working out of LZ Dottie. In Mar70, Medina was charged with murder but cleared of all charges in Sep70. In Apr69, Medina's 1st Plt Ldr, Lt William Calley, was charged with murdering 102 Viet civilians and convicted on 29Mar71 for the premeditated murder of at least 22 Viets and sentenced to life at hard labor. In Aug71, his sentence was reduced to 20 years and, in Apr74 to 10 years. Then, in Nov75 his sentence was commuted by Presidential Order(?). Although incident represents absolute worst US troop behavior, it also produced some of best when WO-1 Hugh Thompson and his 2 door gunners landed their Huey between civilians and advancing US Troops after realizing a tragedy was unfolding. Thompson ordered his gunners to fire on the Americans if they attempted to harm the civilians, and then had an orbiting gunship land to extract the civilians in several sorties while his ship stayed on ground protecting the innocents until all had been extracted. He and his crew also landed to rescue a living baby from a pile of victims and flew it to safety. Thompson's calls for help/investigation went unheeded, and nothing was done until Ron Ridenour (non-participant who heard participants' stories while in VN), gathered evidence and presented it to 30 Congressman (2 years later). In 1998, the Thompson crew was awarded the Army's Soldier Medal for their heroism in rescuing the civilians (in addn to DFC awarded in '69 for presumably protecting civilians from "enemy" force). Recommended reading is *My Lai 4*. See Son Thang-4. Son My Dist, Quang Ngai Pr, I Corps.

My Lai CAP (BS 73-77?)
CAP 1-4-6. Cited in Jim Champion's *Combined Action Platoons*, p 52, per CAP Website. Grid for My Lai ville complex, not CAP site. Quang Ngai Pr, I Corps.

My Lan (AT 875-175)
Apx 44 km due W Tam Ky and 8 km SSW Hiep Duc. Americal list. Quang Tin Pr, I Corps.

My Loc Basecamp (YD 305-680)
Apx 5 km W mouth Cua Viet River, 16 km NNE Quang Tri and 8 km E QL-1. Apr-May68. Quang Tri Pr, I Corps.

My Loc II Outpost (AT 912-513)
A.k.a. My Loc (2) Outpost. Apx 2 km S Song Thu Bon River, 5 km NE An Hoa AF and 26 km SSW Da Nang AB. Aug67. 3d Mar Div elements here late '66, during Op Mississippi. In op, civilians of Hiep Duc (Antenna Valley) relocated to My Loc (2). Detailed discussion of site in *Not Going Home Alone*, Chp 5. Quang Nam Pr, I Corps.

My Loc (2) Outpost (AT 912-513)
See My Loc II Outpost. Quang Nam Pr, I Corps.

My Phu, Battle of (CQ 1-3?)
Near Tuy Hoa, Mar66. Took place in Tuy Hoa Rice Bowl, and involved Bn of 1st Bde/101st Abn engaging NVA Bn as it prepared to attack a US FSB. During battle, 101st's Tiger Force LRRP element was inserted at night to supt heavily engaged US Bn in what some claim was 1st night helo assault of US war (however, 1st Cav reinforced a unit near LZ Mary with night CA in Nov65). Discussed in *Rangers At War*, p. 154. Phu Yen Pr, II Corps.

My Phuoc Tay (XS 203-598)
Along Kinh Muo Hai Canal apx 33 km NW My Tho and 8 km NNW Cai Lay. 5th SF Operating Bases (SFOB) Det A-411 (was A-424) here. 9th Inf Div units fought fierce battle nearby in Oct68, per *Doc: Platoon Medic*, p 15. Dinh Tuong Pr, IV Corps.

My Phuoc Tay Heliport (XS 203-598)
Along Kinh Muo Hai Canal, apx 33 km NW My Tho and 8 km NNW Cai Lay. Heliport #619, alt 7', sod pad. Land E or W. Road by tower, orbit approach over agricultural ville, per Feb73 TAD. Dinh Tuong Pr, IV Corps.

My Phuoc Tay SF Camp (XS 2006-5984)
Along Kinh Muo Hai Canal, apx 33 km NW My Tho and 8 km NNW Cai Lay. 5th SF camp, and base for 2d/60th Inf, 9th Div per Jim Stone. Battle discussed in *Doc: Platoon Medic*, p 15. Transferred to RF/PF. Info/grid per *SF Order of Battle*. 9th Inf Div units fought fierce battle nearby, Oct68, per *Doc: Platoon Medic*, p 15. Mentioned in *Dispatches*, p. 257. Dinh Tuong Pr, IV Corps.

My Thanh Airfield (BS 545-730)
See Thuan Hoa AF. Quang Ngai Pr, I Corps.

My Tho (n/a)
Mapsheet name of L-7014-6229-1. SVN.

My Tho (XS 49-45)
On N bank of Mekong River, apx 84 km NE Soc Trang and 50 km SW Saigon. Home of 7th ARVN Inf Div Advsy Det, Advsy Team 75 at Monastery Cmpd (had been French monastery until abnd in mid '50s). 1,200' AF used by Army Caribou acft for resupply. Founded by Chinese refugees fleeing Taiwan, town became 1 of SVN's 6 autonomous municipalities in Sep70. Taken by VC during Tet68, and heavily damaged by US bombing and Arty when retaken. Population of about 100,000 at time. Map is L-7014-6229-1, per Jim Stone. Capitol, Dinh Tuong Pr, IV Corps.

My Tho Airfield (XS 463-523)
See Ben Tranh AF. Dinh Tuong Pr, IV Corps.

My Tho Heliport (XS 492-449)
At My Tho, N the Mekong River and roughly 50 km SW Saigon. "Heliport #620, alt 7', gravel/tar pad, Ammo-7.62, 2.75" rockets. Apx 250' tower apx 1/2 mile SE heliport. Arty advsy-Dong Tam 222.7, 42.6. At: 10°21'15"N-106°22'00"E," per Feb73 TAD. Map is L-7014-6229-1, per Jim Stone. Dinh Tuong Pr, IV Corps.

My Tho Leper Colony (XS 4-4?)
At My Tho, apx 50 km SW Saigon. C Bty 3d/34th Arty, 9th Inf MRF made $90 monthly contributions to this facility during '68-69. Per MRF Assn website at www.mrfa.org 3_34th.htm. See Giong Trom pagoda. Dinh Tuong Pr, IV Corps.

My Tho New Airfield (XS 478-450)
See Binh Duc AF. Dinh Tuong Pr, IV Corps.

My Tho NSA (XS 48-44)
On Mekong River, apx 6 km E Dong Tam. USN Supt Activity, '66-69. Per MRF Assn. Dinh Tuong Pr, IV Corps.

My Tho PBR Base (XS 48-44?)
On Mekong River, apx 6 km E Dong Tam. River Div 53, TF-116, USN Gamewarden base here, per MRF Assn website at www.mrfa.org. Map is L-7014-6229-1, per Jim Stone. Dinh Tuong Pr, IV Corps.

My Tho Province (WS/XS)
In what later became known as IV Corps and absorbed into what became primarily Go Cong and Dinh Tuong Pr?, Thought to have ceased existence shortly before or during early US presence? Actual dates of existence unknown.

My Tho River (XS 75-37)
See Thoi Son Island. IV Corps.

My Thoi Airfield (WS 521-416)
See Long Xuyen AF. Chau Doc Pr, IV Corps.

My Thuan Ferry Landing (WS 985-358)
Ferry across Mekong River, apx 8 km WNW Vinh Long and 15 km E Sa Dec. Sa Dec/Dinh Tuong Pr, IV Corps.

My Thuoc Tay (XS 203-598)
See My Phuoc Tay. Dinh Tuong Pr, IV Corps.

My Trang Outpost (BS 832-337?)
Near QL-1 and apx 6 km SSE Duc Pho AF. NPIA grid. Cited in *Locator* section of Dec00 *Veteran* Mag, p 39. See *McKean, USS*. Quang Ngai Pr, I Corps.

My Yen, FSB? (XS 69-81)
Just E My Yen, apx 3 km NW Binh Chanh and 20 km SW Tan Son Nhut AB. Listed as unknown 199th LIB FSB; however, My Yen is closest ville to site. 199th LIB FSB/patrol base grid courtesy the 199th LIB Assn. Long An or Gia Dinh Pr, III Corps.

Myles C. Fox, USS (n/a)
DD-829, per Ralph Fries.

Myron, FSB (YU 03-40?)
If grid correct, was just inside Cambodia at point where QL-14A crossed border, apx 7 km NE Bu Dop AF, 6 km SW Phum Leu 47 km due E Snuol. Per 199th LIB Assn, was at listed grid and 5th/12th Inf here during Cambodian Incursion, May70. Data per www.redcatcher.org/Cambodia.html. Also listed at YU 063-445. Cambodia.

Myron, FSB (YU 063-445?)
Along Rte 14A in Cambodia, apx 3 km SSE Phu Sre Preah, 30 km WNW Djamap AF/Bu Gia Map, 17 km NNE Bu Dop, 6 km due N FSB Brown/Bu Dop, and 10 km N SVN border. On 8May70, D/2d/12th Cav CA'd to clearing N Myron where it discovered and secured "Rock Island East", a huge NVA/NLF basecamp and supply depot. Named to honor Maj Myron Diduryk, KIA 24Apr70, when shot on Bn CO's CC Bird as it was lndg in what was thought to be an abnd FSB. [375] C Bty, 2d/12th Arty here

with six-155mm howitzers. AO of 1st Cav, 11th ACR and 199th LIB; 5th/12th Inf, 199th LIB. Grid and some data per *11th ACR Cambodia Invasion AAR, 1st Cav Div, May-Jun70*, courtesy Lou Rochat. [376] Also listed at YU 069-436 and 03-40? Another source puts FSB Brown at YU 063-445? Cambodia.

Mystery, FSB (YT 251-714)
A.k.a. FSB Mystery Hill. Apx 8 km WSW FSB Green, 17 km ESE Dong Xoai, 18 km S Bunard AF and 16 km N Rang Rang. Opened or reopened 1Sep70; closed 9Sep70 by 1st/7th Cav. Reopened 25Sep70, closed 14Oct70 by 1st/7th. Name/data per *1st Cav Div Op Rpt, ending 31Oct70*, courtesy Peter Cole. Phuoc Long Pr, III Corps.

Mystery Hill, FSB (YT 251-714)
See Mystery, FSB for location. Opened or reopened 1Sep70, closed 9Sep70, by 1st/7th Cav. Reopened 25Sep70, closed 14Oct70 by 1st/7th. Name/data per *1st Cav Div Op Rpt, ending 31Oct70*, courtesy Peter Cole. Mike Pautler, B Bty (DS), 1/21st Arty, recalls this as mini FSB built along on steep saddle-top that could barely hold its three 105s and two 81mm mortars. 105s/mortars were on one peak of saddle (with FDC sometimes at edge of crest), while smaller peak held bunker and .50 Cal MG. Saddle used as helo pad. "B-1/21 suptd the 1st/7th Cav, 1st Cav after they moved to this AO following the Cambodian Invasion. We fired M-102s and had two vehicles on firebase: a 3/4 ton pickup and a mule. It only existed 2 to 4 months." Paulter also remembers site being given this name because hill wasn't on map, and recalls survey teams trying to survey site were prevented from doing so by monsoonal cloud-cover. Phuoc Long Pr, III Corps. [377]

Mystic Dagger (BP 03-18?)
See Pra Lean Signal Site. Tuyen Duc Pr, II Corps.

November

Facility/Feature Name, Grid Coordinate, a.k.a. Name/History/Province/CTZ

Unless otherwise stated, 6-digit grid coordinates reference DMA L-7014, L-7015 or L-7016 series, 1:50,000 scale maps, while 2- and 4-digit coordinates reference AMS/DMA/NIMA 1:250,000, 1:500,000 and 1:1,000,000 scale maps. Unless otherwise stated, all heights are in meters. To convert meters to feet, multiply by 3.2808; feet to meters, multiply by .3048.

Na Bo (Moc Chau) (n/a)
Mapsheet L-7014-5950-4. Full sheet name: Moc Chau (Na Bo). NVN only.

Na Bua Airfield (QV 0-0)
At 17°11'00"N-100°53'00"E. NIMA data. Thailand.

Na Cham (n/a)
Mapsheet name of L-7014-6353-3. NVN/China.

Na Dao Airfield (UG 40-47)
LS-70. Apx 185 km NE Vientiane. CIA/SF, per *Air Facilities Data-Laos*. El. 2,700'. Laos.

Na Fac (n/a)
Mapsheet name of L-7014-6153-1. NVN only.

Na Khang Airfield (UH 41-10)
LS-36. CIA/SF per *Air Facilities Data-Laos*. El. 4,400'. Overrun by elements of 316th PAVN Div, early '69, per *War in Laos*, p 24. Laos.

Na Krong Bolah River (XD/YD)
See Ya Krong River. Quang Tri/Thua Thien Pr, I Corps.

Na Kung (n/a)
Mapsheet name of L-7014-6055-2. NVN/China.

Na Lang Airfield (QV 26-59)
LS-286 and Na Leng. Per *Air Facilities Data-Laos.*

Na Lay (n/a)
Mapsheet name of L-7014-6055-3. NVN/China.

Na Leng Airfield (QV 26-59)
LS-286 and Na Lang AF. Per *Air Facilities Data-Laos.*

Na Luang Airfield, New (TF 71-91)
LS-252. CIA/SF, per *Air Facilities Data-Laos.*

Na Nong (n/a)
Mapsheet name of L-7014-6054-3. Covers NVN.

Na Poung Airfield (TG 55-48)
LS-78. CIA/SF, per *Air Facilities Data-Laos.*

Na San (various)
Common Viet place-name. Grid squares inc: VM 2-2, VM 2-2, TK 9-2, XK 6-3, WL 1-2, XL 5-1, UK 5-6, UK 6-6, XK 5-4, VJ 0-4VJ 1-6, UJ 9-4 and VH 4-6. NVN/SVN.
Na San Airfield (VJ 01-46)
A.k.a. Ban Loi AF. Major AF apx 5 km W Ban Loi and I85 km WNW Hanoi. Per ONC-J-11. El. 2,050'. NVN.
Na San (VJ 02-46)
On plateau between Red and Nam Ma Rivers, apx 185 km W Hanoi. French hastily built airheads at Lai Chau and Na San in order to aid and supply Col Bigeard's 6th Paras as they retreated from battle at Tu Le, Oct52. Was held by 4 Inf Bns, 1 Arty grp that were airlifted in over 4-day period. Per *Street Without Joy*, p 77. NVN.
Na Vat Airfield (n/a)
Apx 380 km NNW Vientiane. El. 1,772'. Laos.
Na Wiang Airfield (QV 2-1)
At 17°17'00"N-101°09'00"E. NIMA data. Thailand.
Na Xieng Airfield (UG 53-48)
LS-181. CIA/SF, per *Air Facilities Data-Laos.*
NAAPTB, FSB (CP 034-510)
Apx 2-3 km SSW Nha Trang AF, 3 km due W Thon Thuong Tay and perhaps 1 km W Vinh Truong. A Bty, 2d/17th Arty, Nov70-Apr71. Meaning of acronym unknown. Grid and arty info per Nolan Putman. Khanh Hoa Pr, II Corps.
Nac, FSB (AT 921-795)
Apx 3 km SW Red Beach AF, 11 km WNW Da Nang AB and 3 km W QL-1. XXIV Corps grid per Don Armstrong. Quang Nam Pr, I Corps.
Nack, FSB (AT 921-795)
See Nac. Quang Nam Pr, I Corps.
Nag, FSB (AT 921-785)
Apx 11 km NW Da Nang AB and 4 km SW Red Beach AF. Oct70. Quang Nam Pr, I Corps.
Nagor Rjasima (SB 8-5)
See Korat AB, Thailand.
Nai, Dam (BN 8-8)
Lagoon at 11°37'N-109°02'E. On NC49-01 JOG. Ninh Thuan Pr, II Corps.
Nai, Lagune de (BN 8-8)
A.k.a. Dam Nai. Lagoon at 11°37'N-109°02'E. On NC49-01 JOG. Ninh Thuan Pr, II Corps.
Nai, Mui (CQ 3-2)
A.k.a. Cape Varella. At 12°54'N-109°26'E. On ND49-13 JOG. Khanh Hoa Pr, II Corps.
Nai, Mui (VS 3-4)
Coastal point at 10°22'N-104°27'E. On NC48-06 JOG. Kien Giang Pr, IV Corps.
Nai Lagoon (BN 8-8)
A.k.a. Dam Nai. Lagoon at 11°37'N-109°02'E. On NC49-01 JOG. Ninh Thuan Pr, II Corps.
Nai Van Heliport (AT 933-915)
See Hai Van Heliport Thua Thien Pr, I Corps.
Nail, LZ (BR 643-824)
Apx 25 km SW Bong Son and 41 km NNE An Khe. Mar66. Binh Dinh Pr, II Corps.
Nail, FSB (YS 282-836)
A.k.a. Nails. Apx 22 km WNW Binh Gia, 31 km SW Xuan Loc, and 17 km ESE Long Thanh AF. 11-31Jan68. Also listed YS 275-804? Bien Hoa Pr, III Corps.
Nails, FSB (YS 275-804)
A.k.a. Nail. Apx 19 km WNW Binh Gia, 33 km SW Xuan Loc, and 20 km SE Long Thanh AF. 11-31Jan68. Also listed YS 282-836? Bien Hoa Pr, III Corps.
Naked Fanny (n/a)
See Nakhon Phanom West. Nickname for USAF's major AB, a.k.a. NKP. Thailand.
Nakhon Phanom Airfield (VE 7-2)
Minor AF just W the Mekong River and Laotian border, 610 km NE Bangkok, 210 km E Udorn AB, 10 km ENE NKP major AB and 7 km WNW Thakhek AF (Laos), per ONC-J-11. At 17°25'00"N-104°46'00"E. NIMA data. El. 490'? Thailand.
Nakhon Phanom West AF (VE 6-2)
A.k.a. NKP and Naked Fanny. Apx 600 km NE Bangkok, 220 km NE Khon Kane AF, 220 km SE Vientiane, 190 km E Udorn AB, 120 km from SVN border, 16 km WSW NKP minor AF, 17 km W the Mekong and 90 km N Savannakhet AB. USAF Fighter/FAC base, that for many years was kept secret. Also the major US AB in an area populated with four AFs. Jet capable rwy exceeded 8,000'. Per *A Better War*, p 366, between '73-75, was HQ of US Supt Activities Group (nicknamed "MACV in Exile") under cmd of Gen Ira Hunt.[378] At 17°23'00"N-104°39'00"E Per ONC-J-11. NIMA data. El. 579'. Thailand.
Nakhon Rachasima Airfield (SB 8-5)
See Korat AB. Thailand.
Nakhon Ratchasima Airfield (n/a)
See Khorat AB. Feb67 Natl Geo map. El. 729'. Thailand.
Nakhon Sawan Airfield (PT 1-2)
Along Chao Phraya River at 15°38'00"N-100°07'00"E, or apx 220 km N to NNW Bangkok per Feb67 Natl Geo map. NIMA data. El. 91'. Thailand.
Nakhon Si Thammarat AF (PK 0-3)
Near coast, apx 585 km S to SSW Bangkok per Feb67 Natl Geo map. 8°28'00"N-99°57'00"E per NIMA. Thailand.
Nam, Mui (BN 9-7)
A.k.a. Do, Hon. Coastal point at 11°34'N-109°08'E. On NC49-01 JOG. Ninh Thuan Pr, II Corps.
Nam, Mui (CP 0-1)
Coastal point at 11°51'N-109°14'E. On NC49-01 JOG. Khanh Hoa Pr, II Corps.
Nam, Pointe de Mui (CP 0-1)
Mui Nam. Coastal point at 11°51'N-109°14'E. On NC49-01 JOG. Khanh Hoa Pr, II Corps.
Nam Bac Airfield (TH 35-83)
LS-203. CIA/SF, per *Air Facilities Data-Laos.*
Nam Bu Airfield (PD 99-08)
LS-125. CIA/SF, per *Air Facilities Data-Laos.*
Nam Can (n/a)
Mapsheet name of L-7014-5926-1. SVN.
Nam Can Airfield (VQ 988-674)
On Cau Mau Peninsula and southernmost AF on mainland SVN. Apx 285 km SW Saigon and 32 km NE Mui Bai Bung. 20 km SE Binh Hung AF, 50 km SSW Quan Long's two AF's and 8 km E Cau Son Bay Hap Bay. Per TPC K-10D. El. 7', 2,800' rwy. At 08°45'N 104°59'E.
Nam Can Forest (WQ)
An Xuyen Pr, IV Corps.

Nam Can Heliport (WQ 02-78)
Apx 13 km NNE Nam Can AF, 5 km SW Xom Cai Keo and 18 km E Binh Hung AF. "Heliport #621, El. 3'. Inside cmpd, bldgs and wires on N, W and E. At 08°5I'N 105°01'E," per Feb73 TAD. An Xuyen Pr, IV Corps.

Nam Can Navy Base (VQ 98-67)
On Song Cua Lon River apx 24 km due W Tan An, 32 km ENE the tip of Cau Mau Peninsula. USN Mobile Facility, '69-71. Per MRF Assn Website. An Xuyen Pr, IV Corps.

Nam Chon, Baie de (AT 9-8)
Bay at 16°09'N-108°09'E. ND49-01 JOG. Quang Nam Pr, I Corps.

Nam Chong Airfield (TG 63-41)
LS-17. CIA/SF, per *Air Facilities Data-Laos.*

Nam Dinh (n/a)
Mapsheet name of L-7014-6249-4. NVN only.

Nam Dinh (XH 23-50)
Apx 75 km SE to SSE Hanoi and 25 km W QL-1. Power plants, rail yards, naval facilities, barracks, and heavy industrial plants here struck by Carrier TF-77 attempts to blunt NVA Tet '68 offensive. French garrison here involved in Battle of Day River, 29May-18Jun51. See *Street Without Joy*, Chp 2, map at p 46. NVN.

Nam Dong Airfield (YC 868-840)
See Ruong Ruong AF. Thua Thien Pr, I Corps. [379]

Nam Dong CIDG Camp (YC 865-838)
See Nam Dong SF Camp. Thua Thien Pr, I Corps.

Nam Dong SF Camp (YC 865-838)
A.k.a. "Five Cents" SF Camp, and Nam Duc SF Camp(?). Apx 56 km WNW Da Nang AB, 30 km due S Phu Bai and 3 km SSE FSB Pistol. SF Det A-726 was here, site of 4Jul64 battle in which Capt. R. C. Donlan became 1st recipient of MOH in VN. Closed. In Vietnamese "Nam Dong" meant 5 Dong or Dong #5, and because the "Dong" was a unit of Viet currency apx equiv to US cent, SF troops apparently adopted nickname "Five Cents." Grid per *SF Order of Battle*. Thua Thien Pr, I Corps. [380]

Nam Duc SF Camp (YC 8650-8380)
A.k.a. Nam Dong SF Camp? See Nam Dong SF camp for detail. Thua Thien Pr, I Corps.

Nam Hoa, FSB (YD 762-129)
At Nam Hoa Dist HQ, apx 9 km due S Hue, 1.8 km SE Pohl Bridge. ARVN/RF/PF position in Spring70, and author is not aware US forces (apart from Adv) were ever stationed here. 31Oct69. Thua Thien Pr, I Corps.

Nam Hoa Bridge (YD 755-144)
A.k.a. Pohl Bridge or Hwy 547 Bridge. Apx 1.5 km NNW Nam Hoa and 8 km S Hue Citadel AF. Secured by 1st/505th Inf, and other elements of 82d Abn between Mar-Sep68, and then 2d Bde/101st Abn, '69-71. See Pohl Bridge for more detail. Thua Thien Pr, I Corps.

Nam Hoa Dist HQ (YD 763-128)
At Nam Hoa, apx 10 km due S Hue Citadel AF and 12 km W Phu Bai. ARVN, RF/PF cmpd. Thua Thien Pr, I Corps.

Nam Hang Airfield (UH 16-43)
LS-278. CIA/SF, per *Air Facilities Data-Laos.*

Nam Hou River (TJ 43-35)
At confluence of Nam Pak and Nam Hou Rivers, apx 65 km SW Dien Bien Phu. See Muong Khoua. Laos.

Nam Houn Airfield (TJ 51-96)
LS-243. CIA/SF, per *Air Facilities Data-Laos.*

Nam Keng Airfield (n/a)
Apx 185 km NE Vientiane. Natl Geo map. El. 4,800'. Laos.

Nam Keo Airfield (n/a)
190 km SE Vientiane, 20 km SW the NVN border. Per ONC-J-11. El. 4,626'. Laos.

Nam Lan Airfield (UG 55-85)
LS-07. CIA/SF, per *Air Facilities Data-Laos.*

Nam Lieu Airfield (PC 65-75)
LS-118A and Nam Yu. CIA, per *Air Facilities Data-Laos.*

Nam Luong (n/a)
Fictional name used by *The Green Berets* author to represent either an actual camp or composite of SF Camps visited during his 6-month visit to VN, '64 or '65. Referenced base unknown.

Nam Ma River (VJ)
A.k.a. Ma River. See Na San. NVN.

Nam Moh Airfield (TF 82-87)
LS-207. CIA/SF, per *Air Facilities Data-Laos.*

Nam My Relocation Camp (AT or BT?)
Listed at BT 847-015, but that point well out in ocean? Possibly AT or BS grid zone; however, either of those grids puts site on mtn and likely incorrect. NPIA Gaz lists Nam My (1) at AT 860-855, and Nam My (2) at AT 897-816, both of which are in valley NW of Da Nang and more likely setting. Quang Nam Pr? I Corps.

Nam Na (n/a)
Mapsheet name of L-7014-5653-2. NVN only.

Nam Nang (XK 3-9?)
See Namnang. NVN.

Nam O Beach (AT 94-84?)
Beach presumably E Nam O Bridge, perhaps 8 km NNW Da Nang AB and immed N Red Beach. BLT 2d/26th made a practice amphib lndg here Sep69. Quang Nam Pr, I Corps.

Nam O Bridge (AT 934-834)
QL-1 bridge over the Song Cu De (also sp Ca De?) at N end Red Beach, apx 1 km NNW Da Nang AB and 2 km W ocean. Destroyed Apr67. On 8Mar65, 1st major US ground force (3d Bn/9th Marines) landed on beach just S this bridge. Later same day, another Bn was landed at Da Nang by C-130s via Okinawa. With H-34 helos of HMM-162 providing log supt, these units formed the 9th MEF whose mission was to protect Da Nang and its AF from VC. An enclave at Phu Bai AF (15 km S Hue) soon followed, then another at Ky Ha, just S Tam Ky. Also listed at AT 927-842, per XXIV Corps index, III MAF, 6Apr70. Quang Nam Pr, I Corps.

Nam O Village (AT 94-83)
A.k.a. Ap Nam O. On QL-1 about 1 km S of Nam O Bridge and directly W of Red Beach. Quang Tri Pr, I Corps.

Nam O, Pointe de (AT 9-8)
See Pointe Nam O. Quang Nam Pr, I Corps.

Nam Pak River (TJ 43-35)
At confluence of Nam Pak and Nam Hou Rivers, a point apx 65 km SW Dien Bien Phu. See Muong Khoua. Laos.

Nam Pha Noi Airfield (TF 80-96)
LS-218. CIA/SF, per *Air Facilities Data-Laos.*

Nam Phong Airfield (TD 8-4)
Apx 415 km NE Bangkok and 80 km SSE Udorn AB, per ONC-J-11 and Feb67 Natl Geo maps. Major AF and

USMC fixed-wing/helo AB here reopened or created in response to '72 NVA Easter Offensive (and after Marine Air had departed Vietnam in '69). HMM-36 moved here from ships in South China Sea. Listed as abnd in '66 NIMA data. El. 787'. Thailand.

Nam Phong SF Camp (TD 8-4)
Possibly apx 415 km NE Bangkok and 80 km SSE Udorn AFB. SF camp or AO per *SF Order of Battle*. Thailand.

Nam Phung Dam, Camp (UD 90-78?)
See Nam Pung Dam, Camp. Thailand.

Nam Phung Dam North AF (UD 90-78)
See Nam Pong Dam AF. Thailand.

Nam Pong Dam Airfield (UD 90-78)
A.k.a. Nam Phung Dam North AF. Apx 30 km SW Sakon Nakhon (New/Army) AF. El. 1050'. Thailand.

Nam Poune Airfield (TF 98-87)
LS-344. CIA/SF, per *Air Facilities Data-Laos*.

Nam Pung Dam, Camp (UD 90-78?)
A.k.a. Nam Phung Dam and Nam Pong Dam. If grid correct, was apx 30 km SW Sakon Nakhon (New or Army) AF. SF camp, *SF Order of Battle*. Thailand.

Nam Quet (n/a)
Mapsheet name of L-7014-6154-1. NVN/China.

Nam Rom River (TJ 93-60)
See Nam Yum River. NVN.

Nam Sathay River (YA 66-42)
Joined Se San River at listed grid, roughly 24 km NW Duc Co. River formed part of Cambodian/SVN border. Pleiku Pr, II Corps.

Nam Song Airfield (UG 76-21)
LS-199. CIA/SF, per *Air Facilities Data-Laos*.

Nam Tan Airfield (QB 61-04)
LS-268. CIA/SF, per *Air Facilities Data-Laos*.

Nam Tang Airfield (QB 83-14)
LS-73. CIA/SF, per *Air Facilities Data-Laos*.

Nam Tha (QD 50-19?)
Nam Tha AF is shown on Feb67 Natl Geo map as apx 350 km NNW Vientiane? During '61 crisis in Laos, anti-sub supt carrier *Bennington* (CVS 20) took fourteen H-34 helos to Gulf of Siam for transfer to friendly Lao forces fighting the Pathet Lao. Calm followed during late '61 and early '62, but was shattered when Pathet Lao overran pro-US defenders of Nam Tha, 6May62, renewing fears the Communists would succeed in war. Laos.[381]

Nam Tha Airfield (QD 50-19)
A.k.a. L-100. Roughly 350 km NNW Vientiane on Feb67 Natl Geo map. El. 1,968'. CIA/SF, per *Air Facilities Data-Laos*. Laos.

Nam Thinh (n/a)
Mapsheet name, L 701-6675-3. NVN/China.

Nam Thom Airfield (VG 14-17)
LS-47. CIA/SF, per *Air Facilities Data-Laos*.

Nam Thuam Airfield (TH 25-68)
LS-176. CIA/SF, per *Air Facilities Data-Laos*.

Nam Trach Region (n/a)
Mekong Delta, no data available? IV Corps.

Nam Tram, Cape (BT 6-0)
See Cape Nam Tram. Quang Tin Pr, I Corps.

Nam Tram, Mui (BT 6-0)
Coastal point at 15°25'N-108°50'E, SE Da Nang. On ND49-01 JOG. Quang Tin Pr, I Corps.

Nam Tram, Mui (BT 66-05)
A.k.a. Cape Nam Tram. Apx 13 km E and ESE Chu Lai CB, and 34 km NNE Quang Ngai. Site of Hill 141 and Bty C/2d LAAM Bn Hawk AA Missile base. See Hill 141 and LAAM Sites. Quang Tin Pr, I Corps.

Nam Ve Airfield (TF 72-95)
LS-335. CIA/SF, per *Air Facilities Data-Laos*.

Nam Yon Airfield (TF 77-95)
LS-288 and Nam Yong. CIA, per *Air Facilities Data-Laos*.

Nam Yong Airfield (TF 77-95)
LS-288 and Nam Yon. CIA, per *Air Facilities Data-Laos*.

Nam Youm River (TJ 93-60)
See Nam Yum River. NVN.

Nam Yu Airfield (PC 65-75)
LS-118A and Nam Lieu. Per *Air Facilities Data-Laos*.

Nam Yum Rats, The (TJ)
See Nam Yum River. NVN.

Nam Yum River (TJ 93-60)
A.k.a. Nam Youm in Thai, and Nam Rom in Vietnamese. Ran through Muong Thanh Valley (Dien Bien Phu) apx 290 km WNW Hanoi. Notorious for its "Nam Yum Rats," the est 3,000 deserters who lived in holes and caves along its banks during DBP siege, scavenging for food and stealing supplies from French garrisons and errant air drops of supplies. Apparently a depraved and wild lot whose ranks were filled mostly by Vietnamese tribal partisans, North African, Moroccan and Vietnamese deserters, many of whom had lost their nerve or were shell-shocked. Also spelled Namyuoum River. NVN.

NAMBO Interzone (n/a)
See Interzone NAMBO.

Namnang (XK 3-9?)
A.k.a. Nam Nang. At *Poste Kilomtre* 28 (PK 28) along R.C. 4 in northern Tonkin. In late 1950, designated mtg point of forces abandoning Cao Bang (under Col Charton) and relief forces (4 Bns of Moroccans under Col LePage) moving to rescue from Lang Son. Before abandoning Cao Bang, reinforcements were flown in and defenses improved in order to deceive Vietminh into thinking site was meant to be held. Col Charton asked wisely to escape to SW along R.C. 3 so that his men could be extracted by air, but was overruled. To reach PK 28/Cao Bang garrison, LePage's men had to fight way to That Khe (where 1st Bn of Moroccans was exchanged for most famous of all French units, the 1st BEP of Foreign Legion Paras) but still had 96 km of contested R.C. 4 to traverse before reaching PK 28. At now Vietminh-controlled Dong Khe, they were stopped cold, forced to leave R.C. 4 and evade cross-country through trackless and incredibly dense jungle. Charton's forces waiting in vain at PK 28 then had to escape via the Quangliet (or Quang Liet) Track, a long-abandoned trail and their only hope of survival. See Quangliet Track, Coxha Gorge and Cao Bang. NVN.

Namo Bridge (AT 927-842)
See Nam O Bridge. Quang Nam Pr, I Corps.

Namyuoum River (n/a)
See Nam Yum River. NVN.

Nan (PA 8-7?)
Apx 535 km N Bangkok. SF camp or AO per *SF Order of Battle*. Thailand

Nan, LZ (XS 509-945)
Apx 9 km WSW Duc Hoa AF and 31 km W Bien Hoa AB. Mar66. Hau Nghia Pr, III Corps.
Nan Airfield (PA 8-7)
Along Rte 7 at 18°48'00"N-100°47'00"E, or apx 560 km N Bangkok. Feb67 Natl Geo map. El. 800'. Thailand.
Nan Dong Airfield (YC 868-840)
See Ruong Ruong AF. Thua Thien Pr, I Corps.
Nancy, FSB (XT 564-383?)
Listed at both YT and XT 564-383? If XT correct, was apx 12 km SE Dau Tieng/Tri Tam, 22 km due W Lai Khe AF, 32 km ESE Tay Ninh and 47 km NW Tan Son Nhut AB. If YT correct, it was within a few km of QL-20, apx 18 km WNW Vo Dat AF and Xa Vo Dat, 31 km NNE Xuan Loc and 80 km NE Saigon. Attacked Apr or May70 by 120 man Sapper Bn. [382] 4th/12th Inf, 199th LIB '70. Grid per 199th LIB Assn. 1st Cav ORLL lists grid as XT 564-383. Binh Duong Pr, III Corps.
Nancy, FSB (YT 564-383?)
See Nancy at XT 564-383. Long Khanh Pr, III Corps.
Nancy, FSB (XT 607-112)
Apx 6 km SW Cu Chi CB and 11 km NE Khiem Cuong. Sep67. Hau Nghia Pr, III Corps.
Nancy, LZ (BR 752-583)
In narrow river valley, apx 27 km NE An Khe and 9 km ENE Vinh Thanh ville. Oct66. Binh Dinh Pr, II Corps.
Nancy, LZ (BS 915-229)
Apx 3 km from ocean and 2 km W QL-1, some 10 km NNE Gia An and 18 km SSE Duc Pho AF. May67. Binh Dinh Pr, II Corps.
Nancy, LZ/FSB (YD 425-395?)
A.k.a. FSB My Chanh. If grid correct, was apx 5 km SE Quang Tri, 3 km E La Vang AF and 4 km W QL-1. Occupied by elements of 1st Cav and later 1st Bde/5th Mech Div, whose TAOR included lowlands and piedmont of Quang Tri Pr from DMZ S to Thua Thien Pr border. 3d Mar Div elements also apparently here. By Lam Son 719, was ARVN FSB My Chanh (1st ARVN Inf Rgt), per HQ 3d Bde/101st Abn Op Rpt of 30Apr71. Also listed at YD 435-395, 445-395, 422-394 and 434-304 in XXIV Corps index per Don Armstrong. Quang Tri Pr, I Corps.
Nancy, LZ (YD 434-304)
If grid correct, was apx 12 km W Camp Evans and 33 km WNW Hue Citadel AF. Quang Tri Pr, I Corps.
Nancy, LZ (YD 442-394)
A.k.a. FSB My Chanh. If grid correct, site was in coastal lowlands, apx 11 km ESE Quang Tri, 4 km NE Hai Lang and 8 km SW Wunder Beach/ocean. Likely built by 1st Cav in late 67 or early '68. 2d Bde/1st Cav HQ here. Army's 5th/4th Arty suptd 1st Bde/5th Mech Div from FSBs Sharon, Hai Lang and Nancy in '69. By Lam Son 719, was ARVN FSB My Chanh (1st ARVN Inf Rgt) per HQ 3d Bde/101st Abn Op Rpt of 30Apr71. Apr-Oct70. Listed at YD 422-394 (apx 2 km W site indicated above, and some 3 km W QL-1) in XXIV Corps index, per Don Armstrong. Also listed at YD 400-440, 1Nov68; YD 430-390, 30Apr69; YD 435-395, Jan69-Jan70; YD 440-395, 16Aug68; YD 445-404, 1Aug68; YD 448-511, 10Mar68. Map is L-7014-6442-3, per Ken Burrington. Quang Tri Pr, I Corps.
Nancy, LZ (YD 639-271?)
Apparent grid error. Grid is for LZ Sally and author doubts Sally was ever known as LZ Nancy? 1Nov67. Thua Thien Pr, I Corps.
Nang Buk Airfield (AS 983-417)
See Mang Buk AF. Kontum Pr, II Corps.
Nang Son Airfield (AT 879-396)
See Phouc Binh AF. Quang Nam Pr, I Corps.
Nangle, SF Camp (BR?)
Possibly Camp Plei Ta Nangle at BR 332-274? Listed as such in DA Chief, Mil Hist records summary which also indicates Det A-422 here '64. Binh Dinh Pr, II Corps?
Nape Airfield (WF 09-23)
LS-43. CIA/SF facility. Grid per *Air Facilities Data-Laos.* Feb67 Natl Geo map. 1700'. Laos.
Nape Pass (WF 16-36)
A.k.a. Deo Keo Nu'a. Along NVN/Lao border apx 65 km SW Vinh, near 18°23'00"N-105°09'00"E. One of 3 major passes of the HCMT. 1st Attacked by USAF planes during Barrel Roll, Mar65. NVN/Laos.
Napoleon/Saline, Operation (n/a)
29Feb-9Dec68. USMC op along Cua Viet River suptg ops in Dong Ha AO. 3,495 rptd enemy KIA, per *Vietnam Order of Battle*, pp 9-14. Quang Tri Pr, I Corps.
Narai, Fort (SU 9-9?)
SF camp or AO per *SF Order of Battle.* Thailand.
Narathiwat Airfield (RH 0-2)
At 6°31'00"N-101°44'00"E. NIMA data. Thailand.
Nash, LZ (BR 555-505)
A.k.a. or adj site of LZ Buick. Apx 10 km NW An Khe and 9 km ENE Tien Thuan. Oct65. Binh Dinh Pr, II Corps.
Nashua, FSB (XT 988-325)
A.k.a. FSB Nassau? Just S of Ku Tru Mat, apx 17 km due N Bien Hoa AB and 23 km ESE Lai Khe. Apparently HQ of 4th/12th and 2d/3d Inf Rgts, 199th LIB. Apr-Dec67. Also listed at XT 991-326. Bien Hoa Pr, III Corps.
Nashville, LZ (YD 264-047)
Remote site apx 50 km WSW Hue, 3 to 4 km from Laos, and 18 km NW Ta Bat. Apr70 XXIV Corps grid per Don Armstrong. Quang Tri Pr, I Corps.
Nassau, FSB (XT 988-325)
See FSB Nashua. Bien Hoa Pr, III Corps.
Nasty, Camp (n/a)
Derisive nickname for Korat AB. See Korat. Thailand.
Natalie, LZ (BP 359-806)
Apx 4 km due W Biam Tiam, 60 km ESE Ban Me Thuot and 38 km ENE Lac Thien AF. Apr67. Darlac Pr, II Corps.
Natalie, LZ (BQ 895-609)
Apx 10 km SSW Dong Tre AF and 2 km NW Phuoc Hoa Name/grid per Dan Gillotti. Phu Yen Pr, II Corps.
Natasha, DZ (TJ 94-67)
See Dien Bien Phu, Battle of. NVN.
Natasha, LZ (TJ 94-67)
A.k.a. DZ Natasha. See Dien Bien Phu, Battle of. NVN.
Natchez, LZ (AT 939-915)
Apx 23 km NW Da Nang AB, 9 km due W the Hai Van Pass and 18 km WSW Q Phu Loc. Apr70 XXIV Corps grid per Don Armstrong. Quang Nam Pr, I Corps.
Nathan, LZ (YS 390-860)
A.k.a. FSB Berryman. Apx 12 km SSW Blackhorse AF, 18 km NNW Nui Dat and 11 km NW Binh Gia. Mar66. Phuoc

Tuy Pr, III Corps.
National Police (n/a)
See White Mice in Glossary.
National Priority Area 1 (AT/BT)
See NPA-1. Quang Nam Pr, I Corps.
National Salvation Committee, The (n/a)
See Glossary.
Navajo, LZ (BS 815-175)
Apx 9 km NW Gia An, 22 km due S Duc Pho AF and 8 km NE Thuan An. Feb67. Binh Dinh Pr, II Corps.
Navajo, LZ (YA 864-005)
On W side of Chu Pong Massif apx 3 km WSW its peak, 26 km WSW Plei Me, 51 km W Phu Nhon AF and 17 km SSE Plei Girao Kla. 2d Bde/4th Div apparently here, Apr69. Cited in and grid from, *Time Heals No Wounds*, p 184's 1st/12th Inf Radio Log excerpt of 24Apr69 that indicates it was likely opened near same date. 4th Div FSB. Pleiku Pr, II Corps.
Navajo, FSB (YD 269-732)
In coastal sands apx 20 km NNW Quang Tri, 9 km WNW Cua Viet, 4 km inland and 4 km due E Gio Linh. Apr70 XXIV Corps grid per D. Armstrong. Quang Tri Pr, I Corps.
Naval Forces Vietnam HQ (n/a)
See US Naval Forces Vietnam in Major HQs Section.
Navan, Baie de (BN 8-7)
A.k.a. Vung Phan Rang. Bay at 11°34'N-109°04'E. On NC49-01 JOG. Ninh Thuan Pr?, II Corps.
Navarre Plan (n/a)
See Glossary.
Navarro, USS (n/a)
APA-215. Amphib Attack, Transport, per Ralph Fries.
Navasota, USS (n/a)
AO-106. Aux Oiler, per Ralph Fries.
Navel, FSB (BR 6-8?)
Possibly in vic of FSB Challenge, as both are listed as subjects of NARA film: NWDNM(m)-111-LC-55634. Challenge was at BR 628-822, apx 17 km W Ha Tay AF and 32 km SW LZ English. 4th Inf Div, Apr70. Binh Dinh Pr?, II Corps.
Navy Binh Thuy Airfield (WS 81-13)
Minor AF apx 6 km NW Can Tho, 2 km SW the Mekong River and immed SE Binh Thuy AF, some 120 km SW Saigon. 1 of 2 major and 1 minor AFs near Can Tho. TPC K-10D. El. 7'. Phong Dinh Pr, IV Corps.
Navy Nam Cam Noc (n/a)
Call sign for Nam Cam AF Control.
Naw Nuen Airfield (SG 95-35)
LS-79. CIA/SF, per *Air Facilities Data-Laos.*
Nay, Mui (CQ 3-2)
Coastal point at 12°55'N-109°28'E. On ND49-13 JOG. Khanh Hoa Pr, II Corps.
NC, LZ (XT 676-788)
6 km SE Tonle Cham. 30Jun66. Binh Long Pr, III Corps.
Ncoc (generally)
See Ngoc and Ngok.
Ncoc Run Ridge (ZB 143-401)
See Ngok Run Ridge. II Corps.
NDB An Loc (YT 43-12)
On N side of QL-1, apx 5 km WNW Xuan Loc. Long Khanh Pr, III Corps.
NDB Battambang (UV 07-48)
At Battambang AF, Batdambang. Cambodia.
NDB Can Tho (WS 83-12)
Apx 3 km NW Can Tho and 6 km SE TACAN NDB Binh Thuy. Phong Dinh Pr, IV Corps.
NDB Da Nang (BT 01-63)
Apx 4 km S Da Nang AB. See VOR DME Da Nang. Quang Nam Pr, I Corps.
NDB Dalat (BN 14-99)
At Dalat/Lien Khuong AF. Tuyen Duc Pr, II Corps.
NDB Duong Dong (US 86-31)
On coast of Phu Quoc Island at Duong Dong AF. Kien Giang Pr, IV Corps.
NDB Kampong Cham (WU 48-30)
Just S Phum Kav Ramuol, Cambodia.
NDB Ninh Hoa (BP 97-83)
At Ninh Hoa AF. Khanh Hoa Pr, II Corps.
NDB Pakse (WB 78-73)
At Pakse AF, Cambodia.
NDB Phan Thiet (AN 94-08)
On S edge of Phan Thiet and along coast apx 3 km NE Phan Thiet AF. Binh Thuan Pr, II Corps.
NDB Phnom Penh (VT 85-78)
Apx 3 km NE Phnom Penh AP and VOR NDB Phnom Penh. Cambodia.
NDB Phu Bai (1) (YD 89-15)
A.k.a. NDB Phubai 1. Phu Bai AF. Thua Thien Pr, I Corps.
NDB Phu Bai (2) (YD 96-18)
A.k.a. NDB Phubai 2. Phu Bai AF. Thua Thien Pr, I Corps.
NDB Qui Nhon (CR 08-23)
At Qui Nhon AB, along NE edge of Qui Nhon. Binh Dinh Pr, II Corps.
NDB Ream Kampong Saom (US 52-69)
Apx 16 km ESE Kampong Saom AF, and 5 km from Gulf of Thailand. Cambodia.
NDB Saigon (XS 81-87)
Along S edge of Saigon, apx 10 km S Tan Son Nhut AB. Gia Dinh Pr, III Corps.
NDB Soc Trang (XR 06-59)
At Soc Trang AB. Ba Xuyen Pr, IV Corps.
NDB Vung Tau (YS 30-47)
At Vung Tau AF. Phuoc Tuy Pr, III Corps.
Nds Mae Sot Airfield (MU 5-4)
At 16°42'00"N-98°33'00"E. NIMA data. Thailand.
Ne, Mui (BN 0-0)
Cape near Hai Long, at 10°55'N-108°17'E. On NC48-08 JOG. Binh Thuan Pr, II Corps.
Neal, FSB (YU 122-523)
A.k.a. FSB Neil. Along road connecting O Rang and Snuol, apx 2 km W Phum Phnum Krang, 58 km ENE Snuol, 26 km WSW O Rang, 8 km NE FSB Myron and 15 km from SVN. 1st Cav Cambodian Incursion FSB, May70. In AO of 1st Cav, 11th ACR and 199th LIB FSB. Grid also listed as YU 125-525, per *11th ACR Cambodia Invasion AAR, 1st Cav Div, May-Jun70*, courtesy Lou Rochat. [383] Mentioned in *Pleiku*. Cambodia.
Nee Soon (n/a)
New Zealand Military garrison in Singapore. Briefly mentioned in *Vietnam Gunners* (p 114) where hilarious description of morning following 161 Bty RNZA's

departure from VN (and stop in Singapore en-route NZ) is heartily recommended to the reader.

Neil, FSB (YU 122-523)
See FSB Neal. Cambodia.

Nelson, FSB (YS 253-754)
On QL-15, apx 18 km WNW Nui Dat, 10 km SE FSB Archer, 38 km NNW Vung Tau. 161 Bty, RNZA (Hitching's Bty 14Apr68-18Mar69) FSB set here 27Oct-2Nov68 (right section). Grid per 1ATF NCO trng map, courtesy John Hollett. Site may have shifted after '68-69? Also listed at YS 21-81. Phuoc Tuy Pr, III Corps.

Nelson, FSB (YT 049-659)
Apx 10 km S Dong Xoai and 18 km NNE Phouc Vinh AF. Feb71. Phuoc Long Pr, III Corps.

Nelson Inn (YT 04-07)
Annex #4, USARV Mess Assn at Long Binh Post. Named to honor Sp6 Leon G Nelson, EOD specialist, 133d Ord Det, 6th Ord Bn, KIA 1Jul67, while defusing ammo that had been scattered by massive explosion (21Jun67) which destroyed Duc Pho ammo supply point. Data per *Vietnam Military Lore, 1959-1973*. Bien Hoa Pr, III Corps.

Neptune NCO Club (CP 04-53?)
Nha Trang. Khanh Hoa Pr, II Corps.

Neptune, LZ (XD 888-538)
On Nui Tia Pong Hill Mass, apx 12 km NW Ca Lu, 13 km NNE Khe Sanh CB and 35 km WSW Dong Ha. Apr70 XXIV Corps grid per D. Armstrong. Quang Tri Pr, I Corps.

Nettle, USCGS (n/a)
WAK 169. USCG Cargo vessel.

Neva West, SS (n/a)
Merchant ship under govt contract, per Ralph Fries.

Nevada Eagle, Operation (n/a)
17May68-28Feb69. 101st Abn. 3,299 rptd NVA/VC KIA, per *VN Order of Battle*, pp 9-14. Thua Thien Pr, I Corps.

Neville, FSB (XD 790-573)
Apx 55 km W to WNW Quang Tri, 33 km due W Cam Lo, 10 km WSW FSB Russell, 15 km due E FSB Argonne and 17 km due N Khe Sanh CB. H/2d/4th Marines and Bty G/3d/12th Marine Arty attacked and partially overrun here 25Feb69, by 200 raiders and sappers of 246th NVA Rgt, resulting in 11 US KIA, 29 WIA. On map at p 58, *US Marines in Vietnam-1969*. 101st Abn inactive FSB grid per Don Armstrong. Quang Tri Pr, I Corps.

New, LZ (BR 807-627)
Apx 20 km NNW Phu Cat AB, 37 km ENE An Khe and 9 km W QL-1. Oct66. Binh Dinh Pr. II Corps.

New, USS (n/a)
DD-818, per Ralph Fries.

New Dak To (ZB 007-215)
At W edge of Dak To 2 AF, apx 42 km NW Kontum. Nature of site unknown. 31Oct68. Kontum Pr, II Corps.

New Discovery, FSB (YS 608-687)
Apx 17 km E Nui Dat, 1 km NE FSB Beth and 7 km N FSB Mardi. On 1ATF NCO trng map per John Hollett. Phuoc Tuy Pr, III Corps.

New French Fort, The (XD 858-387)
A.k.a. French Fort (Khe Sanh). Old French fortifications near Khe Sanh Ville. Cited in index of *Valley of Decision* but no page reference listed and no other data found. Map is L-7014-6342-3, per Ken Burrington. See Khe Sanh SF Camp. Quang Tri Pr, I Corps.

New Hau Duc (BT 073-064)
Apx 10 km NNE Old Hau Duc, 27 km WSW Tam Ky and 10 km SSW Tien Phuoc AF. Americal List. Quang Tin Pr, I Corps.

New Hope, Operation (n/a)
21-27Oct65. 173d Abn, Di An, Phu Loi. 2/503d Inf and B/3/319th clearing Op securing and preparing the area for arrival of 1st Inf Div. III Corps.

New Indigo, FSB (YS 060-380?)
Location unknown as listed grid is in ocean? If in "YT" zone, site was 26 km NNE Bien Hoa AB. If grid were instead YS 060-880, then site was 9 km SW Long Thanh AF and 25 km SSE Bien Hoa AB? Possibly Bien Hoa Pr?, III Corps.

New Jersey, USS (n/a)
BB 62. Only US Battleship to serve in Vietnam War. Raided NVN coast with 16" gunfire for one month, Oct-Nov66, as part of Op Sea Dragon. Her 16-inch guns were in action again fromOct68 and early '69, as well, departing VN CTZ for last time in Mar69. *Webster's Dictionary of the VN War* repts that in all, she fired apx 12 million pounds of ordnance suptg allied forces. See Barsanti Affair in Glossary. NVN & I Corps.

New Life, Operation (n/a)
21Nov-17Dec65. 173d Abn, La Nga River Valley. 3 Inf Bns, 4 Arty Btys, a Cav Trp and CP moved by air to Vo Dat. Mission was to deny VC access to rice harvest. 1st use Long Range Patrols (LRPs) by 173d. III Corps.

New Life, Operation
23Apr-16Oct75. Creation of VN evacuee camps on Guam. During evac of Saigon/SVN at end of American War, US moved many refugees to Guam. Initially, evacuees were settled in apts around island, but huge influx quickly overwhelmed capacity and drastic expansion required. 1st expansion was Tin City, which opened in vacant troop barracks at Anderson AFB. USMC then opened Camp Asan in former civilian contractor employee housing cmpd at ville of Asan, while Navy Seabees cleared 500 acres at Orote Point (abnd AF on USN Base that was battle site in WWII) to erect several thousand tents a.k.a. Tent City. Apx 115,000 evacuees (25,000 more than Guam's normal population) processed through camps. Most moved-on to US, but apx 500 became permanent residents. Data per, and detail/photos at: www.mississippi.net/~comcents/tendertale.com/ttonl/newlife.html. Island of Guam.

New Life Hamlet (AT 898-772)
Apx 12 km WNW Da Nang AB. Jun-Jul66. Quang Nam Pr, I Corps.

New Life Hamlets (n/a)
See Glossary.

New Life Village, Chu Lai (BT 53-05?)
Refugee camp built near Chu Lai AB. Site of Dickey Chapelle Dispensary. Quang Tin Pr, I Corps.

New London County, USS (n/a)
LST-1066 and *USNS New London County*. To MSTS, Feb67. SVN.

New Mexico, FSB (XT)
Name or nickname of 25th Inf Div FSB/Patrol base somewhere in Tay Ninh Pr. *Suicide Charlie* author Norman Russell called this New Mexico, "because the arid late-dry season terrain reminded me of Southwest." He went on to

say base "was a well-established army base with a resident battery of 155s that had civilized the wilderness. It also had a dump that was enclosed by barbed-wire and that we had to guard from the children of a nearby village." May or may not be actual name of this base. Tay Ninh Pr, III Corps. [384]

New Orleans, FSB (YT 19-23?)
A.k.a. FSB Choctaw. Apx 4 km due E FSB Bunker Hill, 22 km NE Bien Hoa AB, 17 km NE Plantation AF, 29 km NW Xuan Loc and 18 km E FSB Choctaw. 5th/12th and 3d/7th Inf, 199th LIB, '68. Bien Hoa Pr, III Corps.

New Orleans, USS (n/a)
LPH 11, Amphibious Landing Platform, Helicopter. See Op End Sweep.

New Plei Djereng (YA 873-457)
Apx 36 km W Pleiku and 4 km SE Plei Djereng New AFJan67-Jan70. Also listed at YA 855-457, 870-455 870-465. Pleiku Pr, II Corps.

New Plei Djereng, FSB (YA 855-475)
Along SE edge Plei Djereng and at S edge Plei Djereng New AF, some 37 km W Pleiku. C Bty 6th/29th Arty here May70. Name/4th Div 31Jul70 ORLL grid, per Jim Henderson. Pleiku Pr, II Corps.

New Port (XS 870-930)
See Newport. Gia Dinh Pr, III Corps.

New Prince BOQ (XS 8-9)
At 700-706 Tran Hung Dao St., Saigon. Per R. Bows' *Vietnam Military Lore, 1959-1973.* Gia Dinh Pr, III Corps.

New Sharon, FSB (n/a)
No data. 7th/8th Arty. Name per Dan Gillotti. III Corps.

New Xieng Dat Airfield (TG 63-51)
LS-117. Apx 160 km N Vientiane. CIA/SF, per *Air Facilities Data-Laos.*

New York (n/a)
See Glossary.

New York, LZ (BR 370-460)
Just S An Dinh/QL-19, apx 11 km due W An Khe. Jan66. Binh Dinh Pr, II Corps.

New Zealand, Forces of (n/a)
See Major HQs Section.

Newark, LZ (AT 937-767)
Apx 7 km WNW Da Nang AB and 4 km due S Red Beach AF. Apr70 XXIV Corps grid per Don Armstrong. Quang Nam Pr, I Corps.

Newark, Operation (n/a)
18-30Apr67. 173d Abn, War Zone D. III Corps.

Newbie (n/a)
See Glossary.

Newell, USS (n/a)
DER-322. DD-Escort, Radar, per Ralph Fries.

Newport (XS 870-930)
See Newport Naval Port. Gia Dinh Pr, III Corps.

Newport BOQ (XS 824-940)
At 1 Vo Tanh St., Saigon. Per R. Bows' *Vietnam Military Lore, 1959-1973.* Gia Dinh Pr, III Corps.

Newport Bridge (XS 892-941)
Crossed Song Saigon, apx 6 km SSW Thu Duc and 7 km ESE Tan Son Nhut, at NE corner of Saigon. HQ 3d ARVN Ranger Grp here. Also listed at XS 865-968, 873-980, 890-940, 896-938. Gia Dinh/Bien Hoa Pr, III Corps.

Newport Heliport (XS 890-950)
At Saigon's Newport, apx 7 km ENE Tan Son Nhut AB. "Heliport #758, 120'. Offl Bus Only, 2 hr PPR tel 922-3103/3201/4405. Black area with yellow 'H', cntr of vehicle pkg area S hwy. At 10°48'N 106°44'E," per 73 TAD. Gia Dinh Pr, III Corps.

Newport Naval Port (XS 890-935)
60-acre facility along NE edge of Saigon just below Bien Hoa Hwy Bridge, apx 2 km N to NE the docks of Saigon and 4 to 5 km N the commercial port of Saigon. A deep-water draft port under control of US Army Transport Cmd and constructed to accommodate military shipping and to free Saigon Port for civilian shipping. Completed in '67, it cost over $25 million, could handle simultaneously 4 ocean-going and 4 shallow-draft lndg vessels, and 7 barges. Facility included 4 berths for deep draft (ocean going) vessels, 4 barge sites, 2 LST slips and one LCU slip. Because of depth limitations at Newport, ships discharging there were Class C-2 or smaller. 71st Trans Bn's 5 terminal service Cos, the 154th, 368th, 561st, 567th and 551st Serv Cos, operated facility. After completion, it was handling more than 150,000 tons of supplies every month. Author of text at 4th Trans Cmd website adds that, "also at Newport was a large mess hall that served 4 excellent meals a day, the 4th being at midnight, a chapel, the HQ for 71st Trans Bn, the 4th Trans Cmd Cargo Accounting Div and a computer center." [385] Good map of site in *Vietnam Studies, Base Development in South Vietnam*, p144. Also listed at XS 870-930. See Saigon Seaports and Saigon, Port of. Gia Dinh Pr, III Corps. [386]

Newport News, USS (n/a)
CA-148. Cruiser. In Jun68, *Newport News* severely slowed flow of ammo/supplies to desperate post-Tet NVA troops hanging on in Quang Tri Pr, when it destroyed major NVA logistics complex N the Cua Viet River. On 10May72, its 8" guns hit targets near Hanoi from position off Do Son Peninsula, while Cruisers *Oklahoma City*, *Providence* and 3 destroyers suppressed NVA counter-bty fire. In Aug72, *Newport News*, *Rowan* (DD 782) and naval air sank 2 PT boats that attacked US ships off Haiphong. [387]

Nga Ba Airfield (YC 868-840)
See Ruong Ruong AF. Thua Thien Pr, I Corps.

Nga Ba Dinh SF Camp (VQ 937-8570)
A.k.a. FOB Binh Hung. Apx 20 km NNW Nam Can AF and 10 km ENE Binh Hung AF. 5th SF. Info/grid per *SF Order of Battle.* An Xuyen Pr, IV Corps.

Nga Ba Heliport (YD 141-693)
Apx 2 to 3 km N Phu Phuong, 7 km W QL-1 and 26 km NW Quang Tri."Heliport #623, 16', at 16°54'00"N-107°01'00"E," per Feb73 TAD. Quang Tri Pr, I Corps.

Ngai Fong Tion (n/a)
Mapsheet name of L-7014-5854-3. NVN/China.

Ngai Giao (YS 47-81)
Along QL-2 apx 12 km NNE Nui Dat and 18 km SSE Blackhorse Basecamp. Apparently elements of ANZAC 1ATF here, or was a significant terrain feature of their AO. Phuoc Tuy Pr, III Corps.

Ngai Ha Valley (BT 05-35)
On NE side of Que Son mtns, generally 6 km S Pagoda Valley, 10 km SW LZ Baldy and 20 km SW Hoi An. Site of LZ Ross. Quang Nam/Quang Tin Pr border, I Corps.

Ngan Cau Refugee Camp (BT 068-688)
Along Rte 543, apx 8 km SE Da Nang AB and 5 km S Marble Mtn AF. NPIA data. Quang Nam Pr, I Corps.
Nghi Ha Valley (BT 0-3)
Apx 12 km SW LZ Baldy and 5 km N FSB Ross. Quang Nam Pr, I Corps.
Nghi Xuan (n/a)
Mapsheet name of L-7014-6146-2. NVN only.
Nghia Do Tong (n/a)
Mapsheet name of L-7014-5853-1. NVN only.
Nghia Duc (Gia Nghia) (n/a)
Mapsheet L-7014-6532-4. Full sheet name: Gia Nghia (Nghia Duc).
Nghia Hanh (BS 614-641)
Apx 9 km due S Quang Ngai AF, 6 km W QL-1 and 15 km NW Mo Duc AF. Americal list indicates battle site nearby at BS 60-61. AF also here. Also listed at BS 618-642, BS 611-625 and BS 616-640. Quang Ngai Pr, I Corps.
Nghia Hanh Airfield (BS 62-64)
Apx 9 km due S Quang Ngai AF, 6 km W QL-1 and 15 km NW Mo Duc AF. El. 30' Quang Ngai Pr, I Corps.
Nghia Hung (n/a)
Mapsheet name of L-7014-6047-1. NVN only.
Nghia Lo (n/a)
Mapsheet name of L-7014-5952-3. NVN only.
Nghia Lo (VJ 48-89)
Apx 145 km WNW Hanoi. French garrison in T'ai region of Tonkin. In late Sep51, Vietminh 312th Div crossed Red River Valley near Yen Bay (Yen Bai) in order to split French defensive line in its center. Attack marked opening of "The Battle for Indochinese Highlands." On 11Oct52, 700-man French garrison again became target, when 308th, 312th, and 316th VM Divs attacked across Red River at 3 points N of Yen Bay in "Battle for T'ai Hill Country." VM attacked at 1700 hrs and within 1 hour, town had fallen. Per *Street Without Joy*, pp 47, 62-65; map at p 67. NVN.
Nghia Lo Airfield (WJ 4-9)
Feb67 Natl Geo map. El. 886'. NVN.
Nghia Tin (n/a)
Mapsheet name of L-7014-6533-3. SVN.
Ngo Quyen, FSB (XT 549-866)
Apx 24 km ESE Katum, 3 km N Rte 248, 6 km SW tip of Fishhook and 22 km due W An Loc. Grid per *11th ACR Cambodia Invasion AAR, 1st Cav Div, May-Jun70*, courtesy Lou Rochat. [388] Tay Ninh Pr, III Corps.
Ngo Tung Airfield (WS 027-635)
See That Son AF. Chau Doc Pr, IV Corps.
Ngo Xa Dong CAP (YD?)
A.k.a. Ngo Xa East. CAP 4-3-7, 4th CAG per Tim Duffie. Quang Tri Pr, I Corps.
Ngo Xa Dong, Thon (n/a)
Mapsheet L-7014-6442-1. Full sheet name: Thon Ngo Xa Dong. SVN.
Ngo Xa Tay CAP (YD?)
A.k.a. Ngo Xa West. CAP 4-3-7, 4th CAG per Tim Duffie. Quang Tri Pr, I Corps.
Ncoc (generally)
See also Ngok entries.
Ngoc Ho, OP (YD 692-158)
A.k.a. OP Tiger, OP Viper and LZ Chicken. Apx 6 km SW Hue, 7 km due N FSB Birmingham. Grid per 1Feb70, 101st Abn rpt, per Don Armstrong. Quang Tri Pr, I Corps.
Ngoc Linh Mountain (ZB 21-68)
A.k.a. Hill 2597. Apx 40 km SE Dak Gle, 80 km due W Quang Ngai and 115 km S Da Nang near 15 degrees N Latitude, 108 degrees W Longitude. At 8,524', the highest point in SVN. Curiously, Natl Geo map of Sep55, lists it as being 10,761' in height, or 3,280 meters? Fan Si Pan was tallest Mtn in all of VN. Kontum Pr, II Corps.
Ngoc Run Ridge (ZB 143-401)
See Ngok Run Ridge. II Corps.
Ngoc Son (n/a)
Mapsheet name of L-7014-6632-4. SVN.
Ngoc Thap (WJ 23-74)
Apx 10 km NNE Phu Tho and Red River, some 75 km NW Hanoi. Vietminh Supply point that was one objective of Op Lorraine. See Lorraine. NVN.
Ngok (generally)
See also Ngoc entries.
Ngok Bor Beang Mountain (YB 98-15)
Hill 1338. Apx 6 km SSW Dak To 2. Kontum Pr, II Corps.
Ngok Dorlang Mountain (YB 920-140)
Hill 882. Apx 12 km SW Dak To 2. Kontum Pr, II Corps.
Ngok Ian Drang Mountain (YB 911-028)
See Hill 1570. Kontum Pr, II Corps.
Ngok Jrong Mountain (ZB 002-372)
See Hill 1748. Kontum Pr, II Corps.
Ngok Kom Leat Mtn (YB 840-200)
Apx 17 km W Dak To 2 AF. Nov67. Kontum Pr, II Corps.
Ngok Kom Leat Mountains (YB 850-105)
Mtn chain W and SW Dak To, and S Ben Het. Scene of heavy fighting during late '67. See Dak To, Battle of. Kontum Pr, II Corps.
Ngok Kring Mtn Range (YB 820-150)
Was between 10 and 15 km SSE Ben Het, and included Hills 889 and 882. Cited in *Dak To*, p 211. Grid is near center of mass. Kontum Pr, II Corps.
Ngok Krinh Mountain (AS 920-340)
A.k.a. Hill 2066. A 6,778' high mtn overlooking and 11 km SW Mang Buk AF, 36 km ENE Dak To and 26 km NW Plateau Gi. Kontum Pr, II Corps.
Ngok Lang Grang Mtn (YB 830-120)
Apx 22 km SW Dak to 2 AF. Oct67. Kontum Pr, II Corps.
Ngok Lang Lo Mountain (YB 790-446)
See Hill 903. Kontum Pr, II Corps.
Ngok Ngo Airfield (BS 081-145)
See Plateau Gi AF. Kontum Pr, II Corps.
Ngok Pong Der Mountain (YB 793-542)
See Hill 1051. Kontum Pr, II Corps.
Ngok Ring Rong Mtn (YB 930-220)
Apx 8 km W Dak To 2 AF. Kontum Pr, II Corps.
Ngok Run Ridge (ZB 143-401)
A.k.a. Ngoc Run and Ncoc Run Ridge. Ridge adj to Dak Tan Kan Valley near Toumorong, apx 31 km NW Dak To 2 AF and 11 km NW Dak Ben Fighting here during Op Hawthorne involved 2d/502d and 1st/327th Inf, 101st Abn and 24th NVA Rgt, 2-13Jun 66. II Corps.
Ngok Sie Mountain (YA 836-444)
See Hill 1255. Kontum Pr, II Corps.

Ngok Tahun Mountain (YB 894-016)
See Hill 1274 and also Ngok Tolum. Kontum Pr, II Corps.
Ngok Tang Mountain (YB 950-170)
Apx 7 km SW Dak To 2. Kontum Pr, II Corps.
Ngok Tavak (YC 96-01?)
A.k.a. FOG Ngok Tavak (Forward Operating Grp. An old French Fort apx 5 km SW Kham Duc and used as SF Camp. Apparently overrun May68. Americal List. Quang Tin Pr, I Corps.
Ngok Tavak Airfield (YC 964-020)
Apx 10 km SSW Kham Duc and 75 km WSW Tam Ky, per TPC K-10A. Also listed at YC 968-013, and as "Insecure, abnd, partly overgrown, 29Jan67, AF # VA1-75," in Aug69 TAD per Frank Penk, Jr. Not in Feb73 TAD. El. 1,450'. Quang Tin Pr, I Corps.
Ngok Tavak SF Camp (YC 9640-0091)
A.k.a. FOB Kham Duc. Adj to Ngok Tavak AF, apx 10 km SSW Kham Duc, and 75 km WSW Tam Ky. 5th SF. Info/grid per *SF Order of Battle*. Quang Tin Pr, I Corps.
Ngok Toba Mountain (YB 820-100)
Mtn mass apx 23 km SW Dak To 2 AF and near Hill 875. Was staging area for elements of 66th NVA Rgt and 40th NVA Arty Rgt in early '71. See Polei Kleng Ranger Camp. Kontum Pr, II Corps.
Ngok Tolum Mountain (YB 893-016)
A.k.a. Ngock To Lum, Ngok Tahun, LZ Ouachita and Hill 1274. Overlooking Plei Trap Valley, apx 24 km SSW Dak To 2 AF, 16 km NW Polei Kleng AF and 2 km NW LZ Delaware. Per *Time Heals No Wounds*, p 172. 4th Div AO, 2d Bde/4th Inf operated out of this location, early '69. Cited in *Time Heals No Wounds*, p 172. Plei Trap Valley area of Kontum Pr, II Corps.
Ngok Wan Mountain (ZB 132-314)
See Hill 1416. Kontum Pr, II Corps.
Ngokti Heliport (YB 930-860)
Apx 4 km E Laos, 25 km SSW Kham Duc and 17 km N Dak Pek AF. Heliport #624, El. 4,724', at 15°14'00"N-107°44'00"E, per Feb73 TAD. Quang Tin Pr, I Corps.
Ngot, Nuoc (CR 0-6)
Dam Nuoampoc Ngot. Lagoon at 14°09'N-109°11'E. On ND49-05 JOG. Phu Yen Pr?, II Corps.
Ngu Hanh Son Pacification Area (AT/BT)
Pilot pacification program site in 9th Marines TAOR S Da Nang in latter half of '65. Map showing area in US Marines in Vietnam, 1966, p 46, discussed at p 38. See NPA I. Quang Nam Pr, I Corps.
Nguoi Rung (n/a)
See Glossary.
Nguon Rao (n/a)
Mapsheet name of L-7014-6342-4. SVN, NVN, Laos and DMZ also covered.
Nguyan Thi Thi Plantation (AR 785-390)
A.k.a. Nguyen Thi Thi? Tea plantation to N of Camp Enari. Pleiku Pr, II Corps.
Nguyen Ai Quoc (n/a)
See Glossary.
Nguyen Binh (n/a)
Mapsheet name of L-7014-6154-2. NVN only.
Nguyen Binh (WL 9-0)
Apx 175 km N Hanoi. Involved in French Op Lea, Oct47. On map in *Street Without Joy*, p 31. NVN.
Nguyen Binh Outpost (WL 9-0)
Apx 180 km N Hanoi. French Frontier outpost abnd in 1950 as Vietminh under Giap gained strength. See Cao Bang. Northern Tonkin, NVN.
Nguyen Cao Ky (n/a)
See Glossary.
Nguyen Dinh Quat, Plantation de (XT 8-4)
A.k.a. Don Dien Nguyen Dinh Quat. Binh Duong or Phuoc Long Pr, III Corps.
Nguyen Dynasty Wall (YD?)
During the 1630's, the Vietnamese Nguyen Dynasty attempted to create an earlier version of McNamara's Wall in vain effort to prevent invasions from N. By odd coincidence, these two 20' high walls were also built near 17th Parallel. See McNamara's Wall.
Nguyen Trai, FSB (YU 369-261)
Apx 13 km SSE Djamap/Bu Gia Map and 25 km NE Song Be City AF. 30Apr70. Also listed at YU 363-262, May70. Phuoc Long Pr, III Corps.
Nguyen Tat Thanh (n/a)
See Glossary.
Nguyen The Patriot (n/a)
See Glossary.
Nguyen Trai, FSB (YU 369-261)
See FSB Lolita. Phuoc Long Pr, III Corps.
Nguyen Van Be (n/a)
See Glossary
Nguyen Van Nhut, Camp (YS 300-473)
Formerly Army AF and 36th Evac Hosp complex at Vung Tau. Transferred to 3d Corps ARVN, 19Nov70, and named Camp Nguyen Van Nhut. Phuoc Tuy Pr, III Corps.
Nguyen Van Tan SF Camp (CP 310-518?)
At Nha Trang. 5th SF Det B-52 HQ apparently here. Opened 15May64, closed Aug70. Grid per *SF Order of Battle*. Khanh Hoa Pr, II Corps.
Nguyen Van Troi (n/a)
See Glossary.
Nguyen Van Troi Bridge (BT 03-76)
At Da Nang. Formerly the Han River Bridge, but renamed after war's end. See Nguyen Van Troi for interesting history. Quang Nam Pr, I Corps.
Nha Bang (WS 03-72?)
A.k.a. Nga Ba Lam? SW and within 15 km of Chau Doc AF. Grid is est. Chau Doc Pr, IV Corps.
Nha Be (XS 94-80?)
Along W bank of Song Nha Be, apx 16 km SE Tan Son Nhut AB, and 10 km SE Saigon. Home of Game Warden Ops, Naval Supt Activity Detachment. "Game Warden" was operational name for allied river patrol ops of Mekong delta waterways, a combined USN and 9th Inf Div US Army op in IV Corps. Also petroleum refinery here that was partially destroyed by VC sabotage, date unknown. Gia Dinh Pr, III Corps.
Nha Be Base (XS 94-80?)
Along W bank of Song Nha Be, apx 16 km SE Tan Son Nhut and 8 km SE Saigon. 4th/39th and 6th/31st Inf, 9th Div basecamp, per Jim Stone. Gia Dinh Pr, III Corps.

Nha Be Heliport (XS 937-798)
On W shore of Song Nha Be River, apx 9 km SSE Saigon, 3 km SE Nha Be and 10 km ENE Ap Phuoc Khanh "Heliport #746, El. 5', 705' x 80' (M8A1) 11-29 Fuel-J4, Ammo-7.62, 2.75", .50, .30, 40mm. Hvy tfc all hrs. CAUTION-20' bunker/tower 15' from SW cor of rwy intersection, lighted. Tower-257.8, 44.45, 42.05, Contact 5 min out. Opr 2300-1100Z Arty advsy-285.0, 40.90, at 10°40'10"N-106°46'15"E," per Feb73 TAD. Gia Dinh Pr, III Corps.
Nha Be NSA (XS 9-8)
Apx 10 km SSE Saigon. USN Supt Activity, '66-72, per MRF Assn Website. Basecamp of 4th/39th Inf and 6th/31st Inf, 9th Inf Div apparently also here, per Jim Stone. Gia Dinh Pr, III Corps.
Nha Be Point (XS 94-80)
USN Seals and Avn here. On W shore of Song Nha Be River where the Song Dong Tranh River branches off to SE, apx 9 km SSE Saigon, 3 km SE Nha Be and 10 km ENE Ap Phuoc Khanh. Grid courtesy 199th LIB Assn. Gia Dinh Pr, III Corps.
Nha Be River PBR Base (XS 9-8)
Apx 10 km SSE Saigon. River Div 54, TF-116, USN Game Warden base here per MRF Assn website at www.mrfa.org. Gia Dinh Pr, III Corps.
Nha Be Signal Site (XS 9-8?)
No data. Gia Dinh Pr?, III Corps.
Nha Be Tank Farm (XS 910-820)
Petroleum stg facility on W shore of Song Nha Be River where Song Dong Tranh River branches off to SE, apx 9 km SSE Saigon, 3 km SE Nha Be and 10 km ENE Ap Phuoc Khanh. Gia Dinh Pr, III Corps.
Nha Be, FSB (XS 91-82)
2d/3d, 199th LIB, III Corps.
Nha Hai River (YS?)
Possibly a.k.a. Song Nga Bay? Flows through the Rung Sat Zone SE Saigon and to E both the Dong Tran River and Nha Be (Saigon) River. III Corps?
Nha Phu, Dam (CP 0-7)
Bay at 12°25'N-109°13'E. On ND49-13 JOG. Khanh Hoa Pr, II Corps.
Nha Trang (CP 04-55)
On coast astride Nha Trang Bay, apx 190 mi N Saigon and 24 km N Cam Ranh Bay. Pop of 195,000 in '71. Its 8 km-long beach regarded as one of most beautiful in Far East and area was originally developed by French as seaside resort. Giant White Buddha sits on hilltop overlooking the city. Military facilities included I Field Force VN HQ (IFFV), Nha Trang Sub Area Cmd, Camp J. F. McDermott, Long Van Cmpd, Reich Trng Ctr (Hon Tre Island), Nha Trang Commando Ctr (US SF troops were trng at Ctr as early as '57), 1st SF Grp Det C-3 (HQ), Nha Trang 5th SF Grp HQ, 5th SF Grp Det B-52 (Project Delta), 1st SF att 5th SF Grp, Det. B-2, A-111, A-131 Dec64 Det B-52 (was B-220) Project DELTA, 5th SF FOB, Oct65, B-50 Project OMEGA, SF Det 36. Nha Trang MAAG Cmpd, MACV Adv team, CORDS-Nha Trang, Nha Trang AB, MACV-SOG, USARV Special Missions Adv Grp (SMAG), also the MACV-SOG USARV Trng Advsy Grp (TAG) suptg SMAG, 864th Engr Bn. Made one of 6 autonomous municipalities of SVN, Oct70. APO for SF HQ here was APO 96240. Capitol, Khanh Hoa Pr, II Corps. [389]
Nha Trang (n/a)
Mapsheet name of L-7014-6833-3. SVN.
Nha Trang, Baie de (CP 0-5)
Bay at 12°15'N-109°12'E. On ND49-13 JOG. Khanh Hoa Pr, II Corps.
Nha Trang, HQ (CP 038-522)
At Nha Trang AF, apx 1 km SE the NW end of main rwy. Oct66. Khanh Hoa Pr, II Corps.
Nha Trang 5th SF HQ (CP 0310-5180)
Apx 1 km SSE the NW end of Nha Trang AF main rwy. HQ, 5th SF Grp, SF Vietnam. HHC, E Co SF Recondo School also at this site. Det B-52 here with 169 CSF (Camp Strike Force) personnel and 1,381 MSF personnel attached. Khanh Hoa Pr, II Corps.
Nha Trang AFB Hospital (CP 040-523)
Apparently a.k.a. 8th Field Hospital? 8th Field in the Long Van Cmpd, apx 1.2 km ESE the NW end of Nha Trang AF main rwy and 500 meters from ocean. See USAF Hospitals. Khanh Hoa Pr, II Corps.
Nha Trang Airfield (CP 039-520)
A.k.a. Camp McDermott AF and Long Van AF. Major AF, on coast and at southern edge of that city, 40 km SSE Duc My AF, 22 km due N Dong Ba Thin AF and 32 km S Ninh Hoa AF and 5 km W the E end Hon Tre Island. Between Nha Trang and Camp J. F. McDermott. Served USAF, Army and VNAF units with its 6,100 asph rwy. Managed by 14th Combat Supt Grp. El. 16', 6,166' asph rwy. Khanh Hoa Pr, II Corps.
Nha Trang Army Logistical Center (CP 037-504)
Apx 1.5 km SW SE end Nha Trang AF's main rwy. Khanh Hoa Pr, II Corps.
Nha Trang Basecamp (CP 04-53)
At Nha Trang. Site of Det B-55 cmpd, See Davan Cmpd for history. Khanh Hoa Pr, II Corps.
Nha Trang Buddha (CP 034-568)
On Hon San Mtn (Hill 160), apx 4 km due N the NW end Nha Trang AF main rwy. Giant White Buddha that sits on hilltop overlooking Nha Trang. Khan Hoa Pr, II Corps.
Nha Trang Cham Temple (CP 05-49?)
If grid correct, overlooked the USN base and commercial port at end of peninsula on SE edge of city, apx 2 km SE the SE end of AF's main rwy. Per journalist Lawrence Holmberg, Jr,: "I made a trip to VN in 1996...Inside the 11th century Cham temple above the harbor in Nha Trang, I noticed a tarnished silver bowl with the following inscription: *Moreau Bowl. Dedicated to memory of SSgt Eugene Moreau and all of those in Project Delta that made the supreme sacrifice*. Khanh Hoa Pr, II Corps. [390]
Nha Trang Commando Center (CP 031-518?)
At Nha Trang SF Trng Facility, and possibly near listed grid at NW end of main rwy? Elements of US 1st SF Grp (Okinawa) were providing advisors and instructors to this SVN govt commando training center as early as 1957. Khanh Hoa Pr, II Corps.
Nha Trang Commercial Port (CP 054-497)
See Nha Trang Seaport. Khan Hoa Pr, II Corps.
Nha Trang IFFV HQ (CP 042-534)
Overlooking beach, apx 2.4 km NE the NW end of Nha Trang AF main rwy. Per Don Truitt, was in Grand Hotel at

Nha Trang, '68-69, and CG then was Lt Gen. Peers. Khanh Hoa Pr, II Corps.

Nha Trang Lighthouse (CP 065-501)
Apx 4 km SE Nha Trang AF. Per *Team Sergeant*, p 21, was manned by USCG personnel. Khanh Hoa Pr, II Corps.

Nha Trang MAAG Compound (CP 033-546?)
Overlooked ocean, apx 2.5 km NE the NW end Nha Trang AF main rwy. Khan Hoa Pr, II Corps.

Nha Trang Naval Facilities (CP 054-497)
Apx 2.4 km SSE SE end of Nha Trang AF main rwy. Nha Trang's port facility. Khan Hoa Pr, II Corps.

Nha Trang Navy Base (CP 052-496)
Apx 2.3 km SSE SE end of Nha Trang AF main rwy. USN Operating Station, '65-71 Per MRF Assn Website. Khanh Hoa Pr, II Corps.

Nha Trang POL Facility (CP 053-500)
Apx 1.4 km SSE SE end of Nha Trang AF main rwy and immed S Camp McDermott. Pipeline ran from facility N to POL stg bladders at CP 038-523 (immed W the 8th Field Hosp). Khanh Hoa Pr, II Corps.

Nha Trang Recondo School (CP 031-518)
Apx 1 km S the NW end Nha Trang main rwy and just N Nha Trang SF HQ/Trng Facilities. Khan Hoa Pr, II Corps.

Nha Trang SATCOM (CP 035-498)
A.k.a. Nha Trang STRATCOM commo site. Apx 2 km SW SE end of Nha Trang AF main rwy and on N bank of Song Tau River's mouth. Nha Trang's port facility. Khan Hoa Pr, II Corps.

Nha Trang Seaport (CP 064-496)
At tip of peninsula at SE edge of city, apx 2.5 km SE the SE end Nha Trang AF main rwy. Berthing Feet: 600 lineal feet, Draft Max: 40', Cargo Capacity: 1,000 tons/day, Storage Covered w/in 5 km: 306,000 ft^2, Storage Uncov, w/in 5 km:51,000 yd^2. Khanh Hoa Pr, II Corps. [391]

Nha Trang SF Camp (CP 0310-5180)
Apx 1 km SSE the NW end of Nha Trang AF main rwy. A.k.a. "The SFOB." Per *Team Sergeant*, p 5, was adj Nha Trang AB. Det B-52 here with 169 CSF personnel and 1,381 MSF personnel attached. In *The Green Berets*, p 77, author Robin Moore described base in early '64 as being "dominated by five huge white warehouses that dwarfed the complex of one-story barracks and offices; in them were stored the supplies for 40 A detachments." The PCOD (personnel coming off duty) lounge was open to both officers and EM and known as the Playboy Club. Khanh Hoa Pr, II Corps.

Nha Trang STRATCOM (CP 035-498)
See Nha Trang SATCOM. Khan Hoa Pr, II Corps.

Nha Trang TACAN NDB (CP 03-52)
Tactical Air Navigation and Non-Directional air navigation beacon site. At Nha Trang AB. Khanh Hoa Pr, II Corps.

Nha Trang VFW Post (CP 05-49?)
See VFW Post 8316, Saigon. II Corps.

Nhan Bieu Airfield (YD 328-525)
See Quang Tri 1 AF. Quang Tri Pr, I Corps.

Nhan Dan (n/a)
See Glossary.

Nhan Hung SF Camp (VS 995-7640)
Apparently a.k.a. Cai Kit SF Camp? Apx 3 km from Cambodia, 62 km ENE Ha Tien, 16 km WSW Chau Phu/Chau Duc AF and 13 km NNW That Son AF. 5th SF. Info/grid per *SF Order of Battle*. See FOB Tien Binh SF Camp. Kien Tuong Pr, IV Corps.

Nhan Vi Billets (XS 8-9)
At 43 Nhan Vi, Oct 63, 84 rms. Per R. Bows' *Vietnam Military Lore, 1959-1973.* Gia Dinh Pr, III Corps.

Nhan Vi BOQ Annex (XS 832-896)
At 43 Tran Hoang Quan St., Aug 65-68, 31 rms, Saigon. Per *VN Military Lore, 1959-1973.* Gia Dinh Pr, III Corps.

Nhaques (n/a)
See Glossary.

Nhi Binh (XT 75-03)
See FSB Hoc Mon. Gia Dinh or Binh Duong Pr, III Corps.

Nhi Ha, Battle of (YD 272-703)
In coastal sands apx 18 km NNW Quang Tri, 7 km WNW Cua Viet, 4 km inland and 6 km W QL-1. Took place-15May68 and involved elements of 2d/31st Inf, 196th LIB. NVA tank attack against 2d/31st near Nhi Ha, 8May68, per *Into The Valley*, p 292. Map is L-7014-6442-2, per Ken Burrington. See Dai Do. Quang Tri Pr, I Corps.

Nhio Mui (BN 2-2)
Pointe Guio. Coastal point at 11°03'N-108°28'E. On NC49-01 JOG. Binh Thuan Pr, II Corps.

Nho Na, Baie de (BS 7-9)
A.k.a. Vung Nho Na. Bay at 15°20'N-108°52'E. On ND49-01 JOG. Quang Ngai Pr, I Corps.

Nhon CAP, The (BT 0-5?)
See CAP 2-3-10. 2d CAG, Quang Nam Pr, I Corps.

Nhon Co (YU 80-25)
Apx 65 km ENE Song Be and 13 km WSW Gia Nghia AF. SF camp and AF here. A Bty, 1st/92d Arty here Dec69, per 31Jan70, 4th Div ORLL. Quang Duc Pr, II Corps.

Nhon Co Airfield (YU 800-261)
Apx 13 km WSW Gia Nghia AF, 53 km NW Tan Phat AF, 66 km ENE Song Be and 30 km SSE Bu Prang AF. Per TPC K-10D. El. 2,230', 4,200' asph rwy. Also listed at YU 804-250. Quang Duc Pr, II Corps.

Nhon Co SF Camp (YU 804-250)
Apx 13 km WSW Gia Nghia AF, 66 km ENE Song Be and 30 km SSE Bu Prang AF. Det 39, 5th SF, Det A-235, here Oct66. 1st/92d attached to 17th Arty here 3-21Dec69, and 17th had Bn Light Cmd Post here, per Jack Picciolo. Transferred to RF/PF. Grid per *SF Order of Battle*. Quang Duc Pr, II Corps.

Nhon Duc, FSB (XS 87-80)
Apx 8 km due S Saigon, 4 km SW Nha Be, 5 km due W Nhe Be Point Tank Farm and 6 km ENE Ap Phuoc Khanh. 2d/3d Inf, 199th LIB, '69. Grid per 199th LIB Assn. Gia Dinh Pr, III Corps.

Nhon Due (XS 87-80)
See Nhon Duc. Gia Dinh Pr, III Corps.

Nhon My Refugee Camp (BR 895-393)
Apx 4 km due S Phu Cat AB and 3 km W QL-1. Binh Dinh Pr, II Corps.

Nhon Ninh Heliport (XS 044-746)
Apx 25 km W to WSW Thuy Phong AF and 17 km S Moc Hoa. "Heliport #724, El 13', sod," per Feb73 TAD. Kien Tuong Pr, IV Corps.

Nhon Ninh (XS 08-68)
Ville apx 72 km WSW Saigon and 47 km NW My Tho. Kien Tuong Pr, IV Corps.

Nhon Trach (YS 14-83)
Along Rte 319, apx 12 km due S Long Thanh AF and 14 km NW Phu My. 3d/7th, 199th LIB, III Corps.
Nhon Trach (Pu Thanh) (n/a)
Mapsheet name of L-7014-6330-2. SVN.
Nhona Bay (BS 7-9)
A.k.a. Vung Nho Na. Bay at 15°20'N-108°52'E. On ND49-01 JOG. Quang Ngai Pr, I Corps.
Nhot Phat Airfield (UH 67-43)
LS-179. CIA/SF, per *Air Facilities Data-Laos.*
Nhuong Ban (n/a)
Mapsheet name of L-7014-6245-4. NVN only.
Nhut, Bai (XQ 7-5)
See Bai Nhut, Bai.
NIAGARA (n/a)
See Glossary.
Niagara, LZ (BR 421-820)
A.k.a. LZ Mattie (?) and also spelled Niagra. Apx 38 km due W Ha Tay AF, 36 km N An Khe, and 36 km WSW Bong Son. 4th Div AO, '70. Mentioned on 129th AHC's webpage at vhfcn.org/129th/ 129thhist.htm. Name/grid per Jim Claeys. Also listed at BR 521-820, but that is thought to be an error. Apr-Oct70. Binh Dinh Pr, II Corps.
Niagara/Cedar Falls, Op (XT)
5-25Jan67. 173d Abn Bde in Cau Dinh Jungle and Iron Triangle of VC MR 4. With other units in blocking positions, the 3d Bde's 3 Inf Bns swept Iron Triangle. 51st Chemical Det, 173d Engr Co, and tunnel rats explored numerous VC tunnels, finding large weapon/supply caches. Some 1,000 tons of rice, plus over 200 crew-served/individual weapons were also captured. More importantly, 65 POWs taken. Est 85 VC KIA, with E Trp, 17th Cav credited with 73 of those in one action.
Niagara Falls, USS (n/a)
AFS-3. Aux Refrig, per Ralph Fries.
Nicholas, FSB (XD 858-479)
Apx 8 km due N Khe Sanh CB, 24 km W Mai Loc and 47 km W Quang Tri. 101st Abn inactive FSB grid per Don Armstrong. Quang Tri Pr, I Corps.
Nichole, LZ (ZA 173-784)
See Nicole. Kontum Pr, II Corps.
Nicolas, FSB (XD 858-479)
See Nicholas, FSB. Quang Tri Pr, I Corps.
Nicole, LZ (ZA 173-784)
Along secondary road, apx 12 km SSW Kontum, 25 km ENE Chu Pa Mtn and 5 km W QL-14. 4thInf Div LZ said to have been near LZ Carmen. Cited in *Time Heals No Wounds*, at pp 227-228. C/1st/12th Inf, 4th Div here, May69. 10th Cav and at least one 155mm Bty at site. Grid per S-3 Daily Journal/Op rpts of 31 July-1Sep69, courtesy Bob Patsfield. Aug-Nov69. Kontum Pr, II Corps. [392]
Nicholes, USS (n/a)
DD-449. 7th Flt Destroyer, per Ralph Fries.
Night of The Pagodas (n/a)
See Glossary.
Niles BOQ (XS 8-9)
On Lot 52, Phu Tho Hoa St., Saigon. Per R. Bows' *Vietnam Military Lore, 1959-1973.* Gia Dinh Pr, III Corps.
Nimitz, LZ (BT 005-480)
In Que Son Mtns, apx 14 km due W LZ Baldy, 38 km NW Tam Ky and 31 km due S Da Nang AB. Apr70 XXIV Corps grid per Don Armstrong. Quang Nam Pr, I Corps.
Nina, LZ (n/a)
1st Cav FSB/LZ. No data. Name per Jim Claeys. Pleiku or Binh Dinh Pr?, II Corps.
Nine Dragons, The (n/a)
See Cuu Long Son and Do Son Beach. NVN.
Nine Yards, FSB (YD 9-0?)
Apparently near QL-1 between Phu Bai and FSB Anzio but its precise location is unknown. 1st/508th Inf, 82d Abn in Sep68. Thua Thien Pr, I Corps.
Nineteenth Hole, LZ (YA 83-21?)
A.k.a. LZ 19th Hole, and spelled "Nineteen Hole" in one text. Apx 3 km N Plei Girao Kla, 7 km SSW Duc Co SF Camp, 18 km NNW Chu Pong Mtn, 8 km E Cambodia, 8 km N LZ Golf and 35 km NW Plei Me. 1st Cav. On map in *The Rise and Fall of the American Army*, pp 368-369, and also mentioned in *Incursion* (map at p 252). Grid is est. Pleiku Pr, II Corps.
Ninh Binh (n/a)
Mapsheet name of L-7014-6149-1. NVN only.
Ninh Binh (XH 03-40)
Along QL-1, apx 88 km SSE Hanoi, 60 km N Thanh Hoa. French garrison here involved in Battle of Day River, 29May-18Jun5, being overrun, 29May51. Son of Cmd Gen. Marshal de Lattre, Lt Bernard de Lattre, was KIA here. See *Street Without Joy*, Chp 2, map at p 46. NVN. [393]
Ninh Binh (various)
Common Viet place name, See grid squares: XH 0-3, BP 8-8, WH 8-3, AT 8-3. NVN/SVN.
Ninh Giang (Vinh Ninh) (n/a)
Mapsheet L-7014-6250-2. Sheet name: Vinh Ninh (Ninh Giang). NVN only.
Ninh Heup Highway Strip (n/a)
Apx 80 km NNW Vientiane. ONC-J-11. El. 700'. Laos.
Ninh Hoa (n/a)
Mapsheet name of L-7014-6833-4. SVN.
Ninh Hoa (BP 980-830)
Apx 32 km N Nha Trang AF, 13 km WNW Ninh Hoa AF, 20 km from coast and 30 km SW Van Ninh AF. HQ Rep of Korea 9th Inf "White Horse" Div, Oct66-Mar73. Khanh Hoa Pr, II Corps.
Ninh Hoa Airfield (BP 983-830)
NE Ninh Hoa, apx 32 km N Nha Trang AF, 13 km WNW Ninh Hoa AF, 20 km from coast and 30 km SW Van Ninh AF. ROK Army controlled this field in '73. Per TPC K10-B. El. 20', 1,600' rwy. At 12°30'16"N-109°08'48"E. Khanh Hoa Pr, II Corps.
Ninh Hoa Bypass (BP 971-799)
Ql-1 alternate road that skirted E side of Ninh Hoa, bypassing city center, apx 27 km NNW Nha Trang. Khanh Hoa Pr, II Corps.
Ninh Hoa NDB (BP 97-83)
Non-Directional air navigation Beacon site at Ninh Hoa AF. Khanh Hoa Pr, II Corps.
Ninh Lam (n/a)
Mapsheet name of L-7014-6834-2. SVN.
Ninh Ma Fort (CQ 22-16)
Apx 2 km NE Ninh Ma. Khanh Hoa Pr, II Corps.

Ninh Phuoc (n/a)
Mapsheet name of L-7014-6833-1. SVN.
Ninh Thanh (XT 245-505)
Ville that formed NE part of Long Hoa ville complex along southern edge of Tay Ninh. Attacked and occupied by elements of 33d and 88th NVA Rgts night of 10-11Sep, during 2d phase of Battle for Tay Ninh.
Ninh Thuan PFTC (BN 7-8?)
RVNAF Popular Force Trng Ctr, apparently near Phan Rang. Ninh Thuan Pr, II Corps.
Ninh Thuan Province (BP/BN)
One of 12 north-central provs forming II Corps (II CTZ).
Nita, LZ (BP 655-613)
Apx 38 km WNW Nha Trang AB and 15 km WSW Dien My. Apr67. Khanh Hoa Pr, II Corps.
Nixon Project, The (n/a)
See Glossary.
NKP (VE 7-2)
See Nakhon Phanom West AF. Thailand.
NMCB-9 Camp (BT 06-73)
See Camp Adenir. Quang Nam Pr, I Corps.
No Bomb Line (n/a)
See NBL in Glossary.
No Dak, FSB? (XU 448-033)
Apx 17 km NW tip of Fishhook, 2 km NNW Phum Dong, 17 km NE Katum and 29 km WSW Loc Ninh. Cambodian Incursion ville or FSB site. 11th ACR/1st Cav here. Grid per *11th ACR Cambodia Invasion AAR, 1st Cav Div, May-Jun70*, courtesy Lou Rochat. [394] Cambodia.
No Drink Creek (YD 0-6)
Apx 12 km SW Con Thien, 7 km N QL-9 and 27 km WNW Dong Ha. Significance of site unknown. Apx location shown on *Leatherneck* Magazine map at: www.monboys. com. Quang Tri Pr, I Corps.
No Name Island (BT 084-567?)
If grid correct, was immed N Go Noi Island and apx 4 km W Hoi An? cleared by 2d/1st Marines, 1st Mar Div, Apr-May69. Also listed at BT 084-667, but no island at that grid? Quang Nam Pr, I Corps.
No Ngoc Tau, SF Camp (XT 958-001?)
See Ho Ngoc Tau SF Camp. Sp variant of Ho Ngoc Tau. in DA Chief, Mil Hist records summary which indicates Det A-314 (a.k.a. 301) here '65, and B-56 Sigma here '66. Gia Dinh Pr, III Corps.
No Slack, LZ (YB 997-067?)
If grid correct, was apx 31 km NW Kontum, 16 km SSW Dak To 2 AF, 3 km E Dak Su River and 14 km NNW Polei Kleng. Listed at ZB 997-067 but grid does not exist. Possibly YB 097-067, and if so, was 4 km W tri Dao and 18 km SSE Dak To 2 AF? Americal list. Photos/map at http://1-14th.com/maps.html. Kontum Pr, II Corps. [395]
Noah, FSB (YT 644-824)
Remote site overlooked river valley apx 13 km NE FSB Leo, 32 km SE Duc Phong, 56 km ENE Dong Xoai, 43 km W Bao Loc AF and 94 km NE Bien Hoa AB. Opened or reopened 19Aug70, closed 2Sep70. 1st/5th Cav. Data in *1st Cav Div Op Rpt, ending 31Oct70*, per Peter Cole. Photos/ maps at http://1-14th.com/maps.html. Phuoc Long Pr, III Corps.
Noble, FSB (YT 423-751)
In mnts, apx 32 km due S Duc Phong AF and SF Camp, 35 km due E Dong Xoai and 74 km NE Bien Hoa AB. Phuoc Also listed at YT 434-749, which is 21 km SE Bunard AF. Long Khanh/Phuoc Long Pr border, III Corps.
Noble, USS (n/a)
APA-218. Amphib Attack, Transport, per Ralph Fries.
Nocona (n/a)
Apr70, XXIV Corps proposed 101st Abn FSB name.
Noi Bai Airfield (WJ 83-47)
Apx 20 km due N Hanoi, per ONC J-11. El. 49'. NVN.
Noi Go Choi Mtn (BR 860-790)
Apx 17 km SSW Bong Son. Binh Dinh Pr, II Corps.
Nola, FSB (YD 617-302)
Also spelled Nora? Adj to Ap Bo Dien along N bank of Song Bo River apx 700 meters WSW the An Lo Bridge and 3.5 km NW Van Xa/LZ Sally AF. 1st/502d, 101st Abn here Mar68. Thua Thien Pr, I Corps.
Nola, FSB (YS 346-708)
Apx 10 km WNW Nui Dat, 300 meters SSE site of FSB Gimlet, 1 km SW FSB Thornton and 16 km SW FSB Dampier. On 1ATF NCO trng map per John Hollett. Phuoc Tuy Pr, III Corps.
Nolte, LZ (YD 630-208)
Apx 3 km E the Song Bo River, 2 km WNW FSB T-Bone (Nui Hon Vuon), 5 km SSE Ap Lai Bang. Apr70 XXIV Corps grid per Don Armstrong. Thua Thien Pr, I Corps.
Non Son Airfield (AT 879-396)
See Phouc Binh AF. Quang Nam Pr, I Corps.
Nong Het Airfield (UG 94-56)
LS-03. Apx 220 km NE Vientiane on Feb67 Natl Geo map. CIA/SF, per *Air Facilities Data-Laos*. El.? Laos.
Nong Kala Airfield (UG 07-34)
LS-338. CIA/SF, per *Air Facilities Data-Laos.*
Nong Kha Airfield (UF 08-93)
LS-333. CIA/SF, per *Air Facilities Data-Laos.*
Nong Khai Airfield (TE 6-7)
Along Mekong River at Laotian border, apx 515 km NNE Bangkok, and 20 km ESE Vientiane (Laos), near 17°51'44"N-102°44'52"E, on Feb67 Natl Geo map (ONC J-11 also). NIMA data. El. 525'. Thailand.
Nong Khang Airfield (VH 05-81)
L-52. CIA/SF, per *Air Facilities Data-Laos.*
Nong Luang Airfield (QV 27-68)
LS-322. CIA/SF, per *Air Facilities Data-Laos.*
Nong Mek Airfield (n/a)
Apx 15 km W of Laos, 90 km SE Ubon AB, per TPC K-10A. El. 180'. Thailand.
Nong Pet Airfield (SF 98-79)
LS-154. CIA/SF, per *Air Facilities Data-Laos.*
Nong Railroad Bridge (YD 926-101)
A.k.a. Railroad Bridge #2. Parallel to QL-1 bridge at same site, apx 17 km SE Hue and 20 km NW Q Phu Loc. Apr60. Thua Thien Pr, I Corps.
Nong Saeng Airfield (WB 5-2)
Apx 85 km SE Ubon AB, 8 km W of Laos, at 14°43'00"N-105°29'00"E. Grid/data per NIMA and TPC K-10A. El. 590'. Thailand.
Nong Seang Airfield (WB 5-2)
See Nong Saeng AF. Thailand.

Nong Sakhe Airfield (QB 55-33)
LS-106. CIA/SF, per *Air Facilities Data-Laos.*
Nong Son, FSB/LZ (AT 814-383)
A.k.a. Nong Son Outpost/CB. Near site of Nong Son Coal Mine, only producing coal mine in SVN, apx 40 km SSW Da Nang, 4 km WSW Phouc Binh AF and 48 km WNW Tam Ky. 5th SF CIDG A-105, USMC and Americal units here. USMC outpost here provided security for mine. F/5th Mar manned 2 positions and kept 81mm mortar section that included two 4.2" mortars on hill overlooking mine. Heavily attacked 3Jul67, and in ensuing battle, PFC Melvin Lewis was awarded the MOH. Recon Mtn was within close proximity to mine and this post. Map is L-7014-6640-3. Quang Nam Pr, I Corps.
Nong Son Airfield (AT 879-396)
See Phouc Binh AF. Quang Nam Pr, I Corps.
Nong Son Coal Mine (AT 81-38)
Apx 40 km SSW Da Nang, 4 km WSW Phouc Binh AF and 48 km WNW Tam Ky. Only producing coal mine in SVN. See An Hoa Industrial Complex and FSB Nong Son. Map is L-7014-6640-3. Quang Nam Pr, I Corps.
Nong Son Heliport (1) (AT 823-394)
Apx 5 km W Phuoc Binh AF, 4 km due E Khuong Trung and 40 km SSW Da Nang. Heliport #625, El. 131' per Feb73 TAD. Quang Nam Pr, I Corps.
Nong Son Heliport (2) (AT 876-399)
At or adj to Phuoc Binh AF, apx 37 km SSW Da Nang. Heliport #626, alt 66', at 15°43'30"N-108°05'00"E, per Feb73 TAD. Quang Nam Pr, I Corps.
Nong Son Outpost (AT 814-383)
See FSB Nong Son. Quang Nam Pr, I Corps.
Nong Son Mountain (AT 816-380)
A.k.a. Recon Mtn? Roughly 40 km SSW Da Nang and 4 km WSW Phouc Binh AF. Aug67. Quang Nam Pr, I Corps.
Nong Son Combat Base (AT 822-388)
See Nong Son, FSB/LZ. Quang Nam Pr, I Corps.
Nong Son SF Camp (AT 814-383)
Apx 40 km SSW Da Nang, 4 km WSW Phouc Binh AF and 48 km WNW Tam Ky. 5th SF CIDG A-105 camp near only producing coal mine in SVN. Transferred to 78th Border Rangers. Possible sp variant of Nong Song. Grid per *SF Order of Battle.* Quang Nam Pr, I Corps.
Nong Song Outpost (AT 81-38?)
See Nong Son Outpost. Quang Nam Pr, I Corps.
Nong Takoo (QR 8-2 or TB 8-1?)
SF camp or AO per *SF Order of Battle.* Thailand.
Nong Thoi (YS 5-6)
A.k.a. Ap Nong Thoampoi. Vicinity of Dat Do, NE Vung Tau. Phuoc Tuy Pr, III Corps.
Nong Troung Nam Dong (YC 8-8)
In Ruong Ruong Valley, apx 54 km WNW Da Nang and 38 km SSE Hue. 16°07'00"N-107°41'00"E. On map L-7014-6541-3. Thua Thien Pr, I Corps.
Nong Truong Nam Dong (n/a)
Mapsheet name of L-7014-6541-3. SVN.
Noose Island (XS 474-715)
Terrain feature resembling hangman's noose. Apx 10 km NW Tan An, and formed by channel of Song Vam Co Tay River. Jul70. Long An or Kien Tuong Pr?, III Corps.
Nora, Fort (AN 958-297)
See Fort Nora. Binh Thuan Pr, II Corps.
Nora, FSB (YD 617-302?)
Also spelled Nola? Adj to Ap Bo Dien along N bank of Song Bo River apx 700 meters WSW the An Lo Bridge and 3.5 km NW Van Xa/LZ Sally AF. 1st/502d, 101st Abn here Mar68. Thua Thien Pr, I Corps.
Nora, Ft. (AN 958-297)
See Fort Nora. Binh Thuan Pr, II Corps.
Nord Est, Baie du (XQ 8-6)
A.k.a. Vinh Dong Bac. Bay at 8°43'N-106°39'E. On NC48-11 JOG. NVN.
Nord Est, Pointe du (XQ 8-6)
See Pointe Nord Est. IV Corps.
Nord Ouest, Pointe (US 7-4)
See Pointe Nord-Quest. Kien Giang Pr, IV Corps.
Norma, FSB (YT 348-272)
Along QL-20, apx 7 km W Xa Binh Hoa and 20 km NNW Xuan Loc. Aug69. Long Khanh Pr, III Corps.
Norma, LZ (BQ 275-614)
Apx 24 km due W Phu Tuc, 3 km SE peak of Hill 1229 and 5 km ESE Ban Kdiel. 2d/17th Arty here supt 1st Cav, 16Jul66. Data per Jack Picciolo. Phu Bon Pr, II Corps.
Norman, LZ (YS 370-950)
Apx 16 km SSW Xuan Loc, 6 km W Blackhorse and 17 km E to ENE Ap Binh Son. Mar66. Long Khanh Pr, III Corps.
Normandy, FSB (XT 904-318)
Apx 8 km W to WSW Khu Tru Mat, 15 km ESE Lai Khe AF and 18 km NNW Bien Hoa AB. Aug-Oct68. Binh Duong Pr, III Corps.
Normandy, FSB (YD 690-017)
Apx 21 km SSW Hue, 24 km SW Phu Bai, 12 km W FSB Brick, 8 km SSE FSB Checkmate and 8 km SSW FSB Birmingham. 101st Abn AO '68-71, and used by 1st Bde during Op Spokane Rapids. Also listed at YD 688-017. 101st Abn inactive FSB grid per Don Armstrong. May68-Nov69. Also listed at YD 697-012 and 639-271(Nov69?). Thua Thien Pr, I Corps.
Normandy I, FSB (XT 828-338)
Apx 7 km SE Lai Khe AF and 7 km WNW FSB Normandy. Jan68. Binh Duong Pr, III Corps.
Normandy II, FSB (XT 911-319)
On site of original FSB Normandy. See FSB Normandy. Jun-Jul68. Binh Duong Pr, III Corps.
Normandy III, FSB (XT 904-318)
On site of original FSB Normandy. See FSB Normandy. Oct69-Jan70. Binh Duong Pr, III Corps.
Norodom Palace (XS 857-915)
A.k.a. Independence Palace and Presidential Palace See Presidential Palace. Gia Dinh Pr, III Corps.
Norris, USS (n/a)
DD-859, per Ralph Fries.
North, FSB (YT 75-53)
A.k.a. FSB Terry Lynn? Along QL-20, apx 6 km NE Xa Phuong Lam, 95 km NE Saigon, 19 km N Vo Dat and 37 km SW Bao Loc. 1st Cav and 4th/12th Inf, 199th LIB here. Long Khanh Pr, III Corps.
North, LZ (BS 725-907)
On Batangan Peninsula, apx 2 km from coast, 3 km SSE An Cuong, 18 km NNE Quang Ngai and 12 km W QL-1.

Per Americal list author, was bad area and at one time near 2d NVA Div's HQ. Americal list. Quang Ngai Pr, I Corps.

North, LZ (XT 462-038)
Along Song Vam Co Dam, apx 16 km ESE Duc Hua AF, 6 km WSW Khiem Cuong and 36 km WNW Tan Son Nhut. Apr66. Hau Nghia Pr, III Corps.

North 1, FSB (XU 505-226?)
If grid correct, site was along Rte 7 in Cambodia, apx 13 km SSW Snuol, 27 km NW Loc Ninh, 3 km SW the sharp point of Angel's Wing. 11th ACR's grid is XU 525-262, and listed grid may not be accurate? See North 1 at XU 525-262. Data per Frank Penk, Jr. Cambodia.

North 1, FSB (XU 525-262)
Along Snuol/Memot road (Rte 7), apx 2 km NW the sharp point of Angel's Wing, 8 km SSW Snuol, 27 km NW Loc Ninh, 5 km S Phum Rohar and 42 km NNE Katum. Described as clearing along Rte 7, apx 6 km S Snuol and 4 km S largest cache found in war, a.k.a. "The City." Also listed at XU 505-226, which is some 13 km S Snuol in SVN? Opened (?) 3May70, by 1st/5 Cav, 1st Cav as Incursion FSB. Possibly 1st Cav, 25th Inf, 11th ACR or ARVN elements here at various times. Grid and some data per *11th ACR Cambodia Invasion AAR, 1st Cav Div, May-Jun70*, courtesy Lou Rochat.[396] Cambodia.

North 2, FSB (XU 494-175)
At road junction on Rte 7 between Memot and Snuol, apx 26 km WNW Loc Ninh SVN, 7 km SW FSB North 1, 16 km SSW Snuol and 23 km NE Memot. Incursion FSB, May and/or Jun70. Possibly 1st Cav, 25th Inf, 11th ACR or ARVN elements here at various times. Data per Frank Penk, Jr. Cambodia.

North Dakota, FSB (YS 248-753)
On QL-15, apx 20.5 km WNW Nui Dat, 10.5 km SSE FSB Archer, 2 km SE FSB Doody and 3 km NW FSB Gladstone. On 1ATF NCO trng map per John Hollett. Phuoc Tuy Pr, III Corps.

North Dakota, FSB (XU 489-033)
Apx 6 km from SVN border, 20 km ESE Memot AF, 25 km WSW Loc Ninh AF and 16 km N tip of Fishhook. Apparent Cambodian Incursion base. Cambodia.

North English, LZ (BS 883-056)
A.k.a. or near site of LZ Zager or Zaeger (BS 883-068), and possibly an old ARVN FSB called LZ Tom. In valley of An Lao River, on a hilltop near coast at Bong Son and just N LZ English. It could be seen from LZ English (BS 877-077), and according to *Charlie Ranger* author, "was surrounded by some of most beautiful country-side I'd ever seen." 2d/503d Inf, 173d Abn here as was 4th/173d Engrs. 19th Engr Bn's HQ, A and 137th (LE) Engr Cos were at this base in mid-68. Map is L-7014-6838-3 (Tam Quan). Also listed at BS 881-058. Grid and map data per Ray Smith. See LZ Zaeger. Binh Dinh Pr, II Corps.

North Hue LCU Ramp (YD 760-250)
See Hue LCU Ramp North. Thua Thien Pr, I Corps.

North Hills, SS (n/a)
Commercial ship under US govt contract, per Ralph Fries.

North One, FSB (XU 5-2)
See FSB North 1. Cambodia or III Corps.

North Pole BOQ (XS 833-893)
At 48 Hong Bang St., Saigon, prior to Jul 62. Had 32 rms. Per R. Bows' *Vietnam Military Lore, 1959-1973.* Gia Dinh Pr, III Corps.

North SAR Station (YH 10-12)
See SAR North. Gulf of Tonkin. NVN.

North Two, FSB (XU 494-175)
See North 2. Cambodia.

Northeast Bay (XQ 8-6)
A.k.a. Vinh Dong Bac. Bay at 8°43'N-106°39'E. On NC48-11 JOG. NVN.

Northeast Pointe (XQ 8-6)
See Pointe Northeast. IV Corps.

Northern Artillery Cantonment (AT 921-799)
Apx 10 km NW Da Nang AB and 4 km WSW Red Beach AF. Nov-Dec69. 1st Mar Div and 2 Btys 1st/13th Arty moved to FSB Los Banos from this site after having 1st being here following initial lndg in SVN, '69. Fired in supt 1st and 2d Bns, 26th Marines. Quang Nam Pr, I Corps.

Northampton, USS (n/a)
CC-1. Cruiser, per Ralph Fries.

Northwest Operational Group (TJ 94-66)
See GONO in Glossary.

Northwest Point (US 7-4)
See Point Northwest. Kien Giang Pr, IV Corps.

Notawi (n/a)
SF camp or AO per *SF Order of Battle*. Thailand (or Cambodia?).

Notre Dame Rock (WJ 3-2)
A.k.a. Ap Da Chong. Terrain feature along E bank of Black River, apx 55 km W Hanoi, and just E Tu Vu. Bernard Fall wrote, "Probably the bloodiest river battles since the American Civil War were fought out between the French and Vietminh in confines of Black River around Notre Dame Rock." On 12Jan52, the Vietminh ambushed an entire river convoy S of the rock, severely damaging nearly every ship, while sinking 4 patrol boats and one LSSL. Ambush ended French attempts to resupply its troops in Hoa Binh area by river. Per *Street Without Joy*, pp 54-55; map at p 50. NVN.

Nouvelles du Nord-Viet-Nam (n/a)
See *Caravelle* and *Indochine-Sud-Est Asiatique.*

November, FSB (XT 590-420)
See Firebase N. Binh Duong Pr, III Corps.

November, FSB ? (XT 645-302)
Apx 1 km W song Saigon, 16 km SW Lai Khe and 3 km ESE Xa Duoc. Nature of site unknown. Jun66. Binh Duong Pr, III Corps.

November, FSB (YA or ZA)
Apparently SE Ben Het and apx 20(?) km NNW Pleiku. Pleiku Pr?, II Corps.

November Revolution, The (n/a)
See Glossary.

Noxubee, USS (n/a)
AOG-56. Aux Oiler, per Ralph Fries.

NPA-1 (AT/BT)
National Priority Area 1. In Feb66, the Ngu Hanh Son Pacification Area (pilot pacification prgm zone in 9th Marines TAOR S of Da Nang in latter half of '65) was expanded to include all of Hao Vang and parts of Hieu Duc and Dien Ban Districts, and renamed NPA-1. Map showing

area in *US Marines in Vietnam, 1966*, p 46, discussed at p 45. Quang Nam Pr, I Corps.

Nrai, Camp (n/a)
One home of Royal Thai Army Special Warfare Ctr; the other being Camp Erawan. Cited in *Rangers at War*, p 273. Lopburi Pr, Thailand.

NSA Hospital, Da Nang (BT 008-754?)
Naval Support Activity Hosp at Da Nang AB, a.k.a. G-4 NSA Hosp. See USN/USMC Hosp, Da Nang. Grid is for AB. Quang Nam Pr, I Corps.

NSA, Saigon (XS 852-917)
On Thi Diem St., apx 1 km WSW US Embassy. Gia Dinh Pr, III Corps.

NSAD Cua Viet (YD 33-69)
See Cua Viet NSA. Quang Tri Pr, I Corps.

NSAD Hue (YD 785-230)
See Hue NSAD. Thua Thien Pr, I Corps.

NSAD Tan My (YD 83-34)
See Tan My. Thua Thien Pr, I Corps.

Nue Hoac (BT 07-22)
See Nui Hoac.

Nueces, USS (n/a)
A.k.a. APB-40. Launched 6May45. Departed US for VN in late '68, arriving at Vung Tau. Soon moved into Mekong Delta suptg MRF, TF-117. Left VN in '70, per MRF Assn at www.mrfa.org navy_index.htm. Also spelled Nuecess? III, IV Corps.

Nui A Van (AT 94-92)
See Hill 724. Quang Nam Pr, I Corps.

Nui Ao Ho (CP 091-149)
Hill mass at S end of Cam Ranh Peninsula, apx 9 km SSE main AF and 2.5 km W Howell Beach. Apx 500 meters at max height and consisting of five distinct peaks. Khanh Hoa Pr, I Corps.

Nui Ba Mountain (CQ 061-695)
Apx 14 km E Dong Tre AF. Jan69. Phu Yen Pr, II Corps.

Nui Ba Dai (CQ 276-260)
A.k.a. Hill 706. Apx 19 km SSE Phu Hiep AF, 4 km due N Phong So and 2 km E QL-1. Phu Yen Pr, II Corps.

Nui Ba Dan (YT 920-170)
A.k.a. Hill 731 (2,398'). Apx 12 km SSW Tanh Linh AF. Binh Tuy Pr, III Corps.

Nui Ba Den (XT 283-583)
A.k.a. Black Virgin Mountain, Retrans and Hill 986. A 3,000' high monolith that rose sharply from otherwise flat plain, 10 km NE Tay Ninh and apx 96 km NW Saigon. Derived name from legend in which young woman died while in search of her lover on its slopes. "Black Virgin Mtn" is literal English translation of Viet name. An important US Radio Relay "Retrans" (as in radio re-transmission) facility and possibly 25th Inf, 1st Inf, 196th LIB and 1st Cav FSB at its peak. Was notable as most (if not only) significant terrain feature within a 80 km (?) radius of Tay Ninh, and crucial to both land/air navigation/commo. 1st captured by allies in May64, when SF 3d Mobile Strike Force took summit. During WWII, Japanese had signal relay site here beginning in 1940, and occupied it for 7 years(?). Under pressure from French, Japanese abnd site and Viet Minh apparently moved in to replace them. In '69, was run by NBD Provisional Co as relay site for almost every unit operating in III Corps (call sign: "Lonely Summit."). Most staff were volunteers and standard tour on hill only 90-days, though many extended their stay. Despite repeated efforts to clear them, VC/NVA also maintained significant presence on mtn, and slopes between crest and base generally belonged to enemy without pause during war. 88th NVA Rgt occupied caves between Jan-Aug68, using mtn as radio relay site also. On 18Aug68, during Battle for Tay Ninh, US cmpd attacked by est Co in effort to disrupt commo in supt of assault on Tay Ninh, but met elements of 3d/22d Inf who stopped them after portion of perimeter was breached (8 US KIA). [397] Per Frank Penk, Jr, Nui Ba Den, Nui Ba Ra and Nui Chua Chan all had radio relay sites at their summit. "No arty but a defensive perimeter and chopper pads on all three. Nui Chua Chan's pad was large enough for four Hueys. As I recall, there were no names for these locations, just the name of mtn, or they might have gone by radio call-sign." 4th/23d Inf, 25th Inf Div patrolled base of mtn regularly. 4th/9th Inf and possibly 199th LIB here also. SF A-Team Camp, SF Det 56, 5th SF, Det A-325B (was 303), Oct65. On mapsheet L-7014-6231-4 (Tay Ninh). See White Virgin Mtn. Tay Ninh Pr, III Corps. [398]

Nui Ba Den, FSB (XT 288-565)
Apparently at Nui Ba Den Quarry site. See Nui Ba Den Quarry. 31Oct69. Tay Ninh Pr, III Corps.

Nui Ba Den Quarry (XT 275-560)
Apx 3-4 km due S peak of Nui Ba Den Mtn, near Ap Thanh Son and 6 km NNE Tay Ninh. 588th Engrs/20th Engr Bde worked quarry. Grid per Frank Penk, Jr. Tay Also listed at XT 260-574 and 288-565, Apr67-Jan70. Ninh Pr, III Corps.

Nui Ba Den Radio Relay (XT 281-581)
See Nui Ba Den. Tay Ninh Pr, III Corps.

Nui Ba Den SF Camp (XT 281-582)
See Nui Ba Den. Grid per *SF Order of Battle.* Tay Ninh Pr, III Corps.

Nui Ba Den Signal Site (XT 281-581)
See Nui Ba Den. Tay Ninh Pr, III Corps.

Nui Ba Doi (WS 01-55)
See Hill 261. Chau Doc? Pr, IV Corps.

Nui Ba Hao Mountains (YT 2-4)
Mtn range at 11°15'N-107°05'E. On NC48-04 JOG. Phuoc Long Pr, III Corps.

Nui Ba Ho (YD 028-479?)
See FSB Sarge? Quang Tri Pr, I Corps.

Nui Ba Hon? (AN 731-050)
A.k.a. Hill 164. Apx 10 km WSW Phan Thiet, 6 km from coast, 3km S QL-1. Binh Thuan Pr, II Corps.

Nui Ba Lon (CP 18-98)
A.k.a. Hill 567. On Hon Lon Island, 45 km NNE Nha Trang. Khanh Hoa Pr, II Corps.

Nui Ba Ra Airfield (YU 182-109)
See Song Be AF. Phuoc Long Pr, III Corps.

Nui Ba Ra Mountain (YU 184-068)
A.k.a. Hill 723 (2,372') Phuoc Binh Mtn and "White Virgin Mtn." Apx 46 km ENE An Loc and W the Song Be River, 2k km E Song Be/Phuoc Binh, 4 km due W Song Be AF and 4 km due S Song Be City AF. Held commanding view of both Song Be AF's from S. Likely nicknamed White Virgin Mtn in reference to its relative prominence with Nui Ba Den as a terrain feature (see LRRP Company

Command, p 67). Site of Nui Ba Ra Signal Site and French-era penal colony. Phuoc Long Pr, III Corps.

Nui Ba Ra Penal Colony (YU 165-075)
French apparently had notorious prison for political prisoners at base of Nui Ba Ra Mtn, and possibly at Phuoc Binh. Discussed in *Mobile Guerrilla Force*, p 47. Near listed grid. Phuoc Long Pr, III Corps.

Nui Ba Ra Signal Site (YU 184-068)
A.k.a. Hill 723 and possibly Phuoc Binh and/or White Virgin Mtn Signal Site? Apx 4 km due W Song Be AF and 4 km due S Song Be City AF. Per Frank Penk, Jr, Nui Ba Den, Nui Ba Ra and Nui Chua Chan were all signal sites, "No arty but a defensive perimeter and chopper pads on all three. Nui Chua Chan's pad was large enough for four Hueys. As I recall, there were no names for se locations, just the name of mtn or, they might have gone by radio call-sign." 194th MPs and elements of 1st Signal Bde here. Phuoc Long Pr, III Corps.

Nui Ba Vi (WJ 38-27)
See Ba Vi. NVN.

Nui Bach Ma (ZC 040-900)
A.k.a. Hill 1408 (4,630'). See Dong Bach Ma and Bach Ma. Thua Thien Pr, I Corps.

Nui Bai Cay Tat (YD 52-23)
A.k.a. Hill 647. See FSB Meredith. Thua Thien Pr, I Corps.

Nui Bai Voi, Battle of (VS 58-29?)
See Nui Sai Voi. Kien Giang Pr, IV Corps.

Nui Ban Nu (BS 920-180)
Binh Dinh Pr, II Corps.

Nui Bang Lim (BT 0-1)
W of and overlooking Tien Phuoc SF Camp. Quang Ngai Pr, I Corps.

Nui Batangan (BS 790-890)
Quang Ngai Pr, I Corps.

Nui Be (YS 88-90)
A.k.a. Hill 874. Major terrain feature jutting from flat plain apx 100 km due E Saigon, 70 km NE Vung Tau and 12 km NW Ham Tan AF. Phuoc Tuy Pr, III Corps.

Nui Bi Doup (BP 460-373)
A.k.a. Hill 2287 (7,503'). Apx 24 km NE Dalat. Tallest peak in southern 1/2 of SVN? Tuyen Duc Pr, II Corps.

Nui B'Nom M' Hai (ZT 07-54)
A.k.a. Hill 1642 (5,387'). Apx 27 km S Bao Loc. Binh Tuy or Lam Dong Pr?, III Corps.

Nui Bo (AT 878-576)
See Hill 65. Quang Nam Pr, I Corps.

Nui Bo Bo (AT 967-617)
See Hill 55. XXIV Corps grid.

Nui Braian (AN 91-78)
A.k.a. Hill 1874 (6,148'). Apx 36 km due E Bao Loc. Lam Dong Pr, II Corps.

Nui Cai Muong (XD 329-337?)
See FSB Barbara. Quang Tri Pr, I Corps.

Nui Cai Tong (ZC 192-952)
Apx 13 km ESE Phu Loc and 36 km SE Phu Bai. Thua Thien/Quang Nam Pr, I Corps.

Nui Cam Linh (CP 123128)
A.k.a. Hill 222. At SE tip of Cam Ranh Peninsula overlooking South Beach. Khanh Hoa Pr, I Corps.

Nui Cam Mountain (WS 05-64)
A.k.a. Hill 259. Apx 4 km ENE That Son AF, 22 km SW Chau Duc AF, 15 km SE Cambodia and 8 km NE peak of Dop Chompa Mtn. Possibly FSB here which one text called FSB Nui Can (sic). Chau Doc Pr, IV Corps.

Nui Can Linh (n/a)
Mapsheet name of L-7014-6832-1. SVN.

Nui Can Mountain, FSB (BS 3-7 or WS 05-64?)
Possibly on Nui Can Mtn in BS grid zone, which is generally NW Ha Thanh AF and roughly 30 km W Quang Ngai? Or possibly on Nui Cam Mtn in in WS zone, which is apx 4 km ENE That Son AF. Quang Ngai or Chau Doc Pr, I or IV Corps.

Nui Cat Airfield (XT 630-664)
See Minh Thanh AF. Binh Long Pr, III Corps.

Nui Cau Hai (BP 985-450)
A.k.a. Hill 978 and Grand Sommet Mtn. Apx 8 km SW Nha Trang AF. Khanh Hoa Pr, II Corps.

Nui Cay Tre Mountain (XD 968-617)
A.k.a. Hill 484. Part of major ridgeline known as Mutter's Ridge and scene of very heavy fighting for 3d/4th Marines, 3d Mar Civ, during Op Prairie, Aug66. See Mutter's Ridge. Quang Tri Pr, I Corps.

Nui Cay Tre Ridge (XD 945-624 to XD 999-615)
A.k.a. Mutter's Ridge. 5 km-long ridge that formed the N edge of Razorback Valley, roughly 5 km N the Rockpile. During Op Prairie, scene of some heaviest fighting in VN up to Oct66. See Mutter's Ridge. Quang Tri Pr, I Corps.

Nui Cha Pa (UK 7-7)
See Fan Si Pan. NVN.

Nui Chau (BP 97-62)
A.k.a. Hill 682. Apx 11 km WNW and overlooking Nha Trang. Khanh Hoa Pr, II Corps.

Nui Chau Chan Mountain (YT 61-11)
See Nui Chua Chan. Long Khanh Pr, III Corps.

Nui Chau Chan Signal Site (YT 61-11?)
See Nui Chua Chan. Long Khanh Pr, III Corps.

Nui Chau Hin (BP 98-46)
A.k.a. Hill 976. Apx 8 km SE and overlooking Nha Trang. Khanh Hoa Pr, II Corps.

Nui Che Ket (BN 31-60)
A.k.a. Hill 1017 (or 3,337'). Apx 15 km ENE Song Mao AF. Binh Thuan Pr, II Corps.

Nui Choi Hill Mass (BS 63-49)
Peak roughly 10 km SW Mo Duc. Center of mass at BS 67-46. Nui Nham-Nui Choi Hill masses dominated Mo Duc region W and SW Mo Duc, and 1st infiltrated by *Dac Cong* patrols during Op Golden Fleece, Sep-Oct66. See *Dac Cong* for detail. Quang Ngai Pr, I Corps.

Nui Chom Mountain (AT 09-32)
Situated 46 km SSW Da Nang in Que Son Mtns. Part of rugged ridgeline that formed the northern edge of Hiep Duc (a.k.a. Death) Valley. Quang Nam Pr, I Corps.

Nui Chua Chan Mountain (YT 61-11)
A.k.a. Hill 837, and apparently Signal Mtn Relay. Apx 3 km SE Gia Ray, 4 km N Suoi Cat, 15 km E Xuan Loc and about 70 km ENE Saigon. Long Khanh Pr, III Corps.

Nui Chua Chan Signal Site (YT 61-11)
Apparently a.k.a. Signal Mtn Relay. Apx 75 km ENE Saigon and 15 km E Xuan Loc. Per William Glascher, a signal site manned by 313th Sig Co was set atop this peak,

and FSB Mace was along mtn's S base. Per Frank Penk, Jr, Nui Ba Den, Nui Ba Ra and Nui Chua Chan all had radio relay sites. "No arty but a defensive perimeter and chopper pads on all three. Nui Chua Chan's pad was large enough for four Hueys. As I recall, there were no names for se locations, just the name of mtn, or they might have gone by radio call-sign." Long Khanh Pr, III Corps.

Nui Co To (VS 99-47)
A.k.a. Nui Coto or Hill 614 or Million Dollar Hill or Million Dollar Knoll. On Nui Coto Mtn and site of major battle against 510th VC Bn, waged by 5th SF 521st Mobile Strike Force, 16-26Mar69. One of 7 peak grp rising from flat, mangrove plain generally E Ha Tien and N Rach Gia and collectively known as "Seven Sisters." Included Hue Duc Mtn (Hill 220), Nui Co To (Hill 61, just S Tri Tron), Dop Chompa (actually two separate peaks, highest of which is 710 meters, SW That Son AF), Hill 232 (near Chau Phu) and Hill 296 (5 km from Cambodia and 10 km N That Son). Chau Doc Pr, IV Corps.

Nui Con Thien (YD 113-703)
A.k.a. Con Thien, the Hill of Angels and Hill 158. From it, observation was unfettered for 15 km to coast in E, the Annamite mtns to W and DMZ to N. Strategically important but extremely vulnerable USMC base. NVA arty (130mm and 152mm) across DMZ often pummeled base with impunity because it had greater range than US arty and was generally immune to counter-battery fire. After the second Indochina War ended, the Viet govt built what is known as Trung Son Cemetery near this hill. That cemetery contains 10,000 graves containing the remains of NVA soldier who died or MIA in Quang Tri area. See Con Thien. Quang Tri Pr, I Corps.

Nui Coto (VS 99-47)
See Nui Co To. Chau Doc Pr, IV Corps.

Nui Da (ZT 08-17 and ZT 17-22)
Nui Da Mtns are shown at both grids, roughly 10 km apart and generally 40 km ESE Vo Dat. Binh Tuy Pr, III Corps.

Nui Da Bac (BN 74-59)
A.k.a. Hill 649 (2,130') or Hill 644. Apx 22k SSW Phan Rang and apx 6 km from ocean. Ninh Thuan Pr, II Corps.

Nui Dagai (AN 912-438)
A.k.a. Hill 356. On N edge of coastal lowland-plain, apx 18 km NNE Thien Giao and 34 km NNE Phan Thiet. Binh Thuan Pr, II Corps.

Nui Dai (VS 95-58)
A.k.a. Hill 549. Apx 50 km E Ha Tien, 5 km SW Dop Chompa Mtn and 9 km SW That Son. One of Seven Sisters and twin peak to Dop Chompa. Chau Doc Pr, IV Corps.

Nui Dang (BS 7-0)
A.k.a. Hill 140. Twin peaked hill overlooking and immed E of Duc Pho and W Tra Cau River inlet. Op Desoto in this area, the southernmost district of Quang Ngai Pr, I Corps.

Nui Dang S' Ruin (ZT 053-256)
A.k.a. Hill 1304 (4,277'), Hill 1302 and Nui Ong. Apx 12 km due E Tanh Linh AF. Binh Tuy Pr, III Corps.

Nui Dap (BS 708-608)
See Nui Dep. Quang Ngai Pr, I Corps.

Nui Dat (Dust Off) Pad (YS 435-668)
At or near Nui Dat/Luscombe AF. "Heliport #736, alt 115', apx 200' long conc, uncontrolled. Pads marked with red cross. Rubber trees on 3 sides, open to N. Two 185' ant within 600' SW pad, lgtd O/R to Phuoc Tuy Arty. Refueling at Kangaroo Heliport. Arty advsy-Phuoc Tuy, 369.6 40.7," per Feb73 TAD. Phuoc Tuy Pr, III Corps.

Nui Dat 1 (YS 436-676?)
See Nui Dat Basecamp. Phuoc Tuy Pr, III Corps.

Nui Dat 2 (YS 48-67?)
See Nui Dat Basecamp. Apx 5 km East and 1 km N 1ATF basecamp. Phuoc Tuy Pr, III Corps.

Nui Dat 3 (YS 58-68?)
See Nui Dat Basecamp. Apx 16 km E Nui Dat. Grid is est based on rptd location. Phuoc Tuy Pr, III Corps.

Nui Dat Airfield (YS 437-681)
See Luscombe AF. Phuoc Tuy Pr, III Corps.

Nui Dat Basecamp (YS 436-676)
On Rte-2, apx 60 km ESE Saigon, 35 km NNE Vung Tau, 8 km NE Ba Ria and 14 km SSW Ngai Giao. On site of abnd rubber plantation. Apparently consisted of 3 installations: Nui Dat (1) the 1 ATF base; Nui Dat (2) 5 km E and 1 km S of 1ATF base; and Nui Dat (3), apx 16 km ESE Nui Dat (2) and 2 km NNW Xuyen Moc.[399] Hill at Nui Dat (1) was about 100-meters high and roughly 800-meters wide on its N to S axis, and 600 meters wide on its E to W axis. 1ATF base was apx 4 km N to S and 2 km W to E, and surrounded the hill. Nui Dat (2) was 126-meters high and apx 9 km N Dat Do and FSB for 1ATF, RAR, RNZR and RNZA. 161 Bty, RNZA FSB and HQ set here with Bty Ready (Kenning's Bty) 5Jun66, after permanent move from Bien Hoa that day. On 25-29Jul66, 3-6Nov66 and 18Nov66, the 161 Bty was 3 km SW Nui Dat at YS 46-65. Luscombe AF also at or near this site. Bty 161 set up golf driving range here (also built a 3-hole course inside FSB Serle). In apx Jun70, Helo pad was poured in concrete to eliminate dust (had large, white Kiwi insignia painted on it). Eddie Tricker tells us his 7 Bn, RAR book says 8" guns working at Nui Dat were part of A Bty, 7th/8th US Arty. Apparently elements of 199th LIB and possibly 9th Inf Div also here. On 1ATF NCO trng map per John Hollett. Phuoc Tuy Pr, III Corps.[400]

Nui Dat Mountain (BN 757-882)
A.k.a. Hill 180 (594'). On Phan Rang AB and 2 km NW the main rwy. Basecamp of 3d/506th Inf was at western base of hill. Ninh Thuan Pr, II Corps.

Nui Dat Mountain (YS 434-674)
A.k.a. Hill 101. At Luscombe AF apx 22 km WNW the other Nui Dat Mtn just NW Xuyen Moc. HQ of 1ATF here. Phuoc Tuy Pr, III Corps.

Nui Dat Mountain (YS 648-700)
A.k.a. Hill 93. Horseshoe-shaped hill apx 1 km NW Xuyen Moc Heliport and 22 km ENE the other Nui Dat Mtn at 1ATFs Luscombe AF on LTL-2. Phuoc Tuy Pr, III Corps.

Nui Dat Playboy Club (YS 436-676)
A.k.a. the Nui Dat 1ATF POW Cmpd. On Rte-2, 60 km ESE Saigon, 35 km NNE Vung Tau, 8 km NE Ba Ria and 14 km SSW Ngai Giao. Entrance sign read: *Club Members Only-Exclusively for NVA/VC*. Phuoc Tuy Pr, III Corps.

Nui Dat POW Compound (YS 436-676)
See Nui Dat Playboy Club.

Nui Dau (BS 873-324)
A.k.a. Hill 164 and 163. Along E side of QL-1, apx 8 km SSE Duc Pho AF and 25 km SSE Mo Duc. Overlooked Red Beach (assault beach of TF Delta BLT during Op

Double Eagle), and recon OP, Jan-Feb66. Secured by 2d/4th Mar & 4th ARVN Rgt, 27Jan66, per *USMC in Vietnam, '66*, p 23, 27, map p 20. Quang Ngai Pr, I Corps.

Nui Den (CR 15-32)
A.k.a. Hill 361. On Qui Nhon Peninsula apx 8 km NE, overlooked Qui Nhon. Binh Dinh Pr, II Corps.

Nui Dep (BS 708-608)
A.k.a. Hill 68. Apx 7 km NNW Mo Duc AF, 800 meters Hill 105 and 500 meters W QL-1. See LZ Snoopy. Quang Ngai Pr, I Corps.

Nui Dinh (YS 336-655)
Hilltop on Nui Thi hill mass, apx 10 km WSW Nui Dat and 7 km NW Ba Ria. Apparently elements of ANZAC 1ATF here or a significant terrain feature of their AO in Phuoc Tuy Pr, III Corps.

Nui Dinh Mountains (YS 340-650)
Generally between 10 and 15 km W to WSW Nui Dat and Luscombe AF. A VC sanctuary offering them good observation of traffic on Inter-provincial Rte-2 (Xuan Loc-Nui Dat-Long Dien) and along QL-15 (Vung Tau-Saigon). Phuoc Tuy Pr, III Corps.

Nui Dinhs, FSB (YS 29-64)
Apx 4 km WSW Nui Dinh, 10 km WSW Nui Dat and 7 km NW Ba Ria. Bty 161, RNZA (Honner's Bty 13Jun66-13May67) set here 16-18Jul66. Phuoc Tuy Pr, III Corps.

Nui Doc Mountains (YT 5-2)
Mtn range at 11°04'N-107°21'E. On NC48-04 JOG. Long Khanh Pr, III Corps.

Nui Dong De (BS 630-855)
A.k.a. LZ Dottie and Hill 102. Apx 19 km S Chu Lai, E QL-1, and N Ham Giang River. Also listed by arty ORLL at BS 630-856. Americal list. Quang Ngai Pr, I Corps.

Nui Dong Hoai (YD 798-107)
See FSBs Arrow and Panther II. Thua Thien Pr, I Corps.

Nui Dong Lam (AT 824-606)
Apx 25 km SW Da Nang AB. Quang Nam Pr, I Corps.

Nui Dong Tranh (BS 36-96)
A.k.a. Hill 1362. Major terrain feature and hill mass 24 km S Tam Ky and overlooking the Batangan Peninsula some 30 km to E. Quang Tin Pr?, I Corps.

Nui Flat, FSB (YT 43-28)
Just NE Xa Binh Hoa, near or in rubber plantation along QL-20 apx 18 km NNW Xuan Loc and 45 km ENE Binh Hoa AB. Word "Flat' is thought not to be Vietnamese origin, which suggests use here was possibly a sarcastic reference to fact site was flat? 4/12th Inf, 199th LIB here. Long Khanh Pr?, III Corps.

Nui Giai (VS 99-72)
A.k.a. Hill 266. Immed SE Hill 282 (Nui Ta Bac), 7 km SE Cambodian border and 598 km ENE Hat Tien. Chau Doc Pr, IV Corps.

Nui Giang-Yang Brai Mountain Ridge (AT/ZC 0-3)
Ridgeline that along with adj Ong Thu slope ridgeline was portion of Base Area 112, near Song Cai River, and SW An Hoa. Quang Nam Pr, I Corps.

Nui Gio, OP (YD 601-189)
A.k.a. OP Lion. Apx 12 km W of Hue, 6 km SE Ap Thanh Tan and 14 km NW FSB Birmingham. Grid per 1Feb70, 101st Abn rpt, per Don Armstrong. Thua Thien Pr, I Corps.

Nui Gioc Lon Mountains (YT 1-2)
Mtn range at 11°06'N-106°59'E. On NC48-04 JOG. Bien Hoa Pr, III Corps.

Nui Hai Van (AT 94-92)
See Hill 724. Quang Nam Pr, I Corps.

Nui Ham Rong (US 868-488)
See Ham Rong Mtn. Phu Quoc Island, IV Corps.

Nui Hao Chu Hi (BP 82-04)
A.k.a. Hill 1451 (4,761'). Apx 18 km ENE Phan Rang AF. Ninh Thuan Pr?, II Corps.

Nui Hoa Ngan (AT 82-43)
A.k.a. Hill 662. Apx 6 km NW Phuoc Binh and 38 km SW Da Nang. Quang Nam Pr, I Corps.

Nui Hoac (BT 075-225)
A.k.a. Hill 352. Apx 9 km NNW Tien Phuoc AF and 22 km W Tam Ky. Americal list puts near Kham Duc; however it apx 54 km ENE Kham Duc. Quang Tin Pr, I Corps.

Nui Hoan Gay (YD 750-086)
See Banana Mtn. Thua Thien Pr, I Corps.

Nui Hoat Mountains (BS)
Mtn Range bordering Song Ve River Valley in Americal AO. Quang Ngai Pr, I Corps.

Nui Hoc Nom (CP 16-28)
A.k.a. Hill 524. Apx 12 km SW Phu Hiep AF. Khanh Hoa Pr, II Corps.

Nui Hon Chau (AT 82-43)
See Hill 675. Quang Nam Pr, I Corps.

Nui Hon Cha Mountain (BR 986-239)
Apx 10 km W Qui Nhon AF. Binh Dinh Pr, II Corps.

Nui Hon Sec Mountain (VS 903-225)
Apx 26 km NW Rach Gia. Kien Giang Pr, IV Corps.

Nui Hop (AN 736-315)
A.k.a. Hill 801. Part of large hill mast apx 25 km NNE Phan Thiet and 14 km NW Thien Giao. 3rd/506th Inf AO. Binh Thuan Pr, II Corps.

Nui Ke (CP 070-240)
Small hill on Cam Ranh Peninsula, 6.5 km NE the Ammo unloading dock and about 1 km SE the S end of main rwy of Cam Ranh Bay AF. Khanh Hoa Pr, II Corps.

Nui Ke (YD 760-055)
A.k.a. Hill 618, LZ Satan II, Satan OP, LZ Greek and OP Satan. Apx 16 km due S Hue, 16 km SW Phu Bai, 8 km SE FSB Birmingham, 6 km WSW FSB Arsenal and 7 km due S Nam Hoa District HQ. Site of '68 battle involving the 82d Abn Bde and HQ of 5th NVA Rgt. On 25-26May68, 82d Abn's 3d Bde used Brick as staging area for attack on HQ of 5th NVA Rgt on Hill 618, to its NW. 1st/508th Inf then assaulted Nui Ke and, on successive days of battle, its B Co fixed bayonets and carried out 2 of very few bayonet charges of war, killing 13 NVA in 1st attack and 92 in attack of 26May68. Small valley along Nui Ke's E slope was known as Rocket Valley. See LZ Satan II, LZ Greek and the Bone Yard. Thua Thien Pr, I Corps.

Nui Khe Thut (YJ 4-3)
A.k.a. Grand Sommet des Mines. NVN.

Nui Khinh (AN 758-213)
A.k.a. Hill 238. Small hill mass 3.5 km SW Nui Tio Ha, 5 km SSE Nui Ong, 11 km ESE Thien Giao and 15 km NW Phan Thiet. 3rd/506th Inf AO. Binh Thuan Pr, II Corps.

Nui Kim Son CAP (BT?)
CAP 2-4-2, 2d CAG. Quang Nam Pr, I Corps.

Nui Kim Son CAP (BT?)
Delta 1, 2d CAG. Quang Nam Pr, I Corps.
Nui Lang Bian (BP 218-327?)
A.k.a. Hill 2167 and Lang Bian Signal Site. Apx 8 km due N Dalat and 5 km WNW Ap Lat. Site of major US Signal facility of 566th Signal Co. Tuyen Duc Pr, II Corps.
Nui Lang Hon Mountains (AN 8-3)
Mtn range at 11°12'N-108°08'E. On NC49-01 JOG. Binh Thuan Pr, II Corps.
Nui Lang Ram (BS 53-18)
See Hill 1103. Quang Ngai Pr, I Corps.
Nui Le Quarry (XT 687-068)
Apx 16 km NW Tan Son Nhut AB. Oct70. Hau Nghia Pr, III Corps.
Nui Liet Kiem (AT 990-251)
A.k.a. Hill 440, Mtn of Leeches and LZ West. Apx 9 km E Hiep Duc, 6 km SSW LZ Dragon Base and 31 km W to WNW Tam Ky. Overlooked Song Chang River to S and Hiep Duc Valley to NW. In Hiep Duc Valley to N was Song Lau River and Old French Road (Hwy 535), while to E was Nui Lon Mtn. Quang Tin Pr, I Corps.
Nui Loc Son (BT 022-228)
A.k.a. Nui Loc Son Base and LZ Motor Pool. On hill complex overlooking Que Son Valley, apx 25 km WNW Tam Ky. Remote Marine outpost/FSB of 2d/1st Marines and 1st/11th Mar Arty in Que Son Mtns S An Hoa. In '67 an ARVN outpost, and HQ of F/1st Bn, 1st Mar during Op Union in fight with 2d NVA Div's, 3d and 21st Rgts. Later renamed LZ Motor Pool under Americal Div. Americal list puts it 13 km W battle site at BT 15-28. Grid per *Bonnie-Sue*. Map is L-7014-6640-3. See Que Son Valley and Motor Pool. Quang Tin Pr, I Corps.
Nui Loc Son Base (BT 022-228)
See Nui Loc Son and Motor Pool. Quang Tin Pr, I Corps.
Nui Loc Son Basin (BT 0-3?)
A.k.a. Que Son Valley or Death Valley. See Que Son Valley for detailed information. Quang Tin/Quang Nam Pr border, I Corps.
Nui Lon (YS 269 465)
A.k.a. Hill 245, Vung Tau Signal Site, VC Hill and Ghost Mountain? On the Vung Tau Peninsula at Vung Tau, immed NW city, 1 km from ocean and apx 4 km NNW Nui Nho. Phuoc Tuy Pr, III Corps.
Nui Lon Mtns (BS 670-470)
Generally 10-15 km SW Mo Duc. Quang Ngai Pr, I Corps.
Nui Loo Bridge (YT 058-206)
Apx 10 km NE Bien Hoa AB, if grid correct? Dec68. Bien Hoa Pr, III Corps.
Nui M'Neun Pantar (AN 84-68)
A.k.a. Hill 1664 (5,459'). Apx 30 km ESE Bao Loc. Lam Dong Pr, II Corps.
Nui Mang (ZC 02-77)
See Hill 1712. Quang Nam Pr, I Corps.
Nui Marrai (BP 66-24)
A.k.a. Hill 1637 (5,371'). Apx 40 km due E Cam Ranh Bay AB. Ninh Thuan Pr, II Corps.
Nui Mai Nha (YD 604-100)
See Hill 316. Thau Thien Pr, I Corps.
Nui Mat Rang Mountain (AT 17-44)
A.k.a. Hill 845. Is SE Antenna Valley and 32 km due S Da Nang, in Que Son Mtns. Quang Nam Pr, I Corps.
Nui May Tao (YS 74-92)
Apx 40 km NE Nui Dat and 30 km ESE Blackhorse basecamp. Apparently 1ATF position here at one time. Phuoc Tuy Pr, III Corps.
Nui Meu Mountains (BR 9-7)
See Nui Mieu. Binh Dinh Pr, II Corps.
Nui Mieu Mountains (BR 9-7)
Small mtn mass along coast generally 25 km SSE Bong Son. At center/top of map L-7014-6837-3, per Ken Burrington. Binh Dinh Pr, II Corps.
Nui Mieu Mountain (BR 980-760)
Apx 11 km NE Phu My and 5 km E QL-1. Also sp Nui Miou. Also listed at BR 986-678 and BR 996-687 and CR 051-737. Binh Dinh Pr, II Corps.
Nui Miou (BR 980-680)
See Nui Mieu. Binh Dinh Pr, II Corps.
Nui Miou (CR 051-737)
A.k.a. Hill 142. On coast apx 16 km ENE Phu My/QL-1. Binh Dinh Pr, II Corps.
Nui Nai, Pointe (VS 3-4)
See Pointe Nui Nai. Kien Giang Pr, IV Corps.
Nui Ne Mountains (BS?)
Swept by 198th LIB and 6th ARVN Rgt during Op Geneva Park, Apr67. Quang Ngai Pr?, I Corps.
Nui Nghe (YS 390-730)
Apx 6 km NW Nui Dat and 4 km WSW Binh Ba. Apparently elements of ANZAC 1ATF here or a significant terrain feature of their AO in Phuoc Tuy Pr, III Corps.
Nui Ngoc (BT 132-203)
See Hill 488. Quang Tin Pr, I Corps.
Nui Nham Hill Mass (BS 64-54)
A.k.a. Nui Cham, Hill 513, LZ Tiger and LZ Bulldog. Center of mass roughly 7 km W Mo Duc, overlooking Song Ve valley to N. Nui Nham-Nui Choi Hill masses dominated region W and SW Mo Duc, and 1st infiltrated by *Dac Cong* patrols during Op Golden Fleece, Sep-Oct66. See *Dac Cong* in Glossary. Quang Ngai Pr, I Corps.
Nui Nhiao (BR 97-73)
See Hill 602. Binh Dinh Pr, II Corps.
Nui Nho (YS 286-418)
A.k.a. Hill 136. On the Vung Tau Peninsula at Vung Tau, apx 4 km SSE Nui Lon. Phuoc Tuy Pr, III Corps.
Nui Ong (AN 732-253)
A.k.a. Hill 906. Apx 14 km due W Thien Giao and 19 km NW Phan Thiet. VC used hill mass as staging area and OP for rocket attacks in Phan Thiet AO. 3rd/506th Inf AO. [401] Binh Thuan Pr, II Corps.
Nui Ong (ZT 053-256)
A.k.a. Dang S'Ruin Mtn, Hill 1302 and 1304 (4,277'). Apx 12 km due E Tanh Linh AF. Binh Tuy Pr, III Corps.
Nui Ong Mountains (various)
Common Mtn name in VN. Mtns with this name are in following grid squares: YT 9-2, WF 8-4, VJ 9-8, VJ 7-5, BS 3-9, BQ 9-9, BN 9-9, ZT 0-2, AN 7-2, XT 5-5, CQ 0-2. NVN, I, II and II Corps.
Nui Ong Ta (YT 16-18)
A.k.a. Hill 57. Small Hill apx 9 km NE Plantation AF, 4 km N QL-1 and roughly 34 km NE Saigon.

Nui Ong Trinh (YS 32-71)
Apx 38 km SE Saigon, 7 km SE Phu My. 3 km ESE Nui Thi Vai and 7 km E QL-15. One peak of a twin-peak monolith jutting out of plain SE Saigon. See Hill 467. Bien Hoa Pr, III Corps.

Nui Pho Tinh (BS 648-936)
Apx 5 km E QL-1, some 17 km SSE Chu Lai and 20 km due N Quang Ngai. Apparent FSB position. Americal list. Quang Ngai Pr, I Corps.

Nui Pon Mountain (YB 862-483)
See Hill 976. Kontum Pr, II Corps.

Nui Quan Do (BP 20-12)
A.k.a. Hill 1812. 8 km S Dalat. Tuyen Duc Pr, II Corps.

Nui Quoc Phu (AN 902-099)
A.k.a. Hill 105. Apx 600 meters from coast, 6 km due E Phan Thiet and 2 km E mouth of Song Cai River. Binh Thuan Pr, II Corps.

Nui Rat Mang (AT 17-44)
See Hill 845. Likely misspelling of Nui Mat Rang. Quang Nam Pr, I Corps.

Nui Sa Leo Mountains (CQ 1-3)
Mtn range at 12°56'N-109°19'E, per ND49-13. Phu Yen and/or Khanh Hoa Pr, II Corps.

Nui Sa Mui (XD 699-589)
A.k.a. Hill 1550. Apx 3 km NE FSB Argonne. Quang Tri Pr, I Corps.

Nui Sa Truc (YD 740-065)
A.k.a. Hill 416. Apx 17 km WSW Phu Bai, 2 km WNW Nui Ke (Hill 618), 2 km SSW Nui Hoan Gay (Hill 434) and 5 km SE FSB Birmingham. Thua Thien Pr, I Corps.

Nui Sai Voi, Battle of (VS 583-295)
A.k.a. Hill 142, and sp "Nui Bai Voi" in one text. Apx 22 km SSE Ha Tien, 7 km N Hon Chong and about 3 km inland from coast near 10°13'00"N-104°37'00"E. Took place 27Sep-20Nov70, and involved 42d and 44th ARVN Ranger Bns under ARVN 9th Div. In Mekong Delta and described by Shelby Stanton as "craggy mtn fortress held by Viet Cong troops." Numerous caves and intricate rock formations made clearing op very difficult, and high casualties resulted. See *Rangers At War*, p 269-270. Kien Giang Pr, IV Corps.

Nui Sam (WS 09-80)
A.k.a. Hill 230. Apx 7 km WSW Chau Duc AF, 3 km SE Cambodian border and right in middle of LTL-10. Chau Duc Pr, IV Corps.

Nui Se Gai (BP 82-48)
A.k.a. Hill 1118 (3,668'). Apx 24 WSW Nha Trang. Khanh Hoa Pr, II Corps.

Nui Soc Lu (YT 34-18)
A.k.a. Hill 418. Apx 52 km NE Saigon and 36 km E Bien Hoa AB. Bien Hoa Pr, III Corps.

Nui Ta Bac (VS 94-68)
A.k.a. Hill 282. Apx 8 km NNW That Son AF, 20 km SW Chau Duc and 5 km SE Cambodia. Described as "strategic hilltop" employed for MAC-SOG ops. On map at p 89 in *War In The Shadows* vol of *Vietnam Experience* series. Apparently radio relay/listening site and OP that may have also been a "White Radio" facility. Chau Doc Pr, IV Corps.

Nui Ta Dom (AN 925-223)
A.k.a. Hill 386 and possibly also Tittie or Titty Mtn. Apx 7 km ESE Thien Giao and 16 km NW Phan Thiet. A lone sentinel in large coastal lowland-plain N and W Phan Thiet. Likely OP or possible FSB. LZ Sandy possibly near its base. 3rd/506th Inf AO. Binh Thuan Pr, II Corps.

Nui Ta Dung (AP 78-13)
A.k.a. Hill 1982 (6,503'). Apx 40 km WSW Dalat. Lam Dong Pr, II Corps.

Nui Tac Huong CAP (BT 282-225?)
A.k.a. Nui Tac Huong. Home of CAP 1-1-2, 1st CAC, 1st CAG 10Jan68. May or may not be proper grid, but if same as Hill 38 on Americal Website list, it was on W outskirts of Tam Ky. Quang Tin Pr?, I Corps.

Nui Takou (ZS 17-97)
A.k.a. Hill 694 (2,277'). Apx 22 km SW Phan Thiet. Binh Tuy Pr?, III Corps.

Nui Tam Cap Mountains (BS)
Apparently along coast near Mo Duc/Quang Ngai? Quang Ngai Pr, I Corps.

Nui Tam Dao (WJ 5-9)
Peak at 21°38'00"N-105°30'00"E. See Tam Dao. NVN.

Nui Tha La (XT 50-57)
See Razorbacks. Binh Duong Pr, III Corps.

Nui Thi (YS 36-67)
A.k.a. Hill 504. Apx 10 km SW Nui Dat/Luscombe AF, and 20 km N Vung Tau. Phuoc Tuy Pr, III Corps.

Nui Thi Signal Site (YS 36-67)
Grid based on presumption site was at peak of Nui Thi Mtn (Hill 504), apx 8 km WSW Nui Dat/Luscombe AF. Phuoc Tuy Pr, III Corps.

Nui Thi Vai (YS 29-72)
A.k.a. Hill 467. Hilltop apx 14 km WNW Nui Dat and 5 km SE Phu My and 47 km SE Saigon. Apparently 1ATF here or significant terrain feature. Phuoc Tuy Pr, III Corps.

Nui Thi Vai Hills (YS 35-65)
Hill mass apx 10 km SW Nui Dat, with Nui Thi as its highest peak. Phuoc Tuy Pr, III Corps.

Nui Thien An (BS 659-754)
A.k.a. Hill 101, Buddha Hill/Mtn, Little Round Top and Mountain of Heavenly Peace. Immed N Rte 521, apx 2.5 km NNE Quang Ngai and 2 km E QL-1. See Buddha Mnt for detail. Grid is est. Quang Ngai Pr, I Corps.

Nui Tia Pong (XD 9-5)
Major hill mass apx 9 km NW FSB Vandegrift and 13 km NNE Khe Sanh CB. Quang Tri Pr, I Corps.

Nui Tien Du (CP 045-809)
A.k.a. Hill 771. Apx 6 km E Ninh Hoa 6 km SW coast. Khanh Hoa Pr, II Corps.

Nui Toc Tien (YS 31-71)
Hilltop apx 7 km SE Phu My, immed ESE Nui Thi Vai and 13 km WNW Nui Dat. 1ATF here or significant terrain feature of its AO. Phuoc Tuy Pr, III Corps.

Nui Toi Ha (AN 783-239)
A.k.a. Hill 349 and FSB Bartlett. Apx 8.5 km W and slightly S of Thien Giao, 18 km NW Phan Thiet and 4 km N of QL-1. 5th/27th Arty, 3rd/506th Inf here, per Jerry Berry. Binh Thuan Pr, II Corps.

Nui Trun (AU 84-06)
See Hill 88, FSB. Thua Thien Pr, I Corps.

Nui Tuong (VS 89-61)
A.k.a. Hill 145. Adj to Nui Tuong SF Camp, apx 46 km ENE Ha Tien, 13 km WSW That Son AF, 34 km SW Chau Duc AF, 4 km SE Cambodia and Chau Doc Pr, IV Corps.

Nui Tuong SF Camp (VS 905-595)
At SE base of Nui Tuong and Dop Chompa Hill mass, apx 5 km from Cambodian border, 47 km ENE Ha Tien and 13 km WSW That Son AF. 5th SF. See Ba Chuc. Info/grid per *SF Order of Battle.* Chau Doc Pr, IV Corps.

Nui Vi Tha Hills (YS 30-72)
Apx 11 km WNW Nui Dat. Swept by elements of 8 RAR during Apr68. Phuoc Tuy Pr, III Corps.

Nui Vien Nam (WJ 46-26)
A.k.a. Hill 1931. Apx 40 km W Hanoi, between the Black and Song Day Rivers. Per *Street Without Joy*, Chp 2; map at p 50. NVN.

Nui Vinh Phong (ZD 150-067)
A.k.a. Hill 482. Part of prominent hill mass on W edge of Dam Cau Hai Bay, at N end of the Hai Van Pass. Hill 592, Dong Nhut, was other major peak of hill mass. Both overlooked FSB Roy, FSB Tomahawk and ocean. 101st Abn AO, '69-71. Thua Thien Pr, I Corps.

Nui Vong (BS 702-601)
A.k.a. Hill 105. Apx 8 km NNW Mo Duc AF, 1 km W QL-1 and 14 km SSE Quang Ngai. Americal list. See LZ Snoopy. Quang Ngai Pr, I Corps.

Nui Vu (BT 132-203)
A.k.a. Hill 488, LZ 1, LZ 2, Howard's Hill, LZ East and LZ Mary Lou. Apx 43 km WNW Chu Lai, and 17 km W Tam Ky. See Howard's Hill. Quang Tin Pr, I Corps.

Nui Vung Ro (CQ 319-235)
A.k.a. Hill 302. Apx 2 km SSW Lang Tuong and 16 km SE Phu Hiep AF. Phu Yen Pr, II Corps.

Nui Xa Rong (BR 83-67)
See Hill 701. Binh Dinh Pr, II Corps.

Nui Xa To (AN 898-291)
A.k.a. Hill 251. Apx 75 km NW Thien Giao and 20 km NW Phan Thiet. Small hill mass rising alone in large plain N and W Phan Thiet. Likely an OP and possible FSB location. 3rd/506th Inf AO. Binh Thuan Pr, II Corps.

Nui Xuong (BS 75-43)
Just W the QL-1 RR tracks apx 12 km SSE Mo Duc, 7 km NW Duc Pho AF, 2 km W QL-1 and 2 km NW Tra Cau River QL-1 Bridge. Per *USMC in Vietnam, 1966*, p 27, map at p 20. Quang Ngai Pr, I Corps.

Nui Ya Bo (BN 59-77)
A.k.a. Hill 1031 (3,383'). Apx 20 km WSW Phan Rang AB. Ninh Thuan Pr?, II Corps.

Nui Yok Nam Lao (ZU 14-42)
A.k.a. Hill 951 (or 3,120'). 25 km NE Gia Nghia AF and 60 km WNW Dalat. Lam Dong Pr?, II Corps.

Nui Yon (BT 248-169)
A.k.a. Hill 84/93. Apx 5 km WSW Tam Ky, 2 km W Trung Dan and 3 km S Rte 533. OP overlooking W approach to Tam Ky. *Battle of Nui Yon* apparently took place 13May69, when est Co attacked and possibly overran elements of C/3d/21st Inf, 196th LIB here. MIA, Sp4 Larry D. Aiken was badly wounded and taken prisoner, but sometime later, a Hoi Chanh rptd his location in hospital camp apx 27 km SW Tam Ky, and elements of 5th/2d ARVN and US helo crews rescued Aiken, per 29Jul *Southern Cross* Newspaper. Quang Tin Pr, I Corps.

Nui Yon, OP (BT 248-169)
See Nui Yon. Quang Tin Pr, I Corps.

Nui Youk Nam Rmay (AP 857-380)
A.k.a. Hill 1442 (4,731') and Y Nam Rmay. Apx 38 km WNW Dalat. Tuyen Duc Pr, II Corps.

Nuinai Point (VS 3-4)
See Point Nuianai. Kien Giang Pr, IV Corps.

Number 30, LZ (XD 58-46)
See 30, LZ. Laos.

Number 31, LZ (XD 51-46)
See 31, LZ. Laos.

Nung (n/a)
See Glossary.

Nuoampoc Man, Dam (BS 9-2)
Lagoon at 14°41'N-109°04'E. On ND49-05 JOG. Binh Dinh Pr, II Corps.

Nuoampoc Ngot, Dam (CR 0-6)
Baie de Nuoc Ngot. Lagoon at 14°09'N-109°11'E. On ND49-05 JOG. Binh Dinh Pr, II Corps.

Nuoampoc Van (YS 1-5)
Coastal point at 10°27'N-106°56'E. On NC48-07 JOG. Gia Dinh Pr, III Corps.

Nuoc Hai (n/a)
Mapsheet name of L-7014-6254-3. NVN only.

Nuoc Moc (n/a)
Mapsheet name of L-7014-5951-2. NVN only.

Nuoc Ngot, Lagune de (CR 0-6)
Dam Nuoampoc Ngot. Lagoon at 14°09'N-109°11'E. On ND49-05 JOG. Binh Dinh Pr, II Corps.

Nuoc Ngot, Vinh (CR 0-6)
See Nuoc Ngot, Lagune de. Binh Dinh Pr, II Corps.

Nuoc Ngot Bridge (ZD 153-010)
QL-1 bridge apx 7 km due E Q Phu Loc and 31 km SE Phu Bai. Apr68-Feb69. Thua Thien Pr, I Corps.

Nuoc Vang Bridge (XT 991-510)
LTL-1A bridge apx 3 km ENE Phuoc Vinh AF and 36 km due N Bien Hoa AB. Dec65. Binh Duong Pr, III Corps.

Nuoc Vang SF Camp (XT 995-510)
Apx 4 km ENE Phuoc Vinh AF and 37 km due N Bien Hoa AB. 5th SF camp/FOB relocated to Bu Ghia Map. *SF Order of Battle* lists grid as XT 395-510, but that is an error. Tay Ninh/Binh Duong Pr border, III Corps.

Nuog Ngot, Bai (CR 0-6)
A.k.a. Dam Nuoampoc Ngot. Lagoon at 14°09'N-109°11'E. On ND49-05 JOG. Binh Dinh Pr, II Corps.

Nurses BOQ, Tan Son Nhut (XS 826-938)
At 3d Field Hosp, Hosp Cmd, Tan Son Nhut AB. Data per *Vietnam Military Lore, 1959-1973.* Grid is for hospital proper. Gia Dinh Pr, III Corps.

Nutmeg, LZ (BR 224-380)
Apx 27 km WSW An Khe, 10 km SW QL-19, 12 km ESE Chu Rran Mtn and 31 km ENE Plei Do Lim AF. 4th Div AO, '70. Name/grid per Jim Claeys. Pleiku Pr, II Corps.

Nutmeg, LZ (YD 114-303)
Overlooked Khe Ta Laou Valley apx 4 km SE Ta Laou, 11 km SSW Ba Long AF and 31 km SW Quang Tri. Apr70 XXIV Corps grid per D. Armstrong. Quang Tri Pr, I Corps.

Nuts, FSB (YC 757-855)
W of the Ruong Ruong Valley apx 32 km SSW Phu Bai, 36 km WSW Phu Loc and 8 km WSW FSB Fist. Evidently 101st Abn FSB named to honor CG of 101st Abn surrounded at Bastogne during WWII, who upon demand for surrender by Germans sent note back in response that

read simply "Nuts." During Lam Son 720, the 3d ARVN Rgt worked nearby beginning mid Jul71, while 2d/11th and 2d/320th Arty fired in supt from Blitz and Normandy. 101st Abn inactive FSB grid per Don Armstrong. Thua Thien Pr, I Corps.

NVA Air Force Bombing (n/a)
See Glossary.

NVA Base Areas (generally)
See Base Areas.

NVA Helicopters (n/a)
See Glossary.

NVA Operational Area 101 (YD 4-4?)
See Base Area 101. Quang Tri Pr, I Corps.

NVA Operational Area 'A' (YD 01-66)
VC/NVA Area of Ops, generally 35 km NW Quang Tri. Quang Tri Pr, I Corps.

NVA Operational Area 'B' (YD 54-17)
VC/NVA Area of Ops, generally 20 km W of Hue. Thua Thien Pr, I Corps.

NVA Operational Area 'C' (AT 97-52)
VC/NVA Area of Ops, generally 23 km S Da Nang. Quang Nam Pr, I Corps.

NVA Operational Area 'D' (BT 18-18)
VC/NVA Area of Ops, generally 14 km WSW Tam Ky. Quang Tin Pr, I Corps.

NVA Operational Area 'E' (BS 39-73)
VC/NVA Area of Ops, generally 25 km W Quang Ngai. Quang Ngai Pr, I Corps.

NVA Operational Area 'F' (BS 70-57)
VC/NVA Area of Ops, generally 16 km SSE Quang Ngai. Quang Ngai Pr, I Corps.

NVRS Transmissions (n/a)
See Glossary.

Nye County, USS (n/a)
LST-1067 and *USNS Nye County*. To MSTS, 27Mar67.

Nyot Mo Airfield (TG 94-02)
LS-321. CIA/SF, per *Air Facilities Data-Laos.*

OSCAR

Facility/Feature Name, Grid Coordinate, a.k.a. Name/History/Province/CTZ

Unless otherwise stated, 6-digit grid coordinates reference DMA L-7014, L-7015 or L-7016 series, 1:50,000 scale maps, while 2- and 4-digit coordinates reference AMS/DMA/NIMA 1:250,000, 1:500,000 and 1:1,000,000 scale maps. Unless otherwise stated, all heights are in meters. To convert meters to feet, multiply by 3.2808; feet to meters, multiply by .3048.

O, The (ZA 114-275)
Nickname of Oasis AF. See Oasis AF. Pleiku Pr, II Corps.

O D, LZ (BS 786-368)
See LZ OD. Quang Ngai Pr, I Corps.

O Lang, Dam (CQ 1-6)
A.k.a. Dam O Loan. Lagoon at 13°16'N-109°16'E. On ND49-09 JOG. Phu Yen Pr, II Corps.

O Lang Lagoon (CQ 1-6)
A.k.a. Dam O Loan. Lagoon at 13°16'N-109°16'E. On ND49-09 JOG. Phu Yen Pr, II Corps.

O Loan, Dam (CQ 1-6)
Lagoon at 13°16'N-109°16'E. On ND49-09 JOG. Phu Yen Pr, II Corps.

O Mon (Phong Phu) (n/a)
Mapsheet L-7014-6129-3. Full sheet name: Phong Phu (O Mon). SVN.

O Rang Airfield (YU 35-65)
A.k.a. Ban Nham AF and possibly Thumi Dak Dam? Apx 7 km N SVN border, 14 km SSW Mondol Kiri City AF, 35 km WNW Bu Prang SVN, per TPC K-10A. El. 2,428'. See FSB David. Cambodia.

O Rang, FSB? (YU 365-640)
Ville or 1st Cav/11th ACR position during Cambodian Incursion. At O Rang AF, apx 2 km E FSB David (YU 346-653), 17 km NW Bu Krak, 14 km SSW Mondol Kiri City AF, 9 km ENE FSB Speer and 28 km N Djamap/Bu Gia Map. Grid per *11th ACR Cambodia Invasion AAR, 1st Cav Div, May-Jun70*, courtesy Lou Rochat. Cambodia.
O Ro, Pointe (XS 9-7)
See Pointe O Ro. Gia Dinh Pr?, III Corps.
O'Brien, USS (n/a)
DD-725, per Ralph Fries.
O'Cannon, USS (n/a)
USN Destroyer. On 10Oct69, suptd D/3d/506th Inf during amphibious assault by LCU. USCG escort vessel also involved. SVN.
O'Conner, LZ (AT 934-243)
On hilltop apx 3 km due E Hiep Duc, 36 km W Tam Ky and 25 km SSE An Hoa CB. Americal Assn list author indicates base was named to honor 1st Cav pilot taken POW near DMZ in Feb68. Apr70 XXIV Corps grid per Don Armstrong. Quang Tin Pr, I Corps.
O'Keefe, FSB (YT 197-839)
A.k.a. FSB Remagen VIII. Along QL-14, apx 14 km NE Dong Xoai and 9 km SW Bunard AF. 2d/12th Cav, 1st Cav here Jul-69 per Frank Penk, Jr. Cited in 1st Cav VN *Yearbook* Aug65-Dec69, p 278, per Peter Cole. Phuoc Long Pr, III Corps.
O'Reilly, FSB (YD 324-258)
A.k.a. Hill 542. Apx 26 km due S Quang Tri, 20 km SW My Chanh and 41 km W Hue. 2d/506th Inf and ARVN here in supt FSB Ripcord during op Chicago Peak, Apr-Jul71. ARVN, 1st Cav and 2d Bde 101st Abn, I Corps. 101st Abn inactive FSB grid per Don Armstrong. Thua Thien Pr, I Corps.
Oa Ho, Lac (CP 080-150)
A.k.a. Lac Ao Ho. Freshwater lake at 11°54'N-109°14'E, which is at S end of Cam Ranh Peninsula, and apx 10 km S the main rwy of the AB. On NC49-01 JOG. Khanh Hoa Pr, II Corps.
Oachita, LZ (YB 893-016)
See Ouachita. Kontum Pr, II Corps.
Oaho Lake (CP 0-1)
Lac Ao Ho. Freshwater lake at 11°54N-109°14'E. See Oa Ho, Lac. Khanh Hoa Pr, II Corps.
Oak, FSB (XT 274-775)
A.k.a. FSB Vicki. Apx 2 km SE Prek Klok, 13 km SSW Katum and 18 km due N Nui Ba Den. Apr67. Also listed at XT 270-770 and 278-785. Tay Ninh Pr, III Corps.
Oak, LZ (YD 953-005)
Apx 23 km due W Q Phu Loc, 17 km SSE Phu Bai and 28 km SE Hue. Jul68. Thua Thien Pr, I Corps.
Oakland, SS (n/a)
Commercial transport under govt contract, per Ralph Fries.
Oasis, FSB (ZA 112-275)
Either at the Oasis AF or a FSB built within or adj to it. D Bty, 5th 16th Arty here dec69, B Bty, 7th/15th Arty here, Apr-Oct71. See Oasis for location. Grid and arty info per Nolan Putman. 4th Div 31Jan70 ORLL grid per Jim Henderson. Pleiku Pr, II Corps.
Oasis, LZ (ZA 103-277)
See Oasis AF for location. Possibly original position of what later became Oasis AF? Elements of 2d/17th arty here '65. Also listed at ZA 105-271, ZA 113-271. Data per Jack Picciolo. Pleiku Pr, II Corps.
Oasis Airfield (ZA 104-274)
A.k.a. LZ Tuttle AF. Near Thanh An, apx 27 km due E Duc Co AF, 28 km due W Plei Do Lim AF, 25 km SW Pleiku, 12 km SW Catecka AF and E Plei Rongol. Per TPC K-10A. Alt 1,770', 3,500' laterite rwy. At 13°148'00"N-107°52'16"E. Also listed at ZA 114-275 per 4th Div Ops Rpt for period ending 31Jan69. Origin of LZ Tuttle name not known. Pleiku Pr, II Corps.
Oasis SF Camp (YA 8460-2493)
A.k.a. Duc Co SF Camp? Along QL-19B, at or near Duc Co AF, apx 26 km W Oasis AF, and 44 km SW Pleiku. 5th SF. Info/grid per *SF Order of Battle.* See Duc Co. Pleiku Pr, II Corps.
Oasis, The (ZA 114-275)
A.k.a. LZ Oasis, LZ Tuttle, The Oasis, Oasis Basecamp and FSB Oasis. At Thanh An, apx 24 km SSW Pleiku, 12 km SW Catecka AF, and built by 1st Cav in '65, during 1st Ia Drang campaign and then abnd soon after. Reopened in May66 by TF Walker under BGen Glenn Walker using 3 Bns of 25th Inf Div (inc 1st/14th, 1st/35th Inf), 1 Armored Cav Trp, 1 Air Cav Trp, 1 Bn of 105mm howitzers, 1 Bty each of 155mm, 175mm (C Bty, 7th/15th Arty), and 8" cannons. Attacked and partially overrun 11May69 (Mother's Day), resulting in at least 25 US KIA and 3 MIA (later released during Op Homecoming). Per Larry Kline, "The Oasis was hit at 0100 hrs, 11May69 by 600+ NVA/sappers. Battle lasted until Puff arrived at about 0330 or 0400. When daylight came it looked like Custer's Last Stand--bodies everywhere! We got overrun at a bunker about 200 yards to [our] left...but I don't know how much of 'O' was actually occupied by enemy. I was told there were over 400 enemy dead. I don't know why they didn't get all of us but luck was with us." Americal arty was here at one time, working in 4th Div's AO. B Bty, 7th/15th Arty here, Apr-Oct71, per Nolan Putman. Abnd by US forces in Summer of '71 and unknown if ARVN then reopened or demolished it. Discussed in *Battles in the Monsoon*, pp 262-265, 268-269, 315. 1st Cav, Task Force Walker, 4th Div, Americal. Grid per 4th Div Ops Rpt for period ending 31Jan69. Per J. R. Wright, C/227th AHC, is on map L-7014-6536-1, at ZA 10-27, with parking ramp at NE end of rwy at ZA 108-277. On TPC K-10A, site is 107° 20'E, 13° 48'N. Pleiku Pr, II Corps. [402]
Oates, LZ (XD 928-434)
Apx 18 km WSW Mai Loc and 42 km WSW Quang Tri. Mar68. Quang Tri Pr, I Corps.
Oauchita, LZ (YB 893-016)
A.k.a. Hill 1274, LZ Oachita and Ngok Tolum Mtn. Overlooking Plei Trap Valley, apx 24 km SSW Dak To 2 AF, 16 km NW Polei Kleng AF and 2 km NW LZ Delaware. Per *Time Heals No Wounds*, p 172. 4th Div AO, 2d Bde/4th Inf operated out of this location, early '69. Grid per *Time Heals No Wounds*, p 172. 2d Bde/4th Inf operated out of this base in early '69. Kontum Pr, II Corps.
Observation Posts (generally)
See OP and also IOD.

Ocala, LZ (YD 147-463)
Along Hwy 557, apx 5 km SW Chau Lang, 18 km WSW Quang Tri. Apr70 XXIV Corps grid per Don Armstrong. Quang Tri Pr, I Corps.

Ocean Cloud, SS (n/a)
Commercial transport under govt contract, per Ralph Fries.

Ocean View, FSB (YD 291-751)
A.k.a. Ocean View Outpost. Apx 8 km NW Cua Viet, 23 km NNW Quang Tri, 8 km SE mouth of Ben Hai River. Apr70 XXIV Corps grid per Don Armstrong. Aug68. On map at http://wmcbride. space.swri.edu/visit/maps/cuamap.jpg. Quang Tri Pr, I Corps.

Ocean View Outpost (YD 291-751)
See FSB Ocean View. Quang Tri Pr, I Corps.

Oceanside, LZ (YD 028-664)
On S edge of DMZ, apx 7 km W Thon An Hoa, 12 km NW Cam Lo and 22 km WNW Dong Ha CB. Apr70 XXIV Corps grid per Don Armstrong. Quang Tri Pr, I Corps.

Oceanview, FSB (YD 291-751)
See Ocean View, FSB. Quang Tri Pr, I Corps.

OD, LZ (BS 786-368)
A.k.a. LZ Olive Drab. W of QL-1 RR tracks, apx 3 km W Duc Pho, 6 km SE Nui Xuong (LZ Liz) and 18 km SSE Quang Hien/Mo Duc. 1st/35th Inf, 4th Div fwd FSB, 15Apr-4Oc67, per Dick Arnold. Quang Ngai Pr, I Corps.

OD Lake (BS 78-36)
Apx 3 km SW Duc Pho AF and 2 km W QL-1. Per Dick Arnold, this 1.5 x .5 km lake was within view of, and SE LZ OD. Arnold recalls farmers/fisherman along lake would quickly row to its center to avoid his unit whenever it was checking ID cards. OD meant Olive Drab in GI lingo, and it may be name simply reflected lake's color. Americal list. Quang Ngai Pr, I Corps.

Odessa, FSB (XT 063-754?)
If grid correct, was apx 30 km WSW Katum and 7 km SSW Thien Ngon AF. 2d/505th Inf, 82d Abn moved here apx 1Feb69, to provide security for entry of 3d Bde/1st Cav into III Corps, and worked opcon to 2d Bde/1st Cav until 11Feb69, when 505th left for FSB Joe. 1st/7th Cav, 1st Cav here '68 per Frank Penk, Jr., who lists grid as YT 078-758? Also listed at YT 063-754? Tay Ninh Pr, III Corps.

Odessa, FSB (YT 063-754?)
If grid correct, was apx 5 km WSW Dong Xoai, 30 km SE An Loc. 2d/505th Inf, 82d Abn moved here apx 1Feb69, to provide security for entry of 3d Bde/1st Cav into III Corps, and worked opcon to 2d Bde/1st Cav until 11Feb69, when 505th left for FSB Joe. 1st/7th Cav, 1st Cav here '68 per Frank Penk, Jr., who lists grid as YT 078-758? Also listed at "XT" 064-253? Phuoc Long Pr, III Corps.

Odessa, FSB (YT 078-758?)
If accurate, was at SE edge of Dong Xoai, apx 3 km W Dong Xoai AF and 28 km NNE Phuoc Vinh AF. 1st/7th Cav, 1st Cav here '68. Grid/unit data per Frank Penk, Jr. Also listed at YT 063-754? Phuoc Long Pr, III Corps.

Odessa East, FSB (YT 137-785?)
A.k.a. FSB June? If grid correct, was apx 8 km E to ENE Odessa at YT 063-754? Cited in 1st Cav *Cavilair* newspaper. 1st/12th Inf, 1st Cav here, Jan '69. Grid est. Phuoc Long Pr, III Corps.

Odessa East, FSB (XT 137-785?)
If grid correct, was apx 8 km E to ENE Odessa at XT 063-754? Cited in 1st Cav *Cavilair* newspaper. 1st/12th Inf, 1st Cav here, Jan '69. Grid est. Phuoc Long Pr, III Corps.

Odin, FSB (YT 362-517)
Apx 40 km E Phuoc Vinh AF, 15 km ESE Rang Rang, 42 km NW Vo Dat and 45 km NNW Xuan Loc. Opened 27Jul70, unit unknown, closed 6Aug70, by 1st/12th Cav. Reopened 16Sep70, closed 19Sep70, by 2d/7th Cav Data per *1st Cav Div Op Rpt, ending 31Oct70*, courtesy Peter Cole. Also listed at YT 362-515. Long Khanh Pr, III Corps.

Odonek Airfield (n/a)
Featured 5,800' rwy, 45 km NNW Phnom Penh. Per TPC K-10D. El. 25'. Cambodia.

Ogden, USS (n/a)
LPD 5, Lndg. Platform, Dock. See End Sweep, Op.

Oh Jac Kyo I, Operation (n/a)
7Mar-18Apr67. Largest ROK op to that date. Linked to ROK AOs along central coast of II Corps. 831 rptd NVA/VC KIA, per *Vietnam Order of Battle*, pp 9-14. Binh Dinh (et al) Pr, II Corps.

Ohi Airfield (XS 8-9)
A.k.a. Tan Son Nhut AB? In Saigon, and presumably the main Saigon AF during WWII. Was either Japanese built or expanded, and Ohi possibly its Japanese name. See *Vietnam Military Lore, Legends, Shadows, and Heroes*, pp 1, 11, 14. Gia Dinh Pr, III Corps.

Ohio, LZ (YD 161-121)
Apx 30 km SW to WSW Ba Long AF, 13 km W FSB Cunningham and 7 km WSW Tou Rout. Apr70 XXIV Corps grid per Don Armstrong. Quang Tri Pr, I Corps.

Ohu Sa Ngop Airfield (UF 09-90)
LS-270 and Phia Louang. CIA, *Air Facilities Data-Laos.*

OK Corral Hill (ZB 1-5?)
See Carpenter's Hill. Kontum Pr, II Corps.

OK Corral Compound (XS 95-94?)
At Thu Duc. Possibly near listed grid. See Thu Duc. Gia Dinh Pr, III Corps.

Okanogan, USS (n/a)
APA-220. Amphib Attack, Transport, per Ralph Fries.

Okie (n/a)
A.k.a. "The Rock." Marine and SF slang for Okinawa.

Okinawa, USS (n/a)
LPH 3. Lndg. Platform, Helo. During '72 Easter Offensive, landed SVN Marines far behind NVA lines in I Corps. [403]

Oklahoma, FSB (XT 832-525)
At crossroads, apx 13 km WNW Phuoc Vinh AF and 12 km SSE Chonh Thanh AF. Oct69. Binh Tuy Pr, III Corps.

Oklahoma, FSB (XU 427-095)
Adj to or a.k.a. Phu Xuan. Apx 4 km NE Phum Khcheay, 14 km ENE Memot AF, 23 km NNE Katum and 31 km due W Loc Ninh and 15 km from SVN at closest point. Grid per *11th ACR Cambodia Invasion AAR, 1st Cav Div, May-Jun70*, courtesy Lou Rochat. [404] Cambodia.

Oklahoma, LZ (ZA 102-169)
Apx 32 km NW Phu Nhon AF, 33 km SSW Pleiku and 14 km N Plei Me. 1st/12th Cav, 1st Cav here during early stages of 1st Ia Drang Battle, Nov65. Cited in *Pleiku*, p 134. Pleiku Pr, II Corps.

Oklahoma City, USS (n/a)
CL-5, Guided Missile Light Cruiser. On 16Apr72, during Easter Offensive, the *Oklahoma City* and three destroyers hit targets on Do Son Peninsula, which guarded approaches to Haiphong Harbor. Was armed with 6-inch/47-Cal. guns, eff to 22,000 yds. Deployed vicinity of SVN in '62?

Oklahoma Hills, Operation (n/a)
1Mar-29May69. USMC 7th and 26th Mar Rgts working SW Da Nang. 596 rptd enemy KIA, per *Vietnam Order of Battle*, pp 9-11. Quang Nam Pr, I Corps.

OL-A (XS 819-962)
USAF Rescue Coordination Center. At Tan Son Nhut AB (call-sign Queen), Saigon. Gia Dinh Pr, III Corps.

Olang, Lagune de (CQ 1-6)
A.k.a. Dam O Loan. Lagoon at 13°16'N-109°16'E. On ND49-09 JOG. Phu Yen Pr, II Corps.

Old Baldy (YB 890-273)
Apx 4 km NE Ben Het. Nature of site unknown. Possibly hill or LZ? Jul69. Kontum Pr, II Corps.

Old Chu Lai (BT 53-06)
See Chu Lai, Old. Quang Tin Pr, I Corps.

Old Embassy, The (XS 8-9)
At 39 Ham Nghi St., Saigon. Building known as the "Old Embassy" and site of Coco Club (destroyed by a terrorist bomb, 30Mar65). Per R. Bows' *Vietnam Military Lore, 1959-1973.* Gia Dinh Pr, III Corps.

Old French Factory, The (XT 350-320)
See French Factory, The. Tay Ninh Pr, III Corps.

Old French Fort (various)
See French Fort and Old French Fort.

Old French Fort (XT 542-376)
Apx 11 km SSE Dau Tieng/Tri Tam. Aug69-Jan70. Binh Duong Pr, III Corps.

Old French Fort (Dau Tieng), The (XT 430-460?)
Near Boundary Road and Michelin Rubber Plantation, apx 12 km from Dau Tieng. Cited in *Low Level Hell*, p 319. Tay Ninh Pr, III Corps.

Old French Fort (Kham Duc), The (ZC 060-080)
See Kham Duc SF Camp. Quang Tin Pr, I Corps.

Old French Fort (Khe Sanh), The (XD 858-38)
A.k.a. The Alamo. In '62, SF A Det occupied the abnd French post (concrete structures built in apx '52) just off Rte 9 near Khe Sanh ville. Facilities became known as The Old French Fort and also nicknamed "The Alamo" by SF advisors here. See Alamo, BV-33 and Khe Sanh SF Camp (Old) for detailed history. Also listed at XD 859-383. Quang Tri Pr, I Corps.

Old French Fort (Rach Cat), The (XS 786-847?)
Apparently old French Fort at Rach Cat. If NPIA grid accurate, was apx 12km S Tan Son Nhut AB and 8 km NE Binh Chanh. Gia Dinh or Go Cong Pr?, III or IV Corps.

Old French Fort, The (Vinh Thanh) (BR 620-580?)
Near BR 62-58. At N end of Vinh Thanh Valley (a.k.a. Happy Valley) and along Song Con Creek, 2.5 km NW Vinh Than apx 22 km NE An Khe. CIDG base in this crumbling, old fort involved in Op Crazy Horse, May66. See *Battles in the Monsoon*. Binh Dinh Pr, II Corps.

Old French Fort, The (AT or BT?)
SW or near Da Nang? ARVN/US prisoner interrogation facility. Quang Nam Pr, I Corps.

Old French Fort, The (AT 916-582)
See Hill 37. Quang Nam Pr, I Corps.

Old French Road, The (AT)
A.k.a. Rte 534 near Hiep Duc, the Song Lau River and Nui Chom Mtn. Americal AO. Quang Tin Pr, I Corps.

Old French Fort Base (XT 275-683)
Along TL-4, apx 10 km N Nui Ba Den. Feb67. Tay Ninh Pr, III Corps.

Old Ha Thanh (BS 39-71?)
A.k.a. Son Ha. Possibly near listed grid? Americal list. Quang Ngai Pr, I Corps.

Old Ham (YS 988-841)
See Ham Tan. Binh Tuy Pr, III Corps.

Old Hau Duc (BS 024-979)
Apx 53 km WSW Chu Lai, 8 km SSW New Hau Duc/LZ Mildred (BT 048-043) 37 km SW Tam Ky. Americal List. Quang Tin Pr, I Corps.

Old Hickory, FSB (ZD 088-008)
At Phu Loc (Q Phu Loc), apx 2 km W FSB Tomahawk, 37 km SE Hue, 40 km NW Da Nang and 300 meters N QL-1. Apr70 XXIV Corps grid per Don Armstrong. Thua Thien Pr, I Corps.

Old Karen, LZ (AQ 825-185)
Apx 3 km NW Quang Nhieu and 14 km N to NNE Ban Me Thuot City AF. Feb66. Darlac Pr, II Corps.

Old Lang Vei (XD 848-417)
See Lang Vei, Old SF Camp and BV-33. Quang Tri Pr, I Corps.

Old MacDonald Had a Farm (n/a)
See *Canberra, USS.*

Old Man's Trail (n/a)
A.k.a. Infantry Route One, the Truong Son Trail and the Transportation Corridor; all were NVA nicknames for the Ho Chi Minh Trail complex. See Ho Chi Minh Trail for more detail.

Old Plei Djereng (YA 865-531)
Apx 40 km WNW Pleiku, 7 km N Plei Djereng New AF and 3 km S Ya Krong Bolah River. Also listed at YA 859-534. Apr67-Jan70. Pleiku Pr, II Corps.

Old Quarter (n/a)
The older portion of Hanoi, N Hoan Kiem Lake, and known to French as *Ceti Indigene*. NVN.

Oleson, FSB (XT 023-697?)
A.k.a. FSB Olesen or LZs Olsen or Olson? 1st Cav FSBs Olsen and Olson both listed at XT 023-697, and they may be sp variants of this name. If that is true, then site was apx 22 km NW Tay Ninh West AF, 5 km E Cambodian border and 14 km SSW Thien Ngon AF. Possibly named to honor either SFC Ronald A. Olesen, KIA, 22Jul70, or 1Lt Joseph Oleson Jr., KIA 9Jun68 (note last name sp variance). 2d/32d Arty, 23d Grp here '71. Name per Dan Gillotti, 15th Arty Assn. Tay Ninh Pr, III Corps.

Olesen, FSB? (XT 023-697?)
See FSBs Oleson and Olsen. Tay Ninh Pr, III Corps.

Olive, LZ (BR 882-738)
Apx 3 km S Lac Son, 6 km NNW Phu My and 4 km W QL-1. Oct 66. Binh Dinh Pr, II Corps.

Olive Chapel (XT 98-13?)
Chapel at Camp Zinn, Bien Hoa AB, basecamp of 173d Abn. Named to honor PFC Milton L. Olive, III, 2d/503d Inf, 173d Abn, KIA 22Oct65, who threw himself on

grenade to save others and was awarded MOH. Army regulations preclude chapels being named for individuals; however, exception was made here. Bien Hoa Pr, III Corps.

Olive Drab, LZ (BS 786-368)
See OD. Quang Ngai Pr, I Corps.

Olive Theater (YT 04-07?)
At Long Binh Post, NE Saigon. Named to honor PFC Milton L. Olive (see Olive Chapel). Bien Hoa Pr, III Corps.

Ollie, LZ (BR 9119-8464)
Per Ken Burington, was apx 1 to 2 km W QL-1, 2 km SW Van An, 13 km SSE Bong Son, 40 km due N Phu Cat AB and 11 km E Ha Tay (17Jun67). A Bty/2d/17th FA here 30Sep67, suptg 1st/77th FA. On mapsheet L-7014 6837-4. Some data per Jack Picciolo. Binh Dinh Pr, II Corps.

Ollie, LZ (YD or XD?)
No data. Map reference suggests site was no less than 30 km NW to WNW Hue? Map is L-7014-6442-3. Thua Thien or Quang Tri Pr, I Corps.

Olsen, FSB (XT 023-697)
A.k.a. FSB Olson, Oleson or Olesen? Apx 22 km NW Tay Ninh West AF and 14 km SSW Thien Ngon AF. 1st Cav. See FSB Oleson. Tay Ninh Pr, III Corps.

Olson, FSB (XT 023-697)
See FSBs Olsen and Oleson. III Corps.

Omaha, FSB (YD 683-335)
In coastal sands just S Ap Trang Luc, 12 km NNW Hue. E/1st/502d Inf, 101st Abn listed as being here 16Nov68, per '68 1st/502d Bn An Hist Supp. 101st Abn inactive FSB grid per Don Armstrong.

Omaha, LZ (YA 945-084)
Apx 46 km SW Pleiku, 43 km WNW Phu Nhon and 10 km NE peak of Chu Pong mtn. 21Aug66. Data per Jack Picciolo. Pleiku Pr, II Corps.

Omega, Operation (n/a)
See Glossary

On (n/a)
Mapsheet name of L-7014-6352-3. NVN only.

On Guard, Operation (XT)
17-21 Jan66. 173d Abn, Di An, Phu Loi. III Corps.

ONC (n/a)
See Glossary.

Onderko Commo Site (BT 06-84)
A.k.a. Monkey Mtn Signal Site and Hill 621 (2,037'). On the Tien Sha Peninsula, apx 12 km NE Da Nang AB, 4 km WNW Son Tra Mtn and 11 km NNE Marble Mtn AF. Apparently on ridge perhaps 2 km S peak of Hill 621 rather than at its top. Dedicated as "Onderko Integrated Communications Systems Site," and previously a.k.a. ICS-64. Named to honor Capt. John P. Onderko, USA, KIA 4Feb68, Tet '68, after breaking through enemy lines to install replacement generator at besieged MACV Cmpd(?) in Hue. Quang Nam Pr, I Corps.

One, LZ (BN 828-628)
On coast at Thon Son Hai, apx 17 km S Phan Rang and 14 km E Ql-1. Mar67. Ninh Thuan Pr, II Corps.

One Hundred P Alley (XS 82-96)
A.k.a. 100 P Alley and 100 Piaster Alley. Labyrinth of muddy alleys across from main gate at Tan Son Nhut AB. Described as somewhat dangerous area populated by military misfits, AWOLs and deserters. Purportedly named for nominal fee AWOL troops would to pay Viet villagers to put them up for night until curfew was over and they could sneak back onto base. Grid is for Tan Son Nhut AF. Gia Dinh Pr, III Corps.

One Oh Worst Pad (BT 173-078)
See 1-Oh-Worst Pad. Quang Tin Pr, I Corps.

One Zero (n/a)
See Glossary.

Ong Doc, Vam Song (VQ 80-99)
See Song On Doc. An Xuyen Pr, IV Corps.

Ong Doi Mui (US 9-0)
Coastal point at 10°00'N-104°03'E. On NC48-05 JOG. Kien Giang Pr, IV Corps.

Ong Doi, Pointe (US 9-0)
A.k.a. Mui Ong Doi. Coastal point at 10°00'N-104°03'E. On NC48-05 JOG. Kien Giang Pr, IV Corps.

Ong Doi, Pointe (US 9-0)
See Pointe Ong Doi. Kien Giang Pr, IV Corps.

Ong Linh Airfield (XT 949-261)
See Xong Ong Linh AF. Bien Hoa Pr, III Corps.

Ong Que Airfield (YS 392-994)
Apx 12 km SW Xuan Loc, 15 km due E Long Thanh North AF and 6 km NW Blackhorse Basecamp. "Pvt AF # VA3-140," in Aug69 TAD per Frank Penk, Jr. Not in Feb73 TAD. Long Khanh Pr, III Corps.

Ong Que Combat Base (YS 390-990)
Apx 12 km SW Xuan Loc, 15 km E Long Thanh North AF and 6 km NW Blackhorse AF Aug-Oct66. Long Khanh Pr, III Corps.

Ong Que Rubber Plantation (YS 390-980)
Apx 11 km SW Xuan Loc, 15 km E Long Thanh North AF and 6 km NW Blackhorse AF. Long Khanh Pr, III Corps.

Ong Thay, Xong (n/a)
Mapsheet L-7014-5729-1. Sheet Name: Xong Ong Thay. SVN/Cambodia.

Ong Thin Bridge (XS 815-775)
Along LTL-15 at Ap Phuoc Khanh, apx 6 km NNW Can Guioc and 10 km S Saigon. Gia Dinh Pr, III Corps.

Ong Thu Slope (ZC 0-3/AT)
Near the Song Cai River, SW of An Hoa. Ridgeline that along with adj Nui Giang/Yang Brai ridgeline was portion of Base Area 112. Quang Nam Pr, I Corps.

Ong Loc (XT 868-103?)
A.k.a. Hung Loc? Enemy held ville a few km S Phu Loi. Discussed in *Ambush*, pp 174-75. Gia Dinh or Binh Duong Pr, III Corps.

Ong Thay, Mui (VS 5-2)
A.k.a. Mui Ong Thoa. Cape at 10°08'N-104°36'E. On NC48-06 JOG. Kien Giang Pr, IV Corps.

Ong Thoa, Mui (VS 5-2)
Cape at 10°08'N-104°36'E. On NC48-06 JOG. Kien Giang Pr, IV Corps.

Ongthai, Cape (VS 5-2)
A.k.a. Mui Ong Thoa. Cape at 10°08'N-104°36'E. On NC48-06 JOG. Kien Giang Pr, IV Corps.

Ong Coc, Da (WG 8-2)
See Da Ong Coc. NVN.

Ong Qui, Mui (US 7-3)
Coastal point at 10°17'N-103°53'E. On NC48-05 JOG. Kien Giang Pr, IV Corps.

Ong Trang, Mui (VQ 8-6)
Coastal point at 8°42'N-104°50'E. On NC48-15 JOG. An Xuyen Pr, IV Corps.

Ong Dien Mui (CQ 1-8)
Coastal point apx 40 km SSE Qui Nhon. On ND49-09 JOG. Phu Yen Pr, II Corps.

Ong Dien, Pointe (CQ 1-8)
See Pointe Ong Dien. Phu Yen Pr, II Corps.

Ong, Mui (XE 6-8)
Coastal point at 17°57'N-106°31'E. NE48-12 JOG. NVN.

Ong Que, Plantation de (YS 36-98)
A.k.a. Don Dien Ong Que. Apx 6 km WNW Blackhorse AF. Long Khanh Pr, III Corps.

Onion, The (XT)
Apx 10 km ESE Dau Tieng, 20 km WNW Lai Khe and immed S FSB Gela. Onion-shaped terrain feature and aerial landmark discussed in *Low Level Hell* (shown on inside-cover 1st Div TAOR map). 1st Inf Div AO, '69. Binh Duong Pr, III Corps.

OP 1 (BS 515-780)
A.k.a. Observation Post #1. Apx 3 km E Ba Gia AF and 15 km NW Quang Ngai. Mortar attacks on lndg helos common here. On map L-7014-6739-3. Also listed at BS 516-778. Americal list. Quang Ngai Pr, I Corps.

OP 3 (BS 754-421)
A.k.a. Observation Post #3. On Nui Xuong, apx 7 km NW Duc Pho and 12 km S Mo Duc. Americal List. Quang Ngai Pr, I Corps.

OP 7 Heliport (BT 164-233)
Apx 15 km due W Tam Ky. Heliport #627, alt 525', per Feb73 TAD. Quang Tin Pr, I Corps.

OP 10 (BT 0-6?)
A.k.a. OP Panther. Apparently USMC OP near Cau Ha CB and Marble Mtn. Described as having been "Along Cau Do River near 1st. Tank Bn." Photos of site in May69 at: www.lbjlib.utexas.edu/shwv/images/ a_ground.htm. Quang Nam Pr, I Corps.

OP 10 Outpost (ZA 220-465)
Apx 3 km SW Pleiku and 7 km WSW Camp Holloway. Oct68. Pleiku Pr, II Corps.

OP 55 (YD 549-086)
Apx 22 km WSW Hue, 15 km due W FSB Birmingham, 5 km N Hwy 547. Apr70 XXIV Corps grid per Don Armstrong. Thua Thien Pr, I Corps.

OP 56 (YD 855-133)
Apx 3 km WSW Camp Hochmuth/Phu Bai, 11 km SE Hue and 7 km ENE Nam Hoa. Rick Schmierer recalls the OP being hit by lightning storm in '70 or '71, "that set off all its Fougasse in one, very large and spectacular blossom of fire." 101st Abn Inactive FSB grid per Don Armstrong. Thua Thien Pr, I Corps.

OP 60 (n/a)
See Glossary.

OP Ann-Margaret (XT 64-15?)
See Ann Margaret, OP. Hau Nghia Pr, III Corps.

OP Apache (YD 629-223)
A.k.a. Hill 285 or The' Bai Mtn. Apx 2 km E Song Bo River, 4 km SE Ap Lai Bang1.5 km SW Hwy 598 and 7 km W Hue. 101st Abn inactive FSB grid per Don Armstrong. Thua Thien Pr, I Corps.

OP Castle (YD 663-225)
A.k.a. Ya Do Mtn or Hill 140? Apx 3.5 km due E OP Apache, 500 meters N Hwy 598, 6 km ESE Ap Lai Bang and 4 km W Hue. 101st Abn inactive FSB grid per Don Armstrong. Thua Thien Pr, I Corps.

OP Checkmate (YD 633-083)
A.k.a. FSB Checkmate and Hill 342. On S side Hwy 547 apx 1.5 km SSE FSB Bastogne, 5 km and NW FSB Normandy and 15 km SW Hue. Apparently used primarily as radio relay site and/or OP? By early May72, during Easter Offensive, FSB's Bastogne and Checkmate had fallen after what Gen Abrams considered an admirably stubborn defense by ARVN. In 2d Bde/101st Abn AO, 68-72. Thua Thien Pr, I Corps.

OP Chickie Pie (AT 8-4?)
Apparently a.k.a. Hill 457. Vic of An Hoa and overlooking the Song Thu Bon River Valley. 5th Marines, '67? Quang Nam Pr, I Corps.

OP D (XT 628-304)
Along LTL-15, immed S Xa Ba Phuoc and 1.5 km S the Song Saigon near Xa Duoc, apx 17 km WSW Lai Khe AF. Name/grid per Dan Gillotti, 15th Arty Assn. 25th Div. Binh Duong Pr, III Corps.

OP Dong Den (AT 873-828)
A.k.a. Hill 868 and LZ Dong Den. See Dong Den for detailed history. Quang Nam Pr, I Corps.

OP Duong Uoi (BT 148-122)
In valley of Song Chang River apx 5 km SE Tien Phuoc AF and 19 km SW Tam Ky. Reported to have been attacked and overrun by VC/NVA force on 5May70. Americal list. Quang Tin Pr, I Corps.

OP Durham (AT 988-508)
A.k.a. Orange West. On same mtn as FSB Hardcore, 16 km WSW Hoi An, 25 km S Da Nang AB. Apr70 XXIV Corps grid per Don Armstrong. Quang Nam Pr, I Corps.

OP Eagle's Eye (AT 9-8?)
Overlooked Song Cu De River and was manned by 3d/26th Marines in Oct69, and 9th MAB before that time. Quang Nam Pr, I Corps.

OP George (BS 739-606?)
A.k.a. Hill 64? Overlooked An Phong (I), apx 7 km due N Mo Duc AF. Home of USMC Cap 1-3-9. Unit awarded Navy MUC for Action of 13Sep69, when CAP 1-3-9 and its PF forces engaged an estimated NVA Bn. Element assigned to OP George, which overlooked An Phong (I), was also attacked. In hand-to-hand fighting, NVA were finally forced to withdraw. Part of 1st CAG, III MAF. Quang Ngai Pr, I Corps.

OP Hill (YA 956-859)
A.k.a. Hill 1124. Apx 28 km W Kontum, 12 km SW Polei Kleng AF and 1.2 km NW FSB/LZ Brillo-Pad. An OP used by 4th Div LRRPs in conjunction with the Inf/Arty units on Brillo-Pad. Overrun night of 15May68, during an attack in which NVA used flame-throwers. Grid per Kevin Rafferty, B/1st/14th Inf, 4th Div. Map is L-7014-6537-4. See LZs Alamo, Bunker-Hill, Bingo, XYZ Pad and Brillo-Pad. Kontum Pr, II Corps.

OP Hill 250 (AT or BT)
See Hill 250. Quang Tin Pr?, I Corps.

OP Juliet (BT 077-273)
In the Song Chang River Valley apx 6 km NNW Tien Phuoc, and 23 km WSW Tam Ky. Americal list. Quang Tin Pr, I Corps.

OP Lake (BS 78-36)
See OD Lake. Quang Ngai Pr, I Corps.

OP Legionnaire, LZ (n/a)
A.k.a. LZ Legionnaire. Near Laotian border, and apparently 82d Abn Bde arty base used for observation of Ho Chi Minh Trail. No location data. I or II Corps.

OP/LZ Legionnaire (BT 15-25)
In mtns apx 17 km WNW Tam Ky and 12 km ESE Binh Son. Quang Tin Pr, I Corps.

OP Lion (YD 601-189)
A.k.a. Nui Gio. Apx 12 km due W Hue, 6 km SE Ap Thanh Tan and 14 km NW FSB Birmingham. Grid per 1Feb70, 101st Abn rpt, per Don Armstrong. Thua Thien Pr, I Corps.

Op Nui Yon (BT 248-169)
See Nui Yon. Quang Tin Pr, I Corps.

Op Ord 13-70, Operation (n/a)
See Jefferson Glenn/Op Ord 13-70, Op.

Op Ord 17May65, 7May-9Jul65 (n/a)
1st op of war for 173d Abn, in which it was assigned the defense of Bien Hoa AB. Bde conducted company-sized sweeps up to 15 km from base. Bien Hoa Pr, III Corps.

OP Orange West (AT 988-508)
See OP Durham. Quang Nam Pr, I Corps.

OP Panther (BT 0-6?)
See OP 10. Quang Nam Pr, I Corps.

OP Reno (AT 884-747)
Observation Point Reno. In foothills overlooking Song Cu De River Valley apx 12 km WSW Da Nang AB. 3d/26th Marines, '69. See FSB Reno. Quang Nam Pr, I Corps.

OP Sarge (YD 028-479?)
Precise location unknown. Possibly near Dong Ha/Camp Horn. Perhaps later known as FSB Sarge? Grid is for FSB Sarge and may not be correct. Quang Tri Pr, I Corps.

OP Satan (YD 761-056)
A.k.a. Hill 618 or Nui Ke. See Nui Ke for location and more detail. 101st Abn inactive FSB grid per Don Armstrong. Thua Thien Pr, I Corps.

OP Sugar Mill Hill (BS 613-735)
In or near Quang Ngai AF (along its S edge), 4 km SW Quang Ngai and immed NE Thu Pho. Americal List. Quang Ngai Pr, I Corps.

OP Sunrise (AT)
A.k.a. Hill 425. Precise location unknown; however was apparently generally E Spider Lake, SE Phu Loc and SSW Phu Nam Tay, in Que Son Mtns and covering Phu Loc and An Hoa Basin approaches to Da Nang. Spider and Alligator lakes nearby and Que Son Mtns to S. 11th Mar Arty Permanent OP (POP) employing Integrated Observation Devices (IOD). Security courtesy 1st Marine Recon Bn in 70. Described as barren sliver of rock, splattered with sandbags and radio antenna overlooking a valley that ran SW to NE out of Thong Duc Mtns into Arizona. See IOD and POP. 1st Mar Div, Quang Nam Pr, I Corps.

OP Three Sisters (YD 808-186)
See Three Sisters. Thua Thien Pr, I Corps.

OP Tiger (YD 692-158)
A.k.a. OP Ngoc Ho, LZ Chicken and OP Viper. Apx 6 km SW Hue, 7 km due N FSB Birmingham. Grid per 1Feb70, 101st Abn rpt, per Don Armstrong. Quang Tri Pr, I Corps.

OP Viper (YD 692-158)
A.k.a. OP Ngoc Ho, LZ Chicken and OP Tiger. Apx 8 km SW Hue, 6 km NNW FSB Birmingham and 3 km NE Hon Dun Mtn. XXIV Corps grid. Thua Thien Pr, I Corps.

Opal, FSB (XD 982-547)
Along S side of QL-9, apx 35 km due W Quang Tri, 16 km WSW Cam Lo and a few km S the Rockpile. Apr70 XXIV Corps grid per Don Armstrong. Quang Tri Pr, I Corps.

Opal, LZ (BR 966-637)
Apx 7 km ESE Phu My and 22 km NNE Phu Cat AB. Oct66. Binh Dinh Pr, II Corps.

Open Arms (n/a)
See Chieu Hoi Program in Glossary.

Operation (*name*) (n/a)
Military Operation (also Op and Ops in this text) entries are formatted with formal name first, followed by a comma and the word Operation or Op. For example, Cedar Falls, Operation. There were literally thousands of named ops conducted during war, and those listed in this manuscript are but a sampling of the more significant ops.

Operational Area 101 (YD 4-4?)
See Base Area 101. Quang Tri Pr, I Corps.

Operational Area 'A' (YD 01-66)
See NVA Operational Area A. Quang Tri Pr, I Corps.

Operational Area 'B' (YD 54-17)
See NVA Operational Area B. Thua Thien Pr, I Corps.

Operational Area 'C' (AT 97-52)
See NVA Operational Area C. Quang Nam Pr, I Corps.

Operational Area 'D' (BT 18-18)
See NVA Operational Area D. Quang Tin Pr, I Corps.

Operational Area 'E' (BS 39-73)
See NVA Operational Area E. Quang Ngai Pr, I Corps.

Operational Area 'F' (BS 70-57)
See NVA Operational Area F. Quang Ngai Pr, I Corps.

Operations North (n/a)
See Ops North. Quang Tri Pr, I Corps.

OPORD (n/a)
Operational order.

OPORD 13-70, Operation (n/a)
See Jefferson Glenn/Op Ord 13-70, Op.

OPORD 17May65, 7May-9Jul65, Op (n/a)
See Op Ord 17May65. Bien Hoa Pr, III Corps.

Opium Usage (n/a)
See Drug Abuse in Glossary.

Ops North (YD 24-59?)
USMC Helicopter ops CP at Dong Ha in '66. Said to have been nothing more than small shack on dusty strip at time. Quang Tri Pr, I Corps.

Oran, FSB (XT 628-504)
Apx 4 km NW FSB Picardy, 20 km NW Lai Khe and 16 km ENE Dau Tieng. 3d Bde1st Inf Div FSB on S side of "Boundary Road" at W edge of Michelin Rubber plantation. Per *Hamburger Hill* author Sam Zaffiri, was attacked by 101st NVA Rgt, 1Feb69, with 2 US KIA/33 US WIA and 11th Avn Bn Gunship shot down. 1st/26th and 1st/28th Inf here '69. Named after WWII 1st Inf Div European battle site. On *Low Level Hell's* 1st Div TAOR

map. Also listed at XT 613-490. Jan-Feb69. Binh Duong Pr, III Corps.

Oran II, FSB (XT 629-507)
See FSB Oran. Apparent later incarnation of Oran on same site. May69. Binh Duong Pr, III Corps.

Orange, FSB/LZ (BR 818-883)
In valley apx 7 km SE Bong Son, 7 km NNE Ha Tay AF and 8 km W QL-1. 173d Abn, '70. Cited in *Rangers at War*, p 192, and also mentioned in '70 Bn Annual Hist Supp of 3/503d Inf, 173d Abn, on net at www.gasparot.com/nammedic. Map is L-7014-6737-1 (Hoai An), per Ray Smith. Binh Dinh Pr, II Corps.

Orange, LZ (BR 809-878)
Apx 9 km SE Bong Son, and E of QL-1. Oct66. Also listed at BR 818-883, Jul68. Binh Dinh Pr, II Corps.

Orange, LZ (XT 015-730)
Apx 12 km SW Thien Ngon AF and 5 km E Cambodia. 29Apr66. Tay Ninh Pr, III Corps.

Orange, LZ (YD 058-585)
Overlooked Cam Lo River and QL-9, apx 1.5 km N QL-9, 6 km due W Cam Lo, 18 km W to WSW Dong Ha and 4 km WSW Xom Quat Xa. Apr70 XXIV Corps grid per Don Armstrong. Quang Tri Pr, I Corps.

Orange, LZ (YS 632-615)
Apx 20 km ESE Nui Dat and 3 km N the ocean. 5Apr66. Phuoc Tuy Pr, III Corps.

Orange, LZ (YT 445-109)
Along QL-1, apx 3 km NW Xuan Loc. 22Feb66. Long Khanh Pr, III Corps.

Orange, LZ (ZA 020-230)
Apx 7 km ESE Plei Luong Ya Rang, 33 km SW Pleiku, 17 km ESE Duc Co, and 1.5 km E LZ Pink. Per Don Shutt, was major 1st Cav battle site during Op Paul Revere II, 30Jul-2Aug66. At 1st light following ground and mortar assault, a Cav Plt was inserted in nearby LZ Pink and were virtually annihilated. Grid deduced from map in article entitled *Paul Revere II*, 1st Cav '66 *Yearbook*, per Mr. Shutt. See LZ Pink. Pleiku Pr, II Corps.

Orange Beach (BT 264-438)
Apx 4 km E Thang Binh, 5 km NNW Hiep Hung and 22 km NNW Tam Ky. Nov65. Quang Ngai Pr, I Corps.

Orange Highway (XT/YT)
See Route Orange. III Corps.

Orange West, OP (AT 988-508)
See OP Durham. Quang Nam Pr, I Corps.

Ord, FSB (XT 084-816)
At or adj to Thien Ngon AF, apx 34 km NNW Tay Ninh. Feb68-Nov69. Tay Ninh Pr, III Corps.

Ordway, LZ (BT 114-371)
A.k.a. LZ Colt. Was W of Rte 543, apx 5 km WSW Quy Thanh, 9 km SSW LZ Baldy, 26 km NW Tam Ky, 5 km ENE Cang Dong, 8 km W QL-1, and about 20 km NW Hawk Hill. Also listed at BT 113-327, BT 002-371 and BT 115-371. Map is L-7014-6640-2. Americal List. Photos-maps of base at http://1-14th.com/maps.html. Quang Tin/Quang Nam Pr border, I Corps. [405]

Oregon BOQ (XS 8-9)
At 84 Bis, Ba Huyen Thanh Quan, Saigon. Data per *Vietnam Military Lore, 1959-1973*. Gia Dinh Pr, III Corps.

Oregon Trail, The (BR 6-6 to 8-7)
Nickname of apparent NVA infiltration route in 4th Div AO that ran from Vinh Thanh Valley to vicinity Hoi San. Ran generally from BR 61-64, NE to BR 84-71. Per *Rites of Passage*, p 236, the 1st/14th Inf/25th Div was at LZ Alpha-Alpha (adj trail), Jan67. Binh Dinh Pr, II Corps.

Oreilly, FSB (YD 324-258)
See O'Reilly. Thua Thien Pr, I Corps.

Oriental Richelieu of Vietnam, The (n/a)
See Madame Nhu in Glossary.

Oriental River (XT 435-054)
A.k.a. Song Vam Co Dong. Listed grid in river near Duc Hoa, apx 38 km NW Saigon. See Oriental River Front. Hau Nghia/Long An Prvs, III Corps.

Oriental River Front (XS 60-90)
Enemy staging and base area S of Duc Hoa and along Song Vam Co Dong River. Long An Pr, III Corps.

Oriskany, USS (n/a)
A.k.a. CV-34. Deployed with CVW-19 16Sep75-3Mar76; with CVW 19 14May71-18Dec71; with CVW-19 14Apr69-17Nov69; with CVW-19 14May70-10Dec70; with CVW-19 18Oct73-5Jun74; with CVW-19 5Jun72-30Mar73; with CVW-16 16Jun67-31Jan68; with CVW-16 26May66-16Nov66; with CVW-16 5Apr65-16Dec65; with CVW-16, 1Aug63-10Mar64. Serious fire off VN, 26Oct66, when a flare being stored in locker at starboard fwd corner of hangar deck ignited. Locker contained 650 flares and resulting fire killed 25 naval aviators and 19 other officers and men. Entire fwd section from hangar floor up also gutted. Data per www.uss-salem.org/features/fires/. In Sept65 attack sqdns from Carriers *Oriskany*, *Constellation*, *Coral Sea*, and *Intrepid* hit previously off-limits areas in Haiphong and smaller ports of Hon Gai and Cam Pha. [406]

Orleck, USS (n/a)
DD 886. 7th Fleet destroyer.

Orote Point Refugee Camp (n/a)
A.k.a. Tent City. Anderson AFB, Guam. See Operation New Life.

Oscar, FSB (XT 540-451)
Apx 6 km ESE Dau Tieng. Apr67. Binh Duong Pr, III Corps.

Oscar, LZ ? (XT 652-285)
Apx 15 km W Lai Khe and 16 km SE Dau Tieng/Tri Tam. Nature of site unknown. Jun66. Binh Duong Pr, III Corps.

Oscar CAC (XD)
See CAC listings, and also CAP 0-1 and 0-2. I Corps.

Oscar CAP (XD)
See CAP Oscar listings. Quang Tri Pr, I Corps.

Osceola, SS (n/a)
Contract ocean tugboat of MSC. See Evacuation of Da Nang, and Frequent Wind, Op.

Ou Neua Airfield (QE 88-69)
A.k.a. L-26. Apx 485 km NNW Vientiane on Feb67 Natl Geo map. CIA/SF facility. Grid per *Air Facilities Data-Laos*. El. 2,592'. Laos.

Ouachita, LZ (YB 893-016)
A.k.a. Hill 1274 and Ngok Tahun Mtn. Overlooking the Plei Trap Valley, apx 24 km SSW Dak To 2 AF, 16 km NW Polei Kleng AF and 2 km NW LZ Delaware (Hill 1483). Per *Time Heals No Wounds*, p 172. 2d Bde/4th Inf

Div here early '69. Cited in *Time Heals No Wounds*, p 172. Kontum Pr, II Corps.

Ouest, Lagune de le (YD 7-3)
A.k.a. Pha Tam Giang. Lagoon at 16°36'N-107°32'E. On NE48-16 JOG. Thua Thien Pr, I Corps.

Ouest, Pointe (XQ 7-5)
See Pointe Ouest. IV Corps.

Our Lady of Peace, SS (n/a)
Commercial transport under govt contract, per Ralph Fries.

Outagamie County, USS (n/a)
LST-1073. SVN.

Outlaw, LZ/FSB (AT 808-858)
Along Hwy 548 and in Elephant Valley, to E Ruong Ruong Valley, apx 44 km WNW Da Nang AB and 17 km SSE Q Phu Loc. Apr70 XXIV Corps grid per Don Armstrong. Quang Nam Pr, I Corps.

Outpost 7 Mountains (WS 027-636?)
See Seven Mountains. Chau Doc Pr, IV Corps.

Outpost Curless (YC 905-947)
See Curless, Outpost. Thua Thien Pr, I Corps.

Outpost Cutlass (YD)
See Cutlass entries. Thua Thien Pr, I Corps.

Outpost Seven Mountains (WS 027-636?)
See Seven Mountains. Chau Doc Pr, IV Corps.

Outrider, LZ (ZA 204-214)
Apx 3 km due E Plei La Meur, 26 km SSW Pleiku, 16 km SE Camp Enari and 19 km WSW Plei Do Lim AF. 4th Div. Name/grid per Jim Claeys. Also listed at ZA 200-170. Pleiku Pr, II Corps.

Over The Fence (n/a)
See Glossary.

Overseas Rose, SS (n/a)
Commercial transport under govt contract, per Ralph Fries.

Owasco, USCGC (n/a)
WHEC 39. 23Jul68-21Mar69. Sqdn 3 CGC, during Coast Guard's 3d deployment.

Owl, LZ (AT or BT?)
7th Marine Rgt used LZs Owl and Hawk for searching 10 sq-km area S of Hill 55, between Rte 4 and Song Thu Bon River, during Op Linn River. 1st/7th and 2/26th Marines, 28-29Jan69. 1st Mar Div. Quang Nam Pr?, I Corps.

Owl, LZ (YD 243-592)
At S edge of Dong Ha AB/CB, apx 11 km NW Quang Tri and 1.5 km W QL-1. Apr70 XXIV Corps grid per Don Armstrong. Quang Tri Pr, I Corps.

Oxen, LZ (XD 817-534)
Apx 2 km NW peak Dong Voi Mep (Hill 1739), 14 km NNW Khe Sanh CB and 5 km ESE Lang Ha. Apr70 XXIV Corps grid per Don Armstrong. Quang Tri Pr, I Corps.

Oxford, USS (n/a)
AGTR-1. Aux Ship, per Ralph Fries.

Oyster, LZ (YD 270-308)
Apx 14 km SE Ba Long AF and 22 km SSW Quang Tri. Apr70 XXIV Corps grid per Don Armstrong. Thua Thien Pr, I Corps.

Ozbourn, USS (n/a)
DD 846. Saw duty off VN, Aug-64-Dec65, and again with TF 77.6 beginning apx 20Aug65, in III/IV Corps area, and in Oct65, her gunfire in Rung Sat Zone helped halt a VC attack. In Jul66, began 2-year tour with 7th Flt's DesRon 9, suptg ground ops in SVN, and shelling enemy supply/commo in NVN. On 25Mar67 and 4Dec67, received direct shore fire. Returned to US on 6Sep68, and re-deployed to WESTPAC, Sep69-70. [407]

PAPA

Facility/Feature Name, Grid Coordinate, a.k.a. Name/History/Province/CTZ

Unless otherwise stated, 6-digit grid coordinates reference DMA L-7014, L-7015 or L-7016 series, 1:50,000 scale maps, while 2- and 4-digit coordinates reference AMS/DMA/NIMA 1:250,000, 1:500,000 and 1:1,000,000 scale maps. Unless otherwise stated, all heights are in meters. To convert meters to feet, multiply by 3.2808; feet to meters, multiply by .3048.

P A & E Hotels (Various)
Pacific Architects & Engrs primary housing facility. PA&E were civilian contractors who performed maintenance services for military installations throughout VN.

P A & E Saigon (XS 833-957)
Apx 1 km ENE MACV HQ and at E side of Tan Son Nhut AB. Pacific Architects & Engrs. Gia Dinh Pr, III Corps.

Pa Doung Airfield (UG 02-12)
LS-05. Apx 140 km NNE Vientiane, per ONC-J-11. CIA/SF, per *Air Facilities Data-Laos.* El. 4,770'. Laos.

Pa Doung Noi Airfield (UF 06-89)
LS-340. CIA/SF, per *Air Facilities Data-Laos.*

Pa Duong Airfield (n/a)
See Pa Doung AF. Laos.

Pa Ka Airfield (TG 63-17)
LS-51 and Pha Khe. CIA/SF, per *Air Facilities Data-Laos.*

Pa Kha (n/a)
Mapsheet name of L-7014-5854-2. NVN/China.

Pa Seu Lung (VJ 5-1)
Mtn range at 20°57'N-104°33'E. Grid per DMA L-1501 map NF48-14.

Pa Wai Airfield (QU 1-8)
Listed as abnd in '66 NIMA data. At 17°00'00"N-101°02'00"E. NIMA data. Do not confuse with Pawai AF (at PS 7-3). Thailand.

Pa Wai Airfield (QU 2-7)
Listed as abnd in '66 NIMA data. At 16°59'00"N-101°04'00"E. NIMA data. Do not confuse with Pawai AF (at QU 1-8). Thailand.

Pace, FSB (XT 06-84)
Apx 3 km S Cambodia, 4 km NW Thien Ngon AF, 27 km WSW Katum and 34 km NNW Tay Ninh. Apparently built sometime between '70-72? Apparently a mutiny of some sort here at one time? Tay Ninh Pr, III Corps.

Pacific Exchange (n/a)
See PACEX Glossary.

Pacific, LZ (XD 908-675)
On S edge of DMZ, apx 32 km WNW Cam Lo, 26 km NNW Khe Sanh CB and 12 km NNE peak of Dong Voi Mep (Hill 1739). Apr70 XXIV Corps grid per Don Armstrong. Quang Tri Pr, I Corps.

Package (n/a)
See Glossary.

Padaran, Baie de (BN 6-4)
Bay at 11°15'N-108°50'E. On NC49-01 JOG. Binh Thuan Pr, II Corps.

Padaran, Cap (BN 8-5)
A.k.a. Mui Dinh. Cape at 11°22'N-109°01'E. On NC49-01 JOG. Ninh Thuan Pr, II Corps.

Paddock Compound (AT 946-812)
A.k.a. 18th Engr Bde Cmpd. At Red Beach, apx 8 km NW Da Nang AB. Named to honor 1Lt David A Paddock, USA, Bn S-2/Recon Officer, 19th Engr Bn/18th Engr Bde, KIA by mine 7Jun68, while on recon mission. See Red Beach. Quang Nam Pr, I Corps.

Paddock/Westrate Bridge (BS 78-43)
A.k.a. the Song Tra Cau QL-1 Bridge. Apx 14 km SE Mo Duc and 5 km N Duc Pho. Named to honor 1Lt David A. Paddock and Sgt Robert K. Westrate, KIA 7Jun68. Data per Ray Bows. Quang Ngai Pr, I Corps.

Page, Tim (n/a)
See Point Welcome, CGC.

Page County, USS (XS 8-9)
LST-1076 (also listed as 1096?). On15May70, and aboard this vessel in Saigon harbor, Adm Zumwalt gave COMNAVFORV (Cmdr Naval Forces Vietnam) to Vice Adm Jerome H. King, Jr, and left VN to become Chief, Naval Operations. See *Brown Water, Black Berets*, p 352. Gia Dinh Pr, III Corps.

Pagoda Inn, FSB (XT 873-186)
Apx 23 km N Saigon, 21 km SE Lai Khe, 4 km NE Phu Loi, 4 km NNW FSB Venable Heights and 15 km due S FSB Holiday Inn. 1st Div, 69. On *Low Level Hell's* TAOR map. Also listed at XT 883-197. Binh Duong Pr, III Corps.

Pagoda Valley (BT 05-45)
Was apx 15 km SSW Hoi An, 8 km SSW LZ Baldy and 6 km N Ngai Ha Valley. Named for many pagodas on valley floor. Quang Nam and Quang Tin Pr border, I Corps.

Pagoda, Pointe de la (CP 0-1)
See Pointe Pagoda. Khanh Hoa Pr, II Corps.

Pagode, Pointe (YJ 5-5)
See Pointe Pagode. NVN.

Pai Airfield (MB 3-3)
At 19°21'00"N-98°25'00"E. NIMA data. Thailand.

Pailin Airfield (n/a)
Apx 285 km NW Phnom Penh and 12 km from Thai border on Feb67 Natl Geo map. El. 580'. Cambodia.

Paint, LZ (BR 97-95?)
Near coast, apx 4 km SE LZ Stud, 10 km ESE Bong Son and 3 km NE LZ Colt. Used during Op Masher/White Wing, 28Jan-6Mar66. Discussion of Ops Masher/White Wing and this LZ in *A Contagion of War* vol, *Vietnam Experience* series, pp 32-48, with map showing site at p 38. 1st/8th Cav. 1st Cav LZ. Grid is only an estimate based on location description. Binh Dinh Pr, II Corps.

Pair-Off Operations (BN)
Joint 44th ARVN Rgt, Regional Force, US Op program created by 3d/506th Inf, 101st Abn (Sep), that began

1Apr69. Involved COBRAA (Combined Reconnaissance American-ARVN) missions. Initial focus was area NE LZ Betty/Phan Thiet, in Binh Thuan Pr, II Corps.

Pak Chong Airfield (QS 7-1)
At 14°36'00"N-101°35'00"E. NIMA data. Thailand.

Pak Chong? Airfield (n/a)
Said to have been an SF AF in Mekong Delta near Bet My Tho? (My Tho is at XS 50-45). No other data available; however, NIMA lists a Pak Chong AF at QS 7-1 in Thailand. Thailand or IV Corps.

Pak Chung (QS 7-1?)
Spelling variant of Pak Chong? SF camp or AO per *SF Order of Battle*. Thailand?

Pak Mouei Airfield (TF 64-93)
LS-273. CIA/SF, per *Air Facilities Data-Laos.*

Pak San Airfield (n/a)
5,300' rwy, on Cambodian border apx 120 km ENE Vientiane, per ONC-J-11. El. 515'. Laos.

Pak Song Airfield (XB 3-7?)
Apx 480 km SE Vientiane. Natl Geo map. El. 3,100'. Laos.

Pak Song SF Camp (XB 3-7?)
Possible sp variant of Paksane (UF 59-34) or Pak San? SF camp when Lao neutrality declared, 23Jul62. FTT 29, 34, 35 and 45 here, per *Special Forces at War*. MR4, Laos.

Paka (n/a)
Mapsheet name of L-7014-6053-1. NVN only.

Paklay Airfield (QA 55-16)
A.k.a. L-09. Apx 130 km WNW Vientiane on Feb67 Natl Geo map. CIA/SF. *Air Facilities Data-Laos.* El. 917'. Laos.

Paksane Airfield (UF 59-34)
A.k.a. L-35. Along Mekong River, apx 120 km ENE Vientiane on Feb67 Natl Geo map. CIA/SF, per *Air Facilities Data-Laos.* El. 100'? Laos.

Paksane SF Camp (UF 59-34)
Along Mekong River, apx 120 km ENE Vientiane. SF camp when Lao neutrality declared, 23Jul62. FTT 8, 11, 37 and ATT 5 here. Per *Special Forces at War*. MR5, Laos.

Pakse (WB 8-7)
Largest city in Military Region IV of Laos. Was also Regional HQ for "Raven" FACs based at Pakse AF there. Discussed in *Da Nang Diary*, p 74. Laos.

Pakse Airfield (WB 84-73)
A.k.a. L-11. Major AF on N bank of Mekong River and W of Pakse, apx 30 km E the Thai border, per Dec67 DMA TPC K-10A and Feb67 Natl Geo maps. CIA/SF facility. El. 330' or 295'. Grid per *Air Facilities Data-Laos.*

Pakse NDB (WB 78-73)
Non-Directional air navigation Beacon. Pakse AF, Laos.

Pakse/Moung Kau SF Camp (WB 84-73?)
SF camp when Lao neutrality declared, 23Jul62. Apparently on N bank of Mekong River and W of Pakse, apx 30 km E the Thai border. Det BD, ATT 2 and Provincial FTT 2 here then. Per *Special Forces at War.* MR4, Laos.

Paksong Airfield (XB 43-94)
L-05. CIA/SF, per *Air Facilities Data-Laos.*

Paksong Airfield, New (XB 33-77)
LS-180. CIA/SF, per *Air Facilities Data-Laos.*

Palace Hotel, Dalat (BP 23-24?)
See Dalat Palace Hotel. Tuyen Duc Pr, II Corps.

Palm Beach, Operation (n/a)
6Jan-31May67. 9th Inf Div op. 570 NVA/VC KIA, per *VN Order of Battle*, pp 9-14. Dinh Tuong Pr, IV Corps.

Palm Springs, FSB (XT 913-167)
Apx 7 km WNW Bien Hoa, 20 km NNE Saigon, 5 km due E Phu Loi AF, and 11 km N Di An. 1st Inf Div, Jan-Mar69. On *Low Level Hell's* TAOR map. Bien Hoa Pr?, III Corps.

Palms, LZ (YD 040-584)
Overlooked Song Cam Lo/QL-9, apx 8 km due W Cam Lo, 21 km W Dong Ha and 9 km NW Mai Loc. Apr70 XXIV Corps grid per Don Armstrong. Quang Tri Pr, I Corps.

Pam, FSB (YS 540-770)
A.k.a. FSB Terry? Along LTL-25, Apx 3 km E Xa Binh Gia, 8 km E LTL-2 and 15 km NE Nui Dat/Luscombe AF. Jan68. Phuoc Tuy Pr, III Corps.

Pam, LZ (BR 902-730)
Apx 4 km due N Phu My, 23 km SSE Bong Son and 2 km W QL-1. Oct66. Binh Dinh Pr, II Corps.

Pam, LZ? (YA 611-525)
At S entrance to Plei Trap Valley, apx 4 km from Cambodia, 23 km W Old Plei Djereng and 7 km due E Phum Hay (C). Jan66. Kontum Pr, II Corps.

Pamela, FSB (XT 423-974)
Apx 12 km NE Katum AF (SVN), 4 km NE Phum Beong Chruong Kraom and 5 km SW Phum Dong (both in Cambodia). Cambodia.

Pamela, FSB (XT 546-229)
Apx 12 km NW Cu Chi and 7 km SE Xom Rung Cay. Sep67. Hau Nghia Pr, III Corps.

Pamela, FSB (YS 483-924)
Just S the Suoi Ran and SW the Suoi Nhac Rivers, NE Rte 2 and SW Cam Tiem, apx 25 km NNE Nui Dat and 12 km E FSB Wattle. 3 RAR ANZAC HQ and A/3d Cav here during Op Overlord, 5-14Jun71. On 1ATF NCO trng map per John Hollett. Long Khanh Pr, III Corps.

Pamela, LZ (ZA 065-701)
Apx 6 km NW Plei Mrong and 26 km SW Kontum. Sep69. Kontum Pr, II Corps.

Panama Control (n/a)
See Glossary.

Panther, FSB/LZ (XT 130-940)
Apx 13 km NNE Thien Ngon AF, 20 km WNW Katum AF, 5 km NE FSB Mustang, 3 km E Cambodia, and 3 km NE junction of QL-22/Rte 246. 3d/21st Inf here, during Op Junction City 22Feb-17Mar6. Tay Ninh Pr, III Corps.

Panther, FSB (YD 787-167)
Along N side of Hwy 547 between Eagle and Pohl bridge, apx 1.5 km WNW Camp Eagle and 4 km ENE Pohl Bridge. Likely built by elements of 3d Bde/82d Abn during Op Carentan, possibly Mar68. 101st Abn inactive FSB grid per Don Armstrong. Possibly a.k.a. FSB Panther 1? Thua Thien Pr, I Corps.

Panther, FSB (YS 465-845)
Apx 17 km NNE Nui Dat, 7 km ESE FSB Coolah, 1 km NE Camp Lynch and 1 km E LTL-2. On 1ATF NCO trng map per John Hollett. Phuoc Tuy Pr, III Corps.

Panther, LZ (BR 958-970)
Apx 8 km ESE LZ English, 10 km ENE Bong Son AF and 3 km S the An Lao River. Oct66. Binh Dinh Pr, II Corps.

Panther, LZ (ZA 156-065?)
If grid correct, was apx 41 km SSW Pleiku, 22 km WNW Phu Nhon AF and just E Plei Me SF Camp. Also listed at ZB 156-065, and unknown which grid is correct? May-Jul69. Pleiku Pr?, II Corps.

Panther, LZ (ZB 156-065?)
If grid correct, was along QL-14, apx 2 km N Tri Dab, 22 km NNW Kontum and 13 km SSE Dien Binh. Also listed at ZA 156-065, and unknown which grid is correct? May-Jul69. Kontum Pr?, II Corps.

Panther I, FSB (YD 787-157)
Along S side of road between Camp Eagle and Pohl Bridge, apx 3 km W Camp Rodriguez, 1.5 km WSW Camp Eagle and 3.3 km NE Pohl Bridge. Built by elements of 2d/505th Inf, 3d Bde/82d Abn during Op Carentan, between 8Ma4-31Mar68. Bty A, 2d/321st Arty fired supt for 2d/505th from this site. Thua Thien Pr, I Corps.

Panther II, FSB (YD 798-107)
A.k.a. FSB Arrow and Nui Dong Hoai. Apx 5 km SE Pohl Bridge, 1 km NW FSB Arsenal and 10 km WSW Phu Bai. Also listed at YD 808-065. Data per Butch Sincock. Jan-Apr69. See FSB Arrow. Thua Thien Pr, I Corps.

Panther III, FSB (YD 810-060)
A.k.a. Hill 46. On E bank of Song Ta Trach River apx 2 km due S FSB Arsenal, 15 km SSE Hue and 11 km SW Phu Bai. 2d/505th Inf and 2/321st Arty, 82d Abn here during Op Mot. Attacked by 50-man sapper unit night of 29Aug68, who penetrated wire under barrage of RPGs. Hand-to-hand fighting ensued, with 8 US KIA and 21 WIA. Data per *All the Way-The 3d Brigade, 82d Abn Div, Vietnam, 1968*, pp 33-35. Other data puts it on site of what later became FSB Arsenal, at YD 812-080, so base may have been moved? Also listed at YD 808-078. See FSB Arsenal. Thua Thien Pr, I Corps.

Panther III, FSB (YD 808-078)
See FSB Arsenal Thua Thien Pr, I Corps.

Panzer, FSB (n/a)
No data. 10th Cav, 4th Div here, per Bob Patsfield. Possibly Binh Dinh or Pleiku Pr, II Corps.

Papa, LZ (BR)
Near Luong Tho, apx 2 km NW LZ 4, some 2 km W QL-1 and 12 km due N Bong Son. Used during Op Masher-White Wing, 28Jan-6Mar66. 1st/7th Cav. Discussion of Ops Masher/White Wing and this LZ in *A Contagion of War* vol, *Vietnam Experience* series, pp 32-48, with map showing site at p 38. Binh Dinh Pr, II Corps.

Papa CAC (YD or XD?)
See CAC Listings. I Corps.

Papa CAP (n/a)
See CAP Papa listings. I Corps.

Paradise, LZ (BS 700-967)
On Batangan Peninsula and along cliff or bluff overlooking ocean S of Chu Lai, apx 2 km from coast, 10 km N Pinkville, 5 km NNW An Cuong, 11 km W QL-1 and 24 km NNE Quang Ngai. To its W about 1.2 km was Le Thuy 2, and to E was Phuoc Thuan 1 (home of CAP 1-3-5 Team). Co of 5th/46th Inf, 196th LIB possibly took over this LZ in '68? Data per CAP 1-3-5 Webpage at: www.capmarine.com/cap1-3-5/1-3-5log.htm. Apr70 XXIV Corps grid per Don Armstrong. Also listed at BS 705-972. Quang Ngai Pr, I Corps.

Parakeet, LZ (XD 987-343)
In valley, apx 14 km S Ca Lu, 19 km WSW Ba Long AF, 8 km ENE Lang Klung and 17 km WSW Khe Sanh CB. Apr70 XXIV Corps grid per Don Armstrong. Quang Tri Pr, I Corps.

Parakeet Flights (n/a)
See Glossary.

Parasol/Switchback, Operation (n/a)
See Glossary.

Paratroop Mafia (TJ 94-67)
See Glossary.

Parfums, Riviere des (YD 8-3)
See Perfume River, Song Huu Trach and Song Ta Trach. Thua Thien Pr, I Corps.

Paricutin, USS (n/a)
AE-18. Aux Explosive.

Paris, FSB (XD 808-237)
In Vietnam Salient, 5 km SW Lang Chei, 3 km from Laos, 20 km SSW Khe Sanh CB, 62 km SW Quang Tri and 13 km WSW Lang Klung. 101st Abn inactive FSB grid per Don Armstrong. Quang Tri Pr, I Corps.

Paris, FSB (YT 13-09)
Apx 13 km ESE Bien Hoa AB, 6 km ESE Plantation AF and 27 km NE Saigon. 5th/12th Inf, 4th/12th Inf and 3d/7th Inf, 199th LIB. Bien Hoa or Gia Dinh Pr, III Corps.

Paris, LZ (BS 480-828)
A.k.a. LZ Clemson. Apx 3 km N Ba Gia AF, 3 km NW Xuan Hoa, an 18 km NW Quang Ngai. Apr70 XXIV Corps grid per Don Armstrong. Also at same grid on Americal Assn list. Quang Ngai Pr, I Corps.

Paris, LZ ? (ZA 025-057)
Apx 15 km ENE Chu Pong Mtn, 45 km SSW Pleiku13 km due W Plei Me SF Camp. Nov65. Listed simply as Paris, and nature of site unknown. Pleiku Pr, II Corps.

Paris Control (n/a)
See Glossary.

Paris Peace Accords (n/a)
See Glossary.

Park, LZ (YS 716-755)
Apx 22 km WSW Xa Binh Gia, 20 km SW Nui Be and 9 km NE Xuyen Moc. Apr66. Phuoc Tuy Pr, III Corps.

Park County, USS (n/a)
LST-1077. USN Landing Ship, Tank. SVN service with 9th Inf Div/MRF. See www.mrfa.org. III/IV Corps?

Parker, FSB (XS 200-510)
Along QL-4, apx 2.5 km W Lai Cay and 31 km WNW My Tho. Apr68. Dinh Tuong Pr, IV Corps.

Parramatta (n/a)
Australian Escort ship serving under US 7th Flt.

Parrot, LZ/FSB (XD 972-412)
Apx 12 km due E Khe Sanh CB, 8 km SSW Ca Lu and 2 km SE Lang Ruou/QL-9. Apr70 XXIV Corps grid per Don Armstrong. Quang Tri Pr, I Corps.

Parrot, LZ (YD 147-773)
Along S bank of Ben Hai River, apx 30 km NNW Quang Tri and 12 km WSW mouth of Ben Hai River. May67. Quang Tri Pr, I Corps.

Parrot's Beak, The (XT 30-93)
Distinct Cambodian/SVN border feature apx 50 km due W Saigon and jutting well into SVN. Offered NVA/VC a major sanctuary and convenient access to major population

center of SVN. Invaded by ARVN forces during joint US/ARVN incursion into Vietnam May-Jun70. Grid is at tip of beak. Kien Tuong and Long An Pr, III Corps.

Parrot's Beak, The (AU 83-08)
See Mui Chon May Dong. Thua Thien Pr, I Corps.

Parry, FSB (XT 490-750)
Along Rte 244, apx 7 km S its junction with Rte 244 some 30 km W An Loc, 11 km ENE FSB Gold, 15 km NW Minh Thanh and 7 km W the Song Saigon. Built 22-23Mar67 by 173d Abn during Op Junction City. 173d was attached to 1st Inf Div 20Mar67 with mission to secure staging area at Minh Thanh and conduct airmobile assaults into eastern War Zone C, beginning 23 March. From 23Mar-7Apr, the Bde worked SW, W and NW Parry and from 9-11Apr67 worked to its S and SE. Data per *Cedar Falls-Junction City*, p 126. Tay Ninh Pr, III Corps.

Parsons, USS (n/a)
DD-949, per Ralph Fries.

Parsons, USS (n/a)
DDG-33. Guided-Missile DD, per Ralph Fries.

Partisans, Pass of (WL 0-5/UK 0-1)
Col des Partesans and Col des Partisans. NIMA data. NVN.

Partridge, LZ (AT 998-602)
Along RR tracks, apx 16 km S Da Nang AB and 4 km NNW Dien Ban. Oct69. Quang Nam Pr, I Corps.

Paseau Airfield (SG 94-95)
LS-315. CIA/SF, per *Air Facilities Data-Laos.*

Pass, LZ (BS 492-039)
Apx 27 km WSW Thuan An, 38 km W LZ English and 26 km SSE Gia Vuc AF. Mar66. Binh Dinh Pr, II Corps.

Pass of Cannons (YD 1-5)
Col de Canons. NIMA data. Quang Tri Pr, I Corps.

Pass of Vents (WK 9-7)
A.k.a. Deo Vents and Col des Vents. NIMA data. NVN.

Passe des Hydress (YH 2-9)
Hydress Pass. NIMA data. NVN.

Passport, FSB (XD 796-227)
A.k.a. LZ Passport. In SW edge of Vietnam Salient, apx 63 km WSW Quang Tri, 3 km SSE, FSB Paris, 32 km SW Vandegrift CB and 3 km W of Laos. On map at p 65, *US Marines in Vietnam-1969*. USMC '69. 101st Abn inactive FSB grid per Don Armstrong. Quang Tri Pr, I Corps.

Pat (various)
See Patt entries.

Pat, FSB (XT 680-990)
Apx 10 km SSW Loc Ninh AF and 3 km W QL-13. Jan68. Binh Long Pr, III Corps.

Pat, FSB (XT 902-609)
Apx 6 km W Chon Thanh AF and 21 km NE Dau Tieng. 1st Inf Div, 68. Data per Dan Gillotti, 15th Arty Assn. Phuoc Long Pr, III Corps.

Pat, FSB (YS 613-815)
Apx 32 km NE Nui Dat, 17 km ENE Duc Tanh/Rte-2 and14 km N FSB Discovery. Described as old, mosquito infested FSB. 161 Bty, RNZA (Andrew's Bty 18Sep69-6Sep70) FSB set here 16Feb-11Mar70. 106 Bty RAR also here 13Feb70. Pr, III Corps. On 1ATF NCO trng map per John Hollett. Also listed at YS 61-82. Phuoc Tuy or Long Khanh Pr, III Corps.

Pat, LZ (BS 330-475)
Just N Lang Baout, apx 40 km SW Quang Ngai and on ridgeline 2,300 meters from abnd airstrip at Ta Ma in Song Re Valley. 2d/8th Cav, 1st Cav CA'd her here 9Aug67, with 2 helos shot down in process. Grid per Dan Gillotti, 15th Arty Assn. Quang Ngai Pr?, I Corps.

Patch, LZ (BS 438-574)
Apx 12 km NW Minh Long AF, 26 km SW Quang Ngai and 13 km SSE Ha Thanh AF. Apr70 XXIV Corps grid per Don Armstrong. Also listed at BS 436-635 on Americal Assn FSB list. Quang Ngai Pr, I Corps.

Patch Compound (XS 040-331)
USAF cantonment at Vinh Long AF, apx 95 km SW Saigon. Named to honor Capt. Donald C Patch, USAF, 602d Fighter Sqd, KIA 2Oct65, A1E crash 32 km W Qui Nhon. Data *per Vietnam Military Lore, 1959-1973.* Vinh Long Pr, IV Corps.

Patch, Gen., USS MSTS (n/a)
A.k.a. *USS Patch.* Troop transport that saw duty from WWII to Vietnam. Carried troops to SVN in at least '66-67. In Dec66, it carried 1st Bde of 9th Inf Div from Oakland Army Terminal on 2 week trip to SVN, stopping at White Beach Okinawa en route, then offloading at Vung Tau. For detailed look at voyage, see *Two Weeks Before The Mast*, article by Michael Mark in Mar2000 issue of *Military* Mag, pp 5-8.

Patricia, LZ (BR 383-425)
Apx 10 km WSW An Khe, 6 km SE An Dinh/QL-19. Aug69-Jan70. 10th Cav, 4th Div here, per Bob Patsfield. Binh Dinh Pr, II Corps.

Patriots League, Sacred Sword of (n/a)
See Project Urgency in Glossary.

Patrol Base Austin (XT 2-3?)
See Austin, FSB. Tay Ninh Pr, III Corps.

Patrol Base Blue (XT 258-290)
See Blue, FSB. Kien Tuong Pr, IV Corps.

Patrol Base Dong Tien (XT 609-247)
See Dong Tien Patrol Base. Binh Duong Pr, III Corps.

Patrol Base Dragon (XT 636-286)
See Dragon, FSB. Binh Duong Pr, III Corps.

Patrol Base Harris (XT 417-126)
See Harris, Patrol Base. Hau Nghia Pr, III Corps.

Patrol Base Hunsley (XT 597-270)
See Hunsley, PB. Binh Duong Pr, III Corps.

Patrol Base J (XT 544-210)
See J, Patrol Base. Hau Nghia Pr, III Corps.

Patrol Base Kotrc (XT 358-148)
See Kotrc, Patrol Base. Hau Nghia Pr, III Corps.

Patrol Base Mole City (XT 1-3?)
See FSB Mole City. Tay Ninh Pr, III Corps.

Patrol Base Rittgers (XT 358-148)
See Rittgers, PB. Hau Nghia Pr, III Corps.

Patrol Bases, Instant (n/a)
See Instant Patrol Bases in Glossary.

Patsy, LZ (ZA 080-215)
Apx 2 km S LZ Fig, at S edge of Xuong Kuang, apx 29 km SW Pleiku and 7 km SSW the Oasis. Per Dick Arnold, 4th Div op rpts indicate Patsy was demolished by 2d/35th Inf, 5Aug69. A Bty, 6th/29th Arty here Dec69. 31Jan70 grid per Jim Henderson. Pleiku Pr, II Corps.

Patt, FSB/LZ (ZA 097-834)
Apx 15 km WSW Kontum, 2 km E the Krong Poko River and 9 km due S Polei Krong AF. Apparently near Dak Bla River. 4th Div and 173d Abn AO. Kontum Pr, II Corps. [408]

Pattani (QH 3-5)
SF camp or AO per *SF Order of Battle*. Thailand.

Pattani Airfield (QH 3-5)
At 6°47'00"N-101°09'00"E. NIMA data. Feb67 Natl Geo map. El. 30'. Thailand.

Pattaya (QQ 0-1)
Pattaya Beach in listed grid square. SF camp or AO per *SF Order of Battle.* Thailand.

Patti, FSB (XT 226-873)
Apx 12 km WSW Katum AF, 35 km due N Tay Ninh and 14 km S Cambodia. Tay Ninh Pr, III Corps.

Patti Mission, The (WJ 88-25)
See Glossary.

Patton, FSB/LZ (BR 823-828)
Apx 3 km ESE Ha Tay AF and 14 km SSW Bong Son. Oct66. Binh Dinh Pr, II Corps.

Patton, FSB (XT 580-190)
Along Rte 237 apx 7 km NW Cu Chi CB and immed E Patton II. Was also near Gia Be and on N edge of Trung Lap. Had open field to its N (Trung Lap sat on rising curve coming up from small river, so outer bunkers of Patton II had slight high-ground advantage). Built in haste and to contour of site, bunkers varied widely in shape and meandered through base in random pattern that was not circular. Cmd bunkers were scattered throughout, and its 6(?) tube, 155mm SP howitzer Bty could barely maneuver within site. As a result and because it was too close to ville, Patton II was built and this site demo'd May/Jun69. Engrs designed Patton II as "beautiful, symmetrical circle." Cited in *1st Cav Op Rpt, May-Jul70*, p 38, and 2d/7th Cav Unit History '70-71, p 4, per Peter Cole. Info/grid per Kirk Ramsey, 2d/14/th Inf/25th Inf Div. Appears Patton, I, and II were always in same general location and likely given numerical variations to mark reincarnations; a common practice in III Corps. Oct68-Sep69. Also listed at XT 592-216, 492-214, 692-214, 582-195, 590-210, and 593-217? Hau Nghia Pr, III Corps. [409]

Patton, LZ (YD 286-184)
Apx 17 km SE Ba Long AF and 22 km SSE Quang Tri. Apr70 XXIV Corps grid per Don Armstrong. Thua Thien Pr, I Corps.

Patton I, FSB (XT 592-214)
See FSB Patton. Nov68-Jan70. Hau Nghia Pr, III Corps.

Patton I, FSB (XT 492-214)
See FSB Patton at XT 595. Nov68-Jan70 Also listed at XT 592-214, and 593-217. Hau Nghia Pr, III Corps.

Patton II, FSB (XT 582-195)
See FSB Patton. Nov68-Jul69. Also listed at XT 580-190 and 593-217. Hau Nghia Pr, III Corps.

Patton II, FSB (XT 595-215)
Along TL-7A, apx 9 km NW Cu Chi, 8 km due S Ben Suc. Constructed or reconstructed May or Aug69 (by A/2d/14th Inf and others inc E Co's 4.2" mortar section) to replace Patton I due to its poor design and close proximity to Trung Lap. Built as "a beautiful, symmetrical circle," with 24 fighting bunkers. Also had six-155mm SP guns. 2d/49th ARVN Rgt and 1st Cav also here? Data per Kirk Ramsey, 2d/14th Inf/25th Inf Div. Nov68-Jan69. Also listed at XT 582-195 and 593-217. Hau Nghia Pr, III Corps. [410]

Patty (n/a)
6Apr70, XXIV Corps proposed Americal FSB name.

Patty, FSB (XT 226-873)
See Patti. Tay Ninh Pr, III Corps.

Paul, LZ (BS 912-172)
Apx 4 km N Gia An, 23 km NNE Bong Son and 1 km W QL-1. Feb-May67. Also listed at BS 920-214. Binh Dinh Pr, II Corps.

Paul, LZ (XT 283-670)
Along LTL-4, apx 9 km N Nui Ba Den and 23 km SSW Katum AF. Apr67. Also listed at XT 281-685. Tay Ninh Pr, III Corps.

Paul Doumer Bridge (WJ 89-27)
A.k.a. the Long Bien Bridge. 5,532' railroad bridge built as premier achievement of French rail system at start of 20th Century. During War, provided Hanoi's sole means of rail supply/transportation, as it was only major bridge over Red River within 50 km city. Although heavily defended with arsenal of anti-aircraft guns and SAM missiles, was finally destroyed 11Aug67 with 100 tons of 3,000 lb. bombs delivered by F-105 Thuds/F-4 Phantoms of 355th TFW out of Takli AB (Thailand). During that famous mission, MIG fighters flew within 200' under attacking force but did not fire upon it. NVN.

Paul Milius, USS (n/a)
DDG-69, Guided Missile Destroyer. SVN

Paul Revere, USS (n/a)
APA-248. Amphib Attack Transport, per Ralph Fries.

Paul Revere II, Operation (n/a)
1-25Aug66. 1st Cav/ARVN op. 809 rptd NVA/VC KIA, per *Vietnam Order of Battle*, pp 9-14. Pleiku Pr, II Corps.

Paul Revere IV, Operation (n/a)
18Oct-30Dec66. 4th Div's 1st major op(?) of war. 1st Cav and 25th Inf Div elements also participated. 977 rptd NVA/VC KIA, per *Vietnam Order of Battle*, pp 9-14. Near Cambodia, Pleiku Pr, II Corps.

Paul Revere/Than Phong 14, Operation (n/a)
10 May-30Jul66. 3d Bde/25th Inf Div and VN forces screening Cambodian border. 546 rptd NVA/VC KIA, per *Vietnam Order of Battle*, pp 9-14. Pleiku Pr, II Corps.

Paula, LZ (BR 489-408)
Apx 5 km S An Khe/QL-19, and 21 km due W Binh Khe. C Bty, 2d/9th Arty here Feb70. Name/grid per Jim Claeys. Also listed at BR 489-488, a site 8 km N listed grid. Listed grid thought to be correct. Binh Dinh Pr, II Corps.

Pause, LZ (YA 868-889)
Apx 37 km due W Kontum, 17 km WSW Polei Kleng and 7 km SSE Polei Meo. 3d/8th Inf here Feb69, per Jan-Mar69 1st/35th Inf Daily Logs. Name/grid per Dick Arnold. Kontum Pr, II Corps.

Pave Way (n/a)
See Glossary.

Pavie Track/Trail (TJ)
Rugged trail originating at Dien Bien Phu and leading W through wilderness N of Lai Chau (Thai Capitol of '50's). An extension of Rte 41 which ended in Muong Thanh Valley (TJ 93-60) where track began. In 1887, named to honor himself by Auguste Pavie, 1st Gov of DBP. NVN.

PAVN Hospital Fight (ZA 042-026)
See Hospital Fight. Pleiku Pr, II Corps.

Pawai Airfield (PS 7-3)
At 14°46'00"N-100°39'00"E. NIMA data. Do not confuse with Pa Wai AFs (QU 1-8, and QU 2-7). Thailand.

Pawai, Camp (PS 7-3)
SF camp or AO per *SF Order of Battle.* Thailand.

Pawnee, FSB? (XT 921-024)
On N edge of Thu Duc, apx 11 km NE Tan Son Nhut AB. Dec68-Mar69. Simply listed as Pawnee, and presumed to have been LZ or FSB. Gia Dinh Pr, III Corps.

Pawnee, USS (n/a)
Commercial contract ocean tugboat of MSC. See Evacuation of Da Nang.

Payable Hill (XD 979-583)
Described by Tom Mosher as being along road that lead N from Thon Cay Muon at QL-9, and apx 2.3 km due N the Rockpile. He also thinks it may have been named after his CAP Team's call-sign. Apparently L/3d/3d Mar here at one point also. Quang Tri Pr, I Corps.

Payne Compound (BT 31-19?)
MAAG Detachment Cmpd at Tam Ky. Named to honor MAAG Advisor to 2d ARVN Inf Div, KIA by rifle fire while on patrol with the ARVN. Plaque on entrance gate to this facility read, "*Erected by people of Quang Tin Province to honor Captain Lloyd A. Payne killed in action on 15 Dec 63, near Tien Phuoc, QT Pr, RVN.*" [411] Per *Vietnam Military Lore, 1959-1973*. Quang Tin Pr, I Corps.

PCF-15 (n/a)
Patrol Craft, Fast. See *Point Welcome*.

PCF-19 (n/a)
Patrol Craft, Fast. US Swift Boat hit by three rockets and sunk at 0100 hrs 16Aug66. Apparently attack took place just N the DMZ? 4 US and 1 VNN crew KIA. Incident discussed in *Brown Water, Black Berets*, p 114. Market Time TF-115. NVN waters?

PCF-29 (n/a)
Patrol Craft, Fast. Sunk 16Aug68, after being hit by 3 rockets from US Acft, w/5 US KIA. See *Point Welcome*.

Peach (n/a)
See Glossary.

Peach, LZ (XT 267-713)
Along LTL-24, apx 11 km N Nui Ba Den and 19 km SSW Katum AF. Feb-Mar67. Tay Ninh Pr, III Corps.

Peach, LZ (YA?)
No data. Per Peter Cole, cited in Robert Towles' (D/2d/7th Cav) LZ Albany research. Possibly Pleiku Pr?, II Corps.

Peacock, LZ (BS 429-021)
Remote site was apx 38 km due W LZ English, 27 km SSE Gia Vuc AF and 26 km WSW Thua An. Mar66. Binh Dinh Pr, II Corps.

Peacock, LZ (XD 959-379)
Apx 11 km ESE Khe Sanh CB, 4 km due S Lang Ruou/QL-9 and 11 km SSW Ca Lu. Apr70 XXIV Corps grid per Don Armstrong. Quang Tri Pr, I Corps.

Peacock, USS (n/a)
MSC-198. Minesweeper, Coastal, per Ralph Fries.

Peacock, USS (n/a)
1st US Navy ship to visit Vietnam. In 1832, carried Edmund Roberts on trade mission for President Jackson which was also 1st US diplomatic mission to VN. Roberts was reportedly denied entry because his letter of intro from Jackson lacked Emperor Minh Mang's full name, improperly spelled country's name, and because Roberts' own name and titles exceeded those of Minh Mang! Roberts returned in 1836, but soon fell seriously ill and left for Macao before completing negotiations, where he died 20 days later. See *Constitution, USS,* and *Boxer*. [412]

Peacock Control (n/a)
See Glossary.

Peak, LZ (BQ 983-384)
Apx 10 km NNW Buon Ho AF, 38 km NNE Ban Me Thuot and 2 km W QL-14. 1st Cav. Name/grid per Dan Gillotti, 15th Arty Assn. Darlac Pr, II Corps.

Peam Amleang Airfield (n/a)
Apx 65 km WNW Phnom Penh. El. 250'. Cambodia.

Peam Lovek Airfield (n/a)
Along Tonle Sap River apx 35 km NNW Phnom Penh on Feb67 Natl Geo map. El. 25'. Cambodia.

Peanuts, LZ/FSB (XD 811-395)
Apx 5 km SW Khe Sanh and 4 km N Lang Vie. *The Final Formation* indicates site was used by 1st Cav Arty FSB during Op Pegasus. M/3d/4th Mar suffered 3 KIA when apx 100 rnds 130mm NVA arty hit them here, 27May68. [413] Also listed at XD 810-392 on XXIV Corps index of 6Apr70. Quang Tri Pr, I Corps.

Pear, FSB (BT 372-054)
Apx 18 km SSE Tam Ky, 9 km SSE FSB Plum and 15 km due W Chu Lai. 196th LIB here during Op Benton, Aug67. 2d/9th Arty here supt 2d/1stInf, 196th LIB, 14-30Aug67. Name and Grid per Les Hines. Quang Tin Pr, I Corps.

Pearl, LZ (BR 837-637)
Apx 14 km NE Vinh Thanh Ville, 33 km NE An Khe and 7 km SW Hoi San. Oct66. Binh Dinh Pr, II Corps.

Pearl, LZ (XD 896-678)
In DMZ about 1 km S the NVN border, apx 23 km WNW Cam Lo and 22 km NNW Ca Lu. Apr70 XXIV Corps grid per Don Armstrong. Quang Tri Pr, I Corps.

Pearson, LZ (AR 85-14?)
A.k.a. LZ Pierson. Map at 15th Arty website indicates Pierson was near (or a.k.a.) LZ St. George (AR 854-144), and near intersection of QL-14 and road that led SE to Cheo Reo/Hou Bon, roughly 17 km N Phu Nhon AF, 32 km SSE Pleiku and 20 km SSE Camp Enari. 4th Div AO, '70. Pleiku Pr, II Corps. [414]

Pearson, LZ (ZB 125-163)
See Mud, LZ. Kontum Pr, II Corps.

Pearson Community Centre (YS 43-67)
Per Eddie Tricker tells, was at 1ATF HQ at Nui Dat and also known as Pogo's Paradise. "Within its confines were situated a barber's shop; food and drink shops and a PX-type shop where cameras, watches and like were available." Phuoc Tuy Pr, III Corps.

Pechabun (QU 2-1)
A.k.a. Camp Pine and Petchabun. SF camp per *SF Order of Battle*. Thailand.

Pechures, Iles de (CP 1-3)
Fishermen's Island. Khanh Hoa Pr, II Corps.

Pecos, FSB (YT 504-262)
Along the Song La Naa, apx 22 km WSW Vo Dat AF and 16 km NNE Xuan Loc. Jul71. Long Khanh Pr, II Corps.

Pedro, FSB (YD 294-485?)
If grid correct, was apx 4 km WSW La Vang AF, 5 km SW Quang Tri and 3 km NW Thon Nhu Le. Also listed at YD 250-484? XXIV Corps grid. 1st Cav and 101st Abn possibly here. Also listed at YD 248-488, 243-483 and 245-582? Quang Tri Pr, I Corps.

Pedro, LZ (YD 250-484)
Apx 8 km WSW Quang Tri and 18 km ESE Vandegrift CB. 1st/8th Cav, here '68. 1st Mar Div, '69. Also listed at YD 245-484 and 255-485 in 1st/8th Cav Staff Daily Journal of Nov67-Nov68 and in another rpt at YD 294-485? Quang Tri Pr, I Corps.

Pee Wee, LZ (BS 736-338)
Apx 7 km SW Duc Pho AF and QL-1. 1st Cav. Name/grid per Dan Gillotti, 15th Arty. Quang Ngai Pr, I Corps.

Peeler Compound (XS 8-9)
In Cholon, a suburb of Saigon. Named to honor SSgt Glover A. Peeler III, USAF, 377th Trans Sqdn, KIA 19Feb67 by VC terrorist grenade thrown from passing motor scooter. Data per *Vietnam Military Lore, 1959-1973*. Gia Dinh Pr, III Corps.

Peg, LZ (ZT 015-926)
Remote site apx 14 km NNW Tan Phat AF and 23 km W Huong Lam. Feb67. Lam Dong Pr, II Corps.

Pegasus/Lam Son 207, Operation (n/a)
1-15Apr68. US 1st Cav/ARVN Abn and USMC op to relieve siege of Khe Sanh CB. Total of 17 Bns involved. 1,044 rptd NVA/VC KIA, per *Vietnam Order of Battle*, pp 9-14. Quang Tri Pr, I Corps.

Peggy, FSB (YS 436-834)
On N edge of Cu Bi Rubber Plantation, apx 6 km NNW Duc Tanh, 3 km SW FSB Kylie, 16 km due N Nui Dat and 2 km W Rte-2. Unusual in that it was not named for female, but rather to honor LTC Peggy O'Neill, CO of newly arrived 8 RAR, Nov69. 161 Bty, RNZA (Andrew's Bty 18Sep-6Sep70) FSB set here 11Dec69-10Jan70. On 1ATF NCO trng map per John Hollett. Also listed at YS 43-83. Phuoc Tuy Pr, III Corps.

Peggy, FSB (YT 860-330)
Apx 7 km WSW Tanh Linh AF, 45 km ENE Xuan Loc and 17 km SE Vo Dat. 1st Cav? Nov70. Binh Tuy Pr, III Corps.

Peking II, LZ/FSB (XD 936-475)
Apx 7 km W Ca Lu and 10 km NE Khe Sanh CB. Apr70 XXIV Corps grid per D. Armstrong. Quang Tri Pr, I Corps.

Peking, LZ/FSB (XD 943-476)
Apx 6 km W Ca Lu and 11 km NE Khe Sanh CB. Apr70 XXIV Corps grid per D. Armstrong. Quang Tri Pr, I Corps.

Pelican, LZ (XD 923-375)
Apx 9 km ESE Khe Sanh CB, 3 km S QL-9 and 13 km SW Ca Lu. Apr70 XXIV Corps grid per Don Armstrong. Quang Tri Pr, I Corps.

Pen, LZ (BR 733-473)
Apx 16 km WNW Phu Cat AB and 26 km E An Khe. Oct65. Binh Dinh Pr, II Corps.

Pencil, LZ (XD 769-364)
Apx 4 km due E Bao Lao, 1.5 km N QL-1 and 10 km WSW Khe Sanh CB. Apr70 XXIV Corps grid per Don Armstrong. Quang Tri Pr, I Corps.

Pendleton, LZ (YS 350-710)
Apx 7 km WNW Nui Dat/Luscombe AF and 5 km N peak Nui Thi. Mar66. Phuoc Tuy Pr, III Corps.

Penguin, LZ (BS 399-061)
Remote site apx 33 km ESE Plateau Gi AF, 22 km S Gia Vuc AF and 48 km W to WNW LZ English. Mar66. Binh Dinh Pr, II Corps.

Penguin, LZ (YD 900-224)
In coastal sands, apx 15 km E Hue Citadel AF and 7 km due N Phu Bai AF. Mar68. Thua Thien Pr, I Corps.

Penitencier, Baie du (XQ 7-5)
A.k.a. Vinh Con Son. Bay at 8°40'N-106°38'E. On NC48-11 JOG. NVN.

Penney, LZ (ZA 118-722)
See LZ Penny at grid. Kontum Pr, II Corps.

Pennsylvania BOQ (XS 8-9)
At 159-161 Pham Ngu Lao St., Saigon. Per R. Bows' *Vietnam Military Lore, 1959-1973.* Gia Dinh Pr, III Corps.

Penny, FSB (YS 257-687)
On E side of QL-15, apx 18 km NE Nui Dat, 2 km S FSB Stingray and 13.5 km due W FSB Weir. On 1ATF NCO trng map per John Hollett. Phuoc Tuy Pr, III Corps.

Penny, LZ/FSB (ZA 118-722)
Apx 3 km WSW Plei Te, 21 km SSW Kontum and 26 km NNE Pleiku. Per SSgt Lafe Baehr, 3d/8th Inf, after running several patrols off this base 9May69, it came under heavy ground attack by NVA using satchel charges/grenades. Several NVA penetrated NW corner of perimeter and Baehr's squad then took back and held the NW corner bunker until 1st light. "Needless to say, we didn't sleep the following night" he adds. Jay Philbrick, 3d/12th Inf, who was here 21-25Jun69, recalls that it was hell hole of action, near Plei Te. After 3-day period of heavy contact, their Recon Plt was ambushed 13Jun69, and 2 were Cos sent to rescue it (inc D/3d/12th Inf?). 10th Cav here as well. 4th Div AO. Grid per S-3 Daily Journal/Op rpts of 31Jul-1Sep69, courtesy Bob Patsfield. Also listed at ZA 121-725. Kontum Pr, II Corps. [415]

Penny Arcade (BS 3-4 to 3-5)
In the Song Ve River Valley and running between BS 348-450 to BS 348-510, roughly 40 km SW Quang Ngai. Legendary as helicopter shooting gallery of US helos. Americal List. Quang Ngai Pr, I Corps.

Pensacola, LZ (YD 199-278)
Apx 1 km SE peak Dong Ba Le Mtn (Hill 1102), 12 km SSE Ba Long AF and 28 km SSW Quang Tri. Apr70 XXIV Corps grid per Don Armstrong. Quang Tri Pr, I Corps.

Pentagon East (XS 825-953)
At Tan Son Nhut AB. Nickname for HQ MACV, Saigon. Constructed as network of two-story pre-fabricated bldgs that provided air-conditioned workspace for 4,000 personnel. Also inc mortar shelters, security fences and guard towers. See MACV Cmpd #1 and Keopler Cmpd. Gia Dinh Pr, III Corps.

Pentalateral Agreement (n/a)
See SOFA in Glossary.

People's Anti-Corruption Movement (n/a)
See Glossary.

People's Road, Operation (n/a)
See Truong Cong Dinh, Operation.

People's Self Defense Force (n/a)
See Glossary.

Peoria, USS (n/a)
LST 1183. See Frequent Wind.

Pepper, FSB (YD 340-028)
On Dong So Mtn on NW edge of A Shau Valley, apx 3 km ENE Dong Ap Bia (Hamburger Hill), 45 km WSW Quang Tri, 23 km NW A Sap and 10 km due W FSB Eagle's Nest. 1st Cav here '68. Cited in *Anatomy of a Division*, per Peter Cole. Also listed at YD 355-027, a site 1.5 km E listed grid? 101st Abn inactive FSB grid per Don Armstrong. Thua Thien Pr, I Corps.

Pepper, LZ (BS 492-725)
Apx 7 km S Ba Gia AF, 12 km due W Quang Ngai AF and 15 km due W Quang Ngai. Also listed at BS 491-729, and by arty ORLL at BS 496-716. Map is L-7014-6739-3. Apr70 XXIV Corps grid per Don Armstrong. Quang Ngai Pr, I Corps.

Pepper Grinder (n/a)
See Twenty Mike-Mike in Glossary.

Perch, LZ (BR 390-858)
Apx 42 km NNW An Khe, 41 km W Ha Tay AF and 21 km N Kannack AF. Dec65. Binh Dinh Pr, II Corps.

Perch, USS (n/a)
APSS 313, Transport Sub. In early-mid '60s, US recommissioned subs *Perch* (APSS 313) and *Sealion* (APSS 315) to land/supply US SEALs, collect intel, and perform rescue ops in NVN waters. [416]

Percival, Captain John 'Mad Jack' (n/a)
See *Constitution, USS.*

Perdue, Camp (AT 97-74)
On Division Ridge, Hill 327, at Da Nang. Possibly named to honor one of 3 US Marines named Perdue who died in SVN. They were: Sgt Donald M., KIA 25May67; PFC Richard W., KIA 5Apr69; and LCpl William C., who died 29Sep68. Ray Bows thinks it was named for Donald M. Perdue. Sometimes sp Purdue. Quang Nam Pr, I Corps.

Perfume Pagoda (WJ)
Famous tourist attraction in Hanoi. NVN.

Perfume River (YD 81-32)
A.k.a. the Song Huong River, or River of Perfumes. Major, but short river flowing through Hue. Has W branch, the Song Huu Trach, and S branch, the Song Ta Trach, that flow generally from S and W to N, joining to form the Song Huong just N of Nam Hoa and just S the Nam Hoa (Pohl) Bridge, apx 7 km S Hue. US troops were quick to point out that it smelled more of human waste than of perfume once in Hue. Grid is at river's mouth. See Song Huong. Thua Thien Pr, I Corps.

Periera, Camp (n/a)
No data. Possibly named to honor SFC Socorro Periera, KIA 6Jan68. Used by 1st/502d Inf while opcon to Americal Div near Tam Ky during Op Lamar Plain, mid '69. Americal AO. Quang Tin Pr?, I Corps.

Perishing, FSB (XT 513-257)
See Pershing. Hau Nghia Pr, III Corps.

Permanent Observation Posts (n/a)
See Glossary.

Perry Drop Zone (ZA 190-865)
Apx 5 km SW Kontum, 3 km W QL-14 and 9 km SE Polei Breng. Jan67. Kontum Pr, II Corps.

Pershing, FSB/LZ (YD 684-139)
In Valley apx 6 km NW FSB Birmingham, 11 km SW Hue and 24 km due W Phu Bai. Likely named to honor 2d Lt Richard W. Pershing (grandson of WW1 hero Gen John J. "Black Jack" Pershing), KIA 16Feb68, while with 1st Bn/502d Inf, 101st Abn N of Hue. B Bty 1st/8th Arty here '67-68. 101st Abn inactive FSB grid per Don Armstrong. See Pershing Field. Thua Thien Pr, I Corps.

Pershing, FSB (XT 483-468?)
If accurate, site was at or immed S Dau Tieng/Tri Tam. Apr69. Binh Duong Pr, III Corps.

Pershing, FSB (XT 513-257)
Just SE Xom Rung Cay, apx 29 km WSW Lai Khe, 34 km SE Tay Ninh and 18 km NW Cu Chi. 14th Inf, 25th Div here at one point. In '97 visit to site, veteran said no trace whatsoever of it now exists. Grid/Info per Butch Sincock. 25th Inf Div, Aug68. Also listed at XT 518-269, 483-468, 510-250, 515-259, 521-427? Hau Nghia Pr, III Corps.

Pershing, FSB (YT 161-405)
Apx 22 km ESE Phuoc Vinh AF, 28 km NE Bien Hoa and 8 km ESE Bao Phung. Opened or reopened 11Sep70, closed 25Sep70 by 2d/7th Cav. Reopened 1Oct70 by same unit. Data per *1st Cav Div Op Rpt, ending 31Oct70*, courtesy Peter Cole. Also listed at YT 151-405. Long Khanh Pr, III Corps.

Pershing Field (XS 827-943)
In Gia Dinh, a suburb of Saigon, and adj main gate at Tan Son Nhut AB, apx 300 meters NNE 3d Field Hosp, 1 km S MACV HQ Cmpd and 4 km NW Independence Palace. Originally a sports field leased by US Army in early 60's and later administered by USN's HQ Supt Activities. VC bombing of bleachers during baseball game here 12Feb64, killed 2, and wounded 25 (score at time of blast was 2d Air Div Cobras-6, Advsy Grp Supt Branch-1). Later became home of 92d MP Bn, and used as stockade for VC POWs during Tet '68. On 15Mar66, was named to honor Spanish-American/WW1 hero Gen John J. "Black Jack" Pershing (was not named for Gen Pershing's Grandson, 2d Lt Richard W. Pershing, KIA 16Feb68). Pershing Field is only known Army facility lacking an airstrip to be given title "Field" during war. Data per *Vietnam Military Lore, 1959-1973*, pp 201-202. Gia Dinh Pr, III Corps.

Pershing, Operation (n/a)
11Feb67-19Jan68. 1st Cav op to find and destroy the 610th NVA Div and suptg VC elements. Most of 1st Cav moved to Thua Thien and Quang Tri Provs in I Corps following this op. 5,401 NVA/VC KIA, per *Vietnam Order of Battle*, pp 9-14. Binh Dinh Pr, II Corps.

Pershing II, Operation (n/a)
22Jan-29Feb68. Continuation of Op Pershing after most of 1st Cav Div deployed to I Corps. 1,014 est enemy KIA, per *Vietnam Order of Battle*, pp 9-14. Binh Dinh Pr, II Corps.

Persimmon CP (XD 975-565)
Apx 17 km WSW Cam Lo and 9 km NNE Ca Lu and just a few km W of what became Vandegrift CB. Rgtl? CP during Op Prairie. Quang Tri Pr, I Corps.

Persistent, USS (n/a)
MSO-491. Minesweeper, Ocean, per Ralph Fries.

Personnel Feminin de "'Armee de Terre (n/a)
See Glossary.

Perth, HMAS (n/a)
A.k.a. DDG-38. HMAS Perth was 1st of3 guided missile destroyers (DDGs) built in US for Royal Australian Navy. From 67-71, she had 3 tours of duty with US 7thFlt off VN. For her performance, during which she was hit once and

had many near misses, she was awarded USN UC and MUC. Armed with 2-127mm computer-controlled, rapid-fire guns capable of 70 rnds/min w/range of 20 km. Powered by 4-superheated boilers producing 70,000 shaft hp for 2 main engines. Sister ship to *Hobart* and *Brisbane*. See www.hmasperth.asn.au/. SVN/NVN.

Peta Pac (n/a)
Mapsheet name of L-7014-6539-4. SVN/Laos.

Petchabun (QU 2-1)
See Pechabun. Thailand.

Pete, LZ (BR 750-740)
Apx 16 km WNW Phu My/QL-1, 8 km SSW Ha Tay AF and 42 km NE An Khe. Jan66. Binh Ding Pr, II Corps.

Pete, LZ/FSB (XD 977-585)
Apx 5 km due N Elliott CB, 5 km WSW FSB Fuller, 13 km N Vandegrift CB, 14 km due W Cam Lo and 11 km N to NNE Ca Lu. On map at p 58, *US Marines in Vietnam-1969*. 3d/9th Marine, 3d Mar Div, '69. XXIV Corps grid. Quang Tri Pr, I Corps.

Pete, LZ (XT 962-367)
Apx 12 km S Phuoc Vinh AF and 24 km N to NNW Bien Hao AB. May67. Binh Duong Pr, III Corps.

Peter, LZ (BS 923-183)
Along QL-1 at coast, apx 7 km NNE Gia An and 23 km SSE Duc Pho. Feb67. Quang Ngai Pr, I Corps.

Peter Badcoe Club (YS 28-43)
ANZAC in-country R&R Ctr on Cape St. Jacques at Vung Tau. Was in 1st Aussie Supt Cmpd. Named to honor legendary Maj. Peter Badcoe, VC, RAR subsector advisor to Nam Hoa Dist, S of Hue, KIA Apr(?)67, near An Thuan while attacking enemy position with a grenade and in supt of beleaguered ARVN unit. For that and numerous other acts of valor, he was awarded the Victoria Cross, the Aussie's highest award. Paraphrasing Eddie Tricker, "the Club had all the modern facilities of a holiday resort, including a large, modern swimming pool, aptly named 'The Harold Holt Memorial Swimming Pool' (poor old Harold had just about every swimming pool built at time named after him, following his mysterious death at Cheviot Beach in Victoria), and N of it were bldgs like the club's orderly room where rifles and ammo were secured. The 2-story club itself was slightly further N and in front of orderly room, and offered TV lounge rooms, pool and billiard tables and most importantly, upstairs and downstairs, bars where Aussie beer in cans was available (non of that American shit that you drank forever and in end only got a pain in the gut). N of the Badcoe was the huge 'Kevin Wheatley Stadium' (a.k.a. The Wheatly Amphitheater), named to honor Kevin 'Dasher' Wheatley, RAR, awarded Posthumous Victoria Cross, and used only for concert parties on my visits. I was present for 2, one a 'Noggie' show complete with strippers, and the other a concert party complete with dancing girls. Both filled the hall to capacity! A number of tennis courts were built in large area behind the club (N it), though I never saw them used. Many Viets worked at club, which was not the case at Nui Dat. These facilities were appreciated by diggers who usually came out of bush after a long, stressful op and had a couple of days leave for utilising them." Vung Tau Peninsula, Phuoc Tuy Pr, III Corps.

Peterson, USS (n/a)
A.k.a. DD-969. Destroyers *Elliott* and *Peterson* were named to honor USN LtCmdrs KIA on Song Vam Co Dong River during Op Giant Slingshot. See *Brown Water, Black Berets*, p 334. Apparently never in SVN.

Petite Fleur, Le (XD 858-390)
Name given his Coffee plantation by Felix Poilane. See Poilane Coffee Plantation. Quang Tri Pr, I Corps.

Petite Passe (CP 0-1)
A.k.a. Cua Be. Channel near 11°51'N-109°15'E. On NC49-01 JOG. Khanh Hoa Pr, II Corps.

Petrarca, USNS (n/a)
MSTS Transport, per Ralph Fries.

Petticoat Junction (AT 997-737)
Appears to identify the intersection of Rte 540, QL-1 and the QL-1 RR tracks near SW corner of Da Nang AB. Jan68. Quang Nam Pr, I Corps.

Petty, Camp (CR 03-16?)
At Phu Tai, in Pioneer Valley, near Qui Nhon. Cmpd of the 504th Sig Co. Named to honor Sp5 Eugene "Pecker" Petty, 504th Sig Co, 1st Sig Bde, KIA 12Sep67, while trying to retrieve a disabled vehicle with his tow truck near Song Cau. Data per *Vietnam Military Lore, 1959-1973*. Camp at Phu Tai dedicated in his name. Binh Dinh Pr, II Corps.

Peysson, Plantation de (YT 4-0)
A.k.a. Don Dien Peysson. Apx 8 km NW Xuan Loc. Bien Hoa and/or Long Khanh Pr, III Corps.

Ph' Tnaot (XT 16-04)
See Phum Tnaot. Cambodia.

Pha (n/a)
Vietnamese for lagoon. Words Dam and Pha denote lagoons or estuaries.

Pha Bong Airfield (UH 36-53)
LS-76. CIA/SF, per *Air Facilities Data-Laos.*

Pha Deng Airfield (TG 73-03)
LS-341. CIA/SF, per *Air Facilities Data-Laos.*

Pha Du Airfield (VF 53-72)
LS-263. CIA/SF, per *Air Facilities Data-Laos.*

Pha Hang Airfield (UH 75-46)
LS-205. CIA/SF, per *Air Facilities Data-Laos.*

Pha Hom Airfield (VF 42-76)
LS-241. CIA/SF, per *Air Facilities Data-Laos.*

Pha Hong Airfield (TG 43-74)
LS-213. CIA/SF, per *Air Facilities Data-Laos.*

Pha Ka Airfield (VF 38-96)
LS-245. Apx 125 km NNE Vientiane, per ONC-J-11. CIA/SF facility. El. 3,900'. *Air Facilities Data-Laos.*

Pha Khao Airfield (TG 92-05)
LS-14. CIA/SF, per *Air Facilities Data-Laos.*

Pha Khe Airfield (TG 63-17)
LS-51 and Pa Ka. CIA/SF, per *Air Facilities Data-Laos.*

Pha Lai (n/a)
Mapsheet name of L-7014-6251-2. NVN only.

Pha Langmou Airfield (TG 29-67)
LS-170. CIA/SF, per *Air Facilities Data-Laos.*

Pha Mi, Pointe (XS 9-7)
See Pointe Phami. Gia Dinh Pr?, III Corps.

Pha Peung Airfield (UG 38-22)
LS-21. CIA/SF, per *Air Facilities Data-Laos.*

Pha Phai Airfield (UG 18-10)
LS-65. CIA/SF, per *Air Facilities Data-Laos.*

Pha Poon Airfield (QC 08-54)
LS-328. CIA/SF, per *Air Facilities Data-Laos.*
Pha Poun Airfield (UH 32-01)
LS-230. CIA/SF, per *Air Facilities Data-Laos.*
Pha Tam Giang (YD 7-3)
Village. Thua Thien Pr, I Corps.
Pha Tam Giang (YD 96-22)
Long, narrow tidal bay NE of Hue and between Hue and Ocean. Roughly 25 x 3 km in size. Huong Dien was at its N end and it was here that infamous Street Without Joy began its NW projection. See Street Without Joy, Dam Cau Hai Bay, Wunder Beach and Dam Thuy Tu Bay. Thua Thien/Quang Tri Pr, I Corps.
Pha Tang Airfield (n/a)
On Laotian border, apx 20 km WNW Vientiane. Per ONC-J-11. El. 600'. Cambodia.
Phami, Pointe (XS 9-7)
See Pointe Phami. Gia Dinh Pr?, III Corps.
Phan Chau (WS 027-636)
Fictional name used by Robin Moore to represent That Son SF Camp (a.k.a. Seven Mtns Outpost) in *The Green Berets*. He describes it as being 4 miles S (likely N) of Chau Lu (probably Chau Lang or Tri Ton SF Camp), 3 miles E Cambodia, 150 mi (in reality about 140 km or 90 mi) from Soc Trang and 8 miles S of BP 236-581 (which, if accurate, would put base some 100 km E of Cambodia!). [417] An A-Team here is purported to have been under control of fictional SF Det B-520 (Det B-52?). At pp 33-34, Phan Chau is described as square fort, with "Low, white buildings which rose above the mud walls of base, and a tall steel fire-control tower. To W were rocky foothills along both sides of the Cambodian border. Hills and scrub-brush jungle were to N, and to S land was open and bare. AF was one mile E camp." Also a Viet SF HQ here and actual cmdr at time of Moore's visit was legendary Capt. Larry Thorney, a Finnish national later MIA in Cambodia (and subject of *Soldier under Three Flags*). See Phan Chau (old). Chau Doc Pr, IV Corps.
Phan Chau (old) (WS 005-515)
A.k.a. Little Dien Bien Phu. Fictional name used by author Robin Moore at p 34 of *The Green Beret*, as predecessor to Phan Chau (new) SF Camp. He describes it as having been next to Phan Chau, "surrounded by hills on all sides." Was apparently a French camp at one time. Moore told this author that Phan Chau (new) was actually That Son and this author's analysis suggests Phan Chau Old was likely Tri Ton, apx 12 km SSW That Son. See Phan Chau. Chau Doc Pr, IV Corps.
Phan Dinh Phung BEQ (XS 8-9)
At 172 Phan Dinh Phung St., Mar 65-68, 16 rms, Saigon. Per *VN Military Lore, 1959-1973.* Gia Dinh Pr, III Corps.
Phan Huy Quat (n/a)
See Glossary.
Phan Ly Cham (BN 29-43)
Ville apx 3 km SE Hai Ninh, 4 km SE Song Mao AF and 56 km NE Phan Thiet. Binh Thuan Pr, II Corps.
Phan Rang (n/a)
Mapsheet name of L-7014-6732-2. SVN.
Phan Rang (BN 77-86)
On coast and along QL-1, apx 160 NE Saigon, 115 km NE Phan Thiet, 50 km SSW Cam Ranh Bay and 5 km inland from ocean. Phan Rang AB (2 rwys, one being 10,000') was 7 km NNW the city. 1st Bde/101st Abn here at times prior to arrival of 2d Bde in Nov/Dec67. Per Mar98 issue of *ARMY* Magazine, Phan Rang AB is still in use today as Viet military base. [418] Map is L7014-6731-2. Capitol, Ninh Thuan Pr, II Corps.
Phan Rang, FSB (BN 745-870)
Apx 3 km NW Phan Rang AF, 10 km NW Phan Rang City, and apparently near base of Hill 181. HQ Bty and SVC Bty, 5th/22d Arty here Oct-Nov70. Grid and arty info per Nolan Putman. Ninh Thuan Pr, II Corps.
Phan Rang, FSB? (BN 755-882)
Actual name unknown. At W base of Nui Dat (Hill 180), apx 3 km WNW the N end of Phan Rang AB's main rwy and 13 km NNE Phan Rang. Data per Jerry Berry. 3d/506th Inf. Ninh Tuan Pr, II Corps.
Phan Rang AFB Hospital (BN 772-862)
See USAF Hospitals. Ninh Thuan Pr, II Corps.
Phan Rang Airfield (BN 772-862)
A.k.a. Luan Thanh AF, Thop Cham AF and Thap Cham AF. Major, jet capable AF apx 8 km NW Phan Rang, 50 km SW Cam Ranh Bay AF, 67 km NE Song Mao major AF and 10 km from sea, per TPC K-10D. El. 101'. 2 parallel rwys: one 10,000' Conc and one 10,000' PSP. Home of 35th TFG and 35th Combat Supt Grp. At 11°37'47"N-108°57'20"E. Per Mar98 issue of *ARMY* Magazine, Phan Rang AB is still in use today as Vietnamese Military Facility. Ninh Thuan Pr, II Corps.
Phan Rang Heliport (BN 770-830)
Phan Rang (MAAG) Heliport. A few km S Phan Rang AF and apx 5 km NW Phan Rang. Heliport #628, alt 66', per Feb73 TAD. Ninh Thuan Pr, II Corps.
Phan Rang Seaport (BN 84-78)
Berthing Feet: 200 lineal feet, Draft Max: 5', Cargo Capacity: 1,000 tons/day, Storage Covered w/in 5 km: 48,000 ft^2, Storage Uncov, w/in 5 km: 23,000? yd^2. Ninh Thuan Pr, II Corps. [419]
Phan Rang SF Camp (BN 770-830?)
If grid correct, site was a few km S Phan Rang AF, apx 5 km NW Phan Rang, and at or near Nui Tour Cham. 5th SF camp. Info/grid per *SF Order of Battle.* Grid is for Phan Rang Heliport. See Phuoc Thien. Ninh Thuan Pr, II Corps.
Phan Rang TACAN NDB (BN 77-87)
Tactical Air Navigation and Non-Directional air navigation beacon site at Phan Rang AB. Ninh Thuan Pr, II Corps.
Phan Rang, Baie de (BN 8-7)
A.k.a. Vung Phan Rang. Bay at 11°34'N-109°04'E. On NC49-01 JOG. Ninh Thuan Pr, II Corps.
Phan Ri (n/a)
Mapsheet name of L-7014-6731-3. SVN.
Phan Ri, Baie de (BN 3-3)
A.k.a. Vung Phan Ry. Bay at 11°09'N-108°35'E. On NC49-01 JOG. Binh Thuan Pr, II Corps.
Phan Thiet (AN 840-090)
On coast apx 115 km SW Phan Rang, 45 km ENE Ham Tan AF and 150 km E of Saigon. HQ 3rd/506th Inf, 101st Abn here most of its time in VN (only 101st Div unit sent to Cambodian incursion). Binh Thuan Advsy Team 37 and Plt of 1st/69th Armor also here. Per Mar98 issue of *ARMY* Magazine, the US rwy on bluffs overlooking the ocean here "is now a garbage dump where people practice

motoring skills before taking driving tests." [420] Maps: L7014-6630-4 for LZ Betty while area immed N Phan Thiet is on L7014-6631-3 and area immed W Phan Thiet is on L7014-6530-1. Capitol, Binh Thuan Pr, II Corps,

Phan Thiet, Baie de (AN 8-0)
A.k.a. Vinh Phan Thiet. Bay at 10°53'N-108°05'E. On NC48-08 JOG. Binh Thuan Pr, II Corps.

Phan Thiet, LZ (AN 855-100)
Between Phan Thiet and Ap Sung Xuan, apx 6 km ENE Phan Thiet AF/LZ Betty and 2 km E QL-1. 30Apr68. Binh Thuan Pr, II Corps.

Phan Thiet, Xa (n/a)
Mapsheet name of L-7014-6630-4. Actual sheet name is: Xa Phan Thiet. SVN.

Phan Thiet Compound (AN 838-096)
In downtown Phan Thiet, apx 4 km NE Phan Thiet AF/LZ Betty. Mar69. Nature of cmpd unknown, but possibly an SF cmpd? Binh Thuan Pr, II Corps.

Phan Thiet Supply Point (AN 801-068)
At Phan Thiet AF. Dec67. Binh Thuan Pr, II Corps.

Phan Thiet Airfield (AN 801-068)
On coast S QL-1, apx 3 km SW Xa Phan Thiet, 60 km SW Song Mao AF, 46 km SE Tanh Linh AF and adj to LZ Betty. TPC K-10D. El. 203', 3,600' steel-mat rwy. Binh Thuan Pr, II Corps.

Phan Thiet NDB (AN 940-080)
On south edge of Phan Thiet and on coast, apx 3 km NE Phan Thiet AF. Binh Thuan Pr, II Corps.

Phanh Hanh Social Club (YT 04-07)
At Camp Phanh Hanh at Long Binh Post. Organized by Col Le Quang Hien in 67-68 to provide schooling and mtg place for Girl Youth and Boy Youth Groups of 3d ARVN Ranger Grp's family quarters (almost 400 families housed in just 90 buildings). At time, only 25% of educational needs of unit's dependents was being met. See Camp Phanh Hanh. Data per *Rangers At War*, p 262. Bien Hoa Pr, III Corps.

Phanh Hanh, Camp (YT 04-07)
Near intersections of QL-1 and QL-15, just NE the Song Cai River and apx 20 km NE Saigon. Barracks and family quarters of ARVN 3d Ranger Group here; while Grp HQ was at Newport Bridge, just outside Saigon. In *Rangers At War*, at p 261, described in '68 as having been on edge of Long Binh Post, and consisting of "11 rows of wooden shacks and 12 rows of tin and iron-sheet roofed buildings." Despite ongoing construction projects and assistance from 3d Grp's US Adv, the 90 houses and a maternity hospital of Phanh Hanh housed 148 families of 31st ARVN Ranger Bn, and 219 families of 52d Bn! See Hoang Hoa Tham Dependent Quarters. Bien Hoa Pr, III Corps.

Phanom Sarakam (QR 5-2)
Apx 85 km E Bangkok. US Army Supt Cmd facility, Thailand; home of 809th Engr Bn Mar62-Feb71. Thailand.

Phanom Sarakham Airfield (QR 5-2)
Apx 85 km E Bangkok, near 13°45'00"N-101°24'00"E on Feb67 Natl Geo map. NIMA data. El. 450'. Thailand.

Phantom (n/a)
Apr70, XXIV Corps proposed 101st Abn FSB name.

Phat Diem (n/a)
Mapsheet name of L-7014-6249-3. NVN only.

Phat Diem (XH 1-2)
Apx 105 km SSE Hanoi and 10 km E QL-1. French garrison here battled Vietminh's 308 Div during Battle of Day River, 29May-18Jun51. See *Street Without Joy*, Chp 2, map at p 46. NVN.

Phet Buri Airfield (NQ 9-3)
At 12°57'00"N-99°54'00"E. NIMA data. Thailand.

Phetburi (n/a)
A.k.a. Khoa Yoi and Phet Buri. SF camp, per *SF Order of Battle.* Thailand.

Phey Srunh Airfield (AP 895-308)
Along LTL-18, apx 8 km SSE peak of Yook Nam Rmay Mtn (Hill 1442), 17 km S Duc Xuyen AF and 32 km WNW Dalat. "Insecure, abnd ARVNAF 8Feb67, AF # VA2-211," in Aug69 TAD per Frank Penk, Jr. Not in Feb73 TAD. Tuyen Duc Pr, II Corps.

Phey Srunh SF Camp (AP 889-331)
Along LTL-18, apx 8 km SSE peak of Yook Nam Rmay Mtn (Hill 1442), 17 km S Duc Xuyen AF and 32 km WNW Dalat. 5th SF. Moved to An Lac. Info/grid per *SF Order of Battle.* Tuyen Duc Pr, II Corps.

Phi Ho SF Camp (BN 264-415)
A.k.a. FOB Song Mao. Apx 6 km SSE Song Mao AF, 6 km WSW Phan Ly Cham and 52 km NE Phan Thiet. 5th SF camp/FOB "Flying Tiger" site. Info/grid per *SF Order of Battle.* Binh Thuan Pr, II Corps.

Phi Long SF Camp (AN 965-304)
A.k.a. Flying Dragon and FOB Song Mao. Apx 31 km WSW Song Mao AF, 33 km NNE Phan Thiet and 9 km NNW Ap Long Lam/QL-1. 5th SF. Info/grid per *SF Order of Battle.* Binh Thuan Pr, II Corps.

Phi Ma SF Camp (BN 3267-0387)
A.k.a. FOB Song Mao and "Flying Horse" Camp. Along QL-1, apx 10 km SW Song Mao AF, 5 km SSE Phan Ly Cham, and 56 km NE Phan Thiet. Official Army list of SF facilities on-line at www.army.mil/cmh-pg/BOOKS/Vietnam/90-23/90-23ac.htm shows this listing for Phi Ma: "Phi Ma (Plei Me), Binh Thuan [Prov], "A" [Det], 5 Dec 63 closed." 5th SF. Info/grid per *Special Forces of Battle.* See Phi Ho-Flying Tiger. Binh Thuan Pr, II Corps.

Phi Ma, FSB (XT 763-113?)
If grid correct, was apx 6 km WSW Phu Cuong and 14 km NNW Tan Son Nhut AB. Apr70. Also listed at XU 700-113 and unknown which grid is correct? Binh Duong Pr?, III Corps.

Phi Ma, FSB (XU 700-113?)
A.k.a. FSB Ann. Cambodian Incursion base apx 4 km NW N Loc Ninh AF, and 5 km due E Srok Silamite. Closed 3May70. A Bty, 6th/27th Arty here with two-175mms, and C Bty, 2d/12th Arty with six-155mms, per *11th ACR Cambodia Invasion AAR, 1st Cav Div, May-Jun70*, courtesy Lou Rochat. [421] Also listed at XT 763-113, and unknown which grid is correct? Binh Long Pr, III Corps.

Phi Sroin (n/a)
Mapsheet name of L-7014-6633-3. SVN.

Phi Troung Airfield? (n/a)
Location unknown. Mentioned in Jul-Aug99 *Screaming Eagle* 101st Abn Assn newsletter as caption to Apr66 photo digitized by Natl Archives which "shows members of 101st Abn aboard a C-130 at Pham (sic) Thiet AB waiting for an airlift to Phi Troung AB during Op Austin 6.

Possible misspelling of Viet phrase "Phi Truong," which simply means "airport." Presumably in II Corps.

Phia Chan Airfield (PB 87-62)
LS-155. CIA/SF, per *Air Facilities Data-Laos.*

Phia Khan Airfield (VH 00-70)
LS-87. CIA/SF, per *Air Facilities Data-Laos.*

Phia Louang Airfield (UF 09-90)
A.k.a. LS-270 and Ohu Sa Ngop. CIA/SF, per *Air Facilities Data-Laos.*

PHILCAG (XT 175-517)
A.k.a. Philippine Civic Action Cmpd and 1st PHILCAG-V. Adj to the Tay Ninh West AF complex. Per 588th Eng Bn website, 1st PHILCAG was mechanized Engr unit from the Philippines, and their cmpd was triangular in shape and immed E of the AF. "Both basecamps had complete and separate perimeter defenses." Mission was pacification of Thanh Dien Forest region, and its forces inc Inf Security Bn, 105mm Arty Bn, Const Engr Bn, Med-Dental Bn, Log Supt Co and HQ/Services Co. Arrived 14Sep66, departed 13Dec69. Grid per Tay Ninh facilities map at www. mendonet.com/588th/map. htm. See Philippines, Forces of, in Major HQs Section. Tay Ninh Pr, II Corps.

PHILCAG-V (XT 175-517)
See PHILCAG. Tay Ninh Pr, II Corps.

Philippine Civic Action Compound (XT 175-517)
See PHILCAG. Tay Ninh Pr, II Corps.

Philippine Sea, USS (n/a)
A.k.a. CV-47. See *Wasp, USS* for detail.

Philippines, Forces of (n/a)
See PHILCAG in main alpha listing, and Philippine Forces in Major HQs Section.

Philip, USS (n/a)
DD-498. SVN.

Philips, LZ (YA 488-639)
See Phillips. Cambodia.

Phillips, LZ (YA 488-639)
A.k.a. Hill 887. Incursion FSB on Hill 887 and overlooking Stoeng Ta Pok River Valley, apx 14 km NNE LZ Commanche, 63 km WNW Plei Mrong, 10 km W SVN border, 15 km ENE Savanbav and 43 km NE Plei Djereng. Possibly northernmost US FSB of Cambodian Incursion? 4th Div, '70. Named to honor Capt. Robert L. Phillips, CO C/3d/8th Inf, 4th Div, KIA 6May70. Name/grid per Jim Claeys. Also listed at YA 491-636. Cambodia.

Phillips Compound (XS 8-9)
Cmpd of HQ, 525th Mil Intel Bn, Saigon. Named to honor Sgt Samuel C. III Phillips, Sgt, USA, B/519th Mil Intel Bn, KIA 2Oct67, shot down while passenger during an aerial recon. Data per Ray Bows. Gia Dinh Pr, III Corps.

Phitsanulok (PU 3-6)
A.k.a. Pitsanuloke and Pitsanulok. In flat, delta area along Nam River, near 16°50'00"N-100°15'00"E, and apx 340 km N Bangkok. US radar vectoring facility responsible for guiding US fighter and fighter-bomber acft to rendezvous with KC-135 air tankers both en route to, and returning from, bombing missions over NVN. Facility's call-sign was "Dora." Tanker acft were based in southern Thailand, while fighters and fighter-bombers (chiefly F-105 Thuds) were based in throughout Thailand and elsewhere. Per Claude Moutray (Apr68-Apr69), this was very small base that housed only about 121 USAF personnel of 621st Tactical Control Sqdn, Det 8, and small Air Police Det (12-15 personnel). Security for facility was courtesy of RTA. Cited in *SF Order of Battle* as SF camp location as well. Data per Claude Moutray, grid per NIMA. Thailand.

Phitsanulok Airfield (PU 3-5)
Along Nam River near 16°50'00"N-100°15'00"E, and apx 340 km N Bangkok. Natl Geo map. El. 150'. Apparently a secondary AF here, but no data available? Thailand.

Phitscamp (n/a)
A.k.a. Camp Surat Sena. SF camp per *SF Order of Battle.*

Phnom Penh (VT 92-78)
On E bank of Mekong River apx 190 km due W Saigon, 75 km at closest point to SVN and about 135 km at closest Gulf of Thailand. Sits at confluence of Tonle Sap, Song Hau Giang and Mekong Rivers and in center of immense, flat plain. Although apx 100 miles from ocean, elevation is only 40' above sea level. Capitol, Cambodia.

Phnom Penh International Airport (VT 8-7)
A.k.a. Pochentong International and Yean Than Antaracheat Airport. Major AF apx 5 km W Phnom Penh, 65 km W SVN border and 135 km N the ocean at its closest point to those places, per TPC K-10D. At 11°33'00"N-104°51'00"E. NIMA data. El. 39'. Cambodia.

Phnom Penh NDB (VT 85-78)
Non-Directional Air Nav Beacon site. Apx 3 km NE Phnom Penh AF and VOR NDB Phnom Penh. Cambodia.

Phnom Penh VOR NDB (VT 83-76)
Very high frequency Omnidirectional Radio ranging and Non-Directional Air Nav Beacon site. At Phnom Penh AF and 3 km SW NDB Phnom Penh. Cambodia.

Phnom Thbeng Meanchey AF (n/a)
Apx 245 km due N Phnom Penh. El. 200'. Cambodia.

Pho Bang (n/a)
AMS/DMA mapsheet L 701-6080-4. NVN/China.

Pho Binh Gia (n/a)
Mapsheet name of L-7014-6252-1. NVN only.

Pho Chau (n/a)
Mapsheet name of L-7014-6046-2. NVN only.

Pho Lu (n/a)
Mapsheet name of L-7014-5853-4. NVN only.

Pho Lu Outpost (VK 1-6?)
Apx 160 km NE Dien Bien Phu and in shadow of China's Yunnan Province border, along narrow canyon of upper reaches of Red River (Song Coi), 30 km downstream from Lao Kay and 235 km NW Hanoi. French frontier outpost overrun and lost to Vietminh, Spring 1950, during first major test of newly created and trained VM Divs under Nguyen Vo Giap. Described in *To the Last Cartridge* as Godforsaken "primitive little post made of logs...in great primeval forest; a desolate, brooding place," it was bordered by rugged limestone ridges on both the E and W.[422] Here Giap decided to test his newly formed army, and the VM man-handled heavy arty and mortars onto high ground and then pulverized fort as prelude to massive Inf assault (feat to be repeated at DBP). French reacted by dropping in 3d Colonial Para Bn, but it survived only because it landed 30 km from Pho Lu and on opposite side of Song Coi. See Cao Bang and Dong Khe. NVN.

Pho Phisai Airfield (n/a)
See Phon Phisia AF. Thailand.

Pho Thu Airfield (WJ 23-67)
Apx 80 km NW Hanoi. Feb67 Natl Geo map. El. 33'. NVN.
Pho Trach (YD 52-35)
Ville apx 1.5 km NW Camp Evans. Map is L-7014-6442-2, per Ken Burrington. Quang Tri Pr?, I Corps.
Pho Trach Heliport (YD 525-349)
Apx 3 km NW Camp Evans, S of QL-1 and W of Phong Dien. Heliport #629, alt 49', at 16°35'00"N-107°22'00"E, per Feb73 TAD. "Abnd, rwy mortared 30Jul67, AF # VA1-76," in Aug69 TAD per Frank Penk, Jr. Not in Feb73 TAD. Quang Tri Pr?, I Corps.
Pho Trach Railroad Bridge (YD 519-349)
Along QL-1, apx 5 km NW Camp Evans and 23 km SE Quang Tri. XXIV Corps grid. Thua Thien Pr, I Corps.
Pho Yen (n/a)
Mapsheet name of L-7014-6151-1. NVN only.
Phoc Ha Valley (BT 10-35)
See Phuoc Hoa Valley. Quang Tin Pr, I Corps.
Phoebe, USS (n/a)
MSC-199. Minesweeper, Coastal, per Ralph Fries.
Phoenix (n/a)
6Apr70, XXIV Corps proposed Americal FSB name.
Phoenix, LZ (BS 567-878)
Apparently on or near Hill 182, apx 17 km due S Chu Lai and 7 km W QL-1. Quang Ngai Pr, I Corps.
Phoenix, Operation (n/a)
26 Feb-22 Mar 66. 173d Abn. Binh Duong and Bien Hoa Provs, III Corps.
Phoenix, Project (WS 153-814?)
See MACV Adv Team 64. Chau Doc Pr, IV Corps.
Phoenix City, FSB (BR 628-825)
A.k.a. LZ File. Apx 17 km W Ha Tay AF and 40 km NNE An Khe. Mar66. Binh Dinh Pr, II Corps.
Phoenix City BEQ (XS 844-924)
At 155 Truong Minh Giang St., Saigon. Per R. Bows' *Vietnam Military Lore, 1959-1973.* Gia Dinh Pr, III Corps.
Phoenix Program (n/a)
See Glossary.
Phol Bridge (YD 755-144)
See Pohl Bridge. Thua Thien Pr, I Corps.
Phon Mai Dang CAP (YD 3-4)
If grid correct, was S of, and within 10 km of, Quang Tri. Listed as Phon Mai Dang at CAP website, but apparent "proper" spelling is Thon Mai Dang or Mai Dang Phuong. CAP 4-2-8, 4th CAG per Tim Duffie. Hai Lang District, Quang Tri Pr, I Corps.
Phon Phisai Airfield (n/a)
Along Mekong River at Laotian border, apx 540 km N Bangkok, and 50 km ENE Vientiane. Feb67 Natl Geo map. El. 680'. Thailand.
Phon Thon Airfield (n/a)
Apx 465 km NE Bangkok, and 45 km NE Roi Et. Feb67 Natl Geo map. El. 550'. Thailand.
Phone Sai Airfield (TF 62-99)
LS-211. Apx 115 km NNE Vientiane Per ONC-J-11. CIA/SF, per *Air Facilities Data-Laos.* El. 902'. Laos.
Phone Thong Airfield (WB 74-69)
LS-450. Apx 10 km SW Pakse per TPC K-10A. CIA/SF, per *Air Facilities Data-Laos.* El. 330'. Laos.
Phong Bai (n/a)
Mapsheet name of L-7014-6147-4. NVN only.
Phong Cau, Battle of (BQ 96-56)
Ville of Phong Cau is apx 27 km NW Tuy Hoa AB. Took place in forested area known as "The Hub" during Op Geronimo, 9-11Nov66. Involved B/2d/502d Inf and its Recondo Plt. 5th/95th NVA lost 39 KIA/36 POW, while US lost 5 KIA and 15 WIA. Discussed in *Mad Minutes and Vietnam Moments*, Chp 20. Phu Yen Pr, II Corps.
Phong Dien (YD 528-348)
Ville 26 km SE Quang Tri and roughly half way between Quang Tri and Hue. Camp Evans was built apx 2.5 km SSE this town. During Op Carentan II, Apr68, elements of 2d Sqdn, 17th Cav and 2d/501st Inf, 101st Abn cordoned ville and, after night of arty and fighting, found 66 NVA KIA. Quang Tri Pr, I Corps.
Phong Dien, FSB (YD 520-340)
Near Phong Dien/QL-1 Bridge, apx 4 km NW Camp Evans. Apr69. Thua Thien Pr, I Corps.
Phong Dien Airfield (YD 541-318)
A.k.a. Camp Evans AF. 26 km SE Quang Tri. El. 33'. Quang Tri Pr, I Corps.
Phong Dien Bridge (YD 519-348)
Crosses the Song O Lau River at listed grid, immed NW Phong Dien, apx 11.5 km WNW An Lo Bridge and roughly 26 km NW Hue. Thua Thien Pr, I Corps.
Phong Dien Bridge (YD 52-34)
On QL-1, apx 3 km NW Camp Evans and immed NW Thon An Thon. D/1st/502d Inf pulled security here, 10Apr68. Quang Tri or Thua Thien Pr, I Corps.
Phong Dinh Airfield (WS 840-108)
See Can Tho AF. Phong Dinh Pr, IV Corps.
Phong Dinh Province (WS/WR/XR)
One of 16 southern provs forming IV Corps (IV CTZ).
Phong Hong Airfield (TF 27-47)
LS-133. CIA/SF, per *Air Facilities Data-Laos.*
Phong Luc 1 Combat Base (BT 015-627)
A.k.a. FSB Dai Loc, FSB 412, Whiskey Tower and Camp Middlesworth. Apx 12 km due S Da Nang AB and 2.5 km W QL-1. Jul69. Quang Nam Pr, I Corps.
Phong Luc 2 Combat Base (BT 015-627)
See Phong Luc 1. Jul69. Quang Nam Pr, I Corps.
Phong My (n/a)
Mapsheet name of L-7014-6130-3. SVN.
Phong Ngu 2 CAP (BT 0-6?)
See CAP 2-3-8. 2d CAG. Quang Nam Pr, I Corps.
Phong Phu (XS 6-3)
A.k.a. Ap Phong Phu. Ville within 15 km W of My Tho. Kien Hoa Pr, IV Corps.
Phong Phu (O Mon) (n/a)
Mapsheet name of L-7014-6129-3. SVN.
Phong Phu Heliport (WS 688-180)
At or near O Mon, apx 17 km NW Can Tho AF. Heliport #725, alt 7', at 10°07'30"N-105°37'30"E, per Feb73 TAD. Phong Dinh Pr, IV Corps.
Phong Saly (SK 9-0)
See Phongsali. Laos.
Phong Saly Airfield (TK 00-00)
A.k.a. L-15 and Phongsali AF. Apx 410 km NNW Vientiane. CIA/SF, per *Air Facilities Data-Laos.* El. 4,500'. Laos.

Phong So (CQ 26-23)
See Vung Ro Seaport. Khanh Hoa Pr, II Corps.
Phong Tho (Muong So) (n/a)
Mapsheet name of L-7014-5654-2. NVN/China.
Phong Thong Airfield (n/a)
Feb67 Natl Geo map. El. 550'. Cambodia.
Phonghong SF Camp (n/a)
SF camp when Lao neutrality declared, 23Jul62. FTT 30 and ATT 4 here. Per *Special Forces at War*. MR5, Laos.
Phongsali (SJ 95-98)
A.k.a. Phong Saly. Apx 105 km WNW DBP and 80 km NW Muong Khoua in an extremely remote region some 20 km W the Nam Pak River. Northernmost French outpost in Laos during Vietminh, 1953 Spring Offensive. Laos.
Phongsali Airfield (n/a)
A.k.a. Phong Saly AF. Apx 410 km NNW Vientiane. El. 4,500'. Laos.
Phou (n/a)
One of several Viet words for mountain.
Phou Chai Airfield (SG 99-50)
LS-25 and Phou Chia. CIA, per *Air Facilities Data-Laos.*
Phou Chia Airfield (SG 99-50)
LS-25 and Phou Chai. CIA, per *Air Facilities Data-Laos.*
Phou Da Pho Airfield (TG 52-43)
LS-103. CIA/SF, per *Air Facilities Data-Laos.*
Phou Dam Airfield (SH 98-21)
LS-256. CIA/SF, per *Air Facilities Data-Laos.*
Phou Douak Airfield (XB 82-38)
LS-440. CIA/SF, per *Air Facilities Data-Laos.*
Phou Fa Airfield (TG 70-74)
LS-16. CIA/SF, per *Air Facilities Data-Laos.*
Phou Houang Airfield (UG 07-29)
LS-140. CIA/SF, per *Air Facilities Data-Laos.*
Phou Kahm Phouk Airfield (XB 88-51)
LS-166. CIA/SF, per *Air Facilities Data-Laos.*
Phou Kang Neua Airfield (TG 73-09)
LS-337. CIA/SF, per *Air Facilities Data-Laos.*
Phou Khao Khouai Airfield (n/a)
Apx 40 km NE Vientiane. Natl Geo map. El. 2,200'. Laos.
Phou Khe Airfield (UG 19-37)
LS-19. CIA/SF, per *Air Facilities Data-Laos.*
Phou Kheo Airfield (UG 32-72)
LS-115. CIA/SF, per *Air Facilities Data-Laos.*
Phou Khong Airfield (QB 48-49)
LS-42. CIA/SF, per *Air Facilities Data-Laos.*
Phou Kouk Airfield (UH 85-25)
LS-59. CIA/SF, per *Air Facilities Data-Laos.*
Phou Lat Seua Airfield (WB 57-95)
LS-418. On Mekong River at Thai border, apx 35 km NW Pakse. CIA/SF base per *Air Facilities Data-Laos.*
Phou Leang Airfield (QB 58-63)
LS-323. CIA/SF, per *Air Facilities Data-Laos.*
Phou Louang Airfield (XB 78-86)
LS-402. CIA/SF, per *Air Facilities Data-Laos.*
Phou Loutoukou Ridge (XD 635-526)
Rugged, remote and very steep 2,300' high ridgeline apx 500 meters from border and just inside Laos, apx 20 km W Khe Sanh. Overlooked Xe Samou River (E/W course) basin and Valley. Major emergency extraction mission for trapped Recon element (Team 5-2, 3d Force Recon, 26-28Jan67) here described in great detail in *Bonnie-Sue*, pp 274-299. Near listed grid. Laos.
Phou Nam Nhiou Airfield (QB 54-06)
LS-146. CIA/SF, per *Air Facilities Data-Laos.*
Phou Ngieu Airfield (UG 74-26)
LS-232. CIA/SF, per *Air Facilities Data-Laos.*
Phou Nhoi Hill Mass (XD 8-2)
In Vietnam Salient near Lao border generally S FSB Saigon and near 16°30'00"N-106°45'00"E. 3d Marines, 3d Mar Div operated in this area during Op Maine Crag, Mar-May69. Quang Tri Pr, I Corps.
Phou Nong Airfield (UG 58-55)
LS-71. CIA/SF, per *Air Facilities Data-Laos.*
Phou Pang Sang Airfield (QC 28-78)
LS-142. CIA/SF, per *Air Facilities Data-Laos.*
Phou Pha Louom Airfield (UH 61-16)
LS-220. CIA/SF, per *Air Facilities Data-Laos.*
Phou Pha Louom Airfield (UH 92-15)
LS-228. CIA/SF, per *Air Facilities Data-Laos.*
Phou Sai Airfield (TG 73-83)
LS-312. CIA/SF, per *Air Facilities Data-Laos.*
Phou Saly Airfield (TH 93-63)
LS-178. CIA/SF, per *Air Facilities Data-Laos.*
Phou Sam Soun Airfield (UG 82-91)
LS-231. CIA/SF, per *Air Facilities Data-Laos.*
Phou San Airfield (TH 96-07)
LS-336. CIA/SF, per *Air Facilities Data-Laos.*
Phou San Nyai Airfield (TF 75-98)
LS-362. CIA/SF, per *Air Facilities Data-Laos.*
Phou So Airfield (TG 81-74)
LS-57. CIA/SF, per *Air Facilities Data-Laos.*
Phou Soung Airfield (TG 37-56)
LS-156. CIA/SF, per *Air Facilities Data-Laos.*
Phou Ta Beng Airfield (n/a)
Apx 280 km WSW Da Nang. ONC-K-10. El. 1,800'. Laos.
Phou Tai Airfield (UH 43-64)
LS-185. CIA/SF, per *Air Facilities Data-Laos.*
Phou Vieng Airfield (TG 49-58)
LS-197. CIA/SF, per *Air Facilities Data-Laos.*
Phou Vieng Airfield (UG 07-89)
LS-06. CIA/SF, per *Air Facilities Data-Laos.*
Phouc Binh (n/a)
See Phuoc Binh and/or Phuoc Vinh. III Corps.
Phouc Binh Airfield (AT 879-396)
See Phuoc Binh AF. Quang Nam Pr, I Corps.
Phouc Binh Combat Base (YU 144-073?)
See Phuoc Binh CB. Also listed at YU 138-063? Phuoc Long Pr, III Corps.
Phouc Tan Outpost (XT 018-435)
See Phouc Tan RF Post. Tay Ninh Pr, III Corps.
Phouc Tan RF Post (XT 018-435)
Also sp Phuoc Tan. Along Rte 13, apx 2 km E Cambodia, 8 km SW Ben Soi and 17 km WSW Tay Ninh West AF. Stand-off attacks on 17-18Sep68 were followed by all-out assault on 19-20Sep68, however RF and ARVN defenders were able to hold site despite fact it was 90% destroyed. After battle, 35 enemy bodies were found, 19 of which were inside the cmpd. Was again hit night of 26-27Sep68, taking over 2,000 rnds of mortar fire and ground assault. Spooky and defenders accounted for 148 enemy KIA while suffering 1 KIA, 33 WIA. [423] Tay Ninh Pr, III Corps.

Phouc Vinh (n/a)
Common sp variant of Phuoc Binh and Phuoc Vinh. See Phuoc Binh and/or Phuoc Vinh.
Phougas (n/a)
See Glossary.
Phoung Sam Airfield (UH 10-12)
LS-114. CIA/SF, per *Air Facilities Data-Laos.*
Phoung Savan Airfield (UG 13-54)
L-21. CIA/SF, per *Air Facilities Data-Laos.*
Phowachedy Airfield (WD 01-16)
LS-311. CIA/SF, per *Air Facilities Data-Laos.*
Phrae Airfield (PA 2-0)
At 18°08'00"N-100°10'00"E, apx 485 km N Bangkok per Feb67 Natl Geo map. El. 450'. NIMA data. Thailand.
Phu An (various)
Common Viet place-name. See grid squares: XR 1-7, BP 9-5, ZD 1-1, XT 7-2, XH 4-4, BT 1-2, BR 7-3, CR 0-2, AT?, WS 3-8 and XS 0-2. NVN/SVN.
Phu An I, and II (AT 83-52?)
Apx 5 km NW An Hoa CB. Site of battle involving 1st/7th Marines reinforced by elements of 3d/7th and 3d/5th Marines, 1st Mar Div 12Aug69, 5 US KIA, 33 WIA. Grid is est. Quang Nam Pr, I Corps.
Phu Bai (YD 913-118)
Series of villes, Ap Phu Bai I thru Ap Phu Bai VI, that straddled QL-1 apx 22 km SE Hue, and from 2 to 5 km SE Phu Bai CB. Thua Thien Pr, I Corps.
Phu Bai, FSB (YD 882-135)
On S side QL-1, apx 1 km S Phu Bai AF. Possibly arty at this site, which appears to have been within Camp Hochmuth perimeter? Jan69-Apr70. Also listed at YD 880-140. Thua Thien Pr, I Corps.
Phu Bai [1] NDB (YD 89-15)
Non-Directional Air Nav Beacon site. A.k.a. NDB Phubai [1]. Phu Bai AF. Thua Thien Pr, I Corps.
Phu Bai [2] NDB (YD 96-18)
Non-Directional Air Nav Beacon site. A.k.a. NDB Phubai [2]. Thua Thien Pr, I Corps.
Phu Bai Airport (YD 885-149)
Apx 12 km SE Hue, 65 km NW Da Nang AB, and 66 km SE Quang Tri. Thua Thien Pr, I Corps.
Phu Bai Army Airfield (YD 887-148)
A.k.a. Hue/Phu Bai AF. Apx 12 km SE Hue, 65 km NW Da Nang AB, and 66 km SE Quang Tri. 5,600' asph rwy serviced by Army, USAF and Viet civilian air controllers. Provided combat Avn supt in Hue/Phu Bai AO, Army's 85th Evac Hosp was adj rwy. Thua Thien Pr, I Corps.
Phu Bai CAP (YD)
3rd CAG per CAP Website. Thua Thien Pr, I Corps.
Phu Bai Combat Base (YD 885-135)
A.k.a. Phu Bai CB and Camp Hochmuth. Along QL-1, apx 16 km SE of Hue Citadel AF, 62 NW Da Nang, and 76 km SE Dong Ha CB. Site of 3d Mar Div HQ. Built in Spring of '65, its first occupants were the 9th MEB, their ten H-34 helos and 3d Bn/4th Mar. Later, it became home of MAG-39 (over 75 rotary-wing and other fixed-wing acft). Renamed Camp Hochmuth in '68(?) to honor MGen Bruno Hochmuth, KIA 14Nov67. In Apr 70, after 3d Mar Div went home, became HQ of 101st Abn and home to 2d Bde/101st and the 85th Evac Hosp. Phu Bai AF was major USMC AB as well. Overrun in '75 Final Offensive. Per Mar98 *ARMY* Magazine, was still in use by Viets at visit here Oct96. [424] Map is L-7014-6541-4, per Ken Burrington. Thua Thien Pr, I Corps.
Phu Bai Fill Pit (YD 872-118)
See Phu Bai Quarry. Thua Thien Pr, I Corps.
Phu Bai Quarry (YD 872-118)
Apx 4 km SSW Phu Bai AF and 4 km W Ap Phu Bai I. Apr71. Thua Thien Pr, I Corps.
Phu Bai/Hue Airfield (YD 887-148)
See Hue/Phu Bai AF. Thua Thien Pr, I Corps.
Phu Bai/Hue/Tan-My NSA (YD 82-33?)
At Tan My apx 12 km NNE Hue. USN Supt Activity, '65-70. Per MRF Assn Website. Thua Thien Pr, I Corps.
Phu Bon Province (BQ/BR)
One of 12 north-central provs forming II Corps (II CTZ)
Phu Cat (BR 92-50)
Apx 13 km SE Phu Cat Mtns, 32 km N Qui Nhon and 8 km N An Nhon (birthplace of communist movement in SE Asia). Binh Dinh Pr, II Corps.
Phu Cat 2 Airfield (BR 914-456)
Minor AF on E side of QL-1 about 5 km NE the major Phu Cat 1 AB. May have originally been a 1st Cav helicopter laager/fwd operating base in '66 known as "The Rifle Range." On TPC K-10B, El. 55'. Listed as "Insecure, seldom used, AF # VA2-212," in Aug69 TAD per Frank Penk, Jr. Not in Feb73 TAD. Also listed at BR 92-47. See Rifle Range, The. Binh Dinh Pr, II Corps.
Phu Cat AFB Hospital (BR 896-412)
See USAF Hospitals. Binh Dinh Pr, II Corps.
Phu Cat Airbase (BR 896-412)
A.k.a. Base X, Bordner Field and Phu Cat 1 AB. Was larger of two AF's here, and sited apx 5 km SW Phu Cat II, 20 km due E Binh Khe, 40 km due E An Khe AF, 32 km N Qui Nhon and 2 km W QL-1. Had mtns on S, W and E at from 5 to10 km distance and lowlands to N & SE. This jet-capable AF was also 8 km N of An Nhon (birthplace of communist insurgency movement in SE Asia and former VC trng area). Originally known as "Base X" and informally known as Bordner AF to honor LTC William H. Bordner, USAF, KIA 16Feb66. Following info compiled from extensive history at www.fgi.net/~rdoughty/phuhist.htm, and authored by Mr. J. Doughty. Though lengthy, it is meant to provide an example of the logistical and personnel enormities presented by a single major facility during war: Built on high ground surrounded by rice paddies and dense underbrush on rolling terrain. Part of S edge bordered by Song Dap Da River and part of N edge by Song La Vi River. Main N/S railway bordered S and E edges as did QL-1 and separated it from ROK 1st Inf Rgt HQ, 1st Tiger Div basecamp to E. Prior to occupation by US and ROK during Op Pershing, area was VC trng center. Initial survey took place 16Feb66, during which LTC William Bordner was KIA by mine. That site, Hill 151, was later named Bordner Hill. ROK Tiger Div secured area 1May66 as RMK-BRJ arrived to build camp for themselves and ROK. Temp 3,000' strip and some bldgs completed by 1Jun66. AF first used by new USAF C-7A Sqdns that delivered const materials. By 1Aug RMK-BRJ and 150 USAF personnel were in place. On 4Aug66, Capt Robert Sullivan arrived with 53 security police (37th SPS) and 63 RED HORSE (819CES) Engrs. 37th SG activated 19Sep66.

Using rock and gravel supplied by rail, main rwy concrete pour began 20Dec66 with several records set for most concrete poured in single day during war. While const in progress, the 459th and 537th TAS (C-7As); 1041st Police Sqdn, commo, med, maint, aerial port and Engr personnel arrived. 37TFW activated 1Mar67 and attached 7th AF during Jan67. Base Ops began 15Ma67. Base was last home of 12th Tactical Fighter Wing (TFW) in SVN, after moving here 1Apr70 to replace 37th TFW. The 12TFW stood down 17Nov71. 12th TFW included: 12th CSG, 12th FMS, 389th TFS (F-4Ds), 412th MMS, 480th TFS (F-4C/Ds), 12th Dispensary, 12th AMS, 12th HSS, 12th SS, 12th Civ Engr Sqdn, 12th Trans Sqdn, 12th SPS. The 37TFW's combat ops began 15Apr67, w/strikes by 416TFS (F-100Ds orig from Bien Hoa). Det 1, 612TFS (F-100Dst) began ops 8Jun67 (orig from Phan Rang AB). In Jun67, Commando Sabre (Misty) was activated employing F-100Fs as first Fast FACs over NVN. Univ of MD opened classes at base 15 Aug67. 3Feb68, 355TFS (F-100Ds, Myrtle Beach AFB, SC) was attached to 37TFW for 6 mos TDY. By 28Feb68, 37TFW had completed 13,000 combat sorties. 174TFS (four F-100C sqdns from Iowa Air NG, arrived 14May68. As 355TFS completed TDY, ANG from NJ and Wash DC replaced them. By 3Jan69, some 90 acft inc TFW F-100s, HH-43B/R rescue helos, AC-47 gunships, C-7A, EC-47N/P EW, UC-123B/K Ranch Hand defoliation and RF-101C/RF-4C photo recon acft called Phu Cat home. During '69, the F-100s transitioned to F-4s. Det 1, 612TFS (F-100Ds left 13Apr69 and were replaced by 48OTFS (F-4C/Ds from Da Nang). On 11May69, 174TFS (F-100Cs) returned stateside as did 355TFS (F-100Ds) on 15May69. 27May69, the 416TFW (F-100Ds) moved to Tuy Hoa AB. May69, Commando Sabre (Misty-FAC F-100Fs) was inactivated. 389TFS (F-4Ds from Da Nang) arrived 24Jun69, completing transition to F-4s. Also beginning in '69, AC-47 "Spooky" gunships were turned over to VNAF and replaced with AC-119G "Shadow" and then AC-119K "Stinger" gunships. 361st TEWS (EC-47N/Ps from Nha Trang) moved to PCAB and 25th Casualty Staging Flight was inactivated. During 70, 37TFW was deactivated with assets redesignated as 12TFW (orig from Cam Ranh Bay). While at Phu Cat AB, all 12TFW acft used call-sign "COBRA." In Jun70, 459TAS (C-7As) was inactivated and Ranch Hand redesignated "A" Flight 310th TAS, as TAS and Ranch Hand units were consolidated throughout SVN. Until '70, base relatively secure from rocket/mortar and sapper attack due to concentration of ROK and US troops in area. During '71, Ranch Hand mission was moved to Tan Son Nhut. Det 1, 608th MASS was inactivated. Rescue, commo and Weather units were inactivated, downsized, and/or redesignated. 537TAS (C-7Ast) was inactivated assets turned over to VNAF. 429th TS was formed as was VNAF 431TS (C-7As), and 361TEWS (EC-47N/Ps) departed Phu Cat. 8Oct71, 389TFS flew its last combat sortie in SEA. On 15Oct71, 389TFS (name only) was transferred to Mountain Home AFB, ID. 20Oct71, 48OTFS flew the last US combat missions from Phu Cat, which was also the last combat sortie for 12TFW. The mission consisted of four F-4Ds with 12-MK-82 LD bombs each and hit portions of HCMT in Tri-border area. On 26Oct71, the 389TFS deployed to US when first cell of six F-4Ds departed at 0645 hrs. 2d cell left 30 min later. Crews for this historic deployment were selected from F-4 units throughout SEA. Thirteen 12TFW crew members included in deployments. 48OTFS's F-4Ds were redistributed in SEA. Last two F-4Ds of 12TFW departed on 2Nov71 for Clark AB. 12th TFW was inactivated at Phu Cat, 17Nov71. On 18Nov71, 6259th Base Sqdn and Dispensary were activated to service remaining USAF personnel, while deactivation of 12th Security Police Sqdn was delayed until 23Dec71 due to VNAF reluctance to assume base security duties. Base officially turned-over to VNAF 1Jan72. On Mar72, Det 5009, 1005th Spcl Invest Grp (AFOSI) was inactivated (it had provided intel and analysis since Jan67). Other USAF personnel remained as instructors for VNAF C-7A (airlift) and A-37B (tactical fighter) units. During 72 Easter Offensive, VNAF units here were effective in halting NVA attacks down QL-19 from Kontum/Pleiku toward Qui Nhon and also provided supt for ARVN counteroffensive which began Jul72. In 73 VNAF units here reportedly responded to NVA offensive and ARVN needs effectively in Binh Dinh Pr. By 6Mar75, Rte 19 was cut by NVA between Pleiku and Qui Nhon. VNAF 6th Air Div planes from Phu Cat provided fire supt and supplies to retreating ARVN forces. Pleiku was evaced 14Mar75, by VNAF C-130s moving equip/people to Phu Cat. VNAF 6th AD cmdr from Pleiku was then designated senior mil cmdr for area and base became focal point for ARVN ops. A-37Bs from Phu Cat and Phan Rang flew all-out effort regarded by some as best VNAF fight of war; pilots loaded own planes and VNAF fought professionally after ARVN troops pulled out. A-37Bs were hitting targets so close to AF that pilots did not have time to raise lndg gear before dropping ordnance. Finally, acft were evacuated to Bien Hoa and Phan Rang. Phu Cat AB and Qui Nhon fell to NVA forces on 31March75. Address was APO SF 96368. Detailed history of base can be found on internet at www.fgi. net/~rdoughty/phuhist.htm. Serv Bty, 7th/15th Arty here, as was 37th Aeromedical Evac Sqd. Also listed at BR 90-43 and BR 890-470. Map is L-7014-6836-4, per Ken Burrington. El. 101', 10,000' conc rwy. At 13°57'12"N-109°02'48"E. Binh Dinh Pr, II Corps.

Phu Cat ARVN Trng Center (BR 913-459)
At Phu Cat 2 AF, apx 3 km NE Phu Cat AB and 27 km NE Qui Nhon. Mar67. Binh Dinh Pr, II Corps.

Phu Cat Heliport (BR 908-477)
Slightly NE or along NE edge of Phu Cat AB. Heliport #630, alt 49', at 13°59'5"N-109°03'30"E, per Feb73 TAD. Binh Dinh Pr, II Corps.

Phu Cat Mountains (BR/CR)
Small mtn range between Phu Cat and Ocean and due E Phu Cat AB. Binh Dinh Pr, II Corps.

Phu Cat RFTC (BR 8-4?)
RVNAF Regional Force Trng Ctr. Apparently near Phu Cat AB. Binh Dinh Pr, II Corps.

Phu Cat TACAN NDB (BR 88-44)
Tactical Air Navigation and Non-Directional air navigation beacon site. At Phu Cat AB. Binh Dinh Pr, II Corps.

Phu Cat Training Center (BR 913-459)
See Phu Cat ARVN Trng Ctr. Binh Dinh Pr, II Corps.

Phu Cong (XT 81-14)
See Phu Cuong. Binh Duong Pr, III Corps.
Phu Cong Bridge (XT)
Over Saigon River along vital supply corridor between Cu Chi and Saigon/Long Binh/Tan Son Nhut area. Detailed story with photos of this bridge in 23Sep68 issue of *Tropic Lightning News*, Vol. 3, No. 39, pp4-5. Binh Duong and Gia Dinh Prvs, III Corps.
Phu Cu Pass Quarry (BR 881-887)
Along QL-1, apx 7 km SE Bong Son and 6 km NNW Van An. Apr-Oct67. Binh Dinh Pr, II Corps.
Phu Cum Airfield (UH 03-01)
LS-50. CIA/SF, per *Air Facilities Data-Laos.*
Phu Cum Airfield (UH 04-00)
LS-50A. CIA/SF, per *Air Facilities Data-Laos.*
Phu Cuong (XT 81-14)
A.k.a. Camp Crocker or Crocker Cmpd. On eastern bank of Song Saigon apx 17 km due N Tan Son Nhut AB/Saigon and 4 km WSW Lam Son. Home of MACV Advsy Teams 70 and 91 (also rptd as being at Thu Dat Mot, Binh Dinh Pr). On E shore of Saigon River along QL-13, 16 km NNW Saigon, 16 km W Bien Hoa 7 km SSW Dog Leg Village. Per *Low Level Hell's* 1st Div TAOR map. Capitol, Binh Duong Pr, III Corps.
Phu Cuong Airfield (XT 862-158)
See Phu Loi AF. Binh Duong Pr, III Corps.
Phu Cuong Bridge (XT 806-136)
QL-13 bridge over Song Saigon at Phu Cuong and near Phu Ha Dong, apx 18 km due N Tan Son Nhut AB, 16 km W Bien Hoa 7 km SSW Dog Leg ville. 1st Inf Div AO, '69. Also spelled "Phu Cong." As it was only major link across Saigon River N of Saigon, 2d/34th Armor provided security here circa Tet '68. The newly completed bridge was a prime VC frogman and sapper target during '68, and 1 lb. blocks of TNT were routinely thrown into river at 10 min intervals all along bridge at night to discourage them. B/2d/14th Inf helped secure it thru Oct and 1st week of Nov68, when 1st/27th Inf, 25th ID took over. Per AARs and Hist Supps at www.en.com/users/kramsey/vnr102.html#. See Phu Ha Dong. Binh Duong Pr, III Corps.
Phu Cuong Navy ASB (XT 81-17)
On Saigon River apx 15 km due N Saigon. USN Advanced Supt Base, '69-70. Per MRF Assn Website. Binh Duong Pr, III Corps.
Phu De Me Airfield (QB 35-44)
LS-105. CIA/SF, per *Air Facilities Data-Laos.*
Phu Dien Chau (n/a)
Mapsheet name of L-7014-6146-4. NVN only.
Phu Dien, Vung (WG 7-0)
Bay at 19°00'N-105°40'E. On NE48-03 JOG. NVN.
Phu Doan (WJ 19-93)
At confluence of Chay and Clear Rivers. One objective of Op Lorraine, Nov52. Large Vietminh caches found around this town during Op. Per *Street Without Joy*, Chp3, map at p 80. NVN.
Phu Duc (n/a)
Mapsheet name of L-7014-6734-1. SVN.
Phu Fa Noi Airfield (TG 65-70)
LS-102. CIA/SF, per *Air Facilities Data-Laos.*
Phu Gia (various)
Common Viet place-name. See grid squares: AU 8-0, XK 4-1, WF 6-1, XE 8-0, BP 9-8 and AT 8-9. NVN/SVN.
Phu Gia, Lagune de (AT 8-9)
A.k.a. Dam Lap An. Lagoon at 16°14'N-108°04'E. Grid per DMA ND49-01 map and NIMA. Quang Nam Pr, I Corps.
Phu Gia CAP (AT 84-99?)
Possible 3d CAG CAP Team site near Phu Loc, SE Hue. Thua Thien Pr, I Corps.
Phu Gia Heliport (AT 845-995)
Along QL-1, at N edge of Dam Lap An Lagoon near Phu Gia, apx 28 km NNW Da Nang and 3 km E FSB Los Banos. Heliport #631, alt 33', per Feb73 TAD. Thua Thien Pr, I Corps.
Phu Gia Pass (AT 833-999)
QL-1 pass, apx 13 km NW Hai Van Pass, 16 km due E Q Phu Loc and 30 km NW Da Nang AB. Also listed at AU 833-000, and both grids are correct as site is on grid zone border. Thau Thien Pr, I Corps.
Phu Gia Pass (AU 833-000)
See Phu Gia Pass. Thau Thien Pr, I Corps.
Phu Ha Dong (XS8-8)
On river bank apx 2 km from main road to Cholon, between Phu Cong Bridge and Cholon, with rice paddies on other 3 sides. ARVN Rgt HQ'd here, but VC still controlled ville and area at night. Gia Dinh Pr, III Corps.
Phu He Airfield (TF 93-77)
LS-255. CIA/SF, per *Air Facilities Data-Laos.*
Phu Hien (WJ 08-98?)
Apx 25 km NNE Yen Bay and 105 km NW Hanoi. As French Armored spearhead pushed N toward Phu Hien during Op Lorraine (Oct-Dec52), a sharp-eyed Lt spotted fresh tire tracks pointed away from Phu Doan-Yen Bay Road and decided to follow them. Tracks led to Soviet Molotov truck park, 1st proof of Soviet assistance to Vietminh in 1st Indochina War. Per *Street Without Joy*, Chp 3, p 92, with map at p 80. NVN.
Phu Hiep (various)
Common Viet place-name. Listed at AN 93-86, BN 00-11, BR 97-61, BR 75-37, BT 15-32, CQ 24-35, XS 17-35, VS 99-72, and WT 14-05. I, II and IV Corps.
Phu Hiep (CQ 26-38)
A.k.a. Hell's Half Acre. On coast, apx 9 km SE Tuy Hoa AF and 6 km E QL-1. 134th AHC here. 268th Avn Bn here and later moved to Tuy Hoa. Phu Yen Pr, II Corps.
Phu Hiep Airfield (CQ 26-38)
On coast, apx 9 km SE Tuy Hoa AF and 5 km E QL-1. Minor AF per TPC K-10B. El. 20'. Phu Yen Pr, II Corps.
Phu Hiep Army Air Field (CQ 245-354)
A.k.a. Phu Hiep AAF. On coast, apx 9 km SE Tuy Hoa AF and 5 km E QL-1. "Secure, hvy helo trfc, US Army, 21Feb69 Closed to A/C larger than OV-1, AF # VA2-298," in Aug69 TAD per Frank Penk, Jr. Not in Feb73 TAD. Phu Yen Pr, II Corps.
Phu Hiep Beach (CQ 244-382)
N Phu Hiep AF, apx 7 km SE Tuy Hoa AF and 5 km E QL-1. Jan69. Phu Yen Pr, II Corps.
Phu Hiep SF Camp (WT 143-052)
A.k.a. FOB An Phu. Immed S Cambodian border, 24 km NNW Chau Doc AF and 90 km NE Ha Tien. 5th SF. Info per *SF Order of Battle.* Chau Doc Pr, IV Corps.

Phu Hiep Signal Site (CQ 26-38?)
If grid correct, was on coast apx 5 km SE Tuy Hoa AF. Also possibly in WT 1-0. Grid est. Phu Yen Pr?, II Corps.

Phu Hoa Airfield (XT 862-158)
See Phu Loi AF. Binh Duong Pr, III Corps.

Phu Hoi (n/a)
Mapsheet name of L-7014-6836-2. SVN.

Phu Houei Mouei Airfield (QB 82-65)
LS-67 and Phu Hua Moui. CIA/SF base per *Air Facilities Data-Laos.*

Phu Houot Airfield (TG 42-31)
LS-99. CIA/SF, per *Air Facilities Data-Laos.*

Phu Hua Moui Airfield (QB 82-65)
LS-67 and Phu Houei Mouei. CIA/SF, per *Air Facilities Data-Laos.*

Phu Khan Hua Airfield (TF 77-82)
LS-251. CIA/SF, per *Air Facilities Data-Laos.*

Phu Khe (CQ 0-9)
N Song Cau along QL-1. Phu Yen Pr, II Corps.

Phu Khe (various) (BT/CQ/YD)
Common Viet place-name. See UTM grid squares BT 3-1, CQ 0-9, CQ 2-3 and YD 7-2. I/II Corps.

Phu Khieo Airfield (SD 9-1)
Apx 70 km W Khon Kaen AF, 135 km SSW Udorn AB, and 340 km NNE Bangkok, per ONC-J-11. 3,400' rwy. Grid per, and listed as abnd in, '66 NIMA. Near 16°22'00"N-102°10'00"E. El. 695' or 754'. Thailand.

Phu Khuong Airfield (XT 343-583)
Apx 7 km E peak of Nui Ba Den, 3 km NE Ap Phuoc Hoa, and 13 km NE Tay Ninh. Listed as "Insecure, abnd 6Dec67, AF # VA3-238," in Aug69 TAD per Frank Penk, Jr. Not in Feb73 TAD. Tay Ninh Pr, III Corps.

Phu Khuong Dist HQ (XT 335-580)
At or near Ap Phuoc Hoa, apx 6 km due E Nui Ba Dean and 14 km NE Tay Ninh. Feb68. Also listed at XT 234-476, apx 10 km S this site? Tay Ninh Pr, I Corps.

Phu Khuong District HQ (XT 234-476)
Just W Long Hoa, apx 2-3 km S Tay Ninh and 7 km SE Tay Ninh West AF. Co sized NVA assault here morning of 18Aug68, during Battle for Tay Ninh.[425] Also listed at XT 335-580, apx 10 km N this site? Tay Ninh Pr, III Corps.

Phu Lac 6 (AT 925-527)
A.k.a. Phu Lac 6 CB and Outpost. Small Marine FSB at Liberty Bridge (spanned Song Thu Bon) along Rte TL-3, apx 25 km SSW Da Nang AB, 8 km NE An Hoa Base and 8 km SE Hill 55. Manned by 1st/5th Mar, 1st Mar Div and D Bty, 1st/11th Arty. Attacked by NVA Bn, 8Mar69. Also listed at BS 692-648, but that may be a different Liberty Bridge? Quang Nam Pr, I Corps.

Phu Lac 6 Combat Base (AT 925-527)
See Phu Lac 6. Quang Nam Pr, I Corps.

Phu Lac 6 Outpost (AT 925-527)
See Phu Lac 6. Jul-Dec69. Quang Nam Pr, I Corps.

Phu Lac 6 Refugee Camp (AT 927-528)
A.k.a. Phu Loc 6 R.C.? Along Song Thu Bon, apx 22 km SSE Da Nang AB. NPIA grid. Quang Nam Pr, I Corps.

Phu Lam (XS 78-89)
Suburb of Saigon. Home of Phu Lam Army STRATCOM Facility near Cholon, a worldwide US defense commo system site. Gia Dinh Pr, III Corps.

Phu Lam Signal Site (XS 78-89)
A.k.a. Long Lines South. Apx 5 km SW Tan Son Nhut AB. Early US VN commo began in small station on 2d flr of old MAAG HQ Bldg (later MACV II Cmpd), Saigon. Estab 1951 by ARMY-MAAG-INDO-CHINA-SIG-I-51-DEV, it served MAAG and US. Embassy. In '56, transmitter moved to former French station on Plantation Rd, with receiver at Ba Queo (2km S the W end of Tan Son Nhut rwy) while commo center stayed at MAAG cmpd. In Nov61, const began for complex that became Phu Lam Sig Site. In '62, was a.k.a. STARCOM Station and later USASTRATCOM. In Nov63, MAAG commo center began its shift to Phu Lam Site, and complete site went into op 7Jan64. Data per Josef Rokus at http://phulam.com/history.htm. See Long Lines North. Gia Dinh Pr, III Corps.

Phu Lam Station (XS 8-9)
At Saigon. Site of US Army STRATCOM Facility near Cholon. Worldwide US defense commo system site. Gia Dinh Pr, III Corps.

Phu Lan Combat Base (BT 030-533)
Apx 17 km ENE An Hoa AF, 10 km WSW Hoi An and 6 km WSW Song Thu Bon QL-1 Bridge. Jul68. Quang Nam Pr, I Corps.

Phu Lang Thuong (n/a)
Mapsheet name of L-7014-6251-4. NVN only.

Phu Loc (various)
Common Viet place-name that can lead to some confusion. Q Phu Loc was at ZD 0-0, on QL-1 about 40 km SE Hue and there were also Phu Loc's at BS 7-8, BS 7-2 (Phu Loc 2), AT 9-4, AT 9-5 (Phu Loc 2), CQ 1-4 and CR 0-7 (Phu Loc 2), WR 8-4, XJ 2-2, WH 6-2, WH 6-0, XE 5-7 and XE 8-0. NVN/SVN.

Phu Loc (AT 9-4 or 9-5)
Village on S side of Hai Van Pass, NE Spider Lake, N Hill 425 and SW Phu Nham Tay. See mapsheet L-7014-6541-1. Quang Nam Pr, I Corps.

Phu Loc (BS 59-93)
N of the Song Tra Bong, W of QL-1, apx 16 km SSE Chu Lai and 22 km N Quang Ngai. A series of villes with this name around listed grid. Quang Ngai Pr, I Corps.

Phu Loc (ZD 084-004)
A.k.a. Q Phu Loc. On S shore of Dam Cau Hai Bay and along QL-1, apx 40 km SE Hue and N of Hai Van Pass. District HQ. Thua Thien Pr, I Corps.

Phu Loc, FSB (ZC 077-987)
Along the Phu Loc-Bach Ma road, just W Q Phu Loc, apx 38 km SE Hue and 25 km SE Phu Bai. Apr68. Possibly ARVN, or 82d and/or 101st Abn? Thau Thien Pr, I Corps.

Phu Loc 6, FSB (AT 9-4?)
No data. 5th Marine and CAP One FSB discussed in *Mot CAP*. Presumably near Chu Lai? Quang Nam or Quang Tin Pr, I Corps.

Phu Loc Airfield (WR 760-412)
Apx 15 km NNW Bac Lieu and 47 km SSE Vi Thanh AF/City. "Insecure, operated on request, pvt AF, 9Jan69, AF # VA4-172," in Aug69 TAD per Frank Penk, Jr. Not in Feb73 TAD. Ba Xuyen Pr, IV Corps.

Phu Loc CAP (AT 9-4?)
CAP 3-1-8, 3rd CAG. Thua Thien Pr, I Corps.

Phu Loc CAP (AT 9-5?)
CAP 3-2-5, 3rd CAG. Thua Thien Pr, I Corps.
Phu Loc District HQ (ZD 085-003)
Along QL-1 at Q Phu Loc, apx 37 km SE Hue. Jan68. Also listed at ZD 097-007, Apr69. Thau Thien Pr, I Corps.
Phu Loc Plantation (ZD 175-012)
Coconut or rubber plantation on N side of QL-1 apx 8 km E Q Phu Loc, just E Dam Cau Hai Bay and 6 km E FSB Tomahawk. Thua Thien Pr, I Corps.
Phu Loc Quarry (ZD 027-024)
Along S side QL-1, apx 7 km WNW Q Phu Loc and 18 km SE Phu Bai. Apr71. Also listed at ZD 042-021, Jul70. See also Camp DeShurley. Thau Thien Pr, I Corps.
Phu Loc Railroad Bridge (ZD 099-008)
Apx 1 km E Q Phu Loc and 1 km W FSB Tomahawk. Thau Thien Pr, I Corps.
Phu Loc Rock Crusher (ZD 027-024)
See Camp De Shurley. Thau Thien Pr, I Corps.
Phu Loc Valley (BT 00-47)
Apx 28 km due S Da Nang AB and 14 km due E An Hoa AF. 1st Mar Div. Americal List. Quang Nam Pr, I Corps.
Phu Loi (various)
Common Viet place-name. Sites inc: WR 8-9, XT 8-1, YS 1-5, WJ 9-5, VH 9-7, YS 1-5 and AT 8-5. NVN/SVN.
Phu Loi Advisory Compound (XT 84-18)
A.k.a. Gosney Cmpd. At Phu Loi combat base. Named to honor Maj. Durward D. "Dean" Gosney, KIA 7Oct64, when his chopper was shot down while in supt 5th ARVN Data per *Vietnam Military Lore, 1959-1973*. Div Binh Duong Pr, III Corps.
Phu Loi Airfield (XT 862-158)
A.k.a. Darkhorse Base. Apx 20 km E Cu Chi, 7 km ENE Phu Cuong, 2 km W Phu Loi, 19 km N Saigon and 2 km N Lam Son. N/S rwy was built by Japanese during WWII. 1st Sqd, 4th Air Cav and other 1st Inf Div units here '69. Per *Low Level Hell's* 1st Div TAOR map. Per TPC K-10D. El. 95', 2,800' asph rwy. At 10°59'57"N-106°42'10"E. Binh Duong Pr, III Corps.
Phu Loi Base Camp (XT 84-18)
Along outskirts of Phu Loi, apx 20 km N Saigon. Built in 65, it became basecamp of US 1st Inf (Big Red One) Div its ops in Binh Duong Pr run from this facility. 1st Sqd, 4th Cav (Div Recon) 1st Inf Div, 11th Avn Bn (Combat), 12th Avn Grp (with its 13 Cos, the 12th suptd IIFFV and HQ 82d Abn Bde) and Replacement and R&R centers here also. Per Monte Olsen, the 213th and 205th ASH and 128th AHC (Tomahawks) were housed here. Also apparently a "VC" ville to S that was source of occasional rocket and mortar attacks. Also misspelled Fou Loi by S.L.A. Marshall in *Ambush*, where he adds that 1st/26th, 1st Inf Div here '66-67, p. 174. N/S rwy here was built by Japanese during WWII. Binh Duong Pr, III Corps.
Phu Loi Post (XT 860-156)
Apx 5.5 km ENE Phu Cuong, 24 km NNE Tan Son Nhut AB and 14 km NNE FSB Copperhead. HQ and 3d Bde/82d Abn and elements of 3d/82 Supt Bn here, Oct68-Mar69. In Fall '68, initial fwd cmd post for 3d Bde/82d Abn was at "Tent City" in Bien Hoa basecamp, after Bde moved S from I Corps (Hue AO, beginning Sep-Oct68) in order to work AO covering W and NW approaches to Saigon. Immed became apparent that fwd Bde HQ needed to be closer to actual AO, so site was selected at Camp Red Ball (XS 832-984), along N edge Tan Son Nhut AB. Const of Bde's TOC at Red Ball began 1Oct68, and it was operational by 16Oct68. During same period, a new basecamp for Bde was built at Phu Loi Post (XT 860-155), and occupied on 20Oct68. [426] Binh Duong Pr, III Corps.
Phu Loi NDP (XT 908-167)
Along Rte 313, apx 5 km ESE Phu Loi AF. Occupied 15May68. Binh Duong Pr, III Corps.
Phu Loi Plains (XT 860-200)
Generally 7 km S Phu Loi AF, and 15 km NNE Tan Son Nhut. Binh Duong Pr, III Corps.
Phu Ly (n/a)
Mapsheet name of L-7014-6150-2. NVN only.
Phu Ly (WH 96-72)
A.k.a. Phu Li. Along QL-1, apx 60 km SSE Hanoi. French garrison here fought Vietminh 304 Div during Battle of Day River, 29May-18Jun51. See *Street Without Joy*, Chp 2, map at p 46. Also a Phu Ly at WG 7-9. NVN.
Phu Ly Bridge (BR 885-586)
Bridge over Soui Ca River on QL-1, apx 10 km N Phu Cat, 35 km S Bong Son and 7 km due N LZ Hammond. Binh Dinh Pr, II Corps.
Phu Mieng Mane Airfield (QV 21-55)
LS-96. CIA/SF, per *Air Facilities Data-Laos.*
Phu Moun Airfield (UF 45-90)
LS-212. CIA/SF, per *Air Facilities Data-Laos.*
Phu My (n/a)
Mapsheet name of L-7014-6837-3. SVN.
Phu My (BR 900-673)
Village on QL-1, 27 km SSE Bong Son, 13 km SSE Loc Son and 48 km NNE Qui Nhon. Map is L-7014-6837-3, per Ken Burrington. Binh Dinh Pr, II Corps.
Phu My (YS 26-75)
Along QL-15, apx 20 km WNW Nui Dat, and 27 km SE Bearcat. 1ATF here, or it was simply a significant terrain feature of their AO. 2d Bde/9th Inf Div MRF elements here per Jim Stone. Phuoc Tuy Pr, III Corps.
Phu My, FSB (BR 940-670)
Apx 3 km E Phu My/QL-1, some 24 km NNE Phu Cat AB and 28 km SSE Bong Son. Apr70. Binh Dinh Pr, II Corps.
Phu My Base (YS 260-750)
Along QL-15, apx 20 km WNW Nui Dat, and 27 km SE Bearcat. 2d Bde/MRF basecamp during Rung Sat Swamp ops, per Jim Stone, 2d/39th Inf. Phuoc Tuy Pr, III Corps.
Phu My 2 Airfield (YS 230-771)
See Phu My AF. Phuoc Tuy Pr, III Corps.
Phu My Airfield (YS 230-771)
Along QL-15, apx 4 km NNW Phu My, 23 km WNW Nui Dat and 24 km SE Bearcat. "Abnd ARVN(A), AF # VA3-142," in Aug69 TAD per Frank Penk, Jr. Not in Feb73 TAD. Phuoc Tuy Pr border, III Corps.
Phu My District HQ (BR 899-672)
On W side of QL-1 apx 8.5 km SSW LZ Uplift. SF A-Team situated here and advising a Co of RF/PFs. 1st/69th Armor routinely provided security here. II Corps.
Phu My SF Camp (BR 899-672)
On W side of QL-1 apx 8.5 km SSW LZ Uplift. SF A-Team situated here and advising a Co of RF/PFs. 1st/69th Armor routinely provided security here '68-69 and had no kind words for aggressiveness or ability of SVN militia

there. Was apparently never attacked while the 69th's tanks were there per www.rjsmith.com/6837-iii.html#lzuplift. Binh Dinh Pr, II Corps.

Phu My Thuong Airfield (BT 116-128)
See Tien Phuoc AF. Quang Tin Pr, I Corps.

Phu Nhon (n/a)
Mapsheet name of L-7014-6636-3. SVN.

Phu Nhon Airfield (AQ 870-990)
Flight serv G3 Air, II Corps TOC ARVN(A) 22Dec68, AF # VA2-280

Phu Nhon Airfield (AQ 88-99)
Apx 30 km due S Plei Do Lim AF, 48 km E Chu Pong Mtn (LZ X-Ray), and 40 km NW Cheo Reo AF. El. 1,360'. Pleiku Pr?, II Corps.

Phu Nhon Engineer Camp (AQ 88-99)
Existed for roughly 6 wks in '71, per Mike Young. Was not a named facility. 20th Engr Plt and 155mm Arty section here. Pleiku Pr, II Corps.

Phu Nhon, FSB (AQ 88-99)
A.k.a. FSB/LZ Gray. Apx 50 km SSE Pleiku. Described by Mike Young as, "a small Montagnard ville [on QL-14] S Weigt-Davis [Engr Camp and rock quarry]. 155mm US arty Bty here at one point as well as Engr security forces. Montagnard RF/PFs operated out of Phu Nhon and were noted for ruthlessness. An entire ville of Montagnard were resettled from infiltration rte in nearby valley (apx 7 km to SSW), to what became a new Plei Mei (about the 6th one). 1Nov71 7th/15th Arty ORLL courtesy Nolan Puttman states that site was renamed FSB Gray to honor Lt Richard J. Gray, who died of wounds suffered 12Jun71, when he was one of 11 WIA in rocket attack. Pleiku Pr, II Corps.

Phu Ninh, Battle of (BR 976-790)
At S end of Dam Tra O Lake, apx 3 km E Phuoc Thung, 22 km SSE Bong Son, 37 km NNE Phu Cat AB. Occurred 11Mar67. Map is L-7014-6837-4, per Ken Burrington. Binh Dinh Pr, II Corps.

Phu Nung Nong (n/a)
Mapsheet name of L-7014-5653-1. NVN only.

Phu Pha Thi Airfield (UH 68-60)
LS-85. CIA/SF, per *Air Facilities Data-Laos.*

Phu Quac Airfield (US 870-310)
Misspelling of Phu Quoc. See Duong Dong AF. Phu Quoc Island, IV Corps.

Phu Qui (various)
Common Viet place-name. See UTM grid squares: XE 6-3, BS 7-8, CQ 1-5, WG 4-3, BM 7-6, CP 0-6, BN 7-7, WG 1-6, BT 4-0 and BT 3-2. NVN/SVN.

Phu Qui Ammo Depot (XE 6-3 or WG)
NVA ammo storage area that was 2d target of Rolling Thunder, on 15Mar65. NVN.

Phu Quoc (B-44) SF Camp (US 870-310)
On Dao Phu Quoc Island in South China sea, apx 40 km W Ha Tien. 5th SF CIDG Det B-44, Feb67, SF Det 82. Transferred to RF/PF. Info/grid per *SF Order of Battle*. See Dao Phu Quoc. Kien Giang Pr, IV Corps.

Phu Quoc Airfield (US 870-310)
See Duong Dong AF. Phu Quoc Island, Kien Giang Pr?, IV Corps.

Phu Quoc Island (US 90-40)
A.k.a. Dao Phu Quoc. Apx 45 km due W Ha Tien and point where Cambodia/SVN border meet ocean. At some 50 x 27 km (31 miles x 16.8 miles) is by far largest Island in SVN territorial waters. Hill 565 (1,854') at US 96-47 is tallest peak. Here were 2 AFs (at least one of which was C-130 capable), major SVN govt POW camp (held 35,000 POWs in '68-69), USN NSA base, MP Advsy facility, SF camp, and MAT team IV-44. Per Ben Youmans, USN personnel working waters N of the island said that at low tide, water separating isle from Cambodia (apx 15 km) was only chin deep in most places and, as a result, determined escapees from An Thoi POW Camp (at S end of isle) could wade or swim across with relative ease. See An Thoi for POW camp history. Photos of An Thoi and POW camp at www.petester.com/toc.html. Gulf of Thailand, IV Corps.

Phu Quoc SF Camp (A-441) (US 867-295)
See Phu Quoc SF Camp. Gulf of Thailand, IV Corps.

Phu Quoc SF Camp (A-442) (US 867-295)
See Phu Quoc SF Camp. Gulf of Thailand, IV Corps.

Phu Quoc SF Camp (US 867-295)
On Dao Phu Quoc Island, apx 40 km W Ha Tien. 5th SF, Det A-426, A-427, later respectively changed to Det A-441 and A-442, Oct66 (also Det 82?). Transferred to RF/PF. Grid per *SF Order of* Gulf of Thailand, IV Corps.

Phu Quoc Training Center (US 867-295)
On Dao Phu Quoc Island, apx 40 km W Ha Tien. Grid is guess at likely site. Gulf of Thailand, IV Corps.

Phu Quy Combat Base (BN 740-742)
Along QL-1, apx 8 km SW Phan Rang and 13 km SSW Phan Rang AB. Oct69. Ninh Thuan Pr, II Corps.

Phu Reng, Plantation de (YT 1-9)
See Phu Rieng. Phuoc Long Pr, III Corps.

Phu Rieng (YT 0-9)
A.k.a. Phu Rieng Sron. Phuoc Long Pr, III Corps.

Phu Rieng 1 Airfield (YT 124-916)
Apx 43 km ESE Loc Ninh, 16 km WNW Bunard AF, and 16 km NNE Dong Xoai. Listed as, "Insecure, overgrown, AF # VA3-276," in Aug69 TAD per Frank Penk, Jr. Not in Feb73 TAD. Phuoc Long Pr, III Corps.

Phu Rieng Old Airfield (YT 124-916)
See Phu Rieng 1 AF. Phuoc Long Pr, III Corps.

Phu Rieng Sron (YT 0-9)
A.k.a. Phu Rieng. Phuoc Long Pr, III Corps.

Phu Rieng, Plantation de (YT 1-9)
A.k.a. Don Dien Phu Rieng. Apx 40 km ESE Loc Ninh and 15 km NNE Dong Xoai.Phuoc Long Pr, III Corps.

Phu Sang Nao Airfield (TG 85-87)
LS-80. CIA/SF, per *Air Facilities Data-Laos.*

Phu Sang Noi Airfield (TF 71-95)
LS-244. CIA/SF, per *Air Facilities Data-Laos.*

Phu Se Bott Airfield (UG 74-80)
LS-82. CIA/SF, per *Air Facilities Data-Laos.*

Phu Tai (various)
Common Viet ville name. See grid squares: BS 4-8, BR 9-4?, CR 0-2 and CR 0-1. I & II Corps, SVN

Phu Tai (CR 03-16 or CR 9-4?)
A.k.a. Phu Tai (2). In valley along QL-1, apx 6 km WSW Qui Nhon AF, and 5 km W Qui Hoa. Location of Camps Adams, Addison, Petty, Provide and Vasquez. Was also site of in-processing area for 173d Abn (and of their in-country training area in nearby Cha Rang Valley), per *Charlie Rangers*, p 32. Binh Dinh Pr, II Corps.

Phu Tai Ammo Storage Point (CR 03-16)
Along QL-1 apx 8 km SW Qui Nhon, per 19th Eng article at www.war-stories.com/Incoming.htm. Described as major ammo point for Central Highlands. Binh Dinh Pr, II Corps.

Phu Tai Camp (CR 03-16?)
Apparently in Pioneer Valley (a.k.a. Phu Tai Valley?), apx 6 km SW Qui Nhon? In '70 was renamed Camp Petty. Binh Dinh Pr?, II Corps.

Phu Tai Refugee Camp (BR 986-430)
If grid correct, was apx 10 km due E Phu Cat AB. NPIA data. Binh Dinh Pr, II Corps.

Phu Tai Valley (CR 03-16)
A.k.a. Pioneer Valley? Apx 6 to 8 km W to WSW Qui Nhon. Binh Dinh Pr, II Corps.

Phu Thanh Heliport (YS 032-870)
On LTL-25, apx 12 km WSW Long Thanh N AF and 15 km E Saigon. "Heliport #663, alt?, soccer fld, at 10°44'00"N-106°51'30"E." Bien Hoa Pr, III Corps.

Phu Thanh Valley (CR 02-21)
Apx 6 km inland from Qui Nhon. When USMC BLT 2/7 landed at Qui Nhon, 7Jul65, its HQ, Arty and supply stayed at the AF (while its 4 Inf Cos went W) until 10Jul65, when the HQ CP elements moved here to E of QL-1. Per *Utter's Battalion*, p 101, was "a small valley tucked into the hills near, but not astride [QL-1]." Khanh Hoa Pr, II Corps.

Phu Thien (n/a)
Mapsheet name of L-7014-6636-2. SVN.

Phu Thien SF Camp (BQ 245-929)
A.k.a. FOB Mai Linh. See Mai Linh SF Camp for relative loc. Villes with this name ubiquitous in SVN and, in Phu Bon Pr, alone are near BQ 08-97, BQ 1-8, BQ 1-9, AR 9-0, AR 9-4 and BR 03-00. 5th SF. Name per *SF Order of Battle.* Phu Bon Pr, II Corps.

Phu Tho (n/a)
Mapsheet name of L-7014-6051-4. NVN only.

Phu Tho (WJ 24-66)
On N bank of Red River apx 72 km NW Hanoi and 25 km WNW Viet Tri. One objective of Op Lorraine. See Op Lorraine. NVN.

Phu Tho, FSB? (XS 81-90)
A.k.a. FSB Phu To? Presumably at Phu To Racetrack in downtown Saigon during Tet '68? 3d/7th Inf, 199th LIB here. Gia Dinh Pr, III Corps.

Phu Tho Hoa Airfield (XS 815-905)
A.k.a. the Phu Tho or Saigon Racetrack AF? In center of Saigon, apx 4.5 km WSW Independence Palace and 5 km S Tan Son Nhut AB. Map is L-7014-6330-4, which lists it as "Phu Tho Hoa (abnd AF)." Gia Dinh Pr, III Corps.

Phu Tho Racetrack (XS 815-905)
A.k.a. the Saigon Racetrack and Phu To Racetrack. In center of Saigon, apx 4.5 km WSW Independence Palace and 5 km S Tan Son Nhut AB. Apparently at one time also an AF, as map L-7014-6330-4 lists it as "Phu Tho Hoa (abnd airfield)." Scene of heavy mechanized Inf attacks of VC positions, 31Jan-1Feb68, during Tet '68. 3d/7th Cav, 1st Cav also involved in attack of 275th VC Rgt positions here. Gia Dinh Pr, III Corps.

Phu Thong Hoa (WK 9-6)
Roughly 25 km NNE Bac Kan and 110 km N Hanoi. During Op Lea, beginning 12Oct47, Vietminh stood their ground and fought Moroccan R.I.C.M. armored TF of Groupement "B", in effort to prevent its reinforcing heavily engaged French Paras of Groupement "S" near Bac Kan, Cho Moi and Cho Don. Took Moroccans 3 days of bitter fighting to reach Groupement "S." Per *Street Without Joy*, p 29, and map at p 31. NVN.

Phu To Racetrack (XS 815-904)
See Phu Tho Race Track. Gia Dinh Pr, III Corps.

Phu Tu Peninsula (ZD 00-13)
Peninsula thrusting into NW corner of Dam Cau Hai Bay, apx 25 km ESE Hue. Thua Thien Pr, I Corps.

Phu Tu Road (ZD/YD)
Likely on Phu Tu Peninsula? Road built by 326th Engrs, 101st Abn during Op Lamar Plain, apx Aug69? Thua Thien Pr, I Corps.

Phu Tuc (n/a)
Mapsheet name of L-7014-6735-3. SVN.

Phu Tuc (BQ 510-590)
Apx 35 km SE Cheo Reo AF and 42 km WSW Dong Tre AF. SF Camp and AF here. Phu Bon Pr, II Corps.

Phu Tuc Airfield (BQ 504-598)
At Phu Tuc, apx 35 km SE Cheo Reo AF, 36 km NW Cung Song AF, and 42 km WSW Dong Tre AF, per TPC K-10A. Listed as "Secure (C-123, C-7) MACV 16Jul69, AF # VA2-215," in Aug69 TAD per Frank Penk, Jr. Not in Feb73 TAD. El. 450', 3,100' laterite rwy. At 13°11'46"N-108°41'52"E. Phu Bon Pr, II Corps.

Phu Tuc SF Camp (BQ 510-590)
At Phu Tuc AF, apx 35 km SE Cheo Reo and 42 km WSW Dong Tre. SF Det 27, 5th SF, Det A-224 (was 432), Oct65, A-224 Oct66. Transferred to RF/PF base. Grid per *SF Order of Battle.* Phu Bon Pr, II Corps.

Phu Ty Bridge (BR 885-586)
See Phu Ly Bridge. Binh Dinh Pr, II Corps.

Phu Van, FSB (XT 833-126)
Apx 3 km due S Lam Son AF, 16 km W Bien Hoa AB and 3 km SE Phu Cuong. Apr69. Binh Duong Pr?, III Corps.

Phu Vang (n/a)
Mapsheet name of L-7014-6542-3. SVN.

Phu Vang (YD 783-269)
Along Rte 551, apx 5 km ENE Hue Citadel AF and 9 km SSW Tan My AF. USMC Bn CP, mid '68. D/1st/502d Inf, 101st Abn here Oct68. POL line ran from Tan My/Eagle Beach on coast and along Hwy 551. 101st Abn was responsible for security of line, its pumping stations, the LCU Ramp at Tan My and Hwy 551 itself. Grid at city center and not likely CP site. Thua Thien Pr, I Corps.

Phu Vang District HQ (YD 781-269)
Apx 5 km ENE Hue Citadel AF and 9 km SSW Tan My AF. Apr68. Thua Thien Pr, I Corps.

Phu Vinh (XR 47-98)
Just NE Tra Vinh AF, apx 46 km due S My Tho, 33 km S Ben Tre/Truc Giang and 95 km SSW Saigon. Capitol, Vinh Binh Pr, IV Corps.

Phu Vinh (Tra Vinh) (n/a)
Mapsheet name of L-7014-6228-1. SVN.

Phu Vinh Airfield (XR 459-975)
See Tra Vinh AF. Vinh Binh Pr, IV Corps.

Phu Xuan Airfield (BQ 910-705)
See Dong Tre AF. Phu Yen Pr, II Corps.

Phu Xuan, FSB (XU 426-094)
A.k.a. FSB Oklahoma. Apx 4 km WNW Phum Dong, 15 km NE Katum, 33 km WSW Loc Ninh and 18 km WNW tip of Fishhook. Incursion FSB. Grid per *11th ACR Cambodia Invasion AAR, 1st Cav Div, May-Jun70*, courtesy Lou Rochat. [427] Cambodia.

Phu Yen (various)
Common Viet place-name. Sites in grid squares: WG 6-1, VJ 6-4, WJ 7-3, WJ 6-1, WJ 7-0, WH 8-7, WF 4-8, CQ 0-5, BT 3-2, B-R 1-5, BT 3-2. NVN & SVN.

Phu Yen Aqueduct (CQ 007-353)
Along LTL 7B and Song Da River, apx 21 km WSW Tuy Hoa AB, 2 km ESE Lac My and 8 km WSW Phuoc Thanh. Nov67. Phu Yen Pr, II Corps.

Phu Yen Binh (n/a)
Mapsheet name of L-7014-5952-1. NVN only.

Phu Yen Binh (VK 98-47?)
On Chay River, apx 65 km NNW Phu Doan and 145 km NW Hanoi. On 14Nov42, French armored units reached this point during Op Lorraine; the northernmost point of Op. Gen. Salan then ordered their withdrawal because despite Lorraine, the Vietminh T'ai Highland offensive had reached the Black River, and Lorraine had not eased pressure as anticipated. Data per *Street Without Joy*, p 95, map at p 80. Grid is est. NVN.

Phu Yen Province (BQ/CQ)
One of 12 north-central provs forming II Corps (II CTZ)

Phu Yen Rehab Center (CQ 15-48)
Prison just N of Tuy Hoa North AF and C Bty, 6th/32d Arty's position at that AF. Was object of Tet '68 attack. See Cemetery Hill and Tuy Hoa AF. Phu Yen Pr, II Corps.

Phuc Hao (n/a)
Mapsheet name of L-7014-6354-3. NVN/China.

Phuc Loi (WF 7-6 or UJ 7-5?)
Port attacked by USN carrier-based acft during Pierce Arrow, 2-7Aug64. See Pierce Arrow. NVN.

Phuc Nhac Airfield (XH 1-3?)
At Phat Diem, apx 100 km SSE Hanoi, 50 km NE Thanh Hoa and 20 km from ocean. Per ONC-J-11. NVN.

Phuc Vinh (n/a)
See Phuoc Vinh and Phuoc Binh.

Phuc Vinh, Camp (XT 977-497?)
Sp variant of either Phuoc Vinh or Phuoc Binh SF Camp? Spelled "Phuc Vinh" only in DA Chief, Mil Hist records summary which also indicates Det A-412 here '64, and B-31 in '65. Likely at listed grid as Det A-412 is listed as being at Phuoc Vinh SF Camp. Binh Duong Pr, III Corps.

Phuc Yen (WJ 73-48)
On Road No. 3, apx 25 km NW Hanoi. Likely a French garrison here in 1st Indochina War. See *Street Without Joy*, map at p 46. NVN.

Phuc Yen Airfield (WJ 7-4)
Major AF 20 km N Hanoi. Per ONC-J-11. El. 36'. NVN.

Phuket Airfield (MJ 2-9)
At 8°07'00"N-98°18'00"E. NIMA data. Thailand.

Phum Cham Sla Airfield (n/a)
Apx 140 km due W Phnom Penh. Cambodia.

Phum Chup Airfield (n/a)
A.k.a. Chup Plantation AF? Apx 85 km ENE Phnom Penh on Feb67 Natl Geo map. El. 82'. Cambodia.

Phum Hay (n/a)
Mapsheet name of L-7014-6437-2. SVN/Cambodia.

Phum Kra Sang Airfield (n/a)
Apx 120 km due ENE Phnom on Feb67 Natl Geo map. El. 131'. Cambodia.

Phum Krek Airfield (n/a)
Some 10 km from SVN border, apx 115 km E to ENE Phnom Penh. El. 262'. Cambodia.

Phum Plok Airfield (n/a)
Apx 235 km ENE Phnom Penh. Feb67 Natl Geo map. El. 1,125'. Cambodia.

Phum Preas Ang Airfield (n/a)
Along Mekong River, apx 110 km NE Phnom Penh per Feb67 Natl Geo map. El. 262'. Cambodia.

Phum Svai Antor Airfield (n/a)
Apx 55 km due E Phnom Penh. El. 5'. Cambodia.

Phum Tnaot (XT 16-04)
In Parrot's Beak, apx 4 km NW Chantrea and 17 km NW Moc Hoa. Battle for Ph' Tnaot (Phum Tnaot), 10May70, involving D/6th/31st Inf, 9th Div, during Cambodian Incursion. Followed "Battle of Chantrea" of 2 days earlier involving D Co and other 6th/31st Cos. Cambodia.

Phum Tapeang Airfield (n/a)
Feb67 Natl Geo map. El. 174'. Cambodia.

Phumi Choam Airfield (n/a)
Apx 160 km due W Phnom Penh. El. 853'. Cambodia.

Phung Du Cemetery (BS 8-2)
W of QL-1, apx 10-11 km N and slightly E of Bong Son, and just S LZ 4. Scene of heavy fighting during Op Masher White Wing involving 2d/7th Cav, 1st Cav Div. See LZ 4. Binh Dinh Pr, II Corps. [428]

Phung Duc Airfield (AQ 800-038)
See Ban Me Thuot East AF. Darlac Pr, II Corps.

Phung Hiep (n/a)
Mapsheet name of L-7014-6128-1. SVN.

Phung Hiep Heliport (WR 906-843)
Along QL-4, apx 25 km S Can Tho. Heliport #726, alt 10', at 09°48' 00" N 105°50' 00" E, per Feb73 TAD. Phong Dinh Pr, IV Corps.

Phung Hoang (n/a)
See Glossary.

Phuoampoc Mai, Ban Dao (CR 1-3)
Peninsula at 13°53'N-109°16'E. On ND49-09 JOG. Binh Dinh Pr, II Corps.

Phuoampoc Mai, Presquile de (CR 1-3)
A.k.a. Ban Dao Phuoampoc Mai. Peninsula at 13°53'N-109°16'E. On ND49-09 JOG. Binh Dinh Pr, II Corps.

Phuoampoc Thien, Pointe de (BS 7-9)
See Pointe Phuoampoc Thien. Quang Ngai Pr, I Corps.

Phuoc An, FSB (BQ 093-033)
At Buon Ea Yang AF, apx 28 km due E Ban Me Thuot. 2d/17th Arty here supt 23d ARVN ops. Data per Jack Picciolo. Darlac Pr, II Corps.

Phuoc An Airfield (BQ 504-598)
See Phu Tuc AF. Phu Bon Pr, II Corps.

Phuoc Binh (YU 16-08)
A.k.a. Song Be. Apx 28 km SE Bu Dop. Site of FSB Buttons, SF camps and 2 AF's (Song Be and Song Be City AF). Phuoc Long Prov Advsy Team, 4th/12th, 3d/7th, 199th LIB, 1st Inf and 101st Abn elements also here. Capitol, Phuoc Long Pr, III Corps.

Phuoc Binh Airfield (AT 879-396)
Apx 20 km SE Ha Tan AF, 38 km SSW Da Nang, 32 km SW Hoi An AF, 45 km NW Tam Ky, per TPC K-10A. El. 60'. "Abnd, Overgrown, SVN Directorate of Civ Avn, US Army on airfield, 29Jul67, AF # VA1-77," in Aug69 TAD per Frank Penk, Jr., not 73 TAD. Quang Nam Pr, I Corps.
Phuoc Binh Combat Base (YU 138-063)
A.k.a. Song Be CB. At Song Be AF, apx 28 km SE Bu Dop and 43 km E Loc Ninh AF. Apr68. Also listed at YU 144-073. Phuoc Long Pr, III Corps.
Phuoc Binh SF Camp (AT 8148-3834?)
Apx 7 km WSW Phuoc Binh AF, 38 km WSW Hoi An and 42 km SSW Da Nang. 5th SF camp. Grid per *SF Order of Battle.* See Ba To (old). Quang Ngai Pr, I Corps.
Phuoc Cam Heliport (BT 094-301)
Apx 4 km due E Binh Son and 21 km WNW Tam Ky. Heliport #634, alt 66', at 15°38'20"N-108°17'10"E, per 73 TAD. Quang Tin Pr, I Corps.
Phuoc Chau Heliport (BT 005-095)
Apx 12 km WSW Tien Phuoc, 5 km ESE Ton Bon/FSB Grunt and 33 km WSW Tam Ky. Heliport #635, alt 164', per Feb73 TAD. Quang Tin Pr, I Corps.
Phuoc Chau Island (CR 23-05)
Narrow, 5 km-long isle Gulf of Tonkin, apx 20 km SSE Qui Nhon and 12 km off SVN coast. There is lighthouse here. Phu Yen Provincial waters, II Corps.
Phuoc Chau Island (CR 23-07)
Apx 22 km SE Qui Nhon. Phu Yen Pr, II Corps.
Phuoc Chau Lighthouse (CR 23-06)
On Phuoc Chau Island, apx 23 km SE Qui Nhon. Phu Yen Pr, II Corps.
Phuoc Chi Special Zone (YS)
Target of Op Colby, 20-28Jan67, involving 1 Bde 9 Inf, 3/5 Cav 9 Inf Div. One of 1st ops conducted by newly arrived 9th Inf Div. 2/39th, 4/39th, and 5/60th Inf Bns plus 3/5th Cav participated. Phuoc Tuy Pr, III Corps.
Phuoc Dien (n/a)
Mapsheet name of L-7014-6838-4. SVN.
Phuoc Ha Heliport (BT 036-216)
Just N the Song Chang River, apx 10 km NW Tien Phouc and 26 km due W Tam Ky. Heliport #636, alt 66', per Feb73 TAD. Quang Tin Pr, I Corps.
Phuoc Ha Valley (BT 10-35)
A.k.a. Phouc Hoa Valley. Generally 20 km WNW Tam Ky. Per Col Harvey C. Barnum, Jr., USMC/MOH, on 11Dec65, the 1st VC Rgt withdrew here following heavy fighting with ARVN and USMC forces. On *Phuoc Ha-Que Son Valley* map in *The Rise and Fall of the American Army*, between pp 368-9. Quang Tin Pr, I Corps.
Phuoc Hai Airfield (WR 760-412)
See Phu Loc AF. Ba Xuyen Pr, IV Corps.
Phuoc Hiep (XT 555-170)
Apx 10 km SW Cu Chi, 7 km NNE Kiem Cuong and 29 km SW Tan Son Nhut AB. Cited in 23Jul66 Combat Op AAR, HQ 1st Bde/25th ID, APO SF 96225 for "Op Fargo" on-line at: www.en.com/users/kramsey/vnr102.html#. Also listed at XT 569-170. Hau Nghia Pr, III Corps.
Phuoc Hin District HQ (XT 126-501)
Apx 4 km WSW Tay Ninh West AF and 6 km NE Ben Soi. May68. Tay Ninh Pr, III Corps.
Phuoc Hoa 1 CAP (BT 036-216?)
CAP 1-3-3, 1st CAG. Quang Ngai Pr, I Corps.
Phuoc Hoa Airfield (XT 912-430)
On edge of plantation, apx 14 km ENE Lai Khe AF and 7 km SW Phuoc Vinh AF. "Field unusable, pvt, 2Jul67, AF # VA3-146," in Aug69 TAD per Frank Penk, Jr. Not in Feb73 TAD. Binh Duong Pr, III Corps.
Phuoc Hoa CAP (BT 036-216?)
1st CAG per Tim Duffie. Quang Ngai Pr?, I Corps.
Phuoc Hoa New Airfield (XT 960-495)
See Phuoc Vinh AF. Binh Duong Pr, III Corps.
Phuoc Hoa Old Airfield (XT 912-430)
See Phuoc Hoa AF. Binh Duong Pr, III Corps.
Phuoc Hoa, Lang (YS 29-61)
See Lang Phuoc Hoa. Phuoc Tuy Pr, III Corps.
Phuoc Khanh, Pointe de (XS 9-8)
See Pointe Phuoc Khanh. III Corps.
Phuoc Lam Heliport (BT 073-061)
Along Rte 531, apx 28 km SW Tam Ky and 8 km SSW Tien Phuoc. Heliport #637, alt 279', at 15°25'00"N-108°16'00"E, per Feb73 TAD. Quang Tin Pr, I Corps.
Phuoc Le (YS 43-67)
A.k.a. Xa Phuoc Le or Ba Ria or Baria. Town apx 20 km NNE Vung Tau and 8 km SW Nui Dat. See Ba Ria. Phuoc Tuy Pr, III Corps.
Phuoc Le Airfield (YS 402-613)
See Ba Ria AF. Phuoc Tuy Pr, III Corps.
Phuoc Le Base (YS 38-62)
A.k.a. Ba Ria Base. At Xa Phuoc Le, apx 20 km NNE Vung Tau and 8 km SW Nui Dat. 1st RAR. See Ba Ria. Phuoc Tuy Pr, III Corps.
Phuoc Long (n/a)
Mapsheet name of L-7014-6027-1. Actual sp in DOD listing is Puoc Long, but that is likely a typo. SVN.
Phuoc Long (WR 489-422)
Apx 42 km NE Quan Long and 32 km NW Bac Lieu. ARVN 42d Ranger Bn won US PUC for success in battle here 16Oct64. Bac Lieu Pr, IV Corps.
Phuoc Long (YU 18-08)
A.k.a. Phuoc Binh and Song Be. In *A Better War*, p 374, NVA Col Bui Tin is noted as having said that after Nixon resigned, NVA victory was no longer in doubt. Author also quotes Pham Van Dong as saying that US President Ford was weakest US president ever, so "We tested his resolve by taking Phuoc Long," adding that when Ford did not send B-52's in retaliation, Hanoi decided to mount the Final Offensive (unknown if he meant the city or the province?). Capitol, Phuoc Long Pr, III Corps.
Phuoc Long Airfield (YU 14-07)
See Song Be AF. Phuoc Long Pr, III Corps.
Phuoc Long City Airfield (YU 182-109)
See Song Be City AF. Phuoc Long Pr, III Corps.
Phuoc Long Heliport (WR 489-422)
Apx 42 km NE Quan Long and 32 km NW Bac Lieu. Heliport #638, alt 7', sod. Trees SE & NW. 09°26'00"N-105°26'40"E, per Feb73 TAD. Bac Lieu Pr, IV Corps.
Phuoc Long Province (XU/XT/YU/YT)
One of 11 south-central provs forming III Corps (III CTZ) during most of US War. During early stages of US presence, Phuoc Long was bordered to its S by what was known as Phuoc Thanh Pr, and was about one half its later

size. Somewhere close to 1964, most of Phuoc Thanh Pr was absorbed in Phuoc Long Pr (and other prvs). III Corps.

Phuoc Mai Pen (CR 1-2)
At Qui Nhon. Binh Dinh Pr, II Corps.

Phuoc Ninh Dist HQ (XT 129-504)
Apx 10 km due W Tay Ninh and 5 km WSW Tay Ninh West AF. Attacked 18Aug68 during Battle for Tay Ninh and again night of 10-11Sep68. Tay Ninh Pr, III Corps.

Phuoc Son 1 Heliport (BT 094-201)
Apx 22 km due W Tam Ky and 7 km NNW Tien Phuoc AF. Heliport #639, alt 197', at 15°33'00"N-108°17'15"E, per 73 TAD. Quang Tin Pr, I Corps.

Phuoc Son 2 Heliport (AT 854-217)
Apx 7 km SW Hiep Duc and 46 km W Tam Ky. Heliport #640, alt 164', per Feb73 TAD. Quang Tin Pr, I Corps.

Phuoc Son SF Camp (AT 910-250)
At or adj to Hiep Duc, apx 40 km W Tam Ky and 53 km SSW Da Nang. 5th SF. Moved to Kham Duc. Info/grid per *SF Order of Battle.* Quang Nam Pr, I Corps.

Phuoc Tan Outpost (XT 018-435)
See Phouc Tan RF Post. Tay Ninh Pr, III Corps.

Phuoc Tan RF Post (XT 018-435)
See Phouc Tan RF Post. Tay Ninh Pr, III Corps.

Phuoc Thanh Airfield (XT 960-495)
See Phuoc Vinh AF. Binh Duong Pr, III Corps.

Phuoc Thanh Province (XT/YT)
Thought to have existed early in US presence but absorbed into Phuoc Long and other adj provs before '65. It could be described very roughly as S half of Phuoc Long Pr that existed for most of US participation. III Corps.

Phuoc Thien (various)
Common Viet place-name. Sites inc: BS 714-976, BN 7118-450, ZS 027-803, YT 080-758, YT 086-757, YT 076-752, YS 1-8, YS 022-995, YU 174-105. SVN.

Phuoc Thien Airfield (BN 711-845)
Apx 6 km WSW Phan Rang AB, and 10 km WNW Phan Rang city. On IFFV Engr map prepared by 66th Engr Co in Jun70, but not in Feb73 TAD. Ninh Thuan Pr, II Corps.

Phuoc Thien CAP (BS 7-9?)
Lima 5/CAP 1-3-5, 1st CAG here per Tim Duffie. Quang Ngai Pr, I Corps.

Phuoc Thien SF Camp (BN 71-84?)
If grid correct, was apx 6 km WSW Phan Rang AB and 10 km WNW Phan Rang. Apparently 5th SF camp/FOB here, per *SF Order of Battle.* Moved to Dong Ba Thin. Ninh Thuan Pr, II Corps.

Phuoc Tho (YS 14-82)
Apx 30 km WSW Saigon, 13 km due E Xom Xoai Minh and 12 km due S Long Thanh AF. 2d/3d, D Trp/17th Cav, 199th LIB here. Gia Dinh or Bien Hoa Pr, III Corps.

Phuoc Tho Airfield (YS 14-82?)
A.k.a. Dat Do AF. Presumably at Dat Do, and if so, was roughly 10 km SW Nui Dat/Luscombe AF, 70 km ESE Saigon and 25 km NE Vung Tau. AF # VA3-196. In Aug69 TAD but not Feb73 TAD. Data per Frank Penk, Jr. Phuoc Tuy Pr, III Corps.

Phuoc Thuan CAP (BS 712-972)
See CAP 1-3-5. 1st CAG, Quang Tri Pr, I Corps.

Phuoc Tien Heliport (BT 182-153)
Apx 12 km SW Tam Ky, 3 km SE FSB Professional and 8km ENE Tien Phuoc. Heliport #641, alt 66', 15°30'10"N-108°22'15"E, Feb73 TAD. Quang Tin Pr, I Corps.

Phuoc Tien, FSB (BT 188-157?)
See LZ Young. Quang Tin Pr, I Corps.

Phuoc Tuc, SF Camp (BQ 510-590?)
Variant of Phu Tuc? Spelled Phuoc Tuc in DA Chief, Mil Hist records summary which also indicates Det A-432 (a.k.a. A-224) here '65. See Phu Tuc SF Camp (which is at listed grid). Phu Bon Pr, II Corps.

Phuoc Tuong Heliport (ZD 119-015)
On S side of QL-1, at or near FSB Tomahawk, apx 37 km SE Hue, 3 km E Phu Loc and 2 km inland from Dam Cau Hai lagoon. Heliport #642, alt 66', at 16°16'20"N-107°50'00"E. Some data from Feb73 TAD, which lists grid as ZD 118-013. Thua Thien Pr, I Corps.

Phuoc Tuy Province (YS)
One of 11 south-central provs forming III Corps (III CTZ).

Phuoc Valley (AT 84-34)
A.k.a. Que Son Valley, Nui Loc Son Basin or Death Valley, See Death Valley. Americal list. Quang Nam or Quang Tin Pr, I Corps.

Phuoc Vinh (n/a)
Mapsheet name of L-7014-6331-1. SVN.

Phuoc Vinh (XT 962-488)
Apx 50 km N to NNE Saigon, 35 km due N Bien Hoa AB, 28 km SSW Dong Xoai AF and 22 km NE Lai Khe. Per *LRRP Company Commander*, p 62, base was "Built on a fine, orange sheet of powdered clay. It was everywhere, and got into everything. During the seasonal rains, the dust…turned into a sticky morass of orange mud." 2d, 506th Inf/101st Abn s airlifted here, 1Jan68, to begin Op Uniontown in sweeps around 101st's Basecamp (killing apx 851 VC in resulting battles). 1st Inf Div elements also here and prior to Nov68, was 1st Inf Div Bde HQ. 1st Cav Fwd HQ moved here from Camp Evans (I Corps), 7Nov68 (Div Rear went to Bien Hoa), during Op Liberty Canyon (largest allied intra-theater combat deployment of 2d Indochina war). Also listed XT 967-490 and 966-492. Binh Duong Pr, III Corps.

Phuoc Vinh, FSB (XT 950-490)
At Phuoc Vinh AF, apx 35 km due N Bien Hoa AB. Feb68. Binh Duong Pr, III Corps.

Phuoc Vinh Airfield (XT 960-495)
Apx 28 km SSW Dong Xoai AF, 35 km N Bien Hoa AB, 22 km NE Lai Khe and immed N Xa Vinh Hoa, per TPC K-10D. El. 180', 3,700' asph rwy. Long/Lat 11°17'53"N-106°47'43"E. Binh Duong Pr, III Corps.

Phuoc Vinh Base Camp (XT 967-490)
Apx 28 km SSW Dong Xoai AF, 35 km N Bien Hoa AB and 22 km NE Lai Khe AF. 1st Inf, 101st Abn and 1st Cav basecamp. Binh Duong Pr, III Corps.

Phuoc Vinh SF Camp (XT 960-495)
Apx 35 km N Bien Hoa AB and 22 km NE Lai Khe. Phuoc Long Pr Adv Team 67, 5th SF Grp, Det. A-412, Dec64, Det B-31, Oct65 (some or all of these units possibly here). Moved to Xuan Loc. Grid per *SF Order of Battle.* Also listed at XT 977-497? Binh Duong Pr, III Corps.

Phuoc Vinh SF Camp (XT 977-497)
Apx 3 km E Phuoc Vinh AF and 25 km NE Lai Khe. Phuoc Long Pr Adv Team 67, 5th SF Grp. DA Chief, Mil Hist records summary says Det A-412 here '64, and B-31,

Oct65. Moved to Xom Cat. Grid per *SF Order of Battle* and also listed at XT 960-495? Binh Duong Pr, III Corps.

Phuoc Xuyen Navy ATSB (WS 810-820?)
If grid correct, was near intersection of several canals, apx 18 km NNE Cao Lanh, and 33 km N Sa Dec. USN Adv Tactical Supt Base, '69-71, per MRF Assn Website. Phuoc Xuyen Canal at WS 6-9? John Caughran tells us, "The base was a small 200 ft-square fenced cmpd with 4 guard towers, commo bunker, helo pad, ammo bunker, and 4 ammo barges with hootches built on them." Caughran and Dempsey B. both tell us it was on the Grand Canal (ran from Mekong to Vam Co Tay). "The next base was Thuy Nhon, [and others were] at Ben Luc and Moc Hoa." Turned over to SVN Navy, Apr71. Kien Phong Pr?, IV Corps.

Phuoc Yen (YD 690-276)
Ville apx 3.5 km N Hue and in bend of Song Bo River that resembled sock or stocking. Cordoned by elements of 2d Bde/101st Abn, Black Panther Co of 1st ARVN Div and PF units, 28Apr-1May68, Op Carentan II (considered THE classic cordon of VN War). 8th Bn, 90th NVA Rgt was fixed here while 21st Arty, USAF fighter-bombers and helo gunships devastated target. 419 NVA KIA, and 107 of survivors became largest NVA force to surrender en masse to a US unit during war. Thua Thien Pr, I Corps.

Phuon An (Tien Phuoc) (n/a)
Mapsheet L-7014-6639-1. Sheet name: Tien Phuoc (Phuon An). SVN.

Phuy Tu, Dam (YD 9-1)
A.k.a. Dam Thuy Tu. Lagoon at 16°26'N-107°46'E. On NE48-16 JOG. Thua Thien Pr, I Corps.

Phy My Thuong Airfield (BT 116-128)
See Tien Phuoc AF. Quang Tin Pr, I Corps.

Phylis, FSB/LZ (XT 538-805)
See Phyillis. Tay Ninh Pr, III Corps.

Phyllis, FSB/LZ (XT 537-806)
Apx 11 km SSW tip of Fishhook, 24 km WSW An Loc, 24 km ESE Katum and 43 km NE Tay Ninh. Per Bobby Jackson, Phyllis and Vivian were named after 1st Cav Bn CO's wives (LTCs Unger and Justice respectively), and diary of "Frenchy" Torres, tells us Phyllis was built beginning 3May69. Attacked by NVA 95C RGT in early Jun69 (along with FSBs Barbara, Grant and Jamie) as part of general attack on Tay Ninh. 1st/7th Cav, 1st Cav here Apr69. Per Peter Cole, is cited in *1st Cav Div Op Rpt, Feb-Apr69*, p 4, and "*Incursion*." Also listed at XT 535-815 and XT 542-808. Tay Ninh Pr, III Corps.

Phyllis, LZ (YA 975-499)
Apx 26 km W to WNW Pleiku and 12 km ENE Plei Djereng New AF. LZs Cathy, Helga, Phyllis and Ruby were mutually suptg bases? 4th Div elements here '68 or '69. Name/grid per Dick Arnold. Pleiku Pr, II Corps.

Piastre (n/a)
See Glossary.

PIC Robin Radio (BP 221-190)
See Radio Relay (Pic Robin). Tuyen Duc Pr, II Corps.

Picardy, FSB (XT 659-492)
Apx 18 km ENE Dau Tieng, 17 km NW Lai Khe, 5 km SE FSB Oran, 14 km NW FSB Thunder I, 10 km NNE FSB El Paso. 1st Inf Div, '69. Binh Duong Pr, III Corps.

Pick, LZ (BR 640-833)
Apx 1.5 km SW Tien Thuan and 17 km ENE An Khe. Mar66. Binh Dinh Pr, II Corps.

Pickaway, USS (n/a)
APA-222. Amphib Attack, Transport, per Ralph Fries.

Picking, USS (n/a)
DD-685, per Ralph Fries.

Pico, LZ (YD 202-130)
In Da Krong River Valley along Rte 9222, apx 2 km NW FSB Cunningham, 26 km SSE Ba Long AF and 41 km SSW Quang Tri. Apr70 XXIV Corps grid per Don Armstrong. Quang Tri Pr, I Corps.

Picton, FSB (YS 640-897)
Apx 30 km NE Nui Dat, 4 km NNE FSB Tasman and 1.5 km SSW FSB Tiger. On 1ATF NCO trng map per John Hollett. Phuoc Tuy Pr, III Corps.

Pie Slice, The (CP 051-501)
Apparently a portion of Camp J. F. McDermott. Vic of listed grid. Nha Trang, Khanh Hoa Pr, II Corps.

Piedmont or FSB Piedmont? (BT?)
Apparently name of an area N of Tam Ky, though possibly a FSB name? Americal list, I Corps.

Pien Lieu Airfield (UG 73-93)
LS-31. CIA/SF, per *Air Facilities Data-Laos.*

Pieng Yao (n/a)
Mapsheet name of L-7014-5949-1. NVN only.

Pierce Arrow, Operation (n/a)
7th Fleet air attacks in NVN, 2-7Aug64. Launched from US aircraft carriers *USS Constellation* and *Ticonderoga* against coastal ports cities of (from N to S) Hon Gai, Loc Chau, Phuc Loi, Vinh, and Quang Khe. NVN.

Pierce Field (YT 04-07?)
USARV parade field at Long Binh Post. Named to honor Sgt Larry S Pierce, HHC 1st/503d Inf, 173d Abn, KIA 20Sep65, posthumous MOH. Data per *Vietnam Military Lore, 1959-1973.* Bien Hoa Pr, III Corps.

Pierson, LZ/FSB (ZB 125-163)
See Mud, LZ. Kontum Pr, II Corps.

Pierson, LZ (AR 85-14?)
See Pearson, LZ. Pleiku Pr, II Corps.

Pig Path, The (XT/XU)
Infiltration trail roughly defined by SVN border in Fishhook area. Binh Long, Tay Ninh Prvs, III Corps.

Pike, FSB (YC 664-753)
A.k.a. Hill 885. Apx 3 km S Quang Nam/Thua Thien Pr border, 4 km W Laos, 12 km S FSB Thor, 17 km SE A Shau ville and 55 km SSW Hue. Quang Nam Pr, I Corps. FSBs Fury, Pike, Shield, Whip and Thor were built during Op Massachusetts Striker, 22Mar-8May69, using "Combat Trap" 10,000 lb bombs (if available) to initiate construction until hilltop "was clear enough for rappelling." [429] Also listed at YC 667-747. Thua Thien Pr, I Corps.

Pike, FSB (ZC 18-44)
A.k.a. Hill 214. Apx 14 km W An Hoa, 7 km SW FSB Champagne and 5 km N FSB Spear. Built Dec68 by 2d/5th Marines as part of assault on Base Area 112, Dec68-Feb69. Quang Nam Pr, I Corps.

Pillage, FSB (XS 575-856)
In large plantation along the Song Vam Co Dong, apx 26 km SW Tan Son Nhut AB and 12 km S Duc Hoa AF.

2d/40th Arty, 199th LIB, '68. Name/grid per Dan Gillotti, 15th Arty Assn. Long An Pr, III Corps.

Pillbox (n/a)
Apr70, XXIV Corps proposed 101st Abn FSB name.

Pillow, LZ (YD 052-368)
Apx 7 km NW Ta Laou, 22 km ESE Khe Sanh CB, 11 km WSW Ba Long AF, 32 km WSW Quang Tri. Apr70 XXIV Corps grid per Don Armstrong. Quang Tri Pr, I Corps.

Pilotes, Baie des (XH 8-8)
Bay at 20°42'N-106°48'E. On NF48-16 JOG. NVN.

Pin, LZ (CR 023-718)
Near Cat Tuong, apx 28 km SE Bong So and 30 km NNE Phu Cat AB. Oct66. Binh Dinh Pr, II Corps.

Pine, Camp (n/a)
A.k.a. Pechabun. SF camp. *SF Order of Battle*. Thailand.

Pine, FSB (YS 331-800)
Apx 16 km NW Nui Dat, 1.5 km ESE FSB Colorado, 7.5 km SSW FSB Dampier and 4 km SW FSB Ash. On 1ATF NCO trng map per John Hollett. Phuoc Tuy Pr, III Corps.

Pine, LZ (ZD 085-097)
On Vinh Loc Island, apx 600 meters from Dam Cau Hai Lagoon, 7 km SE Vinh Loc, 10 km due N Phu Loc and 45 km ESE Hue. Jul68. Thua Thien Pr, I Corps.

Pine Island, USS (n/a)
A.k.a. AV-12. Seaplane Tender. See *Currituck, USS*. Role discussed in *Brown Water, Black Berets*, p 92. SVN.

Pine Ridge, FSB (XT 528-588)
Appears to have been on Nui Ong (Hill 284, in the Razorbacks), apx 13 km NNE Dau Tieng/Tri Tam and overlooking Michelin Plantation. Mentioned 187th AHC's website. Unit's Bn Supp extracts at www.kbi.org/187thahc /incident_67.htm. Nov69. Binh Duong Pr, III Corps.

Pineapple, LZ (BS 358-961?)
If grid correct, was at peak of Nui Dong Tranh (a.k.a. Hill 1362), apx 22 km SW Chu Lai, 8 km N Tra Bong AF, 37 km NW Quang Ngai and 25 km SSE Tam Ky. Grid per 10May 70 ORLL, Americal Div. Also listed at BS 356-962 and 371-966? Quang Tin Pr, I Corps.

Pineapple, LZ (BS 371-966?)
If grid correct, was apx 4 km due S peak Nui Dong Tranh Mtn, 20 km SSE Tam Ky and 18 km WSW Chu Lai. Mentioned on 71st AHC's webpage at Americal's Website: www3.servtech.com/americal/saber6.htm. Americal list has grid at BS 358-961? Quang Tin Pr, I Corps.

Pineapple Patch (BT 46-04?)
Terrain feature near Ky Phu in the Song Chang Valley. Swept during Op Double Eagle, 27Feb65. See *Utter's Battalion*, pp 228. Quang Tin Pr, I Corps.

Pineapple Forest (BT 25-22)
W of Tam Ky and running between BT 18-20 to BT 28-20. Center of mass apx 3 km ESE Ky Phu, 2 km SE Cam Khe, 3 km due S Thon Hai 334 km W Hiep Duc. Staging area for 2d NVA Div in coastal lowlands near Chu Lai. On map L-7014-6640-2. Americal AO. Quang Tin Pr, I Corps.

Pineapple Plantation, The (XS 600-870)
Generally 25 km WSW Saigon and 15 km due SSE Duc Hoa. Nickname of large, flat swampy region and VC sanctuary with center of mass between Song Vam Co Dong River (its S edge) and southern border of Gia Dinh Pr, its N edge. Huge caches found here in '68, inc 3,500 bunkers with concrete overhead and 4,500 bed hospital complete with refrigeration and whole blood stg. [430] Roughly rectangular and perhaps 16 x 16 km in size. Grid is at apx center of mass. On *Rangers at War* map, p 326. Also listed at XS 60-83, 590-850 and 630-890. Long An Pr, III Corps.

Pineapple Region (XS 6-8?)
Likely a.k.a. The Pineapple Plantation. SW Saigon and the AO of 2d/3d Inf, 199th LIB in '68. See Pineapple Plantation. Long An (et al) Pr, III Corps.

Pink, LZ (XT 455-553)
Apx 1 km W Song Saigon and 9 km NNW Dau Tieng. 21Jun66. Tay Ninh/Binh Duong Pr border, III Corps.

Pink, LZ (XU or XT 888-111?)
If in XU grid zone, was apx 16 km ENE Loc Ninh AF/QL-13. If in XT, was apx 6 km NNW Di An CB and 10 km WSW Bien Hoa AB. Listed at XJ 888-111 in III Corps, but no such grid exists. Jun66. Binh Duong Pr?, III Corps.

Pink, LZ (XU 593-025)
Apx 16 km SW Loc Ninh AF, 5 km E Cambodia. 1Jul66. Phuoc Long Pr, III Corps.

Pink, LZ (YS 085-563)
Apx 22 km WNW Vung Tau and 40 km SE Saigon. 31Jul66. Gia Dinh Pr, III Corps.

Pink, LZ (ZA 00-23)
Apx 5 km ESE Plei Luong Ya Rang, 8 km W to WNW Xuong Kuang, 34 km SW Pleiku and 16 km ESE Duc Co. Per Don Shutt, was LZ (not FSB) of 1st Cav during Op Paul Revere II and only open a few days. At 1st light (somewhere between 30Jul-2Aug66), following mortar and ground assault of nearby LZ Orange, a Plt dropped into this LZ was virtually annihilated. Grid deduced from map in article entitled *Paul Revere II*, 1st Cav '66 *Yearbook* per Mr. Shutt. Pleiku Pr, II Corps.

Pink Rose (n/a)
See Glossary.

Pink Team (n/a)
See Hunter-Killer in Glossary.

Pink Teams (AT/BT)
In '69, 11th Marine Arty Rgt created a Permanent OP (POP) system to observe the main infiltration routes into Da Nang Vital Area. Sites were set to cover the following: N Da Nang-Hill 190, covering Elephant Valley, Hai Van Pass approaches. W Da Nang-Hill 270, covering routes leading from Happy Valley, Mortar Valley, Sherwood Forest and Charlie Ridge; and, Hills 65 and 250, covering the Thuong Duc Corridor. S Da Nang-Hill 425 (in Que Son Mtns), covering Phu Loc and An Hoa Basin; Hill 119, covering Go Noi Island and Dodge City; and at FSB Ryder to cover Antenna Valley and northern Que Son Valley. These sites employed a very expensive and accurate target locating device called an IOD (Integrated Observation Device). See IOD. Quang Nam Pr, I Corps.

Pinkville (BS 73-77)
A.k.a. My Lai 4. Generally 8-10 km ENE Quang Ngai. Nickname of VC controlled area on Batangan Peninsula that included My Lai. See My Lai 4 and LZ Pinkville. Quang Ngai Pr, I Corps.

Pinkville, LZ (BS 730-775)
Apx 8 km ENE Quang Ngai and about 2 km N My Key. On Batangan Peninsula near site of My Lai massacre (a.k.a. the Pinkville or Song My massacre). See My Lai. Americal list. Quang Ngai Pr, I Corps.

Pinkville Massacre (BS 73-77)
See My Lai 4/Pinkville. Quang Ngai Pr, I Corps.

Pinky, LZ/FSB (YD 688-252)
At Thon Que Chu, between LZ Sally and Thoan La Chu, some 800 meters SW QL-1 and 5 km WNW NW corner of Citadel in Hue. Built prior to 1Mar68 by 1st Cav and named to honor Col Richard M. Winfield, a redhead and CO 1st Cav Arty. Occupied by elements of 2d/501st, B/321st Arty, 101st Abn, Mar68. Per '68 1st/502d Bn Annual Hist Supp of HHC, 1st/502d Inf, was attacked in Mar or Apr68, with 7 US KIA, 21 WIA, 52 NVA/VC KIA and 5 NVA/VC POWs. Ted Jenkins, 1st Cav, 478th Avn Co (Cranes) 67-68, added that his notes indicate grid was YD 689-254 and that radio frequency for Pinky was 38.40. Also listed at YD 686-253 per XXIV Corps list, courtesy Don Armstrong. Thua Thien Pr, I Corps.

Pintail, LZ (XD 848-454)
Apx 4 km due N Khe Sanh CB, 15 km WSW Ca Lu and Just NW peak Hill 1015. Apr70 XXIV Corps grid per Don Armstrong. Quang Tri Pr, I Corps.

Pioneer Commander, SS (n/a)
See Evacuation of Da Nang in Glossary.

Pioneer Contender, SS (n/a)
See Evacuation of Da Nang in Glossary.

Pioneer Myth, SS (n/a)
Commercial transport under govt contract, per Ralph Fries.

Pioneer Valley (CR 03-16 or CR 9-4?)
A.k.a. Phu Tai Valley? Apparently near Phu Tai 1 and 2, apx 6 km WSW Qui Nhon. Binh Dinh Pr, II Corps.

Pipe Smoke Operations (n/a)
See Glossary.

Pippins Hall EM/NCO Club (XT 962-488?)
In Camp Gorvad at Phuoc Vinh, apx 35 km due N Bien Hoa AB. Named to honor Sgt Willie Sr. Pippins, 1st Bn 5th Arty, 1st Inf Div, KIA 24Feb66 during intense battle of Tan Binh while directing fire on bunker line. Dedicated 1Sep66. Data per *Vietnam Military Lore, 1959-1973*. Binh Duong Pr, III Corps.

Pirates, Ile de (YJ 6-4)
Island of Pirates. NIMA data. Khanh Hoa Pr, II Corps.

Pirates, Pointe des (XJ-9-0)
See Pointe des Pirates. NVN.

Pisa, Leaning Tower of (YS 499-548)
See FSB Thrust at grid. Phuoc Tuy Pr, III Corps.

Pistol, FSB (YC 902-902)
A.k.a. FSB Dagger. Apx 22 km SW Phu Loc, 23 km due S Phu Bai and 24 km SSE FSB Arsenal. 101st Abn. Grid per Apr70 XXIV Corps index. Thua Thien Pr, I Corps.

Pistol, LZ (BR 777-913)
Apx 9 km SW Bong Son and 8 km NNW Ha Tay AF. Oct66. Binh Dinh Pr, II Corps.

Pistol Pete (n/a)
See Glossary.

PIT (AR 7-4)
Plantation Indochinoise de The'. A.k.a. LaPIT. Tea plantation somewhere near Pleiku. Site of major engagement for G.M. 100 during 1st Indochina War. French simply referred to it as "PIT." Pleiku Pr, II Corps.

Pitkin County, USS (n/a)
LST-1082. Lndg. Ship, Tank, per Ralph Fries. Apparently in SVN waters in at least '66-67.

Pitong Dien, LZ (YC 015-397)
Apx 15 km SW Mai Loc and 36 km WSW Quang Tri. 8/369th VNMC Bn here 1Jun71 during Op Lam Son 810. Grid/data per Cliff Snyder. Thua Thien Pr, I Corps. [431]

Pitsanulok Airfield (PU 3-5)
See Phitsanulok AF. Thailand.

Pitsanuloke (PU 3-5)
See Phitsanulok AF. Thailand.

Pivot, USS (n/a)
MSO-463. Minesweeper, Ocean, per Ralph Fries.

Pizza, FSB (XS 430-850)
Apx 20 km SW Duc Hoa, 17 km ENE Thuy Dong AF and 40 km WSW Tan Son Nhut. Feb68. Tay Ninh Pr, III Corps.

PK 3, Ambush at (AR 809-460)
A.k.a. Poste Kilometer 3. Presumably 3 km E Pleiku on QL-19. On 28Jun54, as G.M. 42 resumed its journey following ambush at Dak Ya-Ayun Bridge 27Jun54 (and debacle of G.M. 100 in Mang Yang Pass, 17Jun54), it was again heavily ambushed here by 108th Vietminh Rgt reinforced by elite 30th Independent Bn. Brunt of attack fell on 60 exhausted men of 1st Co, 1st Korea Bn, who delayed 500 enemy but were inevitably overwhelmed at cost of 42 KIA. Unlike slaughter at PK 15, French were prepared and could maneuver. 2d Korea counter-attacked under tank and arty fire, and B-26s arrived with napalm, catching Vietminh in open. In 5-days of fighting on QL-19, 1st Korea had lost more dead (101) than during its entire 3 years in Korea. See Dak Ya-Ayun. Data per *Street Without Joy*, pp 222-235, maps at pp 223, 233. Pleiku Pr, II Corps.

PK 15 (BR 223-520)
On QL-19, apx 15 km W An Khe. Main ambush site of G.M. 100 in Mang Yang Pass. See *Groupement Mobile 100* in Glossary. Binh Dinh Pr, II Corps.

PK 17 Airfield (YD 64-28)
See Van Xa AF. Thua Thien Pr, I Corps.

PK 17, FSB (YD 643-286)
A.k.a. Poste Kilometre 17. Adj QL-1's PK-17 km marker apx 17 km NW center of Hue, 5 km ESE Camp Evans and 5 km NW Van Xa/Camp Sally. ARVN Arty base that also held US Arty units at various times. Battered, old concrete tower marked its entrance. Richard Moore, USMC, recalls it was an ARVN cmpd, Jul-Aug66, and had several old French concrete bunkers on its perimeter (ARVN using 1 at gate as their commo shack). "There were about 20-30 Marines, perhaps 200 ARVN, 2 Marine 8" guns, and 2 Army twin 40mm's [Dusters] at PK-17. The 8" were suptg Op Hastings, I believe. There was also a leper colony run by French nuns right across the hwy, and I remember taking them broken-down ammo cases they put to use for some purpose. We were overrun by NVA one night and all the ARVN took off. NVA destroyed everything, including the big guns, and killed the Army crews and all but about 10 people. There were a lot of dead NVA too." [432] C Bty 1st/77th Arty here fired over 5,000 rounds suptg 2d/12th Cav, 1st Cav in Battle of Thon La Chu, Feb68, during Battle for Hue. 2d Bde/1st Cav CP moved here 1Mar68. HQ 3d Rgt, 1st ARVN Div. Map is L-7014-6442-2, per Ken Burrington. Also listed at YD 547-284 (Oct69), 647-284 and 652-280 (Dec67-Jan68). Thua Thien Pr, I Corps.

PK 17 Leper Colony (YD 643-286)
On QL-1, apx 17 km NW center of Hue, apx 5 km ESE Camp Evans and 5 km NW Van Xa/Camp Sally. Richard Moore, USMC at PK 17 in '66, recalls "There was a leper colony run by French nuns right across the hwy, and I remember taking them broken-down ammo cases they put to use." Thua Thien Pr, I Corps.
PK 21 (Military Res.) Airfield (TF 60-00)
A.k.a. LS-364 and Poste Kilometre 21 Military Reservation AF. Lao military AF apx 21 km NE Vientiane, per ONC-J-11.CIA base. El. 700'. Grid per *Air Facilities Data-Laos.*
PK 22 (BR)
Along QL-19, presumably 22 km W An Khe. French 1st Abn Grp position, Jun54, and escape objective for main body of survivors from G.M. 100 after its destruction at the Mang Yang Pass. See *Groupement Mobile 100* in Glossary. Binh Dinh Pr, II Corps.
Pl Ya Bo (n/a)
Mapsheet name of L-7014-6536-3. SVN/Cambodia.
Place de la Theatre (WJ 88-25)
See Patti Mission in Glossary. Hanoi, NVN.
Plain of Reeds (XS 0-7/WS)
A.k.a. *Plaine de Joncs* and, per NIMA Gaz, Dong Thap Muoi. 2,500 sq mi area covering portions of five SVN provs: Kien Tuong, Kien Phong and portions of Hau Nghia, Long An and Dinh Tuong along Cambodian border in Parrot's Beak/Fishhook areas W and SW Saigon. Flat brush-covered zone used as VC/NVA base and staging area. III and IV Corps
Plain of Reeds, Battle of (XS 273-577)
Took place 3Jun68, just NW Xom Chau, and apx 27 km NW My Tho, 8 km NNE Cai Lay, and 7 km N FSB Moore. Major battle involving elements of A and E/2d/39th Inf, 9th Div, when they were ambushed shortly after insertion and walked into heavily fortified VC positions dug into edge of tree line along Kinh Ton Doc Canal, S of Rte 209. US losses were: A Co 14 KIA, E Co 7 KIA, HHC 1 medic KIA (22 KIA total). Data per Jim Stone, 2d/39th Inf, 9th Div. Dinh Tuong Pr, IV Corps. [433]
Plaine de Joncs (XS 0-7)
See Plain of Reeds. III and IV Corps.
Planetree, USCGS (n/a)
WLB 307. USCG Buoy Tender.
Plantation, LZ (ZB 109-165)
Apx 2 to 3 km S Dien Binh (and QL-14), 11 km SE Dak To 2 AF and 32 km NNW Kontum. C Bty, 6th/14th Arty here Jan70. 4th Div 31Jan70 ORLL grid per Jim Henderson. Also listed at ZB 156-065, and grid thought to be in error; however, if correct, was along QL-14 apx 21 km NNW Kontum? Kontum Pr, II Corps.
Plantation, The (WJ?)
See Plantation POW Camp. NVN.
Plantation, The (YT 04-07)
See Plantation Cmpd. Bien Hoa Pr, III Corps.
Plantation, The (WJ?)
See Plantation POW Camp. NVN.
Plantation Airfield (YT 062-115)
Along S side of Hwy 318 at Long Binh Post, apx 7 km ESE Bien Hoa AF, 28 km NE Tan Son Nhut AB and 40 km W Xuan Loc, per DMA TPC K-10D. 12th AVN Grp HQ here. El. 131'. See Plantation Cmpd. Bien Hoa Pr, III Corps.
Plantation Combat Base (YT 048-106)
A.k.a. Long Binh North, Plantation Cmpd or simply "The Plantation." Just N Long Binh Post. HQ II Field Force (IIFFV, originally known as XXII Corps when activated in VN). Was in remains of French Rubber Plantation, 1st occupied in '66 by IIFFV, though possibly used by MACV Adv Team prior to '66. Most of base (inc Red Carpet Heliport) was transferred to RVNAF, 15Jun72, effected through MPCO (meaning of acronym unknown?) 3d ALC, to ARVN 5th Ranger Grp, 6th Ranger Grp and 2d Air Defense Arty Bn. At turnover, was capable of housing some 4,500 personnel. MACV-JGS IG conducted post-turnover inspection of base, 13-15Sep72, at which time ARVN TRAC was occupying central portion including Red Carpet Heliport. Grid is that of Red Carpet Heliport. Bien Hoa Pr, III Corps.
Plantation Compound (YT 048-106)
See Plantation Combat Base. Bien Hoa Pr, III Corps.
Plantation de An Loc (YT 42-11)
A.k.a. Don Dien An Loc. Apx 5 km NE Xuan Loc. Long Khanh Pr, III Corps.
Plantation de An Vieng (YS 2-9)
A.k.a. Don Dien An Vieng. Bien Hoa and/or Gia Dinh Pr, III Corps.
Plantation de Ban Tieu (XS 9-8)
A.k.a. Don Dien Ban Tieu. Gia Dinh Pr, III Corps.
Plantation de Binh Loc (YT 4-1)
A.k.a. Don Dien Binh Loc. Long Khanh and/or Bien Hoa Pr, III Corps.
Plantation de Bodral (AR 9-6)
See De Bodral Plantation. Pleiku Pr, II Corps.
Plantation de Bourgery (AP 9-8)
A.k.a. Don Dien Bourgery. Darlac Pr, II Corps.
Plantation de Cau Khoi (XT 3-4)
A.k.a. Don Dien Cau Khoi. Tay Ninh Pr, III Corps.
Plantation de Courtenay (YS 4-9)
A.k.a. Don Dien Courtenay. The Courtenay Rubber Plantation. Long Khanh Pr, III Corps.
Plantation de Da Kir (YU 0-1)
A.k.a. Plantation Xa Da Kir and Don Dien Da Kir. Phuoc Long Pr, III Corps.
Plantation de Dinh Quat (XT 8-4)
See Plantation de Nguyen Dinh Quat. Binh Duong or Phuoc Long Pr, III Corps.
Plantation de Halle Concession (XT 8-4)
A.k.a. Don Dien Halle Concession (also spelled Hallet). Binh Duong or Phuoc Long Pr, III Corps.
Plantation de Long Thanh (YS 2-9)
A.k.a. Don Dien Long Thanh. Site of *Societe Terras Rouge* (Society of Red Earth or Terrace or Plains?). Bien Hoa and/or Gia Dinh Pr, III Corps.
Plantation de Michelin (XT 5-5)
See Don Dien Michelin. The Michelin Rubber Plantation, site of many battles. Tay Ninh Pr, III Corps.
Plantation de Nguyen Dinh Quat (XT 8-4)
A.k.a. Don Dien Nguyen Dinh Quat. Binh Duong or Phuoc Long Pr, III Corps.
Plantation de Ong Que (YS 3-9)
A.k.a. Don Dien Ong Que. Bien Hoa Pr?, III Corps.

Plantation de Peysson (YT 4-0)
Don Dien Peysson. Bien Hoa or Long Khanh Pr, III Corps.
Plantation de Phu Reng (YT 1-9)
A.k.a. Don Dien Phu Reng. Phuoc Long Pr, III Corps.
Plantation de Phu Rieng (YT 1-9)
A.k.a. Don Dien Phu Rieng. Phuoc Long Pr, III Corps.
Plantation de Sauveterre (YS 4-9)
A.k.a. Don Dien Sauveterre. Long Khanh Pr, III Corps.
Plantation de Souchere (YS 4-9)
A.k.a. Don Dien Souchere. Long Khanh Pr, III Corps.
Plantation de Suzzannah (YT 3-1)
A.k.a. Don Dien Suzzanah. Bien Hoa Pr, III Corps.
Plantation de Thies (XT 3-4)
A.k.a. Don Dien Thies and Don Dien Cau Khoi. Tay Ninh Pr, III Corps.
Plantation de Thuan Loi (YT 0-8)
Don Dien Thuan Loi. Bien Hoa or Gia Dinh Pr, III Corps.
Plantation de Ven Ven (XT 35-32)
A.k.a. Don Dien Ven Ven. Tay Ninh Pr, III Corps.
Plantation de Xuan Loc (YT 4-0)
A.k.a. Don Dien Xuan Loc. Long Khanh Pr, III Corps.
Plantation Indochinoise de La PIT (AR 7-4?)
A.k.a. "La PIT." French tea plantation N Pleiku at which G. M. 100 paused in Feb54. One of many in area. [434])
Plantation Miniport (YT 062-115?)
Heliport apparently adj to Plantation AF, and along S side of Hwy 318 at Long Binh Post. 12th AVN Grp HQ was nearby. "L1 lighting and J4 Fuel avail. Remarks: 12 points, self service. Lctd E side, N end of rwy. Rgt tfc ldg Rwy 05, left tfc ldg Rwy 23. Departures will be made fr the E lane unless departing Rwy 23. Hazards: 40' power lines extend 500 meters parallel dep path Rwy 05 where it intersects with another power line running due E parallel to railroad tracks. Several comm twrs apx 100' AGL lctd apx 450 meters E miniport. 30' concrete bunker 300 meters NE, 50 meters rgt of dep path Rwy 05," per Apr72 TAD. Bien Hoa Pr, III Corps.
Plantation POW Camp, The (WJ?)
Nickname for POW camp near Hanoi. On map at www.soft-vision.com/hanoi/frame.html. NVN.
Plateau de Kontum (AR 8-4)
A.k.a. Plateau des Habans. Plateau generally 10-20 km SW Pleiku. Pleiku Pr, II Corps.
Plateau des Habans (AR 8-4)
See Plateau de Kontum. Pleiku Pr, II Corps.
Plateau Gi (BS 081-145)
A.k.a. Vic Klum. At N edge of II Corps in remote area apx 32 km WSW Gia Vuc AF, 38 km NE Kontum, 54 km ESE Dak To 2 AF. SF Camp and AF here with SF Det 17, 5th SF, Det A-214 Oct65, A-243 Oct66. Transferred to VNSF A-111. Kontum Pr, II Corps.
Plateau Gi Airfield (BS 081-145)
A.k.a. Vic Klum and Ngok Ngo AF. Near I/II Corps border, apx 32 km WSW Gia Vuc AF, 38 km NE Kontum, 54 km ESE Dak To 2 AF, per TPC K-10A. El. 3,875', 2,500' laterite/PSP rwy. At 14°35'22"N-108°17'26"E. Kontum Pr, II Corps.
Plateau Gi SF Camp (BS 081-145)
At N edge of II Corps, apx 32 km WSW Gia Vuc AF, 38 km NE Kontum, 54 km ESE Dak To 2 AF. Transferred to VNSF A-111 camp. Grid per *SF Order of Battle*. Kontum Pr, II Corps.
Plateaux Montagnards (n/a)
Large SVN mtn plateau known as Central Highlands. Covered much of Kontum, Pleiku, Binh Dinh, Phu Bon and Tuyen Duc Provs, as well as portions of other provs. During French War, area was held by 4th Vietnamese Mountaineer Div and suptd by *Groupement Mobile 100* (G.M. 100). See *Street Without Joy*, p 184. II Corps.
Platoon Patrol Base Cougar (XS)
See Cougar, PPB. Dinh Tuong Pr, IV Corps.
Platte, USS (n/a)
AO-24. Aux Oiler.
Playboy, LZ (CR 006-747)
On Nui Mieu hill mass overlooking ocean apx 5 km W Cat Tuong, 25 km SE Bong Son and 5 km from coast at closest point. Oct66. Cited in 1st Cav VN *Yearbook* Aug65-Dec69, p 88, per Peter Cole. Binh Dinh Pr, II Corps.
Playboy Club, The (CP 031-518)
A.k.a. the PCOD (personnel coming off duty) Lounge. At Nha Trang SF Camp. Was apparently open to both Off and EM. See Nha Trang SF Camp. Khanh Hoa Pr, II Corps.
Playboy Club, The (YS 436-676)
See Nui Dat Playboy Club. Phuoc Tuy Pr, III Corps.
Plaza BEQ (XS 857-904)
At 135 Tran Hung Dao St. (Plaza Enlisted Open Mess), Nov 65, 83 rms, Saigon. Data per *Vietnam Military Lore, 1959-1973*. Gia Dinh Pr, III Corps.
Plaza BEQ & E.O.M. (XS 857-904)
In Saigon, apx 6 km SSE Tan Son Nhut AB. Name per *Vietnam Military Lore, 1959-1973*. Gia Dinh Pr, III Corps.
Plaza BEQ Annex (XS 85-90?)
US enlisted billet, Sep63-68, 142 rms, Saigon. Per *Vietnam Military Lore, 1959-1973*. Gia Dinh Pr, III Corps.
Pleasantville, LZ/FSB (BT 051-049)
Near New Hau Duc, apx 11 km SSW Tien Phuoc AF, 3 km NE FSB Mildred and 30 km WSW Tam Ky. Apr70 XXIV Corps grid per Don Armstrong. An LZ Pleasantville also listed at BT 224-311, apx 32 km NNE this site? Unknown if different base or if one grid in error? Quang Tin Pr, I Corps.
Pleasantville, LZ (BT 224-311?)
If grid correct, site was apx 12 km NW Tam Ky and about 3 km W QL-1. Grid very similar to that of Hawk Hill and may be in error? An LZ Pleasantville also listed at BT 051-049, site 32 km SSW this site? Unknown if different site or if one grid in error? Quang Tin Pr, I Corps.
Pledge, USS (n/a)
MSO-492. Minesweeper, Ocean. See *Brown Water, Black Berets*, p 120. Market Time TF-115. SVN.
Plei Brel Dor (AR 89-43)
Ville apx 13 km ESE Pleiku. Data 31Jan70 4th Div ORLL, courtesy Jim Henderson. Pleiku Pr, II Corps.
Plei Broch (ZA 078-477)
Montagnard ville between Pleiku and Plei Djereng, apx 24 km W Pleiku. Cordoned/searched by 1st/12th Inf, 1st Inf Div, early '69. Cordon discussed in and grid per *Time Heals No Wounds*, at pp 81-82. Pleiku Pr?, II Corps.
Plei Buk SF Camp (YU 839-721?)
Possibly a.k.a. Buon Sar Pa? If grid correct, was apx 6 km from Cambodia, 8 km SW Duc Lap AF, just W Duc Lap

and 55 km SW Ban Me Thuot. 5th SF. Data per *SF Order of Battle.* See Buon Sar Pa. Darlac Pr, II Corps.

Plei Cham Neh (AR 806-411)
Ville apx 8 km SSE Pleiku. Per 31Jan70 4th Div ORLL, courtesy Jim Henderson. Pleiku Pr, II Corps.

Plei Chorr (YA 858-475)
Apx 1 km W Rte 509 and 2 km N Plei Djereng New AF. C/1st/14th Inf/25th Div ran Medcap here Nov66. See *Rites of Passage*, p 47. Pleiku Pr, II Corps.

Plei De Chi (ZA 047-383)
Ville apx 21 km WSW Pleiku. Pleiku Pr, II Corps.

Plei de Cong, FSB? (ZA 0-3?)
Described as having been near Hill 848. One source says 4th/42d Arty, 4th Div, was here. Name possibly a play on term Viet Cong? Pleiku Pr?, II Corps.

Plei Djama (n/a)
Mapsheet name of L-7014-6736-3. SVN.

Plei Djerang (YA 86-53?)
Sp variant of Plei Djereng. Grid matches that of Plei Djereng AF, apx 38 km W Pleiku. Pleiku Pr, II Corps.

Plei Djereng (YA 85-45)
A.k.a. Plei Djreng and Plei Djrang. Apx 3 km from Song Ya Krong Bolah, 3 km due W Plei Djereng SF Camp, adj to Plei Djereng (old) AF and 36 km NW Pleiku. Near home of SF Det 19 and 5th SF Grp, Det. A-214, Dec64, A-251 Oct66. Also two airfields in vicinity. SF and 4th Div units here heavily attacked in Oct66. C Bty, 7th/15th Arty here for Hipshoot. Pleiku Pr, II Corps.

Plei Djereng Airfield (YA 857-535)
A.k.a. Plei Djereng Old AF. At Polei Djereng, apx 28 km SW Plei Mrong AF, 8 km N Plei Djereng New AF, 6 km N Plei Djereng and 41 km WNW Pleiku. Listed as" Insecure, abnd, Clsd to all ops ARVN, 20Oct66, AF # VA2-217," in Aug69 TAD per Frank Penk, Jr. Not in Feb73 TAD. Pleiku Pr, II Corps.

Plei Djereng Airfield (YA 859-457)
See Plei Djereng New AF. Pleiku Pr, II Corps.

Plei Djereng Heliport (YA 859-531)
See Plei Djrang Heliport. Pleiku Pr, II Corps.

Plei Djereng New, FSB (YA 855-475)
Along SE edge of Plei Djereng and S edge of Plei Djereng New AF, some 37 km W Pleiku and 8 km S Plei Djereng Old AF. C Bty 6th/29th Arty here May70. Also listed at YA 860-460 and 859-457. 4th Div 31Jul70 grid, per Jim Henderson. Pleiku Pr, II Corps.

Plei Djereng New Airfield (YA 859-457)
Apx 37 km W Pleiku and 8 km S Plei Djereng Old AF. C Bty 6th/29th Arty here May70. El. 955', 3,150' alum mat rwy. Also listed at YA 860-460 and 859-457. 4th Div 31Jul70 grid, per Jim Henderson. Pleiku Pr, II Corps.

Plei Djereng Old Airfield (YA 859-531)
See Plei Djereng AF. Pleiku Pr, II Corps.

Plei Djereng SF Camp (YA 8745-4590)
Apx 3 km due E Plei Djereng (old) AF, and 36 km WNW Pleiku. Home of SF Det 19 and 5th SF Grp, Det. A-214, Dec64, A-251 Oct66. SF and 4th Div units here heavily attacked in Oct66. Moved to Plei Djereng (new). In *Chickenhawk,* p 261, SF soldier here in early '66 described it as "The asshole of world," to which author replied that it was very dusty as well. Soldier then said, "Yeah, we keep it that way on purpose. Keeps the shit from stinking." Also listed at YA 859-531. Grid per *SF Order of Battle.* Pleiku Pr, II Corps.

Plei Djereng SF Camp (new) (YA 859-457)
Immed NE Plei Djereng, apx 38 km due W Pleiku and 8 km S Plei Djereng Old AF. 5th SF. Transferred to 80th Border Rangers. Info/grid per *SF Order of Battle*. Pleiku Pr, II Corps.

Plei Djiring Heliport (AN 810-800)
At S edge of Di Linh, along QL-20, apx 26 km due E Tan Phat AF and 56 km SW Dalat. Heliport #644, El. 3,084', at 11°34'00"N-108°04'00"E, Spelling and grid per Feb73 TAD. Lam Dong Pr, II Corps.

Plei Djrang Heliport (YA 859-531)
Sp variant of Plei Djereng. At Plei Djereng and at or adj to Plei Djereng (old) AF, apx 36 km WNW Pleiku. Heliport #645, alt 853', at 14°02'00"N-107°39'00"E, per Feb73 TAD. Pleiku Pr, II Corps.

Plei Do (AR 812-436)
Village apx 5 km SE Pleiku. Per 31Jan70 4th Div ORLL, courtesy Jim Henderson. Pleiku Pr, II Corps.

Plei Do Lim Airfield (AR 890-284)
Apx 28 km due E Oasis AF, 22 km SSW Pleiku and 30 km due N Phu Nhon, per TPC K-10A. El. 2,180', 2,800' laterite rwy. 13°48'33"N-108°07'24"E. Pleiku Pr, II Corps.

Plei Do Lim Fort (AR 886-281)
Apx 28 km due E Oasis AF, 22 km SSW Pleiku and 30 km due N Phu Nhon AF. Pleiku Pr, II Corps.

Plei Do Lim SF Camp (AR 885-279)
A.k.a. Camp Hardy. Apx 28 km due E Oasis AF, 22 km SSW Pleiku and 29 km due N Phu Nhon AF. 5th SF Grp, Det. A-1, Dec64. Later VNSF. 2d/17th Arty here supt 1st Cav, 14Jan66, per Jack Picciolo. Grid per *SF Order of Battle.* See Camp Hardy. Pleiku Pr, II Corps.

Plei Du Airfield (BR or BQ?)
Tactical AF said to have been here. Grid for Plei Du in NIMA Gaz is BR 2-0, which is roughly 20-30 km N Cheo Reo; however, a Plei Du is also listed at BQ 241-913, which is apx 10 km due N Cheo Reo AF. Both sites in Phu Bon Pr, II Corps.

Plei Gao Thong (ZA 230-376)
Ville apx 7 km S to SSW Pleiku. 31Jan70 4th Div ORLL grid per Jim Henderson. Pleiku Pr, II Corps.

Plei Hlu Klan (AR 840-329)
Apx 5 km SE Camp Enari. Consolidated ville of 4th Div's "Good Neighbor Program," per 4th Div op rpt for period ending 31Jan69 courtesy Craig Miller. See Good Neighbor Program in Glossary. Pleiku Pr, II Corps.

Plei Ho By (AR 819-242)
Ville apx 23 km SSE Pleiku and 8 km WSW Plei Do Lim AF. Per 31Jan70 4th Div ORLL, courtesy Jim Henderson. Pleiku Pr, II Corps.

Plei Kian Ngol (AR 762-263)
Ville along QL-14, apx 21 km due S Pleiku. Per 31Jan70 4th Div ORLL, courtesy J. Henderson. Pleiku Pr, II Corps.

Plei Kleng Airfield (ZA 184-903 or YA 9-9?)
Possibly a.k.a. Polei Kleng AF? If grid correct, was apx 5 km WNW Kontum and 5 km E Polei Breng. Listed grid is per NPIA Gaz. NIMA Gaz has a Plei Kleng at 14°24'00"N-107°44'00"E, and YA 9-9, which puts it perhaps 10 km W Polei Kleng AF? Kontum Pr, II Corps.

Plei Kly Airfield (AQ 870-990)
See Phu Nhon AF. Pleiku Pr, II Corps.
Plei Ko'Tu (AR 952-375)
Village apx 20 km ESE to SE Pleiku. In 31Jan70 4th Div ORLL, per Jim Henderson. Pleiku Pr, II Corps.
Plei Kret Kroit (BR 182-519)
Village along QL-19, apx 16 km ESE Suoi Doi AF and 41 km E to ENE Pleiku. In 31Jan70 4th Div ORLL, per Jim Henderson. Pleiku Pr, II Corps.
Plei Le Anh (AR 840-328)
Ville apx 4 km ESE Camp Enari, 16 km SE Pleiku. Jan70 4th Div ORLL, per Jim Henderson. Pleiku Pr, II Corps.
Plei Me (ZA 163-049)
Apx 44 km SSW Pleiku, 20 km W QL-14 and linked to QL-14 by TL-6C loop (often impassable dirt road). Siege of SF Camp nearby led to 1st Cav's first major battles of in the Ia Drang Valley, 14-16Nov65. Entire ville of Montagnard resettled from NVA infiltration rte in valley adj to LZ Lonely (apx 7 km SSW Phu Nhon) to what later became "New" Plei Mei (perhaps 6th resettlement ville with this name). SF Det 22, 5th SF Grp; Det. A-313, Dec64; A-255 Oct66. Also listed at ZA 12-04? See LZ X-Ray. Pleiku Pr, II Corps.
Plei Me Airfield (ZA 163-057)
Apx 21 km WNW Phu Nhon AF, 6 km due E Plei Me ville and 43 km SSW Pleiku, per ONC K-10. Also listed at ZA 12-04. El. 1, 214', 1,200' clay/laterite rwy. At 13°36'13"N-107°55'23"E. Pleiku Pr, II Corps.
Plei Me I Airfield (ZA 163-057)
See Plei Me AF. Pleiku Pr, II Corps.
Plei Me SF Camp (ZA 163-049)
Apx 1.5 km NNE Chu Ho Mtn (Hill 468), 1 km SSW Hill 403, 44 km SSW Pleiku, 22 km WNW Phu Nhon AF, 20 km W QL-14, and linked to QL-15 by Rte 5. SF Det 22; 5th SF Grp, Det. A-313, Dec64; A-255 Oct66. Transferred to 82d Border Rangers. Grid per *SF Order of Battle*. Also listed at ZA 12-04? See LZ X-Ray. Pleiku Pr, II Corps.
Plei Mrong (n/a)
Mapsheet name of L-7014-6537-2. SVN.
Plei Mrong (ZA 113-673)
Apx 23 km NW Pleiku, 25 km SW Kontum. SF Camp and AF here. Pleiku Pr, II Corps.
Plei Mrong Airfield (ZA 114-670)
Apx 23 km NW Pleiku, 25 km SW Kontum, per Map TPC K-10A. El. 2,100', 1,400' crushed stone/clay rwy. At 14°09'27"N-107°53'04"E. Pleiku Pr, II Corps.
Plei Mrong SF Camp (ZA 112-671)
Apx 23 km NW Pleiku and 25 km SW Kontum. 5th SF Grp, Det. A-334, Dec64, A-212 '65, A-252 Oct66; SF Det 18. Later became 63rd Border Ranger base. A Bty, 2d/9th Arty here Dec69. Grid per *SF Order of Battle.* Also listed at ZA 1125-6700. Pleiku Pr, II Corps.
Plei Mrong, FSB (ZA 117-673)
See LZ Monica. Pleiku Pr, II Corps.
Plei Mui Plantation (AR 77-57)
Apx 10 km due N Pleiku, NE Plei Mui and generally 2-3 km E QL-14N. Likely a tea plantation but actual use and name unknown, given nearest city's name as interim measure. Pleiku Pr, II Corps.
Plei Mui? CIDG Camp (ZA 233-782)
A.k.a. Tan Phu SF Camp? Along QL-14, apx 7 km SSW Kontum and 32 km due N Pleiku. Cited in AAR at: www.grunt.space. swri.edu/aarpt1.htm, which indicates Montagnard Camp here. 2d/8th Inf here. Kontum Pr, II Corps. Kontum Pr, II Corps.
Plei Neh (n/a)
Mapsheet name of L-7014-6637-3. SVN.
Plei Pham Ge (AR 891-293)
Ville immed N Plei Do Lim AF and 22 km SE Pleiku. Per Jan70 4th Div rpt, per Jim Henderson. Pleiku Pr, II Corps.
Plei Piom Refugee Center (AR 885-485)
Along QL-19, apx 12 km W Pleiku. Grid per NPIA. Binh Dinh Pr, II Corps.
Plei Ptao Kla (AR 8-0)
A.k.a. Plei Potao Kla. Ville near 13°38'N-108°07'E. On ND49-09 JOG. Pleiku Pr, II Corps.
Plei Rinh (BR 0-0)
Apx 50 km SE Pleiku. G.M. 100 major engagement with VM here. See *Street Without Joy*, pp 196-198, 244-249; with translated Vietminh document describing attack in great detail from VM point of view. See *Groupement Mobile 100* in Glossary. Phu Bon Pr, II Corps.
Plei Roh POW Compound (AR 762-487)
Along QL-14, immed N Pleiku. NPIA. Pleiku Pr, II Corps.
Plei Roh Refugee Center (AR 762-487)
See Plei Roh POW Compound. Pleiku Pr, II Corps.
Plei Rongol Relocation Center (YA 98-30)
Vicinity of 13°49'00"N-107°46'00"E, along QL-19B and apx 27 km SW Pleiku. Apx 10,000 Montagnard were moved to this facility in early '67, and their security courtesy the 11th ARVN Ranger Bn per *Rangers At War*, at p 256. Grid/data per NIMA. Pleiku Pr, II Corps.
Plei Rung Khung, FSB? (AR 957-498)
Along QL-19, apx 16 km E Pleiku and 10 km SW Suoi Doi. 2d/17th Arty here 4Jan66, B and C Btys, 2d/17th Arty here. Data per Jack Picciolo. Pleiku Pr, II Corps.
Plei Ta Nangle SF Camp (BR 332-274)
A.k.a. Nangle SF Camp? Near LZ SOP, apx 23 km SW An Khe and 76 km W Qui Nhon. 5th SF Grp, Det. A-422, Dec64. Closed and assets moved to Qui Nhon (Liaison Det). Grid per *SF Order of Battle.* Binh Dinh Pr, II Corps.
Plei The Basecamp (YA 820-070)
Adj to Cambodian border, apx 58 km SW Pleiku, 10 km NW Chu Pong Mtn and 20 km SSW Duc Co AF. Described as Rgt-sized basecamp. Pleiku Pr, II Corps.
Plei Toun (YA 873-441)
Apx 1.5 km SSE of Plei Djereng New AF and 3 km W intersection of Rtes 509 and 546. See *Rites of Passage*, p 47. Pleiku Pr, II Corps.
Plei Toun Breng Airfield (YA 859-457)
See Plei Djereng New AF. Pleiku Pr, II Corps.
Plei Trap (YB 784-917)
A.k.a. Plei Trop. Remote hamlet in heart of Plei Trap Valley, apx 46 km W Kontum. Map is L-7014-6537-4. Kontum Pr, II Corps.
Plei Trap Road (YA/YB)
A.k.a. Hwy 615. N/S dirt road that ran length of Plei Trap Valley parallel to Cambodian border W both Kontum and Pleiku. NVA/VC actually used wheeled vehicles on this

road at various times during war. 4th Div AO. Pleiku and Kontum Prvs, II Corps.

Plei Trap Valley (YA/YB)
Along W edge of Central Highlands, running generally from YA 63-47, NNE to YB 88-15. Its N/S course runs roughly parallel to and adj to the Cambodian border. Its N end is perhaps 20 km E and opposite Tri-border area (Laos Cambodia and SVN), WNW of Kontum. Its S end is apx due W Pleiku and lies against Cambodia. Very long, large, and desolate region that was major NVA sanctuary and scene of heavy fighting throughout war. Map covering much of Plei Trap and numerous 4th Div FSBs is L-7014-6537-4. Pleiku and Kontum Prvs, II Corps.

Plei Troeh (n/a)
Mapsheet name of L-7014-6637-2. SVN.

Plei Trop (YB 784-917)
See Plei Trap. Kontum Pr, II Corps.

Plei Ya Pon (YA 956-367)
Ville apx 32 km WSW Pleiku and 6 km E Plei Ya Kavn. 4th Div AO. 1st/69th Armor in battle here, 10Dec68. Pleiku Pr, II Corps.

Plei Yt SF Camp (ZA 050-200)
Apx 35 km SW Pleiku and 7 km SE Plei Luong Ya Rang. 5th SF. Later relocated to Duc Co. Info/grid per *SF Order of Battle*. Pleiku Pr, II Corps.

Pleiku (n/a)
Mapsheet name of L-7014-6636-4. SVN.

Pleiku (AR 780-480)
On plateau at 3,000' El., apx 225 mi NE Saigon, 42 km due S Kontum and 130 km WNW Qui Nhon, at junction of QL-3/QL-14/QL-19. Home of 4th Div's Camp Holloway, Camp Schmidt, Camp Enari, Artillery Hill, as well as Hensel, Pleiku-Cu Hanh, Pleiku Area and Pleiku-Nansteph AF's. ARVN II Corps HQ here. Elements of 173d Abn here, '68-69. W portion of city is in ZA Quad. City described as "mixture of old French colonial buildings and tin huts." in one reference. 5th SF Grp Det 21, A-301, 5th SF Grp Det. C-2, A-311, Dec64, MIKE Force Det A-219 (was 423), Oct65, 8th Psy Ops Bn, MACV Cmpd, 4th/503d Inf, 173d Abn here Jun67, also. On 7Feb65, VC attacked Camp Holloway 9 US KIA and 128 WIA (also hit US positions at Qui Nhon same day, and the 2 incidents became LBJ's justification for committing combat troops to SVN ostensibly to provide security for US installations). City was site of large ARVN/US Army military complex and was target of intermittent rocket/mortar fire, especially in Summer of '67. Heavy fighting occurred here, Tet '68, as well as during '75 Final Offensive. In '75, NVA made diversionary attacks on Pleiku and Kontum and when ARVN took bait, launched main, 3-Div attack against Ban Me Thuot. After BMT fell, Pleiku was abdn and pulled its forces back to Saigon. L-7014-6636-4 map includes Pleiku and QL-19E west of Mang Yang Pass; L-7014-6536-1 shows area W Pleiku Satellite images of Kontum/Pleiku areas at: http://coombs.anu.edu.au/~vern/space.html. Capitol, Pleiku Pr, II Corps. [435]

Pleiku, Operation (n/a)
10Aug65-5Sep65, 173d Abn, Pleiku-Kontum Provs. C-130s and C-123s took Bde in to relieve siege of Duc Co SF CIDG camp, apx 4 km from Cambodia. It also provided security for Thanh Binh Pass. In Sep65, 1/503d was ordered to Kontum. II Corps.

Pleiku Heliport (SF) (ZA 240-501)
Along QL-14 apx 3 km NNW Pleiku and 3 km W Pleiku/Cu Hanh AF. Heliport #649, alt 2,428', 100' ants 100' N. Pad is 1000 meters W Rwy 27, Pleiku AB. Ctc Pleiku Tower 3 NM out. At 14°00'N 108°00'E, per Feb73 TAD. Pleiku Pr, II Corps.

Pleiku/An Khe Pipeline (BR/AR/ZA)
See Pump Station 1 and An Khe-Pleiku Pipeline. Binh Dinh/Pleiku Pr, II Corps.

Pleiku/Cu Hanh Airfield (AR 783-500)
A.k.a. Pleiku AB and Cu Hanh AF. Apx 3 km NE Pleiku, 6 km SE Pleiku/Nansteph AF, 3 km NW Pleiku Area AF, 37 km due S Kontum AF and 22 km SE Plei Mrong. The Major AF at Pleiku. TPC K-10A. El. 2,436', 6,000' asph rwy. At 14°00'11"N-108°01'17"E. Map is L-7014-6636-4. Pleiku Pr, II Corps.

Pleiku/Nansteph Airfield (ZA 228-536)
Minor AF about 6 km NW Pleiku/Cu Hanh major AF and 10 km NW Pleiku Area AF. Per TPC K-10A. El. 2,580', 1,100' graded earth rwy. At 14°02'09"N-107°59'12"E. Also listed at ZA 230-540. Pleiku Pr, II Corps.

Pleiku AFB Hospital (AR 783-500?)
See USAF Hospitals. Pleiku Pr, II Corps.

Pleiku Airbase (AR 783-500)
A.k.a. Pleiku/Cu Hanh AF and Cu Hanh AF. The major AF of several in Pleiku area. Apx 3 km NE Pleiku, 6 km SE Pleiku/Nansteph AF, 3 km NW Pleiku Area AF and 37 km due S Kontum AF. TPC K-10A. El. 2,436', 6,000' aspt rwy. At 14°00'11"N-108°01'17"E. Map is L-7014-6636-4. Pleiku Pr, II Corps.

Pleiku Airfield (AR 81-34)
Originally 4th Div's main AF, apx 15 km S Pleiku. Later renamed Hensel AF to honor WO1 Ernest V Hensel. See Hensel AF. 6,000' asph rwy operated by 633d Combat Supt Grp. Not jet capable until after '65. El. 2529'. Map is L-7014-6636-4. Pleiku Pr, II Corps.

Pleiku Area Airfield (AR 804-470)
A.k.a. Holloway AF or Camp Holloway AF. Apx 3 km SE Pleiku/Cu Hanh AF, 10 km SE Pleiku/Nansteph AF and 2 km due E Pleiku, per TPC K-10A. El. 2,460'. C Bty, 4th/42d Arty here May70. Also listed at AR 810-480Map is L-7014-6636-4. See Holloway AF. Pleiku Pr, II Corps.

Pleiku Ammo Supply Point (ZA 182-527)
If grid correct, was along Pleiku/Plei Mrong road, apx 10 km NW Pleiku and 4 km W Pleiku Nansteph AF? Also listed at ZA 782-527, but grid does not exist. Jan69. Pleiku Pr, II Corps.

Pleiku ARVN Hospital Heliport (AR 770-460)
At SE corner of Pleiku. Heliport #647, alt 2,428'. "Make appr fr W at or below 300 ft above surface. Remain well clear of Pleiku AB extended rwy centerline. Ctc Pleiku Twr 3 miles out. At 13°57'15"N-108°01'00" E," per Feb73 TAD. Pleiku Pr, II Corps.

Pleiku Basecamp (ZA 790-500)
At site of what became Pleiku/Cu Hanh AF, apx 3 km NE Pleiku. Jul66. Kontum Pr, II Corps.

Pleiku Catecka Airfield (ZA 202-341)
See Catecka AF. Pleiku Pr, II Corps.

Pleiku Logistical Center (ZA 200-530)
Apx 7 km NW Pleiku and 3 km WSW Pleiku/Nansteph AF. May69. Pleiku Pr, II Corps.
Pleiku MAAG Heliport (ZA 239-512)
Along QL-14, apx 4 km NNW Pleiku and 4 km W Pleiku/Cu Hanh AF. "Heliport #648, alt 2,526', 30' wires W Pad," per Feb73 TAD. Pleiku Pr, II Corps.
Pleiku MACV Compound (AR 780-480?)
Presumably in Pleiku City. 8th Psy Ops Bn, Mil Assistance Cmd VN. Map is L-7014-6636-4. Mentioned on 43d Signal Bn website at www.43sigws.heidelberg. army.mil/hist.htm. Pleiku Pr, II Corps.
Pleiku North (AR 795-525?)
Mentioned on 43d Signal Bn website at www.43sigws. heidelberg.army.mil/hist.htm. Possibly an Engr or Sig Corps cmpd, or perhaps reference to Pleiku/Cu Hanh AF? Pleiku Pr, II Corps.
Pleiku North Hill (AR 795-525)
Apx 2 km NNE Pleiku/Cu Hanh AF and 5 km N Camp Holloway. Apr72. Pleiku Pr, II Corps.
Pleiku PFTC (ZA/AR?)
RVNAF Popular Force Trng Ctr. Apparently at Pleiku but precise location unknown. Pleiku Pr, II Corps.
Pleiku POL Depot (n/a)
See An Khe Storage Depot. Binh Dinh Pr, II Corps.
Pleiku Province SF Camp (AR 765-502)
Apparently at or just W Pleiku/Cu Hanh AF and apx 3 km N Pleiku. Det A-301, Det 21, 5th SF Grp, 5th SF Grp, Det. C-2, A-311, Dec64, MIKE Force Det A-219 (was 423), Oct65. Later closed and responsibility transferred to ARVN Border Rangers Cmd. Grid per *SF Order of Battle*. See mapsheet L-7014-6636-4. Pleiku Pr, II Corps.
Pleiku Province SF Camp (AR 775-424)
Along QL-14, apx 3 km S Pleiku. Det A-301, Det 21, 5th SF Grp, 5th SF Grp, Det. C-2, A-311, Dec64, MIKE Force Det A-219 (was 423), Oct65. Moved to Kontum Pr. Grid per *SF Order of Battle*. See mapsheet L-7014-6636-4. Pleiku Pr, II Corps.
Pleiku Province (YA/ZA/AR/BR)
YV, ZV AQ and BQ UTMs also touch this Pr. One of 12 north-central provs forming II Corps (II CTZ).
Pleiku Storage Depot (n/a)
55,000 barrel capacity POL stg facility that received POL products via Qui Nhon-An Khe Pipeline and then pumped them on to Pleiku along QL-19. See Pump Station 1 and An Khe-Pleiku Pipeline. Binh Dinh Pr, II Corps.
Pleiku TACAN NDB (AR78-50)
Tactical Air Navigation and Non-Directional air navigation beacon site. At Pleiku/Cu Hanh AF, roughly 3 km NE Pleiku. Pleiku Pr, II Corps.
Pleiku Tea Plantation? (AR 79-40)
A.k.a. La PIT? Large tea plantation on E side of QL-14, apx 10 km S Pleiku. Pleiku Pr, II Corps.
Pliers, LZ (YS 341-871)
Apx 16 km NW Binh Gia, 22 km NNW Nui Dat and 25 km SSW Xuan Loc. Jan68. Long Khanh Pr?, III Corps.
Pluck, USS (n/a)
MSO-464. Minesweeper, Ocean, per Ralph Fries.
Plum, FSB (BT 338-135)
Apx 8 km SSE Tam Ky, 6 km SSE Tam Ky AF, 9 km NNW FSB Pear and 6 km W to WNW Diem Pho. 196th LIB base during Op Benton, Aug67. 2d/9th Arty here supt 1st/14th Inf, 196th LIB, 14-31Aug67. Name/grid per Les Hines. Quang Tin Pr, I Corps.
Plum, FSB (YC 958-863)
Along Yellow Brick Road in valley of Karum Baran River (flowed to W and through the A Shau Valley) and surrounded by tall mtns. Was apx 2 km due S peak Dong Kijao Mtn, 46 km W to WNW Da Nang, 13 km SW Bach Ma Resort and 5 km SSW peak Dong Nom (Hill 1208). XXIV Corps grid. Thua Thien Pr, I Corps.
Plumb?, LZ (YA?)
Spelling variant of Plum? Per Peter Cole, is mentioned in Robert Towles' 2d/7th Cav LZ Albany research. Pleiku Pr?, II Corps.
Pluto, LZ (BR 615-643)
In Vinh Thanh (Happy) Valley just S Dinh Binh, apx 3 to 4 km due N Vinh Thanh AF, 9 km SW LZ John Henry, 23 km NE An Khe, 28 km due W Crystal AF and 36 km NW Phu Cat AB. 4th Div AO, '70. Name/grid per Jim Claeys. 2d/17th Arty here. Also listed at BR 616-634 per Jack Picciolo. Binh Dinh Pr, II Corps.
Pluto, LZ (XD 894-536)
On Nui Tia Pong hill mass, apx 22 km WSW Cam Lo, 12 km NW Ca Lu and 12 km NNE Khe Sanh CB. Apr70 XXIV Corps grid per D. Armstrong. Quang Tri Pr, I Corps.
Pluto Fire Missions (n/a)
See Glossary.
Pochentong International Airport (VT 8-7)
A.k.a. Phnom Penh Intl Airport and Yean Than Antaracheat Airport. At 11°33'00"N-104°51'00"E. NIMA data. Cambodia.
Poet, Camp (XS 8-9)
In Saigon. Japanese POW camp that among other prisoners held 5 US POWs at end of WWII. Was one objective of *Project Embankment*. Data per *Vietnam Military Lore, Legends, Shadows, and Heroes*, p 11. See *Project Embankment,* and Camp 5-E. Gia Dinh Pr, III Corps.
Pogo's Paradise (YS 43-67)
See Pearson Community Centre. Phuoc Tuy Pr, III Corps.
Pohl Bridge (YD 755-144)
A.k.a. Nam Hoa Bridge. Rte 547 bridge over the Song Huong (Perfume River) 7.5 km due S Hue, 1.5 km NW Nam Hoa, 1.2 km NE Minh Mang's Tomb, 6.5 km ENE FSB Birmingham and 8.5 km NW FSB Arsenal. Was named to honor Col Richard S Pohl, a Bde CO in 101st Abn, KIA 24Jun68, in Huey crash or shoot-down. Small Seabee cmpd at E end of bridge housed fresh water pumping station, reportedly the only fresh water supply for Hue. Was secured by 1st/505th Inf, and other elements of 82d Abn between Mar-Sep68. In '69-70, security provided by 1st/502d Inf, 101st Abn, which had Mortar Plt permanently sited here while Inf plts from Bn rotated security duty. Security involved inspecting all boats passing bridge (mostly to mine gravel in shallows of confluence of Song Ta Trach and Song Huu Trach Rivers) and lumber trucks crossing bridge to harvest Teak and Mahogany(?) between FSBs Birmingham and Bastogne. Was destroyed in either '72 or '75 offenses and, as of 1989, had not been replaced. Thua Thien Pr, I Corps. [436]

Poilane Coffee Plantation (XD 858-390)
A.k.a. *Le Petite Fleur*. On Khe Sanh Plateau adj to N edge of QL-9, N and NE the Old French Fort, apx 3 km S Khe Sanh CB. Established by Eugene Poilane in 1919, who built home in what would later become Khe Sanh ville. Eugene fathered 10 children and on 20Apr64, at age 60, he was assassinated by VC while being chauffeured between Khe Sanh and Quang Tri on Rte 9. Plantation was described as "an exotic element of life at Khe Sanh. Felix showed the pilots his pet Deer, chatted casually, gave out small bags of coffee and served Creme de Menthe in cold water." [437] During '67-68 siege, then owner Felix Poilane left plateau but, eager to check plantation for damage after Op Pegasus had lifted siege, he returned aboard a US C-130, 13Apr68. Sadly, the acft lost control upon lndg and Poilane was killed. Detail/map in "*Valley of Decision*," pp 7, 27, 94. Quang Tri Pr, I Corps.

Poilane, Eugene (XD)
See Poilane Coffee Plantation. Quang Tri Pr, I Corps.

Poilane, Felix (XD)
See Poilane Coffee Plantation. Quang Tri Pr, I Corps.

Point Anyen (US 9-1)
Mui An Yen. Coastal point at 10°04'N-104°02'E. On NC48-05 JOG. Kien Giang Pr, IV Corps.

Point Arden, USCGC (n/a)
WPB 82309. CG Sqdn 1, Div 12. Turned over to SVN Navy, 14Feb70.

Point Banks, USCGC (n/a)
WPB 82327. CG Sqdn 1, Div 11. Turned over to SVN Navy, 26May70.

Point Caution, USCGC (n/a)
WPB 82301. CG Sqdn 1, Div 12. Turned over to SVN Navy, 29Apr70.

Point Clear, USCGC (n/a)
WPB 82315. CG Sqdn 1, Div 11. Turned over to SVN Navy, 15Sep69.

Point Comfort, USCGC (n/a)
WPB 82317. CG Sqdn 1, Div 11. Turned over to SVN Navy, 17Nov69. Role discussed in *Brown Water, Black Berets*, p 87. Market Time TF-115. SVN.

Point Cruz, USS (n/a)
T-AKV 19, Converted Escort Carrier. Served as acft ferry for MSTS fleet.

Point Cypress, USCGC (n/a)
WPB 82326. CG Sqdn 1, Div 13. On 15Aug70, the *Point Marone* and *Point Cypress* were the last of 26 USCG cutters turned-over to VNN. Role discussed in *Brown Water, Black Berets*, p 356. Market Time TF-115. SVN.

Point Defiance, USCGC (n/a)
LSD-31. Bracketed by NVA shore battery arty salvos, 18Ma67, Op Hickory/Beau Charger, off NVN near DMZ.

Point Dong Ba (CP 0-4)
Mui Dong Ba. Coastal point at 12°08'N-109°13'E. On ND49-13 JOG. Khanh Hoa Pr, II Corps.

Point Dume, USCGC (n/a)
WPB 82325. CG Sqdn 1, Div 12. Turned over to SVN Navy, 14Feb70. Suffered friendly fire attack, date? See *Point Welcome* and *Boston, USS.*

Point East (XQ 8-6)
A.k.a. Mui Ta Be. Coastal point at 8°42'N-106°40'E. On NC48-11 JOG. IV Corps.

Point Ellis, USCGC (n/a)
WPB 82330. CG Sqdn 1, Div 12. Turned over to SVN Navy, 9Dec69. Role discussed in *Brown Water, Black Berets*, p 117. Market Time TF-115. SVN.

Point Gammon, USCGC (n/a)
WPB 82328. CG Sqdn 1, Div 12. Turned over to SVN Navy, 11Nov69.

Point Ganh Daee (US 7-4)
Mui Ganh Dau. Coastal point at 10°22'N-103°50'E. On NC48-05 JOG. Kien Giang Pr, IV Corps.

Point Garnet, USCGC (n/a)
WPB 82310. CG Sqdn 1, Div 11. Turned over to VNN 16May69, and renamed *Le Phuoc Duc,* one of 26 cutters ultimately given to VNN. Role discussed in *Brown Water, Black Berets*, p 87, 335. Market Time TF-115. SVN.

Point Glover, USCGC (n/a)
WPB 82307. CG Sqdn 1, Div 11. Turned over to SVN Navy, 14Feb70. Role discussed in *Brown Water, Black Berets*, p 110. Market Time TF-115. SVN.

Point Grace, USCGC (n/a)
WPB 82323. CG Sqdn 1, Div 13. Turned over to SVN Navy, 16Jun70.

Point Grey, USCGC (n/a)
WPB 82324. CG Sqdn 1, Div 11. Turned over to SVN Navy, 14Jul70. Role discussed in *Brown Water, Black Berets*, p 127. Market Time TF-115. SVN.

Point Hon Nei (CP 1-2)
Mui Lo Gio. Coastal point at 11°57'N-109°17'E. On NC49-01 JOG. Khanh Hoa Pr, II Corps.

Point Hudson, USCGC (n/a)
WPB 82322. CG Sqdn 1, Div 13. Turned over to SVN Navy, 11Dec70.

Point Interieure (BT 6-0)
Mui Dat Vian Ka. Coastal point at 15°25'N-108°48'E. On ND49-01 JOG. Quang Tin Pr, I Corps.

Point Jefferson, USCGC (n/a)
WPB 82306. CG Sqdn 1, Div 13. Turned over to SVN Navy, 21Feb70.

Point Kailap (US 8-2)
Mui Cai Lap. Coastal point at 10°11'N-103°58'E. On NC48-05 JOG. Kien Giang Pr, IV Corps.

Point Kamao (VQ 75)
Mui Ca Mau. Coastal point at 8°38'N-104°44'E. On NC48-15 JOG. An Xuyen Pr, IV Corps.

Point Kega (CR 1-0)
Mui Ke Ga. Coastal point at 13°34'N-109°18'E. On ND49-09 JOG. Phu Yen Pr, II Corps.

Point Kega (ZS 2-8)
Mui Ke Ga. Coastal point at 10°42'N-107°58'E. On NC48-08 JOG. Binh Thuan Pr, II or III Corps.

Point Kennedy, USCGC (n/a)
WPB 82320. CG Sqdn 1, Div 13. Turned over to SVN Navy, 16Mar70.

Point Khe Ga (CP 0-6)
Mui Cay Ga. Coastal point at 12°18'N-109°15'E. On ND49-13 JOG. Khanh Hoa Pr, II Corps.

Point Kwala (US 9-5)
Mui Kwala. Coastal point at 10°27'N-104°00'E. On NC48-05 JOG. Kien Giang Pr, IV Corps.

Point League, USCGC (n/a)
WPB 82304. CG Sqdn 1, Div 13. Turned over to VNN 16May69, and renamed *La Van Ng*, one of 26 cutters ultimately given to VNN. Role discussed in *Brown Water, Black Berets*, p 355. Market Time TF-115. SVN.

Point Lomas, USCGC (n/a)
WPB 82321. CG Sqdn 1, Div 12. Turned over to SVN Navy, 26May70. See *Point Welcome*.

Point Marone, USCGC (n/a)
WPB 82331. CG Sqdn 1, Div 11. On 15Aug70, the Point Marone and Point Cypress were the last of 26 USCG cutters turned-over to VNN. Role discussed in *Brown Water, Black Berets*, p 110, 111, 356. Market Time TF-115. SVN.

Point Mast, USCGC (n/a)
WPB 82316. CG Sqdn 1, Div 11. Turned over to SVN Navy, 16Jun70.

Point Northeast (XQ 8-6)
A.k.a. Mui Dong Bac. Coastal point at 8°45'N-106°40'E. On NC48-11 JOG. IV Corps.

Point Northwest (US 7-4)
Mui Ganh Dau. Coastal point at 10°22'N-103°50'E. On NC48-05 JOG. Kien Giang Pr, IV Corps.

Point Nuinai (VS 3-4)
A.k.a. Mui Nai. Coastal point at 10°22'N-104°27'E. On NC48-06 JOG. Kien Giang Pr, IV Corps.

Point Orient, USCGC (n/a)
WPB 82319. CG Sqdn 1, Div 12. Released to SVN Navy, 14Jul70. Role discussed in *Brown Water, Black Berets*, p 85, 114, 119. Market Time TF-115. SVN.

Point Partridge, USCGC (n/a)
WPB 82305. CG Sqdn 1, Div 13. Turned over to SVN Navy, 27Mar70.

Point Slocum, USCGC (n/a)
WPB 82313. CG Sqdn 1, Div 13. Turned over to SVN Navy, 11Dec69.

Point Tam Quan (BS 9-1)
Pointe de Kim Bong. Coastal point at 14°35'N-109°05'E. ND49-05. Quang Ngai Pr?, I Corps.

Point Tamkwan (BS 9-1)
Pointe de Kim Bong. Coastal point at 14°35'N-109°05'E. ND49-05. Quang Ngai Pr?, I Corps.

Point Welcome, USCGC (n/a)
WPB 82329. CG Sqdn 1, Div 12. Turned over to SVN Navy, 29Apr70. Attacked by US jets thinking it to be enemy vessel at 0340 hrs on 11Aug66, while patrolling Market Time Sector1A1, adj to DMZ and apx 1 km S 17th Parallel. Noted news photographer Tim Page severely wounded among11 WIA and 2 KIA caused by strafing conducted by B-57 Bomber and two F4C acft in 9 separate runs. 1st hit by "Yellow Bird 18," a B-57 of 8th Bomb Sqdn (on Sky Spot mission at Cua Tung, N of the DMZ). "Blind Bat 02," a C-130 from 21st Trp Carrier Sqdn, okayed target after Spud 13 and Spud 14 (Army OV-l, SLAR Mohawks of 131st Avn Co) alerted Blind Bat to target. Yellow Bird struck at 0340 hrs, expending 800 rnds of 20mm, then made 2d pass, exhausting its ammo. Blind Bat then called-in two F-4Cs (Coyote 91 & 92) of 480th TAS. Coyote 92 dropped two CBU-2As and some bomblets may have hit ship. Coyote 91 dropped two-250 lb bombs but missed. Boat's chief ordered ship abnd, putting WIA on rafts. As survivors neared shore, rifle, mg and mortar fire from SVN Junk base junks (and possibly VC) fell around them. 5 survivors turned back to their burning ship and were rescued by CGC *Point Caution* (WPB-82317) at 0455 hrs. By 0510, fire on *Pt. Welcome* was extinguished and SVN junks took wounded ashore. *Point Lomas* (WPB-82321), *Point Orient* (WPB-82319), PCF-15 and *USS Haverfield* (DER-393) participated in rescue and recovery. *Pt. Welcome* then taken to Da Nang, arriving at 1615 hrs, 11Aug66. See Friendly Fire incidents Involving US Vessels in Glossary. See *Brown Water, Black Berets*, p 112-114, 127. Market Time TF-115. SVN. [438]

Point White, USCGC (n/a)
WPB 82308. CG Sqdn 1, Div 13. Turned over to SVN Navy, 12Jan70. Role discussed in *Brown Water, Black Berets*, p 112. Market Time TF-115. SVN.

Point Young, USCGC (n/a)
WPB 82303. CG Sqdn 1, Div 11. Turned over to SVN Navy, 16Mar70. Role discussed in *Brown Water, Black Berets*, p 111. Market Time TF-115. SVN.

Pointe An Yen (US 9-1)
Mui An Yen. Coastal point at 10°04'N-104°02'E. On NC48-05 JOG. Kien Giang Pr, IV Corps.

Pointe An Yo (BR 9-9)
Coastal point at 14°27'N-109°08'E. On ND49-05 JOG. Binh Dinh Pr, II Corps.

Pointe An-Hoa (BT 5-1)
Mui An Hoa. Coastal point at 15°31'N-108°41'E. On ND49-01 JOG. Quang Tin Pr, I Corps.

Pointe aux Crabes (YJ 0-1)
Coastal point at 20°54'N-106°57'E. NF48-16 JOG. NVN.

Pointe Bai Nom (CP 0-0)
Mui Bai Nom. Coastal point at 11°49'N-109°14'E. On NC49-01 JOG. Khanh Hoa Pr, II Corps.

Pointe Bai Sau (CP 0-1)
Coastal point at 11°54'N-109°13'E. On NC49-01 JOG. Khanh Hoa Pr, II Corps.

Pointe Cai Lap (US 8-2)
Mui Cai Lap. Coastal point at 10°11'N-103°58'E. On NC48-05 JOG. Kien Giang Pr, IV Corps.

Pointe Con Chim (XQ 8-6)
A.k.a. Mui Ta Be. Coastal point at 8°42'N-106°40'E. On NC48-11 JOG. IV Corps.

Pointe Da Nahi (XE 5-5)
A.k.a. Pointe Da Nhai. Coastal point at 17°40'N-106°29'E. On NE48-11 JOG. NVN.

Pointe Da Nhai (XE 5-5)
Coastal point at 17°40'N-106°29'E. NE48-11 Map. NVN.

Pointe Da-Chong (US 9-4)
Mui Da Chong. Coastal point at 10°21'N-104°05'E. On NC48-05 JOG. Kien Giang Pr, IV Corps.

Pointe Dai Mui (XQ 8-6)
Mui Dong Bac. Coastal point at 8°45'N-106°40'E. On NC48-11 JOG. NVN.

Pointe de An Luong (BT 1-5)
Mui An Luong. Coastal point at 15°53'N-108°22'E. On ND49-01 JOG. Quang Nam Pr, I Corps.

Pointe de Ba Lum (CP 0-1)
Mui Con Ke. Coastal point at 11°56'N-109°11'E. On NC49-01 JOG. Khanh Hoa Pr, II Corps.

Pointe de Ba Tien (CP 0-0)
Mui Ca Tien. Coastal point at 11°49'N-109°12'E. On NC49-01 JOG. Khanh Hoa Pr, II Corps.
Pointe de Ca Mau (VQ 7-5)
Mui Ca Mau. Coastal point at 8°38'N-104°44'E. On NC48-15 JOG. An Xuyen Pr, IV Corps.
Pointe de Ca Mau, Baie de la (VQ 7-5)
Vung Mui Ca Mau. Coastal point at 8°38'N-104°44'E. NC48-15 JOG. An Xuyen Pr, IV Corps.
Pointe de Cam Linh (CP 1-1)
Mui Cam Linh. Coastal point at 11°53'N-109°17'E. On NC49-01 JOG. Khanh Hoa Pr, II Corps.
Pointe de Cam Ranh (CP 1-1)
Mui Cam Linh. Coastal point at 11°53'N-109°17'E. On NC49-01 JOG. Khanh Hoa Pr, II Corps.
Pointe de Cua Dai (BT 1-5)
Coastal point at 15°54'N-108°21'E. On ND49-01 JOG. Quang Nam Pr, I Corps.
Pointe de Gia (CR 1-2)
Coastal point at 13°46'N-109°15'E. On ND49-09 JOG. Binh Dinh Pr, II Corps.
Pointe de Go Nhan (BS 7-9)
Coastal point at 15°20'N-108°53'E. On ND49-01 JOG. Quang Ngai Pr, I Corps.
Pointe de Hoi Binh (XR 3-4)
Coastal point at 9°29'N-106°12'E. On NC48-11 JOG. Ba Xuyen Pr?, IV Corps.
Pointe de Ke Ga (ZS 2-8)
Mui Ke Ga. Coastal point at 10°42'N-107°58'E. On NC48-08 JOG. Binh Thuan Pr, II Corps.
Pointe de Kim Bong (BS 9-1)
Coastal point at 14°35'N-109°05'E. On ND49-05 JOG. Quang Ngai Pr?, I Corps.
Pointe de la Batterie (CR 1-2)
Pointe Sud. Coastal point at 13°46'N-109°15'E. On ND49-09 JOG. Binh Dinh Pr, II Corps.
Pointe de la Pagoda (CP 0-1)
Pointe de la Pagode. Coastal point at 11°53'N-109°12'E. NC49-01 JOG. Khanh Hoa Pr, II Corps.
Pointe de la Pagode (CP 0-1)
Coastal point at 11°53'N-109°12'E. On NC49-01 JOG. Khanh Hoa Pr, II Corps.
Pointe de l'Arequier (ZJ 0-6)
Coastal point at 21°24'N-107°58'E. NF48-12 JOG. NVN.
Pointe de Mui Nam (CP 0-1)
Mui Nam. Coastal point at 11°51'N-109°14'E. On NC49-01 JOG. Khanh Hoa Pr, II Corps.
Pointe de Nam O (AT 9-8)
Coastal point at 16°07'N-108°08'E. On ND49-01 JOG. Quang Nam Pr, I Corps.
Pointe de Phuoampoc Thien (BS 7-9)
Coastal point at 15°21'N-108°52'E. On ND49-01 JOG. Quang Ngai Pr, I Corps.
Pointe de Phuoc Khanh (XS 9-8)
Point at 10°40'48"N-106°46'54"E. On NC48-07 JOG. Gia Dinh Pr?, III Corps.
Pointe de Vian Ka (BT 6-0)
Mui Dat Vian Ka. Coastal point at 15°25'N-108°48'E. ND49-01 JOG. Quang Tin Pr, I Corps.
Pointe de Xuan Day (CQ 1-7)
Mui Ganh Den. Coastal point at 13°22'N-109°18'E. On ND49-09 JOG. Phu Yen Pr, II Corps.
Pointe del Est (XS 7-9)
Point at 10°51'00"N-106°34'48"E. On NC48-07 JOG. Gia Dinh Pr?, III Corps.
Pointe Den Phach (US 9-1)
Mui Den Phach. Coastal point at 10°07'N-104°02'E. On NC48-05 JOG. Kien Giang Pr, IV Corps.
Pointe des Mines (YJ 2-1)
Coastal point at 20°55'N-107°09'E. NF48-16 JOG. NVN.
Pointe des Pirates (XJ-9-0)
Coastal point at 20°50'N-106°55'E. NF48-16 JOG. NVN.
Pointe Do Son (XH 8-9)
Coastal point at 20°43'N-106°48'E. NF48-16 JOG. NVN.
Pointe du Binh Loi (XS 9-8)
Point at 10°44'48"N-106°45'54"E. On NC48-07 JOG. Gia Dinh Pr?, III Corps.
Pointe du Feu Rouge (XS 9-8)
Point at 10°43'48"N-106°45'54"E. On NC48-07 JOG. Gia Dinh Pr?, III Corps.
Pointe du Lazaret (XS 9-7)
Point at 10°40'N-106°46'E. On NC48-07 JOG. Gia Dinh Pr?, III Corps.
Pointe du Lazaret (YS 2-4)
Pointe Ganh Rai. Coastal point at 10°23'N-107°04'E. On NC48-07 JOG. Phuoc Tuy Pr?, III Corps.
Pointe du Lombard (XS 7-7)
Point at 10°36'30"N-106°37'24"E. On NC48-07 JOG. Long An Pr?, III Corps.
Pointe du Lombard (YS 0-7)
Coastal point at 10°36'N-106°52'E. On NC48-07 JOG. Gia Dinh Pr, III Corps.
Pointe du Mirador (XS 9-3)
Coastal point at 10°16'N-106°45'E. On NC48-07 JOG. Go Cong Pr?, IV Corps.
Pointe du Nord-Est (XQ 8-6)
A.k.a. Mui Dong Bac. Coastal point at 8°45'N-106°40'E. On NC48-11 JOG. IV Corps.
Pointe du Rach Bao (XS 9-8)
Point at 10°44'36"N-106°45'06"E. On NC48-07 JOG. Gia Dinh Pr?, III Corps.
Pointe du Valero (XS 7-9)
Point at 10°50'42"N-106°37'30"E. On NC48-07 JOG. Gia Dinh Pr?, III Corps.
Pointe Ganh Daee (US 7-4)
Mui Ganh Dau. Coastal point at 10°22'N-103°50'E. On NC48-05 JOG. Kien Giang Pr, IV Corps.
Pointe Ganh Lon (US 8-3)
Mui Ganh Lon. Coastal point at 10°16'N-103°56'E. On NC48-05 JOG. Kien Giang Pr, IV Corps.
Pointe Ganh Rai (YS 2-4)
Coastal point at 10°22'30"N-107°04'00"E. On NC48-07 JOG. Phuoc Tuy Pr?, III Corps.
Pointe Ganh Rai (YS 2-4)
Coastal point at 10°23'N-107°04'E. On NC48-07 JOG. Phuoc Tuy Pr?, III Corps.
Pointe Guio (BN 2-2)
Coastal point at 11°03'N-108°28'E. On NC49-01 JOG. Binh Thuan Pr, II Corps.

Pointe Hant (US 9-0)
Mui Hanh. Coastal point at 10°00'N-104°01'E. On NC48-05 JOG. Kien Giang Pr, IV Corps.
Pointe Hapoix (BT 5-1)
Mui An Hoa. Coastal point at 15°31'N-108°41'E. On ND49-01 JOG. Quang Tin Pr, I Corps.
Pointe Happoix (BT 5-1)
Mui An Hoa. Coastal point at 15°31'N-108°41'E. On ND49-01 JOG. Quang Tin Pr, I Corps.
Pointe Hon Khoi (CP 0-9)
Coastal point at 12°35'N-109°14'E. On ND49-13 JOG. Khanh Hoa Pr, II Corps.
Pointe Hon Lan (CP 0-1)
Mui Hon Luong. Coastal point at 11°53'N-109°12'E. On NC49-01 JOG. Khanh Hoa Pr, II Corps.
Pointe Hon Nai (CP 1-2)
Mui Lo Gio. Coastal point at 11°57'N-109°17'E. On NC49-01 JOG. Khanh Hoa Pr, II Corps.
Pointe Hong Quoy (US 7-3)
Mui Ong Qui. Coastal point at 10°17'N-103°53'E. On NC48-05 JOG. Kien Giang Pr, IV Corps.
Pointe Isabelle (AT 9-8)
Coastal point at 16°10'N-108°09'E. On ND49-01 JOG. Quang Nam Pr, I Corps.
Pointe Lagan (BN 4-3)
Coastal point at 11°10'N-108°42'E. On NC49-01 JOG. Binh Thuan Pr, II Corps.
Pointe Minchac (YJ 6-1)
A.k.a. Pointe Minchao. Coastal point at 20°56'N-107°34'E. On NF48-16 JOG. NVN.
Pointe Minchao (YJ 6-1)
Coastal point at 20°56'N-107°34'E. NF48-16 Map. NVN.
Pointe Mongom (XS 7-7)
Point at 10°37'48"N-106°36'18"E. On NC48-07 JOG. Long An Pr?, IV Corps.
Pointe Nord-Ouest (US 7-4)
Mui Ganh Dau. Coastal point at 10°22'N-103°50'E. On NC48-05 JOG. Kien Giang Pr, IV Corps.
Pointe Nui Nai (VS 3-4)
A.k.a. Mui Nai. Coastal point at 10°22'N-104°27'E. On NC48-06 JOG. Kien Giang Pr, IV Corps.
Pointe O Ro (XS 9-7)
Point at 10°39'30"N-106°48'54"E. On NC48-07 JOG. Gia Dinh Pr?, III Corps.
Pointe Ong Dien (CQ 1-8)
Mui Ong Dien. Coastal point at 13°28'N-109°20'E. On ND49-09 JOG. Phu Yen Pr, II Corps.
Pointe Ouest (XQ 7-5)
A.k.a. Mui Ba Non. Coastal point at 8°40'N-106°33'E. On NC48-11 JOG. IV Corps.
Pointe Pagode (YJ 5-5)
Coastal point at 21°17'N-107°27'E. NF48-12 JOG. NVN.
Pointe Phami (XS 9-7)
Point at 10°40'N-106°46'E. On NC48-07 JOG. Gia Dinh Pr?, III Corps.
Pointe Rouge (US 9-1)
Mui Dat Do. Coastal point at 10°03'N-104°00'E. On NC48-05 JOG. Kien Giang Pr, IV Corps.
Pointe Seche (CP 1-6)
Mui Da Chong. Coastal point at 12°21'N-109°18'E. On ND49-13 JOG. Khanh Hoa Pr, II Corps.
Pointe Sud (BN 9-7)
A.k.a. Do, Hon. Coastal point at 11°34'N-109°08'E. On NC49-01 JOG. Ninh Thuan Pr, II Corps.
Pointe Sud (CR 1-2)
Coastal point at 13°46'N-109°15'E. On ND49-09 JOG. Binh Dinh Pr, II Corps.
Pointe Tamquam (BS 9-1)
Pointe de Kim Bong. Coastal point at 14°35'N-109°05'E. ND49-05. Quang Ngai Pr?, I Corps.
Pointe Tortue (CP 0-6)
Mui Cay Ga. Coastal point at 12°18'N-109°15'E. On ND49-13 JOG. Khanh Hoa Pr, II Corps.
Pointe Tram (YS 6-5)
Mui Ho Tram. Coastal point at 10°28'N-107°27'E. On NC48-08 JOG. Phuoc Tuy Pr, III Corps.
Pointe Vinay (BN 0-0)
A.k.a. Mui Ne. Coastal point at 10°55'N-108°17'E. On NC48-08 JOG. Binh Thuan Pr, II Corps.
Pointe Vung La (CQ 1-8)
Mui Luoi Cay. Coastal point at 13°24'N-109°18'E. On ND49-09 JOG. Phu Yen Pr, II Corps.
Pointes des Mines (YJ 2-1)
Coastal Point at 20°55'N-107°09'E. NF48-16 JOG. NVN.
Polar Bear, LZ (AT 897-472)
Apx 3 km E An Hoa CB, 25 km WSW Hoi An and 30 km SSW Da Nang. Americal list. Quang Nam Pr, I Corps.
Polar Bear II, LZ (AT 939-211)
Apx 6 km SE Hiep Duc, 36 km W Tam Ky, and 28 km SSE An Hoa CB. Map is L-7014-6640-3. Americal List. Quang Tin Pr?, I Corps.
Polara, LZ (XD 864-373)
Apx 13 km W to WSW Ca Lu and 6 km NNE Khe Sanh CB. Apr70 XXIV Corps grid per Don Armstrong. Quang Tri Pr, I Corps.
Pole Bean, Operation (n/a)
See Eldest Son, Op.
Pole Bridge (YD 755-144)
See Pohl Bridge. Thua Thien Pr, I Corps.
Polei, LZ (ZA 027-937)
See LZ Polly. Kontum Pr, II Corps.
Polei Breng (ZA)
Mapsheet name of L-7014-6537-1. SVN.
Polei Breng (ZA 125-90)
A.k.a. Trung Nghia? Along Rte 512, apx 13 km WNW Kontum. In Jun73, after Paris Peace Accords had been signed, NVA Div-sized attack seized city from ARVN, and it took SVN troops until Sep73 to retake it, with heavy losses on both sides. Kontum Pr, I Corps.
Polei Jar Sieng (YA 8-9)
Sheet name of map that includes significant portion of Plei Trap Valley and number of remote 4th Div FSBs in W Kontum Pr. Map is L-7014-6537-4. Kontum Pr, II Corps.
Polei Kleng (ZA 032-934)
Small Montagnard hamlet/SF Camp roughly 16 km due W Kontum near Cambodian border. Initially an SF led CIDG camp later expanded to inc 155mm Bty plus supt elements and Inf security. Its small AF was also expanded to C-130 capable status. Casualties from nearby FSBs Brillo-Pad and LZ Bingo often evaced here first before further evac for surgery. Site of FSB Polly, and LZ Bass/FSB Polei Kleng. SF Det 11, 5th SF, Det A-241, Oct66. Elements of 173d

Abn and 2d Bde/4th Div here, '68-69, HQ for 2/35th Inf. C Bty, 7th/15th Arty here for Hipshoot. Grid per *SF Order of Battle*. See Polei Kleng Ranger Camp for more data. Kontum Pr, II Corps.

Polei Kleng, FSB (ZA 027-934)
See Bass, LZ. Kontum Pr, II Corps.

Polei Kleng Airfield (ZA 029-933)
Apx 8 km WNW Polei Krong AF, 23 km WNW Dak To AF. El. 1,870', 3,500' steel-mat rwy. At 14°23'41"N-107°48'36"'E. See LZ Polly. Kontum Pr, II Corps.

Polei Kleng Ranger Camp (ZA 032-934)
A.k.a. PK Ranger Border Camp. See Polei Kleng for location. 22d ARVN Fwd Tac Cmd Post established here during Op Quang Trung 22F. Was fwd Logistics and hvy Arty base suptd overland via QL-14. Quang Trung 22F was designed to clear the 66th NVA Rgt and 40th NVA Arty Rgt from entire Plei Trap Valley region, 14Feb-31Mar71. 16-18Feb71, 2 additional 175mm cannons (7th/15th US Arty) moved to site to augment two 175s already here, along with 1st/71st and 2/72 ARVN Border Ranger Cos. Kontum Pr, II Corps [439]

Polei Kleng SF Camp (ZA 032-934)
Apx 16 km due W Kontum near Cambodian border. SF Det 11, 5th SF, Det A-241, Oct66. Later became ARVN 62d Border Rangers. Grid per *SF Order of Battle*. Also listed at ZA 0326-9330 and ZA 0258-9352. Kontum Pr, II Corps.

Polei Krong (ZA 100-920)
Roughly 3 km W Polei Breng and 16 km WNW Kontum. SF Camp/AF here. Kontum Pr, II Corps.

Polei Krong Airfield (ZA 100-920)
Apx 8 km ESE Polei Kleng AF, 3 km W Polei Breng and 15 km W Kontum, per TPC K-10A. Also listed at ZA 095-910, and described as "Insecure, abnd, overgrown, 29Jun67, AF # VA2-178," in Aug69 TAD per Frank Penk, Jr. Not in Feb73 TAD. El. 1,700'. Kontum Pr, II Corps.

Polei Krong SF Camp (ZA 090-912)
Apx 3 km W Polei Breng and 16 km WNW Kontum. 5th SF Grp, Det. A-133, Dec64. Closed and assets moved to Bien Dien. Grid per *SF Order of Battle*. Also listed at ZA 009-912 but that is likely error. Kontum Pr, II Corps.

Polei Yome (n/a)
Mapsheet name of L-7014-6537-3. SVN.

Police Field Force (n/a)
See Glossary.

Polie (various)
Common misspelling of Polei. See Polei entries.

Polk County, USS (n/a)
LST-1084. Decom 15Sep74. SVN.

Polka-Dot T'ai (n/a)
See Glossary.

Poll Bridge (YD 755-144)
See Pohl Bridge. Thua Thien Pr, I Corps.

Pollux, USS (n/a)
AKS 4. Amphib Attack. Cargo ship. Served in vicinity of Chu Lai, in at least May-Jun65.

Polly, LZ (BR 002-610)
Apx 3 km WSW Plei Uot, 8 km NNW Suoi Doi AF and 26 km NE Pleiku. Sep69. Pleiku Pr, II Corps.

Polly, FSB (YS 340-840)
Apx 19 km NNW Nui Dat, 7.5 km ESE FSB Digger's Rest and 3.5 km SW FSB Dampier. On 1ATF NCO trng map per John Hollett. Bien Hoa Pr, III Corps.

Polly, LZ (ZA 027-937)
At or adj to Polei Kleng AF, apx 23 km WNW Kontum. Possibly also LZ Polei? Nov67. Kontum Pr, II Corps.

Polygamy (n/a)
See Glossary.

Pomona, LZ (YD 228-597)
Apx 1 km W Dong Ha AF and 12 km NW Quang Tri. '70 XXIV Corps grid per D. Armstrong. Quang Tri Pr, I Corps.

Pon River (XD)
A.k.a. the Xe Pon River. S of and paralleling Rte 9/QL-9 between Tchepone and SVN/Cambodian border. See Xe Pon River. Laos.

Pond, LZ (BN 702-596)
Along QL-1, apx 23 km SSW Phan Rang, 28 km SSW Phan Rang AB and 4 km W peak Nui Da Bac. Mar67. Ninh Thuan Pr, II Corps.

Ponde Rosa Compound (XS 85-94)
See Ponderosa Cmpd. Gia Dinh Pr, III Corps.

Ponder, FSB (YD 977-012)
Apx 16 km SE Phu Bai, 4 km S QL-1 and 8.5 km WSW FSB Roy. 101st Abn AO '69-70. Thua Thien Pr, I Corps.

Ponderosa, FSB (AT 939-747)
Apx 3 km SW Thon Da Son, 6 km due W Da Nang AB and 1 km S Rte 542. XXIV Corps grid per Don Armstrong. Quang Nam Pr, I Corps.

Ponderosa, The (XD 852-418)
Area just W the CIDG camp on the Khe Sanh Plateau and 1st cleared by D/1st/3d Marines, 29Sep66. Was just off what later became the parking apron at E? end of main rwy of Khe Sanh AB. Nickname *The Ponderosa* retained until USMC left plateau in '68. During siege was manned by D/1st/26th Marines. Mislabeled map showing position is at p 344 of *Valley of Decision*. Quang Tri Pr, I Corps. [440]

Ponderosa, The (XS 85-94?)
See Ponderosa Cmpd. Gia Dinh Pr, III Corps.

Ponderosa Compound (XS 85-94)
A.k.a. The Ponderosa. Cmpd of 525th Military Intel Bn in Saigon and adj to Phillips Cmpd. So named because of its huge courtyard. Data per *Vietnam Military Lore, 1959-1973*. Gia Dinh Pr, III Corps.

Pong Hai Airfield (TG 51-31)
LS-361. CIA/SF, per *Air Facilities Data-Laos*.

Pong Ta Airfield (TG 73-04)
LS-229. CIA/SF, per *Air Facilities Data-Laos*.

Pong Tuk Airfield (n/a)
A.k.a. Pong Toek AF. Apx 130 km SSW Phnom Penh and 8 km from coast. Feb67 Natl Geo Map. El. 26'. Cambodia.

Pong Toek Airfield (n/a)
A.k.a. Pong Tuk AF. 4,700' rwy near southern coast, 18 km NW Ha Tien SVN and 130 km SSW Phnom Penh. Per TPC K-10D. El. 26'. Cambodia.

Pontchartrain, USCGC (n/a)
WHEC 70. 9May70-3Sep70. Sqdn 3 CGC, during Coast Guard's 5th SVN deployment.

Pony, LZ (BR 398-292)
Apx 17 km SW An Khe. 13Dec65. Binh Dinh Pr, II Corps.

Pony, LZ (BR 690-630)
Described by Dave Holdorf, 7th/15th Arty, as having been along QL-19 right in center of Binh Khe, apx 22 km due E An Khe/Camp Radcliff. On map at www.landscaper.net/chighmap.jpg. Binh Dinh Pr, II Corps.

Pony, LZ (BR 798-333)
Apx 15 km SW Phu Cat AB and 33 km ESE An Khe. Sep66-Oct70. Also listed at BR 712-758, 800-829 and 808-832. Binh Dinh Pr, II Corps.

Pony, LZ/FSB (BT 033-475)
Apx 13 km SW Hoi An, 17 km due E An Hoa CB, 6 km WSW QL-1 and 28 km due S Da Nang. Sep69. XXIV Corps grid per Don Armstrong. Quang Nam Pr, I Corps.

Pony, LZ (BR 808-832)
At Ha Tay AF, just S intersection of Rte 506 and TL-3A, apx 13 km SSW Bong Son AF, 40 km NNW Phu Cat AB and 6 km ENE Phu Xuan. 1st/12th Cav, 1st Cav, '66, 4th Bn/503d Inf, 173d Abn here '68-69. '70. Per John Linn, was fwd FSB of B/2d/35th Inf/4th Div, Jul70. C Bty, 7th/15th Arty here for Hipshoot. 2d/17th Arty here supt 1st Cav, 11/Nov66, per Jack Picciolo. Name/grid per Jim Claeys. Also listed at BR 798-833, 795-830, 800-833, and 801-832. Map is L-7014-6737-1 (Hoai An), per Ray Smith. Binh Dinh Pr, II Corps.

Pony Airfield, LZ (BR 799-829)
See Ha Tay AF. Binh Dinh Pr, II Corps.

Poor House, LZ ? (AN 854-298)
A.k.a. LZ Poorhouse? Apx 5 km SW Ap An-Lam and 21 km N Phan Thiet. Jan68. True nature of site unknown. Binh Thuan Pr, II Corps.

Poorhouse, LZ ? (AN 854-298)
See Poor House. Binh Thuan Pr, II Corps.

Pop Gun (n/a)
See Glossary.

POP Sites (n/a)
See Glossary.

Pop's Field Airfield (TG 95-50)
LS-120. CIA/SF, per *Air Facilities Data-Laos.*

Pope, FSB (XT 542-310)
Apx 7 km due W Xa Duoc and 17 km NW Cu Chi. Sep68. Tay Ninh Pr, III Corps.

Popular Forces (n/a)
See PF and Ruff/Puff in Glossary.

Porazzo, LZ (n/a)
See Porrazzo. II Corps?

Pork and Shrapnel (n/a)
See Glossary.

Pork Chop Island (BT 48-10)
Likely Ky Hoa Island, a large island in lagoon formed by mouth of Song Ben Vam River and Vung An Hoa Bay. Center of mass apx 7 km NW Chu Lai AF, and 5 km due W Thanh Long. Shape resembled that of a pork-chop. Quang Tin Pr, I Corps.

Porkchop Island (BT 48-10)
See Pork Chop Island. Quang Tin Pr, I Corps.

Porrazzo, LZ (n/a)
Location unknown, but likely in II Corps and in either Binh Dinh, Pleiku or Kontum Pr. Possibly named to honor Louis E. Porrazzo, KIA 27Sep67. 1st Cav, 67-68? Name per Dan Gillotti, 15th Arty Assn. II Corps?

Port de Sylphes (YJ 5-1)
Song Cong Se. NIMA data.

Port Lane (CQ 287-233)
In Vung Ro Bay at Phong So, apx 22 km SSE Tuy Hoa AB. Small ammo port built by 39th Engr Bn to supt Tuy Hoa. Named to honor LTC Ernest E Lane Jr, Cmdr, 39th Engr Supt Bn, KIA 18May66. Col Lane oversaw const of Cam Ranh Bay facilities beginning Dec 65. Library of Congress has detailed map of facility: # 97-688603: 86-694373: US. Army Topo Cmd VN, 1:12,500. Port Lane-Vung Ro, ['71] 1 map: color, 53 cm x 63 cm. Call # is G8022.V9 1969.U5. Also listed at CQ 275-229. Long Khanh, II Corps.

Porter, LZ (AT 983-474)
Apx 30 km S Da Nang AB, 17 km SW Hoi An and 12 km due E An Hoa CB. Apr70 XXIV Corps grid per Don Armstrong. Quang Nam Pr, I Corps.

Porterfield, USS (n/a)
DD-682, per Ralph Fries.

Portland, LZ (YS 350-772)
Apx 12 km due W Xa Binh Gia, 12 km NW Nui Dat/Luscombe. Mar66. Phuoc Tuy Pr, III Corps.

Poste De Bu Prang Airfield (YU 491-559)
See Bu Krak AF. Quang Duc Pr, II Corps.

Poste De Jamap Airfield (YU 340-368)
See Djamap AF. Phuoc Long Pr, III Corps.

Poste Deshayes Airfield (n/a)
Apx 275 km NE to ENE Phnom Penh and 40 km W the SVN border on Feb67 Natl Geo Map. El. 900'. Cambodia.

Poste Kilometre (n/a)
See Glossary.

Poste Kilometer 17 (YD 595-307)
See PK 17. Thua Thien Pr, I Corps.

Poste Kilometer 21 (Mil Res) Airfield (TF 60-00)
See PK 21 Military AF. Laos.

Pot Luck, Project (n/a)
See Project Pot Luck in Glossary.

Potsdam Agreement (n/a)
See Glossary.

Poulo Condore Airfield (XQ 80-66)
See Con Son AF. South China Sea, IV Corps.

Poulo Condore Island (XQ 77-63)
A.k.a. Con Son Island. Apx 120 km SE of Cau Mau Peninsula. Infamous prison and "Tiger Cages" here. Hills 610 (2,001') and 515 (1,690') were isle's two highest points. See Con Son Island for detailed history. South China Sea, IV Corps.

Poulo Wai Island (TS 96-40)
A.k.a. Ko Tang Island. See Ko Tang and Mayaguez Incident. Gulf of Thailand, Cambodia?

Pouthichentong International Airport (VT 8-7)
See Phnom Penh Intl Airport. Cambodia.

Pouvoir (n/a)
See Glossary.

Powder, FSB (YD 975-012)
Apx 11 km due W Phu Loc, 3 km SW QL-1, and 28 km SE Hue. 101st Abn inactive FSB grid per Don Armstrong. Thua Thien Pr, I Corps.

Powder, LZ (BS 635-178)
At NW end of An Lo Valley, apx 14 km NW Thuan An, 28 km NW LZ English and 26 km SW Duc Co. Per John Linn,

was fwd FSB and B/2d/35th Inf/4th Div here Jul70; A Bty, 4th/42d Arty her 21Aug70. 4th Div op rpt grid per Jim Claeys. Also listed at BS 637-179 per Bob Patsfield. 20Nov70. Binh Dinh Pr, II Corps.

Powder Ridge, FSB (YT 807-787)
Overlooking Da Te River Valley, apx 28 km due E Tan Phat AF 18 km WNW Da Hoa/QL-1 and 25 km WNW Bao Loc. Opened or reopened 11Aug70, closed 31Aug70 by 2d/8th Cav, per *1st Cav Div Op Rpt, ending 31Oct70*, courtesy Peter Cole. Same rpt also lists grid as YT 818-789. Aug70-Feb71. Lam Dong Pr, II Corps.

Powell's Ape (n/a)
Vietnamese Yeti or Bigfoot. See Nguoi Rung in Glossary.

Pr'line Mtn Commo Site (BP 030-182)
See Pra Lean Signal Site. Tuyen Duc Pr?, II Corps.

Pra Bong Airfield (BS 34-88)
See Tra Bong AF. Quang Ngai, Pr, I Corps.

Pra Lean Signal Site (BP 03-18?)
A.k.a. Hill 1548, Pra Lean or Pr'line or Praline Mtn Sig site. Apx 17 km WSW Dalat, 6 km N Psourr and 16 km WSW Dalat Cam Ly AF. Per Roy Stearns, Pra Line was manned byArmy's 459th Sig Co (call-sign Mystic Dagger), 52d Sig Bn, 1st Sig Bde, with security per signalmen and 194th MPs.[441] Apx 500 Montagnard soldiers of ARVN 23d Inf Div and their families also defended site. Tropospheric Antennas here. Tuyen Duc Pr, II Corps.

Prachin Buri Airfield (QR 5-5)
Apx 95 km ENE Bangkok, near14°04'00"N-101°23'00"E. Feb67 Natl Geo map. NIMA data. El. 20'. Thailand.

Prachuap Khiri Khan AF (NP 8-0)
Along coast, apx 225 km SSW Bangkok. Feb67 Natl Geo map. Near 11°47'00"N-99°48'00"E. El. 8'. Thailand.

Prairie, Operation (XD/YD)
3Aug66-31Jan67. TF Delta against 304th and 341st NVA Divs. 3d Mar Div op in Con Thien/Gio Linh areas of DMZ. Immed followed Op Hastings, when 1 Hastings Bn was left in field to monitor 324B NVA Div's movements. During op and in some of heaviest fighting of war, 3d Bn/4th Mar pushed NVA off Nui Cay Tre Ridge (Razorback Ridge; inc Hills 400 and 484), Aug-Oct66. When 3d/4th (call-sign "Mutter") took ridge on 5Oct66 after 2 weeks of bloody fighting, it was renamed Mutter's Ridge in their honor. See Mutter's Ridge. 1,397 rptd NVA/VC KIA, per *Vietnam Order of Battle*, pp 9-14. Quang Tri Pr, I Corps.

Prairie II, Operation (XD/YD)
1Feb-18Mar67. 3d Mar Div ops in DMZ. 693 rptd NVA/VC KIA, per *Vietnam Order of Battle*, pp 9-14. Quang Tri Pr, I Corps.

Prairie Fire (n/a)
See Glossary.

Prairie Fire FACs (n/a)
See Glossary.

Prairie Fire Operations (n/a)
See Glossary.

Prairie Fire Radio Relay Site (YB 604-355?)
Possibly Leghorn? Radio relay site said to have been on 7,200' mtn top in Laos and operated by 5th SF Grp personnel assigned to MAC-SOG Prairie Fire and other "Over the Fence" Ops. Could intercept virtually any MAC-SOG Team's line-of-sight radio transmissions and relay them to CCN, MLT-1 or MLT-2. Formal name not cited in *Da Nang Diary* reference to it. See Leghorn entry for likely location. Laos.

Pralean Signal Site (BP 03-18?)
See Pra Lean. Tuyen Duc Pr, II Corps.

Pran Buri Airfield (NP 9-7)
A.k.a. Pranburi. Apx 160 km SSW Bangkok per Feb67 Natl Geo map, near 12°25'00"N-99°53'00"E. NIMA data. El. 90'. Thailand.

Pran Buri SF Camp (NP 9-7)
A.k.a. Pranburi SF Camp. Apx 160 km SSW Bangkok. Per *SF Order of Battle*. NIMA grid. Thailand.

Pranburi Airfield (NP 9-7)
See Pran Buri AF. Thailand.

Pranburi SF Camp (NP 9-7)
See Pran Buri SF Camp. Thailand.

Prance, LZ (YD 330-094)
Apx 34 km SE Ba Long AF and 42 km due S of Quang Tri. Apr70 XXIV Corps grid per Don Armstrong. Thua Thien Pr, I Corps.

Pranchinburi (QR 5-5)
See Prachin Buri. Thailand.

Pratt, Camp (YT 627-122)
Along rail tracks at NE base of Nui Chua Chan Mtn some 3 km NNE its peak, and apx 16 km ENE Xuan Loc AF. Jul70. Long Khanh Pr, III Corps.

Pratt, LZ (AT 9-2 or 9-3?)
Built N of LZ Siberia (AT 901-232), after extension of 4th Div AO into Marine AO was authorized. LZ Siberia was apx 4 km SSW Hiep Duc and 40 km W Tam Ky. Temporary FSB set up by 4th Inf Div, 31Nov70. Americal list. Quang Tin Pr?, I Corps.

Pratt, LZ (YD 196-039)
Apx 13 km SE Tou Rout, 1 or 2 km N of Laos, and 56 km WSW Hue. Apr70 XXIV Corps grid per Don Armstrong. Quang Tri Pr, I Corps.

Preah Vihear Airfield (n/a)
On Cambodian border, apx 95 km SSW Ubon AB and 7 km SW Ban Phumsaron AF. El. 1,673'. Thailand.

Preble, USS (n/a)
DLG-15. Guided Missile DD Ldr, per Ralph Fries.

Precarious, FSB (n/a)
No data. 10th Cav, 4th Div here, per Bob Patsfield. Possibly Binh Dinh or Pleiku Pr, II Corps.

Precinct Five (XS 8-9)
Police District a.k.a. Cholon; a major suburb of Saigon. According to Nguyen Cao Ky, was apx 90% Chinese and some 100,000 of Draft-eligible youth living in precinct were able to evade ARVN Draft through heavy bribes paid by their families to Chief of Police of precinct. Ky says that officers on his VNAF staff often joked that if Ky were to become Premier, rather than appointing them to cabinet posts, they would rather he instead appoint them Chief of Police for Precinct Five. Ky claims that to become any Chief of Police, a bribe of as much as 15 million Piastres was often necessary, and that the investment could be tripled in as little as 2 years by an enterprising chief. Gia Dinh Pr, III Corps.[442]

Prek Klok (XT 270-780)
Along Rte 4 apx 14 km SSW Katum, 21 km due N Nui Ba Den and 30 km NNE Tay Ninh. Site of Battle of Prek Klok I, 28Feb67, during Op Junction City. B/ 1st/16th Inf, 1st

Inf Div fighting 2d Bn, 101st NVA Rgt, 9th VC Div. 25 US KIA, 28 WIA. SF Det 54. Arty Base II nearby, as was ARVN FSB Cayalya. Tay Ninh Pr, III Corps.

Prek Klok, FSB (XT 288-815)
Along TL-4, apx 10 km SSW Katum AF and 23 km N Nui Ba Den. Dec67. Tay Ninh Pr, III Corps.

Prek Klok Airfield (XT 275-787)
Along Rte 4, apx 14 km SSW Katum, 21 km due N Nui Ba Den and 30 km NNE Tay Ninh. Listed as "Insecure, abnd, 30Nov67, AF # VA3-288," in Aug69 TAD per Frank Penk, Jr. Not in Feb73 TAD. Tay Ninh Pr, III Corps.

Prek Klok II, Battle of (XT 27-78?)
Generally along Rte 4, apx 14 km SSW Katum, 21 km due N Nui Ba Den and 30 km NNE Tay Ninh. 10-11Mar67, during Op Junction City. 2/2d Inf/1st Div was at FSPB II apx 32 km NE Tay Ninh near Prek Klok stream when at 2208 hrs, VC initiated mortar attack followed by US counter bty/recon-by-fire and then VC grnd assault. By midnight battle was over. 197 NVA KIA and 5 US WIA. Tay Ninh Pr, III Corps.

Prek Klok River (XT)
Runs through War Zone C from NW to SE, forming S edge of Iron Triangle and joining Song Saigon at Iron T's SE corner, S of Ben Cat about 25 km N Saigon. Tay Ninh Pr, III Corps.

Prek Klok SF Camp (XT 270-780)
Along Rte 4 apx 14 km SSW Katum, 21 km due N Nui Ba Den and 30 km NNE Tay Ninh. 5th SF. Closed and moved to Katum through Trang Sup. Info/grid per *SF Order of Battle.* Tay Ninh Pr, III Corps.

Prep, FSB/LZ (BT 008-148)
Apx 4 km SE Thon Ba, 11 km W to WNW Tien Phuoc AF, and 30 km WSW Tam Ky. Per Les Hines, apparently served CIA helos and Nung mercenaries since both were frequently observed "hanging-out" here. Also listed at BT 009-147 and BT 0000-4148? Apr70 XXIV Corps grid per Don Armstrong. Quang Tin Pr, I Corps.

Prescott, LZ (XD 743-443)
Apx 9 km E Laos, 2 km W Lang Ruon, 10 km WNW Khe Sanh CB and 9 km NNE Lao Bao. Apr70 XXIV Corps grid per Don Armstrong. Quang Tri Pr, I Corps.

President Buchanan, SS (n/a)
Commercial transport under govt contract, per Ralph Fries.

President Garfield, SS (n/a)
Commercial transport under govt contract, per Ralph Fries.

President Jefferson, SS (n/a)
Commercial transport under govt contract, per Ralph Fries.

Presidential Palace (XS 857-915)
A.k.a. Norodom Palace and Palace of Independence. In Saigon, apx 6 km SE Tan Son Nhut AB and 500 meters SW the US Embassy. 1st occupied by Ngo Dinh Diem (1st Premier of SVN, and who formally assumed office on 7Jul54, after Emperor Bao Dai asked him to take job during Geneva Conference, 18Jun54, and he accepted on 21Jun54) when it was named Norodom Palace. Diem quickly renamed it Doc Lap, or Independence Palace. In Feb63, two dissident VNAF pilots bombed and strafed the Palace in attempt to kill President Diem. Attack did destroy one wing of palace; however, none of Diem's family was injured. Some data per *The Unquiet American*, pp 150-152 Gia Dinh Pr, III Corps.

Preston, USS (n/a)
DD-795, per Ralph Fries.

Prey-Nokor (XS 85-95)
See Saigon. Gia Dinh Pr, I Corps.

Prey Veng Airfield (n/a)
Apx 45 km ESE Phnom Penh, perFeb67 Natl Geo map. El. 3'. Cambodia.

Price, Camp (YT 042-115)
A.k.a. Camp W. S. Price. Apx 6 km SE Bien Hoa AB and 2 km WSW Plantation AF. Cmpd of 54th Arty Grp at Long Binh Post. Named to honor LTC William S Price, USA, CO 7th/8th Field Arty (Jun-Dec 67) and Dpty Sr. Adv to 18th ARVN Inf Div (Dec 67 to death), KIA 29Mar68 when hit by grnd fire while on helo suptg 52d ARVN Ranger Bn near Xuan Loc. Cmpd dedicated 29Mar69. Data per *Vietnam Military Lore, 1959-1973*. Bien Hoa Pr, III Corps.

Price, W. S., Camp (YT 042-115)
See Price, Camp. Bien Hoa Pr, III Corps.

PRIME BEEF (n/a)
See Glossary.

Prince BEQ (XS 8-9)
At 187 Pham Ngu Lao St. (pre-68), Saigon. Data per *Vietnam Military Lore, 1959-1973*. Gia Dinh Pr, III Corps.

Princeton BEQ (XS 8-9)
At 215-217 Tran Hung Dao St., Saigon. Data per *Vietnam Military Lore, 1959-1973*. Gia Dinh Pr, III Corps.

Princeton, USS (n/a)
LPH-5, Amphib Assault Ship. In Jan62, *USS Card* (T-AKV 40) carried Army helos/helo transport Co to Subic Bay, which then transferred to *Princeton*, LST 629 and LST 630, for trip to Da Nang. On 15Apr62, she carried USMC HMM 362 off Cau Mau Peninsula, and with cover of aircraft carrier *Hancock's* air grp, HMM 362 deployed to Soc Trang. [443] In 66, carried 3d/5th Marine SLF from Okinawa to VN per *Not Going Home Alone*, p 48.

Prisonner-Interne Militare (n/a)
See Glossary.

Pritchett, USS (n/a)
A.k.a. DD 561. In Oct67, replaced *USS Evans* off Phan Thiet, firing apx 300 five-inch rnds suptg 3/506th Inf, per www.currahee.org/pageb2.html.

Private Delta Force (n/a)
See Glossary.

Privateer (n/a)
See Glossary.

Professional, Camp (AT 860-860?)
Apx 5 km W Da Nang AB. Was transferred from US control to ARVN 3d Inf Div, 13Jun72. At time of transfer, was capable of housing 500 personnel. MACV-JGS IG conducted Post-Transfer Inspection of facility, 29Jun72. Grid is est. Quang Nam Pr, I Corps.

Professional, FSB/LZ (BT 173-078)
A.k.a. Hill 185. Apx 32 km NW Chu Lai, 9 km NNE old Hau Duc and 16 km SW LZ East. 1st/46thInf closed site 22Aug70. Apparently reopened and, George Buckley tells us, closed finally by 4th/3d Inf in Oct71. Tommy Poppell, B/1st/46th Inf, recalls that S-4 helipad here was called the "One-O-Worst Pad." 1st/502d Inf, 101st Abn and other 1st Bde/101st units here Summer '69. while opcon to Americal Div. 1st Cav also here? Apr70 XXIV Corps grid per Don

Armstrong. Also listed at BT 185-053, 176-070, 173-077, 173-076 and 172-078. Quang Tin Pr, I Corps.[444]

Project B-36, Operation (n/a)
See Glossary.

Project B-50 (n/a)
See Glossary.

Project B-56 (n/a)
See Glossary.

Project 404 (n/a)
See Glossary.

Project 406 (n/a)
See Glossary.

Project 603 (n/a)
See Glossary.

Project 9024 (n/a)
See Glossary.

Project 100,000 (n/a)
See Glossary.

Project Arizona (n/a)
See Glossary.

Project Delta, Operation (n/a)
See Glossary.

Project Delta Compound (CP 03-52?)
See MACV Recondo School. Khanh Hoa Pr, II Corps.

Project Douche (n/a)
See Glossary.

Project Dye Marker (n/a)
See Glossary.

Project Embankment (XS 8-9)
See Glossary.

Project Enhance (n/a)
See Glossary.

Project Enhance Plus (n/a)
See Glossary.

Project Illinois City (n/a)
See Glossary.

Project Leaping Lena (n/a)
See Glossary.

Project Omega (n/a)
See Glossary.

Project Phoenix (WS 153-814?)
See MACV Adv. Team 64. Chau Doc Pr, IV Corps.

Project Pot Luck (n/a)
See Glossary.

Project Practice Nine (XD/YD)
See Glossary.

Project Rapid Fire (n/a)
See Glossary.

Project Shining Brass (n/a)
See Shining Brass.

Project Sigma (XS)
See Glossary.

Project Tiger Hound (n/a)
See Glossary.

Project Urgency (n/a)
See Glossary.

Propaganda Leaflets (n/a)
See Glossary.

Prospector, Camp (n/a)
See Prospector's Camp. Kontum Pr, II Corps.

Prospector's Camp, FSB (ZB?)
Map in *Chickenhawk* indicates it was perhaps 3 km WNW Dak To, 10 km SW The Fortress and 40 km NNW Kontum. Helo laager area for 49th AHC (and named for unit's call-sign "Prospector") while suptg 1st Bde/101st Abn in Dak To/Toumorong area during Op Hawthorne, Jun66. Described as being "in a grassy plain south of some low foothills. Our tents were set up in three straight lines paralleling the red-dirt airstrip. A mile from our camp, the 101st bivouacked and maintained security for themselves and for the Prospectors."[445] Kontum Pr, II Corps.

Prosperity Centers (n/a)
See Glossary.

Provide, Camp (CR 03-16 or BR 95-42?)
At Phu Tai, near Qui Nhon. 41st Sig Bn Cmpd and formerly the 173d Bde Supt Bn Cmpd. Was transferred for dismantlement to Binh Dinh Pr HQ, 22Mar72, then shifted to Qui Nhon Peoples Self Defense Force, which began actual demo 23Mar. On 26Mar, Prov Chief reassigned base to 399th PF Co. Was yet again transferred to Pacification Development Council, 20May72. Binh Dinh Pr, II Corps.

Providence, USS (n/a)
CLG 6, Guided Missile Cruiser. Deployed off SVN in '62? In Feb68, *Canberra* (CAG 2). *Providence*, and 7 other ships poured thousands of shells into Hue, inc the Citadel, suptg USMC ground units during Tet '68.

PS Sites (n/a)
See Glossary.

PS 21 (n/a)
PS site (LS site?) described as "desolate looking" and near edge of Bolovens Plateau. Discussed in *Da Nang Diary*, p 74. See PS Sites in Glossary. Laos.

PS 38 (n/a)
PS site (LS site?) described as busiest PS Site of all. Had 3,000' rwy carved from red dirt with a dozen buildings lining either side of rwy at its center. Apparently subjected to frequent probes and attacks. Discussed in *Da Nang Diary*, p 74. See PS Sites in Glossary. Laos.

PS 39 (n/a)
PS site (LS site?) characterized by its partially paved rwy and half-moon shaped perimeter defensive trenching. Discussed in *Da Nang Diary*, p 74. See PS Sites in Glossary. Laos.

PS 71 (n/a)
PS site (LS site?) described as "a triangular-shaped SF "A" team camp with a small dirt airstrip along its side." Discussed in *Da Nang Diary*, p 74. See PS Sites in Glossary. Laos.

Pu Thanh (Nhon Trach) (n/a)
Mapsheet L-7014-6330-2. Sheet name: Nhon Trach (Pu Thanh). SVN.

Pua Airfield (n/a)
Apx 610 km N Bangkok. Natl Geo map. El. 850'. Thailand.

Public Indictment #1 (n/a)
See People's Anti-Corruption Movement in Glossary.

Public Indictment #2 (n/a)
See Glossary.

Puff (n/a)
See Glossary.

Puff the Magic Dragon (n/a)
See Glossary.

Pugh Amphitheater (BP?)
Originally South Beach Amphitheater. On Cam Ranh Bay Peninsula. Named to honor Sp4 Robert E Pugh, USA, 87th Engr Bn, KIA 15De66, while starting up a booby-trapped crane. Dedicated in his name, 2Jul67. Bob Hope, among other notables, performed here. Data per *Vietnam Military Lore, 1959-1973*. Khanh Hoa Pr, II Corps.

Pulaski, FSB (n/a)
Presumed to have existed. No data. III Corps?

Pulaski II, FSB (n/a)
Location unknown. 1st/8th Arty, 25th Inf Div here, 68. Name per Dan Gillotti, 15th Arty Assn. III Corps.

Pulaski County, USS (n/a)
LST-1088. A.k.a. *USNS Pulaski County*. To MSTS, Jul67.

Puma, FSB (YS 444-738)
Apx 1 km W LTL-2, 6 km N Nui Dat, and 2 km NNE FSB Dagger. On 1ATF NCO trng map per John Hollett. Phuoc Tuy Pr, III Corps.

Puma, FSB (YS 895-990)
Along QL-1, apx 4 km WNW Ap Da Mai, 10 km NNE peak Nui Chua Chan and 18 km NW Ham Tan AF. Jan68. Binh Tuy Pr, III Corps.

Puma, FSB (ZA 079-218)
At SW corner of Xuong Kuang, apx 7 km SSW Oasis AF, 8 km W Plei Ya Bo and 28 km SW Pleiku. 10th Cav, 4th Div here, per Bob Patsfield. Name/grid per Jim Claeys. Also listed at ZA 095-232, Jan69, which is apx 2 km NE listed grid. Unknown which grid is correct or if site moved? Pleiku Pr, II Corps.

Puma, FSB (ZA 095-232)
At NE corner of Xuong Kuang, apx 5 km SSW Oasis AF, 7 km W Plei Ya Bo and 27 km SW Pleiku. Also listed at ZA 079-218, and unknown which grid is correct or if site moved? Pleiku Pr, II Corps.

Puma, LZ (BR 928-990)
Apx 1 km S Song An Lao River, 4 km ESE LZ English and 8 km NE Bong Son. Oct66. Binh Dinh Pr, II Corps.

Pump Station 1 (BR 47-44?)
At the POL tank farm in An Khe. One of 5 stations forming the An Khe-Pleiku Pipeline. Under control of 640th QM Co/240th QM Bn/58th Field Depot until Jun68, then assigned to Qui Nhon Supt Cmd, 1st Log thereafter. Data per Conrad Creitz. Binh Dinh Pr, II Corps.

Pump Station 2 (BR 309-457)
Adj to Bridge Site 25, along QL-19 apx 18 km W An Khe. In early May68, security wire was in place but bunkers not built. On 6May68, was hit with 2 mortar and small arms fire attacks; 1st at 0945 hrs inc apx 20 rnds of mortar, 8 of which fell in cmpd, resulting in 1 WIA and minor damage; 2d took place at 1600 hrs, in which 8 rnds were fired but only 1 landed in base with no damage. On 19May68, it was again attacked with small arms and mortars for apx 30 min beginning at 1300 hrs, and resulting in 1 US WIA, minor damage, 6 VC KIA and one captured mortar tube. On 23May68, took 5 mortar rnds and small arms fire with no damage. [446] Rumor was that VC Bn was HQ'd just over a hill SW site. See Pump Station 1. Data per Conrad Creitz. Binh Dinh or Pleiku Pr?, II Corps.

Pump Station 3 (BR 243-494)
Along QL-19, at base of long hill leading to Mang Yang Pass. Apx 24 km W to WNW An Khe. At 1045 hrs, 25May68, received 4 mortar rnds and small arms fire with no damage; at 1045 hrs, 1Jun68, it received 25-30 mortar rnds including 4 in cmpd of 647th QM Co (Petrol OP) that resulted in 2 WIA; on 21Jul68, took small arms fire and 3 mortar rnds with no casualties, and again on 23Jul68, it was hit with 35 mortar rnds but no casualties. [447] See Pump Station 1. Also listed at BR 240-497 and 230-497. Data per Conrad Creitz. Pleiku Pr, II Corps.

Pump Station 4 (BR ?)
Precise location unknown, but somewhere along QL-19 and W of Pump Station 3. See Pump Station 1. Data per Conrad Creitz. Pleiku Pr?, II Corps.

Pump Station 5 (AR 937-480)
Along QL-19 apx 2 km NE ville of Lo Trung, 16 km ENE Pleiku and 32 km due W Pump Station 3. Also listed as PS #9 in 31Jan70 4th Div ORLL (AR 939-480)? On 10Jul68, at 2115 hrs, was hit by small arms fire from 3 directions; however, no damage resulted. A Trp 2d/1st Cav provided mortar fire in supt. [448] See Pump Station 1. See Pump Station 9. Data per Conrad Creitz. Pleiku Pr, II Corps.

Pump Station 6 (BR 461-442)
See Pump Station 8. Due S Camp Radcliff in heavily populated area. In AO of 1st/50th Inf and 1st/69th Armor. Binh Dinh Pr, II Corps.

Pump Station 7 (BR 310-456)
See Pump Station 8. Binh Dinh Pr, II Corps.

Pump Station 8 (BR 243-494)
On QL-19E. One of many pump stations along 6" petro line paralleling QL-19 between Qui Nhon and Pleiku, with break at POL stg tank facility at An Khe and Pump Station 1. Per Conrad Creitz, 647th QM Co manned POL farm, stations and pipeline from An Khe to Pleiku. This particular site was nicknamed "Little DBP" by 1st/69th Armor troops. All QL-19 PSs consisted of wood-framed bldgs that enclosed pumps and Engr/security forces. Each was encircled with large amounts of razor and barbed concertina, liberally seasoned with dozens of Claymore and other defensive mines, trip flares and booby traps. Flame trenches (2' deep and filled with jellied napalm) and Fougasse. Despite isolation, small force and exposure, stations were rarely attacked or taken under direct fire. Map is L-7014-6736-4. Binh Dinh Pr, II Corps. [449]

Pump Station 9 (BR 118-551)
Along QL-19, just W Dinh Dien Dak Quon, apx 33 km ENE Pleiku and 38 km WNW An Khe. Grid per 4th Div 31Jan70 rpt courtesy Jim Henderson, which also indicates A Bty, 4th/42d Arty here Dec69. Pleiku Pr, II Corps.

Pump Station 10 (AR 939-480)
Along QL-19, apx 2 km NE Lo Trung, 16 km ENE Pleiku. Also listed as PS #5? Grid per 4th Div 31Jan70 rpt courtesy Jim Henderson, which also indicates A Bty, 4th/42d Arty here Dec69. Pleiku Pr, II Corps.

Punch-Bowl, LZ (YA 9-8?)
A.k.a. FSB 504C? Described as 25th and 4th Div FSB/LZ in Punch Bowl Valley, a wide-open plain surrounded by mtns and SW LZ Brillo-Pad. Bn-sized FSB opened by 1st/14th Inf, 25th Inf Div apx 25Oct66. Discussed in *Rites of Passage*, p 30-45. Op there described in *Time Heals No Wounds*, at pp 88-91 with photo in photo section. 2d Bde/4th Div worked out of this LZ in early-mid '69. See Punch Bowl Valley for more detail. Kontum Pr, II Corps.

Punch Bowl, The (YD?)
Described as large depression somewhere on floor of A Shau Valley. Per *After Tet*, well-entrenched NVA eng and transport troops put up significant resistance to 1st/8th Cav during 3-day battle here, May68, during Op Delaware. During fight, an NVA tank was destroyed by trooper using M-72 LAW. Thua Thien Pr?, I Corps. [450]

Punch Bowl Valley (YA 95-83?)
A.k.a. Dragon Valley. Described as having been N of Hills 903 and 1005, and as wide-open plain surrounded by mtns SW LZ Brillo-Pad (YA 962-855). 1st/14th Inf/25th Div here, 23Oct66. Per *Rites of Passage*, p 30, "a Bn-level officer had seen it from the air and thought it looked like a punch bowl." On 2Nov66, Bn CO of the 1st/14th Inf (a Col Proctor) dedicated a sign at LZ 504-C (a.k.a. LZ Punch Bow), and renamed valley Dragon Valley. Kontum Pr, II Corps.

Punch-Up at Madame T's, The (YS 28-43)
See Madame T's. Phuoc Tuy Pr, III Corps.

Puncher, FSB (TK 00-00)
In Oct70, Hmong recaptured LS-5 (Ban Na) and then in Dec70 built large FSB code-named Puncher there. In May71, Hmong were forced to abandon base and retreat S. Photos/discussion in *War In Laos*, pp 43-48. See Lao FSBs Lion and Mustang. Laos

Punji Stake Hill (n/a)
Apparently near Da Nang, but precise location unknown. Photo of hill taken Mar67 is in *The Vietnam War* at p 104. Quang Nam Pr?, I Corps.

Punt, LZ (ZA 183-123)
Apx 7 km NW Plei Me SF Camp,38 km SSW Pleiku, 30 km WNW Phu Nhon AF and 24 km ENE peak Chu Pong Mtn. Set up by 2d/12th Cav and B Bty, 2d/17th Arty, 28Oct65, in effort to break siege of Plei Me. LZs Punt and Homecoming were closed by 2d/8th Cav in order to open LZ Con sometime in Oct or Nov65. Cited in *Pleiku*" at p 106, per Peter Cole. See LZ Con. Pleiku Pr, II Corps.

Puntai Airfield (RD 09-68)
A.k.a. L-20 and Bun Taio AF. CIA/SF, per *Air Facilities Data-Laos.*

Puoc Long (n/a)
Mapsheet name of L-7014-6027-1. DOD list sp; however, Phuoc Long is principal city on sheet and listed sp likely in error. SVN.

Purdue, Camp (AT 97-74)
See Perdue, Camp. Quang Nam Pr, I Corps.

Purple, LZ (XT 410-565)
Apx 12 km NE Dau Tieng/Tri Tam and 14 km ESE peak Nui Ba Den. Jun66. Tay Ninh Pr, III Corps.

Purple Heart (n/a)
See Glossary.

Purse, LZ? (BR 851-788)
In 506 Valley, apx 6 km SE Ha Tay AF and 16 km S Bong Son. Feb66. Simply listed as "Purse," and nature of use unknown. Binh Dinh Pr, II Corps.

Purshing, FSB (YT 161-405)
See Pershing, FSB. Long Khanh Pr, III Corps.

Pusan, LZ (YD 042-249)
Apx 19 km SW Ba Long AF, 23 km SSE Ca Lu, 38 km SW Quang Tri. 10, and within 3 km of Laos. Also listed at YD 036-351 (Nov68), apx 13 km NNW listed grid? '70 XXIV Corps grid per D Armstrong. Thua Thien Pr, I Corps.

Putnam Tiger, Operation (n/a)
22Apr-22Sep69. 4th Div. 563 NVA/VC KIA, per *Vietnam Order of Battle*, pp 9-14. Pleiku/Kontum Prvs, II Corps.

Putter, LZ (BR 644-825)
Apx 16 km W Ha Tay AF, 42 km NNE An Khe and 24 km SW Bong Son. 1st Cav. Listed with LZ Bird on USAF Herbicide rpt which states following agents were sprayed within 8 km radius of site: Orange, 50,095 gal; White, zero; Blue, 7,200 gal. 66-67. Binh Dinh Pr, II Corps.

Putting Green (BR 470-485)
Apx 1 km E Golf Course AF and 3 km N An Khe's main AF. Apparently somehow related to AF? 1st Cav/1st Bde 101st Abn. Oct65. Binh Dinh Pr, II Corps.

Pyle Barracks (AR 80-47)
US Advsy Det Cmpd at Camp Holloway, just E of Pleiku. Named to honor Sp5 Jesse A. Pyle, KIA 7Feb65, while on guard duty and fighting VC Sapper attack. His and other deaths that night prompted President Johnson to order Op Flaming Dart. Data per *Vietnam Military Lore, 1959-1973.* Pleiku Pr, II Corps.

Pyramid Island (CP 2-5)
A.k.a. Hon Dung and Pyramid, Ile de. NIMA data. Khanh Hoa Pr, II Corps.

Python, LZ (YC 405-975)
In the A Shau Valley, apx 17 km NW A Sap and 38 km SW Hue. XXIV Corps, 101st Abn inactive FSB list per Don Armstrong. Thua Thien Pr, I Corps.

QUEBEC

Facility/Feature Name, Grid Coordinate, a.k.a. Name/History/Province/CTZ

Unless otherwise stated, 6-digit grid coordinates reference DMA L-7014, L-7015 or L-7016 series, 1:50,000 scale maps, while 2- and 4-digit coordinates reference AMS/DMA/NIMA 1:250,000, 1:500,000 and 1:1,000,000 scale maps. Unless otherwise stated, all heights are in meters. To convert meters to feet, multiply by 3.2808; feet to meters, multiply by .3048.

Q Phu Loc (n/a)
Mapsheet name of L-7014-6541-1. SVN.

Q Phu Loc (ZD 084-004)
A.k.a. Phu Loc. Along QL-1 and S shore of Dam Cau Hai and apx 40 km SE Hue. Thua Thien Pr, I Corps.

Qanh Tach, FSB? (YS 82-97)
A.k.a. FSB Strike or possibly Quan or Quanh Tach? Immed N Nui Be Mtn, 58 km WSW Phan Thiet and near Ap Rung La. 2d/3d, 199th LIB here. Long Khanh Pr, III Corps.

QL (Road Type Identifier) (n/a)
See Glossary.

QL-1 (numerous)
Natl Rte 1. Principal hwy running S from Hanoi generally along coast S and then W to Saigon. From Saigon, it ran generally W to Phnom Penh and S to the Cambodian coast. Much of Rte was asphalt, which was atypical for SVN. Ran ESE from Cambodian border (at point some 35 km SW Tay Ninh on Parrot's Beak) 120 km to Saigon, then E 150 km to Phan Thiet, then turned NE for 130 km to Phan Rang, then NNE for 75 km to Nha Trang, then N for 100 km to Tuy Hoa, then NNE for 80 km to Qui Nhon, then NNW for 150 km to Quang Ngai, then NNW for 130 km to Da Nang, then NW for 90 km to Hue (over the Hai Van Pass), then NW for 50 km to Quang Tri and finally another 35 km NNW to Ben Hai River. Often referred to as the Street Without Joy; however, SWJ was only that portion of QL-1 and Rtes 592/555 running NW/SE from Quang Tri to Huong Dien, NW of Hue.

QL-1A (XT)
Natl Rte 1A. Originates near Phu Cuong (just W Phu Loi), running generally N thru Dog Leg Ville to Claymore Corners where Rtes 2A, 1A and 16 meet, then over Song Be Bridge and thru Phuoc Vinh and Dong Xoai to Song Be. Described in *Low Level Hell* as small, thin road that looked like a "rust-colored snake" from air. Built by French. In Jun69, 1st Engr Bn cleared a 90-mile stretch to depth of 200 meters on both sides in order to eliminate ambushes. Long Khanh/Phuoc Tuy Prvs, III Corps.

QL-2 (YS)
Natl Rte 2. Connected Xuan Loc (at QL-1) to Vung Tau in S. 55 km long. Nui Dat and Blackhorse Basecamp were along QL-2. Long Khanh/Phuoc Tuy Pr, II Corps.

QL-3A (BR)
Natl Rte 3. N/S artery through Vinh Thanh (Happy) Valley that joins E/W QL-19 apx 18 km E An Khe and 25 km W Phu Cat. Vinh Thanh, Vinh Phuc, Din Quang and CIDG Camp in Old French Fort N Vinh Thanh are along its course. Binh Dinh Pr, II Corps.

QL-4 (XS/WS/WR/XR)
Natl Rte 4. Connected Saigon with Ca Mau (a.k.a. Quan Long). Ran from Saigon SW to My Tho, then W to Vinh Long, then SW to Can Tho, then turned SE to Soc Trang, then turned SSW to Bac Lieu, then W to Ca Mau (Quan Long) some 250 km SW Saigon. III/IV Corps.

QL-9 (XD/YD)
Natl Rte 9. Ran W from QL-1 (at point 15 km NE Quang Tri) through Cam Hu, Cam Lu, Camp Carroll, Vandegrift CB, the Rockpile, Khe Sanh, Lang Vei and Khe Sanh, to border of Laos. Main artery between Khe Sanh CB and Dong Ha/Quang Tri area during Lam Son 719. Apx 70 km (road distance) between border of Laos and QL-1. Quang Tri Pr, I Corps.

QL-11 (BP/CP)
Natl Rte 11. Connected Phan Rang (on QL-1) with Dalat, running inland to NW. II Corps.

QL-13 (XT)
A.k.a. Thunder Road and Natl Rte 13. Major N/S artery dividing War Zones C & D in III Corps. Connected Loc Ninh (near Cambodia) with Saigon, some 130 km due S Loc Ninh. An Loc and Lai Khe were important towns along its path. See Thunder Road. III Corps.

QL-14 (numerous)
AQ/BQ/AP/ZU/YU/YT/XT. Natl Rte 14, the main N/S artery of Central Highlands. Connected Inter-provincial route 4 (LTL-4) and Rte 540 at their confluence just SW Da Nang, all the way S along SVN's "spine" to its intersection with QL-13 near Bien Hoa and Saigon. As a practical matter, stretch between Ha Tan (SW Da Nang apx 35 km) and Dak To was not in use or open during much of war. Also connected Dak To with Ban Me Thuot, Pleiku, Ban Blech, Dao Thong Dong Xoai and Phuoc Vinh, though the stretch between Dao Thong and Phuoc Vinh was probably rarely in use. Apx 380 km in length. QL-14S was the major supply rte between Pleiku and Ban Me Thuot while QL-14N was the same between Pleiku and Dak To. I, II/III Corps.

QL-14S and 14N (numerous)
See QL-14. II Corps.

QL-15 (YT/YS)
Natl Rte 15. Connected Bien Hoa with QL-2 to SE, meeting it near Nui Dat and N Vung Tau. Apx 65 km in length. III Corps.

QL-19 (ZA/AR/BR)
Natl Rte 19. Main supply rte between Qui Nhon and Pleiku. Connected Pleiku (on QL-14) in W with Binh Dinh (on QL-1) in E, meeting QL-1 apx 15 km N Qui Nhon. Also ran W from Pleiku to Cambodian border, but that

portion likely saw little use during war. Apx 125 km in length between Pleiku and QL-1, and perhaps 180 km its full length from border to Binh Dinh (QL-1). 10" fuel pipeline and numerous pumping stations at 15 km intervals that ran Hwy's entire length were frequent target of VC/NVA attacks and sabotage. Skirted An Khe, home of both the 1st Cav and 173d Abn. During its course, crossed the An Khe, Deo Mang and infamous Mang Yang Passes. See Mang Yang Pass, Strongpoints, Pump Stations, and *Groupement Mobile 100*. II Corps.

QL-19E and 19W (ZA/AR/BR)
See QL-19. II Corps.

QL-20 (YT/ZT/AN/BN/BP)
Natl Rte 20. Ran NE from its intersection with QL-1 near Xuan Loc some 180 km to NE. Bao Loc, Di Linh and Duc Trong were situated along its route. II/III Corps.

QL-21 (AQ/BQ/BP/CP)
Natl Rte 21. Connected Ban Me Thuot in W with Ninh Hoa on QL-1 N Nha Trang, in E. II Corps.

QL-21A (BP)
Natl Rte 21A. Connected QL-11 with QL-20 just S Dalat, forming triangle with Dalat at N apex, QL-20 running N/S and forming W edge, QL-11 running NW to SE forming E edge and QL-21A running E/W and forming base.

QL-22 (XT)
Natl Rte 22. Connected Tay Ninh with QL-1, meeting it apx 40 km SE Tay Ninh and 60 km NW Saigon. III Corps.

Quail, LZ (AT 998-593)
near rail tracks, apx 2 km S Song Thu Bon Railroad Bridge, 15 km ENE An Hoa AF and 23 km S Da Nang AB. Oct69. Quang Nam Pr, I Corps.

Quail, LZ (BR 693-840)
Apx 11 km W Ha Tay AF and 19 km SW Bong Son. Mar66. Binh Dinh Pr, II Corps.

Quail, LZ (BS 560-047)
Apx 36 km WSW Tam Quan, 27 km due S Ba To AF, and 5 km WSW Lang Doi. Mar66. Quang Ngai Pr, I Corps.

Quail, LZ (BT 060-395)
Apx 18 km due E Phuoc Binh AF and 36 km S to SSE Da Nang AB. May67. Quang Nam Pr, I Corps.

Quam Duc (n/a)
Fictional name used by *The Green Berets* author to represent either an actual camp or composite of SF Camps visited during his 6-month visit to VN, '64 or '65. Is mentioned at p 256. Possibly represented Kham Duc?

Quan (n/a)
See Glossary.

Quan Ba (n/a)
Sheet name of L 701-5980-2 map. NVN/China.

Quan Dao Bai Lao (VS 4-2)
A.k.a. Balau Island or Ile Ba Lua. NIMA data. Kien Giang Pr, IV Corps.

Quan Dau Tieng (Tri Tam) (n/a)
Mapsheet L-7014-6231-1. Sheet name: Tri Tam (Quan Dau Tieng). SVN.

Quan Do An Thomapoi (US 9-0)
A.k.a. Ile d' An Thomapoi. NIMA data. NVN.

Quan Do Mountain (BP 20-12)
A.k.a. Hill 1812 (5,945'). Apx 8 km due S Dalat. Tuyen Duc Pr, II Corps.

Quan Doi Nhan Dan (n/a)
See Glossary.

Quan Lai (XT)
Spelling variant of Quan Loi? 1st Cav website states that on 12Aug69, VC threw simultaneous attacks against many 1st Cav bases in III Corps, including "Quan Lai," LZ Becky, LZ Jon, LZ Kelly and LZ Caldwell. No ville by this name listed in either NIMA or NPIA Gaz. III Corps.

Quan Lan Airfield (WF 05-98)
A.k.a. Quang Lang AF. MIG base apx 75 km NW Vinh, per ONC-J-11. El. 60'. NVN.

Quan Lan, Cape (YJ 5-0)
See Cape Quan Lan. NVN.

Quan Lang Airfield (YJ 6-0?)
See Quan Lan AF. NVN.

Quan Loi Airfield (XT 816-907)
Apx 6 km due E An Loc, 21 km SSE Loc Ninh and 92 km N Saigon. El. 508', 3,900' laterite rwy. At 11°40'07"N-106°40'08"E. Binh Long Pr, III Corps.

Quan Loi Base Camp (XT 820-910)
A.k.a. Rocket City and LZ Andy? In or adj to rubber plantation apx 4 km NE An Loc, 23 km due E tip of Fishhook and 92 km N Saigon. Apparently plantation workers here in 1930's frequently went on strike to protest poor working conditions. French plantation manager once responded to an extended strike by inviting strike leaders to his mansion for negotiations. There the strike leaders were seized and taken to An Loc's beautiful cobble-stone town square where they were disemboweled and beheaded in front of townspeople, thus ending strike. 1st Bde/1st Inf Div HQ in '68, and described in *Father Soldier Son*, at p 33 as "northernmost outpost of 1st Inf Div." 11th ACR here also and, per Tom Skelly, was HQ of 1st Cav's 2d Bde (and later, 3d Bde?), and 2d/7th Cav in late '68-69. 1st Cav moved here from Camp Evans, 27Oct68, as part of move from I Corps during Op Liberty Canyon (largest allied intra-theater combat deployment of American war). On 12Aug69, VC threw simultaneous attacks against many III Corps 1st Cav bases, inc Quan Loi, LZ Becky, LZ Jon, LZ Kelly and LZ Caldwell. Arty elements here moved to Cambodia and border bases to supt Incursion in May-Jun70. Among those were: C Bty, 6th/27th Arty with two-175mms, A Bty, 6th/27th Arty, with two-175mms, A Bty, 2d/35th Arty with six-155s, B Bty, 2d/12th Arty with six-155s, C Bty, 2d ARVN with six-105mms, C Bty, 2d/20 ARA with fourteen AH1G Cobra gunships, per *11th ACR Cambodia Invasion AAR, 1st Cav Div, May-Jun70*, courtesy Lou Rochat.[451] Binh Long Pr, III Corps.

Quan Loi FOB (XT 818-905)
See Quan Loi Basecamp. Also listed at XT 948-905, and if 2d grid accurate, was apx 19 km W An Loc/QL-13. Binh Long Pr, III Corps.

Quan Long (WR 17-14)
A.k.a. Camau or Ca Mau. Apx 26 km S Tan Phu SF Camp. SF B-Team here early 60's, also MAAG Intel element. Also spelled Quang Long in one reference. Capitol, An Xuyen Pr, IV Corps.

Quan Long (Ca Mau) (n/a)
Mapsheet name of L-7014-6027-3. SVN.

Quan Long Airfield (WR 196-142)
At southern tip of Cau Mau Peninsula and southernmost major AF in SVN. Apx 240 km SW Saigon, 2 km E Quan Long/Quan Long City minor AF, 52 km NNE Nam Can AF (southernmost AF of any sort) and 48 km NE Binh Hung AF. El. 16', 3,200' asph rwy. At 09°10'32"N-105°10'46"E. An Xuyen Pr, IV Corps.
Quan Long City Airfield (WR 169-139)
At Quan Long, apx 64 km WSW Bac Lieu AF, 50 km NNE Nam Can AF and 3 km WSW Quan Long AF. "Secure ARVN/CIV, US Army on AF, 6Jun67, AF # VA4-57," in Aug69 TAD per Frank Penk, Jr. Not in Feb73 TAD. El. 10'. An Xuyen Pr, IV Corps.
Quan Tach (YS 82-97)
See FSB Strike. Binh Tuy Pr, III Corps.
Quan Trang, FSB (XT 7-0)
Apx 16 km NE Saigon. A Bty 6th/56th Arty, 97th Arty Grp here Jul67. Gia Dinh or Hau Nghia Pr?, III Corps. [452]
Quan Tro Training Ctr (XT 65-08, 65-69 or 68-05?)
If at XT 650-087, was apx 21 km NW Tan Son Nhut; if at XT 650-687, was apx 4 km NE Minh Thanh AF; and if at XT 68-05, was apx 13 km NW Tan Son Nhut? Per Ray Bows' *Vietnam Military Lore, Legends, Shadows and Heroes*, at p 766, "The 1st basic training center in VN was founded in '53, and originally known as Quan Tro Trng Ctr (Trng Ctr #1). Between '54-and '57, the center [trained] commissioned officers and NCOs. In Sep57, [it] was renamed Quang Trung and became the largest basic training center in VN." Also listed at XT 650-687, which is apx 4 km NE Minh Thanh AF? See Van Kiep Natl Trng Ctr. Hau Nghia Pr?, III Corps.
Quan Xuyen Heliport (XS 962-713)
See Quan Zuyen Heliport. Bien Hoa Pr, III Corps.
Quan Zuyen Heliport (XS 962-713)
Along E bank of Song Nha Be, apx 15 km SSE Nha Be and 23 km SSE Saigon. Heliport #759, alt 5', Cement Pad center of town. Town is on E side of river. At 10°35'N 106°48'E, per Feb73 TAD. Bien Hoa Pr, III Corps.
Quan, Vung (CQ 1-9)
Bay at 13°29'N-109°19'E. Phu Yen Pr, II Corps.
Quang Binh (XE 4-3?)
Ville apx 7-day march from Laos. Starting point for NVA 22d Rgt, Sao Van Div's infiltration into SVN along Ho Chi Minh Trail. NVN.
Quang Da Province (YC/ZC/AT/BT)
In what later became known as I Corps and apparently absorbed into what became primarily Quang Nam Pr. Thought to have ceased existence shortly before or during early US presence in SVN? Actual dates of existence unknown. I Corps.
Quang Dien (YD 674-336)
Apx 13 km NW Hue Citadel AF and 14 km ENE Camp Evans. ARVN Dist HQ, '68, 1/502d Inf, B/321st Arty 101st Abn mid '68. Also listed at YD 681-339 per Gen John Cushman. Thua Thien Pr, I Corps.
Quang Dien, FSB (YD 670-330)
Apx 13 km NW Hue Citadel AF and 14 km ENE Camp Evans. Apr69. Thua Thien Pr, I Corps.
Quang Dien District HQ (YD 687-341)
Just E Hwy 554 at its NE terminus, apx 6.5 km SE ocean 7 km N QL 1 and 10 km NNW Hue. Bn HQ for 1st/502d Inf, 101st Abn on 31Dec68 and in'68-early '69. Quang Dien District, Thua Thien Pr, I Corps.
Quang Duc Province (YU/ZU)
One of 12 north-central provs forming II Corps (II CTZ)
Quang Khe (XE 5-5?)
Apx 25-30 km NE Dong Hoi. Port attacked by USN carrier-based acft during Pierce Arrow, 2-7Aug64. Quang Khe and Xom Bang were 1st targets of Rolling Thunder. See Pierce Arrow. NVN.
Quang Khe Ferries (XE 5-5)
Possibly near listed grid square and on NE48-11 JOG. Key choke-point on HCMT that consisted of 2 ferrying points. Was focus of '68 interdiction campaign and, in addition to conventional bombing/Tac Air sorties, river around ferry points was seeded with Mark 36 mines and adj dry land areas with other types of anti-personnel mines. Data per *A Better War*, p 98. NVN?
Quang Lang 2 Airfield (WR 196-142)
See Quan Long AF/Quan Lan AF. An Xuyen Pr, IV Corps.
Quang Lang Airfield (WF 05-98)
A.k.a. Quan Lan AF. MIG base apx 75 km NW Vinh, per ONC-J-11. El. 60'. NVN.
Quang Liet Track (XK 3-8?)
See Quangliet Track. NVN.
Quang Loc Dong 1 & 2 CAP (BT?)
See CAP 2-3-2. 2d CAG. Quang Nam Pr, I Corps.
Quang Loc Tay 1 & 2 CAP (BT?)
See CAP 2-3-3. 2d CAG. Quang Nam Pr, I Corps.
Quang Loc Tay CAP (BT?)
See CAP 2-3-6. 2d CAG. Quang Nam Pr, I Corps.
Quang Long 1 Airfield (WR 169-139)
See Quan Long City AF. An Xuyen Pr, IV Corps.
Quang Nam (BT 0-5?)
MACV Det 3. Quang Nam Pr, I Corps?
Quang Nam, Operation (n/a)
27Feb-20Jun69. 1st ARVN Ranger Grp op. 688 rptd NVA/VC KIA, per *Vietnam Order of Battle*, pp 9-14. Quang Nam Pr, I Corps.
Quang Nam PFTC (AT?)
RVNAF Popular Force Trng Ctr. Appears to have been near An Hoa. Quang Nam Pr, I Corps.
Quang Nam Province (YC/ZC/AT/BT)
One of the 5 northern provs forming I Corps.
Quang Ngai (BS 647-723)
Major town and trading hub along QL-1 and on S bank of Song Tra Khuc River, apx 10 km from coast and 35 km SSE Chu Lai. 3d most populated area in Vietnam. Home of 2d ARVN Inf Div Advsy Det, Advsy Team 2 and 5th SF Det 3(?). SF Camp and major airfield nearby. On map L-7014-6739-2. Capitol, Quang Ngai Pr, I Corps.
Quang Ngai (n/a)
Mapsheet name of L-7014-6739-2. SVN.
Quang Ngai Airfield (BS 610-720)
Apx 4 km W Quang Ngai/QL-1, and 36 km SSE Chu Lai, per TPC K-10A. Was a tactical airfield. El. 36', 4,900' asph rwy. At 15°06'49"N-108°46'33"E. Also listed at BS 605-719. Map is L-7014-6739-2. Quang Ngai Pr, I Corps.
Quang Ngai City SF Camp (BS 650-730)
Apparently just off QL-1, apx 1 km S Quang Ngai. 5th SF Grp Det3(?). Closed then assets moved to Da Nang. Grid per *SF Order of Battle*. Quang Ngai Pr, I Corps.

Quang Ngai MAAG Det Compound (BS 64-73)
See Kramer Cmpd. Quang Ngai Pr, I Corps.
Quang Ngai Province (AS/BS/BT)
One of 5 northern provs forming I Corps (I CTZ).
Quang Nhieu (AQ 835-175)
New Life Hamlet apx 15 km N to NNE Ban Me Thuot. 4th Div AO. Darlac Pr, II Corps.
Quang Nhieu, LZ (AQ 822-180)
Apx 15 km N Ban Me Thuot/Lac Giao and 2 km W Quang Nhieu and QL-14. 2d/17th Arty here supt ARVN ops, '70. Data per Jack Picciolo. Darlac Pr, II Corps.
Quang Te (n/a)
Mapsheet name of L-7014-6145-4. NVN only.
Quang Te Airfield (WH 5-4?)
Apx 90 km SSW Hanoi, per map in *Vietnam Experience* Series, *Rain of Fire* vol, p. 11. NVN.
Quang Tin Heliport (BT 292-229)
On W edge of Tam Ky, just E QL-1 RR tracks and apx 2 km S Tam Ky Alt AF. Heliport #650, alt 16', at 15°34'30"N-108°28'00"E, per TAD. Quang Tin Pr, I Corps.
Quang Tin Province (XD/YD)
One of 5 northern provs forming I Corps (I CTZ).
Quang Tri (n/a)
Mapsheet name of L-7014-6442-4. SVN/NVN/DMZ.
Quang Tri (YD 34-54)
On E side of QL-1, apx 50 km NW Hue and 28 km SSE mouth of Ben Hai River. Adv Team 4, 3d Mar Div, 1st Bde 1st Cav, 2d Bde/101st Abn and 5th Div (Mech) here at various times. In Apr67, was heavily attacked and occupied by some 1,500 NVA who liberated jail and 250 military/political prisoners. Again occupied by NVA at beginning of Tet '68 Offensive, 31Jan68, and liberated Feb68 by elements of 1st Cav with 2d Bde 101st Abn attached. On 30Mar72, was object of opening blow of '72 Easter Offensive, when 4 NVA Divs attacked via DMZ, and after moving 130mm/152mm arty within range of city. While under siege was protected to some degree by US air power (inc B-52 strikes) until weather closed-in on 27Apr72, restricting air supt and allowing NVA 304th Div to attack in full force. On 1May70, city again fell into NVA hands, followed by balance of entire province a few days later. With help of massive B-52 strikes, NVA attack S finally stalled and ARVN counter-attacked. ARVN suffered over 5,000 casualties in retaking city after vicious house-to-house fighting ending 7Sep72. By that point, however, it was little more than a pile of rubble. Map is L-7014-6442-4, per Ken Burrington. Capitol, Quang Tri Pr, I Corps.
Quang Tri 1 Airfield (YD 328-525)
A.k.a. Nhan Bieu AF, Quang Tri North AF, Riverside AF, and AF# VA1-79. On N bank of Song Thac Han River, to W QL-1, apx 2 km NW La Vang AF and 4 km SSE Quang Tri AF. Listed as "Secure 30Jul67, AF # VA1-79," in Aug69 TAD per Frank Penk, Jr. Not in Feb73 TAD. Also listed at YD 330-540, Jan67. Quang Tri Pr, I Corps.
Quang Tri 2 Airstrip (YD 340-510)
See Quang Tri/La Vang AFJan67. Quang Tri Pr, I Corps.
Quang Tri Agricultural Dev. Center (YD 04-53)
Apx 8 km due W Mai Loc, 4 km S QL-9 and perhaps 15 km SW Cam Lo. May or may not be the Dinh Dien Ag Dev Ctr at YD 090-693. Quang Tri Pr, I Corps.
Quang Tri Airfield (YD 309-556)
Apx 10 km NE La Vang/Quang Tri City AF and on SW bank of Thach Han River apx 3 km NW Quang Tri, SE Dong Ha and on E side of QL-1. Diagram of Ai Tu CB in *The Marines in Vietnam 1954-1973*, p 154, shows location of this AF. Per ONC J-11, El. 36'. 3,500' alum mat rwy. At 16°46'28"N-107°09'58"E. Quang Tri Pr, I Corps.
Quang Tri Army Base (YD 30-50)
Da Nang Diary, p 188-191, describes it as separate facility (in '70) from Quang Tri AB and Marine base at that location. At referenced pages, author describes humorous incident involving the not-so-successful theft of a Pop-Corn popping machine from this facility by Prairie Fire SF Troops, and also notes the 18th MASH Hosp was here (from which same grp apparently stole a jeep). Presumably elements of 5th Mech Div and 3/5th Cav here as well. See 18th Surgical Hosp. Quang Tri Pr, I Corps.
Quang Tri Bridge (YD 330-519)
QL-1 bridge over Song Thac Han River, immed S Quang Tri, apx 1 km N Quang Tri/La Vang AF and 13 km SE Dong HaApr69. Quang Tri Pr, I Corps.
Quang Tri City/La Vang Airfield (YD 343-509)
Immed S of QL-1, apx 10 km SE Quang Tri AF, I Corps. Per ONC J-11. El. 40', 1,900' laterite rwy. At 16°43'40"N-107°11'55"E. Quang Tri Pr, I Corps.
Quang Tri Combat Base (YD 303-541)
W of the RR tracks and QL-1, apx 4 km NW Song Thac Han River QL-1 bridge, 8 km SE Dong Ha, 2 km S Quang Tri AF and 6 km NW Quang Tri/La Vang AF. May69. Quang Tri Pr, I Corps.
Quang Tri Heliport (YD 328-526)
Along QL-1, apx 3 km NNW La Vang AF and 4 km SSE Quang Tri AF. Heliport #651, alt 16', at 16°14'30"N-107°11'00"E, per Feb73 TAD. Quang Tri Pr, I Corps.
Quang Tri North Airfield (YD 328-525)
See Quang Tri 1 AF. Quang Tri Pr, I Corps.
Quang Tri Province (XD/YD)
One of 5 northern provs forming I Corps.
Quang Tri Province Hospital (YD 333-519)
S of QL-1, and immed W La Vang AF. Oct68. Quang Tri Pr, I Corps.
Quang Tri River (YD 30-47)
A.k.a. the Song Tach Han, Song Quang Tri and Riviere de Quang Tri. Headwaters near Khe Sanh CB at XD 92-42, then ran E passing Ba Long AF before turning to the NE passing Quang Tri, where it shifted to NW and then met the Song Mieu Giang to form the Cua Viet River at YD 27-63. Quang Tri Pr, I Corps.
Quang Tro Training Center (XT 687-050?)
See Quan Trung Trng Ctr. Hau Nghia Pr?, III Corps.
Quang Trung (n/a)
See Glossary.
Quang Trung, FSB? (XT 050-687)
Apx 10 km E Cambodia, 27 km NW Tay Ninh, 12 km SSW Thien Ngon AF and 7 km due W Ap Trai Bi. Tay Ninh Pr, III Corps.
Quang Trung 22F, Op (YA/YB)
QT-22F was an ARVN Op designed to clear 66th NVA Rgt and 40th NVA Arty Rgt from entire Plei Trap Valley region, 14Feb-31Mar71. See Polei Kleng Ranger Camp and Firebases A-W. Kontum Pr, II Corps.

Quang Trung NTC (XT 687-050?)
See Quang Trung Natl Trng Ctr. Gia Dinh Pr, III Corps.
Quang Trung Natl Training Center (XT 687-050?)
A.k.a. Quang Trung NTC. ARVN Natl Trng Ctr apx 16 km NW Saigon. Per Ray Bows' *Vietnam Military Lore, Legends, Shadows and Heroes*, at p 766, "The 1st basic training center in VN was founded in 1953, and was originally called Quan Tro Trng Ctr (Trng Ctr #1). Between '54-and '57, the center [trained] commissioned officers and NCOs. In Sep57, [it] was renamed Quang Trung and became the largest basic training center in VN." Had 2 primary areas: "A Bn Area" and "B Bn Area." Design was very similar to US BCT trng bases, as was its 12 week course with 5 and1/2 days per wk allotted to trng. Also listed at XT 650-687? See Van Kiep Natl Trng Ctr. Gia Dinh Pr?, III Corps. [453]
Quang Xuyen Heliport (XS 962-713)
See Quan Zuyen Heliport. Bien Hoa Pr, III Corps.
Quang Yen (n/a)
Mapsheet name of L-7014-6350-1. NVN only.
Quang Yen (XJ 87-16)
On marshy isthmus, apx 15 km NE Haiphong. Home of the Quang Yen Vietnamese Natl Commando Trng School (see also that entry). NVN.
Quang Yen Coal Fields (XJ 6-2/XJ 8-1)
Generally near Haiphong and N. High quality anthracite coal deposits in this region gave it much strategic importance during 1st Indochina War. NVN.
Quang Yen Viet Natl Training Center (XJ 87-16)
On marshy isthmus, apx 15 km NE Haiphong. School built by French to train the Tieu-Doan Kinh Quan; Viet Natl Commando Bns. Per *Street Without Joy*, p 20. See Tieu-Doan Kinh Quan in Glossary. NVN.
Quangliet Track (XK 3-8)
A.k.a. Quang Liet Track. Ancient trail noted on French military maps that suggested possible escape route for Col Charton's 3d Bn Legion Inf and 3d Tabor of Moroccans when trapped at PK 28 (Namnang) on R.C. 4, while attempting escape from Cao Bang, Sep50. The trail had long been abnd and Charton's grp soon found itself mired in trackless wilderness. At 22°26'00"N-106°21'00"E. See Namnang. NVN.
Quangliet Valley (XK 3-8?)
A.k.a. Quang Liet Valley. Along the Quangliet Track in northern Tonkin. Open country, partially cultivated in Sep50, when Col Charton's Cao Bang garrison moved through it under Vietminh MG fire from adjoining ridges. Unit was under heavy pursuit after being ordered to escape Cao Bang via the "Quangliet Track" after Col LePage's relief column from Lang Son was hammered by Vietminh at Dong Khe and prevented from keeping its R.C. 4, PK 28 rendezvous with Charton's grp. See Namnang. NVN.
Quanh Tach, FSB (YS 82-97)
A.k.a. FSB Strike. Also spelled Qanh Tach and Quan Tach. Immed N Nui Be Mtn, apx 58 km WSW Phan Thiet and near Ap Rung La. 2d/3d, 199th LIB here. See FSB Strike. Long Khanh Pr, III Corps.
Quantico, FSB (XD 873-429)
Apx 7 km due W Cates, 3 km NW Khe Sanh AF and 15 km WSW Vandegrift CB. 3d/2d ARVN Rgt and USMC, '69. On map at p 73, *US Marines in Vietnam-1969*. Apr70 XXIV Corps grid per D. Armstrong. Quang Tri Pr, I Corps.
Quatre Cantons, Canal des (WS 3-5)
A.k.a. Khinh Bong Ton. An Giang Pr?, IV Corps.
Que Son (BT 040-345)
Apx 2 km NE LZ Ross16 km SW LZ Baldy and 20 km SE An Hoa. Que Son Dist Capitol and site of Que Son Dist HQ. Nearby FSB Ross commanded the Que Son Valley. Americal list, USMC, 1st Cav. On map L-7014-6640-3. Quang Tin Pr?, I Corps.
Que Son District HQ (BT 038-347)
Near FSB Ross, apx 30 km NW Tam Ky. On map L-7014-6640-3. Quang Nam Pr, I Corps.
Que Son Heliport (BT 042-349)
Apx 2 km SE LZ Ross and 27 km NW Tam Ky. Heliport #652, alt 16', at 15°10'30"N-108°14'15"E, per Feb73 TAD. On map L-7014-6640-3. Quang Nam Pr, I Corps.
Que Son Mountains (BT 00-40)
Mtn mass whose center of mass was apx 15 km ESE to SE An Hoa, 33 km due S Da Nang and 15 km WSW LZ Baldy/QL-1. Quang Nam/Quang Tin Pr border, I Corps.
Que Son Valley (BT 04-35?)
Surrounded by Que Son Mtns roughly 50 km SE Arizona Territory/Go Noi Island areas and a.k.a. Nui Loc Son Basin, Phuoc Valley, or Death Valley. Sat astride Quang Nam/Quang Tin border. In Jan67, F/2d/1st Mar was assigned to secure an outpost on Nui Loc Son, and when it became apparent the 2d NVA Div was planning an all-out assault on position in Apr67, plans to foil that attack took form in Op Union, a multi-Bn sweep of valley to eliminate the VC/NVA threat. Op started 21Apr67, and as F Co swept down from Nui Loc Son in their part of mission, they became heavily engaged near Binh Son. That same day, 3d Bn/1st Marines, 3d Bn/5th Marines and 1st Bn/1st Marines were flown into battle, and next day the enemy fled N and were pursued by Marine and ARVN forces. In Aug67, Op Cochise again swept the valley of renewed NVA forces, and then in Sep67, Op Swift made yet another attempt and resulted in some of heaviest and bloodiest Marine battles of war. During Swift, elements of 1st/5th and 3d/5th Marines were repeatedly ambushed, trapped and decimated 4-6Sep67, and heavy fighting continued until 15Sep67. Per Tom Brizendine, Dragon Valley, Death Valley or Que Son Valley were all names for same valley. Home of 2d NVA Rgt. During Tet '69, the 1st/6th Inf made heavy contact with this unit and during 3-day battle employed the 16-inch guns of Battleship New Jersey. 7th and 26th Marines/1st Mar Div swept area in Aug-Sep69. Quang Nam/Quang Tin Pr border, I Corps.
Quebec, FSB? (XT 655-285)
Apx 37 km NW Bien Hoa AB, 14 km SW Lai Khe. Listed simply as "Quebec," and true nature of use unknown. Hua Nghia Pr, III Corps.
Quebec, LZ (BS 84-08?)
Along W edge of Bong Son Valley, apx 12 km NNE Bong Son, 8 km NNW LZ Dog, 75 km NNE An Khe and 5 km W QL-1. Per *Chickenhawk*, p 272-277, was opened with CA, 31Jan66, and described as 2-acre "narrow strip of brushy, dry sand next to foothills on west side of [Bong Son] valley." Two grunt 2d Lts and at least 1 Helo pilot were KIA in initial assault. Binh Dinh Pr?, II Corps.

Quebec CAP (n/a)
See CAP. No specific listings for Quebec CAP was encountered; however, seems likely it existed.

Queen, LZ (BR 708-924)
Apx 16 km WSW Bong Son and 14 km NW Ha Tay AF. Oct66. Binh Dinh Pr, II Corps.

Queen, LZ (XD 925-306)
Apx 2 km NNE Lang Klung, 13 km SE Khe Sanh CB and 47 km WSW Quang Tri. Apr70 XXIV Corps grid per Don Armstrong. Quang Tri Pr, I Corps.

Queen, LZ (YA 875-130)
Apx 50 km SE Pleiku and 14 km SSE Duc Co AF. Jan66. Pleiku Pr, II Corps.

Queen, LZ (YS 385-758)
Apx 9 km NW Nui Dat/Luscombe AF and 8 km WSW Xa Binh Gia. Mar-Apr66. Also listed at YS 394-758? Phuoc Tuy Pr, III Corps.

Queen's Cobras (n/a)
See Glossary.

Queenfish, USS (n/a)
ASS 393. Submarine. Between '61-64, Vietnamese sailors served short tours on 7th Fleet ships or with combined antisubmarine warfare exercises involving US subs *Bluegill* (SS 242), *Queenfish* (SS 393), and *Capitaine* (AGSS 336).

Queensborough, HMAS (n/a)
Australian ship serving under US 7th Flt, per John Middlesworth.

Qui Hau (n/a)
Mapsheet name of L-7014-6343-2. NVN only.

Qui Nhon (CR 080-230)
Apx 385 km NE Saigon, 28 km SE Phu Cat, 64 km ESE An Khe and W QL-1. Portion of city was on flat peninsula jutting into small bay surrounded by mtns that dropped sharply into sea. Only a small port and fishing ville before the war, it grew to population of apx 190,000 by '70. Harbor here was deepened by US Engrs and then supply and petro depots were added to create major port and military complex suptg over 100,000 US troops at height of war. On 7Jul65, USMC BLT 2/7 landed on beach here via LVTP-5s from ships off-shore. Job was to secure AF and area for subsequent arrival of Army's 1st Bde/101st Abn and 1st Cav Div (Army Engr, supply and motor units already at QN had little infantry security). Waiting on beach for them that day were hundreds of civilians. *Utter's Battalion*, at pp 98-103, describes hectic scene as follows: "The troops were astounded to find the milling throng of [Viets] watching their every move. There they stood, Marines in full combat gear, flack jackets zipped tightly, weapons locked and loaded for combat with no enemy in sight. Instead, [they] found themselves amid hundreds of laughing women and children. Their shock was obvious..." (see "Shit Beach" for unusual aspect of landing). Here were: Qui Nhon AB, Qui Nhon Army Depot, Qui Nhon Port, Cha Rang Valley, Lane Army Field, and Camp Granite, Navy "Market Time" Naval Patrol Facility. Det B-22, 5th SF Grp, Advsy Det 25, also HQ of Rep of Korea's Capitol Div. Capitol, Binh Dinh Pr, II Corps. [454]

Qui Nhon (n/a)
Mapsheet name of L-7014-6836-4. SVN.

Qui Nhon, Baie de (CR 0-2)
A.k.a. Vung Qui Nhon. Bay at 13°50'N-109°14'E. On ND49-09 JOG. Binh Dinh Pr, II Corps.

Qui Nhon, Vinh (CR 0-2)
A.k.a. Vung Lang Mai. Bay at 13°45'N-109°14'E. On ND49-09 JOG. Binh Dinh Pr, II Corps.

Qui Nhon Airbase (CR 082-225)
In heart of Qui Nhon, apx 385 km NE Saigon, and 160 km N Nha Trang. USAF/US Army and Vietnamese Civil Avn control, 5,100' asph rwy. At 13°45'58"N-109°13'35"E. Binh Dinh Pr, II Corps.

Qui Nhon Ammo Supply Point (BR 995-319)
Along Rte 441, apx 3 km NNW Vinh Thanh (1), 2.5 km SSE An Nhon AF and 13 km NW Qui Nhon AF, Mar69. Binh Dinh Pr, II Corps.

Qui Nhon-An Khe Pipeline (BR)
See Pump Station 1 and An Khe-Pleiku Pipeline. Binh Dinh Pr, II Corps.

Qui Nhon Army Depot (CR 080-230)
See Qui Nhon entry for location. US Army Supt Cmd, built by 84th Engr Bn. Binh Dinh Pr, II Corps.

Qui Nhon Bay (CR 09-23)
On N side of Qui Nhon Peninsula and NE Qui Nhon AB. Binh Dinh Pr, II Corps.

Qui Nhon Compound #1 (CR 080-230)
MACV Advsy Det Camp for Qui Nhon Area Adv Det 25. Binh Dinh Pr, II Corps.

Qui Nhon Harbor (CR 106-236)
Apx 3 km NE Qui Nhon AF and at NE corner of city. Binh Dinh Pr, II Corps.

Qui Nhon Harbor Entrance Control (CR 126-217)
A.k.a. Hill 193 and The Hill. At S end of Vung Qui Nhon Peninsula, atop 360' hill with sheer cliffs that fell to ocean, apx 4 km ENE Qui Nhon AF. Manned by USN's Unit 3, Inshore Undersea Warfare Grp-1, W Pacific Det (northernmost IUWG unit). Had single helo pad and was among remnants of old French position. Discussed in *Thanksgiving Dinner Vietnam, 1968*, article in Nov99 *Military* Magazine, pp 14-15. Binh Dinh Pr, II Corps.

Qui Nhon Hospital (CR 101-232)
Immed S QN port and immed W POL Farm, apx 2 km E the N end of main AF rwy. Binh Dinh Pr, II Corps.

Qui Nhon Leper Colony (CR 07-21)
Near coast toward S edge of Qui Nhon, per Duane Good. Binh Dinh Pr, II Corps.

Qui Nhon Lighthouse (north) (CR 13-24)
One of 2 lighthouses on Cape Qui Nhon, apx 4 km ENE Qui Nhon AF. Binh Dinh Pr, II Corps.

Qui Nhon Lighthouse (south) (CR 114-216)
One of 2 lighthouses on Cape Qui Nhon, apx 3 km due E Qui Nhon AF. Binh Dinh Pr, II Corps.

Qui Nhon LST/LCM/LCU Ramps (CR 114-227)
At E end of isthmus apx 3 km due E the N end of main AF rwy., and 1 km SE QN Port. Binh Dinh Pr, II Corps.

Qui Nhon Market Time Facility (CR 126-227)
Due E and across bay from tip of Qui Nhon LST facility, ESE the port and due E Qui Nhon AB. Joint USN/US Coast Guard/VN Navy off shore patrol facility responsible for controlling NVA/VC water-based infiltration into SVN. See Cam Ranh Bay Market Time Facility. Grid is est. See Qui Nhon. Binh Dinh Pr, II Corps. [455])

Qui Nhon NDB (CR 08-23)
Non-Directional Air Nav Beacon site. At Qui Nhon AB, along NE edge of that city. Binh Dinh Pr, II Corps.
Qui Nhon NSA (CR 08-23)
At port of Qui Nhon? USN Supt Activity, '65-71. Per MRF Assn Website. Binh Dinh Pr, II Corps.
Qui Nhon POL Tank Farm (CR 105-235)
Petroleum, Oil and Lubricant stg area on thin isthmus apx 2 km ENE Qui Nhon AF. Binh Dinh Pr, II Corps.
Qui Nhon Port (CR 108-231)
Apx 2.5 km ENE N end of the Qui Nhon AF main rwy. Site of 394th Trans Bn Terminal and operated by that Bn. Apparently built in '65. Berthing Feet: 5,600 lineal feet, Draft Max: 26', Cargo Capacity: 8,300 tons/day, Storage Covered w/in 5 km:1,050,000 ft^2, Storage Uncov, w/in 5 km: 359,000 yd^2. Binh Dinh Pr, II Corps. [456]
Qui Nhon Surgical Rehab Center (CR 086-223)
Apx 600 meters due E the center of the main Qui Nhon AF rwy. Binh Dinh Pr, II Corps.
Qui Nhon RMK-BRJ (CR 079-217)
Immed W the S end of Qui Nhon AF's main rwy. Binh Dinh Pr, II Corps.
Qui Nhon SF Camp (Liaison Det) (CR 088-236)
In Qui Nhon proper, apx 1 km W the Qui Nhon MSF Camp. SF Liaison Det (LD). Det B-22, 5th SF. Later closed and assets moved to Qui Nhon (B-22). II Corps. Grid per *SF Order of Battle.* Binh Dinh Pr, II Corps.
Qui Nhon SF Camp (MSF) (CR 0991-2281)
In Qui Nhon proper, near waterfront and about 1 km E Qui Nhon (LD) SF Camp. Det B-22, 5th SF Grp and Advsy Det 25. Grid per *SF Order of Battle.* Moved to Kontum MSF. Binh Dinh Pr, II Corps.
Qui Nhon SF Camp (CR 0991-2281)
See Qui Nhon (MSF) Camp. 5th SF, Det B-22 (was A-121), Oct65. Advsy Det 25. Later closed and assets moved to Chu Lai (B-11). Grid per *SF Order of Battle.* Binh Dinh Pr, II Corps.
Qui Nhon VFW Post (CR 10-23?)
See VFW Post 8316, Saigon. Binh Dinh Pr, II Corps.
Quiberon, HMAS (n/a)
Australian ship serving under US 7th Flt, per John Middlesworth.
Quick, LZ (BR 931-903)
In Cay Giep Mtns overlooking ocean 6 km to E and QL-1 to 6 km to W, apx 8 km ESE Bong Son and near peak of Hill 641, about 4 km WNW Phu Ha. Image on Army Mil Hist Institute website shows it on a very small, steep-sided round hill top. C/1st/50 Inf, 1st Cav here Oct67. L-7014-6837-4, per Ken Burrington. Binh Dinh Pr, II Corps. [457]
Quick, LZ/FSB (YD 906-028)
Along road that ran S from QL-1 to Ruong Ruong Valley, apx 13 km due S Phu Bai, 7 km SSW road's intersection with QL-1, and 19 km W Phu Loc. Apr70 XXIV Corps grid per Don Armstrong. Thua Thien Pr, I Corps.
Quick I, FSB (YD 911-041)
Apx 14 km SSE Phu Bai, 12 km ENE FSB Brick, and 18 km SE Camp Eagle. 2d Bde/101st Abn AO, '69-71 but likely built in '68. Also listed at YD 905-033, 900-030 and 906-029, Jan-Nov69. Thua Thien Pr, I Corps.
Quick II, FSB (YC 894-994)
At or near Thon Ben Tau, apx 20 km due W Q Phu Loc and 16 km due S Phu Bai. Jan-Apr69. Also listed at YC 890-990, 896-998 and incorrectly at "YD" 993-897 (which is in ocean). Thua Thien Pr, I Corps.
Quoc Nhu (n/a)
See Glossary.
Quoi Xuan (XT 8-0?)
Possibly Quoi Thanh or Quio Than? On 2Mar68, some 48 men of C/4th/9th Inf, 25th Div were KIA near this ville, in one of largest single-event loss-of-life incidents for a US rifle Co of American War. Unit was ambushed by large force on Hwy 248, NE Tan Son Nhut AB, near Quoi Xuan. Enemy was concealed in bunkers and spider holes along road and struck convoy moving through what was thought to be a secure area. C Co also suffered 24 WIA. D Co suffered addnl casualties in rescue effort. SP4 Nicholas J. Cutinha of C Co posthumously awarded MOH for his actions. Data per 4th/9th Inf Manchu Assn website. Gia Dinh or Bien Hoa Pr?, III Corps.
Quyet Chien, Operation (n/a)
17Jul68-4Mar69. 7th, 9th, and 21st ARVN Inf Div Op. 15,953 rptd NVA/VC KIA, per *Vietnam Order of Battle*, pp 9-14. IV Corps.
Quyet Thang, Operation (n/a)
1Jan-31Dec69. ARVN 7th, 9th, 24th Div ops. 37,874 rptd NVA/VC KIA, per *VN Order of Battle*, pp 9-14. IV Corps.
Quyet Thang, Operation (n/a)
11Mar-7Apr68. 22 US and 11 ARVN Bns working around Saigon in largest to-date op of war. Involved were elements of US 9th and 25th Inf Divs, ARVN 5th and 25th Inf Divs, and VNMC. 2,658 rptd NVA/VC KIA. Quyet Thang translates as "Resolve to Win." Per *Vietnam Order of Battle,* pp 9-14. Gia Dinh and other Prvs, III Corps.
Quyet Thang 21/38, Operation (n/a)
29Sep-31Dec69. 32d ARVN Rgt ops. 721 rptd VC KIA, per *VN Order of Battle*, pp 9-14. An Xuyen Pr, IV Corps.
Quyet Thang 22, Operation (n/a)
24Feb-10Mar69. 2d ARVN Div op. 777 rptd enemy KIA, per *Vietnam Order of Battle*, pp 9-14. Quang Ngai, I Corps.
Quyet Thang 25, Operation (n/a)
20-31Mar69. ARVN 4th Rgt op. 592 rptd enemy KIA, per *Vietnam Order of Battle*, pp 9-14. Quang Ngai Pr, I Corps.
Quynh Luu (WG 6-1)
Ville apx 80 km S Thanh Hoa and used as a waypoint along the HCMT. NVN.
Quynh Nhai (n/a)
Mapsheet name of L-7014-5752-4. NVN only.

ROMEO

Facility/Feature Name, Grid Coordinate, a.k.a. Name/History/Province/CTZ

Unless otherwise stated, 6-digit grid coordinates reference DMA L-7014, L-7015 or L-7016 series, 1:50,000 scale maps, while 2- and 4-digit coordinates reference AMS/DMA/NIMA 1:250,000, 1:500,000 and 1:1,000,000 scale maps. Unless otherwise stated, all heights are in meters. To convert meters to feet, multiply by 3.2808; feet to meters, multiply by .3048.

R, FSB (YB 8-1?)
ARVN FSB generally W or SW Dak To. See Firebase A for detail. Kontum Pr, II Corps.

R&R (n/a)
See Glossary.

R.C. (n/a)
See Glossary.

R.C. 4 (XK, et al)
A.k.a. *Route Coloniale 4.* Northern Tonkin major link between Cao Bang at its W terminus and Lang Son on its E during French War. Along its path were the outposts of Dong Khe and That Khe. NVN.

R.C. Ba Na (ZC 206-704)
A.k.a. *Route Coloniale Ba Na.* Apx 15-20 km W/WSW Da Nang, and N of Happy Valley. Road leading to French resort area on Ba Na Mtn (Hill 1467), that later became important strategic position during American War. Mtn held USMC Automatic Radio Re-transmission/OP/Radar Control(?) facility and/or OP. Grid per George Neville, 3d Recon Bn. Quang Nam Pr, I Corps.

Rach (n/a)
Vietnamese word for stream or arroyo.

Rach Ba Dap Creek (XT 543-177)
Flows southward under QL-1 at listed grid, apx 10 km NW Cu Chi. Cited in 23Jul66 Combat Op AAR, HQ 1st Bde/25th ID, for "Op Fargo" on-line at: www.en.com/users/kramsey/vnr102.html#. Hau Nghia Pr, III Corps.

Rach Ba Rai River (XS 1-4)
Apx 25 km W Dong Tam. See NC48-07 JOG. Vinh Long Pr, IV Corps.

Rach Bao Dinh (XS 48-46)
River along N edge of My Tho. Dinh Tuong Pr, IV Corps.

Rach Bao, Pointe du (XS 9-8)
See Pointe Rach Bao. Gia Dinh Pr?, III Corps.

Rach Ben Da (YS 2-5)
Channel near 10°28'N-107°03'E. On NC48-07 JOG. Phuoc Tuy Pr, III Corps.

Rach Ben Nge (XS 88-91)
Stream/Canal that emptied into Saigon River at Port of Saigon. On map at: http://home.epix.net/ ~gramborw/saigon.htm. Gia Dinh Pr, III Corps.

Rach Beng Go River (WT 970-730)
A.k.a. Tonle Roti. Stream used as NVA infiltration rte that formed portion of Cambodian border NW Tay Ninh. Cited in *Rangers At War*, p 151 et al. Tay Ninh Pr, III Corps.

Rach Cat (XS 78-84)
A.k.a. Fort de Rach Cat. Grid square is roughly 25 km due S Saigon. An Old French Fort at this location. No data. Gia Dinh Pr, III Corps.

Rach Gia (n/a)
Mapsheet name of L-7014-6029-3. SVN.

Rach Gia (WS 10-07)
Along W coast of Vietnam, apx 85 km SE Ha Tien, 140 km NNE tip of Cau Mau Peninsula and 190 km WSW Saigon. Home of Kien Giang Pr Adv Team 54, Rach Gia Subsector. Kien Giang Pr, IV Corps.

Rach Gia, Vinh (WS 0-0)
Bay at 10°00'N-105°00'E. On NC48-06 map, and NIMA. Kien Giang Pr, IV Corps.

Rach Gia, Vung (WS 0-0)
A.k.a. Vinh Rach Gia and Baie de Rach Gia. Bay at 10°00'N-105°00'E. NC48-06. Kien Giang Pr, IV Corps.

Rach Gia Airfield (WS 14-00)
See Kien Giang AF. Kien Giang Pr, IV Corps.

Rach Gia City Airfield (WS 105-048)
Minor AF apx 6 km NW Kien Giang major AF, 1 km SE Rach Gia, 60 km SE the Cement Plant AF, 80 km SE Ha Tien and 195 km SW Saigon, per TPC K-10D. 1,400' earth rwy. "Secure, operated on request, light acft only, SVN Directorate of Civ Avn, 2Jun67, AF # VA4-56," in Aug69 TAD per Frank Penk, Jr. Not in Feb73 TAD. At 09°59'47"N-105°05'48"E. El. 5'. Kien Giang Pr, IV Corps.

Rach Gia Heliport (XS 410-153)
Was apx 21 km SSE Truc Giang/Ben Tre, in Kien Hoa Pr. "Heliport #741, alt 7', earth, approach from river, 10°54'00"N-106°17'30"E," per Feb73 TAD. Kien Hoa Pr, IV Corps.

Rach Gia New Airfield (WS 149-004)
See Kien Giang AF. Kien Giang Pr, IV Corps.

Rach Gia Old Airfield (WS 105-048)
See Rach Gia City AF. Kien Giang Pr, IV Corps.

Rach Gia Province (VR/WR/WS)
In what later became known as IV Corps and absorbed into what became primarily Kien Giang Pr. Thought to have ceased existence shortly before or during early US presence in SVN? Actual dates of existence unknown.

Rach Goi (n/a)
Mapsheet name of L-7014-6128-4. SVN.

Rach Kien, FSB (XS 74-69)
Apx 18 km SSW Saigon, 20 km ENE Tan An and 19 km ESE Thu Thua. 4th/12th, 199th LIB here at one point. 2d/39th Inf, 3d/39th Inf, 5th/60th Inf and other 9th Inf Div elements basecamp in '70, per Jim Stone, 2d/39th Inf. Long An Pr, III Corps.

Rach Kien Base (XS 74-69)
See Rach Kien, FSB. Long An Pr, III Corps.

Rach Nui Canal (XS 840-660)
Near Ap Bac, apx 22 km S Saigon. Long An Pr, III Corps.

Rach Ong Keo River (YS 03-78)
Tributary of Song Nga Bay River roughly 18 km SE Saigon. Patrolled by RAS 11, Jun68. AAR on MRF Assn website mentioning action here on at: www.mrf.org/ras11_action.htm. Gia Dinh Pr?, III Corps.
Rach Ruong Canal, Battle of (XS 1-4?)
Near Cai Be. On 4-5Dec67, during Op Coronado IX, the 3d/47th and 4th/47th Inf Bns, 9th Inf Div and 5th Bn VNMC fought 267th and 502d VC Bns, resulting in 9 US KIAs/89 WIA; VNMC 40 KIA/107 WIA and 266 VC KIA. Dinh Tuong Pr, IV Corps.
Rach Soi Advanced Base (WS 149-004)
See Advanced Base Rach Soi. Kien Giang Pr, IV Corps.
Rach Soi Airfield (WS 14-00)
See Kien Giang AF. Kien Giang Pr, IV Corps.
Rach Soi Navy ISB (WS 14-01)
Apx 8 km SE Rach Gia. USN Intermediate Supt Base, '69-71. Per MRF Assn Website. Kien Giang Pr, IV Corps.
Rach Suoi River (YT 3-3)
Small tributary of Song Saigon. Bien Hoa or Phuoc Long Pr, III Corps.
Rach Trang, Mui (CP 2-4)
Coastal point at 12°11'36"N-109°20'48"E. On ND49-13 JOG. Khanh Hoa Pr, II Corps.
Rach Vung Liem (XS 32-16)
See Vung Liem. IV Corps.
Racquel, LZ (BR 506-903)
See LZ Raquel. Binh Dinh Pr, II Corps.
Radcliff, Camp (BR 470-480)
A.k.a. An Khe Basecamp and the Golf Course. Div-sized facility N of QL-19 about 60 km NW Qui Nhon, 60 km ESE Pleiku, immed NW An Khe ville and apx 400 km. N Saigon. Originally named "The Golf Course" when 1st Cav's CG Wright selected site, Aug65, and told advance team to, "Cut brush until we have a Golf Course." 1,000-man advance team arrived here to begin const 25Aug65, while security for their arrival and initial clearing of site were provided by 1st Bde/101st Abn. This 1st Cav HQ was named to honor Maj. Donald G. Radcliff, XO of 1st/9th Cav, KIA 18Aug65, at LZ Blue during Op Starlight (19 km S Chu Lai), when hit by ground fire while suptg Marines with his helo gunship (first 1st Cav soldier to die in VN). Home of 1st Cav during much of war, and site of An Khe Army AF. Also spelled Radcliffe on An Tuc L-7014 map, but that is an error. Its outer perimeter was called The Green Line. An Khe and A Luy 2 were on S tip if its perimeter, while Tan Lai and Tan Phong were along its SW edge. Was N of QL-19, SW Cu'u Dao and An Thach and W An Xuap. Hon Cong Mtn and Tan Tao 2 were within base's perimeter. [458] Cav cut and painted (on PSP, once source says) a huge replica of their Div patch on S face of Hon Cong Mtn and, when 173d Abn took over when Cav moved to Quang Tri (Jan68), the 173d did the same with its patch. Each image was several stories in height and could be seen for many miles. C-130 capable AF/heliport was built at N end of base and just NE Hon Cong mtn, while a smaller AF was built at its SW corner. "Rear Support Base Buffalo" (home of 10th Cav) was also in or near this facility. History/map in *Infantry in Vietnam,* p. 265. 2d/5th Cav; 1st, 2d and 5th Bns, 7th Cav; 2d Bn 8th Cav, 1st Bn 12th Cav; 21st Arty, 8th Engr Bn; 11th Avn Grp; 173d Abn Bde. Map is L-7014-6736-4. El. 1,380'. See An Khe, Sin City, Hon Cong, LZ Logan. Binh Dinh Pr, II Corps. [459]
Radcliff Airfield, Camp (BR 462-478)
A.k.a. Thuan Hoa AF. Apparently the old French and Japanese AF that ran along SW edge of Camp Radcliff. AF # VA2-261?" in Aug69 TAD per Frank Penk, Jr. Not in Feb73 TAD. See An Khe. Binh Dinh Pr, II Corps.
Rade de Vung Lam (CQ 0-8)
See Vung Lam. Phu Yen Pr, II Corps.
Radio Singapore (n/a)
See Glossary.
Radio Relay Hill (AP 822-990)
See Hill, The, at grid. Darlac Pr, II Corps
Radio Relay (Pic ROBIN) (BP 221-190)
Apx 500 meters S Ap Tan Loc, 3 km SSE center of Dalat and overlooking QL-20. Name/grid per Jerry Berry, who also tells us that Pic Robin was the call-sign of commo unit here. Tuyen Duc Pr, II Corps.
Raedy, FSB (XU 855-420?)
See Ready, FSB? Cambodia?
Raglan, FSB (YS 601-802)
Apx 17 km ENE FSB Le Loi, 10 km W FSB Toby, 23 km NE Nui Dat, 11 km ENE Ngai Giao, 11 km S the Long Khanh Pr border, and 16 km E Rte 2. Site was covered with luxuriant shoulder-high grass which was quickly flattened. 161 Bty RNZA fired "Mark Missions" suptg 7RAR (working with US units in area). Named for New Zealand town that supt 161 Bty by sending it gifts every Christmas and throughout its 6 years in SVN. 161 Bty, RNZA (Master's Bty 6Sep70-8May71) FSB set here 19Dec70-2Jan71. On 1ATF NCO trng map per John Hollett. Also listed at YS 60-80. Phuoc Tuy Pr, III Corps.
Rahaeng Airfield (n/a)
A.k.a. Tak AF. Along Ping River, apx 375 km NNW Bangkok per Feb67 Natl Geo map. At 16°53'00"N-99°09'00"E. NIMA data. El. 360'. Thailand.
Raid (n/a)
Apr70, XXIV Corps future-use 101st Abn FSB name.
Raid, LZ (BR 738-904)
Apx 13 km WSW Bong Son and 10 km NW Ha Tay AF. Oct66. Binh Dinh Pr, II Corps.
Railroad Bridge #2 (YD 926-103)
See Nong Railroad Bridge. Thua Thien Pr, I Corps.
Rain, FSB (XT 200-350)
Apx 13 km S Tay Ninh, 7 km NE Cambodia, 2 km SE Ap Van Lang(?) and 6 km WNW Ap Cai Tac. 4th/12th Inf, '68. Grid per 199th LIB Assn. Tay Ninh Pr?, III Corps.
Rainbelt Radio Relay Site (YD 068-556?)
Per George Neville, was apparently on a Hill 250. Manned and secured by elements of 3d Recon Bn, 3d Mar Div. Precise location unknown. Quang Tri Pr?, I Corps.
Rainbow (n/a)
6Apr70, XXIV Corps future-use III MAF FSB name.
Rainier, Camp (XT 495-475)
At Dau Tieng, apx 60 km NW Saigon. In '68, home of 3d Bde/25th Inf Div. Dick Detra, 188th AHC, provided photo of sign at base which read: *Welcome to Dau Tieng-Camp Rainier-Home of the 3d Brigade, 25th Infantry Division.* Also listed at XT 505-470. Binh Duong Pr, III Corps.
Rainier, USS (n/a)
AE-5. Aux Explosive ship, per Ralph Fries.

Rakkasan Road (YD 50-20)
Road built by 326th Engrs that linked FSB Rakkasan with QL-1. Beginning Apr71, during Lam Son 720, the 326th improved the road to FSB Rakkasan (possibly Jul71?). 101st Abn. Thua Thien Pr, I Corps.
Rakkasan, FSB (YD 490-198)
A.k.a. Hill 493 or Dong Cung Cap. Apx 23 km due W Hue, 14 km SW Camp Evans and 8 km ESE FSB Gladiator. During Lam Son 720, beginning in Apr '71, FSBs Fury, Kathryn, Maureen, Gladiator and later Eagle's Nest were all reopened by B/326th Engrs, while elements of 326th also rebuilt and enlarged FSBs Brick, Tennessee, Rendezvous and Rifle and improved all-weather Rte 545, road to FSB Rifle, and also road to this site. 101st Abn. See Rakkasan Road. Thua Thien Pr, I Corps.
Raleigh, LZ (YD 008-398)
On the Dong Cho hill mass, apx 9 km S Ca Lu and 16 km due W Ba Long AF. Apr70 XXIV Corps grid per Don Armstrong. 101st Abn, Apr70. Quang Tri Pr, I Corps.
Ram, LZ (XD 925-498)
Apx 23 km WSW to SW Cam Lo, 18 km W to WSW Mai Loc, 7 km W QL-9, some 6 km NE FSB Tsingtao, 11 km ENE Ap La Vien and 43 km W of Quang Tri. Apr70 XXIV Corps grid per Don Armstrong. Quang Tri Pr, I Corps.
Ramada, FSB (XU 972-327)
A.k.a. Ramada Inn? Just inside Cambodia, apx 2 km from SVN border, 6 km NW Bu Dop, 37 km due E Snuol, 32 km NE Loc Ninh and 4 km NNE FSB Thor. Cited in *1st Cav Op Rpt, May-Jul70*, p 28, 38, per Peter Cole. Grid per *11th ACR Cambodia Invasion AAR, 1st Cav Div, May-Jun70*, courtesy Lou Rochat. [460] Phuoc Long Pr, III Corps.
Ramsey, USS (n/a)
DEG-2. DD-Escort, per Ralph Fries.
Ranch, FSB (XU 938-367?)
Apx 2 km from SVN border, 8 km NNE Bu Dop, 38 km ENE Snuol, 35 km NE Loc Ninh and 5 km NNE FSB Ramada. Also listed at XU 938-638 which, if correct, suggests it was apx 42 km due W O Rang AF, 4 km WSW Phum Pu Amaye and 48 km NW Djamap AF? Grid per *11th ACR Cambodia Invasion AAR, 1st Cav Div, May-Jun70*, courtesy Lou Rochat. [461] Cambodia.
Ranch, FSB (XU 938-683?)
If grid correct, was apx 42 km due W O Rang AF, 4 km WSW Phum Pu Amaye and 48 km NW Djamap AF? Also listed at XU 938-367? Cambodia.
Ranch Hand, Operation (n/a)
See Glossary.
Ranch House, LZ (AT 999-425)
A.k.a. LZ Ranchhouse. In the Que Son Mtns, apx 14 km ESE An Hoa AF and 5 km S Da Nang AB. Jan71. Quang Nam Pr, I Corps.
Ranchhouse, LZ (AT 999-425)
See Ranch House. Quang Nam Pr, I Corps.
Randolph Glen, Operation (n/a)
7Dec69-31Mar70. US 101st Abn and 1st ARVN Inf Div providing security for lowlands of Thua Thien Pr. 670 NVA/VC KIA, per *Vietnam Order of Battle*, pp 9-14. Thua Thien Pr, I Corps.
Randy, FSB (n/a)
Location unknown. 7th/8th Arty here, 70. Name per Dan Gillotti, 15th Arty Assn. III Corps.
Rang Rang Cache, The (YT 2-5?)
In Feb70, a MSF working NE Saigon and apparently near Rang Rang (YT 207-543, roughly 70 km NNE Saigon), discovered series of VC/NVA munitions and supply caches that totaled over 150 tons. 95% of material was identified as having been made in China, but also inc were materials mfgd in Cambodia (tires), Czechoslovakia (field telephones), India (shovels), NVN (rifle grenades), and Romania (RPGs). Data per *A Better War*, p 177. Long Khanh or Phuoc Long Pr, III Corps.
Rang Rang Airfield (YT 207-543)
Along Rte 322, apx 2 km SW Rang Rang, 26 km ENE Phuoc Vinh AF and 66 km NNE to NE Saigon. Listed as "Insecure, abnd 20Apr69, AF # VA3-148," in Aug69 TAD per Frank Penk, Jr. Not in Feb73 TAD. Long Khanh Pr at Phuoc Long Pr border, III Corps.
Rangae Airfield (QE 9-8)
Listed as abnd in '66 NIMA data. At 4°25'00"N-101°42'00"E. NIMA data. Thailand.
Ranger, Camp (YT 046-076?)
If grid correct, was 26 km ENE Tan Son Nhut AB and 8 km SE Bien Hoa AB. 2d Bde/1st Inf Div departed Ft. Riley Kansas, 14Jul65, and then boarded *USS Gordon* for transit to VN. Once in VN, immed began const of Camp Ranger, their basecamp at Long Binh (possibly initial phase for what became Long Binh Post). Bien Hoa Pr, III Corps. [462]
Ranger, FSB (BR 287-998)
Remote site apx 7 km NNE Kon Lok, 26 km SE Plateau Gi AF and 28 km SSW Gia Vuc AF. Name/grid per Dan Gillotti, 15th Arty Assn. Binh Dinh Pr, III Corps.
Ranger, FSB (YD 133-193)
Apx 7 km NNE Tou Rout, 58 km due W Hue and 20 km WSW FSB O'Reilly. Apr70 XXIV Corps grid per Don Armstrong. Quang Tri Pr, I Corps
Ranger, LZ (BS 287-998?)
If grid correct, was apx 24 km WSW Chu Lai AB and 10 km ENE Thanh Truoc. Americal Assn grid is "BT" 287-998; however, that is point is in ocean and in error. 1st/35th Inf, 4th Div here while opcon Americal. Quang Nam/Quang Tin Pr border, I Corps.
Ranger II, FSB (YT 913-319)
On mtn apx 6 km NNW Tanh Linh AF and 47 km NE Xuan Loc. Jul68. Binh Tuy Pr, III Corps.
Ranger, USS (n/a)
CVA-61. Deployed with CVW-2, 14Oct69-1Jun70; with CVW-2, 16Nov72-23Jun73; with CVW-2, 27Oct70-17Jun 71; with CVW-2, 4Nov67-25May68; with CVW-2, 7May74-18 Oct 74; with CVW-2, 26Oct68-17May69; with CVW-14, 10 Dec65-25Au 66; with CVW-9, 5Aug64-6May65. On 17Dec64, A-1H Skyraiders escorted by F-4Bs and followed by RF-8A photo recon acft from *Ranger* flew USN's 1st armed recon mission over eastern Laos. 2d Rolling Thunder op took place15Mar65, as USN sent 64 Skyhawks/Skyraiders and 30 suptg acft from carriers *Hancock* and *Ranger* to hit Phu Qui ammo depot. [463]
Ranger North, FSB (XD 60-55)
Apx 5 km NNE Ranger South, 28 km NW Khe Sanh and 18 km NE Aloui. ARVN FSB during Lam Son 719. ARVN Rangers here. Good Lam Son 719 FSB map at www.americal.org/174/ map4.htm. Laos.

Ranger South, FSB (XD 58-50)
Apx 5 km SSW Ranger North, 28 km WNW Khe Sanh and 12 km NE Aloui. ARVN FSB/LZ during Lam Son 719. ARVN Rangers here. Good Lam Son 719 FSB map at www.americal.org/174/map4.htm. Laos.

Ranger Training Center (XT 592-212)
See Trung Lap Trng Ctr. Hau Nghia Pr, III Corps.

Ranong Airfield (ML 5-7)
Listed as abnd in '66 per NIMA. At 9°46'00"N-98°37'00"E. NIMA data. Feb67 Natl Geo map. El. 14' Thailand.

Ranson, Camp (BT 0-7?)
Somewhere in the Da Nang military complex. Named to honor Cpl David W. Ranson, USMC, KIA 7Apr69. Data per *Vietnam Military Lore, Legends, Shadows, and Heroes*, p 497. Quang Nam Pr, I Corps.

Rao (n/a)
Vietnamese for stream (also Cao, Song, and Khe).

Rao Loa River (YC 47-90)
Primary stream running through center of A Shau Valley and draining W into Laos. Thua Thien Pr, I Corps.

Rao Nai River (YD 50-00/YC)
Provided drainage for western slopes forming the A Shau Valley. Its course ran generally NNE beginning in area S of FSBs Whip and Fury, crossing Hwy 547 near FSB Veghel and joining the Rao Trang River SE FSB Kathryn and NW Hue, to form the Song Bo. See Rao Nai Valley. Thua Thien Pr, I Corps.

Rao Nai Valley (YD/YC)
During Op Delaware, 19Apr-17May68, 1st Bde/101st Abn and 3d ARVN Abn Task Force swept the Rao Nai and Rao Nho River Valleys in preparation for const of FSB Veghel, apx 10 km E the A Shau Valley. In Mar69, during Op Massachusetts Striker, the 2d/501st Inf, 101st Abn swept valley in drive W toward A Shau Valley and Laos. Thua Thien Pr, I Corps.

Rao Nho River (YD 50-00)
Stream draining mtns to E of FSBs Eagle's Nest, Georgia, Berchtesgarden and Zon. Ran generally W to E, and then N to parallel Hwy 547A. Thua Thien Pr, I Corps.

Rao Nho Valley (YD 500-030)
See Rao Nho River. Thua Thien Pr, I Corps.

Rao Qua (n/a)
Mapsheet name of L-7014-6045-1. NVN/Laos.

Rao Quan River Valley (XD 90-30)
Valley of Rao Quan in the Khe Sanh Plateau. Helped carve broad valley in which Khe Sanh CB was located, running from NW to SE on NE side of base. Home of NVA 6th Bn, 95th Rgt, 325(C) Div during siege of Khe Sanh. Quang Tri Pr, I Corps.

Rao Rao Valley (YC 540-960)
Generally 35 km SW Hue and 10 km E A Shau Valley. May68. Thua Thien Pr, I Corps.

Rapides De Houan Repou (YT 5-5)
A.k.a. the Thac Houan Repou. On Song Ngai River apx 45 km NNE Xuan Loc. NIMA data. Long Khanh Pr, III Corps.

Rapides de Lierg Djran (YT 5-5)
Near Lieng Djran. On Song Ngai River apx 45 km NNE Xuan Loc. NIMA data. Long Khanh Pr, III Corps.

Rapides, Canal de (XJ 3-3)
NIMA data. NVN.

Rapier, FSB (YS 658-699)
Apx 22 km ENE Nui Dat, 1 km SW FSB Scobie, 2 km N FSB Alisoun and 6 km NW FSB Feathers. On 1ATF NCO trng map per John Hollett. Phuoc Tuy Pr, III Corps.

Raquel, LZ (BR 506-903)
Apx 27 km NNE Kannack AF, 33 km WSW Bong Son, 14 km NE LZ Niagara, 14 km E LZ Cajun and 3 km NE LZ Welch. LZs Raquel and Welch (BR 498-879) were likely named in tandem to honor Raquel Welch, a buxom film star who toured with Bob Hope Show on several occasions. Often spelled Racquel. Per Jim Hall, 2d/35th Inf built base beginning 15Apr70. B/2d/35th Inf, 4th Div AO in Apr-May, '70, per John Linn. Name/grid per Jim Claeys. Also listed at BR 502-899. Binh Dinh Pr, II Corps.

Raquel, FSB (XT 652-336)
Apx 13 km WSW Lai Khe AF and 21 km SE Dau Tieng and 4 km NE Xa Duoc. 3d Bde/1st Inf Div, 68. Name/grid per Dan Gillotti. Binh Duong Pr, III Corps.

Rat Buri Airfield (NQ 7-9)
A.k.a. Ratburi. Apx 75 km WSW Bangkok per Feb67 Natl Geo map. Near 13°34'00"N-99°44'00"E. NIMA data. El. 150'. Thailand.

Rat Buri SF Camp (NQ 7-9)
A.k.a. Ratburi SF Camp. Apx 75 km WSW Bangkok? SF camp or AO per *SF Order of Battle*. Thailand.

Ratburi Airfield (NQ 7-9)
See Rat Buri AF. Thailand.

Ratburi SF Camp (NQ 7-9)
See Rat Buri SF Camp. Thailand.

Ratchathani Airbase (VB 8-8)
See Ubon AB. Thailand.

Ratchet, LZ (YD 183-140)
Apx 4 km N FSB Cunningham, 26 km S Ba Long AF and 41 km SSW Quang Tri. Apr70 XXIV Corps grid per Don Armstrong. Quang Tri Pr, I Corps.

Ratissages (n/a)
See Glossary.

Rattler, LZ (BT)
On Barrier Island due S Hoi An and straddling the Quang Nam/Quang Tin Pr border. Blue Beach, LZs Cobra, Krait and Rattler were used by ship-based Amphibious Ready Grp, BLT 1st/26th Marines, during Op Bold Pursuit, Jun-Jul69. 1st Mar Div, Americal list. Quang Nam or Quang Tin Pr, I Corps.

Rattlesnake, FSB (ZC 125-650)
A.k.a. Hill 749. Apx 9 km SW R.C. Ba Na, 10 km N FSB Hawk, 26 km W Hill 55 and 37 km WSW Da Nang. On map on p 109, *US Marines in Vietnam-1969*. USMC '69. Apr70 XXIV Corps grid per Don Armstrong. Quang Nam Pr, I Corps.

Raven, LZ (YD 526-437)
Just N Rte 597, apx 9 km N Phong Dien, 32 km NW Hue Citadel AF and 10 km NW LZ Shrike. 2d/4th Mar LZ during Op Jay, Jun66. On map in *USMC In Vietnam, 1966*, p 153. Thua Thien/Quang Tri Pr border, I Corps.

Raven, LZ (AT 904-386)
Just N Ap Hai, apx 3 km E Phuoc Binh AF and 38 km SSW Da Nang. Nov67. Quang Nam Pr, I Corps.

Raven FACs (n/a)
See Glossary.

Rawhide, FSB (AT 879-578)
A.k.a. LZ Rawhide and Hill 65. Along Rte 4, 28 km SW Da Nang, 26 km W Hoi An, 8 km SE FSB Buckskin, 15 km E FSB Hawk and 10 km SW Hill 55 (Camp Muir). USMC '69. Also listed at AT 880-580 and 883-579. 69-70. Quang Nam Pr, I Corps.

Rawlings, FSB (XT)
See Rawlins. Tay Ninh Pr, III Corps.

Rawlins, FSB (XT 296-485)
A.k.a. Rollins, Rawlings, and Rawlins I, II and III. Apx 6 km ESE center of Tay Ninh, 5 km ESE the Cao Dai Temple, 1 km SW LTL-26 and 1.5 km due W Ap Phuoc Binh. Possibly named to honor PFC James P. Rawlins, USA, KIA 17Sep68? Bty 7th/11th Arty here (towed 105s), as was Bn HQ, 4th(Mech)/23rd Inf Div. Site selected by LTC Clifford Neilsen (CO of 4th/23d). 1Lt Morgan Sincock led B/4/23 to site and established initial perimeter in mid-Aug68, just prior to Aug68 offensive. Sincock tells us that in '97 revisit, it remained a Viet Arty base occupied by 'New People's Army,' "keeping those pesky Cambodians at bay." Attacked 22Aug68 during Battle for Tay Ninh, while defended by A and B Cos 4th/23d Inf; with 1 US KIA/10 WIA. Attacked again at 0040 hrs, 27Aug68 by est 2 Bns of 88th NVA/VC Rgt preceded by 200 mortar rnds and fifty 107mm rockets. Spooky/air supt killed 27 NVA. 15 US WIA. On 20Sep68, In unusual daylight attack, 3d Bn, 174th NVA/VC Co hit elements of 4th/23d Inf and 3d/22d Inf, 25th Inf Div. On maps in *The Infantry Brigade in Combat*, pp 5, 13, 18, 20, and TL-7014-6231-4 (Tay Ninh). Also listed at XT 301-502 and 286-498. Tay Ninh Pr, III Corps.

Rawlins I, FSB (XT 301 502)
See FSB Rawlins. Tay Ninh Pr, III Corps.

Rawlins II, FSB (XT 302-507)
See FSB Rawlins. Dec68-May69. Tay Ninh Pr, III Corps.

Rawlins III, FSB (XT 296-485)
See FSB Rawlins. Also Listed at XT 290-480 and 306-521. Tay Ninh Pr, III Corps.

Ray, Camp (XT 99-14)
At Bien Hoa AB, apx 22 km NE Saigon. Apparent home of 101st Abn's SERTS (Screaming Eagle Replacement Trng School; a 1-week orientation given to all new 101st Abn personnel). At Bien Hoa until Spring of '70, and then moved to Camp Evans, Quang Tri Pr. It is unknown if it kept Camp Ray there as well. Bien Hoa Pr, III Corps.

Ray, FSB (XT 415-242)
Along QL-22, apx 2 km ESE Go Dau Ha, 26 km WNW Cu Chi and 27 km SE Tay Ninh. 2d/12th Cav, 1st Cav here '68, per Frank Penk, Jr. Also listed at XT 426-239, which is apx 4 km SE Go Dau Ha and 1 km SE listed grid. Tay Ninh Pr, III Corps.

Ray, LZ (BR 635-481)
If grid correct, was along QL-19, apx 15 km E An Khe and 7 km NW Binh Khe. 5Oct65. Also listed at BR 755-483, 20Oct65? Binh Dinh Pr, I Corps.

Ray, LZ (BR 755-483)
If grid correct, was apx 28 km ENE An Khe and 9 km NE Binh Khe. 20Oct65. Also listed at BR 755-483, 5Oct65? Binh Dinh Pr, I Corps.

Ray, LZ (XT 415-242)
Apx 2 km E Song Vam Co Dong, 13 km NE Duc Hue and 25 km W Cu Chi. Dec68-Jan69. Tay Ninh Pr, III Corps.

Ray, LZ (YV 955-970)
Apx 8 km ENE Hill 534, 8 km SE peak Chu Pong Mtn, 57 km SSW Pleiku, 11 km ENE LZ George and 4 km NE LZ Bill. Opened by 5th Cav/1st Cav Div, Aug66, during Op Paul Revere II. May have existed for only apx 1 week? Arty here thought to have suptd Battle for Hill 534, 14-15Aug66. Grid from map in *Paul Revere II*, 1st Cav '66 *Yearbook* courtesy Don Shutt. Pleiku Pr, II Corps.

Raye, Martha (n/a)
See Glossary.

Rayong Airfield (QP 6-9)
At 12°37'00"N-101°26'00"E. NIMA data. Thailand.

Razor, FSB (YD 142-185)
A.k.a. Dong Tou Trouein? Apx 8 km SE FSB Shiloh, 7 km NW FSB Cunningham, 31 km SE Vandegrift CB, 13 km E Laos and 7 km W FSB Lightning. FSBs Erskine, Razor, and Cunningham and LZ Dallas were built during Op Dawson River South, Jan22-10Feb69, to facilitate attack on Base Area 618. 9th Marines/3d Mar Div, Op Apache Snow, May-Jun69. Also listed 143-187. On map at p 32, *US Marines in Vietnam-1969*. Also listed at YD 143-186. Quang Tri Pr, I Corps.

Razorback, The (XD 96-57)
A.k.a. Razorback Ridge. Sharp ridgeline between XD 954-588 and 968-562. A 1,000' high, 3 km-long ridge that began apx 1 km NW the Rockpile and ran SE to NW. Primarily solid rock with volcanic sides, this jagged ridge was almost completely devoid of vegetation. See Helicopter Valley, Razorback Valley and Song Nang Valley. Quang Tri Pr, I Corps.

Razorback Beach (BS 86-39?)
Built due E LZ Montezuma to supt move of 1st Bde/1st Cav Div to replace USMC units at Duc Pho during Op Lejune, Apr67. Navy LST/LCM port here supplied Cav's Bde-sized basecamp and busy AF at LZ Montezuma. Grid is est. See LZ Montezuma. Quang Ngai Pr, I Corps.

Razorback Ridge (XD 96-57)
See Razorback, The. Quang Tri Pr, I Corps.

Razorback Valley (XD 975-568)
N the Rockpile and E Razorback Ridge, apx 38 km WNW Quang Tri. Large valley that was home to the Rockpile and Razorback Ridge. Quang Tri Pr, I Corps.

Razorbacks, The (XT 50-57)
A.k.a. Nui Tha La hill mass. 15 km-long ridgeline running generally SW/NE along W edge of Michelin Rubber Plantation from XT 47-53 NE to XT 54-60, with S terminus apx 5 km N Dau Tieng and 65 km NW Saigon. Highest peak was Hill 284. See *Low Level Hell* (shown on its 1st Div TAOR map), and *Rangers at War*, p 234. 1st Inf Div AO, '69. Binh Duong Pr, III Corps.

Re-Up Hill (YD 362-165)
A.k.a. Hill 640? Apx 38 km WSW Hue, 3 km SSE FSB ripcord, and 2 km ESE peak Hill 902. Focal point of heavy contact during Siege of FSB Ripcord, Mar-Jul70. Drew its name from fact that numerous men in units fighting here re-enlisted to get out of further combat. Per Ray Blackman, site was "really just an NDP near FSB Ripcord." 3rd Plt/D/2d/501st Inf, 101st Abn sent here to reinforce B Co

of same Bn after C had been involved in nasty, 2-day fight. See FSB Ripcord. Thua Thien Pr, I Corps.

Re-Up Lizard (n/a)
See Glossary.

Ready, FSB (XU 855-420)
Apx 12 km from SVN border, 10 km W Phum Chhaneng, 31 km ENE Snuol, 16 km NW Bu Dop and 35 km NNE Loc Ninh. Also spelled FSB Raedy; however "Ready" likely correct (no KIA with name Raedy in CACF). Cited in *1st Cav Op Rpt, May-Jul70*, p 21, 36, 38, per Peter Cole. Grid per *11th ACR Cambodia Invasion AAR, 1st Cav Div, May-Jun70*, courtesy Lou Rochat. [464] Cambodia.

Really New Life Hamlets (n/a)
See Ap Doi Moi in Glossary.

Ream Kampong Airfield (US 52-69)
Major AF with 6,000' rwy, apx 185 km SW Phnom Penh. Per TPC K-10D. El. 39'. Cambodia.

Ream Kampong Airfield (US 52-69)
Near Gulf of Thailand, apx 180 km SW Phnom Penh, 18 km E Kampong Soam AF and about 100 km from SVN border. Per ONC-K-10. El. 39'. Cambodia.

Ream Kampong Saom NDB (US 52-69)
Non-Directional Air Nav Beacon site. Apx 16 km ESE Kampong Saom AF and 5 km from ocean. Cambodia.

Reaper, USS (n/a)
MSO-467, Mine Sweeper, Ocean. SVN

Rear Support Base Buffalo (BR 483-448?)
See "Buffalo, Rear Support Base." Binh Dinh Pr, II Corps.

Reasoner, Camp (AT 97-74)
A.k.a. Hill 327 and Division Hill. At Da Nang. Named to honor 1Lt Frank S Reasoner, A/3d Recon Bn, 3d Mar Div, KIA 12Jul65 near An Ky, Da Nang Sector, first Marine of VN War to be awarded the MOH. Grid is est. Also listed at AT 86-86. Quang Nam Pr, I Corps.

Reasoner, USS (n/a)
DE 1063. In Task Grp 76.8, during Op Eagle Pull.

Reba, FSB (YD 091-495)
On E side of QL-9 apx 2 km due S Mai Loc, and 24 km W Quang Tri. Apr70 XXIV Corps grid per Don Armstrong. Quang Tri Pr, I Corps.

Rebecca, FSB (YT 325-175?)
Apx 6 km W to WSW Xa Gia Kiem, 17 km NW Xuan Loc and 33 km ENE Bien Hoa AB. Also listed as LZ Rebecca at "YU" 325-175? Long Khanh Pr, III Corps.

Rebecca, LZ (YU 325-175?)
Apx 16 km NE Song Be City AF and 16 km NNW Duc Phong AF/QL-14. 1st Cav. Name/grid per Dan Gillotti. Also listed as FSB Rebecca at "YT" 325-175? Phuoc Long Pr, III Corps.

Reblinn BOQ (XS 8-9)
At 32 Nguyen Hue St., Nov 62, 18 rms, Saigon. Data per *Vietnam Military Lore, 1959-1973*. Gia Dinh Pr, III Corps.

Reclaimer, USS (n/a)
ARS 42. Salvage Vessel like the *Reclaimer* (ARS 42) and Fleet Tug *Lipan, USS* (ATF 85) helped to free many grounded ships, inc destroyer *Frank Knox*, the *Terrell County* (LST 1157), and even some NVA trawlers. [465]

Recon Hill (AT?)
Possibly on Hill 327 (Division Ridge). Home of USMC 1st Recon Bn. Cited in *Reconnaissance Extraction*, Jan 2001 issue of *Military* Mag, p 16. See Recon Mtn. Quang Nam Pr, I Corps.

Recon Mountain (AT 81-38?)
Within 2 km of FSB/Outpost Nong Son, apx 40 km SSW Da Nang, 4 km WSW Phouc Binh AF and 48 km WNW Tam Ky. A steep, sharp ly-pointed hill apparently used for OP by 5th Marines and CAP 1 in '67. See Nong Son Outpost and Recon Hill. Quang Nam Pr, I Corps.

Recondo School, MACV (CP 03-52?)
See MACV Recondo School. Khanh Hoa Pr, II Corps.

Recondo (n/a)
See Glossary.

Red, LZ (BQ 810-337)
Apx 9 km due S Cung Son AF and 14 km WSW Lac Dien. Oct66. Phu Yen Pr, II Corps.

Red, LZ (XT 011-585)
Apx 18 km WNW Tay Ninh West AF and 5 km E Cambodia. 5Apr66. Tay Ninh Pr, III Corps.

Red, LZ (XT 020-640)
Apx 20 km NW Tay Ninh West AF and 3 km E Cambodia. Apr66. Also listed at XT 025-652. Tay Ninh Pr, III Corps.

Red, LZ (XT 270-860)
Apx 6 km SW Katum AF and 30 km NNE Nui Ba Den. 31Mar67. Tay Ninh Pr, III Corps.

Red, LZ (XT 470-515)
Along Song Saigon, apx 5 km NNE Dau Tieng/Tri Tam. 21Jun66. Binh Duong Pr, III Corps.

Red, LZ (XT 523-344)
Apx 14 km SSE Dau Tieng/Tri Tam. 16May66. Binh Duong/Tay Ninh Pr border, III Corps.

Red, LZ (XT 532-358)
Along Song Saigon, apx 13 km SSE Dau Tieng/Tri Tam. 21Feb66. Binh Duong/Tay Ninh Pr border, III Corps.

Red, LZ (XU 657-050)
Apx 7 km SW Loc Ninh AF and 18 km NW An Loc. 2Jul66. Binh Long Pr, III Corps.

Red, LZ (YC 636-943)
Apx 30 km SSW Hue Citadel AF. Feb-Mar66. Also listed at YC 643-943. Thua Thien Pr, I Corps.

Red, LZ (YD 081-606)
Apx 3 km WNW Thon Ba Thung, 4 km WNW Cam Loc and 19 km due W Dong Ha. Apr70 XXIV Corps grid per Don Armstrong. Quang Tri Pr, I Corps.

Red, LZ (YS 377-793)
Apx 13 km NW Nui Dat/Luscombe AF. 3Apr66. Phuoc Tuy Pr, III Corps.

Red, LZ (YT 143-303)
Apx 31 km ENE Bien Hoa AB 26 km SE Phuoc Vinh AF. 12Feb66. Tay Ninh Pr, III Corps.

Red, LZ (YT 197-995)
Apx 8 km SE Song Be AF 26 km NNE Dong Xoai. 29Jun66. Tay Ninh Pr, III Corps.

Red, LZ (YT 896-419)
Just W of Da M'Brim, and apx 17 km ENE Vo Dat AF. 7Jan66. Binh Duong Pr, III Corps.

Red, LZ/FSB (ZT 223-225)
Apx 20 km NW LZ Betty and 22 km WNW Phan Thiet. D/2d/320th Artillery. 3d/506th Inf, 101st Abn AO. Info/grid per Jerry Berry. Binh Thuan Pr, II Corps.

Red Ball, Camp (XS 831-884)
At An Nhon, along N edge of Saigon, immed NE Tan Son Nhut AB, apx 1.8 km due N the NE end of main rwy and on N side Rte TL-15. Basecamp of 3d Bde/82d Abn, Oct68-Mar69. In Fall '68, initial fwd cmd post for 3d Bde/82d Abn was at "Tent City" in Bien Hoa Basecamp after Bde moved S from I Corps (Hue AO), Sep-Oct68 to take up new AO covering W and NW approaches to Saigon. Immed became apparent fwd Bde HQ needed to be closer to its actual AO, so site was found at Camp Red Ball (XS 832-984) along N edge of Tan Son Nhut AB, and const of Bde's TOC here began 1Oct68, and site was operational by 16Oct68. During same period, new Bde basecamp built at Phu Loi Post and occupied 20Oct68. [466] Data per Butch Sincock. Gia Dinh Pr, III Corps.

Red Beach (AT 946-812)
Apx 10 km NW Da Nang AB and 12 km NW Marble Mtn AF. Site of Camp J. J. Books, Camp Haskins and Paddock Cmpd. HQ USMC Force Logistics Cmd, 30th Naval Const Rgt camp/stg area, and USMC III MAF. See also Camps Haskins, Haskins North, Haskins South and Viking. Quang Nam Pr, I Corps.

Red Beach (BS 84-43)
Just N mouth of Tra Cau and Lo Bo Rivers, apx 5 km NE Duc Pho and 17 km SE Mo Duc. Assault beach of USMC TF Delta BLT 3/1 and 2/4, 28Jan66, during Op Double Eagle. USN documentation refers to same beach as Blue Beach. Cited in *USMC in Vietnam, 1966*, p 23, map at p 20. See Hill 163. Quang Ngai Pr, I Corps.

Red Beach (BT 300-370)
Apx 3 km SSE Hiep Hung, 15 km due N Tam Ky and 38 km NW Chu Lai. 2May67. Quang Tin Pr, I Corps.

Red Beach (CR 0-2)
Near Qui Nhon. On map at 15th Arty website at: www. landscaper.net/chighmap.jpg. Binh Dinh Pr, II Corps.

Red Beach Airfield (AT 946-812)
Apx 10 km NW Da Nang AB and 12 km NW Marble Mtn AF. Per ONC J-11 El. 3', 1,800' steel-mat rwy. At 16°05'50"N-108°08'50"E. Quang Nam Pr, I Corps.

Red Beach, Camp (AT 95-82)
A.k.a. Red Beach. Apx 10 km NW Da Nang AB and 12 km NW Marble Mtn AF. Original name of Camp Books? Da Nang, HQ Force Logistics Cmd, USMC. Grid is apx. See Camp Books and Red Beach. Quang Nam Pr, I Corps.

Red Carpet Heliport (YT 048-106)
A.k.a. Heliport #764. Along S side of Hwy 317, roughly midway between Bien Hoa and Plantation AF's in area known as The Plantation CB, or Long Binh North, apx 24 km NE Saigon and just N Long Binh Post. IIFFV HQ here. "200' x 200'. Opr 2300-1000Z. PPR exc Code 7 and above. Tfc pat is 500' AGL NW pad. Apch headings 180° and 030°. Dep headings 360° and 210°. HAZARDS-Bldg with 30' ant 50 meters NW, copter revetments on W edge, 40' pwr line 50 meters S extending to SW 1000 meters. Tower-Red Carpet 322.8, 56.0. Opr Heliport times. Advsy. Arty advsy-Bien Hoa 290.0, 46.7, El. 95'," per Feb73 TAD. See Plantation AF. Bien Hoa Pr, III Corps.

Red Carpet Tower (YT 074-067)
Apx 8 km ESE Bien Hoa AB. Call-sign of control tower at Sanford Army AF. Bien Hoa Pr, III Corps.

Red Catcher Base Camp (YT 056-116)
See RedCatcher. Bien Hoa Pr, III Corps.

Red Catcher, FSB (YS?)
See RedCatcher. Long Khanh Pr?, III Corps.

Red Cross Hospital Ship (German) (n/a)
See *Helgoland*. SVN.

Red Devil, Camp (YD 24-597)
At Dong Ha CB, apx 13 km NW Quang Tri, 14 km E Cam Lo, 63 km NW Hue. US 1st Bde/5th Div's name for their portion of US Marine's Dong Ha CB when 5th was HQ'd here, '69. Quang Tri Pr, I Corps.

Red Devil Road (XD 8-4?)
Alternate to Rte QL-9, between FSB Elliott and Khe Sanh. Quang Tri Pr, I Corps.

Red Devils (n/a)
See Glossary.

Red Dog, FSB? (XT 678-303)
See FSB Red Leg. Binh Duong Pr, III Corps.

Red Fish, USS (n/a)
SS-395. Submarine, per Ralph Fries.

Red Fox, LZ? (n/a)
Location unknown. 173d Abn LZ. Name per Dan Gillotti, 15th Arty Assn. II Corps.

Red Haze Missions (n/a)
See Glossary.

RED HORSE (n/a)
See Glossary.

Red Leg, FSB (BR?)
See Redleg, FSB. Binh Dinh or Pleiku Pr, II Corps.

Red Leg, FSB (XT 678-303)
Apx 12 km SW Lai Khe and 15 km N to NNE Cu Chi. Dec70. Also listed as both FSB Red Dog and Red Log, though "Red Leg" thought to be likely correct spelling? "Red Leg" is traditional term used to identify an artillerymen in the US Army. Binh Duong Pr, III Corps.

Red Log, FSB? (XT 678-303)
See FSB Red Leg. Binh Duong Pr, III Corps.

Red River, The (n/a)
A.k.a. the Song Hong. Flows NW to SE in almost a straight line from Chinese border, through Hanoi and empties in sea near Thuan Nghiep, 110 km SE Hanoi. NVN.

Red Sector (XD 853-418)
Portion of Khe Sanh CB's western perimeter. L/3d/26th Marines here during siege. Quang Tri Pr, I Corps.

Red Watch, Khe Sanh (n/a)
See Khe Sanh Red Watch in Glossary.

RedCatcher, FSB (YS 43-96?)
A.k.a. Camp 398 (significance of numeric designation is unknown). Possibly at or adj to Blackhorse Basecamp, apx 55 km due E Saigon? FSB or Engr camp of 199th LIB apparently built in Jun69, or near that date. Data per the papers of LTC William Coley Jr. (1st/43d Inf, '65-66, 1st Cav '66, and 11th Cav '69), courtesy his son and biographer, Joe Coley. Long Khanh Pr?, III Corps.

RedCatcher Base Camp (YT 056-116)
Along S side of Hwy 316, at or adj to Plantation AF and Long Binh, apx 7 km ESE Bien Hoa AB and 28 km ENE Tan Son Nhut AB. 199th LIB HQ. Bien Hoa Pr, III Corps.

Redding, LZ (YD 209-099)
Apx 2 km W Hwy 548, about 8 km ESE Tou Rout, 53 km WSW Hue. Apr70 XXIV Corps grid per Don Armstrong. Quang Tri Pr, I Corps.
Redhorse, Camp (AT 86-86?)
Apx 5 km W Da Nang. This facility was transferred to ARVN 3d Inf Div, 23Jun72. At that time, it had capacity to house 450 personnel. Occupants prior to transfer were not listed in MACV-JGS IG Post-Turnover Inspection Rpt for 29Jun72 inspection. Grid is est. Data per Ray Bows. Quang Nam Pr, I Corps.
Redleg, FSB (BR?)
No data. 10th Cav, 4th Div here, per Bob Patsfield. "Red Leg" is traditional term used to identify an artillerymen in the US Army. Possibly Binh Dinh or Pleiku Pr, II Corps.
Redleg, FSB ? (XT 678-303)
See FSB Red Leg. Binh Duong Pr, III Corps.
Reed, FSB (BS 764-277)
Apx 3 km NE LZ Tempest, 12 km SSW Duc Pho and 35 km NNW Bong Son. Possibly built Oct70? Americal Assn grid. Quang Ngai Pr?, I Corps.
Reed, FSB (XT 477-125)
Apx 17 km WSW Cu Chi and 16 km ENE Duc Hue AF. Nov68-Feb69. Hau Nghia Pr, III Corps.
Reed, LZ (ZA 173-103)
Apx 22 km NW Phu Nhon AF and 37 km SSW Pleiku. 5Nov65. Pleiku Pr, II Corps.
Reed II, FSB (XT 470-120)
Apx 18 km WSW Cu Chi and 15 km ENE Duc Hue AF. Apr69. Hau Nghia Pr, III Corps.
Reeves, USS (n/a)
DLG-24. Guided-Missile DD Ldr, per Ralph Fries.
Refuge, LZ (n/a)
Location unknown. 1st Cav. Corps?
Rega, FSB (ZT 05-40)
Possibly "Regan?" In mnts apx 33 km ENE Vo Dat, 8 km NE Xa Huy Kiem, 15 km E Da M'Brim and 19 km NE Tanh Linh AF. 5th/12th Inf, 199th LIB here at one time. Binh Thuy Pr?, III Corps.
Regiment de Marche (n/a)
See Glossary.
Regional Force NCO Training Center (YS 43-51?)
On coast at Long Hai and apx 17 km NE Vung Tau. Phuoc Tuy Pr, III Corps.
Regional Forces (n/a)
See Ruff/Puffs in Glossary.
Regional Troops (n/a)
See Glossary.
Regular, LZ (BR 600-233)
Apx 25 km SSE An Khe, 27 km NW Van Canh AF, 47 km Due W Qui Nhon, 1.5 km SW LZ Truman and 13 km SE LZ Lincoln. 4th Div AO, '70. 4th Div op rpt grid per Jim Claeys. Binh Dinh Pr, II Corps.
Regular Hill Base Camp (ZA?)
Near Plei Djereng. Discussed on webpage at http://grunt.space.swri.edu/LouTplei.htm (Lou Talley). Photo on that webpage shows sign made of painted rocks or painted on side of a hill adj to basecamp that read, *Regulars By God.* On 16Feb67, 46 men of A/1st/22d Inf, 4th Div were KIA nearby in major ambush by est Div size NVA element. Presumably in SW Kontum Pr, II Corps.
Regulars By God (n/a)
See Glossary.
Regulatrice Routiere (n/a)
See Glossary.
Reich Training Area (CP 03-52)
See Merrill D Reich Trng Area. Khanh Hoa Pr, II Corps.
Reliable AAF Airfield (XS 408-453)
See Dong Tam AF. Dinh Tuong Pr, IV Corps.
Remagen 1 thru 18 FSB Series (XT)
See Remagen I thru XVIII. III Corps.
Remagen, FSB (YT 005-565)
A.k.a. Remagen I and FSB Karen. Along QL-14, apx 8 km NNE Phuoc Vinh AF. Jan69. Remagen FSB series was built running NE from Phuoc Vinh AF to Dong Xoai along LTL-1A, then NE from Dong Xoai along QL-14 to its intersection with Rte 311, about 9 km N Bunard AF, then NW along 311 almost to Song Be. Numbering sequence started at I in S and increased to XVIII in N. Presumably all 1st Inf Div bases? Binh Duong Pr, III Corps.
Remagen I, FSB (YT 005-565)
See FSB Remagen. Jan69. Binh Duong Pr, III Corps.
Remagen II, FSB (XT 996-547?)
Along LTL-1A, apx 7 km NE Phuoc Vinh AF, 23 km SSW Dong Xoai AF. Grid per Frank Penk, Jr. Also listed at YT 001-611, Jan69, a site 13 km NNE Phuoc Vinh and 16 km SSW Dong Xoai? Binh Duong Pr, III Corps.
Remagen III, FSB (XT 997-595?)
Along LTL-1A, apx 11 km NNE Phuoc Vinh AF, 18 km SSW Dong Xoai AF. Grid per Frank Penk, Jr. Also listed at YT 029-625, Feb69, a site 12 km NNE Phuoc Vinh and 17 km SSW Dong Xoai? Phuoc Long Pr, III Corps.
Remagen IV, FSB (YT 028-628)
Along LTL-1A, apx 14 km NE Phuoc Vinh AF, 16 km SSW Dong Xoai AF. Grid per Frank Penk, Jr. Also listed at YT 058-675, Feb69, a site 22 km NNE Phuoc Vinh AF and 7 km S Dong Xoai AF? Binh Duong Pr, III Corps.
Remagen V, FSB (YT 047-660)
Along LTL-1A, apx 11 km SSW Dong Xoai AF, 26 km NNE Phuoc Vinh AF and 2 km NE FSB Supnet. Grid per Frank Penk, Jr. Also listed at YT 061-720, May69, a site 5 km S Dong Xoai AF? Phuoc Long Pr, III Corps.
Remagen VI, FSB (YT 070-732?)
A.k.a. Odessa? Along LTL-1A, apx 4 km SSW Dong Xoai AF, 26 km NNE Phuoc Vinh AF. Grid per Frank Penk, Jr. Also listed at XT 078-758, site of FSB Odessa, and also at YT 148-798, May69, a site 9 km NE Dong Xoai AF? Phuoc Long Pr, III Corps.
Remagen VIII, FSB (YT 195-835)
A.k.a. FSB O'Keefe. Along QL-14, apx 14 km NE Dong Xoai. May69. Phuoc Long Pr, III Corps.
Remagen X, FSB (YT 254-898)
Apx 21 km NE Dong Xoai and 3 km WNW Bunard AF. May69. Phuoc Long Pr, III Corps.
Remagen XII, FSB (YT 257-967)
Along Rte 311, apx 8 km N Bunard AF and 2.5 km W QL-14. May69. Phuoc Long Pr, III Corps.
Remagen XIV, FSB (YT 266-998)
Along Rte 311, apx 12 km N Bunard AF and 2.5 km W QL-14. Jun69. Phuoc Long Pr, III Corps.

Remagen XVIII, FSB (YU 204-047)
Along Rte 311, apx 19 km NNW Bunard AF, 6 km ESE Song Be AF and 3 km SE peak Phuoc Binh Mtn. Jun69. Phuoc Long Pr, III Corps.
Remora, USS (n/a)
SS-487. Submarine, per Ralph Fries.
Remote Firing Devices (n/a)
See Glossary.
Rendezvous, FSB (YC 432-962)
In the A Shau Valley S of A Luoi and just SW intersection of Hwys 547 and 548, apx 37 km SW Hue. Was 3d Bde 101st Abn HQ during Op Kentucky Jumper (inc Massachusetts Striker, Apache Snow and Montgomery Rendezvous). Closed 24Se69, when 3de Bde moved HQ to Camp Evans. 3d/187th Inf, 101st Abn also here. During Lam Son 720, beginning Apr '71, FSBs Fury, Kathryn, Maureen, Gladiator and later Eagle's Nest were all reopened by B/326th Engrs, while elements of 326th also rebuilt and enlarged FSBs Brick, Tennessee, Rendezvous and Rifle (including rte 545, the road to FSB Rifle). Also listed at YC 433-967. Thua Thien Pr, I Corps.
Rene, LZ/FSB (XD 917-645)
A.k.a. LZ/FSB Renee? On S boundary of DMZ, apx 21 km WNW Cam Lo and 33 km WNW Dong Ha. Apr70 XXIV Corps grid per Don Armstrong. Quang Tri Pr, I Corps.
Renee, LZ (XD 917-645)
See LZ Rene. Quang Tri Pr, I Corps.
Renegade, LZ (YA 678-367)
Along Cambodian border and Ya Krong Bolah River, apx 18 km WSW Plei Djereng new AF and 56 k WSW Pleiku. Jan66. Kontum/Pleiku Pr border, II Corps.
Renegade Woods (XT 29 30)
Generally 18 km SSE Tay Ninh and 22 km SW Dau Tieng. Ran from apx XT 29-30 to XT 30-32, and described as flat, covered with thick, double-canopy jungle, and heavily overgrown with vines. Sanctuary for 271st and 272d Rgts, 9 VC/NVA Div. US 25th Inf Div AO. On L-8020-6231-3 (1:25,000 scale) map. [467]. Also on *Rangers At War* map, pp 324-325. Heiu Thien Dist, Tay Ninh Pr, III Corps.
Reno, FSB (AT 884-747)
A.k.a. Outpost and OP Reno. In foothills overlooking Song Cu De River Valley, apx 12 km WSW Da Nang AB. 3d/26th Marines, '69. Apr-May70. Quang Nam Pr, I Corps.
Reno, Camp (ZA 236 863)
See FOB 2. Kontum Pr, II Corps.
Reno, OP (AT 884-747)
See OP Reno and FSB Reno. Quang Nam Pr, I Corps.
Reno Bar (ZA 236 863)
See FOB 2. Kontum Pr, II Corps.
Renville, USS (n/a)
APA-227. Amphib Attack, Transport ship, per Ralph Fries. In Chu Lai area, at least May-Jun65.
Repeater Aircraft (n/a)
See Glossary.
Replacement Depots (n/a)
See Glossary.
Repose, USS (XD/YD/BT)
A.k.a. AH 16. Hospital ship in SVN waters, 66-70. Was part of 7th Fleet's III MAF TF 73. Painted white with large red crosses on either side, this floating hospital obviated need for const of hospital complexes ashore and substantial ground forces needed to secure onshore facilities. Customers spoke highly of its comforts and staff members. In Quang Tri/Thua Thien Prov waters, though possibly positioned elsewhere as well? Standard complement was medical staff of 24 doctors, 29 nurses and 250 Corpsmen, as well as dental surgeons, Chaplains and ship's crew. See *USS Sanctuary*, *USS Hope* and USN/USMC, USAF and US Army Hospitals. SVN.
Republic of China Forces (n/a)
See Major HQs Section.
Republic of Korea Forces (n/a)
See Major HQs Section.
Republic of Vietnam Forces (n/a)
See Major HQs Section.
Rescue Coordination Center (XS 819-962)
A.k.a. OL-A USAF RCC. At Tan Son Nhut AB (call-sign Queen), Saigon. Gia Dinh Pr, III Corps.
Rescue, Operation (n/a)
See Glossary.
Reserve Forestiere de Cachu (XT 530-325)
At Trang Co, apx 24 km WSW Lai Khe and 15 km NW Cu Chi. Grid at apx center of mass. Tay Ninh Pr?, III Corps.
Resolutions, COSVN (n/a)
See Glossary.
Resor Quarry (XT 974-127)
Along E bank Song Dong Nai, apx 2 km WSW Bien Hoa AB. Jan-Oct70. Bien Hoa Pr, III Corps.
Rest Camp, The (WJ 6-7?)
Reference point on "Thud Ridge," apx 30 km NNW Hanoi. Apparently a resort nicknamed the "Rest Camp" by F-105 Thud pilots. Its large pools of blue water and bungalow clusters were easily seen from air, making it a good check point. Grid is apx. See Thud Ridge. NVN.
Retrans, FSB (XT 281-581)
A.k.a. Nui Ba Den. Apx 8 km NNE Tay Ninh. Apparent nickname of radio relay site on Nui Ba Den Mtn. See Nui Ba Den for detail. Tay Ninh Pr, III Corps.
Retro Molar Pad BOQ (XS 8-9)
At 20 Phung Khac Khoan St., Saigon. Apparently housed dental clinic personnel. Data per *Vietnam Military Lore, 1959-1973*. Gia Dinh Pr, III Corps.
Revolutionary Redevelopment Program (n/a)
See Glossary.
Rex Annex BOQ (XS 86-91)
At 135 Nguyen Hue St., prior to Jul62, 24 rms (in '65 the Rex BOQ annex was in old Tax Building at 31 Le Loi St.), Saigon. Per R. Bows' *Vietnam Military Lore, 1959-1973*. Gia Dinh Pr, III Corps.
Rex BOQ (XS 864-914)
At 147-149 Nguyen Hue St. (Rex Officers Open Mess and Rex Room Bar) prior to Jul 62, 98 rms, Saigon. Data per *Vietnam Military Lore, 1959-1973*. Gia Dinh Pr, III Corps.
Rex BOQ & OOM (864-914?)
See Rex BOQ. Gia Dinh Pr, III Corps.
See Regional Forces and Ruff/Puff in Glossary.
Rhino, LZ (YD 273-322)
Apx 12 km SE Ba Long and 22 km SSW Quang Tri. Apr70 XXIV Corps grid per D. Armstrong. Quang Tri Pr, I Corps.
Rhode Island, FSB (YS 434-766)
Apx 9 km N Nui Dat, 3 km SW FSB Alanbrooke and 2 km W FSB Le Loi/LTL-2. FSBs Maureen, Robin and Rhode

Island all appear to have been within very close proximity to one another and may represent a succession of bases since it is unlikely they would have coexisted. On 1ATF NCO trng map per John Hollett. Phuoc Tuy Pr, III Corps.

Rhodes, Alexandre de (n/a)
See Glossary.

Rhodes, Camp (XD or YD?)
Apparently at Quang Tri; however, also said to have been at Phu Bai? Named to honor Lt Joseph L. Rhodes, USN, Seabee Civil Engrs, NMCB-121, KIA 23Oct67, when his jeep detonated mine near Phu Bai. 1st Naval Civil Engr KIA in VN. MCB-11 Seabees, 9May69-15Jan69. Data per Ray Bows. Quang Tri or Thua Thien Pr, I Corps.

Rhonda, FSB (XT 374-863)
At or near Bo Tuc, apx 8 km SE Katum AF and 36 km due W An Loc. Cited in *2d/7th Cav Unit History* '70-71, p 2, per Peter Cole. Tay Ninh Pr, III Corps.

Rice Bowl, The (AT 99-09)
Valley generally 15 km SSE Hiep Duc. Americal list. Quang Tin Pr, I Corps.

Rice Bowl, The (BS 83-33)
An area generally about 6 km SSE Duc Pho. Site of many rice caches captured by Americal Div, Summer of '70. Quang Ngai Pr, I Corps.

Rice Bowl, The (YT 75-40)
28 sq-km, fertile valley apx 36 km NE Xuan Loc, NW Vo Dat, N Vo Dat AF W of LTL-3 and basin of Lan Nga River, and W of Than Duc. Secured by 2d/503d Inf, 173d Abn during Op New Life, late '65. For discussion see *Infantry in Vietnam*, pp168-175. Long Khanh/Binh Tuy Pr border, III Corps.

Rice Farmer, Operation (n/a)
1Jan-31Aug69. 9th Inf Div and 8th ARVN Rgt op in Mekong Delta. 1,860 rptd NVA/VC KIA, per *Vietnam Order of Battle*, pp 9-14. IV Corps.

Rice Mill, The (XS 8-8)
See Rice Mill Cmpd. Gia Dinh Pr, III Corps.

Rice Mill Compound (XS 808-875)
A.k.a. The Rice Mill. On island in tributary of Saigon River at S edge of Cholon, apx 3 km SSW Phu Tho Racetrack. Home of 79th Ordnance Bn, which occupied warehouse bldgs once part of rice mill/stg facility. Surrounded by high masonry walls, it was considered quite secure. Perhaps because it was only accessible by bridge, it was attacked and held by VC during Tet '68. Gia Dinh Pr, III Corps.

Rice Victory, SS (n/a)
Commercial transport under govt contract, per Ralph Fries.

Rich, USS (n/a)
DD-820, per Ralph Fries.

Rich Forts (n/a)
See French Fort Design in Glossary.

Richard B. Anderson, USS (n/a)
DD 786. On 5Apr72, during Easter Offensive, Destroyers *Joseph Strauss* and *Richard B. Anderson* fired on Ben Hai Bridge and northern half of DMZ. See *Stickell, USS*.[468]

Richard S. Edwards, USS (n/a)
A.k.a. DD 950. See *Morton, USS*.

Richard E. Kraus, USS (n/a)
DD-849, per Ralph Fries.

Richards, LZ (AT 866-214)
Apx 6 km SW Hiep Duc, 20 km due S Phuoc Binh AF and 44 km due W Tam Ky. Americal. Quang Tin Pr, I Corps.

Richelieu of Vietnam (n/a)
See Madame Nhu in Glossary.

Richmond BEQ & Mess (XS 829-952)
In MACV Annex, Tan Son Nhut AB, Saigon, and just E MACV HQ Cmpd. Gia Dinh Pr, III Corps.

Richmond K. Turner, USS (n/a)
DLG-20. Guided-Missile DD Ldr, per Ralph Fries.

Rick, LZ (XD 718-382)
Apx 3 km NW Lao Bao, 13 km WSW Khe Sanh CB and 30 km WSW Ca Lu. Apr70 XXIV Corps grid per Don Armstrong. Quang Tri Pr, I Corps.

Rick, LZ (XT 530-280)
Apx 17 km NW Cu Chi and 4 km NE Xom Rung Cay. Feb66. Hau Nghia Pr, III Corps.

Rickey, LZ (XT 497-757)
Just SW Bau Tram, apx 22 km SE Katum AF and 16 km NW Minh Thanh AF. 1st Cav. Name/grid per Dan Gillotti, 15th Arty Assn. Tay Ninh Pr, III Corps.

Ricky, LZ (XT 497-757)
See LZ Rickey at grid. Tay Ninh Pr, III Corps.

Rider, LZ (AT 952-355)
See LZ Ryder at grid. Quang Nam Pr, I Corps.

Ridgefield Victory, SS (n/a)
Commercial transport under govt contract, per Ralph Fries.

Ridgeway, LZ (BR 775-670)
Apx 3 km W Hoi San and 36 km NE An Khe. Oct66. Binh Dinh Pr, II Corps.

Riffle, LZ (ZA 205-726)
See LZ Ripple. Kontum Pr, II Corps.

Rifle, FSB (YC 863-988)
Apx 25 km ESE Hue, 17 km SE FSB Birmingham and 16 km WSW Phu Bai. C/1st/501st Inf and elements 326th Engrs, 101st Abn attacked here 21May71. During Lam Son 720 and beginning in Apr '71, elements of 326th rebuilt and enlarged FSBs Brick, Tennessee, Rendezvous and Rifle (including Rte 545, the road to FSB Rifle). Also listed at 87-92. 101st Abn, 2d Bde AO. Apr70 XXIV Corps grid per Don Armstrong. Thua Thien Pr, I Corps.

Rifle Range, The (BR 93-47)
Apx 2 km NE Phu Cat and about 14 km NNE An Nhon, 30 km NE Qui Nhon and 1 km E QL-1. 1st Cav fwd operating base and helo laager pad (227th AHC) used in '66. Apparently set up in an old Viet or French rifle range; hence its nickname. Security provided by ROK Army (apx 1,000 men) which surrounded site. May have later become Phu Cat 2 AF. See *Chickenhawk*, p. 269, and map on p. 11. Grid is est. Binh Dinh Pr, II Corps.

Riley, FSB (XT 830-321)
Along on E side Rte 2A, apx 8 km SE Lai Khe and 10 km E Ben Cat. 1st Inf Dive AO, '69. Per *Low Level Hell's* 1st Div TAOR map. Dec68-Apr69. Binh Duong Pr, III Corps.

Rincon, USNS (n/a)
MSTS Transport, per Ralph Fries.

Ringo, LZ (AQ 935-648)
W of QL-14, apx 8 km NW Buon Blech AF and 36 km S Phu Nhon AF. 173d Abn. Name/grid per Dan Gillotti, 15th Arty Assn. II Corps.

Ringo, FSB (YS 530-650)
Apx 11 km ESE Nui Dat/Luscombe AF and 5 km NE Dat Do. Dec67. Phuoc Tuy Pr, III Corps.

Rio, FSB (YD 505-144)
A.k.a. Hill 247? Apx 15 km SE Ap Lai Bang and 8 km S peak Nui Ong Don hill mass (Hills 674, 548 and 600). Also listed at YD 503-147. Thua Thien Pr, I Corps.

Riong Bolieng Airfield (AP 984-063)
See Dam Pau AF. Tuyen Duc Pr, II Corps.

Riot Gas (n/a)
See CN Gas and CS Gas in Glossary.

Ripcord, FSB (YD 343-194)
A.k.a. Hill 927, Cheeseburger Hill, and FSB Carrol. Apx 38 km due W Hue, 12 km NE the N end of A Shau Valley, 12 km NW FSB Maureen, 12 km SSE FSB O'Reilly, 5 km WNW FSB Granite, 2 km WNW Hill 805 and 1 km E Hill 1000. Originally built by 1st Cav as FSB Carrol (or Carol) in '68. 2d/506th Inf, 101st Abn and 2d/1st ARVN Rgt here in Jan69, during Op Ohio Rapids. 2d/506th, again reopened it by ground assault, 11Apr70, during Op Chicago Peak. 2 attempts to secure site beginning 12Mar70 were beaten back by NVA. Its original position was meant to be Hill 902; however, 902 proved to be unsuitable and attention then focused on Hill 927. Built to exploit "The Warehouse" hill mass of Co Pung Mtn (Hill 1615, generally 9 km to S), which served as huge logistical complex for NVA's 29th and 803d Rgts, 324B Div. Provided arty, Tac Air and B-52 Arc Light FO platform for campaign to interdict NVA who'd been unmolested on Co Pung for 2 years and soon became site of last major hill battle for the 101st Abn in VN (Siege of FSB Ripcord), Jun-Jul 70. During 3 week siege, 101st suffered 75 KIA (more dead than lost at Hamburger Hill) and 345 WIA. Among KIA was only professional football player to die in the war, when on 21Jul70, Capt. James R. Kalsu was KIA by mortar while reading a letter he thought was bringing him news of his wife's delivery of their 2d child (it was her due date). Kalsu was an All-American at Oklahoma U and named '69 Rookie-of-the-Year in his 1st season as offensive guard with the Buffalo Bills, joining them after playing in '68 Orange Bowl. An ROTC grad, Kalsu was called to active duty and was with C Bty, 2d/11th Arty at FSB Arsenal when sent to reinforce Ripcord.[469] Per Keith William Nolan, another noted KIA of 2nd/506th here was 26-yr old PFC Wieland C. Norris, KIA 3Jun70, the brother of US movie/TV star Chuck Norris. Siege ended when base abnd 23Jul 70 because its defense was no longer feasible. Dominant physical feature was large boulder nicknamed "Impact Rock," heavily scarred by incoming. 1st/506th, 2d/506th, 2d/501st Inf, 2d/11th, 2d/319th Arty, 4th/77th ARA and 158th Avn Bn among other units here. Map is L-7014-6441-4 (A Luoi). See Hill 605, 805, 902, 1000, Co Pung, Coc Muen, Re-Up Hill, Triple Hill, Cheeseburger Hill and Electric Bunker. Thua Thien Pr, I Corps.[470 471]

Ripple, LZ (ZA 205-726)
A.k.a. LZ Riffle. On QL-14N, apx 24 km N Pleiku, 17 km SSW Kontum and 10 km ENE Plei Mrong. Possibly named to honor Sp4 Joseph H. Riffle, KIA 15Oct68, although no data supports speculation. 4th Div AO, '70. Name/grid per Jim Claeys. Kontum/Pleiku Pr border, II Corps.

Rising Sun, FSB (YT 92-26)
A.k.a. Tanh Li or Tanh Linh. At Tanh Linh/Tanh Linh AF, 47 km NW Phan Thiet, 50 km ENE Xuan Loc and 22 km ESE Vo Dat. 199th LIB here. Binh Tuy Pr, III Corps.

Rita, FSB (YT 735-252)
Apx 18 km NE Nui Chua Chan, 10 km S Vo Dat AF, and 20 km SSW FSB Warrior. 4th/12th, 2d/3d, 199th LIB. Nov69-Jan70. Binh Tuy Pr, III Corps.

Rita, LZ/FSB (XT 499-804)
Apx 8 km SSW FSB Julie, 12 km S Cambodian border, 28 km WSW An Loc and 30 km NE Nui Ba Den. Described as "twin sister of FSB Julie," in *Charlie Company*, pp 68-76 et al. 1st Inf /1st Cav AO. 5th/7th Cav, 2d/8th Cav, 1st Cav here '68 per Frank Penk, Jr. Also listed at XT 500-800 and 502-795. Oct68-Feb69. Tay Ninh Pr, III Corps.

Ritaville Airfield (TF 66-34)
LS-53. Apx 50 km NNE Vientiane, per ONC-J-11. CIA/SF, per *Air Facilities Data-Laos*. El. 1,428'. Laos.

Rittgers, Patrol Base (XT 358-148)
A.k.a. Patrol Base Kotrc. In the An Ninh Corridor, apx 4 km due E southern tip of Angel's Wing, 28 km due W Cu Chi, 34 km SSE Tay Ninh and 6 km WNW Patrol Base Harris. Origin of Rittgers name unknown, as no casualty of that name in CACF. Later renamed PB Kotrc. 25th Inf Div here. Mentioned in AAR at www.army. mil/cmh-pg/ documents/vietnam/vni/232.htm. See Kotrc, PB. Hau Nghia Pr, III Corps.

River Assault Flotilla One (n/a)
See *Benewah, USS* (APB-35).

River Boat South, LZ (BT 621-016)
On W bank and 2 km S mouth of Song Tra Bong, apx 10 km SE Chu Lai AB and 5 km E QL-1. Apr70 XXIV Corps grid per Don Armstrong. Quang Tin Pr, I Corps.

River Raid, the (BT-01-54)
14Jan67 raid of Banh Lanh. Op zone was between BT 010-541 and 014-548, apx 14 km WSW Hoi An and 22 km due S Da Nang AB. See Banh Lanh. Quang Nam Pr, I Corps.

River Run Quarry (YD 701-098)
Along Song Huu Trach River, apx 1 km SW FSB Birmingham and 14 km SSW Hue. Jul69-Jul70. Thua Thien Pr, I Corps.

Rivera, FSB? (ZS 03-79?)
Variant of Riviera? Apx 5 km SSE Ham Tan AF, 3 km W Binh Tuy (a.k.a. Lagi or La Gi), 3 km N ocean and 44 km SSW Phan Thiet. Per John Driscoll, D Bty, 5th/2d Arty was either here or at FSB Riviera during Tet '71, as were elements of 11 ACR. Binh Tuy Pr, III Corps.

Riverboat South (BT 621-013)
Near mouth of Song Tra Bong River and along its W bank, apx 8 km SE Chu Lai, and 27 km N Quang Ngai. Americal list. Quang Tin Pr, I Corps.

Riverside, LZ (YD 231-076)
Along Hwy 548, apx 12 km ESE Tou Rout and 52 km WSW Hue. Apr70 XXIV Corps grid per Don Armstrong. Quang Tri Pr, I Corps.

Riverside Airfield (YD 328-525)
See Quang Tri 1 AF. Quang Tri Pr, I Corps.

Riviera, FSB? (YS 98-84)
A.k.a. Ham Tam. Apx 58 km SE Xuan Loc, 42 km WSW Phan Thiet, 4 km NW Ham Tan and 9 km N the ocean. 2d/3d Inf, 3d/7th Inf, 199th LIB, '70. Per John Driscoll, D

Bty, 5th/2d Arty here at Tet '71, as were elements of 11 ACR. A FSB Rivera is listed at ZS 03-79. Grid per 199th LIB Assn. Binh Tuy Pr, III Corps.

Riviere de Quang Tri (YD 30-47)
A.k.a. Song Quang Tri and Riviere de Quang Tri. Drained area to W and SW Quang Tri. Quang Tri Pr, I Corps.

Riviere de Rao Quan Valley (XD 80-48)
Avenue of approach to Khe Sanh Plateau. See Rao Quan. Quang Tri Pr, I Corps.

Riviere de Sa Ky (BS 7-8)
At southern end of Batangan Peninsula, apx 17 km NE Quang Ngai? 15Jul67, Op here involving 71st AHC and 161st AHC suptg 2 ROK Marine Corps Bde. Quang Ngai or Quang Tin Pr, I Corps.

Riviere des Parfums (YD 8-3)
The Song Huong or River of Perfumes. Passes through Hue. See Song Huong for detail. Thua Thien Pr, I Corps.

RMK-BRJ Cam Ranh Depot (CP 055-212)
On W side of peninsula and due S the S end of main Cam Ranh AB rwy, apx 3 km and 3 km NNE the ammo docks. Khanh Hoa Pr, II Corps.

RMK-BRJ Main Office (XS 91-97?)
A.k.a. The Main Office. Saigon HQ of civilian contracting firm of Raymond, Morrison, Knudson, Brown, Root & Jones. May have been on Island in Song Saigon? Const AFs at numerous SVN locations, inc: Cam Ranh Bay, Phan Rang, Da Nang and Tuy Hoa. Also const deep-water ports such as Newport and Cam Ranh Bay. Operated the Saigon Island Depot. Gia Dinh Pr, III Corps.

RMK-BRJ Qui Nhon (CR 079-217)
Immed W the S end of Qui Nhon AF's main rwy. Binh Dinh Pr, II Corps.

Ro Heliport (ZC 042-233)
Just E the Song Cai River, apx 68 km due W Tam Ky and 15 km NNE Kham Duc SF Camp. Heliport #653, alt 328', per Feb73 TAD. Quang Tin Pr, I Corps.

Ro, Vung (CQ 2-2)
Vung Ro Bay. 12°52'N-109°26'E. Khanh Hoa Pr, II Corps.

Road, LZ (BR 363-457)
Original name of LZ Schueller? See Schueller for location. 2d/17th Arty here supt 1st Cav, 3Sep67. Data per Jack Picciolo. Binh Dinh Pr, II Corps.

Road 4-11 (BS)
Rte 518. Ran from Quang Ngai to FSB/LZ 4-11. Opened beginning 11Sep69 by 26th Engr Bn with 11th LIB security. Quang Ngai Pr, I Corps.

Road No. 6, Battle for (WJ 3-0)
After the 12Jan52 ambush of a river convoy near Notre Dame Rock ended river resupply efforts, Road No. 6 became the main means of re-supplying French defending Hao Binh. Had 10 strongpoints held by 1 Inf Bn, 1 Arty Bn, 2 Armored Bns and an Engr Grp. On 8Jan52, the Vietminh attacked the Xom Pheo strongpoint, overrunning much of it before withdrawing and leaving 700 of its own dead. On 9Jan52, the Vietminh destroyed almost an entire Mobile Bn, forcing closure of road. An Abn TF under Col Gilles then spent 11, very costly days of fighting to reopen Road 6 from Day River to Hoa Binh Salient, committing 12 Inf Bns to task. Gen. Salan, who succeeded the dying Gen. De Lattre in Jan52, realized futility of effort and ordered a complete withdrawal from Hoa Binh Salient. Data per *Street Without Joy*, p 55-, map at p 50. See Hoa Binh, Battle for. NVN.

Road Runner Teams (n/a)
See Glossary.

Rob, FSB (YT 262-916)
Along QL-14 apx 25 km NE Dong Xoai, 4 km NW Bunard AF and 24 km SW Duc Phong. Cited in *1st Cav Op Rpt, Feb-Apr70*, p 68, *1st Cav Op Rpt, May-Jul70*, p 38, per Peter Cole. Phuoc Long Pr, III Corps.

Robert, LZ (XT 508-665)
Apx 13 km due W Minh Thanh AF and 18 km NNE Dau Tieng AF/Tri Tam. Apr67. Tay Ninh Pr?, III Corps.

Robert A. Owens, USS (n/a)
DD-827, per Ralph Fries.

Roberts, LZ (YA 901-931)
On Chu Do Ridge, apx 14 km due W Polei Kleng AF, 3 km E Polei Meo, 3 km W FSB Mile-High. Originally opened 29Apr68 by elements of 1st/14th Inf, per op rpt courtesy Dick Arnold; however it is unknown if Roberts was its name at that time. 2de Bde/4th Div AO in Mar69. Fighting here involving 1st/12th Inf, 4-6Mar69 is described in detail in *Time Heals No Wounds*, p 128 et seq. Apparently 173d Abn here '68-69 (or at LZ with same name). Photos/maps of base at http://1-14th.com/maps.html. Also listed at YA 899-993. Kontum Pr, II Corps.

Roberts, Edmund (n/a)
See Glossary.

Roberts, Camp? (CP 04-54)
See Roberts Compound. Khanh Hoa Pr, II Corps.

Roberts Compound (CP 039-543)
A.k.a. Camp Roberts? Apx 2 km NE the NW end of Nha Trang AF main rwy, 600 meters NNW IFFV HQ and 500 meters W of the ocean. Khanh Hoa Pr, II Corps.

Robin, FSB/LZ (XD 912-333)
At N edge of Vietnam Salient, apx 37 km WSW Quang Tri, 6 km due S Lang Kat and 4 km NNW Lang Klung. Opened 2Jun68 by elements of 1st and 4th Marines, 3d Mar Div during Ops Robin North and Robin South, Jun68, ops against 308th NVA Div's 88th and 102d Rgts. Also listed at XD 907-278, Sep68 and 912-335, Nov68. Apr70 XXIV Corps grid per Don Armstrong. Quang Tri Pr, I Corps.

Robin, FSB (YS 435-764)
Apx 9 km N Nui Dat, 3 km SW FSB Alanbrooke and 2 km W FSB Le Loi/LTL-2. FSBs Maureen, Robin and Rhode Island all appear to have been within very close proximity to one another and may be succession of bases on same site since it is unlikely they would have coexisted. On 1ATF NCO trng map per John Hollett. Phuoc Tuy Pr, III Corps.

Robin, FSB (YT 89-46)
Apx 19 km NNW Tanh Linh AF and 20 km NE Vo Dat. 4th/12th Inf, 199th LIB. Binh Tuy Pr, III Corps.

Robin, LZ (BS 428-024)
Apx 26 km SSE Gia Vuc AF and 45 km due W LZ English/QL-1. Mar66. Binh Dinh Pr, II Corps.

Robin, LZ (XD 9-4?)
Along W side QL-9, apx 3 km WNW Ca Lu, 5 km SW LZ Stud and 10 km E Khe Sanh CB. 2 USMC Cos air assaulted here 3Apr68 during Op Pegasus, then swept W toward Khe Sanh. Quang Tri Pr, I Corps.

Robin, LZ (YD 073-664)
Apx 3 km S southern edge DMZ, 4 km WSW Thon An Hoa, 19 km WNW Dong Ha CB and 1.7 km SE LZ Dove. Was at E end Song Nang Valley (Helicopter Valley), and used during Op Hastings, 16Jul66. Quang Tri Pr, I Corps.
Robin, LZ (YS 111-503)
Near old French fort, apx 2 km from coast of Vinh Ganh Rai Bay, 6 km WSW Can Gio and 17 km WNW Vung Tau. Mar66. Gia Dinh Pr, III Corps.
Robin, LZ (ZC 135-655)
Overlooking Happy Valley, apx 32 km WSW Da Nang, 12 km N Ha Tan AF and 3 km NE FSB Rattlesnake. Used by BLT 3d/26th Marines, 1st Mar Div during Op Oklahoma Hills, 30Mar or 1Apr69. Mar-Apr69. On map at p 109, *US Marines in Vietnam-1969*. Quang Nam Pr, I Corps.
Robin, Operation (n/a)
10-17Oct66. 173d Abn, Phu My/Bearcat. Bde secured QL-15 from Bearcat S to Phu My for newly arrived 3d Bde/4th Div. Phuoc Tuy Pr, III Corps.
Robin, Outpost (AT 905-820)
Apx 5 km WSW Red Beach AF and 12 km WNW Da Nang AB. Jul70. Quang Nam Pr, I Corps.
Robin Grey, SS (n/a)
Commercial transport under govt contract, per Ralph Fries.
Robin Radio Relay (Pic ROBIN) (BP 221-190)
See Radio Relay (Pic Robin). Tuyen Duc Pr, II Corps.
Robinson Hall (XS 83-97?)
At Tan Son Nhut AB. Named to honor LTC Lewis M. Robinson, USAF, KIA 4Jun67. Gia Dinh Pr, III Corps.
Robinson, USNS (n/a)
Primarily an MSC ammunition ship. See *Tears Before the Rain*, p 112. SVN.
Robinson, USS (n/a)
DDG-12. Guided-Missile DD, per Ralph Fries.
Robot (n/a)
Apr70, XXIV Corps future-use 101st Abn FSB name.
Rocher Noir, Baie du (BT 0-8)
Bay at 16°06'N-108°15'E. On ND49-01 JOG. Quang Nam Pr, I Corps.
Rock, Camp (ZT 065-792?)
A.k.a. Bao Loc. Just N II Corps/III Corps border, apx 80 km SW Dalat, 3 km SW Tan Phat AF, SE Nhon Co, NW Phan Thiet and roughly midway between coast and Cambodian border. Basecamp of 3d/503d Inf, 173d Abn in '68-69. See Bao Loc SF Camp. Lam Dong Pr, II Corps.
Rock, FSB (YT 485-349)
Along QL-20 near its crossing of Song La Nga River, apx 8 km WSW Dinh Quan, 3 km WSW Ap 107, 10 km NE Xa Binh Hoa and 26 km N to NNE Xuan Loc. 1st/8th Cav, 1st Cav, May69, AO Commanche Warrior. Grid per Frank Penk, Jr. Cited in 1st Cav VN *Yearbook* Aug65-Dec69, p 290, per Peter Cole. L-7014-6431-2 map? An LZ Rock is at XT 483-553? Long Khanh Pr, III Corps.
Rock, LZ (BR 625-586)
In Vinh Thanh Valley, apx 2 km SE Vinh Thanh AF, 3 km N Vinh Thanh and 21 km NE An Khe. Oct65. Binh Dinh Pr, II Corps.
Rock, LZ ? (XD 978-558)
See Rockpile, The. Quang Tri Pr, I Corps.
Rock, LZ (XT 483-553)
Apx 6 km due N Dau Tieng AF. May69. See FSB Rock at YT 485-349. Binh Duong Pr?, III Corps.
Rock, The (n/a)
See Glossary.
Rock Apes (n/a)
See Glossary.
Rock Crusher, FSB (XT 264-565)
See Rockcrusher, FSB. Tay Ninh Pr, III Corps.
Rock Crusher, FSB (YD 989-041?)
A.k.a. Hill 162 or FSB Greer? Appears to have been apx 17 km SE Phu Bai, WSW FSB Roy, SE FSB Anzio and SW Dam Cau Hai Bay and QL-1. Thua Thien Pr, I Corps.
Rock Crusher, LZ (BT 108-428)
Along Hwy 535, apx 5 km SW LZ Baldy, 35 km SSE Da Nang AB, 15 km SSW Hoi An, 11 km NE Que Son and 7 km NE Gang Dong. Per Americal website list, there was a rock quarry here used by US Engrs that also employed civilians workers. Quang Nam Pr, I Corps.
Rock Crusher, The (AT 94-75?)
Near Dai La Pass. Briefly 7th Marine HQ before move to Hill 10, Aug69. Quang Nam Pr, I Corps.
Rock Crusher, The (AT 938-747)
Apx 7 km W Da Nang AB. Also listed at AT 952-750 and 924-749, 68-69. Quang Nam Pr, I Corps.
Rock Crusher, The (XT 267-565)
A.k.a. 588th Engr Bn Rockcrusher. At base of Nui Ba Den mtn, apx 6.5 km NNE Tay Ninh, 4 km ESE FSB Buell II and 2.3 km SW the Nui Ba Den Signal Site. Source of crushed rock and const materials for bases in Tay Ninh TAOR. Secured by elements of 25th Inf's 1st Bde and operated by 588th Engrs in '68. Good maps of location and discussions of nearby '68 battles in *The Infantry Brigade in Combat*. Also listed at XT 264-565 and 268-566. Listed grid per Butch Sincock. Map is TL-7014-6231-4 (Tay Ninh). Tay Ninh Pr, III Corps.
Rock Crusher, The (YD 805-088)
Apx 1 km NW FSB Arsenal, and 10 km S Hue. Nam Hoa District, Thua Thien Pr, I Corps.
Rock Crusher, The (YD)
A.k.a. Vinh Dai Rock Crusher. On QL-9, E of the Khe Gio Bridge? Quang Tri Pr, I Corps.
Rock Crusher, The (YD 736-135)
Along W bank Song Huong River, apx 10 km due S Hue Citadel AF and 2.5 km NNW Pho/Nam Hoa Bridge. Aug67. Thua Thien Pr, I Corps.
Rock Crusher, The (ZD 021-021)
Apx 8 km WNW Q Phu Loc, 19 km SE Phu Bai AF and 2 km S QL-1. Apr68. Thua Thien Pr, I Corps.
Rock Crusher, The (ZD 027-003)
Apx 7 km W Phu Loc, 20 km SE Phu Bai and perhaps 2-3 km S of QL-1, near Dam Cau Hai Bay. USMC quarry site. Thua Thien Pr, I Corps.
Rock Island East (YU 010-440)
Incursion FSB, May70. Apx 8 km NW Phum Leu, 5 km SE Phum Sre Preah, 10 km N to NNW point where QL-14A met border and 6 km due W FSB Myron. 1st Cav, 11th ACR, 199th LIB. Also listed at YU 030-340? Cambodia.
Rock Pile (various)
See Rockpile.

Rock Pile (BS)
Americal AO, W of Quang Ngai. See Rockpile (one word). No other data. Quang Ngai Pr, I Corps.
Rock Pile POW Camp, The (WH or XH)
See Rockpile POW Camp. NVN.
Rock Quarry (XT 265-565)
See Rock Crusher at listed grid. Tay Ninh Pr, III Corps.
Rock Quarry, FSB (ZA 055-319)
Apx 6 km NW Oasis AF, 15 km WSW Catecka AF and 26 km SW Pleiku. Apparently an Engr quarry that in Nov69 was defended by D Bty, 5th/16th Cav, 4th Div. 10th Cav, and 1st/92d Arty, 4th Div also here, per Bob Patsfield. Grid courtesy Jim Henderson per 4th Div ORLL of 31Jan70. Pleiku Pr, II Corps.
Rock Quarry, The (XD 832-418)
Basalt outcropping apx 1 km W 3d/26th Marine perimeter at SW end of Khe Sanh CB. Detail Bravo of NCBM Unit 301 had a rock crusher here and used the gravel to add a 5" to 8" base to repair erosion caused to rwy by heavy rain. 36-man Det from NSA, Da Nang, trucked gravel to rwy from site beginning 2Sep67. Secured by 1st/9th Marines during siege, '67-68. Mislabeled map showing layout of position is at p 388 (also at p 1) of *Valley of Decision*. Quang Tri Pr, I Corps.
Rock Quarry, The (XT 965-080)
Apx 6 km SW Bien Hoa AB. Also listed at XT 967-077. Bien Hoa Pr, III Corps.
Rock Quarry, The (ZA 057-313)
Apx 6 km NW Oasis AF and 25 km SW Pleiku. Jul68-Jan70. Pleiku Pr, II Corps.
Rockcrusher, FSB? (XT 264-565)
At southern base of Nui Ba Den Mtn, apx 3 km S its peak and 6 km NNE Tay Ninh. Also site of 58th Engr Bn's rockcrusher facility and quarry. Name/grid per Peter Cole. Tay Ninh Pr, III Corps.
Rockcrusher, Operation (n/a)
A.k.a. Thoan Thang 43. Southern Cambodian Invasion of May-Jun70. See Task Force Shoemaker. Cambodia.
Rocket, FSB (YC 398-903)
Along W edge of A Shau Valley, apx 12 km SSE Hamburger Hill, 12 km NW A Sap and 47 km SW Hue. Oct69. Thua Thien Pr, I Corps.
Rocket Box, The (ZA 145-535)
Generally 12 km NW Pleiku, 13 km WNW Pleiku/Cu Hanh AF, 3 km N Plei Blo O'Dung and 15 km SSE Plei Mrong. 4th Div AO, '70. Data per Jim Claeys. Pleiku Pr, II Corps.
Rocket City (BT 03-78)
Nickname for Da Nang. Quang Nam Pr, I Corps.
Rocket City (XT)
25th Inf Div's general nickname for Angel's Wing/Parrot's Beak region of Cambodian border, due W Cu Chi. Tay Ninh/Hau Nghia Prvs, III Corps.
Rocket Pocket (BT 48-03)
Area apx 8 km SW Chu Lai, used by VC/NVA for launching 122mm rockets and mortar fire on Chu Lai area. Quang Tin Pr, I Corps.
Rocket Ridge (BT 42-00)
Ridge to W and overlooking Chu Lai, running from BT 42-00 to BT 54-00. Inc Hills 707 and 747, among others, and was worked at times by elements of 1st/6th Inf, 198th LIB. Quang Tin Pr, I Corps.
Rocket Ridge (YB 970-150)
Apx 8 km SSW Dak To 2 AF, and 40 km NW Kontum. Kontum Pr, II Corps.
Rocket Ridge (YB/ZA)
Ran from YB 93-24 to ZA 08-95, beginning about 10 km W Dak To 2 AF then SSE to point apx 20 km from Kontum. Roughly paralleled QL-14 at 15 km distance. ARVN FSB's 1, 2, 3, 4, 5, 6, 7, Charlie and Delta were lined along ridge and became focus of NVA attacks during '72 Offensive. Discussed in *A Bright Shining Lie*. See also FSB entries mentioned above. Kontum Pr, II Corps.
Rocket Ridge (YB/ZB)
Ran roughly from YB 93-24 SSE to ZA 08-93, generally W of QL-14, between Tan Canh and Kontum. Ridge starts near Ben Het on N, and ends at Polei Kleng on S. There were at least 6 FSBs built along ridge, most of which were primarily ARVN (see Firebase 6). Kontum Pr, II Corps.
Rocket Ridge (YD 52-23)
Apx 9 km due W Hue. Nickname for Nui Bai Cay Tat Mtn hill mass. So named because it was common NVA/VC 122mm Rocket launching zone at the fringe of their maximum eff range. FSBs Helen, Meredith, Rakkasan and Stella were scattered through area. Thua Thien Pr, I Corps.
Rocket Valley (YD 05-52?)
E of FSB Vandegrift. Common nickname for NVA 122mm rocket launching sites in SVN. Quang Tri Pr, I Corps.
Rocket Valley (YD 780-050)
Small valley immed SE Nui Ke, and apx 14 km S Hue. Common name for NVA rocket launching sites throughout SVN. Thua Thien Pr, I Corps.
Rocket, FSB (YC 398-904)
Very remote site along W edge of A Shau Valley, apx 5 km from Laos, 6 km SE Bou Aie Ha, 13 km WNW A Sap and 45 km SW Hue. Apr70 XXIV Corps grid per Don Armstrong. Thua Thien Pr, I Corps.
Rockpile (BS)
See Rock Pile. Quang Ngai Pr, I Corps.
Rockpile, The (XD 979-559)
A.k.a. Thon Khe Tri. Along QL-9, apx 26 km W Quang Tri, and a 16 km S southern edge of DMZ. Famous Marine OP and terrain feature atop 230-meter high, jagged, almost solid-rock, twin-peaked promontory. Was very difficult to attack by ground and entirely manned and supplied by air. Perhaps most significant landmark in I Corps, it dominated horizon between Khe Sanh CB and Camp Carroll in Razorback Valley. Actually comprised of 2 peaks known as "the Wings of Angels" by Viets. 1st unit here was 1st Force Recon, who were inserted 16Jul66, during Op Hastings. See Wings of Angels, Razorback Valley and Little Rockpile. Quang Tri Pr, I Corps.
Rockpile POW Camp, The (WH or XH)
Nickname for POW camp perhaps 40 km SSE to SE Hanoi, and W the Red River, along one of its tributaries. On map at www.soft-vision.com/ hanoi/frame.html. NVN.
Rockpile Radio Relay Site (XD 979-559)
A.k.a. Thon Khe Tri. Along QL-9, apx 26 km W Quang Tri. Described by 3d Recon Bn vet George Neville as, "Probably the most significant" relay site of his tour. During Fall of 66, its call-sign was "Field Clerk Whiskey."

See Angel's Wings, Rockpile and Little Rockpile. Quang Tri Pr, I Corps.

Rocky, LZ (BR 703-872)
In Song Lao River valley apx 12 km WNW Ha Tay, 16 km WSW Bong Son. Oct66. Binh Dinh Pr, II Corps.

Rod, LZ (ZA 015-449)
Along Stream, apx 7 km WSW Ban Duc and 24 km WSW Pleiku. Jan66. Pleiku Pr, II Corps.

Rodeo, LZ (YD 158-049)
Within a few km N Lao border, apx 8 km SSE Tou Rout, 3 km E FSB Bear and 58 km WSW Hue. Apr70 XXIV Corps grid per Don Armstrong. Quang Tri Pr, I Corps.

Rodriguez, Camp (YD 815-148)
A.k.a. Camp Eagle and/or Camp Rodriguez. Along Rte 546, apx 7 km SW Hue and 3 km W QL-1. Built apx 500-1,000 meters SE Camp Eagle beginning 4Mar68, by C/307th Eng, 82d Abn. Named to honor the 3d Bde/82d Abn's first VN casualty, SSG Joe S. Rodriguez, C/1st/505th Inf, KIA 29Feb68. Later its positions were blended into those of Camp Eagle as Eagle grew in size and 82d departed I Corps. Discussion of its const, map, photo of base and its sign can be found in *All The Way-The 3d Bde, 82d Abn Div in Vietnam, 1968*, pp 6-8, which show the 2 bases as separate sites; however, one 82d vet tells us it was simply 1 big camp with 82d responsible for portion of perimeter. Grid/Info per Butch Sincock. 3rd Bde/82d Abn. See Camp Eagle. Thua Thien Pr, I Corps.

Rogers, USS (n/a)
DD 876. With *USS Bainbridge*, assisted *USS Enterprise* (CVAN 65) the carrier's serious fire of 14Jan69. Data per www.uss-salem.org/features/fires/. See also *USS Enterprise* and *Coontz, USS*.

Rogtoampung U Minh (VQ/WQ/WR)
See U Minh Forest. An Xuyen Pr, IV Corps.

Rohr, FSB (XT 005-775)
Apx 5 km from Cambodian border, apx 8 km WSW Thien Ngon AF, 34 km WSW Katum and 36 km NW Tay Ninh. Was also apx 4 km WNW FSB Michael and 3 km NW FSB Disantis. Tay Ninh Pr, III Corps.

Roi Et Airfield (UC 5-7)
Apx 420 km NE Bangkok, 160 km NW Ubon AB, near 16°04'00"N-103°39'00"E, per ONC K-10. Thailand.

ROK Army Airfield (AAF) (BR 948-209)
See ROK Strip. Binh Dinh Pr, II Corps.

ROK Strip Airfield (BR 948-209)
A.k.a. ROK AAF AF. Korean forces' AF apx 12 km due W Qui Nhon. Minor US AF here per TPC K-10B. El. 60', 3,000' steel-mat rwy. At 13°44'57"N-109°06'03"E. Binh Dinh Pr, II Corps.

ROK Valley (BQ or CQ)
Apparently S Qui Nhon, near and W of Song Cau. Likely so named because it was ROK Korean force AO at one time. On Agent Orange FSB Map produced by Grand Lake Nam Vets, courtesy Ken Thompson. Phu Yen Pr, II Corps.

ROKA Army Heliport (CP 022-584)
A.k.a. ROKA (Republic of Korea) Logistical Cmd Army Heliport. Apx 6 km NNW Nha Trang AF, 4 km NNE the Nha Trang city limits and about 2 km S QL-1. "Heliport #760, 66', PSP, Fuel J4, Opr 2400-1000Z. One heliport, 7 pads. Contact gnd con for Ldg instructions 5 min out. Limited tran prkg. Gnd Con-68.05, 381.2, 33.1, 384.0," per Feb73 TAD. Khanh Hoa Pr, II Corps.

ROKA Log Cmd Army Heliport (CP 022-584)
See ROKA Army Heliport. Khanh Hoa Pr, II Corps.

Roker BEQ (XS 8-9)
Saigon enlisted quarters. Possibly named to honor PFC Jonathan C. Roker, USMC 13Jun66. Data per *Vietnam Military Lore, 1959-1973*. Gia Dinh Pr, III Corps.

Rokew BEQ (XS 8-9)
In Saigon. Data per *Vietnam Military Lore, 1959-1973*. Gia Dinh Pr, III Corps.

Roll On-Roll Off Freighters (n/a)
See *Lt Col John U. D. Page* Army Vessel.

Rolland, Camp (YU 6-5)
On SVN border apx 125 km WNW Dalat, 8 km NNW Bu Prang, 85 km SW Ban Me Thuot and 280 km ENE Phnom Penh on Feb67 Natl Geo map. El. 3,000'. Cambodia.

Rolland Airfield, Camp (YU 6-5)
A.k.a. Dak Dam AF. On Cambodia/SVN border apx 125 km WNW Dalat, 8 km NNW Bu Prang, 85 km SW Ban Me Thuot and 280 km ENE Phnom Penh. Feb67 Natl Geo map. El. 3,000'. Cambodia.

Rolling Thunder, Operation (NVN)
Code name for USAF bombing of NVN that began in Mar65 in response to Gulf of Tonkin Incident, and then escalated through 7 phases, each ending with bombing halts, until it ended N of the 19th Parallel, 1Nov68. The White House controlled target selection throughout Rolling Thunder. 3 wks after Op Flaming Dart II, USAF and VNAF started Rolling Thunder with strikes on Xom Bang and Quang Khe. 2d Rolling Thunder op took place 15Mar65, as USN sent 64 Skyhawks and Skyraiders plus 30 suptg acft from TF 77 carriers *USS Hancock* and *Ranger* to hit Phu Qui ammo depot. Over 920 US acft were lost during Op and over 640,000 tons of bombs dropped. Most B-52 strikes of op were flown from Guam.

Rollins, FSB (XT 301-502)
See FSB Rawlins. Tay Ninh Pr, III Corps.

Romanelli, Camp (YD 204-593)
Near Rtes 557 and 559, apx 5 km WSW Dong Ha, 16 km NW Quang Tri and 7 km due E Cam Lo. Possibly named to honor HN Louis V. Romanelli, KIA 16Mar69. USMC and 5th Mech Div base? Aug69. Quang Tri Pr, I Corps.

Rome Plow (n/a)
See Glossary.

Rome Plow Base Camp (BR)
Apparently near LZ Uplift or English. per '70 Bn Annual Hist Supp of 3/503d Inf, 173d Abn at www.gasparot.com/nammedic. Presumably home of Rome Plow Engr units demolishing 173d Abn positions as it stood-down in late '70. Binh Dinh Pr, II Corps.

Rome Plow Camp (generally)
See Glossary.

Rome Plow Camp (XS 883-733)
Apx 35 km ENE Nui Dat/Luscombe AF, 7 km N Binh Chau and coast, and 24 km SW Ham Tan AF. Oct70. Phouc Tuy Pr, III Corps.

Romeo, LZ (BR 763-703)
Apx 15 km WNW Phu My/QL-1, 14 km SSW Ha Tay AF and 37 km NE An Khe. Sep66. Binh Dinh Pr, II Corps.

Romeo CAP (n/a)
See CAP Romeo listings. I Corps.
Ron (n/a)
Mapsheet name of L-7014-6244-1. NVN only.
Ron Ma, Cape Mui (XF 5-0)
A.k.a. Mui Ron. Coastal point at 18°07'N-106°27'E. On NE48-07 JOG. NVN.
Ron Ma, Mui (XF 5-0)
A.k.a. Mui Ron. Coastal point at 18°07'N-106°27'E. On NE48-07 JOG. NVN.
Ron, Cape Mui (XF 5-0)
A.k.a. Mui Ron. Coastal point at 18°07'N-106°27'E. On NE48-07 JOG. NVN.
Ron, Cape (XF 5-0)
See Cape Ron. NVN.
Ron, Mui (XF 5-0)
Coastal point at 18°07'N-106°27'E. NE48-07 Map. NVN.
Rond, Mui (WG 8-4)
Coastal point at 19°24'N-105°47'E. NE48-03 Map. NVN.
Rong, Mui (WF 7-8)
Coastal point at 18°50'N-105°44'E. NE48-07 Map. NVN.
Rong Rong Valley (YC 860-830)
See Ruong Ruong Valley. Thua Thien, I Corps.
Rook, LZ (YA 830-098)
Apx 4 km E Cambodia, 16 km S Duc Co AF and 9 km NNW peak Chu Pong Mtn. Jan66. Pleiku Pr, II Corps.
Rookie, LZ (YD 118-187)
Apx 7 km NNW Tou Rout, 3 km WSW FSB Ranger and 61 km W Hue. Apr70 XXIV Corps grid per Don Armstrong. Quang Tri Pr, I Corps.
Root, LZ (BS 7-0?)
Overlooking and on W side of An Lao River Valley, apx 17 km NW Bong Son, 13 km SW Nuoc Giaoe and 5 km WSW LZ Lion. Used during Op Masher/White Wing, 28Jan-6Mar66. Detailed discussion of Ops Masher/White Wing and this LZ in *A Contagion of War* vol, *Vietnam Experience* series, pp 32-48, with map showing site at p 38. 2d/7th Cav, 1st Cav LZ. Binh Dinh Pr, II Corps.
Rope, LZ (BN 610-523)
Along QL-1 at coast, apx 5 km ENE Vinh Hoa, 35 km SW Phan Rang and 34 km ENE Hai Ninh/Song Mao AF. Mar67. Binh Thuan Pr, II Corps.
Rope, LZ (BR 393-337)
Apx 14 km SW An Khe. Dec65. Binh Dinh Pr, II Corps.
Rope, LZ (BR 615-870)
Apx 8 km WNW Nghia Nhon and 26 km WSW Bong Son. Mar-Oct66. Binh Dinh Pr, II Corps.
Rose, Camp (ZV 025-267)
A.k.a. Camp Gerald B. Rose, Ban Don and Trang Phuc SF Camp. Along TL-1 and immed E the Da Krong (Ea Krong) River, 500 meters W Ban Don AF and 36 km NW Ban Me Thuot. 5th SF camp/FOB with Det. A-3, here Dec64. Renamed Camp Gerald B. Rose to honor Sp5 Gerald Rose, KIA 22Feb65, in ambush on Mang Yang Pass. Chapter devoted to Rose in Ray Bows' *Vietnam Military Lore-Legends, Shadows and Heroes*, p 799-808. Info/grid per *SF Order of Battle*. See Ban Don AF. Darlac Pr, II Corps.
Rose, FSB (XT 206-770)
A.k.a. FSB Sondra? Apx 16 km SW Katum AF, 7 km W Prek Klok, 23 km NNW Nui Ba den and 28 km due N Tay Ninh. Tay Ninh Pr, III Corps.
Rose, LZ (BR 545-533)
Apx 10 km NE An Khe AF and 11 km SSW Vinh Thanh AF. Dec65. Binh Dinh Pr, II Corps.
Rose, LZ (n/a)
No data. Possible misspelling of LZ Ross? Listed in USAF Herbicide gallonage rpt indicates total gallonages of following agents were sprayed within an 8 km radius of this site: Orange, 15405; White, 6720; Blue, 18508. I Corps.
Rose, LZ (XU 590-040)
Apx 15 km WSW Loc Ninh AF, 3 km E Cambodia and 14 km N tip of Fishhook. Jul66. Binh Long Pr, III Corps.
Rose, LZ (YA 612-509)
At S entrance to Plei Trap Valley, apx 2 km N Cambodian border, 6 km NE Phum To Lay and 63 km W Pleiku. Jan66. Kontum Pr, II Corps.
Rosencranz (XT?)
Location unknown. 7th/11th Arty, 25th Div here, '68. Data per Dan Gillotti, 15th Arty Assn. III Corps.
Rosencranz II? (XT?)
Presumed to have existed? III Corps.
Rosencranz III (XT?)
7th/11th Arty, 25th Div said to have been here, '68. Data per Dan Gillotti, 15th Arty Assn. III Corps.
Ross, LZ (BT 025-343)
A.k.a. Hill 51, FSB and CB Ross. Just SE intersection of Rtes 535 and 536 in Que Son Valley, apx 2 km SW Que Son, 27 km SSW Hoi An, 24 km NW Tam Ky and 42 km due S Da Nang. Commanded Que Son Valley region. Author of *Son Thang* described it as situated near Rte 535 and built on 2 low knolls separated by a saddle and defended by two 105mm Btys, two 8" cannons, an 81mm Plt and two M-48 tanks. He said Arty units were positioned on lower, eastern knoll, and 7th Marines cantonment on higher, western knoll. Also had six-50' tall observation towers. 1st, 2d and 3d Bns, 7th Marines, 1st Mar Div rotated through Ross, Ryder and LZ Baldy, '69-70. G Bty, 3d/11th Mar Arty also here. 2d/12th Cav here and on LZ Leslie were heavily attacked at 0140 hrs, 2Jan68. On 6Jan70, 409th Local Force VC Bn attacked at 0130 hrs during monsoon rain. Attack included 200 mortar rnds plus RPGs from 20 sappers who got inside wire, but with fire supt from FSBs Ryder and Baldy, VC were repulsed at 0330, leaving 39 VC KIA, 18 USMC KIA/63 WIA.[472] Elements of 1st Cav overrun here 19Aug72. Used also as Helo refueling point between LZ Baldy and Hiep Duc. Also listed at BT 028-34 and 027-341. Cited in 1st Cav VN *Yearbook* Aug65-Dec69, p 54, 129, 211, per Peter Cole. Quang Nam Pr, I Corps.
Ross 2, LZ (BT 029-341)
A.k.a. FSB Excedrin? Along Hwy 535 at Que Son, apx 17 km SW LZ Baldy, 27 km S Hoi An, 14 km SE FSB Ryder, S Ngai Ha Valley, 24 km NW Tam Ky and ESE Antenna Valley. Apparently an adjunct of LZ Ross and a few hundred meters to its E? This designation may instead simply represent site of a second helicopter pad at Ross? See LZ Ross. Quang Nam Pr, I Corps.
Ross Compound (CP 04-53?)
At Nha Trang. HQ of 1FFV Arty and Camp J. F. McDermott here. Named to honor 1Lt Ronald A Ross, USA, firing plt CO, Bty C, 1st/92d Arty, who was with 5th

Bn/22d Arty before volunteering to replace wounded 92d Arty Off, KIA 31Oct69, during Battle for LZ Kate in Quang Duc Pr, and while carrying wounded Vietnamese to safety. Grid is rough est. Data per *Vietnam Military Lore, 1959-1973*. Khanh Hoa Pr, II Corps.

Rotation Tour Date (n/a)
See Glossary.

Rouge, Pointe (US 9-1)
See Pointe Rouge. Kien Giang Pr, IV Corps.

Round Bottom, LZ (YA 937-852)
Apx 31 km W Kontum and 13 km SW Polei Kleng AF. 4th Div. Near LZs Bunker Hill, Brillo-Pad and Alamo. 3d/12th Inf, Jan69. Also sp Roundbottom. Kontum Pr, II Corps.

Round Rock, FSB (XT 75-63)
See Roundrock, FSB. Binh Duong Pr, III Corps.

Round Top, FSB (YA 962-855)
See Roundtop. Kontum Pr, II Corps.

Round Up, LZ (AT 999-315)
A.k.a. Hill 270. Apx 44 km due S Da Nang AB and 6 km WNW Binh Son. 71. Quang Nam Pr, I Corps.

Roundbottom, LZ (YA 937-852)
See Round Bottom. Kontum Pr, II Corps.

Roundrock, FSB (XT 75-63)
Apx 3 km W Chon Thonh AF, 14 km ESE Minh Thanh AF and 60 km N Saigon. Binh Duong Pr, III Corps.

Roundtop, FSB (YA 962-855)
Near Cambodian border apx 10 km due W Polei Kleng SF Camp, 38 km WNW Kontum and 30 km SSW Dak To. Per Tom Lacombe, in Jan69 this was his unit's primary FSB and was only known to them as Roundtop. Same grid is also used to describe FSB Brillo-pad in number of lists? Map is L-7014-6537-4. Kontum Pr, II Corps.

Roundup (n/a)
6Apr70, XXIV Corps future-use III MAF FSB name, actually built in '71. Quang Nam Pr, I Corps.

Roundup, LZ (AT 999-315)
See Round Up. Quang Nam Pr, I Corps.

Roung Roung Valley (YC 860-830)
See Ruong Ruong Valley. Thua Thien, I Corps.

Route (road system) (N/A)
See Glossary.

Route 1 (numerous)
A.k.a. QL-1 and Highway One. See QL-1. I, II & III Corps.

Route 1A (XT)
See QL-1A. III Corps.

Route 2 (YS)
See QL-2. Long Khanh/Phuoc Tuy Prvs, III Corps.

Route 3A (BR?)
See QL-3A. II Corps.

Route 4 (numerous)
See QL-4 (III, IV Corps), and also LTL-4 (I Corps).

Route 5 (XS)
See LTL-5A. III/IV Corps.

Route 7A (XS/XR)
See LTL-7A. IV Corps.

Route 7B (AR/BQ/CQ)
See LTL-7B. II Corps.

Route 8A (VS/WS/WT)
See LTL-8A. IV Corps.

Route 8B (ZA/AR?)
See LTL-8B. II Corps.

Route 9 (WS/XD/YD)
See QL 9 (I Corps) and LTL-9 (IV Corps).

Route 10 (WS)
See LTL 10. IV Corps.

Route 11 (BP/CP)
See QL-11. II Corps.

Route 13 (XT)
See QL-13. A.k.a. Thunder Road. III Corps.

Route 14 (numerous)
See QL-14. I, II/III Corps.

Route 14S and 14N (numerous)
See QL-14. II Corps.

Route 15 (YT/YS)
See QL-15. III Corps.

Route 19 (ZA/AR/BR)
See QL-19. II Corps.

Route 19E and 19W (ZA/AR/BR)
See QL-19. II Corps.

Route 20 (YT/ZT/AN/BN/BP)
See QL-20. II/III Corps.

Route 21 (AQ/BQ/BP/CP)
See QL-21. II Corps.

Route 21A (BP)
See QL-21A. III Corps.

Route 23 (YS/ZS)
See LTL-23. Phuoc Tuy/Binh Tuy Prvs, III Corps.

Route 24 (XS)
See TL-24. IV Corps.

Route 26 (XS)
See TL-26. IV Corps.

Route 27 (WS/WR/XR)
See LTL-27. IV Corps.

Route 31 (WS/WR)
See LTL-31. IV Corps.

Route 92 (n/a)
Intersected Rte 9 E of Tchepone (after Ql-9 exited SVN near Khe Sanh). Laos.

Route 401 (AN 900-105)
See Highway 401. Binh Thuan Pr, II Corps.

Route 512 (YB 90-27)
Generally E Ben Het. Kontum Pr, II Corps.

Route 516 (BS)
Rtes 516/517 were known as Minh Thanh Road. See Minh Thanh Road. Quang Ngai Pr?, I Corps.

Route 517 (BS)
See Route 516. Quang Ngai Pr?, I Corps.

Route 518 (BS)
A.k.a. LZ 4-11 Road. Ran from Quang Ngai to FSB/LZ 4-11. Opened beginning 11Sep69 by 26th Engr Bn with 11th LIB security. Quang Ngai Pr, I Corps.

Route 534 (BT?)
See Highway 534, The Old French Road. Americal list. Quang Tin Pr, I Corps.

Route 535 (AT/BT)
See Highway 535. The Tien Phuoc Highway, Americal list. Quang Nam/Quang Tin Pr, I Corps.

Route 540 (AT 82-57)
See Highway 540. Quang Tri Pr, I Corps.

Route 545 (YD 87-00)
See. Rifle Road and Highway 545. Thua Thien Pr, I Corps.

Route 547 (YD 755-144)
See Highway 547. Thua Thien Pr, I Corps.
Route 548 (XD/YD)
See Highway 548. Quang Tri Pr, I Corps.
Route 551 (YD 83-31)
Ran from YD 826-312 to YD 780-260. See Highway 551. Thua Thien Pr, I Corps.
Route 554 (YD 690-342)
See Highway 554. Thua Thien Pr, I Corps.
Route 556/558 (YD 121-429)
Within view of Hill 819 Radio Relay Site. Grid is at their intersection. See also India Relay. Quang Tri Pr, I Corps.
Route 559 (YD)
See Highway 559. Quang Tri Pr, I Corps.
Route 561 (YD)
See Highway 561. Quang Tri Pr, I Corps.
Route 598 (YD 608-255)
See Highway 598. Grid is on road at Ap Lai Bang. Thua Thien Pr, I Corps.
Route 614 (YC/ZC/AT?)
See Highway 614. A.k.a. the Yellow Brick Road. Quang Nam and Thua Thien Prvs, I Corps.
Route 615 (YA?)
See Plei Trap Road. II Corps.
Route 922 (XD/YD)
By Jan69, NVA were moving as many as 1,000 vehicles into SVN along Rte 922 and through the Da Krong River valley. XXIV Corps responded with Op Dewey Canyon, a multi-Bde op into Lao border area N of the A Shau to interdict, destroy supply depots and engage NVA in area. During op, USMC captured 1 dozen 122mm arty pieces (1st time found inside SVN) and destroyed some 525 tons of munitions and supplies. Est 1,335 NVA KIA. See Highway 548. Quang Tri Pr, I Corps.
Route 966 (n/a)
In Laos, W Chu Lai.
Route 966 (n/a)
See Highway 966. In Laos, W Chu Lai.
Route Coloniale (n/a)
See Glossary.
Route Coloniale 4 (n/a)
See R.C. 4. NVN.
Route Coloniale Ba Na (n/a)
See R.C. Ba Na. Quang Nam Pr, I Corps.
Route La (n/a)
Location unknown. Rail and vehicle bridges along this route hit during Carrier TF-77 attacks to blunt NVA Tet '68 offensive. NVN.
Route Orange (XT 74-33 to XT 89-02?)
Ran from QL-13 just S Ben Cat, E to Rte 16, passing Tam Binh (XT 89-02?) to its S. Basecamp s 1, 2 and 3 were camps built by and for 1st US Engr Bn, 1st Inf Div Engrs during Op Rolling Stone, 10Feb-3Mar66, to facilitate const of Route Orange. Camps were spread out along proposed path of Orange. All were generally S and SE Lai Khe and were built near Laterite Pits used for mining materials needed for road surfacing. For discussion, see *Infantry in Vietnam,* pp 223-228. Binh Duong Pr, III Corps.
Route Package (n/a)
See Glossary.
Route Packages 1 and 2 (n/a)
See Glossary.
Route R.C. 4 (n/a)
See R.C. 4, *Route Coloniale 4*. NVN.
Route R.C. Ba Na (ZC 206-704)
See R.C. Ban Na. Quang Nam Pr, I Corps.
***Rowan*, USS** (n/a)
DD-782, per Ralph Fries. There were also Destroyers named *Rowan* with hull the #s 42 and 405, but it appears neither served in VN (405 sunk by torpedo in WWII).
Roy, FSB? (YC 835-955?)
Grid is for FSB Brick, not Roy. See FSB Roy at ZD 058-033. Thua Thien Pr, I Corps.
Roy, FSB/LZ (ZD 058-028)
On small isthmus in, and along S edge of Dam Cau Hai Bay, apx 8 km WNW FSB Tomahawk and 3 km NW Phu Loc. Also listed at ZD 805-871, but that grid does not exist. 2d Bde/101st Abn AO 69-71. Thua Thien Pr, I Corps.
Roy, FSB/LZ (ZD 805-871)
Grid per Dan Gillotti and 15th Arty Assn; however, no such grid exists. Apparent that either grid zone is in error or there was a transposition or transcription error.
Royal Thai Army Div HQ (YS 14-98)
See Bearcat. Bien Hoa Pr, III Corps.
Royal Thai Forces (n/a)
See Thailand, Forces of, in Major HQs Section, and also Bearcat in alpha listing. Bien Hoa Pr, III Corps.
Royal Tomb (YD 748-130)
See Minh Mang's Tomb. Thua Thien Pr, I Corps.
RP 1 and 2 (n/a)
See Route Packages 1 and 2. Laos.
RP 1 thru RP 6B (n/a)
Route Package for NVN bombing zones during Op Rolling Thunder. See Route Package in Glossary. NVN [473]
RTA Special Warfare Center (n/a)
See 46th SF Co. Lopburi?, Thailand.
Ruby, LZ (XD 821-450)
Apx 5 km NW Khe Sanh CB and 18 km WSW Ca Lu. '70 XXIV Corps grid per D. Armstrong. Quang Tri Pr, I Corps.
Ruby, LZ (XT 526-625)
Apx 12 km WSW Minh Thanh AF and 15 km NNE Dau Tieng/Tri Tam. Apr67. Binh Duong Pr, III Corps.
Ruby, LZ (YA 995-463)
In river valley, apx 25 km due W Pleiku, and 15 km E Plei Djereng. 4th Div elements here '68 or '69. LZs Cathy, Helga, Phyllis and Ruby were apparently mutually suptg firebases? Data per Dick Arnold. Pleiku Pr, II Corps.
Rufe, LZ (XT 952-611)
Apx 12 km duc N Phuoc Vinh AF, 18 km due E Chonh Thanh AF/QL-13. Jun67. Also listed at XT 950-610 and 955-663? Phuoc Long Pr, III Corps.
Ruff-Puff (n/a)
See Glossary.
Ruffs (n/a)
See Ruff-Puff in Glossary.
Rumor Valley (AT 9-7?)
South of Dai La Pass. Quang Nam Pr, I Corps.
Run Run Valley (YC 860-840)
See Ruong Ruong Valley. Thua Thien Pr, I Corps.

Rung Lang Refugee Camp (BS 615-724)
At or just S of Quang Ngai AF, apx 4 km WSW Quang Ngai/QL-1. NPIA data. Quang Ngai Pr, I Corps.

Rung Rung Valley (YC 860-840)
See Ruong Ruong Valley. Thua Thien Pr, I Corps.

Rung Sat Special Zone (YS 10-70)
A.k.a. the Forest of Assassins and RSSZ. Area consisting of the deltas of the Dong Nai, Nha Be and Saigon Rivers, heavily infiltrated by VC. Gen Westmoreland called it, "One of most savage pieces of terrain in world." The Long Tau River, main shipping channel to Saigon, ran through middle of the zone. Was a vast mangrove swamp and tidal bog from which VC often planted mines in shipping lanes between Saigon and South China Sea. The Song Dong Tranh, Song Nga Bay, Song Ba Gioi and Song Thi Vai Rivers ran through zone and emptied into Vinh Ganh Rai. 1st AO of 2d Bde/9th Div MRF after its arrival in-country, per Jim Stone, 2d/39th Inf. Grid at apx center of mass. Gia Dinh Pr, III Corps. [474]

Rung Sat Swamp (YS 10-70)
See Rung Sat Special Zone. Gia Dinh Pr, III Corps.

Runsley, FSB (XT 590-270)
Apx 13 km NNW Cu Chi and 5 km SW Xa Duoc. Sep69. Hau Nghia/Binh Duong Pr border, III Corps

Runway (XD 932-281)
See FSB Runway at XD 948-281. Quang Tri Pr, I Corps.

Runway, FSB (XD 948-272)
At NE edge of Vietnam Salient, apx 1 km W Laos, 3 km SE Lang Klung, 12 km ENE Lang Chei and 47 km SW Quang Tri. Apr70 XXIV Corps grid per Don Armstrong. Also listed at XD 932-281, a site 1.5 km W listed grid? Quang Tri Pr, I Corps.

Ruong Ruong Airfield (YC 868-840)
In the Ruong Ruong Valley, apx 35 km due S Phu Bai, 50 km W Da Nang and adj Montagnard ville of same name. 1,600' AF cut by French. Had 2 wooden blockhouses that were built at base of nearby Hill 309. Cited in *Bonnie-Sue*, pp 241-246. "Abnd, Overgrown, probably mined, 29Jul67, AF # VA1-177," in Aug69 TAD per Frank Penk, Jr. Not in Feb73 TAD. Thua Thien Pr, I Corps.

Ruong Ruong Airstrip (YC 86-84)
See Ruong Ruong AF. Thua Thien Pr, I Corps.

Ruong Ruong SF Camp (YC 865-838)
A.k.a. Ta Ru or Ta Rhu or Ta Ro SF Camp? In the Ruong Ruong Valley, apx 48 km SSE Hue, 35 km due S Phu Bai and 50 km W Da Nang. 5th SF. Ta Rhu spelling in DA Chief, Mil Hist records summary which also indicates Det A-726 here,'63. Data per *SF Order of Battle* where it is also listed as Ta Ru and Ta Ro. See Nam Dong. Thua Thien Pr, I Corps.

Ruong Ruong Valley (YC 860-840)
Large valley at W end of Elephant Valley, apx 45 km W Nam O Bridge and 48 km SSE Hue. Khe Aroh, Kede and Khe Hai Nhut Rivers merge here. Roughly L-shaped, 15 km in length and varying in width between 1 and 3 km. Base area of 4th NVA Rgt in '68-69. Site of Op Platte Canyon, starting 6Jan69 and involving 2/502 and 1st/327th Inf, 101st Abn. Thua Thien Pr, I Corps.

Rupertus, USS (n/a)
DD 851. Destroyers *Rupertus*, *Samuel N. Moore* (DD 747) and *George K. Mackenzie* fought catastrophic 29Jul67, fire aboard *USS Forrestal* (CVA 59) at Yankee Station, in which 15 were KIA and 63 WIA. Data per www.uss-salem.org/features/fires/.

Rush, USCGC (n/a)
WHEC 723. 28Oct70-15Jul71. Sqdn 3 CGC, during Coast Guard's 7th SVN deployment.

Russ, LZ (YA 991-440)
Apx 14 km ESE Plei Djereng new AF and 26 km WSW Pleiku. Jan66. Pleiku Pr, II Corps.

Russell, FSB (XD 912-592)
Apx 10 km E FSB Neville, 8 km NW Elliott CB, 21 km W Cam Lo, 8 km ENE FSB Neville and apx 4 km S the DMZ. 25Feb69, E, F, and K Cos, 2d/4th Marines, Mortar and H Btys, 3d/12th Mar Arty attacked and partially overrun by 200-man Sapper unit of 27th NVA Rgt, 29 US KIA, 77 WIA. 3d Mar Div. On map at p 58, *US Marines in Vietnam-1969*. Quang Tri Pr, I Corps. [475]

Russia, Forces of (n/a)
See Major HQs Section and Glossary.

Ruth, FSB (XU 97-28?)
Just W QL-14, apx 1 km S Bu Dop, NE Bau Ba Linh and "The Crescent." 2d Sqdn 11th ACR here at one time. Phuoc Long Pr, III Corps.

Ruth, FSB (ZA 168-530)
Apx 8 km NW Pleiku, 4 km ENE Plei Blo O'Dung and 17 km SSE Plei Mrong. Grid per S-3 Daily Journal/Op rpts dated 31Jul-1Sep69, per Bob Patsfield. Pleiku Pr, II Corps.

Ruth Lykes, SS (n/a)
Commercial transport under govt contract, per Ralph Fries.

RVNAF Academies, Colleges & Schools (various)
See ARVN in alpha listing, and RVNAF in Glossary.

RVNAF Military Training Schools (various)
See ARVN in alpha listing, and RVNAF in Glossary.

Ryder, LZ/FSB (AT 952-355)
A.k.a. Hill 675 and Hon Chau Mtn (however, also described as being on Hill 579 in *Son Thang*, p 13?). On Que Son Mtn range's highest peak, apx 48 km W Tam Ky, 14 km NW FSB Ross (Que Son), 7 km SE An Hoa CB, 12 km due S Liberty Bridge, 2 km WSW LZ Baldy and 22 km S Hill 55. Closed and later rebuilt. 1st Mar Div, '69. 11th Mar Arty POP site employing IOD, and covering Antenna and northern Que Son Valley approaches to Da Nang here also, '69. "Bunkers had some big rats", says Tommy Acosta, 11th LIB, '68-69. Also listed at AT 946-342, 949-345, 945-344 and 920-430. Map is L-7014-6640-3. Americal list. Quang Nam Pr, I Corps.

Ryukyu Islands US Army Hospital (n/a)
On Okinawa, not in SVN. Apparently involved in treatment of Marine and Navy VN War casualties.

SIERRA

Facility/Feature Name, Grid Coordinate, a.k.a. Name/History/Province/CTZ

Unless otherwise stated, 6-digit grid coordinates reference DMA L-7014, L-7015 or L-7016 series, 1:50,000 scale maps, while 2- and 4-digit coordinates reference AMS/DMA/NIMA 1:250,000, 1:500,000 and 1:1,000,000 scale maps. Unless otherwise stated, all heights are in meters. To convert meters to feet, multiply by 3.2808; feet to meters, multiply by .3048.

S4, LZ (BR 402-509)
Immed SW Plei Kadjang, apx 11 km NW An Khe. 9Apr67. Binh Dinh Pr, II Corps.

Sa Airfield (PA 8-5)
Along Rte 7 at 18°34'00"N-100°44'00"E, or apx 540 km N Bangkok per Feb67 Natl Geo map. El. 1,000'. Thailand.

Sa Dec (n/a)
Mapsheet name of L-7014-6129-1. SVN.

Sa Dec Airfield (WS 830-373)
Apx 2 km SW Sa Dec, 4 km SW Mekong River, 27 km NNW Can Tho AF, 14 km W Vinh Long AF and 12 km SE Cao Lanh AF. El. 20', 1,600' asph rwy. At 10°17'12"N-105°4'12"E. Map is L-7014-6129-1, per Jim Stone. Sa Dec Pr, IV Corps.

Sa Dec City (WS 84-38?)
On Mekong River apx 30 km due N Can Tho and 110 km WSW Saigon. Battle of Sa Dec here 6Jan69, involving A and B Cos, 2d/39th Inf, 9thInf Div. Map is L-7014-6129-1, per Jim Stone. Capitol, Sa Dec Pr, IV Corps.

Sa Dec Heliport (WS 845-384)
On Mekong River apx 30 km due N Can Tho and 110 km WSW Saigon. Heliport #654, alt 7', 100' x 40', PSP, fuel-J4. Buildings W and S. Approach along canal E side of Pad. At 10°17'45"N-105°46'00"E, per Feb73 TAD. Map is L-7014-6129-1, per Jim Stone. Sa Dec Pr, IV Corps.

Sa Dec NSAD (WS 84-39)
On Mekong River apx 30 km due N Can Tho and 110 km WSW Saigon. USN Supt Activity Detachment, '66-71. Map is L-7014-6129-1, per Jim Stone. Per MRF Assn Website. Sa Dec Pr, IV Corps.

Sa Dec PBR Base (WS 84-39)
On Mekong River apx 30 km due N Can Tho and 110 km WSW Saigon. River Div 52, TF-116, USN Gamewarden base here per MRF Assn website at www.mrfa.org. Moved to Vinh Long. Sa Dec Pr, IV Corps.

Sa Dec Province (WS)
One of 16 southern provs forming IV Corps (IV CTZ).

Sa Hoi, Cape (BS 9-2)
Cape at 14°40'N-109°06'E. Binh Dinh Pr, II Corps.

Sa Hoi, Pointe (BS 9-2)
A.k.a. Sa Hoi, Cap. Cape at 14°40'N-109°06'E. On ND49-05 JOG. Binh Dinh Pr, II Corps.

Sa Huynh (BS 9-3)
Along coast, E QL-1, apx 18 km SE Duc Pho and near 14°40'00"N-109°04'00"E. On ND49-05 JOG. Quang Ngai Pr, I Corps.

Sa Huynh Island (BS 92-22)
Near FSB Charlie Brown (which was on peninsula NE Bong Son), apx 16 km SE Duc Pho. Also spelled Sa Hynh. USN Port nearby. 1st/14th Inf here Dec 67. USN, 4th Div, 1st Cav and Americal AO at various times. Near listed grid. Quang Ngai Pr, I Corps.

Sa Huynh NSAD (BS 93-23)
On small island at mouth of lagoon apx 36 km SSE Mo Duc and 24 km NNE LZ English. USN Supt Activity Detachment, '67-70, per MRF Assn Website. Originally developed as an "Over-the-Beach" resupply port, Apr67(?), by Army Engrs and Trans units to supt Op Malheur (1st Bde/101st Abn). US Army 159th Trans Bn here at one point per Col Charles Sunder, its CO. Map/photo of site in *The Marines in Vietnam 1954-1973*, p 245. *A Better War*, at p 365, tells us that after the Paris Peace accords were signed Mar73, NVA launched Div-sized attack on Sa Huynh and it was then retaken by counterattack of 2d ARVN Div, with heavy casualties on both sides. Quang Ngai Pr, I Corps.

Sa Huynh Port (BS 924-223)
US-built port E of QL-1, apx 14 km NNE Gia An and 18 km SE Duc Pho. HQ for Army's 159th Trans Bn just prior to (or after?) its move to Wunder Beach. USN, 4th Div, 1st Cav and Americal here at various times. LZ Charlie Brown was nearby. *A Better War*, at p 365, tells us that after Paris Peace accords signed, Mar73, NVA launched Div-sized attack on Sa Huynh, and it was taken by counterattack of 2d ARVN Div with heavy casualties on both sides. Near listed grid. Americal list. Map/photo of site in *The Marines in Vietnam 1954-1973*, p 245. Quang Ngai Pr, I Corps.

Sa Huynh POFAC? (BS 929-224)
Apx 500 meters E QL-1 and 18 km SE Duc Pho. Because grid is at point of channel access to Dam Nuocman Bay adj to Sa Huynh Docks, then POFAC acronym apparently means point of access. Oct67. Quang Ngai Pr, I Corps.

Sa Huynh SF Camp (BS 9159-2630)
Along E side QL-1, apx 14 km NNE Gia An and 18 km SE Duc Pho. 5th SF. FOB for Military Region 1 MSF. Info/grid per *SF Order of Battle*. Quang Ngai Pr, I Corps.

Sa Hynh Island (BS)
See Sa Huynh. Binh Dinh Pr, II Corps.

Sa Ky River (BS 7-8)
See Riviere de Sa Ky. Quang Ngai/Quang Tin Pr, I Corps.

Sa Noi Airfield (n/a)
Apx 180 km N to NNE Vientiane. El. 2,800'. Laos.

Sa Pa (UK 8-7)
In 1922, Sa Pa or Sapa was built in beautiful valley of NVN at 1,600 meters above sea level. This remote northern mtn hamlet is noted for its temperate and fog-filled winters. Climate favorable for gardening, growing fruit trees (peaches and plums) and for raising medicinal herbs that

are marketed in Hanoi and Ho Chi Minh City. Its natural attractions include Thac Bac (Silver) Falls and Cau May Bridge (the Cloud Bridge; over Muong Hoa River). Author of *Sparring With Charlie* (1996) found villager here carrying "Boom box radio," which he viewed as evidence that western culture was eroding even most remote Viets. Also spelled Sar Pa. At 22°21'00"N-103°52'00"E. NVN.

Saber (various)
See also Sabre entries.

Saber, FSB (YD 868-278?)
See LZ Sabre at grid. Thua Thien Pr, I Corps.

Saber, FSB (YD 898-187)
Apx 3 km due N Phu Bai AF, 2 km S FSB Lanyard, 10 km WSW Hue and 6 km WNW Xom Moc Duc. Apr70 XXIV Corps grid per D. Armstrong. Also listed at YD 890-180 and 868-278? See FSB Forward. Thua Thien Pr, I Corps.

Saber, FSB (ZC 04-35)
Apx 32 km SW An Hoa, 5 km SW LZ Javelin, 10 km due N FSB Machete, 8 km NW FSB Battle-Ax. Used by USMC Task Force Yankee during assault on Base Area 112, Jan-Feb69. 1st Mar Div. Grid per map in *US Marines in Vietnam-1969*, p 90. Quang Nam Pr, I Corps.

Saber, LZ (YU 864-766)
A.k.a. "Sabre" in some rpts. Apx 5 km WNW Duc Lap AF, 6 km E Cambodia and 51 km WSW to SW Ban Me Thuot. 2d/35th Inf, 4th Div here Sep68, per Don Blankin. Grid per Ben Youmans. Quang Duc Pr, II Corps.

Saber Heliport (XT 901-062)
See Sabre Heliport, Di An. Bien Hoa Pr, III Corps.

Sabot (n/a)
Apr70, XXIV Corps future-use 101st Abn FSB name.

Sabre (various)
See also Saber entries.

Sabre, FSB (XU 575-352)
Apx 3 to 4 km NE Snuol AF, 32 km NNW Loc Ninh, 16 km NE point where QL-13 met border, and 10 km SE FSB Hammerstone. 1st Cav, Cambodian Incursion FSB, May70. 1st Cav, 11th ACR and 199th LIB. Grid per *11th ACR Cambodia Invasion AAR, 1st Cav Div, May-Jun70*, as per Lou Rochat.[476] Also listed at XU 570-340. Cambodia.

Sabre, FSB (YD 868-278?)
A.k.a. FSB Forward. On triangular promontory jutting into lagoon apx 9 km E Phu Vang and 9 km ENE Hue. Built beginning apx 23May68. Beginning 18May68, was night location for what was known as TF Sabre (2/17th Cav element attached to 2d Bde/101st Abn). Became FSB when 2d/17th assigned its own arty w/addition of C/6th/33d Arty. Cav operated out of site for apx 2 months. Also listed at YD 867-272 and 898-187. Thua Thien Pr, I Corps.

Sabre, FSB (YD 897-188)
See FSB Saber at grid. Thua Thien Pr, I Corps.

Sabre, FSB (YS 385-745)
Apx 8.5 km NW Nui Dat, 6 km W FSB Leopard and 6 km N FSB Weir. On 1ATF NCO trng map per John Hollett. Phuoc Tuy Pr, III Corps.

Sabre Heliport, (Di An) (XT 901-062)
Apx 16 km NW Bien Hoa AB, 5 km N Xom Ben San and 10 km NNE Phu Loi AF. "Heliport #765, alt 108', Peneprime, Rwy 18-36 apx 1,000' Lighted, soft dirt base, peneprimed. Rgt tfc Ldg Rwy 18, left tfc Ldg Rwy 36. Fuel W side of rwy, revetments E rwy, rearm NE rwy. Arty advsy-Binh Duong 286.1 40.3." At 10°54'28"N-106°44'24"E, per Feb73 TAD. Bien Hoa Pr, III Corps.

Sacramento, USS (n/a)
AOE 1. Aux. Oiler, Fast Combat Supt Ship.

Sacred Sword of Patriots League (n/a)
See Glossary.

Sad Hoai Cu (BS 9-2?)
Coastal ville that in '60 was defended by NVA 271st Inf Bde. Cited in *Bird*, p 5. There is a Cape Sa Hoi at listed grid. Location unknown. I or II Corps or NVN?

Saddle, LZ (BR 353-301)
Apx 20 km SW An Khe and 18 km NNW Plei Niang. Dec65. Binh Dinh Pr, II Corps.

Saddle, LZ (BR 769-939)
Apx 9 km WNW Bong Son AF. Oct66. Map is L-7014-6837-4, per Ken Burrington. Binh Dinh Pr, II Corps.

Saddle Bag, LZ (ZC 133-655)
See Saddlebag. Quang Nam Pr, I Corps.

Saddlebag, LZ (ZC 133-655)
Apx 3 km SE Phu Hoa, 11 km N to NNW Ha Tan AF and 32 km WSW Da Nang AB. III MAF. Apr70 XXIV Corps grid per Don Armstrong. Quang Nam Pr, I Corps.

Sadec Airfield (WS 830-373)
See Sa Dec AF. Sa Dec Pr, IV Corps.

Safeguard, USS (n/a)
ARS-25. Aux Ship, per Ralph Fries.

Sage, LZ (AT 987-508)
Apx 16 km WSW Hoi An, 14 km ENE An Hoa CB and 25 km due S Da Nang AB. Apr70 XXIV Corps grid per Don Armstrong. Quang Nam Pr, I Corps.

Sagebrush (n/a)
6Apr70, XXIV Corps future-use III MAF FSB name.

Saigon (XS 85-95)
A.k.a. Prey-Nohor, Ho Chi Minh City, The Paris of the Orient or The Pearl of the Orient. Capitol, Republic of SVN from '54-75, and 1 of the 6 autonomous municipalities of SVN. Sat along the Song Saigon River, apx 72 km from ocean. '70 population was apx 1-2 million, and size then was roughly 27 sq miles (today it is 50 sq miles), making it one of most densely populated areas on earth. In 16th Century, area was part of Cambodia and city known as Prey-Nokor. The city we know as Saigon apparently began its life as fishing ville beginning in the mid 1800's. French began calling it "Saigon" in early 1860's, when they landed here to begin colonization. Cholon, one of many suburbs, was called its sister city. In late '67 to early '68, Saigon was put off limits to US military not having official business there, and most military housing billets in pvt bldgs were closed in order to prevent terrorist bombings (had become target of choice). City was infamous for its legions of bars and "Tea" clubs catering to hundreds of thousands of lonely US and ARVN GIs in area. Per Neil Sheehan, there were over 63,000 registered prostitutes in the city at height of US involvement ("and that's not including amateurs," he adds). City was heavily infiltrated/attacked by VC during both Tet '68 and Mini-Tet (May68). Here were Saigon Port, Newport, MACV HQ, US Embassy, Camp Red Ball, Keopler Cmpd, Pentagon East, Camp Davies, Pershing Field, Saigon USO, Saigon VFW, and SF Det 63, among numerous other hotels/pvt residences/apartment buildings

used as BEQs, BOQs, transient quarters, clubs and rec centers. Nearby major US Military installations included Bien Hoa AB, Tan Son Nhut AB and Long Binh Post, which together with Saigon housed nearly half of all US troops in VN at height of war. Numerous ARVN units positioned in city as well. Home to 5th SF Grp, Det. B-320, Dec64. NVA renamed it Ho Chi Minh City in '75. "In 1992, former SVN air force pilot Ly Tong, hijacked a Vietnam Airlines Airbus A310 and parachuted out after forcing it to fly low so he could drop 50,000 anti-Communist leaflets over [city]..."[477] See Precinct Five and Cholon. Gia Dinh Pr, III Corps.

Saigon (Thanh Pho Ho Chi Minh) (n/a)
Mapsheet L-7014-6330-4. Sheet name: Thanh Pho Ho Chi Minh (Ho Chi Minh City). SVN.

Saigon, FSB/LZ (XD 818-277)
In Vietnam Salient and overlooking Rte 616 near Lang Up, apx 15 km SSW Khe Sanh, 27 km SW Vandegrift CB, 6 km from Laos. 3d Mar Div in '69 and apparently in use during Lam Son 719 in'71. On map at p 65, *US Marines in Vietnam-1969*. Also listed at XD 814-272 per XXIV Corps index, courtesy Don Armstrong. Mar-Nov69. Also listed at XD 820-770. Quang Tri Pr, I Corps.

Saigon, Port of (XS 890-903)
Along W edge of Saigon, and apx 70 km of winding river channel from sea. Featured 12 deep-draft quays for ocean-going vessels, 6 of which were used by military and 6 by commercial traffic. There were also 30 buoy-discharge sites in middle of Saigon River and Army Trans Cmd used some 1,500 barges and sampans to shuttle cargo to docks. At start of US war, this was only commercial seaport capable of handling large vessels in SVN. Data per Army Transportation Assn's website. Good map at: http://home.epix.net/~gramborw/saigon.htm. See Saigon Seaports and Newport (5 km N Saigon Port). Gia Dinh Pr, III Corps.

Saigon 7th Day Adv Hospital (XS 841-940)
See 7th Day Adventist Hosp and 3d Field Hospital. Gia Dinh Pr, III Corps.

Saigon Airfield (XS 82-97)
See Tan Son Nhut AB. Gia Dinh Pr, III Corps.

Saigon Buddhist Pagoda (XS 8-9)
On Cong Ly St. in Saigon. In Nov-Dec66, Capt Bo Gritz employed the Khmer-Serei ("Free Cambodia") underground org to recruit 263 Cambodes and other indigenous personnel for 1st MGF (MGF Det A-303). Recruiting held in this Pagoda. Force then trained at Ho Ngoc Tau. Per *Mobile Guerrilla Force*, pp 2-4. Gia Dinh Pr, III Corps.

Saigon Cemetery (XS 85-95?)
Near Tan Son Nhut AB? Scene of heavy fighting with VC, 1Feb68, during Tet '68. Gia Dinh Pr, III Corps.

Saigon Cemetery (French) (XS 810-940)
At W edge of city, 2 km S Tan Son Nhut AB, Saigon. Gia Dinh Pr, III Corps.

Saigon CIA Station (XS 863-922)
Apx 5 km SE MACV HQ, 500 meters NE Independence Palace and just W the Song Saigon. Occupied upper 2 stories of 6-story US Embassy. Gia Dinh Pr, III Corps.

Saigon Commissary (XS 831-895)
Gia Dinh Pr, III Corps.

Saigon Compound (XS 871-965)
Apx 7 km E Tan Son Nhut AB. Nature of cmpd unknown? Gia Dinh Pr, III Corps.

Saigon Free World Heliport (XS 835-912)
See Free World Heliport (Saigon). Gia Dinh Pr, III Corps.

Saigon Ditch, The (XS 8-9)
See Saigon Moat, The. Gia Dinh Pr, III Corps.

Saigon Golf Course (XS 85-95)
Gia Dinh Pr, III Corps.

Saigon Hotel-3 Heliport (XS 810-946)
Apx 1 km SSE Tan Son Nhut AB. "Heliport #707, alt 33', 2 ea 100' diameter (1 asph, 1 sod), Fuel-J4. Official business only. Acft restricted to 30 min prkg unless prior permission obtained from H-3 CO. Tel 924-2722/2258. CH-47 and CH-54 PPR. HAZARDS-96' Lgtd twr 1400' NE heliport. 164' Lgtd ants 850' SSE heliport. 135' Lgtd twr 260' NW. Emerg only. Commo-Capital Ctr-295.9 128.6 58.95 VFR flt flw. Opr 2300-1100Z. 'Paris Con'-347.9, 133.2 (E). Tower-281.1, 131.6, 120.4, 35.5. Arty advsy-239.0, 46.0 Radio/Nav Remarks: Possible freq interference, watch for light signal." At 10°48'24"N-106°39'42"E, per Feb73 TAD. Gia Dinh Pr, III Corps.

Saigon Independence Hall (XS 855-914)
See Independence Hall. Gia Dinh Pr, III Corps.

Saigon Island Depot (XS 91-97?)
Facility in Saigon River(?) operated by civilian contracting firm of Raymond/Morrison, Knudson/Brown, Root & Jones (a.k.a. RMK-BRJ) near Thu Duc. See RMK-BRJ Main Office. Gia Dinh Pr, III Corps.

Saigon Military Citadel (XS 8-9)
In Saigon. In 1859, the French attacked this facility. By 1883 they had completely occupied what became known as French Indochina or *Indochine*, as French called it. In short order, some 15,000 French were ruling apx 6,000,000 Vietnamese. Gia Dinh Pr, III Corps.

Saigon Moat, The (XS 8-9)
Herman Khan, an influential member of Hudson Institute actually proposed const of a defensive moat that would have completely encircled Saigon in order to deny enemy easy access to capitol. Gen Abrams strongly opposed concept and idea was abnd. Data per *A Better War*, p 123. See also McNamara's Wall. Gia Dinh Pr, III Corps.

Saigon MP Billets (XS 8-9)
See Military Police Billets, Saigon. Gia Dinh Pr, III Corps.

Saigon MP Compound (XS 8-9)
See Military Police Cmpd, Saigon. Gia Dinh Pr, III Corps.

Saigon Navy HQ (XS 842-917)
In city center at corner of Doan Thi Diem and Dinh Phung Streets, apx 4 km SE MACV HQ and 700 meters W Independence Palace. USN HQ Supt Activity, and Naval Supt Activity, '50-73. Per MRF Assn Website. Gia Dinh Pr, III Corps.

Saigon NDB (XS 81-87)
Non-Directional Air Nav Beacon site. Along S edge of city apx 10 km S Tan Son Nhut. Gia Dinh Pr, III Corps.

Saigon Newport (XS 87-93)
See Newport. Gia Dinh Pr, III Corps.

Saigon Port (XS 890-903)
See Saigon, Port of. Gia Dinh Pr, III Corps.

Saigon Prison (XS 824-915)
In heart of city, apx 6 km due S Tan Son Nhut AB and 5 km ENE Phu Lam. Gia Dinh Pr, III Corps.
Saigon Racetrack (XS 819-905)
A.k.a. Phu Tho or Phu To Racetrack. In city center, apx 4.5 km WSW Independence Palace and 5 km S Tan Son Nhut AB. Scene of heavy Mech Inf attacks of VC positions, 31Jan-1Feb68, during Tet '68. Gia Dinh Pr, III Corps.
Saigon Radio Station (XS 862-945)
Apx 5.5 km SE Tan Son Nhut AB. Captured by NVA/VC during Tet '68 and held for several days despite heavy attacks by ARVN. VC Broadcast from site while it was in their control. On *Saigon-Bien Hoa-Long Binh* map in *The Rise and Fall of the American Army*, between pp 368-9. Gia Dinh Pr, III Corps.
Saigon River (XT/XS/YS)
A.k.a. The Big Blue. Boundary between 25th and 1st US Inf Div AO. See Song Saigon and Big Blue. III Corps.
Saigon RCTR? (XS 813-905)
Saigon race track? Listed as a "rctr," and meaning of acronym unclear, though it could mean recreation or relocation center? In any case, grid is adj to Phu Tho race track. Gia Dinh Pr, III Corps.
Saigon Rocket Belt (XT)
Area within max eff range of the 122mm rocket. Ran generally from Bien Hoa along a NW radius from Saigon and 10 to 15 km from that city. Gia Dinh Pr, III Corps.
Saigon Seaports (XS 87-92)
Along E and NE edge of Saigon. Berthing Feet: 8,300 lineal feet, Draft Max: 25'-29', Cargo Capacity: 12,400 tons/day, Storage Covered w/in 5 km: 2,399,000 ft^2, Storage Uncov.: 430,000 yd^2. See Newport. Gia Dinh Pr, III Corps.[478]
Saigon SF CLD Camp (XS 8530-9295)
In city center, apx 5.5 km SE Tan Son Nhut AB and 1 km W the Song Saigon. SF Camp, Cmd Liaison Det, Saigon. 5th SF Grp. Moved to Bien Hoa. Gia Dinh Pr, III Corps.
Saigon Textile Mill (XS 787-958)
Apx 2 km W Tan Son Nhut AB. See VinaTexaco Textile Factory. Gia Dinh Pr, III Corps.
Saigon Transport Terminal (XS 87-92?)
Saigon. HQ of Saigon Trans Terminal Cmd (ARVN), Vietnamese Naval Base Saigon. Gia Dinh Pr, III Corps.
Saigon US Army Hospital (XS 8-9)
See US Army Hosp Saigon. Gia Dinh Pr, III Corps.
Saigon US Embassy (XS 863-922)
Apx 5 km SE MACV HQ Cmpd/Tan Son Nhut AB, 500 meters NE Independence Palace and just W the Song Saigon. On 1Jan68, after VC had occupied Embassy during initial Saigon attacks of Tet '68, C/1st/502d Inf, 101st Abn (had been waiting its turn in 2d Bde's deployment to I Corps that had begun 28Jan68) was instead landed on its roof and helped secure bldg, floor by floor, then remained in defensive positions on roof for several(?) more days. Gia Dinh Pr, III Corps.
Saigon USAR Newport Terminal (XS 886-935)
At W Central edge of Saigon and on W bank of Song Saigon, apx 9 km WSW Tan Son Nhut AB. Dec66. See Newport. Gia Dinh Pr, III Corps.
Saigon USO (XS 866-912)
See USO Saigon. Gia Dinh Pr, III Corps.
Saigon VFW Post (XS 87-92?)
See VFW Post 8316. Gia Dinh Pr, III Corps.
Saigon VOR TACAN (XS 82-97)
At Tan Son Nhut AB. Very high frequency Omnidirectional Radio ranging, Tactical Air Navigation beacon site. Gia Dinh Pr, III Corps.
Saigon Water Plant (XS 922-997?)
See Thu Duc Water Plant. Gia Dinh Pr? III Corps.
Saigon Zoo (XS 870-927)
Apx 1.5 km NE Independence Palace and 5.5 km SE Tan Son Nhut AB. Gia Dinh Pr, III Corps.
Saigon/Bien Hoa Bridge (XS 87-97?)
Apx 9 km E Tan Son Nhut AF and 4 km NE the Presidential Palace. Saigon/Bien Hoa Hwy Bridge across Saigon River at NE corner of city. Scene of heavy fighting during Tet '68. Gia Dinh Pr, III Corps.
Saint Barbara, FSB (XT 273-679)
See St. Barbara. Tay Ninh Pr, III Corps.
Saint Clair County, USS (n/a)
LST-1096. Decom 26Sep69. SVN.
Saint Francis River, USS (n/a)
LSMR-525. Landing ship Medium, Repair. Mentioned at MRF Assn website at: www.mrfa.orgnavy_index.htm.
Saint George BEQ (XS 828-887)
At 107 Dong Khanh St., Saigon. Data per *Vietnam Military Lore, 1959-1973*. Gia Dinh Pr, III Corps.
Saint George, LZ (AR 854-144)
See St. George. Pleiku Pr, II Corps.
Saint Jacques, Cape (YS 28-44)
See Cape St. Jacques. Phuoc Tuy Pr, III Corps.
Saint James, Cape (YS 2-4)
A.k.a. Mui Vung Tau. Cape at 10°19'N 107°05'E. On NC48-07 JOG. Phuoc Tuy Pr, III Corps.
Saint Joseph's Church (AT 906-754)
See St. Joseph's Church. Quang Nam Pr, I Corps.
Saint Kilda Heliport (YS 298-438)
On Vung Tau Peninsula near its southernmost tip, and along city's SE edge. "Heliport #747, alt 20', 456' x 286', Bitumen. Official business only. Appr from NE and W. Four 20' x 20' Landing pts on W LZ and three 50' x 125' lndg pts on E LZ. CH-47/CH-54 to land on NE Ldg pt." 10°20'N 107°06'E, per 73 TAD. Phuoc Tuy Pr, III Corps.
Saint Lo, LZ (XT 275-972)
Along Rte 254, apx 2 km S Cambodia and 9 km NW Katum. May66. Tay Ninh Pr, III Corps.
Saint Louis, USS (n/a)
LKA-116. Amphib Attack. Cargo.
Saint Paul, USS (n/a)
CA 73. Heavy Cruiser and flagship Cmdr 7th Fleet, when in Oct60, it visited Saigon to participate in Viet Independence Day celebrations. Was armed with 8-inch/55-caliber guns, eff to 26,000 yds., and 5-inch/38-caliber guns, accurate at 15,000 yds.[479]
Sainte Anne, Cape (WF 7-8)
See Cape Sainte Anne. NVN.
Saint Jacques, Cap (YS 2-4)
See Cape St. Jacques. Phuoc Tuy Pr, III Corps.
Saipan, LZ (YD 053-279)
Apx 16 km SW Ba Long AF, 21 km SSE Ca Lu and 6 km SW Ta Laou. Apr70 XXIV Corps grid per Don Armstrong. Quang Tri Pr, I Corps.

Sake, Mui (CP 1-5)
Coastal point at 12°13'30"N-109°18'16"E. On ND49-13 JOG. Khanh Hoa Pr, II Corps.
Sakhol Nakon SF Camp? (n/a)
Apparent misspelling of "Sakhon Nakon?" Thailand.
Sakhon Nakhon (VE 0-1?)
A.k.a. Sakon Nakhon. Apx 545 km NE Bangkok. US Army Supt Cmd facility, Thailand. At various times occupied by 16th and 54th Engr Cos, Aug67-Feb71. Thailand.
Sakhon Nakhon Airfield (VE 0-1?)
A.k.a. Sakon Nakhon. Major AF apx 540-545 km NE Bangkok, 150 km ESE Udorn AB and 60 km SW Nakohn Phanom West AB. Per ONC-J-11. El. 230'? Thailand.
Sakhon Nakhon SF Camp (VE 0-1?)
A.k.a. Sakon Nakhon. Apx 545 km NE Bangkok and at or near one of two airfields with the same name. SF camp or AO per *SF Order of Battle.* Thailand
Sakon Nakhon AF (New) (VE 0-1)
A.k.a. Sakhon Nakhon AF (New). Major AF apx 540-545 km NE Bangkok, 10 km N Sakon Nakhon Army AF, 5 km NW Sakon Nakhon Old AF and 55 km WSW NKP AB. Per ONC-J-11. El. 550'. Thailand.
Sakon Nakhon Airfield (VE 0-1)
A.k.a. Sakhon Nakhon AF. At 17°17'00"N-104°06'00"E. NIMA data. Feb67 Natl Geo map. El. 563'. Thailand.
Sakon Nakhon Army AF (VE 0-0)
A.k.a. Sakhon Nakhon AAF. Apx 60 km WNW NKP, 10 km S Sakon Nakhon (New) AB. Per ONC-J-11. At 17°11'00"N-104°08'00"E. NIMA data. El. 563'. Thailand.
Sakon Nakhon Old Airfield (VE 0-1?)
A.k.a. Sakhon Nakhon Old AF. Minor AF, apx 5 km SE Sakon Nakhon (New) AF, 15 km SSE Sakon Nakhon Army AF. Per ONC-J-11. El. 500'. Thailand.
Sala Phou Koun Airfield (TG 31-49)
LS-260. CIA/SF, per *Air Facilities Data-Laos.*
Salad Bowl, The (YD 684-045)
Apx 7 km W peak Hill 618 (Nui Ke). A valley so named by elements of 82d Abn in Jun-Jul68 due to its odd shape. Thau Thien Po, I Corps.
Salamat-Po (n/a)
A.k.a. USAF Hospital, Clark AFB. Used extensively as supt/Evac Hosp for VN Casualties in-transit. See USN Hosp, Okinawa, USAF Hospital Kadena AFB and Clark AFB. Philippines.
Salem, LZ (BR 711-846)
On W side Song Lao River Valley, apx 18 km SW Bong Son. Apr-Sep70. Binh Dinh Pr, II Corps.
Salem, LZ (BR 935-805)
Just E QL-1, apx 18 km SSE Bong Son, 2 km NW Phuoc Thung and 13 km NNE Phu My. 2d & 3d/17th Arty here 6-8May68. Data per Jack Picciolo. Binh Dinh Pr, II Corps.
Salem, LZ (YS 270-450)
Along N edge of Vung Tau, apx 3 km SW Vung Tau AF. Mar66. Phuoc Tuy Pr, III Corps.
Salem House (n/a)
See Daniel Boone Operations in Glossary.
Salina, LZ (YS 673-845)
Near small lake, apx 29 km NE Nui Dat/Luscombe AF and 20 km WSW peak Nui Be. Apr66. Phuoc Tuy Pr, III Corps.
Salisbury Sound, USS (n/a)
AV-13. Seaplane Tender. Role discussed in *Brown Water, Black Berets*, p 92. See *Currituck, USS* for detail. SVN.
Sally, Camp (YD 639-275)
See LZ Sally. Thua Thien Pr, I Corps.
Sally, FSB (YT 297-067)
Apx 16 km WSW Xuan Loc, 4 km due W FSB Jilian, 18 km NW FSB Blackhorse Basecamp. On 1ATF NCO trng map per John Hollett. Long Khanh Pr, III Corps.
Sally, FSB (YU 584-022)
Apx 3 km E Poul Bri, 16 km ENE Duc Phong AF/SF Camp, 41 km due E Song Be/Phuoc Binh, 25 km SW Nhon Co AF and 8 km SSE FSB Jeanne. Opened or reopened 30Aug70, closed 17Sep70 by 2d/12th Cav Data per *1st Cav Div Op Rpt, ending 31Oct70*, courtesy Peter Cole. Phuoc Long/Lam Dong Pr border, II or III Corps.
Sally, LZ ? (YD 435-595?)
Likely error as grid matches that of LZ Nancy's location? Quang Tri Pr, I Corps.
Sally, LZ (YD 639-275)
A.k.a. Camp and FSB Sally. Built adj Van Xa, apx 12 km NW Hue, 11 km ESE Camp Evans, 2 km W Thon Van Xa, 3 km SSE An Lo Bridge, and 1 km W QL-1. Possibly built by French, but 1st Cav apparently was first US unit to establish position here. Const of permanent facility apparently began in earnest, 28Feb68. Per LtGen John Cushman, Sally was named after wife of 1st Cav Co Cmdr. By Oct68, permanent bldgs were replacing tents and base had become 2d Bde/101st Abn HQ. Home to elements of 101st Abn, '68-70, 1/321st Arty, C Bty, 2/11th Arty (155mm), until Mar70. In Oct96, LTC Thomas Morgan visited site and found large cement plant operating there; photo and story in Mar98 ARMY magazine. Also listed as YD 649-284. Map is L-7014-6442-2, per Ken Burrington. Thua Thien Pr, I Corps.
Sally, LZ (YA 647-521)
At S entrance Plei Trap Valley, apx 12 km E Phum Hay and 57 km W Pleiku. Jan66. Kontum Pr, II Corps.
Sally Airfield, LZ (YD 639-275)
See Van Xa AF. Thua Thien Pr, I Corps.
Saloon (n/a)
6Apr70, XXIV Corps future-use III MAF FSB name.
Saloon, LZ (n/a)
Location unknown. Per Americal website list, this LZ opened 14Jun71. I Corps.
Salt and Pepper (n/a)
See Glossary.
Salvo (n/a)
Apr70, XXIV Corps future-use 101st Abn FSB name.
Sam, FSB (BR 628-531)
Overlooking Vinh Thanh Valley from W side, apx 16 km ENE An Khe. 5Oct65. Binh Dinh Pr, II Corps.
Sam, FSB (XU 790-120)
Apx 7 km ENE Loc Ninh AF and 6 km ESE Ap Loc Thanh. Jan68. Binh Long Pr, III Corps.
Sam, LZ (XT 714-767)
Apx 6 km due W Tan Khai/QL-13 and 13 km NE Minh Thanh AF. Aug67. Also listed at XT 710-760. Binh Long Pr, III Corps.

Sam Hai (BT 519-114)
Small ville adj to USMC/Americal facilities at Ky Ha. Per Les Hines, most hootch maids working at 123rd Avn Bn at Ky Ha lived here. Quang Tin Pr, I Corps.

Sam Houston, Operation (n/a)
1Jan-5Apr67. 4th and 25th Inf Div border surveillance ops in Pleiku and Kontum Provs. Op Francis Marion followed. 733 NVA/VC KIA, per *Vietnam Order of Battle*, pp 9-14. Kontum and Pleiku Prvs, II Corps.

Sam Neua (VH 6-0)
A.k.a. Samneua. Apx 315 km NE Vientiane and 150 km SE DBP. French Outpost during 1953 Communist Spring Offensive. Laos.

Sam Neua Airfield (VH 03-58)
A.k.a. L-04, and Samneua AF. Apx 315 km NE Vientiane, 18 km W Ban Nakay Neua AF, 195 km WSW Hanoi and 40 km from NVN border. CIA per *Air Facilities Data-Laos*. ONC-J-11 El. 3,346' (3,281' on Natl Geo map). Laos.

Sam Ngao Airfield (n/a)
Along Ping River apx 415 km NNW Bangkok per Feb67 Natl Geo map. El. 490'. Thailand.

Sam Sen Airfield (TG 60-37)
LS-112. CIA/SF, per *Air Facilities Data-Laos.*

Sam Son (n/a)
Mapsheet name of L-7014-6148-2. NVN only.

Sam Song Hong Airfield (UG 84-83)
LS-201. CIA/SF, per *Air Facilities Data-Laos.*

Sam Thong Airfield (TG 79-24)
LS-20. CIA/SF, per *Air Facilities Data-Laos.*

Samae San (n/a)
SF camp or AO per *SF Order of Battle.* Thailand (or Cambodia?)

Samneua Airfield (n/a)
A.k.a. Sam Neua AF. Apx 315 km NE Vientiane, 18 km W Ban Nakay Neua AF, 195 km WSW Hanoi and 40 km from NVN border, per ONC-J-11. El. 3,346' (3,281' on Feb67 Natl Geo map). Laos.

Sample, USS (n/a)
DE-1048. DD-Escort, per Ralph Fries.

Sampan Valley (XT or YT?)
Per *Bloods*, p 120, a "serious place" apparently within normal Huey flying distance of Bien Hoa (or roughly within 50 mile radius of that base). III Corps.

Samrong Airfield (n/a)
Apx 325 km NW Phnom Penh, 65 km W Anlong Veng AF, and 95 km NNW Siemreap. 6,700' rwy, per Dec67 DMA TPC K-10A, El. 138' (300' on Natl Geo map?). Cambodia.

Samuel N. Moore, USS (n/a)
DD 747. Destroyers *Rupertus* (DD 851), *Samuel N. Moore* and *George K. Mackenzie* (DD 836) fought catastrophic Jul67 fire aboard Acft Carrier *Forrestal* at Yankee Station, in which 15 were KIA and 63 WIA.

San Bernardino County, USS (n/a)
LST-1189. SVN.

San Ho, Cape (CR 1-2)
See Cape San Ho. Binh Dinh Pr, II Corps.

San Joaquin County, USS (n/a)
LST-1122. Decom 1May72.

San Jose, USS (n/a)
AFS-7. Aux Refrig, per Ralph Fries.

San Juan Hill, FSB/LZ (BS 634-380)
In mtns apx 18 km due W Duc Pho, 17 km SW Mo Duc/Quang Hien, 34 km S Quang Ngai and 11 km NE Ba To New AF. 6th/11th Arty here. Mentioned at p 82, *Vietnam: Reflexes and Reflections*. Per Americal site, mortar attacks on incoming helos were common here. Also listed at BS 688-328. Quang Ngai Pr, I Corps.

San Louang Airfield (TG 71-49)
LS-41. CIA/SF, per *Air Facilities Data-Laos.*

San Pa Ka Airfield (UH 07-09)
LS-33. CIA/SF, per *Air Facilities Data-Laos.*

San Soak Airfield, Old (VF 63-56)
LS-265. CIA/SF, per *Air Facilities Data-Laos.*

San Tiau Airfield (UG 50-55)
LS-02. CIA/SF, per *Air Facilities Data-Laos.*

Sanakham Airfield (QV 86-83)
L-49. CIA/SF, per *Air Facilities Data-Laos.*

Sanam Bin Changwat Udon Thani Airport (n/a)
A.k.a. Changwat Udon Thani AF. In grid square TE 6-2, at 17°23'00"N-102°47'00"E. NE48-09. NIMA data. Thailand.

Sanam Bin Ubon Ratchathani (VB 8-8)
See Ubon AB. Thailand.

Sanambin Songkhla Airfield (PH 7-9)
See Songkhla. Thailand.

Sanctuary, USS (n/a)
A.k.a. AH 17. Hospital ship that was part of 7th Fleet's III MAF, 66-70. Painted white with large red crosses on each side, this floating hospital obviated need for const of hospital complexes ashore and substantial ground forces needed to secure onshore facilities. Kept off coast, out of arty range and used primarily to treat Marine and Navy casualties, though all branches were welcomed. Customers spoke highly of their comforts and staff members. Normally in I Corps waters, though possibly positioned elsewhere as well. Standard complement was medical staff of 24 doctors, 29 nurses and 250 Corpsmen, in addition to dental surgeons and Chaplains. See USN/USMC, USAF and US Army Hospitals and also *Hope, USS* and *Repose USS.*

Sand, LZ (BS 832-084)
Overlooking coastal plain, apx 8 km WSW Gia An/QL-1 and 9 km NW LZ English. Mar67. Binh Dinh Pr, II Corps.

Sandi, FSB (XT 523-788)
Apx 23 km ESE Katum, 4 km NNE Bau Tram, 25 km WSW An Loc and 37 km NE Tay Ninh. Grid per Frank Penk, Jr. Tay Ninh Pr, III Corps.

Sandra, LZ (BR 923-754?)
If grid correct, was along QL-1, apx 4 km E Lac Son and 21 km SSE Bong Son. Dan Gillotti, 15th Arty Assn, lists grid as BS 923-754, but that grid is well out to sea; "BR" grid zone more likely correct. Binh Dinh Pr, II Corps.

Sandra, LZ/FSB (BS 803-193)
Apx 12 km NW LZ English, 6 km due E Thuan An and 13 km W ocean. Binh Dinh Pr, II Corps.

Sandra, LZ/FSB (XT 204-788)
A.k.a. FSB Rose? Apx 26 km N Tay Ninh East AF, 17 km SW Katum and 13 km ESE Thien Ngon AF. Tay Ninh Pr, III Corps.

Sandra, FSB (ZT 096-195)
Apx 30 km ENE Phan Thiet and 10 km SSE peak Dang Sruin Mtn. Feb71. Binh Tuy Pr, III Corps.

Sands, LZ (BR 847-016)
Along N side Rte 504, apx 25 km due S Bong Son AF, 7 km NW QL-1/Phu My, 5 km NNE peak of Hill 701 (Nui Xa Rong), 14 km SSE Ha Tay and about 20 km W the coast. B/1st/8th Cav/1st Cav here per www.familyville.com /data/lusmyp/ courage/. Per Terry McGee, on 21Mar67, while B/1/8th Cav was at LZ Sands, his Plt of 28 men was sent to ville at base of nearby hill to investigate aerial VR of enemy and, "Within a few minutes of getting there we had only 5 men not wounded or killed." Grid/info courtesy Terry McGee and Jim Claeys. Binh Dinh Pr, II Corps.
Sandy (n/a)
See Glossary.
Sandy, FSB/LZ (AN 846-241)
Near base of Tittie Mtn, apx 15 km due N Phan Thiet, 2.5 km WSW Thien Giao/intersection of Rtes 402 and LTL 8B and 1 km NW QL-1 RR tracks. Elements of 3d/506th Inf, 101st Abn and US 155mm Btys. C Bty, 5th/22d Arty here, Oct-Nov70. Grid and arty info per Nolan Putman. Binh Thuan Pr, II Corps.
Sandy, FSB (BT 133-453)
Apx 28 km NW Tam Ky and 32 km SSE Da Nang, 3 km due W LZ Baldy and 3 km SW QL-1. Apr70 XXIV Corps grid per Don Armstrong. Quang Nam Pr, I Corps.
Sandy, FSB (XT 192-770)
Apx 13 km ESE Thien Ngon AF, 18 km SW Katum, 20 km NNW Nui Ba Den and 26 km N Tay Ninh. 1st Cav, '69. Grid per Frank Penk, Jr. Tay Ninh Pr, III Corps.
Sandy, FSB (XT 523-788)
See Sandi, FSB. Tay Ninh Pr, III Corps.
Sandy, FSB (YD 877-247)
Apx 14 km due E Hue Citadel AF, 9.5 km due N Phu Bai AF and 9 km SE Eagle Beach. 5-point star-shaped FSB built in wide, flat sandy area with no vegetation of any sort within less than 1 km of its perimeter. Perimeter formed of thick berms simply plowed into placed by hvy equip. Extremely difficult to keep weapons/equip clean here due to helo traffic's wind-blown sands. 2d Bde/101st Abn elements here Dec68. Also listed at YD 878-249. Thua Thien Pr, I Corps.
Sandy, LZ (BR 615-435)
Apx 15 km E An Khe and 8 km W Binh Khe. 19Dec65. Also listed at BR 815-445, 18Dec65, and unknown which grid is correct? Binh Dinh Pr, II Corps.
Sandy, LZ (BR 815-445)
Apx 13 km E Binh Khe and 7 km W Phu Cat AB. 18Dec65. Also listed at BR 615-435, 19Dec65, and unknown which grid is correct? Binh Dinh Pr, II Corps.
Sandy, LZ (XD 910-564)
Apx 13 km NW Ca Lu and 44 km W Quang Tri. Sep68. Quang Tri Pr, I Corps.
Sanford Army Airfield (YT 074-067)
Apx 22 km NE Saigon, 12 km SE Bien Hoa AF and 15 km due E Di An AF. Named to honor Maj. Jack W Sanford, USA, A/502d Avn Bn, KIA 16Jun65, when his gunship was shot down by small arms fire, per *Vietnam Military Lore, 1959-1973*. HQ 1st Avn Bde, Long Binh Post. Alt 120', 3,200' asph rwy. At 10°55'00"N-106°54'00"E. Bien Hoa Pr, III Corps.
Sangliers, Ile de (YJ 6-1)
Island of Wild Boar. NIMA data. NVN.
Sansone, Camp (n/a)
Not in VN. Named to honor SFC Dominic Sansone, KIA 10Dec64, per *Vietnam Military Lore, 1959-1973*. Okinawa
Santa, LZ (BR 843-717)
Apx 6 km ESE Ha Tay AF and 14 km due S Bong Son AF. Oct66. Cited in 1st Cav VN *Yearbook* Aug65-Dec69, p 89, per Peter Cole. Binh Dinh Pr, II Corps.
Santana, LZ (n/a)
No data. Cited in 1st Cav VN *Yearbook* Aug65-Dec69, p 288, per Peter Cole. I, II or III Corps.
Santiago, LZ (YD 178-258)
Apx 5 km SSE Ba Long AF, 2 km SSW Sa Ve and 21 km SW Quang Tri. Apr70 XXIV Corps grid per Don Armstrong. Quang Tri Pr, I Corps.
Sao Mai, FSB (YT 86-15?)
If grid correct, was along W side Rte 336 and N of some RR tracks, apx 2 km WNW peak Nui Kiet, 37 km ENE Xuan Loc and 14 km SW Tanh Linh AF. NPIA Gaz lists a Sao-Mai at YS 263-486, which is 3 km W Vung Tau AF? 3d/7th and 2d/3d Inf, 199th LIB. Binh Tuy Pr?, III Corps.
Sao Tri Plantation (AQ 85-03)
On W side of QL-21, apx 5 km E Ban Me Thuot. Grid apx. Darlac Pr, II Corps.
Sao Vang Division (NVA) (n/a)
See Glossary.
Sao, Mui (US 9-3)
Coastal point at 10°15'N-104°05'E. On NC48-05 JOG. Kien Giang Pr, IV Corps.
Sap, LZ (BR 786-470)
Apx 12 km WNW Phu Cat AB and 31 km ENE An Khe. 12Dec65. Binh Dinh Pr, II Corps.
Sapa (UK 8-7)
See Sa Pa. NVN.
SAR North (YH 10-12)
USN Search and Rescue patrol station in Gulf of Tonkin at 20N-107E, apx 100 km SSE Haiphong, 90 km due E Nghia Duc and 170 km SW Hanoi. Gulf of Tonkin. NVN.
SAR South (XG 06-01)
USN Search and Rescue patrol station in Gulf of Tonkin at 19N-106E, a point 220 km SSW Haiphong, and 40 km due E Phu Dien. Gulf of Tonkin. NVN.
Sara, FSB (XT 385-755)
Apx 14 km SSE Katum AF and 32 km NNE Tay Ninh. Mar70. Tay Ninh Pr, III Corps.
Sard, LZ (BR 812-485)
Apx 10 km NW Phu Cat AB and 33 km ENE An Khe. 19Dec65. Binh Dinh Pr, II Corps.
Sara Buri Airfield (QS 00)
A.k.a. Saraburi AF. Apx 95 km NNE Bangkok per Feb67 Natl Geo map., near 14°30'00"N-100°55'00"E. NIMA data. El. 300'. Thailand.
Sara Buri SF Camp (QS 00)
A.k.a. Saraburi SF camp. Apparently apx 95 km NNE Bangkok. SF camp per *SF Order of Battle.* Thailand.
Saraburi Airfield (QS 00)
See Sara Buri AF. Thailand.
Saraburi SF Camp (QS 00)
See Sara Buri SF camp. Thailand.

Sarah, FSB (XT 385-755)
See Sara. Tay Ninh Pr, III Corps.

Sarah II, FSB/LZ (ZA 115-670)
Along TL-3B, at or near Plei Mrong AF, apx 23 km NNW Pleiku and 8 km W QL-14. Name/grid and data per map provided by Patrick "O" Kelly (as per Ben Youmans). See also www.bravecannons.org/stories/C_SO_DP_rktactk_1.html. Grid is apx. Pleiku Pr, II Corps.

Saratoga, LZ (XD 851-339)
Apx 7 km SE Lang Vei (2), 9 km due S Khe Sanh CB and 21 km SW Ca Lu. Apr70 XXIV Corps grid per Don Armstrong. Quang Tri Pr, I Corps.

Saratoga, USS (n/a)
CV-60. Acft Carrier. Deployed with CVW-3, 11Apr72-13 Feb73. [480]

Saratoga, Operation (n/a)
8Dec67-11Mar68. 25th Inf Div op W Saigon and along Cambodian border. Yellowstone and Saratoga were concurrent ops, with the former in northern portion of 25th's AO while the latter was in southern AO. 3,862 rptd NVA/VC KIA, per *Vietnam Order of Battle*, pp 9-14. Tay Ninh/Hau Nghia Prvs, III Corps.

Saravane Airfield (XC 52-37)
A.k.a. L-44. Apx 470 km SE Vientiane. '67 Natl Geo map. CIA/SF facility. Grid, per Kent Spalding. El. 550'. Laos.

Saravane SF Camp (XC 52-37)
Apx 470 km SE Vientiane. SF camp/FOB in Laos when neutrality declared (23Jul62). FTT 4, 6, 12, 17, 31 and 44 here then. Per *Special Forces at War*. MR4, Laos.

Sarge, FSB/LZ (YD 029-478)
A.k.a. FSB Dong Toan, "Xa'c," Nui Dong Toan or Nui Ba Ho, and possibly OP Sarge? Immed SW of and overlooking Vandegrift CB, 32 km W Quang Tri, 3 km due E Ca Lu and 6 km WSW Mai Loc. While manned by ARVN and US Adv, was overrun by NVA, 30Mar72, during Easter Offensive. USMC/5th Div. Also listed at YD 038-478, which if correct, is apx 9 km E listed grid? Apr70 XXIV Corps grid per Don Armstrong. Quang Tri Pr, I Corps. [481]

Satan, OP (YD 761-056)
See OP Satan. Thua Thien Pr, I Corps.

Satan 1, FSB (YD 663-222)
Apx 400 meters ESE OP Castle on Ya Do Mtn, some 7 km SE Ap Lai Bang and 5 km W Hue. 101st Abn AO, '69-71. Thua Thien Pr, I Corps.

Satan II, FSB (YD 761-055)
A.k.a. Nui Ke, Hill 618, LZ Satan II or Satan II OP. Apx 15 km due S Hue, 16 km SW Phu Bai, 7 km SE FSB Birmingham and 6 km due W FSB Arsenal. 3d Bde/82d Abn base during Op Nevada Eagle (82d's portion of op was "Op Mot"). 2d Bde/101st Abn AO, '69-71. See LZ Satan II and Nui Ke. Thua Thien Pr, I Corps.

Satan II, OP (YD 761-055)
See LZ Satan II. Thua Thien Pr, I Corps.

Sattahip (U-Tapao) (n/a)
Along coast of Gulf of Siam, apx 125 km SSE Bangkok. Home of US Army Supt Cmd Facility. At various times occupied by 9th Logistical Cmd, 562d Maint Co, 599th Ord Co, 596th QM Co, 379th Sig Bn, 324th Sig Co, 499th Trans Bn HHD, 165th, 229th, 233d, 260th and 505th Trans Cos. Apparently US SF Camp/FOB here. Thailand.

Sattahip Airfield (QP 1-9)
A.k.a. U Tapao AF? Along coast of Gulf of Siam, apx 125 km SSE Bangkok, per Feb67 Natl Geo map. Near 12°39'00"N-100°57'00"E. El. 23'. Thailand.

Satun Airfield (PH 1-3)
Near Malaysian border, apx 825 km SSW Bangkok. At 6°39'00"N-100°05'00"E. Grid per, and listed as abnd in, '66. Some NIMA data. El. 18'. Thailand.

Saturn, LZ (YD 094-668)
Apx 3 km WNW Thon Bai An, 2 km SW Thon An Hoa, 9 km NNW Cam Lo, and 16 km WNW Dong Ha. Apr70 XXIV Corps grid per D. Armstrong. Quang Tri Pr, I Corps.

Satyr, USS (n/a)
ARL-23. USN Landing Craft Repair Ship. SVN service with 9th Inf Div/MRF. Per www.mrfa.org. III/IV Corps?

Sauveterre, Plantation de (YS 4-9)
A.k.a. Don Dien Sauveterre. Near Blackhorse Basecamp-AF, and S of Xuan Loc. Long Khanh Pr, III Corps.

Savage, FSB (YB 85-18?)
Within 10 km of listed grid. Per 173d Abn AAR dated 7Dec67, was clearly visible from Hill 823 (FSB 15). Hill 823 was at YB 854-186, so it is likely Savage was within 10 km radius of FSB 15. Evidently 4th Div and 173d Abn FSB. Kontum Pr, II Corps. [482]

Savage, USS (n/a)
DER-386. DD-Escort, Radar, per Ralph Fries.

Savannah, LZ/FSB (AT 9-5?)
In general vic of the An Hoa Industrial Complex, SW of Da Nang (AT 92-53). During Op MACON LZ, 6Jul66, 2 full Bns were landed on both LZ Dixie and LZ Savannah. By end of op on 10Jul66, there were 8 US KIA and 33 WIA with 87 NVA KIA. Quang Tri Pr?, I Corps.

Savannakhet Airfield (VD 75-30)
A.k.a. L-39? Major US AF along Mekong River in Laos, and just across border from Cambodia, apx 240 km SE Vientiane, 90 km S NKP AB and directly E Savannakhet ville. CIA/SF facility also? Per ONC-J-11 and Feb67 Natl Geo map. El. 509'. Laos.

Savannakhet Airfield (Minor) (VD 75-30?)
A.k.a. L-39? On border apx 90 km due S Nakhon Phanom AB and 5 km W Savannakhet major AF (that was to E and across border in Laos), per ONC-J-11. CIA/SF Lima Site? El. 443'. Cambodia?

Savannakhet SF Camp (VD 75-30?)
Apx 240 km SE Vientiane and 90 km S NKP AB. SF camp when Lao neutrality declared, 23Jul62. Det BC and ATT 6 here then. Per *Special Forces at War*. MR3, Laos.

Savoy Palace BOQ (XS 826-888)
At 220 Dong Khanh St., Sep 64, 44 rms, Saigon. Data per *Vietnam Military Lore, 1959-1973*. Gia Dinh Pr, III Corps.

Savoy, LZ (BR 612-604)
At or near site of Vinh Thanh AF, immed S Old French (CIDG) Fort in Vinh Thanh (Happy) Valley, 2 km NNW Vinh Thanh and 22 km NE An Khe. 17th and 19th Arty (155mm) elements here suptg LZ Hereford during Op Benning/Crazy Horse, May66. See *Battles in the Monsoon*, pp 48, 54, 66, 70, 77-78. Binh Dinh Pr, II Corps.

Sawang Daen Din Airfield (UE3-3)
At 17°28'43"N-103°27'57"E. NIMA data. Thailand.

Sawyers, Camp (AR 780-480?)
Camp at Engineer Hill near Pleiku. Named to honor SSgt Charles D Sawyers, USA, 1st Plt/B/299th Engr Bn, 4th Div? KIA 11Nov67, shot in neck during ambush on Hwy 14 near Checkpoint 24. 70th Engr Bn. Pleiku Pr, II Corps.
Sayaboury Airfield (QB 86-30)
L-23 Ba Na To AF? Apx 165 km NNW Vientiane on Feb67 Natl Geo map. CIA/SF, per *Air Facilities Data-Laos*. El. 1,070'. Laos.
Sayaboury SF Camp (QB 86-30?)
Apx 165 km NNW Vientiane. SF camp/FOB when Laos neutrality declared, 23Jul62. FTT 1 and 39 here then. Per *Special Forces at War*. MR1, Laos.
Scale, LZ (XD 951-316)
At NE edge of Vietnam Salient, apx 15 km SE Khe Sanh CB and 18 km SSW Ca Lu. Apr70 XXIV Corps grid per Don Armstrong. Quang Tri Pr, I Corps.
Scalp, LZ (BS 849-195)
In valley, apx 8 km NW Gia An/QL-1 and 20 km SSE Duc Pho AF. Feb67. Binh Dinh Pr, II Corps.
Scarf, LZ ? (BR 850-793)
Along Rte 506, apx 6 km SE Ha Tay AF and 16 km due S Bong Son AF. Nature of site unknown. 24Feb66. Binh Dinh Pr, II Corps.
Scarlet, FSB (XT 029-544)
Apx 15 km WNW Tay Ninh W AF, 5 km E Cambodia and 10 km NW Ben Soi. 5Apr66. Tay Ninh Pr, III Corps.
Scarlet, FSB (XT 727-154)
Apx 13 km SE Cu Chi and 12 km NW Tan Son Nhut AB. Aug-Sep67. Also listed at XT 729-145. Binh Duong Pr, III Corps.
Schenectady County, USS (n/a)
LST-1185. Lndg. Ship, Tank, per Ralph Fries.
Scheuler, LZ (BR 363-457)
See Schueller. Binh Dinh Pr, II Corps.
Scheuller, LZ (BR 363-457)
See Schueller. Binh Dinh Pr, II Corps.
Schmidt, Camp (AR 763-517)
Immed NW the N end Pleiku AB rwy. HQ 45th Gen Supt Cmd. Named to honor Maj. Richard H. Schmidt, USA, Civil Affairs Officer, Qui Nhon Supt Cmd, KIA 17May66, in VC ambush while returning from Medcap at Phy My, Binh Dinh Pr. Died in hand to hand combat while covering his mens retreat. Pleiku Pr, II Corps. [483]
Schofield, FSB (XT 403-443)
Along road connecting Dau Tieng with QL-22, apx 9 km WSW Dau Tieng, 3.5 km NE Checkpoint Tango and 14 km ESE Tay Ninh. Established 23Aug68, by elements of 2d Bde/25th. Heavily attacked at 0300 hrs, 24Aug68, while defended by A, B and C Cos, 2d/27th Inf, A Trp 3d Sqdn, 4th Cav, A Bty 1st/8th Arty and C Bty 7th/11th Arty. Several human wave attacks blunted by organic fire and Spooky Gunship. 9 US KIA and 41 WIA with 103 NVA KIA in battle. [484] Elements of 4th Bn.(Mech) 23rd Inf, also here. Grid/Info per Butch Sincock. Also listed at XT 407-440. Tay Ninh Pr, III Corps.
Schofield II, FSB (XT4-4?)
No grid. 1st/8th Arty, 25th Div said to have been here. Data per Dan Gillotti, 15th Arty Assn. Tay Ninh Pr?, III Corps.

Schook, Camp (BS 888-056)
Along QL-1, apx 6 km N LZ English and 8 km SSW Gia An. Possibly named to honor PSgt George Washington Schook, KIA7Aug67. Jul68. Binh Dinh Pr, II Corps.
Schoolhouse Valley (BT 5-0?)
Named for Vietnamese schoolhouse across QL-1 from, and to W of, Chu Lai. Map/discussion of site in *Mot CAP*. In 5th Marine and CAP One AO. Quang Tin Pr, I Corps.
Schrapnel, FSB (XD 857-591)
See FSB Shrapnel. Quang Tri Pr, I Corps.
Schroeder, FSB (XS 140-480)
A.k.a. FSB Dirk. Along QL 4, apx 27 km WNW Dong Tam. 9th Inf originally built as FSB Dirk, Jan69, after FSB Cleopatra was closed. Later in '69 was renamed FSB Schroeder to honor LTC Donald B Schroeder, CO 2d/39th Inf (1st Recondo Bn), 9th Inf Div, KIA 13Feb69 while trying to capture 2 VC, alone and on foot after disembarking his helo. Gen Hank "Gunslinger" Emerson called him greatest battlefield cmdr by far of any he had known in his 2 wars. Map is L-7014-6129-1 (Sa Dec). Data per Jim Stone, 2d/39th Inf. Dinh Tuong Pr, IV Corps.
Schueler, LZ (BR 363-457)
See Schueller. Binh Dinh Pr, II Corps.
Schueller, LZ/FSB (BR 363-457)
Originally LZ Road? Along QL-19E apx 13 km due W An Khe and 2 km WSW An Dinh. Possibly named to honor 1Lt James P. Schueller, KIA 17Jun67. Described as "just some concertina wire surrounding a few sandbagged bunkers, home to one [105mm Bty]." [485] 1st/50th Armor provided security here and at various strongpoints along QL-19E. In '68-69, base was "Dry" (no alcohol), so nightly, 10 km "Beer Runs" were made by 1st/69th Armor to LZ Action, a "wet" FSB. [486] On 10Apr68 major ambush of road near Schueller resulted in 300 NVA KIA, who were later buried in mass grave just below its perimeter (per Jim Walker). 2d/17th Arty here supt 1st Cav prior to '69? Per Jim Claeys, was 4th Div AO, '70. B & B Btys, 7th/15th Arty here, Apr-Oct71, per Nolan Putman. At 13°58'10"N-108°33'33"E. Map is L-7014-6736-4. Also listed at BR 367-458. Photos at: www.landscaper.net/vietnam.html. Binh Dinh Pr, II Corps.
Schultz, FSB (XU)
Incursion FSB. 3d/4th Cav, 11th ACR operated out of this site and FSB Koropey, keeping Rte 7 clear between Memot and Snuol Cambodia, and also the Rome Plow road S to Katum, Jun70. Cambodia.
Schwartz, FSB? (YS 381-992)
Apx 12 km SW Xuan Loc, 7 km NE Blackhorse Basecamp and 24 km due E Long Thanh North AF. Apparently on edge of rubber plantation. Aerial photos of site at: www.users.uswest.net/~huffpapa/Rubber.jpg, website of Doug Huffman. Possibly also spelled Swartz or Shwartz? Long Khanh Pr, III Corps.
Scimitar, FSB (ZC 077-498)
A.k.a. COB Scimitar. Apx 47 km W Hoi An, 5 km NNW FSB Maxwell, 10 km NE FSB Tomahawk. Used in TF Yankee assault on Base Area 112, Jan-Feb69. 1st Mar Div. On map in *US Marines in VN-1969*, p 90. Apr70 XXIV Corps grid per D. Armstrong. Quang Nam Pr, I Corps.

Scobie, FSB (YS 665-706)
Just E LTL-23, apx 23 km ENE Nui Dat, 1 km NE FSB Rapier5 km NW FSB Feathers. RAR and US Arty position. On 1ATF NCO trng map per John Hollett. Conflicting information indicates it was between Rte 2 (LTL-2) and what Aussies called Courtenay Hill (1,000'), just N the Long Khanh/Phuoc Tuy Pr border near Xa Cam My in Xuan Loc District, Long Khanh Pr. [487] May be that it was moved? Listed In Phuoc Tuy Pr, III Corps. [488]

Scofield, FSB (XT 403-442)
See FSB Schofield. Tay Ninh Pr, III Corps.

Scotch, FSB (XD 912-562)
In river valley and near FSB Aries, apx 20 km WNW Mai Loc, 44 km W Quang Tri. Apparent initial occupation was by 2d/9th Marines, 3d Mar Div during Op Arlington Canyon (which also involved 3Jul69 assault into LZ Uranus then occupied by 2d/9th Mar Rgt CP; and 8Jul69 assault by M/2d/9th Marines into LZ Cougar some 6 km NW FSB Uranus, and 10Jul69 assault of K/2d/9th Marines into LZ Scotch). Later became fwd CP for 2 Bns of 101st Abn, 30Sep69. 1st and 2d Bns, 506th Inf landed at old Marine AF here 30-31Sep, to allow3d Mar Div to re-deploy. In 8-Co CA on following day, 506th then built FSBs Scotch and Shrapnel, then left area 31 Oct69, as USMC and 1st ARVN Div returned. Apr70 XXIV Corps grid per Don Armstrong. Quang Tri Pr, I Corps.

Scotch, LZ (XT 485-042)
Apx 13 km NW Duc Hoa AF and 4 km WSW Khiem Cuong. Apr66. Hau Nghia Pr, III Corps.

Scotland, Operation (n/a)
1Nov67-31Mar68. 3d Mar Div op that ended with start of Op Pegasus. 1,561 rptd NVA/VC KIA, per *Vietnam Order of Battle*, pp 9-14. Western Quang Tri Pr, I Corps.

Scotland II, Operation (n/a)
15Apr68-28Feb69. USMC op in Khe Sanh AO. PEGASUS 3,311 NVA/VC KIA, per *Vietnam Order of Battle*, pp 9-14. Quang Tri Pr, I Corps.

Scott (n/a)
6Apr70, XXIV Corps future-use III MAF FSB name.

Scott, Camp (XS 67-63?)
See FSB Tan Tru. Long An Pr, III Corps.

Scott, FSB (XT 265-930?)
Apx 7 km WNW Katum AF and 5 km S Cambodian border. Feb68. Also listed at XT 320-080, Mar68? Tay Ninh Pr, III Corps.

Scott, FSB (XT 320-080?)
At or near Duc Hue AF, apx 33 km WSW Cu Chi and 5 km S southern tip of Angel's Wing. Mar68. Also listed at XT 265-930 in Feb68? Hau Nghia Pr, III Corps.

Scott, FSB (XU 68-24?)
Described as having been SE Snuol and right on border of Cambodia where QL-13 crossed it. 1st Cav, 11th ACR and 199th LIB Incursion FSB, May70. Cited in *11th ACR Cambodia Invasion AAR, 1st Cav Div, May-Jun70*, courtesy Lou Rochat. [489] Grid est based on description. Cambodia.

Scott, LZ (YA 581-573)
Remote site along SW edge of Plei Trap Valley, apx 3 km E Cambodia, 65 km WNW Pleiku, and 26 km WNW Plei Djereng AF. Apparently built to provide fire supt for 4th Div's Cambodia invasion LZs across border to W. A Bty, 6th/26th Arty and A Bty, 1st/92d Arty here May 70. 4th Div 31Jul70 grid, per Jim Henderson. Pleiku Pr, II Corps.

Scott, LZ (YS 353-947)
Apx 8 km WSW Blackhorse AF and 17 km SW Xuan Loc. Mar66. Long Khanh Pr, III Corps.

Scout, FSB (XT 497-954)
Just inside Cambodia at W end of Fishhook, apx 2 to 3 km N the SVN border, 18 km ENE Katum, 23 km SE Memot, and 27 km ESE Loc Ninh, 27 km WNW An Loc. 1st Cav here and possibly others. Cited in *1st Cav Op Rpt, May-Jul70*, p 36, per Peter Cole. Grid per *11th ACR Cambodia Invasion AAR, 1st Cav Div,* courtesy Lou Rochat. [490] Also listed at XT 497-937, per Frank Penk, Jr. Cambodia.

Scout, LZ (YD 329-299)
Apx 21 km due S Quang Tri and 20 km SE Ba Long AF. Apr70 XXIV Corps grid per Don Armstrong. Thua Thien Pr, I Corps.

Screaming Eagle (n/a)
See Glossary.

Screwdriver, LZ (YS 223-834)
Along QL-15, apx 9 km NNW Phu My, 14 km SSE Long Thanh AF. Jan68. Bien Hoa Pr, III Corps.

Se San River (YA 66-42)
Joined Nam Sathay River at listed grid, apx 24 km NW Duc Co. Its upper reaches were known as the Ya Krong Bolah. Met Cambodian border at YA 66-40, and formed portion Cambodian/SVN border, as well as Pleiku and Kontum Pr border. II Corps.

Sea Dragon, Operation (NVN)
USN shore bombardment counterpart to USAF's Op Rolling Thunder. Began Oct66 and ended Oct68. See Task Force 70.8, US Naval Cmd Vietnam and Coastal Surveillance Force in Major HQs Section. NVN.

Sea Float, ATSB (VQ?)
A.k.a. Advanced Tactical Supt Base Sea Float. Apparently at sea near tip of Cau Mau Peninsula. Floating USN base renamed "Solis Anchor" when moved ashore for fwd ops. Suptd Riverine, Seal and ARVN ops. Data per Mike Turner at http://members.xoom.com/mdturner/ vietnam.htm. See Solid Anchor ATSB. An Xuyen Pr, IV Corps.

Sea Lift (n/a)
A.k.a. RO-RO2. Army Transport. See *Lt Col John U. D. Page* for detail.

Sea Train Florida, SS (n/a)
Commercial transport under govt contract, per Ralph Fries.

Sea Train New Jersey, SS (n/a)
Commercial transport under govt contract, per Ralph Fries.

Sea Train Texas, SS (n/a)
Commercial transport under govt contract, per Ralph Fries.

Sea Wolves (n/a)
See Seawolves in Glossary.

Seabee, FSB/LZ (AN 755-487)
See FSB Seebee. Binh Thuan Pr, II Corps.

Seabee Bridge (AT 913-587)
Hwy 540 bridge just N Ai Nghia and Dai Loc, apx 20 km SSW Da Nang AB and 10 km WNW Dien Ban. Aug68. Quang Nam Pr, I Corps.

Seabee, NMCB HQs (n/a)
See USN Seabees in Division Level Commands Section.

SEALs and Seal Teams (n/a)
See Glossary.

Sealion, USS (n/a)
APSS 315, Transport Submarine. In early-mid '60s, subs *Perch* (APSS 313) and *Sealion* (APSS 315) recommissioned to land/supply US SEALs, collect intel, and perform rescue ops in NVN waters. [491]

SEALORDS (n/a)
See Glossary.

Search and Attack (n/a)
See Glossary.

Search and Avoid (n/a)
See Glossary.

Searh and Clear (n/a)
See Glossary.

Search and Destroy (n/a)
See Glossary.

Sebago, USCGC (n/a)
WHEC 42. 2Mar69-16Nov69. Sqdn 3 CGC, during Coast Guard's 4th deployment.

Sec, Cape (CP 1-6)
See Cape Sec. Khanh Hoa Pr, II Corps.

Seche, Pointe (CP 1-6)
See Pointe Seche. Khanh Hoa Pr, II Corps.

Second Holy See (XT 265-463)
See Temple of Holy See (2). Tay Ninh Pr, III Corps.

Second Offensive (n/a)
See Glossary.

Sedang, Kingdom of (n/a)
See Glossary.

Sedgewick, FSB (XT 249-309)
A.k.a. FSB Mole City and also spelled Sedwick and Sedgwick. Apx 15 km due S Tay Ninh, 3 km ENE Ap Cai Tac, 5 km from Cambodia and 14 km W FSB Austin. 25th Inf Div. Also listed at XT 243-309, Jan-May69. See Mole City for more detail. Tay Ninh Pr, III Corps.

Sedgewick II, FSB (XT 240-320)
Apx 10 km N Angel's Wing and Cambodian border, some 3 km NNE Ap Cai Tac and 22 km SSE Tay Ninh West AF. May69. Tay Ninh Pr, III Corps.

Sedgwick County, USS (n/a)
LST 1123. MRF base ship. IV Corps.

Sedgwick, FSB (XT 249-309?)
See Sedgewick. Tay Ninh Pr, III Corps.

Sedwick, FSB (XT 249-309?)
See Sedgewick. Tay Ninh Pr, III Corps.

See, Temple of Holy (XT 241-496)
See Temple of Holy See. Tay Ninh Pr, III Corps.

Seebee, FSB (AN 751-485)
A.k.a. Hill 746. Apx 40 km NW Phan Thiet, 47 km WNW Song Mao and 9 km SE Ap Gia Bac. 3d/506th Inf, 101st Abn. Name per Jerry Berry, who lists it at AN 755-485. Also sp Seabee? Binh Thuan Pr, II Corps.

Segundo, USS (n/a)
SS-389. Submarine, per Ralph Fries.

Seldom Inn (XT 99-13 and YS 84-36)
First at Bien Hoa AB, then moved to Nui Dat. Mess facility/club and watering hole of RNZA, 161 Bty. Its 1st sign was lost to raid by Aussie troops during shift from Bien Hoa to Nui Dat (began 23May66). Recovered in '69, when 161 Bty Officer noticed it hanging in Aussie Engr's Mess tent. In Oct70, BBQ was built in Seldom Inn's garden. Bien Hoa and Phuoc Tuy Prvs, III Corps.

Self, Camp (XT 630-664?)
A.k.a. Camp Irving A. Self. At Minh Thanh, apx 33 km NNW Lai Khe AF, 16 km WNW Chon Thanh AF and 70 km NNW Saigon. Named to honor SSgt Irving A Self, 5th SF Det A-132, KIA 19May64. Binh Long Pr, III Corps.

Self, Irving A., Camp (XT 630-664?)
See Self, Camp. Tay Ninh Pr, III Corps.

Selma, LZ (YS 250-750)
Apx 3 km due N Phu My, 20 km WNW Nui Dat/Luscombe AF and 2 km E QL-15. Mar66. Phuoc Tuy Pr, III Corps.

Seminole, FSB (XS 980-962)
Apx 17 km E Tan Son Nhut AB and 7 km NNE Cat Lai. Dec68-Mar69. Gia Dinh Pr, III Corps.

Seminole, FSB (XT 275-028)
On Cambodian border apx 7 km SSW Duc Hue AF, 29 km WSW Cu Chi, 11 km E Chantrea, and 10 km N tip of Parrot's Beak. CP 6th/31st Inf, 9th Inf Div during Incursion, May-Jun70. Between 7-12May70, during Op Toan Thang 500, the 6th/31st Inf, 9th Inf Div conducted ops here, suffering 7 KIA, 29 WIA, with NVA losses at 159 KIA/18 POW. Per VHPA battle index at www.vhpa.org/info/panel/battle/ 70050700.htm. Cambodia.

Seminole, USS (n/a)
AKA-104. Amphib Attack. Cargo.

Semmes, USS (n/a)
DDG-18. Guided-Missile DD, per Ralph Fries.

Semper, FSB (n/a)
Possibly Semper Fi? No data. Americal list, I Corps.

Sen Kung Airfield (VA)
Apx 12 km SW Thbeng Meanchy AF, 10 km NW Phnum Tbeng Mtn. TPC K-10A. El. 1,542'. Cambodia.

Sen Sai Airfield (QC 13-52)
LS-162. CIA/SF, per *Air Facilities Data-Laos.*

Senate, LZ (YD 010-334)
Just N Hill 891, apx 14 km S Ca Lu, 39 km SW Quang Tri and 17 km WSW Ba Long AF. Nov68. Apr70 XXIV Corps grid per Don Armstrong. Quang Tri Pr, I Corps.

Senmonorom Airfield (n/a)
Apx 265 km ENE Phnom Penh and 20 km N the SVN border on Feb67 Natl Geo map. El. 2,250'. Cambodia.

Seno Airfield (WD 01-43)
A.k.a. L-46/46A. Major AF apx 285 km SE Vientiane, and 90 km SE NKP AB (Cambodia). Originally built by French as fighter-bomber AF, 1953-54, and last French AF to operate in Laos. Released to Lao Neutralists, Dec62. Laos. Also CIA/SF facility. Per ONC-J-11 and Feb67 Natl Geo maps. El. 607'. Laos.

Sepone Airfield (n/a)
A.k.a. Tchepone AF. Apx 410 km SE Vientiane and 50 km WNW Khe Sanh. Laos.

Serges Jungle Highway (XU/XT/YU)
A.k.a. The Song Be Corridor. N/S enemy infiltration rte toward Saigon that generally followed Binh Long, Phuoc Long Pr border SSE from Song Be through Bunard, then swinging to SW, passing S Dong Xoai, and then S toward Phuoc Vinh and Saigon. On Map One in *Rangers At War*, p 324. Binh Long and Binh Duong Prvs, III Corps.

Serignac Valley SF Camp (AP 979-069)
A.k.a. Dam Pau SF Camp and Camp Brotherhood. Apx 8 km NW Thanh Binh, 25 km SW Dalat and 16 km ESE Duc

Trong. 5th SF. Info/grid per *SF Order of Battle.* See Dam Pau. Tuyen Duc Pr, II Corps.

Serle, FSB (YS 538-614)
Along Rte-23, apx 4 km E FSB Horseshoe and 13 km ESE Nui Dat. 161 Bty, RNZA (Horsford's Bty 18Mar69-18Sep69) FSB set here 15-31Aug69. "A generously set out FSB, a factor that allowed the Bty to lay out a [3-hole] golf course" (Bty also built golf driving range at Nui Dat), per *Vietnam Gunners*. Grid per John Hollett. Also listed at YS 53-61. Phuoc Tuy Pr, III Corps.

SERTS (XT 98-13 and YD 53-32)
At Bien Hoa until Spring of '70 and known as "Camp Ray." In '70, was moved to Camp Evans in Quang Tri Pr, but unknown if it kept "Ray" name there. Screaming Eagle Replacement Trng School, the in-country, one-week course held for all new members of 101st Abn. Bien Hoa and Quang Tri Prvs, II Corps and I Corps.

Service Historique de L'Armee (France)
See Glossary.

Services Correctional Establishment (YS 2-4)
1ATF prison at Vung Tau. Precise location unknown. See Playboy Club. Phuoc Tuy Pr, III Corps.

Services Techneques des Constructions (n/a)
See Glossary.

SESU Site (XD 84-54)
On Hill 1739, apx 30 km WSW Cam Lo and 50 km due W Quang Tri. USMC Sig Engr Survey Unit. Created in Apr64, it included 5 officers, 152 EM, plus 3 officers and 27 EM from 1st Radio Co FMF Pacific, G/2d/3d Marines and an 81mm mortar section. Was 1st USMC ground unit to conduct independent ops in VN when it deployed to Radio Recon site on Dong Voi Mep (Tiger Tooth Mtn/Hill 1739). See also LZs Crest and Hill. Quang Tri Pr, I Corps.

Seven Mountains Outpost (WS 027-636?)
Nickname or early name of That Son SF camp? See That Son SF Camp and Phan Chau. Named for "Seven Sisters" nearby Mtn range. Was model for SF camp featured in book and film *The Green Berets*. Fictional base of "Phan Chau" used in film and book was based upon Moore's experiences here in 65-65. Chau Doc Pr, IV Corps.

Seven Pagodas (XJ 48-21?)
On Road No. 18, apx 58 km E Hanoi. French garrison here involved in fighting during 1st Indochina War. See *Street Without Joy*, Chp 2 and p 46. Grid is est. NVN.

Seven Sisters, The (WS 00-60)
Generally about 50 km ENE Ha Tien. 7 Mtn peaks that were virtually only terrain features available for land navigation by ground troops in that area. Grid is roughly in center of grp. See also Nui Coto. Chau Doc/Kien Giang Prvs, IV Corps.

Seven-Step Snake (n/a)
See Seven-Step Snake in Glossary.

Seventeenth Parallel (XD)
See 17th Parallel. NVN/SVN/Laos.

Seventh Day Adventist Hospital (XS 841-940)
See 7th Day Adventist & 3d Field. Gia Dinh Pr, III Corps.

Sgt Andrew Miller, USNS (n/a)
See Evacuation of Da Nang.

Sgt Truman Kimbro, USNS (n/a)
See Evacuation of Da Nang.

Shain Memorial Dining Hall (XT 988-129)
At Bien Hoa AFB. Named to honor USAF Maj. Elwin R. Shain, KIA 28Jul68. Data per *Vietnam Military lore, 1959-1973*. Near listed grid. Bien Hoa Pr, III Corps.

Shakey, FSB (YU 210-517)
Likely a.k.a. Shakey's Hill and Hill 423. Apx 10 km from SVN border, 20 km NW Djamap and 7 km E Phum Phnum Krang. Also slightly NE FSB Neal and 12 km due W FSB 11-Bravo. Incursion base named to honor Sgt Chris A "Shakey" Keffalos, KIA, 21May70. Also listed at YU 212-517, per *11th ACR Cambodia Invasion AAR, 1st Cav Div, May-Jun70*, courtesy Lou Rochat. [492] Cambodia.

Shakey's Hill (YU 210-517?)
See FSB Shakey. Cambodia.

Shanghai, LZ (XD 949-479)
Apx 5 km W Ca Lu and 12 km NE Khe Sanh CB. Apr70 XXIV Corps grid per D. Armstrong. Quang Tri Pr, I Corps.

Shangri La, LZ (ZC 083-553)
Along LTL-4 and N bank of Song Vu Gia, apx 3 km ENE Ha Tan AF and 33 km SW Da Nang. Oct68. See LZ Vulture and An Diem Heliport. Quang Nam Pr, I Corps.

Shangri-La, USS (n/a)
A.k.a. *Shangrila*. CVS-38. Acft Carrier. Deployed with CVW-8, 5Mar70-17Dec70. [493]

Shannon-Wright Compound (XS 040-331)
A.k.a. Wright Cmpd. At Vinh Long Army AF, apx 90 km SW Saigon, 46 km WSW My Tho and 28 km NE Can Tho. Named to honor both Sp5 Wyley Wright, Jr, KIA 9Mar64, in Huey crash in Bassac River, while escorting Secty of Def Robert McNamara on tour. Also honored 1Lt Kenneth A. Shannon KIA 15Mar64 (both of 114th Avn Co). Photo of front gate/sign at. www.familyville. com/data/lusmyp/ knight461/. Data per *Vietnam Military Lore, Legends, Shadows and Heroes*, p 557. Vinh Long Pr, IV Corps.

Shark, FSB (AT 933-885)
A.k.a. LZ Shark? On Mtn overlooking ocean along W side QL-1 just SSW Hai Van Pass, apx 3 km from coast, 4 km due N Ap Kim Lien, 16 km NNW Da Nang AB and 3 km SW FSB Moccasin. Apr70 XXIV Corps grid per Don Armstrong. Pr, I Corps.

Sharon, FSB (XT 541-450)
Apx 7 km ESE Dau Tieng Tri Tam. Aug-Sep69. Binh Duong Pr, III Corps.

Sharon, FSB/LZ (YD 340-497)
A.k.a. La Vang, FSB Tich Tuong and also LZ/FSB Betty-Sharon. W of RR tracks and QL-1 apx 2 km S Quang Tri, 25 km NW Camp Evans and 10 km NE FSB Nancy. Betty and Sharon were initially 2 adj perimeters built adj. Per Mike Cohen, A/1st/8th Cav, his unit helped in initial const (while another 1st Cav unit built Betty) as their 1st FSB following move N from Bong Son, Dec67-Jan68. He recalls old, French, tin-roofed, concrete army barracks were incorporated into perimeter, as well as was circular, French concrete observation tower. 229th AHB here. One text describes site as "somewhere in Khe Chau Valley" and occupied by Army's 1st/11th Inf working with 3d/9th Marines during Op Montana Mauler, Mar-Jul69? Army's 5th/4th Arty suptd 1st Bde/5th Mech Div from FSBs Sharon, Hai Lang and Nancy during '69. Elements of 4th/60th, E/71st and I/29th Inf here late 67-Jan68 (Dusters, Quads, Searchlights); 1st/44th Arty AO, per Paul Kopsick.

Also listed at YD 340-393, 330-490 and 390-495. Quang Tri Pr, I Corps.

Sharp, LZ (BR 710-945)
Apx 15 km W Bong Son and 16 km NW Ha Tay AF. Oct66. Binh Dinh Pr, III Corps.

Sharp, FSB (XU 854-153)
Along QL-14A, apx 17 km NE Loc Ninh and 19 km SW Bu Dop AF. Jan68. Binh Long Pr, III Corps.

Shawnee, LZ (BS 802-203)
Apx 12 km NW Gia An and 18 km S Duc Pho AF. Mar67. Binh Dinh Pr, III Corps.

Shay, Camp (BT 063-826)
See Camp Fay. Quang Nam Pr, I Corps.

Sheffield Village (XT 44-54?)
If grid correct, site was along LTL 14, apx 4 km SW Dau Tieng and 18 km due E Tay Ninh. Americal Div Assn lists name with grid as "OH" 440-540; however, no such grid zone exists in SVN. That list also claims facility was near Tay Ninh, which suggests proper grid zone is XT. Tay Ninh Pr?, III Corps.

Shelly, LZ (XD 936-653)
At S edge of DMZ, apx 19 km WNW Cam Lo and 31 km WNW Dong Ha. Apr70 XXIV Corps grid per Don Armstrong. Quang Tri Pr, I Corps.

Shelton, USS (n/a)
DD-790, per Ralph Fries.

Shenandoah, LZ (XD 688-420)
Apx 1 km E of Laos, 8 km NW Lao Bao and 17 km due W Khe Sanh CB. Apr70 XXIV Corps grid per Don Armstrong. Quang Tri Pr, I Corps.

Shenandoah II, Operation (n/a)
27Sep-19Nov67. 1st Inf Div op. 956 rptd NVA/VC KIA, per *Vietnam Order of Battle*, pp 9-14. Binh Duong and Binh Long Prvs, III Corps.

Shepard, FSB/LZ (XD 934-410)
See Shepherd. Quang Tri Pr, I Corps.

Shepherd, LZ/FSB (XD 934-410)
A.k.a. Fwd Base Sheperd, Sheppard, Shephard and Shepperd. On or near peak of Hill 691, apx 3 km N QL-1 and 18 km SW Mai Loc. 3d Mar Div in '69. On map at p 73, *US Marines in Vietnam-1969*. Jul68-Sep70. Also listed at XD 945-420, which if correct, is apx 10 km E listed grid. Quang Tri Pr, I Corps.

Sheppard, FSB/LZ (XD 934-410)
See Shepherd. Quang Tri Pr, I Corps.

Sherida, FSB/LZ (BR 690-558)
Apx 10 km SE Vinh Thanh AF, 23 km NW Phu Cat AB and 30 km SSW Ha Tay. 4th Div AO, '70. Spelling apparently correct and not a variant of "Sheridan." Also listed at BR 688-560. Binh Dinh Pr, II Corps.

Sheridan, FSB (BR 688-560)
See Sherida. Binh Dinh Pr, II Corps.

Sherman, FSB (YT 220-372)
Apx 27 km SE Phuoc Vinh AF, 23 km NW Xa Binh Hoa and 34 km NE Bien Hoa AB. 1st/12th Cav, 1st Cav? Also listed at YT 216-369, Feb71. Long Khanh Pr, III Corps.

Sherman, USCGC (n/a)
WHEC 720. 22Apr70-25Dec70. Sqdn 3 CGC, during Coast Guard's 6th deployment.

Sherry, FSB/LZ (AN 810-160)
Apx 7 km N Phan Thiet and immed N Ap Tan Long. Housed US 155mm howitzer Btys. Data per Jerry Berry. 3d/506th Inf/101st Abn. Binh Thuan Pr, II Corps.

Sherry, LZ (BN 281-449)
A.k.a. FSB Song Mao. Adj Hai Ninh, apx 2 km SE Song Mao AF, 2 km NW Phan Ly Cham and 50 km NE Phan Thiet. 3d/506th Inf/101st Abn. Info/grid per Jerry Berry. Binh Thuan Pr, II Corps.

Sherry, LZ (BR 490-690)
Apx 9 km NE Kannack AF, 15 km NW Vinh Thanh AF, 44 km SE Bong Son, 26 km N An Khe and 6 km NE Kon Creh. 4th Div AO, '70. C Bty, 2d/9th Arty here Feb70. Data per Jim Claeys. Apr-Oct70. Binh Dinh Pr, II Corps.

Sherry 1, LZ (BS 690-325)
Immed S Lang Khom Kang, apx, 13 km WSW Duc Pho AF, 14 km E Ba to New AF and 1 km W LZ Sherry 2. 1st Cav. Name/grid per Dan Gillotti, 15th Arty Assn. I Corps.

Sherry 2, LZ (BS 700-322)
Apx 1.5 km SE Lang Khom Kang, 12 km WSW Duc Pho AF, 15 km E Ba to New AF and 1 km E LZ Sherry 1. 1st Cav. Name/grid per Dan Gillotti, 15th Arty Assn. I Corps.

Sherwood Forest (AT 90-97)
USMC nickname for AO apx 15-20 km SW Da Nang and immed N Charlie Ridge. *US Marines in Vietnam-1969*, p 98 map puts it near AT 80-70. Quang Nam Pr, I Corps.

Sherwood Forest (n/a)
Generic phrase used by USN sailors to describe several different coastal fishing grounds along coast of SVN. Characterized by tall Bamboo poles holding fish traps and nets that rose above surface giving area the look of a forest. Areas presented numerous navigation and fouling hazards. Cited in *Brown Water, Black Berets*, p 106. SVN.

Sheryl, LZ (BT 302-192)
A.k.a. Cheryl? At or near Tam Ky's major AF, 4 km due S Tam Ky, 12 km NW Diem Pho and 4 km SW QL-1. Americal list. Quang Tin Pr, I Corps.

Shibaura Maru (n/a)
Commercial contract Ocean Tug. See Evacuation of Da Nang and Op Frequent Wind.

Shield, FSB (YC 746-645)
Apx 5 km NW Ai Yin Yong14 km E Laos and 68 km WNW Da Nang. FSBs Fury, Pike, Shield, Whip and Thor were built during Op Massachusetts Striker, 22Mar-8May69, using Combat Trap 10,000 lb bombs (if available) to clear initial site enough for rappelling.[494] XXIV Corps grid per D. Armstrong. Quang Nam Pr, I Corps.

Shields, Camp (BT 555-035)
At Chu Lai CB. Possibly a Seabee cmpd or at the SF camp here? Named to honor CMA3 Marvin G Shields, USN, KIA 9Jun65, in attack of SF Camp at Dong Xoai. Quang Tin Pr, I Corps.

Shields, CM3 Marvin (n/a)
See Glossary.

Shields, USS (n/a)
DD-596, per Ralph Fries.

Shing Scha Airfield (UH 05-03)
LS-339. CIA/SF, per *Air Facilities Data-Laos.*

Shiloh, FSB (YD 107-267)
A.k.a. Hill 347. Near the Ba Long Valley, apx 24 km SSE Vandegrift CB, 7 km SE FSB Tun Tavern, 9 km W Laos

and 15 km SSW Ba Long AF. Re-opened by 3d/9th Marines, 3d Mar Div Jan69. On map at p 32, *US Marines in Vietnam-1969*. Apr70 XXIV Corps grid per Don Armstrong. Nov68-Feb69. Quang Tri Pr, I Corps.

Shining Brass (n/a)
See Glossary.

Ship, LZ (BR 8-6?)
Apparently in Phu My District. Per *Rites of Passage*, p 328, was adj to long narrow valley and a 3-hour hump from LZ Wire. Feb-Mar67, Binh Dinh Pr, II Corps.

Shirley, FSB (AT 873-385)
Adj to or just S Phuoc Binh AF, apx 12 km due S An Hoa CB, 38 km SSW Da Nang AB and 33 km SW Hoi An. Americal list. Quang Nam Pr, I Corps.

Shirley, FSB (YD 836-324)
In sands of narrow Phuoc Vinh Island, apx 3 km ESE Tan My/Eagle Beach, 13 km NE Hue Citadel AF, and at or near Thon Thai Duong Ha. Apr70 XXIV Corps grid per Don Armstrong. Thua Thien Pr, I Corps.

Shirley, LZ (AQ 855-255)
Apx 8 km ENE Quang Nhieu and 22 km NNE Ban Me Thuot City AF. Mar66. Darlac Pr, II Corps.

Shirley, LZ (BS 382-700)
A.k.a. Ha Thanh SF Camp. In valley of Song Tra Khuc River, apx 27 km W Quang Ngai, and apx 1 km W Ha Thanh. Established by 2d/1st Inf, 3Dec70. Americal list, Also listed at BS 395-705? Quang Ngai Pr, I Corps.

Shirley, LZ (BS 395-705?)
If grid correct, was in valley of Song Tra Khuc, apx 26 km W Quang Ngai and immed NE Ha Thanh. Also listed at BS 382-700? Quang Ngai Pr, I Corps.

Shirley, LZ (XT 763 891)
Along QL-13 apx 1 km N An Loc, 18 km due S Loc Ninh AF and 65 km NE Tay Ninh. Binh Long Pr, III Corps.

Shirley, LZ (YT 959-895)
Apx 16 km NW Tanh Phat AF, 14 km NW Bao Loc AF and 11 km SSE Dang Klar. Feb67. Lam Dong Pr, II Corps.

Shirt, LZ ? (BR 870-812)
Apx 15 km SSE Bong Son and 7 km ESE Ha Tay AF. Feb66. Binh Dinh Pr, III Corps.

Shit Beach (BT)
Near Marble Mtn AF and Da Nang. May have been along the Han river or the coast itself? Cited in *Recon Extraction*, Jan 2001 *Military* Mag, p 16. Quang Nam Pr, I Corps.

Shit Beach (CR 08-22)
A.k.a. Sierra Beach. Along S? edge of Qui Nhon. On 7Jul65, USMC's BLT 2/7 arrived in VN and made amphib landing via LVTP-5s on beach at Qui Nhon. Origin of beach's name apparently resulted from this landing, which is described as follows in *Utter's Battalion*, p 100, "For many Marines making the landing, the very first aspect of combat service in the Republic of Vietnam...was the presence of an extremely large volume of human feces on the beach. For some reason, the locals had chosen to use the white sand of the curving, attractive beach as a communal toilet. The leavings of hundreds...lay on the sand where much of it got stuck to the combat boots of the arriving infantrymen and in the tracks of the amphibious tractors. The smell along the otherwise pleasant shore was strong enough to induce nausea." Nickname "Sierra" was more polite name based upon phonetic alpha for letter "S." Name per Duane Good. See Camp Granite and Vung Chau Mtn Signal Site. Binh Dinh Pr, II Corps.

Shock (n/a)
Apr70, XXIV Corps future-use 101st Abn FSB name.

Shock, FSB (YD 518-056?)
FSB apx 3 km NE FSB Cannon, 10 km SE FSB Kathryn and 5 km NW FSB Veghel. Possibly a.k.a. Dong Ong Doi? 101st Airborne Div. Grid is position of Dong Ong Doi. Thua Thien Pr, I Corps.

Shook, Camp (BS 888-056)
See Camp Schook. Binh Dinh Pr, II Corps.

Short Uplift (n/a)
See Glossary.

Short-Timer I (BS 6-1 or BR?)
Near FSB/LZ Powder (BS 637-179)? Short-Timer I and II are described by John Linn as having been very small FSBs used in Co or plt-sized ops, employing single 81mm mortar for fire supt. In 4th Div, similar sites apparently called "hip-shoot" bases. Linn also tells us that B/2d/35th Inf/4th Div was at Short-Timer I, Aug70, and at II, Sep70. Likely Binh Dinh Pr, II Corps.

Short-Timer II (BS or BR?)
See Short-Timer I. Likely Binh Dinh Pr, II Corps.

Shotgun, Operation (n/a)
Per Dick Arnold, although the 3d Bde/25th Inf Div (1st/35th, 2d/35th, 1st/14th) was the Div's first Bde to deploy to VN in late Dec65, a large number of 25th Div men preceded them in specialized role. In early '63, under Op Shotgun, 25th Div volunteers (Div was in Hawaii), served as door gunners for VN Avn units. Plts of 32-40 men were TDY'd to VN for 90-120 days at a stretch, and total of 11 Shotgun Plts preceded the Div to VN (losing 19 KIA). Each received initial trng at 25th's gunnery range in Makuia Valley, Hawaii. Trng of Shotgun 10 also happened to coincide with filming of feature film *Hawaii*, Sep65, and because sounds of choppers and firing were being picked-up on sound track of film, its producers asked that trng be suspended. 25th CG Fred Weyand said "No," but did give principal stars Julie Andrews and Max Von Sydow, rides on gun run over target area.

Shoup, FSB (XD 883-495)
Apx 9 km NNE Khe Sanh CB, 26 km WSW Cam Lo, 20 km due W Mai Loc and 9 km W QL-9. Possibly named to honor LCpl Roy N. Shoup, KIA 16Mar67. Apr70 XXIV Corps grid per Don Armstrong. Quang Tri Pr, I Corps.

Shrapnel, FSB (XD 857-591)
Apx 18 km due N Khe Sanh CB, 25 km WNW Mai Loc and 47 km WNW Quang Tri. Mai Loc became fwd CP for 2 Bns/101st Abn, 30Sep69. 1st and 2d Bn/506th Inf landed at old Marine AF there, 30-31Sep, to allow 3d Mar Div to redeploy elsewhere. In 8-Co CA following day, 506th built 2 Scotch and Shrapnel, then left area 31Oct69, as Marines and 1st ARVN Div returned. Apr70 XXIV Corps grid per Don Armstrong. Quang Tri Pr, I Corps.

Shrike, LZ (YD 63-38?)
Along Rte 597, apx 9 km ENE Phong Dien and 10 km SE LZ Raven. 2d/1st Mar LZ during Op Jay, Jun66. Grid estimated per map in *USMC In Vietnam, 1966*, p 153. Thua Thien/Quang Tri Pr border, I Corps.

Shubiak Bridge (CQ 07-87 or 06-73?)
Apparently on QL-1 between Song Cau and Tuy Hoa. A sign bearing following inscription once stood at this bridge site: *This Bridge Built to honor Sp4 Joseph Shubiak, A Company, 19th Engineer Bn* (*CA*). Shubiak was KIA 17Aug67. Data courtesy Ray Bows. Phu Yen Pr, II Corps.
Shuck (n/a)
Apr70, XXIV Corps future-use 101st Abn FSB name.
Shufly Compound (BT 008-754?)
Built in Da Nang, Summer of '63. Photo of installation is at www.popasmoke./shufly2.html. Grid is for Da Nang AB, but precise location unknown. Quang Nam Pr, I Corps.
Shufly, Operation (XR 058-591)
1st deployment of a Marine Helo Unit to SVN, 15Mar62. On that day, USMC Med helo Sqdn HMM 362 launched its H-34 Sikorskys from deck of *USS Princeton* at point some 25 km from coast of SVN and bound for old, WWII Japanese AF at Soc Trang in Mekong Delta. Soc Trang was apx 140 km WSW Saigon and 25 km E mouth of Mekong River. Unit was under cmd of LTC Archie Clapp and its 1st combat mission took place 18Apr62. Over next 2 years, USMC rotated HMM-362, 163, 261, 364 and 365 through Shufly and Soc Trang. Shufly later replaced by term MUVN, for "Marine Unit, Vietnam." See Soc Trang and Shufly Cmpd Da Nang. [495] Ba Xuyen Pr, IV Corps.
Shuttle X (n/a)
See Shuttle X in Glossary and Katum AF in alpha listings.
Shwartz, FSB (YS 381-992)
See FSB Schwartz. Long Khanh Pr, III Corps.
Si Ching Mai Airfield? (n/a)
Along S bank of Mekong River at Lao border, apx 515 km NNE Bangkok and perhaps 10 km W Vientiane (Laos). Unknown if this is proper name for AF. Thailand.
Si Siang Mai Airfield (UG 00-43)
LS-277. CIA/SF, per *Air Facilities Data-Laos.*
Siberia, LZ (AT 901-232)
On hilltop overlooking Song Chang River, apx 40 km due W Tam Ky, 12 km SE Thach Bich, 2 km SW Hiep Duc and 9 km WSW LZ West/Nui Liet Kiem Mtn. Per Les Hines, site also overlooked resettlement ville for people of Hiep Duc. Apparently built near 19Apr69. Also listed at AT 899-238 and 903-232. Quang Tin Pr, I Corps.
Sicily I through IV, FSB (XT 8-3?)
Presumed to have existed because there was a Sicily V and VI? Binh Duong Pr, III Corps.
Sicily V, FSB (XT 886-368)
Apx 10 km NW Khu Tru Mat and 12 km due E Lai Khe. Jan68. Same grid as Sicily VI. Binh Duong Pr, III Corps.
Sicily VI, FSB (XT 887-369)
Apx 10 km NW Khu Tru Mat and 12 km due E Lai Khe. Jan68. Same grid as Sicily V. Binh Duong Pr, III Corps.
Sickle, LZ (BN 222-743)
A.k.a. Hill 1136. Apx 29 km NNW Song Mao AF, 13 km SW Xieng Tiar and 27 km SSE Dalat/Lien Khuong AF. Mar67. Binh Thuan Pr, II Corps.
Sicovina TFACT (BT 011-728)
At intersection of QL-1 and Hwy 541, apx 3 km SSW Da Nang AB. Meaning of TFACT acronym and nature of site unknown. Possibly a factory or refinery or TF HQ? Quang Nam Pr, I Corps.
Sidewinder, FSB (XT 745-810)
Along Rte 245, apx 7 km SSW An Loc, 5 km S Xa Thanh Binh and 56 km NE Tay Ninh. FSBs Aspen I, Aspen II and Sidewinder sat in row within 8 km An Loc, protecting convoys and that flank of city. 11th ACR here. Cited in *Incursion*, per Peter Cole. Grid per Frank Penk, Jr. Also listed at XT 745-821 and 739-821. Jun-Aug68. Binh Long Pr, III Corps.
Sidney, LZ (YS 435-915)
Apx 23 km N Nui Dat/Luscombe AF, 18 km S Xuan Loc, 5 km S Blackhorse AF and 2 km W LTL-2. Apr66. Long Khanh Pr, III Corps.
Siem Pang Airfield (n/a)
Near Laotian border apx 320 km NE Phnom Penh. Feb67 Natl Geo map. El. 246'. Cambodia.
Siem Reap Airfield (n/a)
Adj to Angkor Wat and apx 225 km NW Phnom Penh. Feb67 Natl Geo map. El. 75'. Cambodia.
Siempang West Airfield (XA 4-6)
On Tonle Kong River, apx 47 km WNW Viracheay AF and 30 km from Thai border. El. 223'. Cambodia.
Siemreap Airfield (UV 7-7?)
Major AF apx 20 km N Tonle Sap Lake at its NW end, 5 km NW Siemreap and 72 km NE Battambang AF. Per TPC K-10A. El. 75'. Cambodia.
Sierra, LZ (BR 635-793)
Apx 17 km WSW Ha Tay AF and 27 km SW Bong Son. Sep66. Binh Dinh Pr, II Corps.
Sierra, LZ/FSB (XD 945-624)
A.k.a. Hill 461. Apx 40 km WNW Quang Tri, 7 km NW FSB Fuller, 3 km S DMZ and W Mutter's Ridge. 3d Mar Div. Re-occupied by 3/4th Marines, 13Mar69, at cost of 10 US KIA, 35 WIA. On map at p 58, *US Marines in Vietnam-1969*. Also listed at XD 946-625 per XXIV Corps index, courtesy Don Armstrong. Quang Tri Pr, I Corps.
Sierra, LZ (XT 625-385)
Apx 16 km W Lai Khe and 17 km ESE Dau Tieng Tri Tam. Dec65. Binh Duong Pr, III Corps.
Sierra Beach (CR 08-22)
See Shit Beach. Binh Dinh Pr, II Corps.
Sierra CAC (YD or XD?)
See CAC entries. I Corps.
Sierra North, LZ (XD 85-65?)
Map at p 58, *US Marines in Vietnam-1969* suggests location was on Hill 695 (Lu Bu Mtn) at S edge of DMZ, apx 28 km WNW Cam Lo and 24 km N KSCB (map is not clear). 3d Mar Div, '69. Quang Tri Pr, I Corps.
Sigma I/Sigma II (n/a)
See Glossary.
Signal Hill (YD 406-036)
A.k.a. FSB Eagle's Nest. Dong Re Lao, Signal Mtn and Hill 1487. Overlooked E edge of A Shau Valley toward its N end, apx 4 km NNE A Luoi, 35 km WSW Hue and 14 km due W FSB Veghel. Originally opened 19Apr68 by LRRP, 8th Eng and 13th Sig Bn elements here during Op Delaware (story of opening in *LRRP Company Command*, p 3, which called it Signal Mtn at that stage) as radio relay site/OP for 1st Cav working A Luoi area in the A Shau. Per Ed Regan, D/2d/8th Cav, here '68., LZ Carol (later FSB Ripcord) was "in the shadow of what they called Signal Hill." Greg Mills, CO D/1st/502d Inf, '68, adds this

recollection: "Eagle's Nest was called 'Signal Hill' for a few days before getting a name. After several days of aborted attempts due to clouds, we landed in a Chinook with the front wheels dangling in air off the sharp peak. Then we went down the ridge about 2 clicks and began clearing. The next day, someone didn't like the location, so we moved down the ridge about 2 more clicks and built FSB Georgia." See also Eagle's Nest and FSB Ripcord. Thua Thien Pr, I Corps.

Signal Mountain (YD 406-306)
See Signal Hill and Eagle's Nest. Thua Thien Pr, I Corps.

Signal Mountain (AR 78-35?)
Apparently site was along S edge of Camp Enari, E QL-14, between Dragon Mtn and Enari's center of mass. Possibly a.k.a. Artillery Hill/Hill 842 (AR 797-348), which was within perimeter of Enari along its W central edge. See 1:50k map of Enari at www. rjsmith.com/topo_map.html. Pleiku Pr, II Corps.

Signal Mountain Relay (YT 60-10?)
Atop Nui Chua Chan Mtn, apx 15 km E Xuan Loc. 199th LIB. See Nui Chua Chan. Long Khanh Pr, III Corps.

Signal Sites (generally)
See name of Signal Site in appropriate alpha list, such as "Vung Tau Signal Site," etc.

Sihanouk Trail (VS, VT, WT, XU)
Companion trail to HCMT which originated on southern coast of Gulf of Thailand. It began at Sihanoukville and port of Kompong Son in Cambodia (US 35-75), and delivered men and supplies from coast to NE along eastern Cambodian frontier to an area generally between Memot and O Rang. Apparently called the Sihanouk Trail in reference to Prince Sihanouk's complicity in allowing its operation. Map can be found in Dept of Army's *Vietnam Studies, Airmobility 1961-1971*, at p 219. Cambodia.

Sihanoukville (US 36-75)
A.k.a. Kompong Soam and Kompong Soam. Cambodian port that was key entry point for NVA supplies and personnel in transit on Sihanoukville Trail. Access through port was unfettered until May70 Cambodian Incursion apparently ended its role in war. See also Sihanoukville Trail. Cambodia.

Sihanoukville Airfield (US 36-75)
See Kampong Soam AF. Cambodia.

Silk, LZ (BQ 354-493)
Apx 34 km ENE Buon Ho, 44 km Son Hoa/Cung Son, and 25 km SW Phu Tuc. 12Jul66, suptg 1st/12th Cav. Data per Jack Picciolo. Phu Bon Pr, II Corps.

Sills Compound (YT 47-09)
At Xuan Lo, apx 64 km ENE Saigon. HQ of 23rd Arty Grp. Named to honor SSgt Tommie L. Sills, an M-107 175mm howitzer Crew Chief, 2/32d Arty, KIA 3Apr66 at Xuan Loc when his 175mm cannon exploded while on fire mission. Sills' crew was 1st ever to fire the 175mm in combat, Nov 65. His name was spelled Tommy on cmpd's entrance sign. Long Khanh Pr, III Corps.

Silver, FSB (YT 829-043)
Apx 35 km ESE Xuan Loc, 90 km E to ENE Saigon, 22 km ESE peak Nui Chua Chan Mtn, and 15 km NNW peak Nui Be Mtn. 2d/3d Inf, 199th LIB here. Opened or reopened 22Sep70, closed 10Oct70, by 2d/5th Cav. Reopened 26Oct70 by 2d/8th Cav. Data in *1st Cav Div Op Rpt, ending 31Oct70*, per Peter Cole. Binh Tuy Pr, III Corps.

Silver, LZ (BQ 958-348)
Apx 17 km ESE Cung Son AF and 7 km NW My Thanh. Oct66. Phu Yen Pr, II Corps.

Silver, LZ (XT 755-330)
Apx 6 km SSW Lai Khe and 2 to 3 km E Ben Cat. Dec65-Jan66. Binh Duong Pr, III Corps.

Silver, LZ (YA 644-494)
On Cambodian border at S entrance to Plei Trap Valley, apx 20 km WSW Plei Djereng (old) AF and 59 km due W Pleiku. Jan66. Kontum Pr, II Corps.

Silver, LZ (YT 8-4?)
On W side Rte 3 NE N Lan Nga River, apx 45 km NE Xuan Loc and immed SW Than Duc. 2d/503d Inf, 173d Abn here during Op New Life, 25Nov65. CA to open site originally planned as parachute assault but when vendors in Bien Hoa began selling parachute wings, it was apparent jump had been compromised and helo assault replaced it. For discussion of battle here, see *Infantry in Vietnam*, pp 168-175. Long Khanh Pr?, III Corps.

Silver Bayonet, Operation (n/a)
23Oct-20Nov 65. 1st Cav and ARVN ops in western Pleiku Pr. Ia Drang Valley campaign resulted, involving 1st Cav's 3d Bde in 1st major engagements of war with NVA at LZs X-Ray and Albany. 1,771 rptd NVA/VC KIA, per *Vietnam Order of Battle*, pp 9-14. Pleiku Pr, II Corps.

Silver City, Operation (n/a)
9-22 Mar66. 173d Abn and elements of 1RAR CA'd vicinity of Song Be River, War Zone D. Discovered and destroyed several large bunker complexes and large amounts of food, ammo and documents. On 7th day, the 2/503d Inf TF was heavily attacked from all directions by 501st VC Bn. Resupply effected by helos at great risk and numerous air strikes required. 1st/503d Inf reinforced the 2d/503d during fight and badly mauled VC broke contact as they arrived (some VC found chained to tripods of their MGs). Battle lasted 4 hrs. 302 VC KIA plus 150 probables, and 7 US KIA. Long Khanh Pr. III Corps.

Silver Dollar (n/a)
6Apr70, XXIV Corps future-use III MAF FSB name.

Silver Dollar Lake (YB 8-6?)
P. J. Martin tells us it was NNW Dak Pek, and "Most beautiful place I've ever seen; a Volcano filled with water." Kontum Pr, II Corps.

Silver Spur (n/a)
6Apr70, XXIV Corps future-use III MAF FSB name.

Silver Star Hill (YA)
Somewhere near or in Plei Trap Valley. A.k.a. Million Dollar Hill, per Tom Lacombe. Apparently not a FSB, but instead a battle site? Kontum Pr?, II Corps.

Silvia, LZ (AR 805-214)
See LZ Sylvia. Pleiku Pr, II Corps.

Simard Coffee Plantation (XD 842-382)
On Khe Sanh Plateau, apx 1/2 km due W CAP Oscar/Dist HQ in Khe Sanh and 3 km due S Khe Sanh CB. Good map on p 27 of *Valley of Decision*. Quang Tri Pr, I Corps.

Simmons BEQ (XS 8-9)
In Saigon. Named to honor Sp5 Wayne C. Simmons, UH1-B Crew Chief, KIA 10Oct64, after leaving chopper to help wounded ARVN soldier. Gia Dinh Pr, III Corps.

Sin City (AQ 793-026)
Nickname for bar/red light recreational district at Ban Me Thuot. Per John Linn, was along main Hwy and within walking distance of US base he describes as fortress surrounded by a tall walls that was well-lit at night and included an NCO Club and PX. Grid is for Ban Me Thuot. Darlac Pr, II Corps.
Sin City (BR 477-435)
A.k.a. Dodge City. Collection of ramshackle bars and bordellos along QL-9 and just outside Camp Radcliff at An Tuc/An Khe Ville. Names and physical makeup of this red light district " bore a striking resemblance to towns featured in old wild west movies. It had dirt streets, with raised and covered wooded sidewalks...GIs going there on pass...were required to wear body armor...steel pots and carry a weapon with ammo [because] the town was subject to attack [and as result] shoot-outs between drunken ARVN soldiers were common. Few occurred between US forces [and those were] mostly confined to basecamp commandos who rarely carried or fired weapons." [496] Grid apx. See *Million Fingers Massage Parlor* for humorous anecdote. Binh Dinh Pr, II Corps.
Sing Ka Airfield (QB 26-92)
LS-92. CIA/SF, per *Air Facilities Data-Laos.*
Singes, Ile de (YJ 8-5)
Island of the Monkeys? NIMA data. NVN.
Singes, Presqu'ile aux (US 9-0)
See Monkey Peninsula. Kien Giang Pr, IV Corps.
Singora Airfield (PH 7-9)
See Songkhla. Thailand.
Sink, LZ (BR 778-640)
Apx 5 km SW Hoi San, 13 km WSW Phu My/QL-1 and 36 km NE An Khe. Oct66. Binh Dinh Pr, II Corps.
Sioux, LZ (BS 885-199)
Apx 37 km N Gia An, 21 km SSE Duc Pho AF and 3 km W QL-1. Feb67. Binh Dinh Pr, II Corps.
Sioux, LZ (YA 885-014)
Apx 3 km E Cambodia, 27 km WSW Plei Me and on W side of Chu Pong massif. Cited in *Time Heals No Wounds*, p 182-183's 1st/12th Inf Radio Log excerpt. 4th Div FSB, Pleiku Pr, II Corps.
Sioux, LZ (YD 236-601)
On N side of or within Dong Ha AF/CB, apx 12 km NW Quang Tri. Apr70 XXIV Corps grid per Don Armstrong. Quang Tri Pr, I Corps.
Sioux City, Operation (n/a)
26Sep-9Oct66. 173d Abn, near Xom Cat. 1st and 2d Bns, 503d Inf and Arty supt deployed 23 km NE Bien Hoa.
Sirin, FSB (YS 272-859)
Apx 25 km NW Nui Dat, 1 km S FSB Digger's Rest and 9 km W FSB Dampier. On 1ATF NCO trng map per John Hollett. 1ATF. Bien Hoa Pr, III Corps.
Sisaket Airfield (VB 2-6)
Apx 435 km ENE Bangkok, 65 km NNW Ubon AB, at 15°06'00"N-104°20'00"E per TPC K-10A. NIMA data. El. 430'. Thailand.
Sisophon Airfield (n/a)
Apx 305 km NW Phnom Penh. El. 65'. Cambodia.
Sisson, FSB (XU 658-295)
N of the Angel's Wing and along Rte 13, apx 5 km NW point road met SVN border, 13 km SE Snuol, 21 km NNE Loc Ninh and near FSBs Compton, Wilma and Scott. From here, 2d/11th ACR patrolled Rome Plow roads around FSB Myron S to Snuol, as well as Hwy 13 E to Loc Ninh in SVN. Possibly named to honor Army Sgt Donald H. Sisson, KIA 23Feb69, and only Army casualty with that last name? Grid per *11th ACR Cambodia Invasion AAR, 1st Cav Div, May-Jun70*, courtesy Lou Rochat. [497] Also listed at XU 656-285. Cambodia.
Site 20 SF Camp (n/a)
See Lima Site 20. Laos
Site 36 (UH 41-10)
See Lima Site-36. Laos.
Site 85 (UH 68-60)
See Lima Site-85. Laos.
Six Shooter, FSB (AT 927-737)
See FSB Sixshooter. Quang Nam Pr, I Corps.
Sixshooter, FSB (AT 923-737)
A.k.a. Six Shooter. Just N Thuan Xuan Loc, apx 2 km SW Ap Dai Lai, 3 km WSW peak of Hill 364, 9 km W Da Nang AB and 4 km WNW Hill 327. Apr70 XXIV Corps grid per Don Armstrong. Quang Nam Pr, I Corps.
Skagit, USS (n/a)
AKA-105. Amphib Attack. Cargo.
Skid Row POW Camp (WJ)
Nickname for POW camp apparently just W Hanoi. On map at www.soft-vision.com/hanoi/ frame.html. NVN.
Skota, LZ (AQ 826-192)
Apx 6 km SSE Ban Me Thuot City AF and 8 km NW Trung Hoa. Feb66. Darlac Pr, II Corps.
Skull Orchard, The (YD 0-6)
Apx 5 km due W Con Thien, 26 km NW Dong Ha and 12 km N QL-9. Significance of site unknown, though presumably a graveyard or battle site. Apx location on *Leatherneck* Magazine map (date unknown) posted on net at: www.monboys.com. Quang Tri Pr, I Corps.
Sky Horse, FSB/LZ (YA/ZA)
A.k.a. ARVN Firebase #2. Apparently near Pleiku, and either along QL-14 N or S, or QL-19? Photo of sign at base is at: www.geocities.com/CapeCanaveral/ 3266/, in link entitled *Ted Ashton's Album*, picture #13. Sign read: *CAN GU HOA LUC II-Fire Base-THIEN MA SON LAM-Sky Horse*. Pleiku or Kontum Pr, II Corps. [498]
Skyspot (n/a)
See Site 85. Laos.
Sledge, FSB (ZC 067-920)
Apx 9 km S Phu Loc, 45 km SSW Hue and 16 km SSW FSB Brick. Built on 4,500' high ridge of Bach Ma (White Horse) Mtn mass overlooking coastal lowlands of Phu Loc Dist. White Horse name from Viet legend related to cloud shapes often obscuring peaks. Site air-assaulted 13Jul69 by 1st/327th, 2d/502d Inf, and 326th Eng of 101st Abn, along with 54th ARVN Rgt, and const of FSB began although hampered by winds as high as 100 mph. Designed as model FSB, it was also one of highest in SVN. Op ended 11Aug69 after VC/NVA vacated area. Over 80 LZs were also prepared for possible future-use during same op. Was reopened Jul71, by elements of 101st Abn during Lam Son 720. Also listed ZC 063-927 and 067-920. See Bach Ma. Thua Thien Pr, I Corps.

Sledge Hammer Relay (YA 810-690)
A.k.a. Sledgehammer, Hill 1438, Cu Grock or Chu Grock Mtn, Cloud 9, and Heavy Drop. Apx 18 km NNW Plei Djereng Old AF, 10 km due W Plei Dei Go, 46 km NW Pleiku and 2o km E Cambodia. Grid per Barry Toll, and others. Home movie taken by Sherman Batman shows sign here that read, *WELCOME TO SLEDGE HAMMER, INTERNATIONAL HELIPAD, ELEVATION, 4,717 FEET*, (1,437 meters). Contrary to Harve Saals' 4-vol SOG history, it was NOT in Cambodia, but well inside SVN and overlooking Plei Trap Valley to W. Apparently opened Mar67, and closed Mar69. Per Steve Sherman, was opened by SOG's CCC, and after closure, resources moved to Hill 1152, apx 8 km SSE Kontum, and reopened Apr69 as Klondike. Paul Wilson, 52d CAB, recalls it as Cloud-9 and Heavy-Drop, in 66-67, and that helo pad was PSP not more that 20' sq. built on top of bunker stairway. Toll tells us it was SOG MSS site on a sheer pinnacle of mtn peak, used as radio relay site for SOG OP-35 (i.e., "Ground Studies Division") ops. Only practical access was air but helos could not land if wind exceeded 15 kts. Built by lopping-off and leveling mtn peak, Toll says, and only apx 150' long x 50' wide and, "To the N and E it was sheer precipice as was part of W side. Only approach to site by foot was from mtn to S, across a deep, very steep saddle. Apparently attacked Feb69(?). Max of 4 US here with apx 25 Montagnard whom CIA/SF had vigorously trained (Hatchet Force). "The Yards were fearless and seemed possessed of super-natural sensibilities enabling them to see in dark and detect danger at great distances, and they were loyal to point of self-sacrifice." On classified maps, site was "No Fire. No Bomb. No Entry." Mike Boster adds that after FOB 5 (Duc Co) was established in '68, CCS also ran some ops off Sledgehammer Relay. "...you could see the [Ya Krong Bolah] river in two directions about 5 to 6 klicks away. We were told it had been a French outpost, and did find evidence of that. We always launched out of Duc Co using Green Hornet choppers and flew NW." In '68 or '69, ARVN pilot, co-pilot, and door gunner, 219th Vietnamese CH-34 "Kingbee" were KIA when their helo crashed [while attempting resupply or medevac while site was being defended by Team Arkansas]. 4th ID 3d Be LRRPs (Later, 3rd Plt/K/75th Rangers) had radio relay team here when SOG elements were opcon'd to SOG-35 FOB 2 in Kontum as result of heavy personnel losses suffered during last half of '68. Entertainer Martha Raye may have secretly visited site. Don Lewis, 170th AHC pilot who flew there often, thinks site was on Hill 1528, some 40 km WSW Kontum and 28 km N Plei Djereng, but photo evidence does not supt that belief. See also Klondike, Leghorn and Hickory Hill. Kontum Pr, II Corps. [499]

Sledgehammer Relay (YA 810-690)
See Sledge Hammer. Kontum Pr, II Corps.

Sleeper, FSB (XU 800-125)
Apx 8 km ENE Loc Ninh AF, 6 km ESE Ap Loc Thanh and 3 km S QL-14A. Jan68. Binh Long Pr, III Corps.

Slick (n/a)
See Glossary.

Slope 30 (YS 4-7?)
Area in Phuoc Tuy Pr near Duc Thanh, from which 7 RAR cleared and relocated all civilians during Op Ainslie. Those displaced were moved to Hamlet 3, a.k.a. Ap Suoi Nghe, apx 14Sep67. Phuoc Tuy Pr, III Corps.

Slot, The (XD)
Terrain feature in vic of Khe Sanh CB. Simply listed as being on map L-7014-6342-3? Quang Tri Pr, I Corps.

Small Chimes?, LZ (AR or BR?)
Apparently near An Khe or Camp Holloway? Cited in query by Bill Beard at http://wae.com/messages/msgs27211.html; however, source may have meant LZ Hard Times? 227th AHC apparently here. Binh Dinh or Pleiku Pr, II Corps.

Smaller Wheel, The (n/a)
See Hinayana in Glossary.

Smash, Operation (YS)
17-23Dec65. 173d Abn, Phuoc Tuy Pr. Took place apx 50 km SE Bien Hoa on Courtenay Rubber Plantation. 1st and 2d Bn/503d Inf saturation patrols in conjunction with 1st/RAR, 1ATF. On 18Dec65, recon plt, 2/503d ran into VC trench system that was heavily defended. B/2d/503d, then overran the position. 62 VC rptd KIA. III Corps.

Smith BEQ (XS 858-905)
At 79 Tran Hung Dao St., 21 Feb 65, 52 rms (see Wabash Inn), Saigon. Data per *Vietnam Military Lore, 1959-1973.* Gia Dinh Pr, III Corps.

Smith, Camp (ZT 023-753)
Along QL-20, apx 3 km SW Ap Cong Hinh, 7 km SW Bao Loc AF and 10 km SW Tan Phat AF. Transferred to SVN govt, with MACV-JGS IG post-transfer inspection of facility, 2May72. Camp Coryell and Camp McDermott inspections mentioned in same rpt. Apr70-Oct71. Lam Dong Pr, II Corps.

Smith, FSB (XD 789-383)
Apx 6 km SW Khe Sanh CB, 6 km ENE Sa Tiac, 3 km N QL-9, 32 km WSW Mai Loc, 7 km SE FSB Geiger and 55 km WSW Quang Tri. 2/12th Arty here and on FSB Geiger suptg 3d Recon Bn, and 2d and 3d Bns, 9th Marines during Op Dawson River West, Jan69. Apr70 XXIV Corps grid per Don Armstrong. Quang Tri Pr, I Corps.

Smith, LZ (YA 988-246)
Apx 13 km WSW Oasis AF, 34 km SW Pleiku and 4 km E Plei Luong Ya Rang. Jan66. Pleiku Pr, II Corps.

Smitty (a unit of measure) (n/a)
See Glossary.

Smitty, LZ (XD 906-277)
In Vietnam Salient, apx 15 km SSE Khe Sanh CB, 22 km SSW Ca Lu and 5 km W of Laos. Apr70 XXIV Corps grid per Don Armstrong. Quang Tri Pr, I Corps.

Smoke, FSB (XS 789-769)
In Binh Chanh Dist just SW Cholon, apx 10 km S Saigon, 5 km SSW Ap Phuoc Khanh and 5 km NW Can Giuoc. 3d/7th Inf, 199th LIB and 2d/3d Inf, 199th LIB here. May68. Gia Dinh Pr, III Corps.

Smokey (n/a)
See Glossary.

Smokey, LZ (n/a)
Possibly FSB Smoke at XS 79-76? Gia Dinh Pr, III Corps?

Snack (n/a)
See Base Area 351. Cambodia.

Snake, LZ (XD 810-378)
Apx 6 km WSW Khe Sanh CB, 2 km N QL-9 and 6 km from Laos. Apr68. Quang Tri Pr, I Corps.

Snake, LZ ? (YA 629-498)
On Cambodian border, apx 7 km ENE Phum To Lay and 61 km W Pleiku. Jan66. Kontum Pr, II Corps.
Snake Hosking Compound (XT 98-13)
See C E "Snake" Hosking Cmpd. Bien Hoa Pr, III Corps.
Snake n' Nape (n/a)
See Glossary.
Snake Pit, The (BT 537-062)
Flight line and flight control center for 71st AHC at Chu Lai AB. Discussed on unit website at: www3.servtech.com/americal/saber6.htm. Quang Tin Pr, I Corps.
Snapper, LZ (XD 845-344)
At N end of Vietnam Salient, apx 7 km due S Khe Sanh CB, 18 km SE Vandegrift CB, 5 km S QL-9 and apx 10 km from Laos. 2d ARVN Div Arty here early '69, suptg Op Maine Crag, Mar-May69. 1st/8th, 1st Cav assaulted into site 5 or 6Apr68, as part of Op Pegasus, the op to break the siege of Khe Sanh CB. 3d Mar Div. On map, p 65 *of US Marines in Vietnam-1969* Map is L-7014-6342-3, per Ken Burrington. Also listed at XD 815-346, 840-340, 841-345 and 842-347 in 1st Cav Staff Daily Journal, 1st/8th Cav per Kevan Mynderup. Quang Tri Pr, I Corps.
Snatch Teams (n/a)
See Glossary.
Sneaky Pete (n/a)
See Glossary.
Sneaky-Pete Operations (n/a)
See Glossary.
Snipe, LZ (BR 693-613)
Apx 4 km due W LZ Arnold's Trail, 1 km S peak Hill 975, 6 km due N LZ Sheridan, 27 km NE An Khe and 26 km NW Phu Cat AB. 4th Div AO, '70. Name/grid per Jim Claeys. Apr-Oct70. Binh Dinh Pr, II Corps.
Sniper, LZ (XD 724-367)
Just N Sa Tiac near Laotian border, apx 7 km WSW FSB Smith, 13 km WSW Khe Sanh CB and 64 km WSW Quang Tri. Apr70 XXIV Corps grid per Don Armstrong. Quang Tri Pr, I Corps.
Sniper's Island (BS 915-087)
Apx 6 km due S Gia An, 7 km NNE LZ English and 2 km E QL-1. Dec67. Binh Dinh Pr, II Corps.
Sniper Valley (BT?)
A.k.a. AO Dog, per *Rites of Passage*, pp 394, 449. Quang Ngai Pr?, I Corps.
Snohomish County, USS (n/a)
LST-1126. On 16Jul65, 8 USCG cutters of CG Sqdn 1 (opcon USN) along with LST *Snohomish County* left Subic Bay bound for Da Nang, where they became part of TF-115 (Market Time). Role discussed in *Brown Water, Black Berets*, p 84. Decom 1Jul70. SVN.
Snoopy, LZ (BS 705-612)
On or adj to both Nui Dep (Hill 68) or Nui Vong (Hill 105). Perhaps 1 km E QL-1, apx 8 km NNW Mo Duc AF and 13 km SSE Quang Ngai. Basecamp of C/39th Engr Bn, 23d Inf Div, with ARVN cmpd nearby. Mortar attacks Dec68-Jan69. Also listed at BS 700-600, 709-608 and 705-610. Americal list. Quang Ngai Pr, I Corps.
Snoopy's Nose (XS 194-410)
Bend in the Rach Bai Rai River at Ap Ho Le, apx 6 km ESE Cai Be/Sung Hieu, and 23 km W Dong Tam. Per Paul Kasper, terrain feature given this nickname by 2d Bde/9th Inf Div. Dinh Tuong Prov, IV Corps.
Snoul (XU 55-35)
See Snuol. Cambodia.
Snowden Hall (ZA 236 863)
Name of Recon orderly room bldg at SOG CCC's FOB 2, Kontum. See FOB 2. Kontum Pr, II Corps.
Snuffy, FSB (XU 336-362)
See Snuffy at "YU" 336-362. Phuoc Long Pr, III Corps.
Snuffy, FSB (YU 336-362)
Small FSB built in scrubby clearing at site of old Bu Gia Map outpost (a.k.a. Djamap AF), apx 36 km ENE Bu Dop AF, 35 km NNE Song Be, 13 km from Cambodia and 66 km ENE Loc Ninh. *Apache Sunrise*, p 179, describes it as on small AF roughly halfway between FSB David in Cambodia and Song Be in VN. Built Feb70-Apr70, B/8th Engrs, 1st Cav. [500] Used as staging area for 5th/12th Inf, 199th LIB, May 70, just prior to their crossing Cambodian border to occupy FSB Brown, 11May70, relieving 5th/7th Cav to move further into Cambodia. Attacked 13May70, with 1 US KIA, 8 WIA. Djamap AF here also. Cited in *1st Cav Op Rpt, Feb-Apr70*, p 14, and *May-Jul70 Rpt*, p 38, per Peter Cole. Phuoc Long Pr, III Corps.
Snuol (XU 552-345)
Apx 30 km W SVN border, 175 km ENE Phnom Penh, 32 km NNW Loc Ninh, 42 km WNW Bu Dop and 51 km NNE Katum. Focus of many activities during Cambodian Incursion, May-Jun70. Huge cache, a.k.a. "The City," was found just S of this town. Grid per *11th ACR Cambodia Invasion AAR, 1st Cav Div, May-Jun70*, courtesy Lou Rochat. [501] Also XU 498-599. Cambodia.
Snuol Airfield (XU 56-34)
Apx 175 km ENE Phnom Penh, 38 km NE Memot AF, 140 km NNW Saigon SVN, 67 km WNW Song Be SVN, 30 km NW Loc Ninh AF (SVN). El. 525'. Cambodia.
Snyder, LZ (BR 762-950)
Overlooking Song An Lao River Valley from W, apx 13 km WSW LZ English and 10 km W to WSW Hoai Nhon/QL-1. Binh Dinh Pr, II Corps.
Snyder, FSB (YU 261-166)
Apx 22 km NW Duc Phong AF and 9 km NE Song Be City AF. Jan68. Phuoc Long Pr, III Corps.
Soc Giang (n/a)
Mapsheet name of L-7014-6254-4. NVN/China.
Soc Trang (XR 07-62)
A.k.a. Khanh Hung. Apx 150 km SW Saigon and in heart of Mekong Delta, apx 56 km SW Tra Vinh AF (Phu Vinh), 25 km E mouth of the Hau Giang River and 53 km SSE Can Tho. Only10' above sea level. Site of Soc Trang AF (3 km SW Khanh Hung). Ba Xuyen Pr, IV Corps.
Soc Trang (Khanh Hung) (n/a)
Mapsheet L-7014-6128-2. Ture sheet name: Khanh Hung (Soc Trang). SVN.
Soc Trang Airfield (XR 058-591)
A.k.a. Khanh Hung AF. Major AF in Mekong Delta apx 2 km SW Khan Hung, 150 km SSW Saigon, 56 km SW Tra Vinh AF (Phu Vinh), 53 km SSE Can Tho and 30 km W mouth of Mekong River. Originally a Japanese fighter base during WWII that included hard-surface rwy and bldgs built by both French and Viets. 1st US unit here was HMM 362 ('62) USMC helo sqdn (one of few USMC sites

outside I Corps) but Marines were quickly replaced by US Army's 93d Trans Co, Jan 62, which was then itself replaced by 121st Avn Co. Aviators out of Soc Trang were known as "Soc Trang Tigers." El. 10', 3,100' asph rwy. At 09°34'45"N-105°57'52"E. See Op Shufly and Tiger's Den for more detail. Ba Xuyen Pr, IV Corps.

Soc Trang NDB (XR 06-59)
Non-Directional Air Nav Beacon site. At Soc Trang AB. Ba Xuyen Pr, IV Corps.

Soc Trang Province (WR/XR)
In what later became known as IV Corps, and absorbed into what became primarily Bac Lieu Pr. Thought to have ceased existence shortly before or during early US presence in SVN? Actual dates of existence unknown.

Soc Trang SF Camp (XR 060-507)
A.k.a. Du Tho SF Camp. Apx 8 km due S Soc Trang AF, 12 km S Khanh Hung and 62 km SSW Tra Vinh AF. 5th SF. Info/grid per *SF Order of Battle*. See also Du Tho. Ba Xuyen Pr, IV Corps.

Societe d' Exploitation Agricole (AQ 95-05)
Societe d' Exploitation Agricole du Darlac. At Klet Gir, on QL-21, apx 15 km E Ban Me Thuot. Apparently an Ag experimentation/trng facility. Darlac Pr, II Corps.

Société de Anonyme des Plantations (XT 3-4)
At Don Dien Theis (Cau Khoi). Tay Ninh Pr, III Corps.

Société des Terres Rouges (YS 2-9)
Society of Red Soils at Don Dien Long Thanh. Per Mr. Jean-Paul Meyer (Délégué aux Affaires Extérieures, et à la Valorisation, CIRAD-FLHOR), Société des Terres Rouges means Red Soils Co. Apparently is still involved in rubber tree plantation business. Gia Dinh Pr, III Corps.

SOG 00 to SOG 99 (n/a)
See Glossary.

SOG Khe Sanh (XD 860-385)
A.k.a. the Old French Fort. Apx 4 km SSE Khe Sanh CB and just SW intersection of QL-9 and Rte 608. SOG MLT (FOB-1) moved here when SF unit here moved to Lang Vei. SF FOB-3 joined SOG here after moving from Khe Sanh ville, Summer '67. Quang Tri Pr, I Corps.

SOG Radio Relay Site (XD?)
Possibly Leghorn? Said to have been a relay station on 7,200' mtn top in Laos operated by 5th SF/MAC-SOG Prairie Fire and other "Over the Fence" Ops. Could intercept virtually any MAC-SOG line-of-sight radio transmission and relay it to CCN, MLT-1 or MLT-2. Its formal name not cited in *Da Nang Diary's* reference. See Leghorn, Hickory Hill, and Sledgehammer. Laos.

Solid Anchor Airfield (VQ 988-674)
See Nam Can AF. An Xuyen Pr, IV Corps.

Solid Anchor, ATSB (VQ 988-674)
A.k.a. Solid Anchor and Advanced Tactical Supt Base Solid Anchor. Along Song Cua Long, at or near old Nam Can, apx 24 km due W Tan An, 33 km ENE tip of Cau Mau Peninsula, and 300 km SW Saigon. Originally a floating base named "Sea Float," and renamed Solid Anchor when moved ashore to supt fwd ops. One of several land and ship facilities used by USN Helo Attack (Light) Sqdn 3, beginning 1Apr67, as part of Op Gamewarden. Suptd Riverine, Seal and ARVN ops. At end of Apr70(?), was also last USN base in SVN turned over to Viets (Op Tran Hung Dao IV?). Had 9 Dets operating at shore bases or on converted LST's anchored in rivers or ocean. Some data per Mike Turner at http://members.xoom.com/mdturner/ vietnam.htm. An Xuyen Pr, IV Corps.

Sommers, USS (n/a)
DD-947. USN Destroyer. SVN.

Son, FSB (XT 681-486)
Apx 19 km E Dau Tieng/Tri Tam and 15 km NW Lai Khe. Oct69. Binh Duong Pr, III Corps.

Son, FSB (YD 472-011)
See FSB Zon. Thua Thien Pr, I Corps.

Son Bla Mla Airfield (BQ 504-598)
See Phu Tuc AF. Phu Bon Pr, II Corps.

Son Dong Airfield (XS 480-347)
See Truc Giang AF. Kien Hoa Pr, IV Corps.

Son Ha (n/a)
Mapsheet name of L-7014-6739-3. SVN.

Son Ha (BS 390-700)
Ville apx 32 km due W Quang Ngai and 3 km SW Ha Thanh, at 15°03'00"N-108°34'00"E. Ha Than AF here or nearby. On L-7014-6739-3 map. Quang Ngai Pr, I Corps.

Son Ha (Cung Son) (n/a)
Mapsheet name of L-7014-6735-2. SVN.

Son Ha Airfield (BS 390-700)
See Ha Thanh AF. Quang Ngai Pr, I Corps.

Son Ha SF Camp (BS 393-714)
Possibly a.k.a. Ha Thanh SF Camp? Adj to Ha Thanh AF, apx 26 km W Quang Ngai. 5th SF. Closed and assets moved to Kannack. Info/grid per *SF Order of Battle.* On map L-7014-6739-3. Quang Ngai Pr, I Corps.

Son Ha, FSB? (BS 39-70?)
See Ha Thanh. Quang Ngai Pr?, I Corps.

Son Hai Company (n/a)
See Glossary.

Son Hai, Thon (n/a)
Mapsheet L-7014-6831-4. Sheet: Thon Son Hai. SVN.

Son Hai, Vung (BN 83-63)
Freshwater lake just SW Son Thon Son Hai and 17 km due S Phan Rang. At 11°25N-109°00'E. On NC49-01 JOG. Ninh Thuan Pr, II Corps.

Son La (n/a)
Mapsheet name of L-7014-5751-1. NVN only.

Son La (VJ 3-2 or UJ 9-5)
Apx 308 km W Hanoi. Populated primarily by hill tribes (Black Thai, Meo, Muong and White Thai). Generally unaffected by outside cultures until late 1950's when French built penal colony here for anti-colonial revolutionaries. Capitol, Son La Pr, NVN.

Son La Airfield (VJ 3-2 or UJ 9-5)
Feb67 Natl Geo map. El.? NVN.

Son La Airfield (BQ 504-598)
See Phu Tuc AF. Phu Bon Pr, II Corps.

Son Lam, Thon (XD 996-560)
See Thon Son Lam. Quang Tri Pr, I Corps.

Son My Massacre (BS 73-77)
See My Lai. Quang Ngai Pr, I Corps.

Son Quang CAP (BS 648-747?)
CAP 1-4-2, 1st CAG per Tim Duffie. NPIA lista a Trai Son Quang at grid, which is N of the Song Tra Kuch, apx 2 km NE Quang Ngai. Quang Ngai Pr, I Corps.

Son Soak Airfield, New (VF 59-59)
LS-126. CIA/SF, per *Air Facilities Data-Laos.*
Son Tay (n/a)
Mapsheet name of L-7014-6151-3. NVN only.
Son Tay (WJ 53-37)
Apx 34 km WNW Hanoi and along SW bank of Red River. Was birthplace of Nguyen Cao Ky and site of Son Tay POW Camp. On map at www.soft-vision.com/hanoi/frame.html. NVN.
Son Tay Airfield (WJ 5-3?)
Feb67 Natl Geo map. El. 200'. NVN.
Son Tay POW Camp (WJ 53-37)
Apx 34 km WNW Hanoi and along SW bank of Red River. At 2 am on 21Nov70, and despite intel that its US prisoners had been moved to Dong Hoi (24 km to E), a joint USAF, SF and Ranger unit code-named TF Ivory raided camp but found it empty. Raid became known as the "Son Tay Raid." As a result, NVA moved most US prisoners to Hanoi Hilton and apparently improved their treatment. Effects of raid discussed in *A Better War*, p 229. Town was also birthplace of Nguyen Cao Ky. On map at www.soft-vision. com/hanoi/ frame.html. NVN.
Son Tay Raid (WJ 53-37)
See Son Tay POW Camp. NVN.
Son Thang-4 (BT 01-34)
A.k.a. Son 4, Thang Tra. In Que Son Valley and sub-hamlet of Son Tra, apx 2 km WSW FSB Ross, 5 km N the Quang Nam/Quang Tin Pr border and roughly 85 km NW My Lai. Son Tra straddled Song Ly Ly River just W Rte 535 and 2 km SW its intersection with Rte 536. Scene of Feb70 massacre of 16 women and children perpetrated by 5-man Killer Team, from B/1st/7th Marines. Incident became known as the "Marine My Lai," and was worst rptd case of war crime associated with USMC during war. With help of one team member under immunity, subsequent trails in SVN convicted 2 and acquitted another 2 (inc patrol leader who ordered killings). Later, disparate sentences of convicted were greatly reduced by Marine Cmdr to compensate for apparent uneven quality of defense counsel. S*on Thang*: *An American War Crime*, published in '97, covers incident in great detail. Que Son District, Quang Nam Pr, I Corps.
Son Tinh, FSB? (BS 607-790)
On small hill immed E of RR tracks, apx 4 km NW Son Tinh, 7 km NNW Quang Ngai, 1 km E Hill 103 and 3 km W QL-1. Jun70. Quang Ngai Pr, I Corps.
Son Tra (BT 01-34)
Ville in Que Son Valley apx 4 km WSW Que Son, 2 km WSW FSB Ross and 5 km N the Quang Nam/Quang Tin Pr border. Straddled the Song Ly Ly just W Rte 535 and 2 km SW its intersection with Rte 536. Son Thang-4, a sub-hamlet of this ville, was scene of Feb70 massacre known as "Marine My Lai." See Son Thang-4. Que Son District, Quang Nam Pr, I Corps.
Son Tra Mountain (BT 10-84?)
A.k.a. Hill 696. 2,283' high mtn on the Tien Sha Peninsula apx 10 km NNE Marble Mtn and 12 km NE Da Nang AB. See Monkey Mtn. Quang Nam Pr, I Corps.
Son Tra, Ban Dao (BT 0-8)
Peninsula at 16°08'N-108°16'E. ND49-01 JOG. Quang Nam Pr, I Corps.
Son Tra, FSB? (BT 622-015)
Near mouth of Song Tra Bong River and just S Hoa Van, roughly 10 km SE Chu Lai and 7 km E QL-1. Americal list. Quang Ngai Pr, I Corps.
Sondra, LZ (XT 204-788)
See Sandra. Tay Ninh Pr, III Corps.
Song Ai Nghai River (AT 9-5)
Apparently near Dai Loc. Also listed in AT 8-5. Quang Nam Pr, I Corps.
Song An Lau River (BS 96-03)
Runs through Bong Son, apx 5 km S LZ English. Grid is river mouth. Quang Ngai Pr, I Corps.
Song Ba Gioi River (YS 17-68)
The Song Dong Tranh, Song Nga Bay, Song Ba Gioi and Song Thi Vai Rivers ran through Rung Sat Special Zone and emptied into Vinh Ganh Rai. Gia Dinh Pr, III Corps.
Song Ba Ren River (BT 1-5)
S of and within 10 km of Hoi An, and 25 km SSE Da Nang. Quang Nam Pr, I Corps.
Song Ba River (BR 469-436)
Flows S through Kannack to An Khe near Camp Radcliff, running along its E side (very thin at that point). Kannack is apx 23 km NNW An Khe. Bridge 20 on QL-19E crossed river at listed grid. Involved in Op Crazy Horse, May66, and discussed in *Battles in the Monsoon*, and in *Bird*, p 11. Also mentioned in *Chickenhawk*, p 72. 1st Cav, Binh Dinh Pr, II Corps.
Song Ba River (BR 4-4 to BQ 2-9)
Ran generally from BR 47-45, just S An Khe, apx 60 km to SSW to BQ 27-98, then S to Hou Bon/Cheo Reo where it joined the Ea Pa River. Grid per Jim Claeys. Binh Dinh and Pleiku? Prvs, II Corps.
Song Ba To River (BS 5-3)
45 km SSW Quang Ngai. Quang Ngai Pr, I Corps.
Song Bam La Airfield (BQ 504-598)
See Phu Tuc AF. Phu Bon Pr, II Corps.
Song Bau Xau River (n/a)
No data. I Corps.
Song Be (YU 19-11)
Apx 2 km SW Phuoc Binh, 110 km NNE Saigon, 36 km WNW Duc Phong, 45 km NE An Loc and 4 km W peak Nui Ba Ra. 173d Abn Div here '65-66, 4th Inf, 1st Cav, SF Det 47, 5th SF, Det B-34 (was B-21), Oct65, 1st Cav, 4th Div. 161 Bty, RNZA (Kenning's Bty 13Jun65-13Jun66) FSB set here 12-13Apr66 and 17Apr66, suptg 1s/503d Inf. Phuoc Long Pr, III Corps.
Song Be?, Camp (YU 9745-2909)
SF camp said to have been at this grid is not at all close to Song Be; hence, name may be error? Possibly Buon Konho or Gia Nghia SF Camp instead? Grid puts site along QL-14, apx 5 km E Gia Nghia AF, 58 km ENE Duc Phong AF and 2 km W Buon Konho. Phuoc Long Pr, III Corps.
Song Be Airfield (YU 141-070)
A.k.a. Farley Field? One of 3 AFs at Song Be, apx 115 km NNE Saigon, 4 km SW Song Be AF, 1 km SW Phuoc Binh, 60 km NNE Phuoc Vinh AF, 33 km N Dong Xoai AF and 40 km due E Loc Ninh AF. 173d Abn Div here, '65-66, 4th Inf, 1st Cav, SF Det 47, 5th SF, Det B-34 (was B-21), Oct65, 1st Cav, 4th Div. 161 Bty, RNZA (Kenning's Bty 13Jun65-13Jun66) FSB set here 12-13Apr66 and 17Apr66, suptg 1s/503d Inf. El. 797', 3,400'

alum-mat rwy. C-130 capable. 11°49'05"N-106°58'09"E. See also Farley Field. Phuoc Long Pr, III Corps.

Song Be Basecamp (YU 140-071)
See Song Be AF. Phuoc Long Pr, III Corps.

Song Be Bridge (XT 925-442)
Rte 1A bridge over the Song Be, apx 10 km SW Phuoc Vinh, 15 km ENE Lai Khe and 10 km NE intersection of Rte 1A/Rte 2A (Claymore Corner), per *Low Level Hell's* TAOR map. Binh Duong Pr, I Corps.

Song Be City Airfield (YU 182-109)
Possibly a.k.a. Farley Field. One of 3 AFs at Song Be, apx 120 km NNE Saigon, 4 km NE Phuoc Binh, 7 km NE Song Be AF, 26 km WNW Duc Phong AF and 38 km NNE Dong Xoai. Per TPC K-10D. El. 722', 2,200' asph rwy. 11°51'04"N-107°00'11"E. See also Farley Field. Phuoc Long Pr, III Corps.

Song Be Corridor, The (XU/XT)
See Serges Jungle Highway. Phuoc Long/Binh Long/Binh Duong Prvs, III Corps.

Song Be Heliport (YU 183-112)
A.k.a. Farley Field? Apparently on N side of Song Be City AF, apx 4 km NE Phuoc Binh, 7 km NE Song Be AF, 26 km WNW Duc Phong AF and 38 km NNE Dong Xoai. "Heliport #655, alt 660', 80' diameter circle, asph. Fuel A+ J4 (J4 tanker avail) Ammo-7.62, 2.75" rockets. Fuel N side of pad. 3 asph pkg ramps adj to pad. 160' x 160' (sod) pkg ramp S side of pad. Pad adj to F/W rwy. All helos W pad. (F/W TFC/E) F/W acft takeoff from N end of rwy and are not visible from pad due to fence on N side of pad. Clear area well for F/W acft before takeoff or Ldg. Do not use rwy unless commo is established with advsy svc. Numerous unlighted ant and obstacles. 65' steeple 1,100' N. 100' unlighted ant 800' NE. 50' Water twr 800' ENE, Hosp 400' E, 120' Lighted ant 700' S. Arty advsy-Phuoc Long 338.9, 39.5." At 11°51'N 107°00'E, per Feb73 TAD. See also Farley Field. Phuoc Long Pr, III Corps.

Song Be North Airfield (YU 173-122)
See Song Be AF. Phuoc Long Pr, III Corps.

Song Be River (XU/XT/YT)
Generally along Phuoc Long/Binh Long Pr border from point near XU 80-23 on Cambodian border (due N of Loc Ninh), to Binh Duong Pr between Long Nguyen Secret Zone and War Zone D. An NVA/VC infiltration that fed NVA toward Saigon that was object of 1st Cav ops in '69. Cited in *Cedar Falls-Junction City*. See *Low Level Hell's* TAOR map, *Rangers At War* p 234, Song Be Bridge and Testicles. Phuoc Long/Binh Long Pr, III Corps.

Song Be Road (XT)
A.k.a. LTL-1A. Originated near Phu Cuong (just W Phu Loi) and ran generally N through Dog Leg Ville to Claymore Corners (meeting point of LTLs 2A, 1A and 16), then over the Song Be Bridge, through Phuoc Vinh and then Dong Xoai to Song Be. *Low Level Hell* says that from air it resembled a "rust-colored snake". Built by colonial French. In Jun69, 1st Engrs Bn cleared 90 mile stretch to a depth of 200 meters on both sides. III Corps.

Song Be SF Camp (YU 176-091)
Near main road, immed S Song Be City AF, apx 36 km WNW Duc Phong and 5 km NE Song Be AF. SF Det 47, 5th SF, Det B-34 (was B-21), Oct65. Closed. Grid per *SF Order of Battle*. Phuoc Long Pr, III Corps.

Song Be South Airfield (YU 148-074)
See Song Be City AF. Phuoc Long Pr, III Corps.

Song Be Signal Site (YU 104-068)
See Nui Ba Ra. Phuoc Long Pr, III Corps.

Song Be U-2 Crash (YU)
See Glossary.

Song Ben Van (BT 47-10?)
River W and NW of Chu Lai. Quang Tin Pr, I Corps.

Song Ben Van (XT 7-3)
Near Lai Khe/Ben Cat. Binh Duong Pr, III Corps.

Song Binh Long (BT 9-6)
SE of Hill 55. Quang Nam Pr, I Corps.

Song Bo Bridge (YD 624-303)
Bridge security position at QL-1 Song Bo River bridge, apx 14 km NW Hue. Apr70 XXIV Corps grid per Don Armstrong. Thua Thien Pr, I Corps.

Song Bo River (YD 730-286)
Running generally SW to NE, apx 15 km WNW Hue, then turning E after crossing QL-1 at An Lo Bridge (near LZ Sally/Van Xa), and joining the Perfume River N of Hue at YD 752-287. River and its valley provided convenient VC/NVA infiltration rte to coastal lowlands N of Hue. During Op Carentan II, Apr68, 2d Bde/101st Abn conducted sweeps along river apx 6 km NW of Hue that netted 200 NVA KIA. Thua Thien Pr, I Corps.

Song Bo Valley (YD 545-160)
Apx 15 km WNW Hue Thua Thien Pr, I Corps.

Song Bo Railroad Bridge (YD 614-278)
Apx 2 km SSW the An Lo Bridge. Thua Thien Pr, I Corps.

Song Bu Lu (ZD 185-063)
River apx 46 km SE Hue, 36 km NNW Da Nang, 11 km ENE Phu Loc. Portion of drainage for N side of the Hai Van Pass. Grid is at mouth. Thua Thien Pr, I Corps.

Song Boung River (ZC 0-5)
Apx 10 km WSW Ha Tan and 45 km SW Da Nang. Quang Tin Pr, I Corps.

Song Buong (YT 07-04)
A.k.a. Song La Buong. E/W stream meets QL-15 at listed grid, apx 3 km SSE of Sanford AF. NC48-07 JOG. Also ville of this name in I Corps? Bien Hoa Pr, III Corps.

Song Ca Lau Bridge (BT 083-550)
QL-1 bridge apx 23 km SSE Da Nang AB, and 5 km WSW Hoi An. Quang Nam Pr, I Corps.

Song Ca Lon (WR 3-7?)
If grid square accurate, this stream or canal was perhaps 15 km SE Chau Duc AF. River Assault Sqdn 15, with 2d VNMC Bn were in ops along Song Cai Tu and Song Ca Lon beginning 11Jan69. Kien Giang Pr, IV Corps.

Song Ca River (WF 80-76)
Major river of NVN by which boat traffic reached the port of Vinh. Grid is at its mouth. NVN.

Song Ca Ty River (AN 840-085)
River whose mouth forms the bay of Phan Thiet at Xa Phan Thiet. Grid is at mouth. Binh Thuan Pr, II Corps.

Song Cai (AN 877-098)
River's mouth is at Ap Thuan Hai apx 4 km due E Xa Phan Thiet. Grid is at its mouth. Binh Thuan Pr, II Corps.

Song Cai Loi (WR 11-97)
River on Cau Mau Peninsula that enters Gulf of Thailand at Rach Gia. Kien Giang Pr, IV Corps.

Song Cai River (AT 80-45?)
If grid is accurate, it was near An Hoa, perhaps 35 km SSW Da Nang. Quang Nam Pr, I Corps.
Song Cai River (CP 05-56)
Drains mtns W of Nha Trang, meeting ocean at Nha Trang. Grid is at mouth. Khanh Hoa Pr, II Corps.
Song Cai River Valley (AT 80-45?)
SW An Hoa and draining the Nui Giang, Yang Brai and Ong Thu Slope ridgelines that were part of Base Area 112. Quang Nam Pr, I Corps.
Song Cai Tu (WR 3-7)
Apx 15 km SE Chau Duc AF. River Assault Sqdn 15, with 2d VNMC Bn were in ops along this and the Song Ca Lon rivers beginning 11Jan69. Chuong Thein Pr, IV Corps.
Song Cam Lo River (YD 13-61?)
River generally near Cam Lo, and drainage for large area W and WNW of that city. Quang Tri Pr, I Corps.
Song Cau (CQ 17-47)
Ql-1 coastal ville apx 30 km S Qui Nhon and 42 km NNW Tuy Hoa. Phu Yen Pr, II Corps.
Song Cau River (CQ 08-88)
Stream that met ocean immed S Song Cau AF, apx 30 km due S Qui Nhon. Phu Yen Pr, II Corps.
Song Cau Airfield (CQ 084-886)
On coast and aside QL-1 at Vung Chau Bay, apx 30 km due S Qui Nhon. Minor US airfield here Per TPC K-10B. El. 10', 2,300' laterite/sand rwy. At 13°27'38"N-109°13'48"E. Phu Yen Pr, II Corp.
Song Cau Bien River (YD 5-4?)
No data. Possibly Song Cau at grid in Thua Thien Pr?
Song Cau Dai River (XS 9-2)
See Song My Tho River. Kien Hoa Pr, IV Corps.
Song Cau Do River (BT 0-7)
Portion of Da Nang/Tourane River drainage system immed S and SW of Da Nang. Quang Nam Pr, I Corps.
Song Cau Do Bridge (AT 998-706)
QL-1 bridge 6 km S Da Nang AB. Quang Nam Pr, I Corps.
Song Cau Lau Bridge (BT 092-552)
QL-1 bridge 23 km SSE Da Nang AB and 5 km WSW Hoi An. Quang Nam Pr, I Corps.
Song Cau Ke (AN 8-1)
Close to and N of Phan Thiet. Binh Thuan Pr, II Corps.
Song Cau Lam (BP 9-7)
Vicinity of Ninh Hoa. Khanh Hoa Pr, II Corps.
Song Cau Lau River (BT 083-550)
Apparently apx 23 km SSE Da Nang, and meeting QL 1 at listed grid. Quang Nam Pr, I Corps.
Song Cau Tieu (XS 92-35)
Meets ocean at listed grid, apx 42 km ESE My Tho. Go Cong Pr, IV Corps.
Song Cau/Tuy Hoa (CQ 17-47)
See Tuy Hoa. Phu Yen Pr, II Corps.
Song Cay Bua Bridge (BS 692-648)
QL-1 bridge apx 2 km NNW the Song Ve bridge and 9 km SSE Quang Ngai. Quang Ngai Pr, I Corps.
Song Chang River (AT 95-24)
Flows generally NW from mtns SE Hiep Duc, and joins the Song Thu Bon on its journey to sea at Hoi An. Valley of river was a.k.a. "AK Valley." Quang Tin Pr, I Corps.
Song Chang Valley (AT 95-24)
A.k.a. AK Valley. Near Hiep Duc and Hiep Duc Valley. VC/NVA staging area and stronghold. Americal list. Quang Tin and Quang Nam Prvs, I Corps.
Song Chay Lake (VK 80-60)
Huge, narrow lake apx 100 km NW Hanoi. Roughly 50 km in length and perhaps avg of 8 km in width. Sat exactly parallel to course of the Red River and about 15 km to its E. Apparently few villes along its shore? NVN.
Song Cho (BT 42-14)
See Cho River. Quang Tin Pr, I Corps.
Song Con (n/a)
Mapsheet name of L-7014-5850-1. NVN/Laos.
Song Con River (BQ 8-4)
In W Phu Yen Pr, near Cung Song (river of same name in Binh Dinh and Quang Nam Prs). Phu Yen Pr, II Corps.
Song Con River (BR 65-55)
Meanders through Vinh Thanh (Happy) Valley and parallel to Rte 3a and QL-19), apx 18 km ENE An Khe. Involved in Op Crazy Horse, May66, and discussed in *Battles in the Monsoon*. LZ Savoy, on W bank near Vinh Than, heavily attacked in battle. Also listed at BR 70-43. 1st Cav '67 AO. See also Song Kon. Binh Dinh II Corps.
Song Con River (ZC 1-5)
In Central Quang Nam Pr, I Corps.
Song Cu De River (AT 9-8)
NW of Hue, and S Hai Van Pass. QL-1 crosses it at Nam O Bridge. Quang Nam Pr, I Corps.
Song Cua Viet River (YD 33-68)
Principal drainage for Cam Lo/Quang Tri area. Mouth was apx 16 km SE mouth of Ben Hai River (SVN border), and 17 km due N of Quang Tri. Quang Tri Pr, I Corps.
Song Da Bach (XJ 8-1)
See Da Bach River. NVN.
Song Da Krong River (XD 95-40)
A.k.a. Riviere de Da Krong. Quang Tri Pr, I Corps.
Song Da Krong Valley (XD 95-40)
S of Vandegrift CB and N of the A Shau Valley. Quang Tri Pr, I Corps.
Song Dai Giang (YD 910-165)
Stream apx 200 meters wide running parallel to QL-1 apx 3 km NE Phu Bai. Dia Giang is Chinese for widening river. Thua Thien Pr, I Corps.
Song Dap Da River (BR 89-41)
S edge of Phu Cat AB was bordered by the Song Dap Da and N edge by the Song La Vi. Binh Dinh Pr, II Corps.
Song Darang (CQ 08-87)
A.k.a. Song Do Rang. Major river flowing past Tuy Hoa and N of the AF. Grid is at mouth. Phu Yen Pr, II Corps.
Song Darang Valley (CQ 002-458)
Generally 17 km SW Tuy Hoa. Phu Yen Pr, II Corps.
Song Day (WJ 75-15)
See Day River. NVN.
Song Dinh (n/a)
Mapsheet name of L-7014-6530-4. SVN.
Song Do Rang River (CQ 19-48)
A.k.a. Song Darang. Major river that drains mtns W of Tuy Hoa and meets the ocean immed S and E Tuy Hoa. Grid is at its mouth. Phu Yen Pr, II Corps.

Song Dong Airfield (XS 480-347)
See Truc Giang AF. Kien Hoa Pr, IV Corps.

Song Dong Nai River (YT/XS/XT)
Ran generally NE to SW through central Long Khanh Pr, passing just W Bien Hoa and Long Binh in Bien Hoa Pr, and becoming border between Gia Dinh and Bien Hoa Prvs before joining the Song Saigon below Saigon. II/III Corps.

Song Dong Nai River Bridge (YT 015-055)
Rte 316 bridge over Dong Nai River apx 7 km S Bien Hoa AB and 11 km NE Thu Duc. Bien Hoa Pr, III Corps.

Song Dong Tranh River (YS 01-77)
A.k.a. the Long Tau Channel. Apx 20-25 km SE Saigon. Patrolled by RAS 11. AAR mentioning action here is at: www.mrf.org/ras11_action.htm, on MRF Assn Home Page. Gia Dinh Pr, III Corps.

Song Dua River (YS 04-74)
A.k.a. the Long Tau Channel. The Song Dong Tranh, Song Nga Bay, Song Ba Gioi and Song Thi Vai Rivers ran through Rung Sat Spec Zone and emptied into Vinh Ganh Rai. Gia Dinh Pr, III Corps.

Song Ga Mountain (AT 870-620)
On Charlie Ridge, apx 20 km SW Da Nang AB. Jan66. Quang Nam Pr, I Corps.

Song Go Ma Bridge (BS 691-646)
On QL-1, 10 km SE Quang Ngai. Quang Ngai Pr, I Corps.

Song Ha River (BT 04-74)
See Song Han. Quang Nam Pr, I Corps.

Song Hac Giang (WJ 33-35)
The Black River. Flows generally N, joining the Red River near Viet Tri and 55 km WNW Hanoi. NVN.

Song Hai River (BQ 7-6?)
Grid square indicates it was between Phu Tuc and Dong Tre. Phu Yen Pr, II Corps.

Song Ham Luong River (XS 7-0)
Exits to South China Sea apx 90 km S Saigon. Kien Hoa (et al) Prvs, IV Corps.

Song Han Giang (YD 20-60)
A.k.a. the Quang Tri River. Quang Tri Pr, I Corps.

Song Han River (BT 00-71)
A.k.a. the Da Nang River, Tourane River or Riviere de Da Nang. Immed SE Da Nang, between that city and Marble Mtn AB. Quang Nam Pr, I Corps.

Song Hau Giang River (XR 4-5)
Exits to South China Sea apx 140 km SSW Saigon. Vinh Binh/Ba Xuyen Pr border, IV Corps.

Song Hau Giang (XR 4-5)
See Bassac River. Vinh Binh Pr, IV Corps.

Song Hoa Airfield (BQ 808-422)
See Cung Son AF. Phu Yen Pr, II Corps.

Song Hong (WJ 95-05)
A.k.a. the Red River. Flows NW to SE from Chinese border through Hanoi, and meets ocean apx 35 km NW Thuan Nghiep, and 110 km SE Hanoi. NVN.

Song Hong Ha River (XH 6-4)
Portion of Red River below Hanoi. Mouth at grid. NVN.

Song Huong River (YD 740-208)
A.k.a. Song Hue, the River of Perfumes, or the Perfume River. Flows through Hue. Formed by its W branch, the Song Huu Trach, which flows W to E along Hwy 547, and its S branch, the Song Ta Trach, which flows S to N and joins the Huu Trach just below Nam Hoa (Pohl) Bridge, apx 7 km S of Hue. Where 2 branches joined was a gravel bed that Viets "harvested" using small boats on daily trips from Hue. Thua Thien Pr, I Corps.

Song Huu Trach (YD 740-103)
W branch of Song Huong River (Perfume River). Flowing W to E, it joins the Song Ta Trach just N Nam Hoa and just S Nam Hoa (Pohl) Bridge apx 7 km S Hue, to form the Song Huong. Thua Thien Pr, I Corps.

Song Khang (AT 05-20)
See Song Chang. Quang Nam Pr, I Corps.

Song Khon (BR?)
A.k.a. the Song Kon River? Apparently near LZ English and in AO of 173d Abn, 70. Binh Dinh Pr?, II Corps.

Song Kon River (BR 74-81)
Possible sp variant of Song Con, Song Khon and/or Song Lon? Valley of this river used as staging/R&R area for NVA's 22d Rgt, Sao Vang Div, in prep for attack on LZ Bird, Dec66. Discussed in *Bird*, p. 6. Also listed at BR 72-87. See Song Con River. Binh Dinh Pr, II Corps.

Song Kon River (CR 0-3)
A.k.a. Song Ha Giao. Near Ba Gi and N Qui Nhon. Sp variant of Song Con and/or Song Lon? Grid per NIMA Gaz. Binh Dinh Pr, II Corps.

Song Ky La River (BQ 9-7)
NE Dong Tre. Phu Yen Pr, II Corps.

Song Ky Lam River (BT 0-5?)
If grid correct, was SE Hill 55, and apx 20 km S Da Nang. Quang Nam Pr, I Corps.

Song La Buong (YT 07-04)
A.k.a. Song Buong. Bien Hoa Pr, III Corps.

Song La Tho River (BT 0-5)
SE of Hill 55 and apx 20 km S Da Nang. 1st Mar Div. Quang Nam Pr, I Corps.

Song La Vi River (BR 89-41)
S edge of Phu Cat AB was bordered by the Song Dap Da and N edge by the Song La Vi. Binh Dinh Pr, II Corps.

Song Lai Airfield (TF 73-98)
LS-318. CIA/SF, per *Air Facilities Data-Laos.*

Song Lo Bo (BS 82-37)
See Lo Bo River. Quang Ngai Pr, I Corps.

Song Lo Dong River (AT 8-6)
Apx 15 km WSW Da Nang. Quang Nam Pr, I Corps.

Song Lo Tho River (BT 0-5?)
If grid correct, was SE Hill 55, roughly 20 km S Da Nang. Quang Nam Pr, I Corps.

Song Lo (WJ 45-75)
See Clear River. NVN.

Song Loi Nong (YD 870-185)
Small stream running from Phu Bai area N through Loi Nong near Hue. Thua Thien Pr, I Corps.

Song Lon River (BR 72-87)
Variant of Song Kon. Apx 40 km N Song Con. May or may not be "Song Kon" cited by S.L.A. Marshall as in valley of river used as staging/R&R area for NVA's 22d Rgt, Sao Vang Div, in prep for its attack on LZ Bird (BR 743-817), Dec66. Discussed in *Bird*, p. 6. See Song Con River. Binh Dinh Pr, II Corps.

Song Lon River (WT, WS, XS, XR)
See Mekong River. IV Corps.

Song Ly Ly River (BT 00-33)
Parallel and between Rtes 534 and 535, apx 2 km S Que Son and some 45 km due S Da Nang. Met QL-1 at BT 14-45. Quang Nam Pr, I Corps.

Song Mao (BN 27-46)
On western outskirts of Hai Ninh, at or near Song Mao AF, apx 5 km NW Phan Ly Cham and 55 km NE Phan Thiet. Home of Song Mao, Binh Thuan Pr Advsy Team 33. Also sp "Song Mau." Binh Thuan Pr, II Corps.

Song Mao, FSB? (BN 268-458)
Actual name unknown. Just N the E end of Song Mao AF rwy, apx 1 km NW Hai Ninh. 3d/506th Inf. Grid per Jerry Berry. Binh Thuan Pr, II Corps.

Song Mao Airfield (BN 264-456)
Major AF apx 67 km SW Phan Rang AF, 56 km NE Phan Thiet and 13 km from coast. Per TPC K-10D, El. 85', 3,500' steel-mat rwy. At 11°15'25"N-108°29'40"E. Also spelled Song Mau. Binh Thuan Pr, II Corps.

Song Mao Mountains (BN 30-57)
Region within 20 km N and NE Song Mao/AF. Contained the Le Hon Phong Forest and were object of Sep69 op to recover a POW camp reportedly containing US/ARVN POWs. Grid is at apx center of mass. See Le Hon Phong Forest. Binh Thuan Pr, II Corps.

Song Mao River (CQ 0-0)
Near coast and Van Ninh, roughly 25 km NNE Ninh Hoa. Khanh Hoa Pr, II Corps.

Song Mao SF Camp (BN 264-456)
Near QL-1 RR tracks, apx 3 km WSW Hai Ninh, and 3 km SW Song Mao AF. 5th SF. Binh Thuan Prov Advsy Team 33. Moved to Dong Ba Thin. Info/grid per *SF Order of Battle.* Binh Thuan Pr, II Corps.

Song Mao, Camp (AN 965-304)
See Phi Long and Phi Ma. Binh Thuan Pr, II Corps.

Song Mao, FSB (BN 269-548)
See FSB Gaiser. Binh Thuan Pr, II Corps.

Song Mao, FSB (BN 281-449)
See FSB Sherry. Binh Thuan Pr, II Corps.

Song Mau (BN 27-46)
See Song Mao. Binh Thuan Pr, II Corps.

Song My Massacre (BS 73-77)
See My Lai. Quang Ngai Pr, I Corps.

Song My Thanh River (XR 28-40)
Mouth apx 160 km SSW Saigon. Ba Xuyen Pr, IV Corps.

Song My Tho River (XS 9-2)
A.k.a. Song Cau Dai. Exits to South China Sea apx 60 km S Saigon. Kien Hoa Pr, IV Corps.

Song Nga Bay River (YS 13-67)
NW Vung Tau, and N Can Gio. The Song Dong Tranh, Song Nga Bay, Song Ba Gioi and Song Thi Vai Rivers ran through the Rung Sat Special Zone and emptied into Vinh Ganh Rai Bay. Gia Dinh Pr, III Corps.

Song Ngan River (XD 98-62 to YD 07-03)
Ran roughly parallel to and just S the southern edge of DMZ, from point apx due N the Rockpile until it turned N and joined the Ben Hai River in DMZ at YD 07-73, NNW Con Thien. Quang Tri Pr, I Corps.

Song Ngan Valley (YD 03-64)
A.k.a. Helicopter Valley. Rugged valley N of Mutter's Ridge running parallel to and just S the southern edge of DMZ. Was 5 km S Hill 208 (CP for 324-B NVA Div) and staging area for 90th NVA Rgt (1,500 men) of 324-B Div. Focus of Op Hastings, Summer '66. See Helicopter Valley for more detail. Quang Tri Pr, I Corps.

Song Nong Bridge (YD 927-103)
On QL-1 over Song Nong River SE of Phu Bai, apx 2 km SE Song Phu Bridge and 24 km SE Hue. Marketplace and villes of Thon An Nong I-IV and Thon An Tach were adj to bridge. Thua Thien Pr, I Corps.

Song Nuoc Luong River (BR 699-871)
Near listed grid, which puts it generally about 70 km NNW Qui Nhon. Hamlet of Hoi Van apparently along this river, as noted in *Bird*, p 14. Binh Dinh Pr, II Corps.

Song O Giang River (YD 45-46)
Joins Song Thac Ma and Song O Lau between Hai Lang in Quang Tri Pr and Phong Dien in Thua Thien Pr. I Corps.

Song O Giang River Bridge (YD 474-422)
Apx 17 km SE Quang Tri and 3 km NE QL-1. Quang Tri Pr, I Corps.

Song O Lau (YD 519-348)
Major river that partially forms border between Quang Tri and Thua Thien Prvs. Flows into Pha Tam Giang Bay at its northernmost point near Ap Hai Lai (YD 60-42). Listed grid is QL-1 bridge immed NW Phong Dien. Song Thac Ma and O Giang Rivers join this river near Thon My Chan Bridge. Thua Thien Pr, I Corps.

Song Ong Doc (n/a)
Mapsheet name of L-7014-5927-2. SVN.

Song Ong Doc (VQ 80-99)
Name of tidal river and ville on W coast of SVN, apx 50 km NNE tip of Cau Mau Peninsula. Apparently small SF camp and USN 572d River Boat Sqdn here. See *Bering Strait*. An Xuyen Pr, IV Corps.

Song Ong Doc Heliport (VQ 804-986)
A.k.a. Song On Duc Heliport. At river mouth near Vam Song Ong Don, apx 40 km WSW Quang Long, 18 km NNW Binh Hung AF and 50 km NNE tip of Cau Mau Peninsula. Heliport #727, alt 7', at 09°03'00"N-104°48'30"E, per Feb73 TAD. An Xuyen Pr, IV Corps.

Song Ong Doc Navy Base (VQ 80-98)
US Navy base at river mouth's. See Song On Doc Heliport for location. An Xuyen Pr, IV Corps.

Song Pha (BP 48-08)
A.k.a. Thon Song Pha. Villes of this name also listed at BP 49-08 and 52-09. Tuyen Duc or Ninh Thuan Pr, II Corps.

Song Phan Airfield (YS 988-841)
See Ham Tan AF. Binh Tuy Pr, III Corps.

Song Phan River (ZS 14-86)
Apx 28 km WSW Phan Thiet. FSB Jo Ann was along this stream. Grid is at mouth. Binh Tuy Pr, III Corps.

Song Phu Bridge (YD 913-118)
QL-1 bridge over the Song Phu at Phu Bai and 22 km SE Hue. Thua Thien Pr, I Corps.

Song Quang Tri River (YD 30-47)
A.k.a. Riviere de Quang Tri. Drained area to W and SW Quang Tri. Quang Tri Pr, I Corps.

Song Rach Cac River (YS 83-70)
Tidal river 10-30 km due S Saigon. Gia Dinh Pr, III Corps.

Song Rai (YS 59-57)
A.k.a. Song Ray River. Significant terrain feature in 1ATF AO. Runs generally S/N, apx 15 km E Nui Dat and roughly

parallels QL-2 at same distance to E. Grid is at its mouth. Phuoc Tuy Pr, III Corps.

Song Rao Vinh River (YD 2-5)
NW and within 10 km of Quang Tri. Quang Tri Pr, I Corps.

Song Ray (YS 59-57)
See Song Rai River. Phuoc Tuy Pr, III Corps.

Song Re River (BS 35-42)
Quang Ngai Pr, I Corps.

Song Re Valley (BS 33-55)
Apx 40 km SW Quang Ngai and focus of Op Vernon Lake, Jan-Feb69. Americal and 1st Cav. See also LZ Pat and Ta Ma AF. Quang Ngai Pr, I Corps.

Song Saigon (XS 88-93)
The Saigon River. Runs from Fishhook area (XT 60-80) S to Dau Tieng, then turns to SE and to Saigon, joining the Song Nha Be at YS 92-88. Acft/helo pilots nicknamed the Song Saigon and Song Thi Tinh, the Big and Little Blue. Per *Low Level Hell*, p 58. Dividing boundary between 25th and 1st US Inf Divs. III Corps.

Song Suoi Co Ca River (AT 9-6 or BT 0-5?)
SE Hill 55. Quang Nam Pr, I Corps.

Song Ta Trach (YD 765-765)
S branch of the Song Huong. Joins the Song Huu Trach N Nam Hoa and just S Nam Hoa (Pohl) Bridge, apx 7 km S Hue, to form the Song Huong. Flows S to N. Nam Hoa Dist HQ was on its E bank apx 8 km S Hue. See Song Huong, Perfume River and Pohl Bridge. Thua Thien Pr, I Corps.

Song Tam Giap River (BT 0-6?)
Generally SE of Hill 55. Quang Nam Pr, I Corps.

Song Tam Ky (BT 26-30)
Stream that ran E of, and roughly parallel to, QL-1, from Tam Ky NW to vic of Thang Binh. Quang Tin Pr, I Corps.

Song Tan Khong River (n/a)
Spelling variant of Song Tan Kong? I Corps.

Song Tan Kong River (BT 4-0?)
Generally W of Happy Valley. Quang Nam Pr, I Corps.

Song Thac Ma River (YD 460-400)
Along QL-1, just NW Thua Thien Pr border. The Thon My Chan Bridge crosses it at listed grid, apx 32 km NW Hue. Quang Tri Pr, I Corps.

Song Thach Han River (YD 2-6)
See Quang Tri River. Quang Tri Pr, I Corps.

Song Thanh Quit River (BT 0-6)
See Song Thanh Quyt. Quang Nam Pr, I Corps.

Song Thanh Quyt River (BT 0-6)
A.k.a. Song Thanh Quit. Generally of E Hill 55 and S of Da Nang. Quang Nam Pr, I Corps.

Song Thi Tinh River (XT 7-2)
Originates apx 10 km NW Ben Cat, then parallels QL-13 to S where it joins the Song Saigon about 12 km S Ben Cat. Acft/helo pilots called Song Saigon and Song Thi Tinh, the Big and Little Blue. Per *Low Level Hell*, p 58. III Corps.

Song Thi Vai River (YS 23-72)
The Song Dong Tranh, Song Nga Bay, Song Ba Gioi and Song Thi Vai Rivers ran through the Rung Sat Spec Zone and emptied into Vinh Ganh Rai. Gia Dinh Pr, III Corps.

Song Thu Bon River (AT 54-85)
Main channel draining mtns W Hoi An. Fed by Song Cai River from W (Ha Thanh area), and by Song Chang River from SW (Hiep Duc and AK valleys). Mouth of river at BT 22-57. Quang Tin/Quang Nam Prvs, Corps.

Song Thu Thua River (XS 43-72)
See Kinh Thu Thua. Long An/Kien Tuong Pr, III/IV Corps.

Song Thuy Loan River (AT 9-6)
If grid correct, was within 15 km SW of Da Nang AB. NIMA sp is "Song Thuy Loan." See Tuy Loan CAP. Presumably in Hieu Duc Dist, Quang Nam Pr, I Corps.

Song Tra Cau QL-1 Bridge (BS 78-43)
A.k.a. the Paddock/Westrate Bridge. Apx 14 km SE Mo Duc and 5 km N Duc Pho. Quang Ngai Pr, I Corps.

Song Tra Khuc River (BS 55-76)
Runs through Quang Ngai. Quang Ngai Pr, I Corps.

Song Tra No River (BS 55-30)
SW to NE Infiltration rte that ran from Gia Vuc to Ba To to Mo Duc/Duc Pho coastal region. Quang Ngai Pr, I Corps.

Song Tram River (BT 13-03)
See Song Tram Valley. Quang Tin Pr, I Corps.

Song Tram Valley (BT 180-000)
Due S Tien Phuoc, apx 22 km SW of Tam Ky and 40 km due W Chu Lai. Runs 15 km S from confluence of Song Tram and Song Chang, then turns E for another 7 km. Portion of Op Lamar Plain here involved elements of 101st Abn opcon to Americal Div. Quang Tin Pr, I Corps.

Song Trang Valley (BR?)
Apparently in NW II Corps and staging area for 22d NVA Rgt infiltration of coastal areas near Phu Cat and Bong Son. Unable to identify river of this name in area described. Binh Dinh Pr, II Corps?

Song Truoi River (YD 985-080)
Drained into W edge of Dam Cau Hai lagoon, apx 26 km SE Hue and 12 km NW Phu Loc. Grid is at mouth. Thua Thien Pr, I Corps.

Song Truoi Bridge (YD 968-063)
Ql-1 bridge apx 13 km NW Phu Loc and 13 km SE Phu Bai AF. Jan68. Thua Thien Pr, I Corps.

Song Truong Giang (BT 33-30)
See Truong Giang River. Quang Tin Pr, I Corps.

Song Tuy Loan River (AT 9-6)
See Song Thuy Loan. Quang Nam Pr, I Corps.

Song Vam Co Dong River (XS 80-58)
Runs NW to SE, passing within 5 km of Tay Ninh and by such towns as Go Dau Ha, Duc Hoa and Ben Luc before reaching the Cua Soirap apx 30 km W Vung Tau. Also at XT 25-40 and 55-90. III Corps.

Song Vam Co Tay River (XS 63-62)
Long river that ran NW to SE, beginning NW Moc Hoa and joining the Song Vam Co Dong apx 15 km ESE Tan An. Kien Tuong and Long An Prvs, III/IV Corps.

Song Ve (BS 72-58)
Ville apx 19 km SSE Quang Ngai and 5 km N Mo Duc AF. Quang Ngai Pr, I Corps.

Song Ve Bridge (BS 695-635)
QL-1 bridge apx 12 km SSE Quang Ngai and 10 km NNW Mo Duc AF. Another Song Ve Bridge is at BS 650-580. Americal List. Quang Ngai Pr, I Corps.

Song Ve Bridge (BS 695-635)
Rte 517 bridge apx 12 km W Mo Duc AF and 7 km ENE Minh Long AF. Another Song Ve Bridge is at BS 695-635. Quang Ngai Pr, I Corps.

Song Ve River (BS 75-70)
Major tributary draining Minh Long and Ba To area. Flows generally SW to NE and intersects QL-1 apx 12 km SSE Quang Ngai. Grid is at mouth. Quang Ngai Pr, I Corps.
Song Ve Valley (BS 61-52)
Bordering the Nui Hoat Mtns generally 13 km W of Mo Duc AF. Quang Ngai Pr, I Corps.
Song Vinh Dien River (BT 0-7)
A.k.a. Vin Dien? SE Hill 55, Quang Nam Pr, I Corps.
Song Vu Gia River (AT 9-9)
SW of Da Nang AB. Quang Nam Pr, I Corps.
Song Vuong River Valley (AT)
See Vuong River Valley. Quang Nam Pr, I Corps.
Song Xe Pon River (XD)
See Xe Pon River. Laos.
Song Yang River (ZC 0-5)
Near Thanh My and to S An Diem, roughly 45 km WSW Da Nang. Quang Nam Pr, I Corps.
Song Yen River (AT 9-6)
NNE of An Hoa and roughly 14 km SE Da Nang. Quang Nam Pr, I Corps.
Songkhla Airfield (PH 6-8)
Along coast, roughly 740 km S Bangkok, near 7°08'00"N-100°32'00"E. NIMA data. Thailand.
Songkhla Airport (PH 7-9)
A.k.a. Sanambin Songkhla and Singora AF. Along coast, apx 740 km S Bangkok per Feb67 Natl Geo map. Near 7°11'00"N-100°37'00"E. NIMA data. El. 13'. Thailand.
Sonnette (n/a)
See Glossary.
Sontay (WJ 53-37?)
See Son Tay. NVN.
Sooner, LZ (AT 876-369)
Apx 4 km due S Phuoc Binh AF, 34 km SW Hoi An and 12 km S An Hoa CB. Also listed by arty ORLL at AT 869-359 and 870-367. Apr70 XXIV Corps grid per Don Armstrong. Quang Nam Pr, I Corps.
Sop, Mui (CP 0-1)
Coastal point at 11°53'N-109°12'E. On NC49-01 JOG. Khanh Hoa Pr, II Corps.
Sop Cop (n/a)
Mapsheet name of L-7014-5750-4. NVN/Laos.
Sop Nao (TJ 78-62?)
Apx 30 km ENE Muong Khoua and perhaps 40 km SE DBP. A satellite French outpost, manned by reinforced Plt under a Lt Grezy. On 3Apr53, the Vietminh surrounded post. Despite overwhelming odds, Grezy's men held until 9Apr53, when Capt. Teullier at Muong Khoua gave them permission to escape and evade. Grezy was aware Vietminh would likely lay ambush to E (which they did), so instead he headed W toward Muong Khoua. When he learned the Vietminh had moved ambush to that area, he turned NW toward remote outpost at Phong Saly, where he met a French canoe river supply convoy coming S on the Nam Hou River. The grp then headed again towards "safety" at Muong Khuoa (where most all would die in siege). On 29-30Jul54, the renewed garrison here was held by a single plt of RTA fled without a fight when they heard an "enemy" unit was approaching (actually it was 80-man force of Black T'ai from Vietnam) and sat in hills for several days observing post and returned when "enemy" did not show. See *Street Without Joy*, pp 117, 130. Laos.
Sop Hao Airfield (VH 43-73)
L-17. CIA/SF, per *Air Facilities Data-Laos.*
Sop Hien Airfield (TF 72-84)
LS-75. CIA/SF, per *Air Facilities Data-Laos.*
Soper, LZ (BR 331-273)
Apx 17 km NW Plei Niang, 11 km NE LZ Mattie, 23 km SW An Khe and 20 km S QL-19. Possibly named to honor either PFC John C. Soper, KIA 6Aug67, or WO Richard O. Soper, KIA 23Aug68. 4th Div AO, '70. Name/grid per Jim Claeys. Apr-Oct70. Binh Dinh Pr, II Corps.
Sophia, LZ (XD 34-40)
A.k.a. Sophia West? Apx 15 km WNW LZ Sophia-2, some 51 km due W Khe Sanh, 18 km W Aloui and 10 km SE Tchepone. 1st ARVN Div LZ during Lam Son 719. Lam Son 719 map at www.americal.org/174/ map4.htm. See also LZ Sophia West. Laos.
Sophia 2, LZ (XD 50-46)
Roughly 15 km ESE LZ Sophia, 36 km WSW Khe Sanh and 4 km SSW Aloui (Laos). ARVN LZ During Lam Son 719. Good map of Lam Son 719 at www.americal.org/174/map4.htm. Laos.
Sophia West, LZ/FSB (XD 34-40?)
A.k.a. LZ Sophia? Overlooked Rte 9 in Laos. Elements of 1st ARVN Div assaulted here and to LZ Lolo, 3-6Mar71 during Lam Son 719. Cited in *Airmobility, 1961-1971*, p 242. Good Lam Son 719 map at www.americal.org/174/map4.htm. See also LZ Sophia. Laos.
Soprai (n/a)
Mapsheet name of L-7014-6631-1. SVN.
Sopt, La Pointe (CP 0-1)
See Pointe La Sopt. Khanh Hoa Pr, II Corps.
Sopt, Mui (CP 0-1)
A.k.a. Mui Sop. Coastal point at 11°53'N-109°12'E. On NC49-01 JOG. Khanh Hoa Pr, II Corps.
Sot, Mui (XF 0-4)
A.k.a. Cape Sot. Coastal point at 18°28'N-105°57'E. NE48-07 Map. NVN.
Souchere, Plantation de (YS 4-9)
A.k.a. Don Dien Souchere. Near Blackhorse basecamp, SW Xuan Loc. Long Khanh Pr, III Corps.
Soui Ca Valley (BR 800-660)
See Suoi Ca. Binh Dinh Pr, II Corps.
Soui Da, FSB (XT 340-583)
See Suoi Da. Tay Ninh Pr, III Corps.
Soui Doi (BR 023-522)
See Suoi Doi. Pleiku Pr, II Corps.
Soui Dai Airfield (BR 040-500)
A.k.a. Suoi Doi? On QL-19, apx 27 km ENE Pleiku. "Abnd, Overgrown 29Jun67, AF # VA2-244." Aug69 TAD, per Frank Penk, Jr. Not 73 TAD. Pleiku Pr, II Corps.
Soui Doi Airfield (BR 034-544)
See Suoi Doi AF. II Corps
Soukhouma Airfield (n/a)
Apx 495 km SE Vientiane. Natl Geo map. El. 252'. Laos.
Source, Baie de la (YJ 6-4)
Bay at 21°12'N-107°34'E. On NF48-12 JOG.
South, FSB (XT 5-9)
See FSBs South I and South II. Tay Ninh Pr, III Corps.

South, LZ (BS 705-832)
Apx 11 km NE Quang Ngai and 7 km ESE LZ Dottie. 11th LIB here. Also listed at BS 700-830 and 702-827. XXIV Corps grid, per of Don Armstrong. Quang Ngai Pr, I Corps.
South, LZ (XD/YD?)
No data. I Corps.
South, LZ (ZA 209-123)
Apx 8 km NE Plei Me SF Camp and 35 km S Pleiku. On 24Oct65, an ARVN armored TF moving to relieve siege of Plei Me SF Camp was ambushed and stalled on Rte 5, about 12 km N Plei Me. This LZ used in relief of column. Secured by A and C Cos, 2d/8th Cav, 1st Cav and B Bty, 2d/19th Arty, suptg ARVN against 32d and 33d NVA Rgts. On map in *Pleiku*, p 88. Pleiku Pr, II Corps.
South I, FSB (XT 515-905)
Apx 19 km due E Katum AF, 8 km W tip of Fishhook, 2 km W FSB South II and 3 km from Cambodia. Incursion FSB, May-Jun70. Possibly 1st Cav, 25th Inf, 11th ACR or ARVN here? Also listed at 50-89? See also FSB South II. Tay Ninh Pr, III Corps. [502] [503]
South II FSB (XT 531-900)
Apx 21 km due E Katum AF, 6 km W tip of Fishhook, 2 km E FSB South I, and 3 km from Cambodia. Incursion FSB, May-Jun70. Possibly 1st Cav, 25th Inf, 11th ACR or ARVN here? Data per Frank Penk, Jr. Also listed at XT 515-905 and 50-89? See South I. Tay Ninh Pr, III Corps.
South Beach (CP 053-166?)
On Cam Ranh Bay Peninsula. Site of AT&B (Alaska Barge and Transport Cmpd), the AT&B Cave Bar and possibly the 6th Convalescent Hosp? [504] See also Howell Beach. Grid is est. Khanh Hoa Pr, II Corps.
South Beach Airfield (CP 053-166)
See Cam Ranh AF. Khanh Hoa Pr, II Corps.
South Beach Amphitheater (CP 05-16?)
Precise location unknown, but apparently near South Beach, at S end of Cam Ranh Bay Peninsula. Later renamed to honor Sp4 Robert E. Pugh. See Pugh Amphitheater. Khanh Hoa Pr, II Corps.
South Dakota, FSB (YS 273-660)
Along E side of QL-15, apx 16.5 km WSW Nui Dat, 2 km SE FSB Janet and 12 km WSW FSB Weir. On 1ATF NCO trng map per John Hollett. Phuoc Tuy Pr, III Corps.
South East Point (CP 2-8)
A.k.a. Mui Ganh. Coastal point at 12°34'N-109°26'E. On ND49-13 JOG. Khanh Hoa Pr, II Corps.
South Hue LCU Ramp (YD 773-225)
See Hue LCU Ramp. Thua Thien Pr, I Corps.
South Point (CR 1-2)
Pointe Sud. Coastal point at 13°46'N-109°15'E. On ND49-09 JOG. Binh Dinh Pr, II Corps.
South Point (CR 1-2)
See Point South. Binh Dinh Pr, II Corps.
South Port, SS (n/a)
Commercial transport under govt contract, per Ralph Fries.
South SAR Station (XG 06-01)
See SAR South. Gulf of Tonkin. NVN.
Southerland, USS (n/a)
DD-743, per Ralph Fries.
Southern, LZ (BP 791-668)
Apx 27 km NW Nha Trang AB and 21 km S to SSW Duc My AF. Apr67. Khanh Hoa Pr, II Corps.
Southern Cross (n/a)
See Glossary.
Southwest Bay (XQ 7-5)
A.k.a. Dam Ben. Bay at 8°39'N-106°34'E. NVN.
Soviet Bloc, Forces of (n/a)
See Major HQs Section.
SP 1 through 15 (BR)
See Strongpoint 1 through 15. Binh Dinh Pr, II Corps.
SP A-2 (YD 213-743)
See A-2, Strongpoint. Quang Tri Pr, I Corps.
SP A-4 (YD 118-701)
See A-4, Strongpoint. Quang Tri Pr, I Corps.
SP C-1 (YD 212-675)
See C-1, Strongpoint. Quang Tri Pr, I Corps.
SP C-2 (YD 135-645)
See C-2, Strongpoint. Quang Tri Pr, I Corps.
Spades, LZ (BS 458-035)
Apx 29 km WSW Thuan An, 25 km SSW Gia Vuc AF and near LZs Hearts and Clubs. Mar66. Binh Dinh Pr, II Corps.
Spain, Forces of (n/a)
See Major HQs Section.
Spanish Beach (BT 032-843)
On the Tien Sha Peninsula, apx 3.5 km WNW Camp Tien Sha, 8 km N Da Nang AB and 7 km W peak Son Tra Mtn. On map at www.ptfnasty.com/images/jpg/ptfdanang1a.JPG. Quang Nam Pr, I Corps.
Spark, FSB (XD 875-238)
In center of Vietnam Salient, apx 7 km SSW Lang Klung, 6 km SE Lang Chei, 18 km SSE Khe Sanh CB and 54 km SW Quang Tri. Reactivated by 2d/9th Marines, 2Jul69, during Op Utah Mesa. On 15Jan69, helo carrying Col Michael Spark, Rgt CO 3d Marines, LTC Ermil Whisman, CO 1st/12th Marines and 3d Rgt Sgt Maj. Ted McClintock was shot down near FSB Maxwell during TF Yankee attack on Base Area 112. FSBs later named after all 3 men. 3d Mar Div. Apr70 XXIV Corps grid per Don Armstrong. Quang Tri Pr, I Corps.
Sparrow, LZ (BS 424-040)
Apx 33 km WSW Thuan An and 23 km SSE Gia Vuc. Mar66. Binh Dinh Pr, II Corps.
Sparrow, LZ (BS 723-424)
Apx 16 km due W Phu Cat AB, 4 km due E Binh Khe and 25 km E An Khe. Feb66. Quang Ngai Pr, I Corps.
Sparrow, LZ (YD 050-648)
Apx 1.5 km S the DMZ, 13 km NW Cam Lo and 24 km WNW Dong Ha. Op Virginia Ridge FSB of 1st/3d Marines, 3d Mar Div, 30Mar69. 1st Bde/5th Div saw heavy contact nearby with 27th NVA Rgt, 22Oct69, which ARVN and 101st Div reinforced. Apr70 XXIV Corps grid per Don Armstrong. Also listed at YD 06-66. On map at p 58, *US Marines in Vietnam-1969*. Quang Tri Pr, I Corps.
Sparrow Hawk Reaction Force (n/a)
See Glossary.
Sparrow Knob, LZ (BT 200-387)
A.k.a. Sparrow's Knob. On QL-1 apx 20 km NNW Tam Ky and 20 km SSE Hoi An. Americal list. Map is L-7014-6640-2. Quang Tin Pr?, I Corps.
Sparrowhawk (TJ 94-67)
French strongpoint at Dien Bien Phu. Cited in *Bonnie-Sue*, at p 423. NVN.

Spartan Heliport (XT 990-105)
See Bien Hoa Heliport. Binh Duong Pr, III Corps.
Spartan, LZ (BR 13-39?)
Per 199th AHC website, in Jun70, was in VC Valley (BR 13-39), somewhere S LZ Blackhawk and QL-19. 4th Div AO. Grid is for VC Valley. Binh Dinh Pr, II Corps.
Spear, FSB (YC 683-921)
Apx 32 km SSW Hue, 31 km SW Phu Bai and 19 km ESE FSB Tennessee, 101st Abn. Also listed at YC 685-925 per XXIV Corps index. Thua Thien Pr, I Corps.
Spear, FSB (YS 666-582)
On coast, Apx 25 km ESE Nui Dat, 7 km SE FSB Mardi and 6.5 km SSE FSB Bruiser. On 1ATF NCO trng map per John Hollett. Phuoc Tuy Pr, III Corps.
Spear, FSB (YU 262-618)
See Speer. Cambodia.
Spear, FSB (ZC 180-390)
A.k.a. Hill 558. Apx 15 km SW An Hoa, 45 km SW Hoi An, and 5 km due S FSB Pike. Built beginning 15Dec68, on very narrow ridgeline as part of USMC TF Yankee's assault on Base Area 112. Const by 1st/3d Marines. Initial const facilitated by USAF 10,000 lb., Combat Trap bomb (see Combat Trap in Glossary). Grid per map in *US Marines in VN-1969*, p 90. Quang Nam Pr, I Corps.
Spear Valley (YD?)
Location unknown, but apparently in 101st Abn AO, and possibly near A Shau Valley? 5th NVA Rgt found here by 101st Abn LRRPs. Cited in *Rangers at War*, p 170. Thua Thien Pr, I Corps.
Spearhead, LZ (YA 519-471)
Cambodian Incursion FSB. Apx 6 km WNW Plei To Lav, 15 km NE Phum Chuoy, 2 km from SVN and 73 km due W Pleiku. 4th Div, '70, and C Bty, 4th/42d Arty here may70. Also listed at YA 516-471. Name/grid per Jim Claeys. Cambodia.
Special Capital Zone (XS/XT)
Combat Tactical Zone (CTZ) that included Saigon and much of Gia Dinh Pr. One of five CTZs in SVN, the others being I, II, III and IV Corps.
Special Forces BOQ (XS 8-9)
At 11 Dang Duc Sieu St., Saigon. Data per *Vietnam Military Lore, 1959-1973*. Gia Dinh Pr, III Corps.
Spectre (n/a)
See Glossary.
Speedy Express, Operation (n/a)
1Dec68-31May69. Gen 9th Inf Div ops throughout IV Corps. 10,899 rptd NVA/VC KIA, per *Vietnam Order of Battle*, pp 9-14. Multi-Prvs, IV Corps.
Speer, FSB (YU 262-618)
Often misspelled "Spear." Apx 10 km WSW O Rang/FSB David in Cambodia, 25 km WNW Bu Krak AF, 26 km NNW Djamap AF and 10 km from SVN. Possibly named to honor Army Lt Richard M. Speer, KIA 22Apr70. 2d/12th Cav, 1st Cav 23May70, also C/1st/77th Arty, A/1st/30th Arty. Incursion base, May-Jun70. Also listed at YU 260-618 per *11th ACR Cambodia Invasion AAR, 1st Cav Div, May-Jun70*, courtesy Lou Rochat [505] and at YT 262-618 (likely in error). Cambodia.
Spencer, USCGC (n/a)
WHEC 36. 11Feb69-30Sep69. Sqdn 3 CGC, during Coast Guard's 4th deployment.
Sphinx, USS (n/a)
ARL-24. USN Landing Craft Repair Ship. SVN with 9th Inf Div/MRF. See www.mrfa.org. III/IV Corps?
Spider (n/a)
See Glossary.
Spider Lake (AT 9-4?)
NW of Da Nang. Alligator Lake was to E, Hill 425 (OP Sunrise) was to E, with Phu Son Chin and Phu Loc to NE. Man-made/dammed key terrain feature in Phu Loc Basin. Quang Nam Pr?, I Corps.
Spider Web, The (XT 755-175)
A.k.a. Spiderweb and Spider's Web. Nickname of geographic area along Saigon River, apx 22 km NNW Tan Son Nhut AB. Also listed at XT 745-164. Binh Duong Pr, III Corps.
Spike, LZ (YS 082-795)
Along LTL-25, apx 33 km SW Tan Son Nhut AB, 15 km SSW Long Thanh AF and 9 km ESE Xoai Minh. Jan66. Bien Hoa Pr, III Corps.
Spillman, Camp (YD 243-597?)
At Dong Ha Basecamp. Named to honor BU1 Charles O. Spillman, Seabee Unit 301(?) "Detail Bravo" (const maintained Khe Sanh), KIA 28Feb68, when his re-supply helo shot down on Khe Sanh perimeter. Dedicated, 3Jun68. Data per Ray Bows. Quang Tri Pr, I Corps.
SPK Rubber Plantation? (XU 300-397)
Apx 27 km WNW Snuol and 35 km due N Memot. 31Jul70. Cambodia.
Splendid BOQ (XS 861-916)
At 89-91 Nguyen Du St. (a.k.a. the Splendid Bar), Saigon. Data per *Vietnam Military Lore, 1959-1973*. Gia Dinh Pr, III Corps.
Spoiler, LZ (BR 33-33?)
Very roughly 20 km SSW An Khe and perhaps 6 km NNW LZ Soper (BR 331-273). On map in 4th Div ORLL of 31Jul70, per Jim Henderson, B/1st/33d Inf, 4th Div. Grid is est. Binh Dinh Pr, II Corps.
Spooky (n/a)
See Glossary.
Sportif, Cercle (WJ 8-2)
See Cercle Sportif at grid. Hanoi. NVN.
Sportif, Cercle (XS 855-915)
See Cercle Sportif at grid. Gia Dinh Pr, III Corps.
SPOTLIGHT (n/a)
See Glossary.
Springfield, LZ (BR 759-913)
Apx 10 km WSW Bong Son and 9 km NNW Ha Tay AF. Oct66. Binh Dinh Pr, II Corps.
Spruce, LZ (BT)
Near Tam Ky. Opened and secured by 2d/7th Marines 9Dec65, during Op Harvest Moon. See *Utter's Battalion*, pp 187-192. Quang Tin Pr, I Corps.
Spurs, LZ (BR 345-395)
Less than 1 km W of LZ Boots and apx 15 km WSW An Khe. Oct65. Binh Dinh Pr, II Corps.
Square Pond, The (BT)
Into the Valley, p 311, describes it as square-shaped pond near some vine-covered towers S of the Ly Ly River, NW or WNW Tam Ky? Quang Tin Pr, I Corps.

Squeeze-Bore .50 Cal MG (n/a)
See Glossary.
Sre Mat Airfield (YV)
Apx 26 km SE Lumphat AF, 32 km NNE Kaoh Nhek AF. Per TPC K-10A. El. 376'. Cambodia.
Sroc Con Trang Bridge (XT 62-82?)
210' long Bailey Bridge on Rte246, apx 50 km NNW Lai Khe. Built during Op Junction City by 1st Div Engrs starting 8Mar67. By noon 12Mar67, was open for traffic. Grid is est. Tay Ninh Pr, III Corps.
Sroc Con Trang, FSB (XT 860-550)
A.k.a. FSB "C." On Rte 246, apx 5 km NW the Sroc Con Trang Bridge and roughly 55 km NNW Lai Khe. By 18 Mar67, Rte 246 had been opened to a distance of just over 6 km W bridge site and to turnoff to Sroc Con Trang. By 18Mar67, jungle had been cleared from 1,800' of rwy, and 400' of rwy complete. 1st/26th Inf /1st Inf Div moved by foot to seize Sroc Con Trang and then (along with 36th SVN Ranger Bn) built and secured this base, its AF, the Sroc Con Trang Bridge, some 12 surrounding FSBs (stretching from Lai Khe N to Quan Loi/Rte 246, and S on Rte 244 from its junction with Rte 246). One of largest FSBs established during Junction City. Sustained 11 mortar attacks during Op. Data per p 123, *Cedar Falls-Junction City*. Tay Ninh Pr, III Corps.
Srok Dong (XU 73-03)
On QL-13, apx 16 km N An Loc. During Op El Paso II, 1st Sqdn/4th Cav attacked by 271st VC Rgt here, 30Jun66. Near listed grid. Binh Long Pr, III Corps.
Srok Silamlite II, Battle of (XU 65-11)
At SE end of Angel's Wing, apx 5 km from Cambodia, 8 km WNW Loc Ninh and 24 km NNW An Loc. On 30Oct67, during Op Shenandoah II, elements of 1/18th Inf, 1st Inf Div killed 83 VC in 2d of 3 small battles prior to Srok Silamlite III. Binh Long Pr, III Corps.
SS (Ship's Name) (n/a)
All vessels in this text are listed by name in alphabetical listing with normal prefixes of *SS, USCG, USNS, USS* (and so on) following the formal name, as in *Fairport, SS*.
St. Barbara, FSB (XT 273-679)
A.k.a. The French Fort, The Old French Fort and FSB Bau Co. At Bau Co, apx 9 km due N Nui Ba Den, 18 km NE Tay Ninh West AF and perhaps 3 km W Hwy 4. Per Butch Sincock, perimeter was high berm of compacted dirt with bunkers built into sides of berm. Its helo pad was outside berm and open to VC observation/attack. During Aug68, was cut-off for apx 3 weeks and only re-supplied by helos whose arrival always prompted mortar attacks. Mortar attack night of 10-11Sep68 during battle for Tay Ninh, caused 3 US WIA. Attacked again 13Sep68, receiving 33 rounds and again 16Sep68 with 31 rounds, and again 17-18Sep68 (31 US WIA in last 2 attacks). Four 175s of 1st/27th and 2d/3d Arty here, among other arty. Fired in supt during major attack on FSB Carolyn, 2Jun69. 25th Inf Div here, as were 1st/7th, 1st/8th Cav, 2d/8th Cav, 1st Cav per Frank Penk, Jr. Also listed at XT 274-680, 281-662 and 276-679. Apr68-Mar70. Tay Ninh Pr, III Corps.
St. Barbara, Camp (ZA 230-354 or ZA 230-534?)
If ZA 230-354 grid is accurate, was apx 13 km S Pleiku, 6 km W Camp Enari and 3 km E Catecka AF. If ZA 230-534 is correct, then site was instead along QL-14 immed S Pleiku Nansteph AF, apx 5 km NW Pleiku/Cu Hanh AF and 5 km NNW Pleiku? Pleiku Pr, II Corps.
St. Francis River, USS (n/a)
LSMR-525. See *Saint Francis River, USS*.
St. Clair County, USS (n/a)
LST-1096. See *Saint Clair County, USS*.
St. George BEQ (XS 828-887)
At 107 Dong Khanh St., Saigon. Data per *Vietnam Military Lore, 1959-1973*. Gia Dinh Pr, III Corps.
St. George, LZ/FSB (AR 854-144)
At intersection of QL-14 and LTL-7B (led SE to Cheo Reo/Hou Bon), 4 km S My Thach, 15 km N Phu Nhon, 33 km SSE Pleiku and 20 km SSE Camp Enari. 1st/14th Inf, 4th Div apparently overrun here by sappers 16Nov69, with 9 US KIA. 15th Arty Rgt website at www.landscaper.net/chighmap.jpg shows an LZ Pierson at roughly same spot, so possibly a.k.a. Pierson? 10th Cav, 4th Div also here, per Bob Patsfield. Name/grid per Jim Claeys. Aug69-Oct70. Pleiku Pr, II Corps.
St. Joseph's Church (AT 906-754)
Along Rte 540, apx 10 km due W Da Nang AB. Oct68. Quang Nam Pr, I Corps.
St. Kilda Heliport (YS 298-438)
See Saint Kilda Heliport. Phuoc Tuy Pr, III Corps.
St. Louis, USS (n/a)
LKA-116. Amphib Attack. Cargo.
St. Paul, USS (n/a)
See *Saint Paul, USS*.
STABO Rig (n/a)
See Glossary.
STABS (n/a)
See YRBM 21 and Glossary.
Stadium, The (ZA 207-345)
Along QL-19B at Catecka AF, apx 6 km WSW its intersection with QL-14, and 14 km SSW Pleiku. Became HQ of 1st Bde/1st Cav during siege of Plei Me, Oct65. On 26Oct65, HQ moved to LZ Homecoming in order to coordinate final effort to relieve Plei Me SF Camp. However, when Bde CO realized site was not appropriate, it was moved to what became known as The Stadium, at Catecka, along with its 3 Air Cav Trps (helo supt units). When 3d Bde took over Stadium, they began calling it "Catecka." Road between Pleiku and Catecka was unusual in that it was paved. Pleiku Pr, II Corps.
Staff (n/a)
6Apr70, XXIV Corps future-use III MAF FSB name.
Stag, LZ (XD 926-643)
On S edge of DMZ, apx 20 km WNW Cam Lo and 32 km WNW Dong Ha. Apr70 XXIV Corps grid per Don Armstrong. Quang Tri Pr, I Corps.
Stage Coach, FSB (ZC 189-648)
See Stagecoach. Quang Nam Pr, I Corps.
Stagecoach, FSB (ZC 203-653)
Also "Stage Coach." Apx 22 km W Hill 55 (Camp Muir), 10 km N FSB Hawk, 7 km S Ba Na Mtn and 34 km SW Da Nang. Used during Op Oklahoma Hills, 1st Mar Div, '69. On map at p 109, *US Marines in Vietnam-1969*. Apr70 XXIV Corps grid per Don Armstrong. Also listed at ZC 189-648? Quang Nam Pr, I Corps.

Stalk, LZ (BR 739-775)
Apx 7 km SW Ha Tay AF and 18 km SSW Bong Son. Feb66. Binh Dinh Pr, II Corps.

Stallion, FSB (AT 923-691?)
A.k.a. Hill 10. Apx 5 km SW Hill 327, 15 km SW Da Nang, 10 km NW Hill 55 (Camp Muir), 4 km NW Hill 40 and 27 km NW Hoi An. 2d/7th Marines used site during Op Oklahoma Hills, Mar-May69. Alpha Bty, 1st Bn/11th Marine Arty, 1st Mar Div, 1st Cav. Apr70 XXIV Corps grid per Don Armstrong. Also listed at AT 923-691? Quang Nam Pr, I Corps.

Stallion, LZ (BR 698-849)
Apx 11 km W to WNW Ha Tay AF and 19 km SW Bong Son. Feb66. Binh Dinh Pr, II Corps.

Stallion, LZ (YA 757-386)
Apx 7 km W Plei Beng, 12 km from Cambodia and 48 km WSW Pleiku. Jan66. Pleiku Pr, II Corps.

Stallion, LZ (YC 373-994)
See LZ Stallion at YD 386-003. Thua Thien Pr, I Corps.

Stallion, LZ (YD 386-003)
At the abnd AF and former SF camp at A Luoi 1, in N end of A Shau Valley, apx 10 km ENE Dong Ap Bia (Hamburger Hill). Seized and reopened as LZ Stallion by 1st Bde/1st Cav 24-26Apr68, during Op Delaware. [506] 1st Bde HQ then. Also listed at YC 385-993 and YC 373-994 (which are also correct). Thua Thien Pr, I Corps.

Stark, LZ (BR 667-733)
Apx 3 km due W Nghia Dien and 28 km SW Bong Son. Oct66. Binh Dinh Pr, II Corps.

Starlight, Operation (BT)
A.k.a. Op Starlight. One of 1st US military ops of war and 1st using US Armor units (tanks) in war. 18-21Aug65 preemptive strike at 1st VC Rgt (as it prepared to attack Chu Lai) S of Chu Lai, resulting in 700 VC casualties. Involved 3 Marine BLT Bns, each suptd by tank plt of 3d Marine Tank Bn. 3d Tank Bn was 1st US Armored unit in VN, arriving 8Jul65. Quang Tin Pr, I Corps.

Starlight, Task Force (n/a)
See Task Force Starlight.

Starlight Scope (n/a)
See Glossary.

Starling, LZ (AT 899-882)
Apx 9 km NNW Red Beach AF, 4 km WSW Hai Van Pass and 17 km NW Da Nang AB. Apr70 XXIV Corps grid per Don Armstrong. Thua Thien or Quang Nam Pr, I Corps.

Starling, LZ (BS 390-000)
Apx 48 km W LZ English and 27 km S Gia Vuc AF. Mar66. Binh Dinh Pr, II Corps.

Starlite Scope (n/a)
See Glossary.

Starlite, Operation (BT)
See Starlight. Quang Nam/Quang Tin Pr, I Corps.

State of Vietnam, The (n/a)
See Glossary.

Statesman (n/a)
Apr70, XXIV Corps future-use 101st Abn FSB name.

Station Ham Tam (ZS 03-79)
See Ham Tam Station. Binh Tuy Pr, III Corps.

Station Lang Co (AT 88-97)
See Lang Co Bridge. Thua Thien Pr, I Corps.

Statler, LZ (XD 995-484)
Adj to or at. Ca Lu AF. At Ca Lu, apx 1 km E QL-9 and 34 km W to WSW of Quang Tri. Apr70 XXIV Corps grid per Don Armstrong. Quang Tri Pr, I Corps.

Steel, FSB (BS 572-153)
Apx 16 km WNW Thuan An, 35 km NW Bong Son and 33 km SW Duc Pho AA. Binh Dinh Pr, II Corps.

Steel Recorder, SS (n/a)
Commercial transport under govt contract, per Ralph Fries.

Steel Tiger Operations (n/a)
See Glossary.

Steve, LZ (AR 855-556)
Apx 2 km SE Plei Neh and 11 km NE Pleiku. Sep69. Binh Dinh Pr, II Corps.

Stein, USS (n/a)
DE-1065. DD-Escort, per Ralph Fries.

Steinaker, USS (n/a)
DD-863. On 27Jul68, replaced *USS Epperson* off Binh Thuan Pr, suptg TF 3d/506th Inf per www.currahee.org/pageb2.html. SVN.

Stella, FSB (n/a)
No data. 10th Cav, 4th Div here, per Bob Patsfield. Binh Dinh, Kontum or Pleiku Pr?, II Corps.

Stella, FSB (YD 465-244)
Apx 15 km WSW LZ Sally and 25 km WNW Hue. 1st Cav '68? 101st Abn AO, '69-71. Thua Thien Pr, I Corps.

Step-and-a-Half Snake (n/a)
See Glossary.

Stephanie, FSB (XS 75-90)
Apx 5 km W the SW corner of Saigon and 10 km SW Tan Son Nhut AB. 199th LIB FSB? Gia Dinh Pr, III Corps.

Stewart, FSB (XT 498-196)
See FSB Stuart at grid. Hau Nghia Pr, III Corps.

Stewart, LZ (BR 731-803)
A.k.a. or near site of LZ Bird (726-809). Just E the Song Lon River, apx 15 km SW Bong Son, 10 km NW Ha Tay and 7 km NNE Nghia Nhon. A Bty 2d/17th Arty here 21Nov67, suptg 5th/7th and 2d/12th Cav. Data per Jack Picciolo. Binh Dinh Pr, II Corps.

Stewart II (XT 4-1?)
See FSB Stuart II. Hau Nghia Pr?, III Corps.

Stewart III, FSB (XT 490-190)
See FSB Stuart III at grid. Hau Nghia Pr, III Corps.

Stickell, USS (n/a)
DD 888. As early as Mar50, the 7th Fleet cmdr, with destroyers *Stickell* (DD 888) and *Richard B. Anderson* (DD 786), visited Saigon while 60 acft from *Boxer* (CVA 21) over flew city. In Oct53, the 4 ships of Destroyer Div 30 conducted similar show at Saigon. [507]

Stiletto, FSB (ZC 134-357)
Apx 15 km WSW Phuoc Binh, 48 km SW Da Nang and 62 km WNW Tam Ky. Apr70 XXIV Corps grid per Don Armstrong. Quang Nam Pr, I Corps.

Stilwell, Operation (YB/ZB)
18-22Jun67. 173d Abn, Dak To/Kontum. The Battle of Slopes began when A/2/503d's point squad bumped into several NVA. A Co perimeter then came under hvy attack as NVA separated the Pltns. 2 more assaults were made on A Co's CP before C Co could reinforce, but 24th NVA Rgt prevented C Co from linking with A Co's lost Plt, which was annihilated during night. 43 out of 76 of the 173d's

KIA were executed (shot in back of head). See Dak To, Battle of. Kontum Pr, II Corps.

Sting Ray, Operation (n/a)
6-10Mar69. 173d Abn. An Khe. Binh Dinh Pr, II Corps.

Stingray, FSB (YS 257-707)
Apparently a.k.a. or very close to sites of FSBs Bravo (YS 250-700) and Hope (YS 253-704). Along E side of QL-15, apx 18 km WNW Nui Dat, 1.5 km SSE FSB Gail and 2 km N FSB Penny. On 1ATF NCO trng map per John Hollett. Phuoc Tuy Pr, III Corps.

Stingray, Operation (n/a)
6-10Mar69. 173d Abn. Binh Dinh Pr, II Corps.

Stinson, LZ/FSB (BS 539-824)
A.k.a. LZ Buff and Buff-Stinson. Apx 13 km NW Quang Ngai, 5 km N the Song Tra Khuc River, 24 km due S Chu Lai, 5 km SSW LZ Phoenix, 5 km ENE Xuan Hoa, 7 km NE Ba Gia AF and 9 km W QL-1. Prior to 21May69 was named LZ Buff, but then renamed to honor LTC William Stinson, Jr, KIA near Hau Duc 3MAR69 on A/123d Avn Co's Helo #737 (Americal list). Also listed at BS 539-824. Map is L-7014-6739-3. Quang Ngai Pr, I Corps.

Stirrup, LZ (BR 982-684)
Apx 8 km WNW Phu My/QL-1 and 30 km SSE Bong Son. Oct66. Binh Dinh Pr, II Corps.

Stoddard, USS (n/a)
DD-566, per Ralph Fries.

Stokes, Camp (BT 01-76?)
Near Da Nang AB. Home of USMC 1st MP Bn. Quang Nam Pr, I Corps.

Stomp, Operation (CP)
See CS Gas Incident in Glossary.

Stone BEQ (XS 828-887)
Saigon enlisted Quarters apparently on corner of Ham Tu and Ngo Quyen Streets, apx 4 km SW Independence Palace and 2 km SSE Phu Tho Racetrack. Data per *Vietnam Military Lore, 1959-1973*. Gia Dinh Pr, III Corps.

Stone BOQ (XS 828-887)
At 26 Ngo Quyen St., Sep 65-68, 42 rms, Saigon. Data per *VN Military Lore, 1959-1973*. Gia Dinh Pr, III Corps.

Stone County, USS (n/a)
LST-1141. SVN.

Stoneman, FSB (XT 300-370)
A.k.a. Patrol Base Stoneman. N of QL-1 apx 15 km NW Go Dau Ha and 12 km SE Tay Ninh. Photo at www.oregoncoast.com/willy/msp-9.jpg. '69-70, 4/9th Inf, 25th Div here, per Manchu Mike Smith. Tay Ninh Pr, III Corps.

Stork, LZ (XD 934-553)
Overlooked Khe Trinh Hin River Valley, apx 6 km due W Thon Son Lam (at QL-9), 10 km NW Ca Lu and 40 km W to WNW of Quang Tri. Apr70 XXIV Corps grid per Don Armstrong. Sep68. Quang Tri Pr, I Corps.

Storm, LZ (XT 36-31)
Along N edge of Parrot's Beak, apx 10 km from Cambodia between QL-1(?) and Song Vam Co Dong River, apx 20 km SE Tay Ninh, 5 km NNW Go Dau Ha and 56 km NW Saigon. 199th LIB, 4th Div. Tay Ninh Pr, III Corps.

Stormes, USS (n/a)
DD 780. In Sep68, she was credited with over 200 enemy KIA in 3-hours of suptg fire. By Nov68, she had fired nearly 40,000 rnds. Attached to Surface Grp TF, which was credited with 3,000 enemy KIA and destroying apx 35,000 structures for year '68. SVN.

Stormy, FSB (XD 945-425)
Apx 8 km SW Ca Lu, 50 km WSW Quang Tri and 1 km S QL-9. Sep-Oct68. Quang Nam Pr, I Corps.

Straight Edge Woods, The (XT 13-34)
Forested area along Cambodian border apx 18 km SW Tay Ninh. 2 NVA Bns destroyed by B-52 strikes here, Summer '68, as US tried to preempt NVA offensive against Tay Ninh that later took place 17Aug-27Sep68. [508] Also XT 150-350. Tay Ninh Pr, III Corps.

Straps (n/a)
See Glossary.

STRATCOM Facility (XS 78-89)
Near Phu Lam Station in Cholon, at SW corner of Saigon. Army worldwide US defense commo system site. See Nha Trang STARCOM. Gia Dinh Pr, III Corps.

Strategic Hamlets (n/a)
See Glossary.

Strategic Transportation Corridor, The (n/a)
Hanoi's formal name for what we called the Ho Chi Minh Trail. See Ho Chi Minh Trail.

Straus, USS (n/a)
DE-408. DD-Escort, per Ralph Fries.

Street Without Joy (YD 60-44 to YD 40-55)
Area just inland from coast and running generally NW from Huong Dien (at N end of narrow Pha Tam Giang Bay) to area NE Quang Tri. Apparently consisted of Rte 555, a portion of QL-1 and Rtes 592, 602 and 603. Made famous by writer Bernard Fall as the *La rue sans jolie* or *The Street Without Joy*. Contrary to widely held belief, the SWJ was not simply QL-1 throughout VN, but rather a series of dirt roads and QL-1 that Fall loosely referred to as "Route 1." While some consider QL-1 for its entire length be the SWJ, it is this author's belief Bernard Fall only meant it to be that portion in Quang Tri Pr involved in Op Camargue (*Utter's Battalion*, at p 101, makes same claim). See Camargue and Street. The. See also Chp 7, pp 146-7, of *Street Without Joy* (4th ed., '67) for detailed map and description. Quang Tri/Thua Thien Pr, I Corps.

Street, The (YD)
101st Abn/1st Cav nickname for same area known as The Street Without Joy. Was area between Quang Tri on N and Lai Ha on S, with QL-1 on W, and Ocean on E. Quang Tri/Thua Thien Prvs, I Corps.

Streeter, LZ (YD 301-649)
Apx 2 km W Giao Liem, 7 km SW mouth of Cua Viet River, and 11 km NNW Quang Tri. Apr70 XXIV Corps grid per Don Armstrong. Thua Thien Pr, I Corps.

Stribling, USS (n/a)
DD-867, per Ralph Fries.

Strike Forces (n/a)
See Glossary.

Strike, FSB (YD 576-172)
A.k.a. Nui Khe Thai. In bend of the Song Bo, apx 17 km WSW Hue Citadel AF and 11 km SW LZ Sally. C/D Cos/1st/502d Inf, 101st Abn const beginning 19Mar68. Also listed at YD 577-170, 615-235, 608-235 (May68) and 705-013 (Jul68)? May68-Jan70. Thua Thien Pr, I Corps.

Strike, FSB (YD 615-235?)
If grid correct, overlooked Song Bo River apx 14 km W Hue Citadel AF and 6 km SW LZ Sally. See FSB Strike at YD 576-172. Thua Thien Pr, I Corps.
Strike, FSB (YD 705-013?)
This is the grid for FSB Birmingham and improperly associated with Strike. See FSB Strike at YD 576-172. Thua Thien Pr, I Corps.
Strike, FSB (YS 82-97)
A.k.a. FSB Qanh Tach or Quan Tach? Immed N Nui Be Mtn, 58 km WSW Phan Thiet and near Ap Rung La. 2d/3d Inf, 199th LIB here. Lam Dong Pr, III Corps.
Strike, FSB (YT 058-205)
A.k.a. FSB Killer, Feb69. Apx 9 km NE Bien Hoa AB, 1 km N the Song Dong Nai River and 4 km W Ap Mot. 1st/7th Cav AO, Mar69, Co sized LZ during Op Cheyenne Saber. Grid per Frank Penk, Jr. Bien Hoa Pr, III Corps.
Strikers (n/a)
See Glossary.
Strip, LZ (CR 040-717)
On coast, apx 2 km ESE Cat Tuong, 32 km NNE Phu Cat AB and 13 km E QL-1. Oct66. Binh Dinh Pr, II Corps.
Strong, USS (n/a)
On 1May68 was off coast of Binh Thuan Prov suptg TF 3d/506th Inf, per www.currahee.org/pageb2.html.
Strongpoint (DBP) (TJ 9-6)
See Glossary.
Strongpoint 1 (BR 352-448)
A.k.a. SP 1. On QL-19E, apx 1.5 km SW LZ Schueller. See Strongpoint 15 for detail. Binh Dinh Pr, II Corps.
Strongpoint 2 (BR 348-451)
A.k.a. SP 2. On QL-19E, apx 1.6 km WSW LZ Schueller. See Strongpoint 15 for detail. Binh Dinh Pr, II Corps.
Strongpoint 3 (BR 344-454)
A.k.a. SP 3. On QL-19E, apx 2 km W LZ Schueller. II Corps. Strongpoints 3 and 5 are described as least defensible and most dangerous Strongpoints in 1st/69th Armor's AO at www.rjsmith.com. See Strongpoint 15 for detail. Binh Dinh Pr, II Corps.
Strongpoint 4 (BR 334-453)
A.k.a. SP 4. On QL-19E, apx 2.8 km W LZ Schueller. Separated from SPs # 3 and 5 by a ridgeline and dense vegetation. See Strongpoint 15. Binh Dinh Pr, II Corps.
Strongpoint 5 (BR 328-460)
A.k.a. SP 5. On QL-19E, apx 3.5 km W LZ Schueller. At 13°58'25"N-108°31'25"E per www.rjsmith.com. SPs 3 and 5 are described as least defensible and most dangerous Strongpoints in 1st/69th Armor's AO at same website. See Strongpoint 15 for detail. Binh Dinh Pr, II Corps.
Strongpoint 6 (BR 304-458)
A.k.a. SP 6. On QL-19E, apx 6 km W LZ Schueller. Protected bridge 25. See Strongpoint 15. At 13°58'20"N-108°30'15"E per www.rjsmith.com. Binh Dinh Pr, II Corps.
Strongpoint 7 (BR 290-459)
A.k.a. SP 7. On ridge overlooking QL-19E from N side, and covering a blind spot the ridge created for traffic crossing bridge 26. Described as relatively safe since it had excellent fields of fire and observation. See Strongpoint 15. At 13°58'10"N-108°30'30"E per 1st/69th Armor Website. Binh Dinh Pr, II Corps.
Strongpoint 8 (BR 281-459)
A.k.a. SP 8. On S side of QL-19E, apx 2.3 km SE LZ Action and 1 km NW Bridge 26. Described as relatively secure position. Graphic showing view from SP 8 at www.rjsmith.com/ lz_action.html. See Strongpoint 15. Binh Dinh Pr, II Corps.
Strongpoint 9 (BR 279-463)
A.k.a. SP 9. On S side of QL-19E, apx 1.6 km SE LZ Action and just 300 meters NW SP 8. See Strongpoint 15 for detail. Binh Dinh Pr, II Corps.
Strongpoint 10 (BR 274-469)
A.k.a. SP 10. On S side of QL-19E, apx 1 km E LZ Action. Described as having excellent fields of fire and observation and "favorite" SP of 1st/69th Armor at its website. Apparently site of frequent enemy sightings/contact. See Strongpoint 15. Binh Dinh Pr, II Corps.
Strongpoint 11 (BR 266-465)
A.k.a. SP 11. Along S side of QL-19E, apx 500 meters due S LZ Action. Described as safest strongpoint on QL-19 by 1st/69th Armor website. See Strongpoint 15 for detail. Binh Dinh Pr, II Corps.
Strongpoint 12 (BR 256-484)
A.k.a. SP 12. On N side of QL-19E 1.8 km NW LZ Action and 1.5 km NW Bridge 27. At entrance (base) of Mang Yang Pass and described as less dangerous than Strongpoints further up pass to W. See Strongpoint 15. Binh Dinh Pr, II Corps.
Strongpoint 13 (BR 237-498)
A.k.a. SP 13. On QL-19E. At E entrance to Mang Yang Pass. See Strongpoint 15. Binh Dinh Pr, II Corps.
Strongpoint 14 (BR 227-508)
A.k.a. SP 14. On QL-19E. Described as an eerie and forbidding location and 2d only in vulnerability to Strongpoint 15. Was lower than SP 15, and apparently armored units assigned security did not like it. [509] See Strongpoint 15 for detail. Binh Dinh Pr, II Corps.
Strongpoint 15 (BR 228-513)
A.k.a. SP 15. On QL-19E. Described as highest, westernmost and most vulnerable OP Strongpoint outpost on QL-19. [510] 1st/50th Inf and 1st/69th Armor operating out of FSBs Action, Schueller, An Khe and Pleiku (among others), would apparently move to various "Strongpoints" lining QL-19 between Pleiku and Qui Nhon during daylight hours to protect convoys and 10" petroleum pipeline that paralleled the hwy. At night they would return to firebases. Each Strongpoint was assigned a numerical designation. Detailed maps and discussions of QL-19E's Strongpoints at www.rjsmith.com. Binh Dinh Pr, II Corps.
Strongpoint A-1 (YD 270-734)
See A-1, FSB. Quang Tri Pr, I Corps.
Strongpoint A-2 (YD 213-734)
See A-2, FSB. Quang Tri Pr, I Corps.
Strongpoint A-3 (YD 173-722)
See A-3, FSB. Quang Tri Pr, I Corps.
Strongpoint A-4 (YD 118-701)
See A-4, FSB. Quang Tri Pr, I Corps.
Strongpoint A-5 (YD 077-663)
See A-5, FSB. Quang Tri Pr, I Corps.
Strongpoint C-1 (YD 213-674)
See C-1, FSB. Quang Tri Pr, I Corps.

Strongpoint C-2 Bridge (YD 128-671)
See C-2 Bridge. Quang Tri Pr, I Corps.
Strongpoint C-2 (YD 135-645)
See C-2, FSB. Quang Tri Pr, I Corps.
Strongpoint C-3 (YD 143-614)
See C-3, FSB. Quang Tri Pr, I Corps.
Strongpoint C-4 (YD 314-724)
See C-4, FSB. Quang Tri Pr, I Corps.
STTC (XS 875-925)
Saigon Transportation Terminal Cmd (ARVN). Apparently at the Viet Naval Base, Saigon. Gia Dinh Pr, III Corps.
Stuart, FSB (XT 498-196)
A.k.a. Stewart? Along QL-1, apx 13 km ESE Go Dau Ha and 16 km WNW Cu Chi. Also listed at XT 484-196, 490-190, and 501-194. Mar68-Apr69. Hau Nghia Pr, III Corps.
Stuart II, FSB? (XT 4-1?)
A.k.a. Stewart II? Location unknown, but since FSBs Stuart and Stuart II are at XT 498-156 and 490-190 respectively, it seems likely Stewart II was part of the Stuart series. 7th/11th Arty/25th Div said to have been here in '68, and Stewart II name per Dan Gillotti, 15th Arty Assn. Hau Nghia Pr?, III Corps.
Stuart III, FSB (XT 490-190)
A.k.a. Stewart III? Within 1 km SW listed position of FSB Stuart and apx 17 km WNW Cu Chi. Apr69. Hau Nghia Pr, III Corps.
Stuart, HMAS (n/a)
Australian Escort ship serving under US 7th Flt.
Stud, LZ (BR 95-96?)
In Mtns, apx 7 km E Bong Son, 4 km W ocean, 3 km NW LZ Paint and 9 km ENE LZ Two-Bits. Used during Op Masher/White Wing, 28Jan-6Mar66. Detail of Ops Masher and White Wing and this LZ in *A Contagion of War* vol, *Vietnam Experience* series, pp 32-48, with map showing site at p 38. 1st/5th Cav, 1st Cav. Grid is est based on described location. Binh Dinh Pr, II Corps.
Stud, LZ/FSB (YD 002-493)
On E side QL-9, apx 5 km NNE Ca Lu, 15 km ENE Khe Sanh CB and perhaps 8 km NE LZ Cates. Built apx Mar68, under direction of BG Oscar Davis, Asst Div Cmdr, 1st Cav. Used as main staging area and pivotal point of air assaults during Op Pegasus, the relief of Khe Sanh CB, 1-8Apr68. 2d/12th Cav here 3Apr68, as were numerous other Cav and ARVN units. Cited in Michael Herr's *Dispatches*, p. 257. Also mentioned in 1st Cav VN *Yearbook* Aug65-Dec69, p 55, 99, 123, 129, 270, 291, per Peter Cole. Also listed at XD 995-483 and YD 01-45. Map is L-7014-6342-2, per Ken Burrington. Quang Tri Pr, I Corps.
Stud, FSB (YD 473-264)
If grid correct, was apx 8 km SW Camp Evans and 28 km WNW Hue Citadel AF. 31Jul70. Thau Thien Pr, I Corps
Stud Airfield, LZ (XD 999-479)
See Ca Lu AF. Quang Tri Pr, I Corps.
Stung Treng Airfield (n/a)
Along Mekong River, apx 240 km NNE Phnom Penh on Feb67 Natl Geo map. El. 137'. Cambodia.
SU-7 (CAP) (XD)
Per Jim Taylor, Oscar Co/III MAF was originally designated "SU-7." Detailed accounting of CAP Oscar units at Khe Sanh can be found in *Valley of Decision*. See also CAC Oscar. Quang Tri Pr, I Corps.
Subic, LZ (YD 171-246)
In valley of Khe Ba Le River, apx 16 km due S Ba Long AF and 31 km SW Quang Tri. Apr70 XXIV Corps grid per Don Armstrong. Quang Tri Pr, I Corps.
Sud, Ile du (BM 75-65)
Possibly uninhabited island, apx 1.5 km by .5 km in size, and in South China Sea apx 110 km ESE Phan Thiet. Cu Lao Hon Island, 100 km ESE Phan Thiet, has 2 small islands off its N end and 2 off its S end as well, one of which is Il Du Sud.
Sud, Pointe (BN 9-7)
See Pointe Sud. Ninh Thuan Pr, II Corps.
Sud, Pointe (CR 1-2)
See Pointe Sud. Binh Dinh Pr, II Corps.
Sud-Ouest, Baie du (XQ 7-5)
A.k.a. Ben Dam. Bay at 8°39'N-106°34'E. NVN.
Sue, FSB (XT 918-956)
Immed ENE of Srok Phu Mieng, apx 16 km ENE An Loc and 26 km NW Dong Xoai. 2d/7th Cav, 1st Cav here Dec68, per Frank Penk, Jr. Also listed at XT 920-950. Binh Long Pr, III Corps.
Sue, LZ (BP 373-787)
Apx 3 km SW Ban Tiam and 37 km SE Buon Ea Yang AF. Apr67. Darlac Pr, II Corps.
Sue, LZ (BS 678-877)
Apx 16 km NNE Quang Ngai and 6 km E QL-1. Dec67. Quang Ngai Pr, I Corps.
Sue, LZ (BS 9-2?)
Immed N An Do, apx 25 km due N Bong Son, 7 km NNE LZ Gold, 4 km due W QL-1 and 5 km due W ocean. Used during Op Masher/White Wing, 28Jan-6Mar66. Detailed discussion of Ops Masher/White Wing and this LZ in *A Contagion of War* vol, *Vietnam Experience* series, pp 32-48, with map showing site at p 38. 2d/12th Cav, 1st Cav LZ. Binh Dinh Pr, II Corps.
Sue, LZ (BS 554-674)
Apx 7 km SW Quang Ngai AF, 12 km SW Quang Ngai, 7 km NW Nghia Hanh AF and 13 km NE LZ Bronco. Also listed at BS 566-877. Americal list. Quang Ngai Pr, I Corps.
Sue, LZ/FSB (XT 918-956)
See FSB Sue at grid. Binh Long Pr, III Corps.
Sue, LZ (YA 648-481)
On Cambodian border at S entrance to Plei Trap Valley, apx 58 km due W Pleiku. Also listed at YA 644-485. Kontum Pr, II Corps.
Sugar Mill, The (XT 441-058)
Sugar mill along Song Vam Co Dong River, apx 13 km ESE Duc Hue AF, 8 km due W Khiem Cuong and 25 km WSW Cu Chi. Hau Nghia Pr, III Corps.
Sugar Mill Hill, OP (BS 613-735)
See OP Sugar Mill Hill. Quang Ngai Pr, I Corps.
Suicide Dam (AT 88-46?)
Area consisting of a Hydroelectric power unit, water purification plant and fertilizer plant complex, a.k.a. the An Hoa Industrial Complex. See An Hoa Industrial Complex Quang Nam Pr, I Corps.
Suicide Zone (YB/YC)
Nickname for interior mtns toward Laotian border in Americal Div's LRRP Recon Zone. Per *Rangers at War*, p 39. Quang Nam and Quang Tin Pr, I Corps.

Suim Ngok Tu Mountain (ZB 018-258)
See Mortar Mountain. Kontum Pr, II Corps.
Summer, FSB (YD 098-443)
A.k.a. Hill 660? Apx 3 km NW FSB Holcomb and 25 km WSW Quang Tri. Quang Tri Pr, I Corps.
Summit County, USS (n/a)
LST-1146. SVN.
Sumner, Allen M., USS (n/a)
DD-692. 7th Flt Destroyer, per Ralph Fries.
Sumner County, USS (n/a)
LST-1148. Decom 15Sep74. SVN.
Sumter, LZ (AQ 832-206)
Apx 3 km N Quang Nhieu and 16 km N Ban Me Thuot City AF. Feb66. Darlac Pr, II Corps.
Sumter County, USS (n/a)
LST-1181. SVN.
Sun, FSB (YD 472-011)
See FSB Zon. Thau Thien Pr, I Corps.
Sunder Beach (YD 494-565)
See Wunder Beach. Quang Tri Pr, I Corps.
Sung Hieu (XS 14-43)
See Cai Be. Dinh Tuong Pr, IV Corps.
Sung Hieu Heliport (XS 134-424)
See Cai Be Heliport. Dinh Tuong Pr, IV Corps.
Sung Trau, Mui (BN 7-4)
Coastal point at 11°18'N-108°55'E. On NC49-01 JOG. Ninh Thuan Pr, II Corps.
Sungtran, Mui (BN 7-4)
A.k.a. Mui Sung Trau. Coastal point at 11°18'N-108°55'E. On NC49-01 JOG. Ninh Thuan Pr, II Corps.
Sunrise, OP (AT)
See OP Sunrise/Hill 425. Quang Nam Pr, I Corps.
Suoi Ba Hoa River (XT)
River running NW to SE just below the Fishhook. Joins the Song Saigon apx 10 km NNW Dau Tieng. In AO of Op Junction City, Mar-Apr67. Tay Ninh Pr, III Corps.
Suoi Ca River (BR 91-47)
Flows from NW to SE, meeting QL-1 just N of Phu Cat. Involved in Op Crazy Horse, May66, and discussed in *Battles in the Monsoon*. Grid is at QL-1 bridge site. Binh Dinh Pr, II Corps.
Suoi Ca Tung River (BR 366-459)
Bridge 24 on QL-19E crossed this river near listed grid, apx 13 km due W An Khe. Binh Dinh Pr, II Corps.
Suoi Ca Valley (BR 82-65)
A.k.a. Happy Valley and sometimes spelled Soui Cai. Valley of Suoi Ca River, apx 20 km NW Phu Cat and 30 km S Bong Song. 22d NVA Rgt (among other units) infiltration rte to Bong Son coastal plains. On NE 1/4 of mapsheet L-7014-6737-2, per Ken Burrington. See also Happy Valley. Binh Dinh Pr, II Corps.
Suoi Cao, FSB (XT 450-290)
At edge of plantation, apx 8 km NE Go Dau Ha and 25 km NW Cu Chi. Tay Ninh Pr, III Corps.
Suoi Cat (BP 8-4 and 9-4))
3 villes with this name were roughly 15 km SW Nha Trang (BP 898-483, 888-494, 905-485). Khanh Hoa Pr, II Corps.
Suoi Cat (YT 585-064)
Along QL-1, E of Blackhorse Basecamp, apx 50 km E Saigon, and 7 km SW Gia Ray. Battle of Suoi Cat here, 2 Dec66. See Claymore Corner. Long Khanh Pr, III Corps.
Suoi Cut (XT 487-788)
Near FSB Burt, apx 1.5 km W Rte 244 and 4 km S Rte 246, some 20 km SE Katum AF. Battle of Suoi Cut took place 1-2Jan67. See also FSB Burt. Tay Ninh Pr, III Corps.
Suoi Da (BN 908-998)
Apx 23 km NNE Phan Rang. Ninh Thuan Pr, II Corps.
Suoi Da (XT 33-57)
Near Suoi Da SF Camp, apx 7 km E Nui Ba Den, 2 km SSW Ap Phuoc Hoa and 12 km NE Tay Ninh. Adj VC/NVA staging area during Battle for Tay Ninh, 17Aug-27Sep68. Tay Ninh Pr, III Corps.
Suoi Da, FSB (XT 340-583)
Just NE Suoi Da SF Camp, apx 8 km E Nui Ba Den and 13 km NE Tay Ninh. Nov68-Dec67. Tay Ninh Pr, III Corps.
Suoi Da Airfield (XT 343-583)
See Phu Khuong AF. Tay Ninh Pr, III Corps.
Suoi Da Bang River (BR 522-462)
Bridge 19 (QL-19E) crossed river at listed grid, apx 5 km E Camp Radcliff. Binh Dinh Pr, II Corps.
Suoi Da Base (XT 343-578)
Along TL-4, apx 8 km E Nui Ba Den and 13 km NE Tay Ninh. Feb-Mar67. Tay Ninh Pr, III Corps.
Suoi Da Heliport (XT 331-575)
On TL-4 near Ap Phuoc Hoa, apx 6 km E Nui Ba Den and 12 km NE Tay Ninh. Heliport #656, 80', at 11°22'20"N-106°13'00"E, per Feb73 TAD. Tay Ninh Pr, III Corps.
Suoi Da Lchg Airfield (XT 343-583)
See Phu Khuong AF. Tay Ninh Pr, III Corps.
Suoi Da SF Camp (XT 331-575)
Along TL-4, apx 2 km S Ap Phuoc Hoa, 7 km E Nui Ba Den, 4 km NE Ap Thanh Son and 11 km NE Tay Ninh. 5th SF Grp, Det. A-114, Dec64. Moved to Dak Sut. Grid per *SF Order of Battle*. Tay Ninh Pr, III Corps.
Suoi Dai Airfield (BR 040-500)
See Soui Doi AF? Pleiku Pr, II Corps.
Suoi Doi (BR 023-522)
Along QL-19, apx 26 km ENE Pleiku, 45 km WNW An Khe and 7 km WSW Dinh Dien Dak Quon. AF and other military facilities here and nearby, including FSB Blackhawk. Pleiku Pr, II Corps.
Suoi Doi Airfield (BR 039-541)
A.k.a. Soui Dai AF. Apx 28 km ENE Pleiku, 45 km WNW An Khe's major AF, per TPC K-10A. El. 2,400'. "Abnd, overgrown ARVN 29Jun67, AF # VA2-245," in Aug69 TAD per Frank Penk, Jr. Not in Feb73 TAD. Also spelled Soui Doi. Also listed at BR 034-544. Pleiku Pr, II Corps.
Suoi Doi Heliport (BR 030-510)
S of QL-19, apx 4 km SSW Suoi Doi AF, 26 km ENE Pleiku and 45 km WNW An Khe. Data in Aug69 TAD, per Frank Penk, Jr. Pleiku Pr, II Corps.
Suoi Doi SF Camp (BR 039-541)
Apx 26 km ENE Pleiku, 45 km WNW An Khe and 8 km W Dinh Dien Dok Quan. 5th SF. Moved to Plateau Gi. Info/grid per *SF Order of Battle*. Pleiku Pr, II Corps.
Suoi Doi, FSB (BR 034-535)
Along Ql-19, slightly S of what later became Suoi Doi AF, apx 27 km ENE Pleiku. 1st/92d Arty elements here Dec68. Data in 4th Div/1st/92d Arty op rpt per Craig Miller. Pleiku Pr, II Corps.

Suoi Kon River (BR 48-96)
A.k.a. the Dak Kron Bung River. Binh Dinh Pr, II Corps.
Suoi Kon River Valley (BR 600-750)
Generally 35 km SW Bong Son, 30 km NNE An Khe. Was valley immed N of, and drained into, Vinh Thanh (Happy) Valley. Binh Dinh Pr, II Corps.
Suoi Tan River (BR 444-434)
Grid is at QL 19E Bridge 21 over the Suoi Tan at SW edge of An Khe. Binh Dinh Pr, II Corps.
Suoi Tre, Battle of (XT 385-705)
Took place at FSB Gold near Suoi Tre, 21Mar67, and during Op Junction City. During battle, elements of 3d/22d Inf, 25th Inf Div were being overrun until C/2d/22d Inf and other units reinforced. See FSB Gold for detail and location. Tay Ninh Pr, III Corps.
Suoi Voi River (BR 539-461)
Bridge 18 on QL-19E crossed this river at listed grid, apx 5 km E Camp Radcliff/An Khe. Binh Dinh Pr, II Corps.
Super Gaggle (XD)
See Glossary.
Superspook, The (n/a)
See Glossary.
Superstition Mountain, LZ (n/a)
Said to have been a 4th Div Bde Radio Relay Station, Apr69. Location unknown, but is mentioned in *Time Heals No Wounds*, p 188 and p 194's 1st/12th Inf Radio Log excerpt of 26Apr69. Pleiku or Binh Dinh Pr?, II Corps.
Supnet, FSB (YT 041-651)
Along QL-14 between FSBs Remagen 4 and 5, apx 11 km SSW Dong Xoai, 18 km NNE Phuoc Vinh and 70 km NNE Saigon. Likely named to honor Sp4 Emilio C. Supnet, Jr., KIA 16May70. Opened or reopened 3Aug70 by 1st/7th Cav, closed 8Aug70 by 2d/5th Cav. Data per *1st Cav Div Op Rpt, ending 31Oct70*, courtesy of Peter Cole. Phuoc Long Pr, III Corps.
Supper (n/a)
See Base Area 704. Cambodia.
Supplementary Routes (n/a)
See Route in Glossary.
Surat Sena, Camp (PU 3-6)
See Phitscamp and Phitsanulok. SF camp or AO per *SF Order of Battle*. Thailand.
Surat Thani Airfield (NL 3-0)
A.k.a. Ban Don AF. Near coast, apx 525 km SSW Bangkok per Feb67 Natl Geo map. Near 9°08'00"N-99°21'00"E. NIMA data. El. 15'. Thailand.
Surfbird, USS (n/a)
ADG-383. Aux Ship, per Ralph Fries.
Surikan, Camp (n/a)
US Army and SF camp on Okinawa, not in Vietnam.
Surin Airfield (UB 3-4)
Apx 340 km ENE Bangkok, 150 km SSW Ubon AB and 52 km N Cambodia, at 14°53'00"N-103°30'00"E, per TPC K-10A. NIMA data. El. 465'. Thailand.
Susan, FSB (BR 478-908?)
See LZ Susie at grid. Binh Dinh Pr, II Corps.
Susan, FSB (XU 437-142)
A.k.a. or near site of FSB Susie listed at XU 413-102? Along Rte 7, apx 17 km NE Memot, 24 km SSW Snuol, 30 km WNW Loc Ninh and 27 km NNE Katum. Incursion FSB, May-Jun70. 3d Sqdn/11th ACR kept Rte 7 open S to Snuol, Cambodia, while operating out of this FSB. M Co, 3d/11th suffered a mortar attack here19Jun70. Grid per *11th ACR Cambodia Invasion AAR, 1st Cav Div, May-Jun70*, courtesy Lou Rochat. [511] Cambodia.
Susan, FSB (YD 079-623)
Apx 27 km WNW Quang Tri, 6 km NW Cam Lo and 3 km SE FSB Annette. Grid per XXIV Corps index, 5th Div, 6Apr70, courtesy Don Armstrong. Quang Tri Pr, I Corps.
Susan, FSB (YS 283-649)
On E side QL-15 apx 16 km WSW Nui Dat, 300 meters N FSB Tess and 11.5 km WSW FSB Weir. On 1ATF NCO trng map per John Hollett. 1ATF. Phuoc Tuy Pr, III Corps.
Susan, LZ (XT 654-484)
Apx 16 km E Dau Tieng AF/Tri Tam and 14 km WNW Ap Bau Bang. Jun66. Also listed at XT 660-580? Binh Duong Pr, III Corps.
Susan, LZ (YC 797-923)
In the Khe Lo Moi Valley, apx 30 km S Hue and 13 km SW Thon Ben Tau. Feb-Mar69. Thau Thien Pr, I Corps.
Susie, FSB (XU 413-102)
See Susan at grid. Cambodia.
Susie, FSB (YD 271-423)
A.k.a. LZ Susie, LZ Suzie and Suzy. Apx 13 km SSW Quang Tri and 18 km SE Mai Loc. Also listed at YD 270-424, YD 270-443 (and at YD 267-442 per 1st/8th Cav Daily Staff Journal of 3Mar68). Elements of 4th/60th, E/71st and I/29th here late 67-Jan68 (Dusters, Quads, Searchlights); 1st/44th Arty and others, per Paul Kopsick. Quang Tri Pr, I Corps.
Susie, LZ (BR 478-908)
On plateau just NE Dak Som River, apx 3 km due W LZ Raquel, 35 km WSW Bong Son AF and 45 km due N An Khe. 4th Div AO. A Bty/2d/9th and C Bty/1st/92d Arty here Feb70. 10th Cav, 4th Div here, per Bob Patsfield. Grid per Jim Claeys. See LZ Susan listed at BR 576-909? Binh Dinh Pr, II Corps.
Sutter County, USS (n/a)
LST-1150. Decom 15Sep74.
Suzie, LZ (YD 271-423)
See FSB Susie at grid. Quang Tri Pr, I Corps.
Suzie, LZ (BR 478-908)
See LZ Susie at grid. Binh Dinh Pr, II Corps.
Suzie, LZ (BR 576-909)
Apx 25 km WNW Ha Tay AF and 29 km ESE Bong Son AF. 173d Abn Bde, 68-71. Name/grid per Dan Gillotti. See LZ Susie listed at BR 478-908? Binh Dinh Pr, II Corps.
Suzy, LZ (BR 478-908)
See LZ Susan at grid. Binh Dinh Pr, II Corps.
Suzy, LZ (YD 271-423)
See FSB Susie at grid. Quang Tri Pr, I Corps.
Suzzanah, Plantation de (YT 3-1)
A.k.a. Don Dien Suzzanah. Apx 10 km W to WSW Xuan Loc. Bien Hoa Pr, III Corps.
Svay Rieng Airfield? (n/a)
Alternate name for Kompong Chak AF? Apx 60 km NW the tip of Parrot's Beak, 15 km SW SVN border, 105 km ESE Phnom Penh and 35 km SE Tay Ninh on Feb67 Natl Geo Map. El. 23'. Cambodia.
Swampy, Camp (BQ 192-134)
Along QL-21, apx 14 km NE Buon Ea Yang AF and 42 km ENE Ban Me Thuot. Jan-Sep70. Darlac Pr, II Corps.

Swampy, Camp (BR?)
Geographic feature "above the Mang Yang Pass" along QL-19, per Ted Ashton. Pleiku Pr?, II Corps.

Swan (n/a)
Australian Escort ship serving under US 7th Flt.

Swann, Camp (BT 42-13?)
Marine CAC (CAP) cmpd at Ky Khuong, along QL-1, apx 13 km NW Chu Lai and 14 km SE Tam Ky. Named to honor Sgt H. E. Swann, KIA 9Jun67, while aiding an Army Patrol. Sgt Swann was Ky Khuong CAC team leader at time. Quang Tin Pr, I Corps. [512]

Swartz, FSB (YS 381-992)
See FSB Schwartz. Long Khanh Pr, III Corps.

Sweat, LZ (YD 109-394)
On Dong Cho hill mass, apx 6 km ESE Lang Ruou (on QL-9), 9 km due S Ca Lu and 16 km ESE Khe Sanh CB. Apr70 XXIV Corps grid per D. Armstrong. Quang Tri Pr, I Corps.

Sweet Pea, FSB (n/a)
Apparently a fictitious FSB? Cited in Larry Heinemann's *Paco's Story*.

Swenson, Lyman K., USS (n/a)
DD-797, per Ralph Fries.

Swift, LZ (YA 818-855)
Apx 8 km WNW LZ Bunker Hill, 14 km SW Polei Kleng (described in one text as having been 21 km SW Polei Kleng?) and 33 km W Kontum. 3d/12th Inf, 4th Div here at one time. Kontum Pr, II Corps.

Swift, Operation (n/a)
4-15Sep67. US 1st Mar Div op. 517 rptd NVA/VC KIA, per *Vietnam Order of Battle*, pp 9-14. Quang Nam/Quang Tin Prvs, I Corps.

Swift Boats (PCF) (n/a)
See Glossary.

Swift Play, Operation (n/a)
See *Thomaston, USS.*

Swift Sabre, Operation (n/a)
See *Thomaston, USS.*

Swinger, LZ (YA 837-965)
Apx 2 km N Polei Meo, 19 km WNW Polei Kleng, 7 km NW LZ Roberts, and 42 km WNW Kontum. Per Dick Arnold, 1st/14th Inf AARs say const began 17/18Apr68. 3d/12th Inf, 4th Div attacked here, 1Mar69, resulting in 30 NVA KIA, but only 1 US KIA. 1st/92d Arty here Spring '69, per Craig Miller. Per Tom Lacombe, was also listed at YA 837-835, 837-985, 835-966 and 814-864. It may be base was relocated several times? Photos/maps of base at http://1-14th.com/maps.html. Kontum Pr, II Corps.

Swinger II, LZ (YA 814-864)
Apx 3 km WSW site of LZ Swinger, 4 km WNW Polei Meo and 43 km WNW Kontum. Kontum Pr, II Corps.

Swiss, LZ (YD 137-469)
Apx 4 km ESE Ca Lu, 2 km NE Quan Thua (on Rte 556) and 7 km SW Mai Loc. Apr70 XXIV Corps grid per Don Armstrong. Quang Tri Pr, I Corps.

Switch, LZ (BS 374-266)
Adj Gia Vuc AF, apx 18 km WSW Ba To New AF, and 46 km WSW Duc Pho. 2d/17th Arty here suptg 1st Cav, 6Aug67. Data per Jack Picciolo. Quang Ngai Pr, I Corps.

Switchback, Operation (n/a)
See Glossary.

Switchback-Parasol (n/a)
See Parasol/Switchback in Glossary.

Sword, FSB (YD 425-312)
In lowland plain, apx 10 km due W Camp Evans and 30 km NW Hue. Opened 14Feb69, and attacked by sappers 23Feb69, in 1st/506th AAR of 30Apr69, per Dick Arnold. Also listed at YD 427-311, 420-310 and 423-312. Apr-Oct69. Thua Thien Pr, I Corps.

Sword of Patriots League (n/a)
See Glossary.

Sydney, HMAS (YS)
During Op Tanton, *Sydney* delivered Fld Arty Bty, an Engrs Trp, 161 Recon Flight, a Sig Trp and addns to existing HQ & Log Supt Co to Vung Tau. Departed Sydney 11Sep65, and from Brisbane 14Sep65, arriving at Vung Tau, at 0630 hours on 28Sep65. There Engrs and Recce Flt came under 1RAR to form 1RAR Grp, with 161 Fld Arty Bty (RNZA) already in direct supt of 1RAR. The 105 Fld Arty Bty remained under Australian Army Force VN (COMAAFV) and placed opcon to US 3rd/319th Art, suptg 173 Abn Bde. Logistics transport ship initially manned by civilians, but later commissioned into Royal Aussie Navy due to union bans. *Sydney*, *Boonaroo* and *Jesparit* made total of 42 trips to VN carrying almost 200,000 DW tons of cargo, per www.navy.gov.au/4_history/vietnam.htm. Per Eddie Tricker, *Sydney* routinely offloaded supplies for ANZAC's at Vung Tau. Phuoc Tuy Pr, III Corps.

Sylphes, Ile de (YJ 5-1)
Island of Sylphs. NIMA data. NVN.

Sylvia, LZ (AR 805-214)
Along QL-14, apx 12 km SW Plei Do Lim AF, 27 km SSE Pleiku and 6 km NM My Thach. 10th Cav, 4th Div here, per Bob Patsfield. Aug69-Jan70. Pleiku Pr, II Corps.

Sylvia, FSB (YS or ZS?)
Per John Mowat, was near Ham Tan. Ham Tan is apx 6 km inland from coast, 45 km SE Phan Thiet and 75 km ENE Vung Tau. John Driscoll thinks small AF here was used almost exclusively by Air America, and says there was a small Seabee cmpd here and a well-appointed MACV cmpd (had running water, bar etc.) apx 8 km from base (unclear if description applied to Sylvia or Ham Tan?). Binh Tuy Pr, III Corps.

Syracuse, LZ (XD 953-659)
On S edge of DMZ, overlooking Khe Kui River valley, apx 18 km WNW Cam Lo and 29 km WNW Dong Ha. Apr70 XXIV Corps grid per D. Armstrong. Quang Tri Pr, I Corps.

TANGO

Facility/Feature Name, Grid Coordinate, a.k.a. Name/History/Province/CTZ

Unless otherwise stated, 6-digit grid coordinates reference DMA L-7014, L-7015 or L-7016 series, 1:50,000 scale maps, while 2- and 4-digit coordinates reference AMS/DMA/NIMA 1:250,000, 1:500,000 and 1:1,000,000 scale maps. Unless otherwise stated, all heights are in meters. To convert meters to feet, multiply by 3.2808; feet to meters, multiply by .3048.

T-3, FSB (YA 850-455?)
See Tango Three. Kontum Pr?, II Corps.

T-12 (WF)
Apx 35 km down river (SW or S?) from Vinh. A commo-liaison waypoint on HCMT that became vital radio traffic intercept resource for MACV/ARVN intel gathering beginning early '68. Commo between this site and Binh Tram 8 was particularly vital to US intel. See also Binh Tram in Glossary. Data per *A Better War*, pp 48-52. NVN.

T Bone, FSB (YD 652-202)
A.k.a. FSB Nui Hon Vuon, Hill 309 and FSB An Do. Visible from and apx 6.5 km due S of LZ Sally, 1.5 km S Hwy 598, 7 km SE Ap Lai Bang and 6 km due W Hue. In 20Mar68 battle, D/2d/501st Inf, 101st Abn cleared hill as eventual site for T-Bone. Strategic value was its commanding view of Hue. Also listed at YD 650-200, 659 203 and 567-223. Thua Thien Pr, I Corps.

T. C. Miller (AQ 870-998)
Along QL-14, at or near Phu Nhon AF. Nature of site and meaning of initials T.C. unknown. However, 1st/92d Arty here '71, and a PFC Thomas C. "TC" Miller was KIA 1Feb71. Possibly named in his honor? Pleiku Pr, II Corps.

T Stations (n/a)
See Glossary.

T'ai Highlands (n/a)
Region between the Black and Red Rivers. Cleared by 2 French T'ai Mountaineer Bns in late 1940's at cost of some 9,500 casualties, and kept relatively clear of Vietminh for some 5 years as result. Per *Street Without Joy*, p 30.

T'ai Hill Country, Battle for the (n/a)
Began 11Oct52, when 148th, 308th, 312th and 316th Vietminh Divs launched offensive along 40 mile front, advancing in 3 columns across the Red River N of Yen Bay and toward Than Uyen, Nghia Lo and Tu Le. 1st hit was 700-man French garrison at Nghia Lo, with mortar attack at 1700 hrs 11Oct, and at 1730 hrs with ground assault that in 1 hour had overwhelmed defenders. Next attack took place at Tu Le, a small garrison reinforced with Bigeard's 6th Para to cover its withdrawal ahead of advancing Vietminh. Tu Le was in small plain surrounded by jungle when Vietminh arrived 18Oct52, and then struck at 0300 on 20Oct52 in weather preventing air supt. After suffering mightily, 6th Para tried to withdraw toward the Black River in 40-mile fighting retreat. After losing 60% of unit's strength, its survivors reached safety on 22Oct52. After moving through Than Uyen, the 148th Div continued heading SW through Dien Bien Phu and then on to Muong Khoua in Laos, and then to the Plain of Jars. After Nghia Lo and Tu Le, the 308th, 312th and 316th joined near Na San punching SW toward Xieng Khouang in Laos (just E the Plain of Jars and where French counter-attacked). Data per *Street Without Joy*, Chp 3; map at p 67. NVN/Laos.

T'ai Tribes (n/a)
See Glossary.

Ta Bat (YD 39-99?)
In A Shau Valley, apx 20 km NNW A Shau/A Sap, 6 km ENE Dong Ap Bia (Hamburger Hill) and 40 km WSW Hue. SF CIDG Camps and AFs along Rte 548 at A Luoi, Ta Bat and A Shau in the A Shau Valley were closed Mar66 due to enemy pressure. See A Shau Valley for more detail. Thua Thien Pr, I Corps.

Ta Bat (new) SF Camp (YC 388-992)
A.k.a. A Luoi SF Camp/AF. In A Shau Valley, apx 20 km NNW A Shau/A Sap, 6 km ENE Dong Ap Bia (Hamburger Hill) and 40 km WSW Hue. 5th SF. Grid per *SF Order of Battle*. See A Luoi. Thua Thien Pr, I Corps.

Ta Bat (old) SF Camp (YC 421-942)
In A Shau Valley, apx 6 km SSE Ta Bat (new)/A Luoi SF Camp/AF, 14 km NNW A Sap/A Shau ville/AF, and 40 km SW to WSW Hue. 5th SF Grp, Det. A-324, Dec64. Info/grid per *SF Order of Battle*. Moved to A Shau. Thua Thien Pr, I Corps.

Ta Bat (old), Camp (YC 499-837)
See Camp A Shau. Thua Thien Pr, I Corps.

Ta Bat Airfield (YC 423-951)
A.k.a. A Luoi SF Camp/AF. In A Shau Valley, apx 6 km SSE Ta Bat (new)/A Luoi SF Camp/AF, 14 km NNW A Sap/A Shau ville/AF, and 40 km SW to WSW Hue. Reopened or established 29Apr69 by 1st/12th Cav, 1st Cav. In Jun69, 326th Engrs/101st Abn const 1,500' C-7A Caribou AF here in what was their largest const proj to that point. Job was completed in 54 hours and 1st C-7A landed 13Jun69. "Abnd, probably mined. No friendly forces within 11 nautical miles, AF # VA1-80," in Aug69 TAD per Frank Penk, Jr. Not in Feb73 TAD. Also spelled Tabat. Near that grid. Thua Thien Pr, I Corps.

Ta Be, Mui (XQ 8-6)
Coastal point at 8°42'N-106°40'E. NC48-11. IV Corps.

Ta Cath (n/a)
Mapsheet name of L-7014-6232-3. SVN/Cambodia.

Ta Chong CAP (XD)
See CAP Oscar 3. Quang Tri Pr, I Corps.

Ta Cong (XD 84-41?)
Ville on S side Rte 9, S of Khe Sanh CB. Was original site of CAP 0-3 Team. Also a Ta Cong at YD 085-518? See also CAP 0-3. Quang Tri Pr, I Corps.

Ta Cong CAP (XD 842-410)
See CAP Oscar 3. 1st CAG, Quang Tri Pr, I Corps.

Ta Fa Airfield (PC 97-61)
LS-216. CIA/SF, per *Air Facilities Data-Laos*.

Ta Khli Airbase (PS 3-8)
A.k.a. Ban Ta Khli and Takhli AB. At 15°16'00"N-100°18'00"E, or apx 170 km N Bangkok per Feb67 Natl Geo map. NIMA data. El. 112'. Thailand.
Ta Ko (n/a)
Mapsheet name of L-7014-6440-1. SVN/Laos.
Ta Ko SF Camp (YC 470-470)
If grid is accurate, this camp was certainly one of most remote SF camps in SVN, being roughly 125 km WSW Da Nang, 65 km NW Kham Duc and less than 1 km from Laos. 5th SF. Moved to Ba To (new) thru Kham Duc. Info/grid *per SF Order of Battle*. Quang Nam Pr, I Corps.
Ta Kong Tul River (XT?)
Apparently NW An Loc? Cited in *Ambush*, pp 216-217.
Ta Luong Heliport (YD 553-027)
On N edge of Hwy 547, apx 27 km SW Hue, 1 km due S FSB Veghel and 10 km SW FSB Bastogne. Heliport #658, alt 787', at 16°17'30"N-107°23'30"E, per Feb73 TAD. Thua Thien Pr, I Corps.
Ta Lus, Mui (WG 8-3)
Coastal point at 19°16'N-105°47'E. NE48-03 JOG. NVN.
Ta Ma Airfield (BS 249-486)
Remote site apx 29 km W Minh Long AF, 46 km WSW Quang Ngai and 10 km WNW Lang Baout. Described as abnd AF in Song Re Valley when 2d/8th Cav assaulted to nearby LZ Pat, 9Aug67. Listed as "Abnd, Overgrown 28Jul67, AF # VA1-109," in Aug69 TAD per Frank Penk, Jr. Not in Feb73 TAD. Quang Ngai Pr, I Corps.
Ta Nagl Airfield (n/a)
Apx 85 km NE Phnom Penh. El. 158'. Cambodia.
Ta Ngan Island (YD 773-236)
Boat-shaped, 1.7 km x 300 meters, N/S island and ville in Perfume River just NW the Hue Citadel. Linked by bridge to S shore but not to N shore. Thua Thien Pr, I Corps.
Ta Phing (n/a)
Mapsheet name of L-7014-5653-4. NVN/China.
Ta Rau (YC 910-890)
Apx 1 km W Nong Truong Hai Dong, 6 km NNE Ruong Ruong, 2 km SE FSB Rifle and 25 km S Phu Bai AF. Nature of site unknown; listed only as "Tarau." Dec63-Jan64. Also listed at YC 876-840, 29Dec63? See also Ta Ru. Thua Thien Pr, I Corps.
Ta Rau SF Camp (YC 865-838)
See Ruong Ruong SF Camp and also Nam Dong. Name/grid per *SF Order of Battle*. Thua Thien Pr, I Corps.
Ta Rhu, Camp (YC 865-838?)
See Ruong Ruong SF Camp. Ta Rhu spelling in DA Chief, Mil Hist records summary which also indicates Det A-726 here,'63. Thua Thien Pr?, I Corps.
Ta Ro SF Camp (YC 865-838)
See Ruong Ruong SF Camp. Name/grid per *SF Order of Battle*. Thua Thien Pr, I Corps.
Ta Trach River (YD 80-07)
See Song Ta Trach. Thua Thien Pr, I Corps.
Ta Trach Valley (YC 845-991)
Generally 25 km SSE Hue and 25 km due W Phu Loc. Valley of Song Ta Trach. May68. Also listed as Tra Trach valley. Thua Thien Pr, I Corps.
Ta Viang Airfield (UG 32-04)
LS-13. CIA/SF, per *Air Facilities Data-Laos.*

Tabat (YC 42-94)
See Ta Bat. Thua Thien Pr, I Corps.
Table Head Cape (VS 6-2)
See Table, Cape. Kien Giang Pr, IV Corps.
Table, Cap de la (VS 6-2)
See Table, Cape. Kien Giang Pr, IV Corps.
Table, Cape (VS 6-2)
A.k.a. Table Head Cape, Mui Cai Ban and Cap del al Table. Cape at 10°08'N-104°39'E. On NC48-06 JOG. Kien Giang Pr, IV Corps.
Tac Van Heliport (WR 296-130)
Apx 13 km ESE Quan Long and 62 km WSW Bac Lieu. Heliport #728, alt 7', per 73 TAD. An Xuyen Pr, IV Corps.
TACAN (n/a)
See Glossary.
TACAN NDB Ban Me Thuot East (AQ 87-02)
At Ban Me Thuot East AF, apx 7 km E Ban Me Thuot. Darlac Pr, II Corps.
TACAN NDB Bien Hoa (XT 98-13)
At Bien Hoa AB. Bien Hoa Pr, III Corps.
TACAN NDB Binh Thuy (WS 79-15)
At Binh Thuy AF, apx 8 km NW Can Tho and 6 km NW NDB Can Tho. Phong Dinh Pr, IV Corps.
TACAN NDB Nha Trang (CP 03-52)
At Nha Trang AB. Khanh Hoa Pr, II Corps.
TACAN NDB Phan Rang (BN 77-87)
At Phan Rang AB. Ninh Thuan Pr, II Corps.
TACAN NDB Phu Cat (BR 88-44)
At Phu Cat AB. Binh Dinh Pr, II Corps.
TACAN NDB Pleiku (AR 78-50)
At Pleiku/Cu Hanh AF. Pleiku Pr, II Corps.
Tachikawa AFB Hospital (n/a)
See USAF Hospitals.
Tactical Urgent (n/a)
See Glossary.
Tadak Pong Airfield (n/a)
Apx 120 km W Phnom Penh. TPC K-10A. 6,000' rwy, El. 82'. Cambodia.
Tai Tribes (n/a)
See Glossary.
Tailwind, Operation (n/a)
See Glossary.
Taiwan, Forces of (n/a)
A.k.a. Republic of China Forces. See Major HQs Section in Glossary for detail.
Tak, FSB (XS 120-890)
Apx 10 km ESE Moc Hoa, 18 km W the tip of Parrot's Beak and 22 km WNW Thuy Dong AF. Jul68. Kien Tuong Pr, IV Corps.
Tak Airfield (NU 1-6)
A.k.a. Rahaeng AF. Along Ping River, apx 375 km NNW Bangkok, per Feb67 Natl Geo map. At 16°53'00"N-99°09'00"E. El. 360'. Thailand.
Tak Police Airfield (MU 9-5)
At 16°44'00"N-98°59'00"E. NIMA data. Thailand.
Tak Xa Airfield (YT 062-753)
See Dong Xoai AF. Phuoc Long Pr, III Corps.
Takeo Airfield (n/a)
Apx 70 km SSW Phnom Penh. El. 20'. Cambodia.

Takhek Airfield (n/a)
See Thakhek AF. Laos.
Takhek New Airfield (n/a)
See Thakhek AF. Laos.
Takhek SF Camp (n/a)
See Thakhek SF Camp. Laos.
Takhli Airbase (PS 3-8)
A.k.a. Ban Ta Khli and Ta Khli AB. Apx 175 km N Bangkok, 180 km WNW Korat AB and some 840 km NW Saigon, per map in *Vietnam Experience* Series, *Rain of Fire* vol, p. 11. Major US bomber and fighter-bomber base. Feb67 Natl Geo. Map, at 15°16'00"N-100°18'00"E. Grid/data per NIMA. El. 112'. Thailand.
Tako Heliport (YC 530-525)
Adj to A Hoi, apx 5 km from Laotian border, 20 km NW of A Ro AF and 105 km SW Da Nang. Heliport #659, alt 3,937', per Feb73 TAD. Quang Nam Pr, I Corps.
Tall Star (n/a)
6Apr70, XXIV Corps future-use III MAF FSB name.
Talladega, USS (n/a)
APA-208. Amphib Attack, Transport, per Ralph Fries.
Tally Ho, Task Force (n/a)
See Task Force Tally Ho.
Talon Heliport (YC 886-325)
At head of a river valley, apx 8 km SW Ben Giang, 26 km NNW Kham Duc and 70 km SW Da Nang. Heliport #660, alt 459', at 15°39'45"N-107°41'30"E, per Feb73 TAD. Quang Nam Pr, I Corps.
Talon Vise (YS/XS)
Original name of Operation Frequent Wind. See Frequent Wind for detailed history. SVN.
Taluga, USS (n/a)
AO-62. Aux Oiler, per Ralph Fries.
Tam (n/a)
Vietnamese for River.
Tam, Cua (AD 8-6)
Channel near 21°24'N-108°00'E. NVN.
Tam An Airfield (YS 135-935)
See Long Thanh AF. Bien Hoa Pr, III Corps.
Tam Binh Heliport (XS 090-118)
In plantation, apx 8 km ESE Tru Khu Mat, 22 km due S Vinh Long and 40 km WNW Tra Vinh. "Heliport #661, alt 7', sod, S town, do not fly E canal." At 10°03'30"N-105°59'40"E, per Feb73 TAD. Vinh Long Pr, IV Corps.
Tam Canh Signal Site (ZB 0-2 or XS 8-9?)
Variant of Tan Canh? NIMA nor NPIA lists and town with listed spelling, but do list a Tan Canh at ZB 063-225 and XS 824-933? Kontum or Gia Dinh Pr?, II or III Corps?
Tam Dao (WJ 6-7)
French called Tam Dao Hill Station (Hill 930) the *Cascade d' Argent* (Silver Cascade). Built as resort by French in 1870(?) to escape the heat of Red River Delta. Site of one of earliest Vietminh attacks, when they hit a Japanese garrison here in WWII. Area's cool weather and superb views apparently make it a much desired vacation spot. Sometimes called the "Dalat of North," and also noted for its giant ferns (some 30' tall), camellias, orchids, birds, butterflies, deer, monkeys, wild pigs, tortoises and rare snakes. Peak at listed grid per NIMA (21°28'00"N-105°38'00"E). Nui Tam Dao is in WJ 5-9 (21°38'00"N-105°30'00"E. NVN.
Tam Dao Massif (WJ 5-9 or 6-7)
Mtn mass generally 40 km NNW Hanoi that was staging area for Vietminh offensive (force of 81 Bns of Inf, 12 Hvy weapons Bns and8 Engr Bns) toward Vinh Yen (apx 40 km NW Hanoi), beginning 13Jan51. NVN.
Tam Dien Refugee Center? (YD 749-372)
On isthmus apx 8 km NW Tam My and 15 km N of Hue Citadel AF. Listed as Tam Dien R.C.? NPIA data. Thua Thien Pr, I Corps.
Tam Giang, Pha (YD 7-3)
Lagoon at 16°36'N-107°32'E. On NE48-16 JOG. Thua Thien Pr, I Corps.
Tam Hiep Airfield (XS 463-523)
See Ben Tranh AF. Dinh Tuong Pr, IV Corps.
Tam Hoa (CR 0-4)
Ville at 13°56'00"N-109°09'00"E, near Qui Nhon. Binh Dinh Pr, II Corps.
Tam Hoa CAP (BT?)
Possibly Tan Hoa? CAP 2-2-4, 2d CAG, and Charlie 4, 2d CAG here per Tim Duffie. Tan Hoas are listed at BT 024-786, BT 018-783, BT 054-801, Dai Loc District, Quang Nam Pr, I Corps.
Tam Ky (BT 310-225)
Between Chu Lai and Hoi An River, apx 62 km SSE Da Nang. Maps are L-7014-6640-2 (W side) and L-7014-6740-3 (E side). Capitol, Quang Tin Pr, I Corps.
Tam Ky (East) (n/a)
Mapsheet name of L-7014-6740-3. SVN.
Tam Ky (West) (n/a)
Mapsheet name of L-7014-6640-2. SVN.
Tam Ky Airfield (BT 309-186)
Just W of QL-1, apx 5 km S Tam Ky Alternate AF and about 1 km due S Tam Ky, per TPC K-10A. El. 33', 4,000' asph rwy. At 15°34'32"N-108°28'30"E. Also listed at BT 305-199 per Americal list. Quang Tin Pr, I Corps.
Tam Ky Alternate Airfield (BT 302-245)
Just W QL-1 about 1 km N W Tam Ky and 5 km N Tam Ky AF. El. 16', 600' sod rwy. Quang Tin Pr, I Corps.
Tam Ky CAP (BT 3-2?)
CAP 1-1-3, 1st CAG. Quang Tin Pr, I Corps.
Tam Ky CAP (BT 3-2?)
Precise location unknown. Home of India 1 CAP, 1st CAG, per T. Duffie's CAP website at www.capmarine.com. Quang Tin Pr, I Corps.
Tam Ky Heliport (BT 307-216)
In heart of Tam Ky City, W QL-1, and 62 km SSE Da Nang. Heliport #662, alt 16', per Feb73 TAD. Quang Tin Pr, I Corps.
Tam Ky MAAG Compound (BT 31-22?)
At Tam Ky, apx 62 km SSE Da Nang. Named to honor Capt. Lloyd A. Payne, MAAG Advisor to 2d ARVN Inf Div, KIA by rifle fire while on patrol with the ARVN, 15Dec63. Data per *Vietnam Military Lore, 1959-1973*. See also Payne Cmpd. Quang Tin Pr, I Corps.
Tam Ky Provincial Airfield (BT 302-245)
See Tam Ky Alternate AF. Quang Tin Pr, I Corps.
Tam Lan, FSB (YD 063-547)
See Carroll, Camp. Quang Tri Pr, I Corps.

Tam Lich Heliport (YD 197-727)
Apx 3 km W Gio Linh, 3 km E FSB A-1, and 24 km NNW Quang Tri. Heliport #663, alt 98', at 16°55'30"N-10P03'30"E, per Feb73 TAD. Quang Tri Pr, I Corps.
Tam My 4 CAP (BT 329-202?)
If grid correct, was along W side of QL-1, apx 3 km NE Tam Ky AF and 3 km SE Tam Ky. CAP 2-3-6, 2d CAG per Tim Duffie. Grid per NPIA Gaz. Dien Banh District, Quang Nam Pr, I Corps.
Tam Quan (n/a)
Mapsheet name of L-7014-6838-3. SVN.
Tam Quan, 2d Battle of (BR 893-135)
Battle site was near a RR line W of the Soui Son Thanh River, apx 10 km NE Vanh Canh, 18 km WSW Qui Nhon and 9 km SW ROK AF. Took place 6-17Dec67. Map is L-7014-6838-3, per Ken Burrington. Binh Dinh Pr, II Corps.
Tam Quan, Battle of (BR 8-1?)
Took place near FSB Mahoney, apx 15 km N LZ English and 70 km N Phu Cat AB during Op Pershing, 6-20Dec67. Apparently largest battle of that op when 22d NVA Rgt stood its ground against 1st/9th, 2d/8th and 1st/12th Cav (among others units) of 1st Cav. 661 NVA KIA. Binh Dinh Pr, II Corps.
Tam Quan Bridge (BS 905-130)
QL-1 bridge at S edge of Tam Quan, apx 16 km NNE Bong Son. Also a QL-1 Tam Quan bridge NE of town at BS 920-140. Binh Dinh Pr, II Corps.
Tam Quan Bridge (BS 920-140)
QL-1 and RR bridge, immed NE Tam Quan and 17 km NNE Bong Son. Also a QL-1 Tam Quan bridge S of town at BS 905-130. Binh Dinh Pr, II Corps.
Tam Quan Point (BS 9-1)
See Point Tam Quan. Binh Dinh Pr, I Corps.
Tam Soc Operating Base (WR 91-57)
Apx 32 km NNE Bac Lieu and 14 km WSW Soc Trang. See Freeman-Anderson Cmpd. Ba Xuyen Pr, IV Corps.
Tame the West, Operation (n/a)
The invasion of northern Cambodia, May-Jun 70. See Task Force Shoemaker. Cambodia.
Tamkwan Point (BS 9-1)
See Point Tamkwan. Binh Dinh Pr, I Corps.
Tampa, LZ (YD 230-088)
Apx 5 km SE FSB Cunningham, 31 km SSE Ba Long and 44 km SSW Quang Tri. Apr70 XXIV Corps grid per Don Armstrong. Quang Tri Pr, I Corps.
Tamquam, Pointe (BS 9-1)
See Pointe Tamquam. Binh Dinh Pr, I Corps.
Tan An (n/a)
Mapsheet name of L-7014-6230-2. SVN.
Tan An (various)
Common Viet place-name. Sites inc: BT 237-463, BR 928-692, CQ 147-631, BN 873-830, AN 840-123, XT 958-065, XS 785-350, WS 423-694, XS 498-418, XS 874-220, XS 638-175, XS 798-085, XS 785-200, XS 435-225, XS 403-147, WS 773-218, WS 660-306, WS 642-264, WS 326-192, WR 160-420, WR 078-006, WS 823-386, WS 634-353 and WS 737-225. All CTZs, SVN.
Tan An (XS 55-66)
Along QL-4, apx 30 km SW Saigon, 23 km NNE My Tho and 19 km ESE Rach Kien. Advsy Team 86, Long An Pr Advisors here, as was HQ 3d Bde/9th Inf Div, Jul69-Oct70. Capitol, Long An Pr, III Corps.
Tan An, Camp (WS 203-058)
See Vinh Xuong. Kien Giang Pr, IV Corps.
Tan An, Camp (WS 271-936)
A.k.a. Tan Chu SF Camp? Along S bank of Mekong River at Tan Chau, apx 17 km NE Chau Phu and 16 km NNE Chau Duc AF. See Tan Chau. Chau Doc Pr, IV Corps.
Tan An (Training Center) Heliport (WS 650-580)
Apx 6 km NW Cao Lanh AF, 115 km WSW Saigon and 28 km NW Sa Dec. "Heliport #666, alt 10' earth, dusty." 10°28'30"N-105°35'30"E. Kien Phong Pr, IV Corps.
Tan An Airfield (XS 524-656)
See Long An AF. Long An Pr, III Corps.
Tan An Base Camp (XS 546-648)
Along QL-4 and N edge of Tan An, apx 30 km SW Saigon and 20 km NNE My Tho. HQ 3d Bde/9th Inf Div Jul69-Oct70. 1st/3d Bdes, 9th Inf Div basecamp, and also site of 3rd Bde (Sep) HQ, per Jim Stone. Long An Pr, III Corp.
Tan An Bridge (XS 549-656)
QL-4 bridge over Song Vam Cotay, at N end of Tan An, apx 30 km SSW Saigon. Long An Pr, III Corps.
Tan An Heliport (WS 204-045)
A.k.a. Vinh Xuong SF Camp Heliport. At Tan An, apx 7 km NE Kien Giang AF and 10 km E Rach Gia. "Heliport #664, alt 7' sod, Trees N and S." At 09°59'30"N 105°11'00"E, per Feb73 TAD. Kien Giang Pr, IV Corps.
Tan An Heliport (XS 543-650)
At Tan An and along QL-4, apx 30 km SW Saigon and 20 km NNE My Tho. "Heliport #665, alt 10' soccer field. Heliport Lctd on W side of Hwy #4, 2 orange fluorescent Lgts along hwy mark pad at night. High wire Lctd E side of Heliport. 162' twr in vicinity, flashing beacon oval O/R. Do not use soccer fld at XS 551-651. Phone." At 10°32'40"N-106°25'00"E, per Feb73 TAD. Long An Pr, III Corps.
Tan An Joint Ops Center (XS 500-650)
Apx 4 km W Tan An and 4 km E Cho Thay Yen. Nov66. Long An Pr, III Corps.
Tan An Navy ATSB (XS 55-65)
On Song Vam Co Tay River, apx 35 km SE Saigon. USN Advanced Tactical Supt Base, '68-69. Per MRF Assn Website. Long An Pr?, III Corps.
Tan An SF Camp (MSF) (XS 5660-6395)
A.k.a. Long An SF Camp? Just SE Tan An, apx 32 km SW Saigon, 22 km NNE My Tho and 4 km ESE Long An AF. 5th SF camp. Later became RF/PF base. Named Moc Hoa SF Camp in *SF Order of Battle*, but that is believed to be incorrect. Long An Pr, III Corps.
Tan Ba Heliport (XT 935-140)
A.k.a. Black Diamond Heliport? On W bank Song Dong Nai, apx 6 km WNW Bien Hoa AB and 22 km NE Tan Son Nhut AB. Heliport #667, alt 23', at 10°58'40"N-106°46'15"E, per Feb73 TAD. Bien Hoa Pr, III Corps.
Tan Canh (ZB 060-220)
A.k.a. Kon Hojao, Tanh Canh, Tan Cann, Tan Kan, and Tancann. At intersection of QL-14N and Rte 512 to Ben Het, apx 5 km E Dak To 2 AF, 2 km ESE Dak To 1 AF, 5k S Dak To ville and 38 km NNE Kontum. Involved in Battle of Toumorong, Jun66, and mentioned in *Battles in the Monsoon*, pp 275-6 (sp Tancann there). 42d ARVN Inf Rgt and MACV Team 23 here '70. 4th Inf and 173d Abn

elements here, as were 7th 15th Arty's 175s. Apparently an ARVN Rgtl or Div HQ as well. Also listed at ZB 051-21 per Nolan Putman. Kontum Pr, II Corps.

Tan Canh Airfield (ZB 044-024)
See Dak To I AF. Kontum Pr, II Corps.

Tan Canh MAAG Heliport (ZB 054-218)
Apparently immed E original Dak To 1 AF, apx 4 km NE Dak To 2 AF and 40 km NNW Kontum. Heliport #668, "alt 2,034', Fuel-J4, 150' flagpole S pad. 50' ants W pad. Approach to W if wind permits. Avail to Dak To 2 Afld, 3000 meters W." At 14°39'N 107°50'E, per Feb73 TAD. Kontum Pr, II Corps.

Tan Canh Quarry (ZB 059-221)
Along QL-14, apx 5 km NW Dien Binh and 6 km due E Dak To 2 AF. Kontum Pr, II Corps.

Tan Canh SF Camp (ZB 043-224)
Apparently immed E the original Dak To 1 AF, apx 4 km NE Dak To 2 AF and 40 km NNW Kontum. 5th SF FOB Dak To. Info/grid per *SF Order of Battle*. Involved in Battle of Toumorong, Jun66. Discussed in *Battles in the Monsoon*, pp 275-6. 42d ARVN Inf Rgt and MACV Team 23 here '70. Also spelled Tan Cann. Kontum Pr, II Corps.

Tan Canh Signal Site (ZB 0-2?)
Likely near Tan Canh and Dak To 2 AF. Spelled Tam Canh; however, neither NPIA nor NIMA lists a name with that spelling. Kontum Pr?, II Corps?

Tan Chau (n/a)
Mapsheet name of L-7014-6030-4. SVN/Cambodia.

Tan Chau Heliport (WS 265-935)
On S bank of the Mekong W of Tan Chau, 16 km NE Chau Phu and 16 km NNE Chau Duc AF. "Heliport #669, alt 13' soccer field," per Feb73 TAD. Chau Doc Pr, IV Corps.

Tan Chau PBR Base (WS 27-94)
On Mekong River, apx 16 km NNE Chau Duc AF and 15 km SE Cambodian border. USN River Patrol Base, '69-70. Per MRF Assn Website. Chau Doc Pr, IV Corps.

Tan Chau SF Camp (WS 231-945?)
Apx 4 km W Tan Chau, 16 km NNE Chau Phu and 16 km NNE Chau Duc AF. 5th SF Grp, Det. A-428, Oct65, A-428 Oct66. Relocated to Tan An. Grid per *SF Order of Battle*. Also listed at WS 271-945? Chau Doc Pr, IV Corps.

Tan Dien, Camp (YD 732-374)
On Pham Tam Giang Peninsula, apx 10 km NW Tan My AF and 16 km N Hue Citadel AF. Oct68. Thua Thien Pr, I Corps.

Tan Ha Heliport (XT 935-140)
See Tan Ba Heliport. Binh Duong Pr, III Corps.

Tan Hei Airfield (XS 463-523)
Tan Hiep AF. Dinh Tuong Pr, IV Corps.

Tan Hiep (various)
Common Viet ville name. Sites inc: BT 3-6, XT 7-0, XS 4-5, WS 2-2. I, III and IV Corps.

Tan Hiep Airfield (XS 463-523)
Apx 8 km NW My Tho. See also Ben Tranh AF. Dinh Tuong Pro, IV Corps.

Tan Hiep SF Camp (XS 46-52?)
A.k.a. Ben Phuoc or Ben Tranh SF Camp? If at or near Tan Hiep AF, was apx 8 km NW My Tho. 5th SF. Moved to Ben Cat. Info/grid per *SF Order of Battle.* Listed as being in Kien Tuong Pr? Grid is in Dinh Tuong Pr, IV Corps.

Tan Hoa (various)
Common Viet place-name and sp variant of Thanh Hoa and Tanh Hoa. Villes of this name near: AQ 9-1, BT 024-786, BT 018-783, BT 054-801, XT 7-1, WS 8-2, WS 2-2, WQ 3-8, XS 8-3 and XS 4-6. All CTZs.

Tan Hoa Airfield (XT 437-071)
See Hiep Hoa AF. III Corps.

Tan Hoa CAP (n/a)
See Tam Hoa CAP. Quang Nam Pr, I Corps.

Tan Hung Heliport (WQ 141-973)
Apx 10 km NW Xom Tang Long, and 16 km SSW Quan Long City/AF. Heliport #729, alt 7', at 09°02'00"N-105°07'20"E, per Feb73 TAD. An Xuyen Pr, IV Corps.

Tan Khan (ZB 06-23)
See Tan Canh. Kontum Pr, II Corps.

Tan Kieu, FSB? (XS 77-84)
Possible name of position listed as "Unknown FSB" on 199th LIB Assn FSB list. Was a few km SW Saigon, along S side of Rte 232, apx 2 km NE Tan Kieu, 4 km ESE My Phu and 14 km SSW Tan Son Nhut AB. Grid per 199th LIB Assn. Gia Dinh Pr, III Corps.

Tan Ky (WG 2-0)
Assembly point of NVA headed for Thanh Hoa and beginning of their trek down HCMT. Nghe An Pr, NVN.

Tan Lap, FSB? (YT 39-08)
Apx 5 km due W Xuan Loc, in rubber plantation apx 6 km due S Hill 395. 2d/3d Inf, 199th LIB here at one time. Long Khanh Pr, III Corps.

Tan Linh (Xa Lac Tanh) (n/a)
Mapsheet name of L-7014-6531-3. SVN.

Tan Linh SF Camp (YT 929-262)
See Tanh Linh SF Camp. Binh Tuy Pr, III Corps.

Tan Linh, FSB (YT 93-26?)
See Tanh Linh SF Camp. Binh Tuy Pr, III Corps.

Tan Mai (n/a)
Mapsheet L 701-6575-4. NVN/China.

Tan My (YD 818-328)
Apx 2.5 km WNW Eagle Beach R&R Ctr/POL Farm, and 13 km NE Hue. Navy Seabee refueling facility, dredge area, lndg supt area and fuel farm, and POL pipeline to Hue. Adj to and/or inc Col Co (a.k.a. Cocoa Beach) and Eagle Beach R&R center. Ferry facilities and USN NSA here as well. Apr70 XXIV Corps grid per Don Armstrong. Thua Thien Pr, I Corps.

Tan My/Phu Bai/Hue NSA (YD 82-33)
On Vinh Loc Island at Tan My, apx 12 km NE Hue. USN Supt Activity, '65-70. Per MRF Assn Website. Thua Thien Pr, I Corps.

Tan My Airfield (YD 815-332)
Apx 2.5 km WNW Eagle Beach R&R Ctr and 13 km NE Hue. W end of rwy at bay's edge. Per DMA L-7014 series map 6542-3 and ONC J-11. El. 3', 2,500' asph rwy. At 16°33'58"N-107°38'06"E. Thua Thien Pr, I Corps.

Tan My Bridge (BN 618-957)
QL-11 bridge over the Song Ga at Ap Tan My, apx 25 km NW Phan Rang and 18 km WNW Phan Rang AB. Ninh Thuan Pr, II Corps.

Tan My Docks (YD 818-324)
Immed S Tan My AF, and on inland side of Vinh Loc Island, apx 12 km NE Hue Citadel AF. Jul70. Thua Thien Pr, I Corps.

Tan My LCU Ramp (YD 826-312)
Adj Tan My AF, apx 12 km NNE Hue. USN ran ferry service from ramp to Vinh Loc Island and POL tank farm/Eagle Beach R&R Ctr. Pvt Vietnamese ferry service also operated to island from this ramp. Likely a USN Seabee cmpd here or nearby as well. POL line ran from tank farm on Vinh Loc Island near Eagle Beach (a.k.a. Col Co Beach), and along Hwy 551 to Hue. 101st Abn (with ARVN/RF/PF units) was responsible for security along line, its pumping stations, the LCU Ramp and Hwy 551 itself. Thua Thien Pr, I Corps.

Tan My NSA (YD 82-33)
On Vinh Loc Island at Tan My, apx 12 km NNE Hue. USN Supt Activity, '65-70. Per MRF Assn Website. Thua Thien Pr, I Corps.

Tan My NSAD (YD 83-34)
Apx 12 km NE Hue Citadel AF on Vinh Loc Island. Site noted on map in *The Marines in Vietnam 1954-1973*, p 243. Thua Thien Pr, I Corps.

Tan Nhut, FSB? (XS 70-84)
Apx 2 km W Tan Nhut, 1 km S the Kinh Sang Canal, 3 km WSW My Phu and 17 km SE Tan Son Nhut AB. Possible name of FSB listed as "Unknown FSB" on 199th LIB Assn list. 199th LIB FSB/patrol base grid courtesy the 199th LIB Assn. Gia Dinh Pr?, III Corps.

Tan Nhy Bridge (BN 618-957)
See Tan My Bridge. Ninh Thuan Pr, II Corps.

Tan Nien Tay Heliport (XS 884-495)
Apx 7 km NE Go Cong and 5 km NE Go Cong AF. "Heliport #670, alt 10', earth road, new post under const. At 10°23'30"N-106°43'30"E," per Feb73 TAD. Go Cong Pr, IV Corps.

Tan Phat Airfield (ZT 100-810)
Major AF apx 76 km SW Dalat, 3 km E Bao Loc AF and 3 km NE Bao Loc Plantation AF. El. 2,800', 4,200' asph rwy. 11°34'N 107°50'E. Lam Dong Pr, II Corps.

Tan Phu (WR 168-394)
Apx 25 km N Quan Long AF/City. Ville immed W of, and on W side of canal separating it from, Tan Phu 5th SF Camp. An Xuyen Pr, IV Corps.

Tan Phu (AR 746-813)
Adj to SF camp at Tan Phu, apx 6 km S Kontum. Housed US 584th Lt Engr Co. Successfully attacked morning of 21Mar69, by apx 40 Sappers while Inf attacked SF camp as diversion. Enemy destroyed the asphalt plant, four 20-ton and three 5-ton dump trucks, a D-7 Bull Dozer and two 2C truck-mounted Cranes in only 15 minutes; suffering only 2 confirmed KIAs themselves. Described in, and grid from, *Time Heals No Wounds*, p 169's ORLL Extract. 4th Div AO. Kontum Pr, II Corps.

Tan Phu Heliport (WR 195-410)
Apx 26 km due N Quan Long AF and city. Heliport #671, alt 7', at 09°25'15"N-105°10'30"E, per Feb73 TAD. An Xuyen Pr, IV Corps.

Tan Phu Refugee Camp (ZA 227-845)
A.k.a. Kontum Refugee Camp. Along QL-14, apx 3 km SW Kontum. Kontum Pr, II Corps.

Tan Phu Secret Zone (XS 6-0?)
See Thanh Phu Secret Z. Kien Hoa Pr, IV Corps.

Tan Phu SF Camp (AR 746-813?)
SF camp not listed in *SF Order of Battle* and apparently about 6 km S Kontum? Kontum Pr, II Corps.

Tan Phu SF Camp (WR 170-394)
Apx 25 km due N Quan Long AF/City, and just SW Tan Phu Heliport. CIDG camp in Mekong Delta along edge of U Minh Forest at intersection of 2 major canals (N and W of the camp) next to an abnd road built by French along S side of canal to N. Ville of Tan Phu was W of the camp and on across canal. Team A-20, followed by A-43, here early 60's; also Viet LLDB unit and from 2 to 4 CIDG Co's. Described in *Tan Phu* as one of most dangerous SF camps in '63 era. Moved to Don Phuoc. Grid per *SF Order of Battle*. An Xuyen Pr, IV Corps.

Tan Phu SF/CIDG Camp? (ZA 233-782)
A.k.a. Plei Mui CIDG Camp? Along QL-14, apx 7 km SSW Kontum and 32 km due N Pleiku. Cited in AAR at: www.grunt.space.swri.edu/aarpt1.htm, which indicates Montagnard Camp here. 2d/8th Inf here. Kontum Pr, II Corps. Kontum Pr, II Corps.

Tan Phu Thuong Airfield (XT 544-050)
See Hau Nghia AF. Hau Nghia Pr, III Corps.

Tan Phung Lighthouse (CR 05-76)
Apx 37 km NNE Phu Cat AB and 2 km N Tan Phung. Binh Dinh Pr, II Corps.

Tan Qui Tay Outpost (XS 741-805)
Along QL-4, apx 3 km NE Binh Chanh and 18 km SSW Tan Son Nhut AB. Gia Dinh Pr, III Corps.

Tan Rai Airfield (ZT 094-874)
See Xa Tan Rai AF. Lam Dong Pr, II Corps.

Tan Rai SF Camp (ZT 058-873)
A.k.a. Camp Tan Rai. Apx 10 km NW Tan Phat AF and 12 km due N Bao Loc. 5th SF Det A-232, Oct66 and SF Det 40. Per *Rangers At War*, p 202, an indigenous Co of SF sent here from II CTZ Mike Force camp at Pleiku to fill-in for US 101st Recon elements when those elements were attached to regular line units of 101st Abn during Op Klamath Falls, Dec67. Later became RF/PF base. Grid per *SF Order of Battle*. Also listed at ZT 958-873, but grid does not exist? Lam Dong Pr, II Corps.

Tan Son Nhut AFB Hospital (XS 819-962)
See USAF Hospitals. Gia Dinh Pr, III Corps.

Tan Son Nhut Airbase (XS 819-962)
A.k.a. Saigon Airport and Ohi AF. Major AF at NW edge of Saigon, apx 24 km SW Bien Hoa AB, 25 km SE Cu Chi and 20 km due E Duc Hoa AF. 3,500 acre (5.46 sq mi) base was used jointly by civilian airlines, Air America, VNAF, USAF, US Army, USN and USMC air forces. Originally built by French Army in 1939, was improved by Japanese during WWII and further expanded by French after they reoccupied the base in 1946. In 1955, RVN took over control/maint of facility, and in '61, it was placed in joint control of RVN and US Overseas Mission (USOM). At end of War, 29Apr75, it became likely the only base in SVN ever bombed by "NVA Air Force" planes, when only a day before NVA entered Saigon, SVNAF pilots in US F-5s(?), who'd gone over to NVA, bombed it in order to prevent further air evac of city. Base featured 2 concrete, commrcial jet-capable rwys and by '67 was considered busiest AF in world based on number of take-offs/lndgs. 1st US Avn unit based here was 2d Air Force Avn Grp

('61), followed by HQ 13th AF and, in '67, HQ of 7th AF. 377th Combat Supt Grp was base's major supt unit. Also here were Camp Alpha, Davis Station, Camp Gaylor, and Camp Hustler. Battle of Tan Son Nhut took place 30Jan68, when3d Sqdn/4th Cav fought major battle here during Tet '68. 12th Avn Grp. El. 33', two 10,000' x 150' wide conc parallel rwys. Good aerial photo of AB at: http://wmcbride.space.swri.edu/visit/maps/ tsn2.jpg. 10°49'02"N-106°39'02"E. See also Ohi AF. Gia Dinh Pr, III Corps.

Tan Son Nhut Heliport (XS 810-946)
Apparently in Gia Dinh suburb of Saigon at site of 3d Field Hosp, Saigon. Apx 1.5 km SSW Tan Son Nhut AB center of mass, and apx 1.5 km E Ba Que. H-3 pad listed as helo maintenance facility; H-4 pad as 3d Field Hosp; H-5 pad as mortuary. Data per Aug69 TAD (not in Feb73 TAD), per Frank Penk, Jr. Gia Dinh Pr, III Corps.

Tan Son Nhut Nurses BOQ (XS 82-96)
At 3d Field Hosp Cmd, at Tan Son Nhut AB. Data per *Vietnam Military Lore, 1959-1973*. Gia Dinh Pr, III Corps.

Tan Son Northwest Airfield (YT 369-487)
See Dong Bo AF. Long Khanh Pr, III Corps.

Tan Tao (n/a)
Mapsheet name of L-7014-6530-3. SVN.

Tan Thanh, Ap (XS 671-614)
See FSB Tan Tru. Long An Pr, III Corps.

Tan Thoi (XS 29-56)
A.k.a. Ap Tan Thoi. VC controlled ville apx 22 km NW My Tho, 3 km from Kinh Song My Canal and 1 km NNE Ap Bac. VC radio transmissions of 261st Main Force Bn monitored from this site in Dec62 led to infamous 1st battle of Ap Bac. See Ap Bac. Dinh Tuong Pr, IV Corps.

Tan Tich Airfield (WS 705-532)
See Cao Lanh AF. Kien Phong Pr, IV Corps.

Tan To CAP, Thon (YD 916-157)
See CAP Alpha 2. Thua Thien Pr, I Corps.

Tan Tru, FSB (XS 654-623?)
A.k.a. Camp Scott and FSB Tan Thanh. See Tan Tru Basecamp for location. Per David Argabright, was "the Long An Province basecamp of 2d/60th Inf, beginning 7Mar67." Apparently destroyed/abnd around 13-15Jul70." Long An Pr, III Corps.

Tan Tru Basecamp (XS 654-623)
Along Rte 226 just N Song Vam Co Tay River, apx 14 km SSE Ben Luc, 10 km ESE Tan An and 36 km SSE Tan Son Nhut AB, Also listed at XS 669-631. See Tan Tru, FSB. Long An Pr, III Corps.

Tan Tru District HQ (XS 666-628)
Apx 12 km E Tan An and 14 km SSE Ben Luc, near Ap Thanh Tan. Aug69. Long An Pr, III Corps.

Tan Tru Heliport (XS 669-631)
Apx 13 km E Tan An and 15 km SSE Ben Luc, adj Ap Tan Thuan (Tan Tru). Heliport #673, alt 5', at 10°31'15"N-106°31'30"E, per Feb73 TAD. Long An Pr, III Corps.

Tan Uyen (Xa Uyen-Hung) (n/a)
Mapsheet name of L-7014-6331-2. SVN.

Tan Uyen Heliport (XT 965-230)
Along N bank of Song Dong Nai River, apx 6 km NE Xom Ben San and 10 km NNW Bien Hoa AB. "Heliport #674, alt 17', at 11°03'30"N-106°48'00"E," per Feb73 TAD. Bien Hoa Pr, III Corps.

Tan Uyen, FSB (XT 965-230?)
Along Song Dong Nai River near W edge of War Zone D, apx 14 km NNW Bien Hoa, 32 km NNE Saigon and 6 km due S FSB Luke's Castle. 161 Bty, RNZA (Kenning's Bty 13Jun65-13Jun66) FSB set here 29-30Jan66. 1st Inf Div/11th ACR AO. '69. Bien Hoa Pr, III Corps.

Tan Xuan Airfield (BP 835-845)
See Duc My AF. Khanh Hoa Pr, II Corps.

Tancann (ZB 060-220)
See Tan Canh. Kontum Pr, II Corps.

Tanee, FSB (YS 283-934)
Along S side Rte 320, apx 24 km SW Xuan Loc, 15 km WSW Blackhorse AF and 3 km E Binh Son Plantation. Dec70. Bien Hoa Pr, III Corps.

Taney, USCGC (n/a)
WHEC 37. 14May69-31Jan70. Sqdn 3 CGC, during Coast Guard's 4th deployment.

Tang Hoa Heliport (XS 880-408)
Just SE Tang Hoa, apx 8 km SE Go Cong and 5 km SSW Xom Go Me. "Heliport #675, alt 17', earth road. Land in front of Post. Rough." Feb73 TAD. Go Cong Pr, IV Corps.

Tang Hung Airfield (XB 68-77)
LS-167. CIA/SF, per *Air Facilities Data-Laos.*

Tango, Checkpoint (XT 371-423)
See Checkpoint Tango. Tay Ninh Pr, III Corps.

Tango, FSB (XS 96-71)
Along E Bank Song Nha Be River, apx 32 km SE Tan Son Nhut AB, 14 km SSE Nha Be, 14 km E to ESE Can Giuoc and 24 km SE Saigon. 3d/34th Arty here during Op Coronado, 20-21-Jul67, in supt 3d and 4th/47th Inf, US 9th Div (as well as 3d Bn VNMC and 3d/46th ARVN). Grid estimated. Gia Dinh Pr, III Corps. [513]

Tango, LZ ? (XT 655-273)
Along the Song Saigon, apx 12 km N Cu Chi and 16 km SW Lai Khe. 27Jun66. See Tango, Patrol Base, at XT 554-236. Binh Duong Pr, III Corps.

Tango, LZ (ZA 035-663)
Apx 27 km NW Pleiku, 8 km W to WSW Plei Mrong AF, and 6 km SSW Plei Doi. 1st/92d Arty, 4th Div here suptg 24th STZ, 6Jan69, per 4th Div/1st/92d Arty op rpt courtesy Craig Miller (site apparently unnamed at that time). Became 1st/35th Inf fwd FSB from 1-17-69 to 1-23-69. Ill-fated assault on Chu Pa Mtn launched from this LZ, 21Jan69, per Jan-Mar69 1st/35th Inf Bn daily logs. Data per Dick Arnold. Pleiku Pr, II Corps.

Tango, LZ (ZA 0-9)
One of initial sites proposed for 7th Cav, 1st Cav's assault on Chu Pong Massif during 1st Ia Drang Valley Campaign. LZs Tango, Victor, Whiskey, X-Ray and Yankee were 5 proposed sites but only X-Ray and Yankee were large enough to handle a Bn. Visual recon found Yankee was surfaced with tall tree stumps, so LZ X-Ray was chosen. Per Peter Cole, is discussed in *Pleiku,* pp 188, 191, etc. Pleiku Pr, II Corps.

Tango, Patrol Base (XT 554-236)
Apx 8 km WNW Cu Chi CB and 7 km ESE Trang Bang. 14mar69. See also LZ Tango at XT 655-273. Hau Nghia Pr, III Corps.

Tango Three, FSB (YA 850-455?)
A.k.a. FSB T-3 and Three Church. Near Plei Djereng. 1st/22d Inf, 4th Div in '66-67. Picture/discussion at

http://grunt.space.swri. edu/LouTplei.htm. Possibly named after call-sign of A/1st/22d Inf? Apparently an SF camp nearby. Kontum Pr?, II Corps.

Tanh Canh (ZB 06-23)
See Tan Canh. Kontum Pr, II Corps.

Tanh Hoa (WG 8-8)
Spelling variant of Thanh Hoa, a NVN village. NVN.

Tanh Kanh (ZB 06-23)
See Tan Canh. Kontum Pr, II Corps.

Tanh Li (YT 92-26)
Variant of Tanh Linh on 199th LIB Assn list? See Tanh Linh and FSB Rising Sun. Binh Tuy Pr, III Corps.

Tanh Linh, FSB (YT 93-26)
A.k.a. FSB Rising Sun. Apx 44 km NNE Ham Tan, at S edge of Tanh Linh, 46 km NW Phan Thiet, 12 km due W Dang S'Ruin Mtn (Hill 1302), 50 km ENE Xuan Loc and 22 km ESE Vo Dat. 199th LIB and 2d/40th Arty here. Pronounced "Tin Yawn." Binh Tuy Pr, III Corps.

Tanh Linh Airfield (YT 935-256)
Apx 46 km NW Phan Thiet AF, 58 km SSW Tan Phat AF and 92 km WSW Song Mao AF at S edge of Tanh Linh. El. 240', 2,000' steel-mat rwy. Pronounced "Tin Yawn." Binh Tuy Pr, III Corps.

Tanh Linh SF Camp (YT 929-262)
A.k.a. Tan Linh SF Camp. Apx 44 km NNE Ham Tan, at S edge of Tanh Linh, 46 km NW Phan Thiet and 12 km due W Dang S'Ruin Mtn (Hill 1302). 5th SF camp, Det A-304 (was 235), Oct65, A-312, Oct66, SF Det 42. Moved to Ben Cat. Grid per *Special Forces Order of Battle*. Pronounced "Tin Yawn." Binh Tuy Pr, III Corps.

Tank Battles (various)
See A Shau Valley, An Loc, Lang Vei, Nhi Ha, Polei Kleng, and Lam Son 719. See also "Firsts" in Glossary.

Tank Hill (YA or ZA or AR?)
Per Don Truitt, 54th Sig Bn IFFV, "Tank Hill was at Pleiku. All I can recall about it is that it was a fairly isolated position built on top of a hill serviced by a newly built asphalt hwy that Charlie used unchallenged because nobody wanted tear up what was some really fine construction! The hill was topped by a very large concrete bunker that was originally built for some Gen but declared inadequate after Charlie employed a new, larger rocket. Was then turned over to 167th Radio Relay and they used it as cmd center (?). I remember visiting the bunker and being shown around. As I recall, it had 6 ft steel I-beams and looked like it could withstand anything the enemy had. Was a standing joke, in that it showed just how terrified the Gen and his staff must have been." Pleiku Pr, II Corps.

Tanker Valley (YT 04-07)
Somewhere in Long Binh Post, and home to at least the 47th Trans Co. Data per Apr/May 2000 VETERAN Mag Locator, p 38. Bien Hoa Pr, III Corps.

Tannee, FSB (YS 278-937)
Apx 7 km E FSB Bulsan, 16 km WSW Blackhorse Base Camp, 8 km WNW FSB Wattle and 3 km WNW FSB Burke. On 1ATF NCO trng map per John Hollett. Also listed at YS 288-937. Bien Hoa Pr, III Corps.

Tanner, USS (n/a)
AGS-15. Hydrographic Survey Ship.

Tanton, Operation (YS)
See *Sydney, HMAS.*

Tao-Tsieng, Mui (ZJ 0-6)
A.k.a. Pointe de l' Arequier. Coastal point at 21°24'N-107°58'E. On NF48-12 JOG. NVN.

Tape, LZ (BS 745-125)
Apx 9 km NW Van Canh AF, 36 km WSW Qui Nhon and 17 km SE of LZ Regular. In 4th Div op rpt grid per Jim Claeys. Also listed at BS 745-134. Nov69-Jan70. Binh Dinh Pr, II Corps.

Tappahannock, USS (n/a)
A-043. Aux Oiler. Apparently in SVN waters during at least '66-67.

Tappy, LZ (BR 534-604)
Apx 8 km WNW Vinh Thanh ville, 5 km ENE De Ponang and 17 km NNE An Khe. Aug69. Binh Dinh Pr, II Corps.

Tarau (YC 910-890)
See Ta Rau, Ta Rhu and Ta Ro. Thua Thien Pr, I Corps.

Tarawa, LZ (YD 098-232)
Apx 2 km NNE Pa Lar, 5 km SE Ba Noa, 18 km SSW Ba Long AF, 7 km NW FSB Razor, 4 km ESE FSB Pusan, 5 km NE FSB Tuba. 3d Mar Div. Apr70 XXIV Corps grid per Don Armstrong. On map at p 73, *US Marines in Vietnam-1969.* Quang Tri Pr, I Corps.

Target Boxes (n/a)
See Choke Point Bombing in Glossary.

Tarpon (n/a)
Apr70, XXIV Corps future-use 101st Abn FSB name.

Tarzan, LZ (BR 200-300)
Apx 32 km WSW An Khe and 15 km SE peak Chu Ran Mtn. Sep69. Binh Dinh Pr, II Corps.

Tarzan, LZ (BS 481-073)
Apx 27 km WSW Thuan An and 22 km SSE Gia Vuc AF. Mar66. Binh Dinh Pr, II Corps.

Tarzan, LZ (XD 987-645)
In Khe Kui River Valley, 1 km S south edge of DMZ, apx 14 km WNW Cam Lo and 26 km WNW Dong Ha. Numerous LZs built nearby, inc Bazooka, Camel, Champ, Deacon, Hackney, Parakeet, Amber and FSB Toledo. XXIV Corps grid per D. Armstrong. Quang Tri Pr, I Corps.

Task Force (n/a)
See also Task Group.

Task Force 70.8 (n/a)
USN contingents responsible for naval shore bombardment from mid '65 to late '67. Primary craft used were Hvy Cruisers and Destroyers; however, Battleship *New Jersey* spent six months as part of TF in '68-69. Bombarded coastal targets in both SVN and NVN. See also Sea Dragon, Operation.

Task Force 73 (n/a)
USN 7th Fleet's logistic supt unit.

Task Force 76 (n/a)
USN 7th Fleet's Amphibious unit. See Frequent Wind.

Task Force 76.4 (n/a)
A.k.a. Amphibious Ready Grp Alpha. See Eagle Pull and Task Group 76.4.

Task Force 76.5 (n/a)
See Task Group 76.5.

Task Force 76.9 (n/a)
31st Marine Amphibious Unit. See Eagle Pull and Task Group 76.9.

Task Force 77 (n/a)
USN 7th Fleet's aircraft carrier attack unit.

Task Force 78 (n/a)
See End Sweep, Op.
Task Force 115, 114 & 117 (n/a)
USN small craft Divs used for inland Water and Coastal patrol operations and under Naval Forces Vietnam. TF 116 and 117 were assigned to MRF with the 2d Bde 9th US Inf Div and 7th ARVN Inf Div beginning Jun67. See Mobile Riverine Force in Division Command Section, and Market Time and Game Warden in Glossary.
Task Force 333 (n/a)
ARVN TF that included at least the 36th and 52d ARVN Ranger Bns, 3d ARVN Ranger Recon Co and 5th ARVN Cav Rgt (14 M-41 tanks) which attacked into Cambodia, 29Apr70. Op AO included areas W Svay Rieng, Krek and Chup Rubber Plantation along Hwy 7. On 21May70, the NVA made an all-out attack on TF HQ. Op discussed in *Rangers At War*, p 268. Cambodia and SVN.
Task Force 3-506 (n/a)
Operational and nickname of 3d Bn, 506th Inf, 101st Abn, which operated independently of Div during most of its VN tour. At various times, was opcon to Americal Div, 173d Abn, 1st Bde/4th Div, among possibly other units. Only unit of 101st Abn to participate in Cambodian Incursion, May70. In late '70 or early '71, finally moved N to join 101st Div in I Corps for 1st time since its arrival in VN. See also 3d/506th Inf in Major Units/Divisions section.
Task Force Alpha, Operation (n/a)
Program of electronic sensor info analysis from sensors along Ho Chi Minh Trail. Started in '67, under 7th Air Force at Tan Son Nhut and later moved to NKP. In *Da Nang Diary* (p 203), author describes this facility as enormous concrete building at NKP AB, filled with intel analysts and sophisticated electronic gear that deciphered relayed "Igloo White" acoustical sensor data monitoring vehicle traffic on HCMT in Laos. These sensors were so sensitive the unit could track individual trucks and pinpoint their locations for targeting air strikes. See Igloo White, Dutch Mill, Muscle Shoals, Repeater Aircraft, Spotlight and Gravel Mines in Glossary. Thailand.
Task Force Black (YB)
1 of 2 TFs created by LTC David Schumacher, Bn CO, 1st/503d Inf, 173d Abn during Battle for Dak To. TF Black consisted of C/4th/503d and two plts of D Co. TF Blue contained A Co and other 2 plts of D Co. These two TFs maneuvered while Bn's B Co pulled security for FSB 15. TF Black was heavily attacked 11-12Nov67, by 8th and 9th Bns, 66th NVA Rgt, and C/4th/503d was brought 12Nov67 to save it from annihilation. TF Black suffered 20 KIA, 154 WIA and 2 MIA, and C/4/503d 30 WIA but no dead. Data per Dak To, pp 179-211. Kontum Pr, II Corps.
Task Force Blue (YB)
See Task Force Black. Kontum Pr, II Corps.
Task Force Clearwater (YD)
A.k.a. River Security Group, I Corps. Elements of Brown Water Navy with HQ at Cua Viet from Feb68 until TF terminated. Was Broken into two groups, Dong Ha River Security Group and Hue River Security Group (Tan My?/Eagle Beach?). Per *Brown Water, Black Berets*, p 278. Quang Tri/Thua Thien Prvs, I Corps.
Task Force Delta (n/a)
TF under Marine Gen Lowell English during Op Hastings in '66. Forward CP was at Cam Lo.
Task Force Gimlet (n/a)
See Artillery Firsts in Glossary.
Task Force Hay (n/a)
Originally known as Hurricane Forward, this HQ was sent to Saigon in order to counter Tet '68 attack, then kept to supt Saigon area until Mar73. A.k.a. Task Force Hay, after Gen John Hay, its first Cmdr. See CMAC, HQ in Major Headquarters Section.
Task Force Ivory (n/a)
Code name of Son Tay POW Camp raid, 21Nov70.
Task Force McQuarrie (n/a)
See Hill 1338. Kontum Pr, II Corps.
Task Force Oregon (n/a)
See 23d Inf Division, and Task Force Oregon in Division Commands Section.
Task Force Oregon, Operation (n/a)
See 23d Inf Div, Americal, and Task Force Oregon in Division Command Section.
Task Force Privette (n/a)
Combined armored elements of 11th ACR and Royal New Zealand Army operating out of Long Binh/Bien Hoa in mid-68. Was under Capt. William Privette, with RNZA Capt. Martin Steeds as 2d in cmd. Used Scout Section of Rgt HQ Trp as its HQ, and was made up of fast moving gun jeeps and ACAVs. Conducted recon-in-force ops with 36th ARVN Rangers and local RF/PF Forces. III Corps.
Task Force Russia (n/a)
See Glossary.
Task Force Shoemaker (n/a)
Code name for 10,000 US and 5,000 ARVN troops that invaded Cambodia 1May-30Jun70, in op known as Op Toan Thang 43/Rockcrusher in Fishhook, Parrot's Beak area. The Invasion further north by 4th Div elements and attached units was Op Tame the West.
Task Force South, Operation (n/a)
See Task Force South in Division Command Section.
Task Force Starlight (n/a)
River patrolling technique that combined 9th Inf Div LRRP teams and Vietnamese Natl Police operating together aboard heavily armed USN Monitor water craft.
Task Force Sunder (n/a)
US Army Transportation TF under LTC Charles Sunder, shipped via LSD from Qui Nhon to Quang Tri Pr, Mar68, to establish a USN ship logistical off-loading facility at Omaha Beach (a.k.a. Wonder Beach and Sunder Beach). Was created in response to Tet '68 attacks and need to resupply 1st Cav and 101st Div elements that had been sent to Quang Tri to reinforce the Marine elements. See Wunder Beach. Quang Tri Pr, I Corps.
Task Force Tally Ho (n/a)
See Glossary.
Task Force Tyson (n/a)
Named for a Maj. Tyson of 2d/35th Inf, 4th Div. Involved in Battle for LZ 10 Alpha, May-Jun66. See LZ 10-Alpha for detail. Pleiku Pr, II Corps.
Task Force Vietnam (n/a)
See Glossary.

Task Force Walker (n/a)
Force organized under BGen Glenn Walker during Op Paul Revere, May-Jun66. Assigned an area in II Corps W Pleiku that was 80 km wide by 40 km. Zone ran SW to Chu Pong Mtns and NW as far as outpost at Duc Co. Its eastern border was on a line with Plei Me and western limit was Cambodian border. Job was to monitor activity in infamous Ia Drang Valley. Its element included 3 Inf Bns from 25th Inf Div (1st/14th, 1st and 2d of 35th Inf) one Co of medium armor, one armored Cav Trp, one Air Cav Trp, one Bn of 105 howitzers and 1 Bty each of 155mm, 175mm and 8" cannons. See *Battles in the Monsoon*, pp 261 et seq. Pleiku Pr, II Corps.
Task Force Winner (AR/BR)
In Dec68?, elements of 2d Bde/4th Div, ARVN and an MSF swept the Dak Payou Valley (a.k.a. VC Valley) and Dak Doa Valley (AR 9-7) in Kontum Pr, E LZ Blackhawk and in Chu Drou Mtns (BR 1-4). Op ended 3Jan69. See also listed valleys. Kontum and Pleiku Prvs?, II Corps.
Task Force Yankee (n/a)
Created Dec65, by III MAF to initiate assault on Base Area 112, generally SW An Hoa. TF was 1st Mar Div under Cmd of BGen Ross T. Dwyer. Op lasted through Feb69. Quang Nam Pr, I Corps.
Task Group (n/a)
See also Task Force.
Task Group 76.4 (n/a)
Movement Transport Grp Alpha. See Frequent Wind.
Task Group 76.5 (n/a)
Movement Transport Grp Bravo. See Frequent Wind.
Task Group 76.9 (n/a)
Movement Transport Grp Charlie. See Frequent Wind.
Tasman, FSB (YS 632-861)
Apx 27 km NE Nui Dat, 4 km SSW FSB Picton and 7 km NNE FSB Raglan. On 1ATF NCO trng map per John Hollett. Also listed at YS 340-870 and possibly at both locations? Phuoc Tuy Pr, III Corps.
Tasman, FSB (YS 340-870)
Apx 3 km NW FSB Dampier, 5 km SSW FSB Wattle, 22 km NNW Nui Dat and 11 km W Rte-2. 161 Bty, RNZA (Horsford's Bty 18Mar69-18Sep69) FSB set here 7-8Apr69. Also listed at YS 632-861 and possibly in both locations? Bien Hoa Pr, III Corps.
Tau O Bridge (XT 765-729)
QL-13 bridge, apx 12 km due N Chonh Thanh and 15 km S An Loc. Jul66. Binh Long Pr, III Corps.
Taussig, USS (n/a)
DD-746. SVN
Tay (n/a)
Vietnamese word for the direction "West" when used following (or possibly also preceding?) a place name, such as "Ngo Xa Tay," meaning Ngo Xa West.
Tay Ninh (n/a)
Mapsheet name of L-7014-6231-4. SVN.
Tay Ninh (XT 24-47)
Apx 100 km NW Saigon, 10 km S Nui Ba Den (Black Virgin Mtn), 4 km SE Tay Ninh West AF, 5 km N Song Vam Co Dong River, 25 km W Dau Tieng/Tri Tam, 50 km NW Ben Cat and 22 km E Cambodia. Originally home of 196th LIB and later elements of 25th Inf Div. Series of VC/NVA attacks known as Battle of Tay Ninh occurred between 17Aug-27Sep69, resulting in 137 US KIA and 755 WIA, 138 ARVN KIA and 370 WIA, in exchange for est 2,489 enemy KIA and 71 POW. [514] Was also site of SF Det 57(?), Bty C, 7th Bn, 11th Arty (25th Div), 5th SF Grp Det B-32 (was B-120), Oct65, III Corps. Adv Team 90, Tay Ninh Pr Advs; 1st Philippine Civic Action Grp. Map is TL-7014-6231-4. Facilities map at www.mendonet.com/588th/map.htm. See also Nui Ba Den. Capitol, Tay Ninh Pr, III Corps.
Tay Ninh Basecamp (XT 143-518)
Along LTL-13, apx 3 km WSW Tay Ninh West AF and 8 km W Tay Ninh. '68-70. Also listed at XT 164-516, Nov66. Tay Ninh Pr, III Corps.
Tay Ninh Bridge Site (XT 270-458?)
Blocking position for A & B/4th/23d Inf, 25th Inf, per AAR, Battle of Tay Ninh (17Aug-27Sep68), HQ 25th ID, 2Feb69, p 14. Tay Ninh Pr, III Corps.
Tay Ninh Airfield (XT 203-510)
See Tay Ninh City AF. Tay Ninh Pr, III Corps.
Tay Ninh City Airfield (XT 203-510)
At NW edge of Tay Ninh, apx 4 km ESE Tay Ninh West AF. 1,900' PSP rwy. At 11°18'55"N-106°06'08"E. El. 39'. Tay Ninh Pr, III Corps.
Tay Ninh Combat Base (XT 158-513)
A.k.a. Tay Ninh West. Apx 6 km W Tay Ninh. 1st Bde/1st Cav HQ, 196th LIB, 25th Inf Div all here. During Cambodian Incursion, arty units here were moved to various positions adj to or within Cambodia, among which were: B Bty, 1st/27th Arty, six 155s, and B Bty, 2d/4th Arty with six-105mms. Grid/some data in *11th ACR Cambodia Invasion AAR, 1st Cav Div, May-Jun70*, per Lou Rochat. [515] Tay Ninh facilities map at www. mendonet.com /588th/map.htm. Also listed at grid XT 202-508, 160-510 and 158-513? Tay Ninh Pr, III Corps.
Tay Ninh East (XT 202-508)
A.k.a. FSB Tay Ninh East and Tay Ninh City East AF? At NW edge of Tay Ninh, apx 4 km ESE Tay Ninh West AF, and at same location as Tay Ninh City AF. Wallace Cmpd and MACV Team 90 here. 1st Cav. Tay Ninh Pr, III Corps.
Tay Ninh I Airfield (XT 203-510)
See Tay Ninh City AF. Tay Ninh Pr, III Corps.
Tay Ninh III Airfield (XT 168-518)
Along road to Ben Soi, apx 2 to 3 km SW Tay Ninh City East AF and 7 km W Tay Ninh. See Tay Ninh West AF. Tay Ninh Pr, III Corps.
Tay Ninh PA&E Compound (XT 24-47?)
Pacific Architects & Engineers, civilian construction contractor facility. Tay Ninh Pr, III Corps.
Tay Ninh Province (XT/WT)
One of 11 south-central provs forming III Corps (III CTZ).
Tay Ninh Provincial HQ (XT 198-506)
On western outskirts of Tay Ninh. Attacked 18Aug68 during Battle for Tay Ninh. Tay Ninh Pr, III Corps.
Tay Ninh SF Camp (XT 204-509)
Astride Hwy 4, apx 4 km ESE Tay Ninh West AF. 5th SF. Later closed and assets moved to ? Grid per AAR, *Battle of Tay Ninh* (17Aug-27Sep68), HQ 25th ID, 2Feb69, courtesy Butch Sincock. *SF Order of Battle* lists grid as XT 2045-5087. Tay Ninh Pr, III Corps.

Tay Ninh West Airfield (XT 168-518)
Major AF apx 6 km W Tay Ninh, 40 km SSW Katum AF, 18 km NE Cambodia, and 31 km W Dau Tieng AF. Per TPC K-10D. El. 300', 3,800' asph rwy. Tay Ninh Pr, III Corps. Also listed at XT 178-515. Tay Ninh Pr, III Corps.
Tay Ninh West (XT 178-515)
A.k.a. Tay Ninh CB. Apx 6 km NNW Tay Ninh city proper, 20 km E Cambodia. 12 km SW Nui Ba Den. Transferred to SVN Govt 4Sep70, at which time it had been previously occupied by US 25th Inf Div and could supt 7,300 troops. For some reason, transfer agreement stipulated that ARVN 25th Inf Div would replace US 25th Inf Div and operate Tay Ninh West as combat base.[516] MACV-JGS IG conducted a post-transfer inspection, 10-12Oct72. Also listed at XT 202-508, 160-510 and 158-513? Map is TL-7014-6231-4. Facilities map at www.mendonet.com/588th/map.htm. Tay Ninh Pr, III Corps.
Tay Thinh Canal (AT 987-663)
Apx 11 km SSW Da Nang AB. Quang Nam Pr, I Corps.
Taylor, LZ (BR 808-625)
Apx 1 km S LZ Gavin, 12 km SW Phu My/QL-1 and 21 km NNW Phu Cat AB. Oct66. Binh Dinh Pr, II Corps.
Taylor, FSB (XS 410-950)
Apx 19 km W to WSW Duc Hoa AF and 16 km SE Duc Hue AF. Mar67. Hau Nghia Pr, III Corps.
Taylor Common, Operation (n/a)
6Dec68-7Mar69. 1st Mar Div op. 1,299 rptd NVA KIA, per *VN Order of Battle*, pp 9-14. Quang Nam Pr, I Corps.
Tchepone (XD 27-48)
Apx km 50 km WNW Khe Sanh, and 410 km SE Vientiane. Major objective of Lam Son 719. See Lam Son 719, and Binh Tram in Glossary. Laos.
Tchepone Airfield (XD 27-48)
A.k.a. L-38 and Sepone AF. Apx 410 km SE Vientiane and 50 km WNW Khe Sanh on Feb67 Natl Geo map. CIA/SF facility. Grid per *Air Facilities Data-Laos.*
TDKQ (n/a)
See Glossary.
Te Nau Bay (YA 97-43?)
Freshwater lake at 13°55N-107°45'E. ND48-12. NVN.
Tea Plantation, The (ZA 199-340)
Adj to and a.k.a. Catecka AF, apx 14 km SSW Pleiku. Jan66. Pleiku Pr, II Corps.
Tea Plantation, The (AR 7-8?)
Along W side QL-14, apx 8 km due S Camp Holloway and adj to "The Turkey Farm." A Co/1st Cav helo laager area. Used by 1st Cav as fwd op base during first Ia Drang Campaign, Oct-Nov65. French-owned Tea Plantation (Catecka?) also adj to these camps. See also Catecka, Stadium and Turkey Farm. Pleiku Pr, II Corps.
Teal, FSB (XD 805-443)
Apx 5 km E FSB Geiger, 7 km NW Khe Sanh CB, 35 km WSW Cam Lo and 54 km WSW Quang Tri. Apr70 XXIV Corps grid per Don Armstrong. Quang Tri Pr, I Corps.
Team Breaker Site (XD 756-532)
See Hill 665 at grid. Quang Tri Pr, I Corps.
Tear Gas (n/a)
See CN Gas and CS Gas in Glossary.
Tears of Spring (n/a)
See Madame Nhu in Glossary.
Tecksu Island (VS 83-02)
See Hon Tre Island. Kien Giang Pr, IV Corps.
Tee, LZ/FSB (YA 88-09?)
Apx 3.5 km SE LZ Golf, 17 km SSE Duc Co SF Camp, 8 km due N Chu Pong Mtn, 9 km E Cambodia and 2 km N the Ia Drang River. 1st Cav. On *Ia Drang Valley* map in *The Rise and Fall of the American Army*, between pp 368-9. Grid is est. Pleiku Pr, II Corps.
Telstar, FSB (XD 855-454?)
Apparently near listed grid and on Hill 1015, apx 48 km WSW Quang Tri, and 16 km WSW Ca Lu. Data per *The Final Formation*, p 148, Quang Tri Pr, I Corps.
Temnara, FSB (XD 826-352)
Apparent misspelling of Tenaru (XD 827-316)? Apx 7 km SSW Khe Sanh AF, 5 km SW Khe Sanh Ville, 3 km S QL-9 and 22 km WSW Ca Lu. Quang Tri Pr, I Corps.
Tempest, LZ (BS 745-280)
Apx 14 km SSW Duc Pho, 3 km NNE Sa Long, 15 km due N Thuan An, 17 km W the coast and 2 km due S Nui Hoc Hoa. Built to supt 1st/14th Inf, 4th Div during Op Catnip. 173d Abn also here, '68-69. Photos/maps at http://1-14th.com/maps.html. Quang Ngai Pr, I Corps.
Temple Lake, LZ (XD 877-257)
Apx 7 km SSE Khe Sanh CB, 18 km SW Ca Lu and 5 km SE Khe Sanh ville. Apr70 XXIV Corps grid per Don Armstrong. Quang Tri Pr, I Corps.
Temple of Literature (WJ 8-2)
In Hanoi. A fixture of French Colonial rule. NVN.
Temple of Holy See (2) (XT 265-463)
A.k.a. the Second Temple of Holy See. Apx 2.5 km E the Great Temple of Holy See (minor of the 2) and 2 km from SE corner of Tay Ninh. During Battle for Tay Ninh City, 17Aug-27Sep68, a US Mech squad investigating grp of refugees here had its APC destroyed by RPG fire from NVA hiding in temple when it arrived and, in fight that ensued, 17 refugees were killed. Tay Ninh Pr, III Corps.
Temple of Holy See (XT 241-496)
A.k.a. the Great Temple of Holy See. Apx 95 km NW Saigon. Cao Dai Sect's famous temple in town of Long Hoa, near Tay Ninh. During Battle of Tay Ninh, 17Aug-27Sep69, was attacked or occupied by enemy forces and used as refuge by civilian refugees. Grid in AAR, Battle of Tay Ninh (17Aug-27Sep68), HQ 25th ID, 2Feb69, per Butch Sincock. Tay Ninh Pr, III Corps.
Ten Alpha, LZ (YA 7-2?)
See LZ 10-Alpha. II Corps.
Tenaru, FSB (XD 827-316)
Apx 5 km WSW FSB Snapper, 4 km E of Laos, 15 km W FSB Whisman, 15 km SW FSB Cates, E Lang Vei and just N the Vietnam Salient. I/9th Marines, 3d Mar Div attacked here by 2 Cos of NVA on 27Jun69. On map p 73, *US Marines in VN-1969.* Also spelled Tenearu and Temnara? Also listed at XD 826-352? Quang Tri Pr, I Corps.
Tenko, FSB? (n/a)
Said to have been 7th/8th Arty base in III Corps. Data per Dan Gillotti, 15th Arty Assn. III Corps.
Tennessee, FSB (XT 582-392)
In river-bend terrain feature of Song Saigon known as The Mushroom, apx 15 km SE Dau Tieng and 10 km SW FSB El Paso. 1st Inf Div AO, '69. On *Low Level Hell's* 1st Div

TAOR map. Grid per Frank Penk, Jr. Also listed at XT 583-333, Aug69-Jan70. Binh Duong Pr, III Corps.
Tennessee, FSB (YC 552-961)
Apx 27 km SW Hue and 18 km SW FSB Birmingham. During Lam Son 720, beginning Apr '71, FSBs Fury, Kathryn, Maureen, Gladiator and later Eagle's Nest were reopened by B/326th Engrs, while elements of 326th also rebuilt/enlarged FSBs Brick, Tennessee, Rendezvous and Rifle (including rte 545, road to FSB Rifle). 101st Abn. Thua Thien Pr, I Corps.
Tennessee Ernie Ford (n/a)
See American Radio Service in Glossary.
Tennessee Valley (YD or YC?)
Location unknown. Said to have been in 101st Abn AO and possibly near FSB Tennessee? Presence of Chi Thieu Sapper Bn confirmed here by 101st LRRP Team "New Zealand." Per *Rangers at War*, p 167, 170, Ranger Team Ferrari suffered 6 WIA and barely escaped from its northern rim, 6Jul70. Thua Thien Pr, I Corps.
Tent City (XS 82-96?)
A.k.a. Camp Alpha. Transient troop billet just outside Tan Son Nhut AB. Built beginning 5May65 and first named Tent City, then Tent City Alpha when other billet-tent cities were built at Pershing Field and Camp Davies. Grid is for Tan Son Nhut AB. Gia Dinh Pr, III Corps.
Tent City (82d Abn) (XT 99-12)
At Bien Hoa. Basecamp that served as initial fwd cmd post for 3d Bde/82d Abn when it moved S from I Corps (Hue AO), beginning in Sep-Oct68, to take up its new AO covering the W and NW approaches to Saigon. It immed became apparent fwd Bde HQ needed to be closer to its actual AO, so site was found at Camp Red Ball (XS 832-984) along N edge of Tan Son Nhut AB. Const of TOC at Camp Red Ball began 1Oct68, and it was operational by 16Oct68. During same period, new basecamp for Bde was built at Phu Loi Post (XT 860-155), and occupied on 20Oct68. [517] Bien Hoa Pr, III Corps.
Tent City Alpha (XS 82-96?)
A.k.a. Camp Alpha. Transient troop billet just outside Tan Son Nhut AB. First named "Tent City," then "Tent City Alpha" when other billet-tent cities built at Pershing Field and Camp Davies. Grid is est. Gia Dinh Pr, III Corps.
Tent City Charlie (XS 87-93?)
A.k.a. The Fish Market, and later Camp Charlie. An area on outskirts of Saigon at NE edge of Saigon Port. Erected by US Army QM Depot from Ft. Bragg, NC. Administered by 543d QM Grp beginning '65. In '66, renamed Camp Charlie and then Camp Davies. Housed 506th Field Depot, the largest military Field Depot in World. When 506th moved to Long Binh, the 4th and 125th Trans Cmds took over Camp Davies. Grid apx. Gia Dinh Pr, III Corps.
Tent City Refugee Camp (n/a)
A.k.a. Orote Point, Guam. See Operation New Life.
Terendak, Camp (n/a)
Australian Army base in Malaya, not Vietnam.
Tern, LZ (AT 936-748)
Apx 7 km due W Da Nang AB and 8 km SSW Red Beach. Sep69. Quang Nam Pr, I Corps.
Terrace, LZ (BR 572-753)
On W edge of plateau overlooking N end of Vinh Thanh (Happy) Valley, apx 30 km NNE An Khe, 19 km NE Kannack AF and 15 km NNW Vinh Thanh AF. 4th Div AO, '70. C Bty, 4th/42d Arty here 1-22Aug70, suptg 1st/22d Inf, 4th Div. Name/grid per Jim Claeys. Also listed at BR 572-758. Binh Dinh Pr, II Corps.
Terrell County, USS (n/a)
LST-1157. USN Landing Ship, Tank. SVN service with 9th Inf Div/MRF. Discussed on MRF Assn website at www.mrfa.org. At one point was grounded and apparently freed by harbor tugs/salvage vessels of Harbor Clearance Unit 1. [518] III/IV Corps?
Terri, FSB (XT 421-168)
Just E of a plantation and on E side Song Vam Co Dong River, apx 42 km NW Saigon and 24 km WSW Cu Chi. 2d/12th Cav, 1st Cav here Jan-69, per Frank Penk, Jr. Also listed as FSB Terry at XT 425-131, some 3 km S listed grid. Hau Nghia Pr, III Corps.
Territorial Forces (n/a)
See RF, PF, and People's Self Defense Force in Glossary.
Terry, FSB (XT 421-168)
See FSB Terri at grid. Hau Nghia Pr, III Corps.
Terry, LZ (XT 423-169)
See Terri. Hau Nghia Pr, III Corps.
Terry, LZ (XS 423-172?)
XS grid zone thought to be in error and proper grid zone likely XT? However, if listed grid accurate, site was apx 20 km NNW Tar Vinh AF/Phu Vinh. See also LZ Terri at XT 423-172. Kien Hoa Pr, IV Corps.
Terry, LZ (YS 530-770)
A.k.a. FSB Pam? On LTL-25, apx 3 km E Xa Binh Gia, 8 km E LTL-2 and 15 km NE Nui Dat/Luscombe AF. Apr66. Phuoc Tuy Pr, III Corps.
Terry, LZ (ZA 008-654)
Apx 11 km W-WSW Plei Mrong AF, 6 km SE peak Chu Pa Mtn and 30 km NW Pleiku. 1st/35th Inf, 4th ID here Apr-May69. Name/Grid per Dick Arnold. Pleiku Pr, near Kontum Pr border, II Corps.
Terry Ann, FSB (XU 929-081)
A.k.a. Fort Granite. Along Song Be River, apx 20 km ESE Loc Ninh, 23 km WSW Song Be AF/Phuoc Binh and 20 km NE An Loc. 1st/8th Cav, 1st/12th Cav, 1st Cav, '69, AO Commanche Warrior. Grid per Frank Penk, Jr. Binh Long Pr?, III Corps.
Terry Lynn, FSB/LZ (XU 53-32?)
A.k.a. FSB North 1. If grid correct, was W of Rte 7, apx 5 km SSW Snuol. 1st Cav FSB originally named LZ Terry Lynn, then renamed "North One" by 1st/5th Cav, 1st Cav, 4May70. Used During Cambodian Incursion, May-Jun70. Clearing for base was created 1May70 at 0630 hrs by USAF drop of 15,000 lb. bomb (a.k.a. Daisy Cutter and Commando Vault) in order to provide LZ for ARVN Abn initial assault into Cambodia. LZ East also blown by Daisy Cutter at same time and for same reason. Grid is est. Cited in *Incursion*, per Peter Cole. Cambodia.
Tess, FSB (YS 282-646)
Along E side of QL-15, apx 16 km WSW Nui Dat, 300 meters S FSB Susan, 2 km SE FSB South Dakota and 2 km NW FSB Cook. On 1ATF NCO trng map per John Hollett. Phuoc Tuy Pr, III Corps.
Tess, Typhoon (n/a)
See Typhoon Tess. I Corps.

Testicles, The (XT 99 40)
Between XT 97-40 and YT 01-40. Terrain feature resembling the male scrotum and formed by course of Song Be apx 10 km SE the Song Be Bridge on Rte 1A, 15 km NE FSB Holiday Inn, 22 km due E Lai Khe, 48 km NNE Saigon and 8 km S Phuoc Vinh. Aerial landmark discussed in *Low Level Hell* and on inside-cover 1st Div TAOR map. 1st Inf Div AO, '69. Bien Hoa Pr, III Corps.
Tet (n/a)
See Glossary.
Tet 68 Offensive (n/a)
Major VC/NVA offensive launched 30-31Jan68. Hit 34 of 44 provincial capitols and 5 of the 6 major cities in SVN. Tremendous psychological victory for enemy and probably single-most important factor in galvanization of US anti-war movement and eventual withdrawal of US forces from war. However, was also staggering military defeat for enemy, who failed almost completely in military objective of holding major cities and precipitating overthrow of Saigon govt. Est 80% of VC forces became casualties and VC as nationwide force was so greatly depleted that it was unable recover sufficient strength to renew major ops until perhaps '71 (Mini-Tet in May68, the exception). Of est 84,000 VC/NVA committed, apx 45,000 est KIA and 24,000 WIA (equiv to 3 entire US Divs). ARVN lost apx 2,300 KIA, while US lost apx 1,100 KIA in some of most bitter fighting of war. Also during Tet '68, acft from TF-77 (carriers *Coral Sea, Kitty Hawk, Enterprise, Ticonderoga, Ranger, Bon Homme Richard, and Oriskany*) hit targets of opportunity and mined river mouths and other strategic points along NVN coast S of Vinh in order to blunt NVA thrust. Near end of Mar68, the TF detected a 100+ truck convoy on the HCMT and 98 were destroyed. Additionally, TF-77 hit rail and vehicle bridges along vital Rte La at Long Ngoc, Thanh Hoa, and Dong Phong, as well as AFs at Haiphong and Kien An, Vinh, Ke Sat, Cat Bi, and Bai Thuong. Other targets inc power plants, rail yards, naval facilities, barracks, and heavy industrial plants at Hanoi, Haiphong, Nam Dinh, Hai Duong, Hon Gai, and Cam Pha. See Year of Decision and First, Second, and Third Offensives. SVN. [519]
Texaco, LZ? (BR 840-055)
Along QL-1, apx 2 km S Van Canh AF and 30 km SW Qui Nhon. May have been a Texaco refinery or POL site here instead of an LZ? Binh Dinh Pr, II Corps.
Texaco Textile Factory (XS 787-958)
See VinaTexaco. Gia Dinh Pr, III Corps.
Texas, FSB (YD 020-356)
Apx 33 km W Camp Evans, 20 km SE Mai Loc and 24 km SSW Quang Tri. See LZ Texas listed at YD 468-236. Quang Tri Pr, I Corps.
Texas, LZ (YD 468-236)
Apx 10 km W to WSW Ap Thanh Tan, 27 km due W Hue and 12 km SW Camp Evans. Apr70 XXIV Corps grid per Don Armstrong. Thua Thien Pr, I Corps.
Texas, LZ (ZA 082-167)
Apx 8 km WSW Plei Meun, 33 km SSW Pleiku and 26 km NE peak Chu Pong. 1st/12th Cav, 1st Cav here during Ia Drang campaign in Nov 65. Cited in *Pleiku*, p 134. Nov65. Pleiku Pr, II Corps.
Texas BOQ (XS 8-9)
At 179 Le Van Duyet, St., Saigon. Data per *Vietnam Military Lore, 1959-1973*. Gia Dinh Pr, III Corps.
Texas Star, Operation (n/a)
1Apr-5Sep70. Adjunct of Randolph Glen in which only 1 Bde of 101st Abn assumed entire responsibility for securing lowlands and training RF/RF forces while the other 2 Bdes of Div were involved in offensive ops in western Thua Thien/Quang Tri Provs. 1,782 rptd NVA/VC KIA, per *Vietnam Order of Battle*, pp 9-14. Quang Tri/Thua Thien Prvs, I Corps.
Texas Thor, FSB? (n/a)
No data. Possibly Op Texas-Thor and not a FSB?
Texas/Lien Ket 28, Operation (n/a)
20-24Mar66. USMC/ARVN/VNMC op to retake An Hoa outpost. 623 rptd NVA/VC KIA, per *Vietnam Order of Battle*, pp 9-14. Quang Nam? Pr, I Corps.
Textile Factory (XS 787-958)
See VinaTexaco. Gia Dinh Pr, III Corps.
TF (Generally)
See also Task Force and Task Group.
TF-115 (n/a)
See Task Force 115 and Market Time.
TF-116 (n/a)
See Task Force 115 and Game Warden.
TF-117 (n/a)
See Task Force 115, MRF and Mobile Riverine Force.
Tha Akatsayan Don Muang Airfield (PR 7-3)
See Don Muang AP and Bangkok Intl AP. Thailand.
Tha Bo Airfield (n/a)
Along Mekong River at Laotian border, apx 505 km NNE Bangkok, and 15 km SSW Vientiane on Feb67 Natl Geo map. El. 550'. Thailand.
Tha Lin Noi Airfield (UG 34-51)
LS-18. CIA/SF, per *Air Facilities Data-Laos.*
Tha Tam Bleung Airfield (TG 88-27)
LS-72. CIA/SF, per *Air Facilities Data-Laos.*
Tha Thom Airfield (UG 53-00)
LS-11. Apx 155 km NE Vientiane. CIA/SF facility. El. 850'. Grid per *Air Facilities Data-Laos.*
Tha Yang Airfield (n/a)
Apx 110 km SW Bangkok per Feb67 Natl Geo map. El. 40'. Thailand.
Thac Ba Camp (n/a)
Island POW Camp where US POW Bobby Garwood claims to have seen some 30 live US POWs in 1977. Discussed in *Prisoners of Hope*, p 79. NVN.
Thac Houan Repou (YT 5-5)
Rapides De Houan Repou. Rapids in the Song Dong Nai River, SW Loi Tan and perhaps 20 to 25 km NW Vo Dat. Long Khanh Pr, III Corps.
Thac Nuc Heliport (ZC 029-229)
Along QL-14, and in valley of Song Cai River apx 14 km NNE Kham Duc and 73 km due W Tam Ky. Heliport #676, alt 787', at 15°34'00"N-107°49'30"E, per Feb73 TAD. Quang Tin Pr, I Corps.
Thach Ban Airfield (AT 874-475)
See An Hoa AF Quang Nam Pr, I Corps.

Thach Han Bridge (YD 33-52)
QL-1 bridge over Thach Han River at S edge of Quang Tri. Quang Tri Pr, I Corps.
Thach Han River (YD)
A.k.a. Quang Tri River. The Cua Viet River is formed by confluence of Mieu Giang, Thach Han and Vinh Phuoc Rivers. All Join NW Quang Tri. Quang Tri Pr, I Corps.
Thach Khe (n/a)
Mapsheet name of L-7014-6836-3. SVN.
Thach Tru (BS 76-46)
Along QL-1, apx 29 km S Quang Ngai. Triangular fort here of either French or Vietnamese origin was heavily attacked by elements of 95th NVA Rgt, 325th Alpha Div, 22 Nov 65, resulting in 71 friendly KIA, 74 WIA and 175 VC KIA. At time of attack, RF/PF and 2 Cos of ARVN Ranger Bn here, with another 2 Cos nearby. Quang Ngai Pr, I Corps.
Thach Tru QL-1 Bridge (BS 771-461)
QL-1 bridge apx 9 km SSE Mo Duc and 9 km NNW Duc Pho. In mid '68, VC removed 4' x 6' decking and five 6' x 16' stringers from bridge. Quang Ngai Pr, I Corps.
Thai Binh (n/a)
Mapsheet name of L-7014-6249-1. NVN only.
Thai Binh (XH 3-6)
In Red River Delta, apx 80 km SE Hanoi. French garrison here involved in Battle of Day River, 29May-18Jun51. See *Street Without Joy*, Chp 2, with map at p 46. NVN.
Thai Binh (WJ 20-84?)
See Chan Muong Gorge. NVN.
Thai Hoa (XT 190-505)
Along Hwy 22 bypass road and at NW corner of Tay Ninh, apx 2 km E Tay Ninh West AF. Seized by NVA night of 10-11Sep68, during Battle for Tay Ninh. On 11Sep68, RF forces on N side of road made at least 4 attacks to displace NVA entrenched on S edge of road. During those attacks, and in what an AAR of the battle notes as a major curiosity of the war, 2 US convoys passed between the opposing forces but was not fired upon. [520] Tay Ninh Pr, III Corps.
Thai Nguyen (WJ 87-88)
French outpost 55 km due N Hanoi and 36 km NNE Phuc Yen and Phuc Yen AF. 21°36'00"N-105°50'00"E. NVN.
Thai Nguyen (n/a)
Apx 70 km due N Hanoi, 70 km ESE Tuyen Quang. Involved in French Op Lea, Oct47. On map in *Street Without Joy*, p 31. NVN.
Thai Thien Airfield (YS 230771)
See Phu My AF. Phuoc Tuy Pr, III Corps.
Thai Thong (XT 191-502)
See Ap Thai Thong. Tay Ninh Pr, III Corps.
Thai Thuy (n/a)
Mapsheet name of L-7014-6350-3. NVN only.
Thailand, Forces of (YS 14-98)
See Major HQs Section.
Thakhek (West) Airfield (VE 81-24)
A.k.a. L-40A, Khammouane AF, and sometimes spelled Takhek AF. On Thai border, apx 10 km NW Takhek New AF, 20 km E Nakhon Phanom major AF, apx 240 km ESE Vientiane (Laos), per ONC-J-11 and Feb67 Natl Geo maps. CIA/SF facility. Grid per *Air Facilities Data-Laos.* 4,400' rwy, El. 492' or 450'? Laos.
Thakhek New (East) Airfield (VE 85-21)
A.k.a. L-40. On Thai border, 10 km SE Takhek (old) AF and 25 km E NKP AB (Thailand), per ONC-J-11. CIA/SF facility. Grid per *Air Facilities Data-Laos.* El. 500'. Laos.
Thakhet SF Camp (VE 8-2)
Apparently at or near Thakhek AF, apx 240 km ESE Vientiane. SF camp when Lao neutrality declared, 23Jul62. FTT 20 here then. Per *Special Forces at War.* MR3, Laos.
Tham Lo Airfield (UF 11-94)
LS-316. CIA/SF, per *Air Facilities Data-Laos.*
Tham Sorm Airfield (TG 41-33)
LS-74. CIA/SF, per *Air Facilities Data-Laos.*
Than Binh SF Camp (WS 409-854)
On E bank of Mekong River, apx 27 km ENE Chau Phu, 12 km SSE Hong Ngu and 140 km due W Saigon. 5th SF. See An Long? Data per *SF Order of Battle.* Spelling variant of Thanh Binh? Thuong Pr, IV Corps.
Than Heup Airfield (TG 77-44)
LS-238. CIA/SF, per *Air Facilities Data-Laos.*
Than Phong 14, Operation (n/a)
See Paul Revere/Than Phong 14.
Than Phu (ZA 234-825)
Ville along QL-14, apx 6 km S Kontum. Ops in area Aug68. Kontum Pr, II Corps.
Than Phu Airfield (XR 370-990)
Apx 8 km WNW Tra Vinh AF/Phu Vinh. "Abnd, capable of suptg C-7 ex when wet, AF # VA4-290," in Aug69 TAD (not 73 TAD) per Frank Penk, Jr. Vinh Binh Pr, IV Corps.
Than Quit CAP (BT 0-6)
See Thanh Quyt. Quang Nam Pr, I Corps.
Than Quyt CAP (BT 0-6)
See Thanh Quyt. Quang Nam Pr, I Corps.
Than Tri Airfield (WR 760-412)
See Phu Loc AF. Ba Xuyen Pr, IV Corps.
Than Uyen (n/a)
Mapsheet name of L-7014-5752-1. NVN only.
Than Uyen Airfield (UK 8-3)
Apx 225 km WNW of Hanoi. Feb67 Natl Geo map. El. 1,903'. NVN.
Thang Binh (BT164-414)
Apx 27 km NW Tam Ky, 36 km SSE Da Nang AB, 16 km S Hoi An and 2 km W QL-1. LSA (Log Supt Area) manned by elements of USMC BLT 2d/7th plus 4th/11th Arty was at a Thang Binh during Op Harvest Moon, per *Utter's Battalion*, p 188. Home of ARVN HQ in at least Dec65, for units such as 1st Bn, 5th ARVN Rgt, 11th ARVN Ranger Bn. [521] Also listed at BT 175-419. Map is L-7014-6640-2. Quang Tin Pr, I Corps.
Thang Binh, FSB (BT 17-42?)
If grid correct, was near Thang Binh, apx 27 km NW Tam Ky, 2 km W QL-1. Americal List. Quang Tin Pr, I Corps I.
Thang Long, FSB (XU 510-040)
At NW end of Fishhook, apx 3 km from SVN border, 23 km WSW Loc Ninh, 22 km ENE Katum and 23 km ESE Memot. Possible FSB or simply ville used for Incursion. Elements of 11th ACR and 1st Cav apparently here sometime in May-Jun70. Grid per *11th ACR Cambodia Invasion AAR, 1st Cav Div, May-Jun70*, courtesy Lou Rochat. [522] Cambodia.

Thang Phong II, Operation (n/a)
See Masher/White Wing, Op.
Thanh Am (n/a)
Thanh An? Mapsheet name of L-7014-6351-1. NVN only.
Thanh An (ZA 10-27)
Site of Oasis and Oasis AF. Pleiku Pr, II Corps.
Thanh An (Le Thanh) (n/a)
Mapsheet name of L-7014-6536-4. SVN.
Thanh Binh Heliport (WS 545-660)
Along LTL-30, apx 21 km NNE Long Xuyen, and 18 km NW Cao Lanh AF. "Heliport #677, alt 10', sod (hard), at 10°33'00"N-105°29'40"E," per Feb73 TAD. Kien Phong Pr, IV Corps.
Thanh Binh Pass (ZA 10-33?)
NVA infiltration point and withdrawal rte near Duc Co. Blocked by 173d Abn during op in Aug-Sep65. See *Dak To*, p 27. Pleiku Pr?, II Corps.
Thanh Dien Forest? (XT 15-40?)
Heavily forested area generally 10 to 15 km SW Tay Ninh. May or may not be correct name. AO of 25th Inf Div. Tay Ninh Pr, III Corps.
Thanh Dien Forestry Preserve (XT 60-50)
Jungle reserve in War Zone D that is N of Ben Suc, NE the Boi Loi Woods, 7 km W and NW Ben Cat and 10 km W Lai Khe. 25th Inf Div and 196th LIB AO, swept during Op Cedar Falls, Jan-Feb67. Binh Duong Pr, III Corps.
Thanh Giao (n/a)
Resettlement ville in 4th Div AO, '68. Pleiku Pr?, II Corps.
Thanh Hai (n/a)
Mapsheet name of L-7014-6832-3. SVN.
Thanh Hoa (n/a)
Mapsheet name of L-7014-6148-1. NVN only.
Thanh Hoa (WG 82-90)
Coastal ville apx 150 km S Hanoi and 15 km inland. Considered by NVA as starting point of HCMT. Rail and vehicle bridges here hit by Carrier TF-77 attempts to blunt NVA Tet '68 Offensive. See Ham Rong Bridge. NVN.
Thanh Hoa A, B & C (XT 85-10)
Hamlets at XT 852-103, 855-104 and 847-100 respectively. Along QL-4, apx 4 km NE Tan Son Nhut AB. Mar69. Gia Dinh Pr, III Corps.
Thanh Hoa Heliport (BT 328-115)
Apx 10 km due S Tam Ky and 8 km W Diem Pho and QL-1. Heliport #678, alt 66'. 73 TAD. Quang Tin Pr, I Corps.
Thanh Hoa Prison (YT 0-1 or 1-1?)
See Ho Nai Prison. Bien Hoa Pr?, III Corps.
Thanh Hoa Province (BP/CP)
In what later became known as II Corps. Appears to have been renamed or absorbed into what became primarily Khanh Hoa Pr. Thought to have ceased existence shortly before/during early US presence in SVN? Actual dates of existence unknown. II Corps.
Thanh Hoa RR/Hwy Bridge (WG 83-93)
A.k.a. the Ham Rong Bridge and Dragon's Jaw. A 56' wide bridge across the Song Ma River at Thanh Hoa. Carried country's only N-S rail line and its main N-S hwy, QL-1. Heavily attacked by US acft, 3Apr65, the same day Dong Thuong Bridge was attacked. Despite heavy bombing beginning in '67, this bridge did not fall until 13May72, during Op Linebacker and with 1st-ever combat-use of "Smart Bombs." NVN.
Thanh Hung (WS 919-420?)
Town at 10°00'00"N-105°23'00"E. On map NC48-06. Thanh Hung also listed in XS and WR grid zones. Kien Giang Pr, IV Corps.
Thanh Lam, Dam (YD 8-2)
Lagoon at 16°31'N-107°41'E. On NE48-16 JOG. Thua Thien Pr, I Corps.
Thanh Lam, Lagune de (YD 8-2)
Dam Thanh Lam. Lagoon at 16°31'N-107°41'E. On NE48-16 JOG. Thua Thien Pr, I Corps.
Thanh Mai, FSB (BN 019-172)
Apx 18 km ENE Phan Thiet, 4 km NNE Ap Thien Son and 600 meters E of Ap Phu Hiep and Hill 208. Name/grid per Jerry Berry. Binh Thuan Pr, II Corps.
Thanh My (various)
Common Viet place-name. Sites inc: AT 9-5, BT 103-508, 454-033; BP 952-788; WS 838-048, WR 4-8, 7-9, 740-895; XR 4-8, XS 9-9, YS 16-6575, ZC 0-4, 026-439; ZS 2-8, 139-865. All SVN.
Thanh My Heliport (ZC 026-439)
Along QL-14, apx 8 km WNW Phuoc Binh AF, and 10 km SW An Hoa. Heliport #679, alt 66', at 15°45'30"N-107°50'00"E, per Feb73 TAD. Quang Nam Pr, I Corps.
Thanh My Tay Outpost (XS 873-935)
Along W edge Saigon and W bank of the Song Saigon, apx 8 km ESE Tan Son Nhut. Feb68. Gia Dinh Pr, III Corps.
Thanh Noi (Hue City) AF (YD 748-230)
See Hue (Thanh Noi) Airfield. Thua Thien Pr, I Corps.
Thanh Pho Ho Chi Minh (Saigon) (XS)
Mapsheet name of L-7014-6330-4. SVN.
Thanh Phong (XR 760-863)
At mouth of tributary of the Mekong River, apx 30 km WSW Tra Vinh AF/Phu Vinh, and 100 km due S Saigon. Bob Kerrey (MOH, later US Senator and candidate for Pres) led Navy Seal mission here night of 25Feb69, in which apparently 13-20 unarmed civilians died when his unit is said to have returned enemy fire and later discovered the tragic results. Kien Hoa Pr, IV Corps.
Thanh Phu Heliport (XR 668-999)
Along TL-30, apx 19 km E Tra Vinh AF/Phu Vinh and 48 km SSE My Tho, near mouth of Mekong. "Heliport #680, alt 10' soccer field," per 73 TAD. Kien Hoa Pr, IV Corps.
Thanh Phu Secret Zone (XS/XR)
Bty A and B, 34th Arty established 2 FSBs in this VC AO, Nov68. On23Nov, Bty A made 1st arty transit of Mo Cay Ville. 3d/34th suptd 8 major ops during Nov68. In 2 mortar attacks, its C Bty working off paddy platforms at Giong Trom, suffered 1 KIA and 6 WIA. Newly established "Eagle Prep" technique used widely as 3rd/34th smothered helo LZs with prep fire. Cited in An Hist Rpt of 3d/34th Arty for 1Apr68-31Jan69, on MRF Assn Website at: www.mrfa.org3_34th. htm. Kien Hoa Pr, IV Corps.
Thanh Quit (BT 042-622)
See Thanh Quyt. Quang Nam Pr, I Corps.
Thanh Quyt CAP (BT 04-62)
CAP 2-7-2, 2-7-4 per CAP website at www.capmarinecom. Dien Banh District, Quang Nam Pr, I Corps.
Thanh Quyt (1) CAP (BT 04-62)
See CAP 2-7-2. 2d CAG. Quang Nam Pr, I Corps.
Thanh Quyt (2) & (5) CAP (BT 04-62)
CAP 2-7-4. 2d CAG. Quang Nam Pr, I Corps.

Thanh Quyt (3) CAP (BT 04-62)
CAP 2-7-4 per CAP Website. Dien Banh District, Quang Nam Pr, I Corps.

Thanh Quyt (5) CAP (BT 04-62)
CAP 2-7-4 per CAP Website. Dien Banh District, Quang Nam Pr, I Corps.

Thanh Quyt River (AT/BT)
A.k.a. Song Thanh Quit. The Cau Do, Yen, Tuy Loan La Tho, Thanh Quyt, Vu Gia, Cau Lau and Thu Bon Rivers all formed part of drainage that becomes the Da Nang River. All were S or SW Da Nang. Quang Nam Pr, I Corps.

Thanh Son 2, Battle of (BS 858-120?)
6-7May66, during Op Davey Crockett. Described as having been N of Bong Son. Listed grid is from NPIA and, if correct, is apx 16 km N Bong Son, 5 km SW Gia An, 3 km SW Mahoney AF and 5 km W QL-1. Involved 2d/7th Cav and NVA's Qyet Tan Rgt/325th NVA Div. Discussed in *Baptism*, Chp 25 (entitled *Bong Son II*). Est 355 NVA KIA, 22 POW. Binh Dinh Pr, II Corps.

Thanh Taxy CAP (BT 169-578)
See CAP 2-4-3. Quang Nam Pr, I Corps.

Thanh Tay CAP (BT 169-578)
See Thanh Taxy CAP. Quang Nam Pr, I Corps.

Thanh Tay Relocation Camp (BT 124-571)
Just NW of Hoi An, apx 21 km SSE Da Nang AB and 6 km E QL-1. Jul68. Quang Nam Pr, I Corps.

Thanh Tri SF Camp (XS 0575-9953)
A.k.a. FOB Moc Hoa. Apx 3 km from Cambodia, 10 km NNE Moc Hoa AF and 75 km W Saigon. 5th SF CIDG Det A-414, Mar68. Transferred to 67th ARVN Border Rangers. Grid per *SF Order of Battle.* Kien Tuong Pr, IV Corps.

Thap Cham Airfield (BN 772-862)
See Phan Rang AF. Ninh Thuan Pr, II Corps.

That Khe (XK)
Mapsheet name of L-7014-6253-1. NVN only.

That Khe Airfield (XK 52-62)
Apx 150 km NE-NNE Hanoi. El. 596'. NVN.

That Khe Outpost (XK 52-62?)
Along R.C. 4 in northern Tonkin, between Cao Bang and Lang Son, apx 150 km NE-NNE Hanoi, 53 km NW Lang Son, 48 km from Cao Bang and 15 km W China. Frontier outpost of French War. 3d Colonial Paras pushed out from this fort to meet Col Charton at PK-28, after Charton was forced to abandon Cao Bang. See Cao Bang. NVN.

That Son Airfield (WS 027-635)
NE the Dop Chompa hill mass, apx 12 km from Cambodia, 22 km SSW Chau Duc AF, 60 km ENE Ha Tien, 58 km NNW Rach Gia and 53 km NW Xuyen Long AF, 180 km WSW Saigon. Per TPC K-10D. El. 100', 2,000' steel-mat rwy. At 10°31'38"N-105°01'29"E. Chau Doc Pr, IV Corps.

That Son Heliport (WS 020-650)
NE the Dop Chompa hill mass, apx 12 km from Cambodia, 22 km SSW Chau Duc AF, 180 km WSW Saigon. "Heliport #681, alt 30', sod, N side of rwy in grass, at 10°32'15"N-105°01'00"E," per Feb73 TAD. See That Son AF. Chau Doc Pr, IV Corps.

That Son SF Camp (WS 027-636)
NE the Dop Chompa hill mass, apx 12 km from Cambodia, 22 km SSW Chau Duc AF, 180 km WSW Saigon. Camp used as model for fictional base of Phan Chau in Robin Moore's *The Green Berets* and focus of John Wayne movie of same name. The actual cmdr at time of Moore's visit was Capt. Larry Thorney, a Finnish Natl later MIA in Cambodia. 5th SF. Info/grid per *SF Order of Battle.* See akso Chi Lang and Phan Chau. Chau Doc Pr, IV Corps.

Thateng Airfield (XC 48-07)
LS-210. CIA/SF, per *Air Facilities Data-Laos.*

Thayer II, Operation (n/a)
25Oct66-12Feb67. 1st Cav op in coastal plains and Kim Son and Luoi Ci Valleys. 1,757 NVA/VC KIA, per *Vietnam Order of Battle*, pp 9-14. Binh Dinh Pr, II Corps.

Thbeng Meanchy Airfield (VA)
Apx 12 km SW Thbeng Meanchy AF, 55 km S the Thai border. Per TPC K-10A. Cambodia. El. 330'.

The (place name) (various)
See formal name of objective its alpha listing. Most such entries are listed last-name first, followed by a comma, then word "The" as in "Catcher's Mitt, The."

The' Bai Mountain (YD 629-223)
See OP Apache. Thua Thien Pr, I Corps.

The Hill Radio Relay (AP 822-990)
Apx 3 km due S Ban Me Thuot, 5 km S Ban Me Thuot City AF and 7 km WSW Ban Me Thuot East AF. Per SF expert Steve Sherman, The Hill was 2 km south of SOG CCS and SOG CCS's radio relay site. Darlac Pr, II Corps.

The List of Adrian Messenger (XS 8-9)
See Kinh Do Movie Theater. Gia Dinh Pr, III Corps.

Thelma, LZ (n/a)
Location unknown. Cited in *Dispatches*, p. 10. SVN.

Theodore E. Chandler, USS (n/a)
DD-717. 7th Flt Destroyer, per Ralph Fries.

Thi Ngu Yen (n/a)
Mapsheet name of L-7014-6152-2. NVN only.

Thi Thi Tea Plantation (AR 785-390)
A.k.a. Nguyan (or Nguyen?) Thi Thi Plantation. Tea plantation to N of Camp Enari. Pleiku Pr, II Corps.

Thi Tinh River (XT)
N to S flowing river that originates NW of Lai Khe, passes Ben Cat and generally parallels QL-13 until its confluence with the Song Saigon 25 km NNW Saigon. Per *Low Level Hell's* 1st Div TAOR map. III Corps.

Thich Tam Chau (n/a)
See Glossary.

Thien Ngon Airfield (XT 084-815)
Apx 25 km WSW Katum, 7 km S Cambodia, 34 km NNW Tay Ninh. Per TPC K-10D. El. 66', 2,900' laterite/steel-mat rwy. At 11°35'31"N-105°59'38"E. Also listed at XT 086-813. Tay Ninh Pr, III Corps.

Thien Ngon CIDG Camp (XT 087-814)
Apx 25 km WSW Katum, 7 km S Cambodia, 34 km NNW Tay Ninh. Attacked 1Se68 during Battle for Tay Ninh. 5th SF Grp CIDG Det A-323, Feb68. Transferred to 73rd ARVN Border Rangers, per *SF Order of Battle,* which lists grid at XT 0869-8162. Co A 5th SF Grp received twenty 122mm rockets and sixty 82mm mortar rnds in one incident, suffering 6 KIA, and employed Spooky to repulse enemy. [523] Tay Ninh Pr, III Corps.

Thien Ngon SF Camp (XT 087-816)
Apx 35 km NNW Tay Ninh. Hit by 400 rounds mortar fire on 26Sep68, then by ground attack of 271st NVA/VC Rgt resulting in 2 US KIA and 11 WIA. Grid on AAR, 5th SF Grp CIDG Det A-323, Feb68. Battle of Tay Ninh (17Aug-

27Sep68), HQ 25th ID, 2Feb69, per Butch Sincock. Tay Ninh Pr, III Corps.

Thien Ngon, FSB (XT 086-813)
Apx 25 km WSW Katum, 7 km S Cambodia, 34 km NNW Tay Ninh. SF CIDG Camp. 105s here suptg FSB Illingworth when it was attacked by Bn of NVA 272d Rgt, 1Apr70. Tay Ninh Pr, III Corps.

Thien Nhan, Nui (WF 5-5)
Mtn range at 18°34'N-105°32'E. Grid per DMA L-1501 map NE48-07. NVN.

Thien Phuoc Heliport (BT 113-137)
See Tien Phuoc Heliport. Quang Tin Pr, I Corps.

Thien Phuoc SF Camp (BT 105-102)
See Tien Phuoc SF Camp. Quang Tin Pr, I Corps.

Thies, Plantation de (XT 3-4)
A.k.a. Don Dien Thies and Don Dien Cau Khoi. Generally about 10 km E Tay Ninh and 14 km due W Dau Tieng. Tay Ninh Pr, III Corps.

Thiet Son (n/a)
Mapsheet name of L-7014-6244-4. NVN only.

Thieu Hoa (Tri Can) (n/a)
Mapsheet name of L-7014-6148-4. NVN only.

Thinh Tri Quang (n/a)
See Glossary.

Third Country Nationals (n/a)
See Glossary.

Third Offensive (n/a)
See Glossary.

Third Vietnam, The (n/a)
See Glossary.

Thirty Minute Island (BN 63-42)
See 30 Minute Island. Binh Tuan Pr, II Corps.

Thistle, LZ (BS 641-278 or BR 641-278?)
If "BS" grid correct, then site was apx 10 km ESE Ba To New AF, 3 km W Con Doc and 19 km SW Duc Pho AF/QL-1. 1st Cav. If grid properly "BR," then site was apx 43 km W and slightly N of Qui Nhon. Listed grid per Dan Gillotti, 15th Arty Assn. Quang Ngai Pr, I Corps.

Tho An (BS 474-954)
Apx 13 km SW Chu Lai. See LZ Thrush for more detail. Quang Tin Pr, I Corps.

Tho Binh, LZ (BR 845-945)
Apx 3 km SW of Bong Son and 4 km W of QL-1. Binh Dinh Pr, II Corps.

Tho Duc SF Camp (XT 958-001 or YT 5-1?)
Possible sp variant of Thu Duc? If Thu Duc correct, see Thu Duc SF Camp for detail. If Tho Duc is correct, then grid possibly in YT 5-1, and apx 10 km SE Xuan Loc. Tho Duc sp in DA Chief, Mil Hist records summary which also indicates Det A-413 here '64. Gia Dinh or Long Khanh Pr?, III Corps?

Tho Lam (YT 7-4?)
Typical French *de Lattre Line* Bunker position here, per *Street Without Joy*, p 177. NVN.

Thoampoi Island (US 95-05?)
See An Thoampoi island. Kien Giang Pr, IV Corps.

Thoeng Airfield (PB 3-7)
At 19°41'00"N-100°15'00"E, apx 665 km N Bangkok and 25 km from Lao border. NIMA data. El. 1,500'. Thailand.

Thoi Binh (n/a)
Mapsheet name of L-7014-6027-4. SVN.

Thoi Binh (WR 12-33?)
If grid correct, was apx 3 km SE Ap Thoi Duc and 20 km NNW Quan Long City/AF. Thoi Binh District HQ and ARVN outpost holding two 155mm howitzers in '63. Map is L-7014-6027-4. An Xuyen Pr, IV Corps.

Thoi Binh Heliport (WR 109-335)
Apx 20 km NNW Quan Long and 68 km due S Rach Gia. "Heliport #730, alt 10', Pad on west end of sod strip. Arty position to W," per Feb73 TAD. An Xuyen Pr, IV Corps.

Thoi Hoa Airfield (WS 477-155)
Apx 30 km ENE Rach Gia and 48 km WNW Can Tho. "Flight Serv, contact G3 Air, IV Corps TOC MACV 5Jul68, AF # VA4-174," per Aug69 TAD courtesy Frank Penk, Jr. Not in Feb73 TAD. Phong Dinh Pr, IV Corps.

Thoi Son Island (XS 4-4?)
In the My Tho River S of Dong Tam. If grid correct, Thoi Son isle was roughly 1 km x 300 meters, with center of mass apx 5 km WSW My Tho. Cordoned and searched by 9th Div MRF, 3Jan69, during Op Water Trap, 3-7Jan69. Dinh Tuong Pr, IV Corps.

Thom Tchay (n/a)
Mapsheet name of L-7014-6154-3. NVN only.

Thomas Open Mess (XS 8-9)
See Murrel D. Thomas Open Mess. Gia Dinh Pr, III Corps.

Thomaston, USS (n/a)
LSD-28. Served with 7th fleet, 22Apr-5May63, and again Aug-Sep63. In Nov64, moved a dredge from Saigon to Da Nang. Was at initial landings of USMC at Da Nang and Chu Lai, Apr65, leaving WESTPAC in Jun65. She again arrived SVN waters, 5 Feb66, operating around Chu Lai and Da Nang. During Op Deckhouse III, she landed Marines N Vung Tau and then acting as primary control ship in Op Deckhouse IV, landing Marines just S the DMZ, and also operated convoys carrying supplies apx 16 km up the Cua Vet River to Dong Ha. In Mar67, she returned to SVN after stay in Philippines. During Op Deckhouse V, on 5Jan67, she dropped anchor off mouth of Song Co Chien River and oversaw ops aimed at delta of Kien Hoa Pr. Was relieved at Vung Tau by *Point Defiance* (LSD-31) on 6Mar67. After major overhaul at San Diego, she joined Amphib Ready Grp off I Corps, Feb68. During Mar68, she made supply runs between Da Nang and Cam Ranh Bay in supt SLF, and also suptd 1st Cav and 101st Abn at Thon My Thuy (Wunder Beach). She later joined Op Badger Catch III (withdrawal of SLF from Cua Viet River), then Op Swift Sabre (near Da Nang 8Jun68); then Op Eager Yankee, 9Jul68; then Swift Play (S Da Nang) during which she came under shore battery fire briefly. For next 5 years, she conducted troop and cargo lifts in SVN and, during her 15th WESTPAC deployment, SVN finally fell. On 2Mar75, she departed Subic Bay for Op Eagle Pull (evac of Cambodia), but on 5Apr75 was ordered to Phu Quoc Island to assist evacuees from Da Nang area, transferring food and medical supplies via LCU's and LCM-8s to refugees on MSC vessels anchored there. Op Eagle Pull began 11Apr75, with ship as plane guard on station to S. On 18Apr75, she was diverted from Philippines to assist in evac of Saigon, Op Frequent Wind, which began 19Apr75, during which she boarded 811 Vietnamese in 9 hours and

landed evac helos as large as CH-46's. She returned to San Diego 6Jun75. Data per http://lsd-28.homepage.com/ history.html. See also Op Eagle Pull.

Thompson Compound (CP 04-33)
US Army cantonment at Dong Ba Thin AF, apx 4 km NW Cam Ranh Bay AB. HQ 97th MP Bn. Named to honor Maj. Farley D. Thompson. While inspecting MP facilities in his AO, Thompson became ill with fever and was medevaced to Philippines where he died, 23Dec66. Beloved by his men, the cmpd was renamed only days later but not dedicated until 2Jul67. Data per *Vietnam Military Lore, 1959-1973*. Khanh Hoa Pr, II Corps.

Thon An Thai (YD 36-54?)
Ville just E of Quang Tri. On 1Feb68, after NVA/VC had taken Quang Tri, 4 Cos of 1st/5th and 1st/12th Cav, 1st Cav, began their attack to liberate Quang Tri here during Battle for Quang Tri. Tet '68. Grid apx. NIMA Gaz indicates site was near 16°44'00"N-107°13'00"E and in UTM YD 3-5. Quang Tri Pr, I Corps.

Thon Bach Thach CAP (ZD 038-023)
On S side of QL-1, apx 20 km SE Phu Bai, 2 km WSW FSB Roy and within 1 km of shore of Dam Cau Hai Bay. Hotel 4, 3rd CAG per CAP Website. Phu Loc District, Thua Thien Pr, I Corps.

Thon Ben Tau (YC 890-990)
Apx 18 km due W Phu Loc and 15 km due S Phu Bai. Position of 82d Abn in '68. Thua Thien Pr, I Corps.

Thon Dien Sanh (Hai Lang) (n/a)
Mapsheet L-7014-6442-2. Full sheet name is: Hai Lang (Thon Dien Sanh)

Thon Doc Kinh (n/a)
Mapsheet name of L-7014-6342-2. SVN/Laos.

Thon Ha Vung (Ba Long) (n/a)
Mapsheet name of L-7014-6442-3. Full sheet name: Ba Long (Thon Ha Vung). SVN.

Thon Huynh An (YD 882-172)
See CAP Alpha 1. Thua Thien Pr, I Corps.

Thon Khe Tri Mountain (XD 979-559)
See Rockpile. Quang Tri Pr, I Corps.

Thon Kim Doi (YD 754-313)
Apx 8 km W Tan My/Eagle Beach, 1.5 km E the N bank Song Huong, 2 km N point where Song Bo River joins the Song Huong and 6 km N Hue. During Op Carentan II, Apr68, the 2d/501st Inf, 101st Abn, followed 2 VC here and were ambushed by NVA Co. 101st Abn's 2d Bde then cordoned ville and airstikes/arty accounted for 100 NVA KIA. Thua Thien Pr, I Corps.

Thon La Chu (YD 694-244)
Ville apx 4 km WNW the NW corner Hue Citadel, 7 km SE LZ Sally and 1.5 km SW QL-1. Major battle here Feb68, with NVA protecting their N flank after occupying Hue, and 3d Bde/1st Cav with 2d Bde/101st Abn attached, during Battle for Hue. 2/12th Cav, 1st Cav, with C Bty/1st 77th Arty, suptg from PK-17, saw extremely heavy fighting here. Thua Thien Pr, I Corps.

Thon Ma Ty (n/a)
Mapsheet name of L-7014-6732-1. SVN.

Thon Mai Dang CAP (YD 3-4?)
Was apparently S of and within 10 km of Quang Tri. Listed as Phon Mai Dang at CAP website but possible correct sp is Thon Mai Dang or Mai Dang Phuong? CAP 4-2-8, 4th CAG per Tim Duffie. Quang Tri Pr, I Corps.

Thon Me Thuy (XK 7-0?)
Bombing target? Significance unknown. NVN.

Thon My Chanh Bridge (YD 460-400)
A.k.a. Rao Thac Ma Bridge. On Ql-1 across Rao Thac Ma River, apx 9 km SE Hai Lang, 9 km NW Phong Dien and 20 km NW An Lo Bridge. Map is L-7014-6442-2, per Ken Burrington. Quang Tri/Thua Thien Pr border, I Corps.

Thon My Chanh (YD 465-403)
Along QL-1, apx 9 km SE Hai Lang. See My Chanh. Quang Tri Pr, I Corps.

Thon Ngo Xa Dong (n/a)
Mapsheet name of L-7014-6442-1. SVN.

Thon Sam Lam (XD 996-560)
See Thon Son Lam. Quang Tri Pr, I Corps.

Thon Son Hai (n/a)
Mapsheet name of L-7014-6831-4. SVN.

Thon Son Lam (XD 996-560)
Possible FSB or security position here? Hamlet on W side of Rte 9 where it turned S above Ca Lu and LZ Stud, SE of the Rockpile and 14 km WSW Cam Lo. Near 16°46'00"N-106°52'00"E. Apr70 XXIV Corps grid per Don Armstrong. Quang Tri Pr, I Corps.

Thon Tan To CAP (YD 916-157)
See CAP Alpha 2. Thua Thien Pr, I Corps.

Thoan Thang 43/Rockcrusher (n/a)
The invasion of southern Cambodian, May-Jun70. See Task Force Shoemaker. Cambodia.

Thon To Da CAP (YD 916-157)
See CAP Alpha 2. Thua Thien Pr, I Corps.

Thon Trung Kien (n/a)
Mapsheet name of L-7014-6641-4. SVN.

Thon Van Xa (YD 665-280)
Ville/AF just S of the Song Bo River, apx 12 km NW Hue and on the E side of QL-1. Was just W of Van Xa AF/LZ Sally. Map is L-7014-6442-2. Thua Thien Pr, I Corps.

Thon Vu Bon (n/a)
Mapsheet name of L-7014-6731-1. SVN.

Thon Xuan Hoa Heliport (YD 111-700)
See Xuan Hoa Heliport. Quang Tri Pr, I Corps.

Thong Bon Tri (YD 695-218)
Apx 2 km NW the Song Huong (Perfume) River, 4 km W Hue and 1.5 km NE peak of Nui Nha Nhan. On *Hue-A Shau Valley* map in *The Rise and Fall of the American Army*, between pp 368-9. Thua Thien Pr, I Corps.

Thong Khamo Airfield (n/a)
Apx 40 km SSW Luang Prabang. El. 2,100'. Laos.

Thong Khen Airfield (TF 95-90)
LS-317. CIA/SF, per *Air Facilities Data-Laos.*

Thong Miang Airfield (TF 89-87)
LS-266. CIA/SF, per *Air Facilities Data-Laos.*

Thong Nhat Piers (BT 03-84)
A.k.a. Thong Nhat (Allied) Piers. Apx 7 km WNW Red Beach and 7 km NNE Da Nang AB. Docking facility at W end of Tien Sha Peninsula and immed N the Market Time Swift Boat Base. On map in *The Marines in Vietnam 1954-1973*, p 238. Quang Nam Pr, I Corps.

Thong Noi Airfield (TF 94-83)
LS-330. CIA/SF, per *Air Facilities Data-Laos.*

Thonh Gia Le CAP (YD 821-183)
See Gia Le CAP. Thua Thien Pr, I Corps.
Thop Cham Airfield (BN 772-862)
See Phan Rang AF. Ninh Thuan Pr, II Corps.
Thor, FSB (XU 912-284)
On border apx 6 km due W Bu Dop, 28 km NE Loc Ninh, 26 km ESE Snuol and 4 km SSW FSB Ramada. Grid in *11th ACR Cambodia Invasion AAR, 1st Cav Div, May-Jun70*, per Lou Rochat. [524] Per Peter Cole, is in *1st Cav Div Op Rept for May-Jul70*, p 37, 38, and 1st Cav *Yearbook*, Aug 65/Dec69. Phuoc Long Pr/Cambodia. III Corps.
Thor, FSB (YC 665-835)
On W side of the S end of the A Shau Valley and overlooking "Yellow Brick Road" apx 8 km E Be Loung, 38 km SSW Hue and 14 km ESE FSB Fury. Apr70 XXIV Corps grid per Don Armstrong. Thua Thien Pr, I Corps.
Thor, LZ/FSB (XD 898-403)
A.k.a. LZ Mark. Along QL-9 at Ra Co Ap, apx 6 km ESE Khe Sanh CB and 3 km W LZ Mike. 2d/7th Cav, 1st CA'd here, Op Pegasus, 1-8Apr68. Quang Tri Pr, I Corps. [525]
Thornton, FSB (YS 358-716)
Apx 8 km WNW Nui Dat, 4 km NNW Nui Thi and 10 km SE FSB Nelson. Named to honor New Zealand's "Gunner General," CDS LtGen Sir Leonard Thornton, who became NZ's Chief of Defense, '68. [526] Was apparently an arty gunner in his early years of service. 161 Bty, RNZA (Hitching's Bty 14Apr68-18Mar69) FSB set here 21-23Apr68. On 1ATF NCO trng map per John Hollett. Also listed at YS 350-710. Phuoc Tuy Pr, III Corps.
Thot Not Heliport (WS 588-352)
On W bank of Mekong River, apx 25 km WSW Sa Dec AF and 11 km SE Long Xuyen AF. "Heliport #683, alt 7' sod. VC to S." At 10°16'15"N-105°32'00"E, per 73 TAD. An Giang Pr, IV Corps.
Thot Not Operations (n/a)
See Daniel Boone Operations in Glossary.
Thousand Ghost Valley (YA 93-04)
See Valley of a Thousand Ghosts and Ia Drang River. Pleiku Pr, II Corps.
Thoy Dong Airfield (WS 477-155)
See Thoi Hoa AF. Phong Dinh Pr, IV Corps.
Three, LZ (BN 825-585)
See 3, LZ. Ninh Thuan Pr, II Corps.
Three Bees, The (n/a)
See Glossary.
Three Church, LZ/FSB (YA 850-455?)
See Three Tango. Pleiku Pr, II Corps.
Three Forks Area (YD 500-120)
Apx 25 km WSW Hue. Point where Song Bo, Rao La and Rao Trang Rivers meet. Grid per Dan Gillotti, 15th Arty Assn. Thua Thien Pr, I Corps.
Three Frontiers, Fort (YU 6-5)
See Fort of the Three Frontiers. Quang Duc Pr, II Corps.
Three Sisters (YD 810-184)
A.k.a. Hill 78, FSB Three Sister and/or OP Three Sisters? On small, 3-peaked outcropping 300 meters SW QL-1, apx 3 km SE Hue, 1 km NW Gia Le, and 8 km NW Phu Bai. Listed at YD 808-186 on 101st Abn inactive FSB list per Don Armstrong. Thua Thien Pr, I Corps.
Three Sisters, FSB (YD 808-186)
See Three Sisters. Thua Thien Pr, I Corps.
Three Sisters Mountain (YD 068-653)
Apx 30 km NW Quang Tri and 8 km NW Cam Lo/QL-9. Mar67. Quang Tri Pr, I Corps.
Three Sisters, OP (YD 808-186)
See Three Sisters. Thua Thien Pr, I Corps.
Three Tango, LZ/FSB (YA 450-455?)
A.k.a. LZ 3t and LZ Three Church? If grid correct, was appx 3 km SW Plei Djereng New AF, 2 km S of Rte 567 and 38 km W of Pleiku. 1st/22d Inf, 4th Div in '66-67. Picture and discussion at http://grunt.space.swri.edu/LouTplei.htm. Possibly named after call-sign of A/1st/22d Inf. Apparently also an SF camp nearby. Listed grid is for an LZ 3t, Mar-Apr67. Pleiku Pr, II Corps.
Thrush, LZ (BT 190-140)
Apx 13 km SW Tam Ky and 8 km ENE Tien Phuoc AF. Feb66. Quang Tin Pr, I Corps.
Thrush, LZ (BS 48-95)
Apx 400 meters E(?) Tho An, and 13 km SW Chu Lai. Open 19-20Apr66. F/2d/7th Marines in battle here. See *Utter's Battalion*, p 301-310 for detailed account. Quang Tin Pr, I Corps.
Thrush, LZ (XD 948-474)
On the Dong Ca Lu hill mass, apx 5 km WSW Ca Lu and 11 km ENE Khe Sanh CB. Apr70 XXIV Corps grid per Don Armstrong. Quang Tri Pr, I Corps.
Thrust, FSB (XT 499-800)
Along Rte 244, apx 1,500 meters S its junction with Rte 246, 12 km SE Bo Tuc, 7 km SE Ap Gu, 28 km WSW An Loc and 5 km from Cambodia. Built by 173d Abn beginning 29Mar67. Fired supt for LZ George during Battle of Ap Gu, 31Mar-1Apr67, during Op Junction City. Also XT 499-800. Tay Ninh Pr, III Corps.
Thrust, FSB (YS 499-548)
Along S edge Rte 326, apx 23 km NE Vung Tau, 4 km S Dat Do, 4 km NW of the coast and 15 km SSE Nui Dat. Built 1 Mar69, as model FSB and upon sand so dazzling "gunners formed permanent squints." 161 Bty, RNZA (Horsford's Bty 18Mar69-18Sep69) base set here 11May-15Jun69. 9 RAR also here. Hit by 30 mortar rounds, 5Jun69, resulting in 1 9RAR KIA and 9 WIA. 40' high, sandbagged NOD tower here was nicknamed "Leaning Tower of Pisa." [527] On 1ATF NCO trng map per John Hollett. Also listed at YS 50-54. Phuoc Tuy Pr, III Corps.
Thu Bon River (AT/BT)
Cau Do, Yen, Tuy Loan La Tho, Thanh Quyt, Vu Gia, Cau Lau and Thu Bon Rivers all formed drainage that became Da Nang River. All were just S or SW Da Nang. Quang Nam Pr, I Corps.
Thu Dat Mot (XT 86-16)
A.k.a. Phu Loi. Ville apx 32 km N Saigon and home of MACV Advsy Teams 70 and 91. Crocker Cmpd here. Binh Duong Pr, III Corps.
Thu Dau Mot Airfield (XT 862-158)
See Phu Loi AF. Binh Duong Pr, III Corps.
Thu Duc (XS 922-997)
Along QL-1, apx 10 km NE Tan Son Nhut, 7 km SW Di An and 13 km SSW Bien Hoa AB. Home of 5th SF Grp Det B-56 (Project Sigma), 5th SF Grp, Det. A-413, Dec64, Ho Ngoc Tau CIDG SF Camp, 4th/12th, 199th LIB. Cav task force of students and faculty from SVN Armor School here defeated VC elements in this Saigon Suburb during

Tet '68, during difficult street fighting. Cordoned by 2d/16th Inf, 1st Inf Div, 11Dec66. Elements of 4th/12th, 199th LIB also here. Also listed at XS 91-00 and XS 95-94. Gia Dinh Pr, III Corps.

Thu Duc 2, FSB? (XT or YT 91-00?)
If in XT, was apx 9 km ENE Tan Son Nhut AB in Gia Dinh Pr. If in YT, was at SE base of Hill 234, apx 17 km NNW Ham Tan in Binh Tuy Pr?, 4th/12thInf, 199th LIB here at one time. III Corps.

Thu Duc Heliport (XT 922-000)
Apx 10 km ENE Tan Son Nhut AB. "Heliport #761, alt 30', wood and sand pad in soccer field, center of town," per Feb73 TAD. Gia Dinh Pr, III Corps.

Thu Duc SF Camp (XT 958-001)
Apx 14 km ENE Tan Son Nhut AB. Data per *SF Order of Battle.* See Ho Ngoc Tau. Spelled "Tho" Duc SF Camp in DA Chief, Mil Hist records summary which also indicates Det A-413 here '64. Gia Dinh Pr, III Corps.

Thu Duc VNMC Boot Camp (XT 9-0?)
Presumably in Thu Duc and, if so, was roughly 10 km ENE Tan Son Nhut AB. Gia Dinh Pr, III Corps.

Thu Duc Plant? (XS 918-950)
Nature of site unknown; possibly the water filtration plant? Also listed at XS 940-998. Gia Dinh Pr, III Corps.

Thu Duc Power Plant (XS 940-998)
Along Rte 316, apx 13 km ENE Tan Son Nhut and 3 km E Thu Duc. Gia Dinh Pr, III Corps.

Thu Duc Water Plant (XS 918-950?)
A.k.a. the Saigon Water Plant. On E side of Song Saigon apx 10 km E Tan Son Nhut AB and 4 km S Thu Duc. Per *Low Level Hell's* 1st Div TAOR map. $20 million facility. 2d/18th Inf, 1st Inf Div, '68-69. Gia Dinh Pr, III Corps.

Thu Due (XS 9-9)
See Thu Duc. Binh Duong Pr, III Corps.

Thu Duong CAP (YD?)
3rd CAG per CAP Website. Thua Thien Pr, I Corps.

Thu Huong (n/a)
See Glossary.

Thu Luat Cape (YD 25-90)
Prominent cape surrounded by coral reef and jutting into Gulf of Tonkin, apx 10 km N mouth of Ben Hai River and NVN/SVN border. NVN.

Thu Pass (BR)
Listed at BR 887-781; however, there is no pass at that grid. Possibly at BR 863-765, which is a small pass on Rte 506 apx 19 km due S of Bong Son, or BR 888-879, which is a small pass on QL-1 apx 8 km SSE Bong Son. Binh Dinh Pr, II Corps.

Thu Thua Canal (XS 43-72)
See Song Thu Thua. Long An Pr, III Corps.

Thu Thua, FSB (XS 43-72)
Near listed grid, apx 7 km N Tan An, 2 km NE Song Vam Co Tay River and 30 km WSW Saigon. C Bty, 5th/42d Arty (155 mm) IIFFV here. Long An Pr, III Corps. [528]

Thua Dat Mot (n/a)
Home of 5th French Cuirassers (Armor) during 1st Indochina War. Per *Street Without Joy*, p 20. NVN.

Thua Duc (n/a)
Mapsheet name of L-7014-6329-2. SVN.

Thua Lang, Mui (YD 3-8)
Cape at 17°01'N-107°10'E. Quang Tri Pr, I Corps.

Thua Luu Bridge (ZD 197-010)
QL-1 bridge, apx 12 km E Q Phu Loc and 33 km ESE Phu Bai. Thua Thien Pr, I Corps.

Thua Thien Province (YC/YD/ZD/ZC)
One of 5 northern provs forming I Corps (I CTZ). Hue, Phu Bai and A Shau Valley in this province.

Thua Tich, FSB? (YS 62-80)
Apx 22 km NE Nui Dat, 13 km NNW Xuyen Moc and 15 km W OL-2. Elements of ANZAC 1ATF here or significant terrain feature of their AO? Phuoc Tuy Pr, III Corps.

Thua Tua CAP (n/a)
Hotel 7, 3rd CAG here per T. Duffie's CAP Vets website at www.capmarine.com. Thua Thien Pr, I Corps.

Thuan An (various)
Common Viet place-name. Villes/features with this name near: AN 886-125, BR 858-946, BS 7-7, BT 185-544, BT 266-265, BT 2-0, BT 023-763, BT 3-0, BT 032-345, BT 4-1, BT 5-1, CR 024-741, WR 555-683, XH 4-5, XT 401-392, YD 7-3 and YD 8-3, YU 146-115.

Thuan An (BT 2-2)
Listed grid is near Que Son, Quang Tin Pr. There is also a Thuan An listed in BS 7-7, Quang Ngai Pr. I Corps.

Thuan An Navy ISB (WR 555-683?)
Possibly on Song Cai Lon River, apx 15 km SW Vi Thanh AF? USN Intermediate Supt Base in '71, per MRF Assn Website. Chuong Thien Pr?, IV Corps?

Thuan Chau (Ban Pan) (n/a)
Mapsheet name of L-7014-5751-4. NVN only.

Thuan Hoa (n/a)
Mapsheet name of L-7014-6026-1. SVN.

Thuan Hoa, FSB (XT 05-85)
Apx 18 km SW Bien Hoa and 10 km due N Saigon. 161 Bty, RNZA (Kenning's Bty 13Jun65-13Jun66) FSB set here 18Apr66. Gia Dinh Pr, III Corps.

Thuan Hoa Airfield (BS 545-730)
A.k.a. Thuon Hoa AF. Apx 7 km NW Quang Ngai AF, 3 km S the Song Kha Truc River and 10 km W to WNW Quang Ngai. "Abnd, overgrown 28Jul67, AF # VA1-111," in Aug69 TAD per Frank Penk, Jr. Not in Feb73 TAD. Quang Ngai Pr, I Corps.

Thuan Hoa Heliport (WR 893-648)
Apx 2 km SW Tam Soc and 15 km WSW Soc Trang AF. Heliport #731, alt 10', at 09°37'30"N-105°48'30"E, per Feb73 TAD. Ba Xuyen Pr, IV Corps.

Thuan Loi Airfield (YT 059-817)
Along LTL-1A and E edge Don Dien Thuan Loi Plantation, apx 6 km NNW Dong Xoai, 6 km due N Dong Xoai AF, 31 km ESE An Loc and 86 km NNE Saigon. Listed as "Insecure, abnd, unusable, pvt AF, 23Jun67, AF # VA3-154," in Aug69 TAD per Frank Penk, Jr. Not in Feb73 TAD. Phuoc Long Pr, III Corps.

Thuan Loi, Plantation de (YT 0-8)
A.k.a. Don Dien Thuan Loi. See Thuan Loi AF for location. Phuoc Long Pr, III Corps.

Thuan Nhon Heliport (WR 648-971)
Apx 9 km due E Ap Truong Thuan and 23 km SW Can Tho AF. "Heliport #732, alt 7', low fence around pad, at 09°56'30"N-105°36'00"E." Phong Dinh Pr, IV Corps.

Thuan Trung Heliport (WR 476-156)
Apx 6 km SW Gia Rai and 33 km WSW Bac Lieu AF. "Heliport #733, alt 7', pad N of sod strip, at 09°12'30"N-105°26'00"E," per Feb73 TAD. Bac Lieu Pr, IV Corps.

Thuc Thuy (n/a)
Mapsheet name of L-7014-6052-1. NVN only.

Thuc, Vung (CP 0-7)
A.k.a. Dam Nha Phu. Bay at 12°25'N-109°13'E. On ND49-13 JOG. Khanh Hoa Pr, II Corps.

Thud Ridge (WJ 66-78)
Apx 32 km N Hanoi. A narrow, 24 km-long, 5,000' high hill mass pointing at Hanoi from NW and running roughly parallel to Red River. The river and city itself were 2 of 3 major landmarks relied upon by F-105 Thunderchief (a.k.a. "Thud") acft in attacking area. 3d was this ridge. US acft hugged N slope of ridge in order to evade radar controlled SAMs, AA-guns and MIGs, and it was most common route for both approach/escape. Other approaches were less desirable because they were table-flat for miles and lined with thousands of anti-acft and SAM sites. Ridge's peaks and rugged terrain were inaccessible to vehicles and it posed a major problem for Hanoi's defense until '67, when AA guns were finally emplaced. Noted feature of ridge was "the Rest Camp" whose large pools of blue water and bungalow clusters were easily seen from air, making it a good check-point. NVN.

Thuin Dhua (VR 8-5?)
Atypical Viet spelling, and no ville of this name, or anything like it, listed in NPIA or NIMA Gaz. Possible variant of Tieu Dua, which is in listed grid square along W coast of Cau Mau Peninsula, S of Rach Gia? Home of MAT-13. Kien Giang Pr?, IV Corps.

Thuitrieu Lagoon (CP 03)
Bau Can Lo Than. Lagoon at 12°03'N-109°11'E. On ND49-13 JOG. Khanh Hoa Pr, II Corps.

Thuk, Vung (CP 0-7)
A.k.a. Dam Nha Phu. Bay at 12°25'N-109°13'E. On ND49-13 JOG. Khanh Hoa Pr, II Corps.

Thumb, The (XT 57-42)
Apx 10 km SE Dau Tieng/Tri Tam, 23 km W Lai Khe and 50 km NNW Saigon. Terrain feature created by edge of a rubber plantation just W the Song Saigon. Grid per Eric Weil, 7th Cav, 1st Cav. Binh Duong Pr, III Corps.

Thunder, FSB (YD 216-176)
Apx 52 km W Hue, 14 km N the Laotian border and 10 km NE Tou Rout and 5 km NW the NW end of A Shau Valley. Thua Thien Pr, I Corps.

Thunder, FSB (ZA 143-897)
See Thunder, LZ, at grid. Kontum Pr, II Corps.

Thunder 1 thru 11, FSB (XT)
See Thunder I thru XI and "Caisson" FSB series. Binh Duong/Binh Long Pr, III Corps.

Thunder, LZ (BS 872-325)
A.k.a. LZ Debbie, LZ Debbie-Thunder and LZ Thunder Mtn. On hill apx 3 km W of the coast, 8 km SE Duc Pho and 20 km NNW Gia An. Was, "Hell of a hill to climb after a day long patrol," says Tommy Acosta, 1st/20th, 11th LIB, '68-69. Americal, 173d Abn '68-69. 4th Div apparently also here '70? Also listed at BS 868-318, 869-319, 874-325, 870-325 and by arty ORLL at BS 870-321. Map is L-7014-6838-4 (Phuoc Dien), per Ray Smith. Photos/maps of base at http://1-14th.com/ maps.html. See also LZ Debbie Thunder. Quang Ngai, I Corps.

Thunder, LZ (XT 524-346)
Along Rte 238, apx 12 km SSE Dau Tieng. May66. Tay Ninh Pr, III Corps.

Thunder, LZ/FSB (ZA 147-897)
S of Rte 511, apx 3 km ESE Polei Breng, 10 km WNW Kontum and 1 km N Dak Bla River. Per Dick Arnold, 4th Div AARs indicate LZs Muriel, Ingrid, Thunder and Irma Jay were built by 1st/14th Inf, early-mid Jul68, and while LZ Bass was being demolished. Elements of 2d/9th, 1st/69th and 1st/92d Arty here. Also listed at ZA 146-898. Name/grid per Craig Miller. Kontum Pr, II Corps.

Thunder I, FSB (XT 788-464)
A.k.a. LZ Alpha and possibly FSB Tom? On E side QL-13, at SE edge of Ap Bau Bang, apx 8 km NNE Lai Khe, 49 km due N Tan Son Nhut AB and 17 km S to SSE Chon Thanh AF. On *Low Level Hell's* TAOR map and map in *Charlie Company,* p 6. 1st Inf Div AO, '69. Grid per Frank Penk, Jr. See also Caisson FSBs. Binh Duong Pr, III Corps.

Thunder II, FSB (XT 785-553)
E side QL-13, apx 18 km NNE Lai Khe, 7 km SSE Chon Thanh AF and 10 km due N FSB Thunder I. On *Low Level Hell's* 1st Div TAOR map. Apparently largest of Thunders series strung out along QL-13. I Trp, 11th ACR here immed prior Cambodian Incursion. On map in *Charlie Company,* p 6, and map in *Rangers At War*, p 324. 2d Bde/1st Inf Div '68-69. Cited in *11th ACR Cambodia Invasion AAR, 1st Cav Div, May-Jun70*, courtesy Lou Rochat. [529] Grid per Frank Penk, Jr. See also Caisson FSBs. Binh Duong Pr, III Corps.

Thunder III, FSB (XT 772-653)
Along E side of QL-13 its intersection with LTL-13, apx 11 km NNW FSB Thunder II, 4 km N Chon Thanh AF, 23 km due S An Loc, 28 km N Lai Khe and 5 km SW Xom Ruong. On *Low Level Hell's* 1st Div TAOR map and map in *Charlie Company* at p 6. 2d/2d Mech Inf, 1st Inf Div attacked and almost overrun here 5Sep69; 23 NVA KIA inside perimeter. Grid per Frank Penk, Jr. Also listed at 768-655. See also Caisson FSBs. Binh Long Pr, III Corps.

Thunder IV, Basecamp (XT 116-890)
If grid correct, was apx 8 km NNE Thien Ngon AF, 2 km SE Bo Cay Sai and 5 km from Cambodia? Jan69. Tay Ninh Pr, III Corps.

Thunder IV, FSB (XT 760-793)
Along E side of QL-13, apx 9 km S An Loc, 18 km N Chon Thanh AF and 4 km NNE Xa Tan Khai. On *Low Level Hell's* 1st Div TAOR map and map in *Charlie Company* at p 6. 1st Inf Div AO, '69. (Frank Penk, Jr. thinks the grid was XT 760-893, which puts it on N side of An Loc at precisely same point others claim was Thunder V? Also listed at XT 772-656. 763-892 and 782-556? See also Caisson FSBs. Binh Long Pr, III Corps.

Thunder V, FSB (XT 760-893?)
A.k.a. Camp Alpha, An Loc Basecamp, and possibly Thunder IV? If grid correct, was on QL-13 (Thunder Road) immed N An Loc, apx 18 km S Loc Ninh and 33 km NW Dong Xoai. Per *Father Soldier Son*, p 9 and 167, in Aug68, was a Bde or Bn HQ of 1st Inf Div and/or 1st/28th Inf. Described in detail throughout that book, but author notes that when his unit was there, it was on a red clay knoll that

was a "revolting mess of garbage and putrid water-filled holes and rats." See also Caisson FSBs. Also listed at XT 773-615? Binh Long Pr, III Corps.

Thunder V, LZ (XT 773-615)
Along QL-13 at Chon Thanh AF, apx 23 km N Lai Khe. Jan68. Binh Long Pr, III Corps.

Thunder VI, LZ (XT 767-686)
Along QL-13, apx 19 km S An Loc, 8 km N Chon Thanh. Jan68. Binh Long Pr, III Corps.

Thunder VII, LZ (XT 764-764)
Along QL-13 at Tan Khai, apx 12 km S An Loc, 16 km N Chon Thanh. Jan68. Binh Long Pr, III Corps.

Thunder VIII, LZ (XT 767-730)
Along QL-13, apx 16 km S An Loc, 12 km N Chon Thanh. Jan68. Binh Long Pr, III Corps.

Thunder X, LZ (XT 744-819)
Apx 7 km SSW An Loc, 20 km N Chon Thanh. Jan68. Binh Long Pr, III Corps.

Thunder XI, LZ (XT 763-891)
Along QL-13 at N edge An Loc, apx 20 km S Loc Ninh AF. Jan68. Binh Long Pr, III Corps.

Thunder Mountain (BS 872-325)
A.k.a. LZ Debbie-Thunder. See LZ Thunder at grid and Debbie-Thunder. Quang Ngai, I Corps.

Thunder Road (XT)
Nickname of QL-13 between Lai Khe and Loc Ninh. Origin of name was 11th ACR's call-sign, "Thunder." Reflected the many thunderous convoys along the corridor and the many thunderous ambushes they encountered. Formed boundary between War Zone C to W and War Zone D to E. Binh Long/Binh Duong Prvs, III Corps.

Thunder Road, Battle of (XT)
12Aug69-6Sep69. Involved 1st Inf Div units: 1st/4th Cav, 2d/34th Armor, 2d/2d (Mech) Inf, 1st Engrs, as well as 11th ACR Sqdns opcon to 1st Inf Div (all of which suffered frequent ambushes along QL-13). C/2d/2d (Mech) Inf was at FSB Thunder III when it responded to ambush of nearby convoy; 73 NVA were killed in 2 hr battle that followed. Within 10-day period, QL-13 was ambushed 3 times costing enemy 110 KIA. An attack on FSB Thunder II, and on yet another convoy, resulted in 78 more enemy dead. Binh Long Pr, III Corps.

Thunder Run (n/a)
See Glossary.

Thunder Run, FSB (XT?)
No data. Likely along QL-13 in III Corps.

Thung Chang Airfield (PB 9-4)
At 19°24'00"N-100°53'00"E. NIMA data. Thailand.

Thung Peeut Airfield (UF 99-96)
LS-262. CIA/SF, per *Air Facilities Data-Laos.*

Thung Peeut Airfield (VF 00-95)
LS-202. CIA/SF, per *Air Facilities Data-Laos.*

Thung Song Airfield (NK 7-0)
At 8°10'00"N-99°43'00"E. NIMA data. Thailand.

Thuon Hoa Airfield (BS 545-730)
See Thuan Hoa AF. Quang Ngai Pr, I Corps.

Thuong Duc (ZC 140-520)
Apx 42 km SW Da Nang and 3 km SW Ha Tan AF. Site of 5th SF CIDG Camp Oct 66. 7th Marines, 1st Mar Div AO. Quang Nam Pr, I Corps.

Thuong Duc (Ha Tan) (n/a)
Mapsheet name of L-7014-6540-1. SVN.

Thuong Duc Airfield (ZC 152-540)
See Ha Tan AF. Quang Nam Pr, I Corps.

Thuong Duc SF Camp (ZC 152-540)
Along N fork of Song Thu Bon River, apx 6 km E Ha Tan, 32 km SW Da Nang, 36 km W Hoi An and 12 km NW An Hoa. 5th SF Grp CIDG Camp, Det A-109, Oct 66. Transferred to 79th ARVN Border Rangers. Info/grid per *SF Order of Battle.* Quang Nam Pr, I Corps.

Thuong Duc Valley (ZC 13-52)
Apx 45 km SW Da Nang and 5 km SW Ha Tan AF. Included Thuong Duc and portions of Rte 4, 7th Marines, 1st Mar Div AO. Quang Nam Pr, I Corps.

Thuong Giang (BT 3-3)
A.k.a. Truong Giang. Lagoon at 15°40'N-108°30'E. On ND49-01 JOG. Quang Tin Pr, I Corps.

Thuong Li Station (XJ 7-0)
One of 2 major railway stations within Haiphong's city limits: The Thuong Li Station (W part of city), and Hai Phong Station (city center). See Haiphong. Likely heavily bombed. NVN.

Thuong Thoi Airfield (WS 313-955)
Along N bank of Mekong River apx 12 km S Cambodia and 21 km WSW Don Phuoc AF. AF # VA4-294, in Aug69 TAD per Frank Penk, Jr. Not in Feb73 TAD. Kien Phong Pr, IV Corps.

Thuong Thoi SF Camp (WS 3140-9565)
On N bank of Mekong River apx 12 km S Cambodia, 21 km WSW Don Phuoc AF, 22 km NE Chau Phu/Chau Duc AF. SF Det 75, 5th SF, Det A-425, Oct66. Flooded-out and moved to Chi Lang Trng Ctr. Grid per *SF Order of Battle.* Listed in Kien Tuong Pr in that text; however, appears to be in Kien Phong Pr, IV Corps.

Thuy Dong Airfield (XS 283-777)
A.k.a. Tuyen Nhon AF. Apx 2 km W Tuyen Nhon, 52 km WSW Saigon, 27 km NW Long An AF, 28 km ESE Muc Hoa AF. Listed as "Flight serv SF Can Tho (C-123) (C-7 ARVN(A) 21Jul69, AF # VA4-38," in Aug69 TAD per Frank Penk, Jr. 2,000' laterite/clay rwy. 10°39'08"N-106°10'20"E. El. 13'. Kien Tuong Pr, IV Corps.

Thuy Dong SF Camp (XS 2787-7758)
See Thuyen Nhon. Kien Tuong Pr, IV Corps.

Thuy Hien (n/a)
Mapsheet name of L-7014-6150-3. NVN only.

Thuy Long CAP (YD 882-172)
See CAP Alpha 1. Thua Thien Pr, I Corps.

Thuy Luong CAP (YD?)
Alpha 1, 3rd CAG. Thua Thien Pr, I Corps.

Thuy Phuoc Refugee Center? (YD 770-200)
At S edge of Hue, apx 3 km S Hue Citadel AF and 3 km W of QL-1. Listed as Thuy Phuoc R.C. Possibly a refugee center? NPIA data. Thua Thien Pr, I Corps.

Thuy Tan CAP (n/a)
Alpha 2, 3rd CAG. Thua Thien Pr, I Corps.

Thuy Thac Relocation Camp (BS 869-316)
On QL-1, apx 47 km SSE Quang Ngai, 9 km SE Duc Pho and 17 km NNW Gia An. Oct68. Quang Ngai Pr, I Corps.

Thuy Trieu, Lagune de (CP 0-3)
A.k.a. Bau Can Lo Than. Lagoon at 12°03'N-109°11'E. On ND49-13 JOG. Khanh Hoa Pr, II Corps.

Thuy Tu, Dam (YD 9-1)
Lagoon at 16°26'N-107°46'E. On NE48-16 JOG. Thua Thien Pr, I Corps.
Thuyen Nhon ATSB (XS 273-773?)
See Tuyen Nhon ATSB. Kien Tuong Pr, IV Corps.
Ti Oan, Cape (YS 4-4)
See Cape Ti Oan. Phuoc Tuy Pr, III Corps.
Ti Ti Woods (YD 695-240)
Apx 6 to 7 km SE LZ Sally, 1 to 2 W QL-1, and 6 km WNW Citadel AF. 68. Thua Thien Pr, I Corps.
Tich An (BT 305-328)
Apx 11 km due N Tam Ky, 6 km E QL-1 and 3 km W the coast. VC controlled ville and object of C Trp/17th Cav Recon, '67. Quang Tin Pr, I Corps.
Tich Phu CAP (AT 935-600?)
If grid correct, was apx 16 km SSW Da Nang AB, 4 km NE Dai Loc/Ai Nghia and 2 km E Rte 540. CAP 1-2-3, 1st CAG. Tich Phu (3) at listed grid. Quang Nam Pr, I Corps.
Tich Phu CAP (AT 935-600?)
CAP 1-3-2, 1st CAG. Quang Nam Pr, I Corps.
Tich Tuong, FSB (YD 340-493)
See FSB Sharon. Quang Tri Pr, I Corps.
Ticonderoga, LZ (YD 001-354)
In valley of Khe Ta Laou River, apx 2 km WSW Lang Ran (3), 13 km due S Ca Lu and 17 km ESE Khe Sanh. Apr70 XXIV Corps grid per D. Armstrong. Quang Tri Pr, I Corps.
Ticonderoga, USS (n/a)
CVA-14 (and CVS 14). Acft Carrier. Deployed with CVW-16, 1Feb69-18 Sep69; with CVW-19, 28Dec67-17Aug68; with CVSG-53, 17May72-29Jul72; with CVSG-59, 11Mar71-6Jul71; with CVW-5, 14Apr64-15Dec64; with CVW-19, 15Oct66-29May 67; 14 with CVW-5, 28Sep65-13May66. During Fall '61 crisis, planes from *Ticonderoga* conducted photo recon over Central Highlands, and with *Constellation* also suptd Destroyers *Maddox* and *C. Turner Joy* during Gulf of Tonkin Incident. [530]
Tiem Ton? (XS 7-0?)
Possibly Tien Ton or Tiem Tan? Near Ba Tri (XS 7-0), and apparently on Mekong River near its mouth? ARVNN Junk river patrol unit here at least '64-65. Data per *A Mekong Delta Junkie*, Military Magazine, Oct2000, p 5-8. No ville by this name in either NPIA or NIMA Gazetteers, and spelling may be phonetic? Kien Hoa Pr, IV Corps.
Tien Binh SF Camp (VS 953-712)
Apx 3 km SE Cambodia, 9 km NW That Son and 23 km SE Chau Duc and 55 km ENE Ha Tien. 5th SF. Later closed and assets moved to ? Info/grid per *SF Order of Battle*. Chau Doc Pr, IV Corps.
Tien Binh, Camp (WS 071-809)
See Ba Bai. IV Corps.
Tien Bo, Operation (n/a)
24Aug-9Sep68. ARVN 23d Div Op. 1,091 rptd VC KIA, per *VN Order of Battle*, pp 9-14. Quang Duc Pr, II Corps.
Tien Cha Peninsula (BT 05-80)
A.k.a. the Tien Sha Peninsula and Ban Dao Son Tra. This spelling may have only applied to thin portion of peninsula immed opposite Da Nang and below Monkey Mtn (that, or Tien Cha was anglicized into Tien Sha)? Site of Marble Mtn and Camp Tien Sha. At 16°08'N-108°16'E. On ND49-01 JOG. Quang Nam Pr, I Corps.
Tien Don Suc, FSB (YT 93-21)
Apx 5 km SSW Tanh Linh AF, 5 km N peak Nui Da Ban Mtn (Hill 731), 48 km WNW Phan Thiet, 45 km ENE Xuan Loc and 23 km SE Vo Dat AF. 2d/3d Inf, 199th LIB, '70. Grid per 199th LIB Assn. Binh Tuy Pr, III Corps.
Tien Don Sue (YT 93-21)
See Tien Don Suc. Binh Tuy Pr, III Corps.
Tien Len (n/a)
See Glossary.
Tien Phuoc (BT 116-138)
Apx 24 km SW Tam Ky and 64 km SSE Da Nang AB. AF, SF camp and at least one FSB/LZ here During '72 Easter Offensive, NVA seized this city, but revitalized ARVN 3d Div retook it after bitter fight that ended late Sep72. For map see DMA L-7014-6639-1. Quang Tin Pr, I Corps.
Tien Phuoc, LZ (BT 115-135)
At Tien Phuoc AF, apx 24 km SW Tam Ky and 64 km SSE Da Nang. Sep70. Quang Tin Pr, I Corps.
Tien Phuoc (Phuon An) (n/a)
Mapsheet name of L-7014-6639-1. SVN.
Tien Phuoc Airfield (BT 116-128)
Apx 20 km WSW Tam Ky. El. 197', 2,000' steel-mat rwy. At 15°29'16"N-108°18'36"E. Quang Tin Pr, I Corps.
Thien Phuoc Heliport (BT 113-137)
A.k.a. Thien Phuoc Heliport. Apx 3 km N Tien Phuoc SF Camp, 20 km WSW Tam Ky. Heliport #682, alt 115'. 73 TAD. Quang Tin Pr, I Corps.
Tien Phuoc Highway (BT)
See Highway 535. Quang Tin Pr, I Corps.
Tien Phuoc Refugee Camp (BT 110-130)
Immed SW Tien Phuoc AF, apx 25 km WSW Tam Ky and 65 km SSE Da Nang. Jul68. Quang Tin Pr, I Corps.
Tien Phuoc SF Camp (BT 105-102)
SF/CIDG Camp along Rte 585 in Song Chang/Song Tien River Valley, apx 20 km WSW Tam Ky AF and 43 km W to WNW Chu Lai. During Battle of Tien Phuoc, was heavily attacked evening of 22Feb69, partially overrun at 0200, but recaptured early next day. KIA-1 US SF, 54 CIDG, 1 ARVN, 30 civilians; WIA-12 US SF, 3 ARVN SF, 1 USN, 136 CIDG, 12 ARVN, 60 civilians. NVA continued harassing camp until Mar69. Per *Green Berets at War*, p 201. 5th SF Grp Det A-102 here beginning 1Mar66, through '70. Per Americal website & Army SF history, was converted to ARVN Ranger base, Oct70. Also listed at BT 104-144 and 105-142. 5th SF Grp Det A-102, A-233, Oct66, 5th SF Det 4. Map is L-7014-6639-1, per Les Hines. Quang Tin Pr, I Corps. [531]
Tien Phuoc SF Camp (BT 1057-1435)
Just W Tien Phuoc AF, apx 22 km WSW Tam Ky. 5th SF. Transferred to 77th ARVN Border Rangers. Info/grid per *SF Order of Battle*. Map is L-7014-6639-1, per Les Hines. Quang Tin Pr, I Corps.
Tien Phuoc, LZ (BT 108-142)
Apx 22 km WSW Tam Ky. Apr70 XXIV Corps grid per Don Armstrong. Quang Tin Pr, I Corps.
Tien Sa, Ban Dao (BT 0-8)
A.k.a. Son Tra, Ban Dao and Mui Da Nang. Peninsula at 16°08'N-108°16'E. Quang Nam Pr, I Corps.
Tien Sha (BT 1-8)
A.k.a. Mui Da Nang. Cape at 16°07'N-108°19'E. On ND49-01 JOG. Quang Nam Pr, I Corps.

Tien Sha, Camp (BT 060-828)
On Tien Sha Peninsula, adj to Camp Fay, apx km 8 km NNE Da Nang AB and 4 km WSW peak Son Tra Mtn. On map at www.ptfnasty.com/images/jpg/ ptfdanang1a.JPG. Quang Nam Pr, I Corps.

Tien Sha, Presquile de (BT 0-8)
A.k.a. Son Tra, Ban Dao. Peninsula at 16°08'N-108°16'E. On ND49-01 JOG. Quang Nam Pr, I Corps.

Tien Sha City (BT 04-84)
On SW edge of Tien Sha Peninsula, W of Monkey Mtn, 10 km NNE Da Nang AB and 12 km due E the Nam O Bridge. Quang Tri Pr, I Corps.

Tien Sha LAAM Site (BT)
See LAAM Sites. C Bty, 1st LAAM here in '66. Quang Nam Pr, I Corps.

Tien Sha Peninsula (BT 10-84)
A.k.a. Tien Cha Peninsula (at least thin portion of peninsula opposite Da Nang at BT 0-8 had that name) and Ban Dao Son Tra. Immed NE Da Nang. Site of Son Tra, Monkey Mtn, Marble Mtn, Camp Fay and Camp Tien Sha. See Da Nang entry for history related to *USS Constitution's* 1845 visit here. Quang Nam Pr, I Corps.

Tien Sha Ramp (BT 04-83)
Along SW edge of Tien Sha Peninsula apx 1 km due E the Market Time Swift Boat Base. Apx 7 km NNE Da Nang AB. On map in *The Marines in Vietnam 1954-1973*, p 238. Quang Nam Pr, I Corps.

Tien Tan (XS 70-07?)
See Tiem Ton. Kien Hao Pr, IV Corps.

Tien Thuan (BR 6-9)
Mapsheet name of L-7014-6737-2. SVN.

Tien Ton (XS 70-07?)
See Tiem Ton. Kien Hao Pr, IV Corps.

Tien Tra (Hau Duc) (n/a)
Mapsheet L-7014-6639-4. Sheet: Hau Duc (Tien Tra)

Tien Yen (n/a)
Mapsheet name of L-7014-6451-1. NVN only.

Tien Yen, Rade de (YJ 5-5)
Anchorage at 21°15'N-107°30'E. On NF48-12 JOG. NVN.

Tientsin, LZ (XD 898-347)
Apx 10 km SSE Khe Sanh CB and 27 km WSW Ba Long AF. Apr70 XXIV Corps grid per Don Armstrong. Quang Tri Pr, I Corps.

Tieu Atar Airfield (ZV 020-622)
Apx 48 km due W Buon Blech AF, 22 km E Laos, 35 km due N Ban Don AF, 65 km NNW Ban Me Thuot. El. 558', 1,500' laterite rwy. At 13°12'48"N-107°47'02"E. *Time Heals No Wounds*, lists grid as ZV 021-622, p 185. 4th Div AO. Darlac/Pleiku Pr border, II Corps.

Tieu Atar Mountain (ZV 117-762)
A.k.a. Hill 405. Solitary peak apx 14 km NNE Tieu Atar AF. Pleiku Pr, II Corps.

Tieu Atar SF Camp (ZV 0220-6235)
Apx 48 km due W Buon Blech AF, 22 km E Laos, 35 km due N Ban Don AF, 65 km NNW Ban Me Thuot. 5th SF CIDG Det A-231. Transferred to 71st ARVN Border Rangers. Grid per *SF Order of Battle*. Darlac Pr, II Corps.

Tieu Can (XR 31-84)
Town apx 35 km NE Soc Trang and 19 km SW Tra Vinh AF. Per Bill Hunt, portion of MACV Det 72 was here sometime between Oct71-Sep72. Vinh Binh Pr, IV Corps.

Tieu Can Heliport (XR 305-845)
Apx 35 km NE Soc Trang and 19 km SE Tra Vinh AF. "Heliport #685, alt 7', sod (hard). Next to arty pieces." At 09°48'30"N-106°11'05"E Vinh Binh Pr, IV Corps.

Tieu Teo (n/a)
Mapsheet name of L-7014-6535-1. SVN.

Tieu Teo Mountain (ZV 058-820)
A.k.a. Hill 471 and 7 km W Hill 711. Pleiku Pr, II Corps.

Tieu-Doan Kinh Quan (n/a)
See Glossary.

Tiger, FSB/LZ (BS 368-552)
Apx 28 km SW Quang Ngai, 17 km WNW Minh Long AF, 15 km S Ha Thanh AF and 6 km S Lang Re. 31Oct70 ORLL indicates Tiger built 1Apr70. Americal list. Quang Ngai Pr, I Corps.

Tiger, FSB (YD 253-091)
A.k.a. Co A Nong Mtn, FSB Turnage, Hill 1228 and perhaps Upper LZ Tiger? Along Rte 548 at extreme N end A Shau Valley, apx 6 km N Laos, 5 km NE Hill 1224, 32 km SSE Ba Long AF and 49 km WSW Hue. 2d/1st ARVN here during Op Apache Snow, 10May-7Jun69. On map at p 32, *US Marines in Vietnam-1969*. 5th/7th Cav, 1st Cav air assaulted here 19Apr68 on 1st day Op Delaware/Lam Son 216. There are references to an Upper LZ Tiger and a Lower LZ Tiger in the A Shau, but these may refer to different portions or helo pads of same FSB? Cited in 1st Cav VN *Yearbook* Aug65-Dec69, p 78, per Peter Cole. XXIV Corps grid. Also listed at YD 282-086, and perhaps this is the Lower LZ Tiger? Thua Thien Pr, I Corps.

Tiger, FSB (282-086)
A.k.a. Lower LZ Tiger? At NW end of the A Shau Valley, apx 1 km N Lan Lam, 13 km NW A Luoi and 46 km WSW Hue. Also listed at YD 253-091? Thua Thien Pr, I Corps.

Tiger, FSB (YS 646-913)
Apx 32 km NE Nui Dat, 5 km NNE FSB Tasman and 12 km ENE FSB Flinders. On 1ATF NCO trng map per John Hollett. 1ATF. Long Khanh Pr, III Corps.

Tiger II, FSB (XS 620-270)
Near Ap Dong Nhon, apx 11 km ESE Truc Giang/Ben Tre. Jan69. Kien Hoa Pr, IV Corps.

Tiger, Lower, LZ (282-086?)
See FSB Tiger at grid. Thua Thien Pr, I Corps.

Tiger, LZ (BS 478-478?)
Apx 10 km SW Minh Long AF and 30 km SSW Quang Ngai. See LZ Lion. Quang Ngai Pr, I Corps.

Tiger, LZ/FSB (BS 638-552)
A.k.a. LZ Bulldog, Hill 513 and Nui Nham. On Hill 513 overlooking Song Ve River Valley and coast, apx 8 km WNW Mo Duc AF and 18 km due S Quang Ngai. Built 1Apr70. Americal list. Quang Ngai Pr, I Corps.

Tiger, LZ (YA 819-609)
Apx 10 km NW Plei Djereng (old) AF, 13 km SW Plei De Go and 52 km SW Kontum. Jan66. Pleiku Pr, II Corps.

Tiger, LZ (YD 251-086)
See FSB Tiger at YD 253-091. Thua Thien Pr, I Corps.

Tiger, OP (YD 692-158)
See OP Tiger. Thua Thien Pr, I Corps.

Tiger, Upper LZ (YD 253-091?)
See FSB Tiger at grid. Thua Thien Pr, I Corps.

Tiger 5 Heliport (YS 438-685)
At or near Luscombe Field/Nui Dat CB, apx 28 km NE Vung Tau and 60 km ESE Saigon. "Heliport #748, alt 195', 300' x 150' Uncontrolled. LZ oriented E/W. 4 Lndg points on S side of LZ. Arty advsy-Phuoc Tuy 369.6, 40.7, at 10°34'N 107°14'E," per 73 TAD. Phuoc Tuy Pr, III Corps.
Tiger Attacks (various)
See Glossary.
Tiger Beer (n/a)
See Glossary.
Tiger Cages (XQ 77-63)
See Glossary.
Tiger Division (BR/CR)
See Glossary.
Tiger Hound Operations (n/a)
See Glossary.
Tiger Island (BN 0-0)
A.k.a. Hon Lao. Small island, apx 22 km E of Phan Thiet and only 2 km off coast, at 10°54'00"N-108°18'00"E. NC48-08 JOG. Binh Thuan Pr, II Corps.
Tiger Island (YD 49-98)
A.k.a. Ile du Tigre and Dao Con Co Island. Apx 28 km NE the mouth of the Ben Hai River. Weapons installation several km N DMZ and just off coast. Attacked by 24 VNAF Skyraider acft, 14Mar65, as part of Op Rolling Thunder. Island at grid may not be Tiger Island, though NIMA does put it in YD 4-9. At 17°10'00"N-107°20'00"E. On NE48-12 JOG. NVN.
Tiger Lake (CP 08-15)
On Cam Ranh Peninsula, several km S of the main AF. Apparently recreational and/or water supply? Photo: www. petester.com/steve/slentz47. html. Khanh Hoa Pr, II Corps.
Tiger Mountain (BR 930-930)
Apx 8 km ESE Bong Son and 7 km W of QL-1. Oct70. Binh Dinh Pr, II Corps.
Tiger Mountain (YD 239-118)
A.k.a. Hill 1228 or Co A Nong Mtn. Apx 50 km WSW Hue and 12 km ESE Tou Rout. Thua Thien/Quang Tri Pr border, I Corps.
Tiger Mountain (XD 83-54)
See Tiger Tooth Mtn. Quang Tri Pr, I Corps.
Tiger Papa Three CAP (YD 21-63)
Per Tom Flynn, TP3 CAP was at Cam Hu, apx 8 km W Dong Ha and 100 meters N QL-9. CAC HQ for TP3 was at Cam Lo. Flynn was in start-up crew of 1st TP3 team, apx Mar68(?) and overrun twice. Was also severely wounded in hand-to-hand combat in 1 of those incidents (May68). Grid is only an approximation based on point 8 km W Dong Ha. 4th CAG, Quang Tri Pr, I Corps. [532]
Tiger Tooth Mountain (XD 83-54)
A.k.a. Dong Voi Mep, Hill 1739 and Tiger Mtn. Apx 10 km NW Khe Sanh CB, at 16°46'00"N-106°44'00"E. At 5,705 feet, the highest terrain feature in northern I Corps. Photo as seen from Hill 861 in pictorial following p 168 of *Valley of Decision* (captioned Hill 1371?) clearly indicating origin of nickname. May have also been a MAC-SOG "strategic hilltop" with code name Hickory Hill? On NE48-16 JOG. See also LZ Crest, LZ Hill, Advsy Team One and SESU. Quang Tri Pr, I Corps.
Tiger Tower (n/a)
See Glossary.
Tiger's Den (XR 058-591)
The bar of the 93d Helicopter Co at Soc Trang AF, apx 100 mi S Saigon. Said to have been named to honor the mongrel mascot dog of the 93d. Tiger is known to have flown along on at least 10 helo combat assaults; just 10 missions short of qualifying for the Air Medal; however, no written record of his having received the award was found, and his fate is otherwise unknown. Ba Xuyen Pr, IV Corps.
Tigre, Ile (BN 0-0)
See Tiger Island at grid. II Corps.
Tigre, Ile du (YD 49-98)
See Tiger Island at grid. NVN.
Tim, FSB (YU 154-169)
Apx 7 km NNW Song Be City AF, 8 km N Phuoc Binh, 10 km N Song Be AF. 2d/12th Cav, 1st Cav, '69. Cited in *1st Cav Op Rpt, Feb-Apr70*, p 13, per Peter Cole. Grid per Frank Penk, Jr. Phuoc Long Pr, III Corps.
Tim, LZ (XD 880-360)
Apx 4 km SW Lang Rai, 17 km SW Ca Lu and 48 km WSW Quang Tri. Apr68. Quang Tri Pr, I Corps.
Timber, FSB (YT 692-687)
In bend of Song Dong Nai River, apx 36 km WSW Bao Loc, 36 km due N Vo Dat and 63 km ESE Dong Xoai. Opened 29Jul70, closed 19Aug70, by 1st/5th Cav Data per *1st Cav Div Op Rpt, ending 31Oct70*, courtesy Peter Cole. Also mentioned in *1st Cav Op Rpt, May-Jul70*, p 38. Long Khanh Pr, III Corps.
Timbuktu, FSB (YT 779-658)
Overlooked river valley and QL-1 to S, apx 32 km SW Bao Loc and 32 km NNE Vo Dat. Also listed at YT 79-66. Also spelled Timbuctu. Lam Dong Pr, II Corps.
Time, LZ (XD 699-623)
Apx 2 km S the southern edge DMZ, 4 km E Laotian border, 25 km NNW Khe Sanh CB and possibly the northwestern-most US LZ/FSB of war. Apr70 XXIV Corps grid per Don Armstrong. Quang Tri Pr, I Corps.
Tin Bong Airfield (TG 50-20)
LS-90. CIA/SF, per *Air Facilities Data-Laos.*
Tin City Refugee Camp (n/a)
At Anderson AFB, Guam. See Operation New Life.
Tin Mines, Ban Phon (n/a)
See Ban Phon Tin Mines.
Tin Quan Ca (n/a)
See Glossary.
Tin Trunk (n/a)
See Glossary.
Tin Yawn (YT 929-262)
See Tanh Linh. Binh Tuy Pr, III Corps.
Tina, FSB (XT 415-829)
Near the Fishhook, apx 15 km SE Katum, 5 km SE Bo Tuc and about 10 km S Cambodia. Cited in *1st Cav Op Rpt, Feb-Apr70*, p 7, and in *Incursion*, per Peter Cole. Tay Ninh Pr, III Corps.
Tinche (n/a)
Mapsheet name of L-7014-5948-2. NVN Laos.
Tinh (n/a)
See Glossary.
Tinh Bien Advance Base (VS 953-712?)
On the Vinh Te border canal near Cambodian border, apx 55 km ENE Ha Tien and 24 km SW Chau Phu. PBR base

with prominent watch tower. River Dets using YRBM 20 and YRBM 16(?) also used this base while patrolling Vinh Te Canal. Photos/data at: http://hawley.interspeed.net/vietnam/a_base.htm. See also YRBM-16 and and YRBM-20. Chau Doc Pr, IV Corps.

Tinh Bien Airfield (VS 960-720)
A.k.a. Tinh Bien Highway Strip AF. Apx 3 km from Cambodian border, 57 km ENE Ha Tien and 23 km SW Chau Phu. AF # VA4-249, in Aug69 (not Feb73) TAD, per Frank Penk, Jr. Chau Doc Pr, IV Corps.

Tinh Bien Heliport (VS 940-725)
Apx 3 km from Cambodia, 55 km ENE Ha Tien and 24 km WSW Chau Duc AF. "Heliport #686, alt 10', earth, VC to S and E," per Feb73 TAD. Chau Doc Pr, IV Corps.

Tinh Bien Highway Strip AF (VS 960-720)
See Tinh Bien AF. Chau Doc Pr, IV Corps.

Tinh Bien SF Camp (VS 940-725)
Apx 3 km from Cambodia, 55 km ENE Ha Tien and 24 km WSW Chau Phu/Chau Duc AF. Tinh Bien SF Camp here. SF Det 77, 5th SF Grp, Det. A-331, Dec64, 5th SF Grp, Det. A-423 (was 134), Oct65. Chau Doc Pr, IV Corps.

Tinh Xuyen (n/a)
Mapsheet name of L-7014-6147-1. NVN only.

Tinville North, LZ (BS 595-810)
Apx 9 km N Quang Ngai AF, 12 km E Ba Gia AF and 4 km W QL-1. Americal list. Quang Ngai Pr, I Corps.

Tinville South, LZ (BS 610-797)
On small hill apx 7 km N Quang Ngai AF, 10 km NNW Quang Ngai, 13 km E Ba Gia AF and 3 km W QL-1. Americal list. Quang Ngai Pr, I Corps.

Tioga County, USS (n/a)
LST-1158 and *USNS Tioga County*. USN Landing Ship, Tank. SVN service with 9th Inf Div/MRF discussed on MRF Assn website. To MSTS, 72. III/IV Corps?

Tittie Mountain (AN 925-223)
A.k.a. Whiskey Relay Nui Ta Dom and Hill 386. Apx 16 km NE Phan Thiet, 2 km NE Ap Hoa Thanh (1) and 1 km E QL-1. Apparent OP and radio relay site for 3d/506th Inf. Nickname likely based on profile of mtn and its resemblance to portion of the female anatomy. LZ Sandy was at mtn's base. 3d/506th Inf, 101st Abn AO. Data per Jerry Berry. Binh Thuan Pr, II Corps.

Titty Mountain (AN 925-223?)
See Tittie Mountain. Binh Thuan Pr, II Corps.

Titty Mountain (AR 780-368)
A.k.a. Dragon Mtn. Just S 4th Div's Camp Enari. See Dragon Mtn for detail. Pleiku Pr, II Corps.

Titus Tavern (WR 170-394)
See Hepatitis Tavern. An Xuyen Pr, IV Corps.

Tiwan, Cape (YS 4-4)
See Cape Tiwan. Phuoc Tuy Pr, III Corps.

TL (Road System) (n/a)
See Glossary.

TL-1 (ZV/AQ/AP)
Short rte between Ban Don and Ban Me Thuot. Runs NW from QL-14 just S Ban Me Thuot. Darlac Pr, II Corps.

TL-2A (XT)
Short NE to SW road joining TL-16 (S Phuoc Hoa) and QL-13 (S Ben Kat, N Lam Son). Binh Duong Pr, III Corps.

TL-2B (YS/ZS)
Short, N/S road that ran S from QL-1 to Ham Tan and Coast. Binh Tuy Pr, III Corps.

TL-2D (BQ/CQ)
Joined Dong Tre with QL-1 roughly midway between Song Cau and Tuy Hoa. Phu Yen Pr, II Corps.

TL-2E (BR/BQ)
Ran NE to SE from QL-14 at An Khe through Cheo Reo to QL-14 at Buon Blech. Binh Dinh/Phu Bon Prvs, II Corps.

TL-3A (BR)
Left QL-1 just below Bong Son and ran SW to join QL 19 at point E An Khe. Binh Dinh Pr, II Corps.

TL-3B (ZA)
Connected Kontum with Pleiku via Plei Morong. To W of and leaving and joining QL-14 near those 2 cities. Kontum and Pleiku Pr, II Corps.

TL-4 (XT)
Ran N/S. Joined Katum/Tay Ninh. Tay Ninh Pr, III Corps.

TL-5A (XS)
N/S road that ran from Saigon S to Go Cong Pr. Gia Dinh, Long An, Go Cong Prvs, III Corps.

TL-6C (ZA)
Joined QL-14 to Plei Me. Pleiku Pr, II Corps.

TL-7C (AR)
Short rte that left QL-19 apx 18 km E Pleiku, running NE to SW to join QL-14 (near Camp Enari), thus bypassing Pleiku. Pleiku Pr, II Corps.

TL-8A (XT)
W to E running road that joined Lam Son (on QL-13), with TL-10 near Boa Tria, through Cu Chi. Binh Duong and Hau Nghia Prvs, III Corps.

TL-9A (XT/XS)
Ran SSW from QL-1 near Hoc Mon, in arc that swung to W and then back to E to join QL-4 NE Tan An. Gia Dinh, Hau Nghia, Long An Prvs, III Corps.

TL-9B (BQ)
Ran S from Son Hoa/Cung Son to Khanh Duong/Ban M'Drak. Phu Bon Pr, II Corps.

TL-10 (XT/XS)
NW to SE running road that ran SE from QL-1 near Trang Bang to join QL-4 S of Saigon. Hau Nghia and Gia Dinh Prvs, III Corps.

TL-13 (WR/XR)
E/W road that joined Thuan Hoa with QL-4 at point just N Soc Trang. Ba Xuyen Pr, IV Corps.

TL-18 (XS)
Short road that joined LTL-5A with QL-4SW Can Giouc and Saigon. Long An Pr, III Corps.

TL-20 (XS)
Road ran apx from Vinh Long in W, ESE to Mo Cay and LTL-6A in E. Roughly paralleled branch of Mekong River. Kien Hoa Pr, IV Corps.

TL-23 (WS)
Paralleled branch of Mekong River, running roughly from vic of Thanh Binh to vic of Vinh Long. Kien Phong and Sa Dec Prvs, IV Corps.

TL-24 (XS)
E/W road that connected My Tho with Go Cong (30 km gap). Parallel to and N of the Mekong River. IV Corps.

TL-26 (XS)
NW/SE road that connected Ham Long in W and Truc Giang with Ba Tri to SE. Kien Hoa Pr, IV Corps.
TL-28 (XR)
Ran apx 20 km SE from Soc Trang/QL-4. Ba Xuyen Pr, IV Corps.
TL-30 (XS)
Joined LTL-6A at Mo Cay with Thanh Phu at SW tip of Kien Hoa Prov at ocean. Kien Hoa Pr, IV Corps.
TL-34 (XS/XR)
NE/SE road that spanned Vinh Binh Pr and joined 2 branches of Mekong River, passing by Tra Vinh in NE and Tieu Can in SW. Vinh Binh Pr, IV Corps.
TL-37 (WS/XS/XR)
NW/SE running road that paralleled branch of Mekong River, running roughly from Lap Vo to Tra On. Sa Dec and Vinh Long Prvs, IV Corps.
TL-38 (XR/WR)
Ran roughly parallel to coast of Bac Lieu Pr from QL-4 at Bac Lieu, to vic of Vinh Chau and eastern tip of Bac Lieu Pr, IV Corps.
TL-39 (XS/XR)
N to S rte that joined LTL-7A with TL-37 near Tra On, and ended near Dal Ke. Vinh Long/Vinh Binh Pr, IV Corps.
TL-42 (WR/XR)
Ran in long, southerly and then easterly arc from Long My in N until it joined QL-4 at point just N Soc Trang in E. Ba Xuyen Pr, IV Corps.
TL-48 (WT)
Joined LTL10 and LTL-9, passing through That Son and Seven Sister Mtns near Cambodian border. Chau Doc Pr, IV Corps.
TL-59 (XR)
Ran from Soc Trang, NE to Mekong River at Ba Xuyen/Vinh Binh Pr border. IV Corps.
TL-7014 Series (n/a)
See L-7014 Series in Glossary.
Tnaot Airfield (XV)
Apx 55 E the Mekong River, 82 km SW Lumphat AF and 62 km WSW Kaoh Nhek AF. El. 30'. Cambodia.
To Cham (VS 4-4)
Possibly a.k.a. To Chao? To Cham was apparently original name of Camp Toth, near Ha Tien. The SF camp was renamed to honor PFC William Toth, KIA 27Oct64, when shot in chest during VC ambush while on river patrol. Kien Giang Pr, IV Corps.
To Chao SF Camp (CIDG) (VS 419-495)
At or a.k.a. Ha Tien AF, 3 km NE Ha Tien, 4 km S Cambodia, 80 km NW Rach Gia and about to 2 km E the Gulf of Thailand. Westernmost mainland-based US military installation in SVN. SF Det 81, 5th SF Grp, Det. A-332, Dec64. See Ha Tien (Old). Info/grid per *SF Order of Battle.* Kien Giang Pr, IV Corps.
To Chao SF Camp (FOB) (VS 419-495)
A.k.a. FOB Ha Tien (new). See To Chao SF Camp (CIDG) for location and detail. Grid per *SF Order of Battle.* Kien Giang Pr, IV Corps.
To Chao SF Camp (MGF) (VS 4560-4552)
At Ha Tien South AF, apx 1 km from coast, 9 km SE point where SVN/Cambodia borders meet ocean, 245 km WSW Saigon, 3 km SE Ha Tien and 7 km SE Ha Tien AF. Relocated to Moc Hoa. Info/grid per *SF Order of Battle.* Kien Giang Pr, IV Corps.
To Chau SF Camp (MSF) (VS 566-639)
Immed S Cambodian border, apx 22 km NE Ha Tien45 km due W That Son AF and 15 km ESE Kampong Thrach. Moved to Can Tho. Grid per *SF Order of Battle.* Phong Dinh Pr, IV Corps.
To Chau SF Camp (new) (VS 4560-4552)
See To Chao SF Camp (MGF) for location. 5th SF. Info/grid per *SF Order of Battle.* Transferred to 66th ARVN Border Rangers. Kien Giang Pr, IV Corps.
To Cau Bridge (BT 017-675)
On QL-1, apx 6 km S Da Nang AB and just N the Ba Ren Bridge. 7th Marine AO while it was holding S flank of 1st Mar Div in '69 (which abutted Americal's N flank). XXIV Corps grid per Don Armstrong. Quang Nam Pr, I Corps.
To Da CAP, Thon (YD 916-157)
See CAP Alpha 2. Thua Thien Pr, I Corps.
Toan Thang (n/a)
See Glossary.
Toan Thang I, Operation (n/a)
NW of Saigon, 8Apr-31May68. 2d/14th Inf, 25th Inf Div, et al. III Corps.
Toan Thang, Operation (n/a)
8Apr-31May68. 3d ARVN Corps and IIFFV combined op that was largest op to that date of war. 42 US and 37 ARVN Bns involved. 7,645 rptd NVA/VC KIA. Per *Vietnam Order of Battle,* pp 9-14. Gia Dinh Pr, III Corps.
Toan Thang 41, Operation (n/a)
ARVN Cambodian invasion op, 14-17Apr71. See also Angel's Wing. Cambodia.
Toan Thang 42, Operation (n/a)
Major Cambodian invasion by 3 ARVN armored TFs to destroy enemy/supplies in Svay Rieng Pr. Began at 0710 on 29Apr70, w/out any US advsy supt and ended in little known disaster 4 months later with 1 ARVN TF cut-off below Snuol. 3d ARVN Armored Bde attacked S toward Snuol to rescue the cut-off TF and, after finally reaching its survivors, fled in complete disarray back to SVN through gauntlet of fire. So many vehicles destroyed that there were 35 men aboard every remaining track when TF reached safety. Action received little press because it was overshadowed by Lam Son 719 debacle. III Corps, Parrot's Beak area of Cambodia.
Toan Thang 43/Rockcrusher (n/a)
Southern Cambodian Invasion, May-Jun70, a.k.a. Rockcrusher. Adjunct of Thoan Thang 43. See also Task Force Shoemaker.
Toan Thang 500, Operation (XT 3-9?)
During Op, 6th/31st Inf, 9th Inf Div, conducted ops around FSB Seminole, suffering 7 KIA, 29 WIAs and 159 NVA KIA, 18 POW. III Corps.
Toast, LZ (XT 7-4?)
Said to have been in 1st Inf Div's AO, apparently near FSB Lorraine (XT 709-409). Cited in *Low Level Hell*, p 99. A/2d/12th Inf in heavy contact here apx 26Apr69. Binh Duong Pr?, III Corps.
Toba, LZ (AQ 818-172)
A.k.a. Tuba or Kona? Apx 2 km W Quang Nhieu and 13 km due N Ban Me Thuot AF. Feb66. Darlac Pr, II Corps.

Toby, FSB (YS 713-796)
Along Rte-329, apx 5 km SW FSB Lynx, 13 km SSW Hill 704 and 30 km NE Nui Dat. 161 Bty, RNZA (Master's Bty 6Sep70-8May71) FSB set here 21-29Mar70 (left section). Site of Battle of Grand (See also Madame T). On 1ATF NCO trng map per John Hollett. Also listed at YS 71-79. Phuoc Tuy Pr, III Corps.

Toilet Bowl, The (ZT 25-15)
Area apx 16 km NW Phan Thiet and NW QL-1 railroad tracks up to base of Mtns. Described as flat and sparsely vegetated. Info per D Trp, 2d/1st Cav, web page at www.sirinet.net/~flohr/eddie.htm. Binh Thuan Pr, II Corps.

Tolavana, USS (n/a)
AO-64. Aux Oiler, per Ralph Fries.

Toledo, LZ (XD 988-481)
In valley along QL-9, apx 10 km W Mai Loc, 16 km SW Cam Lo and 33 km W Quang Tri. Numerous FSBs built nearby, including: LZs Bazooka, Camel, Champ, Deacon, Hackney, Parakeet, Amber and Tarzan. Apr70 XXIV Corps grid per Don Armstrong. Quang Tri Pr, I Corps.

Toledo, LZ (ZC 114-521)
On N side QL-14, apx 40 km SW Da Nang, 5 km SW Ha Tan AF. Oct68. Quang Nam Pr, I Corps.

Toledo, Operation (n/a)
10Aug-7Sep66. 173d Abn Bde found est 125,000 rnds of small arms ammo, 50 tons of rice, 10 basecamp s, 75 huts and 5 tunnel systems in May Tao Secret Zone. Phuoc Tuy and Binh Tuy Prvs, III Corps.

Toledo, USS (n./a)
CA-133. Heavy Cruiser. In Oct60, visited Saigon to participate in Independence Day celebrations. [533]

Tom, FSB (YS 650-760)
A.k.a. FSB Xuyen Moc. Apx 23 km due E Nui Dat, 18 km NE Dat Do and apx 12 km N ocean. Renamed FSB Tom in '67. 161 Bty, RNZA (Martin's Bty 28Apr67-6Apr68) here 8-15Jul67 See Xuyen Moc. Phuoc Tuy Pr, III Corps.

Tom, LZ (BN 783-558)
On Nui Da Bac Hill mass, overlooking ocean apx 8 km SSW Thon Son Hai and 23 km due S Phan Rang. Mar67. Ninh Tuan Pr, II Corps.

Tom, LZ (BR 790-535)
Apx 14 km NW Phu Cat AB, 32 km ENE An Khe. Dec65. Binh Dinh Pr, II Corps.

Tom, LZ (BS 900-090)
Possibly a.k.a. LZ North English or LZ Zaeger? Apx 3 km from coast and within sight of LZ English, 4 km S Gia An, 6 km SSW LZ Lowboy and 15 km NNE Bong Son. ARVN/173d Abn here as was 1st Cav, 2d Bn/173d Abn, A Bty, 7th/15th Arty. On map at www.landscaper.net/chighmap.jpg. Map is L-7014-6838-3 (Tam Quan). Data per Ray Smith. Cited in *1st Cav Div Op Rpt, May-Jul67*, p 19, per Peter Cole. Apr67-Oct68. Binh Dinh Pr, II Corps.

Tom, LZ (XD 900-345)
Apx 8 km SE Khe Sanh CB, 3 km SW LZ Thor, 14 km WSW Ca Lu and 3 km S Rte 9. 2d/5th Cav, 1st Cav CA'd here and swept W toward Khe Sanh CB during Op Pegasus, 1-8Apr68. Map is L-7014-6342-2, per Ken Burrington. Also listed at "YD" 898-347 in error? Quang Tri Pr, I Corps.

Tom, LZ (XT 789-457)
Near or a.k.a. FSB Thunder I and/or LZ Alpha? Along QL-13, apx 7 km N Lai Khe. Jul67. Binh Duong Pr, III Corps.

Tom, LZ (XU 666-239)
Just S Cambodia, apx 17 km NNW Loc Ninh and 16 km SE Snuol. 20May66. Binh Long Pr, III Corps.

Tom, LZ (XU 725-016)
Along QL-13, apx 7 km S Loc Ninh and 13 km NNW An Loc. 22Dec67. Binh Long Pr, III Corps.

Tom, LZ (YD 898-347 or XD 898-347)
Listed grid is in ocean and in error. If by chance proper grid zone is XD, then site was apx 8 km SE Khe Sanh CB and 2 km ENE Lang Haren. Quang Tri Pr, I Corps.

Tom, LZ (YT 487-351)
Apx 5 km NE Blackhorse Basecamp and 8 km due S Xuan Loc. Long Khanh Pr, III Corps.

Tom Green County, USS (n/a)
LST-1159. USN Landing Ship, Tank. SVN service with 9th Inf/MRF. Per www.mrfa.org. III/IV Corps?

Tomahawk, FSB (ZC 020-420)
Apx 60 km WSW Hoi An, 30 km W An Hoa, 8 km WSW FSB Maxwell and 7 km N FSB Saber. Used during attack on Base Area 112, Dec68-Feb69. 1st Mar Div MOH awarded to 3d/5th Marines, 1st Mar Div soldier here for 1Mar69 action. Grid per map in *US Marines in Vietnam-1969*, p 90. Quang Nam Pr, I Corps.

Tomahawk, FSB (ZD 117-014)
A.k.a. Hill 132 or Tomahawk Hill. Along S side QL-1 near northern approach to Hai Van Pass, apx 2 km E Q Phu Loc and 40 km SE Hue. Noted for its breathtaking view of Dam Cau Hai Bay/Ocean. Elements C/2/501st Inf, 101st Abn, overrun here 19Jun69, by 72d Sapper Co, 4th NVA Rgt, resulting in 13 US KIA and 45 WIA; three 155mm howitzers destroyed and 1 rendered inoperable. 6 dead were from Bty C, 138th Arty, (1 of handful of Reserve units called to active duty during war) were from Bardstown, KY. Elements C & E/327th Inf involved in mop-up. 2d Howitzer Bn, 138th Kentucky Ntl Guard also helped construct base, '68 or '69. Also listed at ZD 118-013. Thua Thien Pr, I Corps. [534]

Tomahawk, LZ (BS 822-229)
Apx 16 km due S Duc Pho AF and 23 km NNW LZ English. Mar67. Binh Dinh Pr, II Corps.

Tomahawk Hill (ZD 117-014)
A.k.a. Hill 132 or FSB Tomahawk. Hill upon which FSB Tomahawk was built. Thua Thien Pr, I Corps.

Tomb, The (n/a)
See Glossary.

Tombstone, FSB (YD 392-588)
In coastal sands along the Street Without Joy, apx 5 km from ocean and 7 km NE Quang Tri. XXIV Corps grid per D. Armstrong. Also listed at YD 390-580, Jan-Nov69. Quang Tri Pr, I Corps.

Tombstone, LZ (YD 812-154)
A.k.a. the LZ El Paso which later became Camp Eagle? HQ and main basecamp of 101st Abn in '68-69. Originally established about 17Jan68 by 1st Cav, following its re-deployment to I Corps from LZ Two Bits in III Corps. Was briefly 1st Bde/1st Cav CP. Also listed at YD 808-162. Map is L-7014-6541-4, per Ken Burrington. See Camp Eagle. Thua Thien Pr, I Corps. [535]

Tommie L. Sills Compound (YT 47-09)
See Sills Compound. Long Khanh Pr, III Corps.
Ton Dung Airfield (BS 565-324)
See Ba To AF. Quang Ngai Pr, I Corps.
Tong Airfield (WJ)
Apx 35 km WNW Hanoi. El. 34'. NVN.
Tong Cong (n/a)
Mapsheet name of L-7014-6148-3. NVN only.
Tong Doc Long, Kinh (WS 9-4)
See Kinh Tong Doc Long. Go Cong Pr, IV Corps.
Tong Hang Airfield (TF 91-83)
LS-173. CIA/SF, per *Air Facilities Data-Laos.*
Tong Le Chon Basecamp (XT 625-810)
Apx 15 km SW An Loc, 50 km NE Tay Ninh and 10 km SSE Fishhook. Jan69. Tay Ninh Pr, III Corps.
Tong Le Chon Ranger Camp (XT 6222-8103)
See Tong Le Chon SF Camp. Spelling variant of Tonle Cham? Tay Ninh Pr, III Corps.
Tong Le Chon SF Camp (XT 6222-8103)
See Tonle Cham SF Camp. Tay Ninh Pr, III Corps.
Tong Pa How Airfield (PC 62-33)
LS-250 and Ban Rosie. CIA per *Air Facilities Data-Laos.*
Tong Prang Airfield (QC 46-74)
LS-145. CIA/SF, per *Air Facilities Data-Laos.*
Tong Too Airfield (TH 05-67)
LS-186. CIA/SF, per *Air Facilities Data-Laos.*
Toni, LZ (YA 798-458)
Apx 7 km W Plei Djereng New AF and 45 km W Pleiku. Jan66. Pleiku Pr, II Corps.
Tonkin (n/a)
Annam, Cochin China and Tonkin were three major regions of Vietnam as named by French.
Tonkin, Gulf of (AC 8-1)
A.k.a. Vinh Bac Bo. 20°00'00"N-108°00'00"E. NF49-13. Grid is in NVN waters.
Tonle Cham, FSB? (XT 625-810?)
Apx 14 km SW An Loc, 38 km NNE Dau Tieng and apx 8 km SE very tip of Fishhook. Tay Ninh Pr, III Corps.
Tonle Cham Airfield (XT 625-822)
Just S Rte 248, apx 14 km SW An Loc, 38 km NNE Dau Tieng and apx 8 km SE tip of Fishhook, per ONC K-10. Per essay on Internet by Sam McGowan, Katum AF and Tonle Cham AF were forward AFs dreaded by C-130 pilots and aircrews assigned to visit them. [536] At Tonle Cham, rwy was very short and approaches/takeoffs apparently very difficult. El. 33', 3,000' laterite rwy. See also Katum AF and Shuttle X. An Xuyen Pr, IV Corps.
Tonle Cham Basecamp (XT 625-810)
See Tong Le Chon. Tay Ninh Pr, III Corps.
Tonle Cham SF Camp (XT 6222-8103)
A.k.a. Tong Le Chon SF Camp and FSB Jake? At or near Tonle Cham AF/Heliport and FSB Jake? Just S Rte 248, apx 15 km SW An Loc, 50 km NE Tay Ninh and 10 km SSE tip of Fishhook. SF Det 52, 5th SF Grp CIDG Det A-334, May '67. Transferred to 92d ARVN Border Rangers. In Mar73, and soon after Paris Peace Accords signed, small Bn of ARVN Border Rangers defending site was hit by NVA Div-sized attack but held gallantly for almost 1 month. Took NVA 20 grnd attacks and 300 shellings of some 10,000 rnds arty, rocket and mortar fire before it fell. Some data/grid per *SF Order of Battle*, other data per *A Better War*, p 370. Tay Ninh Pr, III Corps.
Tonle Chon Ranger Camp (XT 6222-8103)
See Tonle Cham SF Camp. Tay Ninh Pr, III Corps.
Tonle Roti (WT 970-730)
See Rach Beng Go River. Tay Ninh Pr, III Corps.
Tonle Thom River (WT, WS, XS, XR)
See Mekong River. IV Corps.
Tonto, LZ (BR 855-470)
Apx 4 km NW Phu Cat AB, 6 km W QL-1 and 17 km ENE Binh Khe. LZs Tonto and Trigger were part of Op Clear House, 1st/8th Cav, 18-20Dec65. Binh Dinh Pr, II Corps.
Tonueng Prong (AR 77-55)
See Tonueng, Lac. Pleiku Pr, II Corps.
Tonueng, Lac (AR 77-55)
A.k.a. Bien Ho, Lac. Freshwater lake about 2 x 3 km in size, apx 7 km N Pleiku and just to E QL-14 at 14°03N-108°00'E. On ND49-05 JOG. Pleiku Pr, II Corps.
Tony, LZ (YA 798-458)
See LZ Toni. Pleiku Pr, II Corps.
Toong Cha Airfield (TF 99-90)
LS-334. CIA/SF, per *Air Facilities Data-Laos.*
Toong Set Airfield (XB 37-81)
LS-449. Apx 240 km SW Da Nang SVN, and 50 km ENE Pakse, per TPC K-10A. CIA/SF, per *Air Facilities Data-Laos.* El. 4,120'. Laos.
Tooth Lake (BS 528-752)
1 km diameter lake apx 1 km S the Song Tra Khuc River, 13 km WNW Quang Ngai and 8 km WNW Quang Ngai AF. Significance unknown. Americal list. Map is L-7014-6739-3. Quang Ngai Pr, I Corps.
Top Hat, The (XT?)
Terrain feature mentioned on webpage of 187th AHC's Bn Hist Supps at www.kbi.org/187thahc/incident_67. htm. Apparently near Tay Ninh and possibly formed by course of the Song Vam Co Dong River? Tay Ninh Pr, III Corps.
Topaz, LZ (BR 955-617)
Apx 8 km SE Phu My, 24 km NNE Phu Cat AB and 6 km E QL-1. Oct66. Binh Dinh Pr, II Corps.
Topeka, LZ (AT 935-764)
Along Rte 542, apx 4 km NW Hill 327 and 7 km due W main rwy at Da Nang AB. Apr70 XXIV Corps grid per Don Armstrong. Quang Nam Pr, I Corps.
Topeka, USS (n/a)
CLG 8, Guided Missile Light Cruiser. Armed with 6-inch/47-caliber guns, eff to 22,000 yds.
Torch, LZ (XD 911-278)
Near Lang Up 2, apx 14 km SSE Khe Sanh CB and 6 km SE LZ Loon. Built 7Jun68 by 3d/9th Marines 3d Mar Div during Ops Robin North and Robin South (ops against 308th NVA Div's 88th and 102d Rgts). Also used during Op Maine Crag, Mar-May69. On map p 65, *US Marines in Vietnam-1969*. Also listed at XD 907-278 and 906-279. Quang Tri Pr, I Corps.
Torch Hill (XT 873-219)
Apx 10 km NW Phu Loi AF, 14 km ENE Cu Chi and 2 km W QL-13Dec68-Feb69. Binh Duong Pr, III Corps.
Tornado, LZ (YD 22-13?)
Described as having been 4 km NE FSB Cunningham; which, if accurate, means site was N Rte 922, about 37 km SSW Quang Tri. Used by K/3d/9th Mar, 3d Mar Div

during const of FSB Lightning, 1Feb69, USMC. Grid is est. Quang Tri Pr, I Corps.

Torpedo, LZ (XD 781-392)
Apx 2 km N FSB Smith, 7 km WSW Khe Sanh CB, 6 km SSW La Vien and 12 km due W Lang Kat. Apr70 XXIV Corps grid per Don Armstrong. Quang Tri Pr, I Corps.

Torrens (n/a)
Australian Escort ship serving under US 7th Flt.

Tortilla Flats, LZ (ZC 103-530)
On Mtn, overlooking and apx 6 km WSW of Ha Tan AF, 42 km SW Da Nang AB. Oct68. Quang Nam Pr, I Corps.

Tortue, Ile (VS 83-02)
See Hon Tre Island. Kien Giang Pr, IV Corps.

Tortue, Pointe (CP 0-6)
See Pointe Tortue. Khanh Hoa Pr, II Corps.

Tortuga, USS (n/a)
LSD-26. USN Landing Ship, Dock. Supt 9th Inf Div/MRF in '66, per MRF Assn at www.mrfa.org. III/IV Corps?

Torture Island (VS 83-02)
See Hon Tre Island. Kien Giang Pr, IV Corps.

Toth, Camp (VS 4-4)
Originally Camp To Cham, near Ha Tien. Renamed to honor PFC William Toth, KIA 27Oct64, when shot during VC ambush while on river patrol. Kien Giang Pr, IV Corps.

Tou Morong (various)
A.k.a. Tou Morong and To Mo Rong. Tou Morongs listed at: ZB, 188-476, 190-460 and 102-476, with To Mo Rong at ZB 179-504. Kontum Pr, II Corps.

Tou Morong (ZB 19-48)
A.k.a. Toumorong. Apx 22 km NNE Dak To ville, 22 km ENE Dak Seang AF and 33 km NE Ben Het. Remote CIDG outpost in W Central Highlands, l. Kontum Pr, II Corps.

Touchdown, LZ (ZA 150-155)
Apx 5 km S Plei Meun, 31 km ENE peak Chu Pong and 32 km SSW Pleiku. Oct65. Pleiku Pr, II Corps.

Toughie, LZ (BR 553-680)
At N end of 1.5 km diameter lake, apx 15 km NE Vinh Thanh, 6 km ESE LZ Sherry, 12 km WSW LZ John Henry and 25 km NNE An Khe. 4th Div AO, '70. A Bty, 2d/9th Arty here Jan70, C Bty 6th/29th Arty here Aug70, and B/2d/35th Inf also here '70. Name/grid per Jim Claeys. Aug69-Oct70. Binh Dinh Pr, II Corps.

Toumorong (various)
A.k.a. Tou Morong and To Mo Rong. Tou Morong at: ZB, 188-476 and 190-460 and 102-476, with To Mo Rong at ZB 179-504. Kontum Pr, II Corps.

Toumorong (ZB 19-48?)
A.k.a. Tou Morong and To Mo Rong. Apx 22 km NNE Dak To ville, 22 km ENE Dak Seang AF and 33 km NE Ben Het. Remote CIDG outpost in W Central Highlands. Kontum Pr, II Corps.

Toumorong CIDG Camp (ZB 188-475?)
Remote CIDG outpost at 5000', apx 33 km NE Dak To 2 AF and 16 km NE Kon Honong. Under siege May66, and center of relief effort known as Battle of Toumorong, involving elements 1st Bde/101st Abn opcon to 1st Cav, and 1st Cav, Jun66. See *Battles in the Monsoon,* pp 271-279. Also spelled "Toumoroung" and "Tou Mrong." See also LZs Jenny and Lima Zulu. Kontum Pr, II Corps.

Tounorong? SF Camp (ZV 130-360?)
If grid correct, site was apx 13 km NE Ban Don AF and 36 km NW Ban Me Thuot. Possible misspelling of Toumorong and, if so, grid zone should be ZB, not ZV. Jul66. Darlac Pr?, II Corps.

Tour of Duty (n/a)
See Glossary.

Tour Extensions (n/a)
See Glossary.

Tourane (BT 04-78)
A.k.a. Touron and Da Nang. [537] See Da Nang. Quang Nam Pr, I Corps.

Tourane Airfield (BT 01-76)
See Da Nang AB. Quang Nam Pr, I Corps.

Tourane River (BT-03-73)
French name for Song Ha River, a.k.a. the Da Nang River. Quang Nam Pr, I Corps.

Tourane, Baie de (AT 9-8)
A.k.a. Vinh Da Nang. Bay at 16°08'N-108°11'E. Quang Nam Pr, I Corps.

Tourane, Cape (BT 1-8)
A.k.a. Mui Da Nang. Cape at 16°07'N-108°19'E. On ND49-01 JOG. Quang Nam Pr, I Corps.

Touron (BT 04-78)
A.k.a. Tourane and Da Nang. See Da Nang. Quang Nam Pr, I Corps. [538]

Tower, LZ (XD 701-364)
Close to Laotian border, near point where QL-9 crossed it a few km W Sa Tiac, and apx 15 km WSW Khe Sanh CB and 65 km WSW Quang Tri. Apr70 XXIV Corps grid per Don Armstrong. Quang Tri Pr, I Corps.

Tower of Pisa (YS 499-548)
See FSB Thrust at grid. Phuoc Tuy Pr, III Corps.

Towers, USS (n/a)
DDG-9. Guided-Missile DD, per Ralph Fries.

Towhee, USS (n/a)
AGS 28. Hydrographic Survey Ship. Also spelled *Towher*?

Towher, USS (n/a)
AGS-28. Hydrographic Survey Ship. Also spelled *Towhee*? Per Ralph Fries.

Town House BEQ (XS 8-9)
At 39 Hai Ba Trung St. (Mess and Club), Saigon. Nov 65, 46 rms (HQ Supt Activity). Data per *Vietnam Military Lore, 1959-1973*. Gia Dinh Pr, III Corps.

Townes, Camp (BR 972-252)
Along LTL-6B, apx 12 km WNW Qui Nhon AF, 6 km NE the ROK AF and 3 km ESE LTL-6B's intersection with QL-1. Said to have been basecamp of 1st/30th Arty. Per Ray Bows, was named to honor 1Lt Morton E. Townes, Jr., KIA 3Feb67, and was HQ for 4th/60th Arty and E Bty/41st Arty. Grid per Dan Gillotti. Binh Dinh Pr, II Corps.

Tra Bong (BS 344-884)
Ville apx 40 km NW Quang Ngai. FSB A-107 here, as was SF camp. In Aug 70, reportedly converted to ARVN Ranger or VN SF camp. Before 28Aug65, camp apparently at another location. AF and heliport here as well. Americal list. Map is L-7014-6739-4. Also listed at BS 338 878, 341-880 and 343-883. Quang Ngai Pr, I Corps.

Tra Bong (n/a)
Mapsheet name of L-7014-6739-4. SVN.

Tra Bong, LZ (BS 340-900)
Apx 28 km SW Chu Lai AF, 16 km NW Ba Gia AF and 34 km S Tam Ky. Apr70 XXIV Corps grid per Don Armstrong. Quang Tin Pr, I Corps.
Tra Bong-LZ Cindy (BS 35-38?)
See LZ Cindy. Quang Ngai Pr?, I Corps.
Tra Bong (new) SF Camp (BS 3455-8838)
Apx 28 km SW Chu Lai AF, 16 km NW Ba Gia AF and 34 km S Tam Ky. SF Det 6, 5th SF CIDG Det A-107, Oct65 and Det A-107, Oct66. Transferred to 61st ARVN Border Rangers. Grid per *Special Forces Order of Battle*. Quang Ngai Pr, I Corps.
Tra Bong (old) SF Camp (BS 3455-8838)
See Tra Bong (new) for location and unit data. Moved to Plei Do Lim. Info/grid per *Special Forces Order of Battle.* Quang Ngai Pr, I Corps.
Tra Bong Airfield (BS 34-88)
Apx 28 km SW Chu Lai AF, 16 km NW Ba Gia AF and 34 km S Tam Ky. El. 131' Quang Ngai Pr, I Corps.
Tra Bong Heliport (BS 348-378)
At or just SE of Tra Bong AF/SF Camp. Heliport #687, alt 919', at 14°48'00"N-108°32'00"E. Quang Ngai Pr, I Corps.
Tra Cu (n/a)
Mapsheet name of L-7014-6228-2. SVN.
Tra Cu ATSB (XS 47-97)
Along Song Vam Co Dong River, apx 13 km WNW Duc Hoa AF and 33 km due W Tan Son Nhut AB. USN Advanced Tactical Supt Base, '68-71, per MRF Assn Website. Long An Pr, III Corps.
Tra Cu Canal (XS 442-951)
Apx 15 km W Duc Hoa AF and 38 km W Saigon. Jan69. Hau Nghia Pr, III Corps
Tra Cu SF Camp (XS 478-985)
On N bank of the Song Vam Co Dong, apx 33 km due W Tan Son Nhut AB and 6 km SW Khiem Cuong. A-Team Camp. SF Det 67, 5th SF Grp CIDG Det A-326, Jan67. 25th Div Arty ground surveillance 5-man teams using TPS-25 ground scanning radar here at times. Transferred to 64th ARVN Border Rangers. Also listed at XS 471-973. Some data/grid per *SF Order of Battle.* See http:// pacer.calpoly.edu/Tri/radar.html for detailed info. Long An Pr, III Corps.
Tra Lang SF Camp (WR 755-665)
A.k.a. Long Phu SF Camp. Apx 32 km WNW Soc Trang, 45 km SSE Can Tho, 27 km SE Vi Thanh AF and at same grid as Long Phu Heliport/SF Camp. 5th SF. Grid per *SF Order of Battle.* Ba Xuyen Pr, IV Corps.
Tra Linh (n/a)
Mapsheet name of L-7014-6254-1. NVN/China.
Tra Ma Airfield (BS 0-9?)
Location? Possible variant of "Tra My?" Its 830' dirt rwy was built for Army's Caribou acft and notorious for being shortest Caribou rwy in VN, and sandwiched in valley requiring very steep approach. 1st lndg here made by Capt. E. M. Gross, who touched down 12' from one end and stopped 8' from other on his 3d try, after which it became obvious rwy need lengthening! [539] A Tra Mi is in BS 0-9, and Tra My at BS 014-972. Quang Tin Pr?, I Corps.
Tra My Airfield (BS 016-970)
See Hua Duc AF. Quang Tin Pr, I Corps.
Tra My SF Camp (BS 014-972)
In Valley of Nam Nim River near Old Hau Duc, apx 54 km WSW Chu Lai and 20 km SW Tien Phuoc SF Camp/AF. 5th SF. Moved to Kham Duc. Info/grid per *SF Order of Battle.* Quang Tin Pr, I Corps.
Tra O, Dam (BR 9-8)
Lagoon at 14°19'N-109°06'E. On ND49-05 JOG. Binh Dinh Pr, II Corps.
Tra On (XS 0-0)
Along N bank of the Mekong, apx 17 km SE Can Tho and 43 km N Soc Trang AF. Vinh Long Pr, IV Corps.
Tra On Airfield (XS 019-009)
Along N bank of the Mekong, apx 17 km SE Can Tho, 43 km N Soc Trang AF, 44 km due W Tra Vinh AF (Phu Vinh) 32 km due S Vinh Long major AF, 65 km SW My Tho, and 120 km SW Saigon, per TPC K-10D. Listed as "Abnd, AF # VA4-250," in Aug69 TAD per Frank Penk, Jr. Not in Feb73 TAD. El. 8'. Vinh Long Pr, IV Corps.
Tra On Heliport (XS 016-014)
Adj to Tra On AF along N bank of Mekong River apx 17 km SE Can Tho. "Heliport #688, alt 7', soccer field, VC to S, at 09°58'00"N-105°56'00"E." Vinh Long Pr, IV Corps.
Tra Phu SF Camp (VS 533-551)
A.k.a. or assets moved to FOB Ha Tien (new)? Apx 3 km E Cambodia, 13 km NE Ha Tien and 7 km NE Xom Vam Hang. 5th SF. Info/grid per *SF Order of Battle.* Also listed at VB 533-551, but that is error. Kien Giang Pr, IV Corps.
Tra Tien Forest (VS 640-440)
Generally about 20 km ESE Ha Tien AF. Jul70. Kien Giang Pr, IV Corps.
Tra Trach Valley (YC 845-991)
See Ta Trach Valley. Thua Thien Pr, I Corps.
Tra Vinh (Phu Vinh) (n/a)
Mapsheet L-7014-6228-1. Full sheet name: Phu Vinh (Tra Vinh). SVN.
Tra Vinh Airfield (XR 459-975)
Major AF in Mekong Delta just SW Phu Vinh, 38 km due S Truc Giang AF, 48 km S My Tho and 100 km SSW Saigon. El. 7', 3,600' asph rwy. Vinh Binh Pr, IV Corps.
Tra Vinh Province (WR/XR)
In what later became known as IV Corps and absorbed into what became primarily Vinh Binh Pr. Thought to have ceased existence shortly before or during early US presence in SVN? Actual dates of existence unknown. IV Corps.
Trac, FSB (YT)
No data. III Corps.
Tracer, LZ (AR 846-592)
Apx 4 km NE Plei Neh, 15 km NE Pleiku, 12 km NE Cu Hanh AF and 21 km WNW Suoi Doi AF. 4th Div AO, '70. Name/grid per Jim Claeys. Pleiku Pr, II Corps.
Tracey, LZ (XT?)
Per *LRRP Company Commander*, p 118, was in War Zone D and relatively close to the Cambodian border (8Jan69). Possibly was the FSB Tracy listed at XT 440-072? Tay Ninh Pr?, III Corps.
Traci, FSB (XT?)
Cited in *Incursion*, per Peter Cole. Apparently Cambodian Incursion FSB. Possibly FSB Tracy at XT 440-072? In either III Corps or Cambodia?

Tracy, LZ/FSB (XT 440-072)
A.k.a. LZ/FSB Traci and Tracey. On E bank Song Vam Co Dong River, 36 km WNW Saigon, 22 km SW Cu Chi and 12 km ESE Duc Hue AF. 1st/8th Cav, 1st Cav here Jan-69, per Frank Penk, Jr. Occupied by 1st/505th Inf, 82d Abn 17Mar69, who were assigned AO from Tracy to Cambodian border between Angel's Wing and Parrot's Beak. [540] Cited in *1st Cav Op Rpt Feb69/Apr69*, p2, *1st Cav Op Rpt Nov68/Jan69*, p 97, per Peter Cole. Also listed at XT 439-071 and XS 440-072? Hau Nghia Pr, III Corps.
Trai, Cape (US 7-4)
A.k.a. Mui Da Trai. On W edge Phu Quoc Island near 10°22'N-103°50'E. On NC48-05 JOG.
Trai Bi Base (XT 112-709)
Adj Trai Bi SF camp, apx 23 km NNW Tay Ninh, 20 km NW Nui Ba Den and 14 km SSE Thien Ngon AF. Feb67. Tay Ninh Pr, III Corps.
Trai Bi Forward Support Base (XT 120-700)
Along QL-22 apx 23 km NNW Tay Ninh and 20 km NW Nui Ba Den. Here Mar67. Tay Ninh Pr, III Corps.
Trai Bi SF Camp (XT 116-698)
Along QL-22 apx 23 km NNW Tay Ninh, 20 km NW Nui Ba Den and 14 km SSE Thien Ngon AF. SF Det 55, 5th SF, Det A-323, Oct66. Moved to Thien Ngon. Grid per *SF Order of Battle*. Tay Ninh Pr, III Corps.
Trai Ca Airfield (BP 941-138)
See Ba Ngoi. AF. Khanh Hoa Pr, II Corps.
Trai Cu CIDG Camp (XT or XS?)
Spelling variant of Tar Cu? There is a Trai Cu at BS 7-2, which is SSW Duc Pho in Quang Ngai Pr, and another at AN 813-807 in Lam Dong Pr; however, one text puts site in Hau Nghia Pr, which suggests Tra Cu is correct name.
Trai Dao, FSB (ZB 156-057)
Along QL-14 at Trai Dao, apx 20 km NNW Kontum and 22 km SE Dak To 2 AF. A Bty 1st/92d Arty here 24Mar69. Name/grid in 4th Div Op rpt per Craig Miller, Kontum Pr, II Corps.
Trai Hut (n/a)
Mapsheet name of L-7014-5952-4. NVN only.
Train Compound (XT 99-14?)
At Bien Hoa AB. Named to honor 1Lt William F Train, III, KIA 16Jun62 with Capt. Walter McCarthy (McCarthy BOQ) during ambush of convoy near Ben Cat SF Camp, 34 km N Saigon. Grid is est. Data per *Vietnam Military Lore, 1959-1973*. Bien Hoa Pr, III Corps.
Training Center #1 (XT 65-08, 65-69 or 68-05?)
A.k.a. Quan Tro Trng Ctr. If at XT 650-087, was apx 21 km NW Tan Son Nhut; if at XT 650-687, was apx 4 km NE Minh Thanh AF; and if at XT 68-05, was apx 13 km NW Tan Son Nhut? One list put site at XT 050-687; however, that grid is in Cambodia and likely error. Listed grid est from description of site. See also Quan Tro and Quang Trung Trng Centers. Hau Nghia Pr?, III Corps.
Trains, Div (82d Abn) (XS 798-862)
See Division Trains. Gia Dinh Pr, III Corps.
Trains, FSB (BR 9-4 or CR 1-4?)
Near Phu Cat AB, 31Jan67. 1st/14th Inf/25th Div here then. Per *Rites of Passage*, p 224, the 1st Cav called area near FSB Trains & Bronco Beach. Binh Dinh Pr, II Corps.
Tram (n/a)
Vietnamese for lake or pool.
Tram Da Mi, Xa (n/a)
Mapsheet L-7014-6531-2. Sheet: Xa Tram Da Mi. SVN.
Tram Vang Heliport (XT 414-270)
Apx 3 km NE Go Dau Ha, 24 km SE Tay Ninh and 27 km NW Cu Chi. Heliport #689, alt 23', at 11°05'30"N-106°17'30"E, per Feb73 TAD. Tay Ninh Pr, III Corps.
Tram, Pointe (YS 6-5)
See Pointe Tram. Phuoc Tuy Pr, III Corps.
Tran Dinh (TJ 94-66)
Vietminh name for Muong Thanh (DBP) Valley. NVN.
Tran Hung Dao, Operation (n/a)
5-17Feb68. Tet '68 op in Saigon area involving VNMC, 4 ARVN Ranger and 5 ARVN Abn Bns. 953 rptd VC KIA, per *VN Order of Battle*, pp 9-14. III Corps.
Tran Hung Dao Heliport, Camp (XS 825-945)
Pad apparently inside Tan Son Nhut AB at the JGS HQ. Was Joint Gen Staff's heliport. "Heliport #768, Saigon (JGS Cmpd/High Cmd Cmpd). 700' x 300', PPR. Tel. Air Tfc coordinator at 923-4667/4160. No waiting in lndg areas. Prkg areas at N end of pad mrkd H. Prkg near revetment NW side of pad prohibited. Overflt of Cmpd prohibited between Vo Tonh St on diagonal line starting at Boi Lo Vo Di Nguy St, extending across golf course and cemetery to access road to MACV Annex on N, to Vo Tonh St on W. Pad located in center of Cmpd. No ITS or RDO facilities." At 10°48'N 106°40'E, El. 33', per Feb73 TAD. Gia Dinh Pr, III Corps.
Tran Hung Dao II, Operation (n/a)
17Feb-8Mar68. Extension of Op Tran Hung Dao in Saigon AO. 713 rptd NVA/VC KIA, per *Vietnam Order of Battle*, pp 9-14. Gia Dinh et al Prvs, III Corps.
Tran Le Xuan Le (n/a)
See Glossary.
Tran Quan Khai HQ-2 (n/a)
See CGC *Bering Strait*.
Trang, Camp (n/a)
A.k.a. Camp Carrow. SF camp, per *SF Order of Battle*. Thailand.
Trang Airfield (n/a)
Apx 705 km SSW Bangkok, and 110 km WNW Songkhla AF. El. 60'. Thailand.
Trang Bang (XT 49-19)
Ville apx 15 km WNW Cu Chi, and 47 km NW Saigon. Hau Nghia Pr, III Corps.
Trang Bang Bridge (XT 501-194)
Along vital supply corridor between the Cu Chi, Saigon, Long Binh and Tan Son Nhut areas, apx 15 km NW Cu Chi and 47 km NW Saigon, Story/photos of site in 23Sep68 issue of *Tropic Lightning News*, Vol. 3, No. 39, pp 4-5. Secured by B Trp, 3d/4th Cav, 25th Inf Div during Tet '68. Also listed at XT 520-190. Hau Nghia Pr, III Corps.
Trang Bang Heliport (XT 490-190)
At NE corner Trang Bang near intersection TL 10 and QL-1, apx 16 km WNW Cu Chi and 40 km NW Tan Son Nhut AB. "Heliport #690, alt 30', soccer field, at 11°01'30"N-106°21'40"E," per Feb73 TAD. Hau Nghia Pr, III Corps.
Trang Bang Joint Ops Center (XT 490-190)
At Trang Bang Heliport. Apx 16 km WNW Cu Chi and 40 km NW Tan Son Nhut. Nov66. Hau Nghia Pr, III Corps.

Trang Bang Outpost (XT 493-201)
Apx 1 km NE Trang Bang Heliport and 17 km WNW Cu Chi. Feb68. Hau Nghia Pr, III Corps.

Trang Bao Laager Site (XT 614-226)
See US/ARVN Laager Site. Binh Duong Pr, III Corps.

Trang Bao On (XT 625-227)
A.k.a. Xa Trang Bao On. Apx 7 km NNW Cu Chi CB and 22 km SW Lai Khe. 2d/14th US Inf and 2d/49th ARVN Rgt, joint ops here Summer '69. Data per www.en.com/users/kramsey/dragons.html. Binh Duong Pr, III Corps.

Trang Boa On (XT 625-227)
See Trang Bao On. Binh Duong, III Corps.

Trang Bom Airfield (YT 192-112)
Along N edge of QL-1, apx 20 km E Bien Hoa AB and 15 km NNE Long Thanh N AF. Bien Hoa Pr, III Corps.

Trang Bong Airfield (YT 192-112)
See Trang Bom AF. Bien Hoa Pr, III Corps.

Trang Co (XT 535-315)
A.k.a. Xa Trang Co. Apx 30 km SE Tay Ninh, 6 km WSW Ben Suc and 8 km from Cambodia. Site of Cachu Forest Reserve. Tay Ninh Pr, III Corps.

Trang Lon Airfield (XT 168-518)
See Tay Ninh West AF. Tay Ninh Pr, III Corps.

Trang Phuc Airfield (ZV 032-268)
See Ban Don AF. Darlac Pr, II Corps.

Trang Phuc SF Camp (ZV 025-265)
A.k.a. Camp Rose, Ban Don SF and Trang Phuoc SF Camp. Along TL-1 and immed E the Da Krong (Ea Krong) River, 500 meters W Ban Don AF and 36 km NW Ban Me Thuot. 5th SF Det 31, CIDG Det A-233 here. Transferred to 72d ARVN Border Rangers. Also listed at ZV 0366-2671, which is AF grid. Feb-Dec67. Grid per *SF Order of Battle*. See also Ban Don. Darlac Pr, II Corps.

Trang Phuoc SF Camp (ZV 025-267)
See Trang Phuc SF Camp. Darlac Pr, II Corps.

Trang Sup Heliport (XT 177-550)
Apx 4 km N Tay Ninh West AF, 7 km NW Tay Ninh and 10 km WSW Nui Ba Den. Heliport #691, alt 25', at 11°21'00"N-106°04'30"E. Due N Tay Ninh West apx 3.5 km, Data per Feb73 TAD. Tay Ninh Pr, III Corps.

Trang Sup SF Camp (XT 1688-5550)
Apx 4 km N Tay Ninh West AF, 7 km NW Tay Ninh and 10 km WSW Nui Ba Den. 5th SF Det 58, Det A 411, Dec64; Det A-323 (was 111), Oct65. Transferred to 65th ARVN Border Rangers. Info/grid in *SF Order of Battle*. AAR, Battle of Tay Ninh (17Aug-27Sep68), HQ 25th ID, 2Feb69 (per Butch Sincock) lists grid as XT 170-555. Tay Ninh Pr, III Corps.

Trang Sup, Camp (XT 395-247)
See Go Dau Ho. III Corps.

Trans Caribbean, SS (n/a)
Spelled *Trans CCarbbea*, but that is likely error. Possibly *Trans Carbbea*? Commercial contract ship. *CCarbbea* spelling found at www. vietnamunitmemorial.org site.

Trans CCarbbea, SS (n/a)
See *Trans Caribbean, SS.*

Trans Colorado, SS (n/a)
A.k.a. *Tanscolorado*. Commercial transport under govt contract, per Ralph Fries.

Trans Globe, SS (n/a)
Commercial transport under govt contract, per Ralph Fries.

Transcolorado, SS (n/a)
A.k.a. *Trans Colorado*. See Evacuation of Da Nang in Glosssary.

Trapeang Rung Airfield (n/a)
Apx 180 km W Phnom Penh. 3,500'. rwy. El. 35'. Cambodia.

Trapeze, The (CQ 1-6)
A.k.a. Le Trapeze. Coastal point at 13°15'N-109°19'E. ND49-09 JOG. Phu Yen Pr, II Corps.

Trapezoid, The (XT 60-40)
Arrowhead-shaped terrain feature that ran from NW to SE, with it's pointed southern end roughly 6 km due W An My and 16 km N Saigon. Michelin Plantation and Suoi Ho Da River formed its NW edge, the Song Saigon River roughly its SW edge, and the Rach Thi Thinh River its NE edge. FSBs Gela and El Paso were to its S/SW, while FSBs Oran and Picardy were to its N/NW. "The Mushroom" was within this feature. Discussed in *Low Level Hell* and on its 1st Div TAOR map. Also on map in *Rangers At War*, p 234. Grid is apx center of mass. Binh Duong Pr, III Corps.

Traps, The (n/a)
See Glossary.

Trat Airfield (TU 2-5)
At 12°15'00"N-102°31'00"E. NIMA data. Thailand.

Trathen, USS (n/a)
DD-530, per Ralph Fries.

Trau Nam, Mui (US 9-5)
Coastal point at 10°27'N-104°00'E. On NC48-05 JOG. Kien Giang Pr, IV Corps.

Trau Nam, Vung (CQ 1-1)
Bay at 12°47'N-109°20'E. On ND49-13 JOG. Khanh Hoa Pr, II Corps.

Trddug Giang (BT 3-3)
A.k.a. Truong Giang. Lagoon at 15°40'N-108°30'E. On ND49-01 JOG. Quang Tin Pr, I Corps.

Tre, Mui (CP 1-5)
Coastal point at 12°13'30"N-109°19'18"E. On ND49-13 JOG. Khanh Hoa Pr, II Corps.

Tres Sommets, Ile des (YJ 1-0)
Island of Three Summits. NVN.

Tri Bac Station (YD 887-148)
At Phu Bai. Home of 8th Radio Research Unit. Prior to Fall of '68, was known as 8th Radio Research Field Station. Was front for ASA (Army Security Agency) secret ops. Grid is for AF. Thua Thien Pr, I Corps.

Tri Border Area (YB 75-25)
Apx 27 km WNW Dak To, and along Kontum Prov border. Area surrounding point where the borders of Cambodia, Laos and SVN all meet. Kontum Pr, II Corps.

Tri Can (Thieu Hoa) (n/a)
Mapsheet L-7014-6148-4. Full sheet name: Thieu Hoa (Tri Can). NVN only.

Tri-Comers, FSB (YT 20-12)
See Tri-Corners. Bien Hoa Pr, III Corps.

Tri-Corners, FSB (YT 20-12)
Near intersection of QL-1 and minor rd that ran NE to Ap Thanh Dang and Xa Binh Hoa, apx 1 km N Trang Bom AF, 27 km W Xuan Loc, 15 km due E Plantation AF, 14 km NNE Long Thanh North AF and 22 km ESE Bien Hoa AB. 3d/7th and 4th/12th Inf, 3d/7th Inf, 199th LIB. Grid per 199th LIB Assn. Bien Hoa Pr, III Corps.

Tri Le (n/a)
Mapsheet name of L-7014-6046-4. NVN only.
Tri Quang (n/a)
See Thinh Tri Quang in Glossary.
Tri Quyet Thang (YS 17-00?)
A.k.a. Bearcat SF Camp. See Bearcat for detailed history. Bien Hoa Pr, III Corps.
Tri Tam (XT)
Ville in War Zone C where Rte 245 meets the Song Saigon River, apx 25 km E Tay Ninh, 20 km due W Ap Bau Bang, 18 km NW Ben Cat and 18 km SW Minh Thanh. Tay Ninh Pr?, III Corps.
Tri Tam (Quan Dau Tieng) (n/a)
Mapsheet name of L-7014-6231-1. SVN.
Tri Tom, Camp (WS 005-515)
See Tri Ton SF Camp. Kien Giang Pr, IV Corps.
Tri Ton (n/a)
Mapsheet name of L-7014-6029-4. SVN.
Tri Ton (various) (WS/VS)
Common Viet place-name. See grid squares WS 2-7, VS 8-2 (Thon Tri Ton), VS 9-2 (Xom Tri Ton).
Tri Ton Heliport (WS 005-520)
Apx 5 km due N Nui Co To and 46 km NNW Rach Gia. “Heliport #692, alt 10', soccer fld, at 10°25'00"N-105°00'00"E,” per Feb73 TAD. Chau Doc Pr, IV Corps.
Tri Ton SF Camp (WS 005-515)
Apx 12 km SSE That Son SF Camp and AF, 63 km ENE Ha Tien and 54 km NNW Rach Gia. 5th SF Grp, Det. A-427, Oct65. Moved to Phu Quoc. Spelled “Tri Tom” in DA Mil Hist records summary. Grid per *SF Order of Battle*. See Phan Chau (old). Kien Giang Pr, IV Corps.
Tri Ton, Xom (n/a)
Mapsheet L-7014-5929-2. Xom Tri Ton. SVN.
Trident, LZ (ZC 184-401)
Apx 22 km due W Phuoc Binh AF, 6 km SW Ha Tan AF and 48 km SW Da Nang AB. XXIV Corps index per Don Armstrong. Quang Nam Pr, I Corps.
Triem Duc (n/a)
Mapsheet name of L-7014-6735-1. SVN.
Triem Trung 1 CAP (n/a)
See CAP 2-3-4. 2d CAG. Quang Nam Pr, I Corps.
Trieu Ai CAP (YD 2-5 or 3-5?)
Generally SW Quang Tri CB. Papa 2, 4th CAG per Tim Duffie. Quang Tri Pr, I Corps.
Trieu Chau 2 CAP (BT 1-5?)
See CAP 2-3-9. 2d CAG. Quang Nam Pr, I Corps.
Trieu Phuong Heliport (YD 340-533)
N edge of Quang Tri. Heliport #693, alt 33', at 16°45'00"N-107°11'30"E, per Feb73 TAD. Quang Tri Pr, I Corps.
Trieu Relocation Ville (YD 403-574)
In Street Without Joy area, apx 7 km NE Quang Tri, 12 km SSE mouth Cua Viet and 4 km from coast. Oct69. Quang Tri Pr, I Corps.
Trigger, LZ (BR 645-885)
Apx 22 km WSW Bong Son and 17 km WNW Ha Tay AF. LZs Tonto and Trigger were used in Op Clear House, 1st/8th Cav, 18-20Dec65. Mar66. Binh Dinh Pr, II Corps.
Triple Hill (YD 331-203)
Apx 1.5 km NW FSB Ripcord and 37 km W Hue. Significant terrain feature during siege of FSB Ripcord, May-Jun70. Consisted of 3 hilltops closely aligned along same ridge. 1:50k map image of site in *Ripcord, Screaming Eagles Under Siege, Vietnam 1970*, p 206. See also FSB Ripcord. Thua Thien Pr, I Corps.
Tripoli, USS (n/a)
LPH-10. Lndg. Platform, Helo, per Ralph Fries.
Trish, FSB (YS 526-889)
A.k.a. FSB Flinders? Apx 23 km NNE Nui Dat, 11 km WNW Tasman and 3.5 km ESE FSB Bass. On 1ATF NCO trng map per John Hollett. 1ATF. Phouc Tuy Pr, III Corps.
Tro Voi, Ru (WF 5-5)
A.k.a. Nui Thien Nhan. Mtn range at 18°34'N-105°32'E. On NE48-07 JOG. NVN.
Trooper, LZ (BR 894-841)
Apx 11 km SSE Bong Son and 3 km W QL-1. Oct68. Binh Dinh Pr, II Corps.
Tropic Lightning (n/a)
See Glossary.
Tropic Lightning News (n/a)
See Glossary.
Tropo Hill (AR?)
Per Tom Rethard, was N of Pleiku, “where we had a pair of very large Tropospheric antennas in place; you could see them for miles.” Likely N Pleiku, E QL-14 N, and from Arty Hill was “within 600 mils to left of II Corps HQ.” Similar antennas on Dragon Mtn. Pleiku Pr, II Corps.
Tropo Hill Signal Site (AR?)
See Tropo Hill. Pleiku Pr, II Corps.
Troposcatter Signal Sites (n/a)
See Glossary.
Troung Hoa RF outpost (XT 268-452)
See Truong Hue. Tay Ninh Pr, III Corps.
Troung Hue RF outpost (XT 268-452)
See Truong Hue. Tay Ninh Pr, III Corps.
Trout, LZ (YS 059-473)
At Dong Hoa, near mouth of Cua Soirap, southernmost point of Gia Dinh Pr, apx 22 km W Vung Tau. Jul66. Gia Dinh Pr, III Corps.
Tru, Bai (CP 0-5)
Bay at 12°14'N-109°15'E. Khanh Hoa Pr, II Corps.
Truc Giang (XS 52-32)
A.k.a. Ben Tre. Apx 60 km SSW Saigon and 13 km S My Tho. See also Ben Tre. Capitol, Kien Hoa Pr, IV Corps.
Truc Giang Base (XS 52-32)
A.k.a. Ben Tre Base. Apx 60 km SSW Saigon and 13 km S My Tho. 2d Bde/9th Inf and USN MRF basecamp, per Jim Stone, 2d/39th Inf. Kien Hoa Pr, IV Corps.
Truc Giang (Ben Tre) (n/a)
Mapsheet name of L-7014-6229-2. SVN.
Truc Giang Airfield (XS 480-347)
On Truc Giang Island in Mekong Delta, 3 km NW Truc Giang, 10 km S My Tho, 10 km SE Dong Tam AF and 62 km SW Saigon. El. 10', 2,800' alum-mat rwy. At 10°15'46"N-106°21'03"E. Kien Hoa Pr, IV Corps.
Truc Giang Heliport (XS 513-317)
See Ben Tre Heliport. Kien Hoa Pr, IV Corps.
Truc Giang Hotel (XS 8-9)
In downtown Saigon. Gia Dinh Pr, III Corps Capital Zone.
Truman, LZ (BR 607-223)
About 1.5 km NE LZ Regular (BR 600-233), and apx 25 km SSE An Khe, 13 km SE LZ Lincoln, 27 km NW Van

Canh AF and 47 km Due W Qui Nhon. 4th Div AO, '70. 4th Div op rpt grid per Jim Claeys. Binh Dinh Pr, II Corps.

Trunc Phuc SF Camp (n/a)
Misspelling of Trang Phuc or Trung Phuoc? Listed in DA Chief, Mil Hist records summary as Camp Trunc Phuc and as Trung Phuc. Trang Phuc SF Camps at ZV 0366-2671 and ZV 052-265; Trung Phuoc at AT 95-91, Trung Phu (BT 07-57, CR 09-22, XS 15-48, WS 33-44), and Trung Phuong at BT 21-54? SVN.

Truncheon (n/a)
6Apr70, XXIV Corps future-use III MAF FSB name.

Trung, FSB (YT 32-00)
Apx 45 km E of Saigon, 15 km E of Long Thanh N AF and 25 km SW of Xuan Loc. 2d/3d Inf, 199th LIB here. Bien Hoa Pr?, III Corps.

Trung, LZ (AR 92-47)
A.k.a. LZ Lo Trung. Apx 3 km WSW Lo Trung, 2 km S QL-19 and 13 km due E Pleiku. Data in 4th Div ORLL of 20Nov70, per Bob Patsfield. Pleiku Pr, II Corps.

Trung An (YD 1-7)
Deserted hamlet near Con Thien. Heavy contact, May67, during Op Hickory/Beau Charger. Quang Tri Pr, I Corps.

Trung Doi Phong Khong (n/a)
See Glossary.

Trung Dung SF Camp (BP 9370-5571)
At Dien Khanh, apx 10 km due W Nha Trang. SF Det 35, Det A-501 (was 218), 5th SF Operating Base (SFOB), Oct65. Later became RF/PF base? Grid per *SF Order of Battle.* Khanh Hoa Pr, II Corps.

Trung Khanh Phu (n/a)
Mapsheet name of L-7014-6354-4. NVN/China.

Trung Kien, Thon (n/a)
Mapsheet L-7014-6641-4. Full sheet name: Thon Trung Kien. SVN.

Trung Lap (various)
Common Viet place-name. See grid squares WH 5-0, WG 6-1, YD 1-8, XT 5-2, XT 588-204, 590-198, 595-210 and 592-204. NVN/SVN.

Trung Lap (XT 595-215)
A.k.a. Thruong Lap and Truong Lap and site FSB Patton I. Apx 7 km NW Cu Chi CB and 12 km ESE Xom Rung Cay. 2d/14th Inf, 2d/49th ARVN Rgt, joint ops here Summer '69. 1st/506th Inf, 101st Abn established basecamp nearby, mid-68. Original FSB Patton built on N edge of ville but soon moved. ARVN Trung Lap Ranger Trng Ctr here. Data per www.en.com/users/ kramsey/dragons.html. Map is L-7014-6231-2. See Patton I and II. Hau Nghia Pr, III Corps.

Trung Lap, FSB (XT 60-20?)
Grid estimated; however, if accurate, then site was apx 5 km WNW Cu Chi. Villes with this name are at: XT 588-204, 590-198, 595-210 and 592-204. See FSB Patton, Patton II, Trung Lap Trng Ctr. Hau Nghia Pr, III Corps.

Trung Lap Airfield (XT 591-213)
Apx 7 km NW Cu Chi CB, 12 km ESE Xom Rung Cay and 6 km NNE QL-1. El. 39'. Map is L-7014-6231-2. Hau Nghia Pr, III Corps.

Trung Lap ARVN Training Center (XT 592-212)
A.k.a. Trung Lap ARVN Ranger Trng Ctr. Along TL-7A, apx 9 km NNW Cu Chi and 6 km NE QL-1. On 3Jun66, elements from trng center were ambushed at XT 593-210, by 20-40 VC. Cited in 23Jul66 Combat Op, HQ 1st Bde/25th ID, for Op Fargo at: www.en.com/users/kramsey/vnr102. html#. L-7014-6231-2. Hau Nghia Pr, III Corps.

Trung Lap Ranger Station (XT 591-214)
See Trung Lap ARVN Trng Ctr. Hau Nghia Pr, III Corps.

Trung Luong (CQ 038-721?)
Ville NE of Dong Tre, SE of La Hai SF Camp and NNW Tuy Hoa. Map in *The Fields of Bamboo*, p 13 et al. Phu Yen Pr, II Corps.

Trung Luong Relocation Camp (BR 842-947)
On S bank of the Song An Lao, within 2 km SW Bong Son AF. Relocation camp Jul68-Jan69. Binh Dinh Pr, II Corps.

Trung Luong Valley (BQ 93-75?)
Described as being "short chopper ride" from Tuy Hoa. Trung Luong, Dong Tre and La Hai SF Camp here. Battle of Dong Tre here, during Op Nathan Hale, Jun66. II Corps. Per *The Fields of Bamboo*, p 28. Phu Yen Pr, II Corps.

Trung Nghia (ZA 125-905)
A.k.a. Polei Breng? Along Hwy 512, apx 13 km WNW Kontum. In Jun73, after Paris Peace Accords had been signed, an NVA Div-sized attack seized city, and it took ARVN until Sep73 to retake it; w/heavy losses on both sides. Grid per NPIA Gaz, but unknown if correct. Data per *A Better War*, p 365.

Trung Phuc, Camp (n/a?)
In DA Chief, Mil Hist records summary as Camp Trunc Phuc (atypical VN spelling) and as Trung Phuc, but no SF camp of either spelling is listed in *SF Order of Battle.* Likely variant of either Trang Phuc SF Camp (ZV 0366-2671 and ZV 052-265); or of Trung Phuoc (AT 95-91), or Trung Phu (BT 07-57, CR 09-22, XS 15-48, WS 33-44), or Trung Phuong (BT 21-54)? SVN.

Trung Phuoc (AT 8-3)
Ville within 10 km of and SW An Hoa and Phuoc Binh. Possible SF camp location? Quang Nam Pr, I Corps.

Trung Son Cemetery (YD 11-70)
See Truong Son Cemetery.

Trung Son Mountains (n/a)
See Truong Son Mtns. NVN/SVN.

Trung Thanh (BR 96-67?)
Villes of Trung Thuan 1 thru 5 are around listed grid, which is on Rte 504 apx 6 km E Phu My/QL-1. Described as having been immed S of LZ Apple, SW Trung Luong, SW LZ Eagle and NNW Tuy Hoa. 80th VC Main Force Bn trapped here during Op Nathan Hale, Jun66. Discussed in *The Fields of Bamboo*, pp 149, 152-156 et al. II Corps.

Truoi (YD 9-0)
A.k.a. Thon Xuan An. On W side of QL-1, SE Phu Bai, NW Phu Loc, and roughly midway between those 2 villes. Site of 101st Abn battle in '68. Thua Thien Pr, I Corps.

Truoi Lagoon (ZD 0-0)
A.k.a. Dam Cau Hai. Lagoon at 16°20'N-107°52'E. On NE48-16 JOG. Thua Thien Pr, I Corps.

Truoi River Bridge (YD 97-06)
QL-1 bridge over the Truoi River, just W Dam Cau Hai Bay, apx 16 km SE Phu Bai and 13 km NW Phu Loc. 2d/9th Mar secured site during Op Troy, 2-3Mar66. Info per *USMC in Vietnam, 1966*, p 54, on map at p 55. Thua Thien Pr, I Corps.

Truoi River Valley (YC 993-952)
Apx 12 km WSW Q Phu Loc and 24 km SSE Phu Bai AF. Feb69. Thua Thien Pr, I Corps.
Truong Cong Dinh, Operation (n/a)
1Mar-30Jul68. Joint ARVN and US 9th Div op that on 21 May68 was combined with Op People's Road. Dinh Tuong and Kien Tuong Prvs, IV Corps.
Truong Giang (BT 3-3)
Lagoon at 15°40'N-108°30'E. On ND49-01 JOG. Quang Tin Pr, I Corps.
Truong Giang River (BT 33-30)
A.k.a. the Song Truong Giang. Portion of tidal(?) river paralleling coast, and just inland from it. Ran from Hoi An in N, SE some 65 km to tidal bay just above Chu Lai. Quang Tin Pr, I Corps.
Truong Hoa RF outpost (XT 268-452)
See Truong Hue. Tay Ninh Pr, III Corps.
Truong Hue RF outpost (XT 268-452)
A.k.a. Ap Truong Hue RF Outpost. Guarded SE approach to Tay Ninh city complex. Ground assault overran it in just 15 minutes, beginning at 0245 hrs, 18Aug68, during battle for Tay Ninh. [541] Tay Ninh Pr, III Corps.
Truong Lap (XT 595-215)
See Trung Lap. Hau Nghia Pr, III Corps.
Truong Lap Laager Site (XT 614-226)
See US/ARVN Laager Site. Binh Duong Pr, III Corps.
Truong Son Cemetery (YD 11-70)
After American War ended, the Vietnamese govt built what is known as Trung Son Cemetery near Con Thien (the Hill of Angels). Over 10,000 graves here contain the remains of NVA who were KIA or missing in the Quang Tri area. Thought to be near listed grid. Quang Tri Pr, I Corps.
Truong Son Mountains (n/a)
Major chain of the Annamite Cordillera and "spine" of Vietnam. Runs through both North and SVN. Along its southern slopes lies the 20,000 sq mile plateau known as the Central Highlands. See Ho Chi Minh Trail in Glossary for more detail. NVN/SVN.
Truong Son Trail (n/a)
A.k.a. Infantry Route One, the Transportation Corridor and The Old Man's Trail. All NVA nicknames for HCMT complex. See Ho Chi Minh Trail in Glossary.
Truxton, USS (n/a)
DLG(N)-35. Guided-Missile DD Ldr, per Ralph Fries.
Tsingtao, FSB (XD 874-445)
Apx 5 km NE Khe Sanh CB, 26 km WSW Cam Lo and 6 km NNW Lang Kat. Apr70 XXIV Corps grid per Don Armstrong. Quang Tri Pr, I Corps.
Tsinh Ho (UK 1-7)
Platoon-sized French outpost near Lai Chau. Two BMC prostitutes volunteered to take 30-mile jungle trek to this outpost in order to bring comfort to lonely troops there. The 2 performed well under fire during an ambush on return trip and were recommended for the *Croix de Guerre* by patrol's cmdr; however, French Army declined to award the medals out of political concerns. See Dien Bien Phu and BMC. NVN.
TSQ-81 (n/a)
See Site 85. Laos.
Tu Bong (CQ 1-1)
Along QL-1 and NE Van Ninh AF, apx 25 km S Tuy Hoa. Vic of 12°46'00"N-109°18'00"E. On ND49-13 JOG. Khanh Hoa Pr, II Corps.
Tu Cam Heliport (BT 175-225)
Along Rte 533, apx 12 km due W Tam Ky and 11 km NE Tien Phuoc. Heliport #694, alt 164', at 15°34'00"N-108°21'30"E, per Feb73 TAD. Quang Tin Pr, I Corps.
Tu Cau Bridge (BT 033-648)
QL-1 bridge near Tay Viem, apx 12 km SSE Da Nang AB. 1st Marines, 1st Mar Div provided security, '69. Quang Nam Pr, I Corps.
Tu Ca Refugee Camp (BT 050-658)
A.k.a. Tu Cau Refugee Camp? Apx 11 km SSE Da Nang AB, 1 km SE Tu Cau and 3 km W QL-1. NPIA grid. Quang Nam Pr, I Corps.
Tu Cau Refugee Camp (BT 050-658)
See Tu Ca Refugee Camp. Quang Nam Pr, I Corps.
Tu Chanh (various) (AT/BT)
Common Viet place-name. Sites inc: AT 8-2, AT 8-3, AT 9-3, BT 2-2 and BT 2-3. All I Corps.
Tu Dai (n/a)
See Glossary.
Tu Duc, FSB? (XT 170-930)
Apx 15 km WNW Katum AF, 12 km NNE Thien Ngon AF, 10 km S Cambodia and 40 km due W tip of Fishhook. Tay Ninh Pr, III Corps.
Tu Le (VK 27-10)
In small plain surrounded by jungle apx 160 km NW Hanoi, 20 km NE Nghia Lo and 12 km NW Gia Hoi. Small French garrison here overwhelmed 20Oct52, during Battle for T'ai Highlands. Position was reinforced with Col Bigeard's 6th Para to cover its withdrawal ahead of advancing Vietminh that had overrun nearby Nghia Lo, 17Oct52. Vietminh arrived 18Oct52. Bigeard decided to wait until 19Oct52, in hope of recovering Co-sized unit from Gia Hoi before retreating. He was ordered to leave Tu Le at 2100 hrs, 19Oct52, but again postponed retreat and wait until 20Oct for missing Gia Hoi contingent. At 0300 on 20Oct52, Vietminh struck Tu Le in weather that prevented air supt. After suffering mightily, 6th Para left 110 of its wounded at Tu Le and withdrew toward the Black River but was repeatedly ambushed en route (2 of its rear-guard Cos were annihilated). When survivors reached the river, 22Oct52, after 40 mile fighting retreat, it had lost 60% of its strength. [542] Data per *Street Without Joy*, pp66-71, map at p 67.
Tu My Refugee Camp (BS 620-717)
Perhaps 2 km S Quang Ngai AF, 4 km W QL-1 and 4 km SW Quang Ngai. NPIA grid. Quang Ngai Pr, I Corps.
Tu Vu (WJ 3-2)
Along Road No. 6, and on W bank of Black River (near Notre Dame Rock) at its confluence with the Ngoi Lat River, apx 55 km WSW Hanoi. French Moroccan garrison here heavily attacked and overrun by 3 Rgts of Vietminh 308th and 312th Divs, 9Dec51, during Battle for Hao Binh. Survivors fled to island in river and returned following day to find apx 400 Vietminh dead. Per *Street Without Joy*, Chp 2; map at p 50. NVN.

Tua Moi Bay (AU 7-0)
A.k.a. Vung Chon May. Bay at 16°20'N-108°00'E. On ND49-01 JOG. Thua Thien Pr, I Corps.
Tuamoi, Baie de (AU 7-0)
See Tau Moi Bay. Thua Thien Pr, I Corps.
Tuan Giao (n/a)
Mapsheet name of L-7014-5652-2. NVN only.
Tuan Tuong (n/a)
Mapsheet name of L-7014-6245-3. NVN only.
Tub, LZ (YD 080-270)
Possibly of LZ Tuba? Apx 36 km SW Quang Tri, 6 km W Laos, 15 km SSW Ba Long, 16 km NNW Tou Rout,16 km E Lang Klung and 22 km SSE Vandegrift CB. Nov68. Listed as LZ Tub on Apr70 XXIV Corps list per Don Armstrong. Listed as Tuba on map at p 65, *US Marines in Vietnam-1969*. Quang Tri Pr, I Corps.
Tuba, LZ (AQ 818-172)
A.k.a. Tub or Kona? Apx 2 km W Quang Nhieu and 13 km due N Ban Me Thuot AF. Feb66. Darlac Pr, II Corps.
Tuba, LZ (YD 080-270)
Possibly of LZ Tub? Apx 36 km SW Quang Tri, 6 km W Laos, 15 km SSW Ba Long, 16 km NNW Tou Rout,16 km E Lang Klung and 22 km SSE Vandegrift CB. Nov68. Listed as LZ Tub on Apr70 XXIV Corps list per Don Armstrong. Listed as Tuba on map at p 65, *US Marines in Vietnam-1969*. Quang Tri Pr, I Corps.
Tuc Fln (n/a)
See Glossary.
Tuc Trung SF Camp (YT 740-331)
At or adj to Vo Dat AF, SW edge of Xa Vo Dat, apx 35 km NE Xuan Loc. 5th SF. Moved to Minh Thanh. Grid per *SF Order of Battle.* Long Khanh Pr, III Corps.
Tucson, LZ (AT 894-823)
Along Hwy 545, apx 5 km due W Ap Nam O/Red Beach, and 14 km WNW Da Nang AB. Apr70 XXIV Corps grid per D. Armstrong. Quang Nam or Thua Thien Pr, I Corps.
Tucumcari, USS (CP 0-2)
A.k.a. PGH-2. Hydrofoil gunboat. Part of Coastal Sqdn 3, out of Cam Ranh Bay, later Coastal Flotilla 1. Arrived SVN in '67? Role discussed in *Brown Water, Black Berets*, p 91. Market Time TF-115. Khanh Hoa Pr, II Corps.
Tuffy, LZ (BR 553-680)
See LZ Toughie. Binh Dinh Pr, II Corps.
Tugboat, LZ (AT 966-687)
Apx 8 km SW Da Nang AB and 5 km W QL-1. '70 XXIV Corps grid per D. Armstrong. Quang Nam Pr, I Corps.
Tugboat YTB-784 (n/a)
USN ship APL-26 served as mother ship for Tugs *YTB-784* and *YTB-785*, in at least Apr67, plying the waters of Mekong Delta and Rung Sat Special Zone as part of MRF. These two tugs possibly only "Olive Drab" painted tugs in USN. III, IV Corps.
Tugboat YTB-785 (n/a)
See Tugboat YTB-784. III, IV Corps.
Tui Loan CAP (n/a)
Delta 3, 2d CAG per CAP Vets website at www. capmarine.com. Hieu Duc Dist, Quang Nam Pr, I Corps.
Tuk Chup Knoll (VS 99-47)
A.k.a. Million Dollar Hill or Million Dollar Knoll. On Nui Coto Mtn and site of major battle against 510th VC Bn, involving 5th SF's 521st MSF, 16-26Mar69. See Davan Cmpd. Chau Doc Pr, IV Corps.
Tuk Fin (n/a)
See Tuc Fin in Glossary.
Tulare, USS (n/a)
LKA-112. Amphib Attack. Cargo.
Tule (n/a)
Mapsheet name of L-7014-5852-1. NVN only.
Tulsa, FSB (XD 808-237)
In Vietnam Salient apx 18 km SSW Khe Sanh, 3 km NE FSB Passport and 13 km S Lang Vie. Apparently also used during Lam Son 719, Apr71. Apr70 XXIV Corps grid per Don Armstrong. Quang Tri Pr, I Corps.
Tun Tavern, FSB (YD 059-328)
A.k.a. Hill 613. Near Ta Lou, apx 33 km SW Quang Tri, 8 km due S FSB Henderson, 17 km SE Vandegrift CB and 8 km E Lao border. Named for tavern that was birthplace of the USMC. 9th Mar/3d Mar Div here early '69. Map at p 32, *US Marines in Vietnam-1969*. Quang Tri Pr, I Corps.
Tunny, USS (n/a)
APSS 282, Transport Submarine. Part of Logistic Supt Force 73. Carried USN/VNN UDTs, SEALs and VNMC to prospective lndg beaches in NVN.
Tuoan, Cape (YS 4-4)
See Cape Tuoan. Phuoc Tuy Pr, III Corps.
Tuong Duc Bridge (AT/BT?)
On Rte 4 between Hill 52 and Thuong Duc. Cleared and repaired by USMC 1st Engr Bn in concert with 1st/7th Marine, 1st Mar Div, May69. Quang Nam Pr, I Corps.
Turan, Cape (BT 1-8)
A.k.a. Mui Da Nang. Cape at 16°07'N-108°19'E. On ND49-01 JOG. Quang Nam Pr, I Corps.
Turkey, LZ (BP 666-922)
Apx 19 km WNW Duc My AF, 20 km SSE Khanh Duong New AF and 34 km WNW Ninh Hoa. Feb67. Khanh Hoa Pr, II Corps.
Turkey, LZ (XD 834-417)
Apx 2 km due W Khe Sanh CB and Rte 608, some 51 km WSW Quang Tri. Cited in *The Final Formation*, p 122. CH-46 #YR-31 of HMM-161 had a cargo parachute entangle its rotors at touchdown here, 19Jun68, resulting in death of pilot and co-pilot. Apr70 XXIV Corps grid per Don Armstrong. Also listed at XD 849-417? See also Turkey Ridge. Quang Tri Pr, I Corps.
Turkey, LZ (ZA 240-520)
Along QL-14, apx 3 km N Pleiku, 3 km due W Pleiku/Cu Hanh AF and 5 km SSE Pleiku Nansteph AF. Aug66. Pleiku Pr, II Corps.
Turkey Farm, The (AR 81-47?)
Apparently W of Ql-14 and just N QL-19, apx 3 km due E Pleiku and intersection of those roads. Also due N Camp Holloway. Helicopter laager and resupply area for 1st Cav helo assets during 1st Ia Drang Campaign, Oct-Nov65. Possibly at site of what later became Pleiku Area AF? Discussed extensively in *Chickenhawk;* map at p 11. See Catecka, Stadium and Tea Plantation. Pleiku Pr, II Corps.
Turkey Hill (YD 03-60?)
See Turkey Ridge. Northern Quang Tri Pr, I Corps.
Turkey Ridge (YD 03-60?)
A.k.a. Turkey Hill and possibly Marine Hill? Per Dennis Rees, was just E of FSB Fuller (Dong Ha Mtn), N of QL-9

and WNW Cam Lo. Also described as having been near Camp Red Devil (YD 243-597). It consisted of at least Hills 222 and 249 and possibly a.k.a. Marine Hill. On Thanksgiving eve, 27Nov69, elements of A & C Cos, 1st/11th Inf were waiting to be flown to rear for Turkey dinner but instead were tasked to assault NVA positions on this ridge to relieve 1st/61st Inf element pinned down on S face of Hill 222. Hill 222 was hit 1st, then Hill 249 in the relief effort. Quang Tri Pr, I Corps. [543]

Turnage, FSB (YD 252-090)
A.k.a. Co A Nong Mtn, FSB Tiger, and Hill 1228. Apx 52 km WSW Hue, N of and on line with center axis of the A Shau Valley, 15 km ESE Tou Rout and 6 km from Laos. ARVN here during Op Apache Snow, 10May-7Jun69. On map p 32, *US Marines in Vietnam-1969*. Likely named to honor Navy Adm Turnage of WWII fame. Also listed at YD 253-091 and 240-090. Thua Thien Pr, I Corps.

Turner Joy, USS (n/a)
DD 951 and *C. Turner Joy*. See also *Maddox*, *USS*.

Turtle, FSB? (YT 079-044)
Apx 5 km NNE Long Thanh North AF, 21 km ESE Bien Hoa AB and 7 km S QL-1. Apparent 199th LIB FSB/PB per 199th LIB Assn list. Feb68. Bien Hoa Pr, III Corps.

Tuscaloosa County, USS (n/a)
LST 1187. See Frequent Wind.

Tuttle Airfield (ZA 104-274)
See Oasis AF. Pleiku Pr, II Corps.

Tutuila, USS (n/a)
ARG-4. USN repair ship launched 12Sep43. In WWII served as floating advance base. In May or Jun65, arrived at An Thoi, Phu Quoc Island, Gulf of Thailand, to supt Op Market Time along SW coast or SVN. Relieved *USS Krishna* (APL-28) and on 19Jul65, began servicing PCF's (Swift boats), attached to USCG Div 11. WPB's of Div 11 also based on this craft. During Op Seamount (Army op to clear enemy from southern Phu Quoc Is.), landed ARVN at 4 sites and suptd helo medevacs. In Oct65, *Krishna* returned and *Tutila* moved to Vung Tau to supt Ops Market Time, Game Warden, and Stable Door through '66. In early 67, began suptg MRF by preparing ASPB's and patrol craft until *USS Askari* assumed that duty. In Apr67, moved to mouth of Mekong to service LST's of MRF and supt USCG Coastal Div 13. In late '71, transferred to Rep of China Navy. Left SVN, 1Jan72, after 6 years war duty. Data per MRF Assn at www.mrfa.orgnavy_index.htm. III, IV Corps.

Tuy An (Phu Tan) (n/a)
Mapsheet L-7014-6835-1. Full sheet name: Tuy An (Phu Tan). SVN.

Tuy An (Phu Tan) (n/a)
Mapsheet name of L-7014-6835-1. SVN.

Tuy An Airfield (CQ 112-675)
On coast and E side QL-1 at Vung Chao Bay, apx 22 km S Song Cau AF, 27 km NNW Tuy Hoa AB. Listed as "Secure, MACV subsector camp N field ARVN(A) 25Feb67, AF # VA2-253," in Aug69 TAD per Frank Penk, Jr. Not in Feb73 TAD. El. 164'. Phu Yen Pr, II Corps.

Tuy Hoa (CQ 17-47)
Coastal city on QL-1, midway between Qui Nhon and Nha Trang and apx 90 km due S Qui Nhon. One of few US bases const by USAF under its own direction and using own assets. Longest of its 2 rwys was 9,000' and each surfaced differently. Was not made jet capable until '65. Per Mar98 *ARMY* Magazine, all that remains of base today are some large pyramidal-shaped fighter-bomber shelters and rwy itself, now used for herding cattle. [544] Was HQ and home of 1st Bde/101st Abn for most of period '65-67. At 0200, 31Jan68, 5th/95th NVA Rgt attacked Tuy Hoa, its prison (Phu Yen Rehab Ctr, just S 6th/32d Arty position) and US arty positions. Bty C, 6th/32d Arty (8" and 175 mm Bty) at Tuy Hoa North AF were inc. At 0700, 4th/503rd Inf, 173rd with Bn of Korean 28th Regt was sent to reinforce 6th/32d, and together pushed NVA from cmpd. NVA suffered heavy casualties and survivors fled to hamlet immed S of the prison and at base of hill nicknamed "Cemetery Hill" (likely a Viet cemetery there?). 32d Arty Bn CO, LTC Robert Whitbeck was KIA in fight. 4th/503rd's own CO later personally led charge on NVA in ville followed by air strikes, which ended battle (19 US KIA, 39 WIA; few NVA survived). VC Bn also made 2 attacks against Tuy Hoa city and were stopped by 2 Bns, 47th ARVN Rgt. ARVN retook remaining NVA strongholds on 5-6Feb68. Phu Yen Pr, II Corps.

Tuy Hoa (Chau Thanh) (n/a)
Mapsheet name of L-7014-6835-2. SVN.

Tuy Hoa AFB Hospital (CQ 21-43)
See USAF Hospitals. Phu Yen Pr, II Corps.

Tuy Hoa Airbase (CQ 200-428)
On coast apx 90 km due S Qui Nhon. Major US AB. El. 28', 9,500' conc rwy. At 13°02'46"N-109°2018"E. See also Tuy Hoa. Phu Yen Pr, II Corps.

Tuy Hoa Area FSB (CQ 150-489)
Along QL-1, apx 3 km NW Tuy Hoa, 1.5 km N Tuy Hoa AF and 7 km NNE Phu Lam. 2d/17th Arty here in supt 1/8th Cav. Data per Jack Picciolo. Phu Yen Pr, II Corps.

Tuy Hoa Bac Airfield (CQ 154-481)
See Tuy Hoa North AF. Phu Yen Pr, II Corps.

Tuy Hoa Basecamp (CQ 240-350)
On coast at Phu Hiep AF, apx 7 km SE Tuy Hoa AF and 6 km E QL-1. Jul66. Phu Yen Pr, II Corps.

Tuy Hoa Chop Chai Airfield (CQ 154-481)
See Tuy Hoa North AF. Phu Yen Pr, II Corps.

Tuy Hoa MAAG Heliport (CQ 180-480)
Along coast and N bank Song Do Rong River at its mouth, apx 6 km N to Tuy Hoa AB, immed E Tuy Hoa and 3.5 km E to ESE Tuy Hoa North AF. Heliport #695, alt 197', at 13°05'00"N-109°17'30"E. 73 TAD. Phu Yen Pr, II Corps.

Tuy Hoa Nam Airfield (CQ 200-428)
See Tuy Hoa AF. Phu Yen Pr, II Corps.

Tuy Hoa North Airfield (CQ 154-481)
Apx 8 km NW Tuy Hoa AF, 1 km NW Tuy Hoa, 19 km S Tuy An AF and on W side QL-1 some 3 km from coast. El. 30', 3,700' steel-mat rwy. At 13°05'40"N-109°17'49"E. Phu Yen Pr, II Corps.

Tuy Hoa South Airfield (CQ 200-428)
See Tuy Hoa AF. Phu Yen Pr, II Corps.

Tuy Hoa South Beach (CQ 247-373)
Beach immed E Phu Hiep AF, apx 8 km SE Tuy Hoa AF and 7 km E QL-1. Jan-Apr67. Phu Yen Pr, II Corps.

Tuy Loan CAP (AT 944-701?)
If grid correct, was apx 6 km SW Da Nang AB and immed W of Ap Thach Nham/Rte 540. CAP 3-1 (Originally CAC

3-1), 3rd CAG, Hieu Duc Dist here per Tim Duffie. A.k.a. Thuy Loan? Thua Thien Pr, I Corps.

Tuy Loan River (AT/BT)
The Cau Do, Yen, Tuy Loan La Tho, Thanh Quyt, Vu Gia, Cau Lau and Thu Bon Rivers all formed part of drainage that became the Da Nang River. All were S or SW Da Nang. Quang Nam Pr, I Corps.

Tuy Phong (BN 5-4 or CR 0-0)
NPIA lists Tuy Phong (7) at CR 078-084; Tuy Phong (8) at CR 090-050; and Tuy Phong at BN 543-425 and BN 562510. Binh Dinh and Binh Thuan Pr, II Corps.

Tuy Phong (BN 53-42)
Large coastal town apx 25 km E to ESE Song Mao AF/Hai Ninh, and 47 km SW Phan Rang. Binh Thuan Pr, II Corps.

Tuy Phuoc SF Camp (BS 015-971)
Near Old Hau Duc, apx 19 km SW Tien Phuoc AF and 36 km SW Tam Ky. 5th SF, Det A-122, Oct65. Turned over to ROK forces, and SF assets moved to Vinh Thanh. Data per *SF Order of Battle*. Quang Tin Pr, I Corps.

Tuyen Duc Province (AP/AN/BP/BN)
One of 12 north-central provs forming II Corps (II CTZ). Dalat was its capitol city.

Tuyen Nhon (n/a)
Mapsheet name of L-7014-6230-3. SVN.

Tuyen Nhon Airfield (XS 283-777)
See Thuy Dong AF. Kien Tuong Pr, IV Corps.

Tuyen Nhon ATSB (XS 273-773)
Along the Kinh Lagrange Canal, apx 2 km W the Song Vam Co Tay River and Tuyen Nhon, apx 50 km WSW Saigon, 3 km SSW Xom Thong Xoai and 28 km NW Long An AF. USN Advanced Tactical Supt Base, here '69-71. Data per, and spelled "Thuyen Nhon" on MRF Assn website. Kien Tuong Pr, IV Corps.

Tuyen Nhon SF Camp (XS 2787-7758)
A.k.a. Thuy Dong SF Camp? Along the Kinh Lagrange Canal, apx 2 km W the Song Vam Co Tay River and Tuyen Nhon, apx 50 km WSW Saigon, 3 km SSW Xom Thong Xoai and 28 km NW Long An AF. SF Det 68, 5th SF Grp, Det. A-415 (was 322), Oct65. Transferred to 75th ARVN Border Rangers. Info/grid per *SF Order of Battle*. Kien Tuong Pr, IV Corps.

Tuyen Nhon, Camp (XS 200-825)
See Hoi Dong Chieu. IV Corps.

Tuyen Quang (WK 2-1)
Ville on Clear River apx 110 km due NW Hanoi, 45 km WSW Cao Bang and 30 km S Chiem Hoa. Involved in Op Lea, Oct47. Was lndg point of riverborne French TF Groupement "C," during that Op. Per *Street Without Joy*, p 31 (also map). NVN.

Twelve-Alpha, LZ (YA)
See 10-Alpha. Pleiku Pr, II Corps.

Twenty Alternate (n/a)
A.k.a. 20-A. Gen Van Pao's Meo Guerrilla and CIA HQ in northern Laos.

Twenty Mike-Mike (n/a)
See Glossary.

Twenty-Two, FSB (XS 83-86)
A.k.a. FSB 22. Along LTL-5A, apx 5 km S Saigon, 8 km N Ap Phuoc Khanh and 8 km NNW Nha Be. 5th/12th Inf, 3d/7th Inf, 199th LIB. III Corps.

Twenty-Two Step Snake (n/a)
See Glossary.

Twin Boobs, The (WD or XD?)
Terrain feature of Xe Krong River in northern Laos. Cited in *Da Nang Diary*, at p 38. Laos.

Two, LZ (BN 819-623)
See 2, LZ. Ninh Thuan Pr, II Corps.

Two Alfa, LZ (BN 826-613)
Near coast, apx 2 km S Thon Son Hai, 18 km S Phan Rang and 12 km E QL-1. See LZs 2 and 3. 9Mar67. Ninh Thuan Pr, II Corps.

Two Bits, LZ (BR 846-947)
Apx 2 km W intersection of QL1 and Hwy 514, adj Bong Son AF, 50 km NE An Khe, 9 km SSW LZ English, 52 km N Phu Cat AB, 46 km S Duc Pho and 70 km NNW Qui Nhon. Gen John Tolson's 1st Cav tactical CP, Apr-Dec67, and before move to I Corps (Div rear was at An Khe). 1st Cav moved to Quang Tri and LZ Tombstone early Jan67 and immed preceding Tet '68. 4th Div AO '70. Per John Linn, was 4th Div fwd FSB and B/2d/35th Inf here Jul70. Also listed at BR 845-945. Map is L-7014-6837-4 (Bong Son). Binh Dinh Pr, II Corps.

Two Bits Airfield, LZ (BR 846-947)
See Bong Son AF. Binh Dinh Pr, II Corps.

Two Bits I, LZ (BR 837-955)
Possibly the LZ Two Bits listed at BR 846-947? At Bong Son, apx 75 km NNE Qui Nhon and 8 km SSW LZ English. 4th Div AO, '70. Grid on 4th ID op rpts per Jim Claeys. Binh Dinh Pr, II Corps.

Two Monks, Isle of (XJ 7-5)
Ile des Deux Freres. NIMA data. NVN.

Two Songs, Island of (XJ 7-2)
Ile des Deux Songs. NIMA data. NVN.

Typhoon (n/a)
See Glossary.

Typhoon Tess (n/a)
Hit I Corps, 11Jul69. Came within 50 miles of Camp Eagle and Eagle received 3.13" of rain (greater amounts to S) plus 45 knot winds in short period. Caused severe flooding in coastal plains and destroyed many homes. In 21 years of record keeping, was 1st tropical storm to hit Hue area in month of Jul. [545]

UNIFORM

Facility/Feature Name, Grid Coordinate, a.k.a. Name/History/Province/CTZ

Unless otherwise stated, 6-digit grid coordinates reference DMA L-7014, L-7015 or L-7016 series, 1:50,000 scale maps, while 2- and 4-digit coordinates reference AMS/DMA/NIMA 1:250,000, 1:500,000 and 1:1,000,000 scale maps. Unless otherwise stated, all heights are in meters. To convert meters to feet, multiply by 3.2808; feet to meters, multiply by .3048.

U-1 Secret Base Area (YT or YS)
No data on boundaries. Cited in *Rangers at War,* p 227 as VC Staging area in Bien Hoa Pr, III Corps.

U-2 Crash near Song Be (YU)
See Glossary.

U Minh Forest (WR 2-6)
A.k.a. Rogtoampung U Minh. At southern tip of SVN with center of mass roughly at WR 2-6. An extensive inundated region along W coast of Cau Mau Peninsula generally inaccessible by land and a haven for VC. Ops here in early '69 marked 1st military ops in region since French War. At 9°37'00"N-105°11'00"E. NC48-10 JOG. See also Base Area 483. An Xuyen Pr, IV Corps.

U Ta Pao (QQ 1-0)
See U Tapao AF. Thailand.

U Tapao Airbase (QQ 1-0)
A.k.a. Sattahip and U Taphao, U Tapao and U Tap Pao AF. Near coast apx 130 km SSE Bangkok, 420 km WNW Phnom Penh, 250 km SSE Korat AB and 640 km WNW Saigon. Major USAF Bomber/Fighter-bomber base. On map in *Vietnam Experience* Series, *Rain of Fire* vol, p. 11. 566th Civ Engrs, RED HORSE Sqdn also here. At 12°41'00"N-101°01'00"E. El. 59'. Thailand.

U Taphao Airfield (QQ 1-0)
See U Tapao AF. This spelling on Natl Geo Map. Thailand.

Ubon (VB85-85)
A.k.a. Udorn-Ubon. Apx 490 km ENE Bangkok, 125 km from point where borders of Laos, Cambodia and Thailand converge. US Army Supt Cmd facility, USAF Fighter and FAC Base nearby. 5th SF camp/AO per *SF Order of Battle.* See also Udorn. Thailand.

Ubon (major) Airfield (VB 87-87)
A.k.a. Ubon Ratchathani AF and Sanam Ban Ubon Ratchathani AF. Major AB apx 2 km E Ubon Northwest AF, at NE corner of Ubon Ratchathani and N the Lam Nam Chi River, 125 km from point where the borders of Laos, Cambodia and Thailand converge. Wolfpack F-4s of 8th TAC fighter Wing, F-105s and SAR HH-3 helicopters here. At 15°15'00"N-104°52'00"E. El. 405'. Thailand.

Ubon Northwest Airfield (VB 87-84)
The minor of the 2 Ubon area AFs. Apx 490 km ENE Bangkok, and 2 km W Ubon AB and at NW corner of Ubon Ratchathani, per TPC K-10A. At 15°15'00"N-104°51'00"E. NIMA data. El. 394'. Thailand.

Ubon Ratchathani Airfield (VB 8-8)
Apx 490 km ENE Bangkok. El. 410'. Thailand.

Ubon Ratchathani, Sanam B. (VB 8-8)
See Ubon AB. Thailand.

Ubon VOR TACAN NDB (VB 86-86)
At Ubon Northwest AF. Very high frequency Omnidirectional Radio ranging, Tactical Air Navigation and Non-Directional Air Nav Beacon site. Thailand.

Udon Airfield (TE 6-2)
See Udorn AF. Thailand.

Udon Thani Airfield (TE 6-2)
See Udorn AF. Thailand.

Udon Border Police Airfield (TE 7-2)
See Udorn Border Police AF. Thailand.

Udorn Airfield (TE 6-2)
A.k.a. Udon Thani AF and Udon AF. Apx 65 km SSE Vientiane, and 475 km NNE Bangkok. Major, jet-capable AF immed S Udon Thani and used by US throughout war. See ONC-J-11 and Feb67 Natl Geo maps. At 17°23'10"N-102°47'21"E. NIMA data. El. 584'. Thailand.

Udorn Border Police Airfield (TE 7-2)
A.k.a. Udon Border Police AF. Apx 5 km due W Udorn AF (major), 6 km SE Udon Thani and 475 km NNE Bangkok. Near 17°23'10"N-102°47'21"E. El. 592'. Thailand.

Udorn-Ubon (n/a)
USAF Fighter and FAC Base. US Army Supt Cmd facility, Thailand here and home of USASTRATCOM Sig Bn (Provisional). Thailand.

UFO Sightings (n/a)
See Glossary.

Uhnmann, USS (n/a)
A.k.a. DD 687. On 4May68, replaced *USS* Strong off Binh Thuan Pr suptg TF 3d/506th Inf, per www.currahee.org/pageb2.html.

Umphang STOL Strip Airfield (MT 8-7)
At 16°01'00"N-98°52'00"E, per NIMA. Thailand.

Under the Southern Cross (n/a)
See Glossary.

Unicorn, LZ (XD 745-439)
A.k.a. FSB Geiger. Apx 7 km E Laos, 12 km WNW Khe Sanh CB, 7 km WSW Ap La Vien and 36 km WSW Mai Loc AF. Apr70 XXIV Corps grid per Don Armstrong. See also FSB Geiger. Quang Tri Pr, I Corps.

Uniform, LZ ? (XT 655-278)
Apx 16 km SW Lai Khe and 13 km N Cu Chi. Jun66. Binh Duong Pr, III Corps.

Union, FSB (n/a)
Cited in *1st Cav Ops Rpt, May-Jul70*, p 28, 38, per Peter Cole. During that period, Cav was in western III Corps/Cambodia. Cambodia or III Corps?

Union, LZ (ZA 112-680)
Apx 2 km N Plei Mrong/ Plei Mrong AF, and 25 km NNW Pleiku. Jun66. Pleiku Pr, II Corps.

Union, Operation (n/a)
21Apr-17May67. USMC 1st Mar Div op. 865 NVA/VC KIA, per *Vietnam Order of Battle*, pp 9-14. Quang Nam and Quang Tin Prvs, I Corps.

Union, USS (n/a)
AKA 106. See also *Vancouver, USS.*

Union II, Operation (n/a)
25May-5Jun67. 1st Mar Div op. 701 rptd NVA/VC KIA, per *Vietnam Order of Battle*, pp 9-14. Quang Nam and Quang Tin Prvs, I Corps.

Uniontown, Operation (n/a)
17Dec67-8Mar68. 199th LIB op over Tet68. 922 rptd NVA/VC KIA, per *Vietnam Order of Battle*, pp 9-14. Bien Hoa Pr, III Corps.

United Seaman's Service Clubs (n/a)
See Glossary.

University of Maryland (n/a)
See Glossary.

Unnamed Mapsheet (n/a)
Mapsheet name of L-7014-6053-3. NVN only.

Unnamed Mapsheet ((n/a)
Mapsheet name of L-7014-6351-2. NVN only.

Unnamed Mapsheet (n/a)
Covers Da Nang. Sheet name of L-7014-6641-3. SVN.

Up Tight, LZ (BS 727-856)
Also spelled "Uptight." On Batangan Peninsula, Apx 4 km inland, 2 km N Hwy 522, 2 km WSW Chau Binh, 9 km E LZ Dottie, 6 km N My Lai 4, and 14 km NE Quang Ngai. Also listed at BS 720-780, 731-840, 726-857. Americal, 173d Abn, '68-69. Apr70 XXIV Corps grid per Don Armstrong. Photos/maps of base at http://1-14th.com/maps.html. Quang Ngai Pr, I Corps.

Uplift, LZ (BR 924-752)
A.k.a. Deo Nhong Pass. Along QL-1, apx 8.5 km NNE Phu My, 10 km N Crystal AF and 12 km SSE Bong Son. Les White thinks B/8th Engr Bn, 1st Cav built original base and says it was very primitive site when they arrived after Xmas, '66. Per Ray Smith, was "a dreary, sprawling firebase located directly on Hwy 1 (no kidding, the road ran through the base)." Per Ralph Bunten (call-sign Short Uplift) an Adv in '65-66, site was originally known as Deo Nhong Pass, but when he returned in '68, was known as LZ Uplift on all maps. Apparently drew name from call-sign of US Advisors at site early in war. Maps and discussion at 1st/69th Armor webpage. 4th Div AO, '70 with HH Bty and B Bty, 7th/15th Arty, 173d Abn, '68-69, 1st/50th Inf, 1st/69th Armor also here. Also listed at BR 918-753, 920-746, 926-754, 927-757, and 925-754. Photos at www.landscaper.net/vietnam.html. Map is L-7014-6837-3, per Ken Burrington. Binh Dinh Pr, II Corps. [546]

Upper LZ Tiger (YD 25-09?)
See FSB Tiger. Thua Thien Pr, I Corps.

Upper Tiger, LZ (YD 25-09?)
See FSB Tiger. Thua Thien Pr, I Corps.

Upshua, USNS (n/a)
MSTS Transport, per Ralph Fries.

Uptight, LZ (BS 727-856)
See Up Tight. Quang Ngai Pr, I Corps.

Upton Airfield (XS 040-331)
See Vinh Long AF. Vinh Long Pr, IV Corps.

Uranus, LZ (XD 886-538)
Apx 20 km W Mai Loc, 45 km due W Quang Tri and 3 km SSW FSB Aries. Apparently in mutual supt with LZ Cougar and Vandegrift CB? Apr70 XXIV Corps grid per Don Armstrong. USMC '69. Quang Tri Pr, I Corps.

Urgency, Project (n/a)
See Glossary.

Urgent Medevac (n/a)
See Glossary.

US/ARVN Laager Site (XT 614-226)
Apx 7 km NW to NNW Cu Chi Base and near villes of Trang Bao On and Truong Lap. Aug69. 2d/14th Inf, 2d/49th ARVN Rgt. Data per www.en.com/users/kramsey/dragons.html. Binh Duong Pr, III Corps.

US Armed Forces Institute (n/a)
See Glossary.

US Army Boats in Vietnam (n/a)
See Glossary.

US Army Headquarters Area Cmd (n/a)
See AHAC in Major HQs Section.

US Army Hospital, Camp Zama (n/a)
In Japan. Apparently not same as the 249th Gen Hosp, though also at Camp Zama?

US Army Hospital, Japan (n/a)
See 249th Gen and US Army Hosp, Camp Zama. Japan.

US Army Hospital, Okinawa (n/a)
See Ryukyu Islands.

US Army Hospital, Ryukyu Islands (n/a)
See Ryukyu Islands.

US Army Hospital, Saigon (XS 841-940)
Apx 2 km SE Tan Son Nhut AB and 3 km NNW Independence Palace. An adjunct of 3d Field Hosp under cmd of the US Army Health Services Grp. When US left in Mar73, it became the Seventh Day Adventist Hosp. Only open May72-Mar73. Gia Dinh Pr, III Corps.

US Army POW Hospital (YT 04-07)
Prisoner of War Hosp on Long Binh Post. Operated by 74th Field Hosp until Aug69, when 24th Evac Hosp took over control. Presumably treated enemy POWs. Grid is for Long Binh Post, not the hospital. Bien Hoa Pr, III Corps.

US Defender, SS (n/a)
Commercial transport under govt contract, per Ralph Fries.

US Embassy Annex (XS 869-908)
At 39 Ham Nghi St., Saigon, 100 meters W of the Saigon River and 1.2 km ESE of Independence Palace. In bldg known as "Old Embassy." Site of Coco Club which was destroyed by terrorist bomb, 30Mar65. Data per *Vietnam Military Lore, 1959-1973.* Gia Dinh Pr, III Corps.

US Embassy Heliport (XS 863-922)
See Embassy Heliport. Gia Dinh Pr, III Corps.

US Embassy, Saigon (XS 863-922)
At E edge of downtown Saigon, apx 800 meters NE Independence Palace, 1 km W the Saigon River, 5 km SE MACV HQ Cmpd, 6 km SE Tan Son Nhut AB and 3.5 km NE the Y-Bridge. On 1Jan68, after VC had occupied embassy at outset of Tet '68, C Co, 1st/502d Inf/101st Abn (which had been awaiting its turn in 2d Bde's deployment to Phu Bai/Quang Tri area) was landed on its roof and helped secure site floor-by-floor, then remained in on roof for several days. Gia Dinh Pr, III Corps.

US Explorer, SS (n/a)
Commercial transport under govt contract, per Ralph Fries.
US Naval Forces Vietnam (n/a)
See Glossary and Major HQs section.
US Support Activities Group (VE 6-2)
A.k.a. USSAG or SAG. At Nakhon Phanom West AF (a.k.a. NKP or Naked Fanny), apx 220 km SE Vientiane, 190 km E Udorn AB, and 120 km from SVN border. Per *A Better War*, p 366, between '73-75, nicknamed "MACV in Exile" and under cmd of Gen Ira Hunt.[547] NE Thailand.
US Tourist, SS (n/a)
Commercial transport under govt contract, per Ralph Fries.
USAF Hospital, Bien Hoa (XT 988-129)
On Bien Hoa AB. Open '65-72. Supt/Evac Hosp often used for casualties and other patients in-transit to major hospitals outside VN. Bien Hoa Pr, III Corps.
USAF Hospital, Binh Thuy (WS 80-13?)
At Binh Thuy AF. Open '66-70. Supt/Evac Hosp often used for casualties and other patients in-transit to major hospitals outside VN. Phong Dinh Pr, IV Corps.
USAF Hospital, Cam Ranh (CP 066-261)
At Cam Ranh Bay AB. Open '65-72. II Corps. Supt/Evac Hosp often used for casualties and other patients in-transit to major hospitals outside VN. Khanh Hoa Pr, II Corps.
USAF Hospital, Clark AFB (n/a)
Philippines. Supt/Evac Hosp for VN Casualties in-transit.
USAF Hospital, Da Nang (BT 008-754)
At Da Nang AB. Open '65-72. Supt/Evac Hosp often used for casualties and other patients in-transit to major hospitals outside VN. Quang Nam Pr, I Corps.
USAF Hospital, Hickam (n/a)
At Hickam Field, Honolulu Hawaii, and adj to Pearl Harbor. Supt/Evac Hosp for VN casualties in-transit. USA.
USAF Hospital, Kadena (n/a)
At Kadena AFB, Okinawa. Supt/Evac Hosp for VN casualties in-transit. See also USN Hosp Okinawa and Camp Butler.
USAF Hospital, Nha Trang (CP 039-520)
At Nha Trang AB. Open '62-69. II Corps. Supt/Evac Hosp often used for casualties and other patients in-transit to major hospitals outside VN.
USAF Hospital, Phan Rang (BN 772-862)
At Phan Rang AB. Open '66-72. Supt/Evac Hosp often used for casualties and other patients in-transit to major hospitals outside VN. Ninh Thuan Pr, II Corps.
USAF Hospital, Phu Cat (BR 896-412)
At Phu Cat AB. Open '66-67. Supt/Evac Hosp often used for casualties and other patients in-transit to major hospitals outside VN. Binh Dinh Pr, II Corps.
USAF Hospital, Pleiku (AR 783-500?)
Grid is for Pleiku/Cu Hanh AB, main Pleiku USAF facility, and thought to be location of facility. May have been at Camp Holloway? Open '67-71. Pleiku Pr, II Corps.
USAF Hospital, Tachikawa (n/a)
At Tachikawa AFB, Japan. Supt/Evac Hosp for VN Casualties in-transit.
USAF Hospital, Tan Son Nhut (XS 819-962)
Near or within perimeter of Tan Son Nhut AB, Saigon. Open 62-72. Gia Dinh Pr, III Corps.
USAF Hospital, Tuy Hoa (CQ 21-43)
At Tuy Hoa AB. Open 66-70. Supt/Evac Hosp often used for casualties and other patients in-transit to major hospitals outside VN. Phu Yen Pr, II Corps.
USAF Rescue Coordination Center (XS 81-96)
A.k.a. OL-A USAF RCC. At Tan Son Nhut AB (call-sign Queen), Saigon. Gia Dinh Pr, III Corps.
USAID #1, Saigon (XS 853-909)
On No Tung Chau St. Gia Dinh Pr, III Corps.
USAID #2, Saigon (XS 847-916)
On Ngo Thoi Nhiem St. Gia Dinh Pr, III Corps.
USAID #3, Saigon (XS 855-901)
On Hung Dao St. Gia Dinh Pr, III Corps.
USARV BEQ #2 (XS 8-9)
At 309 Cach Mang St., Saigon. Data per *Vietnam Military Lore, 1959-1973*. Gia Dinh Pr, III Corps.
USARV BEQ #3 (XS 8-9)
At 189-193 Vo Tanh St., Saigon. Data per *Vietnam Military Lore, 1959-1973*. Gia Dinh Pr, III Corps.
USARV BEQ #4 (XS 8-9)
At 9-11 Cao Ba Nha St., Saigon. Data per *Vietnam Military Lore, 1959-1973*. Gia Dinh Pr, III Corps.
USARV BEQ #I (XS 8-9)
In Saigon. Data per *Vietnam Military Lore, 1959-1973*. Gia Dinh Pr, III Corps.
USARV BOQ #1 (XS 8-9)
At 210 Vo Tanh St., Saigon. Data per *Vietnam Military Lore, 1959-1973*. Gia Dinh Pr, III Corps.
USARV Detachment BOQ (XS 8-9)
In Saigon per *Vietnam Military Lore, 1959-1973*, but grid unknown. Gia Dinh Pr, III Corps.
USARV HQ (XS 82-96 and YT 038-056)
A.k.a. the Headshed or Head Shed. At Long Binh Post, along S side of Hwy 319, apx 11 km SE Bien Hoa AB, 26 km WNW Tan Son Nhut AB and 13 km due E Di An city. Originally at Tan Son Nhut AB, US Army VN HQ moved to Long Binh, Jul67. Was responsible for cmd and control of all US Army units in VN and fell directly under MACV cmd. By virtue of being Army generals, Gen Westmoreland and Creighton Abrams were <u>simultaneously</u> the MACV and USARV Cmdrs during their tenure. USARV HQ at Long Binh Post was 26 km from Saigon, over 25 sq mi in size, housed over 50,000 permanent cadre and initial cost exceeded $100 million. Also listed at YT 040-064. Gia Dinh and Bien Hoa Prvs, III Corps.
USARV HQ Heliport (YT 038-056)
A.k.a. the Headshed or Head Shed Heliport. At Long Binh Post, on S side Hwy 319, apx 11 km SE Bien Hoa AB, 25 km ENE Tan Son Nhut AB and 13 km NW Long Thanh North AF. "Heliport #744, alt 105', asph, 300' x 600' .02-20" Closed. W tfc pattern at 500'. Aprch and depart fr A, B, or main Cross pads. Panel 1 for DCG USARV only. Panel 2 for pickup or drop off only. No shutdown excpt code 6 above. Panels 3-4 pickup or dropoff, 0-10 min. prk. Panels 5-8 reserved for UH-1 prk. Panels 11-14 reserved for OH-6A and OH-58 acft. CH-47 and larger copter proh. Do not overfly HQ or general's quarters. Arty advsy-Bien Hoa 290.0 46 7. At 10°54'N 106°52'E, per Feb73 TAD. Originally at Tan Son Nhut AB. Bien Hoa Pr, III Corps.
USARV Individual Training Groups (various)
See Glossary.

USARV Newport Terminal (XS 886-935)
See Saigon USAR Newport Terminal. III Corps.

***USCGC* (*Ship's Name*)** (n/a)
All vessels in this text are listed by name in alphabetical listing with normal prefixes of *USCG, USNS, USS* (and so on) following the formal name, as in *Maddox, USS.*

USN Hospital, Okinawa (n/a)
On Okinawa. Supt/Evac Hosp for VN Casualties in-transit. See USAF Hosp Kadena and Camp Butler.

USN Hospital Ship *Hope* (n/a)
See *Hope, USS.* AH-7. SVN.

USN Hospital Ship *Repose* (n/a)
See *Repose.* SVN.

USN Hospital Ship *Sanctuary* (n/a)
See *Sanctuary.* SVN.

USN/USMC Hospital, 1st Mar Med Bn (AT/BT?)
Open 66-70. At Da Nang? Quang Nam Pr, I Corps.

USN/USMC Hospital, 3d Mar Med Bn (YD 8-1)
Open 65-69. At Phu Bai. Thua Thien Pr, I Corps.

USN/USMC Hospital, Da Nang (BT 008-754?)
At or near Da Nang AB. Open '66-70. Grid is for AB. Quang Nam Pr, I Corps.

USN Hospital, *USS Hope* (n/a)
See *Hope, USS.* AH-7. SVN.

USN/USMC Hospital, *USS Repose* (n/a)
See *Repose, USS.* SVN.

USN/USMC Hospital, *USS Sanctuary* (n/a)
See *Sanctuary, USS.* SVN.

***USNS* (*Ship's Name*)** (n/a)
All vessels in this text are listed by name in alphabetical listing with normal prefixes of *USCG, USNS, USS* (and so on) following the formal name, as in *Maddox, USS.*

USO Saigon (866-912)
At 119 Nguyen Hue St., Saigon, and apx 800 meters SE of Independence Palace. Facility of United Service Org that provided some of only direct telephone service to continental US, as well as free food, pool tables, and lounges (USO was sponsored by US military to provide recreation and boost troop morale worldwide, but was not a military agency itself). Also had vending machines, slot machines and a pay-as-you-go snack bar. Data per *Vietnam Military Lore, 1959-1973.* Gia Dinh Pr, III Corps.

USO Vung Tau (YS 28-43)
At Vung Tau R&R Ctr. Apx 72 km SE Saigon. See also Vung Tau R&R Ctr. Phuoc Tuy Pr, III Corps.

***USS* (*Ship's Name*)** (n/a)
All vessels in this text are listed by name in alphabetical listing with normal prefixes of *USCG, USNS, USS* (and so on) following the formal name, as in *Maddox, USS.*

USS Forest Fire (n/a)
See *Forrestal, USS.*

USS Benny Maru (n/a)
See *Bennington, USS.*

Utah, LZ (YD 218-175)
Apx 51 km due W Hue, 7 km ESE FSB Ranger and 11 km NE Tou Rout. Apr70 XXIV Corps grid per D. Armstrong. Quang Tri Pr, I Corps.

Utah Beach (YD 494-565)
A.k.a. Wonder, Wunder and Sunder Beach. On coast near Thon Me Thuy and Hai Lang, apx 16 km E to ESE Quang Tri, 40 km NW Hue, and adj FSB Hardcore. Utah was its original name, eff 2Mar68. USN ship offloading facility here grew out of need to resupply 1st Cav and 101st Abn during Tet '68. Opened/operated by 159th Trans Bn, under Col Charles Sunder (TF Sunder), with 14th Engr Bn and 363d Truck Co also here. 1st Cav provided initial security, followed by 101st Abn and then 3d/26th Marines (17Apr68). Also listed at YD 467-528 and 488-551. See Wunder Beach and Utah Beach. Quang Tri Pr, I Corps.

Utah/Lien Ket 26, Operation (BT)
4-8Mar66. USMC/ARVN op near Quang Ngai against NVA/VC MF units. 632 NVA/VC KIA, per *Vietnam Order of Battle*, pp 9-14. See Chau Ngai. Quang Ngai Pr, I Corps.

Utapao Airbase (n/a)
See U Tapao. Thailand.

Ute, LZ (BR 355-705)
N of and overlooking the Song Ba River, 9 km NW Kannack AF, 10 km N Plei Ko Re, 13 km SSW LZ Niagara, 26 km NNW An Khe and 5 km WNW Hill 666. 4th Div AO, '70. B Bty, 4th/42d Arty here, Jun70. Name/grid per Jim Claeys. Also listed at BR 355-709. Apr-Oct70. Binh Dinh Pr, II Corps.

UTM Grid Zones (n/a)
See Glossary and Map Reading Section.

Uttaradit Airfield (PV 3-5)
Along San River at 17°40'00"N-100°14'00"E, apx 430 km N Bangkok. Feb67 Natl Geo map. El. 700'. Thailand.

Uttaradit Northwest Airfield (PV 1-4?)
At 17°38'00"N-100°05'00"E, roughly 430 km N Bangkok. NIMA data. Thailand.

Uyen Binh (Bo Tuc) (n/a)
Mapsheet name of L-7014-6232-2. Full sheet name is: Bo Tuc (Uyen Binh)

Uyen-Hung, Xa (Tan Uyen) (n/a)
Mapsheet name of L-7014-6331-2. Full sheet name is: Tan Uyen (Xa Uyen-Hung). SVN.

VICTOR

Facility/Feature Name, Grid Coordinate, a.k.a. Name/History/Province/CTZ

Unless otherwise stated, 6-digit grid coordinates reference DMA L-7014, L-7015 or L-7016 series, 1:50,000 scale maps, while 2- and 4-digit coordinates reference AMS/DMA/NIMA 1:250,000, 1:500,000 and 1:1,000,000 scale maps. Unless otherwise stated, all heights are in meters. To convert meters to feet, multiply by 3.2808; feet to meters, multiply by .3048.

V, LZ (BR 544-960)
Remote site, apx 26 km SW Thuan An. 17Mar66. Binh Dinh Pr, II Corps.

V Interzone (n/a)
See Interzone V.

Vagabond Crossing (n/a)
See Glossary.

Valentine, LZ (ZA 21-68?)
A.k.a. Vallentine (Jan-Mar69 1st/35th Inf, 4th Div rpts). Said to have overlooked a "long, wide valley with SF camp near valley's W or S end (camp often attacked, May-Jun69)." *Ivy Leaves* (4th Div) article supplied by Don Blankin puts it on E side QL-14, apx 23 km N Pleiku; however, Lee Vernitskiy puts it on plateau E of Kontum and to E of, and within 155mm range of, FSB Mary Lou. (ZA 228-829). James Marsh recalls it being SW Kontum and E Pleiku? Apparently built by 2d/35th Inf and one of 1st FSBs const in area. 1st/35th Inf involved in big battle here in which FSB Mary Lou provided vital fire supt. Blankin tells us it was near base of the Chu Pong mtns, Feb69, and "We heard many rumors from the 'world' that a renowned psychic had predicted one of last big battles of war would be fought on or around an LZ called Valentine." Listed grid est per *Ivy Leaves'* description. Some data per Dick Arnold. Pleiku Pr, II Corps.

Valero, Pointe du (XS 7-9)
See Pointe Valero. Gia Dinh Pr?, III Corps.

Valhalla, LZ (AQ 990-610)
Apx 2 km NW Buon Blech AF, 60 km NNE Ban Me Thuot, 7 km NNE Buon Brieng AF and 2 km E QL-14. Jul66. Darlac Pr, II Corps.

Valkyrie, LZ (YA 516-416)
Apx 6 km NE the Tonle San River, 27 km NNE Ba Kev AF, 14 km W SVN border, 73 km due W Pleiku and 6 km S LZ Spearhead. 4th Div Incursion FSB, May-Jun70. Also listed at YA 516-417 and 516-471 (latter grid apparent transposition error). Name per Jim Claeys and grid per James Henderson. Cambodia.

Vallentine, LZ (ZA 21-68?)
See Valentine. Kontum Pr, II Corps.

Valley 506 (BR 80-84 to 86-77)
See 506 Valley. Binh Dinh Pr, II Corps.

Valley 515 (BS 68-42)
See 515 Valley. Quang Ngai Pr, I Corps.

Valley A (CR 0-1?)
A.k.a. 19th Engr Bn Logistics Depot. Apparently near Qui Nhon. Original home of 19th Engr Bn, later moved to Long My Valley (Valley F), Mar67. Discussed at www.war-stories.com/Incoming.htm. See also Long My Valley. Binh Dinh Pr, II Corps.

Valley F (CR 0-1?)
Apparently close to Qui Nhon. See also Long My Valley and 19th Engr Bn cantonment. Binh Dinh Pr, II Corps.

Valley Forge, USS (n/a)
A.k.a. (LPH-8). Lndg. Platform, Helo.

Valley of a Thousand Ghosts (YA 93-04)
Viet superstitious nickname for the Ia Drang Valley. So named because of the many thousands of NVA/VC soldiers MIA here. Heavily bombed by B-52 Arc Lightd, particularly during and after 1st Ia Drang Battles at LZ X-Ray and LZ Albany, Nov65. Pleiku Pr, II Corps.

Vammen, USS (n/a)
DE-644. DD-Escort, per Ralph Fries.

Vampire, HMAS (n/a)
Australian Escort serving under US 7th Flt.

Van, Cua (CP 2-9)
Bay at 12°39'N-109°23'E. Khanh Hoa Pr, II Corps.

Van, FSB (n/a)
Cited in *1st Cav Op Rpt, Feb-Apr70*, p 12, per Peter Cole. During period, Cav was in W and central III Corps.

Van Alstine Mess (CR 08-23)
At Qui Nhon. Named to honor SF SSgt Merle O. Van Alstine, KIA 10Feb65, as 1 of 24 US personnel killed by VC terrorist bombing of Qui Nhon Military Hotel bar. Data per *VN Military Lore, 1959-1973*. Binh Dinh Pr, II Corps.

Van Ba (n/a)
See Glossary.

Van Ban (n/a)
Mapsheet name of L-7014-5853-3. NVN only.

Van Buren, Operation (n/a)
19Jan-21Feb66. 1st Bde/101st Abn, ROK 2d Mar Bde, and 47th ARVN Rgt providing security for rice farmers. 679 NVA/VC KIA, per *Vietnam Order of Battle*, pp 9-14. Phu Yen Pr, II Corps.

Van Canh (new) SF Camp (BR 840-064)
Apx 53 km SE An Khe AF, 30 km SW Qui Nhon and 31 km NW Song Cau AF. SF Det 26, 5th SF Grp CIDG Det A-223, Oct66. Transferred to Qui Nhon, MSF. Grid per *SF Order of Battle*. Binh Dinh Pr, II Corps.

Van Canh (old) SF Camp (BR 841-078)
Apx 52 km SE An Khe AF, 30 km SW Qui Nhon and 32 km NW Song Cau AF. SF Det 26, 5th SF Grp CIDG Det A-223, Oct66. Transferred to ARVN. Grid per *SF Order of Battle*. Binh Dinh Pr, II Corps.

Van Canh Airfield (BR 833-064)
Apx 52 km SE An Khe AF, 30 km SW Qui Nhon, 18 km SSW ROK AAF, 70 km NNW Tuy Hoa and 32 km NW

Song Cau AF, per TPC K-10A. El. 190'. Listed as "Secure, SF ARVN(A) 5Apr68, AF # VA2-114," in Aug69 TAD per Frank Penk, Jr. Not in Feb73 TAD. Binh Dinh Pr, II Corps.

Van Canh Heliport (BR 835-070)
Apx 52 km SE An Khe AF, 30 km SW Qui Nhon and 32 km NW Song Cau AF. Heliport #696, alt 16', at 13°37'30"N-108°59'45"E. Binh Dinh Pr, II Corps.

Van Fong, Baie de (CP 1-8)
A.k.a. Vung Van Phong. Bay at 12°33'N-109°18'E. On ND49-13 JOG. Khanh Hoa Pr, II Corps.

Van Gia (n/a)
Mapsheet name of L-7014-6834-3. SVN.

Van Hoa (n/a)
Mapsheet name of L-7014-6551-3. NVN only.

Van Hoa (various)
Common Viet place-name. Villes with it in grid squares: BQ 9-3, BS 6-7, BS 7-0, WJ 8-9, YD 3-5 and YJ 6-4.

Van Hoa CAP (YD 3-5)
Apparently within 10 km of Quang Tri. NPIA lists Van Hoa Xuan at YD 754-337, which is near Hue? CAP 4-3-4, 4th CAG per Tim Duffie. Quang Tri Pr, I Corps.

Van Kiep National Training Center (YS 402-608)
A.k.a. Van Kiep NTC or ARVN Ntl Trng Ctr. Along N edge Xa Phuoc Le, apx 17 km SSW Nui Dat, 8 km WNW Dat Do and 62 km ESE Saigon. Per *Vietnam Military Lore, Legends, Shadows and Heroes*, at p 766, "The 1st basic training center in VN was founded in 1953, and was originally called "Quan Tro Trng Ctr" (Trng Ctr #1). Between '54-'57, the center [trained] commissioned officers and NCOs. In Sep57, [it] was renamed Quang Trung and became largest BCT center in VN." Created to assume Quan Tro's prgms, inc special unit tactics and AIT. Australian-sponsored LRP trng class for ARVN recon elements began here Jun68. Discussed in *Rangers At War*, p 259. Phuoc Tuy Pr, III Corps.

Van Ly (n/a)
Mapsheet name of L-7014-6249-2. NVN only.

Van Ly Airfield (BS 718-425)
See An Thin AF. Quang Ngai Pr, I Corps.

Van Ninh Airfield (CQ 075-032)
Along coast just E of QL-1, W of Ben Goi Bay, 40 km SSW Tuy Hoa, 28 km NE Duc My AF, 52 km due N Nha Trang AF and NNE Ninh Hoa AF. Minor AF here, per TPC K-10B and TPC K-10A. El. 10', 1,100' laterite rwy. At 12°41'21"N-109°13'40"E. Khanh Hoa Pr, II Corps.

Van Pak Len Airfield (PC 16-51)
LS-267. CIA/SF, per *Air Facilities Data-Laos.*

Van Phong, Vung (CP 1-8)
Bay at 12°33'N-109°18'E. Khanh Hoa Pr, II Corps.

Van Thien (3), Battle of (BR 863-603)
At base of a hill mass apx 3 km NW Van Tien, 16 km NNW Phu Cat AB, 9 km SSW Phu My and 4 km W QL-1. Took place 21Jun67. Map is L-7014-6837-3, per Ken Burrington. Quang Ngai Pr, I Corps.

Van Toan, General (n/a)
See Glossary.

Van Tuong Peninsula (BS 75-85?)
Apx 19 km SE Chu Lai, 12 km NNE Quang Ngai. See Batangan Peninsula. Quang Ngai Pr, I Corps.

Van Xa (YD 638-274)
Ville and AF apx 12 km NW Hue and 1 km W QL-1. Was site of LZ/Camp Sally. Thon Van Xa (YD 665-280) was on E side of and along QL-1, just E Van Xa. Map is L-7014-6442-2. Thua Thien Pr, I Corps.

Van Xa Airfield (YD 639-275)
Adj to LZ/Camp Sally, apx 12 km NW Hue and on W side of QL-1. El. 100', 1,100' laterite rwy. At 16°30'58"N-107°28'18"E. Thua Thien Pr, I Corps.

Van Yen (n/a)
Mapsheet name of L-7014-5951-3. NVN only.

Vance, USS (n/a)
DER-387. DD-Escort, Radar. Incident involving *Vance* discussed in *Brown Water, Black Berets*, p 102. Market Time TF-115. SVN.

Vancouver, USS (n/a)
LPD 2. Lndg Platform, Dock. On 26Feb65, LBJ authorized deployment of 2 USMC BLTs to Da Nang. TF inc HMM sqdn and HQ 9th MEB. At 0600 on 8Mar65, Rear Adm Donald Wulzen, cmdr 7th Fleet Amphibious TF, gave order to, "Land the lndg force," upon which ships *Vancouver* (LPD 2), *Mount McKinley* (AGC 7), *Henrico* (APA 45), and *Union* (AKA. 106) began disembarking the BLTs. Between 0902-0918 hrs, 3d Bn/9th Marines became 1st US Bn-sized element deployed in War. To their surprise, waiting on shore was a gaggle of journalists, photographers and Vietnamese who welcomed them with flowers rather than bullets! Quang Nam Pr, I Corps.

Vandegrift, FSB (XD 984-484)
Along QL-9 and W of Vandegrift CB, apx 2.5 km NW Ca Lu and 46 km W Quang Tri. Possibly a 5th Mech Div base? Jul70. Quang Tri Pr, I Corps.

Vandegrift Combat Base (YD 003-488)
Along QL-9 and at base of hill that was site of FSB Sarge, apx 3 km N Ca Lu, 34 km W Quang Tri, 10 km WSW Mai Loc and 12 km NW FSB Henderson. 9th Mar/3d Mar Div here'69. Originally 1st Cav base (name unknown) built '68, to provide arty supt for Marines besieged at Khe Sanh. Later USMC named it to honor MGen Alexander A. Vandegrift, WWII CG 1st Mar Div and 1st Marine to achieve 4-star rank. 2d/2d ARVN Inf Div dismantled it in Oct69, and left over materials used in const at Camp Carroll. Also listed at XD 999-478. Quang Tri Pr, I Corps.

Vandegrift Combat Base #3 (XD 997-483)
Meaning of numbering assigned to Vandegrift CB on XXIV Corps facility list is unknown; however, may have designated helo lndg pad sites within base. Pad #3's grid is immed W and adj to grid listed for main facility (YD 003-488), while that of #4 is adj to and slightly SW main grid? May also have signified areas assigned to other units apart from USMC? Apr70 XXIV Corps grid per Don Armstrong. Quang Tri Pr, I Corps.

Vandegrift Combat Base #4 (XD 990-477)
See Vandegrift CB #3. Quang Tri Pr, I Corps.

Vandergrift (YD 003-488)
Common misspelling of Vandegrift. Quang Tri Pr, I Corps.

Vanfong Bay (CP 1-8)
A.k.a. Vung Van Phong. Bay at 12°33'N-109°18'E. On ND49-13 JOG. Khanh Hoa Pr, II Corps.

Vang Lai (CP 04-56)
Possible military facility here? At or near Nha Trang. Grid only apx. Khanh Hoa Pr, II Corps.
Vang Tau Signal Site (YS 26-46?)
A.k.a. VC Hill? Possible misspelling of Vung Tau? If site was at Vung Tau, it was likely atop VC Hill/Hill 245, immed N Vung Tau, and apx 1 km from ocean. Phuoc Tuy Pr, III Corps?
Vang Veng Airfield (TF 32-94)
See Vang Vieng AF. Laos.
Vang Vieng Airfield (TF 32-94)
A.k.a. L-16 and Vang Veng AF. Apx 110 km N to NNE Vientiane. CIA/SF facility. Spelled "Vang Veng" on ONC-J-11, and "Van Vieng" on Feb67 Natl Geo map Grid per *Air Facilities Data-Laos.* 5,200' rwy, El. 722'. Laos.
Vanguard, FSB (BS 576-433)
Apx 25 km WNW Duc Pho and 10 km N Ba To. Americal List. Quang Ngai Pr, I Corps.
Vann, John P, Crash Site (ZA 20-68?)
See John Paul Vann. Pleiku/Kontum Pr, II Corps.
Varalla, Cape (CQ 3-2)
See Varella, Cape. Khanh Hoa Pr, II Corps.
Varela, False (CN 0-9)
A.k.a. Mui Da Vach. Coastal point at 11°43'N-109°14'E. Ninh Thuan Pr, II Corps.
Varella, Cape (CQ 3-2)
Cape at 12°54'N-109°26'E. On ND49-13 JOG. Khanh Hoa Pr, II Corps.
Varella, Mui (CQ 3-2)
Mui Ke Ga. Coastal point at 12°53'N-109°28'E. On ND49-13 JOG. Khanh Hoa Pr, II Corps.
Vasquez, Camp (CR 03-16? or BR 95-42?)
A.k.a. US Army 27th Trans Bn Cmpd. At Phu Tai, near Qui Nhon and CR grid thought to be most likely location. Transferred to VNAF/SVN Govt, 24Mar72, and, at turnover, consisted of 134 buildings, capable of suptg 900 troops. 2d ARVN Trans Bn replaced US units here. The MACV/JGS IG conducted a pre-turnover inspection, 13Nov71, and post-turnover inspection 30-31May71. Data per Ray Bows. Binh Dinh Pr, II Corps.
Vaunt (n/a)
Apr70, XXIV Corps future-use 101st Abn FSB name.
Vayama (n/a)
Thailand (or Cambodia?), per *SF Order of Battle.*
VC/NVA Propaganda Leaflets (n/a)
See Glossary.
VC Hill (YS 26-46??)
A.k.a. Vang Tau or Vung Tau Signal Site? If site was at Vung Tau, it is likely Hill 245, immed N Vung Tau and 1 km from ocean. Phuoc Tuy Pr?, III Corps?
VC Island (YS 13-95)
Large island in the Song Nha Be apx 17 km E Saigon and 18 km S Bien Hoa. Apx 8 x 2.5 km in size. VC staging area and sanctuary. Discussed in *Low Level Hell* and on its 1st Div TAOR map. Gia Dinh Pr, III Corps.
VC Lake (various)
See Glossary.
VC Valley (BR 130-390)
A.k.a. Dak Payou or Dak Pihao Valley. Northern reaches Dak Payou River Valley, apx 37 km ESE Pleiku, 35 km WSW An Khe, 13 km SSE Suoi Doi AF and generally S FSB Blackhawk. Named no doubt for its use as VC staging area and proliferation of VC based there. Grid per Jim Claeys. Pleiku Pr, II Corps.
VC Valley (BR 900-935)
NW side Cay Giep Mtns, apx 8 km ESE Bong Son. Map is L-7014-6837-4, per K. Burrington. Binh Dinh Pr, II Corps.
VC Valley (BT?)
Per *Rites of Passage*, p 453, its author apparently gave area this name. Apparently in Quang Ngai Pr, I Corps.
VC Valley (YA 857-540)
Valley of Ya Krong Bolah in vic Plei Djereng (old), apx 40 km WNW Pleiku. Pleiku/Kontum Pr border, II Corps.
Veal Vang Airfield (UU 10-34)
See Veal Veng AF. Cambodia.
Veal Veng Airfield (UU 10-34)
Apx 195 km WNW Phnom Penh and 112 km S Battambang AF, and 110 km SW Krakor AF, per TPC K-10D/TPC K-10A. 3,100' rwy, and El. 1,903'. Also spelled Veal Veng on Feb67 Ntl Geo map. Cambodia.
Vega, USS (n/a)
AF 59, Storeship. Part of TG 76.8, during Op Eagle Pull.
Vegas, LZ (AT 932-762)
Along Hwy 540, apx 4 km SW Red Beach AF and 8 km NW Da Nang AB. Apr70 XXIV Corps grid per Don Armstrong. Quang Nam Pr, I Corps.
Veghel, FSB (YD 549-036)
Along Rte 547 at its intersection with Rte 547a, apx 10 km WSW FSB Bastogne, 16 km WSW FSB Birmingham, 24 km WSW Nam Hoa Dist HQ and 27 km SW Hue. Site consisted of 2 peaks with a saddle between them. On 16Apr68, 1st/327th Inf began attack of NVA Bn entrenched on hill that later became Veghel. Paraphrasing Steve Patterson: "It took 3 days of almost constant fighting to take the hill. On 19Apr at about 5:00 pm, a plt from C Co captured one peak (led by my friend Lt Fred Raymond) and I was the Plt Ldr of the point Plt for A Co that captured the other peak. Both peaks were taken within 30 minutes of one another. The 1/327th suffered 60% casualties in that fight." [548] Const began soon after. Remote site in AO of 1st/2d Bdes, 101st Abn during Ops Nevada Eagle and Sherman Peak. Was captured from ARVN during '72 Easter Off. 1st/327th, 2d/501st Inf, 1st/502d Inf, among others here. Thua Thien Pr, I Corps.
Vehgel, FSB (YD 549-036)
See Veghel. Thua Thien Pr, I Corps.
Velvet Hammer, Operation (n/a)
See Glossary.
Vema, FSB (YT 273-103)
See Verna. Bien Hoa Pr, III Corps.
Vemable Heights, FSB (XT 88-18?)
See Venable Heights. Binh Duong Pr, III Corps.
Ven Ven (XT 350-324)
Along QL-1, apx 34 km NW Cu Chi and 20 km SE Tay Ninh. ARVN 3d Abn Div HQ moved here from Tan Son Nhut AB on 14Sep68, as part of Battle for Tay Ninh. Tay Ninh Pr, III Corps.
Ven Ven, Plantation de (XT 350-320)
A.k.a. Don Dien Ven Ven. Along QL-1, apx 34 km NW Cu Chi and 20 km SE Tay Ninh. Tay Ninh Pr, III Corps.

Ven Ven Rubber Plantation (XT 395-550)
Apx 15 km NW Tay Ninh. Tay Ninh Pr, III Corps.
Venable Heights, FSB (XT 902-176)
Likely proper spelling of base a.k.a. Vemable Heights. Apx 10 km WNW Bien Hoa AB, 4 km ENE Phu Loi AF and 13 km due N Di An. 1st Inf Div AO, '69. Per *Low Level Hell's* 1st Div TAOR map. Possibly named to honor one of 3 men: Sgt Elton Venable, KIA 26Aug68; SGM Joseph Venable, KIA13Sep68; or PFC Westovel Venable, KIA25Jan66. Jan-Aug69. Binh Duong Pr, III Corps.
Venus, LZ (XD 908-535)
Apx 11 km NW Ca Lu, 13 km NNE Khe Sanh CB and 10 km WNW Thon Son Lam. Apr70 XXIV Corps grid per Don Armstrong. Quang Tri Pr, I Corps.
Vera, FSB/LZ (YA 835-172)
On E side Plei Girao Kla, apx 6 km from Cambodia, 50 km SW Pleiku, 8 km S Duc Co AF and 42 km WSW Oasis AF. Built Nov68 by 1st/35th Inf, 4th Div. African-American 1st Sgt Kahn Carley Jr., 37, who DEROS'd 11/68, told Dick Arnold that when he arrived in VN, "I had a fire base named in my honor because I'd spent more time in the field than any 1st Sgt in 4th Div." Carley apparently asked it be named for his wife. Arnold also tells us Bn Op rpts indicate site was reopened by A/1st/35th Inf, 23Oct68, and hit by sappers 13Nov68. During reopening, numerous casualties suffered from mines apparently planted by site's previous occupants (ARVN or RF/PF?). NVA tanks had been confirmed nearby in Cambodia, so LZs Jean and Vera were soon reinforced with two 106 mm RR', special concertina, wire and tank anti-intrusion devices. Became true Bn FSB, so 3d/8th Inf sent here a week later, with A/1st/35th opcon to them. On 12Nov68, 3d/8th left, leaving A Co to man 2-co perimeter with 1 Co while awaiting the 1st/22d Inf to reinforce. NVA took immed advantage of situation and at 0100 on 13Nov68, hit base with mortars, recoilless rifles and sappers (LZs Jean and Joan mortared simultaneously). Sappers penetrated perimeter (2 KIA inside), leaving explosives and sub-MGs strewn about base. US Inf lost 4 KIA, and 2d/9th Arty lost 2 KIA plus 1 vehicle destroyed. The next morning, A Co requested 2,000 sandbags for reconstruction. A/1st/35th Inf, also attacked here 13Nov68, with 5 US KIA, 38 WIA, and 6 NVA KIA. 10th Cav also here, per Bob Patsfield, as was1st/92d Arty. Also listed at YA 834-178. Pleiku Pr, II Corps. [549] [550]
Verd, Cape (CP 1-7)
A.k.a. Mui Ban Thang. Cape at 12°24'N-109°20'E. On ND49-13 JOG. Khanh Hoa Pr, II Corps.
Verdun, LZ (XT 236-922)
Apx 10 km WNW Katum AF and 6 km S Cambodia. 8May66. Tay Ninh Pr, III Corps.
Verna, FSB (YT 273-103)
A.k.a. FSB Bau Ca. Along QL-1 apx 18 km W Xuan Loc, 29 km ESE Bien Hoa AB, 34 km NE Saigon and 17 km NE Long Thanh North AF. 2d/3d and 5th/12th Inf, 199th LIB position '68 or '69. Sometimes spelled "Vema." Grid per 199th LIB Assn. Nov69-Jan70. Bien Hoa Pr, III Corps.
Vendetta, HMAS (n/a)
Australian DD or Escort serving under US 7th Flt.
Vernon County, USS (n/a)
LST-1161. USN Landing Ship, Tank. SVN service with 9th Inf Div/MRF. See www.mrfa.org. III/IV Corps?
Vernon Sturdee, HMAS (n/a)
AV-1355. Australian LSM serving under US 7th Flt. Originally *USS LSM-315* when sold to Australia, '60. Assigned to Aust Army Royal Engrs, 32 Small Ship Sqdn.
Vert, Cape (CP 1-7)
A.k.a. Mui Ban Thang. Cape at 12°24'N-109°20'E. On ND49-13 JOG. Khanh Hoa Pr, II Corps.
Vesole, USS (n/a)
DD 878. See *Barry, USS* (DD 933).
Vesperhell, LZ (XD 895-410)
Just N QL-9 and adj to Ra Co Ap, apx 6 km E to ESE Khe Sanh CB and 12 km SW Ca Lu. Apr70 XXIV Corps grid per Don Armstrong. Quang Tri Pr, I Corps.
Vesuvius, USS (n/a)
AE-15. Aux Explosive.
VFW Post 8316, Saigon (XS 87-92?)
The Veterans of Foreign Wars (federally chartered private US veterans organization) actually operated VFW posts in VN during war. Saigon post was 1st VFW in VN, chartered 21Nov65, and was later followed by posts in all major seaports. Catered to US military, Merchant Marines and other civilian personnel who were vets of earlier wars and the VN War. Other VFW posts were at Nha Trang, Cam Ranh Bay, Qui Nhon, Da Nang and Bien Hoa. Bien Hoa was exception to seaport rule because of large troop concentration there. All post charters in VN were revoked 20Oct66, after evidence of "improprieties" surfaced (specifics unknown, but speculation is it involved misuse of slot machine profits or club proceeds). Data per *Vietnam Military Lore, 1959-1973*. Gia Dinh Pr, III Corps.
VHPA Battle Index (n/a)
See Glossary.
Vi An (WR 497-800)
Ville apx 5 km SW Vi Thanh AF and 15 km E Ap Luc. Chuong Thien Pr, IV Corps.
Vi Thanh (WR 54-83)
Apx 50 km ESE Rach Gia and 40 km SW Can Tho. Home of 3d/31st, 21st ARVN Div and MACV Team 51, '65. Capitol, Chuong Thien Pr, IV Corps.
Vi Thanh (Duc Long) (n/a)
Mapsheet L-7014-6028-1. Sheet: Duc Long (Vi Thanh)
Vi Thanh (Old) Airfield (WR 521-816)
Along N side LTL-31 at Duc Long/Vi Thanh, apx 2 km W Vi Thanh New AF, and 46 km ESE Rach Gia. "Afld ops on request, O-1 type only, AF # VA4-175," in Aug69 TAD per Frank Penk (not 73 TAD). Chuong Thien Pr, IV Corps.
Vi Thanh 2 Airfield (WR 521-816)
See Vi Thanh (Old). Chuong Thien Pr, IV Corps.
Vi Thanh Airfield (WR 537-822)
In Mekong Delta apx 2 km E Vi Thanh (Duc Long), 55 km NW Soc Trang AF, 78 km NNE Quan Long city/AF, 42 km SW Can Tho, 49 km SE Rach Gia and 245 km SW Saigon, per TPC K-10D. El. 7', 2,300' steel-mat rwy. Chuong Thien Pr, IV Corps.
Vi Thanh New Airfield (WR 537-822?)
See Vi Thanh AF. Chuong Thien Pr, IV Corps.
Vian Ka, Mui (BT 6-0)
A.k.a. Mui Dat Vian Ka. Coastal point at 15°25'N-108°48'E. ND49-01 JOG. Quang Tin Pr, I Corps.
Vian Ka, Pointe de (BT 6-0)
See Pointe Vian Ka. Quang Tin Pr, I Corps.

Vic, FSB (YC 632-868)
On Laotian border, apx 80 km due W Da Nang and 20 km NW Yavour. Thua Thien Pr, I Corps.
Vic, LZ (BR 615-610)
Apx 13 km SSW Quang Ngai and 14 km NW Mo Duc AF. Oct66. Binh Dinh Pr, II Corps.
Vic, LZ (YC 630-870)
Apx 35 km SSW Hue and 8 km NE Be Luong. '70 XXIV Corps grid per D. Armstrong. Thua Thien Pr, I Corps.
Vic Klum (BS 081-145)
A.k.a. Plateau Gi. See Plateau Gi for location. Site of 1st known NVA attack in SVN. 2 NVA Bns attacked arty position here night of 26Apr62. US Adviser MSgt Rube A. Freeman was KIA in attack. Data per *Vietnam Military Lore, 1959-1973*. Kontum Pr, II Corps.
Vic Klum Airfield (BS 081-145)
See Plateau Gi AF. Kontum Pr, II Corps.
Vicki, FSB (XT 270-770)
A.k.a. FSB Vicky and FSB Oak? Apx 2 km SE Prek Klok, 21 km ESE Thien Ngon AF, 14 km SSW Katum and 18 km due N Nui Ba Den. Apparently ARVN FSB and possibly 1st Cav, '69. Cited in *Incursion,* per Peter Cole. Grid per Frank Penk, Jr. Tay Ninh Pr, III Corps.
Vicki, LZ (YD 282-114)
Apx 57 km WSW Hue and 16 km E Tou Rout. Apr68. 1st/7th Cav, 1st Cav CA'd here 19Apr68, during 1st day of Op Delaware/Lam Son 216. Although initial lndg unopposed, heavy AA fire greeted subsequent acft. Heavy weather then set-in preventing resupply or extraction, so Bn was forced to move overland to LZ Goodman, 6 km to S, a trek in heavy rain that took 4 days. Cited in 1st Cav VN *Yearbook* Aug65-Dec69, p 70, 259, per Peter Cole Quang Tri Pr, I Corps.
Vicky, FSB (XT 402-732)
Apx 18 km NE Nui Ba Den, 19 km ESE Katum AF and 3 km SE Ta Yen. Jan71. Tay Ninh Pr, III Corps.
Vicky, LZ (YD 282-114)
See LZ Vicki at grid. Quang Tri Pr, I Corps.
Victor, FSB (XT 164-922)
A.k.a. FSB Cao Thang. At Ky Dong, apx 7 km SE Cambodia, 17 km W to WNW Katum, 13 km NE Thien Ngon AF and 43 km N Tay Ninh. Apparently existed 5-8Mar70, and was 1of 7 FSBs opened and closed in 7 weeks by 2d/8th Cav, 1st Cav, prior to Cambodian Incursion (7 were: Jamie, Mary Gwen, Heather, Victor, Flashner, Drum and Illingworth). Cited in *Anatomy of a Division*, and *Pleiku*, p 188 et al, per Peter Cole. Tay Ninh Pr, III Corps.
Victor, LZ (YV 964-994)
Apx 3 km ESE LZ X-Ray, 5 km SSE LZ Albany, 6.5 km SW LZ Falcon and 55 km SW Pleiku. 1st Cav LZ during 1st Ia Drang Battle, Nov65. 2d/5th Cav CA'd here 14Nov65. Had 2 btys 105mm suptg battle at LZ X-Ray, 14-17Nov65. See also LZ Tango. Pleiku Pr, II Corps.
Victor Charlie (n/a)
See Glossary.
Victor Sites (n/a)
See Glossary.
Victoria BOQ (XS 8-9)
At 937 Tran Hung Dao St., Saigon. US military billet, Nov 63, 126 rms. Data per *Vietnam Military Lore, 1959-1973.* Gia Dinh Pr, III Corps.
Victory, FSB (XD 942-476)
Apx 16 km WSW Mai Loc, 5 km WNW Ca Lu and 38 km W to WSW of Quang Tri. Apr70 XXIV Corps grid per Don Armstrong. Quang Tri Pr, I Corps.
Victory, FSB (YD 813-080?)
Listed at this grid 1Nov69, but is thought to be incorrect because this was site of FSB Arsenal in Nov69? Arsenal was apx 11 km WSW Phu Bai AF, 11 km ESE FSB Birmingham and 7 km SE Nam Hoa Dist HQ. Thua Thien Pr, I Corps.
Viem Tay 1 CAP (BT 030-637)
See CAP 2-7-10. 2d CAG. Quang Nam Pr, I Corps.
Viem Tay 3 CAP (BT 03-64?)
See CAP 2-7-1. 2d CAG. Quang Nam Pr, I Corps.
Vien Pou Kha Airfield (QC 14-88)
LS-152. Apx 335 km NW Luang Prabang and 520 km NE Bangkok. CIA/SF. El. 2,130. *Air Facilities Data-Laos.*
Vientiane Airfield (TE 43-88)
A.k.a. L-08. Major AF in Laos near Thai border and Lao capitol city. Apx 210 km SSE Luang Prabang and 520 km NE Bangkok. Per ONC-J-11 and Feb67 Natl Geo maps. CIA/SF facility. Near 17°58'00"N-102°36'00"E. Grid per *Air Facilities Data-Laos.*
Vientiane SF Camp (TE 43-88?)
Along Mekong River, apx 210 km SSE Luang Prabang and 520 km NE Bangkok. SF camp/FOB in Laos when it declared neutrality (23Jul62). Team Control and FTT 36 here then. Per *Special Forces at War*. MR5, Laos.
Viet An Heliport (BT 028-286)
Apx 4 km WSW Binh Son, 12 km ENE Hiep Duc and 4 km ENE Phuoc Tuy. Heliport #697, alt 131', at 15°37'30"N-108°13'30"E. Quang Nam Pr, I Corps.
Viet An Outpost (BT 018-270)
Apx 12 km ENE Hiep Duc, 3 km NE Phuoc Tuy, 30 km WNW Tam Ky and 18 km SE Phuoc Binh AF. ARVN outpost here during Op Harvest Moon, 13Dec65. See *Utter's Battalion*, pp 199-200. Quang Tin Pr, I Corps.
Viet Cong (n/a)
See Glossary.
Viet Dac Military School (n/a)
NVA Military school in Thai Nguyen Prov. Basic Trng took 1st 3 months, then 60 days of Platoon Leader's School for typical NVA officer. Cited in *Bird*, pp. 3-4. NVN.
Viet Kich (n/a)
See Glossary.
Viet Minh (n/a)
See Glossary.
Viet Nam (n/a)
See Glossary.
Viet Thanh, Baie de (BT 7-0)
A.k.a. Vung Viet Thanh. Bay at 15°22'N-108°52'E. On ND49-01 JOG. Quang Ngai Pr, I Corps.
Viet Thanh, Vung (BT 7-0)
See Viet Thanh, Baie de. Quang Ngai Pr, I Corps.
Viet Tri (n/a)
Mapsheet name of L-7014-6051-1. NVN only.
Viet Tri (WJ 45-56)
On Road No. 2, apx 20 km W Vinh Yen and 58 km NW Hanoi. Focus of an attack by Vietminh 308 Div, 13Jan51, during Battle of Vinh Yen. See Chp 2, *Street Without Joy*, at p 39. NVN.

Vietminh (n/a)
See Glossary.
Vietnam (n/a)
See Glossary.
Vietnam, State of (n/a)
See Glossary.
Vietnam Campaign Medal (n/a)
See Glossary.
Vietnam Combat Zone, The (n/a)
See Glossary.
Vietnam National Army (n/a)
VNA. See Glossary.
Vietnam Presse (n/a)
See Glossary.
Vietnam Salient (XD 85-25)
That portion of SVN border in Quang Tri Prov that protrudes S into Laos near FSB Passport and SW Vandegrift CB. Grid at its apx center. Was immed W the Laotian Salient. Quang Tri Pr, I Corps.
Vietnam Service Medal (n/a)
See Glossary.
Vietnam Shower (n/a)
See Glossary.
Vietnam Tour Extensions (n/a)
See Glossary.
Vietnamese Joint General Staff HQ (XS 825-945)
Along S edge of Tan Son Nhut AB. Gia Dinh Pr, III Corps.
Vietnamese Military Schools (n/a)
See ARVN and RVNAF listings.
Viking, Camp (BT 94-83?)
At Red beach, immed N Camp Haskins, on coast apx 8 km NNW Da Nang AB. Per John Doherty, here 69-70, "The S boundary of Camp Viking was the N boundary of Camp Haskins. Viking was home of the 58th Trans Bn, Feb68-Apr72. Camp Haskins was a Navy Seabee base until late 70 or early 71, when an Army Engr Bn moved in. I do know that Viking was built by the Seabees at Haskins. On the other side of QL-1 by Haskins was USMC FLC. These were the only cmpds close by." Turned over to RVNAF-SVN Govt, 24Mar72, and MACV-JGS IG conducted a post-turnover inspection of facility, 26-27Sep72. Prior to transfer, had been occupied by US 57th Trans Bn, 1st Avn Bde, and subsequent to transfer by ARVN 102d Arty Bn (175mm). At turnover, facility consisted of 433 structures and could supt a force of 1,150 troops. Some data per 174th AHC site at http://www. americal.org/174/lutgrn16. htm. Quang Nam Pr, I Corps.
Viking, Camp (XS 470-440)
A.k.a. Viking South? On N shore of Mekong River at or near Binh Duc AF, apx 3 km W My Tho. Possibly the home of the 86th Eng Bn, who were also known as the Vikings. Dinh Tuong Pr, IV Corps.
Viking South (Camp?) (BT or XS)
Possibly a.k.a. or adj to Camp Haskins North (at Red Beach on coast apx 8 km NNW Da Nang AB)? Or possibly at Chu Lai or west of My Tho? Turned over to RVNAF-SVN Govt, 20Mar72, and MACV-JGS IG conducted post-turnover inspection of facility, 28Sep72. At transfer, consisted of 27 structures and could supt force of 250 men. Prior to transfer, it had been occupied by A/39th Engr Bn (attached 84th Engr Bn); and subsequent to transfer, by ARVN 118th Trans Co, 1st Trans Grp. Quang Nam or Quang Tin or Dinh Tuong Pr, I or IV Corps.
Viking Surprise (n/a)
See Glossary.
Vil Bu (XD)
Per Jim Taylor, USMC's CAC Oscar and SF units near Khe Sanh CB recruited Bru tribesmen from villes of Vil Bu, Vil Ch'eng, Vil Tacun and Vil C'on. While many VN vets hold the SVN military in low regard, Taylor offered this view of his indigenous counter parts: "Oscar was the only company (to my knowledge) that worked with the Bru (a Montagnard tribe). These ethnic Mon Khmer were NOT Vietnamese, but rather earlier ethnic aborigines displaced by south Chinese invaders...They are linguistically and ethnically related to Laos, Cambodes and Thai, especially the Hmong Tribe. They were cheerful, courageous (without being stupid) and honest; a pleasure to work with! Oscar worked with Bru tribesman from villes [listed above]." When CAC Oscar withdrew to KSCB after the initial attacks on their positions outside the CB during Tet '68, the Marines did not want Oscar-2's Bru comrades in the base, so the CAC team asked for and received a position in the perimeter of SF's FOB-3, outside the defensive wires along KSCB's S edge and QL-9. Quang Tri Pr, I Corps.
Vil C'on (XD)
See Vil Bu. Quang Tri Pr, I Corps.
Vil Ch'eng (XD)
See Vil Bu. Quang Tri Pr, I Corps.
Vil Tacun (XD)
See Vil Bu. Quang Tri Pr, I Corps.
Villa Rosa, Camp (BT 065-738?)
A.k.a. Marble Mtn SF Camp? At Marble Mtn, apx 5 km SE Da Nang AB. Apparently the cmpd of SOG CCN, and named to honor SFC Paul H. Villa Rosa, KIA 4Jan68. Data per Ray Bows. Quang Nam Pr, I Corps.
VinaTexaco Textile Factory (XS 787-958)
Along QL-1, apx 1 km due W the W end of main rwy of Tan Son Nhut AB. Site of heavy fighting when it was occupied by VC forces during battle of Tan Son Nhut, 31Jan68 (Tet '68). Grid apx. Gia Dinh Pr, III Corps.
Vinay, Pointe (BN 0-0)
See Pointe Vinay. Binh Thuan Pr, II Corps.
Vinell, Inc. (n/a)
See Glossary.
Vinh (n/a)
Vietnamese word for ocean, sea or a large lake.
Vinh (n/a)
Mapsheet name of L-7014-6146-3. NVN only.
Vinh (WF 71-64)
Major port/industrial and war material supply center apx 230 km NW the 22Jul54 SVN border, 15 km SW mouth of Song Ca River and 12 km at its closest point to Gulf of Tonkin. Inland port used as waypoint for NVA moving S to the Ho Chi Minh Trail. Repeatedly bombed by both US and French during 2 wars. One writer rptd that in 1996 it had only 2 of its pre-1940 buildings still intact. Frequently used as northernmost boundary of various restricted bombing campaigns during war. and it is presumed military targets here suffered heavy attack (likely one of most heavily bombed areas in NVN). Attacked by USN carrier-based acft during Pierce Arrow, 2-7Aug64. AFs here also

struck by Carrier TF-77 attempts to blunt NVA Tet '68 Offensive. See also Pierce Arrow. NVN.

Vinh Airfield (WF 72-72)
On coast, apx 160 km NW Dong Hoi, 245 km due S Hanoi and 10 km N Vinh. El. 68'. NVN.

Vinh An Bridge (BT 379-174)
Apx 3 km SW Tam Ky AF, along provincial rte (532?) that led SW to Hau Duc. Apparently attacked or destroyed in Apr70. Quang Tin Pr, I Corps.

Vinh Bac Bo (AC 8-1)
The Gulf of Tonkin. Center of mass at roughly 20°00'00"N-108°00'00"E. NF49-13 JOG. NVN.

Vinh Bac Phan (AC 8-1)
A.k.a. Vinh Bac Bo. The Gulf of Tonkin.

Vinh Bac Phan (WK 0-3)
Region of NVN.

Vinh Binh (XS 728-933)
See Vinh Loc Pacification Hamlets. Gia Dinh Pr, III Corps.

Vinh Binh Province (XR/XS)
One of 16 southern provs forming IV Corps (IV CTZ). In some texts is also erroneously spelled "Binh Binh."

Vinh Chau (n/a)
Mapsheet name of L-7014-6127-1. SVN.

Vinh Chau (Various)
Common Viet place name. Sites inc: BT 130-558, CP 005-548, XS 675-325, WR 9-2, 9-3, 9-5, XR 0-2, 0-3, 1-3. 1-4, 2-0. I/II/IV Corps.

Vinh Chau (XR 08-31)
Ville near intersection of Rtes 113 and 116, apx 30 km due S Soc Trang AF and 3 km N of coast. ARVN 42d Ranger Bn won its 2d US PUC for success against VC in battle here, 17May66. Bac Lieu Pr, IV Corps.

Vinh Chau CAP (BT or AT?)
CAP 2-4-2, 2d CAG. Quang Nam Pr, I Corps.

Vinh Chau Heliport (XR 082-311)
Slightly S of Rte 113, apx 30 km S Soc Trang AF and 3 km N the coast. "Heliport #698, alt 10', town square, houses all sides, at 09°22'00"N-105°00'30"E," per Feb73 TAD. Bac Lieu Pr, IV Corps.

Vinh Da Nang (BT 00-85)
Da Nang Bay. Quang Tri Pr, I Corps.

Vinh Dai CAP (YD 0-5 or BT 4-1?)
Papa 3, 4th CAG per T. Duffie's CAP Vets website at www.capmarine.com. (a Vinh Dai is in grid square BT 4-1). Quang Tri or Quang Tin Pr?, I Corps.

Vinh Dai Rock Crusher (YD?)
On QL-9 E(?) of Khe Gio Bridge. Quang Tri Pr, I Corps.

Vinh Ganh Rai (YS 20-54)
Bay immediately NW the Vung Tau Peninsula. Phuoc Tuy/Gia Dinh Pr, III Corps.

Vinh Gia Heliport (VS 766-609)
Apx 3 km S Cambodian border, 35 km ENE Ha Tien and 26 km W That Son AF. "Heliport #699, alt 10', earth, at 10°30'N 104°47'E." Feb73 TAD. Chau Doc Pr, IV Corps.

Vinh Gia SF Camp (VS 7622-6090)
Apx 3 km S Cambodia, 35 km ENE Ha Tien and 26 km W That Son AF. 5th SF Grp, Det. A-7, Det. A-321, Dec64, A-422 Oct66, SF Det 79. Transferred to VNSF A-144?, then 93rd ARVN Border Rangers. Grid/data per *SF Order of Battle.* Chau Doc Pr, IV Corps.

Vinh Gia, Camp (VS 564-639)
See Gian Thanh. IV Corps.

Vinh Hanh (XS 715-976)
See Vinh Loc Pacification Hamlets. Gia Dinh Pr, III Corps.

Vinh Hoa (XS 717-949)
See Vinh Loc Pacification Hamlets. Gia Dinh Pr, III Corps.

Vinh Kim Heliport (XS 369-477)
Apx 6 km NW Dong Tam. "Heliport #700, alt 7', earth, wires to NW." At 10°21'N 106°15'E. Data per Feb73 TAD.

Vinh Kim, FSB (XS 27-51 or 36-44 or 43-43?)
Possibly ARVN FSB once known as FSB Moore? If XS 27-51 grid accurate, then site was apx 3 km E Cai Lay, 24 km WNW My Tho, 17 km WNW Dong Tam, 1 km NW FSB Fels and 500 meters N QL-4. If at XS 36-44, was apx 1 km W Vinh Thanh/Cho Gru. If at XS 43-43, was at Tan Phu, apx 5 km WSW My Tho. Vinh Kim was name of area W of My Tho, so FSB name may have been unrelated to a ville's name? Dinh Tuong Pr, IV Corps.

Vinh Linh (YD 15-87)
Apx 38 km NNW Quang Tri, 10 km W Cape Thu Luat and about 5 km at its closest point to ocean. Immed N the DMZ. Attacked by carrier and Da Nang based US and VNAF acft during Op Flaming Dart I, 7-8Feb65. See also Flaming Dart I. NVN.

Vinh Linh Airfield? (YD 15-87?)
Apx 38 km NNW Quang Tri. Feb67 Natl Geo map. NVN.

Vinh Linh Special Zone (XD/YD)
Military region extending an avg of apx 25 km N of the SVN/NVN border. NVN. [551]

Vinh Lo (Ho Xa) (n/a)
Mapsheet name of L-7014-6443-3. NVN only.

Vinh Loc (YD 049-122)
On Vinh Loc Island and along N edge of Dam Cau Hai Lagoon, apx 16 km ESE Phu Bai AB and 14 km NNW Q Phu Loc. Thua Thien Pr, I Corps.

Vinh Loc Bell (XS 73-95)
Nickname for telephone/commo system installed by 58th Signal Co, 82d Abn, at Vinh Loc, a 6-hamlet ville in AO of 1st/508th Inf, NW Saigon. Connected village chief with his hamlets and a TV set was installed at each ville as well. See Vinh Loc Pacification Hamlets. Gia Dinh Pr, III Corps.

Vinh Loc Island (YD 81-33 to ZD 13-11)
Long, narrow island E and SE Hue. Was apx 40 km long and avg of 2.5 km wide. Ran NW to SE and parallel to mainland. Eagle Beach and Tan My Naval POL facility were at its N end. VC haven for many years, the author recalls remarkable tunnels built into sand here S of Tan My, where bamboo strips had been laced together to keep sand from caving-in. In 10 day classic op sweeping island, elements of 101st Abn killed 154 and captured 374 enemy. Vinh Loc is at ZD 84-12. Thua Thien Pr, I Corps.

Vinh Loc Pacification Hamlets (XS 73-95)
Group of 6 pacification/relocation hamlets generally around listed grid and between 6 km and 9 km WNW to WSW Tan Son Nhut AB, and 2 km to 6 km W to NW FSB Hardcore. Villes were: Vinh Hanh (XS 715-976), Vinh Phuoc (XS 735-970), Vinh Thana (XS 733-956), Vinh Hoa (XS 717-949), Vinh Tin (708-938) and Vinh Binh (XS 728-933). See Vinh Loc Bell. Gia Dinh Pr, III Corps.

Vinh Loc, FSB? (ZD 049-122)
Just E Vinh Loc on Vinh Loc Island, apx 27 km ESE Hue, 17 km ESE Phu Bai and about 3 km inland from Dam Cau Hai Lagoon. Apr70 XXIV Corps grid per Don Armstrong. Thua Thien Pr, I Corps.
Vinh Loi (Bac Lieu) (n/a)
Mapsheet name of L-7014-6127-4. SVN.
Vinh Loi Airfield (WR 791-281)
See Bac Lieu AF. Bac Lieu Pr, IV Corps.
Vinh Loi BOQ (XS 8-9)
In Saigon. US officers billet, Jun 64-68, 52 rms. Data per *Vietnam Military Lore, 1959-1973.* Gia Dinh Pr, III Corps.
Vinh Loi Heliport (XS 734-437)
Adj to or in Vinh Binh, apx 9 km WSW Go Cong and 43 km SSW Saigon. "Heliport #701, alt 5', paved rd, at 10°20'40"N-106°35'00"E," per Feb73 TAD. Go Cong Pr, IV Corps.
Vinh Loi SF Camp (XS 720-455)
Apx 2 km NW Vinh Binh, 12 km WSW Go Cong and 42 km S Saigon. 5th SF, Det A-321, Dec64. Moved to Tan Hiep. Grid per *SF Order of Battle.* Go Cong Pr, IV Corps.
Vinh Long (XS 07-34)
Along the Mekong River, apx 90 km SW Saigon and 46 km WSW My Tho. The Vinh Long AF and Army Installation (a.k.a. Shannon-Wright Cmpd) were situated apx 3 km W the city. Capitol, Vinh Long Pr, IV Corps.
Vinh Long Airfield (XS 040-331)
A.k.a. Vinh Long Army AF and Gauvin-Upton AF. Major AF in Mekong Delta apx 3 km W Vinh Long, 48 km WSW My Tho, 38 km WSW Dong Tam, 30 km NE Can Tho and 95 km SW Saigon, per TPC K-10D. Named the Gauvin-Upton AF to honor Capt. Roger E Gauvin and Sp5 Carelton W. Upton of the 114th Avn Co, both KIA 15Mar64, in fiery crash of their helicopter, per *Vietnam Military Lore, Legends, Shadows and Heroes*, p 557. 114th Avn Co and A/502d Avn Bn were here and Shannon-Wright Cmpd (a.k.a. Vinh Long Installation) was next to them. Patch Cmpd here as well. El. 10', 3,000' asph rwy. At 10°14'51"N-105°56'53"E. Vinh Long Pr, IV Corps.
Vinh Long Army Installation (XS 040-331)
See Shannon-Wright Cmpd. Vinh Long Pr, IV Corps.
Vinh Long Basecamp (XS 040-330)
Apx 45 km WSW My Tho and 88 km SW Saigon. 2d Bde/9th Inf MRF TF basecamp, per Jim Stone, 2d/39th Inf. Oct68. Vinh Long Pr, IV Corps.
Vinh Long Navy Base (XS 04-34)
On Mekong near Vinh Long, apx 45 km WSW My Tho and 88 km SW Saigon. USN Facility, '66-71, per MRF Assn Website. 2d Bde/9th Div MRF basecamp also here. Vinh Long Pr, IV Corps.
Vinh Long PBR Base (XS 07-34)
On Mekong near Vinh Long, apx 45 km WSW My Tho and 88 km SW Saigon. River Div 52, TF-116, USN Gamewarden base here per MRF Assn at www.mrfa.org. Moved here from Sa Dec. Vinh Long Pr, IV Corps.
Vinh Long PFTC (XS)
RVNAF Popular Force Trng Ctr. Appears to have been near Vung Lien or Tam Binh? Vinh Long Pr, IV Corps.
Vinh Long Province (WS/XS/XR)
One of 16 southern provs forming IV Corps (IV CTZ)
Vinh Long Signal Site (XS?)
No data. Possibly at Vinh Long AF or the Shannon-Wright Cmpd? Vinh Long Pr, IV Corps.
Vinh My (n/a)
Mapsheet name of L-7014-6127-3. SVN.
Vinh Ninh (Ninh Giang) (n/a)
Mapsheet name of L-7014-6250-2. NVN only.
Vinh Ninh Airfield (CQ 08-04)
E side of Ql-1, apx 40 km SSW Tuy Hoa AB and 52 km N Nha Trang. TPC K-10B. El. 10' Khanh Hoa Pr, II Corps.
Vinh Phan Thiet (AN 835-075)
Phan Thiet Bay. At mouth of Song Ca Ty River. Binh Thuan Pr, II Corps.
Vinh Phuc (BR 62-62)
Apx 5 km due N of Vinh Thanh in Happy (Vinh Thanh) Valley, apx 27 km NE An Khe. A collection of hamlets known as Vinh Phuc 1 through 6 involved in Op Crazy Horse and discussed in *Battles in the Monsoon*, pp 23-27. Vinh Puc (1) is at BR 62-61, (2) at 63-64, (6) at 63-62. 1st Cav. Binh Dinh Pr, II Corps.
Vinh Phuoc (XS 735-970)
See Vinh Loc Pacification Hamlets. Gia Dinh Pr, III Corps.
Vinh Phuoc Bridge (YD 270-570)
QL-1 bridge over the Song Vinh Phuoc, NW Quang Tri and apx 5 km SE Dong Ha. Quang Tri Pr, I Corps.
Vinh Phuoc River (YD 27-63)
The Cua Viet River is formed by confluence of Mieu Giang, Thach Han and Vinh Phuoc Rivers. All joined NW Quang Tri. Grid is at confluence. Quang Tri Pr, I Corps.
Vinh Quoi Heliport (WR 660-570)
Apx 48 km W Soc Trang AF, 13 km due S Long My and 28 km ENE Kien Long AF. Heliport #734, alt 7', at 09°34'00"N-105° 31'00"E, per Feb73 TAD. Chuong Thien Pr, IV Corps.
Vinh Son (n/a)
Mapsheet name of L-7014-6344-4. NVN only.
Vinh Te Canal (WS 13-85)
Joined Bassac River N Chau Duc. River Dets assigned to YRBM 20 and YRBM 16(?) patrolled this French-built canal, which ran from the Bassac to Ha Tien (Gulf of Thailand) past Tinh Bien Adv Base and along Cambodian border within SVN. Chau Doc Pr, IV Corps. [552]
Vinh Thana (XS 733-956)
See Vinh Loc Pacification Hamlets. Gia Dinh Pr, III Corps.
Vinh Thanh (n/a)
Mapsheet name of L-7014-6130-4. SVN/Cambodia.
Vinh Thanh Airfield (BR 614-606)
Apx 20 km ESE Kannack AF, 22 km NE An Khe's major AF and 30 km SW Ha Tay AF. El. 190', 1,900' asph rwy. At 14°06'26"N-108°47'23"E. Binh Dinh Pr, II Corps.
Vinh Thanh BEQ (XS 8-9)
At 258 Ben Chuong Duong Quay St., Saigon. US military billet, Apr 65, 42 rms. Data per *Vietnam Military Lore, 1959-1973.* Gia Dinh Pr, III Corps.
Vinh Thanh Mountain (BR 69-62)
A.k.a. Hill 975 and LZ Chris. On E side of and overlooking Vinh Thanh (Happy) Valley, apx 7 km E to ENE Vinh Thanh AF and 6 km E Vinh Phuc (2). Op Crazy Horse, May66. Binh Dinh Pr, II Corps.

Vinh Thanh SF Camp (BR 615-606)
Apx 20 km ESE Kannack AF, 22 km NE An Khe AF and 30 km SW Ha Tay AF. SF Det 24, and later A-120, RF/PF. Det A-228, Oct66, is listed as being at Vinh Tranh in II Corps and that may be a misspelling of this base? Grid per *SF Order of Battle.* Binh Dinh Pr, II Corps.
Vinh Thanh Valley (BR 82-63)
See Happy Valley. Binh Dinh Pr, II Corps.
Vinh Tin (XS 708-938)
See Vinh Loc Pacification Hamlets. Gia Dinh Pr, III Corps.
Vinh Tranh (BR 615-606?)
Variant or misspelling of Vinh Thanh? Apparently 5th SF, Det A-228 here Oct66. II Corps.
Vinh Truong, FSB (CP 034-510)
See NAAPTB, FSB. Khanh Hoa Pr, II Corps.
Vinh Tuy (BS/WR)
Common Viet place-name in both NVN/SVN. See SVN grid squares BS 4-8, BS 8-3, BS 9-1, WR 3-7 and WR 4-6.
Vinh Tuy Valley (BS 46-85)
Apx 15 km WSW Binh Son, S of Rte 539 and 21 km NW Quang Ngai. See also Hill 141. Quang Ngai Pr, I Corps.
Vinh Xuong (various)
Villes of this name in grid squares BP 9-5, 9-7, CP 0-5, 0-6, 0-7, YD 5-4, XS 5-6, 7-3, and WT 2-0. II/III/IV Corps.
Vinh Xuong SF Camp (WS 203-058)
A.k.a. FOB Tan An and Tan An Heliport. Apx 11 km due E Rach Gia and 8 km NE Kien Giang AF. Grid per *SF Order of Battle*. 5th SF. Kien Giang, IV Corps.
Vinh Yen (n/a)
Mapsheet name of L-7014-6151-4. NVN only.
Vinh Yen (various)
Common Viet place-name. Sites in: WJ 6-5, WG 7-1, XK 3-2, WG 8-8, WG 5-3, WF 2-8, XF 3-0, WF 7-7, BS 7-4, XK 3-2. NVN & SVN.
Vinh Yen (WJ 63-57)
Along Road No. 2, apx 38 km NW Hanoi, 8 km S the Tam Dao River and 14 km WNW Phu Yen. NVN.
Vinh Yen, Battle of (WJ 6-5)
On Road No. 2, apx 38 km NW Hanoi, 8 km S the Tam Dao River and 14 km WNW Phu Yen. Focus of Vietminh offensive launched from Tam Doa massif beginning 13Jan51. Battle here 13-17Jan51 was one of few set-piece battles of 1st Indochina War. Battle centered around series of hills NE the city: Hills 210, 101, 47, 75 and 157. Marshal de Lattre de Tasigny personally took charge of French here whereupon he ordered a number of reserve Bns flown from southern VN (1,000 km trip) and also ordered Mobile Group 1 (3 Bns of crack N Africans) to smash through VM lines and bring in resupply and reinforce G.M. 3. 1st ever VM use of "Human Sea Wave" tactic here almost overwhelmed French completely, but when De Lattre realized just how serious threat was, he ordered all available acft capable of dumping bombs or napalm to Vinh Yen and into what became most massive aerial bombardment of 1st Indochina War. VM survivors described it as "wall of napalm." On morning of 17Jan51, G.M. 2 was added to mix and, at noon that day, Giap decided to disengage after having suffered stunning defeat, costing VM over 6,000 dead and 500 captured in brutal hand-to-hand fighting. See Chp 2 of *Street Without Joy*, and map on p 38, and also Bao Chuc and Dao Tu. NVN. [553]

Violin, LZ (YD 043-659)
Apx 2 km N Helicopter Valley, 10 km NW Cam Lo and 20 km WNW Dong Ha. Apr70 XXIV Corps grid per Don Armstrong. Quang Tri Pr, I Corps.
Viper (n/a)
Apr70, XXIV Corps proposed 101st Abn FSB name.
Viper, OP (YD 692-158)
See OP Viper. Thua Thien Pr, I Corps.
Viracheay Airfield (XA)
A.k.a. Virachei AF? Along Tonle Son River, apx 47 km SSE Siempang West AF, per TPC K-10A. El. 302' (98' on Feb67 Natl Geo map?). Cambodia.
Virachei Airfield (XA)
A.k.a. Viracheay AF? Along San River apx 340 km NE Phnom Penh. El. 98' (302' on TPC K-10A?). Cambodia.
Vireo, USS (n/a)
MSC-205. Minesweeper, Coastal, per Ralph Fries.
Virgin, LZ (YA 939 991?)
Overlooking Ya Ray River Valley, apx 33 km WNW Kontum, 11 km NW Polei Kleng AF, 3 km WSW Hill 1713 and 6 km N LZ Mile High. Per Ben Youmans, was "On a knob across saddle of ridge from LZ Mile High" (YA 937-931). LZs Mile High and Virgin were at end of ridgeline overlooking N end of Plei Trap Valley, and on same ridge to S was LZ Incoming. Built by 2d/35th in Apr-May68, and2d Bde/4th Inf operated off LZ, Apr69. In late Apr68, 2 Cos of 1st/35th Inf left wire at LZ Mile High, moving across a saddle on Hill 1198 to secure and cut clear a knob only 600 meters to N. That knob was to be LZ Virgin. Unfortunately, an HQ of NVA 325C Div awaited them on the knob and, in vicious ambush, both Cos were badly mauled. C/2d/35th secured site next day and, after digging in, was hit by typhoon that injured 3 more men. Soon after its const, LZ was hit twice by Rgt-sized attacks only to be saved by heavy arty/air supt. Per one witness, "In May68, 37 arc lights in 7 days were dropped within a 10 km radius and Stars and Stripes carried headline, *Heaviest B-52 Strikes of the War.* " On 26May68, a C/2d/35th patrol is said to have heard noises coming from the mouth of a cave just 200 meters down-slope from the perimeter. Cave then hit with an air strike and subsequent BDA revealed an NVA Corps Cmdr and staff had been KIA; apparently the only confirmed death of an NVA Corps Cmdr (Maj Gen) in the war. [554] Also listed at YA 935-991; however, listed grid per Kevin Rafferty (1st/14th Inf), who adds, "YA 935 991 puts it on side of a hill [and] YA 939 991 a more likely location for an LZ given the terrain." MACV Team 23 also here. Map is L-7014-6537-4. Kontum Pr, II Corps.
Virginia, FSB (YS 437-802)
Apx 12.5 km due N Nui Dat, 3 km NW FSB Alanbrooke and 7 km SE FSB Coolah. On 1ATF NCO trng map per John Hollett. Phuoc Tuy or Bien Hoa Pr, III Corps.
Virginia Lee, LZ/FSB (YA 841-091)
In the Ia Drang Valley, apx 5 km from Cambodia, 54 km SW Pleiku, and 9 km NNW peak Chu Pong Mtn. Per Dick Arnold, site was occupied briefly mid-Oct'68 by C, 1st/35th Inf. 10th Cav, 4th Div here also, per Bob Patsfield. Grid per D. Arnold. Pleiku Pr, II Corps.

Virginia Ridge, Operation (n/a)
1May-16Jul69. USMC 9th Marines along DMZ. 560 rptd NVA/VC KIA, per *Vietnam Order of Battle*, pp 9-14. Quang Tri Pr, I Corps.
Vista, LZ (YD 028-642)
Apx 2 km S the DMZ, 11 km WNW to NW Cam Lo and 21 km WNW Dong Ha. Apr70 XXIV Corps grid per Don Armstrong. Quang Tri Pr, I Corps.
Vivian, FSB (XU 909-011)
Apx 20 km ESE Loc Ninh, 25 km S Cambodia and 25 km ESE Song Be. Per Ed Torres, was built beginning 13Jul69. Bobby Jackson, HQ 1st/7th Cav, notes that FSBs Phyllis and Vivian were named after 1st Cav Bn CO's wives (LTC Unger and LTC Justice, respectively). Per Frank Penk, Jr., 1st/8th Cav, 1st/5th Cav, 1st Cav here'69, AO Commanche Warrior. Cited in 1st Cav VN *Yearbook* Aug65-Dec69, p 125, 185, 267, per Peter Cole. Also listed at XU 918-038. Binh Long Pr, III Corps.
Vo Dat (YT 73-33)
Trade center apx 80 km ENE Bien Hoa and 35 km NE Xuan Loc. 161 Bty, RNZA (Kenning's Bty, 13Jun65-13Jun66) FSB set here 21-25Nov65 (25-29Nov65, were 6 km NW Vo Dat at Chinh Duc). Long Khanh Pr, III Corps.
Vo Dat, FSB (YT 730-330)
At or near Vo Dat AF, near SW corner Xa Vo Dat, apx 35 km NE Xuan Loc, 75 km ENE Bien Hoa AB and 21 km WNW Tanh Linh AF. 4th/12th Inf, 199th LIB here '69. Grid per 199th LIB Assn. Binh Tuy Pr, III Corps.
Vo Dat Airfield (YT 720-325)
At SW corner of Vo Dat, apx 35 km NE Xuan Loc, 24 km WNW Tanh Linh AF, and 75 km ENE Bien Hoa AB. El. 443', 3,700' laterite rwy. Binh Tuy Pr, III Corps.
Vo Dat Basecamp (YT 723-327)
At Vo Dat AF, apx 36 km NE Xuan Loc and 20 km WNW Tanh Linh AF. Long Khanh Pr, III Corps.
Vo Dat I Airfield (YT 720-325)
See Vo Dat AF. Binh Tuy Pr, III Corps.
Vo Dat II SF Camp (YT 740-331)
Within Vo Dat, apx 80 km ENE Bien Hoa and 35 km NE Xuan Loc. 5th SF. Info/grid per *SF Order of Battle.* See also Tuc Trung. Binh Tuy Pr, III Corps.
Vo Dinh Airfield (YT 418-180)
See Binh Loc AF. Long Khanh Pr, III Corps.
Vo Thanh, FSB (XT 475-866)
Ville or FSB position of 11th ACR and/or 1st Cav during Cambodian Incursion, May-Jun70. Apx 4 km S Cambodian border, 13 km ESE Katum, 30 km due W An Loc, 34 km SW Loc Ninh and 14 km WSW tip of Fishhook. Grid per *11th ACR Cambodia Invasion AAR, 1st Cav Div, May-Jun70*, courtesy Lou Rochat. [555] Tay Ninh Pr, III Corps.
Vo Xu (YT 81-38)
Apx 8 km NE Vo Dat, 44 km NE Xuan Loc. 161 Bty, RNZA (Kenning's Bty 13Jun65-13Jun66) FSB here 29Nov65-13Dec66. On 1Apr70, D Trp, 17th Cav was ambushed near Vo Xu by 33d NVA Rgt. During action, BGen William Bond landed his C&C bird to lead a search party but was KIA by sniper. [556] Binh Tuy Pr, III Corps.
Vodka, LZ (XT 450-008)
Apx 14 km WNW Duc Hoa AF and 25 km SW Cu Chi and 16 km ESE Duc Hue AF. Apr66. Hau Nghia Pr, III Corps.
Voice of America (Manila) (n/a)
See Glossary.
Volunteer, LZ (BS 348-593)
On mtn peak apx 4 km SW Lang Re, 20 km WNW Minh Long AF and 26 km ENE Nghia Hanh AF. Americal list. Quang Ngai Pr, I Corps.
Volunteers of Death (n/a)
See Glossary.
Von Sydow, Max (n/a)
See Shotgun, Operation.
VOR NDB Phnom Penh (VT 83-76)
At Phnom Penh Airport and 3 km SW of NDB Phnom Penh. Cambodia.
VOR TACAN NDB Da Nang (BT 02-75)
A.k.a. VOR DME Da Nang. At Da Nang AB. See NDB Da Nang. Quang Nam Pr, I Corps.
VOR TACAN NDB Ubon (VB 86-86)
At Ubon Northwest AF. Ubon Ratchathani, Thailand.
VOR TACAN Saigon (XS 82-97)
At Tan Son Nhut AB. Gia Dinh Pr, III Corps.
Voting Machines (n/a)
See Glossary.
VR-6 (n/a)
Designated sector of the HCMT in Laos restricted to Da Nang's "Covey" FACs (20th TASS). Presumably there were many other VR numeric zones assigned to other FAC units in SEA. Laos.
Vu Bon, Thon (n/a)
Mapsheet name of L-7014-6731-1. Thon Vu Bon. SVN.
Vu Gia River (AT/BT)
The Cau Do, Yen, Tuy Loan La Tho, Thanh Quyt, Vu Gia, Cau Lau and Thu Bon Rivers all formed part of drainage that became the Da Nang River. All were S or SW Da Nang. Quang Nam Pr, I Corps.
Vulture, LZ (ZC 088-574)
Along LTL-4 and on N bank Song Vu Gia near An Diem, apx 7 km ENE Ha Tan AF and 39 km SW Da Nang AB. Apr70 XXIV Corps grid per Don Armstrong. Oct68. See LZ Shangri-La near this grid. Quang Nam Pr, I Corps.
Vung (n/a)
Vietnamese word and name-prefix meaning "Bay."
Vung Cam Ranh (CP 00-15)
Cam Ranh Bay. TPC K-10D. Khanh Hoa Pr, II Corps.
Vung Chao Bay (CQ 10-88)
Large bay on central coast, apx 30 km S Qui Nhon and 30 km N Tuy Hoa. 13°27'N-109°15'E. Phu Yen Pr, II Corps.
Vung Chao, Baie de (CQ 1-8)
See. Vung Chao Bay. Phu Yen Pr, II Corps.
Vung Chau Commo Site (CR 03-23?)
See Vung Chau Mtn Signal Site. II Corps.
Vung Chau Mountain (CR 030-210)
Large Mtn mass overlooking Qui Nhon. At peak was US Vung Chau Commo Site of 41st Signal Bn and "Long Lines North." Consisted of small cantonment, club, main commo bldg, and 60' radio tower. Binh Dinh Pr, II Corps.
Vung Chau Mtn Signal Site (CR 03-23?)
On Vung Chau Mtn overlooking Camp Granite and Qui Nhon. Sp5 Jerry Ault (here for "11 mos/25 days without R&R!"), describes site as: "Visible to S/SW from any point in Qui Nhon were large antenna arrays here. 4 were 60' billboard-type Tropospherics used for REL2600 equip that

relayed all IWCS traffic.Was "Lit up like Christmas every night of year" per one source. Manned by 3 Sig grps, as well as AFVN TV (Chan 11) and AFRTS. Major unit was 1st Sig Bde STRATCOM Long Lines North, whose apx 25 personnel handled long distance radio traffic between Monkey Mtn in N, to Saigon in S. 518th Sig Co (10-12 men) handled VHF/local traffic and had large van buried in sand bags connected to cable that ran down mtn to another relay station in Qui Nhon (why VC never cut it is a mystery to me). Microwave Det called "36-Deuce" or 362d Sig. Co (10-12 men) also here with old TRC29 microwave gear in vans dug into hill (handled VF traffic) and smaller microwave shots to Anh Khe, Phu Bai and Phu Lam, etc. Units did own guard duty and built own defenses. Also MP unit of apx 5 men here, who guarded front gate and manned mortar pit. Was hit twice(?) in '68, with one killing several people. At foot of mtn was small ville called 'Boom Boom' ville for obvious reasons. Site overlooked all of Qui Nhon, including Shit Beach, the airport, and power ship in bay that supplied back-up AC power. At least twice, ammo dump below site detonated; a fire works spectacle never to be forgotten." Binh Dinh Pr, II Corps.

Vung Chau Signal Site (CR 15-4?)
See Vung Chau Commo Site. Binh Dinh Pr?, II Corps.

Vung Chua (XE 6-8)
A.k.a. Baie de Vung Chau and Vung Chua Bay. Bay at 17°56'N-106°31'E. On NE48-12 JOG. NVN.

Vung Chua, Baie de (XE 6-8)
See Vung Chua. NVN.

Vung Dam Chinh (CP 2-4)
Coastal point at 12°11'36"N-109°20'48"E. On ND49-13 JOG. Khanh Hoa Pr, II Corps.

Vung Gang, Baie de (CN 0-9)
Island bay near 11°43'N-109°12'E. On NC49-01 JOG. Ninh Thuan?, II Corps.

Vung Han, Baie de (XF 4-0)
A.k.a. Vung Han. Bay at 18°07'N-106°24'E. NVN.

Vung La, Pointe (CQ 1-8)
A.k.a. Mui Luoi Cay. At 13°24'N-109°18'E. On ND49-09 JOG. Phu Yen Pr, II Corps.

Vung Lam, Rade de (CQ 0-8)
Anchorage at 13°24'00"N-109°14'30"E. On ND49-09 JOG. Phu Yen Pr, II Corps.

Vung Liem (n/a)
Mapsheet name of L-7014-6229-3. SVN.

Vung Liem (XS 304-158)
At intersection of LTL-7A and Rte 171, apx 3 km SW the Mekong River, 30 km SW My Tho and at 10°06'00"N-106°13'00"E. On NC48-07 JOG. Vinh Long Pr, IV Corps.

Vung Liem Heliport (XS 304-158)
Apx 24 km NW Tra Vinh AF/PhuVinh, and 36 km SSW My Tho. "Heliport #702, alt 7', sod, soccer field, white H. Has been mined." Feb73 TAD. Vinh Long Pr, IV Corps.

Vung Phan Rang (BN 90-75)
Phan Rang Bay. TPC K-10D. Ninh Thuan Pr, II Corps.

Vung Phan Ri (BN 40-35)
Large bay 60 km NE Phan Thiet. Binh Thuan Pr, II Corps.

Vung Phan Thie (BN 85-05)
Phan Thiet Bay. TPC-K10D. Ninh Thuan Pr, III Corps.

Vung Qui Nhon Bay (CR 10-30)
Large, 12 km x 4 km N/S bay, along central coast of SVN, with Qui Nhon at its narrow mouth. Grid at bay's apx center of mass. See also Qui Nhon. Binh Dinh Pr, II Corps.

Vung Qui Nhon (CR 15-35)
Qui Nhon's 20 km long peninsula. Binh Dinh Pr, II Corps.

Vung Ro Bay (CQ 269-226)
Bay at 12°52'N-109°26'E. On ND49-13 JOG. Phu Yen/Khanh Hoa Pr, II Corps.

Vung Ro Incident (CQ 2-2)
See Glossary.

Vung Ro Mountain (CQ 319-235)
See Nui Vung Ro. Phu Yen Pr, II Corps.

Vung Ro Mtn Tropo Site (CQ 267-260?)
A.k.a. Vung Ro Mtn Tropospheric Commo Site. Precise location unknown, but possibly on Hill 706, Nui Ba Dai, apx 20 km SSE Tuy Hoa AF? US and Korean (White Horse Rgt) site, '69. Phu Yen Pr?, II Corps.

Vung Ro Seaport (CQ 26-23?)
Apparently Port Lane. At Phong So in Vung Ro Bay, apx 15 km SSE Phu Hiep AF and 22 km SSE Tuy Hoa AB? Berthing Feet: 1,100 lineal feet, Draft Max: 32', Cargo Capacity: 1,600 tons/day, Storage Covered w/in 5 km: 88,000 ft^2, Storage Uncov, w/in 5 km: 233,000 yd^2. See Port Lane. Khanh Hoa Pr, II Corps. [557]

Vung Tau (YS 28-43)
Resort city and in-country R&R center on Cape St. Jacques Peninsula, apx 62 km SE Saigon. Surrounded by high coastal hills and fabled for its beautiful scenery, climate regarded as perhaps best in VN due to moderate temps and low rainfall. Its beauty, relative security and climate made it a major recreation area for both Vietnamese and military. Folklore has it that VC/NVA took R&R here as well, and that there was understanding between belligerents that area was off-limits to fighting/terrorist activities. US sites inc: Vung Tau R&R Ctr, Black Beach, AAFES-V (Army & Air Force Exchange System), USO Vung Tau, Vung Tau Port (main supply point for southern SVN) and Vung Tau AF. 1ATF's Services Correctional Establishment (Prison) also here. One of SVN's 6 autonomous municipalities, and 5th largest city (In '70, apx 40,000). Phuoc Tuy Pro, III Corps.

Vung Tau, Mui (YS 28-44)
The Vung Tau Peninsula, a.k.a. Cape St. Jacques, Cape Vung Tau and Mui Vung Tau. At 10°19'N-107°05'E. Phuoc Tuy Pr, III Corps.

Vung Tau, Xa (Cap Saint Jacques) (YS)
Mapsheet name of L-7014-6429-4. Full sheet name is: Xa Vung Tau (Cap Saint Jacques). SVN.

Vung Tau Airfield (YS 300-473)
A.k.a. Cap St. Jacques AF and Vung Tau Army AF. Major AF apx 3 km N Vung Tau, 23 km SW Luscombe AF, 62 km SSW Xuan Loc AF and 60 km SE Saigon. Per TPC K-10D. El. 13', 4,900' asph and 1,800' PSP rwys. At 10°22'23"N-107°05'59"E. Phuoc Tuy Pr, III Corps.

Vung Tau Army Airfield (YS 300-473)
A.k.a. Cap St. Jacques AF and Vung Tau AF. 4,900' asph rwy run by Army and used primarily to transport US personnel to and from Vung Tau in-country R&R Ctr. Also home to 53d Supt Grp, the 765th Trans Bn and 330th Trans Co's "Booze Box Saloon" (a.k.a. The Fang, and named

after "Fang the Wonder Dog," the unit's black mongrel mascot). Phuoc Tuy Pr, III Corps.

Vung Tau Detail (Provisional) (YS 2-4)
See Vung Tau Seaport. Phuoc Tuy Pr, III Corps.

Vung Tau Lighthouse (YS 279-427)
On Nui Nho Mtn, immed S of Vung Tau. Phuoc Tuy Pr, III Corps.

Vung Tau Mountains (YS 26-45 and 28-42)
Nui Lon and Nui Nho. Phuoc Tuy Pr, III Corps.

Vung Tau NDB (YS 30-47)
Non-Directional navigation Beacon site. At Vung Tau AF. Phuoc Tuy Pr, III Corps.

Vung Tau NSAD (YS 2-4)
At Vung Tau, on Vung Tau Peninsula, apx 60 km SE Saigon. USN Supt Activity Det, '65-71. Per MRF Assn Website. Phuoc Tuy Pr, III Corps.

Vung Tau R&R Center (YS 27-43?)
On the Cap St. Jacques Peninsula at Vung Tau Bay and overlooked by coastal hills, apx 62 km SE Saigon. Major in-country R&R facility at Vung Tau operated by Vung Tau Sub Area Cmd of 1st Logistics Cmd. Its climate was regarded as perhaps the best in VN due to moderate temps and low rainfall. Because of its beauty, security and climate, was major recreation area for Vietnamese civilians and military alike. Folklore has it that VC/NVA took R&R there as well and that it was understood by both sides that area was off-limits to fighting or terrorist activities. Was home of Beachcomber Club and various AAFES-V facilities. Phuoc Tuy Pr, III Corps.

Vung Tau Rock Quarry (YS 2-4?)
Location unknown. 544th Engrs apparently worked this quarry, '67-68. Phuoc Tuy Pr, III Corps.

Vung Tau Seaport (YS 27-45?)
SVN's southernmost major seaport facility on the ocean. Was main source of supplies and war materials for allies in southern SVN during war. Run by US Army Trans Bn Vung Tau Detail (Provisional) under 4th Trans Cmd. Terminal inc 2 deep-draft berths, 5 anchorage berths and 3 LST/LCU berths. Berthing Feet: 2,000 lineal feet, Draft Max: 28', Cargo Capacity: 3,100 tons/day, Stg Covered w/in 5 km: 67,000 ft^2, Stg Uncov, w/in 5 km: 135,000 yd^2 See Vung Tau. Phuoc Tuy Pr, III Corps.[558]

Vung Tau Signal Site (YS 269 465)
A.k.a. Nui Lon, Hill 245, VC Hill and Ghost Mtn? Also listed as Vang Tau Signal Site, a likely misspelling. If site was at Vung Tau, it is likely VC Hill was Hill 245, immed N of the city and 1 km from ocean. See Vung Tau South? Phuoc Tuy Pr, III Corps.

Vung Tau South (YS 28-43?)
Possibly connected with, or same as, Vung Tau Signal site? Facility was transferred to ARVN Signal School and ARVN Veterans Admin, 28Feb70. At time of transfer, was capable of housing 1,500 personnel. MACV/JGS IG conducted post-transfer inspection on 14 and 22Jun72. Data per Ray Bows. Phuoc Tuy Pr, III Corps.

Vung Tau USO (YS 27-43?)
See Vung Tau R&R Ctr. Phuoc Tuy Pr, III Corps.

Vung Trau, Mui (BN 7-4)
Coastal point apx 30 km SSW Phan Thiet. At 11°18'N-108°55'E. On NC49-01 JOG. Ninh Thuan Pr, II Corps.

Vung Trich, Mui (CQ 1-9)
Coastal point at 13°30'N-109°18'E. Phu Yen Pr, II Corps.

Vung Xuan Doi (CQ 12-80)
Bay apx 12 km SSE Song Cau and 45 km S Qui Nhon. Phu Yen Pr, II Corps.

Vungchua, Cape (XE 6-8)
See Cape Vungchua. NVN.

Vunggang Bay (CN 0-9)
A.k.a. Baie de Vung Gang. Island bay at 11°43'N-109°12'E. Ninh Thuan Pr?, II Corps.

Vuong River Valley (AT)
Apparently in the An Hoa Basin. Site of Op Cass Park I, 29Mar-30Jun69, which was followed by Cass Park II, then Trojan Horse I and II, which hit NVA/VC strongholds in An Hoa basin. B-52 SF Det, 101st Abn and 282d AHC involved. Quang Nam Pr, I Corps.

WHISKEY

Facility/Feature Name, Grid Coordinate, a.k.a. Name/History/Province/CTZ

Unless otherwise stated, 6-digit grid coordinates reference DMA L-7014, L-7015 or L-7016 series, 1:50,000 scale maps, while 2- and 4-digit coordinates reference AMS/DMA/NIMA 1:250,000, 1:500,000 and 1:1,000,000 scale maps. Unless otherwise stated, all heights are in meters. To convert meters to feet, multiply by 3.2808; feet to meters, multiply by .3048.

W, LZ (YA 692-832) Apx 32 km SW Polei Kleng. Built 16-18Feb71 by elements 2/42 ARVN to exploit sightings and engagements by US B Trp/7th/17th Air Cav. Two-105mm howitzers here as part of Op Quang Trung 22F. Kontum Pr, II Corps. [559]

W. S. Price, Camp (YT 04-07?)
54th Arty Grp Cmpd at Long Binh Post. Named to honor LTC William S. Price, USA, CO 7th/8th FA (Jun-Dec 67) and Dpty Sr. Advisor to 18th ARVN Inf Div (Dec 67-death), KIA 29Mar68 when hit by ground fire aboard a suptg helicopter during battle involving 52d ARVN Ranger Bn near Xuan Loc. Cmpd dedicated 29Mar69. Data per *Vietnam Military Lore, 1959-1973*. Bien Hoa Pr, III Corps.

Wabash, USS (n/a)
A.k.a. AOR-5, Attack Oiler Replentisher. Served along coast of VN, delivering fuel, oil, aviation gas, bombs and bullets to Carrier Grps working near Yankee Station and other vessels. Data per Guy McCammon.

Wabash Inn (XS 858-905)
At 97 Tran Hung Dao St., Saigon. US military billet, Feb 65, 24 rms (see also Smith BEQ). Data per *Vietnam Military Lore, 1959-1973*. Gia Dinh Pr, III Corps.

Wachusett, USCGC (n/a)
WHEC 44. 10 Sep-1Jun69. Sqdn 3 CGC, during Coast Guard's 3d deployment.

Waco, LZ (YD 164-136)
Apx 29 km due S Ba Long AF and 5 km SE Tou Rout. '70 XXIV Corps grid per D. Armstrong. Quang Tri Pr, I Corps.

Waco, Operation (n/a)
25Nov-2Dec66. Near Bien Hoa. 173d Abn's return to Bien Hoa TAOR. III Corps.

Wade, FSB (XU 732-086)
At or just N of Loc Ninh AF, apx 22 km N An Loc, 43 km E Memot, 32 km SE Snuol and 24 km NE tip of Fishhook. Per John Driscoll, "Wade had a C-130 capable airstrip with an ARVN cmpd at one end of Runway and a Ranger cmpd at other end. There was also a French Villa nearby with a swimming pool, tennis courts and beautiful house, none of which had ever received scratch. Its owner had his own plane. Also had 175mm there to supt the Cambodian Invasion." 23rd Arty Grp and 2d/5th Cav occupied site in Jun70, per *11th ACR Cambodia Invasion AAR, 1st Cav Div, May-Jun70*, courtesy Lou Rochat. [560] Also listed at XT 732-086, but XT grid zone likely in error. Binh Long Pr, III Corps.

Wagon Wheel, The (XS 581-346)
Immed S of Ap Tan Thanh and apx 7 km ENE of Ben Tre. 2nd Bde/9th Inf Div nickname for terrian feature roughly resembling the spoke and hubs of a wagon wheel. Name/location per Paul Kasper. Kien Hoa Prov, IV Corps.

Wainwright, FSB (XT 061-773)
Apx 5 km SSW Thien Ngon AF, 28 km NNW Tay Ninh West AF and 10 km S Cambodia. Possibly named to honor Sgt Michael A. Wainwright, KIA, 17May70; or possibly Cpl Michael J. Wainwright, KIA 29Mar70? B Bty, 2d/19th Arty here per *11th ACR Cambodia Invasion AAR, 1st Cav Div, May-Jun70*, courtesy Lou Rochat. [561] Also listed at XT 060-771, per Peter Cole. Often spelled Waynewright; but Wainwright thought to be correct. Tay Ninh Pr, III Corps.

Wainwright, FSB (XT 288-509)
Apx 4 km NE Tay Ninh, 12 km E Tay Ninh West AF and 8 km SSE Nui Ba Den. Also listed at XT 282-528 and, if correct, was 2 km N of listed position? Feb-Apr68. Tay Ninh Pr, III Corps.

Wainwright II, FSB (XT 288-509)
Apparently built on same site as original FSB Wainright. Feb68. Tay Ninh Pr, III Corps.

Wainwright, USS (n/a)
CG-28. Cruiser, per Ralph Fries.

Wainwright, USS (n/a)
DLG-28. Guided-Missile DD Ldr, per Ralph Fries.

Wake-Davis, Camp (AR 896-116)
See Weigt-Davis. Pleiku Pr, II Corps.

Waldron, USS (n/a)
DD-699, per Ralph Fries.

Walke, USS (n/a)
DD-723, per Ralph Fries.

Walker, Operation (n/a)
16Jan68-31Jan69, 173d Abn, An Khe. II Corps.

Walker's Hill (BR 6-7 or 7-5?)
Per Jim Claeys and Ed Buckley, this hill was in '70 AO of 4th Div, and apparently near LZ John Henry/LZ Football. No other data. Binh Dinh Pr, II Corps.

Wall, Camp/FSB (BT 537-062)
At Chu Lai CB, apx 27 km SE Tam Ky. Grid for AF and only apx. Quang Tin Pr, I Corps.

Wallace Compound (XT 202-508)
At Tay Ninh East. Named to honor SSgt Gilbert E Wallace, USA, Advsy Team 90, KIA 1Nov69, when Huey carrying him crashed or was shot down during a Recon mission near Mo Cong. Tay Ninh Pr, III Corps.

Wallace L. Lind, USS (n/a)
DD-703, per Ralph Fries.

Walling BEQ (XS 854-905)
At 275 Pham Ngu Lao St., Saigon. Named to honor Sgt Harry A. Walling, US Army, KIA 19Jun64. Data per *Vietnam Military Lore, 1959-1973*. Gia Dinh Pr, III Corps.
Wallowa, Operation (n/a)
See Wheeler/Wallowa, Op.
Walrus, LZ (XD 715-444)
Along Rte 6068, apx 13 km due W Khe Sanh CB, 3 km E the Lao border and 5 km NNE Lao Bao. Apr70 XXIV Corps grid per Don Armstrong. Quang Tri Pr, I Corps.
Walt (n/a)
6Apr70, XXIV Corps future-use Americal FSB name.
Walton, USS (n/a)
DE 361. USN Destroyers *Wiseman* and *Walton* (DE-361) were deployed to SVN 27Feb62, to train VNN in blue-water surveillance ops. [562]
Wanon Niwat Airfield (n/a)
Apx 555 km NE Bangkok. El. 520'. Thailand.
War Horse, LZ (XT 324-377)
See Warhorse. Tay Ninh Pr, III Corps.
War of Vast Empty Spaces, The (n/a)
See Glossary.
War Zone C (XT)
Was W of War Zone D and included the NW 1/4 of Binh Duong and W 1/2 of Binh Long Prvs. Was bounded on S edge by Tay Ninh and Ben Cat, on E by QL/13 running between Ben Cat and Loc Ninh, and by Cambodian border N and W. Map in *Rangers At War,* pp 324-325. Primarily Tay Ninh Pr, but also portions of Binh Duong and Binh Long Prvs, III Corps.
War Zone D (XT/YT)
Was E of War Zone C and included southern Phuoc Long, northern Long Khanh, NW Binh Duong and NE Bien Hoa Prvs. Bounded on S and E by Song Dong Nai River above Bien Hoa, on N by QL/14 (which runs to NE through Dong Xoai), and on W by QL/13. Some say the northern boundary ran all the way to Cambodia. Map in *Rangers,* pp 324-325. Phuoc Long, Long Khanh, Bien Hoa and Binh Duong Prvs, III Corps.
Warbler, USS (n/a)
MSC-206. Minesweeper, Coastal, per Ralph Fries.
Ware, Charles R., USS (n/a)
DD-865, per Ralph Fries.
Ware, FSB (XT 591-266)
Apx 22 km WSW Lai Khe and 12 km NNW Cu Chi. Oct68. Binh Duong Pr, III Corps.
Warehouse, The (YD 335-107)
Nickname for the hill mass of Co Pung Mtn (Hill 1615). Apx 43 km WSW Hue, 5 km NW Dong Ngai Mtn, 3.5 km NE La Dut(1), 4 km E the N end of A Shau Valley and 9 km due S FSB Ripcord. Was NVA supply area just S FSB Goodman and Dong Tien Cong Mtn, on E side of A Shau Valley. Given nickname by 101st Abn troops because it served as huge logistical complex for NVA's 29th and 803d Rgts, 324B Div. Was objective of Op Chicago Peak, Apr70, and soon after, Op Texas Star, which led to siege of FSB Ripcord. Ripcord was built early 70 as arty, Tac Air and B-52 airstrike FO platform for interdicting NVA who'd been unmolested here for 2 yrs. See also FSBs Ripcord and Co Pung. Thua Thien Pr, I Corps.
Warhorse, LZ (XT 324-377)
On edge of plantation apx 11 km SE Tay Ninh, 5 km ENE Ap Van Long and 19 km WSW Dau Tieng. Name/grid per Kevan Mynderup. Tay Ninh Pr, III Corps.
Warlock, FSB (BP 303-211)
Apx 5 km E to ESE Dalat and 8 km NNW Xuan Truong. 2d/17th Arty here supt 53d Rgt/23d ARVN Div, 7Oct70. Data per Jack Picciolo. Tuyen Duc Pr, II Corps.
Warnes, Catherine Anne (n/a)
See Glossary.
Warning (n/a)
Apr70, XXIV Corps future-use 101st Abn FSB name.
Warrington, USS (n/a)
DD 843. In Jul72, struck what was later determined to be a US mine. Degree of damage unknown. [563]
Warrior, FSB (YT 83-42)
Near river valley apx 10 km NE Vo Dat, 48 km NE Xuan Loc and 4 km W Mepu. 4th/12th Inf, 199th LIB here at one time. Binh Tuy Pr, III Corps.
Warrior, LZ (BR 322-558)
Near Plei Brang Klah, 18 km NW An Khe, 16 km SW Kannack AF and 10 km NW An Dinh/QL-1. 4th Div AO, '70, and B Bty, 4th/42d Arty here Feb70. Per John Linn, was fwd FSB and B/2d/35th Inf here Jul70. Name/grid per Jim Claeys. Apr-Oct70. Binh Dinh Pr, II Corps.
Warrior, LZ/FSB (BS 400-540)
On peak apx 14 km WNW Minh Long AF, 28 km SW Quang Ngai AF and 14 km due S Ha Thanh AF. Also listed at BS 398-536 and also at "BT" 400-540, but the BT grid is in the ocean? Americal list. Quang Ngai Pr, I Corps.
Washburn, USS (n/a)
AKA-108. Amphib Attack Cargo.
Washington, FSB (AN 864-589?)
Apx 43 km WNW Song Mao/Hai Ninh and 7 km SE Tan Phat/Bao Loc. At listed grid, Jul68. Jerry Berry thinks grid was AN 964-589, which is 10 km E of listed grid and 33 km WNW Song Mao AF. Lam Dong Pr, II Corps.
Washington, FSB (XT 097-765)
Apx 7 km S Thien Ngon AF, 26 km SW Katum AF and 30 km NNW Tay Ninh. 15Aug70. Tay Ninh Pr, III Corps.
Washington, FSB (XT 123-526)
Apx 4 km W Tay Ninh W AF10 km 16 km WSW Nui Ba Den. 8Apr68. Tay Ninh Pr, III Corps.
Washington, FSB (XT 147-567)
Apx 4 km NW Tay Ninh West AF, 12 km NW Tay Ninh and 13 km WSW Nui Ba Den. Attacked 19Jun69, while occupied by 3d/22d Inf, 25th Inf Div (The Regulars). Also apparently 1st Cav FSB. Dec68-Jan70. Also listed at XT 140-560 and 148-568. Tay Ninh Pr, III Corps.
Washington, LZ (BQ 672-705)
Apx 25 km due W Dong Tre, 10 km NE Ban Chan Dong, 46 km WSW Song Cau AF and 67 km SW Qui Nhon. 4th Div AO, '70. Grid per Jim Claeys. 173d Abn, '70. Cited in '70 Bn Annual Hist Supp of 3/503d Inf, 173d Abn, on-line at www.gasparot.com/nammedic. Apr-Oct70. Phu Yen/Phu Bon Pr, II Corps.
Washington III, FSB (XT 101-595)
Apx 10 km NW Tay Ninh West AF, 10 km S Ap Trai Bi and 17 km W Nui Ba Den. Nov68. Tay Ninh Pr, III Corps.

Washington Green, Operation (n/a)
15Apr69-1Jan71. 173d Abn pacification op in An Lao Valley. 1,957 rptd NVA/VC KIA, per *Vietnam Order of Battle*, pp 9-14. Binh Dinh Pr, II Corps.

Washoe County, USS (n/a)
LST-1165. USN Landing Ship, Tank. SVN service with 9th Inf Div/MRF. See www.mrfa.org. To MSTS, '75. III/IV Corps?

Washtenaw County, USS (n/a)
LST-1166. USN Landing Ship, Tank. SVN service with 9th Inf Div/MRF. See www.mrfa.org. Decom 30Aug73. III/IV Corps?

Wasp, LZ (XD 862-540)
Apx 4 km ESE peak Dong Voi Mep (Hill 1739), 12 km NNE Khe Sanh CB and 26 km WSW Cam Lo. Apr70 XXIV Corps grid per Don Armstrong. See Dong Voi Mep and SESU. Quang Tri Pr, I Corps.

Wasp, USS (n/a)
A.k.a. CVA 18. In spring of '54, during Battle for Dien Bien Phu, US President Eisenhower deployed an aircraft carrier TF and suptg units to Gulf of Tonkin as show of support. The *Wasp* (CVA 18), *Essex* (CVA 9), *Boxer,* and *Philippine Sea* (CV 47) all patrolled off coast of Vietnam at various times and were prepared to launch aircraft against Viet Minh besieging DBP. Apparently these carriers never actually participated in the battle? [564]

Waste Land, The (WT)
Area described as having been across the border and into Cambodia, NNE Saigon. Cambodia.

Wat Phu Airfield (WB 91-42)
A.k.a. L-107 and Champassak. CIA/SF, per *Air Facilities Data-Laos.*

Wat Po (PR 7-3?)
In or near Bangkok. Site of "Reclining Buddha." Was frequently visited by US troops on R&R in Bangkok who were not otherwise "occupied." Thailand.

Water, LZ (XD 793-619)
Apx 6 km S the southern edge of DMZ, 5 km NNE Lang Ha and 32 km W to WNW Cam Lo. Apr70 XXIV Corps grid per Don Armstrong. Quang Tri Pr, I Corps.

Water Cannons (n/a)
See Glossary.

Water Plant, Saigon (XS 922-997?)
See Saigon Water Plant. Gia Dinh Pr, III Corps.

Water Point, The (YD 380-424)
See Waterpoint. Quang Tri Pr, I Corps.

Water Trap, Operation (XS 4-4?)
3-7Jan69. Cordon and search of Thoi Son Island in My Tho River S Dong Tam by 9th Div MRF. If grid correct, Thoi Son was island roughly 1 km long by 300 meters wide with center of mass apx 5 km WSW My Tho. Kien Hoa or Dinh Tuong Pr?, IV Corps.

Waterboy Control (YD 24-59)
A.k.a. an ASRAT Site. Call sign and cmpd name of 620th Tac Control Ctr (TCS), Det 1, Dong Ha, Jun-Jul66. A/1st Force Recon. 3d Recon Bn vet George Neville (Dong Ha '66-67) and his comrades quickly discovered this facility, "had nice beer garden with mixed drinks, in glass, with ice cubes." USAF personnel here admitted to Neville that prior to Marine's arrival, "they watched the NVA march across the airstrip in formation. They said they had an unwritten rule: They didn't shoot at NVA and the NVA did not shoot at them!" Possibly involved in "Skyspot" radar bombing control ops. Grid apx. Quang Tri Pr, I Corps.

Waterman Quarry (AR 833-567)
A.k.a. Connell Quarry. Apx 9 km NE Pleiku and 4 km W Plei Neh. Jan67. Binh Dinh Pr, II Corps.

Waterpoint, The (YD 380-424)
Apx 10 km ENE LZ Anne, 4 km SW QL-1 and 12 km SSE Quang Tri. Apparently waterpoint used by 1st/8th Cav in '68. Name/grid per Kevan Mynderup, as per Daily Staff Journal. Quang Tri Pr, I Corps.

Watson Army Airfield (BT 29-23?)
A.k.a. Blue Ghost AF. At Tam Ky, apx 60 km SSE Da Nang. Named to honor Capt. Richard B Watson, Trp F, 8th Cav Sqd, 16th Avn Grp, KIA 3Jun69, after being shot down while flying an OH-A6 near Quang Ngai. Was shot and killed on ground while carrying one of his crew members to safety from burning acft. Listed grid is for Tam Ky Alternate AF, which is thought to be same field. If site was Tam Ky AF, grid should be BT 31-19. Americal Div. Quang Tin Pr, I Corps.

Watthana Nakhon Airfield (n/a)
Apx 190 km E Bangkok and 30 km W of the Laotian border, per Feb67 Natl Geo map. Thailand.

Wattle, FSB (YS 358-918)
Apx 6 km W Rte-2/Courtenay Rubber Plantation, 25 km NNW Nui Dat and 6 km N FSB Dampier. 161 Bty, RNZA (Horsford's Bty 18Mar69-18Sep69) FSB set here 2-11Apr69. On 1ATF NCO trng map per John Hollett. Also listed at YS 350-910. Long Khanh Pr, III Corps.

Wayne, Fort (XT)
Refers to Operation Fort Wayne, not a facility. 1-4May67. 173d Abn, War Zone D. III Corps.

Wayne, FSB (XT 283-428)
Apx 7 km NE Ap Co Tac, 23 km SE Tay Ninh West AF, 25 km SW Dau Tieng and 13 km NW Go Dau Ha. Apr68. Tay Ninh Pr, III Corps.

Wayne Grey, Operation (n/a)
1Mar-14Apr69. 4th Div op. 608 rptd NVA/VC KIA, per *Vietnam Order of Battle*, pp 9-14. Kontum Pr, II Corps.

Wayne Stab II, Operation (n/a)
Op to free US and ARVN POWs involving 3 Bns and "Highland Rangers" of 4th Div, mid-Feb70. Acting on intel, the 3 Bns were inserted to surround camp and Rangers inserted to capture it. Rangers reached site and, after clash with NVA, did succeed in releasing one ARVN POW. Survivor said other prisoners had been moved shortly before US troops arrived. Cited in *Rangers*, p 104.

Waynewright, FSB (XT 061-773?)
See Wainwright, FSB. Tay Ninh Pr, III Corps.

Weaver, LZ ? (ZA 185-115?)
If grid correct, was apx 36 km SSW Pleiku, 22 km NW Plei Do Lim AF and 7 km NNE Plei Me. Listed in "AZ" UTM, but that grid zone does not apply to SVN and is presumed to be a transposition. Nov65. Pleiku Pr, II Corps.

Webb, Bruce E, Camp (BT 53-07)
See Webb, Camp. Quang Tin Pr, I Corps.

Webb, Camp/FSB (BT 53-07)
A.k.a. Camp Bruce E. Webb. In 3rd Bn/3rd Marine sector of Chu Lai. Named to honor Capt. Bruce Webb, CO I/3d/3d Mar, KIA 18Aug65, at Van Tuong (BS 704-948?)

during Op Starlight, by VC casualty feigning death who tossed a grenade at the Co's cmd grp after it had passed by his position and within minutes of Webb admonishing a Plt Sgt to stop shooting the "already dead" VC they were encountering. Grid apx only. Data per R. Bows' *Vietnam Military Lore, 1959-1973*. Quang Tin Pr, I Corps.

Wedderburn, USS (n/a)
DD-684, per Ralph Fries.

Wedding Cake Hill (AT 8-2?)
Somewhere along Song Lau River and NE Million Dollar Hill. Americal list. Quang Nam or Quang Tin Pr, I Corps.

Weight-Davis (AR 896-116)
See Weigt-Davis. Pleiku Pr, II Corps.

Weigle, USS (n/a)
A.k.a. *USNS Gen. William Weigel*. In Oct67, carried some 5,000 men of 101st Abn to SVN, inc the 3d/506th, per Frank Griffo, Jr. See *Gen. William Weigel, USNS*.

Weigt-Davis (AR 896-116)
Apx 12 km NNE Phu Nhon, 9 km SE My Thach, 37 km SSE Pleiku and 16 km S Plei Do Lim, near Plei Kuong. Small Army Engr cmpd/rock quarry, variously misspelled Weight-Davis, Waite-Davis and Wake-Davis. Apparently could not be seen from adj road as it was over a small hill on downslope from it. Mystery of proper spelling/name origin was solved by Ken Williamson, who noted that it was named to honor Sp4 Stephen L. Weigt, and Sp4 Robert S Davis, both KIA 21Mar69, at Kontum. Ken also said quarry was built in '69 by D/815th Engrs, 937th Engr Grp (Pleiku IIQ) and element of 102d Engr Supt Co, to supply crushed rock for asphalt being used to resurface QL-14 and QL-19. Mike Young, recalls, "It was primarily a rock crushing plant and base of ops for 20th Engr Bn in its road building capacity. Also hauled sand from river in Kontum about an equal distance N Pleiku to make asphalt for road." In'70-71, 584th Engr Co was part of 20th Engr Bn here but Young does not recall any arty. Per Bob Clark, site included a "Rock quarry, asphalt plant and small supt elements such as 2 Dusters, some 4.2" mortars, a dump truck Co and later on some big guns (105, 155, 175mm)." Nickname of 584th was "Wooly Bullies," and its men wore patch with that slogan. In Dec69, the 584th supt plt ran quarry. Asphalt plant built after Dec69 caught fire immed after putting out first load; however, no fire fighting equip was available and plant severely damaged. Legendary civilian named "Smokey" maintained 5 Cubic Yd Front-End Loaders and D-9 Bulldozers (painted bright camouflage yellow!), and often "ran the road" to Pleiku in an old Chevy pickup, his sawed-off shotgun at his side, and had a place on CPO road in Pleiku where many a wild parties were held." Also listed at AR 905-114. Grid per Cliff Snyder. Pleiku Pr, II Corps. [565]

Weir, FSB (YS 391-688?)
Apx 4 km WNW Nui Dat, 5 km NE Nui Thi and 33 km NNE Vung Tau. 161 Bty, RNZA (Honner's Bty 13Jun66-13May67) FSB set here 27Apr67. Likely named to honor Sir Stephen Weir, NZ's Ambassador to Thailand and SVN, who had been a gunner himself and was very supportive of 161 Bty. One night (apx 22Oct68) when a US arty unit was passing through, there were 72 arty pieces set up here. Grid also listed as YS 45-74 in *Vietnam Gunners,* but that grid thought to be in error since map in same text puts it at YS 391-688? Phuoc Tuy Pr, III Corps.

Weir, FSB (YS 45-74?)
If grid correct, was along LTL-2, apx 5 km SSW Ngai Giao and 5 km NNE Nui Dat. See Weir listed at YS 391-688? Phuoc Tuy Pr, III Corps.

Weiss, USS (n/a)
APD 135. In Jan62, *USS* Cook (APD 130) conducted beach surveys along SVN coast from Quang Tri to Vung Tau. In Feb-Mar63, the *Weiss* did same thing. VC sometimes fired on shore parties from *Weiss*.

Welch, LZ (BR 494-879)
A.k.a. Welsh. N of and overlooking the Dak Som River apx 2.5 km SW LZ Raquel, 3 km SE LZ Susie, 44 km due N An Khe, 36 km WSW Bong Son and 30 km NNW Vinh Thanh AF. Nearby LZs Raquel and Welch likely named in tandem to honor Raquel Welch, a beautiful film starlet who toured SVN with the Bob Hope USO show on several occasions. 4th Div AO in '70, and 2d/35th Inf, 4th ID here Apr-May70? Name/grid per Jim Claeys. Binh Dinh Apr-Oct70. Pr, II Corps.

Welch, USS (n/a)
A.k.a. PG-93. Patrol Gunboat that worked "Sherwood Forest" area; a network of coastal fishing grounds where tall poles holding fish traps and nets rose above surface and presented numerous navigation/fouling hazards. Role discussed in *Brown Water, Black Berets*, p 106. Market Time TF-115. SVN.

Wells, FSB (YS 660-694)
N of Xuyen Moc, apx 1 km N FSB Janet, 23 km E Nui Dat, 18 km NE Dat Do and 13 km SE FSB Wilton. 161 Bty, RNZA (Horsford's Bty 18Mar69-18Sep69) FSB set here 31Aug-10Sep69. On 1ATF NCO trng map per John Hollett. Also listed at YS 65-69. Phuoc Tuy Pr, III Corps.

Welsh, LZ (BR 494-879)
See LZ Welch. Binh Dinh Pr, II Corps.

Wescot, FSB/LZ (XT 06-89 or 95-94)
See FSB Wescott. Cambodia or Phuoc Long Pr, III Corps.

Wescott, FSB (XT 952-941)
A.k.a. Westcot, and FSB/LZ Jill. Apx 26 km SE Loc Ninh, 23 km SW Song Be AF and 6 km E Srok Phu Mieng. 2d/7th Cav, 1st Cav here '68, when named LZ Jill, and reopened as FSB Wescott by 1st/8th Cav, Jul69. 1st/7th Cav, 1st Cav, here Sep69. On 12Nov68, 2d/505th Inf, and Bty B 2/321st Arty, 82d Abn were airlifted to FSB Eleanor (XT 916-736) in order to block elements of 5th VC Div, and on 14 Jan69, the Bn shifted to FSB Jill. Grid per Frank Penk, Jr. Per Frank Penk, Jr, "A sign at LZ Wescott's VIP pad (imagine a mud hole in jungle with a VIP pad) read: *LZ Wescott, Named to honor SFC Robert Wescott A Co. 1/8 Killed in Action 29 Apr 69*." C Bty, 1st 30th Arty here '69. 3d Bde/82d Abn here per Butch Sincock. Also listed at XT 955-905, which is apx 20 km E and slightly N An Loc. Cited in 1st Cav VN *Yearbook* Aug65-Dec69, p 125, 245, 290, and 1st Cav Op Rpt for Aug69/Oct69, p 21, per Peter Cole. Phuoc Long Pr, III Corps.

Wescott LZ (XT 059-888)
May or may not be same FSB Wescott as that listed at XT 952-941? If grid correct, site was apx 27 km due W Katum AF and within 2 km of SVN border. Cambodia.

West, LZ/FSB (AT 990-251)
A.k.a. Nui Liet Kiem (Mtn of Leeches), and Hill 440 (or Hill 445). Overlooked Song Chang River to S, and dominated SE end of Hiep Duc Valley, apx 9 km E Hiep Duc, 6 km SSW LZ Dragon Base and 31 km W to WNW Tam Ky. Opened '67 by 196th LIB. LZs Center, East and West were 196th LIB bases of period, and built in line from E to W, spaced roughly 7 km apart. Center was likely so named because it was roughly centered between LZ's East and West. 4th/31st Inf, 23d Inf Div (Americal), 196th LIB HQ, and 2d/35th Inf 4th Div here. 7th Marines/1st Mar Div, also saw heavy fighting in adj Hiep Duc Valley, 21-29Aug69. Listed as Hill 445 in *Through the Valley*, p 31. On map L-7014-6640-3. Also listed at AT 988-249 and 990-025. Quang Tin, Pr, I Corps.

West, LZ (BR 687-891)
Apx 13 km NW Ha Tay AF and 17 km WSW Bong Son. Feb66. Binh Dinh Pr, II Corps.

West 1, FSB (XT 328-970?)
Listed grid may be incorrect, but if accurate, site was just inside Cambodia, apx 8 km due N Katum, 27 km WNW tip of Fishhook and 9 km SSE Memot. Incursion FSB, May-Jun70. Possibly 1st Cav, 25th Inf, 11th ACR or ARVN elements here. Data per Frank Penk, Jr. Also listed at XT 374-950 and 375-950 and, in *1st Cav Div Ops Rpt for May-Jul70*, p 20, at 347-934, per Peter Cole? Cambodia.

West I, FSB (XT 375-950?)
On border, apx 7 km NE Katum, 15 km SE Memot and 21 km WNW tip of Fishhook. C Bty, 1st ARVN here with six-105mms, A Bty, 46th ARVN with three-155s, and B Bty, 2d/12th US Arty here with six-155s. Grid and unit data per *11th ACR Cambodia Invasion AAR, 1st Cav Div, May-Jun70*, courtesy Lou Rochat. [566] Also listed at XT 347-934, XT 328-970 and at XT 374-950. See also addnl FSB West 1 entries, but XT 375-950 is thought to be correct grid for base despite wide variance. Tay Ninh Pr at Cambodian border, III Corps.

West I, FSB (XT 342-943)
If grid correct, was apx 1 km N site of FSB West II. 31Jul70. Tay Ninh Pr, III Corps.

West II, FSB (XT 346-935)
Apx 4 km NE Katum, 25 km due W tip of Fishhook, and 16 km SSE Memot. Incursion FSB, May-Jun70. Possibly 1st Cav, 25th Inf, 11th ACR or ARVN elements here. B Bty, 2d/19th Arty here with six-105mms, and B Bty, 2d/4th Arty with six-105mms, per *11th ACR Cambodia Invasion AAR, 1st Cav Div, May-Jun70*, courtesy Lou Rochat. [567] Cited in *1st Cav Ops Rpt May70/Jul70*, p 38, per Peter Cole. Also listed at XT 335-925 per Frank Penk, Jr. Tay Ninh Pr, III Corps.

West III through VIII, FSB (XT?)
May or may not have existed. Tay Ninh Pr, III Corps.

West IX, FSB (XT 344-932)
See FSB West II. Jul70. Tay Ninh Pr, III Corps.

West Lagoon (YD 7-3)
A.k.a. Pha Tam Giang. Lagoon at 16°36'N-107°32'E. On NE48-16 JOG. Thua Thien Pr, I Corps.

West of Jack, FSB? (YD 474-260)
Apx 10 km SW Camp Evans and 27 km WNW Hue Citadel AF. Apr70. Thua Thien Pr, I Corps.

Westchester County, USS (XS)
LST-1167. USN Landing Ship, Tank. Supt and barrack ship for elements of 9th Inf Div MRF. Was attacked by VC frogmen 1Nov67 (during Op Coronado IX), who planted mines as she lay at anchor on the My Tho River. Blast resulted in 25 US KIA, 27 WIA and 4 MIA. Discussed on MRF Assn website at www.mrfa.org. III/IV Corps.

Westcott, FSB (Various)
See Wescott. III Corps and Cambodia.

Westfall, FSB (YT 380-835)
Apx 3 km S Bo Tuc, 10 km SE Katum AF and 35 km NNE Tay Ninh. Tay Ninh Pr, III Corps.

Wexford County, USS (n/a)
LST-1168. SVN.

Wharton, LZ (XD 878-364)
Apx 2 km NNE Lang Haren, 7 km SE Khe Sanh CB and 47 km WSW Quang Tri. 2d/5th Cav air assaulted here 3Apr68 during Op Pegasus, then swept to S, W and N. The Old French Fort at intersection of Rte 9 and road N to Khe Sanh was one of its objectives. Cited in 1st Cav VN *Yearbook* Aug65-Dec69, p 99, per Peter Cole. Mar-Apr68. Quang Tri Pr, I Corps.

Wheatley Amphitheater (YS 27-44?)
A.k.a. Kevin Wheatley Stadium. At Vung Tau and named to honor Kevin "Dasher" Wheatley, RAR, who was awarded posthumous Victoria Cross. Grid apx. See Peter Badcoe Club. Phuoc Tuy Pr, III Corps. [568]

Wheeler/Wallowa, Operation (n/a)
11Nov67-11Nov68. Americal Div op. 10,000 rptd NVA/VC KIA, per *Vietnam Order of Battle*, pp 9-14. Quang Nam/Quang Tin Prvs, I Corps.

Where the Dragon Descends to the Sea (NVN)
See Ha Long Bay. NVN.

Whip, FSB (YC 589-877)
At S end A Shau Valley, apx 39 km SSW Hue, 10 km SSE FSB Tennessee and 12 km SE FSB Spear. Built beginning 22Mar69, by elements of 326th Engrs/101st Abn during Op Massachusetts Striker. Heavy weather prevented its resupply, so relief force was landed to W on abnd FSB Veghel (2d/327th+ C/1st/502d Inf). FSBs Fury, Pike, Shield, Whip and Thor were built during same op, 22Mar-8May69, using "Combat Trap" 10,000 lb bombs (if available) so that hilltop "was clear enough for rappelling." [569] Also listed at YC 590-878 (and YC 389-877 in error). Thua Thien Pr, I Corps.

Whipcrack (n/a)
Apr70, XXIV Corps proposed 101st Abn FSB name.

Whipporwill, USS (n/a)
MSC-207. Minesweeper, Coastal, per Ralph Fries.

Whire Beach (BT 743-883)
On coast of Batangan Peninsula, apx 3 km SE An Cuong, 18 km NE Quang Ngai and11 km W QL-1. Grid per Dan Gillotti, 15th Arty Assn. Quang Ngai Pr, I Corps.

Whiskey, FSB (XS 046-350)
On island in the Mekong River, apx 3 km NW Vinh Long, 46 km WSW My Tho and 3 km N Vinh Long AF. Feb68. Vinh Long Pr, IV Corps.

Whiskey, LZ (XT 545-048)
Apx 3 km E Khiem Cuong, 8 km Duc Hoa AF and 15 km SE Cu Chi. Apr66. Hau Nghia Pr, III Corps.

Whiskey, LZ (YA 9-0)
See LZ Tango. Pleiku Pr, II Corps.
Whiskey, Checkpoint (ZB 153-124)
Along QL-14, apx 7 km SSE Dien Binh, 16 km SE Dak to AF and 26 km NNW Kontum. Oct68-Jul769. Kontum Pr, II Corps.
Whiskey India Alpha (n/a)
See Glossary.
Whiskey Mountain (AM or AN or ZS or ZT?)
Per Jerome Lohman, was near Phan Thiet, and 73d Engrs, here at least May70-Mar71. Binh Thuan Pr, II Corps.
Whiskey Relay (YD 516-219)
Possibly at listed grid, which is Hill 674, apx 11 km WSW Ap Lai Bang, 6 km WSW Ap Thanh Tan, 11 km SSW Camp Evans and 22 km due W Hue. Radio relay site operated by elements of 3d Recon Bn, 3d Mar Div in at least 66-67. Info per Steve Laktash, 3d Recon Bn. Quang Tri Pr, I Corps. [570]
Whiskey Relay (AN 925-220)
See Tittie Mtn and Nui Ta Dom. Binh Thuan Pr, II Corps.
Whiskey Tower (BT 0128-6268)
A.k.a. FSB Dai Loc, FSB 412, Camp Middlesworth, and possibly FSBs Phong Luc I & II. Apx 9 km S Da Nang, 6 km ENE Hill 55, immed N An Tu 2, SE Phong Luc 2 and 2 km W QL-1. In '69, was home of A Bty/1st/11th Marine Arty. On map L-7014-6640-4. Info per Ex-PFC John Middlesworth. Dai Loc Dist, Quang Nam Pr, I Corps.
Whisman, FSB (XD 973-333)
On S slope Dong Cho Mtn and immed SE Da Ban Heliport, apx 14 km SSW Vandegrift CB and 12 km SSE FSB Snapper. Built by 2d/9th Marines beginning 29May69(?) during Op Cameron Falls, and attacked 1Jun69. Attack unusual in that NVA mounted assault within hours of FSB's completion. Col Michael Spark, Rgt CO 3d Marines, LTC Ermil Whisman, CO 1st/12th Marines and 3d Rgt Sgt Maj. Ted McClintock were shot down and KIA 15Jan69 near FSB Maxwell during TF Yankee (Base Area 112 attack). Separate FSBs later named to honor each. On maps at pp 65, 73, *US Marines in Vietnam, 1969*. Quang Tri Pr, I Corps.
Whispering Death (n/a)
See Glossary.
White, Capt. John (n/a)
See First Americans to Visit Vietnam in Glossary.
White, FSB (XT 235-305)
Apx 18 km WSW Minh Thanh AF and 17 km ENE Nui Ba Den. Apr70. Tay Ninh Pr, III Corps.
White, FSB (XT 340-900)
Apx 2 km E Katum AF and 7 km S Cambodia. Mar67. Tay Ninh Pr, III Corps.
White, FSB/LZ (XT 455-623)
Apx 25 km NE Tay Ninh, 18 km WSW Minh Thanh AF, 3 km W the Song Saigon and 5 km WNW Hill 248. 1st/8th Cav/1st Cav here in'68, per Frank Penk, Jr. Also listed at XT 444-625, 458-627, 463-632. Tay Ninh Pr, III Corps.
White, LZ (BR 745-877)
Apx 13 km WSW Bong Son and 8 km NE Ha Tay AF. Oct66-Jan67. Binh Dinh Pr, II Corps.
White, LZ (XU 657-037)
Apx 9 km SW Loc Ninh AF and 18 km NNW An Loc. Jul66. Binh Long Pr, III Corps.
White, LZ (YD 048-585)
Apx 7 km W Cam Lo, 5 km due W Thon Quai Xa and 3 km N QL-9. Apr70 XXIV Corps grid per Don Armstrong. Quang Tri Pr, I Corps.
White Beach (BT 743-883)
On Batangan Peninsula, apx 19 km NE Quang Ngai and 4 km SE An Cuong. Americal list. Quang Ngai Pr, I Corps.
White BEQ (XS 828-887)
Saigon enlisted quarters at 24 Ngo Quyen St. Named to honor PFC John W. White, KIA 9Jun65, at Gia Ray. Per *Vietnam Military Lore, 1959-1973.* Gia Dinh Pr, III Corps.
White Christmas, I'm Dreaming of a (n/a)
See American Radio Service in Glossary.
White Elephant (BT)
A.k.a. III MAF NSA Da Nang, the Wooden Elephant and White Elephant. Apparently near BT 03-80 and BT 06-77 in succession. HQ of NSA (Naval Supt Activities), Da Nang. Was apparently1st in Da Nang, 15Aug69, and housed in facility nicknamed "the White Elephant." Later moved to China Beach Public Works Cmpd in Da Nang East, where it was renamed "The Wooden Elephant." Quang Nam Pr, I Corps.
White Elephant BEQ (XS 8-9)
At 72 Tran Tan Phat St., Saigon. US enlisted billet. Data per *VN Military Lore, 1959-1973.* Gia Dinh Pr, III Corps.
White Horse Division (n/a)
See Glossary.
White Horse (ZC 06-93)
See Bach Ma. Thua Thien Pr, I Corps.
White House, The (CP 0-5)
Nickname for SVN presidential retreat at Nha Trang. Nguyen Cao Ky called it Vietnam's Camp David, and described it as, "A magnificent, dazzling-white villa on spacious grounds, with a private beach, that had been built for Emperor Bao Dai in Nha Trang, one hour's flight from Saigon." [571] Khanh Hoa Pr, II Corps.
White House BOQ (XS 861-916)
A.k.a. The White/Blair House. At 93 Nguyen Do St., Saigon. US officers billet, Jul 63, 6 rms (Annex also on Nguyen Du). Data per *Vietnam Military Lore, 1959-1973.* Gia Dinh Pr, III Corps.
White Mice (n/a)
See Glossary.
White Owl (n/a)
See Glossary.
White Plains, USS (n/a)
AFS-4. Aux Refrig, per Ralph Fries.
White Radio (n/a)
See Black and White Radio.
White River, USS (n/a)
LSMR-536. Landing Ship Medium, Repair. Launched 14Jul45. On 9May65, she left Japan for SVN, arriving off I Corps, 25May65, and immed began gunfire supt for Op Mobile. She then shifted to supt ARVN 2d Div near Quang Ngai for 2 months, and then added gunfire and rocket supt for 3 other ops, inc USMC Deckhouse III (amphib lndg). In Sep66, she worked off northern II Corps. Returned to I Corps, 9Feb67, then to Cam Ranh Bay and then Rung Sat Zone (III Corps) in succession. Returned to northern SVN waters 11Jun67, working shores of I and II Corps until 31Oct67. In '68, deployed 4 times to provide fire supt off

SVN. In '70, and as a reward for her faithful duty, she was sold for scrap. Data per MRF Assn at www.mrfa.org navy_index.htm. SVN.

White Star (n/a)
See Glossary.

White Star Mobile Training Team (n/a)
See Glossary.

White Star, Operation (n/a)
See Glossary.

White T'ai (n/a)
See Glossary.

White Thai Position (TJ 93-60)
Small defensive position on W bank of Nam Yum River apx 1 mi SSE Dien Bien Phu main CP, immed S the main ammo point, due E strongpoint C3. In Muong Thanh Valley apx 290 km W Hanoi. French position during Op Castor, 20Nov53-7May54. NVN.

White Virgin Mountain (YU 184-068)
See Nui Ba Ra Mtn. Phuoc Long Pr, III Corps.

White Wing/Masher, Op (n/a)
See Masher/White Wing. I/II Corps.

Whitfield County, USS (n/a)
LST-1169. USN Landing Ship, Tank. SVN service with 9th Inf Div/MRF. See www.mrfa.org. III/IV Corps?

Whittier Victory, SS (n/a)
Commercial transport under govt contract, per Ralph Fries.

Wichita, USS (n/a)
A.k.a. AOR-1, Attack Oiler Replentisher. Served along coast of VN, delivering fuel, oil, avn gas, bombs and bullets to Carrier Grps working near Yankee Station and other ships. Data per Guy McCammon.

Widder, Camp (XS 66-93?)
A.k.a. Camp David Widder. In plantation at Hoan Quan, apx 16 km W Saigon, 8 km SSE Duc Hoa AF, and 13 km due N Ben Luc. SF B-Team here. Named to honor Capt. David John Wick Widder, KIA 24Mar65. Grid is est. Gia Dinh (or Long An) Pr, III Corps.

Widder, Camp David (XS 66-93?)
See Widder, Camp. Gia Dinh or Long An Pr, III Corps.

Widgeon, USS (n/a)
A.k.a. MSC-208. Communication vessel that served as commo link during attack described in *Camp, USS* entry. Role discussed in *Brown Water, Black Berets*, p 121. SVN.

Widow-Maker Alley (XS 3-4)
Described as the road that ran between Dong Tam and Vinh Kim. See *Doc: Platoon Medic*, p 66. Dinh Tuong Pr, IV Corps.

Widows Village (YT 050-110)
Adj to Long Binh Post. Small hamlet of shacks across road from Long Binh complex. Govt-pensioned widows and children of deceased ARVN soldiers were its principal residents. Apparently the widows took in laundry from troops at Long Binh in order to augment meager pensions and drying laundry typically filled streets of ville. On 31Jan68, VC took residence here as well in effort to breach Long Binh Post perimeter and attack IIFFV HQ. Sent to stop them was 2d/47th Inf (Mech), 9th Div, soon reinforced first by Recon Plt, 2d/47th, and then by B/4th/39th Inf (defending Binh Son Rubber Plantation at time). Per Larry O'Neill, 6th/56th Arty, his unit was awarded Vietnam Cross of Gallantry when they engaged Bn of VC/NVA here during Tet '68. Discussed at: www.mrfa.org widow.htm. Oct66-Apr68. Bien Hoa Pr, III Corps.

Wiegle, USS (n/a)
A.k.a. *USS* or *USNS* or *MSTS Wiegle*? Troop transport that carried elements of 9th Inf Div (orig from Ft. Riley, KS) departing US, 1Dec66, and arriving SVN, 23Dec66.

Wigwam, LZ (YD 131-299)
Apx 19 km due S Ca Lu and 19 km SW Ba Long AF. '70 XXIV Corps grid per D. Armstrong. Quang Tri Pr, I Corps.

Wild People, The (n/a)
See Moi Tribes in Glossary.

Wildcat, LZ (YA 595-525)
Apx 3 km E Cambodia, 6 km ESE Phum Hay, 6 km NNE Phum Ta Lav, 17 km ESE LZ Currahee and 25 km W Plei Djereng AF. Cambodian Incursion FSB. 3d/506th Inf, 101st Abn and 4th Div elements here, May70. Name/grid per Jim Claeys. Pleiku Pr, II Corps.

Wildcat, LZ/FSB (YS 817-965)
Apx 8 km NW peak Nui Be, 21 km NW Ham Tan AF and 12 km WSW Ap Da Mai. Dec67-Jan68. Also listed at YS 810-960. Long Khanh Pr, III Corps.

Wilderness, Operation (XT)
1Jan-31Dec68. 2d/14th Inf, 11Mar68-7Apr68. Near XT 634-244, and 716-030, Bn NDPs for 2d/14th Inf, 25th Inf Div during Op. Per 3Sep69. AAR of 2d/14th Inf (Golden Dragons), 25th Inf Div, on-line at: www.en.com/users/kramsey/vnr102.html#. III Corps.

Wilhoite, USS (n/a)
A.k.a. DER-397. Along with *USCGC Point Orient*, *USS Gallup* and *PCF-79*, intercepted enemy Trawler #497 on night of 15Jul67, placing it under heavy fire when it refused to stop. #497 lost control and ran aground near mouth of Sa Ky River, where its crew attempted to return fire. Additional attacks put it ablaze and, when searched the next morning by VNN, several tons of munitions were discovered. Trawler #497 was then towed to sea and sunk. Incident discussed in *Brown Water, Black Berets*, p 119-120. Market Time TF-115. SVN.

Wilkinson, Camp (YD 830-144)
A.k.a. Gia Le Seabee Basecamp. Apx 5 km due W Phu Bai AF, 2 km SE Camp Eagle, 3 km NW Hill 80 and 9 km SE Hue. Named to honor CM1 Jack W Wilkinson, USN, NMCB-3, KIA 30Aug67, by stray US Army 105mm Arty round. Data per Ray Bows. Thua Thien Pr, I Corps.

Will, LZ (ZT 184-483)
Remote site apx 33 km SSE Tan Phat/Bao Loc AFs and 33 km NE Tanh Linh AF. Feb67. Lam Dong Pr, II Corps.

William, LZ (ZA 022-249)
Apx 32 km SW Pleiku and 18 km due E Duc Co AF. Jan66. Pleiku Pr, II Corps.

Williams Cove (AT or BT?)
At or near Da Nang? Quang Nam Pr, I Corps.

Willard Keith, USS (n/a)
DD-775, per Ralph Fries.

Willard Lowry, USS (n/a)
DD-770, per Ralph Fries.

William C. Lawe, USS (n/a)
DD-763, per Ralph Fries.

William V. Pratt, USS (n/a)
DLG-13. Guided-Missile DD Ldr, per Ralph Fries.

Willow Run, LZ (XT 310-470)
Apx 16 km due W Dau Tieng and 15 km ESE Tay Ninh West AF. May66. Tay Ninh Pr, III Corps.

Wilma, FSB (XU 689-317)
Apx 14 km ESE Snuol, 23 km NNW Loc Ninh, 3 km S Stoeng Chrey Meang River and 7 km N point where QL-13 crossed SVN border. In general vic FSBs Compton, Sisson and Scott. Grid per *11th ACR Cambodia Invasion AAR, 1st Cav Div, May-Jun70*, courtesy Lou Rochat. [572] Cambodia.

Wilson, Camp (AR 763-530)
Apx 5 km N Pleiku, 3 km WNW Pleiku/Cu Hanh AF and 1 km E QL-14. Sep70. Pleiku Pr, II Corps.

Wilson, FSB (YS 545-768?)
Variant of Wilton? Phouc Tuy Pr?, III Corps.

Wilton, FSB (YS 545-768)
Apx 2 km E FSB Longreach, 15 km NE Nui Dat, 4 km E Ngai Giao and 9 km E Rte-2. 161 Bty, RNZA (Hitching's Bty 14 Apr69-18Mar69) FSB set here 22-26Oct68. On 1ATF NCO trng map per John Hollett. Also listed at YS 54-76. Phuoc Tuy Pr, III Corps.

Wilson, Henry B., USS (n/a)
A.k.a. DDG 7. In May68, her gunfire decimated an NVA Bn in northern I Corps, killing 82. See Eagle Pull.

Wiltsie, USS (n/a)
DD-716, per Ralph Fries.

Winchester, FSB (WR 2-7?)
Said to have been apx 24 km from ocean and 68 km SW Can Tho. When built, was deepest penetration of area by US Forces in SVN. In Aug68, 34th Arty and other elements MRF here suptd 2d Bde/5th VNMC and local RF/PF forces. During week of 4Aug68, Bty B and C, 34th Arty occupied 4 different FSBs in very close proximity to this site and along Song Cai Loi River. On 24Aug68, all 3 btys 34th Arty and Bn GP were airlifted from water craft and placed in 3 different FSPB's suptg 7th ARVN Div and 9th Inf. Div. Kien Giang Pr, IV Corps. [573]

Winchester, LZ (BR 781-905)
Apx 9 km SW Bong Son and 8 km NNW Ha Tay AF. Oct66. Binh Dinh Pr, II Corps.

Winchester, LZ (XD 905-588)
Apx 22 km due W Cam Lo and 18 km NNE Khe Sanh CB. Photos/stories of troops here featured in 25Oct68 *LIFE* Magazine, pp76-77. Photo indicates C-shaped perimeter, triple-canopy jungle nearby, at least 2 arty btys and, by all appearances, an ill-chosen, almost indefensible site. Apr70 XXIV Corps grid per D. Armstrong. Quang Tri Pr, I Corps.

Winchester, LZ (ZB 046-208)
Apx 17 km due E Dak Sut and 36 km NNE Dak To 2 AF. Nov67. Kontum Pr, II Corps.

Winchester, Operation (n/a)
23-31May67. 173d Abn, Pleiku.

Winchester, Operation (n/a)
8Oct-4Dec66. 173d Abn in Da Nang AO. 4th, 503d Inf's assumed 2d Bn, 26th Marines' responsibility for securing the Da Nang TAOR. Mission lasted 58 days.

Windham Bay, USNS (n/a)
MSTS Transport, per Ralph Fries.

Windham County, USS (n/a)
LST-1170. USN Landing Ship, Tank. SVN service with 9th Inf Div/MRF. See www.mrfa.org. III/IV Corps?

Winds of Laos (n/a)
See Glossary.

Windy, FSB (BP 675-505)
Apx 36 km W to WSW Nha Trang and 7 km SE Thach Trai. 2d/17th Arty here suptg 22d ARVN Ranger ops, 7Sep70. Data per Jack Picciolo. See also FSB Big Windy. Khanh Hoa Pr, II Corps.

Windy, LZ (BR 158-244)
See FSB Big Windy. Pleiku Pr, II Corps.

Wine, LZ (XS 535-967)
Apx 6 km due W Duc Hoa AF and 28 km due W Bien Hoa AB. 2d/503d, 173d Abn was 1st unit to operate in Mekong Delta and 1st to assault W of the Oriental River when it CA'd to this site 1Jan66. Apr66. Hau Nghia Pr, III Corps.

Wing, LZ (YA?)
On Bank of Ia Meur River between the Ia Meur and Ia Tae Rivers. LZ used during 1st Ia Drang Valley Battle, Nov65. 2d/8th Cav, 1st Cav here. Cited in 1st Cav VN *Yearbook* Aug65-Dec69, p 203, and in *Pleiku,* at pp 168, 169, 170, per Peter Cole. Pleiku Pr?, II Corps.

Wings of Angels (XD 979-559)
See Rockpile, The, at grid. Quang Tri Pr, I Corps.

Winnebago, USCGC (n/a)
WHEC 40. 20Sep68-19Jul69. Sqdn 3 CGC during Coast Guard's 3d deployment.

Winnie, LZ (BR 524-334)
Apx 13 km SSE An Khe, 20 km SW Binh Khe and 3 km NE LZ Lincoln. 4th Div AO, '70. 4th Div op rpt grid per Jim Claeys. Apr-Oct70. Binh Dinh Pr, II Corps.

Winona, USCGC (VQ/WQ)
WHEC 65. 25Jan68-17Oct68. Sqdn 3 CGC during CG's 2d deployment. 29Feb68 action 7 mi off coast of An Xuyen Pr is discussed in *Brown Water, Black Berets*, 131 (index incorrectly cites p 181). Market Time TF-115. IV Corps.

Winquat (n/a)
MSTS tug, per Ralph Fries.

Winston, USS (n/a)
AKA-94. Amphib Attack. Cargo, per Ralph Fries. In Chu Lai area at least May-Jun65.

Wire, LZ (BR 8-6?)
Apparently in Phu My District of Binh Dinh Pr. Per *Rites of Passage*, pp 278, 328, was 3-hour hump from LZ Ship. Binh Dinh Pr, II Corps.

Wire Beach (BT 743-883)
See Whire Beach. Quang Ngai Pr, I Corps.

Wiseman, USS (n/a)
DE 667. USN Destroyers *Wiseman* and *Walton* (DE-361) were deployed to SVN 27Feb62, and assigned to train VNN in blue-water surveillance ops. [574]

Wishman, FSB (XD 97-33)
See FSB Whisman. Quang Tri Pr, I Corps.

Women Combatants in Vietnam (n/a)
See Glossary.

Wonder Beach (YD 494-565)
See Wunder Beach and Utah Beach for location and history. Quang Tri Pr, I Corps.

Wood, FSB (XT 044-796)
Apx 5 km E Cambodia, 4 km SW Thien Ngon AF and 34 km NW Tay Ninh. Built by 5th/7th Cav/1st Cav, May70, and holding B/1st/77th Arty after its move from FSB Illingworth, 4Apr70, immed prior Cambodian Incursion. B

Bty/1st/27th Arty also apparently here with six-155s during Incursion, per *11th ACR Cambodia Invasion AAR, 1st Cav Div, May-Jun70*, courtesy Lou Rochat. [575]Also listed at XT 049-801 in 1st Div Op Rpt for Feb-Apr70, p 68, per Peter Cole. Tay Ninh Pr, III Corps.

Wood, FSB (XT 464-379)
Apx 8 km SSW Dau Tieng/Tri Tam and 12 km WNW Xom Bung Binh. Nov68-Jun69. Also listed at XT 405-378 (likely error), 439-359, 440-340, 441-347 and 465-379. Tay Ninh Pr, III Corps.

Wood II, FSB (XT 465-378)
Apparently built on same site as orig FSB Wood. Nov68-Apr69. Also listed at XT 460-370. Tay Ninh Pr, III Corps.

Wood III, FSB (XT 442-345)
Apx 13 km SSW Dau Tieng/Tri Tam, 11 km W Bung Binh and 3 km SSW orig FSB Wood/Wood II. Nov69-Jan70. Tay Ninh Pr, III Corps.

Wood North, FSB (XT ?)
Apparently near Tay Ninh. Mentioned on 187th AHC's website. Unit's Bn Supp extracts are at: www.kbi.org/187 thahc/incident_67.htm. Tay Ninh Pr?, III Corps.

Wooden Elephant (BT)
See White Elephant. Quang Nam Pr, I Corps.

Woodpecker, USS (n/a)
MSC-209. Minesweeper, Coastal, per Ralph Fries.

Woodson Compound (XT 99-13?)
A.k.a. Honour-Smith Cmpd. At Bien Hoa AB. Named to honor Capt. Richard E Woodson, USAF, KIA 1Aug66, when his F-100 was hit by ground fire while strafing enemy positions. Later "unofficially" renamed the Honour-Smith Cmpd after the Army's 145th Avn Bn (which moved there May68) was denied permission by MACV to change the name. Unofficial name was likely meant to honor LTC Charles M. Honour and Capt. Albert A. Smith, both KIA 18Feb66, in non-hostile helo crash in which Smith was the pilot. Grid apx only. Bien Hoa Pr, III Corps.

Woodstock, FSB (BS 660-569)
If grid correct, was roughly 8 km NW Mo Duc AF, 3 km NE Hill 513, and 3 km S the Son Ve River. Americal List. Quang Ngai Pr, I Corps.

Woody, LZ (YD 048-585?)
If grid correct, was apx 28 km WNW Quang Tri, 18 km due W Dong Ha and 9 km NNW Mai Loc. Listed at XD 048-585, but that grid presumed to be in error as it is deep in Laos. 5th Div, Apr70. Also listed at XD 999-515. Quang Tri Pr, I Corps.

Woody, LZ (XD 999-515)
If grid correct, was in valley of Khe Trinh Hin River, apx 11 km WNW Ca Lu and 43 km due W of Quang Tri. Apr70 XXIV Corps grid per Don Armstrong. Also listed at XD 048-585 (in error) and YD 048-585. Quang Tri Pr, I Corps.

Wooly Bullies (n/a)
See Glossary.

Wooly Bully, Camp (AR 765-816?)
See Wooly Bully Basecamp. Kontum Pr, II Corps.

Wooly Bully, LZ (AR 765-816)
Along QL-13, apx 8 km S Kontum and 34 km N Pleiku. Oct69. Also listed at ZA 235-812 (both grids correct as site straddles ZA and AR grid zones). See also Wolly Bully Basecamp. Kontum Pr, II Corps.

Wooly Bully, LZ (ZA 235-812)
See Wooly Bully at AR 765-816. Kontum Pr, II Corps.

Wooly Bully II Quarry (AR 765-816)
Along QL-13, apx 8 km S Kontum and 34 km N Pleiku. Apr-Jul69. Kontum Pr, II Corps.

Wooly Bully Basecamp (AR 765-816)
Along QL-13, apx 8 km S Kontum and 34 km N Pleiku. Per CSM Steve "Sapper 7" Walls, in '69 was Army Engr cmpd later used to house Engr units and their hvy equip for major resurfacing project on QL-14 between Dak To-Kontum. Apx 1/3 of living space was underground while other 2/3ds was built with 55 gallon drums surrounded with sandbags. Had 2 perimeters; a primary exterior perimeter which inc motor pool, rock crushers and asphalt plant; and an interior perimeter with living areas and only two 81 mm mortars for defense. NVA Sapper once threw satchel charge into rock crusher jaws (unaware of fact explosives were routinely used to clear jams) and, in Young's words, "did little more than remove some rust!" "Wooly Bully" was nickname of 584th Engrs and source of camp's name. Elements 815th Engr Bn also likely here. 584th Engrs/20th Engr Bn worked quarry just S base. CSM Walls recalls site was next to SF Mike Force trng base with only concertina separating camps. Says SF camp was overrun and abnd late '68 or early '69, and 1st notice of its evac came when during attack, SF troops blew Bangalore torpedoes buried under their camp and the debris and NVA bodies from blast started falling into Wooly Bully! See Weigt Davis, Kontum Quarry, Wooly Bully II and footnote to Engineer Hill. Kontum Pr, II Corps.

Wooly Bully II Basecamp (AR 78-89?)
Described in 17Nov69 *Castle Courier* (newspaper of 815th Engr Bn and/or 20th Engrs) as having been "just N Kontum," and that "HQ of 815th Engr Bn is still based on Engineer Hill, but Kontum is going to be where the action is for next 7 or 8 months. [When Monsoons ended in Oct69], the Bn shifted most of its units northward to Wooly Bully II Basecamp …The 815th [has] one goal - making a top grade Hwy out of QL-14, the road that joins Kontum to Dak To." Data per Ken Williamson. Kontum Pr, II Corps.

Wooly Bully Quarry (AR 78-89?)
Near Kontum and cut into side of hill near Wooly Bully cmpd itself. Top of hill was heavily jungled and security measures were taken to prevent attack from above. Per CSM Steve Walls, at night, an LP/OP was put on hill, "because the VC liked booby-trap the rocks in quarry. When that became a severe problem for drill and blast teams, a PSG named Ivy, came up with a novel solution. Was forbidden for US troops to put out mines or booby traps unless directly suptg a FSB, and even then those had to be cmd detonated, so to meet the letter of law, a hard week at drilling prepared the quarry for a 'secondary blasting.' When intel suggested a VC probe was imminent, the holes (hundreds of them) were packed with explosives and it was rptd to 'higher up' that there might be some 'secondary blasting' during the week. An escape 'bomb shelter' bunker was built about 100 yds from LP site, and on 3d night of alert, the VC made their move. When the LP rptd a 'large' probe, its men were told to head for the bunker and, 45 minutes later, 1,200 lb. of dynamite was remotely detonated. 12 bodies and several blood trails were

found the next day. The VC never bothered the site again." Some data per Frank Canaga. Also listed at ZA 057-315? See footnote to Engineer Hill. Kontum Pr, II Corps.

Wooly Bully Quarry (ZA 057-315)
Apx 26 km SW Pleiku and 7 km NE Oasis AF. Oct67-Oct69. Also listed at AR 78-89, but that quarry thought to be different site with same name? Pleiku Pr, II Corps.

Worden, USS (n/a)
DLG 18, Guided Missile Frigate.

Worden, USS (n/a)
DLG-18. Guided Missile Frigate. See End Sweep. SVN

World, The (n/a)
See Glossary.

Worth Ridge (AT 85-66)
Ridgeline running roughly W to E, apx 20 km SW Da Nang and immed N of, and parallel to, Charlie Ridge. NVA/VC used its as base area for attacks on Da Nang, An Hoa, Hoi An and the Arizona. Characterized by single, double and triple canopy jungle and dense undergrowth covering high, narrow hills cut by numerous steep-sided valleys, ravines and gorges. Grid per map on p 109, *US Marines in Vietnam-1969*. Quang Nam Pr, I Corps.

Wratten Memorial Hospital (XT 168-518)
A.k.a. 45th Surgical Hosp. Named to honor Maj. Gary P. Wratten, Cmdr 45th Surgical Hosp MUST Unit (Medical Unit Self-contained portable Hosp), KIA by mortar fire while supervising its installation W of Tay Ninh. While surgical resident at Walter Reed, Wratten attended Gen Douglas MacArthur and became his friend. Grid is for Tay Ninh West AF. Tay Ninh Pr, III Corps.

Wren, LZ (AT 918-910)
Apx 25 km NW Da Nang AB, 13 km W the Hai Van Pass and 3 km SE LZ Dark. Apr70 XXIV Corps grid per Don Armstrong. Thua Thien Pr?, I Corps.

Wren, LZ (AT 962-552)
Along N bank of Song Thu Bon, apx 21 km SSW Da Nang AB and 12 km NE An Hoa AF. Quang Nam Pr, I Corps.

Wren, LZ (BS 421-026)
Apx 46 km due W LZ English and 25 km SSE Gia Vuc AF. Mar66. Binh Dinh Pr, II Corps.

Wren, LZ (BT 384-123)
Apx 3 km SW Diem Pho/QL-1 and 15 km SSE Tam Ky. Also listed at BT 372-125. Apr68. Quang Tin Pr, I Corps.

Wren, LZ (YS 833-797)
Apx 13 km SSW peak Nui Be and 16 km WSW Ham Tan AF. Aug66. Binh Tuy Pr, III Corps.

Wright, LZ (BS 821-287)
Apx 10 km due S Duc Pho AF, 7 km W QL-1 and 18 km NNW Gia An. Apr70 XXIV Corps grid per Don Armstrong. Quang Ngai Pr, I Corps.

Wright, USS (n/a)
CC-2. Cruiser, per Ralph Fries.

Wright Compound (XS 040-331)
See Shannon-Wright Cmpd. Vinh Long Pr, IV Corps.

Wrong Hole, NDP (BS 738-805)
Near coast apx 12 km NE Quang Ngai, 6 km N mouth Song Tra Khuc River and 11 km E QL-1. Sep-Oct70. Also listed at BS 742-808. Quang Ngai Pr, I Corps.

Wunder Beach (YD 494-565)
A.k.a. Utah Beach, Wonder Beach and Sunder Beach. On coast near Thon Me Thuy and Hai Lang, apx 16 km E to ESE Quang Tri, 40 km NW Hue and adj FSB Hardcore. Originally opened as Utah Beach, 2Mar68, then later became Wonder and/or Wunder Beach. Ship offloading facility opened/operated by TF Sunder as L.O.T.S. facility to resupply elements of 1st Cav and 101st Abn during Tet '68. Origin of Wunder name is not entirely clear, but, John Chandre, 363rd Trans Co, in '68, thought proper name was Sunder Beach and meant to honor LTC. Charles Sunder, CO 159th Trans Bn and Task Force Sunder, while Cliff Snyder at NARA was told it was named after a Jeep. Interestingly, elements of fact are found in both accounts because Col Sunder himself (telecon with author) tells us that in Fall '67, while 159th was at Qui Nhon before move to Quang Tri Pr, 2 of his men died in ship fire, which, along with other problems, led to poor unit morale. To boost esprit, he, his officers and NCO's decided to call themselves "Sunder's Wonders," and then had name stenciled in Gold paint on all the unit's vehicles. To his great surprise, morale improved considerably by time 159th was moved N by LSD *Comstock* to open what was 1st called Utah Beach, lndg there 2Mar68. Col Sunder has photograph of sign at Beach which clearly reads, *WELCOME-WONDER BEACH-HOME OF SUNDER'S WONDERS-19th TRANS. BN.* 2d name was for a while at least spelled Wonder Beach. How it became Wunder is not clear, although Gen Jack Cushman (CO 2d Bde/101st Abn '68) reports the name was changed from Utah to Wunder on 3Apr68. Possibly renamed Wunder due to typo perhaps, but whatever the reason, most official XXIV Corps rpts list it as Wunder Beach. 14th Engr Bn also here. 1st Cav Bn provided initial security (Col Sunder says its CO, LTC Robert Runkle, was KIA 4Apr68). Elements 2d/501st/101st Abn shortly followed in that role and security finally handed to 3d/26th Marines, 17Apr68. Also listed at YD 467-528 and 490-560. Map is L-7014-6442-1, per Ken Burrington. Quang Tri Pr, I Corps. [576]

Wyoming Hook Pad (YD?)
Apparently CH-47 log pad at either FSB Birmingham, LZ Sally or Phu Bai? Cited in 101st Abn ORLL for period ending 31Jul69, p 25, at: http://carlisle-www.army.mil/usamhi/DL/chron.htm#AVietnamWar19601973. Thua Thien Pr, I Corps.

X-RAY

Facility/Feature Name, Grid Coordinate, a.k.a. Name/History/Province/CTZ

Unless otherwise stated, 6-digit grid coordinates reference DMA L-7014, L-7015 or L-7016 series, 1:50,000 scale maps, while 2- and 4-digit coordinates reference AMS/DMA/NIMA 1:250,000, 1:500,000 and 1:1,000,000 scale maps. Unless otherwise stated, all heights are in meters. To convert meters to feet, multiply by 3.2808; feet to meters, multiply by .3048.

X, LZ (YA 9-5?)
S of Hill 903? A and C/1st/14th Inf/25th Div here, 22-23Oct66. See *Rites of Passage*, p 29. Pleiku Pr, II Corps.
X-Cache Route, The (XT)
NVA/VC infiltration corridor filtering enemy toward Saigon that ran NW to SE along an axis from Cambodian border at XT 06-87, SE to vic of Song Saigon and Michelin Plantation at XT 53-55. On map in *Rangers at War*, p 324. Tay Ninh/Binh Duong Prvs, III Corps.
X-Ray, FSB (XS 88-62)
Apparently a.k.a. The French Fort (Ap Long Ninh). On island along Cua Soirap just E Ap Long Ninh, 13 km due E Can Duoc, 17 km NNE Go Cong, and 30 km S Saigon. 2d/35th Arty here during Op Coronado, 20-21-Jul67, in supt of 3d and 4th/47th Inf, US 9th Div (as well as 3d Bn VNMC and 3d/46th ARVN). E/2d/39th here, 1Jun68, per Jim Stone, 2d/39th. Grid est from map on 199th LIB Assn website. Long An Pr, III Corps. [577]
X-Ray, FSB/LZ (XU 356-013)
A.k.a. LZ X-Ray II. In Cambodia apx 26 km WNW tip of Fishhook, 12 km NNE Katum, 38 km WSW Loc Ninh and 8 km SE Memot. Incursion LZ used by 2d/7th Cav, 1st Cav for 1st US air assault on day-one of Incursion. C/2d/27th Inf, 25th Inf Div, apparently secured its const beginning 1May70? Opened 2May70, by 2d/5th Cav or 2d/7th Cav? Grid and some data per *11th ACR Cambodia Invasion AAR, 1st Cav Div, May-Jun70*, courtesy Lou Rochat. [578] Also listed at XU 342-022 per Frank Penk, Jr. Cited in *Incursion*. Cambodia.
X-Ray, LZ (XD 860-370)
Apx 1 km S Huonh Hoa, 2.5 km SE Khe Sanh ville and 6 km SSE Khe Sanh CB. Apr70 XXIV Corps grid per Don Armstrong. Quang Tri Pr, I Corps.
X-Ray, LZ (XT 959-680)
Apx 13 km SW Dong Xoai AF, 16 km due E Xom Ruong and 5 km S LTL-13. Jun67. Phuoc Long Pr, III Corps.
X-Ray, LZ (YA 935-010)
In the Ia Drang River Valley at western base of Chu Pong Mtn, apx 5 km E peak of Chu Pong, 55 km SW Pleiku, 3 km SSW LZ Albany, 18 km WSW Plei Me and 12 km E Cambodian border. Site of 1st major engagement of US with the NVA, and 1st major test of 1st Cav's helo Airmobility concept. Battle fought, 14-16Nov65. Involved were LTC Hal Moore's 1st/7th Cav, and also 2d/7th Cav, plus elements 2d/5th Cav. Excellent and profound account of battle here and at LZ Albany in *We Were Soldiers Once...And Young*. On map in *Infantry in Vietnam*, p. 143. For detailed account of helo supt of battle, see *Chickenhawk*, *The Ia Drang Valley* Chp, pp 164-229. Pleiku Pr, II Corps.
X-Ray Alfa (YD 3-7?)
US name for SVN Junk Force base north of or near mouth Cau Viet River. Quang Tri Pr, I Corps.
X-Ray II, LZ/FSB (XU 356-013)
See X-Ray, FSB, at listed grid. Cambodia.
X-Ray Missions (n/a)
See Glossary.
X-Rays (n/a)
See Glossary.
Xa An Nhut (YS 46-59?)
Ville cordoned and searched for VC and ARVN deserters by 1ATF RAR elements during Op King Hit, 5-8Dec68. Phuoc Tuy Pr, III Corps.
Xa An Relocation Camp (BT 167-552)
A.k.a. Xl Relocation Camp. Apparently on island in the Song Thu Bon apx 4 km WSW its mouth at Cua Dai and 4 km ESE Hoi An. NPIA data. Quang Nam Pr, I Corps.
Xa Ba Sau Airfield (XT 949-261)
See Xong Ong Linh. Bien Hoa Pr?, III Corps.
Xa Binh Ba (n/a)
Mapsheet name of L-7014-6430-3. SVN.
Xa Cat Rubber Plantation (XT 75-85?)
Apx 6 km S of An Loc. Site of FSB Caisson IV and Battle of Xa Cat, 67. Binh Long Pr, III Corps.
Xa Cat, Battle of (XT 7-8)
Took place at Xa Cat Rubber Plantation, apx 6 km S An Loc. On 10Dec67, elements 1st/18th Inf, 1st/4th Cav, and A/6th/15th Arty, 1st Inf Div were at FSB Caisson VI when at 0200 FSB, they received heavy mortar fire followed by ground assault of 2d/165th NVA Rgt, several of whom got in the perimeter. 205 NVA KIA. Binh Long Pr, III Corps.
Xa Gia Kiem (n/a)
Mapsheet L-7014-6431-3. SVN.
Xa Huynh, FSB? (n/a)
Variant of Sa Huynh? Possible FSB, or ARVN or US SF camp here? See also Sa Huynh at BS 93-23?
Xa Lac Tanh (Tan Linh) (n/a)
Mapsheet L-7014-6531-3. Full sheet name: Tan Linh (Xa Lac Tanh). SVN.
Xa Lang Miet Heliport (XD 818-486)
See Xa Miet Heliport. Quang Tri Pr, I Corps.
Xa Long Hai Airfield (YS 432-512)
See Long Hai AF. Phuoc Tuy Pr, III Corps.
Xa Miet Heliport (XD 818-486?)
A.k.a. Xa Lang Miet Heliport. If grid correct, was along Rte 608, apx 7 km NNW Khe Sanh CB, 2 km NNE Ap La Vien and 8 km SSW peak Hill 1739 (Dong Voi Mep).

Listed in 14Aug69 TAD at "ZD" 818-486, which is in error as no such grid exists (not listed in Feb73 TAD). Name and '69 TAD info per Frank Penk. Quang Tri Pr, I Corps.

Xa Phan Thiet (n/a)
Mapsheet name of L-7014-6630-4. SVN.

Xa Phuoc Le (YS 43-67)
See Ba Ria or Baria. Phuoc Tuy Pr, III Corps.

Xa Tan Rai Airfield (ZT 094-874)
Apx 3 km S Tan Phat AF and 2 km E Bao Loc AF. "Secure, 5th SF Nha Trang ARVN(A) 12Apr69, AF # VA2-227," in Aug69 TAD per Frank Penk, Jr. Not in Feb73 TAD. Lam Dong Pr, II Corps.

Xa Tram Da Mi (n/a)
Mapsheet name of L-7014-6531-2. SVN.

Xa Uyen-Hung (Tan Uyen) (n/a)
Mapsheet name of L-7014-6331-2. Full sheet name: Tan Uyen (Xa Uyen-Hung). SVN.

Xa Vung Tau (Cap Saint Jacques) (YS)
Mapsheet name of L-7014-6429-4. SVN.

Xa Xuan Loc (n/a)
Mapsheet name of L-7014-6430-4. SVN.

Xam Cam My (n/a)
Mapsheet name of L-7014-6430-1. SVN.

Xam Tai Airfield (VH 62-11)
A.k.a. L-47. CIA/SF, per *Air Facilities Data-Laos.*

Xaum Hoa National Police HQ (AT 997-779)
A.k.a. Xuam Hoa I NPHQ. Along N edge Da Nang at bay's edge, apx 3 km NNW Da Nang AB. Apr69. Apparently Viet Natl Police HQ for area? Quang Nam Pr, I Corps.

Xay Dung Nong Thon (n/a)
See Glossary.

Xe (n/a)
Among several Vietnamese words that mean river.

Xe Banhiang River Valley (XD 60-50)
In Laos W of Khe Sanh, apx 70-90 km W of Quang Tri. Used as an avenue of approach to/from the HCMT. Laos.

Xe Krong River (WD 6-5)
A.k.a. Xe Kong? Laotian terrain feature in sector known as VR-6 of the Steel-Tiger portion of Tiger Hound/Commando Hunt ops. Cited in *Da Nang Diary*, at p 37-38. Northern Laos.

Xe Pon River (XD)
Parallels Rte/QL-9 in Laos and which forms a portion of the border between Laos and SVN where it reaches the SVN border and turns S, apx 15 km due W Khe Sanh. ARVN's Op Lam Son 719 launched along this river and Rte 9, 8Feb-6Apr71. Good Lam Son 719 map at www.americal. org/174/ map4.htm. Laos.

Xe Samou Valley (XD 665-627)
Apx 20 km W Khe Sanh CB. Major emergency extraction mission for trapped recon element (Team 5-2, 3d Force Recon, 26-28Jan67) on ridge adj this valley described in *Bonnie-Sue*, pp 274-299. Laos.

Xeno SF Camp (n/a)
US SF camp when Lao neutrality declared, 23Jul62. FTT 21, 27, 28 and 43 here then. Per *Special Forces at War.* MR3, Laos.

Xeon (XT 95-05)
Misspelling of Di An (1st Div's main basecamp) due to Viet pronunciation of Di An (sounds like "Zee-On"). No facility with this spelling is known to have existed. See Di An entries. Bien Hoa Pr, III Corps.

Xepon (XD 27-48)
Apparent spelling variant for Tchepone. On Rte 9, W of Khe Sanh. See Tchepone and Lam Son 719. Laos.

Xien Sone SF Camp (n/a)
SF camp when Lao neutrality declared, 23Jul62. FTT 13 and 15 here then, per *Special Forces at War*. MR3, Laos.

Xieng Dat Airfield (TG 60-49)
A.k.a. LS-26. CIA/SF facility apx 160 km N Vientiane. Grid per *Air Facilities Data-Laos.* El. 2,500'. Laos.

Xieng Dat Airfield, New (TG 63-51)
LS-117. Apx 160 km N Vientiane. CIA/SF, per *Air Facilities Data-Laos.*

Xieng Khouang (UG 06-51?)
To E of Plain of Jars and apparently about 170 km NE Vientiane. Here French counter-attacked elements of Vietminh during 1st Indochina War. Laos.

Xieng Khouang Airfield (UG 06-51)
A.k.a. L-22. Apx 170 km NE Vientiane. CIA/SF facility. Grid per *Air Facilities Data-Laos.* El. 3,117'. Laos.

Xieng Khouang Ville Airfield (UG 27-40)
A.k.a. L-03. CIA/SF, per *Air Facilities Data-Laos.*

Xieng Lom Airfield (PB 91-73)
A.k.a. LS-274. Apx 260 km NW Vientiane on Feb67 Natl Geo map. CIA/SF facility. Grid per *Air Facilities Data-Laos.* El. 2,050'. Laos.

Xieng Ngeun Airfield (TG 04-87)
A.k.a. LS-354. CIA/SF, per *Air Facilities Data-Laos.*

Xing Than Airfield (TJ 63-24)
A.k.a. LS-288. CIA/SF, per *Air Facilities Data-Laos.*

XI Relocation Camp (BT 167-552)
See Xa An Relocation Camp. Quang Nam Pr, I Corps.

Xo Tho Thanh (n/a)
Mapsheet name of L-7014-6534-2. SVN.

Xom (n/a)
Vietnamese word for village (A, Ap Thon, Thon and Xuan are also place-name prefixes meaning village).

Xom Ba Hon Airfield (VS 599-353)
See Cement Plant AF. Kien Giang Pr, IV Corps.

Xom Bang (XD 8-9?)
Quang Khe and Xom Bang were 1st targets of Rolling Thunder. Another grid possibility is VJ 7-4? NVN.

Xom Bau (n/a)
Mapsheet name of L-7014-6047-2. NVN only.

Xom Ben San Leprosarium (XT 907-213)
See Ben San Leprosarium. Bien Hoa Pr, III Corps.

Xom Bo (various)
Common Viet place-name. Sites in grid squares: YD 5-4, WJ 6-9, XT 9-6, XT 0-4, XT 8-5, ZT 1-3, WQ 1-9 and XT 5-2. Also at grids XS 769-426, XT 396-338. NVN/SVN.

Xom Bo II (XT 956-657?)
Apx 64 km NNE Saigon, and 10-15 km N Phuoc Vinh. Battle at Xom Bo II triggered 17May67 when 1st Inf Div units decided to walk into planned helo LZ after intel rptd 4 Cos of 271st VC Rgt had ambush prepared there. Enemy was completely surprised by grnd move, losing some 222 casualties. Tactic saved many US lives as LZ was heavily mined and enemy was waiting to ambush helos as suspected. See Xom Bo for other possible grid locations. Binh Duong, Binh Long or Phuoc Long Pr?, III Corps.

Xom Cai Nuoampoc (WR 1-8)
See Cai Nuoc. Kien Giang Pr, IV Corps.
Xom Cat Airfield (YT 153-287)
Apx 22 km NE Bien Hao AB. "Abnd 15Feb67, AF # VA3-255," in Aug69 TAD per Frank Penk, Jr. Not in Feb73 TAD. See FSBs Drennan, Charger and LZ Blue. Bien Hoa Pr, III Corps.
Xom Cat Doi Vam Airfield (VQ 849-818)
See Binh Hung AF. An Xuyen Pr, IV Corps.
Xom Cat SF Camp (YT 135-285)
Apx 3 km N the Song Dong Nai River, 22 km NE Bien Hoa AB and 26 km WNW Xa Gia Kiem. 5th SF, Det A-312, Oct66. Moved to Bunard. Grid per *SF Order of Battle.* Binh Duong Pr, III Corps.
Xom Chai (n/a)
Mapsheet name of L-7014-6051-3. NVN only.
Xom Cham Airfield (XD 849-418)
See Khe Sanh AF. Quang Tri Pr, I Corps.
Xom Duong Dong SF Camp (US 87-31?)
On Phu Quoc Island, near 10°13'00"N-103°58'00"E. Listed as 5th SF camp in DA Chief, Mil Hist records summary but not in other texts? Same summary also indicates Det B-230 (a.k.a. A-426) here '65. IV Corps.
Xom Giau (n/a)
Mapsheet name of L-7014-5927-1. SVN.
Xom Go (n/a)
Mapsheet name of L-7014-6149-4. NVN only.
Xom Go Jungle (XT)
Jungle area swept during Op Cedar Falls, Jan67. Possibly near XT 5-2 or XT 9-1? Tay Ninh Pr?, III Corps.
Xom Luoampoi, Ao (CQ 0-8)
Bay at 13°23'N-109°14'E. Phu Yen Pr, II Corps.
Xom Moi 1 (XT 626-218)
Roughly 7 km NNW Cu Chi CB. 2d/14th Inf, 2d/49th ARVN Rgt, joint ops here and at Xom Moi 2 in Summer '69, per www.en.com/users/kramsey/dragons.html. Binh Duong Pr, III Corps.
Xom Moi 2 (XT 617-221)
See Xom Moi 1. Binh Duong Pr, III Corps.
Xom Nui Trau Airfield (VS 599-353)
See Cement Plant AF. Kien Giang Pr, IV Corps.
Xom Ong Trang (n/a)
Mapsheet name of L-7014-5926-2. SVN.
Xom Pheo (WJ 2-2)
On Road No. 6, apx 55 km WSW Hanoi. On 8Jan52, entire Vietminh 304th Div plus Rgt 88 of 308th Div attacked strongpoint at Xom Pheo held by crack 2d Bn, 13th Half Bde, French Foreign Legion. [579] Vietminh shadowed close behind 2 French ambush patrols as they returned to hill position at 0110 hrs, thus being guided in their attack. By 0400, most of hill had been overrun, but VM withdrew by morning, leaving some 700 of their own dead. Per *Street Without Joy*, pp 56-58; maps at p 50 and 57. NVN.
Xom Ruong (n/a)
Mapsheet name of L-7014-6331-4. SVN.
Xom Tam Quarry (XT 978-123 or XS?)
If grid correct, was the quarry located at SW edge of Bien Hoa AB. FSB Ben Luc (XS 635-765) and Xom Tam Quarry are subjects of NARA film NWDNM(m)-111-LC-54455, May69. Bien Hoa or Long An Pr?, III Corps.
Xom Tri Ton (n/a)
Mapsheet name of L-7014-5929-2. SVN.
Xong Ong Linh Airfield (XT 949-261)
Along LTL-16, apx 13 km NNW Bien Hoa AB, 21 km SE Lai Khe and 32 km NNE Saigon. Listed as "Abnd, rwy overgrown 2Jul67, AF # VA3-150," in Aug69 TAD per Frank Penk, Jr. Not in Feb73 TAD. Bien Hoa Pr, III Corps.
Xong Ong Thay (n/a)
Mapsheet name of L-7014-5729-1. SVN/Cambodia.
Xuan (n/a)
One Vietnamese word for village.
Xuan Binh (CR or BR)
Small fishing ville apx 80 km N Qui Nhon. Elements of 2d/8th Cav, 1st Cav operated from site, Fall of '66. Binh Dinh Pr, II Corps.
Xuan Dai, Baie de (CQ 1-8)
See Xuan Dai, Vung. Phu Yen Pr, II Corps.
Xuan Dai, Vung (CQ 1-8)
A.k.a. Baie de Xuan Dai. Bay at 13°25'N-109°15'E. Phu Yen Pr, II Corps.
Xuan Day, Pointe de (CQ 1-7)
See Pointe Xuan Day. Phu Yen Pr, II Corps.
Xuan Hoa (various)
Common Viet place name. Sites inc: AT 992-778, BS 505-805, BS 517-812, BS 507-805, BT 002-779, YD 111-700, and YD 788-229. All in I Corps.
Xuan Hoa Heliport (YD 111-700)
A.k.a. Thon Xuan Hoa. At base of Con Thien/Hill 158/FSB A-4, apx 12 km WSW Gio Linh, 5 km NW Phu Phuong and 28 km NW Quang Tri. Heliport #703, alt 459', at 16°54'20"N-lC6°59'00"E. 73 TAD. Quang Tri Pr, I Corps.
Xuan Huong, Ho (BP 23-22)
See Ho Xuan Huong. Tuyen Duc Pr, II Corps.
Xuan Loc (YT 47-09)
Apx 60 km ENE Saigon, 46 km E Bien Hoa AF and 40 km due N Nui Dat. What has been described as bloodiest battle of war and one of ARVN's most remarkable performances took place here during Final Offensive in '75 when ARVN 18th Div under BGen Le Minh Dao destroyed 3 of 4 NVA Divs attacking it, holding their ground gallantly for most of month before being overrun. Home of 18th ARVN Inf Div Adv Det, Adv Team 87, 5th SF, Det AB-31, Oct66. 11th ACR, 199th LIB and 2d Bde/25th Inf Div here also as was FSB Husky. Capitol, Long Khanh Pr, III Corps.
Xuan Loc, Plantation de (YT 4-0)
A.k.a. Don Dien Xuan Loc. Long Khanh Pr, III Corps.
Xuan Loc, Xa (n/a)
Map name of L-7014-6430-4. "Xa Xuan Loc." SVN.
Xuan Loc Airfield (YT 460-082)
Major AF apx 60 km ENE Saigon, 46 km E Bien Hoa AF, 13 km N Blackhorse AF and 40 km due N Luscombe AF. Per TPC K-10D. El. 525', 3,500' asph rwy. At 10°55'17"N-107°15'20"E. Long Khanh Pr, III Corps.
Xuan Loc Basecamp (YT 460-090)
N of Xuan Loc AF and apx 60 km ENE Saigon. Apr68-Jan69. Long Khanh Pr, III Corps.
Xuan Loc Compound (YT 474-094)
Immed N Xuan Loc AF, apx 15 km W peak Nui Chua Chan. Oct70. Long Khanh Pr, III Corps.
Xuan Loc City Airfield (YT 460-082?)
A.k.a. Xuan Loc AF? Long Khanh Pr, III Corps.

Xuan Loc Heliport (YT 460-094)
N of Xuan Loc AF and apx 60 km ENE Saigon. "Heliport #704, alt 525', earth. Main pad on N side of Rwy 28. Addnl pads NE and S Rwy 28. Two 170' radio towers 700' N W end of rwy. Rgt hand tfc pad to N radio twr. Arty advsy-Long Khanh 238.1, 39.4. At 10°56'00"N-107°15'00"E," per Feb73 TAD. Long Khanh Pr, III Corps.

Xuan Loc SF Camp (YT 461-085)
Apx 60 km ENE Saigon, 46 km E Bien Hoa AF, 13 km N Blackhorse Basecamp and 40 km due N Nui Dat. 5th SF camp/FOB, Det AB-31, Oct66; close, assets moved to B-36 at Nui Ba Den? Data per *SF Order of Battle*. Long Khanh Pr, III Corps.

Xuan Loc Signal Site (YT)
No data. If on hilltop, was likely on one of 3 prominent terrain features near Xuan Loc. Alternatives inc: Nui Chau Chan (Hill 837 at YT 61-10) apx 14 km to E; Nui Soc Lu (Hill 418 at YT 3416,) apx 15 km to NW; or Hill 396 (YT 28-13), 8 km to WNW. Long Khanh Pr, III Corps.

Xuan Loc, FSB (YT 46-08?)
11th ACR base possibly a.k.a. FSB Husky? If it was Husky, then site was near listed grid and at or near Xuan Loc AF, apx 13 km NNE Blackhorse Basecamp and 47 km ESE Bien Hoa AB. Long Khanh Pr, III Corps.

Xuan Mai (WJ)
Apx 30 km WSW Hanoi. French strongpoint marking main line of defense in the *de Lattre Line* along Road No. 6. Was also ending point of the withdrawal of the Hao Binh Salient during Op Aramanth, Feb52. NVN.

Xuan Truong Orphanage (XT 932-020)
Along QL-1, apx 1 km NE Thu Duc and 13 km NE Tan Son Nhut AB. Jan68. Gia Dinh Pr?, III Corps.

Xuandai Bay (CQ 1-8)
See Xuan Dai, Vung. Phu Yen Pr, II Corps.

Xuanday, Mui (CQ 1-7)
A.k.a. Mui Ganh Den. Coastal point at 13°22'N-109°18'E. On ND49-09 JOG. Phu Yen Pr, II Corps.

Xuong Kuang (n/a)
Mapsheet name of L-7014-6536-2. SVN.

Xuyen Moc (n/a)
Mapsheet name of L-7014-6430-2. SVN.

Xuyen Moc, FSB (YS 65-76)
A.k.a. FSB Tom and/or Janet? Apx 23 km due E Nui Dat, 18 km NE Dat Do and apx 12 km N the coast. Rgt-sized base. US 9th Inf Div, 1st Bde here for ops in Jul66 against 274th VC Rgt. Contained 1ATF 4th Field HQ, Arty TAC, 108 Bty RAA, 161 Bty RNZA, B Bty, 1st/11th US Arty and howitzer Bty of 1st/11th ACR. 161 Bty, (Honner's Bty 13Jun66-13May67) FSB set here 25-27Nov66 (on 27Nov-1Dec66, Bty was 5 km NW Xuyen Moc at YS 60-70, and on 1-3Dec66 was at YS 65-68). FSB Janet also at Xuyen Moc, 24-31Aug69. Phuoc Tuy Pr, III Corps.

Xuyen Moc Airfield (YS 658-681)
Apx 17 km NE Dat Do, 22 km E Nui Dat and 46 km NE Vung Tau. "VDCA(A) 12Sep68, AF # VA3-162," in Aug69 TAD per Frank Penk, Jr. Not in Feb73 TAD. Phuoc Tuy Pr, III Corps.

Xuyen Moc Heliport (YS 655-690)
Just N Xa Xuyen Moc, apx 17 km NE Dat Do, 22 km E Nui Dat and 46 km NE Vung Tau. Heliport #705, alt 148', at 10°34'00"N-107°25'40"E, per Feb73 TAD. Phuoc Tuy Pr, III Corps.

XXII Corps (n/a)
See Corps Level Command Section.

XXIV Corps (n/a)
See Corps Level Command Section.

XXX Corps (n/a)
See Corps Level Command Section.

XYZ Pad (YA 96-85?)
A.k.a. LZ XYZ. Per Patrick Dudney, was 4th Div LZ near Kontum and within 1 km of FSB Brillo Pad. If description is accurate, then was possibly a.k.a. Hill 1124, OP Hill or LZ Alamo. 3d/12th Inf, 4th Div here, among other units. Grid apx. Kontum Pr, II Corps.

XYZ, LZ (YA 96-85?)
See XYZ Pad, 4th Div. Kontum Pr, II Corps.

YANKEE

Facility/Feature Name, Grid Coordinate, a.k.a. Name/History/Province/CTZ

Unless otherwise stated, 6-digit grid coordinates reference DMA L-7014, L-7015 or L-7016 series, 1:50,000 scale maps, while 2- and 4-digit coordinates reference AMS/DMA/NIMA 1:250,000, 1:500,000 and 1:1,000,000 scale maps. Unless otherwise stated, all heights are in meters. To convert meters to feet, multiply by 3.2808; feet to meters, multiply by .3048.

Y, LZ (BR 535-929)
A.k.a. Hill 736. Remote site, apx 27 km SW Thuan An. 17Mar66. Binh Dinh Pr, II Corps.

Y Bridge, The (XS 845-886)
Y-shaped bridge at south-central edge of Saigon, and scene of heavy fighting during Tet '68. Was on connecting road between QL-5(?) and QL-15. Per Jim Stone, 2d/39th Inf, also site of major battle involving elements of 3d Bde/9th Inf Div, during Mini-Tet, May68. Excellent photo in *Vietnam Experience* series, *Nineteen Sixty-Eight* vol, p 159. Gia Dinh Pr, III Corps.

Youk Nam Rmay (AP 857-380)
See Nui Youk Nam Rmay. Tuyen Duc Pr, II Corps.

Ya Bo Mountain (BN 59-77)
A.k.a. Hill 1031 (3,383'). Apx 20 km W Phan Rang AB. Ninh Thuan Pr, II Corps.

Ya Do Mountain (YD 663-225)
See OP Castle. Thua Thien Pr, I Corps.

Ya Krong Bolah River (YA 86-60)
Major river passing Plei Djereng 40 to 50 km WNW Pleiku. Its lower portion (as it approached Cambodia) was known as the Se San River. In Cambodia, it was the Tonle San River. The Se San/Ya Krong Bolah formed portion of Cambodian/SVN border (met border at YA 66-40), as well as portion of the Pleiku-Kontum Pr border. II Corps.

Ya Krong Bolah Valley (YA 86-60)
Valley of Ya Krong Bolah River, roughly 40 km W Pleiku in Kontum/Pleiku Prvs, II Corps.

Ya Lop (n/a)
Mapsheet name of L-7014-6535-4. SVN/Cambodia.

Ya Loup SF Camp (ZV 105-946)
Apx 7 km W Plei Bai, 27 km WSW Phu Nhon AF and 55 km SSW Pleiku. 5th SF. Info per *SF Order of Battle.* See also Ea Soup. Darlac Pr, II Corps.

Yacht, LZ/FSB (BR 165-435)
A.k.a. LZ Frodo. Apx 33 km due W An Khe, 18 km SE Suoi Doi AF, 6 km ESE peak of Chu Rran Mtn and 10 km S QL-19. Thought to have been renamed "Yacht" after only short period as "Frodo?" 3d/8th Inf, 4th Div here at one point in Jun70. Grid and info per Jim Claeys. Near Binh Dinh/Pleiku Pr border, II Corps.

Yakutat, USCGC (n/a)
WHEC 380. Deployed to VN twice, 4May67-1Jan68 and 17May70-31Dec70. [580]

Yala Airfield (QH 4-2)
Apx 810 km due S Bangkok, near 6°32'00"N-101°14'00"E, per Feb67 Natl Geo map. Southernmost Thai AF. Grid per, and listed as abnd in,'66 NIMA data. El. 50'. Thailand.

Yang Talat Airfield (UD 2-1)
At 16°25'00"N-103°21'00"E. NIMA data. Thailand.

Yankec Heliport (BP 010-460)
Apx 13 km ESE Duc Xuyen AF and 29 km SSE Lac Thien. Heliport #706, El. 837', at 12°10'00"N-108°15'00"E. Tuyen Duc Pr, II Corps.

Yankee, FSB (XS 167-403)
On N edge of island in Mekong River, apx 5 km SW Sung Hieu/Cai Be, 14 km NE Vinh Long and 25 km WSW Dong Tam. Feb68. Vinh Long Pr, IV Corps.

Yankee, FSB (YB 999-130)
A.k.a. Artillery Hill and Hill 1314. Apx 1 km due W Dak To 2 AF (possibly within its perimeter?) and 6 km W Tanh Can. AF? Grid per Nolan Putman. Kontum Pr, II Corps.

Yankee, LZ (XT 952-664)
Apx 15 km SW Dong Xoai AF and 16 km due N Phuoc Vinh AF. Jun67. Phuoc Long Pr, III Corps.

Yankee, LZ (YA 9-0)
Proposed but unused Ia Drang campaign LZ. See also LZ Tango for detail. Pleiku Pr, II Corps.

Yankee, LZ (YD 13-58)
Apparently along QL-9 at or near Cam Lo, and 23 km WNW Quang Tri. Was Op Lam Son 719 LZ, '71. Grid per Lam Son 719 FSB map at www.americal.org/174/map4.htm. Quang Tri Pr, I Corps.

Yankee, Operation (n/a)
A.k.a. Op Yankee Team. Joint USN/USAF op that began 21May64, when two RF-8A Crusaders doing photo recon off Carrier Kitty Hawk (CVA 63), discovered NVA in Plain of Jars region. One plane hit by antiaircraft fire. [581]

Yankee Ammo Storage Area (CR 066-261?)
On Cam Ranh Bay Peninsula, apx 3 km SW the S end of main AF rwy. 1 of 3 ammo stg areas here renamed on 12Jul69 for 3 EOD personnel KIA while disarming ordnance. See also Black, McKinley or Moore Ammo Stg Areas. Khanh Hoa Pr, II Corps.

Yankee Heliport (BP 010-460)
See Yankec Heliport. Tuyen Duc Pr, II Corps.

Yankee Station (n/a)
In Gulf of Tonkin at 17°30'N 108°30'E, apx 190 km due E Dong Hoi, NVN, and 150 km NE Hue, SVN. Northern staging area of US 7th Fleet's TF 77 after '66. See also Dixie Station.

Yankee Team, Operation (n/a)
See Yankee, Operation.

Yao San Meo (n/a)
AMS/DMA mapsheet L 701-5679-2. NVN/China.

Yard (n/a)
See Glossary.

Yarra, HMAS (n/a)
Australian Escort ship serving under US 7th Flt.
Yasothon Airfield (n/a)
Apx 450 km NE Bangkok. Thailand.
Yean Than Antaracheat AF (VT 8-7)
A.k.a. Phnom Penh Intl Airport. At 11°33'00"N-104°51'00"E. NIMA data. Cambodia.
Year of Decision, The (n/a)
See Glossary.
Yellow, LZ (BQ 883-383)
Apx 6 km WNW Lac Dien and 10 km SE Cung Son AF. Oct66. Phu Yen Pr, II Corps.
Yellow, LZ (BR 545-432)
Apx 8 km ESE An Khe and 15 km due W Binh Khe. Aug66. Binh Dinh Pr, II Corps.
Yellow, LZ (n/a)
Apparent ARVN Cambodian Incursion LZ. Website of 119th AHC indicates it extracted some 2,000 ARVN of 47th ARVN Rgt from this site, 24May70. Cambodia?
Yellow, LZ (XT 415-528)
Apx 9 km NW Dau Tieng/Tri Tam and 18 km ENE Tay Ninh. Jun66. Tay Ninh Pr, III Corps.
Yellow, LZ (XU 725-013)
Along QL-13, apx 9 km S Loc Ninh AF and 13 km NNW An Loc. Jul68. Binh Long Pr, III Corps.
Yellow, LZ (YC 798-923)
Apx 21 km S Hue and 17 km SSW Phu Bai. Apr70 XXIV Corps grid per Don Armstrong. Thua Thien Pr, I Corps.
Yellow Brick Road (YC/ZC/AT)
Apparently consisted of portions of Hwys 545 and 548. Road generally leading from S end of the A Shau Valley toward the Da Nang area. Said to have traversed Elephant Valley as Hwy 545, then became QL-548 as it turned N and into the A Shau. During Op Massachusetts Striker, over 100 tons of enemy supplies discovered in caches along this road by 1st/502d Inf, 101st Abn beginning 20Apr69. Quang Nam/Thua Thien Prvs, I Corps.
Yellow Dog, LZ, (BS 811-211)
Apx 12 km NW Gia An, 18 km S Duc Pho AF and 12 km W QL-1. Mar67. Binh Dinh Pr, II Corps.
Yellowstone, Operation (n/a)
8Dec66-24Feb68. 25th Inf Div Op. 1,254 rptd NVA/VC KIA, per *Vietnam Order of Battle*, pp 9-14. Per 1Jan-1Dec68r Annual Hist Supp for2d/14th Inf 25th ID (7Dec67-10Mar68), at: www.en.com/users/kramsey/dragons.html, Op began 7Dec67 with 2d/14th Inf (plus 2d Plt, Co B, and 65th Engr Bn) into Katum, near Cambodian border. Tay Ninh Pr, III Corps.
Yen Bai (VJ 86-99)
See Yen Bay. NVN.
Yen Bai Airfield (VK 86-03)
Apx 110 km NW Hanoi, per map in *Vietnam Experience* Series, *Rain of Fire* vol, p. 11. NVN.
Yen Bai, FSB? (XD 832-221)
In S end of the Vietnam Salient, apx 4 km SE FSB Paris, 6 km due S Lang Chei, 13 km SW Lang Klung and 58 km SW Quang Tri. Apr70 XXIV Corps grid per Don Armstrong. Quang Tri Pr, I Corps.
Yen Bay (n/a)
Mapsheet name of L-7014-5952-2. NVN only.
Yen Bay (VJ 86-99)
A.k.a. Yen Bai. NVN town on Red River, apx 120 km NW Hanoi. See *Street Without Joy*, Chp 3; with map at p 80. See also Nghia Lo. NVN.
Yen Binh (n/a)
Mapsheet name of L-7014-5953-4. NVN only.
Yen Chau (n/a)
Mapsheet name of L-7014-5851-2. NVN only.
Yen Cu Ha (XH)
E of QL-1, apx 95 km SSE Hanoi. French garrison here involved in Battle of Day River, 29May-18Jun51. See *Street Without Joy*, Chp 2, with map at p 46. NVN.
Yen Cu (various)
Common Viet place-name. Sites inc: WJ 5-9, WJ 3-3, YJ 0-1, YD 3-6, VS 9-6, WF 6-5, WF 7-5. NVN & SVN.
Yen Dinh (n/a)
Mapsheet name of L-7014-6149-3. NVN only.
Yen Duyen, Nui (WH 9-2)
Mtn range at 20°07'N-105°55'E. On NF48-15 JOG. NVN.
Yen Lac (n/a)
Mapsheet name of L-7014-6253-3. NVN only.
Yen Phu (various)
Common Viet place-name. Sites inc: XJ 5-5, XJ 45, WJ 9-4, WJ 8-2, XJ 0-1, WH 9-6, WG 7-2, WG 5-0, WF 3-9, WF 6-9, WF 2-9. NVN
Yen Phu Power Plant (WJ 8-2?)
In or near Hanoi? Portions of plant were used as US POW Camp. NVN.
Yen River (AT/BT)
The Cau Do, Yen, Tuy Loan La Tho, Thanh Quyt, Vu Gia, Cau Lau and Thu Bon Rivers all formed part of drainage that became the Da Nang River. All were S or SW Da Nang. Quang Nam Pr, I Corps.
Yen The, Camp (n/a)
Map at p 89 of, *War In The Shadows*, of *Vietnam Experience* series indicates base was NE Saigon; however, a Yen The is listed near XU 56-01, a point apx 2 km from Cambodia, 11 km NNW tip of Fishhook, and 19 km WSW Loc Ninh? Described as "strategic hilltop" employed for MAC-SOG ops. Apparently radio relay/listening site and/or OP that may have also been a "White Radio" facility. Yen The also listed in NVN at XJ 1-7. III Corps.
Yen The, FSB (XU 558-008)
Possibly a.k.a. FSB East I (XU 536-008 or XU 562-005)? Apx 2 km from Cambodia, 11 km NNW tip of Fishhook, 19 km WSW Loc Ninh and 23 km WNW An Loc. 11th ACR/1st Cav here during Cambodian Incursion. Grid per *11th ACR Cambodia Invasion AAR, 1st Cav Div, May-Jun70*, courtesy Lou Rochat.[582] Phuoc Long Pr, III Corps.
Yen, Mui (CR 1-2)
A.k.a. Cap de Hirondelles. Coastal point at 13°45'N-109°18'E. On ND49-09 JOG. Binh Dinh Pr, II Corps.
Yeti Sightings (n/a)
See Glossary.
YFNB-2 (n/a)
USN Non Self-Propelled Barge. SVN.
YFR-889 (n/a)
USN Refrigerated Stg Craft supt MRF. SVN
YFU-78 (n/a)
USN Harbor Utility Craft. SVN

Yna, LZ (BR 348-309)
A.k.a. LZ Ina. Apx 20 km SW An Khe and 14 km S QL-19. Sep69. Binh Dinh Pr, II Corps.
Yna, LZ (XT 607-621)
See LZ Ina. Binh Long Pr, III Corps.
Yok Mbre (n/a)
Mapsheet name of L-7014-6535-3. SVN/Cambodia.
Yok Mria Mountains (ZU 1-6)
Mtn range at 12°22'N-107°53'E. On ND48-16 JOG. Quang Duc Pr, II Corps.
Yok Nam Lao Mountain (ZU 14-42)
A.k.a. Hill 951 (3,120'). Apx 25 km NE Gia Nghia AF and 60 km WNW Dalat. Quang Duc Pr, II Corps.
Yok Ngiang Mountains (ZU 0-6)
A.k.a. Yuk Ngiang Mtns. Mtn range at 12°20'N-107°50'E. On ND48-16 JOG. Quang Duc Pr, II Corps.
Yonkers, FSB (AT 945-405)
A.k.a. LZ Ike. Apx 12 km SE An Hoa, 35 km SSW Da Nang and 7 km due E Phuoc Binh. On 6Apr70, XXIV Corps Americal FSB future-name list, so possibly built after that date. Quang Nam Pr, I Corps.
Yorktown, LZ (YD 149-318)
In Khe Ta Laou River Valley, apx 7 km ESE Ta Laou, 27 km SW Quang Tri and 8 km SSW Ba Long AF. Apr70 XXIV Corps grid per D. Armstrong. Quang Tri Pr, I Corps.
Yorktown, Operation (n/a)
23 Jun-8 Jul66. 173d Abn. AO 60 km E Bien Hoa. A, 2d/503d Inf fought 75-100 VC. Long Khanh Pr, II Corps.
Yorktown, USS (n/a)
CVS-10. Acft Carrier. Deployed with CVSG-55, 28Dec67 to 5Jul68; with CVSG-55, 23Oct64 to 16May65; with CVSG-55, 6Jan66 to 27Jul66. [583]
You Bet Your Life FTX (CP 03-52?)
See MACV Recondo School. Khanh Hoa Pr, II Corps.
Youk Nam Rmay Mtn (AP 86-38)
See Nui Youk Nam Rmay. Tuyen Duc Pr, II Corps.
Young, LZ (BT 188-157)
A.k.a. FSB Phuoc Tien? Apx 12 km SE Tam Ky, 8 km ENE Phuoc An/Tien Phuoc and 36 km WNW Chu Lai. Heliport also here. Per Tommy Poppell, was on road to Phuoc Tien and apx 2 km to its SE. Les Hines tells us this was "a very bad place" due to enemy activity in '68 (NVA Div HQ was apparently nearby). 1st/46th Inf here. Also listed at BT 188-168, 182-146 and 189-159. Map is L-7014-6640-2. Apr70 XXIV Corps grid per Don Armstrong. Quang Tin Pr, I Corps. [584]
Young American, SS (n/a)
Commercial transport under govt contract, per Ralph Fries.
Young Heliport (BT 188-157)
See LZ Young at grid. Quang Tin Pr, I Corps.
Young Turks, The (n/a)
See Glossary.
Ypsilanti BEQ (XS 8-9)
At 33 Phu Tho Hoa St., Saigon. US enlisted military billet prior to '68. Data per *Vietnam Military Lore, 1959-1973*. Gia Dinh Pr, III Corps.
YRBM-16 (n/a)
Brown Water Navy "Yard, Repair, Berthing and Messing" facility. 1st sited at Tan Chau near Cambodia. Used as Barracks Barge (non self-propelled) and MRF base ship suptg 9th Div and other units. In '67 moved to Can Tho on Bassac River, where it suptd building of Binh Thuy PBR Base. It then moved to Ben Tre on Ham Luong River and it was here on 26Nov67, that VC frogmen planted a mine that killed 8 USN personnel and caused severe damage. *YRBM 16* was then towed to Dong Tam for a temporary patch, then towed to Japan for a refit (was almost lost in heavy seas during trip). Returned to Chau Doc, Fall of '69 and left in '70. See also *YRBM 16* Bombing. IV Corps.
***YRBM-16* Bombing** (XS 5-3)
8 US servicemen were KIA when mine exploded against hull of *YRBM-16* at 0115 hrs, Thanksgiving Day, 26Nov67, while it was moored in the Ham Luong River at Ben Tre (Truc Giang). VC swimmer planted mine near bulkhead separating PBR Crew Quarters and Diesel Tank. Damage well-illustrated in photos at: http://hawley.interspeed.net/vietnam/YRBM16c.htm. Fire/flooding damaged much of interior. [585] See *YRBM-21*. Kien Hoa Pr, IV Corps.
YRBM-17 (n/a)
USN Repair, Berthing, and Messing Barge (non-self-propelled). MRF base ship. IV Corps.
YRBM-20 (n/a)
A.k.a. The Delta Hilton. Brown Water Navy base, '69-70, on Bassac River (tributary of Mekong) S of Chau Duc, near Cambodia. River Dets assigned to this craft patrolled French-built border canals nearby. One canal ran between Bassac River and Tinh Bien, another ran to Mekong River. Had sizable Freezer and Refrigeration capacity and was often referred to as "best dining spot in Chau Doc Province." 19Jul70 its pusher barge caught fire. The barge was carrying 13,000 gal gasoline, 100 drums Oil, some 15,000 2.75" rockets and several cases of grenades (used to deter underwater attacks). Refueling of a night watch boat went awry so barge was cut loose and floated away sporting 20' high flames. 200' from YRBM-20, the grenades exploded, creating spectacular, red mushroom-shaped cloud. 3 men were injured trying to quell blaze after barge beached itself. Photos/data at: http://hawley.interspeed. net/vietnam/ YRBM_20.htm. [586]
YRBM-21 (n/a)
Brown Water Navy "Yard, Repair, Berthing and Messing" facility. At 0730 hrs, 9May70, ten days after ground forces invaded Cambodia, a SEALORDS force, inc a combined Vietnamese-American naval TF, steamed up the Mekong into Cambodia as well. The flotilla was in Cmd of a VNN officer and included US PCFs, ASPBs, PBRs, HAL-3 and VAL-4 acft, *USS Benewah*, *Askari*, *Hunterdon County*, *YRBM 16*, *YRBM 21* and 10 strike assault boats (STAB) of Strike Assault Boat Sqdn 20 (a fast-reaction unit created by Admiral Zumwalt in '69).
YTB- 84, USS (n/a)
Harbor Tug for MRF base ships. IV Corps.
YTB- 85, USS (n/a)
Harbor Tug for MRF base ships. IV Corps.
YTB-762 (n/a)
USN, Large Harbor Tug Boat. SVN
YTB-779 (n/a)
USN, Large Harbor Tug Boat. SVN
YTB-784, USS (n/a)
See Tugboat YTB-784. III, IV Corps.
YTB-785, USS (n/a)
See Tugboat YTB-785. III, IV Corps.

Yuk Ngiang Mountains (ZU 0-6)
See Yok Ngiang. Mtns. Quang Duc Pr, II Corps.
Yuma, FSB (AT 934-663)
Near NE tip of Charlie Ridge, apx 2 km W Rte 540, 13 km SW Da Nang AB and 24 km ENE Ha Tan AF. '70 XXIV Corps grid per D. Armstrong. Quang Nam Pr, I Corps.
Yung Tuia Airfield (TJ 44-21)
LS-217. CIA/SF, per *Air Facilities Data-Laos.*
Yvonne, LZ (AR 896-116)
A.k.a. or adj to Weigt-Davis Engr Camp/Quarry. Apx 13 km NNE Phu Nhon AF, 38 km SSE Pleiku and 10 km SE My Thach. 10th Cav, 4th Div here, per Bob Patsfield. May69. Pleiku Pr, II Corps.

ZEBRA

Facility/Feature Name, Grid Coordinate, a.k.a. Name/History/Province/CTZ

Unless otherwise stated, 6-digit grid coordinates reference DMA L-7014, L-7015 or L-7016 series, 1:50,000 scale maps, while 2- and 4-digit coordinates reference AMS/DMA/NIMA 1:250,000, 1:500,000 and 1:1,000,000 scale maps. Unless otherwise stated, all heights are in meters. To convert meters to feet, multiply by 3.2808; feet to meters, multiply by .3048.

Z, LZ (BR 500-968)
Apx 3 km NW Nuoc Trinh and 2 km W the Dak Kron Bung (Suio Kon) River. 17Mar66. Binh Dinh Pr, II Corps.
Zaeger, LZ (BS 883-068)
See Zager. Binh Dinh Pr, II Corps.
Zager, LZ (BS 883-068) Also spelled Zaeger. Apparently a.k.a. or near LZ North English (BS 883-056) and described as being E of LZ Tom. Was in the An Lao River Valley, and on hilltop near Bong Son coast just N of LZ English. C Bty, 4th/42d Arty here Dec69. 4th Div 31Jan70 ORLL grid per Jim Henderson. See also LZ North English. Binh Dinh Pr, II Corps. [587]
Zama, Camp (n/a)
In Japan. Home of the 249th Gen Hosp and US Army Hospital, Camp Zama. These hospital facilities were major component of US Army's treatment program for the more serious of its VN War casualties. Patients were routinely transferred here from the Evac hospitals of VN, and treated here until it was felt they were stable enough to endure the rigors of the final leg of their long journey home. [588]
Zebra, LZ (BR 626-635)
In Vinh Thanh Valley, just S Dinh Binh and apx 3 km N Vinh Thanh AF, 7 km NNW Vinh Thanh and 23 km NNE An Khe. Oct66. Binh Dinh Pr, II Corps.
Zebra, LZ (XD 807-671)
Along S edge DMZ, apx 26 km NNE Khe Sanh CB and 44 km WNW Dong Ha. Apr70 XXIV Corps grid per Don Armstrong. Quang Tri Pr, I Corps.
Zeon Basecamp (XT 95-05)
Misspelling of Di An (1st Div's main basecamp), due to Viet pronunciation of Di An (sounds like "Zee-On"). No facility with this spelling is known to have existed. See Di An entries. Bien Hoa Pr, III Corps.
Zeus, FSB (YT 142-373)
Apx 22 km ESE Phuoc Vinh, 29 km NNE Bien Hoa AB and 5 km NE FSB Mars. Opened or reopened 6Aug70, closed 7Sep70 by 1st/12th Cav, per *1st Cav Div Op Rpt, ending 31Oct70*, per Peter Cole. Bien Hoa Pr, III Corps.
Zewert, FSB/LZ (AN 793-136)
Apx 44 km due W Song Mao AF, 16 km NW Ap An Lam, 12 km SWW Ap Gia Bac. Built during Op Double Eagle IV, between 7 and 25Jan69, by 3d/506th Inf. Named to honor CSF/LRRP, Sp4 Edward J. Zewert, Jr, KIA 26Apr68. On 10Oct69, A Co reopened Zewert, while B, C and D Cos, plus Recon elements assaulted nearby. Name/grid per Jerry Berry; data per *Currahee History, 1Feb69-31Dec69*, p 26 and 46. Just inside Binh Thuan Pr border, II Corps.
Ziggie, FSB (YS 613-811)
Apx 32 km NE Nui Dat, 1.5 km NE FSB Raglan, 300 meters S FSB Pat and 5 km SSW FSB Tasman. On 1ATF NCO trng map per John Hollett. Phuoc Tuy Pr, III Corps.
Zindermeuf, FSB (XS 71-79)
See Zinderneuf. III Corps.
Zinderneuf, FSB (XS 712-795)
Apx 2 km W Binh Chanh, 8 km ENE Ben Luc and 9 km SW the SW corner of Saigon. 2d/3d Inf, 3d/7th Inf, 4th/12th Inf, 199th LIB. Origin of name unknown (no KIA by this name). Also spelled Zindermeuf. Grid per 199th LIB Assn. Feb68. Long An/Gia Dinh Pr border, III Corps.
Zinn, Camp (XT 988-129)
At Bien Hoa AB. 1st basecamp of 173d Abn in VN. Named to honor Capt. Ronald, L. Zinn, 1st West Point grad to participate in Olympics (see Zinn, Ronald, in Glossary). Was also apparently home to some 1st Bde/101st Abn units. Bien Hoa Pr, III Corps.
Zinn, Ronald, Capt. (XT 988-129)
See Glossary.

Zion, FSB (YD)
Possible variant of Zon (YD 472-011)? Said to have been in or near the A Shau Valley. Per John Barmann, was opened in '69 as short-term arty-raid FSB of 321st Arty. Was meant to only exist for a few hours; however, weather closed in and "cannons became buried in mud along with everything else" such that raiding team could not be extracted for 3 days. Four 105mms were dropped into hot LZ at its birth, and all involved in that initial assault were awarded the Air Medal by Gen Abrams as a result. Thua Thien Pr, I Corps.

Zircon, LZ (YD 306-310)
Apx 17 km SE Ba Long AF and 22 km S to SSW Quang Tri. Apr70 XXIV Corps grid per Don Armstrong. Thua Thien Pr, I Corps.

Zodiac, LZ (XD 781-656)
Apx 1 km S of DMZ, 24 km NNW Khe Sanh and 46 km WNW Dong Ha. Apr70 XXIV Corps grid per Don Armstrong. Quang Tri Pr, I Corps.

Zon, FSB (YD 472-011)
Often spelled FSB "Son" or "Sun" in error. Apx 33 km SW Hue, 8 km WSW FSB Veghel, 5 km due E FSB Berchtesgarden, 16 km due N A Sap and 7 km from E edge of A Shau Valley. 1st/502d Inf, 101st Abn here '68-69. Also listed at YD 622-095 in error (grid is for FSB Bastogne). See also FSB Zion. Thua Thien Pr, I Corps.

Zone A (YD 91-16)
In '65, this was name assigned to area immed N and E the Phu Bai AF perimeter. The USMC (3d/4th Marines, 3d Mar Div) guarding base were restrained from patrolling or from firing and arty missions into this zone. Apparently the ARVN imposed the restrictions, claiming the area was pacified and under control; however, the Marines defending the base angrily recall the VC using the zone to regularly mortar and attack them. Thua Thien Pr, I Corps.

Zoo, The (WJ?)
Inmates' derisive nickname for a POW camp somewhere near Hanoi. Cited in *Bloods*, p 134. NVN.

Zoo POW Camp, The (WJ?)
See Zoo, The. NVN.

Zulu, LZ ? (BR 802-290)
Apx 28 km WNW Qui Nhon, 18 km SSW Phu Cat AB and 6 km NNW An Truong. Nov65. Binh Dinh Pr, II Corps.

Zulu, LZ (XS 536-892)
Apx 22 km E Katum AF, 5 km W Fishhook's tip and 22 km W An Loc. Mar66. Long An Pr, III Corps.

Zulu, LZ (YD 526-136)
Apx 18 km due S Hue, 10 km SSE FSB Birmingham and 22 km SW Phu Bai. XXIV Corps, 101st Abn inactive FSB list, per Don Armstrong. Thua Thien Pr, I Corps.

Zulu Time (n/a)
See Glossary.

Endnotes for Alphabetical Listings

---

[1] Vietnam Studies, *Airmobility 1961-1971*, Tolson, Lt. Gen John J, Dept of Army, 1973, p 195
[2] From article entitled *LZ 10-ALFA*, 35th Inf Div website at: www.cacti68.com/35thinf/_disc4/0000000c.htm
[3] Marshall, S.L.A., *Battles In the Monsoon*, William Morrow and Company, NY, 1967, pp 267-268.
[4] Unusual list of ARVN Officers KIA at this base is on net at: www.viet.org/e-kia.htm
[5] Vietnam Studies, *Airmobility 1961-1971*, Tolson, Lt. Gen John J, Dept of Army, 1973, p 195
[6] Schild, LTC James, *For Garry Owen in Glory*, Auto Review Publishing, Florrisant MO, 1989, p. 43.
[7] Strukey, Marion, *Bonnie-Sue: A Marine Corps Helicopter Squadron in Vietnam*, pp 18-24
[8] Great photo of full length of the A Shau on internet at: www.ameritech.net/users/cnurse/stories.htm#currahee
[9] For a concise but comprehensive look at history of A Shau ops, see introduction to Keith William Nolan's *RIPCORD*.
[10] FSB Aachen discussed on internet at: www2.okstate.edu/wcross/artillery.htm
[11] FSB Aachen discussed on internet at: www2.okstate.edu/wcross/artillery.htm
[12] Data courtesy Ann Kelsey, Special Services employee at Cam Ranh and Dong Ba Thin.
[13] Per website www.rjsmith.com/lz_action.html"
[14] Bows, Ray, *Vietnam Military Lore, 1959-1973*, p 112
[15] Prados/Stubbe, *Valley of Decision*, Houghton-Mifflin, NY, pp 20-21
[16] Per USN Historical Center data at www.history.navy.mil/seairland/
[17] Prados/Stubbe, *Valley of Decision*, pp 13-15
[18] Newman, Lt. D.S., *Vietnam Gunners, 161 Bty RNZA, South Vietnam, 1965-71*. Wellington, New Zealand, Moana Press, 1988, p 107
[19] Bows, Ray, *Vietnam Military Lore, 1959-1973*, pp 237-38
[20] An 800-page documentation for 11th ACR's Cambodian Incursion PUC, May-Jun70.
[21] The Goolden tiger incident is discussed, and a 1:50,000 scale map showing location of FSB Alpine is online at www.3rdrecon.org/Snakey.htm
[22] Per USN Historical Center data at www.history.navy.mil/branches/ordbat.htm
[23] Data per 10Jul71 AAR of Lam Son 487 and 720 (U), MACMR-11D-54R, MACJ3-32, courtesy Cliff Snyder, NARA.
[24] 1:50,000 scale map (DMA's 'An Tuc' sheet, stock # TL-7014-6736-4) of An Khe/Camp Radcliff area on 1st/69th Armor website at: www.rjsmith.com/camp_radcliff_0.html
[25] Data per undated "*A History of the 64th Quartermaster Company (Petroleum Operations),* 1Jan68-1Dec68, compiled by Capt. Robert Stockfelth and 1Lt Eridc Dohogne, 240th QM Bn (Petrol Ops), US Army Support Command, Qui Nhon. Document courtesy Conrad G. Creitz, 647th QM Co, 68-69.
[26] According to a 4th Div list, this valley is located generally from BR 685-430 N to BR 62-64; however, that grid range appears to be in error as it defines the Vinh Thanh River Valley or Happy Valley? 4th Div grid per official 4th ID list perJim Claeys.
[27] Detailed discussion of Operation Masher/White Wing can be found in *A Contagion of War* vol, *Vietnam Experience* series, pp 32-48. Good map of operation at p 38.
[28] Data per *Father Soldier Son*, p 164.
[29] A very unusual first-person account entitled *The Battle for An Loc* and written by Mark A. Smith (a.k.a. Capt. Zippo) who describes himself as ground cmdr for much of the fight, at http://lzsally.com/zippo.html
[30] According to Youmans, in Nov or Dec68, over 30 prisoners dug a 6' deep, 150 yard-long escape tunnel using soup spoons. Entrance was under a bed pallet and dirt from the excavaction was scattered daily during prisoners' soccer and volleyball games (ala the movie *Great Escape*). Youmans was told later that an NVA officer POW had seen the movie while at college in US and simply adopted the techniques used by US troops at Stalag 17 during WWII.
[31] Per USN Historical Center data at www.history.navy.mil/seairland
[32] Per www.thehistorynet.com/Vietnam/articles/1096_text.htm
[33] An 800-page documentation for 11th ACR's Cambodian Incursion PUC, May-Jun70.
[34] Grauwin, Paul, *Doctor at Dien Bien Phu*, Stratford Press, 1955, p19
[35] Sheehan, Neil, *A Bright Shining Lie*, p262
[36] Data per AAReport, *Battle of Tay Ninh* (17Aug-27Sep68), HQ 25th ID, 2Feb69, p 28
[37] Data per AAReport, *Battle of Tay Ninh* (17Aug-27Sep68), HQ 25th ID, 2Feb69, p 28
[38] Bows, Ray, *Vietnam Military Lore, 1959-1973*, pp 118-20
[39] Excellent map of Artillery Hill and Pleiku can be found in Ray Bows' *Vietnam Military Lore, 1959-1973*, pp 624
[40] Data per Feb70-Apr70, 8th Eng Bn, 1st Cav, Ops Rpt, p 31, courtesy Peter Cole.
[41] Data per Feb70-Apr70, 1st Cav. Quart. Rpt, 2d Bde Os, p 12, courtesy Peter Cole.
[42] Grid, and opening closing data per 1st Cav Operational Rpt, ending 31Oct70, courtesy Peter Cole.
[43] *USMC In Vietnam, 1966*, p 23
[44] *The Rise & Fall of the American Army,* p 228
[45] Per *A Better War*, p 376.
[46] An 800-page documentation for 11th ACR's Cambodian Incursion PUC, May-Jun70.
[47] Post-war data per per www.nvr.navy.mil/nvrships/details/SS580.htm.
[48] Sortie/tonnage data per *The War In The Shadows*, Boston Pub Co's *Vietnam Experience* series, p141
[49] Sortie/tonnage data per *The War In The Shadows*, Boston Pub Co's *Vietnam Experience* series, p141
[50] Sortie/tonnage data per *The War In The Shadows*, Boston Pub Co's *Vietnam Experience* series, p141
[51] Sortie/tonnage data per *The War In The Shadows*, Boston Pub Co's *Vietnam Experience* series, p141
[52] Sortie/tonnage data per *The War In The Shadows*, Boston Pub Co's *Vietnam Experience* series, p141
[53] Sortie/tonnage data per *The War In The Shadows*, Boston Pub Co's *Vietnam Experience* series, p141
[54] Mentioned repeatedly in 4th Div After Action Report/News Release dated 23Mar69, and on internet a: "http://grunt.space.swri.edu/aarrpt1.htm.
[55] Dukes, a writer with the *China Times* (Beijing) was with the unit that opened Bastogne. "I was attached to Co. C, 2/502 as an FO when we flew in with the 1st helicopter lift to what became Bastogne shortly after 26Mar68. That day, Cpl Craig Averill, a close friend, died in firefight west of Nam Hoa with Co. B, 2/502. I was on mortar base at that time and fired supt for the Co at max rang/load using 81mms. When we arrived at

Bastogne, there were no emplacements or foxholes of any kin. We secured the hill and 105s were brought in at top. Later, 155s were placed below the crest. Within a month, they were joined by 8" and 175's, while I was on a road clearing op where we got nailed about three km E the FSB. I have Polaroids of the tracked howitzers rolling by.

[56] By early May72, during Easter offensive, FSB's Bastogne and Checkmate along Hwy 547 had fallen after what Gen Abrams considered an admirably stubborn defense by ARVN.

[57] It is the author's understanding that Pierre Schoendoerffer's remarkable black & white documentary *The Anderson Platoon* ('67) features some footage of the 1st Cav's fighting on Batangan (or possibly in nearby Bong Son area). Notable about the terrain in film was the presence of cacti, which were otherwise uncommon in SVN, we believe.

[58] The names of these 7 Mechant Marines do not appear on National Vietnam Veterans Memorial because they were civilians, not military employees of the Dept of Defense.

[59] Data per http://academic.uofs.edu/faculty/ gramborw/atav/5tc.htm, and http://lists.village.virginia.edu/sixties/HTML_docs/Texts/Narrative/Flynn_Street_Joy.html

[60] Grauwin, Paul, *Doctor at Dien Bien Phu*, p19

[61] Per *LRRP Company Commander*, p 231, in 69 was hit by major 2-day NVA assault that lasted 2 nights and 1 day and resulted in "dozens of US dead, scores of US wounded and hundreds of NVA dead."

[62] Data per AAReport, *Battle of Tay Ninh* (17Aug-27Sep68), HQ 25th ID, 2Feb69, p 24

[63] Data per AAReport, *Battle of Tay Ninh* (17Aug-27Sep68), HQ 25th ID, 2Feb69, various pages

[64] Per USN Historical Center data at www.history.navy.mil/branches/ordbat.htm

[65] White, HCSM Joe, *The Vietnamization of WHEC-382*, Military Magazine, Dec 98, pp 24-25

[66] An 800-page documentation for 11th ACR's Cambodian Incursion PUC, May-Jun70.

[67] An 800-page documentation for 11th ACR's Cambodian Incursion PUC, May-Jun70.

[68] According to Delmar S. Hilliar, "We did it to ourselves. The B-57s were parked tip to tip and armed with 500 lb bombs. A black powder cartridge used to start the engines spun a small starter turbine which had a nasty habit of spinning loose and coming out its housing like a buzz saw. In this case it came out and hit the fuse of a bomb. I think we lost 24 B-57s abd their crews 24 VNAF A-1s destroyed and some damaged; several VNAF KIA and US ground crew KIA; and some US A-1s also damaged. One USN jet fighter was destroyed. The pilot was USAF Maj. Bell on an exchange tour with the USN. He had a hung bomb and they would not let him back on carrier with it. He was standing on wing of his plane at time. Ee found was his name tag, and it took 3 days to ID him. Col 'Wild Bill' Beatha (Cmdr, 34 Tac Ftr Gp) said he was in cmd of the worst US military disaster since Pearl Harbor."

[69] Wade, Leigh, *Tan Phu: Special Forces Team A-23 in Combat*, p 49

[70] Data per Annual Hist. Report, HQ 3rd/34th Arty, dated 14April69, for 1Apr68 to 31Jan69, at: www.mrfa.org3_34th.htm

[71] Location and Hill# per Plans Summary, 1st/327th Inf, dated 17May71, courtesy Cliff Snyder, NARA.

[72] Per *Fast Rifles* CAP website at: www.capmarine.com/gazette/fastrfls.htm

[73] Detailed discussion of Ops Masher/White Wing and this LZ in *A Contagion of War* vol, *Vietnam Experience* series, pp 32-48, with map showing this site at p 38.

[74] Map is part of four map series entitled *MR Major Road Net & AFs*, that is available at Library of Congress Geography and Map Div. Call number is G8021.P2 svar.U51 (#3 0f 4).

[75] Per USN Historical Center data at www.history.navy.mil/branches/ordbat.htm

[76] Newman, Lt. D.S., *Vietnam Gunners, 161 Bty RNZA, South Vietnam, 1965-71*, p 103

[77] Per 10Dec67, Combat Ops After Action Report, *Battle of Dak To*, 29th Hist Det, 4th Div, courtesy 173d Abn Assn.

[78] An 800-page documentation for 11th ACR's Cambodian Incursion PUC, May-Jun70.

[79] Per 10Dec67, Combat Ops After Action Report, *Battle of Dak To*, 29th Hist Det, 4th Div, courtesy 173d Abn Assn.

[80] Per 10Dec67, Combat Ops After Action Report, *Battle of Dak To*, 29th Hist Det, 4th Div, courtesy 173d Abn Assn.

[81] An 800-page documentation for 11th ACR's Cambodian Incursion PUC, May-Jun70.

[82] An 800-page documentation for 11th ACR's Cambodian Incursion PUC, May-Jun70.

[83] Data per US Army History of SF in vietnam online at www.army.mil/cmh-pg/books/vietnam/90-23/90-23ad.htm

[84] Newman, Lt. D.S., *Vietnam Gunners, 161 Bty RNZA, South Vietnam, 1965-71*, p 90

[85] Per '*The Battle of Bunker Hill 10*,' www.afa.org/magazine/valor/0185valor.html

[86] An 800-page documentation for 11th ACR's Cambodian Incursion PUC, May-Jun70.

[87] Prados/Stubbe, *Valley of Decision*, p 272

[88] When CAC Oscar withdrew to Khe Sanh CB after the intial attacks against their vulnerable positions outside the base in late '67/early '68, the Marines did not want to accept O-2's Bru, so CAC Oscar asked for and received a spot in defese perimeter of the SF's FOB-3, outside the main defensive wires along Khe Sanh CB's southern edge and QL-9. While many Vietnam vets hold the South Vietnamese military in low regard, Jim Taylor, a CAP Oscar vet, offered this view of his indigenous counter parts: "Oscar was the only company (to my knowledge) that worked with the Bru (a Montangard tribe). These ethnic Mon Khmers were NOT Vietnamese, but rather earlier ethnis aborigines displaced by south Chinese invaders...They are linguistically and ethnically related to Laos, Cambodes and Thai, especially the Hmong Tribe. They were cheerful, courageous (without being stupid) and honest. A pleasure to work with!-Oscar 2 worked with Bru tribesman from the villages of Vil Bu, Vil Ch'eng, Vil Tacun and Vil C'on"

[89] Specific data found on CAP Website at www.capmarine.com/2dcag/command/68chron.htm

[90] Morgan, LTC Thomas L., *Rendezvous in Vietnam*, Mar 98, ARMY Magazine, pp 34-38

[91] Excellent map of the facilities at Cam Ranh Bay can be found in Ray Bows' *Vietnam Military Lore, 1959-1973*, pp 620, 621

[92] For a very detailed and remarkable look at history of Cam Ranh Bay compiled by Tom Beauvais, and Andrew Hartsook (518th Personnel Serv Co/USA Supt CMd, '72), go to www.petester.com/html/CRB_historical_notes.html

[93] Morgan, LTC thomas, *Rendezvous inVietnam*, Army Magazine, Mar98, p 37

[94] Detailed maps of various seaports at: http://academic.uofs.edu/faculty/gramborw/atav/maps.htm

[95] Per Fall, Bernard, *Street Without Joy*, Stackpole Co, Harrisburg PA, 67, pp 144-173. Op got its name from the area's similarity with the swampy coastal plani of France, W Marseilles.

[96] An 800-page documentation for 11th ACR's Cambodian Incursion PUC, May-Jun70.

[97] Roberts, Craig, *Combat Medic-Vietnam*, Pocket Books-Simon & Schuster, NY, 1991, p 132
[98] Detailed maps of various seaports at: http://academic.uofs.edu/faculty/gramborw/atav/maps.htm
[99] Craig, William, *Team Sergeant*, Ivy Books, NY, 1998, p 2-3
[100] Data per Feb70-Apr70, 8th Eng Bn, 1st Cav, Ops Rpt, p 31, courtesy Peter Cole.
[101] Data pcr Fcb70-Apr70, 1st Cav. Quart. Rpt, 2d Bde Os, p 12, courtesy Peter Cole.
[102] Cited in: 1st Cav. Operational reports for Feb-Apr70, at p 12, and in May-Jul70 report at p 38, according to Peter Cole.
[103] Per documents at www.capmarine.com/cap2-7-1/death.htm
[104] Specific data found on CAP Website at www.capmarine.com/2dcag/command/68chron.htm
[105] Per e-mail correspondence with George "Cordman' Clancy dated 14Mar98
[106] While many Vietnam vets hold the South Vietnamese military in low regard, Taylor offered this view of his indigenous counter parts: "Oscar was the only company (to my knowledge) that worked with the Bru (a Montangard tribe). These ethnic Mon Khmers were NOT Vietnamese, but rather earlier ethnic aborigines displaced by south Chinese invaders...They are linguistically and ethnically related to Laos, Cambodes and Thai, especially the Hmong Tribe. They were cheerful, courageous (without being stupid) and honest; a pleasure to work with! Oscar worked with Bru tribesman from the villages of Vil Bu, Vil Ch'eng, Vil Tacun and Vil C'on" When CAC Oscar withdrew to Khe Sanh CB after the intial attacks against their positions outside Khe Sanh CB during Tet '68, the Marines did not want to accept O-2's Bru comrades, so CAC Oscar asked for and received a spot in defense perimeter of the SF's FOB-3, outside the main defensive wires along Khe Sanh CB's southern edge and QL-9.
[107] An 800-page documentation for 11th ACR's Cambodian Incursion PUC, May-Jun70.
[108] An 800-page documentation for 11th ACR's Cambodian Incursion PUC, May-Jun70.
[109] Per *LRRP Company Commander*, p 162, NVA 95C Rgt hit the 2d/8th Cav, 1st/30th and 2d/19th (?) in May69 (on day after MGen E.B. Roberts became Div CG), overrunning a portion of perimeter. Per same book, p 62, FSBs Carolyn Eleanor and Grant were intentionally built on enemy infiltration corridors, with FSBs Billy, Buttons, Dot, Ike, Jamie and Mud firing in supt of them.
[110] The initial four tubes of 175mm moved to Carroll and manned by Army's 6th/27th Arty marked the 1st introduction of a major Army unit into I Corps, which had previously been almost exclusively a Marine AO. Rer Prados/Stubbe, *Valley of Decision,* p50
[111] Bows, Ray, *Vietnam Military Lore, 1959-1973*, p 228-29
[112] For detailed information regarding Army Transportation Command seaports, bases and units, visit their website at: http://academic.uofs.edu/faculty/gramborw/atav/
[113] For detailed information regarding Army Transportation Command seaports, bases and units, visit their website at: http://academic.uofs.edu/faculty/gramborw/atav/
[114] Cited in 1st Cav VN *Yearbook* Aug 65 to Dec69. at p 292, per Peter Cole.
[115] An 800-page documentation for 11th ACR's Cambodian Incursion Presidential Unit Citation (PUC), May-Jun70.
[116] *Facing the Phoenix*, p 66
[117] *Facing the Phoenix*, p 66
[118] Vetter, Larry, *Never Without Heroes*, Ivy Books, NY, 1996, p 36
[119] Per *Time Heals No Wounds*, pp 91, 101, and referenced to 2d/9th Arty, 4th Div ORLL for "Operation Binh Tay-MacArthur, period ending 1Jan69On 19Jan69),
[120] Excellent map of the facilities at Cholon/Saigon can be found in Ray Bows' *Vietnam Military Lore, 1959-1973*, pp 626-7
[121] Americal was only 'named' Div in US Army until '69, when redesignated as 23d Inf Div. Was given Americal name during WWII by Gen Doug MacArthur who combined words 'American' with 'New Caledonia.'
[122] An 800-page documentation for 11th ACR's Cambodian Incursion PUC, May-Jun70.
[123] For detailed information regarding Army Transportation Command seaports, bases and units, visit their website at: http://academic.uofs.edu/faculty/gramborw/atav/
[124] BT related the existence of this location to author in conversation not long before Brien's death in 1993. S.L.A. Marshall misspelled Brien's name as 'Bryant,' in his epic *Battles in the Monsoon*, where BT is mentioned at pp 82, 84 and 91.
[125] Unknown whether Ordway or Colt was 1st name of base; however, while Ordway, it likely named to honor of 2d Lt William D. Ordway, USA, KIA 18Jan68.
[126] An 800-page documentation for 11th ACR's Cambodian Incursion PUC, May-Jun70.
[127] Per USN Historical Center data at www.history.navy.mil/branches/ordbat.htm
[128128] Percival's nickname has roots in his unpredictable behaviour. For example, he is said to have had a coffin filled with Chinese tea in his cabin and, during diplomatic meetings there, apparently had the rather distracting habit of speaking to coffin as though it were a person! Per *The Vietnam Guidebook*, pp 50-51.
[129] The following was paraphrased from article by Peter J. Kneisel posted at: www.state.ma.us/veterans/ancientmariner.htm:
Landsman William Cooke (or Cook) was a ship's musician aboard *USS Constitution* and played in her 22-piece band. He entered the Navy near Baltimore and joined the crew of *Constitution* in Norfolk, VA. He died of dysentery while at sea on May 11, 1845, apparently as *Constitution* entered Da Nang Bay. USN archives tell us where Cook was buried, but not what instrument he played. Crew journals from the era include sketches of Monkey Mtn and water color paintings of a pagoda where Cooke was buried. They also tell us his burial cost two US dollars. Just 2 days after Cooke's burial at the foot of what we call Monkey Mtn, Capt 'Mad Jack' Percival, took the 53-years old *Constitution* into battle in response to word a French missionary was under sentence of death at Hue. Percival apparently fired his cannons into the city (killing and wounding and unknown number of civilians) in what was the 1st ever US shelling of Vietnam. He is also said to have held for a prisoner exchange local officials aboard ship when the trouble started, captured some junks, fired on the city, and otherwise behaved badly for a sailor on a 'Good Will' tour. 16 (or 23?) days after its arrival and with its rescue mission a failure, *Constituion* pulled anchor and fired a departing salvo at, but missing, the harbor's fortifications. Upon reaching Boston, the USN gave Percival an official reprimand but apparently left him in cmd? In a letter delivered 4 years later, President Zachary Taylor apologized to the Emperor for Percival's behavior, adding, "...may no more blood be spilled between our two peoples." In 1858, the French are said to have demolished both the Pagoda and fort. Records indicate the graveyard itself was sparred, and is located in a small cove beneath what had been the ramparts of the Viet fort. It was also here that *Constitution* is said to have renewed her fresh water stores. According to the MA Dept of Vets Affairs, the 'People's Committee of the City of Da Nang' has agreed to help create a memorial to Cooke in the cove.
[130] See *The Vietnam Guidebook*, pp 50-52.

[131] According to John Eastman (D/1/502d Inf, 69-70), "The *Constitution* anchored in Da Nang Bay and sent a company of US Marines ashore, who then moved overland to Hue. Their mission was to free a French Bishop who had been imprisoned by Vietnamese; America's apparent first VN combat involvement. 120 years later two Bns of US Marines returned to same port. In 1847, French vessels apparently also bombarded Da Nang." John adds, "An ancestor of mine, John Glover, was a First Mate on *Constitution*, we think. During the Revolutionary War, he leased the *Hannah* to US as first ship of the Continental Navy. In the film '*Crossing*', it startled me to see how much Glover and his men were involved in Battle of Trenton (acting as first Marines)."
[132] Per USN Historical Center data at www.history.navy.mil/seairland/
[133] Per USN Historical Center data at www.history.navy.mil/branches/ordbat.htm
[134] Per USN Historical Center data at www.history.navy.mil/seairland/
[135] The *USS Albemerle* later became the *Corpus Christi*: On 7Aug64, Albemerle was transferred for conversion to floating helo maintenance facility. On 27Mar65, renamed and reclassified as *Corpus Christi Bay* (T-ARVH-1), and transferred MSC 11Jan66. Was converted at Charleston Naval Shipyard, and emerged only faintly resembling her former self. "Gone was prominent seaplane ramp aft, replaced by built-up superstructure, topped by a helo pad measuring 50' by 150'." Helos previously sent back to US for repair, were now repaired in CZ, after being barged out and put aboard by two 20-ton capacity cranes. Crew of 129 was fraction of ship's original complement. Accompanying ship on 1st deployment to VN was Army's 1st Trans Corps Bn (Seaborne), inc 308 aircraft techs. Operated primarily out of Cam Ranh Bay during 66. Data per http://www.hazegray.org/danfs/auxil/av5.htm.
[136] An 800-page documentation for 11th ACR's Cambodian Incursion PUC, May-Jun70.
[137] Memories of 1ATF RAR veteran Eddie Tricker at: "http://users.mildura.net.au/users/marshall/tales/tales.htm
[138] Smith, Robert B, *To The Last Cartridge*, Avon Books paperback, NY, 1994, pp 313-314
[139] Prados/Stubbe, *Valley of Decision*, pp 20-21
[140] This action described in detail in M. Sturkey's *Bonnie-Sue: A Marine Corps Helicopter Squadron in Vietnam.*
[141] K-Tel Records produced an audio cassette entiled *Rock Radio Vietnam-1970*, on which can be found and ad for Cu Chi U, among other surprises. It may be still available from K-Tel.
[142] Story about Currahee and marvellous photo of the A Shau Valley at: www.ameritech.net/users/cnurse/stories.htm#currahee. See 101st Abn HQ ORLL for period ending 31Jul69, dated 9Dec69 online at: http://carlisle-www.army.mil/usamhi/DL/chron.htm#AVietnamWar19601973.
[143] According to John Eastman: "The Constitution anchored in Da Nang Bay and sent a company of US Marines ashore, who then moved overland to Hue. Their mission was to free a French Bishop who had been imprisoned by Vietnamese; America's apparent first VN combat involvement. 120 years later two Bns of US Marines returned to same port. In 1847, French vessels apparently also bombarded Da Nang."
[144] According to Ray Bows, a musician named Cooke died during *USS* Constitution's journey to Tourane, and was buried at foot of Monkey Mtn on Tien Sha Peninsula. Apparently in part due to Bows' efforts, the Vietnamese now care for grave.
[145] Touron mentioned as name in *River Road to China, The Search for the Source of the Mekong, 1866-73*, by Milton Osborne, p 38.
[146] Excellent map of the facilities at Da Nang can be found in Ray Bows' *Vietnam Military Lore, 1959-1973*, pp 621
[147] Detailed maps of various seaports at: http://academic.uofs.edu/faculty/gramborw/atav/maps.htm
[148] Per 4th Div After Action Report/News Release dated 23Mar69, on internet a: "http://grunt.space.swri.edu/aarrpt1.htm.
[149] Fall, Bernard, *Street Without Joy*, Stackpole Co, Harrisburg PA 4th ed, May67, p 208
[150] Per 10Dec67, Combat Ops After Action Report, *Battle of Dak To*, 29th Hist Det, 4th Div, courtesy 173d Abn Assn.
[151] Per 10Dec67, Combat Ops After Action Report, *Battle of Dak To*, 29th Hist Det, 4th Div, courtesy 173d Abn Assn.
[152] Per 10Dec67, Combat Ops After Action Report, *Battle of Dak To*, 29th Hist Det, 4th Div, courtesy 173d Abn Assn.
[153] Per 4th Div After Action Report/News Release dated 23Mar69, on internet a: "http://grunt.space.swri.edu/aarrpt1.htm.
[154] Roberts, Craig, *Combat Medic-Vietnam*, p 153
[155] Translation courtesy Mark Richardson and his wife Toah (who is Banhar and from Kontum).
[156] *Vietnam Experience* series, *A Contagion of War* volume, pp 168-185
[157] Per 10Dec67 Combat Ops After Action Report, *Battle of Dak To*, 29th Hist Det, 4th Div, courtesy 173d Abn Assn, and 6Dec67 Combat Ops After Action Report, *Battle of Dak To*, HQ 173d Abn (Sep) from same source
[158] This data from and an in-depth discussion is available at '*Imagining Vietnam*,' by Robert Templer, apparently published in Richmonfd Review, and available on-line at www.demon.co.uk/review/features/temple01.html
[159] Newman, Lt. D.S., *Vietnam Gunners, 161 Bty RNZA, South Vietnam, 1965-71,* p 104
[160] Data per Annual Hist. Report, HQ 3rd/34th Arty, dated 14April69, for 1Apr68 to 31Jan69, at: www.mrfa.org3_34th.htm
[161] *Suicide Charlie*, p 123-5
[162] Attack discussed in *Army Reporter* article of 11May70, Vol 6, No. 19 as quoted on internet at: http://home.ptd.net/~trward/pagen.htm
[163] Russell, Norman L., *Suicide Charlie*, p 95
[164] Russell, Norman L., *Suicide Charlie*, p 139
[165] Russell, Norman L., *Suicide Charlie*, p 139
[166] Hunt, Christopher, *Sparring With Charlie-Motorbiking Down the Ho Chi Minh Trail*, p.215 et seq
[167] Grids and data per *All The Way-The 3d Bde, 82d Abn Div In Vietnam 1968*, p 37-41.
[168] Data per Feb70-Apr70, 1st Cav. Quart. Rpt, 2d Bde Os, p 12, courtesy Peter Cole.
[169] Also described as being apx 16 km SSE Da Nang City and formed by QL-1 on E, and Song Ky Lam and Song La Tho River S to N, S and W.
[170] Detailed discussion of Ops Masher/White Wing can be found in *A Contagion of War* vol, *Vietnam Experience* series, pp 32-48, with map showing this LZ/FSB at p 38.
[171] Grauwin, Paul, *Doctor at Dien Bien Phu*, p19
[172] Prados/Stubbe, *Valley of Decision*, pp 137-188, 444-447
[173] Smith, Robert B, *To The Last Cartridge*, 1994, pp 304-318
[174] 9th Inf Div left VN Aug69 (leaving behind its 3d Bde until Oct70), shortly after being pulled from IV Corps and shifted over to eastern III Corps. Was deactivated Aug69.
[175] Detailed maps of various seaports at: http://academic.uofs.edu/faculty/gramborw/atav/maps.htm
[176] Hunt, Christopher, *Sparring With Charlie-Motorbiking Down the Ho Chi Minh Trail*, p. 7
[177] Per Richard Weaver, at 4th Div website guestbook. The 362d Signal Company has a webpage at www.jbeck@iwaynet.net

[178] A number of interesting photos of Enari from Dragon Mtn and Dragon Mtn from Enari are on internet at www.coil.com/~rickw/
[179] The author recalls seeing some 3' and 4' long lizards along banks of the Song Ta Trach River (south branch of the Perfume River) S Nam Hoa and S FSB Arsenal. On one occasion, his squad mistook an extremely large lizard for a crocodile in what was known as Rocket Valley, several km from that river and W FSB Arsenal perhaps 4 km.
[180] Tolson, Gen John J, *Airmobility, 1961-1971*, Vietnam Studies, Dept of the Army, 1973, p 160.
[181] Per unpublished memoirs of Gen John Cushman, 2d Bde, 101st Abn CO, Dec67-Jun68.
[182] Per 101st Div HQ ORLL for period ending 31Jul69, dated 9Dec69, online at: http://carlisle-www.army.mil/usamhi/DL/chron.htm#AVietnamWar19601973
[183] Morgan, LTC thomas, *Rendezvous inVietnam*, Army Magazine, Mar98, p 37
[184] Ken Burington, C Co, 2d/5th Cav, 1st Cav, 67-68 confirmed the transition in names of the baseas follows: "The 1st Cav moved its divisional cmd post north to I Corps during period 19Jan68-31Jan68. The CP moved into LZ Tombstone, which was soon renamed LZ El Paso. When the 101st Abn took over the LZ, it was renamed Camp Eagle."
[185] According to Rich Kirchner, the 27th Combat Eng Bn was known as Tiger Bn and "We were located just inside the Gia Le gate that was the 1st entrance to Eagle (Phu Bai side). Our HQ surrounded a Russian bulldozer captured during Lam Son 719. We commandeered a tank retriever and loaded dozer on a truck (shortly after the 101st stood down-Jan. '72), for stateside shipping from Da Nang. Don't know if it ever made it to states, but we sure had fun riding around on that huge retriever! After the 101st left Eagle, a skeleton crew of Engrs was left (8 of us) with a squad of CID to erase all the names carved in hootches and to burn any paper with english on it. We also picked up all brass and destroyed anything mechanical left behind. It took 3 days. After the 27th went home, we were sent to 84th Const Bn, in Da Nang, on beach...permanent R&R! A month later, flew back to Eagle with an ARVN Col (ARVN Huey ride) after turning over the rock quarry near Langco to him and ARVN Eng. Eagle was by then totally an ARVN base. I couldn't recognize it. They had sucked the perimeter in big time, scrapped over half the hootches, and were running a ghost town. Laundry hanging everywhere, kids and mamasans everywhere. Maybe they saw the futility of sitting on a defoliated hill waiting to be overrun?
[186] Per 10Dec67, Combat Ops After Action Report, *Battle of Dak To*, 29th Hist Det, 4th Div, courtesy 173d Abn Assn.
[187] The 101st Abn *1969 Yearbook* ended its description of the beach with the overly generous and amusing assessment that, "for the men who fought in twisted jungles of Thua Thien and northern I Corps, only the best is good enough."
[188] An 800-page documentation for 11th ACR's Cambodian Incursion PUC, May-Jun70.
[189] Per USN Historical Center data at www.history.navy.mil/seairland
[190] Greg Mills, CO, D/1st/502d Inf, '68, adds this recollection: "Eagle's Nest was called 'Signal Hill' for a couple days before getting a name. After several days of aborted attempts due to clouds, we landed in Chinook with the front wheels dangling in air off the sharp peak. Then we went down the ridge a couple clicks and began clearing. The next day, someone didn't like the location, so we went down a couple more clicks and built FSB Georgia. There were NVA vehicle convoys in valley below running at night with lights on. We were out of arty range except for 175s at FSB Bastogne for first 2 days, so we hid until the site was finalized and construction began. D-1/502(Abn) was opcon 1Bde, 101 for about 30 days in Jul-Aug68.
[191] An 800-page documentation for 11th ACR's Cambodian Incursion PUC, May-Jun70.
[192] Data per Feb70-Apr70, 8th Eng Bn, 1st Cav, Ops Rpt, p 31, courtesy Peter Cole.
[193] An 800-page documentation for 11th ACR's Cambodian Incursion PUC, May-Jun70.
[194] Grauwin, Paul, *Doctor at Dien Bien Phu*, p19
[195] David Argabright tells us this amusing anecdote about Elois: "After the [2d/60th] came out of Cambodia, they apparently had to construct FSB Elois in Tay Ninh [Prov] from scratch (don't ask why we needed another FSB in Tay Ninh by mid-1970, surely the artillery fans from the existing FSB's were adequate by then. Go figure!) The 25th Inf Div airlifted in bulldozer and some Engr types to assist. Well there is a running commentary [in the unit journals] about needed bulldozer parts, missing parts, damaged parts, airlifting parts from CONUS, airlifting in new dozers, TOC to Bde messages about how many hours of operation the dozer logged each day, threats to go directly to division CG to get the dozer operational, etc., etc. This goes on in journals for almost 3 months. It must have been so very Army-like.
[196] Image and info re FSB Emory at: www.users.uswest.net/~huffpappa/
[197] "Leaving the Cu Chi Hilton, we drove past our Bn area, down one street after another until we left Cu Chi itself, and then turned east on a major highway. 15 minutes later we arrived at FSB Base Emory. Ramsey, Kirk, *Tales of a War Far Away*, illustrated on-line memoir of the 2d/14th Inf, 25th Inf at: www.en.com/users/ kramsey/default.html.
[198] A number of interesting photos of Enari from Dragon Mtn and Dragon Mtn from Enari are on internet at www.coil.com/~rickw/.
[199] Per USN Historical Center data at www.history.navy.mil/seairland.
[200] During Op End Sweep, Apr73, the MSS-2 (an old, decommissioned LST converted to temporary minesweeping duties in VN) was filled with foam and other shock absorbing materials, and several brave volunteers made 8 runs up the Haiphong channel to ensure that all the aerial mines had been cleared! Per USN Historical Center data at www.history.navy.mil/seairland.
[201] HQ for 15thEng was on Engineer Hill and for 584th Eng was at Enari. According to Frank Canaga, who served with both the 584th was preferred for personal safety/comfort even though no one was KIA (?) with the 15th. In Sep-Oct67, 12-15 men were moved from 584th to 15th. At time, those at 584th's Quarry were sleeping in tents with wood floors, had an EM club camp at Enari was well built w/cement floors, wood bldgs & good maintenance facility. 15th's cmpd at Dak To had few creature comforts left and was living in underground bunkers after it had been completely destroyed when adj Ammo dump was ignited by enemy fire. As result, Eng tape formed sidewalks, with other areas off limits due to unexploded ordnance blown from dump. Only 3 tents (mess hall, orderly rm and CO), remained. The 584th had cots, 24-hr card games and 12 hr shifts. 15th's bunkers had 6" water in bottom, troops slept on bunker tops, had guard duty every night, restricted to area 3 pm-9 am, had cans filled with hot coals in bunkers for heat, music through battery-powered children's 45 RPM record players and bathed from helmets. Men of 15th carried weapon at all times and maintained 5 meter interval in chow line. Rocket/mortar fire or infiltration were daily events. Said Frank Canaga, "We would listen to shrapnel hitting front of the bunker we thought was from our own H&I fire. We soon learned it was from NVA rockets fired from Cambodia."
[202] Per 19th Eng Bn website at: http://home.earthlink.net/~engr19/dlaugoct68.html
[203] Map showing LZ English AO is at www.nexus.net/~911gfx/vietnam/maps/nd49-05/nd49_05c.jpg. See photos/maps of base at http://1-14th.com/maps.html.
[204] Per 19th Eng Bn website at: http://home.earthlink.net/~engr19/dlaugoct68.html

---

[205] Per USN Historical Center data at www.history.navy.mil/branches/ordbat.htm

[206] Report indicating origin of camp Evan's name was published as "Locator" request in Oct/Nov99 issue of *VETERAN* magazine, at p 40. There, a Ronald Chism, who served with I Co, 3d/26th Marines, Oct-66-Oct67, tells us that its namesake was "Paul D. Evans."

[207] Morgan, LTC Thomas L., *Rendezvous in Vietnam*, ARMY Magazine, pp 34-38. Map courtesy Butch Sincock, Galaxy Tours.

[208] Account of the detonation of Evans' ammo dump is available on net at: www.toad.net/~n3tef/page7.html

[209] Bows, Ray, *Vietnam Military Lore, Legends and Shadows*, p 497-8.

[210] An 800-page documentation for 11th ACR's Cambodian Incursion PUC, May-Jun70.

[211] Per USN Historical Center data at www.history.navy.mil/seairland/

[212] According to Peter Cole, base mentioned in 1st Cav Operational Report for May-Jul70, pp 18, 38.

[213] An 800-page documentation for 11th ACR's Cambodian Incursion PUC, May-Jun70.

[214] Detailed discussion of battle in 19May71 2d Reg Asst Grp HQ, AAR for Operation Quang Trung 22F.04-Phases I thru IV courtesy Dan Gillotti, 30th FA Assn.

[215] In Mar71, FSB 6 was overrun by NVA and UPI carried the following "SAIGON (UPI). (excerpts) 30Mar71-The communist victory near Laos-Cambodian border 160 miles below the recent Laotian operation was the fourth major Communist attack this week...The South Vietnamese base...was the first ever totally overrun by Communists in [Tri-border area]. Spokesmen said the [NVA] drove off the [ARVN], killing 7 of the defenders and 6 Americans and [also] capturing the ARVN's 105 mm howitzers, which had been spiked...However, the Reds repaired the guns and turned them [against the ARVN] later today. 2 American helicopters were shot down in rescue attempts, killing a 7th American and wounding one-the third and fourth American helicopters reported shot down today. Two other Americans were missing. By late today, spokesmen said, fighting still raged around the area despiteB-52 strikes. The base was Fire Support Base No. 6, manned by two Cos of the independent 42d ARVN Rgt, a Bn of 105mm howitzers. U.S. Advisors and a US chemical sniffer outfit. The Communists opened up at 6 a.m. Wednesday with a barrage of 122mm rocket and 75mm recoilless rifle fire and stormed the base. The [ARVN] removed the sights and breech blocks from their howitzers and fled, U.S. military sources said." [According to Tom Rethard, 4th Div FO attached to 42d ARVN Rgt, "the 'chemical sniffer outfit' actually a 3 man IOS (Improved Observation System) team-early version of the designator for laser-guided bombs and artillery shells. Neither that equipment, its transport boxes, its documentation nor its crew were recovered. The initial attack came directly through the IOS team's bunker"]. Detailed discussion of battle in 19May71 2d Reg Asst Grp HQ, AAR for Operation Quang Trung 22F.04-Phases I thru IV courtesy Dan Gillotti, 30th FA Assn.

[216] Per 10Dec67, Combat Ops AAR, *Battle of Dak To*, 29th Hist Det, 4th Div, courtesy 173d Abn Assn.

[217] Per 10Dec67, Combat Ops AAR, *Battle of Dak To*, 29th Hist Det, 4th Div, courtesy 173d Abn Assn.

[218] Per 10Dec67, Combat Ops AAR, *Battle of Dak To*, 29th Hist Det, 4th Div, courtesy 173d Abn Assn.

[219] Per 10Dec67, Combat Ops AAR, *Battle of Dak To*, 29th Hist Det, 4th Div, courtesy 173d Abn Assn.

[220] 4th Div Op rpt for period ending 31Jan69 (per Craig Miller) describes the attacks thusly: 2Nov68-C/1st/8th at FSB 29 received 135 rnds of 120mm mortar resulting in 4 US WIA; 4Nov68-FSB 29 received in excess of 100 rndsof mixed arty, recoilless rifle and 82mm mortar with 6 US WIA; 10Nov68-FSB 29 recieved 2 mortar and 75mm RR attacks invoving 22 rnds that resulted in 4 US WIA; 11Nov68-FSB29 hit by apx 125 rnds of mixed arty, RR and mortar fire with 2 US WIA.

[221] Data per 19May71 2d Reg Asst Grp HQ, AAR for *Op Quang Trung 22F.04-Phases I thru IV*, courtesy Dan Gillotti, 30th FA Assn., p 9-11

[222] Data per 19May71 2d Reg Asst Grp HQ, AAR for *Op Quang Trung 22F.04-Phases I thru IV*, courtesy Dan Gillotti, 30th FA Assn., p 9-11

[223] Data per 19May71 2d Reg Asst Grp HQ, AAR for *Op Quang Trung 22F.04-Phases I thru IV*, courtesy Dan Gillotti, 30th FA Assn., p 4, 6

[224] Data per 19May71 2d Reg Asst Grp HQ, AAR for *Op Quang Trung 22F.04-Phases I thru IV*, courtesy Dan Gillotti, 30th FA Assn., p 5, 7

[225] Data per 19May71 2d Reg Asst Grp HQ, AAR for *Op Quang Trung 22F.04-Phases I thru IV,* courtesy Dan Gillotti, 30th FA Assn., p 6, 9-11

[226] Data per 19May71 2d Reg Asst Grp HQ, AAR for *Op Quang Trung 22F.04-Phases I thru IV*, courtesy Dan Gillotti, 30th FA Assn., p 9

[227] Data per 19May71 2d Reg Asst Grp HQ, AAR for *Op Quang Trung 22F.04-Phases I thru IV,* courtesy Dan Gillotti, 30th FA Assn., p 4

[228] From the recolletions of Capt. Peter Grasser, 1st SF Grp, 5th SF Grp and D Co, 1st/502d Inf

[229] According to Jim Taylor, CAC Oscar (CAP O-2) vet, the team worked with Bru tribesman from the villages of Vil Bu, Vil Ch'eng, Vil Tacun and Vil C'on. When CAC Oscar withdrew to Khe Sanh CB after the intial attacks against their vulnerable positions outside the base in late '67/early '68, the Marines did not want to accept O-2's Bru comrades, so CAC Oscar asked for and received a spot in defese perimeter of the SF's FOB-3 along Khe Sanh CB's southern edge.

[230] Per USN Historical Center data at www.history.navy.mil/branches/ordbat.htm

[231] An 800-page documentation for 11th ACR's Cambodian Incursion PUC, May-Jun70.

[232] Foxy and C-7 airstrip construction mentioned in 101st Abn ORLL for period ending 31Jul69, dated 9Dec69, p 40-41. Rpt is online at: http://carlisle-www.army.mil/usamhi/DL/chron.htm#AVietnamWar19601973.

[233] An 800-page documentation for 11th ACR's Cambodian Incursion PUC, May-Jun70.

[234] Per USN Historical Center data at www.history.navy.mil/seairland/

[235] An 800-page documentation for 11th ACR's Cambodian Incursion PUC, May-Jun70.

[236] Info re this area in great detail on internet at website www.rjsmith.com/an_khe_pass.html".

[237] Op Coronado data per Army and Navy in Can Giuoc, Sep 2000, Military Magazine, pp 10-12. Also map showing location of FSB X-Ray, FSB Tango and Mobile Riverine Base (MRB) location at time on p 10.

[238] Per1st/69th Armor website www.rjsmith.com/topo3.html".

[239] Data per Ray Bows' *Vietnam Military Lore, 1959-1973.*

[240] Per USN Historical Center data at www.history.navy.mil/seairland

[241] Russell, Norman L., *Suicide Charlie*, p 142 and Chp 13

[242] per e-mail to author dated 8Jun00

[243] Per 101st Abn Combat Ops *AAR* of 25May69.

[244] Grauwin, Paul, *Doctor at Dien Bien Phu*, p19

[245] Greg Mills, CO of D/1/502d in '68 adds this: "During 3 wks from start to evac on FB Georgia, the company had 7 plts plus attachments. 2Bde CO said he'd provide whatever we asked for, so I gave him a list and he did exactly that: We had 5 rifle plts (extra 2 from the 501st); a wpns plt with 4-81mms plus 90mm RR's; and 106 RR (with flechette rounds used on nearby snipers); 1 Eng plt with 3 dozers (used as reserve at night-worked their asses off during day); 1 quad-.50 mounted on a turret (NVA convoys running in valley with headlights on scarred the heck out of us

and we needed firepower since we were at max range for 175 guns). A USAF Air Traffic Controller staff (not FAC-there was so much air traffic we couldn't handle it on our net) also joined us, sorted it out and did a great job. The wind currents were hell on pilots carrying heavy loads; one huey crashed and a sky crane almost crashed and had to drop a dozer blade. A Ground Radar Unit attached to us picked up a force moving on us one night, but our arty was slow to fire (something about clearance-we got in big argument), so I called our mortar plt and they gave'em about 100 rounds-end of movement. The arty guys were not happy. One thing I wish I had donc. I should havc buricd a bottle (case) of whiskey up there for a day in future we'd all returned for a reunion and dug it up."

[246] Sturkey, M, *Bonnie-Sue: A Marine Corps Helicopter Squadron in Vietnam*, pp 398-399

[247] Data per Annual Hist. Report, HQ 3rd/34th Arty, dated 14April69, for 1Apr68 to 31Jan69, at: www.mrfa.org3_34th.htm

[248] Prados/Stubbe, *Valley of Decision*, p 118

[249] An 800-page documentation for 11th ACR's Cambodian Incursion PUC, May-Jun70.

[250] *All The Way-The 3d Bde, 82d Abn Div In Vietnam 1968*, p 42

[251] Some data per www.seabee.navy.mil/nmcb4/Welcome/history.htm

[252] Data per Annual Hist. Report, HQ 3rd/34th Arty, dated 14April69, for 1Apr68 to 31Jan69, at: www.mrfa.org3_34th.htm

[253] An 800-page documentation for 11th ACR's Cambodian Incursion PUC, May-Jun70.

[254] Per USN Historical Center data at www.history.navy.mil/branches/ordbat.htm

[255] Detailed 1:50,000 scale map image of Hanoi (1965 Army Map Service) at: www.lib.berkeley.edu/EART/digital/topo.html

[256] Hunt, Christopher, *Sparring With Charlie-Motorbiking Down the Ho Chi Minh Trail*, 1996

[257] *All The Way-The 3d Bde, 82d Abn Div In Vietnam 1968*, p 42

[258] An 800-page documentation for 11th ACR's Cambodian Incursion PUC, May-Jun70.

[259] Stubbe, Ray W, *The Final Formation*, softback special ed of Khe Sanh Veteran Magazine, 1995, p 136

[260] Data per S.L.A. Marshall's *Battles in the Monsoon*, pp 43, 46, 55, 63-65, 69-74 et al. Mapsheet is L-7014-6837-3, per Ken Burrington. Cited in 1st Cav VN *'Yearbook'* Aug 65-Dec 69, p 58, 83, 87, 92, per Peter Cole.

[261] Wade, Leigh, *Tan Phu: Special Forces Team A-23 in Combat*, p 191-193

[262] Sturkey, M, *Bonnie-Sue: A Marine Corps Helicopter Squadron in Vietnam*, pp 398-399

[263] Prados/Stubbe, *Valley of Decision*, pp 20-21

[264] Sturkey, M, *Bonnie-Sue: A Marine Corps Helicopter Squadron in Vietnam*, p 312

[265] Data per a 1st/7th Cav site at: www.metronet.com/~harryb/1st_team/7th_rgmt/7thndx04.html

[266] Prados/Stubbe, *Valley of Decision*, p 435

[267] 1:50,000 scale map showing location of FSB Alpine is online at www.3rdrecon.org/Snakey.htm

[268] Images of Whiskey Relay at www.gruntspace.swri.edu/images/vn/reco/steve1.jpg and steve2.jpg

[269] Prados/Stubbe, *Valley of Decision*, pp 137-188, 444-447

[270] Per 10Dec67, Combat Ops After Action Report, *Battle of Dak To*, 29th Hist Det, 4th Div, courtesy 173d Abn Assn.

[271] Prados/Stubbe, *Valley of Decision*, p 91

[272] Prados/Stubbe, *Valley of Decision*, p 90

[273] Per 10Dec67, Combat Ops After Action Report, *Battle of Dak To*, BGen Leo Schweiter, 173d Abn (Sep) courtesy 173d Abn Assn.

[274] Prados/Stubbe, *Valley of Decision*, p 203-204

[275] Data per 19May71 AAR for *Operation Quang Trung 22F.04-Phases I thru IV*, courtesy Dan Gillotti, 30th FA Assn., p 7

[276] An interesting discussion of that attack by MajGen Ben Harrison, 3d Bde CO at time, can be found in Summer 1998 issue of the *Ripcord Report*, p 8

[277] An 800-page documentation for 11th ACR's Cambodian Incursion Presidential Unit Citation (PUC), May-Jun70.

[278] Detailed story with photos of this bridge in 23Sep68 issue of the *Tropic Lightning News*, Vol 3, No. 39, pp4-5

[279] Mason, Robert, *Chickenhawk*, Penquin Books, 1984, pp 250-253

[280] The 1st Cav patch on this mountain is featured in Pierre Schoendeorfer's classic documentary, *The Anderson Platoon*, which won the Academy Award for best documentary of 1967.

[281] The Boeing Company (VERTOL Division) once produced a 15" by 18" color print of one of their CH 47's hovering over the peak. The print clearly shows the huge 1st Cav patch painted on side of the hill and signal site's fortifications. Print was entitled*: Chinook Over Heliport-Hong Kong Mountain, Vietnam.*

[282] See footnotes to Hon Cong Hill.

[283] An 800-page documentation for 11th ACR's Cambodian Incursion Presidential Unit Citation (PUC), May-Jun70.

[284] Per USN Historical Center data at www.history.navy.mil/branches/ordbat.htm

[285] Info courtesy of Noel Izzi at izzi@cyberalink.com.au

[286] Per 282d AHC History 1Jan-31Dec68 wrtten by 1LT Thomas Prince

[287] According to Kirk Ramsey, PB Hunsley was similar in design to PB Dragon. In remote, enemy-held area, but terrain was a bit different. Was small, having just 2 Cos to defend it. Tall grass covereded surrounding fields and a thin forest began apx 300 meters away in 2 directions. "I sensed a darkness all about. Even at Dragon, with the constant danger, the booby-traps and direct confrontations with Charlie, the terrain had an open, airy feel to it. It did not seem sinister. This did. There was a hovering presence, a nearness of doom..." Earth was pushed by dozers into a segmented-wall with holes left in 3' high berm apx every 10' for bunker construction. A 20' foot tower was sat in its center with 2-105 Howitzwers sitting back-to-back against the tower and covering 180 degrees each of perimeter. The low 3' high perimeter berm allowed the guns to fire directly over them by leveling the tubes to fire point-blank at any ground attack. "One might even say inviting it! I started thinking about the possibilities of requesting a transfer." Per Ramsey, Kirk, *Tales of a War Far Away*, illustrated memoir of 2d/14th Inf, 25th Inf at: www.en.com/users/ kramsey/default.html.

[288] Province names in paranthesis are provinces that existed during US involvement (typically between 1959-1964) but were either renamed or blended into other provinces. Other listed names are thought to have seen use for most of the US experience.

[289] Lehrack, Otto J., *No Shining Armor: The Marines at War Vietnam, An Oral History*, story/photo of Camp I.V. Long sign in that entry.

[290] Province names in paranthesis are provinces that existed during US involvement (typically between 1959-1964) but were either renamed or blended into other provinces. Other listed names are thought to have seen use for most of the US experience.

---

[291] Province names in paranthesis are provinces that existed during US involvement (typically between 1959-1964) but were either renamed or blended into other provinces. Other listed names are thought to have seen use for most of the US experience.
[292] The only Army casualty named Ingalls was Sp4 George A. Ingalls, KIA 16Apr67. FSB was possibly named in his honor, although the time frame differences suggest that was no the case?
[293] Per USN Historical Center data at www.history.navy.mil/branches/ordbat.htm
[294] An 800-page documentation for 11th ACR's Cambodian Incursion Presidential Unit Citation (PUC), May-Jun70.
[295] Province names in paranthesis are provinces that existed during US involvement (typically between 1959-1964) but were either renamed or blended into other provinces. Other listed names are thought to have seen use for most of the US experience.
[296] An 800-page documentation for 11th ACR's Cambodian Incursion Presidential Unit Citation (PUC), May-Jun70.
[297] Mentioned on webpage of the 187th AHC. Unit's Bn Supplement extracts are at: www.kbi.org/187thahc/incident_67.htm.
[298] Report on file at www.army.mil/cmh-pg/documents/vietnam/reneg/rtxt.htm. See that report for detailed info.
[299] Leninger, Jack, *Time Heals No Wounds,* Ivy Books, NY, 1993, p51
[300] Data per Feb70-Apr70, 8th Eng Bn, 1st Cav, Ops Rpt, p 31, courtesy Peter Cole.
[301] Newman, Lt. D.S., *Vietnam Gunners, 161 Bty RNZA, South Vietnam, 1965-71,* p 87
[302] Data per Feb70-Apr70, 1st Cav. Quart. Rpt, 2d Bde Os, p 12, courtesy Peter Cole.
[303] Leninger, Jack, *Time Heals No Wounds,* p51
[304] Per USN Historical Center data at www.history.navy.mil/seairland/
[305] Cited in *1st Cav Op Rpt, Feb70/Apr70*, p 12, & 1st Cav VN *Yearbook* Aug 65-Dec 69, p 185, 278, per Peter Cole.
[306] Data per Leninger, Jack, *Time Heals No Wound,* p51
[307] On Internt at: www.spectrumwd.com/c130/articles/katum.htm
[308] Data per AAReport, *Battle of Tay Ninh* (17Aug-27Sep68), HQ 25th ID, 2Feb69, p 34
[309] Per USN Historical Center data at www.history.navy.mil/branches/ordbat.htm
[310] Per 25 October 1968, Lessons Learned summary at www.en.com/users/kramsey/vnll6801.html
[311] "Keene was built on a slight mound, with a ragged line of dirt walls and sandbag bunkers circling the base. A single stucco bldg sat in its center, remnant of a former owner's estate. Ground was lumpy, and covered with a well-trampled layer of grass/patches of charcoal-colored earth. 3-105 howitzers were placed in triangle on one side of the rise. Beyond the walls lay stacked coils of concertina wire to help keep out the riffraff." Per Ramsey, Kirk, *Tales of a War Far Away*, illustrated on-line memoir of 2d/14th Inf, 25th Inf at: www.en.com/users/ kramsey/default.html.
[312] Data per 242d ASHC webpage at: www.vhpa.org/crash.htm.
[313] An 800-page documentation for 11th ACR's Cambodian Incursion Presidential Unit Citation (PUC), May-Jun70.
[314] The stadium was named to honor WO2 Kevin A. Wheatley. On 13Nov66, Wheatley accompnied a SVN CIDG Co into the Tra Bong valley, apx 15 km E Tra Bong SF Camp, Quang Ngai Prov. After being engaged by a VC Company, Wheatley refused to abandon his dying comrade, a WO Swanton (after his CIDG plt fled under fire), and tried dragging him to safety while under heavy MG and AW fire, assisted bya lone CIDG Pvt named Dinh Do. Dinh urged him to abandon Swanton when the VC came within 10 meters, but Kevin refused, and last seen alive after having pulled the pins on 2 grenades, calmly awaiting the VC, one frag in each hand. Soon, two explosions were followed by rifle fire. The 2 bodies were recovered the next day.
[315] *Americal Log, Vietnam,* Military Magazine, Vol XV, No. 6, Nov 1998, p 11-12
[316] Stubbe, Ray W, *The Final Formation*, p 6 (includes very detailed accounting of all casualties related to siege of Khe Sanh CB; an important reference, see bib for ordering address.)
[317] Prados/Stubbe, *Valley of Decision*, pp 261-263
[318] Location and Hill# per Plans Summary, 1st/327th Inf, dated 17May71, courtesy Cliff Snyder, NARA.
[319] Per USN Historical Center data at www.history.navy.mil/branches/ordbat.htm
[320] Data per Annual Hist. Report, HQ 3rd/34th Arty, dated 14April69, for 1Apr68 to 31Jan69, at: www.mrfa.org3_34th.htm
[321] Data per HQ 52d Arty Grp memorandum of 2June68, courtesy Craig Miller.
[322] Satellite images of Kontum and Pleiku areas at: http://coombs.anu.edu.au/~vern/space.html.
[323] An 800-page documentation for 11th ACR's Cambodian Incursion Presidential Unit Citation (PUC), May-Jun70.
[324] An 800-page documentation for 11th ACR's Cambodian Incursion Presidential Unit Citation (PUC), May-Jun70.
[325] Data per 19May71 2d Reg Asst Grp HQ, AAR for *Op Quang Trung 22F.04-Phases I thru IV*, courtesy Dan Gillotti, 30th FA Assn., p 5
[326] An 800-page documentation for 11th ACR's Cambodian Incursion PUC, May-Jun70.
[327] An 800-page documentation for 11th ACR's Cambodian Incursion Presidential Unit Citation (PUC), May-Jun70.
[328] Per *CAP One Website* at: www.capmarine.com/ky_hoa/dayone.html
[329] More info on this position and a photo of the sign at Ky Khuong can be viewed at http;//w3.one.net/~timd/cap/gazette/sgtswan.htm
[330] Fall, Bernard, *Street Without Joy*, Stackpole Co, Harrisburg PA 4th ed, May67, p 191
[331] While on a squad-sized patrol in Jan70, out of pure curiosity, the author's squad broke the off-limits rule and entered the grounds. The patrol observed no war damage of any sort within the compound, which gave credence to rumors it was a no-combat zone for both friend and foe, and they were soon approached by an older, and very amiable caretaker who gave the impression he was not at all anxious about their presence. The caretaker introduced the men to his very beautiful 16-year-old daughter and offered them all tea as if it were an everyday occurrence. The author recalls being stunned by the pastoral, serene and unblemished beauty found just inside the walls of the compound, as it contrasted with the filthy, hostile, shell and bullet shattered landscape that surrounded the compound only a step outside its gate. That contrast gave the experience a very surreal and other-worldly feeling.
[332] Moore, Robin, *The Green Berets*, Crown Publishers, NY, 1966, p 235
[333] Newman, Lt. D.S., *Vietnam Gunners, 161 Bty RNZA, South Vietnam, 1965-71,* p 103. See Choo Choo Train Insertion in Glossary for equally unusual patrol inserion.
[334] In a footnote in *Street Without Joy*, at p 29, Bernard Fall explains that Nazis were working with the Japanese when both were captured by Vietminh and choose to cooperate with them, rather than face trial as war criminals at hands of the allied forces of WWII.
[335] Per *Street Without Joy*, p 28.
[336] Per USN Historical Center data at www.history.navy.mil/seairland/
[337] Data per *Dictionary of American Fighting Ships* at: www.hazegray.org/danfs/amphib/apa195.htm

[338] Rat data at www.viet.org/ratbase.htm
[339] Per USN Historical Center data at www.history.navy.mil/seairland/
[340] Data per Feb70-Apr70, 1st Cav. Quart. Rpt, 2d Bde Os, p 12, courtesy Peter Cole.
[341] Position easily plotted on 1:50,000 scale map (DMA's 'An Tuc' sheet, stock # TL-7014-6736-4) of An Khe/Camp Radcliff area on 1st/69th Armor website at: www.rjsmith.com/camp_radcliff_0.html
[342] Data per Feb70-Apr70, 8th Eng Bn, 1st Cav, Ops Rpt, p 31, courtesy Peter Cole.
[343] Data per Feb70-Apr70, 1st Cav. Quart. Rpt, 2d Bde Os, p 12, courtesy Peter Cole.
[344] An 800-page documentation for 11th ACR's Cambodian Incursion Presidential Unit Citation (PUC), May-Jun70.
[345] Morgan, LTC Thomas L., *Rendezvous in Vietnam*, ARMY Magazine, pp 34-38
[346] A large, black & white and very detailed copy of a site plan map of Long Binh Post prepared by 66th Engr. Co. (Topo) (Corps) can be purchased from the Library of Congress, Geography and Maps Div. Request "Long Binh Post, Call No. G8024, .L6, 1972, .L6".
[347] For detailed information regarding Army Transportation Command seaports, bases and units, visit their website at: http://academic.uofs.edu/faculty/gramborw/atav/. See article entitled "Controlling the Rung Sat Special Zone" in Oct96 issue of VIETNAM Magazine.
[348] Stubbe, Ray W, *The Final Formation*, p 118. At same page, Stubbe adds parenthetically that C C/1/4 Marines assaulted Loon on 17Jun68 at 0900hrs, but the remark seems out of context?
[349] Per USN Historical Center data at www.history.navy.mil/seairland/
[350] Data per Feb70-Apr70, 8th Eng Bn, 1st Cav, Ops Rpt, p 31, courtesy Peter Cole.
[351] Data per Dennis Rees in personal letter to author dated 8/7/00
[352] Data per Feb70-Apr70, 8th Eng Bn, 1st Cav, Ops Rpt, p 31, courtesy Peter Cole.
[353] An 800-page documentation for 11th ACR's Cambodian Incursion Presidential Unit Citation (PUC), May-Jun70.
[354] According to excerpts of the diary of Lt. Joseph Abodeely, 2d/7th Cav, 1st Cav, dated 8Apr68, and published in *The Mammoth Book of War Diaries & Letters*, at pp 464-470, LZ Thor was known both as Thor and LZ Mark, and had been "named after the CO's son. Presumably the CO's son was named Mark, although it's not clear whether Abodeely meat his company or Bn or ? CO.
[355] An 800-page documentation for 11th ACR's Cambodian Incursion Presidential Unit Citation (PUC), May-Jun70.
[356] A Mar66 nigt CA during Battle of My Phu was thought by some to be 1st night helo CA; however, it appears 1st Cav's night CA to LZ Mary in Nov65 was earliest.
[357] Info regarding construction was supplied by Gary Noller, President (97/98), Americal Div Assn in form of an article from the Jul70 AMERICAL Newspaper, an in-country publication of the Americal Div, pp 14-17
[358] Photo and other info re Mary Ann available on net at: www3.maryann2.htm
[359] This LZ/FSB mentioned repeatedly in 4th Div After Action Report/News Release dated 23Mar69, and on internet a: "http://grunt.space.swri.edu/aarrpt1.htm. Map of AO at: www.nexus.net/~911gfx/vietnam/maps/nd48-08/nd48_08h.jpg
[360] An 800-page documentation for 11th ACR's Cambodian Incursion Presidential Unit Citation (PUC), May-Jun70.
[361] Suggested reading: *River Road to China, The Search for the Source of the Mekong, 1866-73*, by Milton Osborne, Atlantic Monthly Press, NY, 1975, 1996
[362] Per USN Historical Center data at www.history.navy.mil/seairland
[363] Per 1st Cav website at: www.metronet.com/~harryb/1st_team/1stndxo4.html
[364] An 800-page documentation for 11th ACR's Cambodian Incursion PUC, May-Jun70.
[365] Per 1st Cav website at: www.metronet.com/~harryb/1st_team/1stndxo4.html
[366] Photo of sign at www.manchu.org/mole_city/index7.htm
[367] Russell, Norman l., *Suicide Charlie*, pp 54, 95
[368] "On 18Dec68 the men of the 4th/9th Infantry Manchus constructed a patrol basecamp, nine and a half miles south of Tay Ninh City. In a single day, Company A, 65th Eng., transformed 186,000 lbs of building materials hauled in by 27 helicopter sorties into a well fortified position dubbed Patrol Base Mole City." Quote per www.manchu.org/mole_city/
[369] Russell, Norman l., *Suicide Charlie*, p 162
[370] An 800-page documentation for 11th ACR's Cambodian Incursion PUC, May-Jun70.
[371] Base site shown clearly on map at http://all-media-inc.com/1bn14inf/ maps.html.
[372] Per USN Historical Center data at www.history.navy.mil/seairland/
[373] Per USN Historical Center data at www.history.navy.mil/seairland
[374] Hunt, Christopher, *Sparring With Charlie-Motorbiking Down the Ho Chi Minh Trail*, p. 7
[375] Maj. Diduryk had earlier distinguished himself as Plt Ldr during 1st Ia Drang Valley battle at L-Z X-Ray, SW Pleiku, Nov65.
[376] An 800-page documentation for 11th ACR's Cambodian Incursion PUC, May-Jun70.
[377] Data per e-mail correspondence with Mr. Paulter dated 14-15Sep00
[378] Author Lewis Sorely also pointed out that Hunt was amazed by performance of the ARVN after the US pulled-out of SVN, saying that although the NVA initiated almost all actions, the ARVN "cleaned their clocks" for two years.
[379] Nickname based upon the literal anglicized translation of Nam Dong, which was 'five dong.' The dong was a Vietnamese monetary increment roughly equivalent to US cent.
[380] See Nam Dong AF footnote.
[381] Per USN Historical Center data at www.history.navy.mil/seairland/
[382] Attack discussed in Army Reporter article of 11May70, Vol 6, No. 19 as quoted on internet at: http://home.ptd.net/~trward/pagen.htm
[383] An 800-page documentation for 11th ACR's Cambodian Incursion PUC, May-Jun70.
[384] Russell, Norman L., *Suicide Charlie*, p 123-5
[385] Per http://academic.uofs.edu/faculty/gramborw/atav/4tc.htm
[386] Detailed maps of various seaports at: http://academic.uofs.edu/faculty/gramborw/atav/maps.htm
[387] Per USN Historical Center data at www.history.navy.mil/seairland
[388] An 800-page documentation for 11th ACR's Cambodian Incursion Presidential Unit Citation (PUC), May-Jun70.
[389] Excellent map of the facilities at Nha Trang can be found in Ray Bows' *Vietnam Military Lore, 1959-1973*, pp 623

[390] According to Lawrence O. Holmberg, Jr. and Steve Sherman, Moreau was part of an SF recon team (4 CIDG, 2 US) who made contact with the VC in Tay Ninh Prov near Cambodian border, 27Aug66. At 1530 hrs a resupply bird was unable to establish commo and when it flew over the rendezvous point, observed a red panel, red smoke, and a signal mirror flashing 700 meters SW the panel. At mirror position they saw 2 men lying on ground. At 1617 hours a pick up chopper found Sgt. Johnny Varner, wounded in chest and leg. The medic, Tim O'Connor, recovered Varner then attempted to retreive Sgt. Eugene Moreau's body, but due to intense ground fire, could not and was wounded in leg himself. At 1633 hours, a CIDG team member was spotted and rescued. The 91st Abn Ranger Bn was reaction force arrived at site by air at 1830, and recovered the bodies of Sgt. Moreau and Cpl Mo at 1920 hours.
[391] Detailed maps of various seaports at: http://academic.uofs.edu/faculty/gramborw/atav/maps.htm
[392] According to Tom Lacombe, the 29Jun69 issue of 4th Div newspaper states that LZs Penny, Nicole and Joyce gave given arty supt to B Co, 1st/12th Inf in contact 8 km S Highlander Heights (Mary Lou), and also for B Co, 2d/35th. Penny was described as being 10 miles S Kontum City.
[393] In *Street Without Joy*, p 45, Bernard Fall mentions that his son's death virtually destroyed Marshal de Lattre. Fall also adds that sons of 20 French generals or marshals were killed during their war.
[394] An 800-page documentation for 11th ACR's Cambodian Incursion PUC, May-Jun70.
[395] Cited in 4th Div After Action Report/News Release dated 23Mar69, and on internet a: "http://grunt.space.swri.edu/aarrpt1.htm.
[396] An 800-page documentation for 11th ACR's Cambodian Incursion PUC, May-Jun70.
[397] Data per AAReport, *Battle of Tay Ninh* (17Aug-27Sep68), HQ 25th ID, 2Feb69, p 13
[398] Detailed article with good photos in Thunder, Vol 1, No. 2, Fall 1969, Official Publication of the 25th Inf Div, pp 6-11
[399] Nui Dat 1, 2 and 3 Info courtesy of izzi@cyberalink.com.au
[400] During Aug69, 161 Bty became likely the 1st and only arty unit ever to fire in retaliation of its own firing. While setting defensive targets near Ba Ria one afternoon, a charge 2 was inadvertantly substituted for a charge three and several rounds fell short in town of Ba Ria. The DT was set and Bty was going about its business the call came in that Ba Ria was thought to be under attack, so it then began firing a counter-battery mission on nearby suspected enemy mortar site! Unfortunately, two civilians were killed in Ba Ria. Per Newman, Lt. D.S., *Vietnam Gunners, 161 Bty RNZA, South Vietnam, 1965-71*, p 91
[401] The best friend of the author's highschool years, Lawrence Lee Keister, was KIA 26Jan69, on slope of this mountain at AN 745-264 while serving as Machine Gunner with B Co' 3d/506th Inf
[402] Russ "Gus" Reynolds has an interesting story of the Mother's Day, 1969 attack at: www.war-stories.com/LZOasis.htm
[403] Per USN Historical Center data at www.history.navy.mil/seairland
[404] An 800-page documentation for 11th ACR's Cambodian Incursion PUC, May-Jun70.
[405] Unknown whether Ordway or Colt was 1st name of base; however, while Ordway, it likely named to honor of 2d Lt William D. Ordway, USA, KIA 18Jan68.
[406] Per USN Historical Center data at www.history.navy.mil/seairland
[407] Data per *Dictionary of American Fighting Ships* at: www.hazegray.org/danfs/destroy/dd846txt.htm
[408] Grid per webpage at: "grunt.space.swri/edu/aarpt1.htm
[409] Data per Kirk Ramsey's, *Tales of a War Far Away*, illustrated on-line memoir of the 2d/14th Inf, 25th Inf at: www.en.com/users/kramsey/default.html.
[410] Some data per 14Sep69, 2d/14th Inf QUARTEVAL Feeder Report at www.en.com/users/kramsey/vnr102.html#.
[411] Photo of gate and additonal data is found in *Vietnam Military Lore, legends, Shadows, and Heroes,* p 437. Photo of another plaque honoring Payne in Tam Ky at p 439.
[412] The Vietnamese apparently thought his sudden departure was very rude! *The Vietnam Guidebook*, p 51.
[413] Stubbe, Ray W, *The Final Formation*, p 113
[414] See map at www.landscaper.net/chighmap.jpg
[415] According to Tom Lacombe, the 29Jun69 issue of 4th Div newspaper states that LZs Penny, Nicole and Joyce gave arty supt to B Co, 1st/12th Inf in contact 8 km S Highlander Heights (Mary Lou), and also for B Co, 2d/35th. Penny was described as being 10 miles S Kontum City in that article.
[416] Per USN Historical Center data at www.history.navy.mil/seairland/
[417] Moore, Robin, *The Green Berets*, p 37
[418] Morgan, LTC Thomas L., *Rendezvous in Vietnam*, Mar98, ARMY Magazine, pp 34-38
[419] Detailed maps of various seaports at: http://academic.uofs.edu/faculty/gramborw/atav/maps.htm
[420] Morgan, LTC Thomas L., *Rendezvous in Vietnam*, Mar 98, ARMY Magazine, pp 34-38
[421] An 800-page documentation for 11th ACR's Cambodian Incursion PUC, May-Jun70.
[422] Smith, Robert B, *To The Last Cartridge*, pp 317
[423] Data per AAReport, *Battle of Tay Ninh* (17Aug-27Sep68), HQ 25th ID, 2Feb69, p 34
[424] Morgan, LTC Thomas, *Rendezvous inVietnam*, Army Magazine, Mar98, p 37
[425] Data per AAReport, *Battle of Tay Ninh* (17Aug-27Sep68), HQ 25th ID, 2Feb69, p 13
[426] Grids and data per *All The Way-The 3d Bde, 82d Abn Div In Vietnam 1968*, p 37-41.
[427] An 800-page documentation for 11th ACR's Cambodian Incursion PUC, May-Jun70.
[428] Detailed discussion of Operation Masher/White Wing can be found in *A Contagion of War* vol. *Vietnam Experience* series, pp 32-48. Good map of operation at p 38.
[429] Per 101st Abn Combat Ops *AAR* of 25May69.
[430] Cache discovery data per *A Better War*, p 42.
[431] Data per 10Jul71 AAR of Lam Son 487 and 720 (U), MACMR-11D-54R, MACJ3-32, courtesy Cliff Snyder, NARA.
[432] Moore reflects "I never held the ARVN in high regard. We would give them some ground we'd taken and they would lose it, then we'd have to go back and re-take it. One of them "accidentally" took a shot at me once. The bullet missed my right ear by about 4" from the way it sounded. I was around them at Con Thien and Dong Ha also and I don't know who I hated more, the NVA or ARVN? Oh well."
[433] As per 9th Inf Div ORLL for period ending 31Jul68
[434] Fall, Bernard, *Street Without Joy*, 4th ed, p 191
[435] Excellent map of the facilities at Pleiku/Camp Holloway can be found in Ray Bows' *Vietnam Military Lore, 1959-1973*, pp 624

[436] Data from author's personal experience. The Seabees based here (perhaps a dozen men?) also had 14' boats with outboard motors and would sometimes water ski near bridge ala "Apocalypse Now!" In Spring, '70, one such skier was run over by his tow and was medevaced from the bridge. As far as author knows, the bridge was never attacked even though it provided a vital link to Hue/Phu Bai area and was used as resupply route for a number of US FSBs along Hwy 547
[437] Prados/Stubbe, *Valley of Decision*, p 147
[438] Portions of this entry compiled from article entitled, "Friendly Target," by Master Chief William R. Wells II, online at http://members.aol.com/rhassard/Friendly_Target.html
[439] Data per 19May71 2d Reg Asst Grp HQ, AAR for Operation Quang Trung 22F.04-Phases I thru IV courtesy Dan Gillotti, 30th FA Assn., p 4
[440] Prados/Stubbe, *Valley of Decision*, p 53
[441] Stearns was a reporter with NBC affiliate KCRA TV-3 in Sacramento, who was instrumental in supporting the construction of the California Vietnam Veterans memorial there. He was an officer in 459th Sig Co at Pr'line Mtn.
[442] Per Nguyen Cao Ky's *Twenty Years and Twenty Days*, p 106
[443] Per USN Historical Center data at www.history.navy.mil/seairland/
[444] Americal Assn says vet who visited the site in Mar95 thinks listed grid coordinate is wrong. Same vet added that: the upper part of hill has eroded such that two feet of mud now cover the former helipads; that top of hill is much smaller now; and that area had been thoroughly scavenged leaving only remnants of sandbags.
[445] Mason, Robert, *Chickenhawk*, pp 400-401
[446] Per 9May68, 24May68 and 25may68 AARs of the 647th QM Co (PETROL OP), signed by Hugh J. Cary, Capt, Cmdg
[447] Per 25May68, 2Jun68, 21Jul68 and 24 Jul68 AARs of the 647th QM Co (PETROL OP), all signed by Hugh J. Cary, Capt, Cmdg
[448] Per 15Jul68 AAR of the 647th QM Co (PETROL OP), signed by Hugh J. Cary, Capt, Cmdg
[449] Creitz also added that, "the 647th QM Co. was under the 240th QM Bn which was at Phu Tai. The 240th also had a pipeline from Qui Nhon to Phu Cat AB that only pumped JP-4..." Creitz related that he was sent TDY to 647th in May68, and initially assigned to help build and secure Pump Station 2. At his arrival there was only a pump shed, a one story wooden bldg and a single bunker under construction. "The bunkers used 6" or larger beams in what they call a 'post and beam' method then covered with 'PSP' with heavy sheet metal for decking. Then the bunkers were covered with sandbags 4 or 5 layers deep... When I left after two months, they had nine bunkers...and a trench that zigzagged from bunker to bunker. The sleeping quarters were built with a 1/2 round culvert on a wooden platform and were covered with sandbags. Everytime we were attacked, we got motivated to add another layer of sandbags!"
[450] Spector, Ronald H., *After Tet*, The Free Press, NY, 1993, p 140. Spector tells us the LAW was fired by Sgt Hillery Craig, D/1st/8th Cav.
[451] An 800-page documentation for 11th ACR's Cambodian Incursion PUC, May-Jun70.
[452] Info from and image of at: http://carlisle-www.army.mil/cgi-bin/usamhi/pixdata/searchpix-photo RE123S.
[453] Apparently the name of the facility in Vietnamese was "Trung Taâm Huaán Luyeän Quang Trung." That information was found at: www.freeviet.org/forum/text/viw-kn0008.html. According to that same source, "In the middle of March 1976, communists mobilized secretly around 100,000 young, "energetic" and unexeperienced students of universities and high schools in Saigon and sent them to former Quang Trung Training Center." Ostensibly, this was for training as commercial proprieter investigators to monitor illegal trade and sales practices in Ho Chi Minh City. We have no independent proof to verify this claim.
[454] Excellent map of the facilities at Qui Nhon can be found in Ray Bows' *Vietnam Military Lore, 1959-1973*, pp 625
[455] Excellent map of QN Market Time Facility can be found in Ray Bows' *Vietnam Military Lore, 1959-1973*, pp 625
[456] Detailed maps of various seaports at: http://academic.uofs.edu/faculty/gramborw/atav/maps.htm
[457] Info from and images of at: http://carlisle-www.army.mil/cgi-bin/usamhi/pixdata/searchpix-photo G123S.
[458] Originally, Hon Cong Mtn was not included within the outer perimeter (Green Line); however, after US signal site atop the mtn was overrun in about Feb66, the perimeter was enlarged to include the mtn and apparently the site was never attacked again as result.
[459] Excellnt quality 1:50,000 scale maps (DMA TL-7014 series) of An Khe/Camp Radcliff area on 1st/69th Armor website at: www.rjsmith.com/camp_radcliff_0.html
[460] An 800-page documentation for 11th ACR's Cambodian Incursion PUC, May-Jun70.
[461] An 800-page documentation for 11th ACR's Cambodian Incursion PUC, May-Jun70.
[462] Data per Sep99 issue of MILITARY Magazine, *16th Infantry Association Regimental History-Vietnam, 1965-1970*, pp26-27.
[463] Per USN Historical Center data at www.history.navy.mil/seairland
[464] An 800-page documentation for 11th ACR's Cambodian Incursion PUC, May-Jun70.
[465] Per USN Historical Center data at www.history.navy.mil/seairland/
[466] Grids and data per *All The Way-The 3d Bde, 82d Abn Div In Vietnam 1968*, p 37-41.
[467] Detailed report of operation in this area at US Center for Military History on file at www.army.mil/cmh-pg/documents/vietnam/reneg/rtxt.htm.
[468] Per USN Historical Center data at www.history.navy.mil/seairland
[469] Palmer, Laura, *Shrapnel in The Heart*, Random House, NY, 1987, pp 150-157.
[470] Marshal, Tom, *Rescue from FSB Ripcord*, Vietnam Magazine, June '98, p 34-40.
[471] Recommended reading: *Ripcord, Screaming Eagles Under Siege, Vietnam 1970,* by Keith William Nolan, *Presidio Press*, Novato, CA, 2000. 1:50,000 scale map image of site and surrounding positions at p 206.
[472] In Son Thang 4, at p 18, author Gary Solis reports, "Immed after the assault, there was an investigation to determine how the VC had penetrated Ross's presumably solid defense. Major Theer...thought [the investigator] 'was looking for someone to blame.' Eight days after Ross was overrun, LTC Clark [its CO, who was in Hawaii at time of attack] was relieved of cmd. [Maj. Richard] Theer bitterly recalls being told not to submit award recommendations he had prepared: the division commander had directed that there would be no medals, other than purple Hearts, for defenders of Ross."
[473] Map showing Rolling Thunder route packages at p 125 in *Thunder from Above*, a vol of the *Vietnam Experience* series.
[474] See excellent article entitled "Controlling the Rung Sat Special Zone" in Oct96 issue of *VIETNAM* Magazine.
[475] Website devoted to FSB Russell features *Stars & Stripes* article about attack at: www.swnm.com/dol/lzrussell/ documents/, as well as pictures of the base at: www.swnm.com/dol/lzrussell/picsite/
[476] An 800-page documentation for 11th ACR's Cambodian Incursion PUC, May-Jun70.

[477] Per Reuters wire service article, "*Philippine Hijacker Found Dead; Parachute Failed*" http://dailynews.yahoo.com/h/nm/20000526/wl/philippines_hijack.html, posted Fri 26May00. According to Tuck Boys, an almost identical took place in early 2000, when a former VNAF pilot dropped anti-communist leaflets over Havana. "The FAA was helpless to respond, and it took considerable chutzpah for guy to do this thing!"
[478] Detailed map of Saigon Port at http://home.epix.net/~gramborw/saigon.htm, and other ports at: http://academic.uofs.edu/faculty/gramborw/atav/maps.htm
[479] Per USN Historical Center data at www.history.navy.mil/seairland/
[480] Per USN Historical Center data at www.history.navy.mil/seairland/
[481] According to Rich Kirchner, "The 30Mar72 overrun of FSB Sarge resulting in 2 US MIA's (Gary Westcott & Bruce A. Crosby Jr.) from 8th RRFS (Radio Research Field Station), who worked inside air-conditioned, self contained field "vans" filled with top secret electronic eavesdropping devices. The 27th Eng built two bunkers to house these things, one on Sarge and another at Camp Evans. I reconned the sites, designed the bunkers and one of our platoons buried them in sandbags after the framework and then the "van" were airlifted into place." "The ASA web-page posted a picture of a of Soviet Helicopter on FSB Sarge in Jun(?)99 with members of JTFFFA looking for remains of Wescott and Crosby. Go to: http://asa.npoint.net/fsbsarge99.jpg and http://asa.npoint.net/fsbsarge99.jpg."
[482] Per 7Dec67, Combat Ops After Action Report, *Battle of Dak To*, BGen Leo Schweiter, 173d Abn (Sep) courtesy 173d Abn Assn.
[483] Data about and map of Camp Schmidt and Pleiku can be found in Ray Bows' *Vietnam Military Lore, 1959-1973*, pp 624
[484] Data per AAReport, *Battle of Tay Ninh* (17Aug-27Sep68), HQ 25th ID, 2Feb69, p 20, 35
[485] Per website www.rjsmith.com/".
[486] Per website www.rjsmith.com/".
[487] Memories of 1ATF RAR veteran Eddie Tricker at: "http://users.mildura.net.au/users/marshall/tales/tales.htm
[488] "I did a lot of work setting up FSB "Scobie" with Alpha Bty, 2d/35th US Artillery. 'Arse Kicking Alpha,' was amongst the many signboards they had. The unit consisted of mobile 155mm artillery pieces and would have been stationed at Nui Dat. Per Eddie Tricker, 1 1ATF Fwd Scout.
[489] An 800-page documentation for 11th ACR's Cambodian Incursion PUC, May-Jun70.
[490] An 800-page documentation for 11th ACR's Cambodian Incursion PUC, May-Jun70.
[491] Per USN Historical Center data at www.history.navy.mil/seairland/
[492] An 800-page documentation for 11th ACR's Cambodian Incursion PUC, May-Jun70.
[493] Per USN Historical Center data at www.history.navy.mil/branches/ordbat.htm
[494] Per 101st Abn Combat Ops *AAR* of 25May69.
[495] Strukey, Marion, *Bonnie-Sue: A Marine Corps Helicopter Squadron in Vietnam*, pp 6-8.
[496] Per 1st/69th Armor website www.rjsmith.com/topo4.html".
[497] An 800-page documentation for 11th ACR's Cambodian Incursion PUC, May-Jun70.
[498] Drs. Van Hanh Hoang of UC Davis offered following translations for FSB Sky Horse sign: 'Ca(n Cu+' Ho?a Lu+.c II' means 'Fire Base # 2'; 'Thien Ma' translates to 'Sky Horse'; 'Son Lam' means 'Mountain and/or Forest'; hence, Thien Ma Son likely translates to 'Sky Horse Mountain'. 'Thie^n Ma? So+n La^m' also translates to: 'The Forest of the Sky Horse Mountain'. Dr Hoang tells us the literal translation of each word as: Thie^n = God or King or Sky; Ma? = Horse; So+n = Mountain, La^m = Forest. Tony Nguyen (www.beerguy.com) offered the following "My Father says it describes a a firebase within a region. Can Cu Hoa Luc Thien Ma Son Lam, is Firebase "Sacred Horse in Mountain's Forrest."
[499] Data per e-mail correspondence with Mr. Toll dated 15-16Sep00. He once spent 45 days on Sledgehammer while most MSS missions apparently only ran appx. two week.
[500] Data per Feb70-Apr70, 8th Eng Bn, 1st Cav, Ops Rpt, p 31, courtesy Peter Cole.
[501] An 800-page documentation for 11th ACR's Cambodian Incursion PUC, May-Jun70.
[502] Frank Penk, Jr tells us: "Just to confuse everything even more, Keith William Nolan's *Into Cambodia* has a line drawing on p 102, that shows FSB South 1 as due N FSB Burkett and FSB South 2 to W South 1!"
[503] Cited in Pleiku, by J. D. Coleman, p 86, 88, per Peter Cole.
[504] Data courtesy Ann Kelsey, Special Services employee at Cam Ranh and Dong Ba Thin.
[505] An 800-page documentation for 11th ACR's Cambodian Incursion PUC, May-Jun70.
[506] Schild, LTC James, *For Garry Owen in Glory*, p. 43.
[507] Per USN Historical Center data at www.history.navy.mil/seairland
[508] Data per AAReport, *Battle of Tay Ninh* (17Aug-27Sep68), HQ 25th ID, 2Feb69, p 7
[509] Per website www.rjsmith.com/topo1.html
[510] Per website www.rjsmith.com/topo1.html
[511] An 800-page documentation for 11th ACR's Cambodian Incursion PUC, May-Jun70.
[512] More info on this position and a photo of the sign at Ky Khuong can be viewed at http://w3.one.net/~timd/cap/gazette/sgtswan.htm
[513] Op Coronado data per Army and Navy in Can Giuoc, Sep 2000, Military Magazine, pp 10-12. Also map showing location of FSB X-Ray, FSB Tango and Mobile Riverine Base (MRB) location at time on p 10.
[514] See Combat After Action Report, *Battle of Tay Ninh* (17Aug-27Sep68), HQ 25th ID, 2Feb69
[515] An 800-page documentation for 11th ACR's Cambodian Incursion PUC, May-Jun70.
[516] Per Fact Sheet: MACIG-INS, Summary of Combined MACV-JGS IG Post-Turnover Inspection of Tay Ninh CB, Tay Ninh Pr, MR 3, 10-12Oct70. Sheet not dated.
[517] Grids and data per *All The Way-The 3d Bde, 82d Abn Div In Vietnam 1968*, p 37-41.
[518] Per USN Historical Center data at www.history.navy.mil/seairland/
[519] Interestingly, Hanoi claimed that some 43,000 Americans had been killed in Tet Offensive alone. Rather an extraordinary claim when we know that only 58,000 Americans died in entire war, and only 47,000 of those through hostile action. Suggested reading is Lewis Sorely's *A better War*, in general and pp 31-59 in particular.
[520] Data per AAReport, *Battle of Tay Ninh* (17Aug-27Sep68), HQ 25th ID, 2Feb69, p 26
[521] Per www.thehistorynet.com/Vietnam/articles/1096_text.htm
[522] An 800-page documentation for 11th ACR's Cambodian Incursion PUC, May-Jun70.
[523] Data per AAReport, *Battle of Tay Ninh* (17Aug-27Sep68), HQ 25th ID, 2Feb69, p 22

[524] An 800-page documentation for 11th ACR's Cambodian Incursion PUC, May-Jun70.
[525] According to excerpts of the diary of Lt. Joseph Abodeely, 2d/7th Cav, 1st Cav, dated 8Apr68, and published in *The Mammoth Book of War Diaries & Letters*, at pp 464-470, LZ Thor was known both as Thor and LZ Mark, and had been "...named after the CO's son. Presumably the CO's son was named Mark, although it's not clear whether Abodeely meat his company or Bn or ? CO.
[526] Newman, Lt. D.S., *Vietnam Gunners, 161 Bty RNZA, South Vietnam, 1965-71,* p 76
[527] Newman, Lt. D.S., *Vietnam Gunners, 161 Bty RNZA, South Vietnam, 1965-71,* p 89
[528] Info from and images of at: http://carlisle-www.army.mil/cgi-bin/usamhi/pixdata/searchpix-photo G123S.
[529] An 800-page documentation for 11th ACR's Cambodian Incursion PUC, May-Jun70.
[530] Per USN Historical Center data at www.history.navy.mil/branches/ordbat.htm
[531] Synopsis of battle at: www3.servtech.com/vhpa/info/panel/battle/69022220.HTM
[532] Per e-mail correspondence with Thomas P. Flynn, Port Richey FL, dated 10Mar98
[533] Per USN Historical Center data at www.history.navy.mil/seairland/
[534] Action discussed in 101st Abn ORLL for period ending 31Jul69, dated 9Dec69, and online at: http://carlisle-www.army.mil/usamhi/DL/chron.htm#AVietnamWar19601973. Was also focus of: *The Sons of Bardstown: 25 Years of Vietnam in an American Town*, by Jim Wilson, Crown Publishers 1994
[535] Tolson, Gen John J, *Airmobility, 1961-1971*, Vietnam Studies, Dept of the Army, 1973, p 160.
[536] On Internt at: www.spectrumwd.com/c130/articles/katum.htm
[537] Per *River Road to China, The Search for the Source of the Mekong, 1866-73*, by Milton Osborne, p 38.
[538] Per *River Road to China, The Search for the Source of the Mekong, 1866-73*, by Milton Osborne, p 38.
[539] Tolson, Gen John J, *Airmobility, 1961-1971*, Vietnam Studies, Dept of the Army, 1973, p 160.
[540] *All The Way-The 3d Bde, 82d Abn Div In Vietnam 1968*, p 57
[541] Data per AAReport, *Battle of Tay Ninh* (17Aug-27Sep68), HQ 25th ID, 2Feb69, p 13
[542] Of the 110 wounded left at Tu Le, only 4 survived to be released in 1954. Per *Street Without Joy*, at pp 70-71
[543] Data per Dennis Rees in personal letter to author dated 8/7/00
[544] Morgan, LTC Thomas L., *Rendezvous in Vietnam*, Mar 98, ARMY Magazine, pp 34-38
[545] Discussed in 101st Abn ORLL for period ending 31Jul69, dated 9Dec69, p 21-22, online at: http://carlisle-www.army.mil/usamhi/DL/chron.htm#AVietnamWar19601973.
[546] Map of LZ Uplift AO at www.nexus.net/~911gfx/vietnam/maps/nd49-05/nd49_05g.jpg
[547] Author Lewis Sorely also pointed out that Hunt was amazed by performance of the ARVN after the US pulled-out of SVN, saying that although the NVA initiated almost all actions, the ARVN "cleaned their clocks" for two years.
[548] Data per, and poigniant discussion of battle at, http://screamingeagles-327thvietnam.com/first327th/interesting/just_a_brief_history_of_fb_veghe.htm
[549] Leninger, Jack, *Time Heals No Wounds*, p51
[550] 4th Div Op rpt for period ending 31Jan69 (per Craig Miller) states that on 13Nov68 Vera (held by A/1st/35th and B/3d/8th) was hit by 40 rnds of 60mm mortar and ground probe that resulted in 5 US KIA and 38 WIA; 14Nov68-Vera received 60 rnds of 75mm RR, 82mm mortar, 122mm rocket and 105mm mortar fire (no casualties mentioned).
[551] On map at www.vietvet.org/visit/maps/mapB.jpg
[552] Data per http://hawley.interspeed.net/vietnam/YRBM16c.htm
[553] In *Street Without Joy*, ay p 40, Bernard Fall reported that during Battle of Vinh Yen, civilian porters supporting the Vietminh invested over 2 million man days to deliver some 5,000 tons of supplies and ammo to battlefield. Although his troops lost the battle, Gen. Giap heaped praise on effort of those porters.
[554] Incident cited in *Time Heals No Wounds*, p 183's 1st/12th Inf Radio Log excerpt.
[555] An 800-page documentation for 11th ACR's Cambodian Incursion PUC, May-Jun70.
[556] Data per *Rangers At War, LRRPs in Vietnam*, at p. 237
[557] Detailed maps of various seaports at: http://academic.uofs.edu/faculty/gramborw/atav/maps.htm
[558] Detailed maps of various seaports at: http://academic.uofs.edu/faculty/gramborw/atav/maps.htm
[559] Data per 19May71 2d Reg Asst Grp HQ, AAR for Operation Quang Trung 22F.04-Phases I thru IV courtesy Dan Gillotti, 30th FA Assn., p 6
[560] An 800-page documentation for 11th ACR's Cambodian Incursion PUC, May-Jun70.
[561] An 800-page documentation for 11th ACR's Cambodian Incursion PUC, May-Jun70.
[562] Per USN Historical Center data at www.history.navy.mil/seairland/
[563] Per USN Historical Center data at www.history.navy.mil/seairland
[564] Per USN Historical Center data at www.history.navy.mil/seairland/
[565] From Jan70-Aug71, the 20th Eng Bn (consisting of 584th, 15th and 509th Eng LE Cos) provided almost all the Engr supt for central highlands. Its AO ran from Dak To in N, to Ban Me Thuot in S, and from Cambodia to An Khe, E to W. During that period, the Bn's mission transitioned from 4th Div combat supt to line of communication construction.
[566] An 800-page documentation for 11th ACR's Cambodian Incursion PUC, May-Jun70.
[567] An 800-page documentation for 11th ACR's Cambodian Incursion PUC, May-Jun70.
[568] On 13Nov66, WO2 Kevin A. Wheatley accompanied a CIDG Co into the Tra Bong Valley, apx 15 km E Tra Bong SF Camp, Quang Ngai Prov. When engaged by VC Co and his CIDG plt fled the battlefield, Wheatley refused to abandon his dying comrade (WO Swanton) and tried dragging him to safety while under heavy MG and AW fire while assisted by a lone CIDG Pvt named Dinh Do. Dinh urged him to abandon Swanton when the VC came within 10 meters, but Kevin refused and he was last seen alive after having pulled the pins on 2 grenades, calmly waiting for the VC with one frag in each hand. Two explosions were heard later, followed by rifle fire. Swanton's and Wheatley's bodies were recovered the next day.
[569] Per 101st Abn Combat Ops *AAR* of 25May69.
[570] Images of Whiskey Relay at www.gruntspace.swri.edu/images/vn/reco/steve1.jpg and steve2.jpg
[571] Per Nguyen Cao Ky's *Twenty Years and Twenty Days*, p 85
[572] An 800-page documentation for 11th ACR's Cambodian Incursion PUC, May-Jun70.

[573] Data per Annual Hist. Report, HQ 3rd/34th Arty, dated 14April69, for 1Apr68 to 31Jan69, at: www.mrfa.org3_34th.htm
[574] Per USN Historical Center data at www.history.navy.mil/seairland/
[575] An 800-page documentation for 11th ACR's Cambodian Incursion PUC, May-Jun70.
[576] Also spelled Wunder Beach in Gen William Westmoreland's *Report on the War in Vietnam*, p 172
[577] Op Coronado data per Army and Navy in Can Giuoc, Sep 2000, Military Magazine, pp 10-12. Also map showing location of FSB X-Ray, FSB Tango and Mobile Riverine Base (MRB) location at time on p 10.
[578] An 800-page documentation for 11th ACR's Cambodian Incursion PUC, May-Jun70.
[579] These units had been armed with all new Chinese equipment and new US equipment captured by Chinese from the Americans in Korea. Per *Street Without Joy*, p 55
[580] Per USN Historical Center data at www.history.navy.mil/seairland
[581] Per USN Historical Center data at www.history.navy.mil/seairland/
[582] An 800-page documentation for 11th ACR's Cambodian Incursion PUC, May-Jun70.
[583] Per USN Historical Center data at www.history.navy.mil/branches/ordbat.htm
[584] It is possible "Tien" and "Phuoc" were transposed by list creator, and it that were true, proper grid would be Tien Phuoc AF at BT 12-14, and 8 km WSW listed grid?
[585] Dick Strandberg wrote: "I was on YRBM-16 when the explosion ripped a 30' wide hole in its hull. Each Thanksgiving the memories can flood back; being trapped inside a burning ship filling with smoke, burn victims screaming for help and you unable to help them."
[586] Near Easter '70, for an apx 72 hr period, a large NVA force was engaged moving near YRBM-20. Hueys/Cobras landed on deck for a hot reloads w/mini-gun, MG ammo and rockets. Pilots given quick bite of food/soda while still sitting in aircraft. After liftoff, helos would begin firing just beyond river banks. Crewmen passed ammo from docked ammo supply ship hand-over-hand to flight deck for loading. 4 large mortars were manned on push barge and men were standing by to cut and drop the anchor chain if NVA got past the air cover.
[587] On map at www.landscaper.net/chighmap.jpg on 15th Arty homepage
[588] After being WIA 16Sep70, and following 7 days in the ICU of the 85th Evac at Phu Bai, the author was himself a patient at the 249th from 22Sep70 to 9Oct70. He recalls huge one-story wards stuffed with 100 patients each. He also recalls with some fondness the overall high levels of morale and good-natured kidding he observed among the patients despite the often staggering severity of their wounds. Each bed had its own headphone jack and patients could listen to radio all night long, if they so wished. TVs were also mounted on the ceilings at various points and a nightly Thai Kickboxing show seemed a particular favorite among many of the troops.

Appendix A

Airfields and Heliports of South Vietnam

Per DMA ONC/TPC Maps and DOD/DMA Tactical Aerodrome Directories

During the war, eight airfields designed to accommodate jet aircraft were constructed at: Da Nang, Chu Lai, Phu Cat, Tuy Hoa, Cam Ranh Bay, Phan Rang, Bien Hoa and Tan Son Nhut. These were extremely large facilities that often included multiple, 10,000-foot concrete runways, as well as a wide range of related facilities including: administrative buildings, bunker lines, barracks, control towers, fire stations, hangars, hospitals, mess halls, mortar shelters, security fences and warehouses. Tan Son Nhut Airbase consisted of over 3,500 acres (5.46 sq. mi.) and, based upon the number of daily take-offs and landings, was considered one of the busiest airports in the world at the height of American involvement.

By 1967, apart from those eight jet-capable airfields, there were at least 90 other airfields in SVN using asphalt, aluminum matting or compacted earth for their runway surface. Of those 90 others, eleven were capable of handling jet fighters and 62 capable of landing C-130, four-engine, medium cargo aircraft. Additionally, there were hundreds of isolated dirt strips throughout SVN, many of which were capable of landing C-7s or C-123s, as well as smaller observation aircraft and helicopters.

The names and detail that follow in many of the various airfield and heliport listings here were compiled primarily from a Department of Defense DMA TAD (Defense Mapping Agency, Tactical Aerodrome Directory). This TAD was published by the DMA Aerospace Center (St. Louis, MO) in 1973, and effective 1Feb73. Apparently, it was the last TAD issued during the American War.

TADs (also known as Flip Charts) include overhead photographs of the most significant airfields, runway schematics, as well as highly detailed radio, artillery advisory, hazard, fuel, ammo and taxiing information. They also provide an extensive listing of heliports with similarly detailed data but lacking photographic images or schematics. The TAD itself is 5" by 8" by 1/2" in size, and printed on light-weight newsprint. They are a treasure if one can be found.

Paul Whetzel, a retired USAF Officer who flew numerous missions in Vietnam, unhesitatingly offered to loan the author his copy of the 1Feb73 TAD and, in doing so, gifted the reader with the grid coordinates and other detail for at least 300 airfields and another 322 heliports. Pinpointing these facilities also helped locate numerous associated facilities and firebases, thus compounding the benefit immeasurably. Our chance meeting in 1997 was a Godsend indeed, and Mr. Whetzel's exceedingly generous and selfless gesture contributed greatly to the knowledge found among these pages.

Additional listed airfield data was compiled from a 15Aug69 TAD in the possession of Frank Penk, Jr. (a helicopter pilot who flew for the 1st Cav Div and 20th Eng Bn over several tours). Of his own accord, Mr. Penk compared the 1973 data with the 1969 data, and generously transcribed for the author that 1969 information not found in the 1973 version. Like Whetzel, his gift contributed greatly to the knowledge found in this text. Such selfless actions were common among the many contributors who helped construct *Where We Were*.

Air Control Call Signs:

Panama Control, Vietnam: USAF flight control operations center served the following airfields: Da Nang, Hue/Phu Bai and Marble Mountain. Service provided by USAF Tac Weapons Controller personnel H24, on frequencies 367.8, 133.2.

Paris Control, Vietnam USAF flight control operations served the following airfields: Tan Son Nhut, Bien Hoa, Vung Tau (as well as radar vector assistance to numerous Army airfields). Service provided by USAF Tac Weapons Controller personnel H24, on frequencies 347.9, 133.2.

Peacock Control, Vietnam: USAF Flight control operations served the following airfields: Pleiku (USAF/VNAF) and Phu Cat (VNAF). Service by USAF Tac Weapons Controller personnel H24, on frequencies 345.0, 248.6, 133.2.

South Vietnam Aerodrome, Airfield and Heliport Synopsis by Military Region

Fields Listed Alphabetically by Military Region/CTZ/Corps

For detailed locational and other historical information about any of the airfield or heliport listed in this section, refer to the corresponding listing in the main alphabetical listings in this text. The following list was compiled primarily from the 1Feb73 Tactical Aerodrome Directory (TAD). Additional data was also compiled from the 15Aug69 TAD and provided by Frank Penk, Jr.

Explanation of AF# - ALOREP System:

The airfield and heliport numbering system used in the TAD is referred to as the **ALOREP** numbering system (Airlift Operational Reporting System). While airfields are listed with the full ALOREP number displayed (such as VA1-223), only the numeric portion of the number are displayed in heliport listings (such as Heliport #501); heliports are not listed as say VH2-501, as one might expect. Presumably the ALOREP was/is the DOD's (and/or DMA's) worldwide identification system for all U.S., or U.S.-used military airfields.

The Airfield ALOREP identification number is broken down as follows:

Bold Type Indicates Primary Name, e.g. A Shau
Light Type indicates alternate name, e.g. A Sap

V	A	1	223
Country (SVN)	Airfield	Mil Region	Airfield Number

For Example: Nhan Bieu, VA1-79
Ban Me Thuot West, VA2-12
Ban Me Thuot East VA2-12 *

*Airfields with multiple formal or informal names are all listed under the same ALOREP number. They were distinguished from one another in the Tactical Aerodrome Directory by printing the current formal name of the airfield in bold text, while all other name variants of the same airfield were in plain text. That practice is continued in the listing that follows.

Heliports:

In the TAD, heliports were simply assigned a (presumably) sequential number that included first the Military Region/CTZ, followed by a number. It does not appear that they were divided into primary and alternate names by bold text as was the case for the airfield listings:

For Example:	Khe Sanh	MR 1 # 594
	Chan Thanh	MR 3 # 551
	Gia Ria	MR 4 # 567

Airfields and Heliports Listed Alphabetically by Military Region/CTZ/Corps

With ALOREP or Heliport Number

I Corps

A Luoi	**VA1-59,** per 69 TAD
A Ro	**VA1-268,** per 69 TAD
A Sap	VA1-60, per 69 TAD
A Shau	**VA1-60,** per 69 TAD
Ai Tu	VA1-78
An Diem	MR 1, Heliport # 500
An Hoa	**VA1-257,** per 69 TAD
An Hoa	MR 1, Heliport # 501
An Lau	MR 1, Heliport # 502
An Lo	VA1-69
An Thinh	**VA1-115,** per 69 TAD
Aroh	MR 1, Heliport # 507
Atou	MR 1, Heliport # 508
Ba Gia	**VA1-82,** per 69 TAD
Ba Long	VA1-64, per 69 TAD
Ba Long	MR 1, Heliport # 510
Ba Long	**VA1-64,** per 69 TAD
Ba To	**VA1-84,** per 69 TAD
Ba To New	VA1-272
Bach Ma	MR 1, Heliport # 514
Baldy	**VA1-63,** per 69 TAD
Ban Long	VA1-64, per 69 TAD
Bao To	VA1-84, per 69 TAD
Be Loung	MR 1, Heliport # 516

Ben Giang	MR 1, Heliport # 518	LZ Stud	VA1-181, per 69 TAD
Binh Son	**VA1-230,** per 69 TAD	LZ Tuttle	VA2-252
Ca Lu	**VA1-181**, per 69 TAD	Mai Loc	VA1-72
Ca Lu	MR 1, Heliport # 532	Marble Mountain	VA1-195
Cam Lo	**VA1-98**, per 69 TAD	Mau Ca	MR 1, Heliport # 613
Camp Eagle	MR 1, Heliport # 751	Miet Xa	MR 1, Heliport #?
Camp Evans	VA1-143 (listed *VA3-143*)	**Minh Long**	VA1-102
Cau Soi	MR 1, Heliport # 546	**Mo Duc**	**VA1-209**, per 69 TAD
Chu Lai	VA1-194	Mu Duc	MR 1, Heliport # 617
Cu Lao Re Island	VA1-93	My Chanh	MR 1, Heliport # 618
Cua Viet	MR 1, Heliport # 547	My Thanh	VA1-111, per 69 TAD
Da Bac	MR 1, Heliport # 553	Nai Van	MR 1, Heliport # 622
Da Dan	MR 1, Heliport # 554	Nam Dong	VA1-177, per 69 TAD
Da Nang	**VA1- 3**	Nan Dong	VA1-177, per 69 TAD
Da Nang East	VA1-195	Nang Son	VA1-77, per 69 TAD
Da Nang	MR 1, Heliport # 513	Nga Ba	VA1-177, per 69 TAD
Da Nang/Marble Mt.	VA1-195	Nga Ba	MR 1, Heliport # 623
Dai An	VA1-68	**Ngok Tavak**	**VA1-75**, per 69 TAD
Dai Phong	VA1-77, per 69 TAD	Ngokti	MR 1, Heliport # 624
Dak Lane	VA1-75, per 69 TAD	Nhan Bieu	VA1-79, per 69 TAD
Dak Nhe	VA1-45	Non Son	VA1-77, per 69 TAD
Diem Truong	MR 1, Heliport # 559	Nong Son	VA1-77, per 69 TAD
Dong Ha	**VA1-22**	Nong Son	MR 1, Heliport # 625
Duang Hoa Thuang	VA1-81, per 69 TAD	Nong Son	MR 1, Heliport # 626
Duc Long	MR 1, Heliport # 716	Op # 7	MR 1, Heliport # 627
Duc Pho	**VA1-201**	**Pho Trach**	**VA1-76**, per 69 TAD
Duc Pho	MR 1, Heliport # 564	Pho Trach	MR 1, Heliport # 629
Dung Long	MR 1, Heliport # 565	**Phouc Binh**	**VA1-77**, per 69 TAD
Foxy	YC 405-975? (A Shau)	Phu Bai	VA1-6
Gia Vuc	VA1-43	Phu Gia	MR 1, Heliport # 631
Gio Linh	**VA1-67**, per 69 TAD	Phu My Thuong	VA1-239
Ha Tan	VA1-68	Phuoc Cam	MR 1, Heliport # 634
Ha Thanh	VA1-204	Phuoc Chau	MR 1, Heliport # 635
Hai Lang	MR 1, Heliport # 573	Phuoc Ha	MR 1, Heliport # 636
Hau Duc	VA1-81, per 69 TAD	Phuoc Lam	MR 1, Heliport # 637
Hawk Hill (Hill 29)	MR 1, Heliport # 714	Phuoc Son 1	MR 1, Heliport # 639
Hiep Duc	MR 1, Heliport # 576	Phuoc Son 2	MR 1, Heliport # 640
Hiep Khanh	VA1-69	Phuoc Tien	MR 1, Heliport # 641
Hieu Duc	MR 1, Heliport # 577	Phuoc Tuong	MR 1, Heliport # 642
Hieu Duc	MR 1, Heliport # 578	PK-17	VA1-69
Hill 40	MR 1, Heliport # 580	**Quang Ngai**	**VA1-23**
Hill 59	MR 1, Heliport # 531	Quang Tin	MR 1, Heliport # 650
Hill 60	MR 1, Heliport # 582	**Quang Tri**	VA1-78
Hill 63	VA1-63, per 69 TAD	**Quang Tri 1**	**VA1-79**, per 69 TAD
Hill 69	MR 1, Heliport # 583	Quang Tri North	VA1-79, per 69 TAD
Hill 76	MR 1, Heliport # 584	Quang Tri	MR 1, Heliport # 651
Hoa Cam	MR 1, Heliport # 585	Quang Tri/La Vang	VA1-263
Hoa Long	MR 1, Heliport # 586	Que Son	MR 1, Heliport # 652
Hoi An	VA1-206	**Red Beach**	**VA1-24**
Hoi An	**VA1-206,** per 69 TAD	Riverside	VA1-79, per 69 TAD
Hoi An	MR 1, Heliport # 588	Ro	MR 1, Heliport # 653
Hua Duc	**VA1-81,** per 69 TAD	**Ruong Ruong**	**VA1-177**, per 69 TAD
Hue	VA1-6	Son Ha	VA1-204
Hue Citadel	VA1-70	**Ta Bat**	**VA1-80**, per 69 TAD
Hue Thanh Noi	VA1-70	Ta Luong	MR 1, Heliport # 658
Hue/Phu Bai	**VA1-6**	**Ta Ma**	**VA1-109**, per 69 TAD
Kham Duc	**VA1-45**	Tako	MR 1, Heliport # 659
Khan Duc	VA1-45	Talon	MR 1, Heliport # 660
Khe Sanh	**VA1-44,** per 69 TAD	**Tam Ky**	**VA1-40**
Khe Sanh	MR 1, Heliport # 594	Tam Ky Alternate	VA1-246
Khe Tre	MR 1, Heliport # 595	Tam Ky Provincial	VA1-246
Ky Ha	MR 1, Heliport #?	Tam Ky	MR 1, Heliport # 662
La Hierre	VA1-60, per 69 TAD	Tam Lich	MR 1, Heliport # 663
La Vang/Quang Tri	VA1-263	Tan My	VA1-62
Lang Chanh	MR 1, Heliport # 602	Thac Nuc	MR 1, Heliport # 676
Lao Bao	**VA1-71,** per 69 TAD	Thach Ban	VA1-257, per 69 TAD
Li Tinh	MR 1, Heliport # 604	Thanh Hoa	MR 1, Heliport # 678
Ly Son	VA1-93	Thanh My	MR 1, Heliport # 679
LZ Foxy	YC 405-975? (A Shau)	Thien Phouc	MR 1, Heliport # 682
LZ Sally	VA1-69	**Thuan Hoa**	**VA1-111**, per 69 TAD

Thuong Duc	VA1-68
Tien Phuoc	VA1-239
Ton Dung	VA1-84, per 69 TAD
Tourane	VA1-3
Tra Bong	MR 1, Heliport # 687
Tra My	VA1-81, per 69 TAD
Trieu Phoung	MR 1, Heliport # 693
Tu Cam	MR 1, Heliport # 694
Van Ly	VA1-115, per 69 TAD
Van Xa	VA1-69
Viet An	MR 1, Heliport # 697
Vinh Long	**VA1-20**
Xom Cham	VA1-44, per 69 TAD
Xuan Hoa	MR 1, Heliport # 703

II Corps

An Khe	**VA2-29**
An Khe AAF	VA2-29
An Khe/Golf Course	**VA2-261,** per 69 TAD
An Lac	VA2-97
An Tuc	VA2-29
Ba Gi	**VA2 189,** per 69 TAD
Ba Mla	VA2-215
Ba Ngoi	**VA2-83,** per 69 TAD
Ba Ngoi/Hane Cohe	VA2-54
Ba Ngoi/Trai Ca	VA2-83, per 69 TAD
Bac Lac	VA2-37, per 69 TAD
Ban Bich	VA2-215
Ban Blech	VA2-104
Ban Don	**VA2-39**
Ban Ho	VA2-85, per 69 TAD
Ban Me Thuot City	**VA2-86,** per 69 TAD
Ban Me Thuot East	VA2-12
Ban Me Thuot West	**VA2-12,** per 69 TAD
Ban Trap	VA2-101, per 69 TAD
Bao Loc	VA2-260
Bao Loc	VA2-37
Bao Loc City	VA2-260
Bao Loc New	VA2-260, per 69 TAD
Bao Loc Plantation	**VA2-37**
Bao Loc Plantation	**VA2-37, per 69** TAD
Ben Het	VA2-179
Binh Khe	**VA2-185,** per 69 TAD
Blao Hinh Da	VA2-37
Boa Loc New	VA2-301
Boc Lo New	VA2-301, per 69 TAD
Bom Am Bla	VA2-215
Bon Sar Pa	VA2-95, per 69 TAD
Bong Son	**VA2-87,** per 69 TAD
Bu Brang	VA2-176, per 69 TAD
Bu Glao	**VA2-270,** per 69 TAD
Bu Krak	**VA2-176,** per 69 TAD
Bu Krak South	VA2-270, per 69 TAD
Bu Prang	MR 2, Heliport # 531
Bu Prang New	VA2-107
Bun Son	VA2-28
Buon Ba Mia	VA2-215, per 69 TAD
Buon Beng	MR 2, Heliport # 526
Buon Blech	VA2-104
Buon Bon Bla	VA2-215
Buon Brieng	**VA2-188,** per 69 TAD
Buon Brieng New	VA2-215
Buon Ea Yang	**VA2-190,** per 69 TAD
Buon Ea Yang 2	VA2-190, per 69 TAD
Buon Ha	**VA2-88,** per 69 TAD
Buon Hai	VA2-88, per 69 TAD
Buon Ho	**VA2-85,** per 69 TAD
Buon Mi Ga	**VA2-55,** per 69 TAD
Buon Tsuke	VA2-89
Buu Son	VA2-28
Cam Ranh	**VA2-54**
Cam Ranh AAF	VA2-56, per 69 TAD
Cam Ranh Bay	VA2-192
Cam-Ly	VA2-8
Camp Enari	VA2-219
Camp McDermott	VA2-7, per 69 TAD
Camp McDermott	MR 2, Heliport #?
Camp McDermott	VA2-7
Camp Radcliff	VA2-261, per 69 TAD
Can Tach Tria	VA2-8
Canh Van	VA2-279
Cat	**VA2-266,** per 69 TAD
Catecka	**VA2-90,** per 69 TAD
Cheo Reo	**VA2-27**
Chudron	VA2-91
Chuong Nghia	VA2-92
Con Tach Tria	VA2-8, per 69 TAD
Crystal	**VA2-296,** per 69 TAD
Cu Hanh	VA2-4
Cung Son	VA2-46
Dak Doa	MR 2, Heliport # 555
Dak Pek	VA2-42
Dak Rode	MR 2, Heliport #?
Dak Sak	VA2-293
Dak Seang	VA2-283
Dak Sut	MR 2, Heliport #?
Dak To	VA2-34
Dak To 1	VA2-110
Dak To II	VA2-34
Dak To/Tan Canh	VA2-110
Dal Pek	VA2-42
Dalat /Cam-Ly	**VA2-8**
Dalat/Lien Khuong	**VA2-9**
Dam Pau	**VA2-49,** per 69 TAD
De Duc	VA2-232
Di Linh	VA2-48, per 69 TAD
Djiring	**VA2-48,** per 69 TAD
Dog	VA2-232
Dong Ba	MR 2, Heliport # 739
Dong Ba Thin	VA2-198
Dong Toc	VA2-113
Dong Tre	VA2-199
Dong Tre	MR 2, Heliport # 561
Dragon Mountain	VA2-219
Duc Co	VA2-91
Duc Lap	VA2-293, also VA2-95?
Duc Lap	**VA2-95,** also VA2-293?
Duc Lap #2	VA2-293
Duc Lap 2	**VA2-293,** per 69 TAD
Duc My	**VA2-96**
Duc My	**VA2-96,** per 69 TAD
Duc Xuyen	VA2-97
DZ Donna	VA2-218, per 69 TAD
DZ Kent	VA2-199, per 69 TAD
English	VA2-232
Fimnon	VA2-9
Gia Nghia	VA2-202
Giang Tay	**VA2-233,** per 69 TAD
Ha Tay	**VA2-300,** per 69 TAD
Ham Tan (MAAG)	MR 2, Heliport # 575
Hammond	**VA2-234,** per 69 TAD
Hau Bon	VA2-27
Hau Nghia	VA3-182
Hensel	VA2-219
Hoai Nhon	VA2-87, per 69 TAD
Holloway	**VA2-25**
Joyce	**VA2-152,** per 69 TAD
Kala	VA2-48, per 69 TAD

Kannack	**VA2- 99,** per 69 TAD
Khanh Duong	**VA2-235,** per 69 TAD
Kon Hojao	VA2-110
Kon Hojao West	VA2-34
Kon Mahar	MR 2, Heliport # 600
Kon Plong	**VA2-92**
Kontum	**VA2-15**
Kontum (22d Div Fwd)	MR 2, Heliport # 506
Kontum (District)	MR 2, Heliport # 597
Kontum (MAAG)	MR 2, Heliport # 601
Kontum (Sector)	MR 2, Heliport # 591
Krong No	VA2-97, per 69 TAD
Krong No	VA2-97
Labonte	VA2-300, per 69 TAD
Lac Thien	**VA2-208,** per 69 TAD
Lac Tien	VA2-208, per 69 TAD
Lane (An Son) Army	MR 2, Heliport # 713
Lang Dak Sang	VA2-283
Le Thant	VA2-252
Lien Khuong	VA2-9
Litts	VA2-152, per 69 TAD
Long Van	VA2-7
Luan Thanh	VA2-28
Luong Son	**VA2-228,** per 69 TAD
LZ Cat	**VA2-266,** per 69 TAD
LZ Crystal	**VA2-296,** per 69 TAD
LZ Dog	VA2-232
LZ Joyce	**VA2-152,** per 69 TAD
LZ Litts	VA2-152, per 69 TAD
LZ Pony	VA2-300, per 69 TAD
M'Drak	**VA2-100,** per 69 TAD
Mahoney AAF	**VA2-282,** per 69 TAD
Mang Buk	VA2-41
Mewal	**VA2-101,** per 69 TAD
Min Rong Sakang	VA2-227, per 69 TAD
Nang Buk	VA2-41
Ngok Ngo	VA2-92
Nha Trang	**VA2-7**
Nhon Co	**VA2-21**
Ninh Hoa	VA2-103
Oasis	VA2-252
Phan Rang	**VA2-28**
Phan Rang (MAAG)	MR 2, Heliport # 628
Phan Thiet	**VA2-11**
Phey Srunh	**VA2-211,** per 69 TAD
Phu Cat	VA2-213
Phu Cat	MR 2, Heliport # 630
Phu Cat 2	**VA2-212,** per 69 TAD
Phu Hiep AAF	**VA2-298,** per 69 TAD
Phu Nhon	**VA2-280,** per 69 TAD
Phu Tuc	**VA2-215,** per 69 TAD
Phu Tuc	VA2-215
Phu Xuan	VA2-199
Phung Duc	VA2-12
Phuoc An	VA2-215
Plateau Gi	**VA2-92**
Plei Djereng	**VA2-217,** per 69 TAD
Plei Djereng	VA2-285
Plei Djereng New	VA2-285
Plei Djiring	MR 2, Heliport # 644
Plei Djrang	MR 2, Heliport # 645
Plei Do Lim	**VA2-221**
Plei Kly	VA2-280, per 69 TAD
Plei Me	VA2-218
Plei Me I	VA2-218
Plei Mrong	VA2-106
Plei Toun Breng	VA2-285
Pleiku	VA2-4
Pleiku (ARVN Hosp)	MR 2, Heliport # 647
Pleiku (MAAG)	MR 2, Heliport # 648
Pleiku (SF)	MR 2, Heliport # 649
Pleiku Area	VA2-25
Pleiku Catecka	VA2-90, per 69 TAD
Pleiku/Cu Hanh	VA2-4
Pleiku/Nansteph	VA2-229
Polei Kleng	VA2-241
Polei Krong	**VA2-178,** per 69 TAD
Pony	VA2-300, per 69 TAD
Poste De Bu Prang	VA2-176, per 69 TAD
Qui Nhon	**VA2-13**
Riong Bolieng	VA2-49, per 69 TAD
ROK AAF	VA2-279
ROKA Logistical Cmd	MR 2, Heliport # 760
Son Bla Mla	VA2-215
Son La	VA2-215
Song Bam La	VA2-215, per 69 TAD
Song Cau	VA2-108
Song Hoa	VA2-46
Song Mao	**VA2-18**
Soui Dai	**VA2-244,** per 69 TAD
Soui Doi	**VA2-245,** per 69 TAD
South Beach	VA2-54
Suoi Doi	MR 2, Heliport #?
Tan Canh	VA2-110
Tan Canh (MAAG)	MR 2, Heliport # 668
Tan Phat	VA2-301
Tan Rai	VA2-227, per 69 TAD
Tan Xuan	VA2-96
Thop Cham	VA2-28, (Thap Cham?)
Tieu Atar	VA2-265
Tra Bong	VA2-112
Trai Ca	VA2-83, per 69 TAD
Trang Phuc	VA2-39
Trung Lap	VA2-? (XT 591-213)
Tuttle	VA2-252
Tuy An	**VA2-253,** per 69 TAD
Tuy Hoa	**VA2-113**
Tuy Hoa (MAAG)	MR 2, Heliport # 695
Tuy Hoa Bac	VA2-19
Tuy Hoa Chop Chai	VA2-19
Tuy Hoa Nam	VA2-113
Tuy Hoa North	**VA2-19**
Tuy Hoa South	VA2-113
Two Bits	VA2-87, per 69 TAD
USNS Corpus Christi Bay	MR 2, Heliport # 742
Van Canh	**VA2-114,** per 69 TAD
Van Canh	MR 2, Heliport # 696
Van Ninh	**VA2-224**
Vinh Thanh	VA2-259
Xa Tan Rai	**VA2-227,** per 69 TAD
Yankee	MR 2, Heliport # 706

III Corps

An Loc	**VA3-47,** per 69 TAD
Ap Tan Hoa	VA3-267, per 69 TAD
Ap Thonh Nguyen	VA3-136
Ba Ria	MR 3, Heliport # 511
Ba Ria	VA3-216
Ba Xuyen	VA4-16
Bao Trai	**VA3-182,** per 69 TAD
Bao Trai	MR 3, Heliport # 515
Bearcat	MR 3, Heliport # 738
Ben Cat	MR 3, Heliport # 517
Ben Cat	VA3-135
Ben Keo	MR 3, Heliport # 519
Ben Luc	MR 3, Heliport # 766
Ben Nam	VA3-125, per 69 TAD
Ben Suc	MR 3, Heliport # 520

Bien Hoa (Spartan)	MR 3, Heliport # 522
Bien Hoa	**VA3-2**
Bing Duong	VA3-214
Binh Ba II	**VA3-118,** per 69 TAD
Binh Ba South	VA3-118, per 69 TAD
Binh Chanh	MR 3, Heliport # 754
Binh Duong	VA3-214
Binh Gia	MR 3, Heliport # 524
Binh Gia	VA3-258
Binh Loc	**VA3-119,** per 69 TAD
Binh Long	VA3-133
Binh Phuoc	MR 3, Heliport # 525
Binh Son	**VA3-120,** per 69 TAD
Blackhorse	MR 3, Heliport # 763
Blackhorse	**VA3-240**
Bo Mua	VA3-50
Bu Dang	MR 3, Heliport # 527
Bu Dang	VA3-269
Bu Dong Srei	VA3-269
Bu Dop	MR 3, Heliport # 528
Bu Dop	VA3-121
Bu Ghia	MR 3, Heliport # 529
Bu Ja Map	VA3-130
Bu Ja Mo	MR 3, Heliport # 530
Bunard	VA3-297
Bung Bung	VA3-50
Camp 77	MR 3, Heliport # 539
Camp Evans	*VA3-143, should be VA1-143*
Camp Tran Hung Dao (Saigon?)	MR 3, Heliport #?
Can Dot	VA3-247
Can Duoc	MR 3, Heliport # 540
Can Gio	MR 3, Heliport # 541
Can Giuoc	MR 3, Heliport # 542
Cao Song Be	VA3-286, per 69 TAD
Cap St. Jacques	VA3-5
Castle	MR 3, Heliport #?, per 69 TAD
Cau Cay	VA3-148, per 69 TAD
Cau Lay	VA3-148, per 69 TAD
Cay Gao	**VA3-125,** per 69 TAD
Chan Thanh	MR 3, Heliport # 551
Chi Linh	**VA3-286,** per 69 TAD
Cho Gao	MR 3, Heliport # 549
Chon Than Hwy Strip	VA3-126
Chon Thanh	VA3-126
Chua Chan	VA3-131
CORDS Roof Top	MR 3, Heliport # 756
Courtenay	**VA3-127,** per 69 TAD
Cruickshank	MR 3, Heliport #?
Cu Chi AAF	VA3-207
Cu Chi	MR 3, Heliport # 552
Dakkir	**VA3-128,** per 69 TAD
Dat Do	**VA3-196**, per 69 TAD
Dau Tieng	VA3-129
DEPCORDS Trac	MR 3, Heliport # 767
Di An AAF	**VA3-278,** per 69 TAD
Di An	VA3-278
Dinh Quan	VA3-289
Dinh Thanh North	VA3-129
Dinh Thauh	VA3-129
Djamap	VA3-130
Don Luan	VA3-149
Dong Bo	**VA3-138,** per 69 TAD
Dong Hoa	MR 3, Heliport # 757
Dong Xoai	MR 3, Heliport # 562
Dong Xoai	VA3-149
Dozier	VA3-135
Duan Loc	VA3-119, per 69 TAD
Duc Hoa	MR 3, Heliport # 563
Duc Hoa	VA3-200
Duc Hue	VA3-94
Duc Phong	VA3-269
Duc Phuong	VA3-269
Eagle Bay	MR 3, Heliport # 743
Eagle Farm	MR 3, Heliport # 743
Free World	MR 3, Heliport # 750
Gia Ray	MR 3, Heliport # 566
Gia Ray	VA3-131
Go Cong	MR 3, Heliport # 570
Go Dau Ha	**VA3-299,** per 69 TAD
Go Dau Ha	MR 3, Heliport # 571
Ham Tan	VA3-132
Hau Nghia	VA3-**182**
Headquarters, USARV	MR 3, Heliport # 744
Hiep Hoa	**VA3-267,** per 69 TAD
Hieu Liem	MR 3, Heliport # 579
Hoa Binh	MR 3, Heliport # 718
Hoc Mon	MR 3, Heliport # 587
Hon Quan	MR 3, Heliport # 589
Hon Quan	VA3-133
Kangaroo Hospital	MR 3, Heliport # 737
Katum	VA3-287
Kien Phuoc	MR 3, Heliport # 598
Kieng Phuoc	MR 3, Heliport # 598
Lai Khe	MR 3, Heliport # 753
Lai Khe	VA3-135
Lam Son	MR 3, Heliport # 632
Lam Son	VA3-214
Lassiter	MR 3, Heliport # 755
Li Lich	VA3-138, per 69 TAD
Loc Ninh	MR 3, Heliport # 605
Loc Ninh	**VA3-31**
Long An	VA3-247
Long Binh (24th Evac)	MR 3, Heliport #?
Long Binh AAF	VA3-61
Long Binh Ammo Depo 1	MR 3, Heliport #? (2 pads)
Long Binh Ammo Depo 2	MR 3, Heliport #? (2 pads)
Long Binh Dustoff	MR 3, Heliport #?, 69 TAD
Long Giao	VA3-240
Long Hai	MR 3, Heliport # 607
Long Hai	VA3-274
Long Thanh	VA3-136
Long Thanh I	**VA3-136**
Long Thanh II	VA3-137
Long Thanh North	VA3-137
Long Thanh South	VA3-142, per 69 TAD
Luscombe (Nui Dat)	VA3-284
Minh Thanh	**VA3-139**
Moi Loi	MR 3, Heliport # 709
Newport MR 3, Heliport	MR 3, Heliport # 758
Nha Be	MR 3, Heliport # 746
Nui Bara	VA3-30
Nui Cat	VA3-139
Nui Dat (Dust Off)	MR 3, Heliport # 736
Nui Dat (Luscombe)	VA3-284
Nui Dat	VA3-284
Ohi (a.k.a. **Tan Son Nhut**)	**VA3-1**
Ong Linh	VA3-150, per 69 TAD
Ong One	VA3-140, per 69 TAD
Ong Que	**VA3-140,** per 69 TAD
Phu Cuong	VA3-153
Phu Hoa	VA3-153
Phu Khuong	**VA3-238,** per 69 TAD
Phu Loi	VA3-153
Phu My	**VA3-142,** per 69 TAD
Phu My 2	VA3-142, per 69 TAD
Phu Tho Hoa (Phu Tho racetrack)	n/a
Phu Rieng 1	**VA3-276,** per 69 TAD

Phu Rieng Old	VA3-276, per 69 TAD
Phu Thanh	MR 3, Heliport # 633
Phuoc Hoa	**VA3-146,** per 69 TAD
Phuoc Hoa New	VA3-50
Phuoc Hoa Old	VA3-146, per 69 TAD
Phuoc Le	VA3-216
Phuoc Long City	VA3-243
Phuoc Long	VA3-30
Phuoc Thanh	VA3-50
Phuoc Tho	VA3-196, per 69 TAD
Phuoc Vinh	VA3-50
Poste De Jamap	VA3-130, per 69 TAD
Prek Klok	**VA3-288,** per 69 TAD
Quan Loi	VA3-147
Quan Xuyen	MR 3, Heliport # 759
Rang Rang	**VA3-148,** per 69 TAD
Red Carpet	MR 3, Heliport # 764
Sabre MR 3, Heliport	MR 3, Heliport # 765
Saigon (Hotel 3)	MR 3, Heliport # 707
Saigon	VA3-1
Saint Kilda	MR 3, Heliport # 747
Sanford AAF	**VA3-61**
Song Be City	VA3-243
Song Be	MR 3, Heliport # 655
Song Be	**VA3-30**
Song Phan	VA3-132
Suoi Da	VA3-238, per 69 TAD
Suoi Da Lchg	VA3-238, per 69 TAD
Suoi Da	MR 3, Heliport # 656
Tak Xa	VA3-149
Tam An	VA3-136
Tan An	MR 3, Heliport # 665
Tan An	VA3-247
Tan Ba	MR 3, Heliport # 667
Tan Hoa	VA3-267, per 69 TAD
Tan Nien Tay	MR 3, Heliport # 670
Tan Phu Thuong	VA3-182
Tan Son Nhut	MR 3, Heliport #?, 69 TAD
Tan Son Nhut	**VA3-1**
Tan Son Northwest	VA3-138, per 69 TAD
Tan Tru	MR 3, Heliport # 673
Tan Uyen	MR 3, Heliport # 674
Tang Hoa	MR 3, Heliport # 675
Tanh Linh	VA3-248
Tay Ninh City	VA3-151
Tay Ninh I	VA3-151
Tay Ninh III	VA3-256
Tay Ninh West	VA3-256
Tay Ninh	VA3-151
Thai Thien	VA3-142, per 69 TAD
Thien Ngon	**VA3-35**
Thu Dau Mot	VA3-153
Thu Duc	MR 3, Heliport # 761
Thuan Loi	**VA3-154,** per 69 TAD
Tiger 5	MR 3, Heliport # 748
Tonle Cham	VA3-292
Tram Vang	MR 3, Heliport # 689
Trang Bang	MR 3, Heliport # 690
Trang Bom	VA3-?
Trang Lon	VA3-256
Trang Sup	MR 3, Heliport # 691
U.S. Embassy	MR 3, Heliport # 749
Vinh Loi	MR 3, Heliport # 701
Vo Dat	VA3-159
Vo Dat I	VA3-159
Vo Dinh	VA3-119, per 69 TAD
Vung Tau	**VA3-5**
Xa Ba Sau	VA3-150, per 69 TAD
Xom Cat	**VA3-255,** per 69 TAD
Xong Ong Linh	**VA3-150,** per 69 TAD
Xuan Loc	MR 3, Heliport # 704
Xuan Loc	VA3-226
Xuyen Moc	**VA3-162,** per 69 TAD
Xuyen Moc	MR 3, Heliport # 705

IV Corps

An Giang	VA4-169
An Hiep	**VA4-180,** per 69 TAD
An Long	**VA4-33,** per 69 TAD
An Long	MR 4, Heliport # 503
An Phu	MR 4, Heliport # 504
An Thoi	VA4-264
An Xuan Cu	VA4-57, per 69 TAD
An Xuyen	VA4-57, per 69 TAD
Ap Bac	MR 4, Heliport # 505
Ap Long Thonh	VA4-169
Ba Dua	MR 4, Heliport # 509
Ba Hon	VA4-166
Ba Tri	VA4-180, per 69 TAD
Ba Tri	MR 4, Heliport # 512
Bac Lieu	VA4-58
Be Duc	VA4-183
Ben Tranh	MR 4, Heliport # 710
Ben Tranh	**VA4-26**
Ben Tre	MR 4, Heliport # 521
Ben Tre	VA4-14
Bin Hung	VA4-163, per 69 TAD
Bing Hung	VA4-163, per 69 TAD
Binh Dai	**VA4-184,** per 69 TAD
Binh Dia	MR 4, Heliport # 23
Binh Duc	**VA4-183**
Binh Hung	**VA4-163,** per 69 TAD
Binh Tan Tan	MR 4, Heliport # 12
Binh Tan	MR 4, Heliport # 711
Binh Thanh Thon	VA4-186
Binh Thuy Heliport	MR 4, Heliport # none
Binh Thuy	**VA4-187**
Ca Mau (New)	VA4-10
Ca Mau Moi	VA4-10
Ca Mau Old	VA4-57, per 69 TAD
Ca Mau	VA4-10
Cai Be	MR 4, Heliport # 533
Cai Cai	MR 4, Heliport # 534
Cai Cai	VA4-191
Cai Doi Van	VA4-163, per 69 TAD
Cai Lay	MR 4, Heliport # 535
Cai Mon	MR 4, Heliport # 536
Cai Nhum	MR 4, Heliport # 537
Cai Nuoc	MR 4, Heliport # 538
Can Tho (Old)	VA4-17
Can Tho New	VA4-187, per 69 TAD
Can Tho	**VA4-17**
Can Tho	VA4-187
Cao Lanh	MR 4, Heliport # 543
Cao Lanh	VA4-53
Cau Ke	MR 4, Heliport # 544
Cau Ngang	MR 4, Heliport # 545
Cement Plant	VA4-166
Chau Doc	MR 4, Heliport # 48
Chau Doc	VA4-193
Chau Duc	VA4-193
Chau Lang	**VA4-164,** per 69 TAD
Chau Phu	VA4-193
Chi Lang Trng Center	VA4-173
Cho Lach	MR 4, Heliport # 50
Con Son	**VA4-32**
Dai Dien	MR 4, Heliport # 715
Dam Doi	MR 4, Heliport # 558

Dan Phuc	VA4-197, per 69 TAD
Dinh Thanh	MR 4, Heliport # 560
Don Phuc	VA4-197
Don Phuoc	VA4-197
Dong Phuoc	VA4-197, per 69 TAD
Dong Phuoc	VA4-197
Dong Tam	MR 4, Heliport # 752
Dong Tam	VA4-295
Duong Dong	VA4-165
Gauvin-Upton (Vinh Long AF)	VA4-? (XS 040-331)
Gia Ria	MR 4, Heliport # 567
Giao Duc	MR 4, Heliport # 568
Giong Trom	MR 4, Heliport # 569
Go Bac Chien	VA4-51
Go Cong	**VA4-203**
Go Do	VA4-174, per 69 TAD
Go Quao	MR 4, Heliport # 717
Ha Tien South	VA4-273
Ha Tien	**VA4-36**
Hai Yen	VA4-163, per 69 TAD
Ham Long	MR 4, Heliport # 574
Hong Chong	VA4-166
Hong Ngu	MR 4, Heliport # 590
Huong My	MR 4, Heliport # 592
Ke Sach	MR 4, Heliport # 719
Khai Quang	MR 4, Heliport # 593
Khanh Duong New	VA4-291
Kien Binh	MR 4, Heliport # 596
Kien Cung	MR 4, Heliport # 720
Kien Giang	VA4-167
Kien Hoa	VA4-l4
Kien Long	**VA4-236**
Kien Tien	MR 4, Heliport # 599
Lap Vo	MR 4, Heliport # 603
Long Dinh	MR 4, Heliport # 606
Long Khanh	MR 4, Heliport # 608
Long Khot #2	VA4-262
Long Khot	MR 4, Heliport # 609
Long Khot	VA4-186
Long My	MR 4, Heliport # 722
Long Phu	MR 4, Heliport # 610
Long Phu	MR 4, Heliport # 723
Long Toan	**VA4-168,** per 69 TAD
Long Toan	MR 4, Heliport # 611
Long Xuyen	MR 4, Heliport # 612
Long Xuyen	VA4-169
Me Ann	MR 4, Heliport # 614
Mo Cay	MR 4, Heliport # 616
Moc Hoa	VA4-51
My An	MR 4, Heliport # 708
My Phuoc Tay	MR 4, Heliport # 619
My Tho New	VA4-183
My Tho	MR 4, Heliport # 620
My Tho	VA4-26
My Thoi	VA4-169
Nam Can	MR 4, Heliport # 621
Nam Can	VA4-302
Ngo Tung	VA4-173
Nhon Ninh	MR 4, Heliport # 724
Phong Dinh	VA4-17
Phong Phu	MR 4, Heliport # 725
Phu Loc	**VA4-172,** per 69 TAD
Phu Quoc	VA4-165
Phu Vinh	VA4-52
Phung Hiep	MR 4, Heliport # 726
Phuoc Hai	VA4-172, per 69 TAD
Phuoc Long	MR 4, Heliport # 638
Poulo Condore	VA4-32
Quan Long	**VA4-10**
Quan Long City	**VA4-57,** per 69 TAD
Quang Lang 2	VA4-10
Quang Long 1	VA4-57, per 69 TAD
Rach Gia City	**VA4-56,** per 69 TAD
Rach Gia New	VA4-167
Rach Gia Old	VA4-56, per 69 TAD
Rach Gia	MR 4, Heliport # 741
Rach Gia	VA4-167
Rach Soi	VA4-167
Reliable AAF	VA4-295
Sa Dec	MR 4, Heliport # 654
Sadec	VA4-242
Soc Trang	**VA4-16**
Solid Anchor	VA4-302
Son Dong	VA4-14
Song Dong	VA4-14
Song On Doc	MR 4, Heliport # 727
Tac Van	MR 4, Heliport # 728
Tam Binh	MR 4, Heliport # 661
Tam Hiep	VA4-26
Tan An (Training Center)	MR 4, Heliport # 666
Tan An	MR 4, Heliport # 664
Tan Chau	MR 4, Heliport # 669
Tan Hei	VA4-26
Tan Hiep	VA4-26
Tan Hung	MR 4, Heliport # 729
Tan Phu	MR 4, Heliport # 671
Tan Tich	VA4-53
Than Phu	**VA4-290,** per 69 TAD
Than Tri	VA4-172, per 69 TAD
Thanh Binh	MR 4, Heliport # 677
Thanh Phu	MR 4, Heliport # 680
That Son	MR 4, Heliport # 681
That Son	VA4-173
Thoi Binh	MR 4, Heliport # 730
Thoi Hoa	**VA4-174,** per 69 TAD
Thot Not	MR 4, Heliport # 683
Thoy Dong	VA4-174, per 69 TAD
Thuan Hoa	MR 4, Heliport # 731
Thuan Nhon	MR 4, Heliport # 732
Thuan Trung	MR 4, Heliport # 733
Thuong Thoi	**VA4-294,** per 69 TAD
Thuy Dong	**VA4-38,** per 69 TAD
Thuy Dong	**VA4-38**
Tieu Can	MR 4, Heliport # 685
Tinh Bien	**VA4-249,** per 69 TAD
Tinh Bien Highway Strip	VA4-249, per 69 TAD
Tinh Bien	MR 4, Heliport # 686
Tra On	**VA4-250,** per 69 TAD
Tra On	MR 4, Heliport # 688
Tra Vinh	VA4-52
Tri Ton	MR 4, Heliport # 692
Truc Giang	**VA4-14**
Tuyen Nhon	VA4-38
Upton (Vinh Long AF)	VA4-? (XS 040-331)
Vi Thanh	**VA4-225**
Vi Thanh (Old)	**VA4-175,** per 69 TAD
Vi Thanh 2	VA4-175, per 69 TAD
Vi Thanh New	VA4-225
Vinh Chau	MR 4, Heliport # 698
Vinh Gia	MR 4, Heliport # 699
Vinh Kim	MR 4, Heliport # 700
Vinh Loi	VA4-58
Vinh Long AF (Gauvin-Upton)	**VA4-? (XS 040-331)**
Vinh Quoi	MR 4, Heliport # 734
Vung Liem	MR 4, Heliport # 702
Xom Ba Hon	VA4-166
Xom Cat Doi Vam	VA4-163, per 69 TAD
Xom Nui Trau	VA4-166

U.S. Military Medium to Large Airfields and Passenger Jet Capable Airports

Compiled from *Vietnam Studies, Base Development in South Vietnam 1965-1970*, Department of the Army, 1972, p 66.

I Corps:

An Hoa - Tactical AF
Camp Evans - Tactical AF
Chu Lai - Tactical AF
Da Nang - **Jet Capable AP**
Dong Ha - Tactical AF
Duc Pho - Tactical AF
Gia Vuc - Tactical AF
Hue/ Phu Bai - Tactical AF
Kham Duc - Tactical AF
Khe Sanh - Tactical AF
Marble Mtn. - tactical AF
Plateau Gi - Tactical AF
Quang Ngai - Tactical AF
Quang Tri - Tactical AF
Tam Ky - Tactical AF
Tra Bong - Tactical AF

II Corps:

An Khe Golf Course - Tactical AF
Ban Blech - Tactical AF
Ban Don - Tactical AF
Ban Me Thuot - Tactical AF
Bao Loc - Tactical AF
Cam Ranh Bay - **Jet capable AP**
Camp Holloway - Tactical AF
Cheo Reo - Tactical AF
Cung Son - Tactical AF
Da Lat Cam Ly - Tactical AF
Da Lat Lien Khuong - Tactical AF
Dak Pek - Tactical AF
Dak To - Tactical AF
Dong Ba Thin - Tactical AF
Dong Tre - Tactical AF
Duc Co - Tactical AF
Duc Lap - Tactical AF
Hammond - Tactical AF
Hensel Army Airfield - Tactical AF
Khanh Duong - Tactical AF
Kontum - Tactical AF
LZ English - Tactical AF
Nha Trang - Tactical AF
Nhon Co - Tactical AF
Phan Rang - **Jet capable AP**
Phan Thiet - Tactical AF
Phu Cat - **Jet capable AP**
Phu Hiep - Tactical AF
Phu Nhon - Tactical AF
Phu Tuc - Tactical AF
Plei Djereng - Tactical AF
Plei Du - Tactical AF
Plei Kleng - Tactical AF
Plei Mrong - Tactical AF
Pleiku - Tactical AF
Qui Nhon - Tactical AF
Song Mao - Tactical AF
The Oasis - Tactical AF
Tuy Hoa - **Jet capable AP**
Van Canh - Tactical AF

III Corps:

Bien Hoa - **Jet capable AP**
Long Thanh - Tactical AF
Bu Nard - Tactical AF
Chi Linh - Tactical AF
Courtenay - Tactical AF
Cu Chi Army Airfield
Dau Tieng - Tactical AF
Di An - Tactical AF
Dinh Quan - Tactical AF
Dong Xoai - Tactical AF
Duc Phong - Tactical AF
Ham Tan - Tactical AF
Katum - Tactical AF
Lai Khe - Tactical AF
Loc Ninh - Tactical AF
Minh Thanh - Tactical AF
Phuoc Vinh - Tactical AF
Phu Loi - Tactical AF
Quan Loi - Tactical AF
Song Be - Tactical AF
Tan Son Nhut - **Jet Capable**
Ohi (A.k.a. Tan Son Nhut)
Tanh Linh - Tactical AF
Tay Ninh West - Tactical AF
Thien Ngon - Tactical AF
Tonle Cham - Tactical AF
Vo Dat - Tactical AF
Vung Tau - Tactical AF
Xuan Loc - Tactical AF**I**

IV Corps:

An Long - Tactical AF
Binh Tuy - Tactical AF
Moc Hoa - Tactical AF
Phu Vinh - Tactical AF
Quan Long - Tactical AF
Rach Gia - Tactical AF
Soc Trang - Tactical AF

Airfields in North Vietnam

Per DMA/NOAA Aeronautical Charts

Airfield	Remarks
Bac Giang Airfield	Feb67 Natl Geo. map. El. 50'. NVN.
Bac Mai (Hanoi) Airfield	Major airport on the S edge of Hanoi and 6 km SW of Gia Lam AF, the other major airfield of Hanoi area, per ONC J-11. NVN. El 16'.
Bai Thuong Airfield	MIG base, appx 35 km WNW of Thanh Hoa and 130 km SSW of Hanoi, per Oct75 ONC-J-11. NVN. El 73'.
Ban Nam Nam	Feb67 Natl Geo. map. El. 656'. NVN.
Ben Loi Airfield	75 km SSE of Vinh and 95 km NW of Dong Hoi, per ONC J-11. NVN. El 54'.
Cai Bi (Hai Phong) Airfield	Major airfield 95 km ESE of Hanoi and 5 km SE of Hai Phong. One of two major fields near the port of Hai Phong, per Oct75 ONC-J-11. NVN. El 15'.
Cao Bang Airfield	Feb67 Natl Geo. map. El. 750'. NVN.
Dang Son Airfield	3600' runway 130 km NE of Hanoi, 110 km N of Hai Phong and 20 km S of China border, per ONC J-11. NVN. El 840'.
Dien Bien Phu Airfield	5 km N of Dien Bien Phu hamlet, 17 km N of Ban Cong Den hamlet, 10 km E of Laotian border and 290 km WNW of Hanoi. Dien Bien Phu Valley is appx 20 km in length and 7 km in width, running N-Sand parallel to the border, per ONC J-11. NVN. El 1821'.
Dong Hoi Airfield	MIG base on the coast, 165 km SE of Vinh, per ONC J-11. NVN. El 65'.
Dong Suong Airfield	25 km SW Hanoi, per ONC J-11. NVN. El 81'.
Gia Lam (Hanoi) Airfield	One of two major fields in the Hanoi area, the other being Bac Mai. On the N side of the Red River (Song Hong), 5 km NE of Hanoi and 8 km NE of Bac Mai Airport, per ONC J-11. NVN. El 25'.
Ha Giang Airfield	Feb67 Natl Geo. map. El. ?'. NVN.
Kep Airfield	75 km NNE of Hanoi, per map in *Vietnam Experience* Series, *Rain of Fire* volume, p. 11.
Kep Ha Airfield	Feb67 Natl Geo. map. El. 60'. NVN.
Khe Phat Airfield	45 km NW of Dong Hoi and 135 km SSE of Vinh, per ONC J-11. NVN. El 60'.
Kien An (Hai Phong) Airfield	Major airfield 10 km SW of Hai Phong and 85 km ESE of Hanoi. One of two major fields near the port of Hai Phong, per ONC-J-11. NVN. El 15'.
Lai Chau Airfield	Feb67 Natl Geo. map. El. 591'. NVN.
Lang Son Airfield	Feb67 Natl Geo. map. El. ?'. NVN.
Lao Cai Airfield	Feb67 Natl Geo. map. El. 295'. NVN.
Mong Cai Airfield	On border with China where it meets the ocean in NW NVN, appx 224 km ENE of Hanoi. On the S edge of village with the same name and appx 5 km N of the coast, per ONC J-11. NVN. El 33'
Na San Airfield	Major airfield 5 km W Ban Loi village and I85 km WNW of Hanoi, per ONC J-11. NVN. El 2050'.
Nghia Lo Airfield	Feb67 Natl Geo. map. El. 886'. NVN.
Pho Thu Airfield?	Feb67 Natl Geo. map. El. 33'. NVN.
Phuc Nhac Airfield	At Phat Diem, 100 km SSE of Hanoi, 50 km NE of Thanh Hoa and 20 km from the ocean, per ONC J-11. NVN. El ?
Phuc Yen Airfield	Major airfield 20 km due N of Hanoi, per ONC J-11. NVN. El 36'.
Quan Lan Airfield	MIG base appx 70 km NW of Vinh, per ONC J-11. NVN. El 60'.
Quang Te Airfield	90 km SSW of Hanoi, per map in Time/Life Vietnam Experience Series, *Rain of Fire* volume, p. 11.
Son La Airfield	Feb67 Natl Geo. map. El. ?'. NVN.
Son Tay Airfield	Feb67 Natl Geo. map. El. 200'. NVN.
Than Uyen Airfield	Feb67 Natl Geo. map. El. 1903'. NVN.
That Khe Airfield	Feb67 Natl Geo. map. El. 596'. NVN.
Tong Airfield	35 km WNW of Hanoi, per ONC J-11. NVN. El 34'.
Tuyen Quang Airfield	Feb67 Natl Geo. map. El. 80'. NVN.
Vinh Airfield	On the coast, 160 km NW of Dong Hoi, 245 km due S of Hanoi and 10 km N of Vinh, per ONC J-11. NVN. El 68'
Vinh Linh Airfield?	Feb67 Natl Geo. map. NVN.
Yen Bai Airfield	110 km NW of Hanoi, per map in Time/Life Vietnam Experience Series, *Rain of Fire* volume, p. 11.
Yen Khanh Airfield?	Feb67 Natl Geo. map. El. 6'. NVN.

Airfields In Cambodia

Per DMA/NOAA Charts

Data here compiled from DMA/NOAA aeronautical charts ONC J-11, ONC K-10, TPC K-10A TPC K-10B, TPC K-10D, and the Feb67 *National Geographic Magazine* Vol. 131, No. 2. insert: *Vietnam, Cambodia, Laos and Thailand*, 1,980,000 scale map, and *Air Facilities Data: Laos* (official airfield guide for Air America pilots and similar to the DMA TAD). For detailed locational and other historical information for any airfield listed in this section, refer to the corresponding listing in the main alphabetical section of this text.

Cambodian Airfields and Airports

Aeroport de Pochentong
Amleang AF
Andaung Pech AF
Anlong Veng AF
B. *(universal abbr for 'Ban'}*
Ba Kev AF
Ba Na Ku AF
Ban Chuang AF
Ban Kaeng Nang AF
Ban Nham Airstrip
Ban Pu Kroy AF
Baray AF
Baray Highway Strip
Batdambang AF
Battambang AF
Bo Khco AF
Boung Long AF
Buong Long AF
Camp Rolland AF
Chamkar Leu AF
Chamkar Leu AF
Cheom Ksan AF
Chhep AF
Choam KhsamAF
Choam Khsan AF
Chup Plantation AF?
Dak Dam AF
Deshayes AF
Kampon Chhnang AF
Kampone Spoe AF
Kampong Cham AF
Kampong Cham AF
Kampong Chhnang AF
Kampong Saom AF
Kampong Soam AF
Kampong Sralu AF
Kampong Thum AF
Kampong Thum Hwy Strip
Kampong Thum Hwy Strip
Kampong Thum South AF
Kampot AF
Kampot AF
Kaoh Nhek AF
Kep AF
Khemarak Phouminville AF
Khlong Yai AF
Khon Kaen AF
Koh Kong Southeast AF
Kompong Chak AF
Kompong Cham AF
Kompong Chhnang AF
Kompong Sralao AF
Kompong Thom AF
Krakor AF
Kratie AF
Leong Nok Tha AF
Lomphat AF
Lumphat AF
Marech AF
Memot AF
Mimot AF
Mondol Kiri City AF
Muong AF
Nam Pong Dam AF
O Rang AF
Odonek AF
Pailin AF
Peam Amleang AF
Peam Lovek AF
Pha Tang AF
Phnom Penh Intl Airport
Phnom Thbeng Meanchey AF
Phong Thong AF
Phum Cham Sla AF
Phum Chup AF
Phum Kra Sang AF
Phum Krek AF
Phum Plok AF
Phum Preas Ang AF
Phum Svai Antor AF
Phum Tapeang AF
Phumi Choam AF
Pochentong Intl Airport
Pong Tuk AF
Pong Toek AF
Poste Deshayes AF
Pouthichentong Intl Airport
Prey Veng AF
Ream Kampong AF
Sakhon Nakhon AF
Sakon Nakhon AF (New)
Sakon Nakhon Army AF
Sakon Nakhon Old AF
Samrong AF
Savannakhet AF (Major)
Savannakhet AF (Minor)
Sen Kung AF
Sen Kung AF
Senmonorom AF
Siem Pang AF
Siem Reap AF
Siempang West AF
Siemreap AF
Sihanoukville AF
Sisophon AF
Snuol AF
Sre Mat AF
Stung Treng AF
Svay Rieng AF?
Ta Nagl AF
Tadak Pong AF
Takeo AF
Thbeng Meanchy AF
Tnaot AF
Trapeang Rung AF
Veal Vang AF
Veal Veng AF
Viracheay AF
Virachei AF
Yean Than Antaracheat AF

Airfields In Laos

Per DMA/NOAA Charts

Data here compiled from DMA/NOAA aeronautical charts ONC J-11, ONC K-10, TPC K-10A TPC K-10B, TPC K-10D, Feb67 *National Geographic Magazine* Vol. 131, No. 2. insert: *Vietnam, Cambodia, Laos and Thailand*, 1,980,000 scale map, and *Air Facilities Data: Laos* (official airfield guide for Air America pilots and similar to the DMA TAD). For detailed locational and other historical information for any airfield listed in this section, refer to the corresponding listing in the main alphabetical section of this text.

The L- and LS- numbers following many of these entries is an Air America (CIA) airfield numbering system for what that company referred to as Lima Sites. Lima was simply the military phonetic alphabet for the letter 'L' used as shorthand for the word Laos. Some texts suggest LS meant Listening Site, and although they may have served as electronic eavesdropping sites, that apparently was not the official intent of the designation L or LS for airfields in Laos.

Recommended reading: *Air Facilities Data: Laos*, a reproduction of Air America official airfield guide (author unknown). Complete listing of all Lima Sites used by Air America, Continental Air Services and USAF Ravens flying in Laos. Data given individually for each of the over 350 sites that includes: Number and name of airfield, length/width, construction, geographic coordinates, map reference, runway orientation, elevation and much more. This publication can be orderd from K&S Militaria, PO Box 9630, Alpine TX 79831, tel. 915-837-5053, fax 915-837-5021. Order number is *BO 842*.

Laotian Airfields and Airports

Attopeu (LS-10)
B. *(universal abbr for 'Ban'}*
Ba Na
Ba Na Puong
Ba Na Then
Ba Phu Lun (LS-136)
Ba Ta Ngane
Ban 'Y' (LS-187)
Ban An (L-110)
Ban Ban
Ban Ban (LS-10)
Ban Beecher (LS-100)
Ban Bo Mei (LS-194)
Ban Bonong (LS-12)
Ban Boua Mu (LS-367)
Ban Bouac (LS-34)
Ban Bouac New (LS-116)
Ban Bungxang (LS-296)
Ban Chomhat (LS-295)
Ban Chuk Chung (LS-138)
Ban Da Bom (LS-64)
Ban Done
Ban Done (East)
Ban Done (LS-163)
Ban Done (West)AF
Ban Dong (LS-28)
Ban Dong Hene (LS-54)
Ban Dong Khan Khou (LS-304)
Ban Donge (LS-163)
Ban Hang Khang
Ban Hong Non
Ban Houana (LS-302)
Ban Houaymun (LS-310)
Ban Houei Dionne (LS-123)
Ban Houei Keng (LS-226)
Ban Houei Kong
Ban Houei Kong
Ban Houei Lao (LS-147)
Ban Houei Lung
Ban Houei Pamone (LS-272)
Ban Houei Sai (L-25)
Ban Houei Sai Citadel (LS-283)
Ban Houei Sane (LS-189)
Ban Houei Sane North
Ban Houei Sou
Ban Hquaymun
Ban In Thi
Ban Kagnontang
Ban Keng Sai (LS-84)
Ban Keng Tanga (LS-298)
Ban Kengpe (LS-292)
Ban Keun
Ban Keun (LS-44)
Ban Kha (LS-94)
Ban Khami (LS-39)
Ban Kho
Ban Khoanag (L-41)
Ban Khok Mai (LS-171)
Ban Khok May
Ban Khok Tong
Ban Kia Maa (LS-314)
Ban Kong Mi
Ban Konghang
Ban Kongmi (LS-407)
Ban Kout Lamphong
Ban Koutlamphong (LS-447)
Ban La Tee
Ban La Tee (LS-190)
Ban Lahanam (LS-301)
Ban Lao Ngam
Ban Laong Hwy Strip
Ban Lee (LS-233)
Ban Lee 2 (LS-253)
Ban Lou (LS-248)
Ban Mai (LS-329)
Ban Maya (LS-234)
Ban Moung (LS-177)
Ban Moung Ngan (LS-236)
Ban Muong Mo
Ban Muong Ngat
Ban Na
Ban Na (LS-15)
Ban Na Kala Hwy Strip
Ban Na Khai 30
Ban Na Kouang (LS-281)
Ban Na Luang (LS-66)
Ban Na Tai (L-50)
Ban Na Tan (LS-237)
Ban Na Tao
Ban Na Then (LS-249)
Ban Na Ti (LS-287)
Ban Na To
Ban Na Woua (LS-109)
Ban Nachalit (LS-297)
Ban Nakay Neua
Ban Nakhua
Ban Nalay (LS-291)
Ban Nam Bac
Ban Nam Chuam (LS-290)
Ban Nam Deng (LS-110)
Ban Nam Dua (LS-143)
Ban Nam Feng (LS-223)
Ban Nam Hin (LS-104)
Ban Nam Kama
Ban Nam Keng (LS-108)
Ban Nam Kueung (LS-150)
Ban Nam Luang (LS-313)
Ban Nam Na (LS-20A)
Ban Nam Nhion
Ban Nam Nhion (LS-149)
Ban Nam Pao
Ban Nam Song (LS-363)
Ban Nam Thao (LS-161)
Ban Nam Thouei (LS-118)
Ban Nam Tieng (LS-165)
Ban Nam Xao (LS-208)
Ban Nam Xao (LS-240)

Ban Nam Yon Nea (LS-307)
Ban Nathom (LS-343)
Ban Naty (LS-287 and Ban Na Ti)
Ban Naty North (LS-327)
Ban Ngang
Ban Nong Bok (LS-183)
Ban Nong Boua
Ban Nong Boua (LS-134)
Ban Nong Bqua
Ban Nong Dao (LS-83)
Ban Nong Lao
Ban Nong One (LS-101)
Ban Nong Tong (LS-209)
Ban Nong Vien
Ban Nong Vien
Ban Nongla (LS-214)
Ban Nongsa (LS-446)
Ban Nou Kha Chok (LS-148)
Ban Padou (LS-419)
Ban Pak En (LS-97)
Ban Pak Ham (LS-306)
Ban Pak Mi
Ban Pawi (LS-285)
Ban Peung (LS-95)
Ban Pha Ka (LS-40)
Ban Pha Kao (LS-308)
Ban Pha Nop
Ban Pha Thong (LS-169)
Ban Pha Thong (LS-247)
Ban Phak Khagna (LS-303)
Ban Pham Khao
Ban Phan Hop (L-53)
Ban Phang (LS-239)
Ban Phone Sai (LS-309)
Ban Phoungmay (LS-222)
Ban Poung (LS-324)
Ban Rosie (LS-250)
Ban Sa Noi (LS-119)
Ban Sa Phout (LS-151)
Ban Samet
Ban San Tiott
Ban San Tong
Ban Saphat
Ban Saphat (LS-175)
Ban Sapi (LS-60)
Ban Se (LS-225)
Ban Si
Ban Sing Keo (LS-332)
Ban Sok (LS-420)
Ban Sok West
Ban Song (LS-29)
Ban Song Hac
Ban Song Khone (LS-77)
Ban Sop Siem (LS-269)
Ban Soukhouma (L-45)
Ban Sun Kang (LS-349)
Ban Ta Viang
Ban Talan Nua
Ban Tang
Ban Tangvay (LS-299)
Ban Tha
Ban Tha (LS-52)
Ban Tha Si
Ban Tha Si (LS-61)
Ban Tham Tat (LS-81)
Ban Thamloup
Ban Than Lay (L-105)
Ban Thang (LS-275)
Ban Ton Phung (LS-305)
Ban Vieng (LS-135)
Ban Vieng (LS-89)
Ban Xani (LS-294)
Ban Xiang Khai (LS-293)
Ban Xien Kok
Ban Xieng Lom (LS-69)
Ban Xon
Ban Xon (LS-246)
Ban Xon (LS-272)
Ban Xot
Ban Y (LS-187)
Bolovens (LS-55)
Borikhane (LS-129)
Bouam Long (LS-32)
Boum Lao (LS-174)
Boun Loum (LS-88)
Boun Neua (L-30)
Buam Vang (LS-242)
Bun Taio (L-20)
Buon Neua
Buon Neua (L-30)
Champassak (L-107)
Chavane
Chinaimo (LS-279)
Chong Ha (LS-48)
Doi Seang (LS-160)
Don's Strip (LS-219)
Dong Hene
Fort Carnot
Ft. Carnot
Gang Sa Ni (L-45)
Grove Jones (LS-141)
Grove Jones 2 (LS-141A)
Happy's Strip (LS-264)
Har Due (LS-366)
Hat Khon (LS-271)
Hin Heup (LS-365)
Hong Non (LS-86)
Hong Non New (LS-122)
Hong Sa (LS-62)
Hong Sa (LS-62A)
Hongsa (LS-62)
Hongsa (LS-62A)
Houei Hinsa (LS-215)
Houei Hok (LS-198)
Houei Hong (LS-200)
Houei Kah Moun (LS-111)
Houei Ki Nin (LS-38)
Houei Kong (L-56)
Houei Ma (LS-107)
Houei Mai (LS-325)
Houei Moun (LS-221)
Houei Nam Om (LS-224)
Houei Sa An (LS-127)
Houei Sa An (LS-23)
Houei Sai (LS-284)
Houei Sang (LS-206)
Houei Soi (LS-164)
Houei Thom (LS-27)
Houei Tong Ko (LS-184)
Hua Moung (LS-58)
Huei Thong (LS-196)
Jennifer's Strip (LS-259)
Jom Mog (LS-345)
Ken Thao (L-06)
Kene Thao
Keng Ka Boa (LS-235)
Keng Kaboa (LS-235)
Keng Kok (LS-139)
Keo Sa Khai Neua (LS-331)
Kha Phu (LS-35)
Khammouane
Khang Hong (LS-68)
Khang Khai (LS-08)
Khang Kho (LS-204)
Khang Ko (LS-204)
Khieu Manang (LS-192)
Khong
Khong Island (L-07)
Khong Sedone (LS-289)
Kiou Ca Cham (LS-04)
Kiou Cacham (LS-04)
Klahan (LS-326)
Kok Kieng (LS-282)
La Khong Pheng (LS-159)
La Ta Sin (LS-130)
Lak Sao (LS-49)
Lakhonpeng
Lao Bao
Lao Ta (LS-121)
Lat Houang (LS-09)
Lat Khai (LS-280)
Lat Sen (LS-276)
Long Keo (LS-172)
Long Pot (LS-132)
Long Chien (LS-20A/30/98)
Long Tieng (LS-20A/30/98)
Luang Prabang (L-54)
Mahaxay (L-57)
Mak Phout (LS-137)
Mary's Strip (LS-258)
Moang Soum (LS-157)
Mok Lok (LS-131)
Mok Plai (LS-193)
Moung Ao Neua (LS-227)
Moung Cha (LS-113)
Moung Chim (LS-56)
Moung Hai (L-41)
Moung Het (L-13)
Moung Hiem (LS-48A)
Moung Houn (L-34)
Moung Kassy (LS-153)
Moung Khao (LS-128)
Moung Kheung (L-109)
Moung Lem (LS-320)
Moung Met (LS-158)
Moung Mo (LS-182)

Moung Moe (LS-46)
Moung Moungw (LS-93)
Moung Ngai (LS-01)
Moung Ngeum (LS-168)
Moung Nham (LS-63)
Moung Ou Tay (L-02)
Moung Oum (LS-22)
Moung Pa (LS-342)
Moung Peun (L-31)
Moung Phalane (L-61)
Moung Phalane SW (L-61A)
Moung Phanh (L-106)
Moung Phieng (LS-124)
Moung Phun (LS-37)
Moung Sai (L-27)
Moung Sam (LS-24)
Moung Sao (LS-319)
Moung Sing (L-42)
Moung Sol (L-60)
Moung Son (L-59)
Moung Soui (L-108)
Moung Sung (L-01)
Moung Tiouen (LS-91)
Muang Kay
Muang Kout (LS-195)
Muang Met
Muang Phine (LS-300)
Muang Phon Savan
Muang You (LS-261)
Muong Cassy
Muong Cha
Muong Et
Muong Hai
Muong Han
Muong Houn
Muong Kassy
Muong Khao
Muong Mugne
Muong Nane (LS-254)
Muong Ngeun
Muong Ngoi
Muong Nong (L-19)
Muong Ou Tay
Muong Peun
Muong Phalane
Muong Sai
Muong Sing
Muong Soi
Muong Son
Muong Soui
Muong Soum
Muong Tiouen
Na Dao (LS-70)
Na Khang (LS-36)
Na Lang (LS-286)
Na Leng (LS-286)
Na Luang New (LS-252)
Na Poung (LS-78)
Na Vat
Na Xieng (LS-181)
Nam Bac (LS-203)
Nam Bu (LS-125)
Nam Chong (LS-17)
Nam Hang (LS-278)
Nam Houn (LS-243)
Nam Keng
Nam Keo
Nam Lan (LS-07)
Nam Lieu (LS-118A)
Nam Moh (LS-207)
Nam Pha Noi (LS-218)
Nam Poune (LS-344)
Nam Song (LS-199)
Nam Tan (LS-268)
Nam Tang (LS-73)
Nam Tha (L-100)
Nam Thom (LS-47)
Nam Thuam (LS-176)
Nam Ve (LS-335)
Nam Yon (LS-288)
Nam Yong (LS-288)
Nam Yu (LS-118A)
Nape (LS-43)
Naw Nuen (LS-79)
Nhot Phat (LS-179)
Ninh Heup Hwy Strip
Nong Het (LS-03)
Nong Kala (LS-338)
Nong Kha (LS-333)
Nong Khang (L-52)
Nong Luang (LS-322)
Nong Pet (LS-154)
Nong Sakhe (LS-106)
Nyot Mo (LS-321)
Ohu Sa Ngop (LS-270)
Old San Soak (LS-265)
Ou Neua (L-26)
Pa Doung (LS-05)
Pa Doung Noi (LS-340)
Pa Ka (LS-51)
Pak Mouei (LS-273)
Pak San
Pak Song
Paklay (L-09)
Paksane (L-35)
Pakse (L-11)
Paksong (L-05)
Paksong New (LS-180)
Paseau (LS-315)
Pha Bong (LS-76)
Pha Deng (LS-341)
Pha Du (LS-263)
Pha Hang (LS-205)
Pha Hom (LS-241)
Pha Hong (LS-213)
Pha Ka (LS-245)
Pha Khao (LS-14)
Pha Khe (LS-51)
Pha Langmou (LS-170)
Pha Peung (LS-21)
Pha Phai (LS-65)
Pha Poon (LS-328)
Pha Poun (LS-230)
Phia Chan (LS-155)
Phia Khan (LS-87)
Phia Louang (LS-270)
Phone Sai (LS-211)
Phone Thong
Phone Thong (LS-450)
Phong Hong (LS-133)
Phong Saly (L-15)
Phongsali (L-15)
Phou Chai (LS-25)
Phou Chia (LS-25)
Phou Da Pho (LS-103)
Phou Dam (LS-256)
Phou Douak (LS-440)
Phou Fa (LS-16)
Phou Houang (LS-140)
Phou Kahm Phouk (LS-166)
Phou Kang Neua (LS-337)
Phou Khao Khouai
Phou Khe (LS-19)
Phou Kheo (LS-115)
Phou Khong (LS-42)
Phou Kouk (LS-59)
Phou Lat Seua (LS-418)
Phou Leang (LS-323)
Phou Louang (LS-402)
Phou Nam Nhiou (LS-146)
Phou Ngieu (LS-232)
Phou Nong (LS-71)
Phou Pang Sang (LS-142)
Phou Pha Louom (LS-220)
Phou Pha Louom (LS-228)
Phou Sai (LS-312)
Phou Saly (LS-178)
Phou Sam Soun (LS-231)
Phou San (LS-336)
Phou San Nyai (LS-362)
Phou So (LS-57)
Phou Soung (LS-156)
Phou Ta Beng
Phou Tai (LS-185)
Phou Vieng (LS-06)
Phou Vieng (LS-197)
Phoung Sam (LS-114)
Phoung Savan (L-21)
Phowachedy (LS-311)
Phu Cum (LS-50)
Phu Cum (LS-50A)
Phu De Me (LS-105)
Phu Fa Noi (LS-102)
Phu He (LS-255)
Phu Houei Mouei (LS-67)
Phu Houot (LS-99)
Phu Hua Moui (LS-67)
Phu Khan Hua (LS-251)
Phu Mieng Mane (LS-96)
Phu Moun (LS-212)
Phu Pha Thi (LS-85)
Phu Sang Nao (LS-80)
Phu Sang Noi (LS-244)
Phu Se Bott (LS-82)
Pien Lieu (LS-31)
PK 21 (LS-364)

PK 21 Military Res.
Pong Hai (LS-361)
Pong Ta (LS-229)
Pop's Field (LS-120)
Poste Kilometre 21(LS-364)
Puntai (L-20)
Ritaville (LS-53)
Sa Noi
Sala Phou Koun (LS-260)
Sam Neua (L-04)
Sam Sen (LS-112)
Sam Song Hong (LS-201)
Sam Thong (LS-20)
Samneua
San Louang (LS-41)
San Pa Ka (LS-33)
San Tiau (LS-02)
Sanakham (L-49)
Saravane (L-44)
Savannakhet (L-39)
Savannakhet (Major)
Savannakhet (Minor)
Sayaboury (L-23)
Sen Sai (LS-162)
Seno (L-46/46A)
Sepone
Shing Scha (LS-339)
Si Siang Mai (LS-277)
Sing Ka (LS-92)
Son Soak New (LS-126)
Song Lai (LS-318)
Sop Hao (L-17)
Sop Hien (LS-75)
Soukhouma
Ta Fa (LS-216)
Ta Viang (LS-13)
Takhek
Tang Hung (LS-167)
Tchepone (L-38)
Tha Lin Noi (LS-18)
Tha Tam Bleung (LS-72)
Tha Thom (LS-11)
Thak Hek
Thakhek
Thakhek New
Thakhet East (L-40)
Thakhet West (L-40A)
Tham Lo (LS-316)
Tham Sorm (LS-74)
Than Heup (LS-238)
Thateng (LS-210)
Thong Khamo
Thong Khen (LS-317)
Thong Miang (LS-266)
Thong Noi (LS-330)
Thung Peeut (LS-202)
Thung Peeut (LS-262)
Tin Bong (LS-90)
Tong Hang (LS-173)
Tong Pa How (LS-250)
Tong Prang (LS-145)
Tong Too (LS-186)
Toong Cha (LS-334)
Toong Set (LS-449)
Van Pak Len (LS-267)
Vang Veng
Vang Vieng
Vang Vieng (L-16)
Vien Pou Kha (LS-152)
Vieng Pou Kha (LS-152)
Vientiane (L-08)
Wat Phu (L-107)
Xam Tai (L-47)
Xieng Dat (LS-26)
Xieng Dat New (LS-117)
Xieng Khouang (L-22)
Xieng Khouang Ville (L-03)
Xieng Lom (LS-274)
Xieng Ngeun (LS-354)
Xing Than (LS-288)
Yung Tuia (LS-217)

Airfields In Thailand

Per DMA/NOAA Charts

Data here compiled from DMA/NOAA aeronautical charts ONC J-11, ONC K-10, TPC K-10A TPC K-10B, TPC K-10D, the Feb67 *National Geographic Magazine* Vol. 131, No. 2. insert: *Vietnam, Cambodia, Laos and Thailand*, 1,980,000 scale map, and *Air Facilities Data: Laos* (official airfield guide for Air America pilots and similar to the DMA TAD). For detailed locational and other historical information for any airfield listed in this section, refer to the corresponding listing in the main alphabetical section of this text.

Thai Airfields and Airports

B. (*universal abbr for Ban*)
Ban Bo Han AF
Ban Chai Buri AF
Ban Chiang Klang AF
Ban Don Tan SF
Ban Fang Lum AF
Ban Hong Ten AF
Ban Huai Kaeo AF
Ban Kut Kho Kan AF
Ban Lampang Luang AF?
Ban Mae Kon Ken AF
Ban Mae Thalop AF
Ban Muang Phrae AF
Ban Nong Saeng AF
Ban Pru Yai AF
Ban Sak Ngoi AF
Ba Na Muang AF
Ban A Ham AF
Ban Bung Khla AF
Ban Dan AF
Ban Don AF
Ban Hae Don New AF
Ban Hin Taek AF
Ban Hong Thong AF
Ban Huai Khi Nu AF
Ban Kapchoen AF
Ban Khe Don New AF
Ban Khemarat AF
Ban Khok Huai AF
Ban Kop AF
Ban Kut Khae Don AF
Ban Kut Khaen AF
Ban Le Kho AF
Ban Mae Lana AF
Ban Mae Sao AF
Ban Mae Tan AF
Ban Maeo Thap Boek AF
Ban Mai AF
Ban Muang Chet Ton AF
Ban Muang Pok AF
Ban Na Khu AF
Ban Na Wai AF
Ban Naeng Mut AF
Ban Nam Muap AF
Ban Nong Khan Yaeng AF
Ban Nong Lom Hwy Airstrip
Ban Pak Chom AF
Ban Phumsaron AF
Ban Poeng Khloeng AF
Ban Pru Yai AF
Ban Pua AF
Ban Samrong AF
Ban Siwilai AF
Ban Sop Han AF

Ban Takhli Airbase
Ban Tha Chang AF
Ban Tha Ta Fang AF
Ban That AF
Ban The Pang AF
Ban Tin Tok AF
Ban Yot Don Chi AF
Bangkok AF
Bangkok Intl Airport
Barnae AF
Bau Rai AF
Ben Khemmarat AF
Bung Kan AF
Buntharick AF
Buriram AF
Camp Nasty
Chainat AF
Chaiyaphum AF
Changwat Udon Thani Sanam Bin
Chanthaburi AF
Chiang Kham AF
Chiang Khan AF
Chiang Khong AF
Chiang Mai AF
Chiang Rai AF
Chiang Saen AF
Chiayaphum AF
Chong Mek AF
Chumphon AF
Crossroads AF
Dean's Strip AF
Don Muang AF, Bangkok
Don Muang Air Force Base
Don Muang Airbase
Don Muang, Tha Akatsayan
Don Muang, Tha Akatsayan AF
Hat Yai Intl AF
Hin Luk AF
Hua Hin AF
Huai San AF
Kabin Buri AF
Kalasin AF
Kamphaeng Saen AF
Kanchanaburi AF
Khao Saphan Nak ArmyAF
Khemmara AF
Khiri Khan, PrachuapAF
Ko Kha AF?
Khak Pho AF
Khok Krathiam AF
Khon Kaen AF
Khorat AF
Khorat Army AF
Khun Yuam AF
Korat AF
Korat Airbase
Korat Army AF
Krung Thep AF
Kuchinairai AF
Kukhan AF
Lahan Sai AF
Lam Na AF
Lampang AF
Lao Na AF
Leon Nok Tha AF
Leong Nok Tha AF
Loei AF
Lomsak AF
Lom Sak AF
Lop Buri AF
Mae Hong Son AF
Mae Rim AF
Mae Sai AF
Mae Sariang AF
Mae Sot AF
Maha Sarakham AF
Maruk AF
Mukdahan AF
Na Bua AF
Na Wiang AF
Nagor Rjasima
Nakhon Phanom AF
Nakhon Phanom West AF
Nakhon Rachasima AF
Nakhon Ratchasima AF
Nakhon Sawan AF
Nakhon Si Thammarat AF
Nam Phong AF
Nam Phung Dam North AF
Nam Pong Dam AF
Nan AF
Narathiwat AF
Nds Mae Sot AF
NKP
Nong Khai AF
Nong Mek AF
Nong Seang AF
Nong Seang AF
Pa Wai AF
Pa Wai AF
Pai AF
Pak Chong AF
Pattani AF
Pawai AF
Phanom Sarakham AF
Phet Buri AF
Phitsanulok AF
Phon Phisai AF
Phrae AF
Phu Khieo AF
Phuket AF
Prachin Buri AF
Prachuap Khiri Khan AF
Pran Buri AF
Preah Vihear AF
Pua AF
Rahaeng AF
Rangae AF
Ranong AF
Rat Buri AF
Ratchathani Airbase
Rayong AF
Roi Et AF
Sa AF
Sakhon Nakhon AF
Sakon Nakhon AF
Sakon Nakhon Army AF
Sam Ngao AF
Samrong AF
Sanam Bin Changwat Udon Thani Airport
Sanam Bin Ubon Ratchathani
Sanambin Songkhla AF
Sara Buri AF
Sattahip AF
Satun AF
Sawang Daen Din AF
Si Ching Mai AF?
Singora AF
Sisaket AF
Songkhla AF
Songkhla Airport
Surat Thani AF
Surin AF
Ta Khli Airbase
Ta Klhi AF
Tak AF
Tak Police AF
Takhli Airbase
Taklhi AF
Tha Akatsayan Don Muang
Tha Akatsayan Don Muang AF
Tha Bo AF
Tha Yang AF
Thai Airfields (continued)
Thoeng AF
Thoeng AF
Thung Chang AF
Thung Song AF
Trang AF
Trat AF
U Ta Pao Airbase
U Tapao Airbase
U Taphao AF
Ubon (major) AF
Ubon Northwest AF
Ubon Ratchathani AF
Ubon Ratchathani, Sanam B.
Udon AF
Udon Border Police AF
Udon Thani AF
Udorn AF
Udorn Border Police AF
Umphang STOL Strip AF
Uttaradit AF
Uttaradit Northwest AF
Wanon Niwat AF
Watthana Nakhon AF
Yala AF
Yang Talat AF
Yasothon AF

NDB, VOR, TACAN And DME Radio Guidance Facilities/Sites

Data compiled from DMA 1:500,000 scale maps: TPC J-11D, K-10A, K-10B, K-10D

Term Definitions:

NDB	n/a	Non Directional Air Navigation Beacon site.
DME	n/a	Directional Measuring Equipment site.
TACAN	n/a	Tactical Air navigation. An ultra-high frequency electronic air navigation system providing continuous bearing and slant range to a selected station. Acronym derived from phrarse: **Tac**tical **A**ir **N**avigation.
VOR	n/a	Air navigational radio aid which uses phase comparisons of a ground transmitted signal to determine bearing. Acronym derived from phrase: **V**ery high frequency **O**mnidirectional **R**adio range.

Sites Sorted by Facility Type:

NDB An Loc	YT 43-12	N of QL-1, apx 5 km WNW of Xuan Loc. Long Khanh Prov, III Corps.
NDB Battambang	UV 07-48	At Battambang AF. Cambodia.
NDB Can Tho	WS 83-12	Apx 3 km NW Can Tho and 6 km SE of TACAN NDB Binh Thuy. Phong Dinh Prov, IV Corps.
NDB Da Nang	BT 01-63	Apx 4 km S of Da Nang AB. See also VOR DME Da Nang. Quang Nam Prov, I Corps.
NDB Dalat	BN 14-99	At Dalat/Lien Khuong AF. Tuyen Duc Prov, II Corps.
NDB Duong Dong	US 86-31	On Phu Quoc Island at Duong Dong AF. Kien Giang Prov, IV Corps.
NDB Kampong Cham	WU 48-30	Just S of Phum Kav Ramuol. Cambodia.
NDB Ninh Hoa	BP 97-83	At Ninh Hoa AF. Khanh Hoa Prov, II Corps.
NDB Pakse	WB 78-73	At Pakse AF, Cambodia.
NDB Phan Thiet	AN 94-08	Apx 3 km NE of Phan Thiet AF. Binh Thuan Prov, II Corps.
NDB Phnom Penh	VT 85-78	Apx 3 km NE of Phnom Penh AF/VOR NDB Phnom Penh. Cambodia.
NDB Phu Bai [1]	YD 89-15	A.k.a. NDB Phubai [1]. At Phu Bai AF. Thua Thien Prov, I Corps.
NDB Phu Bai [2]	YD 96-18	A.k.a. NDB Phubai [2]. Thua Thien Prov, I Corps.
NDB Qui Nhon	CR 08-23	At Qui Nhon AB. Binh Dinh Prov, II Corps.
NDB Ream Kampong Saom	US 52-69	Apx 16 km ESE of Kampong Saom AF, and 5 km from ocean. Cambodia.
NDB Saigon	XS 81-87	Apx 10 km S Tan Son Nhut. Gia Dinh Prov, III Corps.
NDB Soc Trang	XR 06-59	At Soc Trang AB. Ba Xuyen Prov, IV Corps.
NDB Vung Tau	YS 30-47	At Vung Tau AF. Phuoc Tuy Prov, III Corps.
TACAN NDB Ban Me Thuot East	AQ 87-02	At Ban Me Thuot East AF, apx 7 km E of Ban Me Thuot.
TACAN NDB Bien Hoa	XT 98-13	At Bien Hoa AB. Bien Hoa Prov, III Corps.
TACAN NDB Binh Thuy	WS 79-15	At Binh Thuy AF, 8 km NW of Can Tho and 6 km NW of NDB Can Tho. Phong Dinh Prov, IV Corps.
TACAN NDB Nha Trang	CP 03-52	At Nha Trang AB. Khanh Hoa Prov, II Corps.
TACAN NDB Phan Rang	BN 77-87	At Phan Rang AB. Ninh Thuan Prov, II Corps.
TACAN NDB Phu Cat	BR 88-44	At Phu Cat AB. Binh Dinh Prov, II Corps.
TACAN NDB Pleiku	AR78-50	At Pleiku/Cu Hanh AF, apx 3 km NE Pleiku. Pleiku Prov, II Corps.
VOR TACAN NDB Da Nang	BT 02-75	A.k.a. VOR DME Da Nang. At Da Nang AB. See also NDB Da Nang. Quang Nam Prov, I Corps.
VOR NDB Phnom Penh	VT 83-76	At Phnom Penh Airport and 3 km SW of NDB Phnom Penh. Cambodia.
VOR TACAN NDB Ubon	VB 86-86	At Ubon Northwest AF, Ubon Ratchathani, Thailand.
VOR TACAN Saigon	XS 82-97	At Tan Son Nhut AB. Gia Dinh Prov, III Corps.

Sites Sorted Alphabetically by Location:

An Loc NDB	YT 43-12	N of QL-1, apx 5 km WNW of Xuan Loc. Long Khanh Prov, III Corps.
Ban Me Thuot East TACAN NDB	AQ 87-02	At Ban Me Thuot East AF, apx 7 km E of Ban Me Thuot.
Battambang NDB	UV 07-48	At Battambang AF, Batdambang, Cambodia.
Bien Hoa TACAN NDB	XT 98-13	At Bien Hoa AB. Bien Hoa Prov, III Corps.
Binh Thuy TACAN NDB	WS 79-15	At Binh Thuy AF, 8 km NW of Can Tho and 6 km NW of NDB Can Tho. Phong Dinh Prov, IV Corps.
Can Tho NDB	WS 83-12	Apx3 km NW Can Tho and 6 km SE of TACAN NDB Binh Thuy. Phong Dinh Prov, IV Corps.
Da Nang NDB	BT 01-63	Apx 4 km S of Da Nang Airport. See also VOR DME Da Nang.
Da Nang VOR DME	BT 02-75	A.k.a. Da Nang TACAN DME and VOR TACAN NDB Da Nang At Da Nang AB. Quang Nam Prov, I Corps.
Da Nang VOR TACAN NDB	BT 02-75	A.k.a. Da Nang TACAN DME and VOR TACAN NDB Da Nang. At Da Nang AB. Quang Nam Prov, I Corps.
Dalat NDB	BN 14-99	At Dalat/Lien Khuong AF. Tuyen Duc Prov, II Corps.
Duong Dong NDB	US 86-31	On the coast of Phu Quoc Island at Duong Dong AF. Kien Giang Prov, IV Corps.
Kampong Cham NDB	WU 48-30	Just S of Phum Kav Ramuol, Cambodia.
Nha Trang TACAN NDB	CP 03-52	At Nha Trang AB. Khanh Hoa Prov, II Corps.
Ninh Hoa NDB	BP 97-83	Khanh Hoa Prov, II Corps.
Pakse NDB	WB 78-73	At Pakse AF, Cambodia.
Phan Rang TACAN NDB	BN 77-87	At Phan Rang AB. Ninh Thuan Prov, II Corps.
Phan Thiet NDB	AN 94-08	Binh Thuan Prov, II Corps.
Phnom Penh NDB	VT 85-78	Apx 3 km NE of Phnom Penh AP and VOR NDB Phnom Penh. Cambodia.
Phnom Penh VOR NDB	VT 83-76	At Phnom Penh AP and 3 km SW of NDB Phnom Penh. Cambodia.
Phu Bai [1] NDB	YD 89-15	A.k.a. NDB Phubai [1]. At Phu Bai AF. Thua Thien Prov, I Corps.
Phu Bai [2]NDB	YD 96-18	A.k.a. NDB Phubai [2]. Thua Thien Prov, I Corps.
Phu Cat TACAN NDB	BR 88-44	At Phu Cat AB. Binh Dinh Prov, II Corps.
Pleiku TACAN NDB	AR78-50	At Pleiku/Cu Hanh AF, roughly 3 km NE Pleiku. Pleiku Prov, II Corps.
Qui Nhon NDB	CR 08-23	At Qui Nhon AB, along NE edge of that city. Binh Dinh Prov, II Corps.
Ream Kampong Saom NDB	US 52-69	Apx 16 km ESE of Kampong Saom and AF and 5 km from the Gulf of Thailand. Cambodia.
Saigon NDB	XS 81-87	Apx 10 km S of Tan Son Nhut AB. Gia Dinh Prov, III Corps.
Saigon VOR TACAN	XS 82-97	At Tan Son Nhut AB. Gia Dinh Prov, III Corps.
Soc Trang NDB	XR 06-59	At Soc Trang AB. Ba Xuyen Prov, IV Corps.
Ubon VOR TACAN NDB	VB 86-86	At Ubon Northwest AF, Ubon Ratchathani, Thailand.
Vung Tau NDB	YS 30-47	At Vung Tau AF. Phuoc Tuy Prov, III Corps.

Appendix B
Military Facility and Geographical Data

Major U.S. Military Base Camps [1]

An Khe - II Corps

Housing for on base cadre - **Officers: 1,950**
" " **Enlisted: 12,000**
Admin. Building Square Footage: 259,730 sq. ft
Storage Area Covered: 225,492 sq. ft
Storage Area Uncovered: 107,761 sq. yds
Maintenance Space Square Footage: 188,942 sq. ft

Bearcat - III Corps

Housing for on base cadre - **Officers: 972**
" " **Enlisted: 7,615**
Admin. Building Square Footage: 125,132 sq. ft
Storage Area Covered: 60,987 sq. ft
Storage Area Uncovered: 64,207
Maintenance Space Square Footage: 117,778 sq. ft

Bien Hoa - III Corps

Housing for on base cadre - **Officers: 815**
" " **Enlisted: 8,407**
Admin. Building Square Footage: 134,597 sq. ft
Storage Area Covered: 91,972 sq. ft
Storage Area Uncovered: 3,333 sq. yds
Maintenance Space Square Footage: 136,353 sq. ft

Black Horse (Long Giao) - III Corps

Housing for on base cadre - **Officers: 307**
" " **Enlisted: 4,537**
Admin. Building Square Footage: 79,320 sq. ft
Storage Area Covered: 30,302 sq. ft
Storage Area Uncovered: 5,333 sq. yds
Maintenance Space Square Footage: 6,824 sq. ft

Cam Ranh Bay - II Corps

Housing for on base cadre - **Officers: 1,479**
" " **Enlisted: 17,173**
Admin. Building Square Footage: 440,900 sq. ft
Storage Area Covered: 873,425 sq. ft
Storage Area Uncovered: 622,844 sq. yds
Maintenance Space Square Footage: 377,795 sq. ft

Camp Enari - II Corps

Housing for on base cadre - **Officers: 1,023**
" " **Enlisted: 9,223**
Admin. Building Square Footage: 300,420 sq. ft
Storage Area Covered: 85,600 sq. ft
Storage Area Uncovered: 58,200
Maintenance Space Square Footage: 218,898 sq. ft

Can Tho - IV Corps

Housing for on base cadre - **Officers: 131**
" " **Enlisted: 1,915**
Admin. Building Square Footage: 41,419 sq. ft
Storage Area Covered: 32,782 sq. ft
Storage Area Uncovered: 28,050 sq. yds
Maintenance Space Square Footage: 48,643 sq. ft

Chu Lai - I Corps

Housing for on base cadre - **Officers: 1,595**

[1] *Vietnam Studies, Base Development in South Vietnam 1965-1970*, Department of the Army, 1972, pp 135-136.

" " **Enlisted: 10,337**
Admin. Building Square Footage: 76,165 sq. ft
Storage Area Covered: 101,881 sq. ft
Storage Area Uncovered: 56,587 sq. yds
Maintenance Space Square Footage: 262,949 sq. ft

Cu Chi - III Corps

Housing for on base cadre - **Officers: 1,512**
" " **Enlisted: 12,616**
Admin. Building Square Footage: 207,261 sq. ft
Storage Area Covered: 125,036 sq. ft
Storage Area Uncovered: 91,560 sq. yds
Maintenance Space Square Footage: 191,800 sq. ft

Da Nang - I Corps

Housing for on bas cadre - **Officers: 671**
" " **Enlisted: 4,865**
Admin. Building Square Footage: 106,500 sq. ft
Storage Area Covered: 21,634 sq. ft
Storage Area Uncovered: 89,617 sq. yds
Maintenance Space Square Footage: 114,425 sq. ft

Dalat - II Corps

Housing for on base cadre - **Officers: 7**
" " **Enlisted: 579**
Admin. Building Square Footage: 3,821
Storage Area Covered: 17,767
Storage Area Uncovered: 373 sq. yds
Maintenance Space Square Footage: 1,760

Dong Ba Thin - III Corps

Housing for on base cadre - **Officers: 563**
" " **Enlisted: 2,430**
Admin. Building Square Footage: 38,192 sq. ft
Storage Area Covered: 7,600 sq. ft
Storage Area Uncovered: 0 sq. yds
Maintenance Space Square Footage: 25,220 sq. ft

Dong Tam - IV Corps

Housing for on base cadre - **Officers: 1,193**
" " **Enlisted: 10,995**
Admin. Building Square Footage: 160,210 sq. ft
Storage Area Covered: 89,189 sq. ft
Storage Area Uncovered: 11,247
Maintenance Space Square Footage: 212,266 sq. ft

Lai Khe - III Corps

Housing for on base cadre - **Officers: 532**
" " **Enlisted: 3,760**
Admin. Building Square Footage: 72,326
Storage Area Covered: 17,038
Storage Area Uncovered: 105,350
Maintenance Space Square Footage: 26,216

Long Thanh North - III Corps

Housing for on base cadre - **Officers**: 189
" " **Enlisted**: 933
Admin. Building Square Footage: 21,808 sq. ft
Storage Area Covered: 28,880 sq. ft
Storage Area Uncovered: 27,710 sq. yds
Maintenance Space Square Footage: 70,050 sq. ft

Long Binh - III Corps

Housing for on base cadre - **Officers: 5,855**
" " **Enlisted: 36,987**
Admin. Building Square Footage: 1,085,544 sq. ft
Storage Area Covered: 992,655 sq. ft
Storage Area Uncovered: 1,269,901 sq. yds
Maintenance Space Square Footage: 917,734 sq. ft

MACV-Saigon-Tan Son Nhut - III Corps

Housing for on base cadre - **Officers: 10,768**
" " **Enlisted: 23,288**
Admin. Building Square Footage: 1,143,452 sq. ft
Storage Area Covered: 1,453,945 sq. ft
Storage Area Uncovered: 64,813 sq. yds
Maintenance Space Square Footage: 221,155 sq. ft

Nha Trang - II Corps

Housing for on base cadre - **Officers: 438**
" " **Enlisted: 7,958**
Admin. Building Square Footage: 257,407
Storage Area Covered: 306,605 sq. ft
Storage Area Uncovered: 51,840 sq. ft
Maintenance Space Square Footage: 154,541 sq. ft

Phan Rang - II Corps

Housing for on base cadre - **Officers: 220**
" " **Enlisted: 4,487**
Admin. Building Square Footage: 48,119 sq. ft
Storage Area Covered: 48,075 sq. ft
Storage Area Uncovered: 230 sq. yds
Maintenance Space Square Footage: 11,176 sq. ft

Phu Bai - I Corps

Housing for on base cadre - **Officers: 754**
" " **Enlisted: 5,800**
Admin. Building Square Footage: 93,784 sq. ft
Storage Area Covered: 127,983 sq. ft
Storage Area Uncovered: 9,777 sq. yds
Maintenance Space Square Footage: 48,532 sq. ft

Phu Loi - III Corps

Housing for on base cadre - **Officers: 932**
" " **Enlisted: 5,721**
Admin. Building Square Footage: 81,032 sq. ft
Storage Area Covered: 36,716 sq. ft
Storage Area Uncovered: 149,055 sq. yds
Maintenance Space Square Footage: 481,013 sq. ft

Pleiku - II Corps

Housing for on base cadre - **Officers: 611**
" " **Enlisted: 9,521**
Admin. Building Square Footage: 119,497 sq. ft
Storage Area Covered: 112,669 sq. ft
Storage Area Uncovered: 5,916
Maintenance Space Square Footage: 100,547 sq. ft

Qui Nhon - II Corps

Housing for on base cadre **Officers: 1,870**
" " **Enlisted: 20,980**
Admin. Building Square Footage: 519,200 sq. ft
Storage Area Covered: 1,050,499 sq. ft
Storage Area Uncovered: 359,242 sq. yds
Maintenance Space Square Footage: 499,128 sq. ft

Saigon Ports - III Corps

Housing for on base cadre - **Officers: 218**
" " **Enlisted: 1,379**
Admin. Building Square Footage: 163,582 sq. ft
Storage Area Covered: 945,499 sq. ft
Storage Area Uncovered: 365,231 sq. yds
Maintenance Space Square Footage: 61,093 sq. ft

Tuy Hoa - II Corps

Housing for on base cadre - **Officers:**	**1,002**
" " **Enlisted:**	**6,765**
Admin. Building Square Footage:	116,345 sq. ft
Storage Area Covered:	88,438 sq. ft
Storage Area Uncovered:	233,550 sq. yds
Maintenance Space Square Footage:	92,063 sq. ft

Vinh Long - IV Corps

Housing for on base cadre - **Officers:**	**365**
" " **Enlisted:**	**2,435**
Admin. Building Square Footage:	11,544 sq. ft
Storage Area Covered:	25,951 sq. ft
Storage Area Uncovered:	0 sq. yds
Maintenance Space Square Footage:	46,582 sq. ft

Vung Tau - III Corps

Housing for on base cadre - **Officers:**	**294**
" " **Enlisted:**	**8,182**
Admin. Building Square Footage:	136,390 sq. ft
Storage Area Covered:	267,757 sq. ft
Storage Area Uncovered:	135,068 sq. yds
Maintenance Space Square Footage:	331,035 sq. ft

TOTALS - All Major Base Camps

Housing for on base cadre - **Officers:**	**36,266**
" " **Enlisted:**	**240,870**
Permanent cadre:	**277,136 Personnel**
Admin. Building Square Footage:	5,844,179 sq. ft
Storage Area Covered:	7,120,483 sq. ft
Storage Area Uncovered:	3,916,852 sq. yds
Maintenance Space Square Footage:	4,964,533 sq. ft

"Construction materials for use in [construction of camp facilities in SVN's] Corps...were supplied, with few exceptions, by the U.S. Navy. Materials for II, III and IV Corps...were stored in four depots located at Qui Nhon, Cam Ranh Bay, Long Binh and Vung Tau. Each of these depots had an engineer construction materials yard operated by civilian contractors. Bulk assets were, in general, distributed with approximately 25% to Qui Nhon, 26% to Cam Ranh Bay, 33% to Long Binh and 16% to Vung Tau. Army Operations and Maintenance (OMA) assets were stored according to demand experience or in forecast amounts for each individual depot. Certain items, such as lumber, asphalt products and cement were stored in a common location in each depot and issued according to immediate requirements without regard to funding sources." [2] See also Adams Huts in Glossary.

Major Military Seaports: [3]

Cam Ranh Bay:	
Berthing Feet:	6,500'
Draft Max:	34'
Cargo Capacity:	8,300 tons/day
Storage Covered w/in 5 km:	881,000 ft^2
Storage Uncov, w/in 5 km:	377,000 yd^2
Can Tho:	
Berthing Feet:	300'
Draft Max:	8'

[2] *Vietnam Studies, Base Development in South Vietnam 1965-1970,* p. 117

[3] All data as of 23Apr69 and includes berthing footage/cargo capacity both completed and under construction that date. *Vietnam Studies, Base Development in South Vietnam 1965-1970*, p 60.

Cargo Capacity:	800 tons/day
Storage Covered w/in 5 km:	32,000 ft^2
Storage Uncov, w/in 5 km:	28,000 yd^2

Chu Lai:

Berthing Feet:	1,400'
Draft Max:	18'
Cargo Capacity:	2,100 tons/day
Storage Covered w/in 5 km:	175,000 ft^2
Storage Uncov, w/in 5 km:	91,000 yd^2

Da Nang:

Berthing Feet:	7,100'
Draft Max:	34'
Cargo Capacity:	10,700 tons/day
Storage Covered w/in 5 km:	21,000 ft^2
Storage Uncov, w/in 5 km:	89,000 yd^2

Dong Tam:

Berthing Feet:	800'
Draft Max:	15'
Cargo Capacity:	1,200 tons/day
Storage Covered w/in 5 km:	89,000 ft^2
Storage Uncov, w/in 5 km:	11,000 yd^2

Nha Trang:

Berthing Feet:	600'
Draft Max:	40
Cargo Capacity:	1,000 tons/day
Storage Covered w/in 5 km:	306,000 ft^2
Storage Uncov, w/in 5 km:	51,000 yd^2

Qui Nhon:

Berthing Feet:	5,600'
Draft Max:	26'
Cargo Capacity:	8,300 tons/day
Storage Covered w/in 5 km:	1,050,000 ft^2
Storage Uncov, w/in 5 km:	359,000 yd^2

Phan Rang :

Berthing Feet:	200'
Draft Max:	5'
Cargo Capacity:	1,000 tons/day
Storage Covered w/in 5 km:	48,000 ft^2
Storage Uncov, w/in 5 km:	23,000? yd^2

Saigon:

Berthing Feet:	8,300'
Draft Max:	25'-29'
Cargo Capacity:	12,400 tons/day
Storage Covered w/in 5 km:	2,399,000 ft^2
Storage Uncov, w/in 5 km:	430,000 yd^2

Vung Ro:

Berthing Feet:	1,100'
Draft Max:	32'
Cargo Capacity:	1,600 tons/day

Storage Covered w/in 5 km:	88,000 ft^2
Storage Uncov, w/in 5 km:	233,000 yd^2

Vung Tau:

Berthing Feet:	2,000'
Draft Max:	28'
Cargo Capacity:	3,100 tons/day
Storage Covered w/in 5 km:	267,000 ft^2
Storage Uncov, w/in 5 km:	135,000 yd^2

"Privately owned U.S. flag merchant ships delivered 65 percent of the dry cargo shipments to support American forces in Vietnam, and government-owned ships carried the balance. The Maritime Administration activated 172 World War II era Victory ships from its National Defense Reserve Fleet. Some 15,000 U.S. citizen merchant mariners crewed the vessels. Cargoes totaled more than 85 million measurement tons." [4]

For a detailed overview of seaport construction and unit assignments during the war, visit the Internet site of the *Army Transportation Association Vietnam*, at http://academic.uofs.edu/faculty/gramborw/atav/ default.html. Seaport histories are at http://academic.uofs.edu/faculty/gramborw/atav/4tc.htm

An excellent map of the port of Saigon is available on-line at: http://home.epix.net/~gramborw/saigon.htm.

The *Army Transportation Association Vietnam* website also includes a very detailed and substantial listing of U.S. Army water craft that served in Vietnam. The list attempts to identify every Army vessel in the war; everything from from huge floating cranes and tankers down to the smallest patrol craft and tugs. Its address is: http://134.198.33.115/hulltypes.htm.

USN Support Activity (NSA), PBR, River Division and Tactical Bases in South Vietnam

All data per Mobile Riverine Force Association website at: at www. mrfa.org/

An Thoi	NSA, '65-71.
Ben Keo	USN Advanced Tactical Support Base, '69-71.
Ben Luc	USN Support Base, '68-71.
Binh Thuy	NSA, '66-72.
Binh Thuy/Can Tho	River Division 51, TF-116, USN Gamewarden base here.
Cam Ranh Bay	USN Base, '65-71.
Can Tho	NSA, '66-72.
Can Tho/Binh Thuy	River Division 51, TF-116, USN Gamewarden base here.
Cat Lai	USN Intermediate Support Base, '65-71.
Cat Lo	USN Combat and Logistics Base, '65-71.
Cho Moi	USN Logistics Installation, '69-71.
Chu Lai	NSA, '64-71.
Cua Viet	NSA, '67-70.
Da Nang	River Division 55, TF-116, USN Gamewarden base here.
Da Nang	NSA, '64-73.
Dong Ha	NSA '67-70.
Dong Tam	NSA, '66-71.
Go Dau Ha	USN Advanced Base, '69-71.
Ha Tien	USN River Patrol Boat Staging Area, '68-70.
Hiep Hoa	USN Advanced Tactical Support Base, '69.
Hoi An	USN Patrol Boat Base, '69-71.
Hue-Tan-My-Phu Bai	NSA, '65-70.
Kien An	USN and RVN Forces Operating Base, '69-70.
Long Binh	USN River Forces Operating Base, '69-70.
Long Phu	USN Intermediate Support Base, '69-71.
Long Xuyen	USN Advanced Support Base, '66-71.
Moc Hoa	USN Advanced Tactical Support Base, '68-71.

[4] Quote Per: http://marad.dot.gov/ support_forces.html - U.S. Maritime Administration, America's Merchant Marine.

My Tho	River Division 53, TF-116, USN Gamewarden base here.
My Tho	River Division 53, USN TF 116.
My Tho	NSA, '66-69.
Nam Can	USN Mobile Facility, '69-71.
Nha Be River	River Division 54, TF-116, USN Gamewarden base here.
Nha Be River	River Division 54, USN TF 116
Nha Be	NSA, '66-72.
Nha Trang	USN Operating Station, '65-71
Phu Bai-Hue-Tan-My	NSA, '65-70.
Phu Cuong	USN Advanced Support Base, '69-70.
Phuoc Xuyen	USN Advanced Tactical Support Base, '69-71.
Qui Nhon	NSA, '65-71.
Rach Soi	USN Intermediate Support Base, '69-71.
Sa Dec	River Division 52, TF-116, USN Gamewarden base here and later moved to Vinh Long.
Sa Dec	River Division 52, USN TF 116 (later moved to Vinh Long)
Sa Dec	NSA Detachment, '66-71.
Sa Huynh	NSA Detachment, '67-70.
Saigon	USN HQ Support Activity, & Naval Support Activity, '50-73.
Tam My	NSA, '65-70.
Tan An	USN Advanced Tactical Support Base, '68-69.
Tan Chau	USN River Patrol Base, '69-70.
Tan-My-Phu Bai-Hue	NSA, '65-70.
Thuan An	USN Intermediate Support Base, '71.
Thuyen Nhon	USN Advanced Tactical Support Base, '69-71.
Tra Cu	USN Advanced Tactical Support Base, '68-71.
Vinh Long	USN Facility, '66-71.
Vinh Long	River Division 52, TF-116, USN Gamewarden base here. Moved here from Sa Dec.
Vung Tau	NSA Detachment, '65-71.

Military POL (Petroleum, Oil and Lubricants) Facilities [5]

(Private commercial storage not included)

	Facility	Storage Capacity Barrels	# of Tanks	Pump Capacity Barrels/Day	Incoming Pipeline in Miles
I Corps:					
	Camp Evans			18,000	18 miles
	Dong Ha	3,000		18,000	5 miles
	Duc Pho	16,000	6		
	Hue/Tan My			36,000	7 miles
	Phu Bai	24,000	2	18,000	11 miles
	Quang Tri	59,000	8	18,000	20 miles
II Corps:					
	An Khe	69,000	10	18,000	53 miles
	Cam Ranh Bay	579,000	51	210,000	22 miles
	Dalat	4,500			
	Dau Tieng	1,500	3	18,000	20 miles
	Dong Ba Thin				
	Nha Trang	72,000	10		
	Phan Rang/AFB	6,000	2	43,000	22 miles
	Phan Thiet	7,500	3	8,250	2 miles
	Phu Cat AFB			18,000	20 miles
	Pleiku	59,000	3	18,000	63 miles
	Qui Nhon	324,000	27	145,740	11.5 miles
	Tay Ninh	9,000	3		

[5] *Vietnam Studies, Base Development in South Vietnam 1965-1970*, p. 128-130

Tuy Hoa	13,000	6	43,000	4 miles
Vung Ro				
Xom My Ca				2 miles?
III Corps:				
Binh Loi				
Dong Nai				
Long Bien	86,000	10	81,000	54 miles
Long Bien Power Plant	12,000		8,000	2 miles
Newport			38,000	1.5 miles
Phu Loi				7 miles?
Tan My An				
Tan Son Nhut				
Vung Tau	25,000	13		
IV Corps:				
Can Tho/Binh Thuy	3,000	3		
Dong Tam	12,000	6		
Soc Trang	2,500	3		
Vinh Long	9,000	5		

"Since pipeline movement of fuel and oil was more efficient and economical than highway transport when an area was secure enough for its use, a military construction program was undertaken, and by 1968, over 270 miles of pipeline were in use throughout Vietnam." [6]

"Monthly consumption of oil products increased from over 500,000 barrels a day in July, 1965 to over 3 million barrels per day in 1968. During the same period, storage rose to 2.6 million barrels. In the absence of sufficient storage tank resources, collapsible tanks (primarily 10,000, 20,000 and 50,000-gallon capacity) proved to be an effective and highly useful. By October 1969, over $27 million worth of collapsible bladders had been shipped to Vietnam." [7]

Major Headquarters, Corps, Divisional and Regimental Commands

Data compiled primarily from Shelby Stanton's *Vietnam Order of Battle*, 1986, Galahad Books.

Major Headquarters & Advisory Commands

1st Australian Task Force
See Australian Task Force, HQ in this section.

1st Special Forces
See 5th SF Grp.

5th Special Forces Group
Actually, 5th SF Grp, 1st Special Forces. Arrived 1Oct64, departed 3Mar71. Replaced U.S. Army Special Forces Vietnam (Provisional) command. Auth troop strength grew from 28 men in '64, to 383 in '68. Tasked to conventionalize the CIDG program built by predecessors, with high priority given to border regions. Numerous older SF camps were closed as a result and new camps built along Cambodian/Laotian borders. Simultaneously, hamlet militias were disbanded and CIDG troops retrained for border interdiction. At peak, there were apx 45,000 indigenous troops under SF control.

7th Air Force/SAC
HQ, Guam. See U.S. Air Force, Vietnam, in this Section. Casualties: KIA-1,739, WIA-3,475.

7th Fleet/U.S. Naval Forces Vietnam
HQ, Hawaii. See U.S. Navy Naval Forces, Vietnam. Casualties: KIA-1,626, WIA 10,406.

AAAGV
Australian Army Assistance Group, Vietnam: In Vietnam 6Mar72-31Jan73, HQ, Saigon.

AAFV, HQ
HQ Australian Army Forces, VN: In VN 2May65-2May66. HQ at Bien Hoa, Bien Hoa Pr suptg 1st Bn RAR at Bien Hoa. 1RAR was supt by Log supt Co arriving May/Jun65, followed by suptg Arty, Armor and Avn assets in Sep65. Attached to U.S. 173d Abn Bde working War Zone D. 1RAR returned to Australia Jun66, after being replaced by 1st Australian Task Force. Simultaneously, HQ AAFV was enlarged to include naval and airforce commands and renamed HQ, AFV, May66.

AATTV
Australian Army Training Team, VN. In VN 31Jul62-18Dec72. 1st Aussie forces to serve. Originally a 30 officer contingent (grew to 100+ by '72) assisting U.S. Adv providing op training/leadership to ARVN and VNSF. Primarily in I Corps. 4 received Victoria Cross.

---

[6] *Vietnam Studies, Base Development in South Vietnam 1965-1970*, p. 129-30

[7] *Vietnam Studies, Base Development in South Vietnam 1965-1970*, p. 129

AFV, HQ
HQ, Australian Forces VN. In VN 1Apr66-12Mar72. HQ at Saigon. Was combined HQ of all Australian forces, air/sea/land, in VN. Created May66 by combining its predecessor, HQ AAFV, with air and Naval asset Cmds. This HQ remained responsible for cmd until Aussie forces left VN.

AHAC, HQ
U.S. Army Headquarters Area Command, Long Binh, Apr66-May72, Authorized strength: 472.

Australian Task Force, HQ
A.k.a. ATF 1ATF, 1RATF, HQ AAFV, HQ AFV and 1st Royal Australian TF. Between 25May65-2May66 was known as HQ AAFV, with its HQ'd in Saigon suptg 1 Bn RAR at Bien Hoa AB (and attached to U.S. 173d Abn Bde). From 3May66-15Mar72 was given own Phuoc Tuy Pr TAOR and HQ moved to Nui Dat/Luscombe AF. Major elements were: 1st Australian TF HQ, 161st Battery RNZ Arty, which included 1st Aust. Log Supt Grp, 1st, 2d, 3d, 4th, 5th, 6th, 7th, 8th and 9th Bns, RAR (Inf), 1st Armored Pers Carrier Trp (redesignated, A Sqdn 4th Cav Rgt), B Sqdn 3d Cav Rgt, A, B, & C Sqdns/1st Armored Rgt, 104th & 105th Field Arty Batteries, 1st, 4th and 12th Arty Rgts, 3d Field Trp 1st Field Sqdn, 1st Field Sqdn-, 1st-, 2d- & 3d- Special Air Services Sqdns, as well as numerous Sig & Supt Trps/Sqdns, 161st Bty RNZ Arty, V & W Cos RNZ Inf, NZ SAS Commandos. Combined elements a.k.a. ANZAC; the Australian/New Zealand Army Corps. Estimated 59,000 Aussie/NZ troops served in VN. Casualties: KIA-469 (all ANZAC dead), WIA - 2,348. See also AAAGV, AAFV HQ AATTV, and AFV in this section.

China, Communist Forces of
Per John Swensson (De Anza College), the book *China And The Vietnam Wars, 1950-75,* tells us these "facts" about the Sino-Vietnamese relationship during French and American Wars: 1) Chinese military assistance was critical to Viet Minh in their war against the French (which the U.S. funded) while concurrently helping the North Koreans. 2) The Chinese sent 320,000 troops to NVN between 1965-68, and over 1000 of them were killed. 3) Mao was prepared to fight the U.S./ARVN had they invaded NVN. 4) After '68, Chinese influence diminished and Soviet influence blossomed. 5) The Chinese had difficulty explaining Nixon's visit to Beijing in 1972, so they stepped up military aid to NVN.

China, Republic of, Forces
See Taiwan, Forces of.

CINCPAC
Commander-in-Chief, Pacific, PACOM. The Individual and in charge of all forces and commands operating in the Vietnam theater. See COMPAC.

CMAC, HQ
Capital Military Assistance Command, Saigon, Jun68-Mar73, originally known as Hurricane Forward, the HQ sent to Saigon to counter the Tet '68 attack and then kept to support the Saigon area until Mar73. Hurricane Forward was also known as Task Force Hay, after General John Hay, its first Cmdr. Auth Strength: 359 in '68, 378 in '71.

Coastal Surveillance Force
The U.S. 7th Fleet creation designed to control enemy infiltration along SVN's 1,200 mi long coast. Code named Market Time.

CORDS, HQ
See MACV CORDS, HQ.

COSVN
The NLF's elusive and legendary mobile HQ, formed in '62 by combining Interzone V and NAMBO Interzone NLF regional commands into a single cmd. Hunted relentlessly and without success by allied forces throughout the war. Acronym for Central Office of South Vietnam.

French Union Forces
French Union Forces at height of their war numbered 287,000. When Japanese attacked across border at Lang Son and Dong Dang on 22Sep40, France had some 70,000 troops in VN, armed with just 15 modern fighter planes and one tank (*Street Without Joy*, p 22). Throughout entire French War, they suffered apx 95,000 KIA (only 25,000 of French blood), inc 4 Generals, 1,300 Lts and mix of French, French Foreign Legion, Cambodian, Lao, Algerian, Moroccan and Sengalese troops. French Foreign Legion troops did not exceed 20,000 at any point. French Army's experience can be researched at *Service Historique de L'Armee*; a facility that houses historical archive of French War in Indochina and is within massive walls of Fort de Vincennes, on outskirts of Paris (*Street Without Joy*, p 16).

III Marine Amphibious Force (MAF)
Located at Camp Horn, and later Camp Haskins, Da Nang, Quang Nam Prov. Exercised control over all Marine and Army ground and air forces in I Corps.

JOAEG, HQ
Joint Operations & Evaluation Grp, HQ: Saigon, Aug62-Apr64, responsible for developing counter-insurgency tactics & philosophies under MACV. Feb64, became part of the JRATA (Joint Research & Test Activities).

Joint General Staff HQ
Located at XS 825-945. Vietnamese Military HQ. Located on S edge of Tan Son Nhut Airbase. Gia Dinh Prov, III Corps.

Korean Forces, Vietnam
Republic of Korea Forces serving in Vietnam were: The Capital Tiger Div, operating in Qui Nhon-Binh Khe area Sep65-Mar73, the Korean 9th Inf White Horse Div, operating in Ninh Hoa area Oct66-Mar73, Korean 2d Marine Corps Blue Dragons Brigade, Sep65-Feb72 operating initially in Cam Linh Peninsula-Dong Ba Thin areas in 65 and then in Hoi An area of I Corps. Casualties: KIA-4,407.

MAAG, Indochina, HQ
Military Assistance Advsy Group; Cholon, Sep50-Oct55.

MAAG, Vietnam, HQ
Military Assistance Advisory Group; Saigon, Nov55-May64, 1,606 authorized personnel.

MACV CORDS, HQ
MACV Civil Operations & Rural Development Support, Saigon, May67-Mar73, authorized strength: 6,437 in '70. Successor to the Office of Civil Operations, that was under control of the U.S. Embassy from Nov66 to May67.

MACV, HQ
Military Assistance Command, Vietnam; Saigon, Tan Son Nhut, Feb62-Mar73, subordinate to Cmdr-in-Chief, Pacific (Navy Admiral). Authorized strength was: 1,488 in '66; 6,407 in '68; 13,095 in '71; 6,681 in '72. Constructed near

Tan Son Nhut Airbase as a network of two-story pre-fabricated buildings that provided air-conditioned working space for 4,000 personnel. In addition to utilities and cantonments, it included mortar shelters, security fences and guard towers. see also MACV Compound #1 and the Keopler Compound. III Corps.

MACV-FAE HQ

Field Advisory Element, MACV; Senior U.S. Army Advisors, one for each CTZ, Jun64-Mar73 for the IV Corps FAE, and Jun66-Mar73 for the other three CTZ FAEs. Authorized strength was: 4,741 in '64, 5,394 in '66, 9,430 in '68, 1,486 in '71.

MACV-JGS IG BTI Team

Inspector General, Joint General Staff, Military Assistance Command Vietnam, Base Inspection Turnover Team. A Joint ARVN and U.S. Inspector General's office created Oct71, and charged with inspecting all pre and post-turnover inspections of U.S. facilities to ARVN/VNAF/SVN Govt control. Inspections included facilities that transferred both prior to and subsequent to its creation.

MACV-SOG, HQ

MACV Studies and Observation Group, Long Binh, Apr66-May72. Although its name implied it was composed of scientists and technicians, SOG was really a very sensitive and very secretive child of the 5th SF Group. Its primary duties were intelligence gathering operations in SVN, Cambodia Laos, the DMZ and NVN using small recon teams. Operation Prairie Fire's AO, for example, extended 33 km into Laos and the same distance N of the DMZ. Commonly referred to as MAC-SOG or simply SOG. See also Ban Me Thuot, Chi Lang, Da Nang, Dong Ba Thin, Long Hai, Kontum, Nha Trang, Phuoc Tuy, Prairie Fire Operations. CCN, CCS, CCS and MLT. See also MACV-SOG in Alpha Listing.

Marine Unit, Vietnam

MUVN. The operational name of USMC helicopter support in Vietnam operating out of Soc Trang immediately succeeding Op Shufly. Shufly began 16Apr62 and its name was changed to MUVN soon thereafter. See Operation Shufly in main alpha listing.

MUVN

See Marine Unit, Vietnam.

New Zealand, Forces of

New Zealand V Force arrived in Vietnam 21Jul65 and withdrew in stages from Nov70-Jun72.Hq was located at: Nui Dat, Phuoc Tuy Province, III Corps, in support of 1st Australian Task Force, both attached to the U.S. 173d Abn Bde. Major elements were: 161st Arty Bty, V and W Rifle Companies, Royal New Zealand Inf, Number 4 Trp, Royal NZ Special Air Service (SAS) and other support and Admin elements. The first NZ force to be sent to Vietnam was the 161st Bty Royal NZ Arty, which was attached to and supported the 1st Australian TF/U.S. 173d Abn elements working in Phuoc Tuy Prov. Although the NZ 28th Commonwealth Bde was seeing service in Malaysia during the Vietnam war, it provided its V Rifle Co 11May67, and W Rifle Co 17Dec67 which together with the an Australian Bn formed an ANZAC Bn (ANZAC-Australian/ New Zealand Army Corps). The SAS company provided Recon. It is interesting that initially, the tour requirements for RNZ troops were different for married and single troops. Married Soldiers were assigned a 9 month tour, while single troopers were given 18 month tours. It was not until after May67 that serious morale problems caused by that imbalance and pay disparities led to a 12 month tour for both groups and other reforms. [8] Casualties: KIA-469 (inc. all ANZAC forces).

NEWZARM

New Zealand Army Headquarters, Singapore.

Office of Civil Operations

The predecessor of CORDS. Created Nov66 by Ambassador Henry Cabot lodge, Jr. to conduct pacification and rural development programs, it remained under Embassy of the Republic of Vietnam Control until CORDS was created in May67 under MACV control.

PACOM

Pacific Command, a joint HQ located in Hawaii and responsible for joint ops in Asia and the Pacific. 4 individuals served as CINCPAC during the war: Adm Harry Felt until Jun64, Adm Ulysses Sharp Jun64-Jul68, Adm John McCain Jul68-Sep72, Adm Noel Gaylor Sep72 to the end of the war.

PHILCAG-V

Philippine Civic Action Group, Vietnam. See Philippines, Forces of, and PHILCAG in main alpha listing.

Philippines, Forces of

SEATO Philippine forces (known as PHILCAG-V) included an Infantry Security Bn, a 105mm Arty Bn, a Construction Eng Bn, a Medical and Dental Bn, a Logistical Support Compound & a HQ & Services Co. Arrived 14Sep66, departed 13Dec69. See Philippine Civic Action Compound. Primary AO was in Thanh Dien Forest of Tay Ninh Prov, III Corps.

Regional Assistance Command, HQs

Four regional assistance command HQs (RACs), known as FRAC (First RAC - Da Nang, Apr72-Mar73), SRAC (Second RAC - Nha Trang, Pleiku Apr71-Mar73), TRAC (Third RAC - Long Binh, Apr71-Mar73) and DRAC (Delta RAC - Can Tho, Apr71-Mar73). Each command included Advisors (averaging about 750 per RAC) and CORDS personnel (avg. of about 1,000+ for each RAC).

Republic of China Forces

See Taiwan, Forces of.

Russia, Forces of (n/a)

The Russians, as did the Chinese, furnished advisors to NVA and, apparently, a few combat troops who flew MIG fighters as well. The author was unable to find any data indicating how many casualties they may have suffered.

Spain, Forces of

Under the SEATO alliance, Spain provided a very small contingent of advisors who served in a support role. Total Spanish commitment never exceeded 13 troops in any given year and ranged from 7 to 13 between '66 and '70. [9]

Taiwan, Forces of

Under SEATO alliance, the Republic of China provided small advsy grp who served primarily in supt role. Total force never exceeded 31 troops in any year and ranged

---

[8] Newman, Lt. S. D., *Vietnam Gunners - 161 Battery RNZA, South Vietnam, 1965-1971*, p 41

[9] A *Contagion of War* volume, Time/Life *Vietnam Experience* series, pp 90-91

from 20 to 31 between '64 and '70. Data per *Contagion of War* vol., *Vietnam Experience* series, pp 90-91.

Thailand, Forces of

Bearcat Base Camp, Tri Quyet Thang, Bien Hoa Province, home of the Royal Thai Army Expeditionary Force (Black Panthers, later renamed the Royal Thai Army Volunteer Force), arrived at Bearcat in Fall of 1967, and eventually built into an entire, 3 Bde Div consisting of the 1st, 2d and 3d Brigades, 4 Bns RTA Div Arty, an Armored Cav Sqd, support Avn, MPs, Div HQ and a LRP Co. One crack Thai Inf Rgt was known as the Queen's Cobras. III Corps. Casualties: KIA-351, WIA-?

U.S. Air Force, Vietnam

Primarily the 7th Air Force, but also elements of the 5th AF, 13thAF HQ (in the Philippines) and 14th AF, operating out of Guam, SVN, Thailand and the Philippines during the war. The 2d Air Division, in control of all tactical air support in SEA, was originally under the 13th AF, the Philippines, until reorganized into the 7th AF in early '66. The SAC B-52s operating out of Guam maintained a semi-autonomous status throughout the war. See also Operations Ranch Hand, Rolling Thunder, Menu, Babylift, Steel Tiger and Tiger Hound.

U.S. Army Headquarters Area Cmd

See AHAC.

U.S. Army Special Forces, VN, Provisional

Created Sep62, departed Sep64 when 5th SF Grp took over SF ops in SVN, 1Oct64. U.S. Army 1st Special Forces (Okinawa was providing advisors to the Nha Trang Commando Center as early as 1957. This function was expanded into an country-wide command structure originally formed at Saigon (under CIA control) to advise/assist SVN govt in creating, training and equipping a CIDG force (its HQ later relocated to Nha Trang). This Provisional unit was staffed by 1st SF Grp on Okinawa, and 5th and 7th SF from Ft. Bragg, NC, using men on 6-month only tours. The very 1st CIDG camp was built near Ban Me Thuot in '61. On 1Jul63, the CIA turned over complete control of the CIDG program (and on 26Oct63, its border surveillance program) to this unit.

U.S. Naval Forces Vietnam

Office of the Commander, Naval Forces Vietnam, 1Apr66-29Mar73, Directed USN forces along coast of SVN, controlling USN TFs 115, 116 and 117 (Mobile Riverine Force) river ops, Coast Guard and Seabee NMCBs. 7th Fleet ops in open ocean were under control of CINCPAC, in Hawaii. See also Op Sea Dragon, Task Force 70.8, Dixie Station, Yankee Station and Coastal Surveillance Force.

USARV, HQ

U.S. Army, Vietnam; Long Binh, Jul65-May72. Authorized strength: 808 in '66, 1,329 in 68, 1,521 in 70, 559 in '71. In May '72, became known as Headquarters, USARV/MACV when those two major commands were consolidated. USARV Headquarters was constructed at Long Binh Post, apx 26 km from Saigon. It was 25 square miles in size, housed over 50,000 permanent cadre, and its initial cost was over $100 million. III Corps.

USARV/MACV, HQ

May72-Mar73, Long Binh, consolidated HQ of the two major U.S. commands in Vietnam shortly before U.S. departure. Auth Strength: 425.

USASC, Vietnam, HQ

US Army Support Command, Saigon Mar65-Jul65, an expansion of the U.S. Army Support Group ('62-64). Auth. strength: 508.

USASG, Vietnam, HQ

U.S. Army Support Group, Saigon-Cholon, Apr62-Mar64. Created from the 9th Logistical Cmd which was under the overall Cmd of "U.S. Army, Ryukyu Islands" (although under operational control of MACV). Renamed U.S. Army Support Command in Mar64. Auth strength: 462 in '63.

Vietnamese Joint General Staff HQ

HQ for the entire SVN military establishment. Located on S edge of Tan Son Nhut Airbase at XS 825-945. Gia Dinh Prov, III Corps.

Corps Level Commands and Attached Divisions/Support Elements

Data compiled primarily from Shelby Stanton's *Vietnam Order of Battle*, 1986, Galahad Books

Field Force Vietnam

FFV. According to LTC Elmer Goetsch, 54th Sig Bn XO, was, "organized in Sep65, and redesignated as IFFV on 15Mar66. The designation Field Force was used in part because normal Army corps had only tactical, not logistical, functions while the FFV's had tactical, logistical, pacification, and advisory roles." It's also true that the ARVN used the term Corps to define multi-divisional units, while the U.S. Army used it for the same purpose, so in part also to avoid confusion, Field Force was adopted to describe a Corps equivalent force. First Field Force Vietnam (IFFV) and Second Field Force Vietnam (IIFFV) are two other examples; however, MACV also created a number of corps level commands during the war using the conventional designation (the XXII Corps, the XXIV Corps and the XXX Corps. See IFFV and IFFV. [10]

IFFV HQ

Located at Nha Trang, Mar66-Apr71. Army Corps level command that included: 1st Cav Div (until Oct 68 move to IIFFV), 4th Inf Div, 3d Bde 25th Inf Div, 1st Bde 101st Abn Div, 173d Abn Bde (after May67 move from IIFFV), 3d Bn 506th Inf 101st Abn, 1st Bn 50th Inf, 7th Sqdn 17th Cav, 17th Avn Grp, 41st Arty Grp, 52d Arty Grp, Task Force South, B Co 5th SF. IFFV exercised operational control of allied forces in II Corps CTZ and provide assistance to the ARVN forces in that area. According to LTC Elmer Goetsch, 54th Sig Bn XO, "IFFV was originally just FFV, organized in Sep65, and redesignated as IFFV on 15Mar66."

IFFV Artillery HQ

Located at Qui Nhon, Dalat and Nha Trang. A Cmd apart from IFF, which exercised control over U.S. Arty forces in

[10] Murphy, Edward, *Dak To*, Pocket books, NY, 1993, p 369

II & III Corp. Arrived in VN as the XXX Corps Arty, became the IFFV Arty (Forward) Dec66-Apr67. In Dec70 a Provisional IFFV Arty was detached to Dalat as a separate command apart from IFFV Arty. In Apr 71, its assets were used to from SRAC Arty & in Jun71 became USAATYF, MR 2 Arty (U.S. Army Artillery Force, Military Region 2).

IFFV, Artillery (Forward) HQ

Qui Nhon, Dec66-Apr67. See IFFV Arty

IIFFV HQ

Located at Bien Hoa-Long Binh, Mar66-May71. Army Corps level command that included: 1st Cav Div (after Oct68 move from IFFV), 1st Inf Div, 9th Inf Div, 25th Inf Div, 3d Bde 82d Abn Div, 3d Bde 101st Abn Div, 173d Abn Bde (until May67 move to IFFV), 196th LIB, 199th LIB, 11th Armored Cav Rgt, 3d Sqdn 17th Cav, 12th Avn Grp, 23d Arty Grp, 54th Arty Grp, A Co 5th SF Grp. IIFFV, the largest Army Cmd in VN, exercised operational control of allied forces in III Corps CTZ and provided assistance to the ARVN in that area. Was created from the assets of the XXII Corps. See also Plantation Compound.

III Marine Amphibious Force

In VN 7May65-14Apr71. Headquartered at Camp Horn, and later Camp Haskins, Da Nang, Quang Nam Prov. The 3d MAF was a Corps Level HQ responsible for all Marine and Army forces operating in I Corps. The amphibious concept was meant to provide logistical support of ground maneuver units via ships at sea and without the need for constructing fixed facilities at ports, airbases or basecamps. MACV-Forward HQ (that later became the XXIV Corps HQ) was created in Feb68 to accommodate the large increase in Army units working in I Corps.(1st Cav, 101st Abn & Americal) but although it held control of Army forces there, overall control remained with II MAF. All Marine Div & units in Vietnam were under the Cmd of the USN (CINCPAC), Pacific, HQ'd in Hawaii. Casualties: KIA-13,082, WIA-88,633 (the USMC did not report breakdown of casualties at Rgtl or Div levels. These figures include total III MAF casualties).

XXII Corps

Predecessor of II Field Force (IIFFV), when IIFFV, originally was activated in VN, Long Binh Post, Bien Hoa Prov. See also IIFFV and Plantation Compound.

XXIV Corps HQ

In existence from Aug68-Jun72. Originally located in Phu Bai, '68, and was then in Da Nang after '70. An Army Corps level command that included: III Marine Amphibious Force, 3d Mar Div, 23d Inf (Americal) Div, 101st Abn Div, 3d Bde 82d Abn Div, 1st Bde 5th Inf Div (Mech), C Co 5th SF Grp. Activated 15Aug68, consolidated with the Provisional Corps, VN, which had been created 10Mar68 using assets of MACV Forward (created 9Mar68, an Army HQ created to counter the '68 Tet Offensive in Saigon area). Was under the operational control of the III Marine Amphibious Force. Deactivated 30Jun72 and its assets given to FRAC.

XXX Corps Artillery HQ

Located at Qui Nhon, Nov66-Dec66. See IFFV Arty

Division, Regimental and Separate Brigade Level Commands

Data compiled primarily from Shelby Stanton's *Vietnam Order of Battle*, 1986, Galahad Books.

1st CAG

1st Combined Action Group, USMC. TAOR included all of Quang Tin and Quang Ngai Provs. I Corps.

2d CAG

2d Combined Action Group, USMC. HQ was located ENE of An Hoi city center and apx 1 km SW of CAP 2-4-3 location. Its geographic TAOR included all of Quang Nam Province, including Da Nang and Hoi An cities. Portion of L-7014 series 1:50,000 scale map of the Cap 2-4-3 and 2d CAG HQ AOs can be found at CAP website, http://w3.one.net/~timd/cap /cap2-4-3/pcktmap.htm. Quang Nam Prov, I Corps.

3d CAG

3d Combined Action Group, USMC. TAOR included all of Thua Thien Prov. I Corps.

4th CAG

4th Combined Action Group, USMC. TAOR included all of Quang Tri Prov. I Corps.

1st Cavalry Division

In VN Sep65-Apr71. HQs at: An Khe Sep65-Jun67, An Khe/Bong So Jul67-Jan68, An Khe/Hue Feb68, An Khe/Phong Dien Mar68-Oct68, An Khe/Quang Tri May68, An Khe/Phong Dien Jun68-Oct68, An Khe/Phuoc Vinh Nov68-Apr69, Bien Hoa/Phuoc Vinh May69-Apr71.

Major elements were: 1st/5th, 2d/5th, 1st/7th, 2d/7th, 5th/7th, 1st/8th, 12/12th and 2/12th Cavalry Rgts; 1st Sqdn 9th Air Cav, 11th Avn Grp & 228th & 229th Avn Bns, 2d/17th, 2d/19th, 2d/20th, 1st/21st, 1st/30th, 1st/77th Artillery, Co E 52d LRP, Co H 75th Inf Rangers among others.

1st full Div of the U.S. Army sent to VN and the first Army Div to fight in all four CTZs during the war. Oct-Nov65, it fought the U.S. forces 1st major battle in the Ia Drang Valley of far western Pleiku Prov, which was also the 1st field test of the Airmobile helicopter concept. For next 13 months, it fought widely through II Corps. In Spring '66, it was assigned to clear Binh Thuan Prov. and in Aug66 to Pleiku Prov, while some of its Bns continued fighting in Binh Thuan Prov. from Aug66-Jan68. From Oct66-to Feb 67, it worked to clear the northern coastal plains of Kim Son & Luoi Ci Valleys around Bong Son, Binh Dinh Prov. In Spring of '66 it participated in 1st. large cross-border, multi provincial op, when USMC units crossed into Binh Dinh to join the 1st Cav. In Aug 66, the Div moved to Pleiku and fought in that area until Jan68. Throughout 67, the Div battled the VC & NVA 610th Div in II Corps.

In Jan68 it was ordered to Quang Tri, I Corps. to blunt the expected major attack of Khe Sanh while some elements remained in Binh Dinh Prov. In Apr68, the Div moved to Khe Sanh to relieve the besieged Marine base there. During Tet 68 it also fought south into Thua Thien Prov to relieve the NE portions of Hue in Battle for Hue. In

Apr-May 68 it fought in A Shau valley of western Thua Thien Prov, protecting Hue from further attack and for the balance of 68, it remained on the borders of Thua Thien/Quang Tri Provinces. In Oct68, it was sent to III Corps and northwestern parts of IV Corps along the Cambodian border and in 69 suffered heavy losses in attacks on 1st Cav FSBs in western III Corps area. May-Jun70 it participated in the invasion of Cambodia and was sent home, April71 minus its 3d Bde which was left behind.

On 28Jun68, USARPAC issued Gen Order 325 redesignating 1st Cav to be the "1st Air Cavalry Division" (thereby making official its popular nickname) eff 1Jul68. However, "Air Cavalry Division" was revoked by DOA directive issued 26Aug68, and thereafte, official name became "1st Cavalry Div (AMBL)." Same orders affected 101st Abn Div.[11] Casualties: KIA-5,444, WIA-26,592.

1st Cavalry Division, 3d Bde (Sep)

Bien Hoa, Apr71-Jun72. Was built around the 1st/7th Cav Rgt after the bulk of the Div was sent home in Apr71. Its elements consisted of: 2d/5th, 1st/7th, 2d/8th & 1st/12th Cav Rgts, 229th Avn Bn, 36d Avn Co, F Trp, 9th Air Cav, 2d Sqdn 11th ACR, 1st Bn 21st Arty, and Bty F's from the 26th, 77th & 7th Arty. Casualties: See 1st Cav Div.

1st Infantry Division

In VN from Oct65-Apr70. HQs at: Bien Hoa Oct65-Jan66, Di An Feb66-Jan67, Di An/Lai Khe Feb67-Sep67, Lai Khe Oct66-Oct69, Di An Nov69-Apr70.

Major elements were: 1st/2d, 2d/ 2d (Mech), 1st/16th (Mech), 2d/16th, 1st/18th, 2d/18th, 1st/26th, 2d/28th and 5th/60th Inf (Mech) Inf Rgts and 3d Sqdn 11th ACR; 1st/5th, 8th/6th, 1st/7th, 6th/15th, 2d/33d, and Bty D 25th Artillery Rgts; 1st Avn Bn, 162d & 173d Avn Cos, C Trp 16th Air Cav; 1st Sqdn 4th Cav (Armored), F Co 52d Inf LRP, I Co 75th Inf Rangers.

The 2d Bde of the "Big Red One" arrived in VN 2Oct65 followed quickly by the remaining two Bdes. The Div was assigned to III Corps and in mid-66 was fighting in Binh Long Prov. with the 9th VC Rgt. In the Fall of 66, the 1st Inf Div swept War Zone C in Tay Ninh Prov along with elements of the 4th Inf Div (et al) in Op Attleborro. In late 67 through to Tet 68, it operated in the Loc Ninh area of Binh Long Prov. During Tet 68, the 1st was pulled in to the Saigon area in defense and counter-attacks to regain control of that city. From mid-69 until it left VN, it worked closely with the ARVN 5th Inf Div in what was called Dong Tien (Progress Together) Operations. It returned home, 15Apr70. Casualties: KIA-3,146, WIA-18,019.

1st Marine Division

In Vietnam 23Feb66-14Apr71. Its HQs at: Chu Lai Feb66-Nov66, Da Nang Feb66-Apr71. Major elements were: The 1st, 5th and 7th Marine Regiments, which consisted of the following Battalions: 1st/1st, 2d/1st, 3d/1st, 1st/, 2d/5th and 3d/5th Marine Rgt; 1st/7th, 2d/7th and 3d/7th Marine Regiment, all of the 1st Mar Div; also the 1st/26th, 2d/26th and 3d/26th Marine Rgt, and the 1st/2d, 2d/27th and 3d/27th Marine Rgt, all of the 5th Marine Div and attached to the 1st Div; 1st Recon Bn, 1st Force Recon Bn, 1st Tank Bn, 1st Amphibian Tractor Bn, 1st Armored Amphibian Co, 1st anti-tank Bn; 11th Artillery Rgt (1st, 2d, 3d and 4th Bns, 11th Arty); 1st Marine Air Wing. Casualties: see III MAF

1st Marine Regiment

In VN Jan66-May71. Rgt HQs located at: Chu Lai Jan66-Jun66, Da Nang Jun66-Oct67, Quang Tri Oct67-Feb68, Hue Feb68, Khe Sanh Apr68-Aug68, Gio Linh Aug68-Sep68, Dan Nang Sep68-May71.

3d Marine Division

In VN 6May65-30Nov69. HQs were located at: Da Nang May65-Oct66, Hue Oct66-Mar68, Quang Tri Mar68-Jun68, Dong Ha Jun68-Nov69, Da Nang Nov69. Major elements were: 3d, 4th and 9th Marine Rgts, which included the following Battalions: 1st/3d, 2d/3d and 3d/3d Marine Rgt; 1st/4th, 2d/4th and 3d/4th Marine Rgt; 1st/9th, 2d/9th and 3d/9th Marine Rgt; 3d Tank Bn, 3d Amphibian Tractor Bn, 3d Anti-Tank Bn, 3d Recon Bn, 3d Force Recon Bn, 12th Marine Artillery Rgt (1st, 2d, 3d and 4th Bns, 12th Arty and, the 1st and 2d Bns, 13th Arty); 1st Marine Air Wing. Casualties: see III MAF.

3d Marine Regiment

In VN Apr65-Sep69. Rgt HQ at: Da Nang Apr65-Dec66, Hue Dec66-May67, Dong Ha May67-Jan68, Camp Carroll Jan68-Feb68, Dong Ha Feb68-Aug68, Cam Lo Aug68-Dec68, Dong Ha Dec68-Jun69, Khe Sanh? Jun69-Sep69

4th Infantry Division

In VN Sep68-Dec70. HQs located at: Pleiku Sep66-Feb68, Dak To Mar68, Pleiku Apr68-Feb70, An Khe/Pleiku Mar70, An Khe Apr70-Dec70.

Major elements were: 1st/8th, 2d/8th, 3d/8th, 1st/12th, 2d/12th (sent to 25th Inf Div, Aug67), 3d/12th, 1st/14th (came from 25th Inf Div, Aug67), 1st/22d, 2d/22d (sent to 25th Inf Div, Aug67), 3d 22d (sent to 25th Inf Div, Aug67), and the 1st/35th and 2d/35th Inf Rgts (both came from 25th Inf Div, Aug67); 2d/34th and 1st/69th Armored Rgts; 2d/9th, 5th/16th, 6th/29th, 4th/42d and 2d/77th Artillery Rgts; 1st Sqdn 10th Cav, E Co 20th Inf (LRP), E Co 58th Inf (LRP), K Co 75th Inf Rangers.

Arrived in VN 25Sep66, with two Bdes being sent to II Corps and one (the 3d) reinforced Bde being sent to II Corps. In Aug 67, the 3d Bde was exchanged for elements of the 25th Inf Div's 3d Bde (the only major interdivisional unit switch of the war). That Bde became the 3d Bde of the 25th and was immediately attached to Task Force Oregon, then HQ'd in I Corps at Duc Pho. The Div's first op was Attleborro, Sep-Nov66, and it saw heavy action from the outset. from Dec66 and into 67, the Div worked the Cambodian border in Pleiku and Kontum Provs. During that same period, its 3d Bde was in Op Junction City, War Zone C, Feb-May67. The Div saw heavy action in Central Highland border areas throughout 68/69 and in June70, participated in the Invasion of Cambodia. The 3d Bde was sent home as part of Increment III of the U.S. withdrawal and the other two Bdes returned as part of Increment V. Casualties: KIA-2,531, WIA-15,229.

4th Marine Regiment

In VN May65-Nov69. Rgt HQs located at: Hue May65-Jan68, Phong Dien Jan68-Feb68, Camp Carroll Feb68-Jul68, Khe Sanh Jul68-Dec68, Cam Lo Dec68-Nov69.

5th Infantry Division, 1st Bde (Mech)

In VN Jul68-Aug71. HQs located at Quang Tri and Dong Ha (Camp Red Devil. Major elements were: 1st/77th Armored Rgt, 1st/11th and 1st/61st Inf Rgts; A Trp 4th

[11] Vietnam Studies, *Airmobility 1961-1971*, Tolson, Lt. Gen John J, Dept of Army, 1973, p 195

Sqdn/12th Cav, P Co 75th Inf Rangers, 3d Sqdn/5th Cav, 3d/187th Inf Rgt (opcon from 101st Abn). Operated in northern I Corps in area immediately south of the DMZ. Assigned the coastal lowlands and piedmont from the DMZ S to the Quang Tri/Thua Thien Provs. Often worked in concert with the 3d Mar Div. In Jan71, it launched an attack to clear QL-9, & reopen Khe Sanh for Lam Son 719, the disastrous ARVN invasion of Laos. Casualties: KIA-504, WIA-3,648.

5th Marine Division

The 5th Mar Div did not operate in VN as an independent Div; however, its 26th and 27th Rgts were attached to the 1st Marine Div (Feb66-Apr71) during the war and saw significant action, including the Battle for Khe Sanh. Casualties: See III MAF (the USMC did not brake down casualties by division).

5th Marine Regiment

In VN May66-Apr71. Rgt HQs located at: Chu Lai May66-Jun67, Da Nang Jun67-Jan 68, Hoi An Jan68, Hue Feb69, Phu Loc Mar69-Aug68, Da Nang Aug68-Apr71.

7th Marine Regiment

In VN Aug65-Oct70. Rgt HQs located at: Chu Lai Aug65-May67, Da Nang May67-Oct70.

9th Infantry Division

In VN Dec66-Aug69. HQs located at: Bearcat Dec66-Jul68, Dong Tam Aug68-Aug69. Main elements were: 6th/31st, 2d/39th, 3d/39th, 4th/39th, 2d/47th (Mech), 3d/47th (Riverine), 4th/47th (Riverine), 2d/60th, 3d/60th(Riverine), 5th/60th (Mech), 3d Sqdn/5th Cav, E Co 50th Inf (LRP), E Co 75th Inf Rangers; 9th Avn Bn; 2d/4th, 1st/11th, 3d/34th, 1st/84th and H Bty 29th Artillery Rgts.

1st VN Op was Op Palm Beach, Jan66-May67, a sweep through Dinh Tuong and Log An Provs. Beginning in '67, its 2d Bde was assigned to Mobile Riverine Force ops with the USN, the 1st time since the civil War an Army unit became amphibious and completely afloat. That Bde trained in Rung Sat swamps, 67, then moved to its HQ at Dong Tam (near My Tho), a base created by building a 600 acre Island in Mekong River. The MRF operated also with the SVN Marines, Navy Seals, ARVN 7th Inf Div & River Assault Grps. Elements participated in bitter III Corps fighting in vicinity. of Saigon during Tet 68 and throughout IV Corps. Div left VN Aug69, leaving behind its 3d Bde until Oct70. Casualties: KIA-2,624, WIA-18,831.

The following synopsis of the 9th Inf Div's Vietnam history was provided by Jim Stone, E/2d/39th in '68: "Only the 2d Bde of the U.S. 9th Inf Div (3d/47th, 4th/47th & 3d/60th) was considered Riverine Infantry. The 2d Bde was also part of the joint Army/Navy task force, known as 'The Mobile Riverine Force'. While the 2d Bde mostly operated from water craft, it also built dry-land bases in the Mekong Delta of IV Corps. The 9th Div's 1st and 3d Bdes were comprised of 7 other Inf Bns. The 9th also had two, strictly land-based Mech Bns (2d/47th and 5th/60th Inf).

One 9th Div unit operated in I Corps near the DMZ. This was the 3d Sqdn/5th Cavalry (consisting of 3 mechanized ground recon Troops). This unit, less its Air Cav Troop, operated in support of the 101st Abn in '69-70, and also in the A Shau Valley. [It may have supported 5th Inf (Mech) and 3d Mar Div also.]

During '67, the 4th/39th Inf operated briefly in II Corps, while the main elements of the Div (1st and 3d Bdes) were based at Camp Bearcat (a.k.a. Camp Martin Cox), in III Corps, E of Saigon. Later that year, the 3d Bde moved to Tan An Base, Long An Prov, SE of Saigon. The 3d/39th was assigned briefly to the SW coast of SVN at Rach Gia as well. During all of 1967, the 2d BDE/USN MRF was headquartered at Dong Tam, Dinh Tuong Prov, while also operating from naval vessels further S in the Mekong Delta.

In early '68, the 1st Bde was moved to Dong Tam, while the 2d Bde/USN MRF set up a land base at Mo Cay, further S in the Delta. Later in '68, the 1st and 3d Bdes swapped AO's, with the 1st Bde, moving up to Tan An and Long An Prov. The 2d/39th was headquartered in a town named Rach Kien. Other 1st/3d Bde bases or outposts were located at: Binh Chanh, Binh Phuoc, My Tho, Ben Luc, Tan Tru, Can Giouc, Nha Be, My Phouc Tay and An Nhut Tan. At the end of '68, 1st Bde moved back along QL 4 in Dinh Tuong Prov, building several FSBs W of Cai Lay.

Most 9th Div FSBs and base camps were eventually shifted to the ARVN beginning in late '68, and proceeding until July/Aug69, when the 9th Inf Div was pulled out of Vietnam. The 3d Brigade, consisting of 4 Inf Bns (6/31, 2/47 Mech, 2/60, and 5/60) was left behind until it too was pulled out in Oct70. The 3d Bde (Separate) had its main base camp at Tan An, and was opcon to 25th Inf Div, operating primarily in the southern III CTZ, SW of Saigon. It also participated in the Cambodian Incursion, May70.

9th Infantry Division, 3d Bde

In VN Dec 66-Oct70. HQ located at Tan An. Major elements were: 6th/31st, 2d/47th (Mech), 2d/60th, and 5th/60th Inf Rgts; D Trp 3d Sqdn/5th Air Cav, E Co 75th Inf Rangers; 2d/4th Artillery, 39th Cav Plt (Air Cushioned Vehicles). 3d Bde was left behind when 9th Inf Div went home in Aug69, and served Opcon to the 25th Inf Div in southern III Corps until Oct70. Casualties: (see 9th Div's.)

9th Marine Amphibious Bde

Arrived in VN 8Mar65, and originally called the 9th Marine Expeditionary Bde, but name changed to remove the French-Colonial association with the word "expeditionary."

The 9th MEB's two Battalion Landing Teams (BLT), 3d/9th and 1st/3d Marine Rgts were sent to VN in Mar65, as a security force for the Airbase at Da Nang. In 72 it was again deployed as a ship based force to counter the Easter Offensive of 1972. Its helicopter assets were sent ashore to support the ARVN and it deployed a BLT of Marine Infantry to guard Bien Hoa AB and Nam Phong (Thailand) AB, out of which some of the Marine's air support operated.

Was also involved in Op Frequent Wind, the evacuation of U.S. personnel at the fall of Saigon, 29-30Apr75, providing ground security and the 68 helicopters necessary to Evac 1000's of people from the U.S. Embassy and Tan Son Nhut Airbase. 9th MAB also supplied the 200 man force that invaded Ko Tang Island during the Mayaguez incident 14May75, during which it suffered 15 KIA and 50 WIA, the last USMC VN War casualties.

9th Marine Expeditionary Force (n/a)

A.k.a. 9th MEF and 9th MEB. On 8Mar65, the 1st U.S. major ground force (3d Bn/9th Marines) landed on Red Beach just S Nam O Bridge. Later that day, C-130s from Okinawa delivered another Bn (1st/3d Marines?) at Da Nang. With H-34 helos of HMM-162 providing log supt, these units formed 9th MEF. Purpose was to protect Da Nang and its AF from VC. An enclave at Phu Bai AF (15 km S Hue) soon followed, then another at Ky Ha, SE of Tam Ky. Name later became 9th Marine Amphibious Bde, in order to remove French-Colonial association with the word "expeditionary."

9th Marine Expeditionary Bde

A.k.a. 9th MEB and 9th MEF. In VN 8Mar65-6May65. Original name of what became the 9th Marine Amphibious Bde, but name changed to remove the French-Colonial association with the word "expeditionary." Its two Bn Landing Teams (BLT), 3d/9th and 1st/3d Marine Rgts were sent to VN as a security force for the Airbase at Da Nang in Mar65.

9th Marine Regiment

In VN Jul65-Aug69. Rgt HQ located at: Da Nang Jul65-May67, Dong Ha May67-Feb68, Con Thien Feb68-May68, Cam Lo May68-Nov68, Khe Sanh Nov68-Feb69, Cam Lo Feb69-Aug69.

11th Armored Cavalry Regiment

In VN 8Sep66-5Mar71. HQ located at: LZ Blackhorse, War Zone C, Long Giao, Hau Nghia Prov, was home of the 11th Armored Cavalry Rgt, 1967. Known as the Black Horse Regiment, it operated under the II FFV mostly in III Corps area (War Zone C, Tay Ninh Prov.), and in Apr69-Jun70 was opcon to the 1st Cav Div for the Cambodian Invasion. Oct-Nov70 was attached to the 25th Inf Div. Left its 2d Sqdn behind when the Rgt left in Mar71 and the 2d Sqdn returned to U.S. Apr72. 50 tanks, 300 APCs, 50 helicopters and 3,900 personnel at peak of its strength. Do not confuse with the 11th LIB of the 23d (Americal) Div. Casualties: KIA-728, WIA-5,761.

11th Infantry Brigade (Light)

In VN Dec67-Nov71. BDE HQ at Duc Pho Dec 67-Jun71, The Loi, Jul71-Nov71 (Bde HQs), and Chu Lai (Div HQ) while with the 23d Inf Div. Major elements were: 3d/1st, 4th/3d, 1st/20th, 4th/21st Inf Rgts; 6th Bn 11th Artillery Rgt. Arrived in-country 19Sep67 to become part of the newly formed 23d Inf Div (Americal) 19Feb67 (along with the newly arrived 198th LIB). The Bde operated in the coastal areas of Quang Ngai & Quang Tin Provs. in southern I Corps. Casualties: Unknown; incorporated in 23d Inf Div casualties.

11th Marine Regiment

Provided artillery support for the 1st Marine Division. 11th Arty Rgt consisted of: 1st, 2d, 3d and 4th Bns, 11th Arty.

12th Marine Regiment

Provided artillery support for the 3rd Marine Division. 12th Arty Rgt consisted of: 1st, 2d, 3d and 4th Bns, 12th Arty

13th Marine Regiment

The 1st and 2d Bns, 13th Arty, were attached to 12th Marine Arty Regt, supporting the 3rd Marine Division.

23d Infantry Division (AMERICAL)

In VN Sep67-Nov71. HQs at Chu Lai that entire time. Major elements were: 2d/1st, 3d/1st, 4th/3d, 1st/6th, 1st/20th, 3d/21st, 4th/21st, 4th 34th, 5th/46th and 1st/52d Inf Rgts; F Trp 8th Air Cav, E Trp 1st Armored Cav, F Trp 17th Armored Cav, E Co 51st Inf (LRP), Americal scout Inf, H Trp 17th Cav; 1st Sqdn 1st Armored Cav, Chu Lai Prov's Defense Cmd; 6th/1th, 1st/14th, 3d/16th, 3d/18th, 1st/82d, 3d/82d & G Bty 55th Arty Rgts.

The Americal was the only "named" Div to serve in VN. It was originally formed from elements of Task Force Oregon, Apr67-Sep67, brought in to support the Marine Divs operating in I Corps so that they might concentrate their units closer to the DMZ). On 25Sep67, Task Force Oregon was reconstituted into the 23d Inf Div (Americal) (originally named Americal by Gen Doug MacArthur by combining "American" with "New Caledonia," it location during WWII. Though officially the 23d Inf Div, it was almost universally referred to as the Americal Div. Though it operated primarily in southern I Corps (Quang Nam, Quang Ngai & Quang Tin Prvs), it also fought in Quang Tri Prov in 67. Wheeler/Wallowa was its 1st op, with 2 Bdes in Quang Nam & Quang Tri and 1 Bde in Quang Ngai Provs, Nov67-Nov68. In 69-70, the Div fought in the Duc Pho, Chu Lai & Tam Ky areas. Casualties: KIA-808, WIA-8,237 (Inc 11th Inf Bde & 198th LIB, but not the 196th LIB).

25th Infantry Division

In VN Mar66-Dec70. HQs at Cu Chi that entire period. Major elements: 1st/5th(Mech), 4th/9th, 2d/12th (from 4th ID, Aug 67), 1st/14th (to 4th Inf Div, Aug 67), 2d/14th, 2d/22d (Mech) (from 4th Inf Div, Aug 67), 3d/22d (from 4th Inf Div, Aug 67), 4th/23d, 1st/27, 1st/35th (to 4th Inf Div, Aug 67), and 2d/35th(to 4th Inf Div, Aug 67), Inf Rgts; 2d/34th Armor, 1st/69th Armor, 3d Sqdn/4th Armored Cav, F Co 50th Inf (LRP), F Co 75th Rangers, 25th Avn Bn; 1st/8t, 2d/9th, 7th/11th, 3d/13th, 2d/77th, 6th/77th Artillery Rgts.

Div's 3d Bde sent to VN Dec65 & posted in the central highlands at Pleiku, II Corps. Elements of the 3d Bde were later sent to the 4th Inf Div in exchange for 4th Div units that had been in III Corps. When the Div arrived in Mar66, it was sent to operate in III Corps near the Cambodian border and to the Saigon area. In Jan67 it entered the enemy stronghold of the Iron Triangle, followed by Op Junction City near Tay Ninh in War Zone C, Feb-May67, and very heavy fighting. From May67-Dec67, it swept Hau Nghia Prov, and then in Dec67 it again entered War Zone C and parts of southern III Corps W of Saigon until Feb68. On 12Apr67, the 3d Bde of the 25th was sent north to Quang Ngai and Quang Tin Prov to work with the 1st Bde of the 101st Abn and 196th LIB as part of Task Force Oregon, thus making the 25th Div to be one of the few U.S. divisions to serve in all four CTZs.

During Tet 68, it was committed to the Saigon area counter-offensive, then operated in the Cu Chi are until the Spring of '70. In May 70, it became part of the Cambodian invasion and was sent home in Dec of that year, leaving behind its 2d Bde until Apr71. Division nickname was *Under the Southern Cross*. Casualties: KIA-4,547, WIA-31,161.

25th Infantry Division, 2d Bde(Sep)

In Vietnam Jan66-Nov70, as part of the 25th Inf Div and then Nov70-Apr71 as a separate Bde attached to the IIFFV in III Corps. HQs at Long Binh & Xuan Loc. Major elements were: 1st/5th (Mech), 2d/12th, 3d/22d, and 1st/27th Inf Rgts; 1st/8th Artillery Rgt; F Trp 4th Air Cav, F Co 75th Inf Rangers. Casualties: Inc. with 25th Inf Div's.

26th Marine Regiment

In VN Apr67-Mar70. Rgt HQs located at: Da Nang Apr67-Jun67, Dong Ha Jun67-Dec67, Khe Sanh Dec67-May68,

Hoi An May68-Aug68, Phu Loc Aug68-Nov68, Da Nang Nov68-Mar70.

27th Marine Regiment

In VN Feb68-Sep68. Rgt HQs located at: Da Nang Feb68-Sep68.

82d Airborne Division, 3d Bde

In Vietnam, Feb68-Dec69. HQs at Hue/Phu Bai, Phu Loi/Saigon. Major elements were: 1st/505th, 2d/505th and 1st/508th Inf Rgts; 2d/321st Artillery; A Co 82d Avn Bn.

Airlifted to VN on Valentine's day '68, it landed at Chu Lai and was soon moved to I Corps and attached to the 101st Abn Div and given the task of defending the approaches to city of Hue during Tet 68. In Sep 68, it was moved to Saigon and was attached to the Capitol Military Assistance Cmd. There it secured the Western approaches to Saigon from rocket & mortar attack until returned home in Dec69 to rejoin its Div as a worldwide Strategic Reserve for the U.S. Although plans were made to send the entire 82d Abn to VN, they never materialized. Casualties: KIA-184, WIA-1,009.

101st Airborne Division (AMBL)

The Div's 1st Bde was in VN Mar66-Mar72, while the 2d & 3d Bdes were there Nov67-Mar72. HQs were: Bien Hoa Nov67-Feb68, Bien Hoa/Phu Bai Mar68-Feb69, Bien Hoa/Gia Le May69-Sep69, Bien Hoa/Hue/Phu Bai Oct69-Nov69, Hue/Phu Bai Dec69-Mar72.

Major elements were: 3d/187th, 1st/327th, 2d/327th, 1/501st, 2d/501st, 1st/502d, 2d/502d, 1st/506th, 2d/506th, 3d/506th Inf Rgts; F Co 58th Inf (LRP), L Co 75th Inf Rangers, 2d Sqdn/17th Air Cav; 2d/11th, 1st/39th, 4th/77th, 2d/319th, 2d/320th, 1st/321st and A BTY 377th Artillery Rgts; 101st Avn Grp (formerly 106th Avn Grp), 101st Avn Bn, 158th Avn Bn, 159th Avn Bn, 163d Avn Co, 478th Avn Co.

Officially changed from Airborne Div to an Airmobile (AMBL) Div, 1Jul69. 1st Bde sent to VN in Jul65 and opconed to IFFV in II Corps in vicinity. of Phan Rang, until it rejoined the 101st in Apr68. The remaining 2 Bdes of the Div arrived, Nov67 and were committed to III Corps in Dec67. In Feb68, the 2d Bde was Opcon'd to the 1st Cav Div in Quang Tri Prov. to counter the Tet 68 offensive in I Corps. Apr-May68 the Div worked in the coastal lowlands of Quang Tri and Thua Thien Provs, and was engaged at Hue. It sent its 3d Bde to Dak To in mid-68, which then moved to reinforce the 25th Inf Div near Saigon while the rest of the Div swept Thua Thien Prov under control of the XXIV Corps. In Sep68, the 3d Bde rejoined the Div at Phong Dien near Hue.

In the Spring of 69, 2d Bde drove W from the Da Nang area to the A Shau Valley, uncovering some of the largest caches found by the Div. May-Aug69, portions of the 2d Bde were opcon to the Americal Div and involved in heavy fighting in the Tam Ky/Duc Hau areas. Elements of the Div fought at Hamburger Hill in '69 and at the siege of FSB Ripcord in May-Jul70. The 3rd Bn/505th Inf, that remained opcon to the 25th Inf Div throughout most of the war operated primarily out of Phan Thiet in III Corps and was the only 101st Abn Div element involved in the 1970 Cambodian Invasion. The Div's Avn and Arty assets participated in the Spring '71 invasion of Laos, Lam Son 719. From 1Dec71-31Jan 72, the bulk of the Div was re-deployed to the U.S. as part of Increment X.

Note: On 28Jun68, U.S. Army, Pacific issued Gen Order 325 which reorganized the 101st Abn into Army's second Airmobile (AMBL) Div (1st Cav being the first). Same order redesignated Div as "101st Air Cavalry Division" eff 1Jul68. However, term "Air Cavalry Division" was revoked by a Dept of Army directive issued 26Aug68, and thereafter, official name was 101st Airborne Division (Airmobile). Same order affected 1st Cav Div. [12]Casualties: KIA-4,011, WIA-18,259.

101st Airborne Div, 1st Bde (Sep)

In Vietnam from Jul65-Nov67 as a separate Bde attached to the IFFV in II Corps. HQ locations were: Bien Hoa/Vung Tau Jul65-Sep65, Cam Ranh Bay Oct65, Ma Ca Nov 65, Phan Rang Dec65-May67, Duc Pho June67, Phan Rang/Duc Pho Jul67-Nov67.

Major elements were: 1st/327th, 2d/327th, 2d/502d Inf Rgts, A Trp, 2d Sqdn/17th Armored Cav; 2d Bn 320th Arty. It rejoined the Div when the remaining two Bdes deployed to VN in Nov67. While with the IFFV, it helped clear Phu Yen Prov. in early 66, and then moved to Kontum in Western II Corps. In May67 the Bde was attached as part of Task Force Oregon (which later became the Americal Div) until the 101st came in-country, Nov67. Casualties: See 101st Abn Div.

173d Airborne Bde

In VN May65-Aug71. HQs were located at: Bien Hoa May65-Oct67, An Khe Nov67-Apr69, Bong Son May 69-Aug71.

Major elements were: 1st/503d, 2d/503d, 3d/503d, 4th/503d Inf Rgts; D Co 16th Armor, E Trp 17th Armored Cav; 3d Bn 319th Arty [13]; 335th Avn Co; attached units: 1st Bn Royal Australian Army, 3d/506th Inf (101st Abn).

First major U.S. ground unit sent to Vietnam (arrived 7May65). Deployment was intended to be temporary; however, the Bde stayed in VN most of the period U.S. was involved. Generally regarded as an elite unit, it was the only? major element to maintain its pure "Airborne" status while in-country, and on, its 2d Bn/503d Inf became the only Army battalion to make an actual combat parachute jump during the war.

The Bde gained major fame during the Battle for Hill 875, Nov67, during the overall Battle for Dak To. In some of the most bitter contact of the war, it took very heavy casualties and captured Hill 875 on Thanksgiving Day, '67. It was originally sent to VN to provide security for Bien Hoa Airbase but in Sep-Nov66 was committed to heavy fighting in War Zone C and then returned to that location in early '67. During '68-69, the Bde was committed to ops in Binh Thuan & Binh Dinh Provinces (II Corps), providing security for QL-1 and pacification in the An Lo Valley. Between 69-71, the Bde continued similar ops, returning home 25Aug71. Major ops during war included Attleboro & Junction City. Casualties: KIA-1,748, WIA-8,747.

196th Infantry Brigade (Light)

In Vietnam Aug66-Jun72. Was attached to the Americal Division. HQs were located at : Tay Ninh Aug66-May67, Chu Lai Jun67-Oct67, Tam Ky Nov67-Mar68, Phong Dien

---

[12] Vietnam Studies, *Airmobility 1961-1971*, Tolson, Lt. Gen John J, Dept of Army, 1973, p 195

[13] According to Dan Gillotti, the 3d/319th FA, while supporting the 173rd Abn, fired the 1st U.S. <u>Army</u> Arty round (105mm), 12May65.

Apr68-May68, Hoi An Jun68, Chu Lai Jul68-Mar71, Da Nang Apr71-Jun72.

Major elements were: 2d/1st, 1st/46th, 5th/46th, 1st/52d Inf Rgts; F Trp 8th Air Cav, F Trp 17th Armored Cav; 3d Bn 82d Artillery.[14] The Bde arrived in VN, 26Aug66, and sent to western II Corps, War Zone C, Tay Ninh Prov. After fighting a major battle in Oct66, the Bde was selected as one of the Inf Bdes used to form Task Force Oregon in Apr 67. It was then moved to I Corps in order to release USMC units to migrate north toward the DMZ. In Sep67, Task Force Oregon was redesignated the 23d Inf (Americal) Div and the 196th remained attached until Feb69, when it became an official part of the Americal. While with that Div it operated widely throughout I Corps until Apr71, when it was fixed in Da Nang to provide security until sent home 29Jun72. Casualties: KIA-1,004, WIA-5,591.

198th Infantry Brigade (Light)

In Vietnam Oct67-Nov71. HQs were located at: Duc Pho Oct67-Nov67, Chu Lai Dec67-Nov71.

Major elements were: 1st/6th, 1st/46th, 5th/46th and 1st 52d Inf Rgts; H Trp 17th Armored Cav; 1st/14th Arty. Originally slated for securing the development of Secty of Defense Robert MacNamara's proposed physical and electronic barrier along the DMZ that was code named *Practice Nine* Because of that the Bde became known as the *Practice Nine Barrier Brigade*. Although partially constructed in '67, the project was abandoned as too costly and impractical and the Bde was instead sent to VN, 21Oct67 to become part of Task Force Oregon, a makeshift division formed from three borrowed Bdes operating in southern I Corps to release USMC units north toward the DMZ. In Sep67 the Task Force was redesignated the 23d Infantry Division (Americal Div) and remained with that Div throughout its stay in VN. Casualties: Unknown (inc. in those of 23d Inf Div).

199th Infantry Brigade (Light)

In Vietnam 10Dec66-11Oct70. HQs located at: Long Binh/Cat Lai Dec66-Dec67, Bien Hoa Jan68-Apr68, Long Binh/Duc Hoa May68-Jul69, Xuan Loc Aug69-Jun70, Long Binh/Gia Ray Jul70-Oct70.

Major elements were: 2d/3d, 3d/7th, 4th/12th and 5th/12th Inf Rgts; D Trp 17th Armored Cav, F Co 51st Inf (LRP), M Co 75th Inf Rangers; 3d Sqdn/11th Armored Cav; 2d/40th Arty. The 199th arrived in VN 10Dec66 and was assigned to III Corps where it remained for its entire tour. Operating jointly with ARVN force, it worked the Saigon area during '67, then moved to Bien Hoa in Dec67. The Bde was heavily engaged with the VC 275th Rgt, which attacked its IIFFV perimeter 31Feb68, during the Tet 68, Battle for Saigon. During that battle, its 3d Bn/7th Inf attacked and cleared the VC CP at the Phu Tho Racetrack and then fought house-to-house through the Cholon Dist. The Bde then conducted numerous sweeps around Duc Hoa/Long Binh and in '69 was responsible for the northern and eastern security for Saigon. It left VN 11Oct70. Casualties: KIA-754, WIA-4,679.

502d Light Infantry Bde

Col Hank Emerson's amusing name for makeshift unit used in reopening of Bn Mia Gap Airfield in May66. Consisted of: one platoon of the 326th Engineers, a 17-man element from an RF Company from Bu Prang, 30 Montagnard porters, a squad of VN National Police who were interpreters and Third Co, 4th Bn, 9th ARVN Rgt, its Recondo Platoon, 30 Montagnard Trackers (the Apache Platoon) and its U.S. and U.S. SF Advisors. Reopening discussed in S.L.A. Marshall's *Battle in the Monsoon*, pp 228-229.

A Teams

Tactical level and the bottom of Army Special Forces unit hierarchy. Under the direct command of SF B-Teams. There were four B-Teams, one located in each CTZ (Corps), and each B-team had 4 or 5 A-Teams under its command. Strike Forces were indigenous units put together and advised by the A-Teams. In the early 60's, commo between A and B Teams was by Morse code sent encrypted on what was known as a "one-time pad," while at the tactical level A-teams used voice radio. [15]

Americal Division

See 23d Infantry Division.

B Teams

Mid level of Army Special Forces unit hierarchy and under command of the C-Team at Nha Trang. There were four B-Teams, one located in each CTZ (Corps), and each B-team had 4 or 5 A-Teams under its command. Strike forces were indigenous units put together and advised by the A-Teams. In the early 60's, commo between A and B Teams was by Morse code sent encrypted on what was known as a "one-time pad," while at the tactical level the A-teams used voice radio.[16]

C-Teams

Highest level of Army SF unit hierarchy. The C-Team was the command and control element HQ'd at Nha Trang. It was in command of a B-Team (one in each CTZ), while each B-Team ran 4 or 5 A-Teams and associated indigenous Strike Force elements at the tactical level. [17]

Mobile Riverine Force

In Vietnam Jun67-1969. HQs Located at, Vung Tau and later, Dong Tam. Major elements were: 2d Bde U.S. 9th Inf Div, U.S. Navy Task Forces 115, 116 and 117), Navy Seal Teams, SVN Marines, and the 7th ARVN Div/River Assault Grps.

The Mobile Riverine Force included apx 5,000 troops, with a high degree of mobility. Its headquarters originally located in Vung Tau, but moved to a the 600 acre, man-made Island of Dong Tam (apx 9 km from My Tho) after that Island was dredged from the Mekong River. Numerous of this forces facilities and "fire support bases" were on board ships and floating platforms throughout the delta.

Op Game Warden (Navy Task Force 116) was created in '65 to interdict VC guerrilla forces operating in the Mekong Delta. In 1967, Task Force 117 was added to expand coverage of the Mekong Delta and the Rung Sat Swamp area. These forces employed fiberglass PBRs, air-cushioned vehicles, WWII landing craft, LSTs, LSMs,

[14] According to Dan Gillotti, B Bty, 3d/82nd FA, Task Force Gimlet, 196th LIB, fired the last U.S. Army arty round of the VN War, 10Aug72.

[15] Wade, Leigh, *Tan Phu: SF Team A-23 in Combat*, p 31

[16] Wade, Leigh, *Tan Phu: SF Team A-23 in Combat*, p 31

[17] Wade, Leigh, *Tan Phu: SF Team A-23 in Combat*, p 31

motorized junks, and various amphibious personnel carriers to negotiate the waterways of the Mekong and to deliver and support Mobile Riverine Force troops.

The MRF assets gradually migrated to the ARVN between 1969-71, after bulk of the 9th Inf Div went home and its 3d Bde moved to III Corps in '69. See also Dong Tam, Game Warden, Market Time and U.S. Naval Forces VN (Major Command Section) and 9th Inf Div (Divisional Command Section).

Nung

Mercenary soldiers, mostly of Chinese ancestry, employed and trained by the U.S. In *Ambush*, S.L.A. Marshall described them as "prodigious guzzlers of beer" and stated that any group party they held that did not go on for at least 5 hours and include a 10 course meal was deemed a failure! Noted for their skill and prowess as very effective soldiers. Any male Nung was supposed to be at least 2d generation military. Nung riflemen were paid 5,100 Piasters/month in 66/67, about $43 U.S., with an extra 400 Piaster family allowance and an additional 1,000 Piasters if they were rated as a paratrooper. Of that pay, 300 Piasters was deducted for rations. See also C-3 Compound.

Task Force 70.8

The U.S. Navy contingents responsible for naval shore bombardment mid '65 to late '67. Primary craft used were Cruisers and Destroyers, however, the Battleship New Jersey spent six months as a part of the TF in '68/'69. Supported Allied forces in SVN and also bombarded coastal targets in NVN. See also Op Sea Dragon.

Task Force 73

USN 7th Fleet's logistic support unit.

Task Force 76

USN 7th Fleet's Amphibious unit.

Task Force 77

USN 7th Fleet's aircraft carrier attack unit.

Task Force Oregon

In VN Apr67-Sep67, a provisional Div-sized element deployed to southern Quang Tin Prov. and Quang Ngai Prov, I Corps, in order to release Marine units protecting those areas to move further north toward the DMZ. Its HQ was at Chu Lai.

Major elements were: 3d Bde 25th Inf Div, 1st Bde 101st Abn Div, and the 196th LIB. In Sep 67, the 11th Inf Bde and the 198th LIB joined the task force, thereby releasing the 1st Bde 101st Abn & 3d Bde 25th Inf for duty elsewhere. At that point, TFO became the 23d Infantry Division (Americal). The division was composed of Bdes and other elements borrowed from other Divs already in-country. Although officially redesignated the 23d Infantry Div in Sep67, it remained known universally as the "Americal" Division. With the arrival of two its own new Bdes from the U.S. in Sep67, it was able to release the borrowed Bdes back to their original assignments.

The subsequent history of the Americal is one checkered with ill fortune and lack of esprit due to in part to the makeshift nature of the unit, its lack of experience and bad luck. The Division suffered a high percentage of casualties to mines and booby traps without ever seeing the enemy and that frustration led to additional problems. Casualties: (see 23d Inf Div).

Task Force South

Vietnam Jul68-Oct70. HQ Locations, Dalat & Phan Thiet. Major elements: 1st/50th (Mech), 3d/503d (82d Abn), 3d/506th (101st Abn) Inf Rgts, 2d Sqdn/1st Armored Cav, C Co 75th Inf Rangers; 5th/22d, 5th/27th, Bty C 3d/319th, Bty D 2d/320th Artillery Rgts. (1st/50th replaced the 3/503d Inf, Sep69.) Organized by the IFFV in Jul68 to pressure VC/NVA elements in the 4 southern provinces of II Corps after Tet 68 and "Mini-Tet" in May 68, and in order to relieve pressure on Saigon. Its CP was located with that of the ARVN 23d Inf Div in order to facilitate cooperation and mutual support. In May 70 various of its elements participated in the invasion of Cambodia. Casualties: Unknown

Task Force Walker

Force organized under BG Glenn Walker during Op Paul Revere, May-Jun66. Assigned an area in II Corps W of Pleiku that was 80 km wide and 40 km tall. Zone ran SW to the Chu Pong Mountains and NW as far as the outpost at Duc Co. Its eastern border was on a line with Plei Me and the western limit was the Cambodian border. Job was to monitor activity in the infamous Ia Drang Valley. Its element included 3 Inf Bns from the 25th Inf Div (1st/14th, 1st & 2d of the 35th Inf) one Co of medium armor, one armored Cav Trp, one Air Cav Trp, one Bn of 105 howitzers and on Bty each of 155mm, 175mm and 8" cannons. See S.L.A. Marshall's *Battle in the Monsoon*, pp 261 et seq. II Corps.

U.S. Navy Seabees

A.k.a. NMCBs, Naval Mobile Construction Battalions (term "Seabee" is derived from initials "CB," for Construction Battalion). In '54, Amphibious Construction Bn 1 was constructing refugee camps at various locations in Vietnam, including Hanoi. Between '62 and '65, Seabees were used to construct Special Forces Camps in VN, many of which were located in very remote sites. In May '65, the navy began landing NMCB, usually under the control of the II MAF, with each Bn having an authorized strength of about 25 officers and 740 enlisted men. Most NMCBs were limited to about and average of a 10 month tour in-country. Major Navy Const elements were: 3d Naval Const Bde, 30th Naval Const Rgt, 32d Naval Const Rgt, 1st Amphibious Const Bn and: NMCBs #1 through 12, 22, 40, 53, 58, 62, 71, 74, 121, 128 and 133.

U.S. Military Casualties by Province

Subtotals by Province per DOD Combat Area Casualty File (CACF)

Province	# of Reported Casualties
An Giang	30
An Xuyen	65
Ba Xuyen	82
Bac Lieu	18
Bien Hoa	1,328
Binh Dinh	2,351
Binh Duong	2,758
Binh Long	942
Binh Thuan	303
Binh Thuy	195
Chau Doc	1
Chuong Thien	39
Con Son Island	1
DMZ	1
Darlac	192
Dinh Tuong	835
Gia Dinh	1,316
Go Cong	71
Hau Nghia	1,441
Khanh Hoa	447
Kien Giang	124
Kien Hoa	462
Kien Phong	77
Kien Tuong	159
Kontum	1,683
Lam Dong	166
Long An	1,018
Long Khanh	576
Ninh Thuan	189
Phong Dinh	198
Phu Bon	32
Phu Quoc Island	1
Phu Yen	319
Phuoc Long	685
Phuoc Tuy	236

Area	# of Reported Casualties
Pleiku	1,084
Quang Duc	178
Quang Nam	8,084
Quang Ngai	2,972
Quang Tin	2,986
Quang Tri	7,532
Sa Dec	32
Tay Ninh	2,675
Thua Thien	4,278
Tuyen Duc	80
Vinh Binh	71
Vinh Long	169
SUB-TOTAL	48,482
Military Region 1	30
Military Region 2	28
Military Region 3	54
Military Region 4	29
Offshore, Military Region 1	91
Offshore, Military Region 2	29
Offshore, Military Region 3	8
Offshore, Military Region 4	47
Offshore, Province unknown	182
SUB-TOTAL	498
Unknown	6,413
Unknown (LZ)	722
Unknown (NY)	420
Unknown (NZ)	624
Unknown/Not Reported	1,009
SUB-TOTAL	9,687
TOTAL	58,667

U.S. Military Casualties [18] [19]	# Serving	Battle Dead	Other Dead	Wounds not Mortal [20]
Total All Branches	8,744,000	47,378	10,799	303,635
U.S. Army	4,368,000	30,922	7,273	96,802
U.S. Navy	1,842,000	1,631	931	4,178
U.S. Marines	794,000	13,084	1,753	51,392
U.S. Air Force	1,740,000	1,741	842	931

[18] Per official U.S. Dept of Defense statistics at: http://web1.whs.osd.mil/mmid/m01/SMS223R.HTM. Number serving covers the period 4Aug64, through 27Jan73, (date of cease-fire).

[19] According to Dick Arnold, the 2d week of May '68 was the most deadly week of the war; 616 Americans died that week. Arnold also notes that 173d Abn Div apparently holds the tragic distinction of suffering the most KIA in a single company in one day, when A Co, 2d/503d lost 75 KIA, 22Jun67, in Kontum Prov.

[20] Wounds not mortal include 153,303 hospitalized and 150,332 wounds not requiring hospital care. Known status of casualties is as of 30Sep95. IMPORTANT: This does NOT mean that 303,635 Americans were wounded in the war. 303,635 is the total number of incidents of wounding. Many individuals, particularly in the Infantry, were wounded multiple times, and individuals receiving 2, 3, 4, 5, 6 or even more Purple Hearts was not at all uncommon. It is the author's estimate that the actual total number of INDIVIDUALS wounded in the war was perhaps only half of the 303,635 wound incidents. It is interesting to also note that the U.S. military had a policy whereby an individual who was wounded three times during any tour was sent back to the U.S. regardless of the time remaining in their one-year obligation unless the individual could convince the authorities otherwise.

Major Army Unit KIA (all causes) Casualty Totals

Per National Archives TAGCEN Database [21]
(Data Courtesy of Constance Menefee and Gary Rousch)

Unit/Command	Total KIA (all causes)	TAGCEN Unit Code ID
1st Aviation Brigade	1,637	FA
1st Cavalry Division (AMBL)	5,367	FC
1st Field Force	340	FF
1st Infantry Division	3,094	FI
1st Logistic Command	586	FL
1st Signal Brigade	189	FS
9th Infantry Division	2,586	IN
11th Armored Cavalry	715	AC
11th Light Infantry Brigade	1,095	EI
2d Field Force	76	TF
4th Infantry Division	2,496	IF
5th Infantry Division (Mech)	520	IM
25th Infantry Division	4,486	TI
82d Airborne Division	223	EA
101st Airborne Division (Ambl)	3,906	OA
173rd Airborne Brigade	1,717	AB
196th Light Infantry Brigade	1,171	IB
198th Light Infantry Brigade	949	BI
199th Light Infantry Brigade	741	LI
Americal (23rd Infantry Div) [22]	773	AD
Engineering Command	63	EC
MACV Advisors	997	MV
Other	2,942	XX
Special Forces	739	SF
U.S. Army Republic of Vietnam	809	UV

Disabled U.S. Veteran Statistics of the Vietnam War

Wounded requiring treatment:	303,678 (total incidence, not # of individuals) [23]
Wounded requiring hospitalization	151,000 (total incidence, not # of individuals) [24]
Severely disabled:	75,000
100% disabled:	23,214
Lost limbs:	5,283
Sustained multiple amputations:	1,081

Amputation or crippling wounds to the lower extremities were 300% higher than in WWII and 70% higher than in Korea. Multiple amputations occurred at the rate of 18.4% compared to 5.7% in WWII (per www.pbr-fva.org/statist.html)

[21] The TAGCEN file is an electronic casualty file maintained by the National Archives and Records Administration Center for Electronic Records in Adelphi, MD. It contains a comprehensive and detailed accounting of all casualties (wounded, injured and KIA, world-wide) for all Army personnel during the period 1961-1981. The data for wounded has been kept confidential because it includes the Social Security Numbers of still living veterans; otherwise, the data for KIA can be purchased in electronic or hard copy formats. NARA CER will provide information in electronic form or in hard copy form arrayed in a number of different formats (i.e., by unit by date, by name by unit, by date, by name and etc.

[22] This total is misleading because the Americal Division was composed of a number of units and its composition varied over time. See Major Unit Section entries for the Americal and 23d Infantry Division.

[23] Each wounding of an individual counted seperately; i.e. total individuals wounded is a much lower figure.

[24] Each wounding of an individual counted seperately; i.e. total individuals wounded is a much lower figure.

Non-U.S. Casualties of the Vietnam War [25] [26]

South Vietnamese Military:	185,000	499,026
Viet Cong/NVA:	924,048	?
Vietnamese Civilian SVN & NVN:	415,000	935,000
Australian/New Zealand:	475	2,348
Communist Chinese[27]	1,000+	?
Philippines:	?	?
Republic of China (Taiwan):	?	?
Republic of Korea:	4,407	?
Royal Thai Army:	350	?
Russia (Soviet Bloc):	?	?
Spain:	?	?

French Casualties of the First Indochina War

95,000 KIA (25,000 of whom were of French blood) including 4 Generals, 1,300 Lieutenants and a mix of French, French Foreign Legion, Cambode, Laotian, Algerian, Moroccan and Sengalese troops.

Campaign Periods and Awards of the Vietnam War

Any member of the U.S. Armed Forces who served in Vietnam, its contiguous waters or air space in accordance with the appropriate DOD regulations authorizing the award of the Vietnam Service Medal (VSM). See detail below) is also authorized to wear a "bronze battle star" on their VSM Ribbon for each specified campaign period he or she served in Vietnam. The bronze battle star is a small five-pointed star approximately 1/8th" in diameter and the award of five such bronze battle stars can be represented by a silver battle star used in their place. There were a total of seventeen campaign periods assigned for the VSM between 15Mar62 and 28Jan73.

The Campaign periods for which a bronze battle star is authorized are:

Advisory	15Mar62	7Mar65
Defense	8Mar65	24Dec65
Counteroffensive	25Dec65	30Jun66
Counteroffensive Phase II	1Jul66	31May67
Counteroffensive Phase III	1Jun67	29Jan68
Tet Counteroffensive	30Jan68	1Apr68
Counteroffensive Phase IV	2Apr68	30Jun68
Counteroffensive Phase V	1Jul68	1Nov68
Counteroffensive Phase VI	2Nov68	22Feb69
Tet 69 Counteroffensive	23Feb69	8Jun69
Summer-Fall 1969	9Jun69	31Oct69
Winter-Spring 1969	1Nov69	30Apr70
Sanctuary Counteroffensive	1May70	30Jun70
Counteroffensive Phase VII	1Jul70	30Jun71
Consolidation I	1Jul71	30Nov71
Consolidation II	1Dec71	29Mar72
Cease Fire	30Mar72	28Jan73

[25] Compiled from *The Vietnam War, An Alamanc*, p 358

[26] Dougals Pike esitmates SVN civilian casualties were 465,000 KIA and 935,000 WIA, and that NVN civilian casualties were but only a small fraction of those totals. Data per *A Better War*, pp 46-47.

[27] According to Professor John Swensson (De Anza College), *China And The Vietnam Wars, 1950-75*, tells us Chinese sent 320,000 troops to NVN between 1965-68, and over 1,000 of them were killed.

Vietnam Service Medal:

A.k.a. the VSM. Established by executive Order # 11231, 8Jul65. U.S. Campaign medal awarded to all who served in or over the Vietnam Combat Zone. On 24Apr64, President Kennedy signed an executive order retroactively allowing U.S. Servicemen wounded in SVN to receive the Purple Heart effective 15Mar62. Although the VSM was not created until 8Jul65, it also became retroactive to 1Jul58 for those personnel who had been awarded the Armed Forces Expeditionary Medal and wished to exchange it for the VSM. The VSM award period therefore effectively began 1Jul58 and ended 28Jan73; however, the campaign Bronze Star attached to the ribbon (one per campaign period served) was only authorized between 15Mar62 and 28Jan73. The "Cease Fire" campaign period (last of 17 campaigns in the VN War) ended 28Jan73. Although that dates marks the end of the award period, Camp Alpha (at Tan Son Nhut AB) was the very last U.S. military facility to close at the end of the U.S. involvement in SVN, and its flag was actually lowered in a ceremony occurring 29Jan73. Per Ray Bows' *Vietnam Military Lore, 1959-1973*, pp 237-238, an honor guard of apx 50 U.S. personnel gave a final salute as the U.S. flag was lowered and then the base officially turned-over to the SVN Govt. Moments after the ceremony ended, "Vietnamese looters, both military and civilian, ransacked the camp and carried off everything in Camp Alpha that wasn't securely affixed." Later the looters tore down most of the buildings and fixtures as well, and left the facility in ruins."

Armed Forces Expeditionary Medal:

Campaign Medal awarded for Service between 1Jul58(?) and the effective date of the Vietnam Service Medal, 8Jul65. Although the VSM was not created until 8Jul65, it also became retroactive to 1Jul58 for those personnel who had been awarded the Armed Forces Expeditionary Medal and wished to exchange it for the VSM. If exchanged, personnel are not authorized to wear both ribbons unless their AFEM was awarded for other then Vietnam Service.

Republic of Vietnam Campaign Medal:

Medal awarded by the Vietnamese government (<u>not</u> U.S. government). Where U.S. forces were concerned, it was awarded to anyone who served for <u>a minimum of six-months</u> within Vietnam, its surrounding waters or in air support against an armed enemy in Vietnam between March 1, 1961 and March 28, 1973. The time limit was waived if the recipient was killed, wounded or captured at any Time before the fulfilling the 6-month minimum. The medal was also awarded to other SEATO member nation troops supporting the South Vietnamese, as well as the troops of the South Vietnamese Government itself. Time limits and regulations apart from U.S. participation are not known. Presumably the small, metal scroll attached to the medal and engraved "*1960-*" was meant to someday include the final year of the war as well. The fall of the SVN government in '75 apparently precluded any final revision to that scroll.

The Vietnamese Cross of Gallantry:

Medal awarded by the Vietnamese government to units or individuals for courage under fire against an armed enemy force which varied in name by branch of service. Attachments to the award represent the level at which it was awarded. For Army personnel, a "Palm" represented an entire armed force level award, a Gold star represented a Corps level award; the Silver Star a Division level award, and the Bronze Star a Bde or Rgtl level award. The physical shape of the attachments changed when the same award was Presented to Navy and Air Force personnel; a similarly colored wing was attached to the Air Gallantry Cross and similarly colored anchors to the Navy Gallantry Cross. (Some data per *Vietnam Military Lore, 1959-1973*, pp 254.)

Vietnamese Meritorious Unit Commendation:

A.k.a. the Vietnamese Gallantry Cross with palm and frame. According to Marine Author George Neville, was apparently awarded to personnel who served on land and in country but not off-shore participation for the period 8Feb62-28Mar73. However, we were unable to confirm this peculiar distinction from other variations of the Gallantry Cross award which were presented for naval participation?

Executive (Presidential) Orders Defining the Vietnam Combat Zone and other Combat Zone Related Documents

The Vietnam Combat Zone

Executive Order 11216, which established the original Vietnam Combat zone and defines it in detail is found in Section 112 of the Internal Revenue Code and is entitled: *Certain Combat Pay of Members of the Armed Forces*. It's location emphasizes the fact that the primary purpose for defining a combat zone is to establish IRS exemptions and eligibility for combat pay. The text is available at: www.tns.lcs.mit.edu/uscode/TITLE_26/Subtitle_A/ CHAPTER_1/Subchapter_B/PART_III/ Sec._112.html

Ex. Ord. No. 11216. Designation Of Vietnam And Adjacent Waters As Combat Zone:

Ex. Ord. No. 11216, Apr. 24, 1965, 30 F.R. 5817, provided:

"Pursuant to the authority vested in me by section 112 of the Internal Revenue Code of 1954 (now I.R.C. 1986), I hereby designate, for the purposes of that section, as an area in which Armed Forces of the United States are and have been engaged in combat: Vietnam, including the waters adjacent thereto within the following-described limits: From a point on the East Coast of Vietnam at the juncture of Vietnam with China southeastward to 21 N Lat., 108 15 E Long.; thence southward to 18 N Lat., 108 15 E Long.; thence southeastward to 17 30 N Lat., 111 E Long.; thence southward to 11 N Lat., 111 E Long.; thence southwestward to 7 N Lat., 105 E Long.; thence westward to 7 N Lat., 103 E Long.; thence northward to 9 30 N Lat., 103 E Long.; thence northeastward to 10 15 N Lat., 104 27 E Long.; thence northward to a point on the West Coast of Vietnam at the juncture of Vietnam with Cambodia. The date of the commencing of combatant activities in such area is hereby designated as January 1, 1964." - Lyndon B. Johnson

Termination Of Vietnam Combat Zone Issued By President Clinton 14MAY96

(no identifying number apart from the date is given)

THE WHITE HOUSE
Office of the Press Secretary
For Immediate Release, May 14, 1996

EXECUTIVE ORDER

TERMINATION OF COMBAT ZONE DESIGNATION IN VIETNAM AND WATERS ADJACENT THERETO

"By the authority vested in me as President by the Constitution and the laws of the United States of America, including section 112(c)(3) of the Internal Revenue Code of 1986 (26 U.S.C. 112(c)(3)), June 30, 1996, as of midnight thereof, is hereby designated as the date of termination of combatant activities in the zone comprised of the area described in Executive Order No. 11216 of April 24, 1965." - William Jefferson Clinton

Executive Orders As They Relate To Medals And Awards

Armed Forces Expeditionary Medal: "The Armed Forces Expeditionary Medal (AFEM) was established by Executive Order 10977, dated 4 December 1961 (DA Bull. 1, 1962) and Executive Order 11231, 8 July 1965. This medal is authorized for U.S. military operations, U.S. operations in direct support of the United Nations, and U.S. operations of assistance for friendly foreign nations. Operation, area of operations, and direct support are defined in the Glossary." Designated U.S. ops of assistance for a friendly foreign nation included:

1. Laos. From 19Apr61 to 7Oct62.
2. Vietnam. From 1Jul58 to 3Jul65.
3. Cambodia From 29Mar73 to 15Aug73.
4. Thailand (only those in direct support of Cambodia ops). From 29Mar73 to 15Aug73."
   (data per http://132.94.50.31/army/D1-123/awards/afem.htm)

Vietnam Service Medal:

"a. The Vietnam Service Medal (VSM) was established by Executive Order 11231, 8 July 1965. It is awarded to all members of the Armed Forces of the United States serving in Vietnam and contiguous waters or airspace thereover, after 3 July 1965 through 28 March 1973. Members of the Armed Forces of the United States in Thailand, Laos, or Cambodia, or the airspace thereover, during the same period and serving in direct support of operations in Vietnam are also eligible for this award."

Individuals qualified for the Armed Forces Expeditionary Medal for reason of service in Vietnam between 1 July 1958 and 3 July 1965(inclusive) shall remain qualified for that medal. Upon request (unit personnel officer) any such individual may be awarded the VSM instead of the Armed Forces Expeditionary Medal. In such instances, the Armed Forces Expeditionary will be deleted from the list of authorized medals in personnel records. No person will be entitled to both awards for Vietnam service."

(NOTE: Technically then, an individual is not authorized to wear both the VSM and the AFEM at the same time if both medals were awarded for service in Vietnam. Interesting too is the fact that the AFEM regulation contains no language alerting a recipient to the corresponding restriction in the VSM regulation?) (Data per http://132.94.50.31/army/D1-123/awards/vsm.htm.)

Other Legal Citations

The following citation was found at: www.hsba.org/Hawaii/Admin/Ag/op91-4.htm. It is an excerpt from the letters of the State of Hawaii's Attorney General, and offers other legal citations that may be of interest:

> "The Vietnam Era is defined as a 'period of war' and as a 'period of conflict' and has been described as 'combatant activities' and an 'armed conflict.' 38 U.S.C.A. 101 and I note that various conflicts and hostilities after World War II have usually not been 'wars' within the constitutional meaning. Although commonly denoted as the 'Korean War' and the 'Vietnam War,' no congressional declaration of war was made in either conflict. Both of these conflicts are defined as 'periods of war' in 38 U.S.C.A. 101 and 501 (West 1979). The Executive Order setting the termination date of the Korean conflict spoke only of 'combatant activities,' not a war. Executive Order 10585 (January 1, 1955), 1955 U.S. Code Cong. & Ad. News 1048.
>
> Similarly, Executive Order 11216 (April 24, 1965), 1965 U.S. Code Cong. & Ad. News 4381, designated Vietnam and its vicinity only as 'an area of combatant activities.' In setting the last day of the Vietnam Era, President Ford spoke only of conflict and combatant activities. Proclamation No. 4373 (May 7, 1975), 1975 U.S. Code Cong. & Ad. News 2500. 501 (West 1979) and 26 U.S.C.A. 112 (West 1984), respectively. As discussed above, the statutory definition of active duty in the United States armed forces includes active duty for training and, except for a limited exception regarding benefits, the courts have generally equated active duty for training with active military service."

Appendix C

Military Topographical Maps and Map Resources

How to Acquire Copies of Military Topographical Maps (From the USGS, National Archives, Library of Congress and NOAA)

USGS Catalog of NIMA Public Sale Topographic Maps, Publications, and Digital Products:

The Department of the Interior, U.S. Geological Survey (USGS), is the distributor of public sale *National Imagery and Mapping Agency* (NIMA) topographic maps, publications, and digital products. Their catalog of available products contains descriptions, availability, currency, and ordering procedures for NIMA produced topographic maps and publications. Copies of this catalog and further information on NIMA products can be obtained from any *Earth Science Information Center* (ESIC), or by calling 1-888-ASK-USGS, or by calling USGS's 24 hour-a-day Ask USGS fax service at 703-648-4888 and identifying those materials one would like (which are then faxed to a number the caller specifies). For Internet information on the subject, go to http://mac.usgs.gov/mac/nimamaps/index.html.

Still another source of product information is USGS's Internet home page at: www.usgs.gov, and e-mail inquires can be direced to the USGS at: ask@usgs.gov.

USGS Catalog of NIMA Public Sale Topographic Maps For Vietnam (et al):

The following was compiled from http://mac.usgs.gov/mac/nimamaps/topo.html and/or http://mac.usgs.gov/mac/nimamaps/topo.html#Vietnam to view this catalog. Two primary products featured there are:

Southeast Asia Briefing Map, Series 5213, Scale 1:2,000,000
Type: Topographic; multicolor
Format: Approximately 15° N-S by 10° E-W; Lambert Conformal Conic projection; geographic grid
Sheet Size: 24" by 35" (61 cm by 89 cm)
Symbols: NIMA
Source: Prepared by NIMAOG from NIMAAC 1:1,000,000 ONC, current as of 1981.
Characteristics: International boundaries delineated; relief indicated by 1,000 foot contours with 250 and 500 foot supplementary contours; heights in feet; populated places classified by importance; principal roads shown; airfields symbolized; drainage shown. Countries depicted include Cambodia, Laos, and Vietnam. Parts of Burma, China, and Thailand are also depicted.
USGS Stock Number: T5213XSEABRM

L-7014 Series 1:50,000 scale maps (Index and complete list of stock numbers)
Type: Topographic; multicolor
Format: 15° N-S by 15° E-W, Transverse Mercator projection; 1,000 meter UTM Grid
Sheet Size: 22.5" x 29"
Symbols: NIMA and Vietnamese
Source: Photo-revised and format conversion from stereo-compiled 1:50,000 NIMA Series 701
Characteristics: Relief shown by contours at 5, 10, and 20 meter intervals with 5 or 10 meter supplementary contours, at 25 meter intervals with 12.5 meter supplementary contours, at 40 meter intervals and by form lines; elevations in meters; foreshore and offshore detail shown: depths in meters; drainage symbolized; standing water area indicated, international, phan, and tinh boundaries. Provisional Military Demarcation Line delineated; quan boundaries delineated in Index to Boundaries south of 17°, populated places symbolized and classified by importance; roads classified by weatherability, surface, and width; railroads classified by gauge and number of tracks; airfields delineated and classified by weatherability; vegetation symbolized, trilingual marginal data (English, French, Vietnamese).

L-7014 Series 1:50,000 Scale, Military Topographical Maps:

The DMA L-7014 Series Maps are the very same 1:50,000 scale, color, topographical, Defense Mapping Agency maps used at the platoon and company level in Vietnam.

These maps were de-classified by the Department of Defense in about 1995, and can now be purchased by the public through the USGS (U.S. Geological Survey) Map Center in Denver, Colorado (the Defense Mapping Agency [DMA, now NIMA - the

National Imagery and Mapping Agency], no longer sells maps directly to the public). These are very high quality maps of very high detail, and are an invaluable resource for locating places or terrain features in Vietnam.

- Each L-7014 Series map covers approximately 28 kilometers on its vertical axis and 27 kilometers on its horizontal axis, for a total surface area of just under 756 square kilometers per map.
- At 1:50,000 scale, 1 inch equals about 1.22 kilometers.
- The contour interval between contour lines is 20 meters (with supplemental contours of five meters) in elevation.
- The maps are apx 22 3/8" by 28 7/8" in size.

Because of their 1:50,000 scale, over 300 separate L-7014 maps are required to cover South Vietnam alone. At current prices, the entire SVN set would cost roughly $1,800. It has been rumored that a number of private vendors plan to digitize the entire set and make it available onCD-ROM at a much lower cost in the future.

Ordering L-7014 Series DMA/NIMA Maps From USGS

As of December, 2000, the L-7014 series maps were $7.00 each, plus a shipping & handling charge of $3.50 per order (i.e., total shipping charge per order is $3.50 regardless of the number of maps in a given order). Maps can be ordered directly from the USGS or through vendors listed in the yellow pages under "Map Dealers." A current price list of USGS topographic products is at: http://mapping.usgs.gov/mac/isb/pubs/ forms/nimaplof.pdf. NOTE: Request an L-7014 INDEX Map before ordering.

The USGS's own, rather poor index map to the L-7014 series can be accessed on-line at http://mapping.usgs. gov/mac/nimamaps/topo.html. A black & white copy (better quality than USGS's index) can also be ordered from the Library of Congress or the National Archives. The index is also available at: www.rjsmith.com/images/kelley/Index-L7014s.jpg.

USGS Phone Orders: Order five maps maximum per call using a credit card at: 1-888-ASK-USGS (275-8747).

USGS Fax Orders: If more than five maps are needed, or one simply prefers the alternative, orders can be faxed or mailed to USGS. To order from USGS by fax, first print an order form from the Internet at:http://mapping.usgs.gov/ esic/to_order.html, or simply print the order with all appropriate data on a sheet of paper and fax it to: 303-202-4693. Include credit card type, number, expiration date and include a signature.

USGS Mail Orders: Send credit card, check or money order to:

USGS Information Services
Box 25286. Denver Federal Center, Denver CO 80225-0046
Tel: 303-202-4200; Fax 303-202-4695

Unfortunately, little information regarding the L-7014 series maps can be found on USGS's otherwise amazing website. One should not be discouraged if a visit to their website produces no results because the maps are available. Recent conversations with USGS staff suggested detailed L-7014 map information would be available eventually. Go to: http://mapping.usgs.gov/esic/.

USGS apparently now offers the entire 300 map L-7014 series set (covering all of what was South Vietnam). Their listing of available maps does include a few that cover areas immediately above the DMZ/17th Parallel. Keep in mind that the limit for cross-border "Prairie Fire" operations was set 33 kilometers north of the DMZ and 33 kilometers west of the Lao border as well, so available maps should satisfy most needs since they appear to cover as far north of the DMZ as 60 kilometers.

These North Vietnam maps were identified among USGS's list of available L-7014 maps:

TL-7014-6243-1	Co Trang
TL-7014-6243-2	Lang Mo
TL-7014-6243-4	Ben Karai
TL-7014-6343-1	An Dinh
TL-7014-6343-2	Qui Hau
TL-7014-6343-3	My Duc
TL-7014-6343-4	Dong Hoi
TL-7014-6443-3	Vinh Linh (Ho Xa)

The DMZ is covered by following map sheets:

Vinh Linh	TL-7014 6443 III
Qui Hau	TL-7014 6343 II (small portion)
Quang Tri	TL-7014 6442 IV

Cam Lo	TL-76014 6342 I
Nguon Rao	TL-7014 6342 IV

The following L-7015 series maps cover portions of the DMZ adjacent to the Laotian border:

TL-7015-6243-3	Ban Vang-Ala
TL-7015-6440-3	Ban Tangyoun
TL-7015-6440-4	Ban Alot
TL-7015-6441-3	Ban Ko

Ordering Other U.S. Geological Survey Products

Apart from the L-7014 Series of 1:50,000 scale topographical maps, the USGS offers many other products. The phone book's Yellow Pages will list the nearest commercial dealers offering USGS products, but one may also call the USGS directly at 1-888-ASK-USGS (1-888-275-8747) to product information.

To contact any USGS Earth Science Information Center by mail, write:

USGS Information Services
Box 25286
Denver, CO 80225

Other products offered by USGS include, but aren't limited to:

- **USGS Digital Cartographic Data and Aerial Photography products**: Visit the *USGS Status Graphics* website at http://mapping.usgs.gov/www/products/status.html, for the current availability of selected.

- **Map Indexes**: Indexes can be requested calling 1-888-ASK USGS. Ask for their *Defense Mapping Agency - Public Sales of Topographic Maps Publications and Digital Products* catalog ISBN 0-607-62418-3

- **Aerial Photographs**: To obtain Aerial Photographs Fact Sheet: Call 1-888 ASK USGS or contact any *Earth Science Information Center*. *National Aerial Photography Program* photos can be searched and ordered using WebGLIS

- **Satellite Images**. These are available on the Internet or contact:

  Customer Services, U.S. Geological Survey
  EROS Data Center
  Sioux Falls, SD 57198
  Tel: 605-594-6151
  Email: custserv@edcmail.cr.usgs.gov

- **Digital Data from USGS Topographic Maps**:

  Metadata (data descriptions). Digital data online.
  Digital Raster Graphics (scanned topographic maps) can be searched and ordered using WebGLIS.
  U.S. GeoData Available Through the Internet Fact Sheet.
  Spatial Data Transfer Standard Fact Sheet.
  1:100,000-scale Digital Line Graph Data available in SDTS Format

For more information call **1-888-ASK-USGS** (1-888-275-8747) or contact any Earth Science Info Center.

To order from USGS directly by Fax, select, print, and complete one of the on-line forms at http://mapping.usgs.gov/esic/to_order.html, and then fax the order to: 303-202-4693. One must include their credit card type, credit card number, expiration date and include a signature on the fax. In the alternative, mail an order and check or money order to:

USGS Information Services
Box 25286
Denver Federal Center
Denver CO 80225-0046   Tel: 303-202-4200; Fax 303-202-4695

Library of Congress and National Archives L-7014 Series Map Products

The cartographic branches of both the Library of Congress and the National Archives hold massive map collections, and their staffs are most helpful in navigating those resources. It is also true that both offer black & white, 1:1 photo copies of the L-7014 Series DMA, 1:50,000 large-scale maps, as well as of most all the maps in their collections.

Smaller scale L-607 series (1:100,000) and L-509 Series (1:250,000 scale) maps are also available at both intitutions. It is important to realize that most copies are in black & white; however, color hard-copies or scanned electronic copies are available, but tend to be <u>much</u> more costly than the corresponding black & white images (at least that was the case in year 2000).

The Black & white copies offered are relatively inexpensive and the quality of reproduction quite good. The images are a typical photoduplicate-on-bond, and are both durable and long-lived compared to similar thermal or blue line copies.

(NOTE: It is recommended that one acquire an L-7014 Index Map before attempting to order L-7014 maps unless one knows the specifically the stock numbers and/or sheet names of the maps needed. In the past, the index was provided at no charge. A high quality image of the actual DMA L-7014 Index map is also available at: www.rjsmith.com/images/kelley/Index-L7014s.jpg)

Order maps from:

Cartographic & Architectural Branch (NNSC)
National Archives & Record Administration (NARA)
8601 Adelphi Road
College Park MD 20740-6001 (Feb '95)
(The author has little personal experience with this resource but found it inconvenient that orders are sent to one address but payment to a completely different address.)

or:

Geography & Map Division, Library of Congress
Washington, DC 20540
202-707-6277
202-707-8531 FAX
(Accepts faxed credit card orders. Orders are billed before(?) shipping and cost was $2 per lineal foot in 1999)

Where the Library of Congress is concerned, one may request quotes by phone or by fax. To order by mail, send a check made out to the Library of Congress, or fax them a credit card number along with its expiration date, the card-holder's signature and a daytime phone number. The charge in year 2000 was $2.00 per lineal foot,and, if that is still the case, and L-7014 series, 1:50,000 scale map will cost between $4.00 and $6.00. It would be a good idea to include a request for L-7014 series index with your first order, if one does not already possess th eindex. In the past, the index was provided free of charge, and the staffing <u>most</u> helpful, courteous and professional.

L-509 Series, DMA Joint Operation Graphics maps are also available from both agencies. The L-509's (later superseded by the L-1501 series) are 1:250,000 in scale and cover a great deal more territory than the L-7014 maps do. For example, sheet # NE-48-16, entitled "Hue" (Indochina & Laos, 1962) covers an area from the Hai Van Pass north to above the DMZ and west to beyond the Vietnamese/Laos border. L-509 and L-1501 JOG provide good topographic detail and are an excellent resource by any measure; in fact, the author regards them as the best all-around map resource for those with a limited budget.

<u>Library of Congress Map Holdings Generally</u>:

(Following was transcribed/edited from http://lcweb.loc.gov/rr/geogmap/guide/gmillgen.html)

"European colonial powers were the first to undertake large-scale topographic surveys in other parts of the world. The British established the *Survey of India* in 1767, but it was not until 1802 that a geodetic triangulation of the subcontinent was begun and the first period of topographic surveys initiated. The *Dutch Topographic Service* began mapping in the Netherlands East Indies (Indonesia) in the 1860s. Similarly, the first official topographic maps of Cambodia, Laos, and Vietnam were prepared by the *French Army's Topographic Bureau* in 1886. Most other national topographic mapping programs were created in the twentieth century. For historical research, these series are especially valuable because individual sheets were revised periodically to reflect internal improvements such as canals, roads, and railroads, growth of urban areas, boundary and name changes.

A large number of the multi-sheet map series were also produced during World War II. All of the major military belligerents devoted extensive resources to compiling maps. The primary topographic map-producing organizations for the Allies were the British Directorate of *Military Survey, War Office, Geographical Section, General Staff (GSGS),* and the *U.S. Army Map Service (AMS).* In an unprecedented example of cooperation, Great Britain assumed primary responsibility for mapping the Eastern Hemisphere, while the United States focused on the Western Hemisphere and the western Pacific. Their combined production totaled more than one billion printed sheets covering most of Europe, North Africa, and East and South Asia.

Following World War II, the Library acquired a considerable number of German and Japanese military multi-sheet maps captured by American military units, particularly maps of Europe produced by the German *Generalstab des Heeres* (General Staff of the Army) and of northern and eastern China and Manchuria surveyed by the *Japanese Kwantung Army*, the *Japanese General Staff*, and the *Japanese Imperial Survey* during the 1930s. Among the captured maps are tactical and operational map series produced by the *Soviet General'nyy Shtab Krasnoy Armii* (General Staff of the Red Army), the *Glavnoye Upravleniye Geodezii i Kartografii (GUGK),* and the *Narodyy Komissariat Vnutrennykh Del (NKVD)* which had been initially captured by German forces, including some which contain German military maps printed on the verso.

Military map series prepared for American units in Korea and Vietnam are also housed in the division. The 1:50,000 scale maps for Vietnam (L7014 series) prepared by the *Defense Mapping Agency (DMA)* are available for reference use but most large-scale military maps are restricted to official use. This restriction also applies to other DMA topographic series covering selected Third World countries.

L-509/1501 Series DMA/NIMA Maps on the Internet:

Some quite beautiful and very detailed 1:250,000 scale Defense Mapping Agency topographic maps are available at: www.nexus.net/~911gfx/SVNmap.html, and color printers should provide excellent copies.

L-7014 and L-701 Series DMA/NIMA North and South Vietnam Map Stock Numbers & Sheet Names

The following is a complete L-7014 series map sheet listing for both South and North Vietnam in two formats:

1. Sorted by Map Sheet Stock Number
2. Sorted by Map Sheet Name

These lists were transcribed from DOD historical files provided by military historian George Neville (3d Recon Bn, 3d Marine Division, 1966-67). Mr. Neville's exceedingly thoughtful and generous assistance has been greatly appreciated.

NOTE: An L-7014 series index map is available at: www.rjsmith.com/images/kelley/Index-L7014s.jpg

1. Vietnam L-7014 and L-701 Maps Sorted by Stock Number

Stock Number, Sheet Name, Territories Covered:

TL 7014-5453-1, Giang Mung Pho, NVN/China only

TL 7014-5454-2, Ban Me Rang, NVN/China only

TL 7014-5552-1, Muong Cha, NVN & Laos

TL 7014-5553-1, Muong Boum, NVN/China only
TL 7014-5553-2, Muong No, NVN only
TL 7014-5553-3, Muong Tong, NVN & Laos only
TL 7014-5553-4, Muong Te, NVN only

TL 7014-5554-3, Ban Sa Lin, NVN/China only

TL 7014 5650-1, Ban Pou Sung, NVN & Laos only

TL 7014-5651-1, Ban Muong Lan, NVN only
TL 7014-5651-2, Ban Kha, NVN only
TL 7014-5651-3, Ban Na Phai, NVN & Laos only
TL 7014-5651-4, Dien Bien Phu, NVN only

TL 7014-5652-1, Ban Nam Nen, NVN only
TL 7014-5652-2, Tuan Giao, NVN only
TL 7014-5652-3, Muong Ang, NVN only
TL 7014-5652-4, Muong Tong, NVN only

TL 7014-5653-1, Phu Nung Nong, NVN only
TL 7014-5653-2, Nam Na, NVN only
TL 7014-5653-3, Lai Chau, NVN only
TL 7014-5653-4, Ta Phing, NVN/China only

TL 7014-5654-2, Phong Tho (Muong So), NVN/China only

TL 7014-5728-1, Hon Thom, SVN

TL 7014-5729-1, Xong Ong Thay, SVN & Cambodia
TL 7014-5729-2, Duong Dong, SVN & Cambodia

TL 7014-5750-1, Muong Hung, NVN & Laos only
TL 7014-5750-4, Sop Cop, NVN & Laos only

TL 7014-5751-1, Son La, NVN only
TL 7014-5751-2, Mai Son, NVN only
TL 7014-5751-3, Muong Lam, NVN only
TL 7014-5751-4, Thuan Chau (Ban Pan), NVN only

TL 7014-5752-1, Than Uyen, NVN only
TL 7014-5752-2, Muong Trai, NVN only
TL 7014-5752-3, King Khoai, NVN only

TL 7014-5752-4, Quynh Nhai, NVN only

TL 7014-5753-1, Lao Kay, NVN only
TL 7014-5753-2, Chom Chang, NVN only
TL 7014-5753-3, Muong Khoa, NVN only
TL 7014-5753-4, Ban Kol La, NVN only

TL 7014-5754-3, Muong Hum, NVN/China only

TL 7014-5847-1, Cu Rao, NVN only
TL 7014-5847-2, Ban Tem, NVN & Laos only
TL 7014-5847-4, Muong Sen, NVN & Laos only

TL 7014-5848-2, Ban Tha Lang, NVN & Laos only
TL 7014-5848-3, Ban Huoi Heo, NVN & Laos only

TL 7014-5850-1, Song Con, NVN & Laos only

TL 7014-5851-1, Ban Luu, NVN only
TL 7014-5851-2, Yen Chau, NVN only
TL 7014-5851-3, Ban Lot, NVN only
TL 7014-5851-4, Ban Ang, NVN only

TL 7014-5852-1, Tule, NVN only
TL 7014-5852-2, Muong Chen, NVN only
TL 7014-5852-3, Ban Na Tong, NVN only
TL 7014-5852-4, Kim Noi, NVN only

TL 7014-5853-1, Nghia Do Tong, NVN only
TL 7014-5853-2, Bao Ha, NVN only
TL 7014-5853-3, Van Ban, NVN only
TL 7014-5853-4, Pho Lu, NVN only
TL 7014-5854-2, Pa Kha, NVN/China only
TL 7014-5854-3, Ngai Fong Tion, NVN/China only

TL 7014-5926-1, Nam Can, SVN
TL 7014-5926-2, Xom Ong Trang, SVN

TL 7014-5927-1, Xom Giau, SVN
TL 7014-5927-2, Song Ong Doc, SVN

TL 7014-5928-1, Dong Thai, SVN
TL 7014-5928-2, Dong Hung, SVN

TL 7014-5929-1, Ba Chuc, SVN
TL 7014-5929-2, Xom Tri Ton, SVN
TL 7014-5929-3, Hon Chong, SVN
TL 7014-5929-4, Kien Luong, SVN & Cambodia

TL 7014-5946-1, Ban Tai, NVN & Laos only

TL 7014-5947-1, Ban Na Ca, NVN only
TL 7014-5947-2, Con Cuong, NVN only
TL 7014-5947-3, Khe Bo, NVN & Laos only
TL 7014-5947-4, Ban Xieng Lip, NVN only

TL 7014-5948-1, Ban Xen Con, NVN & Laos only
TL 7014-5948-2, Tinche, NVN & Laos only
TL 7014-5948-3, Muong Lam, NVN & Laos only

TL 7014-5949-1, Pieng Yao, NVN only
TL 7014-5950-1, Lang Chum, NVN only
TL 7014-5950-2, Ban Na Sun, NVN only
TL 7014-5950-3, Muong Lat, NVN & Laos only
TL 7014-5950-4, Moc Chau (Na Bo), NVN only

TL 7014-5951-1, Ban Chau, NVN only
TL 7014-5951-2, Nuoc Moc, NVN only
TL 7014-5951-3, Van Yen, NVN only

TL 7014-5951-4, Ban Buc, NVN only

TL 7014-5952-1, Phu Yen Binh, NVN only
TL 7014-5952-2, Yen Bay, NVN only
TL 7014-5952-3, Nghia Lo, NVN only
TL 7014-5952-4, Trai Hut, NVN only

TL 7014-5953-1, Bac Quang, NVN only
TL 7014-5953-2, Bao Ha, NVN only
TL 7014-5953-3, Luc An Chau, NVN only
TL 7014-5953-4, Yen Binh, NVN only

TL 7014-5954-1, Ha Giang, NVN only
TL 7014-5954-2, Lang Zoi, NVN only
TL 7014-5954-3, Haong Su Phi, NVN only

TL 7014-6026-1, Thuan Hoa, SVN
TL 7014-6026-3, Duong Keo, SVN
TL 7014-6026-4, Cai Nuoc, SVN

TL 7014-6027-1, Puoc Long, SVN
TL 7014-6027-2, Gia Rai, SVN
TL 7014-6027-3, Quan Long (Ca Mau), SVN
TL 7014-6027-4, Thoi Binh, SVN

TL 7014-6028-1, Duc Long (Vi Thanh), SVN
TL 7014-6028-2, Kien Hung (Go Quao), SVN
TL 7014-6028-3, Dong Hoa, SVN
TL 7014-6028-4, Chau Thanh, SVN

TL 7014-6029-1, Long Xuyen, SVN
TL 7014-6029-2, Co Do, SVN
TL 7014-6029-3, Rach Gia, SVN
TL 7014-6029-4, Tri Ton, SVN

TL 7014-6030-1, Hong Ngu, SVN & Cambodia
TL 7014-6030-2, An Long, SVN
TL 7014-6030-3, Chau Phu (Chau Doc), SVN & Cambodia
TL 7014-6030-4, Tan Chau, SVN & Cambodia

TL 7014-6045-1, Rao Qua, NVN only, Laos
TL 7014-6046-1, Cam Ngoc, NVN only
TL 7014-6046-2, Pho Chau, NVN only
TL 7014-6046-3, Ban Ka Long, NVN & Laos only
TL 7014-6046-4, Tri Le, NVN only

TL 7014-6047-1, Nghia Hung, NVN only
TL 7014-6047-2, Xom Bau, NVN only
TL 7014-6047-3, Lang Rao, NVN only
TL 7014-6047-4, Ban Dan, NVN only

TL 7014-6048-1, Bai Thuong, NVN only
TL 7014-6048-2, Dong Tau, NVN only
TL 7014-6048-3, Ke Bon, NVN only
TL 7014-6048-4, Ban Pang, NVN only

TL 7014-6049-1, Lang Be, NVN only
TL 7014-6049-2, Lang Tung, NVN only
TL 7014-6049-3, Lang Chan (Lang Chieng Trai), NVN only
TL 7014-6049-4, Hoi Xuan, NVN only

TL 7014-6050-1, Hoa Binh, NVN only
TL 7014-6050-2, Lang Tam, NVN only
TL 7014-6050-3, Ban Bang, NVN only
TL 7014-6050-4, Cho Bo, NVN only

TL 7014-6051-1, Viet Tri, NVN only
TL 7014-6051-2, Hoang Xa, NVN only
TL 7014-6051-3, Xom Chai, NVN only
TL 7014-6051-4, Phu Tho, NVN only

TL 7014-6052-1, Thuc Thuy, NVN only
TL 7014-6052-2, Le My, NVN only
TL 7014-6052-3, Doan Hung, NVN only
TL 7014-6052-4, Tuyen Quang, NVN only

TL 7014-6053-1, Paka, NVN only
TL 7014-6053-2, Chiem Hoa, NVN only
TL 7014-6053-3, (Unknown, or sheet not named), NVN only
TL 7014-6053-4, Lang Dat, NVN only

TL 7014-6054-1, Ban Le, NVN only
TL 7014-6054-2, Bac Me, NVN only
TL 7014-6054-3, Na Nong, NVN only
TL 7014-6054-4, Muong Cha, NVN only

TL 7014-6055-2, Na Kung, NVN/China only
TL 7014-6055-3, Na Lay, NVN/China only

TL 7014-6127-1, Vinh Chau, SVN
TL 7014-6127-2, Giong Giua, SVN
TL 7014-6127-3, Vinh My, SVN
TL 7014-6127-4, Vinh Loi (Bac Lieu), SVN

TL 7014-6128-1, Phung Hiep, SVN
TL 7014-6128-2, Khanh Hung (Soc Trang), SVN
TL 7014-6128-3, Long My, SVN
TL 7014-6128-4, Rach Goi, SVN

TL 7014-6129-1, Sa Dec, SVN
TL 7014-6129-2, Can Tho, SVN
TL 7014-6129-3, Phong Phu (O Mon), SVN

TL 7014-6129-4, Cao Lanh, SVN

TL 7014-6130-1, Moc Hoa, SVN & Cambodia
TL 7014-6130-2, My An, SVN
TL 7014-6130-3, Phong My, SVN
TL 7014-6130-4, Vinh Thanh, Cambodia

TL 7014-6144-1, Kim Lu Xa, NVN only
TL 7014-6144-2, Hung Trung, NVN & Laos only

TL 7014-6145-1, Ha Tinh, NVN only
TL 7014-6145-2, Lakhe Thon, NVN only
TL 7014-6145-3, Huong Khe, NVN & Laos only
TL 7014-6145-4, Quang Te, NVN only

TL 7014-6146-1, Hon Nieu, NVN only
TL 7014-6146-2, Nghi Xuan, NVN only
TL 7014-6146-3, Vinh, NVN only
TL 7014-6146-4, Phu Dien Chau, NVN only

TL 7014-6147-1, Tinh Xuyen, NVN only
TL 7014-6147-3, Cho Giat, NVN only
TL 7014-6147-4, Phong Bai, NVN only

TL 7014-6148-1, Thanh Hoa, NVN only
TL 7014-6148-2, Sam Son, NVN only
TL 7014-6148-3, Tong Cong, NVN only
TL 7014-6148-4, Thieu Hoa (Tri Can), NVN only

TL 7014-6149-1, Ninh Binh, NVN only
TL 7014-6149-2, Mai Xa, NVN only
TL 7014-6149-3, Yen Dinh, NVN only
TL 7014-6149-4, Xom Go, NVN only

TL 7014-6150-1, Ha Dong, NVN only
TL 7014-6150-2, Phu Ly, NVN only
TL 7014-6150-3, Thuy Hien, NVN only
TL 7014-6150-4, Luong Son, NVN only

TL 7014-6151-1, Pho Yen, NVN only
TL 7014-6151-2, Ha Noi (Hanoi), NVN only
TL 7014-6151-3, Son Tay, NVN only
TL 7014-6151-4, Vinh Yen, NVN only
TL 7014-6152-1, Cho Moi, NVN only
TL 7014-6152-2, Thi Ngu Yen, NVN only
TL 7014-6152-3, Dai Tu, NVN only
TL 7014-6152-4, Cho Chu, NVN only

TL 7014-6153-1, Na Fac, NVN only
TL 7014-6153-2, Bac Kan, NVN only
TL 7014-6153-3, Cho Don, NVN only
TL 7014-6153-4, Cho Ra, NVN only

TL 7014-6154-1, Nam Quet, NVN/China only
TL 7014-6154-2, Nguyen Binh, NVN only
TL 7014-6154-3, Thom Tchay, NVN only
TL 7014-6154-4, Bao Lac, NVN only

TL 7014-6227-4, Lac Hoa, SVN

TL 7014-6228-1, Phu Vinh (Tra Vinh), SVN
TL 7014-6228-2, Tra Cu, SVN
TL 7014-6228-3, Long Phu (Bang Long), SVN
TL 7014-6228-4, Cau Ke, SVN

TL 7014-6229-1, My Tho, SVN
TL 7014-6229-2, Truc Giang (Ben Tre), SVN
TL 7014-6229-3, Vung Liem, SVN
TL 7014-6229-4, Khiem Ich (Cai Lay), SVN

TL 7014-6230-1, Duc Hoa, SVN
TL 7014-6230-2, Tan An, SVN
TL 7014-6230-3, Tuyen Nhon, SVN
TL 7014-6230-4, Duc Hue, SVN & Cambodia

TL 7014-6231-1, Tri Tam (Quan Dau Tieng), SVN
TL 7014-6231-2, Hieu Thien (Go Dau Ha), SVN
TL 7014-6231-3, An Thanh, SVN & Cambodia
TL 7014-6231-4, Tay Ninh, SVN

TL 7014-6232-2, Bo Tuc (Uyen Binh), SVN
TL 7014-6232-3, Ta Cath, SVN & Cambodia

TL 7014-6243-1, Co Trang, NVN & Laos only
TL 7014-6243-2, Lang Mo, NVN & Laos only
TL 7014-6243-4, Ban Karai, NVN & Laos only

TL 7014-6244-1, Ron, NVN only
TL 7014-6244-2, Guang Khe, NVN only
TL 7014-6244-3, Cah Noi, NVN only
TL 7014-6244-4, Thiet Son, NVN only

TL 7014-6245-2, Ky Anh, NVN only
TL 7014-6245-3, Tuan Tuong, NVN only
TL 7014-6245-4, Nhuong Ban, NVN only

TL 7014-6248-4, Cua Day, NVN only

TL 7014-6249-1, Thai Binh, NVN only
TL 7014-6249-2, Van Ly, NVN only
TL 7014-6249-3, Phat Diem, NVN only
TL 7014-6249-4, Nam Dinh, NVN only

TL 7014-6250-1, Hai Duong, NVN only
TL 7014-6250-2, Vinh Ninh (Ninh Giang), NVN only
TL 7014-6250-3, Hung Yen, NVN only
TL 7014-6250-4, Ke Sat, NVN only

TL 7014-6251-1, Luc Nam, NVN only
TL 7014-6251-2, Pha Lai, NVN only
TL 7014-6251-3, Bac Ninh, NVN only
TL 7014-6251-4, Phu Lang Thuong, NVN only

TL 7014-6252-1, Pho Binh Gia, NVN only
TL 7014-6252-2, Lang Met, NVN only
TL 7014-6252-3, Mo Trang, NVN only
TL 7014-6252-4, La Gieo, NVN only

TL 7014-6253-1, That Khe, NVN only
TL 7014-6253-2, Fac Ta, NVN only
TL 7014-6253-3, Yen Lac, NVN only

TL 7014-6253-4, Ban Cao, NVN only

TL 7014-6254-1, Tra Linh, NVN/China only
TL 7014-6254-2, Cao Bang, NVN only
TL 7014-6254-3, Nuoc Hai, NVN only
TL 7014-6254-4, Soc Giang, NVN/China only

TL 7014-6328-3, Con Son, SVN
TL 7014-6328-4, Ba Dong, SVN

TL 7014-6329-1, Can Gio, SVN
TL 7014-6329-2, Thua Duc, SVN
TL 7014-6329-3, Binh Dai, SVN
TL 7014-6329-4, Go Cong, SVN

TL 7014-6330-1, Bien Hoa, SVN
TL 7014-6330-2, Nhon Trach (Pu Thanh), SVN
TL 7014-6330-3, Can Giuoc, SVN
TL 7014-6330-4, Thanh Pho Ho Chi Minh (*Saigon*), SVN

TL 7014-6331-1, Phuoc Vinh, SVN
TL 7014-6331-2, Tan Uyen (Xa Uyen-Hung), SVN
TL 7014-6331-3, Ben Cat, SVN
TL 7014-6331-4, Xom Ruong, SVN

TL 7014-6332-1, Phuoc Binh (Ap Son Thuy), SVN
TL 7014-6332-2, Don Xoai, SVN
TL 7014-6332-3, An Loc (Hon Quan), SVN
TL 7014-6332-4, Loc Ninh, SVN & Cambodia

TL 7014-6342-1, Cam Lo, SVN, NVN & **DMZ**
TL 7014-6342-2, Thon Doc Kinh, SVN & Laos
TL 7014-6342-3, Huong Hoa, SVN & Laos
TL 7014-6342-4, Nguon Rao, SVN, NVN, Laos & **DMZ**

TL 7014-6343-1, An Dinh, NVN only
TL 7014-6343-2, Qui Hau, NVN only
TL 7014-6343-3, My Duc, NVN only
TL 7014-6343-4, Dong Hoi, NVN only

TL 7014-6344-3, Ly Hoa, NVN only
TL 7014-6344-4, Vinh Son, NVN only

TL 7014-6349-4, Cua Tra Ly, NVN only

TL 7014-6350-1, Quang Yen, NVN only
TL 7014-6350-2, Do Son, NVN only
TL 7014-6350-3, Thai Thuy, NVN only
TL 7014-6350-4, Hai Phong (Haiphong), NVN only

TL 7014-6351-1, Thanh Am, NVN only
TL 7014-6351-2, (Unknown, or sheet not named), NVN only
TL 7014-6351-3, Dong Trieu, NVN only
TL 7014-6351-4, Chu, NVN only

TL 7014-6352-1, Lang Son, NVN/China only
TL 7014-6352-2, Don Quan, NVN only
TL 7014-6352-3, On, NVN only
TL 7014-6352-4, Dong Dang, NVN/China only

TL 7014-6353-3, Na Cham, NVN/China only

TL 7014-6354-3, Phuc Hao, NVN/China only
TL 7014-6354-4, Trung Khanh Phu, NVN/China only

TL 7014-6429-1, Cho Phuoc Hai, SVN
TL 7014-6429-4, Xa Vung Tau (Cap Saint Jacques), SVN

TL 7014-6430-1, Xam Cam My, SVN
TL 7014-6430-2, Xuyen Moc, SVN
TL 7014-6430-3, Xa Binh Ba, SVN
TL 7014-6430-4, Xa Xuan Loc, SVN

TL 7014-6431-1, Loi Tan, SVN
TL 7014-6431-2, Dinh Quan, SVN
TL 7014-6431-3, Xa Gia Kiem, SVN
TL 7014-6431-4, Ap Cau Cay, SVN

TL 7014-6432-1, Duc Phong (Bu Bang), SVN
TL 7014-6432-2, B Rdu, SVN
TL 7014-6432-3, Dia Diem Bunard, SVN
TL 7014-6432-4, Dong Sre Viet, SVN

TL 7014-6433-2, Ap Doan Van, SVN & Cambodia
TL 7014-6433-3, Bu Gia Map, SVN & Cambodia

TL 7014-6437-2, Phum Hay, SVN & Cambodia

TL 7014-6440-1, Ta Ko, SVN & Laos
TL 7014-6440-2, A Ro, SVN & Laos

TL 7014-6441-1, Ap Lai Bang,
TL 7014-6441-2, A Sap, SVN & Laos
TL 7014-6441-4, A Luoi, SVN & Laos

TL 7014-6442-1, Thon Ngo Xa Dong, SVN
TL 7014-6442-2, Hai Lang (Thon Dien Sanh), SVN
TL 7014-6442-3, Ba Long (Thon Ha Vung), SVN
TL 7014-6442-4, Quang Tri, SVN & NVN, **DMZ**

TL 7014-6443-3, Vinh Lo (Ho Xa), NVN only

TL 7014-6450-1, Ile Longue, NVN only
TL 7014-6450-3, Cat Ba, NVN only
TL 7014-6450-4, Hong Gai, NVN only

TL 7014-6451-1, Tien Yen, NVN only
TL 7014-6451-2, Cam Pha, NVN only
TL 7014-6451-3, Lang Troi, NVN only
TL 7014-6451-4, Chau Son, NVN only

TL 7014-6452-2, Binh Lieu, NVN/China only
TL 7014-6452-3, Dinh Lap, NVN/China only

TL 7014-6530-1, Ap Dinh Ba, SVN
TL 7014-6530-2, Ham Tan, SVN
TL 7014-6530-3, Tan Tao, SVN
TL 7014-6530-4, Song Dinh, SVN

TL 7014-6531-1, Cirlao Da Srang, SVN
TL 7014-6531-2, Xa Tram Da Mi, SVN
TL 7014-6531-3, Tan Linh (Xa Lac Tanh), SVN
TL 7014-6531-4, Madagui, SVN

TL 7014-6532-1, Kro Layu, SVN

TL 7014-6532-2, Bao Loc (Blao), SVN
TL 7014-6532-3, B Dan Deung, SVN
TL 7014-6532-4, Gia Nghia (Nghia Duc), SVN

TL 7014-6533-1, Duc Xuyen, SVN
TL 7014-6533-2, Ban Ndoh, SVN
TL 7014-6533-3, Nghia Tin, SVN
TL 7014-6533-4, Duc Minh, SVN & Cambodia

TL 7014-6534-1, Ban Don, SVN
TL 7014-6534-2, Xo Tho Thanh, SVN
TL 7014-6534-3, Bon Dak Ndrot, SVN & Cambodia
TL 7014-6534-4, Bon Drang Phok, SVN & Cambodia

TL 7014-6535-1, Tieu Teo, SVN
TL 7014-6535-2, Buon Ya Soup, SVN
TL 7014-6535-3, Yok Mbre, SVN & Cambodia
TL 7014-6535-4, Ya Lop, SVN & Cambodia

TL 7014-6536-1, Bao Duc, SVN
TL 7014-6536-2, Xuong Kuang, SVN
TL 7014-6536-3, Pl Ya Bo, SVN & Cambodia
TL 7014-6536-4, Thanh An (Le Thanh), SVN

TL 7014-6537-1, Polei Breng, SVN
TL 7014-6537-2, Plei Mrong, SVN
TL 7014-6537-3, Polei Yome, SVN
TL 7014-6537-4, Polei Jar Sieng, SVN & Cambodia

TL 7014-6538-1, Kon Honong (Kon Henong), SVN
TL 7014-6538-2, Dak To, SVN
TL 7014-6538-3, Dak Mot Lap, SVN, Laos & Cambodia
TL 7014-6538-4, Dak Sut, SVN & Laos

TL 7014-6539-1, Kason Mai, SVN
TL 7014-6539-2, G Rieng, SVN
TL 7014-6539-3, D Go Kram, SVN & Laos
TL 7014-6539-4, Peta Pac, SVN & Laos

TL 7014-6540-1, Thuong Duc (Ha Tan), SVN
TL 7014-6540-2, Ben Giang, SVN
TL 7014-6540-3, Muang Bac, SVN
TL 7014-6540-4, Atiun, SVN

TL 7014-6541-1, Q Phu Loc, SVN
TL 7014-6541-2, Bach Ma, SVN
TL 7014-6541-3, Nong Truong Nam Dong, SVN
TL 7014-6541-4, Hue, SVN

TL 7014-6542-3, Phu Vang, SVN

TL 7014-6550-1, Ile Cu X, NVN only
TL 7014-6550-4, Ile De La Table, NVN only

TL 7014-6551-1, Ha Coi, NVN only
TL 7014-6551-2, Ile Tching Lan Xan, NVN only
TL 7014-6551-3, Van Hoa, NVN only
TL 7014-6551-4, Dam Ha, NVN only

TL 7014-6630-1, Hai Long (Ap Long Linh), SVN
TL 7014-6630-4, Xa Phan Thiet, SVN
TL 7014-6631-1, Soprai, SVN
TL 7014-6631-2, Ap Luong Tay, SVN
TL 7014-6631-3, Ham Thuan Bac, SVN
TL 7014-6631-4, Ap Gia-Bac, SVN

TL 7014-6632-1, Da Lat, SVN
TL 7014-6632-2, Dai Ninh, SVN
TL 7014-6632-3, Di-Linh, SVN
TL 7014-6632-4, Ngoc Son, SVN

TL 7014-6633-1, Buon Ja Ea Kuat, SVN
TL 7014-6633-2, Ban Kia, SVN
TL 7014-6633-3, Phi Sroin, SVN
TL 7014-6633-4, Buon Dong Bak, SVN

TL 7014-6634-1, Buon Ho, SVN
TL 7014-6634-2, Ban Ti Srenh, SVN
TL 7014-6634-3, Ban Me Thuot, SVN
TL 7014-6634-4, Buon Trap, SVN

TL 7014-6635-1, Cheo Reo (Hau Bon), SVN
TL 7014-6635-2, Ban Suk Hdrah, SVN
TL 7014-6635-3, Ban Drang, SVN
TL 7014-6635-4, Ban Tsham, SVN

TL 7014-6636-1, Chu Rpan, SVN
TL 7014-6636-2, Phu Thien, SVN
TL 7014-6636-3, Phu Nhon, SVN
TL 7014-6636-4, Pleiku, SVN

TL 7014-6637-1, Kon Mahar, SVN
TL 7014-6637-2, Plei Troeh, SVN
TL 7014-6637-3, Plei Neh, SVN
TL 7014-6637-4, Kontum, SVN

TL 7014-6638-1, Dak Ninh Kola, SVN
TL 7014-6638-2, Chuong Nghia, SVN
TL 7014-6638-3, Kong Roman, SVN
TL 7014-6638-4, Mang Buk, SVN

TL 7014-6639-1, Tien Phuoc (Phuon An), SVN
TL 7014-6639-2, Gi Lang, SVN
TL 7014-6639-3, Lac Trom Dong, SVN
TL 7014-6639-4, Hau Duc (Tien Tra), SVN
TL 7014-6640-1, Hoian [Hoi An], SVN
TL 7014-6640-2, Tam Ky (West), SVN
TL 7014-6640-3, Hiep Duc, SVN
TL 7014-6640-4, Dai Loc, SVN

TL 7014-6641-2, Khu Pho Nam Tho, SVN
TL 7014-6641-3, Da Nang (west)? (sheet not named), SVN
TL 7014-6641-4, Thon Trung Kien, SVN

TL 7014-6731-1, Thon Vu Bon, SVN
TL 7014-6731-3, Phan Ri, SVN
TL 7014-6731-4, Hai Ninh, SVN

TL 7014-6732-1, Thon Ma Ty, SVN
TL 7014-6732-2, Phan Rang, SVN
TL 7014-6732-3, Ma Noi
TL 7014-6732-4, Don Duong, SVN

TL 7014-6733-1, Buon Thach Trai, SVN
TL 7014-6733-2, E Lam Thuong, SVN
TL 7014-6733-3, B Du Damour, SVN
TL 7014-6733-4, Lak Ea Gam, SVN

TL 7014-6734-1, Phu Duc, SVN
TL 7014-6734-2, Buon Ea Thi, SVN
TL 7014-6734-3, Ban M Trong, SVN
TL 7014-6734-4, Ban M Gam, SVN

TL 7014-6735-1, Triem Duc, SVN
TL 7014-6735-2, Son Ha (Cung Son), SVN
TL 7014-6735-3, Phu Tuc, SVN
TL 7014-6735-4, Buon Thoat, SVN
TL 7014-6736-1, Binh Khe (Binh Lien), SVN
TL 7014-6736-2, Canh Tien, SVN

TL 7014-6736-3, Plei Djama, SVN
TL 7014-6736-4, An Tuc (An Khe), SVN

TL 7014-6737-1, Hoai An, SVN
TL 7014-6737-2, Tien Thuan, SVN
TL 7014-6737-3, Kan Nak, SVN
TL 7014-6737-4, Kon Giong, SVN

TL 7014-6738-1, Mo Duc, SVN
TL 7014-6738-2, An Lao, SVN
TL 7014-6738-3, Gia Vuc, SVN
TL 7014-6738-4, Ba To, SVN

TL 7014-6739-1, Binh Son, SVN
TL 7014-6739-2, Quang Ngai, SVN
TL 7014-6739-3, Son Ha, SVN
TL 7014-6739-4, Tra Bong, SVN

TL 7014-6740-3, Tam Ky (East), SVN
TL 7014-6740-4, Cu Lao Cham, SVN

TL 7014-6831-4, Thon Son Hai, SVN

TL 7014-6832-1, Nui Can Linh, SVN
TL 7014-6832-3, Thanh Hai, SVN
TL 7014-6832-4, Cam Ranh, SVN

TL 7014-6833-1, Ninh Phuoc, SVN
TL 7014-6833-2, Hon Tre, SVN
TL 7014-6833-3, Nha Trang, SVN
TL 7014-6833-4, Ninh Hoa, SVN

TL 7014-6834-1, Ban Nham, SVN
TL 7014-6834-2, Ninh Lam, SVN
TL 7014-6834-3, Van Gia, SVN
TL 7014-6834-4, Lien Thach, SVN

TL 7014-6835-1, Tuy An (Phu Tan), SVN
TL 7014-6835-2, Tuy Hoa (Chau Thanh), SVN
TL 7014-6835-3, Dong Cam, SVN
TL 7014-6835-4, Dong Xuan, SVN

TL 7014-6836-1, Hai Dong, SVN
TL 7014-6836-2, Phu Hoi, SVN
TL 7014-6836-3, Thach Khe, SVN
TL 7014-6836-4, Qui Nhon, SVN

TL 7014-6837-3, Phu My, SVN
TL 7014-6837-4, Bong Son, SVN

TL 7014-6838-3, Tam Quan, SVN
TL 7014-6838-4, Phuoc Dien, SVN
L 701-5679-2, Yao San Meo, NVN & China
L 701-5779-3, Ban Mac, NVN & China
L 701-5879-3, Muong Khuong, NVN & China
L 701-5979-3, Hoang Su Phi, NVN & China
L 701-5980-2, Quan Ba, NVN & China
L 701-6080-2, Dong Van, NVN & China
L 701-6080-4, Pho Bang, NVN & China
L 701-6180-3, Luong Mang, NVN & China
L 701-6377-4, Bi Nhi, NVN & China
L 701-6476-3, Chi Ma, NVN & China
L 701-6575-4, Tan Mai, NVN & China
L 701-6675-3, Nam Thinh, NVN & China

2. Vietnam L-7014 & L-701 Maps Sorted Alphabetically by Sheet Name

NOTE: An L-7014 series index map is available at: www.rjsmith.com/images/kelley/Index-L7014s.jpg.

Sheet Name , Stock Number, Countries Covered:

Sheet Name	Stock Number, Countries
A Luoi	TL 7014-6441-4. SVN, Camb
A Ro	TL 7014-6440-2. SVN, Camb
A Sap	TL 7014-6441-2. SVN, Camb
An Dinh	TL 7014-6343-1. NVN
An Khe (An Tuc)	TL 7014-6736-4. SVN
An Lao	TL 7014-6738-2. SVN
An Loc (Hon Quan)	TL 7014-6332-3. SVN
An Long	TL 7014-6030-2. SVN
An Thanh	TL 7014-6231-3. SVN, Camb
An Tuc (An Khe)	TL 7014-6736-4. SVN
Ap Cau Cay	TL 7014-6431-4. SVN
Ap Dinh Ba	TL 7014-6530-1. SVN
Ap Doan Van	TL 7014-6433-2. SVN, Camb
Ap Gia-Bac	TL 7014-6631-4. SVN
Ap Lai Bang	TL 7014-6441-1. SVN
Ap Long Linh (Hai Long)	TL 7014-6630-1. SVN
Ap Luong Tay	TL 7014-6631-2. SVN
Ap Son Thuy (Phuoc Binh)	TL 7014-6332-1. SVN
Ap Son Thuy (Phuoc Binh)	TL 7014-6332-1. SVN
Atiun	TL 7014-6540-4. SVN
B Dan Deung	TL 7014-6532-3. SVN
B Du Damour	TL 7014-6733-3. SVN
B Rdu	TL 7014-6432-2. SVN
Ba Chuc	TL 7014-5929-1. SVN
Ba Dong	TL 7014-6328-4. SVN
Ba Long (Thon Ha Vung)	TL 7014-6442-3. SVN
Ba To	TL 7014-6738-4. SVN
Bac Kan	TL 7014-6153-2. NVN
Bac Lieu (Vinh Loi)	TL 7014-6127-4. SVN
Bac Me	TL 7014-6054-2. NVN
Bac Ninh	TL 7014-6251-3. NVN
Bac Quang	TL 7014-5953-1. NVN
Bach Ma	TL 7014-6541-2. SVN
Bai Thuong	TL 7014-6048-1. NVN
Ban Ang	TL 7014-5851-4. NVN
Ban Bang	TL 7014-6050-3. NVN
Ban Buc	TL 7014-5951-4. NVN
Ban Cao	TL 7014-6253-4. NVN
Ban Chau	TL 7014-5951-1. NVN
Ban Dan	TL 7014-6047-4. NVN
Ban Don	TL 7014-6534-1. SVN
Ban Drang	TL 7014-6635-3. SVN
Ban Huoi Heo	TL 7014-5848-3. NVN, Laos
Ban Ka Long	TL 7014-6046-3. NVN, Laos
Ban Karai	TL 7014-6243-4. NVN, Laos
Ban Kha	TL 7014-5651-2. NVN
Ban Kia	TL 7014-6633-2. SVN
Ban Kol La	TL 7014-5753-4. NVN
Ban Le	TL 7014-6054-1. NVN
Ban Lot	TL 7014-5851-3. NVN
Ban Luu	TL 7014-5851-1. NVN
Ban M Gam	TL 7014-6734-4. SVN
Ban M Trong	TL 7014-6734-3. SVN
Ban Mac	L 701-5779-3. NVN, China
Ban Me Rang	TL 7014-5454-2. NVN, China
Ban Me Thuot	TL 7014-6634-3. SVN
Ban Muong Lan	TL 7014-5651-1. NVN

Ban Na Ca	TL 7014-5947-1. NVN
Ban Na Phai	TL 7014-5651-3. NVN, Laos
Ban Na Sun	TL 7014-5950-2. NVN
Ban Na Tong	TL 7014-5852-3. NVN
Ban Nam Nen	TL 7014-5652-1. NVN
Ban Ndoh	TL 7014-6533-2. SVN
Ban Nham	TL 7014-6834-1. SVN
Ban Pan (Thuan Chau)	TL 7014-5751-4. NVN
Ban Pang	TL 7014-6048-4. NVN
Ban Pou Sung	TL 7014 5650-1. NVN, Laos
Ban Sa Lin	TL 7014-5554-3. NVN, China
Ban Suk Hdrah	TL 7014-6635-2. SVN
Ban Tai	TL 7014-5946-1. NVN, Laos
Ban Tem	TL 7014-5847-2. NVN, Laos
Ban Tha Lang	TL 7014-5848-2. NVN, Laos
Ban Ti Srenh	TL 7014-6634-2. SVN
Ban Tsham	TL 7014-6635-4. SVN
Ban Xen Con	TL 7014-5948-1. NVN, Laos
Ban Xieng Lip	TL 7014-5947-4. NVN
Bang Long (Long Phu)	TL 7014-6228-3. SVN
Bao Duc	TL 7014-6536-1. SVN
Bao Ha	TL 7014-5853-2. NVN
Bao Lac	TL 7014-6154-4. NVN only
Bao Loc (Blao)	TL 7014-6532-2. SVN
Ben Cat	TL 7014-6331-3. SVN
Ben Giang	TL 7014-6540-2. SVN
Ben Tre (Truc Giang)	TL 7014-6229-2. SVN
Bi Nhi	TL 701-6377-4. NVN, China
Bien Hoa	TL 7014-6330-1. SVN
Binh Ba, Xa	TL 7014-6430-3. SVN
Binh Dai	TL 7014-6329-3. SVN
Binh Khe (Binh Lien)	TL 7014-6736-1. SVN
Binh Lien (Binh Khe)	TL 7014-6736-1. SVN
Binh Lieu	TL 7014-6452-2. NVN, China
Binh Son	TL 7014-6739-1. SVN
Blao (Bao Loc)	TL 7014-6532-2. SVN
Bo Tuc (Uyen Binh)	TL 7014-6232-2. SVN
Bon Dak Ndrot	TL 7014-6534-3. SVN, Camb
Bon Drang Phok	TL 7014-6534-4. SVN, Camb
Bong Son	TL 7014-6837-4. SVN
Bu Bang (Duc Phong)	TL 7014-6432-1. SVN
Bu Gia Map	TL 7014-6433-3. SVN, Camb
Buon Dong Bak	TL 7014-6633-4. SVN
Buon Ea Thi	TL 7014-6734-2. SVN
Buon Ho	TL 7014-6634-1. SVN
Buon Ja Ea Kuat	TL 7014-6633-1. SVN
Buon Thach Trai	TL 7014-6733-1. SVN
Buon Thoat	TL 7014-6735-4. SVN
Buon Trap	TL 7014-6634-4. SVN
Buon Ya Soup	TL 7014-6535-2. SVN
Ca Mau (Quan Long)	TL 7014-6027-3. SVN
Cah Noi	TL 7014-6244-3. NVN
Cai Lay (Khiem Ich)	TL 7014-6229-4. SVN
Cai Nuoc	TL 7014-6026-4. SVN
Cam Lo	TL 7014-6342-1. SVN, NVN, **DMZ**
Cam Ngoc	TL 7014-6046-1. NVN
Cam Pha	TL 7014-6451-2. NVN
Cam Ranh	TL 7014-6832-4. SVN
Can Gio	TL 7014-6329-1. SVN
Can Giuoc	TL 7014-6330-3. SVN
Can Tho	TL 7014-6129-2. SVN
Canh Tien	TL 7014-6736-2. SVN
Cao Bang	TL 7014-6254-2. NVN
Cao Lanh	TL 7014-6129-4. SVN
Cap Saint Jacques (Vung Tau)	TL 7014-6429-4. SVN
Cat Ba	TL 7014-6450-3. NVN
Cau Cay, Ap	TL 7014-6431-4. SVN
Cau Ke	TL 7014-6228-4. SVN
Chau Doc (Chau Phu)	TL 7014-6030-3. SVN, Camb

Chau Phu (Chau Doc)	TL 7014-6030-3. SVN, Camb
Chau Son	TL 7014-6451-4. NVN
Chau Thanh (Tuy Hoa)	TL 7014-6835-2. SVN
Chau Thanh	TL 7014-6028-4. SVN
Cheo Reo (Hau Bon)	TL 7014-6635-1. SVN
Chi Ma	TL 701-6476-3. NVN, China
Chiem Hoa	TL 7014-6053-2. NVN
Cho Bo	TL 7014-6050-4. NVN
Cho Chu	TL 7014-6152-4. NVN
Cho Don	TL 7014-6153-3. NVN
Cho Giat	TL 7014-6147-3. NVN
Cho Moi	TL 7014-6152-1. NVN
Cho Phuoc Hai	TL 7014-6429-1. SVN
Cho Ra	TL 7014-6153-4. NVN
Chom Chang	TL 7014-5753-2. NVN
Chu Rpan	TL 7014-6636-1. SVN
Chu	TL 7014-6351-4. NVN
Chuong Nghia	TL 7014-6638-2. SVN
Cirlao Da Srang	TL 7014-6531-1. SVN
Co Do	TL 7014-6029-2. SVN
Co Trang	TL 7014-6243-1. NVN, Laos
Con Cuong	TL 7014-5947-2. NVN
Con Son	TL 7014-6328-3. SVN
Cu Lao Cham	TL 7014-6740-4. SVN
Cu Rao	TL 7014-5847-1. NVN
Cua Day	TL 7014-6248-4. NVN
Cua Tra Ly	TL 7014-6349-4. NVN
Cung Son (Son Ha)	TL 7014-6735-2. SVN
D Go Kram	TL 7014-6539-3. Laos
Da Lat	TL 7014-6632-1. SVN
Da Nang west (sheet unnamed)	TL 7014-6641-3. SVN
Dai Loc	TL 7014-6640-4. SVN
Dai Ninh	TL 7014-6632-2. SVN
Dai Tu	TL 7014-6152-3. NVN
Dak Mot Lap	TL 7014-6538-3. SVN, Laos, Camb
Dak Ninh Kola	TL 7014-6638-1. SVN
Dak Sut	TL 7014-6538-4. SVN, Laos
Dak To	TL 7014-6538-2. SVN
Dam Ha	TL 7014-6551-4. NVN
Dau Tieng, Quan (Tri Tam)	TL 7014-6231-1. SVN
Dia Diem Bunard	TL 7014-6432-3. SVN
Dien Bien Phu	TL 7014-5651-4. NVN
Di-Linh	TL 7014-6632-3. SVN
Dinh Ba, Ap	TL 7014-6530-1. SVN
Dinh Lap	TL 7014-6452-3. NVN, China
Dinh Quan	TL 7014-6431-2. SVN
Do Son	TL 7014-6350-2. NVN
Doan Hung	TL 7014-6052-3. NVN
Doan Van, Ap	TL 7014-6433-2. SVN, Camb
Doc Kinh, Thon	TL 7014-6342-2. SVN, Laos
Don Duong	TL 7014-6732-4. SVN
Don Quan	TL 7014-6352-2. NVN
Don Xoai	TL 7014-6332-2. SVN
Dong Cam	TL 7014-6835-3. SVN
Dong Dang	TL 7014-6352-4. NVN, China
Dong Hoa	TL 7014-6028-3. SVN
Dong Hoi	TL 7014-6343-4. NVN
Dong Hung	TL 7014-5928-2. SVN
Dong Sre Viet	TL 7014-6432-4. SVN
Dong Tau	TL 7014-6048-2. NVN
Dong Thai	TL 7014-5928-1. SVN
Dong Trieu	TL 7014-6351-3. NVN
Dong Van	TL 701-6080-2. NVN, China
Dong Xuan	TL 7014-6835-4. SVN
Duc Hoa	TL 7014-6230-1. SVN
Duc Hue	TL 7014-6230-4. SVN, Camb
Duc Long (Vi Thanh)	TL 7014-6028-1. SVN
Duc Minh	TL 7014-6533-4. SVN, Camb
Duc Phong (Bu Bang)	TL 7014-6432-1. SVN

Duc Xuyen	TL 7014-6533-1. SVN
Duong Dong	TL 7014-5729-2. SVN, Camb
Duong Keo	TL 7014-6026-3. SVN
E Lam Thuong	TL 7014-6733-2. SVN
Fac Ta	TL 7014-6253-2. NVN
G Rieng	TL 7014-6539-2. SVN
Gi Lang	TL 7014-6639-2. SVN
Gia Kiem, Xa	TL 7014-6431-3. SVN
Gia Nghia (Nghia Duc)	TL 7014-6532-4. SVN
Gia Rai	TL 7014-6027-2. SVN
Gia Vuc	TL 7014-6738-3. SVN
Gia-Bac, Ap	TL 7014-6631-4. SVN
Giang Mung Pho	TL 7014-5453-1. NVN, China
Giong Giua	TL 7014-6127-2. SVN
Go Cong	TL 7014-6329-4. SVN
Go Dau Ha (Hieu Thien)	TL 7014-6231-2. SVN
Go Quao (Kien Hung)	TL 7014-6028-2. SVN
Guang Khe	TL 7014-6244-2. NVN
Ha Coi	TL 7014-6551-1. NVN
Ha Dong	TL 7014-6150-1. NVN
Ha Giang	TL 7014-5954-1. NVN
Ha Noi (Hanoi)	TL 7014-6151-2. NVN
Ha Tan (Thuong Duc)	TL 7014-6540-1. SVN
Ha Tinh	TL 7014-6145-1. NVN
Ha Vung, Thon (Ba Long)	TL 7014-6442-3. SVN
Hai Dong	TL 7014-6836-1. SVN
Hai Duong	TL 7014-6250-1. NVN
Hai Lang (Thon Dien Sanh)	TL 7014-6442-2. SVN
Hai Long (Ap Long Linh)	TL 7014-6630-1. SVN
Hai Ninh	TL 7014-6731-4. SVN
Hai Phong (Haiphong)	TL 7014-6350-4. NVN
Ham Tan	TL 7014-6530-2. SVN
Ham Thuan Bac	TL 7014-6631-3. SVN
Hanoi (Ha Noi)	TL 7014-6151-2. NVN
Haong Su Phi	TL 7014-5954-3. NVN
Hau Bon (Cheo Reo)	TL 7014-6635-1. SVN
Hau Duc (Tien Tra)	TL 7014-6639-4. SVN
Hiep Duc	TL 7014-6640-3. SVN
Hieu Thien (Go Dau Ha)	TL 7014-6231-2. SVN
Ho Chi Minh, Thanh Pho	TL 7014-6330-4. SVN
Ho Xa (Vinh Lo)	TL 7014-6443-3. NVN
Hoa Binh	TL 7014-6050-1. NVN
Hoai An	TL 7014-6737-1. SVN
Hoang Su Phi	TL 701-5979-3. NVN, China
Hoang Xa	TL 7014-6051-2. NVN
Hoi An (Hoian)	TL 7014-6640-1. SVN
Hoi Xuan	TL 7014-6049-4. NVN
Hoian [Hoi An]	TL 7014-6640-1. SVN
Hon Chong	TL 7014-5929-3. SVN
Hon Nieu	TL 7014-6146-1. NVN
Hon Quan (An Loc)	TL 7014-6332-3. SVN
Hon Thom	TL 7014-5728-1. SVN
Hon Tre	TL 7014-6833-2. SVN
Hong Gai	TL 7014-6450-4. NVN
Hong Ngu	TL 7014-6030-1. SVN, Camb
Hue	TL 7014-6541-4. SVN
Hung Trung	TL 7014-6144-2. NVN Laos
Hung Yen	TL 7014-6250-3. NVN
Huong Hoa	TL 7014-6342-3. Laos
Huong Khe	TL 7014-6145-3. NVN, Laos
Ile Cu X	TL 7014-6550-1. NVN
Ile De La Table	TL 7014-6550-4. NVN
Ile Longue	TL 7014-6450-1. NVN
Ile Tching Lan Xan	TL 7014-6551-2. NVN
Kan Nak	TL 7014-6737-3. SVN
Kason Mai	TL 7014-6539-1. SVN
Ke Bon	TL 7014-6048-3. NVN
Ke Sat	TL 7014-6250-4. NVN
Khanh Hung (Soc Trang)	TL 7014-6128-2. SVN
Khe Bo	TL 7014-5947-3. NVN, Laos
Khiem Ich (Cai Lay)	TL 7014-6229-4. SVN
Khu Pho Nam Tho	TL 7014-6641-2. SVN
Kien Hung (Go Quao)	TL 7014-6028-2. SVN
Kien Luong	TL 7014-5929-4. SVN, Camb
Kim Lu Xa	TL 7014-6144-1. NVN
Kim Noi	TL 7014-5852-4. NVN
King Khoai	TL 7014-5752-3. NVN
Kon Giong	TL 7014-6737-4. SVN
Kon Henong (Kon Honong)	TL 7014-6538-1. SVN
Kon Honong (Kon Henong)	TL 7014-6538-1. SVN
Kon Mahar	TL 7014-6637-1. SVN
Kong Roman	TL 7014-6638-3. SVN
Kontum	TL 7014-6637-4. SVN
Kro Layu	TL 7014-6532-1. SVN
Ky Anh	TL 7014-6245-2. NVN
La Gieo	TL 7014-6252-4. NVN
Lac Hoa	TL 7014-6227-4. SVN
Lac Tanh, Xa (Tan Linh)	TL 7014-6531-3. SVN
Lac Trom Dong	TL 7014-6639-3. SVN
Lai Bang, Ap	TL 7014-6441-1. SVN
Lai Chau	TL 7014-5653-3. NVN
Lak Ea Gam	TL 7014-6733-4. SVN
Lakhe Thon	TL 7014-6145-2. NVN
Lang Be	TL 7014-6049-1. NVN
Lang Chan (Lang Chieng Trai)	TL 7014-6049-3. NVN
Lang Chan (Lang Chieng Trai)	TL 7014-6049-3. NVN
Lang Chum	TL 7014-5950-1. NVN
Lang Dat	TL 7014-6053-4. NVN
Lang Met	TL 7014-6252-2. NVN
Lang Mo	TL 7014-6243-2. NVN, Laos
Lang Rao	TL 7014-6047-3. NVN
Lang Son	TL 7014-6352-1. NVN, China
Lang Tam	TL 7014-6050-2. NVN
Lang Troi	TL 7014-6451-3. NVN
Lang Tung	TL 7014-6049-2. NVN
Lang Zoi	TL 7014-5954-2. NVN
Lao Kay	TL 7014-5753-1. NVN
Le My	TL 7014-6052-2. NVN
Le Thanh (Thanh An)	TL 7014-6536-4. SVN
Lien Thach	TL 7014-6834-4. SVN
Loc Ninh	TL 7014-6332-4. SVN, Camb
Loi Tan	TL 7014-6431-1. SVN
Long My	TL 7014-6128-3. SVN
Long Phu (Bang Long)	TL 7014-6228-3. SVN
Long Xuyen	TL 7014-6029-1. SVN
Luc An Chau	TL 7014-5953-3. NVN
Luc Nam	TL 7014-6251-1. NVN
Luong Mang	TL 701-6180-3. NVN, China
Luong Son	TL 7014-6150-4. NVN
Luong Tay, Ap	TL 7014-6631-2. SVN
Ly Hoa	TL 7014-6344-3. NVN
Ma Noi	TL 7014-6732-3. SVN
Ma Ty, Thon	TL 7014-6732-1. SVN
Madagui	TL 7014-6531-4. SVN
Mai Son	TL 7014-5751-2. NVN
Mai Xa	TL 7014-6149-2. NVN
Mang Buk	TL 7014-6638-4. SVN
Mo Duc	TL 7014-6738-1. SVN
Mo Trang	TL 7014-6252-3. NVN
Moc Chau (Na Bo)	TL 7014-5950-4. NVN
Moc Hoa	TL 7014-6130-1. SVN, Camb
Muang Bac	TL 7014-6540-3. SVN
Muong Ang	TL 7014-5652-3. NVN
Muong Boum	TL 7014-5553-1. NVN, China
Muong Cha	TL 7014-5552-1. NVN, Laos
Muong Cha	TL 7014-6054-4. NVN
Muong Chen	TL 7014-5852-2. NVN
Muong Hum	TL 7014-5754-3. NVN, China
Muong Hung	TL 7014-5750-1. NVN, Laos
Muong Khoa	TL 7014-5753-3. NVN

Muong Khuong	L 701-5879-3. NVN, China
Muong Lam	TL 7014-5751-3. NVN
Muong Lam	TL 7014-5948-3. NVN, Laos
Muong Lat	TL 7014-5950-3. NVN, Laos
Muong No	TL 7014-5553-2. NVN
Muong Sen	TL 7014-5847-4. NVN, Laos
Muong So (Phong Tho)	TL 7014-5654-2. NVN, China
Muong Te	TL 7014-5553-4. NVN
Muong Tong	TL 7014-5553-3. NVN, Laos
Muong Tong	TL 7014-5652-4. NVN
Muong Trai	TL 7014-5752-2. NVN
My An	TL 7014-6130-2. SVN
My Duc	TL 7014-6343-3. NVN
My Tho	TL 7014-6229-1. SVN
Na Bo (Moc Chau)	TL 7014-5950-4. NVN
Na Cham	TL 7014-6353-3. NVN, China
Na Fac	TL 7014-6153-1. NVN
Na Kung	TL 7014-6055-2. NVN, China
Na Lay	TL 7014-6055-3. NVN, China
Na Nong	TL 7014-6054-3. NVN
Nam Can	TL 7014-5926-1. SVN
Nam Dinh	TL 7014-6249-4. NVN
Nam Na	TL 7014-5653-2. NVN
Nam Quet	TL 7014-6154-1. NVN, China
Nam Thinh	TL 701-6675-3. NVN, China
Ngai Fong Tion	TL 7014-5854-3. NVN, China
Nghi Xuan	TL 7014-6146-2. NVN
Nghia Do Tong	TL 7014-5853-1. NVN
Nghia Duc (Gia Nghia)	TL 7014-6532-4. SVN
Nghia Hung	TL 7014-6047-1. NVN
Nghia Lo	TL 7014-5952-3. NVN
Nghia Tin	TL 7014-6533-3. SVN
Ngo Xa Dong, Thon	TL 7014-6442-1. SVN
Ngoc Son	TL 7014-6632-4. SVN
Nguon Rao	TL 7014-6342-4. SVN, NVN, Laos, **DMZ**
Nguyen Binh	TL 7014-6154-2. NVN
Nha Trang	TL 7014-6833-3. SVN
Nhon Trach (Pu Thanh)	TL 7014-6330-2. SVN
Nhuong Ban	TL 7014-6245-4. NVN
Ninh Binh	TL 7014-6149-1. NVN
Ninh Giang (Vinh Ninh)	TL 7014-6250-2. NVN
Ninh Hoa	TL 7014-6833-4. SVN
Ninh Lam	TL 7014-6834-2. SVN
Ninh Phuoc	TL 7014-6833-1. SVN
Nong Truong Nam Dong	TL 7014-6541-3. SVN
Nui Can Linh	TL 7014-6832-1. SVN
Nuoc Hai	TL 7014-6254-3. NVN
Nuoc Moc	TL 7014-5951-2. NVN
O Mon (Phong Phu)	TL 7014-6129-3. SVN
On	TL 7014-6352-3. NVN
Ong Thay, Xong	TL 7014-5729-1. SVN, Camb
Pa Kha	TL 7014-5854-2. NVN, China
Paka	TL 7014-6053-1. NVN
Peta Pac	TL 7014-6539-4. SVN, Laos
Pha Lai	TL 7014-6251-2. NVN
Phan Rang	TL 7014-6732-2. SVN
Phan Ri	TL 7014-6731-3. SVN
Phan Thiet, Xa	TL 7014-6630-4. SVN
Phat Diem	TL 7014-6249-3. NVN
Phi Sroin	TL 7014-6633-3. SVN
Pho Bang	TL 701-6080-4. NVN, China
Pho Binh Gia	TL 7014-6252-1. NVN
Pho Chau	TL 7014-6046-2. NVN
Pho Lu	TL 7014-5853-4. NVN
Pho Yen	TL 7014-6151-1. NVN
Phong Bai	TL 7014-6147-4. NVN
Phong My	TL 7014-6130-3. SVN
Phong Phu (O Mon)	TL 7014-6129-3. SVN
Phong Tho (Muong So)	TL 7014-5654-2. NVN, China
Phu Dien Chau	TL 7014-6146-4. NVN
Phu Duc	TL 7014-6734-1. SVN
Phu Hoi	TL 7014-6836-2. SVN
Phu Lang Thuong	TL 7014-6251-4. NVN
Phu Ly	TL 7014-6150-2. NVN
Phu My	TL 7014-6837-3. SVN
Phu Nhon	TL 7014-6636-3. SVN
Phu Nung Nong	TL 7014-5653-1. NVN
Phu Thien	TL 7014-6636-2. SVN
Phu Tho	TL 7014-6051-4. NVN
Phu Tuc	TL 7014-6735-3. SVN
Phu Vang	TL 7014-6542-3. SVN
Phu Vinh (Tra Vinh)	TL 7014-6228-1. SVN
Phu Yen Binh	TL 7014-5952-1. NVN
Phuc Hao	TL 7014-6354-3. NVN, China
Phum Hay	TL 7014-6437-2. SVN, Camb
Phung Hiep	TL 7014-6128-1. SVN
Phuoc Dien	TL 7014-6838-4. SVN
Phuoc Vinh	TL 7014-6331-1. SVN
Phuon An (Tien Phuoc)	TL 7014-6639-1. SVN
Pieng Yao	TL 7014-5949-1. NVN
Pl Ya Bo	TL 7014-6536-3. SVN, Camb
Plei Djama	TL 7014-6736-3. SVN
Plei Mrong	TL 7014-6537-2. SVN
Plei Neh	TL 7014-6637-3. SVN
Plei Troeh	TL 7014-6637-2. SVN
Pleiku	TL 7014-6636-4. SVN
Polei Breng	TL 7014-6537-1. SVN
Polei Jar Sieng	TL 7014-6537-4. SVN, Camb
Polei Yome	TL 7014-6537-3. SVN
Pu Thanh (Nhon Trach)	TL 7014-6330-2. SVN
Puoc Long	TL 7014-6027-1. SVN
Q Phu Loc	TL 7014-6541-1. SVN
Quan Ba	TL 701-5980-2. NVN, China
Quan Dau Tieng (Tri Tam)	TL 7014-6231-1. SVN
Quan Long (Ca Mau)	TL 7014-6027-3. SVN
Quang Ngai	TL 7014-6739-2. SVN
Quang Te	TL 7014-6145-4. NVN
Quang Tri	TL 7014-6442-4. N/SVN, **DMZ**
Quang Yen	TL 7014-6350-1. NVN
Qui Hau	TL 7014-6343-2. NVN
Qui Nhon	TL 7014-6836-4. SVN
Quynh Nhai	TL 7014-5752-4. NVN
Rach Gia	TL 7014-6029-3. SVN
Rach Goi	TL 7014-6128-4. SVN
Rao Qua	TL 7014-6045-1. NVN, Laos
Ron	TL 7014-6244-1. NVN
Sa Dec	TL 7014-6129-1. SVN
Saigon (Thanh Pho HCMC)	TL 7014-6330-4. SVN
Sam Son	TL 7014-6148-2. NVN
Soc Giang	TL 7014-6254-4. NVN, China
Soc Trang (Khanh Hung)	TL 7014-6128-2. SVN
Son Ha (Cung Son)	TL 7014-6735-2. SVN
Son Ha	TL 7014-6739-3. SVN
Son Hai, Thon	TL 7014-6831-4. SVN
Son La	TL 7014-5751-1. NVN
Son Tay	TL 7014-6151-3. NVN
Song Con	TL 7014-5850-1. NVN, Laos
Song Dinh	TL 7014-6530-4. SVN
Song Ong Doc	TL 7014-5927-2. SVN
Sop Cop	TL 7014-5750-4. NVN, Laos
Soprai	TL 7014-6631-1. SVN
Ta Cath	TL 7014-6232-3. SVN, Camb
Ta Ko	TL 7014-6440-1. SVN, Laos
Ta Phing	TL 7014-5653-4. NVN, China
Tam Ky (East)	TL 7014-6740-3. SVN
Tam Ky (West)	TL 7014-6640-2. SVN
Tam Quan	TL 7014-6838-3. SVN
Tan An	TL 7014-6230-2. SVN
Tan Chau	TL 7014-6030-4. SVN, Camb

Tan Linh (Xa Lac Tanh)	TL 7014-6531-3. SVN
Tan Mai	L 701-6575-4. NVN, China
Tan Tao	TL 7014-6530-3. SVN
Tan Uyen (Xa Uyen-Hung)	TL 7014-6331-2. SVN
Tay Ninh	TL 7014-6231-4. SVN
Thach Khe	TL 7014-6836-3. SVN
Thai Binh	TL 7014-6249-1. NVN
Thai Thuy	TL 7014-6350-3. NVN
Than Uyen	TL 7014-5752-1. NVN
Thanh Am	TL 7014-6351-1. NVN
Thanh An (Le Thanh)	TL 7014-6536-4. SVN
Thanh Hai	TL 7014-6832-3. SVN
Thanh Hoa	TL 7014-6148-1. NVN
Thanh Pho Ho Chi Minh	TL 7014-6330-4. SVN
That Khe	TL 7014-6253-1. NVN
Thi Ngu Yen	TL 7014-6152-2. NVN
Thiet Son	TL 7014-6244-4. NVN
Thieu Hoa (Tri Can)	TL 7014-6148-4. NVN
Thoi Binh	TL 7014-6027-4. SVN
Thom Tchay	TL 7014-6154-3. NVN
Thon Dien Sanh (Hai Lang)	TL 7014-6442-2. SVN
Thon Doc Kinh	TL 7014-6342-2. SVN, Laos
Thon Ha Vung (Ba Long)	TL 7014-6442-3. SVN
Thon Ma Ty	TL 7014-6732-1. SVN
Thon Ngo Xa Dong	TL 7014-6442-1. SVN
Thon Son Hai	TL 7014-6831-4. SVN
Thon Trung Kien	TL 7014-6641-4. SVN
Thon Vu Bon	TL 7014-6731-1. SVN
Thua Duc	TL 7014-6329-2. SVN
Thuan Chau (Ban Pan)	TL 7014-5751-4. NVN
Thuan Hoa	TL 7014-6026-1. SVN
Thuc Thuy	TL 7014-6052-1. NVN
Thuong Duc (Ha Tan)	TL 7014-6540-1. SVN
Thuy Hien	TL 7014-6150-3. NVN
Tien Phuoc (Phuon An)	TL 7014-6639-1. SVN
Tien Thuan	TL 7014-6737-2. SVN
Tien Tra (Hau Duc)	TL 7014-6639-4. SVN
Tien Yen	TL 7014-6451-1. NVN
Tieu Teo	TL 7014-6535-1. SVN
Tinche	TL 7014-5948-2. NVN, Laos
Tinh Xuyen	TL 7014-6147-1. NVN
Tong Cong	TL 7014-6148-3. NVN
Tra Bong	TL 7014-6739-4. SVN
Tra Cu	TL 7014-6228-2. SVN
Tra Linh	TL 7014-6254-1. NVN, China
Tra Vinh (Phu Vinh)	TL 7014-6228-1. SVN
Trai Hut	TL 7014-5952-4. NVN
Tram Da Mi, Xa	TL 7014-6531-2. SVN
Tri Can (Thieu Hoa)	TL 7014-6148-4. NVN
Tri Le	TL 7014-6046-4. NVN
Tri Tam (Quan Dau Tieng)	TL 7014-6231-1. SVN
Tri Ton	TL 7014-6029-4. SVN
Tri Ton, Xom	TL 7014-5929-2. SVN
Triem Duc	TL 7014-6735-1. SVN
Truc Giang (Ben Tre)	TL 7014-6229-2. SVN
Trung Khanh Phu	TL 7014-6354-4. NVN, China
Trung Kien, Thon	TL 7014-6641-4. SVN
Tuan Giao	TL 7014-5652-2. NVN
Tuan Tuong	TL 7014-6245-3. NVN
Tule	TL 7014-5852-1. NVN
Tuy An (Phu Tan)	TL 7014-6835-1. SVN
Tuy An (Phu Tan)	TL 7014-6835-1. SVN
Tuy Hoa (Chau Thanh)	TL 7014-6835-2. SVN
Tuyen Nhon	TL 7014-6230-3. SVN
Tuyen Quang	TL 7014-6052-4. NVN
Unnamed	TL 7014-6053-3. NVN
Unnamed	TL 7014-6351-2. NVN
Unnamd (Da Nang west?)	TL 7014-6641-3. SVN
Uyen Binh (Bo Tuc)	TL 7014-6232-2. SVN
Uyen-Hung, Xa (Tan Uyen)	TL 7014-6331-2. SVN
Van Ban	TL 7014-5853-3. NVN
Van Gia	TL 7014-6834-3. SVN
Van Hoa	TL 7014-6551-3. NVN
Van Ly	TL 7014-6249-2. NVN
Van Yen	TL 7014-5951-3. NVN
Vi Thanh (Duc Long)	TL 7014-6028-1. SVN
Viet Tri	TL 7014-6051-1. NVN
Vinh Chau	TL 7014-6127-1. SVN
Vinh Lo (Ho Xa)	TL 7014-6443-3. NVN
Vinh Loi (Bac Lieu)	TL 7014-6127-4. SVN
Vinh My	TL 7014-6127-3. SVN
Vinh Ninh (Ninh Giang)	TL 7014-6250-2. NVN
Vinh Son	TL 7014-6344-4. NVN
Vinh Thanh	TL 7014-6130-4. SVN, Camb
Vinh Yen	TL 7014-6151-4. NVN
Vinh	TL 7014-6146-3. NVN
Vu Bon, Thon	TL 7014-6731-1. SVN
Vung Liem	TL 7014-6229-3. SVN
Vung Tau. Xa (Cap St Jacques)	TL 7014-6429-4. SVN
Xa Binh Ba	TL 7014-6430-3. SVN
Xa Gia Kiem	TL 7014-6431-3. SVN
Xa Lac Tanh (Tan Linh)	TL 7014-6531-3. SVN
Xa Phan Thiet	TL 7014-6630-4. SVN
Xa Tram Da Mi	TL 7014-6531-2. SVN
Xa Uyen-Hung (Tan Uyen)	TL 7014-6331-2. SVN
Xa Vung Tau (Cap St Jacques)	TL 7014-6429-4. SVN
Xa Xuan Loc	TL 7014-6430-4. SVN
Xam Cam My	TL 7014-6430-1. SVN
Xo Tho Thanh	TL 7014-6534-2. SVN
Xom Bau	TL 7014-6047-2. NVN
Xom Chai	TL 7014-6051-3. NVN
Xom Giau	TL 7014-5927-1. SVN
Xom Go	TL 7014-6149-4. NVN
Xom Ong Trang	TL 7014-5926-2. SVN
Xom Ruong	TL 7014-6331-4. SVN
Xom Tri Ton	TL 7014-5929-2. SVN
Xong Ong Thay	TL 7014-5729-1. SVN, Camb
Xuan Loc, Xa	TL 7014-6430-4. SVN
Xuong Kuang	TL 7014-6536-2. SVN
Xuyen Moc	TL 7014-6430-2. SVN
Ya Lop	TL 7014-6535-4. SVN, Camb
Yao San Meo	L 701-5679-2. NVN, China
Yen Bay	TL 7014-5952-2. NVN
Yen Binh	TL 7014-5953-4. NVN
Yen Chau	TL 7014-5851-2. NVN
Yen Dinh	TL 7014-6149-3. NVN
Yen Lac	TL 7014-6253-3. NVN
Yok Mbre	TL 7014-6535-3. SVN, Camb

NIMA - National Imagery And Mapping Agency Resources

NIMA (formerly the Defense Mapping Agency or DMA), is the map maker for the U.S. Department of Defense and U.S. military. Most of its current products are either classified or simply not available for public purchase. However, a number of very important and helpful NIMA Nautical and Aeronautical products related to the Vietnam era are available for public purchase indirectly through other government agencies or private vendors, though not directly through NIMA itself. For information on the availability of NIMA maps and publications, go to their products Internet page at: http://164.214.2.59/poc/public.html.

Sale of many of NIMA's nautical, aeronautical, hydrographic charts and publications and Flight Information Publication (FLIP) products is the responsibility of the National Ocean Service (NOS) and/or NOAA. Also available from NOS are nautical charts of coastal waterways of the continental U.S., Hawaii, Alaska and the U.S. territories. To purchase products contact:

NOS Distribution Branch N/CG33
National Ocean Service
6501 Lafayette Avenue
Riverdale, Md. 20737-1199

Toll free phone: 1 (800) 638-8972
Commercial: (301) 436-6990
Internet address: http://chartmaker.ncd.noaa.gov

NIMA Topographic Maps:

The U.S. Geological Survey (USGS) is responsible for public sale of NIMA's Vietnam topographic maps, gazetteers and other publications (topographic maps of the U. S. produced by the USGS are also available at USGS):

USGS - Information Services
Map and Book Sales
Federal Center, Building 41
Box 25286
Denver, Colo. 80225
Toll free: 1-888-ASK-USGS (1-888-275-8747)
Commercial: (303) 202-4700
Internet address: www.usgs.gov

NIMA (DMA) Public Sale catalog:

NIMA's (DMA) public sale catalog is free. Order it by stock number TUS5668. It includes a rather poor L-7014 Series Map index that is only marginally helpful. It does however contain helpful explanations and other information related to reading maps and is useful for that reason. In fact, all USGS topographic indexes are free upon request as well.

Gazetteer of Vietnam Place-Names - NIMA/USGS

NIMA's Gazetteer of Vietnam Place names is now accessible on the Internet and for purchase on CD-ROM in .htm format (read easily in one's Internet browser) through the USGS, Denver. The Gazetteer of foreign place names includes the name of every geographic feature (city, village, mountain, river, bay and so on) printed on likely every 1:250,000 scale map DMA or NIMA has produced. In hard copy, the gazetteer for Vietnam alone comes in two volumes and each volume costs $80.

The complete hard-copy, two-volume Gazetteer for Vietnam is roughly 2,000 pages in length. Today one can access the same information on the net for no charge, or one can purchase NIMA's Gazetteer of the entire world (excluding the USA and Alaska) for a mere $15.00 ($11.50 plus $3.50 Shipping). The CD includes literally tens of thousands of pages of data for only $15.00; truly one of the greatest bargains on the planet.

Each entry in the Gazetteer includes the following important data:

Name (Column 1):
Normally the formal name first, followed by a comma and the surname. For example "Song Ta Trach" would be listed "Ta Trach, Song." In this example, "Song" is Vietnamese for river.

Feature Designation (Column 2):
Normally an abbreviation such as RIV, MTN for river and mountain, and so on. Since many geographic terms are subject to different interpretations, the sense in which these designations are used and the range of features to which they are applied may vary.

Latitude/Longitude (Columns 3 and 4):
Latitude and Longitude of the feature, such as: 11°15'25"N, 108°29'40"E.

Area Code (Column 5)
In a nutshell, this 2-letter, 2-numeric code identifies the Province or Major Municipality in which the feature is located (for example, VM29 refers to Quang Nam-Da Nang Province). Unfortunately, the codes on this disk refer to the post-war provinces as reorganized by the Vietnamese communist government, and are of limited usefulness for historical purposes. NIMA's own definition reads: "The fifth column indicates the first-order administrative division in which the coordinates listed for each feature are located. General area codes ending in -00 are used for features of shared sovereignty, and for features crossing administrative boundaries. These area codes generally correspond to the those issued in the Federal Information Processing Standard 10, *Countries, Dependencies, Areas of Special Sovereignty, and Their Principal Administrative Divisions* (FIPS 10), maintained by the National Imagery and Mapping Agency and published by the National Institute of Science and Technology, U.S. Department of Commerce."

UTM Grid Zone (Column 6):
The Universal Transverse Mercator (UTM) Grid Reference: This reference consists of a two-letter, UTM 10,000 square kilometer (100 by 100 km) grid-square identification, followed by a two-digit numeric. The two-digit number identifies the southeast corner of the 100 square kilometer (10 km by 10 km) grid-square (within that UTM 10,000 sq. km grid-square) which contains the geographic feature listed. For example "YD 37" should be read as YD 30-70, and this particular grid reference would mean the listed feature is located in the 100 sq. km grid-square immediately to the NE (upper right) of the intersection of the YD 30 vertical grid line and the YD 70 horizontal grid line. This grid is only a general guide similar in application to map grid location indexes found in all standard U.S. road maps.

Map Reference (Column 7):
Defined on NIMA's website as: "JOG Sheet Number - The map sheet numbers which accompany all name entries are based upon the Joint Operations Graphic (Series 1501) worldwide map sheet numbering scheme. While each sheet number is derived from the geographic coordinates in the third and fourth columns of the entry, the feature name may not actually appear on the referenced map sheet. The listing of a Series 1501 map sheet number in this column does not necessarily indicate that the map sheet actually exists or is available."

The CD ROM Gazetteer is known as: Digital Interim Geographic Names Data

Series:	GAZGN
Item:	DIGNAMES
Edition:	002
NSN:	7644014174141
NIMA Ref. No.:	GAZGNDIGNAMES

NIMA/USGS's CD-ROM stock number is: 68-DIGNAMES. Its price was $11.50 plus $3.50 handling charge (June, 1999).

<u>Ordering NIMA's CD ROM Place-Names Gazetteer</u>:

USGS Information Services
Box 25286
Denver, CO 80225-0286
tel. 1-888-ASK-USGS (1-888-275-8747)

<u>Hard-Copy Versions of the NIMA Vietnam Gazetteer</u>:

Vietnam (over 50,000 listings), version date 1986:
Volume I: A-K...................68-VIETNAMV1....$83.95 (December '99 price)
Volume II: L-Z...................68-VIETNAMV2....$83.95 (December '99 price)

USGS Foreign Geographic Names (hard-copy) Gazetteer Ordering Instructions:

1. A list of foreign geographic names gazetteers in hard-copy volumes, including prices, is available on the *Foreign Gazetteer Price List*. The order form can be printed using your browser software or requested from the *EarthFax* Fax-On-Demand system at 1-888-ASK-USGS (press 4 and request document 3806).
2. Payment (VISA, Mastercard, check, money order, or Govt account #) must accompany order. Make all drafts payable to "Dept. of the Interior - USGS." Do not send cash or e-mail your credit card information. Customers outside the U.S. must remit by credit card, international money order, or check drawn on a U.S. bank in U.S. dollars.
3. Delivery is via U.S. Postal Service First Class, or UPS Ground service. Provide a courier account number if shipping is requested through a specific courier service. A $5.00 handling charge is applied to all orders (12/99).
4. Print, complete, and fax or mail the order form to:

   U.S.G.S. Information Services
   Box 25286
   Denver, CO 80225
   Fax: 303-202-4693 (Credit Card Orders Only)

5. For more information on foreign geographic names products, telephone 703-648-4544 or 1-888-ASK-USGS.

NIMA Place-Name Gazetteers on-line at their GEOnet Names Server:

The GEOnet Names Server (GNS) provides access to the National Imagery and Mapping Agency's (NIMA) database of foreign geographic feature names. Approximately 20,000 of the databases 3.5 million features are updated monthly with names information approved by the U.S. Board on Geographic Names (U.S. BGN).

Geographic names of a particular country are current to the date displayed after the country name in the Database Query Form. This date represents the publication date of the most recent NIMA gazetteer of that country. or the date after which at least 10% of the data for that country had been modified or major additions were made. The information in this database is based in part on copyrighted source material. Copyright restrictions continue to exist.

To access the world gazetteer search engine on the Internet go to: www.nima.mil/geospatial/geospatial.html and/or http://gnpswww.nima.mil/geonames/GNS/. To visit NIMA's Home Page, go to: www.nima.mil.

Operational Navigation And Tactical Pilotage Charts Available Through NOAA

NOAA/NOS/NIMA Aeronautical and Nautical Charts and Publications

National Oceanic and Atmospheric Administration/National Ocean Service (NOAA/NOS, www.noaa.gov/ and www.nos.noaa.gov/ are respective home pages) produces charts and publications primarily of United States airspace and waterways. NIMA produces charts and publications primarily of areas outside the United States.

NACO also prints and distributes all NOAA nautical charts and related products, as well as National Imagery and Mapping Agency (NIMA) public sale aeronautical and nautical charts; and maps compiled by the National Weather Service. Product distribution is achieved through a network of more than 4,000 FAA Authorized Chart Sales Agents throughout the world, plus 40,000 subscribers, and thousands of one-time sales. Both NOAA/NOS and NIMA produced products are now available from NOAA/NOS Aeronautical and Chart Sales Agents located worldwide or from the NOAA/NOS address shown below:

NIMA public sale charts and miscellaneous products are available through the FAA's *Aeronautical Chart Distribution* system.

ONC & TPC Aeronautical Charts:

Operational Navigation (ONCs) and Tactical Pilotage Charts (TPCs) were printed by the Defense Mapping Agency (Now NIMA) and were available for purchase from them up until about 1995, when DMA stopped sales to civilians. NIMA now only directly supplies the Department of Defense; however, ONCs and TPCs are still available to the public through NOAA (National Oceanographic and Atmospheric Administration) and are readily accessible and, just as importantly, relatively inexpensive (ordering instructions follow).

ONCs are 1:500,000 scale, while the TPCs have much greater detail at their 1:250,000 scale. Each ONC is subdivided into four TPCs of the same physical dimensions, and each also carries a legend at its base noting the four TPCs included in the parent ONC's coverage. Most all of Vietnam, North & South, is covered by two primary ONC's: ONC K-10 and ONC J-11.

ONC K-10 is comprised of TPCs K-10A, B, C and D. ONC J-11 is comprised of TPCs J-11A, B, C and D. In each case, the "A" TPC map is the upper-left quadrant, the "B" map is the upper-right quadrant, the "C" map is the lower-right quadrant and the "D" map is the lower-left quadrant of their corresponding ONC "parent" map.

ONC/TPC K-10 and ONC/TPC J-11 Aeronautical Chart Series Coverage:

ONC J-11 Covers the DMZ, all of North Vietnam, plus portions of Laos and Thailand.
ONC K-10 Covers most of South Vietnam and part of Cambodia.

TPC J-11A Covers all of NVN from 200 km S of Hanoi N to China, and the NE corner of Laos.
TPC J-11B Covers Southern China (but none of Vietnam)
TPC J-11C Covers Hainan Island and Southern China (but none of Vietnam).
TPC J-11D Covers NVN from 200 km S of Hanoi to just below Da Nang in SVN, Central Laos and a portion of the NE corner of Thailand. Includes northern I Corps and the DMZ.

TPC K-10A Covers SVN from just N of Da Nang to a point 25 km S of Nha Trang. It does NOT include a small strip of the central SVN coast that is instead found on TPC K-10B. Also covers southern 1/4 of Laos, the northern 2/3ds of Cambodia and a small portion of the SE corner of Thailand. Southern I Corps and most of II Corps are covered.
TPC K-10B Covers a small strip of the central coast of SVN from a point about 30 km North of LZ English in II Corps, South to Cam Ranh Bay Airfield. 90% of this map is water only.
TPC K-10C Not needed? - Covers only an extremely small portion of the central coast of SVN from Cam Ranh Bay Airfield S a few km. Almost all its data is also duplicated on TPC K10D. 99% of this map is water.
TPC K-10D Covers all of southern SVN from Nha Trang south (including the Fishhook and Parrot's Beak border areas). Also includes the southern 1/3d of Cambodia.

ONC & TPC Indexes:

An online index of TPC maps is available at: www.omnimap.com/cgi-bin/omni/graphic.pl?images/ind-for/tpc-afr.gif. ONC & TPC international indexes plus other topo maps are listed at: www.omnimap.com/catalog/int/topo.htm#p1.

ONC & TPC Products and Pricing:

Operational Navigation Charts (ONC) are available on paper, or as "ADRG" CD-ROMs
Worldwide, paper $4.00 per chart
Worldwide, CD-ROM $12.00 per chart (one chart per disk only)

Tactical Pilotage Charts (TPC) are available on paper, or as "ADRG" CD-ROMs
Worldwide, paper $5.75 per chart
Worldwide, CD-ROM $12.00 per chart (one chart per disk only)

Free NIMA Catalogs available from NOAA upon request:
1) Catalog, NIMA Public Sale Aeronautical Charts & Products
2) Dates of Latest Editions, NIMA Public Sale Aeronautical Charts

Ordering ONC & TPC Aeronautical Charts:

NOAA Ordering instructions: http://acc.nos.noaa.gov:80/orderCharts.htm
NOAA/NOS Map Search Engine: http://search.nos.noaa.gov/compass
Catalog of World Aeronautical Charts, 1,000,000 scale: http://acc.nos.noaa.gov/Catalog/WAC.html
NIMA Aeronautical Charts price list: http://acc.nos.noaa.gov:80/PriceLists/PricesNIMAAero.html
Agents/Vendors selling NIMA ONC's and TPC's: http://acc.nos.noaa.gov:80/Aero/AeroAgents.html

Phone orders: ONCs/TPCs toll free at: 1-800-638-8972, or (301) 436-8301, or by FAX at (301) 436-6829

Mail orders: NOAA Distribution Division (N/ACC33)
National Ocean Service
6501 Lafayette Avenue
Riverdale, MD 20737-1199
Phone: 302-436-6990 or 1-800-638-8972

E-mail orders: Distribution@[140.90.121.10]

Walk-in sales: NOAA/National Ocean Service
Chart Sales Office, 6501 Lafayette Avenue
Riverdale, MD 20737-1199

(Requests for other NIMA publications that are no longer available through the FAA should be sent to: Superintendent of Documents, PO Box 371954, Pittsburgh, PA 15250-1954, or on-line at http://bookstore.gpo.gov, or by calling 202-512-1800, fax 202-512-2250.)

NIMA, ARC Digitized Raster Graphics (ADRG):

The ONCs and TPCs on CD-ROM first became available from NOAA's Office of Aeronautical Charting and Cartography on July 1, 2000. The ADRG is an image format developed by NIMA for use with available commercial applications to provide a raster background display of a scanned map image. Most of the following NIMA Aeronautical Chart Products are now available in ADRG format on CD-ROM:

- Tactical Pilotage Charts (TPC)
- Operational Navigation Charts (ONC)
- Global Navigation and Planning Charts (GNC)
- Jet Navigation Charts (JNC)

One chart is provided on each CD-ROM. Price per CD-ROM is $12.00. ADRG documentation can be downloaded from the NIMA website at:http://164.214.2.59/publications/specs/printed/89007/89007_ADRG.pdf

To order ADRGs, provide the product name, stock number, the current price and number of copies on a separate sheet of paper or an order form. Adding a "D" to the beginning of the paper chart stock number indicates that an ADRG CD-ROM is desired, rather than a paper chart. For example, to order *Tactical Pilotage Chart E-3-A* in ADRG format, the stock number is DTPCE3A.

Include room or apartment number on your delivery address, and a daytime phone number should questions arise concerning your order. Payment must be included with your order. Remittance must be in U.S. funds: by check payable to "NOAA," on a U.S. bank; by international money order; or by providing VISA, MasterCard or Discovery Card account information. All sales are final unless an error is made by their office in filling the order.

One may place an order by calling (800) 638-8972 or (301) 436-8301. Send mail orders and payment to:

NOAA Distribution Division, N/ACC3
National Ocean Service
6501 Lafayette Avenue
Riverdale, MD 20737-1199

Miscellaneous Map Resources

The Vietnam Map Book

The Vietnam Map Book is a very rare and very large soft-cover publication that contains a complete set of 1:500,000 scale maps of SVN in black and white, as well as all the reported mission dates and grid coordinates between which Agent Orange spraying missions were flown during the war. It was produced by the Agent Orange Advisory Committee, Winter Soldier Archives in Berkeley, CA, sometime around 1982? It authors were Clark Smith and Don Watkins and the book is approximately 20" by 24" in size. The Sacramento Vet Center has a copy in their library and it may be that a copy is kept in all Vet Centers?

The following address and phone numbers were printed in the book but likely no longer valid: Agent Orange Advisory Committee, 2000 Center Street, PO Box 1251, Berkeley, CA 94704. 415-540-6175, 415-527-0616.

***National Geographic's* February, 1967 Indochina Map:**

The February, 1967 issue of *National Geographic Magazine* included a widely-used and treasured fold-out map of Vietnam and Southeast Asia. Many American families adopted it as their primary reference for following the course of the war and their sons' or daughters' tour. As a result, it is relatively scarce now and, if one is unable to locate a copy at a used bookstore specializing in *National Geographic* back-issues, there is the possibility the Society now has reprints available. The author is aware that the Society has recently published CD-ROM compilations of every issue of the magazine ever published; presumably, this map is included in that collection.

The author was successful in acquiring copies of the map over the Internet by searching with employing "*National Geographic Maps*" (in quote marks) as a search phrase. One used-map vendor very helpful and efficient in locating copies was *New World Maps, Inc*, of Apple Hill Road, Bennington, VT 05201-9544 (Internet orders were accepted). Their web address is: http://pages.prodigy.com/FL/maps4sale/natgeo3.html

The Map Catalog:

A unique reference entitled *THE MAP CATALOG* (2d Ed. 1990, Vintage/Tilden Press, NY), offers a tremendous number of map resources and is an excellent primer for understanding and locating maps of just about any source. Out of print now, copies or subsequent editions (if they exist) may be available in used books stores. Unfortunately, much of the address and phone number data contained therein is likely now obsolete; however, a treasure worthy of some effort to locate nonetheless.

CIA Maps:

The Central Intelligence Agency also markets remarkably useful reference maps as well. Their maps are generally focused on political, economic, and agricultural characteristics and boundaries, rather than militarily significant terrain and topographical features. One may request a free catalog, *CIA Maps and Publications Released to the Public*, from the following address:

The Central Intelligence Agency
Public Affairs Office
Washington, DC 20505
703-351-2053 (address & tel # as of 1990)

Among Vietnam War-related maps the CIA offers are the following maps (the series includes separate maps for each military region/CTZ, as well as for Cambodia and Laos, and is also avilable from the Library of Congress):

Vietnam 1 - Nha Dia-du' Quoc-Gia. RVN Administrative map, 38" x 27". color. 1:1,000,000 scale (also available in black & white from Library of Congress; Call# G8020 1967. V4).
Vietnam 2 - U.S. CIA South Vietnam. 1969. color. 24" x 29". 1:1,760,000 scale. Six maps of various economic, demographic and economic distributions (also available from the Library of Congress; Call# G8020 1969. U52).

Vietnam - 4: I Corps	Lib. of Cong. Call # G8021.F7 1969 .U5 (missing from file at last try)
Vietnam - 5: II Corps	Lib. of Cong. Call # G8021.F7 1969 .U51
Vietnam - 6: III Corps	Lib. of Cong. Call # G8021.F7 1969 .U52
Vietnam - 7: IV Corps	Lib. of Cong. Call # G8021.F7 1969 .U53
Cambodia - 1	Lib. of Cong. Call # G8010 1972 .U5
Laos - 1	Lib. of Cong. Call # G8010 1968 .L3

CIA World Fact Book:

"The World Factbook is prepared by the Central Intelligence Agency for the use of U.S. Government officials, and the style, format, coverage, and content are designed to meet their specific requirements. Information was provided by the American Geophysical Union, Bureau of the Census, Central Intelligence Agency, Defense Intelligence Agency, Defense Nuclear Agency, Department of State, Foreign Broadcast Information Service, Maritime Administration, National Imagery and Mapping Agency, National Maritime Intelligence Center, National Science Foundation (Antarctic Sciences Section), Office of Insular Affairs, U.S. Board on Geographic Names, U.S. Coast Guard, and other public and private sources.

The Factbook is in the public domain. Accordingly, it may be copied freely without permission of the Central Intelligence Agency (CIA). The official seal of the CIA, however, may NOT be copied without permission as required by the CIA Act of 1949 (50 U.S.C. section 403m). Misuse of the official seal of the CIA could result in civil and criminal penalties." (Data per www.odci.gov/cia/publications/factbook/info-frame.html.)

Other CIA Maps and Publications related to Vietnam:

a) 1996, Vietnamese Storage of Remains of Unaccounted U.S. Personnel, PB-96-928009, $19.50
b) 1994, Communist Party of the Socialist Republic of Vietnam (wall chart), LDA 94-10035, PB-94-927902, $10.00
c) Government Structure of the Socialist Republic of Vietnam (wall chart), LDA 94-10036, PB-94-927901, $10.00
d) 1993, Vietnam, Map # 802035, PB-93-928311, $7.00

e) 1990, Government Structure of the Socialist Republic of Vietnam: The Machinery of State: A Reference Guide, LDA 90-11785, PB-90-927906, $12.50
f) 1988, Directory of Officials of Vietnam, LDA 88-13512, PB-88-927911 $13.95
g) 1980, Directory of Officials of the Socialist Republic of Vietnam, PB-80-927912, $35.00
h) 1978, Socialist Republic of Vietnam Party and Government Structure (wall chart). Library of Congress
i) 1977, Council of Ministers of the Socialist Republic of Vietnam. Library of Congress
j) Socialist Republic of Vietnam Party and Government Structure (wall chart). Library of Congress
k) 1976, Socialist Republic of Vietnam Party and Government Structure. Library of Congress
l) 1975, Democratic Republic of Vietnam Party and Government Structure (wall chart). Library of Congress
m) 1974, Democratic Republic of Vietnam Party and Government Structure (wall chart). Library of Congress

Commercial Vendor Vietnam Map Sales:

According to Courtney Frobenius of *Vietnam-Indochina Tours*, the 1:1,000,000 scale map of Vietnam published by *ITMB Publishing* of Vancouver, B.C., Canada, is the most current map available, and was created in association with the Vietnamese Cartographic Society of Hanoi. It can be ordered from ITMB at: www.itmb.com/Catalog.htm

A wide variety of Vietnam Topo and other maps from 1:50,000 scale and larger scale are available for purchase from *Omni Maps* at: www.omnimap.com/catalog/int/vietnam.htm. An online index of TPC maps is also available from the same company at www.omnimap.com/cgi-bin/omni/graphic.pl?images/ind-for/tpc-afr.gif, while ONC & TPC international indexes plus other topo maps are listed at: www.omnimap.com/catalog/int/topo.htm#p1.

Civilian And Military Maps Of Vietnam Available On The Internet

Internet Map Sites:

Internet searches using the phrases "Map of Vietnam" or "Maps of Vietnam" or "Vietnam Maps" or "Vietnam War Maps" are quite effective as there are literally thousands of maps available. The following is a small sampling of sites offering everything from large-scale, highly detailed maps, to very small-scale maps:

www.vietvet.org/maps.htm
http://grunt.space.swri.edu/visit.htm
www.rjsmith.com/topo_map.html
www.multimap.com/index/VM1.htm
www.informatik.uni-leipzig.de/~duc/ban_do/maps.html
www.ehistory.com/vietnam/maps/index.cfm

The following site offers a plethora of historical maps of Vietnam and its cities, including some military city maps. Some areas are covered by a progression of maps that cover decades and even centuries. A wonderful site, indeed, if still running: http://quebec.eds-ingevision.fr/bando/bando.htm

L-1501 Series DMA JOG maps on the Internet:

Henthorn Site: The L-509 series of 1:250,000 scale maps was superseded by the L-1501 series at or near the end of the war, and one can access virtually all Indochina-related L-1501 Joint Operations Graphics (Air) of these quite beautiful and very detailed DMA topographic maps at the following, very remarkable site (created by Jim Henthorn): www.nexus.net/~911gfx/SVNmap.html.

I Corps index map: www.nexus.net/~911gfx/ICorps.html
II Corps index map: www.nexus.net/~911gfx/IICorps.html
III Corps index map: www.nexus.net/~911gfx/IIICorps.html
IV Corps index map: www.nexus.net/~911gfx/IVCorps.html

Henthorn has also scanned most of the L-1501 series maps covering Laos, Cambodia and Thailand as well:

L-1501 maps of North Vietnam: www.nexus.net/~911gfx/NVNmap.html

L-1501 maps of Laos: www.nexus.net/~911gfx/Laos.html [28]
L-1501 maps of Cambodia: www.nexus.net/~911gfx/Cambodia.html
L-1501 maps of Thailand: www.nexus.net/~911gfx/Thailand.html

RedCatcher Site: Tom Ward's remarkable 199th LIB *RedCatcher Association* website has posted a great deal of excellent map and firebase location information. This major resource is at: www.redcatcher.org/. The graphics at the RedCatcher site are very memory intensive and time-consuming to download, but if one has a color printer, will provide quite handsome copies.

For 1;250,000 scale DMA JOG's go to www.redcatcher.org/AO.html
For 1:50,000 maps, go to www.redcatcher.org/AO50.html (note that the assn. e-mails the visitor these maps upon request in .tif format, and the file sizes are apx 10 megabytes per map.)

Other Sites of Interest:

- Good, basic, zoomable map of SVN: http://staff.feldberg.brandeis.edu/~minh_le/vsa/vn_map_zoom.html
- Vietnam-related map and satellite image resource links:: http://coombs.anu.edu.au/WWWVLPages/VietPages/WWWVL-Vietnam_07.html
- Satellite images of Kontum and Pleiku areas: http://coombs.anu.edu.au/~vern/space.html
- Satellite images of Vietnam (Australia Vietnam Science-Technology Link): http://coombs.anu.edu.au/ ~vern/space/ space2.html
- Kontum Province and Quang Nam Mountains satellite images: http://coombs.anu.edu.au/~vern/space/kontum.html
- Ban Do Viet Nam ancient and recent maps files: 07 http://quebec.eds-ingevision.fr/bando/bando.htm
- Very clear and detailed 1:50,000 scale map of Hanoi (1965 Army Map Service map scan): www.lib.berkeley.edu/ EART/digital/topo.html
- Map of Mekong Delta / SEALORDS Area of Ops:www.history.navy.mil/seairland/ch165big.gif
- Yankee Station/Dixie Station map: www.history.navy.mil/seairland/ch67big.gif
- NVN Coast and Capes Map: www.history.navy.mil/seairland/ch44big.gif
- Americal Area of Ops maps in varying scalest: http://greene.xtn.net/~wingman/index.html

Firebase Information on the Internet:

At publication there were few websites featuring comprehensive firebase data, although some do exist.

1. Some excellent firebase maps and a large firebase listing are available on the home page of the Americal Division Association at: www.americal.org. Several, excellent I Corps firebase maps are there at www.americal.org/174/maps.htm, while maps of Americal/Marine and Lam Son 719 Laotian firebase locations in I Corps and Laos are posted in a variety of image types and magnifications. These are high-quality images that sometimes include firebase locations noted in grease pencil. There are approximately eight separate maps covering the area from Da Nang south to the northern end of the II Corps area below Quang Ngai. The A Shau Valley is also featured in a separate map, as are the firebases of Lam Son 719. Americal website map files are very large (600K to 700K and more), so long download-times should be expected.

2. www.rjsmith.com/ provides a very large number of excellent maps, and this incredible resource is in a constant state of expansion. The site is the home page of the *1st Battalion, 69th Armor Association*, a unit that was responsible for the defense of QL-19's vital role as an east/west commercial and military link between Qui Nhon on the coast, and the Pleiku/Kontum areas of operation in the west. Its maps primarily focus on the QL-19 corridor (with base locations well marked) between Kontum and Qui Nhon. Firebases, strongpoints, bridges and pump stations are clearly marked on L-7014, 1:50,000 scale images of high-quality that often require significant download times.

---

[28] Incredibly, Henthorn has also plotted (in red lettering) the location of all of the approximate 400 Lima-Site airfields in Laos this map.

3. Some Americal AO FSBs are marked on maps at http://greene.xtn.net/~wingman/index.html

4. The Vietnam Helicopter Pilots Association (VHPA) has some firebase information at www3.servtech.com/vhpa/

5. A site calling itself *WAR-RECORDS* has a somewhat limited interactive firebase listing where one can search for other relevant data, in addition to viewing the list. Go to: www.InsideTheWeb.com/mbs.cgi/mb982251. The *WAR-RECORDS* home page address is at www.war-records.com/War-Records.index.htm.

6. An excellent site containing detailed maps and photos of II Corps/4th Inf Div FSBs/LZs is at the home page of the 1st/14th Infantry Regiment; http://1-14th.com/index.html, and http://1-14th.com/maps.html. The site includes both 1:250,000 scale and 1:50,000 map images.

7. A remarkable set of base location and other maps are available on the 199th LIB *Red Catcher Association* website built by Tom Ward. Anyone interested in III Corps base locations and other detailed 1:250,000 and 1:50,000 scale maps should visit www.redcatcher.org/.

8. Incredibly, Jim Henthorn has also plotted (in red lettering) the location of all 400 or so Lima-Site Airfields in Laos on 1:250,000 L-1501 JOG map images that he has installed on his website at: www.nexus.net/~911gfx/Laos.html.

U.S. Geological Survey Map website:

Go to: http://mapping.usgs.gov/

Appendix D

Researching the Vietnam War

Researching and Acquiring U.S. Military Historical Unit and Personnel Records

Obtaining U.S. Army Historical and Personnel Records

U.S. Army Battalion Daily Staff Journals, Annual Historical Supplements, Operational and After-Action Reports

Historical records vital to reconstructing the daily activities of an Army battalion during its Vietnam tour (or any other period of its history) are now available at the National Archives. The Archives and the U.S. Army Center for Military History also store other Battalion, Brigade, Divisional, Corps and Army Group operational, annual historical, lessons learned and after action reports as well (and likely a wealth of other information), that any determined effort will uncover if one is persistent, considerate and courteous in their search.

A typical Battalion Annual Supplement contains a short paragraph outlining each day's principal events (perhaps an average of 8 days per page). The entries include grid coordinate data and other important general information such as casualty detail. Most Bn Annual Supplements are about 45 to 80 pages in length.

The "Daily Staff Journal or Duty Officer's Log" (also known as form AR 220-346) includes and hour by hour account of the entire battalion's activities and normally include very detailed and precise information about unit locations down to the squad level throughout the day. As a result of its extensive detail, a Daily Journal can average about 8 to 20 pages per DAY, depending on how heavy the action may have been on a given day!

There is a charge for copies provided to civilians and the rates are fairly steep (but worth every cent). The author recommends one first fax a request outlining the nature of the data being sought in as much detail as possible. Contact:

The National Archives, Archives II, Textual Reference
8601 Adelphi Road
College Park MD 20740-6001
301-713-7482 FAX

Army Battalion Annual Historical Supplements and Battalion Daily Journals are available for charges that decline as the volume of material being reproduced increases (50 cents per page for small orders was typical in 1999). In one's request, they should carefully outline the information needed, while at the same time being as specific as possible about unit designations and the dates involved in the request. It is recommended that one fax their initial request. Once the request is received, the NARA will review their files and then advise the requestor in writing as to availability and approximate reproduction cost.

U.S. Army Unit Rosters and Company Morning Reports

Army unit rosters and Morning Reports are available from the NPRC in St. Louis. As with Battalion Daily Journals, there are charges for civilians acquisitions but not for official Army inquiries. Many of the records are on microfilm and some are barely legible. It would not be overly difficult to reconstruct a complete record of practically every person who served with a particular unit during a particular period if copies of every roster on file at the NPRC for that period are purchased. The rosters include Service Numbers up to mid 1969, then Social Security Numbers thereafter. Social Security Numbers are confidential, so NPRC blackens them out of rosters that contain them.

Prior to 1961, it is our understanding that Army units were required to file unit rosters on a monthly basis. After 1961, the requirement was modified to quarterly filings. During the Vietnam War, and particularly during its late years, filings often became rather erratic and the required quarterly filings were not always submitted.

When requesting unit rosters it is wise not to be too specific. NPRC will only provide exactly what is requested and if say a roster was requested for the month of February 1968, and the NPRC had rosters for January 1968 and May 1968 on file but none for February, they would send nothing. It is best to set wide parameters for a request, such as "any rosters issued in '68."

Morning reports were filed by each Army company every day and listed details of a unit's strength and the disposition of its personnel assets. They may be thought of as a sort of daily report card, and the comings and goings of individuals can often be tracked using such reports. Accordingly, they are very voluminous and may be costly to acquire as a result.

Unit rosters and morning report records are very extremely vital resources for tracking down individuals who might have important data in their possession. NPRC is a wonderful resource but responses are normally very slow (one to six months), and one must keep in mind that government budgets are very lean and that the NPRC receives more than 200,000 requests for documents monthly! Be patient and don't take your frustration out on NPRC staff. Contact the NPRC at:

National Personnel Records Center, Army Records Branch
9700 Page Blvd, St. Louis, MO 63132
NPRC website: www.nara.gov/regional/stlouis.html
(301) 713-7482 FAX (recommended, normally speeds up the process significantly)

U. S. Army Center for Military History

Do not overlook the U.S. Army Center for Military History in the Washington DC area. Its Internet address is www. army.mil/cmh-pg. The site contains links to the Army Military History Institute (MHI) at Carlisle Barracks, as well as the huge web site of the National Archives and other resources.

Contacting the U.S. Army Military History Institute (MHI):

Website http://carlisle-www.army.mil/usamhi/

Contacting MHI by e-mail or phone:

http://carlisle-www.army.mil/usamhi/ContactMHI.html
For inquiries relating to photographs or artifacts / MHI-SC@awc.carlisle.army.mil
For inquiries relating to archival collections / MHI-AR@awc.carlisle.army.mil
For other historical inquiries / MHI-HR@awc.carlisle.army.mil
For administrative requests / AWCC-DMH@awc.carlisle.army.mil
Telephone: +1-717-245-3611
FAX: +1-717-245-3711

National Archives Military Films, Document and Photograph Search Engine:

www.nara.gov/nara/searchnail.html

Vietnam on Film and in Television Documentaries at the Library Of Congress:

To view a very extensive filmography of both film and TV documentaries at the LOC (compiled by Victoria E. Johnson, and dated July, 1989), go to: gopher://marvel.loc.gov/00/research/reading.rooms/motion.picture/mopic.tv/mpfind/vietnam

Frequently Asked Questions on the U.S. Army Homepage:
(www.dtic.mil/armylink/faq/#01.htm) as of 10/98

Q. How may a member of the general public obtain government publications?
A. The office of the Superintendent of Documents carries a free catalog of all its documents and their cost. To request a catalog or document, call (202) 512-1800, or write to : Superintendent of Documents, PO Box 371954, Pittsburgh, PA 15250-7954. The National Technical Information Service (NTIS) also carries government publications. To contact NTIS, call (703) 487-4600, or write to: 5285 Port Royal Road, Springfield, VA 22161.

Q. How may I obtain a copy of my military personnel record?
A. Request a copy of your military record by writing The National Personnel Records Center; Military Personnel Records; 9700 Page Avenue; St. Louis, MO 63132-5100. Or call (800) 318-5298. At minimum, please include the service member's complete name, social security number and/or serial number, and the requester's return address.

Q. How may I obtain a copy of my military medical record?

A. Medical records are maintained at one of 58 regional Veterans Administration (VA) centers around the country or at the national Veterans Administration Records Management Center in St. Louis. Call (800) 827-1000 for information on your regional VA Center. The national VA Records Management Office can be reached by calling (314) 263-2800.

Q. How may I obtain historical information about the Army?
A. For historical information, such as a the history of an Army unit or a retired general's military biography, please contact the Center for Military History (CMH). (www.army.mil/cmh-pg/)

> **CMH Historical Services available to the Public**: The Center's art and documents collections, library facilities, and reference services are open to private researchers. Official priorities permitting, its historians, curators, and archivists advise researchers on military history topics and stand ready to share their expertise concerning the location of sources. Its Art and Exhibits Branch arranges temporary loans of paintings and drawings from the Army Art Collection to private organizations that agree to display the art publicly in accordance with Army regulations. The Army's museums and historical holdings throughout the country and abroad are open to the public, and their curators are also available to answer reference questions. Specific inquiries about these programs and services should be addressed to the Center's Executive Officer:
>
> > **Mailing Address**: Executive officer, Attn: DAMH-ZAX, U.S. Army Center of Military History, 103 Third Avenue, Ft. McNair, DC 20319-5058
> > **Physical Location**: Building 35, 102 Fourth Avenue, Fort Lesley J. McNair, Washington, DC

Q. How may I obtain historical operational information about a particular Army unit?
A. The National Archives has historical operational information on Army units. For military information preceding the year 1941, please contact the National Archives One at (202) 501-5390. For military information from 1942 and later, please contact the National Archives Two at (301) 713-7250.

Q. How can I locate a former Army soldier?
A. The Privacy Act of 1974 prohibits releasing the last known address of former Army members without their written consent. However, the agency identified below will assist your search by forwarding your letter to the service member's last known address. To pursue locating a former Army soldier:

1. Write a letter to the soldier. Place letter in a sealed/stamped envelope, including your full name and return address.
2. Write a letter addressed to the National Personnel Records Center requesting their assistance with your search. Be sure to include the service member's name, serial number and/or social security number, and date of birth if available.
3. Place your envelope addressed to the service member AND the letter to the National Personnel Records Center in ONE envelope. Address this envelope to: National Personnel Records Center, 9700 Page Boulevard, St. Louis, MO 63132-5200. Please note current addresses for discharged service members are not maintained at the records center - this center only has the service member's last officially recorded address. Letters to service members the record center can not identify or who are known to be deceased will be returned to the requestor.

Obtaining U.S. Marine Corps Historical and Personnel Records

The following information was provided by Ann Kelsey, who served in Vietnam as a civilian volunteer with Army Special Services, Library Branch, as an administrative librarian in Cam Ranh Bay, Dong Ba Thin, Nha Trang, and Saigon from August 1969 to August 1970. Ms. Kelsey is currently Associate Director, Learning Resource Center, County College of Morris, Randolph, New Jersey.

> "The Marine Corps Historical Center Archives and Reference Section located in Building 58 at the Navy Yard in Washington, DC has command chronologies, after-action reports and other related records. If you provide them with unit information along with a date or date range, they can often locate useful material.
>
> Unit diaries, which include rosters, through 1966 are located at the Marine Corps Historical Center. The records are arranged by month and year, and list the officers and enlisted personnel within a unit at the company level or the battalion/squadron level. These documents may be examined in person or may be requested in writing, one month and one year per letter. As soon as one request has been fulfilled, another may be submitted. Specify exact unit information and state the request is being made under the Freedom of Information Act. Send fax or written requests to: The Marine Corps Historical Center, Reference Section, Building 58, Washington Navy Yard, Washington, DC 20374-0580. Tel 202-433-3483, 202-433-4691 fax.

Unit diaries and rosters from 1967 forward are available by written request only. The procedure above also applies. Send requests to CMC HQ Marine Corps, Records Service Section, Code MMSB-10 "Unit Diaries", HQ U.S. Marine Corps, 2008 Elliott Rd, Ste 201, Quantico, VA 22134-5030. Tel 703-784-3934 (or 784-3935, 3939, or 3940).

Marine Corps operation reports, including plans, diaries, command chronologies and after action reports from 1964 on are located at the Marine Corps Historical Center, Archives Section, Building 58, Washington Navy Yard, Washington, DC 20374-0580. Tel 202-433-3439. If you are planning to visit, it is a good idea to call and speak with the archivist about the material you are looking for before you go. Bring a National Archives Researcher Card or any photo identification, for example, a driver's license or passport, with you. You will need these for admittance into the section containing the Archives."

For USMC Personnel Records, send a completed "Standard Form 180" to the address listed below. The SF 180 can be printed from the internet at: www.nara.gov/regional/mprsf180.html. It can also be requested by phone at 314-538-4141 (form requests only, staff will not respond to questions), and a faxback phone number for requesting it is 314 538-4175.

National Personnel Records Center
Navy, USMC & CG Records
9700 Page Blvd, St. Louis, MO 63132

For award information, refer to the Section entitled: "Obtaining U.S. NAVY and U.S. COAST GUARD Records"

Obtaining U.S. Navy Historical and Personnel Records

For access to U.S. Naval and Coast Guard historical records and Ship's Musters, send requests to:

U.S. Navy & U.S. Coast Guard Records, Naval Historical Center
Operational Archives
Bldg 57, Washington Navy Yard
Washington, DC 20374

The following was transcribed from the official Navy website at: www.chinfo.navy.mil/navpalib/questions/awards.html:

"To obtain copies of awards earned, write to the National Personnel Records Center at the below address. This office will identify any awards you've earned and provide replacement awards as necessary. It is helpful to include a copy of your Discharge Certificate (DD 214). If a DD 214 is not available, include your full name, service number, social security number, date of birth and as much additional pertinent information as possible."

Navy Liaison Office, National Personnel Records Center
9700 Page Avenue
St. Louis, MO 63132-5100

To obtain information about unit awards earned, contact the Chief of Naval Operations, Awards and Special Projects Branch at the below address. This office can identify awards earned by Navy units. Additionally, that office can provide a DD 215 (correction to DD 214) if necessary, which can then be used to acquire respective awards by sending to the National Personnel Records Center.

Chief of Naval Operations, Awards and Special Projects Branch (Code N09B33)
2000 Navy Pentagon, Washington, DC 20350-2000

Veterans are entitled to one replacement set of their medals. To request medals, send a Standard Form 180, which can be obtained from the National Personnel Record Center web site (www.nara.gov/regional/mprsf180.html), to the Naval Liaison Office, National Personnel Records Center, 9700 Page Boulevard, St. Louis, Missouri 63132-5100. Please write "Do not open in mailroom" on the outer envelope.

For Navy Personnel Records contact:

National Personnel Records Center, Navy, USMC & CG Records
9700 Page Blvd, St. Louis, MO 63132
(or telephone the Navy, USMC & CG Records Section at 314-538-4141)"

Navy Historical Research and Ships' Histories:

From the U.S. Navy's official website: "One of the best sources of the histories on the ships of the U.S. Navy is *The Dictionary of American Naval Fighting Ships*, an eight-volume reference set published by the Naval Historical Center and available in most major public and university libraries. If the local library does not have a copy of this set, one can ask their librarian to request a photocopy of the appropriate pages from the Interlibrary Loan (ILL) and have the copies sent via fax. Some responding libraries will charge for this service. The Naval Historical Center is at www.history.navy.mil. Write the center at:

Department of the Navy
Naval Historical Center, Ships' Histories Branch
901 M Street SE, Washington, DC 20374-5060

Obtaining U.S. Air Force Historical and Personnel Records

For access to U.S. Air Force historical records, send requests to:

Office of Air Force History
Bldg 5681, Bolling AFB
Washington, DC 20332
202-767-5088

For personnel records contact:

National Personnel Records Center, USAF Records
9700 Page Blvd, St. Louis, MO 63132
(or phone the Air Force Records Section at 314-538-4243)

Obtaining U.S. Coast Guard Historical and Personnel Records

For access to U.S. Naval and Coast Guard historical records and Ship's Musters, send requests to:

U.S. Navy & U.S. Coast Guard Records
Naval Historical Center
Operational Archives
Bldg 57, Washington Navy Yard
Washington, DC 20374

Other historical resources listed at the USCG's official website (www.uscg.mil/dotinfo/uscg/welcome.html) includes the following contact points:

U.S. Coast Guard Historian's Office (G-CP-4)
2100 2d Street, SW
Washington, DC 20593
(202) 267-0948

U.S. Coast Guard Curatorial Services
7945 Fernham Lane
Forestville, MD 20747
(301) 763-4008

U.S. Coast Guard Museum
Waesche Hall
15 Mohegan Avenue
New London, CT 06320
(860) 444-8511

For Coast Guard Personnel Records contact:

National Personnel Records Center
Navy, USMC & CG Records
9700 Page Blvd, St. Louis, MO 63132
(or telephone the Navy, USMC & CG Records Section at 314-538-4141)

Appendix E
Internet Reference Resources

1AFH Assn: www.callsignvampire.org.au/
1st AFH: www.callsignvampire.org.au/
1st Australian Field Hospital (John Lyle): www.ozdocs.net.au/users/johnlyle/index.html
1st Australian Field Hospital Assn: www. callsignvampire.org.au/
1st Avn Bde, 1st Infantry Division: www.angelfire.com/wa2/palmeracres/1stavnbn.html
1st Bde, 1st Cav Flying Circus: www.fbvfw.org/circus/
1st Bde, 101st Abn Division: www.101stabndiv1stbrigade.com/
1st Bn RAR: www.firstbattalion.au
1st Cavalry Division Assn. home page: www.vvm.com/~firstcav/home.html
1st Cavalry Division: www.1stcav.org
1st Cavalry Division Assn. page: www.metronet.com/~harryb/1st_cav.html
1st Marine Tank Bn: www.usmctanker.com
1st Infantry Division: www.xnet.com/~fdmuseum/
1st/4th Marine Rgt: www.geocities.com/Pentagon/Barracks/2230/
1st/8th Cavalry Jumping Mustangs, 1st Cavalry Division**:** www.familyville.com/data/lusmyp/courage/
1st/9th Bullwhip Sqd Assn: www.bullwhipsquadron.org
1st/9th, 1st Air Cav, B Trp: www.geocities.com/b19loretta/
1st/9th, C Trp, 1st Air Cav: www.RealCav.org
1st/14th Infantry, Golden Dragons: http://1-14th.com/
1st/20th Inf, B Co: www.angelfire.com/pa3/bravo1bn20vietnam/
1st/22d Inf: www.eatel.net/~22inf/
1st/50th Infantry (Mech): www.ichiban1.org/
1st/69th Armor: http://rjssmith.com. Numerous high-quality maps of QL-19 II Corps area and firebases/strongpoints between Kontum and Qui Nhon are here along with descriptive text. A remarkable site by any measure
1st/92d Field Arty Assn: www.bravecannos.org
1st/502d Inf, D Co, Assn: http://pone.com/dc/index.htm
1st/503d Infantry, B Co, 173rd Airborne Bde: http://members.aol.com/gkozdron/web/index.htm#Home
2d/14th Infantry Golden Dragons award-winning: www.en.com/users/kramsey/dragons.html
2d/17th Air Cav, B Trp Banshees: www.ameritech.net/users/dschave/B2nd17th.html
2d/17th Cav, A Trp Assault: http://home.sprintmail.com/~karig/realcav.html
2d/1st Cav, D Trp: www.sirinet.net/~flohr/
2d/1st Marines Assn: www.express-news.net/mikerod/21mar/21home.html
2d/20th ARA, 1 Cav, F Trp/79th CAV Blue Max: www.bluemax-ara-assoc.com/
2d Sqdn/1st Cav: www.2-1cavalry.com
3d/17th ACR Assn: http://members.aol.com/sirdruid/ACR317.htm
3d/17th Cav, A Trp Silver Spurs: http://members.aol.com/bear317/spurs.htm
3d/17th Cav, C Trp & D Trp 3d/5th Cav: www.geocities.com/pentagon/7063/
3d/4th Marines Assn: www.concentric.net/~reddawg
3d/5th Cav: http://pone.com/bk/index.htm
3d/5th Air Cav Sqdn, D Trp War Wagons: http://named.dalton.net/~warwagon19/
3d/5th Cav, D Trp & C Trp 3d/17th Cav: www.geocities.com/pentagon/7063/
3d Recon Battalion, 3rd Marine Division: http://grunt.space.swri.edu (Tremendous resource)
4th Bn RAR: http://users.mildura.net.au/users/marshall/4RAR.htm
4th Infantry Division Assn: www.4thID.org (links to all the Regimental websites of the Div here also.)
4th/77th, 101st Abn Dragons/Toros/Griffins: www.ameritech.net/users/cnurse/aerialarty.htm
5th Bn RAR: www.netspace.net.au/~harrison
5th/60th Inf, 9th Div: www.5thbattalion.org/
6th Bn RAR: http://msnhomepages.talkcity.com/ReportersAlley/garymcmahon/6rar.htm
7th Bn, 15th Artillery Regiment: www.landscaper.net/vietnam.html
7th Cavalry Regiment: www.metronet.com/~harryb/1st_team/7th_rgmt/7thndx06.html
7th Marines: www.marzone.com/
7th/17th Air Cav Ruthless Riders: http://members.tripod.com/aircavalry17/
8th Bn RAR (alt site): http://members.tripod.com/~BAZILBRUSH/index-4.html
8th Bn RAR: www.pcug.org.au/~cmt
8th Transportation Group: http://academic.uofs. edu/faculty/gramborw/atav/8tc.htm
8th Air Cav, F Trp Blueghosts: http://members.aol.com/BluGhstGrn/odgreen.html
9th Infantry Division: www.oldreliable.org/
9th Infantry Division, Flamethrowers site: http://msnhomepages.talkcity.com/lagrangeln/r_a_camaro/
9th Infantry Regiment Manchu Assn: www.manchu.org/
9 Sqdn RAAF (Peter Robinson): www.iinet.net.au/~rob7299/
14th Infantry Rgt: http://1-14th.com/

15th Artillery Regiment: www.landscaper.net/. Large resource, excellent site
15th Engineers: http://15thengineer.www8.50megs.com/index.html
15th Medical Bn, Medevac: www.vabch.com/mssb/snore/index.htm
16th Infantry Regiment Assn: http://users.jerseycape.com/deaton/regiment/regiment.htm
16th Infantry Regiment Assn: www.16thinfantry-regiment.org
19th Engineer Battalion Assn: http://home.earthlink. net/~engr19/index.html
19th Combat Engineer Battalion Assn: http://home.earthlink.net/~engr19
22nd Infantry Regiment (4th and 25th Divisions): www.22ndinfantry.org/
25th Avn Bn, A & B Cos: http://members.tripod.com/ronleonard/index.htm
25th Infantry Division Assn: www.25thida.com
31st Trans. (H-34) Co: www.ecr.net/ahh/31Trans.htm
35th Infantry Regiment: www.cacti68.com/35thinf/
43d Signal Battalion: www.43sigws.heidelberg.army. mil/hist.htm
48th AHC Bluestars: www.raydon.com/48ahc/
52d Combat Avn Bn and 119th Avn Co Dragons: www.megsinet.com/cjlsr/index.html
57th AHC Gladiators: www.geocities.com/Pentagon/Bunker/7051
60 s Project, Vietnam Generation: http://jefferson.village.virginia.edu/sixties
61st AHC: www.metrocast.net/~jsbeach/
69th Armor Assn: www.rjsmith.com/69_hist.html
70th Combat Engineer Battalion (constructed Camp Radcliff): http://saturn.vcu.edu/~dmouer/70th.htm
71st AHC Rattlers/Firebirds: www.rattlers.org
75th Ranger Regiment Assn: www.75thassoc.org/index.html
79th Cav, F Trp & 2d/20th ARA 1st Cav Blue Max: www.bluemax-ara-assoc.com/
92nd AHC: www.geocities.com/Pentagon/Base/3031/
101st Avn, Co. A (AHC), 101st Abn Comancheros: www.a101avn.org
114th AHC Knights/Cobras: www.angelfire.com/tx/114thAvnCo/
116th AHC: www.pauljenkins.com/hornets/
117th AHC: http://members.tripod.com/plaroue/Warlords.html
117th AHC Beachbums: www.geocities.com/Pentagon/Barracks/1719/index.html
118th AHC: www.gorilla.net/~118ahc
119th AHC Gators/Crocs: www.geocities.com/Pentagon/Quarters/1534/
119th AHC: www.geocities.com/Pentagon/Quarters/1534/
11th ACR Avn: www.uticaweb.com/blackhorse/
120th Avn Co: www.georgenville.com/razorback.htm or http://members.xoom.com/_XMCM/razorback947/index.html
121st AHC Tigers/Vikings: www.benchmarkcomputer.com/vietnam/index.htm
128th AHC Tomahawks/Gunslingers: www.vietnamexp.com/
129th AHC Bulldogs/Cobras: www.129th.net
134th AHC: http://home1.gte.net/dsoul/demon.htm
135th AHC EMU s: www.135ahc.com/
138th Trans. Det: www.ecr.net/ahh/31Trans.htm
145th Combat Aviation Battalion: http://userzweb.lightspeed.net/~rojobob/145cab.html
155th AHC: www.geocities.com/pentagon/quarters/1517/
158th Avn, A Co, 101st Abn Ghostriders: www.ghostriders-online.org/
158th Avn, B Co, 101st Abn Lancers: http://members. tripod.com/dmussey/
161 Reconnaissance Flight (Recce Flt) Possums: www.161recceflt.org.au
161st AHC: www.161ahc.org/
162d AHC Vultures: http://162AHC.Vultures.com/
170th AHC Bikinis/Buccaneers: www.170thahc.org
170th AHC: www.170thahc.org
173d Airborne Brigade: http://sunsite.unc.edu/173abn/173abn.html
173rd Airborne Brigade, Firebase 173 Newspapers**:** http://hometown.aol.com/a46piodet/index.htm
173rd Airborne Brigade: http://metalab.unc.edu/173abn
173rd Airborne Brigade: www.olywa.net/sdotctho/sdotctho.html
173rd Airborne Div Assn: www.173rdAirborne.com
173rd AHC Robinhoods: www.robinhoods.net
174th AHC Dolphins/Sharks: www.americal.org/174/. (Excellent maps and extensive I Corps FSB list here)
196th Light Infantry Brigade Assn: www.americal.org/196
199th Light Infantry Brigade: http://home.ptd.net/~trward
199th Light Infantry Brigade (Red Catcher) official: www. redcatcher.org/. Official mailing address for 199th LIB Assn. Is: Redcatcher, PO Box 199, Mclean VA, 22101-0199
227th AHC, Company C: http://members.dialnet.net/jarw/cmpr.htm
242d Assault Helicopter Company (ASHC): www.vhpa.org/crash.htm
362d Signal Company webpage: www.jbeck@iwaynet.net
588th Trans Bn: www.mendonet.com/588th/map
Agent Orange (and herbicide) useage and effect: see Herbicide
Air America: www.air-america.org/

Air Commando Assn: http://home.earthlink.net/~aircommando1
Air Force Assn: www.afa.org/afafcts.html
Air Force Historical Research: www.au.af.mil/au/afhra/
Air Force History Support: www.airforcehistory.hq.af.mil/
Air Force Sergeants Assn: www.association.com/AFSA/mainmenu.shtml
Air Force Unit Assns: www.vets.com/inside/alumni.htm (large database, all branches)
Air Force: see also U.S. Air Force
Aircraft of the Vietnam War: www.petester.com/html/vnraircraft.html
Airfield Defence Assn: www.geocities.com/adghome_au/adg_home_page.html
Americal Division Assn: www.americal.org. List of Americal, Marine, 101st Abn and 1st Cav Div FSBs in I Corps and some of II and III Corps
Americal Division, Historical Records: http://rattlers.org/history/toc.htm (large resource)
American Battle Monuments Commission: www.abmc.gov
American Forces Vietnam Network Detachment 5, Quang Tri, Vietnam: www.geocities.com/Eureka/Gold/6654/quangtri.html
American Historical Assn: http://web.gmu.edu/chnm/aha
American Legion National Headquarters: www.legion
American Society of Naval Engineers: www.jhuapl.edu/ASNE
American Veterans Assn: www.amvets.org
An Loc, The Battle for, Mark A. Smith (a.k.a. Capt. Zippo): http://lzsally.com/zippo.html. (unusual account by man who describes himself as ground cmdr for much of the fight)
Archival Research, commercial resources: Pike Military Research (a.k.a. Archival Research International, Inc.), Military Histories, Maps and Photographs: www.militaryunits.com. (e-mail: milhist@erols.com)
Archives, Univ of Texas Vietnam Archives: www.lbjlib.utexas. edu/shwv/
Army Alumni Assns: www.army.mil/vetinfo/vetloc.htm
Army and Navy Union of the U.S.A: www.armynavy.net
Army Flight School (unofficial) site: www.armyflightschool.org
Army Historical Foundation: www.armyhistoryfnd.org
Army Institute of Heraldry: www-perscom.army.mil/tagd/tioh/tioh.htm
Army Military History Institute: http://carlisle-www.army. mil/usamhi/
Army Quartermaster Military Museum and History Links: www.qmmuseum.lee.army.mil/links.html
Army Ranger Assns: www.ranger.org/~ranger/index.html
Army Security Agency Vets: http://members.gnn.com/asavets/asa.htm
Army Transportation Assn. Vietnam Home Page: http://academic.uofs.edu/faculty/gramborw/atav/default.html
Army Unit Assns: www.vets.com/inside/alumni.htm (large database, all branches)
Army War College: http://carlisle-www.army.mil/
Army: See also U.S. Army
Art: National Vietnam Veterans Art Museum: www.nvvam.org/home.htm
ASA Veterans: http://members.gnn.com/asavets/asa.htm
Association of Air Force Missileers: www.thebook.com/missileers
Association of Former Intelligence Officers: http://euphoria.mercy.edu/afio
Association of Graduates of the U.S. Military Academy: www.aog.usma.edu
Association of Military Flight Surgeon Pilots: http://members.aol.com/iamfsp/index.html
Association of Naval Services Officers: www.ids. net/~cisneroj/anso/anso.htm
Association of the U.S. Army (AUSA): www.ausa.org/
Australia/Australians in Vietnam:

- 161 Reconnaissance flight (Recce Flt) Possums: www.161recceflt.org.au
- 1AF Hospital Assn. (John Lyle): www.ozdocs.net.au/users/johnlyle/index.html
- American Veterans Traveling Tribute: www.avtt.org/
- Australian Airfield Defence Assn: www.geocities.com/adghome_au/adg_home_page.html
- Australian Forces at War: www.australiansatwar.gov.au/(companion to TV series launched May 2001
- Australian Forces in Vietnam, History of: www.vietvet.org/aussie1.htm
- Dept of Veterans Affairs: www.dva.gov.au
- Diggers: www.diggerz.org/
- Ex-Military Resources Centre Peter Badcoe Club: www.xmrc.com/
- Far Eastern Strategic Reserve: www.dashmark.com.au/fesr
- In Vietnam, Analysis of: http://rubens.anu.edu.au/student.projects/vietnam/public html/home.htm
- in Vietnam: http://users.mildura.net.au/users/marshall/
- Medevac Units: www.callsignvampire.org.au/
- National Centre for War Related PTSD: www.austin.unimelb.edu.au/NCPTSD/
- Naval Assn: www.navalassoc.org.au/
- Navy, history of in Vietnam and ships list: www.navy.gov.au/4_history/vietnam.htm
- Navy, HMAS Perth Assn: www.hmasperth.asn.au
- Ntl Univ, Vietnam Virtual Library: http://coombs.anu.edu.au/WWWVLPages/VietPages/WWWVL-Vietnam.html
- Ordnance Field Park: http://web.logicworld.com.au/~4seasons/index/index.htm
- Regular Defence Force Welfare Assn: www.rdfwa.org.au
- Veterans on the Net (AusVets): www.ausvets.powerup.com.au/

Veterans, Entitlement Act 1986: http://scaleplus.law.gov.au
Vietnam Veterans Mortality Listing: www.fan.net.au/~lonestar/
Vietnam Veterans Organization Links: http://grunt.space.swri.edu/ozorgs.htm
Vietnam Veterans: www.vvaa.org.au/
Vietnam War Veterans Trust: www.accsoft.com. au/~vvt
Vietnam, War Links: www.vvaa.org.au/links.htm
VVAA Museum: www.vietnamvetsmuseum.org/
VVAA of South Australia: http://vvaa-sa.asn.au/
War Memorial: www.awm.gov.au

Aviation, Military Aircraft of the Vietnam War:www.petester.com/html/vnraircraft.html
Military Aircraft, links: www.landings.com/_landings/pages/military.html

Battle Index, VHPA: www.vhpa.org/info/panel/battle/. (large chronological resource)
Battlefield Vietnam, PBS TV Series: www.pbs.org/battlefieldvietnam/index.html
Bibliographies,
Edwin Moise: http://hubcap.clemson.edu/~eemoise/bibliography.html (massive resource)
Women in Vietnam War: http://servercc.oakton.edu/~wittman/women.htm
Women Nurses in Vietnam: www.illyria.com/nursebib.html

Brown Water Navy Pages (Kent Hawley): http://hawley. interspeed.net/vietnam/links.htm
By Sea, Air, and Land, History of the U.S. Navy in Vietnam: www.history.navy.mil/seairland/
CACF: www.no-quarter.org/html/crunch.html (excellent resource for researching casualties and data)
Cam Ranh Bay, History, Photos and more: www.petester.com (large resource)
Cambodian Holocaust:
www.yale.edu/cgp
Dith Pran site: www.dithpran.org
http://edweb.gsn.org/sideshow/index.html
www.cybercambodia.com/dachs/index.html

Camp Holloway Assn: www.megsinet.com/cjlsr/index.html
Camp Holloway: www.megsinet.net/~cjlsr/
Canadian Vietnam Veterans Organization Links: http://grunt.space.swri.edu/canvets.htm
CAP - Marine Combined Action Platoon Website - www.billnimmo.co; has links to other CAP related sites
CAP Veterans Assn: www.capmarine.com (excellent resource, plus other CAP links)
Casualty Information/Statistics:
Casualty search engine: www.no-quarter.org/html/crunch.html
NARA CACF and TAGCEN Files: www.nara.gov/nara/electronic/vnstat.html
NARA CER Combat Area Casualty File info: www.nara.gov/nara/electronic/vnstat.html
State-level casualty lists (1956 to present): www.nara.gov/nara/electronic/korvnsta.html
www.army.mil/cmh-pg
www.rjsmith.com/kia_tbl.html

CIA:
Home Page: www.odci.gov/cia/
World Fact Book: www.odci.gov/cia/publications/factbook/info-frame.html
www.odci.gov/cia/
www.odci.gov/cia/publications/factbook/info-frame.html

CID Agents Assn: www.randomc.com/~german/cidaa.html
Coast Guard:
Unit Assns: www.vets.com/inside/alumni.htm (large database, all branches)
History of in Vietnam: www.uscg.mil/hq/g-cp/history/h_tulichvietnam.html
History: www.uscg.mil/hq/g-cp/history/collect.html
www.uscg.mil

Combat Area Casualty File (CACF): www.no-quarter.org/html/crunch.html
Combat Infantrymens Assn: www.2-60inf.com/cia.htm
Command and General Staff College: www-cgsc.army.mil/
Congressional Medal of Honor Society: www.awod.com/gallery/probono/cmhs
Constitution, USS, 1845: www.state.ma.us/veterans/ancientmarin
Corps of Engineers Office of History: www.hq.usace.army.mil/history/
Counterinsurgency, U.S.: www.parascope.com/articles/0497/phoenix.htm
DAV: www.dav.org
Defense Language Institute, Office of the Command Historian**:** http://pom-www.army.mil/atzp_/mh/default.htm
Department of Veterans Affairs: www.va.gov/
Dictionary and Gazetteer: http://dns.advnet.net/gdmoore/vnwords1.htm
Dictionary of American Fighting Ships: www.hazegray.org/danfs/
Dien Bien Phu-French Perspective: www.dienbienphu.org/english/index.htm
Disabled American Veterans: www.dav.org
DMA, Defense Mapping Agency: see NIMA
Documents, Vassar College: http://students.vassar.edu/~vietnam/index.html
DOD Directorate for Information: http://web1.whs.osd.mil/

DUSTOFF Assn. (medevac): www.fbg.net/dustoff
Edwin E. Moïse Vietnam War Bibliography: http://hubcap.clemson.edu/~eemoise/bibliography.html
Embassy, Vietnamese in U.S.: www.vietnamembassy-usa.org
Enlisted Assn. of the National Guard of the U.S.: www.eangus.org
Fast Rifles CAP Website - www.capmarine.comgazette/fastrfls.htm
Film and Films:
 www.sru.edu/depts/artsci/engl/dpitard/vietnamfilms.htm
 Filmography/TV docs, Lib of Congress: gopher://marvel.loc.gov/00/research/reading. rooms/motion.picture/mopic.tv/mpfind/vietnam
 NARA films search engine: www.nara.gov/nara/searchnail.html
Fire Support Base Development, article by Maj. Robert V. Nicoli, September. 1969, posted on the net: http://members.aol.com/warlibrary/vwfsb.htm
Firebase Info/Maps, online:
 199th LIB Red Catcher Assn. II Corps FSB locations: www.redcatcher.org/
 1st/69th Armor QL-19 corridor: www.rjsmith.com/
 Americal AO FSBs: http://greene.xtn.net/~wingman/index.html
 Americal Division Assn: www.americal.org. List of Americal, Marine, 101st Abn and 1st Cav Div FSB I, II and III Corps http://members.aol.com/warlibrary/vwfsb.htm
 Jim Henthorn s Lima Site locations in Laos: www.nexus.net/~911gfx/Laos.html.
 Navy Bases in Vietnam: www.mrfa.org/bases.htm
 War Records site: www.InsideTheWeb.com/mbs.cgi/mb982251
 War-Records: www.war-records.com/War-Records.index.htm
 Vietnam Helicopter Pilots Assn. (VHPA): www3.servtech.com/vhpa/
 www.americal.org/174/maps.htm
 1st/14th Infantry Rgt: http://1-14th.com/index.html and http://1-14th.com/maps.html
Fleet Reserve Assn: www.va.gov/vso/fra.htm
French Experience in Indochina:
 Edwin E. Moïse's bibliography of 1st Indochina War: http://hubcap.clemson.edu/~eemoise/bibliography.html.
 Edwin E. Moïse's bibliography, French involvement: http://hubcap.clemson.edu/~eemoise/firstwar.htm.
 War Archive Info: www.sedet.cicrp.jussieu.fr/sedet/Afrilab/orgdoc.htm
 Dien Bien Phu: www.dienbienphu.org/english/index.htm
 Historical records of Vietnam Experience at: www.sedet.cicrp.jussieu.fr/sedet/Afrilab/orgdoc.htm
Gazetteers:
 Geographical place names (NIMA): www.nima.mil/geospatial/geospatial.html
 Geographical place names: http://gnpswww.nima.mil/geonames/GNS/
Glossary of Slang: www.vietvet.org/glossary.htm
Government Forms: www.va.gov/forms/index.htm
Government Printing Office (GPO):
 Ordering info/catalogs available: https://orders.access.gpo.gov/su_docs/sale/prf/prf.html
 Publications generally, ordering information: https://orders.access.gpo.gov/su_docs/sale/prf/prf.html
 Publications, search/order: https://orders.access.gpo.gov/su_docs/sale/prf/prf.html
GPO: see Government Printing office
Helicopter, History of in Vietnam War on CD-ROM: see Vietnam Helicopter History
Herbicide usage and effect (Operation Ranch Hand): http://dns.advnet.net/gdmoore/ao_info1.htm, and
 http://dns.advnet.net/gdmoore/ao_info1.htm#Webs, and http://njaoc.org/
Historical Records and Documents:
 Americal Division (large resource): http://rattlers.org/history/toc.htm
 Archival Research, commercial, Pike Military Research (a.k.a. Archival Research International, Inc.), Military Histories, Maps and Photographs: www.militaryunits.com. E-mail: milhist@erols.com
 Electronic files: www.nara.gov/nara/electronic/def.html#dia
 Electronic, NARA CER: www.nara.gov/nara/electronic/types.html
 Government Printing Office: https://orders.access.gpo.gov/su_docs/sale/prf/prf.html
 LBJ Library Vietnam Resources: www.lbjlib.utexas.edu/shwv/
 Library of Congress Search: http://lcweb.loc.gov/catalog/
 Mobile Riverine Force: www.mrfa.org/mrfrepts.htm
 NARA CER electronic files: www.nara.gov/nara/electronic/def.html#dia
 Nixon Project: http://metalab.unc.edu/lia/president/nixon.html
 Presidential Libraries: http://scribers.midwest.net/nixon/sites.htm
 Presidential Libraries: www.pipeline.com/~weberr/EdSites/Library.html
 Vassar College: http://students. vassar.edu/~vietnam/index.html
 VHPA Battle Index: www.vhpa.org/info/panel/battle/ (large chronological resource)
 Vietnam Veteran Database (2.7 million names): www.militaryUSA.com
 Vietnam Veterans Home Page: www.vietvet.org/index.htm
 www.nara.gov/regional/stlouis.html
 www.va.gov/forms/index.htm
 www.vietvet.org/infoindx.htm
 www.vietvet.org/records.htm

History Department, U.S. Military Academy, Selected Vietnam Battle Sites: www.dean.usma.edu/history/ap_bac/apbachome.htm
History Department, U.S. Military Academy: www.dean.usma. edu/history/home.html
History of the Vietnam War:

25 Years After (*AP*): http://wire.ap.org/APpackages/vietnam/index.html
25 Years After the War (*LA Times*): www.latimes.com/news/nation/reports/vietnam
25 Years After, DOD site: www.defenselink.mil/specials/vietnamtrip
25 Years After, Echoes of War (*CNN*): www.CNN.COM/SPECIALS/2000/vietnam
25 Years After: http://salon.com/news/special/vietnam/index.html
25 Years After: www.vietnam25.org/index-ie-f.html
Archives, Univ of Texas Vietnam Archives: www.lbjlib.utexas.edu/shwv/
Battles, VHPA Battle Index: www.vhpa.org/info/panel/battle/ (large chronological resource)
Film, Drama and historical: www.sru.edu/depts/artsci/engl/dpitard/vietnamfilms.htm
Film, Tet 68 Remembered: http://woub.org/wanderingsouls
French War: www.sedet.cicrp.jussieu.fr/sedet/Afrilab/orgdoc.htm
General, Assoc Colleges of the South**:** www2.centenary.edu/vietnam
General, Australian Navy in Vietnam: www.navy.gov.au/4_history/vietnam.htm
General, De Anza College: http://saturn.fhda.edu/instructor/swensson/ewrt2vn.html
General, DOD Alumni Search Form: www.army.mil/vetinfo/
General, Helicopters in Vietnam: see Vietnam Helicopter History
General, Herbicide usage and effect: see Herbicide
General, LBJ Library Vietnam Resources: www.lbjlib.utexas.edu/shwv/
General, NARA Films, Document And Photograph Search Engine: www.nara.gov/nara/searchnail.html
General, Naval Historical Center: www.history.navy.mil
General, U.S. Army FAQ s: www.dtic.mil/armylink/faq/#01.htm
General, U.S. Army Military History Institute: http://carlisle-www.army.mil/usamhi/
General, U.S. Army: www.army.mil/cmh-pg/
General, U.S. Coast Guard in Vietnam: www.uscg.mil/hq/g-cp/history/h_tulichvietnam.html
General, U.S. Navy vessels and units: see Navy Vessels
General: http://icarus.shu.edu/gallery/V_Portfolio
General: http://web20.mindlink.net/vets
General: www.lbjlib.utexas.edu/shwv/shwvhome.html
General: www.oakton.edu/~wittman
General: www.shss.montclair.edu/english/furr/vietnam.html#TOC
General: www.vietnamwar.net
General: www.vietvet.org/infoindx.htm
General: www.vwam.com/vets/hisintro.html
General: www1.shore.net/~vietnam
John Birch Society perspective**:** www.jbs.org/vietnam/index.htm
Library of Congress**:** http://lcweb2.loc.gov/frd/cs/vntoc.html
Oral History & Folklore Project**:** www. buffalostate.edu/~fishlm/folksongs
Oral History Project, U of Ca**:** http://globetrotter.berkeley.edu/conversations
Oral, Interviews with McNamara, Ellsberg, Oliver Stone, Harry G. Summers, etc: http://globetrotter.berkeley.edu/PubEd/research/vietnam.html
Oral, www.csn.net/~nulevich/vietnam.html
Oral, PBS: www.pbs.org/pov/stories/vietnam/
PBS Links: www.pbs.org/pov/stories/vietnam/links.html
Phu Cat Airbase**:** www.fgi.net/~rdoughty/phuhist.htm, Doughty, J, author
Quotes, Timelines and Analysis**:** www.historyplace.com/unitedstates/vietnam
Sound Recordings, Vietnam War Sounds: www.manchu.org/sounds/
TV (PBS): www.pbs.org/newshour/bb/asia/vietnam/index.html
TV, Vietnam: A Television History: www.pbs.org/wgbh/pages/amex/vietnam/index.html
USMA Dept of History: www.dean.usma.edu/history/dhistorymaps/Vietnam%20Pages/VietnamToC.htm
Vietnam Veteran Database (2.7 million names of VN vets): www.militaryUSA.com

Hmong: www.stolaf.edu/people/cdr/hmong
Ia Drang Battle: www.lzxray.com/index.htm
Jim Henthorn, 1:250,000 scale Maps of Indochina: www.nexus. net/~911gfx/SVNmap.html (Massive and invaluable collection of 1:250,000 scale L-1501 JOG maps. Very important resource)
Kent State: www.emerson.edu/acadepts/cs/comm/may4.html
Khe Sanh Battle, Historical Documents: http://members. easyspace.com/airdrop/
Khe Sanh Veterans Assn: www.geocities.com/~khesanh/
Khmer Experience: http://allithai.mekong.net/cambodia
L-1501 Maps: www.nexus.net/~911gfx/SVNmap.html
L-509 Maps: www.loc.gov/rr/geogmap/gmpage.html (Geography and Maps Division)
L-7014 DMA map series Index Map, high quality image of the original can be seen: www.rjsmith.com/images/kelley/Index-L7014s.jpg
LBJ Library Vietnam Resources FAQ Links: www.lbjlib.utexas. edu/shwv/link-faq.html

Library of Congress:
Maps: www.loc.gov/rr/geogmap/gmpage.html (Geog & Maps Div)
Search document & photo holdings of: http://lcweb.loc.gov/catalog
Research Services: http://lcweb.loc.gov/rr/
Lyndon Johnson Presidential Library, Vietnam Resources: www.lbjlib.utexas.edu/shwv/
LZ Russel: www.swnm.com/dol/lzrussell/
LZ Sally: www.lzsally.com/
M-16, History of: http://jdumong.net/delta/m-16Part1.htm
Manchu Assoc (9th Inf Div): www.manchu.org/
Maps of Indochina and Vietnam, Online:
1:50,000 scale map of Hanoi: www.lib.berkeley.edu/EART/digital/topo.html
1:50,000 scale maps of Quang Tri Province: www.georgeneville.com/maps.htm
1:50,000 scale maps of QL-19 Corridor, II Corps: http://rjssmith.com
1:250,000 scale L-1501 JOG maps: www.nexus. net/~911gfx/SVNmap.html.
199th LIB Red Catcher Assn. DMA JOG s: www.redcatcher.org/AO.html
199th LIB Red Catcher Assn. L-7014 1:50,000 scale maps: www.redcatcher.org/AO50.html
199th LIB Red Catcher Assn. maps: www.redcatcher.org/
1st/69th Armor Collection. High-quality images of QL-19 II Corps area and firebases and strongpoints between Kontum and Qui Nhon here along with descriptive text. Remarkable site by any measure: http://rjssmith.com
Americal AO maps in varying scales: http://greene.xtn.net/~wingman/index.html
Ban Do Viet Nam ancient and recent maps files: 07 http://quebec.eds-ingevision.fr/bando/bando.htm
Cambodia, L-1501: www.nexus.net/~911gfx/Cambodia.html
Commercial vendors: www.itmb.com/Catalog.htm
Commercial vendors: www.omnimap.com/catalog/int/vietnam.htm
Commercial vendors: www.omnimap.com/cgi-bin/omni/graphic.pl?images/ind-for/tpc-afr.gif
DMA, Defense Mapping Agency, see NIMA
Firebases: see Firebase Info/Maps, online
Gazetteer of geographical place names (NIMA): www.nima.mil/geospatial/geospatial.html
Gazetteer of geographical place names: http://gnpswww.nima.mil/geonames/GNS/
Grunt Space: http://grunt.space.swri.edu/visit/maps/maps.htm
http://grunt.space.swri.edu/visit.htm
http://home.vnd.net/english/map/
http://quebec.eds-ingevision.fr/bando/bando.htm
www.georgeneville.com/maps.htm
Jim Hentorne: 1:250,000 scale L-1501 JOG Indochina maps: www.nexus.net/~911gfx/SVNmap.html. Important resource
L-509 JOG maps: See L-1501
L-1501 DMA JOG maps for I, II, III and IV Corps: www.nexus.net/~911gfx/ICorps.html; www.nexus.net/~911gfx/IICorps.html; www.nexus.net/~911gfx/IIICorps.html; and www.nexus.net/~911gfx/IVCorps.html (respectively)
L-1501 JOG maps of Indochina: www.nexus. net/~911gfx/SVNmap.html. Important resource
L-7014 DMA map series Index Map, high quality image original: www.rjsmith.com/images/kelley/Index-L7014s.jpg
Laos, L-1501: www.nexus.net/~911gfx/Laos.html
Library of Congress Search http://lcweb.loc.gov/catalog/
Mekong Delta/SEALORDS Operational area: www.history.navy.mil/seairland/ch165big.gif
MRF Assn: www.mrfa.org
National Imagery and Mapping Agency (NIMA), Catalog of Public Sale Topographic Maps, Publications, and Digital Products (: http://mac.usgs.gov/mac/nimamaps/index.html)
NIMA (formerly the DMA) Public Sale Topographic Maps, Tecchnical Publications, and Digital Products Catalog: http://mapping.usgs.gov/mac/nimamaps/index.html
NIMA aeronautical charts price list: http://acc.nos.noaa.gov:80/PriceLists/PricesNIMAAero.html
NIMA List of agents selling ONC s and TPC s: http://acc.nos.noaa.gov:80/Aero/AeroAgents.html
NIMA ONC & TPC price list: http://acc. nos.noaa.gov:80/PriceLists/PricesNIMAAero.html#MiscDOD
NIMA TPC s and ONCs, order: http://acc.nos.noaa.gov:80/orderCharts.htm
NIMA, ARC Digitized Raster Graphics (ADRG); TPC, ONC, GNC and JNC aeronautical charts on CD-ROM. Documentation: http://164.214.2.59/publications/specs/printed/89007/89007_ADRG.pdf
NIMA, National Imagery Mapping Agency (formerly DMA) Home Page: www.nima.mil
NOAA/NIMA Aeronautical and Nautical Charts/Publications: www.noaa.gov/
NOAA/NOS Catalog of World Aeronautical Charts, 1,000,000 scale: http://acc.nos.noaa.gov/Catalog/WAC.html
NOAA/NOS Map Search Engine: http://search.nos.noaa.gov/compass
North Vietnam, L-1501: www.nexus.net/~911gfx/NVNmap.html
NOS/NIMA Aeronautical and Nautical Charts/Publications: www.nos.noaa.gov/
NVN Coast/Capes Map: www.history.navy.mil/seairland/ch44big.gif
ONC & TPC international chart indexes: www.omnimap.com/catalog/int/topo.htm#p1
Quang Tri Province key towns and points, 1:50k: www.georgeneville.com/maps.htm
Satellite and aerial maps/photos (many of which are available for purchase): http://mapping.usgs.gov/
satellite Images: http://coombs.anu.edu.au/~vern/space/space2.html
Thailand, L-1501: www.nexus.net/~911gfx/Thailand.html

TPC chart index: www.omnimap.com/cgi-bin/omni/graphic.pl?images/ind-for/tpc-afr.gif
USGS e-mail inquiries: ask@usgs.gov
USGS Official Home Page: www.USGS.gov/
USGS order form: http://mapping.usgs.gov/esic/order_forms/map_order.html
USGS ordering info: http://mapping.usgs.gov/esic/to_order.html#map
USGS s NIMA Catalog of Public Sale Topographic Maps For Vietnam (et al): http://mac.usgs.gov/mac/nimamaps/topo.html and/or http://mac.usgs.gov/mac/nimamaps/topo.html#Vietnam
USGS Status Graphics; current availability of selected USGS Digital Cartographic Data/Aerial Photo products site: http://mapping.usgs.gov/www/products/status.html.
Vets with a Mission: www.vwam.com/vets/nprojects.html
Vets with a Mission: www.vwam.com/vets/nprojects.html
Vietnam Veterans Home Page: www.vietvet.org/
www.ehistory.com/vietnam/maps/index.cfm
www.informatik.uni-leipzig.de/~duc/ban_do/maps.html
www.loc.gov/rr/geogmap/gmpage.html (Geography and Map Div, Library of Congress)
www.multimap.com/index/VM1.htm
www.rjsmith.com/topo_map.html
www.vietvet.org/maps.htm
Yankee and Dixie Station: www.history.navy.mil/seairland/ch67big.gif
Zoomable map of SVN: http://staff. feldberg.brandeis.edu/~minh_le/vsa/vn_map_zoom.html

Marine Corps Assns: www.vets.com/inside/alumni.htm (large database, all branches)
Marine Corps League: www.pos.net/Marine
Marines: See also USMC and U.S. Marines
Merchant Marines: http://marad.dot.gov/support_forces.html
MIA, Library of Congress POW/MIA database**:** http://lcweb2.loc.gov/pow/powhome.html
Military Assns., DOD Alumni Search Form: www.army. mil/vetinfo/
Military Aviation Links: www.landings.com/_landings/pages/military.html
Military Chaplains Assn: www.mvpsoa.org/military_chaplains.html
Military History Institute: http://carlisle-www.army.mil/usamhi/
Military Intelligence Corps Assn: www.primenet.com/~usamica
Military Order of the Purple Heart: http://washington.xtn.net/~grunt/moph
Military Police Home Page: www.primenet.com/~burchel/milpol.html
Military Police Organizations and units: www.pima.edu/dps/Mil.htm
Military Records:
Army/Air Force: www.nara.gov/regional/stlouis.htm
Naval Historical Center: www.history.navy.mil
Search Engines: www.free-people-search-engines.com/mil.htm
U.S. Navy Historical Research and Ships Histories: www.history.navy.mil
U.S. Navy Records: www.chinfo.navy.mil/navpalib/questions/awards.html
USCG official: www.uscg.mil/dotinfo/uscg/welcome.html:
USMC Records: www.chinfo.navy.mil/navpalib/questions/awards.html

Military Search Engines: www.free-people-search-engines.com/mil.htm
Military Unit Asssociations: See Association name
Military Unit Associations: www.vets.com/inside/alumni.htm (large database, all branches)
Mobile Riverine Force Assn: www.mrfa.org/
Mobile Riverine Force, Historical records: www.mrfa.org/mrfrepts.htm
Mohawks, OV-1 Assn: www.ov-1.com
Moise s Bibliographies of Vietnam War History: http://hubcap.clemson.edu/~eemoise/bibliography.html
Monkey Mountain: http://members.dynasty.net/lauray/Aerial_Vietnam/msp00125.htm, and www.geocities.com/CapeCanaveral/Runway/4426/index33.html
MRF: www.mrfa.org/
Museums: http://members.aol.com/mraffin/vnmuseum.htm
Music, etc, Country Joe: www.dnai.com/~borneo/index.html#who
My Lai Massacre:
Comprehensive overview: www.law.umkc.edu/faculty/projects/ftrials/mylai/mylai.htm
www.asiapac.org.fj/cafepacific/resources/aspac/viet.html
www.derechos.org/mlcc
www.pathfinder.com/photo/essay/mylai/mylaihp.htm

NARA: See National Archives
National Alliance of Families for the Return of America s Missing Servicemen: http://pages.prodigy.com/ALLIANCE/naf1.htm
National Archives and Records Administration (NARA)
Home Page: www.nara.gov/
Center for Electronic records: www.nara.gov/nara/electronic/types.html
Electronic Records Collection: www.nara.gov/nara/electronic/def.html#dia
Military film, photo and textual files search engine: www.nara.gov/nara/searchnail.html
Military Films, Document And Photograph Search Engine: www.nara.gov/nara/searchnail.html

Search engine: www.nara.gov/nara/searchnail.html
National Guard Assn: www.ngaus.org
National Personnel Records Center (NPRC): www.nara.gov/regional/stlouis.html
Native American Vietnam Veterans: www.corpcomm.net/~redeye/vietnamVets.html
Naval Assn. of Australia: www.navalassoc.org.au/
Naval Historical Center: www.history.navy.mil
Naval Reserve Assn: www.cais.com/nra/
Naval Vessel Registry: www.nvr.navy.mil/nvrships/
Naval Vessel Registry: www.nvr.navy.mil/nvrships/
Naval Vessels of Australian Navy serving in Vietnam: www.navy.gov.au/4_history/vietnam.htm
Navy Associations: http://members.aol.com/kwjaccard/associations.htm
Navy Bases in Vietnam: www.mrfa.org/bases.htm
Navy Enlisted Reserve Assn: www2.thefuture.net/~users/wjpelka
Navy Historical Center: www.history.navy.mil/
Navy League of the U.S.: www.navyleague.org/index.htm
Navy Unit Assns: www.vets.com/inside/alumni.htm (large database, all branches)
Navy Vessels and Navy Units in Vietnam:
www.hazegray.org/danfs/ (Dictionary of American Fighting Ships)
www.mrfa.org/ (Mobile Riverine Force Assn)
www.vietnamunitmemorialmon.org/(Ralph Fries' remarkable resources)
www.vietnamunitmemorialmon.org/naval_ships_commads_at_sea.htm,
www.vietnamunitmemorialmon.org/usn_uscg_units.htm
Navy: See U.S. Navy
NCO Assn: www.kols.com/ncoa.htm
NCOC Assn. (Non-Commissioned Officer Candidates), Budd Russell: http://w3.ime.net/~ncocloca/MCOC-1~1.htm
E-mail: ncocloca@ime.net
New Zealand:
RNZIR, V Co,: http://ourworld.compuserve.com/homepages/rhimona/vietnam/indexv.htm
Vietnam Veterans Organization Links: http://grunt.space.swri.edu/nzorgs.htm
Vietnam Veterans: www.vietvet.org/nzorgs.htm
NIMA, National Imagery Mapping Agency (formerly DMA) Home Page: www.nima.mil
Nixon Project: http://metalab.unc.edu/lia/president/nixon.html
NOAA Home Page: www.noaa.gov/
Non Commissioned Officers Assn: www.kols.com/ncoa.htm
NOS Home Page: www.nos.noaa.gov/
NPRC: www.nara.gov/regional/stlouis.html
Office of Army Medical History: www.armymedicine. army.mil/history/
Oral History:
Interviews with McNamara, Ellsberg, Oliver Stone, Harry G. Summers, etc:
http://globetrotter.berkeley.edu/PubEd/research/vietnam.html
Oral History & Folklore Project: www.buffalostate.edu/~fishlm/folksongs
Oral History Project, U of Ca: http://globetrotter.berkeley.edu/conversations
Tales of a War Far Away, Ramsey, Kirk, (on-line memoir, 2d/14th Inf, 25th Inf): www.en.com/users/kramsey/default.html. (Illustrated)
www.csn.net/~nulevich/vietnam.html
www.mindspan.com/vets/hisintro.html
Ordnance Field Park: http://web.logicworld.com.au/~4seasons/index/index.htm
OV-1 Mohawks Assn: www.ov-1.com
PBR Forces Veterans Assn. (PBRFVA): www.pbr-fva.org/ (Patrol Boat, River Assn., Navy River Detachments)
Personnel, Vietnam Veteran Database (2.7 million names of VN vets): www.militaryUSA.com
Perth, HMAS: www.hmasperth.asn.au
Pete Peterson, 1st postwar ambassador to VN: www.pbs.org/hanoi
Photo journal, USMC: www.woodlot.com/vietnam/start.html
Photo journal: www.ionet.net/~uheller/vnbktoc.html
Photo Journalism (Tim Page): http://dspace.dial.pipex.com/leuhusen/nam/index.shtml
Photographs:
NARA photograph archive search engine: www.nara.gov/nara/searchnail.html
See also National Archives, U.S. Army Center for Mil Hist, U.S. Army Mil Hist Inst, as well as historical divs for each branch.
www.mindspan.com/vets/photos.html
Phu Cat Airbase: History www.fgi.net/~rdoughty/phuhist.htm, Doughty, J, author
POW (film): www.pbs.org/wgbh/amex/honor
POW/MIA:
Library of Congress POW/MIA database: http://lcweb2.loc.gov/pow/powhome.html
National Alliance of Families for the Return of America s Missing Servicemen: http://pages.prodigy.com/ALLIANCE/naf1.htm
Operation Homecoming**:** http://seamonkey.ed.asu.edu/~holmlund/index.html
Presidential Libraries:
http://scribers.midwest.net/nixon/sites.htm

www.pipeline.com/~weberr/EdSites/Library.html
Presidential Service Assn: http://users.aol.com/presserv/text/psa.html
Propaganda from NVN Project (U of WI): www.library.wisc. edu/guides/SEAsia/vnimage/
Quotes, Timelines and Analysis**:** www.historyplace com/unitedstates/vietnam
RAAF-Phan Rang (David Foote): www.is-1.net.au/~dfoote/vietstuf.html
Ranch Hand Herbicide usage and effects: see Herbicide
Ranger Assns: www.ranger.org/~ranger/index.html
RAR Assn., Queensland Division: www.rar.org.au
RAR Assn: www.rarfoundation.org.au/
Recordings of Vietnam War Sounds: www.manchu.org/sounds/
Red Catchers, 199th LIB: www.redcatcher.org/
Red River Valley Fighter pilots Assn: www.eos.net/rrva/
Research Services, Library of Congress: http://lcweb.loc.gov/rr/
Reserve Officers Assn. of the U.S.: www.afi.org/roa.htm
Retired Officers Assn: www.troa.org
RNZIR, V Co,: http://ourworld.compuserve.com/homepages/rhimona/vietnam/indexv.htm
Royal Australian Air Force, 9 Sqdn RAAF (Peter Robinson): www.iinet.net.au/~rob7299/
Royal Australian Air Force, Phan Rang (David Foote): www.is-1.net.au/~dfoote/vietstuf.html
Royal Australian Army Service Corps: www.raasc.org.au/
Royal Australian Engineers Association., WA Branch: www. auswebtech.com.au/rae.htm
Royal Australian Navy Net (Bob Yorke): www.powerup.com.au/theyorks/rannet.html
Royal Australian Rgt Assn., Queensland Div: www.rar.org.au
Royal Australian Rgt Assn: www.rarfoundation.org.au/
Royal Australian Rgt Foundation: www.rarfoundation.org.au
Royal Canadian Legion: www.westvikingc.nf.ca/legion1.htm
Royal New Zealand Inf Rgt, V Co,: http://ourworld.compuserve.com/homepages/rhimona/vietnam/indexv.htm
Search Engines, Military: www.free-people-search-engines.com/mil.htm
Ships/Naval Vessels:
 Australian Navy serving in Vietnam: www.navy.gov. au/4_history/vietnam.htm
 Dictionary of American Fighting Ships: www.hazegray.org/danfs/
 Reunion List: www.me.pdx.edu/~jgriffin
 Ships Serving in the Vietnam CTZ: see Navy Vessels
 Surface Navy Assn: www.cais.com
 U.S. Naval Vessel Registry: www.nvr.navy.mil/nvrships/
Sixties Project, Vietnam Generation: http://jefferson.village.virginia.edu/sixties
Social History, War, Vietnam, LBJ Library Vietnam Resources: www.lbjlib.utexas.edu/shwv/
Society for Military History: www.smh-hq.org/**:** www.uscmh.org
Sound Recordings of Vietnam War/Combat: www.manchu.org/sounds/
Special Forces Histories: www.greenberet.net/books
Special Services Assn: www.riverwolf.net/reflections/vietnam/
Study guides:
 VVMF, Inc, educational site**:** www.teachvietnam.org
 www.refstar.com/vietnam/index.html
 www.refstar.com/vietnam/online_study.html
Surface Navy Assn: www.cais.com
***Tales of a War Far Away*,** Ramsey, Kirk, (on-line memoir, 2d/14th Inf, 25th Inf): www.en.com/users/kramsey/default.html. Illustrated
Tet 68 Remembered (film): http://woub.org/wanderingsouls
The Institute of Heraldry: www-perscom.army.mil/tagd/tioh/tioh.htm
Timelines, Quotes, and Analysis: www.historyplace.com/unitedstates/vietnam
Unit Associations,
 DOD Alumni Search Form: www.army.mil/vetinfo/
 Substantial listing of unit reunions/associations at: www.vfw.org/
 Substantial listing of unit reunions/associations at: www.militaryusa.com/
 www.vets.com/inside/alumni.htm (large database, all branches)
University of Texas Vietnam Archives: www.lbjlib.utexas. edu/shwv/
U.S. Air Force
 Unit Assns: www.vets.com/inside/alumni.htm (large database, all branches)
 Aircraft of the Vietnam War: www.petester.com/html/vnraircraft.html
U.S. Army Center for Military History: www.army.mil/cmh-pg
U.S. Army:
 ASA Veterans: http://members.gnn.com/asavets/asa.htm
 Center for Military History: www.army.mil/cmh-pg
 FAQ s: www.dtic.mil/armylink/faq/#01.htm
 Historical Info: www.army.mil/cmh-pg/
 Institute of Heraldry: www-perscom.army.mil/tagd/tioh/tioh.htm
 Military History Institute: http://carlisle-www.army.mil/usamhi/

Quartermaster History Page: www.lee.army.mil/quartermaster/history/index.html
Quartermaster: www.lee.army.mil/quartermaster/history/index.html
Ranger Assns: www.ranger.org/~ranger/index.html
Special Services Assn: www.riverwolf.net/reflections/vietnam/
Unit Assns: www.vets.com/inside/alumni.htm (large database, all branches)
U.S. Army Military History Institute, Contacting the: http://carlisle-www.army.mil/usamhi/ContactMHI.html
Administrative requests E-mail: AWCC-DMH@awc.carlisle.army.mil
Historical inquiries E-mail: MHI-HR@awc.carlisle.army.mil
Inquiries re: archival collections E-mail: MHI-AR@awc.carlisle.army.mil
Inquiries re: photographs or artifacts E-mail: MHI-SC@awc.carlisle.army.mil
Warrant Officers Assn: www.genstar.net/mil-link/localorg/awoa/awoa.htm

U.S. Coast Guard:
History: www.uscg.mil/hq/g-cp/history/collect.html
Official Home Page: www.uscg.mil/dotinfo/uscg/welcome.html:
Unit Assns: www.vets.com/inside/alumni.htm (large database, all branches)
Vietnam History: www.uscg.mil/hq/g-cp/history/h_tulichvietnam.html
www.uscg.mil

U.S. Department of Veterans Affairs: www.va.gov/
U.S. Government Forms: www.va.gov/forms/index.htm
U.S. Government Printing Office (GPO) ordering info and catalogs available: https://orders.access.gpo.gov/su_docs/sale/prf/prf.html

U.S. Marine Corps:
Associations: http://grunt.space.swri.edu/marine.htm
Associations: www.vets.com/inside/alumni.htm (large database, all branches)
Associations: www.vets.com/inside/alumni.htm (large database, all branches)
CAP units: see CAP
Historical Center: www.usmc.mil/historical.nsf/table+of+contents
Official Home Page: www.usmc.mil/
Records: www.chinfo.navy.mil/navpalib/questions/awards.html

U.S. Maritime Administration, America s Merchant Marine: http://marad.dot.gov/support_forces.html
U.S. Naval Cryptologic Veterans Assn: http://userwww. qnet.com/~kolbod/ncva/ncvahome.html
U.S. Naval Fire Support Assn: www.usnfsa.com
U.S. Naval Submarine Force: www.subnet.com
U.S. Naval Vessel Registry: www.nvr.navy.mil/nvrships/
U.S. Naval Vessel Registry: www.nvr.navy.mil/nvrships/

U.S. Navy:
Associations: http://members.aol.com/kwjaccard/associations.htm
Bases in Vietnam: www.mrfa.org/bases.htm
By Sea, Air, and Land, online history of the U.S. Navy in Vietnam: www.history.navy.mil/seairland/
Historical Center Index: www.history.navy.mil/index.html
Historical Center: www.history.navy.mil
Historical Research and Ships Histories: www.history.navy.mil
Naval Historical Center: www.history.navy.mil/
Official Home page: www.navy.mil
Records: www.chinfo.navy.mil/navpalib/questions/awards.html
SEALS: http://The-South.Com/TheTeams
Ships Reunion List: www.me.pdx.edu/~jgriffin
Ships, Vessel Registry: www.nvr.navy.mil/nvrships/
Unit Assns: www.vets.com/inside/alumni.htm (large database, all branches)
Vessles and Units in VN. Lists of, see Navy Vessels

USCG: see U.S. Coast Guard
USGS (U.S. Gelogical Survey) Home Page: www.USGS.gov/
USMC: see U.S. Marine Corps
***USS Constitution's* Vietnam Visit**: www.state.ma.us/veterans/ancientmarin
VA (Veterans Administration or USDVA) Home Page: www.va.gov/
Veteran Database (2.7 million names of VN vets): www.militaryUSA.com

Veteran Locators:
http://grunt.space.swri.edu/locators.htm
www.militaryusa.com
www.vfw.org/magazine
www.vva.org

Veterans Administration: www.va.gov/
Veterans Home Page: www.vietvet.org
Veterans of Foreign Wars: www.vfw.org
Veterans of the Vietnam War, Inc: www.vvnw.org/vvnw
Vets With A Mission: www.vwam.com. (Tremendous resource of Vietnam War history stored here)
VFW: www.vfw.org

VHPA Battle Index: www.vhpa.org/info/panel/battle/
Victorian Vietnam Veterans: http://home.pacific.net.au/~vicsec/
Vietnam Dog Handlers Assn: www.vdhaonline.org
Vietnam Experience, WGBH Boston PBS: www.pbs.org/wgbh/pages/amex/vietnam/101ts.html
Vietnam Helicopter Crew Members Assn: Homepage at www.vhcm.org/. See also http://tarnhelm.blu.org/vhcma/; www.blu.org/vhcma/
Vietnam Helicopter History, by Gary Roush, Mike Law, Mike Sloniker, et al. Very comprehensive resource available for purchase on CD-ROM. Call 1-800-505-VHPA, or use order form at www.vhpa.org/products_form.html
Vietnam Helicopter Pilots Assn: www.vhpa.org/
Vietnam Magazine: www.thehistorynet.com/Vietnam
Vietnam Military Lore: www.namlore.com/ (Ray Bows)
Vietnam Ministry of Foreign Affairs: www.mofa.gov.vn/english/index.html
Vietnam News Agency: www.vietnamnews.vnagency.com or http://vietnamnews.vnagency.com
Vietnam Security Police Assn: www.vspa.com/
Vietnam Studies, U.S. Army Special Forces 1961-1971, available in its entirety at www.army.mil/cmh-pg/books/vietnam/90-23/90-23c.htm)
Vietnam Veteran Database (2.7 million names of VN vets): www.militaryUSA.com
Vietnam Veterans Against the War: www.prairienet.org/vvaw
Vietnam Veterans Foundation of Texas: http://grunt.space.swri.edu/vvft.htm
Vietnam Veterans Home Page: www.vietvet.org/index.htm Massive resources & many links available here.
Vietnam Veterans In Canada: www.vvic.org/
Vietnam Veterans Memorial Fund: www.vvmf.org/index.html
Vietnam Veterans of America: www.vva.org
Vietnam Veterans of Australia: www.vvaa.org.au/
Vietnam Veterans Oral History and Folklore Project: www.buffalostate.edu/~fishlm/folksongs/index.htm
Vietnam Veterans War Memorial: http://thewall-usa.com
Vietnam War Bibliography, Edwin E. Moïse: http://hubcap. clemson.edu/~eemoise/bibliography.html
Vietnam War on Film: www.sru.edu/depts/artsci/engl/dpitard/vietnamfilms.htm
Vietnam War Memorial, National Park Service: www.nps. gov/vive/index2.htm
Vietnam War Resource Links: LBJ Library: www.lbjlib. utexas.edu/shwv/link-faq.html
www.vietvet.org/resour.htm
Vietnam War Stories: www.war-stories.com/
Women in Military Service for America: www. womensmemorial.org/
Women in Vietnam War:
Bibliography: http://servercc. oakton.edu/~wittman/women.htm
http://grunt.space.swri.edu:80/women.htm
http://tlc.discovery.com/tlcpages/vietnam/vietnam.html
Nurses, Bibliography: www.illyria.com/nursebib.html
Nurses: www.mbc.edu/academic/disciplines/econ/net/morris/Angels.html
Women In-Country: http://grunt.space.swri.edu:80/women.htm
Women Marines Assn: www.inc.com/users/wma1.html
Women Veterans: www.spencergroup.net/vwv
www.illyria.com/vnwomen.html
Women In-Country: http://grunt.space.swri.edu:80/women.htm
Women Marines Association: www.inc.com/users/wma1.html
Women Nurses in Vietnam, Bibliography: www.illyria.com/nursebib.html
Women Nurses in Vietnam: www.mbc.edu/academic/disciplines/econ/net/morris/Angels.html
Women Veterans of VN: www.spencergroup.net/vwv

Appendix F
Glossary, Abbreviations, Acronyms and Minutiae

1ATF - 1st Australian Task Force.
1st Indochina War - For purposes of this text, the French War with the Vietminh, 1946-1954.
2d Indochina War - For purposes of this text, the SVN and American War with the Viet Cong/NLF and NVA, 1965-75.
3 Bees, The - See Three Bees.
3d Vietnam - See Third Vietnam.
4-H Division - Nickname for U.S. 4th Infantry Div, as were "Famous Fighting 4th," and "Funny 4th."
4 Noes - See Four Noes.
4.2" Mortar - A.k.a. 107mm and Four-Deuce mortar. See also M-30 Mortar.
8" SP Howitzer - Self-propelled, track-mounted 8" cannon. Same M-107 chassis could mount the less accurate, but longer range, 175mm cannon barrel, and barrels quickly alternated as need arose.
9 RAR Handshake - New Zealand Forces (Kiwi) nickname for fragging. Apparently, the 1st ANZAC fragging incident involved officer of 9th RAR murdered with a grenade.
17th Parallel - See main alpha listing.
20 Mike-Mike - See Twenty Mike-Mike.
20mm - See Twenty Mike-Mike.
22 Step Snake - See Twenty-Two Step Snake.
40mm Grenade Launcher - See M-79 Grenade Launcher, XM-174 Auto Grenade Launcher, M 203, XM-143, and Hand-Cranked Grenade launcher.
40 Mike-Mike - Twin 40mm, auto-loading, WWII naval AA gun mount fitted to tank chassis and used both defensively and offensively. Typically mounted in M-42 Duster, a tracked, armored vehicle. Very eff and well-liked weapon. The 40mm, M-79 Grenade Launcher (hand-held, breech-loading weapon that fired an explosive, shotgun or CS gas projectile apx 400 meters), was also sometimes referred to by this name.
40mm - See 40 Mike-Mike.
57mm Recoilless Rifle - NVA/VC crew-served, portable recoilless weapon firing a 57mm rocket-propelled projectile similar to U.S. Bazooka and LAW.
60mm Mortar - See M-19 Mortar and 82mm Mortar.
66mm - See M-72 LAW.
81mm Mortar - See M-29 Mortar.
82mm Mortar - NVA standard mortar, along with 60mm "Knee Mortar." The 82mm bore had advantage of being able to fire U.S. 81mm mortar shells, but 82mm shell could not be fired in U.S. 81mm mortar.
90mm Recoilless Rifle - See M-67 Recoilless Rifle.
105mm Howitzer - See M-101A howitzer and M-102 howitzer.
105s - See M-101A howitzer and M-102 howitzer.
106mm Recoilless Rifle - See M-40A1 Recoilless Rifle.
107mm Rocket - NVA ground-to-ground missile. Weighed 90 lbs, had a 35 lbs warhead and range of 10,000 meters.
122mm Rocket - NVA ground-to-ground missile of Soviet-bloc manufacture that had no internal guidance mechanism Was simply aimed and fired much like an arty piece would be. Warhead and rocket motors were in separate sections of roughly equal weight (apx 95 lbs. each?) for ease of transport, and the 2 sections screwed together at launch site, then fired from relatively crude launcher-aiming mechanism. Very inaccurate (but more accurate than the 140mm) and used more to terrorize than to destroy specific targets. 140mm rocket was apparently larger version of 122. Range of the 122 was 10,100 meters, and that of the 140 some 8,800 meters.
120mm Mortar - NVA's heavy mortar.
130mm Field Gun - The M-46 130mm field gun. NVA arty piece employed widely along the DMZ and Lao border. Later deployed in SVN during '72 Easter Offensive and Final Offensive of '75. Fired a 74-pound shell up to 27,000 meters. Widely considered superior to most U.S. arty pieces.
140mm Rocket - See 122mm Rocket.
152mm Field Gun - NVA 130mm and 152mm arty pieces were employed widely along the DMZ and Lao border. Later deployed in SVN during '72 Easter Offensive and Final Offensive of '75. Many consider the 152 to have been the NVA's best arty piece.
155mm Howitzer - See M-114A1 and M-109 SP howitzer.
165mm Demolition Gun - Short-barreled 165mm cannon mounted on M-48A3 tank Chassis as M-728 Combat Engr Vehicle. This indirect-fire weapon had range of 4,870 meters and presumably used principally to demolish fortifications/clear mines with special munitions. See M-728 Combat Eng Vehicle.
175mm Cannon - See M-107 SP 175mm.
175s - See M-107 SP 175mm.
240mm Rocket - NVA indirect fire rocket that was largest in NVA arsenal. Warhead was much larger that rocket body and resembled oversized RPG. Photo in *A Better War*, at p. 327.
4181 May Bay My - Not a place but the inscription on North Vietnamese Stamp which translates literally as: "4,181 U.S. Planes Shot Down." U.S. DOD records indicate that number was wild exaggeration used for propaganda purposes.
A - Army; (A) or U.S. Army (TAD).
A - One Viet word for "village."
A/D - Aerodrome (TAD).
A/G - air/ground (TAD).
A-1 Skyraider - U.S. single-eng, prop-driven close air ground supt bomber acft with 1,270 mi rnge, 310 kts top spd. mfgd by Douglas Acft. Of WWII/Korean War vintage but did a yeoman's job in VN war. Carried hvy payload and could remain airborne for extended periods. Used extensively in supt of SAR ops.
A-1H Skyraider - Propeller-driven, fixed-wing fighter-bomber of WWII(?) and Korean War Vintage. Used widely in ground supt and SAR rescue roles by both USAF and SVNAF. Noted for its massive load carrying capability, long range, dependability, accuracy and durability. Many considered it far superior to jet acft in every aspect except speed. Were nicknamed "Spads," and their pilot's "Spad Drivers." SAR ops call-sign typically "Sandy."
A-3 Skywarrior - U.S. jet acft with 1,050 mi rnge, 610 kts top spd. mfgd by Douglas Acft.
A-4 Skyhawk - U.S. single-jet eng carrier-based fighter acft with 2,000 mi rnge, 680 kts top spd. mfgd by Douglas Acft.
A-6 Intruder - U.S., twin-jet eng, all-weather fighter-bomber acft with 1,860 mi rnge, 545 kts top spd. mfgd by Grumman Avn.

A-7 Corsair II - U.S. single-jet eng, carrier-based fighter-bomber with 4,000 mi rnge, 700 kts top spd. mfgd by Chance-Vought.
A-22, A-23, A-24 - These alpha-numeric designators were used by MACV HQ to denote various intelligence agents (spies) working in NVA/VC infrastructure, circa '68. See Superspook.
A-26 Invader - U.S. twin-eng, prop-driven acft with 1,400 mi rnge, 350 kts top spd. Of WWII design. mfgd by Douglas Acft.
A-37 Dragonfly - U.S. acft with 4,100 mi rnge, 505 kts top spd. mfgd by Cessna.
A Team - Tactical level and lowest rung of Army SF unit hierarchy. 12-man detachment (inc Capt, 1st Lt XO and 10 highly trained EM/NCO's) under direct cmd of SF B-Team HQ. There were 4 B-Team HQs in SVN, 1 in each CTZ (Corps), and each B-team had 4 or 5 A-Teams under its cmd. Strike Forces were indigenous units put together and advised by A-Teams. In early 60's, commo between A and B Teams was by Morse Code sent encrypted on what was known as "one-time pad," while at tactical level A-teams used voice radio. Indigenous personnel working for an A-team were often called "Strikers." Data per *Tan Phu*, p 31
AA - Anti Aircraft.
AAA - Anti- Aircraft Artillery.
AAF - Army Airfield (TAD).
AAFV - Australian Armed Forces, Vietnam.
AAR - After Action Report.
AB - Airbase (TAD).
AB&T - Alaska Barge and Transport. One of several major civilian contractors, along with Vinell, RMK-BRJ and PA&E, that were involved in building and maintaining U.S. facilities in SVN. AB&T had a significant presence at Cam Ranh Bay.
ABFC - Advanced Base Functional Components system. A complete system developed by USN that inc prefabricated structures, equip and packaging for advanced base const.
Abn - Airborne.
Abnd - Abandoned.
AC - Air Crew or Acft. Also A/C and a/c.
AC- 47 Gunship - A.k.a. "Puff." Gunship version of C-47, twin-eng, prop-driven air transport of WWII vintage used for transport and airdrop throughout SEA. Also had gunship role as "Puff the Magic Dragon."
AC-119 Shadow-Stinger - U.S. C-119 Flying Boxcar converted to an aerial gunship platform employing 20mm Gatling guns and even 105 arty pieces. Had 900 mi rnge, 245 kts top spd. mfgd by Fairchild Acft. See also C-119.
ACAV - Armored Cavalry Assault Vehicle.
ACC - Area Control Center (TAD).
Accelerated Pacification Campaign - The APC. Approved by President Thieu Jul68, and initiated 1Nov68, after NVN bombing halt and SVN govt launched concerted effort to pacify previously VC controlled areas. Goal was to raise security level of 1,000 contested hamlets in 3-month period, but bar was soon raised to 1,330 hamlets, and by Jan69, various ARVN and RF/PF forces had been moved to 1,320 of those. Data per *A Better War*, p 65. SVN.
Accessory Pack, C-Ration - One of these units was found inside most C-Ration meals. Was a small, sealed, foil-coated-plastic bag that contained salt, pepper, coffee, tea, sugar, cocoa, matches, toilet paper, a P-38 can opener, a napkin, a plastic knife, fork and a spoon. See also C-Rations.
Acft - Acft (TAD).
Acoubuoy Sensor - See Muscle Shoals System.
ACTOC - Accelerated Turnover Plan (USN).
ACTOV - Accelerated Turnover to the Vietnamese.
ACTOVLOG - Accelerated Turnover to the Vietnamese, Logistics (USN).
AD - Armored Division.
AD - Destroyer Tender (USN).
ADAMS Huts - Acronym for Advanced Design Aluminum Military Shelter. One type of prefab bldg design used widely in Long Binh area. Developed in Australia, Adams Huts were of all-aluminum construction featuring louvered sections in walls and windows for max ventilation. Easy to erect on concrete slabs but required on-site drilling of many holes in order to assemble.
ADIZ - Air Defense Identification Zone (TAD).
Admin - Administrative or Administration.
ADR - Advisory Route (TAD).
Adrian Messenger, The List of - See Kinh Do Theater in main alpha listing.
Adnl - Additional
Addnl - Additional
ADSID Sensors (n/a)
Air Delivered Seismic Anti-Intrusion Device. Actually a miniature seismometer capable of detecting very minute vibrations. See Muscle Shoals and Igloo White.
Adv - Advisor or Advisory.
Advanced Tactical Bases - Naval Base term. For example, see Solid Anchor, ATSB in main alpha section.
advs - advise, advised (TAD) or advisor.
advsy - advisory (TAD).
AE - Ammunition Ship.
Aeroportes - Guerrilla units armed and led by French commando special forces of GIM, *Groupement Mixtes d'Intervention*. 1st Indochina War.
AF - Air Force; USAF (TAD).
AF - Airfield.
AF - Store Ship.
AFDL - Small Auxiliary Floating Dry-Dock (non-self-propelled).
AFRTS - Armed Forces Radio & Television Service. See AFVN and American Radio Service.
AFS - Combat Store Ship.
AFVN - Armed Forces Vietnam Network (radio). Broadcast throughout SEA. Included 1-hour periods separately devoted to various music formats: Country, Big Band, Polka, Jazz and Rock, although Country and Western may have had edge on air time. Its format was much like that of a U.S. station but all ads pushed public service type announcements. News of war was heavily censored. There was also an AFVN TV station (Channel 11) which broadcast daily from ground facilities and orbiting acft transmitters, but viewing was only available after 2:30 pm and ended with feature movie starting at 10:05 PM. Schedules were listed in *The Army Reporter*. (K-Tel Records produced an audio cassette entitled *Rock Radio Vietnam-1970*, which features AFVN broadcasts and among other ads, an ad for Cu Chi U. May be still be available from K-Tel.) For more info/photos of AFVN facilities in Quang Tri, go to: www.geocities.com/Eureka/Gold/6654/quangtri.html. See also Hensel AF entry in main alpha listing.
AFVN TV- Armed Forces Vietnam Network TV. A.k.a. Channel 11. See AFVN and, for info/pics of AFVN in Quang

Tri, see *American Forces Vietnam Network Detachment 5-Quang Tri*, at: *www.geocities.com/Eureka/Gold/6654/quangtri.html.*

AGAS - A.k.a. Air-Ground Air Service. In '44 or '45, U.S. "AGAS" teams began arriving in VN to assist in rescue and return of downed WWII U.S. fliers. See also JANIS and Deer Mission.

AGC - Amphibious Force Flagship (USN).

Agence France Presse - French News Service. Cited in *A Better War*, p 208, for releasing statement by Prince Sihanouk shortly after Cambodian Incursion in which for 1st time he publicly acknowledged presence of NVA troops in Cambodia. At time, Hanoi was insisting no NVA were there and that all fighting was being done by Cambode revolutionaries.

Agrovilles - After French defeat in '54 and country was partitioned, U.S. continued aid to new SVN govt under Diem regime through SEATO. U.S. provided funds for land reform and President Eisenhower also sent Gen J. Lawton Collins to oversee start of military trng program. Land reforms were designed to aid refugees from NVN, as well as peasantry of SVN, by opening land and creating communities in central highlands, and in former swamp/jungle areas. These communities were called "Agrovilles" and "Prosperity Centers." Few enjoyed success and inhabitants moved elsewhere. Per *Twenty Years and Twenty Days*, p 121.

AGS - Surveying Ship (USN).

AGSS - Auxiliary Submarine (USN).

AH - Hospital Ship (USN).

AH-1 Huey Cobra - U.S. gunship helicopter with 165 mi rnge, 170 kts top spd. mfgd by Bell Helicopter. For history/specs, go to www-acala1.ria.army.mil/acala/sma/asa/AAHIST.HTM

AHB - Assault Helicopter Battalion.

AHC - Assault Helicopter Company.

AHCO - Aviation Helicopter Company (USN).

AID - Agency for International Development, a.k.a. USAID. See also USOM.

Aigle Azur - *Aigle Azur* and Air Viet-Nam were the 2 civilian airlines flying in Indochina during French War.

Air America - In Aug50, the CIA purchased all assets of Civil Air Transport (CAT), adding an air transport capability to facilitate and disguise covert ops in Asia. CAT was company founded by Gen. Claire Chennault and W. Willauer in China following WWII. CAT continued to operate as pvt airline after acquisition, but flight-crews simultaneously ran covert ops. Used wide variety of acft and, according to *A Better War*, p 368, its final flight left Udorn 30Jun74, with flight log showing only one crew member by name of Rhyne. History and photo gallery at: www.air-america.org/.

Air Cofat - See Air Cofat and COFAT Cmpd in main alpha index..

Air Ground Air Service - A.k.a. AGAS. In '44(?), U.S. AGAS teams began arriving in VN to assist in rescue/return of downed WWII U.S. fliers. See also JANIS and Deer Mission. NVN.

Air Laos - The major civilian airline of Laos during French War.

AIR VIAT ? - See AIR VIET.

AIR VIET - Early civil air transport service of SVN used by CIA to drop para-agents into NVN during early 60's. Spelled VIAT in *Twenty Years and Twenty Days*, p 25, and either a misspelling or possible acronym for Vietnam Indochina Air Transport? See Nguyen Cao Ky.

Air Viet-Nam - *Aigle Azur* and Air Viet-Nam were the two civilian airlines flying in Indochina during French War.

Airborne Resupply Companies - French force assigned to air dropping of supplies during 1st Indochina War. Often worked in concert with C-119 flying boxcars and other air assets courtesy "CAT," Gen. Chennault's Civil Air Transport air wing that evolved into Air America.

AIT - Advanced Infantry Training (U.S. Army). Immediately followed Basic Combat Training (BCT) for the 11B infantry MOS.

AK - Cargo Ship (USN).

AK 47 - A.k.a. the Kalishnakov-47. Standard individual weapon of VC/NVA forces throughout war. Weighed apx 9 lbs., was 34.25" in length (heavier but shorter than the U.S. M-16) and fired a 7.62mm bullet. Was capable of semi or fully automatic fire via a curved (banana clip) 30-rnd magazine, and was noted for its durability, dependability, ruggedness and ease of maintenance. On rare occasions some U.S. troops and special ops troops used them in the field. Was designed by the Soviets and mass-produced by Chinese for NVA.

AKA - Attack Cargo Ship (USN).

AKD - Cargo Ship, Dock (USN).

AKL - Light Cargo Ship (USN).

AKR - Vehicle Cargo Ship (USN).

AKS - Stores Issue Ship (USN).

Akuna Jack - CIA nickname for an alleged POW/MIA alleged scam artist by name of Jack Bailey. See Op Rescue.

AKV - Acft Ferry (USN).

Alaska Barge and Transport - A.k.a. AB&T. One of several major civilian contractors (along with Vinell, RMK-BRJ and PA&E) involved in building and maintaining U.S. facilities in SVN. AB&T had a significant presence at Cam Ranh Bay, including a unique bar called AB&T Cave Bar built inside natural cave at AB&T Cmpd on South Beach.

Albatross - Trade name for HU-16B acft w/2,850 mi rnge, 235 kts top spd. mfgd by Grumman Avn.

ALCC - Airlift Control Center (TAD).

ALCE - Airlift Control Element (TAD).

Alexandre de Rhodes - See Rhodes, Alexandre de.

All Americans - Nickname for the U.S. 82d Airborne Div.

Alley Cat - A call-sign of the 282d AHC.

ALOREP# - Airlift Operational Reporting System Number. Acronym for DOD's airfield/heliport numbering system. Presumably DOD's worldwide system. For example, Tan Son Nhut AB's ALOREP# was "VA3-1" while Lai Khe Heliport was known as "Heliport # 753."

ALS - Approach Light System (TAD).

ALSG - Australian Logistical Supt Group (Vung Tau).

alt - altitude (TAD).

altn - alternate (TAD).

AM-2 - Aluminum runway matting (TAD).

AM-2 - Aluminum runway matting (TAD).

AMBL - Airmobile.

AMBL - Military abbreviation of "Airmobile." Designation assigned to Infantry Divs primarily trained for and using helicopter-borne assets and ops.

American Radio Service - A.k.a. ARS. At 9 Hong Thap Tu St., Saigon, 6 blocks from U.S. Embassy. Civilian run radio service in SVN that replaced Armed Forces Radio Network Vietnam (a.k.a. AFRTS) when U.S. went home in '73.

Operated out of same facilities and used same equip as had been used by its military staff. According to Chuck Neil, a civilian broadcaster there at fall of Saigon, it was decided that Bing Crosby's song, *I'm Dreaming of a White Christmas*, coupled with the announcement: "The temperature in Saigon is 105 degrees and rising," would be secret code signal to Americans in Saigon that evacuation of Saigon had begun and they should move to prearranged pickup points. The code was thought necessary in order to avoid civilian panic or SVN govt interference with U.S. evac. The idea of using ARS for notice is attributed to Ann Bottorf, PAO at DAO (Ms Bottorf later died in C-5 crash during Op Babylift). Neil was unable to find Bing Crosby version of song, but did find one by U.S. singer Tennessee Ernie Ford (has always been rptd that song actually broadcast was Bing Crosby's version, but apparently that was not case). He then recorded it on a tape cartridge along with coded announcement. On 29Apr75, between 11:30 and 11:40 AM, the DAO called Neil and told him to evacuate immediately, upon which Neil loaded cartridge into a "Gates Automatic Programmer," hit "start" button and left. Data per *Tears before the Rain*, pp 198-206.

Amphibious Ready Group Alpha - A.k.a. USN Task Grp 76.4. See Eagle Pull in main alpha listing.

AMS - Army Map Service. Predecessor to the DMA and NIMA.

AN - Antonov Transport (USN).

AN - Net Laying Ship (USN).

AN/MPQ4 - Counter-mortar radar unit. U.S. Army and USMC.

AN/PRC-10 - A.k.a. "Prick 10." 26 lb., back-pack, plt radio. Had 170 channels and range of apx 5 to 8 km on level ground. Used early in war and soon replaced by transistorized PRC 25.

AN/PRC-25 - A.k.a. the "Prick 25." Back-pack style, transistorized 920 channel FM platoon radio. Heavy and vulnerable moisture. Had a small whip antenna, and a large pole antenna of apx 10' length that could be deployed when stationary. Its batteries were quite heavy and short-lived. Was replaced by longer-range and somewhat more reliable AN/PRC-77.

AN/PRC-77 - A.k.a. the "Prick 77." Very similar to the less-reliable AN/PRC-25 it replaced, but had greater range and was capable of secure transmissions with use of a special attachment.

AN/PRC9 - Helmet-mounted receiver of a 2-piece squad radio in concert with the AN/PRT4 hand-held transmitter. Awkward to use, vulnerable to moisture, and with limited range of apx 1.5 km, the unit enjoyed limited use and success. Picture of this radio combo is in *Vietnam Order of Battle*, p 304.

AN/PRS-3 - Metallic-mine detector carried by an individual and employed widely by combat engrs in VN. Consisted of a backpack power/electronic module, earphones and hand carried wand.

AN/PRT4 - See AN/PRC9.

AN/PVS 2 - See "Starlight Scope."

AN/TVS 2 – Enlarged version of AN/PVS 2 "Starlight Scope." Used for fixed-position observation and mounting on larger, crew-served weapons. See also AN/PVS 2 and Starlight Scope.

AN-2 - Soviet built acft used by NVN. 560 mi rnge, 160 kts top spd. mfgd by Antonov.

AN-24 - Soviet built acft used by NVN. 340 mi rnge, 295 kts top spd. mfgd by Antonov.

Angel of Dien Bien Phu, The - During Siege of Dien Bien Phu, a C-47 medevac was destroyed by arty leaving a nurse, Genevieve de Galard-Jerraube, stranded at base. She stayed through battle, caring for wounded and was captured at its end, earning title "Angel of Dien Bien Phu," and both a *Croix de Guerre* and Knight's Cross of Legion of Honor. Genevieve flew over 149 medevac missions, inc 40 to Dien Bien Phu. See also Dien Bien Phu, Battle of, in main alpha listing.

ANGLICO - U.S. Marine Air and Naval Gunfire Liaison Company.

Annam - Annam, Cochin China and Tonkin were the 3 major regions of Vietnam as named by French. Annam covered apx 57,000 sq miles adjoining Cambodia and Laos, and included cities of Quang Tri (its capital) Hue, Da Nang, Binh Dinh and Vinh.

Annual Hist Supp - See Daily Journal.

Anti-Corruption Movement - See People's Anti-Corruption Movement.

AO - Oiler (USN).

AOE - Fast Combat Supt Ship (USN).

AOG - Gasoline Tanker (USN).

AP - Airport (but not if "Ap").

Ap - One Viet word for "village."

Ap Do Moi - "Really New Life" Hamlet Program. One of CORDS rural hamlet development programs that began with the Strategic Hamlet Program and evolved in name and concept to "New Life," and later, the "Really New Life" (a.k.a. Ap Doi Moi) programs. All involved relocating civilian populations (mostly against their will) to end VC access to them. All were apparently dismal failures.

APA - Attack Transport.

Apache Platoon - SF CIDG unit consisting of 30 Montagnard trackers. See Bu Gia Map in main alpha list.

APB - Self Propelled Barracks Ship (USN).

APC - All Purpose Capsule. U.S. military medicine's standard analgesic. Contained combination of Aspirin and Caffeine.

APC - Armored Personnel Carrier. See M-113 and Flame Tracks.

APC - See Accelerated Pacification Campaign.

apch - approach (TAD).

APD - High-speed Transport (USN).

APL - Auxiliary Personnel, Light. USN Non-Self-Propelled barracks ship/barge.

APL - Barracks Craft (non-self-propelled).

APP - Accelerated Pacification Campaign.

App - approach (TAD).

APP CON - Approach Control (TAD).

appr - approach (TAD).

apr - approach (TAD).

aprch - approach (TAD).

APSS - Transport Submarine (USN).

apt - apartment or apartments.

apx - approximate.

AR - Repair Ship (USN).

AR-15 - Predecessor to the M-16 Rifle. Tested successfully and well-liked by SF troops in '64-65. However, revised gun-powder formula, bolt/buffer problems led to disaster when it evolved into the M-16 replaced the M-14 as the standard U.S. infantry weapon. See also M-16.

ARC LAPES - Low Level Parachute Extraction System (LAPES) variant designed by the Aerospace Research Corp. (ARC); hence, ARC-LAPES. See also LAPES and GPES.

Arc Light - Code name for B-52 bombing strikes employing 250 lb., 500 lb., 1,000 lb. bombs along with various other munitions such as CBUs. Typically 2 "sticks" of three B-52s dropping ordnance that effectively covered an area one by three grid squares (1 x 3 km). Of all U.S. weapons, by far NVA feared Arc Light most, calling them "The Whispering Death" because planes and their bombs could be neither seen nor heard until actually impacting on target. Rarely used tactically (LZ X-Ray and Op Iron Triangle are some exceptions), most missions were pre-planned weeks in advance, automatically guided and bombs automatically released. VC soldier Truong Nau Tang recalled heavy B-52 strike campaign of '69-70 in III Corps as, "Invisible predators," and noted in awe that they precipitated "undiluted psychological terror" among his comrades (*A Better War*, p 122). It has long been rumored that NVA spies within SVN govt were relaying missions data to NVA throughout war and that Arc Light effectiveness suffered greatly as result. Per *A Better War*, pp 120-122, CINCPAC had control over all Arc Light mission assignments, and U.S. ambassadors to Laos (H. Sullivan and G. McCurtie Godley) frequently went over MACV's head to CINCPAC in order to orchestrate strikes of their own design. This angered and frustrated MACV HQ because it felt targeting intel for Laos was notoriously unreliable or non-existent and assets wasted as result. Nonetheless, Vientiane often vetoed missions near crucial Tchepone terminus of the HCMT. When bombing halt cutbacks shifted control of Route Packages 1 & 2 from CINCPAC to MACV in '69, Gen Creighton Abrams gained control of all Arc Lights below the 20th Parallel and soon unleashed what was known as the "Great B-52 Deluges of '69 and '70." In Main alpha listings and Glossary, see Khe Sanh Red Watch, Niagara, Route Package, Ho Chi Minh Trail, Iron Triangle Op, and Khe Sanh Air Strike Data. See also, Pink Rose.

Archimedes Patti, Major - See Patti Mission.

ARCR-10 - ARCR-10 and URC-68 were both hand-held radios.

ARG - Amphibious Ready Group.

ARG - Internal Combustion Engine Repair Ship (USN).

ARL - Auxiliary Repair, Light. Landing Craft Repair Ship.

Armed Forces Council - Org of SVN military leaders created to advise and oversee SVN govt's activities in 60's and prior to its 1st elected govt. Council inc what became known as "The Young Turks;" the younger, more liberal generals and marshals of ARVN (among them Nguyen Cao Ky and Gen Thieu) who took a greater hand in decision making process as time went by. Replaced Military Revolutionary Council in Jan65 (apparently only a name change). See also Military Council, Military Revolutionary Council, Committee of Natl Leadership and Nguyen Cao Ky. Per *Twenty Years and Twenty Days*, p 29.

Armed Forces Institute - See Cu Chi Univ in main alpha listing..

Armed Forces Radio and TV - See AFVN.

Armed Forces Expeditionary Medal - U.S. campaign medal awarded for service in VN between 1Jul58(?), and the eff date of the Vietnam Service Medal, 8Jul65. Although the VSM was not created until 8Jul65, it became retroactive to 1Jul58 for those personnel who had been awarded the Armed Forces Expeditionary Medal and wished to exchange it for the VSM. The VSM award period therefore effectively began 1Jul58 and ended 28Jan73; however, the campaign Bronze Star attached to the ribbon (one per campaign period served) was only authorized between 15Mar62 and 28Jan73 (In other words, it is possible to have served in Vietnam, awarded the VSM by exchanging one's Armed Forces Expeditionary Medal for it, but not be authorized to add any campaign star devices because one was only there between 1Jul58 and start of the "Advisory" campaign period on 15Mar62). See also Vietnam Service Medal.

Arm'ee Clandestine - Gen Vang Pao's Laotian rebel forces suptd by CIA/Air America Projects 404, 406 and 603, '59-62?

Army Boats in Vietnam - See U.S. Army Boats in Vietnam.

Army Education Center - See Cu Chi University.

Army Reporter, The - Official magazine of U.S. Army in Vietnam. Its banner read: *The largest Army newspaper in the world.* Published by U.S. Army Info Office, VN, APO 96375 (tel. Long Binh, 4204/4819), and printed by *Pacific Stars & Stripes*. In '68. Its byline indicated that 95,000 copies were printed each issue.

ARP - Aerial Rifle Platoon. Ready reaction units normally associated with Air Cav recon units assigned to each Div.

arpt - airport (TAD).

ARS - American Radio Service.

ARS - Salvage Ship (USN).

ARTCC - Air Route Traffic Control Center (TAD).

Article 15 - Non-judicial punishment exercised by a CO, and a level of punishment below more formal Courts Martial. Could be exercised at unit cmdr's discretion to expedite swift penalties for minor infractions. Penalties could include loss of pay, loss of rank, restriction to quarters, but generally not jail time. Typically an Army term. USMC/Navy equiv was "Captain's Mast."

Artillery Firsts - See Firsts.

Arty - Artillery.

ARVH - Acft Repair Ship (Helicopter) (USN).

ARVN - Army, Republic Vietnam. Pronounced "Arvin" and used as GI slang to denote SVN soldiers of any branch of service. "Marvin the Arvin" was typical variant. See also Ruff-Puff.

ARVN Military Training Schools - Vietnamese military training was focused in number of schools, academies and colleges spread throughout SVN. In '56, there was but one Natl Trng Ctr (NTC) and by '70, there were 35. RVNAF school system totaled 25 facilities by end of war. Additionally, a number of Popular Force/Regional Force training centers opened as RF/PF prgm expanded after '68. In '67, Natl Defense College in Saigon was created and Natl Military Academy at Dalat was permanently expanded from a 2-yr to 4-yr prgm. Detailed history of RVNAF trng systems is available in Dept of Army's *Vietnam Studies*, *The Development and Training of the South Vietnamese Army, 1950-1972.* Most NTCs, RTCs, PFTCs and RFTCs are identified on map pp 81and 107 of that text. See ARVN in main alpha listing.

ARVNAF - Army, Republic Vietnam Air Force.

ARVNF - Army, Republic Vietnam Forces.

AS - Air Station (TAD).

ASA - Army Security Agency.

ASB - Advanced Supt Base (USN).

ASCO - Australian Services Canteen Operation. Equivalent to U.S. AAFES, or Armed forces Exchange Service. Supplied troops with retail goods and services.

ASHB - Assault Support Helicopter Battalion.

ASP - Asphalt (TAD).
asph - asphalt.
ASPB - Assault Supt Patrol Boat (USN). The only naval craft designed and built specifically for Mobile Riverine Force warfare in SVN. Primary duties were fire supt and mine sweeping. Data per *Brown Water, Black Berets*, p 245.
ASRAT - Air Strike Radar Assistance Team?
Assault - Call-sign for A Trp, 2d Sqdn, 17th Cav.
ASW - Antisubmarine Warfare (USN).
ATC - Air Traffic Control (TAD).
ATC - Armored Transport Craft (USN).
ATC - Armored Troop Carrier (USN). USN barges and small landing craft, a.k.a. "Monitors," which had armored super-structures built atop their hulls. Was adaptation primarily for MRF river warfare in Mekong Delta and swamps of southern III and IV Corps. Many resembled boxy looking barges, but were produced in a wide variety of shapes and sizes.
ATC(H) - Armored Troop Carrier (Helicopter) (USN).
ATF - Australian Task Force.
ATF - Fleet Ocean Tug (USN).
ATSB - Advanced Tactical Supt Base. USN.
Att - Attached.
ATZ - Air Traffic Zone (TAD).
AU-23A Peacemaker - U.S. acft with 555 mi rnge, 165 kts top spd. mfgd by Fairchild Acft.
AU-24A - U.S. gunship acft with 410 mi rnge, 160 kts top spd. mfgd by Helio. According to essay entitled *Gunships*, "The Helio AU-24A was the gunship version of the H550A Stallion, with a PT6A-114 turboprop, equipped with a GE XM-197, three-barreled 20mm Gatling gun mounted in left cargo door. Also had 5 under-wing and fuselage hard points. Of 17 built, 14 or 15 were sold to Cambodian (Khmer) Air Force." Per: www.ais.org/~schnars/texte/
gunships.htm.
Australian Army Training Team - A.k.a. AATTV. In mid '62, 1st contingent of apx 30 Aussie Adv were dispersed through northern provs to work with U.S. Adv teams (and also independently) in trng ARVN and VNSF. Contingent grew to 100+ by '72. In VN 31Jul62-18Dec72. Data per *SF Order of Battle*. See Australian Task Force HQ in Major Command Section.
auth - authorized (TAD).
Aux - Auxiliary
AV - Seaplane Tender (USN).
avbl - available (TAD).
Avenger - A call-sign of the 189th AHC and/or 604th Trans Det.
Avn - Aviation.
AW - Automatic weapons.
AWOL - Absent Without Leave (not equiv to desertion).
B Units - See C-Rations.
B.G.I. Beer - Hanoi-brewed beer common to French occupation.
B-1, B-2, B-3 Units - See C-Ration.
B-4 Bag - Nickname and nomenclature for hand-carried equipment and helmet bag used by USAF pilots.
B-26 Bomber - Twin engine, prop driven light bomber of WWII vintage used widely by French in 1st Indochina War. In all, French employed 90 of these acft. In '51, U.S. began supplying acft and other military goods (including loan of Acft Carrier *Belleau Woods*) to the French under the Military Assistance Prgm (MAP). Data per *Street Without Joy*, p 263. See also *USS Belleau Woods* in main alpha listing.
B-36 Project Rapid Fire - See Project Rapid Fire. III Corps.
B-40 Rocket - An explosive, shaped-charge projectile for Soviet/Chinese produced shoulder-fired RPG (Rocket-Propelled Grenade). Used extensively by NVA/VC forces, it was very effective against armor, bunkers and personnel. Unlike the "one-shot" U.S. M-72 LAW, it could be reloaded and fired indefinitely. A much-feared weapon. See also RPG.
B-50 Project - See Project Omega.
B-52 Stratofortress - A.k.a. "The BUFF." U.S. eight-jet eng hvy bomber with 7,370 mi rnge and 575 kts top spd. mfgd by Boeing Acft. Was major workhorse and, without question, the most devastating weapon of the American War. According to *A Better War*, p 283, according to Richard Funkhauser, by end of '71, all Vietnamese hoped from the U.S. after it pulled-out was B-52's, money, and Rome Plows. During 72 Easter Offensive, Gen Abrams masterminded an extremely eff tactic that devoted MACV's entire B-52 assets for a single day to each of the 3 key battle points: 11May72 at Kontum; 12May at Hue, and 13May at An Loc. During those strikes, 3 B-52 sorties were hitting the target every 55 minutes for 24 hours, and tactic broke the back of NVA attack at all 3 sites. The acft could carry very large load of 250, 500 or 1,000 lb. bombs, as well as other ordnance (inc as many as 44,000 CBU's in a single load). See also Ho Chi Minh Trail, Choke Point Bombing, Island Tree, Pink Rose and Khe Sanh Air Campaign.
B-56 Project - See Project Sigma.
B-57 Canberra – U.S. twin-jet eng light bomber with 2,200 mi rnge, 580 kts top spd. mfgd by Martin. See FSB Birmingham and Clark AFB in main alpha listing.
B-66 Destroyer - Carrier-based ECM/ASW twin-jet eng recon and electronics platform. mfgd by Douglas Acft.
B Team - Mid-level of U.S. Army's SF unit hierarchy under the C-Team at Nha Trang. There were four B-Teams; one in each CTZ (Corps), and each had 4 or 5 A-Teams under its cmd. Strike forces were indigenous units assembled/advised by A-Teams. In early 60's, commo between A and B Teams was by Morse Code sent encrypted on what was known as "one-time pad," while at tactical level, A-teams used voice radio. Data per *Tan Phu: Special Forces Team A-23 in Combat*, p 31.
Bac Ho - Uncle Ho. Affectionate Viet nickname for Ho Chi Minh, the revolutionary nationalist-communist leader of NVN between 1944 and his death in '69.
Bac Si - Vietnamese word for Doctor or Medic. Also frequently used as an affectionate nickname for combat medics.
Backlog Bird - GI slang for a helicopter (Log Bird) returning soon after an initial re-supply mission to pickup dirty uniforms, outgoing mail, broken equipment and the like, in order to return them to rear for cleaning, repair or disposal. See also Log Bird.
Bamboo Viper - A.k.a. the "Step-and-a-Half" or the "Two Step" Snake. See Two-Step.
Ban G. I. Beer - Hanoi-brewed beer common to French War.
Bandit Net - A.k.a. "The Bullshit" Net. The highest frequency ("push") on military FM band of standard field radios (75.95 mhz), such as the PRC 25 and PRC 77. Used frequently by clandestine, would-be disk-jockeys and/or sometimes political activists in various basecamps (rear areas) to broadcast music, information and commentary. Ordinarily on the air only at night and scheduling was erratic due to efforts by military to

eradicate them. Such broadcasts were strictly against regulations and their "owners" kept varying broadcast points and times to avoid triangulation. Even infantry and maneuver troops could call-in requests using this push! Such unauthorized commo likely did not flourish widely until the late in war. This author recalls listening-in (and actually requesting/receiving a Jimi Hendrix tune) while on ambush in Summer, '70. NPR aired segment about the net in Nov92(?).

Banshee - Call-sign for B Trp, 2d Sqdn, 17th Cav.

BAR - Browning Automatic Rifle. W.W.I vintage automatic, magazine-fed rifle used widely by SVN in early years of war.

Barky - Call-sign for USAF FACs suptg 1st Bde/5th Mech Inf Div, out of Quang Tri. TOC was known as "Barky Ops."

Barrelhouse - Call-sign of USMC's HMM 161, Medium Helicopter Sqdn.

Barsanti Affair, The - (XT 98-13) Dennis Vassey has a remarkable anecdote posted at www.a101avn.org/unitcitations.htm. During his tour in '68 as Avn Safety Officer for A/101st Avn, an unusual incident took place at Bien Hoa AB(?) that got little media attention. It seems that MG Barsanti (CG 101st Abn) decided to punish a Lt who'd been fouling things up and had either threatened to jail the man in a CONEX, or had in fact put him in the CONEX. At any rate, Vassey and staff could see the suspected POW CONEX and its guards from A/101st Avn's maintenance area nearby. By great coincidence, not only was the hapless Lt's father an officer aboard the *USS Missouri* (likely the *USS New Jersey* instead, as it was only BB to serve in VN), but that battleship was also patrolling off the coast of VN at the time! Apparently Barsanti brushed-off the father's inquiries, and soon thereafter, a Navy CH-46 carrying several Seals landed in A/101st Avn's maintenance area. The Seal team ldr asked permission for his team to use the helo pad for staging an op and, after receiving it from his unsuspecting hosts, moved-out to explore the site. Within an hour of its arrival, the CH-46 suddenly went into action against the suspected CONEX, 1st hooking a line to it and then disappearing over the horizon. "We got a good look at the VIP departure which went off without a hitch," notes Vassey dryly. "Apparently the Lt was reunited with his father aboard the [*New Jersey*] as a liaison officer. Whether he was in the CONEX or in a guarded tent isn't clear. What is clear is that the CONEX left without a shot being fired."

Bartender - A call-sign of the 271st AHC.

BAS - Battalion Aid Station.

Base Turnover Program - As U.S. withdrew from SVN in late '71, 750 facilities, FSBs, LZs and basecamps were given to SVN govt. Per *A Better War*, p 277. See also Camp Eagle.

Baseball Grenade - See M-26 and M-33 Frag.

Basketball – Call-sign/code name for C-130 flare ship acft capable of providing battlefield illumination over extended periods of time (up to 8-hours). See also Moonglow.

Bataillion de Marche Indochinois - See BMI.

Batallion de Coree - Element of French Army's famous Korean Rgt; elite Korean War vets who'd served with U.S. 2d Inf Div during that war at places like Chipyong Ni, Wonju and Arrowhead Ridge. 1st and 2d Korea Bns were transferred to southern Indochina in Jul53, and reinforced with 2 Viet Bns, 2d Grp 10th Colonial Arty Rgt, and *Batallion de Marche* (B.M.) of 43d Colonial Inf (unit composed of experienced Cambodian and French Jungle fighters). See *Street Without Joy*, p 186.

Batallion de Marche - A.k.a. "B.M." French Army "March Units" normally assembled for specific purpose and roughly equiv to a U.S. Army Task Force, but often became permanent fixtures. French had 2 B.M.s in Indochina, as well as French Foreign Legion's famous *Regiment de Marche*. See *Street Without Joy*, p 186.

Batallion Medical de Campagne - BMC. Medical Field Bn of French Army.

Batallion Volontaire-33 - See BV-33 in main alpha listings.

Battalion - A.k.a. "Bn." The typical Army Infantry Battalion consisted of six companies (Cos), a Headquarters (HHC or HQ) Co, as well as A, B, C, D and E (or Recon) Cos. Each Army Infantry Co typically contained 3 to 4 platoons and a total of about 160 men at fully-authorized strength. USMC Battalions were very similar in makeup to Army's Bn, but contained other elements and variations. Marine Rgts typically contained same 3 to 5 Bns that U.S. Army Rgt did, but differed in how individual Cos were identified. Marine Cos were lettered alphabetically such that no two Co's in a Rgt bore the same letter of the alphabet. For example, the 1st(Bn)/9th Marine (Rgt) might consist of A, B, C, D, and E Cos, while 2d/9th Marines would continue the progression up alphabet with F, G, H, I and J Cos. In Army Rgts, each Bn typically consisted of A, B, C, D and E Co's, with the same progression repeating itself through each Bn (in author's opinion, the Marine nomenclature system makes good sense. In heat of battle, were one to ask a Marine his Co and "India Co" his response, one would instantly know the man was with the Rgt's 2d Bn. Given same scenario with an Army Rgt, if answer was "Bravo Co," the man's Bn remains unclear). It was rare for any Marine or Army Bn to enjoy a full complement during the war. In 101st Abn Div in '69-70, this author would est that on any given day, most Cos averaged perhaps 100 men or less. See also "Company."

Battalion Daily Journal - See Daily Journal.

Battle Index, VHPA - See VHPA Battle index.

Bau - One Viet word for "lagoon" or "lake."

BB - Battleship (USN).

BC - Body count.

bcn - beacon (TAD).

bcst - broadcast (TAD).

BCT - Basic Combat Training (U.S. Army). Standard initial training for all Army personnel. Immediately preceded Advanced Infantry Training. (AIT) for the 11B infantry MOS.

BD Cranes - 8 Army heavy cranes served in SVN. Their hulls were classified as "BD Cranes," and 4 of the 8 were 100-ton cranes, while remaining 4 were 60-ton cranes. Were used at Army seaports to lift items that ships' equipment could not, such as tanks, bulldozers, locomotives and other large vehicles or machinery and equipment. Data per and pictures/discussion at: http://academic.uofs.edu/faculty/gramborw/atav/4tc.htm. See also "Big John."

BDA - Bomb Damage Assessment.

Bde - Brigade (see Battalion).

bdry - boundary (TAD).

Bearcats - U.S. carrier-based, prop-driven fighter-bomber (along with the Corsair, Hellcat and Helldiver) used by French in the '50's. In '51, the U.S. began supplying acft and other military goods (including loan of Acft Carrier *Belleau Woods*) to the French under the Military Assistance Program (MAP). Data per *Street Without Joy*, pp 261. See also *USS Belleau Woods* in main alpha listing.

Beehive Round - See Canister Rounds.
Beer Runs - See FSB Schueller in main alpha listing.
Ben - One Viet word for "bay."
BEQ - Bachelor Enlisted Quarters.
Berm - A dike or ledge. Also an earthen wall built into the perimeter of an FSB to protect occupants from direct fire.
BG - Brigadier General.
BGen - Brigadier General.
BGI beer - Hanoi brewed beer common to French War.
Bien - One Viet word for "lake."
Bier La Rue – A.k.a. Tiger Beer. Local SVN beer noted for its harsh taste and formaldehyde hangovers.
Biet Dong Quan - ARVN Rangers. Created in '60 as counter-guerrilla force consisting of light Cos. Mission was to track VC and hit them in their home bases. 1st U.S. training sites for BDQ were built in '60 at Da Nang, Nha Trang and Song Mao. Original course at Duc My (Nha Trang), later became ARVN's Duc My Ranger Trng Center. Data per *Rangers At War*, pp 251-252.
Biet Hai - Coastal Force commandos of VNN/VNMC. During '63-64, SEAL Team 1 Dets were in SVN to train U.S. Advrs, SVN "frogmen" (LDNN or Lien Doi Nguoi Nhai) and Coastal Force Biet Hai commandos.
Biet Kichs - See main alpha listing.
Big Minh - SVN Gen. Duong Van Minh, nicknamed "Big Minh" because he was physically quite large. An influential political figure throughout the war. Was Chairman of Revolutionary Military Council, 63-64, and briefly president of Vietnam, 1Nov63-30Jan64 after Diem was murdered in coup. In exile after losing the presidency, he ran unsuccessfully for job again in '66 and '71. He was again briefly president from 28Apr-30Apr75, after president Tran Van Huong appointed him as his replacement. Minh surrendered SVN Govt to NVA forces 30Apr75, was then arrested and sent to re-education camps. In 1983, he moved to France.
Big Red One - Nickname of U.S. 1st Infantry Div.
Big Windy - A call-sign of the 180th AHC.
Bigfoot Sightings - See Nguoi Rung.
Bikini - A call-sign of the 170th AHC.
Binh Tram - NVA way stations, waypoints and checkpoints along HCMT. These sites were assigned various alpha-numeric designators by MACV based on their function. Primary Binh Trams were simply numbered in sequence, such as 1, 2, 3 and so on. Commo-liaison sites controlled by primaries sites were called "T-Stations" and numbered T-1, T-2 and so on. Additionally, there were "K-Intervals," which were permanent supply depots, built near each of which were cemeteries. Each primary Binh Tram was typically manned by regimental-sized supt unit. Beginning in 67/68, US/SVN intel gained ability to intercept and decode radio traffic between some of various facilities along HCMT (known as NVRS transmissions, or NVN Rear Services transmissions). As a result and for balance of war, MACV HQ and ARVN HQ were receiving quite accurate data on size, destination and progress of all personnel in the pipeline, as well as the volume of supplies being moved and stored. Binh Tram 33 in Base Area 604 near Tchepone, Laos, was one of 1st to fall victim to intercepts, as was Binh Tram 19. Later, commo between Binh Tram 8 and T-12 became a key intercept. 1st intercept took place 1Nov67, and it referenced several groups along trail (by Mar68, 14 grps had been identified in movement). Through Mar-Apr68, 114 groups were identified (over 66,000 troops) as they moved toward Mini-Tet '68, and then in Jun68, large groups of wounded and sick of 304th Div were detected going north. By May70, Binh Trams 14, 18, 32 and 33 were added to MACV intercept list. During Cambodian Incursion, more than 1 million pages of documents and 32 boxes of cryptographic material were captured that, among other things, verified accuracy of Binh Tram radio traffic intercepts by confirming arrival of over 93% of units in Cambodian AO that intercepts had indicated would arrive in Jan-May70. NVA rptd that by end of '71, supplies of Binh Trams of 559th Grp (in charge of that portion) rose to 6,000 tons each, which they est could supply 50,000 to 60,000 troops for 4 months. Another 30,000 tons of supplies were also stored along the Transportation Corridor (HCMT). See NVRS, T-Stations and K-Intervals. Data per *A Better War*, pp 47-50, 208-209, 238.
Bird Dog - See L-19 Bird Dog and O-1 Bird Dog.
Bitrex - Chemical agent that rendered food inedible but not toxic. Employed by MACV-SOG. SOG chief Singlaub wanted to use on NVA rice caches found along HCMT but U.S. State Dept initially blocked use because it was considered chemical warfare even though non-toxic. SOG eventually got permission, but its effectiveness is not discussed in our references. Spread over rice caches, it apparently made the grain very bitter such that it was "enough to gag a maggot" as one source reports. Was mixed with water and poured over the foodstuff so application was noiseless and did not alert enemy, making it the ideal solution for destroying large caches of rice that could not be moved. Data per Jim Jones as gleaned from *SOG and The Secret War Against Hanoi*.
Black Ace - Call-sign of 21st Recon Airplane Co (RAC).
Black and White Radio - 2 varieties of long-range, MAC-SOG radio commo and intel gathering equip suptg 34-Alpha Program. White Radios were sited in Saigon and capable of reaching well into NVN. Black Radios were sited on mtn peaks in northern Quang Tri Prov and adj to DMZ. Both used for commo with SVN commando operatives (spies) that had been inserted into NVN. Data per *Gulf of Tonkin Revisited*, by Gregory Johnson, in Jan 2000 issue of *MILITARY* Mag, pp 5-8.
Black Cat - Call-sign of 213th AHC, 282d AHC and 282d AHC.
Black Khmer, The - A.k.a. Buller. Nickname of McKinley Nolan, 1st U.S. soldier to openly defect after the Korean War. He escaped from Long Binh Jail 9Nov67, where he was being held on drug charges. Initially he allied himself with local VC, composing poorly written leaflets and making statements for Radio Hanoi. Nolan worked in some SVN POW camps but efforts of POWs to communicate with him were shunned. In '73, he and his Vietnamese wife had falling out with VC over poor treatment, were arrested in SVN, then escaped, and then fled to SE Cambodia were until '75 they apparently lived with the Khmer Rouge (and probable U.S. Defector named Chaigar) on coffee plantation near Memot. See also Chaigar. Data per *Prisoners of Hope*, pp 62-64.
Black T'ai - See T'ai Tribes in Glossary.
Black Widow - A call-sign of the 188th AHC?
Black Widow - Call-sign for C Co 101st Avn Bn.
Blackbird - Trade name for SR-71, ultra-secret twin-jet, high-altitude, high-spd, recon and spy acft. Had 3,250 mi rnge, 2,215 kts top spd. mfgd by Lockheed Acft.
Blackhawk - A call-sign of the 187th AHC.

Blick - MACV acronym for "Water-borne Logistics Craft," i.e., a boat of any sort.
BLT - Battalion Landing Team (USMC).
BLU-82-B - Official USAF designation for what was known as the "Daisy Cutter," a 15,000 lb. conventional, iron bomb used mostly to create instant helicopter LZs. Code name was "Commando Vault." See also Daisy Cutter and Combat Trap.
Blue – U.S. radio code/slang used to describe a stream or river.
Blue Max - A call-sign of the 20th ARA (1st Cav), and F Trp 7th/9th Cav? Apparently also the call-sign of 1st Cav's 79th AHC Cobra gunships (1st unit in history to destroy an enemy tank with a helicopter). See also An Loc, Battle of.
Blueghost - A call-sign of F Trp, 8th Air Cav.
Bluestar - A call-sign of the 48th AHC.
BM - *Batallion de Marche*. See also *Batallion de Coree.*
BMC - *Batallion Medical de Campagne*. Medical field Bn of French Army. A humorous takeoff of this acronym was assigned to mobile bordellos kept by French, which were also labeled BMC, for *Bordel Mobile de Campagne*.
BMC - *Bordel Mobile de Campaigne*. Field brothels of French Army, 2 of which were sited at Dien Bien Phu. Vietnamese women staffed one, while other was staffed by North African women of Ouled Nai'l Tribe (who by tribal custom were prostitutes in their native land until they'd accumulated enough wealth to allow marriage). There were also at least 73 known French women who served as prostitutes in Indochina. Women of BMC also often performed heroically in battle, as did many during siege of Dien Bien Phu and also near a remote outpost at Tsinh Ho, a plt-sized French outpost near Lai Chau (2 volunteered to take 30-mile jungle trek to this outpost in order to bring comfort to lonely troops there. They performed so well under fire during an ambush on return trip that they were recommended for the *Croix de Guerre* by patrol's cmdr; however, French Army declined to award the medals due to political concerns. As a general rule, this fixture of French Army was kept out of sight of American journalists and officials. See also Dien Bien Phu, Battle.
BMI - *Bataillion de Marche Indochinois*. Composite unit of Europeans, Cambodes, and Viet Mountaineers, considered one of best units in Indochina. Fought valiantly at battle of Chan Muong Gorge. See Chan Muong Gorge, and *Street Without Joy*, p 97.
Bn - Battalion. See Battalion for definition.
Bn Ann Hist Supp - Battalion Annual Historical Supplement. An annual historical summary prepared by many Army Bns during the war. See Table of Contents, *Researching the Vietnam War* entry.
Boat Dock - A call-sign of the 179th AHC.
BOHICA - Acronym for slang, "Bend Over, Here It Comes Again." Per USN Cmdr Joe Gerber, this standard GI euphemism was celebrated with actual metal emblems worn proudly on uniforms of various members of RC-A5-A unit flying off the *USS Enterprise* in '74-75. It represented their resignation to fact the *Enterprise* always seemed to be stuck with the toughest assignments or extended tour because other carriers were unable to take on various missions. The ship's Capt was at first unaware of its meaning and raised no objection; however, the perplexed Capt immediately got on ship's PA system and forbade it's further display when was told its translation. The pilots then simply moved emblem under flight suits for appropriate display in private.
BOHICA, Operation - Not a military Op. Was privately-funded, post-war POW rescue "mission" of POW/MIA movement. See also Grand Eagle, Op.
Bombing by NVA Air Force - See Determined to Win, Op.
Bonanza Beechcraft QU-22B - See QU-22 Beechcraft.
Bong Son Bomber - 173d Abn Bde nickname for a very large Marijuana cigarette available in '70 around LZ English and North English in Bong Son area of Binh Dinh Prov, II Corps. Described in *Charlie Rangers*, p 42. In Phu Bai/Hue AO of 101st Abn in '70, similar cigarettes were called "White Owls," and as one trooper aptly put it, "One of them baby's could stone an entire platoon!"
Bonnie-Sue - Call-sign for USMC's HMM 265, Medium Helicopter Sqdn.
Booby-Traps - See Mines.
Boomerang - A call-sign of the 191st AHC.
Boonie Rat - Slang for an infantryman or anyone else out in the boonies looking for Charlie.
Boonies, The - The deep jungle, or generally any remote area..
BOQ - Bachelor Officer's Quarters.
Bordel Mobile de Campaigne - See BMC in Glossary.
Borneo design Battery - RNZA nomenclature for a form of Arty battery using only four guns instead of normal six. Specifically, it meant four, L-5 (105mm) pack howitzers served by 89 gunners, 13 reinforcements and a 17 man logistical Det. 161 Bty RNZA was also allowed a 5th tube when it deployed to VN which was supposed to be a spare; however, it was used as part of Bty makeup almost from start and without the permission of New Zealand Govt, as extra firepower was needed and prudent. The Borneo configuration was standard for 161 Bty RNZA from '65 until 2Jul66, when a 6-gun battery was finally authorized. Later, the U.S. M2A2 105mm howitzer replaced the lighter, shorter-ranged and less durable L-5s. Until the arrival of Chinook helos in large numbers, the New Zealander's L-5 was only howitzer deployable by UH-1 helo
Bostos Cigarettes - Viet cigarette brand with purple wrapper that cost apx 2 cents per pack. Jim Vincent remembers them from tour as USN Adv with a "Junk Div" at Tiem Ton, Kien Hoa Prov.
Bounty Hunter - A call-sign of the 191st AHC.
Boxcar - A call-sign of the 178th AHC and 400th TC Co?
Brandy – A.k.a. "Brandy Ghost." Call-sign for 2d Bde HQ Hueys/LOHs flying in supt of 101st Abn (et al) in I Corps.
Brandy Ghost - See Brandy.
brg - bearing (TAD).
Bright Light Missions - A.k.a. Brightlight. Code name for specially-trained 12-man MAC-SOG SF teams (associated with Op Prairie Fire and other ops) whose mission was recovery of POWs and downed pilots (or their remains) in NVN, Cambodia and Laos. See *Rangers At War*, p 194 for discussion of Feb71 Brightlight Tiger mission.
Brokenwing, Operation - The 5th POW rescue mission organized by Bo Gritz to rescue alleged U.S. POWs in Laos. Launched in Jan85, Lao contacts were supposed to deliver POWs to a waiting Gritz along Mekong River. Gritz claims POWs actually made it to river, had conversations with him but 2 attempts at linkage were disrupted 1st by a powerboat that sunk boats ferrying POWs across river, and on 2d night by rocket fire at Gritz's riverbank position. Gritz claims mission was abandoned due to publicity it generated. Discussed in *Prisoners of Hope*, pp 148-150.

Bronco - OV-10, twin-engine reconnaissance and ground supt acft. Had 190 mi rnge and 280 kts top spd. mfgd by North American. Normally only armed with marking rockets but sometimes with HE rockets and multiple versions of M-60 MG for limited offensive role. Normally a daylight acft, while O-2 (Oscar Deuce) was used for same role at night. *Da Nang Diary* provides detailed look at TASS ops. See also Oscar Deuce, TASS and SCAR.

Brother Buck - U.S. Vice President Al Gore's nickname while serving in Vietnam. See FSB Blue in main alpha listing.

Browning .50 Cal MG - See M-2 Machine Gun.

BS - Border Surveillance.

btn - between (TAD).

Bty - Battery (as in Artillery Battery).

BUFF - Nickname for B-52 Bomber. Acronym for Big Ugly Friendly Fellow (or less politely, Big Ugly Fat Fucker).

Buffalo - In at least the 2d/7th Cav, 1st Cav ('65 and '66), "Buffalo" was 1st radio code word for a wounded soldier (WIA). Code for a KIA was "Elephant" Data per *Baptism*, p 256.

Buffalo City – Call-sign of USMC HMM-165 helicopter Sqdn.

Bulldog - A call-sign of the 129th AHC.

Buller - See Black Khmer.

Bullshit Bombers - Rather derisive nickname for O-1, O-2, OV-10 and other acft configured for dropping propaganda or "Chieu Hoi" leaflets and broadcast of related psyops messages over bulky loudspeakers mounted to acft.

Bullshit Net - Military FM Radio frequency 75.95 mhz. See Bandit Net in Glossary for detail.

Bunds - RAR/RNZA name for sandbagged defensive Arty positions employed because it was impossible to dig down in their AO without striking water.

Buong Incident, The - During Op Frequent Wind, 29-30Apr75, the USN Task Force sent to evacuate Saigon was approached by a mass of helos (30Apr) for which it had no warning and with which it had no commo. Acft carrier *USS Midway* (among others) quickly began landing the helos, then shoving them overboard as they were emptied of their Viet pilots and families (one helo had 54 people crammed aboard it!). After exodus had ended, the *Midway* was approached by a lone O1-Birdog acft. It made several passes over ship attempting to drop note to ship. On 4th try, a note wrapped in a wrench finally landed on deck. It said pilot was Maj. Buong and that he and his wife and 5 kids wished to land. The Capt ordered all remaining helos pushed to one end of flight deck, and then to total amazement of crew, Buong put plane on deck, bounced twice and stopped. A huge cheer rang out for his incredible feat and, when he exited acft and someone yelled, "Where in hell did you learn to Fly?," he replied, "In Texas!" At that, another great cheer went up! Per *Tears Before the Rain*, pp 168-171.

bus - business (TAD).

Bushmasters – Tactic for infantry units in which they would stay out in bush for extended periods, hiding by day and moving at night to set up ambushes.

Butt-Pack - See LBE.

BX - Base Exchange. Also PX (Post Exchange). Retail outlet.

C-1A Trader - U.S. acft with 875 mi rnge and 228 kts top spd. mfgd by Grumman Avn.

C-2 Greyhound - U.S. acft with 1,900 mi rnge and 310 kts top spd. mfgd by Grumman Avn.

C-4 Explosive - White, plastic high-explosive. Detonated at apx 21,000 feet/sec. Used in claymore mine and also available in bricks or in plastic tubing (a.k.a. Det Cord), for general demolition. Was revered for its very hot flame, when small portions were broken off to heat C-rations (generating acrid fumes that were painful to inhale). Care also had to be taken not to extinguish the burning cmpd using pressure (such as by stomping on it) because it could detonate (and take off a soldier's foot).

C-47 Skytrain - A.k.a. DC-3 and Dakota. Twin-eng, prop-driven air transport of WWII vintage used for transport/airdrops throughout SEA and also in gunship role as "Puff the Magic Dragon."

C-5A Galaxy - U.S. 4-eng hvy-lift jet transport with 2,729 mi rnge, 515 kts top spd. mfgd by Lockheed Acft. Was largest acft in use during war. See also Operation Babylift. At war's end, one crashed (or was sabotaged) during Op Babylift, taking lives of hundreds of Amerasian children; the only loss of a C-5 during war.

C-119 Flying Boxcar - U.S., twin-eng. propeller-driven acft with 900 mi rnge, 245 kts top spd. mfgd by Fairchild Acft. Saw duty as cargo transport/paratroop carrier in both U.S. and French wars, and as a gunship platform in U.S. war. See AC-119 Shadow/Stinger.

C-123 Provider - USAF, HC-123 dual-eng. prop-driven STOL cargo acft that was noted for its high load capacity and remarkably short takeoff and landing capability. Was gradually replaced by the C-130, but kept in use for short runways. Had 1,470 mi rnge and 175 kts top spd. mfgd by Fairchild Acft.

C-124 Globemaster II - U.S. 4-eng, prop-driven hvy transport acft 4,030 mi rnge, 230 kts top spd. mfgd by Douglas Acft.

C-130 Hercules - USAF, HC-130, Hercules, 4-engine turbo-prop acft. Had 1,830 mi rnge and 355 kts top spd. mfgd by Lockheed Acft. Noted for it STOL capability, durability, long range, dependability and large load capacity. Certainly one of most important, ubiquitous and best-loved cargo acft of war. Also used as weapons platform in grnd-supt attack and flareship mode known as Spectre. Nicknamed Herky Birds. See also Spectre.

C-133 Cargomaster – U.S. 4-eng turboprop(?) transport acft with 4,360 mi rnge and 300 kts top spd. mfgd by Douglas Acft.

C-141A Starlifter - A.k.a. "Starlighter?" Four-eng, jet transport used in cargo and medevac roles. Did extensive medevac work. 4,080 mi rnge and 570 kts top spd. mfgd by Lockheed Acft.

C's - Slang for C-ration canned meals. See C-Rations.

C Rations - Referred to simply as "Cs," or "C-Rations," the "Meal, Combat, Individual." Was 1st ration adopted to meet the subsistence concept of supplying nutritionally balanced meals rather than simply as "rations." It replaced the "Ration, Combat, Individual (C Ration)" of WWII/Korea era. Older Cs were issued until their supplies were depleted, and early in the Vietnam War, C-Rations of WWII and Korean War vintage were not uncommon. Vietnam era Cs could be issued in individual units (a small box) as a meal or in multiples of 3-boxes as a daily ration, or typically, by the case. Design emphasized utility, flexibility, and variety. 12 meals were included in each case, and each meal contained 1 canned meat item; 1 canned fruit, bread or dessert item; one B unit (an accessory packet containing cigarettes, matches, chewing gum, toilet paper, coffee, cream, sugar, and salt; and a spoon). Each case also inc 4 P-38 can openers. Cs could be eaten cold, but were much better heated. Each meal furnished apx 1/3 minimum nutrition prescribed by Army Regs. Per: www.lee.army.mil/quartermaster/history/ index.html. See also LRRP Rations.

C Team - Highest level of Army SF unit hierarchy and 1st cmd and control element HQ'd at Nha Trang. Was in cmd of a B-Team (one in each CTZ), while each B-Team ran 4 or 5 A-Teams and their associated indigenous Strike Force elements at tactical level. Per *Tan Phu: Special Forces Team A-23 in Combat*, p 31.

CA - Combat Assault. Normally a helicopter-borne assault on an objective or to an undefended LZ.

CA - Heavy Cruiser (USN).

CAC - Combined Action Company, a.k.a. CAP. Original acronym for USMC plt (or smaller) sized units permanently situated with, and working with, RF/RF/ARVN units based in rural locations. Were isolated from and independent of other, larger Marine forces in same area and, as such, were often at great risk. According to Jim Taylor, CAP Oscar vet, the terms CAC and CACO were replaced by term CAP (Combined Action Platoon) when laughter of civilians passing CAC cmpd signs was traced to fact that in Viet those terms sounded same as, and meant same, as "penis" did in English. Tim Duffie added to legend by pointing out that original CAC identity badges also apparently contained phrase "Sou CAC," and it was later discovered the Viet word "Sou" meant "Strong." Generally viewed as very successful program that many analysts argue might have brought war to different conclusion had it been expanded nationwide and become the focus of U.S. effort. See also CAP, CAG, and CUPP.

CACO - Combined Action Company. Synonymous with CAP (combined Action Platoon). See CAC for detail and also CAP, CAG and CUPP.

CAG - Combined Action Grp. USMC assigned geographical TAOR groupings of CAP, CAC or CUPP (Combined Unit Pacification Program) Teams. There were 4 CAG regions in I Corps: 1st CAG included all of Quang Tin and Quang Ngai Provs; 2d CAG was all of Quang Ngai Prov; 3d CAG was all of Thua Thien Prov and 4th CAG all of Quang Tri Prov.

CAG - Guided Missile Heavy Cruiser.

Cai Tang - Not a place but widely misunderstood Viet custom of exhuming and re-burying the dead. When conditions forced burial in sites not appropriate, the Viets would later reclaim their family member's bones, wash them and then re-bury them in more suitable location.

Cambodian Incursion - Joint U.S./ARVN invasion of Cambodian Sanctuaries, May-Jun70. Captured were: 10,000 tons of rice, enough to feed 25,000 troops for 1 year; individual weapons that would have supplied 33 full Bns; mortar, rocket and recoilless rifle ammo for 9,000 "typical" attacks against U.S. forces. Est 11,400 enemy KIA and 2,000 captured, and for next 14 months there were apparently no significant VC/NVA actions in SVN. Invasion also delivered bonus when more than 1 million pages of documents and 32 boxes of cryptographic material were captured that, among other things, verified accuracy of Jan-May70 Binh Tram radio traffic intercepts by confirming arrival of over 93% of units that intercepts indicated would arrive (per *A Better War*, pp 208-209). Though not well known, river and naval forces were also involved in invasion. At 0730 hrs, 9May70, 10 days after grnd forces invaded Cambodia, SEALORDS forces including combined Viet-American naval TF steamed up Mekong into Cambodia as well. Flotilla was in Cmd of VNN officer and included U.S. PCFs, ASPBs, PBRs, HAL-3 and VAL-4 acft, *USS Benewah*, *Askari*, *Hunterdon County*, *YRBM 16*, *YRBM 21* and 10 strike assault boats (STAB) of Strike Assault Boat Sqdn 20, a fast-reaction unit created by Admiral Zumwalt in '69. See also Binh Tram.

Camerone Day - April 30. Anniversary of legendary French Foreign Legion "to-the-last-man" stand in Mexico.

Camh Sat - SVN Natl Police. A.k.a. NP or White Mice.

Camp - Term "Camp" typically designated a permanent military facility that was much larger than a permanent LZ or FSB. Camps (often known as basecamps) typically housed multi-Bn, multi-Bde or even Div-sized elements, their HQs and suptg units. Terms "Landing Zone" (LZ), "Firebase" (FSB) and "Camp" were often used interchangeably and many bases known by all three names simultaneously, or at different stages in their history. "Landing Zone" often simply referred to anyplace a helicopter might land, i.e., an undefended clearing in jungle. Such LZs often later grew into FSBs with addn of Arty and, later, into full-fledged and permanent Landing Zones. General distinction between a permanent LZ and FSB was that an LZ was usually much larger than a FSB and, although it may have also provided Arty fire supt as one of its functions, typically contained facilities designed to house helos and their suptg units, ground transport, POL facilities, engr elements, ammo dumps, medical and even recreational facilities, most of which were absent or minimal on a FSB. Camps were often simply the last evolutionary stage of an installation as it grew from an LZ to a firebase, then to a permanent LZ, and then to a camp or basecamp. See also Fire Support Base.

Camp de Maries - Settlements built within or adj to French forts, and for dependents and *congai* of French soldiers. Meant to protect dependents from Vietminh reprisals. Per *Street Without Joy*, p 140.

Can Bo - "Revolutionary Development" personnel of SVN Govt. Sometimes worked with USMC CAP teams.

Can Bo Platoons - RVN 60-man rural reconstruction units that were part of Ngu Hanh Son Pacification Prgm S of Da Nang in '65. Phrase *Can Bo* was of Chinese origin and used by Viet Minh in WWII to denote highly motivated troops operating against French and Japanese. See U.S. *Marines in Vietnam, 1966*, p 38.

Can Hoa - Viet phrase for "Firebase." Dr. Van Hanh Hoang offered this translation: "Ca(n Cu+' Ho?a Lu+.c ll = Fire Base."

Canberra - See B-57.

Candle Stick Operations - C-123 flare ships (designed for long-term, ground-supt night illum) flying out of NKP Thailand. These particular acft performed modified FAC missions over the HCMT at night looking for trucks, and when found, night-capable fighter-bombers were launched and the C-123 would drop ground marks, flares and then direct their strikes. Acft carried huge flare loads and could loiter on target for many hours. See *Da Nang Diary*, p 175.

Canister Rounds - A.k.a. Flechette Round and Beehive Round. Devastating antipersonnel arty and tank round available in various calibers (76mm, 90mm, 105mm, 155mm, 8" and also used in 90mm recoilless rifle and 2.75" aerial rockets). Contained thousands of shot or flechette darts. After being fired, it was designed to open just beyond the muzzle using a secondary charge to disperse its contents in wide fan (much like a shotgun) that was very effective against ground frontal assaults. Its design required weapon's barrel to be depressed parallel to ground and, in most cases, was used as "last resort" option, as enemy was about to overrun a position. Its use required advance warning so that friendly elements defending the perimeter in its path could take cover. Called the "Beehive Round" for sound it made when fired and for volume of shrapnel it produced. Perhaps one of the more successful munitions designs of war. The 90mm Tank Flechette rnd could contain either 1,280 shot, or 5,600-10,000 flechette-shaped darts. Per *Mad Minutes and Vietnam Moments,* p 313, its 1st use in combat took place 7Nov66, during Op Geronimo, when Capt Joe Jenkin's 2d/320th arty used it to break NVA grnd assault.

Cao - One Viet word for "stream" or "river."

Cao Dai -Religious sect centered in Tay Ninh Prov (apx 200,000 of Prov's 310,000 population), with its principal temple, Great Temple of Holy See, built in Long Hoa near Tay Ninh. At one time, sect had its own 50,000 man army and was one of leading political forces in SVN. See also Temple of Holy See.

CAP - Civil Action Patrol (U.S. Army).

CAP - Combined Action Platoon. Successor acronym to CAC and CACO (Combined Action Company) for Marine plt (or smaller) sized units permanently situated with and working with RF/RF/ARVN units based in rural civilian populations and villes (see also CAC entry). Very 1st CAP Team was apparently created 14May66 when LtGen Victor Krulak secretly returned to VN against the orders of Gen Westmoreland. That day, a 14-man squad of 3d plt (India Company, 3d Bn, 1st Marines) + two Corpsman and a mortar team was designated the 1st CAP team in Chu Lai area and separated from its company completely. Krulak told them to remain at Ky Hoa indefinitely and not to join in ops with any other units, then he and India Co left them to fend for themselves. Team was one of first 37 "semi-secret" CAP teams formed at end of '66, although "official" USMC records show no teams created before '67 (per www.capmarine.com/ky_hoa/dayone.html). It is little known that U.S. army also had a CAP program (See CAP Teams, U.S. Army). See also Ky Hoa CAP, CAC, CAG and CUPP.

CAP Teams (U.S. Army) - U.S. Army Civil Action Patrol Team. Similar to USMC CUPP Teams but on smaller scale; however, Army CAP Teams (in 101st Abn, at any rate) did not live with SVN units or among civilians. In 101st, each 3-man team had an officer (Lt), RTO and instructor. CAP team with which author served for 2 wks in Jun70 for example, was created in Summer of '70, and billeted at 101st's Eagle Beach R&R facility E of Hue.

CAP Teams (USMC) - Combined Action Platoons. See CAC.

CAP, Mobile Teams - See Mobile CAP Teams.

Capital Regiment, The - Vietminh 112th Rgt (later 304th Div and "Bde Doc-Lap") engaged during Op Ceinture, Nov-Dec47.

CAPT - Captain.

Capt. - Captain.

CAR 15 - See XM-177E2.

CAR 16 - See XM-177E2.

Caravelle - *Caravelle* and *Nouvelles du Nord-Viet-Nam* were weekly news magazines published by French during '50's. French soldiers placed ads in them to find other troops willing to swap jobs, a practice allowed by French Army. *Street Without Joy*, refers to them as "Gold mines of information" (pp 15, 16).

CARE - Co-operative for American Relief Everywhere.

Cargomaster - Trade name for C-133 acft. 4,360 mi rnge and 300 kts top spd. mfgd by Douglas Acft.

Caribou - Trade name For U.S. DHC-4, twin-eng, prop-driven, STOL acft. 242 mi rnge, 215 kts top spd. mfgd by D. H. Canada.

Casevac'd - RNZA/RAR expression equivalent to U.S. term "Medevaced," for medical evacuation.

Castan, Sam - (BR 64-62?) 32-year old senior editor for *Look* Magazine, killed along with most of a Plt of C C/1st/12th Cav, 1st Cav Div, when overrun on LZ Hereford (NE Vinh Thanh Valley), 22May66, during Op Crazy Horse. Rolls of film inc photos taken of doomed plt only minutes before attack were found on body of NVA soldier in later battle. See photos in *Men Facing Death* Chapter of *Battles in the Monsoon*, pp 114-136.

Castle Courier - Newspaper of 815th Engr Bn and/or 20th Engrs. See Wooly Bully II Basecamp in main alpha listing.

Casualty Landmarks - Per Dick Arnold, 2d week of May '68 was most deadly week of war, with 616 Americans KIA. He also notes that 173d Abn Div apparently holds tragic distinction of suffering most KIA in single company in one day, when A Co, 2d/503d lost 76 KIA, 22Jun67 (see Operation Stilwell in main alpha list).

cat - category (TAD).

CAT - Civil Air Transport Co. Founded by Gen. Claire Chennault and W. Willauer in China following WWII. In Aug50, purchased by CIA as cover for covert intel ops. See also Air America.

Cat Fours - A.k.a. Category Four Enlistees. See Project 100,000.

Cat Killer - Call-sign of 220th Reconnaissance Airplane Co (RAC). Operated out of Quang Ngai, '67.

Catalina - U.S. Amphib acft (flying boat) used by French for coastal surveillance and Junk interdiction in '50's. Per *Street Without Joy*, pp 261. See *Belleau Woods* in main alpha listing.

Category Four Enlistee - A.k.a. Cat Fours. See Project 100,000.

CATO - Combat Arms Trng Organization. Initial U.S. sponsored SVN military trng effort that began in '55, per *How We Got There*, by Ray Bows in Dec99 *Military* Mag, pp 20-21.

Cayuse - Trade name for OH-64, light observation helicopter (LOH), affectionately nicknamed "Loach." 380 mi rnge, 150 kts top spd. mfgd by Hughes Avn. See also "Loach."

CB - Combat Base.

CB - Navy Mobile Construction Bn personnel. A.k.a. "Seabees."

CBU - See Cluster Bomb Unit.

CBU-24 - Cluster Bomb Units dropped by F-4 Phantom acft (et al) that, after being dropped, split in half apx halfway to target, releasing hundreds of spin-armed, baseball-sized bomblets that exploded on impact. Per *Da Nang Diary,* p 182, explosion "resembled a giant doughnut with a hollow center." A B-52 could carry 44,000 CBU's in single load. See Cluster Bomb Unit.

CBU-25 - 2.75" Rocket borne CBU. See Cluster Bomb Unit.

CC - Command & Control, sometimes C&C.

CCB - Command Communications Boat (USN). Typically a Monitor ATC vessel configured primarily for commo with 9th Inf MRF units on land and other ships.

CCC - Command & Control Central (MACV-SOG).
CCN - Command & Control North (MACV-SOG).
CCS - Command & Control South (MACV-SOG).
CCW - counter-clockwise (TAD).
CD - Coastal Division (USN).
Civilian Defense Corps - See Hue Civilian Defense Corps.
CDR - Commander (USN rank).
Cdr - Commander (USN rank).
CEC - Civil Engineer Corps.
Centipedes - Centipedes were as feared by many U.S. ground troops as was enemy! Some varieties were very large, from 6" to 12" in length, and bite apparently both extremely painful and potentially dangerous. See *Baptism*, pp 246-247.
CG - U.S. Coast Guard.
CGC - Coast Guard Cutter. See also USCG.
CGN - Guided Missile Cruiser (nuclear-powered).
CH - Channel (TAD).
CH-21 Shawnee - U.S. twin-rotor, medium helicopter a.k.a. "The Banana." Had 300 mi rnge, 130 kts top spd. mfgd by Piasecki. . See: www.acala.ria.army.mil/acala/sma/asa/ AAHIST.htm.
CH-47 Chinook - U.S. twin-rotor transport helicopter with 115 mi rnge, 130 kts top spd. mfgd by Boeing Acft. Could carry apx 30 fully equipped Inf troops and crew of 4. Often carried external loads of supplies, dozers, arty pieces and other acft/helos. . See: www.acala.ria.army.mil/acala/sma/ asa/AAHIST.htm.
CH-54 Tarhe - U.S. Twin-rotor, heavy-cargo lift helicopter with 230 mi rnge, 125 kts top spd. mfgd by Sikorsky. Heaviest payload capacity of all helos in war, and also had fasted vertical acceleration. Could lift hvy dozers, 155mm arty pieces and even deliver 10,000 lb Combat Trap bombs for instant LZ creation. See: www.acala1.ria.army.mil/acala/sma/ asa/AAHIST.htm.
Chaigar - Alleged U.S. defector. Reportedly fought actively against U.S. troops in SVN, and later with Khmer Rouge in Cambodia, where it is said he died fighting ARVN. This tall, red-headed man is said to have been a USMC deserter. See also Black Khmer. Data per *Prisoners of Hope*, p 64.
Chaine - "mountain range."
Cham - Cambodian sect fighting with the KKK and SF MGFs. KKK were apparently composed primarily of Khmer-Serei and Cham. Khmer Serei where a.k.a. the Free Cambodians and were intent on ridding Cambodia of Prince Sihanouk's control. Cham were mostly Muslim. See *Mobile Guerrilla Force* p 157.
Champa - Region of central ancient VN between the Red River Delta and Mekong Delta. An Indianized-kingdom that until 15th century withstood advance of Viet expansion for 1,000 years.
Charles-Marie David de Mayréna - See Kingdom of Sedang.
Charlie Sites - A.k.a. Charley Sites. According to Kent Spalding, Lima Sites were CIA/USAF secret AFs/positions in Laos, "Charlie Sites" those in Cambodia, and "Victor Sites" those in SVN. See also LS and Lima Sites.
Chasseur Laottiens - Laotian Light Inf serving under French.
Chasseurs Blindes - French for "Armored Cavalry." HQ for the *1st Chasseurs Blindes* and Airborne Grp 1 was in Hanoi.
Chat and Gravel - An explosive material that resembled ordinary gravel. When wet, it was harmless, but when dry, the pressure of a man's footstep could detonate it. SVNAF piloted acft suptg MAC-SOG's 34-Alpha Prgm dropping ARVN spies into NVN sometimes carried a "wet" supply of material. After their ARVN spy cargo had been dropped over NVN, the acft would then dump the "Chat" along Ho Chi Minh Trail during return leg. Data per *Gulf of Tonkin Revisited*, by Gregory Johnson, in Jan 2000 issue of *MILITARY* Mag, pp 5-8.
Chatterbox - Call-sign, USMC Med Helo Sqdn HMM 364.
Chau - One Viet word for "island."
CHC - Chaplain Corps (USN).
Cherry – See FNG.
Chiang Kai-Shek - See Potsdam Agreement.
Chicken of the Sea-See *Helgoland* in main alpha section.
Chieu Hoi Program – Program that encouraged VC/NVA to defect. Chieu Hoi translated literally as "Open Arms." Many million of leaflets and/or safe conduct passes were air-dropped on enemy-controlled areas. Many Psy Ops acft and vehicles were also employed to broadcast Chieu Hoi messages throughout SVN. Generally regarded as marginally successful prgm. Those who surrendered/defected under prgm were a.k.a. "Hoi Chanh" and often trained for integration into allied units working same areas in which individual had been captured. Many contributed greatly to the effectiveness of U.S. units and often distinguished themselves otherwise, earning decorations as high as Silver Star. See also Hoi Chanh and FSB Buffalo.
Chieu Tich Chung - Legendary PF unit cmdr who sported a black Khaki outfit complete with pair of pearl-handled pistols. See Biet Kichs in main alpha listing..
Chin Si - Vietnamese phrase meaning "War Hero."
China Boy Battalion - Nung mercenary unit w/U.S. Advisors. See C-3 Cmpd in main alpha listings.
China, Forces of - Both Taiwan (ROC) and Communist China contributed forces to war. See Major Command Section.
Chinook - Trade name for CH-47 twin-rotor helicopter. 115 mi rnge, 130 kts top spd. mfgd by Boeing Acft.
Cho - One Viet word for "market."
Choctaw - Trade name for H-53, single-rotor SAR helicopter (USAF). 180 mi rnge, 120 kts top spd. mfgd by Sikorsky.
Choke Point Bombing - USAF adaptation to greatly-reduced Congressional funding in late '70 to early '71. Because HCMT network had expanded tremendously in concert with reduced aerial resources as U.S. withdrew from conflict, MACV decided to ignore most of the trail and instead focus all 7th AF sorties on several "Choke Points" where NVA transport options were narrowed or were channeled by terrain. Four "Target Boxes" were selected at the Mu Gia, Ban Karai and Ban Raving Passes, as well as another site immed W of the DMZ (each apx 1 km by 2 km in size). A series of sophisticated sensor devices new to war were then planted around sites and monitored by high-altitude unmanned drones that forwarded sound/seismic data to various relay stations and other, manned acft. Based on that data, each point was then scheduled for twenty-seven B-52 sorties plus between 125 to 150 Tac Air sorties every single day over a 60-day period such that Target Boxes would be receiving incoming bombs, CBUs and other ordnance every 20 minutes, 24 hours a day! Per *A Better War*, p 239.
Choo Choo Train Insertion - Certainly one of strangest recon team insertions of war. Per Dave Robin, in early '69, elements of Recon plt/B/1st/26th Marines was inserted by train (via QL-1 railway) near base of Hai Van Mtn on mission to locate rocket launching sites. When unit arrived at the train station near Camp Reasoner ("all decked-out like Rambo"), civilian authorities would not allow boarding until all had purchased a

proper ticket! After dutifully paying their fare, the patrol disembarked train as it passed through tunnel near the objective. See also FSB Le Loi for equally unusual patrol insertion method.
Chopper - Helicopter.
Christmas Bombing, The - A.k.a. Linebacker II, the bombing of targets in NVN, 18-31Dec68. In part, an attempt to lighten NVA pressure on Khe Sanh CB. NVN.
Chu Luc - See Du Kich in Glossary.
CIA - Captured in action.
CIA - Central Intelligence Agency.
CID - Criminal Investigation Division (U.S. Army).
CIDG - Civilian Irregular Defense Group.
CILHI - Central Identification Lab, Hawaii. U.S. govt agency charged with identifying recovered remains of U.S. MIAs. See *Prisoners of Hope*, pp 110-121.
Cinnamon General, The - Derisive nickname for Gen. Van Toan, CG, 2d ARVN Div. Per Nguyen Cao Ky, while Ky was Prime Minister in '66, Gen Toan made millions of dollars on black market by peddling stolen cinnamon being produced in mtns south of Da Nang; the area in which Toan's troops were operating. Ky forced him to abandon practice but kept him as general because he was a brave and aggressive leader in battle. Per Nguyen Cao Ky's *Twenty Years and Twenty Days*, p 109.
CINCPAC - Commander in Chief, Pacific.
CINCPACAF - Commander in Chief, Pacific Air Force.
CINCPACFLT - Commander in Chief, U.S. Pacific Fleet.
CINCSAC - Commander in Chief, Strategic Air Command.
civ - civilian (TAD).
CIV - Civilian agencies (TAD).
ck - check (TAD).
Civil Air Transport - See CAT.
Civil Air Transport Company - See Air America and CAT.
CLA - Cambodian Liberation Army. See *Agence France Presse*.
Class I Supplies - Food (USMC).
Class V Supplies - Ammo (USMC).
Class Six Store - A.k.a. Class VI Store. U.S. military liquor stores. Required minimum rank of E-6 (NCO) and special ration cards for their use in SVN. Hard liquor could be purchased there at very heavily discounted prices. (author recalls a quart of *Beefeaters* Gin or *Canadian Club* whiskey being priced at $1.15? each).
Claymore Mine - See M-18 A1 Anti-Personnel Mine.
CLC - Combat Leadership Course (Army).
CLD - Command Liaison Detachment. A Special Forces term.
CLG - Guided Missile Light Cruiser (USN).
Click - Slang for kilometer. See also "klick."
CLITC - Chi Lang Individual Training Center.
clnc - clearance (TAD).
clsd - closed (TAD).
Cluster Bombs - A.k.a. CBUs or Cluster Bomb units. Acft and Arty delivered anti-personnel munitions that upon impact distributed hundreds of bomblets that were scattered over a large area from the main point of impact and then in turn exploded, sending steel pellets in all directions (initial primary distribution explosive could be set to either go off on impact or at a preset altitude just above the ground). Very lethal, effective and much feared weapon, "It was pure misery," said NVA Col Luc in a 1996 interview (per *Sparring With Charlie*, p. 27). Was also made in 2.75" rocket borne format as well.
CM - Construction Mechanic (USN).
Cmd - Command.
Cmdr - Commander. The boss, or a Naval rank.
Cmnd - Command.
Cmpd - Compound.
CN Gas - Standard tear-gas riot agent. Unlike CS, had no vomit agent. Grenade form was common. See also M-79 Grenade Launcher, E-158 Canister and CS Gas; all in Glossary.
CNO - Chief of Naval Operations.
Cntrl - control.
CO - Commanding Officer.
Coach - A call-sign of the 155th AHC.
Coastal Surveillance Force - enemy infiltration along SVN's 1,200 mi-long coast. U.S. 7th Fleet creation designed to control A.k.a. Market Time.
COB - Combat Operations Base.
Cobra - A call-sign of the 114th Avn and 129th AHC.
Cobra - Nickname of AH-1 *Bell* Huey Cobra Helo Gunship. 1st helicopter designed exclusively as a weapons platform. See AH-1.
COBRAA - Combined Reconnaissance American-ARVN. Sister prgm to "Pair-Off Operations." Initiated by 3d/506th Inf, Apr69, and involving 3d/506th Inf, 101st Abn (Sep) plus elements of 44th ARVN Rgt and RF in Binh Thuan Pr, II Corps.
Cochin China - Annam, Cochin China and Tonkin were three major regions of Vietnam as named by French.
COFRAM Rounds - Controlled Fragmentation Ordnance. An experimental anti-personnel arty rnd (similar to Beehive Rnd) that retro-fired about 100 golf ball-sized impact grenades after impacting or soon after leaving the muzzle of cannon. Top secret weapon when introduced in late '67(?), one of 1st recorded combat uses occurred at 0035 hrs 7Feb68, when Lang Vei SF Camp near KSCB was overrun. 4th Div arty units 1st used them at Polei Kleng in '68. Initial tests showed them to be erratic but very effective against NVA ground assaults. Nicknamed "Firecracker" Rounds because the secondary bomblets exploding sounded very much like a string of firecrackers exploding.
Colt Commander - 9mm version of M-119A .45 caliber pistol. Only issued to General Offs and some SF troops. See M-119A1.
Colt Commando - See XM-177E2.
Comanchero - Call-sign for A Co 101st Avn Bn.
Combat Trap - USAF code name for its MK-121, 10,000 lb. bomb. Used primarily for clearing vegetation for LZs or initial stage of FSB const. FSBs Mace and Spear in Quang Nam Pr were cleared by device as part of TF Yankee's assault on Base Area 112, Jan-Feb69. See also Daisy Cutter and Commando Vault.
Combined Action Groups - CAG Cos and Plts. See CAG, CAC, CAP and CUPP.
Comm – Commercial or communication.
comm - communication (TAD).
Command Chronologies - USMC cmd historical chronologies. See Table of Contents, *Researching the Vietnam War*.
Commando Bergerol - Small French commando unit assigned to GM 100, Nov53. Such units were typically given last name of their cmdg officer. See *Street Without Joy*, p 186.
Commando Club - See Commando Club in main alpha index.
Commando Hunt Operation - Air campaign designed to place constant umbrella of air control/FAC/SCAR missions over 2,000 sq. mi. sector of HCMT in Laos and contiguous to SVN. Initiated Nov68. See also Steel Tiger, Barrel Roll and Tiger Hound.

Commando Sabre - Code name of op employing F-100Fs as 1st Fast FACs over NVN. Call-sign was Misty. Began Jun67, w/flights out of Phu Cat AB. Misty was inactivated in late May69. See also Phu Cat AB in main alpha listing.
Commando Units, French - Small, specialized French units of 1st Indochina War typically assembled for specific purpose and typically given last name of their cmdg officer.
Commando Vault - Code name for USAF's conventional 15,000 lb. iron bomb. See Daisy Cutter and Combat Trap.
Committee of National Leadership - Organization of ARVN military generals that set national and military policies during the various military regimes that followed ouster of Diem. See also Military Council, Armed Forces Council, Military Revolutionary Council, and Nguyen Cao Ky.
Communal Routes - HL road designation. The least improved of road systems in SVN and identifiable by use of a diamond box to enclose a two-digit numeric identifier. Typically joined small towns with one another and ordinarily did not cross provincial borders/ Were almost all dirt roads. See also QL, LTL, TL, Route, Highway, HL, R. C., *Route Colonial*, as well as the Principal Roadways of South Vietnam Section.
COMNAVFORV - Commander U.S. Naval Forces, Vietnam.
Company - A.k.a. "Co." At infantry level for both USMC and Army, a unit commanded by a Capt or 1Lt, and containing 3 to 4 platoons. Each Co also inc rear elements providing clerical, equip, supplies, arms and personnel supt. Could vary in size from as little as perhaps 50 to many as 240 men, but in combat situation, typically 100 to 150 men. See also Battalion.
Compd - Compound.
COMUSMACV - Cmdr U.S. Military Assistance Cmd, Vietnam.
Con - One Viet word for "island."
conc - concrete.
cond - condition(s) (TAD).
Condor - Call-sign for C Trp, 2d Sqdn, 17th Cav.
Congai - Common law wives/concubines of French soldiers during 1st Indochina War. Not infrequently spies planted by Vietminh.
Congrints - USMC slang for "Congressional Interest" or "Congressional Inquiry."
Connie Francis Snake - In '67, the Inf security at 584th's Eng Co's quarry (Weigt-Davis?) was playing a Connie Francis record on child's battery-powered record player when a guard someone approaching and challenged them. There was no response, so the guard opened fire. Turns out the figure was a King Cobra apparently attracted by music! It got passed guard and into a bunker where it was dispatched via .45 pistol. Snake was "as long as dump truck's bed," according to one witness.
Consolidated RVNAF Improvement/Modernization - See CRIMP.
const - construction (TAD).
Continental Air Services - Apparent adjunct of Air America's CIA-run air service operating in Indochina.
convl - conventional (TAD).
Cooke, Able Seaman - See *USS Constitution* in main alpha list.
Cooper-Church Amendment - Amendment to Defense Appropriations bill passed in '70 that denied funding for U.S. ground ops in Laos or Cambodia. See *A Better War*, p 228.
Copperhead - A call-sign of the 162d AHC.
copter - helicopter (TAD).
Corps - Combat Tactical Zones (CTZs) designated as: I Corps, II Corps, III Corps, IV Corps and Special Capitol Zone. Ran from N to S, with I Corps the northernmost Corps. Corps were re-designated "Military Regions" (MRs 1 through 4), as of 1Jul70. Corps also describes a military unit comprised of any number of Divs under cmd of a single Corps Cmdr (several Corps would form an "Army"). See Military Region Section.
Corps - Military Region, or multi-Division unit.
Corral Program - A.k.a. Op Corral? Per David Graham, 29th Arty FDC at Dak To, '68-69, the prgm involved hush-hush 175mm arty missions in Tri-border area of Laos and Cambodia to W Dak To. 4th Div HQ would send coded grids to FDC at Dak To, which would then decode and then re-shackle them in another form. then transmit target info to 175mm Btys within range of targets. Were likely fired on targets designated by SOG or LRRP Teams operating "over the fence" in those countries, or targets found by Covey and/or other forms of aerial or electronic surveillance. Kontum Prov, II Corps.
Corral, Operation - See Corral Program.
Corsair II - Trade name for A-7 acft. 4,000 mi rnge, 700 kts top spd. mfgd by Chance-Vought.
Corsairs - U.S. carrier-based, prop-driven fighter-bomber used by French in the '50's. See Bearcats in Glossary.
COSVN - Acronym for "Central Office of South Vietnam," the NLF's (VC) elusive and legendary mobile HQ. Formed in '62 by combining Interzone V and NAMBO Interzone NLF regional Cmds into a single cmd. Hunted relentlessly but without success by allies throughout war. See Major Command Section.
COSVN Directive 38 - Issued by COSVN in conjunction with 3Oct71 general election in SVN. Approved VC participation in electoral process but called for paramilitary ops to disrupt election and embarrass SVN govt.
COSVN Guy, The - Possibly a.k.a. "Superspook A-22"? SVN intel agent inside VC infrastructure circa '68. See Superspook.
COSVN Resolution Nine - Major policy statement of NVA/VC high cmd captured after Tet '68, that was an admission of how badly they had been hurt in offensive, and indicated they would be incapable of any sustained ops for what CIA analysis found would be at least 2 years. See *Facing the Phoenix*, p 30.
Cougar - A call-sign of the 57th AHC.
Cougar - Trade name for TF-9J jet acft. 600 mi rnge, 705 kts top spd. mfgd by Grumman Avn.
Coup Troops - Derisive nickname for ARVN armored forces because their units were always involved in coup attempts. ARVN tanks/armor were also referred to sarcastically as "Voting Machines" because of their use during elections.
Covey - Call-sign for special mission, USAF FACs of 20th TASS (et al?) flying sorties "over the Fence" into Laos from Pleiku and Da Nang. Their ops later in war are detailed in *Da Nang Diary*.
Cowboy - Call-sign of the 335th AHC.
CP - Command Post.
Cpl - Corporal.
Crash at Marble Mountain "O" Club - On 14Sep66, CH-46 #EP-165 (bureau #152506) of HMM-265 suffered "In-Flight Control System Failure" at 700' over ocean and immediately in front of Marble Mtn Officer's Club. It broke in half and crashed in 5' of water. Miraculously, all aboard survived, in part due to quick reaction of off-duty pilots lounging on nearby beach. Per *Bonnie-Sue*, pp 158-163.

CRB - Cam Ranh Bay
CRIMP - Consolidated RVNAF Improvement and Modernization Prgm. Approved by Washington Jun70, plan was designed to expand SVN's military complement to 12 ground combat Divs (10 Inf, 1 Abn, and 1 Marine Div), 50 air sqdns, 1,200+ naval vessels, and increase RF/PF forces to more than 50% of all SVN's military strength. Between '68 and '72, RVNAF's strength grew from 700,000 to more then 1.1 million men, per *A Better War*, p 214-5.
CRIP - Combined Reconnaissance and Intelligence Platoon. Acronym employed by at least the 25th Inf Div. '68.
Croc - A call-sign of the 119th AHC.
Crocodiles in Vietnam - Wide distribution. 2 species of Croc are native to VN, the freshwater Croc (C. siamensis) and saltwater Croc (C. porosus). In Spring '70, this author encountered a huge Croc (20' long?) in the Song Ta Trach River, apx 17 km SSE Hue (near YD 813-040) and generally W Nui Mo Tau, though his comrades did not believe him at time (despite his soiled shorts)! Because animal's head was not visible as it shot under his patrol boat (he at first thought it to be torpedo of some sort), he did not realize it was a Croc, but '97 query to Viet govt Biologist revealed creature's identity (and further soiling of shorts). Per www.pownetwork.org/bios/t/t046.htm, on 13Jan70, LRRP Sgt Glenn Tubbs was on patrol on the Cambodian border when, while attempting to cross a stream, lost his balance and was swept away by strong current. Witnesses said he went under 5 times and, that further downstream, he was "being attacked by alligators [likely Crocs]. The team members located hundreds of the creatures [seems an unlikely number] downstream as they searched for anything left of Glenn Tubbs." Incident occurred at YA 675-330, which is in Se San/Tonle San River near Phum Ban Phinay, apx 18 km WNW Duc Co and 23 km SW Plei Djereng. Prior to '75, Viets apparently rarely ventured into deep forest to capture wild Crocs, so there were still substantial numbers to that point. In 80's and 90's however, VN and Cambode smugglers began selling Croc skins in neighboring countries and Crocs became endangered in VN. Since '92, Croc hunting has been prohibited in VN. Cambodian Crocs sometimes migrate via Mekong into VN. See also Roberts, Edmund. Some data per *Crocodile Specialist Group Newsletter 144B* at www.flmnh.ufl.edu/natsci/herpetology/newsletter/news144b.htm, and Tubbs MIA data per Dick Arnold.
Crook, Edward, 1st Sgt - 1960 Olympics boxing gold medalist. Served with C/4th/503d Inf, 173d Abn Bde, and involved in TF Black's major battle of 11-12Nov67, vicinity of Hills 823 and 889 during Battle for Dak To.
Crosby, Bing - See American Radio Service.
Cross of Gallantry - See Vietnamese Cross of Gallantry.
Crossbow - A call-sign of the 173d AHC.
crs - course (TAD).
Crusader - A call-sign of the 187th AHC.
Crusader - Trade name of U.S. F-8, single eng jet, carrier-based fighter-bomber. Had 453 mi rnge, 1,230 kts top spd. mfgd by Chance-Vought.
CS Gas - Standard tear-gas riot agent mixed with vomit inducing agent. Available in grenades, M-79, mortar and arty rnds. Also came in powdered form (provided long-term dispersal and often used to render tunnel complexes unusable indefinitely). See also M-79 Grenade Launcher and E-158 Canister in Glossary.
CS Gas Incident - International outcry was triggered when *TIME* Mag ran story (apparently based on a Peter Arnett AP report) of 2d/7th Marine's use of gas grenades to clear VC bunkers/caves near Qui Nhon during Op Stomp, 5-7Sep65. Story's title was *Tears of Death,* and writer inferred gas was poisonous. World press then attacked in full force, declaring Marines to be inhumane and barbarians. Hanoi chimed-in, claiming U.S. was using toxic agents to murder Viet civilians. A Bn ammo Sgt had suggested using tear gas grenades (supply on hand for possible riot control) to flush enemy from caves/bunkers instead of blasting them out and, with Bn staff and chaplain approval, idea was adopted as means of saving lives of both sides. 48 grenades were used in the op and results were described as "Spectacular" in that enemy cleared caves immediately and surrendered without a fight. USMC would have fired 2/7's CO (LTC Leon Utter) over incident had not Army LtGen Stanley "Swede" Larsen intervened. See Chp 8, *Utter's Battalion* for discussion, and where author correctly points out that later in war CS and tear-gas agents were widely used in both gas and powder forms. See also CS Gas and Red Devils.
CSC - Coastal Surveillance Center (USN).
CSF - Camp Strike Force.
CSWC - Crew Served Weapons captured.
ctc - contact (TAD).
CTF - Commander Task Force (USN).
CTG - Commander Task Group (USN).
ctl - control (TAD).
CTLZ - Control Zone (TAD).
Ctr - Center.
ctrl - control.
CTU - Commander Task Unit (USN).
CTZ - Corps (sometimes, "Combat") Tactical Zones. See Corps.
Cua - Vietnamese word for estuary, or river mouth.
Culao - One Viet word for "island."
CUPP - Combined Unit Pacification Program. USMC successor to or adjunct to CAP pacification prgm. Per Ed Saragoza, 3d CAG and CUPP vet, was apparently 1st initiated in '70, and differed from CAP ops in that all activities (Medcaps, training and etc.) took place in secure areas and teams did not patrol or pull ambush duties outside assigned villes. See also CAC, CAP and CAG.
Custer - Per *Rites of Passage*, in '67 was 1st/14th Inf/25th Div radio code for an ambush position, as was term "Peach," among others. 3d Bde/25th Div periodically changed code word to confuse enemy.
CV - Aircraft Carrier (USN).
CVA - Attack Acft Carrier (USN).
CVAN - Attack Acft Carrier, Nuclear-Powered) (USN).
CVS - Antisubmarine Warfare Supt Acft Carrier (USN).
CVSQ - Carrier Antisubmarine Warfare Air Group (USN).
CW - Clockwise or continuous wave (TAD).
D - Destroyer (USN).
DA - Department of the Army.
Da Nang Anti-Infiltration System - A.k.a. DIAS. Covered portions of both AT and BT grid zones in an arc around Da Nang. Brainchild of III MAF; was project similar to McNamara's DMZ Wall. Was 1st line of defense for Da Nang Vital Area (the city, its military facilities and surrounding population within 122mm rocket range), and to eliminate rocket/mortar attacks. In Jun68, 1st Mar Div began const of this 12 kilometer-long physical barrier along outer edge of "Rocket Belt" in semi-circle centered on Da Nang and with

radius equal to max range of 122mm rocket. Was 500 meter wide strip of land cleared of all vegetation and habitation, containing 2 barbed-wire fences, concertina wire, 23 observation towers, numerous land mines and sophisticated electronic sensors. Work tapered off and halted in late '68 due to other demands but was resumed by Mar69. By Jun69, Marine, ARVN and Korean engrs had completed clearing entire 500 meter wide swath but remaining elements of design were only partially completed before Marines departed in late '69. Thereafter they project fell into disarray. Was III MAF's intention that DAIS would require only 1,800 Marines to operate effectively (two 105mm Arty Btys, and 5 rifle companies of 2d and 3d Bns, 7th Marines) thereby freeing over 5,000 other Marines to conduct ops in Quang Nam/Quang Tin Provs. Like MacNamara's wall, apparently a general failure. Quang Nam Prov, I Corps.

Da Nang Vital Area - Any of Da Nang, its military facilities and surrounding population that were within NVA 122mm rocket range. See Da Nang Anti-Infiltration System.

Da Nang, Evacuation of - Mar75. Op to evac U.S. and allied personnel from Da Nang and other ports along coast of SVN. On 24Mar75, as NVA approached Da Nang, USN Military Sealift Cmd (MSC; formerly MSTS), deployed 5 tugs, pulling total of six barges, from Vung Tau toward Da Nang to assist in evac of that city. Tugs were: *Asiatic Stamina*, *Chitose Maru*, *Osceola*, *Pawnee*, *Shibaura Maru*. On 25Mar75, 11 more ships were alerted for evac op; they were: *SS American Racer, SS Green Forest, SS Green Port, SS Green Wave, SS Pioneer Commander, SS Pioneer Contender, SS Transcolorado, USNS Greenville Victory, USNS Sgt Andrew Miller, USNS Sgt Truman Kimbro, Boo Heung Pioneer* (Korean-flag LST). See also Op Frequent Wind in main alpha listing, as well as Buong Incident, Final Offensive and American Radio Service in Glossary. Some data per USN Historical Center data at www.history.navy.mil/seairland.

Dac Cong - Elite NVA Combat Engr unit. Also name of special ARVN observation units supplemented by USMC patrols successfully employed during Op Golden Fleece, Sep66, in Nui Nham-Nui Choi Hill mass (Mo Duc Dist, Quang Ngai Prov), and much farther W than VC anticipated. Discussed in *USMC in Vietnam, 1966*, p 236-7.

Dai Doi Du-Kich - Vietnamese term for peasant Vietminh Militia of 1st Indochina War.

Dai Doi Phong Khong - A Vietminh Anti-Aircraft Co. Normally equipped with a 20mm cannon, four .50 Cal MGs and 2 BARs. See also Trung Doi Phong Khong. Per *Street Without Joy*, p 266.

Dia Phong - Also Dia Phong. See Du Kich in Glossary.

Daily Journal – A.k.a. the *Battalion Daily Staff Journal or Duty Officer's Log* (Form AR 220-346). A daily and very highly detailed 24-hour summary of Army battalion's daily activities and radio traffic. See Table of Contents, *Researching the Vietnam War* entry.

Daisy Cutter - Nickname for largest non-nuclear bomb in USAF inventory during VN era. Official designation was BLU-82-B. This 15,000 lb. bomb's code name was "Commando Vault," and it was used primarily to clear vegetation for LZ/FSB const. Term "Daisy Cutter" was also generic for any long, pipe-like extension attached to fuse of a bomb to facilitate an above-ground level detonation. See also "Combat Trap."

Dak - One Viet word for "stream."

Dakota C-47 - See C-47 and AC-47 acft.

Dam - One Viet word for "lagoon" or "bay."

Dan Vang Quang, General - Per Nguyen Cao Ky, Quang was an ARVN 4th Corps General notorious for his dealings in black market opium and rice. Ky had some difficulty persuading President Thieu to fire Quang, but not long after he did, Thieu brought the corrupt Quang back as one of his right-hand men. In his new position, Quang was in charge of granting passports and exit visas, charging $5,000 as bribe to issue a passport, and then increasing the fee to $20,000 per passport as war's end approached and it became obvious the NVA would win. Per Nguyen Cao Ky's *Twenty Years and Twenty Days*, p 110

Dan Ve - Militia units of Diem Govt created in late 50's-early 60's. Predecessor of RF/PF (or Ruff/Puffs) concept.

Daniel Boone Operations - Covert SF ops in Cambodia using 2 or 3 man teams operating with 10 indigenous Viets. Authorized in Jun66 but not operational until May67. Ended in '71. Over those years, 1,835 missions were run and 24 prisoners captured. Ops were kept hidden from Congress. Renamed "Salem House" in Dec68 and "Thot Not" in '71. Cambodia.

dans le Baton - French phrase meaning "in the concrete." Used to describe those French forces assigned to, or pinned-down within, the "suicidal" bunkers of *de Lattre Line*.

DAO - Defense Attaché Office.

Dap - Handshake ritual common among U.S. African-American troops in latter years of war.

Dapsone - Experimental anti-malarial tablet given to U.S. troops in SVN. Meant to prevent Falciparum Malaria, its most virulent form. Was small white pill.

Dapzone - See Dapsone.

Darkhorse - Nickname and/or call-sign of D Trp 1st /4th Air Cav, 1st Inf Div, and C Trp, 16th Air Cav?

DASC - Direct Air Supt Center (TAD).

DASC - Division Air Supt Coordination Center.

Dau Tran Strategies - Literally, "armed struggle movement." Gen Giap's various grand strategies for conducting the war.

daylt - daylight (TAD).

DBP - Dien Bien Phu.

DBST - Double Bituminous Surface Treatment (Asphalt treated crushed rock) (TAD).

DBTITC - Special Forces Dong Ba Thin Individual Training Center. See Dong Ba Thin.

DC - Dental Corps (USN).

DC-3 Skytrain - See C-47 and AC-47 acft.

DD - Destroyer (USN).

DD-214 – Standard form issued to U.S. military personnel upon their discharge from active duty.

DDG - Guided Missile Destroyer (USN).

DDR - Radar Picket Destroyer (USN).

DE - Destroyer Escort (USN).

De - One Viet word for "dike."

de Lattre Line - Beginning in '51, Marshal de Lattre de Tassigny ordered massive const project to build what became known as the '*de Lattre Line.* Project consumed over 51 million cubic yds of concrete and resulted in string of some 2,200, concrete, "pillbox-type" bunkers (nicknamed "tombs") and 900 forts built along a triangular-shaped "Indochina Maginot Line" that was roughly400 km in length and meant to deny Vietminh some 7,500 sq miles of Red River Delta's heart, SE and E Hanoi. Line began at eastern Chinese border, apx 30 km N Mao Cai, then ran generally WSW and parallel to coast, to point apx 60 km N Haiphong where it turned WNW generally following Road No. 2 N of the Red River and Hanoi to Viet Tri. At a point just W Viet Tri, it turned to a course of SSE all the way to ocean, at point perhaps 50 km SW Haiphong. Small, individual concrete bunkers with small firing ports replaced traditional French forts by '51. (see '*de Lattre* Bunkers for more detail). Noted for their isolation/vulnerability, these 9-man bunkers were often out of arty/air supt range and, if attacked, had to survive until help could arrive from nearest main fort. Serving in the bunkers was referred to as *dans le Baton* (In the concrete). Many of the bunkers were wiped-out during war. Like its predecessors in WWII and its successor in the McNamara Line, the *de Lattre line* failed it purpose. Data per *Street Without Joy,* Chp 8, map at p 67.

de Lattre Line Bunkers - A.k.a. "the Tombs." One of some 2,200, concrete, pillbox-type bunkers built along the triangular-shaped *de Lattre* Line that ran roughly 400 km in length and was meant to deny the Vietminh the heart of Red River Delta, SE and E Hanoi. Their const consumed over 51 million cubic yds of concrete and thousands of laborers. The bunkers evolved in design as did French forts, varying from round, to hexagonal, to square in shape, and were fitted with small firing ports to which were added armored covers and doors over time. Their strength and armor coatings increasing over time as well: in Spring '51, the multi-chambered block was built; in mid-'51, design evolved to 3-chambered block; in late '51, the round block emerged with a solidly-built cmd center added; in '52, an easier to build hexagon arrived; in '53 small, square attachments were added to hexagon; finally, in '54, the square, small-block type emerged that was dense enough to absorb direct hits from a 105mm or even a 155mm, and which had armored-steel covers over its portholes and doors. In the later designs, a 4' x 6' centrally located, heavily reinforced and armored radio room was added (aptly nicknamed The Tomb). Each bunker also had the letters PK (Poste Kilometre) painted in white on their exterior, followed by a number that corresponded to its distance in kilometers from main French Fort or major town in area (such as PK-22). Most were staffed by only a 9-man squad that included 1 NCO. Typically, each bunker was allotted but a small ration of ammo for main guns (30 rnds or less). Data per *Street Without Joy,* Chp 8, map of Line at pp 67, 176.

de Maries, Camp – See *Camp de Maries.*

Deadbone - Call-sign for 1st Bde/101st Abn HQ helos.

Deadlock - Call-sign for USMC's VMO-2 Huey Gunships in '66.

Death Volunteers - Militant Buddhists armed with U.S. weapons acquired by joining ARVN and then deserting with the weapons after training. Opposed the Ky military govt in '66, and were in part reason Prime Minister Ky attacked Buddhist strongholds in Da Nang, May66. Per *Twenty Years and Twenty Days*, p 92.

Declination - Map reading term indicating degree of variation between true N and magnetic N for a given location. Annotated on most topo maps and necessary for orienting them to true N. Amount of declination varies over time because magnetic N moves. For most of SVN, declination was/is very small (apx 1°) and, as result, orientation was relatively simple process during war. This fortunate circumstance no doubt resulted in far fewer "friendly fire" casualties due to ease of reporting accurate locations without complicated and confusing magnetic N adjustments.

Decom - decommissioned (TAD).

Deer Mission, The - On 16Jul45, U.S. Army Maj. Allison K. Thomas, 2 other Americans and a French Officer parachuted from China-based acft into Vietminh territory N of Hanoi(?). They were on a commando mission to establish U.S. Advisory Grp in VN that became known as the Deer Mission. A Vietminh official greeted team at DZ, then escorted it to Vietminh trng cmpd whose Bamboo-gated entrance held banner reading: *Welcome to Our American Friends.* Ho Chi Minh soon arrived to greet the team. Fearing French were only interested in re-colonization, he had them sent back to China. Maj Thomas' orders were to establish guerrilla trng center and to build 100-man commando unit that would interdict Japanese supply and commo lines. The existing training facility was suitable for task and he quickly recruited the needed men from Vietminh's own cadre. However, before his newly-trained commandos could go into action, the Vietminh accepted Japan's surrender (just 1 month after Mission's arrival).

DeLong Floating Piers - Patented product of DeLong Corp., used in constructing several deep-draft ports in SVN, among which were Qui Nhon, Vung Tau, Cam Ranh Bay, Vung Ro and Da Nang. Piers were sectional and fabricated outside war zone in wide variety of shapes and sizes, then towed to site and quickly emplaced, thus allowing completion in remarkably short time.

Delta Dagger - Trade name for F-102 jet fighter. 500 mi rnge, 825 kts top spd. mfgd by Convair.

Delta Tangos - Defensive Targets, a.k.a. "DTs." Firing and plotting of arty registrations of pre-set defensive targets. Normally fired and plotted during daylight on likely avenues of enemy approach, DTs were typically assigned numbers and/or letters so that units could quickly call for fire missions simply by calling the number to their arty supt without usual, time-consuming adjustments/commo ordinarily needed to adjust fire to a new target. See Also Tin Trunk.

Demon - A call-sign of the 134th AHC.

Deo - One Viet word for "mountain pass."

Deo Van Long – Head of the T'ai Federation of T'ai tribes of the T'ai Highlands. His HQ was NW Hanoi at Lai Chau throughout French War. See T'ai Tribes.

dep - depart (TAD).

DEP CON - Departure Control (TAD).

DePuy Bunker - Bunkers of a flawed perimeter design credited to 1st Div CG DePuy in '67-68, and later called "Hay Bunkers" after his successor continued its use. Involved 2 circles of bunkers, one just inside the other, and in which occupants covered areas only at 45 degree angles to left and right, but in which no one could see to their direct front. Frontal zones were theoretically covered by the 45 degree fire of suptg bunkers to left, right and rear. Its flaws are discussed in *Platoon Bravo Company*, pp 32-33.

DER - Destroyer Escort, Radar. Radar Picket Ship (USN).

DEROS - Date of Estimated Return from Over Seas; i.e., date one's Vietnam tour was scheduled to end. Standard tour for all military branches except U.S. Marines was 365 days. Tour for a Marine was 13 months. As a matter of course, 30-day and six-month extensions were offered with various incentives. A 6-month extension usually brought with it a 30-day stateside leave before returning to SVN to complete the extension. Despite nature of war, a very significant percentage of troops (even in infantry) decided to extend their tours for any number of reasons, not all of which involved a reward or incentive bonus. Other incentives included "Early-Outs," promotions and pay or shortened enlistment periods, although many troops elected to stay simply because they liked the perks of combat zone duty or the combat environment in general. Many choose to stay because they felt adjusting to stateside life/duty would be too difficult, while others stayed because they felt a strong comradeship for or a strong sense of responsibility toward those left behind. Not all U.S. troops were eager to return home, as one might expect. *A Better War*, at p 288, also notes that at highest level, U.S. troop turnover rate hit 120% per year.

Desoto Missions - Covert USN spy ops that began in early 50's to monitor activities in China, Korea and Soviet Bloc. Destroyer *USS Maddox* was on such a mission when Gulf of Tonkin Incident occurred. See also Desoto Patrols.

Desoto Patrols - USN intel and surveillance patrols in NVN waters that included patrol which led to Gulf of Tonkin Incident and Resolution. In Sep64, 1st Desoto Patrol following Gulf of Tonkin Incident was initiated, and on 17-18Sep64, destroyers *Morton* and *Richard S. Edwards* cruised within 20 mi of NVN. On night of 18Sep64, both fired on what they thought were high-speed vessels in attack. Later investigation left doubt on reality of attack due to lack of firm evidence. Thereafter, Desoto Patrols were discontinued in NVN waters. See also Maddox. Per USN Historical Center data at www.history.navy.mil/seairland/.

destn - destination (TAD).

Destroyer - Trade name for B-66 ECM twin-eng carrier based jet acft mfgd by Douglas Acft.

Det - Detachment.

Determined to Win, Operation - Code name for only confirmed incidence of an NVA airstrike in SVN during American War. At apx 6 pm evening of 28Apr75, a formation of five A-37s arrived over Tan Son Nhut AB (from Phan Rang AB) at 5,000' and went into steep dives, dropping bombs along string of VNAF planes parked on main rwy. Control tower frantically requested acft to identify themselves, but only response was: "These are American-made aircraft!" Three AC-119 gunships and several C-47's were destroyed in attack. Pilots were led by Capt. Nguyen Thanh Trung (who'd defected 8Apr75, as VNAF Lt), and who'd trained a small grp of NVN MIG pilots rudimentary elements of flying the A-37 Dragonfly. NVN Gen Dung told grp they would have only 1 day and 1 chance to make attack. By coincidence, flight left Phan Rang at 5:15 pm 28Apr75, as then President Huong was making his resignation speech. Data per *Vietnam Experience* series, *Fall of the South* vol, pp 158-161, and in *Tears Before The Rain*.

Dets - Detachments.

Devil - A call-sign of the 134th AHC.

DEWS - Duck Early Warning System, or Goose EWS. VC/NVA developed notable reputation for ability to approach U.S. perimeters undetected prior to attack, or to steal deployed mines and other defensive devices for future use. They also sometimes turned claymores around to face perimeter, retreated to cover and then made noises which prompted defenders to detonate mines upon themselves. Legend has it that the DEWS system was born in IV Corps, when it was observed that at night it was all but impossible to approach a domestic duck or goose without it sounding an alarm. Trait was exploited by tethering ducks or geese near mines. If an alarm sounded, claymore was detonated. Apparently device was virtually 100% effective, albeit often fatal for alarm mechanism, hence a serious drain on supply of the poor birds. In *A Better War*, p. 27, author relates an anecdote in which Gen Creighton Abrams recalled an event in mid '68 where the ARVN decorated a goose: "That's right," exclaimed the general, "They put him in pen outside the outpost. And there's no way to sneak up on a goose at night. And this goose alerted the outpost, they'd made a successful defense, and Vietnamese were decorating the goose. And by God nobody was laughing!"

DFC - Distinguished Flying Cross.

DHC-4 Caribou - U.S. Twin-eng, prop-driven STOL acft with 242 mi rnge, 215 kts top spd. mfgd by D. H. Canada.

DIA - Defense Intelligence Agency.

Dia Phong - Also Dai Phong. See Du Kich in Glossary.

Dich Board - Casualty Tally Board. 9th Div term.

Dimmer – Call-sign of Marine Med Helicopter Sqdn HMM 463.

Dinassaut - *Divisions navales d'assuaut*, a.k.a. DNA. Naval Assault Divs of French Union forces. Per *Street Without Joy*, p 44, the typical "DNA" consisted of apx 12 ships: an armored LSSL (Landing Ship Supt, Large) flagship, 2 armored "Monitor" firebase LCM's, 6 addnl LCM's (each armed with 81mm mortar btys, supplies and 1 to 2 Marine commandos Cos). Some of Red River Delta's DNA's had 20 or more water craft, their own recon acft and vehicle complement carried aboard LCT's.

Diplomat and Warrior - 1st Bde, 101st Abn Div's weekly newsletter until 21July67, then renamed *The Screaming Eagle*.

Dinh - The community house of a Vietnamese village.

Dinner - Code name for Enemy Base Area 352 in Cambodia. See Base Area 352 in main alpha index.

Dir - Directorate or Director.

DIS - Defense Investigative Service.

dist - distance (TAD).

Div - Division.

Divisions navales d'assuaut - *Dinassaut*. French VN Naval Assault Divs.

DLG - Guided Missile Frigate (USN).

dly - daily (TAD).

DMA - Defense Mapping Agency.

DMAC - Delta Military Assistance Command (TAD).

DME - Directional Measuring Equipment Site.

DMZ - Demilitarized Zone.

DNA - *Dinassaut*, or *Divisions navales d'assuaut*.

Do Ke Giai, General - At one time the infamous CG of ARVN 18th Div HQ'd at Xuan Loc. Per *A Better War*, p 378, Gen Abrams once described him as "not only the worst general in Vietnamese Army, but the worst general in any army!" By contrast, his successor, BG Le Minh Dao led 18th in one of most gallant stands of war during final Offensive at Xuan Loc, where his troops destroyed 3 of 4 NVA Divs attacking them and held ground for almost a month before being overrun. SVN.

DOA - Dead on Arrival.

DOA or DoA - Department of the Army.

Doan - NVA infiltration grps. NVA normally moved men south in 3 to 5-man cells called "Doan." Cells would gather into a full unit strength only when unit was moving in tactical manner. During late '69 and much of '70 (and as result of staggering losses suffered in Tet '68 and Tet '69), the Doan concept was applied to men already operating as units in I Corps (at least). That phase of enemy's ops greatly reduced their casualty rates, allowing them to regroup and train replacements.

Doc Lap Brigade - The Independence Bde. An offshoot of Vietminh Capital Rgt and 304th Div. Later became the 308th Div.
DOD - Department of Defense.
Dog, The - Nickname of H-34 Sikorsky piston-driven medium helicopter that was a primary USMC transport/supply helo '65 to '68, when UH-1H Huey replaced it. Though it had very limited lift and speed compared to Huey, it was loved for its reliability and ability to withstand abuse and enemy fire yet still fly. Its pilots were nicknamed Dog Drivers.
Dog Drivers - See Dog, the.
Dogs of Note - See Camp Hill, Camp Land, Tiger's Den, and Vung Tau Army AF in main alpha listing.
Dogwood 6 - Apparently radio code for KIA in some units of 101st Abn Div. "Dogwood 8" said to have meant WIA.
Dogwood 8 - See. Dogwood-6.
Dolphin - A call-sign of the 174th AHC.
Dolphins – Call-sign of 176th Avn Co.
Domino Theory - Theory that if communism were allowed to take Vietnam, then balance of Indochina and Malaysia would fall under their domination in rapid sequence. That mindset in great degree contributed to America's supt of French in 1st Indochina War, and later, its own entry into VN. Phrase is attributed to President Dwight Eisenhower, who when drawing an analogy between Indochina situation and a set of dominoes said; "knock over the first one and what will happen to last one is the certainty that it will go over quickly." Per *The Unquiet American*, p 139.
Dong - Vietnamese for "East" when used following a name.
Dong - One Viet word for "hill" or "mountain" when used before a place name.
Dong - Vietnamese unit of currency roughly equiv of one cent in the 60's and 70's.
Dong Nai Boats - Small Styrofoam craft used by the VNMC for amphibious landing ops off LSTs in the Cau Mau Peninsula, '63 and designed for use in swampy areas.
Dong Tien - Program known as "Progress Together" involving cooperation between ARVN 5th Inf Div and U.S. 4th Div, '69-70.
Dora - Call-sign of Phitsanuloke Thailand, radar vectoring facility of USAF 621st Tactical Control Sqdn. See Also Pitsanuloke.
Douche Boats - During Op Giant Slingshot, certain ATC vessels of "Project Douche," known as "Douche Boats" (9th Inf Div/MRF) were equipped with 2 high-pressure pumps (in well deck) capable of pumping water through nozzle (cannon) at 3,000 PSI. Stream could eat through concrete bunkers and these water cannons were used as both defensive and offensive weapon. Op Slingshot was turned over to VNN, May 70. Photo and data in *Brown Water Black Berets*, p 305.
Doughnut Dollies - GI nickname for young women working for the Red Cross or Special Services who were flown from FSB to FSB, entertaining troops with games and other distractions meant to give the men a short break from rigors of combat duty. Were rarely at a base more than a few hours. Also called "Heavy Blues," due to blue and white pen-striped dresses they often wore.
DRAC - Delta Regional Assistance Command (TAD).
Draft, The (SVN) - In General Mobilization Act (GMA) of 1968 (reaction to the '68 Tet Offensive), the SVN govt raised military draft age to a range of 19-38 years of age, where it had previously been 19-28. Ultimately, it also raised size of military from 600,000 to 1,100,000 (per *A Better War*, pp14-15). Curiously then, the brutality and terror tactics employed by attacking NVA/VC forces during Tet '68 appear to have had exactly opposite of their intended effect, turning many former communists to support the SVN govt, because the GMA was met with little opposition and most required to serve did so. Still, during war, hundreds of thousands of SVN's Draft-eligible youth evaded service. In many or perhaps most cases, evasion was apparently effected through bribes paid to the chief of police in one's home police precinct. Nguyen Cao Ky claims evasion was most widespread in Cholon (90% Chinese at time), where over 100,000 evade the draft as a result of huge bribes paid by their merchant families. According to Ky, at one point standard bribe was 100,000 Piastres (apx $1,000 US), and corruption so widespread that while playing poker, wives of the govt officials that controlled conscription would call out, "I'll raise you a soldier" as equiv of a 100,000 Piastre bet (*Twenty Years and Twenty Days*, p 105). See Chp 9 (*Corruption*) of *Twenty Years and Twenty Days*. See also Precinct Five.
Draft, The (US) - Overall, only about 25% of those who served in Vietnam were Drafted, while other 75% volunteered (the opposite of WWII stats). While certainly patriotism and a yearning for adventure was often the basis for volunteering, it is also true that many people joined the military to avoid combat. As odd as that might sound, enlisting for periods greater than the two-year Draft requirement guaranteed specialized schooling and a resulting access to lower-risk jobs outside the combat arms. On the other hand, possibly as many as 90% of those Drafted were placed in the Infantry, where risk was of injury or death was much higher. For example, according to *The Perfect War*, p 121, Draftee deaths as percentage of all deaths rose steadily during war: '65-16%; '66-21%; '67-34%, '69-40%. Where only U.S. Army Draftees (vast majority of those Drafted) KIAs are concerned, percentages were: '69-62%, and '70-70%. According to *The Vietnam War, An Almanac*, p 358, of some 15 million Draft-eligible Americans during the war, apx 250,000 did not register, 1 million apparently broke some Selective Service law, and apx 25,000 were indicted but only about 3,250 actually served any prison time.
Dragon - A call-sign of the 52d Avn Bn, and 119th Avn Co, and A Bty, 4th/77th ARA gunships.
Dragon Lady - See U-2 Spy Plane and Madame Ngu
Dragonfly - Trade name for A-37 acft. 4,100 mi rnge, 505 kts top spd. mfgd by Cessna.
Drive-On Rag – See Drive-On Towel.
Drive-On Towel - A.k.a. "Drive-On Rag." A green towel commonly worn around the neck by infantryman and used to wipe sweat and debris from one's face.
Drug Abuse - Illegal drug usage by U.S. troops between '65-69 appears to have been very low; while use of marijuana, heroin, opium, speed and other illegal drugs reached epidemic levels between ,70-73 (and in concert with steadily declining morale, esprit and discipline). Often overlooked however is fact alcohol abuse was much more widespread during war and had even been institutionalized to some extent by the military. Access to alcohol was provided through clubs and BXs at extremely low prices (for example: beer at 10 cents/can, hard liquor at 25 cents/shot, and quarts of spirits such *Beefeaters* or *Canadian Club* at merely $1.15 a bottle) and, while those in cmd and of the "old Army" hung their heads in dismay at use

of other drugs, they looked the other way where Agent Alcohol was concerned. This author's personal observation was that in '70 at least, alcohol abuse was far more problematic than that of other drugs because alcohol users were far more prone to aggressive, violent and destructive behavior. Brawls common to EM and NCO clubs at the time were invariably fueled by booze, while users of most other illegal drugs tended to be passive and non-confrontational. Some units even rationed free beer to troops (even those in the field) at 2 cans/day. Per *A Better War*, p 292, a study of prisoners convicted of fragging in SVN done by Dr. Thomas Bond, (Chief, Psychiatry Ft. Leavenworth) found that all admitted to drug usage of various sorts in SVN, and that 87.5% said they were "acutely intoxicated" at time of crime. Unfortunately no explanation of what Dr. Bond meant by that phrase was listed, but presumably alcohol intoxication was included in many, if not most, of those cases. At same page, it is rptd that in all of '69, only 16 deaths were attributed to drug overdoses, but in Jul70 there were 14; in Aug70, 23; in Sep70, 26; and, in 1st 18 days of Oct70, 35. The Oct rate suggests a rate of 700 overdose deaths/yr if trend steadied at that point! Also in '70, MACV surveyed troops arriving in VN and found that over 50% admitted to having used marijuana (MACV also rptd that by '71, fully 15% of U.S. troops in VN were addicted to heroin!). Many rpts claim NVA/VC trafficked in drugs, pricing them very cheaply in order to hook U.S. troops and disrupt their morale and efficiency. The NVA/VC also apparently used drugs, as there are numerous rpts of marijuana and other drugs being found on bodies of those killed in grnd assaults, while other rpts indicate attacking NVA often appeared to be "hopped-up" on drugs due to suicidal nature of attacks and fact some shot repeatedly would not slow their advance or otherwise display ill effects from hits that would normally drop a man. Levels of drug use among French troops in their war are unclear, though opium was widely available and used by many of French as recreational drug. Popular among the French was a Vietnamese cigarette named "Melia Jaune," but author does not know if product actually contained the drug? See also Fragging, and Melia Jaune.

DRV - Democratic Republic of Vietnam (North Vietnam).

DSC - Distinguished Service Cross.

Du Kich - The Du Kich were the VC's Local Force Units; the Dia Fong its Regional Force units (described as great diggers); and the Chu Luc its Interprovincial units (described as well-trained, brave and very tough). Per *Utter's Battalion*, pp 140, 169.

Duck Butt - Over-water, precautionary orbit flown by rescue acft.

Duck Early Warning System - See DEWS in main alpha listing.

Duffel Bag Team - Code name for remote sensor reading units monitoring enemy movements electronically in at least Binh Dinh Prov during '70. Term widely used in '70 Bn Annual Hist Supp of 3/503d Inf, 173d Abn Bde at www.gasparot.com/nammedic. Binh Dinh Prov, II Corps.

Dummy Extractions - A tactic similar to dummy insertions, only in this case a unit already in the field moved to a conspicuous LZ while an equal-sized unit was loaded on helicopters at a rear base. The heli-borne unit would then lay flat on the floor of the helo so enemy observers would think the landing helos empty. When the helos landed, the waiting unit would walk out to them but upon reaching them, would lay down on the ground instead of boarding, while at the same instant, those already on the birds would sit up and the helo would depart as if just fully loaded. The scenario was repeated until entire ground unit appeared to have been extracted. The unit on the ground would lay still for a few minutes and then crawl slowly back to cover, where it resumed its patrol or ambush in hopes the ruse would lull enemy into thinking area was clear.

Dummy Insertions - Common helo CA or recon team insertion tactic in which any number LZs were prepped by arty and/or escorting attack acft but the team/unit was inserted at only one of the selected sites. In another variant, helos inserting a recon element would land at a series of several LZs both before and after the LZ of actual insertion to confuse enemy as to actual point of insertion, forcing them to split forces to recon all apparent sites.

Dummy Rangers - Six Mannequins, replete with camouflage paint and fatigues, that were employed by the "Red Devil" Ranger LRRPs of the 5th Mech Inf Div in I Corps. The mannequins were used to facilitate and disguise LRRP Team insertions in '70. Quang Tri Prov, I Corps.

Dung, Madame - Pronounced "Zung." Viet woman from Thanh Hoa who was much sought-after for her beauty and influence during 1st Indochina War. Bernard Fall relates that she worked her way to position of great power through series of affairs with increasingly influential French and Vie military officers and officials. Was rumored she could advance or block virtually any promotion. Owned villa in Hanoi, convertible Peugeot and a "courtesy customs pass" that let her deal unfettered in lucrative Hong Kong currency and gold trade. She moved to SVN when French lost influence, gaining friends among the Americans that soon followed. See *Street Without Joy*, pp138-140.

dur - during (TAD).

Dust Off - Became standard term for any helicopter medevac early in war. Per *Doc: Platoon Medic*, p 105, its origin was originally a tribute to Maj. Charles Kelly (call-sign, "Dustoff"), a medevac pilot KIA during a medevac, 1Jul64.

Dustoff - See Dust Off.

DUTCH MILL - Code name for Cmdr of TF Alpha, the Igloo White sonic-sensor interpretation unit at NKP in Thailand. In 67-68, it was USAF BG William McBride. See Gravel Mines, Igloo White and Muscle Shoals. NKP AB, Thailand. Data per *Valley of Decision*, pp 300-301

Duty Officer's Log - See Daily Journal.

DW - Dry Weight.

DX - Army infantry slang meaning "to get rid of something," or throw something away. Could apply to anything, inc people.

E - East.

E-1B Tracer - U.S. acft with 875 mi rnge, 225 kts top spd. mfgd by Grumman Avn.

E-2 Hawkeye - U.S. acft with 1,900 mi rnge, 310 kts top spd. mfgd by Grumman Avn.

E-8, 35mm Tear Gas Launcher - Non-lethal, CS-Gas dispenser area weapon consisting of 16-tube, 35mm-rocket launcher that fired small missiles containing CS anti-riot gas. Provided wide dispersion and was employed to disable and disorient enemy in a fixed position. Also used for crowd control. Could be vehicle-mounted or carried by individuals in a back-pack configuration.

E-158 Canisters - 50- pound canisters of CS Gas mounted on Huey Helos to facilitate LRRP team extractions. Discussed in *Rangers At War, LRRPs in Vietnam*, p 250.

ea - each (TAD).
Eagle Dustoff - Call-sign for 326th Med Bn Medevacs HQ'd at Phu Bai(?) AF and 85th Evac Hosp (saved author's life, Sep70).
Eagle Prep - 9th Inf Div/MRF tactic in which 9th Inf Div LZs were smothered with prep arty fire before insertion. Mentioned in rpt of 3d/34th Arty, dated 14Apr69, for period 1Apr68-31Jan69, on MFR Assoc Website at: www.mrfa.org/3_34th.htm.
Earl McGovern - A.k.a. "Earthquake McGoon." Served as U.S. Civil Air Transport pilot helping French resupply during 1st Indochina War. When hit by flak at Dien Bien Phu, he choose to stay with the acft radioing, "I'm riding her in!" as his last words.
Earthquake McGoon - See Earl McGovern.
Easter Offensive - Major NVA invasion of SVN, beginning 30Mar72. In MR1, began with over 4,000 rounds of arty/mortar/rocket fire, followed on 31Mar72 with grnd attacks by 10 NVA Inf and 5 Arty Rgts of 304th and 308th Divs on Quang Tri and Cam Lo. For 1st time, NVA armor attacked S across Ben Hai River and DMZ, as well as down QL-9. By early May72, FSB's Bastogne and Checkmate along Hwy 547 had fallen after what Gen Abrams considered a stubborn defense by ARVN. Many important SVN Capitols were captured, but ARVN regrouped and put up surprisingly good fight behind renewed U.S. bombing/air supt and pushed NVA back. At An Loc (NVA called it Binh Loc), NVA mounted 3 ground/armor assaults, losing 1/2 of their tanks and very large number of troops in vain effort to dislodge ARVN defenders in what Douglas Pike referred to as possibly most important battle of war. Gen Abrams masterminded an extremely effective tactic that devoted MACV's entire B-52 assets for a single day to each of 3 key battle points: 11May72 at Kontum; 12May at Hue, and 13May at An Loc. During those strikes, three B-52 sorties were hitting the target every 55 minutes for 24 hours, and this massed firepower broke the back of attacks on all 3 sites. B-52 and naval gunfire badly mauled NVA forces at My Chanh River defensive line (Quang Tri/Thua Thien Pr border) where ARVN had stalled them. ARVN 3d Div retook Tien Phuoc after bitter fight that ended in late Sep72. For 1st time in war, offensive prompted Nixon to mine Haiphong and other NVN harbors on 9May72. 9 USN acft from *USS Coral Sea* took only 1 minute to drop 36 Mk-52 mines (magnetic mines weighing 1,100 lbs. each and packed w/625 lbs. of explosive) in approaches to Haiphong harbor, all set to activate at 9 am 12May72. In that minute, the U.S. accomplished what MACV had been requesting for 8 years, and as result, not a single ship entered/left Haiphong until mines cleared as part of Paris Peace Accords in '73. Est 100,000 NVA troops were casualties, roughly 50% of attacking force (with 40,000 KIA), while ARVN lost apx 8,000 KIA, 24,000 WIA and 3,500 MIA (during same period, 53,000 volunteered for ARVN duty while 40,000 deserted!). Hanoi was so fearful of an amphib assault on NVN to disrupt offensive, they held back 2 Divs in NVN as reserve; a tactic that contributed to their subsequent defeat. Some data per *A Better War*, pp 330-339, map at p 320. See also An Loc, Battle for, Project Enhance, and Project Enhance Plus.
EC/RC-135 - U.S. 4-eng jet ECM and electronic surveillance acft based on the KC-135 chassis. Had 3,450 mi rnge, 530 kts top spd. mfgd by Boeing Acft.
EC-121 Warning Star - A.k.a. the Super Connie. U.S. 4-eng, prop-driven electronic surveillance and weather acft based on the *Super Constellation* commercial chassis of post WWII vintage. Noted for its triple tail configuration and sleek aerodynamic chassis. Had 20 hrs range, and 320 kts top spd. mfgd by Lockheed Acft.
eff - effect, effective (TAD).
El. - elevation.
Electric Strawberry - Nickname for 25th Inf Div. See Tropic Lightning.
Elephant - Call-sign for Lao *Batallion Volontaire-33* (BV-33). Also, in 2d/7th Cav, 1st Cav Div ('65 and '66), "Elephant" was radio code for a KIA. Code for a WIA was "Buffalo." Data per *Baptism*, p 256..
elev - elevation (TAD).
emerg - emergency (TAD).
Emu - A call-sign of the 135th AHC and acronym for "Experimental Military Unit" originally assigned to that unit. Apparently only U.S. helo supt unit to serve ANZAC forces in III Corps, Phuoc Tuy, Long Khanh and other provs?
EMU - Experimental Military Unit.
End Sweep, Operation - See main alpha index.
ENE - East North East.
eng - engine (TAD).
Eng and Engs - Engineer or Engineers.
Engineer LZs - Term used by 20th Engr Bde. Referred to temporary Eng encampments built during road and bridge const projects. Typically existed only a week or so, per Frank Penk, Jr. Penk does not recall any being named; instead, sites were simply referred to by call-sign of unit occupying them.
Engrs - Engineers.
Engs - Engineers.
ENS - Ensign (USN rank).
EOD - Explosive Ordnance Disposal.
EOM - Enlisted Open Mess.
eqpt - equipped or equipment (TAD).
Equip - equipment.
ESE - East South East.
Essayons - French for "We Will Try." Motto of U.S. Army Engineer Corps.
est - estimate or estimated.
et al - Latin for "and others."
et seq. - Latin phrase "et sequitor," meaning "and those following."
ev - every (TAD).
Evac - Evacuation.
exc - except (TAD).
excld - excluded (s) (TAD).
Executive order 10977 - Officially defined eligibility for Armed Forces Expeditionary Medal (AFEM) as established by Exec Order 10977, dated 4Dec61, and Exec Order 11231, dated 8Jul65.
Executive Order 11216 - Officially established and defined VN Combat Zone for pay and IRS purposes, eff 24Apr65. LBJ.
Executive Order 11231 - Officially established/defined eligibility for VN Service Medal eff 8Jul65. See Vietnam Service Medal.
Expeditionary Medal, Armed Forces - See Armed Forces Expeditionary Medal.
Extensions, Vietnam Tour - See DEROS.
extv - extensive (TAD).
F-4 Phantom II - Fighter-bomber widely used in both grnd supt and bombing role. Both grnd and carrier-based versions employed. Gradually replaced F-100 as the main close-air,

grnd-supt bomber. Originally designated the F-110 Spectre. 1,750-2300 mi rnge, 1500 kts top speed. mfgd by McDonnell.
F-5 Freedom Fighter - 215 mi rnge, 925 kts top spd. mfgd by Northrop.
F-8 Crusader - 453 mi rnge, 1,230 kts top spd. mfgd by Chance-Vought.
F-10 Skynight - Large twin-eng, straight-wing, U.S. night fighter. Originally the F3D. Powered by two J34 engines. Used for ECM until '69. 1,150 mi rnge, 490 kts top spd. mfgd by Douglas Acft.
F-111A Raven - U.S. all-weather, twin-jet, fighter-bomber that was supposed to be low-level contour capable, but early intro to SVN saw numerous crashes and it was withdrawn until flaws fixed. Was very effective once bugs worked-out. Saw limited use only. 3,165 mi rnge, 570 kts top spd. mfgd by Gen Dynamics.
F-100 Super Sabre - U.S. high-spd, single-eng jet fighter-bomber. Saw wide use as both a bomber and close air ground supt acft until the F-4 gradually replaced it in that role. 550 mi rnge, 865 kts top spd. mfgd by North American.
F-102 Delta Dagger - U.S. single-eng jet fighter. Saw limited use in the war. 500 mi rnge, 825 kts top spd. mfgd by Convair.
F-104C Starfighter - U.S. high-spd, single-eng jet fighter. Saw limited use in the war. 1,000 mi rnge, 1,450 kts top spd. mfgd by Lockheed Acft.
F-105 Thunderchief - 2,390 mi rnge, 1,480 kts top spd. mfgd by Republic Acft.
F/W - Fixed Wing.
F.O.M - French equiv of U.S. C-Ration; individually packaged meals for the individual soldier.
FA - Field Artillery. U.S. Army term.
fac - facility (TAD).
FAC - Forward Air Control.
Falcon - A call-sign of the 155th AHC.
Falcon - Falcon and Stagecoach were call-signs if the 155th AHC.
Fall, Bernard - Author of classic *Street Without Joy*, ironically KIA on the Street Without Joy, 21Feb67, while on patrol with A/1st/9th Marines, apx 22 km NW Hue. USMC Photo A-188262 shows his body after blast. Per *Bonnie-Sue*, p 308.
Famous Fighting Fourth - Nickname of U.S. 4th Inf Div. Often shortened to "Famous Fourth" and "Fighting Fourth."
Fan Song - Radar homing GCI device used to target NVA SAM missile launches. SAM radar signal was detected by ECW acft which then fired radar-seeking missile that homed-in on GCI signals. Once the NVA became wise to practice, they devised a successful countermeasure in which their GCI was activated for only 20 seconds prior to launch, then immediately switched off. Data per *A Better War*, p 313.
FAR - *Forces Arme'es du Royaume* (Royal Laotian Army).
Farm Gate - (XT 98-13) Det-2, 4400th Combat Crew Trng Sqdn and later USAF commando unit at Bien Hoa AFB. In '61, President Kennedy authorized increased military assistance inc part of 4400th CCTS USAF (code name Farm Gate), under guise that it was to familiarize SVNAF pilots with T-28 trainer. By Feb62, U.S. Farm Gate crews were flying combat and even 1st defoliation missions. Bien Hoa Prov, III Corps.
Fast FACs - See Misty.
Fast Mover - Grunt nickname for any jet acft providing grnd supt.
Father & Son Combinations - Fathers and sons serving in VN were rather common. In fact, at least 2 sets are known to have died there: Leo C. Hester (KIA 10Mar67) and Leo C. Hester, Jr, (KIA 2Nov69); and also Richard Fitzgibbon Jr (died 8Jun56, by coincidence earliest name listed on memorial and only added in May99) and his son Richard B. Fitzgibbon III, (KIA 7Sep65). In likely most unusual example, during his 2d VN tour, Medevac pilot Michel J. Novosel (WWII vet & VN MOH recipient) and his son both flew in same Dustoff unit and, within 1 week period, each rescued the other from hostile LZs (See *DUSTOFF: The Memoir of an Army Aviator,* Presidio Press, '99)! The stepson of a 1st/502d Inf Bn Cmdr was KIA with same Bn in helo crash, 3Sep69 (stepfather learned of tragedy while visiting crash site). Also, USMC 1Lt Ronald McLean, stepson of actor Jimmie Stewart was KIA, 8Jun69.
Fatherland Front, The - Mat Tran To Quoc. See Viet Cong.
FDC - Fire Direction Control. The command center of an arty or mortar element.
FDRD Navigation System - Fool proof navigation system known among 20th Eng Bde pilots as: "Follow Da Road, Dummy," per Frank Penk, Jr. III Corps.
Feet Dry - Code phrase/pilot jargon which meant an acft had transitioned from flying over water to flying over dry land.
Feet Wet - Code phrase/pilot jargon which meant an acft had transitioned from flying over dry land to flying over water.
Fence, The - Pilot, LRRP, SF and SOG jargon for border of Laos, Cambodia or NVN. Cross-border missions were often referred to as "Going over the Fence," or "Crossing the Fence."
FFEAF - French Far Eastern Air Force. French air force of the 1st Indochina War. See *Street Without Joy*, pp 260-267.
FFSB - Forward Fire Supt Base.
Field Force Per LTC Elmer Groetsch, 54th Sig Bn XO, "The designation 'Field Force' was used in part because normal Army corps had only tactical, not logistical, functions while the FFV's had tactical, logistical, pacification, and advisory roles." It's also true that the ARVN used the term "Corps" to define multi-divisional units, while the U.S. Army used it for the same purpose, so in part also to avoid confusion, "Field Force" was adopted to describe a "Corps" equiv force. Field Force Vietnam (FFV), First Field Force Vietnam (IFFV) and Second Field Force Vietnam (IIFFV) are examples; however, MACV also created several Corps level cmds during war that used conventional "Corps" designation (XXII Corps, XXIV Corps and XXX Corps). See IFFV and IFFV in Major Commands Section. Some data per *Dak To*, p 369.
Fighting Fourth - See Famous Fighting Fourth.
FIGMO - Soldier slang for "Fuck it, I've got my orders."
Final Offensive, The -The Ho Chi Minh Campaign of '75, in which SVN was finally defeated. Lasted only 4 days, 26-30Apr75. In Jan75, NVA took Phuoc Long Prov, the 1st entire province to fall to communists since French war. Per *A Better War*, p 374, NVA Col Bui Tin said that after Nixon resigned, NVA victory was no longer in doubt. Sorely also quotes Pham Van Dong as saying U.S. President Ford was the weakest U.S. president ever, "so we tested his resolve by taking Phuoc Long," adding that when Ford did not send B-52's in retaliation, Hanoi decided to mount an all-out final offensive. Under cmd of Gen. Van Tien Dung, during Mar and Apr75, 18 NVA Divs were positioned to attack Saigon around 300 degree radius apx 40 miles from city. On 10Mar75, 3 NVA Divs (25,000 men) attacked the 1,200 ARVN defending Ban Me Thuot, overwhelming them in matter of days and ending any hope of defending Kontum and Pleiku. On 14Mar74, Thieu ordered Pleiku and Kontum Provs abandoned. At Xuan Loc took place what has been described as bloodiest battle of war, where ARVN 18th Div under BG Le Minh Dao gallantly

destroyed 3 of 4 NVA Divs attacking it and held their ground for almost a month before being overrun. When launched, plan worked perfectly and though some ARVN units fought gallantly, they were simply overwhelmed by force of thrust and, by 30Apr75, NVA had taken Saigon and war was over. Chp 19, pp 203-231, of *Twenty Years and Twenty Days* provides interesting perspective of events leading to end of war, while *The Fall of The South* vol of *Vietnam Experience* series discusses Final Offensive in detail. Per *A Better War,* p 366, Gen Ira Hunt (CG U.S. Activities Supt Grp at NKP Thailand '73-75) was amazed by performance of the ARVN after the U.S. pulled-out of SVN in '73, saying that although NVA initiated most actions, ARVN "cleaned their clocks" for two years. See also Operation Frequent Wind in main alpha listing, and Buong Incident, Evacuation of Da Nang and American Radio Service in Glossary.

FIR - Flight Information Region (TAD).

Fire Cracker Rounds - A.k.a. M-449 COFRAM Rounds (Controlled Fragmentation). Arty anti-personnel rnds containing numerous secondary bomblets dispersed over a large area as round impacted, creating a rapid series of secondary explosions that sounded much like a string of firecrackers exploding. 1st/92d Arty op rpt for courtesy Craig Miller mentions that 1st/92d test-fired this round for 1st time on 26May68, firing 24 rnds on target at 9,400 meters in supt of FSB 14 (YA 939-0912), where A/3d/8th and A Bty 6th/29th were hit by a 2 Bn force using flame-throwers. The FO reported excellent coverage and effect. See COFRAM.

Fire Support Base - A.k.a. FB, FSB, FSSB, FSPB or Firebase, and in Vietnamese, "Can Hoa." Ground installations designed to house Arty units firing in supt of maneuvering infantry elements and of other bases within its Arty range. FSBs also housed infantry security and communication elements as well. Most were generally circular in design (or built in any shape necessary to conform to terrain), and contained any number of Arty pieces and/or mortars defended by exterior concertina wires and a system of trenches and sand-bagged bunkers/foxholes. Although landing pads for helicopters were normally built within or adj to most FSBs, acft were not normally based or maintained upon them. Some firebases existed for only a few days or hours and others evolved into permanent positions that remained open for many years. In some areas, firebase were seasonally opened, closed and reopened in concert with the monsoon rains on a cyclical basis. Some FSBs were built in one location and then moved to several other locations but retained the same name. Others remained in one location yet were given new names several times during their life span. Others still were reclassified periodically from LZs to FSBs to Camps and to Basecamp s in concert with their changing size, available facilities or at whims of new tenants or cmdrs. The terms "Landing Zone" (LZ) and "FSB" were often used interchangeably and many bases were known both as LZs, and FSBs at same time or at different stages during their history. The term "Landing Zone" also often simply referred to any place a helicopter might land; i.e., an undefended clearing in jungle. In some cases, small LZs later grew into firebases with the addition of Arty and still later into a full-fledged and permanent Landing Zones. The general distinction between a permanent Landing Zone and FSB was that LZs were usually much larger than FSBs and, although it may have also provided Arty fire supt as one of its functions, an LZ typically included facilities house helos and their suptg units, ground transportation, POL facilities, Eng elements, ammo supply dumps, medical and even recreational facilities, most of which were absent on a FSB. Term "Camp" was usually assigned to a permanent facility even larger than a permanent LZ often large enough to house multi-Bn, multi-Bde or even Div-sized elements. In Sep69 essay, *Fire Support Base Development*, by USMC Maj. Robert V. Nicoli, the term 'Firebase' is defined in this manner "Very basically, a FSB is a rapidly constructed artillery position defended by a minimum of infantry. the infantry & tactical elements operate within the protective fan of the artillery, and as presently applied in [3d Mar Div] the FSB's themselves offer overlapping artillery supt to each other and protection for several Landing Zones," per http://members.aol.com/warlibrary/vwfsb.htm. Per Peter Cole, 1st Cav Div 68-69, the name of virtually any permanent position of the 1st Cav Div was preceded by "LZ" until September, 1969, when Lt Gen Julian Ewell, IIFFV CG, ordered that any fortified position designated as an 'LZ,' would thereafter be called a Fire Support Base (FSB). Cole also points out that in *Incursion*, at p 47, "Ewell"'s orders angered the airmobile purists in [1st Cav] division, who disliked the term firebase as common to regular infantry divisions and certainly not appropriate for use by Air Cav." "Can Hoa" and/or "Can Cu Hoa Luc" are apparently Viet phrases equiv to 'Firebase,' per Dr. Van Hanh Hoang of UC Davis. See also Landing Zone and French Fort Design.

Firebase 173 - Newspaper of 173d Airborne Bde. Printed by *Pacific Stars & Stripes*, Tokyo, Japan, and its mailing address was "Firebase 173, 173d Abn Bde, APO 96250."

Firebird - A call-sign of the 71st AHC.

Firecracker Rounds, M-449 - See Fire Cracker.

Firefly - See *Luciole.*

Firefly - Code name for night-illumination mission helicopters employing a 1,750,000 candlepower xenon spot-light. Firefly acft nicknamed "The Bug" by 121st AHC at Soc Trang Army AF. Apart from spotlight and people sensors, it was equipped with a .50 caliber machine-gun, 2 M-60s and 40mm grenade launchers.

First Americans to Visit Vietnam - Apparently were Capt. John White and men of ship *Franklin*, who in 1820 arrived at Vung Tau, and requested permission to sail up Dong Nai River to Saigon. After month of bureaucrat confusion, officials decided Smith must instead secure Emperor's permission (at Hue), so *Franklin* sailed to Da Nang (closest port). There, bureaucracy required more paperwork (13 copies of inventory/crew data) before Emperor finally granted request, and *Franklin* sailed back to Saigon. Smith's account, *History of a Voyage to the China Sea*, mentions great skill of Viet boatmen and ubiquitous crocodiles on Dong Nai River. At Saigon, Smith was hosted by French Cochinchina governor and took on load of cane sugar for return trip. Data per *The Vietnam Guidebook*, p 50.

First Artillery Rounds fired in VN - Per Dan Gillotti, the 3d/319th FA (suptg 173rd Abn) fired 1st U.S. Army Arty round (105mm), 12May65, and B Bty, 3d/82nd FA, TF Gimlet, 196th LIB, fired last U.S. Army arty round, 10Aug72. The 11th Marines (possibly A Bty) may have fired 1st U.S. Arty rnd of entire war, shortly after their landing at Red Beach in early '65. 1st U.S. arty fired on VN apparently took place when *USS Constitution* fired on Tourane in 1845. See also Canister Round, and *Constitution, USS.*

First CAP Teams - See Ky Hoa Cap in main alpha listing.

First Helicopter kill of Tank in Combat - In Jan68, Air America Flight-Mechanic in back seat of civilian model Bell 205 Huey shot down 1 of 2 PAVN Antonov AN-2 biplanes it was pursuing after the AN-2s had surprised, bombed/rocketed mtn base of Phuo Pha Thi (a.k.a. Phu Ph Thi and LS-85). Apparently 1st ever shoot-down of fixed-wing acft by a helicopter. Photos/text in *War In Laos*, pp 24, 26, 29. See Lima Site 85. Laos.

First Helicopter kill of Fixed-Wing Afct - See main alpha listing.

First Human Wave Attack by Vietminh - See Vinh Yen, Battle of., in main alpha listing.

First in Vietnam - Motto of the 1st Avn Bde.

First Indochina War - For purposes of this text, the French War against the Vietminh, 1946-1954.

First Mining of NVN Ports - See Ops Linebacker and End Sweep in main alpha listing, as well as Tet '68 and *MSS-2*.

First Night Helicopter Assault - See LZ Mary (YA 82-09, 1st Cav, Nov65) and My Phu, Battle of (Mar66) in main alpha listing. **First NVA Armor Attack in SVN** - See Lang Vei (old) SF Camp in main alpha list.

First NVA Attack in SVN - See Vic Klum.

First Offensive - NVA/VC's Jan-Mar68 Tet Offensive. Est 45,000 NVA/VC KIA resulted. See Year of Decision, and Tet 68.

First Person Awarded Silver Star on 2 Consecutive Days - See Hill 700 in main alpha listing.

First Proof NVA Supplying VC by Sea - See Vung Rio Incident in Glossary.

First Tactical Use of B-52s in Supt of Ground Troops - Took place apx 8-14Oct65, in supt of 173d Abn. See Operation Iron Triangle in main alpha listing.

First Tank-Unit to-Tank Unit Battle (major) - See Lam Son 719 in main alpha list.

First U.S. Armored Unit in VN - See Operation Starlite in main alpha listing.

First U.S. Diplomat to Vietnam - See main alpha listing.

First U.S. Inflicted Vietnamese Casualties - See *Constitution, USS*, in main alpha listing.

First U.S. Navy Ship to Visit Vietnam - See *Peacock* in main alpha listing.

First U.S. Navy Ship Bombed by NVA Acft - See Higbee, USS, in main alpha listing.

First U.S. Shelling of Vietnam - See main alpha listing.

First US Tank-vs.-Tank Engagement - 1st known direct engagement between US and NVA tanks took place 3-4Mar69, and involved B/1st/69th Armor (att 2d APC of the B-3 Front were employed (convoy of from 8 to 15 addnl vehicles were also observed near base). US tank fire destroyed 2 PT-76s and personnel carrier. One US tank was hit by NVA tank fire. B Co lost 2 KIA and 2 WIA, but no tanks.

First Use of Smart Bombs - See Operation Linebacker and Thanh Hoa RR/Hwy Bridge in main alpha listing.

First Use of Tanks by U.S. Forces - See Operation Starlite in main alpha listing.

First USMC Independent Ground Unit in SVN - See SESU Site in main alpha listing..

First USMC Helo Unit in SVN - See Shufly, Operation, in main alpha listing. Ba Xuyen Pr, IV Corps.

First Vietnam Veterans - See main alpha listing.

First Vietnamese Ambassador to U.S. - Bui Vien was 1st Ambassador to U.S. (1873), sent by Emperor Tu Duc to secure help in quelling French expansion, but although President Ulysses S. Grant was sympathetic, Congress was not. Possibly was also 1st Viet ever to visit U.S. as well? See *The Vietnam Guidebook*, pp 52.

First Vietnamese to Visit U.S. - Apparently Bui Vien was 1st Viet to visit US. Was also its 1st Ambassador here. Data per *The Vietnam Guidebook*, pp 52.

FIS - French Information Service. Bridgette Friang, an FIS reporter, parachuted into the desperate battle at Tu Le with French 6th Paras. See also IPSA, PFAT and Women In Vietnam.

Fishbed - Code name for Mig-21 Fighter Aircraft.

FL - Flight Level (TAD).

Flame Bath - 55 gallon drums of napalm dropped by helo on enemy bunker location as both an offensive weapon and to eliminate vegetation concealing positions or potential positions. One use described in HQ 2d/14th Inf, 25th Inf Div (Golden Dragons) AAR of 6Oct69, at: www.en.com/users/ kramsey/ dragons.html. Also found in 18th Mil Hist Det, 25th Inf Div, rpt for 2-6Apr70 (Rpt on file at www.army.mil/cmh-pg/documents/ vietnam/reneg/rtxt.htm), 3d Bde, 25th Inf Div AAR within following quote: "At 1500 hours LTC Custer's Command and Control Ship engaged and killed one enemy with three flame baths at XT296301." See also Pink Rose.

Flame Drop - 101st Abn term. Quantities of 55 gal drums containing napalm dropped from CH-47 helos and then strafed by cobra gunships to ignite their contents. Used to defoliate troublesome sites and deny the enemy usage. Believed to have been 1st employed in '70. Author witnessed and participated in on-ground BDA of Flame Drop in Rocket Valley near Nui Ke, Summer '70. See also Pink Rose.

Flame Platoon - A.k.a. Zippo Zappers. Armored Flame Platoons such as 2d Bn (Mech), 22d Inf, 25th Inf Div. In '68, its first Flame Plt was created. Plt consisted of 4 sections, each mounted in an APC (200 gal napalm tank) with refueling unit mounted in 5-ton truck (later on a track carrier). Essentially, these were giant flame-throwers used to clear foliage or destroy enemy positions and bunkers. See 9th Div Flame-throwers website at: http://msnhomepates.talkcity.com/ lagrangeln/r_a_camaro/.

Flame Tanks - Tanks equipped to spray napalm. See also Flame Platoon for APC version of same weapon/tool.

Flame Tracks - M-113 APCs designed to carry napalm dispensers. See Flame Platoon. Flame Track website at: http://msnhomepages.talkcity.com/lagrangeln/r_a_camaro/.

Flaming Arrow - SF A-Team code word indicating that a tactical emergency airstrike was urgently needed and that pilot should look for a "Flaming Arrow" on grnd and pointing toward enemy. Each A-Team camp had large arrow composed of tin cans filled with sand and gasoline mounted on a turntable. Arrow was put in an open area and could easily be seen by acft. Pilots would know to deliver ordnance in direction it was pointed, and number of burning pots in tail portion of arrow was an indicator of distance to enemy in 100 meter increments. Data per *Tan Phu*, p 49.

Flareship - Any acft used or designed for long-term, grnd-supt night illum role. C-47, C-119, C-123 and C-130 fixed-wing acft filled that role and roles as specialized weapons platforms throughout war. CH-47 Medium helo was also used in role by 1st Inf Div early in war. Gunship and Flareship roles were often combined in one acft. The parachute-borne flares used were very large, extremely bright and could burn for as long as four minutes(?). Larger acft could provide almost constant

battlefield illum for hours at a time. See also Basketball, Candlestick, Spectre, Spooky and Puff the Magic Dragon.
FLC - Fleet Logistics Cmd. Major Cmd HQ'd at Da Nang. Quang Nam Pr, I Corps.
fld - field (TAD).
Flechette Round - Anti-personnel arty rnd a.k.a. the "Beehive Round" or "Canister Round." Also variety of 2.75" aerial arty rockets used same principle but contained hundreds of 1.5" finned nails for its shrapnel. See also Canister Round for detail.
Flechettes - The 1.5" finned-nails used in 2.75" aerial arty rocket that contained hundreds of these "nails" for its shrapnel. Also term used to describe shrapnel element of conventional arty "Canister" rnds of different form than the 2.75 rocket version. See Canister Round for more detail.
Flt - Fleet
Flt - Flight
FLT CON - Flight Control (TAD).
Flying Boxcar - Trade name for C-119 twin-eng, prop, cargo transport. 900 mi rnge, 245 kts top spd. mfgd by Fairchild Acft.
Flying Circus - Call-sign of USMC HMM-365. A.k.a., the "Magnificent Flying Circus."
Flying Circus, The - Nickname of 1st Bde, 1st Cavalry Div.
Flying Dragon - A call-sign or nickname of 52d Combat Avn Bn?
Flying Tiger - A call-sign of USMC HMM-361.
Flying Tiger Airlines - Contract troop commercial airline that flew many U.S. servicemen to and from combat zone. Also prominent during evac of Da Nang and Saigon when its flamboyant owner ignored warnings not to land in Da Nang after it had fallen to enemy. Dramatic accounts of those events can be found in *Tears before the Rain*.
FMF - Fleet Marine Force?
FNG - Fucking New Guy. Generally derisive U.S. GI slang denoting newly-arrived replacement personnel. Equiv terms "Newbie", "FNG" and "Cherry" were widely used and universally abhorred by those to whom they were applied.
FO - Forward Observer. Provided expert fwd Arty control with infantry units in jungle and adjusted fire by actual visual observation. ANZAC equivalent was "FOO."
FOB - Forward Operating Base. Generally an SF designation assigned to some of their fwd positions and camps. For info regarding specific FOBs, see FOB in main alpha listing.
FOC - Flight Operations Control (TAD).
FOD - foreign object damage (TAD).
FOIA - Freedom of Information Act. Use discussed in *Prisoners of Hope*, pp 105, 177-178, and extensively in *Stolen Valor*.
FOM (short or long) - French River Patrol Boat, Short. A.k.a. *France Outre Mer*.
FOM Rations - French equiv of U.S. C-Ration. That is, the food ration packaged for individual soldier.
fone - telephone (TAD).
FOO - ANZAC acronym for an arty Forward Observation Officer and the equivalent of FO (Forward Observer) in U.S. Military.
Force Fed Fire Support System - Brainchild of MajGen Ellis Williamson, CG 25th ID, '68-69. System of FSB/Patrol base const designed as offensive strategy in which they were built directly in path of NVA infiltration/lines-of-march, thereby inviting enemy to attack. Per *Suicide Charlie*, p 95, "Williamson also altered the shape of patrol bases from ellipses to circles, and had them built smaller so they could be manned by one or two line companies." His theory was that NVA would only attack such bases individually, allowing the 25th ID to concentrate all available suptg fires to destroy the massed enemy. FSB Mole City was 1st base hit as result of this prgm (4th/9th Inf, 22Dec68), and 2d was Diamond I (2d/27th Inf, 23Feb69), in an apparent disaster where NVA overran base and it took 10hrs to drive them off. Photo of FSB Mole City that typifyies concept is at: www.manchu.org/mole_city/index13.htm.
Ford, Tennessee Ernie - See American Radio Service.
Foreign Legion, French - See French Foreign Legion.
Form-180 - Standard U.S. Dept. of Defense form used for requesting copies of military records. Is available on website of the National Personnel Center (St. Louis, MO)
Form-214 - See DD-214.
Form-AR 220-346 - See Daily Journal.
Fortify Elm - Type of emergency Tac-Air immediate action response employed by Tactical Air Cmd for rptd enemy concentrations. Cited in 4th Inf Div news release dated 23Mar69, at: http://grunt. space.swri.edu/aarrpt1.htm.
Forty Mike-Mike - 40MM. See 40 Mike Mike.
Fougas - See Phougas.
Fougasse - See Phougas.
Fountainebleau Conference - 1946 meetings between French (whom under the aegis of WWII's victorious allies had been allowed to reclaim control of VN) and Ho Chi Minh's new Vietnamese govt. Ended without an agreement. As result, by late '46, French were at war with Ho's Vietminh Army in what became known as the 1st Indochina War.
Four Noes, The - SVN President Thieu often responded to suggestions he compromise with NVA or form a coalition govt with what he called, "The Four Nose:" no coalition, no neutralization, no territorial concessions, no communist forces allowed to operate openly in SVN. As per *A Better War*, p 342.
Foxtrot Owl - Call-sign for Dong Ha Airfield Control.
FPF-5 Radar - Ground scanning portable radar unit. In Late Dec, early Jan 69, 3d/34th Arty placed FPS-5 surveillance radar on an LCM-8 boat that proved a successful adaptation of equip. In part due to its use during 1st 4 months suptg 9th Inf Div's 2d Bde MRF, over 1,500 VC KIA and 100% increase in Hoi Chanhs resulted. Per Ann Hist Rpt of 3d/34th Arty, period 1Apr68-31Jan69, at: www.mrfa.org/3_34th.htm.
fr - from (TAD).
Fr - French.
FRAC - First Regional Assistance Command (TAD).
Frag - Nickname for any hand grenade Also used as a verb to denote act of pre-mediated murder by any means.
Fragging - Slang denoting act of attempted or actual pre-mediated murder by hand grenade (and other means). Grenades (a.k.a. "Fragmentation Grenade" and "Frag" for short) were common weapon of choice; however, the term was often used quite loosely to refer to any homicide attempt regardless using a weapon. Per *The Perfect War*, p 472, for Army alone documented fraggings were 126 in '69, 271 in '70, and 321 in '71 resulting in 85 deaths. It is likely actual totals were slightly higher due to fact that by design, some could not be distinguished from enemy actions. Per *A Better War*, p 292, a study done by Dr. Thomas Bond, (Chief of Psychiatry at Ft. Leavenworth Disciplinary Barracks) of prisoners convicted of fragging in SVN found that all admitted to drug usage of various sorts in SVN, and that 87.5% said they were "acutely intoxicated" at time the crime was committed. Unfortunately, Sorely did not discuss what Dr. Bond meant by term "acutely

intoxicated," but presumably alcohol intoxication was included. It was not uncommon for disarmed grenades to be tossed into, or placed conspicuously within, a targeted individual's billet or office as warning. See next entry.

Fragging, French v. U.S. - *Facing the Phoenix* rpts that according to Ed Landsdale, between 1954-56, "A group of soreheads among the French in Saigon undertook a spiteful terror campaign against American residents [in which] grenades were tossed at night into yards of houses where Americans lived. American-owned automobiles were blown-up or booby-trapped." Lansdale traced effort to a French colonel (chief of staff, American-French trng mission, no less) and some underlings, then told the man of his knowledge and, that same night, grenades landed in yards of various French suspects. French protested to U.S. ambassador and Lansdale was ordered to cease any retaliation, despite fact Lansdale showed him that Viet police had apprehended 3 French officers in act, "with the explosives in their jeep and a list of American targets." Soon thereafter, Lou Conein was apparently told to toss a grenade into yard of the new U.S. ambassador; an act designed shock him and focus suspicion on French. It apparently did just that, because the next day barricades were installed around the ambassador's residence and French Gen Ely ordered a halt to the foolishness. See also Fragging. *Per Facing The Phoenix*, pp 125-127 author cites an eye witness to Conein incident as follows: " 'It was around nine in evening,' Elyette [Bruchot] recalled. 'We were driving slowly past the home of the American Ambassador. Lou took something-I didn't know what it was, it was hissing-and threw it. BOOM! He had thrown a hand grenade in ambassador's yard. I couldn't believe it...We drove away and luckily nobody came after us.' " Courtney Frobenius relates another possible example: "I recall that soon after Le Clerc's landing and advance, a U.S. major was mysteriously blown up outside Saigon. Though blamed on Viets, it seems rather strange that a U.S. major riding a jeep with a U.S. flag (then Ho's delight) would be blown up by Viets."

France Outre Mer -A.k.a. FOMs. French River Patrol boats.

Free Fire Zone - Any defined geographic area in which U.S. troops were free to fire on any target without the inordinate time delays and (sometimes malicious) interference associated with securing clearance from SVN govt/ARVN officials or Viet Dist authorities. Presumption was that anyone inside these zones was the enemy and could be engaged at will. See also Gook Box

Freedom Fighter - Trade name for F-5, twin-jet fighter also used in light bombing and ground supt role. 215 mi rnge, 925 kts top spd. mfgd by Northrop.

French Casualties, 1st Indochina War - French Union Forces at height of French War numbered 287,000. Throughout their war, they suffered apx 95,000 KIA (only 25,000 of whom were of French blood), inc 4 Generals, 1,300 lieutenants and a mix of French, French Foreign Legion, Cambodian, Laotian, Algerian, Moroccan and Sengalese troops. French Foreign Legion troops, which numbered perhaps 40,000 worldwide, did not exceed 20,000 in Indochina at any point.

French Civilians in Vietnam - French had over 80,000 dependents in Indochina: admin personnel, truckers, const workers, teachers, doctors and the like. In French Natl school exams, the children among them scored as well as, if not better than, their peers in France, and they also regularly won the Natl high school swimming championship. Per *Street Without Joy*, p 131.

French Far Eastern Air Force - French air forces of 1st Indochina War. See *Street Without Joy*, pp 260-267.

French Foreign Legion - French Foreign Legion troops, which numbered perhaps 40,000 worldwide, did not exceed 20,000 in Indochina at any point.

French Fort Design - *Street Without Joy* devotes much of Chp 8 to discussion of French fort designs, techniques and curiosities. Apparently they ranged from copies of earlier, African, Beau Geste types (elaborate, with crenelated towers) to more modern, utilitarian sorts (ugly, squat, dug-in bunker type). Some later forts were elaborate models resembling those of American War to come, with their own arty, armor, airstrips and even their names spelled out on painted rocks or tiles placed atop a roof for ease of aerial recognition. Such forts were nicknamed "Rich Forts" by Fall (who offered Ke Sat as example). Fortifications in Indochina, Fall says, had their "architectural periods just like any other works of man, based on local terrain, availability of building materials, the enemy's combat potential, and state of art of military Engineering." In SVN, terrain and enemy's lack of hvy weapons allowed tall observation towers (square, concrete belfry-types) to be added with trees placed around the base of tower to absorb Bazooka fire. As southern enemy acquired recoilless rifles (the SKZ), the towers were incorporated into concrete bunker systems, while still others were built atop concrete bunkers using armored observation points placed atop a metal framework similar to that of an oil derrick. Many French forts became standardized and were even assigned model numbers. Fall cites an example: FTSV-52, which translates as French Ground Forces Fort Model #52 (with 52 being year of intro). By '49, the Beau Geste-type fort was obsolete and only used for daytime observation or barracks. By '51, small, individual concrete bunkers with small firing ports replaced traditional forts Marshal de Lattre de Tassigny's massive const project known as the *de Lattre Line* evolved (some 2,200 pillbox bunkers built in the prgm). Like French forts, de *Lattre* bunkers also evolved in design over time (see also *de Lattre Bunkers* and *de Lattre Line* for detail). Data per *Street Without Joy,* Chp 8.

French Union Forces – See French Union Forces in Major Commands Section.

Friendly Fire incidents Involving U.S. Vessels - *Point Welcome, USCGC*, WPB 82329, attacked by U.S. jets thinking it to be enemy vessel at 0340 hrs on 11Aug66, while patrolling Market Time Sector1A1, adj to DMZ and apx 1 km S 17th Parallel. Noted news photographer Tim Page severely wounded among11 WIA and 2 KIA caused by strafing conducted by B-57 Bomber and two F4C acft in 9 separate runs (see *Point Welcome* in main alpha listing for detail). Other friendly-fire incidents involving U.S. ships include: 16Aug68, when PCF-29 was sunk by 3 rockets w/5 KIA; the *Point Dume* (WPB-82325) and *PCF-12* were hit by an unidentified acft, *USS Boston* (CAG-1) and HMAS *Hobart* (DLG-39) also suffered air attacks with loss of life. See *Brown Water, Black Berets*, p 112-114, 127. See also *Friendly Target*, online at http://members.aol. com/rhassard/Friendly_Target.html.

freq - (radio) frequency (TAD).

FSB - Fire Support Base, or Artillery Fire Supt Base.

FSCC - Fire Support Coordination Center (USMC).

FSPB - Fire Support Patrol Base.

FSS - Flight Service Station.
FSSE - Forward Service & Supt Element.
FTX - Field Training Exercise. See also MACV Recondo School.
FUBAR - Fouled-Up (or Fucked-up) Beyond All Recognition.
Fuck You Bird - Bird whose song sounded remarkably like the phrase that became its nickname. Described in Jack Leninger's *Time Heals No Wounds*, at page28.
Fuck-You Lizard - A.k.a. the "Re-Up" Lizard. Lizard that at night frequently repeated a call (likely a mating call) that sounded remarkably like the phrase that became its nickname. Described in *Time Heals No Wounds*, at page28.
Fullbright-Aiken Amendment - Amendment to '73(?) Defense Appropriations Bill that, among other things, mandated: "On or after 15Aug73, no funds may be obligated or expended to finance indirectly or directly U.S. military forces in, over or off-shore of South Vietnam, North Vietnam, Laos or Cambodia," per *A Better War*, p 364. See also Cooper-Church and Paris Peace Accords.
FUO - Fever of Unknown Origin. Common diagnosis of fever related illnesses in VN.
FWMAF - Acronym for Free World Military Assistance Forces. The allied forces fighting with RVN Govt.
G-2 - Assistant chief of staff for military intelligence at an army, corps (field force in Vietnam), or division HQ.
Galard-Jerraube, Genevieve de - See Angel of Dien Bien Phu.
G. B. - See *Groupement Blinde* in Glossary.
G. M. 100 - See *Groupement Mobile 100* in Glossary.
Galaxy - Trade name for C-5A, 4-jet eng cargo transport acft (largest in use during VN War). 2,729 mi rnge, 515 kts top spd. mfgd by Lockheed Acft.
Game Warden, Operation – A.k.a. USN Task Force 116. Was created in '65 to interdict VC guerrilla forces of Mekong Delta. In '67, TF 117 was added to expand coverage of Mekong Delta and Rung Sat Swamp. Forces employed fiberglass PBRs, air-cushioned vehicles, WWII landing craft, LSTs, LSMs, motorized junks, and various amphib personnel carriers to negotiate waterways and to deliver/supt MRF of U.S. 9th Div and ARVN forces. MRF was created in '67 using a Bde of 9th Inf Div and TFs 116 and 117, and gradually shifted to ARVN between '69-71 (bulk of 9th Div went home in '69). See also MRF, Market Time, USN Forces VN (Major Cmd Section) and 9th Inf Div (Divisional Cmd Section).
Gap-2 - Nickname of French Army LTC Pierre Langlais, Cmdr Abn Grp at Dien Bien Phu. See Dien Bien Phu, Battle of.
Garand - The M-1 Rifle. See M-1.
GATAC - *Groupement Aeriens Tactiques*. Any one of 4, French, regional tactical air cmds in French War, each of which was cmd by a BG. They were: GATAC North (inc northern VN and northern Laos), GATAC Central (inc central VN and southern Laos), GATAC South (inc all of Cochinchina, Cambodia and south-central VN); and GATAC LAOS (existed in '53-54 only). Data per *Street Without Joy*, p 262.
GATAC Central - See GATAC.
GATAC Laos - See GATAC.
GATAC North - See GATAC.
GATAC South - See GATAC.
Gator - A call-sign of the 119th AHC.
Gauloise Troupe - Popular French cigarettes of 1st Indochina War. Noted for their harsh, black tobacco.
GB - See *Groupement Blinde* in Glossary.
GCA - Ground Control Approach radar used to facilitate landings.
GCI - USAF acronym for Ground Control Intercept Radar.
GCMA -*Groupement de Commandos Mixtes*. French commandos who lived with indigenous populations across N and central highlands. The GCMA controlled some 15,000 guerrillas at height of French War. In Spring 1954, some 5,000 partisans were operating with under GCMA in NW Tonkin, northern Tonkin and NE Laos. Their war was called, *Le Guerre des Grandes Vides* ("the war of vast empty spaces"), and they operated almost without resupply or commo of any kind. As late as '59, some were still fighting, apparently unaware war had ended or unwilling to give up. Later in war, name changed to GIM (*Groupement Mixtes d'Intervention*). *Street Without Joy* discusses post-war plight of those GCMA lost or left in far reaches of NW Tonkin in detail. It notes: "French officers recall with a shudder the last radio message picked up somewhere from North Vietnam nearly two years after the fighting had officially stopped. The voice was a French voice and message was addressed to French. It said: 'You sons of bitches, help us! Help us! Parachute us at least some ammunition, so that we can die fighting instead of being slaughtered like animals!' " Per *Street Without Joy*, p 278. See also *Aeroportes*.
GD or Gd - Guard.
GDRA - General Directorate of Rear Services. NVA office in charge of traffic control on the HCMT. NVA's 559th Trans Grp (HQ'd in Base Area 604 near Tchepone, Laos), was responsible for managing trail, and it is est that some 40,000 troops were assigned its operation. Data per *A Better War*, pp 48-53. See also Binh Tram, T-Stations, and K-Intervals.
General Mobilization Act -See Draft, The (SVN), in Glossary.
Genevieve de Galard-Jerraube - See Angel of Dien Bien Phu.
Ghost Riders - Call-sign for A Co, 158th Avn Bn.
Ghost Ship, The - Huey gunship (#702), that flew supt for 101st Abn and 49th Avn Co slicks during Op Hawthorne, Jun66. Per *Chickenhawk*, p 407, after mission to rescue trapped ARVNs, 702 radioed it had been hit, but no further commo followed. Long after its ETA, it was heard approaching the unit's pad at Prospectors' Camp, NW of Dak To. It then made very rough lndg, and "With a collective sigh of relief, the [waiting] crowd began to break up. I stopped outside with some others because something odd was happening with 702. Nobody was getting out. The ship just stood there hissing. Its rotors swung lazily. Somebody ran over to ship and started waving frantically, calling for Doc. All four people on board were unconscious from wounds."
Ghosting - GI slang for goofing off and/or avoiding/hiding-out from field duty or work.
Ghostrider - A call-sign of the 189th AHC and/or 604th Trans Det, as well as A Co, 158th Avn Bn (supt 101st Abn (et al) in Thua Thien/Quang Tri Prov, I Corps).
GIB - Guy In Back. Nickname for back-seat navigation and weapons officer of the F-4 Phantom acft.
GIM - Guerrilla units originally known as *Aeroportes*, who were armed and led by French commandos in what later became known as GIM, or *Groupement Mixtes d'Intervention*. 1st Indochina War. See also GCMA.
Gladiator - A call-sign of the 57th AHC.
Globemaster II - Trade name for C-124, 4-eng. Prop driven cargo transport acft. 4,030 mi rnge, 230 kts top spd. mfgd by Douglas Acft.
GM 100 - See *Groupement Mobile 100* in Glossary.

gnd - ground (TAD).
GND CON - Ground Control (TAD).
Go Go Bird - Heavily armed experimental Chinook CH-47 helo created for and tested by 1st Cav Div early in war. Was armed with two 20mm Vulcan cannons (Gatling guns), a 40mm grenade launcher and .50 cal machine guns. 3 were produced, but although troops loved them and enemy always fled at their arrival, no more were built and the 3 apparently pulled from inventory.
Going Over The Fence - Special ops code phrase for crossing the border into Laos, Cambodia or NVN.
Golden BB, The - Pilot jargon for that single, lucky shot that might down an aircraft.
GONO -*Groupement Operationne du Nord-Ouest*, or Northwest Operational Group. The Dien Bien Phu Cmd.
Good Deal Company – Motto/call-sign of B Co, 227th AHB.
Good Neighbor Program - Prgm designed to reduce number of hamlets in AO of 4th Div by concentrating civilian populations presumably as means of improving the efficiency of defending them against VC/NVA infiltration/tax collections. By Jan69, prgm reduced overall # of hamlets in 4th Div's AO from 58 to 41. For example, villes of Plei Pham Ho (AR 854-336), Plei Le Anh (AR 824-324) and Plei Gyum were consolidated to form Plei Hlu Klan (apx 16 km SSE Pleiku and 5 km SE Camp Enari). Data per 4th Div op rpt for period ending 31Jan69 courtesy Craig Miller.
Gook - Slang for the NVA or VC or Vietnamese in general. While often derisive in use, it was more the author's experience that such slang words were used in everyday conversation simply as nouns to denote the enemy. They were less frequently used in the pejorative sense or as an intentional slur, despite the inference one might draw from simply looking at such words. Words such as Gook, Slope, Dink, NVA, VC, Little People, Charlie, Chuck, Chuck and the Boys, Charles, Sir Charles, Rice Eaters and the like were used interchangeably in casual conversation and, odd though it may seem, often out of respect and awe for enemy's significant accomplishments and courage (for example: "Damn, those gooks sure kicked our butt today!" or, "Sir Charles is the Man!" or "Screw with Charlie and Charlie will screw with you!") Although one text claims the word "Gook" was the Korean word for "Person," the author of *Son Thang* (at p 115), tells us that while the word "Gook" was used widely by U.S. troops in WWII/Korean War and is presumed to refer primarily to Asians, it was originally used to describe Nicaraguan rebels during the 1912 Nicaraguan Banana Wars. Adding, at p 116, "The mind-set illustrated by the mere Gook Rule, however, was common in conversation among U.S. forces of all ranks in SVN and reflected casual, unthinking racism and cultural arrogance." During the 1st Indochina War, rich Viets or their children attending school in France were derisively referred to as "Mites;" contraction of the word "Annamite" (per J. Middlesworth, appears in *Secrets of the Viet Cong*). French also used term "Nhaques," meaning "peasant," though origin is unclear. See also Mere Gook Rule.
Gook Box - Per *Apache Sunrise*, p 239, was 1st Air Cav slang for "Free Fire Zone." See Free Fire Zone.
Goose Early Warning System - See DEWS in main alpha listing.
Gophers - Per Eddie Tricker, was Aussie nickname for soft drinks.
Gorwoody Antenna - Consisted of stnd PRC 25 or PRC 77 short-whip antenna cut at 1st joint, to which flexible, silver-coated, wires (with loop at the end so that they could be hung in bushes or trees) was attached. Wires were apparently cut at specific lengths to match certain radio frequencies. Invented in Aug68 by, and named for, Sp4 William Gorris and SFC Jason Woodworth. Discussed in and data per *Rangers At War, LRRPs in Vietnam*, p 287. See McGuire Rig and STABO Rig.
GP - General Purpose. Military nomenclature assigned to many things, such as the GP-tent.
GP-Tent - General Purpose Tent. Stnd military, green-canvas tent used for just about anything including housing, storage, medical treatment and dining.
GPES - Ground Proximity Extraction System. Innovation created by necessity to overcome very hazardous resupply of Khe Sanh CB during its '67-68 siege. Similar to LAPES system, but involved grnd equip to aid in extracting cargo from C-130's doing touch-and-go resupply landings. See also LAPES.
GPO - Government Printing Office.
Graham Report - James Graham was CIA's lead analyst of Sihanouk Trail data and in his rpt he stubbornly refused to acknowledge that port of Sihanouk was primary ingress point for NVA/VC supplies and personnel suptg III and IV Corps ops. His intransigence drove MACV intel analysts to distraction because their data clearly showed it was major supply route and that Cambodian govt was complicit in its operation. Graham insisted he was correct until late '69, when interdiction bombing of the HCMT had strangled southbound supplies to only 8 tons per day (an amount that couldn't possibly meet needs) yet NVA ops continued unabated. Graham's position may have had more to do with the political predicament into which Cambodia had maneuvered itself than with his belief in the numbers. See *A Better War*, p 102.
Graham's Folly - Minefield laid to S of FSB Horseshoe (apparently under direction of CO named Graham) from which VC made regular habit of stealing ANZAC mines. PF in area failed to properly patrol access to minefield and author of *Vietnam Gunners* speculates that more allied soldiers in Phuoc Tuy Pr may have died from these mines than died from VC bullets. See Horseshoe in main alpha listing for location.
Grand Eagle, Operation - A.k.a. Operation BOHICA. 2d POW rescue mission into Laos organized by Bo Gritz, who also gave it the code name BOHICA. Followed Op Velvet Hammer after that op was canceled in 1981. Collapsed soon after it was initiated when Gritz's claimed financial backers denied any involvement. Discussed in *Prisoners of Hope*, pp 136, 151-2.
Gravel and Chat - See Chat and Gravel.
Gravel Mines - The XM-41E. Air-seeded anti-personnel mine designed to wound feet/legs, and originally proposed for extensive use ('65-66) in what was known as "The Laotian Barrier" (an adjunct of McNamara's Wall). Large numbers could be dispensed by each metal air-dropped metal canister. Consisted of 3" cloth bag filled with an explosive and plastic pellets. Could not be detected with mine detectors and its pellets could not be seen on X-rays. Used in conjunction with the sensor technologies of Igloo White and Muscle Shoals Ops. See *Valley of Decision*, pp 142, 300-301.
Greater Wheel, The - See Mahayana.
Green Dragons - VC gave this nickname to camouflaged APCs firing their MGs and on the attack.

Grey Eight – Nickname of 8 Royal Australian Army Rgt (8 RAR).

Greyhound - A call-sign of the 240th ASHC.

Greyhound - Trade name for C-2 acft. 1,900 mi rnge, 310 kts top spd. mfgd by Grumman Avn.

Griffin - Call-sign for C Bty, 4th/77th ARA gunships.

Groupement Blinde - A.k.a. G.B. Basic French Armored Group.

Groupement de Commandos Mixtes - French Commando Special Forces. See GCMA.

Groupement Mixtes d'Intervention - French Commando Special Forces originally known as GCMA. See GIM and GCMA.

Groupement Mobile 100 - A.k.a. G.M. 100. French armored composite unit that on 24Jun54 was ambushed and annihilated by 803d Vietminh Rgt in the Mang Yang Pass on QL-19 between An Khe and Pleiku. Unit consisted of famous and battle-hardened 1st and 2d *Batallion de Coree* (transferred from Korea Jul53), reinforced by 2 Bns of Viet Inf, 2d Grp/10th Colonial Arty Rgt, *Batallion de Marche* of 43d Colonial Inf (skilled Cambodian and French Jungle fighters), Commando Bergerol, and reinforced with 3d Sqdn/5th (Royal Poland) Armored Cav. Unit was 1st brought together at Gia Dinh, near Saigon, and activated 15Nov-29Nov53. TF was assigned mission of clearing central highlands of Vietminh along QL-14, which was generally invulnerable to French aerial bombing and observation. It left Gia Dinh 29Nov53 (with 3,498 men) and endured steady string of murderous ambushes until was virtually annihilated at Mang Yang Pass. Sites of major engagements inc: Dak Doa, La PIT, Plei Rinh, Kon Brai, An Khe, PK 15 on QL-19, Cu Dreh Pass on QL-14. Final ambush took place near PK 15, apx 15 km W An Khe and along QL-19 just W the Kon Bar road intersection, and at point where QL-19 emerged into small plain covered with dense, 6' high elephant grass (and exact point of similar deadly ambush of 4Apr54). Aerial recon had warned column that rocks had been placed across road at PK 15, but otherwise saw no evidence of enemy. After main ambush at PK 15, the escape objective for main body of survivors was PK 22, where French 1st Abn Grp had position. Fighting through series of ambushes, exhausted elements of 1st Korea Bn met and embraced the 1st Abn Grp at PK 22 at 11:30 am, 25Jun54. At bridge over Dak Ya Ayun River on 27Jun54, the 803d Vietminh Rgt then hit the 1st Korea Bn of G.M. 42 as it was escaping W toward Pleiku with survivors of G.M. 100. 1st Korea broke through with help of tanks and camped at bridge that night after losing 20 KIA. On 28Jun54, as column approached Pleiku, they were again heavily ambushed at PK 3, this time by 108th VM Rgt, reinforced by elite 30th Independent Bn. 2d Korea Bn counter-attacked under tank and arty fire, and B-26s arrived with napalm, catching Vietminh in open. When survivors reached Pleiku, 29Jun54, HQ Co had lost 138 of its 222 men; the 1st Korea, 382 of its 834 (overall, 1st Korea Bn lost 62 KIA in 5-days of fighting on QL-19; more dead than during its entire 3 years in Korea); the 2d Korea, 337 of its 834; Batallion de Marche of 43d Colonials, 489 of its 834 men; 2d Grp of 10th Colonial, 259 of its 474 men (a total of over 1,600 dead and missing); 85% of all vehicles; an entire armored car plt; 100% of its Arty; 68% of all signal equip and 1/2 of all its automatic weapons and machine guns. For years afterwards, the white crosses of French dead could be seen from below Mang Yang pass and served as stark warning of its potential. Sadly, its survivors were soon back in combat where they again suffered mightily during Op Forget Me Not, the last French Op of war. On 1Aug54, after the Armistice had been signed on 20Jul54, the remnants of G.M. 100 marched to Saigon and Vung Tau, where it was dissolved 1Sep54. In main alpha listing, see also Dak Ya Ayun, PK 3, Plei Rinh, Mang Yang Pass, French Tank, Dak Jappur, Op Forget Me Not and Buon Ho Tea Plantations. See *Street Without Joy* for detailed history, Chp 9, *Death of a Task Force*, pp 185-250; maps at pp 187, 213.

Groupement Operationne du Nord-Ouest - See GONO.

Grp - Group.

GS - Glide Slope (TAD).

GSW - Gun shot wound.

GTC - General Classification Test. U.S. Military's rough equiv to IQ test. Score of 100 considered avg; score of 120 minimum for officer candidates. See Project 100,000 and Category Four.

Guard Channel - Radio frequency used for emergencies only. USAF FACs and pilots used other channels to communicate but monitored guard channel simultaneously.

Gulf of Tonkin Incident - Incident involving U.S. DDs *Maddox* and *C. Turner Joy* that began night of 31Jul65 and ended night of 4Aug71. *Maddox* was part of Op Desoto and monitoring NVA naval activities when attacked by 2 torpedo boats, 31Jul65, apx 28 mi from NVN in Gulf of Tonkin. PT boats launched 2 torpedoes but only one PT boat suffered any damage. *Maddox* was joined by *C. Turner Joy,* and in bad weather on night of 4Aug, thought it was again attacked by five radar contacts. Witnesses testified they saw torpedo wakes and jets from *USS Ticonderoga* rptd sinking two PT boats but that evidence has since been challenged. As a result, on 5Aug65 President Johnson ordered retaliatory strikes against NVN PT boat bases, during which 2 U.S. acft were shot down resulting in 1st U.S. POW the war (Lt Edward Alvarez), and ultimately the committal of 1st U.S. ground forces that same month.

Gun Line, The - NGS or naval gunfire supt provided by USN warship TFs for grnd ops along coast. See also ANGLICO.

Gunfighter - Call-sign for F-4s Phantoms of 8th(?) TFW, flying out of Da Nang. I Corps.

Gunflint - Gen Westmoreland's secret code name for an inspection tour of ANZAC positions at Nui Dat and throughout III Corps in Aug67.

Gunner - Call-sign for B Bty, 377th Arty.

Gunner - Nickname for individuals assigned to man most any sort of gun, inc arty pieces and machine guns. Standard nickname for infantry squad's M-60 Machine Gunner as well. "AG" was standard nickname for gunner's assistant gunner.

Gunners' Day - 26May. Anniversary of birth of 161 Royal New Zealand Arty. See "Gunner's Day" main alpha entry.

Guy Fawkes Night - New Zealand celebration first held in VN 5Nov65 (and each 5Nov thereafter), when 161 Bty, RNZA fired 240 rounds of illum, smoke and HE into air above War Zone D. Puzzled U.S. cmd, ignorant of significance of event, urgently queried Kiwis as to nature of enemy contact and then relayed to higher U.S. HQ that "the Kiwis are celebrating some Guy named Fox." Data per, *Vietnam Gunners.*

GVN – Government, Republic of Vietnam.

GYROJET Pistol - Tested by SOG in Laos with mixed results. Made mostly from stamped steel and plastic, it weighed but a few ounces. Fired small, 13mm mini solid fuel-propelled rocket. Gases jetting from projectile made it spin for accuracy and also made it sound like "Roman Candle" fireworks. Was recoilless, inaccurate, but also impressive. Per *SOG,* "In one test, a rocket round punched through an old truck door and into a water filled 55-gallon drum, almost exiting its opposite side."

H-2 Seasprite - U.S. single-rotor(?) helicopter with 445 mi rnge, 165 kts top spd. mfgd by KAMAN.

H-3 Sea King - Aka SH-3 Sea King. U.S. single-rotor helicopter with 625 mi rnge, 162 kts top spd. mfgd by Sikorsky Helicopter. See also SH-3 Sea King.

H-46 Sea Knight - A.k.a. CH-46. U.S. Twin-rotor helicopter with 110 mi rnge, 120 kts top spd. mfgd by Boeing Acft.

H-53 Choctaw - U.S. single-rotor SAR helicopter with 180 mi rnge, 120 kts top spd. mfgd by Sikorsky Helicopter.

H-53 Sea Stallion - A.k.a. CH-53. U.S. single-rotor SAR helicopter with 255 mi rnge, 170 kts top spd. mfgd by Sikorsky Helicopter.

Hac Bo - The elite Black Panther Co of 1st ARVN Div.

HACOM, U.S. **Army** - See main alpha listing.

Hai Quan - South Vietnamese Navy.

HAL - Helicopter Attack Light (UH-1 Hueys) (USN).

Ham and Motherfuckers - Derisive nickname of "Ham and Lima Beans" C-Ration meal. See also LRRP Rations.

Hamlet Evaluation System - A.k.a. HES. MACV's analytical guidelines employed to evaluate pacification success and enemy activity in rural SVN. See also NPIA.

Hamlet Operational Base(?) - See HOB.

Hand-Crank Grenade Launcher - A.k.a. Honeywell Hand-Cranked 40mm Grenade Launcher. See also XM-174.

Hangi - New Zealand forces term for a celebration. Of Maori (NZ) origin, and has certain traditions associated with it that only a Kiwi could explain. Typically, hole is dug in ground, huge fire is started in hole and then rocks are placed in the coals to heat. Excess coals are removed and basket of food items surrounded with banana leaves or damp cloth is lowered into the fire pit and covered by earth from original hole. Food is cooked primarily by steam and a work party is tasked with keeping steam trapped by covering any leaks that develop. Entire process can take as long as 24 hrs. "The food (bloody delicious) is served as a feast most having already enjoyed a few beers." Activities accompanying a Hangi vary greatly. Info per Noel Izzy at izzi@cyberalink.com.au.

Hanoi, French Forces in - HQ of *1st Chasseurs Blindes* (Armored Cav), and Airborne Group 1, among others.

Hanoi Hannah - A.k.a. Trinh Thi Ngo. Certainly Hanoi's most prominent propagandist during Vietnam War. Tried to convince U.S. soldiers they were fighting an immoral war and that America was exploiting them. Her voice has been described as smooth as silk and her English impeccable. Each broadcast would begin with "This is Thu Huong calling American servicemen in South Vietnam" (Thu Huong was alias that meant "Autumn Fragrance"). During broadcasts, she read news of U.S. anti-war protest and, on Fridays, names of U.S. KIA taken from the *Stars and Stripes*. Per David Lamb of LA Times, "Her scripts were written by propagandists in the North Vietnamese army who lifted their material from articles in magazines such as *Time* and *Newsweek* and newspapers such as The New York Times that North Vietnamese diplomats stationed abroad had sent home." Members of U.S. anti-war movement also brought articles to NVN, among them activist Tom Hayden and actress Jane Fonda. Reports aired were often so wildly exaggerated (entire Divs being annihilated or hundreds of planes shot down in single day) that U.S. troops rarely took news seriously, although many did enjoy the current rock and roll music interspersed throughout each show. Her last 30-minute broadcast was made in1973. She moved to Ho Chi Minh City in '75 where today she lives near former Presidential Palace with her engineer husband. Ngo was awarded the First-Class Resistance Medal by Vietnamese Govt.

Hard Rice - Hard Rice and Hard Rice Deliveries were CIA code phrases and slang for ammunition and ammo supply missions carried-out by Air America in Laos and etc.

Harbor Clearance Unit 1 - Medium and Light Lift USN craft used to recover vessels sunk in inland waterways of SVN.

Harbor Defense and Surveillance Units - Units sited at ports of Vung Tau, Cam Ranh Bay, Qui Nhon, Nha Trang, and Vung Ro.

Hard Spots - Per Bill Noyes, in '68 and '69, the 25th Div built number of FSBs called "hard spots." "They were small, durable positions meant to control important terrain and to lure enemy into costly attacks." Each site could accommodate a full Mech Co, and units rotated routinely through sites each week. See Ben Cui Hardspot in main alpha list and Instant Patrol Base in Glossary.

Harry the Hairy Ape - Song by Ray Stevens. See FSB/PB Frontier City entry in main alpha index.

Hardcore - Mongrel mascot dog at Gio Linh/Camp Hill. See FSB Gio Linh in main alpha listing for interesting anecdote.

***Hawaii,* (the movie)** - See Shotgun, Op, in main alpha index.

Hawk - Call-sign for D Co 101st Avn Bn.

Hawk Missile - A surface-to-air anti-aircraft missile (LAAM) employed widely only in I-Corps at what were called LAAM sites. Was apx 20' in length and could reach targets to a max altitude of 38,000 ft. None were ever fired at enemy acft during war, although apparently there was one accidental firing. See LAAM Sites.

Hawkeye - Trade name for E-2 1 acft. 900 mi rnge, 310 kts top spd. mfgd by Grumman Avn.

Hawkeye Teams - Per *Rangers At War*, p 88, were created by Maj. Gen Peers, CG 4th Inf Div, and based upon success of SF patrols employing indigenous troops. 2 Div Recondo troops were paired with 2 Rhade tribesman chosen for their hunting skills and knowledge of terrain. Each team went through 10-day course designed to increase mutual communication skills. Teams had 3 main functions: trail watching, terrain analysis, and screening for line troop movements.

Hawks - 173d Abn slang/code for night ambushes.

Hay Hole - See DePuy Bunker.

HB, M-2 .50 Cal MG - See M-2 Machine Gun.

HC-1 - Helicopter Combat Supt Squadron One. Suptd USN Brown Water forces.

HCMC - Ho Chi Minh City (Saigon).

HCMT - Ho Chi Minh Trail.

hdg - heading (TAD).

HE Bird - High Explosive or UFO Bird. Described in *Time Heals No Wounds*, page 35, as a "Giant Black Bird with an orange beak and a wing span of 8 to 10 feet."

He Who Shines - See Ho Chi Minh.

HEAT - High Explosive, Anti-Tank. Arty, or tank, or recoilless rifle round.

HEAT Round - High Explosive, Anti-Tank Round. See M-72.

Heavy Blues - See Doughnut Dollies.

HECP - Harbor Entrance Central Post (USN).

HEDSUPPACT, USN - See main alpha listing.
Hegdahl, Doug - See *Canberra, USS*, in main alpha index.
Helatkatron - Helatktron and Seawolf were call-signs of Det 8 of Seawolves HA(L)-3. Described as most decorated USN Sqdn.
Helicopter Bug - Bug described as being size of a plum with 2 sets of wings whose wings made sound similar to that of a helicopter. See p 27 of *Time Heals No Wounds*.
Helicopters, NVA - See NVA Helicopters.
Hellcats - U.S. carrier-based, prop-driven fighter-bomber used by French in 1950's. See Bearcats in Glossary.
Helldivers - U.S. carrier-based, prop-driven fighter-bomber used by French in '50's. See Bearcats in Glossary.
Hercules - HC-130 USAF Acft. See C-130 for detail.
Herky Bird - Nickname for USAF's C-130 Hercules Acft.
Hero's Day - (AR) June 21. Pleiku festival that was the idea of Gen Vinh Loc, ARVN II Corps CG in '66. Chosen as time to honor the 2 outstanding fighters of each Div and Bde. Among 1st recipients of Vietnam's highest award at 1st festival were Capt. William Carpenter Jr (The Lonesome End) and PFC David Dolby, who also later received the U.S. MOH for their heroism in Op Crazy Horse, May66. Pleiku Prov, II Corps.
Heroin Usage - See Drug Abuse.
HES - See Hamlet Evaluation System.
HH-43 Huskie - U.S. twin-rotor SAR helicopter with 235 mi rnge, 120 kts top spd. mfgd by Kaman Avn.
hi - high (TAD).
Hinayana - One of 2 main sects of Buddhist religion in SVN. Two were: "The Greater Wheel" or Mahayana, which was centered in central and northern SVN, and "The Smaller Wheel," or Hinayana which was strong in southern SVN. Greater Wheel Buddhists believed anyone could attain the enlightenment of Buddha, while those of Smaller Wheel sect believed enlightenment was only possible for a very few. See also Thinh Tri Quang and *Twenty Years and Twenty Days*, pp 87-88.
High Clerical Association - One of 2 organizations formed by SVN Buddhists in '66, in order to exert pressure on SVN govt reform and put end to discrimination against Buddhists. Under control of Thinh Tri Quang, Assn was considered hard-line. The Institute for Propagation of Buddhist Faith, under control of Thich Tam Chau, was considered more moderate. Discussed in *Twenty Years and Twenty Days*, pp 87-88. See also Thinh Tri Quang.
High Explosive Bird, The - See HE Bird.
Highway (generally) - Highway and Route are terms used interchangeably and informally in this text to identify Provincial Routes (TLs), and Supplementary Routes in particular, but often also for any road that is identified. See also QL, LTL, TL, Route, Highway, HL, R. C., *Route Colonial*, as well as "Principal Roadways of South Vietnam" Section.
Hillsborough - Tactical call-sign for USAF abn C&C C-130 acft controlling fighter supt over part of Laos for TASS FACs (et al).
Hip Shoot LZs - Apparently a 4th Inf Div term used to describe tactical strategy of rapidly-built, quickly abnd Plt-sized, FSBs or LZs manned by single Plt armed with 81mm mortars (or possibly 1 or 2 tubes of 105mm) in supt of company-sized ops nearby. Presumably facilitated fast deployment and wide-area saturation of force in an effort to find or harass enemy when enemy did not want to engage. Paralleled "Art Raid" strategy of 101st Abn Div. Per John Linn, B/2d/35th Inf, LZs Short-Timer I and II are examples.
Hist - Historical
HM - Helicopter Squadron (USN).
HMAS - Her Majesty's Australian Ship.
HMH - Marine Heavy Lift Helicopter Squadron (USMC).
HMM - Marine Medium Helicopter Squadron (USMC).
HMR - Marine Transport Helicopter Squadron (USMC).
HMV - Her Majesty's vessel (Aussie/NZ).
Ho - Possibly a Vietnamese word for "lake?"
Ho Chi Minh - Born in central Vietnam May 19, 1890, as Nguyen Sinh Cung. During his early life, Ho adopted numerous pseudonyms, among which were: Nguyen Ai Quoc (Nguyen The Patriot); Ho Chi Minh (He Who Shines); Nguyen Tat Thanh and Van Ba. Attended school in Hue, then moved S in 1909, where he taught school and called himself, "Van Ba." Beginning in 1911, traveled world for 3 years (would not return to VN until 1941) as cabin boy and ship's cook on a French freighter, afterwards living 1 year in U.S. (Brooklyn NY). He then moved to London, calling himself "Nguyen Tat Thanh," then to Paris where he attended school and became founder of French Communist Party in 1920. In 1924, he moved to Moscow where he received formal communist schooling for several months and then on to Canton, China. Between 1924-40, he formed number of political orgs and traveled throughout Asia. In May41, he returned to VN now calling himself "Ho Chi Minh." On 2Sep45, he declared Viet independence using language from U.S. Declaration of Independence for much of his own proclamation. After French returned to VN under aegis of WWII's allied victors, he tried to reach an agreement with them at Fountainebleau Conference, but failed. By late '46, his Vietminh Army, which had fought the Japanese invaders, was at war with French. In May '54, after French were defeated at Dien Bien Phu, true independence was finally achieved. His reform polices in NVN were often brutally imposed, and many thousands of landed middle and upper class were murdered or executed under his regime. Despite that unfortunate circumstance and American War that followed, Uncle Ho (Bac Ho) was revered by most Viets, NVN and SVN alike. Interestingly, he died 2Sep69, the anniversary of his original declaration of independence.
Ho Chi Minh Sandals - Footwear of choice for many NVA/VC troops. Fabricated from used vehicle tires and very durable.
Ho Chi Minh Trail - Known to NVA variously as the Transportation Corridor, Infantry Route One, the Old Man's Trail, the Truong Son Trail (after Truong Son Mtn Range it traversed), and (Hanoi's official designation) as the Strategic Transportation Corridor. Actually a large network of trails and roads used by NVA to funnel troops/supplies back and forth between NVN and SVN. Originated in several passes along NVN's Lao border, then ran generally S through eastern border areas of Laos and Cambodia, fanning E into border of SVN at hundreds of different locations. Initial const began in 1959, when 5 soldiers were assigned task of cutting it. 6 months later, and at point just below the Ben Hai River, the 1st delivery of arms and supplies were handed to VC troops. 1 year later, NVA began expanding trail to W in order to avoid detection. By end of war, trail consisted of grid of roads and trails over 20,000 km in length. Its primary roads were numbered: Rte 9, 10, 13, 14, 15, 16, 20and 71. To reach trailhead in Laos, NVA crossed the Truong Son mtn range through several key passes (Mu Gia, Ban Karai and Ban Raving). As result, U.S. focused large, round-the-clock

bombing campaign on those choke-points. 1st known published account of trail's use appeared in Wilfred Burchett's *Vietnam: Inside Story of the Guerrilla War* (early 60's). MACV est that avg speed of troops on trail was 10.5 to 12.2 km per day, and that avg infiltration grp numbered 565 to 570 (though only avg of 420 would complete journey). Captured data suggested casualty rate along trail averaged 22%. Avg travel times were apx: 120 days from NVN to COSVN in II Corps; 60 days to B-3 Front in central highlands; 45 days to Quang Tri/Thua Thien region; and 20-25 days to western DMZ. In May68, 3,000 sorties were flown against trail; 6,500 in Jul68, 8,000 in Aug68; and 6,400 in Sep68. Highest observed traffic rate was Jul68, when avg of 1,100 trucks/day observed. USAF est that it cost $15,000 a ton to "kill" a truck, but only $1,000 a ton to halt supplies by trail blockage techniques. Over entire war, 75% of all bombing missions were flown in SVN, 15.25% in Laos, 3% in Cambodia, and only 6.7% in NVN. The HCMT had a southern counterpart; the Sihanouk Trail, which originated on S coast of Cambodia at Sihanoukville, delivering men and supplies to NE along E Cambodian frontier to area generally between Memot and O Rang. Creighton Abrams est that 90% of supplies entering N end of the HCMT were destroyed or interdicted en route, but that virtually all supplies entering through Sihanoukville reached destination until Cambodia Incursion of May70 closed it completely. See also Binh Tram, Door of Death, Laboy Ford, and Sihanouk Trail. Some data per *Sparring With Charlie*, pp 6, 7. HCMT statistical data per *A Better War*, pp 48-52, 82-83.

Hoa Long Dance, The - Hoa Long (YS 42-63) was VC-controlled ville apx 8 km WNW 1st ATF FSB Horseshoe. As practical joke, newly arrived ANZAC replacements were told to dress up in their best uniform and rpt to base's main gate for bus that would take them to "Hoa Long Dance." Dutifully, many would show up and mill about, waiting for a bus that never came! Per *Vietnam Gunners, 161 Bty RNZA, South Vietnam, 1965-71*, 1988 p 67. Phuoc Tuy Pr, III Corps.

HOB - Possibly "Hamlet Operational Base?" Per John Rochelle, 704th Maint Bn, was term used to describe ARVN/RF/PF FSBs/positions in western II Corps.

Hobos - Call-sign of 20th SOS lift Hueys (USAF).

Hog - See M-60 Machine Gun.

Hogs - Nickname for Huey UH-1 Gunship models. Huey helos were often used as weapon platforms, taking on roll of attack helos or "Gunships" (nicknamed Hogs) after being fitted with various combinations of multiple M-60 machine guns, 7.62 mini-guns, .50 Cal, rocket pods and/or M-79 grenade launchers.

Hoi – One Vietnamese word for "stream" (among many others).

Hoi Chanh - NVA or VC soldier who defected to U.S. or ARVN forces under Chieu Hoi Prgm. See Chieu Hoi and FSB Buffalo.

Homecoming, Operation - Return of US/allied POWs beginning 11Feb73 when U.S. C-130 landed at Gia Lam Airport, Hanoi, with first load of POW escorts. Ended 14Mar73(?), some 3 weeks later. 118 missions flew 591 POWs to freedom. Final peace agreement signed 27Jan73, required NVN to release all POWs within 60 days, with 1st release set for 12Feb73. All former prisoners taken 1st to Clark AFB in Philippines before continuing to US. Marine Bombardier/Navigator Larry Friese described his release as follows: "It was the strangest day of my life [14Mar73]. There I was in stinking cell that morning, and I ended the day with a fistful of $20 bills in one hand and a nice cold bottle of Michelob in other." Larry Friese quote and other data from Feb98 *The Retired Officer* Mag article, *The Journey Home*, pp 33-40.

Hon - Vietnamese for hill or mountain (& Dong, Nui, Phu).

Hon - Vietnamese for island or islands.

Honeywell Grenade Launcher - Honeywell hand-cranked 40mm grenade launcher. See XM-174 Automatic Grenade Launcher.

Honolulu Conference - Giving Nguyen Cao Ky just 2 days' notice, President Johnson called for high level conference in Hawaii about war to begin 6Feb66. Was Johnson's 1st meeting with Prime Minister Ky, and attending with Ky were generals Thieu and Nguyen Huu Co (Ky's Defense Minister). On American side were Dean Rusk, Robert McNamara, John McNaughton, McGeorge Bundy, Orville Freeman, Generals Earle Wheeler, William Westmoreland, Maxwell Taylor, Admiral U. S. Grant Sharp, Ambassador Henry Cabot Lodge, Averell Harriman and Leonard Unger. After listening to Ky's 1st speech, Johnson praised him by exclaiming, "Boy, you speak just like an American." Thereafter, Ky and Johnson got along quite well, Data per *Twenty Years and Twenty Days*, p 83.

Hop Tac – 1964 Saigon area pacification effort launched by Gen Westmoreland. Intent was for ARVN to clear areas and then deliver supplies to civilians and, in process, win peoples' hearts and minds. ARVN failed to clear assigned areas and kept the supplies for themselves, so program quickly failed.

Hornets - Call-sign 116th Avn Co Slicks, and of the 20th SOS Gunships (USAF).

Hosp -Hospital.

Hotel - Radio code for "Hour," Created by simply substituting military phonetic alphabet for first letter of whatever word it represented.. As such, minute became "Mike," second became "Sierra" and so on.

Hotfoot, Operation - See Hotfoot/White Star.

Hotfoot/White Star - SF ops in Laos, 1959-62. Hotfoot ran from Jul59-Apr61, and in 4 grps: Grp I, Jul59-Dec59 under Bull Simons; Grp II, Dec59-Jun60 under Bull Simons; Grp III Jun60-Nov60 under Magnus Smith; Grp IV, Nov60-Apr61 under Shark Little. A 12 man Psy-war team under Charles Murphy began ops as part of Hotfoot on 28Jan61. In Apr61, mission name changed to White Star, which included 3 grps: Grp V, Apr61-Oct61 under Charles Murray (or Little?); Grp VI, Oct61-Mar62 under Bull Simons; Grp VII, Mar62-Oct62. Laos declared neutrality 23Jul62 and SF ops were terminated there as result. 48 teams were withdrawn 21-28Sep62, four B-Dets were withdrawn 27Sep-2Oct62, and Control Team was withdrawn 6Oct62. Data Per *Special Forces at War*, and *SF Order of Battle*.

Howtar - M-98 Howtar was the unusual combination of a 4.2" mortar tube mounted on wheeled-chassis of WWII vintage 75mm pack howitzer. Used by USMC in parts of I Corps.

HPE - Harbor Patrol Element (USN).

hp - Horse power.

Hpt - heliport (TAD).

HQ - Headquarters.

HQ - Vietnamese Navy. Derived from Viet phrase, "Hai Quan."

HSAS - Headquarters Supt Activity, Saigon.

HU-16B Albatross - U.S. Twin-engine amphibious acft with 2,850 mi rnge, 235 kts top spd. mfgd by Grumman Avn.
HU21-B - A.k.a. the H-21 helicopter. A.k.a. "the Flying Banana." Discussed in *The Green Berets*, p 234 et al.
Hue Civilian Defense Corps - Organized by Hue University science professor Ngo Dong, following Tet '68 NVA takeover of Hue. Trng began mid-Apr68, after Nguyen Van Thieu visited city to distribute 1st batch of several thousand weapons. By Sep68, more than 9,000 men and women had been trained for Corps. Story/photos in *The Army Reporter*, 21Sep68, Vol 4, No. 38, p 12.
Huey - "Slick" and "Huey" were common nicknames for the Bell UH-1 utility helicopter; the most widely used helicopter of the American War in VN.
Huey Cobra - See AH-1 Huey Cobra.
Human Sea Wave Attacks - First employed by Vietminh against French in set-piece action during Battle of Vinh Yen. VM came close to overrunning French completely, but when Marshal de Lattre realized how serious threat was, he ordered reserve Bns flown-in from SVN, additional armored grps, plus all available acft capable of dumping bombs or napalm into what became most massive aerial bombardment of 1st Indochina War. Some VM survivors described it as a "wall of napalm." See Vinh Yen, Battle.
Hunter-Killer Team - AH-1 Cobra helo gunship was often worked in purely offensive mode in combination with other helos to independently locate and attack enemy apart from role as direct supt weapon protecting/augmenting grnd ops. A pair of Cobras working with an OH-6 Cayuse was known as a Pink Team, while a single Cobra working with an OH-6 was known as Hunter-Killer Team. Such teams often patrolled enemy-controlled areas and attacked targets of opportunity.
Huong - Vietnamese word for village (among many others).
Hurricane - Call-sign for CH-54 Skyhooks of 478th Avn Co. Suptd 101st Abn (et al) in I Corps.
Hurricane Forward – An HQ sent to Saigon in order to counter Tet '68 offensive, then kept to supt Saigon area cmd until Mar73. Also known as "Task Force Hay," after Gen John Hay, its 1st Cmdr. See CMAC, HQ, in Major Command Section.
Huskie - Trade name for HH-43 twin-rotor SAR helicopter. 235 mi rnge, 120 kts top spd. mfgd by Kaman Avn.
hvy - heavy (TAD).
Hz - hertz (cycles per sec) (TAD).
I & I - Intercourse and Intoxication. Humorous GI spin on the term "R&R" (Rest and Recreation), that perhaps recognized more closely what most R&Rs really involved. See R & R.
I'm Dreaming of a White Christmas - See American Radio Service in main alpha list.
IA - Immediate Action.
IAD - Immediate Action Drill. Practice of prescribed responses to various ambush scenarios by U.S. Army and USMC recon/SF.
IC - Innocent Civilian.
ICAO - International Civil Aviation Organization. Responsible for phonetic alphabet adopted by the U.S. military in 1956.
ICP - Indochinese Communist Party.
ID - Infantry Division.
IFF - Identification Friend or Foe (TAD).
IFR - Instrument Flight Rules.
IFS - Inshore Fire Supt Ship (USN).
IFFV - 1st Field Force Vietnam. See term Field Force in Glossary and IFFV in Corps Level Cmd Section.
IFSS - International Flight Service Station (TAD).
Igloo White - Code name for string of sophisticated acoustical and seismic sensors strung-out along the HCMT in Laos. Specially equipped acft orbiting trail monitored sensor's transmissions and relayed them to what was known as TF Alpha at NKP for analysis. See also Dutch Mill, Muscle Shoals, Repeater Aircraft, Spotlight, Gravel Mines and Task Force Alpha.
IIFFV - 2d Field Force Vietnam. See term Field Force in Glossary and IIFFV in Corps Level Cmd Section.
Illum - Illumination.
ILS - Instrument Landing System (TAD).
Immed - Immediate or immediately.
In articulo mortis - Latin for posthumous(?) or "in the approach of death?" Used in *Street Without Joy*, p 215, when in midst of slaughter of G.M. 100 in the Mang Yang Pass, Col Barrou awarded Officer's Cross of Legion of Honor to dying Capt. Fievet.
inbd - inbound (TAD).
Independence Brigade - See Doc Lap Brigade. Vietminh.
Indian Country - Generally meant any enemy controlled area.
Indiana Rangers - Per Shelby Stanton, the Indiana Rangers of D Co (LRP), 151st Inf, were only U.S. Natl Guard Inf unit to serve in VN. Called into service 13May68, they arrived in-country, Dec68. After trng period with 199th LIB, and the IIFFV LRP Co at Camp Atterbury East, unit ran its first solo combat patrol 8Feb69 in southern War Zone D/U-1 VC Secret Base Area. Suffered 1st WIA, 28Feb69, when 3 men WIA during fierce firefight (per *Rangers at War*, p 225). See also Atterbury East.
Indictment #1, Public - See People's Anti-Corruption Movement.
Indictment #2, Public - See People's Anti-Corruption Movement.
Indochine-Sud-Est Asiatique - French magazine similar to *LIFE*, that Bernard Fall felt was best first-hand record of French War available anywhere (ceased pub Aug54). Per *Street Without Joy*, p 16. See also *Caravelle* and *Nouvelles du Nord-Viet-Nam.*
Inf - Infantry, or Inf Rgt, or Inf Div.
Infantry Route One - See Ho Chi Minh Trail.
Innkeeper - A call-sign of the 271st AHC.
inop - inoperative (TAD).
Insect Armies, The - Bernard Falls' description of burgeoning Vietminh in early 1950's, as a swarm "moved by revolutionary slogans and dialectic, responsive to a single will."
Inshore Undersea Warfare Units - A.k.a. IUWU #s 1, 2, 3, 4, and 5, respectively, operated total of 16 large personnel landing craft, 25 Boston Whalers, and 8 picket boats as part of Op Stable Door. The 45' picket boats 1st arrived SVN Jun67, had crew of 1 Off, 5 EMs, and were armed w/ twin-mounted .50-Cal. MGs.
inst - instrument (TAD).
Instant Patrol Bases - 25th Inf Div program used to const certain types of FSBs such as Frontier City (Apr69). Once site selected and secured by Inf in morning, 1 or 2 dozers were delivered. Then a 130-foot rope tied to stake at center was used to sketch bases' circular perimeter. 24 prefab packages were then flown in and lowered around the etched bunker line. Each consisted of a shaped cratering-charge, 2 sheets of PSP, plus sandbags. Holes were blasted, the Inf squared them off and

then using the materials built 9' high bunkers, usually completing task in 9 hrs. Dozers created berms between bunkers while Inf was at work. Simultaneously, fields of fire were cut, concertina and apx 300 claymore mines installed. Prefab 20' observation tower then was flown in, sandbagged and equipped with radar/large starlight scope. Job normally took 21 CH-47 sorties, inc delivery of two 105s and their ammo. By sundown base would be complete. See also Hard Spots.

int - intersection (TAD).

Interprovincial Routes - See LTL.

Interzone NAMBO - See main alpha listing.

Interzone V - See main alpha listing.

Intl - International (TAD).

Intrepid Four, The - In '67, four young, U.S. sailors on leave in Tokyo from carrier *USS Intrepid*, were talked into deserting by Japanese group called Beheiren (a.k.a. Peace to Vietnam). Were 1st taken to Russia where they were exploited by KGB, then, disillusioned, all 4 settled in Sweden. One, Craig Anderson, returned to U.S. in '70. Data per *Prisoners of Hope*, pp 24-26.

Intruder - A call-sign of the 281st AHC.

Intruder - Nickname of USN's A-6, all-weather fighter-bomber. A twin-eng carrier-based, jet acft unusual in that pilot and bombardier/navigator sat side-by-side rather than fore and aft. Noted for its large payload capacity. Had 1,860 mi rnge, 545 kts top spd. mfgd by Grumman Avn.

ints - intense, intensity, intensive (TAD).

Invader - Trade name for A-26 acft. 1,400 mi rnge, 350 kts top spd. mfgd by Douglas Acft.

IOD - Integrated Observation Device. A 400 pound, $225,000 observation instrument that consisted of very large pair of ship's optical binoculars coupled with Infrared night vision and laser range-finding capabilities. 1st used in '69 by USMC in several Permanent Observation Points (POPs) as part of Da Nang Barrier system. Could pinpoint target at 30 km in daylight (4 km at night) such that arty fire could be called in directly on target (within 5 meters and 1 mil of angle) without firing registering or adjustment rounds that gave enemy time to take cover.

IOS - Improved Observation System. Per Tom Rethart, was an arty fire direction observation crew. Perhaps also name of site employing an IOD? See IOD.

IOS - Integrated Observation Site(?).

IPSA - French acronym for Flying Nurse Corps. One member was Paule DuPont Isigny, pilot with over 4,200 flying hours, and paratrooper with over 30 combat missions (awards inc: Indochina *Croix de Guerre* w/2 palms, *Croix de Guerre 1939-1945* w/1 palm and *Legion of Honor* for Military Valor. Per *Street Without Joy*, pp 136-138. See also PFAT, FIS and Women In Vietnam.

Iroquois Huey - A.k.a. Huey and Slick. Trade name for UH-1 utility helo. 125 mi rnge, 145 kts top spd. mfgd by Bell Helo.

ISB - Intermediate Supt Base (USN).

Island Tree - U.S. air campaign initiated Aug71. Unique in that it targeted specific NVA units infiltrating along HCMT rather than vehicular traffic, fords, bridges and choke points. Binh Tram commo intercepts combined with enhanced sensor technology were so successful they spawned this prgm. Probable bivouac areas were seeded with air-dropped seismic and acoustic sensors of great sensitivity that were monitored by unmanned, high altitude drones. Though Gen Abrams was initially very skeptical about prgm's potential, acoustic sensors provided graphic proof of its success and he came to view it as one of most important and successful air campaigns of war. Data per *A Better War*, p 278. See also Binh Tram, Choke Points, and Target Boxes.

IUWG - Inshore Undersea Warfare Group (USN).

IUWU - See Inshore Undersea Warfare Units for detail (USN).

Ivy Leaf - See *Steadfast and Loyal.*

IWC - Individual Weapon Captured.

J-2 - Assistant chief of staff for military intelligence, MACV.

J BAR - Jet Barrier (TAD).

JANIS - Joint Army-Navy Intelligence Service. In Aug45 as WWII ended, "JANIS" teams under Col Steven L. Nordlinger deployed in Vietnam to facilitate the repatriation of Japanese-held U.S. POWs. See also AGAS and Deer Mission.

Japanese Invasion of Vietnam- The Japanese invaded and occupied Vietnam between Sep40 and VJ Day, Aug45. Invasion began with an attack across NVN border at Lang Son and Dong Dang, 22Sep40, aimed at French Forts along a 45 mile front between and around those two cities. At time, occupying French Army forces had some 70,000 troops serving in Indochina (armed with just 15 modern fighter planes and one tank, per *Street Without Joy*, p 22). On 24Sep40, Japanese planes bombed Haiphong, and landed troops there that night. 800 French died in two days of fighting, at which point an agreement was signed to allow Japanese occupation. In surprise attack 9Mar45, the Japanese overwhelmed, captured and destroyed all remaining French forces, and on 11Mar45, they forced the Emperor of Annam to proclaim an end to French Protectorate. In one of their earliest offensive actions, the Vietminh attacked Japanese at mtn resort of Tam Dao. At end of WWII, the Japanese surrendered to Ho Chi Minh's Vietminh government, and on 2Sep45, Vietnam was proclaimed a Republic. In Feb46, however, the Western allies allowed 2 Divs of French Expeditionary Force to reestablish French control of VN.

JATO - Jet Assisted Takeoff.

JCS - Joint Chiefs of Staff.

Jerraube, Genevieve de Galard-Jerraube - See Angel of Dien Bien Phu.

Jesus Nut, The - The huge threaded nut that holds rotor to the rotor shaft of a Huey UH-1 and other helicopters.

JGS - Joint General Staff.

JOG - Joint Operations Graphics. DOD/DMA/NIMA 1:250,000 scale topo charts available in both aeronautical (alt. in feet) and ground navigation (alt. in meters) versions. They provide great detail (inc private AF's) and are much more detailed than ONC or TPC charts. See also L-7014, L-1501, L-509, TPC, ONC and Map Reading section. JOGs are available for purchase through the USGS.

Joint Operations Graphics Maps - See JOG.

Joker - Call-sign for USAF Joint Rescue Coordination Center.

Jolly - Call-sign and nickname for long range HH-3 and HH-53 SAR air-sea rescue helicopters. Where capable of flying well into Laos or NVN and remain on station for extended periods.

Jolly Green Giant - Nickname for HH-3 and HH-53 Heavy helicopters used primarily in SAR role.

Junkers-52 - German Tri-motor acft assembled from body parts found in Germany after WWII and employed by French Far Eastern Air Forces during French War. Until 1950, were considered backbone of French transport and "bomber" force. Major disadvantage was that supplies and bombs had to be tossed out of side doors by hand. Per *Street Without Joy*, p 261.

Junkies - Short version of the general nickname "Junkmen" used to describe any ARVN or USN Advsy personnel assigned to the "Junk" river patrol divisions such as that at Tiem Ton(sp?).
Junkmen - See Junkies.
K Intervals - MACV designation for permanent supply depots along HCMT. Each was had a cemetery. See Binh Tram. Per *A Better War*, p 49.
Kalishnakov-AK 47 - See AK-47.
Kalsu, James Robert, Capt. - Only professional football player to die in Vietnam War. KIA 21Jul70, by mortar fire while serving with C Bty, 2d/11th Arty, 101st Abn, during siege of FSB Ripcord. Kalsu had been voted most valuable player in his rookie year with the Buffalo Bills, '69. See also FSB Ripcord.
Kampuchea Krom - Ancient Cambodian name for Mekong Delta.
Karst - Large, irregular limestone formations typical of SEA and particularly ubiquitous in Laos. Though it might seem unlikely, they were often covered with jungle and other forms of vegetation.
KBA - Killed By Air. Enemy dead attributed to helicopter or fixed-wing acft of any sort.
KC-135A Stratotanker - US, 4-eng, jet tanker with 3,450 mi rnge, 530 kts top spd. mfgd by Boeing Acft.
Keystone Robin, Operation - Staged withdrawal of U.S. combat forces from SVN theater under President Nixon's order.
KHA - Killed by Hostile Action.
Khe – One Vietnamese word for "stream" (among others).
Khe Sanh Air Strike Data - Per *Valley of Decision*, the bombing campaign in supt of Khe Sanh (Dec67 to Apr68), delivered a stunning volume of sorties and bomb tonnage: Fighter-bombers of 7th USAF flew 9,691 sorties and dropped 14,223 tons of bombs; 1st MAW acft flew 7,078 sorties dropping 17,015 tons; USN acft flying off acft carriers flew 5,337 sorties dropping 7,941 tons of ordnance; Arc Lights totaled 2,548 sorties flown out of Guam and Utapao, delivering 55,542 tons of bombs. Overall, 98,721 tons of bombs were dropped in 24,654 sorties (see remarkable aerial photo of bomb damage surrounding Khe Sanh plateau on pp 84-85 of *Air Power and the Fight for Khe Sanh*).. *Valley of Decision* notes that tonnage was apx equiv of a thousand-ton nuclear bomb being dropped at Khe Sanh every day of siege, and arty tonnage is not inc in these figures (per *Valley of Decision*, p 297). See Khe Sanh Red Watch, Niagara, and Super gaggle for more detail.
Khe Sanh Red Watch - Code name for special MACV HQ intel unit created in '67 by Gen Westmoreland to monitor only the Khe Sanh situation. Unit was tasked to provide sufficient targeting data such that a cell of 3 B-52s were on target every 90 minutes. Was also told that more bomb tonnage would be dropped in supt of Khe Sanh than in all of WWII (an exaggeration, but not by much). As practical matter, request was soon reduced to 6 targets every 3 hours. Arc Lights flown in supt of Khe Sanh totaled 2,548 sorties flown out of Guam and Utapao, delivering 55,542 tons of ordnance. Only 881 of those missions were flown before mid Feb68. B-52 campaign in supt of Khe Sanh CB was considered to have been very effective overall. Discussed extensively in *War Without Windows* and *Valley of Decision*, p 297. See also Khe Sanh Air Strike Data, Niagara and Super Gaggle.
Khe Sanh Stamp - NVN issued postage stamp commemorating Khe Sanh Battle featuring date "1968," and image of NVA male soldier firing mortar while being assisted by female counterpart wearing a necklace of flowers. A U.S. soldier is shown crouching inside a trench. At top edge are words: *Chien Thang-Khe Sanh-1968*, and at bottom, *12 xu, Viet-Nam-Dan Chu Cong Hoa, Huy-Khanh 69*. Huy Khanh possibly stamp's designer. Photo of stamp is at page 361 of *Valley of Decision*.
Khmer-Serei - "Free Cambodia." An Underground Cambodian organization employed by Capt Bo Gritz to recruit 263 Cambodes and other indigenous personnel for the first MGF (MGF Det A-303), Nov-Dec66. Recruiting held in Buddhist Pagoda on Cong Ly Street, Saigon. Many served with the KKK and U.S. SF MGFs, apparently doing so not out of any concern for the Vietnamese (whom they hated and distrusted), but to free Cambodia of Prince Sihanouk's control. The Cham also served with the KKK and MGFs. Data per *Mobile Guerrilla Force*, pp 2-4.
Khi Trau Sightings - Lao for Buffalo Monkey or big monkey (a.k.a. Yeti or Bigfoot). See Nguoi Rung.
kHz - kilohertz (TAD).
KIA - Killed in Action.
Killer Teams - Tactic employed by 7th Marine Rgt in '69-70, involving squad-sized or five-man, roving ambush teams that at night patrolled up to 2 km from Co or larger sized NDPs/FSBs. Teams covered much larger areas than typical fixed ambush positions and risks were higher for its participants as result. One such team was involved in Feb70 massacre at Son Thang-4 near FSB Ross. See also Son Thang.
Kilo India Alpha - Military slang/standard radio phrasing denoting terms "killed-in-action" and "wounded-in-action" were "Kilo India Alpha" and "Whiskey India Alpha."
King - Call-sign for special C-130 acft that oversaw and coordinated all SAR (Search and Rescue Operations) for downed pilots in NVN and Laos.
King Bee - Call-sign of ARVN H-34's supt SOG ops in CCC.
Kingdom of Sedang - Founded in 1888 by Frenchman Charles-Marie David de Mayréna. Reign of King Marie the First, as he called himself, lasted only 2 years, ending with his death, 11Nov 1890, at Tioman in Malaya, while returning to Sedang from diplomatic mission. Mayréna was an adventurer who first roamed the central highlands of Vietnam making treaties with highland tribes. Apparently very persuasive man, he eventually managed to convince number of tribal chiefs and tribes to form new kingdom with himself as its king! On 3Jun 1888, Mayréna was elected as king by chiefs of Sedang, Bahnar, and Rengao tribes at ville of Kon Gung, and Kingdom of Sedang was born. Marie the First, soon began travels throughout world (England, Europe and Hong Kong) awarding medals, titles of nobility, and knighthood to many who offered supt. His kingdom even issued postage stamps (now quite rare and sought after). King Marie died without heir or successor, and Sedang ceased to exist. Data per www.sedang.com/.
Kingsman - Call-sign for B Co and B Co Guns, 101st Avn Bn.
Kinh - Vietnamese for canal.
Kiowa - Trade name for OH-1 single-rotor helicopter. 265 mi rnge, 138 kts top spd. mfgd by Bell Helicopter.
KITDFBS – Acronym for Kept In The Dark, Fed Bullshit.
Kiwis - Nickname for troops of New Zealand Artillery (161 Bty) and RNZR Infantry. See New Zealand and Australian Forces in Major Command Section.

KKK - Chamber Kampuchea Kron. Cambodian bandits that worked border area. Described as mercenaries who fought only for money and loyal to no one. Cited in *The Green Berets*, at p-35.
Klick - Slang for one kilometer or 1,000 meters. Also a windage or elevation adjustment on the rear sight of a rifle.
Klondike - Call-sign For USMC's VMO-6 Huey Gunship Sqdn.
km - Kilometer, or 1,000 meters.
Knight - A call-sign of the 114th Avn.
Knightrider - A call-sign of USMC HMM-164.
Ko – One Vietnamese word for mountain.
Kool-Aid - Per *Rites of Passage*, in '67 was 1st/14th Inf/25th Div radio code for "Killed in Action" or KIA.
KSCB - Khe Sanh Combat Base.
Kts - Knots, or Nautical miles per hour.
Kum Sah - Vietnamese for Marijuana? Also possibly "Tuc Fin."
KY 28 - Secure electronic radio gadget that scrambled radio calls for TASS Prairie Fire FACs (and other acft). Mentioned in *Da Nang Diary*, p 195.
L-5 Howitzer – 105mm pack howitzer used by 161 Bty RNZA when it deployed to SVN in '65. Was replaced by the longer-ranged, more durable but heavier U.S. M2A2 105mm howitzer, 2Jul66. Until arrival of Chinook helos in large numbers, the L-5 was only 105 deployable by UH-1. See Borneo Design Battery.
L-5 - French Reconnaissance/Liaison acft employed during French War. At most, French had only about 85 such acft during the entire war; among which were the Morane, the L-5, the Siebel and etc. Data per *Street Without Joy*, pp 263.
L-19 Bird Dog - Light, single-eng, prop-driven observation acft (Cessna?) used by both the Army and USAF. Was of WWII/Korean war vintage but its slow speed and excellent visibility (wing over), made its wide use as a FAC acft advantageous. Its slow max airspeed also made it highly vulnerable to ground fire as well. See also O-1 Bird Dog.
L-509 Series - 1:250,000 scale JOG topo maps that preceded the L-1501 series. See JOG for detailed description. See also L-7014, L-1501, L-509, TPC and ONC. Are available for purchase through the USGS.
L-1501 Series - 1:250,000 scale JOG topo maps that superseded the L-509 series. See JOG for detailed description. See also L-7014, L-1501, L-509, TPC and ONC. Are available for purchase through the USGS.
L-7014 Series - A.k.a. TL-7014 (USGS Stock#). Military map series covering Vietnam that was produced by the DMA for tactical use. Large-scale, highly-detailed, 1:50,000 scale (1" = apx 1.25 km), color, topo maps used at the Plt and Co level. In other words, these are the maps with which most Infantrymen were intimately familiar. Generally speaking, are most detailed maps of Vietnam available in any volume. USGS has added the letter "T" to its L-7014 stock numbers such that all begin with TL-7014. These maps are available for purchase through the USGS or the Library of Congress (see Table of Contents).
L Sites - Lima Site or Laos Site. See main alpha listing.
L'asphyxie par le vide - French term for Vietminh tactic known as "*a choking-off by creating a void.*" Typically preceded by absence of farmers and other vendors near French position, then by absence of any nearby inhabitants. See *Street Without Joy*, p 119.
***L'homme Sauvage* Sightings** -Viet Yeti/Bigfoot. See Nguoi Rung.

LAAM - Light Anti-Aircraft Missile Bns or Btys employing the Hawk Anti-Acft Missile. See LAAM Sites in main alpha section.
LAAM Sites - See LAAM Sites in main alpha section.
Lach - Vietnamese for marine channel.
Lancer - Call-sign for B Co, 158th Avn Bn.
Land Mines - See Mines, Land.
Land of the Big PX - U.S. troop slang for home; the USA.
Land to the Tiller Program - Initiated by President Thieu in Mar70. Prgm in which over 1.5 million acres (1/3d of all cultivated land in SVN) was shifted from landed-populace and divided among farmers who'd been working it as tenants (and paying 50% of their crops as rent for privilege). Was more land than had been moved to peasantry during previous 7 years under other prgms. "In one fell swoop," said John Paul Vann, "the program eliminated [land] tenancy in Vietnam." Between '70-72, some 400,000 farmers were given title to parcels of land that averaged almost 4 acres per farmer. 500,000 families who'd been paying land rent saw that practice ended completely. Data per *A Better War*, p 194.
Landing Zone - Generally shortened to "LZ" in common usage. Term "LZ" was used either in either formally to designate a specific base such as LZ Sally, or informally to designate any spot where helicopters might land to deliver or pick-up-troops (PZ or Pick-up Zone). The distinction between formally named LZs and FSBs (Fire Support Bases) is very blurry; however it can generally be said (with many exceptions) that long-term LZs normally included facilities designed to house helos and their suptg units in addition to their roles of housing and suptg infantry/arty units, while FSBs were primarily designed for arty supt. Although landing pads for helo were built at all FSBs, helos were rarely based or maintained upon them as well. Terms LZ and FSB were often used interchangeably without apparent distinction as well. LZs were often also called "Lima Zulu's," using military alphabet conversion of initials. Per Peter Cole, most all permanent bases of the 1st Cav Div were called LZs until Sep69, when IIFFV CG LtGen Julian Ewell, ordered that any fortified positions designated as LZs, would thereafter be called FSBs. Per *Incursion*, p 47, "Ewell's orders greatly angered the airmobile purists in the division, who disliked the term firebase as common to regular infantry divisions and certainly not appropriate for use by Air Cav." See also Camp and Fire Support Base.
Landshark Bravo - Call-sign of the Air Control Center at Dong Ha (which had a fwd detachment at Khe Sanh).
Landslide - Nickname given Col Edward Landsdale (of CIA) by Indian Ambassador to Philippines after Landsdales's influence and counsel helped Ramon Magsaysay to huge victory over incumbent Elpidio Quirino in '53 Philippine elections. The ambassador wryly observed that the election "should cause a certain American colonel to change his name to Landslide," per *The Unquiet American*, p 131.
Lang – A Vietnamese word for "tomb" or "grave."
Lang - As in "Lang of rice" was NVA allocation of rice-ration roughly equiv to 1 and 1/3d ounces.
Laotian Military Regions - During SF Ops Hotfoot & White Star, 1959-62, U.S. military designated five military regions in Laos calling them MR1 (containing Luang Prabang); MR2 (containing Xiangkhoang); MR3 (containing Khammouane); MR4 containing Saravane and Vapikham Thuong) and MR5, much as they would later divide-up SVN. These MR's divided

country into 4 horizontal strips with MR1 at N end, and MR4 at S end. MR 2 was split in half vertically by MR5, with MR5 (containing Vientiane) in the SW and MR2 in the NW.
LAPES - Low Altitude Parachute Extraction System. Innovation created by necessity for very hazardous resupply of Khe Sanh CB during 67/68 siege. Parachutes were used to extract loads as C-130 did a high speed touch and go landing on Khe Sanh rwy, rather than having the plane stop to unload. The chutes would drag the load out and it would skid to a halt on rwy while the A/C applied power and regained the air. System greatly minimized exposure to enemy fire. LAPES variant designed by Aerospace Research Corp. was designated ARC-LAPES. See also GPES.
LARC - Lighter, Amphibious Resupply Cargo.
Laterite Soil - Red, ferruginous soil containing iron and alumina and common throughout much of SVN.
Laterite Lantern, The - See main alpha listings.
LAU-68 Pods - Stnd 2.75" rocket pods adapted to FAC O-2s and OV-10s, and likely many other USAF acft.
LAW - Light Anti-Tank Weapon. See M-72 LAW.
Lazarus Omega, Operation - 4th attempt organized by Bo Gritz to rescue alleged POWs at secret POW camp in Laos. Gritz's grp apparently made it to Thailand but may never made it into Laos, although they claimed to have been there and to have seen U.S. POWs. Data per *Prisoners of Hope*, pp 138-141.
Lazarus, Operation - 3d and most elaborate of Bo Gritz's POW rescue missions into Laos. Was aimed at POW camp called Fort Apache. This rather bizarre mission collapsed as funding and intrigue cut it apart. Gritz's small band of 19 men apparently actually set foot in Laos but gave up effort when they were ambushed by Laotian forces and one man was captured. See also Op Grand Eagle, Velvet Hammer and Lazarus Omega. Data per *Prisoners of Hope*, pp 136-138.
LBE - Load Bearing Equipment, a.k.a. "Web Gear." Stnd-issue waist-borne web pistol belt and attached shoulder straps that carried a multitude of attached ammo pouches, canteens, frags, etc., as well as small pack known as. a "butt-pack."
LBJ - Initials of U.S. President Lyndon Baines Johnson. Also acronym of, and slang for, infamous "Long Binh Jail."
LCA - Landing Craft Assault (USN).
LCC - Amphibious Command Ship (USN).
LCDR - Lieutenant Commander (USN).
LCI - Landing Craft, Infantry (USN).
lcl - local (TAD).
LCM - Landing Craft, Mechanized or Medium (USN).
LCM(M) - Landing Craft, Mechanized Minesweeper (USN).
LCpl - Lance Corporal.
LCpl - Landing Craft Personnel (Large) (USN).
LCS - Landing Craft Supt (USN).
LCT - Landing Craft, Tank (USN).
lctd - located (TAD).
LCU - Landing Craft, Utility.
LCVP - Landing Craft, Vehicles and Personnel (USN).
lczr - localized beacon (TAD).
ldg - landing (TAD).
LDNN - Lien Doi Nguoi Nhai. SVN military "frogmen," and UWDT's. Roughly equiv to U.S. SEALs. During '63-64, SEAL Team 1 Dets were sent to SVN to train U.S. Advisors, the LDNN and Coastal Force Biet Hai commandos.
Le Guerre des Grandes Vides – "The war of vast empty spaces." Term used by GCMA French commandos to describe their war against Vietminh in vast wilderness of NE Laos, N and NW Tonkin during French war. See also GCMA and GIM.
Le Guerre sans fronts – "The War Without Fronts." French War expression cited in *Street Without Joy*.
Les pieges – "The Traps." Nickname given to the acft flown by French pilots of the 1st Indochina War.
Lefevre, Monsignor -See *Constitution*, *USS*, in main alpha listing.
Leeches – This author is familiar with 2 distinct types in Thua Thien Province. There was the typical water-borne leech; black and up to 3 inches in size. There was also some referred to as a "dry-land" (or tree) leech, found in trees/brush/wet grass. The dry-land type headed toward prey upon sensing heat, and by either dropping from above, or moving along ground in same motion as that of the inch worm. Dry-land type was smaller and more ubiquitous than water-borne cousin, though both were equally dreaded by troops in the field. Good description of dry-land type in *Gone Native*, pp 130-131.
LHITC - Long Hai Individual Training Center.
LI-2 - Soviet built acft used by NVN. 1,550 mi rnge, 175 kts top spd. mfgd by Lisunov.
LIB - Light Infantry Brigade.
Liberty City - Code name for secret, post-war ('81) POW rescue mission training camp funded by *Soldier of Fortune* Magazine publisher Bob Brown, and organized with help of Bo Gritz's rivals Fred Zabitosky, Earl Bleacher and James Monaghan. Was in Laos, W of the Mekong River and close Thailand. Opened in Jul81 and closed under pressure of Thai Govt in Nov81. Data per *Prisoners of Hope*, pp 138-141.
Lien So - Vietnamese phrase meaning Soviet personnel and tourists (Russian and East German).
Lima Lima - Military phonetic alphabet abbreviation for Land-Line. Meant commo by telephone (hard wire), as opposed to radio wireless commo.
Lima Sites - See main alpha listing.
Lima Zulu - Landing Zone. U.S. acronym of the initials "LZ" per military phonetic alphabet. See LZ.
Line One - 1st Air Cav Avn unit slang for KIA, with "Line Two" meaning WIA.
Line Two - See Line One.
Lion – Call-sign of Ubon Airfield GCI site.
Little People - Common GI slang for NVA/VC soldiers and the Vietnamese in general.
LKA - Amphibious Cargo Ship (USN).
LL-14 - Soviet built acft used by NVN. 250 mi rnge, 260 kts top spd. mfgd by Llyshin.
LL-28 - Soviet built acft used by NVN. 1,300 mi rnge, 560 kts top spd. mfgd by Llyshin.
LLBD - Luc Luong Dac Biet. The SVN SF. In *The Green Berets*, the acronym was anglicized as "Lousy Little Dirty Bug-Outs!"
Loach - See LOH.
LOC - Lines of Communication.
Local Force VC - Lowest organized component of Viet Cong Forces, generally not exceeding Plt or Co strength. Sometimes LF units were numbered (i.e., C-61 Co, D-368, K-10, etc.) and often simply named after the ville or area from which they came (i.e., the Ben Cat Co). See also Main Force VC.
LOD - Line of Departure.
Log - Logistic or logistical.

Log Bird - GI slang for a resupply (or logistical resupply) helicopter. Typically brought mail, clean uniforms, ammo, food and replacement equip. See also Backlog Bird.
LOH - Any Light Observation Helicopter.
LOH - Hughes 500 Light Observation Helicopter, a.k.a. the OH-6 Cayuse. Pronounced "Loach," and GI's affectionate nickname for this tear-drop shaped observation helo.
Lonely Summit - Call-sign for Nui Ba Den Provisional Co's Radio Relay facility at peak of Nui Ba Den Mtn.
Lonesome Polecat - Call-sign of the 192d AHC's slick (Huey) plt.
LPD - Amphibious Transport Dock (USN).
LPH - Amphibious Assault Ship (USN).
LPSS - Amphibious Transport Submarine (USN).
LRP - Long Range Patrol.
LRPD - Long Range Patrol Detachment.
LRRP - Long Range Reconnaissance Patrol.
LRRP Rations - A.k.a. "Meal, Quick-Serve." Freeze-dried meals in dark-brown, vacuum-packed, foil-coated plastic pouches. Originally intended for recon units but found their way into line Co menus as well. Inside outer casing was a plastic bag with a formed paper base to which a cup or more of hot water was added. Cold water could be used, but absorption period was much greater and taste much worse if done that way. Principal advantage was their extreme light weight while principal disadvantage was that they required significant quantities of potable water for proper use, and in some locales, water was very scarce and carrying it for hydrating rations apart from normal water needs very problematic. Its Chile Con Carne meal was affectionately known as "Pork and Shrapnel" in the 101st Abn Div. Other meals included Spaghetti with Meat and Tomato Sauce, Chicken with Rice, and a beef stew of sorts. There were only several varieties available in '70.
LS Sites - Lima Site or Laos Site. See main alpha listing.
LSA - Logistical Supt Area (USMC).
LSA - Lubricant designed specifically for the M-16 rifle.
LSD - Landing Ship, Dock.
LSIL - Landing Ship, Infantry, Large (USN).
LSM - Landing Ship Medium (USN).
LSMR - Landing Ship, Medium, Repair.
LSMR - Landing Ship, Medium, Rocket (USN).
LSSC - Light Seal Supt Craft (USN).
LSSL - Landing Supt Ship, Large (USN).
LST - Landing Ship, Tank. U.S. Naval vessel designation. WWII vintage craft used extensively to supt 9th Inf Div MRF ops in IV Corps. Served as barracks, supply points, floating firebases and provided transportation as well. It seems unlikely tanks were transported by them much at all during American War.
LT - Lieutenant.
ltd - limited (TAD).
ltg - lights or lighted (TAD).
LtGen - Lieutenant General.
LTJG - Lieutenant, Junior Grade (USN).
LTL - Designator used to Identify Inter-Provincial roads of SVN road system. LTL rtes were secondary to QL rtes (major and international roads), and 2d highest level of system. Normally identified by 2 digits enclosed in circular map symbol. See also QL, LTL, TL, Route, Highway, HL, R. C., *Route Colonial*, as well as *Principal Roadways of South Vietnam* Section.
Luciole - French for "Firefly." Also French code name for a C-47 Dakota acft that nightly dropped flares over DBP, Mar-Jun54.
Lucrezia Borgia - See Madame Nhu.
Luke The Gook - Nickname of very persistent and very brave NVA sniper positioned in spiderhole within 120 meters of U.S. positions on either Hill 881-S or 881-N during Siege of Khe Sanh. Although his fire was inaccurate, it was extremely annoying, so numerous attempts were made to silence his position over a week-long period. To amazement of Marines, he somehow managed to survive everything thrown at him, inc arty fire. In frustration, Marines finally called in an airstrike of napalm, 22Feb68, but after flames died down, sniper pushed his rifle from hole and defiantly fired a round to signal his survival. The Marines were so taken by his courage and tenacity that thereafter firing at his position was forbidden and he was given this nickname as measure of respect (data per *Bonnie-Sue*, p 448). Was common slang throughout war and it is possible its use began as result of this incident.
LVT - Landing Vehicle, Tracked.
LVTP-5 - Amphibious Tractor used by USMC BLTs for amphib landings along coast. See Shit Beach in main alpha listing.
Ly Tong - Per Reuters wire service article, *Philippine Hijacker Found Dead; Parachute Failed*: "In 1992, former SVN Air Force pilot Ly Tong, hijacked a Vietnam Airlines Airbus A310 and parachuted out after forcing it to fly low so he could drop 50,000 anti-Communist leaflets over Ho Chi Minh City"
LZ - See Landing Zone. A.k.a. "Lima-Zulu."
M - meters (or "magnetic" if after a compass bearing) (TAD).
M-1 Garand Rifle - .30 Caliber, 8-rnd, clip-fed, gas-operated semi-auto rifle originally developed for U.S. forces of WWII, and used widely there and later in Korea. ARVN and RF/PF militia of the SVN were widely equipped with M-1 early in war. Was primary weapon for early Korean forces in SVN as well. SVN were transitioned to the M-16 as quickly as possible after it was available because its lighter weight and smaller size better suited their small physical stature.
M-1 Maneuver - Tactic employed by fighter pilots to avoid blackout during high G-force turns. Involved pushing-out stomach as hard as possible and grunting loudly.
M-2 Machine Gun - Stnd Browning mfgd U.S. .50 caliber heavy machine gun. Crew-served weapon of extreme range and effectiveness that was either vehicle or tripod mounted as a defensive and/or offensive weapon. Its 2,500 meter eff range made it useful as a sniper rifle and it was often employed in a single-shot capacity, and mounted with a scope for that purpose. See also .50 Caliber and Quad 50.
M-7A2 Anti-Tank Mine - WWII vintage anti-tank mine employed by both sides in conflict. Mentioned in *Rangers at War, LRRPs* in *Vietnam*.
M-7 Portable Flame-thrower - Flame-throwing unit that was carried and operated by individual soldier as a backpack-mounted unit. Had hand-held delivery/ignition nozzle for directing flame. Backpack unit weighed apx 50 pounds but could only deliver about a 6 to 9 second stream of flaming gas out to max range of apx 130'-165'. Due to heavy weight and short periods of effectiveness, it was rarely used in Vietnam and almost never carried in field as a stnd weapon. If need arose for it to clear enemy bunkers, a request was made and M-7s with trained operators were airlifted to scene.
M-8A1 - Light duty steel runway matting (anti-skid) (TAD).

M-8C Rifle - Experimental .50 Caliber spotting rifle that was sometimes attached to the M-40A1 Recoilless Rifle, and used to fire tracer adjustment/spotting rounds for adjusting RR's aim before firing its main 106mm round. See also M-40A1.

M-14 A1 Rifle - Fully auto version of M-14 rifle.

M-14 Anti-Personnel Mine - Small anti-personnel mine sometimes employed by LRRP units to delay enemy tracking them. Possibly a.k.a. "Toe Popper," which was designed to wound rather than kill. Mentioned in *Rangers at War, LRRPs* in Vietnam.

M-14 Rifle - Standard Infantry rifle of the Army and Marines until phased-out entirely during '65 and '66. Magazine fed (15 rnds), 7.62mm, semi-auto (M-14-A1 was full auto, but rare) rifle with an eff range of about 500 meters. Loved for its accuracy and durability, weapon was sorely missed when replaced by much lighter and but labor-intensive and jam-prone M-16. When it became apparent early M-16 version had severe flaws, troops would beg, borrow and steal to get an M-14 replacement. Both the weapon and its 7.62mm ammo was apx twice weight of the M-16, and that was its main disadvantage. Weighed 11.2 lbs. fully loaded.

M-16 Rifle – Stand U.S. individual infantry weapon of the Vietnam War. Introduced in '66 as the M-16E1, and modified to the M-16A1 in '67. Magazine fed (20 or 30 rounds), semi or fully auto rifle, with very high rate of fire on auto (20 rounds/1.5 seconds). Mfgd by Colt Arms, weapon had very checkered reputation early in war after it replaced the M-14. Disadvantageous powder change coupled with bolt design and buffer problems caused frequent jamming, and significant number of Marines and Army infantryman died as a direct result of this weapon's failures. Many troops felt the military, Colt Arms and DuPont (manufacturer of the problematic gunpowder used in 5.56mm ball ammo) were criminally negligent in their stubborn unwillingness to recognize/correct its flaws. Once problems were resolved, it proved to be an effective weapon for close-in jungle fighting and was loved for its extreme light weight, light weight of its ammo (roughly half that of 7.62 mm) and distinctive carrying handle. Was 1st stnd U.S. Army rifle to employ plastics entirely in lieu of wood for its stock and hand grips. Derisively referred to as being "Made by Mattel," in reference to plastic toy manufacturer of era. Weighed 7.01 lbs. fully loaded, had eff range of apx 400 meters and muzzle velocity of 3,280 fps. For critical analysis of its early problems in war, see: http://jdumong.net/delta/m-16Part1.htm. For remarkable criticism, see letter to Congress quoted in *The Perfect War*, p 210 (footnote #151); pp 194-196.

M-18 Smoke Grenade - Stnd signal smoke of U.S. and allied forces. Came in red, green, yellow and purple colors. Red was ordinarily used to denote landing zone or unit that was under fire. Green was typically used to denote a "cold" LZ, i.e., landing zone not under fire. Smokes most commonly used to alert acft to grnd positions of units and to provide wind direction info. Also used to hide movements and to blind enemy troops fixed in bunkers.

M-18A1 Anti-Personnel Mine – Famous and infamous claymore mine. Actually developed at end of Korean War, but before it could see service there. Contained 700 steel pellets, weighed 3.5 lbs. including apx 2 lbs. of C-4 plastic explosive. Its kill-zone was over a 60 degree horizontal fan to apx 8' in height and its eff range was about 165'. Could be detonated using electrical or mechanical fuses and "daisy-chained" together in unlimited numbers using Det Cord. Had both defensive and offensive roles, and used widely in what were known as "Mechanical Ambushes" (unattended and remotely placed mines set-up by maneuvering Inf units that were detonated by trip wires attached to batteries or stand grenade fuse; essentially booby-traps). Very devastating and effective weapon held in high regard by men who used them.

M-19 Mortar - Small, light-weight 60mm mortar used widely by USMC. Had been phased out of U.S. Army inventory, but its significantly lighter weight as compared to 81mm mortar resulted in its reintroduction to many line units during war. Carried in field by maneuvering Inf.

M-20 Rocket Launcher - Vietnam version of the WWII Bazooka. Crew-served, reloadable 3.5" rocket launcher used almost exclusively by U.S. Marines (Army troops relied almost exclusively on M-72 LAW, which while not reloadable, but lighter and operated by a single person). Nicknamed the "Super Bazooka," it fired an 89mm (3.5') projectile to max range of 3,937 yards(?), was 61" long and tube alone weighed 12 lbs.

M-21 Rifle - Sniper version of M-14 rifle, with scope attached.

M-21 Sniper Rifle - XM-21 Sniper Rifle.

M-29 Mortar - Stnd 81mm mortar of U.S. Army/USMC during war. Range apx 3,500 meters. Some Inf units carried it in the field, though its weight and weight of its ammo placed significant burdens on troops. NVA employed an 82mm mortar that could also use the U.S. 81mm shell, but reverse was not true.

M-30 Mortar - A.k.a. 107mm Mortar. Heavy, 4.2" mortar commonly referred to as the "Four-Deuce." Had 60" barrel, was 672 lbs. in weight and had range of 5,650 meters.

M-33 Grenade - A.k.a. the "Baseball Grenade." See M-26 Frag.

M-35 Incendiary Bomb - See Pink Rose.

M-34 "4x4" Jeep - Stnd 3-person, 4-wheel drive vehicle used for transportation by U.S. forces. Differed from WWII jeep in that it had independent suspension on all 4 wheels. M-151 was apparently version of the same vehicle?

M-36 Mortar - NVA's Soviet-designed 82mm mortar. Very similar to U.S. 81mm mortar and capable of using U.S. ammo (reverse was not true) when necessary. Weighed 57.4 lbs., had range of 3,100 meters and used both HE and smoke rounds.

M-40A1 - U.S. 106mm Recoilless Rifle. Typically vehicle mounted in single and multiple barreled versions. See also M-8C and Ontos.

M-42 Duster - A.k.a. "Dusters," and 40 Mike-Mike's. Track-mounted, dual-40mm cannon armored vehicle. 40mm, auto, anti-acft, WWII naval gun mounts fitted to tank chassis and used in both defensive and offensive roles. Very effective weapon.

M-26 Grenade - Stnd U.S. Army hand-grenade for much of war. Unlike very rough looking "pineapple" grenades of WWII and Korea, it was smooth-sided, elliptically-shaped and its shrapnel agent was a notched-wire coiled around explosive core designed to fragment into hundreds of small pieces that would wound rather than kill. Later replaced by heavier M-33 "baseball" grenade which studies revealed was more lethal and could be thrown farther due to its baseball shape and troops baseball-throwing heritage.

M-46 130mm Field Gun - See 130mm Field Gun.

M-48 A3 Patton Tank - Stnd U.S. heavy tank of war. Armed with 90mm cannon, coaxial 7.62mm MG and turret mounted .50 caliber MG. Weighed 104,000 lbs. and had a top speed of 30 MPH. Basic load was 64 rounds of 90mm cannon shells.

M-55 Quad .50 - Four M-2 Browning .50 Cal MGs.

M-56 SP Anti-Tank Gun - Light, track-mounted, open-chassised 90mm cannon SPAT (Self-Propelled Anti-Tank) vehicle that saw brief duty in SVN. Simply a 90mm tank without its armored turret. Lightly protected crew deck was extremely vulnerable to sniper and direct fire, so vehicle was quickly removed from service.

M-60 Machine Gun - 7.62mm, air-cooled, belt fed, crew-served Machine Gun capable of 100 rounds/min eff rate of fire, and sustained rate of apx 600 rounds/min. Typically there was one M-60 per Inf squad in Army. Frequently vehicle-mounted on jeeps, trucks, tracks and helos as both defensive and offensive weapon. Had interchangeable barrel. Nicknames were 'the 60,' "Pig" and "Hog." Weighed 23.1 lbs and had an eff range of 3,280'.

M-61 Vulcan Cannon - Acft-mounted 20mm version of GE's M-134 Gatling gun. Its six barrels could deliver up to 6,600 rnds/min. Used by AC-130, the F-4, the A-7A, the F-104 and F-111 acft.

M-67 Recoilless Rifle - U.S. 90mm, crew-served recoilless rifle. Occasionally carried by Inf units in field, but due to it's 35 lb. weight plus weight of its individual rnds, was relegated almost exclusively to defensive role. Also sometimes mounted on a vehicle or fixed mount in FSB defense. Fired self-propelled rnd equiv to a heavy tank rnd but produced no recoil. Had both HE and Beehive rnds. Was 53" long, had range of 13,123 yards and apx 5 rnds/min rate of fire.

M-72 LAW - "Light Anti-Tank Weapon." Shoulder-fired, single shot, disposable, 62mm shaped-charge anti-tank rocket similar to enemy's RPG and U.S. bazooka except that it was not reloadable. Frequently carried by Inf for use against enemy bunkers. Weighed 5.1 lbs. loaded, was 32" long when extended, and had an eff range of about 400-600 meters. Noted for its unreliability due to a vulnerability to wet, Viet climate.

M-73 Mini-Gun - 7.62 mm, six-barreled MG operated by an electric motor and capable of firing apx 6,000 rnds/min. Mounted in acft, vehicles and fixed positions; distribution in other than acft limited to latter stages of war. See also M-132 and Mini-Gun.

M-79 Grenade Launcher - Breech-loaded, single-shot, 40mm grenade launcher that fired variety of rnds inc, HE (most common), shotgun, flare and CS gas. Eff range of 400 meters. Well-loved weapon that was very eff in delivering direct and indirect fire on enemy positions. Noted for its significant kick and propensity to scar thumbs with its recoil. Disadvantage was weight of its ammo. Typical grenadier carried between 25 and 75 HE rnds (depending on anxiety level). HE rnd was problem in dense jungle because it armed only after apx 30 feet of flight and was not eff close-in for that reason (rnds sometimes exploded prematurely after hitting foliage en route to target, injuring grenadier and not enemy!). Its ammo and barrel were 40mm in diameter and it looked like a short, fat, sawed-off shotgun. Typically one or two M-79 grenadiers per squad in U.S. Army ('70). Weighed 6.5 lbs. loaded, was 29" long, had 249 fps muzzle velocity and its HE round had an 18' kill radius. See also XM-174 Auto Grenade Launcher, M-203, XM-143 and Hand-Cranked Grenade Launcher.

M-88 Armored Recovery Vehicle – Tracked, heavy-vehicle recovery platform mounted on medium tank chassis. Carried crew of 4 and was capable of 30 mph. Photo in *Vietnam Order of Battle*, p 308.

M-101A 105mm Howitzer - A.k.a. the "Split-Trail" howitzer. Most common indirect fire supt towed-105mm howitzer of war. Of WWII/Korean War vintage w/range of 11,500 meters. Gradually replaced by lighter and more maneuverable M-102 howitzer.

M-102 Howitzer - Newer, lighter, and more maneuverable of the U.S. stnd towed-105mm howitzers. Gradually replaced WWII and Korean War vintage M-101A 105mm howitzer during war.

M-106A1 4.2" Mortar Track - Variant of the M-113 APC that carried a 107mm (4.2") mortar. Unlike M-125 SP 81mm Mortar track, M-106A1 carried base plate and mortar tube of 107mm externally. When employed, mortar was removed from vehicle for firing. Data per *Vietnam Order of Battle*, p 311 (photo at p 310).

M-107 SP 175mm - Self-propelled, track-mounted 175mm cannon. 32,600 meter range was longest of any U.S. arty piece, but accuracy was sacrificed for extreme range. Same chassis could mount more accurate, but shorter-ranged 8" cannon barrel, and weapon readily switched from one barrel to the other as needed.

M-108 105mm SP Howitzer - Self-propelled, track-mounted 105mm howitzer. Had range of 11,500 meters.

M-108 Flamegun - Flame-throwing cannon (napalm) frequently mounted on M-113 chassis in variant known as M-132 "Flame Track." Photo in *Vietnam Order of Battle*, p 308. See also M-132.

M-109 SP 155mm - Self-propelled, track-mounted 155mm howitzer. Had range of 14,600 meters.

M-110 SP 8" Howitzer - Self-propelled, track-mounted 8" howitzer. Had range of 16,800meters, crew of 5 and was regarded as the most accurate arty piece in the American arsenal.

M-113 APC - Stnd armored personnel carrier (APC) of VN War. Track mounted amphibious vehicle noted for propensity of its aluminum armor to burn when hit by RPGs. Some were powered by 283 cubic inch GM gasoline eng, and later models were diesel or turbine(?) powered. Used more to carry food, ammo and supplies than to carry men. Due to intense heat of climate and its weakness to RPG, troops ordinarily rode atop it or walked beside it. Had crew of 3, weighed 22,900 lbs. and top speed of a40 mph on land; 3 1/2 mph in water. See also M-132 Flame-thrower, M-557A1 Cmd Track, XM-174 Vulcan Track, XM-174, M-113AI Porta-Bridge, M-106A1 4.2" Mortar and M-125 SP 81mm Mortar.

M-113A1 Porta-Bridge - Only used in Vietnam, this variant of the M-113 APC carried folding, 30' bridge mounted in a scissors-like configuration above chassis. Bridge could carry vehicle traffic up to light armor. Photo in *Vietnam Order of Battle*, p 308.

M-114A1 155mm Howitzer - Heavy, indirect-fire supt arty piece used widely by U.S. Army/USMC during war. Had 14,600 meter range, and was normally operated by crew of 11. Weighed 12,700 lbs. An accurate and very effective weapon.

M-119A1 Pistol - See M-1911A1 Pistol and Colt Commander.

M-125 SP 81mm Mortar - M-113 APC chassis modified to carry a pivot-mounted 81mm mortar, its crew and basic ammo load. Hinged roof was opened to employ weapon. Data per *Vietnam Order of Battle*, p 310 (Photo at same page).

M-132 Flame-thrower - M-113 APC variant employing M-108 Flamegun with removable flame-thrower (napalm) turret. Had range of 300'-600' and M-113 tracks carrying it were often called Zippo Tracks or Flame Tracks. Many of these units were also armed with an M-73 Mini-Gun capable of

firing 6,000 rnds/min. Photo in *Vietnam Order of Battle*, p 308. See also XM-45E1 Flame-Thrower Service Unit and M-113 APC.
M-134 Minigun – GE's 7.62mm, six-barreled Gatling gun designed for use in helo, acft and vehicle-based weapons platforms. With rate of fire of from apx 1,000 to 6,000 rnds/min; was very eff and much-feared weapon. Driven by 28-volt electric motor, and weighed apx 265 lbs. XM-214 was lighter-weight version (only 35 lbs.) designed for use in boats and other vehicles. Both were noted for their destructive force and distinct pepper-grinder howl when in use. Widely used by Huey Cobra gunships in concert with 2.75" rocket pods and auto M-79 Grenade Launcher. Photo of jeep-mounted version at p 303, *Vietnam Order of Battle*.
M-134 Weapons package - 7.62mm mini-gun coupled with seven-tube, 2.75" rocket pod designed for helo gunships.
M-151 Quarter-Ton Jeep - See M-34 "4x4" Jeep and M-151A1.
M-151A1 LUT – A.k.a. the Mutt. Stnd 4x4 Jeep, Light Utility Truck of war. Featured rugged seating for 3-persons, 4-wheel drive and independent suspension. Replaced very famous Jeep of WWII vintage. Often modified to carry weapons ranging from M-60 MG to .50 Cal MG, to the Hand-Cranked 40mm Grenade Launcher, 106mm recoilless rifles and etc. See also M-34 Jeep.
M-174 Grenade Launcher - See XM-174 grenade launcher.
M-177 Rifle - CAR 15 and CAR 16 automatic 5.56mm Rifle. See XM-177E2 for detail.
M-203 Rifle - Combined over-and-under M-16A1 Rifle and 40mm grenade launcher in individual weapon employed widely by U.S. beginning apx '70. Was preceded by XM-148 and XM-203. See XM-148 and XM-203 for more detail.
M-214 Minigun - A.k.a. XM 214 Minigun. See M-134 Minigun.
M-274 Mechanical Mule - Small, 1/2 ton load, single-seat, flat-bed, 4 wheel-drive utility vehicle/light weapons carrier perhaps 10 ft by 5 feet, used to ferry supplies and personnel for short distances. Had only driver's seat and was powered by small gas eng. Bed only sat apx 24" above grnd. Saw wide use during war, principally in moving supplies to and from helo landing pads. Photo in *Vietnam Order of Battle*, p 319.
M-449 Firecracker Round - See Firecracker Round.
M-551 Sheridan - M-551 Sheridan Tank was very light-weight (33,460 lbs.) and very fast (43 mph) track-driven tank, armed with short-barreled 152mm cannon capable of firing conventional rounds as well as wire guided missiles. Its complex electronic systems (inc night vision capability) proved extremely vulnerable to SVN's weather and to RPGs because its light armor and highly volatile ammo were easily ignited by an RPG hit. Entered war Jan69, and although it had most powerful tank gun ever built, was not considered a successful weapon.
M-557A1 Cmd Track - The M-113 APC modified to act as CP for mobile unit cmd. Had additional body height and elaborate commo equip added. Photo in *Vietnam Order of Battle*, p 308. See also M-113 and M-132 Flame-Thrower.
M-576 Buckshot Round – A cannister anti-personnel rnd for M-79 Grenade Launcher. Each rnd contained 27 double-ought buckshot pellets held in a small cup atop large plastic plug that filled weapon's 40mm bore. Had very short eff range and often rnd of choice while unit was on move in thick vegetation.
M-578 LRV - Track-mounted recovery vehicle designed for light vehicle recovery duty. Armed with .50 Cal MG, and capable of 37 mph. Photo in *Vietnam Order of Battle*, p 308.
M-728 Combat Eng. Vehicle - Combat Engr vehicle designed for clearing minefields and general hoist work. Featured unusual, short-barreled 165mm Demolition Gun coupled with hoist beam and winch mechanism (capable of 17,500 lb lift, and 25,000 lb pull) mounted on M-48A3 tank chassis. See also 165mm Demolition Gun. Data/photo in *Vietnam Order of Battle*, pp 326-7.
M-1911A1 Pistol - A.k.a. "The Rust Bucket" and ".45 Caliber Anchor." Colt .45 caliber pistol first introduced to military in 1911 with its basic design unchanged thereafter. Stnd sidearm of U.S. Army/USMC. Clip-fed (9 rnds?), heavy, and its ammo was also very heavy (50 rnds = apx 5 lbs). Loved by many and hated by just as many. Its short range, high maintenance, propensity to rust and abominable accuracy (author's opinion) limited its usefulness. Renowned for its alleged "stopping power," but hitting target to stop it was often very problematic! Only people it could be depended on to stop were those unfortunate enough to have to carry it and its basic load in a tropical climate. Also produced in a limited 9mm version known as "Colt Commander," which was apparently only issued to General Officers and some SF troops. In 101st Abn Div during this author's tour, was SOP that all M-60 gunners carry also the .45 with 50 rnds of ammo; however, as a practical matter, the significant additional weight only added insult to injury and many M-60 gunners "farmed-out" their .45's to eager "John Wayne" types in the unit. Some data per *Vietnam Order of Battle*, p 301.
M.R. - Military Region.
MAAG - Military Assistance Advisory Group.
MAB - Marine Amphibious Brigade.
MAC-SOG - A.k.a. MACV-SOG. Military Assistance Command, Vietnam-Special Observation and Studies Group. Although name implied it was composed of scientists and technicians, SOG was very secret child of 5th SF Group. Primary duties were intel gathering ops in Cambodia, Laos, the DMZ and NVN using small recon teams. Op Prairie Fire's AO, for example, extended 33 km into Laos and same distance N of the DMZ. Commonly referred to as MAC-SOG or simply SOG. Mailing address was: *MACV-SOG, APO San Francisco 96307*. See also Ban Me Thuot, Chi Lang, Da Nang, Dong Ba Thin, Long Hai, Kontum, Nha Trang, Phuoc Tuy, Prairie Fire Operations. CCN, CCS, CCS and MLT. See also MACV-SOG in Major Commands Section.
MAC-SOG Operational Divisions - See SOG-00 et seq.
MACV - Military Assistance Command, Vietnam.
MACV Objectives Plan - After taking cmd of MACV, Creighton Abrams adopted concepts of Washington-based study urging an end to big unit search and destroy ops in favor of shift to attacking VC infrastructure, seeking-out and destroying enemy supply caches, while also refocusing forces to provide security at village level. Study had been written by Don Marshall prior to Gen Westmoreland's exit. Data per *A Better War*, pp 123-124.
MACV-JGS - MACV Inspector Gen, Joint Gen Staff.
MACV-JGS IG BTI Teams - Inspector Gen, Joint Gen Staff, Military Assistance Cmd VN, Base Turnover Inspection teams. Joint ARVN/US Inspector General's Office created in Oct71, and charged with conducting all pre and post-turnover inspections of U.S. facilities to SVN Govt control. Inspections included facilities that transferred both prior to and subsequent to its creation.
MACV-SOG - MACV Special Observation & Studies Grp.

MAC-SOG Operational Divisions - See SOG-00 et seq.
Mad Dog - A call-sign of the 240th AHC.
Mad Dog - A call-sign of the 240th ASHC.
Mad Minute - Practice of having perimeter guards of base or unit's NDP fire weapons and throw grenades into surrounding terrain at pre-selected random times during hours of darkness. Done in order to foil potential enemy assaults or trigger premature response of any force gathering to attack. On 101st Abn Div FSBs occupied by 2d Bde in late '69 through '70, was SOP to schedule 3 random mad minutes every night. 1st known use of tactic in VN apparently took place during 1st Ia Drang Battle at LZ X-Ray, Nov65. There Col Hal Moore ordered his beleaguered men to fire a "mad minute" just before dawn on one morning of battle. His trick worked, surprising NVA moving into position, killing many and forcing others to attack prematurely (thinking battle had started). In any case, one can surmise that a great deal of ammo was expended using technique, but a Godsend when it worked. See *Baptism*, p 123, for discussion of 1st Cav's early use of tactic.
Madame Nhu - A.k.a. Tran Le Xuan Le (maiden name), the Dragon Lady, Lucrezia Borgia and the Oriental Richelieu of Vietnam, among other derisive nicknames. Notorious wife of President ('54-63) Ngo Dinh Diem's reputedly evil, venal and ruthless Brother, Ngo Dinh Nhu. Born 1911, as Tran Le Xuan Le, which meant "Tears of Spring." Because Pres. Diem was single/celibate and his chief advisor/brother was her husband Nhu, Madame Nhu became the 1st lady of Vietnam by default. Very opinionated and talkative, she was also noted for her beauty, enormous influence and ruthlessness, and became frequent subject of press reports and much gossip. Per Nguyen Cao Ky, on 8May63 (Buddha's Birthday), she "uttered the words that made her one of most despised women of our age" when, after a Buddhist monk committed sacrificial suicide by burning himself to death in protest of Diem's policies, she remarked on camera, "I would clap my hands at seeing another monk barbecue now." Behind her back, Ky says, she was called Lucrezia Borgia. When her husband was murdered in Nov63, she went into exile in Rome but remained focus of news media until end of war. Data per *Twenty Years and Twenty Days*, pp 31-35.
MAF - Marine Amphibious Force.
Mag - Magazine.
MAG - Marine Air Group.
Mahayana - One of 2 main sects of Buddhist religion in SVN. See Hinayana for detail and also Thinh Tri Quang.
Main Force VC Units - Highest level of organized Viet Cong Forces. Up to regimental-sized strength. See Local Force VC.
Maj - Major.
MajG - Major General.
MajGen - Major General.
Man Tribes - Highland tribe of the downslopes of northern Tonkin Mtns. Loyal to French during 1st Indochina War. See also Moi and Montagnard, Meo, and Tai Tribes.
MAP - Military Assistance Program. U.S. prgm that provided various acft to French during 1st Indochina war, beginning in '51.
Mar – Marine(s), Marine Rgt, or Marine Div.
Marechaux d' Empire - Marshal de Lattre's jaunty nickname for group of Colonels defending the Red River Valley and his *'de Lattre Line*. Data per *Street Without Joy*, p 60.
Marie-Rose M. - French woman discussed in *Street Without Joy*, p 140, who lost her 1st husband to Germans, May40; her 2d husband to Japanese in Indochina, 9Mar45; and her 3d husband (an Army Doctor) to plane crash in French West Africa. She requested reassignment to Indochina and found romance with BG Hartemann, North Air Cmdr. On 27Apr51, he talked her into a ride on a B-26, arguing that there was no such thing as fate and that her bad luck had run out. 1 hour later, plane was shot down by AAA fire over Cao Bang, killing all aboard.
Marijuana Dogs - Dogs used by MP Cos to search for contraband drugs among troops, their personal goods and particularly mail being sent home. Image of 101st MP Co, 101st Abn, Marijuana Dog searching mail at Phu Bai APO on net at: http://carlisle-www.army.mil/cgi-bin/usamhi/pixdata/searchpix-RG123S.
Marijuana Usage - See Drug Abuse.
Marine Unit, Vietnam - MUVN. Operational name of USMC helicopter supt in VN operating out of Soc Trang and immediately succeeding Op Shufly. Shufly began 16Apr62 and its name was changed to MUVN soon thereafter. See also Op Shufly.
Mark-36 Mine - See Mk-36.
Mark-52 Mine - See Mk-52.
Mark-82 Bomb – See Mk-82.
Mark-117 Bomb – See Mk-117.
Mark Mission - ANZAC nomenclature for what U.S. arty called a marking rnd. A single arty shell (usually smoke or white phosphorous, fired on given grid intersection to give FO a fixed point of reference for adjusting fire.
Market Time, Operation - U.S. 7th Fleet's Coastal Surveillance Force, TF 115. Created to control enemy infiltration along SVN's 1,200 mi-long coast. See also Game Warden and MRF in Glossary, and U.S. Naval Forces in Major Command Section.
Marlin - Trade name for SP-5B 2 acft,050 mi rnge, 250 kts top spd. Mfgd by Martin.
MARS - Military Amateur (Affiliated?) Radio Service. U.S. Signal Corps Ham Radio operators who provided "telephone service to U.S. by linking through Ham operators around the world to telephone system in US." Troops at larger basecamp s could sometimes make appointments at MARS stations for calls home. Service was erratic, sound quality often poor. Normal radio procedure also had to be followed during conversations (i.e., each party had to say "over" at end of each statement).
Marston Matting - Interlocking steel or aluminum metal plates used to surface rwys and other for other purposes such as bunker roofing/siding. Similar to or same as PSP.
Marvin the Arvin - U.S. GI slang for ARVN soldiers generally ("Army, Republic Vietnam" anglicized by U.S. troops as "Arvin"). Sometimes meant derisively. See also Ruff-Puff.
MAS - Marine Air Squadron.
MASH - Mobile Army Support Hospital.
MASS - Marine Air Supt Squadron.
mat - matting.
MAT - Mobile Advisory Teams. Per Bill Hunt, MACV-Team 72/85, these were MACV-owned and typically attached to hamlet forces. "The Popular Forces (PFs) probably had these guys available to go out with them on patrol, until the program was abandoned." Jim Alkek, MACV-Team 46, tells us: "Normally, they worked out of District MACV team HQ. We had an assigned MAT team that had their "permanent" bunks in a team house behind our villa, but usually they were situated

at one of the RF/PF locations working on fortifications, training, night ambushes, etc. We partied together, but not generally together otherwise. District advisory teams were assigned to work with the RF/PF and district HQ and other allied units in the area (ROK, SF). The MAT people had their own MAT II designation, although they were officially part of the district advisory team. They were sometimes moved around districts by the province HQ." Described in *Father Soldier Son*, at p 179, as 5-man Army advsy teams that operated like SF units. May have also been SF term?

Mat Tran To Quoc - The "Fatherland Front." See Viet Cong.

MATS - Military Air Transportation Servicc.

Maverick - A call-sign of the 175th AHC.

MAW - Marine Air Wing.

max - maximum (TAD).

Max Von Sydow - See Operation Shotgun in main alpha listing.

May Bay My, 4181 - An inscription on NVN Stamp which translated as: *4,181 U.S. Planes Shot Down*.

MB1 - Mobile Supt Base One (USN).

MB2 - Mobile Supt Base Two (USN).

MC - Marine Corps or USMC.

MCAF - Marine Corps Air Facility.

MCB - Mobile Construction Battalion.

McGuire Rigs - Rope assembly designed by SF Project Delta Sgt Maj Charles McGuire. Was used for tactical emergency extractions of recon, SF and SOG teams when LZs were not available. Consisted of a rope, knotted with several loops near its base, and weighted with sandbags. Was simply dropped through jungle canopy from hovering helo to team on grnd. Awaiting team removed sandbags, then put one foot into an available loop and, as safety valve, secured themselves to rig using D-Ring (even if wounded while on rig, a man could stay attached). Used only as last resort when teams were in great danger and could not reach suitable LZ. See also STABO Rig and Gorwoody Antenna.

McNamara's Wall - See main alpha listings.

MDMAF - Mekong Delta Mobile Afloat Base.

Meal Combat, Individual - See C-Rations.

Meal, Quick-Serve - See LRRP Rations.

MEB - Marine Expeditionary Bde.

Mech - Mechanized.

Mechanical Ambush - See M-18 A1 Anti-Personnel Mine.

MEDCAP - Medical Civic Action Program. USMC/Army prgm in which medics and doctors made routine periodic visits to rural villes in order to provide primary medical care and dispense basic medicines as sincere goodwill gesture. Seriously ill Viets who visited MEDCAP were often then evaced for proper care.

Melia Jaune - Viet cigarette common to French War. Unknown whether name was simply a parody of marijuana, or if this product actually included the drug in its tobacco? U.S. *Lucky Strike* brand was also popular among French.

Meng Ho - Common ARVN op name. Meant 'Fierce Tiger.'

Meo Tribes - N Tonkin tribe of Eskimo heritage. Opium farmers who believed they were descendants of "The Great Holy Dog."

Mere Gook Rule - Manifestation of war's nature given a name by cynical troops. It characterized attitude of minority of troops who viewed Viets as less than human, or at least of a lower stature than themselves. Author of *Son Thang* (p. 115) tried to define it as an attitude in which, "It was no crime to kill or torture or rob or maim a Vietnamese because he was a mere Gook." See also Gook.

METAR - Avn Routine Weather Report (TAD).

meter – Equal to 3.2808 feet.

Metro, The - French nickname for underground network of tunnels and bunkers at Dien Bien Phu.

Metro Station – Apparently used to denote form of standardized commo or radar facility. 101st Abn ORLL for period ending 31Jul69, indicates such facilities were at FSB Currahee and other I Corps FSBs, Jun69.

Mfg - Manufacture or manufacturing.

Mfgr - Manufactured.

Mfgd - Manufactured.

MG - machine gun.

MGs- machine guns.

MGF - Mobile Guerrilla Force.

Mgr - Manager.

MGR - Acronym for "Mere Gook Rule." See Mere Gook Rule.

Mhz - megahertz (TAD).

mi - Mile. Equal to 1.609 km.

MI-4 - Soviet built acft used by NVN. 155 mi rnge, 130 kts top spd. mfgd by MIL.

MIG - Russian-made jet-fighter acft.

MIG-15UT L1 - Soviet built acft used by NVN. 885 mi rnge, 630. mfgd by Mikoyan.

MIG-17F - Soviet built fighter acft used by NVN. 1,230 mi rnge, 710 kts top spd. mfgd by Mikoyan.

MIG-19SF - Soviet built fighter acft used by NVN. 425 mi rnge, 830 kts top spd. mfgd by Mikoyan.

MIG-21 - Soviet built fighter acft used by NVN. 670 mi rnge, 1,320 kts top spd. mfgd by Mikoyan.

MIGCAP - Anti-MIG acft air patrol.

Mike - Radio lingo or code for word "Minute." Created by simply substituting military phonetic alphabet for first letter of whatever word it represented. As such, Hotel replaced "hour," Sierra replaced "second" (or south), Whiskey replaced "west" and so on.

mil - military (TAD).

Military Council, The - Secret SVN org formed by generals of Committee of Natl Leadership under a non-constitutional framework, and just before the 1st national elections in '67. Inc were all generals, as well as the Minister of Defense, the President and Vice President. Council took upon itself right to set national policy and promote civilian/military authorities. Chair also given authority to issue directives to elected pres. In effect, was hidden government of VN and, since then elected Nguyen Cao Ky was appointed chair, he actually had more power than President Thieu. See Armed Forces Council, Military Revolutionary Council. Committee of Natl Leadership and Nguyen Cao Ky.

Military Operations - See Op's name in main alpha listing. Entries are formatted with name first, followed by comma and then word Operation or Op. For example, "Cedar Falls, Operation."

Military Regions - Corps Tactical Zones (CTZs) designated as I Corps, II, Corps, III Corps, IV Corps and Special Capitol Zone running from N to S, with I Corps the northernmost. These were re-designated as Military Regions (MR's) 1 through 4, eff 1Jul70. Laos and Cambodia were divided into MRs as well.

Military Revolutionary Council - Organization of SVN military leaders set up to advise and oversee SVN government's activities in 1960's prior to an elected govt. Inc what became known as "The Young Turks," younger, more liberal ARVN generals and marshals (inc Nguyen Cao Ky and Gen Thieu) who took greater hand in decision making process as time went by. In Jan65, name became Armed Forces Council. See also Military Council, Armed Forces Council, Committee of National Leadership and Nguyen Cao Ky. Per *Twenty Years and Twenty Days*, p 59.

Millpoint - Call-sign of USMC HMM 363, Medium Helo Sqdn.

min - minimum (TAD).

Mines, Gravel - See Gravel Mines.

Mines, Land - According to DOD stats, apx 75% of all U.S. vehicle losses during the Vietnam War were the result of mines. As were 73% of tank losses and 77% of APC losses. Mines and booby-traps also accounted for high percentage of U.S. personnel losses and, in '67, were responsible for 17% of all casualties.

Mini-Gun - See M-73, M-134, M-214 and Twenty Mike-Mike.

Mining of NVN Waters - See Tet '68 Offensive, and Operations Linebacker and End Sweep, and *MSS-2*.

Mini-Tet – 2d major VC attack of Saigon area, May68. Follow-up to Jan-Feb Tet '68 offensive. Major fighting in city, Cholon and Saigon cemetery ensued but eventually ended in VC's defeat and more staggering casualty totals being added to their Jan defeat.

Mins - Vietnamese/French word for "Mines." Likely origin was French minefield signs of 1st Indochina War. VC often posted "Mins" signs adj to booby-trapped/mined areas to warn civilians of risk or their presence. Sometimes simply used as ruse to either deflect U.S. ops away, or to draw them into ambush, or channel them into real danger zones when they maneuvered to avoid the supposed mined area. See also Tu Dai.

Minuteman – Call-sign of the 176th Avn Co Slicks. Suptd Americal Div in I Corps.

Missing On Purpose - GI slang used for those troops who were AWOL, or who had deserted of their own free will.

Misty - Call-sign of F-100 Fast FACs of Operation Commando Sabre and flying out of Phu Cat AB. See also detailed history of Phu Cat AB in main alpha listing.

Mites - Per Ex-PFC John Middlesworth, *Secrets of the Viet Cong* tells us that during French War, rich Vietnamese or there children attending school in France were derisively referred to as "Mites;" a contraction of word "Annamite." The French also used the term "Nhaques," which was a word for "peasant," though its origin is unclear. See also Gook.

MIUWS - Mobile Inshore Undersea War Surveillance (USN).

Mk-36 Mines - Air-dropped anti-shipping mine. See Quang Khe Ferries in main alpha listing.

Mk 52 Mines - See Easter Offensive in Glossary.

Mk-82 Bomb - USAF's standard 500 lb iron bomb.

Mk-117 Bomb - USAF's standard 250 lb(?) iron bomb.

mkr - marker (TAD).

MLMS - Minesweeping Launch (USN).

MLS - Mobile Launch Site?

MLT - Mobile Launch Team.

mm - Millimeter(s).

MMAF - Marble Mountain Air Facility.

Mobile CAP Teams - USMC Combined Action Platoons that were mobile and not attached to any specific location as was otherwise the norm for CAP. Teams depended upon frequent, unpredictable movement for survival and operated more like an Inf Plt in that they were always patrolling within their AO and avoiding predictable patterns of movement.

Mobile Launch Teams -MACV-SOG MLT's. CCN and presumably (CCC and CCS also) operated permanent sites controlling its ops in VN, Cambodia, Laos, the DMZ and NVN (Prairie Fire, et al). See also MLT-1 and MLT-2 in main alpha listing, and Prairie Fire in Glossary.

Mobile Riverine Force - A.k.a. MRF. Created in Jun67 using combined elements of 2d Bde/9th Inf Div and USN TFs 115, 116 and 117), Navy Seal Teams, SVNMC, and 7th ARVN Div/River Assault Grps. Force inc apx 5,000 very mobile troops. Its HQ was originally in Vung Tau, but moved to the 600 acre, man-made Island of Dong Tam (apx 9 km W My Tho). Many of force's facilities and "FSBs" were ship-borne and on floating platforms throughout the Mekong Delta, while its ops were carried-out from various small boats, PBRs, WWII landing craft, as well as various amphib and air-cushioned vehicles. Operated in IV and southern III Corps. Assets gradually turned-over to ARVN between '69-71, after bulk of 9th Inf Div had left VN in '69. See also Dong Tam, Game Warden, Market Time, U.S. Naval Forces VN (Major Cmd Section) as well as 9th Inf Div (Divisional Cmd Section).

Mobile Strike Force Camps - See 1st CTZ MSF Camp and 2d CTZ MSF in main alpha listing.

Mobile Strike Force Cmds - A.k.a. Mike Forces. '65-71 MACV project which established Strike Force Cmd for each of 4 major CTZs, and at 5th SF Grp HQ in Nha Trang. Each Mike Force consisted of a 12-man SF A-Team, several CIDG Bns, a recon Co, and a Nung or Cambode Abn Co.

Mobilization Act of 1968 - See General Mobilization Act.

MOH - Medal Of Honor, Highest U.S. Award for Valor.

Mohawk - Army reconnaissance acft built by Grumman Acft. Powered by 2-Lycoming T-53 L-3 turboprops of 1,000 hp each. Capable 317 mph at 5,000' alt.

Mohawk - Trade name of U.S. OV-1, twin-eng, prop-driven recon acft. 1,300 mi rnge, 295 kts top spd. mfgd by Grumman Avn.

Moi - Vietnamese word meaning "Wild People." Collective and derisive ethnic appellation for northern Tonkin Hill tribe peoples and those of central highlands (generally the Montagnard). Held in contempt by Vietnamese, the Montagnard naturally allied with French and U.S. of both the 1st and 2d Indochina Wars. See also Montagnard, Meo, Man and Tai Tribes.

Monsignor Lefevre - See *Constitution, USS*, in main alpha listing.

Monitor - Armored Troop Carrier (ATCs) vessels. USN barges and small landing craft with armored super-structures built on their hulls as adaptation to MRF warfare of Mekong Delta and swamps of IV and southern III Corps. Many resembled boxy looking barges, but came in wide variety of shapes and sizes.

Montagnard - Literal translation of Montagnard in Vietnamese is "Mountain People." Commonly "Moi" (Wild People, a derisive name for highland tribes of both SVN and NVN used by "native" Viets. "Cordially detested by Vietnamese," as one author puts it, the Montagnard naturally allied with French and U.S. of 1st and 2d Indochina Wars. Often simply "Yards" in U.S. GI slang and always held in high regard by those who served with them. Described by U.S. SF as exceedingly honest, generous, fearless, loyal and fierce. In '64, the Yards revolted against 5 CIDG camps in II Corps, killing dozens of ARVN before U.S. SF was able to negotiate halt to 3-week revolt. See also Moi and Meo, Man and Tai Tribes.

Moon Beam – Call-sign of night counterpart to "Hillsborough Control," a USAF abn C & C C-130 acft controlling fighter supt over part of Laos for TASS FACs. See also Hillsborough.

Moonglow - Nickname/call-sign of C-47 Flareships operating over I Corps in early '68 (at least). Standard load was 96 multimillion-candle power, 3-min flares capable of illuminating battlefield for up to 4 1/2 hrs. Cited in *Through the Valley*. See also Basketball.

MOOSE - Move Out Of Saigon Expeditiously. See Operation Moose in main alpha list.

MOP - Missing On Purpose.

Morane - French recon/Liaison acft employed during French War. At most, French had only about 85 of this type of recon acft during entire war; among which were the Morane, the L-5, the Siebel and etc. Data per *Street Without Joy*, pp 263.

More Flags Program - See SEATO.

Mortar Magnet - Nickname of C-130 transport acft, and any other acft that tended to draw enemy attention once it had landed.

MP - Maintenance period (TAD).

MP - Military Police.

MPC - Military Payment Certificates. A.k.a. "Scrip" or "Script." Used in lieu of U.S. greenbacks to avoid political and economic impact on local economies. During VN war, several series and designs were employed, one superseding the other without warning, in order to disrupt black market activities.

MPQ4 - See AN/MPQ4.

MR - Military Region (TAD).

MR1, MR2, MR3 and MR4 - Military Regions in SVN. See main alpha listings, and Military Regions, Corps and CTZ in Glossary.

MR1, MR2, MR3, MR4, MR5 - Military Regions in Laos. See Laotian Military Regions in Glossary.

MRF - See Mobile Riverine Force.

mrkd - marked (TAD).

MSB - Minesweeping, Boat (Non-Magnetic) (USN).

MSB - Minesweeping, Boat (Non-Magnetic).

MSC - Military Sealift Command. Succeeded MSTS.

MSC - Minesweeper, Coastal (Non-Magnetic) (USN).

MSF - Minesweeper, Fleet (USN).

MSF - Mobile Strike Force.

MSgt - Master Sgt

MSL - Minesweeper, Light (USN).

MSM - Minesweeper, Medium (USN).

MSO - Minesweeper, Ocean (USN).

MSO - Minesweeper, Ocean.

MSR - Minesweeper Patrol (USN).

MSR - Minesweeper, River.

MSS - Minesweeper, Special (USN).

MSS - Mission Support Site (MAC-SOG). For examples see Leghorn, Hickory Hill and Sledgehammer in main alpha listing.

MSTS - Military Sea Transport Service (USN). Preceded MSC.

mt - mountain(s), mount, motor, meters (TAD).

mtg – meeting.

mtgs – mettings.

mtn - mountain(s), mount.

MUC - Meritorious Unit Commendation (USN).

Mui - Vietnamese word for cape or point.

Mule - See M-274 Mechanical Mule.

Mule Teams - Units providing USAF logistical supt early in war.

Muleskinner - A call-sign of the 242d ASHC.

Muong/Nung - Hill Tribes of Central and NVN Highlands. Recruited by French as GCMA mercenaries. French moved many to mnts near Dalat and were loyal to them and respected their fighting skills and spirit, as did U.S. SF advisors who followed.

MUSCLE SHOALS System - Air dropped acoustic (Acoubouy) and seismic (ADSID) sensors of Igloo White Op deployed in supt of Khe Sanh CB, Jan68(?) and monitored by Igloo White and Dutch Mill. Sensors' transmissions were monitored by modified EC-121's acft (called "repeater aircraft") in constant orbit over area and then amplified/retransmitted to Igloo White facility at NKP in Thailand for interpretation. Activated sensors were rptd under code name SPOTLIGHT to target info center at Khe Sanh, that would in turn request arty, air strikes or Arc Light missions on rptd targets. By Fe68, USN and USAF a/c had flown 72 sorties dropping nine arrays of 316 sensors in 44 "strings." In 1st ten days alone, seismic sensors were activated 197,501 times and acoustic sensors 105,007 times! Dutch Mill computers made 52,356 analyses of data and Khe Sanh target center scheduled 99 strikes in response. Sensors could detect activity within 10 meter radius but since they were air-dropped, precise location of sensors was difficult to ascertain (built-in location transmitters often disabled by impact) and targeting accuracy was initially off by as much as 1 km; however accuracy improved as time went by and other measurements were employed. Discussed extensively in *Valley of Decision*. See also Task Force Alpha, Igloo White, Dutch Mill, Khe Sanh Red Watch and Gravel Mines in main alpha listing and in Glossary. Some data per *Valley of Decision*, pp 300-301.

Musket - Call-sign of 176th AHC Gunships. Suptd Americal Div.

MUST Unit - Medical Unit Self-contained Transportable Hospital.

Mutt - See M-151A1.

MUVN - Marine Unit Vietnam. See Op Shufly in main alpha sect.

MX19 - Aluminum runway matting (TAD).

M-X19 - Aluminum runway matting (TAD).

My - Viet word for "American." Pronounced "My-eeee."

Mystic Dagger - Call-sign of Pra Lean Mtn signal site near Dalat.

N - North.

N - U.S. Navy; (N) means U.S. Navy in TAD).

N-Day - VC code phrase for the launch day of Tet '68.

n/a - Not available or, not applicable.

NAG - Naval Advisory Group (USN).

Nail - Call-sign for FAC acft operating out of USAF's 2d (or 23d?) TASS at NKP AB, Thailand. (*Da Nang Diary* states that "Nails" was call-sign of 23d TASS?).

Nailing - Aerial Rocket Arty term for tactic of clearing an LZ using 2.75" flechette rockets which contained thousands of 1.5" finned, nail-like Flechettes for its shrapnel element.

Nam Bo - NVA term for the South, i.e., SVN.

Nam Yum Rats, The - The est 3,000 deserters of French forces who lived in holes and caves along shores of Nam Yum River during battle for Dien Bien Phu, scavenging for food and stealing supplies from French garrisons and errant air drops of supplies. Nam Yum ran through Muong Thanh Valley in which Dien Bien Phu was located. "Rats" were reportedly a depraved and wild lot whose ranks were filled mostly by Viet Tribal partisans, North African, Moroccan and Viet deserters,

many of whom had lost their nerve or were shell-shocked. See also Nam Yum River and Dien Bien Phu in main alpha listing.
NAP - Non Airborne Personnel. "Official" term in 101st Abn Div HQ during 67-68, used to describe troops who were not parachute-qualified (used instead of more derisive "Leg" slang commonly used by paratroops). However, Div was redesignated from true "Airborne" status to "Airmobile" (AMBL) status on 28Jun68, and thereafter, most of men who served with it were not paratroopers or jump-qualified.
Napalm – A.k.a. Nape. Jellied gasoline in form of salts of Naphthaenic and Palmitic Acids. Primarily air-dropped, the exploding napalm canisters produced intense heat that not only cleared vegetation and incinerated enemy troops, but could also kill by removing oxygen from air. Was also delivered by tank and track mounted flame-thrower units and by the backpack mounted flame-thrower units carried by individual soldiers. Produced huge and dramatic ball of fire, and thick black smoke. While controversial weapon and considered inhumane by some, it was nonetheless very effective. See also Flame Tracks, Zippo Tracks, M-132 and M-7 flame-throwers.
Nape - See Napalm.
NARA - National Archives and Records Administration. In this text, typically refers to the Archives II, Textual Reference Branch (College Park, MD) , which is repository for most all VN War Army unit archives (except unit rosters and personnel records, which are at the NPRC), inc Bn Annual Hist Supp, Daily Staff Journals, Op summaries, AARs, ORLLs and various other rpts.
NAS - Naval Air Station.
Nasty Class Patrol Boats - Norwegian-built PT boats refitted with U.S. equip. Diesel-powered, fiberglass hulled, 80' craft capable of 41-knots and ideal for SEA. Sent to VN circa 64-66? Per USN data at www.history.navy.mil/seairland/.
Natl - National.
Natl Geo Map - Reference specific to map of Indochina published as insert in Fe67, issue of *National Geographic Magazine*. This excellent resource is entitled: *Viet Nam, Cambodia, Laos, And Thailand*, and its scale is 1:1,900,800 (1 inch equals 30 miles). During war, many families of those serving relied on this map to track whereabouts of their relatives. It is perhaps the best single-map war-related resource one could possess.
National Salvation Committee, The - On 27Mar75, Nguyen Cao Ky reentered political scene to form this committee, an org that sought to replace President Thieu and stop NVA Final Offensive before it reached Saigon.
nav - navigation (TAD).
NAV-CAV - Elements of 1st Cav working with USN in IV Corps, and along Cambodian border in late '68 to early69.
navaid - navigation aid (TAD).
Navarre Plan - According to John F. Dulles, "provided that French were to break the organized body of communist aggression by end of 1955 'fighting season,' leaving the task of mopping-up the remaining (presumably disorganized) guerrilla grps to progressively stronger armies of Cambodia, Laos and Thailand." Per *Street Without Joy*, p 103.
NAVFORV - Naval Forces, Vietnam.
Navy Nam Cam Noc - Call-sign for Nam Cam Airfield Control.
NBL - No Bomb Lines. Designated areas in Indochina indicated on maps by squares drawn with lines labeled *NBL*. Terrain within those lines was reserved exclusively for top-secret Prairie Fire Ops and their suptg FACs. No bombing or arty was allowed within those zones without specific authority.
NC - Nurse Corps (USN).
NCB - Naval Mobile Construction Battalion, & CB's.
NCO - Non-Commissioned Officer.
NDB - Non Directional Beacon (TAD).
NDB - Non Directional Beacon Site.
NE - Northeast.
Neptune - Trade name for P-2 acft (USN). 3,685 mi rnge, 410 kts top spd. mfgd by Lockheed Acft.
Never by Never Trench - Slang term used to describe trench dug as punishment in Army. Offender was sentenced to dig a 6' deep hole with no limit to its other 2 dimensions, and told not to stop until ordered to do so. Apparently common to 101st Abn, but its use elsewhere is otherwise unknown.
New Life Hamlets - Part of CORDS rural hamlet development prgm which began with Strategic Hamlet Program and evolved in name and concept to "New Life" and later "Really New Life" (a.k.a. Ap Doi Moi) prgms. All involved relocating civilian populations (mostly against their will) to end VC access to them, but all were regarded as dismal failures.
New York - SOG code name for NVN and secret ops there.
Newbie – See FNG.
NEWZARM - New Zealand Army Headquarters, Singapore.
NG - National Guard.
Ngok - Vietnamese/Lao for Mountain.
NGS - Naval Gunfire Supt Unit. A.k.a. "The Gun Line."
NGSA - Naval Gunfire Supt Unit. Naval task forces that provided gunfire for grnd units. See also ANGLICO.
ngt - night (TAD).
Nguol Rung - Viet Forest People, or Yeti, or Yerin, or Chinese Wildman, or *L'Homme Sauvage*, Khi Trau (Laotian for Buffalo Monkey or big monkey), and Powell's Ape. Viet equiv of elusive Yeti or Bigfoot. Descriptions sound very much like those of an Orangutan, putting size at that of human or smaller, and color from gray through shades of brown to reddish-brown to black. There are rpts compiled by westerners of Yeti-like humanoids having been observed in Tri-border area as early as 1947. Sightings were so common during war, that in '74, Gen Hoang Minh Thau (CG Central Highland Forces) requested a scientific study. 27Apr70 *Army Reporter* article, *Ape Story Lingers*, notes that 3 years earlier ('67), a weary guard on Cam Ranh Bay perimeter sighted and fired upon Yeti-like creature one night, and footprint and blood trail were found at daylight. Depot CO, a Capt Powell, then found his name forever associated with the photo of footprint, and it became thereafter "Powell's Ape." Lt Al Szpilla and WO Darryl Santella 101st Abn helo pilots, frequently spotted unusually large footprints from air and one day landed to investigate some. They measured stride at 4' and print size at 18" long by 8" wide. In '82 and on Chu Mo Ray (Mom Ray) Mtn in Kontum Prov, Prof. Tran Hung Viet took cast of footprint measuring 28 by 16 centimeters. This author's unit found what appeared to be a dead Orangutan on LZ on Nui Mo Tau SW of Hue in '70, and later were told there were no Orangutan in SVN. Compiled from discussion/links of Vern Weitzel at: http://coombs.anu.edu.au /~vern/wildman.html. Per Paul Grandy, see also www.ultranet.ca/ bcscc/yiren.htm. See also Khi Trau Sightings.
Nguyen Ai Quoc - See Ho Chi Minh.
Nguyen Cao Ky - One of the "Young Turks" of SVN military, Ky was born in Son Tay, 34 km WNW Hanoi.

Between 1944-45, his father (teacher and farmer) acted as liaison between Vietminh (fighting Japanese) and their contacts in Son Tay and Hanoi. At age of 12, he ran away from home in attempt to join Vietminh, but was intercepted by Japanese and returned to his Mother. During 1st Indochina War, he entered Viet National Army, was trained as an officer by French, and briefly served as plt leader at small post in Red River Delta. He soon joined Vietnamese Air Force, taking his pilot training at French base in Morocco, followed by 2-years of advanced training as DC-3 (C-47) pilot in France, returning to VN in '54 just as war ended. His family moved to Saigon when country was partitioned, and in late '50s flew DC-3's for fledgling SVNAF. In '60, at age 30, became airbase or wing cmdr near Saigon. In '63, he was asked to fly top-secret missions dropping VN agents into NVN for CIA (On each mission, parachutists and aircrews were each handed 100 U.S. dollars to be used only if plane was forced down in foreign country. When crews or agents returned to Saigon, money had to be returned. Per *Twenty Years and Twenty Days*, pp 25-26). In that role, his unit switched to DC-3's of SVN's civil AIR VIET. He became both VNAF Gen and Air Marshal and, in Jun65 and because "no one else wanted the job," the Armed Forces Council appointed him as Prime Minister. As PM for 2 years, he gave SVN its first relatively stable military govt and, in May67, ordered national elections. After some coaxing by military leaders, Ky agreed to run as VP on former Gen. Nguyen Van Thieu's Presidential ticket, winning handily in popular elections. At same time, he was appointed chair of secret Military Council created by Committee for National Leadership just before election to effectively run country no matter who was elected, and as result, Ky had more power and authority than did Thieu. By '71, U.S. State Dept asked Ky to run against Thieu for presidency, but Ky claimed it impossible under Thieu's tight grip. In Oct71, Thieu ran for reelection unopposed and without Ky or anyone else as VP on ticket. From '72 until Mar75, Ky was out of political scene. Although he retained rank of Marshal and kept residences at both Tan Son Nhut and his farm in Khanh Duong, he had no authority or official duties. On 27Mar75, he reentered politics to form the National Salvation Committee, an org that sought to replace President Thieu and stop NVA Final Offensive before it reached Saigon. On 29Apr79, only hours before NVA entered Saigon, he flew his helicopter loaded with fellow officers to Carrier *USS Midway* and was later transferred to *USS Blue Ridge*, which carried him to US. Ky moved his family to Virginia, where he became a rancher. Though flamboyant, Ky was noted for his courage and apparent aversion to corruption. When Ky married his wife Mai in '64, then PM Huong gave Ky 200,000 Piastres and his own, second-hand 1960 Ford Falcon auto as wedding gifts. When Ky himself was appointed PM in '65, on his 1st day in office, he was asked him which car he would like to order as his "official vehicle" and told a Mercedes would be appropriate. Much to everyone's surprise, Ky responded by insisting he would use the '60 Ford Falcon Huong had given him; a promise he apparently kept (per *Twenty Years and Twenty Days*, pp 72-73).

Nguyen Dynasty Wall - See main alpha listing and McNamara's Wall in Glossary.

Nguyen of the North - GI nickname for NVA troops.

Nguyen Tat Thanh - One of Ho Chi Minh's many pseudonyms.

Nguyen The Patriot - See Ho Chi Minh.

Nguyen Van Be - NVA/VC teenager captured by U.S. or ARVN whom NVA glorified for propaganda purposes by declaring him a "Hero of The Revolution." NVN published many stories, books, billboards and leaflets claiming he'd taken a claymore mine from his captors and then martyred himself by detonating it above his head (taking 69 U.S. troops with him in blast). SVN govt scored great counter-propaganda coup when his still very healthy face was recognized in NVA propaganda photo by ARVN jailer at My Tho Prison. To great embarrassment of enemy, SVN Govt widely advertised fact Nguyen was alive and well and had cried like a baby when captured! Per *Bonnie-Sue*, p 375-377.

Nguyen Van Troi - Celebrated Viet hero and electrician who planted cmd-detonated bomb on route of U.S. Secty of Defense Robert McNamara's motorcade. Bomb was discovered and Troi executed, but his last words brought him everlasting respect. He said, "Long live Vietnam. Long live Ho Chi Minh," just before a firing squad ended his days as an electrician. Many towns, streets and buildings now bear his name. Viets struck medal in his honor and an image of it courtesy Bob Peragallo is at www.vwam.com/ vets/nvameds/ m4.html. Apparently Troi had been rejected as NLF member but was quickly adopted by NLF as martyr soon after his death. See also Dien Ban (birthplace), and Han River Bridge. Per *Sparring With Charlie*, p.215 et seq.

Nhan Dan - Newspaper of Lao Dong Party.

Nhaques - Per Ex-PFC John Middlesworth, *Secrets of the Viet Cong* tells us that during 1st Indochina War, rich Viets or their children attending school in France were derisively referred to as "Nhaques," a word equiv to "peasant" Also used derisively was term "Mites," a contraction of word "Annamite." See also Mites and Gook.

NHC - Naval Historical Center.

Nho - Vietnamese word for youth of a village.

NIAGARA - Massive bombing campaign initiated by Gen Westmoreland in Jan '67 as response to increasing enemy pressure on Khe Sanh. Was 2 phase SLAM op and 1st phase was extensive air-ground scouting and recon phase using everything from air recon to MACV-SOG (2d phase was bombing itself). 1 great success of op was apparent annihilation of major NVA HQ in Laos just W of Khe Sanh when, on 30Jan68 (or possibly 24Jan68), the largest Arc Light of war to that point (36 B-52s in morning strike followed by nine B-52's in night strike). Data per *Valley of Decision*, pp 220-223 and 298, and War *Without Windows*. See also, Muscle Shoals, Arc Light, SLAM and Igloo White, Khe Sanh Red Watch and Khe Sanh Air Strike

Night of The Pagodas - 21Aug63. On that date, Ngo Dinh Nhu ordered SVN forces to storm Buddhist pagodas around SVN in order to quell growing and influential dissent among religion's monks. Over 1,400 monks were jailed. Per Nguyen Cao Ky, the phone lines to U.S. embassy were cut just before assault in order to ensure Americans would not interfere with plan. Data per *Twenty Years and Twenty Days*, pp 35-36. SVN.

Nightrider - A call-sign of USMC HMM-164.

NILO - Naval Intelligence Liaison Officer.

NIMA - National Imagery and Mapping Agency (formerly the DMA). Most references in this book using term NIMA, refer to a NIMA Gazetteer of place names available for purchase on CD-ROM from the USGS, Denver CO.

Nixon Project, The -Because of the Nixon impeachment proceedings, all or most of Nixon's papers and letters related to the war are stored in what is known as the "Nixon Project" at the National Archives II, in College Park, MD. For more detail, go to: http://metalab.unc.edu/lia/president/nixon.html.
NLF - National Liberation Front. The Viet Cong.
NM - Nautical Miles (TAD).
NMCB - Naval Mobile Construction Battalion, & NCB.
NNE – North-North East.
NNW – North-North West.
no - number (TAD).
No Bomb Line - See NBL.
NOD - Night Observation Device. A.k.a. AN/TVS 2. Very large and powerful version of the Starlight Scope. Designed for mounting in fixed positions or on vehicles. In use as early as '68, and early use is described in *Father Soldier Son*, at p 135. See also Starlight Scope, AN/TVS 2 and POP Sites.
Nomad - Trade name for T-28 acft. 900 mi rnge, 285 kts top spd. mfgd by North American.
Nomads of Vietnam - Nickname of the 1st Bde, 101st Abn Div.
Northbrook - Call-sign for USMC Helo Sqdn HMM-164.
Northwest Operational Group - See GONO.
November Revolution, The – The coup that deposed Ngo Dinh Diem's regime on 1Nov63, became known as "The November Revolution."
NP - National Police.
NPIA - National Police Infrastructure Analysis Gazetteer, 1971-1973. The Hamlet Evaluation System (HES) electronic file held by NARA's CER. Originally compiled by the Viet Natl Police. A detailed and large file that, among other things, contains 6-digit grid coordinates for apx 12,500 SVN villages and relocation camps, as well as the corresponding VC/NVA name for each location. Available for purchase from: www.nara.gov/nara/electronic/def.html#armystaff.
NPRC - National Personnel Records Center. See also NARA.
nr - number (TAD).
NSA - Naval Support Activity (USN).
NSAD - U.S. Naval Support Activity Detachment.
ntc - notice (TAD).
NTC - RVNAF National Training Center.
Ntl - National.
Nui - Vietnamese word for mountain (as are Dong, Hon and Phu).
Nung - Mercenary soldiers, mostly of Chinese ancestry, employed and trained by US. In *Ambush*, S.L.A. Marshall described them as "prodigious guzzlers of beer" and stated that any group party they held that did not go on for at least 5 hours and include a 10 course meal was deemed a failure! Noted and respected for their skill and prowess as soldiers. Any male Nung was supposed to be at least 2d generation military. Nung riflemen were paid 5,100 Piasters/month in '66-67 (about $43 US), with an extra 400 Piasters as family allowance and addnl 1,000 Piasters if paratrooper-rated. Of that pay, 300 Piasters was deducted for rations. See also China Boy Battalion and C-3 Cmpd.
NVA - North Vietnamese Army (equivalent of PAVN).
NVA Air Force Bombing - See Determined to Win, Op.
NVA Helicopters - At various times during war, recon teams and others rptd what appeared to be NVA helos operating inside SVN. Apart from those rpts, to best of author's knowledge, no physical evidence has been provided to establish fact that NVA helo ops took place in SVN, even during the Final Offensive of Spring '75. However, *Tears Before the Rain* relates story of MSTS ship's Capt (Clinton Harriman, Jr), who rushed back to VN to rescue his Viet family and witnessed what he insists was an NVA helicopter op. Taking his family by back road from Saigon to Vung Tau, where he planned to meet USNS *Greenville Victory* for passage home, the group saw 2 helos land somewhere near Vung Tau. Harriman says, "Now I don't give a shit what some historian of this war will tell you, but I was there in that car and I know what I saw. I saw uniformed North Vietnamese soldiers with AK-47s getting out of helicopters" (per *Tears Before the Rain*, p 115). Dick Arnold notes that 1st/35th Inf, 4th Div logs rpt radar sightings of unknown aircraft, thought to have been NVA helos, W of Duc Co, in late Oct68. "They actually scrambled some 7th/17th Cav gunships at around 0400, and in ensuing 'dogfight,' Cav claimed to have shot down one chopper and possibly 'another unidentified aircraft.' Downed chopper was said to be in terrain too thick to get a fix on it. No mention of subsequent search, which seems odd, so may have been over the fence?" See also UFO Sightings.
NVA/VC propaganda leaflets - Wide variety of US, ARVN, NVA and VC leaflet samples can be found in *Vietnam Military Lore, 1959-1973*, pp 651-695, and on the internet at: www.en.com/users/ kramsey/propag1.html.
NVAF - North Vietnamese Air Force.
NVRS Transmissions - North Vietnamese "Rear Services" radio transmissions between waystations along the HCMT, and under the control of "Commo-Liaison Bureau." Beginning in '67-68, US/SVN intelligence gained ability to intercept and decode radio traffic between some of Binh Trams along trail. As a result, and for balance of war, MACV/ARVN HQ received quite accurate data on size, destination and progress of all personnel in pipeline, as well as volume of supplies being moved and stored. 1st intercept took place 1Nov67, and it referenced a number of grps in transit. By Mar68, 14 groups had been identified in transit. Through Mar-Apr68, 114 groups were identified (over 66,000 troops) as they moved toward Mini-Tet '68, and then in Jun68, large grps of wounded/sick of 304th Div were detected going N. See also Binh Tram, T-Stations and K-Intervals. Per *A Better War*, pp 47-50.
NW - Northwest.
O/R - on request (TAD).
O/S - out of service (TAD).
O-1 Bird Dog - Single eng, Cessna recon acft of WWII and Korean War vintage. Had 530 mi rnge, 115 kts top spd. mfgd by Cessna. Used throughout war by both U.S. and ARVN FACs.
O-2 Super-Skymaster - USAF recon acft. See Oscar Deuce.
obs - observe or observation.
obsn - observation (TAD).
obst - obstruction (TAD).
ODP - Orderly Departure Program for Vietnamese. Evac prgm created in 1980's to end dangerous and chaotic exodus of refugees from VN.
Officer's Cross-Legion of Honor - See *In articulo mortis*.
OH-1 Kiowa - 265 mi rnge, 138 kts top spd. mfgd by Bell Helo.
OH-64 Cayuse – Single-rotor observation helo, a.k.a. "Loach." Had 380 mi rnge, 150 kts top spd. mfgd by Hughes Acft.
OIC - Officer in Charge.
Old MacDonald Had a Farm -See *USS Canberra* in main alpha listing.
Old Man's Trail - See Ho Chi Minh Trail.

Old Reliables, The - Nickname of U.S. 9th Inf Div. Given that name by V Corps Cmdr Gen Huebner in dispatch during WWII, after 9th had captured Schwammennauel Dam, 12Feb45.
Old Tiger - A call-sign of USMC HMM 262.
Omega, Operation - Not a military Op, but privately-funded, post-war, alleged POW rescue mission. See also Lazarus, Op.
ONC - Operational Navigation Chart. Produced by DMA and currently marketed through NOAA. 1:1,000,000 scale, color, topo, aeronautical charts in which colors denote altitude rather than terrain composition. 1 inch equals apx 26 km on these charts.
One Zero - Call-sign for team leader of MAC-SOG recon team, (a.k.a. Prairie Fire team), and also used by their Cobra Supt Helo Team Leaders as well.
OOM - Officer's Open Mess.
OP - Observation Post or Outpost.
Op - Operation.
OP 60 - Code name for SOG's commo Div. Its advanced cryptographic gear maintained secure radio traffic with MACVSOG units in field. Was also testing pad for NSA's intercept-manipulate-block radio systems that interfered with NVA commo, in supt of SOG and other unrelated ops. Data per Jim Jones as gleaned from *SOG* and *The Secret War Against Hanoi*. See also Leghorn and MSS.
Opcon - Operational Control. Term meaning that unit was under the "operational control" of a unit to which it was not normally attached; typically a temporary solution as tactical needs arose. It was not unusual for Cos or Bns or even Rgts to be detached from a Div and sent to supt another Div (for example, elements of 502d Inf Rgt/101st Abn were opcon to Americal Div's 46th Inf Rgt during Op Lamar Plain, in '69).
Operation (*name*) - See operation's formal name in main alpha listing. Military operation (also Op and Ops in this text) entries are formatted with name first, followed by a comma and then the word "Operation" or "Op" (for example, "Cedar Falls, Operation"). There were literally thousands of named ops run during war, and those in this text are but a sampling of the more significant ones.
OPORD - Operational Order.
opr - operate, operator, operated (TAD).
OPS - Operations (TAD).
Ops - Operations.
Ord - Ordnance.
org - organization.
orgs - organizations.
Oriental River Front - See main alpha listing.
Orion - Trade name for P-3A, four-eng, turbo-prop, weather and ASW acft. 475 kts top spd. mfgd by Lockheed Acft.
ORL - Same as ORLL.
ORLL - Operational Report, Lessons Learned.
Oscar Deuce - Nickname for USAF O-2 recon acft and military version of a civilian acft. Was twin boom, push/pull acft, a.k.a. the "Cessna 337 Super Skymaster." Also nicknamed the "Push-Me-Pull-You" or "Suck and Blow" for its two 210 hp reciprocal engines, one mounted in nose (pulling) and other mounted at rear of the fuselage (pushing). Used by TASS sqdns in SCAR/FAC roles. "It was ordered by the USAF as a stop-gap after delivery of the OV-10 Bronco was delayed. The O-2A is used as FAC, the O-2B as psychological-ops acft." Per: http://topedge.com/panels/acft/sites/gustin/us/O2CESSNA.html. O-2 was often relegated to night ops while OV-10 was acft of choice for day ops. Had 1,060 mi rnge, 145 kts top spd. *Da Nang Diary* has detailed look at TASS ops and the OV-10.
OSS - Office of Strategic Services (precursor of the CIA).
OT - other times (TAD).
Outlaw - A call-sign of the 175th AHC.
OV-1 Mohawk - 1,300 mi rnge, 295 kts top spd. mfgd by Grumman Avn.
OV-10 Bronco - U.S. twin-eng, recon acft with 190 mi rnge, 280 kts top spd. mfgd by North American. See Oscar Deuce.
Over The Fence - Term signifying US/ARVN ops over SVN border in NVN, Laos or Cambodia.
overflt - overflight (TAD).
ovrn - overrun (TAD).
P - Civil aerodromes open to transient military acft (TAD).
P-2 Neptune - 3,685 mi rnge, 410 kts top spd. mfgd by Lockheed Acft.
P-3A Orion - U.S. 4-eng turboprop ASW and all-weather acft with 475 kts top spd. mfgd by Lockheed Acft.
P-5 Marlin Seaplane - See *Currituck, USS* (AV-7), for detail.
PACEX - Pacific Exchange. Mail order catalog service for U.S. forces featuring heavily discounted retail goods such as Japanese cameras, stereos, small household goods, jewelry and watches. Prices were very reasonable and much lower than stateside. Delivery could be taken in Vietnam or products sent to U.S.
Pachyderm - Call-sign for CH-46s of A Co, 159th Avn Bn.
Package - Term describing the various fixed-wing and helo assets used in MAC-SOG ops such as Prairie Fire. Each element of op was given a 2-letter alpha call-sign (i.e., Bravo-Lima, Delta-Echo, Foxtrot-Romeo, and so on) and, to ensure security, call-sign of each element was changed every day.
PACV - Patrol Air Cushion Vehicle (USN). See SK-5 PACV.
Page, Tim - See *Point Welcome* in main alpha list.
Pair-Off Operations - See main alpha listing.
Panama Control - USAF flight control ops serving following I Corps AFs: Da Nang, Hue/Phu Bai and Marble Mtn. Service courtesy USAF Tac Weapons Controller personnel H24, on frequencies 367.8, 133.2. See also Peacock and Paris Control.
Panther - Call-sign of 361st AWC Sqdn.
PAP - Pierced Aluminum Plank runway surface material.
Parakeet Flights - 9th Inf Div LRRP variant of Eagle Flight. Per *Rangers At War*, p 121, involved 4-man recon teams operating on Huey UH-1s that performed surprise boat inspections along IV Corps waterways. 1st Parakeet Team included Sgts Joseph Florio, and Bruce Sartwell, and SP4s Ralph Harter and Larry Huges.
Parasol/Switchback, Operation - 1963 program that supplied funding for CIDG program in VN. See also Op Switchback.
Paratroop Mafia - Para commandos of Col Langlais at Dien Bien Phu, who on 24Mar54 took cmd away from Gen de Castries after he suffered a mental breakdown and was ineffectual.
Paris Control - USAF Flight control operations serving following III Corps AFs: Tan Son Nhut, Bien Hoa, Vung Tau (radar vector assistance to numerous Army airfields). Service courtesy USAF Tac Weapons Controller personnel H24, on frequencies 347.9, 133.2. See also Panama and Peacock Control.
Paris Peace Accords - Formally known as "Agreement on Ending the War and Restoring Peace in Vietnam." Initialed on 23Jan73, and signed 27Jan73, ending 4 years and 9 months of negotiations in what Lewis Sorely called "The longest peace

negotiations of the century." Involved 202 open sessions and 24 pvt meetings. As a result, 591 U.S. POWs were released, and at its signing, only 27,000 U.S. troops remained in SVN. Final increment of U.S. troops left VN 29Mar73, leaving behind only a Defense Attaché Office (DAO). At time, there were also about 13 NVA Divs and 75 Rgts still in SVN (apx 160,000 troops), and during '73, NVA added 100,000 more. Per *A Better War*, the flood south became so bad that NVA were moving in open during daylight hours and huge traffic jams were occurring along QL-1 in I Corps as result. By 14Mar73, Henry Kissinger had become so agitated by NVA's blatant disregard for treaty that he sent formal memo to President Nixon requesting permission to reintroduce B-52 bombing immediately after 3d contingent of U.S. POWs was released on 16Mar73 (but inexplicably, before 4th and last contingent was to be released?). Nixon actually approved plan and initialed the memo "Approve." It is not clear what happened after that, although we do know it was not executed. Soon after accords were signed, Div-sized attacks were launched against: Cua Viet; Sa Huynh (later retaken by 2d ARVN with hvy losses); Hong Ngu (ARVN soon pushed NVA back to Cambodia); Tong Le Chan (a.k.a. Tonle Cham) ARVN Border Ranger Camp (defended by 1 ARVN Bn under siege for a month beginning Mar73, that only fell after 20 grnd attacks and 300 shellings of 10,000 rnds of arty, rocket and mortar fire); Trung Nghia (a.k.a. Polei Breng,. Took ARVN until Sep70 to dislodge NVA here with hvy losses on both sides). SVN govt rptd that during '73, some 80,000 ARVN had been KIA in post-Paris Peace Accord fighting; surprisingly the ARVN's greatest troop lost in any year. See also Fullbright-Aiken Amendment. Data per *A Better War*, pp 362-370.

pat - pattern (TAD).

Patti Mission, The - On 22Aug45, OSS officer named Lou Conein parachuted near Hanoi's *Place de la Theatre* in order to determine whether Japanese still holding capitol would honor Japan's coming surrender and allow landing of the 2 acft that had dropped him in. Acft were carrying what became known as Patti Mission under cmd of U.S. Army Maj Archimedes Patti. He and most of U.S. OSS team came in on 1st acft, while Jean Sainteny (whom Charles de Gaulle had named "Commissioner of Indochina") and Free French officials anxious to regain control of VN came in on 2d. Japanese allowed U.S. OSS to roam Hanoi freely, but put French contingent under armed guard. After Ho Chi Minh and his Vietminh cmd entered Hanoi 26Aug45, Ho and Patti had many mtgs, in one of which Ho asked Patti for copy of U.S. *Declaration of Independence*. Patti had no copy but related much of it from memory, which Ho then used in his own *Declaration of Vietnam Independence*. Mission was terminated 1Oct45. For discussion of Patti Mission and its principals see, *Facing the Phoenix*, pp 43-76.

Pave Way - Code name for laser-guided 2,000 lb. bomb introduced in '70(?). Required target designator acft that bathed target with laser while attack acft maneuvered to roll in directly over target-designator acft and release bomb into path of laser. Bomb then locked on beam and flew along it to target. Noted for its precise accuracy but necessary choreography put acft in jeopardy from AAA fire by forcing them into fixed and predictable patterns. Per *Da Nang Diary*, p 41.

PAVN - People's Army of Vietnam (a.k.a. NVA).

pax - passengers or personnel (TAD).

PBR - Patrol Boat River. A.k.a. Mark II PBR, and smaller than the PCF (Swift Boat). Due to small size, generally restricted to rivers and canals, though apparently used for close-in coastal waters also.

PBR - Patrol Boat, River.

PC - Submarine Chaser (Patrol Craft) (USN).

PC - Submarine Chaser.

PCE - Patrol Escort (USN).

PCER - Rescue Escort (USN).

PCF - Patrol Craft, Fast, a.k.a. "Swift Boats." Used in Mekong Delta to interdict contraband, provide fire supt for maneuvering grnd troops, and deliver and extract (sometimes under fire) troops along the many river/canal banks of area. Larger than the PBR.

PCOD Lounge - Personnel Coming Off Duty Lounge. SF nomenclature for their on-base clubs/bars.

PCS - Permanent Change of Station.

Peacemaker - Trade name for AU-23A acft. 555 mi rnge, 165 kts top spd. mfgd by Fairchild Acft.

Peach - Per *Rites of Passage*, in '67 was 1st/14th Inf/25th Div radio code for an ambush position, as was term "Custer," among other words. 3d Bde/25th Div periodically changed word to confuse enemy.

Peacock Control, Vietnam - USAF Flight control operations serving following II Corps AFs: Pleiku (USAF/VNAF) and Phu Cat (VNAF). Service courtesy USAF Tac Weapons Controller personnel H24, on frequencies 345.0, 248.6, 133.2. See also Panama and Paris Control.

Pedro - Call-sign of HH-43 Husky local base rescue acft.

Pelican - A call-sign of the 161st AHC.

People's Anti-Corruption Movement - Conference of some 300 SVN Catholic Priests formed in Jun74. Grp called for end to widespread corruption evident at all levels of SVN govt, and issued declaration accusing the "Government Mafia" of black market speculation and control of such commodities and sidelines as prostitution, gambling, drug traffic, fertilizer, insecticides, rice, raw materials, pharmaceuticals, "in order to plunder the people and enrich the wealthy." In Hue 2 months later, their leader, Father Tran Huu Thanh issued what was called "Public Indictment #1;" leveling charges of graft, heroin smuggling and illegal dealings in rice and fertilizer trade at President Thieu, his family, and number of ministers. Catholic demonstrations were broken up and Thieu confiscated all editions of newspapers that printed the indictment; however, he also acted by promising reform and soon had fired a number of generals, 4 cabinet ministers. His Defense Ministry also fired 377 corrupt Army Cols. Instead of easing pressure in response, Father Thanh then issued "Indictment #2," accusing Mrs., Thieu of corrupt land speculation and President Thieu of treason. Thieu again responded by confiscating or suppressing any newspapers that printed #2, and by arresting 18 journalists. Data per *Twenty Years and Twenty Days*, p 111-113.

Peoples' Self Defense Force - The PSDF. SVN hamlet-based self-defense org that by end of '69 had grown to 1,300,000 armed men and women, plus addnl 1,750,000 women, children and elderly in supt role. During '69, SVN govt sponsored nationwide, 4-day trng sessions for units. PSDF was meant to augment territorial forces of RF/PF. Gen Abrams thought RF/PF in concert with PSDF were an key component if hampering VCI ops was to succeed. Data per *A Better War*, p 172. SVN.

Percival, Captain John "Mad Jack" - See *Constitution, USS*, in main alpha listing.
perm - permanent (TAD).
Permanent Observation Posts - See POP Sites.
perms - permission (TAD).
pers - personnel (TAD).
Personnel Feminin de "'Armee de Terre - See PFAT.
Pets of Note - See Camp Hill, Camp Land, Tiger's Den, and Vung Tau Army AF in main alpha listing.
PF - Popular Forces.
PFAT - *Personnel Feminin de "'Armee de Terre*. French Army Women Soldiers Corps. By 1953, over 2,000 women were working with French grnd forces in Indochina. An additional 120 were in Air Force, 30 in Navy, while apx 470 officers'/officials' wives were hired by Army as civilian assistants. Almost 100 these troops were KIA during French War. French also had different approach to problem of pregnancy than U.S. military. Rather than dismiss their pregnant soldiers, they built special camps where troops continued as productive contributors in clerical and other appropriate positions until children were born and, if practical, soldier then returned to original post. See *Street Without Joy*, Chp 6, and also IPSA, Women Combatants, and FIS.
PFF - See Police Field Force and White Mice. SVN.
PFOD - Presumptive Finding of Death. DOD reclassification review process of MIA cases frequently resulted in this determination, which terminated a missing casualty's MIA status and military's economic supt of surviving family. Was very contentious issue among POW/MIA advocates in 70's and 80's.
PFSV - Pilot Forecast Service (TAD).
PFTC - RVNAF Popular Force Training Center.
PG - Patrol Gunboat.
PGH - Patrol Gunboat Hydrofoil (USN).
PGH - Patrol Gunboat.
PGM - Motor Gunboat (USN).
Pha - Dam and Pha were Viet words for "lagoon" or "estuary."
Phan Huy Quat - Briefly Prime Minister of SVN. Following Gen. Phat's failed attempt to oust PM Gen Khanh's govt on 18Feb65, the Armed Forces Council replaced Gen Khanh (who had been appointed PM by council only weeks earlier to replace PM Huong) with Phan Huy Quat. Quat did not like job and resigned 12Jun65. Nguyen Cao Ky then succeeded him and remained PM until Ky ordered national elections in May67.
Phantom – Trade name for U.S. F-4 Fighter-Bomber.
Phantom II - Trade name for F-4 twin-jet fighter-bomber; land and carrier-based. Provided close air supt, bombing and bomber escort duties. 1,750-2300 mi rnge, 1500. mfgd by McDonnell.
PHILCAG-V - Philippine Civic Action Group, Vietnam. See PHILCAG in Major Cmd Section
Phoenix – Call-sign of C Co, 158th Avn Bn.
Phoenix Program - A.k.a. "Phuong Hoang" (the all-seeing bird). Super-secret counter-terrorist op run principally by ARVN SF operatives assisted by U.S. SF and CIA. In Jul68, general concept of attacking VCI directly was approved by President Thieu when he signed document creating the Accelerated Pacification Campaign (began 1Nov68 following NVN bombing halt and primarily an SVN op). That concept evolved into Phoenix Prgm as U.S. CIA gradually increased its participation. Arguably Phoenix was one of most effective (if also most controversial) U.S. ops of war where stopping VC/NVA aggression was concerned. Designed to attack VCI at individual level rather than on battlefield, by rooting it out where it lived via intricate intel web. Rumors that over 20,000 Vies were "murdered" by Phoenix appear to have been greatly exaggerated, as were most other body counts of war. In any case, while abuses may have occurred to some degree, it nonetheless proved to be extremely effective, a point emphasized by NVA after war's conclusion. In '71-72, MACV Advs (such as MACV Adv Team 72, Muc Hoa) apparently suptd prgm. For more data, see *A Better War, Facing the Phoenix*, and particularly *Slow Burn* (by Orrin DeForest, who was III Corps CIA intel chief in '68). Data per *A Better War*, pp 65-69.
Phou – One of several Vietnamese words for "mountain."
Phougas - A.k.a. Fougas and Fougasse. Napalm (jellied gasoline) deployed as perimeter defensive weapon. Was an area weapon typically consisting of 55-gal, napalm-filled drums placed strategically around perimeters of a base. Were cmd-detonated by detonation of claymore mines strapped to drums.
Phu – One of several Vietnamese words for mountain.
Phung Hoang - RVNAF name for their portion of Phoenix Program. Targeted elimination of VC infrastructure (VCI). See Phoenix Program.
Phuong – One of several Vietnamese words for village.
Piastre - Unit of SVN currency. In '65, one Piaster (or Piaster) was equiv of apx one U.S. cent. Exchange-rate went as high as 160 Piasters per U.S. dollar, per *VN Military Lore, 1959-1973*, p 276.
Pig - See M-60 Machine Gun.
PIM - French acronym for *Prisonner-Interne Militare* (POW).
Pink Rose - Forest fire research project in which UC-123B's 1st sprayed area with defoliant, then B-52Ds carpeted area with M-35 Incendiaries set to detonate at various levels within foliage. Tests run Jan67, apx 16 km N of Tay Ninh and 8 km W An Loc. Similar tests conducted Feb66 on Chu Pong Mtn in Ia Drang Valley (perhaps more to punish NVA for LZ X-Ray/Albany battles than to test tactic). See also Flame Drop and Flame Bath.
Pink Team - See Hunter-Killer.
Pink Teams – POP-based teams that observed main infiltration rtes into the Da Nang Vital Area. See Pink Team in main alpha list, and IOD in Glossary.
Pipe Smoke Operations - Code name of downed-acft recovery missions employing CH-47 Chinook and CH-54 Tahre heavy lift helos. CH-47 proved especially valuable in program, recovering apx 12,000 acft valued at over $3 billion during war. Per: www.acala1.ria.army.mil/acala/sma/asa/AAHIST.HTM#CH47
PIRAZ - Positive Identification Radar Advisory Zone.
Pistol Pete - A call-sign of USMC HMA-369.
Pistol Pete - Per John Cushman (CO 2d Bde/101st Abn '67-68), Pistol Pete was call-sign of USN Swift Boat (or unit) patrolling the Song Huong (Perfume) River from Hue to ocean (call-sign may have been "Sweet Banner 65"?).
PIT - Plantation Indochinoise de The´.
Play Time - Time-span over which fighter acft could loiter over a target. Normally only about 5-10 min.
Playtex - Call-sign for CH-46s of C Co/159th Avn Bn.
Plt - Platoon.
Plt Ldr - Platoon Leader.

Pluto Fire Missions - Royal Australian and RNZA Arty's nickname of what were called H&I (Harassment and Interdiction) missions by U.S. Arty.
PN - Prior Notice Required (TAD).
POL - Petroleum, Oil, Lubricants.
Polecat - A call-sign of the 192d AHC.
Police Field Force - A.k.a. "PFF." Per *A Better War*, p 147, during '68, apx 10,000 men were added to Viet Natl Police to create this division (upping force to 80,000). Its purpose was to increase focus of that org on getting at heart of VC Infrastructure. Historically, Natl Police had been a colonial force acting to preserve govt from the people, but this novel change gradually shifted it to providing protection and law and order to the people, which apparently increased its effectiveness and popularity markedly.
Polka-Dot T'ai – See T'ai Tribes in Glossary.
Polygamy - Practice of taking multiple wives was legal in Vietnam until '58. Per *Street Without Joy*, p 131.
Pop - Population or populace.
Pop Gun - FAC pilot nickname for M-60 MGs mounted on FAC OV-10 Broncos and other FAC acft. See *Da Nang Diary*, p 195.
Pop Gun - See main alpha listing.
POP Sites - In '69, 11th Marine Arty Rgt developed "Permanent Observation Post" system to observe main infiltration rtes into Da Nang Vital Area. Sites were set to cover following areas: N Da Nang/Hill 190 covering Elephant Valley and Hai Van Pass approaches; W Da Nang/Hill 270, covering approaches from Happy Valley, Mortar Valley, Sherwood Forest and Charlie Ridge; and, Hill 65/Hill 250, covering Thuong Duc Corridor; S Da Nang/Hill 425 (in Que Son Mtns), covering Phu Loc and An Hoa Basin; Hill 119, covering Go Noi Island and Dodge City; and FSB Ryder covering Antenna Valley and N Que Son Valley. Sites employed very expensive and accurate target locating device called an IOD (see IOD for detail).
Pork and Shrapnel - Nickname for LRRP ration meal labeled "Chile Con Carne." See also LRRP Rations and C-Rations.
Porter's Bull - A call-sign of USMC HMM-261.
Possums - Call-sign of 161 Reconnaissance Flight (161 Recce Flt www.161recceflt.org.au).
Poste Kilometre - Typically abbreviated "PK." Concrete "mileage" markers lining major roadways of Vietnam and spaced exactly 1 km apart. Were numbered in sequence as they moved away from major cities. Military facilities in VN were named in relation to PK nearest them, particularly during French War. See also French Fort Construction, *de Lattre Line*, and PK.
Potsdam Agreement - During the Potsdam meetings of Jul45, the combined chiefs of staff of western allies agreed that southern part of VN would be put under cmd of British Adm Lord Montbatten (then Supreme Cmdr of Southeast Asia Theater). Was also decided that Nationalist Chinese under cmd of Generalissimo Chaing Kai-Shek (Chinese were ready to accept Ho Chi Minh's new govt) would move to Hanoi to accept Japanese surrender. British however wanted French to regain control (for fear its own empire might collapse from example of a free VN), and on 12Sep45, landed a Ghurka Bn and a Co of Free French in Saigon and, 11 days later, helped French overthrow Saigon's Vietminh govt putting SVN back in French hands. Per *Facing the Phoenix*, p 55.
Pouvoir - Motto of 227th AHB. Is French word for "Power" and roughly equiv to "Can Do."
POW - Prisoner of War.
Power Glide – Call-sign for USMC's HMM 263, H-34 Medium Helicopter Sqdn.
PPB - Platoon Patrol Bases. 9th Inf Div term for small pltn-sized defensive positions that did not include arty. Mentioned in *Doc: Platoon Medic*, p 35.
PPB - Platoon Patrol Bases. See main alpha listing.
PPR - Prior Permission Required (TAD).
Pr - Province.
Prairie Fire - Term "Prairie Fire" used as phrase in radio traffic by a Prairie Fire LRRP Team was code its mission had been compromised, team was in great danger and required immediate extraction. See also Prairie Fire Ops.
Prairie Fire FACs – Specially selected 6-pilot element of 20th TASS (call-sign "Covey") that flew top-secret FAC missions "across the fence" in supt of MAC-SOG Prairie Fire Ops. See also MLT-2, Prairie Fire Ops, Covey CCN and MACV-SOG.
Prairie Fire Operations - Code name for very sensitive and very secret cross-border MAC-SOG/SF recon missions in Laos, NVN and DMZ. Joint-service project for gathering intel in those places using small LRRP teams. Its AO extended 33 km into Laos and same distance N of DMZ. 5th SF Grp personnel generally ran these ops in conjunction with "Covey" (20th TASS, Da Nang) FAC cover. Phrase "Prairie Fire" as used in radio traffic was code indicating Prairie Fire Team's mission had been compromised and that it was in great danger requiring immediate extraction.
PRC-9 - See AN/PRC9.
PRC-10 - See AN/PRC-10.
PRC-25 - See AN/PRC-25.
PRC-77 - See AN/PRC-77.
Precinct Five - See main alpha listing.
prgm - program
PRIME BEEF - "Prime Base Engineer Emergency Force." Engr teams drawn from USAF resources prior to '66, and augmented by apx 300 Viet civilian workers. Prgm was replaced by RED HORSE prgm. See Red Horse.
Prisonner-Interne Militare - French phrase meaning POW, and abbreviated as PIM by French forces.
Private Delta Force - Privately-funded POW rescue grp formed in 1985 by former Army Ranger, Mike Van Atta. Was disbanded after several months of media-hype and fruitless fundraising. Discussed in *Prisoners of Hope*, pp 145-148.
Privateer - Long-range, French naval acft used in VN beginning in 1951. Eight were used ineffectively by French Far Eastern AF in bomber roll. See *Street Without Joy*, p 261.
prk - park (TAD).
prkg - parking (TAD).
proh - prohibited (TAD).
Project 100,000 - After a 1964 federal TF found military was annually rejecting 600,000 men based on low GCT scores, and concluded at least some of those 600,000 were really qualified, a prgm known as "Project 100,000" was instituted to expand available pool of manpower. Experiment required Army and USMC enlist at least 100,000 low-scoring individuals annually. Oddly enough, under prgm it was necessary for military to turn-away better-qualified volunteers. Troops brought-in were called "Category Four Enlistees" or "Cat Fours." Beginning in Oct66, DOD required military to accept 40,000 Cat Fours, and 100,000 each year thereafter. Prgm was universally regarded as an unmitigated disaster, especially by Judge Advocate Corps who later dealt with manifold legal

problems that resulted. MGen R. Tompkins, CG of 3rd Mar Div, noted dryly that a Category Four soldier "was a guy who could see lightning and hear thunder, maybe." Per *Son Thang Four*, pp 131-133.

Project 404 - U.S. "civilian" mission in Vientiane Laos that oversaw Lao bombing campaigns from '66 on. Apparently included CIA and USAF officers masquerading as civilians or U.S. State Dept officials. Projects 406 and 603 were apparently adjuncts of Project 404. See also *Arm'ee Clandestine*.

Project 406 - See Project 404 and *Arm'ee Clandestine*. CIA/Air America ops in Laos.

Project 603 - See Project 404 and *Arm'ee Clandestine*. CIA/Air America ops in Laos.

Project 9024 - In Feb67, 11th Marine Engrs initiated Project 9024 to repair and reopen QL-9 from Cam Lo to Khe Sanh, after it had been closed by flooding and washouts since '64. On 27Mar67, a "Rough Rider Convoy of some 76 heavily laden vehicles made the first (and unopposed) convoy to Khe Sanh. See QL-9.

Project Arizona - SOG code for Cambodia and secret ops there.

Project B-36, Operation - See B-36 and Rapid Fire.

Project B-50 - See Project Omega.

Project B-56 - See Project Sigma.

Project Delta, Operation - Nha Trang, 5th SF Grp Det B-52 (Project Delta). SOG code name for early clandestine ops in Laos, Cambodia and NVN. Originally a MACV-SOG project to train CIDG troops that was launched in May64. Transferred to 5th SF in '68, and renamed Project Delta (a.k.a. Det B-52). Had 450 troops split into dozen recon teams dressed as VC and NVA (to infiltrate enemy units). Also consisted of Nung troops and 91st ARVN Ranger Bn. After Sep66, Project Delta also trained U.S. Inf in LRRP tactics. See also Shining Brass, New York and Arizona.

Project Douche - See Water Cannons.

Project Dye Marker - Jul67 revised code-name for McNamara's Wall. See McNamara, and Projects Practice Nine and Illinois City.

Project Embankment - Code name for advance element of OSS under cmd of 1Lt Emile R. Connase, who with 6 other agents parachuted into Saigon, 1Sep45. Objective was to locate U.S. POWs held by Japanese at Camp Poet (5 POWs) and Camp 5-E (209 POWs). Unit set up in Continental Palace Hotel and made it a neutral safe-haven for French civilians evading Viet anti-French demonstrations and rioting that erupted 2Sep45. On 4Sep45, Maj Dewey flew into Ohi AF and took cmd of unit. Data per *Vietnam Military Lore, Legends, Shadows, and Heroes*, p 11. See also Camp Poet and Camp 5-E in main alpha listing.

Project Enhance - As U.S. troop levels plummeted to 69,000 in Jun72, and 49,000 in Jul72 as U.S. withdrew, MACV initiated ambitious prgm to replace staggering equip/supply losses suffered by SVN during '72 Easter Offensive, and to prepare SVN for America's complete departure. It gave ARVN large number of M-48 tanks, TOW anti-tank missiles and 175mm cannons, among other things. Was followed by 2d phase known as "Enhance Plus." See also Enhance Plus. Data per *A Better War*, pp 343-349.

Project Enhance Plus - 2d phase of "Project Enhance." Both projects were designed to replace equip/supplies lost by ARVN during '72 Easter Offensive. Toward the end of '72 during 2d phase, 100,000 tons of equip, 9 sqdns of acft and 36 amphib vehicles were added to tanks, missiles and cannons of 1st phase, in frantic, last-minute effort to equip SVN before restrictions of Paris Peace Accords became effective (and, some say to assuage U.S. guilt). Soviet-bloc responded to same needs of NVA by shipping twice the materials to NVN in '72 as it had shipped in '71. Data per *A Better War*, pp 343-349.

Project Illinois City - Jun67 code name for McNamara's Wall. See McNamara, Project Practice Nine and Project Dye Marker.

Project Leaping Lena - See Project Delta.

Project Omega - 5th SF Grp, Det B-50. Consisted of 900 CIDG and 125 U.S. SF personnel. Originally based at Nha Trang and later moved to Ban Me Thuot. Was meant to have an ARVN Ranger Bn attached but SF were unhappy with arrangement and instead provided its own Mike Force Cos (three), calling them Commando Cos. B-50 conducted raids, exploited small unit contacts, acted as reaction force, gathered intel and later evolved into Mobile Guerrilla Force concept in '67, and then into MACV-SOG in Nov67. B-50 had 8 recon teams (later increased to 16) as well as 4 (and later 8) Road Runner Teams. Road Runners consisted of 4 indigenous troops posing as VC who operated in enemy areas gathering intel. In '68, Road Runner teams were moved to Det B-57. Ethnic Chinese, Rhade Montagnard, Cham, Sedang and Jah tribal members were recruited for such units. B-50 initiated, Jul66.

Project Phoenix – See main alpha listing.

Project Pot Luck – In late '68, MACV CG Gen Creighton Abrams ordered 525th Military Intel Grp to secretly train in firing NVA's, 107mm, 122mm and 140mm rockets in hope of firing some into Cambodia to disrupt NVA staging areas. 122s had a range of roughly 7,000 yards and were accurate to between 200-800 meters. Purpose of using enemy munitions was they could not be traced back to US. 1 officer and 10 EMs were assigned task, and once team had familiarized itself with large supply of rockets captured during Tet-68, Abrams choose an NVA basecamp near Fishhook as first target due a paucity of civilians in that area. He then asked JCS for permission to fire 20, delay-fused 122s across border and into camp. Apparently JCS wasn't amused by plan and said "Hell no," so Abrams ordered all records of short-lived adventure be destroyed. Data per *A Better War*, pp 95-96.

Project Practice Nine - (XD/YD) Original Code name for McNamara's Wall. See McNamara. Also code named Project Dye Marker and Project Illinois City at various times.

Project Rapid Fire - A.k.a. B-36 Project Rapid Fire. IIFFV SF transient special warfare/recon unit created at Gen Westmoreland's request and designed to provide recon screen around Saigon until regular LRRP Co could be trained/assigned to task. Created in Fall of 67(?) by shifting all 173d Abn Bde LRRPs from 173d to IIFFV cmd just before 173d moved from III to II Corps. III Corps.

Project Shining Brass - See Shining Brass.

Project Sigma - Created Aug66, 5th SF Det B-56 project using apx 900 CIDG and 125 U.S. SF personnel. Conducted special raids, did BDAs, gathered intel and later evolved into MGF and then into MACV-SOG in Nov67. Originally at H Ngoc Nau near Saigon.

Project Tiger Hound - See Tiger Hound Operation.

Project Urgency - Apparent top-secret MAC-SOG U.S. op detailed in national security historian Richard Schulz Jr's, *The Secret War Against Hanoi*. According to Schulz, op involved planting incriminating evidence in clothing of hand-picked NVA POW's, who were then choppered or parachuted back into NVN. Incriminating materials/documents were sewn or hidden in men's clothing for potential discovery by NVA/NVN when POW made his way back to NVN completely unaware he had been framed. Presumably, these innocent victims would then be charged with espionage and executed. Apparent purpose was to confuse and demoralize NVA into thinking many more spies had infiltrated NVN than imagined. Schulz also notes MAC-SOG conducted similar op in which NVN fishermen were kidnapped, blindfolded and spirited to SVN island (disguised as NVN ville) which they were told was HQ of the *Sacred Sword of the Patriots League,* a fictitious anticommunist org made up of SVN govt operatives. 3 weeks later, fishermen were again blindfolded and returned to point of capture. Hope was that after this indoctrination the men would then disseminate news that rebel force had "liberated" a portion of NVN. Schulz says that between '64 and '68, as many as 1,000 NVN civilians were kidnapped and run through this bizarre prgm. Data per *New York Times* article by James Risen, reprinted in 4Nov99 *Sacramento Bee* Newspaper, p A-8.

Propaganda Leaflets - Wide variety of US, ARVN, NVA and VC samples is in *Vietnam Military Lore, 1959-1973*, pp 651-695, and on internet at: www.en.com/users/kramsey/propag1.html.

Prospector – Call-sign of the 49th Avn Co working out of Phan Rang and Dak To, '65-66.

Prosperity Centers - See Agrovilles.

Prostitutes Recommended for the *Croix de Guerre* - See Tsinh Ho in main alpha listing.

Prostitution - See BMC-*Bordel Mobile de Campaigne* in Glossary and FOB 2, Hazel's Whorehouse, Meat Market, Million Fingers Massage Parlor, Saigon, and Sin City in main alpha listing.

Prov - Province.

Provs - Provinces.

Provider - Trade name for C-123 twin-eng, prop-driven STOL transport 1,470 mi rnge, 175 kts top spd. mfgd by Fairchild Acft.

PRS-3 - See AN/PRS-3 AN/PRS-3.

PRT4 - See AN/PRC9.

Prvs - Provinces.

PS Sites – Variant or typo error of "LS." Said to have been SF/CIA clandestine AFs scattered throughout Laos and on Bolovens Plateau in supt Royal Loa Forces against Pathet Lao and encroaching NVA. Were focal point of Air-America and SF activities, and drew many attacks as result. Each was simply designated by two letters "PS" (likely LS) followed by numerical reference such as "PS-39." See Also X-Ray Ops, and Raven FACs. Origin "PS" abbreviation unknown and this author suspects it is typo of LS. See also LS Sites.

PSD - Personal Seismic Detectors.

PSDF - Peoples Self-Defense Force.

PSP - Pierced Steel Planking.

PSP - Pierced Steel Planking. Prefab metal panels used to construct rwys and in bunker const throughout war zone.

PSYOPS - Psychological Operations.

PT - Motor Torpedo Boat.

PT - Patrol Torpedo, a.k.a. Motor Torpedo Boat (USN).

pt - point(s) (TAD).

PTF - Fast Patrol Boat (USN).

Public Indictment #2 - See People's Anti-Corruption Movement.

PUC - Presidential Unit Citation.

Puff - Popular Force militia. See Ruff/Puff. Also slang for "Puff the Magic Dragon" AC-47 Gunship.

Puff the Magic Dragon - Spooky, Spectre and Shadow were respective code names for AC-47, AC-130 and AC-119 fixed-wing gunships of USAF. Noted for their awesome multi mini-gun (even 105mm howitzer) firepower, and also for their ability to provide long-term air and flare supt. Greatly feared by enemy. Generic name for all was often "Puff the Magic Dragon" after a popular *Peter, Paul and Mary* folk song of era.

Pukin' Buzzards - Humorous nickname for the 101st Abn Div, derived from image of screaming eagle on its Div patch.

Purple Heart - A.k.a. the "PH" or "wound medal." During VN war, decoration was awarded to any soldier for wounds received in action against a hostile force in an area defined as being within the VN combat zone by Presidential Order. On 24Apr64, President Kennedy signed Exec order retroactively allowing U.S. Servicemen wounded in SVN to receive the PH effective 15Mar62. At least 303,000 PHs were awarded to U.S. servicemen during War. See Also Vietnam Service Medal.

Push-Me-Pull-You - See Oscar Deuce.

PVS 2 - See AN/PVS 2.

Pvt – Private (rank).

pvt – private (ownershp).

pvtly – privately.

PX - Post Exchange.

QGO - International Morse Code signal for low visibility.

QL - (Rte Type Identifier) Designator for major Natl/Intl roads of VN's transportation system. Were highest quality roads and typically inc one or two-digits enclosed in shield map symbol. See also QL, LTL, TL, Route, Highway, HL, R. C., *Route Colonial* (all in Glossary).

QM - Quartermaster.

QRF - Quick Reaction Force.

qtrs - quarters (TAD).

QU-22B Beechcraft - Military version of twin-eng, 6-place, Bonanza Beechcraft acft used in various intel ops (including Pave Eagle) though few knew it ever served in VN. In '68, some were modified for remote control and flown on pilotless intel missions over the HCMT in Laos.

quad - quadrant (TAD).

Quad Fifties - A.k.a. Quad .50. Track or vehicle-mounted 4-barreled .50 caliber heavy machine guns that traversed from a single pedestal and fired simultaneously by one gunner. See LZ Mustang at BR 770-980 for example of one mounted on pedestal in fixed position of FSB perimeter.

Quan - Viet word for "District." Was political subdivision of a Prov. For example, Quan Nam Hoa is district of Thua Thien Prov. See also Thinh.

Quan Doi Nhan Dan - Newspaper of People's Army. NVN.

Quarter Cav - Nickname of U.S. 1st/4th Armored Cavalry.

Queen - Call-sign for OL-A, the USAF Rescue Coordination Center at Tan Son Nhut AB.

Queen's Cobras - Per *Webster's New World Dictionary of the Vietnam War*, was nickname for Rgt of RTA forces that were part of Thailand's SEATO contingent in VN. The Royal Thai Army Expeditionary Force (a.k.a. the Black Panthers, and later renamed Royal Thai Army Volunteer Force) arrived Fall of '67, and eventually grew into three Bde Div consisting of 1st, 2d and 3d Bdes, 4 Bns RTA Div arty, an armored cav sqdn, supt avn, MPs, Div HQ and a LRP Co.

Quiet Star - See YO-3A Quiet Star.

Quoc Nhu - "The National Language." Modern Latin-based Viet alphabet was introduced by Alexandre de Rhodes in the early 1600s, but it was not until 1920 that 1st dictionary using "Quoc Nhu" was published. See also Rhodes, Alexandre.
R&R – A.k.a. Rest & Recreation or Rest & Recuperation. An out-of-country 7-day leave given to each soldier during their VN tour. Only one per tour was allocated, though other R&Rs could be had if need for personnel was light in a given unit, one had leave time on the books, and space was available on flight. Transportation was free, but lodging and food were normally at soldier's expense. Bangkok, Tokyo, Taipei, Sydney, Hong Kong and Hawaii were among authorized sites; however, only married soldiers were allowed to take R&R in Hawaii (DOD was concerned that R&R on U.S. soil might lead to higher desertion and AWOL rates). There were also in-country R&R sites at places like Eagle Beach, China Beach, Cam Ranh Bay and Vung Tau, where stays were usually limited to 2-3 days. See also I & I.
R in C - Rest in Country. ANZAC equiv to U.S. in-country R&R.
R. C. - *Route Coloniale.* Colonial French prefix for road identification common on early maps of Vietnam.
R.I.C.M. - *Regiment d' Infanterie du Coloniale Maroc.* Motorized Moroccan Colonial Armored Infantry of 1st Indochina War. Key force during Op Lea, Oct47, per *Street Without Joy*, p 29. NVN.
R/W - Rotary Wing (TAD).
RA - Regular Army.
RA-5C Vigilante - A-5 Vigilante configured to fly aerial recon missions. Had 3,200 mi rnge, 1,385 kts top spd. mfgd by North American. Introduced in '58, and designed for long-range, single nuclear weapon delivery, but proved unsuitable to task. Its twin engines were capable of Mach 2.5 and it's bomb bay was converted to carry pod containing photo, electronic and several forms of SLAR. Proved to be excellent for this role. USN Cmdr Joe Gerber was among the last, or very last, U.S. pilot to fly recon missions over VN when, in '75, he flew number of recons over Saigon area as part of Op frequent Wind, Apr75.
RAA - Royal Australian Artillery.
RAC - Reconnaissance Airplane Company.
Rach - Stream or arroyo (& Cao, Khe, Song, Rao).
rad - radius (TAD).
RAD - River Assault Division (USN).
Radio Singapore - When at altitude during 1st Indochina War, U.S. pilots of CAT would often tune in British news broadcasts from Singapore. They could also tune in musical "jam sessions" on Voice of America broadcasting from Manila. Per *Street Without Joy*, pp 108-109.
RAF - River Assault Force.
RAFO - River Assault Flotilla One.
RAG - River Assault Group.
RAID - River Assault-Interdiction Div. A.k.a. Riverine Assault Interdiction Division. (USN).
RAIR - Royal Australian Infantry Rgt.
Ranch Hand, Operation - USAF chemical defoliation and herbicide missions flown by C-123, C-130 and other acft between Jan62-Feb71, designed to rob enemy of forest cover and food resources. During those 10 years, some 19.7 million gallons of herbicides (Agent Orange among others) were sprayed over some 5.7 million acres of SVN and Laos (Laos Ranch Hand Ops ran between Dec65-Sep69).
Rao – One Viet word for stream.
RAPCON - Radar Approach Control (USAF/TAD).
RAR - Royal Australian Rgt.
RAS - River Assault Squadron (USN).
Ratissages - French for "mop-up."
Rattler - A call-sign of the 71st AHC.
Raven - Call-sign of USAF FAC acft operating in Laos.
Raven - Trade name for F-111A all-weather, twin-eng jet fighter-bomber. 3,165 mi rnge, 570 kts top spd. mfgd by Gen Dynamics.
Raven FACs - Small elite grp of USAF FACs stationed in Laos and posing as civilian employees of various U.S. State Dept Agencies. Had regional HQ at Pakse AF. Unit's primary recon acft was O-1 Bird Dog, a single-eng Cessna of WWII and Korean War vintage, which they flew in civilian clothes against Pathet Lao and NVA troops in Laos, and in supt Royal Lao Army. Rumored to have suffered 50% casualty rate. Laos.
Raye, Martha - "Maggie," as entertainer Martha Raye was affectionately known, made numerous visits to troops in VN (particularly SF/SOG units) over 9-yr period (some visits as long as 6 months) and, while a civilian, actually assisted on some medevac missions where her nursing background was put to use. Given honorary rank of LTC, and many "unofficial" military awards and ribbons (including BSM and PH, or so legend says). Awarded U.S. Presidential Medal of Freedom in '93, and buried with full military honors at Ft Bragg NC, '94. Press generally paid little attention to her visits, while other entertainers who rarely visited the remote/dangerous bases she did were lavished with coverage. Brendan Lyons, 5th SF Grp (Abn), wrote of her: "Now Maggie; she loved to visit the boondocks where 'her' troops lived, fought and died, but her exploits were generally ignored! On a personal note, in 29 months I spent toting a rifle and rucksack in VN, I had many a drink with Maggie (she always won), but never came close to even seeing Mr. Hope, since he just didn't go to where we were, nor did he associate with the same crowd as I, but then again, that was his loss!" Some data per www.colonelmaggie.com/awards.htm. See also Leghorn and Sledge Hammer in main alpha listing.
Razorback - A call-sign of the 120th AHC.
RB-47H Stratojet - U.S. bomber with 4,300 mi rnge, 555 kts top spd. mfgd by Boeing Acft.
RBn - Radio beacon (TAD).
RC-3 - Peneprime runway surface (TAD).
rcvr - receiver (TAD).
RCVSQ - Readiness Carrier Antisubmarine Warfare Air Grp
RCVW - Readiness Attack Carrier Air Wing (USN).
rdo - radio (TAD).
Re-Up - "Re-Up" was GI slang for process of re-enlistment in military. Re-enlisting was sometimes a means of escaping a particular job or unit because, by accepting a longer term in the military, certain perks and rewards were offered. In some cases, troops re-enlisted to get out of combat rather than into it. See also Re-Up Hill in main alpha listing.
Re-Up Lizard - A.k.a. the "Fuck-You" Lizard. Small lizard that at night made sound (likely a mating call) remarkably similar to phrase that became its nickname. Described in *Time Heals No Wounds*, at page28.
Recce - Reconnaissance.
Recon - Reconnaissance.
Recondo - Per Paul Brubaker, Gen Westmoreland himself coined term in '66 for school of advanced LRRP/jungle combat trng he ordered built to alleviate shortage of LRRP-

qualified troops in IIFFV. Legend has it that phrase "Recon-Do" began as contraction of term "Recon Doughboy," while staff and students of the MACV Recondo School adopted Japanese meaning of word "Do" (way) as related to its use in fighting arts of Judo, Kendo, Bushido and Aikido. See also MACV Recondo School in main alpha list.
Red Carpet Tower - Sanford Army AF control tower call-sign.
Red Crown - Call-sign of C&C for SAR rescue missions in NVN.
Red Devils - Powerful blowers employed by USMC Engrs to force CS Gas powder into tunnel complexes. *Utter's Battalion*, p 147.
Red Haze Missions - Arty missions fired based upon infra-red intel photos showing suspected VC positions hidden by jungle (as revealed by red heat spots on film).
RED HORSE – USAF's "Rapid Engineer Deployable Heavy Operational Repair Sqdn, Engineering." 1st sent to VN in '66, consisted of apx 400 men. Each Red Horse Sqdn also employed 660-1,000 Viet civilians. Prior to Red Horse Ops, USAF was using 60 man PRIME BEEF units for engineering needs. One Red Horse Sqdn was also kept in Thailand (U-Tapao), Jul66-Aug69).
Redskin - Call-sign for D Co, 158th Avn Bn.
Refrig - Refrigeration
Regiment - A.k.a. "Rgt." See Battalion.
Regiment de Marche - French Foreign Legion's famous "March Units." Typically assembled for specific purpose and roughly equiv to U.S. Army TF. Such temp units often became permanent fixtures. In addn to Legion's Rgt, French had 2 other *Batallion de Marche* in Indochina.
Regional Forces -See Ruff/Puffs.
Regional Troops - Semi-regular Vietminh forces of 1st Indochina War. See *Street Without Joy*, p 49.
Regulars By God - Huge sign of 4th Inf Div Rgtl motto installed on face of hill that was site of Regular Hill Basecamp. See that facility in main alpha listing.
Regulatrice Routiere - French Army traffic control personnel. Wore white helmets with green bands.
Remote Firing Devices - Experimental radio-remote detonating mechanism 1st tested in VN by N Co, 75th Rangers, 173d Abn Bde. Daisy-chained claymores were linked to an electronic trigger box that could be activated via remote signal from hand-held control. Functioned at distance of up to 1 km. Effectiveness was increased by combining them with "Personal Seismic Detectors." In some cases, concussion grenades were detonated in this manner in hope they would stun enemy and facilitate POW snatches. Data per *Rangers At War*, p 188.
Repeater Aircraft - EC-121 acft of Igloo White/Muscle Shoals.
Repel Depels - See Replacement Depot.
Replacement Depots - A.k.a. "Repel-Depels." There were 2 major Repl-Depots in SVN: the 22d at Cam Ranh Bay and 90th at Long Binh Post. Were very large facilities designed for in-processing and distribution of newly arrived replacement troops to units in need of personnel. See those facilities in main numeric listing.
Repo Depots - See Replacement Depot.
Republic of Vietnam Campaign Medal - Medal awarded by Viet govt (not U.S. govt). Where U.S. forces were concerned, was awarded to anyone who served for minimum of 6-months within the VN CTZ between 1Mar61 and 28Mar73. Time limit was waived if recipient was KIA or WIA or captured at any time before 6-months. Was also awarded to other SEATO member troops suptg South Viets, as well as to ARVN troops. Periods of eligibility and regs apart from U.S. participation are not known. Had alternating green and white-stripped sash and small, metal scroll bearing inscription: *1960-*. Presumably scroll was meant to someday include final year of war as well, but NVN victory apparently precluded that addn.
Republic of Vietnam Forces - A.k.a. DRV or Democratic Republic of Vietnam Forces. SVN forces, 1955-75. See Major Cmd section, ARVN, AFRVN and State of Vietnam.
RESCAP - Rescue Combat Air Patrol.
RESCORT - Rescue Escort.
Rescue, Operation - Non-profit org founded by retired USAF safety officer named Jack Bailey (a.k.a. "Akuna Jack"). Bailey secured old smuggling ship, the *Akuna III*, and plied waters of South China Sea to rescue Viet Boat People fleeing VN and dabbling in various POW/MIA recovery schemes. Allegedly bilked supporters of some $3.2 million. In *Prisoners of Hope*, he is alleged to have been an unflappable liar, charlatan and scam artist of extraordinary skill.
Resolution (#)- See COSVN Resolutions.
Revolutionary Redevelopment Program - "Xay Dung Nong Thon" pacification prgm presented to Ambassador Lodge and Secty McNamara by premier Nguyen Cao Ky, Jul65. Viet phrase meant "Rural Construction or Rural Reconstruction."
RF - Regional Force, see Ruff/Puff.
RF/PF - "Ruff Puff," Regional Force/Popular.
RF-101 Voodoo - U.S. twin-eng, fighter/recon acft with 2,200 mi rnge, 1100 kts top spd. mfgd by McDonnell.
RF-4 - Recon version of F-4 Phantom, fighter-bomber.
RFTC - RVNAF Regional Force Training Center.
Rgt - Regiment.
rgt - right (TAD).
Rhodes, Alexandre de - Generally thought to have been 1st Frenchman to visit Vietnam when he arrived as Jesuit priest (under Portuguese control) in 1627, to introduce Catholicism. Before his expulsion in 1630 (another source says 1647), he is credited with converting complex VN language into its current Latin-based alphabet by creating series of diacritical markings that recognized its wide tonal range. Per Courtney Frobenius, prior to conversion, language was "written in modified form of Chinese ideographs configured to express the Vietnamese language. Since the 1st-century AD, Chinese was both the official language of court and that used by elite; the appearance of modified Chinese ideographs emerged in 14th-century(?) through some scholars seeking to counter the Chinese cultural hegemony. Prior to that time, there was no written Vietnamese language, it existed only orally. Until the collapse of Vietnamese court in Aug45, Chinese was the official language." Per *Webster's Dictionary of the Vietnam War*, Rhodes never returned to Vietnam, "but spent much of remainder of his life promoting the French Missionary effort there." For more detail, see: *Vietnam: A Political History*, pp 62-64, and *Voyages et Mission* (1884).
Ricky Rifle - Recoilless Rifle.
RID - River Interdiction Division (USN).
Riviere - French for "river" that saw ubiquitous use on French colonial era maps of VN, as well as some use on later U.S. military maps. Vietnamese words "Song" or "Dak" or "Khe" or "Tonle" often precede a river's name in alpha index.
RLO - Slang for Real Live Officer.
RM - See *Regiment de Marche*.

rmks - remarks.
Rnge - Range.
RNZA - Royal New Zealand Artillery.
RNZIR - Royal New Zealand Infantry Rgt.
RNZR - Royal New Zealand Rgt.
Road Runner Teams - See Project Omega.
Roadrunner - Call-sign for 163d Avn Co.
Roberts, Edmund - 1st U.S. diplomat to VN, 1832. See *Peacock* in main alpha listing.
Robin Hood - A call-sign of the 173d AHC.
Rock, The - Marine and SF slang for Okinawa. A.k.a. Okie.
Rock Apes - Encounters with what were generally referred to as "Rock Apes" were common in I and II Corps. These members (4 to 4 1/2 feet tall?) of primate family lived and roved in small grps, and sometimes very large grps. This author witnessed an encounter on Nui Mo Tau (S of Hue) where apx eight walking upright collided with a squad eating its lunch and, due to their size, color and fact they were on foot, were mistaken for the enemy. Other rpts (see Dong Den in main alpha listing) describe frantic encounters with grps of perhaps hundreds that overran U.S. positions, while others rpt rock-throwing exchanges and other forms of aggressive/defensive behavior by the animals. Per *Utter's Battalion*, at p 102, when USMC's BLT 2/7 arrived at Qui Nhon, 7Jul65, there was much initial confusion about rules/procedure for dealing with Viet populace; however, author adds, "Worse, no one had mentioned anything, ever, about rock apes. Often the checkpoints on [QL-1] were established in choke points where rock outcroppings made it easy to channel ground movement to the road. At night, when a rock ape would fling a stone or feces at the American intruders, the Marines would leap into a high state of alert. Everyone would be ready for an attack, but rock apes do not attack, they just annoy. Like little boys who had cried 'Wolf,' the [security troops] feared they would not be believed when they reported a real [VC] attack...They [also] correctly reasoned that if a rock ape could toss a stone or handful of shit, any passing [VC] could just as easily toss a grenade." Per Dr. Lou Grivetti of UC, Davis, "Vietnamese copy of *Animals of Vietnam* (which I can't read), but the passages list geographical regions where each is found and several primates have ranges that cover the area west of Hue. These are: *Macaca arctoides* (Khi Mat Do); *Macaca indochinesis* (Khi Duoi Lon); *Simia nemaeus* (Vooc Va). All the others have habitat ranges in North Vietnam." To help in identification of any Rock Apes the reader may have encountered, see: www.undp.org.vn/ themes/ wildtrade/index.htm, and open link to wild animal guide. See also Dong Den and Nguoi Rung.
ROE - Rules of Engagement.
ROK - Republic of Korea and their forces.
ROKA - Republic of Korea Army.
Roll O-Roll Off Freighters - See *Lt Col John U. D. Page Army Vessel* in main alpha index.
Rome Plow - A.k.a. D7E Tractor, mfgd by Caterpillar. Modified with huge, curved, sharp cutting blade (mfgd by Rome Co of Rome GA) that could rapidly clear large areas of vegetation and trees up to 1 meter or more in diameter. Perhaps one of most successful, controversial and devastating weapons of war, it was used to cut roads through otherwise impassable jungle and to strip hundreds of sq mi of terrain, thereby denying VC sanctuary and ambush positions. Enemy base area in Iron Triangle suffered mightily from its use, as did coastal lowlands N Hue immediately following Tet '68. Per *A Better War*, p283, Richard Funkhauser said that by end of '71, that what the Viets hoped for most after U.S. pulled-out was B-52's, money, and Rome Plows. He and SVN govt were well aware of plows ability to instantly convert VC jungle sanctuary into farmland, and he observed wryly that a Rome Plow "Was worth its weight in U.S. Advisors."
Rome Plow Camps – Apparently there were many such camps in SVN; however, little data in their regard was found in research for this text. Most were apparently short-term Engr camps built to house Rome Plow bulldozers, earth movers and other hvy equip used in land clearing and/or road building ops. Common in grid zones BR, XT and YT, II/III Corps.
RON - Remain Overnight (TAD).
RONONE - River Operations North(?), Sqdn One (USCG).
Rose-Ann - Call-sign for USMC's MAG 16.
Rotation Tour Date - A.k.a. RTD. USMC equiv of term DEROS. Was date a Marine's Vietnam tour was to end.
Route - Formal designator for "Supplementary Road" system in SVN; a system one step above the communal road system in quality. Typically signified by rectangular map symbol with three-numeric identifier. See QL, Highway, LTL, TL, Route, HL, R. C., *Route Colonial*, as well as *Principal Roadways of South Vietnam* Section for general discussion.
Route Coloniale - French Colonial roads built before and during 1st Indochina War, then secured by French Army during their war. On maps, typically "R.C." followed by numeral, as in "R. C. 4."
Route Package - A.k.a. RP. Numbered, geographically-defined strategic bombing zones both in and outside SVN. For example, NVN was divided into seven separate bombing route packages. During Op Rolling Thunder, these zones where numbered RP's 1, 2, 3, 4, 5, 6A, and 6B, with RP 1 immediately N of the DMZ and zone numbers increasing in sequence as they went farther N. Jurisdiction over each of these RP's was assigned as follows: USAF - 5 and 6A; USN - 2, 3, 4 and 6B; COMUSMACV - RP 1. Map of Rolling Thunder RP's is in, *Thunder from Above*, a *Vietnam Experience* series vol, at p 125.
Route Packages 1 and 2 - Code names for portions of secret bombing campaign in Laos (and perhaps the southern NVN) known as "Tiger Hound." Laos was divided into 3 zones for bombing of infiltration routes/supt of Royal Lao Army in its fight with communist Pathet Lao. Zones were Barrel Roll, Tiger Hound and Steel Tiger (see any of those entries for more detail). Map with Rolling Thunder Rte packages is on p 125 of *Thunder from Above* vol of the *Vietnam Experience* series.
RPC - River Patrol Craft (USN).
RPD - NVA/VC light machine gun that drew its ammo from round drum-style magazine and featured built-in front bipod.
RPG - River Patrol Group(USN).
RPG - Rocket propelled Grenade. Shoulder-fired, reloadable rocket launcher that fired shaped-charge heat round capable of punching through several inches of armor. Used against personnel and structures/vehicle. Very effective and much feared weapon similar to U.S. LAW, but far superior in durability, versatility, fire-power and because it could be reloaded (LAW was one shot only). Ammo was B-40 Rocket. See also B-40.
RPG 2 - Chinese-made rocket launcher. See RPG.
RPG 7 - Chinese-made rocket launcher. See RPG.

RPK - NVA/VC light, magazine fed machine gun that used same 7.62mm ammo as the AK-47. Very similar in design to AK-47, but with a longer barrel and added bipod. It weighed only 10.5 pounds (less than half weight of U.S. M-60 MG's 23 lbs), and was 41" in length (versus M-60's 43.75").
rpt - report (TAD).
rptd - reported.
Rpts - reports.
rqr - require (TAD).
RR - Radio Relay.
RSB - Rear Support Base. For example, see Buffalo, RSB Base, in main alpha section.
RSDU - Radar Storm Detection Unit, surface (TAD).
RSG - River Security Group. Elements of Brown Water Navy TF Clearwater. HQ of TF Clearwater was at Cua Viet from Feb68 until TF terminated. Had 2 grps: Dong Ha River Security Grp and Hue River Security Grp (at Tan My/Eagle Beach).
RSS - River Supt Squadron (USN).
rstd - restricted (TAD).
RT - A.k.a. "Romeo Tangos." MAC-SOG recon teams.
RTA - Royal Thai Army.
RTB - Return To Base (Pilot terminology).
RTC - RVNAF Regional Training Center.
RTD – See Rotation Tour Date.
RTNZ - Return To New Zealand. See main alpha listing.
RTO - Radio Telephone Operator. A unit's radio man.
Rubber Lady – GI nickname for air mattresses.
ruf. - Rough (TAD).
Ruff-Puff - U.S. slang for "PF/PF" which stood for "Popular Force-Regional Force" The were SVN militia troops and units. Popular Forces were lowest level of SVN military and militia structure. Villagers volunteering for PF duty were guaranteed service within their home district in exchange for a lifetime enlistment. RFs were the next, better-trained level of militia and were guaranteed service within a specified region in exchange for an commitment to age 65(?). Enlistment as regular ARVN required commitment to age 55(?) but ARVN could be deployed anywhere in country and risks of death or injury were much higher with ARVN.
Ruffs - See Ruff-Puff.
Russia, Forces of – See Major Commands Section.
Ruthless Rider - A call-sign of the 7th/17th Air Cav.
RVAH - Reconnaissance Attack Squadron (USN).
RVN - Republic of Vietnam.
RVNAF - Republic of Vietnam Armed Forces, or Air Forces.
RVNAF Military Training Schools - SVN military training was focused in number of schools, academies and colleges spread throughout SVN. In '56 there was one National Trng Center (NTC) and by '70, there were 35. RVNAF school system totaled 25 facilities by end of war. Additionally, a number of Popular Force/Regional Force training centers opened as RF/PF prgm expanded rapidly after '68. The National Defense College in Saigon was created in '67, and National Military Academy at Dalat was permanently expanded from a 2-yr to 4-yr prgm in '67 also. For detailed history of RVNAF trng prgms, see *Vietnam Studies, The Development and Training of the South Vietnamese Army, 1950-1972*. Maps of most NTCs, RTCs, PFTCs and RFTCs on pp 81 and 107 of that text. See RVNAF/ARVN in main alpha listings generally as well.
RVR - Runway Visual Range (TAD).
Rwy - Runway.
RZ - Reconnaissance Zone.
S - South.
S and S - Service and Supply.
S&S - Service and Supply.
S-2 - OIC of military intelligence section of Bde or smaller unit.
S-3 - OIC operations & training section of Bde or smaller unit.
S-4 – OIC of logistics of Bde or smaller unit.
S-5 – OIC of Civil affairs of Bde or smaller unit.
SA-2, SA-3 and SA-7 – A.k.a. SAMs. Soviet surface-to-air missiles. SA-2 "Guideline" had 40 km range. SA-3 "Goa" mobile, low-altitude SAM. SA-7 "Grail" hand-held heat-seeker provided to NVA and Khmer Rouge in '72.
Sabreliner - Trade name for T-39 jet acft. 1,950 mi rnge, 595 kts top spd. mfgd by North American.
Sacred Sword of Patriots League - See Project Urgency.
SAG - See U.S. Supt Activities Group's main alpha entry.
Saigon Moat, The - See main alpha entry.
Salt and Pepper - Mythical pair of U.S. defectors alleged to have operated with NVA on numerous missions against U.S. forces. Sightings were so common and descriptions so consistent that MACV had military artist draw composite sketches and distributed a "wanted poster" for pair throughout SVN. ABC News even broadcast sketch (per *Prisoners of Hope*, pp 69-70)! While presumption has been these men were U.S. deserters, that seems unlikely. Many French who fought during 1st Indochina War were from North Africa, and it is likely some either fathered Black children in VN or stayed behind themselves after the French exit. Various other nationalities of mercenaries serving with French Foreign Legion/Army no doubt fathered children of all races (who would have been of military age by American War) as well. It is also true that Soviet Bloc advisors or observers worked with the NVA as well, so it is this author opinion that while such sightings may have been legitimate, they likely of non-Americans.
SAM - Surface-to-Air missile. See SA-2 (et al).
Sandy - Call-sign of A-1 Skyraider SAR unit located at NKP and other airfields dedicated to SAR missions.
Sao Vang Division - NVA Div responsible for offensive in Bong Son coastal areas of II Corps in late '66. Its 22d Rgt attacked LZ Bird, 25-26Dec66 in one of bloodiest U.S. battles of war. See LZ Bird in main alpha listing. Discussed in *Bird*, 1st Chapter.
SAR - Search and Rescue.
SARCAP - Search & Rescue Combat Patrol.
SAS - Special Air Service.
SATS - Short AF for Tactical Support. Prefabricated system of portable rwys and facilities for service, landings and take-offs. Used AM-2 aluminum inter-locking matting and mobile control equip for rapid airfield installation.
SC - Submarine Chaser (USN).
SC - Supply Corps (USN).
SCAR Strike Control and Recon. FAC responsibilities of USAF's Tactical Air Supt Sqdns, such as 20th TASS (Coveys) at Da Nang and 23d TASS (Nails) at NKP. *Da Nang Diary* provides detailed look at TASS ops. See also TASS.
SCATTOR - Small Craft Assets, Training, and Turnover of Resources. A part of Vietnamization process and U.S. withdrawal.
Screaming Eagle - 101st Abn Div's weekly newspaper (and 101st Abn Div Assn's Newsletter). Until 21Jul67 issue (and

while only 1st Bde was in VN), title was *Diplomat and Warrior*.
Screaming Eagles – 101st Abn Div. See also Pukin' Buzzards.
SDF - The Self-Defense Forces and SSDF (Secret Self-Defense Forces) were units of VC Infrastructure (VCI).
SE - Southeast.
SEA - Southeast Asia.
Sea Devil - A call-sign of HC-7, USN Helo Combat Supt Sqdn 7.
Sea King - Trade name for H-3 SAR helicopter. 625 mi rnge, 162 kts top spd. mfgd by Sikorsky Helicopter.
Sea Knight - Trade name for H-46 twin-rotor cargo helo (USMC-USN). 110 mi rnge, 120 kts top spd. mfgd by Boeing Acft.
SEA LORDS - See SEALORDS.
Sea Stallion - Trade name for H-53 single-rotor SAR helo (USN). 255 mi rnge, 170 kts top spd. mfgd by Sikorsky Helicopter.
Sea Wolf - See Sea wolf in main alpha listing.
Seabee - Nickname for USN hvy const engr units known as Mobile Construction Battalions. Name derived from initials "CB" and, over time, became official occupation designation.
SEAL – Sea, Air, Land Team. Naval commando personnel roughly equiv to Army's SF soldiers.
Seal Teams - Teams 1 & 2 were only to see service in SVN.
SEALORDS - South East Asia Lake, Ocean River, Delta Strategy. As part of Vietnamization program, beginning in Feb69, the USN began turning over to SVN its flotilla of river patrol and other craft formerly employed by USN's TFs 116, 117 and the MRF.
Search and Attack - See Search and Destroy.
Search and Avoid - Cynical play on term "Search & Destroy." Described ARVN ops in general and some U.S. ops as well. ARVN were generally thought of as timid and unwilling to fight, though in reality, for many ARVN units that was not true. Was also used describe U.S. ops in later, demoralized, stages of war ('70 and later) when some units avoided contact as well.
Search and Clear - See Search and Destroy.
Search and Destroy - Standard USARV/MACV/III MAF tactical term denoting purpose of certain grnd ops during initial phases of war. As war dragged on, phrase was changed to "Search and Clear," in politically-correct effort to make war more palatable to American public. Specific op names were even changed under political pressure as well. For example. Soon after Op Masher was publicized, Pentagon was told to change name to something less graphic. New name then became "White Wing," but level of its violence was unfettered by switch. "Search and Attack" was a term used in 101st Abn Div during '67-68.
SEASHARP - SE Asia Semi-Permanent Harbor Protection.
Seasprite - Trade name for H-2 acft. 445 mi rnge, 165 kts top spd. mfgd by KAMAN.
SEATO - Southeast Atlantic Treaty Organization. Under his "More Flags" campaign, President Lyndon Johnson pressured SEATO members to join U.S. in defense of SVN. Countries participating and year of greatest commitment were: Australia, 7,672 ('68); Korea, 50,003 ('68): Thailand, 11,586 ('70), New Zealand, 552 ('69); The Philippines, 2,061 ('66); Taiwan (Rep of China) 31 ('67 and '70); Spain, 13 ('66 and '67). Data per *A Contagion of War* vol, *Vietnam Experience* series, pp 90-91.
Seawolf - Helatktron and Seawolf were call-signs of Det 8 of Seawolves HA(L)-3. Described as most decorated USN Sqdn.
Seawolves - A call-sign of HA(L)-3. USN Helicopter Attack (Light) Sqdn 3. See also Helatktron.
sec – second.
secd - secondary (TAD).
Second Indochina War - SVN/American War against Viet Cong (NLF) and North Vietnamese Army (PAVN), Apr65-May73.
Second Offensive - NVA/VC's May68 offensive known as Mini-Tet. See Year of Decision and Tet '68 Offensive. SVN.
sect - section.
Sedang, Kingdom of - See Kingdom of Sedang.
SELCAL - Selective Calling System (TAD).
SERTS - Screaming Eagle Replacement Training School.
Service Historique de L'Armee – the historical archives of the French War - are kept in this facility behind massive walls of Fort de Vincennes, on outskirts of Paris. Per *Street Without Joy*, p 16.
Services Techneques des Constructions -STCAN. *Services Techneques des Constructions et Armes Navales.* French Patrol Craft used by VNN.
SERVPAC - Service Force, U.S. Pacific Fleet.
SESU - Signal Engineering Survey Unit.
Seven-Step Snake - Variant of Two-Step and Twenty-Two Step Snake. See those entries in Glossary.
Seventeenth Parallel - See 17th Parallel in main Alpha listing.
sfc - surface (TAD).
SFOB - Special Forces Forward Operating Base.
Sgt - Sergeant.
SH-3 Sea King - Large, single-rotor helicopter used for long-range SAR (search and rescue) missions "over the fence" in Laos, Cambodia and NVN. First sent to Vietnam in '66.
Shadow - USAF AC-119 gunship platform. See Spooky for detail.
Shadow-Stinger - Trade name for AC-119 acft. 900 mi rnge, 245 kts top spd. mfgd by Fairchild Acft.
Shark - A call-sign of the 174th AHC.
Shark - Call-sign of the 176th AHC.
Shawnee - Trade name for CH-21 twin-rotor, "Banana" helicopter. 300 mi rnge, 130 kts top spd. mfgd by Piasecki.
Sheridan Tank - See M-551 Sheridan Tank.
Shields, CM3 Marvin - 1st USN sailor awarded the MOH in Vietnam War. Seabee with Team 1104 when VC attacked his work site at Dong Xoai, Jun65.
Shining Brass - SOG code name for clandestine Project Delta ops. See also Projects Delta, New York and Arizona.
Ships' Histories - USN historical documents available on the internet as the *Dictionary of American Fighting Ships* at www.hazegray.org/danfs/. See also Table of Contents: *Researching the Vietnam War*.
Ships' Musters - U.S. Navy rosters of ships' personnel. See Table of Contents, *Researching the Vietnam War*.
Shotgun, Operation - See Shotgun, Op, in main alpha index.
Short Range Patrol Screen - See SRP.
Short Uplift - Call-sign of U.S. Advisor Ralph Bunten, 65/66, while he was working Deo Nhong Pass at what later became known as LZ Uplift (named per call-sign). See LZ Uplift.
Shuttle X - USAF term which meant "Shuttle as required" between two position. See Katum AF in main alpha listing.
Siebel - French recon/liaison acft employed during 1st Indochina War. At most, French had only about 85 such recon acft during entire war; among which were the Morane, the L-5, the Siebel and etc. Data per *Street Without Joy*, pp 263.

Sierra - Radio code for word "south" or "second." Created by simply substituting military phonetic alphabet for1st letter of whatever word was being replaced or coded. As such, Mike replaced "minute," Hotel replaced "hour" and so on.
SIF - Selective Identification Feature (TAD).
Sig - Signal (i.e., communication unit).
Sigma I/Sigma II - Sigma I was war game sponsored by U.S. JCS in '63. It predicted that over 500,000 U.S. troops would be needed to beat VC. Sigma II in '64 produced much the same result.
Sigma, Project - See Project Sigma.
Silver Spur - A call-sign of A trp, 3d/17th Air Cav.
Sin Loi - Anglicized spelling for Vietnamese phrase that was roughly equiv to "sorry about that," or "I am sorry" or "excuse me." Also spelled Xin Loi.
Sitrep or Sit Rep - Situation Report. Periodic radio rpts between sub-units and their parent cmds which provided info about position, direction of movement, proposed objectives, contact with or absence of enemy. For example, SOP in 2d Bde/101st Abn Div, required that every 15 minutes during every night, plt CPs were to call their squad and ambush positions for sitrep. All positions responded by "breaking squelch" (pressing transmit button without speaking) twice for all clear, and once if movement was being observed). Calls kept everyone up to date, but also helped to ensure that someone at each position was awake and on guard.
SK-5 PACV - Patrol Air Cushion Vehicle. Very large, prop-driven air-cushion transport carried crew of 6 and 20 passengers. Was capable of 75 knots max speed. Operated with mixed results, principally in delta region of IV Corps and with the Mobile Riverine Forces of the 9th Inf Div.
sked - Schedule (TAD).
SKS - Standard issue Soviet 5-shot semi-auto rifle. Had built-in magazine and some had built-in folding bayonets. Of both Russian and Chinese manufacture.
Sky Raider - See A-1H Skyraider.
Sky Soldiers - Nickname of the U.S. 173d Airborne Bde.
Skyhawk - Trade name for A-4 acft. 2,000 mi rnge, 680 kts top spd. mfgd by Douglas Acft.
Skynight - Trade name for F-10 acft. 1,150 mi rnge, 490 kts top spd. mfgd by Douglas Acft.
Skyraider - Trade name for A-1 fighter-bomber. 1,270 mi rnge, 310 kts top spd. mfgd by Douglas Acft.
Skyspot - See Site 85 in main alpha listing.
Skytrain - C-47 (a.k.a. DC-3, or Dakota) twin-eng, prop-driven air transport of WWII vintage used as a transport and airdrop acft throughout SEA. Used also in gunship role (AC-47) as "Puff the Magic Dragon" or "Puff." Had 2,100 mi rnge, 230 kts top spd. mfgd by Douglas Acft.
Skywarrior - Trade name for A-3 acft. 1,050 mi rnge, 610 kts top spd. mfgd by Douglas Acft.
SKZ - Soviet-mfgd recoilless rifle used by Vietminh and NVA.
SLAM - Search Locate, Annihilate and Monitoring; brainchild of MajG Norman Anderson, 1st MAW CG. Aerial bombardment ops launched during and after Battle of Con Thien, Jul-Dec67. Combined B-52, Tac Air, Arty, and Naval gunfire to focus on apx 130 enemy arty sites (some holding 152mm cannons). Inc elements from all air assets of U.S. and VNAF. After 6 months, only est 40% of enemy sites had been destroyed.
SLAR - Side-Looking Airborne Radar.
SLF - Special Landing Force.
SLG - Special Landing Group.
Slick - Slick and Huey were common nicknames or slang for the Bell UH-1 utility helicopter.
SM - Statute Mile (TAD).
Smart Bombs - Bombs that could be laser-guided to their targets after release. Not available until '72, their value was immed demonstrated by very high success rate in destroying targets which extensive conventional bombing could not. Required a bomb-release acft and laser-targeting acft. Laser acft was vulnerable to ground fire because it had to run straight and steady in order to keep laser on target, and missions could only be flown when cloud cover and weather were minimal. See Linebacker and Thanh Hoa RR/Hwy Bridge in main alpha listing.
Smitty, A - Unit of measurement equal to apx 5'. Named to honor Ray Smith, 1st/69th Armor. During flooding of Typhoon Hester in '69, Smith was on foot guiding his tank down QL-19 (flooding had made roadbed invisible to driver and, to prevent tank from plunging off shoulder, Smith was marking its position). When Smith entered water up to his chin, he hollered to his tank cmdr, "Lieutenant, I can't swim and I'm not going any farther." The cmdr in turn informed HQ that column was stalled because water was now a "Smitty" deep.. HQ of course asked what the hell a "Smitty" was, so the Lt yelled to Smith, "How tall are you Smitty?" and Smith hollered back that he was 5"-2" tall. The Lt then advised HQ that "Smitty" was equiv to 5 feet. Thereafter in 1st/69th Armor, distances were often measured and rptd in "Smitties." Data per Ray Smith, 1st/69th Armor Assn.
Smokey - Legendary civilian who maintained 5 cubic yd front-end Loaders and D-9 Dozers (painted bright, camouflage yellow!) at Weigt-Davis rock quarry N of Phu Nhon. Per Bob Clark, Hvy Equip Operator with 584th Engrs, Smokey "Sometimes 'ran the road' to Pleiku in an old Chevrolet pickup, his sawed-off shotgun at his side, and had a place on CPO road in Pleiku where many wild parties were held." See also Weigt-Davis.
Snack - See Base Area 351 in main alpha section.
Snake - A call-sign of C Co, 227th AHB.
Snake - Nickname for AH-1G Bell Cobra gunship. See also Cobra.
Snake n' Nape - Slang for "Strafe and Napalm." Application of fighter-borne acft mini-gun and napalm in supt of grnd ops.
Snake, The - AH-1G Cobra Attack Gunship Helicopter. Long, narrow, highly maneuverable and naturally ferocious looking helo with crew of 2. Body was but 36" wide and acft capable of very high speeds in a dive. This heavily armed weapons platform was feared by the enemy and loved by the troops it suptd. Normally armed with two-2.75" rocket pods, a 7.62mm mini-gun and a 40mm automatic grenade launcher (or any number of variants or multiples of that basic equip). Often used in pairs with a OH-6 helo (a Pink Team) or singly with an OH-6 (Hunter-Killer Team), in an air-cav offensive mode to locate and attack enemy. Once introduced, Cobras also normally covered all troop insertions, pick-ups and medevac flights in a defensive mode as well.
Snatch Teams - Created by 2d/14th Inf/25th Div for rapid response to intel. When VC cadre located, a 5-ship lift of plt-size element would be quickly ferried to site in what became known as "Snatch Teams." Unit literally landed at VC's door step. Element of surprise prevented escape and tactic proven successful when 20 confirmed VC were caught during inaugural month.

Sneaky Pete -Generic nickname for units (or their electronic equip) involved in placing grnd electronic surveillance sensors. Missions often escorted/secured by Inf. See also Sneaky Pete Ops.
Sneaky-Pete Operations - Top-secret MAC-SOG and other surveillance flights know as "Prairie Fire" ops (and likely other names). Missions were flown over Laos and NVN in supt of SOG teams operating outside SVN. In 20th TASS at Da Nang, this element was composed of only 6 pilots prohibited from sharing their stories even with other TASS pilots. Most TASS FAC KIA-WIA and lost acft were involved in Sneaky Pete missions.
SOFA - Status of Force Agreement. Stnd agreement between U.S. Govt and host foreign nations that govern responsibilities, restrictions upon, and obligations of, U.S. military forces based on host nation's soil. No such agreement was ever signed with SVN govt. To define legal jurisdictional boundaries in SVN, the 6-page *Agreement for Mutual Defense Assistance in Indochina* (a.k.a. *The Pentalateral Agreement* between VN, France, Cambodia, Laos and US) signed in 1950, became the guide. The Pentalateral agreement initially gave U.S. forces no immunity from Viet criminal prosecution, but in 1958 an amendment granted U.S. exclusive jurisdiction over prosecution of criminal behavior by its troops. Data per *Son Thang, An American War Crime*, pp 211-212.
SOG - Special Operating Group (USN).
SOG - Special Operations Group.
SOG - Studies and Observations Group. A.k.a. MAC-SOG and MACV-SOG (see also those entries). USN acronym meant "Special Operating Group."
SOG 00 - Chief, SOG.
SOG 01 - Deputy Chief, SOG.
SOG 02 - SOG Executive Officer (XO).
SOG 03 - Special Assistant to the Chief, SOG.
SOG 04 - SOG IG.
SOG 10 - SOG Personnel and Admin.
SOG 20 - SOG Intel Div.
SOG 30 - SOG Operations/Training Studies.
SOG 31 - SOG Maritime Branch.
SOG 32 - SOG Air Studies Branch.
SOG 33 - Psychological Operations Studies Branch.
SOG 34 - Ground Studies Branch.
SOG 35 - Ground Studies Group.
SOG 36 - Airborne Studies Group.
SOG 37 - Maritime Studies Group.
SOG 38 - Training Studies Group.
SOG 39 - Psychological Operations Studies Group.
SOG 40 - SOG Logistics Div.
SOG 50 - SOG Plans Div.
SOG 60 - SOG Communications Div.
SOG 70 - Radio Studies Group.
SOG 75 - Air Studies Group.
SOG 80 - Recovery Studies Group.
SOG 90 - SOG Comptroller Div.
SOI - Signal Operation Instructions (TAD).
Son Hai Company - CIDG Co consisting of 90 Hre tribesmen from Quang Ngai that became famous for its defense of Kannack outpost, in '65. For part of '66, defended Mang Yang Pass on QL-19, and was later responsible for finding enemy in initial battles of Op Crazy Horse (Vinh Thanh Valley, NE An Khe). See *Battles in the Monsoon*, pp 26-27, 175.
Song – One several Viet words for river or stream.
Sonnette - French name for what U.S. forces referred to as LPs or OPs (listening posts or observation posts). Literal translation is "Door Bell," which reflects their purpose in providing advance warning of enemy's approach.
Southern Cross - Newspaper of the Americal Division (Div's motto was *Under the Southern Cross*.
Soviet Bloc, Forces of - See Russia in Major Command Section.
SP - Self Propelled. Frequently to describe track-mounted arty pieces such as the 8", 155mm and 175mm howitzers/cannons.
Sp - Spelling or spelled.
Sp? - Spelling unknown or in doubt.
SP-5B Marlin - Amphibious acft. 2,050 mi rnge, 250 kts top spd. mfgd by Martin.
Spad - Call-sign for A-1 Skyraider SAR supt acft at Da Nang AB (later "Sandy"). Particularly Skyraiders suptg MAC-SOG ops.
Spad - See A-1H Skyraider; particularly those suptg MAC-SOG.
Spad Sauce - Traditional alcohol concoction used in celebrations, rituals, or initiations, or whenever Spad (A-1 Skyraider SAR) pilots were letting off steam. Per *Da Nang Diary*, was mixture of Beer, Scotch, Bloody Mary mix, Creme de Menthe and Brandy.
Sparrow Hawk Reaction Force – 3d Mar Div's ready reserve reaction force.
SPARS - Significant Problem Areas Reports. SF term.
SPAT - Self-Propelled Anti-Tank. See M-56 SP Anti-Tank Gun.
Special Capital Zone - See main alpha entry.
Spectre - Call-sign for USAF AC-130 fixed-wing gunship platform. See Spooky for detail.
Speedy Four - Army slang for rank of Sp4 (E-4).
Spider - A call-sign of C Co 101st Avn?
Spider - Per *Rites of Passage*, was 1st/14th Inf/25th Div radio code word for a stream or river.
Spike Teams - One of 2 basic SOG missions working out of FOB-1 MLT site at Khe Sanh (HQ'd at Phu Bai). Teams consisted of 3 U.S. personnel accompanied by 5 to 7 indigenous SF troops under aegis of Op Prairie Fire. Indigenous troops dressed in enemy garb and carried NVA equip/arms so they could act as though escorting U.S. POWs if need arose.
Spitfire IX - British WWII fighter acft employed by the French Air Force early in their war. French had 60 of them, but wood and canvas const was ill-suited to climate and "components literally rotted off the acft in mid-flight," per *Street Without Joy*, p 261.
Splintex - Australian/New Zealand Arty's anti-personnel, 105mm cannon round apparently equiv to U.S. Beehive round. See Beehive Round or Flechette Round for detail.
Split Battery Echelon - See main alpha listing.
Split Battery Echelon – Arty tactic in which 6-tube arty bty is split into 2-tube/3-tube elements. Developed to accommodate rapidly moving deployments of 9th Inf Div/MRF units in IV Corps, late '68. For example, on 20Dec98, a bty was alerted for movement to Can Tho, re supplied with rations, fuel and water, and departed all in space of 3 hours. During dry season in Mekong Delta, 34th Arty conducted 2-split bty ops in which plts of 105s were towed off paddy platforms and moved by road to FSBs in Giong Trom area. Data per Annual Hist Rpt of 3d/34th Arty, for 1Apr68-31Jan69, on at: www.mrfa.org 3_34th.htm.
Spooky - See "Puff the Magic Dragon."
Spot Rep - See Spotrep.
SPOTLIGHT - Code Name for sensor activation of Muscle Shoals sensor system deployed around the Khe Sanh CB. See Muscle Shoals for much greater detail.

Spotrep or Spot Rep - Spot Report. USMC equiv of Army's Sitrep or Sit Rep. Periodic radio reports between sub-units and their parent cmds which provided info about position, direction of movement, proposed objectives and contact with, or absence of, the enemy. See also "Sitrep."
Spud 13 and 14 - Call-signs of Army OV-l SLAR Mohawks of 131st Avn Co. See also *Point Welcome* in main alpha listing.
Sqd - Squad or squadron.
Sqdn - Squadron.
Squawk - Air traffic control term that meant pilot should set a specific sequence of numbers on acft's transponder. Sequence allowed grnd radar to scan transponder's signal to ID the acft.
Squeeze-Bore .50 Cal MG - .50 Cal machine gun variant tested by 9th Inf/MRF and Brown Water Navy during Op Giant Slingshot. Barrel narrowed from .50 Cal at breech to .30 Cal at muzzle, thereby squeezing bullet to .30 Cal. size when fired. Theory was this increased coverage for .50 by reducing its range near civilian populations where it could not otherwise be fired. Per *Brown Water, Black Berets*, p 305. Success unknown.
SR - sunrise (TAD).
SR-71 Blackbird - US, ultra-secret twin-jet, high-altitude, high-spd, recon and spy acft. 3,250 mi rnge, 2,215 kts top spd. mfgd by Lockheed Acft.
SRAG - Second Regional Advisory Group (also Second Regional Assistance Cmd). Under cmd of John Paul Vann.
SRP - See main alpha listing.
SRP - Short Range Patrol Screen. 4th Inf Div innovation involving four-man defensive teams put out apx 3 km from FSB and set aside trails or likely routes of approach for 48-hr periods. Basically a poor man's recon team using regular Inf. During Oct68, daily avg of 150 SRPs were deployed. Per *Time Heals No Wounds*, p36.
SS - Steamship (USN).
SS - Submarine (USN).
SS - sunset (TAD).
SSB - Single Side Band radio (TAD).
SSDF – See SDF (Self-Defense Forces).
SSgt - Staff Sgt
STAB - Seal Team Assault Boat, or Strike Assault Boat (USN).
STABO Rig - Successor to McGuire Rig as a ranger/recon/LRRP team extraction device. 1st demonstrated 1Oct68, Shelby Stanton hails it as one of most useful recon hardware innovations to emerge from VN War. Apparently worn as harness-belt combo that enabled hands-free hookup to an extraction rope. Developed by, and named to honor, Maj Robert Stevens, Capt John Knabb and SFC Cliff Roberts. Data per *Rangers At War*, p 287. See also McGuire Rig and Gorwoody Antenna.
STABS - Strike Assault Boat Squadron (fast-reaction unit created by Adm Zumwalt in '69). See YRBM 21 in main alpha list.
Stagecoach – Falcon & Stagecoach were call-signs of 155th AHC.
Stalin Organs - Soviet Katyusha multiple rocket launchers. Named for distinct sound made when fired. Giap's forces used between 12 and 16 of them at Dien Bien Phu in 1954.
Stallion Gunship - Trade name for AU-24A acft. 410 mi rnge, 160 kts top spd. mfgd by Helio. See AU-24A for detail.
Starfighter - Trade name of U.S. F-104C, high-spd, single-eng jet fighter. 1,000 mi rnge, 1,450 kts top spd. mfgd by Lockheed.
Starlighter - Trade name for C-141A, 4-jet eng transport acft. 4,080 mi rnge, 570 kts top spd. mfgd by Lockheed Acft.
Starlite Scope - A.k.a. the AN/PVS 2. Night vision device capable of magnifying available light 40,000 times. Introduced early in war, they were a classified and rigidly controlled item. In U.S. Army, one hand-carried version was usually issued to each Inf Plt. It could be hand-held or attached to a rifle and was about one foot long, 5" in diameter and weighed apx 8 lbs. (its weight and battery maintenance was problem in field). Its $3,000 price tag and loss in combat could result in major recovery op and $3,000 bill to soldier who lost it! Unit was bulky, awkward, vulnerable to wet climate and excess light could blind unit temporarily. Its weight, thirst for batteries, replacement cost, and ultra top-secret nature made its use problematic. While antiquated by current standards, it was a remarkable tool in its day. Another, larger version (AN/TVS 2) was employed in fixed defensive positions and on crew-served weapons such as .50 Cal MG and etc. See also AN/TVS 2.
STAT - Seabee Technical Assistance Team (USN).
State of Vietnam, The - Fragile, primarily fictitious govt under Emperor Bao Dai created by French (in '54?) following French defeat in 1st Indochina War. See *The Unquiet American*, p 137.
Stats - statistics.
STCAN - *Services Techneques des Constructions et Armes Navales* (French Patrol Craft used by VNN).
STCAN/FOM - *Services Techneques des Constructions et Armes Navales*. French designed patrol craft used by VNN.
std - standard (TAD).
stnd - standard.
Steadfast and Loyal - Motto of the "Famous Fighting Fourth Infantry Div." Also name of its official newspaper from May69 to end of war. *Ivy Leaf* was name of 4th Div's newspaper until May69, when it became *Steadfast and Loyal* to match Div's motto and because it was felt "a closer association between the newspaper and the tradition of the division" would result. The 18May69 *Steadfast and Loyal* (Vol 1. No. 1), announced change.
Steel Tiger Operations - Code name for secret air ops over the Ho Chi Minh Trail in northern Lao panhandle. Was divided into 3 zones: Tiger Hound, Steel Tiger and Barrel Roll. Steel Tiger was original name of Ho Chi Minh Trail bombing op. USAF/USN missions began Apr65, from bases in SVN, Thailand and 7th fleet acft carrier grps. In late '65, Gen Westmoreland requested and received control over portion of Steel Tiger adj to SVN and apx 100 km W into Laos (renamed Tiger Hound). Balance of Steel Tiger AO retained orig name. See Tiger Hound and Barrel Roll.
Step-and-a-Half Snake - See Two-Step Snake.
Stg - Storage.
Stinger - USAF C-119 gunship. See C-119 and Spooky.
Stingers - Call-sign 116th Avn Co Gunships.
Stnd - Standard
STOL - Short Take-Off & Landing and acft capable of them. Army's (and later USAF's) C-7 Caribou, Air America's Porter Pilatus and to some degree USAF C-123 are examples.
Straps - Air Cav slang used to describe rear echelon troops "who stayed in rear, away from the fighting, and wrote phony

war stories home," according to *Apache Sunrise*, p 206. Equiv of REMF.
Strategic Hamlets – Element of CORDS Rural Hamlet Dev Prgm which began with Strategic Hamlet Prgm and evolved in name and concept to "New Life" and later "Really New Life" (a.k.a. Ap Doi Moi) programs. All these involved relocating civilian populations (mostly against their will) to end VC access to them, and all were regarded as dismal failures.
Strategic Transportation Corridor - See Ho Chi Minh Trail.
Stratofortress - Trade name for B-52 bomber. 7,370 mi rnge, 575 kts top spd. mfgd by Boeing Acft.
Stratojet - Trade name for RB-47H bomber, a.k.a. the B-47. 4,300 mi rnge, 555 kts top spd. mfgd by Boeing Acft.
Stratotanker EC-135 - U.S. EC/RC-135, ECM version of KC-135 and used for electronic surveillance and countermeasures. 3,450 mi rnge, 530 kts top spd. mfgd by Boeing Acft.
Stratotanker KC-135 - Trade name for KC-135A jet fuel tanker. 3,450 mi rnge, 530 kts top spd. mfgd by Boeing Acft.
Street Without Joy - See main alpha listing.
Stevens, Ray - See FSB/PB Frontier City in main alpha Index.
Strike Forces - Units composed of indigenous personnel organized and advised by SF A-Teams. See A-Team and Strikers.
Strikers - Nickname for indigenous forces working with SF A-Teams derived from their "Strike Force" designation. See A-Team.
Strongpoints - Generic term for most any fortified or defended position. Common among French positions at DBP, U.S. Army positions along QL-19 in Binh Dinh/Pleiku Provs, and some USMC/ARVN positions in Quang Tri Prov. Where U.S. forces concerned, these positions were sometimes either only defended at night or only during daylight hours. Dien Bien Phu strongpoints were named for officers' wives or girlfriends (tradition carried fwd to U.S. War). See Dien Bien Phu (layout), Dien Bien Phu (Battle of), A1 through A5, Ann-Marie, Bald Hill, Beatrice, C1 through C-5, Claudine, Dominique, D1 through D3, Eliane, E1 through E4, Gabrielle, Huguette, H1 through H6, Junon, Isabelle, 2d Thai, The Five Hills, White Thai.
SU-7BM - Soviet built fighter acft used by NVN. 200 mi rnge, 1,055 kts top spd. mfgd by Sukhoi.
Suck and Blow - See Oscar Deuce.
Suicide Zone - Nickname for interior mtns near Lao border in Americal Div's LRRP Recon Zone. Per *Rangers at War*, p 39.
Super Connie - Nickname of EC-121 Warning Star, 4-eng, prop-driven acft. 20 hrs range, 320 kts top spd. See EC-121.
Super Courier - Trade name for U-10 transport acft. Had 660 mi rnge, 165 kts top spd. mfgd by Helio.
Super Gaggle - (XD) Special USMC tactic created to overcome voluminous and accurate grnd and AA fire thrown at helo trying to resupply/reinforce hill positions (861, 881-S and 881-N) around Khe Sanh during siege of 67/68. System involved twelve A-4 Skyhawk Fighter-Bombers from Chu Lai, twelve USMC CH-46 Helos, four Huey gunships and a TAC or FAC in another acft to direct jet acft to target (29 acft in all). Acft were scheduled for mission such that they would all arrive simultaneously over Khe Sanh. 8 Skyhawks would begin show by bombing (iron bombs and napalm) and then strafing (20mm cannons) known enemy positions, then 2 Skyhawks would disperse tear gas over positions and then last 2 Skyhawks would lay down a smoke screen across approach pattern planned for CH-46s. CH-46s would then land or hover at hill positions while gunships providing close-in cover and Skyhawks flew a "Racetrack" pattern (constantly pelting enemy with bombs/20mm cannon fire). Tactic greatly reduced helo losses and casualties. Was considered one of most effective innovations of Khe Sanh Siege. Described in great detail in M. Sturkey's *Bonnie-Sue*, pp 446-447.
Super Sabre - Trade name for F-100 fighter-bomber. 550 mi rnge, 865 kts top spd. mfgd by North American.
Superchief - Nickname for the Sikorsky H-34, piston-driven medium helicopter. Used extensively for ARVN and USMC grnd ops between '62 and '68.
Super-Skymaster - Trade name for Cessna O-2, twin-eng, prop-driven observation acft. See O-2 for more detail. 1,060 mi rnge, 145 kts top spd. mfgd by Cessna.
Superspook, The - MACV HQ generic term for their agents working within the NVA and VC infrastructure. Presumably all or most were under control of ARVN, and during '68, the quality of intel gathered by these spies is rptd to have grown tremendously (and confirmed by ops and radio intercepts). Superspook was also apparently name of a particular agent as well. It seems such agents were typically given alpha-numeric designators, and Gen Davidson once labeled agents A-22, 23, 24, the "COSVN Guy" (possibly A-22?), and "Superspook" as particularly effective. Data per *A Better War*, p 47. SVN.
Supp - Supplement.
Supps - Supplements.
Supt - Support or Supporting.
Suptd - Supported.
Suptg - Supporting
Suptng - Supporting.
sur - surrounding(s) (TAD).
SVAF - South Vietnam Armed Forces.
svc - service (TAD).
svcg - servicing (TAD).
SVN - South Vietnam.
SVNAF - South Vietnam Air Force.
SVNMC - South Vietnam Marine Corps.
SVNN - South Vietnam Marine Navy.
SVNSF - South Vietnam Special Forces.
SW - Southwest.
SWIFT BOAT - Inshore (PCF).
Swift Boats (PCF) - Inshore PCF. Modified USN patrol boat used in conjunction with grnd force ops. Designed by Stewart Seacraft Co., of LA. These 50' long, 23-knot boats armed with .50-Cal. MGs and an 81mm mortar, became the workhorse of USN coastal survei1 1ance forces. Operated under Boat Sqdn 1 (later Coastal Sqdn 1), Boat Divs 101, 102, 103, 104, and 105 (redesignated Coastal Divs 11, 12, 13, 14, and 15 on 1Jan67) operating from bases at An Thoi, Da Nang, Cat Lo, Cam Ranh Bay, and Qui Nhon, respectively. In Jun67, Coastal Div16 at Chu Lai was added.
Switchback, Operation - Op in which U.S. Army began assuming responsibility for U.S. participation in CIDG program, Nov62-Jul63. See also Op Parasol-Switchback.
Sword of Patriots League - See Project Urgency.
T - A prefix for some USNS Ships (USN).
T-17 - Coated nylon membrane runway surface (TAD).
T-28 Nomad - A.k.a. T-28 Trojan? Version of USAF prop-driven Trainer acft configured in grnd supt role primarily for VNAF (particularly between'62-65, and operating out of Soc Trang, among other bases). In '61, President Kennedy authorized increased military assistance inc deployment of

portion of USAF's 4400 Combat Crew Trng Sqdn (code name Farm Gate), under guise that it was to familiarize SVAF pilots with the T-28 trainer. By Feb62 U.S. Farm Gate crews were flying combat (and even 1st defoliant) missions. Had 900 mi rnge, 285 kts top spd. mfgd by North American. Role transitioned to A-1 Skyraider. Difference between T-28s made under Trojan and Nomad names unknown?

T-28 Trojan – See T-28 Nomad.

T-39 Sabreliner - 1,950 mi rnge, 595 kts top spd. mfgd by North American.

T Stations - Commo-liaison sites along the HCMT were known as "T-Sites," and numbered T-1, T-2 and so on. Data per *A Better War*, pp 48-49. See Binh Tram in Glossary.

T'ai Tribes - Valley dwellers of T'ai Highlands W and NW Hanoi, who were primarily farmers and rice growers, and blood cousins to Siamese. Regarded by westerners as a graceful, handsome and charming people. "Their sub-tribes were distinguished from one another by color of their women's blouse, Black Tai, White Tai [there was once even a Polka-Dot T'ai] and so on," per *To The Last Cartridge*, p 352. Tribes. Described by Bernard Fall as graceful, tall, frank, and hospitable. The T'ai Federation's HQ was at Lai Chau, and its head throughout French War was Deo Van Long, per *Street Without Joy*, p 268. See also Moi, Montagnard, and Meo.

TAC AIR - Tactical Air Supt. Fighter and Bombers dropping bombs, napalm and strafing in supt of ground units.

TAC E - Tactical Emergency.

TACAIR - Tactical Air Support.

TACAN - Tactical Air Navigation. Military navigational radio transmissions that provide pilots with bearing and distance from a particular ground site. "An ultra-high frequency electronic air navigation system, able to provide continuous bearing and slant range to a selected station," per DOD Acronym file.

TAC-E - Tactical Emergency.

Tactical Urgent - Medevac priority based upon tactical situation of unit in field. Minor and non-life or limb-threatening injuries normally were given low priority for helo medevacs. However, if minor injury threatened a unit's mission, or put the unit at inordinate risk, then priority could be upgraded to this level. Was one step below an Urgent Medevac in priority.

TAD - Tactical Aerodrome Directory (DMA).

TAFD - Tactical Airfield Directory. Variant of TAD.

TAFDS - Tactical Airfield Fuel Dispensing System. Self-contained unit designed to facilitate rapid deployment of helos or small acft units to remote locations at short notice. USMC used it to for initial opening of Soc Trang AF by HMM-362, 15Apr62, as well as other AFs. Per *Bonnie-Sue*.

Tailwind, Operation - In Jun98, CNN/Time alleged and then later retracted a story that a top-secret MAC-SOG op in Sep70 had used Sarin gas. The CNN/Time rpt also claimed Adm Thomas Moorer (Chief, Naval Ops in VN) had said op was approved by President Nixon and the CIA. 1Lt Robert Van Buskirk, who made the accusation, was quoted as having said his team attacked a ville basecamp in Laos after observing what appeared to be U.S. defectors working for enemy there. He also claimed the toxic agent Sarin was used to prep site for SF raid and then to cover its extraction, but that it was not determined if targeted personnel were killed. Buskirk also claimed that Capt. Eugene McCarley, the Tailwind leader, told his men to, "Put on funny faces [code name for gas masks] because "War Daddy" [apparent call-sign of air cover] said we are coming in with gas." Both McCarley and other team members insisted mission was NOT aimed at defectors and that Sarin was NOT used. Subsequent indignant outcry from SF community led to an investigation and complete retraction by CNN/Time. Apparently gas used was CS, defectors were not op's target (in any case, conventional gas masks would not have been effective against Sarin) and story was simply figment of Buskirk's imagination and addled memories.

Taipan - A call-sign of the 134th AHC. See also EMU.

Taiwan, Forces of – See Major Commands Section.

TALO - Tactical Airlift Liaison Officer (TAD).

Tam – One Vietnamese word for "river."

Tank Battles - See A Shau Valley, An Loc, Lang Vei, Nhi Ha, Polei Kleng, and Lam Son 719 in main alpha listings. See also "Firsts" in Glossary.

TAOI - Tactical Area of Operational Interest.

TAOR - Tactical Area of Responsibility.

Tarhe - Trade name for CH-54 single rotor cargo helicopter. 230 mi rnge, 125 kts top spd. mfgd by Sikorsky Helicopter.

TASG - Tactical Air Supt Grp. 504th TASG was at Cam Ranh Bay, for example.

Task Force Russia - DOD office that investigated claims U.S. POWs had been shipped to Russia during and after VN war. Cited in *Prisoners of Hope*, at p 106.

Task Force Tally Ho - Code name for portion of Op Tiger Hound flying FAC/intel missions into DMZ, Laos and NVN. See also Tiger Hound, Steel Tiger, Baton Rouge and Barrel Roll.

Task Force Vietnam - After Gen Edward G. Landsdale had returned from fact-finding trip to SVN in Jan61 (he'd been sent by Secty of Defense, Thomas S. Gates, Jr.), Dpty Sec of Defense, Roswell Gilpatric was put in charge of an inter-department TF later known as "Task Force, Vietnam." Its assignment was to delineate actions JFK's new administration would take in VN. This action followed the 3Apr61 signing of "Treaty of Amity and Economic Relations" (3 wks before Diem was elected), and VP Johnson's subsequent 11May61 visit to Diem and 13May61 announcement of addnl economic/military aid to Diem Govt. Some data per *Viet-Nam; How We Got There*, Aug99 *Military* Mag, pp 22-23.

TASS - USAF Tactical Air Supt Sqdn. Recon and supt FAC acft (O-1 Bird Dog, 0-2 Skymaster/Oscar Deuce and OV-10 Bronco) that provided fwd air control supt for grnd troops and/or directed independent offensive air ops against grnd targets in SEA. The 20th TASS (Coveys) at Da Nang and the 23d TASS (Nails) at NKP are examples of such units. *Da Nang Diary* provides a very detailed look at TASS ops and SCAR (Strike Control & Recon) missions in general.

Tay - Vietnamese for "West."

TCN - See Third Country Nationals in Glossary.

TCS - Tactical Control Center.

TDKQ – Acronym for "Tieu-Doan Kinh Quan," or Viet National Commando Bns. The French built school to train select Viet Natl troops to out-guerrilla the guerrilla using Vietminh's own tactics in order to draw enemy out where arty and air power could decimate them. 1st graduating Bns were assigned to Bui Chi sector at S edge of Red River Delta to counter 2 Vietminh Rgts in that area. Recognizing real threat the org represented, the Vietminh responded by thoroughly hammering the young, untried Bns in order to embarrass their reputations forever (successfully). School was at Quang Yen, a city on marshy, isolated isthmus apx 15 km NW Haiphong

(another such school was also built in SVN). Data per *Street Without Joy*, p 183. NVN.
TDY - Temporary Duty.
tel - telephone (TAD).
Term - Terminal.
TERM - Temporary Equipment Recovery Mission. Apparently U.S. military op in VN in during '54-55, that violated terms of May54 Geneva Accords. Once the TERM Op was completed, its staff stayed in SVN and formed part of the 20th MAAG. Data per *How We Got There*, Dec99 *Military* Mag, pp 20-21.
Tess, Typhoon - See Typhoon Tess in main alpha listings.
Tet - 1st week of Viet Lunar New Year and most important annual holiday period for them. Dates vary from year to year.
Tet 68 Offensive - See main alpha entry.
TF-115 – USN Task Force 115. See Market Time.
TF-116 - USN Task Force 116. See Game Warden.
TF-117 - USN Task Force 117. See Mobile Riverine Force.
TF-9J Cougar - 600 mi rnge, 705 kts top spd. mfgd by Grumman Avn.
tfc - traffic (TAD).
TFG - Tactical Fighter Group (USAF).
TFO - Task Force Oregon.
The List of Adrian Messenger - See "Kinh Do Movie Theater" in main alpha listings.
TFW - Tactical Fighter Wing (USAF).
TG - Task Group (USN).
Thich Tam Chau - Buddhist leader of Institute for Propagation of Buddhist Faith. See High Clerical Association and Thinh Tri Quang in Glossary.
Thinh Tri Quang - Buddhist leader antagonistic to military govt of SVN in '66. Described by Nguyen Cao Ky as unscrupulous and more a politician than a religious leader. In Mar66, only month after the Honolulu Conference, Ky decided to clamp down on Buddhists opposing his govt. Tri Quang headed the High Clerical Assn of Buddhists (a doctrinal org), and was considered a militant anti-American and a "hard-liner." In May66, Ky attacked and seized key points in Da Nang from Buddhist (and pro-Buddhist unit's of ARVN 1st Corps) control, and then cut off all means of resupply to main Buddhist HQ in Hue. Tri Quang and Gen Nhuan soon surrendered soon, and Hue and Da Nang returned to govt control. Thereafter, Tri Quang was held under house arrest at a Saigon hospital. For detailed look at Ky's response Buddhist activism, see *Twenty Years and Twenty Days*, Chp 8, pp 87-100.
Third Country Nationals - A.k.a. "TCNs." DAO/US Embassy term describing civilian and military staff from countries other than SVN and U.S. (such as those from Korea and Philippines).
Third Offensive - NVA/VC's Aug68 offensive. Primarily "attacks by fire" and "stand-off attacks" using indirect fires, but very few grnd assaults (due in part to numerous U.S. preemptive strikes). Resulted in est 22,000 NVA VC KIA nonetheless. See Year of Decision, and Tet '68 Offensive.
Third Vietnam, The - Hanoi's name for territories captured and held after '72. Easter Offensive. Per *A Better War*, p 342.
thld - threshold (TAD).
Thon – One of several Viet words for "village."
Three Bees, The – "Blind them. Burn them. Blast them." A USMC doctrine taught to its recruits during '60s.
Three-Quarter Cav - Nickname of 3d Bn, 4th Armored Cavalry.
thru - through (TAD).
Thu Huong - See Hanoi Hannah.
Thunder - Call-sign for 3d Bde/10st Abn HQ Hueys/LOHs.
Thunder Run - Armored Cav's version of "mad minute." Tactic in which armored columns would roll down roads at full throttle firing into likely avenues of approach in deliberate attempt to draw fire. Apparently common along QL-19E between LZs Schueller and Action. Data per Ray smith at www.rjsmith.com/topo3.html.
Thunderbird - A call-sign of the 119th AHC.
Thunderchief - Trade name for F-105, single eng, jet fighter bomber, a.k.a. "Wild Weasels." 2,390 mi rnge, 1,480 kts top spd. mfgd by Republic Acft.
TIC – "Troops In Contact" (with the enemy).
Tien Len - Vietminh, NVA and VC equiv to battle-cry "forward" or "charge." Per *Chickenhawk*, p 107.
Tieu-Doan Kinh Quan - See TDKQ.
Tiger - A call-sign of the 121st AHC.
Tiger - Mongrel mascot dog at Soc Trang who may have earned the Air Medal. See Tiger's Den in main alpha listing for detail.
Tiger Attacks – A significant number fatalities/injuries resulted from tiger attacks during war, particularly among recon teams. Same was true of line Marine/Army units working mtns of Thua Thien and Quang Tri Provs, as well as in the central highlands. For example, in '68, near FSB Alpine, a 3d Mar Div soldier was killed by tiger and later, a 3d Recon Bn team member was badly mauled near Alpine by perhaps same tiger. In 2d incident, tiger was shot and killed, but not before inflicting wounds that led to medical retirement of Richard P. Gooding. Following is excerpt from 1st/502d Inf/101st '69 Hist Supp: "5 Feb[69]...A-1/501 became opcon 1/502d. A Co conducted RIF from T-Bone to YD 642-187. At 1420 hours vicinity YD 644-191 the pointman was attacked by a tiger. There were [no] U.S. casualties and tiger was wounded" On front page of 26Jan69, *Ivy leaf* is article and picture of 300-lb "man-eating" tigress tracked and killed by elements of Civil Affair Sect, 3d/8th Inf/4th Inf Div, climaxing 2-month hunt. Tiger had apparently molested livestock and citizens of Plei Breng Keng and Plei Donau. 4th Div Op rpt for period ending31Jan69 (per Craig Miller) states that on 2Nov68, Tiger attacked and killed "member of an SRP from Co A, 2d(Mech)/8th Inf," near ZA 056-224. Other incidents also discussed in *Time Heals No Wounds*, at pp 38, 67. See also LZ Charmaine in main alpha listing.
Tiger Beer - See *Bier La Rue*.
Tiger Cages - (XQ77-63) Nickname for infamous SVN prison cells of Con Son Island. On Poulo Condore Islands, a 5-isle grp in South China Sea, apx 85 km from SVN coast, and 200 km E tip of Cau Mau Peninsula. See also Con Son Island. IV Corps.
Tiger Division - (BR/CR) Republic of Korea's Capital Div. In VN Sep65-Mar73. HQ was Qui Nhon. Operated primarily between Phu Cat and Phan Rang, II Corps. See also White Horse Div and Korean Forces.
Tiger Hound Operations - U.S. secret air ops in Laos were divided into 3 zones: Tiger Hound, Steel Tiger and Barrel Roll. Tiger Hound was area immediately adj to SVN that ran roughly from DMZ, S to Cambodian border and about 100 km W into Laos. Was considered part of "extended battleground." In late '65, area was carved from Steel Tiger's zone and put under control of MACV, while remainder of Steel Tiger retained original name. See also Steel Tiger and Barrel Roll.

Tiger Shark - Call-sign of the 192d AHC's gunships.
Tiger Tower - Call-sign of ROK Airfield Control.
Tigershark - A call-sign of the 192d AHC's gunships.
til - until (TAD).
Tin Quan Ca - Natl Anthem of NVN. Means "Forward Soldiers."
Tin Trunk - RNZA nomenclature for firing arty registrations of pre-set defensive targets (DF task registrations), or Delta Tangos, as they were known by U.S. forces. See also Delta Tango.
Tinh - Vietnamese word for "Province." See also Quan.
tkof - takeoff (TAD).
TL (Road System) - Designator for provincial routes of SVN road system. Typically represented by 2 digits in triangle-shaped map symbol. Third in hierarchy of road identifiers behind major Natl/International roads (QL's) and Inter-Prov roads (LTL's). Were step in quality above Supplementary Roads (Routes). See also QL, LTL, Route, Highway, HL, R. C., *Route Colonial*, as well as "Principal Roadways of South Vietnam" Section.
Toan Thang - Vietnamese for "Complete Victory." Many ARVN ops were named Toan Thang (followed by numeric designator).
TOC - Tactical Operations Center. Electronic commo and/or C&C center of a military unit. Also used generally as reference to bunker or bldg in which that element was located.
TOE - Table of Organization & Equipment.
Tomb, The - Sardonic nickname for 4' x 6', centrally-located, heavily-reinforced and armored radio room that was part of each *de Lattre Bunkers* of *de Lattre Line*.
Tonkin - See main alpha entry.
Toro - Call-sign for B Bty, 4th/77th ARA gunships.
Topo - Topographical.
TOSB - Tactical Operations Supt Base. 25th Inf Div nomenclature for Bde-sized or larger basecamp.
Tour Extensions - See DEROS.
Tour of Duty - Stnd VN tour of duty for all U.S. military branches (except USMC) was one year. Stnd tour for USMC was 13 months (USMC added addnl month to distinguish themselves from other branches as symbol of their esprit, toughness and dedication perhaps?). Practice was probably single-most disruptive, imprudent and deadly prgm instituted by MACV/DOD during entire war. It contributed greatly to sad outcome by robbing U.S. military of trained, competent officers, NCOs and EMs, destroying unit cohesiveness, esprit and morale. It was also no doubt directly responsible for much needless loss of life. Gen Westmoreland is often blamed for the practice, but claim seems improbable since a decision of such gravity more likely trickled down from the JCS and/or President Johnson. Per *A Better War*, p 288, at its highest level, U.S. troop turnover hit 120% per year. See DEROS.
TPC - Tactical Pilotage Chart. Produced by DMA/NIMA and marketed through NOAA. 1:500,000 scale, color, topographical, aeronautical charts in which color denotes altitude rather than vegetation type. 1"= apx 13 km on a TPC. See also ONC.
TPC-25 Radar - Personnel movement detecting radar equip used by ANZAC forces(and presumably US). 1st employed by 1ATF, Aug70, on slopes of Nui Dat and FSB Horseshoe to alert arty and RAR ambush units to enemy movements and their location.
TRAC - ARVN Third Regional Assistance Cmd (TAD).
Tracer - Trade name for E-1B acft. 875 mi rnge, 225 kts top spd. mfgd by Grumman Avn.
Trader - Trade name for C-1A acft. 875 mi rnge, 228 kts top spd. mfgd by Grumman Avn.
Tram – One Vietnamese word for lake or pool.
tran - transient (TAD).
Tran Le Xuan Le - See Madame Nhu.
trans - transport, transmit, transmitter, transmitting.
Transportation Corridor - See Ho Chi Minh Trail.
Traps, The – See *Les pieges*.
Trench, Never by Never - See Never by Never Trench.
Trng - Training.
Trojan - See T-28.
Tropic Lightning - Nickname of the 25th Inf Div, whose Div patch features a lightning bolt over a red field. Unofficial nickname was "The Electric Strawberry."
Tropic Lightning News - Newspaper of the 25th Inf Div in Vietnam. Was published by "Information Office, 25th Inf Div, APO 96225," and printed in Tokyo by the *Pacific Stars & Stripes*.
Tropo – Troposhperic or Troposcatter.
Troposcatter Signal Sites - Sites using large, round Tropospheric commo antennas. Normally built on tallest terrain feature in given area. Tropo Hill and Dragon Mtn Signal Sites are examples.
Trp - Troop.
Trps - Troops.
Trung Doi Phong Khong - Vietminh Anti-Aircraft Platoon. Normally equipped with 2 machine guns and 1 BAR. Data per *Street Without Joy*, p 266. See also Dai Doi Phong Khong.
Truong Son Trail - See Ho Chi Minh Trail.
TSN - Tan Son Nhut.
Tu Dai - Viet phrase for "Danger Zone" or "Kill Zone." VC often posted such signs in booby-trapped and mined areas to warn civilians and other VC of danger. Often, they were posted simply as psychological/tactical ploy in areas that were actually free of mines or, in some instances to channel US/ARVN into, rather than away from, mined or booby-trapped area as unit maneuvered around posted area and into a mined area or ambush. See Mins.
Tuc Fin - Apparent phonetic interpretation of Viet phrase for Marijuana. Also said to be "Kum Sah?"
Twenty Mike-Mike - Nickname for 20mm cannon and/or its ammo. Typically an acft-mounted mini-gun (Gatling gun); a six-barreled machine gun operated by a GE electric motor that could deliver incredibly high rates of fire (1,000 to 6,000 rnds/min). A.k.a. "Pepper Grinders," a nicknamed derived from deep-throated grating sound they produced when fired. AH-1 Cobras (and other fixed-wing acft and helos) employed a 7.62mm version of gun. See also M-73, M-134, M-214.
Twenty-Two Step Snake - Per *Rites of Passage*, p 322, was viper whose venom was so potent that when bitten, victim would last but 30 seconds or 22-paces, whichever came first. See also Two-Step and Seven-Step Snakes.
Two-Man Rule - 5th SF Grp rule that there could be no less than 2 U.S. SF personnel on patrol with any CIDG or Mike Force unit. Cited in *Team Sergeant*, p 139.
Two-Step Snake - Bright-green Bamboo Viper whose venom was so potent it spawned myth that when bitten, person would be dead within 2 steps. See also Twenty-Two Step and Seven Step Snakes.
twr - tower (TAD).
twy - taxiway (TAD).
Typhoon - Monthly newsletter/magazine of IFFV.
Typhoon Tess - See main alpha entry.

U-2 - U.S. single-jet eng, high-altitude, long rnge recon and spy acft. 4,750 mi rnge, 530 kts top spd. mfgd by Lockheed Acft. CIA code name was "Dragon Lady."

U-2 Crash near Song Be - In Dec66 (or Jan67), a U-2 spy plane (Dragon Lady) crashed near Song Be and Capt Bo Gritz's newly-formed (1st ever MGF) Det A-303's 1st assignment was to find wreckage and its ultra-secret ECM 13A black box. Despite fact the U-2 fell in 440 sq. mi. area, MGF found and recovered the ECM 13A. See *Mobile Guerrilla Force*, pp 4-7.

U-10 - The Heliocourier. Single eng, high-winged, multi-passenger acft used almost exclusively by CSG (Combined Studies Group, a.k.a. SOG), an arm of the CIA. mentioned in *The Green Berets*. 660 mi rnge, 165 kts top spd. mfgd by Helio.

U-21 Ute - 1,215 mi rnge, 265 kts top spd. mfgd by Beechcraft.

U-22 - 200 mi rnge. mfgd by Beechcraft.

UC - Unit Commendation (USN).

UCMJ - Uniform Code of Military Justice. Laws governing military criminal law in all branches of U.S. military. Otherwise known as Chapter 47, Title 10, U.S. Code. 1st instituted in May51, and later significantly amended in Aug69 and Sep84.

UDT - Underwater Demolition Team. See Seal and Seal Teams.

UFFLPLL - United Front of Lao People for Liberation of Laos. Org headed by Lao Deputy Premier, Gen Phuomi Nosavon, who joined CIA in attempted coup and later set up exiled cmd in Bangkok. Gen apparently spent many years milking POW/MIA hunters and families with promises of assistance (inc a contract with Bo Gritz to supply troops for Op Lazarus). After his death, Nosavon's son Phoumi took-over org and apparently continued father's POW scams. See *Prisoners of Hope*, pp 209-212.

UFN - Until Further Notice (TAD).

UFO Bird, The - See HE Bird.

UFO Sightings – An unknown number of UFO's sightings were rptd during war. For example, in Jan69, a UFO was spotted from LZ Charmaine (YA 998-217) by 2d/9th Arty troops (per *Time Heals No Wounds*, pp 91, 101), and later that same night was rptd circling at ZA 10-27, ZA 08-22 and ZA 01-23, where it was said to have had a red light but no sound. It then landed near YA 975-267 and arty was fired at it, upon which it moved to YA 964-276, where arty was again employed. Subsequent sweeps of those sites found nothing. On 31Jan69, four more UFOs with one blinking white beacon were spotted from LZ Charmaine. 4th Div Op Rpt for period ending 31Jan69, contains following entry at p 5: "(1)(b) Numerous sightings of unidentified acft near LZs Joan (YA 842-280) Charmaine, and Lanetta (YA 852-457) by both visual and electronic means. No tactical significance can be attached to these sightings [at present]. On specific occasions the acft sighted were identified as Soviet K-18 (Hog), a Yak-24 medium helicopter, and a Czech HC-2 Trainer." Dick Arnold also notes that 1st/35th Inf logs rpt radar sightings of "unknown aircraft," thought to be NVA choppers, W of Duc Co, in late Oct68. "They actually scrambled some 7th/17th Cav gunships at around 0400, and in ensuing "dogfight" the Cav claimed to have shot down one chopper and possibly 'another unidentified acft.' Claimed the downed chopper was in terrain too thick to get a fix on it. No mention of a subsequent search, which seems odd, so may have been across the fence?" See also LZ Charmaine. As far as author can discern, no rpts of alien abductions or crop circles were recorded.

Ugly Angel - A call-sign of USMC HMM-362.

UH-1 Iroquois Helicopter - A.k.a. Hueys, Slicks, and Bell UH-1 Utility helicopter. By far, most widely-used helo of the American War. The C, D and H models were the most common models used. Some Hueys were also used as weapons platforms, taking on role of attack helos or "gunships" (nicknamed "Hogs") after being fitted with various combos of multiple M-60 MGs, 7.62 mini-guns, .50 Cal MGs, rocket pods and 40mm grenade launchers. Had 125 mi rnge, 145 kts top spd. mfgd by Bell Helicopter.

UITG - USARV Individual Trng Grp. See main alpha listing.

Under the Southern Cross – Americal Div's motto.

Unit Diaries - USMC official unit histories. See Table of Contents: *Researching the Vietnam War*.

Unit Rosters - U.S. Army unit rosters. See Table of Contents: *Researching the Vietnam War*.

United Seaman's Service Clubs - Operated clubs for Merchant Marines at most major ports in VN, including Da Nang, Cam Ranh, Qui Nhon, Saigon and New Port.

University of Maryland - U of Maryland provided an extensive array of college correspondence courses that were widely used throughout U.S. Military and for those troops in VN with the time, facilities and logistical supt sufficient to attend those courses. A number of larger bases had education centers providing high school and college level courses. See also Cu Chi University in main alpha listings.

unk - unknown (TAD).

unltgd - unlighted (TAD).

unmrk - unmarked (TAD).

unrel - unreliable (TAD).

unsvc - unserviceable (TAD).

URC-10 - Hand-held emergency UHF radio employed by SF and LRRP troops. Photo of this radio is in *Vietnam Order of Battle*, p 304. See also URC-68.

URC-68 – The ARCR-10 (URC-10?) and URC-68 were both UHF hand-held radios used by LRRP and SF units. See also URC-10.

Urgency, Project - See Project Urgency.

Urgent Medevac - Highest priority for Medevac helicopter assistance. See also Tactical Urgent.

US Armed Forces Institute - A.k.a. USAFI. See Cu Chi University in main alpha listing and Univ of Maryland in Glossary.

US Army Boats in Vietnam - Very detailed and substantial listing of U.S. Army water craft serving in VN is available on Army Transportation Assn website at http://academic.uofs.edu/ faculty/ gramborw/atav/ default.html, with the file address of http:// 134.198.33.115/hulltypes.htm. List attempts to identify every Army vessel in war, from huge floating cranes and tankers down to smallest patrol craft and tugs.

US Naval Forces Vietnam – See Major Commands Section.

US Support Activities Group - See main alpha entry.

USA - U.S. Army.

USACTIV - U.S. Army Concept Team In Vietnam.

USAF - U.S. Air Force.

USAFI - U.S. Armed Forces Institute. Educational institution providing college level training in wide variety of subjects. See also Cu Chi University and University of Maryland.

USAID - U.S. Agency for International Development. Created in '61 and, by '65, had budget of $2 billion and over 15,000

civilian employees. In '67, its VN budget alone was $550 million. After '68, its apparent failures and rumors of CIA involvement helped slowly eroded agency to apx 6,000 people by '75.
USARPAC - U.S. Army, Pacific.
USARV - U.S. Army, Republic of Vietnam.
USARV Individual Training Groups - UITGs or USARVITG. SF trng courses for SVN forces created near end of war. UITGs were at Chi Lang, Lang Hai and Dong Ba Thin. See those locations in main alpha listing for more detail.
USB - Upper Side Band (TAD).
USCG - U.S. Coast Guard.
USCGC - U.S. Coast Guard Cutter.
USCGS - U.S. Coast Guard Ship.
USMC - U.S. Marine Corps.
USN - U.S. Navy.
USNR - U.S. Naval Reserve.
USNS - U.S. Naval Ship.
USOM - United States Operations Mission. A.k.a. USAID.
USSAG - U.S. Support Activities Group.
Ute - Trade name for U-21 acft. 1,215 mi rnge, 265 kts top spd. mfgd by Beechcraft.
UTM Grid Zones - Universal Transverse Mercator projection, grid zone system. Global military grid overlay used for most map reading in VN and source for all grid coordinates noted in this publication. The 2-character alpha designators preceding the numeric portion of a grid coordinate designate the UTM grid zone to which the numeric portion of grid relates. To view the UTM Zones overlying SVN and NVN, refer to UTM Grid Zone maps in map section of this text.
VA - Attack Squadron (USN).
VA - Veterans Administration.
Vagabond Crossing - Call-sign for Tuy Hoa Airfield Control.
VAH - Heavy Attack Squadron (USN).
VAL - Light Attack Squadron (USN).
Vampire - Call-sign of 1st Australian Hospital medevac units.
Van Ba - See Ho Chi Minh.
Van Toan, General - See Cinnamon General.
VAP - Heavy Photographic Squadron (USN).
VAQ - Tactical Electronic Warfare Squadron (USN).
VARS - Visual Airborne (Recon) (USN).
Varsity - Call-sign for CH-46 Chinooks of B Co, 159th Avn Bn.
VAW - Carrier Airborne Early Warning Sqdn (USN).
VC - Victoria Cross.
VC - Viet Cong. SVN communist/NLF guerrilla forces. Generally grouped into Main Force VC and Local Force VC depending on mission, quality, armament and trng. See Viet Cong.
VC/NVA propaganda leaflets - Leaflet examples at: www.en.com/users/kramsey/propag1.html. See also numerous examples pictured in *Vietnam Military Lore, 1959-1973*.
VC Lake – Most any shallow inland body of water was euphemistically as a "VC Lake" by USN's Seawolves helo pilots.
vcnty - vicinity (TAD).
VDCA - Vietnam Directorate of Civil Aviation (TAD).
Velvet Hammer, Operation - 1st post-war, privately-funded POW rescue mission. Organized by activist and former U.S. SF soldier, Bo Gritz, in '80s. Goal was to find and release U.S. POWs held at POW camp in Laos called "Fort Apache," with assistance of a Psychic named Karen Page. Gritz canceled mission in '81. Discussed in *Prisoners of Hope*, pp 131-136.
vert - vertical (TAD).
VF - Fighter Squadron (USN).
VFP - Light Photographic Squadron(USN).
VFR - Refrigerated Covered Lighter, self-propelled. (USN).
VFR - Visual Flight Rules.
VHPA Battle Index - Large chronological index of ops, acft losses and battles available on homepage of Vietnam Helicopter Pilots Assn at www.vhpa.org/info/panel/battle/.
vic – Vicinity, or "in vicinity of."
Victor Charlie - The Viet Cong, or generally any enemy troops. Slang derived from military phonetic alphabet for initials "VC." See also Viet Cong.
Victor Sites – SVN AFs. Per Kent Spalding, Lima Sites designated CIA/USAF secret AFs and positions in Laos, "Charley Sites" those in Cambodia, and "Victor Sites" those in SVN. See also LS and Lima Sites. SVN.
Viet Cong - Derisive nickname originally given to southern communist element of NLF (officially the National Liberation Front, and in Vietnamese: Mat Tran Dan Toc Giai Phong Mien Nam) by SVN President Ngo Dinh Diem sometime after NLF was formed by Ho Chi Minh, 20Dec60 (another text puts date at 31Dec60). NLF was secret org designed to replace the Mat Tran To Quoc (the "Fatherland Front"). Phrase "Viet Cong" literally meant "Vietnamese Communists." Term became a euphemism for enemy and took on various forms such as VC or Victor Charlie or Victor Charles that were born in military phonetic alphabetic initials for "V" and "C." Other slang (and sometimes racist) variants included: Charlie, Chuck, Chuck and his Boys, Dink, Gook, Little People, Slopes and Nguyen of the North.
Viet Kich - SVN government's "People's Action Team."
Viet Minh - Per Sep52 issue of *National Geographic Magazine*, the term Viet Minh translated as "the Association of People." Was also nickname for org named "Viet Nam Doc Lap Dong Minh Loi," a.k.a. "League for Independence of Vietnam." Established May41, by 8th Plenum of Indochinese Communist Party, whose leader was the resilient and popular Ho Chi Minh. Its major victory over French at Dien Bien Phu, May54, led to end of French occupation and partitioning of VN into NVN/SVN under Geneva Accords. Guerrilla forces in SVN were called Vietminh (or Viet Minh) until about 1960, when President Diem derisively nicknamed them the "Viet Cong" (Vietnamese Communists).
Viet Nam - See Vietnam.
Vietminh - See Viet Minh.
Vietnam - One source country's "Viet Nam" name was of Chinese origin and meant "cross over to south." Sep52 issue of *National Geographic Magazine* cites it as historic name meaning "People of South," apparently revived during French occupation. In *The Unquiet American*, p 143, Cecil Currey tells us name was derived from term "Nam Viet," which in Chinese was "Yueh-Nan" (Chinese southern province of Kwangtung's ancient name), meaning "land of south," "distant south" or "south of Yeuh."
Vietnam, The State of - The fragile, primarily fictitious government under Emperor Bao Dai created by French following their defeat by Vietminh. See *The Unquiet American*, p 137.
Vietnam Campaign Medal - See Republic of Vietnam Campaign Medal.
Vietnam Combat Zone - Officially established and defined by President Lyndon B. Johnson's Exec Order. No. 11216, 24Apr65, "30 F. R. 5817" which stated, "Pursuant to authority

vested in me by section 112 of Internal Revenue Code of 1954 (now I.R.C. 1986), I hereby designate, for purposes of that section, as an area in which Armed Forces of United States are and have been engaged in combat: Vietnam, including the waters adj thereto within the following-described limits: From a point on East Coast of Vietnam at juncture of Vietnam with China southeastward to 21 N Lat., 108 15 E Long.; thence southward to 18 N Lat., 108 15 E Long.; thence southeastward to 17 30 N Lat., 111 E Long.; thence southward to 11 N Lat., 111 E Long.; thence southwestward to 7 N Lat., 105 E Long.; thence westward to 7 N Lat., 103 E Long.; thence northward to 9 30 N Lat., 103 E Long.; thence northeastward to 10 15 N Lat., 104 27 E Long.; thence northward to a point on West Coast of Vietnam at juncture of Vietnam with Cambodia. The date of commencing of combatant activities in such area is hereby designated as January 1, 1964."

Vietnam National Army - A.k.a. VNA. French name for its unenthusiastic creation of Viet Natl military to counter the Vietminh. Organizing began in '50 but by '51, only 38,000 of planned 115,000 man force had been recruited and concept never fully developed before French were ousted in '54.

Vietnam Presse - Vietnamese governmental bulletin of 1st Indochina War.

Vietnam Service Medal - A.k.a. the VSM. Established by Exec Order # 11231, 8Jul65. Was U.S. campaign medal awarded to all who served in or over the Vietnam Combat Zone. On 24Apr64, President Kennedy signed an Exec order retroactively allowing U.S. Servicemen wounded in SVN to receive the Purple Heart effective 15Mar62. Although the VSM was not created until 8Jul65, it also became retroactive to 1Jul58 for those personnel who had been awarded the Armed Forces Expeditionary Medal and wished to exchange it for VSM. VSM award period therefore effectively began 1Jul58 and ended 28Jan73; however, the campaign stars attached to ribbon (one per campaign period served) was only authorized between 15Mar62 and 28Jan73. The "Cease Fire" campaign period (last of 17 campaigns in VN War) ended 28Jan73. Although that dates marks the end of award period, Camp Alpha at Tan Son Nhut AB was very last U.S. military facility to close at end of U.S. involvement in SVN, and its flag was actually lowered in ceremony occurring 29Jan73. Per *Vietnam Military Lore, 1959-1973*, pp 237-238, an honor guard of apx 50 U.S. personnel gave a final salute as U.S. flag was lowered and then the base officially turned-over to SVN Govt. Moments after ceremony ended, "Vietnamese looters, both military and civilian, ransacked the camp and carried off everything the in Camp Alpha that wasn't securely affixed." Later, looters tore down most of buildings and fixtures as well, and left facility in ruins.

Vietnam Shower - RNZA gunner's nickname for bathing technique used during mid May-Nov monsoons. Involved stripping inside a tent, stepping out to get wet, stepping inside again to lather and then stepping out again to rinse! Per *Vietnam Gunners*.

Vietnam Tour Extensions - See DEROS.

Vietnam Tour of Duty - See Tour of Duty.

Vietnamese Cross of Gallantry - Medal awarded by SVN Govt to units or individuals for courage under fire against an armed enemy force. Attachments to award represent the level at which it was awarded and varied in type by branch of service. For Army personnel, a "Palm" represented an entire armed force level award, a Gold star represented a Corps level award; a Silver Star a Div-level award, and Bronze Star a Bde or Rgtl-level award. The shape of attachments changed when same award was presented to Navy and Air Force personnel where a similarly colored "wing" was attached to Air Gallantry Cross and similarly colored "anchor" to Navy Gallantry Cross. Some data per *Vietnam Military Lore, 1959-1973*, pp 254. See also Vietnamese Meritorious Unit Commendation.

Vietnamese Meritorious Unit Commendation - A.k.a. the Vietnamese Gallantry Cross with palm and frame. Per George Neville, was awarded to personnel who served on land and in country (but not off-shore participation) for period 8Feb62-28Mar73 (author was unable to confirm if there was a similarly unique form of Gallantry Cross awarded for naval participation as well?). See also Vietnamese Cross of Gallantry.

Vigilante - See RA5-C.

Viking - Call-sign of the121st AHC.

Viking Surprise - Nickname for Firefly missions of 121st AHC. See also Firefly.

Vinell, Inc. - One of several major civilian contractors (along with Alaska Barge & Transport, RMK-BRJ and PA&E), that were involved in building and maintaining U.S. facilities in SVN.

Vinh Loc Bell - See Vinh Loc Bell and Vinh Loc Pacification Hamlets in main alpha listing.

vis - visibility (TAD).

VM - Vietminh.

VMA - Marine Attack Squadron(USMC).

VMF - Marine Fighter Squadron (USMC).

VN - Vietnam or Vietnamese.

VNA - Vietnamese National Army (TAD).

VNAF - Vietnamese Air Force (TAD).

VNAF - Vietnamese Air Force.

VNN - Vietnamese Navy (TAD).

VNSF - Vietnamese Special Forces.

Voice of America, Manila - When at altitude during 1st Indochina War, U.S. pilots of CAT would often tune in British news broadcasts from Singapore. Could also tune in musical "jam sessions" on Voice of America broadcasting from Manila. Per *Street Without Joy*, pp 108-109.

Volunteers of Death - Vietminh equiv to Japanese Kamikaze. Volunteers who strapped satchel charges to their bodies and hurled themselves against French positions (inc doors of *de Lattre Line* bunkers). Were very effective in Battle of Mao Khe.

Von Sydow, Max - See Operation Shotgun in main alpha listing.

Voodoo - Trade name for RF-101, twin-jet fighter acft 2,200 mi rnge, 1100 kts top spd. mfgd by McDonnell.

VOR – Acronym for "Very-high-frequency Omnidirectional Radio-range." Air navigational radio aid which uses phase comparison of grnd transmitted signal to determine bearing, per DOD Acronym file.

Voting Machines - Sarcastic nickname for ARVN tanks and other armored vehicles because of their frequent use to intimidate in most every change of govt. ARVN Armor nicknamed "Coup Troops" for same reason.

VP - Patrol Squadron (USN).

VQ - Fleet Air Reconnaissance Squadron (USN).

VR - Air Transport Squadron (USN).

VR - Visual Recon. Infantry unit leaders would often recon their planned line of movement from air using helo supt.

VRC - Air Transport Squadron (USN).

VSF - Antisubmarine Fighter Squadron (USN).

Vulture - A call-sign of the 162d AHC.

Vung - Vietnamese for bay.
Vung Ro Incident - On 3Mar65, helo pilot James Bowers spotted an island moving in Vung Ro bay, near Cape Varella and S of Qui Nhon. Closer look revealed that a trawler had been camouflaged with potted trees. As a result, ship and nearby beaches were attacked and craft captured. The 100-ton trawler was carrying some 1 million rnds small arms ammo, 1,000 grenades, 500 lbs of satchel charges, 2,000 rnds 81mm, 500 RPG rnds, 3,600 rifles, 500 lbs of medical gear and proof crew/materials were from NVN. Provided 1st solid proof NVN was supplying VC and infiltrating troops/advisors by sea. Led to creation of Op Market Time. Data per *Brown Water, Black Berets*, p 76-79.
W - West.
w/ - with.
War Daddy - See Operation Tailwind.
War of Vast Empty Spaces - See *Le Guerre des Grandes Vides*.
War Zone C - see main alpha listing.
War Zone D - see main alpha listing.
Warnes, Catherine Anne - Australian USO entertainer shot and killed by Sgt James W. Killen, 20Jul69, while she was entertaining troops at Da Nang. Was thought Killen meant to shoot Maj Roger E. Simmons, CO 1st Recon Bn (Killen's unit), but no disciplinary or other action had been taken by Simmons against Killen, and no other apparent motive could be identified. Killen was convicted at 1st trial, but acquitted on appeal.
Warning Star - See EC-121.
Warrior - A call-sign for 145th CAB(?), and 336th AHC.
Water Cannons - See Douche Boats. IV Corps.
Water Pump - Call-sign and nickname of Det 6, USAF 1st Air Commando Wing, deployed to Thailand in '64. Was later call-sign of Det 1, 56th Spec Ops Wing at Udorn AFB, Thailand.
Waterboy Control - (YD 24-59) Call-sign for 620th Tactical Control Center (TCS), Dong Ha. See also main alpha listing.
Web Gear - See LBE.
WHA - Wounded, Hostile Action.
WHEC - High Endurance Cutter Craft (USCG term).
Whiskey India Alpha - See Kilo India Alpha.
Whispering Death - NVA nickname for B-52 Arc Light bombing. Also USAF nickname for the F-111 Fighter-Bomber.
White Christmas, I'm Dreaming of a - See American Radio Service.
White Horse Division - Republic of Korea's 9th Inf Div. In VN 27Sep66-16Mar73. See also Tiger Div in Glossary and Korean Forces in Major Command Section.
White Mice - A.k.a. Cham Sat or NP. Derisive nickname for SVN Natl Police, who wore impeccably clean white uniforms but who paradoxically were also noted for their brutality and incompetence. Per *A Better War*, pp 147-148, during '68, over 10,000 men were added to Natl Police in Div known as the "Police Field Force" (PFF). See Police Field Force for more detail.
White Owl - Nickname for cigar-sized Marijuana cigarette available in the Hue/Phu Bai area circa 1970. In the Bong Son area around LZs English and North English in Binh Dinh Prov, such cigar-sized joints were called "Bong Son Bombers" (per *Charlie Rangers*, p 42). As one trooper so aptly put it, "One of them baby's could stone an entire platoon!"
White Star - See Hotfoot/White Star, SF ops in Laos, 1959-62.
White Star Mobile Training Team - SF unit tasked to train Laotian forces beginning Jul59, and withdrawn in '62. At peak in '62, over 500 U.S. troops were training Lao soldiers and Hmong tribesman under this prgm. See also Hotfoot/White Star.
White Star, Operation - See Hotfoot/White Star.
White T'ai - See T'ai Tribes in Glossary.
White, Capt. John - See "First Americans to Visit Vietnam."
WIA - Wounded In Action.
Wide Minnow Control - Call-sign of 24th Evac Hosp, Qui Nhon.
WIEU - Weekly Intelligence Estimate Updates. Conducted by MACV HQ and pronounced "woo."
Wild People, The - See Moi.
Willie Peter - A.k.a. White Phosphorous. Available in arty and mortar rnds, as well hand grenades and conventional bombs. Primarily an incendiary and anti-personnel weapon, but often used to mark positions or to mask movement using smoke screen provided by its dense, billowing, pure-white smoke. Was infamous in anti-personnel role because phosphorous ignites when exposed to oxygen and is very difficult to extinguish. As a result, it continued burning inside wound for an extended period, causing extreme agony unless somehow cut-off from oxygen by some means (such as packing wound with mud). See Mark Missions.
Winds of Laos - Seasonal phenomena in I Corps. These westerly winds (often exceeding 45 knots) blew in from Laos and created severe turbulence along ridges that often hampered air ops. In Jun-Jul69, they affected AO of 101st Abn with 30-45 knot winds recorded at Camp Eagle, per 101st Abn Div ORLL of 9Dec69, p 22, online at: http://carlisle-www.army.mil/usamhi/DL/chron.htm #AVietnamWar19601973.
Winged Assault - A call-sign of the 229th AHB.
Winged Warrior 1 - Motto or call-sign of 228th AHB (a.k.a. "Guns-a-Go-Go").
Winged Warrior 2 - Motto or call-sign of 228th ASHB.
wk - week(s) (TAD).
wkd - weekday(s) (TAD).
wng - warning (TAD).
WNW - West North West.
WO - Warrant Officer.
Wolfpack – Call-sign for 8th Tactical Fighter Wing, Da Nang.
Women Combatants - Unfortunately, no precise figures are available for number of women who served in U.S. military during American War; however, estimates are that between 7,000 and 14,000 served. The vast majority of those served as nurses in Medical Corps, while others served in Signal Corps as well as other non-combat branches. Many also served in civilian capacities, notably those in Special Services and "Doughnut Dollies" of the Red Cross. Eight women serving with the Dept of Defense died in war and have their names engraved on U.S. National Memorial. Only 1 women serving in U.S. military was killed by enemy action (Sharon Lane, an Army nurse killed by NVA mortar fire). As for French war, women serving the military at that time belonged to the PFAT (*Personnel Feminin de' Armee de Terre*), the French Army Women Soldier's Corps (see PFAT for detailed stats of their participation), and almost 100 of them were KIA. See also PFAT, FIS and IPSA.
Wooly Bullies - 584th Engineers' nickname. Per Robert Clark of that unit, men wore patches bearing that slogan. See also Weigt-Davis and Wooly Bully in main alpha listing.
World, The - U.S. GIs' affectionate nickname for the USA, or simply for "home."
WPB - Patrol Craft (USCG term).
WSW - West South West.

wt - weight (TAD).
wx - weather (TAD).
X-Ray Missions – Ops in which TASS FACs flying on 3-day rotations out of Ubon AB were assigned clandestine, "back-seater," Lao nationals recruited and trained by U.S. CIA. Whenever operatives got wind of or saw a good NVA or Pathet Lao target, they would alert CIA contact and clandestine Air-America pick-up would be arranged for the operative, who was then delivered to FAC at Ubon. Operative would board acft and assist pilot in navigating to and marking target for airstrike. Flown in supt of Royal Lao Troops deployed around various CIA/SF controlled PS-site airfields in Laos. Per *Da Nang Diary*, p 72-75. See also X-Ray and Steel Tiger.
X-Rays - Code name for Lao nationals trained to fly FAC missions for target validation in Steel Tiger Ops.
Xay Dung Nong Thon - Pacification prgm presented to Ambassador Lodge and Defense Secty McNamara by premier Nguyen Cao Ky in Jul65. In Vietnamese, phrase meant "rural construction" or "rural reconstruction." U.S. leaders dubbed it "Revolutionary Redevelopment."
Xe – One of several Vietnamese words for "river."
Xin Loi - See Sin Loi.
XM-16 Rifle – Early, experimental version of the M-16 Rifle.
XM-161 Vulcan Cannon – GE's electric motor-driven, 6-barrel cannon capable of firing 6,000 rnds of 20mm ammo/min. Designed originally by GE for acft platforms and later adapted to vehicles and some fixed hardpoints. See XM-174 Vulcan Track, Vulcan and Mini-Gun.
XM-21 Sniper Rifle - Experimental U.S. sniper rifle based on the M-14, 7.62mm rifle that inc highly refined "match grade" components and ammo. Was mounted with a Redfield 3X scope. Also available were a bipod and silencer for the weapon.
XM-41E Gravel Mine - See Gravel Mines.
XM-45E1 Flame-Thrower - A.k.a. XM-45E1 Flame-Thrower Service Unit. Variant of an M-113 APC designed as large napalm reservoir used to supply the M-132 Flame-Thrower Track. Data per *Vietnam Order of Battle*, p 319 (photo on p 318). See also M-132 Flame track and M-113 APC.
XM-148 Grenade Launcher - Precursor of the XM-203 and M-203 rifle/grenade launchers. Was 1st attempt to wed the M-16A1, 5.56mm stnd Army rifle with the M-79 40mm grenade launcher. See also M-203 and XM-203. Photo of this weapon in *Vietnam Order of Battle*, p 298.
XM-163 Vulcan - Modified version of the acft-mounted M-161A 20mm Vulcan cannon adapted for land vehicular use such as on the XM-741 (M-113 APC variant) tracked-vehicle. The Vulcan was six-barreled Gatling gun capable of firing 6,000 20mm rnds/min. Picture vehicle in *Vietnam Order of Battle*, p 309.
XM-174 Grenade Launcher - A.k.a. XM-174 Automatic Grenade Launcher. Experimental "machine gun-style version of the M-79 40mm Grenade Launcher. Was mounted on tripod of the M-60 MG and featured a 12-round magazine with trigger assembly very similar to that of the old U.S. .30 caliber WWII era MG. Regarded as very accurate and very versatile weapon; however was not introduced until late in war and/or its distribution was very limited (few troops ever saw it or knew of its existence). A hand-cranked version known as the "Honeywell Hand-Cranked 40mm Grenade Launcher" also saw limited use in a vehicle-mount configuration. Photos of each in *Vietnam Order of Battle*, at pages 299 and 303.
XM-174 Vulcan Track - An XM-174 tracked- chassis (modified version of M-113 APC) armed with XM-163A Vulcan 20mm Cannon (an electric motor-driven, six-barreled cannon capable of firing 6,000 rnds of 20mm ammo/min. Photo of vehicle in *Vietnam Order of Battle*, p 309. See also XM-163.
XM-177E2 - Experimental, sawed-off, sub-machine gun version of the M-16A1 Rifle adapted as special-use, commando weapon known as the M-177(?) Colt Commando. Nicknamed the CAR 15 and CAR 16, weapon's barrel was only 11 1/2" in length, and it featured a telescoping metal stock, modified hand-grip and an improved flash suppresser not available on the M-16. Its reduced weight and size made it the weapon of choice for many LRP, LRRP and special ops units. Shorter barrel length, however, greatly reduced its accuracy at ranges over 100 meters and best-suited for use in thick jungle and for close-in fighting. It also sometimes made its way into regular Army line units through means of questionable legality. Regarded as a "very cool" weapon and much sought after by those not authorized to use it!
XM-203 - Revised experimental version of earlier XM-148 Grenade Launcher/M16A1, combo over-and-under wedding of M-79 Grenade Launcher to the M-16 rifle. XM-148 is thought to have been introduced in VN as early as '65 or '66, and later redesignated the M-203. Apparently widely used as replacement for the M-79 in some units, '69-70 and later.
XM-571 - Articulated all-terrain vehicles tested in swampy areas by 25th Inf Div in '68 and during Op Yellowstone(?)
XM-706 Security Vehicle - Amphibious, armored, 4-wheeled, security vehicle used primarily by U.S. military police. *Vietnam Order of Battle* has a photo of one at p 307.
Xom - One several Vietnamese words for "village."
Xuan - One several Vietnamese words for "village."
Yard - Non-derisive U.S. GI slang for "Montagnard" troops and tribesmen. See Montagnard.
YC - Open Lighter(USN).
Yeager, Chuck - First man to break the speed of sound was also a B-57 pilot during war. See Clark AFB in main alpha listing.
Year of Decision, The - NVA/VC name for Tet '68 Offensive and '68 campaign in general. Consisted of 3 offensives: The First Offensive (Jan-Feb68 Tet, which inc hvy grnd assaults on major installations and prov capitols throughout SVN); the Second (May68 Mini-Tet); and Third (Aug68, which consisted primarily of "attacks by fire" and "stand-off attacks" using indirect fires, but very few ground assaults, yet resulted in est 22,000 NVA VC KIA nonetheless). See *A Better War*, pp 37-54. SVN.
Yellow Bird 18 - Call-sign of B-57 from 8th Bombardment Sqdn. See *Point Welcome* in main alpha listing.
Yeti Sightings - See Nguoi Rung and Rock Apes in glossary.
YFNB - Non Self-Propelled Barge (USN).
YFR - Refrigerated Storage Craft (USN).
YFRN - Refrigerated Covered Lighter, non self-propelled (USN).
YFU - Harbor Utility Craft, self-propelled (USN).
YMS - Auxiliary Motor Minesweeper (USN).
YO-3A Quiet Star - Extremely quiet, multi-blade, single-prop "Silent Aerial Surveillance Acft" used experimentally in VN. In May70, Army's 73rd Avn (Airplane) Co became sponsoring unit for its evaluation project. Its YO-3A platoon, a pioneer in area of silent aerial recon, proved a great asset. Acft had 6-hour range and 160 kts top spd and was mfgd by

Lockheed Acft. Info/photos available on OV-1 Mohawk website at: www.ov-1.com.
YOG - Gasoline Barge, self-propelled (USN).
You Bet Your Life FTX - See MACV Recondo School in main alpha listing.
Young Turks, The - Term applied loosely to younger and more liberal generals and marshals of ARVN and VNAF Military Revolutionary Council and its successor, the Armed Forces Council. Noted for their dash and daring, they were much more liberal and progressive politically than their elders and took a greater and greater hand in decision making process as time went by. Eventually one of their own, Nguyen Cao Ky was appointed Prime Minister by Armed Forces Council, after it decided then PM Huong was incompetent and Huong's immediate successors, Gen. Khanh and then Phan Huy Quat proved unworthy or unwilling. Ky notes that by '65, the Young Turks were, "the power behind the throne." In May67, the military govt was replaced by an elected president, former Gen Thieu, with Ky stepping down as appointed PM to be Vice Pres. Per *Twenty Years and Twenty Days*, p 59.
YRBM - Yard, Repair, Berthing and Messing" non-self-propelled USN/MRF barge. Diesel outboards tied to stern provided propulsion. Helo platform on deck used for re-supplying helos/gunships. Radio call-sign in '70 was "JATO One-Six." Data per: http://hawley.interspeed.net/vietnam/YRBM16c.htm.

YTB - Large Harbor Tug Boat (USN).
YTL - Small Harbor Tug Boat (USN).
Z - Greenwich Mean Time (if preceded by numeric grouping).
ZANO - French acronym for "Autonomous Zone North West." Official name of ill-fated Lai Chau airhead behind Viet Minh lines.
Zinn, Ronald, Capt - 1st West Point grad to participate in Olympics and only U.S. Olympian known to have died in War. Finished 19th in '60 Olympics' 20 km walk, and also held U.S. records for 2 mi, 3 mi, 4 mi, 5 mi and 4 km walks at time. In '62 set U.S. record for mile at 6 min 18.3 sec, and finished 6th in '64 Olympics. KIA 7Jul65, by machine-gun fire while a Plt Ldr of 3d Plt/B/2d/503d Inf/173d Abn Bde. Camp Zinn at Bien Hoa AB (XT 988-129) was named in his honor.
Zipper Heads – Also "Zip Heads." U.S. GI slang for Vietnamese.
Zippo Zappers - Armored Flame Platoons such as 2d Bn (Mech), 22d Inf/25th Inf Div. See also Flame Platoon.
Zulu Time - Greenwich Mean Time. Also "Z Time."

Appendix G

Acknowledgments

A very heartfelt thanks is extended to those many generous contributors, circle of dear friends and associates without whom this book would have been merely a lifeless, empty shell.

Regretfully, particular individuals who helped with this project in its infancy may have been overlooked here because contributors' names were not generally recorded until the formal decision to actually commit our collective knowledge to a book had been reached. It's also the case that I've often been unable to see the forest for the trees and find myself haunted by the prospect that some major contributors will likely go unrecognized here. I ask your forgiveness for any oversights, and pray those of you hurt by my failures will find solace in the certainty that many readers will benefit greatly from your thoughtfulness and labors—the true reward this vast body of knowledge we all helped compile will reap.

In any case, I offer my sincere apologies to those very deserving individuals and other contributors who may have been omitted or overlooked in these acknowledgments due to my negligence. Among those valued contributors' whose names and generosity I did record are:

A. J. Light, U.S. Army War College. Mr. Light pointed us toward a History Channel documentary covering an attack on FSB Ferdinand.

Alan Lee, former LAN Manager and IT specialist with the Sacramento County Assessor's Office. Alan shared with me his remarkable computer skills and expert guidance in the formatting of Word text.

Ann Kelsey, civilian volunteer with the Army Special Services Library Branch as an administrative librarian in Cam Ranh Bay, Dong Ba Thin, Nha Trang and Saigon from August 1969 to August 1970. Ann graciously shared her many memories and colorful detail of the Cam Ranh Bay area. Ann also provided audiotapes of AFVN radio music broadcasts as well as expert instructions for finding and obtaining Marine Corps records. Ms. Kelsey is currently Associate Director, Learning Resource Center, County College of Morris, Randolph, NJ.

Barry Toll, 3d Bde/4th Div LRRP, K/75th Rangers. Barry generously provided very vivid, often humorous and enlightening recollections of SOG 35 operations and various SOG signal sites, including Sledge Hammer and Hickory Hill.

Ben Youmans, Secretary/Treasurer, 35th Inf Rgt (CACTI) Association, 2d/35th/4th Inf Div '68-69, and MACV Team 23 in '70. Ben regaled us with numerous recollections regarding the construction date of LZ Virgin and other details for LZ's such as Mile High, 1-Alpha, LZ Saber, LZ Jackie, An Thoi POW Camp, and Phu Quoc Island.

Bernie Davies, D Bty/2d/320th Arty. Through Roger Ables, provided some history for FSB Kim Qui.

Bernie Edelman, Combat Photographer. A dear friend for many years, noted author and veterans advocate, editor of the acclaimed *Dear America: Letters Home from Vietnam*, co-producer of the documentaries *Dear America* and *Memorial: Letters Home From American Soldiers* (Academy Award Nominee), and author of the soon to be published *War Without End*, provided remarkable detail about FSB Brown and his eventful visit there during the Cambodian Incursion.

Bill Boe, 4th Inf Div, 1968. Photos and news clips related to his stay on LZ Brillo-Pad and in the Polei Kleng AO, as well as great detail regarding casualties of notewere his gifts to the effort.

Bill Hunt, Special Agent, Military Intelligence, MACV Team 72, Muc Hoa and Tuyen Bien District Phung Hoang Advisor. My thanks for his treasured friendship, keen and sensitive perspective into the Vietnam experience and for sharing a series of very personal memories transcribed in his unpublished and extraordinarily candid manuscript, *Log, RVN, October 1971-September 1972*. Bill is remarkable also for his caring, intelligence and integrity, and was author of one of my favorite quotes: "War eats good and evil for lunch."

Bill Kelley, U.S. Navy Corpsman attached to the 1st MAW, flying on medevacs out of Ky Ha/Chu Lai (HMM-262, MABS 36/MAG 36 and MABS 12/MAG 12, Dec66-Dec67). Bill is my older brother and I've admired his courage since our high school years when, with unsettling regularity, he'd find the strength to stand up to the rather autocratic whims of our father by simply saying, "No" (a word that rarely crossed my trembling lips in response to any of Major Dad's commands). I'm certain that courage served him and his comrades well in Vietnam, as well, and I'm also certain he was a good soldier and fine medic. Bill provided the project with his memories of the Chu Lai and Ky Ha airfields that were his home during the war.

Bill Noyes, "Tripleducer," 2d/22d Inf (Mech)/25th Inf Div. Noyes provided a detailed description of the location and history for the Ben Cui Hardspot.

Bob Clark, 584th Eng Hvy Equip operator, '69. Evocative memories of the Weigt-Davis Eng Compound north of Phu Nhon, and of the asphalt fire started soon after it was built were among his contributions. Bob also related a number of very colorful memories regarding a civilian who provided maintenance for the unit's 5-cubic-yard, front-end loaders and D-9 bulldozers.

Bob Lindgren, Medic with the 2d/1st Marines south of Marble Mountain in '69. Graphic descriptions of Ca Hau Combat Base and the Leprosarium company patrol base were his gift. Bob's photos of these sites are on the internet at: www.lbjlib.utexas.edu/shwv/images/ a_ground.htm .

Bob Patsfield, C-19 mortar track, 1st Plt, C Trp/1st/10th Cav/4th Inf Div, Mar69-Mar70. A number of 4th Div FSB/LZ names and associated grid coordinates were among his notable contributions. I'm very appreciative of his thoughtful and generous help.

Bob Peragallo, B/1st/9th Marines, 3d Mar Div, and *Vets With a Mission* Co-founder. Bob illuminated the record with recollections of the early years of the 1st/9th Marines. He also inundated me with numerous items of interest that he scavenged during recent trips to Vietnam in support of VWAM's missions there. Among very rare memorabilia he simply handed me as gifts were a king's ransom in NVA/VC/ARVN military awards, several maps and a huge map index apparently published by the ARVN. Bob is an exceedingly generous, compassionate, and thoughtful man, and *Vets With a Mission* does very good things in Vietnam that are deserving of our support. If you'd like to help build medical clinics and/or provide health training in Vietnam, contact VWAM at www.vwam.com.

Bob Race, D/1st/502d/101st Abn. My thanks for his comradeship, general support and for information regarding FSB sites of the 502d Inf generally, and some along the Yellow Brick Road during Op Massachusetts Striker.

Bob Witt, 2d/227th AHC. Provided detail regarding Camp Evans' May68, massive ammo dump explosion.

Bobby Jackson, 1st/7th Cav, Jan-Aug69, 1st Cav Div HQ, 69. Bobby unveiled the origin of the names for LZ/FSB's Phyliss, Vivian and Joy, the location of LZ Dot, and a very precise grid coordinate for LZ Joy. The 1st/7th Cav built at least six LZ/FSBs and occupied another three or four existing FSBs during his tour, and Jackson tells us the Bn was very mobile, covering several AOs and Opcon at one time or another to all 3 brigades in the division.

Boots Malone, the family cat. Boots was unrelenting in his attempts to attract my attention every time my hard drive was spinning. His penchant for thrusting his head over the keyboard resulted in many interesting misspellings and sentence fragments. In my absences, he also apparently enjoyed experimenting with the "10,000 Monkey's typing" theory during uninvited strolls over the keyboard. Sadly, Boots moved on to cat heaven in 2000.

Bud Harton, 4th Inf Div. Bud alerted us to the existence and whereabouts of LZ Gypsy.

Budd Russell, manager of the NCOC Association (Non-Commissioned Officer Candidates, aka Shake-n-Bakes). Bud was extremely supportive of this project and quick to share firebase data in his possession. Bud is also well known for his steadfast and industrious efforts to catalog and locate every graduate of the Army's NCOC program. The Association's website is at http://w3.ime.net/~ncocloca/MCOC-1~1.htm.

Butch Sincock, of Galaxy Tours and long ago a 19-year old 1Lt mortar Plt Ldr with A & B/4th/23d Inf Mech/25th Inf Div, and MAT-III Corps #84, May68-May69, Long An Prov. His exceedingly generous contributions included extensive recollections and data related to the 25th Inf Div and 82d Abn FSBs service in I &III Corps, a map of Camp Enari and a copy of the AAR, *The Battle for Tay Ninh Aug68*. Butch also gave the project a copy of *All the Way - The 3d Brigade 82d Abn in Vietnam, 1968* (reprints may still be available. Contact Rich O'Hare, Golden Brigade Chapter, 4075 Old River Trail, Powhatan, VA 23139-4112).

Charles Dukes, 2d/502d/101st Abn. His detail regarding the early history of FSB Bastogne was much appreciated.

Charles Sunder, LTC, USA Ret, and former CO of the 159th Trans Bn (Sunder's Wonders), and TF Sunder. My thanks for his most helpful and generous assistance with the history of the 159th and its involvement with Sa Huynh Port, Omaha Beach, Wonder Beach and Sunder Beach.

Charlotte Houtz, Information Specialist with the Library of Congress. Ms. Houtz was able to locate and provide us with a very rare original copy of the L-7014 Map series Index Map. Years of frustration came to an end with her discovery and I will be forever grateful to her and to the staff of the Geography and Maps Div of the Library of Congress for the index and their always gracious assistance and expert counsel.

Chris Taylor, A/4th/503d/173d Abn Bde and Hill 875 vet. Chris provided grid coordinates and an L-7014 map sheet for Hill 875.

Chuck Hawkins, C.O. A/2d/506th/101st Abn. Chuck provided much-needed general support, technical advice/analyses, as well as details about his unit's involvement in the siege of FSB Ripcord.

Chuck Schwiderski. Provided data regarding location of MACV Advisory teams.

Claude Moutray, USAF, Apr68-Apr69 (and brother of my former platoon-mate, Gary Moutray). My thanks for his detailed memories of Phitsanulok Airbase, and for his and his wife Angie's wonderful hospitality.

Cliff Snyder, National Archives. Words are inadequate to express my appreciation for his exceedingly professional, always patient, courteous and thoughtful service and guidance. Cliff provided frequent assistance in helping locate relevant materials among the vast NARA Vietnam-era holdings and, once discovered, did everything in his power to facilitate their acquisition for me. His contributions to the accumulation of knowledge found among these pages are far too great in number and value to illuminate or quantify properly here, but let it suffice to say that they were voluminous and critical to whatever success it may enjoy. I suspect no finer nor more conscientious public servant has ever walked the halls of the National Archives.

Connie Menefee. My heartfelt thanks goes out to her for much-needed encouragement, her insightful and thoughtful reflections generally, and also for her generous assistance with access to, and analysis of, casualty file data and anything else I might have needed. In my judgment, Connie is also without question among the very best poets to have emerged from the Vietnam experience.

Conrad Creitz, 554th Maintenance and 647th QM Companies, May68 to ? Detailed and very helpful data concerning the An Khe-Pleiku, QL-19 pipeline, Pump Stations 1 through 5, and the units assigned to operate that pipeline, were his thoughtful contributions.

Courteny "Frog" Frobenius, Plt Ldr B/3d/60th/9th Inf Div and owner of Indochina Tours. My sincere thanks for his comradeship, unflagging support and many eloquent explorations into the geography, history and culture of Vietnam. Few Americans know as much about the country or its history than Frog, and his knowledge has been an invaluable contribution to this project.

Craig Miller, B Bty, 1st/92d Arty (Pleiku, Kontum, Dak To), 155mm artilleryman, 3/68-4/69. Craig alerted us to names and/or grids for FSBs such as 1, 6, 7, 14, 15, 20, 23, 29, Irma J, Muriel, Mary Lou, Brillo Pad, Impossible, Incoming and Thunder, among other important detail.

Curt Knapp, HHC/2Bde/101st Abn helicopter pilot. Curt very generously provided a number of excellent aerial photos of LZ Sally (Van Xa) and the surrounding areas, as well as his general recollections and support.

Dan Gillotti, 3d/319th FA in VN, and now 15th Arty Rgt Historian with the 30th FA Assn. My thanks to Dan for sharing with us a very informative and invaluable copy of the 19May71, 22d ARVN Div AAR for Quang Trung-22F-04-Phase I-IV, which detailed the overrun of FSB 6, 31Mar71. In that fight, 7 U.S. helo crewmembers were KIA, 2 U.S. Advisors KIA and 2 U.S. IOS operators MIA. Facts regarding those units firing the first and last U.S. Army arty rounds of the war (see Artillery Firsts entry) were also among his gifts.

Daniel Evans, 4th/39th/9th Div(?). My thanks for his graphic detail relating of the history and physical nature of FSB Danger.

Dave Fogg, 1st/35th/4th Div. A noted 35th Inf Rgt historian, Dave provided detail regarding the location, construction date and spelling of LZ's Marietta and Lanetta. He also assisted Dick Arnold with other data that found its way among these pages through Dick.

Dave "Hack" Hackworth. Dave's remarkable contributions to the history of the war and betterment of the soldiers' lot go well beyond his support of this and other of my projects. Hack's unwavering devotion to duty was an inspiration to me, as were those memories of Vietnam he recorded in his epic, *About Face*. I will forever remain grateful for his thoughtfulness and generosity toward me. A better or more dedicated warrior likely has never walked this planet.

Dave Aitchison, Aussie veteran of the Battle for FSB Coral. Data regarding the locations of Coral and other ANZAC positions in AO Surfers and AO Manly were Dave's contribution.

Dave Holdorf, 7/15th Arty in RVN and editor of *The Highlander* (www.execpc.com/~hidavo) regimental newsletter. Dave gifted us with significant detail and a number of maps for those bases occupied or used by the 7th/15th Arty Rgt in Vietnam. The 7th/15th's very remarkable website contains many high-quality Vietnam maps, photos, and a detailed regimental history of the unit from its WWII service to the present.

Dave Robin, B/1st/26th Marines. A most fascinating description of perhaps the most unusual recon team insertion of the war, the Choo Choo train Insert, was Robin's addition to the mix.

David Argabright. Our thanks for his detail regarding Tan Tru basecamp and other facilities.

David Graham, an old friend and sidekick who served in the FDC of the 29th Arty/4th Inf Div, at Dak To, Ben Het, Polei Kleng (among others), in 68-69. Dave introduced me to the history of the Corral Program and, over the years, numerous graphic and often humorous memories of his days with the 4th.

David Schill, "Mr. Can Do," USN Seabees, 70-71, and Editor of *Vietnam Era Seabees* Newsletter (PO Box 36781, Richmond, VA 23235). Dave's contributions to this manuscript are far too numerous to list and there is no way I could ever adequately thank him for all he's done. His unrivaled expertise at identifying casualty's units, as well as his extensive knowledge of Seabee deployments and their history in our war were frequently plumbed, to say the least. No matter the complexity, Dave never refused a request and was always forthcoming with more data than I could have hoped for, and I will forever remain in his debt. It is Schill's ultimate goal, I believe, to identify the unit of every single casualty of the war and publish that database in some format, and I'm certain he will succeed.

Deanna Shlee Hopkins, a principal of the Vietnam Veteran's home page at http://vets.appliedphysics.swri.edu/infoindx.htm. Deanna's kind encouragement and thoughtful guidance are freely graced upon anyone who happens to contact her, as they were upon me often during the construction of this manuscript. The website she represents also contains a wealth of resources and important links for vets and historians alike.

Dempsey L. Bumpass, SWCS (E-8) USN retired (gunner on Strike Assault Boat 001, STAB Sqdn 20; call-sign "Racing Danger 1"). Dempsey helped us pin down the location of the USN facility at Phuoc Xuyen, and provided interesting anecdotal information regarding the history of FSB Gettysburg.

Dennis Rees, A/1st/11th/5th Inf Div (Mech). Threw in his help with information regarding Turkey Ridge and Marine Hill.

Dennis Williams, B/1st/502/10st Abn. Dennis very generously photocopied and mailed us a significant archive of Screaming Eagle newspaper articles from early 1968. His data helped us identify the Frank Doezema Compound among other sites in the general vicinity of Cu Chi, as well as being helpful in tracing the 2d Bde/101st Abn's history during its first year in Vietnam.

Dick Arnold, M-60 Gunner with A Co, 1st/35th/4th Div, May67-May68. Dick helped clear-up the mystery of the location of LZ Montezuma and its eventual renaming as LZ Bronco, and also provided the names and/or grids of LZs Lillie, Hilga, Ianetta, Ingrid, Jane, Mary Etta, Pause, FSB 30, and FSB 34. Along with his support and dedication as the secretary of the 35th Inf Rgt's Cacti Association, Dick's contributions and support of this project have been exceedingly valuable. Today, Dick is an engineer with Eli Lilly and Co, a relentless seeker of knowledge, and also very articulate and observant advocate for the Vietnam veteran.

Don "Cavman" Armstrong, 604th Trans, 52 CAB, Pleiku, Apr-July 68, D Troop 3/5 Cav, Bearcat / Dong Tam, Jul-68 May 69. Boundless generosity and unswerving support are the primary characteristics of Dave's contributions. Notable among his many gifts was a very important and very comprehensive 1970, XXIV Corps listing of I Corps. FSBs and proposed FSB names that he unearthed at the National Archives. The list included some 900 entries, was critical to the overall success of this project, and I simply cannot thank him enough for his efforts on our behalf.

Don Blankin, 2d/9th Arty and FO with C/2d/35th Inf, late 68-early 69. Don provided for descriptions/locational data for LZ's Bridgit and Valentine. He also shared with us photocopies of various articles from the 4th Inf Div's *Ivy Leaves* Newspaper that further illuminated the history of those and other positions.

Don Shutt. Provided data regarding LZ Pink and major 1st Cav battle at LZ Orange.

Donald Lewis, "Bikini 25," 170th AHC, '67-68. Lewis helped in our frustrating search to determine the otherwise very elusive grid for SOG CCC's Sledge Hammer Radio Relay site, and he also identified SOG operational zones Juliet-9, Hotel-9 and Charlie-50.

Doug "Manny" Fisher, D and E Co, 2d/501st/101st Abn (Delta Raiders) and former moderator of the *Guard Channel*. For many years, a deluge of e-mail messages bearing firebase names, locations, contact resources and other important data where his contribution. Sadly, Doug passed away during the construction of this book. His loyal friendship, Semper Fi spirit, generosity and counsel is greatly missed by all who knew him.

Doug Durham, Alpha Company, 3d Recon Bn/3d Marine Div, '65-66. Doug regaled us with various riveting accounts of events such as the Battle at the Bamboo Fence on Charlie Ridge, his days scouting the Elephant Valley and Song Bo River Valleys, but most particularly for his incredible retelling of the infamous Battle of Dong Den Mountain, during his many trials and (often humorous) tribulations as a Recon Marine in Quang Tri, Thua Thien and Quang Nam Provinces. Some of those stories may even have been completely truthful, we understand? Co-founder of the San Joaquin County Vietnam Veterans Association, his group raised more money than any other single organization toward the $2 million construction cost of the California Vietnam Veterans Memorial now standing in Sacramento's Capitol Park. While an associate member of the California Commission, I first met Doug while we both were absorbed in our mutual obsessions to build a memorial. We have been close friends ever since, and he and his (very tolerant) wife Mary frequently joined to break bread and share a friendship my wife and I treasure. Notable for his humility, mild manner, even temper, tolerance for injustice and his unwavering aversion to hurting anyone's feelings, Doug is a remarkable man by any measure.

Doug Huffman, 1st/5th (Mech)/25th Inf Div. Among other things, Doug detailed for us the location of FSB Devin. He also has very good (and often humorous) photos of that site (and many others in the Cu Chi/Dau Tieng AO) posted on his webpage at: www.users.uswest.net/~huffpapa/vietnam.html

Duane Duden. Provided data for LZ Lane at Ple Djereng.

Duane Good. Duane helped us pinpoint locations for Camp Granite, Shit Beach and Vung Chau Mtn.

Ed Buckley, 4th Inf Div. Along with Jim Claeys, was helpful with his data for such facilities as Walker Hill, et al.

Ed Escoffier, D Bty/44th Arty Dusters. Ed's colorful and accurate verbal sketches of FSB sites along QL-1 between Hue and Da Nang were a great help, as was his data regarding positions at the Lang Co Bridge and Hill 88.

Ed Regan, D/2d/8th Cav(?), '68. Provided helpful detail about the 1st Cav at Signal Hill and LZs Dolly and Carol (later Ripcord).

Ed Saragoza, CAP 3-5-1, 3d CAG veteran, 70-71. His memories and data for CAP 3-5-1 and the An On 1 & 4 CUPP Teams from his tour with 3d CAG were greatly appreciated.

Eddie Tricker, D & E Plt (Defence & Employment), HQ Company, 1st Royal Australian Task Force, Nui Dat, 13May70-12Aug71, Forward Scout, 2 Section, 18Jun70-12Aug71. Eddie's often very amusing memories of his tour with the RAR generally, and specifically the construction of FSB Scobie, of the 2d/35th Arty's "Arse Kickin" Alpha' sign at that base, and data regarding the transport *Jesparit* and *HMAS Sydney* were a significant and welcome contribution to this manuscript, as were other recollections of the Peter Badcoe Club and its general environs.

Elmer G. Goetsch, LTC U.S. Army Ret, 54th Sig Bn XO. Col Goetsch illuminated for us the origin of the term 'Field Force,' and also thoughtfully provided us with portions of the early history of FFV, IFFV and IIFFV.

Emmett Ramey, owner and publisher of Hellgate Press. It is difficult to properly express my appreciation of the fact that from the moment he first saw this manuscript's proposal, Emmett embraced my vision for what *Where We Were* could become. He then shouldered a project most other publishers felt to be far too complex, far too voluminous and far too ambitious for their taste. I am extremely grateful for the trust he extended to me, and for his belief in soundness of this endeavor. I'm also grateful for his patient and expert guidance throughout the project.

Eric Hammel, author of some thirty military histories and owner/publisher of Pacifica Military History Press. Eric's contributions are manifold. Not only did I glean important data from his many remarkable histories of the Vietnam War, but his personal contributions overshadow even those. I will remain forever grateful for his mentoring, learned counsel and frankness. Eric suffered my naiveté, ignorance and impetuousness very patiently, and his kindness and thoughtfulness will always fill my memories of the man.

Eric Schroeder, Ph.D., Professor of English, UC, Davis, author of *Vietnam, We've All Been There,* and a treasured friend. His many, many years of steadfast encouragement, support, good humor and healthy cynicism have been greatly appreciated.

Eric Weil, 7th Cav/1st Cav Div, archivist and military researcher. Eric shared a good deal of data regarding several key military operations that were quite helpful. Apparently he's also compiled a very large and important database covering several thousand military operations sifted from a huge collection of operational and AARs amassed by him over the years in both hard-copy and microfiche formats.

Erin Elizabeth Kelley, an extraordinarily talented graphic and fine artist. Erin expertly provided several very handsome and professionally-crafted cover design options (including the actual cover) for this book. Her frequent consults in helping me master the rudiments of PhotoShop and the various other programs employed to produce the graphics and text found herein, were both remarkable in their scope and greatly appreciated by her father. Her help was invaluable to this effort, and her support and love simply treasured. Among other things, Erin designs CD covers for record companies, as well as billboards and printed designs and logos of every sort. Her company, Zinc Designs, can be reached at zincdesign@hotmail.com. In the spring of 2002, she will also grace her mother and me with the biggest gift of all, our first grandchild!

Eve Sinaiko, a Senior Editor at Harry N. Abrams Books. Eve's loyal support and invaluable counsel into the intricacies of the publishing world were greatly appreciated and will never be forgotten. She also deserves recognition for her marvelous accomplishment in producing the very remarkable and landmark Vietnam War art book, *Vietnam Reflexes and Reflections*.

Frank Canaga. My thanks for vivid recollections contrasting his service with the 15th Engineers and that of the 584th Engineers during late 1967, both at the place that would become Wooly Bully, and at Dak To.

Frank Penk Jr, helicopter pilot with C/229th Aviation Bn supporting the 1st Cav Div, Jun68-Jan69, 1st Cav/3rd Bde's Aviation Section (Snoopy Flights) Jan69-Jan70, and finally with the 20th Eng Bde, Jan70-Aug70. Frank generously and unhesitatingly shared with us a very extensive listing of 1st Cav Div FSBs/LZs in III Corps. With great devotion, Frank also contributed many hours of patient research in helping us resolve data conflicts and in confirming grids for III Corps and Cambodian FSB/LZ locations. We are all in his debt.

Frenchy Torres, D/1st/7th Cav. Generously supplied access to his diary entries for LZs Joy, Phyliss, Vivian and Libby, among others.

Garry Adams, 2 Plt, A Co, 6th Bn, Royal Australian Rgt, 1st ATF, 1969-70. Scanned image of a portion of the DMA L-7014 series, 1:50,000-scale map of the Vung Tau Peninsula (see map section), were among his thoughtful and very helpful contributions.

Gary Adams, USMC. His memories of Dau Mau Base are now part of this record.

Gary Rousch, Historian for the Vietnam Veterans Helicopter Pilots Association. My sincere thanks for his and the VHPA's support, and for patiently responding to my numerous requests for assistance. Gary also provided CACF casualty data and access to the huge VHPA battle index now available on the VHPA's website.

George "Georgie" Neville, 3d Recon Bn/3d Marine Div (1966-67; Silver Star). Despite the fact I often gave him nothing but trouble, George was unflagging in his friendship, tolerance, counsel, voluminous and exceedingly generous assistance with base information and copies of impossible-to-find MACV intelligence and other documents. George was also very helpful in extracting for us data pinpointing 3d Recon Bn positions and radio relay sites in northern I Corps. Neville's skills as researcher and finder of truth are as legendary as they are remarkable. Among other important offerings, he provided a complete DOD listing of all DMA L-7014 series map sheet names and stock numbers (transcribed in this text), and was also apparently an invaluable cog in Larry Vetter's effort to create the 3d Recon Bn's Vietnam history, *Never Without Heroes*. Neville is himself nearing completion of a manuscript covering the history of Operation Hastings. A Marine's Marine, he would give a needful friend the shirt off his back. A finer comrade and friend would indeed be difficult to find.

George Clancy, Marine CAP 3-2 vet. Provided data regarding CAP 3-2's position in The Basin, and other CAP units/locations in I Corps.

George Critter, H&HTrp 1st/10th Cav. Supplied data regarding LZ Hart, among others.

George Lepre. An extensive knowledge of fraggings generally (his Doctoral thesis covers the subject), and remarkably detailed accountings of various fragging incidents that sometimes led us to facility names such as Camp I. V. Long and the Ivory Tower Bar, were his among his generous and welcome contributions.

George W. Ritter, HH Trp 1st/10th Cav. Provided data regarding LZ Hart and other II Corps FSBs.

Gus Reynolds, 4th Div. who proffered his recollections of the layout of Cam Enari, among other data.

Hal Moore, Battalion C.O., 1st/7th Cavalry at LZ X-Ray during the 1st Ia Drang Battle and co-author of *We Were Soldiers Once...and Young*. General Moore provided much-needed information and grid coordinate data for LZs X-Ray, Albany, Columbus and Falcon, among others.

Hank Anthony, 176th Avn Co, 14th Avn Bn. Hank gave us an unsolicited gift of two copies of *Diplomat and Warrior*, the weekly newspaper of the 1st Bde/101st Abn Div; the 10Jul67 and 21Jul67 issues (coincidentally the Jul67 issue was the last before the newsletter's name became *The Screaming Eagle*).

Harley Patrick, publicist and editor for Hellgate and Oasis Press. Apart from the many other hats he wears at PSI-Research/Hellgate Press, Harley also provided the bulk of the editing for this text. His thoughtful suggestions, sharp eye and expertise greatly improved the quality and integrity of the final product. I must also add my sincere thanks for his steadfast support, good cheer and counsel throughout the various trials and tribulations that attended the journey to publication. Harley was a Godsend.

Harry Dilkes, 1st/12th (Red Warriors)/4th Inf Div, '67-68. A number of maps and excerpts from his book-in-progress (*Five Years To DEROS*) helped us identify the locations of LZ's Brillo Pad, Bunker Hill, Alamo, OP Hill and several others locations.

Harvey C. Barnum, Jr., Col USMC/MOH. Provided data regarding Marine ops in Phuoc Ha Valley.

Herb Artora. Gave us his memories of FSB Leopard.

Hoang Nguyen, a teenager during the battle for Hue and whose family suffered terribly during that fight. My thanks for his memories, translation skills and indomitable spirit.

J. D. Wetterling, USAF F-100 pilot in '68, for his colorful memories of Dusty's Pub at Tuy Hoa AB.

J. H. Binford Peay, Gen, USA Ret. General Peay generously shared memories as an arty battery commander on Firebase Brillo Pad during its 1968 siege. Though embroiled in the complexities surrounding his retirement from the Army (Commander, Central Command) at the time of our first contact (Sep97), General Peay promptly and personally returned my calls and letters.

J. P. Martin. Provided data regarding the location and colorful surroundings of FOB-2, including Hazel's Whorehouse.

J. R. Wright, C/227th AHC website manager. JR provided substantial assistance with FSB grids in the vicinity of The Oasis and other locations in II Corps.

Jack Picciolo, 2d/17th FA, 65-66. A wealth of data that confirmed the grids for perhaps thirty 1st Cav Div FSBs/LZs were his thoughtful gift. Among those were LZ's Apollo, Duc, Lee, Ollie, and Juliet. Jack proudly notes, "We were a general support 105 howitzer unit for the Cav, and I was in the FDC section as a computer. In fact, our unit fired the first arty round for the Cav in Vietnam!" His unit also supported the 2d/19th. 1st/77th and 1st/21st Arty at many different bases and on many different occasions between 1965-1972.

James "Jimmy C" Cartmill, 15th Engrs/9th Inf Div. Jimmy provided information showing regarding the locations of FSBs Lambert and Brown, along QL-4.

James Henderson, B/1st/22d/4th Inf Div, '69-70. Grids for a number of 4th Inf Div sites were Jim's welcome contribution, and included LZs Valkyrie in Cambodia, Fran, Zager (or Zaeger?), Lois, Bison II, Ada, Kraus, Marie, Beaver, the Rock Quarry at ZA 055-319; Patsy, Marlene, April, Plantation, Camp Fidel, Blue, Lynn, Gloria Ann, Edap Enang, Cunningham, FSB New Plei Djereng, Pump Stations 9 and 10. Henderson's generosity in also providing copies of a substantial number of 4th Div Arty ORLLs and Staff Daily Journals from 69-70 was also greatly beneficial and much appreciated.

James Marsh, "Gambler 19," 4th Avn Guns. James provided instructive and colorful recollections of the Vinh Thanh Valley AO, LZ Valentine and LZ Five Fingers, as well as support and encouragement for the project.

Jay D. Trina, Marine CAP vet. Jay provided the location of CAP Hotel 1, 3d CAG.

Jean-Paul Meyer (*Délégué aux Affaires Extérieures, et à la Valorisation, CIRAD-FLHOR, France*). Mr.Meyer educated me about the *Société des Terres Rouges* (Society of the Red Soils or, Red Soils Company) as it related to rubber tree and other plantations in Vietnam. The *Société des Terres Rouges* was recently purchased by the BOLLORE Group, he noted.

Jerome Lohman, 73d Engrs(?). For helping with data regarding Whiskey Mountain near Phan Thiet.

Jerry Ault (Sp5, MOS 26V20 OB2, Fixed Station Microwave Radio Repair, REL2600 tropo, Long Lines North, Vung Chua). Delightful descriptions of Vung Chau Signal Site, its environs and tenants were his notable contribution.

Jerry Berry. My thanks for his kind and helpful assistance with recollections of arty emplacements at LZs Bartlett and Sherry and other FSBs.

Jerry Wood. Provided data regarding the location of LZ Furr and the origin of its name.

Jim "Bagpipes" Taylor. Jim gave a detailed history of his tour with Oscar Company CAP, III MAF. While many U.S. soldiers hold their South Vietnamese counterparts in low regard, Jim offered these remarks about the indigenous troops that worked with CAP Oscar: "Oscar was the only company (to my knowledge) that worked with the Bru (a Montagnard tribe). These ethnic Mon Khmer were NOT Vietnamese, but rather earlier ethnic aborigines displaced by the south Chinese invaders...They are linguistically and ethnically related to the Laos, Cambodes and Thai, especially the Hmong Tribe. They were cheerful, courageous (without being stupid) and honest. A pleasure to work with! When CAC Oscar withdrew to the Khe Sanh CB after the initial attacks against their positions in early '68, the Marines did not want to accept Oscar-2's Bru comrades, so CAC Oscar asked for and received a spot in the defense perimeter of the SF's FOB-3, along Khe Sanh's southern edge and QL-9."

Jim "Dusty" Henthorn, 21st SOS. Nov. '67-May '69. For several years, this project relied heavily on almost daily use of a huge database of 1:250,000 scale, L-1501 Series DMA JOG topo maps Jim has scanned and posted on the net for anyone to access at no charge. It cannot be emphasized enough just how important and useful his creation was to the construction of this manuscript, nor just how valuable it is still to vets generally. Through several layers of clickable maps at his site, complete 1:250k map coverage for every country in SEA is available in its entirety (go to www.nexus.net/~911gfx)! His thoughtfulness and generosity for providing this service are remarkable by any measure, and we are all in his debt.

Jim "Hockey-Puck" Zwit, D/2d/501st/101st Abn, '70-71. Jim is a dear friend and fellow Screaming Eagle, and for his loyal friendship, support and assistance in this and other causes, I am both very appreciative and honored. Jim's selfless heroism during one of the last major battles of the 101st Abn in Vietnam was featured in an article of mine entitled *Delta Raiders Costly Recovery Mission*, published in the Jun99 issue of *VIETNAM* Magazine. Though we served in different units (D/2d/501 and D/1st/502), our connection goes back to the war and a wonderful man named Dr. Charley Carroll, the surgeon who by coincidence managed to save both of our lives during a 6-month interval while he was assigned to the 85th Evac Hospital, Phu Bai. Jim and Charley are very special people and in a class apart from most of us who have the privilege to know them.

Jim Chaffee, Marine CAP veteran. Jim pointed us toward the Marine Corps Historical Society and other resources related to the USMC CAP program.

Jim Claeys (H&S Bty 6th/29th Arty; FO for B/3d/8th and 2d/11th Arty/101st Abn Div, 69-70, Pleiku-An Khe-Bong Son-Phu Bai). Jim's overwhelming and extremely helpful efforts to assist me with 4th Div firebase names and grids (per operational reports he's collected over the years) were invaluable in my research. Jim also constantly scavenged the Internet for Vietnam place and facility names and, with a certain amount of perverse glee I think, frequently buried me with the mountains of information he'd collected! Jim is one of the largest contributors to this project and we all owe him a huge debt of gratitude for his selfless and tireless efforts on our behalf. He provided extensive listings of bases in Kontum, Pleiku and Binh Dinh Provinces, as well as Cambodia, among which were LZs Alma, Assault, Badger, Baker, Caldera, Crystal, Dauntless, Digger, Football, Irma, Lincoln, Logan, Nina, Powder, Regular,

Tape, Truman, Two Bit I, Washington and Winnie. I'm unable to find words adequate to properly express my gratitude for Jim's unflagging support, his integrity and his generosity.

Jim Corbett, A/326th Engrs. Provided us with the name and some history of LZ 101.

Jim "Doc" Hall, 2d/35th/4th Div. My thanks for his memories of LZ Raquel.

Jim Hooper, author of an upcoming book about the 220th Reconnaissance Airplane Company (aka the *Catkillers*). Jim provided assistance and data regarding the 21st RAC and 220th RAC.

Jim Jones (C Company, 1st Recon Bn and one of the swimmers who did the initial recon for the Chu Lai Landing, May65), Webmaster for the 3d Recon Battalion Association. A steady stream of resource leads, internet links and firebase names were Jim's gracious and much-appreciated gift.

Jim Stone, E/2d/39th/9th Div, and his cohorts, Bob Fischer (9th Div Band) and Dave Seefeldt (driver with 9th Div's S & T). Stone and Seefeldt gave the project a substantial body of information regarding 9th Div firebases, their evolution during 1968 and early 69, as well as a *tour de force* overview of the history of the 9th Div in Vietnam. Jim and Dave are themselves compiling a resource that will eventually identify the location of all 9th Div facilities throughout the war. Among the bases credited to these gentlemen are FSB's Cleopatra, Dirk, Fels (or Fells?), Camp Mohawk, Binh Long and Fort Dent.

Joe Coley. Joe provided a fascinating look at the conceptual levels and ultimate construction of Camp RedCatcher, along with grids for FSBs Holiday Inn and Bandit Hill. He came upon that data while thumbing through his father's (LTC William Coley Jr. 1st/43d Inf 65/66, 1st Cav Div 66 and 11th Cav 69) papers and while in the midst of compiling a history of his father's many notable military exploits.

Joe Galloway, the only journalist on the ground with the 1st/7th Cavalry throughout the first Battle of the Ia Drang Valley (Nov65), a good friend, very decent, honorable man, and an extraordinarily gifted writer. For his friendship, encouragement, sage wisdom, journalistic advice and for pointing us toward several important Ia Drang campaign data resources, I will remain eternally grateful. Among those important resources which he pointed our way was General Hal Moore. Joe was a Senior Writer with U.S. *News and World Reports* and co-author with Gen Moore of the classic *We Were Soldiers Once...and Young.* (now a feature film starring Mel Gibson and scheduled for release in 2002).

Joe Gerber, Cmdr USN Ret, among the very last pilots to fly RA-5C Vigilante recon flights over NVN. Many thanks for his colorful stories of carrier life (particularly the BOHICA incident), his flights and how he single-handedly won the air war over NVN.

John Alejandro, 1st Cav Div/196th LIB/F Trp, 8th Cav, '70-71. Provided detail regarding LZ Dragon/FSB Head.

John Barmann, 321st Arty. John's recollections of FSB Zion are now part of this record.

John Caughran, USN. John helped pinpoint Phuoc Xuyen ATSB, providing a detailed description of that base and the Grand Canal.

John Chandre. John helped us unravel the origins and history of Wunder (a.k.a. Wonder) Beach.

John Doherty. John confirmed that Camp Viking was at Red Beach and adjacent to Camp Haskins, and that it was home to the 58th Trans Bn.

John Driscoll, D Bty/5th/2d Arty. His remarkably detailed and vivid recall of FSBs Wade, Haymaker, Sylvia and Ham Tan, was very helpful.

John Eastman, my dear friend and comrade from D/1st/502d/ 101st Abn, 1969-70. John's contribution was his typically learned and razor-sharp counsel on a stupendously wide range of topics, including that of the history of the *USS Constitution's* 1845 journey to Da Nang, FSB Professional and LZ Sally, among others. John's tour with D/1st/502 was of particular note in that he somehow managed to get himself shot down during his very first helicopter ride en-route to join the unit while it was opcon to Americal Div's 1st/46th Inf near Tam Ky (Jun69). He became the stuff of even greater legend when, on 3Sep69, as LZ Sally came under heavy rocket and ground attack, he emerged on the run from his humble domicile (somewhat befuddled and marginally terrified, he readily admits) wearing only his jungle boots and his birthday suit. As the door slammed behind him, and by a most propitious stroke of incredible coincidence, John's trajectory intersected with that of our beloved 1st Sgt, "Top" Henry Hudson. Startled by the unearthly and rather unorthodox appearance of his charge's unusual battle-dress, Hudson screeched to a halt, almost at a loss for words. Almost. "Eastman!" he bellowed, unable to think of a more appropriate command. And John, recognizing the voice and authoritative tone unique to a two-war, battle-hardened Army NCO, dutifully stumbled to a halt himself, turning to present himself to the 1st Sgt, and in doing so coming practically to attention. With the surreal nature of moment no doubt exaggerated by the ethereal, shimmering glow and shadows cast by the many illumination flares then beginning to fill the sky above the base, Top stood there for a few moments carefully studying the trembling apparition before him from head to toe. Finally, extending his M-16 toward John as a teacher might point a yardstick for emphasis, "Eastman," the bemused 1st Sgt added dryly, "what are you gonna do, fuck 'em to death?"

John Forgette, Bellingham, WA. John has published a very comprehensive and informative history of Phu Cat Airbase on the Internet (see Append. H) that was an important resource for the Phu Cat entry.

John Grocki, B/1st/35th Inf/4th Inf Div. His lively memories of the harsh environments that were LZ Gypsy and LZ Cathy were a joy to read and most helpful in this effort.

John Hollett, 1st Australian TF. My very sincere thanks to John for his unwavering support over the years. John steered me toward numerous, valuable RAR and RNZR resources, educated me extensively about the Aussie involvement and also supplied us with an invaluable copy of a 1ATF NCO trng map that included the names and positions of perhaps 130 1ATF firebases. His contributions were major and much appreciated.

John Linn, B/2d/35th/4th Inf Div, 69/70 (infantry and mortars, including the Cambodian invasion May70). Linn gifted us a number of 4th Inf Div firebase name and grid data that had been listed inside the cover of a New Testament of the Bible that was his constant companion throughout his tour! We also offer our thanks for his recollections of the physical nature and locations of LZ/FSB Short-Timer-I and Short-Timer II, and for bringing the term Hip-Shoot firebase to our attention.

John Meyers. Provided data regarding FOB-1 & FOB-6.

John Middlesworth (a.k.a. "Ex PFC Wintergreen" and, if only for a brief, surreptitious and enervating few hours on a supply run to Da Nang, "1st Lt Middlesworth"), Cpl, Alpha Battery, 1st/11th Marine Arty, '69. John's ubiquitous, lively and humorous recollections of his days in and around such places as Dai Loc, Whiskey Tower, Frenchy's, Camp Middlesworth, Da Nang were an invaluable resource in my research. I am also particularly grateful for his loyal friendship, counsel, encouragement and wonderful sense of humor. We've been close friends for many years and survived together a series of harrowing events in northeastern Washington DC, an eventful visit to Senator Cranston's office, the Civil War battlefields of the DC area, a veterans parade in Los Angeles where he personally introduced me (and himself) to Mayor "Yorty" (whom at the time was actually Mayor Bradley), and one or two death-defying cab rides through our Nation's capital. Best of all, we frequently gather to laugh at life, ourselves and to break bread together. A good, loyal, trusted and much admired friend, I thank him from the bottom of my heart for his support and for all the good times we've had together. John also contributed his editorial skills to the manuscript and helped me stay the course when my energies would flag. He is also a remarkable poet of the war and, in my judgment, among the very best to emerge from the Vietnam experience.

John Mowat, 71st Arty Quad 50's, '70. My thanks for his detailed and very helpful data regarding LZ Sylvia near Ham Tan, and FSB Haymaker in Cambodia, among others.

John Rochelle, 1st Lt with the 704th Maint Bn, '68-69. Among other important data, John provided data that helped pinpoint locations for FSB Mary Lou/Highland Heights and for the Grand Bungalow, a famous hunting lodge used as an SF Camp in Ban Me Thuot.

John Salinger, HMCM (Ret), CAP 2-3-7 veteran. His valuable and very detailed listing of 2d CAG CAP Team locations was greatly appreciated.

John Swensson, friend, author, screenwriter, USMA grad and Professor of English at De Anza College. John contribution was his loyal friendship, a Helmut-full of Vietnam war-era stamps, and his recollections of a number of 25th Inf Div facilities which served as his home over two tours.

Keith William Nolan, deservedly noted author and historian of the Vietnam experience. Keith provided me with much-appreciated sage advice and insight into the publishing world, as well as a ton of firebase and LZ data absorbed indirectly through his many wonderful war histories. Keith's remarkable candor in reporting the war as it was, warts and all, sets him well apart from his peers and at the same time provides some of the most illuminating, honest and unfettered perspectives on the Vietnam experience anyone is ever likely to encounter.

Ken Burington, C/2d/5th Cav/1st Cav Div, '67-68. We are in Ken's debt for an extensive listing of I and II Corps FSBs and terrain features as they relate to L-7014 series map sheets which he unhesitatingly and very generously offered to this project. He also identified the location for FSB Ollie in Binh Dinh Province, for us.

Ken Williamson, a photographer with the 815th Engrs in Pleiku and then 26th Engrs PIO in Long Binh. Ken provided the key information that resolved the long-standing mystery of the proper spelling and name-origin of Weigt-Davis, a 20th Eng base near Phu Nhon. Data for other similar installations such as Wooly Bully and Wooly Bully II, were also among his gifts.

Kenneth Thompson, Jr, Special Operations Association. Mr. Thompson graciously sent us the "Agent Orange map of SVN" originally produced by the Grand lakes Nam Vets. This widely reproduced map has upon it the general location and names of a host of FSBs/LZs and base camps.

Kent Spalding of K&S Militaria. My thanks for his trust in sharing with me a number of rare and very important documents, as well as for his insights into, and background information about, Air America/CIA/Continental Air Services operations in Laos. Kent also provided explanations for a number of terms and conventions used by Air America, particularly those related to L-Sites, Lima Sites, Charlie Sites and Victor sites. Mr. Spalding markets a reproduction of an Air America Laotian airfield facilities guidebook entitled *Air Facilities Data-Laos* that is a remarkable resource that should be in any serious historian's library. Ordering information for the book is available in our Appendix II entry for it.

Kevan Mynderup, Secretary of the "Jumping Mustangs" association of C/1st/8th Cav/1st Cav Div. A list of 1st Cav LZ's in the Quang Tri and Tay Ninh area that added LZ Cold, LZ Huckleberry, a waterpoint and LZ Warhorse to our listings, were among his very helpful contributions.

Kevin Rafferty, B/1st/14th Inf/4th Div. Helped pinpoint the grid for LZ Brillo-pad, among other LZs.

Kirk Ramsey, 2/14th/25th Inf Div veteran. Kirk's comprehensive listing of 25th Inf Div FSBs and his eloquent descriptions of 25th Div FSBs, Emory, Keene, Patton II, Patrol Bases Hunsley and Dragon, among others other pertinent data, were extremely helpful to this project, as was his wise counsel. I strongly recommend readers visit his 2d/14th Inf Golden Dragons award-winning website at: www.en.com/users/kramsey/dragons. html. Be sure to also visit and read his well-crafted memoir, *Tales of a War Far Away*, at www.en.com/users/ kramsey/default.html.

Lafe Baehr, SSgt with B/3d/8th Inf. Lafe generously shared with me his memories of LZ Penny and other data.

Larry "Bear" Criteser, a "6th generation Oregonian" and 4th/9th Inf Manchu. Larry's general suggestions and detailed memories of several III Corps, 25th Inf Div bases were greatly appreciated.

Larry "Mitch" Mitchell, 4th/9th Inf Manchu. Mitchell generously proffered his recollections, reflections Katum

Basecamp, as well as a .jpg of the 1st Bde, 25th Inf sign at the entrance to that base.

Larry Kline, 4th Inf Div. My thanks for his memories of the 11May69 attack of LZ Oasis.

Larry O'Neill, HHB and D Bty 6th/56th Arty, Jul67-Jul68. Larry provided the name and other data related to Widow's Village and Widow's Valley.

Lawrence Holmberg, Jr., journalist and aide to Gen. Abrams. My thanks to Larry for his very interesting story about the Moreau Bowl at the Nha Trang Cham Temple and for his delightful memories of Gen. Abrams.

Leroy "M'Boy" Pittman, 6th/31st/9th Div and 25th Inf Div, 1970-71. A most dear friend and long-time compadre, Lee anted-up information helpful in determining the location and physical makeup of FSB Gettysburg. He also shared with us his almost limitless knowledge of the history of our war and unlimited access to his voluminous library. Most of all, I thank him for his wonderful friendship and delightful sense of humor.

Les Hines, 123d Aviation Co. Les invested countless hours in identifying the names and grids for several hundred I Corps firebases generally that he posted on the Americal Div Assn's website (we understand he was assisted by maps supplied by the following individuals: Mr. McCaig, Bill Staffa, Frank Stefancic, and Tony May, so our thanks to them as well.) Les also transcribed the 1969 Battalion Annual Historical Supplement of the 1st/502d Inf/101st Abn for us and provided access to the transcribed content of almost every *The Army Reporter* ever published during the Vietnam War. We also benefited from several video tapes covering a number of topics including the NVA capture of Kham Duc, a college seminar exploring the My Lai Massacre and yet another showing firebases along the coast near Chu Lai (as they were in a 1997 visit). No person helped me more or gave more of himself to this project than did Les Hines. All of us are deeply in his debt.

Les White, B/8th Engr Bn(?), '66. My thanks for his input into the origins and history of LZ Uplift.

Lou "Rocket" Rochat 'x]:-})' 1st/9th Air Cav, '70-71, Cobra & Loach Pilot. A host of new and confirming grids for dozens of firebases in NW III Corps and Cambodia as well as access to the Apr69 DMA Tactical Aerodrome Directory were Lou's very important contributions. He was exceedingly helpful and generous in his assistance, to say the very least.

Marc Leepson. Marc is a treasured friend, relentless seeker of truth and a master of the written word. Among many things, I'm exceedingly grateful for his honest appraisals, unreserved encouragement and marvelous sense of humor throughout this and other of my projects. Among other important contributions, he was able to provide a substantial firebase listing compiled from data accumulated over the years. Ex-Sp5 Leepson is the very talented and widely respected Arts Editor for VVA's *VETERAN* Magazine. He is also the editor of a very important reference volume, *Webster's New World Dictionary of the Vietnam War*, released in January1999, and his own, *Saving Monticello,* a non-fiction history now receiving wonderful reviews, was released in Nov 2001.

Mark and Toah Richardson. My sincere thanks for their information on the translation of the Bahnar name 'Dak To' as meaning Hot Water. Toah is Bahnar and was born in Kontum, SVN.

Megan, our beloved Cocker Spaniel and my constant sidekick. She sat loyally at my feet for all the years this text was under construction and accompanied me regularly on neighborhood inspection tours when breaks were needed. In all respects, her companionship fulfilled my life in every waking minute and calmed my soul when nothing else could. A better more loyal friend could not exist.

Michael Belis, C/1st/22d Inf, '70-71. His memories of Rear Support Base Buffalo, at An Khe, were enlightening and appreciated.

Mike "Iron Mike" Boster, SOG CCS. I am very grateful for his often quite humorous and evocative recollections of SOG CCC's Sledge Hammer Relay and his deadly battles with the VC (Varmint Cong) rat population of that site.

Mike Cohen, Ph.D., a friend and veteran of A Company, 1st/8th Cav, 1st Cav Div, 67-68. His very precise recollections of the building of FSB Mustang in the An Lao Valley, FSB Sharon (aka Betty-Sharon) and of the 7Dec67 battle at Dai Dong village, near Bong Son were his gifts to this effort.

Mike Gacek, 321st Arty. His data on FSB Bastogne and its Boom Boom Room were his significant contribution to the historical record here.

Mike Pautler, B Bty (DS)/1st/21st Arty. Mike added a graphic and very interesting description of Mystery Hill to the project.

Mike Turner, (ex) USN 68-74, RVN 70-71. Among other things, Turner contributed descriptions of ATSB Solid Anchor, Sea Float, Camp Hurt, and also provided other important data found on his very informative and well-designed website at: http://members.xoom.com/mdturner/vietnam.htm

Mike Young, 44th Arty helped with detail regarding FSB Los Banos.

Mike Young, an officer with B Co, 20th Engineer Bn (Combat). I am very appreciative for his assistance in pinpointing the location and actual spelling of Weigt-Davis, and for his interesting descriptions and memories of LZ Lonely and Phu Nhon. According to Mike, the 20th Engr Bn (Combat) consisted of the 584th, the 15th, and the 509th LE Cos in addition to the standard 4 Cos of an Engr Bn. There were 7 Cos in total and 42 officers (he recalls being the 2d lowest ranking and 6th oldest officer, and only one of 3 graduate engineers in the unit during his tour from Dec70, until the unit stood down in Aug71.

Monte Olsen contributed data regarding 25th Inf Div FSB Blue and helo units at Phu Loi.

Nolan Putman, 5th/22d, 2d/17th and 7th/15th Arty, as well as liaison to ARVN 22d and 42d Rgts. Nolan was responsible for solving the mystery of Firebase 6's actual grid coordinates for us and was very helpful in providing grid and arty unit data for FSBs 5, Foxtrot, 101, Ban Me Thuot, Aquarius, Doris K, Bannister, Colgan, Sandy, Gaiser, Apollo and LZ Mud (aka Pierson). His generosity, persistence and devotion to accuracy were remarkable, to say the least, and greatly appreciated by me.

Norman McCormick, my former D/1/502d Inf platoon-mate, treasured friend and constant correspondent. Norm's wildly entertaining letters, thoughtful and often profound insight into the foibles of the Vietnam experience offered great and welcome respite from the drudgery of research. He also gifted to us some official Army photos of firebases Arsenal, Birmingham and Bastogne that he apparently "borrowed" from the U.S. Army while in-country, and one of which that was used in the cover design.

Pam Vanee, of the Geography and Maps Div of the Library of Congress. Pam's a always exemplary professionalism and thoughtful guidance were an enormous help in navigating the intricacies of the Library's map archives, thereby greatly facilitating acquisition of map copies and other documents available through the Library of Congress.

Patrick Dudney, 3d/12th Inf(?), 4th Inf Div. Among his contributions was information pertaining to FSB LZ D-Handle, Flexer and the XYZ Pad near FSB Brillo Pad.

Paul Brubaker. Provided data regarding the MACV Recondo School.

Paul Kasper, Flame Thrower APCs, 15th Combat Engrs, 9th Inf Div., 67-68. Paul helped us by providing the names and general locations for the Wagon Wheel and Snoopy's Nose terrain features.

Paul DeCillis, creator of the De Anza College Library's DeCillis Collection of Vietnam War films, books and memorabilia. Throughout this project, Paul very generously provided numerous video documentaries on firebases and other related topics, as well as other important data regarding his own recollections of II Corps. His support and encouragement were most helpful and my appreciation of his thoughtfulness is very great.

Paul Dinardo, 173d Abn Bde Association. Paul was exceedingly helpful in the search for firebases generally, directing me toward many valuable resources and by often also directing those resources towards me! His contributions were numerous and I'm very appreciative of his assistance.

Paul Kopsick, pointed use toward some excellent resources for FSB/LZ locations in the Central Highlands and along QL-19, among which was the website of the 7th/15th Arty and its detailed history and maps. Paul also provided the name and grid of LZ Mirla, near Quang Tri, as well as alternate grids for LZs Ann, Jane, Suzy and Sharon.

Paul Grandy, 1st/327th Inf/101st Abn, '71, two-tour vet. Helped us identify the precise location of FSB Kim Quy.

Paul Shaffer, A/1st/327th Inf/101st Abn, 71-72. The location of I Corps FSBs Kim Quy and Binh Dinh were a mystery until with Paul's assistance and memories, much of the mystery was dissipated. Paul also provided some photos taken atop Kim Quy and guided us toward other veterans with more data.

Paul Whetzel, USAF retired C-130 pilot. When Paul discovered the nature of this project in casual conversation, he immediately and unhesitatingly offered us the use of his copy of a very rare, 1Feb73 DMA Tactical Aerodrome Directory. In doing so, he thereby provided grid coordinate and other important detail for some 300 airfields and another 322 heliports in one stroke! Our chance meeting was a Godsend, and his generous and thoughtful gesture contributed greatly to the knowledge found among these pages. Unfortunately, I was unable to return the favor with a resolution to his frustrations in dealing with the bureaucracy of California county government, though I tried very hard to help. Needless to say, I am very grateful for his vital contributions.

Peter Cole, 1st Cav Div Aviation, 1968-70. Pete was exceedingly generous in sharing with us a very extensive and well-documented listing of firebases occupied by the 1st Cav in I, II and III Corps, as well as in Cambodia. Numerous entries throughout this text are the result of Pete's resourcefulness and caring, and I am both very grateful and appreciative of his very significant contributions.

Phil Landis, 4th Inf Div. My thanks for his vivid and colorful memories of LZs Mile-High, Brillo-Pad and other helpful data that were his gifts.

Ralph Bunten, U.S. Advisor, 65/66, call-sign "Short Uplift." Ralph's illuminating history of a position known originally as Deo Nhong Pass (which later became LZ Uplift) was his much-appreciated contribution here.

Ralph Fries, Director of the *USN/USCG Vietnam Unit Memorial Monument/Boat Display Project* (www.vietnamunitmemorialmon.org). Ralph unhesitatingly shared with us an enormous listing of Vietnam-service U.S. Navy and commercial vessels, approximately 425 of which were added to those I'd already compiled. Mr. Fries spent over seven tears compiling his information as part of an ongoing effort to erect a memorial to honor the U.S. Navy, Coast Guard and other associated units of the Vietnam war. Be sure to visit the organization's remarkable website and dip into its wealth of information.

Randy K., provided information regarding FSB Woods.

Ray Blackman, D/2d/501st Inf, 101st Abn Delta Raider. My thanks for his general support and guidance, as well as for data regarding Re-Up Hill, FSB Ripcord and others locations in the Ripcord AO.

Ray Bows, 3d Transportation Center and 25th Inf Div. I will forever be in debt to Ray for our long friendship and his very generous and very substantial contributions to this work (see *Preface*).

Ray Smith, Webmaster for and creator of the home page of the 1st/69th Armor. Ray's contributions on our behalf were enormous by any measure, and I'm extremely grateful for his thoughtful and generous assistance. Among other things, Ray was the source for some of the maps presented here, and for a whole host of firebase, strongpoint, pump station, bridge sites and other facility names and grid coordinates for installations built along the QL-19 corridor between Qui Nhon and Pleiku. The 1st/69th website is among the very best and most important sites visited during the research for this book, and I would urge the reader visit it to plumb an absolute wealth of maps, history and other reference materials. The address is www.rjsmith.com/my_unit.html. His very extensive collection of interactive 1:50,000 and other scale maps is at: www.rjsmith.com/topo_map.html. Information for ordering L-7014 series 1:50,000 scale military topo maps is also posted there, and includes a copy of the original L-7014 map series INDEX

Map, which in and of itself is a extremely important resource .

Richard Brown, former S-2 of the 6th/15th FA (R-2d/21st FA/1st Cav and R-7th/11th FA/25 Div) at Thien Ngon and Katum, War Zone C; Target Acq Bty CO with II Field Force Arty FDO for 1st/77 FA, 1st Cav at LZ Buttons (Song Be). My thanks to Richard for providing us with locational data for a number of for 1st Cav Div FSBs.

Richard Moore, USMC. His very colorful and frank discussion of PK-17 and the fighting there in '66 was very illuminating and helpful.

Richard Shand. My sincere thanks go to Richard for his data regarding FSB Gray, and for his general support in helping to dispel the Vietnam vet suicide myth by installing an article on the subject on his website at http://home.fireplug.net/~rshand/reflections/vietnam/suicide.html.

Richard Weaver, Jr., 362d and 24th Signal Companies. Information regarding Camp Enari and the Tropospheric antennas of Dragon Mountain Troposcatter Signal Site were his significant contribution to this effort.

Richard White, 3/d/5th Cav and 1st.502d Inf, and Webmaster for the D/1st/502d Inf Assn's webpage at: http://pone.com/dc/ index.htm. I am exceedingly grateful for Richard's very important contributions to the knowledge found herein and for his steadfast and loyal support. His colorful memories of the last days of the 1st/502d/101st Abn in Vietnam, his very comprehensive historical knowledge generally, and his always insightful and candid analysis were also very much appreciated. Richard is also Webmaster for a 3d/5th Armored Cavalry website as well.

Rick Harris helped with data regarding MACV Advisory Team 67 at Song Be.

Rob LeFreniere. Rob was very helpful in our attempts to identify the location of an alleged radio relay site by the name of Ghost Mountain.

Rick Schmierer, D/1st/502d Inf. My thanks to my old friend for his colorful recollections of an explosion at OP 56, and for all the other support and interesting material he has provided.

Robert Clark, 584th Engineers (Wooly Bullies) in '70. Bob added colorful memories and descriptions of Weigt-Davis to the effort.

Robert D. Tuke, a Marine CAP veteran with the law firm Tuke, Yopp Sweeny. His very helpful information regarding USMC CAP Team locations in the Hieu Nhon District east of Hoi An in Quang Nam Province was very much appreciated.

Robert Shrake, C Co, 4th/31st Inf/196th LIB, '68-69. Detailed .jpg map images of FSBs locations and terrain features SW of Hoi An were his important contributions to the project.

Robin Moore, author of *The Green Berets*. Mr. Moore very graciously provided his help in identify the actual locations of the bases assigned fictional names in his book. Interestingly enough, *The Green Berets* was recently re-released and can be ordered through the author's website at www.robinmoore.com (see also Appendix H).

Rod Barber, D/229th Avn Bn, 69-70. Rod offered his help in determining the location of LZ Dolly.

Roger Ables. Helped with some background history of FSB Kim Qui.

Ron Flint, C/1st/14th Inf/4th Div. Provided detail regarding FSB 32 & 34.

Ron Johnson, my dear friend and Vietnam War comrade of the 3rd Platoon, D/1st/502d/101st Abn Div. Ron helped keep me alive on a singularly bad day in September, 1970. If that weren't enough, over the years he's also been providing me with much-needed support generally. During this project, he also shared with us with a good deal of information related to firebases generally and particularly that of the Firebase Ripcord siege, May-Jul70. I will never forget what you did for me, brother Ron. Never.

Roy Stearns (a.k.a. Col Roy and Blue Canyon Roy), KCRA TV NBC Channel 3, Sacramento, 459th Signal Company, 52d Signal Bn/1st Signal Bde. Roy shared with us a detailed and informative look at the Pr'line (a.k.a. Pra Lean) Mountain Signal Site. Many thanks also for his good cheer, encouragement and for his unwavering support of the California Vietnam Veterans Memorial since 1984.

Russ Richardson, C Bty/1st/83d Arty. Provided helpful data regarding the history of the 83d Arty at FSBs Blaze, Bastogne, Birmingham and Camp Eagle.

Russell "Gus" Reynolds, 4th Inf Div. I'm very thankful for the detailed memories and photos of the Oasis, Camp Enari, Dragon Mountain and Signal Hill that Russ shared with us. He also very thoughtfully rustled-up a hornet's nest of other friends and contacts who pitched-in with other significant contributions as well.

Stan Devin. Stan's recollections regarding the numbered firebase series near Dak To/Ben Het, plus the details of his arty unit's support of Mike Force, A and B teams in '69/70 were helpful and appreciated.

Stan Lyman, B Bty, 1st/92d Arty. Stan assisted us in locating Firebase 6 and the record its history.

Steve Laktash, 3d Recon Bn/3d Mar Div. Information posted by Lyman at www.grunt.spac.swri.edu/ images/vn/ recon/steve1.jpg and steve2.jpg was both educational and very helpful.

Steve Sherman, noted SF historian (Radix Press), author and Vietnam map expert. A special thanks goes to Steve for the invaluable proffered throughout this project. Not only did he unhesitatingly give me a listing of eight-digit grids for most SF camp locations, but he then generally became my mentor where gazetteer and other map related resources were concerned. His help was a Godsend, his patience and generosity much appreciated, and his friendship will be forever treasured.

Steven Walls, CSM USA Ret, 584th Engineers. Among the much-appreciated data Walls shared with us were humorous and entertaining descriptions of the 20th Eng Bn's quarry at Kontum, the Wooly Bully compound, and the events surrounding the closure of the Kontum SF Mike Force compound adj to Wooly Bully in late 68 or early 69. He also provided a number of excellent .jpg files with various views of those locations.

Ted Ashton, 4th Inf Div. Ted very generously shared a number of audio tapes of enemy contact along QL-19, as well as his memories of Weigt-Davis and Camp Swampy.

Ted Hull at NARA CER. My sincere thanks his very his thoughtful assistance and expert guidance in navigating the various MACV electronic files available through the Center for Electronic Records.

Terry McGee, B/1st/8th Cav/1st Cav Div. Ted's recollections of LZ Sands and actions nearby in Mar67 were among his welcomed contributions.

Tim Duffie, CAP team website creator and a genuinely good-hearted man. My sincere thanks go to Tim for his general support and encouragement, as well as his bountiful assistance in helping compile CAP, CAC and CUPP Team sites for the historical record (much of which we gleaned from the voluminous historical CAP data posted on or linked to his CAP webpage at: http://capmarine.com.

Timothy Carr, who lost his brother on FSB Birmingham. My thanks for his very interesting and very unusual data regarding the history of the apparent accidental B-57 bombing of FSB Birmingham, 16Mar68, in which his brother was killed.

Tom Brizendine, 101st Abn, B/1st/6th Inf/198th LIB and A/75th Rangers. Tom shared with us very illuminating and much-appreciated detail and data regarding 198th LIB FSB locations in I Corps.

Tom "Desert Jake" Jacobs (a.k.a. Jardog), 3d Recon Bn/3d Mar Div. My thanks for his comradeship, playful wit, sharp mind, and for keeping me in line when it was necessary. I'm also grateful for data he provided regarding "The Backyard" and other terrain features and facilities of the 3d Mar Div's AO in Quang Tri Province generally.

Tom Dilley, 4th Div. Proffered data regarding LZ Baldie and Mile-High.

Tom Flynn, CAP Marine "Tiger Pappa 3." Flynn was quick to share important information regarding CAP locations and actions along QL-9, and I'm also very grateful for the signed copy of his CAP memoirs, *A Voice of Hope*, that he gave to us as a gift. (A review of his book was at one time available at www.capmarine.com/)

Tom Hanson, Capt, USA (2d Bde HQ/101st Abn). My sincere thanks and a "First Strike" go to Tom for the exceedingly loyal and unflagging support he provided throughout the project. Among other remarkable gifts that periodically showed-up in the mail unannounced was the 1968 Battalion Annual Historical Supplement for the 1st/502d Inf, that he somehow tracked-down when no one else could (neither the HQ of the 101st Abn nor 101st Abn Div Assn museum nor National Archives nor U.S. Army were able to accomplish the feat!). Copies of the 1969 and 1970 supplements were also among his thoughtful and greatly appreciated contributions.

Tom Lacombe. My thanks for his much-needed data regarding FSB Roundtop, LZ Joyce and Silver Star Hill/Million Dollar Hill.

Tom Mosher, USMC CAP team vet. Tom generously provided a number of excellent maps and recollections of bases in the Cam Lo area, as well as quite valuable data regarding Payable Hill and Cap Teams near the Rockpile in Quang Tri Province.

Tom Rethard, C/7th/15th FA(heavy). Tom's contribution was a remarkably thoughtful, able and persistent torrent of data and analysis that helped pinpoint places like FSB 6, Wooly Bully. Detailed descriptions of the locations and access points to Camp Enari, Dragon Mountain and the Pleiku Tropospheric signal site on Tropo Hill were also among the significant additions to the historical record that were his gifts.

Tom Skelly, 1st/12th Cav/1st Cav Div. Skelly provided the much-appreciated unit history and the physical makeup for a number of 1st Cav Div LZs, among which were Carol, Grant and Lee.

Tom Ward and the 199th Light Inf Bde RedCatchers Association. Tom's and the RedCatcher rendered vital assistance through their greatly appreciated contribution of data and grids for numerous 199th LIB positions and FSBs in Tay Ninh, Gia Dinh, Bien Hoa, Phuoc Tuy and Long Khanh Provinces. Their unofficial website is at www.redcatcher.org, and this remarkable site has evolved into a major map and firebase resource that all should visit, particularly those who served in III Corps. The official mailing address for the RedCatcher Association: RedCatcher, PO Box 199, Mclean VA, 22101-0199.

Tommy Acosta, 1st/20th/11th LIB, '68-69. Provided a colorful background for LZ Debbie-Thunder.

Tommy Poppell, B/1st/46th Inf, 196th LIB, Americal Div, 70-71. Tom graciously shared with us the name of the S-4 pad at FSB Professional (1-Oh -Worst Pad) and also his able assistance in pinpointing the correct locations for FSB Mary Ann, LZ Siberia, LZ Young and LZ Judy.

Wayne Gass, A/1/35th/4th Inf Div. Gave us data regarding LZ Gypsy.

William Gaschler. Bill thoughtfully helped establish the grid for FSB Mace and also gave us details regarding the Nui Chau Chan Signal Site, just north of Mace.

William Robert "Weird" Stanley, B/229th AHB, 1st Cav, Mar68-69. Stanley gifted us with a very important 1:100,000 scale war era Army Map Service map marked with 1st Cav Div and 101st Abn Div positions in Quang Tri Province circa 1968. I'd also like to particularly thank him for the very generous and thoughtful gift of a masterful Walnut carving of my 502d Inf regimental crest. Among other things, Stanley is now a woodcarver of the first caliber.

Appendix H
Recommended Readings

12, 20 & 5-A Doctor's Year in Vietnam, Parrish, John, MD, E. P. Dutton & Co, NY, 1972
13th Valley, see *The 13th Valley*
365 Days, Glasser, Ronald J., George Braziller, NY, 1971
A Bright, Shining Lie, Sheehan, Neil, Random House, NY, 1988
A Rumor of War, Caputo, Philip, Holt/Renehart/Winston, NY, 1977, Fiction
About Face, Hackworth, David, Simon & Schuster, NY, 1989
After Tet - The Bloodiest Year in Vietnam, Spector, Ronald H., Free Press, NY, 1993
Air Facilities Data: Laos, apparent reproduction of official *Air America* airfield guide, author and date unknown. Contains a complete listing of all Lima Sites used by Air America, Continental Air Services and the Air Force Ravens flying in Laos. Data given individually for each of the over 350 sites that includes: No. and name of airfield, length/width, construction, geographic coordinates, map reference, runway orientation, elevation and much more. Order from K&S Militaria, PO Box 9630, Alpine TX 79831, 915-837-5053, 915-837-5021 Fax. Order number is BO 842
Air Power and the Fight for Khe Sanh, Nalty, Bernard C, Office of Air Force History, Wash. DC, 1973 (incredible aerial photo of the bomb damage patterns surrounding Khe Sanh plateau at pp 84-85)
All The Way:The 3d Brigade 82d ABN Div In Vietnam 1968, Porter, Capt. William R., and Fairful, Capt. Thomas M, Image Public Relations, Ltd, Tokyo and Toronto (pub date ?) (reprints available at $10 each with check made out to 'Golden Brigade Chapter,' and mailed to: Rich O'Hare, 4075 Old River Trail, Powhatan, VA 23139-4112)
Ambush Valley-I Corps, Vietnam, 1967, A Marine Infantry Battalion's Battle for Survival, Hammel, Eric, Presidio Press, Novato, CA, 1990
Ambush, Marshall, S. L. A., Cowles Education Corp., 1969
American Fighting Ships, Dictionary of, complete text online at www.hazegray.org/danfs/
Anatomy of a Division - See The First Cav in Vietnam
Anatomy of a War, Kolko, Gabriel, The new Press, 1985, NY
Apache Sunrise, Boyle, Jerome, Ivy Books, 1994, NY
Assault on Dak Pek, Wade, Leigh, Ivy Books, NY, 1998
Australian's War in Vietnam, Frost, Frank, Allen & Unwin, Australia (PTY 959.704'34'0994), 1987
Baptism: A Vietnam Memoir, Gwin, Larry, Ballentine Publishing Group/Ivy Books, 1999
Battle For Hue, Nolan, Keith William, Presidio Press, Novato CA, 1983
Battles In the Monsoon, Marshall, S. L. A., William Morrow & Company, NY, 1967
Bird-The Christmastide Battle, Marshall, S. L. A., Cowles Education Corp., 1968
Bloods: An Oral History of the Vietnam War by Black Vets, Wallace Terry, Random House, 84
Bonnie-Sue: A Marine Corps Helicopter Squadron in Vietnam, Strukey, Marion, Heritage Press International, Plum Branch SC, 1996. (May be ordered by mail at HIP, PO Box 333, Plum Branch SC, 29845
Brown Water, Black Berets, Cutler, LCDR Thomas J, USN, Naval Institute press, 1988
Brown Water Navy Pages Of Kent Hawley, RVN 69-70, at: http://hawley.interspeed.net/vietnam/links.htm
By Air Sea and Land, by Marolda, Edward J., Dept. of the Navy, Naval Historical Center, entire text (but only a portion of the 500 photos in the hard copy version) is online at: www.history.navy.mil/seairland/index.html
CAP Mot, The Story of a Marine Special Forces Unit in Vietnam, 1968-1969, Goodson, Barry L, Univ of N Texas Press, Denton TX, 1997
Cedar Falls-Junction City: A Turning Point, Maj. Gen Bernard W. Rogers, U.S. Army Center for Military History, 1974, 1989; 172 pages, chart, maps, illustrations, glossary, index, CMH Pub 90-7 (Available in its entirety on at the USA-CMH site at: www.army.mil/cmh-pg/books/vietnam/90-7/cont.htm
Charlie Company, What Vietnam Did to Us, Goldman, P./Fuller, T., Wm Morrow & Company, NY, 1983
Charlie Ranger, Ericson, Don and Rotundo, John L., Ivy Books paperback, NY, Feb 1989
Chickenhawk, Mason, Robert, The Viking Press, NY, 1983
China And The Vietnam Wars, 1950-75, by Qiang Zhai, 2000
Choppers, Coleman, J. D., St. Martin's Paperbacks, NY, 1988
Combat Medic - Vietnam, Roberts, Craig, Pocket Books - Simon & Schuster, NY, 1991
Da-Nang Diary, Yarborough, Col Tom, Saint Martins Press, NY, 1990
Dak To, Murphy, Edward F., Pocket Books, NY 1993
Dear America: Letters Home From Vietnam, Edelman, Bernie, Ed., W. W. Norton & Co, NY, 1985
Death Valley, Nolan, Keith William, Presidio Press, Novato CA, 1987
Dictionary of American Fighting Ships, online at www.hazegray.org/danfs/
Dictionary of the Vietnam War, Olson, James A., Editor, Peter Bedrick Books, 1987, NY, NY
Directory of Names - Vietnam Veterans Memorial, Vietnam Veterans Memorial Fund, Inc, 1988, Washington DC
Dispatches, Herr, Michael, Alfred A. Knopf, NY, 1978 (Pulitzer Prize)
Dictionary of American Fighting Ships at: www.hazegray.org/danfs/
Doc: Platoon Medic, Evans, Daniel E. Jr, and Sasser, Charles, Pocket Books, NY, 1998
Doctor at Dien Bien Phu, Gauwin, Paul, Stratford Press, 1955
DUSTOFF:The Memoir of an Army Aviator, Novosel, Michael J., Presidio Press, 1999
Edwin E. Moïse Vietnam War Bibliography, at: http://hubcap.clemson.edu/~eemoise/bibliography.html

End of the Line: The Siege of Khe Sanh, Pisor, Robert, Ballentine Books, NY 1982

Everything We Had, Santoli, Al, Random House, NY, 1981, Oral History

Facing the Phoenix, Grant, Zalin, W.W. Norton & Co, NY 1991

Father Soldier Son, Memoir of a Platoon Leader in Vietnam, Tripp, Nathaniel, Steerforth Press, South Royalton, VT, 1998 paperback

Fighting The North Vietnamese - 1967, Telfer, Maj. Gary L. & Rogers, LTC Lane, USMC, History & Museums Division Headquarters, U.S. Marine Corps, 1984, Washington DC

Fire In The Streets: The Battle For Hue, TET 1968, Hammel, Eric, Contemporary Books, Chicago, 1991

Fire Support Base Development, article by Maj. Robert V. Nicoli, September. 1969, posted on the net at: http://members.aol.com/warlibrary/vwfsb.htm

For Garry Owen In Glory, Schild, LTC James, Auto Review publishing, Florissant, MO, 1991

Former Inmate Returns to Phuu Quoac Island, article by Phaim Bau Nhieau, in 23Aug98 issue of Vietnam News Service. On Internet at: http://vietnamnews.vnagency.com.vn/1998-08/1998-08-23/Stories/05.htm

Friendly Fire, Bryan, C.D.B., G.P. Putman's Sons, NY 1976

Gone Native: An NCO's Story, Cornett, Alan G., Ballentine Books, NY, 2000, PB

Hamburger Hill: May 11-20, 1969, Zaffiri, Sam, 1987

History of a Voyage to the China Sea, Capt. John White, 1820(?)

Incursion: From America's Choke-hold on the NVA Lifelines to the Sacking of the Cambodian Sanctuaries, (TAD abbr.), J. D. Coleman, St. Martin's Mass Market Paperback; 1992

Infantry in Vietnam: Small Unit Actions in the Early Days: 1965-66, Garland, LTC Albert, The Battery Press, Nashville, 1982

Into Cambodia: Spring Campaign, Summer Offensive, 1970, Nolan, Keith William, Presidio Press, Novato CA, 1990

Into Laos: The Story of Dewey Canyon II/Lam Son 719, Nolan, Keith William, Presidio Press, Novato CA, 1991

Inventaire des archives de la guerre, Service historique Armée, serie N, 1920-1940. Vincennes: Ministere de la defense, Etat-major de l'Armee de terre, Service historique, 1981- . SML Stacks CD1206 1981 (LC)

Khe Sanh Battle, Historical Documents online at: http://members.easyspace.com/airdrop/

Khe Sanh, Siege In the Clouds, Hammel, Eric, Oral History

L-7014 DMA map series Index Map, high quality image of the original can be seen at: www.rjsmith.com/images/kelley/Index-L7014s.jpg

Last Reflections On A War, Fall, Bernard, Schocken Books, NY, 1967

Lima-6: A Marine Company Commander in Vietnam, Hammel, Eric, Antheneum Press, NY, 1989

Log, RVN - October 1971 to September 1972, Hunt, William D, 1997, unpublished memoir, re: Advisory Team 72, Muc Hoa, Kien Tuong Province. Also on-line: http://saturn.fhda.edu/instructor/swensson/hunt.html.

Low Level Hell: A Scout Pilot in the Big Red One, Mills, Hugh L. Jr./Anderson, Robert A., Dell Books, NY, 1992

LRRP Company Command, Jorgenson, Kregg P.J., Ballantine Publishing, SB, 2000

MACV Command History Reports, 1968-1971

Mad Minutes And Vietnam Months, A Soldier's Memoir, Clodfelter. Michael, Pinnacle Books, Kensington Publishing Corp., Zebra Books, Windsor Publishing Group, NY, 1988 (may have been originally released as *Pawns of Dishonor*?)

Magnificent Bastards-The Joint Army/Marine Defense of Dong Ha, 1968, Nolan, Keith William, Presidio Press, Novato, CA, 1994

Marines & Helicopters 1962-1973, Fails, LTC William R, USMC, History & Museums Division Headquarters, U.S. Marine Corps, 1978, Wash. DC

Memoirs of LtGen. John Cushman, 2d Bde, 101st Abn Div CO, Dec67-Jun68 (Unpublished), 1996

Military, The Press of Freedom, various issues, MHR Publishing, 2122 28th St., Sacramento, CA 95819-1999, 916- 457-8990

Mobile Guerilla Force, With The Special Forces In War Zone D, James C. DonahueSt. Martin's Paperbacks, NY, 1996

My Lai 4, Hersh, Seymour, Random House, NY, 1970

National Geographic Magazine, various articles and maps from Oct35, Oct50, Apr51, Sep52, Feb67, et al issues. The Indochina map in the Feb67 issue is a classic.

Nerve Gas Used on Defectors, AP article re: use of Sarin in Laos, The Sacramento Bee, 8Jun98, p A-4

Never Without Heroes, Vetter, Lawrence C Jr., Ivy Books, NY, 1996

New World Maps, Inc, Apple Hill Road, Bennington, VT 05201-9544 (map resource, not a book)

New Zealand Army Museum, PO Box 45, Main Road, Waiouru, New Zealand

No Shining Armor: The Marines at War Vietnam, An Oral History, Lehrack, Otto J., Univ Pr of Kansas, 1992, oral history of the 3d Bn, 3d Marines in Vietnam

Not Going Home Alone, Kirschke, James J., Ballentine Books, NY, 2001, PB

Officer's Guide-1967-68 Edition, Reynolds, MGen Russell B, USA Ret, Stackpole Books, Harrisburg PA, 1967

On Point, A Rifleman's Year in the Boonies: Vietnam 1967-1968, Hayes, Roger, Presidio Press, Novato, CA, 2000

Once Upon a Distant War, Prochnau, William, Times Books, 1995, London

One Day Too Long: Top Secret Site 85 and the Bombing of North Vietnam, by Castle, Timothy, Columbia Univ Press, 1999

Operation Buffalo: USMC Fight for the DMZ, Nolan, Keith William, Presidio Press, Novato, CA, 1991

Paco's Story, Heinemann, Larry, Farrar, Straus & Giroux, NY, 1986, Fiction (National Book Award)

Parallels: The Soldiers' Knowledge and the Oral History of Contemporary Warfare, Hansen, Madden & Owens, Aldine De Gruyter, NY, '92

Phantom Over Vietnam: Fighter Pilot, USMC, Trotti, John, Presidio Press, Novato, CA, 1984

Phu Cat Airbase History, located at www.fgi.net/~rdoughty/phuhist.htm, Doughty, J, author

Platoon Bravo Company, Hemphill, Robert, St. Martin's Paperbacks, NY, 1998

Pleiku, Coleman, J. D., St. Martins Press, 1988, NY

Prisoners of Hope, Keating, Susan Katz, Random House, NY, 1994

Rain of Fire, Time/Life's *The Vietnam Experience*, Boston Publishing, 1985

Rangers at War, LRRPs in Vietnam, Stanton, Shelby, Ivy Books, NY, 1992 (soft bound)

Red Thunder, Tropic Lightning: The World of a Combat Division in Vietnam, Bergerud, Eric M, Reprint Ed, Penguin USA (Paper) Mar94 ISBN: 0140235450

Reflexes and Reflections: The National Vietnam Veterans Art Museum, Sinaiko, Eve (Ed.), Anthony F. Janson (Ed.), Hardcover, Harry N Abrams, NY, Oct 1998, ISBN: 0810939452

Reluctant Warrior, Hodgins, Michael C, Ivy Books, NY, 1996 (1st Recon Bn, 1st Mar Div in '70)

Rendezvous With Destiny, Fall 1971, 101st Abn Div official publication, 40 pages

Rendezvous With Destiny, Summer 1970, 101st Abn Div official publication, 31 pages

Report on Operations in South Vietnam, Westmoreland, Gen W.C., Government Printing Office, Washington DC, 1968, Appendix L. pp. 281-289

Rescue from FSB Ripcord, Marshal, Tom, article in Vietnam Magazine, June '98, p 34-40

Ripcord, Screaming Eagles Under Siege, Vietnam 1970, by Nolan, Keith William, *Presidio Press*, Novato, CA, 2000

Ripcord Report, periodical published by the FSB Ripcord Assoc, 13140 Lakehill Dr, Nokesville, VA 20181-3328

Rites of Passage: Odyssey of a Grunt, Peterson, Robert, Ballantine Books, NY, 1997

River Road to China, The Search for the Source of the Mekong, 1866-73, Osborne, Milton, Atlantic Monthly Press, NY, 1975, 1996

Riverine: A Pictorial History of the Brown Water War in Vietnam, Lesko, Jim, Squadron/Signal Publications

Roster Of Army Unit Associations, Dept. of the Army, HQDA. Available for purchase through: (SAPA-CR), Washington, DC 20310, or by calling (202) 694-0739. Was discontinued by DA Public Affairs but taken over by private individual who sells list for $12 (1997 cost of duplication). HQDA will tell you where it can be purchased.

Sappers In The Wire, Nolan, Keith William, Presidio Press, Novato CA, 1996

Search & Rescue in Southeast Asia, Tilford, Earl H. Jr., Office of Air Force History, Wash DC, 1980

Secrets of the Viet Cong, McCoy, J. W., Hippocrene Press, NY, 1992

Setting the Stage, volume of *The Vietnam Experience* series, Boston Publishing, 1985

SF Order of Battle, See *Special Forces Order of Battle*

Shrapnel In the Heart: Letters & Remembrances From The Vietnam Veterans Memorial, Palmer, Laura, Random House, NY, 1987, Oral History

Slow Burn: The Rise and Bitter Fall of American Intelligence in Vietnam, DeFores, Orrin and Chanoff, David, Simon & Schuster, 1990. De Forest was Chief of CIA intelligence activities, III Corps in '68.

Small Unit Action in Vietnam - Summer 1966, West, Capt. Franci J. Jr, USMCR, History & Museums Division Headquarters, U.S. Marine Corps, 1967, Wash. DC

SOG: The Secret Wars of America's Commandos in Vietnam, Plaster, John L., Onyx Press

Son Thang: An American War Crime, Solis, Gary D, Bantam Books, Sep 1998, NY

Sparring With Charlie: Motorbiking Down the Ho Chi Minh Trail, Hunt, Christopher, Anchor Books, NY, 1996

Special Forces Order of Battle, Sherman, Steve, The RADIX Press, 2314 Cheshire Ln, Houston, TX 77018, (713) 683-9076 (this and other esoteric SF publications available at that address), www.greenberet.net/books

Street Without Joy, Fall, Bernard, The Stackpole Co, Harrisburg, PA, 4th Ed, 1967

Suicide Charlie: A Vietnam War Story, Norman, Russell L. Pocket Books (Simon & Schuster), NY, 1993

Tales of a War Far Away, Ramsey, Kirk, (complete, on-line memoir of 2d/14th Inf, 25th Inf) at: www.en.com/users/kramsey/default.html. Illustrated

Tan Phu: Special Forces Team A-23 in Combat, Wade, Leigh, Ivy Books, NY, 1997

Team Sergeant: A Special Forces NCO at Lang Vei and Beyond, Craig, William T., Ivy Books, NY, 1998

The 101st Airborne 1968 Yearbook. 101st Abn Div PIO, Vietnam, 1969 (reprinted by Paseo Press Oklahoma City OK, 1985)

The 101st Airborne 1969 Yearbook. 101st Abn Div PIO, Vietnam, 1970 (soft cover reprint, available from 101st Abn Div Assn.; 1968 and 1969 Yearbook reprints also available through that organization)

The 13th Valley, Del Vecchio, John M., Bantam Books, 1978, NY (excellent I Corps firebase map on inside cover)

The Advisory & Combat Assistance Era, Whitlow, Capt. Robert H., USMC, History & Museums Division Headquarters, U.S. Marine Corps, 1977, Wash. DC

The Army Reporter ('The Largest Army Newspaper in the World'), various issues, U.S. Army Information Office, Vietnam, APO 96375 (tel Long Binh, 4204/4819, printed by Pacific Stars & Stripes

The Battle for An Loc, Smith, Mark A. (a.k.a. Capt. Zippo), at http://lzsally.com/zippo.html. (unusual account by man who describes himself as the ground cmdr for much of the fight)

The Battle of Coral: Vietnam Fire Support Bases Coral & Balmoral, May 1968, McAulay, Lex, Arrow Books, London, 1990

The Battle of Dien Bien Phu, Roy, Jules, Carroll & Graf Publishers, Inc., NY, 1963 (PB)

The Battle of Long Tan, McAulay, Lex, Aussies in Vietnam

The Development and Training of the South Vietnamese Army, 1950-1972, Vietnam Studies, Collins, BG James Lawton, Dept of the Army, Wash. DC, 1975

The Easter Offensive: The Last American Advisors Vietnam 1972, Turley, G. H., Presidio Press, 85

The Fields of Bamboo: Three Battles Just Beyond the South China Sea, Marshall, S. L. A., The Dial Press, NY, 1971 (Also Published as Three Battles)

The Final Formation, Stubbe, Ray W, soft back special edition of the *Khe Sanh Veteran Magazine*, 1995, (includes very detailed accounting of all KIA related to the siege of Khe Sanh CB. To order, contact author at 8766 Park View CT, Wauwatosa, WI, 53226-2729

The First Cav in Vietnam: Anatomy of a Division, Stanton, Shelby L., June 1999 Presidio Press; ISBN: 0891416862

The French Experience in Indochina: For an extensive bibliography on the First Indochina War, go to Edwin E. Moïse's Vietnam War Bibliography at: http://hubcap.clemson.edu/~eemoise/bibliography.html. The section covering the French involvement in Indochina is entitled, 'World War II and the First Indochina War' and is located at: www.hubcap/ clemson.edu/~eemoise/firstwar.htm

The Green Berets, Moore, Robin, Crown Publishers, Inc, NY, 1965 (*The Green Berets* was recently re-released and autographed copies can be ordered from the author for $14.95 at: www.robinmoore.com or by sending a check or money order to 179 Nashawtuc Rd, Concord, MA 01742)

The History of the 3d Bde, 82d Airborne Div: February 1968 to March 1969, Porter, Capt. William R, Fairfull, Capt. Thomas M, Image Public Relations Ltd., Toronto, available from the 'Golden Bde Chapter', 82d Airborne Div Association

The Infantry Brigade in Combat, Wolf, Duquesne A, Sunflower University Press, Manhattan, Kansas, 1984 (ISBN 0-89745-053-1)

The Lost Battalion, Krohn, Charles A., Praeger Publishing, Westport, CT, 1993

The Mammoth Book of War Diaries & Letters, Lewis, Jon E., Carroll and Graf, Inc., NY 1999

The Map Catalog, 2d Ed., Vintage/Tilden Press, NY, 1990

The Marines in Vietnam 1954-1973: An Annotated Bibliography, 2d ed., History & Museums Division, USMC, Washington DC, 1985

The Perfect War-Techno War In Vietnam, Glackin, James William, Atlantic Monthly Press, 1986

The Rise and Fall of the American Army, Stanton, Shelby, Presidio Press, 1995 paperback edition, Novato, CA

The Secret War Against Hanoi, Schulz Jr., Richard, Harper-Collins, NY, 1999

The Sons of Bardstown: 25 Years of Vietnam in an American Town, Wilson, Jim, ASIN: 0517577372, 1994, Crown Publishers

The Unquiet American, Currey, Cecile B., Brassey's Books, Dulles VA, 1998

The United States Coast Guard in South East Asia During the Vietnam Conflict, Tulich, Eugene N., USCG, complete text online: www.uscg.mil/hq/gcp/history/ h_tulichvietnam.html

The U.S. Marines in Vietnam, High Mobility and Standdown, 1969, Smith, Charles R. History & Museums Division Headquarters, U.S. Marine Corps, 1988, Wash. DC

The Vietnam Experience, Boston Publishing Co, 1985, a 24-volume series

The Vietnam Guidebook, Cohen, Barbara, 2d Ed., Houghton-Mifflin, NY, 1991

The Vietnam Map Book, Smith, Clark and Watkins, Don, Published by the *Agent Orange Advisory Committee*, Berkeley, CA, date unknown, but circa 1980. Very rare and very large publication. Approximately 20" by 24" in size. Contains a complete set of 1:500,000 (?) scale maps covering SVN in black and white as well as all the dates and reported grids between which USAF Agent Orange missions were flown.

The Vietnam War, Smithmark-US Media Holdings, Inc, NY, 1996 ed

These Good Men: Friendship Forged in War, Norman, Michael, Crown Publishers, NY, 1985

Third Brigade, Ninth Infantry Division, Vietnam 1970 Orientation Brochure, 9th Inf Div official publication

Through The Valley: Vietnam 1967-1968, Humphries, James F., Lynne Rienner Publishers, Inc., Boulder CO, 1999

Thunder From Above, Time/Life's The Vietnam Experience, Boston Publishing, 1985

Thunder, Vol. 1, No. 2, Fall 1969, Official Publication of the 25th Inf Div, 48 pages

Time Heals No Wounds, Leninger, Jack, Ivy Books, NY, 1993. Many details re: 4th Div bases in western II Corps, including many grid coordinates and Divisional/Company Operational Report/Radio Journal excerpts

Tropic Lightning News, Magazine of the 25th Inf Div in Vietnam (various issues), Information Office, 25th Inf Div, APO 96225, 1968

Twenty Years and Twenty Days, Nguyen Cao Ky, Stein & Day publishers, NY, 1976

Unknown Warriors: Canadians in the Vietnam War, Gaffen, Fred, Dundurn Press, Toronto, 1990

U.S. Army Center for Military History website, www.army.mil/cmh-pg

U.S. Army Special Forces Order of Battle, Sherman, Steve, The RADIX Press, 2314 Cheshire Ln, Houston, TX 77018, (713) 683-9076 (this book and other esoteric SF publications available at that address), www.greenberet. net/books

US Marines in Vietnam: ighting the North Vietnamese, 1967, Telfer, Maj. Gary L. and Rogers, LTC Lane, History & Museums Division Headquarters, U.S. Marine Corps, 198?, Wash. DC

US Marines in Vietnam: High Mobility and Standdown, 1969, Smith, Charles R., History & Museums Division Headquarters, U.S. Marine Corps, 1988, Wash. DC

US Marines in Vietnam: The Landing and the Buildup, 1965, History & Museums Division Headquarters, U.S. Marine Corps, 198?, Wash. DC

Utter's Battalion: 2/7 Marines in Vietnam 1965-66, Lee, Alex, Lt Col (Ret.), Ballantine Books (PB), NY, 2000

Valley of Decision, Prados, John/Stubbe, Ray W, Houghton Mifflin, NY 1991

Vietnam: A Political History, Buttinger, Joseph, Praeger, 1969

Vietnam - Reflexes and Reflections : The National Vietnam Veterans Arts Museum, Sinaiko, Eve/Janson, Anthony F. (Editors), Harry N. Abrams Books, NY, 1998

Vietnam Diary, Tregaskis, Richard, Holt, Rinehart & Winston, NY, 1963, one of earliest looks at VN

Vietnam Gunners, 161 Battery RNZA, South Vietnam-1965-1971, Newman, Lt D. S., Moana Press, Tauranga and Wellington, New Zealand, 1988

Vietnam Military Lore: 1959-1973, Bows, Ray A., Bows & Sons Pub. 1988, Hanover MA

Vietnam Military Lore: Legends, Shadows and Heroes, Bows, Ray A., Bows & Sons Pub. 1997, Hanover MA

Vietnam Odyssey, *The Story of the 1st Bde, 101st Abn Division in Vietnam*, 101st Abn Div Assoc, 1967

Vietnam Order of Battle, Stanton, Shelby, 1986, Galahad Books, NY

Vietnam Primer, Hackworth, David/Marshall, S.L.A., Dept of the Army Pamphlet 525-2, 1967

Vietnam Reflexes and Reflections: The National Vietnam Veterans Art Museum, Sinaiko, Eve/Janson, Anthony F. (Editors), hard cover, Harry N Abrams, NY, Oct 1998, ISBN: 0810939452

Vietnam Studies: Cedar Falls, Junction City, A Turning Point, Roger, LtGen Bernard W, Department of the Army, Wash DC, 1974

Vietnam Studies: Base Development 1965-1970, Dunn, LtGen Carroll H, Department of the Army, Wash DC, 1972

Vietnam Studies: Mounted Combat in Vietnam, Starry, Gen Don A, Dept of the Army Vietnam Studies, 1978, Wash. DC

Vietnam Studies: The Development and Training of the South Vietnamese Army, 1950-1972, Collins, BG James Lawton, Dept of the Army Vietnam Studies, Wash. DC, 1975

Vietnam Studies: U.S. Army Special Forces 1961-1971, Pub 90-23, Center for Military History, Wash DC, 1989 (available in its entirety on the internet at www.army.mil/cmh-pg/books/vietnam/90-23/90-23c.htm)

Vietnam War Bibliography, Edwin E. Moïse, at: http://hubcap.clemson.edu/~eemoise/bibliography.html

Vietnam War Stories website at: www.war-stories.com/

Vietnam: A History, Karnow, Stanley, The Viking Press, NY, 1982

Vietnam: From Cease-Fire to Capitulation, Le Gro, Col William E., U.S. Army Center for Military History, 1988, Wash. DC

Village At War: An Account of Revolution in Vietnam, Trullinger, James Walker Jr., Longman, Inc., 1980; Reprinted as **Village at War**, The Stanford University Press, Stanford, CA, 1994; civilian perspective

VN Order of Battle. See Vietnam Order of Battle.

Voice of Hope, Flynn, Tom, Voice Book Productions; ISBN: 1561671339, 1994 (available through Amamzon.com and www.capmarine.com/)

War in Laos - 1954-1973, Conboy, Kenneth, Squadron/Signal Publications, Carrollton TX, 1994

War In The Shadows, Asprey, Robert B, Doubleday, NY, 1975

War of Numbers, Adam, Sam, Steerforth Press, S. Royalton, VT, 1994

War Without Windows, Jones, Bruce, NY, Vanguard Press, 1988

Webster's New World Dictionary of the Vietnam War, Leepson, Marc, Editor, with Hannaford, Hellen, Simon & Schuster Macmillan, NY, 1999 (recommended as standard reference)

We Were Soldiers Once...And Young, Galloway, Joseph and Moore, Harold, Random House, NY 1992 (Maxwell Perkins Prize)

West To Cambodia, Marshall, S. L. A., Cowles Education Corp., 1968

Where the Ashes Are: The Odyssey of a Vietnamese Family, Nguyen Qui Duc, 1994

Year of the Horse: Vietnam, Mertel, Col Kenneth D., Schiffer Publishing Co, 4th Printing, hard back, 1996. Covers 1st Cav in Vietnam, 1965-66 and 1970